SHAKESPEARE

MAJOR PLAYS

and the Sonnets

EDITED BY G. B. HARRISON

University of Michigan

HARCOURT, BRACE AND COMPANY, *NEW YORK*

COPYRIGHT, 1948, BY
HARCOURT, BRACE AND COMPANY, INC.

[k · 9 · 58]

PRINTED IN THE UNITED STATES OF AMERICA

CONTENTS

CONTENTS

APPENDICES

PREFACE

THIS edition of *Shakespeare: Major Plays and the Sonnets* has been produced for college students in the hope that it will help them to understand, appreciate, and enjoy the works for themselves. It is not intended for the scholar, who is amply served elsewhere.

The choice of a text gave considerable difficulty. When the volume was first planned there was hot controversy whether to use the familiar Globe text or to print a text which closely followed the original quarto or folio, on the lines of my Penguin Shakespeares. It was therefore agreed to submit the problem to a plebiscite of professors and to abide by their judgment. The vote was decisively in favor of the Globe, and this decision I accepted. As the work of editing progressed, I have been the more convinced that the decision was right for the purpose of this edition. However, the Globe text (with its more scholarly original, the Cambridge text), published by W. G. Clark and W. Aldis Wright in 1864, is no longer modern, and I have not hesitated to follow current American usage in spelling, punctuation, and capitalization. Again with the student in mind, I have preferred to use a diacritical mark to denote the accented *ed,* and to abandon the earlier (and never consistent) practice of omitting *e* when silent; thus we prefer *determined* to *determin'd;* when the final syllable is accented, we print it *determinèd*. There is no one way to edit a classic; each reader prefers the text most suited to his needs. The text which gives most help will best suit the student who is studying Shakespeare as literature. When he becomes a scholar, nothing but the folio should satisfy him, but meanwhile to insist that he use a text prepared according to the current notions of bibliographers would be sheer pedantry.

The Notes are full, because I have tried consistently to explain words, phrases, customs, and objects which are not readily comprehensible to the normally alert student of today. I have also offered some guidance through the more obscure passages; and certain topics which needed larger annotation than was convenient for a footnote have been gathered into the Appendices. But I resisted (as far as was humanly possible) the temptation to theorize about Shakespeare or his plays; nor have I commented often on textual matters, or listed variant readings, which are a matter rather for the scholar than for the student.

As editor I echo the words of Dr. Johnson: " After the labours of all the editors, I found many passages which appeared to me likely to obstruct the greater number of readers, and thought it my duty to facilitate their passage. It is impossible for an expositor not to write too little for some, and too much for others. He can only judge what is necessary by his own experience; and how long soever he may deliberate, will at last explain many lines which the learned will think impossible to be mistaken, and omit many for which the ignorant will want his help. These are censures merely relative, and must be quietly endured. I have endeavoured to be neither superfluously copious, nor scrupulously reserved, and hope that I have made my authour's meaning accessible to many who before were frighted from perusing him, and contributed something to the publick, by diffusing innocent and rational pleasure." Yet Notes, no matter how full or how carefully compiled, are useless if they pass unnoticed. They are therefore placed at the bottom of each column of the text. Further, the symbol ° is used throughout to denote a word, phrase, or passage which is annotated. Text and Notes are thus linked, and the student need neither despair at searching for help which does not exist nor accept his own guess when an explanation is below.

Students often miss much because they are unfamiliar with the appearance of many things which were part of everyday life in Shakespeare's England. The Plates have therefore been chosen to illustrate the text rather than to beautify the volume. They are an essential part of the commentary, and should be used accordingly. Whenever reference is made to a Plate, the Note on that Plate (see pp. 91–99) should also be consulted.

The reader should observe that each cross reference is not merely to a certain page, but to a specific column on that page, the left column being denoted *a,* the right, *b.* Thus the search is considerably narrowed. The line numbering of the plays follows the Globe edition.

The General Introduction is intended to give the student a knowledge of the background to Shakespeare which he will find useful in studying individual plays. In the chapter "Shakespeare and the Critics," it seemed better to offer pertinent passages from a dozen of the most significant critics than to present a list of a hundred names and dates. In the Reading List I have included those works which are likely to stimulate or be useful to the college student; I have deliberately omitted many more erudite studies which are better suited to the scholar. Instructors who feel that I have unfairly neglected or omitted works which they themselves regard more highly will doubtless supply the omissions in their teaching.

My thanks are due to the many scholars who have given valuable advice, especially to Dr. Frank C. Baxter, Dr. W. E. Farnham, Mr. Anton A. Raven, the late Dr. G. G. Sedgewick, Dr. R. G. Shedd, the late Dr. Theodore Spencer, Dr. Harold R. Walley, and Dr. Virgil K. Whitaker. For help in gathering the illustrations I wish especially to express my gratitude to Dr. C. T. Currelly (formerly Director of the Royal Ontario Museum), and to Miss Elizabeth Maw, who made the drawings from which the line cuts were reproduced; to Dr. James G. McManaway and Dr. Giles E. Dawson; to Dr. J. C. Adams for generously allowing me to make use of the photograph of the model of the stage of the Globe playhouse; to Dr. Louis B. Wright, and to Dr. Herman R. Mead; and though last yet perhaps most to my friend Mr. M. R. Holmes, FSA, Assistant Keeper of the London Museum, for stimulating counsel at all times. Acknowledgment for individual illustrations is made in the Notes on the Plates (pp. 91–99). I want to thank The Macmillan Company for permission to use the quotation from Bradley's *Shakespearean Tragedy* printed on p. 83a–b. I would also like to thank the users of this book who have pointed out errors or misprints; these have been set right in the various successive reprintings. In this printing the Reading List has been revised and paperback editions have been noted.

October, 1958   G. B. H.
University of Michigan
Ann Arbor, Michigan

GENERAL INTRODUCTION
and the Plates

GENERAL INTRODUCTION

THE PLATES

1. The Universality of Shakespeare

It is a common belief that there is some mystery about the life of William Shakespeare and that scholars, for all their bibliographies and footnotes, really know nothing about him. When the scholars protest that they do know more about the facts of Shakespeare's life than about that of any other Elizabethan dramatist, they are met with the incredulous retort that the facts are commonplace; somehow the author of *Hamlet* must have towered above his fellows. Can they produce nothing more interesting than the plump, staring bust on the Stratford monument, or the disreputable legend that Shakespeare stole deer from Charlecot Park, or the fact that he left the second-best bed to his widow? It is well to face this problem clearly and objectively.

Literary persons, even the greatest, are seldom spectacular. The man who leads a life of heroic action has neither the time nor usually the desire, even if he has the ability, to express himself in writing. Those who gallop down valleys of death do not sing about that experience; they leave it to gentle poets living comfortably in country retreats. Moreover, to be a great writer a man must spend much of his time at a table in the laborious but wholly prosaic act of writing. Few writers attract a Boswell, and unless the details of their lives, their sayings, and their oddities happen to be preserved in writing, they soon become little more than a name. Even with all the elaborate apparatus of modern publicity, few readers could without notice write more of the biography of any living writer than could be contained on a postcard. The work is always so much greater than the man.

Nevertheless all great works of literary art reflect and reveal their authors. We need no biography to tell us that the personality and environment of Jane Austen differed from that of Charles Dickens, or that Alfred Tennyson's habits, thoughts, and desires were not the same as the habits, thoughts, and desires of Robert Burns. And as soon as we are aware of these facts, we can go further and distill something of the experiences, the personality, and the attitude toward life of an author. We must not, of course, attempt too much. We cannot expect to discover from a comparison of "Tam o' Shanter" with "The Passing of Arthur" whether Burns had a more tranquil private life than Tennyson; but by studying their works as a whole we can legitimately and with some accuracy deduce their differing likes and prejudices, their beliefs and negations, their views on life and conduct, on God, on man, and on woman. No man can write a good book or play without revealing something of himself to the expert reader, and of all forms of writing drama is often the most revealing, because it is talk and thought. For even though the words of each character must naturally be appropriate, the author wrote the words; the sentiments have first occurred in his mind.

For the past three hundred and fifty years Shakespeare has been regarded as the greatest writer in the English tongue, and since it is unusual for one generation to worship the gods of its fathers, it follows that he has been admired for very different reasons, and that his plays possess an enduring vitality. This quality in art we call universality. When we try to analyze the universality of Shakespeare, we find that he is not particularly original as a thinker, nor is he the only great English writer. Others, in various ways, have written poetry as memorable. But he is the most universal of all, because he is the wisest; that is, he can understand and sympathize more than other men. He can see the whole picture of humanity and re-create it so that men of every kind, country, creed, and generation understand. Knowing humanity as no one else ever did, he is nevertheless neither a mocking nor a weeping philosopher. He views life with zest, and he is so great that he can refrain from moral judgments.

Accordingly when we read Shakespeare's plays we are always meeting our own experiences and are constantly surprised by some phrase which expresses what we thought to be our own secret or our own discovery. It is for this reason that so often, consciously or unconsciously, we can find no words more apt than his to express ourselves in exultation or depression, in holiday mood, in love, or in the very pit of sorrow:

> Why should a dog, a horse, a rat have life
> And thou no breath at all? Thou'lt come no
>   more,
> Never, never, never, never, never!

Anyone who has suffered bereavement knows that experience, and has felt it almost in those words.

Shakespeare is thus continually reminding us of our own experiences and expressing them for us. Moreover, as we grow older and the range of our experience widens, so his range grows too. He is always giving us back our own, so that we understand his plays more and ourselves better. The reward of the study of literature is that we are constantly deepening our own experience and understanding, and of all English literature the study of Shakespeare is the most valuable. It gives us the power of detaching ourselves from ourselves and seeing our own lives as part of universal life, as players playing out our own seven acts on the universal stage, and at the same time enjoying the experience of the play as players on the stage and as critics in the audience.

Now it follows that a man who can touch so many in so large a range of emotional experience must himself have lived a full life. Shakespeare was born in April 1564 at Stratford-on-Avon, an important little town in the west of England, for it stood at the crossing of the river Avon. His father was a man of influence in the town, and in time held most of its chief offices. His mother was of gentle birth; her home still stands, a substantial house of people of means. At eighteen he married; at nineteen he was a father, at twenty the father of twins; and then for seven years there is a gap in the records until, in 1592, he writes a play —*I Henry VI*— which is the success of the season. Thereafter we can trace the outline of his life firmly. In 1593 he writes *Venus and Adonis,* which puts him at once into the first rank of English poets. By 1598 he is recognized as the finest writer of drama yet produced by the English. We can watch him too, in sober records of fact, as a senior partner in the Lord Chamberlain's Company of players, helping to finance the building of the Globe playhouse and later the Blackfriars, and then in middle age returning to Stratford

as a man of means, to retire. On April 23, 1616, he died, leaving a very full will and a comfortable estate. It is the record of a prosperous career.

To some romantic readers it may seem disappointing that a great dramatist should have been nothing more than a prosperous actor. Nevertheless there is some hope, even for the romantic. Shakespeare was nearly twenty-eight when he first attracted notice as a writer, and we do not know what he had been doing in the previous seven years. A man achieves most of his vigorous experiences between the ages of eighteen and twenty-eight, and Shakespeare lived in a world as stirring for a young man as our own world of the 1940's. When Shakespeare was twenty-three, Drake sailed into the Cádiz Harbor and burned a Spanish fleet. When he was twenty-four, the Spanish Armada came and went. When he was twenty-five, the English admirals led a great expedition into Portugal. When he was twenty-seven, an expeditionary force was helping the French King to subdue his rebellious subjects. It may be that Shakespeare did not spend all his time between twenty and twenty-eight holding horses outside the theater, or stealing deer in Charlecot Park, or teaching school in the country.

When we come to look closely into Shakespeare's plays, it is clear that he had an extraordinary knowledge of soldiers. Critics have not appreciated this in the past because one needs to have been a soldier to realize it. It is not only that Shakespeare can express the heroics of battle, as in Henry V's great speech before Harfleur:

> Once more into the breach, dear friends, once
>   more. . . .

Any poet who has a proper flow of words can write heroics. It is rather that he knows how soldiers think and how they behave, as in the little scene in *Henry V* when the King wanders in disguise amongst his soldiers and hears some home truths from the company lawyer. This intimate knowledge is seen again and again in some casual image — " like a rich armor, worn in heat of day, that scalds with safety." Anyone who has served in a tank in a tropical climate knows the significance of that line. Or it may be a chance question, as in *Coriolanus,* to a messenger in battle: " How could'st thou in a mile confound an hour? " The first thing that a young recruit learns about messages is that he must always ascertain the time of origin. This is not the kind of fact that the heroic poet even dreams of, yet somehow Shakespeare came by such a knowledge of soldiering.

As notable is his use of the imagery of the sea, which recurs constantly throughout his plays. There are certain remarkable set pieces, such as Clarence's dream in *Richard III* or the shipwreck in *The Tempest*. These are not necessarily very significant. Any writer who wishes to create such effects can find his material. Far more important as reflections of Shakespeare's mind are the casual images of the sea used sometimes to illustrate something quite different:

Will all great Neptune's ocean wash this blood
Clean from my hand? No, this my hand will
    rather
The multitudinous seas incarnadine,
Making the green one red.

                Behold the threaden sails,
Borne with the invisible and creeping wind,
Draw the huge bottoms through the furrowed
    sea. . . .

For do but stand upon the foaming shore,
The chidden billow seems to pelt the clouds,
The wind-shaked surge, with high and monstrous
    mane,
Seems to cast water on the burning Bear,
And quench the guards of the ever-fixèd
    Pole. . . .

If after every tempest come such calms,
May the winds blow till they have wakened
    death!
And let the laboring bark climb hills of seas
Olympus-high, and duck again as low
As Hell's from Heaven!

Surely Shakespeare's vision of the sea was something greater than can be picked up from an afternoon's cruise on a summer vacation.

Or take a longer passage. King Henry IV, restless and troubled, addresses Sleep:

Wilt thou upon the high and giddy mast
Seel up the ship boy's eyes, and rock his brains
In cradle of the rude imperious surge
And in the visitation of the winds,
Who take the ruffian billows by the top,
Curling their monstrous heads and hanging them
With deafening clamor in the slippery clouds,
That with the hurly, death itself awakes?

Canst thou, O partial Sleep, give thy repose
To the wet sea boy in an hour so rude,
And in the calmest and most stillest night,
With all appliances and means to boot,
Deny it to a king?

How did Shakespeare come by the incident of the ship boy sleeping in the crow's-nest during the storm? It can only have been in one of three ways. He read of it, or he heard of it, or he saw it.

These images of the sea — and there are about two hundred of them — prove nothing; but they show that Shakespeare was sensitive and receptive to anything that had to do with the sea. A man does not use the sea to illustrate his thoughts unless such images are familiar and spontaneous to him, unless the sea has been an experience. Shakespeare is not the kind of author who is forever reshuffling in his own work phrases or ideas collected in reading. Pope was such a collector, as was Milton, and their work can be annotated accordingly.

So in our analysis of Shakespeare's poetry we can say that there are traces of a considerable knowledge of soldiers and of the sea. Until some lucky researcher finds Shakespeare's name in the records of a campaign or a voyage, we can go no further; but it follows that either he was — as George Bernard Shaw has drawn him in *The Dark Lady of the Sonnets* — a man with a notebook, jotting down everything he heard, or else he saw many more things with his own eyes than his biographers have hitherto recorded.

All this, however, is speculation. We are more firmly set when we try to recover Shakespeare's fundamental beliefs, his attitudes toward life. He had little use for those high-sounding proverbs of conduct or consolation which drip so readily from the lips of the professionally respectable, and he put into the mouth of Polonius a wonderful collection of such pearls of wisdom, which are often admiringly quoted by those ignorant of their context and of their irony.

Shakespeare himself had no rigid system of rules, of religion, of conduct, or of morality. He had no particular theories of any kind, but certain very marked instincts. While he never codified his thoughts into rules of right and wrong, he has certainly left us his prejudices and fundamental instincts, as shown, for instance, in his views on love and marriage.

Here he is normally sane, conventional almost, in his instincts, differing thereby from the smart dramatists of his own day, or of the Restoration, or of modern Broadway. He regards marriage as the natural end and fulfillment of love between man and woman. Love outside marriage is disastrous. None of the lovers whom Shakespeare likes — and surely we can see who they are — falls in love without the most honorable intentions. Even in *Romeo and Juliet,* his one great story of youth overwhelmed by elemental, irresistible, passionate love, hero and heroine marry before they mate. Shakespeare goes to great trouble to make the story entirely respectable. The disaster which comes to them is not their fault or of their making. It comes because of the stupidity of their parents; and in Shakespeare's plays most parents, especially fathers of daughters, are incredibly stupid. His other favorite lovers, Rosalind and Orlando, Benedick and Beatrice, march naturally forward to love in wedlock. And in his later plays — *The Winter's Tale* and *The Tempest* — Florizel and Perdita, Ferdinand and Miranda, pairs of lovers whom Shakespeare abundantly blesses, have the nicest regard for the sanctity of marriage.

In this attitude Shakespeare differs noticeably from his contemporaries. Beaumont and Fletcher and others play with themes of love outside marriage, and regard infidelity as a natural topic for comedy. Shakespeare does not. He has plenty of jokes about cuckold's horns, as have all Elizabethan dramatists, but he sees nothing comic in unfaithfulness or unchastity, which always bring disaster. In *Measure for Measure* all the troubles which descend so freely on the chief persons are first caused by Claudio's unchastity. Angelo, having wronged Mariana, is made to offer her the only possible restitution in marriage. In *Troilus and Cressida,* the fickle Cressida is presented not as amusing or even particularly attractive, but as essentially rotten to all decent men.

Infidelity brings disaster. Even a suspicion of infidelity brings disaster on Hero, Desdemona, Imogen, and Hermione. Shakespeare apparently condones the behavior of the wronged lovers; yet he has at the same time a horror of suspicion. He thus instinctively accepts normal morality not because it accords with any rigid code or sanction, but because his instinct tells him that moral customs are founded on that system of conduct which has been found to work best.

As for his religion, all sects of Christianity have claimed him, Roman Catholics, Anglicans, even Puritans. There is a fairly early tradition that he died a Catholic, and there is some evidence that his parents were Catholics, even if secretly. Shakespeare's sympathies in his plays are usually with the older faith. He toned down the Protestant exuberance in the old play of *King John,* which he rewrote. The few friars in his plays are sympathetically treated. They are grave, wise, patient men, such as Friar Laurence in *Romeo and Juliet* or Friar Francis in *Much Ado about Nothing* or the priest in *Twelfth Night.* Shakespeare's parsons are few. Parson Evans in *The Merry Wives of Windsor* is amusing, and so is Sir Nathaniel, the curate in *Love's Labor's Lost;* but neither is a spiritual character. The parson in *As You Like It* is definitely a scamp. But all these are characters in plays. They speak their parts, and perhaps no more.

Shakespeare's own religion is neither Catholic, Anglican, nor Puritan. He belongs to no sect. His characters from time to time utter the phrases of conventional piety, but he has little conception of God as a loving Father, nor does he regard Him as a revenging Jehovah. At its most optimistic his faith is that:

> There's a divinity that shapes our ends,
> Roughhew them how we will.

At its most pessimistic:

> As flies to wanton boys are we to the gods,
> They kill us for their sport.

His general belief seems to have been halfway between the extremes:

> There's special providence in the fall of a sparrow.
> If it be now, 'tis not to come; if it be not to come,
> it will be now; if it be not now, yet it will come.
> The readiness is all. Since no man has aught of
> what he leaves, what is't to leave betimes?

Like Tennyson, he faintly trusts the larger hope.

His religion may be summed up as fulfillment. He seems not to have been greatly interested in the insoluble problems. He has none of Faustus's curiosity in the ultimate incomprehensibles, but he has an insatiable zest for all varieties of men and women. The universe is man's stage, but man holds the center, and it is a sign that Hamlet has lost his balance in the depths of despair when he finds that he can no longer appreciate humanity:

What a piece of work is a man! How noble in reason! How infinite in faculty! In form and moving how express and admirable! In action how like an angel! In apprehension how like a god! The beauty of the world! The paragon of animals! And yet, to me, what is this quintessence of dust? Man delights not me — no, nor woman neither.

Shakespeare had very little hope, or indeed interest, in any glorious or unending immortality. His one ghost who comes back to report on conditions hereafter gives a very gloomy picture of the next world. To Hamlet, death is a consummation devoutly to be wished so long as it means "to die, to sleep — no more." His fear is lest the sleep of death may be disturbed by those terrible dreams which make Claudio frantic when confronted by death. With Edgar in *Lear,* in dejection, the conclusion is that:

> Men must endure
> Their going hence, even as their coming hither.
> Ripeness is all.

Nevertheless, Shakespeare does not brood, as Donne or Marston or Webster brooded, on the horrors of physical death. He made his contributions to the literature of the charnel house in *Hamlet,* as might be expected, but even here in the gravedigging scene he is always sane. Hamlet in some of his moods is hypersensitive:

To what base uses we may return, Horatio. Why may not imagination trace the noble dust of Alexander, till he find it stopping a bunghole?

But Horatio's reply is:

'Twere to consider too curiously, to consider so,

and this seems also to have been Shakespeare's comment on all unprofitable speculations.

In *The Tempest* Shakespeare, if ever, speaks directly and deliberately out of part through Prospero. He sees the universe ultimately dissolving, to leave not a rack behind:

> We are such stuff
> As dreams are made on, and our little life
> Is rounded with a sleep.

Life is a flicker of consciousness between two eternities of oblivion. The thought is not original; the expression is superbly his own.

As for Shakespeare's social beliefs and political instincts, they are from time to time clearly revealed. Certain instincts lie deep in the Englishman's character; one is a horror of civil disorder. The long Wars of the Roses were brought to an end on Bosworth Field (1485) when Henry Tudor established himself as undisputed King. In the days of his grandchildren, King Edward VI and Queen Mary, it seemed for a while that anarchy would return, but thereafter for some forty years peace at home had been symbolized in the person of Queen Elizabeth. Most sane men hoped that this state would continue and most feared that it would not. It is not, therefore, surprising that Shakespeare believed in the divinity of kings. Nevertheless, he saw that kings, if officially divine, were also in fact human — and seldom admirable; but yet they had a terrible responsibility and loneliness. Shakespeare was one of the very few Englishmen who saw that behind the pomp lay the intolerable burden:

> Upon the King! Let us our lives, our souls,
> Our debts, our careful wives,
> Our children, and our sins lay on the King!
> We must bear all. Oh, hard condition,
> Twin-born with greatness, subject to the breath
> Of every fool, whose sense no more can feel
> But his own wringing!

To Shakespeare, as to many of his contemporaries, the universe was an ordered system, a chain or pyramid (see App. 1). At the apex was God; on earth the Sovereign was God's own immediate deputy; and below, ranged in degrees and orders down to the least, came lesser men. This fundamental belief he expressed in one of his finest philosophical utterances, Ulysses' great speech on degree or natural order in *Troilus and Cressida.* Everything, says Ulysses, from the planets and the sun and downward, observes degree. Once degree is broken, chaos follows. When Shakespeare wrote this speech, men's minds were troubled by threats at home of some vast revolution that was likely at any time to break down natural order. He wrote for the understanding of his contemporaries. Yet this speech is a fine instance of Shakespeare's universality; it means even more to our generation when degree and natural order and decency are still in the balance:

Take but degree away, untune that string,
And hark what discord follows! Each thing meets
In mere oppugnancy. The bounded waters
Should lift their bosoms higher than the shores,
And make a sop of all this solid globe.
Strength should be lord of imbecility,
And the rude son should strike his father dead.
Force should be right, or rather, right and wrong,
Between whose endless jar justice resides,
Should lose their names, and so should justice too.
Then everything includes itself in power,
Power into will, will into appetite,
And appetite, a universal wolf,
So doubly seconded with will and power,
Must make perforce a universal prey,
And last eat up himself.

When a man has so clearly indicated his political, religious, and social instincts, we can surely say we know something about him; and with a little patience in reading his plays we can discover for ourselves much more of the personality of the man Shakespeare. We may not always agree with what we find, as so often we disagree in our estimates of living acquaintances, but "the purpose of playing" — and of all creative literary art — " at the first and now was and is to hold as 'twere the mirror up to Nature," and it is the function of a mirror to give us back our own reflections. We look into Shakespeare's plays and find ourselves; it is for this reason that he is of all writers the most universal.

2. Records of the Life of Shakespeare

Apart from the legends, inferences, interpretations, and deductions of scholars and critics, the actual facts of Shakespeare's life, duly authenticated in indisputable records, are considerable. A student of Shakespeare should know where fact ends and guessing begins. In this chapter, facts only are given. The more important records, most of which mention Shakespeare by name, are as follows:[1]

1564. APRIL 26. The parish register of the Stratford-on-Avon church records the baptism of "Gulielmus filius Johannes Shakspere" — William son of John Shakspere.

There is no record of the date of birth, though Shakespeare's birthday is celebrated at Stratford-on-Avon and elsewhere on April 23, principally because this happens also to be the day of Saint George, the patron saint of England.

John Shakespeare had come to Stratford in the 1550's. He is variously described in records as yeoman (that is, a landowner), glover, and whitawer (one who cured glove skins). He had married Mary Arden, whose family were Roman

Catholic gentlefolk living at Wilmcote near Stratford. John Shakespeare became a leading citizen of Stratford. In 1564 he was chosen alderman, and in 1568 bailiff — the highest civic office in the town, the modern mayor. After 1577 the records show that he was disposing of his property and had ceased to attend meetings of the corporation. In 1587 another was chosen alderman in his place. In 1592 his name appeared in the list of those in Stratford who absented themselves from church, and it was noted that he and others "came not to church for fear of process for debt."

1582. NOVEMBER 28. A license was issued by the Bishop of Worcester to " William Shagspere " and " Anne Hathwey of Stratford " to solemnize matrimony upon once asking of the banns, provided that there was no legal objection.

The law required that the banns of marriage should be read out in church for three successive Sundays before the marriage. This was to enable anyone to show cause (such as precontract) why the marriage could not lawfully take place. When for any reason the parties wished to hasten the marriage, a special license from the bishop was required.

According to the inscription on the grave of Anne Shakespeare, she died on August 6, 1623, aged sixty-seven years. She was therefore born in 1556, and was thus eight years older than her husband.

1583. MAY 26. The parish register of the Strat-

---

[1] The spellings in records noted within quotes are original. There is no significance in the different spellings of Shakespeare's name; his contemporaries were very free in such matters. Indeed, I have encountered a case where a Lord Lieutenant of a county signed his own name in three different spellings on the same day in one set of documents. Marlowe's name appears in different documents as Marlo, Marle, Marley, Marlin, Merling, Marling, Morley. In Shakespeare's will, the scribe spelt the name "Shackspeare" on the first sheet and "Shackspere" on the third. Shakespeare himself signed the three sheets: on the first he wrote "William Shakspere," on the second "Willm Shakspere," on the third "By me William Shakspeare."

ford-on-Avon church records the baptism of Susanna, daughter to William Shakespeare.

1585. FEBRUARY 2. The parish register of the Stratford-on-Avon church records the baptism of " Hamnet & Judeth, sonne and daughter to William Shakspere."

1588. MICHAELMAS. John and Mary Shakespeare claiming to some property formerly mortgaged to Edmund Barton, Mary Shakespeare's brother-in-law, joined their son William as a party in the suit.

1592. MARCH 3. Henslowe [2] records that he received £3 16s. 8d. at the first performance of *Harry the Sixth.* The play was repeated on March 7, 11, 16, 28, April 5, 13, 21, May 4, 9, 16, 22, 29, June 12 and 20. For the fifteen performances the gross takings were £32 8s. 6d. or an average of £2 3s. 3d. a performance. The average for all others plays over the period of three and three-quarter months was £1 14s. 10d.

It seems likely that this is Shakespeare's *I Henry VI.* Nashe in *Piers Penniless His Supplication to the Devil,* entered for publication (see p. 66a) on August 8, 1592, commented:

How would it have ioyed braue *Talbot* (the terror of the French) to thinke that after he had lyne two hundred yeares in his Tombe, hee should triumphe againe on the Stage, and haue his bones newe embalmed with the teares of ten thousand spectators at least (at seuerall times) who, in the Tragedian that represents his person, imagine they behold him fresh bleeding?

SEPTEMBER 3. Robert Greene, the pamphleteer, poet, and playwright, died in poverty (see p. 39a). Among his papers was a letter addressed " To those Gentlemen his quondam acquaintance, that spend their wits in making plaies," who are usually identified with Marlowe, Nashe, and Lodge. Greene's complaint was that the professional players had battened on the brains of university men like himself, and now they had forsaken him. He continued:

Base minded men all three of you, if by my miserie you be not warnd: for vnto none of you (like mee) sought those burres to cleaue: those Puppets (I meane) that spake from our mouths, those Anticks garnisht in our colours. Is it not strange, that I, to whom they all haue beene beholding: is it not like that you, to whome they all haue beene beholding, shall (were yee in that case as I am now) bee both at once of them forsaken? Yes trust them not:

for there is an vpstart Crow, beautified with our feathers, that with his *Tygers hart wrapt in a Players hyde,* supposes he is as well able to bombast out a blanke verse as the best of you: and beeing an absolute *Iohannes fac totum,* is in his owne conceit the onely Shake-scene in a countrey. O that I might intreat your rare wits to be imploied in more profitable courses: & let those Apes imitate your past excellence, and neuer more acquaint them with your admired inuentions.

The phrase " Tygers hart wrapt in a Players hyde" is a parody of a line in *III Henry VI* — "O tiger's heart wrapped in a woman's hide!" — and Greene's passage is a bitter attack on Shakespeare. The letter was printed in Greene's *Groatsworth of Wit,* a short collection consisting of an unfinished novel and other scraps, and put together for the press by Henry Chettle. It was entered on September 20, 1592. Marlowe had been pointedly referred to in the letter as an atheist and warned to repent in time; he and Shakespeare apparently protested. On December 8, 1592, Chettle's *Kind Heart's Dream* was entered. To this book Chettle added a prefatory epistle in which he wrote:

With neither of them that take offence was I acquainted, and with one of them I care not if I neuer be: The other, whome at that time I did not so much spare, as since I wish I had, for that as I haue moderated the heate of liuing writers, and might have vsed my owne discretion (especially in such a case) the Author beeing dead, that I did not, I am as sorry as if the originall fault had beene my fault, because my selfe haue seene his demeanor no lesse ciuill than he exelent in the qualitie he professes: Besides, diuers of worship haue reported his uprightnes of dealing, which argues his honesty, and his facetious grace in writing that aproues his Art.

From these records it seems likely that the Talbot scenes in *I Henry VI* were among the first that Shakespeare wrote. Further, if Shakespeare had been writing plays for some years, Greene could have hardly referred to him as an " upstart," nor could Chettle, in the very small world of the London theater, have pleaded that he had not previously known of him. Shakespeare therefore probably first began to write plays in 1591 or 1592; but some scholars dispute this and claim that he had been actor and playwright since 1587.

1593. APRIL 18. *Venus and Adonis* was entered

for publication and was printed with the title page:

VENUS AND ADONIS

Vilia miretur vulgus: mihi flauus Apollo
Pocula Castalia plena ministret aqua.[3]

The poem was dedicated

To the Right Honourable Henrie Wriothesley,[4] Earle of Southampton, and Baron of Titchfield.

Right Honourable, I know not how I shall offend in dedicating my vnpolisht lines to your Lordship, nor how the worlde will censure mee for choosing so strong a proppe to support so weake a burthen, onelye if your Honour seeme but pleased, I account my selfe highly praised, and vowe to take aduantage of all idle houres, till I haue honoured you with some grauer labour. But if the first heire of my inuention proue deformed, I shall be sorie it had so noble a god-father: and neuer after eare so barren a land, for feare it yeeld me still so bad a haruest. I leave it to your Honourable suruey, and your Honor to your hearts content, which I wish may alwaies answere your owne wish, and the worlds hopefull expectation.

Your Honors in all dutie,
WILLIAM SHAKESPEARE.

The Earl of Southampton was at this time nineteen years old. He was regarded as a young man of considerable promise and was conspicuous among the Queen's courtiers for his beauty and intelligence.

Venus and Adonis, though regarded by the sober-minded as an improper poem, established Shakespeare's reputation as a poet. It was reprinted at least nine times during his lifetime.

1594. MAY 9. *The Rape of Lucrece* was entered for printing. This poem too was dedicated

To the Right Honourable, Henry Wriothesley, Earle of Southampton, and Baron of Titchfield.

The loue I dedicate to your Lordship is without end: wherof this Pamphlet without beginning is but a superfluous Moity. The warrant I haue of your Honourable disposition, not the worth of my vntutord Lines makes it assured of acceptance. What I haue done is yours, what I haue to doe is yours, being part in all I haue, devoted yours. Were my worth greater, my duety would shew greater, meane time, as it is, it is bound to your

Lordship; To whom I wish long life still lengthened with all happinesse.

Your Lordships in all duety.
WILLIAM SHAKESPEARE

From the tone of the dedication it may be inferred that Southampton had shown considerable favor to Shakespeare during the previous twelve months.

1594. DECEMBER 26 AND 27. Payment for performances at Court was made to "William Kempe, William Shakespeare, & Richarde Burbage, seruantes to the Lord Chamberleyne." This is the first record which definitely names Shakespeare as a member of the company. Subsequent payments for Court performances were made to John Heminges, who seems to have acted as treasurer for the company.

1596. AUGUST 11. The parish register of the Stratford-on-Avon church records the burial of "Hamnet filius William Shakspere."

OCTOBER 20. William Dethick, Garter Principal King of Arms, granted to John Shakespeare the privilege of bearing a coat of arms, viz.:

Gould, on a Bend Sables, a Speare of the first steeled argent. And for his creast or cognizaunce a falcon his winges displayed Argent standing on a wrethe of his coullers: supporting a Speare Gould steeled as aforesaid sett vppon a helmett with mantelles & tasselles as hath ben accustomed and doth more playnely appeare depicted on this margent: Signefieing hereby & by the authorite of my office aforesaid ratefieing that it shalbe lawfull for the said John Shakespeare gentilman and for his children yssue & posterite (at all tymes & places convenient) to beare and make demonstracon of the same Blazon or Atchevment vppon theyre Shieldes, Targetes, escucheons, Cotes of Arms, pennons, Guydons, Seales, Ringes, edefices, Buyldinges, vtensiles, Lyveries, Tombes, or monumentes or otherwise for all lawfull warlyke factes or ciuile vse or exercises, according to the Lawes of Armes, and customes that to gentillmen belongethe without let or interruption of any other person or persons for vse or bearing the same.

Thus William Shakespeare in the right of his father was henceforward entitled to call himself "gentleman."

1596. NOVEMBER 29. In the Controlment Rolls of the Queen's Bench in the Public Record Office in London occurs an entry that William Wayte craved sureties of the peace against William Shakespeare, Francis Langley, Dorothy

---

[3] The crowd admires vile things; for me may yellow-haired Apollo prepare cups full of Castalian water (i.e., from the Muses' spring on Mount Parnassus). [4] Pronounced and occasionally spelled "Risley."

Soer, wife of John Soer, and Anne Lee for fear of death and so forth. A writ of attachment was issued to the Sheriff of Surrey, returnable on November 29.

This entry was discovered by Dr. Leslie Hotson and published in his *Shakespeare versus Shallow* (1931). Of the persons mentioned, Langley was owner of the Swan playhouse, which he had built about two years earlier. Wayte was the stepson of a rascally magistrate named William Gardener. Langley himself had claimed sureties of the peace against Gardener and Wayte less than a month earlier. Dr. Hotson discovered many details about Wayte and Gardener, but was unable to find how Shakespeare came into the business or how he had caused anyone to be in fear of his life.

1597. MAY 4. William Shakespeare purchased from William Underhill a house with two barns and two gardens in Stratford-on-Avon for £60 sterling.

This property, known as New Place, was a large house in the center of Stratford. It was then about a hundred years old, built of brick and timber, and of fair size, with a frontage of sixty feet and a depth of seventy feet. Only the foundations now remain.

AUGUST 29. Andrew Wise entered *Richard II* for publication. It appeared soon afterward with the title *The Tragedie of King Richard the second. As it hath beene publikely acted by the right Honourable the Lorde Chamberlaine his Seruants.* No author's name was given in the 1597 edition, but the play was twice reprinted in 1598 with the addition of *By William Shake-speare.*

OCTOBER 20. Andrew Wise entered for publication " The tragedie of kinge Richard the Third with the death of the Duke of Clarence," which appeared with the title *The Tragedy of King Richard the Third. Containing, His treacherous Plots against his brother Clarence: the pittiefull murther of his innocent nephewes: his tyrannicall usurpation: with the whole course of his detested life, and most deserued death. As it hath been lately acted by the Right honourable the Lord Chamberlaine his seruants* (see Pl. 14a). No author's name was given in the 1597 edition, but in a second edition dated 1598 is added *By William Shake-speare.*

NOVEMBER 15. The commissioners appointed to collect the subsidy in the ward of Bishopsgate, London, sent in a list of those who had failed to pay their contribution to the subsidy. Included in the names was " William Shackspere," assessed to pay 5*s.* on £5. Shakespeare's name reappeared in several later lists, but the tax was apparently paid in 1600. These records show that before 1596 Shakespeare had lived in the parish of St. Helen's, near Bishopsgate, but afterward went to live on the south side of the Thames.

1598. FEBRUARY 4. Owing to a general shortage of corn due to bad summers, there was considerable hoarding of corn. A survey was made of the corn and malt held by individuals in Stratford-on-Avon. Among them it was found that " Wm. Shackespere " held ten quarters.[5]

FEBRUARY 25. Andrew Wise entered for publication " The historye of Henry the iiij^th with his battaile of Shrewsburye against Henry Hotspurre of the Northe with the conceipted mirthe of Sir John Ffalstoff," which was published under the title *The History of Henrie the Fourth; With the battell at Shrewsburie, betweene the King and Lord Henry Percy, surnamed Henrie Hotspur of the North. With the humorous conceits of Sir Iohn Falstaffe.* No author's name was given in the edition of 1598, but in the second edition printed in 1599 the words *Newly corrected by W. Shake-speare* were added.

JULY 22. James Roberts entered in the Stationers' Register " a booke of the Marchaunt of Venyce, or otherwise called the Jewe of Venyce, Prouided, that yt bee not prynted by the said James Robertes or anye other whatsoeuer without lycence first had from the Right honorable the lord Chamberlen." This is an example of a " blocking entry " (see p. 66a) whereby the players arranged with Roberts to enter a play to avoid its publication.

SEPTEMBER 7. *Palladis Tamia: Wit's Treasury* by Francis Meres was entered for publication. This book was a large collection of " similitudes " or parallel passages from a vast number of authors. Meres added " A comparatiue discourse of our English Poets with the *Greeke, Latine, and Italian Poets.*" Shakespeare was mentioned more frequently than any of the other English writers, as one of eight by whom " the English tongue is mightily enriched, and gorgeouslie inuested in rare ornaments and resplendent abiliments," as one of six who had raised *monumentum aere perennius,* as one of

---

[5] 1 quarter = 8 bushels. "Corn" here means wheat, rye, and oats.

five who excelled in lyric poetry, as one of thirteen "best for Tragedie," as one of seventeen "best for Comedy." Shakespeare was also picked out for special mention not given to the others:

As the soule of *Euphorbus* was thought to liue in *Pythagoras:* so the sweete wittie soule of *Ouid* liues in mellifluous & hony-tongued *Shakespeare,* witnes his *Venus* and *Adonis;* his *Lucrece,* his sugred *Sonnets* among his priuate friends, &c.

As *Plautus* and *Seneca* are accounted the best for Comedy and Tragedy among the Latines: so *Shakespeare* among the English is the most excellent in both kinds for the stage; for Comedy, witnes his *Gentlemen of Verona,* his *Errors,* his *Loue Labors lost,* his *Loue labours wonne,* his *Midsummers night dreame,* & his *Merchant of Venice:* for Tragedy his *Richard the 2. Richard the 3. Henry the 4. King Iohn, Titus Andronicus* and his *Romeo* and *Iuliet.*

As *Epius Stolo* said, that the Muses would speake with *Plautus* tongue, if they would speak Latin: so I say that the Muses would speak with *Shakespeares* fine filed phrase, if they would speake English.

Meres's remarks are important; they show that by 1598 — even before the greatest tragedies were produced — Shakespeare had already firmly established his reputation; and they give a list of twelve plays already written — a valuable piece of evidence for establishing the dates of some of Shakespeare's plays. *Love's Labor's Won* has apparently been lost, unless it is an earlier title of one of the comedies.

SEPTEMBER 20. The Chamberlain's Men acted Ben Jonson's *Every Man in His Humor.* In the 1616 collection of his plays Jonson added the note:

This Comoedie was first Acted, in the yeere 1598. By the then L. Chamberlayne his Seruants. The principall Comoedians were.

Will. Shakespeare.	Ric. Burbadge.
Aug. Philips.	Ioh. Hemings.
Hen. Condel.	Tho. Pope.
Will. Slye.	Chr. Beeston.
Will. Kempe.	Ioh. Duke.

OCTOBER 25. Richard Quiney, a citizen of Stratford, being in London on business, partly private and partly on behalf of the corporation, wrote a letter from the Bell in Carter Lane asking for a loan of £30, addressed "To my Loveinge good ffrend & countreymann Mr. W^m. Shackespere." As the sum of £30 in cash was considerable at this time, the letter shows that Shakespeare was a man of some means.

During this year was printed, but without entry in the Stationers' Register, *A Pleasant Conceited Comedie Called, Loues labors lost. As it was presented before her Highnes this last Christmas. Newly corrected and augmented by W. Shakespere.*

1599. FEBRUARY 21. Documents in a lawsuit dated April 28, 1619, show that a lease of the ground on which the Globe playhouse was being built was agreed between Nicholas Brend on the one part, and on the other Cuthbert Burbadge, Richard Burbadge, William Shakespeare, Augustine Phillipps, Thomas Pope, John Heminges, and William Kempe. The details of the shares of the takings in the playhouse to be received by each are also recorded.

During this year appeared *The Passionate Pilgrime By W. Shakespeare.* The book was published by W. Jaggard and contains twenty poems, two of which are sonnets by Shakespeare and three poems from *Love's Labor's Lost.* The rest of the poems are by different writers. It was an indication of Shakespeare's reputation that a printer should pass off such a volume as entirely his.

1600. AUGUST 23. Andrew Wise and William Aspley entered for publication "Muche a Doo about nothinge" and "the second parte of the history of Kinge Henry the IIIJth with the humours of Sir John Falstaff: Wrytten by master Shakespere." This was the first time that Shakespeare's name was entered in the Stationers' Register. The plays appeared with the titles: *Much Adoe about Nothing. As it hath been sundrie times publikely acted by the right honourable, the Lord Chamberlaine his seruants. Written by William Shakespeare;* and *The Second part of Henrie the fourth, continuing to his death, and coronation of Henrie the fift. With the humours of sir John Falstaffe, and swaggering Pistoll. As it hath been sundrie times publikely acted by the right honourable, the Lord Chamberlaine, his seruants. Written by William Shakespeare.*

OCTOBER 8. Thomas Fisher entered for publication "A booke called A mydsommer nightes Dreame." The play appeared with the title: *A Midsommer nights dreame. As it hath beene sundry times publickely acted, by the Right honourable, the Lord Chamberlaine his seruants. Written by William Shakespeare.*

OCTOBER 28. Thomas Hays by consent of James

Roberts entered "a booke called the booke of the merchant of Venyce." The play appeared with the title: *The most excellent Historie of the Merchant of Venice. With the extreame crueltie of Shylocke the Iewe towards the sayd Merchant, in cutting a iust pound of his flesh: and the obtayning of Portia by the choyse of three chests. As it hath beene diuers times acted by the Lord Chamberlaine his Seruants. Written by William Shakespeare* (see Pl. 14b).

1601. SEPTEMBER 8. The parish register of the Stratford-on-Avon church records the burial of " Mr. Johannes Shaksper." This was Shakespeare's father.

1602. JANUARY 18. John Busby entered, but immediately assigned to Arthur Johnson, " A booke called An excellent and pleasant conceited commedie of Sir John Faulstof and the merry wyves of Windesor." The quarto which followed is entitled: *A Most pleasaunt and excellent conceited Comedie, of Syr Iohn Falstaffe, and the merrie Wiues of Windsor, Entermixed with sundrie variable and pleasing humors, of Syr Hugh the Welch Knight, Iustice Shallow, and his wise Cousin M. Slender. With the swaggering vaine of Auncient Pistoll, and Corporall Nym. By William Shakespeare. As it hath bene diuers times Acted by the right Honorable my Lord Chamberlaines seruants. Both before her Maiestie, and else-where.*

The text of the play printed in this edition is a garbled and pirated version, very different from the play as known in the first folio.

MAY 1. William Combe and John Combe of Stratford-on-Avon sold to " William Shakespere " one hundred and seven acres of arable land in old Stratford for the sum of £320. The deed was delivered to Gilbert Shakespeare " to the use of the within named William Shakespere." Gilbert was Shakespeare's younger brother, and Shakespeare himself seems to have been in Stratford-on-Avon at the time.

JULY 26. James Roberts entered in the Stationers' Register " A booke called the Revenge of Hamlett Prince Denmarke as yt was latelie Acted by the Lord Chamberleyne his servantes." No edition of 1602 is known. This was apparently another " blocking entry " (see p. 66a).

SEPTEMBER 28. Walter Getley transferred a cottage in Walkers Street (alias Dead Lane) in Stratford-on-Avon to " William Shackespere."

1603. MAY 19. Queen Elizabeth died on March 24. The new King, James I, took over the Lord Chamberlain's players as the King's Men. A license was accordingly issued to " our Servauntes Lawrence Fletcher, William Shakespeare, Richard Burbage, Augustyne Phillippes, Iohn Heninges, Henrie Condell, William Sly, Robert Armyn, Richard Cowly, and the rest of theire Assosiates freely to vse and exercise the Arte and faculty of playing Comedies, Tragedies, histories, Enterludes, moralls, pastoralls, Stageplaies and Suche others like as theie haue alreadie studied or hereafter shall vse or studie aswell for the recreation of our lovinge Subjectes as for our Solace and pleasure when wee shall thincke good to see them duringe our pleasure."

During this year was acted Jonson's *Sejanus*. In the collected edition of 1616, Jonson stated that the principal tragedians were:

Ric. Burbadge.	Will. Shake-Speare.
Aug. Philips.	Ioh. Hemings.
Will. Sly.	Hen. Condel.
Ioh. Lowin.	Alex. Cooke.

During this year was printed a garbled and pirated version of *Hamlet* entitled: *The Tragicall Historie of Hamlet Prince of Denmarke By William Shake-speare. As it hath beene diuerse times acted by his Highnesse seruants in the Cittie of London: as also in the two Vniuersities of Cambridge and Oxford, and else-where.*

1604. MARCH. King James made a royal progress through the City of London, with his various servants in attendance. The players being Grooms of the Chamber, four yards of red cloth for liveries was given to " William Shakespeare, Augustine Phillips, Lawrence Fletcher, John Hemminges, Richard Burbidge, William Slye, Robert Armyn, Henry Cundell, and Richard Cowley."

During this year was printed a second version of *Hamlet* entitled: *The Tragicall Historie of Hamlet, Prince of Denmarke. By William Shakespeare. Newly imprinted and enlarged to almost as much againe as it was, according to the true and perfect Coppie* (see Pl. 14d). As copies of this version are dated 1604 and 1605, it was probably issued late in 1604.

1605. MAY 4. Augustine Phillips, one of the King's Men, made his will and died shortly afterward, leaving " to my Fellowe William Shakespeare a thirty shillings peece in gould."

To other members of the company he also left money, thirty shillings to Henry Condell and Christopher Beeston, and twenty shillings each to Lawrence Fletcher, Robert Armin, Richard Cowley, Alexander Cook, and Nicholas Tooley.

JULY 24. Ralph Huband, in consideration of the sum of £440, assigned to "William Shakespear" a half of all the tithes of Stratford, Old Stratford, Welcombe, and Bushopton, and half the tithes of the parish of "Stratford-upon-Avon." This investment yielded Shakespeare about £60 a year.

1607. JUNE 5. The parish register of the Stratford-on-Avon church records the marriage of "M. John Hall gentleman & Susanna Shaxspere." Susanna was Shakespeare's elder daughter, born in 1583. John Hall was a doctor of medicine well known in the neighborhood.

NOVEMBER 26. Nathaniel Butter and John Busby entered in the Stationers' Register a book called "Master William Shakespeare his historye of Kinge Lear, as yt was played before the Kinges maiestie at Whitehall, vppon Sainct Stephens night at Christmas Last [that is, December 26, 1606] by his maiesties servantes playinge vsually at the Globe on the Banksyde." A quarto was published in 1608.

1608. FEBRUARY 21. The parish register of the Stratford-on-Avon church records the christening of "Elizabeth dawghter to John Hall gentleman." This was Shakespeare's first grandchild.

AUGUST 9. William Ostler, gentleman, of London agreed to rent the Blackfriars playhouse to Richard Burbage, John Hemings, William Shakespeare, Cuthbert Burbage, Henry Condell, and Thomas Evans for a period of twenty-one years.

SEPTEMBER 9. The parish register of the Stratford-on-Avon church records the burial of "Mayry Shaxspere, wydowe." This was Shakespeare's mother.

DECEMBER 17. "William Shackspeare," gentleman, began to take proceedings in the Stratford court against John Addenbrooke, gentleman, to recover a debt of £6. The case went on for some months.

1609. JANUARY 28. Richard Bonion and Henry Walleys entered for publication "a booke called the history of Troylus and Cressida," which appeared under the title: *The Historie of Troylus*

and Cresseida. As it was acted by the Kings Maiesties seruants at the Globe. Written by William Shakespeare.

A second issue appeared in the same year with the title: *The Famous Historie of Troylus and Cresseid. Excellently expressing the beginning of their loues, with the conceited wooing of Pandarus Prince of Licia. Written by William Shakespeare.*

MAY 20. Thomas Thorpe entered for publication "a Booke called Shakespeares sonnettes," which appeared under the title "*Shakes-speares Sonnets. Neuer before Imprinted.*

During the year also appeared: *The Late, And much admired Play, Called Pericles, Prince of Tyre. With the true Relation of the whole Historie, aduentures, and fortunes of the said Prince: As also, The no lesse strange, and worthy accidents, in the Birth and Life, of his Daughter Mariana. As it hath been diuers and sundry times acted by his Maiesties Seruants, at the Globe on the Banck-side. By William Shakespeare.*

1611. JANUARY. "William Shackspeare" and others started a suit in the Court of Chancery arising out of the ownership of the tithes which Shakespeare had purchased in 1605.

SEPTEMBER 11. The name of "Mr. William Shackspere" occurs in a list of those contributing toward the prosecuting of a bill in Parliament for the better repair of the highways.

1612. MAY 11. "William Shakespeare" of Stratford-on-Avon in the County of Warwick, gentleman, of the age of forty-eight years or thereabouts, gave evidence in London in the case of Belott vs Mountjoy. The evidence in the case shows that in 1604 Shakespeare was lodging in the house of Christopher Mountjoy, a wigmaker of Huguenot origin, in Cripplegate Ward in the City of London. Shakespeare had helped to negotiate a marriage between Christopher Mountjoy's daughter Mary and Stephen Belott, Mountjoy's apprentice. At the time Mountjoy had promised a dowry, which was not paid. Belott therefore sued his father-in-law, and Shakespeare was summoned as witness to the promises made at the betrothal. Shakespeare however in his evidence could not remember the details. Shakespeare's signature was appended to his deposition; he signed his name as "Willm. Shakp."

1613. MAY 11. John Combe of Stratford

left £5 in his will to "Mr. William Shackspere."

MARCH 10. Henry Walker, citizen and minstrel of London, in consideration of the sum of £140 conveyed a dwelling house erected over the great gate of the former Blackfriars Monastery to "William Shakespeare of Stratford Vpon Avon in the Countie of Warwick gentleman, William Johnson, citizein and Vintener of London [and host of the Mermaid Tavern], John Jackson, and John Hemmyng of London gentlemen." Shakespeare paid the money; the other three were apparently acting as his trustees. One copy of the agreement, now in the Guildhall, London, bears Shakespeare's signature, in which he spelled his name "William Shakspē."

MARCH 31. The steward of the Earl of Rutland recorded in his accounts the payment "to Mr. Shakspeare in gold about my Lorde's impreso, xliiijs; to Richard Burbage for paynting and making yt, in gold xliiijs."

This "impresa" was a symbolic device with appropriate motto borne on the shield of those taking part in a tilt or tournament. These tilts were usually held on the anniversary of the Sovereign's accession (Queen Elizabeth, November 17; King James, March 24). Burbage was well known as a painter as well as an actor.

OCTOBER 28. An agreement was made between "William Shackspeare, of Stretford in the county of Warwicke, gent," and William Replingham of Great Harborough in the County of Warwick that Replingham would recompense Shakespeare for any decrease in his yearly value of tithes which might occur by reason of any enclosure or decay of tillage meant and intended by the said William Replingham. Hereafter Shakespeare's name occurs several times in various Stratford records concerning tithes and enclosures.

1616. FEBRUARY 10. The parish register of the Stratford-on-Avon church recorded the marriage of "M. Tho Queeny tow Judith Shakspere," Shakespeare's younger daugher.

MARCH 25. William Shakespeare made his will. The will was written on three large sheets of parchment, and is now in Somerset House, London. The principal bequests were to his younger daughter Judith, £150, with a further £150 on trust; to his sister Joan Hart, £20, all wearing apparel, and the use for life of the house which she occupied; £5 to each of his nephews; to Elizabeth Hall, his granddaughter, all his plate except the broad silver-gilt bowl, which went to Judith; money to buy memorial rings to five Stratford friends; 26s. 8d. each to his fellows John Heminges, Richard Burbage, and Henry Condell to buy rings; to his wife his second-best bed, with its furniture; to his daughter Susanna Hall of New Place two houses in Henley Street, and all other lands; and the residue, including all plate and household goods, to Susanna Hall and her husband.

The will was much corrected and revised, and signed at the foot of each of the three pages. Shakespeare's bequest of the second-best bed, and nothing else, to his wife has been much discussed. As widow she was entitled to a third of the income of the estate and to remain in the house. There is therefore no reason to suppose the bequest of the second-best bed, made as an interlinear afterthought, was necessarily a sign either of contempt or of especial affection for the widow.

APRIL 23. The monument in the Stratford church records that Shakespeare died on April 23.

APRIL 25. The register in the Stratford church records the burial of "Will. Shakspere, gent."

Shakespeare was buried within the church in the chancel, and over the grave was laid a stone with the inscription:

GOOD FREND FOR IESVS SAKE FORBEARE,
TO DIGG THE DVST ENCLOASED HEARE!
BLESTE BE YE MAN YT SPARES THES STONES,
AND CURST BE HE YT MOVES MY BONES.

A tablet was erected on the north wall of the chancel which contains a bust within an arch (see Pl. 1b). The inscription reads:

IVDICIO PYLIVM, GENIO SOCRATEM, ARTE MARONEM:
TERRA TEGIT, POPVLVS MÆRET, OLYMPVS HABET.

STAY PASSENGER, WHY GOEST THOV BY SO FAST?
READ IF THOV CANST, WHOM ENVIOVS DEATH HATH PLAST,
WITH IN THIS MONVMENT SHAKSPEARE: WITH WHOME,
QVICK NATVRE DIDE: WHOSE NAME DOTH DECK YS TOMBE,
FAR MORE THEN COST: SIEH ALL, YT HE HATH WRITT,
LEAVES LIVING ART, BVT PAGE, TO SERVE HIS WITT.
OBIIT AÑO DOI 1616
ÆTATIS · 53 DIE 23 APR.

The records thus give a clear outline of Shakespeare's life. He was born in Stratford-on-Avon in 1564, married at the age of eighteen and a half, and was the father of three children at twenty. There is a gap until 1592, when he wrote a play which was successful, followed by two popular poems. From 1594 onward he wrote plays which were acted by the company first known as the Lord Chamberlain's Men and later as the King's Men. He was a principal shareholder in this company. He made money, and in his later years lived in his native town, where he died on April 23, 1616. The records are not in themselves exciting, and they tell little of the personality or intimate experience of the man. Much more may be inferred or deduced from other evidence, but these are sober records of fact.

3. Shakespeare's England

London

Shakespeare was born at Stratford-on-Avon in Warwickshire, but he made his name in London, which was then, as now, the heart of England. At the end of the sixteenth century London was a city of about 200,000 inhabitants; few other English cities exceeded 15,000. The old medieval city of London was at that time still surrounded by walls; indeed, the names of some of the gates survive today as stations on the Inner Circle of the Underground Railway system — Aldgate, Bishopsgate, Moorgate, Aldersgate. To the East, and downstream of the River Thames, stood (and still stands) the Tower of London, a great fort protecting the city from any invasion from the sea. The Tower was also a royal palace, though no longer used as such, a prison for offenders who had incurred the displeasure of the Sovereign, and the chief arsenal of the realm. At the West End, the city was entered by Ludgate, though the city boundary stretched farther west to Temple Bar, where Fleet Street joins the Strand.

Farther west and two miles upstream lay the Royal City of Westminster. Here was the Palace of Whitehall, the principal residence of the Queen, the Abbey Church of St. Peter (now called Westminster Abbey), where the Kings and Queens of England are crowned and where also many are buried, and the Parliament House and Westminster Hall, where the Queen's Courts of Justice sat to determine civil lawsuits. The City of Westminster and the City of London were legally and geographically quite distinct. Westminster (like Washington) was the seat of the national Government; London (like New York) was the center of trade, commerce, and wealth. The two cities were connected by the Strand, which ran parallel to the River Thames and was fringed by a double row of houses. To the north and beyond, there was park land or open country.

The city of London had many privileges, jealously guarded. The Sovereign did not enter the city without invitation, and although relations between Court and city were close and friendly during Shakespeare's lifetime, the city was quick to resent anything that might seem to infringe upon its privileges — an attitude which considerably affected the position of players and dramatists. The city itself was quite small; it was less than a square mile in area, and its boundaries were fixed.[1] The suburbs to the north were growing fast, but they were controlled by the magistrates of the County of Middlesex and not by the city authorities.

The River Thames was the main highway for traffic, and watermen with rowboats took the place of the modern taxi. South of the Thames was the suburb of Southwark in the County of Surrey. Southwark clustered around the south end of London Bridge, the only bridge over the Thames and therefore of great strategic importance. The bridge was one of the wonders of Elizabethan England. It had been built on brick piles as early as 1209. By Shakespeare's time the piles had been enlarged, and a double row of shops ran along the length of the bridge, which was broken by a drawbridge (see Pl. 3). The piers held back the waters of the river, which at high and low tide flowed through with great force. Under one of the piers was set the wheel which turned the city's corn mills.

---

[1] Nowadays the *City* of London is a small but highly privileged island in the vast area of Greater London. In Shakespeare's time the suburbs were not extensive.

St. Paul's

In the city itself, with its many churches, the great Cathedral of St. Paul's — known as Paul's — towered over all. The old building was a large Gothic church with a squat tower (see Pl. 2a). It was the social center for all classes. Here at eight o'clock every Sunday morning the Lord Mayor and the Aldermen came in state to hear the weekly Paul's Cross sermon, which was preached in the open air when the weather allowed. The sermon was an important event, for it brought the principal citizens together. Moreover the preacher was often inspired by the Government to deliver official news or views. Here, for instance, on February 15, 1601, was preached the official account of Essex's rebellion by Dr. John Hayward. A fortnight later Dr. William Barlow preached on Essex's trial and condemnation. On November 10, 1605, Dr. Barlow also gave from the same pulpit the first public account of the Gunpowder Plot.

The Gunpowder Plot was the most sensational event at home during Shakespeare's lifetime. When James I came to the English throne in 1603, both Catholics and Puritans expected that the restrictions on liberty of worship would be relaxed, but they soon realized that they had been misled. Some of the more desperate Catholics thereupon plotted to bring about a revolution. They rented a cellar under the Parliament House, where they accumulated a great store of gunpowder with the intention of exploding it when the King was addressing the Lords and Commons on the opening day. Had it succeeded, the plot would have destroyed in one blow the entire executive of government — the King, the Prince of Wales, all the nobility, the bishops, the Privy Council, and a large number of the principal gentlemen. The plot was timed for the state opening of Parliament of November 5, 1605; it was discovered less than twelve hours before the explosion was due. Few events in English history have caused more universal horror and consternation. On this occasion Dr. Barlow's Paul's Cross sermon was below his usual standard; he had not recovered from the shock of his own narrow escape, for he would himself "have been one of the hoisted number."

On weekdays Paul's was a regular meeting place. Unemployed servants stuck up bills there declaring their qualifications; lawyers met their clients; professional perjurers (known as "knights of the post") offered their services to dishonest litigants who required evidence for a doubtful case; needy gentlemen waited hopefully by "Duke Humphrey's" tomb for a free meal; pickpockets hovered about the unwary countryman as he looked around at the tombs, confused by the noise and bustle. Dekker complained:

At one time, in one and the same rank, yea, foot by foot and elbow by elbow, shall you see walking, the knight, the gull [sucker], the gallant, the upstart, the gentleman, the clown, the captain, the apple squire [pimp], the lawyer, the usurer, the citizen, the bankerout [bankrupt], the scholar, the beggar, the doctor, the idiot, the ruffian, the cheater, the puritan, the cut-throat, the high-man, the low-man, the true-man, and the thief; of all trades and professions some, of all countries some.

The City

The city of London was governed by the Lord Mayor and the Council of Aldermen, by whom the Lord Mayor was elected annually from their own body. It was a most important office, for the smooth working of the administration of the state depended largely on the co-operation of the citizens of London through their representative, the Lord Mayor. To be Lord Mayor of London was the ambition of every wealthy merchant; but it was not an easy office, for Londoners were notoriously rowdy. There was, for instance, every year trouble over the slaying of meat in Lent. It was a regular practice of the Privy Council, renewed annually, to order that no cattle should be killed in Lent except for invalids; able-bodied Christians were expected to eat fish.

The Council's motive was not religious but economic, for it was hoped by this means to encourage the fishermen, who were so urgently needed to serve in the navy, and also to preserve the stock cattle. Accordingly, during Lent only six butchers were licensed for the whole City, and the rest, as well as innkeepers and victualers, were strictly forbidden to sell meat. The inspection and control of these regulations was entrusted to the wardens and members of the Fishmongers' Company as the most interested parties. But the butchers were always defiant, even when they were severely punished; in fact, the

Council was so wearied by the struggle that its printed orders, issued annually, began with this pessimistic sentence: "First her Majesty's pleasure is, upon her understanding of the great disorders heretofore, and *especially the last Lent. . . .*" Nevertheless the black market in meat flourished, and disobedient hostesses, such as Mrs. Quickly, continued to set legs of mutton before their guests.

Riots in the city and the suburbs were frequent, for there were always unruly apprentices, masterless men for whom no one was responsible, and unemployed ex-soldiers ready for trouble on the least provocation. There was no regular police force. The sheriffs were responsible for order in the city, which was divided into parishes. In each parish the constable represented the law; he was assisted by the watch, composed of responsible citizens who reluctantly took their turn at patrolling their parish by night. These amateur watchmen were much derided by unruly young gentlemen. Indeed they sometimes acted with incredible stupidity; but their behavior was unpredictable; on occasion they were just obstinately honest. In great emergency, the trained bands — a rudimentary form of militia — could be called out, for it was the duty of every fit man to be trained as a soldier. The training was not very burdensome; it consisted of one annual parade at Mile End on Midsummer Day.

Plague

Many of the troubles in the city were due to overcrowding. Statesmen realized that the continual drift of farm laborers away from the country would be disastrous, but they did not know how to stop it. Regulations were constantly made that no new houses should be built in the city of London, but rules were easily evaded. Men with large houses rented them room by room as apartments, and hovels were knocked together on any piece of unoccupied ground. As a result, the city was pestered by an ill-controlled, filthy, slum population. Bubonic plague broke out frequently. It is known nowadays that the plague was communicated by fleas carried by the rats which bred in the innumerable muck heaps; but in Shakespeare's time, though a few doctors, more intelligent than the rest, associated plague with dirt and stench, most people re-

garded it as the direct sign of God's anger toward a wicked people. Stray dogs were considered to be carriers, and during an epidemic they were destroyed in large numbers, with the result that the rats bred more freely than usual. There were two violent outbreaks during Shakespeare's lifetime. In 1592 and 1593 more than 22,000 died of plague, and in 1603 — the year that King James came to the throne — over 30,000; that is, in two epidemics within eleven years a quarter of the city's population died from plague. Plague was thus a constant fear to the civic authorities.

Sanitation

The city was incredibly dirty. Most of the houses, many of them very old, were built close together in dark, narrow, airless lanes. Moreover, there were no sewers or drains except for the gutter which ran down the middle of the street. Garbage pails were emptied into the gutter and the filth accumulated until the next heavy rain, when it drifted down into one of the ditches — such as the Fleet ditch or the Moor ditch — which became proverbial for their foul stench. Night soil was, however, collected into carts and carried out to sea in barges.

Nevertheless, in many ways Tudor London was singularly beautiful. There were no smoke fogs to reduce the buildings to a uniform grime. Many of the houses were half-timbered, and the Thames, which still ran clear and silver, was fringed with the great mansions and gardens of noblemen and men of wealth. Today little remains of Shakespeare's London, for the old city was almost completely wiped out in the Great Fire of 1666.

Country Life

In the country, life was simple. The parish was the unit of local administration. The chief persons in the village were the squire, who was sometimes also a magistrate, the parson, and a few farmers; often the rest of the villagers lived and died without ever going more than twenty miles from home. In the village the church, surrounded by its churchyard, was the center of community life. It was used as a place of worship on Sundays and holy days, and at other times for public meetings of all kinds. In the churchyard were buried most of the dead; men of wealth with their families were buried inside the church itself, often beneath large and elaborate monuments. The officers of the church were the parson, assisted by the clerk or sexton, and the churchwardens, who were responsible for the administration of the affairs of the parish, such as collection of dues, repairs to roads, relief of the poor, and maintenance of the church fabric.

The Church of England

The right to appoint a minister to a "living" or "cure of souls" was a private property which could be bought and sold. The owner or "patron" had the right to present the living to any duly ordained minister of the Church of England quite regardless of the wishes of the congregation, who were not even consulted. Livings were in the gift of all kinds of patrons — the Sovereign, the bishop of the diocese, colleges and universities, and private individuals. The living was usually endowed with an income drawn from the proceeds of some investment, almost invariably the rents from lands or houses. The parson had the free use of a house and land; he had also the right to exact a tithe, or one-tenth of the produce, of his parishioners. Tithe could, however, be alienated from the living and purchased from the owner. Shakespeare himself (see page 14a) bought tithes as an investment.[2]

The parson had many privileges and few heavy responsibilities. Once appointed to a living he was entitled to enjoy its income for life and he could be turned out only if convicted in an ecclesiastical court of some gross offense against morals or doctrine. Usually he was a graduate of one of the two universities of Oxford and Cambridge, and sometimes he was a scholar; but on the whole the village parson was seldom a man of much distinction. Indeed, very

little was demanded of him. He had to conduct a certain minimum of services in the church and baptize, marry, or bury his parishioners. He was required to preach a sermon on four occasions during the year, and for those who were incapable of original composition a *Book of Homilies* was prescribed. The reason for this generally low level of ability was that the Church was a safe and comfortable profession and attracted the timid and unambitious. A curious illustration of this occurs in a sermon preached against simony in 1597. In attacking those patrons who appropriated for themselves part of the income of the livings in their gift, the preacher argued that such an action would ruin the universities. Men, he declared, underwent the expense of a university training because they expected at the end to be rewarded with a vicarage worth £40 to £50 a year. If the value of livings went down, then the university degree would no longer be a good investment.

Roads

Communication between villages and the nearest town was poor. Roads were bad; there was some attempt to keep them in order, but as each parish was responsible for its own section of road, the state of repair depended on the zeal of the parish officers. There was, however, little wheeled traffic except for farm carts and the few lumbering springless coaches used by men of wealth. Most traffic was by means of pack horses. Travelers rode on horseback or walked. Since communication was so difficult, the local markets, held weekly at the nearest town, or the fairs, held annually at the greater cities, became important places for the exchange of goods of all kinds.

Family Life

Under such conditions men and women seldom moved far from their homes. Family life was therefore strong, and the father of a large family an important person. Women had few legal rights of their own. A married woman owned no property; at marriage her possessions passed into the control of her husband. As a result an unmarried woman with money of her own had a wide choice of husbands, and none need remain alone for long.

---

[2] The terms used for the clergy of the Church of England sometimes cause confusion. A minister was first ordained to the probationary rank of deacon; after a year's service he was ordained priest and entitled to administer all the sacraments. A rector was a priest in full charge of a cure and enjoying all the privileges, including the collection of tithes. A vicar was a priest in charge of a cure, but with curtailed privileges. The word "parson" is applied to both vicars and rectors. A curate was any minister in charge of a cure, but the term was most commonly used for a minister substituting for the rector. It was a common abuse for one man to hold several cures and to pay a small stipend to a curate to carry out the duties in each.

Scandals and abuses were common. The law recognized that a legal contract of marriage had been made when the two parties agreed before witnesses to take each other as man and wife. Such betrothals were neither registered nor officially recorded, but either party could claim the fulfillment of the bargain and all that it implied. If either married some other party, that marriage was void. Should a dispute arise, it was taken to the courts; the parties produced their witnesses and the court decided. Marriage in church was the proper and conventional form of contract and gave additional safeguards in that it was a public ceremony before many witnesses and a record of the marriage was entered by the parson in the parish register. Betrothal, however, was regarded by many as equally binding, and many such marriages were consummated before or even without the blessing of the Church.

So easy a form of contract led to many abuses. It was not difficult to entrap one of the parties into some statement before unscrupulous witnesses which could be construed as a binding betrothal. A woman with property was thus an easy prey, and naturally she found a legal protector as soon as possible.

Elizabethan widows were notorious for the rapidity with which they remarried. There is a story told in the *Hundred Merry Tales* of a certain woman whose husband died leaving her with great wealth. A young gentleman thought that she would be a desirable match, but having nice feelings, he waited until the funeral of the late husband. Then he knelt beside the widow, who was at her prayers, and in a whisper asked if she would marry him. She replied that she was sorry but she was already bespoken. In this case, however, the lady had failed to observe the proper etiquette, for it was not considered seemly for a widow to accept a proposal so long as the corpse of her late husband was still in the house.

In theory, and usually in practice, the father was the supreme head of the family, and had the right to dispose of his daughters in marriage.[3] Indeed the elders usually negotiated marriages for their children, though it naturally gave the greatest satisfaction to all concerned if the young people's desires coincided with those of their parents. But since the purpose of marriage was

[3] See App. 8, " The Ballad of Ulalia Page."

the procreation of children to prolong the family and increase its possessions, it was regarded as of first importance that the young wife should be able to bear healthy children and " to bring meat in her mouth."

Relations between fathers and their children were therefore without much sentiment, and though there were many happy marriages, in real life romantic love was discouraged. The good son addressed his parents as " sir " or " madam," and treated them with formal respect and reverence. Nor was there much sentiment between sons and mothers; no Elizabethan poet ever sang songs about his dear old mammy. The successful mother ruled her sons, and they obeyed her. There are indeed so many stories of shrews that it is clear that the mother was often the real ruler of the household. Women were by no means slaves. In the home they were in fact predominant, and formed their own freemasonry; the menfolk worked and found their own society outside.

The Queen

As the father was in theory the head of the family, so the Queen was the head of the state. Within the state, each person had his proper place in the whole pattern (see p. 7b). The child looked to the father, the servant to the master, the master to the lord, the lord to the Sovereign, who was directly under God. Queen Elizabeth was emphatic in the claim, which she often asserted, that she was responsible to God alone, and she quite genuinely believed that He was always personally concerned with her welfare. One of her proclamations begins with the words:

For as much as it is manifestly seen to all the world how it hath pleased Almighty God of His most singular favour to have taken this Our Realm into His special protection these many years, even from the beginning of Our reign, in the midst of the troubled estate of all other kingdoms next adjoining, with a special preservation of Our own person, as next under his Almightiness, supreme Governor of the same . . .

This conception of the Queen as God's vicegerent and a semidivine being was fostered by the elaborate ceremonial of the Court. A German who was present there in 1598 thus describes Queen Elizabeth going to her private chapel on a Sunday morning:

We were admitted by an order from the Lord Chamberlain into the presence-chamber, hung with rich tapestry, and the floor after the English fashion strewed with hay, through which the Queen commonly passes on her way to chapel: at the door stood a gentleman dressed in velvet, with a gold chain, whose office was to introduce to the Queen any person of distinction, that came to wait on her: it was Sunday, when there is usually the greatest attendance of nobility. In the same hall were the Archbishop of Canterbury, the Bishop of London, a great number of Councillors of State, officers of the Crown, and gentlemen, who waited the Queen's coming out; which she did from her own apartment, when it was time to go to prayers, attended in the following manner. First went gentlemen, Barons, Earls, Knights of the Garter, all richly dressed and bareheaded; next came the Chancellor, bearing the seals in a red-silk purse, between two; one of which carried the royal sceptre, the other the sword of state, in a red scabbard, studded with golden *fleurs de lys,* the point upwards: next came the Queen, in the sixty-fifth year of her age, as we were told, very majestic; her face oblong, fair, but wrinked; her eyes small, yet black and pleasant; her nose a little hooked; her lips narrow; and her teeth black (a defect the English seem subject to, from their too great use of sugar); she had in her ears two pearls, with very rich drops; she wore false hair, and that red; upon her head she had a small crown, reported to be made of some of the gold of the celebrated Lunebourg table; her bosom was uncovered, as all the English ladies have it, till they marry; and she had on a necklace of exceeding fine jewels; her hands were small, her fingers long, and her stature neither tall nor low; her air was stately, her manner of speaking mild and obliging. That day she was dressed in white silk, bordered with pearls of the size of beans, and over it a mantle of black silk, shot with silver threads; her train was very long, the end of it borne by a Marchioness; instead of a chain, she had an oblong collar of gold and jewels. As she went along in all this state and magnificence, she spoke very graciously, first to one, then to another, whether foreign ministers, or those who attended for different reasons, in English, French, or Italian; for besides being well skilled in Greek, Latin, and the languages I have mentioned, she is mistress of Spanish, Scotch, and Dutch: whoever speaks to her, it is kneeling; now and then she raises some with her hand. While we were there, W. Slawata, a Bohemian Baron, had letters to present to her; and she, after pulling off her glove, gave him her right hand to kiss, sparkling with rings and jewels, a mark of particular favour: wherever she turned her face, as she was going along, everybody fell down on their knees. The ladies of the court followed next to her, very handsome and well shaped, and for the most part dressed in white; she was guarded on each side by the gentlemen pensioners, fifty in number, with gilt battle-axes. In the ante-chapel next the hall where we were, petitions were presented to her, and she received them most graciously, which occasioned the acclamation of, "Long live Queen Elizabeth!" She answered it with, "I thank you, my good people." [4]

Queen Elizabeth was no figurehead, and in so far as any one ruler or government is responsible for the fate of a nation, to her belongs the credit for the greatness of England at the end of the sixteenth century. The epoch is justly named the Elizabethan Age.

Just as the Queen was the head of her family of subjects, so she belonged to the family of rulers of other peoples; rulers were all brethren, especially chosen by God, and accordingly bound to each other by the special code of kingly behavior. Queen Elizabeth held, and said, that kings must behave as kings; and when other sovereigns did not come up to her standards, she did not hesitate to rebuke them. She was especially annoyed with Philip II of Spain because he so far forgot himself as to send assassins to murder her, and with King James VI of Scotland because he failed to keep his subjects in proper order.

Religion

In such a conception of society, there is a fundamental instinct for order. Among the more conservative this instinct was the stronger because Englishmen had not forgotten the generations of anarchy during the Wars of the Roses. At all costs order must be preserved, and since the Sovereign was the apex of human society and God's Deputy on earth, to rebel against the Sovereign was to rebel against God. This belief explains also why religious persecution was regarded as natural and right. In theory the structure of the state was founded on God's will and command, as expressed in the Scriptures and in the divine institution, the Church. But the Church of England, by law established under

---

[4] Quoted in *Shakespeare's England*, ed. by Sir Walter Raleigh. 2 vols., I, 91.

Queen Elizabeth, was itself a compromise. England had been a Roman Catholic country until the time of Henry VIII, who, in his quarrel with the Pope over his first divorce, had decreed that he was himself the Head of the Church of England. He had further widened the schism by dissolving the monasteries and religious houses and redistributing their enormous wealth among his own followers. He did not, however, encourage changes in doctrine, and the Church of England in its practice and dogma remained Catholic. At the death of Henry VIII in 1547, the guardians of his young son Edward VI began a thorough Protestant reform of the English Church, which involved the destruction of many of the finest specimens of English ecclesiastic art of the Middle Ages. When the boy King died in 1553, he was succeeded by his elder sister, Queen Mary. She was a zealous and conscientious Roman Catholic. She accepted the superiority of the Pope in ecclesiastical matters and married Philip II, King of Spain, the most powerful of the Catholic Sovereigns; but her zeal for the old faith was without much success, because too many of her wealthiest subjects had profited from the plunder of the abbeys and were not willing to disgorge their spoils. Queen Mary died in 1558, and was succeeded by her half-sister, Queen Elizabeth. After three upheavals in twenty-five years Englishmen were ready for a compromise.

Queen Elizabeth was no zealot in religious matters and was not much interested in the subtleties of theology. At her accession, the Anglican Church reverted to independence from the Pope, but in church practice and ritual much of the old ceremony remained. Foreign visitors noted that outwardly the ceremony in English churches (at least in London) was very much the same as in Catholic churches on the Continent, except that the language used was English and not Latin. The Queen's compromise was accepted by most Englishmen without disturbance, though many were secretly in sympathy with the old faith. Zealous Puritans, on the other hand, were eager for much wider reforms. Extremists of both parties rejected compromise. Catholics hoped that the old order would be restored so that England might remain inside the structure of Catholic Europe. If so, the Queen would have to accept the Pope's supremacy. Some zealots, including the Jesuit

propagandist Father Parsons, were even willing to force the issue by bringing over foreign soldiers and by murdering the Queen.

Extreme Puritans, however, were held to be the greater danger at home, for they put forward the most advanced democratic views. They claimed that the Church of England, with its bishops and ecclesiastical organization, was anti-Christian, and they proposed to reorganize society on a Scriptural basis. Each congregation was to elect elders; the elders were to form local consistories; these would elect provincial synods; finally there would be a National Synod, which would be the supreme court for all affairs, political, religious, moral, and social. No important matter was to be decided without the consent of the National Synod, and the Queen was to be subject to its censure if she did not obey its wishes. The Puritans were indeed the champions of liberty of conscience, but it was for their own kind of liberty; they were as eager as any other sect to force everyone to conform with their views. The Queen and her Ministers felt that such views were alarming and revolutionary and that they should be suppressed accordingly.

Although the three main divisions of Christianity superficially disagreed on matters of interpretation of Scripture, their differences were as much political and social as doctrinaire. Those who wished to reform society justified their theories not by the teaching of economists or political scientists but by the Scriptures. Men were therefore perforce religious, for at any time a man might have to suffer for his religious opinions. Interest in theological controversy was strong. Sermons were eagerly heard and theological argument was keenly followed. This can be well seen from the *Diary* of John Manningham, a barrister, who went twice every Sunday to hear a sermon, which he summarized with comments. On the other six days of the week he was chiefly interested in gossip and jokes of the kind that editors indicate with a row of stars.

Organization of the State

There were as yet no political parties in England. The Queen was the head of the state and personally decided all matters of policy. Queen Elizabeth was a keen and energetic businesswoman, familiar with every detail of the machinery of state. Hundreds of her letters survive; they cover every kind of state business. The Queen chose her own Ministers to carry out her policies in their several departments. They were palace officials, and formed her Privy Council. The government could not therefore be rejected or overthrown except by rebellion or murder, or if the Sovereign was weak, by seizing his person and providing him with new Ministers. The Sovereign could, however, dismiss a Minister, though in fact Queen Elizabeth kept her chief Ministers until they died. The only Councilor to betray or desert her was the Earl of Essex, who was executed on February 25, 1601.

Robert Devereux, Earl of Essex

For a period of ten years before his death Robert Devereux, Earl of Essex, was the most conspicuous figure next to the Queen. He was born in 1566 or 1567, and first attracted notice at Court as the protégé of his stepfather, the great Earl of Leicester. After Leicester's death in 1588, he became conspicuous. As a young man he was intelligent, romantic, ambitious, and flamboyantly brave, and soon became the Queen's favorite. He took part in the expedition known as the Portugal Voyage, and in 1591 was in nominal command of the English forces taking part in the siege of Rouen (see p. 29a). At the early age of twenty-six he was made a member of the Privy Council, and was soon regarded as the natural champion of professional soldiers and Puritans with a grievance. His greatest triumph was at the expedition to Cádiz in 1596, where he shared the command with the old Lord Admiral, Lord Charles Howard, and where his bravery and chivalry were much noted. But chivalry soon degenerated into jealous vanity. He was, indeed, no great leader of men and was easily influenced, especially by anyone who flattered him. Moreover, to the Queen's annoyance, he courted the popularity of the citizens of London. After 1597 his fortunes declined rapidly. He lost much reputation over the expedition to the Azores of which he was commander. Indeed the failure of that expedition was due largely to his incompetent leadership. Thereafter he drifted into the dangerous position of being the natural leader of all malcontents.

Essex was the last of Queen Elizabeth's favorites. The Queen, who liked handsome and promising young men, promoted him before he was ready for responsibility, and granted him excessive favors which he came to regard as his own right. The relations between Essex and the Queen were always uneasy. Essex was very sensitive and resented criticism; the Queen was always more prone to blame than to praise. There were constant quarrels and emotional reconciliations.

The climax in their relationship occurred in the summer of 1598. There had recently been a great disaster in Ireland, and it was essential that a competent commander should be sent over to take charge. The problem of the Irish command was discussed by the Queen, Essex, Lord Charles Howard, and Sir Robert Cecil. Essex obstinately insisted that his own candidate should be chosen, and when the Queen refused he insolently turned his back on her. Thereupon she gave him a box on the ear and told him to go and be hanged. The horrified Lord Admiral shuffled Essex out of the chamber. This crude and embarrassing quarrel upset public business for two months, as neither would apologize. Ultimately a reconciliation was patched up, but Essex had been so critical of all candidates suggested for the Irish command that he found himself in the embarrassing position of being selected.

He went over to Ireland in March 1599 in command of a large army of over sixteen thousand men, and he failed completely. He frittered his army away in unnecessary forays and then continually wrote home demanding reinforcements and complaining bitterly that he was being betrayed. At last, instead of attacking Tyrone, the rebel leader, he came to terms with him and, in spite of direct orders to the contrary, suddenly left his command and appeared in London with a small party of his followers. The Court at the time was at Nonesuch in Surrey. Thither Essex and his party rode. Essex went straight into the palace and up to the Queen's private apartments unannounced. He broke into her bedchamber and found her newly out of bed and not yet made up. She was astonished to see him and at first greeted him kindly, but when she had recovered from the shock she ordered that he remain a prisoner under close arrest. For the next nine months he was banished from Court, and then in June 1600 he was brought before the Privy Council and publicly censured. After this humiliation he was released, but forbidden to come to Court.

Essex's fortunes were now perilous. He had long since mortgaged all his private estate, and his income depended on the grant of a tax on sweet wines which the Queen had given him some years before. This grant lapsed in October 1600, and everyone waited to see whether the Queen would renew it or reduce Essex to beggary. After some hesitation she declared that the grant would not be renewed. This was generally taken to be a sign that she had finally broken with him. For a while he was in great depression, but his followers, many of them men of desperate fortunes, urged him to take revenge. As Christmas came near it was clear that some seditious plan was being hatched in Essex House. Extreme Puritans were allowed to preach dangerous sermons, and men of broken fortune were his chief friends.

The suspicions of the Council increased, and on Saturday, February 7, 1601, it was noticed that the Chamberlain's Men put on the play of *Richard II* before a large and enthusiastic audience of Essex's followers (see p. 45a). That night an official messenger was sent to summon Essex to the Court to explain his conduct. He refused to go, declaring it was a plot to murder him. Essex now sent for his friends to gather at Essex House in the morning. About two hundred of them had assembled by ten o'clock on Sunday when a deputation of Privy Councilors from the Court presented itself at Essex House. They were admitted. Essex led the deputation into his library and ordered them to be held captive. Then he went down into the courtyard and with his particular friend, the Earl of Southampton, put himself at the head of his followers and began to march toward the city of London.

Essex fully expected that the citizens would rise and join him. No one stirred. Meanwhile loyal supporters of the Queen's party were gathering. By afternoon Essex realized that his position was hopeless and, after some fighting near Paul's, with a small party of his followers he went down to the river and was rowed back to Essex House. Late that night Essex, Southampton, and the rest of his party surrendered to a little army commanded by the Lord Admiral Howard. The rebellion caused the greatest excitement and alarm, although it was some days before the truth was known. It seemed incredible that such a movement could have occurred without wide preparations for a general revolution. On February 19 Essex and Southampton were brought to trial for high treason before a special commission in Westminster Hall. The trial lasted all day and Essex was allowed great freedom in his defense. Nevertheless, both Earls were condemned to death. Southampton was reprieved, but six days later Essex was beheaded in the Tower before a select audience of about one hundred persons.

Essex, as can now be seen, was not a great man, but his death caused a vast wave of feeling in England. His rise and fall was not merely the story of one man's folly and ruin. It affected the nation more deeply than any event since the Great Armada. Essex had long seemed to stand out as a symbol of nobility in a corrupted universe, for he had never lost that early charm of manner which distinguished him as a young courtier. Everywhere there was a growing sense of disappointment, failure, and frustration. The Puritans cried out against the Anglican clergy; the Catholics lamented the deaths of their martyrs and were quarreling among themselves; men of wealth found the burden of taxation intolerable. Intelligent young men who had grown up under the shadow of this interminable war against Spain were cynical and contemptuous of the older generation. With Essex's death vanished the last hope of a brave new world. It is more than coincidence that *Hamlet* as we now know it was written in the last months of Essex's decline and fall.

The Privy Council

After Essex's death the Privy Council was reduced to ten members. Four months later three new Councilors were appointed. The thirteen members were John Whitgift, Archbishop of Canterbury (and administrative head of the Established Church); Sir Thomas Egerton, Lord Keeper of the Great Seal (that is, administrative head of the legal profession); Lord Buckhurst, Lord Treasurer; Charles Howard, Earl of Nottingham, Lord High Admiral (responsible for all naval affairs); the Earl of Shrewsbury; the Earl of Worcester, Master of the Horse (or as he would now be called, Minister for War);

Lord Hunsdon, Lord Chamberlain (responsible for the organization of the palace and the royal household); Sir William Knollys, Controller of the Household; Sir John Stanhope, the Vice-Chamberlain; Sir Robert Cecil, the Queen's Principal Secretary (and as such the Minister most intimate with the Queen); Sir John Stanhope, Chancellor of the Exchequer; Sir John Popham, Lord Chief Justice; and Mr. John Herbert, one of the Queen's secretaries and assistant to Sir Robert Cecil.

The Privy Council was the supreme governing body in the state, and functioned in much the same way as the modern Cabinet. Privy Councilors were greatly privileged. Only Councilors had the right of direct access to the Queen herself; other men had to petition for an audience through a Councilor or one of the Queen's personal attendants. The Council was a hard-working body, and met in committee most days, sometimes under the chairmanship of the Queen herself. Many of its letter books survive and show how much business was transacted. Thus in a typical and quite uneventful week in March 1592, the agenda for the first concerned reinforcements to be levied from the city of London; precautions against desertion from the draft; instructions for Sir Roger Williams, commanding the troops in France; relief for a poor man unable to pay his taxes; action to be taken against a crafty attorney. On the second, the Council considered a change in the command of one of the companies. On the third, the Council was concerned with the Free School at Newark; circular letters to the Lords Lieutenant of thirteen counties concerning military munitions, with other similar letters to thirteen other counties; directions to the Warden of the Fishmongers Company concerning the supervision of butchers during Lent. On the fifth, the agenda dealt with a stay of proceedings in a case at Bedford; the repair of the church at Wymondham; a fraud in the City; a French merchant's complaint; the complaint of a widow of New Sarum; the case of a poor prisoner who had been unjustly kept in prison; relief from taxation of a poor man in Essex; protection of a debtor; a complaint in the Court of Chancery; the claims of an orphan in Ireland; a letter to the muster-master in Normandy concerning pay rolls; evasions of public duties by citizens dwelling in the suburbs; a passport for a German citizen;

the private affairs of Sir Hugh Hopton; warrants for the arrest of two suspects; three questions from Ireland; the renewal of the commissions of the commissioners against Catholic recusants in three Lincolnshire towns; complaints against the Lord President and Council in the Welsh Marches; a charge of seditious speech. On the seventh, the only business concerned deserters hiding in London and a special warning to Sir Edmund York not to allow any of his reinforcements to desert.

Such a volume of business could only be transacted when the members of the Council were punctilious and exact in attending to its affairs, as is shown by the record of attendance. Lord Burleigh was present at some two hundred meetings each year. The Council also sat as a supreme court of law in the notorious Star Chamber — so called because the ceiling was decorated with stars — where it tried cases which did not come within the ordinary procedure of the civil or criminal courts. It decided such matters as cases of riot, seditious behavior, perjury, or offenses committed by noblemen. It could fine offenders, or send them to the pillory, or condemn them to lose their ears; but it did not punish by death. Cases of high treason, especially when committed by persons of rank, were usually tried by a special commission.

The Council issued orders through the Lords Lieutenant of the counties or the Lord Mayor of London or, for particular matters, through the local magistrate or mayor immediately concerned. The system worked well. Although to modern notions it may seem undemocratic, it could only function with the willing co-operation of all, for there was no regular police force or standing army to enforce commands. In practice it meant that no regulations were put into force which were against the general wish of the majority.

Noblemen

Next to the Queen in order of importance came the peers or noblemen of England. In Shakespeare's earlier days there were three degrees of nobility — Earl, Viscount, Baron. The highest degree, that of Duke, was at the moment not held by anyone, but that rank was restored when King James came to the throne in 1603. Noblemen were created as a peculiar mark of favor by a special patent bestowed by the Sovereign. The patent was an imposing document sealed with the Great Seal of England (see Pl. 11b). The patent bestowed a title of honor, which descended to the eldest son in perpetuity. Noblemen were beings apart and were treated with much respect and ceremony. They had great estates, many servants, and considerable responsibility. They enjoyed various privileges and special places at Court according to their degree; they were exempt from trial in the ordinary courts of law and could be tried only by their peers; but they were also expected to serve the state without reward whenever required. Privy Councilors were often promoted to the ranks of the nobility as a reward for their services and to give them greater dignity. Indeed the English nobility has always contained a number of noblemen who began life as commoners. When Parliament met, the peers sat apart in their own House, the House of Lords. With them sat the Lords Spiritual, the bishops.

The Bishops

Bishops in the sixteenth century had great power and ranked as noblemen, though their privileges did not pass to their children. The bishop was appointed by the Sovereign and was responsible for the spiritual welfare of his diocese. He had his own ecclesiastical court of law, before which offenders against accepted doctrine and morality were summoned and, if condemned, punished by fine or imprisonment. These courts were particularly hated by the Puritans because they gave the hated " anti-Christian " bishop supreme control over all matters of worship and belief. The bishops were richly rewarded: they had their palaces, and many servants and great estates; they controlled the clergy in their dioceses, and therefore wielded great influence and authority. Occasionally spiritually minded men were chosen, but the quality chiefly required of a bishop was the administrative ability to organize and keep in check a very miscellaneous flock of clergy.

Knights and Gentlemen

Next to the nobility in the chain of order came the knights and gentlemen. A man was made knight either by the Sovereign in person, or by her deputy, such as the general in the field. He then bore the title " Sir " before his name. The honor, which was personal and not hereditary, was given for many different reasons — for political services, for gallant service in the wars, or as a mark of esteem to rich men who had shown public spirit. Queen Elizabeth was particular in bestowing the honor, and it was one of her major causes of annoyance with the Earl of Essex that when in command of her armies he had made knighthood cheap by giving it away too easily. When King James came to the throne, he bestowed so many knighthoods in his first years that the title became a joke.

Next to knights were the gentlemen. Legally a gentleman was a person of good birth and independent means who was not employed in any trade or profession. A man became officially a " gentleman " when a coat of arms was granted to him by the College of Heralds (see p. 10b and App. 9). A gentleman was expected to set an example to his neighbors by giving much of his time freely to the public service, and by undertaking such duties as serving as a justice of the peace or representing his shire in Parliament as a member of the House of Commons.

Parliament

Parliament in Queen Elizabeth's time was of less importance than it became later. It met every three or four years to amend old laws, to make new ones, and to agree as to taxes to cover the extraordinary expenses of the wars. The normal expenses of the state were met out of the Queen's private income, which amounted only to about £300,000 in money of the time.[5] Parliament was not, as the Queen told its members, a standing council, and liberty of speech was not always allowed. In the Parliament of 1593, for instance, the Queen gave orders that members should not discuss the question of her successor. When one member named Peter Wentworth insisted on bringing up the matter, he was sent to the Tower, and remained there without trial until his death three years later. Parliament, however, was a very valuable means of discovering the state of public opinion, especially since members were not controlled by party bosses in their votes or speeches.

[5] Equivalent to about $12,000,000 in modern American money. See App. 27.

A notable instance of this ability of Parliament to reflect the temper of the people occurred in 1601, when the Queen and the Council were made aware of the bitter feelings caused by the excessive granting of monopolies to deal in certain commodities. It had long been a privilege of the Sovereign to grant, as a reward for faithful service, a monopoly or sole right to deal in certain commodities, but the privilege had been abused and extended to cover necessities. There were patents for currants, vinegar, coal, brushes, pots, oils of various kinds, and even salt. The indignation of the House of Commons was reported to the Queen. She sent for the Speaker and told him that measures should immediately be taken to remedy the abuse. When the Speaker reported to the House, they enthusiastically agreed that a deputation should go to the Queen to give her thanks. About a hundred and fifty members appeared before her in Whitehall Palace. When the Speaker finished his speech, the Queen answered him at length with great eloquence and feeling. Then she ended with these words:

To be a King and wear a crown is more glorious to them that see it than it is pleasure to them that bear it. For myself, I was never so much enticed with the glorious name of a King, or royal authority of a Queen, as delighted that God hath made me this instrument to maintain His truth and glory, and to defend this Kingdom from peril, dishonour, tyranny and oppression. There will never Queen sit in my seat with more zeal to my country, care to my subjects, and that will sooner with willingness yield and venture her life for your good and safety than myself. And though you have had and may have many Princes more mighty and wise sitting in this seat, yet you never had or shall have any that will be more careful and loving. Should I ascribe anything to myself and my sexly weakness, I were not worthy to live then, and of all most unworthy of the mercies I have had from God, Who hath ever yet given me a heart which never yet feared foreign or home enemies. I speak it to give God the praise as a testimony before you, and not to attribute anything to myself. For I, O Lord, what am I, whom practices and perils past should not fear! O what can I do — and these words she spake with great emphasis — that I should speak for any glory! God forbid.

This, Mr. Speaker, I pray you deliver unto the House, to whom heartily recommend me. And so I commit you all to your best fortunes and further counsels.

Thereafter the House returned with increased zeal to its business of lawmaking.

Crime and Punishment

Elizabethan laws, especially against crime, were harsh, and many crimes were punished with death. In theory, public punishments provided a warning to the young of the end which awaited the wicked; in fact, they were highly appreciated as spectacles. Many crimes were punished by hanging, usually on the three-cornered gallows at Tyburn, which stood near the present Marble Arch. Murderers and those who had committed notable acts of high treason were sometimes executed as near as possible to the scene of the crime. Women who poisoned their husbands were burned alive.

Those found guilty of high treason were condemned to be hung, drawn, and quartered. They were dragged through the city on hurdles to the place of execution, where after much speech-making and some prayers by the minister, and sometimes unseemly wrangling, the condemned was made to mount the ladder and then "turned off." Before he was unconscious he was cut down, his parts and entrails were cut out and burned in a fire, the body was then dismembered and dipped into boiling tar, and the pieces were displayed in various parts of the city. Traitors' heads were stuck up on top of London Bridge (see Pl. 3). The barbarity of this sentence was sometimes mitigated, for there was a recognized custom that when the condemned acted with notable courage, piety, and decorum, he was allowed to hang until he was dead, or at least insensible. Beheading with the ax was a privilege reserved for noblemen and gentlemen of high standing.

Another form of punishment was that known as peine forte et dure, or pressing to death. This was the penalty for "standing dumb at the bar," or refusing to plead guilty or not guilty. Without a plea the trial could not proceed, and thus the prisoner avoided legal condemnation, which carried with it forfeiture of all his goods to the Queen. By taking this course some hardy individuals saved their families from poverty, but it was an act of considerable heroism and self-sacrifice. The victim was stretched out upon spikes, then a board was laid on him and heavy weights piled on until he was pressed to death.

With such elementary police organization as existed, it is surprising that criminals were so often caught. But when a crime was discovered, everyone took a hand in aiding justice. A "hue and cry" was raised, and the whole parish turned out to chase the offender. If he ran into another parish, the pursuit was taken up from parish to parish until he was caught or escaped. Escape was not easy; in a small community the stranger is conspicuous and suspected.

Violent death was frequent, particularly as the result of the many fights with weapons which occurred. Marlowe was twice involved in a fatal quarrel. On the first occasion he and the poet Watson killed a man called Bradley; on the second he was himself the victim. Ben Jonson killed a fellow actor in 1598 (see p. 42b). Jonson was tried for manslaughter and found guilty, but he escaped by pleading "benefit of clergy," a survival of the times when "clerks" (that is, educated men who could read) were so valuable that they were given a second chance. The accused was required to read aloud a passage from the Psalms — known as the "neck verse" — in Court, and was then branded on the thumb with a T and released with the loss of his goods.

Lesser crimes and frauds were often the work of professional crooks, known as conycatchers (from "cony"; that is, a rabbit, or "sucker"). A most interesting account of these experts was written by Robert Greene in a series of pamphlets which were published in 1591–92. They worked in fraternities, and were regularly organized. Conycatching was a form of cardsharping, but the profession included "crossbiters," "courbers," "nips," and "foists." The crossbiter and his moll (known as a "traffic") lured men into brothels and there stripped them under threats of violence or blackmail. Courbers went round the city at night and where they found an open window they thrust in a fishing rod with a hook at the end and drew out what they could catch. Nips and foists both worked on purses; the nip used a knife, cutting the purse from the girdle, but the foist used his hand and picked the pocket. Foists regarded themselves as belonging to a higher profession than the others, for to use a tool was the mark of a tradesman, and no gentleman practiced a trade.

These experts were members of the city fraternities. In the country there were other branches, such as wandering beggars who called at cottages or farms when the menfolk were away at work. Of these, the bedlam beggars were the fiercest and most terrifying; they were lunatics discharged from Bedlam (Bethlehem Hospital, the London madhouse). There were other unlawful travelers on the roads, of whom the Statute against Vagabonds gives a long catalogue; it includes fencers, bearwards (who trailed a tame performing bear), common players not licensed by a lord, minstrels, jugglers, peddlers, tinkers, scholars from the universities begging for money to finish their education, and shipwrecked sailors.

Sailors were not welcomed in the country, and sober citizens regarded them as likely to be thieves and pirates, as indeed many of them were. Modern romantic notions about the Elizabethan seamen were not shared by their countrymen; although the more farsighted realized that the sea was England's greatest asset, it is significant that while in Elizabethan plays there are many soldier characters, there is no seaman of any importance. The few that appear are either minor rogues or convenient captains who answer such questions as "What country, friend, is this?" Soldier characters are plentiful because the wars came close to every man. England was occupied with major wars for the last eighteen years of the Queen's reign.

The Wars

The most sensational event in the long war with Spain was the defeat of the Spanish Armada in 1588. Historians looking back are prone to take a complacent view of the Spanish danger, as if the destruction of the Armada ended the anxiety of Englishmen and the war thereafter died away. In fact, the defeat of the Armada in August 1588 may be compared with the defeat of the German Air Force in the Battle of Britain in August and September 1940. Both victories were decisive in the history of the world, but at the time each seemed to Englishmen to be but the prelude to greater dangers. Among Shakespeare's contemporaries the first feeling was one of incredible relief, quickly followed by the sobering thought that next time the Spaniards would not repeat their mistakes.

The war continued actively in 1589, when a naval and military force under the command of

Sir Francis Drake was sent to Portugal with the object of restoring Don Antonio, the former King, to the throne from which the Spaniards had driven him — the expedition known as the Portugal Voyage. It was not a success; the Portuguese were not prepared to support Antonio, and although Corunna and Lisbon were sacked, the losses by disease were heavy. In the same year the Queen sent aid to the Protestant French King Henry of Navarre who was fighting the Catholic League of Frenchmen who were allied with the Spaniards. In 1590 while English troops were helping the Dutch in the Low Countries in the struggle against the Spaniards, the Spaniards were slowly advancing in Brittany. In 1591 two small English expeditions were fighting in France — one in Brittany and the other in Normandy, where Essex was in command of a force aiding Henry at the unsuccessful siege of Rouen. In 1593 Henry came to terms with his Catholic subjects. He was converted to Catholicism and so brought an end to the civil war in France. For a time it appeared as if he might be about to abandon the war against the Spaniards, perhaps even to join with them, but he remained true to his alliance with Queen Elizabeth. In 1594 a second expedition to Brittany succeeded in capturing Brest; 1595 was a year of great danger and alarm. Intelligence reports showed that a new Spanish Armada was being made ready. At the same time the alliance with Henry was weakening, as he was quite unable to continue the war. But in the winter of that year orders went out that a large English fleet should be prepared for an expedition in the spring. The alliance continued for the next few months, and in April the Spaniards besieged Calais. Essex at the time was at Dover supervising the assembly of ships. He begged to be allowed to carry over such troops as he could raise to go to the rescue of Calais. On April 9, which was Good Friday, the Lord Mayor was suddenly called away from the Paul's Cross sermon and ordered to collect and dispatch one thousand soldiers at once, but the order was countermanded the same night. Two days later, on Easter Sunday, troops were again ordered. Officers were sent round to the city churches as the people were making their Easter communion and the parish constables shut the church doors until they had collected the necessary numbers. On April 14, the noise of the cannonading outside Calais was heard all day in London, but before the expedition could sail news came that Calais had fallen.

The preparations for the great expedition then went on, and fleet and army were assembled at Plymouth. The expedition, which consisted of more than one hundred and fifty ships and ten thousand soldiers, set sail at the beginning of June. On July 19 news reached London that a magnificent victory had been won. By luck and good generalship the English fleet had entered the Bay of Cádiz, where it destroyed three great Spanish galleons and captured two others. The army then landed, and after a brief fight occupied Cádiz, which was completely sacked and burned. The great fleet of Spanish merchantmen was destroyed by fire. The Queen, however, was very dissatisfied with the expedition. Although every man who took part had helped himself to rich plunder, her own share turned out to be meager.

In 1597 another expedition was prepared under the command of Essex to raid the coast of Spain, but the weather throughout the early part of the summer was stormy and tempestuous and the ships were scattered. It was not until August 19 that the fleet set out to raid the islands of the Azores and to wait for the Spanish treasure fleet from South America. The expedition was a failure. There had been constant bickering between the naval men under Ralegh and the military under Essex, and very little was accomplished. Meanwhile there was a great danger at home, for it was learned that a new Spanish Armada was at sea. It was, however, scattered by tempest before reaching the English coast.

It may be noted that Shakespeare wrote *I Henry IV* while London was still swarming with returned soldiers and captains from the Islands Voyage.

In 1598 the war with Spain languished as the situation on the Continent was uncertain. Henry IV, though nominally an ally, was effecting very little, and in April, without consulting his allies, he made a separate peace with the Spaniards. Meanwhile the situation in Ireland, always uneasy, was worse than usual. For some years the Irish had been in a state of unrest and sporadic rebellion, and the control of the English, except in the district around Dublin called the English Pale, was uncertain. Irish rebels at this time were led by Hugh O'Neill, Earl of Tyrone. In the summer of 1598 the small English forces which garrisoned the Pale were sent out against Tyrone, and in a disastrous battle near Armagh were cut to pieces. Rebellion quickly spread through the rest of Ireland, and by the end of the year it appeared likely that all Ireland would be lost.

In 1599 Essex was sent to Ireland with a model army of sixteen thousand men and failed completely, but in 1600 a new force under Charles Blount, Lord Mountjoy, was sent over. Mountjoy, by establishing garrisons and continually harassing the rebels, gradually regained control.

In 1601 the war both on the Continent and in Ireland was fiercer than ever. There was renewed activity in the Low Countries, where the Spaniards were besieging Ostend. They also sent a small expedition of three thousand men which occupied Kinsale in Ireland. Nevertheless, at the end of the year there were great victories on both fronts. Mountjoy defeated the Irish rebels and forced the Spaniards in Kinsale to surrender, while the Anglo-Dutch force under Sir Francis Vere, consisting of only twelve hundred men, utterly defeated an assault by ten thousand Spaniards.

There were no decisive actions in 1602, but by the end of the year Tyrone, the leader of the Irish rebels, admitted defeat and asked for terms of surrender. The war between Spain and England ceased suddenly in 1603 when Queen Elizabeth died. Wars in those days were the private quarrels of kings, and her successor, James of Scotland, had no quarrel with the Spaniards. Peace was therefore soon negotiated, and was confirmed in 1604.

The burden of war during Shakespeare's manhood was thus heavy and continuous and, particularly after 1598, men were constantly being demanded from the counties. In July 1601 no less than eight thousand men were required. At a time when armies were small and "total war" still unknown this was a considerable reinforcement for a country of about four million people. The wars touched everyone, and many literary men of the time had some experience of war at first hand, among others, including Edmund Spenser, Thomas Lodge, Ben Jonson, Thomas Campion, John Donne, and Walter Ralegh.

The popular notion of the Elizabethan period

that after the defeat of the Armada peace reigned supreme is thus false to facts. Actually Englishmen passed through as great a period of anxiety as at any time in their history. It is not surprising, therefore, that the plays of the time should abound in military characters. Shakespeare drew many, of all kinds, types, and sizes, from Falstaff, who was a supreme example of the shady side of war, to Othello, Coriolanus, and Henry V.

Nevertheless, in spite of the wars, there was still no regular standing army, though there were always available a number of officers with considerable battle experience. When a campaign was to be fought, armies were levied either by calling for volunteers or by "impresting" men from the cities or the counties. The Council would send a demand for soldiers, who were equipped by the local authorities. Their quality depended on the honesty of the selecting magistrate, but since compulsory service was always unpopular and casualties were heavy, especially through sickness, a fine opportunity was provided to clear the jails or to rid a village of its most unruly bums.

The Army

The unit of the army was the company, commanded by a captain, with a lieutenant and an ensign. The captain was commissioned to collect his hundred men; he drew their pay and was allowed to keep 10 per cent, known as "dead pays." The system was easily and often abused. Dishonest captains, such as Falstaff, conscripted men of good class and then accepted bribes to let them go, or else claimed pay for men who were dead or sometimes men who had no existence except on a nominal roll; these were known as "shadows." In an attempt to keep a check, the mustermaster from time to time inspected the men and compared the nominal rolls with those on parade; but men could be borrowed from other companies for the occasion. In the Irish wars it was even a practice to borrow men from the enemy; they often ran away with their arms after the parade. The discipline of an army depended on the general in command, and such abuses were rare under the leadership of such keen soldiers as Charles Blount, Lord Mountjoy, or Sir Francis Vere. On the whole, the English soldiers fought well, though there were some regrettable incidents.

The best soldiers were the volunteers. Volunteers were not difficult to obtain when a campaign promised good loot. Distinguished noblemen recruited special companies from their own followers. Many gentlemen of good family accompanied Essex on his expeditions to Rouen, Cádiz, and the Azores, among them John Donne the poet. But it is not surprising that army service was unpopular. Although the pay was for the times good (see App. 27), and usually forthcoming, disabled soldiers received no regular pension, and at the end of the campaign were left to shift for themselves. The unemployed ex-soldier was always a problem; for it is a quite modern notion that the veteran deserves special rehabilitation grants or educational facilities.

Education

Elizabethan Englishmen were amply aware of the value of education, and in most places of any consequence schools were available. In London the headmasters of the three great schools — St. Paul's, Merchant Taylors, and Westminster — were men of distinction, whose indirect influence on English life and thought through their pupils was very considerable; and in the country grammar schools too the schoolmaster was often an eminent scholar. Hence not only were most men of any social standing in the provinces literate; many of them were highly cultured. Of the friends, for instance, of the Shakespeare family at Stratford-on-Avon, one was a Master of Arts of Oxford University and another read Latin for pleasure.

The universities, then as now, were the main avenues to preferment for the clever boy, but the prizes were far fewer than the applicants, and many young graduates who began with the highest ambitions had to content themselves in the end with insignificant and degrading occupations. In a play called *The Pilgrimage to Parnassus* performed at the University of Cambridge in 1597 two hopeful young freshmen who are about to enter Parnassus (Cambridge) are thus addressed by a disillusioned scholar:

What, I travel to Parnassus? Why, I have burnt my books, splitted my pen, rent my papers and cursed the cosening hearts that brought me up to no better fortune. I, after many years' study, having

almost brought my brain into consumption, looking still when I should meet with some good Maecenas that liberally would reward my deserts. I fed so long upon hope till I had almost starved. Why, our empty-handed satin suits do make more account of some foggy falconer than of a witty scholar, had rather reward a man for setting a hair than a man of wit for making of a poem; each long-eared ass rides on his trappings and thinks it sufficient to give a scholar a majestic nod with his rude noddle. Go to Parnassus? Alas, Apollo is bankrupt, there is nothing but silver words and golden phrases for a man; his followers want the gold, while tapsters, ostlers, carters, and cobblers have a foaming pouch, a belching bag that serves for a chair of estate for *Regina Pecunia*. See'st thou not my host Johns of the Crown, who lately lived like a mole six years under the ground in a cellar, and cried, " anon, anon, sir," now is mounted upon a horse of 20 marks, and thinks the earth too base to bear the weight of his refined body. Why would it not grieve a man of good spirit to see Hobson [the famous Cambridge hostler] find more money in the tails of 12 jades than a scholar in 200 books?

These are the complaints of a man who has found out for himself the universal truth that

Learning and poverty will ever kiss.

While those who were disillusioned in their material hopes blamed the general prevalence of " barbarism " for their own misfortunes, others who had no need to earn a living were equally disappointed because the university failed to satisfy their intellectual longings and questionings. Lampatho, in Marston's play *What You Will* (1601) envies the ignorant fool who is undisturbed by such problems:

I was a scholar. Seven useful springs
Did I deflower in quotations
Of crossed opinions 'bout the soul of man.
The more I learned the more I learned to doubt.
Knowledge and wit, faith's foes, turn faith about.

The Inns of Court

After leaving the university, the richer student came to London to finish his education by the study of law at one of the Inns of Court, which were the center of the intellectual life of the country. The junior members were the pick of the universities, belonged to the best families, and were not too much occupied with their studies, so that writers and dramatists found in them their best patrons. The peculiar position of the Inns of Court is well seen in the " revels " which the gentlemen of Gray's Inn held in the winter of 1594–95, when they elected one of themselves as " Prince of Purpool " and for several weeks kept up an elaborate and at times impudent parody of the Court and ceremonies of the realm. Moreover, the members of the Privy Council, far from standing on their dignity, attended the revels with great satisfaction and amusement, the Lord Mayor of London asked the " Prince " to make a progress through the city and entertained him at a banquet, and the highmaster of St. Paul's School set his head boy to compose some Latin verses of welcome. The proceedings came to an end with a tournament at Court at which the " Prince," having greatly distinguished himself, was very kindly complimented by Queen Elizabeth herself.

Amongst the ceremonies was the establishment of a mock order of knighthood, and one of the articles imposed on new " knights " was that they should read all fashionable authors and also " frequent the Theatre, and such like places of experience; and resort to the better sort of ordinaries for conference, whereby they may not only become accomplished with civil conversations and able to govern a table with discourse, but also sufficient, if need be, to make epigrams, emblems and other devices appertaining to his Honour's learned revels." It is significant that during this time and for the next forty years many of the best poets and dramatists came from the Inns of Court. Here a man with new ideas could hope for an intelligent hearing, but he might also expect severe and sarcastic criticism. Here, too, the players and booksellers found their best customers.

Books

For the spread of new ideas the booksellers were not of less importance than intelligent readers, and the English mind is accurately reflected in the books which were published. Many of the booksellers' shops were situated by St. Paul's Churchyard. About two hundred publications of all kinds came out each year, of which about a quarter were concerned with current news, presented in various forms from the account of an eyewitness of some battle or state pageant to the doleful ballads which were

composed for the execution of criminals. So far the newspaper had not been invented, but a few new pamphlets contained one or more letters from foreign parts, and the art of headlines was well advanced. One of these news pamphlets bears this alluring title: *A true relation of the French King his good success in winning from the Duke of Parma his forts and trenches, and slaying 500 of his men, with the great famine that is now in the said Duke's camp. With other intelligences given by other letters since the second of May 1592. A most wonderful and rare example, the like whereof never happened since the beginning of the world, of a mountain in the Isle of Palme which burned continually for five or six weeks, with other both fearful and strange sights seen in the air over the same place*. The ballad in doggerel verse set to some well-known tune was, however, the most popular way of circulating news.[6]

Nevertheless Elizabethan Englishmen suffered greatly from lack of regular and reliable information. The issue of news pamphlets was quite erratic, and the most important news, especially when it was liable to embarrass the Council, was suppressed. From the first invention of printing, English printers were very carefully controlled by and through their trade organization, the Worshipful Company of Stationers. Printing was allowed only at London and the two university towns, Oxford and Cambridge, and the London printers and their printing presses were limited in number. In theory it was difficult for a seditious book to be issued, for the printer had first to get the book " allowed " by some responsible authority, then to enter its title in the Hall Book of the Company (better known as the Stationers' Register) and so secure his copyright. But, as with other Elizabethan regulations, these rules were often neglected, and many quite harmless books were published unentered; no one cared until some notorious book got abroad, and then there would be an inquiry, possibly a punishment, and for a few weeks the rules would be kept. It was not easy to publish a complete book in secret, but scurrilous ballads, printed on a single sheet, could be rapidly set up, printed off, and distributed; and a most effective means of annoying the Council was to sing rude songs about its members or praises of those whom it liked.

It is difficult in modern times to imagine a world without radio, telegraph, newspapers, or other means of rapidly dispersing news or opinion; but in Shakespeare's England most men had to rely on hearsay rumor and gossip. The chief members of the Council kept in touch with foreign affairs through regular reports from the ambassadors at the various European Courts. Some kept private correspondents abroad to maintain an information service; the most elaborate of these services was organized by Anthony Bacon for the Earl of Essex, whose influence in the Council was partly due to the fact that he was better informed on foreign affairs than anyone else in the kingdom. Returned travelers were expected to report to the Council on what they had heard and seen, and through them and their own agents the principal merchants in the city of London kept in touch with commercial affairs on the Continent. Such news was circulated daily by word of mouth at the Exchange. The gossipmonger with a friend at Court was much in demand. Londoners thus lived in a constant state of rumor, excitement, and panic.

Shakespeare has drawn a picture of such panic in *King John* (IV. ii. 185–202):

Old men and beldams in the streets
Do prophesy upon it dangerously.
Young Arthur's death is common in their
  mouths,
And when they talk of him, they shake their
  heads
And whisper one another in the ear;
And he that speaks doth gripe the hearer's wrist
Whilst he that hears makes fearful action,
With wrinkled brows, with nods, with rolling
  eyes.
I saw a smith stand with his hammer thus
The whilst his iron did on that anvil cool,
With open mouth swallowing a tailor's news,
Who, with his shears and measure in his hand,
Standing on slippers which his nimble haste
Had falsely thrust upon contráry feet,
Told of a many thousand warlike French
That were embattailèd and ranked in Kent.
Another lean unwashed artificer
Cuts off his tale and talks of Arthur's death.

Next in popularity to news pamphlets came sermons, for which there was a good market. In Shakespeare's lifetime the most widely read author was the Reverend Henry Smith, rector of St. Clement's Dane in London. He began to publish his sermons only late in 1589, and he died in 1591, yet a hundred and twenty-seven editions of his works in various forms appeared before 1640; in the same period ninety-three of Shakespeare's and ninety-seven of Greene's works appeared.

A number of volumes of poetry were put out each year, but the poetry-reading public was select. Poetry for better-class readers was usually printed with considerable care in roman type, and some of the books are charming little editions for the pocket. On the other hand, romantic fiction and news pamphlets were hurriedly turned out and generally printed in the old black-letter type, which was still the normal type for popular reading. The fashion of publishing plays for the educated was rapidly spreading, and though at first these were roughly printed and intended rather for the ballad-reading public, by the end of the sixteenth century they were evidently attracting a more cultured type of reader.

Literary vogues were quite noticeable. The Elizabethan general reader, like the modern, had his whims and fancies. During the 1580's he was content with novels which followed the fashion set by Lyly in his *Euphues* and Sidney in the *Arcadia;* at the end of 1591 he turned to Greene's realistic *Conny-catching Pamphlets,* which were more successful than anything Greene had yet written. Six months later both Greene and Nashe produced allegorical prose satires — *The Quip for an Upstart Courtier* and *Piers Penniless* — which attracted much attention by their scurrilous attacks on recognizable persons, especially Dr. Gabriel Harvey, the Cambridge scholar with whom Nashe kept up a paper war between 1592 and 1599, when the Archbishop of Canterbury ordered that the books should be seized and no more printed. Another fashion which began in the 1590's was for commonplace books — collections of pithy sayings, either original or culled from old authors; of these the most famous is the first edition of Bacon's *Essays* in 1597.

Similarly in poetry, the publication of Sidney's sonnet sequence *Astrophel and Stella* in 1591 stirred all the other society poets to examine their own emotions under the stress of unsuccessful love. This phase lasted for about four years, and then long narrative poems came into fashion; of these the most famous are Shakespeare's *Venus and Adonis* and Marlowe's *Hero and Leander*. At the end of the decade, poets turned from introspection to invective satire aimed at their fellow creatures, either in lengthy imitations of Juvenal or in terse, scurrilous, and at times exceedingly witty epigrams.

Most of these poems were written by young gentlemen of good social position, for authorship was still scarcely a paying profession. There is very little record of the payments given to popular authors, though the fees paid to a dramatist varied from about £6 to £10 for a play, and a hard-working playwright might make about £60 a year (roughly $2400; see App. 27). But authors had a double means of profiting by their own work; they received something from the publisher, but they hoped also to make a little by a judicious dedication to some nobleman or rich patron who might be expected to reward the compliment. Most often, however, the author tried to attract notice by his efforts and so secure some post in a great man's household. Many of the well-known Elizabethan writers, such as Drayton, Daniel, Chapman, Nashe, Jonson, Marlowe, and probably Shakespeare, were supported at some time or other in this way. With the possible exception of Greene and one or two ballad-makers, such as Elderton or Deloney, few writers can have made a living solely from their publications.

The Traveler

Intelligent men, however, gained their views of life from other sources than books. Many of them had seen something of the world by travel. Greene had made the journey to Italy, Lodge served in Cavendish's unfortunate expedition to the South Seas, Donne was present at the capture of Cádiz, Jonson volunteered for the Lowlands, Marlowe had served as a government spy, Campion took his degree abroad. Elizabethan

literature is virile because its authors had lived varied and exciting lives.

Travel was encouraged by statesmen, for the information on foreign affairs given by returned travelers was valuable. But in popular opinion travel was bad for a man; at the worst it infected him with foreign vices and atheism, and even if he escaped these dangers he was likely to come back affecting a foreign accent, or else making ostentatious use of such effeminate toys as a toothpick or a fork to use instead of dipping his fingers in the common dish like a man. Says Rosalind to Jaques,

Farewell, Monsieur Traveler. Look you lisp, and wear strange suits. Disable all the benefits of your own country, be out of love with your nativity, and almost chide God for making you that countenance you are, or I will scarce think you have swam in a gondola.

Travel was supposed to have another ill effect — the returned traveler came back to criticize, and a man who criticized his country was suspected of being a malcontent, and therefore dangerous.

Nevertheless it is a mistake to imagine that Englishmen lived in a state of perpetual uneasy suppression, or even that they were crude or uncivilized. A generation which produced such men as Philip Sidney, Bacon, Ralegh, Drake, Spenser, Hooker, Marlowe, Chapman, Jonson, Donne, not to mention Shakespeare or Queen Elizabeth herself, can stand comparison with any. Nor should an age be judged solely by its sensational events. History is more often the record of the abnormal than of the usual. Normal decency and the uneventful daily round provide no copy for the newspaperman. In Shakespeare's England most men were humane, tolerant, decent, and honest, faithful to their wives, fond of their children, genuinely charitable, reasonably patriotic, and they died in their beds as peacefully as their physicians would allow them.

4. Elizabethan Drama

Mysteries and Moralities

Plays have been acted in England from the earliest times. By the fifteenth century the act-

ing of little religious dramas was frequent, popular, and elaborate; such dramas covered the whole story of the Christian faith from the creation of the world to the "Harrowing of Hell," when Jesus descended into Hell in the days between the Crucifixion and the Resurrection. A surprisingly large number of the texts of these playlets, known as mysteries, have survived. Apart from isolated episodes, there are four complete cycles, each of thirty to forty episodes, which were performed in the cities of Chester, York, Coventry, and Wakefield. As well as mystery plays dealing with the Christian story, there were also plays on the lives of the saints, which naturally portrayed their miracles and are accordingly called miracle plays.

Mystery plays were acted principally in one of two ways. In some places there was an arena or an auditorium where various houses or little stages were set up to represent such localities as Heaven, Hell, Solomon's Temple, and the like, and the action moved from house to house. In other cities carts were used, each being the stage for one episode. Each cart was drawn around to various locations in the city where the episode was repeated. It was often the custom for one of the trade guilds to take up an appropriate episode and present it. In the Chester cycle, for instance, the story of the Flood was appropriately acted by the water-drawers. There was thus healthy local rivalry between the various groups of actors. Moreover, since the population of a medieval city was seldom greater than five thousand, there was all the excitement of a college play where the chief players are well known to everyone in the audience.

Subjects were at first taken from the Bible, but though the Bible is full of good stories, there is usually little characterization or dialogue. So the script-writers began to expand and to improve on their sources. Certain characters were popular — Herod, for instance, was presented as a raging, roaring tyrant. One episode which particularly appealed — as it has to children of all ages — was the story of the Deluge, of Noah, his ark, and its miscellaneous freight. It was generally agreed that Noah's wife must have been a shrew, and Noah was presented as a patient, henpecked husband. Noah and the Flood were at least Scriptural, but though Noah's wife and children are mentioned in Genesis, no details of their home life are recorded.

Before long the Scriptures were not enough, and bolder writers freely invented entirely new episodes. One of the most famous and interesting is the story of Mack and the shepherds.

Mack was a rogue who stole a sheep from the shepherds of Bethlehem as they watched their flocks by night, and the whole story was dramatized as a farce occurring before the shepherds passed on to adore the Holy Babe. Englishmen in the fifteenth century took their religion joyously. Writers of mystery plays had some sense of the tragic, but far more of the comic.

Meanwhile toward the end of the fifteenth century another form of drama, known as the morality, was developed. A morality was an allegorical play wherein qualities, virtues, vices, and other abstract ideas were personified as characters; such plays appealed rather to the more intellectual audience. On the whole, except for an occasional work of genius, such as the play of *Everyman,* moralities are tedious.

Thus by the beginning of the sixteenth century the acting of plays was popular and universal — long before academic persons began to discuss theories of drama. In the earlier decades of the sixteenth century the interest in acting increased. New subjects and kinds of play were introduced, and by the middle of the century acting had become a profession. In the households of noblemen, plays were performed at Christmas time and, as the records show, the players would sometimes ask their lord for a license to repeat the show elsewhere. Sometimes the performances were given at Court before the Queen. So rivalries developed, and as the standard of acting improved, more time and care were needed for rehearsals, until playing became a full-time occupation.

At this time, and indeed until long after Shakespeare's death, professional actors were officially the servants of some great lord who was responsible for their good behavior. They wore his livery or badge, and when they traveled they carried his license. If they were in trouble, he would usually protect them as a matter of personal prestige, but the patron had no further responsibility for his players. Though he could call on them for a play on some special occasion, he did not pay them regular wages or allowances.

The First Theaters

By 1570 professional players had become so popular that the authorities of the city of London regarded them, for a number of good reasons, as a public nuisance. Plays, it was complained, contained unchaste speeches and seditious matter. They attracted great crowds, especially of young men, who wasted their time and money and neglected churchgoing. Where there were crowds there were also pickpockets, quarrels, improper assignations, and above all the risk of spreading the plague. The Lord Mayor and his brethren decided that if they could not forbid players to perform in the city, they would control them by severe regulations.

At this time the great Earl of Leicester's company of players was led by James Burbage, a violent, truculent, and not overhonest man. But Burbage had ideas; he realized that the best way to evade the Lord Mayor was to build his own playhouse in the suburbs of London, outside the legal limits of the city, where the Lord Mayor could not touch him. Accordingly, in 1576 Burbage borrowed money from his brother-in-law, rented a piece of ground in Shoreditch, north of the city, and there set up the first English playhouse, which he called the Theater. The speculation was a success, and soon another playhouse, called the Curtain, was erected near by.

The plays first acted in these playhouses were still crude, and gentlemen of culture did not patronize them; but in the same year, 1576, another kind of theater was opened. The choirboys of the Queen's Chapel Royal and of St. Paul's were often summoned to Court to give musical and dramatic entertainments, which required much rehearsal. The masters of the two choirs hit on the bright notion of giving these rehearsals to a select public who should pay for the privilege of a preview. A hall was rented in the old Blackfriars' Monastery in the city, and was converted into a small private playhouse.

For some years this playhouse prospered. The principal playwright for the boys was John Lyly, who had recently made a name for himself by his two novels, *Euphues* (1579) and *Euphues and His England* (1580). Lyly's plays are delicate trifles, founded on mythical stories and full of songs, witty dialogue, and long speeches in his own peculiar "euphuistic" style; they were never intended for the hearty public that thronged the Theater, and they had little influence on drama written for the public stage. This first Blackfriars Theater lasted until 1589, when the boys became involved in a controversy

which greatly excited Englishmen. The Puritans had succeeded in setting up a secret printing press and publishing a number of pamphlets against the bishops of the Church of England, alleged to be written by "Martin Marprelate," which were very witty and scurrilous, and highly entertaining to the ungodly. The press was harried from place to place, but it still continued to function in spite of the Archbishop of Canterbury and his zealous searchers. It was then decided that wit must be countered with wit. Professional writers, including Lyly, were brought in and a number of attacks appeared from the press with such fancy names as *Pap with a Hatchet, An Almond for a Parrot,* and *A Whip for an Ape.* The players were likewise encouraged, particularly the Paul's Boys. None of the anti-Martin plays have survived, but some of the incidents can be discovered from the pamphlets. Playwrights and players entered into the contest with such zest that they soon became a bigger nuisance even than Martin, and as a result the Boys and their playhouse were suppressed.

Edward Alleyn

Meanwhile the professional players were thriving. A third playhouse, called the Rose, had been erected outside the city limits, across the river on the Bankside in the disreputable suburb of Southwark (see p. 16b). Certain of the younger professional players were becoming famous; of these the greatest was Edward Alleyn, the first star actor in the English theater. Alleyn was a good businessman, and he realized that he needed better plays than had hitherto been available. He had the luck to acquire two which made a considerable sensation. They were Thomas Kyd's *Spanish Tragedy* and Christopher Marlowe's *Tamburlaine.*

Thomas Kyd

The *Spanish Tragedy* (c. 1586) is the first surviving specimen of the revenge play, and it remained a favorite for fifty years. The story tells how young Horatio, son of Hieronimo, the Chief Councilor of the King of Spain, is treacherously murdered in his father's orchard, how the old father ultimately finds out the murderers, and how he achieves a ghastly dramatic vengeance. The play was competently put together and full of incident: a ghost, a midnight murder by hanging, an assassination by pistol, a public execution, several mad scenes, a suicide, and in the final scene three murders and two suicides in quick succession. Apart from these exciting episodes, Kyd had considerable skill in blank verse, and Alleyn made the most of his opportunities in the part of the afflicted old father.

Not very much is known of Thomas Kyd. His father was a scrivener — that is, one who drew up legal documents — and the son was educated at St. Paul's School in London under the great headmaster Richard Mulcaster. Kyd apparently did not go up to either of the universities.

Christopher Marlowe

Far more is known of Christopher Marlowe. His father was a shoemaker in the city of Canterbury, a man of good standing and comfortable means. Christopher was baptized on February 26, 1564, and was thus two months older than Shakespeare. He went up to the University of Cambridge in 1581, took his Bachelor's degree in 1584, and then began to study for his M.A. He was ready to apply for his degree in the spring of 1587, but the university hesitated. Rumors were circulating that he, like many other discontented young graduates, was preparing to go abroad to one of the Catholic colleges. Actually he was at this time employed by the Privy Council on some secret mission, probably as a spy on the Catholics. The Council therefore intervened and Marlowe's degree was granted. Then Marlowe came to London and there attracted the notice of Sir Walter Ralegh. He became one of Ralegh's circle of intellectuals, who were greatly suspected of holding atheistic beliefs and committing other enormities.

Marlowe's *Tamburlaine* was as popular as the *Spanish Tragedy*. As a stage play it is far less successful, but Marlowe's verse was more sonorous, astounding, and magnificent than anything that had hitherto been heard on the stage. The character of the Scythian shepherd, who by the power of his personality and his utter ruthlessness conquered the world, gave Alleyn another sensational part, wholly suited to his noisy and robustious style of acting. The first part of *Tamburlaine* was soon followed by a second which carried the story to the death of Tamburlaine.

The third play which Marlowe wrote was *The Jew of Malta*. As a drama it was a great improvement, for Marlowe by this time had learned a good deal about the theater. The play opens with a prologue spoken by the ghost of Machiavelli, who claims the Jew as one of his own special pupils. Then the curtains at the back of the stage are drawn aside and Barabas the Jew is discovered in his countinghouse with his treasures about him. The opening soliloquy effectively creates an impression of enormous and princely wealth. Then comes the conflict. To pay their ransom to the Turk the Christian Maltese seize the Jew's wealth and convert his house into a nunnery. But Barabas has a daughter called Abigail, whom he persuades to pretend that she wishes to be converted to Christianity. She enters the nunnery and recovers a bag of jewels from a secret hiding place. So once more Barabas begins to prosper. His hate of Christians by this time has grown gigantic. Unfortunately, his daughter has two Christian lovers: Lodovic, her chosen, and Mathias, who is unwelcome. Barabas brings it about that the two men fight and kill each other. This so distresses Abigail that she turns nun indeed. Barabas is so angry that to punish his daughter and prevent her from revealing the murder of Lodovic he sends poisoned rice to the nuns and so wipes out the whole nunnery. Meanwhile, Barabas's fortunes are still rising, and when the Turks enter Malta they make him governor. Nevertheless he promises the Maltese that he will destroy the Turkish leader at a banquet by means of a trapdoor through which the Turk shall fall into a caldron of boiling water. The Maltese, however, betray him. Barabas is caught in his own trap and dies in agony. The end of the play is not as good as the beginning, but it is lusty, rousing melodrama. It gave Alleyn another fine part.

Robert Greene

Soon a third writer of repute was attracted to drama. This was Robert Greene, the best known of all popular writers at this time. Greene, born in 1558, took his Bachelor's degree at Cambridge in 1578, and for some months traveled abroad in Italy and Spain. He came back to Cambridge and took his Master's degree in 1583. Thence he went up to London and became the first successful professional novelist. He wrote a number of novels in the style of Lyly and was soon well known, but as much for his wild life and odd pranks as for his books. At first Greene refused to write for the stage; he considered it beneath the dignity of a scholar. But his needs were always greater than his means, and when he saw the success of Marlowe, he was persuaded to turn playwright.

Greene's first plays were written in imitation of Marlowe's style. They were *Alphonsus of Aragon, A Looking Glass for London* (in which he collaborated with Thomas Lodge), and *Orlando Furioso.* Of these, *A Looking Glass for London* is the most interesting. The play dramatizes the Book of Jonah. It opens with the wickedness of the Ninevites, shown in a series of episodes, some fantastic, others realistic and founded on the sordid experiences of the author. Then the prophet Jonas appears and so effectively denounces the Ninevites for their sins that all turn to repentance and fasting, except Adam the clown, who hides food and drink in his baggy breeches until the searchers find them and carry him off to be hanged, in spite of his protest that *"modicum non nocet ut medicus daret"* ("a little drop won't hurt so long as the doctor orders it"). Finally Jonas comes forward and addresses the audience, warning them that London is as wicked as Nineveh and may likewise expect destruction. *A Looking Glass* had no claims to be considered fine drama, but it was first-class entertainment.

Greene also wrote *James the Fourth, King of Scotland,* which, in spite of its title, has nothing to do with history but is a wild melodrama, and *Friar Bacon and Friar Bungay,* his most frequently read play. Friar Bacon, the famous Oxford scholar, and Edward, Prince of Wales, were historical persons, but the play is a mixture of legendary incidents, such as Friar Bacon's famous magical Head of Brass which spoke, and of romance, such as the love of Lacy, Earl of Lincoln, for the lowly-born daughter of the keeper of Fressingfield. Indeed, Greene's plays almost without alteration would serve as scenarios for Hollywood. Plays about magicians were popular; and not long afterward Marlowe wrote his most famous play, *The Tragedy of Dr. Faustus.*[1]

In February 1592 Alleyn came to act at the

[1] See the edition of the play by F. S. Boas.

Rose Theater, which was owned by Philip Henslowe. Henslowe was a good example of the shrewd boy who prospered by making the most of his opportunities. He had been apprenticed in the leather trade to a certain Master Woodward. On the death of his master, he married the widow and took over her considerable property, part of which he invested in the playhouse. A few months later Alleyn married Henslowe's stepdaughter, and thereafter the two worked together in partnership. As owner of the playhouse, Henslowe drew a share of the daily takings, and being a careful man of business, he entered each day in his account book the name of the play acted and the sum received. This book, known as Henslowe's *Diary* (see p. 65a), still survives, and is one of the most interesting and important documents in the history of the English stage, for it gives a complete record of the plays acted by one company for a period of five years. Later Henslowe acted as banker to the companies playing at his theaters, and he then recorded the sums paid out for new plays, costumes, properties, and other expenses. With the aid of the *Diary* it is possible to date with certainty the plays acted at Henslowe's house, for he noted the first performance of each new play. Unfortunately, there are only scattered and fragmentary records for the other playhouses and companies. Except probably for a few months in 1592, Shakespeare was not connected with Henslowe's ventures.

Shakespeare's First Plays

On March 3, 1592, Alleyn put on a new play called *Harry the Sixth,* which is almost certainly the first part of Shakespeare's *Henry VI.* The play was a great success. Indeed at its first performance the takings were the largest ever recorded in Henslowe's *Diary.* The scenes which showed the heroic English knight Sir John Talbot were especially popular.

Shakespeare at this time was almost twenty-eight years old. He was learning his business as a playwright working for Alleyn and his company, and his first models were Alleyn's great successes: *The Spanish Tragedy, Friar Bacon, Tamburlaine,* and *The Jew of Malta.* It is not surprising that with Alleyn's voice and presence constantly before him, Shakespeare in his earliest plays should have imitated his masters. In

Titus Andronicus he outdid even the horrors of the *Spanish Tragedy,* and in *Richard III* he copied the technique of *The Jew of Malta.*

Alleyn's venture came to an abrupt end on June 11. There had been serious rioting in Southwark caused by apprentices trying to rescue a prisoner from the Marshalsea Prison. As the apprentices had gathered at the Rose on the pretext of watching a new play, the Council ordered all playing to cease until Michaelmas. Alleyn therefore took his company on tour. Soon afterward the plague broke out in London; at such times no playing was allowed.

The Deaths of Greene and Marlowe

Meanwhile, Robert Greene was dying in great poverty from the dropsy brought on by his excessive living. All his friends had left London because of the plague, and he grew very bitter as he contemplated the prosperity of the players who had grown rich on the products of university men like himself. Shakespeare's success especially seemed to upset him, and his annoyance may have been partly increased by the fact that *Henry VI* had been drawing far better houses than his own plays. It was in this mood that he penned the famous letter to his fellow playwrights warning them against "the upstart Crow, beautified with our feathers" (see p. 9b). Greene died on September 2, 1592.

Alleyn came back to London just before Christmas and playing began again at the Rose. The repertory then included *The Spanish Tragedy, The Jew of Malta, Titus Andronicus, Friar Bacon,* and, as new plays, Marlowe's *Massacre at Paris* — a dramatization of the massacre of St. Bartholomew's Day — and *The Jealous Comedy,* which some scholars believe to be the origin of the play afterward rewritten as *The Merry Wives of Windsor.* The plague, however, was still lurking, and in February 1593 the playhouses were again closed.

Marlowe survived Greene by only nine months. His end was sensational. It was a time of general uneasiness, and the Council suspected that some revolutionary movement was about to break out. Mysterious libels were being circulated warning the Flemish traders living in London to get out of the country. As a preliminary measure all writers who might be sus-

pected were apprehended, and Thomas Kyd found himself in jail. When his papers were examined, some pages of a disputation denying the divinity of Jesus Christ were discovered. Kyd was asked to explain how he came to possess such a suspicious document. He declared that it was Marlowe's property and had been left behind when the two men had shared a study two years before. Marlowe was therefore summoned to appear before the Council and to explain himself. On May 30, 1593, while he was still awaiting further instructions, Marlowe, in company with three men named Frizer, Skeeres, and Poley, went to eat and drink in an eating-house in Deptford on the Thames. During the evening Marlowe and Frizer began to quarrel. Marlowe seized Frizer's dagger, but in the scuffle he himself was jabbed in the eye and killed.[2] As Marlowe had the reputation of being a violent and foul-mouthed atheist, the godly regarded his end as highly appropriate. Kyd also died before the end of 1594.

The plague continued all through the summer and autumn of 1593, and it was not until the late spring of 1594 that the players began to drift back to London. For a while the players of the Lord Admiral and the Lord Chamberlain united to play at a small theater in the suburb of Newington Butts. Their plays included *The Jew of Malta, Titus Andronicus, Hamlet,*[3] and *The Taming of the Shrew.* The arrangement, however, only lasted for a few days. Alleyn then went back to the Rose and there reorganized the Admiral's Men; the others combined to form a new Lord Chamberlain's Company. By autumn both companies were firmly established.

The Lord Chamberlain's Players

The Lord Chamberlain at this time was Henry Carey, first Lord Hunsdon. He died on July 22, 1596, and his players then took service with his son, George Carey, second Lord Hunsdon. They were thus for a time officially known as the Lord of Hunsdon's Servants and are so described on the title page of the first quarto of *Romeo and Juliet.* They resumed their former title when the second Lord Hunsdon was ap-

---

[2] The report of the inquest was discovered by Dr. Leslie Hotson in the Public Record Office in London and published in 1925. [3] In the early version. See *Haml* Intro. pp. 600b–601a.

pointed Lord Chamberlain on March 17, 1597.

In the new Lord Chamberlain's Company the leading members were Richard and Cuthbert Burbage, sons of James Burbage, the builder of the Theater, Will Kempe, and Shakespeare. Richard Burbage was beginning to make a reputation as a tragic actor almost as great as Alleyn's, Kempe had long been famous as a clown, and Shakespeare was now without a rival as a dramatist. It was a strong team.

By this time Shakespeare had written the three parts of *Henry VI, Richard III, Titus Andronicus, The Two Gentlemen of Verona, The Taming of the Shrew, The Comedy of Errors,* and *Love's Labor's Lost. Richard III* was one of the earliest successes of the Chamberlain's Men. Shakespeare followed it up with *Romeo and Juliet,* which was immediately popular and much quoted by connoisseurs of poetry. In the Christmas holidays of 1594 the Chamberlain's Men played at Court; they also acted *The Comedy of Errors* for the young gentlemen of Gray's Inn, as a contribution to the elaborate revels of that Christmas (see p. 32a).

Shakespeare next wrote *A Midsummer Night's Dream* — probably in 1595 — presumably for some society wedding, and *Richard II,* which was an attempt to rival Marlowe's *Edward the Second.* As Marlowe's play had been printed in 1593, Shakespeare had the pattern in print before him. The patriotic speeches of John of Gaunt were much noted and are quoted in collections of pearls from the poets. Apart from these two plays, this seems to have been a poor year for drama. No plays of note were produced at the Rose, and once more the playhouses suffered from interference from the authorities.

The summer of 1594 had been disastrously wet and the crops failed. The price of food rose; there were serious riots in the city; and on June 26 the playhouses were again shut for two months. In September the Lord Mayor made another attempt to persuade the Council to suppress plays altogether, on the ground that plays were responsible for instilling young persons with "lewd demeanors." There was, indeed, a general air of uneasiness and gloom, especially as it was widely (and accurately) believed that the Spanish were preparing a new and greater Armada to invade England.

The Lord Admiral's Men

Nevertheless in 1596 several notable plays were produced. On February 12, the Admiral's Men put on *The Blind Beggar of Alexandria,* written by George Chapman, in which Alleyn took the part of a shepherd's son who, by disguising himself successively as a duke, a beggar, a moneylender, and a swashbuckling count called Hermes, lives a quadruple life with a different wife fitted to each personality. It was a fantastic play, even for the Rose, but it has some importance in the history of drama because Count Hermes is the first notable specimen of a "humor" character, his particular humor [4] or whim being to wear a patch over one eye, to shroud himself in a large cloak in cold weather or hot, and to carry a pistol with which to emphasize his humor by shooting up his enemies.

To this year also is usually assigned Shakespeare's *King John,* which was a rewriting of an old anti-Catholic play that had belonged to the now defunct Queen's Players and had been published five years earlier. *King John* is a very uneven play, but it contains some good topical speeches which directly reflect the general alarms of this anxious year. It was followed by *The Merchant of Venice,* a play which owed a little to Marlowe's *The Jew of Malta.*

Meanwhile, the Chamberlain's Men had their troubles. The twenty-one years' lease of the ground on which the Theater had been built was due to lapse in 1597, and the landlord, whose name was Giles Alleyn (no relation to the player), was reluctant to renew it. Old James Burbage, whose business instincts were as keen as ever, realized that conditions in the playing profession were fast changing. In the last seven years the standard of plays had so vastly improved that gentlemen of means were now keen patrons of the playhouses. Burbage decided to revive the idea of a private playhouse where plays could be acted indoors, at a high price, to an exclusive audience. He therefore acquired the lease of the old dining hall of the Blackfriars' Monastery and, at great expense, converted it into a small theater. It was almost ready for opening when the aristocratic residents in the neighborhood objected to the presence of a playhouse and petitioned the Council to prohibit the scheme. Burbage was forbidden

[4] See App. 3.

to proceed with his plan and was thus left with a considerable loss. He died a few weeks later, leaving the Theater property to his son Cuthbert and the Blackfriars to Richard.

In March 1597 the Admiral's Men produced at the Rose another play by Chapman, *A Humorous Day's Mirth,* which was very well received. This was the first notable example of a " comedy of humors." In plays of this kind the author aimed at presenting on the stage contemporary types of folly. The particular types caricatured by Chapman were an elderly jealous husband, Count Labervele; his newly married young wife, Florilla, who was a Puritan; a foolish gentleman called Master Blanuel, who tries to show his good breeding by copying the mannerisms of gallants; and Dowsecer, a melancholic man. Dowsecer is the first conspicuous specimen of the melancholic character who scorns the world and stands conspicuously apart, wrapped in a large black cloak and his own bitter thoughts. The play is a good indication of the change of public taste; it was intended for an intellectual and sophisticated audience.

Ben Jonson

About the same time a new competitor appeared to rival both the Admiral's Men and the Chamberlain's Men. From each company some actors broke away to form a new company under the patronage of the Earl of Pembroke. They acted at the Swan playhouse on the Bankside, with some success. But they rashly chose to put on a new play, *The Isle of Dogs,* the work of Thomas Nashe, the most vitriolic of all the Elizabethan satirists, and one of the actors in the company, Benjamin Jonson, who for the first time became conspicuous. The play was a bitter satire and so full of " seditious and slanderous matter " that the Council took stern action. They caused all playhouses to be shut up forthwith, and then sent Jonson and two of his fellow players, Gabriel Spencer and Robert Shaw, to prison. Pembroke's Men thereupon dissolved, but the chief actors agreed that when they came out of prison they would join the Admiral's Men at the Rose.

The offenders were released in October, and both the Admiral's Men and the Chamberlain's Men began again to play. During the restraint,

Shakespeare's *Richard II* had been published, and was so popular that at least three editions were printed during the next year. Soon afterward, Shakespeare continued the story in *I Henry IV.* When the play first appeared the fat knight was named Sir John Oldcastle. The real Oldcastle had been burned as a Lollard heretic during the reign of Henry V, and was thus regarded as one of the first Protestant martyrs. Oldcastle, by right of marriage, had acquired the title of Lord Cobham. The contemporary Lord Cobham, an unpleasant young man who had newly succeeded to the title, objected to the appearance of his predecessor in so disreputable a guise. Shakespeare was therefore obliged to alter the name to Falstaff, who became the most popular of all his characters.

By this time, the rivalry between the Chamberlain's Company and the Admiral's Men was becoming keen, and in the scene where Falstaff acts the part of the King rebuking his prodigal son he assumes the tragic mannerisms of the great Alleyn in a heavy role. The first part of *Henry IV* was so successful that Shakespeare followed it with a second part, probably first produced in the early months of 1598. The parodies in the second part were more conspicuous; Ancient Pistol, a new character, ranted about the stage in a close imitation of Alleyn's mannerisms, uttering bombastic and unintelligible phrases which were culled from the more extravagant plays in the repertoire of the Rose playhouse. Falstaff, Pistol, Bardolph, and the rest of the gang were themselves " humor " characters, and in the list of persons printed in the first folio in 1623 (see p. 66b) are labeled " irregular humorists."

Shakespeare's next play was *Much Ado about Nothing,* the first of the three mature romantic comedies; it was probably produced during the summer of 1598. By this time, the Chamberlain's Men were acting at the Curtain playhouse, for the dispute between the Burbages and their landlord was still unsettled and they had to abandon the Theater.

Meanwhile, since his release from prison Ben Jonson had been writing plays for the Admiral's Men. Ben was the most colorful of the Elizabethan dramatists, and much is known of his life. According to his own account, given to the Scottish poet William Drummond of Hawthornden in 1619, his grandfather was a gentleman from the County of Cumberland; his father had been imprisoned in the time of Queen Mary, lost his estates, and then turned clergyman. Jonson himself was born in London in 1573, a month after his father's death. He was taught at Westminster School by the famous scholar William Camden; but his schooling was interrupted when his mother married a bricklayer, and Ben was put to the trade, which he disliked. Accordingly, he went as a soldier to the Low Countries and there — so he claimed — he killed one of the enemy in single combat. Then he came back to England and turned player. As a young man, he was self-opinionated, conceited, and quarrelsome.

The Comedy of Humors

Jonson's first connection with the Admiral's Men lasted only a few months, and in the late summer of 1598 he sold his first successful play to the Chamberlain's Men. It was called *Every Man in His Humor,* and was produced at the Curtain in September.

The version best known to students differs considerably from the play as first acted, for Jonson revised and rewrote it for the first collected volume of his plays, published in 1616. In the final version the play is set in London and the characters bear English names. In the first version the locality was nominally Florence, but the characters were nevertheless typical Londoners, each representing a different type very familiar to the audience at the Curtain.

Jonson was a student of the classics. He approved Aristotle's theories of drama as expressed in the *Poetics* — and misinterpreted by the Italian critics, who invented the "theory of the three unities" of time, place, and action. They held that drama should present an action which happened in one place and occupied the same time on the stage as the events took in real life. Jonson did not follow these rules too rigidly, but he took great care to plan his plays so that all the events occurred within a single day in the same city and all the characters might reasonably have met each other in the course of their natural occupations. Moreover he held, as did most serious critics of the time, that all literature had a moral purpose. The particular purpose of comedy was to chastise folly by making it ridiculous. Accordingly, in his plays he created char-

acters which were contemporary types, and so plotted the story that each "humor" (see App. 3) displays his own particular folly and is suitably punished for it.

In the early version of *Every Man in His Humor,* Lorenzo, Senior (afterward renamed Edward Knowell, Senior), was an overanxious father who suspected that his son, Lorenzo, Junior, was wasting his time in writing poetry and in the company of a young gentleman called Prospero (renamed Wellbred). Two foolish gentlemen join them: Stephano (Master Stephen), a wealthy fool from the country who wants to learn how to be a gentleman, and Matheo (Master Matthew), a young townsman who writes bad poetry and tries to pass himself off as an aesthete and an intellectual. Matheo is a great admirer of Signor Bodadilla (Bobadil), who poses as a professional soldier of great military experience and distinction. The plot is further elaborated by Thorello (afterward Master Kitely), a merchant inordinately jealous of his young wife. Most of the complications are effected by Brainworm, Lorenzo, Senior's, man-servant, who is full of mischief and ingenuity.

This conception of comedy was not new. It was indeed a direct adaptation of Latin comedy, but the characters and the situations were entirely English. Each character in turn reveals his foolishness in an intricate plot, which keeps to the unities of time and action. Finally, all are brought together in the house of a magistrate, Dr. Clement, and appropriately rewarded or punished.

Every Man in His Humor, especially in the revised version, is still an excellent stage play, though seldom acted, and it set Jonson in the first rank of Elizabethan dramatists. After the first production, there was an unhappy sequel Gabriel Spencer, now one of the Admiral's Players and only a few months before Jonson's companion in misfortune because of *The Isle of Dogs* (see p. 41a), waited for him when the play was over. The two fell to quarreling and went off to the fields to settle the matter with swords. Jonson was wounded, but he killed Spencer. He was arrested and tried for manslaughter, but he pleaded benefit of clergy (see p. 28a) and was released. Thus the Admiral's Men had first lost a promising poet and now **an experienced player.**

The Globe Playhouse

About this time the dispute between the Burbages and their landlord Giles Alleyn reached a climax. In the original lease of 1576 James Burbage had agreed that if the lease of the ground was not renewed at the end of the twenty-one years' occupancy, either the buildings were to be removed or they would become the property of the landlord. As Alleyn had promised to renew the lease, Cuthbert Burbage let the Theater stand. Finally, Alleyn produced a new lease, but the terms were impossible and Burbage refused to sign. This was Alleyn's intention. He proposed to seize the Theater, demolish it, and use its valuable timber. When the Burbages realized Alleyn's plan, they took counsel with the chief sharers in the Chamberlain's Company — Shakespeare, Heminges, Phillips, Pope, and Kempe — and all agreed to finance a new playhouse. They rented a piece of ground south of the Thames, not far from the Rose. Then, during the Christmas holidays, with a party of men armed with swords and other weapons they set about the old Theater, tore it down, and transported the materials to the new site. Here, seven months later, arose the new playhouse, the Globe, the finest theater that had yet been seen in England.

Meanwhile, in the spring of 1599 Shakespeare's *Henry V* was put on at the Curtain. A year had passed since *II Henry IV,* wherein Shakespeare promised to continue Falstaff; but now he allowed Falstaff to die off stage, though the rest of his gang continued — with the addition of a new character, Corporal Nym, who was forever prating of his humors.

The Globe was ready for occupancy about July, and thither the Chamberlain's Men moved. Three of their first plays were *As You Like It,* Jonson's *Every Man out of His Humor,* and *Julius Caesar. As You Like It* was another romantic comedy, but in Jaques Shakespeare created a specimen of the melancholic humor which was now becoming so fashionable.

Every Man out of His Humor was a failure. After the success of *Every Man in His Humor,* Jonson became very arrogant, and he prefaced the new play with an induction or introductory piece in which three characters, apparently spectators, come onto the stage to discuss his theory of the humors and the purpose and history of comedy. The play itself was not so good as its predecessor; the portraits of the humors were too exact and the plot too involved. Jonson also committed a gross error of taste by introducing Queen Elizabeth on the stage, probably idealized as Cynthia or Astraea, to bring the play to a close. This offending episode was dropped when the play was printed. After this failure, Jonson went back to the Admiral's Men and collaborated with Dekker in various pieces of hack writing which have not survived. Thomas Dekker had for some time been writing busily for the Admiral's Men, and in 1599 sold them one of his happiest plays, *The Shoemaker's Holiday.*

Now that the Chamberlain's Men were playing at the Globe and were therefore near neighbors of the Admiral's Men at the Rose, the rivalry between the two companies became more bitter. The parodies in the Falstaff plays especially irked the Admiral's Men. Accordingly, in October 1599 they planned to retaliate. They tried to revive the ill feeling caused two years before, when Shakespeare's fat knight had first appeared as Oldcastle,[5] by producing a play on the real Oldcastle. In the prologue they unctuously claim:

> It is no pampered glutton we present,
> Nor aged counselor to youthful sin.

The authors of the play were Munday, Drayton, Wilson, and Hathaway, and in writing it they borrowed a good deal from Shakespeare's Falstaff. This competition, however, between the two companies did not last much longer; both were threatened with dangerous rivals elsewhere.

The Paul's Boys and John Marston

In the autumn of 1599 after a break of ten years the Paul's Boys (see p. 36a) were reestablished. They were financed by William Stanley, Earl of Derby, who was a keen amateur of the drama. The Boys were immediately popular. They played in a little private house in the precincts of St. Paul's, where a gentleman could be sure of the quality of the audience; he would not " be choked with the stench of garlic, nor pasted to the barmy jacket of a beer-brewer." Their dramatist was John Marston.

[5] See *1 Hen IV* Intro. p. 335a-b.

John Marston, a young man of good family, was the son and heir of John Marston, a bencher of the Middle Temple; that is, a lawyer of high standing. The son was born in 1576, took his degree in the University of Oxford in 1594, and came to London to study law; but he was more attracted to poetry. In 1597 he published a little volume called *The Metamorphosis of Pygmalion's Image and Certain Satires*. He followed this in 1598 with another book of satires called *The Scourge of Villainy*. This was the most popular of all the satires which appeared in the 1590's, but it was an extravagant, ranting book. Marston experimented with words and phrases and created a new kind of poetic language, furious, bombastic, and abounding with strange words.

Marston was a gentleman of means. He would not have condescended to write plays for the professional players at the Globe or the Rose, but there was no disgrace in writing for the genteel audiences which patronized the little theater of the Paul's Boys.

Marston's plays in some ways were as extravagant as his satires. He was, nevertheless, a dramatist of considerable skill, particularly in creating scenes of horror. In the new playhouse, plays were acted by artificial light, and Marston was able to produce vivid effects by the use of a single flickering torch. Among his first plays were *Antonio and Mellida,* and its gory, dismal sequel, *Antonio's Revenge.* Both of these appeared in the autumn of 1599.

By Christmas the Admiral's Men realized that the old Rose could no longer compete with the new Globe. Accordingly, Edward Alleyn decided to move. On January 8, 1600, he and Henslowe signed a contract with Peter Street, who had built the Globe, to erect a new playhouse for them in the parish of St. Giles Cripplegate, north of the City. There were many vexatious delays, which can be traced in Henslowe's *Diary,* but the new house was at last finished in August 1600. It was called the Fortune.

Many difficulties came to the Chamberlain's Men in 1600. In the general uneasiness of the times (see p. 24b), players were obliged to be cautious, and for a while by order of the Council playing was even reduced to two performances a week. Moreover, it had long been the regulation that playing should cease altogether during Lent, and although hitherto the rule had been as much neglected as obeyed, it seemed unsafe this year to incur the anger of the authorities. During this period of enforced idleness Will Kempe, the clown of the company, thought to make some money on the side by betting that he would dance from London to Norwich, a distance of about a hundred miles. He set out on February 10 and reached his destination in nine stages. On his arrival the Mayor and chief citizens gave him a civic reception. It was a triumphant progress and was talked of for years. Kempe was so greatly elated by his success that he planned a much more ambitious venture: to dance over the Alps to Rome. He therefore sold his share in the Globe Theater, left the Chamberlain's Men, and set out. The loss of their clown, always one of the most popular attractions of their playhouse, was serious.

The Children of Blackfriars

Soon after the Admiral's Men had moved into the Fortune, the Chamberlain's Men suffered from a new and far more dangerous rival company. The indoor playhouse in the Blackfriars which James Burbage had built at such expense in 1596 (see p. 40b) was still empty, and Richard Burbage had to find the rent. He was approached by a certain Henry Evans, a Welsh lawyer who had once been a sharer in Lyly's ventures. Burbage agreed to rent the playhouse to Evans, who was in league with Nathaniel Giles, choirmaster of the Queen's Chapel Royal, and the two planned to establish a second boys' company. They were joined by Ben Jonson, who had again parted from the Admiral's Men.

Ben had always longed to write exclusively for audiences of gentlemen and courtiers, and here was his chance. He produced for the Children of the Chapel a play called *Cynthia's Revels,* somewhat after the pattern of one of Lyly's plays, part satire, part masque, part allegory, which would — so he hoped — be produced at Court. The play has the usual crowd of humor characters — foolish courtiers with their fashionable ways, and another melancholic, Crites, the upright judge who neither fears nor favors fools. Crites, indeed, was intended as an idealized portrait of Jonson himself.

Essex's Rebellion

The two boys' companies soon became the fashion and drew off the best part of the usual audiences of the professional players. Moreover, the Chamberlain's Men were involved in trouble which might have been disastrous. By Christmas 1600 it was obvious to observers at Court that the Earl of Essex and his followers were hatching some plot which would soon break (see p. 24a). Shakespeare's *Richard II* had become linked in a curious way with Essex's fortunes. When first published in 1597, the play sold well because contemporaries saw a parallel, not so obvious nowadays, between Queen Elizabeth and King Richard II, with Essex as Bolingbroke. The parallels became more conspicuous when John Hayward brought out his book called *The First Part of the Life and Reign of King Henry the Fourth*. On February 6, 1601, some of Essex's friends went over the river to the Globe playhouse and there saw Phillips, one of the players. They asked that *Richard II* might be played on the next afternoon, which was a Saturday. The players were dubious. *Richard II,* they said, was an old play and would not draw an audience, but they foolishly consented when Essex's friends promised to add forty shillings to the takings. So the play was acted before a large party from Essex House. Next morning, Essex made his disastrous attempt to raise the city of London against the Queen.

The Council took a very serious view of the playing of *Richard II,* which was much stressed at the trials of the conspirators. The Chamberlain's Men were not, however, considered to be involved in the rebellion; indeed, they played at Court on February 24, the night before Essex's execution.

The War of the Theaters

The growing rivalry between the two boys' companies was soon increased by a personal quarrel between Marston and Jonson, their respective playwrights. Jonson disliked Marston and regarded his peculiar style as outrageous. Accordingly, in successive plays these two struck out at each other, and their hostility developed into a regular "war of the theaters." Jonson began the war by introducing into *Every Man out of His Humor* a pair of gulls who try to pass themselves off as wits by speaking in Marston's peculiar manner. In *Jack Drum's Entertainment* Marston retorted with

> . . . bombast wits,
> That are puffed up with arrogant conceit
> Of their own worth, as if Omnipotence
> Had hoisted them to such unequaled height
> That they surveyed our spirits with an eye
> Only create to censure from above.

Jonson followed, in *Cynthia's Revels,* by calling Marston "a strange arrogating puff." Marston in his next play, *What You Will,* which came out in the spring of 1601, replied more fiercely. He prefaced the play with an induction wherein, without mentioning names, he attacked Jonson for his pedantic insistence on rules and his insolent contempt for all who disagreed with him:

> Music and poetry were first approved
> By common sense, and that which pleasèd most,
> Held most allowèd pass. Know rules of art
> Were shaped to pleasure, not pleasure to your
> rules.

Jonson was furious. He determined to make Marston so ridiculous that he would be silent forever. Jonson was a slow writer, and hitherto he had produced a new play at intervals of about ten months. His next play was written in fifteen weeks. It was called *Poetaster, His Arraignment,* a clever, witty comedy, telling of the Court of the Roman Emperor Augustus, with its brilliant circle of artists, including the poets Virgil, Horace, and Ovid. In the play, Horace, as everyone knew, was Jonson himself. Horace is harassed by two inferior wits, Crispinus and Demetrius, whom he finally causes to be condemned after a public trial before the Emperor. As a punishment Crispinus (alias Marston) is given an emetic which makes him vomit up his turgid words; he is then dismissed with a warning to mend his manners. The play was acted by the Children of the Chapel at the Blackfriars in the early autumn of 1601.

Jonson had made many enemies, for apart from Crispinus other characters whom he satirized were recognizable individuals; he had also taken to sneering at the professional players. Before *Poetaster* appeared, the Chamberlain's Men heard of Jonson's forthcoming revenge and hired

Dekker to make an answer. Dekker was a very rapid writer, and soon he had the reply ready. It was called *Satiromastrix; or, The Untrussing of the Humorous Poet.*[6] As a play it was a fantastical hodgepodge. The main story told of the English King, William Rufus (1087–1100), and his lust for the bride of Sir Walter Tyrrel. The underplot was a comedy of contemporary middle-class intrigue. In the midst walked Roman Horace (alias Jonson), who was most viciously abused and finally crowned with nettles and made to swear that he would thereafter behave himself. Dekker knew Jonson well, and his Horace is a brutal but vivid and most amusing caricature. *Satiromastrix* was acted by the Chamberlain's Men and by the Paul's Boys. It brought an end to the stage war; Jonson was bitterly offended and withdrew from writing plays altogether for the time being.

Shakespeare himself took a hand in the stage war. At Christmas time the students at St. John's College, Cambridge, acted a play called *The Second Part of the Return from Parnassus,* in which two students played the parts of Richard Burbage and Will Kempe. Kempe was made to say:

Few of the university pen plays well, they smell too much of that writer Ovid and that writer Metamorphosis, and talk too much of Proserpina and Jupiter. Why, here's our fellow Shakespeare puts them all down — aye, and Ben Jonson too. Oh, that Ben Jonson is a pestilent fellow, he brought up Horace giving the poets a pill, but our fellow Shakespeare hath given him a purge that made him bewray his credit.

The incident has not been identified. It may be that a passage from one of Shakespeare's known plays — *Troilus and Cressida* or *Hamlet* are the most likely — has disappeared. It may be that in a play which has not survived there was an uproarious scene in which a close stool was the principal property.

Little is known of the other plays produced by the Chamberlain's Men in 1601. Parts of *Hamlet,* in the version now known, were certainly written during this year, and probably also *Twelfth Night,* but as a whole the year was the worst for the professional players since the plague years of 1592–94, and there was little call for new plays.

Business improved considerably in 1602. On February 2 the Chamberlain's Men played *Twelfth Night* before the members of the Middle Temple. In this year Shakespeare probably wrote *Othello* and *All's Well That Ends Well.* Business with Henslowe and Alleyn also improved. By this time they had a strong team of writers. Dekker had returned to work for them and two newcomers appear in the *Diary,* John Day and John Webster. During the year twenty new plays were ordered for the Fortune.

In this year also another new company was formed under the patronage of the Earl of Worcester. Their most important actor was Will Kempe, who had returned to England in the previous September. Although he had fulfilled his bet to dance to Rome, the venture was not a success and now he was back in London; but he did not rejoin his old colleagues. Worcester's Men began to act at the Rose in August. Their most interesting play was Thomas Heywood's domestic tragedy *A Woman Killed with Kindness.*

The King's Players

The next year, 1603, was a turning point in the fortunes of the players. At first the prospects were gloomy. By the middle of March it was clear to the Council that Queen Elizabeth was dying, and in the general anxiety every precaution was taken to prevent disturbances. On the nineteenth, orders were sent out that all playing should cease. The Queen died on March 24. By midday King James of Scotland had been proclaimed in London as true and lawful King of England. Immediately there was a scramble for offices under the new King. Among the lucky ones were the Lord Chamberlain's Players, who on May 19 were granted a patent appointing them to be the King's Players and Grooms of the Chamber Extraordinary (see p. 13b). For Shakespeare's fellows this was a great change in fortune. Hitherto the profession of playing had been precarious. Players existed only by favor of the Queen, for the official reason given to the Lord Mayor of London and others when they petitioned that the theaters should be suppressed was that since the Queen enjoyed plays, the players must be allowed to keep in practice. Now all was changed; henceforward the players became royal servants and favorites who were constantly in demand at Court. In the last four years of Queen Elizabeth's reign the Chamberlain's Men played at Court fourteen times; in the first four years of the new reign they played forty-one times.

In the general excitement Ben Jonson forgot his grievances and emerged from retirement. He was reconciled with the King's Men, who produced his latest play, a tragedy called *Sejanus*. This was a most scholarly production, full of minute and accurate details of Roman customs, and based on wide reading in the Roman classics. The historical Sejanus was a favorite of the Emperor Tiberius, who allowed him to obtain such power in the state that Sejanus became a very real danger. The Emperor, thus forced to scheme against his favorite, persuaded the Senate to turn against him, and Sejanus was brutally executed. This play was another of Jonson's unlucky ventures. It was dull and overbookish, and the audience did not like it. Moreover, some members of the Council were disturbed by the theme. It was hardly more than two years since Essex had been beheaded, and a play on the rise and fall of a royal favorite seemed too close to recent events. Jonson was summoned before the Council to explain himself.

The bright hopes of the spring were soon disappointed. As summer came on the plague broke out in London and all the playhouses were closed. The King's Men abandoned the Globe and went on tour in the country. The plague lasted all through the summer and autumn, but by mid-November the weekly record of deaths had fallen to a hundred. The Court during these months had been on progress, and at the beginning of December King James came to Wilton, near Salisbury, the great house of the Earl of Pembroke. Hither the King's Players were summoned to perform before King James, and for their trouble and expense they were allowed £30.

By their appointment as players to the King, the Chamberlain's Men were marked out as the leading company. At the end of the year recognition came also to the Admiral's Men and to the Children of the Blackfriars; the young Prince Henry became the patron of Alleyn's company; the Children of the Chapel were appointed Children of the Queen's Revels, and Samuel Daniel, the poet, was made their overseer.

Unfortunately Henslowe had by this time ceased to record his theatrical transactions in his *Diary,* and henceforward dramatic records of all kinds are so scanty that no continuous history of the London companies is possible. Apart from scattered incidents and details, the account must necessarily be slight and haphazard.

There was much activity for the King's Men in the year 1604. On March 15 King James made a progress in state through the city of London, beginning at the Tower and ending at Ludgate. The King's Men walked in the procession, wearing their red liveries as Grooms of the Chamber. In August they were called on to attend the Spanish Commissioners, who had come to London to take part in the formal ceremonies of swearing the peace between England and Spain. Several new plays came out this year, including probably Shakespeare's *Measure for Measure*. In November the King's Men acted *Othello* for the King and the Court in Whitehall Palace, but in December they caused some offense by putting on a play called *The Tragedy of Gowry* — a dramatization of a sensational attempt to murder King James in 1600 — in which one of the players took the part of King James himself. In the Christmas holidays they played before the King *Measure for Measure, The Comedy of Errors, Love's Labor's Lost, Henry V,* and *Every Man out of His Humor.*

Of the plays acted by other companies in 1604 the best was John Marston's *Malcontent*. This was produced and owned by the Children of the Queen's Revels at the Blackfriars. It was also brought out by the King's Men — although the play was not theirs — in retaliation for the fact that the Children had acted one of their plays.

In the new reign Ben Jonson's fortunes likewise rose. Queen Anne, the Danish wife of King James, was especially fond of masques, and she and her ladies from time to time acted in them. The masque was an elaborate and costly form of entertainment presented by young courtiers of both sexes. Based on a mythological story in verse, the masque was usually intended as a compliment either to the royal family or to the special occasion, such as a marriage, for which it was written. The story was made the excuse for much singing, dancing, elaborate and extravagant costumes, and ingenious scenery. Ben Jonson was particularly successful in writing the kind of poetic dialogue and lyric required for masques. The costumes, scenery, and complicated devices necessary for the production were mostly designed by Inigo Jones, but the partnership between Jonson and Jones was uneasy, as each was very jealous of the other.

During the year 1605 the King's Men continued to display their repertory before their master, and on Sunday, February 12, they acted *The Merchant of Venice*. This so delighted King James that he ordered the performance to be repeated on the following Tuesday.

"Eastward Ho"

Now that the old restraints had been removed, the players grew bolder and held the mirror more closely up to nature. The Children especially were encouraged to comment on their betters. This led to troubles. In September the Children of the Queen's Revels acted a new play by Jonson, Chapman, and Marston called *Eastward Ho*. *Eastward Ho* is a very moral story of life in London. The chief characters are a goldsmith, his two prentices, and his two daughters. One of the apprentices is an extravagant spendthrift, the other is a very proper, hard-working, thrifty young man, who marries the younger daughter and prospers. The other daughter is a giddy creature and is encouraged by her mother to marry a shiftless knight called Sir Petronel Flash. Sir Petronel immediately spends his wife's money, and to avoid her indignation goes on board a ship that is about to sail to Virginia. He is joined by the extravagant apprentice, and when the ship is wrecked in the Thames they are both imprisoned for debt until, after edifying repentance, they are finally delivered by the kindhearted goldsmith. The story in itself was harmless enough, but in speaking of the disreputable Sir Petronel, one of the characters, mimicking King James's Scots accent, remarked: "I ken the man weel. He is one of my thirty-pound knights." And of Virginia, Seagull, the dishonest captain, declared that it was as pleasant a country as ever the sun shined on:

And then you shall live freely there, without sergeants, or courtiers, or lawyers, or intelligencers, only a few industrious Scots, perhaps, who indeed are dispersed over the face of the whole earth. But as for them, there are no greater friends to Englishmen and England, when they are out on't in the world, than they are. And for my part, I would a hundred thousand of 'em were there, for we are all one countrymen now, ye know, and we should find ten times more comfort of them there than we do here.

The King was very angry. Marston ran away, but Jonson and Chapman in spite of their indignant protests of innocence were for a while sent to prison.

This year, also, the King's Men probably acted a domestic comedy called *The London Prodigal*, which was published with Shakespeare's name as its author on the title page, though there is no other reason to believe that Shakespeare took any hand in it.

On November 5, the great Gunpowder Plot was discovered (see p. 17a). The horror and the general feeling of unrest and disillusion of the times are well reflected in the plays which came out during the months following. Early in 1606 the Children of the Blackfriars played a cynical and satirical comedy called *The Isle of Gulls*, the work of John Day. The play is interesting as a comment on the mood of the year and the increasing difficulties of dramatists with an audience that now had grown hypercritical. Nowadays, complained the prologue, spectators are of three kinds: either they insist on satire and invectives, or they call for bawdry, or else nothing will content them but furious and bombastic language. And if the play is not to their liking, they rise in the middle of the action and go out of the theater, leaving the poor Children to speak their lines to an empty house.

Although Ben Jonson was now mostly occupied with writing masques, he produced in 1606 a comedy for the King's Men which — just to show what he could do when he tried and to answer those who had mocked him for only writing one play a year — he completed in five weeks, without any assistance. It was called *Volpone; or, The Fox* and was Ben's bitterest satire on humanity.

During this year, Shakespeare wrote two of his greatest plays, *Macbeth* and *King Lear*. It is possible that *Macbeth* was written in a hurry as one of the three plays which the King's Men acted before the King of Denmark on a memorable state visit. *King Lear* was acted on December 26 as one of the plays presented during the Christmas holidays. There are many indications that Shakespeare had written it during the previous nine months.

About this time a new dramatist appeared, a

young man of about twenty-one named Francis Beaumont. His first play, called *The Woman-Hater* (1606), was one of the last to be acted by Paul's Boys, who had not received any special encouragement in the new reign and soon afterward disappeared entirely from the records. In the following year, Beaumont wrote *The Knight of the Burning Pestle* for the Children of the Queen's Revels. It is his best-known play and gives a most entertaining picture of drama in the private playhouses. Into the auditorium there stray a grocer, his wife, and their two apprentices. While the Children endeavor to perform their own play, the grocer insists that his apprentices shall also act a romantic drama in honor of grocers. The play, however, was a failure at its first production, probably because it satirizes the audience as well as the citizen; intellectual audiences do not always appreciate humor at their own expense.

During these months (1607–08) it is probable that the King's Men acted Shakespeare's *Antony and Cleopatra* and *Coriolanus*. Of plays by other dramatists, one of the most remarkable and powerful was *The Revenger's Tragedy* by Cyril Tourneur. In this play the idea of the humors is applied to tragedy, each of the principal characters in the play representing a type of vice.

The King's Men and the Blackfriars Playhouse

In March 1608 there occurred a scandal which had far-reaching and unfortunate effects on drama. From the very beginning the Children of the Queen's Revels had been very impudent. Many of their plays openly satirized prominent persons, and from time to time there had been trouble. In spite of the indignation which had been caused by *Eastward Ho,* Chapman and the Children offended again and more seriously with a play called *The Conspiracy and Tragedy of Biron.* The real Biron, who had occupied much the same position in France as Essex in England, visited Queen Elizabeth in 1601, and his execution in France in 1602 caused a great sensation. The play thus dealt with French history and scandal only six years old. In one scene Henri IV, the reigning French King, was brought onto the stage together with his wife and his mistress, Madame de Verneuil. The ladies quarreled and the Queen gave hard words

and blows to her rival. The French ambassador protested to the Earl of Salisbury, and the Children were ordered not to repeat the play; but in spite of this, as soon as the Court was moved out of London, they acted it again.

Once more all theaters were closed, and some of the chief offenders were sent to prison. This was hardly fair to the other companies, who indeed, according to the French ambassador's dispatch to his King, offered 100,000 francs to be allowed to resume playing. As a result of this scandal, those in charge of the Children were obliged to give up the private Blackfriars Theater, which in August reverted to Burbage and the King's Men. Henceforward, the King's Men decided to use it as a winter playhouse and to retain the Globe for use only during the summer. The Globe, as they had learned from experience, had several disadvantages: in wintertime the spectators were obliged to cross the river by boat or to trudge over London Bridge; the location was inconvenient, and the approach muddy. As a result of the change, the King's Men found that their profits greatly increased. Henceforward, they naturally preferred to cater to the one-class, moneyed audience which frequented the Blackfriars.

In 1608 Shakespeare probably wrote *Timon of Athens,* the last of his misanthropic plays, and *Pericles,* the first of a batch of four which deal with two generations, wherein the wrongs committed by the elders are set right by the children.

Francis Beaumont and John Fletcher

From about this time dates the most famous of dramatic partnerships, when Francis Beaumont and John Fletcher began to write plays together. Fletcher was the son of a former Bishop of London. Very little is known of him, but the partnership was much noted because the friendship between the two seemed remarkably close. According to gossip, Beaumont and Fletcher lived together on the Bankside, not far from the playhouse; they were both bachelors and shared everything in common — clothes, cloaks, and even a mistress. Their partnership lasted for about five years, until 1613, when Beaumont married an heiress and thereafter ceased to be actively interested in drama. Although in published editions a large number of plays appear as the work of "Beaumont & Fletcher," they can, in fact, have collaborated on only about half a dozen; the rest were the work of Fletcher after Beaumont had left him.

In 1609 Jonson returned to the theater with a comedy called *Epicoene; or, The Silent Woman,* which was acted by the Children of the Queen's Revels; but *The Alchemist,* which he wrote in 1610, was acted by the King's Men. In publishing this play he added a list of those who had taken the chief parts. Shakespeare's name was not included, for by this time he was taking little part in the affairs of the theater.

Beaumont and Fletcher were now working for the King's Men, who produced *Philaster; or, Love Lies a-Bleeding,* one of the best specimens of that kind of play called tragicomedy, in which these two dramatists specialized, a play full of incident, sometimes tragic, yet ending happily for the chief persons concerned. It is a type of drama which has been popular ever since on the stage and in the films. The story of *Philaster* is a kind of mixture of *Hamlet* and *Twelfth Night.* The King is a usurper, but he dares not do away with Prince Philaster, who is the true heir to the throne. To oust Philaster, however, he brings in Pharamond, a Spaniard, to marry Arethusa, his daughter and heir. But Arethusa is in love with Philaster. So Philaster gives Arethusa his adoring page, a youth called Bellario, whom he had found in the country, to be the go-between in their secret love. Meanwhile, the Spanish Prince, having no success with his wooing of Arethusa, becames involved in scandal at Court. Arethusa's obvious liking for the page also causes scandal and misunderstanding, until, after a long series of excitements, it is revealed that the page was in fact the daughter of the King's Chief Councilor, who doted on Philaster and hoped to live near him. The play was quite fantastic, but excellent entertainment. Beaumont and Fletcher have none of the depth of Shakespeare, but they have great skill in writing dialogue, and an excellent stage sense. No one could sit in the theater and watch Shakespeare's greatest tragedies unmoved; Beaumont and Fletcher kept the audience interested and mildly excited from beginning to end, but they never seared the emotions. It is more than a coincidence that Shakespeare's next play, *Cymbeline,* with its enormous complexity, false emotion, and interminable explanation and reconciliation, should bear some resemblance to *Philaster.*

Shakespeare's Last Plays

In 1611 Shakespeare wrote *The Winter's Tale* and *The Tempest,* and Jonson tried his hand at another classical tragedy called *Catiline.* Beaumont and Fletcher's *King and No King,* another melodrama, was also put on by the King's Men. In the autumn of 1612, the great preparations being made for the marriage of the Princess Elizabeth with the Elector Palatine of Bohemia were for a while disturbed by the death of the young Prince of Wales in November. Nevertheless the King's Men acted as usual at Christmas, when their plays included the two parts of *Henry IV, Julius Caesar, Much Ado about Nothing, Othello, The Winter's Tale, The Tempest,* Jonson's *Alchemist,* and Beaumont and Fletcher's *Philaster, The Maid's Tragedy,* and *King and No King.* The wedding of the young Princess took place on February 14 — St. Valentine's Day — and during the days which followed the King's Men acted fourteen times.

On June 29, 1613, they suffered a great misfortune — the Globe playhouse was burned to the ground. There are several descriptions of this disaster. The most famous occurs in a letter written by Sir Henry Wotton:

Now, to let matters of state sleep, I will entertain you at the present with what has happened this week at the Bank's side. The King's players had a new play, called *All is True,* representing some principal pieces of the reign of Henry VIII, which was set forth with many extraordinary circumstances of pomp and majesty, even to the matting of the stage; the Knights of the Order with their Georges and garters, the Guards with their embroidered coats, and the like: sufficient in truth within a while to make greatness very familiar, if not ridiculous. Now, King Henry making a masque at the Cardinal Wolsey's house, and certain chambers [small cannon] being shot off at his entry, some of the paper, or other stuff, wherewith one of them was stopped, did light on the thatch, where being thought at first but an idle smoke, and their eyes more attentive to the show, it kindled inwardly, and ran round like a train [fuse], consuming within less than an hour the whole house, to the very grounds. This was the fatal period of that virtuous fabric, wherein yet nothing did perish but wood and straw, and a few forsaken cloaks; only one man had his breeches set on fire, that would perhaps have broiled him, if he had not by the benefit of a provident wit put it out with bottle ale.

The destruction of the Globe Theater was symbolical. During the fourteen years of its existence Shakespeare's greatest plays had first been produced on its stage; he had now ceased to write for the theater. A new Globe soon rose from the ashes, but it belonged to another generation, and catered to the taste of a new audience.

5. The Elizabethan Playhouse[1]

Of all forms of literary art, that called drama is most affected by external and material influences. An acted play needs a combination of all kinds of artists. At its most elaborate there is a company of professional players to present the characters and speak their words; a stage with scenery, lighting, and equipment; experts responsible for designing and manipulating the settings; designers and makers of costumes; musicians for the orchestra. Above all, a producer or director is needed to mold all these activities into unity. Even in the most elementary form of drama a number of players must combine to act a play in harmony.

The dramatist is thus confined by limitations which do not hamper other forms of art; his play needs living actors and a stage. He must therefore write a play which can be acted on that stage. If he is confined to a stage ten feet square, his characters must be few. Moreover, if his players are professionals and need wages, he must not write a play which will require more actors than the receipts will warrant. A place for the spectators is also needed; and as there are many or few spectators, so the whole structure of the play will be changed. A pageant to be acted in a stadium will require very different treatment from intimate comedy in a small college theater.

When Shakespeare was a boy, players were content with the simplest of equipment. They toured the country and acted wherever they could find a stand or attract an audience. Plays were performed in all kinds of places — churchyards, innyards, halls, and great houses. But London was their natural home, for only in London was there a population large enough to provide regular audiences.

Before playhouses were built, certain inns became associated with the playing companies.

The medieval inn was built on a standard pattern. Rooms were grouped around four sides of a courtyard, from which the street was reached by passing under an arch. The chambers of the guests opened onto a gallery which looked down into the courtyard (see Pl. 4a). At the farther end of the courtyard lay the stables. In the courtyard the players erected their stage on trestles or barrels, and there gave their show. They gathered money from the spectators in the yard; the innkeeper took his share by collecting from his guests in the gallery. Such a stage was bare and primitive, with no possibility for liberty of action or scenic devices. It was natural, therefore, for hearty and noisy speechmaking to take the place of subtle action. Very few inns of this kind survive in England, but in the city of Gloucester there is still the New Inn, built in the fourteenth century, which preserves the old form and is known to have been used by Elizabethan players.

Players also acted in great halls, the Court, and the Inns of Court. The medieval great hall, of which many specimens survive, was also built to a pattern (see Pl. 4b). It was intended chiefly as a community dining hall. Overhead there was a beamed roof. At one end was a dais, or raised platform, with a long table running across. There the chief persons sat. Below the platform in the main hall the tables ran lengthwise; there sat the servants and less important members of the household. Halls of this kind are still used daily in the colleges at Oxford and Cambridge. At the lower end of the hall ran a screen of paneled oak which occupied the whole width and was pierced by two wide doors through which the servers brought the food. Over the screen there was a gallery used by musicians and spectators on great occasions. With this screen as background, the players entertained the guests after the feast.

The pattern for the Elizabethan playhouse

[1] This chapter owes much to two modern studies of first rate importance, *The Globe Playhouse* by John C. Adams (1942) and *Shakespeare's Audience* by Alfred Harbage (1941).

was set by the first English playhouse, the The-
ater, built by James Burbage in 1576 (see p. 36a).
Burbage combined the seating arrangements of
the inn with the stage arrangements of the great
hall. This general pattern was modified and im-
proved in the later playhouses, and by the time
the Globe was built in 1599 the playhouse had
become quite elaborate, with much stage ma-
chinery and many conveniences to enable the
play to be acted quickly and effectively.

Although scholars are generally agreed about
the arrangement and plan of the Elizabethan
playhouse, direct information from contempo-
rary accounts is meager. The details have been
assembled by much patient and elaborate re-
search from many sources, of which the chief
are:

1. PICTURES: There is only one contemporary
picture of an Elizabethan stage (see Pl. 5a).
This is a sketch of the Swan Theater made in
1596 from memory by a Dutch traveler called
De Witt; but his memory was as slight as the
drawing, and some of the details are demonstra-
bly wrong. There are also two or three small
engravings of plays in progress, dating from
about two generations later.

2. BUILDING CONTRACTS: Among the papers of
Philip Henslowe (see p. 65a) are two contracts,
the first for building the Fortune playhouse in
1600, the second for building the Hope in 1613.

3. STAGE DIRECTIONS IN PLAYS AND CASUAL REF-
ERENCES: Much can be deduced from a careful
observation of the original editions of Eliza-
bethan plays. For instance, in *Antony and Cle-
opatra*, which was first printed in the folio of
1623, there appear the following:

*Flourish. Enter Pompey, at one doore with Drum
and Trumpet: at another Caesar, Lepidus, An-
thony, Enobarbus, Mecenas, Agrippa, Menas with
Souldiers; Marching.*

*Enter Ventidius as it were in triumph, the dead
body of Pacorus borne before him.*

*Enter Agrippa at one doore, Enobarbus at an-
other.*

*Camidius Marcheth with his Land Army one
way over the stage, and Towrus the Lieutenant of
Caesar the other way: After their going in, is heard
the noise of a Sea fight. Alarum. Enter Enobarbus
and Scarus.*

Musicke of the Hoboyes is under the Stage.

*Enter Cleopatra, and her Maides aloft, with
Charmian & Iras.*

They heave Anthony aloft to Cleopatra.

From the stage directions in this one play
alone it is clear that the stage for which *Antony
and Cleopatra* was written had at least two doors
by which characters entered and which were
wide enough to admit bearers carrying a corpse;
that there was a place under the stage where
the musicians could play their oboes; that there
was a place aloft large enough for Cleopatra
and her maids, and solid enough to withstand
the heaving-up of Antony. By collecting all such
stage directions from the earliest texts [2] and the
many passages in dialogues which indicate ac-
tion, a fairly accurate picture can be recon-
structed of the playhouse and its arrangements.

The Fortune contract gave a number of meas-
urements in detail. The playhouse was a square
frame building with an outside measurement of
eighty feet on each side.[3] Inside, the yard was
fifty-five feet square, the space between outer
wall and yard being occupied by spectators' gal-
leries. There were three tiers of galleries, the
lowest twelve feet high, the second eleven feet,
the third nine feet, each gallery jutting over the
one below. The stage was forty-three feet wide
and extended to the middle of the yard. Unfor-
tunately, no plan survives, but the stage of the
Fortune was "contrived and fashioned like unto
the stage of the said playhouse called the Globe,"
and was built by the same builder.

The Globe, the most famous of all Elizabethan
playhouses, was, however, an octagonal build-
ing. On the outside each of the eight sides was
approximately thirty-six feet, and the diameter
of the whole was eighty-four feet. It was a frame
building, standing on low brick supports, and
the roof was thatched with straw. It was about
thirty-three feet high to the eaves. Inside ran
three galleries, one above the other, surround-
ing the yard, which was fifty-six feet in diam-
eter. The galleries looked down upon the stage,
which was at one end and occupied about a
third of the yard. Three sections of the octagon

---

[2] The student must always consult the original quartos or
the first folio, because many of the stage directions in the modern
texts were first inserted by editors of the eighteenth century who
knew nothing of the methods of staging in Shakespeare's day.
[3] The reader will better appreciate the smallness of the play-
house if he takes the measurements of any familiar hall or large
room.

were used for backstage and the needs of the players; the remaining five sections were used for the spectators. The yard was open to the sky and the stage was lit by daylight.

A spectator entered from the street by a door facing the stage. If he wished to stand in the yard to watch the play, he placed one penny in a box held by the gatherer and went straight in. If he desired a seat in one of the upper galleries, he paid a second penny and went up by one of the staircases to the right or left. If he wished to go into the lowest and most expensive gallery, he paid a third penny. Spectators who stood in the yard were known as the "groundlings." They were the noisiest, cheapest, and least desirable patrons. In the galleries the spectators sat. In addition, on the lowest gallery on either side of the stage, there were "gentlemen's rooms" reserved for the more distinguished spectators, who had also the privilege of sitting on a cushion. And for a time it was fashionable for gallants to sit or sprawl on the stage itself.

There has been considerable argument among scholars about the capacity of the Elizabethan playhouse. Dr. Harbage points out that in the Fortune the space available for spectators was 1842.5 square feet in the yard and 5725.32 square feet in the galleries. Since a man standing requires on an average 2.5 square feet and a man sitting 3.75 square feet, the total capacity of the Fortune was: standing, 818, sitting, 1,526, a total of 2,344 persons. Other evidence suggests that a full house held between two thousand and three thousand spectators and that on an average day some 1,250 attended each of the playhouses. This means that in 1595, when the Chamberlain's Men and the Admiral's Men were playing in London, about fifteen thousand patrons attended their theaters weekly. Ten years later, when five companies were acting regularly, the weekly number rose perhaps to twenty-one thousand. Thus one in ten or even more of the population of London came to the theater weekly. The proportion of town dwellers nowadays who go weekly to the movies is far greater.

The audience at the playhouse was a fair cross section of the citizens of London; that is, much the same type of audience as now visits the theater in New York or Chicago. A play was the most democratic form of gathering of men and women of all classes. No one had any particular rights over the other; firstcomers got the best places, and there was no advanced booking of seats. Hence the audience was in its place and eager when the play began. There was none of that trampling over the toes of those in the front seats which disturbs a modern play for the first ten minutes. It was a keen audience and well trained. Some critics regret that Shakespeare had to demean himself to please the mob. This is a foolish criticism. Shakespeare's audience was his greatest asset, for it was composed neither wholly of half-wits nor wholly of highbrows, but was a well-proportioned mixture of all levels of taste. It had its intellectuals, young gentlemen from the Inns of Court, and the gallants, but it had also many citizens and their wives and prentices, and the latter, especially in the more skilled trades, had already received an education in rhetoric and the classics which would dumfound most modern high-school boys. After all, an audience which appreciated Shakespeare's plays and encouraged him to write for them is hardly to be despised.

On the other hand the theater had many enemies. Apart from the Puritans, who objected to the theater on moral grounds, the Council was always suspicious. Any form of entertainment that attracts crowds will also attract the parasites that prey on crowds — pickpockets, touts, and prostitutes — and the enemies of the stage were loud in their complaints. Drama, being an intelligent form of entertainment, attracts intelligent and critical spectators. It could therefore be used as propaganda, and in those times government did not approve of methods of propaganda which it could not wholly control. For this reason, the theaters were closely watched, and whenever there was any likelihood of disturbance, they were immediately closed. But, taking the records as a whole, it is surprising that there were so few cases of disturbance in the playhouses at a time when general disorder was common.

The stage differed considerably from the modern stage in its arrangements and in its conventions, and as a result the whole theory of Elizabethan drama differed. In the modern theater the stage resembles a picture frame covered with a curtain. When the play begins, the auditorium lights go out, leaving the stage bright in contrast with the surrounding darkness. There is thus a psychological barrier between spectators and actors. In theory, modern actors pretend to be living their parts oblivious of the audience, who are, as it were, spies through a fourth wall. When the act is finished, the curtain descends, the lights go up, and the audience is abruptly cut off from the world of illusion. Scenery is realistic, properties and costumes are as accurate as possible. Convention demands that the actors shall speak and behave naturally. In the modern theater, if we are to understand what is going on in a character's mind, some natural means must be taken to show it. We become self-conscious if the character thinks aloud, or reads letters audibly, or turns aside to comment in a stage whisper. Nevertheless, modern realism is itself a convention. Spectators willingly allow themselves to pretend that the actors are in reality the people whom they represent, and that the wall before them is made of bricks and not of canvas and plywood.

Elizabethan conventions were quite different. The stage jutted out into the yard and was surrounded on three sides by spectators. There was no curtain to conceal or reveal the main stage, no light but daylight. Hence contact between actors and spectators was close and intimate; both shared in one experience. As there was little attempt at scenery, so there was no realistic setting. All the illusion nowadays created by the electrician and the scene-painter had to be effected by the dramatist and the actors. Words and gestures alone kindled the imagination. When the modern director requires dawn or moonlight, he calls on the electrician. When Shakespeare needed dawn, he suggested it in the dialogue: '

> But, look, the morn, in russet mantle clad,
> Walks o'er the dew of yon high eastward hill.

For night, the modern stage has its cyclorama with little electric lights that twinkle. Shakespeare, in *The Merchant of Venice,* evokes moonlight in words:

> How sweet the moonlight sleeps upon this bank!
> Here will we sit and let the sounds of music
> Creep in our ears. Soft stillness and the night
> Become the touches of sweet harmony.
> Sit, Jessica. Look how the floor of heaven
> Is thick inlaid with patines of bright gold.
> There's not the smallest orb which thou behold'st
> But in his motion like an angel sings,
> Still quiring to the young-eyed cherubins.

This is romantic moonlight and rather obvious. Far more subtle was his creation in *Macbeth* of the atmosphere of grim night, when there was neither moon nor stars:

> BAN. How goes the night, boy?
> FLE. The moon is down, I have not heard the clock.
> BAN. And she goes down at twelve.
> FLE.   I tak't 'tis later, sir.
> BAN. Hold, take my sword. There's husbandry in heaven,
> Their candles are all out. Take thee that too.
> A heavy summons lies like lead upon me,
> And yet I would not sleep. Merciful powers,
> Restrain in me the cursèd thoughts that nature
> Gives way to in repose!

We owe the poetry of Shakespeare's plays to the barrenness of the Elizabethan stage and to the appreciation of the Elizabethan audience.

Although the playhouse was small, the main stage was large — a platform jutting out into the yard like an apron (see Pl. 5a). Here most of the action of the play was staged. On either side of the stage there were doors, the main entrances through which characters came on and went off. The doors themselves could be used symbolically. In a history play, one side of the stage might be France, the other England. One door at least had a knocker and a grille and was used as the door of a house, a tavern, a nunnery, a prison, or a tomb, or the gate of a city. As for scenery, since the spectators were accustomed to using their imaginations, all that was necessary was to indicate the locality. This was done not by sets or program notes but in the course of the dialogue. One reason why Shakespeare's plays are so vivid to read or to broadcast is that so much of the action is described and embedded in the words.

Thus in *Lear:*

> CORN. Bind fast his corky arms.
> GLO. What mean your Graces? Good my friends, consider
> You are my guests. Do me no foul play, friends.
> CORN. Bind him, I say.
> REG. Hard, hard. O filthy traitor!
> GLO. Unmerciful lady as you are, I'm none.
> CORN. To this chair bind him. Villain, thou shalt find——
> GLO. By the kind gods, 'tis most ignobly done
> To pluck me by the beard.

Or in *Macbeth* as Macduff hears the news of the murder of his wife and children, Malcolm comments:

> Merciful heaven!
> What, man! Ne'er pull your hat upon your brows.
> Give sorrow words. The grief that does not speak
> Whispers the o'erfraught heart and bids it break.

Or in *Coriolanus* when Volumnia demonstrates to her son the proper action for winning back the people:

> I prithee now, my son,
> Go to them, with this bonnet in thy hand,
> And thus far having stretched it, here be with them,
> Thy knee bussing the stones — for in such business
> Action is eloquence, and the eyes of the ignorant
> More learnèd than the ears — waving thy head,
> Which often thus, correcting thy stout heart,
> Now humble as the ripest mulberry
> That will not hold the handling. Or say to them
> Thou art their soldier, and being bred in broils
> Hast not the soft way which, thou dost confess,
> Were fit for thee to use as they to claim,
> In asking their good loves. But thou wilt frame
> Thyself, forsooth, hereafter theirs, so far
> As thou hast power and person.

Or Hamlet begging his friends to keep the secret of the Ghost:

> But come,
> Here, as before, never, so help you mercy,
> How strange or odd soe'er I bear myself,
> As I perchance hereafter shall think meet
> To put an antic disposition on,
> That you, at such times seeing me, never shall,
> With arms encumbered thus, or this headshake,
> Or by pronouncing of some doubtful phrase,
> As " Well, well, we know," or " We could an if we would,"
> Or " If we list to speak," or " There be, an if they might,"
> Or such ambiguous giving out, to note
> That you know aught of me. This not to do,
> So grace and mercy at your most need help you,
> Swear.

Or again when Hamlet takes a recorder from one of the players:

HAML. Oh, the recorders! Let me see one. To withdraw with you —— Why do you go about to recover the wind of me, as if you would drive me into a toil?

GUIL. O my lord, if my duty be too bold, my love is too unmannerly.

HAML. I do not well understand that. Will you play upon this pipe?

GUIL. My lord, I cannot.

HAML. I pray you.

GUIL. Believe me, I cannot.

HAML. I do beseech you.

GUIL. I know no touch of it, my lord.

HAML. 'This as easy as lying. Govern these ventages with your fingers and thumb, give it breath with your mouth, and it will discourse most eloquent music. Look you, these are the stops.

There is no need for stage directions to tell the actor or the reader what is happening.

Over the stage, supported on two lofty pillars and running parallel with the roof, was the " shadow," which protected the players from the rain. The pillars themselves were also a useful adjunct to the stage; they were often used as trees, masts, and the like. Beneath the stage there were trapdoors, one large main trapdoor and four subsidiaries; through the trap ghosts and spirits appeared.

Behind the main stage there was an inner stage or recess, sometimes called the " tiring house " or " the place behind the stage," or the " study." [4] It occupied one section of the octagon. Within this inner stage, which was frequently used, were played indoor scenes requiring properties, such as a Court scene with a throne; a Council chamber with a table and stools; a tavern, a tomb, a cave, a prison, or a study. When not required, the inner stage was concealed by curtains, a natural place to conceal eavesdroppers. When Claudius and Polonius retire to overhear Hamlet's conversation with Ophelia, they step through these curtains and stand behind them. At the back of the inner stage was a door, and behind this door a staircase which led up to the second level.

On the second level, parallel with the second gallery and part of it, was the " chamber." [4] When not required, this also was covered with a curtain. In front of it there jutted out a balcony which was used to represent the walls of a castle or a town. Here Richard II, as from the walls of Flint Castle, addresses Bolingbroke, who stands on the stage beneath. The chamber itself was the same size as the recess and could be used for a bedchamber or the living room in a house,

[4] This is Dr. J. C. Adams' term.

or for any other purpose when the dramatist required characters on the upper level. On either side of the chamber there were windows. From one of these, in *The Merchant of Venice* Jessica speaks to Lorenzo before she elopes with him. The gallery was also useful as part of the main stage. As it jutted out, it provided a roof of sorts, which could become the eaves of a house, or a shed. Here, for instance, Conrade and Borachio, in *Much Ado about Nothing,* hold the conversation which is overheard by the Watch.

On the third level there was another chamber, normally used by the musicians, but available occasionally for scenes. The man who describes Othello's ship on the horizon presumably stands in this third chamber.

On the fourth level was the turret. It contained a bell frequently used to ring an alarum or to toll a knell. Here were created the sound effects. Cannon balls were rolled on boards to imitate thunder, and the noises of " alarums and excursions " were produced with drums and trumpets.

The most effective way of visualizing the production of plays on the Elizabethan stage is to follow one play through and endeavor, so far as is possible, to reconstruct its staging. *Romeo and Juliet* is a good example, because in the two early quartos the stage directions are very much fuller than usual.[5] In the following analysis of the action — which must necessarily be conjectural — are included stage directions from the first and second quartos. Those from Q1 are shown in italics and single quotes ('), those from Q2 in italics and double quotes (").

ACT I, SC. i:
" *Enter Sampson and Gregory with swords and bucklers of the House of Capulet,*" by the RIGHT door. At the LEFT door enter Abraham and Balthasar of the Montagues. Benvolio enters at the RIGHT door. Tybalt enters by the LEFT door. During the fight, " *enter three or four citizens with clubs or partisans,*" through the CURTAIN of the RECESS. " *Enter old Capulet, in his gown, and his wife,*" by the RIGHT door. " *Enter old Montague and his wife,*" by the LEFT door. " *Enter Prince Escalus with his train,*" through the CENTER. The Prince

goes out through the CENTER. Capulet and his party go out through the RIGHT door, leaving Montague, Lady Montague, and Benvolio. Romeo enters through the BACK curtain. Benvolio draws attention to his approach with the phrase: " See where he comes! So please you, step aside." (Some such phrase as " See where he comes " is the usual method of drawing attention to a character who is entering from the *rear* of the stage.) Montague and his wife go out by the LEFT door; after some talk Benvolio and Romeo follow them.

ACT I, SC. ii:
Capulet and Count Paris, followed by Peter, enter by the RIGHT door and go out again, leaving Peter. Benvolio and Romeo enter by the LEFT door and read the letter. At the end of the scene, Peter goes out RIGHT; Romeo and Benvolio go out LEFT.

ACT I, SC. iii:
The curtains in the CHAMBER above are opened, revealing Lady Capulet and Nurse. Juliet joins them. A servingman enters to say that the guests have arrived. The curtains over the CHAMBER are closed.

ACT I, SC. iv:
By the RIGHT door, " *enter Romeo and Mercutio, Benvolio and five or six other Maskers, torchbearers.*" After a while, " *they march about the stage and Servingmen come forth with napkins* " through the curtain of the RECESS. They remain on the stage, as

[ACT I, SC. v:][6]
the curtains on the RECESS are opened and at the back of the stage enter old Capulet with " *all the guests and gentlewomen to the Maskers. Music plays and they dance.*" Tybalt goes out RIGHT. At the end of the scene, Capulet's party goes out, on either side at the back of the RECESS. The others go out by the RIGHT and LEFT doors. The curtains of the RECESS are closed.

ACT II:
The Chorus comes through the curtains at the BACK, advances to the center of the stage, delivers his lines, and goes back.

ACT II, SC. i:
" *Enter Romeo alone,*" by the LEFT door. He advances to the front of the stage and says:
" Can I go forward when my heart is here?
Turn back, dull earth, and find thy center out.'
As he moves toward the back of the stage, Benvolio and Mercutio enter by the LEFT door. Romeo hides

---

[5] This demonstration should be followed with the aid of the illustration (Pl. 5b). "Right" means as the actor faces the audience; i.e., the reader's left. The reader will find it an interesting problem in Elizabethan staging to work over other plays in this manner, especially with the aid of the stage directions in a reprint of the original quarto or folio text.

[6] The scenes set off in brackets have been created by editors; in the original texts the action is not interrupted.

by the right pillar (i.e., he keeps the pillar between himself and the other two). Benvolio and Mercutio go out LEFT.

[ACT II, SC. ii:]
When they have gone, Romeo is about to continue his move to the back when Juliet opens the WINDOW and looks out. Romeo pauses and then goes toward her. They converse. A voice calls for Juliet; she goes from the WINDOW, but quickly returns. The lovers bid good night. Juliet closes the WINDOW, and Romeo goes out RIGHT.

ACT II, SC. iii:
"Enter Friar alone with a basket," through the curtains of the RECESS; he comes forward. Romeo enters by the RIGHT door. They go out together through the curtains of the RECESS.

ACT II, SC. iv:
Benvolio and Mercutio enter by the LEFT door. Romeo enters through the curtain of the RECESS. "Enter Nurse and her man" by the RIGHT door. Benvolio and Mercutio go out by the LEFT door. After his conversation with the Nurse, Romeo goes out LEFT, and she goes out RIGHT.

ACT II, SC. v:
The curtains in the CHAMBER above are opened, revealing Juliet. The Nurse enters. At the end of the scene the curtains of the CHAMBER are closed.

ACT II, SC. vi:
The curtains of the RECESS are opened revealing Friar Laurence and Romeo. The recess is now the Friar's cell. Through the door at the back of the RECESS 'enter Juliet, somewhat fast, and embraceth Romeo.' As the Friar prepares to marry the lovers the curtains of the RECESS are closed.

ACT III, SC. i:
"Enter Mercutio, Benvolio and men," by the LEFT door. By the RIGHT door, enter Tybalt and others. Romeo enters through the RECESS curtains. Tybalt draws attention to his entry with "Here comes my man." Tybalt and Mercutio fight; 'Tybalt under Romeo's arm thrusts Mercutio, in and flies' through the RIGHT door. The page goes out by the LEFT door. Mercutio, supported by Benvolio, goes out through the LEFT door, whence Benvolio emerges to say that Mercutio is dead. Tybalt re-enters by the RIGHT door. Romeo and Tybalt fight and Tybalt is slain. Romeo runs out by the LEFT door. The citizens enter through the curtains of the RECESS, followed by the Prince. Capulet and his wife enter by the RIGHT door. Montague and his wife enter by the LEFT. At the end of the scene, all

go out by the ways in which they have entered, the body of Tybalt being carried out through the RIGHT door.

ACT III, SC. ii:
The curtains of the CHAMBER above are opened, revealing Juliet alone. 'Enter Nurse, wringing her hands, with the ladder of cords in her lap.' At the end of the scene the curtains of the CHAMBER are closed.

ACT III, SC. iii:
The curtains of the RECESS are opened; the recess once more represents the Friar's cell. The Friar calls to Romeo, who comes in from the side. The Nurse knocks at the back of the door of the RECESS; she enters through the door at the back of the RECESS. At the end of the scene, the Nurse goes out by the door in the RECESS, and the curtains are closed.

ACT III, SC. iv:
Capulet, Lady Capulet, and Paris enter by the RIGHT door. Paris goes out by the RIGHT door as Capulet and Lady Capulet go out through the curtains of the RECESS.

ACT III, SC. v:
The curtains of the CHAMBER above are opened. 'Enter Romeo and Juliet at the window.' 'He goeth down' by the ladder of cords and goes out LEFT. Juliet pulls up the ladder; 'she goeth down from the window.' She shuts the window and passes into the CHAMBER as Lady Capulet enters. Capulet and the Nurse come to them and go out again. The Nurse goes out, leaving Juliet alone. The curtains of the CHAMBER are closed.

ACT IV, SC. i:
The curtains of the RECESS are opened, disclosing Friar Laurence and Paris, as if in Friar Laurence's cell. Juliet enters by the door at the back of the RECESS. Paris goes out through the door at the back of the RECESS. The Friar closes the door at Juliet's words: "Oh, shut the door." At the end of the scene, the curtains are closed over the RECESS.

ACT IV, SC. ii:
"Enter Father Capulet, Mother, Nurse and Servingmen, two or three," by the RIGHT door. The Servingmen go out RIGHT. Juliet enters through the curtain at the back of the stage: "See where she comes from shrift with merry look." Juliet and the Nurse go out through the curtains of the RECESS. Capulet and his wife go out by the RIGHT door.

ACT IV, SC. iii:
The curtains of the CHAMBER above are opened, revealing Juliet and the Nurse laying clothes on

the bed. Lady Capulet enters. She goes out with the Nurse. Juliet takes the potion; ' *she falls upon her bed within the curtains.*' The curtains of the CHAMBER are closed.

ACT IV, SC. iv:

The curtains of the RECESS are opened; the inner stage has now become the hall of Capulet's house. Enter Lady Capulet and Nurse, ' *with herbs.*' Capulet enters. Lady Capulet and the Nurse go out at the side of the RECESS. "*Enter three or four with spits and logs and baskets,*" who pass across the RECESS and go out. Capulet calls for the Nurse, who comes back. He tells her to make haste to call the bride. She goes up the STAIRS at the back of the RECESS.

[ACT IV, SC. v:]

The Nurse from within opens the curtains of the CHAMBER. Juliet is revealed lying on her bed. The Nurse tries to awaken Juliet and at her cries Lady Capulet and then Capulet go up the STAIRS at the back of the RECESS and appear in the CHAMBER. The Friar and the Count enter the CHAMBER. After their lamentations, ' *they all but the Nurse go forth, casting rosemary on her and shutting the curtains.*' In the act of closing the curtains of the CHAMBER, the Nurse is left standing on the BALCONY in front of the closed curtains. Musicians enter on the stage below. She looks down from the balcony and speaks to them and then she passes into the CHAMBER through the closed curtains. Peter enters at the back of the RECESS, and talks to the musicians, who go out by the RIGHT door. The curtains of the RECESS are closed.

ACT V, SC. i:

Romeo enters by the LEFT door. ' *Enter Balthasar, his man, booted* ' — thereby indicating that he has come a long journey on horseback. Balthasar goes out by the LEFT door. Romeo goes over to the RIGHT door (which now becomes the entrance to the Apothecary's shop) and knocks. The Apothecary comes out; he delivers the poison to Romeo, goes back, and shuts the door. Romeo goes out by the LEFT door.

ACT V, SC. ii:

Friar John comes in by the RIGHT door as Friar Laurence enters through the curtains of the RECESS. Each goes out as he came in.

ACT V, SC. iii:

By the RIGHT door, ' *enter County Paris and his Page with flowers and sweet water.*' Paris goes up to the LEFT door (which now becomes the entrance to the burial vault of the Capulets). ' *Paris strews the tomb with flowers.*' The Page whistles. Paris steps forward in front of the left pillar to watch. By the RIGHT door, ' *enter Romeo and Balthasar, with a torch, a mattock, and a crow of iron.*' Romeo goes up to the LEFT door. His man Balthasar crosses the stage as if to go out by the RIGHT door, but comes back and hides by the pillar. ' *Romeo opens the tomb*'; i.e., he puts his crowbar to the LEFT door and pries it open at the words "Thus I enforce thy rotten jaws to open." Paris steps forward. They fight. The Page runs out by the RIGHT door. As Paris dies, he says: "Open the tomb, lay me with Juliet." Romeo picks up the body, and at the words "I'll bury thee in a triumphant grave" passes through the open LEFT door. The curtains of the RECESS are opened, revealing Juliet lying on a bier, and the shrouded corpse of Tybalt. Romeo appears in the RECESS and lays Paris's body down. He takes the poison and falls dead. By the RIGHT door, "*enter Friar with lanthorn, crow and spade.*" He crosses the stage. ' *Friar stoops and looks on the blood and weapons.*' He goes in through the open LEFT door and reappears in the RECESS as Juliet begins to stir. Friar Laurence comes forward and runs away by the RIGHT door. Juliet speaks to her dead lover and as the boy and the Watch come in through the RIGHT door she stabs herself.

By the RIGHT door then enter, in succession, Balthasar, Friar Laurence and Watchmen, the Prince, Capulet and his wife, Montague. They pass to the back of the stage and stand round the bodies in the RECESS.

The Prince then leads them forward and commands: "Seal up the mouth of outrage for a while." At these words, the curtains across the RECESS are closed, concealing the four bodies, and the LEFT door is also closed. After Friar Laurence's tale and the closing words of the Prince, all go out in procession by the RIGHT door.

From this analysis of the action, it will be seen that an Elizabethan play proceeded rapidly, without pauses for change of scenery. It was thus possible for Shakespeare to have twenty or even more scenes in one play.

But although there was little attempt to indicate scenery, there were properties which took the place of scenery. Chairs or stools suggested a living room or a tavern. A bed denoted a bed chamber. A man wearing riding boots had come on a journey by horseback. A watchman with a torch or a lantern indicated nighttime. Properties in the Elizabethan theater were many and varied, and among Henslowe's papers there still exists a complete inventory of the properties belonging to the Admiral's Men in 1598. They include: a rock, a cage, three tombs, a Hell mouth, a bedstead, a beacon, a heifer, the City of Rome, a golden fleece, a lion's skin, a bear's skin, various heads and limbs, a tree of three golden apples, a number of foils, helmets, and shields, two coffins, a dragon, a lion, a great horse, a black dog, and a device for a realistic beheading. It is not known how "Hell mouth" or the "City of Rome" were represented.

Costumes were lavish and magnificent. Henslowe's companies carried a large stock of general costumes, but for most plays they added something special, and there are many entries in the *Diary* recording the purchases of materials of the finest quality.

Not much is known of the style of costuming, but if the picture of *Titus Andronicus* (see Pl. 13a) is in any way accurate, it suggests that plays were produced with a wild mixture of styles. Shakespeare certainly did not greatly care. His Romans in *Julius Caesar* and in *Coriolanus* wore Elizabethan doublets, cloaks, and large black hats. At the same time, it should not be assumed that Elizabethan players lacked all sense of period. Ben Jonson made painful and pedantic efforts to see that his details were accurate in the Roman tragedy *Sejanus;* he is not likely to have approved of doublets for Tiberius and the Senate. There are also occasional details in the records which show that, spasmodically, Elizabethan players had a feeling for accuracy. The well-known account of the burning of the Globe Theater (see p. 50b) reveals the particular care taken that *Henry VIII* should be staged realistically.

There are other instances of accurate costuming not so well known. In 1601, shortly after the execution of the Earl of Essex, Charles, Duke of Biron, paid a state visit to Queen Elizabeth, with a large train of followers. It was much noted at Court that the Frenchmen wore black without any kind of decoration. Sir Walter Ralegh spent all that night with his tailor and appeared at Court next morning with a black taffeta suit and a black saddle. A year later, Biron himself was executed, and within a few weeks the Admiral's Men put on a play about him (see p. 49a). Henslowe's *Diary* records the purchase of a black satin suit for this play.

Another example may be noted. In the reign of King Richard II, men's fashions were very extravagant. Gallants wore shoes with enormously long toes, attached to the knee with a chain. There exists a manuscript play called *Thomas of Woodstock* in which a courtier is brought on wearing a pair of these shoes. On the whole, however, the Elizabethan player costumed his plays without any regard for historical accuracy.

Elizabethan audiences liked noise. The early texts of plays abound with notes for different kinds of trumpet calls, such as sennets, tuckets, and flourishes. No king or royal person enters in state without a flourish on the trumpets. There is a whole series of noises for battles, such as alarums and retreats. In the prologue before Act III of *Henry V,* "chambers" (small cannon) were shot off to rouse the audience into the proper mood of excitement. These noises had considerable psychological effect. Some stage effects were elaborate. In the play *Arden of Faversham* there was a fog, caused presumably by smoke sent up through one of the traps. Lightning was produced by flashes of gunpowder. Wet blood is often indicated in scenes of killing.

The Elizabethan acting company was a "fellowship." It consisted of ten to fifteen sharers who formed the company, with perhaps another ten or dozen extras, three or four boys, who would ultimately become full sharers, money gatherers, who were sometimes women, stage hands, and the like. The members of the company remained constant, as in the modern repertory company. When, therefore, Shakespeare wrote a play, he had to think in terms of his company. He could not, like the modern playwright, expect the director to gather from the theatrical agencies a special cast for each new play. Being a practical working dramatist, Shakespeare made use of the physical features and talents of the individuals in his company. This is particularly noticeable in some of the women's parts. As yet there were no actresses; young women's parts were taken by boys, and Shakespeare wrote to suit the type and capacity of each boy actor. Thus in the three romantic comedies, *Much Ado about Nothing, As You Like It,* and *Twelfth Night,* all of which were written within a few months, one of the women is always small. Hero is "too low for a high praise, too brown for a fair praise, and too little for a great praise"; she is "Leonato's short daughter." Celia is "low and browner than her brother"—that is, Rosalind. Maria is the "little villain," "the youngest wren of nine." It is clear that the same boy took all three parts, and probably a second boy played Rosalind, Beatrice, and Viola. In contrast to the little "lady" is the tall, thin man with a hatchet face who often appears. He is Private Shadow in *II Henry IV* — "this same half-faced fellow, Shadow. Give me this man. He presents no mark to the enemy, the foeman may with as great aim level at the edge of a penknife." He reappears in *Twelfth Night* as Sir Andrew Aguecheek, "as tall a man as any's in Illyria," and also "a thin-faced knave." He is Master Slender in *The Merry Wives of Windsor* "a latten bilbo," a man with "a little wheyface." There was also a bright little boy who took the part of Falstaff's Page in *II Henry IV*. After Falstaff's death, he transferred his services to Pistol in *Henry V*.

Then there was the clown of the company. He was the low comedian and most plays gave him a chance to play a comic servant, or a watchman, or a gravedigger, or to indulge in some business of his own. In fact, the clown was so important a member of the cast that in stage directions in early texts he is usually designated as "clown" regardless of the part which he represents. When the Chamberlain's Men were formed in the autumn of 1594, their first clown was Will Kempe (see p. 39b). Kempe, who was older than the other chief members of the company, had already won a great reputation. His name survives in some of the stage directions in the early quartos. In *Much Ado about Nothing*, for instance, there is a stage direction "enter Kempe and Cowley," where the modern editions read "enter Dogberry and Verges." He also took the part of Peter in *Romeo and Juliet*. Kempe, however, fell foul of his fellows. He was an individualist, and a great favorite with the groundlings. He was particularly famous for his jigs, which he performed after the play was over. When the tone of plays improved and the players began to take themselves more seriously, Kempe became a nuisance. He left the company in 1600. Shakespeare's severe remarks on the clown in *Hamlet,* written after Kempe joined a rival company, were clearly directed against him. After Kempe's departure, a more intelligent and refined kind of clown is noticeable in Shakespeare's plays — Touchstone in *As You Like It,* Feste in *Twelfth Night,* and Lear's singing Fool. These parts were taken by Robert Armin.

The chief member of the Chamberlain's Men was Richard Burbage, the youngest son of the James Burbage who had built the Theater. Burbage first made his name in the part of Richard III, and his rendering of Richard's cry of despair

A horse! A horse! My kingdom for a horse!

was particularly famous. He also is known to have taken the parts of Hamlet, Lear, and Othello.

The Chamberlain's Men remained friends throughout their fellowship. Shakespeare first worked in partnership with Richard Burbage in 1594. Twenty-one years later, when he made his will, Shakespeare left to Burbage and two others of his surviving fellows twenty-two shillings and eightpence to buy rings as mementos. Of Burbage's style as an actor we know little, but we can guess much from Hamlet's advice to the players. Shakespeare could hardly have been so severe a critic of robustious playing had Burbage been a "ham" actor.

Plays were acted on the repertory system. Each afternoon a different play was presented, and the company kept in their program a series of plays to which they were constantly adding. If the lists of plays in Henslowe's *Diary* are any guide to general practice, they show that the average life of a play was about ten performances. Popular plays were acted more often; unsuccessful plays passed out of the repertory after the first or second performance. This meant that the company was constantly in rehearsal and was able to put on a new play very quickly. There is a tradition that Shakespeare wrote *The Merry Wives of Windsor* in a fortnight to please Queen Elizabeth; it may quite likely be true. It follows that the players can have had little time for elaborate production, but they did have the advantage of being a team, always playing together and, at a pinch, able to improvise. The Elizabethan play was thus a very live form of entertainment.

If by some miracle we could be transplanted to a holiday performance at the Globe, we should be surprised in many ways. The playhouse would strike us as very small, uncomfortably crowded, and far more intimate than any modern theater. The presentation would at first seem noisy and crude, but we should soon become used to the trumpet calls and the lack of scenery. The acting might appear embarrass-ingly emotional, but very slick and competent. Shakespeare is not the only dramatist to speak of the "two hours' traffic of the stage." Since the average play contains from eighteen thousand to twenty thousand words, there can have been little dawdling; the rate of speech must have been at least from a hundred and sixty to a hundred and eighty words a minute. Such pace is only possible when the audience is sensitive, keen, and alert. Indeed the greatest contrast to our modern theater would be in the spectators, who responded quickly and violently, unashamedly demonstrating their grief, pleasure, or amusement, and at times — if dissatisfied with the performance or the play — their anger. Shakespeare was lucky in his environment. He would doubtless have succeeded under any conditions, but as it happened, the kind of play which best suited his theater and his audiences needed also the highest kind of poetry.

6. The Study of the Text

Students are often bewildered by the amount of space and energy which an editor of Shakespeare devotes to textual problems. They can seldom find much satisfaction or interest in such a note as this on *Hamlet*, I.i.63:

> 63. the sledded Polacks (Malone): the sleaded pollax (Q1 Q2 Q3); the sleaded Pollax (Q4 Q5); the sledded Pollax (F1 F2); the sledded Polax (F3); the sledded Poll-Ax (Q 1683); the sledded Poleaxe (F4); the sledded Polack (Pope).

Indeed, of all forms of study, textual notes are the dreariest until the reader has some firsthand knowledge of the facts and problems briefly summarized in these mysterious formulae.

Modern readers sometimes forget that the text in which they read a play of Shakespeare is very different in a variety of small ways from Shakespeare's own manuscript or from the first printed version of the play. The differences can best be realized by some examples.

1. HAMLET:

There are three early texts of *Hamlet*: The first quarto (Q1) of 1603, a pirated, garbled version; the second quarto (Q2) of 1604-05, probably set up by the printer from Shakespeare's own manuscript; and the text of the play as it appears in the first folio (F1) of 1623.

A typical example of the differences between the three versions occurs in III.iv; i.e., toward the end of the closet scene. Hamlet is here upbraiding his mother. The ghost of his father has appeared and speaks to him. The Queen sees nothing. In Q1 the text reads:

> *Ham.* Why doe you nothing heare?
> *Queene.* Not I.

> *Ham.* Nor doe you nothing see?
> *Queene.* No neither.
> *Ham.* No, why see the king my father, my father, in the habite
> As he liued, looke you how pale he lookes,
> See how he steales away out of the Portall,
> Looke, there he goes.   *exit ghost.*
> *Queene.* Alas, it is the weakenesse of thy braine,
> Which makes thy tongue to blazon thy hearts griefe:
> But as I haue a soule, I sweare by heauen,
> I neuer knew of this most horride murder:
> But Hamlet, this is onely fantasie,
> And for my loue forget these idle fits,
> *Ham.* Idle, no mother, my pulse doth beate like yours,
> It is not madnesse that possesseth Hamlet.
> O mother, if euer you did my deare father loue,
> Forbeare the adulterous bed to night,
> And win your selfe by little as you may,
> In time it may be you wil lothe him quite:
> And mother, but assist mee in reuenge,
> And in his death your infamy shall die.
> *Queene.* Hamlet, I vow by that maiesty,
> That knowes our thoughts, and lookes into our hearts,
> I will conceale, consent, and doe my best,
> What stratagem soe're thou shalt deuise.
> *Ham.* It is enough, mother good night:
> Come sir, I'le prouide for you a graue,
> Who was in life a foolish prating knaue.
>   *Exit Hamlet with the dead body.*
>
>   *Enter the King and Lordes.*
> *King.* Now Gertred, what sayes our sonne, how doe you finde him?

In Q2 the text reads:

> *Ham.* Doe you see nothing there?
> *Ger.* Nothing at all, yet all that is I see.

Ham. Nor did you nothing heare?

Ger. No nothing but our selues.

Ham. Why looke you there, looke how it steales away,

My father in his habit as he liued,

Looke where he goes, euen now out at the portall.

        Exit Ghost.

Ger. This is the very coynage of your braine,

This bodilesse creation extacie is very cunning in.

Ham. My pulse as yours doth temperatly keepe time,

And makes as healthfull musicke, it is not madnesse

That I haue vttred, bring me to the test,

And the matter will reword, which madnesse

Would gambole from, mother for loue of grace,

Lay not that flattering vnction to your soule

That not your trespasse but my madnesse speakes,

It will but skin and filme the vlcerous place

Whiles ranck corruption mining all within

Infects vnseene, confesse your selfe to heauen,

Repent what's past, auoyd what is to come,

And doe not spread the compost on the weedes

To make them rancker, forgiue me this my vertue,

For in the fatnesse of these pursie times

Vertue it selfe of vice must pardon beg,

Yea curbe and wooe for leaue to doe him good.

Ger. O *Hamlet* thou hast cleft my hart in twaine.

Ham. O throwe away the worser part of it,

And leaue the purer with the other halfe,

Good night, but goe not to my Vncles bed,

Assume a vertue if you haue it not,

That monster custome, who all sence doth eate

Of habits deuill, is angell yet in this

That to the vse of actions faire and good,

He likewise giues a frock or Liuery

That aptly is put on to refraine night,

And that shall lend a kind of easines

To the next abstinence, the next more easie:

For vse almost can change the stamp of nature,

And either the deuill, or throwe him out

With wonderous potency: once more good night,

And when you are desirous to be blest,

Ile blessing beg of you, for this same Lord

I doe repent; but heauen hath pleasd it so

To punish me with this, and this with me,

That I must be their scourge and minister,

I will bestowe him and will answere well

The death I gaue him; so againe good night

I must be cruell only to be kinde,

This bad beginnes, and worse remaines behind.

One word more good Lady.

Ger. What shall I doe?

Ham. Not this by no meanes that I bid you doe,

Let the blowt King temp't you againe to bed,

Pinch wanton on your cheeke, call you his Mouse,

And let him for a paire of reechie kisses,

Or padling in your necke with his damn'd fingers.

Make you to rouell all this matter out

That I essentially am not in madnesse,

But mad in craft, t'were good you let him knowe,

For who that's but a Queen, faire, sober, wise,

Would from a paddack, from a bat, a gib,

Such deare concernings hide, who would doe so,

No, in dispight of sence and secrecy,

Vnpeg the basket on the houses top,

Let the birds fly, and like the famous Ape,

To try conclusions in the basket creepe,

And breake your owne necke downe.

Ger. Be thou assur'd, if words be made of breath

And breath of life, I haue no life to breath

What thou hast sayd to me.

Ham. I must to *England,* you knowe that.

Ger. Alack I had forgot.

Tis so concluded on.

Ham. Ther's letters seald, and my two Schoolefellowes,

Whom I will trust as I will Adders fang'd,

They beare the mandat, they must sweep my way

And marshall me to knauery: let it worke,

For tis the sport to haue the enginer

Hoist with his owne petar, an't shall goe hard

But I will delue one yard belowe their mines,

And blowe them at the Moone: ô tis most sweete

When in one line two crafts directly meete,

This man shall set me packing,

Ile lugge the guts into the neighbour roome;

Mother good night indeed, this Counsayler

Is now most still, most secret, and most graue,

Who was in life a most foolish prating knaue.

Come sir, to draw toward an end with you.

Good night mother.   *Exit.*

  Enter King, and Queene, with Rosencraus

        and Guyldensterne.

King. There's matter in these sighes, these profound heaues,

You must translate, tis fit we vnderstand them,

Where is your sonne?

In F1 the text reads:

Ham. Do you see nothing there?

Qu. Nothing at all, yet all that is I see.

Ham. Nor did you nothing heare?

Qu. No, nothing but our selues.

Ham. Why look you there: looke how it steals away:

My Father in his habite, as he liued,

Looke where he goes euen now out at the Portall.

        Exit.

Qu. This is the very coynage of your Braine,

This bodilesse Creation extasie is very cunning in.

Ham. Extasie?

My Pulse as yours doth temperately keepe time,

And makes as healthfull Musicke. It is not madnesse

That I haue vttered; bring me to the Test
And I the matter will re-word: which madnesse
Would gamboll from. Mother, for loue of Grace,
Lay not a flattering Vnction to your soule,
That not your trespasse, but my madnesse speakes:
It will but skin and filme the Vlcerous place;
Whil'st ranke Corruption mining all within,
Infects vnseene. Confesse your selfe to Heauen,
Repent what's past, auoyd what is to come,
And do not spred the Compost or the Weedes
To make them ranke. Forgiue me this my Vertue,
For in the fatnesse of this pursie times,
Vertue it selfe, of Vice must pardon begge,
Yea courb, and woe, for leaue to do him good.

   Qu. Oh *Hamlet*,
Thou hast cleft my heart in twaine.

   Ham. O throw away the worser part of it,
And liue the purer with the other halfe.
Good night, but go not to mine Vnkles bed,
Assume a Vertue, if you haue it not, refraine to
   night;
And that shall lend a kinde of easinesse
To the next abstinence. Once more goodnight,
And when you are desirous to be blest,
Ile blessing begge of you. For this same Lord,
I do repent: but heauen hath pleas'd it so,
To punish me with this, and this with me,
That I must be their Scourge and Minister.
I will bestow him, and will answer well
The death I gaue him: so againe, good night.
I must be cruell, onely to be kinde;
Thus bad begins and worse remaines behinde.

   Qu. What shall I do?

   Ham. Not this by no meanes that I bid you do:
Let the blunt King tempt you againe to bed,
Pinch Wanton on your cheeke, call you his Mouse,
And let him for a paire of reechie kisses,
Or padling in your necke with his damn'd Fingers,
Make you to rauell all this matter out,
That I essentially am not in madnesse,
But made in craft. 'Twere good you let him know,
For who that's but a Queene, faire, sober, wise,
Would from a Paddocke, from a Bat, a Gibbe,
Such deere concernings hide, Who would do so,
No in despight of Sense and Secrecie,
Vnpegge the Basket on the houses top:
Let the Birds flye, and like the famous Ape
To try Conclusions in the Basket, creepe
And breake your owne necke downe.

   Qu. Be thou assur'd, if words be made of breath,
And breath of life: I haue no life to breath
What thou hast saide to me.

   Ham. I must to England you know that?

   Qu. Alacke I had forgot: 'Tis so concluded on.

   Ham. This man shall set me packing:
Ile lugge the Guts into the Neighbor roome,
Mother goodnight. Indeede this Counsellor

Is now most still, most secret, and most graue,
Who was in life, a foolish prating Knaue.
Come sir, to draw toward an end with you.
Good night Mother.

       Exit Hamlet tugging in Polonius.
       Enter King.

   King. There's matters in these sighes.
These profound heaues
You must translate; Tis fit we vnderstand them.
Where is your Sonne?

A comparison of these three versions shows
that there are many differences. In Q1 the Queen
swears that she had known nothing of the mur-
der and further that she will help Hamlet in
whatever he devises. There is nothing of this in
the other versions. When F1 is compared with
Q2, it will be seen that Hamlet's speeches have
been considerably altered; F1 omits nineteen
lines that occur in Q2. Further, the version in
Q2 is so lightly punctuated that at times the
sense is obscure. F1 is a more carefully prepared
version, but probably not a direct printing from
Shakespeare's manuscript. There is discrepancy
also between the two versions at the end of the
scene. In Q2, the scene ends at *Exit* and the next
scene begins with: *" Enter King, and Queene,
with Rosencraus and Guyldensterne,"* as if the
Queen had gone out and come in again. In F1,
Gertrude is left alone at the end of the scene for
a few moments, and then the King enters alone.
Rosencranz and Guildenstern do not enter un-
til the King calls for them, at line 32.

Which version should an editor of a modern
text prefer? Actually, editors ignore Q1 as a
spurious text and produce a text which contains
all passages omitted in Q2 or in F1; and where,
as often happens, there is a difference in reading
between the two versions, they choose that which
seems to them to give the better sense.

2. KING LEAR:

Similar problems occur in *Lear*. Here there is
a first quarto (1608) and the text as printed in
F1. Q1 is more complete than F1, but the text
is very corrupt, although apparently not a pi-
rated version of the same kind as the *Hamlet* of
Q1. There are indeed about five hundred dif-
ferences between the two texts, but yet Q1, for
all its shortcomings, will often give a better read-
ing than F1. A typical passage illustrating the dif-
ferences between the two occurs in III.vi.92–122.

In Q1, the text reads:

Glost. Come hither friend, where is the King
my maister.

Kent. Here sir, but trouble him not his wits are
gon.

Glost. Good friend — I prithy take him in thy
armes,

I haue or'e heard a plot of death vpon him,

Ther is a Litter ready lay him in't, & driue to-
wards Douer frend,

Where thou shalt meet both welcome & protection,
take vp thy master,

If thou should'st dally halfe an houre, his life with
thine

And all that offer to defend him stand in assured
losse,

Take vp the King and followe me, that will to
some prouision

Giue thee quicke conduct.

Kent. Oppressed nature sleepes,

This rest might yet haue balmed thy broken sin-
ewes,

Which if conuenience will not alow stand in hard
cure,

Come helpe to beare thy maister, thou must not
stay behind.

Glost. Come, come away.   *Exit.*

Edg. When we our betters see bearing our woes:
we scarcely thinke, our miseries, our foes.

Who alone suffers suffers, most it'h mind,

Leauing free things and happy showes behind,

But then the mind much sufferance doth or'e scip,

When griefe hath mates, and bearing fellowship:

How light and portable my paine seemes now,

When that which makes me bend, makes the King
bow.

He childed as I fathered, *Tom* away,

Marke the high noyses and thy selfe bewray,

When false opinion whose wrong thoughts defile
thee,

In thy iust proofe repeals and reconciles thee,

What will hap more to night, safe scape the King,

Lurke, lurke.

In F1, the text reads:

Glou. Come hither Friend:

Where is the King my Master?

Kent. Here Sir, but trouble him not, his wits are
gon.

Glou. Good friend, I prythee take him in thy
armes;

I haue ore-heard a plot of death vpon him:

There is a Litter ready, lay him in't,

And driue toward Douer friend, where thou shalt
meete

Both welcome, and protection. Take vp thy Master,

If thou should'st dally halfe an houre, his life

With thine, and all that offer to defend him,

Stand in assured losse. Take vp, take vp,

And follow me, that will to some prouision

Giue thee quicke conduct. Come, come, away.

                                        Exeunt.

Here F1 is a far better text than Q1. The verse
lines are correctly divided and the punctuation
is good, yet F1 omits nineteen lines. Scholars
have not yet satisfactorily explained why these
great differences should exist or how Q1 was
put together. From a close comparison of the
two versions, it seems clear that F1 was set up
from a copy of Q1 which had been very care-
fully corrected.

In *Lear* also the editor will probably prefer
to base his text on the folio; when there is a
marked difference between F1 and Q1, he must
decide which to choose.

3. ROMEO AND JULIET:

An example of a different kind of problem
occurs in *Romeo and Juliet*, V.iii.101-21. There
are two quartos of this play. Q1 (1597) has long
puzzled editors, for though it differs in many
places from Q2, it is not corrupt in the same
way as the Q1 of *Hamlet*. Q2 was probably
printed from Shakespeare's manuscript. The
text in F1 was printed from a corrected copy
of Q2. In Q2 (and in F1) Romeo's last speech
appears thus:

              Ah deare *Iuliet*

Why art thou yet so faire? I will beleeue,

Shall I beleeue that vnsubstantiall death is amor-
ous,

And that the leane abhorred monster keepes

Thee here in darke to be his parramour?   [5]

For feare of that I still will staie with thee,

And neuer from this pallat of dym night.

Depart againe, come lye thou in my arme,

Heer's to thy health, where ere thou tumblest in.

O true Appothecarie!   [10]

Thy drugs are quicke. Thus with a kisse I die.

Depart againe, here, here will I remaine,

With wormes that are thy Chamber-maides: O
here

Will I set vp my euerlasting rest:

And shake the yoke of inauspicious starres, [15]

From this world wearied flesh, eyes looke your
last:

Armes take your last embrace: And lips, O you

The doores of breath, seale with a righteous kisse

A datelesse bargaine to ingrossing death:

Come bitter conduct, come vnsauoury guide, [20]

Thou desperate Pilot, now at once run on

The dashing Rocks, thy seasick weary barke:
Heeres to my Loue. O true Appothecary:
Thy drugs are quicke. Thus with a kisse I die.

It will be noted that the final phrases, "O true Appothecary . . . die" are printed twice, at lines 10–11 and 23–24. This repetition is left out by modern editors. The natural inference is that Shakespeare rewrote the last speech. In the first version, the speech ended at line 11: "Thus with a kisse I die." Later Shakespeare revised the play and expanded the last lines, beginning at "pallat of dym night (line 7)," but the printer failed to notice that the last thirteen lines should have directly followed "dym night" and that the next four lines (8–11) should have been omitted.

These are but three examples of the kind of difficulty often encountered in editing any text of Shakespeare. They arise because in Shakespeare's time few dramatists were greatly concerned with the literary value of their plays. The manuscript of a play was sold outright to the players, and there the matter ended. The players were usually anxious to keep their plays from being printed, because there was no acting copyright and nothing to prevent the play from being acted by another company.

Toward the end of Shakespeare's career, it became a fashion for gentlemen to collect and read plays. Some authors, notably Ben Jonson, then grew jealous for their literary fame; Shakespeare seems not to have greatly cared. Certainly he never took any steps to have his plays carefully printed, and had it not been for the zeal of his surviving friends, many would have been lost.

Much information can be gathered from Henslowe's *Diary,* which records many payments to dramatists. Plays were offered or ordered. An author who had a good idea for a play explained the plot to the company; and if they approved, he was commissioned to write it. Many plays were written by syndicates of two, three, or four writers, sometimes in great haste. The price paid for plays was good for the times. It varied from £6 to £10 (about $240 to $400 in modern money).[1] This is a high price when it is remembered that the average life of a play was not much more than ten performances.

The history of a play manuscript was compli-

cated. It had first to be written by the author or authors. Sometimes, indeed, when they were short of money, they sold it act by act as it was finished. A play manuscript as delivered was not always in a fit condition for performance, so the prompter went over it and prepared it for production by adding the necessary notes of stage business. Next, the manuscript was handed to a copyist to prepare the parts for the individual actors. These were written out, as is still the custom, giving the actor's full part and the last few words of the previous speech as a cue. Among the Henslowe papers there still survives a part prepared for Edward Alleyn when he played Orlando in Greene's *Orlando Furioso.* It was originally in the form of a continuous roll which at rehearsals Alleyn held in his left hand while gesturing with his right.

The next stage was to have the play licensed. The Master of the Revels, the Court official responsible for entertainments, was the official censor. The play was sent to him for reading. If he disapproved, he noted on the manuscript the alterations which he required. If he was satisfied, he wrote a certificate to this effect in the manuscript itself, which was thus formally licensed for performance. The play then went into rehearsal and was acted, the original manuscript being used in the theater as prompt copy. When the play had ceased to be popular, the manuscript was put away, or possibly sold to a printer. In some instances, therefore, the text which reached the printer was the original manuscript copy.

It is generally believed nowadays by scholars that the texts of *Romeo and Juliet* (Q2), *Much Ado about Nothing,* and *Hamlet* (Q2), among others, were set directly from Shakespeare's own manuscript and therefore reproduce some of the peculiarities of his spelling.

Printers, as well as actors, were bound by government regulations. When printing was first invented at the end of the fifteenth century, it was soon clear to the Government of the day that an uncontrolled printing press could be a very dangerous instrument of propaganda. Printers were therefore organized into their own Guild, the Stationers' Company. No one was allowed to own a press or print a book who was not a member of that company. Before books were printed they had first to be licensed by an official appointed by the Archbishop of

[1] See App. 27.

Canterbury or by the Master of the Stationers' Company. When a printer had obtained his license, he took the book along to the Stationers' Hall and there entered it in the Stationers' Register, paying a fee of sixpence. This entry gave him the sole right to print the book; any other printer who stole his copyright was liable to be heavily punished by the Stationers' Company. The Stationers' Register still exists and is thus a most valuable record of all early printed books, but by no means all books were entered. Sometimes a printer, knowing that he had a salable book which might or might not be allowed, risked prosecution. At other times, he was casual (as were all Elizabethans) in obeying the law. From a third to a quarter of the books printed during Shakespeare's lifetime were never entered in the Stationers' Register.

It seems also to have been the custom for the Lord Chamberlain's Men occasionally to come to an arrangement with a printer called James Roberts, whereby he would enter the title of one of their plays in the Stationers' Register as his own property, but not print it. In this way the players were protected against unauthorized printing. Modern scholars call this method of control "blocking entry."

Most plays were printed in the form known as quarto; that is, the original sheet of paper was folded twice to form four leaves or eight pages. This was the normal form for printing small books. Plays were usually badly printed and full of mistakes. The printer set up the manuscript more or less as it lay before him. He did not expend much care on tidying it for press. As a result, early quartos preserve many of the peculiarities of the play manuscript. There is seldom any division into acts or scenes, and no indication of the place of the action. Punctuation is light, sometimes effective but often quite impossible. Spelling is quite arbitrary. English spelling as yet was not fixed, and printers either followed the odd spellings of their authors or spelled words to suit their own convenience. As a result, play quartos are usually very slovenly.

When Shakespeare died, fourteen of his plays had been regularly printed in properly authorized quartos. They were: *Richard III, Titus Andronicus, Love's Labor's Lost, Romeo and Juliet, A Midsummer Night's Dream, Richard II, Merchant of Venice, Henry IV* (both parts),

Much Ado about Nothing, Troilus and Cressida, Hamlet, Lear, Pericles. Othello was printed in 1622. Pirated quartos had also appeared of *Romeo and Juliet, Henry V, The Merry Wives of Windsor,* and *Hamlet.* These piracies are interesting, although of no great value as texts. As Shakespeare's fame grew, the demand for his plays in print became considerable. Since the players were unwilling to release the manuscript, dishonest printers sometimes "acquired" a stolen version. Pirated texts were vamped together from various sources. Sometimes a shorthand report was obtained. The pirated quarto of *Hamlet* is apparently based on the part of Marcellus, and it seems likely that one of the lesser players was bribed to produce as much of the original play as he could remember.

In 1623 appeared the first folio; it includes in one volume all Shakespeare's undisputed plays with the exception of *Pericles.* Heminges and Condell, who were mainly responsible for the collection, took considerable care, but they were not scholars, and as soon as the texts in the folio are carefully examined, it is clear that copy of different kinds was sent to the printer. Where a play had already appeared in quarto, this quarto was used, possibly with such changes as had been made in the theater since the play was first written. For some plays, it is likely that Shakespeare's own manuscript was used; but for others (such as *The Winter's Tale*) it is clear that the copy had been carefully prepared by a professional copyist. In some plays the proper division of acts and scenes is made; in others there is no division from beginning to end. A few even have a list of characters. Divisions of verse lines are more accurate than in the quartos, and the punctuation especially has been vastly improved.

Elizabethan punctuation is interesting. Authors and copyists punctuated not as in modern times to indicate the syntax of a sentence, but to "point" it for delivery. The result is that in reading a play in the folio, the punctuation at times enormously increases the pleasure of reading. It is very doubtful, however, whether Shakespeare himself was responsible for this punctuation. If the quartos are any guide, his own method was to punctuate very lightly.

These somewhat haphazard methods of publication sufficed for readers of Shakespeare's generation. After the Restoration, when Rowe brought out his edition of 1709, printers and readers had become far more particular. Rowe took great care to make his text orderly and smooth for the reader. He made the divisions into acts and scenes where these were wanting; he added place headings, and adopted a consistent punctuation. This practice has been followed ever since. For the general reader, many difficulties have been smoothed away by editors, though the scholar prefers to get back to the original quarto or folio.

Editing Shakespeare's texts is thus full of difficulty. The curious notes on textual problems which disturb the student in his early days are a record of the ceaseless care and ingenuity which has gone to the making of the modern text. The note quoted at the beginning of this chapter concerns the famous "crux" in *Hamlet* (see I.i.62–64, *n*):

> So frowned he once when, in an angry parle,
> He smote *the sledded Polacks* on the ice.

The formula shows that Malone (1790) was the first editor to read "sledded Polacks," which most editors have since followed. The phrase in Q1 (1603), Q2 (1604), and Q3 (1611) appears as "the sleaded pollax"; in Q4 (undated) and Q5 (1637) it became "the sleaded Pollax." In F1 (1623), followed by F2 (1632) the reading is "sledded Pollax," which in F3 (1664) became "sledded Polax"; a quarto of 1683 read "sledded Poll-Ax," while F4 (1685) printed "sledded Poleaxe." Pope in his edition (1725) was the first to emend the text to read "sledded Polack," which Malone altered to "Polacks."

7. The Development of Shakespeare's Art

The Early Period

Shakespeare learned his craft in the best of schools, the theater itself. When he began to write, Edward Alleyn was the leading star actor, and his favorite parts, Marlowe's Tamburlaine and the Jew of Malta and Kyd's Hieronimo, set a standard. At first Shakespeare copied his masters, but he soon learned to develop his own techniques, and to the end of his career he was constantly experimenting. The changes in his style are indeed so noticeable that his plays can be approximately dated by style alone.

Shakespeare's poetic style can conveniently be divided into four periods: Early, Balanced, Overflowing, and Final.

To the Early Period belong *I, II, III Henry VI, Richard III, Richard II, Titus Andronicus, Love's Labor's Lost, The Two Gentlemen of Verona, The Comedy of Errors, The Taming of the Shrew, Romeo and Juliet,* and *A Midsummer Night's Dream.* Plays of this period have certain common characteristics. The plots are, on the whole, well worked out; but except in *Romeo and Juliet* the characterization is usually superficial, the psychology seldom subtle, and the dialogue inclined to be stiff, artificial, and overlong. There is an abundance of such rhetorical devices as repetition of phrase, question, exclamation, alliteration, and excess of punning and word play. Thus at their first appearance in *Romeo and Juliet* (I.i.169), Benvolio and Romeo exchange the following conversation:

BEN. What sadness lengthens Romeo's hours?
ROM. Not having that, which, having, makes them short.
BEN. In love?
ROM. Out ——
BEN. Of love?
ROM. Out of her favor where I am in love.
BEN. Alas that love, so gentle in his view,
Should be so tyrannous and rough in proof!
ROM. Alas that love, whose view is muffled still,
Should without eyes see pathways to his will!
Where shall we dine? Oh me! What fray was here?
Yet tell me not, for I have heard it all.
Here's much to do with hate, but more with love.
Why then, O brawling love! O loving hate!
O anything, of nothing first create!
O heavy lightness! Serious vanity!
Misshapen chaos of well-seeming forms!
Feather of lead, bright smoke, cold fire, sick health!
Still-waking sleep, that is not what it is!
This love feel I, that feel no love in this.

There is an excess of poetic imagery, often self-conscious, elaborate, and clever rather than illuminating. Thus in *A Midsummer Night's*

Dream (III.ii.201–16) Helena tearfully protests against Hermia's unkindness, so cruel after their schoolgirl affection:

> Oh, is it all forgot?
> All school days' friendship, childhood innocence?
> We, Hermia, like two artificial gods,
> Have with our needles created both one flower,
> Both on one sampler, sitting on one cushion,
> Both warbling of one song, both in one key —
> As if our hands, our sides, voices, and minds
> Had been incorporate. So we grew together,
> Like to a double cherry, seeming parted
> But yet a union in partition —
> Two lovely berries molded on one stem.
> So, with two seeming bodies, but one heart,
> Two of the first, like coats in heraldry,
> Due but to one, and crownèd with one crest.
> And will you rent our ancient love asunder,
> To join with men in scorning your poor friend?

The imagery of the double cherries and the coat of arms is altogether too elaborate to illustrate the simple idea of long-established friendship, unless — as is very possible — Shakespeare is here deliberately parodying a failing common in his own early work.

Rhyme is very common, verse lines are monotonously regular, stresses even, and verse and sentence usually end together. At first Shakespeare composed his speeches line by line as if he were laying bricks one on top of the other; and he had an excessive taste for puns. These traits can be seen from a typical passage in *Richard II,* in the episode where the King visits the dying Gaunt (II.i.72–85). Richard asks: "What comfort, man? How is't with aged Gaunt?" To which Gaunt replies:

> Oh, how that name befits my composition!
> Old Gaunt indeed, and gaunt in being old.
> Within me grief hath kept a tedious fast,
> And who abstains from meat that is not gaunt?
> For sleeping England long time have I watched,
> Watching breeds leanness, leanness is all gaunt.
> The pleasure that some fathers feed upon
> Is my strict fast — I mean, my children's looks —
> And therein fasting, hast thou made me gaunt.
> Gaunt am I for the grave, gaunt as a grave,
> Whose hollow womb inherits naught but bones.

On all possible occasions characters are given long poetic speeches which may be admirable in themselves but are not always suitable in their context, and often retard the movement of the plot. Two good examples of this habit are the account of Clarence's dream in *Richard III* (I.iv.1–63) and Mercutio's outburst on Queen Mab in *Romeo and Juliet* (I.iv.53–103).

At this stage in his career, Shakespeare did not always have much to say, but he said it at great length, and all the time he was experimenting with the uses of words. He was more a conscious artist than an instinctive dramatist. Nevertheless the artificiality of Shakespeare's verse often has charm, and at times even considerable power. A good example of the early style at its best is to be found in *Richard III* in Gloucester's soliloquy after he has successfully wooed the Lady Anne (I.ii.228–64):

> Was ever woman in this humor wooed?
> Was ever woman in this humor won?
> I'll have her, but I will not keep her long.
> What! I, that killed her husband and his father,
> To take her in her heart's extremest hate,
> With curses in her mouth, tears in her eyes,
> The bleeding witness of her hatred by —
> Having God, her conscience, and these bars
>   against me,
> And I nothing to back my suit at all
> But the plain Devil and dissembling looks,
> And yet to win her, all the world to nothing! . . .
>
> My dukedom to a beggarly denier,
> I do mistake my person all this while.
> Upon my life, she finds, although I cannot,
> Myself to be a marvelous proper man.
> I'll be at charges for a looking-glass,
> And entertain some score or two of tailors,
> To study fashions to adorn my body.
> Since I am crept in favor with myself,
> I will maintain it with some little cost.
> But first I'll turn yon fellow in his grave,
> And then return lamenting to my love.
> Shine out, fair sun, till I have bought a glass,
> That I may see my shadow as I pass.

Here Shakespeare was successfully writing for effect, and though meter and rhythm remain regular, he instills into Richard personality and grim humor.

Another good example is Richard II's speech of renunciation in the deposition scene. Bolingbroke asks, "Are you contented to resign the crown?" To which Richard replies (IV.i.201–22):

> Aye, no; no, aye; for I must nothing be;
> Therefore no no, for I resign to thee.
> Now mark me, how I will undo myself:
> I give this heavy weight from off my head

And this unwieldy scepter from my hand,
The pride of kingly sway from out my heart;
With mine own tears I wash away my balm,
With mine own hands I give away my crown,
With mine own tongue deny my sacred state,
With mine own breath release all duty's rites:
All pomp and majesty I do forswear;
My manors, rents, revenues I forego;
My acts, decrees, and statutes I deny:
God pardon all oaths that are broke to me!
God keep all vows unbroke that swear to thee!
Make me, that nothing have, with nothing
      grieved,
And thou with all pleased, that hast all achieved!
Long mayst thou live in Richard's seat to sit,
And soon lie Richard in an earthy pit!
God save King Harry, unkinged Richard says,
And send him many years of sunshine days!
What more remains?

From the first, however, Shakespeare's comic
dialogue in prose was easy and mature. Bottom,
Quince, and company in *A Midsummer Night's
Dream* are as fully developed as any of the later
clowns, such as Dogberry and Verges in *Much
Ado about Nothing,* the gravedigger in *Hamlet,*
or Stephano and Trinculo in *The Tempest.*

The Early Period passed gradually into the
Balanced Period. At all times Shakespeare wrote
magnificent passages of poetry, but in the early
plays the set piece is noticeably finer than its
surroundings; in the later plays the whole effect
is more even, and the dialogue is less concerned
with fine sayings than with what is immediately
appropriate to the scene. The main difference
between the Early and the Balanced styles is
that as Shakespeare's experience deepened, his
power of expression grew. Speeches are now
written as a whole, in one sweep; run-on lines
become more common, and though the formal
pattern of the verse remains, the stresses no
longer tick like an ill-balanced grandfather
clock.

The Balanced Period

Early and Balanced merge in *The Merchant
of Venice,* which is perhaps the first play where
Shakespeare is completely master of his craft.
There are few long speeches of poetry for its
own sake. The casket scene where Bassanio
wins Portia (III.ii.) is a little drawn-out, but the
effect is deliberate and intentional, and leads up
to the lyric moment when Portia gives herself

to Bassanio. The verse has become easier, the
rhythm more varied, the power and emotion
deeper.

In *I Henry IV,* which was probably his next
play, Shakespeare has achieved complete bal-
ance. The few poetic speeches are short and ap-
propriate, and there is a new sense of humor and
of power. Shakespeare was now so sure of him-
self that he could even venture to parody his
own serious speeches, as Hotspur's excessive
zeal for honor (I.iii.200) is parodied by Falstaff's
cynical self-catechism (V.i.127), or the moving
scene where the King rebukes his erring son
(III.ii) is parodied in advance, and enhanced,
not spoiled, by Falstaff in his extemporary play
(II.iv.409–532).

The characterization also is elaborate and suc-
cessful in *I Henry IV,* and well illustrates Shake-
speare's methods of creating character. There
are three principal methods by which character
can be shown: by what is said of a man by his
friends, and not less important by his enemies;
by what he says of himself, and how he says it;
and by his own actions. Description of a charac-
ter is the most obvious method. Ben Jonson in
his plays made a feature of elaborate descrip-
tions, which mainly occur just before the person
appears. Shakespeare, however, was much more
subtle. He seldom wrote long or elaborate de-
scriptions of his characters. Instead he built up
a character stroke by stroke, revealing each trait
as it was needed. The character of Hotspur is a
good example of his technique.

Hotspur is first mentioned in the first scene
by the King, who sighs enviously that North-
umberland's son should be so much better than
his " young Harry." The King then goes on to
comment on Hotspur's pride in refusing to hand
over his prisoners. The audience is thus given
some notion of Hotspur's character, so that
when he appears in I.iii, and is rebuked by the
King, his angry outburst is not unexpected. His
behavior throughout this scene reveals much: his
impatience and hotheadedness, his waspish sense
of humor, his complete lack of self-control when
roused, his passion for honor, which so obsesses
him that he becomes entirely self-absorbed.
Three scenes later Shakespeare reveals quite a
different side of Hotspur's nature. At home,
sleeping or waking his first thoughts and dreams
are always on war, but he is very fond of his
wife, a gentle, gay, womanly creature, and once

she appears these two tease each other like lovers.

Throughout the play there is a deliberate contrast between Hotspur and Prince Hal. Hotspur is revealed as the showier hero, Hal as the deeper, more intelligent nature. After the scene between Hotspur and his wife, the Prince casually remarks to Poins, "I am not yet of Percy's mind, the Hotspur of the North, he that kills me some six or seven dozen of Scots at a breakfast, washes his hands, and says to his wife, 'Fie upon this quiet life! I want work.' 'O my sweet Harry,' says she, 'how many hast thou killed today?' 'Give my roan horse a drench,' says he, and answers 'Some fourteen' an hour after — 'a trifle, a trifle.'" The description is intentionally a caricature of what has gone before, but yet it adds to our understanding of Hotspur — and of Hal.

Hotspur's next appearance is at the council with Worcester, Mortimer, and Glendower (III.i). Here Shakespeare contrasts four men of very different character in such a way that each reveals his own nature and brings out the character of the others. Hotspur shows himself impatient, rude, and overbearing, contemptuous of anything that he does not understand, a shrewd bargainer until he gets his own way — but, as before, he is redeemed and made lovable at the end by the little conversation with his wife. Finally, in the battle scenes he is true to his name. For a moment he is abashed at the news that his father has deserted him, but he recovers quickly and is eager to try conclusions with Prince Hal. Here he shows himself the lesser nature, for the Prince's challenge is issued with modest sincerity; Hotspur receives it with jealousy and contempt. Even as the two join in fight Hotspur despises his rival as an unworthy opponent. Thus until the end of the play the character is still growing and developing.

The Balanced Period lasted from *Henry IV* to *Othello*, roughly from 1597 to 1603, and includes *Henry V, Much Ado about Nothing, The Merry Wives of Windsor, As You Like It, Julius Caesar, Hamlet, Twelfth Night, Troilus and Cressida, Measure for Measure*, and *All's Well That Ends Well*. During this time Shakespeare's own experience of life was deepening and his power of expression expanding. By the end he could write speeches which were not only full

of the subtlest characterization but, by their choice of vocabulary and rhythm, could express the whole nature of the speaker. Thus the experience of the world now degenerating into a complacent senility in Polonius is perfectly expressed in his instructions to Reynaldo on the best way of finding out whether Laertes is making a fool of himself in Paris (II.i.37–68):

POL. Marry sir, here's my drift,
And I believe it is a fetch of warrant.
You laying these slight sullies on my son,
As 'twere a thing a little soiled i' the working,
Mark you,
Your party in converse, him you would sound,
Having ever seen in the prenominate crimes
The youth you breathe of guilty, be assured
He closes with you in this consequence ——
"Good sir," or so, or "friend," or "gentleman,"
According to the phrase or the addition
Of man and country.
REY. Very good, my lord.
POL. And then, sir, does he this — he does ——
What was I about to say? By the mass, I was about to say something. Where did I leave?
REY. At "closes in the consequence," at "friend or so," and "gentleman."
POL. At "closes in the consequence," aye, marry:
He closes thus: "I know the gentleman.
I saw him yesterday, or t'other day,
Or then, or then, with such, or such, and, as you say,
There was a' gaming, there o'ertook in's rouse,
There falling out at tennis." Or perchance,
"I saw him enter such a house of sale,"
Videlicet, a brothel, or so forth.
See you now,
Your bait of falsehood takes this carp of truth.
And thus do we of wisdom and of reach,
With windlasses and with assays of bias,
By indirections find directions out.
So by my former lecture and advice,
Shall you my son. You have me, have you not?

The breakdown into prose as Polonius loses the thread of his own verbosity is perfect.

There is, however, real poetry in abundance in *Hamlet*, and it is worth comparing Hamlet's soliloquy on suicide (III.i.56–88) with Richard II's soliloquy in prison (V.v.1–66) to see Shakespeare's increased power of writing this kind of philosophic reverie. In *Hamlet* the rhythm is easier and more natural, the imagery terser and sharper, the mind of the speaker more mature and subtle.

The growth of dramatic power can be seen also in Shakespeare's increasing knowledge of human character and a certain change in his interest and point of view. In his early plays, he tended rather to see the whole story objectively. Some characters naturally were more important, but each was treated alike. From about 1599, for the next six or seven years — that is, from *As You Like It* and *Julius Caesar* to *Lear* and *Macbeth* — Shakespeare often selected one or two characters in the play for special treatment, so that we see not only what happens to them, but also the working and development of their minds. Brutus, Hamlet, Iago, Edmund, and Macbeth are given soliloquies in which they lay bare not only their intentions but their very souls.

Soliloquy — where a character left to himself reveals his own mind in a direct speech to the audience — was not a new device. Shakespeare and indeed all Elizabethan dramatists used it frequently, but in his earlier plays soliloquy was used mainly for three purposes: to give necessary information of the speaker's intentions, as when, at the end of the first scene of *A Midsummer Night's Dream,* Helena explains that she will tell Demetrius of Hermia's flight; or to reveal that the speaker is playing a part and is not what he seems, as when Richard of Gloucester gloats over his treachery to his brother Clarence (*Rich III,* I.iii.324); or as an excuse for an outburst of sheer poetry, as when Juliet waiting for Romeo breaks into a lyric ecstasy on night and love (*R & J,* III.ii.1).

In the soliloquies of Shakespeare's more mature plays, as when Brutus ponders whether to join the conspiracy, or Iago broods over the best way to hurt Othello, or Macbeth recoils in horror from the murder of Duncan, we see a mind seething. The interest is not so much in what may ultimately happen as in the working and development of the personality of the speaker. It is as if Shakespeare for a while was more interested in men's motives than in their actions.

The Overflowing Period

When he came to write *Lear,* Shakespeare was again experimenting with language. By this time his thoughts and feelings were coming too thick and powerful for balanced expression. He entered into an Overflowing Period. The metrical line and the formal scheme of five stresses to the line were often neglected. The thought became too intense for clear, logical expression;

the idea in Shakespeare's mind did not always travel along the usual conductor of grammatical sentences, but leapt across in some mighty image which only laborious paraphrase can reduce to everyday speech. *Lear* and *Macbeth* are full of these passages, often packed with a complex imagery which suggests half a dozen different glints and meanings. Thus Lady Macbeth, in her terrible self-dedication to evil (I.v.41–55):

> Come, you spirits
> That tend on mortal thoughts, unsex me here,
> And fill me, from the crown to the toe, topfull
> Of direst cruelty! Make thick my blood,
> Stop up the access and passage to remorse,
> That no compunctious visitings of nature
> Shake my fell purpose, nor keep peace between
> The effect and it! Come to my woman's breasts,
> And take my milk for gall, you murdering ministers,
> Wherever in your sightless substances
> You wait on nature's mischief! Come, thick night,
> And pall thee in the dunnest smoke of Hell,
> That my keen knife see not the wound it makes,
> Nor Heaven peep through the blanket of the dark
> To cry "Hold, hold!"

The language in *Lear* is even more concentrated and overflowing with meaning. Not only with the old King himself at moments of high emotion; the other characters also speak in this concentrated way. Thus Cordelia, while she waits for her father to awake into a feeble sanity, comments (IV.vii.26–42):

> O my dear Father! Restoration hang
> Thy medicine on my lips; and let this kiss
> Repair those violent harms that my two sisters
> Have in thy reverence made! . . .
> Had you not been their father, these white flakes
> Had challenged pity of them. Was this a face
> To be opposed against the warring winds?
> To stand against the deep dread-bolted thunder?
> In the most terrible and nimble stroke
> Of quick, cross lightning? To watch — poor perdu! —
> With this thin helm? Mine enemy's dog,
> Though he had bit me, should have stood that night
> Against my fire, and wast thou fain, poor Father,
> To hovel thee with swine, and rogues forlorn
> In short and musty straw? Alack, alack!
> 'Tis wonder that thy life and wits at once
> Had not concluded all.

There was less of this excessive concentration in *Antony and Cleopatra,* which followed *Macbeth,* but in its place a new sense of poetry, a magnificence, a kind of haunting resonance which occurs nowhere else. The gorgeous account of Antony's first meeting with Cleopatra (II.ii.194–245) was a return to the earlier method of inserting long descriptive passages into the dialogue; but it was necessary to explain Cleopatra's mystery and fascination, which could so enslave the hard-bitten Antony. It was, as it were, the orchestral accompaniment to a play full of word music, which is most conspicuous at the high moments and becomes an echo as Cleopatra prepares to die:

Show me, my women, like a Queen. Go fetch
My best attires. I am again for Cydnus,
To meet Mark Antony. Sirrah Iras, go.
Now, noble Charmian, we'll dispatch indeed;
And when thou hast done this chare I'll give thee
    leave
To play till Doomsday. Bring our crown and all.

In his Overflowing Period, Shakespeare was not only unrestrained in his verse but also in his plots. In *Lear* and in *Antony and Cleopatra* there is an impatience in the construction, or rather an exuberance of incident. There are too many incidents and too much detail for either play to be easily followed. Both require an unusual concentration in reader and playgoer, and both are tributes to the attention and intelligence of Shakespeare's audience. The characterization, however, is as good as anywhere, and the incidents themselves as effective on the stage. And in the use of language, there is less concentration in *Antony and Cleopatra,* and a return to a more balanced manner of writing.

In *Antony and Cleopatra* and *Coriolanus,* both of which were based on North's *Plutarch,* Shakespeare also returned to his earlier manner of construction. He abandoned the elaborate analysis of character and the psychological soliloquy. Though the characterization remains perfect, Shakespeare's intention was now not so much the development of an individual as the presentation of a theme.

Coriolanus is a demonstration of the eternal futility of politicians who in fighting for their own cause destroy not only each other, but the general commonwealth. *Antony and Cleopatra* illustrates the truth expressed in Bacon's Essay of Love:

The stage is more beholding to love than the life of man. For as to the stage, love is ever matter of comedies, and now and then of tragedies; but in life it doth much mischief; sometimes like a siren, sometimes like a fury. You may observe that amongst all the great and worthy persons (whereof the memory remaineth, either ancient or recent), there is not one that hath been transported to the mad degree of love; which shows that great spirits and great business do keep out this weak passion. You must except, nevertheless, Marcus Antonius, the half partner of the empire of Rome, and Appius Claudius, the decemvir and lawgiver; whereof the former was indeed a voluptuous man, and inordinate; but the latter was an austere and wise man; and therefore it seems (though rarely) that love can find entrance not only into an open heart, but also into a heart well fortified, if watch be not well kept.

The Final Period

At the end of his career, Shakespeare reached a Final Period, shown particularly in his last play, *The Tempest,* where he achieved perfect mastery and balance between thought, phrase, and meaning. It is seen in such a speech as Prospero's farewell to his art:

Ye elves of hills, brooks, standing lakes, and
    groves,
And ye that on the sands with printless foot
Do chase the ebbing Neptune and do fly him
When he comes back; you demipuppets that
By moonshine do the green sour ringlets make,
Whereof the ewe not bites; and you whose pastime
Is to make midnight mushrooms that rejoice
To hear the solemn curfew, by whose aid —
Weak masters though ye be — I have bedimmed
The noontide sun, called forth the mutinous
    winds,
And twixt the green sea and the azured vault
Set roaring war. To the dread rattling thunder
Have I given fire, and rifted Jove's stout oak
With his own bolt. The strong-based promontory
Have I made shake, and by the spurs plucked up
The pine and cedar. Graves at my command
Have waked their sleepers, oped, and let 'em
    forth
By my so potent art. But this rough magic
I here abjure, and when I have required
Some heavenly music — which even now I do —
To work mine end upon their senses, that
This airy charm is for, I'll break my staff,
Bury it certain fathoms in the earth,
And deeper than did ever plummet sound
I'll drown my book.

Beyond this the English language cannot reach.

The changes in Shakespeare's style can be felt, but they cannot be exactly or scientifically analyzed, though there was at one time a fashion for reducing Shakespeare's verse to statistics and tables.[1] These figures are of little value except as showing — what is obvious to any sensitive reader — that as Shakespeare developed, his verse was less restrained by metrical rules. But the judgment of style comes late, and only after much reading and experience — and there are no short cuts to the development of taste.

8. Shakespeare and the Critics

Beginnings

The greatness of Shakespeare's plays has been appreciated from the very beginning. The first recorded performance of *I Henry VI* was on March 3, 1592; by 1598, Shakespeare was recognized as the greatest writer yet produced by the English, at least by one young student named Francis Meres (see p. 11b), whose tribute is the more remarkable since it was made before any of Shakespeare's most mature plays were written.

Shakespeare's reputation grew steadily for the next ten years, and then for a while his plays seemed to go somewhat out of fashion. Drama was becoming more and more a genteel amusement for the wealthy, who found the plays of Beaumont and Fletcher and of Ben Jonson more to their taste. Indeed, if it had not been for a lucky chance, Shakespeare might almost have been forgotten, for when he died only fourteen of his plays were in print.

The First Folio, 1623

The beginnings of Shakespeare's literary fame date from the collection of thirty-six of his plays published in 1623 and known as the *First Folio*. It was a great undertaking for all concerned, and was put out as a genuine tribute of affection by those who knew him. The folio is prefaced by a note "To the great Variety of Readers," signed by John Heminges and Henry Condell, two of the surviving members of Shakespeare's company. In this preface they say:

It had been a thing, we confess, worthy to have been wished, that the Author himself had lived to have set forth and overseen his own writings; but

[1] The curious reader will find a whole series of these tables in E. K. Chambers' *William Shakespeare*, II, 397.

since it hath been ordained otherwise, and he by death departed from that right, we pray you do not envy his friends, the office of their care, and pain, to have collected and published them; and so to have published them, as where before you were abused with divers stolen and surreptitious copies, maimed, and deformed by the frauds and stealths of injurious impostors, that exposed them; even those, are now offered to your view cured, and perfect of their limbs; and all the rest, absolute in their numbers, as he conceived them. Who, as he was a happy imitator of Nature, was a most gentle expresser of it. His mind and hand went together: and what he thought, he uttered with that easiness, that we have scarce received from him a blot in his papers.

But the most impressive tribute in the folio is a full-dress ode written by Ben Jonson:

To the memory of my beloved,
The AUTHOR
Mr. WILLIAM SHAKESPEARE:
And
what he hath left us.

The ode itself is an overelaborate performance and poor poetry, except for a few famous lines:

He was not of an age, but for all time!
    And all the Muses still were in their prime,
When like Apollo he came forth to warm
    Our ears, or like a Mercury to charm!
Nature herself was proud of his designs,
    And joyed to wear the dressing of his lines!
Which were so richly spun, and woven so fit,
    As, since, she will vouchsafe no other Wit.
The merry Greek, tart Aristophanes,
    Neat Terence, witty Plautus, now not please;
But antiquated, and deserted lie
    As they were not of Nature's family.
Yet must I not give Nature all: thy Art,
    My gentle Shakespeare, must enjoy a part.
For though the Poets matter, Nature be,
    His Art doth give the fashion. And, that he,

Who casts to write a living line, must sweat,
  (Such as thine are) and strike the second heat
Upon the Muses' anvil: turn the same,
  (And himself with it) that he thinks to frame;
Or for the laurel, he may gain a scorn,
  For a good Poet's made, as well as born.
And such wert thou.

The folio was reprinted in 1632 and further tributes were added, including one by John Milton, then a young man.

Mr. Hales of Eton

Shakespeare's reputation was at its lowest in the 1630's and 1640's, as was but natural. He was not yet established as a classic and he was no longer a modern; to bright young playgoers he appeared just old-fashioned. Nevertheless he always had his champions, and the matter was debated on a famous occasion to which there are several allusions:

In a conversation between Sir John Suckling, Sir William D'Avenant, Endymion Porter, Mr. Hales of Eton, and Ben Jonson, Sir John Suckling, who was a professed admirer of Shakespeare, had undertaken his defence against Ben Jonson with some warmth. Mr. Hales, who had sat still for some time, hearing Ben frequently reproaching him with the want of learning, and ignorance of the Ancients, told him at last, "That if Mr. Shakespeare had not read the Ancients, he had likewise not stolen anything from 'em; (a fault the other made no conscience of) and that if he would produce any one topic finely treated by any of them, he would undertake to show something upon the same subject at least as well written by Shakespeare." [1]

As yet there was little serious attempt at "Shakespearean criticism," nor indeed had any English literary critic of merit appeared. During the period of the Commonwealth, 1642–60, plays were forbidden, but when in 1660 King Charles II was restored to his throne, the theaters were reopened, and naturally Shakespeare's plays were brought out with the others. Playgoers of the new generation were puzzled. They recognized Shakespeare's genius, but they were offended by his irregularities. The latest opinion among literary men was all for classic regularity in the construction of dramas, and there was considerable argument whether ancient or modern plays were to be preferred, and of English writers of the older generation, whether Beaumont and Fletcher or Jonson or Shakespeare were best. The debate developed into an argument about the comparative advantages of "art" and "nature," and critics took sides, each championing his own man, as in Victorian times readers championed either Dickens or Thackeray. For the stage and the theatergoing public of the latter half of the seventeenth century, the plays of Beaumont and Fletcher and of Ben Jonson were indeed more suited.

John Dryden

The first sane and subtle criticism of Shakespeare was written by John Dryden in his *Essay of Dramatic Poesy* (1660), a discussion in dialogue form of the whole controversy. In the dialogue, Neander, one of the speakers, puts forward Jonson's *Silent Woman* as a perfect play, but before he begins his detailed examination he is asked to give his frank opinion whether or not Jonson is greater than all other writers, French or English.

"I fear," replied Neander, "that in obeying your commands I shall draw some envy on myself. Besides, in performing them, it will be first necessary to speak somewhat of Shakespeare and Fletcher, his rivals in poesy; and one of them, in my opinion, at least his equal, perhaps his superior.

"To begin, then, with Shakspeare. He was the man who of all modern, and perhaps ancient poets, had the largest and most comprehensive soul. All the images of Nature were still present to him, and he drew them, not laboriously, but luckily; when he describes anything, you more than see it, you feel it too. Those who accuse him to have wanted learning, give him the greater commendation: he was naturally learned; he needed not the spectacles of books to read Nature; he looked inwards, and found her there. I cannot say he is everywhere alike; were he so, I should do him injury to compare him with the greatest of mankind. He is many times flat, insipid; his comic wit degenerating into clenches, his serious swelling into bombast. But he is always great, when some great occasion is presented to him; no man can say he ever had a fit subject for his wit, and did not then raise himself as high above the rest of poets, *Quantum lenta solent inter viburna cupressi. . . .* [2]

"If I would compare him [Jonson] with Shak-

---

[1] *The Shakspere Allusion-Book: A Collection of Allusions to Shakspere from 1591 to 1700*, edited by John Munro (1909), I, 373.

[2] "As cypresses among lowly shrubs." Virgil, *Eclogues*, I, 26.

speare, I must acknowledge him the more correct poet, but Shakspeare the greater wit. Shakspeare was the Homer, or father of our dramatic poets; Jonson was the Virgil, the pattern of elaborate writing; I admire him, but I love Shakspeare."

Nicholas Rowe

A third reprint of the folio was produced in 1663-64 and a fourth in 1685. In 1709, Shakespeare definitely became a classic when Nicholas Rowe, a Restoration dramatist, brought out the first edited collection of his plays. Shakespeare was now sufficiently ancient for the public to need some information about him, and the taste of readers of plays had grown so much more particular that the earlier and cruder methods of printing were no longer suitable. Rowe added to his edition a short biographical introduction and some commendations of the passages which he most admired. He also considerably revised the text, adding place headings and stage directions. Rowe was largely responsible for the form in which Shakespeare's plays are still normally printed today.

Rowe's attitude toward Shakespeare was a genuine wonder that such greatness could have existed in so crude an age:

But certainly the greatness of this author's genius does nowhere so much appear as where he gives his imagination an entire loose and raises his fancy to a flight above mankind and the limits of the visible world. Such are his attempts in *The Tempest, Midsummer-Night's Dream, Macbeth* and *Hamlet*. Of these, *The Tempest,* however it comes to be placed the first by the former publishers of his works, can never have been the first written by him: it seems to me as perfect in its kind, as almost anything we have of his. One may observe, that the Unities are kept here with an exactness uncommon to the liberties of his writing: though that was what, I suppose, he valued himself least upon, since his excellencies were all of another kind. I am very sensible that he does, in this play, depart too much from that likeness to Truth which ought to be observed in these sort of writings; yet he does it so very finely, that one is easily drawn in to have more faith for his sake, than reason does well allow of. His magic has something in it very solemn and very poetical: and that extravagant character of Caliban is mighty well sustained, shows a wonderful invention in the author, who could strike out such a particular wild image, and is certainly one of the finest and most uncommon grotesques that

was ever seen. The observation, which I have been informed three very great men concurred in making upon this part, was extremely just. " That Shakespear had not only found out a new character in his Caliban, but had also devised and adapted a new manner of language for that character." Among the particular beauties of this piece, I think one may be allowed to point out the Tale of Prospero in the First Act; his speech to Ferdinand in the Fourth, upon the breaking up of the Masque of Juno and Ceres; and that in the Fifth where he dissolves his charms, and resolves to break his magic rod.

Nevertheless, minor critics were often very condescending toward Shakespeare's lack of knowledge of the rules of construction and propriety, which revealed his ignorance of the essentials of a gentleman's education in the classics. Again and again the greatest critics of the age defended Shakespeare against this charge. Thus Addison, in *The Spectator,* No. 592, wrote:

Who would not rather read one of his plays, where there is not a single rule of the stage observed, than any production of a modern critic, where there is not one of them violated? Shakespear was indeed born with all the seeds of poetry, and may be compared to the stone in Pyrrhus's ring, which, as Pliny tells us, had the figure of Apollo and the Nine Muses in the veins of it, produced by the spontaneous hand of Nature, without any help from art.

In the eighteenth century, enthusiasm for Shakespeare grew rapidly, and he soon outstripped all his rivals. In 1616 Jonson had collected the best of his own plays then written in a folio volume; a second folio, with all Jonson's plays, came out in 1640; other editions appeared in 1692 and 1756. Beaumont and Fletcher's collected plays were printed in 1647, 1679, 1711, and 1778. Of Shakespeare's plays, no less than sixty complete editions, including reprints, appeared between 1709 and 1799.

Alexander Pope

After Rowe, Alexander Pope was the next editor; his edition came out during 1723-25. Pope was a highhanded editor. He believed that much rubbish had been foisted into Shakespeare's plays by the actors and he transferred what he regarded as the worst passages to the foot of the page. His preface, however, was full of enthusiasm and common sense:

> Of all English poets Shakespear must be confessed to be the fairest and fullest subject for criticism, and to afford the most numerous, as well as most conspicuous instances, both of beauties and faults of all sorts.

Pope had no respect for Shakespeare's audience, "generally composed of the meaner sort of people," who could have no knowledge or appreciation of "the model of the ancients," but he would not condemn Shakespeare for ignoring the practice of the ancients.

> To judge therefore of Shakespear by Aristotle's rules, is like trying a man by the laws of one country, who acted under those of another. He writ to the People; and writ at first without patronage from the better sort, and therefore without aims of pleasing them: without assistance or advice from the learned, as without the advantage of education or acquaintance among them: without that knowledge of the best models, the ancients, to inspire him with an emulation of them; in a word, without any views of reputation, and of what poets are pleased to call immortality: some or all of which have encouraged the vanity, or animated the ambition, of other writers.
>
> Yet it must be observed, that when his performances had merited the protection of his Prince, and when the encouragement of the Court had succeeded to that of the Town; the works of his riper years are manifestly raised above those of his former. The dates of his plays sufficiently evidence that his productions improved, in proportion to the respect he had for his auditors. And I make no doubt this observation would be found true in every instance, were but editions extant from which we might learn the exact time when every piece was composed, and whether writ for the Town, or the Court.
>
> Another cause (and no less strong than the former) may be deduced from our author's being a Player, and forming himself first upon the judgments of that body of men whereof he was a member. They have ever had a standard to themselves, upon other principles than those of Aristotle. As they live by the majority, they know no rule but that of pleasing the present humour, and complying with the wit in fashion; a consideration which brings all their judgment to a short point. Players are just such judges of what is right, as tailors are of what is graceful. And in this view it will be but fair to allow, that most of our author's faults are less to be ascribed to his wrong judgment as a Poet, than to his right judgment as a Player.

Yet Pope did not agree with those who despised Shakespeare's supposed want of learning:

> I am inclined to think this opinion proceeded originally from the zeal of the partisans of our author and Ben Jonson; as they endeavoured to exalt the one at the expense of the other. It is ever the nature of Parties to be in extremes; and nothing is so probable, as that because Ben Jonson had much the most learning, it was said on the one hand that Shakespear had none at all; and because Shakespear had much the most wit and fancy, it was retorted on the other, that Jonson wanted both. Because Shakespear borrowed nothing, it was said that Ben Jonson borrowed everything. Because Jonson did not write extempore, he was reproached with being a year about every piece, and because Shakespear wrote with ease and rapidity, they cried, he never once made a blot. Nay the spirit of opposition ran so high, that whatever those of the one side objected to the other, was taken at the rebound, and turned into praises; as injudiciously as their antagonists before had made them objections.

Samuel Johnson

Dr. Johnson's edition of Shakespeare's plays appeared in 1765. His Preface is one of the most valuable general estimates of Shakespeare in the eighteenth century. As a critic Johnson regarded himself as a judge of the Supreme Court. His pronouncements were delivered with weight and solemnity, after impartial consideration of the evidence on both sides, but they were always based on common sense and a strong feeling of morality. Johnson's admiration for Shakespeare was immense. In his view, Shakespeare's supreme merit was that he

> . . . above all writers, at least above all modern writers, is the poet of nature; the poet that holds up to his readers a faithful mirror of manners and of life. His characters are not modified by the customs of particular places, unpracticed by the rest of the world; by the peculiarities of studies or professions, which can operate but upon small numbers; or by the accidents of transient fashions or temporary opinions: they are the genuine progeny of common humanity, such as the world will always supply, and observation will always find. His persons act and speak by the influence of those general passions and principles by which all minds are agitated, and the whole system of life is continued in motion. In the writings of other poets a character is too often an individual; in those of Shakespeare it is commonly a species.

Nevertheless, Shakespeare was far from perfect and, having allowed himself to reveal unusual enthusiasm, Johnson felt that he was bound also to censure:

In his comic scenes, he is seldom very successful, when he engages his characters in reciprocations of smartness and contests of sarcasm; their jests are commonly gross, and their pleasantry licentious; neither his gentlemen nor his ladies have much delicacy, nor are sufficiently distinguished from his clowns by any appearance of refined manners. Whether he represented the real conversation of his time is not easy to determine; the reign of Elizabeth is commonly supposed to have been a time of stateliness, formality and reserve, yet perhaps the relaxations of that severity were not very elegant. There must, however, have been always some modes of gaiety preferable to others, and a writer ought to choose the best.

In tragedy his performance seems constantly to be worse, as his labour is more. The effusions of passion which exigence forces out are for the most part striking and energetic; but whenever he solicits his invention, or strains his faculties, the offspring of his throes is tumour, meanness, tediousness, and obscurity.

In narration he affects a disproportionate pomp of diction and a wearisome train of circumlocution, and tells the incident imperfectly in many words, which might have been more plainly delivered in few. Narration in dramatic poetry is naturally tedious, as it is unanimated and inactive, and obstructs the progress of the action; it should therefore always be rapid, and enlivened by frequent interruption. Shakespeare found it an encumbrance, and instead of lightening it by brevity, endeavoured to recommend it by dignity and splendour.

His declamations or set speeches are commonly cold and weak, for his power was the power of nature; when he endeavoured, like other tragic writers, to catch opportunities of amplification, and instead of inquiring what the occasion demanded, to show how much his stores of knowledge could supply, he seldom escapes without the pity or resentment of his reader.

It is always as well to turn to Johnson as a corrective to too much modern enthusiasm, even when, as so often happened, his views were warped by prejudice. Johnson judged Shakespeare by his own standards of universal morality; he would never have admitted, as explanation or excuse, that Shakespeare was bound by the conventions or restrictions of his stage or his generation

Maurice Morgann

With Maurice Morgann, interest shifted from Shakespeare to his creations. Morgann's *Essay on the Dramatic Character of Sir John Falstaff* (1777) is the first important piece of romantic criticism. Morgann set out to prove that Falstaff was not a constitutional coward, and so was led to a full analysis of his character as a real man. Logically and morally Falstaff is reprehensible, if we take his actions one by one; but, Morgann argues, this is not the impression which Falstaff makes on us and

. . . in dramatic composition the impression is the fact; and the writer, who, meaning to impress one thing, has impressed another, is unworthy of observation.

It is a very unpleasant thing to have, in the first setting out, so many and so strong prejudices to contend with. All that one can do in such case, is, to pray the reader to have a little patience in the commencement; and to reserve his censure, if it must pass, for the conclusion. Under his gracious allowance, therefore, I presume to declare it, as my opinion, that cowardice *is not* the *impression,* which the *whole* character of Falstaff is calculated to make on the minds of an unprejudiced audience; though there be, I confess, a great deal of something in the *composition* likely enough to puzzle, and consequently to mislead the understanding. — The reader will perceive that I distinguish between *mental impressions* and the *understanding.* — I wish to avoid everything that looks like subtlety and refinement; but this is a distinction, which we all comprehend. — There are none of us unconscious of certain feelings or sensations of mind, which do not seem to have passed through the understanding; the effects, I suppose, of some secret influences from without, acting upon a certain mental sense, and producing feelings and passions in just correspondence to the force and variety of those influences on the one hand, and to the quickness of our sensibility on the other. Be the cause, however, what it may, the fact is undoubtedly so; which is all I am concerned in. And it is equally a fact, which every man's experience may avouch, that the understanding and those feelings are frequently at variance. The latter often arise from the most minute circumstances, and frequently from such as the understanding cannot estimate, or even recognize; whereas the understanding delights in abstraction, and in general propositions; which, however true considered as such, are very seldom, I had like to have said *never,* perfectly applicable to any particular case. And hence, among other causes, it is, that we often condemn or applaud characters and actions on the credit of some logical process, while our hearts revolt, and would fain lead us to a very different conclusion. . . .

We all like *Old Jack;* yet, by some strange perverse fate, we all abuse him, and deny him the possession of any one single good or respectable quality. There is something extraordinary in this: It must be a strange art in Shakespeare which can draw our liking and good will towards so offensive an object. He has wit, it will be said; cheerfulness and humour of the most characteristic and captivating sort. And is this enough? Is the humour and gaiety of vice so very captivating? Is the wit, characteristic of baseness and every ill quality capable of attaching the heart and winning the affections? Or does not the apparency of such humor, and the flashes of such wit, by more strongly disclosing the deformity of character, but the more effectually excite our hatred and contempt of the man? And yet this is not our *feeling* of Falstaff's character. When he has ceased to amuse us, we find no emotions of disgust; we can scarcely forgive the ingratitude of the Prince in the new-born virtue of the King, and we curse the severity of that poetic justice which consigns our old, good-natured, delightful companion to the custody of the *warden,* and the dishonours of the Fleet.

Charles Lamb

After Morgann, Shakespeare's characters came almost to have an independent life and to be discussed as human beings of whom the play presents some records from which other facts may be deduced. This was Charles Lamb's feeling. Indeed, some of Shakespeare's characters were to him so real that he resented the attempts of actors to impersonate them. He argued his objections in a famous essay *On the Tragedies of Shakspeare, Considered with Reference to Their Fitness for Stage Representation* (1811):

It may seem a paradox but I cannot help being of opinion that the plays of Shakspeare are less calculated for performance on a stage, than those of almost any other dramatist whatever. Their distinguishing excellence is a reason that they should be so. There is so much in them, which comes not under the province of acting, with which eye, and tone, and gesture, have nothing to do. . . .

So to see Lear acted — to see an old man tottering about the stage with a walking-stick, turned out of doors by his daughters in a rainy night, has nothing in it but what is painful and disgusting. We want to take him into shelter and relieve him. That is all the feeling which the acting of Lear ever produced in me. But the Lear of Shakspeare cannot be acted. The contemptible machinery by which they mimic the storm which he goes out in, is not more inadequate to represent the horrors of the real elements, than any actor can be to represent Lear: they might more easily propose to personate the Satan of Milton upon a stage, or one of Michael Angelo's terrible figures. The greatness of Lear is not in corporal dimension, but in intellectual: the explosions of his passion are terrible as a volcano: they are storms turning up and disclosing to the bottom that sea, his mind, with all its vast riches. It is his mind which is laid bare. This case of flesh and blood seems too insignificant to be thought on; even as he himself neglects it. On the stage we see nothing but corporal infirmities and weakness, the impotence of rage; while we read it, we see not Lear, but we are Lear — we are in his mind, we are sustained by a grandeur which baffles the malice of daughters and storms; in the aberrations of his reason, we discover a mighty irregular power of reasoning, immethodized from the ordinary purposes of life, but exerting its powers, as the wind blows where it listeth, at will upon the corruptions and abuses of mankind. What have looks, or tones, to do with that sublime identification of his age with that of the *heavens themselves,* when in his reproaches to them for conniving at the injustice of his children, he reminds them that " they themselves are old." What gesture shall be appropriate to this? What has the voice or the eye to do with such things? But the play is beyond all art, as the tamperings with it show: it is too hard and stony; it must have love-scenes, and a happy ending. It is not enough that Cordelia is a daughter, she must shine as a lover too. Tate has put his hook in the nostrils of this Leviathan,[3] for Garrick and his followers, the showmen of the scene, to draw the mighty beast about more easily. A happy ending! — as if the living martyrdom that Lear had gone through — the flaying of his feelings alive, did not make a fair dismissal from the stage of life the only decorous thing for him. If he is to live and be happy after, if he could sustain this world's burden after, why all this pudder and preparation — why torment us with all this unnecessary sympathy? As if the childish pleasure of getting his gilt robes and sceptre again could tempt him to act over again his misused station — as if at his years, and with his experience, anything was left but to die.

[3] Nahum Tate in 1681 rewrote Shakespeare's *Lear*, keeping about half of Shakespeare's lines and scenes. In this version Edgar falls in love with Cordelia, rescues her from robbers, and ultimately saves her life. The play ends happily with Lear, Gloucester, and Kent retiring to a peaceful old age while Edgar and Cordelia succeed to the throne. Tate's version was acted throughout the eighteenth century. Lamb, it may be noted, never had the opportunity of seeing Shakespeare's *Lear* on the stage.

Lear is essentially impossible to be represented on a stage.

Samuel Taylor Coleridge

To Samuel Taylor Coleridge, Shakespeare was not merely a great dramatist and poet but a divine genius, whose faults were not faults but inspired virtues. In a lecture delivered in 1818, he said:

Let me now proceed to destroy, as far as may be in my power, the popular notion that he was a great dramatist by mere instinct, that he grew immortal in his own despite, and sank below men of second or third-rate power, when he attempted aught beside the drama — even as bees construct their cells and manufacture their honey to admirable perfection; but would in vain attempt to build a nest. Now this mode of reconciling a compelled sense of inferiority with a feeling of pride, began in a few pedants, who having read that Sophocles was the great model of tragedy, and Aristotle the infallible dictator of its rules, and finding that the *Lear, Hamlet, Othello* and other master-pieces were neither in imitation of Sophocles, nor in obedience to Aristotle — and not having (with one or two exceptions) the courage to affirm, that the delight which their country received from generation to generation, in defiance of the alterations of circumstances and habits, was wholly groundless, — took upon them, as a happy medium and refuge, to talk of Shakespeare as a sort of beautiful *lusus naturæ,*[4] a delightful monster — wild, indeed, and without taste or judgment, but like the inspired idiots so much venerated in the East, uttering, amid the strangest follies, the sublimest truths. In nine places out of ten in which I find his awful name mentioned, it is with some epithet of " wild," " irregular," " pure child of nature," &c.

Coleridge indeed demanded almost blind worship from Shakespeare's readers:

Assuredly that criticism of Shakspeare will alone be genial which is reverential. The Englishman, who without reverence, a proud and affectionate reverence, can utter the name of William Shakspeare, stands disqualified for the office of critic. He wants one at least of the very senses, the language of which he is to employ, and will discourse at best, but as a blind man, while the whole harmonious creation of light and shade with all its subtle interchange of deepening and dissolving colours rises in silence to the silent *fiat* of the uprising Apollo. However inferior in ability I may be to

⁴ freak.

some who have followed me, I own I am proud that I was the first in time who publicly demonstrated to the full extent of the position, that the supposed irregularity and extravagances of Shakspeare were the mere dreams of a pedantry that arraigned the eagle because it had not the dimensions of the swan. In all the successive courses of lectures delivered by me, since my first attempt at the Royal Institution, it has been, and it still remains, my object, to prove that in all points from the most important to the most minute, the judgment of Shakspeare is commensurate with his genius — nay, that his genius reveals itself in his judgment, as in its most exalted form.

Coleridge's pronouncements had a profound influence on Shakespearean critics for over a century, and none were more widely quoted than his remarks on *Hamlet:*

In Hamlet he seems to have wished to exemplify the moral necessity of a due balance between our attention to the objects of our senses, and our meditation on the workings of our minds — an *equilibrium* between the real and the imaginary worlds. In Hamlet this balance is disturbed: his thoughts, and the images of his fancy, are far more vivid than his actual perceptions, and his very perceptions, instantly passing through the *medium* of his contemplations, acquire, as they pass, a form and a colour not naturally their own. Hence we see a great, an almost enormous, intellectual activity, and a proportionate aversion to real action, consequent upon it, with all its symptoms and accompanying qualities. This character Shakspeare places in circumstances, under which it is obliged to act on the spur of the moment: — Hamlet is brave and careless of death; but he vacillates from sensibility and procrastinates from thought, and loses the power of action in the energy of resolve. Thus it is that this tragedy presents a direct contrast to that of Macbeth; the one proceeds with the utmost slowness, the other with a crowded and breathless rapidity.

The effect of this overbalance of the imaginative power is beautifully illustrated in the everlasting broodings and superfluous activities of Hamlet's mind, which, unseated from its healthy relation, is constantly occupied with the world within, and abstracted from the world without — giving substance to shadows, and throwing a mist over all commonplace actualities. It is the nature of thought to be indefinite — definiteness belongs to external imagery alone. Hence it is that the sense of sublimity arises, not from the sight of an outward object, but from the beholder's reflection upon it; — not from the sensuous impression, but from the imaginative reflex. Few have seen a celebrated waterfall with-

out feeling something akin to disappointment: it is
only subsequently that the image comes back full
into the mind, and brings with it a train of grand
or beautiful associations. Hamlet feels this; his
senses are in a state of trance, and he looks upon
external things as hieroglyphics. His soliloquy —

"O! that this too too solid flesh would melt, &c."

springs from that craving after the indefinite — for
that which is not — which most easily besets men
of genius; and the self-delusion common to this
temper of mind is finely exemplified in the charac-
ter which Hamlet gives of himself: —

"— It cannot be
But I am pigeon-liver'd, and lack gall
To make oppression bitter."

He mistakes the seeing his chains for the breaking
them, delays action till action is of no use, and dies
the victim of mere circumstance and accident.

Some years later, in his *Table Talk*, Coleridge
made an illuminating comment:

Hamlet's character is the prevalence of the ab-
stracting and generalizing habit over the practical.
He does not want courage, skill, will, or opportu-
nity; but every incident sets him thinking; and it
is curious, and, at the same time strictly natural,
that Hamlet, who all the play seems reason itself,
should be impelled, at last, by mere accident to
effect his object. I have a smack of Hamlet myself,
if I may say so.

William Hazlitt

There was much excellent Shakespearean
criticism in the first quarter of the nineteenth
century. Two writers are particularly important,
William Hazlitt and Thomas De Quincey.
Hazlitt's *Characters of Shakespear's Plays* (1817)
was, in the words of the critic Jeffrey, "written
less to tell the reader what Mr. H. *knows* about
Shakespeare or his writings, than to explain to
them what he *feels* about them — and *why* he
feels so — and thinks that all who profess to
love poetry should feel so likewise."

Hazlitt's book is full of gusto and is always
worth reading. Of Othello he wrote:

It has been said that tragedy purifies the affec-
tions by terror and pity. That is, substitutes imagi-
nary sympathy for mere selfishness. It gives us a
high and permanent interest, beyond ourselves, in
humanity as such. It raises the great, the remote,
and the possible to an equality with the real, the

little and the near. It makes man a partaker with
his kind. It subdues and softens the stubbornness
of his will. It teaches him that there are and have
been others like himself, by showing him as in a
glass what they have felt, thought, and done. It
opens the chambers of the human heart. It leaves
nothing indifferent to us that can affect our com-
mon nature. It excites our sensibility by exhibiting
the passions wound up to the utmost pitch by the
power of imagination or the temptation of circum-
stances; and corrects their fatal excesses in our-
selves by pointing to the greater extent of sufferings
and of crimes to which they have led others. Trag-
edy creates a balance of the affections. It makes us
thoughtful spectators in the lists of life. It is the
refiner of the species; a discipline of humanity. The
habitual study of poetry and works of imagination
is one chief part of a well-grounded education. A
taste for liberal art is necessary to complete the
character of a gentleman. Science alone is hard and
mechanical. It exercises the understanding upon
things out of ourselves, while it leaves the affec-
tions unemployed, or engrossed with our own im-
mediate, narrow interest. — *Othello* furnishes an
illustration of these remarks. It excites our sympa-
thy in an extraordinary degree. The moral it con-
veys has a closer application to the concerns of
human life than that of almost any other of Shake-
spear's plays. "It comes directly home to the
bosoms and business of men." The pathos in *Lear* is
indeed more dreadful and overpowering; but it is
less natural, and less of every day's occurrence. We
have not the same degree of sympathy with the
passions described in *Macbeth*. The interest in *Ham-
let* is more remote and reflex. That of *Othello* is at
once equally profound and affecting. . . .

The character of Iago is one of the supereroga-
tions of Shakespear's genius. Some persons, more
nice than wise, have thought this whole character
unnatural because his villainy is *without a sufficient
motive*. Shakespear, who was as good a philosopher
as he was a poet, thought otherwise. He knew that
the love of power, which is another name for the
love of mischief, is natural to man. He would know
this as well or better than if it had been demon-
strated to him by a logical diagram, merely from
seeing children paddle in the dirt or kill flies for
sport. Iago in fact belongs to a class of character,
common to Shakespear and at the same time pecul-
iar to him; whose heads are as acute and active as
their hearts are hard and callous. Iago is to be sure
an extreme instance of the kind; that is to say, of
diseased intellectual activity, with the most perfect
indifference to moral good or evil, or rather with
a decided preference of the latter, because it falls
more readily in with his favourite propensity, gives
greater zest to his thoughts and scope to his actions.

He is quite or nearly as indifferent to his own fate as to that of others; he runs all risks for a trifling and doubtful advantage; and is himself the dupe and victim of his ruling passion — an insatiable craving after action of the most difficult and dangerous kind. "Our ancient" is a philosopher, who fancies that a lie that kills has more point in it than an alliteration or an antithesis; who thinks a fatal experiment on the peace of a family a better thing than watching the palpitations in the heart of a flea in a microscope; who plots the ruin of his friends as an exercise for his ingenuity, and stabs men in the dark to prevent *ennui*. His gaiety, such as it is, arises from the success of his treachery; his ease from the torture he has inflicted on others. He is an amateur of tragedy in real life; and instead of employing his invention on imaginary characters, or long-forgotten incidents, he takes the bolder and more desperate course of getting up his plot at home, casts the principal parts among his nearest friends and connections, and rehearses it in downright earnest, with steady nerves and unabated resolution.

Thomas De Quincey

De Quincey's appreciation of Shakespeare was subtle and penetrating, and in his essay "On the Knocking at the Gate in Macbeth" (1823) he chose one moment in one play to illustrate Shakespeare's genius:

Or, if the reader has ever been present in a vast metropolis, on the day when some great national idol was carried in funeral pomp to his grave, and chancing to walk near the course through which it passed, has felt powerfully in the silence and desertion of the streets, and in the stagnation of ordinary business, the deep interest which at that moment was possessing the heart of man — if all at once he should hear the death-like stillness broken up by the sound of wheels rattling away from the scene, and making known that the transitory vision was dissolved, he will be aware that at no moment was his sense of the complete suspension and pause in ordinary human concerns so full and affecting, as at that moment when the suspension ceases, and the goings-on of human life are suddenly resumed. All action in any direction is best expounded, measured, and made apprehensible, by reaction. Now apply this to the case in *Macbeth*. Here, as I have said, the retiring of the human heart, and the entrance of the fiendish heart was to be expressed and made sensible. Another world has stept in; and the murderers are taken out of the region of human things, human purposes, human desires. They are transfigured: Lady Macbeth is "unsexed"; Macbeth has forgot that he was born of woman; both are conformed to the image of devils; and the world of devils is suddenly revealed. But how shall this be conveyed and made palpable? In order that a new world may step in, this world must for a time disappear. The murderers, and the murder must be insulated — cut off by an immeasurable gulf from the ordinary tide and succession of human affairs — locked up and sequestered in some deep recess; we must be made sensible that the world of ordinary life is suddenly arrested — laid asleep — tranced — racked into a dread armistice; time must be annihilated; relation to things without abolished; and all must pass self-withdrawn into a deep syncope and suspension of earthly passion. Hence it is, that when the deed is done, when the work of darkness is perfect, then the world of darkness passes away like a pageantry in the clouds: the knocking at the gate is heard; and it makes known audibly that the reaction has commenced; the human has made its reflux upon the fiendish; the pulses of life are beginning to beat again; and the re-establishment of the goings-on of the world in which we live, first makes us profoundly sensible of the awful parenthesis that had suspended them.

O mighty poet! Thy works are not as those of other men, simply and merely great works of art; but are also like the phenomena of nature, like the sun and the sea, the stars and the flowers; like frost and snow, rain and dew, hail-storm and thunder, which are to be studied with entire submission of our own faculties, and in the perfect faith that in them there can be no too much or too little, nothing useless or inert — but that, the farther we press in our discoveries, the more we shall see proofs of design and self-supporting arrangement where the careless eye had seen nothing but accident!

Thomas Carlyle

With De Quincey, as with Coleridge, Shakespeare was elevated into a god; he was still at least a demigod when Carlyle wrote the chapter on "The Hero as Poet" in *Heroes and Hero Worship* (1845):

Whoever looks intelligently at this Shakspeare may recognize that he too was a *prophet,* in his way; of an insight analogous to the Prophetic, though he took it up in another strain. Nature seemed to this man also divine; *un*speakable, deep as Tophet, high as Heaven: "We are such stuff as Dreams are made of!" That scroll in Westminster Abbey, which few read with understanding, is of the depth of any Seer. But the man sang; did not preach except musically. We called Dante the melodious Priest of Middle-Age Catholicism. May we not call Shakspeare the still more melodious Priest of a *true* Catholicism, the "Universal Church" of the Future and of all times? No narrow superstition, harsh asceticism, intolerance, fanatical fierceness or perversion: a Revelation, so far as it goes, that such a thousandfold hidden beauty and divineness dwells in all Nature; which let all men worship as they can.

In "The Hero as Poet" Carlyle drew a romantic picture of the Warwickshire peasant boy for which there was no real foundation in the facts known to scholars. Indeed in sane discussions of a writer long dead, critics and scholars must depend on each other. Until the scholar has established the facts of date and place, the critic is not equipped to discuss the life, the personality, or the development of an author. In Johnson's day, small attempt had been made to discover further facts about Shakespeare, and less to study his environment. Rowe had added a brief biography, but little had been discovered since Rowe's time. But by the end of the eighteenth century Shakespearean scholarship was beginning.

Beginnings of Scholarship

Of the early Shakespearean scholars the greatest was Edmund Malone, a zealous antiquarian who realized that to study Shakespeare a knowledge of his environment was needed. Malone gathered all the contemporary material that he could find and left a large collection of early plays, books, and pamphlets to the Bodleian Library at the University of Oxford. Malone also wrote the first good account of the Elizabethan stage.

In the early years of the nineteenth century, as part of the reaction against the tastes of the eighteenth, there was a considerable revival of interest in the literature of the pre-Restoration period and especially in its drama, but there was as yet no comprehensive collection for study. A studious reader could find, without much difficulty, old editions of the plays of Ben Jonson or of Beaumont and Fletcher or of Massinger, and some of the old plays were collected in Dodsley's *Old Plays* (1744). But there was no complete edition of Ford until 1811, of Marlowe until 1826, of Peele until 1828–39; Webster was first

collected in 1830, Greene in 1831, Middleton in 1840, Heywood in 1842–51, and Dekker so late as 1873.

In 1841 the first Shakespeare Society was founded. The chief interest of its members was to collect and edit records and contemporary books which illustrated Shakespeare's times. This group included John Payne Collier, one of the greatest of all Shakespearean scholars. Payne Collier was a tireless searcher in records, few of which had as yet been catalogued or calendared. Unfortunately his discoveries did not keep pace with his enthusiasm, and when he could not find documents to prove his theories he took to forging them. When his forgeries were exposed in 1853, Shakespearean scholarship received a great setback.

A second or New Shakspere Society was founded in 1873. Its leader was F. J. Furnivall, a medieval scholar, who set his followers to work on the collective project of establishing the order of the writing of Shakespeare's plays by observing all allusions to or within the plays, and by examining statistically the peculiarities of Shakespeare's style. The results, with some modifications, have been generally accepted by scholars. Thus in 1875, when Edward Dowden came to write *Shakspere: A Critical Study of His Mind and Art,* he began with a clear idea of the order in which Shakespeare's plays were written. This was something new in Shakespearean criticism.

Edward Dowden

Dowden was responsible for the conception that Shakespeare's "art life" could be divided into four periods: the years of experiment; the period when "he was gaining a sure grasp of the positive facts of life," shown at first in the *Henry IV* plays and later in *Much Ado about Nothing, As You Like It,* and *Twelfth Night;* the period of the great tragedies; and the last, or tranquil, period when Shakespeare, after some years of turmoil, reached serenity. Dowden thus projected Shakespeare's mental development into his plays, implying that they were a reflection of his own emotional development. The book is a good specimen of Victorian criticism at its best, though Dowden tends to see Shakespeare's artistic development almost as a deliberate and conscious process, uninfluenced by external or material causes. Thus, of *As You Like It* he wrote:

Shakspere, when he wrote this idyllic play was himself in his Forest of Arden. He had ended one great ambition — the historical plays — and not yet commenced his tragedies. It was a resting-place. He sends his imagination into the woods to find repose. Instead of the courts and camps of England, and the embattled plains of France, here was this woodland scene, where the palm-tree, the lioness, and the serpent are to be found; possessed of a flora and fauna that flourish in spite of physical geographers. There is an open-air feeling throughout the play. The dialogue, as has been observed, catches freedom and freshness from the atmosphere. Never is the scene within-doors, except when something discordant is introduced to heighten as it were the harmony. After the trumpet-tones of Henry V comes the sweet pastoral strain, so bright, so tender. Must it not be all in keeping? Shakspere was not trying to control his melancholy. When he needed to do that, Shakspere confronted his melancholy very passionately, and looked it full in the face. Here he needed refreshment, a sunlight tempered by forest-boughs, a breeze upon his forehead, a stream murmuring in his ears.

A. C. Bradley

The last and greatest example of Victorian criticism was A. C. Bradley's *Shakespearean Tragedy* (1904), in which he discusses *Hamlet, Othello, King Lear,* and *Macbeth.* No single volume of criticism has achieved a greater reputation. Bradley's intention was to examine the plays from a single point of view:

Our one object will be what, again in a restricted sense, may be called dramatic appreciation; to increase our understanding and enjoyment of these works as dramas; to learn to apprehend the action and some of the personages of each with a somewhat greater truth and intensity, so that they may assume in our imaginations a shape a little less unlike the shape they wore in the imagination of their creator.

He began with an essay on "The Substance of Shakespearean Tragedy," in which he endeavored to answer the question: "What is Shakespearean tragedy?" He concluded:

Thus we are left at last with an idea showing two sides or aspects which we can neither separate nor reconcile. The whole or order against which the individual part shows itself powerless seems to

be animated by a passion for perfection: we cannot otherwise explain its behaviour towards evil. Yet it appears to engender this evil within itself, and in its effort to overcome and expel it it is agonised with pain, and driven to mutilate its own substance and to lose not only evil but priceless good. That this idea, though very different from the idea of a blank fate, is no solution of the riddle of life is obvious; but why should we expect it to be such a solution? Shakespeare was not attempting to justify the ways of God to men, or to show the universe as a Divine Comedy. He was writing tragedy, and tragedy would not be tragedy if it were not a painful mystery. Nor can he be said even to point distinctly, like some writers of tragedy, in any direction where a solution might lie. We find a few references to gods or God, to the influence of the stars, to another life: some of them certainly, all of them perhaps, merely dramatic — appropriate to the person from whose lips they fall. A ghost comes from Purgatory to impart a secret out of the reach of its hearer — who presently meditates on the question whether the sleep of death is dreamless. Accidents once or twice remind us strangely of the words, "There's a divinity that shapes our ends." More important are other impressions. Sometimes from the very furnace of affliction a conviction seems borne to us that somehow, if we could see it, this agony counts as nothing against the heroism and love which appear in it and thrill our hearts. Sometimes we are driven to cry out that these mighty or heavenly spirits who perish are too great for the little space in which they move, and that they vanish not into nothingness but into freedom. Sometimes from these sources and from others comes a presentiment, formless but haunting and even profound, that all the fury of conflict, with its waste and woe, is less than half the truth, even an illusion, "such stuff as dreams are made on." But these faint and scattered intimations that the tragic world, being but a fragment of a whole beyond our vision, must needs be a contradiction and no ultimate truth, avail nothing to interpret the mystery. We remain confronted with the inexplicable fact, or the no less inexplicable appearance, of a world travailing for perfection, but bringing to birth, together with glorious good, an evil which it is able to overcome only by self-torture and self-waste. And this fact or appearance is tragedy.

From this beginning Bradley proceeded to analyze the four tragedies as records of what passed in the minds of Shakespeare and of the characters. The analysis is long, penetrating, and suggestive. The objection, however, to this kind of criticism is that it ignores the practical facts of Elizabethan stage drama and attributes to

Shakespeare a minute care which he probably never took. Nevertheless, *Shakespearean Tragedy* is still probably the most widely read of all single works of Shakespearean criticism.

Modern Interests

In the last sixty years the mass of Shakespearean studies of every kind has been so vast that no single scholar can now hope to keep abreast of everything that is written about Shakespeare. Yet there are fashions in literary criticism which follow the general changes in taste in other artistic matters. Four branches of research have been especially popular. These are: the exact study of the texts; the Elizabethan theater; the background — historical and intellectual; and the minute analysis of Shakespeare's poetic and dramatic techniques.

Interest in the early texts of the plays was much stimulated by A. W. Pollard, who in *Shakespeare's Fight with the Pirates* (1919) claimed that some of the early quartos were set up by the printer from Shakespeare's own manuscripts and reproduced many of their peculiarities. Interest was further stimulated by Edward Maunde Thompson's claim (in his chapter on "Shakespeare's Handwriting" in *Shakespeare's England* [1916]) that three pages in a manuscript play in the British Museum called *The Booke of Sir Thomas More* were in Shakespeare's handwriting. These and many other studies have sent scholars back to the original texts — quartos and folios — which are now available to the general reader in various facsimiles.

The modern study of the Elizabethan stage and the conditions of acting originated mainly from W. W. Greg's editions (1904–07) of the *Diary* and *Papers* of Philip Henslowe (see p. 65a). Henslowe's *Diary* is one of the most exciting books that a student can encounter; it takes him, as it were, into the manager's office of an Elizabethan playhouse and shows him a host of human details that lie behind the drama. The zeal for reconstructing the actual conditions under which Shakespeare wrote led also to new critical approaches, of which the most important were the *Prefaces* of Harley Granville-Barker (1923–46).

Meanwhile scholars were at work on the historical background of those events and ideas which inevitably find their echo in the plays: of

these studies a few of the more important are recorded in section C of the Reading List (see p. 86a–b).

In criticism, a new movement became conspicuous in the 1930's and is still popular. While the younger poets were evolving new techniques and methods of expression, the universal interest in the processes of the mind, so greatly stimulated by the work of Sigmund Freud, led to a reconsideration of the nature of language itself and of the principles of criticism. It was natural that the New Critics should re-examine Shakespeare's poetic language and his uses of poetic imagery. This approach was especially popularized by Caroline Spurgeon in *Shakespeare's Imagery and What It Tells Us* (1935) and G. Wilson Knight in *The Wheel of Fire* (1930) and other works.

This intensive study of Shakespeare's poetic symbolism is in a way a reaction to earlier methods of criticism. Victorian critics in exalting Shakespeare the poet and universal genius had forgotten that he was also a man of the theater. Critics of the 1920's put Shakespeare back into the Globe playhouse. The latest movement again fetches Shakespeare out of the theater and brings him back into the study — and clinic, for the intricate relationship of image and idea can only be appreciated in close and leisurely reading. Thus Shakespeare the poet and philosopher is once more exalted, while Shakespeare the actor-dramatist is forgotten. If Shakespeare was indeed consciously aware of all that modern critics have found in his plays and deliberately used such symbolism in their structure, it follows that the more intelligent members of his audiences must have been acutely sensitive to verbal subtleties; and if so, it should increase our respect for the Elizabethan audience.

All these "studies" and "approaches" may fill the student with despair at the thought that he must burrow through so huge a pile of conflicting criticism and scholarship. He need not unduly distress himself. With a minimum of learning any intelligent reader can enjoy Shakespeare; but the wider his experience of the various branches of interest, the deeper will be his understanding and his ultimate pleasure — so long as he never commits the fatal error of regarding the commentary as more important than the text.

Reading List

In this short list are included hardback and paperback [1] editions of those volumes which are likely to be of greatest interest and use to the general student. Articles in periodicals are not included; for these the student should consult the bibliographies mentioned in section A. Items in each section are for the most part given in the chronological order of appearance.

A. Bibliography

The Cambridge Bibliography of English Literature, ed. by F. W. Bateson, 4 vols., Cambridge University Press, 1947 (orig. publ. 1940).

For general purposes this is the most useful of all bibliographies for the student. Shakespeare and his contemporaries are included in Volume I. The *Bibliography* includes works published to the end of 1938. A Supplementary Volume (V) carries the *Bibliography* down to the beginning of 1955.

New work is recorded annually in *The Year's Work in English Studies*, Oxford University Press, and *Shakespeare Survey*, Cambridge University Press. Some of the more scholarly works listed below contain useful bibliographies; see for instance E. K. Chambers, *The Elizabethan Stage* and *William Shakespeare*.

B. Texts and Editions

FACSIMILES OF ORIGINAL QUARTOS

a. *The Merchant of Venice, The Merry Wives of Windsor, Hamlet* (Q2), *King Lear, Pericles, Love's Labor's Lost, Henry V, Troilus and Cressida, Hamlet* (Q1), and *Romeo and Juliet* have been reproduced in collotype, ed. by W. W. Greg, Oxford University Press, 1939–57.

b. *Hamlet* (Q1), Harvard University Press, 1931; *Titus Andronicus* (Q1), Scribners, 1936; and *Hamlet* (Q2), Huntington Library, 1938, are collotype reproductions.

PHOTOGRAPHIC FACSIMILES OF THE FIRST FOLIO OF 1623

a. In collotype, ed. by Sidney Lee, Oxford University Press, 1902.

b. By line process, ed. by H. Kökeritz and C. T. Prouty, Yale University Press, 1954. The size of the type has been reduced but the text is adequate for normal use. The process used in the reproduc-

[1] Paperback editions are noted by asterisks.

tion does not give absolute accuracy, for the plates must sometimes be doctored to eliminate imperfections in the original, especially 'show-through' due to too absorbent paper. Though not suitable for the minutest bibliographical research, the volume is a most desirable possession for any serious student.

Photostat and microfilm reproductions of an individual text can usually be obtained by scholars at a reasonable cost from the Folger Shakespeare Library, Washington, D.C.; the Huntington Library, San Marino, California; the British Museum, London; or the Bodleian Library, Oxford.

EDITIONS

Cambridge, ed. by W. G. Clark and W. A. Wright, 9 vols., Macmillan, 1863–66. This edition and its popular version, the *Globe Shakespeare*, Macmillan, 1864, was long, and by many still is, regarded as the "authorized version" of Shakespeare.

New Variorum, ed. by H. H. Furness and others, Lippincott, 1871 — in progress. The more modern volumes of this series are indispensable for advanced students. Each volume is intended to contain in full the material necessary for the serious study of one play: sources, evidences of date, etc., together with copious extracts from the commentators.

Arden, ed. by W. J. Craig and R. J. Case, 39 vols., Heath, 1890–1924. A useful standard edition, a volume to a play. The editors, however, were not of equal ability and the level of editing is uneven. The volumes are being superseded by the *New Arden*, now in process of publication under the general editorship of Una Ellis Fermor.

New, ed. by J. Dover Wilson, Cambridge University Press, 1921 — in progress.

Kittredge, ed. by G. L. Kittredge, Ginn, 1957 (orig. publ. 1936). A plain text, less conservative than most, by one of the greatest of American scholars. Sixteen of the plays, with Kittredge's notes, have also been published, separately and in one collected volume. They are: *The Tempest, Much Ado about Nothing, A Midsummer Night's Dream, The Merchant of Venice, As You Like It, Twelfth Night, Richard II, 1 Henry IV, Henry V, Romeo and Juliet, Julius Caesar, Macbeth, Hamlet, Lear, Othello, Antony and Cleopatra*.

New Cambridge, ed. by W. A. Neilson and C. J. Hill, Houghton Mifflin, 1942. A useful one-volume text for general reading.

C. Shakespeare's Times

Stow, John, *A Survey of London*, London, 1598, ed. by C. L. Kingsford, 2 vols., Oxford University Press, 1908; Dutton (Everyman), 1956. An elaborate contemporary and historical description of London.

Stow, John, *Annales; or, a General Chronicle of England, Begun by John Stow; Continued by Edmund Howes . . . unto . . . 1631*, London, 1631. A contemporary chronicle, year by year, of the most sensational events in English life.

Nichols, John, *The Progresses and Public Processions of Queen Elizabeth*, 3 vols., London, 1823; *The Progresses, Processions, and Magnificent Festivities, of King James the First*, 4 vols., London, 1828.
Both are full and valuable collections of records and contemporary pamphlets dealing with ceremonials, pageants, masques, and entertainments of the Court.

Gardiner, S. R., *History of England from the Accession of James I to the Outbreak of the Civil War, 1603–1642*, new ed., 10 vols., Longmans, Green, 1894–96. With Cheyney (see below), the most comprehensive and generally useful of the longer histories of the period.

Madden, D. H., *The Diary of Master William Silence: A Study of Shakespeare & of Elizabethan Sport*, Longmans, Green, 1897.

Cheyney, Edward P., *A History of England from the Defeat of the Armada to the Death of Elizabeth*, 2 vols., Longmans, Green, 1914–26.

Shakespeare's England, ed. by Walter Raleigh, Sidney Lee, and C. T. Onions, 2 vols., Oxford University Press, 1919. An account of the life and manners of his age. An essential book for any student of Shakespeare. It contains chapters by experts on almost every aspect of life in Shakespeare's England, with particular reference to the plays. There are many illustrations.

Byrne, Muriel St. C., *Elizabethan Life in Town and Country*, British Book, 1954 (orig. publ. 1925). An interesting book for the student.

Harrison, G. B., *The Elizabethan Journals, 1591–1603*, University of Michigan Press, 1955 (orig. publ. 1929, 1931, 1933); *A Jacobean Journal . . . 1603–1606*, Macmillan, 1941; *A Second Jacobean Journal . . . 1607–1610*, University of Michigan Press, 1958. A detailed day-by-day account of those matters great and small which chiefly interested Shakespeare and his contemporaries.

Judges, A. V., *The Elizabethan Underworld*, Kegan Paul, Trench, Trubner, 1930. A useful collection of the more important contemporary pamphlets about Elizabethan rogues and vagabonds.

Wright, Louis B., *Middle-Class Culture in Elizabethan England*, University of North Carolina Press (Huntington Library Publications), 1935. An account of the mentality and culture of the average middle-class citizens who formed the greater part of Shakespeare's audiences.

Black, J. B., *The Reign of Elizabeth, 1558–1603*, Oxford University Press, 1936. A useful general account of the reign in most of its aspects, with a general historical bibliography.

Craig, Hardin, *The Enchanted Glass*, Essential Books, 1952 (orig. publ. 1936). A scholarly account of the intellectual background of the age.

The Letters of John Chamberlain, ed. by N. E. McClure, 2 vols., American Philosophical Society, 1939. John Chamberlain was the best of the Elizabethan letter writers. He had a keen zest for gossip and his letters provide a racy running commentary on the period from 1597 to 1626.

Spencer, Theodore, *Shakespeare and the Nature of Man*, Macmillan, 1942. A discussion of the turmoil of contemporary ideas on man's place in the universe and their reflections in Shakespeare's plays.

Tillyard, E. M. W., *The Elizabethan World Picture*, Macmillan, 1943. An attempt to set out the theory of the universe as understood by Shakespeare's contemporaries.

D. Elizabethan Theatrical Conditions

Henslowe's Diary (2 vols.) and *Henslowe's Papers* (1 vol.), ed. by W. W. Greg, Bullen, London, 1904–08. See Gen. Intro. pp. 38b, 65a, 84a. The accounts and various papers concerning their theatrical ventures left by Philip Henslowe and Edward Alleyn. The most fascinating of all original documents concerning the Elizabethan theater.

Adams, Joseph Quincy, *Shakespearean Playhouses*, Houghton Mifflin, 1917. A lively and interesting account of the various London playhouses.

Chambers, E. K., *The Elizabethan Stage*, 4 vols., Oxford University Press, 1923. An essential work for the advanced student and the scholar. It exhaustively summarizes the facts about Elizabethan plays, dramatists, theaters, and companies, with many extracts from original sources.

Noble, Richmond, *Shakespeare's Use of Song*, Oxford University Press, 1923. Discusses the purpose of the songs in the plays.

Baldwin, T. W., *Organization and Personnel of the Shakespearean Company*, Princeton University Press, 1927. An elaborate and detailed account of the Elizabethan acting company.

Nungezer, Edwin, *A Dictionary of Actors . . . before 1642*, Cornell University Press, 1929. A valuable book of reference.

Greg, W. W., *Dramatic Documents from the*

Elizabethan Playhouses, 2 vols., Oxford University Press, 1931. Facsimiles of the most important documents of stage history. Most valuable and interesting for the serious student.

Naylor, Edward W., *Shakespeare and Music,* rev. ed., Dutton, 1931 (orig. ed., 1896). A useful account of Elizabethan music and musical instruments.

Linthicum, Marie C., *Costume in Elizabethan Drama,* Oxford University Press, 1936. An essential book of reference for all matters of fabrics, colors, and costumes.

Sisson, C. J., *Lost Plays of Shakespeare's Age,* Cambridge University Press, 1936. A record of researches, chiefly in the Public Record Office in London, which throws much light on the murkier corners of Elizabethan social life and the drama. It is, moreover, fascinating and amusing reading.

Harrison, G. B., *Elizabethan Plays and Players,* University of Michigan Press (Ann Arbor *), 1956 (orig. publ. 1940). An account of the chief personalities in Elizabethan dramatic history from 1570 to 1603.

Harbage, Alfred, *Shakespeare's Audience,* Columbia University Press, 1941. An important and stimulating study of the size, social composition, behavior, and intelligence of Shakespeare's audiences.

Adams, John Cranford, *The Globe Playhouse: Its Design and Equipment,* Harvard University Press, 1942. An important study of Shakespeare's theater, an essential book for any serious student.

Smith, Irwin, *Shakespeare's Globe Playhouse,* Scribner, 1957. A modern reconstruction, with text and plans, based upon John Cranford Adams' well-known model (See Pl. 5b).

E. *The Text and Its Problems*

Greg, W. W., *Shakespeare's Merry Wives of Windsor,* Oxford University Press, 1910. The first serious study of a "bad quarto" by a modern scholar.

Pollard, A. W., *Shakespeare's Fight with the Pirates and the Problems of the Transmission of His Text,* 2nd ed., Cambridge University Press, 1937 (orig. publ. 1917). This book, more than any other single volume, was responsible for the modern interest in the exact study of the early texts of Shakespeare. See p. 84a.

Pollard, A. W., Greg, W. W., Thompson, E. M., Wilson, J. Dover, and Chambers, R. W., *Shakespeare's Hand in the Play of "Sir Thomas More,"* Cambridge University Press, 1923.

McKerrow, R. B., *An Introduction to Bibliography for Literary Students,* Oxford University Press, 1927. An indispensable introduction to the scholarly study of the problems of the text.

Willoughby, Edwin E., *The Printing of the First Folio of Shakespeare,* Oxford University Press, 1932. A study of the making of the most important volume in English literature.

McKerrow, R. B., *Prolegomena to the Oxford Shakespeare: A Study in Editorial Method,* Oxford University Press, 1939. Shortly before his death in 1940 McKerrow planned to produce a new text of Shakespeare based on sound bibliographical principles. In this book he laid down the plan he proposed to follow.

Greg, W. W., *The Editorial Problem in Shakespeare,* Oxford University Press, 1954 (orig. publ. 1942). A discussion of the problems and principles of editing the plays. It should be read in conjunction with the preceding.

Duthie, G. I., *The 'Bad' Quarto of Hamlet,* Cambridge University Press, 1941. A full discussion of the origins of the most famous of the "bad quartos."

Hoppe, Harry R., *The Bad Quarto of Romeo and Juliet,* Cornell University Press, 1948. A good example of modern scholarly textual study.

Greg, W. W., *The Shakespeare First Folio: Its Bibliographical and Textual History,* Oxford University Press, 1955. The most generally important and comprehensive of all works on the Shakespeare text.

F. *Sources*

Holinshed, Raphael, *Chronicles of England, Scotland and Ireland,* 2 vols., London, 1577; 2nd ed., 1587. The source book for the History Plays and for *Macbeth.* Copious extracts of the passages Shakespeare used in writing the History Plays are given in *Shakespeare's Holinshed,* ed. by W. G. Boswell-Stone, London, 1896, and *Holinshed's Chronicles as Used in Shakespeare's Plays,* ed., by A. and J. Nicoll, Dutton (Everyman), 1927.

Plutarch, *The Lives of the Noble Grecians and Romans,* transl. from the French by Sir Thomas North, London, 1579, and later editions. See *Caesar* Intro, p. 809b. *Shakespeare's Plutarch,* ed. by W. W. Skeat, Macmillan, 1875, contains the lives used for *Coriolanus, Julius Caesar,* and *Antony and Cleopatra;* the same lives were also edited by R. H. Carr, Oxford University Press, 1932.

Shakespeare's Library, ed. by W. C. Hazlitt, 6 vols., Reeves and Turner, London, 1875. A collection of Shakespeare's source books, which will be superseded by *Narrative and Dramatic Sources of Shakespeare,* ed. by Geoffrey Bullough, Columbia University Press. Volume 1 (1957) covers the early comedies, poems and *Romeo and Juliet;* four other volumes are in preparation.

G. Critical Works

Smith, D. Nichol, ed., *Eighteenth Century Essays on Shakespeare,* MacLehose, Glasgow, 1903.

Smith, D. Nichol, ed., *Shakespeare Criticism* (from the beginnings to Carlyle), Oxford University Press, 1916. A very useful short selection of the most important critical pronouncements, including Rowe, Pope, Johnson, Morgann, Lamb, Coleridge, Hazlitt, and De Quincey. See pp. 73a–82a.

Bradby, Anne, ed., *Shakespeare Criticism, 1919–1935,* Oxford University Press, 1936. A collection of modern critical essays.

Ralli, Augustus, *A History of Shakespearian Criticism,* 2 vols., Oxford University Press, 1932. An elaborate collection of summaries of the critical work on Shakespeare from the beginnings to 1925.

Dean, Leonard F., ed., *Shakespeare: Modern Essays in Criticism,* Oxford University Press,* 1957. Contains twenty-eight selections, most of them from postwar criticism.

Lamb, Charles, *On the Tragedies of Shakespeare Considered with Reference to Their Fitness for Stage Representation,* London, 1811. See pp. 78a–79a.

Coleridge, S. T., *Shakespearean Criticism* (1811–1834), ed. by T. M. Raysor, 2 vols., Harvard University Press, 1930. The standard edition. See also *Lectures on Shakespeare,* Dutton (Everyman), 1907. See pp. 79a–80a. Coleridge was the most important of the critics of the "Romantic Revival," and was largely responsible for the excessive veneration of Shakespeare's genius in the Victorian era.

Hazlitt, William, *Characters of Shakespeare's Plays,* 1817. Included in Vol. IV of the *Complete Works,* ed. by P. P. Howe, 21 vols., Dent, 1932–34; Dutton (Everyman), 1906. See pp. 80a–81a. Sane appreciations of the chief characters, written with much sense and gusto.

Dowden, Edward, *Shakespere: A Critical Study of His Mind and Art,* Kegan Paul, Trench, Trubner, 1875. See pp. 82b–83a. The first critical work based on an accurate knowledge of the general development of Shakespeare's plays.

Moulton, R. G., *Shakespeare as a Dramatic Artist,* Oxford University Press, 1885. A study of the technique of drama and of Shakespeare's methods as a dramatist; a useful book.

Bradley, A. C., *Shakespearean Tragedy,* Macmillan, 1904; Meridian,* 1955. See pp. 83a–84a. The book considers the principles of Shakespearean tragedy, and in detail, *Hamlet, Othello, Lear,* and *Macbeth.*

Raleigh, Walter, *Shakespeare,* Macmillan, 1907; St. Martins,* 1957. A lively and human general introduction to the enjoyment of Shakespeare's plays.

MacCallum, M. W., *Shakespeare's Roman Plays and Their Background,* Macmillan, 1910. Full and elaborate studies of the three Roman tragedies — *Julius Caesar, Antony and Cleopatra,* and *Coriolanus* — with a discussion of Roman stories on the French and English stage.

Quiller-Couch, A. T., *Shakespeare's Workmanship,* Cambridge University Press, 1931 (orig. publ. 1918). Lively, common-sense lectures on the plays as specimens of theatrical art.

Schücking, Levin L., *Character Problems in Shakespeare's Plays,* Harrap, London, 1922. Critical studies from the scholar's point of view.

Granville-Barker, Harley, *Prefaces to Shakespeare,* 2 vols., Princeton University Press, 1946, 1947. See p. 84a. The first of the prefaces was originally published in 1923; others followed at intervals until 1947, the year after Granville-Barker's death. Volume 1, *Hamlet, Lear, Merchant of Venice, Antony and Cleopatra, Cymbeline.* Volume 2, *Othello, Coriolanus, Romeo and Juliet, Julius Caesar, Love's Labor's Lost.* A paperback edition of the *Hamlet* preface was published by Hill & Wang (Dramabooks *) in 1957.

Stoll, Elmer E., *Shakespeare Studies,* Macmillan, 1927. Essays on various topics — including "Literature and Life," "Characterization," "The Ghosts," "Shylock," "The Criminals," "Falstaff" — written in this author's usual pungent style.

Campbell, Lily B., *Shakespeare's Tragic Heroes; Slaves of Passion,* Barnes and Noble, 1952 (orig. publ. 1930). A discussion of the tragic heroes in the light of Elizabethan ideas on moral philosophy and psychology.

Knight, G. Wilson, *The Wheel of Fire,* Oxford University Press, 1930; Meridian,* 1957. A subjective and imaginative interpretation of the ideas suggested by Shakespeare' poetic imagery. It was followed by *The Imperial Theme,* Oxford University Press, 1931, and *The Crown of Life,* Oxford University Press, 1947. See p. 84b.

Lawrence, W. W., *Shakespeare's Problem Comedies,* Macmillan, 1931. Valuable studies of *All's Well, Measure for Measure, Troilus and Cressida,* and *Cymbeline,* particularly considered in the light of medieval and Elizabethan ideas.

Stoll, Elmer E., *Art and Artifice in Shakespeare,* Barnes and Noble, 1933. Considers especially *Othello, Macbeth, Hamlet,* and *Lear.*

Granville-Barker, Harley, and Harrison, G. B., eds., *A Companion to Shakespeare Studies,* Cambridge University Press, 1934. A collection of chapters by different authors on the principal topics which interest modern students of Shakespeare.

Spurgeon, Caroline F. E., *Shakespeare's Imagery and What It Tells Us,* Cambridge University Press, 1952 (orig. publ. 1935); Beacon,* 1958. See p. 84b.

Murry, J. Middleton, *Shakespeare,* Harcourt, Brace, 1936. A general study by a modern critic of the first rank.

Van Doren, Mark, *Shakespeare,* Holt, 1939; Doubleday (Anchor *), 1953. Short stimulating essays on each of the plays and the poems.

Campbell, Oscar James, *Shakespeare's Satire,* Oxford University Press, 1943. A stimulating picture of the varieties of satire in the plays.

Campbell, Lily B., *Shakespeare's " Histories,"* Huntington Library, 1947. A study of the history plays in the light of contemporary ideas on history.

Heilman, R. B., *This Great Stage,* Louisiana State University Press, 1948. An elaborate study of the imagery of *King Lear* and a good example of the latest kind of study of Shakespeare's poetic processes. It was followed by *Magic in the Web* (a study of action and language in *Othello*), University of Kentucky Press, 1956.

Jones, Ernest, *Hamlet and Oedipus,* Norton, 1949; Doubleday (Anchor *), 1954. A psychoanalysis of Hamlet by the biographer of Sigmund Freud. Jones wrote several versions of this, the first of which appeared as an article in *American Journal of Psychology,* XXI, 1910.

Stauffer, Donald, *Shakespeare's World of Images: The Development of His Moral Ideas,* Norton, 1949. A mid-twentieth century version of what Dowden attempted in *Shakespere . . . His Mind and Art* in 1875.

Clemen, Wolfgang H., *The Development of Shakespeare's Imagery,* Harvard University Press, 1951 (orig. publ. in German, 1936). One of the sanest surveys of Shakespeare's use of imagery, and particularly valuable because it makes no extravagant claims.

Fluchère, Henri, *Shakespeare,* trans. by Guy Hamilton, Longmans, Green, 1953; *Shakespeare and the Elizabethans,* Hill & Wang (Dramabooks *), 1957. An excellent introduction to the understanding of Shakespeare's plays as a whole, and especially useful as an introduction to modern criticism.

Hubler, Edward, *The Sense of Shakespeare's Sonnets,* Princeton University Press, 1954. A discussion of the Sonnets and what they say, leading to the contents of Shakespeare's mind.

H. *Shakespeare the Man*

Bagehot, Walter, " Shakespeare, the Man," in *Literary Studies,* Longmans, Green, 1879; Dutton (Everyman), 1911. A sensible short essay by the sanest of Victorian critics, nowadays unjustly neglected.

Adams, Joseph Quincy, *A Life of William Shakespeare,* Houghton Mifflin, 1923. The best of the general biographies.

Fripp, E. I., *Master Richard Quyny, Bailiff of Stratford-upon-Avon and Friend of William Shakespeare,* Oxford University Press, 1924, and *Shakespeare's Stratford,* Oxford University Press, 1928. Good accounts of the social and intellectual background of the Shakespeare family in Stratford-on-Avon.

Hotson, Leslie, *Shakespeare versus Shallow,* Little, Brown, 1931. Dr. Hotson's own account of his discovery of a new fact about Shakespeare. See pp. 10b–11a.

Harrison, G. B., *Shakespeare under Elizabeth,* Holt, 1933; also published as *Shakespeare at Work, 1592–1603,* University of Michigan Press (Ann Arbor *) 1956. An attempt to show how Shakespeare's plays reflected current interest and events.

Hotson, Leslie, *I, William Shakespeare,* Cape, 1937. An account of the man whom Shakespeare appointed as executor of his will and of the circle in which Shakespeare was well known. Valuable for any student interested in Shakespeare's biography and personal background.

Baldwin, T. W., *William Shakspere's Small Latine and Lesse Greeke,* 2 vols., University of Illinois Press, 1944. A vast and illuminating study of education at English schools in Shakespeare's time.

I. *General*

Bartlett, John, *Complete Concordance . . . to . . . Shakespeare,* St. Martins, 1953 (orig. publ. 1889). An essential reference book.

Onions, C. T., *A Shakespeare Glossary,* 2nd rev. ed., Oxford University Press, 1919 (orig. publ. 1911). A most useful reference book for the general student.

Chambers, E. K., *William Shakespeare: A Study of Facts and Problems,* 2 vols., Oxford University Press, 1930. An essential work of reference for any serious student, as it contains all the material for advanced study of the facts and problems of Shakespeare the man and his work. The common reader will find it almost incomprehensibly technical, and even the scholar, while he can rely on the facts, should beware of taking on trust Chambers' curt summaries of theories and opinions with which he disagrees. Nevertheless, it is one of the first books that should be bought for the student's private Shakespearean library.

Munro, J. J., ed., *The Shakspere Allusion Book:*

A Collection of Allusions to Shakspere from 1591 to 1700, 2 vols., Oxford University Press, 1931. Apart from its interest, the collection reveals, so far as is now possible, the contemporary popularity of Shakespeare's plays and characters.

Shakespeare Survey, Cambridge University Press, 1949 —. An annual survey of Shakespearean study and production.

Shakespeare Quarterly, Shakespeare Association of New York, 1950. A quarterly dealing with every kind of Shakespearean interest, particularly on the American continent.

Tilley, Morris Palmer, *A Dictionary of the Proverbs in England in the Sixteenth and Seventeenth Centuries,* University of Michigan Press, 1950. This work, which is especially concerned with Shakespeare's use of proverbs, is one of great value to all students of Shakespeare's language and imagery.

Halliday, F. E., *Shakespeare: A Pictorial Biography,* Crowell, 1957; Nicoll, Allardyce, *The Elizabethans,* Cambridge University Press, 1957. Two picture books of considerable value to any student who is not familiar with the outward appearance of Shakespeare's age.

PLATE I

a. The World as known in 1600

b. William Shakespeare

PLATE 2

a. Shakespeare's London

b. Queen Elizabeth

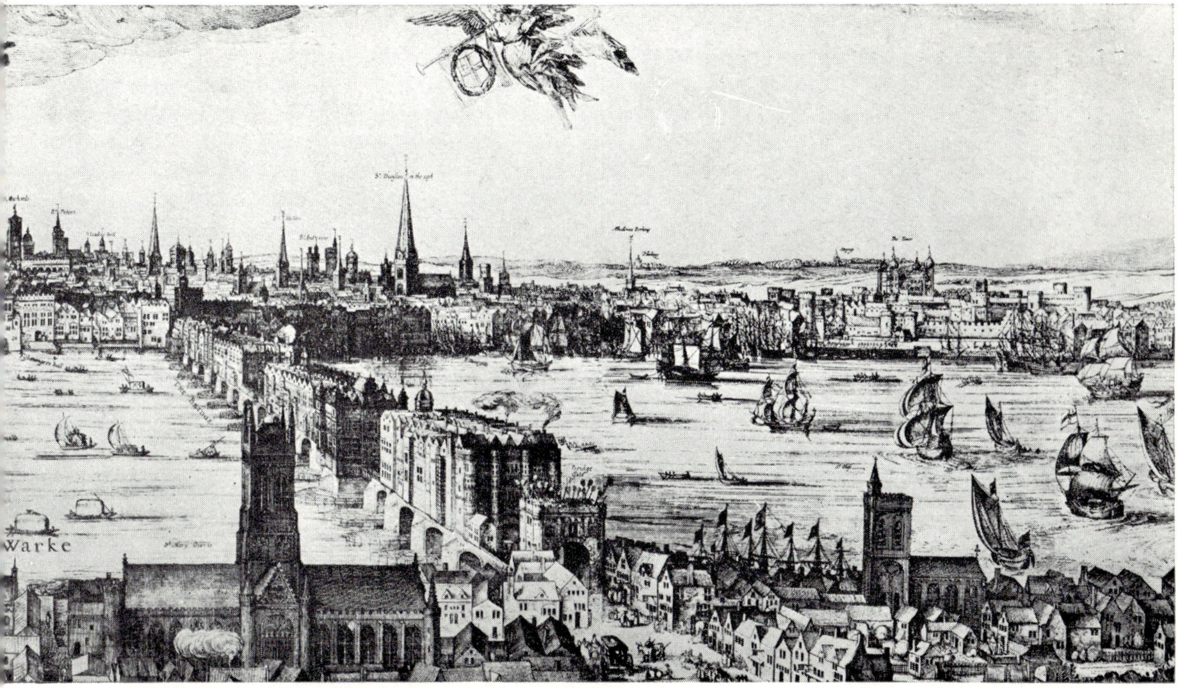

PLATE 3

b. Queen Elizabeth attends a wedding, 1600

PLATE 4

THE EVOLUTION OF THE ELIZABETHAN STAGE

b. The Hall of the Middle Temple

a. The New Inn at Gloucester

PLATE 5

THE EVOLUTION OF THE ELIZABETHAN STAGE

b. The stage of the Globe (Dr. J. C. Adams' model)

a. The Swan playhouse

PLATE 6

a. Jonah and the whale

b. John Harvard's birthplace at Stratford-on-Avon   *c. Bare ruined choirs: Tintern Abbey*

PLATE 7

a. Venus and Adonis

b. Princess Elizabeth leaves England, 1613

PLATE 8   CONTEMPORARY COSTUME

a. Armor

b. A courtier's clothes

c. German slops

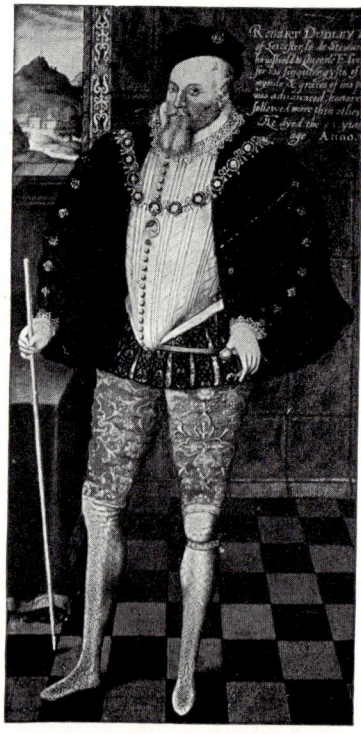

d. The Earl of Leicester

a *b* *c* *d* *e*

a. A military funeral

f *g* *h* *i* *j*

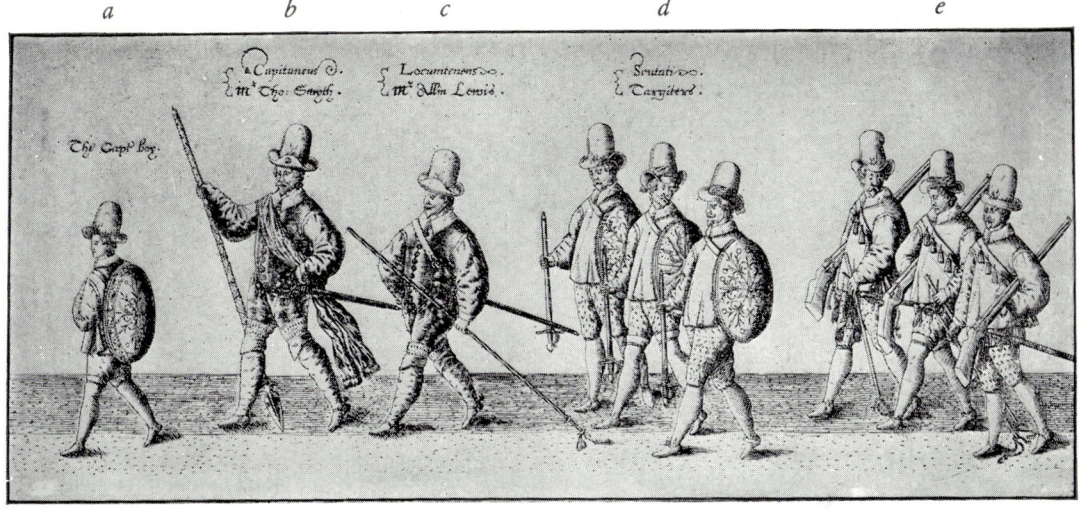

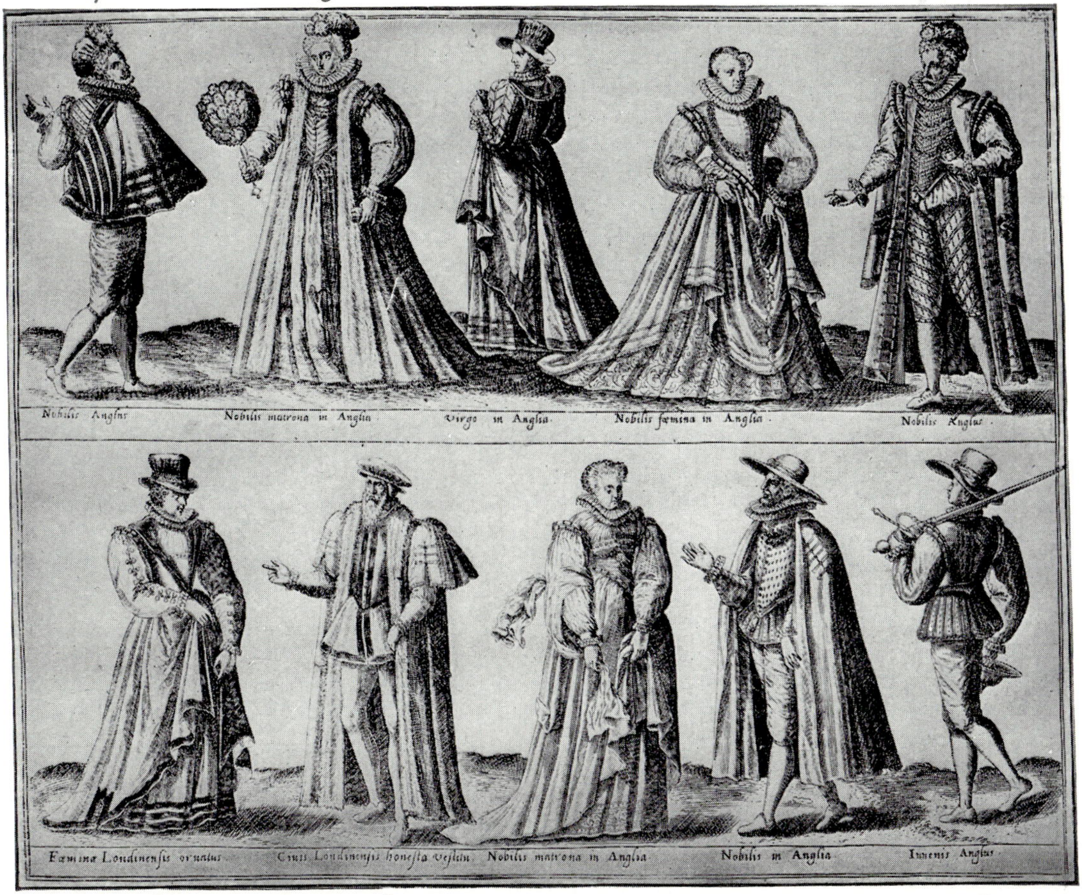

k *l* *m* *n* *o*

b. Elizabethan types

PLATE 10

a. Elizabethan shilling, obverse and reverse   *b. Shilling of James I*

c. Gold angel   *d. Half groat*   *e. Gold half angel*

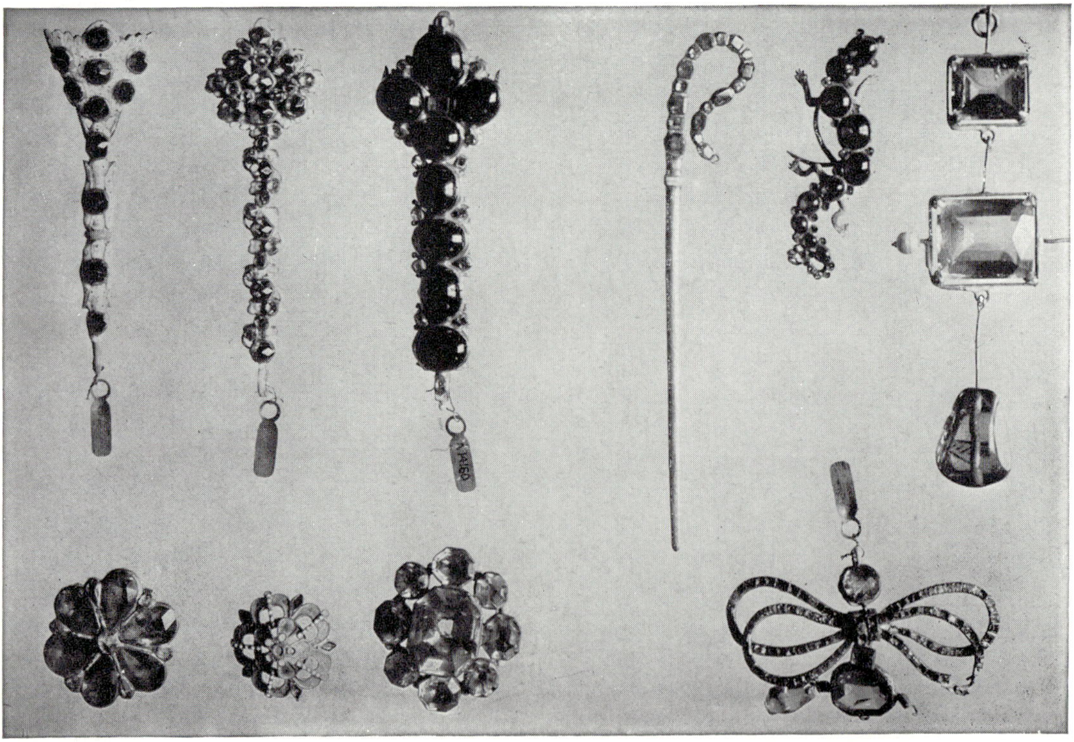

f. Elizabethan jewelry

PLATE II

a. An indenture

b. A patent under the Great Seal

PLATE 12

d. A consort of music

a. The assault

b. A camp

e. The mandrake

c. Macbeth and the Three Weird Sisters

f. The Fool and Death

PLATE 13

a. Elizabethan stage costume: Titus Andronicus

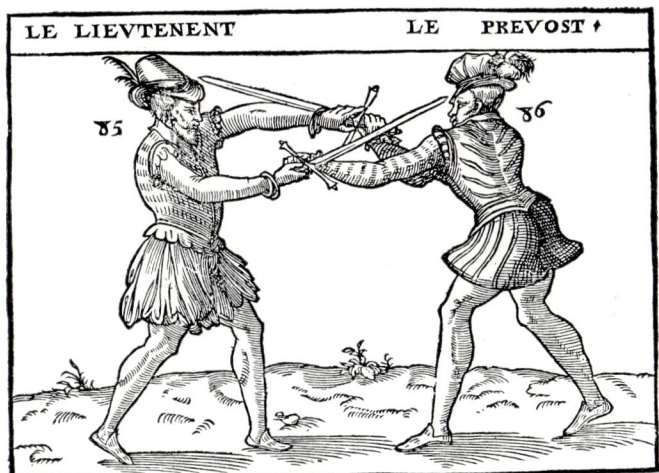

b. The exchange of rapiers

c. A fool and a courtesan

d. Kempe dancing

PLATE 14

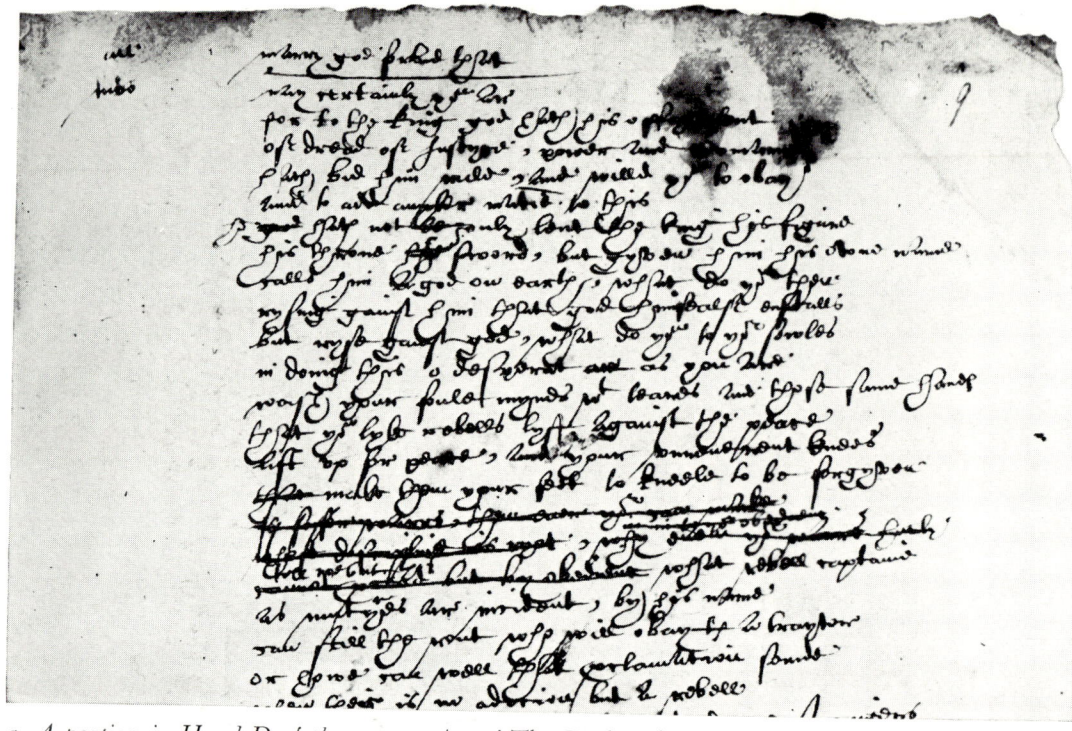

a. A portion in Hand D of the manuscript of The Booke of Sir Thomas More

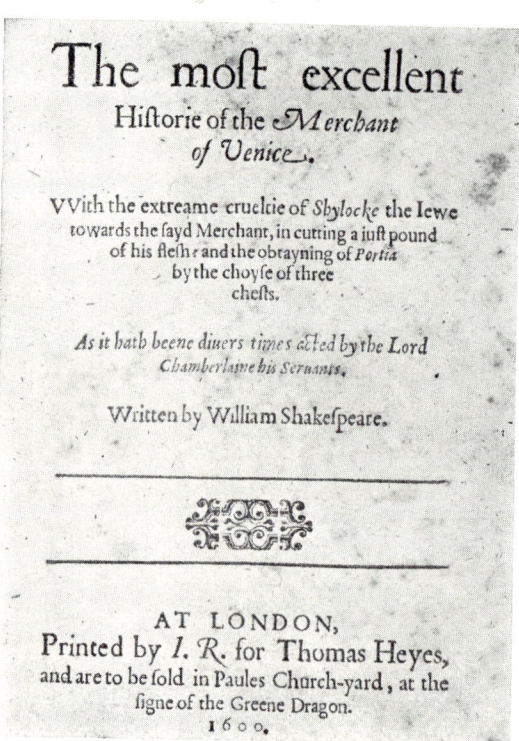

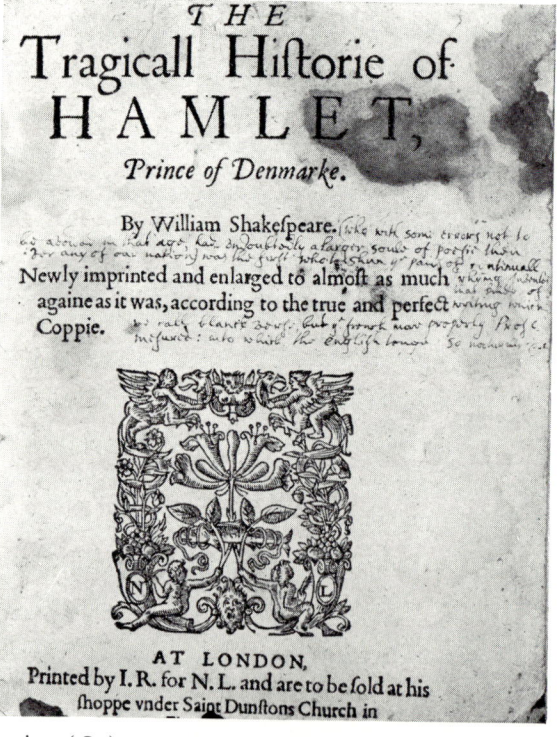

b. Title pages of two quartos: The Merchant of Venice (*Q1*) *and* Hamlet (*Q2*)

PLATE 15

Mr. WILLIAM

SHAKESPEARES

COMEDIES,
HISTORIES, &
TRAGEDIES.

Published according to the True Originall Copies.

Martin Droeshout sculpsit London.

LONDON
Printed by Isaac Iaggard, and Ed. Blount. 1623.

Title page of the first folio

PLATE 16

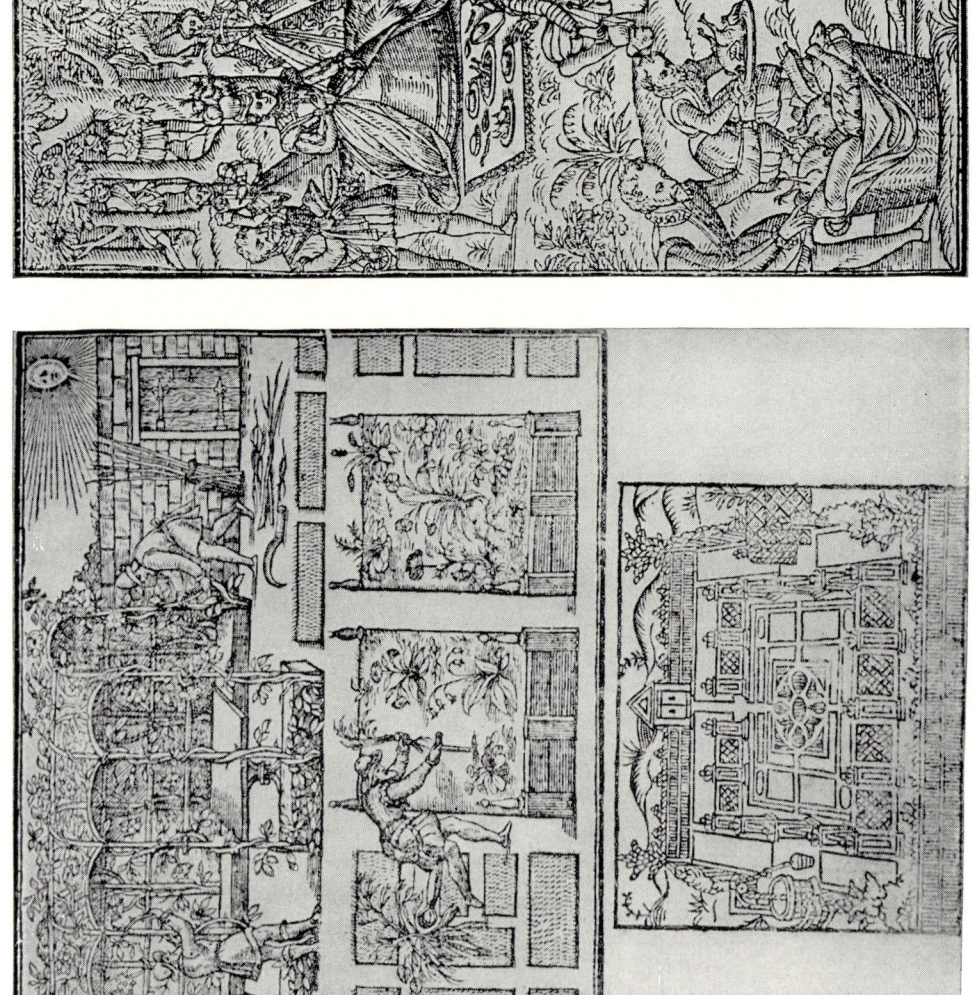

b. The hunting party

a A garden

a. Joint stool   *b. Great bed*   *c. Carved chest*

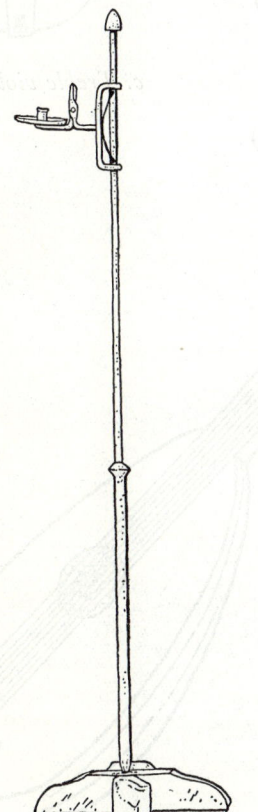

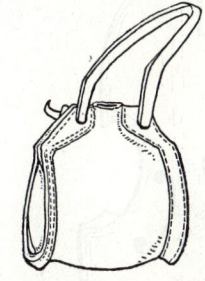

e. Leather bottle (8½″)

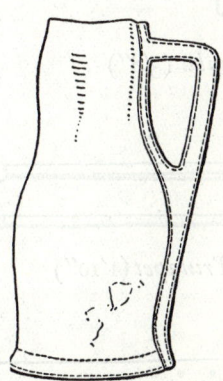

d. Candleholder (3′9″)   *f. Leather bombard* (12⅜″)

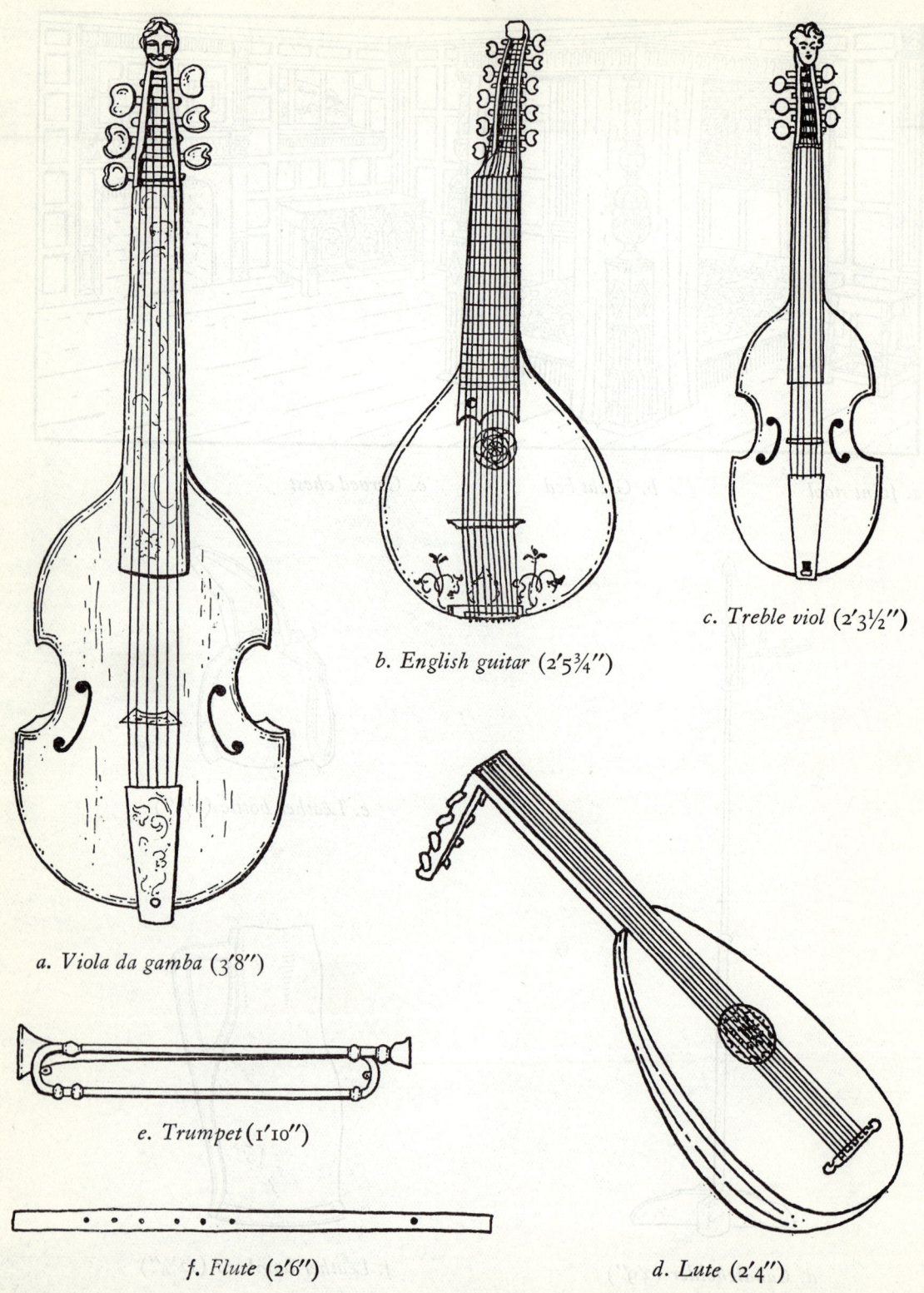

b. English guitar (2′5¾″)

c. Treble viol (2′3½″)

a. Viola da gamba (3′8″)

e. Trumpet (1′10″)

f. Flute (2′6″)

d. Lute (2′4″)

PLATE 19

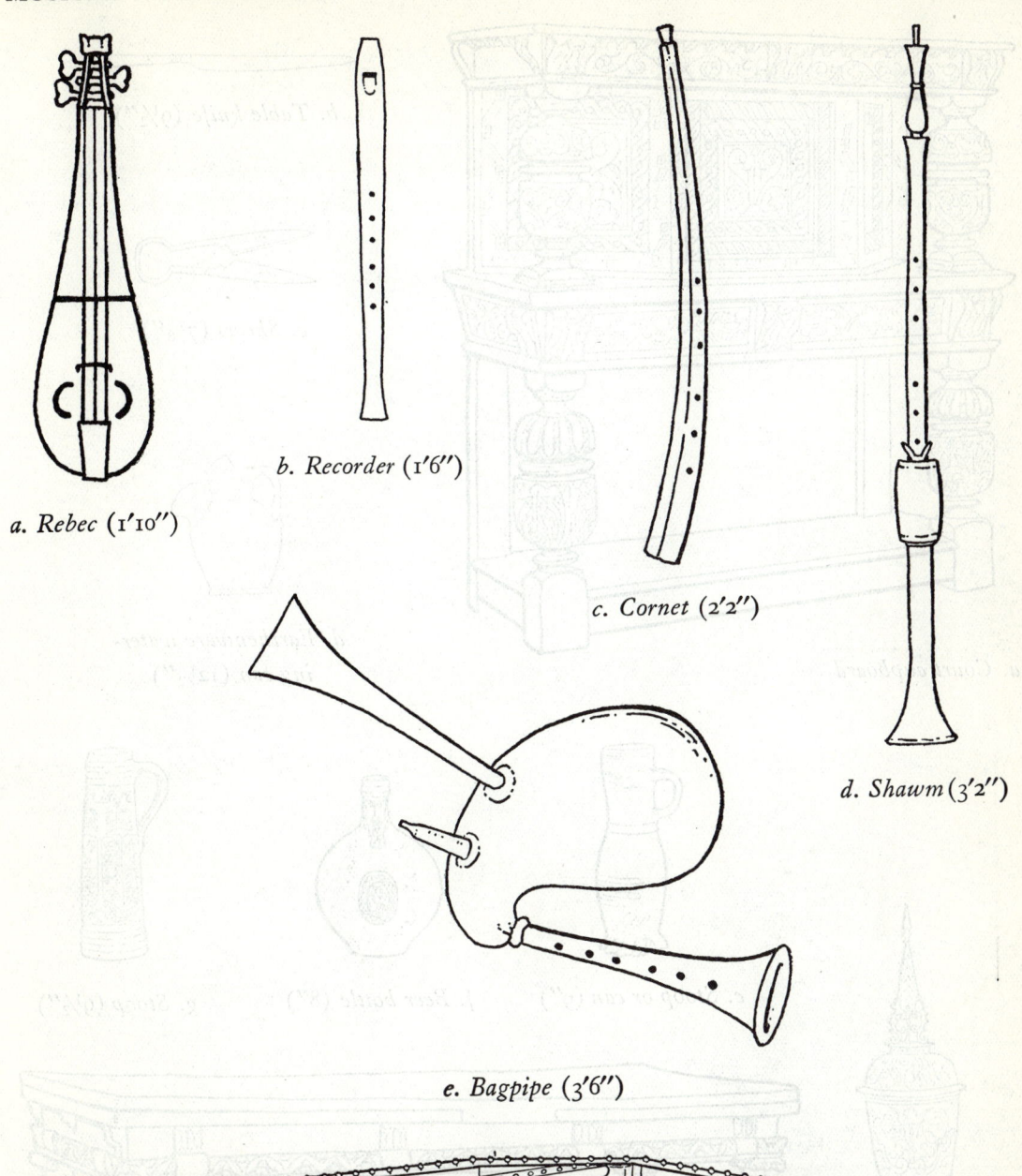

a. Rebec (1′10″)

b. Recorder (1′6″)

c. Cornet (2′2″)

d. Shawm (3′2″)

e. Bagpipe (3′6″)

f. Virginal (5′1⅜″)

PLATE 20   HOUSEHOLD FURNITURE AND UTENSILS: THE DINING ROOM

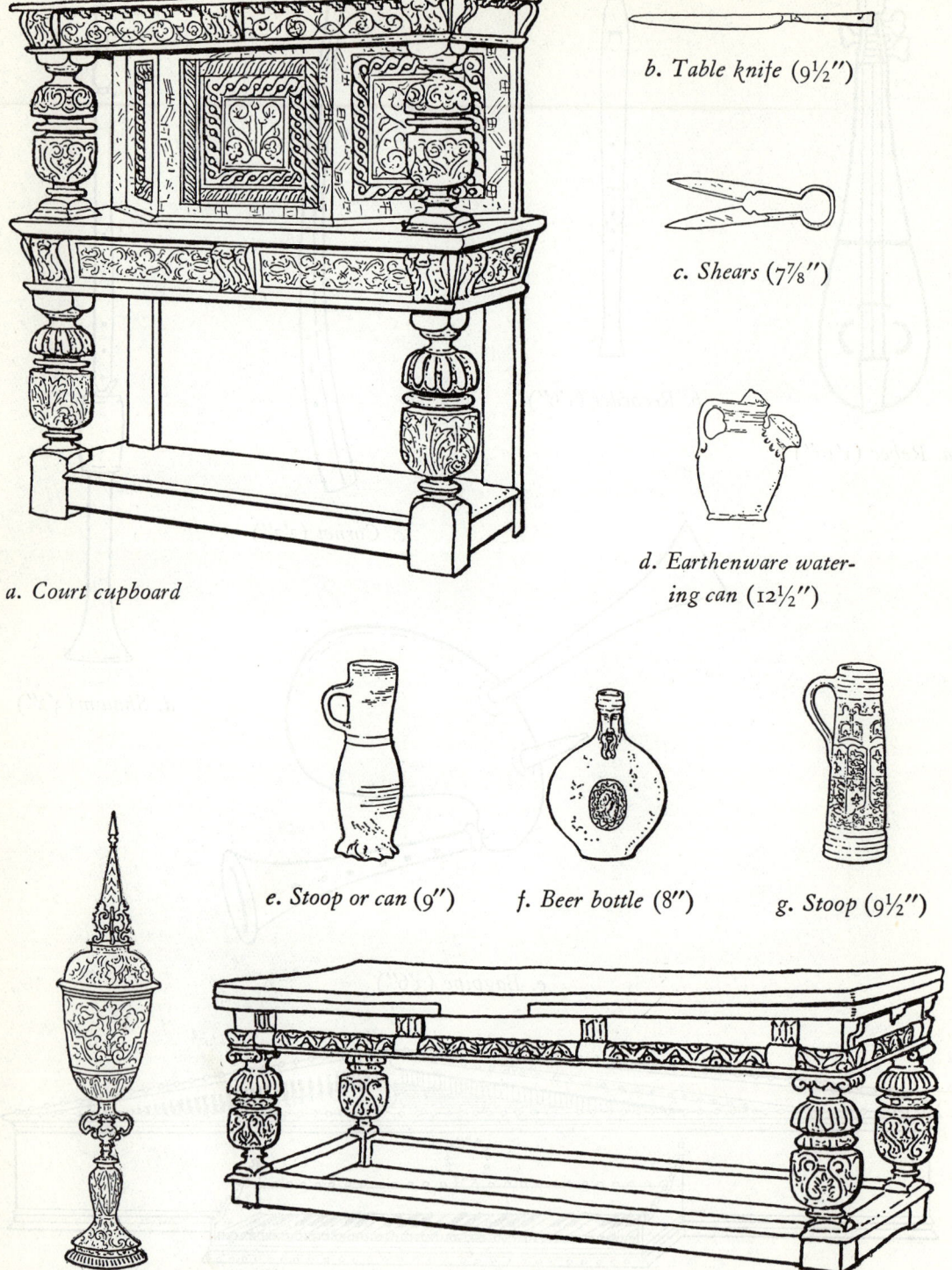

a. Court cupboard

b. Table knife (9½″)

c. Shears (7⅞″)

d. Earthenware watering can (12½″)

e. Stoop or can (9″)

f. Beer bottle (8″)

g. Stoop (9½″)

h. Standing cup (1′8″)

i. Table

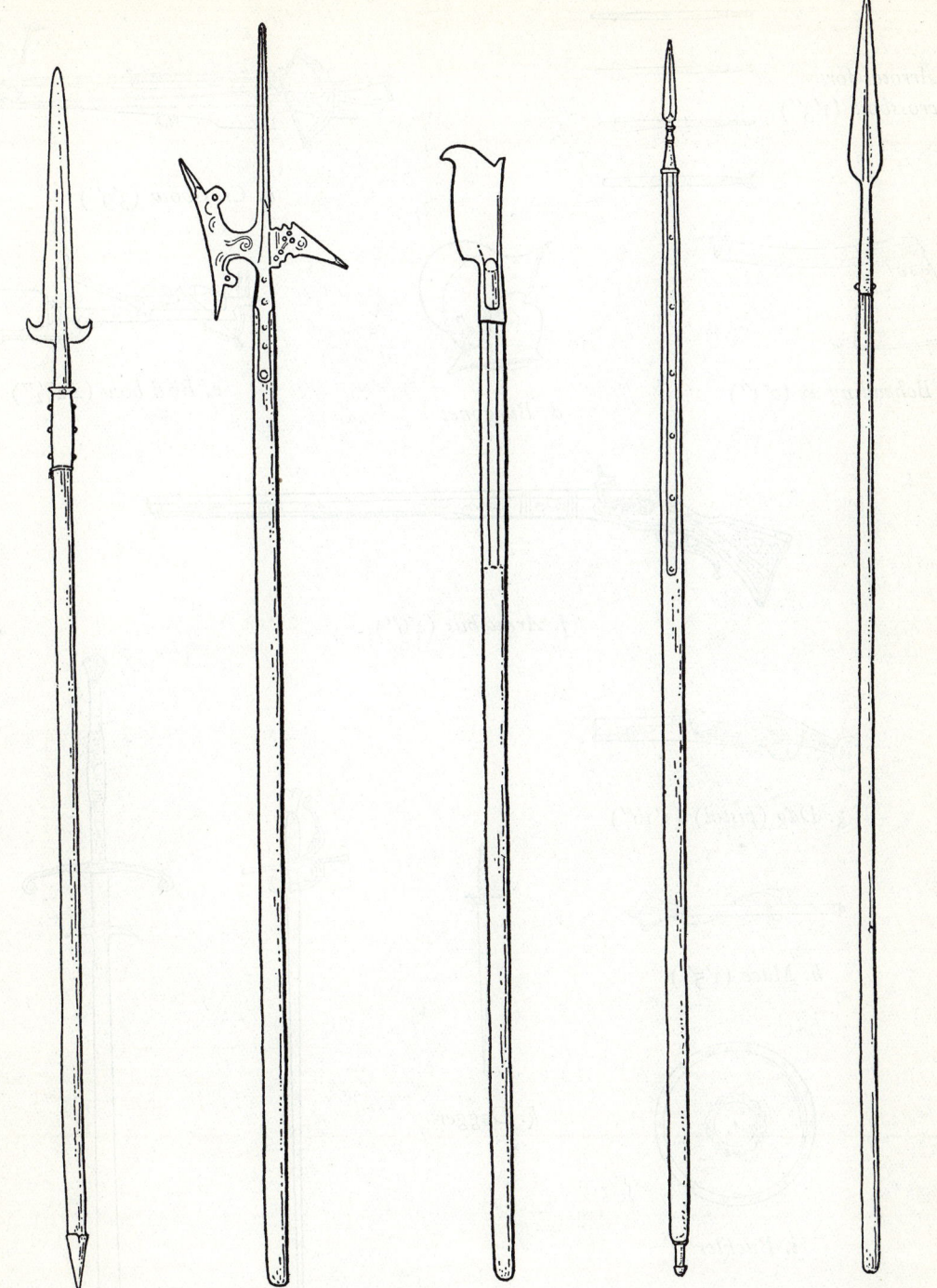

a. Partisan (9′2″) *b. Halberd* (7′2″)   *c. Bill* (6′11″)   *d. Pike* (9′3″)   *e. Hunting spear*
                                                                                        (7′6″)

PLATE 22

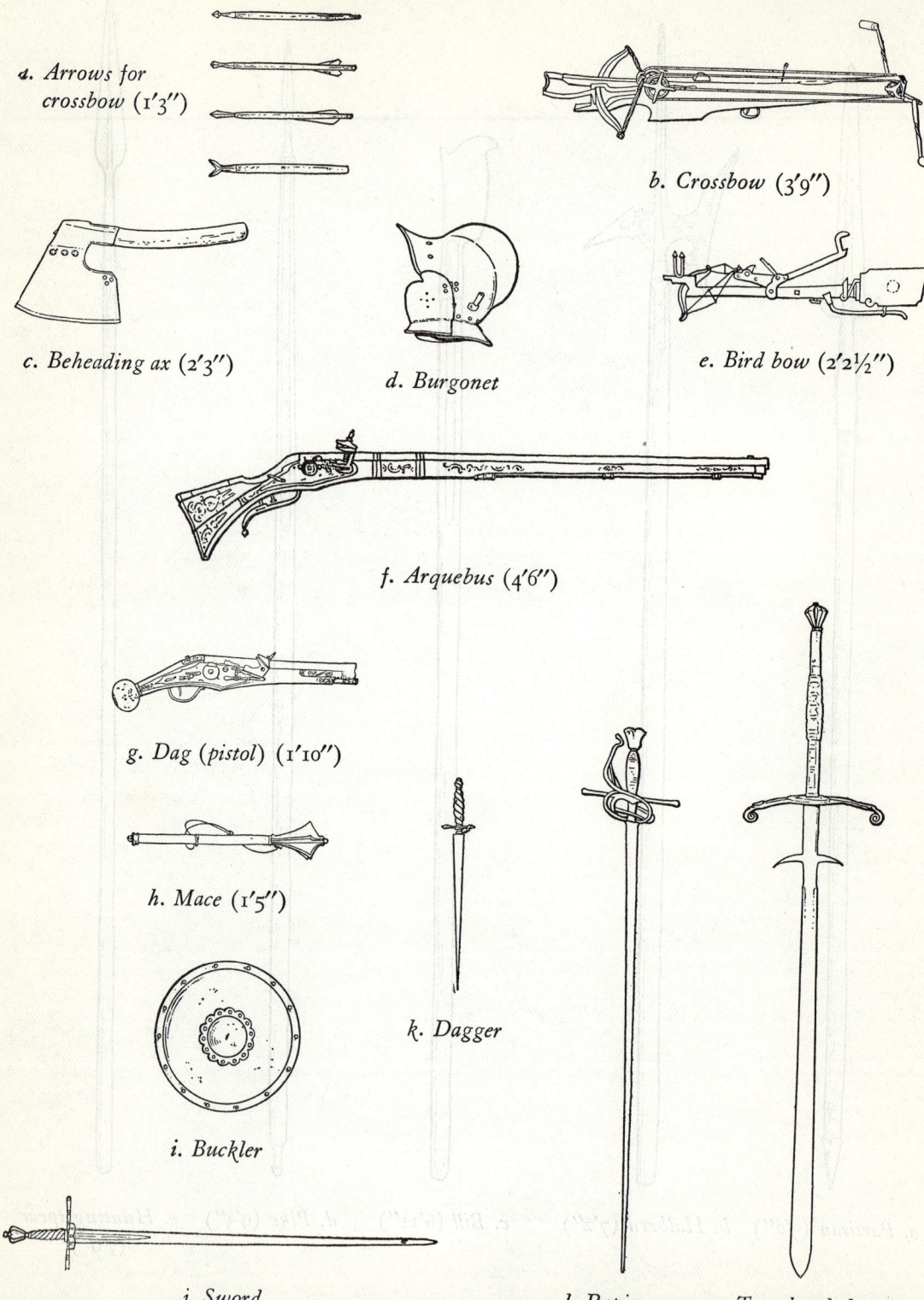

a. Arrows for crossbow (1′3″)

b. Crossbow (3′9″)

c. Beheading ax (2′3″)

d. Burgonet

e. Bird bow (2′2½″)

f. Arquebus (4′6″)

g. Dag (*pistol*) (1′10″)

h. Mace (1′5″)

k. Dagger

i. Buckler

i. Sword

l. Rapier

m. Two-handed sword

NOTES ON THE PLATES[1]

Halftone Reproductions

1a. The World as known in 1600 (Huntington Library)

This map was drawn by Edward Wright, assisted by Richard Hakluyt, the compiler of Hakluyt's *Voyages,* and John Davis, an experienced sea captain. It depicts the world as known to Shakespeare's contemporaries and was the first map to be prepared on the principle known as Mercator's projection — showing the world as flat. Maria compares Malvolio's smiles to the many "rhumb lines" (lines radiating from a point to indicate comparative distances) so conspicuous on the map (*Twelfth Night* III.ii.84). The legend in the top right-hand corner reads:

It appeareth by the discoverie of Francis Gaulle a Spaniard in the yeare 1584 that the sea betweene the west part of America and the east of Asia (which hath bene ordinarily set out as a Straight and named in most maps the Straight of Aman) is above 1200 leagues wide at the latitude of 38 dgr. And that the distance betweene cape Mendocine and cape California which many maps and seacharts make to be 1200 or 1300 leagues is scarse so much as 600.

The legend at the bottom reads:

Thou hast here, gentle reader, a true hydrographical description of so much of the world as hath beene hetherto discovered, and is comme to our knowledge. Which we have in such sort performed, all places herein set downe, have the same positions and distances that they have in the globe, being therein placed in same longitudes and latitudes which they have in this chart; which by the ordinarie seachart can in no wise be performed. The way to finde the position, or course from any place to other herein described, differeth nothing from that which is used in the ordinary seachart. But to finde the distance; if both places have the same latitude, see how many degrees of the meridian taken at that latitude are contayned betweene the two places, for so many score leagues is the distance. If they differ in latitude, see how many degrees of the meridian taken about the midst of that difference are contayned betweene them and so many score leagues is the distance.

[1] The reader when referring to individual plates in the preceding pages should always consult also the relevant note. Notes on particular items of costume are grouped under Pl. 8.

1b. William Shakespeare (Ewing Galloway)

The memorial bust erected on the north wall of the Church of the Holy Trinity at Stratford-on-Avon sometime before 1623. It overlooks Shakespeare's grave in the chancel. The bust was the work of Gerard Johnson (or Janssen), one of a family of monument makers who came originally from Amsterdam. See Gen. Intro. p. 15b. This bust and the engraved portrait in the first folio (Pl. 15) are the only pictures of Shakespeare which are indisputably genuine; both probably derive from the same original sketch or painting, now lost.

2a–3a. Shakespeare's London (Folger Library)

This famous engraving of London was the work of John Visscher in 1616. The city is viewed from a point in Southwark on the south bank of the Thames, which here runs from west to east (i.e., from left to right). St. Paul's is the most conspicuous building. The Guildhall lies away to the north, over the large riverside warehouse known as Coleharbor. On the extreme east can be seen the Tower of London, with its central keep conspicuous with four domed turrets. All along the riverbank stand the warehouses and wharfs belonging to the chief merchants. London Bridge, with its houses and shops, connects north and south banks. The bridge is broken by a drawbridge, which can be seen between the first and second block of buildings. At the south end, the bridge is guarded by the Bridge Gate, above which are exposed the heads of traitors executed for high treason. On the south bank, to the west, the two conspicuous octagonal buildings are the Bear Garden and the Globe playhouse. The large church in the foreground is St. Mary Overeyes; it still stands, and is now known as Southwark Cathedral.

2b. Queen Elizabeth (Reproduced by permission of the Controller of His Britannic Majesty's Stationery Office from the Westminster Abbey volume of the Royal Commission on Historical Documents)

The recumbent marble effigy of the Queen on her tomb in Westminster Abbey, seen from above

3b. Queen Elizabeth attends a wedding, 1600
(Courtesy of Colonel F. J. B. Wingfield Digby, Sherborne Castle, Dorset)

From a painting by Marcus Gheerarts. The wedding took place in the Blackfriars on June 16, 1600, between Anne Russell (one of the Queen's maids of honor) and Lord Herbert, son of the Earl of Worcester. The Queen is seated in a canopied litter borne by courtiers. The other principal persons shown are: Charles Howard, Earl of Nottingham and Lord High Admiral, the white-headed figure looking to the left; George Carey, Lord Hunsdon, the Lord Chamberlain (and patron of Shakespeare's company), bearing his wand of office and with his left hand clasping his rapier, which is supported by a hanger; and Henry Brooke, Lord Cobham (the Queen's host for the occasion), carrying the sword of state. In the foreground, wearing white, is Edward Somerset, Earl of Worcester, the father of the bridegroom. The figure in white supporting the litter is the bridegroom himself. Behind the litter follow the Queen's maids of honor, preceded by the bride (in white) and the bridegroom's mother (shown between bridegroom and bride).

See also General Notes on Contemporary Costume, below.

4a. The New Inn at Gloucester (Raphael Tuck and Sons, Ltd.)

The New Inn was built in the fourteenth century to accommodate visitors to the tomb of Edward II. The illustration shows the typical yard and galleries. See Gen. Intro. p. 51b.

4b. The Hall of the Middle Temple

The Hall was a fine specimen of carved oak paneling of the Elizabethan period. Here on February 2, 1602, *Twelfth Night* was performed. The Hall was very badly damaged during a German air raid in 1940. See Gen. Intro. p. 51b.

5a. The Swan playhouse

A drawing made about 1596 by a Dutch traveler named Johannes de Witt.

5b. The stage of the Globe (Dr. J. C. Adams' model)

See Gen. Intro. pp. 52b–58b.

6a. Jonah and the whale (London Museum)

A Tudor wall painting (*c*. 1560) from an old house at Waltham Cross. It is typical of the kind of scene depicted on " painted cloth " — conventional illustrations of stories from the Bible or classical literature. Jonah is being thrown overboard from the waist of the ship; on the poop a sailor steers with a large oar; another on the forecastle is furling the topsail. The ship itself is of fantastic and semiclassical form, but the vessel in the background shows the usual Elizabethan type.

6b. John Harvard's birthplace at Stratford-on-Avon

This house and the neighboring house were built after a fire which largely destroyed Stratford-on-Avon in 1596. The two are typical town houses of the period, with exposed oak beams, leaded windows, and overhanging upper stories.

6c. Bare ruined choirs: Tintern Abbey

One of the many magnificent abbeys which had been looted and destroyed by the " reformers " in the days of Shakespeare's grandparents. Among folk in general, especially in the country, there was a common feeling that " 'twas never merry world since the friars were put down." See Sonnet 73, l. 4.

7a. Venus and Adonis (Victoria and Albert Museum, London)

The original is a hand-embroidered needlework panel, *c*. 1590. The story is shown in three episodes; the fight with the boar; Venus and her attendants lamenting over the dead youth; Venus returning to heaven in her chariot drawn by swans. Note the elaborate richness and detail of the decoration. Such scenes as these, rather than the nude figures of the Italian masters, were present in the imagination of Sidney, Shakespeare, Marlowe, and Spenser when they retold old tales.

7b. Princess Elizabeth leaves England, 1613

Painting by the Dutch artist Adam Willaerts, 1577–1664. (By permission of the Trustees of the National Maritime Museum, Greenwich, England.)

On February 14, 1613, Princess Elizabeth, daughter of King James I, married Prince Frederick, Elector Palatine and afterward King of

Bohemia. The wedding was the most elaborate of the many Court entertainments in the reign of King James. The picture shows the departure of the bride and bridegroom from Dover, and illustrates the different types of contemporary ships. In the *Tempest* Shakespeare has in mind a ship similar to that in the center of the picture.

8. CONTEMPORARY COSTUME:

General Notes

MEN'S COSTUME

The dress worn by men of rank and wealth was elaborate, richly embroidered, costly, and gay, and was made of various materials. The principal garments and accessories were:

a. DOUBLET. A short close-fitting coat, with fixed or detachable sleeves of various shapes and patterns, and buttoned up the front or sides with many buttons. Pl. 8b shows a fine specimen of actual doublet, elaborately embroidered. Leicester in Pl. 8d is wearing a BIG-BELLY or PEASECOD doublet, so called because it was cut to a point overhanging the stomach and so resembled the end of a pea pod; by contrast, a close-fitting doublet was sometimes called " THIN-BELLY."

b. JERKIN. A short sleeveless coat worn over the doublet. The foremost of the courtiers carrying the litter in Pl. 3b is wearing one. Jerkins of leather were worn by sergeants.

c. CLOAK. Cloaks of various lengths and shapes, often of velvet or other rich material, were worn over the doublet. The specimen shown in Pl. 8b is a short or Spanish cloak; for other specimens see the foremost lords in Pl. 3b, and Pl. 9f and 9n.

d. GOWN. Worn usually by elderly and grave persons; see Pl. 9j and 9l. Gowns worn by the wealthy were trimmed with fur (such as fox or sable) round the neck and down the front; see Pl. 9l.

e. HOSE. This word sometimes causes difficulty, as it was often used to describe any kind of breeches and also the whole set of garments from waist to knee. It was *not* used, as nowadays, for stockings. Of the various garments included under hose, the most common were:

i. ROUND HOSE, called also TRUNK HOSE, FRENCH HOSE, or FRENCH BREECHES. These were very short wide breeches, puffed out with padding, worn immediately below the doublet. See Pl. 8b, 8d, and the men in 3b.

ii. Beneath the round hose and covering the thigh were worn close-fitting breeches called UPPERSTOCKS. See Pl. 8d and the men in 3b.

iii. On the legs were worn stockings called NETHERSTOCKS, drawn up to or over the knee, and sometimes almost to the top of the thighs. See Pl. 8d and 3b.

iv. VENETIANS, called also GASKINS or GALLI-GASKINS, were wide breeches reaching down to the knees. In Pl. 7a Adonis is shown wearing VENETIANS.

v. SLOPS were excessively wide and baggy breeches, worn especially by Germans; see Pl. 8c. The word " slop," however, was sometimes used for any very wide breeches, including TRUNK HOSE. See *Romeo and Juliet,* II.iv.47.

vi. STROSSERS or TROUSERS were long underpants reaching to the ankle, rarely worn by Englishmen.

vii. CODPIECE. The white-bearded man in Pl. 8c wears a codpiece in front of his slops. The codpiece covered the opening in front of the breeches (hose). This accessory to male attire was often indelicately prominent. It was made in various forms, such as a bow of silk, a flap tied to the hose with laces, a small padded sausage-shaped cushion ornamented with pins, or a small bag used as a pocket.

f. STOCKINGS were cut from material and sewn; knitted stockings were however beginning to come into use by the end of the sixteenth century. Stockings were kept up by garters. CROSS GARTERS were passed round the leg beneath the knee, crossed at the back, and tied above the knee; they are being worn by the older man in Pl. 8c. and by the page (drinking) in Pl. 16b.

g. FOOTWEAR.

i. GREAT-BOOTS reaching to the knee were worn by riders or mounted soldiers. See Pl. 9b, 9c, and 12c.

ii. SHOES were of various shapes and patterns. Sometimes they were adorned with rosettes, as in Pl. 3b, or with patterns made in the leather by cutting, slashing, or pinking, as in **Pl. 8c** and **13b.** The modern form of laced shoe was not used.

iii. Buskins were a kind of gaitered boot or sandal, and associated with gods, goddesses, and other ancient personages. They are worn by Titus Andronicus and the Moor in **Pl. 13a.**

h. Shirts were made usually of linen, often embroidered at neck and wrists. Longer shirts were worn as night attire.

i. A nightgown was a long loosely fitting gown, like the modern dressing gown.

j. Neckwear:

i. The ruff or band was a pleated collar, starched to keep it in shape, worn as a kind of frill round the neck, sometimes so wide that the head appeared to be sitting on a plate. See **Pl. 3b, 9f, 9j,** and **9n.**

ii. A falling band was a turned down collar, often ornamented with lace or embroidery; see **Pl. 8d, 9b–9e.**

iii. The whisk was a plain or lace-edged band, semicircular in shape and stiffened with starch; see the portrait of Shakespeare himself on **Pl. 15.**

k. Headgear. Hats were of various kinds and materials. Citizens often wore a flat cap made of wool; see **Pl. 9l.** This kind of hat was known also as a statute cap, because its use on Sunday was compulsory — a measure introduced to compensate hatmakers for the loss of trade caused by the introduction of felt hats. The flat cap was correct wear for apprentices at all times and for citizens when wearing a gown. Hats of this shape are still worn at academic ceremonies by doctors in English universities. Gallants wore hats of many shapes and kinds; see **Pl. 9b, 9f, 9j.** The specimen shown in **Pl. 8b** was called a copintank or copetain hat. Thrummed hats are being worn by the right-hand figure in **Pl. 8c** and the nobleman in **Pl. 9n.** A bonnet was a cap of velvet or other soft material; see **Pl. 8d.**

l. Miscellaneous:

i. Points. Suspenders had not yet been invented. The hose was provided with a series of points (resembling shoelaces), which were inserted from inside into eyelets or loops on the doublet, pulled through and then tied tight.

This process was called trussing. A man taking his ease loosened (or *untrussed*) his points.

ii. Guards were ornamental stripes of braid or trimming sewn to doublet or cloak. The young nobleman in **Pl. 9f** wears a guarded cloak, and **9k** shows the guarded gown traditionally associated with citizens' wives.

iii. Hanger. A device for carrying the sword, consisting of a series of straps hanging from the sword belt. Hangers were often elaborately ornamented and costly. For a specimen see **Pl. 3b.**

WOMEN'S COSTUME

Women's costume was as complicated and elaborate as men's. The chief items of dress were:

a. Body. Above the waist women wore a body (or bodice), often resembling a man's doublet. At one time it was fashionable for unmarried women to wear the front of the body very low. In front was worn a stomacher or placard, a stiff embroidered front worn over the chest and stomach and sometimes ending in a point; see **Pl. 3b.**

b. Kirtle. The outer skirt, called a kirtle, reached to the ground and was very full and voluminous; see **Pl. 9i, 7a.**

c. Farthingale. The kirtle was made to stand out by means of a farthingale, which consisted either of a wire frame (made on the same principle as the hoops fashionable in the eighteenth century and the 1850's) or of a large roll of padding.

d. Petticoat. Over the farthingale and under the kirtle, one or more petticoats were worn. As it was customary to raise the skirt when walking, petticoats were embroidered; see **Pl. 9h, 9i, 9k** and **9m.**

e. Gown. Women's gowns were of various kinds. A sleeveless gown for day wear was worn over body and kirtle, either left open in front as in **Pl. 9g** or gathered at the waist as in **Pl. 16b** or **Pl. 7a** (the kneeling figure with outstretched arms). Elderly ladies who had ceased to care for their figures wore a loose gown as the top garment; see **Pl. 9m.** A nightgown was a long loose coat, much after the fashion of the modern house coat.

f. SMOCK. For night wear, a woman wore a SMOCK, a straight-cut nightshirt of linen embroidered at the neck and wrists. The smock was also used as an undergarment or chemise.

g. SLEEVES. Sleeves were separate from the main garment, to which they were attached by points or pins. Sleeves were usually embroidered and were of various shapes; a sleeve was an appropriate gift from a lover to his lady. A sleeve was Troilus' parting gift to Cressida. The CANNON or LEG-OF-MUTTON sleeve was very full at the shoulder and close-fitting at the wrist. SIDE SLEEVES were long sleeves covering the whole arm; see **Pl. 7a** and **Pl. 9g, 9i, 9k, 9m**. DOWN SLEEVES were open from the shoulder, and worn in addition to side sleeves; Queen Elizabeth is shown wearing them in **Pl. 3b**. The SLEEVEHAND was the ruffle of embroidery worn at the wrist.

h. NECKWEAR. The principal neckwear was the RUFF, either round of similar pattern to that worn by men (see **Pl. 9g, 9i, 9k, 9m**, and **Pl. 13c**) or else open at the throat and supported by a REBATO, a wire frame covered with linen which enabled the ruff to be bent up behind the neck to provide a kind of background to the face; see **Pl. 2b**, and **3b**.

i. Miscellaneous:

i. The PLACKET was the opening in front of the petticoat to enable the wearer to slip it over her head.

ii. CHOPINES were shoes mounted on a very high cork soles.

8a. Armor (Metropolitan Museum)

This suit of armor was made for George Clifford, Earl of Cumberland, about 1590, and used in the tilting contests before Queen Elizabeth. It is of russet steel, very richly decorated, and inlaid with goldsmith's work. Battle armor in the fifteenth and sixteenth centuries was made on the same general pattern, though fashion, details, and shape of different pieces were constantly changing. The technical names for the various protecting pieces are: (a) Head. CLOSE HELMET (CASQUE, ARMET), with the face protected by a visor which can be raised on a pivot. The BEAVER, often used loosely to describe the whole

helmet, was the lowest of the three sections remaining in place about the cheeks and chin when the remainder (the visor proper with its slits for sight, and the MEZAIL with its breathing holes) were raised. The foremost mounted man in **Pl. 12a** is shown with his visor in this position. (b) Throat. GORGET. (c) Shoulders. PAULDRONS. (d) Upper arm. REREBRACE. (e) Elbow. ELBOW COP or COUTER. (f) Forearm. VAMBRACE, or VAUNTBRACE (often used to denote the covering of the whole arm between pauldron and gorget). (g) Hand. GAUNTLET. (h) Chest and stomach. BACK AND BREAST, or "PAIR OF PLATES," from which hung the skirt of plate on the TASSETS, protecting the upper parts of the thighs. (i) Groin. A steel CODPIECE or a fringe of chain mail. (j) Thighs. CUISSES. (k) Knees. KNEECAPS. (l) Legs. GREAVES. (m) Feet. SABBATONS.

8b. A courtier's clothes (London Museum)

One of the very few original suits of Elizabethan clothes still surviving. It consists of embroidered velvet cloak, doublet, trunk hose, copetain hat, and embroidered gloves.

8c. German slops (Victoria and Albert Museum, London)

From Abraham de Bruyn, *Habitas variarum gentium,* 1581. The costumes are characteristically German. The figure on the reader's left is wearing slops, with a codpiece, crossed garters, and slashed or razed shoes.

8d. The Earl of Leicester (From a miniature by Nicholas Hilliard in the Victoria and Albert Museum, London)

Leicester is shown wearing a velvet bonnet, a falling band round his neck, a short velvet cloak with sleeves, a peasecod doublet, trunk hose, embroidered upperstocks, embroidered netherstocks, and shoes. On his left leg is the Order of the Garter, with the collar of the Order round his shoulders (from which hangs the "George" — the badge of Saint George slaying the dragon), and in his right hand the white staff of office. The walls are covered with plain hangings, probably of leather, and the table has a long tablecloth characteristic of the period.

9a. A military funeral

A section from Thomas Lant's engraving of the funeral of Sir Philip Sidney, 1587 (Victoria and Albert Museum, London). (*a*) The Captain's boy carries his master's target, a larger version of the buckler (see **Pl. 22i**). (*b*) The Captain (Thomas Smyth) wears a scarf across his right shoulder to denote his rank, and carries a partisan (see **Pl. 21a**) in his right hand, trailed point to the rear in sign of mourning. (*c*) The lieutenant trails a pike (see **Pl. 21d**). (*d*) Three " targeters " armed with swords and targets. (*e*) Three musketeers, with their muskets muzzle to the rear in sign of mourning. They carry in the other hand the forked rest, which was necessary because of the great weight of the musket, and they wear bandoliers from which are hung little bags, each containing one charge of gunpowder and bullets.

9b. Elizabethan types

From Abraham de Bruyn, *Habitas variarum gentium,* 1581 (Victoria and Albert Museum, London). (*f*) A young nobleman (*g*) An elderly lady of rank. (*h*) A young unmarried woman. (*i*) A noblewoman. (*j*) A nobleman. (*k*) A city matron in her best. (*l*) A London citizen in full dress (i.e., wearing his civic gown). (*m*) An aged noblewoman. (*n*) A nobleman (*o*) A young man carrying sword and spiked buckler (see **Pl. 22 i** and **j**). Note the short Spanish cape of (*f*), the furred and " guarded " gowns of (*j*) and (*l*), the long riding cloak of (*n*), and the short cassocks (the citizens' alternative to the courtly doublet and hose) worn by (*l*) and (*o*). Citizens and servants frequently went about without cloaks, but the wearing or carrying of a cloak, even if it covered only one shoulder, was necessary to any man who claimed to be considered a gentleman.

10a–e. Elizabethan coins (actual size) (Royal Ontario Museum)

(a) Elizabethan shilling, obverse and reverse. (b) Shilling of James I. (c) Gold angel. (d) Half groat. (e) Gold half angel. See App. 27.

10f. Elizabethan jewelry (London Museum)

These are specimens from the Cheapside hoard, discovered in London in 1912. On the left, three examples of jeweled fan holders; below, three hat ornaments; an ornamented pin; on the right, a brooch and two pendants. The hoard contained small vessels of crystal, chains, buttons, ornaments of jewels and enamelwork,

and a quantity of uncut and unset stones. It was probably the stock of a London jeweler about 1600.

11a. An indenture (Folger Library)

See App. 6.

11b. A patent under the Great Seal (Folger Library)

Grants from the sovereign of a title, lands, privileges, etc. were embodied in a document known as letters patent, and sealed with the Great Seal of England.

12a. The assault

This woodcut from Holinshed's *Chronicles* illustrates the assault on a town after the walls have been breached in two places by cannon fire or mines. On the right, the attackers, armed with pikes and swords, are going in to the attack while others mount a scaling ladder. In the left foreground, a musketeer is loading his piece with the aid of a ramrod. In the center, the ordnance, protected by palisades, are being fired by the gunners' applying the lighted match at the end of the linstock. On the right cavalrymen in armor wait their turn. The foremost cavalryman is shown with his visor raised.

12b. A camp

This woodcut from Holinshed's *Chronicles* shows life behind the lines. Note the length of the pikes propped against the tents, the drum, the caliver (center foreground), drinking vessels, etc.

12c. Macbeth and the three Weird Sisters

In this woodcut from Holinshed's *Chronicles* Macbeth is shown wearing full hose and riding boots, with spurs. The costume of the Weird Sisters is quite imaginary.

12d. A consort of music

From Holinshed's *Chronicles.* The consort (or " table ") of music consists of lute, bass viol, virginal, hautboy or recorder, and a singer. See also **Pl. 18** and **19.**

12e. The mandrake (Folger Library)

From John Gerard's *Herbal,* 1597. The mandrake, because of its resemblance to the lower part of the human form, was believed to have magical properties: it flourished best under a gallows, it shrieked when pulled out of the ground, and its screams were so fatal that a dog was tied to the root and forced to draw it forth. In medicine it was used as an anodyne and a soporific.

12f. The Fool and Death

From an initial " A " in Anthony Munday's edition of *Stow's Survey* of London, 1618. The fool is wearing the cap with ass's ears. His bauble — a doll's head on a stick — lies in front under a skull which half conceals an hourglass.

13a. Elizabethan stage costume: *Titus Andronicus* (A drawing in the possession of the Marquis of Bath. Photo from the Cunliffe Collection, by permission of D. Appleton-Century Co.)

From a drawing made in 1595 by Henry Peacham, which in the original is followed by a transcript of *Titus Andronicus* I.i.104–21. The episode shows Tamora vainly appealing to Titus Andronicus to show mercy to her sons, who are about to be sacrificed. If, as is possible, Peacham's drawing was founded on his recollection of an actual performance, it gives some indication of the haphazard method of costuming in the Elizabethan playhouse. The two men on the left holding halberds are in Elizabethan costumes, the first figure being armed with a scimitar or falchion. Titus, Tamora's sons, and Aaron the Moor are in " Renaissance classical " costume, which is common in the better-class engravings of the period and was copied from ancient Roman statues. Tamora is in flowing draperies.

13b. The exchange of rapiers

This cut illustrates the episode in the fencing match in *Hamlet*. See App. 25.

13c. A fool and a courtesan

From the title page of Robert Greene's *Third Part of the Conny-catching*, 1592. The fool wears the cockscomb cap and bells, and the motley dress of his calling, which was particolored — right leg and left breast being of one color, left leg and right breast of another. This is the costume worn by Touchstone in *As You Like It*, Feste in *Twelfth Night*, and the Fool in *Lear*.

In the foreground the tools are a cutpurse's knife and a picklock.

13d. Kempe dancing

Woodcut from the title page of Kempe's *Nine Days' Wonder*, 1601, the pamphlet describing his famous dance to Norwich (see Gen. Intro. p. 44b) The famous clown is shown in morris-dancing costume, with bells tied round his knees. He is accompanied by his taborer, playing pipe and tabor, the typical instruments of shepherds and clowns.

14a. Portion of the *More* manuscript (Trustees of the British Museum). See p. 84a.

14b. Title pages of two quartos: *The Merchant of Venice* (Q1) and *Hamlet* (Q2) (Folger Library)

The last two lines of *Hamlet* have been cut off in the binding. The remarks following *By William Shakespeare* were written in the Old English " secretary " hand about 1660; they read: "(who with some errors not to be avoided in that age, had undoubtedly a larger soule of poesie than for any of our nation) was the first who to shun ye pains of continuall rhyme Invented that kinde of writing which we call blanck verse but ye french more properly Prose mesured: into which the english tonge so nachurally falls."

15. Title page of the first folio (Folger Library)

16a. A garden (From *The Orchard and the Garden, 1594*)

The illustrations show typical contemporary gardens with formal flower beds and covered walks. In such a garden Malvolio was spied upon by the conspirators in *Twelfth Night*, and Benedick and Beatrice were betrayed by overheard conversations.

16b. The hunting party (From George Turberville, *Noble Arte of Venerie*, 1575, as reproduced in *Shakespeare's England*, Vol. II, p. 345)

Queen Elizabeth is shown being served at a picnic dinner in the woods — the kind of scene in Shakespeare's mind in *As You Like It*. Note the hunting horns carried by the gentlemen hunters.

Line Cuts

17. Household furniture and utensils: the bedroom

a. Joint stool. This was the commonest piece of furniture, and used for most sitting purposes; chairs with backs and arms were few and reserved for persons of importance.

b. Great bed, with paneled back, canopy, carved posts, and curtains which were drawn close at night. The fringe round the side was called a valance. In a bed of this kind Desdemona was murdered.

c. Carved chest, used for clothes and linen, and often elaborately ornamented.

d. Candleholder. The candle (or taper) was held in the socket; the pincers were used for holding a rushlight (a taper made of a rush coated thinly with wax) which was used for carrying a light from place to place.

e. Leather bottle (called also a *costrel*), used for carrying liquor by such persons as shepherds, gravediggers, or drunken butlers.

f. Leather bombard, used for carrying liquor from cask to table.

18. Musical instruments

a. Viola de gamba, so called because it was held between the knees like the modern cello

b. English guitar

c. Treble viol

d. Lute, used commonly for the musical accompaniment of songs

e. Trumpet

f. Flute

19. Musical instruments

a. Rebec, a simple form of fiddle

b. Recorder, a popular form of woodwind instrument

c. Cornet, another woodwind instrument

d. Shawm, another woodwind instrument

e. Bagpipe

f. Virginal, played in the same way as the modern piano. In the virginal, however, the strings are plucked by quills held by jacks which are moved by the keys; in the spinet (and modern piano) the strings are struck by hammers.

20. Household furniture and utensils: the dining room

a. Court cupboard of carved oak, used for the display of silver plate

b. Table knife

c. Shears used by tailors for cutting out cloth

d. Earthenware watering can, used for sprinkling rushes and wooden floors to lay the dust

e. Stoop or can, a common stoneware type of drinking vessel, called also a *canater* or *cannikin*

f. Beer bottle of stoneware

g. Stoop or *canette* of stoneware, with the royal arms. These were made in large quantities at Siegburg in Germany for the English market.

h. Standing cup of silverware, 1612, called also a *covered goblet*

i. Table of carved oak, with leaves at either end which can be drawn out to give additional length

21. Weapons

a. Partisan. Carried chiefly by palace guards, a heavy weapon, used for close fighting in rooms and passages.

b. Halberd. The characteristic weapon of the Swiss infantry. It had a threefold purpose: the point was for thrusting, the axhead for a smashing blow, the spike for thrusting down scaling ladders or hooking horsemen from their horses.

c. Bill. Another infantry weapon for miscellaneous fighting. It was adapted from the tool used for cutting down branches of trees or trimming hedges. For use as a weapon it was fixed to a longer shaft and was deadly in the hands of an expert. It was also the normal weapon of a watchman.

d. Pike. The English infantryman's weapon. Pikes were usually mounted on a shaft 16 feet long. For resisting cavalry the butt was thrust into the ground and the point pushed forward. In attack it was used by men in close formation who pushed forward by sheer weight.

e. Hunting spear. In **Pl. 7a** Adonis is shown using a boar spear, which was a hunting spear especially adapted for hunting boar; it had a crossbar below the head to take the weight of a charging animal.

22. Arms and weapons

a. Arrows for crossbow, known also as *bolts,* of various types. The short, blunt kind is a bird bolt for killing small birds.

b. Crossbow. The crossbow has a steel spring too powerful to be bent by hand. It was set by winding up the handle until the string was caught on the projection of the trigger.

c. Beheading ax, used for executions. The specimen shown has a short handle; the handle was sometimes much longer. The blade is very broad and heavy.

d. Burgonet, a type of helmet with an open face used chiefly by horsemen as an alternative to the close helmet

e. Bird bow, a smaller type of crossbow

f. Arquebus. One of the four types of hand firearms, the others being the lighter caliver and the heavy musket (see **Pl. 9e**), and the dag or pistol (**g**). There was still great controversy among military men about the relative merits of the bow and the musket and other firearms. It was admitted that firearms exceeded in weight and effectiveness of the projectile, but they were heavy and cumbersome, and very slow to load; for it was necessary first to pour in the charge of loose gunpowder, then with the aid of a ramrod to tamp it down with a wad, to insert the bullets, and to tamp them down with a wad. To discharge the firearm some loose powder was placed in the little pan beside the butt end of the barrel and lit. There were various methods of discharging the arquebus. The simplest was to apply a lighted match to the touchhole at the base of the barrel and so set off the gunpowder by direct action. In other specimens (as in this plate) a flint, inserted into the hammer, was used; by the action of the trigger the flint struck a steel projection which caused a spark to fall into a little pan of loose gunpowder at the base of the barrel, whereby ignition was conveyed to the charge in the barrel. Gunpowder when discharged gave off a thick cloud of whitish smoke, so that after a volley the troops were completely enveloped in a heavy smoke screen.

g. Dag (pistol)

h. Mace. Carried by horsemen for use in close combat. The heavy end delivered a smashing blow which dented through the helmet and gave the wearer concussion of the brain. A miniature mace was carried by sergeants of the law as a badge of office.

i and **j.** Buckler and sword. The sword was the popular English weapon until superseded by the rapier toward the end of the sixteenth century. The sword was used mainly for a cutting stroke but could also be used for thrusting. The buckler was used with the sword. It was carried in the left hand for warding off the opponent's blows. The specimen illustrated has a flanged rim to catch the sword point and a round leather disk at the back to serve as a pad for the knuckles. Bucklers were sometimes provided with a spike, screwed into the center, for thrusting into the opponent's face; see also **Pl. 9o**.

k. Dagger. Carried in a sheath on the girdle, and used point upward in the left hand for parrying the strokes of the rapier.

l. Rapier. A long, light weapon with a thin blade of very finely tempered steel, introduced from Italy. In Shakespeare's time it was the fashionable weapon of young gallants. It was used mainly for thrusting, though as the blade was flat and as it had a very sharp cutting edge, it could also be used for hamstringing an opponent or slicing him over the eye so that he was blinded by his own blood. A rapier suitable only for thrusting was called an *estoc, stuck,* or *tuck.* Old gentlemen of the old school, such as Capulet (*Romeo and Juliet*) or Antonio (*Much Ado about Nothing*) despised the weapon; but in the hands of an expert it was more than a match for the sword.

m. Two-handed sword. A weapon more common on the Continent, used for a short heavy hammerlike blow.

ACKNOWLEDGEMENTS

The drawings for the line cuts were prepared by Miss Elizabeth Maw of the Royal Ontario Museum. Her sources were original objects and/or photographs from the following collections:

The Royal Ontario Museum, Toronto, Plates 17 a, b, c, d, f, 18; 19; 20 b, c, d; 21

The London Museum, Plates 17 e; 20 e, f, g, h.

The Metropolitan Museum, New York, Plates 20 a, i.

The collection of Mr. M. R. Holmes, FSA, Plates 22 d, i, j, h, k, l, m.

THE PLAYS

and the Sonnets

The Tragedy of
KING RICHARD THE THIRD

Introduction

The Tragedy of King Richard the Third was the fourth and concluding play of the series which Shakespeare began with *I Henry VI*.[1] It was probably written in 1592 or 1593 at a time when Shakespeare was still a learner and an imitator; indeed some scholars have believed that some of the scenes were written by Marlowe.

The main source of the story, as with the other historical plays, was Raphael Holinshed's *Chronicles of England, Scotland, and Ireland,* published in 1577, and reissued in a second edition in 1587. For the events of the life and reign of Richard, Duke of Gloucester, afterward Richard III, Holinshed reprinted almost verbatim from Edward Halle's *Chronicle.* Halle had in turn used Sir Thomas More's life of Richard the Third and Polydore Vergil's *Historia Angliae.* More's life dealt only with the months from the death of Edward IV to the rebellion of Buckingham; Polydore Vergil covered the whole period to the Battle of Bosworth. Shakespeare may have used both chronicles, but he was mainly indebted to Holinshed.

Shakespeare borrowed from his sources freely, selecting a few incidents but inventing others to illustrate the theme that blood will have blood, and to show how the curse laid on the House of Lancaster when Henry IV usurped the throne was at last fulfilled, and how the many troubles caused by that crime were finally purged when Henry of Richmond became King; for by his marriage with Elizabeth of York he united the White Rose and the Red, and thereby became the grandfather of Shakespeare's Queen Elizabeth.

Shakespeare's debt to Holinshed may be illustrated by some extracts:

1. THE CHARACTER OF RICHARD, DUKE OF GLOUCESTER

Richard, the third son, of whom we now intreat, was in wit and courage equal with either of them [Edward IV and Clarence], in body and prowess

[1] For the history behind this play, see Appendix 28.

far under them both; little of stature, ill-featured of limbs, crookbacked, his left shoulder much higher than his right, hard-favored of visage, and such as is in states called " warly " [warlike], in other men otherwise; he was malicious, wrathful, envious, and from afore his birth ever froward. It is for truth reported that the Duchess his mother had so much ado in her travail that she could not be delivered of him uncut; and that he came into the world with the feet forward, as men be borne outward, and (as the fame runneth also) not untoothed . . .

None evil captain was he in the war, as to which his disposition was more meetly than for peace. Sundry victories had he, and sometimes overthrows, but never on default as for his own person, either of hardiness or politic order. Free was he called of dispense, and somewhat above his power liberal; with large gifts he gat him unsteadfast friendship, for which he was fain to pill [pillage] and spoil in other places, and got him steadfast hatred. He was close and secret, a deep dissembler, lowly of countenance, arrogant of heart, outwardly companionable where he inwardly hated, not letting [hindering; that is, allowing himself] to kiss whom he thought to kill; despitious [full of spite] and cruel, not for evil will alway, but ofter of ambition and either for the surety or increase of his estate.

Friend and foe was much what indifferent, where his advantage grew; he spared no man's death whose life withstood his purpose . . .

As he was small and little of stature, so was he of body greatly deformed, the one shoulder higher than the other. His face was small, but his countenance cruel, and such that at the first aspect a man would judge it to savor and smell of malice, fraud, and deceit. When he stood musing, he would bite and chaw busily his nether lip, as who said that his fierce nature in his cruel body always chafed, stirred, and was ever unquiet. Beside that, the dagger which he ware, he would, when he studied [meditated] with his hand pluck up and down in the sheath to the midst, never drawing it fully out. He was of a ready, pregnant, and quick wit, wily to feign, and apt to dissemble. He had a proud mind, and an arrogant stomach, the which accompanied him even to his death; rather choosing to suffer the same by dint of sword than, being forsaken and left helpless of his unfaithful companions, to preserve by cowardly flight such a frail and uncertain life, which by malice, sickness, or condign punishment was like shortly to come to confusion.

2. THE DEATH OF HASTINGS (cf. III.IV)

[On June 13, 1483] many lords assembled in the Tower, and there sat in council, devising the honorable solemnity of the King's [Edward V's] coronation, of which the time appointed then so near approached that the pageants and subtleties were in making day and night at Westminster, and much victuals killed therefor that afterward was cast away. These lords so sitting together communing of this matter, the Protector came in amongst them, first about nine of the clock, saluting them courteously, and excusing himself that he had been from them so long, saying merrily that he had been a sleeper that day.

After a little talking with them, he said unto the Bishop of Ely: " My lord, you have very good strawberries at your garden in Holborn. I require you let us have a mess of them." " Gladly, my lord," quoth he. "Would God I had some better thing as ready to your pleasure as that." And therewithal in all the haste he sent his servant for a mess of strawberries. The Protector set the lords fast in communing, and thereupon, praying them to spare him for a little while, departed thence. And soon after one hour, between ten and eleven, he returned into the chamber amongst them, all changed, with a wonderful sour angry countenance, knitting the brows, frowning, and fretting and gnawing on his lips, and so sat him down in his place.

All the lords were much dismayed, and sore marveled at this manner of sudden change, and what thing should ail him. Then, when he had sitten still awhile, he thus began: " What were they worthy to have that compass and imagine the destruction of me, being so near of blood unto the King, and Protector of his royal person and his realm? " At this question all the lords sat sore astonied, musing much by whom this question should be meant, of which every man wist himself clear. Then the Lord Chamberlain [Hastings], as he that for the love between them thought he might be boldest with him, answered and said that they were worthy to be punished as heinous traitors, whatsoever they were. And all the other affirmed the same. " That is," quoth he, " yonder sorceress my brother's wife, and other with her " (meaning the Queen).

At these words many of the lords were greatly abashed that favored her. But the Lord Hastings was in his mind better content that it was moved by her than by any other whom he loved better [that is, Jane Shore], albeit his heart somewhat grudged that he was not afore made of counsel in this matter

as he was of the taking of her kindred and of their putting to death, which were by his assent before devised to be beheaded at Pomfret this selfsame day; in which he was not ware that it was by other devised that he himself should be beheaded that same day at London. Then said the Protector: " You shall see in what wise that sorceress, and that other witch of her counsel, Shore's wife, with her affinity, have by their sorcery and witchcraft wasted my body." And therewith he plucked up his doublet sleeve to his elbow, upon his left arm, where he showed a weerish [sickly-looking] withered arm, and small as it was never other.

Hereupon every man's mind sore misgave him, well perceiving that this matter was but a quarrel. For they well wist that the Queen was too wise to go about any such folly. And also, if she would, yet would she of all folk least make Shore's wife of her counsel, whom of all women she most hated as that concubine whom the King her husband had most loved. And also no man was there present but well knew that his arm was ever such since his birth.

Naithless, the Lord Chamberlain (which from the death of King Edward kept Shore's wife, on whom he had somewhat doted in the King's life, saving, as it is said, he that while forbear her of reverence toward the King, or else of a certain kind of fidelity to his friend), answered and said: " Certainly, my lord, if they have so heinously done, they be worthy heinous punishment."

" What," quoth the Protector, " thou servest me, I ween, with ' ifs ' and with ' ands.' I tell thee they have so done, and that I will make good on thy body, traitor." And therewith, as in a great anger, he clapped his fist upon the board a great rap. At which token one cried " Treason! " without the chamber. Therewith a door clapped, and in come there men in harness [armor], as many as the chamber might hold. And anon the Protector said to the Lord Hastings: " I arrest thee, traitor! " " What me, my lord? " quoth he. " Yea, thee, traitor! " quoth the Protector. . . .

Then were they all quickly bestowed in divers chambers, except the Lord Chamberlain, whom the Protector bade speed and shrive him [confess his sins and receive absolution] apace, " for by Paul," quoth he, " I will not to dinner till I see thy head off! " It booted him not to ask why, but heavily he took a priest at adventure and made a short shrift; for a longer would he not be suffered, the Protector made so much haste to dinner, which he might not go to until this were done for saving of his oath.

3. THE MURDER OF THE PRINCES (cf. IV.ii AND iii)

Sir James Tyrrel devised that they should be murdered in their beds. To the execution whereof he appointed one Miles Forrest, one of the four that kept them, a fellow fleshed in murder beforetime. To him he joined one John Deighton, his own horsekeeper, a big, broad, square, and strong knave.

Then all the other being removed from them, this Miles Forrest and John Deighton about midnight (the silly [simple, innocent] children lying in their beds) came into the chamber, and suddenly lapping them up among the clothes, so to-bewrapped them and entangled them, keeping down by force the feather bed and pillows hard unto their mouths, that within a while, smothered and stifled, their breath failing, they gave up to God their innocent souls into the joys of Heaven, leaving to the tormentors their bodies dead in the bed. Which after that the wretches perceived, first by the struggling with the pains of death, and after long lying still, to be thoroughly dead, they laid their bodies naked out upon the bed, and fetched Sir James to see them, which, upon the sight of them, caused those murderers to bury them at the stair foot, meetly deep in the ground under a great heap of stones.

Then rode Sir James in great haste to King Richard and showed him all the manner of the murder, who gave him great thanks, and (as some say) then made him knight. But he allowed not (as I have heard) the burying in so vile a corner, saying that he would have them buried in a better place, because they were a King's sons. . . . Whereupon, they say that a priest of Sir Robert Brakenbury's took up the bodies again and secretly interred them in such a place as by the occasion of his death, which only knew it, could never since come to light.

4. RICHARD DREAMS BEFORE BOSWORTH (cf. v.iii)

[The episode of the ghosts which appeared to Richard on the night before he was killed was based on the following paragraph.]

The fame went that he had the same night a dreadful and terrible dream; for it seemed to him being asleep that he did see divers images like terrible devils, which pulled and haled him, not suffering him to take any quiet or rest. The which strange vision not so suddenly strake his heart with a sudden fear, but it stuffed his head and troubled his mind with many busy and dreadful imaginations. For incontinent after, his heart being almost damped, he prognosticated before the doubtful chance of the battle to come, not using the alacrity and mirth of mind and countenance as he was accustomed to do before he came toward the battle. At least that it might be suspected that he was abashed for fear of his enemies, and for that cause looked so piteously, he recited and declared to his familiar friends in the morning his wonderful vision and fearful dream.

5. THE DEATH OF RICHARD AT THE BATTLE OF BOSWORTH (cf. v.iv AND v)

King Richard set on so sharply at the first brunt that he overthrew the Earl's [Richmond's] standard and slew Sir William Brandon his standard-bearer (which was father to Sir Charles Brandon, by King Henry the Eighth created Duke of Suffolk) and matched hand to hand with Sir John Cheney, a man of great force and strength, which would have resisted him; but the said John was by him manfully overthrown. And so, he making passage by dint of sword as he went forward, the Earl of Richmond withstood his violence, and kept him at the sword's point without advantage longer than his companions either thought or judged; which being almost in despair of victory were suddenly recomforted by Sir William Stanley, which came to his succors with three thousand tall men. At which very instant King Richard's men were driven back and fled, and he himself, manfully fighting in the middle of his enemies, was slain, and (as he worthily had deserved) came to a bloody death as he had led a bloody life . . .

When the loss of the battle was imminent and apparent, they brought him a swift and light horse to convey him away. He which was not ignorant of the grudge and ill will that the common people bare toward him, casting away all hope of fortunate success and happy chance to come, answered (as men say) that on that day he would make an end of all battles, or else there finish his life.

Richard III was entered for publication in the Stationers' Register to Andrew Wise on October 20, 1597, as "The tragedie of kinge Richard the Third with the death of the Duke of Clarence." A first quarto appeared in the same year with the title: *The Tragedy of King Richard the Third. Containing, His treacherous Plots against his brother Clarence: the pittiefull murther of his innocent nephewes; his tyrannicall usurpation: with the whole course of his detested life, and most deserved death. As it hath beene lately Acted by the Right Honourable the Lord Chamberlaine his servants.* Other quartos appeared in 1598, 1602, 1605, 1616, and 1622. These were printed one from the other, but when the play was reprinted in the first folio of 1623 the text was set up from a copy corrected from some different original. There are considerable variations between the quarto and folio versions. The folio adds certain passages: I.ii.156-67; II.ii.89-110; II.ii.123-40; III.vii.144-53; IV.iv.221-34; IV.iv. 288-42. As the play is considerably than the average, these passages may have been cut in the acting version. On the other hand, the folio omits IV.ii.101–19 and some shorter passages and there are many minor differences between the two versions. Either the folio text was based on the playhouse copy and the quarto on an inferior original, or the quarto version is the earlier and the folio a revision. The text of the play is thus difficult. The modern text is a compound of both versions, each editor giving the reading which appears to him best.

In writing *Richard III* Shakespeare imitated his predecessors in several ways. The obvious dramatic ironies, the prophecies and curses, the ghosts, and the symbolic figure of the aged Queen Margaret are in the manner of Kyd and of the Roman dramatist Seneca, whom earlier Elizabethan dramatists admiringly copied; but Shakespeare owed most to Marlowe. Like *Tamburlaine* and *The Jew of Malta, Richard III* is a play with one star part; it is the portrayal of a colossal villain. There is little opportunity for other members of the company to distinguish themselves except in individual scenes. The hero, like Barabas in *The Jew of Malta,* is a " Machiavellian," and the play opens in the same way, with the chief character coming forward alone to explain himself in a long soliloquy. Richard as Duke of Gloucester had already shown his ruthless nature in the *III Henry VI,* which ended with Richard murdering King Henry VI in the Tower as King Edward IV was restored to the throne.

Richard III begins with Richard announcing that since he is lame, ugly, and repulsive in body he is " determined to prove a villain." He is thus an unnatural monster who delights in wickedness for its own sake. His first step will be the destruction of his brother Clarence, which he effects by persuading King Edward IV to have Clarence murdered, while at the same time he pretends to Clarence to be his true friend. By the end of the first scene Richard has already shown that his ambitions are leading him to the crown.

His next step is to marry Anne, the daughter of the late Earl of Warwick, even though he had murdered her husband and her father-in-law. In the second scene Richard is shown carrying out this plan: As the funeral of King Henry VI passes by, with the Lady Anne as chief mourner, Richard intercepts the procession and proceeds

first to overcome the loathing of Anne and then to persuade her to accept his monstrous offer of marriage. Richard did in fact marry Prince Edward's widow, but the wooing as shown in the play is wholly unhistorical and highly artificial in conception and dialogue, yet in an extravagant way theatrically effective. It abounds in those devices which mark Shakespeare's early style — puns, conceits, elaborate imagery, repetitions, word play in which one word is used in two or three different meanings, and a general delight in cleverness rather than in psychological insight. Thus Richard addresses Anne (I.ii.75–78):

> Vouchsafe, divine perfection of a woman,
> Of these supposèd evils to give me leave,
> By circumstance, but to acquit myself.

Anne retorts phrase for phrase:

> Vouchsafe, defused infection of a man,
> For these known evils but to give me leave,
> By circumstance, to curse thy cursèd self.

This kind of elaborate cleverness is not to be found in the plays of Shakespeare's maturity.

Richard has made a good beginning, but he is in considerable danger. The King's relations, who occupy the highest offices in the state, loathe him. Further, Edward IV is ailing. While his relations are anxiously debating the King's health, Richard joins them, and during the wrangle that follows there enters the aged Queen Margaret, widow of King Henry VI, and once champion of the House of Lancaster. Her presence among her enemies is quite fantastic, but she is brought in as a prophetess of woe and doom to rain curses on her many enemies of the House of York and to foretell their downfall. Act I ends with the murder of Clarence — a scene which includes a fine piece of epic description in Clarence's account of his dream.

Act II begins with the dying King's vain efforts to bring about a reconciliation between his jarring relatives. Upon Edward's death the women of his family — his wife and his mother — lament for him, but Richard and his ally, Buckingham, at once take steps to seize the boy King, Edward V. At this point Shakespeare interposed a short scene (II.iii) in which two citizens in their conversation reveal the general fears that dangerous times are at hand.

In Act III, Richard and Buckingham, having captured the young King and his brother, the precocious little Duke of York, lead the two boys to the Tower. Richard is now feeling after the crown. The first step is to eliminate possible opponents. Of these the most dangerous is the Lord Chamberlain, Lord Hastings. Richard sends his man Catesby to sound him out; Catesby finds that Hastings, as Richard had suspected, is loyal to the boy King. At a meeting of the Council Richard suddenly denounces Hastings and commands his instant execution. Then he sends Buckingham to try to win over the Lord Mayor and the citizens of London to his support. The citizens are cold, but Buckingham persuades the Lord Mayor to lead a deputation to beg Richard to assume the crown. Richard now becomes King. He sends for Tyrrel, a conscienceless villain, and orders the murder of the two little Princes. Anne dies, evidently by Richard's orders. But new difficulties are showing themselves; Buckingham is no longer as subservient as before. Tyrrel returns with the news of the death of the boys. Then follows a scene where Queen Margaret once more appears to gloat over the downfall of her enemies and to indulge in a contest of lamentation with Elizabeth, widow of Edward IV, and the aged Duchess of York. Though Margaret hates them both, they are at least united in their common hatred of Richard, and they curse him as he passes by. But Richard with his old cynicism approaches Elizabeth and in a long dialogue between them (which parallels the earlier wooing of Anne) tries to win her over to agree to his marriage with her daughter Elizabeth. The tide has now turned; news comes to Richard that his enemies are everywhere rising to join with Henry Richmond, the last survivor of the House of Lancaster and Buckingham is among them. Buckingham, however, is taken.

The last act opens with a brief scene showing Buckingham on his way to execution. He pauses to lament his treacheries, which have now come back on his own head. The scene then shifts to the field of Bosworth on the night before the battle. On either side of the stage the tents of Richard and Richmond are set up. One by one the ghosts of Richard's victims rise — Prince Edward, Margaret's son, Henry VI, Clarence, Rivers, Vaughan, Grey, the two Princes, Anne, Buckingham. They curse Richard, bless Richmond, and disappear. The episode is symbolic and a fitting summary of Richard's career. A short battle scene follows. Richard is killed, Henry Richmond is saluted as King, and the play ends with a prayer that England may be spared another civil war.

To anyone unfamiliar with an intricate period of English history, *Richard III* is difficult to follow in the reading. On the stage it is effective in a melodramatic way; it demands extravagant acting and a certain lack of sophistication in the audience. In its own times it was a popular success, and Burbage's acting of the part of Richard was much admired. Indeed his rendering of Richard's last speech — "A horse! A horse! My kingdom for a horse!" — was almost as much quoted and parodied as some of the famous lines in Kyd's *Spanish Tragedy*. But Shakespeare and his fellows soon abandoned this ranting kind of drama as they came to realize that to make a good play something more was needed than verbal cleverness and a star actor.

Richard III

DRAMATIS PERSONAE

KING EDWARD *the Fourth*
EDWARD, *Prince of Wales, afterward King Edward V* } *sons to the King*
RICHARD, *Duke of York*
GEORGE, *Duke of Clarence* } *brothers to the King*
RICHARD, *Duke of Gloucester, afterward King Richard III*
A young son of Clarence
HENRY, *Earl of Richmond, afterward King Henry VII*
CARDINAL BOURCHIER, *Archbishop of Canterbury*
THOMAS ROTHERHAM, *Archbishop of York*
JOHN MORTON, *Bishop of Ely*
DUKE OF BUCKINGHAM
DUKE OF NORFOLK
EARL OF SURREY, *his son*
EARL RIVERS, *brother to Elizabeth*
MARQUIS OF DORSET *and* LORD GREY, *sons to Elizabeth*
EARL OF OXFORD
LORD HASTINGS
LORD STANLEY, *called also* EARL OF DERBY
LORD LOVEL
SIR THOMAS VAUGHAN
SIR RICHARD RATCLIFF

SIR WILLIAM CATESBY
SIR JAMES TYRREL
SIR JAMES BLOUNT
SIR WALTER HERBERT
SIR ROBERT BRAKENBURY, *Lieutenant of the Tower*
SIR WILLIAM BRANDON
CHRISTOPHER URSWICK, *a priest. Another Priest*
TRESSEL *and* BERKELEY, *gentlemen attending on the Lady Anne*
LORD MAYOR *of London*
SHERIFF *of Wiltshire*

ELIZABETH, *queen to King Edward IV*
MARGARET, *widow of King Henry VI*
DUCHESS OF YORK, *mother to King Edward IV*
LADY ANNE, *widow of Edward Prince of Wales, son to King Henry VI; afterward married to Richard*
A young daughter of Clarence (MARGARET PLANTAGENET)

GHOSTS *of those murdered by Richard III,* LORDS *and other* ATTENDANTS; *a* PURSUIVANT, SCRIVENER, CITIZENS, MURDERERS, MESSENGERS, SOLDIERS, ETC.
SCENE — *England.*

Act I

SCENE I. *London. A street.*

[*Enter* RICHARD, DUKE OF GLOUCESTER, *solus.*]
GLO. Now is the winter of our discontent
Made glorious summer by this sun of York,°
And all the clouds that lowered upon our house
In the deep bosom of the ocean buried.
Now are our brows bound with victorious wreaths,
Our bruisèd arms hung up for monuments,   6
Our stern alarums changed to merry meetings,
Our dreadful marches to delightful measures.°
Grim-visaged war hath smoothed his wrinkled front,°
And now, instead of mounting barbèd° steeds 10
To fright the souls of fearful adversaries,
He capers nimbly in a lady's chamber
To the lascivious pleasing of a lute.°
But I, that am not shaped for sportive tricks,

Nor made to court an amorous looking-glass; 15
I, that am rudely stamped, and want love's majesty
To strut before a wanton ambling nymph;
I, that am curtailed° of this fair proportion,°
Cheated of feature by dissembling° nature,
Deformed, unfinished, sent before my time   20
Into this breathing world, scarce half made up,
And that so lamely and unfashionable
That dogs bark at me as I halt° by them —
Why, I, in this weak piping time° of peace,
Have no delight to pass away the time,   25
Unless to spy my shadow in the sun
And descant° on mine own deformity.
And therefore, since I cannot prove a lover,
To entertain° these fair well-spoken days,
I am determinèd to prove a villain   30
And hate the idle pleasures of these days.
Plots have I laid, inductions° dangerous,
By drunken prophecies, libels, and dreams,
To set my brother Clarence and the King

Act I, Sc. i: **2. sun . . . York:** a triple pun. Edward IV was son of the Duke of York, and bore a sun as his badge. He was also the bright sun of the Yorkist party now in power. **8. measures:** dances. See App. 24. **9. wrinkled front:** frowning forehead. **10. barbed:** armed. **13. lute:** See Pl. 18d.

18. curtailed: cut short. **proportion:** shape. **19. dissembling:** cheating. **23. halt:** limp. **24. piping time:** i.e., when shepherds play their pipes. **27. descant:** warble, "make a song about." **29. entertain:** pass away. **32. inductions:** introductions—the first steps in an undertaking.

In deadly hate the one against the other.   35
And if King Edward be as true and just
As I am subtle, false, and treacherous,
This day should Clarence closely be mewed up,°
About a prophecy, which says that G
Of Edward's heirs the murderer shall be.   40
Dive, thoughts, down to my soul — here Clarence
   comes.
   [*Enter* CLARENCE, *guarded, and* BRAKENBURY.]
Brother, good day. What means this armèd guard
That waits upon your Grace?
   CLAR.   His Majesty,
Tendering my person's safety, hath appointed
This conduct to convey me to the Tower.   45
   GLO. Upon what cause?
   CLAR.   Because my name is George.
   GLO. Alack, my lord, that fault is none of yours.
He should, for that, commit your godfathers.
Oh, belike His Majesty hath some intent
That you shall be new-christened in the Tower.   50
But what's the matter, Clarence? May I know?
   CLAR. Yea, Richard, when I know, for I protest
As yet I do not. But, as I can learn,
He hearkens after prophecies and dreams;
And from the crossrow° plucks the letter G,   55
And says a wizard told him that by G
His issue disinherited should be;
And, for my name of George begins with G,
It follows in his thought that I am he.
These, as I learn, and suchlike toys° as these   60
Have moved His Highness to commit me now.
   GLO. Why, this it is, when men are ruled by
   women.
'Tis not the King that sends you to the Tower;
My Lady Grey his wife, Clarence, 'tis she
That tempers° him to this extremity.   65
Was it not she and that good man of worship,
Anthony Woodville, her brother there,
That made him send Lord Hastings to the Tower,
From whence this present day he is delivered?
We are not safe, Clarence, we are not safe.   70
   CLAR. By Heaven, I think there's no man is secure
But the Queen's kindred and nightwalking heralds
That trudge betwixt the King and Mistress Shore.°
Heard ye not what a humble suppliant
Lord Hastings was to her for his delivery?   75
   GLO. Humbly complaining to her deity
Got my Lord Chamberlain his liberty.
I'll tell you what — I think it is our way,
If we will keep in favor with the King,
To be her men and wear her livery.   80
The jealous o'erworn widow and herself,

Since that our brother dubbed° them gentlewomen,
Are mighty gossips° in this monarchy.
   BRAK. I beseech your Graces both to pardon me —
His Majesty hath straitly° given in charge   85
That no man shall have private conference,
Of what degree° soever, with his brother.
   GLO. Even so, an 't° please your Worship, Brak-
   enbury,
You may partake of anything we say.
We speak no treason, man. We say the King   90
Is wise and virtuous, and his noble Queen
Well struck in years, fair, and not jealous.
We say that Shore's wife hath a pretty foot,
A cherry lip, a bonny eye, a passing° pleasing
   tongue.
And that the Queen's kindred are made gentlefolk.
How say you, sir? Can you deny all this?   96
   BRAK. With this, my lord, myself have naught to
   do.
   GLO. Naught to do with Mistress Shore! I tell
   thee, fellow,
He that doth naught with her, excepting one,
Were best he do it secretly alone.   100
   BRAK. What one, my lord?
   GLO. Her husband, knave. Wouldst thou betray
   me?
   BRAK. I beseech your Grace to pardon me, and
   withal
Forbear your conference with the noble Duke.
   CLAR. We know thy charge,° Brakenbury, and
   will obey.   105
   GLO. We are the Queen's abjects,° and must obey.
Brother, farewell. I will unto the King,
And whatsoever you will employ me in,
Were it to call King Edward's widow° sister,
I will perform it to enfranchise° you.   110
Meantime, this deep disgrace in brotherhood°
Touches me deeper than you can imagine.
   CLAR. I know it pleaseth neither of us well.
   GLO. Well, your imprisonment shall not be long.
I will deliver you, or else lie for you.°   115
Meantime, have patience.
   CLAR.   I must perforce. Farewell.
   [*Exeunt* CLARENCE, BRAKENBURY, *and* GUARD.]
   GLO. Go tread the path that thou shalt ne'er re-
   turn,
Simple, plain Clarence! I do love thee so
That I will shortly send thy soul to Heaven,

---

38. **mewed up:** confined.   55. **crossrow:** alphabet. Boys learned
their alphabet from a printed sheet covered with horn, and
known as the hornbook. As the first sign on the page was a
cross (✠), the alphabet was sometimes called the christcross-
row. 60. **toys:** trifles. 65. **tempers:** molds. 73. **Mistress Shore:**
wife of a London goldsmith and Edward IV's mistress.

82. **dubbed:** promoted.   83. **gossips:** close friends who exchange
gossip. 85. **straitly:** strictly. 87. **degree:** rank. 88. **an 't:** if it.
94. **passing:** exceedingly. 105. **charge:** instructions. 106. **abjects:**
lowly servants, here used ironically for "subjects." 109. **widow:**
the widow whom Edward IV had married — Lady Elizabeth
Woodville. 110. **enfranchise:** set free. 111. **disgrace in brother-
hood:** The phrase, as is common in this play, has various mean-
ings — "unnatural behavior in a brother (the King)," "disgrace
to a brother (Clarence)," and "my own disgraceful conduct."
115. **lie . . . you:** with double meaning — "take your place in
prison" and "tell lies on your behalf."

If Heaven will take the present at our hands.   120
But who comes here? The new-delivered Hastings?
          [*Enter* LORD HASTINGS.]
  HAST. Good time of day unto my gracious lord!
  GLO. As much unto my good Lord Chamberlain!
Well are you welcome to the open air.   124
How hath your lordship brooked° imprisonment?
  HAST. With patience, noble lord, as prisoners
    must.
But I shall live, my lord, to give them thanks
That were the cause of my imprisonment.
  GLO. No doubt, no doubt, and so shall Clarence
    too;
For they that were your enemies are his,   130
And have prevailed as much on him as you.
  HAST. More pity that the eagle should be mewed°
While kites° and buzzards° prey at liberty.
  GLO. What news abroad?   134
  HAST. No news so bad abroad as this at home:
The King is sickly, weak, and melancholy,
And his physicians fear° him mightily.
  GLO. Now, by Saint Paul, this news is bad in-
    deed.
Oh, he hath kept an evil diet long,
And overmuch consumed his royal person.   140
'Tis very grievous to be thought upon.
What, is he in his bed?
  HAST.   He is.
  GLO. Go you before, and I will follow you.
                         [*Exit* HASTINGS.]
He cannot live, I hope, and must not die   145
Till George be packed with post horse° up to
    Heaven.
I'll in, to urge his hatred more to Clarence,
With lies well steeled° with weighty arguments;
And if I fail not in my deep intent,
Clarence hath not another day to live.   150
Which done, God take King Edward to His
    mercy,
And leave the world for me to bustle in!
For then I'll marry Warwick's youngest daughter.
What though I killed her husband and her father?
The readiest way to make the wench amends   155
Is to become her husband and her father —
The which will I, not all so much for love
As for another secret close intent
By marrying her which I must reach unto.
But yet I run before my horse to market.°   160
Clarence still breathes, Edward still lives and
    reigns.
When they are gone, then must I count my gains.
                         [*Exit.*]

SCENE II. *The same. Another street.*

[*Enter the corpse of* KING HENRY *the Sixth,* GENTLE-
MEN *with halberds*° *to guard it,* LADY ANNE *being
the mourner.*]

  ANNE. Set down, set down your honorable load —
If honor may be shrouded in a hearse —
Whilst I awhile obsequiously° lament
The untimely fall of virtuous Lancaster.
Poor key-cold figure of a holy King!   5
Pale ashes of the House of Lancaster,
Thou bloodless remnant of that royal blood!
Be it lawful that I invoke thy ghost
To hear the lamentations of poor Anne,
Wife to thy Edward, to thy slaughtered son,   10
Stabbed by the selfsame hand that made these
    wounds!
Lo, in these windows that let forth thy life
I pour the helpless balm of my poor eyes.
Cursed be the hand that made these fatal holes!
Cursed be the heart that had the heart to do it!   15
Cursèd the blood that let this blood from hence!
More direful hap betide° that hated wretch
That makes us wretched by the death of thee
Than I can wish to adders, spiders, toads,
Or any creeping venomed thing that lives!   20
If ever he have child, abortive° be it,
Prodigious,° and untimely brought to light,
Whose ugly and unnatural aspect°
May fright the hopeful mother at the view,
And that be heir to his unhappiness!°   25
If ever he have wife, let her be made
As miserable by the death of him
As I am made by my poor lord and thee!
Come, now toward Chertsey° with your holy load,
Taken from Paul's° to be interrèd there;   30
And still,° as° you are weary of the weight,
Rest you whiles I lament King Henry's corse.°
                    [*Enter* GLOUCESTER.]
  GLO. Stay, you that bear the corse, and set it
    down.
  ANNE. What black magician conjures up this
    fiend
To stop devoted charitable deeds?   35
  GLO. Villains, set down the corse, or, by Saint
    Paul,
I'll make a corse of him that disobeys.
  GENT. My lord, stand back, and let the coffin pass.
  GLO. Unmannered dog! Stand thou when I com-
    mand.
Advance thy halberd higher than my breast,   40
Or, by Saint Paul, I'll strike thee to my foot

---

125. brooked: endured.   132. mewed: caged.   133. kites: the
lowest of the birds of prey. buzzards: an inferior species of
hawk.   137. fear: fear for, are anxious about.   146. post horse:
See App. 17.   148. steeled: with steel points.   160. I . . . mar-
ket: a proverb like "Count my chickens before they are
hatched."

Sc. ii: s.d., halberds: See Pl. 21b.   3. obsequiously: as be-
fits a mourner with obsequies.   17. hap betide: fortune befall.
21. abortive: unnatural.   22. Prodigious: monstrous.   23. aspect:
look.   25. unhappiness: evil nature.   29. Chertsey: a town in
Surrey.   30. Paul's: St. Paul's Church. See Gen. Intro. p. 17a,
and Pl. 2a.   31. still: meanwhile. as: since.   32. corse: corpse.

And spurn upon thee, beggar, for thy boldness.
ANNE. What, do you tremble? Are you all afraid?
Alas, I blame you not, for you are mortal,
And mortal eyes cannot endure the Devil.   45
Avaunt,° thou dreadful minister° of Hell!
Thou hadst but power over his mortal body,
His soul thou canst not have, therefore be gone.
  GLO. Sweet saint, for charity, be not so curst.°
ANNE. Foul devil, for God's sake, hence, and
    trouble us not,   50
For thou hast made the happy earth thy Hell,
Filled it with cursing cries and deep exclaims.
If thou delight to view thy heinous deeds,
Behold this pattern° of thy butcheries.
O gentlemen, see, see! Dead Henry's wounds   55
Open their congealed mouths and bleed afresh.°
Blush, blush, thou lump of foul deformity,
For 'tis thy presence that exhales° this blood
From cold and empty veins where no blood dwells;
Thy deed, inhuman and unnatural,   60
Provokes this deluge most unnatural.
O God, which this blood mad'st, revenge his death!
O earth, which this blood drink'st, revenge his
    death!
Either Heaven with lightning strike the murderer
    dead,
Or earth, gape open wide and eat him quick,°   65
As thou dost swallow up this good King's blood,
Which his Hell-governed arm hath butchered!
  GLO. Lady, you know no rules of charity,
Which renders good for bad, blessings for curses.
ANNE. Villain, thou know'st no law of God nor
    man.   70
No beast so fierce but knows some touch of pity.
  GLO. But I know none, and therefore am no beast.
ANNE. Oh, wonderful when devils tell the truth!
  GLO. More wonderful when angels are so angry.
Vouchsafe, divine perfection of a woman,   75
Of these supposèd evils to give me leave,
By circumstance,° but to acquit myself.
ANNE. Vouchsafe, defused° infection of a man,
For these known evils but to give me leave,
By circumstance, to curse thy cursèd self.   80
  GLO. Fairer than tongue can name thee, let me
    have
Some patient leisure to excuse myself.
ANNE. Fouler than heart can think thee, thou
    canst make
No excuse current° but to hang thyself.
  GLO. By such despair I should accuse myself.   85
ANNE. And, by despairing, shouldst thou stand
    excused

For doing worthy vengeance on thyself,
Which didst unworthy slaughter upon others.
  GLO. Say° that I slew them not?
ANNE.   Why, then they are not dead.
But dead they are, and, devilish slave, by thee. 90
  GLO. I did not kill your husband.
ANNE.   Why, then he is alive.
  GLO. Nay, he is dead, and slain by Edward's
    hand.
ANNE. In thy foul throat thou liest. Queen Mar-
    garet saw
Thy murderous falchion° smoking in his blood,
The which thou once didst bend against her
    breast,   95
But that thy brothers beat aside the point.
  GLO. I was provokèd by her slanderous tongue,
Which laid their guilt upon my guiltless shoulders.
ANNE. Thou wast provokèd by thy bloody mind,
Which never dreamed on aught but butcheries.   100
Didst thou not kill this King?
  GLO.   I grant ye.
ANNE. Dost grant me, hedgehog?° Then, God
    grant me too
Thou mayst be damnèd for that wicked deed!
Oh he was gentle, mild, and virtuous!
  GLO. The fitter for the King of Heaven, that hath
    him.   105
ANNE. He is in Heaven, where thou shalt never
    come.
  GLO. Let him thank me that holp° to send him
    thither,
For he was fitter for that place than earth.
ANNE. And thou unfit for any place but Hell.
  GLO. Yes, one place else, if you will hear me
    name it.   110
ANNE. Some dungeon.
  GLO.   Your bedchamber.
ANNE. Ill rest betide the chamber where thou
    liest!
  GLO. So will it, madam, till I lie with you.
ANNE. I hope so.
  GLO.   I know so. But, gentle Lady Anne,
To leave this keen encounter of our wits   115
And fall somewhat into a slower method,
Is not the causer of the timeless° deaths
Of these Plantagenets, Henry and Edward,
As blameful as the executioner?
ANNE. Thou art the cause, and most accursed
    effect.°   120
  GLO. Your beauty was the cause of that effect —
Your beauty, which did haunt me in my sleep
To undertake the death of all the world
So I might live one hour in your sweet bosom.
ANNE. If I thought that, I tell thee, homicide,

---

46. Avaunt: be gone. minister: servant. 49. curst: shrewish,
bad-tempered. 54. pattern: example. 56. bleed afresh: It was
popularly supposed that the wounds of a murdered man bled in
the presence of the murderer. 58. exhales: draws out. 65. quick:
aiive. 77. By circumstance: by relating the facts. 78. defused:
diffused, confused. 84. current: genuine.

89. Say: suppose. 94. falchion: curved sword. 102. hedgehog:
an insulting reference to Richard's crest of a wild boar.
107. holp: helped. 117. timeless: untimely. 120. effect: agent.

These nails should rend that beauty from my
   cheeks.   126
GLO. These eyes could never endure sweet
   beauty's wreck.
You should not blemish it if I stood by.
As all the world is cheerèd by the sun,
So I by that. It is my day, my life.   130
ANNE. Black night o'ershade thy day, and death
   thy life!
GLO. Curse not thyself, fair creature — thou art
   both.
ANNE. I would I were, to be revenged on thee.
GLO. It is a quarrel most unnatural
To be revenged on him that loveth you.   135
ANNE. It is a quarrel just and reasonable
To be revenged on him that slew my husband.
GLO. He that bereft thee, lady, of thy husband,
Did it to help thee to a better husband.   139
ANNE. His better doth not breathe upon the earth.
GLO. He lives that loves thee better than he could.
ANNE. Name him.
GLO.   Plantagenet.
ANNE.   Why, that was he.
GLO. The selfsame name, but one of better nature.
ANNE. Where is he?
GLO.   Here. Why dost thou spit at me?   145
ANNE. Would it were mortal poison, for thy sake!
GLO. Never came poison from so sweet a place.
ANNE. Never hung poison on a fouler toad.
Out of my sight! Thou dost infect my eyes.   149
GLO. Thine eyes, sweet lady, have infected mine.
ANNE. Would they were basilisks,° to strike thee
   dead!
GLO. I would they were, that I might die at once,
For now they kill me with a living death.
Those eyes of thine from mine have drawn salt
   tears,   154
Shame their aspéct with store of childish drops.
These eyes, which never shed remorseful tear —
No, when my father York and Edward wept
To hear the piteous moan that Rutland made
When black-faced Clifford shook his sword at him;
Nor when thy warlike father, like a child,   160
Told the sad story of my father's death,
And twenty times made pause to sob and weep
That all the standers-by had wet their cheeks,
Like trees bedashed with rain — in that sad time
My manly eyes did scorn a humble tear.   165
And what these sorrows could not thence exhale,
Thy beauty hath, and made them blind with weep-
   ing.
I never sued to friend nor enemy,
My tongue could never learn sweet smoothing
   words,

But now thy beauty is proposed my fee,°   170
My proud heart sues, and prompts my tongue to
   speak.
Teach not thy lips such scorn, for they were made
For kissing, lady, not for such contempt.
If thy revengeful heart cannot forgive,
Lo, here I lend thee this sharp-pointed sword,   175
Which if thou please to hide in this true bosom
And let the soul forth that adoreth thee,
I lay it naked to the deadly stroke,
And humbly beg the death upon my knee.
Nay, do not pause, for I did kill King Henry.   180
But 'twas thy beauty that provokèd me.
Nay, now dispatch — 'twas I that stabbed young
   Edward,
But 'twas thy heavenly face that set me on.
Take up the sword again, or take up me.
ANNE. Arise, dissembler.° Though I wish thy
   death,   185
I will not be the executioner.
GLO. Then bid me kill myself, and I will do it.
ANNE. I have already.
GLO.   Tush, that was in thy rage.
Speak it again and, even with the word,
That hand which for thy love did kill thy love   190
Shall for thy love kill a far truer love.
To both their deaths shalt thou be accessory.
ANNE. I would I knew thy heart.
GLO. 'Tis figured in my tongue.
ANNE. I fear me both are false.   195
GLO. Then never man was true.
ANNE. Well, well, put up your sword.
GLO. Say, then, my peace is made.
ANNE. That shall you know hereafter.
GLO. But shall I live in hope?   200
ANNE. All men, I hope, live so.
GLO. Vouchsafe° to wear this ring.
ANNE. To take is not to give.
GLO. Look how this ring encompasseth thy finger,
Even so thy breast encloseth my poor heart.   205
Wear both of them, for both of them are thine.
And if thy poor devoted suppliant may
But beg one favor at thy gracious hand,
Thou dost confirm his happiness forever.
ANNE. What is it?   210
GLO. That it would please thee leave these sad
   designs
To him that hath more cause to be a mourner,
And presently° repair to Crosby Place,°
Where, after I have solemnly interrèd
At Chertsey monastery this noble King,   215
And wet his grave with my repentant tears,
I will with all expedient duty see you.

151. **basilisk:** an imaginary creature with a cock's head, an
animal's body, and a snake's tail, hatched out by a toad from a
cock's egg — a very deadly beast able to slay by its mere look.

170. **thy . . . fee:** when your beauty is the proposed reward.
185. **dissembler:** hypocrite.   202. **Vouchsafe:** grant, consent.
213. **presently:** immediately. **Crosby Place:** Richard's house in
London.

For divers unknown reasons, I beseech you
Grant me this boon.°
    ANNE. With all my heart, and much it joys me too   220
To see you are become so penitent.
Tressel and Berkeley, go along with me.
    GLO. Bid me farewell.
    ANNE.   'Tis more than you deserve.
But since you teach me how to flatter you,
Imagine I have said farewell already.   225
    [*Exeunt* LADY ANNE, TRESSEL, *and* BERKELEY.]
    GLO. Sirs, take up the corse.
    GENT.   Toward Chertsey, noble lord?
    GLO. No, to Whitefriars.° There attend° my coming.   [*Exeunt all but* GLOUCESTER.]
Was ever woman in this humor° wooed?
Was ever woman in this humor won?
I'll have her, but I will not keep her long.   230
What! I, that killed her husband and his father,
To take her in her heart's extremest hate,
With curses in her mouth, tears in her eyes,
The bleeding witness of her hatred by° —
Having God, her conscience, and these bars° against me,   235
And I nothing to back my suit at all
But the plain Devil and dissembling looks,
And yet to win her, all the world to nothing!°
Ha!
Hath she forgot already that brave Prince,   240
Edward, her lord, whom I, some three months since,
Stabbed in my angry mood at Tewksbury?
A sweeter and a lovelier gentleman,
Framed in the prodigality of nature,°   244
Young, valiant, wise, and no doubt right royal,
The spacious world cannot again afford.°
And will she yet debase her eyes on me,
That cropped the golden prime of this sweet Prince
And made her widow to a woeful bed?
On me, whose all not equals Edward's moiety?°
On me, that halt and am unshapen thus?   251
My dukedom to a beggarly denier,°
I do mistake my person all this while.
Upon my life, she finds, although I cannot,
Myself to be a marvelous proper° man.   255
I'll be at charges for° a looking-glass,
And entertain some score or two of tailors,
To study fashions to adorn my body.
Since I am crept in favor with myself,
I will maintain it with some little cost.   260
But first I'll turn yon fellow in° his grave,

And then return lamenting to my love.
Shine out, fair sun, till I have bought a glass,
That I may see my shadow as I pass.   [*Exit.*]

SCENE III. *The palace.*

[*Enter* QUEEN ELIZABETH, LORD RIVERS, *and* LORD GREY.]
    RIV. Have patience, madam. There's no doubt His Majesty
Will soon recover his accustomed health.
    GREY. In that you brook it ill, it makes him worse.
Therefore, for God's sake, entertain good comfort,
And cheer His Grace with quick and merry words.
    Q. ELIZ. If he were dead, what would betide of° me?   6
    RIV. No other harm but loss of such a lord.
    Q. ELIZ. The loss of such a lord includes all harm.
    GREY. The Heavens have blessed you with a goodly son
To be your comforter when he is gone.   10
    Q. ELIZ. Oh, he is young, and his minority
Is put unto the trust of Richard Gloucester,
A man that loves not me, nor none of you.
    RIV. Is it concluded he shall be Protector?
    Q. ELIZ. It is determined, not concluded° yet.   15
But so it must be if the King miscarry.
    [*Enter* BUCKINGHAM *and* DERBY.]
    GREY. Here come the Lords of Buckingham and Derby.
    BUCK. Good time of day unto your royal Grace!
    DER. God make your Majesty joyful as you have been!
    Q. ELIZ. The Countess Richmond, good my Lord of Derby,   20
To your good prayers will scarcely say amen.
Yet, Derby, notwithstanding she's your wife,
And loves not me, be you, good lord, assured
I hate not you for her proud arrogance.
    DER. I do beseech you, either not believe   25
The envious slanders of her false accusers,
Or if she be accused in true report,
Bear with her weakness, which I think proceeds
From wayward° sickness, and no grounded malice.
    RIV. Saw you the King today, my Lord of Derby?
    DER. But now the Duke of Buckingham and I
Are come from visiting His Majesty.   32
    Q. ELIZ. What likelihood of his amendment, lords?
    BUCK. Madam, good hope. His Grace speaks cheerfully.
    Q. ELIZ. God grant him health! Did you confer with him?   35

---

219. boon: favor. 227. Whitefriars: a monastery in London. attend: await. 228. humor: mood. 234. witness . . . by: i.e., the corpse of her father-in-law. 235. bars: hindrances. 238. all . . . nothing: against all odds. 244. prodigality of nature: when nature was most generous. 246. afford: produce. 250. moiety: half. 252. denier: small copper coin. 255. proper: handsome. 256. be . . . for: buy. 261. turn . . . in: tip into.

Sc. iii: 6. betide of: become of. 15. determined . . . concluded: settled, but not formally ratified. 29. wayward: perverse.

BUCK. Madam, we did. He desires to make atonement°
Betwixt the Duke of Gloucester and your brothers,
And betwixt them and my Lord Chamberlain,°
And sent to warn° them to his royal presence.
Q. ELIZ. Would all were well! But that will never be.   40
I fear our happiness is at the highest.
[*Enter* GLOUCESTER, HASTINGS, *and* DORSET.]
GLO. They do me wrong, and I will not endure it.
Who are they that complain unto the King
That I, forsooth, am stern and love them not?
By holy Paul, they love His Grace but lightly   45
That fill his ears with such dissentious° rumors.
Because I cannot flatter and speak fair,
Smile in men's faces, smooth, deceive, and cog,°
Duck with French nods and apish courtesy,
I must be held a rancorous enemy.   50
Cannot a plain man live and think no harm
But thus his simple truth must be abused
By silken, sly, insinuating Jacks?°
  RIV. To whom in all this presence speaks your Grace?   54
GLO. To thee, that hast nor honesty nor grace.
When have I injured thee? When done thee wrong?
Or thee? Or thee? Or any of your faction?
A plague upon you all! His royal person —
Whom God preserve better than you would wish! —
Cannot be quiet scarce a breathing-while   60
But you must trouble him with lewd° complaints.
  Q. ELIZ. Brother of Gloucester, you mistake the matter.
The King, of his own royal disposition,
And not provoked by any suitor else —
Aiming, belike, at your interior hatred,   65
Which in your outward actions shows itself
Against my kindred, brothers, and myself —
Makes him to send, that thereby he may gather
The ground of your ill will, and to remove it.
  GLO. I cannot tell. The world is grown so bad   70
That wrens° make prey where eagles dare not perch.
Since every Jack became a gentleman,
There's many a gentle° person made a Jack.
  Q. ELIZ. Come, come, we know your meaning, Brother Gloucester —
You envy my advancement and my friends'.   75
God grant we never may have need of you!
  GLO. Meantime, God grants that we have need of you.
Our brother is imprisoned by your means,
Myself disgraced, and the nobility

Held in contempt, whilst many fair promotions   80
Are daily given to ennoble those
That scarce, some two days since, were worth a noble.°
  Q. ELIZ. By Him that raised me to this careful° height
From that contented hap° which I enjoyed,
I never did incense His Majesty   85
Against the Duke of Clarence, but have been
An earnest advocate to plead for him.
My lord, you do me shameful injury
Falsely to draw° me in these vile suspects.°
  GLO. You may deny that you were not the cause
Of my Lord Hastings' late imprisonment.   91
  RIV. She may, my lord, for ——
  GLO. She may, Lord Rivers! Why, who knows not so?
She may do more, sir, than denying that —
She may help you to many fair preferments,   95
And then deny her aiding hand therein,
And lay those honors on your high deserts.
What may she not? She may, yea, marry,° may she ——
  RIV. What, marry, may she?
  GLO. What, marry, may she! Marry with a king,
A bachelor, a handsome stripling too.   101
I wis° your grandam had a worser match.
  Q. ELIZ. My Lord of Gloucester, I have too long borne
Your blunt upbraidings and your bitter scoffs.
By Heaven, I will acquaint His Majesty   105
With those gross taunts I often have endured.
I had rather be a country servant maid
Than a great queen, with this condition,
To be thus taunted, scorned, and baited at.°
[*Enter* QUEEN MARGARET,° *behind*.] Small joy have I being England's Queen.   110
  Q. MAR. And lessened be that small, God, I beseech Thee!
Thy honor, state, and seat is due to me.
  GLO. What! Threat you me with telling of the King?
Tell him, and spare not. Look, what I have said
I will avouch in presence of the King.   115
I dare adventure to be sent to the Tower.
'Tis time to speak, my pains° are quite forgot.
  Q. MAR. Out, devil! I remember them too well.
Thou slewest my husband Henry in the Tower,
And Edward, my poor son, at Tewksbury.   120
  GLO. Ere you were Queen, yea, or your husband King,

36. atonement: reconciliation. 38. Lord Chamberlain: Hastings.
39. warn: summon. 46. dissentious: troublemaking. 48. cog:
cheat. 53. Jacks: knaves. 61. lewd: vile. 71. wrens: the
smallest of English birds. 73. gentle: of gentle blood.

82. noble: 6s. 8d. See App. 27. 83. careful: full of care.
84. hap: good fortune. 89. draw: involve. suspects: suspicion.
98. marry: Mary, by the Virgin. 102. I wis: certainly. 109. baited
at: harrassed. See App. 5. 110 s.d., Queen Margaret: the
widow of King Henry VI. Her appearance here is quite unhistorical. She is a symbolical figure, the doom of the House of
York. 117. pains: labors.

I was a pack horse in his great affairs,
A weeder out of his proud adversaries,
A liberal rewarder of his friends.
To royalize his blood I spilt mine own.   125
  Q. MAR. Yea, and much better blood than his or
    thine.
  GLO. In all which time you and your husband
    Grey
Were factious° for the House of Lancaster.
And, Rivers, so were you. Was not your husband
In Margaret's battle at St. Albans° slain?   130
Let me put in your minds, if you forget,
What you have been ere now, and what you are;
Withal, what I have been, and what I am.
  Q. MAR. A murderous villain, and so still thou art.
  GLO. Poor Clarence did forsake his father, War-
    wick —   135
Yea, and forswore himself — which Jesu pardon! —
  Q. MAR. Which God revenge!
  GLO. — To fight on Edward's party for the
    crown.
And for his meed,° poor lord, he is mewed up.
I would to God my heart were flint, like Edward's,
Or Edward's soft and pitiful, like mine.   141
I am too childish-foolish for this world.
  Q. MAR. Hie thee to Hell for shame, and leave the
    world,
Thou cacodemon!° There thy kingdom is.   144
  RIV. My Lord of Gloucester, in those busy days
Which here you urge° to prove us enemies,
We followed then our lord, our lawful King.
So should we you, if you should be our king.
  GLO. If I should be! I had rather be a peddler.
Far be it from my heart, the thought of it!   150
  Q. ELIZ. As little joy, my lord, as you suppose
You should enjoy, were you this country's King,
As little joy may you suppose in me,
That I enjoy, being the queen thereof.
  Q. MAR. A little joy enjoys the Queen thereof,
For I am she, and altogether joyless.   156
I can no longer hold me patient.   [Advancing.]
Hear me, you wrangling pirates, that fall out
In sharing that which you have pilled° from me!
Which of you trembles not that looks on me?   160
If not that, I being Queen, you bow like subjects,
Yet that, by you deposed, you quake like rebels?
O gentle villain, do not turn away!
  GLO. Foul wrinkled witch, what mak'st thou in
    my sight?
  Q. MAR. But repetition of what thou hast marred,
That will I make before I let thee go.   166
  GLO. Wert thou not banishèd on pain of death?
  Q. MAR. I was, but I do find more pain in banish-
    ment

Than death can yield me here by my abode.
A husband and a son thou ow'st to me,   170
And thou a kingdom, all of you allegiance.
The sorrow that I have by right is yours,
And all the pleasures you usurp are mine.
  GLO. The curse my noble father laid on thee
When thou didst crown his warlike brows with
    paper,   175
And with thy scorns drew'st rivers from his eyes,
And then, to dry them, gav'st the Duke a clout°
Steeped in the faultless blood of pretty Rutland —
His curses, then from bitterness of soul   179
Denounced against thee, are all fall'n upon thee,
And God, not we, hath plagued thy bloody deed.
  Q. ELIZ. So just is God, to right the innocent.
  HAST. Oh, 'twas the foulest deed to slay that babe,°
And the most merciless, that e'er was heard of!
  RIV. Tyrants themselves wept when it was re-
    ported.   185
  DOR. No man but prophesied revenge for it.
  BUCK. Northumberland, then present, wept to see
    it.
  Q. MAR. What! Were you snarling all before I
    came,
Ready to catch each other by the throat,
And turn you all your hatred now on me?   190
Did York's dread curse prevail so much with
    Heaven
That Henry's death, my lovely Edward's death,
Their kingdom's loss, my woeful banishment,
Could all but answer for that peevish brat?   194
Can curses pierce the clouds and enter Heaven?
Why then, give way, dull clouds, to my quick
    curses!
If not by war, by surfeit° die your King,
As ours by murder, to make him a king!
Edward thy son, which now is Prince of Wales,
For Edward my son, which was Prince of Wales,
Die in his youth by like untimely violence!   201
Thyself a Queen, for me that was a Queen,
Outlive thy glory, like my wretched self!
Long mayst thou live to wail thy children's loss,
And see another, as I see thee now,   205
Decked in thy rights, as thou art stalled° in
    mine!
Long die thy happy days before thy death,
And after many lengthened hours of grief,
Die neither mother, wife, nor England's Queen!
Rivers and Dorset, you were standers-by,   210
And so wast thou, Lord Hastings, when my son
Was stabbed with bloody daggers. God, I pray Him
That none of you may live your natural age,
But by some unlooked accident cut off!
  GLO. Have done thy charm,° thou hateful with-
    ered hag!   215

---

128. factious: active partisans.   130. Margaret's . . . St. Albans:
the second Battle of St. Albans, where Margaret defeated the
Yorkists in 1461.   139. meed: reward.   144. cacodemon: evil
devil.   146. urge: put forward.   159. pilled: pillaged.

177. clout: cloth.   183. that babe: young Rutland.   197. surfeit:
overindulgence.   206. stalled: installed.   215. charm: curse.

Q. MAR. And leave out thee? Stay, dog, for thou
shalt hear me.
If Heaven have any grievous plague in store
Exceeding those that I can wish upon thee,
Oh, let them keep it till thy sins be ripe,
And then hurl down their indignation   220
On thee, the troubler of the poor world's peace!
The worm of conscience still beknaw thy soul!
Thy friends suspect for traitors while thou livest,
And take deep traitors for thy dearest friends!
No sleep close up that deadly eye of thine,   225
Unless it be whilst some tormenting dream
Affrights thee with a Hell of ugly devils!
Thou elvish-marked,° abortive, rooting hog!°
Thou that wast sealed in thy nativity
The slave of nature and the son of Hell!°   230
Thou slander of thy mother's heavy womb!
Thou loathèd issue of thy father's loins!
Thou rag of honor! Thou detested ——
   GLO. Margaret.
   Q. MAR.   Richard!
   GLO.   Ha!°
   Q. MAR.   I call thee not.   234
   GLO. I cry thee mercy, then, for I had thought
That thou hadst called me all these bitter names.
   Q. MAR. Why, so I did, but looked for no reply.
Oh, let me make the period° to my curse!
   GLO. 'Tis done by me, and ends in " Margaret."
   Q. ELIZ. Thus have you breathed your curse
against yourself.   240
   Q. MAR. Poor painted° Queen, vain flourish° of
my fortune!
Why strew'st thou sugar on that bottled° spider
Whose deadly web ensnareth thee about?
Fool, fool! Thou whet'st a knife to kill thyself.
The time will come that thou shalt wish for me
To help thee curse that poisonous bunchbacked°
toad.   246
   HAST. False-boding° woman, end thy frantic
curse,
Lest to thy harm thou move our patience.
   Q. MAR. Foul shame upon you! You have all
moved mine.
   RIV. Were you well served, you would be taught
your duty.   250
   Q. MAR. To serve me well, you all should do me
duty,
Teach me to be your Queen, and you my subjects.
Oh, serve me well, and teach yourselves that duty!
   DOR. Dispute not with her, she is lunatic.

Q. MAR. Peace, Master Marquess, you are mala-
pert.°   255
Your fire-new° stamp of honor is scarce current.
Oh, that your young nobility could judge
What 'twere to lose it, and be miserable!
They that stand high have many blasts to shake
them,   259
And if they fall, they dash themselves to pieces.
   GLO. Good counsel, marry. Learn it, learn it,
Marquess.
   DOR. It toucheth you, my lord, as much as me.
   GLO. Yea, and much more. But I was born so
high,
Our aerie° buildeth in the cedar's top,
And dallies with the wind and scorns the sun.   265
   Q. MAR. And turns the sun to shade, alas! alas!
Witness my son, now in the shade of death,
Whose bright outshining beams thy cloudy wrath
Hath in eternal darkness folded up.
Your aerie buildeth in our aerie's nest.   270
O God, that seest it, do not suffer it.
As it was won with blood, lost be it so!
   BUCK. Have done! For shame, if not for charity.
   Q. MAR. Urge neither charity nor shame to me.
Uncharitably with me have you dealt,   275
And shamefully by you my hopes are butchered.
My charity is outrage, like my shame,
And in that shame still live my sorrow's rage!
   BUCK. Have done, have done.
   Q. MAR. O princely Buckingham, I'll kiss thy
hand,   280
In sign of league and amity with thee.
Now fair befall° thee and thy noble house!
Thy garments are not spotted with our blood,
Nor thou within the compass of my curse.   284
   BUCK. Nor no one here, for curses never pass
The lips of those that breathe them in the air.
   Q. MAR. I'll not believe but they ascend the sky,
And there awake God's gentle-sleeping peace.
O Buckingham, take heed of yonder dog!   289
Look, when he fawns, he bites, and when he bites,
His venom tooth will rankle° to the death.
Have not to do with him, beware of him,
Sin, death, and Hell have set their marks on him,
And all their ministers attend on him.
   GLO. What doth she say, my Lord of Bucking-
ham?   295
   BUCK. Nothing that I respect, my gracious lord.
   Q. MAR. What, dost thou scorn me for my gentle
counsel?
And soothe the devil that I warn thee from?
Oh, but remember this another day
When he shall split thy very heart with sorrow,
And say poor Margaret was a prophetess.   301

---

228. elvish-marked: marked at birth by evil fairies. **hog:**
Richard's badge was a wild boar. **229–30. sealed . . . Hell:** at
your birth nature marked you out as the slave of Hell by making
you deformed.   **234. Ha!:** i.e., you called me?   **238. period:**
end.   **241. painted:** imitation. **vain flourish:** queen merely in
show, as I was once.   **242. bottled:** shaped like a bottle. See
Pl. 20f. **246. bunch-backed:** hunchbacked. **247. False-boding:**
falsely prophesying.

255. malapert: impudent.   **256. fire-new:** newly minted.
264. aerie: the eagle's nest and brood. **282. fair befall:** good
luck come to. **291. rankle:** make fester.

Live each of you the subjects to his hate,
And he to yours, and all of you to God's! [*Exit.*]
    HAST. My hair doth stand on end to hear her
        curses.
    RIV. And so doth mine. I muse why she's at
        liberty.   305
    GLO. I cannot blame her. By God's holy Mother,
She hath had too much wrong, and I repent
My part thereof that I have done to her.
    Q. ELIZ. I never did her any, to my knowledge.
    GLO. But you have all the vantage of° her wrong.
I was too hot to do somebody good   311
That is too cold in thinking of it now.
Marry, as for Clarence, he is well repaid,
He is franked up° to fatting for his pains.
God pardon them that are the cause of it!   315
    RIV. A virtuous and a Christianlike conclusion,
To pray for them that have done scathe° to us.
    GLO. So do I ever — [*Aside*] being well advised.
For had I cursed now, I had cursed myself.
            [*Enter* CATESBY.]
    CAT. Madam, His Majesty doth call for you,   320
And for your Grace, and you, my noble lords.
    Q. ELIZ. Catesby, we come. Lords, will you go
        with us?
    RIV. Madam, we will attend your Grace.
            [*Exeunt all but* GLOUCESTER.]
    GLO. I do the wrong, and first begin to brawl.
The secret mischiefs that I set abroach°   325
I lay unto the grievous charge of others.
Clarence, whom I indeed have laid in darkness,
I do beweep to many simple gulls° —
Namely, to Hastings, Derby, Buckingham —
And say it is the Queen and her allies   330
That stir the King against the Duke my brother.
Now, they believe it, and withal whet me
To be revenged on Rivers, Vaughan, Grey.
But then I sigh, and with a piece of Scripture
Tell them that God bids us do good for evil.   335
And thus I clothe my naked villainy
With old odd ends stolen out of Holy Writ,
And seem a saint when most I play the devil.
[*Enter two* MURDERERS.] But, soft! Here come my
        executioners.
How now, my hardy stout resolvèd° mates!   340
Are you now going to dispatch this deed?
    1. MUR. We are, my lord, and come to have the
        warrant,
That we may be admitted where he is.
    GLO. Well thought upon — I have it here about
        me.   [*Gives the warrant.*]
When you have done, repair to Crosby Place.   345
But, sirs, be sudden in the execution,

Withal obdúrate° — do not hear him plead.
For Clarence is well spoken, and perhaps
May move your hearts to pity if you mark him.
    1. MUR. Tush!   350
Fear not, my lord, we will not stand to prate.
Talkers are no good doers. Be assured
We come to use our hands and not our tongues.
    GLO. Your eyes drop millstones when fools' eyes
        drop tears.
I like you, lads. About your business straight. 355
Go, go, dispatch.
    1. MUR. We will, my noble lord.   [*Exeunt.*]

SCENE IV. *London. The Tower.*

[*Enter* CLARENCE *and* BRAKENBURY.]
    BRAK. Why looks your Grace so heavily today?
    CLAR. Oh, I have passed a miserable night,
So full of ugly sights, of ghastly dreams,
That, as I am a Christian faithful man,
I would not spend another such a night   5
Though 'twere to buy a world of happy days,
So full of dismal terror was the time!
    BRAK. What was your dream? I long to hear you
        tell it.
    CLAR. Methought that I had broken from the
        Tower,
And was embarked to cross to Burgundy,   10
And in my company my brother Gloucester,
Who from my cabin tempted me to walk
Upon the hatches. Thence we looked toward Eng-
        land,
And cited up° a thousand fearful times
During the wars of York and Lancaster   15
That had befall'n us. As we paced along
Upon the giddy footing of the hatches,
Methought that Gloucester stumbled, and in falling
Struck me, that thought to stay° him, overboard,
Into the tumbling billows of the main.   20
Lord, Lord! Methought what pain it was to drown!
What dreadful noise of waters in mine ears!
What ugly sights of death within mine eyes!
Methought I saw a thousand fearful wrecks,
Ten thousand men that fishes gnawed upon,   25
Wedges of gold, great anchors, heaps of pearl,
Inestimable stones, unvalued jewels,
All scattered in the bottom of the sea.
Some lay in dead men's skulls, and in those holes
Where eyes did once inhabit there were crept,   30
As 'twere in scorn of eyes, reflecting gems,
Which wooed the slimy bottom of the deep
And mocked the dead bones that lay scattered by
    BRAK. Had you such leisure in the time of death

---

310. **vantage of:** advantages derived from.   314. **franked up:**
shut up. A frank is a sty for fattening hogs.   317. **scathe:** harm.
325. **set abroach:** set going; lit., tapped, like a cask.   328. **gulls:**
fools.   340. **resolved:** resolute.

347. **obdurate:** hardhearted.
    Sc. iv: 14. cited up: called to mind   **19. stay:** stop.

To gaze upon the secrets of the deep?   35
  CLAR. Methought I had, and often did I strive
To yield the ghost. But still the envious° flood
Kept in my soul, and would not let it forth
To seek the empty, vast, and wandering air,
But smothered it within my panting bulk,   40
Which almost burst to belch it in the sea.
  BRAK. Awaked you not with this sore agony?
  CLAR. Oh no, my dream was lengthened after
    life.
Oh, then began the tempest to my soul,
Who passed, methought, the melancholy flood,   45
With that grim ferryman° which poets write of,
Unto the kingdom of perpetual night.
The first that there did greet my stranger soul
Was my great father-in-law, renownèd Warwick,
Who cried aloud, "What scourge for perjury   50
Can this dark monarchy afford false Clarence?"
And so he vanished. Then came wandering by
A shadow like an angel, with bright hair
Dabbled in blood, and he squeaked out aloud,
"Clarence is come, false, fleeting, perjured Clar-
    ence,   55
That stabbed me in the field by Tewksbury.
Seize on him, Furies, take him to your torments!"
With that, methought a legion of foul fiends
Environed me about, and howlèd in mine ears
Such hideous cries that with the very noise   60
I trembling waked, and for a season after
Could not believe but that I was in Hell,
Such terrible impression made the dream.
  BRAK. No marvel, my lord, though it affrighted
    you.
I promise you, I am afraid to hear you tell it.   65
  CLAR. O Brakenbury, I have done those things,
Which now bear evidence against my soul,
For Edward's sake — and see how he requites me!
O God! If my deep prayers cannot appease Thee,
But Thou wilt be avenged on my misdeeds,   70
Yet execute Thy wrath in me alone.
Oh, spare my guiltless wife and my poor children!
I pray thee, gentle keeper, stay by me.
My soul is heavy, and I fain would sleep.
  BRAK. I will, my lord. God give your Grace good
    rest!   [CLARENCE sleeps.]   75
Sorrow breaks seasons and reposing hours,
Makes the night morning and the noontide night.
Princes have but their titles for their glories,
An outward honor for an inward toil.
And, for unfelt imagination,   80
They often feel a world of restless cares.°
So that, betwixt their titles and low names,
There's nothing differs but the outward fame.

[Enter the two MURDERERS.]
  1. MUR. Ho! Who's here?
  BRAK. In God's name, what are you, and how
came you hither?   85
  1. MUR. I would speak with Clarence, and I came
hither on my legs.
  BRAK. Yea, are you so brief?
  2. MUR. O sir, it is better to be brief than tedious.
Show him our commission.° Talk no more.   91
    [BRAKENBURY reads it.]
  BRAK. I am in this commanded to deliver
The noble Duke of Clarence to your hands.
I will not reason what is meant hereby,
Because I will be guiltless of the meaning.   95
Here are the keys, there sits the Duke asleep.
I'll to the King, and signify to him
That thus I have resigned my charge to you.
  1. MUR. Do so, it is a point of wisdom. Fare you
well.   [Exit BRAKENBURY.]   99
  2. MUR. What, shall we stab him as he sleeps?
  1. MUR. No. Then he will say 'twas done cow-
ardly, when he wakes.
  2. MUR. When he wakes! Why, fool, he shall
never wake till the Judgment Day.   106
  1. MUR. Why, then he will say we stabbed him
sleeping.
  2. MUR. The urging of that word "judgment"
hath bred a kind of remorse in me.   110
  1. MUR. What, art thou afraid?
  2. MUR. Not to kill him, having a warrant for
it, but to be damned for killing him, from which
no warrant can defend us.
  1. MUR. I thought thou hadst been resolute.   116
  2. MUR. So I am, to let him live.
  1. MUR. Back to the Duke of Gloucester — tell
    him so.
  2. MUR. I pray thee stay a while. I hope my holy
humor° will change. 'Twas wont to hold me but
while one would tell° twenty.   121
  1. MUR. How dost thou feel thyself now?
  2. MUR. Faith, some certain dregs of conscience
are yet within me.
  1. MUR. Remember our reward when the deed is
done.
  2. MUR. 'Zounds,° he dies. I had forgot the re-
ward.
  1. MUR. Where is thy conscience now?   130
  2. MUR. In the Duke of Gloucester's purse.
  1. MUR. So when he opens his purse to give us
our reward, thy conscience flies out.
  2. MUR. Let it go. There's few or none will en-
tertain it.   135
  1. MUR. How if it come to thee again?
  2. MUR. I'll not meddle with it. It is a dangerous
thing — it makes a man a coward. A man cannot

---

37. envious: malicious.   **46. grim ferryman:** Charon, who in
classical mythology ferried the souls of the dead across the river
Styx to the underworld.   **80–81. unfelt . . . cares:** they endure
restless cares for the sake of an unreal glory.

91. commission: written instructions.   **120. humor:** mood.
121. tell: count.   **129. 'Zounds:** by God's wounds.

steal but it accuseth him; he cannot swear but it
checks him; he cannot lie with his neighbor's   140
wife but it detects him. It is a blushing shamefast
spirit that mutinies in a man's bosom; it fills one
full of obstacles. It made me once restore a purse
of gold that I found; it beggars any man that keeps
it. It is turned out of all towns and cities for a   145
dangerous thing, and every man that means to live
well endeavors to trust to himself and to live with-
out it.

    1. MUR. 'Zounds, it is even now at my elbow,
persuading me not to kill the Duke.   150

    2. MUR. Take the devil in thy mind, and believe
him not. He would insinuate with° thee but to
make thee sigh.

    1. MUR. Tut, I am strong-framed, he cannot pre-
vail with me, I warrant thee.   155

    2. MUR. Spoke like a tall° fellow that respects
his reputation. Come, shall we to this gear?°

    1. MUR. Take him over the costard° with the
hilts of thy sword, and then we will chop° him in
the malmsey butt° in the next room.   161

    2. MUR. Oh, excellent device! Make a sop of him.

    1. MUR. Hark! He stirs. Shall I strike?

    2. MUR. No, first let's reason with him.   165

    CLAR. Where art thou, keeper? Give me a cup
of wine.

    2. MUR. You shall have wine enough, my lord,
anon.

    CLAR. In God's name, what art thou?

    2. MUR. A man, as you are.   170

    CLAR. But not, as I am, royal.

    2. MUR. Nor you, as we are, loyal.

    CLAR. Thy voice is thunder, but thy looks are
    humble.

    2. MUR. My voice is now the King's, my looks
    mine own.

    CLAR. How darkly and how deadly dost thou
    speak!   175
Your eyes do menace me. Why look you pale?
Who sent you hither? Wherefore do you come?

    BOTH. To, to, to ——

    CLAR. To murder me?

    BOTH. Aye, aye.   179

    CLAR. You scarcely have the hearts to tell me so,
And therefore cannot have the hearts to do it.
Wherein, my friends, have I offended you?

    1. MUR. Offended us you have not, but the King.

    CLAR. I shall be reconciled to him again.

    2. MUR. Never, my lord. Therefore prepare to
    die.   185

    CLAR. Are you called forth from out a world of
    men

To slay the innocent? What is my offense?
Where are the evidence that do accuse me?
What lawful quest° have given their verdict up
Unto the frowning judge? Or who pronounced
The bitter sentence of poor Clarence' death?   191
Before I be convíct by course of law,
To threaten me with death is most unlawful.
I charge you, as you hope to have redemption
By Christ's dear blood shed for our grievous sins,
That you depart and lay no hands on me.   196
The deed you undertake is damnable.

    1. MUR. What we will do, we do upon command.

    2. MUR. And he that hath commanded is the
    King.

    CLAR. Erroneous vassal!° The great King of
    Kings   200
Hath in the tables of His law commanded
That thou shalt do no murder. And wilt thou then
Spurn at His edict, and fulfill a man's?
Take heed, for He holds vengeance in His hands,
To hurl upon their heads that break His law.   205

    2. MUR. And that same vengeance doth He hurl
    on thee,
For false forswearing,° and for murder too.
Thou didst receive the holy sacrament,
To fight in quarrel of the House of Lancaster.

    1. MUR. And, like a traitor to the name of God,
Didst break that vow, and with thy treacherous
    blade   211
Unrip'dst the bowels of thy sovereign's son.

    2. MUR. Whom thou wert sworn to cherish and
    defend.

    1. MUR. How canst thou urge God's dreadful law
    to us
When thou hast broke it in so dear° degree?   215

    CLAR. Alas! For whose sake did I that ill deed?
For Edward, for my brother, for his sake.
Why, sirs,
He sends ye not to murder me for this,
For in this sin he is as deep as I.   220
If God will be revengèd for this deed,
Oh, know you yet, He doth it publicly.
Take not the quarrel from His powerful arm;
He needs no indirect nor lawless course
To cut off those that have offended Him.   225

    1. MUR. Who made thee then a bloody minister
When gallant-springing° brave Plantagenet,
That princely novice,° was struck dead by thee?

    CLAR. My brother's love, the Devil, and my rage.

    1. MUR. Thy brother's love, our duty, and thy
    fault   230
Provoke us hither now to slaughter thee.

    CLAR. Oh, if you love my brother, hate not me.
I am his brother, and I love him well.

---

152. insinuate with: worm his way into. 156. tall: fine. 157. gear:
job. 158. costard: lit., apple, "crack him on the nut." 160. chop:
clap, "chuck." 161. malmsey butt: barrel of malmsey, origi-
nally a Greek wine.

189. quest: jury. 200. vassal: slave. 207. forswearing: perjury.
215. dear: great. 227. gallant-springing: gallant and sprightly.
228. princely novice: young prince.

If you be hired for meed,° go back again,
And I will send you to my brother Gloucester,   235
Who shall reward you better for my life
Than Edward will for tidings of my death.

2. MUR. You are deceived. Your brother Glou-
cester hates you.

CLAR. Oh no, he loves me, and he holds me dear.
Go you to him from me.

BOTH.   Aye, so we will.   240

CLAR. Tell him, when that our princely father
York
Blessed his three sons with his victorious arm,
And charged us from his soul to love each other,
He little thought of this divided friendship.
Bid Gloucester think of this, and he will weep.   245

1. MUR. Aye, millstones, as he lessoned° us to
weep.

CLAR. Oh, do not slander him, for he is kind.°

1. MUR. Right,
As snow in harvest. Thou deceivest thyself.   249
'Tis he that sent us hither now to slaughter thee.

CLAR. It cannot be, for when I parted with him,
He hugged me in his arms and swore, with sobs,
That he would labor° my delivery.

2. MUR. Why, so he doth, now he delivers thee
From this world's thralldom to the joys of Heaven.

1. MUR. Make peace with God, for you must die,
my lord.   256

CLAR. Hast thou that holy feeling in thy soul
To counsel me to make my peace with God,
And art thou yet to thy own soul so blind
That thou wilt war with God by murdering me?
Ah, sirs, consider, he that set you on   261
To do this deed will hate you for the deed.

2. MUR. What shall we do?

CLAR.   Relent, and save your souls.

1. MUR. Relent! 'Tis cowardly and womanish.

CLAR. Not to relent is beastly, savage, devilish.
Which of you, if you were a prince's son,   266
Being pent° from liberty, as I am now,
If two such murderers as yourselves came to you,
Would not entreat for life?
My friend, I spy some pity in thy looks.   270
Oh, if thine eye be not a flatterer,
Come thou on my side, and entreat for me,
As you would beg were you in my distress.
A begging prince what beggar pities not?

2. MUR. Look behind you, my lord.   275

1. MUR. Take that, and that. If all this will not
do,   [Stabs him.]
I'll drown you in the malmsey butt within.
                     [Exit, with the body.]

2. MUR. A bloody deed, and desperately dis-
patched!
How fain, like Pilate, would I wash my hands

Of this most grievous guilty murder done!   280
           [Re-enter FIRST MURDERER.]

1. MUR. How now! What mean'st thou that thou
help'st me not?
By Heavens, the Duke shall know how slack thou
art!

2. MUR. I would he knew that I had saved his
brother!
Take thou the fee, and tell him what I say,
For I repent me that the Duke is slain.   285
                    [Exit.]

1. MUR. So do not I. Go, coward as thou art.
Now must I hide his body in some hole
Until the Duke take order for his burial.
And when I have my meed, I must away,
For this will out,° and here I must not stay.   290
                    [Exit.]

Act II

SCENE I. London. The palace.

[Flourish.° Enter KING EDWARD sick, QUEEN
ELIZABETH, DORSET, RIVERS, HASTINGS,
BUCKINGHAM, GREY, and others.]

K. EDW. Why, so. Now have I done a good day's
work.
You peers, continue this united league.
I every day expect an embassage
From my Redeemer to redeem me hence,
And now in peace my soul shall part to Heaven,   5
Since I have set my friends at peace on earth.
Rivers and Hastings, take each other's hand —
Dissemble° not your hatred, swear your love.

RIV. By Heaven, my heart is purged from grudg-
ing hate,
And with my hand I seal my true heart's love.   10

HAST. So thrive I as I truly swear the like!

K. EDW. Take heed you dally° not before your
King,
Lest He that is the supreme King of Kings
Confound your hidden falsehood, and award
Either of you to be the other's end.   15

HAST. So prosper I as I swear perfect love!

RIV. And I as I love Hastings with my heart!

K. EDW. Madam, yourself are not exempt in this,
Nor your son Dorset — Buckingham, nor you.
You have been factious° one against the other.   20
Wife, love Lord Hastings, let him kiss your hand,
And what you do, do it unfeignedly.

---

234. meed: reward.   246. lessoned: taught.   247. kind: nat-
urally affectionate.   253. labor: work for.   267. pent: shut up.

290. will out: will be revealed.
Act II, Sc. i: s.d., Flourish: trumpet call.   8. Dissemble:
falsely hide.   12. dally: trifle.   20. factious: plotting.

Q. ELIZ. Here, Hastings, I will never more re-
member
Our former hatred, so thrive I and mine!
    K EDW. Dorset, embrace him. Hastings, love
    Lord Marquess.   25
    DOR. This interchange of love I here protest
Upon my part shall be unviolable.
    HAST. And so swear I, my lord.   *[They embrace.]*
    K. EDW. Now, princely Buckingham, seal thou
    this league
With thy embracements to my wife's allies,   30
And make me happy in your unity.
    BUCK. *[To the* QUEEN*]* Whenever Buckingham
    doth turn his hate
On you or yours, but with all duteous love
Doth cherish you and yours, God punish me
With hate in those where I expect most love!   35
When I have most need to employ a friend,
And most assurèd that he is a friend,
Deep, hollow, treacherous, and full of guile
Be he unto me! This do I beg of God
When I am cold in zeal to you or yours.   40
                            [They embrace.]
    K. EDW. A pleasing cordial, princely Buckingham,
Is this thy vow unto my sickly heart.
There wanteth now our brother Gloucester here,
To make the perfect period of this peace.
    BUCK. And in good time here comes the noble
    Duke.   45
             [Enter GLOUCESTER.*]*
    GLO. Good morrow to my sovereign King and
    Queen,
And, princely peers, a happy time of day!
    K. EDW. Happy indeed, as we have spent the day.
Brother, we have done deeds of charity —
Made peace of enmity, fair love of hate,   50
Between these swelling wrong-incensèd peers.
    GLO. A blessed labor, my most sovereign liege.
Amongst this princely heap,° if any here,
By false intelligence, or wrong surmise,
Hold me a foe —   55
If I unwittingly, or in my rage,
Have aught committed that is hardly borne°
By any in this presence — I desire
To reconcile me to his friendly peace.
'Tis death to me to be at enmity,   60
I hate it, and desire all good men's love.
First, madam, I entreat true peace of you,
Which I will purchase with my duteous service.
Of you, my noble cousin Buckingham,
If ever any grudge were lodged between us;   65
Of you, Lord Rivers, and, Lord Grey, of you,
That all without desert have frowned on me —
Dukes, earls, lords, gentlemen, indeed of all.
I do not know that Englishman alive
With whom my soul is any jot at odds   70

More than the infant that is born tonight.
I thank my God for my humility.
    Q. ELIZ. A holy day shall this be kept hereafter.
I would to God all strifes were well compounded.°
My sovereign liege, I do beseech your Majesty   75
To take our brother Clarence·to your grace.
    GLO. Why, madam, have I offered love for this,
To be so flouted in this royal presence?
Who knows not that the noble Duke is dead?
                          [They all start.]
You do him injury to scorn his corse.   80
    RIV. Who knows not he is dead! Who knows he
    is?
    Q. ELIZ. All-seeing Heaven, what a world is this!
    BUCK. Look I so pale, Lord Dorset, as the rest?
    DOR. Aye, my good lord, and no one in this
    presence
But his red color hath forsook his cheeks.   85
    K. EDW. Is Clarence dead? The order was re-
versed.
    GLO. But he, poor soul, by your first order died,
And that a wingèd Mercury° did bear.
Some tardy cripple bore the countermand,
That came too lag to see him burièd.   90
God grant that some, less noble and less loyal,
Nearer in bloody thoughts but not in blood,
Deserve not worse than wretched Clarence did,
And yet go current° from suspicion!
                [Enter DERBY.*]*
    DER. A boon, my sovereign, for my service done!
    K. EDW. I pray thee, peace. My soul is full of
    sorrow.   96
    DER. I will not rise unless your Highness grant.
    K. EDW. Then speak at once what is it thou de-
mand'st.
    DER. The forfeit, sovereign, of my servant's life,°
Who slew today a riotous gentleman   100
Lately attendant on the Duke of Norfolk.
    K. EDW. Have I a tongue to doom my brother's
    death
And shall the same give pardon to a slave?
My brother slew no man. His fault was thought,
And yet his punishment was cruel death.   105
Who sued to me for him? Who, in my rage,
Kneeled at my feet and bade me be advised?
Who spake of brotherhood? Who spake of love?
Who told me how the poor soul did forsake
The mighty Warwick, and did fight for me?   110
Who told me, in the field by Tewksbury,
When Oxford had me down, he rescued me,
And said "Dear brother, live and be a king"?
Who told me, when we both lay in the field
Frozen almost to death, how he did lap me   115

53. heap: gathering.   57. hardly borne: regarded as hard-dealing.

74. compounded: made up.   88. winged Mercury: the messenger
of the gods, who wore winged sandals.   94. current: regarded as
true.   99. forfeit . . . life: the life of my servant forfeited to the
law.

Even in his own garments, and gave himself,
All thin and naked, to the numb cold night?
All this from my remembrance brutish wrath
Sinfully plucked, and not a man of you
Had so much grace to put it in my mind.   120
But when your carters or your waiting vassals
Have done a drunken slaughter, and defaced
The precious image of our dear Redeemer,
You straight are on your knees for pardon, pardon,
And I, unjustly too, must grant it you.   125
But for my brother not a man would speak,
Nor I, ungracious, speak unto myself
For him, poor soul. The proudest of you all
Have been beholding to him in his life,
Yet none of you would once plead for his life. 130
O God, I fear Thy justice will take hold
On me, and you, and mine, and yours for this!
Come, Hastings, help me to my closet.° Oh, poor
Clarence!   [Exeunt some with KING and QUEEN.]
    GLO. This is the fruit of rashness. Marked you
not
How that the guilty kindred of the Queen   135
Looked pale when they did hear of Clarence'
death?
Oh, they did urge it still°unto the King!
God will revenge it. But come, let us in,
To comfort Edward with our company.
    BUCK. We wait upon your Grace.   140
                                    [Exeunt.]

SCENE II. *The palace.*

[*Enter the* DUCHESS OF YORK, *with the two children
of* CLARENCE.]

    BOY. Tell me, good Grandam, is our father dead?
    DUCH. No, boy.
    BOY. Why do you wring your hands, and beat
your breast,
And cry "O Clarence, my unhappy son"?
    GIRL. Why do you look on us and shake your
head,
And call us wretches, orphans, castaways,   5
If that our noble father be alive?
    DUCH. My pretty cousins,° you mistake me much.
I do lament the sickness of the King,
As loathe to lose him — not your father's death.
It were lost sorrow to wail one that's lost.   11
    BOY. Then, Grandam, you conclude that he is
dead.
The King my uncle is to blame for this.
God will revenge it, Whom I will importune
With daily prayers all to that effect.   15

133. closet: private room.   137. still: continually.
    Sc. ii: 8. cousins: kinsmen. The word is used of any blood rela-
tion.

    GIRL. And so will I.
    DUCH. Peace, children, peace! The King doth love
you well.
Incapable° and shallow innocents,
You cannot guess who caused your father's death.
    BOY. Grandam, we can, for my good uncle Glou-
cester   20
Told me the King, provokèd by the Queen,
Devised impeachments° to imprison him.
And when my uncle told me so, he wept,
And hugged me in his arm, and kindly kissed my
cheek —
Bade me rely on him as on my father,   25
And he would love me dearly as his child.
    DUCH. Oh, that deceit should steal such gentle
shapes,
And with a virtuous vizard° hide foul guile!
He is my son — yea, and therein my shame —
Yet from my dugs he drew not this deceit.   30
    BOY. Think you my uncle did dissemble,
Grandam?
    DUCH. Aye, boy.
    BOY. I cannot think it. Hark! What noise is this?
[*Enter* QUEEN ELIZABETH, *with her hair about her
ears;* RIVERS *and* DORSET *after her.*]
    Q. ELIZ. Oh, who shall hinder me to wail and
weep,
To chide my fortune and torment myself?   35
I'll join with black despair against my soul,
And to myself become an enemy.
    DUCH. What means this scene of rude impatience?
    Q. ELIZ. To make an act° of tragic violence.
Edward, my lord, your son, our King, is dead.   40
Why grow the branches now the root is withered?
Why wither not the leaves, the sap being gone?
If you will live, lament; if die, be brief,
That our swift-wingèd souls may catch the King's,
Or, like obedient subjects, follow him   45
To his new kingdom of perpetual rest.
    DUCH. Ah, so much interest have I in thy sorrow
As I had title in thy noble husband!°
I have bewept a worthy husband's death,
And lived by looking on his images.°   50
But now two mirrors of his princely semblance°
Are cracked in pieces by malignant death,
And I for comfort have but one false glass,
Which grieves me when I see my shame in him.
Thou art a widow, yet thou art a mother,   55
And hast the comfort of thy children left thee.
But death hath snatched my husband from mine
arms,
And plucked two crutches from my feeble limbs,

18. Incapable: i.e., of understanding.   22. impeachments: accu-
sations.   28. vizard: mask.   39. act: The Queen continues the
metaphor from drama: "This is an act in a tragedy of violent
deeds."   48. As . . . husband: as I had a claim in your husband
(who was my son).   50. images: i.e. children like himself.
51. semblance: likeness.

Edward and Clarence. Oh, what cause have I,
Thine being but a moiety° of my grief,   60
To overgo° thy plaints and drown thy cries!
  BOY. Good Aunt, you wept not for our father's
    death.
How can we aid you with our kindred tears?
  GIRL. Our fatherless distress was left unmoaned,
Your widow dolor likewise be unwept!   65
  Q. ELIZ. Give me no help in lamentation,°
I am not barren to bring forth complaints.
All springs reduce° their currents to mine eyes,
That I, being governed by the watery moon,
May send forth plenteous tears to drown the world!
Oh, for my husband, for my dear lord Edward!   71
  CHILDREN. Oh, for our father, for our dear lord
    Clarence!
  DUCH. Alas for both, both mine, Edward and
    Clarence!
  Q. ELIZ. What stay° had I but Edward? And he's
    gone.
  CHILDREN. What stay had we but Clarence? And
    he's gone.   75
  DUCH. What stays had I but they? And they are
    gone.
  Q. ELIZ. Was never widow had so dear a loss.
  CHILDREN. Were never orphans had so dear a loss.
  DUCH. Was never mother had so dear a loss.
Alas, I am the mother of these moans!   80
Their woes are parceled,° mine are general.
She for an Edward weeps, and so do I.
I for a Clarence weep, so doth not she.
These babes for Clarence weep, and so do I.
I for an Edward weep, so do not they.   85
Alas, you three, on me threefold distressed
Pour all your tears! I am your sorrow's nurse,
And I will pamper it with lamentations.
  DOR. Comfort, dear Mother. God is much dis-
    pleased
That you take with unthankfulness His doing.   90
In common worldly things, 'tis called ungrateful
With dull unwillingness to repay a debt
Which with a bounteous hand was kindly lent,
Much more to be thus opposite with Heaven,
For it requires the royal debt it lent you.°   95
  RIV. Madam, bethink you, like a careful mother,
Of the young Prince your son. Send straight for
    him.
Let him be crowned, in him your comfort lives.
Drown desperate sorrow in dead Edward's grave,
And plant your joys in living Edward's throne.
[*Enter* GLOUCESTER, BUCKINGHAM, DERBY, HASTINGS,
    and RATCLIFF.]

  GLO. Madam, have comfort. All of us have cause
To wail the dimming of our shining star,   102
But none can cure their harms by wailing them.
Madam my mother, I do cry you mercy,
I did not see your Grace. Humbly on my knee   105
I crave your blessing.
  DUCH. God bless thee, and put meekness in thy
    mind,
Love, charity, obedience, and true duty!
  GLO. [*Aside*] Amen, and make me die a good
    old man!
That is the butt end of a mother's blessing.°   110
I marvel why her Grace did leave it out.
  BUCK. You cloudy princes and heart-sorrowing
    peers
That bear this mutual heavy load of moan,
Now cheer each other in each other's love.
Though we have spent° our harvest of this King,
We are to reap the harvest of his son.   116
The broken rancor of your high-swoln hearts,
But lately splintered, knit and joined together,
Must gently be preserved, cherished, and kept.
Meseemeth good° that, with some little train,° 120
Forthwith from Ludlow° the young Prince be
    fetched
Hither to London, to be crowned our King.
  RIV. Why with some little train, my Lord of
    Buckingham?
  BUCK. Marry, my lord, lest, by a multitude,
The new-healed wound of malice should break
    out.   125
Which would be so much the more dangerous
By how much the estate° is green° and yet ungov-
    erned.
Where every horse bears his commanding rein,
And may direct his course as please himself,
As well the fear of harm as harm apparent,   130
In my opinion, ought to be prevented.°
  GLO. I hope the King made peace with all of us,
And the compact is firm and true in me.
  RIV. And so in me. And so, I think, in all.
Yet, since it is but green, it should be put   135
To no apparent likelihood of breach,
Which haply° by much company might be urged.°
Therefore I say with noble Buckingham
That it is meet so few should fetch the Prince.
  HAST. And so say I.   140
  GLO. Then be it so, and go we to determine
Who they shall be that straight shall post° to
    Ludlow.
Madam, and you, my mother, will you go

---

60. moiety: share. 61. overgo: exceed. 66. Give . . . lamenta-
tion: i.e., I have sorrow enough of my own. 68. reduce: bring.
74. stay: support. 81. parceled: separate. 95. requires . . . you:
asks for the return of the King's life. It is a common idea in
Shakespeare's plays that life is a loan from God to be repaid
when He demands it.

110. butt . . . blessing: that is how a mother's blessing should
end. 115. spent: used up. 120. Meseemeth good: I think it good.
little train: few followers. 121. Ludlow: a castle in Shropshire,
and headquarters of the Lord President of Wales. 127. estate:
state. green: raw. 130–31. As . . . prevented: we should fore-
stall suspected as well as obvious danger. 137. haply: by chance.
urged: provoked. 142. post: go in haste. See App. 17.

To give your censures° in this weighty business?
Q. ELIZ. & DUCH. With all our hearts.   145
[*Exeunt all but* BUCKINGHAM *and* GLOUCESTER.]
BUCK. My lord, whoever journeys to the Prince,
For God's sake, let not us two be behind.
For by the way I'll sort occasion,°
As index to the story we late talked of,
To part the Queen's proud kindred from the King.°
GLO. My other self, my counsel's consistory,°   151
My oracle, my prophet! — My dear cousin,
I, like a child, will go by thy direction.
Toward Ludlow then, for we'll not stay behind.
                                        [*Exeunt.*]

SCENE III. *London. A street.*

[*Enter two* CITIZENS, *meeting.*]

1. CIT. Neighbor, well met. Whither away so
fast?
2. CIT. I promise you I scarcely know myself.
Hear you the news abroad?
1. CIT.   Aye, that the King is dead.
2. CIT. Bad news, by 'r Lady, seldom comes the
better.°
I fear, I fear, 'twill prove a troublous world.   5
[*Enter another* CITIZEN.]
3. CIT. Neighbors, Godspeed!
1. CIT.   Give you good morrow, sir.
3. CIT. Doth this news hold of good King Ed-
ward's death?
2. CIT. Aye, sir, it is too true, God help the
while!°
3. CIT. Then, masters, look to see a troublous
world.
1. CIT. No, no. By God's good grace his son shall
reign.   10
3. CIT. Woe to that land that's governed by a
child!
2. CIT. In him there is a hope of government,
That in his nonage Council under him,
And in his full and ripened years himself,
No doubt, shall then and till then govern well.°   15
1. CIT. So stood the state when Henry the Sixth
Was crowned in Paris but at nine months old.
3. CIT. Stood the state so? No, no, good friends,
God wot,°
For then this land was famously enriched
With politic° grave counsel. Then the King   20
Had virtuous uncles to protect His Grace.

---

144. censures: opinions.   148. sort occasion: find opportunity.
150. To . . . King: i.e., to separate the widowed Queen's family
from the new boy King.   151. consistory: council chamber.

Sc. iii: 4. seldom . . . better: a proverb, meaning "The new
king is usually worse than the old one."   8. God . . . while:
God help us now.   12-15. In . . . well: we may hope for good
government, for a Council will rule during his boyhood (*nonage*).
18. God wot: God knows.   20. politic: prudent.

1. CIT. Why, so hath this, both by the father and
mother.
3. CIT. Better it were they all came by the father,
Or by the father there were none at all,
For emulation° now, who shall be nearest,   25
Will touch us all too near if God prevent not.
Oh, full of danger is the Duke of Gloucester!
And the Queen's sons and brothers haught° and
proud.
And were they to be ruled, and not to rule,
This sickly land might solace° as before.   30
1. CIT. Come, come, we fear the worst. All shall
be well.
3. CIT. When clouds appear, wise men put on
their cloaks.
When great leaves fall, the winter is at hand.
When the sun sets, who doth not look for night?
Untimely storms make men expect a dearth.   35
All may be well, but if God sort° it so,
'Tis more than we deserve, or I expect.
2. CIT. Truly, the souls of men are full of dread.
Ye cannot reason° almost with a man
That looks not heavily and full of fear.   40
3. CIT. Before the times of change,° still is it so.
By a divine instinct men's minds mistrust°
Ensuing dangers, as, by proof, we see
The waters swell before a boisterous storm.
But leave it all to God. Whither away?   45
2. CIT. Marry, we were sent for to the Justices.
3. CIT. And so was I. I'll bear you company.
                                        [*Exeunt.*]

SCENE IV. *London. The palace.*

[*Enter the* ARCHBISHOP OF YORK, *the young* DUKE OF
YORK, QUEEN ELIZABETH, *and the* DUCHESS OF YORK.]

ARCH. Last night, I hear, they lay at Northampton,
At Stony-Stratford will they be tonight.
Tomorrow, or next day, they will be here.
DUCH. I long with all my heart to see the Prince.
I hope he is much grown since last I saw him.   5
Q. ELIZ. But I hear no. They say my son of York°
Hath almost overta'en him in his growth.
YORK. Aye, Mother, but I would not have it so.
DUCH. Why, my young cousin, it is good to grow.
YORK. Grandam, one night, as we did sit at
supper,
My uncle Rivers talked how I did grow   11
More than my brother. "Aye," quoth my uncle
Gloucester,
"Small herbs have grace, great weeds do grow
apace."

---

25. emulation: rivalry.   28. haught: haughty.   30. solace: be
happy.   36. sort: choose.   39. reason: talk.   41. change: rev-
olution.   42. mistrust: suspect.

Sc. iv: 6. my . . . York: her younger son.

And since, methinks I would not grow so fast,
Because sweet flowers are slow and weeds make
    haste.   15
  DUCH. Good faith, good faith, the saying did not
    hold
In him that did object° the same to thee.
He was the wretched'st thing when he was young,
So long a-growing and so leisurely   19
That, if this rule were true, he should be gracious.
  ARCH. Why, madam, so no doubt he is.
  DUCH. I hope so too, but yet let mothers doubt.
  YORK. Now, by my troth,° if I had been remem-
    bered,°
I could have given my uncle's Grace° a flout,°   24
To touch his growth nearer than he touched mine.
  DUCH. How, my pretty York? I pray thee, let me
    hear it.
  YORK. Marry, they say my uncle grew so fast
That he could gnaw a crust at two hours old.
'Twas full two years ere I could get a tooth.
Grandam, this would have been a biting jest.   30
  DUCH. I pray thee, pretty York, who told thee this?
  YORK. Grandam, his nurse.
  DUCH. His nurse! Why, she was dead ere thou
    wert born.
  YORK. If 'twere not she, I cannot tell who told me.
  Q. ELIZ. A parlous° boy. Go to, you are too
    shrewd.°   35
  ARCH. Good madam, be not angry with the child.
  Q. ELIZ. Pitchers have ears.

            [Enter a MESSENGER.]

  ARCH. Here comes a messenger. What news?
  MESS. Such news, my lord, as grieves me to un-
    fold.
  Q. ELIZ. How fares the Prince?
  MESS.   Well, madam, and in health.   40
  DUCH. What is thy news, then?
  MESS. Lord Rivers and Lord Grey are sent to
    Pomfret,
With them Sir Thomas Vaughan, prisoners.
  DUCH. Who hath committed them?
  MESS.   The mighty Dukes
Gloucester and Buckingham.
  Q. ELIZ.   For what offense?   45
  MESS. The sum of all I can I have disclosed.
Why or for what these nobles were committed
Is all unknown to me, my gracious lady.
  Q. ELIZ. Ay me,° I see the downfall of our house!
The tiger now hath seized the gentle hind.°   50
Insulting tyranny begins to jet
Upon° the innocent and aweless° throne.
Welcome, destruction, death, and massacre!

I see, as in a map, the end of all.
  DUCH. Accursèd and unquiet wrangling days,   55
How many of you have mine eyes beheld!
My husband lost his life to get the crown,
And often up and down my sons were tossed,
For me to joy and weep their gain and loss.
And being seated, and domestic broils   60
Clean overblown, themselves, the conquerors,
Make war upon themselves, blood against blood,
Self against self. O preposterous
And frantic outrage, end thy damnèd spleen,°
Or let me die, to look on death no more!   65
  Q. ELIZ. Come, come, my boy, we will to sanctu-
    ary.°
Madam, farewell.
  DUCH.   I'll go along with you.
  Q. ELIZ. You have no cause.
  ARCH.   My gracious lady, go,
And thither bear your treasure and your goods.
For my part, I'll resign unto your Grace   70
The seal° I keep. And so betide° to me
As well I tender° you and all of yours!
Come, I'll conduct you to the sanctuary.   [Exeunt.]

Act III

SCENE I. London. A street.

[The trumpets sound. Enter the young PRINCE, the
DUKES OF GLOUCESTER and BUCKINGHAM, CARDINAL
BOURCHIER, CATESBY, and others.]

  BUCK. Welcome, sweet Prince, to London, to your
    chamber.
  GLO. Welcome, dear Cousin, my thoughts' sov-
    ereign.°
The weary way hath made you melancholy.
  PRINCE. No, Uncle, but our crosses° on the way
Have made it tedious, wearisome, and heavy.   5
I want more uncles here to welcome me.
  GLO. Sweet Prince, the untainted virtue of your
    years
Hath not yet dived into the world's deceit.
Nor more can you distinguish of a man
Than of his outward show, which, God He knows,
Seldom or never jumpeth° with the heart.   11
Those uncles which you want° were dangerous;

---

64. spleen: hatred. 66. sanctuary: the protection of the Church,
which claimed the right to give a place of refuge from pursuers
to any who entered a church. 71. seal: the Great Seal, without
which the highest acts of state cannot be formally ratified. See
Pl. 11b. betide: befall me. 72. tender: care for.

  Act III, Sc. i: 2. thoughts' sovereign: king of my thoughts.
4. crosses: difficulties. 11. jumpeth: agrees. 12. want: lack.
Gloucester, as so often, uses the word with double meaning

---

17. object: apply.   23. troth: truth. remembered: reminded.
24. uncle's Grace: His Grace, my uncle. "Your Grace" is the
courtesy form of address to a Duke. flout: impudent reply.
35. parlous: "perilous," precocious. shrewd: bitter. 49. Ay me:
alas. 50. hind: female deer—a gentle creature. 51–52. jet
Upon: encroach upon. aweless: not provoking awe.

Your Grace attended to their sugared words,
But looked not on the poison of their hearts.
God keep you from them, and from such false
    friends!   15
PRINCE. God keep me from false friends! But they
    were none.
GLO. My lord, the Mayor of London comes to
    greet you.
    [*Enter the* LORD MAYOR *and his train.*]
MAY. God bless your Grace with health and
    happy days!
PRINCE. I thank you, good my lord, and thank
    you all.
I thought my mother and my brother York   20
Would long ere this have met us on the way.
Fie, what a slug is Hastings, that he comes not
To tell us whether they will come or no!
    [*Enter* LORD HASTINGS.]
BUCK. And in good time here comes the sweating
    lord.
PRINCE. Welcome, my lord. What, will our
    mother come?   25
HAST. On what occasion, God He knows, not I,
The Queen your mother and your brother York
Have taken sanctuary. The tender Prince
Would fain have come with me to meet your Grace,
But by his mother was perforce° withheld.   30
BUCK. Fie, what an indirect° and peevish course
Is this of hers! Lord Cardinal, will your Grace
Persuade the Queen to send the Duke of York
Unto his princely brother presently?°
If she deny, Lord Hastings, go with him,   35
And from her jealous arms pluck him perforce.
CARD. My Lord of Buckingham, if my weak
    oratory
Can from his mother win the Duke of York,
Anon expect him here; but if she be obdúrate
To mild entreaties, God in Heaven forbid   40
We should infringe the holy privilege
Of blessèd sanctuary! Not for all this land
Would I be guilty of so deep a sin.
BUCK. You are too senseless-obstinate,° my lord,
Too ceremonious° and traditional.   45
Weigh it but with the grossness of this age,
You break not sanctuary in seizing him.°
The benefit thereof is always granted
To those whose dealings have deserved the place,
And those who have the wit to claim the place.   50
This Prince hath neither claimed it nor deserved it,
And therefore, in mine opinion, cannot have it.
Then taking him from thence that is not there,
You break no privilege nor charter there.
Oft have I heard of sanctuary men,   55

But sanctuary children ne'er till now.
CARD. My lord, you shall o'errule my mind for
    once.
Come on, Lord Hastings, will you go with me?
HAST. I go, my lord.
PRINCE. Good lords, make all the speedy haste
    you may. [*Exeunt* CARDINAL *and* HASTINGS.] 60
Say, Uncle Gloucester, if our brother come,
Where shall we sojourn till our coronation?
GLO. Where it seems best unto your royal self.
If I may counsel you, some day or two
Your Highness shall repose you at the Tower.   65
Then where you please, and shall be thought most
    fit
For your best health and recreation.
PRINCE. I do not like the Tower, of any place.
Did Julius Caesar build that place,° my lord?
BUCK. He did, my gracious lord, begin that
    place,
Which since succeeding ages have re-edified.   71
PRINCE. Is it upon recórd, or else reported
Successively from age to age, he built it?
BUCK. Upon recórd, my gracious lord.
PRINCE. But say, my lord, it were not registered,°
Methinks the truth should live from age to age   76
As 'twere retailed to all posterity,
Even to the general all-ending day.
GLO. [*Aside*] So wise so young, they say, do
    never live long.
PRINCE. What say you, Uncle?   80
GLO. I say, without characters,° fame lives long.
[*Aside*] Thus, like the formal vice Iniquity,
I moralize two meanings in one word.°
PRINCE. That Julius Caesar was a famous man.
With what his valor did enrich his wit,   85
His wit set down to make his valor live.
Death makes no conquest of this conqueror,
For now he lives in fame, though not in life.
I'll tell you what, my cousin Buckingham ——
BUCK. What, my gracious lord?   90
PRINCE. An if° I live until I be a man,
I'll win our ancient right in France again,
Or die a soldier, as I lived a king.
GLO. [*Aside*] Short summers lightly have a for-
    ward spring.
[*Enter young* YORK, HASTINGS, *and the* CARDINAL.]
BUCK. Now, in good time, here comes the Duke
    of York.   95
PRINCE. Richard of York! How fares our loving
    brother?

---

30. perforce: forcibly. 31. indirect: wrong. 34. presently: at
once. 44. senseless-obstinate: foolishly particular. 45. cere-
monious: standing on ceremonies. 46–47. Weigh . . . him: when
you compare this deed with the general lack of morals in this
generation, it is no breach of sanctuary to seize him.

68–69. Tower . . . place: It was a general, but quite erroneous
belief, that the Tower was built by Julius Caesar. See Pl. 3a, and
Gen. Intro. p. 16a. 75. registered: formally recorded. 81. char-
acters: (1) writing, (2) good character. 82–83. the . . . word:
thus like the character of the vice Iniquity in a morality play, I
use the word (character) with two meanings. Richard means: (1)
fame lives with written record, (2) fame lives when the character
(i.e., the man himself) is dead. 91. An if: if.

YORK. Well, my dread lord° — so must I call you
now.
PRINCE. Aye, Brother, to our grief, as it is yours.
Too late° he died that might have kept that title
Which by his death hath lost much majesty.   100
GLO. How fares our cousin, noble Lord of York?
YORK. I thank you, gentle Uncle. Oh, my lord,
You said that idle weeds are fast in growth.
The Prince my brother hath outgrown me far.
GLO. He hath, my lord.
YORK.   And therefore is he idle?
GLO. Oh, my fair cousin, I must not say so.   106
YORK. Then he is more beholding to you than I.
GLO. He may command me as my sovereign,
But you have power in me as in a kinsman.
YORK. I pray you, Uncle, give me this dagger.
GLO. My dagger, little Cousin? With all my
heart.   111
PRINCE. A beggar, brother?
YORK. Of my kind uncle, that I know will give,
And being but a toy,° which is no grief to give.
GLO. A greater gift than that I'll give my cousin.
YORK. A greater gift! Oh, that's the sword to it.°
GLO. Aye, gentle Cousin, were it light enough.
YORK. Oh, then I see you will part but with light
gifts.   118
In weightier things you'll say a beggar nay.
GLO. It is too heavy for your Grace to wear.
YORK. I weigh° it lightly, were it heavier.   121
GLO. What, would you have my weapon, little
lord?
YORK. I would, that I might thank you as you
call me.
GLO. How?
YORK. Little.   125
PRINCE. My Lord of York will still be cross° in
talk.
Uncle, your Grace knows how to bear with him.
YORK. You mean to bear me, not to bear with
me.
Uncle, my brother mocks both you and me.
Because that I am little, like an ape,   130
He thinks that you should bear me on your shoul-
ders.°
BUCK. With what a sharp-provided wit he rea-
sons!
To mitigate° the scorn he gives his uncle,
He prettily and aptly taunts himself.
So cunning and so young is wonderful.   135
GLO. My lord, will 't please you pass along?

Myself and my good cousin Buckingham
Will to your mother, to entreat of her
To meet you at the Tower and welcome you.
YORK. What, will you go unto the Tower, my
lord?   140
PRINCE. My Lord Protector needs will have it so.
YORK. I shall not sleep in quiet at the Tower.
GLO. Why, what should you fear?
YORK. Marry, my uncle Clarence' angry ghost.
My grandam told me he was murdered there.   145
PRINCE. I fear no uncles dead.
GLO. Nor none that live, I hope.
PRINCE. An if they live, I hope I need not fear.
But come, my lord, and with a heavy heart,
Thinking on them, go I unto the Tower.   150
[A sennet.]

[Exeunt all but GLOUCESTER, BUCKINGHAM
and CATESBY.]

BUCK. Think you, my lord, this little prating
York
Was not incensèd° by his subtle mother
To taunt and scorn you thus opprobiously?
GLO. No doubt, no doubt. Oh, 'tis a parlous boy —
Bold, quick, ingenious, forward, capable.°   155
He is all the mother's, from the top to toe.
BUCK. Well, let them rest. Come hither, Catesby.
Thou art sworn as deeply to effect what we intend
As closely to conceal what we impart.
Thou know'st our reasons urged upon the way,
What think'st thou? Is it not an easy matter   161
To make William Lord Hastings of our mind,
For the installment° of this noble Duke
In the seat royal of this famous isle?
CATE. He for his father's sake so loves the Prince
That he will not be won to aught against him.   166
BUCK. What think'st thou, then, of Stanley?
What will he?
CATE. He will do all in all as Hastings doth.
BUCK. Well, then, no more but this. Go, gentle
Catesby,
And, as it were far off, sound thou Lord Hastings,
How he doth stand affected° to our purpose,   171
And summon him tomorrow to the Tower,
To sit about° the coronation.
If thou dost find him tractable to us,
Encourage him, and show him all our reasons.   175
If he be leaden, icy-cold, unwilling,
Be thou so too, and so break off your talk,
And give us notice of his inclination.
For we tomorrow hold divided councils,°
Wherein thyself shalt highly be employed.   180
GLO. Commend me to Lord William. Tell him,
Catesby,

---

97. my . . . lord: now that young Edward is King, his little
brother must treat him respectfully.   99. late: lately.   114. toy:
trifle.   116. to it: to match it.   121. weigh: regard.   126. cross:
perverse.   131. bear . . . shoulders: The domestic fool employed
in a great house sometimes carried an ape on his shoulder.
The boy implies that his uncle is a fool.   133. mitigate: i.e.,
by calling himself ape he "gets away" with calling his uncle
fool.

152. incensed: set on.   155. capable: intelligent.   163. install-
ment: enthroning.   171. affected: favorable.   173. sit about:
sit in council to discuss.   179. divided councils: separate councils.

His ancient knot° of dangerous adversaries
Tomorrow are let blood at Pomfret Castle.
And bid my friend, for joy of this good news,
Give Mistress Shore° one gentle kiss the more. 185

BUCK. Good Catesby, go, effect this business
soundly.

CATE. My good lords both, with all the heed I
may.

GLO. Shall we hear from you, Catesby, ere we
sleep?

CATE. You shall, my lord.

GLO. At Crosby Place, there shall you find us
both.   [Exit CATESBY.] 190

BUCK. Now, my lord, what shall we do if we
perceive Lord
Hastings will not yield to our complots?°

GLO. Chop off his head, man — somewhat we
will do.
And look, when I am King, claim thou of me
The Earldom of Hereford, and the movables° 195
Whereof the King my brother stood possessed.

BUCK. I'll claim that promise at your Grace's
hands.

GLO. And look to have it yielded with all willing-
ness.
Come, let us sup betimes, that afterward
We may digest° our complots in some form. 200
                                    [Exeunt.]

SCENE II. *Before* LORD HASTING'S *house.*

[*Enter a* MESSENGER.]

MESS. What ho! My lord!

HAST. [*Within*] Who knocks at the door?

MESS. A messenger from the Lord Stanley.

[*Enter* LORD HASTINGS.]

HAST. What is 't o'clock?

MESS. Upon the stroke of four.   5

HAST. Cannot thy master sleep these tedious
nights?

MESS. So it should seem by that I have to say.
First, he commends him to your noble lordship.

HAST. And then?

MESS. And then he sends you word   10
He dreamed tonight the boar° had razed his
helm.°
Besides, he says there are two councils held,
And that may be determined at the one
Which may make you and him to rue° at the
other.
Therefore he sends to know your lordship's
pleasure,   15

182. knot: company. 185. Mistress Shore: After the death of
Edward IV she had become Hastings' mistress. 192. complots:
plots. 195. movables: goods. 200. digest: arrange.
  Sc. ii: 11. boar: i.e., Gloucester, whose crest was a boar.
razed , , , helm: shorn off his helmet. 14. rue: be sorry.

If presently you will take horse with him,
And with all speed post with him toward the North,
To shun the danger that his soul divines.

HAST. Go, fellow, go, return unto thy lord.
Bid him not fear the separated councils.   20
His honor and myself are at the one,
And at the other is my servant Catesby,
Where nothing can proceed that toucheth us
Whereof I shall not have intelligence.
Tell him his fears are shallow, wanting instance.°
And for his dreams, I wonder he is so fond°   26
To trust the mockery of unquiet slumbers.
To fly the boar before the boar pursues
Were to incense the boar to follow us,
And make pursuit where he did mean no chase.   30
Go, bid thy master rise and come to me,
And we will both together to the Tower,
Where he shall see the boar will use us kindly.

MESS. My gracious lord, I'll tell him what you
say.   [*Exit.*]

[*Enter* CATESBY.]

CATE. Many good morrows to my noble lord!   35

HAST. Good morrow, Catesby. You are early
stirring.
What news, what news, in this our tottering state?

CATE. It is a reeling world indeed, my lord,
And I believe 'twill never stand upright
Till Richard wear the garland of the realm.   40

HAST. How! Wear the garland! Dost thou mean
the crown?

CATE. Aye, my good lord.

HAST. I'll have this crown of mine cut from my
shoulders
Ere I will see the crown so foul misplaced.
But canst thou guess that he doth aim at it?   45

CATE. Aye, on my life, and hopes to find you
forward
Upon his party for the gain thereof.
And thereupon he sends you this good news,
That this same very day your enemies,   49
The kindred of the Queen, must die at Pomfret.

HAST. Indeed I am no mourner for that news,
Because they have been still mine enemies.
But that I'll give my voice on Richard's side
To bar my master's heirs in true descent —
God knows I will not do it, to the death.°   55

CATE. God keep your lordship in that gracious°
mind!

HAST. But I shall laugh at this a twelvemonth
hence,
That they who brought me in my master's hate,
I live to look upon their tragedy.
I tell thee, Catesby ——   60

CATE. What, my lord?

HAST. Ere a fortnight make me elder,

25. instance: proof. 26. fond: foolish. 55. to . . . death: even
if I should die for it. 56. gracious: holy.

I'll send some packing that yet think not on it.

CATE. 'Tis a vile thing to die, my gracious lord,
When men are unprepared and look not for it. 65

HAST. Oh, monstrous, monstrous! And so falls it
 out
With Rivers, Vaughan, Grey. And so 'twill do
With some men else who think themselves as safe
As thou and I — who, as thou know'st, are dear
To princely Richard and to Buckingham. 70

CATE. The Princes both make high account of
 you —
[*Aside*] For they account his head upon the
 Bridge.°

HAST. I know they do, and I have well deserved
 it.

[*Enter* LORD STANLEY.] Come on, come on, where
 is your boar spear, man?
Fear you the boar and go so unprovided? 75

STAN. My lord, good morrow. Good morrow,
 Catesby.
You may jest on, but, by the holy rood,°
I do not like these several° councils, I.

HAST. My lord,
I hold my life as dear as you do yours, 80
And never in my life, I do protest,
Was it more precious to me than 'tis now.
Think you, but that I know our state secure,°
I would be so triumphant as I am?

STAN. The lords at Pomfret, when they rode from
 London, 85
Were jocund and supposed their state was sure,
And they indeed had no cause to mistrust;
But yet you see how soon the day o'ercast.
This sudden stab of rancor° I misdoubt.
Pray God, I say, I prove a needless coward! 90
What, shall we toward the Tower? The day is
 spent.

HAST. Come, come, have with you. Wot you
 what, my lord?
Today the lords you talk of are beheaded.

STAN. They, for their truth, might better wear
 their heads
Than some that have accused them wear their
 hats. 95
But come, my lord, let us away.

    [*Enter a* PURSUIVANT.°]

HAST. Go on before. I'll talk with this good
 fellow.   [*Exeunt* STANLEY *and* CATESBY.]
How now, sirrah! How goes the world with thee?

PURS. The better that your lordship please to ask.

HAST. I tell thee, man, 'tis better with me now
Than when I met thee last where now we meet.

Then was I going prisoner to the Tower, 102
By the suggestion of the Queen's allies;
But now, I tell thee — keep it to thyself —
This day those enemies are put to death, 105
And I in better state than e'er I was.

PURS. God hold it, to your Honor's good con-
 tent!

HAST. Gramercy, fellow. There, drink that for
 me.   [*Throws him his purse.*]

PURS. God save your lordship.   [*Exit.*]

    [*Enter a* PRIEST.]

PR. Well met, my lord. I am glad to see your
 Honor. 110

HAST. I thank thee, good Sir John,° with all my
 heart.
I am in your debt for your last exercise.°
Come the next Sabbath, and I will content you.

    [*He whispers in his ear.*]

    [*Enter* BUCKINGHAM]

BUCK. What, talking with a priest, Lord Cham-
 berlain?
Your friends at Pomfret, they do need the priest,
Your Honor hath no shriving° work in hand. 116

HAST. Good faith, and when I met this holy man,
Those men you talk of came into my mind.
What, go you toward the Tower?

BUCK. I do, my lord, but long I shall not stay.
I shall return before your lordship thence. 121

HAST. 'Tis like enough, for I stay dinner there.

BUCK. [*Aside*] And supper too, although thou
 know'st it not.
Come, will you go? 124

HAST. I'll wait upon your lordship. [*Exeunt.*]

SCENE III. *Pomfret° Castle.*

[*Enter* SIR RICHARD RATCLIFF, *with halberds,*°
carrying RIVERS, GREY, *and* VAUGHAN
to death.]

RAT. Come, bring forth the prisoners.

RIV. Sir Richard Ratcliff, let me tell thee this:
Today shalt thou behold a subject die
For truth, for duty, and for loyalty.

GREY. God keep the Prince from all the pack of
 you! 5
A knot you are of damnèd bloodsuckers.

VAUGH. You live that shall cry woe for this here-
 after.

RAT. Dispatch. The limit° of your lives is out.

RIV. O Pomfret, Pomfret! O thou bloody prison,
Fatal and ominous to noble peers! 10
Within the guilty closure of thy walls

---

72. account . . . Bridge: Traitors' heads were set up (over the
Bridge Gate) on London Bridge. See Pl. 3a. 77. rood: crucifix.
78. several: separate. 83. secure: Hastings means "safe," but
secure as often means "careless." 89. stab of rancor: premoni-
tion of hatred. 96. s.d., Pursuivant: officer attending on a
herald. See App. 9.

111. Sir John: the courtesy title of "Sir" was usually given
to priests; see *T Night*, IV.ii.20,n. 112. exercise: sermon.
116. shriving: confession and absolution.

 Sc. iii: Pomfret: also called Pontefract Castle. s.d., halberds:
See Pl. 21b. 8. limit: allotted time.

Richard the Second here was hacked to death;
And, for more slander to thy dismal seat,
We give thee up our guiltless blood to drink.

 GREY. Now Margaret's curse is fall'n upon our
  heads,   15
For standing by when Richard stabbed her son.

 RIV. Then cursed she Hastings, then cursed she
  Buckingham,
Then cursed she Richard. Oh, remember, God,
To hear her prayers for them, as now for us!
And for my sister and her princely sons, 20
Be satisfied, dear God, with our true blood,
Which, as thou know'st, unjustly must be spilt.

 RAT. Make haste. The hour of death is expiate.°

 RIV. Come, Grey, come, Vaughan, let us all em-
  brace,
And take our leave until we meet in Heaven. 25
            [Exeunt.]

SCENE IV. *The Tower of London.*

[Enter BUCKINGHAM, DERBY, HASTINGS, *the* BISHOP OF
ELY, RATCLIFF, LOVEL, *with others, and take their
seats at a table.]*

 HAST. My lords, at once,° the cause why we are
  met
Is to determine of the coronation.
In God's name, speak. When is the royal day?

 BUCK. Are all things fitting for that royal time?

 DER. It is, and wants but nomination.° 5

 ELY. Tomorrow, then, I judge a happy day.

 BUCK. Who knows the Lord Protector's mind
  herein?
Who is most inward with the noble Duke?

 ELY. Your Grace, we think, should soonest know
  his mind.

 BUCK. Who, I, my lord! We know each other's
  faces,   10
But for our hearts, he knows no more of mine
Than I of yours —
Nor I no more of his than you of mine.
Lord Hastings, you and he are near in love.

 HAST. I thank His Grace, I know he loves me
  well.   15
But for his purpose in the coronation
I have not sounded him, nor he delivered
His gracious pleasure any way therein.
But you, my noble lords, may name the time,
And in the Duke's behalf I'll give my voice, 20
Which I presume he'll take in gentle part.
       [Enter GLOUCESTER.]

 ELY. Now in good time here comes the Duke
  himself.

 GLO. My noble lords and cousins all, good
  morrow.
I have been long a sleeper, but I hope
My absence doth neglect no great designs 25
Which by my presence might have been concluded.

 BUCK. Had not you come upon your cue, my
  lord,
William Lord Hastings had pronounced your
  part —
I mean, your voice — for crowning of the King.

 GLO. Than my Lord Hastings no man might be
  bolder.   30
His lordship knows me well, and loves me well.

 HAST. I thank your Grace.

 GLO.   My Lord of Ely!

 ELY.   My lord?

 GLO. When I was last in Holborn,°
I saw good strawberries in your garden there.
I do beseech you send for some of them. 35

 ELY. Marry, and will, my lord, with all my heart.
           [Exit.]

 GLO. Cousin of Buckingham, a word with you.
       [Drawing him aside.]
Catesby hath sounded Hastings in our business,
And finds the testy gentleman so hot
As he will lose his head ere give consent 40
His master's son, as worshipful he terms it,
Shall lose the royalty of England's throne.

 BUCK. Withdraw you hence, my lord, I'll follow
  you. *[Exit* GLOUCESTER, BUCKINGHAM *following.]*

 DER. We have not yet set down this day of tri-
  umph.
Tomorrow, in mine opinion, is too sudden, 45
For I myself am not so well provided
As else I would be were the day prolonged.°
     [Re-enter BISHOP OF ELY.]

 ELY. Where is my Lord Protector? I have sent
for these strawberries.

 HAST. His Grace looks cheerfully and smooth
  today.   50
There's some conceit° or other likes° him well
When he doth bid good morrow with such a spirit.
I think there's never a man in Christendom
That can less hide his love or hate than he, 54
For by his face straight shall you know his heart.

 DER. What of his heart perceive you in his face
By any likelihood he showed today?

 HAST. Marry, that with no man here he is of-
  fended,
For, were he, he had shown it in his looks.

 DER. I pray God he be not, I say. 60
   [Re-enter GLOUCESTER *and* BUCKINGHAM.]

 GLO. I pray you all, tell me what they deserve
That do conspire my death with devilish plots

---

23. **expiate:** fully come.
 Sc. iv: 1. **at once:** in a word. 5. **nomination:** naming.

33. **Holborn:** district in London, where the Bishop of Ely had a palace. 47. **prolonged:** postponed. 51. **conceit:** fancy. **likes:** pleases.

Of damnèd witchcraft, and that have prevailed
Upon my body with their hellish charms?

HAST. The tender love I bear your Grace, my
    lord,   65
Makes me most forward in this noble presence
To doom the offenders, whatsoever they be.
I say, my lord, they have deservèd death.

GLO. Then be your eyes the witness of this ill.
See how I am bewitched. Behold, mine arm   70
Is like a blasted sapling, withered up.
And this is Edward's wife, that monstrous witch,
Consorted with that harlot strumpet Shore,
That by their witchcraft thus have markèd me.

HAST. If they have done this thing, my gracious
    lord——   75
GLO. If! Thou protector of this damnèd strumpet,
Tellest thou me of "if"? Thou art a traitor.
Off with his head! Now, by Saint Paul I swear,
I will not dine until I see the same.
Lovel and Ratcliff, look that it be done.   80
The rest that love me, rise and follow me.

   [Exeunt all but HASTINGS, RATCLIFF, and LOVEL.]

HAST. Woe, woe for England! Not a whit for me,
For I, too fond, might have prevented this.
Stanley did dream the boar did raze his helm,
But I disdained it, and did scorn to fly.   85
Three times today my foot-cloth horse° did stum-
    ble,
And startled when he looked upon the Tower,
As loath to bear me to the slaughterhouse.
Oh, now I want the priest that spake to me.
I now repent I told the pursuivant,   90
As 'twere triumphing at mine enemies,
How they at Pomfret bloodily were butchered
And I myself secure in grace and favor.
O Margaret, Margaret, now thy heavy curse
Is lighted on poor Hastings' wretched head!   95

RAT. Dispatch, my lord. The Duke would be at
    dinner.
Make a short shrift.° He longs to see your head.

HAST. O momentary grace of mortal men,
Which we more hunt for than the grace of God!
Who builds his hopes in air of your good looks   100
Lives like a drunken sailor on a mast,
Ready, with every nod, to tumble down
Into the fatal bowels of the deep.

LOV. Come, come, dispatch. 'Tis bootless° to ex-
    claim.

HAST. O bloody Richard! Miserable England!
I prophesy the fearfull'st time to thee   106
That ever wretched age hath looked upon.
Come, lead me to the block, bear him my head.
They smile at me that shortly shall be dead.
                        [Exeunt.]

SCENE V. *The Tower walls.*

[*Enter* GLOUCESTER *and* BUCKINGHAM, *in rotten
    armor, marvelous ill-favored.*]

GLO. Come, Cousin, canst thou quake, and change
    thy color,
Murder thy breath in middle of a word,
And then begin again, and stop again,
As if thou wert distraught and mad with terror?

BUCK. Tut, I can counterfeit the deep tragedian,°
Speak and look back, and pry on every side,   6
Tremble and start at wagging of a straw,
Intending° deep suspicion. Ghastly looks
Are at my service, like enforcèd smiles,
And both are ready in their offices°   10
At any time, to grace my stratagems.
But what, is Catesby gone?

GLO. He is, and see, he brings the Mayor along.
    [*Enter the* MAYOR *and* CATESBY.]

BUCK. Lord Mayor——

GLO. Look to the drawbridge there!   15

BUCK. Hark! A drum.

GLO. Catesby, o'erlook the walls.

BUCK. Lord Mayor, the reason we have sent——

GLO. Look back, defend thee — here are enemies.

BUCK. God and our innocency defend and guard
    us!   20

GLO. Be patient, they are friends, Ratcliff and
    Lovel.

[*Enter* LOVEL *and* RATCLIFF, *with* HASTINGS' *head.*]

LOV. Here is the head of that ignoble traitor,
The dangerous and unsuspected Hastings.

GLO. So dear I loved the man that I must weep.
I took him for the plainest harmless creature   25
That breathed upon this earth a Christian;
Made him my book, wherein my soul recorded
The history of all her secret thoughts.
So smooth he daubed° his vice with show of virtue
That, his apparent° open guilt omitted——   30
I mean, his conversation° with Shore's wife——
He lived from all attainder of suspéct.°

BUCK. Well, well, he was the covert'st sheltered°
    traitor
That ever lived.
Would you imagine, or almost believe,   35
Were 't not that, by great preservation,°
We live to tell it you, the subtle traitor
This day had plotted in the council house
To murder me and my good Lord of Gloucester?

MAY. What, had he so?   40

---

86. **foot-cloth horse:** horse draped with an ornamental cloth
which hung down to the ground on either side, used on cere-
monial occasions. 97. **shrift:** confession in preparation for death.
104. **bootless:** vain.

Sc. v: 5. **deep tragedian:** Shakespeare elsewhere criticizes
"ham" acting. See *Haml.* III.ii.1–40. 8. **Intending:** expressing.
10. **offices:** functions. 29. **daubed:** whitewashed. 30. **apparent:**
well-known. 31. **conversation:** intercourse. 32. **from . . . sus-
pect:** free from all suspicion of dishonor. 33. **covert'st sheltered:**
most secret and hidden. 36. **preservation:** divine protection.

GLO. What, think you we are Turks° or infidels?
Or that we would, against the form of law,
Proceed thus rashly to the villain's death
But that the extreme peril of the case,
The peace of England and our persons' safety,   45
Enforced us to this execution?

MAY. Now fair befall you! He deserved his death,
And you, my good lords both, have well proceeded,
To warn false traitors from the like attempts.
I never looked for better at his hands   50
After he once fell in with Mistress Shore.

GLO. Yet had not we determined he should die
Until your lordship came to see his death,
Which now the loving haste of these our friends,
Somewhat against our meaning, have prevented.°
Because, my lord, we would have had you heard
The traitor speak and timorously confess   57
The manner and the purpose of his treason,
That you might well have signified the same
Unto the citizens, who haply may   60
Miscónstrue° us in him and wail his death.

MAY. But, my good lord, your Grace's word shall
     serve
As well as I had seen and heard him speak.
And doubt you not, right noble Princes both,
But I'll acquaint our duteous citizens   65
With all your just proceedings in this cause.

GLO. And to that end we wished your lordship
     here,
To avoid the carping censures of the world.

BUCK. But since you come too late of our intents,
Yet witness what you hear we did intend.   70
And so, my good Lord Mayor, we bid farewell.
                                    [*Exit* MAYOR.]

GLO. Go, after, after, Cousin Buckingham.
The Mayor toward Guildhall hies° him in all post.
There, at your meet'st advantage° of the time,
Infer the bastardy° of Edward's children.   75
Tell them how Edward put to death a citizen
Only for saying he would make his son
Heir to the crown, meaning indeed his house,
Which, by the sign thereof, was termèd so.
Moreover, urge his hateful luxury°   80
And bestial appetite in change° of lust,
Which stretchèd to their servants, daughters, wives,
Even where his lustful eye or savage heart,
Without control, listed° to make his prey.
Nay, for a need, thus far come near my person.   85
Tell them, when that my mother went with child
Of that unsatiate Edward, noble York,
My princely father, then had wars in France;

And, by just computation of the time,
Found that the issue was not his begot,   90
Which well appearèd in his lineaments,
Being nothing like the noble Duke my father.
But touch this sparingly, as 'twere far off,
Because you know, my lord, my mother lives.

BUCK. Fear not, my lord, I'll play the orator   95
As if the golden fee° for which I plead
Were for myself. And so, my lord, adieu.

GLO. If you thrive well, bring them to Baynard's
     Castle,
Where you shall find me well accompanied   99
With reverend fathers and well-learnèd bishops.

BUCK. I go, and toward three or four o'clock
Look for the news that the Guildhall affords.
                                              [*Exit.*]

GLO. Go, Lovel, with all speed to Doctor Shaw.
[*To* CATESBY] Go thou to Friar Penker. Bid them
     both
Meet me within this hour at Baynard's Castle.   105
                        [*Exeunt all but* GLOUCESTER.]
Now will I in, to take some privy order
To draw the brats of Clarence out of sight,
And to give notice that no manner of person
At any time have recourse unto the Princes. [*Exit.*]

SCENE VI. *The same. A street.*

[*Enter a* SCRIVENER,° *with a paper in his hand.*]

SCRIV. This is the indictment° of the good Lord
     Hastings,
Which in a set hand fairly is engrossed,°
That it may be this day read o'er in Paul's.
And mark how well the sequel hangs together.
Eleven hours I spent to write it over,   5
For yesternight by Catesby was it brought me.
The precedent° was full as long a-doing.
And yet within these five hours lived Lord Hast-
     ings,
Untainted,° unexamined, free, at liberty.
Here's a good world the while! Why, who's so
     gross°   10
That seeth not this palpable device?°
Yet who's so blind but says he sees it not?
Bad is the world, and all will come to naught
When such bad dealing must be seen in thought.°
                                              [*Exit.*]

---

41. Turks: The Turks were regarded as the extreme example of
tyrannical cruelty. **55. prevented:** forestalled. **61. Misconstrue:**
misinterpret. **73. hies:** hastens. **74. meet'st advantage:** fittest
opportunity. **75. bastardy:** See III.vii.12. **80. luxury:** lust.
81. change: i.e., always seeking a new mistress. **84. listed:**
chose.

96. golden fee: crown.
Sc. vi: s.d., Scrivener: professional writer of legal documents.
1. indictment: formal condemnation. **2. engrossed:** written
out in legal form in a fair copy. **7. precedent:** rough copy.
9. Untainted: free from taint, unsuspected. **10. gross:** foolish.
11. palpable device: obvious plot; i.e., the condemnation was
prepared before the trial. **14. seen in thought:** kept quiet.

SCENE VII. *Baynard's Castle.*

[Enter GLOUCESTER *and* BUCKINGHAM, *at several°
doors.]*

GLO. How now, my lord, what say the citizens?

BUCK. Now, by the holy Mother of Our Lord,
The citizens are mum, and speak not a word.

GLO. Touched you the bastardy of Edward's
children?

BUCK. I did, with his contráct° with Lady Lucy,
And his contráct by deputy in France;   6
The insatiate greediness of his desires,
And his enforcement of the city wives;
His tyranny for trifles; his own bastardy,
As being got,° your father then in France, 10
And his resemblance, being not like the Duke.
Withal I did infer° your lineaments,°
Being the right idea° of your father,
Both in your form and nobleness of mind;
Laid open all your victories in Scotland; 15
Your discipline in war, wisdom in peace;
Your bounty, virtue, fair humility —
Indeed left nothing fitting for the purpose
Untouched or slightly handled in discourse.
And when mine oratory grew to an end, 20
I bid them that did love their country's good
Cry " God save Richard, England's royal King!"

GLO. Ah! And did they so?

BUCK. No, so God help me, they spake not a
word,
But, like dumb statuas° or breathing stones, 25
Gazed each on other, and looked deadly pale.
Which when I saw, I reprehended them,
And asked the Mayor what meant this willful si-
lence.
His answer was, the people were not wont
To be spoke to but by the Recorder.° 30
Then he was urged to tell my tale again —
" Thus saith the Duke, thus hath the Duke in-
ferred," —
But nothing spake in warrant from himself.°
When he had done, some followers of mine own
At the lower end of the hall hurled up their caps,
And some ten voices cried, " God save King
Richard! " 36
And thus I took the vantage° of those few —
" Thanks, gentle citizens and friends! " quoth I,
" This general applause and loving shout
Argues your wisdoms and your love to Richard " —
And even here brake off, and came away. 41

GLO. What tongueless blocks were they! Would
they not speak?

BUCK. No, by my troth, my lord.

GLO. Will not the Mayor, then, and his brethren
come?

BUCK. The Mayor is here at hand. Intend° some
fear. 45
Be not you spoke with but by mighty suit.°
And look you get a prayer book in your hand,
And stand betwixt two churchmen, good my lord,
For on that ground I'll build a holy descant.°
And be not easily won to our request. 50
Play the maid's part — still answer nay, and take it.

GLO. I go, and if you plead as well for them
As I can say nay to thee for myself,
No doubt we'll bring it to a happy issue.

BUCK. Go, go up to the leads.° The Lord Mayor
knocks. *[Exit* GLOUCESTER.] 55
[Enter the MAYOR *and* CITIZENS.]*
Welcome, my lord. I dance attendance here.
I think the Duke will not be spoke withal.
[Enter CATESBY.]*
Here comes his servant. How now, Catesby,
What says he?

CATE. My lord, he doth entreat your Grace
To visit him tomorrow or next day. 60
He is within, with two right reverend Fathers,
Divinely bent to meditation,
And in no worldly suit would he be moved
To draw him from his holy exercise.

BUCK. Return, good Catesby, to thy lord again.
Tell him myself, the Mayor, and citizens, 66
In deep designs and matters of great moment,
No less importing° than our general good,
Are come to have some conference with His Grace.

CATE. I'll tell him what you say, my lord. 70
[Exit.]

BUCK. Ah, ha, my lord, this Prince is not an
Edward!
He is not lolling on a lewd day bed,°
But on his knees at meditation;
Not dallying with a brace of courtesans,
But meditating with two deep divines; 75
Not sleeping, to engross° his idle body,
But praying, to enrich his watchful soul.
Happy were England would this gracious Prince
Take on himself the sovereignty thereof.
But sure, I fear we shall ne'er win him to it. 80

MAY. Marry, God forbid His Grace should say
us nay!

BUCK. I fear he will.
[Re-enter CATESBY.]*
How now, Catesby, what says your lord?

CATE.   My lord,
He wonders to what end you have assembled

Sc. vii: s.d., several: separate. 5. contract: betrothal.
10. got: begotten. 12. infer: remark upon. lineaments: features.
13. right idea: very image. 25. statuas: images. 30. Recorder:
the chief legal official of the City of London. 33. in . . . himself:
in his own authority. 37. vantage: advantage.

45. Intend: pretend. 46. mighty suit: urgent petition. 49. des-
cant: argument. See I.i.27,n. 55. leads: rooftop. 68. No . . .
importing: concerned with nothing less. 72. day bed: couch.
76. engross: make fat.

Such troops of citizens to speak with him,   85
His Grace not being warned thereof before.
My lord, he fears you mean no good to him.
  BUCK. Sorry I am my noble cousin should
Suspect me, that I mean no good to him.
By Heaven, I come in perfect love to him,   90
And so once more return and tell His Grace.
                                        [*Exit* CATESBY.]
When holy and devout religious men
Are at their beads, 'tis hard to draw them thence,
So sweet is zealous contemplation.

[*Enter* GLOUCESTER *aloft, between two* BISHOPS.
                     CATESBY *returns.*]

  MAY. See where he stands between two clergy-
men!   95
  BUCK. Two props of virtue for a Christian Prince,
To stay° him from the fall of vanity.
And see, a book of prayer in his hand,
True ornaments to know a holy man.
Famous Plantagenet, most gracious Prince,   100
Lend favorable ears to our request,
And pardon us the interruption
Of thy devotion and right Christian zeal.
  GLO. My lord, there needs no such apology.
I rather do beseech you pardon me,   105
Who, earnest in the service of my God,
Neglect the visitation of my friends.
But, leaving this, what is your Grace's pleasure?
  BUCK. Even that, I hope, which pleaseth God
    above,
And all good men of this ungoverned isle.   110
  GLO. I do suspect I have done some offense
That seems disgracious° in the city's eyes,
And that you come to reprehend my ignorance.
  BUCK. You have, my lord. Would it might please
    your Grace,
At our entreaties, to amend that fault!   115
  GLO. Else wherefore breathe I in a Christian land?
  BUCK. Then know it is your fault that you resign
The supreme seat, the throne majestical,
The sceptered office of your ancestors,
Your state of fortune and your due of birth,°   120
The lineal° glory of your royal house,
To the corruption of a blemished stock
Whilst, in the mildness of your sleepy thoughts,
Which here we waken to our country's good,
This noble isle doth want her proper limbs —   125
Her face defaced with scars of infamy,
Her royal stock graft with ignoble plants,
And almost shouldered° in the swallowing gulf°
Of blind forgetfulness and dark oblivion.
Which to recure, we heartily solicit   130
Your gracious self to take on you the charge

And kingly government of this your land;
Not as Protector, steward, substitute,
Or lowly factor° for another's gain,
But as successively,° from blood to blood,   135
Your right of birth, your empery,° your own.
For this, consorted° with the citizens,
Your very worshipful and loving friends,
And by their vehement instigation,
In this just suit come I to move your Grace.   140
  GLO. I know not whether to depart in silence
Or bitterly to speak in your reproof
Best fitteth my degree° or your condition.°
If not to answer, you might haply think
Tongue-tied ambition, not replying, yielded   145
To bear the golden yoke of sovereignty
Which fondly you would here impose on me.
If to reprove you for this suit of yours,
So seasoned° with your faithful love to me,
Then, on the other side, I checked° my friends.   150
Therefore, to speak and to avoid the first,   151
And then in speaking not to incur the last,
Definitively° thus I answer you.
Your love deserves my thanks, but my desert
Unmeritable° shuns your high request.   155
First, if all obstacles were cut away
And that my path were even° to the crown
As my ripe revenue and due by birth,
Yet so much is my poverty of spirit,
So mighty and so many my defects,   160
As I had rather hide me from my greatness —
Being a bark° to brook° no mighty sea —
Than in my greatness covet to be hid
And in the vapor of my glory smothered.
But, God be thankèd, there's no need of me,   165
And much I need to help you, if need were.
The royal tree hath left us royal fruit,
Which, mellowed by the stealing hours of time,
Will well become the seat of majesty,
And make, no doubt, us happy by his reign.   170
On him I lay what you would lay on me,
The right and fortune of his happy stars,
Which God defend° that I should wring° from
    him!
  BUCK. My lord, this argues conscience in your
    Grace,
But the respects° thereof are nice° and trivial,   175
All circumstances well considered.
You say that Edward is your brother's son.
So say we too, but not by Edward's wife.
For first he was contráct° to Lady Lucy —

97. **stay:** prevent.   112. **disgracious:** disgraceful.   120. **Your . . . birth:** the greatness which is yours through good fortune and right of birth.   121. **lineal:** by right of descent.   128. **shouldered:** pushed over. **gulf:** whirlpool.

134. **factor:** agent.   135. **successively:** by right of succession.   136. **empery:** empire.   137. **consorted:** associated.   143. **degree:** rank.   **condition:** social position.   149. **seasoned:** flavored.   150. **checked:** rebuked.   153. **Definitively:** definitely.   155. **Unmeritable:** unworthy.   157. **even:** level, direct.   162. **bark:** small ship.   **brook:** endure.   173. **defend:** forbid.   **wring:** wrest.   175. **respects:** considerations.   **nice:** unimportant.   179. **contract:** See Gen. Intro. p. 20a.

Your mother lives a witness to that vow —   180
And afterward by substitute betrothed
To Bona, sister to the King of France.
These both put by, a poor petitioner,
A care-crazed mother of a many children,
A beauty-waning and distressèd widow,   185
Even in the afternoon of her best days,
Made prize and purchase° of his lustful eye,
Seduced the pitch and height° of all his thoughts
To base declension° and loathed bigamy.
By her, in his unlawful bed, he got   190
This Edward, whom our manners term the Prince.
More bitterly could I expostulate°
Save that, for reverence to some alive,
I give a sparing limit to my tongue.
Then, good my lord, take to your royal self   195
This proffered benefit of dignity —
If not to bless us and the land withal,
Yet to draw forth° your noble ancestry
From the corruption of abusing times
Unto a lineal true-derivèd course.   200

MAY. Do, good my lord. Your citizens entreat
you.

BUCK. Refuse not, mighty lord, this proffered
love.

CATE. Oh, make them joyful, grant their lawful
suit!

GLO. Alas, why would you heap these cares on
me?
I am unfit for state and majesty.   205
I do beseech you, take it not amiss —
I cannot nor I will not yield to you.

BUCK. If you refuse it — as, in love and zeal,
Loath to depose the child, your brother's son,
As well we know your tenderness of heart   210
And gentle, kind, effeminate remorse,°
Which we have noted in you to your kin,
And egally° indeed to all estates —
Yet whether you accept our suit or no,
Your brother's son shall never reign our King, 215
But we will plant some other in the throne,
To the disgrace and downfall of your house.
And in this resolution here we leave you.
Come, citizens. 'Zounds! I'll entreat no more. 219

GLO. Oh, do not swear, my Lord of Buckingham.

[Exit BUCKINGHAM with the CITIZENS.]

CATE. Call them again, my lord, and accept their
suit.

ANOTHER. Do, good my lord, lest all the land do
rue° it.

GLO. Would you enforce me to a world of care?
Well, call them again. I am not made of stones,

But penetrable to your kind entreats,°   225
Albeit against my conscience and my soul.

[Re-enter BUCKINGHAM and the rest.] Cousin of
Buckingham, and you sage, grave men,
Since you will buckle fortune on my back
To bear her burden whether I will or no,
I must have patience to endure the load.   230
But if black scandal or foul-faced reproach
Attend the sequel of your imposition,
Your mere enforcement shall acquittance° me
From all the impure blots and stains thereof;
For God He knows, and you may partly see,   235
How far I am from the desire thereof.

MAY. God bless your Grace! We see it, and
will say it.

GLO. In saying so, you shall but say the truth.

BUCK. Then I salute you with this kingly title —
Long live Richard, England's royal King!   240

MAY. & CITS. Amen.

BUCK. Tomorrow will it please you to be
crowned?

GLO. Even when you please, since you will have
it so.

BUCK. Tomorrow, then, we will attend your
Grace.
And so most joyfully we take our leave.   245

GLO. Come, let us to our holy task again.
Farewell, good Cousin. Farewell, gentle friends.

[Exeunt.]

Act IV

SCENE I. *Before the Tower.*

[*Enter, on one side,* QUEEN ELIZABETH, DUCHESS OF
YORK, *and* MARQUESS OF DORSET; *on the other,* ANNE,
DUCHESS OF GLOUCESTER, *leading* LADY MARGARET
PLANTAGENET, CLARENCE's *young daughter.*]

DUCH. Who meets us here? My niece Plantagenet
Led in the hand of her kind aunt of Gloucester?
Now, for my life, she's wandering to the Tower,
On pure heart's love to greet the tender Princes.
Daughter, well met.

ANNE.   God give your Graces both   5
A happy and a joyful time of day!

Q. ELIZ. As much to you, good Sister! Whither
away?

ANNE. No farther than the Tower, and, as I
guess,
Upon the like devotion as yourselves,

---

187. purchase: in thieves' language, booty. 188. pitch . . .
height: high flight, a metaphor from the flight of the hawk.
See App. 26. 189. declension: lowering. 192. expostulate:
argue. 198. draw forth: restore. 211. effeminate remorse:
womanly pity. 213. egally: equally. 222. rue: regret.

225. entreats: entreaties. 233. acquittance: acquit.

To gratulate° the gentle Princes there.   10
   Q. ELIZ. Kind Sister, thanks. We'll enter all together.
[*Enter* BRAKENBURY.] And in good time here the Lieutenant comes.
Master Lieutenant, pray you, by your leave,
How doth the Prince, and my young son of York?
   BRAK. Right well, dear madam. By your patience,
I may not suffer you to visit them.   16
The King hath straitly charged the contrary.
   Q. ELIZ. The King! Why, who's that?
   BRAK. I cry you mercy. I mean the Lord Protector.
   Q. ELIZ. The Lord protect him from that kingly title!   20
Hath he set bounds betwixt their love and me?
I am their mother. Who should keep me from them?
   DUCH. I am their father's mother. I will see them.
   ANNE. Their aunt I am in law, in love their mother.
Then bring me to their sights. I'll bear thy blame,
And take thy office from thee,° on my peril.°   26
   BRAK. No, madam, no, I may not leave it so.
I am bound by oath, and therefore pardon me.
                        [*Exit.*]
     [*Enter* LORD STANLEY.]
   STAN. Let me but meet you, ladies, one hour hence,
And I'll salute your Grace of York as mother,   30
And reverend looker-on, of two fair Queens.
[*To* ANNE] Come, madam, you must straight to Westminster,
There to be crownèd Richard's royal Queen.
   Q. ELIZ. Oh, cut my lace° in sunder, that my pent heart
May have some scope to beat, or else I swoon   35
With this dead-killing news!
   ANNE. Despiteful° tidings! Oh, unpleasing news!
   DOR. Be of good cheer. Mother, how fares your Grace?
   Q. ELIZ. O Dorset, speak not to me, get thee hence!
Death and destruction dog thee at the heels.   40
Thy mother's name is ominous to children.
If thou wilt outstrip death, go cross the seas,
And live with Richmond, from° the reach of Hell.
Go, hie thee, hie thee from this slaughterhouse,
Lest thou increase the number of the dead,   45
And make me die the thrall° of Margaret's curse,
Nor mother, wife, nor England's counted Queen.

   STAN. Full of wise care is this your counsel, madam.
Take all the swift advantage of the hours.
You shall have letters from me to my son   50
To meet you on the way, and welcome you.
Be not ta'en tardy° by unwise delay.
   DUCH. Oh, ill-dispersing wind of misery!
O my accursèd womb, the bed of death,
A cockatrice° hast thou hatched to the world,   55
Whose unavoided° eye is murderous!
   STAN. Come, madam, come. I in all haste was sent.
   ANNE. And I in all unwillingness will go.
I would to God that the inclusive verge°
Of golden metal that must round my brow   60
Were red-hot steel, to sear me to the brain!
Anointed let me be with deadly venom,
And die ere men can say God save the Queen!
   Q. ELIZ. Go, go, poor soul, I envy not thy glory.
To feed my humor,° wish thyself no harm.   65
   ANNE. No! Why? When he that is my husband now
Came to me as I followed Henry's corse,
When scarce the blood was well washed from his hands
Which issued from my other angel husband,
And that dead saint which then I weeping followed —
Oh, when, I say, I looked on Richard's face,   71
This was my wish: "Be thou," quoth I, "accursed,
For making me, so young, so old a widow!
And when thou wed'st, let sorrow haunt thy bed,
And be thy wife — if any be so mad —   75
As miserable by the life of thee
As thou hast made me by my dear lord's death!"
Lo, ere I can repeat this curse again,
Even in so short a space, my woman's heart
Grossly grew captive to his honey words,   80
And proved the subject of my own soul's curse,
Which ever since hath kept my eyes from rest.
For never yet one hour in his bed
Have I enjoyed the golden dew of sleep,
But have been wakèd by his timorous dreams.   85
Besides, he hates me for my father Warwick,
And will, no doubt, shortly be rid of me.
   Q. ELIZ. Poor heart, adieu! I pity thy complaining.
   ANNE. No more than from my soul I mourn for yours.
   DOR. Farewell, thou woeful welcomer of glory!
   ANNE. Adieu, pour soul, that takest thy leave of it!   91
   DUCH. [*To* DORSET] Go thou to Richmond, and good fortune guide thee!

Act IV, Sc. i: 10. gratulate: salute. 26. take . . . thee: relieve you of your duty. on my peril: a legal phrase meaning "I will pay all penalties." 34. cut my lace: In Shakespeare's time ladies controlled their figures by tightly lacing themselves within busks or corsets made of whalebone, wood, or even iron. At moments of high emotion drastic relief was sometimes necessary. 37. Despiteful: cruel. 43. from: out of. 46. thrall: slave.

52. ta'en tardy: taken because you are too late. 55. cockatrice: basilisk. See I.ii.151,n. 56. unavoided: if not avoided. 59. inclusive verge: enclosing circle; i.e., the crown. 65. To . . . humor: to satisfy my mood.

[*To* ANNE] Go thou to Richard, and good angels
  guard thee!
[*To* QUEEN ELIZABETH] Go thou to sanctuary, and
  good thoughts possess thee!
I to my grave, where peace and rest lie with me!
Eighty odd years of sorrow have I seen,   96
And each hour's joy wrecked with a week of teen.°
  Q. ELIZ. Stay, yet look back with me unto the
   Tower.
Pity, you ancient stones, those tender babes
Whom envy hath immured° within your walls!
Rough cradle for such little pretty ones!   101
Rude ragged nurse, old sullen playfellow
For tender Princes, use my babies well!
So foolish sorrow bids your stones farewell.
                       [*Exeunt.*]

SCENE II. *London. The palace.*

[*Sennet.*° *Enter* RICHARD, *in pomp, crowned;*
  BUCKINGHAM, CATESBY, A PAGE, *and others.*]

K. RICH. Stand all apart. Cousin of Buckingham!
BUCK. My gracious sovereign?
K. RICH. Give me thy hand. [*Here he ascendeth
  the throne.*]   Thus high, by thy advice
And thy assistance, is King Richard seated.
But shall we wear these honors for a day?   5
Or shall they last, and we rejoice in them?
  BUCK. Still live they, and forever may they last!
  K. RICH. O Buckingham, now do I play the
   touch,°
To try if thou be current gold indeed.   9
Young Edward lives. Think now what I would say.
  BUCK. Say on, my loving lord.
  K. RICH. Why, Buckingham, I say I would be
   King.
  BUCK. Why, so you are, my thrice-renownèd
   liege.
  K. RICH. Ha! Am I King? 'Tis so, but Edward
   lives.   14
  BUCK. True, noble Prince.
  K. RICH.   Oh, bitter consequence,
That Edward still should live true noble Prince!°

Cousin, thou wert not wont to be so dull.
Shall I be plain? I wish the bastards dead,
And I would have it suddenly performed.
What sayest thou? Speak suddenly, be brief.   20
  BUCK. Your Grace may do your pleasure.
  K. RICH. Tut, tut, thou art all ice, thy kindness
   freezeth.
Say, have I thy consent that they shall die?
  BUCK. Give me some breath, some little pause,
   my lord,
Before I positively speak herein.   25
I will resolve° your Grace immediately.   [*Exit.*]
  CATE. [*Aside to a stander-by*] The King is angry,
   See, he bites the lip.
  K. RICH. I will converse with iron-witted fools
And unrespective° boys. None are for me
That look into me with considerate° eyes.   30
High-reaching Buckingham grows circumspect.
Boy!
  PAGE. My lord?
  K. RICH. Know'st thou not any whom corrupting
   gold
Would tempt unto a close exploit° of death?   35
  PAGE. My lord, I know a discontented gentleman
Whose humble means match not his haughty mind.
Gold were as good as twenty orators,
And will, no doubt, tempt him to anything.
  K. RICH. What is his name?
  PAGE.   His name, my lord, is Tyrrel.   40
  K. RICH. I partly know the man. Go, call him
   hither.   [*Exit* PAGE.]
The deep-revolving witty Buckingham
No more shall be the neighbor to my counsel.
Hath he so long held out° with me untired,
And stops he now for breath?   45
[*Enter* STANLEY] How now! What news with you?
  STAN. My lord, I hear the Marquis Dorset's fled
To Richmond, in those parts beyond the seas
Where he abides.   [*Stands apart.*]   49
  K. RICH. Catesby!
  CATE. My lord?
  K. RICH. Rumor it abroad
That Anne, my wife, is sick and like to die.
I will take order for her keeping close.
Inquire me out some mean-born gentleman,
Whom I will marry straight to Clarence' daughter.
The boy is foolish, and I fear not him.   56
Look how thou dream'st!° I say again, give out
That Anne my wife is sick, and like to die.
About it, for it stands me much upon°
To stop all hopes whose growth may damage me.
                   [*Exit* CATESBY.]
I must be married to my brother's daughter,   61

---

97. **each . . . teen:** for every hour of joy I have endured a week
of grief (*teen*).   100. **immured:** walled in.
  Sc. ii: s.d., **Sennet:** trumpet call denoting the approach of a
procession.   8. **play . . . touch:** i.e., play the touchstone. A
touchstone was used by jewelers to ascertain the quality of a
piece of gold. The gold to be tested was rubbed on a stone. An-
other piece of gold of known quality was also rubbed on the
stone. Acid was then applied to both rubbings and the results
were compared.   15–16. **Oh . . . Prince:** This elaborate word
play is typical of Shakespeare's earlier style. At line 10 Rich-
ard says, "Young Edward lives," expecting Buckingham to
reply, "But not for long." Buckingham does not give the re-
quired answer. Richard repeats, "Edward lives." Buckingham
replies, "True, noble Prince." Richard retorts in effect, "That
is not the answer I expected. Now you are calling my rival a
true noble Prince."

26. **resolve:** give a definite answer to.   29. **unrespective:** un-
observant.   30. **considerate:** understanding.   35. **close exploit:**
secret deed.   44. **held out:** kept up.   57. **Look . . . dream'st:** i.e.,
do not betray me in your sleep.   59. **stands . . . upon:** greatly
concerns me.

Or else my kingdom stands on brittle glass.
Murder her brothers, and then marry her!
Uncertain way of gain! But I am in
So far in blood that sin will pluck on sin.   65
Tear-falling pity dwells not in this eye.
[*Re-enter* PAGE, *with* TYRREL.] Is thy name Tyrrel?
   TYR. James Tyrrel, and your most obedient sub-
     ject.
   K. RICH. Art thou, indeed?
   TYR.   Prove me, my gracious sovereign.
   K. RICH. Dar'st thou resolve to kill a friend of
     mine?   70
   TYR. Aye, my lord,
But I had rather kill two enemies.
   K. RICH. Why, there thou hast it. Two deep ene-
     mies,
Foes to my rest and my sweet sleep's disturbers,
Are they that I would have thee deal upon.   75
Tyrrel, I mean those bastards in the Tower.
   TYR. Let me have open means to come to them,
And soon I'll rid you from the fear of them.
   K. RICH. Thou sing'st sweet music. Hark, come
     hither, Tyrrel.
Go, by this token. Rise, and lend thine ear.   80
                 [*Whispers.*]
There is no more but so. Say it is done,
And I will love thee, and prefer° thee too.
   TYR. 'Tis done, my gracious lord.
   K. RICH. Shall we hear from thee Tyrrel, ere we
     sleep?
   TYR. Ye shall, my lord.   [*Exit.*]   85
        [*Re-enter* BUCKINGHAM.]
   BUCK. My lord, I have considered in my mind
The late demand that you did sound me in.
   K. RICH. Well, let that pass. Dorset is fled to Rich-
     mond.
   BUCK. I hear that news, my lord.
   K. RICH. Stanley, he is your wife's son. Well, look
     to it.   90
   BUCK. My lord, I claim your gift, my due by
     promise,
For which your honor and your faith is pawned° —
The Earldom of Hereford and the movables
The which you promisèd I should possess.
   K. RICH. Stanley, look to your wife. If she convey
Letters to Richmond, you shall answer it.   96
   BUCK. What says your Highness to my just de-
     mand?
   K. RICH. As I remember, Henry the Sixth
Did prophesy that Richmond should be King
When Richmond was a little peevish boy.   100
A king, perhaps, perhaps ——
   BUCK. My lord!
   K. RICH. How chance the prophet could not at
     that time
Have told me, I being by, that I should kill him?

82. **prefer:** promote.   92. **pawned:** pledged.

   BUCK. My lord, your promise for the earl-
     dom ——   105
   K. RICH. Richmond! When last I was at Exeter,
The Mayor in courtesy showed me the castle,
And called it Rougemont. At which name I started,
Because a bard of Ireland told me once
I should not live long after I saw Richmond.   110
   BUCK. My lord!
   K. RICH. Aye, what's o'clock?
   BUCK. I am thus bold to put your Grace in mind
Of what you promised me.
   K. RICH.   Well, but what's o'clock?
   BUCK. Upon the stroke of ten.
   K. RICH.   Well, let it strike.   115
   BUCK. Why let it strike?
   K. RICH. Because that, like a Jack,° thou keep'st
     the stroke
Betwixt thy begging and my meditation.°
I am not in the giving vein today.
   BUCK. Why, then resolve me whether you will or
     no.   120
   K. RICH. Tut, tut,
Thou troublest me. I am not in the vein.
           [*Exeunt all but* BUCKINGHAM.]
   BUCK. Is it even so? Rewards he my true service
With such deep contempt? Made I him King for
     this?
Oh, let me think on Hastings, and be gone   125
To Brecknock while my fearful° head is on!
                     [*Exit.*]

SCENE III. *The same.*

[*Enter* TYRREL.]
   TYR. The tyrannous and bloody deed is done,
The most arch° act of piteous massacre
That ever yet this land was guilty of.
Dighton and Forrest, whom I did suborn°
To do this ruthless piece of butchery,   5
Although they were fleshed° villains, bloody dogs,
Melting with tenderness and kind compassion
Wept like two children in their deaths' sad stories.
"Lo, thus," quoth Dighton, "lay those tender
     babes."
"Thus, thus," quoth Forrest, "girdling one another
Within their innocent alabaster arms."   11
Their lips were four red roses on a stalk,
Which in their summer beauty kissed each other.
A book of prayers on their pillow lay,
"Which once," quoth Forrest, "almost changed my
     mind.   15

117. **Jack:** a figure on a clock which strikes the hours.
117–18. **thou . . . meditation:** you keep on mechanically begging
and interrupting my thoughts, like a clock striking.   126. **fear-
ful:** full of fear.
Sc. iii: 2. **most arch:** supremest.   4. **suborn:** procure.
6. **fleshed:** blooded; i.e., who had previously committed murder.

But oh, the Devil " — there the villain stopped
Whilst Dighton thus told on: " We smothered
The most replenishèd° sweet work of nature
That from the prime creation e'er she framed."
Thus both are gone with conscience and remorse.
They could not speak, and so I left them both,   21
To bring this tidings to the bloody King.
And here he comes. [*Enter* KING RICHARD.] All hail,
   my sovereign liege!
K. RICH. Kind Tyrrel, am I happy in thy news?
TYR. If to have done the thing you gave in charge
Beget your happiness, be happy then,   26
For it is done, my lord.
   K. RICH.   But didst thou see them dead?
TYR. I did, my lord.
   K. RICH.   And buried, gentle Tyrrel?
TYR. The chaplain of the Tower hath buried
   them,
But how or in what place I do not know.   30
   K. RICH. Come to me, Tyrrel, soon at after supper,
And thou shalt tell the process of their death.
Meantime, but think how I may do thee good,
And be inheritor of thy desire.
Farewell till soon.   [*Exit* TYRREL.]   35
The son of Clarence have I pent up close,
His daughter meanly have I matched in marriage,
The sons of Edward sleep in Abraham's bosom,°
And Anne my wife hath bid the world good night.
Now, for I know the Breton Richmond aims   40
At young Elizabeth, my brother's daughter,
And, by that knot,° looks proudly o'er the crown,
To her I go, a jolly thriving wooer.
         [*Enter* CATESBY.]
CATE. My lord!
   K. RICH. Good news or bad, that thou com'st in
   so bluntly?   45
CATE. Bad news, my lord. Ely is fled to Rich-
   mond,
And Buckingham, backed with the hardy Welsh-
   men,
Is in the field, and still his power increaseth.
   K. RICH. Ely with Richmond troubles me more
   near
Than Buckingham and his rash-levied° army.   50
Come, I have heard that fearful commenting
Is leaden servitor to dull delay.°
Delay leads impotent and snail-paced beggary,°
Then fiery expedition° be my wing,
Jove's Mercury, and herald for a king!   55
Come, muster men. My counsel is my shield.°
We must be brief when traitors brave the field.
                  [*Exeunt.*]

SCENE IV. *Before the palace.*

[*Enter* QUEEN MARGARET.]
Q. MAR. So now prosperity begins to mellow
And drop into the rotten mouth of death.
Here in these confines° slyly have I lurked,
To watch the waning of mine adversaries.
A dire induction° am I witness to,   5
And will to France, hoping the consequence
Will prove as bitter, black, and tragical.
Withdraw thee, wretched Margaret. Who comes
   here?
[*Enter* QUEEN ELIZABETH *and the* DUCHESS OF YORK.]
   Q. ELIZ. Ah, my young Princes! Ah, my tender
   babes!
My unblown° flowers, new-appearing sweets!   10
If yet your gentle souls fly in the air,
And be not fixed in doom perpetual,
Hover about me with your airy wings,
And hear your mother's lamentation!
   Q. MAR. Hover about her. Say that right for
   right°   15
Hath dimmed your infant morn to agèd night.
   DUCH. So many miseries have crazed° my voice
That my woe-wearied tongue is mute and dumb.
Edward Plantagenet, why art thou dead?
   Q. MAR. Plantagenet doth quit° Plantagenet, 20
Edward for Edward pays a dying debt.
   Q. ELIZ. Wilt thou, O God, fly from such gentle
   lambs,
And throw them in the entrails of the wolf?
When didst Thou sleep when such a deed was
   done?
   Q. MAR. When holy Harry died, and my sweet
   son.   25
   DUCH. Blind sight, dead life, poor mortal living
   ghost,
Woe's scene, world's shame, grave's due by life
   usurped,
Brief abstract and record of tedious days,
Rest thy unrest on England's lawful earth,
              [*Sitting down.*]
Unlawfully made drunk with innocents' blood! 30
   Q. ELIZ. Oh, that thou wouldst as well afford a
   grave
As thou canst yield a melancholy seat!
Then would I hide my bones, not rest them here.
Oh, who hath any cause to mourn but I?
          [*Sitting down by her.*]
   Q. MAR. If ancient sorrow be most reverend,   35
Give mine the benefit of seniory,°
And let my woes frown on the upper hand.

---

18. replenished: perfect.   38. Abraham's bosom: Paradise.
42. knot: marriage.   50. rash-levied: hastily collected.
51–52. fearful . . . delay: cowardly talk leads to stupid delay.
leaden servitor: heavy-footed servant.   53. Delay . . . beggary:
delay leads to poverty.   54. fiery expedition: hot haste.
56. counsel . . . shield: my shield is my councilor.

   Sc. iv: 3. confines: regions.   5. induction: first step.   10. un-
blown: that never bloomed.   15. right . . . right: i.e., by the
murder of her children she is rightly served as I was.   17. crazed:
cracked.   20. quit: pay for, requite.   36. seniory: seniority.

If sorrow can admit society,°
[*Sitting down with them.*] Tell o'er your woes
    again by viewing mine.
I had an Edward — till a Richard killed him.   40
I had a Harry — till a Richard killed him.
Thou hadst an Edward — till a Richard killed him.
Thou hadst a Richard — till a Richard killed him.
  DUCH. I had a Richard too, and thou didst kill
    him.
I had a Rutland too, thou holp'st° to kill him.   45
  Q. MAR. Thou hadst a Clarence too, and Richard
    killed him.
From forth the kennel of thy womb hath crept
A hellhound that doth hunt us all to death.
That dog, that had his teeth before his eyes,
To worry lambs and lap their gentle blood,   50
That foul defacer of God's handiwork,
That excellent grand tyrant of the earth,
That reigns in gallèd° eyes of weeping souls,
Thy womb let loose, to chase us to our graves.
O upright, just, and true-disposing God,   55
How do I thank Thee that this carnal° cur
Preys on the issue of his mother's body,
And makes her pew fellow° with others' moan!
  DUCH. O Harry's wife, triumph not in my woes!
God witness with me, I have wept for thine.   60
  Q. MAR. Bear with me. I am hungry for revenge,
And now I cloy me with beholding it.
Thy Edward he is dead that stabbed my Edward;
Thy other Edward dead, to quit my Edward.
Young York he is but boot,° because both they   65
Match not the high perfection of my loss.
Thy Clarence he is dead that killed my Edward;
And the beholders of this tragic play,
The adulterate Hastings, Rivers, Vaughan, Grey,
Untimely smothered in their dusky graves.   70
Richard yet lives, Hell's black intelligencer,°
Only reserved their factor° to buy souls
And send them thither. But at hand, at hand,
Ensues his piteous and unpitied end.
Earth gapes, Hell burns, fiends roar, saints pray,
To have him suddenly conveyed away.   76
Cancel his bond° of life, dear God, I pray,
That I may live to say, "The dog is dead!"
  Q. ELIZ. Oh, thou didst prophesy the time would
    come
That I should wish for thee to help me curse   80
That bottled° spider, that foul bunch-backed toad!
  Q. MAR. I called thee then vain flourish of my
    fortune.
I called thee then poor shadow, painted Queen,
The presentation of but what I was,

The flattering index° of a direful pageant,   85
One heaved a-high to be hurled down below,
A mother only mocked with two sweet babes,
A dream of what thou wert, a breath, a bubble,
A sign of dignity, a garish° flag
To be the aim of every dangerous shot,   90
A queen in jest, only to fill the scene.
Where is thy husband now? Where be thy brothers?
Where are thy children? Wherein dost thou joy?
Who sues to thee, and cries "God save the
    Queen"?
Where be the bending peers that flattered thee?   95
Where be the thronging troops° that followed
    thee?
Decline all this, and see what now thou art —
For happy wife, a most distressèd widow,
For joyful mother, one that wails the name,
For Queen, a very caitiff° crowned with care,   100
For one being sued to, one that humbly sues,
For one that scorned at me, now scorned of me,
For one being feared of all, now fearing one,
For one commanding all, obeyed of none.
Thus hath the course of justice wheeled about,   105
And left thee but a very prey to time,
Having no more but thought of what thou wert
To torture thee the more, being what thou art.
Thou didst usurp my place, and dost thou not
Usurp the just proportion of my sorrow?   110
Now thy proud neck bears half my burdened°
    yoke,
From which even here I slip my weary neck,
And leave the burden of it all on thee.
Farewell, York's wife, and Queen of sad mischance.
These English woes will make me smile in France.
  Q. ELIZ. O thou well skilled in curses, stay awhile,
And teach me how to curse mine enemies!   117
  Q. MAR. Forbear to sleep the nights, and fast the
    days,
Compare dead happiness with living woe,
Think that thy babes were fairer than they were,
And he that slew them fouler than he is.   121
Bettering thy loss makes the bad causer worse.°
Revolving° this will teach thee how to curse.
  Q. ELIZ. My words are dull. Oh, quicken them
    with thine!
  Q. MAR. Thy woes will make them sharp, and
    pierce like mine.   [*Exit.*]   125
  DUCH. Why should calamity be full of words?
  Q. ELIZ. Windy attorneys to their client woes,
Airy succeeders of intestate joys,°

38. society: partnership. 45. holp'st: helped. 53. galled: sore.
56. carnal: flesh-eating. 58. pew fellow: companion on the same
bench. 65. boot: something given in addition, makeweight.
71. intelligencer: spy. 72. factor: agent; i.e., of Hell. 77. bond:
contract, lease. See II.ii.95,n. 81. bottled: shaped like a bottle.
See Pl. 20f.

85. index: lit., table of contents in the front of a book.
89. garish: gaudy. 96. troops: crowds. 100. caitiff: captive,
slave. 111. burdened: burdensome. 122. Bettering . . . worse:
i.e., by exaggerating your sorrows you may more heavily curse
the cause of them. 123. Revolving: meditating. 127–28. Windy
. . . joys: i.e., words are like pleaders who make windy speeches
on behalf of Woe, their client; words are children who succeed to
a worthless inheritance.

Poor breathing orators of miseries!
Let them have scope. Though what they do impart
Help not at all, yet do they ease the heart.   131
  DUCH. If so, then be not tongue-tied. Go with
    me,
And in the breath of bitter words let's smother
My damnèd son, which thy two sweet sons smoth-
    ered.
I hear his drum. Be copious in exclaims.   135
[*Enter* KING RICHARD, *marching, with drums and
    trumpets.*]
  K. RICH. Who intercepts my expedition?
  DUCH. Oh, she that might have intercepted thee,
By strangling thee in her accursèd womb,
From all the slaughters, wretch, that thou hast done!
  Q. ELIZ. Hidest thou that forehead with a golden
    crown   140
Where should be graven, if that right were right,
The slaughter of the Prince that owed° that crown,
And the dire death of my two sons and brothers?
Tell me, thou villain slave, where are my children?
  DUCH. Thou toad, thou toad, where is thy brother
    Clarence?   145
And little Ned Plantagenet, his son?
  Q. ELIZ. Where is kind Hastings, Rivers, Vaughan,
    Grey?
  K. RICH. A flourish, trumpets! Strike alarum,
    drums!
Let not the Heavens hear these telltale women
Rail on the Lord's anointed. Strike, I say!   150
                            [*Flourish. Alarums.*]
Either be patient, and entreat me fair,
Or with the clamorous report of war
Thus will I drown your exclamations.
  DUCH. Art thou my son?
  K. RICH. Aye, I thank God, my father, and your-
    self.   155
  DUCH. Then patiently hear my impatience.
  K. RICH. Madam, I have a touch of your condition,
Which cannot brook the accent of reproof.
  DUCH. Oh, let me speak!
  K. RICH.   Do then, but I'll not hear.
  DUCH. I will be mild and gentle in my speech.
  K. RICH. And brief, good Mother, for I am in
    haste.   161
  DUCH. Art thou so hasty? I have stayed for thee,
God knows, in anguish, pain, and agony.
  K. RICH. And came I not at last to comfort you?
  DUCH. No, by the holy rood, thou know'st it
    well,   165
Thou camest on earth to make the earth my Hell.
A grievous burden was thy birth to me,
Tetchy° and wayward was thy infancy,
Thy school days frightful, desperate, wild, and fu-
    rious,   169
Thy prime of manhood daring, bold, and venturous,

Thy age confirmed, proud, subtle, bloody, treacher-
    ous,
More mild, but yet more harmful, kind in hatred.
What comfortable hour canst thou name
That ever graced me in thy company?
  K. RICH. Faith, none but Humphrey Hour,° that
    called your Grace   175
To breakfast once forth of my company.
If I be so disgracious in your sight,
Let me march on, and not offend your Grace.
Strike up the drum.
  DUCH.   I prithee, hear me speak.
  K. RICH. You speak too bitterly.
  DUCH.   Hear me a word,
For I shall never speak to thee again.   181
  K. RICH. So.
  DUCH. Either thou wilt die, by God's just ordi-
    nance,
Ere from this war thou turn a conqueror,
Or I with grief and extreme age shall perish   185
And never look upon thy face again.
Therefore take with thee my most heavy curse,
Which in the day of battle tire thee more
Than all the complete armor that thou wear'st!
My prayers on the adverse party fight,   190
And there the little souls of Edward's children
Whisper the spirits of thine enemies
And promise them success and victory.
Bloody thou art, bloody will be thy end.   194
Shame serves° thy life and doth thy death attend.
                                        [*Exit.*]
  Q. ELIZ. Though far more cause, yet much less
    spirit to curse
Abides in me. I say amen to all.
  K. RICH. Stay, madam, I must speak a word with
    you.
  Q. ELIZ. I have no moe° sons of the royal blood
For thee to murder. For° my daughters, Richard,
They shall be praying nuns, not weeping queens,
And therefore level° not to hit their lives.   202
  K. RICH. You have a daughter called Elizabeth,
Virtuous and fair, royal and gracious.
  Q. ELIZ. And must she die for this? Oh, let her
    live,   205
And I'll corrupt her manners, stain her beauty,
Slander myself as false to Edward's bed,
Throw over her the veil of infamy.
So she may live unscarred of bleeding slaughter,
I will confess she was not Edward's daughter.   210
  K. RICH. Wrong not her birth, she is of royal blood.
  Q. ELIZ. To save her life, I'll say she is not so.
  K. RICH. Her life is only safest in her birth.
  Q. ELIZ. And only in that safety died her brothers.

---

175. **Humphrey Hour:** If the reading is correct, it means "dinner-
time for the hungry" when needy gallants in Paul's hoped to
pick up a free meal. See Gen. Intro. p.17b.   195. **serves:** is serv-
ant to.   199. **moe:** more.   200. **For:** as for.   202. **level:** aim.

142. **owed:** owned.   168. **Tetchy:** peevish.

K. RICH. Lo, at their births good stars were opposite. 215

Q. ELIZ. No, to their lives bad friends were contrary.

K. RICH. All unavoided° is the doom of destiny.

Q. ELIZ. True, when avoided grace makes destiny.
My babes were destined to a fairer death
If grace had blessed thee with a fairer life. 220

K. RICH. You speak as if that I had slain my cousins.

Q. ELIZ. Cousins, indeed, and by their uncle cozened°
Of comfort, kingdom, kindred, freedom, life.
Whose hand soever lanced their tender hearts,
Thy head, all indirectly, gave direction. 225
No doubt the murderous knife was dull and blunt
Till it was whetted on thy stone-hard heart,
To revel in the entrails of my lambs.
But that still° use of grief makes wild grief tame,
My tongue should to thy ears not name my boys
Till that my nails were anchored in thine eyes, 231
And I in such a desperate bay of death,
Like a poor bark, of sails and tackling reft,°
Rush all to pieces on thy rocky bosom.

K. RICH. Madam, so thrive I in my enterprise,
And dangerous success° of bloody wars, 236
As I intend more good to you and yours
Than ever you or yours were by me wronged!

Q. ELIZ. What good is covered with the face of heaven,
To be discovered, that can do me good? 240

K. RICH. The advancement of your children, gentle lady.

Q. ELIZ. Up to some scaffold, there to lose their heads?

K. RICH. No, to the dignity and height of honor,
The high imperial type° of this earth's glory.

Q. ELIZ. Flatter my sorrows with report of it. 245
Tell me what state, what dignity, what honor,
Canst thou demise° to any child of mine?

K. RICH. Even all I have — yea, and myself and all —
Will I withal endow a child of thine,
So in the Lethe° of thy angry soul 250
Thou drown the sad remembrance of those wrongs
Which thou supposest I have done to thee.

Q. ELIZ. Be brief, lest that the process of thy kindness
Last longer telling than thy kindness' date.

K. RICH. Then know that from my soul I love thy daughter. 255

Q. ELIZ. My daughter's mother thinks it with her soul.

K. RICH. What do you think?

Q. ELIZ. That thou dost love my daughter from°
thy soul.
So from thy soul's love didst thou love her brothers,
And from my heart's love I do thank thee for it. 260

K. RICH. Be not so hasty to confound my meaning.
I mean that with my soul I love thy daughter,
And mean to make her Queen of England.

Q. ELIZ. Say then, who dost thou mean shall be her King?

K. RICH. Even he that makes her Queen. Who should be else? 265

Q. ELIZ. What, thou?

K. RICH. I, even I. What think you of it, madam?

Q. ELIZ. How canst thou woo her?

K. RICH.   That would I learn of you,
As one that are best acquainted with her humor.

Q. ELIZ. And wilt thou learn of me?

K. RICH.   Madam, with all my heart. 270

Q. ELIZ. Send to her, by the man that slew her brothers,
A pair of bleeding hearts, thereon engrave
" Edward " and " York." Then haply she will weep.
Therefore present to her — as sometime Margaret
Did to thy father, steeped in Rutland's blood — 275
A handkerchief, which, say to her, did drain
The purple sap from her sweet brother's body,
And bid her dry her weeping eyes therewith.
If this inducement force her not to love,
Send her a story of thy noble acts. 280
Tell her thou madest away her Uncle Clarence,
Her uncle Rivers — yea, and, for her sake,
Madest quick conveyance° with her good aunt Anne.

K. RICH. Come, come, you mock me. This is not the way
To win your daughter.

Q. ELIZ.   There is no other way, 285
Unless thou couldst put on some other shape,
And not be Richard that hath done all this.

K. RICH. Say that I did all this for love of her.

Q. ELIZ. Nay, then indeed she cannot choose but hate thee,
Having bought love with such a bloody spoil.° 290

K. RICH. Look, what is done cannot be now amended.
Men shall deal unadvisedly° sometimes,
Which afterhours give leisure to repent.
If I did take the kingdom from your sons,
To make amends, I'll give it to your daughter. 295
If I have killed the issue of your womb,
To quicken your increase, I will beget
Mine issue of your blood upon your daughter.

217. unavoided: unavoidable.   222. cozened: cheated.   229. still: continual.   233. reft: bereft.   236. success: sequel.   244. imperial type: imperial badge; i.e., the crown.   247. demise: convey, a legal phrase.   250. Lethe: river of forgetfulness in the underworld.

258. from: away from; i.e., you hate my daughter.   283. conveyance: removal.   290. spoil: used in a double sense, "plunder" and "massacre."   292. unadvisedly: without stopping to consider.

A grandam's name is little less in love
Than is the doting title of a mother;   300
They are as children but one step below,
Even of your mettle,° of your very blood —
Of all one pain, save for a night of groans
Endured of her for whom you bid° like sorrow.
Your children were vexation to your youth,   305
But mine shall be a comfort to your age.
The loss you have is but a son being King,
And by that loss your daughter is made Queen.
I cannot make you what amends I would,
Therefore accept such kindness as I can.   310
Dorset your son, that with a fearful soul
Leads discontented steps in foreign soil,
This fair alliance quickly shall call home
To high promotions and great dignity.
The King that calls your beauteous daughter wife
Familiarly shall call thy Dorset brother.   316
Again shall you be mother to a king,
And all the ruins of distressful times
Repaired with double riches of content.
What! We have many goodly days to see.   320
The liquid drops of tears that you have shed
Shall come again, transformed to orient pearl,
Advantaging their loan with interest
Of ten times double gain of happiness.
Go then, my mother, to thy daughter go.   325
Make bold her bashful years with your experience,
Prepare her ears to hear a wooer's tale,
Put in her tender heart the aspiring flame°
Of golden sovereignty, acquaint the Princess
With the sweet silent hours of marriage joys.   330
And when this arm of mine hath chastised
The petty rebel, dull-brained Buckingham,
Bound with triumphant garlands will I come
And lead thy daughter to a conqueror's bed,
To whom I will retail my conquest won,   335
And she shall be sole victress, Caesar's Caesar.

Q. ELIZ. What were I best to say? Her father's
brother
Would be her lord? Or shall I say her uncle?
Or he that slew her brothers and her uncles?
Under what title shall I woo for thee,   340
That God, the law, my honor, and her love
Can make seem pleasing to her tender years?

K. RICH. Infer° fair England's peace by this alli-
ance.

Q. ELIZ. Which she shall purchase with still lasting
war.

K. RICH. Say that the King, which may command,
entreats.   345

Q. ELIZ. That at her hands which the King's King
forbids.

K. RICH. Say she shall be a high and mighty
Queen.

302. mettle: material.   304. bid: endured.   328. aspiring flame:
ambitious desire.   343. Infer: argue.

Q. ELIZ. To wail the title, as her mother doth.

K. RICH. Say I will love her everlastingly.   349

Q. ELIZ. But how long shall that title " ever " last?

K. RICH. Sweetly in force unto her fair life's end.

Q. ELIZ. But how long fairly shall her sweet life
last?

K. RICH. So long as Heaven and nature lengthens
it.

Q. ELIZ. So long as Hell and Richard likes of it.

K. RICH. Say I, her sovereign, am her subject
love.   355

Q. ELIZ. But she, your subject, loathes such sover-
eignty.

K. RICH. Be eloquent in my behalf to her.

Q. ELIZ. An honest tale speeds best being plainly
told.

K. RICH. Then in plain terms tell her my loving
tale.

Q. ELIZ. Plain and not honest is too harsh a style.

K. RICH. Your reasons are too shallow and too
quick.   361

Q. ELIZ. Oh no, my reasons are too deep and
dead —
Too deep and dead, poor infants, in their grave.

K. RICH. Harp not on that string, madam. That is
past.

Q. ELIZ. Harp on it still shall I till heartstrings
break.   365

K. RICH. Now, by my George, my Garter,° and
my crown ——

Q. ELIZ. Profaned, dishonored, and the third
usurped.

K. RICH. I swear ——

Q. ELIZ.   By nothing, for this is no oath.
The George, profaned, hath lost his holy honor.
The Garter, blemished, pawned his knightly virtue.
The crown, usurped, disgraced his kingly glory.
If something thou wilt swear to be believed,   372
Swear then by something that thou hast not
wronged.

K. RICH. Now, by the world ——

Q. ELIZ.   'Tis full of thy foul wrongs.

K. RICH. My father's death ——

Q. ELIZ.   Thy life hath that dishonored.   375

K. RICH. Then, by myself ——

Q. ELIZ.   Thyself thyself misusest.

K. RICH. Why then, by God ——

Q. ELIZ.   God's wrong is most of all.
If thou hadst feared to break an oath by Him,
The unity the King thy brother made
Had not been broken, nor my brother slain.   380
If thou hadst feared to break an oath by Him,
The imperial metal circling now thy brow

366. my . . . Garter: Knights of the Garter wore a collar with a
figure of Saint George, and an embroidered garter round the left
knee, with the motto: *Honi soit qui mal y pense*—"Evil be to
him who evil thinks." See Pl. 8d. 3b.

Had graced the tender temples of my child,
And both the Princes had been breathing here,
Which now, two tender playfellows for dust,   385
Thy broken faith hath made a prey for worms.
What canst thou swear by now?

K. RICH.   The time to come.

Q. ELIZ. That thou hast wrongèd in the time
o'erpast,
For I myself have many tears to wash   389
Hereafter time,° for time past wronged by thee.
The children live whose parents thou hast slaugh-
tered,
Ungoverned youth,° to wail it in their age.
The parents live whose children thou hast butchered,
Old withered plants, to wail it with their age.
Swear not by time to come, for that thou hast   395
Misused ere used, by time misused o'erpast.

K. RICH. As I intend to prosper and repent,
So thrive I in my dangerous attempt
Of hostile arms! Myself myself confound!
Heaven and fortune bar me happy hours!   400
Day, yield me not thy light, nor, night, thy rest!
Be opposite all planets of good luck
To my proceedings if with pure heart's love,
Immaculate devotion, holy thoughts,
I tender° not thy beauteous princely daughter!   405
In her consists my happiness and thine.
Without her, follows to this land and me,
To thee, herself, and many a Christian soul,
Death, desolation, ruin and decay.
It cannot be avoided but by this,   410
It will not be avoided but by this.
Therefore, good Mother — I must call you so —
Be the attorney of my love to her.
Plead what I will be, not what I have been —
Not my deserts, but what I will deserve.   415
Urge the necessity and state of times,
And be not peevish-fond° in great designs.

Q. ELIZ. Shall I be tempted of the Devil thus?

K. RICH. Aye, if the Devil tempt thee to do good.

Q. ELIZ. Shall I forget myself to be myself?   420

K. RICH. Aye, if yourself's remembrance wrong
yourself.

Q. ELIZ. But thou didst kill my children.

K. RICH. But in your daughter's womb I bury
them,
Where in that nest of spicery° they shall breed
Selves of themselves, to your recomforture.°   425

Q. ELIZ. Shall I go win my daughter to thy will?

K. RICH. And be a happy mother by the deed.

Q. ELIZ. I go. Write to me very shortly,
And you shall understand from me her mind.

K. RICH. Bear her my true love's kiss, and so fare-
well.   [*Exit* QUEEN ELIZABETH.]   430
Relenting fool, and shallow, changing woman!
[*Enter* RATCLIFF; CATESBY *following*.] How now!
What news?

RAT. My gracious sovereign, on the western coast
Rideth a puissant° navy; to the shore
Throng many doubtful hollow-hearted friends,   435
Unarmed, and unresolved to beat them back.
'Tis thought that Richmond is their admiral,
And there they hull,° expecting° but the aid
Of Buckingham to welcome them ashore.

K. RICH. Some light-foot friend post to the Duke
of Norfolk —   440
Ratcliff, thyself, or Catesby — where is he?

CATE. Here, my lord.

K. RICH. Fly to the Duke. [*To* RATCLIFF] Post°
thou to Salisbury.
When thou comest thither —— [*To* CATESBY]
Dull unmindful villain,
Why stand'st thou still, and go'st not to the
Duke?   445

CATE. First, mighty sovereign, let me know your
mind,
What from your Grace I shall deliver to him.

K. RICH. O true, good Catesby, bid him levy
straight
The greatest strength and power he can make,
And meet me presently° at Salisbury.   450

CATE. I go.   [*Exit.*]

RAT. What is't your Highness' pleasure I shall do
At Salisbury?

K. RICH. Why, what wouldst thou do there before
I go?

RAT. Your highness told me I should post before.

K. RICH. My mind is changed, sir, my mind is
changed.   456
[*Enter* LORD STANLEY.] How now, what news with
you?

STAN. None good, my lord, to please you with the
hearing,
Nor none so bad but it may well be told.

K. RICH. Hoyday,° a riddle! Neither good nor bad!
Why dost thou run so many mile about   461
When thou mayst tell thy tale a nearer way?
Once more, what news?

STAN.   Richmond is on the seas.

K. RICH. There let him sink, and be the seas on
him!
White-livered runagate,° what doth he there?   465

STAN. I know not, mighty sovereign, but by guess.

K. RICH. Well, sir, as you guess, as you guess?

STAN. Stirred up by Dorset, Buckingham, and Ely,

---

390. Hereafter time: time to come.   **392. Ungoverned youth:** children without parents to control them.   **405. tender:** offer. **417. peevish-fond:** obstinately foolish.   **424. nest of spicery:** the allusion is to the nest of spices which the phoenix made, which was both funeral pyre of the old phoenix and birthplace of the new. See *Temp.*, III.iii.23,n.   **425. recomforture:** consolation.

434. puissant: powerful.   **438. hull:** float. **expecting:** awaiting. **443. Post:** ride in haste. See App. 17.   **450. presently:** immediately.   **460. Hoyday:** exclamation of surprise. **465. White-livered runagate:** cowardly traitor.

He makes for England, there to claim the crown.
    K. RICH. Is the chair empty? Is the sword un-
    swayed?   470
Is the King dead? The empire unpossessed?
What heir of York is there alive but we?
And who is England's King but great York's heir?
Then tell me, what doth he upon the sea?   474
    STAN. Unless for that, my liege, I cannot guess.
    K. RICH. Unless for that he comes to be your liege,
You cannot guess wherefore the Welshman comes.
Thou wilt revolt and fly to him, I fear.
    STAN. No, mighty liege, therefore mistrust me not.
    K. RICH. Where is thy power, then, to beat him
    back?   480
Where are thy tenants and thy followers?
Are they not now upon the western shore,
Safe-conducting the rebels from their ships?
    STAN. No, my good lord, my friends are in the
    North.
    K. RICH. Cold friends to Richard. What do they in
    the North   485
When they should serve their sovereign in the west?
    STAN. They have not been commanded, mighty
    sovereign.
Please it your Majesty to give me leave,
I'll muster up my friends, and meet your Grace
Where and what time your Majesty shall please.
    K. RICH. Aye, aye, thou wouldst be gone to join
    with Richmond.   491
I will not trust you, sir.
    STAN.   Most mighty sovereign,
You have no cause to hold my friendship doubtful.
I never was nor never will be false.
    K. RICH. Well,   495
Go muster men. But, hear you, leave behind
Your son, George Stanley. Look your faith be firm,
Or else his head's assurance is but frail.
    STAN. So deal with him as I prove true to you.
                            [*Exit.*]

            [*Enter a* MESSENGER.]
    MESS. My gracious sovereign, now in Devonshire,
As I by friends am well advértisèd,   501
Sir Edward Courtney, and the haughty prelate
Bishop of Exeter, his brother there,
With many moe confederates, are in arms.
         [*Enter another* MESSENGER.]
    2. MESS. My liege, in Kent, the Guildfords are in
    arms,   505
And every hour more competitors°
Flock to their aid, and still their power increaseth.
         [*Enter another* MESSENGER.]
    3. MESS. My lord, the army of the Duke of Buck-
    ingham ——
    K. RICH. Out on you, owls! Nothing but songs of
    death?   [*He strikes him.*]
Take that, until thou bring me better news.   510

       506. competitors: conspirators.

    3. MESS. The news I have to tell your Majesty
Is that by sudden floods and fall of waters
Buckingham's army is dispersed and scattered,
And he himself wandered away alone,
No man knows whither.
    K. RICH.   I cry thee mercy.   513
There is my purse to cure that blow of thine.
Hath any well-advisèd° friend proclaimed
Reward to him that brings the traitor in?
    3. MESS. Such proclamation hath been made, my
    liege.
         [*Enter another* MESSENGER.]
    4. MESS. Sir Thomas Lovel and Lord Marquess
    Dorset,   520
'Tis said, my liege, in Yorkshire are in arms.
Yet this good comfort bring I to your Grace —
The Breton navy is dispersed by tempest.
Richmond, in Dorsetshire, sent out a boat
Unto the shore, to ask those on the banks   52
If they were his assistants, yea or no,
Who answered him they came from Buckingham
Upon his party. He, mistrusting them,
Hoised° sail and made away for Brittany.
    K. RICH. March on, march on, since we are up in
    arms,   530
If not to fight with foreign enemies,
Yet to beat down these rebels here at home.
         [*Re-enter* CATESBY.]
    CATE. My liege, the Duke of Buckingham is taken.
That is the best news. That the Earl of Richmond
Is with a mighty power° landed at Milford   535
Is colder tidings, yet they must be told.
    K. RICH. Away toward Salisbury! While we rea-
    son° here
A royal battle might be won and lost.
Someone take order Buckingham be brought
To Salisbury. The rest march on with me.   540
                       [*Flourish. Exeunt.*]

SCENE V. LORD DERBY's *house.*

     [*Enter* DERBY *and* SIR CHRISTOPHER URSWICK.]
    DER. Sir Christopher, tell Richmond this from me:
That in the sty of this most bloody boar
My son George Stanley is franked up in hold.°
If I revolt, off goes young George's head.
The fear of that withholds my present aid.   5
But, tell me, where is princely Richmond now?
    CHRIS. At Pembroke, or at Ha'rfordwest,° in
    Wales.   10
    DER. What men of name resort to him?

  517. well-advised: thoughtful. **529. Hoised:** hoisted. **535. power:**
army. **537. reason:** argue.
    Sc. v: 3. franked . . . hold: confined in the boar's sty. See
I.iii.314,n. **10. Ha'rfordwest:** Haverfordwest.

CHRIS. Sir Walter Herbert, a renownèd soldier,
Sir Gilbert Talbot, Sir William Stanley,
Oxford, redoubted Pembroke, Sir James Blunt,
And Rice ap° Thomas, with a valiant crew,   15
And many moe of noble fame and worth.
And toward London they do bend° their course,
If by the way they be not fought withal.
DER. Return unto thy lord, commend me to him.
Tell him the Queen hath heartily consented
He shall espouse Elizabeth her daughter.
These letters will resolve him of my mind.   20
Farewell.   [*Exeunt.*]

Act V

SCENE I. *Salisbury. An open place.*

[*Enter the* SHERIFF, *and* BUCKINGHAM, *with halberds,
led to execution.*]

BUCK. Will not King Richard let me speak with
him?
SHER. No, my good lord, therefore be patient.
BUCK. Hastings, and Edward's children, Rivers,
Grey,
Holy King Henry, and thy fair son Edward,
Vaughan, and all that have miscarried   5
By underhand corrupted foul injustice,
If that your moody discontented souls
Do through the clouds behold this present hour
Even for revenge mock my destruction!
This is All Souls' Day,° fellows, is it not?   10
SHER. It is, my lord.
BUCK. Why, then All Souls' Day is my body's
Doomsday.
This is the day that, in King Edward's time,
I wished might fall on me° when I was found
False to his children or his wife's allies.   15
This is the day wherein I wished to fall
By the false faith of him I trusted most.
This, this All Souls' Day, to my fearful soul
Is the determined° respite° of my wrongs.
That high All-seer that I dallied° with   20
Hath turned my feigned prayer on my head,
And given in earnest what I begged in jest.
Thus doth He force the swords of wicked men
To turn their own points on their masters' bosoms.
Now Margaret's curse is fallen upon my head.   25
"When he," quoth she, " shall split thy heart with
sorrow,

Remember Margaret was a prophetess."
Come, sirs, convey me to the block of shame,
Wrong hath but wrong, and blame the due of
blame.   [*Exeunt.*]   30

SCENE II. *The camp near Tamworth.*

[*Enter* RICHMOND, OXFORD, BLUNT, HERBERT, *and
others, with drum and colors.*]

RICHM. Fellows in arms, and my most loving
friends,
Bruised underneath the yoke of tyranny,
Thus far into the bowels of the land
Have we marched on without impediment.
And here receive we from our father Stanley   5
Lines° of fair comfort and encouragement.
The wretched, bloody, and usurping boar
That spoiled your summer fields and fruitful vines
Swills your warm blood like wash, and makes his
trough
In your emboweled° bosoms — this foul swine   10
Lies now even in the center of this isle,
Near to the town of Leicester, as we learn.
From Tamworth thither is but one day's march.
In God's name, cheerly on, courageous friends,
To reap the harvest of perpetual peace   15
By this one bloody trial of sharp war.
OXF. Every man's conscience is a thousand swords,
To fight against that bloody homicide.
HERB. I doubt not but his friends will fly to us.
BLUNT. He hath no friends but who are friends for
fear,   20
Which in his greatest need will shrink from him.
RICHM. All for our vantage. Then, in God's name,
march.
True hope is swift, and flies with swallow's wings,
Kings it makes gods, and meaner creatures kings.
                                 [*Exeunt.*]

SCENE III. *Bosworth Field.*

[*Enter* KING RICHARD *in arms with* NORFOLK, *the* EARL
OF SURREY, *and others.*]

K. RICH. Here pitch our tents, even here in Bos-
worth field.
My Lord of Surrey, why look you so sad?
SUR. My heart is ten times lighter than my looks.
K. RICH. My Lord of Norfolk——
NOR.   Here, most gracious liege.
K. RICH. Norfolk, we must have knocks. Ha! Must
we not?   5
NOR. We must both give and take, my gracious
lord.

---

15. ap: son of.   17. bend: direct.
    Act V, Sc. i: 10. All Souls' Day: November 2.   14. I . . . me:
See II.i.32–40.   19. determined: foreordained. respite: day to
which something is postponed.   20. dallied: played the fool
with.

Sc. ii: 6. Lines: letters.   10. emboweled: ripped up.

K. RICH. Up with my tent there! Here will I lie
tonight.
But where tomorrow? Well, all's one for that.
Who hath descried° the number of the foe?   9
   NOR. Six or seven thousand is their utmost power.
   K. RICH. Why, our battalion° trebles that account.
Besides, the King's name is a tower of strength,
Which they upon the adverse party want.
Up with my tent there! Valiant gentlemen,
Let us survey the vantage of the field,   15
Call for some men of sound direction.°
Let's want no discipline, make no delay,
For, lords, tomorrow is a busy day.   [Exeunt.]
[Enter, on the other side of the field, RICHMOND, SIR
   WILLIAM BRANDON, OXFORD, and others. Some of
   the SOLDIERS pitch RICHMOND's tent.]
   RICHM. The weary sun hath made a golden set,
And by the bright track of his fiery car°   20
Gives signal of a goodly day tomorrow.
Sir William Brandon, you shall bear my standard.
Give me some ink and paper in my tent —
I'll draw the form and model° of our battle,
Limit° each leader to his several° charge,   25
And part in just proportion our small strength.
My Lord of Oxford, you, Sir William Brandon,
And you, Sir Walter Herbert, stay with me.
The Earl of Pembroke keeps° his regiment.
Good Captain Blunt, bear my good night to him,
And by the second hour in the morning   31
Desire the Earl to see me in my tent.
Yet one thing more, good Blunt, before thou go'st —
Where is Lord Stanley quartered, dost thou know?
   BLUNT. Unless I have mista'en his colors much,
Which well I am assured I have not done,   36
His regiment lies half a mile at least
South from the mighty power of the King.
   RICHM. If without peril it be possible,
Good Captain Blunt, bear my good night to him,
And give him from me this most needful scroll.°   41
   BLUNT. Upon my life, my lord, I'll undertake it.
And so, God give you quiet rest tonight!
   RICHM. Good night, good Captain Blunt. Come,
gentlemen,
Let us consult upon tomorrow's business.   45
In to our tent! The air is raw and cold.
              [They withdraw into the tent.]
[Enter, to his tent, KING RICHARD, NORFOLK, RATCLIFF,
          CATESBY, and others.]
   K. RICH. What is 't o'clock?
   CATE.   It's suppertime, my lord,
It's nine o'clock.
   K. RICH.   I will not sup tonight.
Give me some ink and paper.

What, is my beaver° easier than it was,   50
And all my armor laid into my tent?
   CATE. It is, my liege, and all things are in readi-
ness.
   K. RICH. Good Norfolk, hie thee to thy charge.
Use careful watch, choose trusty sentinels.
   NOR. I go, my lord.   55
   K. RICH. Stir with the lark tomorrow, gentle Nor-
folk.
   NOR. I warrant you, my lord.   [Exit.]
   K. RICH. Catesby!
   CATE. My lord?
   K. RICH.   Send out a pursuivant at arms°
To Stanley's regiment. Bid him bring his power   60
Before sunrising, lest his son George fall
Into the blind cave of eternal night. [Exit CATESBY.]
Fill me a bowl of wine. Give me a watch.°
Saddle white Surrey for the field tomorrow.
Look that my staves° be sound, and not too heavy.
Ratcliff!   66
   RAT. My lord?
   K. RICH. Saw'st thou the melancholy Lord North-
umberland?
   RAT. Thomas the Earl of Surrey, and himself,
Much about cockshut time,° from troop to troop   70
Went through the army, cheering up the soldiers.
   K. RICH. So, I am satisfied. Give me a bowl of
wine.
I have not that alacrity of spirit,
Nor cheer of mind, that I was wont to have.
Set it down. Is ink and paper ready?
   RAT.   It is, my lord.   75
   K. RICH. Bid my guard watch. Leave me. Ratcliff,
About the mid of night come to my tent
And help to arm me. Leave me, I say.
        [Exeunt RATCLIFF and the other ATTENDANTS.]
[Enter DERBY to RICHMOND in his tent, LORDS and
                others attending.]
   DER. Fortune and victory sit on thy helm!
   RICHM. All comfort that the dark night can afford
Be to thy person, noble father-in-law!   81
Tell me, how fares our loving mother?
   DER. I, by attorney,° bless thee from thy mother,
Who prays continually for Richmond's good.
So much for that. The silent hours steal on,   85
And flaky darkness breaks within the east.
In brief, for so the season bids us be,
Prepare thy battle early in the morning,
And put thy fortune to the arbitrament°
Of bloody strokes and mortal-staring° war.   90
I, as I may — that which I would I cannot —

<hr/>

Sc. iii: 9. descried: spied. 11. battalion: army. 16. sound
direction: competent leadership. 20. fiery car: i.e., the chariot
of the sun. 24. model: plan. 25. Limit: allot. several: separate,
individual. 29. keeps: stays with. 41. needful scroll: urgent
message.

50. beaver: face piece of the helmet. See Pl. 8a. 59. pursuivant
at arms: herald's officer. 63. watch: guard; or perhaps watch
light, a candle marked to show the time taken in burning.
65. staves: spears. 70. cockshut time: twilight. 83. attorney:
deputy. 89. arbitrament: judgment. 90. mortal-staring: with
deadly looks.

With best advantage will deceive the time,°
And aid thee in this doubtful shock of arms.
But on thy side I may not be too forward,
Lest, being seen, thy brother, tender George,   95
Be executed in his father's sight.
Farewell. The leisure and the fearful time
Cuts off the ceremonious vows° of love,
And ample interchange of sweet discourse,
Which so long sundered friends should dwell upon.
God give us leisure for these rites of love!   101
Once more, adieu. Be valiant, and speed well!
   RICHM. Good lords, conduct him to his regiment.
I'll strive, with troubled thoughts, to take a nap,
Lest leaden slumber peise° me down tomorrow   105
When I should mount with wings of victory.
Once more, good night, kind lords and gentlemen.
                          [*Exeunt all but* RICHMOND.]
O Thou Whose captain I account myself,
Look on my forces with a gracious eye.
Put in their hands Thy bruising irons of wrath,   110
That they may crush down with a heavy fall
The usurping helmets of our adversaries!
Make us Thy ministers of chastisement,
That we may praise Thee in the victory!
To Thee I do commend my watchful soul   115
Ere I let fall the windows of mine eyes.
Sleeping and waking, oh, defend me still!   [*Sleeps.*]
[*Enter the* GHOST OF PRINCE EDWARD, *son to* HENRY *the*
       Sixth.]
   GHOST. [*To* RICHARD] Let me sit heavy on thy soul
       tomorrow!
Think how thou stab'dst me in my prime of youth
At Tewksbury. Despair, therefore, and die!   120
[*To* RICHMOND] Be cheerful, Richmond, for the
       wrongèd souls
Of butchered princes fight in thy behalf.
King Henry's issue,° Richmond, comforts thee.
       [*Enter the* GHOST OF HENRY THE SIXTH.]
   GHOST. [*To* RICHARD] When I was mortal, my
       anointed body
By thee was punchèd full of deadly holes.   125
Think on the Tower and me. Despair, and die!
Harry the Sixth bids thee despair and die!
[*To* RICHMOND] Virtuous and holy, be thou con-
       queror!
Harry, that prophesied thou shouldst be King,   129
Doth comfort thee in thy sleep. Live, and flourish!
       [*Enter the* GHOST OF CLARENCE.]
   GHOST. [*To* RICHARD] Let me sit heavy on thy soul
       tomorrow!
I that was washed to death with fulsome° wine,
Poor Clarence, by thy guile betrayed to death.
Tomorrow in the battle think on me,

And fall thy edgeless sword. Despair, and die!   135
[*To* RICHMOND] Thou offspring of the House of Lan-
       caster,
The wrongèd heirs of York do pray for thee.
Good angels guard thy battle! Live, and flourish!
   [*Enter the* GHOSTS OF RIVERS, GREY, *and* VAUGHAN.]
   GHOST OF RIV. [*To* RICHARD] Let me sit heavy on
       thy soul tomorrow,
Rivers, that died at Pomfret! Despair, and die!   140
   GHOST OF GREY. [*To* RICHARD] Think upon Grey,
       and let thy soul despair!
   GHOST OF VAUGHAN. [*To* RICHARD] Think upon
       Vaughan, and, with guilty fear,
Let fall thy lance. Despair, and die!
   ALL. [*To* RICHMOND] Awake, and think our
       wrongs in Richard's bosom
Will conquer him! Awake, and win the day!   145
       [*Enter the* GHOST OF HASTINGS.]
   GHOST. [*To* RICHARD] Bloody and guilty, guiltily
       awake,
And in a bloody battle end thy days!
Think on Lord Hastings. Despair, and die!
[*To* RICHMOND] Quiet untroubled soul, awake,
       awake!   149
Arm, fight, and conquer, for fair England's sake!
   [*Enter the* GHOSTS OF THE TWO YOUNG PRINCES.]
   GHOSTS. [*To* RICHARD] Dream on thy cousins
       smothered in the Tower.
Let us be lead within thy bosom, Richard,
And weigh thee down to ruin, shame, and death!
Thy nephews' souls bid thee despair and die!
[*To* RICHMOND] Sleep, Richmond, sleep in peace, and
       wake in joy.   155
Good angels guard thee from the boar's annoy!°
Live, and beget a happy race of kings!
Edward's unhappy sons do bid thee flourish.
       [*Enter the* GHOST OF LADY ANNE *his wife.*]
   GHOST. [*To* RICHARD] Richard, thy wife, that
       wretched Anne thy wife,
That never slept a quiet hour with thee,   160
Now fills thy sleep with perturbations.
Tomorrow in the battle think on me,
And fall thy edgeless sword. Despair, and die!
[*To* RICHMOND] Thou quiet soul, sleep thou a quiet
       sleep.
Dream of success and happy victory!   165
Thy adversary's wife doth pray for thee.
       [*Enter the* GHOST OF BUCKINGHAM.]
   GHOST. [*To* RICHARD] The first was I that helped
       thee to the crown,
The last was I that felt thy tyranny.
Oh, in the battle think on Buckingham,
And die in terror of thy guiltiness!   170
Dream on, dream on, of bloody deeds and death.
Fainting, despair; despairing, yield thy breath!

92. **deceive . . . time:** i.e., pretend to be loyal to Richard.
98. **ceremonious vows:** outward demonstrations of friendship.
105. **peise:** weigh down.   123. **issue:** child.   132. **fulsome:** nauseating.

156. **annoy:** hurt.

[*To* RICHMOND] I died for hope ere I could lend thee
    aid.
But cheer thy heart, and be thou not dismayed.
God and good angels fight on Richmond's side, 175
And Richard falls in height of all his pride.
[*The* GHOSTS *vanish.* KING RICHARD *starts out of his*
                        dream.]

  K. RICH. Give me another horse. Bind up my
    wounds.
Have mercy, Jesu! — Soft! I did but dream.
O coward conscience, how dost thou afflict me!
The lights burn blue. It is now dead midnight. 180
Cold fearful drops stand on my trembling flesh.
What do I fear? Myself? There's none else by.
Richard loves Richard; that is, I am I.
Is there a murderer here? No. Yes, I am.
Then fly. What, from myself? Great reason why —
Lest I revenge. What, myself upon myself? 186
Alack, I love myself. Wherefore? For any good
That I myself have done unto myself?
Oh no! Alas, I rather hate myself
For hateful deeds committed by myself! 190
I am a villain — yet I lie, I am not.
Fool, of thyself speak well. Fool, do not flatter.
My conscience hath a thousand several tongues,
And every tongue brings in a several tale,
And every tale condemns me for a villain. 195
Perjury, perjury, in the high'st degree,
Murder, stern murder, in the dir'st degree —
All several sins, all used in each degree,
Throng to the bar, crying all " Guilty, guilty!"
I shall despair. There is no creature loves me, 200
And if I die, no soul shall pity me.
Nay, wherefore should they, since that I myself
Find in myself no pity to myself?
Methought the souls of all that I had murdered
Came to my tent, and every one did threat 205
Tomorrow's vengeance on the head of Richard.
              [*Enter* RATCLIFF.]

  RAT. My lord!
  K. RICH. 'Zounds! Who is there?
  RAT. Ratcliff, my lord, 'tis I. The early village cock
Hath twice done salutation to the morn. 210
Your friends are up, and buckle on their armor.
  K. RICH. O Ratcliff, I have dreamed a fearful
    dream!
What thinkest thou, will our friends prove all true?
  RAT. No doubt, my lord.
  K. RICH.   O Ratcliff, I fear, I fear——
  RAT. Nay, good my lord, be not afraid of shadows.
  K. RICH. By the Apostle Paul, shadows tonight
Have struck more terror to the soul of Richard 217
Than can the substance of ten thousand soldiers
Armèd in proof,° and led by shallow Richmond.
It is not yet near day. Come, go with me. 220

219. **proof:** armor that has been tested.

Under our tents I'll play the eavesdropper,
To see if any mean to shrink from me. [*Exeunt.*]
[*Enter the* LORDS *to* RICHMOND, *sitting in his tent.*]
  LORDS. Good morrow, Richmond!
  RICHM. Cry mercy, lords and watchful gentlemen,
That you have ta'en a tardy sluggard here. 225
  LORDS. How have you slept, my lord?
  RICHM. The sweetest sleep and fairest-boding
    dreams
That ever entered in a drowsy head
Have I since your departure had, my lords.
Methought their souls whose bodies Richard mur-
    dered 230
Came to my tent, and cried on victory.
I promise you, my soul is very jocund
In the remembrance of so fair a dream.
How far into the morning is it, lords?
  LORDS. Upon the stroke of four. 235
  RICHM. Why, then 'tis time to arm and give di-
    rection.
        [*His oration to his* SOLDIERS.]
More than I have said, loving countrymen,
The leisure and enforcement of the time
Forbids to dwell upon. Yet remember this —
God and our good cause fight upon our side; 240
The prayers of holy saints and wrongèd souls,
Like high-reared bulwarks, stand before our faces.
Richard except, those whom we fight against
Had rather have us win than him they follow.
For what is he they follow? Truly, gentlemen, 245
A bloody tyrant and a homicide,
One raised in blood, and one in blood established,
One that made means to come by what he hath,
And slaughtered those that were the means to help
    him —
A base foul stone,° made precious by the foil° 250
Of England's chair,° where he is falsely set,
One that hath ever been God's enemy.
Then, if you fight against God's enemy,
God will in justice ward° you as His soldiers.
If you do sweat to put a tyrant down, 255
You sleep in peace, the tyrant being slain.
If you do fight against your country's foes,
Your country's fat shall pay your pains the hire.
If you do fight in safeguard of your wives,
Your wives shall welcome home the conquerors.
If you do free your children from the sword, 261
Your children's children quit it° in your age.
Then, in the name of God and all these rights,
Advance your standards, draw your willing swords.
For me, the ransom° of my bold attempt 265
Shall be this cold corpse on the earth's cold face.
But if I thrive, the gain of my attempt

250. **foul stone:** valueless jewel. **foil:** tin foil, placed behind a
precious stone to increase its sparkle. 251. **chair:** throne.
254. **ward:** guard. 262. **quit it:** pay it back. 265. **ransom:**
expiation.

The least of you shall share his part thereof.
Sound drums and trumpets boldly and cheerfully.
God and Saint George! Richmond and victory!   270

[*Exeunt.*]

[*Re-enter* KING RICHARD, RATCLIFF, ATTENDANTS
and FORCES.]

K. RICH. What said Northumberland as touching
Richmond?

RAT. That he was never trainèd up in arms.

K. RICH. He said the truth. And what said Surrey
then?

RAT. He smiled and said, " The better for our pur-
pose."   274

K. RICH. He was in the right, and so indeed it is.

[*The clock strikes.*]

Tell° the clock there. Give me a calendar.
Who saw the sun today?

RAT.   Not I, my lord.

K. RICH. Then he disdains to shine, for by the
book
He should have braved the east an hour ago.
A black day will it be to somebody.   280
Ratcliff!

RAT. My lord?

K. RICH.   The sun will not be seen today,
The sky doth frown and lour upon our army.
I would these dewy tears were from the ground.
Not shine today! Why, what is that to me   285
More than to Richmond? For the selfsame heaven
That frowns on me looks sadly upon him.

[*Re-enter* NORFOLK.]

NOR. Arm, arm, my lord, the foe vaunts in the
field.

K. RICH. Come, bustle, bustle. Caparison° my
horse.
Call up Lord Stanley, bid him bring his power.   290
I will lead forth my soldiers to the plain,
And thus my battle shall be ordered:
My foreward° shall be drawn out all in length,
Consisting equally of horse and foot,
Our archers shall be placèd in the midst.   295
John Duke of Norfolk, Thomas Earl of Surrey,
Shall have the leading of this foot and horse.
They thus directed, we will follow
In the main battle, whose puissance on either side
Shall be well wingèd with our chiefest horse.   300
This, and Saint George to boot! What think'st thou,
Norfolk?

NOR. A good direction, warlike sovereign.
This found I on my tent this morning.

[*He showeth him a paper.*]

K. RICH. [*Reads.*] " Jockey of Norfolk, be not too
bold,
For Dickon thy master is bought and sold."   305
A thing devisèd by the enemy.

Go, gentlemen, every man unto his charge.
Let not our babbling dreams affright our souls.
Conscience is but a word that cowards use,
Devised at first to keep the strong in awe.   310
Our strong arms be our conscience, swords our
law.
March on, join bravely, let us to 't pell-mell —
If not to Heaven, then hand in hand to Hell.

[*His oration to his* ARMY.]

What shall I say more than I have inferred?
Remember whom you are to cope withal —   315
A sort of vagabonds, rascals, and runaways,
A scum of Bretons,° and base lackey peasants,
Whom their o'ercloyed° country vomits forth
To desperate ventures and assured destruction.
You sleeping safe, they bring to you unrest.   320
You having lands and blest with beauteous wives,
They would restrain° the one, distain° the other.
And who doth lead them but a paltry fellow,
Long kept in Bretagne at our mother's cost?
A milksop, one that never in his life   325
Felt so much cold as over shoes in snow?
Let's whip these stragglers o'er the seas again,
Lash hence these overweening rags of France,
These famished beggars, weary of their lives,
Who, but for dreaming on this fond exploit,   330
For want of means, poor rats, had hanged them-
selves.
If we be conquered, let men conquer us,
And not these bastard Bretons, whom our fathers
Have in their own land beaten, bobbed,° and
thumped,
And in recórd° left them the heirs of shame.   335
Shall these enjoy our lands? Lie with our wives?
Ravish our daughters? [*Drum afar off.*] Hark! I
hear their drum.
Fight, gentlemen of England! Fight, bold yeomen!
Draw, archers, draw your arrows to the head!
Spur your proud horses hard, and ride in blood.
Amaze the welkin° with your broken staves!   341
[*Enter a* MESSENGER.] What says Lord Stanley? Will
he bring his power?

MESS. My lord, he doth deny to come.

K. RICH. Off with his son George's head!

NOR. My lord, the enemy is past the marsh.   345
After the battle let George Stanley die.

K. RICH. A thousand hearts are great within my
bosom.
Advance our standards, set upon our foes.
Our ancient word of courage, fair Saint George,
Inspire us with the spleen° of fiery dragons!   350
Upon them! Victory sits on our helms.   [*Exeunt.*]

---

276. Tell: count.   289. Caparison: equip with battle harness.
293. foreward: front line.

317. Bretons: Richmond during his exile had lived in Brittany.
318. o'ercloyed: queasy with overfeeding.   322. restrain: seize.
distain: dishonor.   334. bobbed: banged.   335. in record: in
the history book.   341. Amaze . . . welkin: frighten the sky.
350. spleen: wrath.

SCENE IV. *Another part of the field.*

[*Alarum:° excursions.° Enter* NORFOLK *and* FORCES
fighting; to him CATESBY.]

CATE. Rescue, my Lord of Norfolk, rescue, rescue!
The King enacts more wonders than a man,
Daring an opposite to every danger.
His horse is slain, and all on foot he fights,
Seeking for Richmond in the throat of death.   5
Rescue, fair lord, or else the day is lost!

[*Alarums. Enter* KING RICHARD.]

K. RICH. A horse! A horse! My kingdom for a
horse!°
CATE. Withdraw, my lord. I'll help you to a horse.
K. RICH. Slave, I have set my life upon a cast,°
And I will stand the hazard° of the die.   10
I think there be six Richmonds in the field.
Five have I slain today instead of him.
A horse! A horse! My kingdom for a horse!
[*Exeunt.*]

SCENE V. *Another part of the field.*

[*Alarum. Enter* RICHARD *and* RICHMOND; *they fight.*
RICHARD *is slain. Retreat and flourish. Re-enter*
RICHMOND, DERBY *bearing the crown,*
with divers other LORDS.]

RICHM. God and your arms be praised, victorious
friends!
The day is ours — the bloody dog is dead.
DER. Courageous Richmond, well hast thou acquit
thee.°
Lo, here, this long usurpèd royalty°
From the dead temples of this bloody wretch   5
Have I plucked off, to grace thy brows withal.
Wear it, enjoy it, and make much of it.
RICHM. Great God of Heaven, say amen to all!
But tell me, is young George Stanley living?   9

Sc. iv: s.d., Alarum: trumpet call to arms. excursion: battle
movements. 7. A . . . horse!: This line was much admired,
quoted, and imitated by Shakespeare's contemporaries. 9. cast:
throw of the dice. 10. hazard: chance.
Sc. v: 3. acquit thee: given a good account of yourself.
4. royalty: i.e., the crown.

DER. He is, my lord, and safe in Leicester town,
Whither, if it please you, we may now withdraw us.
RICHM. What men of name° are slain on either
side?
DER. John Duke of Norfolk, Walter Lord Ferrers,
Sir Robert Brakenbury, and Sir William Brandon.
RICHM. Inter their bodies as becomes their births.
Proclaim a pardon to the soldiers fled   16
That in submission will return to us.
And then, as we have ta'en the sacrament,
We will unite the white rose and the red.°
Smile Heaven upon this fair conjunction,   20
That long have frowned upon their enmity!
What traitor hears me and says not amen?
England hath long been mad, and scarred herself —
The brother blindly shed the brother's blood,
The father rashly slaughtered his own son,   25
The son, compelled, been butcher to the sire.
All this divided York and Lancaster,
Divided in their dire division,
Oh, now let Richmond and Elizabeth,
The true succeeders of each royal house,   30
By God's fair ordinance conjoin together!
And let their heirs, God, if Thy will be so,
Enrich the time to come with smooth-faced peace,
With smiling plenty and fair prosperous days!
Abate° the edge of traitors, gracious Lord,   35
That would reduce° these bloody days again
And make poor England weep in streams of blood!
Let them not live to taste this land's increase
That would with treason wound this fair land's
peace!
Now civil wounds are stopped, peace lives again.   40
That she may long live here, God say amen!
[*Exeunt.*]

12. name: high rank. 19. We . . . red: i.e., the two warring sides
of York (White Rose) and Lancaster (Red Rose), which was
accomplished when Richmond, as Henry VII, married Elizabeth,
daughter of Edward IV. See App. 28, Table C. 35-36. Abate . . .
again: The closing lines of this speech had special significance
for their original audience. Queen Elizabeth was the grand-
daughter of Richmond and Elizabeth; but she had no heir, and
to many it seemed only too likely that at her death the bloody
story of the civil wars would be repeated. reduce: bring back.

LOVE'S LABOR'S LOST

Introduction

Love's Labor's Lost is at first sight a difficult play; it abounds in inexplicable lines, allusions, topicalities, jokes, and personalities so obscure and unintelligible that they bewilder even the most erudite of commentators. As a result critics tend to leave the play to those who are more interested in literary puzzles than in poetry. This is regrettable, for *Love's Labor's Lost* taken in the right spirit is a most amusing entertainment. It should not be judged according to any critical rules of comedy, or as the work of the sage philosopher who afterward wrote *Hamlet* or *Lear,* but rather as a musical comedy, a revue, a trifle for the amusement of a select audience at a Christmas house party. It is best to consider the play in this light first and the antiquarian matters later.

The theme of *Love's Labor's Lost* is Cupid's revenge, and it is composed in movements almost like an elaborate ballet. The first movement is the opening of the theme. Four normal, lusty, young men — Navarre, Berowne, Longaville, and Dumain — have quixotically agreed to the preposterous proposal that for three years they will forswear love and all earthly delights and devote themselves to study — the kind of resolution a student makes at the beginning of his final year and keeps for the first fortnight. But only Berowne realizes that the pact is impossible; he signs under protest. The first movement also introduces Costard the clown, who is Cupid's servant, since he is in love with Jaquenetta; and Armado, the fantastic Spaniard, who is also trying to resist Cupid.

The second movement opens with the arrival of the Princess of France and her ladies — Rosaline, Maria, and Katharine — escorted by Boyet, her chamberlain. They have come on an embassy to visit Navarre and all are ready to help Cupid; but the edict forbidding love thwarts them, and when Navarre inhospitably leaves them to encamp in the open, all four are eager to become instruments for Love's revenge. Love has already been at work. Berowne is the first traitor to his oath; he has fallen in love with Rosaline of the dark eyes. So he sends a note to his lady by Costard, who is already carrying another from Armado to Jaquenetta. In delivering them Costard mixes up the notes.

Then, before the third movement starts, comes the interlude of Holofernes the schoolmaster and Nathaniel the curate with their learned pleasantries. With the start of the third movement each of the students of philosophy has been caught. They come in one by one reading their love rhymes, each — as he thinks — hiding his shame from the others, until each in turn is betrayed and disgraced. Berowne is the last to be convicted when his letter to Rosaline falls into the hands of Navarre; but Berowne alone has the wit to see that perjury is a less dangerous offense than to deny Cupid's superior power. The new convert now hymns love in a magnificent paean of praise for his lady's eyes. He rallies the lovers, and all are now eager to enter the lists as Cupid's soldiers.

The fourth movement is prefaced by the second interlude of pedant and curate. Then follows a masque of Russians, when the four disguised lovers prepare to attack their ladies; but the women change their masks and confuse their adversaries. The movement is then repeated with a difference. The lovers return without their disguises and in their own persons; the ladies come back escorted by Boyet, and the attacks are resumed. Both groups now join to watch the presentation of the pageant of the Nine Worthies — a very human diversion. The fun is at its highest when there suddenly appears Mercade with the bad news that the King of France is dead. The laughter abruptly ceases, and just as each lover thinks that he has reached the goal, he is thwarted by the barrier of death.

So Cupid is revenged; a penance is laid on the lovers, and the gaiety becomes serious. But this would be too gloomy an ending for so light a play. The antic procession of the owl and the cuckoo, Winter and Spring, enters, and each sings his song. Armado leads his flock away and the sad lovers leave the stage empty. The ending has just that note of interrogation and seriousness with which sometimes Shakespeare ends even a most joyous comedy.

It is often forgotten that Shakespeare's plays as we read them in the text are but a small part of the original experience — the words only. The whole play was a combination of color, music, grouping, dancing, song, voice, and above all, movement. Only the words remain of *Love's Labor's Lost,* like an old record of some lavish opera. Shakespeare, though a poet of incomparable power, was primarily a man of the stage concerned with his plays as a fusion of dialogue and action. His lesser plays cannot be appreciated without action. *Love's Labor's Lost* is not a great play, but on the stage it has lasting qualities and great variety, and above all, poetry in abundance and great variety of meter — sonnets, lyrics, songs, the song of Winter and Spring, Berowne's tirade against learning and love, his praise of love and light, his alarm to Cupid's soldiers, his cameo portrait of Boyet; and with these too there are the humanity and the comedy.

Love's Labor's Lost would be better known if there were fewer difficulties for the ordinary reader. Indeed the problems are so many that the play is quite in a class by itself. Compared with other dramatists Shakespeare was usually sparing with direct topical allusions; *Love's Labor's Lost* abounds with them, but they are so obscure and intimate that nowadays most of them are quite inexplicable. It is thus probable that the play was originally written for a select audience rather than for the general public.

The first definite fact about *Love's Labor's Lost* is that an edition of the play was published in 1598 with the title page: *A Pleasant Conceited Comedie Called, Loues labors lost. As it was presented before her Highnes this last Christmas. Newly corrected and augmented By W. Shakespere. Imprinted at London by W.W. for Cutbert Burby. 1598.* This quarto may originally have been set from the original manuscript. It shows signs that in a few places speeches have been rewritten. The text in the first folio of 1623 was set from a copy of the quarto considerably revised. The words "newly corrected and augmented" on the title page imply that at least one earlier edition had appeared; but if so, no copy survives. A similar note occurs in the second quarto of *Romeo and Juliet,* which differed considerably from the first quarto. The second

quarto of *1 Henry IV* is also described as newly corrected, although the corrections are only of misprints; the third, fourth, and fifth quartos, though reprinted one from the other, were also described as newly corrected.

The date of *Love's Labor's Lost* is doubtful. The quarto establishes that it was written some time before 1598, but scholars are not generally agreed, and their guesses vary from 1588 to 1596. The style of the play — if style in a play so far out of the ordinary is any sure guide — would link it with the Sonnets and the earlier plays such as *Romeo and Juliet;* that is, before 1595. The guess which at present seems likeliest is that of the editors of the New Cambridge Shakespeare (A.T. Quiller Couch and J. Dover Wilson) who state that "in our opinion its first performance had Christmas 1593 for date and for place some great private house, possibly the Earl of Southampton's."

If this guess, and it can only be a guess, is correct, much will follow. In 1593 Shakespeare was twenty-nine. He had already experimented in various kinds of comedy, but in April 1593 his poem *Venus and Adonis* had appeared with a dedicatory letter to the Earl of Southampton. As a result of the poem, which was immediately successful, Shakespeare seems to have received many marks of favor from the young Earl (see Gen. Intro. page 10a–b). Moreover Southampton, to the surprise and annoyance of Lord Burghleigh, his guardian, refused to marry. It is therefore not improbable that love, or rather a disdain for love, was a theme which occupied the witty young men of Southampton's household. The theme of the four young men who despised love was thus ready to hand, and the names of these young men were in themselves topical. Many gallants had served in France with the forces which were aiding Henry of Navarre in 1591 and 1592; among the notable figures in the French campaign were the Marshal de Biron and the Duc de Longueville, two of Navarre's chief commanders, and the Duc de Mayne, his most powerful opponent. It was an amusing notion in itself to bring this ill-assorted company together to study philosophy and to avoid the society of women, especially as the real Navarre was himself a notorious philanderer constantly embarrassed by the demands of his various ladies.

Another topicality which can reasonably be identified occurs at IV.iii.254:

Oh, paradox! Black is the badge of Hell,
The hue of dungeons and the school of night.

In the early 1590's much scandal was caused in
London by a coterie of intellectuals, of whom Sir
Walter Ralegh was chief, who were accused of
discussing obscure and forbidden topics. Other
members of the group were Henry Percy, Earl
of Northumberland, known as the Wizard Earl,
a keen student of the sciences; Thomas Harriott,
one of the greatest mathematicians of his age;
Matthew Roydon, a minor man of letters; and
the two poets Christopher Marlowe and George
Chapman. The discussions of this group were
much suspected; it was said that with Harriott as
their schoolmaster a number of young noblemen
were taught to jibe at the Scriptures, that such
articles of faith as the immortality of the
soul and the future life were ridiculed, and that
scholars taught among other things to spell God
backwards. In 1594 Chapman published an ob-
scure poem called *The Shadow of Night,* which
he dedicated to Roydon.

There are apparently other jibes at this group.
Holofernes with his "foolish, extravagant spirit,
full of forms, figures, shapes, objects, ideas, ap-
prehensions, motions, revolutions" (IV.ii.67–69)
would certainly have reminded the audience of
the mathematician Harriott. Even Ralegh, who
was no friend to the Southampton group, was,
in the view of some scholars, caricatured under
the fantastical Armado. Ralegh was much in the
public eye at the time, but by 1592 he had fallen
from grace. While still flattering the Queen as
of old, he had seduced one of her maids of honor,
whom he subsequently married. The Queen was
so angry that she sent him to the Tower, where

he lapsed into profound melancholy and wrote
her fantastical letters.

However, such identifications can seldom be
proved. Although from time to time characters
utter remarks which would remind the audience
of current gossip, it is rare, even in topical plays,
that a character is a consistent caricature. The
braggart, the pedant, and the witty boy have been
stock figures in comedy from the days of Plautus
and Terence. Such problems, however, have little
to do with the poetical qualities of *Love's Labor's
Lost* and cannot be briefly discussed. Those who
wish to pursue them should consult the works of
scholars (see page 89b).

The story of *Love's Labor's Lost* seems to be
original, for no source has been discovered. But
it is more than a coincidence that in 1592 three of
Lyly's plays were published which gave Shake-
speare a model for witty social comedy written
for select audiences. The true source of *Love's
Labor's Lost* is not, however, any book or play,
but the lively, witty conversation of young men
of high rank, education, and good breeding. The
play is the work of a man who listened eagerly to
good talk and reveled in its wit. We are apt to
forget that conversation is the most potent of all
literary influences.

In the study of most of Shakespeare's plays
some knowledge of the background, source, and
date is essential to full understanding. With
Love's Labor's Lost it is almost the opposite. The
student whose main interest is in drama and
poetry should therefore ignore the obscure lines
and the incomprehensible jokes. If he can regard
the play as a lighthearted trifle he will find that
it is still brimful of the finest poetry and very
comical mirth.

Love's Labor's Lost

DRAMATIS PERSONAE

FERDINAND, *King of Navarre*

BEROWNE
LONGAVILLE } *lords attending on the King*
DUMAIN

BOYET
MERCADE } *lords attending on the Princess of France*

DON ADRIANO DE ARMADO, *a fantastical Spaniard*
SIR NATHANIEL, *a curate*
HOLOFERNES, *a schoolmaster*
DULL, *a constable*
COSTARD, *a clown*

MOTH, *page to Armado*
A FORESTER

THE PRINCESS *of France*
ROSALINE
MARIA } *ladies attending on the Princess*
KATHARINE
JAQUENETTA, *a country wench*

LORDS, ATTENDANTS, ETC.

SCENE — *Navarre*.

Act I

SCENE I. *The King of Navarre's park.*

[*Enter* FERDINAND, *King of Navarre,* BEROWNE,
LONGAVILLE, *and* DUMAIN.]

KING. Let fame, that all hunt after in their lives,
Live registered upon our brazen tombs,
And then grace us in the disgrace of death;
When, spite of cormorant° devouring Time,
The endeavor of this present breath may buy   5
That honor which shall bate° his scythe's keen edge,
And make us heirs of all eternity.
Therefore, brave conquerors — for so you are
That war against your own affections
And the huge army of the world's desires —   10
Our late edict shall strongly stand in force.
Navarre shall be the wonder of the world;
Our Court shall be a little Academe,°
Still and contemplative in living art.°
You three, Berowne, Dumain, and Longaville,   15
Have sworn for three years' term to live with me
My fellow scholars, and to keep those statutes
That are recorded in this schedule here.
Your oaths are passed, and now subscribe your
    names,
That his own hand may strike his honor down   20
That violates the smallest branch herein.
If you are armed° to do as sworn to do,
Subscribe to your deep oaths, and keep it too.
    LONG. I am resolved — 'tis but a three years' fast.
The mind shall banquet though the body pine.   25
Fat paunches have lean pates, and dainty bits
Make rich the ribs, but bankrupt quite the wits.

Act I, Sc. i: **4. cormorant:** a rapacious sea bird. **6. bate:**
blunt. **13. Academe:** society of scholars, from the famous
Athenian Academy at which Plato taught. **14. Still . . . art:**
always pondering over the art of living, which was the main
study of the Stoic philosophers. **22. armed:** resolved.

DUM. My loving lord, Dumain is mortified.°
The grosser manner of these world's delights
He throws upon the gross world's baser slaves.   30
To love, to wealth, to pomp, I pine and die,
With all these living in philosophy.
    BER. I can but say their protestation over.°
So much, dear liege, I have already sworn;
That is, to live and study here three years.   35
But there are other strict observances —
As not to see a woman in that term,
Which I hope well is not enrollèd there;
And one day in a week to touch no food,
And but one meal on every day beside,   40
The which I hope is not enrollèd there;
And then, to sleep but three hours in the night,
And not be seen to wink of° all the day —
When I was wont to think no harm all night,
And make a dark night too of half the day —   45
Which I hope well is not enrollèd there.
Oh, these are barren tasks, too hard to keep:
Not to see ladies, study, fast, not sleep!
    KING. Your oath is passed to pass away from these.
    BER. Let me say no, my liege, an if° you please.
I only swore to study with your Grace,   51
And stay here in your Court for three years' space.
    LONG. You swore to that, Berowne, and to the rest.
    BER. By yea and nay,° sir, then I swore in jest.
What is the end of study? Let me know.   55
    KING. Why, that to know which else we should
    not know.
    BER. Things hid and barred, you mean, from com·
    mon sense?°
    KING. Aye, that is study's godlike recompense.
    BER. Come on, then, I will swear to study so,
To know the thing I am forbid to know.   60
As thus — to study where I well may dine

---

28. mortified: dead to fleshly delights. **33. say . . . over:** repeat.
43. wink of: close the eyes during. **50. an if:** if. **54. By . . . nay:**
assuredly. **57. common sense:** ordinary perception.

When I to feast expressly am forbid;
  Or study where to meet some mistress fine
When mistresses from common sense are hid;
  Or, having sworn too hard a keeping oath,   65
Study to break it and not break my troth.°
If study's gain be thus, and this be so,
Study knows that which yet it doth not know.
Swear me to this, and I will ne'er say no.

KING. These be the stops that hinder study quite,
And train our intellects to vain delight.   71

BER. Why, all delights are vain, but that most vain
Which, with pain purchased, doth inherit pain° —
As painfully to pore upon a book
To seek the light of truth, while truth the while
Doth falsely blind the eyesight of his look.   76
  Light, seeking light, doth light of light beguile;°
So, ere you find where light in darkness lies,
Your light grows dark by losing of your eyes.
Study me how to please the eye indeed,   80
  By fixing it upon a fairer eye,
Who dazzling so, that eye shall be his heed,
  And give him light that it was blinded by.°
Study is like the heaven's glorious sun,
  That will not be deep-searched with saucy looks.
Small have continual plodders ever won,   86
  Save base authority from others' books.
These earthly godfathers of heaven's lights°
  That give a name to every fixèd star
Have no more profit of their shining nights   90
  Than those that walk and wot° not what they are.
Too much to know is to know naught but fame,°
And every godfather can give a name.

KING. How well he's read, to reason against reading!

DUM. Proceeded° well, to stop all good proceeding!   95

LONG. He weeds the corn, and still lets grow the weeding.°

BER. The spring is near, when green geese° are a-breeding.

DUM. How follows that?

BER.   Fit in his place and time.

DUM. In reason, nothing.

BER.   Something, then, in rhyme.°

KING. Berowne is like an envious sneaping° frost
That bites the first-born infants° of the spring.

BER. Well, say I am. Why should proud summer boast   102
Before the birds have any cause to sing?
Why should I joy in any abortive birth?
At Christmas I no more desire a rose   105
Than wish a snow in May's newfangled shows,
But like of each thing that in season grows.
So you, to study now it is too late,°
Climb o'er the house to unlock the little gate.

KING. Well, sit you out. Go home, Berowne. Adieu.   110

BER. No, my good lord, I have sworn to stay with you.
And though I have for barbarism° spoke more
Than for that angel knowledge you can say,
Yet confident I'll keep what I have swore,
And bide the penance of each three years' day.
Give me the paper, let me read the same,   116
And to the strict'st decrees I'll write my name.

KING. How well this yielding rescues thee from shame!

BER. [*Reads.*] "Item, That no woman shall come within a mile of my Court——" Hath this been proclaimed?   120

LONG. Four days ago.

BER. Let's see the penalty. [*Reads.*] "on pain of losing her tongue." Who devised this penalty?   125

LONG. Marry,° that did I.

BER. Sweet lord, and why?

LONG. To fright them hence with that dread penalty.   128

BER. A dangerous law against gentility!° [*Reads.*] "Item, If any man be seen to talk with a woman within the term of three years, he shall endure such public shame as the rest of the Court can possibly devise."
This article, my liege, yourself must break;
  For well you know here comes in embassy   135
The French King's daughter with yourself to speak —
  A maid of grace and complete majesty —
About surrender up of Aquitaine°
To her decrepit, sick, and bedrid father.
Therefore this article is made in vain,   140
  Or vainly comes the admirèd Princess hither.

KING. What say you, lords? Why, this was quite forgot.

BER. So study evermore is overshot.°
While it doth study to have what it would,
It doth forget to do the thing it should;   145
And when it hath the thing it hunteth most,
'Tis won as towns with fire, so won, so lost.°

KING. We must of force dispense with this decree.

---

66. **troth:** faith.   73. **pain . . . pain:** hard labor . . . discomfort. 77. **beguile:** cheat. 82–83. **Who . . . by:** i.e., the dazzling beauty of his lady's eyes may blind him but they also give him light. 88. **earthly . . . lights:** i.e., astronomers who give names to the stars. 91. **wot:** know. 92. **fame:** mere report. 95. **Proceeded:** in the universities of Oxford and Cambridge the word means "has taken his degree," i.e., shown himself a scholar. 96. **weeding:** that which was weeded out. 97. **green geese:** goslings. 98–99. **How . . . rhyme:** Dumain asks Berowne what he means. Berowne replies that his words are quite suitable to such a goose as Dumain. Dumain answers that it does not make sense; to which Berowne retorts that if it is not reason, it is at least in rhyme — a play on the common saying "neither rhyme nor reason." 100. **sneaping:** nipping. 101. **infants:** buds.

108. **to . . . late:** you are past the time for study. 112. **barbarism:** ignorance. 126. **Marry:** Mary, by the Virgin. 129. **gentility:** good manners. 138. **Aquitaine:** a province of France. 143. **overshot:** wide of the mark. 147. **so . . . lost:** i.e., like a town captured after its destruction, not worth having.

She must lie° here on mere° necessity.

BER. Necessity will make us all forsworn°   150
Three thousand times within this three years'
          space;
For every man with his affects° is born,
Not by might mastered, but by special grace.
If I break faith, this word shall speak for me,
I am forsworn on " mere necessity."   155
So to the laws at large I write my name. [*Subscribes.*]
And he that breaks them in the least degree
Stands in attainder° of eternal shame.
Suggestions° are to other as to me,
But I believe, although I seem so loath,   160
I am the last that will last keep his oath.
But is there no quick recreation° granted?

KING. Aye, that there is. Our Court, you know, is
          haunted
With a refinèd traveler of Spain —
A man in all the world's new fashion planted   165
That hath a mint of phrases in his brain;
One whom the music of his own vain tongue
Doth ravish like enchanting harmony;
A man of complements,° whom right and wrong
Have chose as umpire of their mutiny.   170
This child of fancy, that Armado hight,°
For interim° to our studies, shall relate,
In highborn words, the worth of many a knight
From tawny Spain, lost in the world's debate.°
How you delight, my lords, I know not, I,   175
But I protest I love to hear him lie,
And I will use him for my minstrelsy.°

BER. Armado is a most illustrious wight,°
A man of fire-new° words, fashion's own knight.°

LONG. Costard the swain° and he shall be our
          sport,   180
And so to study three years is but short.

[*Enter* DULL *with a letter, and* COSTARD.]

DULL. Which is the Duke's° own person?

BER. This, fellow. What wouldst?

DULL. I myself reprehend° his own person, for I
am His Grace's tharborough.° But I would see his
own person in flesh and blood.   186

BER. This is he.

DULL. Signior Arme — Arme — commends you.
There's villainy abroad. This letter will tell you
more.   190

COST. Sir, the contempts° thereof are as touching
me.

KING. A letter from the magnificent Armado.

BER. How low soever the matter, I hope in God
for high words.   195

LONG. A high hope for a low heaven. God grant
us patience!

BER. To hear? Or forbear laughing?

LONG. To hear meekly, sir, and to laugh moder-
ately — or to forbear both.   200

BER. Well, sir, be it as the style shall give us cause
to climb in the merriness.

COST. The matter is to me, sir, as concerning
Jaquenetta. The matter of it is, I was taken with the
manner.°   205

BER. In what manner?

COST. In manner and form following, sir, all those
three: I was seen with her in the manor house, sitting
with her upon the form,° and taken following her
into the park; which, put together, is in manner and
form following. Now, sir, for the manner — it is the
manner of a man to speak to a woman. For the
form — in some form.   213

BER. For the following, sir?

COST. As it shall follow in my correction, and God
defend the right!

KING. Will you hear this letter with attention?

BER. As we would hear an oracle.

COST. Such is the simplicity of man to hearken
after the flesh.   220

KING. [*Reads.*] " Great deputy, the welkin's° vice-
gerent, and sole dominator° of Navarre, my soul's
earth's god, and body's fostering° patron." ——

COST. Not a word of Costard yet.

KING. [*Reads.*] " So it is " ——   225

COST. It may be so. But if he say it is so, he is, in
telling true, but so.

KING. Peace!

COST. Be to me, and every man that dares not
fight!   230

KING. No words!

COST. Of other men's secrets, I beseech you.

KING. [*Reads.*] " So it is, besieged with sable-
colored° melancholy, I did commend the black-
oppressing humor° to the most wholesome physic of
thy health-giving air; and, as I am a gentleman, be-
took myself to walk. The time when? About the
sixth hour, when beasts most graze, birds best peck,
and men sit down to that nourishment which is
called supper. So much for the time when. Now for
the ground which — which, I mean, I walked upon.
It is ycleped° thy park. Then for the place   240
where — where, I mean, I did encounter that obscene
and most preposterous event that draweth from my

---

149. lie: stay. mere: sheer.   150. forsworn: break our oath.
152. affects: natural inclinations.   158. attainder: condemnation.
159. Suggestions: temptations.   162. quick recreation: lively
sport.   169. complements: refined behavior.   171. hight: named.
172. interim: interlude, pastime.   174. debate: strife.   177. min-
strelsy: band of musicians.   178. wight: man.   179. fire-new:
brand-new. fashion's . . . knight: It was the mark of the accom-
plished courtier to be able to discourse in the latest fashion of
vocabulary. Cf. Osric (*Haml.* V.ii.81–195).   180. swain: coun-
tryman.   182. Duke: Ferdinand in this play is both Duke and
King.   184. reprehend: for "represent." Like other humble
characters in Shakespeare's plays, Costard loves long words but
is not always sure of their meanings.   185. tharborough: third
borough, constable.

191. contempts: for "contents." 204–05. with . . . manner: in
the act.   209. form: bench.   221. welkin: sky.   222. dominator:
ruler.   223. fostering: sustaining.   233. sable-colored: black.
234. humor: See App. 3 and 4.   240. ycleped: called.

snow-white pen the ebon-colored° ink which here thou viewest, beholdest, surveyest, or seest. But to the place where — it standeth north-northeast and by east from the west corner of thy curious-knotted° garden. There did I see that low-spirited swain, that base minnow of thy mirth —— " 251

COST. Me?

KING. [Reads.] "that unlettered small-knowing soul —— "

COST. Me? 255

KING. [Reads.] " that shallow vassal° —— "

COST. Still me?

KING. [Reads.] " which, as I remember, hight Costard —— "

COST. Oh, me! 260

KING. [Reads.] " sorted and consorted, contrary to thy established proclaimed edict and continent canon,° which with — Oh, with — but with this I passion to say° wherewith —— "

COST. With a wench. 265

KING. [Reads.] " with a child of our grandmother Eve, a female; or, for thy more sweet understanding, a woman. Him I, as my ever-esteemed duty pricks me on, have sent to thee to receive the meed° of punishment, by thy sweet Grace's officer, Anthony Dull, a man of good repute, carriage, bearing, and estimation." 273

DULL. Me, an't° shall please you. I am Anthony Dull.

KING. [Reads.] "For Jaquenetta — so is the weaker vessel called which I apprehended with the aforesaid swain — I keep her as a vessel of thy law's fury; and shall, at the least of thy sweet notice, bring her to trial. Thine, in all compliments of devoted and heartburning heat of duty.

DON ADRIANO DE ARMADO." 280

BER. This is not so well as I looked for, but the best that ever I heard.

KING. Aye, the best for the worst. But, sirrah, what say you to this?

COST. Sir, I confess the wench. 285

KING. Did you hear the proclamation?

COST. I do confess much of the hearing it, but little of the marking of it.

KING. It was proclaimed a year's imprisonment to be taken with a wench. 290

COST. I was taken with none, sir. I was taken with a damsel.

KING. Well, it was proclaimed damsel.

COST. This was no damsel neither, sir. She was a virgin.

KING. It is so varied too, for it was proclaimed virgin. 295

COST. If it were, I deny her virginity. I was taken with a maid.

KING. This maid will not serve your turn,° sir.

COST. This maid will serve my turn, sir. 301

KING. Sir, I will pronounce your sentence. You shall fast a week with bran and water.

COST. I had rather pray a month with mutton and porridge. 305

KING. And Don Armado shall be your keeper. My Lord Berowne, see him delivered o'er. And go we, lords, to put in practice that Which each to other hath so strongly sworn.

[Exeunt KING, LONGAVILLE, and DUMAIN.]

BER. I'll lay° my head to any good man's hat, 310 These oaths and laws will prove an idle scorn. Sirrah,° come on.

COST. I suffer for the truth, sir; for true it is I was taken with Jaquenetta, and Jaquenetta is a true girl, and therefore welcome the sour cup of prosperity! Affliction may one day smile again, and till then, sit thee down, sorrow! [Exeunt.]

SCENE II. *The same.*

[Enter ARMADO *and* MOTH *his page.*]

ARM. Boy, what sign is it when a man of great spirit grows melancholy?

MOTH. A great sign, sir, that he will look sad.

ARM. Why, sadness is one and the selfsame thing, dear imp. 5

MOTH. No, no, oh Lord, sir, no.

ARM. How canst thou part° sadness and melancholy, my tender juvenal?°

MOTH. By a familiar demonstration of the working, my tough senior. 10

ARM. Why tough senior? Why tough senior?

MOTH. Why tender juvenal? Why tender juvenal?

ARM. I spoke it, tender juvenal, as a congruent epitheton° appertaining to thy young days, which we may nominate tender.

MOTH. And I, tough senior, as an appertinent title to your old time, which we may name tough. 18

ARM. Pretty and apt.

MOTH. How mean you, sir? I pretty, and my saying apt? Or I apt, and my saying pretty?

ARM. Thou pretty, because little.

MOTH. Little pretty, because little. Wherefore apt?

ARM. And therefore apt, because quick. 25

MOTH. Speak you this in my praise, master?

ARM. In thy condign° praise.

MOTH. I will praise an eel with the same praise.

---

243. ebon-colored: black as ebony. 249. curious-knotted: elaborately laid out with little borders of shrubs. See Pl. 16a. 256. vassal: slave, with a pun on "vessel." 262–63. continent canon: law ordaining continency. 264. passion to say: say with grief. 269. meed: reward. 274. an't: if it.

300. serve . . . turn: help you. 310. lay: wager. 312. Sirrah: term of address used to an inferior.

Sc. ii: 7. part: separate. 8. juvenal: youth, juvenile. 13–14. congruent epitheton: appropriate epithet. 27. condign: worthily deserved.

ARM. What, that an eel is ingenious?

MOTH. That an eel is quick. 30

ARM. I do say thou art quick in answers. Thou heatest my blood.

MOTH. I am answered, sir.

ARM. I love not to be crossed.

MOTH. [*Aside*] He speaks the mere contrary — crosses° love not him. 36

ARM. I have promised to study three years with the Duke.

MOTH. You may do it in an hour, sir.

ARM. Impossible. 40

MOTH. How many is one thrice told?

ARM. I am ill at reckoning, it fitteth the spirit of a tapster.° 44

MOTH. You are a gentleman and a gamester, sir.

ARM. I confess both. They are both the varnish° of a complete man.

MOTH. Then I am sure you know how much the gross sum of deuce-ace° amounts to.

ARM. It doth amount to one more than two. 50

MOTH. Which the base vulgar do call three.

ARM. True.

MOTH. Why, sir, is this such a piece of study? Now here is three studied ere ye'll thrice wink. And how easy it is to put years to the word " three," and study three years in two words, the dancing horse° will tell you.

ARM. A most fine figure!

MOTH. To prove you a cipher. 59

ARM. I will hereupon confess I am in love; and as it is base for a soldier to love, so am I in love with a base wench. If drawing my sword against the humor of affection would deliver me from the reprobate thought of it, I would take Desire prisoner, and ransom him to any French courtier for a new-devised courtesy.° I think scorn to sigh — methinks I should outswear Cupid. Comfort me, boy. What great men have been in love? 68

MOTH. Hercules, master.

ARM. Most sweet Hercules! More authority, dear boy, name more. And, sweet my child, let them be men of good repute and carriage.

MOTH. Samson, master. He was a man of good carriage, great carriage, for he carried the town gates on his back like a porter° — and he was in love. 76

ARM. O well-knit Samson! Strong-jointed Samson! I do excel thee in my rapier as much as thou didst me in carrying gates. I am in love too. Who was Samson's love, my dear Moth? 80

MOTH. A woman, master.

ARM. Of what complexion?°

MOTH. Of all the four, or the three, or the two, or one of the four.

ARM. Tell me precisely of what complexion. 85

MOTH. Of the sea-water green,° sir.

ARM. Is that one of the four complexions?

MOTH. As I have read, sir, and the best of them too.

ARM. Green, indeed, is the color of lovers; but 90 to have a love of that color, methinks Samson had small reason for it. He surely affected° her for her wit.°

MOTH. It was so, sir, for she had a green° wit. 95

ARM. My love is most immaculate white and red.

MOTH. Most maculate° thoughts, master, are masked under such colors.

ARM. Define, define, well-educated infant.

MOTH. My father's wit, and my mother's tongue, assist me! 101

ARM. Sweet invocation of a child, most pretty and pathetical!

MOTH. If she be made of white and red,
   Her faults will ne'er be known; 105
For blushing cheeks by faults are bred,
   And fears by pale white shown.
Then if she fear, or be to blame,
   By this you shall not know;
For still° her cheeks possess the same 110
   Which native° she doth owe.°

A dangerous rhyme, master, against the reason of white and red.

ARM. Is there not a ballad, boy, of " The King and the Beggar? "° 115

MOTH. The world was very guilty of such a ballad some three ages since, but I think now 'tis not to be found; or if it were, it would neither serve for the writing nor the tune.° 119

ARM. I will have that subject newly writ o'er, that I may example° my digression by some mighty precedent. Boy, I do love that country girl that I took in the park with the rational hind° Costard. She deserves well.

MOTH. [*Aside*] To be whipped, and yet a better love than my master. 126

ARM. Sing, boy, my spirit grows heavy in love.

MOTH. And that's great marvel, loving a light wench.

ARM. I say, sing. 130

36. crosses: money, so called because of the cross on the reverse side. See Pl. 10a. 44. tapster: bartender. 46. varnish: outward gloss. 49. deuce-ace: a throw of a pair of dice producing two and one. 57. dancing horse: a famous performing horse called Morocco, owned by a man called Bankes, which performed circus tricks, such as counting money. 65–66. new-devised courtesy: a new Court compliment. 75–76. town . . . porter: the story is told in Judges 16:1–3.

82. complexion: i.e., humor. See App. 3. Moth however takes the word in its literal meaning of color in the face. 86. sea-water green: suffering from green sickness, a form of anemia common with teen-age girls. 92. affected: loved. 94. wit: intelligence. 95. green: raw, immature. 97. maculate: spotted, impure. 110. still: always. 111. native: naturally. owe: own. 114–15. King . . . Beggar: i.e., the story of King Cophetua who married a beggar maid. 118–19. serve . . . tune: i.e., it would not be suitable for your case. 121. example: find a precedent for. 123. rational hind: intelligent peasant.

MOTH. Forbear till this company be past.

[*Enter* DULL, COSTARD, *and* JAQUENETTA.]

DULL. Sir, the Duke's pleasure is that you keep Costard safe. And you must suffer him to take no delight nor no penance; but a'° must fast three days a week. For this damsel, I must keep her at the 135 park. She is allowed for° the day woman.° Fare you well.

ARM. I do betray myself with blushing. Maid.

JAQ. Man.

ARM. I will visit thee at the lodge.   140

JAQ. That's hereby.

ARM. I know where it is situate.

JAQ. Lord, how wise you are!

ARM. I will tell thee wonders.

JAQ. With that face?   145

ARM. I love thee.

JAQ. So I heard you say.

ARM. And so farewell.

JAQ. Fair weather after you!

DULL. Come, Jaquenetta, away!   150

[*Exeunt* DULL *and* JAQUENETTA.]

ARM. Villain, thou shalt fast for thy offenses ere thou be pardoned.

COST. Well, sir, I hope when I do it I shall do it on a full stomach.

ARM. Thou shalt be heavily punished.   155

COST. I am more bound to you than your fellows, for they are but lightly rewarded.

ARM. Take away this villain. Shut him up.

MOTH. Come, you transgressing slave, away!

COST. Let me not be pent up, sir. I will fast, being loose.   161

MOTH. No, sir, that were fast and loose.° Thou shalt to prison.

COST. Well, if ever I do see the merry days of desolation that I have seen, some shall see.   165

MOTH. What shall some see?

COST. Nay, nothing, Master Moth, but what they look upon. It is not for prisoners to be too silent in their words, and therefore I will say nothing. I thank God I have as little patience as another man, and therefore I can be quiet.   171

[*Exeunt* MOTH *and* COSTARD.]

ARM. I do affect the very ground, which is base, where her shoe, which is baser, guided by her foot, which is basest, doth tread. I shall be forsworn, which is a great argument of falsehood, if I love. And how can that be true love which is falsely attempted? Love is a familiar,° Love is a devil. There is no evil angel but Love. Yet was Samson so tempted, and he had an excellent strength; yet was Solomon so seduced, and he had a very good wit. Cupid's 180 butt shaft° is too hard for Hercules' club, and there-

fore too much odds° for a Spaniard's rapier. The first and second cause° will not serve my turn; the passado° he respects not, the duello° he regards not. His disgrace is to be called boy,° but his glory is to subdue men. Adieu, valor! Rust, rapier! Be still, drum! For your manager is in love — yea, he loveth. Assist me, some extemporal god of rhyme, for I am sure I shall turn sonnet. Devise, wit; write, pen; for I am for whole volumes in folio.°   [*Exit.*] 191

Act II

SCENE I. *The same.*

[*Enter the* PRINCESS OF FRANCE, ROSALINE, MARIA, KATHARINE, BOYET, LORDS, *and other* ATTENDANTS.]

BOYET. Now, madam, summon up your dearest° spirits.
Consider who the King your father sends,
To whom he sends, and what's his embassy.
Yourself, held precious in the world's esteem,
To parley with the sole inheritor   5
Of all perfections that a man may owe,
Matchless Navarre; the plea of no less weight
Than Aquitaine, a dowry for a queen.
Be now as prodigal of all dear grace
As Nature was in making graces dear°   10
When she did starve the general world beside,
And prodigally gave them all to you.

PRIN. Good Lord Boyet, my beauty, though but mean,
Needs not the painted° flourish of your praise.
Beauty is bought by judgment of the eye,   15
Not uttered° by base sale of chapmen's° tongues.
I am less proud to hear you tell my worth
Than you much willing to be counted wise
In spending your wit in the praise of mine.
But now to task the tasker. Good Boyet,   20
You are not ignorant, all-telling fame
Doth noise abroad, Navarre hath made a vow,
Till painful° study shall outwear three years,
No woman may approach his silent Court.
Therefore to's° seemeth it a needful course,   25
Before we enter his forbidden gates,
To know his pleasure; and in that behalf,

182. too ... odds: too difficult.   **183. first ... cause:** i.e., technical reasons for a duel. Among gentlemen of fashion the rules and vocabulary of honor were elaborate and exact. See *AYLI,* V.iv.50–108.   **184. passado:** thrust. **duello:** rules of dueling. **185. called boy:** to call a man "boy" was to offer a gross insult. Cf. *M Ado,* V.i.79–91.   **191. in folio:** i.e., books of the largest size.

Act II, Sc. i: 1. dearest: best.   **9–10. dear grace ... graces dear:** best charm . . . beauty scarce.   **14. painted:** artificial. **16. uttered:** put up for sale. **chapmen:** salesmen.   **23. painful:** laborious.   **25. to's:** to us.

---

134. a': he.   **136. allowed for:** assigned to. **day woman:** dairy woman.   **162. fast ... loose:** a cheating game.   **177. familiar:** attendant spirit.   **181. butt shaft:** arrow used for target practice.

Bold of° your worthiness, we single you
As our best-moving° fair solicitor.
Tell him the daughter of the King of France,   30
On serious business craving quick dispatch,
Importunes personal conference with His Grace.
Haste, signify so much while we attend,°
Like humble-visaged suitors, his high will.

    BOYET. Proud of employment, willingly I go.   35
    PRIN. All pride is willing pride, and yours is so.

                   [*Exit* BOYET.]

Who are the votaries,° my loving lords,
That are vow fellows with this virtuous Duke?

    1. LORD. Lord Longaville is one.
    PRIN.   Know you the man?
    MAR. I know him, madam. At a marriage feast
Between Lord Perigort and the beauteous heir   41
Of Jacques Falconbridge, solemnized
In Normandy, saw I this Longaville.
A man of sovereign parts° he is esteemed,
Well fitted in arts, glorious in arms.   45
Nothing becomes him ill that he would° well.
The only soil of his fair virtue's gloss,
If virtue's gloss will stain with any soil,
Is a sharp wit matched with too blunt a will,
Whose edge hath power to cut, whose will still wills
It should none spare that come within his power.   51

    PRIN. Some merry mocking lord, belike, is't so?
    MAR. They say so most that most his humors°
    know.
    PRIN. Such short-lived wits do wither as they
    grow.
Who are the rest?   55

    KATH. The young Dumain, a well-accomplished
    youth,
Of all that virtue love for virtue loved.
Most power to do most harm, least knowing ill;
For he hath wit to make an ill shape good,
And shape to win grace though he had no wit.   60
I saw him at the Duke Alençon's once,
And much too little of that good I saw
Is my report to his great worthiness.

    ROS. Another of these students at that time
Was there with him, if I have heard a truth.   65
Berowne they call him, but a merrier man,
Within the limit of becoming mirth,
I never spent an hour's talk withal.
His eye begets occasion° for his wit,
For every object that the one doth catch   70
The other turns to a mirth-moving jest,
Which his fair tongue, conceit's expositor,°
Delivers in such apt and gracious words
That agèd ears play truant at his tales
And younger hearings are quite ravishèd,   75

So sweet and voluble is his discourse.

    PRIN. God bless my ladies! Are they all in love,
That every one her own hath garnishèd
With such bedecking ornaments of praise?

    1. LORD. Here comes Boyet.

             [*Re-enter* BOYET.]

    PRIN.   Now, what admittance, lord?   80
    BOYET. Navarre had notice of your fair approach.
And he and his competitors° in oath
Were all addressed° to meet you, gentle lady,
Before I came. Marry, thus much I have learned:
He rather means to lodge° you in the field,   85
Like one that comes here to besiege his Court,
Than seek a dispensation for his oath
To let you enter his unpeopled house.
Here comes Navarre.

    [*Enter* KING, LONGAVILLE, DUMAIN, BEROWNE, *and*
                 ATTENDANTS.]

    KING. Fair Princess, welcome to the Court of
Navarre.   90
    PRIN. " Fair " I give you back again, and " wel-
come " I have not yet. The roof of this Court° is too
high to be yours, and welcome to the wide fields too
base to be mine.

    KING. You shall be welcome, madam, to my
    Court.   95
    PRIN. I will be welcome, then. Conduct me thither.
    KING. Hear me, dear lady, I have sworn an oath.
    PRIN. Our Lady help my lord! He'll be forsworn.
    KING. Not for the world, fair madam, by my will.
    PRIN. Why, will shall break it — will, and nothing
    else.   100
    KING. Your ladyship is ignorant what it is.
    PRIN. Were my lord so, his ignorance were wise,
Where now his knowledge must prove ignorance.
I hear your Grace hath sworn out housekeeping.°
'Tis deadly sin to keep that oath, my lord,   105
And sin to break it.
But pardon me, I am too sudden-bold —
To teach a teacher ill beseemeth me.
Vouchsafe to read the purpose of my coming,
And suddenly resolve me in° my suit.   110

    KING. Madam, I will, if suddenly I may.
    PRIN. You will the sooner, that I were away,
For you'll prove perjured if you make me stay.

    BER. Did not I dance with you in Brabant once?
    ROS. Did not I dance with you in Brabant once?
    BER. I know you did.   116
    ROS. How needless was it, then, to ask the ques-
tion!
    BER. You must not be so quick.
    ROS. 'Tis 'long of you° that spur me with such
    questions.

---

28. Bold of: confident in.   **29. best-moving:** most persuasive.
33. attend: await.   **37. votaries:** those who have sworn a vow.
44. sovereign parts: supreme qualities.   **46. would:** would at-
tempt.   **53. humors:** whims.   **69. begets occasion:** finds oppor-
tunity.   **72. conceit's expositor:** commentator on wit.

82. competitors: fellows, partners.   **83. addressed:** ready.
85. lodge: accommodate.   **92. this Court:** i.e., the open sky.
104. housekeeping: hospitality.   **110. suddenly . . . in:** give a
quick answer to.   **119. long of you:** your fault.

BER. Your wit's too hot, it speeds too fast, 'twill
tire.   120
ROS. Not till it leave the rider in the mire.
BER. What time o' day?
ROS. The hour that fools should ask.
BER. Now fair befall your mask!°
ROS. Fair fall° the face it covers!   125
BER. And send you many lovers!
ROS. Amen, so you be none.
BER. Nay, then will I be gone.
KING. Madam, your father here doth intimate
The payment of a hundred thousand crowns,   130
Being but the one half of an entire sum
Disbursèd by my father in his wars.
But say that he or we, as neither have,
Received that sum, yet there remains unpaid
A hundred thousand more; in surety of the which,
One part of Aquitaine is bound to us,   136
Although not valued to the money's worth.
If, then, the King your father will restore
But that one half which is unsatisfied,
We will give up our right in Aquitaine,   140
And hold fair friendship with His Majesty.
But that, it seems, he little purposeth,
For here he doth demand to have repaid
A hundred thousand crowns; and not demands,
On payment of a hundred thousand crowns,   145
To have his title live in Aquitaine;
Which we much rather had depart withal,°
And have the money by our father lent
Than Aquitaine so gelded° as it is.
Dear Princess, were not his requests so far   150
From reason's yielding, your fair self should make
A yielding, 'gainst some reason, in my breast,
And go well satisfied to France again.
PRIN. You do the King my father too much wrong,
And wrong the reputation of your name,   155
In so unseeming° to confess receipt
Of that which hath so faithfully been paid.
KING. I do protest I never heard of it,
And if you prove it, I'll repay it back,
Or yield up Aquitaine.
PRIN.   We arrest your word.°   160
Boyet, you can produce acquittances°
For such a sum from special officers
Of Charles his father.
KING.   Satisfy me so.
BOYET. So please your Grace, the packet is not
come
Where that and other specialties° are bound.   165
Tomorrow you shall have a sight of them.
KING. It shall suffice me. At which interview

All liberal reason I will yield unto.
Meantime receive such welcome at my hand
As honor, without breach of honor, may   170
Make tender of° to thy true worthiness.
You may not come, fair Princess, in my gates;
But here without you shall be so received
As you shall deem yourself lodged in my heart,
Though so denied fair harbor in my house.   175
Your own good thoughts excuse me, and farewell.
Tomorrow shall we visit you again.
PRIN. Sweet health and fair desires consort° your
Grace!
KING. Thy own wish wish I thee in every place!
                                          [*Exit.*]
BER. Lady, I will commend you to mine own
heart.   180
ROS. Pray you, do my commendations. I would be
glad to see it.
BER. I would you heard it groan.
ROS. Is the fool sick?
BER. Sick at the heart.   185
ROS. Alack! let it blood.°
BER. Would that do it good?
ROS. My physic says "aye."
BER. Will you prick't with your eye?
ROS. No point, with my knife.   190
BER. Now God save thy life!
ROS. And yours from long living!
BER. I cannot stay thanksgiving.   [*Retiring.*]
DUM. Sir, I pray you a word. What lady is that
same?   194
BOYET. The heir of Alençon, Katharine her name.
DUM. A gallant lady. Monsieur, fare you well.
                                          [*Exit.*]
LONG. I beseech you a word. What is she in the
white?
BOYET. A woman sometimes, an° you saw her in
the light.
LONG. Perchance light in the light. I desire her
name.
BOYET. She hath but one for herself, to desire that
were a shame.   200
LONG. Pray you, sir, whose daughter?
BOYET. Her mother's, I have heard.
LONG. God's blessing on your beard!
BOYET. Good sir, be not offended.
She is an heir of Falconbridge.   205
LONG. Nay, my choler is ended.
She is a most sweet lady.
BOYET. Not unlike, sir, that may be.
                           [*Exit* LONGAVILLE.]
BER. What's her name, in the cap?
BOYET. Rosaline, by good hap.   210
BER. Is she wedded or no?

---

124. mask: Fashionable ladies at this time often wore masks to
protect their skin from the sun.   125. Fair fall: good luck to.
147. depart withal: part with.   149. gelded: cut.   156. so unseem-
ing: appearing not.   160. arrest . . . word: formally take you
at your word.   161. acquittances: receipts.   165. specialties:
contracts.

171. Make . . . of: offer.   178. consort: accompany.   186. let it
blood: bleeding was a common remedy in many complaints.
198. an: if.

BOYET. To her will, sir, or so.

BER. You are welcome, sir. Adieu.

BOYET. Farewell to me, sir, and welcome to you.

[*Exit* BEROWNE.]

MAR. That last is Berowne, the merry madcap
lord —   215
Not a word with him but a jest.

BOYET.   And every jest but a word.°

PRIN. It was well done of you to take him at his
word.

BOYET. I was as willing to grapple as he was to
board.

MAR. Two hot sheeps, marry.

BOYET.   And wherefore not ships?°
No sheep, sweet lamb, unless we feed on your
lips.   220

MAR. You sheep, and I pasture. Shall that finish
the jest?

BOYET. So you grant pasture for me.

[*Offering to kiss her.*]

MAR.   Not so, gentle beast.
My lips are no common,° though several° they be.

BOYET. Belonging to whom?

MAR.   To my fortunes and me.

PRIN. Good wits will be jangling, but, gentles,
agree.   225
This civil war of wits were much better used
On Navarre and his bookmen, for here 'tis abused.

BOYET. If my observation, which very seldom lies,
By the heart's still rhetoric disclosèd with eyes,
Deceive me not now, Navarre is infected.   230

PRIN. With what?

BOYET. With that which we lovers entitle af-
fected.°

PRIN. Your reason?

BOYET. Why, all his behaviors did make their re-
tire   234
To the court of his eye, peeping thorough° desire;
His heart, like an agate° with your print impressed;
Proud with his form, in his eye pride expressed.
His tongue, all impatient to speak and not see,
Did stumble with haste in his eyesight to be.
All senses to that sense did make their repair,   240
To feel only looking on fairest of fair.
Methought all his senses were locked in his eye,
As jewels in crystal for some prince to buy;
Who, tendering their own worth from where they
were glassed,°   244
Did point you to buy them, along as you passed.
His face's own margent° did quote° such amazes°
That all eyes saw his eyes enchanted with gazes.

I'll give you Aquitaine, and all that is his,
An you give him for my sake but one loving kiss.

PRIN. Come to our pavilion. Boyet is disposed.°

BOYET. But to speak that in words which his eye
hath disclosed.   251
I only have made a mouth of his eye
By adding a tongue which I know will not lie.

ROS. Thou art an old lovemonger, and speakest
skillfully.

MAR. He is Cupid's grandfather, and learns news
of him.   255

ROS. Then was Venus like her mother, for her
father° is but grim.

BOYET. Do you hear, my mad wenches?

MAR.   No.

BOYET.   What then, do you see?

ROS. Aye, our way to be gone.

BOYET.   You are too hard for me. [*Exeunt.*]

Act III

SCENE I. *The same.*

[*Enter* ARMADO *and* MOTH.]

ARM. Warble, child, make passionate my sense of
hearing.

MOTH. [*Singing.*] " Concolinel ——— "°

ARM. Sweet air! Go, tenderness of years. Take this
key, give enlargement to the swain, bring him festi-
nately° hither. I must employ him in a letter to my
love.

MOTH. Master, will you win your love with a
French brawl?°   9

ARM. How meanest thou? Brawling in French?

MOTH. No, my complete master; but to jig off a
tune at the tongue's end, canary° to it with your feet,
humor it with turning up your eyelids, sigh a note
and sing a note, sometime through the throat   15
as if you swallowed love with singing love, sometime
through the nose as if you snuffed up love by smell-
ing love; with your hat penthouse-like° o'er the shop
of your eyes; with your arms crossed on your thin-
belly doublet° like a rabbit on a spit; or your   20
hands in your pocket like a man after° the old paint-

---

216. but a word: i.e., and so worth little.   219. ships: a pun on
sheeps.   223. common: common pasture. several: a pun on
"separated" and "private property."   232. affected: in love.
235. thorough: through.   236. agate: engraved stone of a seal.
244. glassed: enclosed in glass.   246. margent: margin. quote:
note. The notes in learned works were commonly printed in the
margin. amazes: astonishment.

250. disposed: i.e., to mirth.   256. father: i.e., Jupiter.

Act III, Sc. i: 2. Concolinel: probably the name of the song
which Moth sings.   5–6. festinately: hastily.   9. brawl: a French
dance. See App. 24.   13. canary: dance.   18. hat penthouse-like:
pulled down like a roof. To wear a wide-brimmed hat pulled down
over the eyebrows was one of the signs of a melancholy lover.
See App. 4.   19–20. thin-belly doublet: close fitting — without
the padding of the "great belly" doublet. See Pl. 8b, and com-
ment on p. 93a.   21. after: i.e., in.

ing; and keep not too long in one tune, but a snip
and away. These are complements,° these are hu-
mors. These betray nice wenches that would be be-
trayed without these, and make them men of note°
—do you note me?—that most are affected to
these.   26

ARM. How hast thou purchased this experience?

MOTH. By my penny of observation.

ARM. But oh—but oh——

MOTH. "The hobbyhorse° is forgot."

ARM. Callest thou my love "hobbyhorse"?   30

MOTH. No, master, the hobbyhorse is but a colt,
and your love perhaps a hackney.° But have you for-
got your love?

ARM. Almost I had.   35

MOTH. Negligent student! Learn her by heart.

ARM. By heart and in heart, boy.

MOTH. And out of heart, master. All those three I
will prove.

ARM. What wilt thou prove?   40

MOTH. A man, if I live; and this by, in, and with-
out, upon the instant—by heart you love her, be-
cause your heart cannot come by her; in heart you
love her, because your heart is in love with her; and
out of heart you love her, being out of heart that you
cannot enjoy her.   46

ARM. I am all these three.

MOTH. And three times as much more, and yet
nothing at all.

ARM. Fetch hither the swain. He must carry me a
letter.   51

MOTH. A message well sympathized°—a horse
to be ambassador for an ass.

ARM. Ha, ha! What sayest thou?

MOTH. Marry, sir, you must send the ass upon the
horse, for he is very slow-gaited. But I go.

ARM. The way is but short. Away!

MOTH. As swift as lead, sir.

ARM. The meaning, pretty ingenious?
Is not lead a metal heavy, dull, and slow?   60

MOTH. Minimè,° honest master—or rather, mas-
ter, no.

ARM. I say lead is slow.

MOTH.   You are too swift, sir, to say so.
Is that lead slow which is fired from a gun?

ARM. Sweet smoke of rhetoric!
He reputes me a cannon, and the bullet, that's he.
I shoot thee at the swain.

MOTH.   Thump, then, and I flee. [Exit.]

ARM. A most acute juvenal, volable° and free of
grace!   67
By thy favor, sweet welkin,° I must sigh in thy face.
Most rude melancholy, valor gives thee place.

My herald is returned.   70
[Re-enter MOTH with COSTARD.]

MOTH. A wonder, master! Here's a Costard°
broken in a shin.°

ARM. Some enigma, some riddle. Come, thy
l'envoy,° begin.

COST. No egma, no riddle, no l'envoy, no salve° in
the mail,° sir. Oh, sir, plantain,° a plain plantain!
No l'envoy, no l'envoy. No salve, sir, but a plan-
tain!   76

ARM. By virtue, thou enforcest laughter, thy silly
thought my spleen, the heaving of my lungs pro-
vokes me to ridiculous smiling. O pardon me, my
stars! Doth the inconsiderate take salve for l'envoy,
and the word "l'envoy" for a salve?   80

MOTH. Do the wise think them other? Is not
l'envoy a salve?

ARM. No, page, it is an epilogue° or discourse, to
make plain
Some obscure precedence that hath tofore been sain.°
I will example it:
      The fox,° the ape, and the humblebee   85
      Were still at odds, being but three.
There's the moral. Now the l'envoy.

MOTH. I will add the l'envoy. Say the moral again.

ARM. The fox, the ape, the humblebee   90
      Were still at odds, being but three.

MOTH. Until the goose came out of door,
      And stayed the odds° by adding° four.
Now will I begin your moral, and do you follow
with my l'envoy.   95
      The fox, the ape, and the humblebee,
      Were still at odds, being but three.

ARM. Until the goose came out of door,
      Staying the odds by adding four.

MOTH. A good l'envoy, ending in the goose.
Would you desire more?   101

COST. The boy hath sold him a bargain,° a goose,
that's flat.
Sir, your pennyworth° is good, an your goose be fat.
To sell a bargain well is as cunning as fast and
loose.°   104
Let me see, a fat l'envoy—aye, that's a fat goose.

ARM. Come hither, come hither. How did this
argument begin?

MOTH. By saying that a Costard was broken in a
shin.
Then called you for the l'envoy.

COST. True, and I for a plantain. Thus came your
argument in.

22. complements: accompaniments.   24. of note: conspicuous.
29. hobbyhorse: See Haml., III.ii.144,n. The word also meant
"prostitute."   32. hackney: a horse available for common hire.
52. well sympathized: appropriately carried.   61. Minimè: not
in the least.   67. volable: quick-witted.   68. welkin: sky.

71. Costard: head; lit., apple. broken . . . shin: with the skin of
the shin torn.   72. l'envoy: explained at ll. 82–83 below.   73. salve:
healing ointment.   74. mail: bag.   plantain: a broad-leafed weed
growing in grass, believed to be good for bruises.   82. epilogue:
conclusion.   83. sain: said.   85–98. The fox . . . four: These appar-
ently meaningless lines are presumably a topical jest at some-
one's expense.   93. stayed . . . odds: i.e., turned them into evens.
adding: making up the total to.   102. bargain: bad bargain.
103. pennyworth: bargain.   104. fast . . . loose: See I.ii.162,n.

Then the boy's fat l'envoy, the goose that you
    bought,   110
And he ended the market.

ARM. But tell me, how was there a Costard broken
in a shin?

MOTH. I will tell you sensibly.°

COST. Thou hast no feeling of it, Moth. I will
speak that l'envoy.   115
I Costard, running out, that was safely within,
Fell over the threshold, and broke my shin.

ARM. We will talk no more of this matter.

COST. Till there be more matter in the shin.   120

ARM. Sirrah Costard, I will enfranchise° thee.

COST. Oh, marry me to one Frances. I smell some
l'envoy, some goose, in this.

ARM. By my sweet soul, I mean setting thee at
liberty, enfreedoming thy person. Thou wert   125
immured, restrained, captivated, bound.

COST. True, true, and now you will be my purga-
tion, and let me loose.

ARM. I give thee thy liberty, set thee from durance;
and, in lieu thereof, impose on thee nothing but this:
Bear this significant [*Giving a letter.*] to the   130
country maid Jaquenetta. There is remuneration, for
the best ward° of mine honor is rewarding my
dependents. Moth, follow.   [*Exit.*]

MOTH. Like the sequel, I. Signor Costard, adieu.

COST. My sweet ounce of man's flesh! My incony°
Jew!   [*Exit* MOTH.] 136
Now will I look to° his remuneration. Remunera-
tion! Oh, that's the Latin word for three farthings;
three farthings — remuneration. — "What's the
price of this inkle°?" — "One penny." — "No, I'll
give you a remuneration." Why, it carries it.   140
Remuneration! Why, it is a fairer name than French
crown. I will never buy and sell out of° this word.

[Enter BEROWNE.]

BER. O my good knave Costard, exceedingly well
met!   145

COST. Pray you, sir, how much carnation° ribbon
may a man buy for a remuneration?

BER. What is a remuneration?

COST. Marry, sir, halfpenny farthing.

BER. Why, then, three-farthing worth of silk.   150

COST. I thank your Worship. God be wi' you!

BER. Stay, slave; I must employ thee.
As thou wilt win my favor, good my knave,
Do one thing for me that I shall entreat.

COST. When would you have it done, sir?   155

BER. This afternoon.

COST. Well, I will do it, sir. Fare you well.

BER. Thou knowest not what it is.

COST. I shall know, sir, when I have done it.

BER. Why, villain, thou must know first.   160

COST. I will come to your Worship tomorrow
morning.

BER. It must be done this afternoon. Hark, slave,
it is but this:
The Princess comes to hunt here in the park,   165
And in her train there is a gentle lady.
When tongues speak sweetly, then they name her
    name,
And Rosaline they call her. Ask for her,
And to her white hand see thou do commend   169
This sealed-up counsel.° There's thy guerdon.° Go.
    [*Giving him a shilling.*]

COST. Gardon, O sweet gardon! Better than re-
muneration, a 'levenpence farthing better. Most
sweet gardon! I will do it, sir, in print. Gardon!
Remuneration!   [*Exit.*]

BER. And I, forsooth, in love! I, that have been
love's whip —   175
A very beadle° to a humorous° sigh,
A critic, nay, a night-watch constable,
A domineering pedant o'er the boy,
Than whom no mortal so magnificent!   180
This wimpled,° whining, purblind, wayward boy,
This senior-junior, giant-dwarf, Dan Cupid,
Regent of love rhymes, lord of folded arms,
The anointed sovereign of sighs and groans,
Liege° of all loiterers and malcontents,   185
Dread prince of plackets,° king of codpieces,°
Sole imperator and great general
Of trotting 'paritors.° — Oh, my little heart! —
And I to be a corporal of his field,
And wear his colors like a tumbler's° hoop!   190
What! I love! I sue! I seek a wife!
A woman, that is like a German clock,
Still a-repairing,° ever out of frame,°
And never going aright, being a watch,
But being watched that it may still go right!   195
Nay, to be perjured, which is worst of all.
And, among three, to love the worst of all,
A whitely wanton with a velvet brow,
With two pitch balls stuck in her face for eyes —
Aye, and, by Heaven, one that will do the deed   200
Though Argus° were her eunuch° and her guard.
And I to sigh for her! To watch for her!
To pray for her! Go to, it is a plague
That Cupid will impose for my neglect
Of his almighty dreadful little might.   205
Well, I will love, write, sigh, pray, sue and groan.
Some men must love my lady, and some Joan.°
    [*Exit.*]

170. counsel: secret communication. guerdon: reward. 176. bea-
dle: parish officer who whipped offenders. humorous: melan-
choly. 181. wimpled: hooded. 185. Liege: lord. 186. placket:
opening in the petticoat. codpieces: See Pl. 8c and p. 93b.
188. 'paritors: apparitors, officers of the ecclesiastical court who
summoned offenders guilty of moral offenses. 190. tumbler: acro-
bat. 193. Still a-repairing: always needing repair. frame: setting.
201. Argus: the watchman of the gods, who had a hundred eyes.
eunuch: the guardian of a harem. 207. Joan: a country wench.

113. sensibly: feelingly. 121. enfranchise: liberate. 132. ward:
defense. 136. incony: fine. 137. to: at. 139. inkle: piece of
tape. 142. out of: without using. 146. carnation: red.

Act IV

SCENE I. *The same.*

[*Enter the* PRINCESS, *and her* TRAIN, *a* FORESTER,
BOYET, ROSALINE, MARIA, *and* KATHARINE.]

PRIN. Was that the King that spurred his horse so
   hard
Against the steep uprising of the hill?
  BOYET. I know not, but I think it was not he.
  PRIN. Whoe'er a' was, a' showed a mounting
   mind.°
Well, lords, today we shall have our dispatch.   5
On Saturday we will return to France.
Then, forester, my friend, where is the bush
That we must stand and play the murderer in?°
  FOR. Hereby, upon the edge of yonder coppice,
A stand where you may make the fairest shoot. 10
  PRIN. I thank my beauty, I am fair that shoot,
And thereupon thou speak'st the fairest shoot.
  FOR. Pardon me, madam, for I meant not so.
  PRIN. What, what? First praise me, and again say
   no?
Oh, short-lived pride! Not fair? Alack for woe! 15
  FOR. Yes, madam, fair.
  PRIN.   Nay, never paint me now.
Where fair is not, praise cannot mend the brow.
Here, good my glass,° take this for telling true.
Fair payment for foul words is more than due. 19
  FOR. Nothing but fair is that which you inherit.
  PRIN. See, see, my beauty will be saved by merit!
Oh, heresy in fair,° fit for these days!
A giving hand, though foul, shall have fair praise.
But come, the bow. Now mercy goes to kill,
And shooting well is then accounted ill.   25
Thus will I save my credit in the shoot —
Not wounding, pity would not let me do't.
If wounding, then it was to show my skill,
That more for praise than purpose meant to kill.
And, out of question, so it is sometimes   30
Glory grows guilty of detested crimes,
When, for fame's sake, for praise, an outward part,
We bend to that the working of the heart —
As I for praise alone now seek to spill   34
The poor deer's blood, that my heart means no ill.
  BOYET. Do not curst° wives hold that self-
   sovereignty
Only for praise sake, when they strive to be
Lords o'er their lords?
  PRIN. Only for praise. And praise we may afford

To any lady that subdues a lord.   40
  BOYET. Here comes a member of the common-
   wealth.

[*Enter* COSTARD.]

  COST. God dig-you-den° all! Pray you, which is the
head lady?
  PRIN. Thou shalt know her, fellow, by the rest that
have no heads.   45
  COST. Which is the greatest lady, the highest?
  PRIN. The thickest and the tallest.
  COST. The thickest and the tallest! It is so, truth is
truth.
An your waist, mistress, were as slender as my wit,
One o' these maids' girdles for your waist should be
fit.   50
Are not you the chief woman? You are the thickest
here.
  PRIN. What's your will, sir? What's your will?
  COST. I have a letter from Monsieur Berowne to
one Lady Rosaline.
  PRIN. Oh, thy letter, thy letter! He's a good friend
of mine.
Stand aside, good bearer. Boyet, you can carve —
Break up° this capon.   56
  BOYET.   I am bound to serve.
This letter is mistook, it importeth none here,
It is writ to Jaquenetta.
  PRIN.   We will read it, I swear. 58
Break the neck of the wax, and everyone give ear.
  BOYET. [*Reads.*] " By Heaven, that thou art fair is
most infallible, true that thou art beauteous, truth
itself that thou art lovely. More fairer than fair, beau-
tiful than beauteous, truer than truth itself, have
commiseration on thy heroical vassal! The magnani-
mous and most illustrate° King Cophetua set 65
eye upon the pernicious and indubitate beggar
Zenelophon; and he it was that might rightly say,
Veni, vidi, vici; which to annothanize° in the vul-
gar° — O base and obscure vulgar! — videlicet,° He
came, saw, and overcame: he came, one; saw, 70
two; overcame, three. Who came? The King. Why
did he come? To see. Why did he see? To overcome.
To whom came he? To the beggar. What saw he?
The beggar. Who overcame he? The beggar. The
conclusion is victory. On whose side? The King's.
The captive is enriched. On whose side? The 75
beggar's. The catastrophe° is a nuptial. On whose
side? The King's — no, on both in one, or one in
both. I am the King, for so stands the comparison,
thou the beggar, for so witnesseth thy lowliness.
Shall I command thy love? I may. Shall I en- 80
force thy love? I could. Shall I entreat thy love? I
will. What shalt thou exchange for rags? Robes. For

Act IV, Sc. i: **4. mounting mind:** lofty spirit. **7-8. bush . . .
in:** The Princess is about to hunt the deer in the manner prac-
ticed by Queen Elizabeth. The Queen and her ladies, armed
with bows and arrows, took up their stand and the deer were
driven past them well within range. **18. good my glass:** my
good mirror. **22. heresy in fair:** heresy against beauty. **36. curst:**
shrewish.

42. dig-you-den: give you a good evening. **56. Break up:** carve
(a chicken) or open (a letter). **65. illustrate:** illustrious.
68. annothanize: anatomize, dissect. **68-69. vulgar:** common
tongue. **69. videlicet:** viz., namely. **76. catastrophe:** con-
clusion.

tittles?° Titles. For thyself? Me. Thus, expecting thy
reply, I profane my lips on thy foot, my eyes on thy
picture, and my heart on thy every part. Thine,   85
in the dearest design of industry,°
          "DON ADRIANO DE ARMADO"
Thus dost thou hear the Nemean lion° roar   90
  'Gainst thee, thou lamb, that standest as his prey.
Submissive fall his princely feet before,
  And he from forage will incline to play.
But if thou strive, poor soul, what art thou then?
Food for his rage, repasture° for his den.   95
PRIN. What plume of feathers° is he that indited
  this letter?
What vane?° What weathercock? Did you ever hear
  better?
BOYET. I am much deceived but I° remember the
  style.
PRIN. Else your memory is bad, going o'er it ere-
  while.°
BOYET. This Armado is a Spaniard that keeps here
  in Court,   100
A phantasime,° a Monarcho,° and one that makes
  sport
To the Prince and his bookmates.
PRIN.   Thou fellow, a word.
Who gave thee this letter?
COST.   I told you — my lord.
PRIN. To whom shouldst thou give it?
COST.   From my lord to my lady.
PRIN. From which lord to which lady?   105
COST. From my lord Berowne, a good master of
  mine,
To a lady of France that he called Rosaline.
PRIN. Thou hast mistaken his letter. Come, lords,
  away.
[*To* ROSALINE] Here, sweet, put up this. 'Twill be
  thine another day.
                    [*Exeunt* PRINCESS *and* TRAIN.]
BOYET. Who is the suitor?° Who is the suitor?
ROS.   Shall I teach you to know?   110
BOYET. Aye, my continent of beauty.
ROS.   Why, she that bears the bow.
Finely put off!°
BOYET. My lady goes to kill horns, but if thou
  marry,
Hang me by the neck if horns that year miscarry.°
Finely put on!
ROS. Well then, I am the shooter.   115
BOYET.   And who is your deer?

ROS. If we choose by the horns, yourself come not
  near.
Finely put on, indeed!
MAR. You still wrangle with her, Boyet, and she
  strikes at the brow.°
BOYET. But she herself is hit lower. Have I hit her
  now?   120
ROS. Shall I come upon thee with an old saying
that was a man when King Pepin° of France was a
little boy, as touching the hit it?°
BOYET. So I may answer thee with one as old that
was a woman when Queen Guinever° of Britain was
a little wench, as touching the hit it.   126
ROS. "Thou canst not hit it, hit it, hit it,
  Thou canst not hit it, my good man."
BOYET. "An I cannot, cannot, cannot,
  An I cannot, another can."   130
          [*Exeunt* ROSALINE *and* KATHARINE.]
COST. By my troth, most pleasant. How both did
  fit it!
MAR. A mark marvelous well shot, for they both
  did hit it.
BOYET. A mark! Oh, mark but that mark! A mark,
  says my lady!
Let the mark have a prick° in't, to mete° at, if it
  may be.
MAR. Wide o' the bow hand!° I' faith, your hand
  is out.   135
COST. Indeed, a' must shoot nearer, or he'll ne'er
  hit the clout.°
BOYET. An if my hand be out, then belike your
  hand is in.
COST. Then will she get the upshoot° by cleaving
  the pin.°
MAR. Come, come, you talk greasily,° your lips
  grow foul.
COST. She's too hard for you at pricks, sir. Chal-
  lenge her to bowl.   140
BOYET. I fear too much rubbing.° Good night, my
  good owl.   [*Exeunt* BOYET *and* MARIA.]
COST. By my soul, a swain, a most simple clown!
Lord, Lord, how the ladies and I have put him
  down!
O' my troth, most sweet jests, most incony vulgar
  wit!
When it comes so smoothly off, so obscenely,° as it
  were, so fit.   145
Armado o' th' one side — Oh, a most dainty man!
To see him walk before a lady and to bear her fan!

---

83. **tittles:** trifles.   86. **industry:** gallantry.   90. **Nemean lion:**
a fierce beast slain by Hercules.   95. **repasture:** food.   96. **plume
of feathers:** i.e., fantastical gallant.   97. **vane:** weathervane,
with a pun on "vain."   98. **but I:** if I do not.   99. **going . . .
erewhile:** if you have met it before.   101. **phantasime:** fantastic
ass. **Monarcho:** the name of a crazy Italian who haunted Queen
Elizabeth's Court.   110-11. **suitor . . . bow:** with a pun on
"shooter."   112. **Finely . . . off:** well answered.   114. **if . . . mis-
carry:** if horns go short; i.e., if someone is not made a cuck-
old. See App. II.

119. **strikes . . . brow:** aims at your head.   122. **Pepin:** father
of Charlemagne; i.e., a very long time ago.   123. **hit it:** the
name of an old dance tune, given below.   125. **Guinever:** King
Arthur's Queen.   134. **prick:** center of the target. **mete:** aim.
135. **Wide . . . hand:** you're too far to the left.   136. **clout:**
cloth, bull's-eye.   138. **get . . . upshoot:** lit., be hailed as the
best shot. **cleaving . . . pin:** hitting the pin in the center of the
target.   139. **greasily:** indecently.   141. **rubbing:** lit., uneven-
ness on the green.   145. **obscenely:** perhaps for "notoriously,"

To see him kiss his hand! And how most sweetly a'
  will swear!
And his page o' t' other side, that handful of wit!
Ah, Heavens, it is a most pathetical nit!°   150
Sola, sola!°   [*Shout within. Exit* COSTARD, *running.*]

SCENE II.° *The same.*

[*Enter* HOLOFERNES, SIR NATHANIEL, *and* DULL.]

NATH. Very reverend sport, truly, and done in the
testimony of a good conscience.

HOL. The deer was, as you know, *sanguis,*° in
blood; ripe as the pomewater,° who now hangeth
like a jewel in the ear of *caelo,*° the sky, the wel-   5
kin, the heaven, and anon falleth like a crab° on the
face of *terra,* the soil, the land, the earth.

NATH. Truly, Master Holofernes, the epithets are
sweetly varied, like a scholar at the least. But, sir, I
assure ye it was a buck of the first head.°   10

HOL. Sir Nathaniel, *haud credo.*°

DULL. 'Twas not a *haud credo,* 'twas a pricket.°

HOL. Most barbarous intimation! Yet a kind of
insinuation, as it were, *in via,* in way, of explication;
facere, as it were, replication, or, rather, *osten-*   15
tare, to show, as it were, his inclination, after his un-
dressed, unpolished, uneducated, unpruned, un-
trained, or rather unlettered, or ratherest uncon-
firmed fashion, to insert again my *haud credo* for a
deer.°   20

DULL. I said the deer was not a *haud credo,* 'twas
a pricket.

HOL. Twice-sod° simplicity, *bis coctus!*°
O thou monster Ignorance, how deformed dost thou
look!

NATH. Sir, he hath never fed of the dainties that
are bred in a book;   25
he hath not eat paper, as it were; he hath not drunk
ink. His intellect is not replenished, he is only an ani-
mal, only sensible in the duller parts.
And such barren plants are set before us that we
  thankful should be,
Which we of taste and feeling are, for those parts
  that do fructify in us more than he.   30
For as it would ill become me to be vain, indiscreet,
  or a fool,
So were there a patch set on learning° to see him in
  a school.

But *omne bene,*° say I, being of an old father's mind,
Many can brook° the weather that love not the wind.

DULL. You two are bookmen. Can you tell me by
  your wit   35
What was a month old at Cain's birth that's not five
  weeks old as yet?

HOL. Dictynna,° goodman Dull. Dictynna, good-
man Dull.

DULL. What is Dictynna?

NATH. A title to Phoebe, to Luna, to the moon.

HOL. The moon was a month old when Adam was
  no more,   40
And raught° not to five weeks when he came to five-
  score.
The allusion holds in the exchange.°

DULL. 'Tis true indeed, the collusion holds in the
  exchange.

HOL. God comfort thy capacity! I say, the allusion
holds in the exchange.

DULL. And I say, the pollution holds in the ex-
change, for the moon is never but a month old. And
I say beside that 'twas a pricket that the Princess
killed.   49

HOL. Sir Nathaniel, will you hear an extemporal
epitaph on the death of the deer? And, to humor the
ignorant, call I the deer the Princess killed a pricket.

NATH. *Perge,*° good Master Holofernes, *perge,* so
it shall please you to abrogate° scurrility.   55

HOL. I will something affect the letter,° for it
argues facility.
" The preyful Princess pierced and pricked a pretty
    pleasing pricket,
  Some say a sore,° but not a sore till now made
    sore with shooting.
  The dogs did yell. But L° to sore, then sorel°
    jumps from thicket,   60
  Or pricket sore, or else sorel; the people fall
    a-hooting.
  If sore be sore, then L to sore makes fifty sores one
    sorel.
  Of one sore I a hundred make by adding but one
    more L."

NATH. A rare talent!   65

DULL. [*Aside*] If a talent° be a claw, look how he
claws° him with a talent.

HOL. This is a gift that I have, simple, simple; a
foolish extravagant spirit, full of forms, figures,   70
shapes, objects, ideas, apprehensions, motions, revo-
lutions. These are begot in the ventricle° of memory,

---

150. **pathetical nit:** pathetic little louse.   151. **sola:** imitation
of the post boy's horn. See *M of Ven,* V.i.39, and App. 17.
  Sc. ii: In this scene the curious ways of the learned are paro-
died, but it is likely that the original audience recognized Holo-
fernes as a caricature of some well-known person. See *LLL*
Intro. p. 154a.   3. **sanguis:** blood.   4. **pomewater:** a juicy apple.
5. **caelo:** the sky.   6. **crab:** crab apple.   10. **first head:** with its
antlers fully developed, which occurs in the fifth year.   11. **haud
credo:** I don't believe it.   12. **pricket:** buck in its second year.
19-20. **insert . . . deer:** repeat my "*haud credo*" supposing it to
mean a deer.   22. **Twice-sod:** twice-boiled. **bis coctus:** twice-
cooked.   32. **So . . . learning:** if a fool (*patch*) was set to learn.

33. **omne bene:** everything well.   34. **brook:** endure.   37. **Dic-
tynna:** a title of the moon, who is also called Luna or Phoebe.
41. **raught:** reached.   42. **The . . . exchange:** i.e., whether you
speak of Cain or Adam, the saying is still true.   54. **Perge:**
proceed.   55. **abrogate:** refrain from.   56. **affect . . . letter:** in-
dulge in alliteration.   60. **L:** i.e., the Roman numeral for 50. **sorel:**
a buck in the third year.   66. **talent:** with a pun on "talon."   67. **claws:** fondles.
72. **ventricle:** one of the divisions of the brain supposed to hold
the memory.

nourished in the womb of pia mater,° and delivered upon the mellowing of occasion. But the gift is good in those in whom it is acute, and I am thankful for it.   75

NATH. Sir, I praise the Lord for you, and so may my parishioners; for their sons are well tutored by you, and their daughters profit very greatly under you. You are a good member of the common-wealth.   79

HOL. *Mehercle,*° if their sons be ingenuous,° they shall want no instruction; if their daughters be capable, I will put it to them. But *vir sapit qui pauca loquitur,*° a soul feminine saluteth us.

[*Enter* JAQUENETTA *and* COSTARD.]

JAQ. God give you good morrow, Master Parson.

HOL. Master Parson, quasi pers-on.° And if   85 one should be pierced,° which is the one?

COST. Marry, Master Schoolmaster, he that is likest to a hogshead.

HOL. Piercing a hogshead! A good luster of conceit in a turf of earth, fire enough for a flint, pearl enough for a swine — 'tis pretty, it is well.   90

JAQ. Good Master Parson, be so good as read me this letter. It was given me by Costard, and sent me from Don Armado. I beseech you read it.

HOL. *Fauste, precor gelida quando pecus omne sub umbra*   95
     Ruminat° —

and so forth. Ah, good old Mantuan! I may speak of thee as the traveler doth of Venice:

     Venetia, Venetia,
     Chi non ti vede non ti pretia.°   100

Old Mantuan, old Mantuan, who understandeth thee not, loves thee not. Ut, re, sol, la, mi, fa.° Under pardon, sir, what are the contents? Or rather, as Horace says in his —— What, my soul, verses?   105

NATH. Aye, sir, and very learned.

HOL. Let me hear a staff,° a stanze, a verse. *Lege, domine.*°

NATH. [*Reads.*]
" If love make me forsworn, how shall I swear to love?
     Ah, never faith could hold, if not to beauty vowed!   110
Though to myself forsworn, to thee I'll faithful prove;

Those thoughts to me were oaks, to thee like osiers° bowed.
Study his bias° leaves, and makes his book thine eyes,
     Where all those pleasures live that art would comprehend.
If knowledge be the mark, to know thee shall suffice;   115
     Well learned is that tongue that well can thee commend,
All ignorant that soul that sees thee without wonder,
     Which is to me some praise that I thy parts admire.
Thy eye Jove's lightning bears, thy voice his dreadful thunder,
     Which, not to anger bent, is music and sweet fire.   120
Celestial as thou art, oh, pardon love this wrong,
That sings Heaven's praise with such an earthly tongue."

HOL. You find not the apostrophas,° and so miss the accent. Let me supervise the canzonet.°   125 Here are only numbers ratified; but for the elegancy, facility, and golden cadence of poesy, *caret.*° Ovidius Naso was the man. And why, indeed, Naso, but for smelling out the odoriferous flowers of fancy, the jerks of invention? *Imitari* is nothing; so doth the hound his master, the ape his keeper, the tired horse his rider. But, damosella virgin, was this directed to you?   133

JAQ. Aye, sir, from one Monsieur Berowne, one of the strange Queen's lords.

HOL. I will overglance the superscript:° "To the snow-white hand of the most beauteous Lady Rosaline." I will look again on the intellect° of the letter, for the nomination of the party writing to the person written unto: "Your ladyship's in all desired employment, BEROWNE." Sir Nathaniel, this Berowne is one of the votaries with the King. And here he hath framed a letter to a sequent° of the stranger Queen's, which accidentally, or by the way of progression, hath miscarried. Trip and go, my sweet. Deliver this paper into the royal hand of the King — it may concern much. Stay not° thy compliment;° I forgive thy duty.° Adieu.

JAQ. Good Costard, go with me. Sir, God save your life!   150

COST. Have with thee, my girl.

[*Exeunt* COSTARD *and* JAQUENETTA.]

---

73. pia mater: brain.   **80.** *Mehercle:* by Hercules. **ingenuous:** ingenious, quick-witted.   **82–83.** *vir . . . loquitur:* it's a wise man who speaks few words.   **85. quasi pers-on:** as if pronounced "perse one."   **86. pierced:** pronounced "persed."   **95–96.** *Fauste . . . Ruminat:* Faustus, I pray you when all your flock lies feeding under the cool shade — opening lines from the *Eclogues* of Battista Spagnuoli of Mantua which was a prescribed text for schoolboys in Shakespeare's day.   **99–100.** *Venetia . . . pretia:* Venice, Venice, who has not seen you does not prize you — an Italian proverb.   **102. Ut . . . fa:** Here he hums a scale.   **107. staff:** stanza.   **107–108.** *Lege, domine:* read, master.

112. osiers: willows.   **113. bias:** course; lit., of a bowl in the game of bowls.   **123. apostrophas:** apostrophes, poetic omission of a vowel.   **125. canzonet:** short song.   **126–27. Here . . . caret:** i.e., the verses do scan, but the poetry is wanting (*caret*).   **136. superscript:** address.   **138. intellect:** purport, meaning.   **143. sequent:** follower.   **147. Stay not:** do not wait for.   **compliment:** curtsy.   **148. duty:** expression of respect.

NATH. Sir, you have done this in the fear of God, very religiously, and, as a certain father saith ——

HOL. Sir, tell not me of the father, I do fear colorable colors.° But to return to the verses. Did they please you, Sir Nathaniel?

NATH. Marvelous well for the pen.°   158

HOL. I do dine today at the father's of a certain pupil of mine, where, if before repast it shall please you to gratify the table with a grace, I will, on my privilege I have with the parents of the foresaid child or pupil, undertake your *benvenuto;*° where I will prove those verses to be very unlearned, neither   165 savoring of poetry, wit, nor invention. I beseech your society.

NATH. And thank you too; for society, saith the text, is the happiness of life.

HOL. And certes° the text most infallibly concludes it. [*To* DULL] Sir, I do invite you too, you shall not say me nay — *pauca verba.*° Away! The gentles are at their game, and we will to our recreation.   174

[*Exeunt.*]

SCENE III.° *The same.*

[*Enter* BEROWNE, *with a paper.*]

BER. The King he is hunting the deer, I am coursing° myself. They have pitched a toil,° I am toiling in a pitch — pitch that defiles. Defile! A foul word. Well, set thee down, sorrow! For so they say the   5 fool said, and so say I, and I the fool — well proved, wit! By the Lord, this love is as mad as Ajax.° It kills sheep, it kills me, I a sheep — well proved again o' my side! I will not love. If I do, hang me; i' faith, I will not. Oh, but her eye — by this light, but for her eye I would not love her; yes, for her two eyes. Well, I do nothing in the world but lie, and lie in my   12 throat.° By Heaven, I do love, and it hath taught me to rhyme, and to be melancholy; and here is part of my rhyme, and here my melancholy. Well, she hath one o' my sonnets already. The clown bore it, the fool sent it, and the lady hath it. Sweet clown, sweeter fool, sweetest lady! By the world, I would not care a pin if the other three were in.° Here comes one with a paper. God give him grace to groan! [*Stands aside.*]   21

[*Enter the* KING, *with a paper.*]

KING. Aye me!

BER. [*Aside*] Shot, by Heaven! Proceed, sweet Cupid. Thou hast thumped him with thy bird bolt° under the left pap. In faith, secrets!   25

KING. [*Reads.*]
" So sweet a kiss the golden sun gives not
    To those fresh morning drops upon the rose,
As thy eye beams when their fresh rays have smote
    The night of dew that on my cheeks downflows.
Nor shines the silver moon one half so bright   30
    Through the transparent bosom of the deep
As doth thy face through tears of mine give light.
    Thou shinest in every tear that I do weep,
No drop but as a coach doth carry thee,
    So ridest thou triumphing in my woe.   35
Do but behold the tears that swell in me,
    And they thy glory through my grief will show.
But do not love thyself — then thou wilt keep
    My tears for glasses,° and still make me weep.
O queen of queens! How far dost thou excel   40
    No thought can think nor tongue of mortal tell."
How shall she know my griefs? I'll drop the paper.
Sweet leaves, shade folly. Who is he comes here?
[*Steps aside.*]
What, Longaville! And reading! Listen, ear.

BER. Now, in thy likeness, one more fool appear!

[*Enter* LONGAVILLE, *with a paper.*]

LONG. Aye me, I am forsworn!

BER. Why, he comes in like a perjure, wearing papers.°

KING. In love, I hope. Sweet fellowship in shame!

BER. One drunkard loves another of the name.   50

LONG. Am I the first that have been perjured so?

BER. I could put thee in comfort. Not by two that I know.
Thou makest the triumviry,° the cornercap° of society,
The shape of Love's Tyburn° that hangs up simplicity.°

LONG. I fear these stubborn lines lack power to move.   55
O sweet Maria, empress of my love!
These numbers° will I tear, and write in prose.

BER. Oh, rhymes are guards° on wanton Cupid's hose.
Disfigure not his slop.°

LONG.   This same shall go. [*Reads.*]
" Did not the heavenly rhetoric of thine eye,   60

154–155. **colorable colors:** plausible excuses.   158. **pen:** penmanship.   164. *benvenuto:* welcome.   171. **certes:** assuredly. 173. *pauca verba:* few words.

Sc. iii: This scene is more entertaining to watch than to read. As each lover comes in and hides, he is unaware of•the others who have come in before him, and — by stage convention — is supposed not to hear their sarcastic comments.   1–2. **coursing:** chasing.   2. **pitched a toil:** prepared a net.   7. **Ajax:** Ajax, disappointed that the shield of the dead Achilles was not awarded to him, went mad and slew a flock of sheep, supposing them to be his enemies.   12–13. **lie ... throat:** the worst kind of lie.   19. **in:** i.e., also in love.

24. **bird bolt:** short blunt arrow for shooting birds. See Pl. 22a. 39. **glasses:** eyes.   47–48. **perjure ... papers:** Perjurors were condemned to stand in the pillory wearing a paper proclaiming their offense.   53. **triumviry:** party of three. **cornercap:** cap with three or four corners worn by graduates, judges, and divines. 54. **Tyburn:** the place of execution for London criminals where stood the permanent three-cornered gallows. **simplicity:** folly. 57. **numbers:** verses.   58. **guards:** ornamental strips of velvet or braid. See Pl. 9f and 9n, and comment on p. 94b.   59. **slop:** baggy breeches. See Pl. 8–Pl. 8c and comment on p. 93b.

'Gainst whom the world cannot hold argument,
Persuade my heart to this false perjury?
  Vows for thee broke deserve not punishment.
A woman I forswore, but I will prove,
  Thou being a goddess, I forswore not thee.   65
My vow was earthly, thou a heavenly love.
  Thy grace being gained cures all disgrace in me.
Vows are but breath, and breath a vapor is.
  Then thou, fair sun, which on my earth dost
    shine,
Exhalest this vapor vow; in thee it is.   70
  If broken then, it is no fault of mine.
If by me broke, what fool is not so wise
To lose an oath to win a paradise? "
  BER. This is the liver vein,° which makes flesh a
    deity,
A green goose a goddess — pure, pure idolatry.   75
God amend us, God amend! We are much out o'
    the way.°
  LONG. By whom shall I send this? — Company!
    Stay.   [*Steps aside.*]
  BER. All hid, all hid, an old infant play.
Like a demigod here sit I in the sky,
And wretched fools' secrets heedfully o'ereye.   80
More sacks to the mill! Oh, Heavens, I have my
    wish!
[*Enter* DUMAIN *with a paper.*] Dumain transformed!
    Four woodcocks° in a dish!
  DUM. O most divine Kate!
  BER. O most profane coxcomb!°
  DUM. By Heaven, the wonder in a mortal eye!   85
  BER. By earth, she is not, corporal,° there you lie.
  DUM. Her amber hairs for foul hath amber
    quoted.°
  BER. An amber-colored raven was well noted.
  DUM. As upright as the cedar.
  BER.   Stoop, I say.
Her shoulder is with child.°
  DUM.   As fair as day.   90
  BER. Aye, as some days, but then no sun must
    shine.
  DUM. Oh, that I had my wish!
  LONG.   And I had mine!
  KING. And I mine too, good Lord!
  BER. Amen, so I had mine. Is not that a good
    word?
  DUM. I would forget her, but a fever she   95
Reigns in my blood, and will remembered be.
  BER. A fever in your blood! Why, then incision°
Would let her out in saucers — sweet misprision!°

  DUM. Once more I'll read the ode that I have writ.
  BER. Once more I'll mark how love can vary
    wit.   100
  DUM. [*Reads.*]
  " On a day — alack the day! —
    Love, whose month is ever May,
    Spied a blossom passing fair
    Playing in the wanton air.
    Through the velvet leaves the wind,   105
    All unseen, can passage find,
    That the lover, sick to death,
    Wish himself the heaven's breath.
    ' Air,' quoth he, ' thy cheeks may blow.
    Air, would I might triumph so!   110
    But, alack, my hand is sworn
    Ne'er to pluck thee from thy thorn —
    Vow, alack, for youth unmeet,
    Youth so apt to pluck a sweet!
    Do not call it sin in me   115
    That I am forsworn for thee.
    Thou for whom Jove would swear
    Juno but an Ethiope° were,
    And deny himself for Jove,
    Turning mortal for thy love." 120
This will I send and something else more plain,
That shall express my true love's fasting pain.
Oh, would the King, Berowne, and Longaville
Were lovers too! Ill, to example ill,
Would from my forehead wipe a perjured note,   125
For none offend where all alike do dote.
  LONG. [*Advancing.*] Dumain, thy love is far from
    charity,
That in love's grief desirest society.
You may look pale, but I should blush, I know,
To be o'erheard and taken napping so.   130
  KING. [*Advancing.*] Come, sir, you blush, as his
    your case is such.
You chide at him, offending twice as much.
You do not love Maria, Longaville
Did never sonnet for her sake compile,
Nor never lay his wreathèd° arms athwart   135
His loving bosom, to keep down his heart.
I have been closely shrouded in this bush
And marked you both and for you both did blush.
I heard your guilty rhymes, observed your fashion,
Saw sighs reek° from you, noted well your passion.
" Aye me! " says one. " O Jove! " the other
    cries.   141
One, her hairs were gold, crystal the other's eyes.
[*To* LONGAVILLE] You would for paradise break faith
    and troth,
[*To* DUMAIN] And Jove, for your love, would in-
    fringe an oath.
What will Berowne say when that he shall hear   145
Faith so infringèd, which such zeal did swear?

---

74. liver vein: humor of a lover, the liver being regarded as the
seat of love.   76. much . . . way: i.e., we have erred and strayed.
82. woodcocks: i.e., fools.   84. coxcomb: fool.   86. corporal: an
appointment in a regiment corresponding to adjutant, with a pun
on "corporal," human.   87. Her . . . quoted: amber itself has
noted (*quoted*) that her hair is more amber than amber.   90. with
child: burdened; i.e., is not straight.   97. incision: cut for let-
ting blood.   98. misprision: mistake.

118. Ethiope: Ethiopian.   135. wreathed: folded.   140. reek:
steam.

How will he scorn! How will he spend his wit!
How will he triumph, leap and laugh at it!
For all the wealth that ever I did see,
I would not have him know so much by° me.   150
    BER. [*Advancing.*] Now step I forth to whip
        hypocrisy.
Ah, good my liege, I pray thee pardon me!
Good heart, what grace hast thou, thus to reprove
These worms for loving, that art most in love?
Your eyes do make no coaches,° in your tears   155
There is no certain Princess that appears.
You'll not be perjured, 'tis a hateful thing —
Tush, none but minstrels like of sonneting!
But are you not ashamed? Nay, are you not,
All three of you, to be thus much o'ershot?°   160
You found his mote, the King your mote did see,
But I a beam° do find in each of three.
Oh, what a scene of foolery have I seen,
Of sighs, of groans, of sorrow and of teen!°
Oh me, with what strict patience have I sat   165
To see a king transformèd to a gnat!
To see great Hercules whipping a gig,°
And profound Solomon to tune a jig,
And Nestor° play at pushpin° with the boys,
And critic Timon° laugh at idle toys!°   170
Where lies thy grief, oh, tell me, good Dumain?
And, gentle Longaville, where lies thy pain?
And where my liege's? All about the breast.
A caudle,° ho!
    KING.   Too bitter is thy jest.
Are we betrayed thus to thy overview?   175
    BER. Not you to me, but I betrayed by you —
I, that am honest, I, that hold it sin
To break the vow I am engagèd in —
I am betrayed by keeping company
With men like you, men of inconstancy.   180
When shall you see me write a thing in rhyme?
Or groan for love? Or spend a minute's time
In pruning me?° When shall you hear that I
Will praise a hand, a foot, a face, an eye,
A gait, a state,° a brow, a breast, a waist,   185
A leg, a limb?
    KING.   Soft! Whither away so fast?
A true man or a thief that gallops so?
    BER. I post° from love. Good lover, let me go.
       [*Enter* JAQUENETTA *and* COSTARD.]
    JAQ. God bless the King!

---

150. by: concerning.   155. coaches: See l. 34 above.   160. o'er-shot: overshot, wide of the mark.   161–62. mote . . . beam: See Luke 6:41–42: "thou hypocrite, cast out first the beam out of thine own eye and then thou shalt see clearly to pull out the mote [speck of dust] that is in thy brother's eye."   164. teen: grief. 167. gig: spinning top rotated by whipping.   169. Nestor: the oldest and most experienced of the Greek generals. pushpin: a children's game in which each player pushes his pin to cross his opponent's.   170. Timon: the most bitter of all critics of human-ity. toys: trifles.   174. caudle: warm drink, especially for the sick suffering from heartburn.   183. pruning me: preening myself. 185. state: demeanor.   188. post: ride fast.

    KING.   What present hast thou there?
    COST. Some certain treason.
    KING.   What makes treason here?   190
    COST. Nay, it makes nothing, sir.
    KING.   If it mar nothing neither,
The treason and you go in peace away together.
    JAQ. I beseech your Grace, let this letter be read.
Our parson misdoubts° it, 'twas treason, he said.
    KING. Berowne, read it over.   195
                     [*Giving him the paper.*]
Where hadst thou it?
    JAQ. Of Costard.
    KING. Where hadst thou it?
    COST. Of Dun Adramadio, Dun Adramadio.
                [BEROWNE *tears the letter.*]
    KING. How now! What is in you? Why dost thou
        tear it?   200
    BER. A toy, my liege, a toy. Your Grace needs not
        fear it.
    LONG. It did move him to passion, and therefore
        let's hear it.
    DUM. [*Gathering up the pieces.*] It is Berowne's
        writing, and here is his name.
    BER. [*To* COSTARD] Ah, you whoreson logger-
        head!° You were born to do me shame.
Guilty, my lord, guilty! I confess, I confess.   205
    KING. What?
    BER. That you three fools lacked me fool to make
        up the mess.°
He, he, and you, and you, my liege, and I,
Are pickpurses in love, and we deserve to die.   209
Oh, dismiss this audience, and I shall tell you more.
    DUM. Now the number is even.
    BER.   True, true, we are four.
Will these turtles° be gone?
    KING.   Hence, sirs, away!
    COST. Walk aside the true folk, and let the traitors
        stay.   [*Exeunt* COSTARD *and* JAQUENETTA.]
    BER. Sweet lords, sweet lovers, oh, let us embrace!
As true we are as flesh and blood can be.   215
The sea will ebb and flow, Heaven show his face,
    Young blood doth not obey an old decree.
We cannot cross° the cause why we were born,
Therefore of all hands must we be forsworn.
    KING. What, did these rent lines show some love
        of thine?   220
    BER. Did they, quoth you? Who sees the heavenly
        Rosaline
That, like a rude and savage man of Ind,°
    At the first opening of the gorgeous east
Bows not his vassal head and stricken blind
    Kisses the base ground with obedient breast?   225
What peremptory eagle-sighted eye

---

194. misdoubts: suspects.   204. whoreson loggerhead: bastardly blockhead.   206. mess: party of four at a table.   212. turtles: turtledoves; i.e., lovers.   218. cross: thwart.   222. man of Ind: Indian.

Dares look upon the heaven of her brow
That is not blinded by her majesty?
   KING. What zeal, what fury hath inspired thee
    now?
My love, her mistress, is a gracious moon,   230
  She an attending star, scarce seen a light.
   BER. My eyes are then no eyes, nor I Berowne.
Oh, but for my love, day would turn to night!
Of all complexions the culled sovereignty°
  Do meet, as at a fair, in her fair cheek,   235
Where several° worthies make one dignity,
  Where nothing wants that want itself doth seek.
Lend me the flourish of all gentle tongues —
  Fie, painted° rhetoric! Oh, she needs it not.
To things of sale a seller's praise belongs,   240
  She passes praise, then praise too short doth blot.
A withered hermit, fivescore winters worn,
  Might shake off fifty looking in her eye.
Beauty doth varnish age as if newborn,
  And gives the crutch the cradle's infancy.   245
Oh, 'tis the sun that maketh all things shine.
   KING. By Heaven, thy love is black as ebony.
   BER. Is ebony like her? O wood divine!
A wife of such wood were felicity.
Oh, who can give an oath? Where is a book?   250
  That I may swear beauty doth beauty lack
If that she learn not of her eye to look.
  No face is fair that is not full so black.
   KING. Oh, paradox! Black is the badge of Hell,
  The hue of dungeons and the school of night,°
And beauty's crest becomes the heavens well.   256
   BER. Devils soonest tempt, resembling spirits of
    light.
Oh, if in black my lady's brows be decked,
  It mourns that painting and usurping hair
Should ravish doters with a false aspect,°   260
  And therefore is she born to make black fair.
Her favor° turns the fashion of the days,
  For native blood° is counted painting now,
And therefore red, that would avoid dispraise,
  Paints itself black to imitate her brow.   265
   DUM. To look like her are chimney sweepers
    black.
   LONG. And since her time are colliers° counted
    bright.
   KING. And Ethiopes of their sweet complexion
    crack.
   DUM. Dark needs no candles now, for dark is
    light.   269
   BER. Your mistresses dare never come in rain,
  For fear their colors should be washed away.
   KING. 'Twere good yours did, for, sir, to tell you
    plain,

I'll find a fairer face not washed today.
   BER. I'll prove her fair, or talk till Doomsday here.
   KING. No devil° will fright thee then° so much as
    she.   275
   DUM. I never knew man hold vile stuff so dear.
   LONG. Look, here's thy love. My foot and her face
    see.
   BER. Oh, if the streets were pavèd with thine eyes,
  Her feet were much too dainty for such tread!
   DUM. O vile! Then, as she goes, what upward
    lies   280
  The street should see as she walked overhead.
   KING. But what of this? Are we not all in love?
   BER. Nothing so sure, and thereby all forsworn.
   KING. Then leave this chat, and, good Berowne,
    now prove
  Our loving lawful, and our faith not torn.   285
   DUM. Aye, marry, there — some flattery for this
    evil.
   LONG. Oh, some authority how to proceed,
Some tricks, some quillets,° how to cheat the Devil.
   DUM. Some salve for perjury.
   BER.   'Tis more than need.
Have at you, then, affection's men-at-arms.°   290
Consider what you first did swear unto,
To fast, to study, and to see no woman —
Flat treason 'gainst the kingly state of youth.
Say, can you fast? Your stomachs are too young,
And abstinence engenders maladies.   295
And where that you have vowed to study, lords,
In that each of you have forsworn his book,
Can you still dream and pore and thereon look?
For when would you, my lord, or you, or you,
Have found the ground° of study's excellence   300
Without the beauty of a woman's face?
From women's eyes this doctrine I derive:
They are the ground, the books, the academes,
From whence doth spring the true Promethean° fire.
Why, universal plodding prisons up   305
The nimble spirits° in the arteries
As motion and long-during action tires
The sinewy vigor of the traveler.
Now, for not looking on a woman's face,
You have in that forsworn the use of eyes   310
And study too, the causer of your vow;
For where is any author in the world
Teaches such beauty as a woman's eye?
Learning is but an adjunct to ourself,
And where we are our learning likewise is.   315
Then when ourselves we see in ladies' eyes,
Do we not likewise see our learning there?
Oh, we have made a vow to study, lords,
And in that vow we have forsworn our books.

---

234. **culled sovereignty:** selected pre-eminence.   236. **several:** different.   239. **painted:** artificial, insincere.   255. **school of night:** See *LLL* Intro. p. 154a.   260. **aspect:** appearance. 262. **favor:** complexion.   263. **native blood:** natural color. 267. **colliers:** coal men.

275. **No devil:** the devil was believed to be black. **then:** i.e., at Doomsday.   288. **quillets:** subtleties.   290. **affection's men-at-arms:** love's bodyguard.   300. **ground:** foundation.   304. **Promethean:** heavenly. Prometheus stole fire from heaven and gave it to men.   306. **spirits:** vital energy.

For when would you, my liege, or you, or you,   320
In leaden° contemplation have found out
Such fiery numbers as the prompting eyes
Of beauty's tutors have enriched you with?
Other slow arts entirely keep° the brain,
And therefore, finding barren practicers,   325
Scarce show a harvest of their heavy toil.
But love, first learnèd in a lady's eyes,
Lives not alone immurèd in the brain,
But with the motion of all elements
Courses as swift as thought in every power,   330
And gives to every power a double power,
Above their functions and their offices.
It adds a precious seeing to the eye,
A lover's eyes will gaze an eagle blind.
A lover's ear will hear the lowest sound   335
When the suspicious head of theft° is stopped.
Love's feeling is more soft and sensible°
Than are the tender horns of cockled° snails.
Love's tongue proves dainty Bacchus gross in taste.
For valor, is not Love a Hercules,   340
Still climbing trees in the Hesperides?°
Subtle as Sphinx,° as sweet and musical
As bright Apollo's° lute, strung with his hair.
And when Love speaks, the voice of all the gods
Makes Heaven drowsy with the harmony.   345
Never durst poet touch a pen to write
Until his ink were tempered with Love's sighs.
Oh, then his lines would ravish savage ears,
And plant in tyrants mild humility.
From women's eyes this doctrine I derive: 350
They sparkle still the right Promethean fire;
They are the books, the arts, the academes,
That show, contain, and nourish all the world,
Else none at all in aught proves excellent.
Then fools you were these women to forswear,   355
Or keeping what is sworn, you will prove fools.
For wisdom's sake, a word that all men love —
Or for love's sake, a word that loves all men;
Or for men's sake, the authors of these women;
Or women's sake, by whom we men are men —
Let us once lose our oaths to find ourselves,   361
Or else we lose ourselves to keep our oaths.
It is religion to be thus forsworn,
For charity itself fulfills the law,
And who can sever love from charity?   365
    KING. Saint Cupid, then! And, soldiers, to the
        field!
    BER. Advance your standards, and upon them,
        lords,
Pell-mell, down with them! But be first advised

In conflict that you get the sun° of them.
    LONG. Now to plain dealing, lay these glozes° by.
Shall we resolve to woo these girls of France?   371
    KING. And win them too. Therefore let us devise
Some entertainment for them in their tents.
    BER. First, from the park let us conduct them
        thither,
Then homeward every man attach° the hand   375
Of his fair mistress. In the afternoon
We will with some strange pastime solace them,
Such as the shortness of the time can shape;
For revels, dances, masques,° and merry hours   379
Forerun fair Love, strewing her way with flowers.
    KING. Away, away! No time shall be omitted
That will betime, and may by us be fitted.
    BER. Allons! Allons! Sowed cockle reaped no
        corn,°
And justice always whirls in equal measure.   384
Light wenches may prove plagues to men forsworn;
If so, our copper buys no better treasure.
                                        [Exeunt.]

Act V

SCENE I. The same.

[Enter HOLOFERNES, SIR NATHANIEL, and DULL.]
    HOL. Satis quod sufficit.°
    NATH. I praise God for you, sir. Your reasons° at
dinner have been sharp and sententious, pleasant
without scurrility, witty without affection,° audaci-
ous without impudency, learned without opinion,°
and strange without heresy. I did converse this
quondam° day with a companion of the King's who
is intituled, nominated, or called Don Adriano de
Armado.   9
    HOL. Novi hominem tanquam te.° His humor is
lofty, his discourse peremptory, his tongue filed,° his
eye ambitious, his gait majestical, and his general
behavior vain, ridiculous, and thrasonical.° He is
too picked, too spruce, too affected, too odd, as it
were, too peregrinate,° as I may call it.   16
    NATH. A most singular and choice epithet.
                            [Draws out his table book.]
    HOL. He draweth out the thread of his verbosity

---

321. leaden: heavy.   324. keep: dwell in.   336. head of theft: A
much-disputed phrase, variously emended. If correct, it means
the hearing of a thief, who is naturally suspicious of every sound.
337. sensible: sensitive.   338. cockled: in shells.   341. Hes-
perides: where grew the golden apples which Hercules took.
342. Sphinx: a creature half woman, half lion which posed the
riddle to the people of Thebes.   343. Apollo: god of the arts.

369. get . . . sun: come at them when the sun is in their eyes.
370. glozes: pretenses.   375. attach: arrest, take hold of.
379. masques: courtly entertainments.   383. Sowed . . . corn: a
proverb, "If you sow weeds, you won't reap grain." cockle: a
weed which grows in wheat.
    Act V, Sc. i: 1. Satis . . . sufficit: what satisfies is enough.
2. reasons: discourses.   4. affection: affectation.   5. opinion:
arrogance.   7. quondam: former, bygone.   10. Novi . . . te: I
know the man as well as I know you.   11. filed: polished.
14. thrasonical: boastful.   16. peregrinate: foreign.

finer than the staple° of his argument. I abhor   20
such fanatical phantasimes, such insociable and
point-device° companions; such rackers of orthog-
raphy° as to speak dout, fine, when he should say
doubt; det, when he should pronounce debt, — d, e,
b, t, not d, e, t: he clepeth° a calf, cauf; half,   25
hauf; neighbor *vocatur°* nebour; neigh abbreviated
ne. This is abhominable — which he would call
abbominable. It insinuateth me of insanie° — *anne*
intelligis, domine?° To make frantic, lunatic.

NATH. *Laus Deo, bene intelligo.°*   30

HOL. *Bon, bon, fort bon!* Priscian a little
scratched,° 'twill serve.

NATH. *Videsne quis venit?°*

HOL. *Video, et gaudeo.°*

[*Enter* ARMADO, MOTH, *and* COSTARD.]

ARM. [*To* MOTH] Chirrah!   35

HOL. *Quare°* chirrah, not sirrah?

ARM. Men of peace, well encountered.

HOL. Most military sir, salutation.

MOTH. [*Aside to* COSTARD] They have been at a
great feast of languages, and stolen the scraps.   40

COST. Oh, they have lived long on the alms basket°
of words. I marvel thy master hath not eaten thee for
a word; for thou art not so long by the head as
honorificabilitudinitatibus.° Thou art easier swal-
lowed than a flapdragon.°   45

MOTH. Peace! The peal begins.

ARM. [*To* HOLOFERNES] Monsieur, are you not let-
tered?

MOTH. Yes, yes, he teaches boys the hornbook.°
What is a, b, spelt backward, with the horn on   50
his head?

HOL. Ba, *pueritia,°* with a horn added.

MOTH. Ba, most silly sheep with a horn. You hear
his learning.

HOL. *Quis,°* quis, thou consonant?   55

MOTH. The third of the five vowels, if you repeat
them — or the fifth, if I.

HOL. I will repeat them — a, e, i ——

MOTH. The sheep. The other two concludes it —
o, u.   60

ARM. Now, by the salt wave of the Mediterraneum,
a sweet touch, a quick venue° of wit — snip, snap,
quick and home! It rejoiceth my intellect — true
wit!   64

MOTH. Offered by a child to an old man, which is
wit-old.°

HOL. What is the figure? What is the figure?

MOTH. Horns.

HOL. Thou disputest like an infant. Go, whip thy
gig.   70

MOTH. Lend me your horn to make one, and I will
whip about your infamy *circum circa°* — a gig of a
cuckold's horn.

COST. An I had but one penny in the world, thou
shouldst have it to buy gingerbread. Hold, there is
the very remuneration I had of thy master, thou
halfpenny purse of wit, thou pigeon egg° of discre-
tion. Oh, an the heavens were so pleased that   78
thou wert but my bastard, what a joyful father
wouldst thou make me! Go to, thou hast it *ad* dung-
hill,° at the finger's ends, as they say.

HOL. Oh, I smell false Latin — dunghill for
unguem.

ARM. Artsman,° preambulate,° we will be sin-
guled° from the barbarous. Do you not educate
youth at the charge house on the top of the moun-
tain?°   87

HOL. Or *mons,* the hill.

ARM. At your sweet pleasure, for the mountain.

HOL. I do, sans° question.

ARM. Sir, it is the King's most sweet pleasure and
affection to congratulate the Princess at her pavilion°
in the posteriors of this day, which the rude multi-
tude call the afternoon.   95

HOL. The posterior of the day, most generous° sir,
is liable,° congruent, and measurable for the after-
noon. The word is well culled, chose, sweet and apt,
I do assure you, sir, I do assure.   99

ARM. Sir, the King is a noble gentleman, and my
familiar,° I do assure ye, very good friend. For what
is inward° between us, let it pass. I do beseech thee
remember thy courtesy.° I beseech thee apparel thy
head. And among other important and most serious
designs, and of great import indeed too — but   105
let that pass; for I must tell thee it will please His

---

20. staple: lit., fiber of wool.   22. point-device: precise.
22–23. rackers of orthography: torturers of spelling.   25. clepeth:
calleth.   26. vocatur: is called.   28. insinuateth . . . insanie: to
me it suggests lunacy.   28–29. anne . . . domine: do you compre-
hend, master?   30. *Laus . . . intelligo:* praise be to God, I under-
stand well.   31. Priscian . . . scratched: i.e., your Latin is not
too good. Priscian was a famous Latin grammarian about whom
there was a proverb "to break Priscian's head," meaning to
speak bad Latin.   33. *Videsne . . . venit:* do you see who comes?
34. *Video . . . gaudeo:* I see and rejoice.   36. *Quare:* why.
41. alms basket: a basket in which the scraps were collected for
distribution to the poor.   44. *honorificabilitudinitatibus:* The
word was a scholar's joke, as it was the longest word in the Latin
tongue; lit., "in the condition of being loaded with honors."
45. flapdragon: a lighted raisin floated on liquor which had to be
swallowed.   49. hornbook: the first reading book. It was printed
on a single sheet, mounted on a wooden handle, and protected
with transparent horn.   52. *pueritia:* childishness, my little one.
55. *Quis:* who.

62. venue: bout (of fencing).   66. wit-old: with a pun on "wit-
tol," a complacent cuckold.   72. circum circa: round and round.
Theobald's emendation for *unum cita.*   77. pigeon egg: i.e.,
smooth little thing.   80–81. ad dunghill: for *ad unguem* — at the
fingernail; a schoolboy joke.   84. Artsman: scholar. preambul-
ate: walk forth.   85. singuled: separated.   86–87. charge . . .
mountain: This is apparently another topical allusion, now lost.
charge house: probably a school at which a fee is charged (con-
trasted with a free-school).   91. sans: without.   93. pavilion:
tent.   96. generous: well-born.   97. liable: appropriate.
101. familiar: familiar friend.   102. inward: secret.   103. re-
member . . . courtesy: don't forget your manners; i.e., to take
off your hat in the presence of such an important person. But
as a gesture of politeness Armado immediately asks him to put
it on again. See App. 7.

Grace, by the world, sometime to lean upon my poor shoulder, and with his royal finger, thus, dally with my excrement,° with my mustachio — but, sweetheart, let that pass. By the world, I recount no 110 fable. Some certain special honors it pleaseth his greatness to impart to Armado, a soldier, a man of travel, that hath seen the world — but let that pass. The very all of all is — but, sweetheart, I do implore secrecy — that the King would have me pre- 116 sent the Princess, sweet chuck,° with some delightful ostentation, or show, or pageant, or antique,° or firework. Now, understanding that the curate and your sweet self are good at such eruptions and sudden breaking-out of mirth, as it were, I have acquainted you withal, to the end to crave your assistance. 123

HOL. Sir, you shall present before her the Nine Worthies.° Sir, as concerning some entertainment of time, some show in the posterior of this day, to be rendered by our assistants at the King's command, and this most gallant, illustrate,° and learned gentleman, before the Princess, I say none so fit as to present the Nine Worthies. 130

NATH. Where will you find men worthy enough to present them?

HOL. Joshua, yourself; myself and this gallant gentleman, Judas Maccabaeus. This swain, because of his great limb or joint, shall pass° Pompey the Great; the page, Hercules ——

ARM. Pardon, sir, error. He is not quantity enough for that Worthy's thumb. He is not so big as the end of his club. 139

HOL. Shall I have audience? He shall present Hercules in minority° — his enter and exit shall be strangling a snake,° and I will have an apology° for that purpose.

MOTH. An excellent device! So, if any of the audience hiss, you may cry, " Well done, Hercules! Now thou crushest the snake! " That is the way to make an offense gracious, though few have the grace to do it.

ARM. For the rest of the Worthies?

HOL. I will play three myself. 150

MOTH. Thrice-worthy gentleman!

ARM. Shall I tell you a thing?

HOL. We attend.

ARM. We will have, if this fadge° not, an antique. I beseech you, follow. 155

HOL. *Via,*° goodman Dull! Thou hast spoken no word all this while.

DULL. Nor understood none neither, sir.

HOL. *Allons!* We will employ thee.

DULL. I'll make one in a dance, or so, or I will play 160
On the tabor° to the Worthies and let them dance the hay.°

HOL. Most dull, honest Dull! To our sport, away!
                                   [*Exeunt.*]

SCENE II. *The same.*

[*Enter the* PRINCESS, KATHARINE, ROSALINE, *and* MARIA.]

PRIN. Sweethearts, we shall be rich ere we depart
If fairings° come thus plentifully in,
A lady walled about with diamonds!°
Look you what I have from the loving King.

ROS. Madam, came nothing else along with that?

PRIN. Nothing but this! Yes, as much love in rhyme 6
As would be crammed up in a sheet of paper
Writ o' both sides the leaf, margent° and all,
That he was fain to seal on Cupid's name.

ROS. That was the way to make his godhead wax,
For he hath been five thousand years a boy. 11

KATH. Aye, and a shrewd unhappy gallows° too.

ROS. You'll ne'er be friends with him, A' killed your sister.

KATH. He made her melancholy, sad, and heavy,
And so she died. Had she been light,° like you, 15
Of such a merry, nimble, stirring spirit,
She might ha' been a grandam ere she died.
And so may you, for a light heart lives long.

ROS. What's your dark meaning, mouse, of this light word?

KATH. A light condition in a beauty dark. 20

ROS. We need more light to find your meaning out.

KATH. You'll mar the light by taking it in snuff,°
Therefore I'll darkly end the argument.

ROS. Look, what you do, you do it still i' th' dark.

KATH. So do not you, for you are a light wench.

ROS. Indeed I weigh° not you, and therefore light.° 26

KATH. You weigh me not? — Oh, that's you care not for me.

109. excrement: anything growing out of a man, such as hair. **117. chuck:** chick. **118. antique:** grotesque entertainment. **124–125. Nine Worthies:** i.e., the nine great men of history, viz.: Hector of Troy, Alexander the Great, Julius Caesar, Joshua, King David, Judas Maccabaeus, King Arthur, Charlemagne, and Godfrey of Bouillon. Shakespeare, however, includes Hercules and Pompey. **128. illustrate:** illustrious. **135. pass:** enact. **141. in minority:** as a child. **142. strangling a snake:** The infant Hercules began his career as a strongman by strangling two snakes, one in either hand, which attacked him in his cradle. **apology:** explanation. **154. fadge:** be suitable.

156. *Via:* come on.   **161. tabor:** small drum. See Pl. 13d. **hay:** a country dance.
    Sc. ii: **2. fairings:** presents.   **3. lady . . . diamonds:** i.e., a miniature set in diamonds.   **8. margent:** margin.   **12. shrewd . . . gallows:** cunning unlucky rogue.   **15–26. light . . . light:** another elaborate play on the various meanings of *light* — lighthearted, trifling, frivolous, illumination, candlelight, wanton, lightweight. Cf. I.i.72–93. **22. in snuff:** in anger, with a pun on the snuff (smoking wick) of a candle. **26. weigh:** counterbalance.

ROS. Great reason, for "past cure is still past care."

PRIN. Well bandied° both, a set of wit well played.
But, Rosaline, you have a favor° too.   30
Who sent it? And what is it?

ROS.   I would you knew.
And if my face were but as fair as yours,
My favor were as great — be witness this.
Nay, I have verses too, I thank Berowne,
The numbers true; and were the numbering° too,
I were the fairest goddess on the ground.   36
I am compared to twenty thousand fairs.
Oh, he hath drawn my picture in his letter!

PRIN. Anything like?

ROS. Much in the letters, nothing in the praise.   40

PRIN. Beauteous as ink, a good conclusion.

KATH. Fair as a text B° in a copybook.

ROS. 'Ware pencils, ho! Let me not die your debtor,
My red dominical,° my golden letter.
Oh, that your face were not so full of O's!°   45

KATH. A pox of that jest! And I beshrew° all shrows.°

PRIN. But, Katharine, what was sent to you from fair Dumain?

KATH. Madam, this glove.

PRIN.   Did he not send you twain?

KATH. Yes, madam, and moreover
Some thousand verses of a faithful lover,   50
A huge translation of hypocrisy,
Vilely compiled, profound simplicity.

MAR. This and these pearls to me sent Longaville.
The letter is too long by half a mile.

PRIN. I think no less. Dost thou not wish in heart
The chain were longer and the letter short?   56

MAR. Aye, or I would these hands might never part.

PRIN. We are wise girls to mock our lovers so.

ROS. They are worse fools to purchase mocking so.
That same Berowne I'll torture ere I go.   60
Oh, that I knew he were but in by the week!°
How I would make him fawn, and beg, and seek,
And wait the season, and observe the times,
And spend his prodigal wits in bootless° rhymes,
And shape his service wholly to my hests,°   65
And make him proud to make me proud that jests.
So perttaunt-like° would I o'ersway his state

That he should be my fool, and I his fate.°

PRIN. None are so surely caught, when they are catched,
As wit turned fool. Folly, in wisdom hatched,   70
Hath wisdom's warrant and the help of school,
And wit's own grace to grace a learned fool.

ROS. The blood of youth burns not with such excess
As gravity's revolt to wantonness.

MAR. Folly in fools bears not so strong a note   75
As foolery in the wise when wit doth dote,
Since all the power thereof it doth apply
To prove, by wit, worth in simplicity.

PRIN. Here comes Boyet, and mirth is in his face.

[Enter BOYET.]

BOYET. Oh, I am stabbed with laughter! Where's Her Grace?   80

PRIN. Thy news, Boyet?

BOYET.   Prepare, madam, prepare!
Arm, wenches, arm! Encounters mounted are°
Against your peace. Love doth approach disguised,
Armèd in arguments — you'll be surprised.
Muster your wits, stand in your own defense,   85
Or hide your heads like cowards and fly hence.

PRIN. Saint Denis° to° Saint Cupid! What are they
That charge their breath against us? Say, scout, say.

BOYET. Under the cool shade of a sycamore
I thought to close mine eyes some half an hour   90
When, lo! to interrupt my purposed rest,
Toward that shade I might behold addressed°
The King and his companions. Warily
I stole into a neighbor thicket by,
And overheard what you shall overhear —   95
That, by and by, disguised they will be here.
Their herald is a pretty knavish page
That well by heart hath conned° his embassage.
Action and accent did they teach him there —
" Thus must thou speak," and " thus thy body bear."
And ever and anon° they made° a doubt   101
Presence majestical would put him out;
" For," quoth the King, " an angel shalt thou see;
Yet fear not thou, but speak audaciously."
The boy replied, " An angel is not evil.   105
I should have feared her had she been a devil."
With that, all laughed, and clapped him on the shoulder,
Making the bold wag by their praises bolder.
One rubbed his elbow thus, and fleered° and swore
A better speech was never spoke before.   110
Another, with his finger and his thumb,
Cried, " Via! We will do't, come what will come ";

---

29. bandied: exchanged; lit., the exchange of strokes in tennis. **30. favor:** gift. **35. numbers . . . numbering:** meter . . . estimation. **42. text B:** an elaborate initial B. For specimens of elaborate initial, see Pl. 11a, 11b. **44. red dominical:** the red letters used to mark Sundays in all almanacs, with a reference to Katharine's golden hair. See App. 2. Red and gold were not always distinguished in Shakespeare's time. Cf. *Macb,* II.iii.118. **45. O's:** i.e., smallpox scars — a common disfigurement in the sixteenth century. **46. beshrew:** curse. **shrows:** shrews. **61. in . . . week:** a proverbial phrase meaning "completely caught." **64. bootless:** vain. **65. hests:** commands. **67. perttaunt-like:** this is the reading of Q and F and has never been explained, though endlessly emended. It obviously means like a tyrant.

68. fate: destiny. **82. Encounters . . . are:** attacks are prepared. **87. Saint Denis:** patron saint of France. **to:** against. **92. addressed:** directed. **98. conned:** learned. **101. ever . . . anon:** from time to time. **made:** felt, expressed. **109. fleered·** grinned contemptuously.

The third he capered, and cried, "All goes well,"
The fourth turned on the toe, and down he fell.
With that, they all did tumble on the ground, 115
With such a zealous laughter, so profound,
That in this spleen° ridiculous appears,
To check their folly, passion's solemn tears.
    PRIN. But what, but what, come they to visit us?
    BOYET. They do, they do, and are appareled thus,
Like Muscovites or Russians, as I guess. 121
Their purpose is to parle,° to court and dance;
And everyone his love feat° will advance
Unto his several° mistress, which they'll know
By favors several° which they did bestow. 125
    PRIN. And will they so? The gallants shall be
        tasked;°
For, ladies, we will every one be masked,
And not a man of them shall have the grace,
Despite of suit,° to see a lady's face.
Hold, Rosaline, this favor thou shalt wear, 130
And then the King will court thee for his dear.
Hold, take thou this, my sweet, and give me thine,
So shall Berowne take me for Rosaline.
And change you favors too, so shall your loves
Woo contrary, deceived by these removes.° 135
    ROS. Come on, then. Wear the favors most in sight.
    KATH. But in this changing what is your intent?
    PRIN. The effect of my intent is to cross theirs.
They do it but in mocking merriment,
And mock for mock is only my intent. 140
Their several counsels° they unbosom shall
To loves mistook, and so be mocked withal
Upon the next occasion that we meet
With visages displayed, to talk and greet. 144
    ROS. But shall we dance, if they desire us to 't?
    PRIN. No, to the death, we will not move a foot.
Nor to their penned speech render we no grace,°
But while 'tis spoke each turn away her face.
    BOYET. Why, that contempt will kill the speaker's
        heart,
And quite divorce his memory from his part. 150
    PRIN. Therefore I do it, and I make no doubt
The rest will ne'er come in, if he be out.
There's no such sport as sport by sport o'erthrown,
To make theirs ours, and ours none but our own.
So shall we stay, mocking intended game, 155
And they, well mocked, depart away with shame.
              [*Trumpets sound within.*]
    BOYET. The trumpet sounds. Be masked. The
      maskers come.   [*The* LADIES *mask.*]
[*Enter* BLACKAMOORS *with music;* MOTH; *the* KING,
BEROWNE, LONGAVILLE, *and* DUMAIN, *in Russian
      habits,° and masked.*]

MOTH. "All hail, the richest beauties on the
    earth!"
    BOYET. Beauties no richer than rich taffeta.
    MOTH. "A holy parcel of the fairest dames 160
        [*The* LADIES *turn their backs to him.*]
That ever turned their — backs — to mortal views!"
    BER. [*Aside to* MOTH] Their eyes, villain, their
    eyes.
    MOTH. "That ever turned their eyes to mortal
    views!
Out ——"
    BOYET. True, out indeed.   165
    MOTH. "Out of your favors, heavenly spirits,
    vouchsafe
Not to behold ——"
    BER. [*Aside to* MOTH] Once to behold, rogue.
    MOTH. "Once to behold with your sun-beamèd
eyes — with your sun-beamèd eyes ——"
    BOYET. They will not answer to that epithet. 170
You were best call it "daughter-beamèd eyes."
    MOTH. They do not mark me, and that brings° me
    out.
    BER. Is this your perfectness? Be gone, you rogue!
               [*Exit* MOTH.]
    ROS. What would these strangers? Know their
    minds, Boyet.
If they do speak our language, 'tis our will 175
That some plain man recount their purposes.
Know what they would.
    BOYET. What would you with the Princess?
    BER. Nothing but peace and gentle visitation.
    ROS. What would they, say they?   180
    BOYET. Nothing but peace and gentle visitation.
    ROS. Why, that they have, and bid them so be
    gone.
    BOYET. She says you have it, and you may be gone.
    KING. Say to her we have measured many miles
To tread a measure° with her on this grass. 185
    BOYET. They say that they have measured many a
    mile
To tread a measure with you on this grass.
    ROS. It is not so. Ask them how many inches
Is in one mile. If they have measured many,
The measure then of one is easily told. 190
    BOYET. If to come hither you have measured miles,
And many miles, the Princess bids you tell
How many inches doth fill up one mile.
    BER. Tell her we measure them by weary steps.
    BOYET. She hears herself.   196
    ROS.   How many weary steps
Of many weary miles you have o'ergone,
Are numbered in the travel of one mile?
    BER. We number nothing that we spend for you.
Our duty is so rich, so infinite,
That we may do it still without accompt.° 200

---

117. spleen: excess of mirth.   122. parle: converse.   123. love
feat: act of courting.   124. several: particular.   125. favors
several: the particular gifts.   126. tasked: tried.   129. Despite
of suit: in spite of their petition.   135. removes: changes.
141. counsels: secret thoughts.   147. grace: favor.   157. s.d.:
habits: costumes.

172. brings: puts.   185. tread a measure: dance. See App. 24.
200. accompt: reckoning.

Vouchsafe to show the sunshine of your face,
That we, like savages, may worship it.

ROS. My face is but a moon, and clouded too.

KING. Blessèd are clouds, to do as such clouds do!
Vouchsafe, bright moon, and these thy stars, to
shine,   205
Those clouds removed, upon our watery eyne.°

ROS. O vain petitioner! Beg a greater matter.
Thou now request'st but moonshine in the water.

KING. Then in our measure do but vouchsafe one
change.°   209
Thou bid'st me beg. This begging is not strange.

ROS. Play, music, then! Nay, you must do it soon.
                                                   [*Music plays.*]
Not yet! No dance! Thus change I like the moon.

KING. Will you not dance? How come you thus
estrangèd?

ROS. You took the moon at full, but now she's
changed.

KING. Yet still she is the moon, and I the man.
The music plays, vouchsafe some motion to it. 216

ROS. Our ears vouchsafe it.

KING.   But your legs should do it.

ROS. Since you are strangers, and come here by
chance,
We'll not be nice. Take hands. We will not dance.

KING. Why take we hands, then?

ROS.   Only to part friends. 220
Curtsy, sweethearts, and so the measure ends.

KING. More measure of this measure — be not
nice.°

ROS. We can afford no more at such a price.

KING. Prize you yourselves. What buys your com-
pany?

ROS. Your absence only.

KING.   That can never be. 225

ROS. Then cannot we be bought, and so adieu —
Twice to your visor, and half once to you.

KING. If you deny to dance, let's hold more chat.

ROS. In private, then.

KING. I am best pleased with that.
                                                   [*They converse apart.*]

BER. White-handed mistress, one sweet word with
thee.   230

PRIN. Honey, and milk, and sugar — there is
three.

BER. Nay then, two treys,° an if you grow so nice,
Metheglin, wort, and malmsey.° Well run, dice!
There's half a dozen sweets.

PRIN.   Seventh sweet, adieu.
Since you can cog,° I'll play no more with you. 235

BER. One word in secret.

PRIN.   Let it not be sweet.

BER. Thou grievest my gall.°

PRIN.   Gall! Bitter.

BER.   Therefore meet. [*They converse apart.*]

DUM. Will you vouchsafe with me to change a
word?

MAR. Name it.

DUM.   Fair lady——

MAR.   Say you so? Fair lord——
Take that for your fair lady.

DUM.   Please it you, 240
As much in private, and I'll bid adieu.
                                                   [*They converse apart.*]

KATH. What, was your vizard° made without a
tongue?

LONG. I know the reason, lady, why you ask.

KATH. Oh, for your reason! Quickly, sir, I long.

LONG. You have a double tongue within your
mask,   245
And would afford my speechless vizard half.

KATH. Veal, quoth the Dutchman.° Is not " veal "
a calf?

LONG. A calf, fair lady!

KATH.   No, a fair lord calf.

LONG. Let's part° the word.

KATH.   No, I'll not be your half.
Take all, and wean it. It may prove an ox. 250

LONG. Look how you butt yourself in these sharp
mocks!
Will you give horns, chaste lady? Do not so.

KATH. Then die a calf, before your horns do grow.

LONG. One word in private with you, ere I die.

KATH. Bleat softly, then. The butcher hears you
cry.   [*They converse apart.*] 255

BOYET. The tongues of mocking wenches are as
keen
As is the razor's edge invisible,
Cutting a smaller hair than may be seen,
Above the sense of sense. So sensible   259
Seemeth their conference, their conceits° have wings
Fleeter than arrows, bullets, wind, thought, swifter
things.

ROS. Not one word more, my maids. Break off,
break off.

BER. By Heaven, all dry-beaten° with pure scoff!

KING. Farewell, mad wenches, you have simple
wits.

PRIN. Twenty adieus, my frozen Muscovits. 265
        [*Exeunt* KING, LORDS, *and* BLACKAMOORS.]
Are these the breed of wits so wondered at?

BOYET. Tapers° they are, with your sweet breaths
puffed out.

ROS. Well-liking° wits they have — gross, gross;
fat, fat.

---

206. eyne: eyes.   209. change: i.e., of time.   222. nice: dainty,
fussy.   232. treys: throws of three at dice.   233. Metheglin:
mead, a drink made with honey; wort: sweet unfermented beer;
malmsey: a sweet wine. I.e., Berowne replies with three more
"sweets."   235. cog: cheat.

237. gall: sore.   242. vizard: mask.   247. Veal . . . Dutchman:
i.e., the Dutchman's pronunciation of "well" followed by the
inevitable pun on *calf.*   249. part: divide.   260. conceits: witti-
cisms.   263. dry-beaten: beaten without breaking the skin.
267. Tapers: candles.   268. Well-liking: sleek.

PRIN. Oh, poverty in wit, kingly-poor° flout!°
Will they not, think you, hang themselves tonight?
Or ever, but in vizards, show their faces?   271
This pert Berowne was out of countenance quite.
ROS. Oh, they were all in lamentable cases!
The King was weeping-ripe° for a good° word.   274
PRIN. Berowne did swear himself out of all suit.°
MAR. Dumain was at my service, and his sword.
No point, quoth I. My servant straight was mute.
KATH. Lord Longaville said I came o'er his heart,
And trow° you what he called me?
PRIN.   Qualm,° perhaps.
KATH. Yes, in good faith.
PRIN.   Go, sickness as thou art!
ROS. Well, better wits have worn plain statute
caps.°   281
But will you hear? The King is my love sworn.
PRIN. And quick Berowne hath plighted faith to
me.
KATH. And Longaville was for my service born.
MAR. Dumain is mine, as sure as bark on tree.
BOYET. Madam, and pretty mistresses, give ear.
Immediately they will again be here   287
In their own shapes; for it can never be
They will digest this harsh indignity.
PRIN. Will they return?
BOYET.   They will, they will, God knows,   290
And leap for joy, though they are lame with blows.
Therefore change favors, and when they repair,°
Blow° like sweet roses in this summer air.
PRIN. How blow? How blow? Speak to be under
stood.
BOYET. Fair ladies masked are roses in their bud.
Dismasked, their damask° sweet commixture°
shown,   296
Are angels vailing° clouds, or roses blown.
PRIN. Avaunt, perplexity! What shall we do
If they return in their own shapes to woo?   299
ROS. Good madam, if by me you'll be advised,
Let's mock them still, as well known as disguised.
Let us complain to them what fools were here,
Disguised like Muscovites in shapeless gear,°
And wonder what they were and to what end
Their shallow shows and prologue vilely penned,
And their rough carriage so ridiculous,   306
Should be presented at our tent to us.
BOYET. Ladies, withdraw. The gallants are at
hand.
PRIN. Whip° to our tents, as roes run o'er land.
[Exeunt PRINCESS, ROSALINE, KATHARINE, and MARIA.]

[Re-enter the KING, BEROWNE, LONGAVILLE, and
DUMAIN, in their proper habits.]
KING. Fair sir, God save you! Where's the Prin
cess?   310
BOYET. Gone to her tent. Please it your Majesty
Command me any service to her thither?
KING. That she vouchsafe me audience for on:
word.
BOYET. I will, and so will she, I know, my lord.
[Exit.]
BER. This fellow pecks up wit as pigeons peas,
And utters it again when God doth please.   316
He is wit's peddler, and retails his wares
At wakes and wassails,° meetings, markets, fairs.
And we that sell by gross, the Lord doth know,
Have not the grace to grace it with such show.   320
This gallant pins the wenches on his sleeve —
Had he been Adam, he had tempted Eve.
A' can carve° too, and lisp. Why, this is he
That kissed his hand away in courtesy;
This is the ape of form,° monsieur the nice,   325
That, when he plays at tables, chides the dice
In honorable terms. Nay, he can sing
A mean° most meanly, and in ushering,°
Mend° him who can. The ladies call him sweet,
The stairs as he treads on them kiss his feet.   330
This is the flower that smiles on everyone,
To show his teeth as white as whale's° bone;
And consciences that will not die in debt
Pay him the due of honey-tongued Boyet.
KING. A blister on his sweet tongue, with my
heart,   335
That put Armado's page out of his part!
BER. See where it comes! Behavior, what wert thou
Till this madman showed thee? And what art thou
now?   338
[Re-enter the PRINCESS, ushered by BOYET; ROSALINE,
MARIA, and KATHARINE.]
KING. All hail, sweet madam, and fair time of day!
PRIN. "Fair" in "all hail" is foul, as I conceive.
KING. Construe° my speeches better, if you may.
PRIN. Then wish me better. I will give you leave.
KING. We came to visit you, and purpose now
To lead you to our Court. Vouchsafe it, then.
PRIN. This field shall hold me, and so hold your
vow.   345
Nor God, nor I, delights in perjured men.
KING. Rebuke me not for that which you provoke.
The virtue° of your eye must break my oath.
PRIN. You nickname° virtue, vice you should have
spoke,
For virtue's office never breaks men's troth.   350
Now by my maiden honor yet as pure

269. kingly-poor: a bad pun on *well-li-king* (l. 268). flout: jest.
274. weeping-ripe: on the point of bursting into tears. good:
kind. 275. out . . . suit: out of court. 279. trow: know. Qualm:
(pronounced calm), a feeling of sickness. 281. statute caps: flat
woolen caps worn by citizens and apprentices. See Pl. 9l and p. 94a.
292. repair: come again. 293. Blow: open like rosebuds; i.e., un-
mask. 296. damask . . . commixture: pink-and-white complex-
ion. 297. vailing: lowering. 303. gear: stuff. 309. Whip: run.

318. wassails: feasts. 323. carve: be affected. 325. ape of form:
imitator of fashion. 328. mean: tenor. ushering: escorting the
ladies. 329. Mend: surpass. 332. whale's: pronounced as two
syllables here. 341. Construe: interpret. 348. virtue: power.
349. nickname: mention mistakenly.

As the unsullied lily I protest
A world of torments though I should endure,
   I would not yield to be your house's guest,
So much I hate a breaking cause to be   355
Of heavenly oaths, vowed with integrity.
   KING. Oh, you have lived in desolation here,
Unseen, unvisited, much to our shame.
   PRIN. Not so, my lord; it is not so, I swear.
We have had pastimes here and pleasant game.
A mess° of Russians left us but of late.   361
   KING. How, madam! Russians!
   PRIN.   Aye, in truth, my lord,
Trim gallants, full of courtship and of state.
   ROS. Madam, speak true. It is not so, my lord.
My lady, to the manner of the days,   365
In courtesy gives undeserving praise.
We four indeed confronted were with four
In Russian habit. Here they stayed an hour,
And talked apace, and in that hour, my lord,
They did not bless us with one happy word.   370
I dare not call them fools, but this I think —
When they are thirsty, fools would fain have drink.
   BER. This jest is dry to me. Fair gentle sweet,
Your wit makes wise things foolish. When we
   greet,
With eyes best seeing, heaven's fiery eye,   375
By light we lose light.° Your capacity
Is of that nature that to your huge store
Wise things seem foolish and rich things but poor.
   ROS. This proves you wise and rich, for in my
   eye ——
   BER. I am a fool, and full of poverty.   380
   ROS. But that you take what doth to you belong,
It were a fault to snatch words from my tongue.
   BER. Oh, I am yours, and all that I possess!
   ROS. All the fool mine?
   BER.   I cannot give you less.
   ROS. Which of the vizards was it that you wore?
   BER. Where? When? What vizard? Why demand
   you this?   386
   ROS. There, then, that vizard — that superfluous
   case
That hid the worse and showed the better face.
   KING. We are descried.° They'll mock us now
   downright.
   DUM. Let us confess, and turn it to a jest.   390
   PRIN. Amazed, my lord? Why looks your High-
   ness sad?
   ROS. Help, hold his brows! He'll swound! Why
   look you pale?
Seasick, I think, coming from Muscovy.
   BER. Thus pour the stars down plagues for per-
   jury.
Can any face of brass hold longer out?   395

Here stand I. Lady, dart thy skill at me,
   Bruise me with scorn, confound me with a flout,
Thrust thy sharp wit quite through my ignorance,
   Cut me to pieces with thy keen conceit,
And I will wish thee never more to dance,   400
   Nor never more in Russian habit wait.
Oh, never will I trust to speeches penned,
   Nor to the motion of a schoolboy's tongue,
Nor never come in vizard to my friend,
   Nor woo in rhyme, like a blind harper's song!°
Taffeta phrases, silken terms precise,   406
   Three-piled° hyperboles, spruce affectation,
Figures pedantical — these summer flies
   Have blown° me full of maggot ostentation.
I do forswear them, and I here protest,   410
   By this white glove — how white the hand, God
   knows! —
Henceforth my wooing mind shall be expressed
   In russet yeas and honest kersey° noes.
And, to begin, wench — so God help me, la! —
My love to thee is sound, sans° crack or flaw.   415
   ROS. Sans sans, I pray you.
   BER.   Yet I have a trick
Of the old rage.° — Bear with me, I am sick —
I'll leave it by degrees. Soft, let us see.
Write " Lord have mercy on us "° on those three.
They are infected, in their hearts it lies;   420
They have the plague, and caught it of your eyes.
These lords are visited, you are not free,
For the Lord's tokens° on you do I see.
   PRIN. No, they are free that gave these tokens to
   us.   424
   BER. Our states° are forfeit. Seek not to undo us.
   ROS. It is not so, for how can this be true,
That you stand forfeit, being those that sue?
   BER. Peace! For I will not have to do with you.
   ROS. Nor shall not, if I do as I intend.
   BER. Speak for yourselves. My wit is at an end.
   KING. Teach us, sweet madam, for our rude trans-
   gression   431
Some fair excuse.
   PRIN.   The fairest is confession.
Were not you here but even now disguised?
   KING. Madam, I was.
   PRIN.   And were you well advised?
   KING. I was, fair madam.
   PRIN.   When you then were here,   435
What did you whisper in your lady's ear?
   KING. That more than all the world I did respect
   her.

405. Nor . . . song: i.e., the doggerel of a blind ballad singer.
407. Three-piled: the word is normally used for the thickest
velvet.   409. blown: puffed.   413. russet . . . kersey: different
kinds of coarse homespun cloth.   415. sans: without.   417. rage:
poetic fury.   419. Lord . . . us: written over the doors of houses
infected with the plague.   423. Lord's tokens: signs of the plague,
and also the gifts of their lovers which the ladies are wearing.
425. states: estates.

361. mess: party of four.   374–76. when . . . light: i.e., you are
like the sun which blinds by excessive light.   389. descried:
sighted, found out.

PRIN. When she shall challenge this, you will reject her.   438

KING. Upon mine honor, no.

PRIN.   Peace, peace! Forbear.
Your oath once broke, you force not to° forswear.

KING. Despise me when I break this oath of mine.

PRIN. I will, and therefore keep it, Rosaline,
What did the Russian whisper in your ear?

ROS. Madam, he swore that he did hold me dear
As precious eyesight, and did value me   445
Above this world, adding thereto, moreover,
That he would wed me or else die my lover.

PRIN. God give thee joy of him! The noble lord
Most honorably doth uphold his word.

KING. What mean you, madam? By my life, my troth,   450
I never swore this lady such an oath.

ROS. By Heaven, you did, and to confirm it plain,
You gave me this.° But take it, sir, again.

KING. My faith and this the Princess I did give.
I knew her by this jewel on her sleeve.   455

PRIN. Pardon me, sir, this jewel did she wear,
And Lord Berowne, I thank him, is my dear.
What, will you have me, or your pearl again?

BER. Neither of either, I remit both twain.
I see the trick on't. Here was a consent,   460
Knowing aforehand of our merriment,
To dash° it like a Christmas comedy.
Some carrytale, some pleaseman, some slight zany,°
Some mumblenews, some trencher knight,° some Dick
That smiles his cheek in years,° and knows the trick
To make my lady laugh when she's disposed,   466
Told our intents before. Which once disclosed,
The ladies did change favors, and then we,
Following the signs, wooed but the sign° of she.
Now, to our perjury to add more terror,   470
We are again forsworn, in will and error.°
Much upon this° it is. [*To* BOYET] And might not you
Forestall our sport, to make us thus untrue?
Do not you know my lady's foot by the squier,°
And laugh upon the apple of her eye?°   475
And stand between her back, sir, and the fire,
Holding a trencher,° jesting merrily?
You put our page out. Go, you are allowed.°
Die when you will, a smock° shall be your shroud.
You leer upon me, do you? There's an eye   480

Wounds like a leaden° sword.

BOYET.   Full merrily
Hath this brave manage,° this career,° been run.

BER. Lo, he is tilting straight! Peace! I have done.
[*Enter* COSTARD.] Welcome, pure wit! Thou part'st a fair fray.

COST. Oh Lord, sir, they would know   485
Whether the three Worthies shall come in or no.

BER. What, are there but three?

COST.   No, sir, but it is vara fine,
For every one pursents three.

BER.   And three times thrice is nine.

COST. Not so, sir, under correction, sir, I hope it is not so.
You cannot beg us,° sir, I can assure you, sir. We know what we know.   490
I hope, sir, three times thrice, sir ——

BER. Is not nine.

COST. Under correction, sir, we know whereuntil° it doth amount.

BER. By Jove, I always took three threes for nine.

COST. Oh Lord, sir, it were pity you should get your living by reckoning, sir.

BER. How much is it?   499

COST. Oh Lord, sir, the parties themselves, the actors, sir, will show whereuntil it doth amount. For mine own part, I am, as they say, but to parfect° one man in one poor man, Pompion° the Great, sir.

BER. Art thou one of the Worthies?   505

COST. It pleased them to think me worthy of Pompion the Great. For mine own part, I know not the degree° of the Worthy, but I am to stand for him.

BER. Go, bid them prepare.   510

COST. We will turn it finely off, sir, we will take some care.   [*Exit.*]

KING. Berowne, they will shame us. Let them not approach.

BER. We are shameproof, my lord, and 'tis some policy°
To have one show worse than the King's and his company.

KING. I say they shall not come.   515

PRIN. Nay, my good lord, let me o'errule you now.
That sport best pleases that doth least know how,
Where zeal strives to content, and the contents
Dies in the zeal of that which it presents.   519
Their form confounded makes most form in mirth
When great things laboring perish in their birth.°

---

440. force . . . to: do not find it difficult to. 453. this: i.e., the present originally sent by the King to the Princess. 462. dash: make fun of. 463. pleaseman . . . zany: yesman . . . stooge. 464. trencher knight: hanger-on. 465. in years: into wrinkles. 469. sign: outward appearance. 471. will . . . error: deliberately and by mistake. 472. upon this: after this manner. 474. Do . . . squier: i.e., know exactly how to please. squier: rule. 475. laugh . . . eye: jest with her intimately. 477. trencher: wooden plate. 478. allowed: licensed; i.e., a privileged fool. 479. smock: lady's nightdress.

481. leaden: i.e., incapable of wounding. 482. manage: display of horsemanship in the tilting ground. career: charge. 490. beg us: claim us as fools, from the legal procedure in the Court of Wards whereby interested parties begged the court for the custody of a minor or an idiot. 493. whereuntil: whereunto. 502. parfect: for "present." 504. Pompion: pumpkin, for "Pompey." 508. degree: rank. 513. policy: wisdom. 518–21. Where . . . birth: i.e., the unrehearsed results of a too ambitious play are the most amusing.

BER. A right description of our sport,° my lord.

[*Enter* ARMADO.]

ARM. Anointed, I implore so much expense of thy royal sweet breath as will utter a brace of words.   525

[*Converses apart with the* KING, *and delivers him a paper.*]

PRIN. Doth this man serve God?

BER. Why ask you?   528

PRIN. He speaks not like a man of God's making.

ARM. That is all one, my fair, sweet, honey monarch; for I protest the schoolmaster is exceeding fantastical — too too vain, too too vain. But we will put it, as they say, to *fortuna de la guerra.*° I wish you the peace of mind, most royal couplement!°   535

[*Exit.*]

KING. Here is like to be a good presence of Worthies. He presents Hector of Troy; the swain, Pompey the Great; the parish curate, Alexander; Armado's page, Hercules; the pedant, Judas Maccabaeus.   540
And if these four Worthies in their first show thrive, These four will change habits and present the other five.

BER. There is five in the first show.

KING. You are deceived, 'tis not so.

BER. The pedant, the braggart, the hedge priest,° the fool, and the boy.   546
Abate throw at novum,° and the whole world again Cannot pick out five such, take each one in his vein.

KING. The ship is under sail, and here she comes amain.

[*Enter* COSTARD, *for* POMPEY.]

COS. "I Pompey am ——"

BOYET.   You lie, you are not he.   550

COS. "I Pompey am ——"

BOYET.   With libbard's° head on knee.

BER. Well said, old mocker. I must needs be friends with thee.

COS. "I Pompey am, Pompey surnamed the Big ——"

DUM. "The Great."

COS. It is "Great," sir.

"Pompey surnamed the Great, That oft in field, with targe and shield, did make my foe to sweat.
And traveling along this coast, I here am come by chance,
And lay my arms before the legs of this sweet lass of France."
If your ladyship would say, "Thanks, Pompey," I had done.

PRIN. Great thanks, Great Pompey.   560

COST. 'Tis not so much worth, but I hope I was perfect. I made a little fault in "Great."

BER. My hat to a halfpenny, Pompey proves the best Worthy.

[*Enter* SIR NATHANIEL, *for* ALEXANDER.]

NATH. "When in the world I lived, I was the world's commander.   565
By east, west, north, and south, I spread my conquering might.
My scutcheon° plain declares that I am Alisander ——"

BOYET. Your nose says no, you are not, for it stands too right.°

BER. Your nose smells "no"° in this, most tendersmelling knight.

PRIN. The conqueror is dismayed. Proceed, good Alexander.   570

NATH. "When in the world I lived, I was the world's commander ——"

BOYET. Most true, 'tis right, you were so, Alisander.

BER. Pompey the Great ——

COST. Your servant, and Costard.

BER. Take away the conqueror, take away Alisander.

COST. [*To* SIR NATHANIEL] O sir, you have overthrown Alisander the conqueror! You will be scraped out of the painted cloth° for this. Your lion, that holds his poleax sitting on a close-stool, will be   580 given to Ajax:° he will be the ninth Worthy. A conqueror, and afeared to speak! Run away for shame, Alisander. [NATHANIEL *retires.*] There, an't shall please you, a foolish mild man — an honest man, look you, and soon dashed. He is a marvelous good neighbor, faith, and a very good bowler. But for Alisander — alas, you see how 'tis — a little o'erparted.° But there are Worthies a-coming will speak their mind in some other sort.   590

PRIN. Stand aside, good Pompey.

[*Enter* HOLOFERNES, *for* JUDAS; *and* MOTH, *for* HERCULES.]

HOL. "Great Hercules is presented by this imp, Whose club killed Cerberus, that three-headed *canis.*°
And when he was a babe, a child, a shrimp, Thus did he strangle serpents in his *manus.*°
Quoniam° he seemeth in minority,   596

---

522. our sport: i.e., our fiasco of the masque of the Muscovites.
534. *fortuna . . . guerra:* the fortune of war.   535. couplement: pair.   545. hedge priest: low-grade, illiterate priest.   547. Abate . . . novum: except for a throw at novum, a dice game at which the principal throws were five and nine.   551. libbard: heraldic painting of a leopard or lion. The joke has not been satisfactorily explained, but presumably it refers to Pompey's symbolical costume or the coat of arms on his shield.

567. scutcheon: coat of arms.   568. too right: Alexander's head was slightly twisted.   569. nose . . . 'no': the real Alexander was said to have had a sweet smelling skin.   579. painted cloth: See *I Hen IV*, IV.ii.27,n., and Pl. 6a.   579–81. Your . . . Ajax: According to the heraldic experts of the day, the coat of arms of Alexander was a lion sitting in a chair and holding a battle-ax. Ajax was noted among the Greeks for his boasting; among the audience the name was inseparably connected with a privy. See App. 4.   588–89. little o'erparted: hardly up to the part.
593. *canis:* dog.   595. *manus:* hand.   596. *Quoniam:* since.

Ergo° I come with this apology."
Keep some state° in thy exit, and vanish.

           [MOTH *retires*.]

" Judas I am —— "

DUM. A Judas!

HOL. Not Iscariot, sir.   600

" Judas I am, ycliped° Maccabaeus."

DUM. Judas Maccabaeus clipped is plain Judas.

BER. A kissing traitor. How art thou proved
     Judas?

HOL. " Judas I am —— "   605

DUM. The more shame for you, Judas.

HOL. What mean you, sir?

BOYET. To make Judas hang himself.

HOL. Begin, sir, you are my elder.°

BER. Well followed. Judas was hanged on an
     elder.   610

HOL. I will not be put out of countenance.

BER. Because thou hast no face.

HOL. What is this?°

BOYET. A citternhead.°

DUM. The head of a bodkin.°   615

BER. A Death's face° in a ring.

LONG. The face of an old Roman coin, scarce seen.

BOYET. The pommel of Caesar's falchion.°

DUM. The carved-bone face on a flask.

BER. Saint George's half-cheek° in a brooch.   620

DUM. Aye, and in a brooch of lead.

BER. Aye, and worn in the cap of a toothdrawer.
And now forward, for we have put thee in counte-
nance.

HOL. You have put me out of countenance.

BER. False. We have given thee faces.   625

HOL. But you have outfaced them all.

BER. An thou wert a lion, we would do so.

BOYET. Therefore, as he is an ass, let him go.
And so adieu, sweet Jude! Nay, why dost thou stay?

DUM. For the latter end of his name.   630

BER. For the ass to the Jude, give it him. — Jud-as,
away!

HOL. This is not generous,° not gentle, not hum-
ble.

BOYET. A light for Monsieur Judas! It grows dark,
     he may stumble.   [HOLOFERNES *retires*.]

PRIN. Alas, poor Maccabaeus, how hath he been
     baited!°   634

           [*Enter* ARMADO, *for* HECTOR.]

BER. Hide thy head, Achilles. Here comes Hector
in arms.

DUM. Though my mocks come home by me, I will
now be merry.

---

597. *Ergo*: therefore.   598. state: dignity.   602. ycliped: called.
609. you . . . elder: you seem to know more about it than I.
613. this: i.e., indicating his own face.   614. citternhead: the
top of a cittern — a form of guitar. See Pl. 18b and c.
615. bodkin: dagger.   616. Death's face: skull.   618. falchion:
curved sword.   620. half-cheek: side face.   632. generous: noble.
634. baited: tormented.

KING. Hector was but a Troyan° in respect of this.

BOYET. But is this Hector?   641

KING. I think Hector was not so clean-timbered.°

LONG. His leg is too big for Hector's.

DUM. More calf, certain.   645

BOYET. No, he is best indued in the small.°

BER. This cannot be Hector.

DUM. He's a god or a painter, for he makes faces.

ARM. " The armipotent° Mars, of lances the al-
     mighty,   651
     Gave Hector a gift —— "

DUM. A gilt nutmeg.

BER. A lemon.

LONG. Stuck with cloves.

DUM. No, cloven.   655

ARM. Peace! ——

" The armipotent Mars, of lances the almighty,
     Gave Hector a gift, the heir of Ilion,
     A man so breathed° that certain he would fight ye
     From morn till night, out of his pavilion.   660
I am that flower —— "

DUM.   That mint.

LONG.   That columbine.

ARM. Sweet Lord Longaville, rein thy tongue.

LONG. I must rather give it the rein, for it runs
against Hector.

DUM. Aye, and Hector's a greyhound.°   665

ARM. The sweet warman is dead and rotten. Sweet
chucks, beat not the bones of the buried. When he
breathed, he was a man. But I will forward with my
device. [*To the* PRINCESS] Sweet royalty, bestow on
me the sense of hearing.   670

PRIN. Speak, brave Hector. We are much de-
lighted.

ARM. I do adore thy sweet Grace's slipper.   674

BOYET. [*Aside to* DUMAIN] Loves her by the foot.

DUM. [*Aside to* BOYET] He may not by the yard.

ARM. " This Hector far surmounted Hanni-
bal —— "

COST. The party° is gone, fellow Hector, she is
gone,° she is two months on her way.

ARM. What meanest thou?   680

COST. Faith, unless you play the honest Troyan,
the poor wench is cast away. She's quick, the child
brags in her belly already. 'Tis yours.

ARM. Dost thou infamonize° me among poten-
tates? Thou shalt die.   685

COST. Then shall Hector be whipped for Jaque-
netta that is quick by him, and hanged for Pompey
that is dead by him.

DUM. Most rare Pompey!

BOYET. Renowned Pompey!   690

---

640. Troyan: Trojan, gay lad.   642. clean-timbered: clean-
limbed.   646. small: lower part of the leg.   650. armipotent:
powerful in arms.   659. so breathed: with such good wind.
665. greyhound: i.e., a fast runner, as he showed when Achilles
ran after him.   678. The party: i.e., Jaquenetta.   679. gone:
ruined.   684. infamonize: disgrace.

BER. Greater than great, great, great, great Pompey! Pompey the Huge!

DUM. Hector trembles.

BER. Pompey is moved. More Ates,° more Ates! Stir them on! Stir them on!   695

DUM. Hector will challenge him.

BER. Aye, if a' have no more man's blood in's belly than will sup a flea.

ARM. By the North Pole, I do challenge thee.

COST. I will not fight with a pole, like a Northern man, I'll slash, I'll do it by the sword. I bepray°   700 you let me borrow my arms again.

DUM. Room for the incensed Worthies!

COST. I'll do it in my shirt.

DUM. Most resolute Pompey!   705

MOTH. Master, let me take you a buttonhole lower.° Do you not see Pompey is uncasing° for the combat? What mean you? You will lose your reputation.

ARM. Gentlemen and soldiers, pardon me. I will not combat in my shirt.   710

DUM. You may not deny it. Pompey hath made the challenge.

ARM. Sweet bloods, I both may and will.

BER. What reason have you for't?   715

ARM. The naked truth of it is, I have no shirt.° I go woolward° for penance.

BOYET. True, and it was enjoined him in Rome for want of linen. Since when, I'll be sworn, he wore none but a dishclout° of Jaquenetta's, and that a' wears next his heart for a favor.°   722

[*Enter* MERCADE.]

MER. God save you, madam!

PRIN. Welcome, Mercade, But that thou interrupt'st our merriment.   725

MER. I am sorry, madam, for the news I bring Is heavy in my tongue. The King your father ——

PRIN. Dead, for my life!

MER. Even so. My tale is told.

BER. Worthies, away! The scene begins to cloud.

ARM. For mine own part, I breathe free breath. I have seen the day of wrong through the little hole of discretion, and I will right myself like a soldier.

[*Exeunt* WORTHIES.]

KING. How fares your Majesty?   736

PRIN. Boyet, prepare, I will away tonight.

KING. Madam, not so. I do beseech you, stay.

PRIN. Prepare, I say. I thank you, gracious lords, For all your fair endeavors, and entreat,   740 Out of a new-sad soul, that you vouchsafe In your rich wisdom to excuse, or hide, The liberal opposition of our spirits

If overboldly we have borne ourselves In the converse of breath. Your gentleness   745 Was guilty of it. Farewell, worthy lord! A heavy heart bears not a nimble tongue. Excuse me so, coming too short of thanks For my great suit so easily obtained.

KING. The extreme parts of time extremely forms All causes to the purpose of his speed,°   751 And often, at his very loose,° decides That which long process could not arbitrate. And though the mourning brow of progeny Forbid the smiling courtesy of love   755 The holy suit which fain it would convince,° Yet, since love's argument was first on foot, Let not the cloud of sorrow justle it From what it purposed; since, to wail friends lost Is not by much so wholesome-profitable   760 As to rejoice at friends but newly found.

PRIN. I understand you not. My griefs are double.

BER. Honest plain words best pierce the ear of grief, And by these badges° understand the King. For your fair sakes have we neglected time,   765 Played foul play with our oaths. Your beauty, ladies, Hath much deformed us, fashioning our humors Even to the opposèd end of our intents. And what in us hath seemed ridiculous — As love is full of unbefitting strains;   770 All wanton as a child, skipping, and vain; Formed by the eye and therefore, like the eye, Full of strange shapes, of habits and of forms, Varying in subjects as the eye doth roll To every varied object in his glance —   775 Which particoated° presence of loose love Put on by us, if, in your heavenly eyes, Have misbecomed our oaths and gravities, Those heavenly eyes, that look into these faults, Suggested° us to make. Therefore, ladies,   780 Our love being yours, the error that love makes Is likewise yours. We to ourselves prove false By being once false forever to be true To those that make us both — fair ladies, you. And even that falsehood, in itself a sin,   785 Thus purifies itself, and turns to grace.

PRIN. We have received your letters full of love, Your favors, the ambassadors of love, And in our maiden council rated them At courtship, pleasant jest and courtesy,   790 As bombast° and as lining to the time. But more devout° than this in our respects° Have we not been, and therefore met your loves In their own fashion, like a merriment.°

---

694. Ates: goddesses of mischief.   **700. bepray:** beseech. **706–07. take . . . lower:** unbutton your doublet a buttonhole lower. **uncasing:** taking off his coat.   **716. have no shirt:** a confession of extreme poverty in a gallant. **717. go woolward:** wear wool next my skin.   **721. dishclout:** dishcloth.   **722. favor:** love token.

750–51. The . . . speed: i.e., in extremity everything must be done speedily.   **752. at . . . loose:** quite at random.   **756. convince:** win.   **764. badges:** tokens.   **776. particoated:** wearing motley, the fool's dress. See Pl. 13c.   **780. Suggested:** prompted **791. bombast:** padding.   **792. devout:** serious. **respects:** consideration, thoughts.   **794. merriment:** joke.

DUM. Our letters, madam, showed much more
   than jest.   795
LONG. So did our looks.
ROS.   We did not quote° them so.
KING. Now, at the latest minute of the hour,
Grant us your loves.
PRIN.   A time, methinks, too short
To make a world-without-end bargain in.
No, no, my lord, your Grace is perjured much,   800
Full of dear° guiltiness, and therefore this —
If for my love, as there is no such cause,
You will do aught, this shall you do for me.
Your oath I will not trust, but go with speed
To some forlorn and naked hermitage   805
Remote from all the pleasures of the world.
There stay until the twelve celestial signs
Have brought about the annual reckoning.°
If this austere insociable life
Change not your offer made in heat of blood;   810
If frosts and fasts, hard lodging and thin weeds°
Nip not the gaudy blossoms of your love,
But that it bear this trial, and last love —
Then, at the expiration of the year,
Come challenge me, challenge me by these deserts
And, by this virgin palm now kissing thine,   816
I will be thine, and till that instant shut
My woeful self up in a mourning house,
Raining the tears of lamentation
For the remembrance of my father's death.   820
If this thou do deny, let our hands part,
Neither entitled° in the other's heart.
   KING. If this, or more than this, I would deny,
   To flatter up these powers of mine with rest,
The sudden hand of death close up mine eye!   825
Hence ever then my heart is in thy breast.
BER. And what to me, my love? And what to me?
ROS. You must be purgèd too, your sins are
   racked,°
You are attaint° with faults and perjury.
Therefore if you my favor mean to get,   830
A twelvemonth shall you spend, and never rest,
But seek the weary beds of people sick.
DUM. But what to me, my love? But what to me?
A wife?
KATH. A beard,° fair health, and honesty.
With threefold love I wish you all these three.   835
DUM. Oh, shall I say I thank you, gentle wife?
KATH. Not so, my lord. A twelvemonth and a day
I'll mark no words that smooth-faced wooers say.
Come when the King doth to my lady come,
Then, if I have much love, I'll give you some.   840
DUM. I'll serve thee true and faithfully till then.

KATH. Yet swear not, lest ye be forsworn again.
LONG. What says Maria?
MAR.   At the twelvemonth's end
I'll change my black gown for a faithful friend. 844
LONG. I'll stay with patience, but the time is long.
MAR. The liker you.° Few taller are so young.
BER. Studies my lady? Mistress, look on me.
Behold the window of my heart, mine eye,
What humble suit attends thy answer there.
Impose some service on me for thy love.   850
ROS. Oft have I heard of you, my Lord Berowne,
Before I saw you, and the world's large tongue
Proclaims you for a man replete with mocks,°
Full of comparisons and wounding flouts,°
Which you on all estates° will execute   855
That lie within the mercy of your wit.
To weed this wormwood° from your fruitful brain,
And therewithal to win me, if you please —
Without the which I am not to be won —
You shall this twelvemonth term from day to day
Visit the speechless sick, and still° converse   861
With groaning wretches; and your task shall be
With all the fierce endeavor of your wit
To enforce the painèd impotent to smile.
BER. To move wild laughter in the throat of
   death?   865
It cannot be, it is impossible.
Mirth cannot move a soul in agony.
ROS. Why, that's the way to choke a gibing spirit
Whose influence is begot of that loose grace
Which shallow laughing hearers give to fools.   870
A jest's prosperity° lies in the ear
Of him that hears it, never in the tongue
Of him that makes it. Then, if sickly ears,
Deafed with the clamors of their own dear groans,
Will hear your idle scorns, continue then,   875
And I will have you and that fault withal.
But if they will not, throw away that spirit,
And I shall find you empty of that fault,
Right joyful of your reformation.
BER. A twelvemonth! Well, befall what will be-
   fall,   880
I'll jest a twelvemonth in a hospital.
PRIN. [*To the* KING] Aye, sweet my lord, and so I
   take my leave.
KING. No, madam, we will bring you on your way.
BER. Our wooing doth not end like an old play.
Jack hath not Jill. These ladies' courtesy°   885
Might well have made our sport a comedy.°
KING. Come, sir, it wants a twelvemonth and a
   day,

---

796. quote: note, regard.   801. dear: with the double meaning of great and loving.   807–08. twelve . . . reckoning: i.e., a complete year. See App. 1.   811. weeds: garments.   822. entitled: having a claim.   828. racked: tortured.   829. attaint: charged. 834. A beard: i.e., a wish that you'll grow up.

846. The . . . you: like time, you are long; i.e., tall.   853. replete . . . mocks: full of mockery.   854. wounding flouts: bitter jokes which hurt.   855. all estates: men of all kinds.   857. wormwood: bitterness.   861. still: continuously.   871. A . . . prosperity: the success of a jest.   885. These . . . courtesy: i.e., if these ladies had been kind to us.   886. comedy: i.e., a play with a happy ending.

And then 'twill end.

BER.   That's too long for a play.
     [*Re-enter* ARMADO.]

ARM. Sweet Majesty, vouchsafe me ——

PRIN. Was not that Hector?

DUM. The worthy knight of Troy.   890

ARM. I will kiss thy royal finger, and take leave. I
am a votary, I have vowed to Jaquenetta to hold the
plow for her sweet love three years. But, most
esteemed greatness, will you hear the dialogue that
the two learned men have compiled in praise of the
owl and the cuckoo? It should have followed in the
end of our show.

KING. Call them forth quickly. We will do so.

ARM. Holla! Approach. [*Re-enter* HOLOFERNES,
NATHANIEL, MOTH, COSTARD, *and others.*] This   901
side is Hiems, Winter, this Ver, the Spring, the one
maintained by the owl, the other by the cuckoo. Ver,
begin.

THE SONG

SPRING.   When daisies pied° and violets blue
         And lady smocks all silver-white   905
    And cuckoo buds° of yellow hue
       Do paint the meadows with delight,
     The cuckoo° then, on every tree,
     Mocks married men; for thus sings he —
          Cuckoo,   910
   Cuckoo, cuckoo! Oh, word of fear,
   Unpleasing to a married ear!

   When shepherds pipe on oaten straws,
      And merry larks are plowmen's clocks,
   When turtles tread, and rooks, and daws,

904. pied: parti-colored.   905–06. lady smocks . . . cuckoo buds:
wild flowers of the spring.   908. cuckoo: See App. 11.

And maidens bleach their summer
     smocks,   916
The cuckoo then, on every tree,
   Mocks married men; for thus sings he —
        Cuckoo,
Cuckoo, cuckoo! Oh, word of fear,   920
Unpleasing to a married ear!

WINTER.   When icicles hang by the wall,
     And Dick the shepherd blows his nail,°
   And Tom bears logs into the hall,   924
     And milk comes frozen home in pail,
   When blood is nipped and ways be foul,
     Then nightly sings the staring owl —
        Tu-whit,
   Tu-who, a merry note,
   While greasy Joan doth keel° the pot.

   When all aloud the wind doth blow,   931
     And coughing drowns the parson's
       saw,°
   And birds sit brooding in the snow,
     And Marian's nose looks red and raw,
   When roasted crabs° hiss in the bowl,
     Then nightly sings the staring owl — 936
        Tu-whit,
   Tu-who, a merry note,
   While greasy Joan doth keel the pot.

ARM. The words of Mercury° are harsh after the
songs of Apollo.° You that way — we this way.
                       [*Exeunt.*]

923. blows . . . nail: i.e., to warm his fingers.   930. keel: cool.
932. saw: platitude, wise saying.   935. crabs: crab apples.
940. Mercury: the messenger of the gods.   941. Apollo: the god
of the Arts.

The Tragedy of
KING RICHARD THE SECOND

Introduction[1]

The Tragedy of King Richard the Second was probably written in 1594 or 1595. There is no definite evidence, but the style is early, with regular rhythms, elaborate imagery, many conceits, and abundance of rhyme. The play was entered for publication in the Stationers' Register on August 29, 1597, to Andrew Wise, who in the same year brought out a Quarto (Q1) with the title *The Tragedie of King Richard the second. As it hath beene publikely acted by the right Honourable the Lorde Chamberlaine his Seruants.*

A second Quarto (Q2) and a third Quarto (Q3) appeared in 1598, with the added information " By William Shakespeare." None of these quartos included the deposition scene. No further quartos were published during Queen Elizabeth's reign. Shortly after her death the rights in the book were transferred to Matthew Law, but no new edition was published until 1608. This fourth quarto was the first to give the play complete, and in some copies the title page reads *The Tragedie of King Richard the Second: With the new additions of the Parliament Sceane, and the deposing of King Richard, As it hath been lately acted by the Kinges Majesties seruantes, at the Globe. By William Shake-speare.*

A fifth quarto was printed in 1615. The text in the first folio of 1623 was set up from one of the quartos which had been used in the playhouse.

The story of the play was taken mainly from the account of the reigns of Richard II and Henry IV in Raphael Holinshed's *Chronicles.* Richard's reign was so complex that the details needed to be much simplified to make it suitable for a drama. The play covers only the last three years of Richard's life, from which certain events leading to his deposition were selected and very freely adapted. The quarrel between Norfolk and Hereford, the scene at Coventry, York's desertion, the details of Richard's defeat, Carlisle's speech, and the murder of the King were mainly historical. The deposition scene was mostly in-

[1] See also App. 28.

vented, for there was in fact no public ceremony; Richard signed documents in the presence of attorneys. The deathbed speeches of Gaunt, the parting of Richard and his Queen, and Richard's soliloquy before his death were wholly unhistorical. Some extracts from the *Chronicles* will show how Shakespeare used his material.

1. THE QUARREL BETWEEN MOWBRAY AND HEREFORD (cf. 1.i)

Hereupon there were sundry of the nobles that lamented these mischiefs, and especially showed their griefs unto such by whose naughty counsel they understood the King to be misled; and this they did to the end that they being about him might either turn their copies and give him better counsel, or else he, having knowledge what evil report went of him, might mend his manners misliked of his nobles. But all was in vain, for so it fell out that in this Parliament holden at Shrewsbury Henry Duke of Hereford accused Thomas Mowbray Duke of Norfolk of certain words which he should utter in talk had betwixt them as they rode together lately before betwixt London and Brainford, sounding highly to the King's dishonor. And for further proof thereof he presented a supplication to the King, wherein he appealed the Duke of Norfolk in field of battle for a traitor, false and disloyal to the King, and enemy unto the realm. This supplication was read before both the Dukes in presence of the King; which done, the Duke of Norfolk took upon him to answer it, declaring that whatsoever the Duke of Hereford had said against him other than well, he lied falsely like an untrue knight as he was. And when the King asked of the Duke of Hereford what he said to it, he, taking his hood off his head, said: " My sovereign lord, even as the supplication which I took you importeth, right so I say for truth that Thomas Mowbray Duke of Norfolk is a traitor, false and disloyal to your loyal Majesty, your crown, and to all the states of your realm."

Then the Duke of Norfolk being asked what he said to this, he answered: " Right dear lord, with your favor that I make answer unto your cousin here, I say (your reverence saved) that Henry of Lancaster, Duke of Hereford, like a false and disloyal traitor as he is, doth lie, in that he hath or shall say of me otherwise than well." " No more," said the King, " we have heard enough "; and herewith commanded the Duke of Surrey, for that turn Marshal of England, to arrest in his name the two Dukes: the Duke of Lancaster, father to the Duke of Hereford, the Duke of York, the Duke of Aumerle, Constable of England, and the Duke of Surrey, Marshal of the realm, undertook as pledges body for body for the Duke of Hereford; but the Duke of Norfolk was not suffered to put in pledges, and so under arrest was led unto Windsor Castle, and there guarded with keepers that were appointed to see him safely kept.

2. NORFOLK'S DEFENSE (cf. 1.i.83–151)

[On a later occasion both Dukes were brought before the King to justify their words. During the hearing:]

The King then demanded of the Duke of Norfolk if these were his words, and whether he had any more to say. The Duke of Norfolk then answered for himself: " Right dear sir, true it is that I have received so much gold to pay your people of the town of Calais; which I have done, and I do avouch that your town of Calais is as well kept at your commandment as ever it was at any time before, and that there never hath been by any of Calais any complaint made unto you of me. Right dear and my sovereign lord, for the voyage that I made unto France about your marriage I never received either gold or silver of you, nor yet for the voyage that the Duke of Aumerle and I made into Almagne, where we spent great treasure. Marry, true it is that once I laid an ambush to have slain the Duke of Lancaster that there sitteth; but nevertheless he hath pardoned me thereof, and there was good peace made betwixt us, for the which I yield him hearty thanks. This is that which I have to answer, and I am ready to defend myself against mine adversary. I beseech you therefore of right, and to have the battle against him in upright judgment."

3. THE BANISHMENT OF NORFOLK AND HEREFORD (cf. 1.iii.117; 1.iv.65)

The Duke of Hereford was quickly horsed, and closed his beaver, and cast his spear into the rest, and when the trumpets sounded set forward courageously towards his enemy six or seven paces. The Duke of Norfolk was not fully set forward when the King cast down his warder, and the heralds cried " Ho! ho!" Then the King caused their spears to be taken from them, and commanded them to repair again to their chairs, where they remained two long hours while the King and his Council deliberately consulted what order was best to be had in so weighty a cause. Finally, after they had devised and fully de-

termined what should be done therein, the heralds cried silence; and Sir John Bushy, the King's secretary, read the sentence and determination of the King and his Council in a long roll, the effect whereof was that Henry Duke of Hereford should within fifteen days depart out of the realm, and not to return before the term of ten years were expired, except by the King he should be repealed again, and this upon pain of death; and that Thomas Mowbray Duke of Norfolk, because he had sown sedition in the realm by his words, should likewise avoid the realm, and never to return again into England, nor approach the borders or confines thereof upon pain of death; and that the King would stay the profits of his lands till he had levied thereof such sums of money as the Duke had taken up of the King's Treasurer for the wages of the garrison of Calais, which were still unpaid.

When these judgments were once read, the King called before him both the parties, and made them to swear that the one should never come in place where the other was willingly, nor keep any company together in any foreign region; which oath they both received humbly, and so went their ways. The Duke of Norfolk departed sorrowfully out of the realm into Almany, and at the last came to Venice, where he for thought and melancholy deceased; for he was in hope (as writers record) that he should have been borne out in the matter by the King, which when it fell out otherwise, it grieved him not a little. The Duke of Hereford took his leave of the King at Eltham, who there released four years of his banishment; so he took his journey over into Calais, and from thence went into France, where he remained. A wonder it was to see what number of people ran after him in every town and street where he came before he took the sea, lamenting and bewailing his departure, as who would say that when he departed, the only shield, defense, and comfort of the commonwealth was vaded and gone.

4. THE INSTRUMENT OF DEPOSITION TO WHICH RICHARD AGREED

[Shakespeare invented the scene of Richard's deposition but made use of this passage for Richard's speech of renunciation (cf. IV.i.201–20).]

The tenor of the instrument whereby King Richard resigneth the crown to the Duke of Lancaster

In the name of God, Amen: I, Richard by the grace of God King of Engand and of France, &c, Lord of Ireland, acquit and assoil all Archbishops, Bishops, and other prelates, secular or religious, of what dignity, degree, state, or condition soever they be; and also all Dukes, Marquesses, Earls, Barons, Lords, and all my liege men, both spiritual and secular, of what manner or degree they be, from their oath of fealty and homage and all other deeds and privileges made unto me, and from all manner bonds of allegiance, regality and lordship, in which they were or be bounden to me, or any otherwise constrained; and them, their heirs and successors forevermore, from the same bonds and oaths I release, deliver, and acquit, and set them for free, dissolved, and acquit, and to be harmless, for as much as longeth to my person by any manner, way or title of right that to me might follow of the foresaid things, or any of them. And also I resign all my kingly dignity, majesty, and crown, with all the lordships, power, and privileges, to the foresaid kingly dignity and crown belonging, and all other lordships and possessions to me in any manner of wise pertaining, of what name, title, quality, or condition soever they be, except the lands and possessions for me and mine obits purchased and bought. And I renounce all right and all manner of title of possession which I ever had or have in the same lordships and possessions, or any of them, with any manner of rights belonging or appertaining unto any part of them. And also the rule and governance of the same kingdom and lordships, with all ministrations of the same, and all things and every each of them that to the whole empire and jurisdictions of the same belongeth of right, or in any wise may belong. . . .

5. CARLISLE'S SPEECH (cf. IV.i.114–54)

[The speech was actually delivered after Richard's deposition.]

On Wednesday following request was made by the Commons that sith King Richard had resigned and was lawfully deposed from his royal dignity, he might have judgment decreed against him, so as the realm were not troubled by him, and that the causes of his deposing might be published through the realm for satisfying the people; which demand was granted. Whereupon the Bishop of Carlisle, a man both learned, wise, and stout of stomach, boldly showed forth his opinion concerning that demand, affirming that there was none amongst them worthy or meet to give judgment upon so noble a Prince as King Richard was, whom they had taken for their sovereign and liege lord by the space of two and twenty years or more. "And I assure you" (said he) "there is not so rank a traitor, nor so errant a thief, nor yet so cruel a murderer apprehended or detained in prison for his offense, but he shall be brought before the justice to hear his judgment; and will ye proceed to the judgment of an anointed King, hearing neither his answer nor excuse? I say, that the Duke of Lancaster whom you call King hath more trespassed to King Richard and his realm than King Richard hath done either to him or us; for it is

manifest and well known that the Duke was banished the realm by King Richard and his Council, and by the judgment of his own father, for the space of ten years, for what cause ye know, and yet without license of King Richard he is returned again into the realm, and (that is worse) hath taken upon him the name, title, and pre-eminence of King. And therefore I say that you have done manifest wrong to proceed in anything against King Richard without calling him openly to his answer and defense." As soon as the Bishop had ended this tale, he was attached by the Earl Marshal, and committed to ward in the Abbey of St. Albans.

In addition to Holinshed, Shakespeare had a model for his play in Marlowe's *The troublesome reign and lamentable death of Edward the Second,* entered for publication on July 3, 1593. Like Richard, Edward was a weakling who was compelled to abdicate, and who was afterward murdered. There is a general similarity in the speeches of Edward and of Richard when forced to resign the crown, particularly at the climax of Edward's grief:

LEICESTER. My lord, why waste you thus the time away?
They stay your answer. Will you yield your crown?
KING EDWARD. Ah, Leicester, weigh how hardly I can brook
To lose my crown and kingdom without cause —
To give ambitious Mortimer my right,
That, like a mountain, overwhelms my bliss,
In which extreme my mind here murdered is!
But that the Heavens appoint I must obey.
Here, take my crown, the life of Edward too.
Two kings in England cannot reign at once.
But stay awhile. Let me be King till night,
That I may gaze upon this glittering crown.
So shall my eyes receive their last content,
My head, the latest honor due to it,
And jointly both yield up their wishèd right.
Continue ever, thou celestial sun,
Let never silent night possess this clime;
Stand still, you watches of the element —
All times and seasons, rest you at a stay,
That Edward may be still fair England's King!
But day's bright beams doth vanish fast away,
And needs I must resign my wishèd crown.
Inhuman creatures, nursed with tiger's milk,
Why gape you for your sovereign's overthrow?
My diadem, I mean, and guiltless life.
See, monsters, see! I'll wear my crown again.
What, fear you not the fury of your king?
But, hapless Edward, thou art fondly led;
They pass not for thy frowns as late they did,
But seek to make a new-elected King,

Which fills my mind with strange despairing
    thoughts,
Which thoughts are martyred with endless torments.
And in his torment comfort find I none
But that I feel the crown upon my head,
And therefore let me wear it yet awhile.
    TRUSSEL. My lord, the Parliament must have pres-
    ent news,
And therefore say, will you resign or no?
                  [*The King rageth.*]
    KING EDWARD. I'll not resign, but whil'st I live be
    King.
Traitors, be gone, and join you with Mortimer.
Elect, conspire, install, do what you will.
Their blood and yours shall seal these treacheries.

About the same time that Shakespeare wrote his play, Samuel Daniel brought out his narrative poem *Civil Wars between Lancaster and York*. Both Daniel and Shakespeare inserted quite unhistorical accounts of the parting of Richard and his Queen. Although there is little similarity between the two versions, it is likely that either one poet had seen the other's version or that both had seen still another version of the story, possibly a play that has not survived.

Contemporaries, especially followers of the Earl of Essex, saw in the play of *Richard II* certain topical parallels with their own times, which were much marked. As the Earl of Essex became more bitter and critical of Queen Elizabeth, he constantly complained that she was surrounded by evil counselors and refused to admit good advice, while Essex's enemies maintained that he was himself seeking to be a second Bolingbroke; and it is significant that in the quartos of the play published in 1597 and 1598 the deposition scene was omitted, although the deposition scene in Marlowe's *Edward II* had been freely printed in 1593. Essex's great quarrel with the Queen occurred in the summer of 1598; but an uneasy reconciliation was made, and by the end of the year Essex was preparing to take over a great army to quell the rebellion in Ireland. In February, 1599, a young lawyer called John Hayward published a prose history called *The First Part of the Life and Reign of King Henry IV*, which told of the events leading up to the deposition of Richard II. This book was dedicated to Essex in a Latin epistle which contained some curious and significant phrases: *Magnus siquidem es, et praesenti iudicio et futuri temporis expectatione* (You are indeed great, in present judgment and in the expectation of future time). The book further

included a preface signed A. P., pointing out that a study of history afforded " not only precepts but lively patterns both for private direction and for affairs of state." The Privy Council and the Queen herself were very suspicious of the book's inner meaning. Hayward and all concerned with the publication were closely examined, and Hayward was subsequently imprisoned in the Tower. The book itself was very popular, and is still one of the commonest Elizabethan books offered for sale by antiquarian booksellers.

The play of *Richard II* won further and unwelcome notoriety on February 7, 1601, when at the request of certain followers of the Earl of Essex the Chamberlain's Men foolishly revived it on the day before Essex's rebellion (see Gen. Intro. p. 45a).

Richard II had thus certain topical significances which are no longer obvious. The description of Bolingbroke going off to exile seemed at least to one writer to be a picture of Essex. Everard Guilpin, in a book of satires called *Skialethia,* written in 1597–98, imitated the passage with unmistakable and hostile reference to Essex:

For when great Felix passing through the street
Vaileth his cap to each one he doth meet,
And when no broom man that will pray for him
Shall have less truage [2] than his bonnet's brim,
Who would not think him perfect courtesy?
Or the honeysuckle of humility?
The Devil he is as soon. He is the Devil,
Brightly accoustred [3] to bemist [4] his evil.
Like a swartrutter's [5] hose his puff thoughts swell
With yeasty ambition: *Signor Machiavel*
Taught him this mumming [6] trick, with courtesy
To entrench himself with popularity,
And for a writhen [7] face, and body's move,
Be barricadoed in the people's love.

Richard II was the fifth play which Shakespeare wrote dealing with English history. In writing the first four — the three parts of *Henry VI* and *Richard III* — he had come to realize that all the horrors and treacheries of the long Wars of the Roses had their origin in the deposition of Richard II and the usurpation of the throne by Henry Bolingbroke. In *Richard II* Shakespeare went back to show how the story began and to tell how Richard II first wronged his counsin Henry Bolingbroke, who was led thereby to commit the greater wrong of usurping the throne.

In this play Shakespeare tried a new method of

<hr>

[2] acknowledgment.   [3] accoutered.   [4] conceal.   [5] German mercenary.   [6] actor's.   [7] grimacing.

presenting history. The three parts of *Henry VI* were scenes from history. *Richard III* was the portrait of a remorseless, cynical Machiavellian, after the pattern of one of Marlowe's supermen. In *Richard II* Shakespeare presented history as the personal conflict of two individuals. The play is the drama of the failure and death of a King, but Richard's tragedy is not that he came to degradation, misery, and death, but that he wrought his own destruction. Two main causes brought about Richard's ruin: the first was his own character, the second was his cousin, Henry Bolingbroke. Shakespeare had now begun to realize that character is fate.

Richard himself has great charm, but he is weak, selfish, and unscrupulous and, like Narcissus, too easily attracted by his own reflection. He is forever posing. In the first scene he poses as a King who is a stern judge; " We were not born to sue but to command " (I.i.196), he says to Mowbray and Bolingbroke, but neither takes any notice of him. At the lists in Coventry he delights in the dramatic moment when he suddenly stops the combat and attracts attention away from the contestants to himself. He sees himself as the soldier king when he decides to take command of the expedition to Ireland; but in the presence of the dying Gaunt he appears merely mean, and his seizing of Bolingbroke's inheritance is an act of stupid tyranny. He next appears after his return from Ireland. He is now friendless and powerless, yet he takes a morbid delight in the sad spectacle of himself as a wronged and deserted monarch, and he does nothing to resist his enemies except to rant that God will provide angels to fight for him. In the last act of his reign, when he is summoned to make a formal resignation of the crown, he sees himself as a Christ deserted by a host of Judases, and he enjoys to the full the performance of his own tragedy. He keeps up this role in his parting from the Queen. Alone in prison, he plays with fancies of himself as beggar and King, but in the end he dies fighting.

Bolingbroke, Richard's opposite, has none of Richard's weaknesses and none of his charm. He is the strong, silent man of action; yet in the final contest between them, when Richard admits defeat by surrendering the crown, Bolingbroke is the artistic and moral loser. It is an emotional occasion when the plain man is self-conscious and ill at ease and the artist in his element. From his first entry, Richard dominates the scene. As he has nothing now to lose, he has no more to fear. His performance is magnificently dramatic. At the end of the scene, Richard is led away from the presence of the silent King, but he has left behind him the curse on the House of Lancaster.

The theme of the play is thus subtly conceived, and the best scenes — the opening, the lists at Coventry, and the deposition — are effectively planned; but the characterization and the dialogue, except for some high passages of poetry, fall far short.

Indeed, *Richard II* is not a great play. Some of the speeches — especially Gaunt's outburst on England (II.i), Richard's lamentations on his defeat (III.ii and III.iii), his surrender of the crown (IV.i), and his last musings (V.v) — are fine specimens of Shakespeare's earlier poetry. But the characterization is weak. The persons, even Richard himself and Bolingbroke, are not human beings, but mouthpieces for poetic sentiments. A comparison between Henry IV as he appears in Act V of *Richard II* and in Act I of the first part of *Henry IV* (written about two years later) will show how quickly Shakespeare's art of characterization developed. Some of the scenes, indeed, in *Richard II,* particularly those between York, his Duchess, and his son (V.ii.40-116; V.iii.45-146), are unintentionally comic. Nevertheless, in Shakespeare's development the play is important. It was the last of the plays in which he deliberately imitated a model or sacrificed drama to poetry.

Richard II

DRAMATIS PERSONAE

KING RICHARD *the Second*
JOHN OF GAUNT, *Duke of Lancaster* ⎫ *uncles to the*
EDMUND OF LANGLEY, *Duke of York* ⎰ *King*
HENRY, *surnamed* BOLINGBROKE, *Duke of Hereford,*
  son to John of Gaunt; afterward KING HENRY IV
DUKE OF AUMERLE, *son to the Duke of York*
THOMAS MOWBRAY, *Duke of Norfolk*
DUKE OF SURREY
EARL OF SALISBURY
LORD BERKELEY
BUSHY ⎫
BAGOT ⎬ *servants to King Richard*
GREEN ⎭
EARL OF NORTHUMBERLAND
HENRY PERCY, *surnamed Hotspur, his son*
LORD ROSS
LORD WILLOUGHBY

LORD FITZWATER
BISHOP *of Carlisle*
ABBOT *of Westminster*
LORD MARSHAL
SIR STEPHEN SCROOP
SIR PIERCE OF EXTON
CAPTAIN *of a band of Welshmen*

QUEEN *to King Richard*
DUCHESS OF YORK
DUCHESS OF GLOUCESTER
LADY *attending on the Queen*

LORDS, HERALDS, OFFICERS, SOLDIERS, *two* GARDENERS,
  KEEPER, MESSENGER, GROOM, *and other* ATTENDANTS

SCENE — *England and Wales.*

Act I

SCENE I. *London.* KING RICHARD's *palace.*

[*Enter* KING RICHARD, JOHN OF GAUNT, *with other*
NOBLES *and* ATTENDANTS.]

K. RICH. Old John of Gaunt, time-honored°
    Lancaster,
Hast thou, according to thy oath and band,°
Brought hither Henry Hereford, thy bold son,
Here to make good the boisterous late appeal° —
Which then our leisure would not let us hear — 5
Against the Duke of Norfolk, Thomas Mowbray?
  GAUNT. I have, my liege.
  K. RICH. Tell me, moreover, hast thou sounded
    him,
If he appeal the Duke on ancient malice,°
Or worthily, as a good subject should, 10
On some known ground of treachery in him?
  GAUNT. As near as I could sift him on that argu-
    ment,°
On some apparent° danger seen in him
Aimed at your Highness — no inveterate° malice.
  K. RICH. Then call them to our presence. Face to
    face, 15
And frowning brow to brow, ourselves will hear
The accuser and the accusèd freely speak.
High-stomached° are they both, and full of ire,
In rage deaf as the sea, hasty as fire.
    [*Enter* BOLINGBROKE *and* MOWBRAY.]
  BOLING. Many years of happy days befall 20
My gracious sovereign, my most loving liege!
  MOW. Each day still better other's happiness,
Until the Heavens, envying earth's good hap,°
Add an immortal title to your crown!
  K. RICH. We thank you both. Yet one but flatters
    us, 25
As well appeareth by the cause you come;
Namely, to appeal each other of high treason.
Cousin of Hereford, what dost thou object
Against the Duke of Norfolk, Thomas Mowbray?
  BOLING. First — Heaven be the record of my
    speech — 30
In the devotion of a subject's love,
Tendering° the precious safety of my prince
And free from other misbegotten hate,
Come I appellant° to this princely presence.
Now, Thomas Mowbray, do I turn to thee, 35
And mark my greeting well, for what I speak
My body shall make good upon this earth
Or my divine soul answer it in Heaven.
Thou art a traitor and a miscreant,°
Too good to be so,° and too bad to live, 40
Since the more fair and crystal is the sky,
The uglier seem the clouds that in it fly.
Once more, the more to aggravate the note,°

Act I, Sc. i: 1. **time-honored:** venerable. 2. **band:** bond.
4. **appeal:** accusation which the accuser is prepared to justify
by mortal combat. 9. **ancient malice:** long-standing hatred.
12. **argument:** matter, topic. 13. **apparent:** open. 14. **inveter-
ate:** long-established. 18. **High-stomached:** haughty.

23. **hap:** luck. 32. **Tendering:** caring for. 34. **appellant:** one
accusing of treason. 39. **miscreant:** lit., misbeliever, villain.
40. **Too . . . so:** of too high rank to be a traitor. 43. **aggra-
vate . . . note:** make more conspicuous the disgrace.

With a foul traitor's name stuff I thy throat,°
And wish, so please my sovereign, ere I move,   45
What my tongue speaks my right drawn sword may
    prove.
    MOW. Let not my cold words here accuse my zeal.
'Tis not the trial of a woman's war,
The bitter clamor of two eager tongues,
Can arbitrate this cause betwixt us twain.   50
The blood is hot that must be cooled for this.
Yet can I not of such tame patience boast
As to be hushed and naught at all to say.
First, the fair reverence of your Highness curbs me
From giving reins and spurs to my free speech,   55
Which else would post° until it had returned
These terms of treason doubled down his throat.
Setting aside his high blood's royalty,°
And let him be no kinsman to my liege,°
I do defy him, and I spit at him,   60
Call him a slanderous coward and a villain.
Which to maintain I would allow him odds
And meet him, were I tied° to run afoot
Even to the frozen ridges of the Alps,
Or any other ground inhabitable,   65
Wherever Englishman durst set his foot.
Meantime let this° defend my loyalty —
By all my hopes, most falsely doth he lie.
    BOLING. Pale trembling coward, there I throw my
        gage,°
Disclaiming here the kindred of the King,   70
And lay aside my high blood's royalty,
Which fear, not reverence, makes thee to except.
If guilty dread have left thee so much strength
As to take up mine honor's pawn,° then stoop.
By that and all the rites of knighthood else,   75
Will I make good against thee, arm to arm,
What I have spoke, or thou canst worse devise.
    MOW. I take it up, and by that sword I swear
Which gently laid my knighthood on my shoulder,
I'll answer thee in any fair degree   80
Or chivalrous design of knightly trial.
And when I mount, alive may I not light
If I be traitor or unjustly fight!
    K. RICH. What doth our cousin lay to Mowbray's
        charge?
It must be great that can inherit us°   85
So much as of a thought of ill in him.
    BOLING. Look, what I speak, my life shall prove it
        true —
That Mowbray hath received eight thousand nobles°
In name of lendings for your Highness' soldiers,
The which he hath detained for lewd° employments,

Like a false traitor and injurious° villain.   91
Besides, I say and will in battle prove,
Or here or elsewhere to the furthest verge
That ever was surveyed by English eye,
That all the treasons for these eighteen years   95
Complotted and contrivèd in this land
Fetch° from false Mowbray their first head and
    spring.
Further I say, and further will maintain
Upon his bad life to make all this good,
That he did plot the Duke of Gloucester's death,°   100
Suggest° his soon-believing adversaries,   101
And consequently, like a traitor coward,
Sluiced out his innocent soul through streams of
    blood.
Which blood, like sacrificing Abel's, cries
Even from the tongueless caverns of the earth   105
To me for justice and rough chastisement.
And by the glorious worth of my descent,
This arm shall do it or this life be spent.
    K. RICH. How high a pitch° his resolution soars!
Thomas of Norfolk, what say'st thou to this?   110
    MOW. Oh, let my sovereign turn away his face,
And bid his ears a little while be deaf,
Till I have told this slander of° his blood
How God and good men hate so foul a liar.   114
    K. RICH. Mowbray, impartial are our eyes and ears.
Were he my brother — nay, my kingdom's heir —
As he is but my father's brother's son,
Now, by my scepter's awe, I make a vow,
Such neighbor nearness to our sacred blood
Should nothing privilege him, nor partialize°   120
The unstooping firmness of my upright soul.
He is our subject, Mowbray, so art thou.
Free speech and fearless I to thee allow.
    MOW. Then, Bolingbroke, as low as to thy heart,
Through the false passage of thy throat thou liest.
Three parts of that receipt I had for Calais   126
Disbursed I duly to His Highness' soldiers.
The other part reserved I by consent,
For that my sovereign liege was in my debt
Upon remainder of a dear° account   130
Since last I went to France to fetch his Queen.
Now swallow down that lie. For Gloucester's death,
I slew him not, but to my own disgrace
Neglected my sworn duty in that case.
For you, my noble Lord of Lancaster,   135
The honorable father to my foe,
Once did I lay an ambush for your life —
A trespass that doth vex my grievèd soul.
But ere I last received the sacrament
I did confess it, and exactly° begged   140
Your Grace's pardon, and I hope I had it.

44. throat: To give a man "the lie in the throat" was the bitterest insult, which could only be answered by a fight to the death. 56. post: ride fast. See App. 17. 58. Setting . . . royalty: disregarding his royal blood. See App. 28. 59. liege: lord. 63. tied: obliged. 67. let this: i.e., my sword. 69. gage: he throws down a glove as pledge (gage) that he will fight. 74. pawn: pledge. 85. inherit us: make us become inheritor of. 88. nobles: gold coins worth 6s 8d. See App. 27. 90. lewd: base.

91. injurious: insulting. 97. Fetch: derive. 100. Gloucester's death: See App. 28. 101. Suggest: prompt. 109. pitch: lit., the highest point in the flight of the hawk. See App. 26. 113. slander of: disgrace to. 120. partialize: make partial. 130. dear: heavy. 140. exactly: in express terms.

This is my fault. As for the rest appealed,
It issues from the rancor of a villain,
A recreant° and most degenerate traitor.
Which in myself I boldly will defend,   145
And interchangeably° hurl down my gage
Upon this overweening traitor's foot,
To prove myself a loyal gentleman
Even in the best blood chambered in his bosom.
In haste whereof, most heartily I pray   150
Your Highness to assign our trial day.
  K. RICH. Wrath-kindled gentlemen, be ruled by
    me —
Let's purge° this choler without letting blood.
This we prescribe, though no physician.
Deep malice makes too deep incision.   155
Forget, forgive, conclude° and be agreed.
Our doctors say this is no month to bleed.
Good Uncle, let this end where it begun.
We'll calm the Duke of Norfolk, you your son. 159
  GAUNT. To be a make-peace shall become my age.
Throw down, my son, the Duke of Norfolk's gage.
  K. RICH. And, Norfolk, throw down his.
  GAUNT.   When, Harry, when?
Obedience bids I should not bid again.
  K. RICH. Norfolk, throw down, we bid. There is no
    boot.°
  MOW. Myself I throw, dread sovereign, at thy
    foot.   165
My life thou shalt command, but not my shame.
The one my duty owes, but my fair name,
Despite of death that lives upon my grave,
To dark dishonor's use thou shalt not have.   169
I am disgraced, impeached° and baffled° here,
Pierced to the soul with slander's venomed spear,
The which no balm can cure but his heartblood
Which breathed this poison.
  K. RICH.   Rage must be withstood.
Give me his gage. Lions° make leopards tame.
  MOW. Yea, but not change his spots. Take but my
    shame,   175
And I resign my gage. My dear dear lord,
The purest treasure mortal times afford
Is spotless reputation. That away,
Men are but gilded loam or painted clay.
A jewel in a ten-times-barred-up chest   180
Is a bold spirit in a loyal breast.
Mine honor is my life, both grow in one.

144. recreant: traitor. 146. interchangeably: in my turn.
153–57. purge . . . bleed: Richard indulges in an elaborate
metaphor taken from medicine. For many complaints the recog-
nized treatment was bloodletting, for which certain days and
seasons (noted in the almanac) were considered more favorable
than others. choler: excess of bile, anger. See App. 2, 3. incision:
cut, the technical term for bloodletting. 156. conclude: come to
terms. 164. boot: help. 170. impeached: accused. baffled: dis-
graced. The term was used of the degradation of a knight found
guilty of breaking his oath. He was stripped of his armor, his
shield painted with his coat of arms was reversed, and his pic-
ture or effigy hung upside down. 174. Lions: The lion is the
symbol of the English Kings.

Take honor from me and my life is done.
Then, dear my liege, mine honor let me try.°
In that I live and for that will I die.   185
  K. RICH. Cousin, throw up your gage. Do you be-
    gin.
  BOLING. Oh, God defend my soul from such deep
    sin!
Shall I seem crestfallen in my father's sight?
Or with pale beggar-fear impeach my height   189
Before this outdared° dastard?° Ere my tongue
Shall wound my honor with such feeble wrong,
Or sound so base a parle,° my teeth shall tear
The slavish motive° of recanting fear
And spit it bleeding in his high disgrace
Where shame doth harbor, even in Mowbray's face.
                                    [Exit GAUNT.]
  K. RICH. We were not born to sue, but to com-
    mand,   196
Which since we cannot do to make you friends,
Be ready, as your lives shall answer it,
At Coventry, upon Saint Lambert's Day.°
There shall your swords and lances arbitrate   200
The swelling difference of your settled hate.
Since we cannot atone° you, we shall see
Justice design the victor's chivalry.°
Lord Marshal, command our officers-at-arms°   204
Be ready to direct these home alarms.°   [Exeunt.]

SCENE II. *The* DUKE OF LANCASTER'S *palace.*

[*Enter* JOHN OF GAUNT *with the* DUCHESS OF
GLOUCESTER.]
  GAUNT. Alas, the part I had in Woodstock's blood°
Doth more solicit me than your exclaims
To stir against the butchers of his life!
But since correction lieth in those hands
Which made the fault that we cannot correct,   5
Put we our quarrel to the will of Heaven,
Who, when they see the hours ripe on earth,
Will rain hot vengeance on offenders' heads.
  DUCH. Finds brotherhood in thee no sharper spur?
Hath love in thy old blood no living fire?   10
Edward's° seven sons, whereof thyself art one,
Were as seven vials of his sacred blood,
Or seven fair branches springing from one root.
Some of those seven are dried by nature's course,
Some of those branches by the Destinies cut.   15
But Thomas, my dear lord, my life, my Gloucester,
One vial full of Edward's sacred blood,

184. try: make trial of. 190. outdared: defied. dastard: coward.
192. parle: parley; i.e., proposal for peace. 193. motive: instru-
ment; i.e., his tongue. 199. Saint Lambert's Day: September 17.
202. atone: reconcile. 203. design . . . chivalry: designate the
victorious champion; i.e., the man who wins has the just case.
204. Lord . . . arms: See App. 9. 205. alarms: disturbances.
  Sc. ii: 1. part . . . blood: i.e., my brotherhood. part: share.
Woodstock: Thomas of Woodstock, late Duke of Gloucester.
11. Edward: i.e., Edward III.

One flourishing branch of his most royal root,
Is cracked, and all the precious liquor spilt,
Is hacked down, and his summer leaves all faded,
By envy's hand and murder's bloody ax.   21
Ah, Gaunt, his blood was thine! That bed, that
     womb,
That metal, that self-mold,° that fashioned thee
Made him a man; and though thou livest and
     breathest,
Yet art thou slain in him. Thou dost consent   25
In some large measure to thy father's death
In that thou seest thy wretched brother die,
Who was the model° of thy father's life.
Call it not patience, Gaunt, it is despair.
In suffering thus thy brother to be slaughtered, 30
Thou showest the naked pathway to thy life,
Teaching stern murder how to butcher thee.
That which in mean men we entitle patience
Is pale cold cowardice in noble breasts.
What shall I say? To safeguard thine own life,   35
The best way is to venge my Gloucester's death.
     GAUNT. God's is the quarrel, for God's substitute,
His deputy anointed in His sight,
Hath caused his death.° The which if wrongfully,
Let Heaven revenge, for I may never lift   40
An angry arm against His minister.
     DUCH. Where then, alas, may I complain myself?
     GAUNT. To God, the widow's champion and de-
     fense.
     DUCH. Why then, I will. Farewell, old Gaunt.
Thou goest to Coventry, there to behold   45
Our cousin Hereford and fell Mowbray fight.
Oh, sit my husband's wrongs on Hereford's spear,
That it may enter butcher Mowbray's breast!
Or if misfortune miss the first career,°
Be Mowbray's sins so heavy in his bosom   50
That they may break his foaming courser's back
And throw the rider headlong in the lists,
A caitiff° recreant to my cousin° Hereford!
Farewell, old Gaunt. Thy sometimes° brother's wife
With her companion grief must end her life.   55
     GAUNT. Sister, farewell. I must to Coventry.
As much good stay with thee as go with me!
     DUCH. Yet one word more. Grief boundeth where
     it falls,
Not with the empty hollowness, but weight.°
I take my leave before I have begun,   60
For sorrow ends not when it seemeth done.
Commend me to thy brother, Edmund York.
Lo, this is all. — Nay, yet depart not so.
Though this be all, do not so quickly go.

I shall remember more. Bid him — ah, what? —   65
With all good speed at Plashy visit me.
Alack, and what shall good old York there see
But empty lodgings and unfurnished walls,
Unpeopled offices, untrodden stones?   69
And what hear there for welcome but my groans?
Therefore commend me. Let him not come there
To seek out sorrow that dwells everywhere.
Desolate, desolate, will I hence and die.
The last leave of thee takes my weeping eye.
                                        [*Exeunt.*]

SCENE III. *The lists° at Coventry.*

[*Enter the* LORD MARSHAL *and the* DUKE OF
                AUMERLE.]
     MAR. My Lord Aumerle, is Harry Hereford
     armed?
     AUM. Yea, at all points,° and longs to enter in.
     MAR. The Duke of Norfolk, sprightfully° and
     bold,
Stays but the summons of the appellant's° trumpet.
     AUM. Why, then, the champions are prepared, and
     stay   5
For nothing but His Majesty's approach.
[*The trumpets sound, and the* KING *enters with his
     nobles,* GAUNT, BUSHY, BAGOT, GREEN, *and others.
          When they are set, enter* MOWBRAY *in arms,
                defendant,° with a* HERALD.]
     K. RICH. Marshal, demand of yonder champion
The cause of his arrival here in arms.
Ask him his name, and orderly proceed
To swear him in the justice of his cause.   10
     MAR. In God's name and the King's, say who thou
     art,
And why thou comest thus knightly clad in arms,
Against what man thou comest, and what thy quar-
     rel.
Speak truly, on thy knighthood and thy oath,
As so defend thee Heaven and thy valor!   15
     MOW. My name is Thomas Mowbray, Duke of
     Norfolk,
Who hither come engagèd by my oath —
Which God defend° a knight should violate! —
Both to defend my loyalty and truth
To God, my King, and my succeeding issue   20
Against the Duke of Hereford that appeals me,
And, by the grace of God and this mine arm,
To prove him, in defending of myself,
A traitor to my God, my King, and me.
And as I truly fight, defend me Heaven!   25
[*The trumpets sound. Enter* BOLINGBROKE, *appellant,
          in armor, with a* HERALD.]

---

23. **self-mold:** self-same mold.   28. **model:** copy.   37–39. **God's
. . . death:** i.e., since Gloucester's death was caused by the King
(*God's substitute*), it is God's business and not mine to punish
him.   49. **career:** charge.   53. **caitiff:** slave. **cousin:** kinsman;
the word is used of any relation by blood.   54. **sometimes:**
former; i.e., dead.   58–59. **Grief . . . weight:** my complaints re-
bound like a tennis ball from a wall; however, they are not light
like a ball, but heavy.

Sc. iii: s.d., lists: combat ground enclosed by a palisade.
2. **at . . . points:** completely.   3. **sprightfully:** full of spirit.
4. **appellant:** challenger.   6. **s.d., defendant:** i.e., the challenged.
See Pl. 8a.   18. **defend:** forbid.

K. RICH. Marshal, ask yonder knight in arms
Both who he is, and why he cometh hither
Thus plated° in habiliments of war,
And formally, according to our law,
Depose° him in the justice of his cause.   30
    MAR. What is thy name? And wherefore comest
        thou hither
Before King Richard in his royal lists?
Against whom comest thou? And what's thy quar-
        rel?
Speak like a true knight, so defend thee Heaven!
    BOLING. Harry of Hereford, Lancaster, and Derby
Am I, who ready here do stand in arms   36
To prove, by God's grace and my body's valor,
In lists, on Thomas Mowbray, Duke of Norfolk,
That he is a traitor foul and dangerous
To God of Heaven, King Richard, and to me.   40
And as I truly fight, defend me Heaven!
    MAR. On pain of death, no person be so bold
Or daring-hardy as to touch the lists,
Except the Marshal and such officers
Appointed to direct these fair designs.   45
    BOLING. Lord Marshal, let me kiss my sovereign's
        hand,
And bow my knee before His Majesty.
For Mowbray and myself are like two men
That vow a long and weary pilgrimage —
Then let us take a ceremonious leave   50
And loving farewell of our several friends.
    MAR. The appellant in all duty greets your High-
        ness,
And craves to kiss your hand and take his leave.
    K. RICH. We will descend and fold him in our
        arms.
Cousin of Hereford, as thy cause is right,   55
So be thy fortune in this royal fight!
Farewell, my blood, which if today thou shed,
Lament we may, but not revenge thee dead.
    BOLING. Oh, let no noble eye profane a tear°
For me if I be gored with Mowbray's spear.   60
As confident as is the falcon's flight
Against a bird do I with Mowbray fight.
My loving lord, I take my leave of you,
Of you, my noble cousin, Lord Aumerle —
Not sick, although I have to do with death,   65
But lusty, young, and cheerly° drawing breath.
Lo, as at English feasts, so I regreet°
The daintiest last, to make the end most sweet.
O thou, the earthly author of my blood,
Whose youthful spirit, in me regenerate,   70
Doth with a twofold vigor lift me up
To reach at victory above my head,
Add proof unto mine armor with thy prayers,
And with thy blessings steel my lance's point,

That it may enter Mowbray's waxen° coat   75
And furbish° new the name of John-a-Gaunt,
Even in the lusty havior of his son.
    GAUNT. God in thy good cause make thee prosper-
        ous!
Be swift like lightning in the execution,
And let thy blows, doubly redoubled,   80
Fall like amazing° thunder on the casque°
Of thy adverse pernicious enemy.
Rouse up thy youthful blood, be valiant and live.
    BOLING. Mine innocency and Saint George° to
        thrive!
    MOW. However God or fortune cast my lot,   85
There lives or dies, true to King Richard's throne,
A loyal, just, and upright gentleman.
Never did captive with a freer heart
Cast off his chains of bondage, and embrace
His golden uncontrolled enfranchisement,°   90
More than my dancing soul doth celebrate
This feast of battle with mine adversary.
Most mighty liege, and my companion peers,
Take from my mouth the wish of happy years.
As gentle and as jocund as to jest   95
Go I to fight. Truth hath a quiet breast.
    K. RICH. Farewell, my lord. Securely I espy
Virtue with valor couchèd in thine eye.
Order the trial, Marshal, and begin.
    MAR. Harry of Hereford, Lancaster, and Derby,
Receive thy lance, and God defend the right!   101
    BOLING. Strong as a tower in hope, I cry amen.
    MAR. Go bear this lance to Thomas, Duke of Nor-
        folk.
    1. HER. Harry of Hereford, Lancaster, and Derby,
Stands here for God, his sovereign, and himself,
On pain to be found false and recreant,   106
To prove the Duke of Norfolk, Thomas Mowbray,
A traitor to his God, his King, and him,
And dares him to set forward to the fight.
    2. HER. Here standeth Thomas Mowbray, Duke of
        Norfolk,   110
On pain to be found false and recreant,
Both to defend himself and to approve°
Henry of Hereford, Lancaster, and Derby
To God, his sovereign, and to him disloyal,
Courageously and with a free desire   115
Attending° but the signal to begin.
    MAR. Sound, trumpets, and set forward, combat-
        ants.   [A charge sounded.]
Stay, the King hath thrown his warder° down.
    K. RICH. Let them lay by their helmets and their
        spears,
And both return back to their chairs again.   120
Withdraw with us, and let the trumpets sound

---

28. plated: wearing armor. 30. Depose: cause to declare an oath.
59. profane a tear: make unholy lamentation — because if he is
killed it will show that he was a false traitor and so unworthy of
grief. 66. cheerly: cheerfully. 67. regreet: welcome.

75. waxen: as if it were soft as wax. 76. furbish: make
bright. 81. amazing: astounding. casque: helmet. 84. Saint
George: patron saint of England. 90. enfranchisement: liberty.
112. approve: prove. 116. Attending: awaiting. 118. warder:
staff.

While we return these Dukes what we decree.

                    [*A long flourish.*°]

Draw near,
And list what with our Council we have done.
For that our kingdom's earth should not be soiled
With that dear blood which it hath fostered,   126
And for our eyes do hate the dire aspèct
Of civil wounds plowed up with neighbors' sword,
And for we think the eagle-wingèd pride
Of sky-aspiring and ambitious thoughts,   130
With rival-hating envy, set on you
To wake our peace, which in our country's cradle
Draws the sweet infant breath of gentle sleep —
Which so roused up with boisterous untuned drums,
With harsh-resounding trumpets' dreadful bray,
And grating shock of wrathful iron arms,   136
Might from our quiet confines° fright fair peace,
And make us wade even in our kindred's blood.
Therefore we banish you our territories.
You, Cousin Hereford, upon pain of life,   140
Till twice five summers have enriched our fields
Shall not regreet our fair dominions,
But tread the stranger paths of banishment.

    BOLING. Your will be done. This must my comfort
      be,
That sun that warms you here shall shine on me,
And those his golden beams to you here lent   146
Shall point on me and gild my banishment.

    K. RICH. Norfolk, for thee remains a heavier doom,
Which I with some unwillingness pronounce.
The sly slow hours shall not determinate°   150
The dateless limit° of thy dear° exile.
The hopeless word of " never to return "
Breathe I against thee, upon pain of life.

    MOW. A heavy sentence, my most sovereign liege,
And all unlooked for from your Highness' mouth.
A dearer merit,° not so deep a maim°   156
As to be cast forth in the common air,
Have I deservèd at your Highness' hands.
The language I have learned these forty years,
My native English, now I must forgo.   160
And now my tongue's use is to me no more
Than an unstringed viol° or a harp,
Or like a cunning instrument cased up
Or, being open, put into his hands
That knows no touch to tune the harmony.   165
Within my mouth you have enjailed my tongue,
Doubly portcullised° with my teeth and lips,
And dull unfeeling barren ignorance
Is made my jailer to attend on me.
I am too old to fawn upon a nurse,   170

Too far in years to be a pupil now.
What is thy sentence, then, but speechless death,
Which robs my tongue from breathing native
    breath?

    K. RICH. It boots° thee not to be compassionate.°
After our sentence plaining° comes too late.   175

    MOW. Then thus I turn me from my country's
      light,
To dwell in solemn shades of endless night.

    K. RICH. Return° again, and take an oath with
      thee.
Lay on our royal sword your banished hands,
Swear by the duty that you owe to God —   180
Our part therein we banish with yourselves° —
To keep the oath that we administer.
You never shall, so help you truth and God!
Embrace each other's love in banishment —
Nor never look upon each other's face,   185
Nor never write, regreet, nor reconcile
This louring° tempest of your homebred hate,
Nor never by advisèd° purpose meet
To plot, contrive, or complot any ill
'Gainst us, our state, our subjects, or our land.   190

    BOLING. I swear.

    MOW. And I, to keep all this.

    BOLING. Norfolk, so far as to mine enemy.
By this time, had the King permitted us,
One of our souls had wandered in the air,   195
Banished this frail sepulcher of our flesh
As now our flesh is banished from this land.
Confess thy treasons ere thou fly the realm.
Since thou hast far to go, bear not along
The clogging burden of a guilty soul.   200

    MOW. No, Bolingbroke. If ever I were traitor,
My name be blotted from the book of life,
And I from Heaven banished as from hence!
But what thou art, God, thou, and I do know,
And all too soon, I fear, the King shall rue.   205
Farewell, my liege. Now no way can I stray —
Save back to England, all the world's my way.

                        [*Exit.*]

    K. RICH. Uncle, even in the glasses° of thine eyes
I see thy grievèd heart. Thy sad aspèct°
Hath from the number of his banished years   210
Plucked four away. [*To* BOLINGBROKE] Six frozen
    winters spent,
Return with welcome home from banishment.

    BOLING. How long a time lies in one little word!
Four lagging winters and four wanton springs
End in a word. Such is the breath of kings.   215

    GAUNT. I thank my liege, that in regard of me
He shortens four years of my son's exile.

---

122. s.d., flourish: a set of notes on the trumpet.   137. confines:
territories. 150. determinate: end. 151. dateless limit: end to
which no date is assigned. dear: i.e., heavy. 156. dearer merit:
more valuable reward. maim: injury. 162. viol: six-stringed
instrument of the cello type. See Pl. 18c. 167. portcullised: shut
in. The portcullis was a heavy grating, sliding up and down in
grooves, at the entrance to a castle.

174. boots: is of advantage. compassionate: piteous.   175. plain-
ing: complaining. 178–90. Return . . . land: This speech is ad-
dressed to both combatants. 181. Our . . . yourselves: i.e., we
absolve you from allegiance to us. 187. louring: threatening.
188. advised: deliberate. 208. glasses: lenses. 209. aspect:
countenance.

But little vantage shall I reap thereby,
For ere the six years that he hath to spend
Can change their moons and bring their times
    about,   220
My oil-dried lamp and time-bewasted light
Shall be extinct with age and endless night.
My inch of taper° will be burnt and done,
And blindfold° death not let me see my son.
    K. RICH. Why, Uncle, thou hast many years to
    live.   225
    GAUNT. But not a minute, King, that thou canst
    give.
Shorten my days thou canst with sullen sorrow,
And pluck nights from me, but not lend a mor-
    row.
Thou canst help time to furrow me with age,
But stop no wrinkle in his pilgrimage.   230
Thy word is current° with him for my death,
But dead, thy kingdom cannot buy my breath.
    K. RICH. Thy son is banished upon good advice,
Whereto thy tongue a party verdict gave.°
Why at our justice seem'st thou then to lour?   235
    GAUNT. Things sweet to taste prove in digestion
    sour.
You urged me as a judge, but I had rather
You would have bid me argue like a father.
Oh, had it been a stranger, not my child,
To smooth his fault I should have been more mild.
A partial slander° ought I to avoid,   241
And in the sentence my own life destroyed.
Alas, I looked when some of you should say
I was too strict to make mine own away,
But you gave leave to my unwilling tongue   245
Against my will to do myself this wrong.
    K. RICH. Cousin, farewell, and, Uncle, bid him so.
Six years we banish him, and he shall go.

    [*Flourish. Exeunt* KING RICHARD *and* TRAIN.]
    AUM. Cousin, farewell. What presence must not
    know,°
From where you do remain let paper show.   250
    MAR. My lord, no leave take I, for I will ride,
As far as land will let me, by your side.
    GAUNT. Oh, to what purpose dost thou hoard thy
    words,
That thou return'st no greeting to thy friends?
    BOLING. I have too few to take my leave of you
When the tongue's office should be prodigal   256
To breathe the abundant dolor° of the heart.
    GAUNT. Thy grief is but thy absence for a time.
    BOLING. Joy absent, grief is present for that time.
    GAUNT. What is six winters? They are quickly
    gone.   260

    BOLING. To men in joy, but grief makes one hour
    ten.
    GAUNT. Call it a travel that thou takest for pleas-
    ure.
    BOLING. My heart will sigh when I miscall it so,
Which finds it an enforcèd pilgrimage.
    GAUNT. The sullen passage of thy weary steps
Esteem as foil° wherein thou art to set   266
The precious jewel of thy home return.
    BOLING. Nay, rather, every tedious stride I make
Will but remember me what a deal of world
I wander from the jewels that I love.   270
Must I not serve a long apprenticehood
To foreign passages,° and in the end,
Having my freedom, boast of nothing else
But that I was a journeyman° to grief?
    GAUNT. All places that the eye of Heaven° visits
Are to a wise man ports and happy havens.   276
Teach thy necessity to reason thus —
There is no virtue like necessity.
Think not the King did banish thee,
But thou the King. Woe doth the heavier sit   280
Where it perceives it is but faintly° borne.
Go, say I sent thee forth to purchase honor
And not the King exiled thee. Or suppose
Devouring pestilence hangs in our air
And thou art flying to a fresher clime.   285
Look, what thy soul holds dear, imagine it
To lie that way thou go'st, not whence thou comest.
Suppose the singing birds musicians,
The grass whereon thou tread'st the presence°
    strewed,°
The flowers fair ladies, and thy steps no more   290
Than a delightful measure° or a dance.
For gnarling° sorrow hath less power to bite
The man that mocks at it and sets it light.
    BOLING. Oh, who can hold a fire in his hand
By thinking on the frosty Caucasus?   295
Or cloy the hungry edge of appetite
By bare imagination of a feast?
Or wallow naked in December snow
By thinking on fantastic summer's heat?
Oh no! The apprehension of the good   300
Gives but the greater feeling to the worse.
Fell sorrow's tooth doth never rankle° more
Than when he bites, but lanceth not the sore.
    GAUNT. Come, come, my son, I'll bring thee on thy
    way.
Had I thy youth and cause, I would not stay.   305
    BOLING. Then, England's ground, farewell. Sweet
    soil, adieu —

---

223. taper: candle. 224. blindfold: making blind. 231. current: valid; i.e., you can tell Death to take me, but you cannot buy me back from him. 234. party . . . gave: shared in giving the verdict. 241. partial slander: the slander of being partial to my own son. 249. What . . . know: i.e., what you cannot be present to say. 257. dolor: grief.

266. foil: See *Rich III*, V.iii.250,n. 272. foreign passages: wandering in foreign lands. 274. journeyman: hired worker. 275. eye of Heaven: the sun. 281. faintly: faintheartedly. 289. presence: the Presence Chamber where the courtiers assembled. strewed: covered with rushes. 291. measure: formal dance. See App. 24. 292. gnarling: growling. 302. rankle: make fester.

My mother, and my nurse, that bears me yet!
Where'er I wander, boast of this I can,
Though banished, yet a trueborn Englishman.

[*Exeunt.*]

SCENE IV. *The Court.*

[*Enter the* KING, *with* BAGOT *and* GREEN *at one door,
and the* DUKE OF AUMERLE *at another.*]

K. RICH. We did observe. Cousin Aumerle,
How far brought you high Hereford on his way?

AUM. I brought high Hereford, if you call him so,
But to the next highway, and there I left him.

K. RICH. And say, what store of parting tears were
shed?   5

AUM. Faith, none for me, except the northeast
wind,
Which then blew bitterly against our faces,
Awaked the sleeping rheum° and so by chance
Did grace our hollow parting with a tear.

K. RICH. What said our cousin when you parted
with him?   10

AUM. "Farewell."
And, for my heart disdainèd that my tongue
Should so profane the word, that taught me craft
To counterfeit oppression of such grief   14
That words seemed buried in my sorrow's grave.°
Marry, would the word "farewell" have lengthened
hours
And added years to his short banishment,
He should have had a volume of farewells.
But since it would not, he had none of me.   19

K. RICH. He is our cousin, Cousin; but 'tis doubt,
When time shall call him home from banishment,
Whether our kinsman come to see his friends.
Ourself and Bushy, Bagot here, and Green
Observed his courtship° to the common people —
How he did seem to dive into their hearts   25
With humble and familiar courtesy,°
What reverence he did throw away on slaves,
Wooing poor craftsmen with the craft of smiles
And patient underbearing° of his fortune,
As 'twere to banish their affects° with him.   30
Off goes his bonnet to an oyster wench.
A brace of draymen bid God speed him well
And had the tribute of his supple knee,
With "Thanks, my countrymen, my loving friends,"
As were our England in reversion° his,   35
And he our subjects' next degree in hope.

GREEN. Well, he is gone, and with him go these
thoughts.
Now for the rebels which stand out in Ireland,
Expedient manage° must be made, my liege,
Ere further leisure yield them further means   40
For their advantage and your Highness' loss.

K. RICH. We will ourself in person to this war.
And, for our coffers, with too great a Court°
And liberal largess,° are grown somewhat light,
We are enforced to farm° our royal realm,   45
The revenue whereof shall furnish us
For our affairs in hand. If that come short,
Our substitutes at home shall have blank charters,°
Whereto, when they shall know what men are rich,
They shall subscribe° them for large sums of gold
And send them after to supply our wants.   51
For we will make for Ireland presently.

[*Enter* BUSHY.] Bushy, what news?

BUSHY. Old John of Gaunt is grievous sick, my
lord,
Suddenly taken, and hath sent posthaste   55
To entreat your Majesty to visit him.

K. RICH. Where lies he?

BUSHY. At Ely House.°

K. RICH. Now put it, God, in the physician's mind
To help him to his grave immediately!   60
The lining of his coffers shall make coats
To deck our soldiers for these Irish wars.
Come, gentlemen, let's all go visit him.
Pray God we may make haste, and come too late!

ALL. Amen.   [*Exeunt.*]   65

Act II

SCENE I. *Ely House.*

[*Enter* JOHN OF GAUNT *sick, with the* DUKE OF YORK,
etc.]

GAUNT. Will the King come, that I may breathe
my last
In wholesome counsel to his unstaid youth?

YORK. Vex not yourself, nor strive not with your
breath,
For all in vain comes counsel to his ear.

GAUNT. Oh, but they say the tongues of dying men
Enforce attention like deep harmony.   6

Sc. iv: **8.** rheum: moisture. **11–15.** "Farewell" . . . grave:
i.e., I did not wish him to "fare well," so I pretended that my
grief was too strong for words. **24–36.** courtship . . . hope:
There is some disturbance in the text here, which probably in-
dicates that the passage is a later addition. See *Rich II* Intro.
p. 191b. **26.** courtesy: courtly behavior, bending the knee.
29. underbearing: supporting. **30.** banish . . . affects: carry
their affection with him into banishment. **35.** in reversion: by
right of legal succession.

39. Expedient manage: speedy arrangements. **43. too . . .**
Court: by maintaining too many courtiers. **44. largess:** presents
of money. **45. farm:** to let out. To raise ready money the King
took a payment in cash in return for the right to collect taxes.
48. blank charters: documents which rich men were compelled
to sign agreeing to pay the King certain sums of money, the
amount being left blank to be filled in by the King's officers.
50. subscribe: sign. **58. Ely House:** the Bishop of Ely's palace
in London.

Where words are scarce, they are seldom spent in
    vain,
For they breathe truth that breathe their words in
    pain.
He that no more must say is listened more
    Than they whom youth and ease have taught to
      glose.°   10
More are men's ends marked than their lives before.
    The setting sun, and music at the close,
As the last taste of sweets, is sweetest last,
Writ in remembrance more than things long past.
Though Richard my life's counsel would not hear,
My death's sad tale may yet undeaf his ear.   16
    YORK. No, it is stopped with other flattering
      sounds,
As praises, of whose taste the wise are fond,
Lascivious meters, to whose venom sound
The open ear of youth doth always listen —   20
Report of fashions in proud Italy,°
Whose manners still our tardy apish° nation
Limps after in base imitation.
Where doth the world thrust forth a vanity —
So it be° new, there's no respect° how vile —   25
That is not quickly buzzed into his ears?
Then all too late comes counsel to be heard
Where will° doth mutiny with wit's° regard.
Direct not him whose way himself will choose.
'Tis breath thou lack'st, and that breath wilt thou
    lose.   30
    GAUNT. Methinks I am a prophet new-inspired
And thus expiring do foretell of him.
His rash fierce blaze of riot cannot last,
For violent fires soon burn out themselves —
Small showers last long, but sudden storms are short.
He tires betimes° that spurs too fast betimes,   36
With eager feeding food doth choke the feeder.
Light vanity, insatiate cormorant,°
Consuming means, soon preys upon itself.
This° royal throne of kings, this sceptered isle,   40
This earth of majesty, this seat of Mars,
This other Eden, demi-Paradise,
This fortress built by Nature for herself
Against infection° and the hand of war,
This happy breed of men, this little world,   45
This precious stone set in the silver sea,
Which serves it in the office of a wall
Or as a moat defensive to a house
Against the envy° of less happier lands —

Act II, Sc. i: 10. glose: flatter. 21. proud Italy: It was a com-
mon complaint among moralists that young Englishmen who
went to Italy brought back nothing but vicious habits. Hence the
proverb "An Englishman italianate is a devil incarnate."
22. apish: imitating like an ape. 25. So it be: so long as it is.
there's no respect: no matter. 28. will: natural inclination. wit:
wisdom. 36. betimes: soon, early. 38. cormorant: a greedy sea
bird; i.e., a glutton. 40–56. This . . . Son: a passage much ad-
mired by contemporaries and quoted in *England's Parnassus*
(1600), an anthology of English poetry. 44. infection: the
plague. 49. envy: malice.

This blessed plot, this earth, this realm, this Eng-
    land,   50
This nurse, this teeming womb of royal kings,
Feared by their breed and famous by their birth,
Renownèd for their deeds as far from home,
For Christian service and true chivalry,
As is the sepulcher in stubborn Jewry°   55
Of the world's ransom, blessed Mary's Son —
This land of such dear souls, this dear dear land,
Dear for her reputation through the world,
Is now leased out,° I die pronouncing it,
Like to a tenement or pelting° farm.   60
England, bound in with the triumphant sea,
Whose rocky shore beats back the envious siege
Of watery Neptune, is now bound in with shame,
With inky blots and rotten parchment bonds.
That England, that was wont to conquer others,   65
Hath made a shameful conquest of itself.
Ah, would the scandal vanish with my life,
How happy then were my ensuing death!
    [*Enter* KING RICHARD *and* QUEEN, AUMERLE, BUSHY,
           GREEN, BAGOT, ROSS, *and* WILLOUGHBY.]
    YORK. The King is come. Deal mildly with his
      youth,
For young hot colts being raged° do rage the more.
    QUEEN. How fares our noble uncle Lancaster?   71
    K. RICH. What comfort, man? How is't with aged
      Gaunt?
    GAUNT. Oh, how that name befits my composi-
      tion!°
Old Gaunt indeed, and gaunt in being old.
Within me grief hath kept a tedious fast,   75
And who abstains from meat that is not gaunt?
For sleeping England long time have I watched,
Watching breeds leanness, leanness is all gaunt.
The pleasure that some fathers feed upon
Is my strict fast — I mean my children's looks —   80
And therein fasting, hast thou made me gaunt.
Gaunt am I for the grave, gaunt as a grave,
Whose hollow womb inherits° naught but bones.
    K. RICH. Can sick men play so nicely with their
      names?
    GAUNT. No, misery makes sport to mock itself.
Since thou dost seek to kill my name in me,   86
I mock my name, great King, to flatter° thee.
    K. RICH. Should dying men flatter with those that
      live?
    GAUNT. No, no, men living flatter those that die.
    K. RICH. Thou, now a-dying, say'st thou flatterest
      me.   90
    GAUNT. Oh, no! Thou diest, though I the sicker be.
    K. RICH. I am in health, I breathe, and see thee ill.
    GAUNT. Now He that made me knows I see thee
      ill —

---

55. the . . . Jewry: i.e., the Holy Sepulcher in Jerusalem.
59. leased out: i.e., because the King's revenues had been farmed
out. 60. pelting: paltry. 70. raged: enraged. 73. composition:
frame, body. 83. inherits: possesses. 87. flatter: try to please.

Ill in myself to see, and in thee seeing ill.
Thy deathbed is no lesser than thy land,   95
Wherein thou liest in reputation sick.
And thou, too careless-patient as thou art,
Commit'st thy anointed body to the cure
Of those physicians that first wounded thee.
A thousand flatterers sit within thy crown,   100
Whose compass is no bigger than thy head,
And yet encagèd in so small a verge,°
The waste is no whit lesser than thy land.
Oh, had thy grandsire with a prophet's eye
Seen how his son's son should destroy his sons,   105
From forth thy reach he would have laid thy shame,
Deposing thee before thou wert possessed,
Which art possessed° now to depose thyself.
Why, Cousin, wert thou regent of the world,
It were a shame to let this land by lease;   110
But, for thy world enjoying but this land,
Is it not more than shame to shame it so?
Landlord° of England art thou now, not King.
Thy state of law is bondslave to the law,°
And thou ——
    K. RICH. A lunatic lean-witted fool,   115
Presuming on an ague's privilege,°
Darest with thy frozen admonition
Make pale our cheek, chasing the royal blood
With fury from his native residence.
Now, by my seat's right royal majesty,   120
Wert thou not brother to great Edward's son,
This tongue that runs so roundly° in thy head
Should run thy head from thy unreverent shoulders.
    GAUNT. Oh, spare me not, my brother Edward's
        son,
For that I was his father Edward's son.   125
That blood already, like the pelican,°
Hast thou tapped out and drunkenly caroused.
My brother Gloucester, plain well-meaning soul ——
Whom fair befall° in Heaven 'mongst happy
        souls! ——
May be a precedent and witness good   130
That thou respect'st not spilling Edward's blood.
Join with the present sickness that I have,
And thy unkindness be like crooked age,
To crop at once a too-long-withered flower.
Live in thy shame, but die not shame with thee!
These words hereafter thy tormentors be!   136
Convey me to my bed, then to my grave.
Love they to live that love and honor have.

        [*Exit, borne off by his* ATTENDANTS.]

    K. RICH. And let them die that age and sullens°
        have,
For both hast thou, and both become the grave.   140
    YORK. I do beseech your Majesty, impute his words
To wayward sickliness and age in him.
He loves you, on my life, and holds you dear
As Harry Duke of Hereford, were he here.
    K. RICH. Right, you say true. As Hereford's love,
        so his.   145
As theirs, so mine, and all be as it is.

        [*Enter* NORTHUMBERLAND.]

    NORTH. My liege, old Gaunt commends him to
        your Majesty.
    K. RICH. What says he?
    NORTH.   Nay, nothing, all is said.
His tongue is now a stringless instrument.
Words, life, and all, old Lancaster hath spent.   150
    YORK. Be York the next that must be bankrupt so!
Though death be poor, it ends a mortal woe.
    K. RICH. The ripest fruit first falls, and so doth he.
His time is spent, our pilgrimage must be.
So much for that. Now for our Irish wars.   155
We must supplant those rough rugheaded° kerns°
Which live like venom where no venom else
But only they have privilege to live.
And for these great affairs do ask some charge,°
Toward our assistance we do seize to us   160
The plate, coin, revenues, and movables
Whereof our uncle Gaunt did stand possessed.
    YORK. How long shall I be patient? Ah, how long
Shall tender duty make me suffer wrong?   164
Not Gloucester's death, nor Hereford's banishment,
Not Gaunt's rebukes,° nor England's private
        wrongs,
Nor the prevention of poor Bolingbroke
About his marriage,° nor my own disgrace,
Have ever made me sour my patient cheek,
Or bend one wrinkle on my sovereign's face.   170
I am the last of noble Edward's sons,
Of whom thy father, Prince of Wales, was first.
In war was never lion raged more fierce,
In peace was never gentle lamb more mild,
Than was that young and princely gentleman.   175
His face thou hast, for even so looked he,
Accomplished with the number of thy hours.°
But when he frowned, it was against the French
And not against his friends. His noble hand
Did win what he did spend, and spent not that   180
Which his triumphant father's hand had won.
His hands were guilty of no kindred blood,°
But bloody with the enemies of his kin.

---

102. verge: compass. 107–08. possessed . . . possessed: in possession of . . . possessed by an evil spirit. 113. Landlord: i.e.,
because he has rented his kingdom. 114. state . . . law: you are
now subject to the laws as a landlord, and no longer above the
law as King. 116. ague's privilege: i.e., an invalid privileged to
be peevish. ague: fever. 122. roundly: directly; i.e., impudently.
126. pelican: The pelican was believed to feed its young with
blood from its breast, but when the young grew up they attacked
the mother bird. 129. fair befall: may good come to.

139. sullens: sulks. 156. rugheaded: shaggy-headed. kerns:
Irish foot soldiers. 159. charge: expense. 166. Gaunt's rebukes: the rebukes received by Gaunt. 167–68. prevention . . .
marriage: There is nothing further in the play about this incident, which is mentioned by Holinshed. 177. Accomplished
. . . hours: when he was your age. Accomplished: lit., "equipped."
182. kindred blood: blood of his kindred.

O Richard! York is too far gone with grief,
Or else he never would compare between.°   185
   K. RICH. Why, Uncle, what's the matter?
   YORK.   O my liege,
Pardon me, if you please; if not, I, pleased
Not to be pardoned, am content withal.
Seek you to seize and gripe into your hands   189
The royalties° and rights of banished Hereford?
Is not Gaunt dead, and doth not Hereford live?
Was not Gaunt just, and is not Harry true?
Did not the one deserve to have an heir?
Is not his heir a well-deserving son?
Take Hereford's rights away, and take from Time
His charters and his customary rights,°   196
Let not tomorrow then ensue° today.
Be not thyself, for how art thou a king
But by fair sequence and succession?
Now, afore God — God forbid I say true! —   200
If you do wrongfully seize Hereford's rights,
Call in the letters° patents that he hath
By his attorneys general to sue
His livery, and deny his offered homage,
You pluck a thousand dangers on your head,   205
You lose a thousand well-disposèd hearts,
And prick my tender patience to those thoughts
Which honor and allegiance cannot think.
   K. RICH. Think what you will, we seize into our
    hands
His plate, his goods, his money, and his lands.   210
   YORK. I'll not be by the while. My liege, farewell.
What will ensue hereof, there's none can tell,
But by bad courses may be understood
That their events° can never fall out good. [*Exit.*]
   K. RICH. Go, Bushy, to the Earl of Wiltshire
    straight.   215
Bid him repair to us to Ely House
To see this business. Tomorrow next°
We will for Ireland — and 'tis time, I trow.°
And we create, in absence of ourself,
Our uncle York Lord Governor of England,   220
For he is just and always loved us well.
Come on, our Queen. Tomorrow must we part.
Be merry, for our time of stay is short.
   [*Flourish. Exeunt* KING, QUEEN, AUMERLE,
                BUSHY, GREEN, *and* BAGOT.]
   NORTH. Well, lords, the Duke of Lancaster is dead.
   ROSS. And living too, for now his son is Duke.

   WILLO. Barely in title, not in revenues.   226
   NORTH. Richly in both, if justice had her right.
   ROSS. My heart is great,° but it must break with
    silence
Ere't be disburdened° with a liberal° tongue.
   NORTH. Nay, speak thy mind. And let him ne'er
    speak more   230
That speaks thy words again to do thee harm!
   WILLO. Tends° that thou wouldst speak to° the
    Duke of Hereford?
If it be so, out with it boldly, man.
Quick is mine ear to hear of good toward him.
   ROSS. No good at all that I can do for him,   235
Unless you call it good to pity him,
Bereft and gelded of his patrimony.
   NORTH. Now, afore God, 'tis shame such wrongs
    are borne
In him a royal prince and many moe°
Of noble blood in this declining land.   240
The King is not himself, but basely led
By flatterers. And what they will inform,
Merely in hate, 'gainst any of us all,
That will the King severely prosecute
'Gainst us, our lives, our children, and our heirs.
   ROSS. The commons hath he pilled° with grievous
    taxes,   246
And quite lost their hearts. The nobles hath he fined
For ancient quarrels, and quite lost their hearts.
   WILLO. And daily new exactions are devised,
As blanks,° benevolences,° and I wot° not what.
But what, o' God's name, doth become of this?   251
   NORTH. Wars have not wasted it, for warred he
    hath not,
But basely yielded upon compromise
That which his noble ancestors achieved with blows.
More hath he spent in peace than they in wars.   255
   ROSS. The Earl of Wiltshire hath the realm in
    farm.
   WILLO. The King's grown bankrupt, like a broken
    man.
   NORTH. Reproach and dissolution hangeth over
    him.
   ROSS. He hath not money for these Irish wars,
His burdenous taxations notwithstanding,   260
But by the robbing of the banished Duke.
   NORTH. His noble kinsman. Most degenerate
    King!
But, lords, we hear this fearful tempest sing,
Yet seek no shelter to avoid the storm.
We see the wind sit sore upon our sails,   265
And yet we strike not, but securely° perish.
   ROSS. We see the very wreck that we must suffer,

---

185. compare between: make such comparisons. 190. royalties: rights belonging to a member of the royal family. 195–96. Take . . . rights: i.e., if you take Hereford's inheritance you are depriving Time of his rights (viz., the natural law that the son inherits the father's wealth). charters: privileges. 197. ensue: follow. 202–04. letters . . . homage: The lines are taken from Holinshed. letters patent: a grant by the King of some right or privilege. attorneys general: deputies. sue . . . livery: establish his legal right to Gaunt's property. homage: formal acknowledgement of allegiance to the King necessary before Bolingbroke could assume possession. 214. events: sequels, results. 217. Tomorrow next: tomorrow. 218. trow: am sure.

228. great: pregnant, heavy. 229. disburdened: relieved of its burden. liberal: free. 232. Tends: is it your meaning? to: concerning. 239. moe: more. 246. pilled: peeled, stripped. 250. blanks: See I.iv.48. benevolences: loans which the rich were forced to give as "free" offerings. wot: know. 266. securely: overconfidently.

And unavoided° is the danger now
For suffering so the causes of our wreck.
   NORTH. Not so. Even through the hollow eyes of
     death   270
I spy life peering, but I dare not say
How near the tidings of our comfort is.
   WILLO. Nay, let us share thy thoughts, as thou dost
     ours.
   ROSS. Be confident to speak, Northumberland.
We three are but thyself, and, speaking so,   275
Thy words are but as thoughts. Therefore be bold.
   NORTH. Then thus. I have from Le Port Blanc, a
     bay
In Brittany, received intelligence°
That Harry Duke of Hereford, Rainold Lord Cob-
     ham,°   279
That late broke from the Duke of Exeter,
His brother, Archbishop late of Canterbury,
Sir Thomas Erpingham, Sir John Ramston,
Sir John Norbery, Sir Robert Waterton, and Francis
     Quoint —   284
All these well furnished by the Duke of Bretagne
With eight tall° ships, three thousand men of war —
Are making hither with all due expedience°
And shortly mean to touch our northern shore.
Perhaps they had ere this but that they stay
The first departing of the King for Ireland.   290
If then we shall shake off our slavish yoke,
Imp° out our drooping country's broken wing,
Redeem from broking pawn° the blemished crown,
Wipe off the dust that hides our scepter's gilt,
And make high majesty look like itself,   295
Away with me in post to Ravenspurgh.°
But if you faint, as fearing to do so,
Stay and be secret, and myself will go.
   ROSS. To horse, to horse! Urge doubts to them that
     fear.
   WILLO. Hold out my horse, and I will first be
     there.   [*Exeunt.*] 300

SCENE II. *Windsor Castle.*

[*Enter* QUEEN, BUSHY, *and* BAGOT.]
   BUSHY. Madam, your Majesty is too much sad.
You promised, when you parted with the King,
To lay aside life-harming heaviness
And entertain a cheerful disposition.
   QUEEN. To please the King I did, to please myself

I cannot do it. Yet I know no cause   6
Why I should welcome such a guest as grief,
Save bidding farewell to so sweet a guest
As my sweet Richard. Yet again, methinks
Some unborn sorrow, ripe in fortune's womb,   10
Is coming toward me, and my inward soul
With nothing° trembles. At something it grieves
More than with parting from my lord the King.
   BUSHY. Each substance of a grief hath twenty
     shadows,
Which shows like grief itself, but is not so;   15
For sorrow's eye, glazèd with blinding tears,
Divides one thing entire to many objects° —
Like perspectives° which rightly gazed upon,
Show nothing but confusion, eyed awry
Distinguish form. So your sweet Majesty,   20
Looking awry upon your lord's departure,
Find shapes of grief, more than himself, to wail.
Which, looked on as it is, is naught but shadows
Of what it is not. Then, thrice-gracious Queen,
More than your lord's departure weep not. More's
     not seen,   25
Or if it be, 'tis with false sorrow's eye,
Which for things true weeps things imaginary.
   QUEEN. It may be so, but yet my inward soul
Persuades me it is otherwise. Howe'er it be,
I cannot but be sad, so heavy sad   30
As, though on thinking on no thought I think,
Makes me with heavy nothing faint and shrink.
   BUSHY. 'Tis nothing but conceit,° my gracious
     lady.
   QUEEN. 'Tis nothing less. Conceit is still° derived
From some forefather grief. Mine is not so,   35
For nothing hath begot my something grief,
Or something hath the nothing that I grieve.
'Tis in reversion° that I do possess,
But what it is, that is not yet known — what
I cannot name. 'Tis nameless woe, I wot.   40
           [*Enter* GREEN.]
   GREEN. God save your Majesty! And well met,
     gentlemen.
I hope the King is not yet shipped for Ireland.
   QUEEN. Why hopest thou so? 'Tis better hope he
     is,
For his designs crave haste, his haste good hope.
Then wherefore dost thou hope he is not shipped?
   GREEN. That he, our hope, might have retired° his
     power   46
And driven into despair an enemy's hope,
Who strongly hath set footing in this land.
The banished Bolingbroke repeals° himself,

---

268. **unavoided:** unavoidable. 277–78. **I . . . intelligence:** Note
the compression of "real" time here. See App. 22. 279. **Cobham:**
A line is apparently missing after *Cobham*, as is shown by the
passage from Holinshed. He was a son of Richard Earl of
Arundel, who broke from the Duke of Exeter. 286. **tall:** fine.
287. **expedience:** expedition, haste. 292. **Imp:** a metaphor from
falconry; to *imp* is to graft new feathers into a broken wing.
See App. 26. 293. **broking pawn:** the pawnbroker. 296. **Ra-
venspurgh:** in Yorkshire.

Sc. ii: 12. **With nothing:** at nothing. 16–17. **sorrow's . . .
objects:** when the eye is blinded with tears single objects look
double. 18. **perspectives:** ingenious pictures which when viewed
from the front are meaningless, but when seen foreshortened
from the side are clear. 33. **conceit:** imagination. 34. **still:**
continually. 38. **reversion:** destined to be mine later. See
I.iv.35. 46. **retired:** withdrawn. 49. **repeals:** recalls.

And with uplifted arms is safe arrived   50
At Ravenspurgh.
    QUEEN.   Now God in Heaven forbid!
    GREEN. Ah, madam, 'tis too true. And that is
      worse,
The Lord Northumberland, his son young Henry
    Percy,
The Lords of Ross, Beaumond, and Willoughby,
With all their powerful friends, are fled to him.   55
    BUSHY. Why have you not proclaimed Northum-
    berland
And all the rest revolted faction traitors?°
    GREEN. We have. Whereupon the Earl of Wor-
    cester
Hath broke his staff,° resigned his stewardship,
And all the household servants fled with him   60
To Bolingbroke.
    QUEEN. So, Green, thou art the midwife to my
    woe,
And Bolingbroke my sorrow's dismal heir.
Now hath my soul brought forth her prodigy,°
And I, a gasping new-delivered mother,   65
Have woe to woe, sorrow to sorrow, joined.
    BUSHY. Despair not, madam.
    QUEEN.   Who shall hinder me?
I will despair, and be at enmity
With cozening° hope. He is a flatterer,
A parasite, a keeper-back of death,   70
Who gently would dissolve the bands of life,
Which false hope lingers° in extremity.
                 [*Enter* YORK.]
    GREEN. Here comes the Duke of York.
    QUEEN. With signs of war° about his aged neck.
Oh, full of careful° business are his looks!   75
Uncle, for God's sake, speak comfortable words.
    YORK. Should I do so, I should belie my thoughts.
Comfort's in Heaven, and we are on the earth,
Where nothing lives but crosses, cares, and grief.
Your husband, he is gone to save far off   80
Whilst others come to make him lose at home.
Here am I left to underprop his land,
Who, weak with age, cannot support myself.
Now comes the sick hour that his surfeit° made,
Now shall he try° his friends that flattered him. 85
             [*Enter a* SERVANT.]
    SERV. My lord, your son was gone before I came.
    YORK. He was? Why, so! Go all which way it will!
The nobles they are fled, the commons they are cold,
And will, I fear, revolt on Hereford's side.
Sirrah, get thee to Plashy, to my sister Gloucester.
Bid her send me presently° a thousand pound.   91

---

57. revolted . . . traitors: traitors belonging to a conspiracy of
rebels. **59. broke . . . staff:** Court officials carried a white staff
as sign of office. At resignation or the death of the sovereign
the staff was broken. See Pl. 8d. **64. prodigy:** monster.
69. cozening: cheating. **72. lingers:** makes to linger. **74. signs
of war:** armor. **75. careful:** anxious. **84. surfeit:** excess.
85. try: test. **91. presently:** immediately.

Hold, take my ring.
    SERV. My lord, I had forgot to tell your lordship,
Today, as I came by, I called there —
But I shall grieve you to report the rest.   95
    YORK. What is't, knave?
    SERV. An hour before I came, the Duchess died.
    YORK. God for His mercy! What a tide of woes
Comes rushing on this woeful land at once!
I know not what to do. I would to God,   100
So my untruth° had not provoked him to it,
The King had cut off my head with my brother's.
What, are there no posts dispatched for Ireland?
How shall we do for money for these wars?
Come, Sister — Cousin, I would say — pray pardon
    me.   105
Go, fellow, get thee home, provide some carts
And bring away the armor that is there.
               [*Exit* SERVANT.]
Gentlemen, will you go muster men?
If I know how or which way to order these affairs
Thus thrust disorderly into my hands,   110
Never believe me. Both are my kinsmen.
The one is my sovereign, whom both my oath
And duty bids defend. The other again
Is my kinsman, whom the King hath wronged,
Whom conscience and my kindred bids to right.
Well, somewhat we must do. Come, Cousin, I'll
Dispose of you.   117
Gentlemen, go, muster up your men,
And meet me presently at Berkeley.
I should to Plashy too,   120
But time will not permit. All is uneven,
And everything is left at six and seven.°
         [*Exeunt* YORK *and* QUEEN.]
    BUSHY. The wind sits fair for news to go to Ire-
    land,
But none returns.° For us to levy power
Proportionable to the enemy   125
Is all unpossible.
    GREEN. Besides, our nearness to the King in love
Is near the hate of those love not the King.
    BAGOT. And that's the wavering commons. For
    their love
Lies in their purses, and whoso empties them   130
By so much fills their hearts with deadly hate.
    BUSHY. Wherein the King stands generally con-
    demned.
    BAGOT. If judgment lie in them, then so do we,°
Because we ever have been near the King.
    GREEN. Well, I will for refuge straight to Bristol
    Castle.   135
The Earl of Wiltshire is already there.

---

101. So my untruth: so long as it was not disloyalty that.
122. six . . . seven: sixes and sevens, in confusion. **124. none
returns:** At times the wind blew so continuously from the east
that sailing ships could not make the passage from Ireland to
England for several weeks. **133. If . . . we:** i.e., if the commons
condemn the King, they condemn us too.

BUSHY. Thither will I with you, for little office
The hateful commons will perform for us
Except like curs to tear us all to pieces.
Will you go along with us?   140
BAGOT. No, I will to Ireland to His Majesty.
Farewell. If heart's presages° be not vain,
We three here part that ne'er shall meet again.
BUSHY. That's as York thrives to beat back Boling-
broke.
GREEN. Alas, poor Duke! The task he undertakes
Is numbering sands and drinking oceans dry.   146
Where one on his side fights, thousand will fly.
Farewell at once, for once, for all, and ever.
BUSHY. Well, we may meet again.
BAGOT.   I fear me never. [*Exeunt.*]

SCENE III. *Wilds in Gloucestershire.*

[*Enter* BOLINGBROKE *and* NORTHUMBERLAND,
with Forces.]
BOLING. How far is it, my lord, to Berkeley now?
NORTH. Believe me, noble lord,
I am a stranger here in Gloucestershire.
These high wild hills and rough uneven ways
Draws out our miles, and makes them wearisome,
And yet your fair discourse hath been as sugar,   6
Making the hard way sweet and delectable.
But I bethink me what a weary way
From Ravenspurgh to Cotswold will be found
In Ross and Willoughby, wanting your company,°
Which, I protest, hath very much beguiled   11
The tediousness and process of my travel.
But theirs is sweetened with the hope to have
The present benefit which I possess,
And hope to joy is little less in joy   15
Than hope enjoyed. By this the weary lords
Shall make their way seem short, as mine hath done
By sight of what I have, your noble company.
BOLING. Of much less value is my company
Than your good words. But who comes here?   20
        [*Enter* HENRY PERCY.]
NORTH. It is my son, young Harry Percy,°
Sent from my brother Worcester, whencesoever.°
Harry, how fares your uncle?
H. PERCY. I had thought, my lord, to have learned
his health of you.
NORTH. Why, is he not with the Queen?   25
H. PERCY. No, my good lord. He hath forsook the
Court,
Broken his staff of office, and dispersed
The household of the King.
NORTH.   What was his reason?

He was not so resolved when last we spake together.
H. PERCY. Because your lordship was proclaimèd
traitor.   30
But he, my lord, is gone to Ravenspurgh,
To offer service to the Duke of Hereford,
And sent me over by Berkeley, to discover
What power the Duke of York had levied there,
Then with directions to repair to Ravenspurgh. 35
NORTH. Have you forgot the Duke of Hereford,
boy?
H. PERCY. No, my good lord, for that is not forgot
Which ne'er I did remember. To my knowledge,
I never in my life did look on him.
NORTH. Then learn to know him now. This is the
Duke.   40
H. PERCY. My gracious lord, I tender you my serv-
ice,
Such as it is, being tender, raw, and young —
Which elder days shall ripen and confirm
To more approvèd° service and desert.
BOLING. I thank thee, gentle Percy, and be sure
I count myself in nothing else so happy   46
As in a soul remembering my good friends.
And as my fortune ripens with thy love,
It shall be still thy true love's recompense.°
My heart this covenant makes, my hand thus seals
it.   50
NORTH. How far is it to Berkeley? And what stir
Keeps good old York there with his men of war?
H. PERCY. There stands the castle, by yon tuft of
trees,
Manned with three hundred men, as I have heard,
And in it are the Lords of York, Berkeley, and Sey-
mour —   55
None else of name and noble estimate.
        [*Enter* ROSS *and* WILLOUGHBY.]
NORTH. Here come the Lords of Ross and Wil-
loughby,
Bloody with spurring, fiery-red with haste.
BOLING. Welcome, my lords. I wot your love pur-
sues
A banished traitor. All my treasury   60
Is yet but unfelt° thanks, which more enriched
Shall be your love and labor's recompense.
ROSS. Your presence makes us rich, most noble
lord.
WILLO. And far surmounts our labor to attain it.
BOLING. Evermore thanks, the exchequer of the
poor,°   65
Which, till my infant fortune comes to years,
Stands for my bounty. But who comes here?
        [*Enter* BERKELEY.]
NORTH. It is my Lord of Berkeley, as I guess.

---

142. presages: forebodings.
    Sc. iii: 8–10. weary . . . company: i.e., without your company
this will be a very tedious journey for Ross and Willoughby.
21. young . . . Percy: See *I Hen IV*, I.i.92,n. 22. whenceso-
ever: from wherever he may be.

44. approved: tested. 48–49. fortune . . . recompense: as my
fortunes improve, your love shall be rewarded. 61. unfelt: in-
tangible. 65. thanks . . . poor: the poor can repay only with
thanks.

BERK. My Lord of Hereford, my message is to you.
BOLING. My lord, my answer is — to Lancaster,°
And I am come to seek that name in England, 71
And I must find that title in your tongue
Before I make reply to aught you say.
    BERK. Mistake me not, my lord. 'Tis not my meaning
To rase° one title of your honor out. 75
To you, my lord, I come, what lord you will,
From the most gracious Regent of this land,
The Duke of York, to know what pricks you on
To take advantage of the absent time°
And fright our native peace with self-born° arms.
            [*Enter* YORK *attended.*]
    BOLING. I shall not need transport my words by
    you. 81
Here comes His Grace in person. My noble uncle!
            [*Kneels.*]
    YORK. Show me thy humble heart, and not thy
    knee,
Whose duty° is deceivable° and false.
    BOLING. My gracious uncle! 85
    YORK. Tut, tut!
Grace me no grace,° nor uncle me no uncle:
I am no traitor's uncle, and that word " grace "°
In an ungracious mouth is but profane.
Why have those banished and forbidden legs
Dared once to touch a dust of England's ground? 90
But then more " why? " Why have they dared to
    march
So many miles upon her peaceful bosom,
Frighting her pale-faced villages with war
And ostentation° of despisèd° arms? 95
Comest thou because the anointed King is hence?
Why, foolish boy, the King is left behind,
And in my loyal bosom lies his power.
Were I but now the lord of such hot youth
As when brave Gaunt, thy father, and myself 100
Rescued the Black Prince, that young Mars of men,
From forth the ranks of many thousand French,
Oh, then how quickly should this arm of mine,
Now prisoner to the palsy, chastise thee
And minister correction to thy fault! 105
    BOLING. My gracious uncle, let me know my fault.
On what condition stands it, and wherein?
    YORK. Even in condition of the worst degree,
In gross rebellion and detested treason.
Thou art a banished man, and here art come 110
Before the expiration of thy time
In braving arms against thy sovereign.

BOLING. As I was banished, I was banished Hereford,
But as I come, I come for Lancaster.
And, noble Uncle, I beseech your Grace 115
Look on my wrongs with an indifferent° eye.
You are my father, for methinks in you
I see old Gaunt alive. Oh, then, my father,
Will you permit that I shall stand condemned 119
A wandering vagabond, my rights and royalties
Plucked from my arms perforce and given away
To upstart unthrifts?° Wherefore was I born?
If that my cousin king be King of England,
It must be granted I am Duke of Lancaster.
You have a son, Aumerle, my noble cousin. 125
Had you first died, and he been thus trod down,
He should have found his uncle Gaunt a father,
To rouse his wrongs and chase them to the bay.°
I am denied to sue my livery° here,
And yet my letters patent give me leave. 130
My father's goods are all distrained and sold,
And these and all are all amiss employed.
What would you have me do? I am a subject,
And I challenge law. Attorneys are denied me,
And therefore personally I lay my claim 135
To my inheritance of free descent.
    NORTH. The noble Duke hath been too much
    abused.
    ROSS. It stands your Grace upon° to do him right.
    WILLO. Base men by his endowments° are made
    great.
    YORK. My lords of England, let me tell you this.
I have had feeling of my cousin's wrongs 141
And labored all I could to do him right.
But in this kind to come, in braving arms,
Be his own carver and cut out his way,
To find out right with wrong, it may not be. 145
And you that do abet him in this kind
Cherish rebellion and are rebels all.
    NORTH. The noble Duke hath sworn his coming is
But for his own, and for the right of that
We all have strongly sworn to give him aid, 150
And let him ne'er see joy that breaks that oath!
    YORK. Well, well, I see the issue of these arms.
I cannot mend it, I must needs confess,
Because my power is weak and all ill left.
But if I could, by Him that gave me life 155
I would attach° you all and make you stoop
Unto the sovereign mercy of the King.
But since I cannot, be it known to you
I do remain as neuter. So fare you well —
Unless you please to enter in the castle 160
And there repose you for this night.
    BOLING. An offer, Uncle, that we will accept.

---

70. Lancaster: because he is now Duke of Lancaster. 75. rase: erase, omit. 79. absent time: time of the King's absence. 80. self-born: i.e., born by native Englishmen and not by foreigners. 84. duty: act of kneeling. deceivable: full of deceit. 87. Grace . . . grace: A common kind of idiom. See *R & J*, III. v.153. 88. grace: York puns on "grace," a state of grace, and "grace," the courtesy title of a Duke. 95. ostentation: display. despised: despicable.

116. indifferent: impartial. 122. unthrifts: spendthrifts. 128. to . . . bay: to the death. The bay is the death of a deer in the hunt. 129. sue my livery: See II.i.203–04. 138. stands . . . upon: it rests with your Grace. 139. his endowments: i.e., Bolingbroke's possessions. 156. attach: arrest.

But we must win your Grace to go with us
To Bristol Castle, which they say is held
By Bushy, Bagot, and their complices,   165
The caterpillars of the commonwealth,°
Which I have sworn to weed and pluck away.
  YORK. It may be I will go with you. But yet I'll
    pause,
For I am loath to break our country's laws.
Nor friends nor foes, to me welcome you are.   170
Things past redress are now with me past care.
                                            [*Exeunt.*]

SCENE IV. *A camp in Wales.*

[*Enter* SALISBURY *and a Welsh* CAPTAIN.]
  CAP. My Lord of Salisbury, we have stayed ten
    days
And hardly kept our countrymen together,
And yet we hear no tidings from the King.
Therefore we will disperse ourselves. Farewell.   4
  SAL. Stay yet another day, thou trusty Welshman.
The King reposeth all his confidence in thee.
  CAP. 'Tis thought the King is dead. We will not
    stay.
The bay trees in our country are all withered,
And meteors fright the fixèd stars of heaven.   9
The pale-faced moon looks bloody on the earth,°
And lean-looked prophets whisper fearful change.°
Rich men look sad and ruffians dance and leap,
The one in fear to lose what they enjoy,
The other to enjoy by rage and war.
These signs forerun the death or fall of kings.   15
Farewell. Our countrymen are gone and fled,
As well assured Richard their King is dead.   [*Exit.*]
  SAL. Ah, Richard, with the eyes of heavy mind
I see thy glory like a shooting star
Fall to the base earth from the firmament.   20
Thy sun sets weeping in the lowly west,
Witnessing storms to come, woe and unrest.
Thy friends are fled to wait upon thy foes,
And crossly° to thy good all fortune goes.   [*Exit.*]

Act III

SCENE I. *Bristol. Before the Castle.*

[*Enter* BOLINGBROKE, YORK, NORTHUMBERLAND, ROSS,
  PERCY, WILLOUGHBY, *with* BUSHY *and* GREEN,
                    prisoners.]
  BOLING. Bring forth these men.
Bushy and Green, I will not vex your souls —

Since presently your souls must part your bodies —
With too much urging° your pernicious lives,
For 'twere no charity. Yet, to wash your blood   5
From off my hands, here in the view of men
I will unfold some causes of your deaths.
You have misled a prince, a royal King,
A happy gentleman in blood and lineaments,°
By you unhappied and disfigured clean.°   10
You have in manner with your sinful hours°
Made a divorce betwixt his Queen and him,
Broke the possession of a royal bed
And stained the beauty of a fair Queen's cheeks
With tears drawn from her eyes by your foul
    wrongs.
Myself, a prince by fortune of my birth,   16
Near to the King in blood, and near in love
Till you did make him misinterpret me,
Have stooped my neck under your injuries,
And sighed my English breath in foreign clouds,
Eating the bitter bread of banishment,   21
Whilst you have fed upon my signories,°
Disparked° my parks and felled my forest woods,
From my own windows torn my household coat,°
Razed out my imprese,° leaving me no sign   25
Save men's opinions and my living blood
To show the world I am a gentleman.
This and much more, much more than twice all
    this,
Condemns you to the death. See them delivered
    over
To execution and the hand of death.   30
  BUSHY. More welcome is the stroke of death to me
Than Bolingbroke to England. Lords, farewell.
  GREEN. My comfort is that Heaven will take our
    souls
And plague injustice with the pains of Hell.
  BOLING. My Lord Northumberland, see them dis-
    patched.   35
       [*Exeunt* NORTHUMBERLAND *and others,
                          with the prisoners.*]
Uncle, you say the Queen is at your house.
For God's sake, fairly let her be entreated.°
Tell her I send to her my kind commends.°
Take special care my greetings be delivered.
  YORK. A gentleman of mine I have dispatched   40
With letters of your love to her at large.°
  BOLING. Thanks, gentle Uncle. Come, lords,
    away,
To fight with Glendower and his complices.
Awhile to work, and after holiday.   [*Exeunt.*]

---

166. caterpillars . . . commonwealth: a common Elizabethan
metaphor for those who prey on the state, "grafters."
  Sc. iv: 8–10. The . . . earth: all these events were regarded by
the superstitious as omens of disaster. 11. change: revolution.
24. crossly: adversely.

Act III, Sc. i: 4. urging: stressing. 9. happy . . . lineaments:
fortunate in his descent and personal appearance. 10. clean:
completely. 11. in . . . hours: because of your sinful way of life.
22. signories: manors. 23. Disparked: broken-down the enclo-
sures of. 24. household coat: coat of arms in stained glass.
25. imprese: heraldic device. 37. entreated: treated. 38. com-
mends: commendations. 41. at large: at length, fully.

SCENE II. *The coast of Wales. A castle in view.*

[*Drums: flourish and colors.° Enter* KING RICHARD, *the* BISHOP OF CARLISLE, AUMERLE, *and Soldiers.*]

K. RICH. Barkloughly° Castle call they this at
    hand?

AUM. Yea, my lord. How brooks° your Grace the
    air
After your late tossing on the breaking seas?

K. RICH. Needs must I like it well. I weep for joy
To stand upon my kingdom once again.   5
Dear earth, I do salute thee with my hand,
Though rebels wound thee with their horses' hoofs.
As a long-parted mother with her child
Plays fondly with her tears and smiles in meeting,
So, weeping, smiling, greet I thee, my earth,   10
And do thee favors° with my royal hands.
Feed not thy sovereign's foe, my gentle earth,
Nor with thy sweets comfort his ravenous° sense;°
But let thy spiders, that suck up thy venom,
And heavy-gaited° toads° lie in their way,   15
Doing annoyance° to the treacherous feet
Which with usurping steps do trample thee.
Yield stinging nettles to mine enemies,
And when they from thy bosom pluck a flower,
Guard it, I pray thee, with a lurking adder,   20
Whose double tongue° may with a mortal° touch
Throw death upon thy sovereign's enemies.
Mock not my senseless conjuration,° lords.
This earth shall have a feeling and these stones
Prove armèd soldiers ere her native King   25
Shall falter under foul rebellion's arms.

CAR. Fear not, my lord. That Power that made you
    King
Hath power to keep you King in spite of all.
The means that Heaven yields must be embraced,
And not neglected; else, if Heaven would   30
And we will not, Heaven's offer we refuse,
The proffered means of succor and redress.

AUM. He means, my lord, that we are too remiss
Whilst Bolingbroke, through our security,°
Grows strong and great in substance and in power.

K. RICH. Discomfortable° Cousin! Know'st thou
    not   36
That when the searching eye of Heaven is hid

Behind the globe that lights the lower world,°
Then thieves and robbers range abroad unseen
In murders and in outrage, boldly here;   40
But when from under this terrestrial ball
He fires the proud tops of the eastern pines
And darts his light through every guilty hole,
Then murders, treasons, and detested sins,
The cloak of night being plucked from off their
    backs,   45
Stand bare and naked, trembling at themselves?
So when this thief, this traitor, Bolingbroke,
Who all this while hath reveled in the night
Whilst we were wandering with the Antipodes,°
Shall see us rising in our throne, the east,   50
His treasons will sit blushing in his face,
Not able to endure the sight of day,
But self-affrighted tremble at his sin.
Not all the water in the rough rude sea
Can wash the balm° off from an anointed king.   55
The breath of worldly men cannot depose
The deputy elected by the Lord.
For every man that Bolingbroke hath pressed°
To lift shrewd° steel against our golden crown,
God for His Richard hath in heavenly pay   60
A glorious angel. Then, if angels fight,
Weak men must fall, for Heaven still guards the
    right.

[*Enter* SALISBURY.] Welcome, my lord. How far off
    lies your power?°

SAL. Nor near° nor farther off, my gracious lord,
Than this weak arm. Discomfort guides my tongue
And bids me speak of nothing but despair.   66
One day too late, I fear me, noble lord,
Hath clouded all thy happy days on earth.
Oh, call back yesterday, bid time return,
And thou shalt have twelve thousand fighting
    men!
Today, today, unhappy day, too late,   71
O'erthrows thy joys, friends, fortune, and thy state.
For all the Welshmen, hearing thou wert dead,
Are gone to Bolingbroke, dispersed, and fled.

AUM. Comfort, my liege. Why looks your Grace
    so pale?   75

K. RICH. But now° the blood of twenty thousand
    men
Did triumph in my face, and they are fled.
And till so much blood thither come again,
Have I not reason to look pale and dead?
All souls that will be safe, fly from my side,   80
For time hath set a blot upon my pride.

AUM. Comfort, my liege. Remember who you are.

Sc. ii: s.d., colors: i.e., a soldier carrying a flag. **1. Bark-loughly**: The name comes from Holinshed, and is probably a misprint for Harlech, a castle in Wales. **2. brooks**: endures, enjoys. **11. favors**: Richard is saluting the earth by touching it. **13. ravenous**: gluttonous, like a beast of prey. **sense**: nature. **15. heavy-gaited**: heavy-footed, lumbering. **toads**: toads and spiders were considered poisonous. **16. annoyance**: hurt. **21. double tongue**: forked tongue. Adders were believed to sting with the tongue. **mortal**: deadly. **23. senseless conjuration**: attempt to conjure things that have no feeling. **34. security**: lack of care. **36. Discomfortable**: causing discomfort.

37–38. eye ... world: i.e., when the sun (*eye of Heaven*) which lights the world passes behind the earth (*globe*). **49. Antipodes**: the other side of the earth. **55. balm**: consecrated oil used in anointing a king. **58. pressed**: conscripted. **59. shrewd**: malicious. **63. power**: army. **64. near**: nearer. **76. But now**: a moment ago.

K. RICH. I had forgot myself.° Am I not King?
Awake, thou coward Majesty! Thou sleepest.
Is not the King's name twenty thousand names?   85
Arm, arm, my name! A puny subject strikes
At thy great glory. Look not to the ground,
Ye favorites of a King. Are we not high?
High be our thoughts. I know my uncle York
Hath power enough to serve our turn. But who
   comes here?   90

          [*Enter* SCROOP.]

SCROOP. More health and happiness betide° my
   liege
Than can my care-tunèd tongue deliver him!
   K. RICH. Mine ear is open and my heart prepared.
The worst is worldly loss thou canst unfold.
Say, is my kingdom lost? Why, 'twas my care,   95
And what loss is it to be rid of care?°
Strives Bolingbroke to be as great as we?
Greater he shall not be. If he serve God,
We'll serve Him too and be his fellow so.
Revolt our subjects? That we cannot mend.   100
They break their faith to God as well as us.
Cry woe, destruction, ruin, and decay —
The worst is death, and death will have his day.
   SCROOP. Glad am I that your Highness is so armed
To bear the tidings of calamity.   105
Like an unseasonable stormy day,
Which makes the silver rivers drown their shores
As if the world were all dissolved to tears,
So high above his limits° swells the rage
Of Bolingbroke, covering your fearful° land   110
With hard bright steel and hearts harder than steel.
Whitebeards have armed their thin and hairless
   scalps°
Against thy Majesty. Boys with women's voices
Strive to speak big and clap their female joints
In stiff unwieldy arms against thy crown.   115
Thy very beadsmen° learn to bend their bows
Of double-fatal° yew against thy state.
Yea, distaff women° manage° rusty bills°
Against thy seat.° Both young and old rebel,
And all goes worse than I have power to tell.   120
   K. RICH. Too well, too well thou tell'st a tale so ill.
Where is the Earl of Wiltshire? Where is Bagot?
What is become of Bushy? Where is Green?
That they have let the dangerous enemy
Measure° our confines with such peaceful steps?
If we prevail, their heads shall pay for it.   126

I warrant they have made peace with Bolingbroke.
   SCROOP. Peace have they made with him indeed,
   my lord.
   K. RICH. Oh, villains, vipers, damned without re-
   demption!
Dogs, easily won to fawn on any man!   130
Snakes, in my heartblood warmed, that sting my
   heart!
Three Judases, each one thrice worse than Judas!
Would they make peace? Terrible Hell make war
Upon their spotted souls for this offense!
   SCROOP. Sweet love, I see, changing his property,°
Turns to the sourest and most deadly hate.   136
Again uncurse their souls. Their peace is made
With heads and not with hands. Those whom you
   curse
Have felt the worst of death's destroying wound,
And lie full low, graved in the hollow ground.   140
   AUM. Is Bushy, Green, and the Earl of Wiltshire
   dead?
   SCROOP. Aye, all of them at Bristol lost their heads.
   AUM. Where is the Duke my father with his
   power?
   K. RICH. No matter where, of comfort no man
   speak.
Let's talk of graves, of worms and epitaphs,   145
Make dust our paper and with rainy eyes
Write sorrow on the bosom of the earth.
Let's choose executors and talk of wills.
And yet not so, for what can we bequeath
Save our deposèd bodies to the ground?   150
Our lands, our lives, and all are Bolingbroke's,
And nothing can we call our own but death
And that small model° of the barren earth
Which serves as paste° and cover to our bones.
For God's sake, let us sit upon the ground   155
And tell sad stories of the death of kings —
How some have been deposed, some slain in war,
Some haunted by the ghosts they have deposed,°
Some poisoned by their wives, some sleeping killed,
All murdered. For within the hollow crown   160
That rounds the mortal temples of a king
Keeps Death his Court, and there the antic° sits,
Scoffing his state and grinning at his pomp,
Allowing him a breath, a little scene,
To monarchize,° be feared, and kill with looks,   165
Infusing him with self and vain conceit,°
As if this flesh which walls about our life
Were brass impregnable, and humored thus
Comes at the last and with a little pin   169
Bores through his castle wall, and farewell King!

---

83. I . . . myself: This constant change of mood in Richard was imitated from Marlowe's *Edward II*. See *Rich II* Intro. p. 190b. **91. betide:** befall.   **95–96. care . . . care:** responsibility . . . trouble.   **109. limits:** boundaries.   **110. fearful:** full of fear. **112. Whitebeards . . . scalps:** even the most aged have covered their thinning or bald heads with helmets. **116. beadsmen:** old men pensioned to pray for their benefactor. **117. double-fatal:** because the yew is poisonous to cattle and also used for deadly bows. **118. distaff women:** women who spin; the *distaff* is a staff used in spinning. **manage:** wield. **bills:** See Pl. 21c. **119. seat:** throne   **125. Measure:** pace out.

135. property: natural quality.   **153. model:** mold, shape; i.e., the earthly body. **154. paste:** covering like piecrust. **158. ghosts . . . deposed:** i.e., those whom they have deposed and turned into ghosts by murdering them. **162. antic:** buffoon, because Death is represented as a grinning skull. See Pl. 12f. **165. monarchize:** play the monarch. **166. self . . . conceit:** vain self-conceit.

Cover your heads° and mock not flesh and blood
With solemn reverence. Throw away respect,
Tradition, form, and ceremonious duty,
For you have but mistook me all this while.
I live with bread like you, feel want,   175
Taste grief, need friends. Subjected° thus,
How can you say to me I am a king?

    CAR. My lord, wise men ne'er sit and wail their
        woes,
But presently prevent the ways to wail.°
To fear the foe, since fear oppresseth strength,   180
Gives in your weakness strength unto your foe,
And so your follies fight against yourself.
Fear, and be slain. No worse can come to fight.
And fight and die is death destroying death,   184
Where° fearing dying pays death servile breath.

    AUM. My father hath a power. Inquire of him,
And learn to make a body of a limb.

    K. RICH. Thou chidest me well. Proud Boling-
        broke, I come
To change blows with thee for our day of doom.
This ague fit of fear is overblown —   190
An easy task it is to win our own.
Say, Scroop, where lies our uncle with his power?
Speak sweetly, man, although thy looks be sour.

    SCROOP. Men judge by the complexion of the sky
The state and inclination of the day.   195
So may you by my dull and heavy eye —
    My tongue hath but a heavier tale to say.
I play the torturer, by small and small
To lengthen out the worst that must be spoken.
Your uncle York is joined with Bolingbroke,   200
And all your northern castles yielded up,
And all your southern gentlemen in arms
Upon his party.

    K. RICH. Thou hast said enough.
[*To* AUMERLE] Beshrew° thee, Cousin, which didst
        lead me forth
Of that sweet way I was in to despair!°   205
What say you now? What comfort have we now?
By Heaven, I'll hate him everlastingly
That bids me be of comfort any more.
Go to Flint Castle. There I'll pine away.
A king, woe's slave, shall kingly woe obey.   210
That power I have, discharge, and let them go
To ear° the land that hath some hope to grow,
For I have none. Let no man speak again
To alter this, for counsel is but vain.

    AUM. My liege, one word.

    K. RICH.   He does me double wrong   215
That wounds me with the flatteries of his tongue.

---

171. **Cover ... heads:** i.e., cease to show outward respect.
176. **Subjected:** i.e., being a subject to ordinary needs.   179. **pres-
ently ... wail:** take immediate steps to stop the causes of
grief.   185. **Where:** whereas.   204. **Beshrew:** ill luck take.
204–05. **which ... despair:** who falsely encouraged me to leave
the way of despair.   212. **ear:** plow.

Discharge my followers. Let them hence away,
From Richard's night to Bolingbroke's fair day.
                      [*Exeunt.*]

SCENE III. *Wales. Before Flint Castle.*

[*Enter, with drum and colors,* BOLINGBROKE, YORK,
    NORTHUMBERLAND, *Attendants, and Forces.*]

    BOLING. So that by this intelligence we learn
The Welshmen are dispersed, and Salisbury
Is gone to meet the King, who lately landed
With some few private friends upon this coast.

    NORTH. The news is very fair and good, my lord.
Richard not far from hence hath hid his head.   6

    YORK. It would beseem the Lord Northumberland
To say "King Richard." Alack the heavy day
When such a sacred king should hide his head!

    NORTH. Your Grace mistakes. Only to be brief   10
Left I his title out.

    YORK.   The time hath been,
Would you have been so brief with him, he would
Have been so brief with you, to shorten you,
For taking so the head,° your whole head's length.

    BOLING. Mistake not, Uncle, further than you
        should.   15

    YORK. Take not, good Cousin, further than you
        should,
Lest you mistake the heavens are o'er our heads.

    BOLING. I know it, Uncle, and oppose not myself
Against their will. But who comes here?
[*Enter* HENRY PERCY.] Welcome, Harry. What, will
        not this castle yield?   20

    H. PERCY. The castle royally is manned, my lord,
Against thy entrance.

    BOLING. Royally!
Why, it contains no king?

    H. PERCY.   Yes, my good lord,
It doth contain a king. King Richard lies   25
Within the limits of yon lime and stone.
And with him are the Lord Aumerle, Lord Salis-
        bury,
Sir Stephen Scroop, besides a clergyman
Of holy reverence, who, I cannot learn.

    NORTH. Oh, belike it is the Bishop of Carlisle.   30

    BOLING. Noble lords,
Go to the rude ribs° of that ancient castle.
Through brazen trumpet send the breath of parley°
Into his ruined ears, and thus deliver.
Henry Bolingbroke   35
On both his knees doth kiss King Richard's hand
And sends allegiance and true faith of heart
To his most royal person, hither come
Even at his feet to lay my arms and power

Sc. iii: 14. head: title.   **32. rude ribs:** rough walls.   **33. parley:**
summons to parley.

Provided that my banishment repealed°   40
And lands restored again be freely granted.
If not, I'll use the advantage of my power
And lay the summer's dust with showers of blood
Rained from the wounds of slaughtered English-
    men.
The which, how far off from the mind of Boling-
    broke   45
It is such crimson tempest should bedrench
The fresh green lap of fair King Richard's land,
My stooping duty° tenderly shall show.
Go, signify as much while here we march
Upon the grassy carpet of this plain.   50
Let's march without the noise of threatening drum,
That from this castle's tattered° battlements
Our fair appointments° may be well perused.
Methinks King Richard and myself should meet
With no less terror than the elements   55
Of fire and water° when their thundering shock
At meeting tears the cloudy cheeks of heaven.
Be he the fire, I'll be the yielding water.
The rage be his, whilst on the earth I rain
My waters — on the earth, and not on him.   60
March on, and mark King Richard how he looks.
[Parle° without, and answer within. Then a flourish.
    Enter on the walls, KING RICHARD, *the* BISHOP OF
    CARLISLE, AUMERLE, SCROOP, *and* SALISBURY.]
See, see, King Richard doth himself appear,
As doth the blushing discontented sun
From out the fiery portal of the east
When he perceives the envious clouds are bent   65
To dim his glory and to stain the track
Of his bright passage to the Occident.
    YORK. Yet looks he like a king. Behold, his eye,
As bright as is the eagle's, lightens forth
Controlling majesty.° Alack, alack, for woe,   70
That any harm should stain so fair a show!
    K. RICH. [*To* NORTHUMBERLAND] We° are amazed,
        and thus long have we stood
To watch the fearful bending of thy knee,
Because we thought ourself thy lawful king.
And if we be, how dare thy joints forget   75
To pay their awful° duty to our presence?
If we be not, show us the hand of God
That hath dismissed us from our stewardship;
For well we know no hand of blood and bone
Can gripe° the sacred handle of our scepter   80
Unless he do profane, steal, or usurp.
And though you think that all, as you have done,
Have torn their souls° by turning them from us,

And we are barren and bereft of friends,
Yet know my master, God Omnipotent,   85
Is mustering in His clouds on our behalf
Armies of pestilence; and they shall strike
Your children yet unborn and unbegot,
That lift your vassal° hands against my head
And threat the glory of my precious crown.   90
Tell Bolingbroke — for yond methinks he stands —
That every stride he makes upon my land
Is dangerous treason. He is come to open
The purple testament of bleeding war.°
But ere the crown he looks for live in peace,   95
Ten thousand bloody crowns of mothers' sons
Shall ill become the flower of England's face,
Change the complexion of her maid-pale peace
To scarlet indignation, and bedew
Her pastures' grass with faithful English blood.
    NORTH. The King of Heaven forbid our lord the
        King   101
Should so with civil° and uncivil° arms
Be rushed upon! Thy thrice noble cousin
Harry Bolingbroke doth humbly kiss thy hand.
And by the honorable tomb he swears   105
That stands upon your royal grandsire's bones,
And by the royalties of both your bloods,
Currents that spring from one most gracious head,
And by the buried hand of warlike Gaunt,
And by the worth and honor of himself,   110
Comprising all that may be sworn or said,
His coming hither hath no further scope
Than for his lineal royalties,° and to beg
Enfranchisement° immediate on his knees.
Which on thy royal party granted once,   115
His glittering arms he will commend° to rust,
His barbèd° steeds to stables, and his heart
To faithful service of your Majesty.
This swears he, as he is a prince, is just.
And as I am a gentleman, I credit him.   120
    K. RICH. Northumberland, say thus the King re-
        turns:
His noble cousin is right welcome hither,
And all the number of his fair demands
Shall be accomplished without contradiction.
With all the gracious utterance thou hast,   125
Speak to his gentle hearing kind commends.°
[*To* AUMERLE] We do debase ourselves, Cousin, do
    we not,
To look so poorly and to speak so fair?
Shall we call back Northumberland and send
Defiance to the traitor, and so die?   130

AUM. No, good my lord, let's fight with gentle
    words
Till time lend friends and friends their helpful
    swords.
  K. RICH. Oh, God, oh, God, that e'er this tongue of
    mine,
That laid the sentence of dread banishment
On yon proud man, should take it off again   135
With words of sooth!° Oh, that I were as great
As is my grief, or lesser than my name!
Or that I could forget what I have been,
Or not remember what I must be now!
Swell'st thou, proud heart? I'll give thee scope° to
    beat,   140
Since foes have scope to beat both thee and me.
  AUM. Northumberland comes back from Boling-
    broke.
  K. RICH. What must the King do now? Must he
    submit?
The King shall do it. Must he be deposed?
The King shall be contented. Must he lose   145
The name of king? O' God's name, let it go.
I'll give my jewels for a set of beads,°
My gorgeous palace for a hermitage,
My gay apparel for an almsman's° gown,
My figured° goblets for a dish of wood,   150
My scepter for a palmer's° walking-staff,
My subjects for a pair of carvèd saints,
And my large kingdom for a little grave,
A little little grave, an obscure grave.
Or I'll be buried in the King's highway,   155
Some way of common trade,° where subjects' feet
May hourly trample on their sovereign's head;
For on my heart they tread now whilst I live,
And buried once, why not upon my head?
Aumerle, thou weep'st, my tender-hearted cousin!
We'll make foul weather with despisèd tears,   161
Our sighs and they shall lodge° the summer corn
And make a dearth in this revolting land.
Or shall we play the wantons° with our woes,
And make some pretty match° with shedding tears?
As thus, to drop them still° upon one place   166
Till they have fretted° us a pair of graves
Within the earth, and, therein laid — there lies
Two kinsmen digged their graves with weeping
    eyes.
Would not this ill do well? Well, well, I see   170
I talk but idly, and you laugh at me.
Most mighty prince, my Lord Northumberland,
What says King Bolingbroke? Will His Majesty
Give Richard leave to live till Richard die?

You make a leg,° and Bolingbroke says aye.   175
  NORTH. My lord, in the base° court he doth at-
    tend°
To speak with you. May it please you to come down.
  K. RICH. Down, down I come, like glistering
    Phaëton,°
Wanting the manage° of unruly jades.°
In the base court? Base court, where kings grow
    base,   180
To come at traitors' calls and do them grace.
In the base court? Come down? Down, court!
    Down, King!
For night owls shriek where mounting larks should
    sing.   [*Exeunt from above.*]
  BOLING. What says His Majesty?
  NORTH.   Sorrow and grief of heart
Makes him speak fondly,° like a frantic man,   185
Yet he is come.
  [*Enter* KING RICHARD *and his attendants below.*]
  BOLING. Stand all apart,
And show fair duty to His Majesty.
                               [*He kneels down.*]
My gracious lord ——
  K. RICH. Fair Cousin, you debase your princely
    knee   190
To make the base earth proud with kissing it.
Me rather had° my heart might feel your love
Than my unpleasèd eye see your courtesy.
Up, Cousin, up. Your heart is up, I know,
Thus high at least, although your knee be low.   195
  BOLING. My gracious lord, I come but for mine
    own.
  K. RICH. Your own is yours, and I am yours, and
    all.
  BOLING. So far be mine, my most redoubted
    lord,
As my true service shall deserve your love.
  K. RICH. Well you deserve. They well deserve to
    have   200
That know the strong'st and surest way to get.
Uncle, give me your hands. Nay, dry your eyes.
Tears show their love, but want their remedies.°
Cousin, I am too young to be your father,
Though you are old enough to be my heir.   205
What you will have, I'll give, and willing too,
For do we must what force will have us do.
Set on toward London, Cousin, is it so?
  BOLING. Yea, my good lord.
  K. RICH.   Then I must not say no.
                           [*Flourish. Exeunt.*]

---

136. **sooth:** flattery. 140. **scope:** freedom. Here Richard plucks
open his garment. 147. **set of beads:** rosary. 149. **almsman:**
poor man living on charity. 150. **figured:** ornamented. See Pl.
20h. 151. **palmer:** pilgrim. 156. **trade:** tread. 162. **lodge:** beat
flat. 164. **play . . . wantons:** play frivolous tricks. 165. **match:**
competition. 166. **still:** continuously. 167. **fretted:** worn.

175. **make a leg:** curtsy. 176. **base:** lower or outer. **attend:**
wait. 178. **Phaëton:** the son of the sun. He tried to drive his
father's chariot, but the horses were too fierce for him and he was
thrown out. 179. **Wanting . . . manage:** lacking control. **jades:**
horses bad-tempered or in poor condition. 185. **fondly:** foolishly.
192. **Me . . . had:** I would rather. 203. **want . . . remedies:** can-
not remedy.

SCENE IV. *Langley. The* DUKE OF YORK'S
          garden.

[*Enter the* QUEEN *and two* LADIES.]
  QUEEN. What sport shall we devise here in this
    garden
To drive away the heavy thought of care?
  LADY. Madam, we'll play at bowls.°
  QUEEN. 'Twill make me think the world is full of
    rubs,
And that my fortune runs against the bias.   5
  LADY. Madam, we'll dance.
  QUEEN. My legs can keep no measure in delight
When my poor heart no measure° keeps in grief.
Therefore no dancing, girl, some other sport.
  LADY. Madam, we'll tell tales.   10
  QUEEN. Of sorrow or of joy?
  LADY.   Of either, madam.
  QUEEN. Of neither, girl.
For if of joy, being altogether wanting,
It doth remember° me the more of sorrow.
Or if of grief, being altogether had,   15
It adds more sorrow to my want of joy.
For what I have I need not to repeat,
And what I want it boots° not to complain.
  LADY. Madam, I'll sing.
  QUEEN.   'Tis well that thou hast cause.
But thou shouldst please me better wouldst thou
    weep.   20
  LADY. I could weep, madam, would it do you
    good.
  QUEEN. And I could sing would weeping do me
    good,
And never borrow any tear of thee.
[*Enter a* GARDENER, *and two* SERVANTS.] But stay,
    here come the gardeners.
Let's step into the shadow of these trees.   25
My wretchedness unto a row of pins,°
They'll talk of state,° for everyone doth so
Against a change.° Woe is forerun with woe.
             [QUEEN *and* LADIES *retire.*]
  GARD. Go, bind thou up yon dangling apricocks,°
Which, like unruly children, make their sire   30
Stoop with oppression of their prodigal° weight.
Give some supportance to the bending twigs.
Go thou, and like an executioner,
Cut off the heads of too-fast-growing sprays°
That look too lofty in our commonwealth.   35
All must be even° in our government.
You thus employed, I will go root away
The noisome weeds which without profit suck

The soil's fertility from wholesome flowers.
  SERV. Why should we in the compass of a pale°
Keep law and form and due proportion,   41
Showing, as in a model, our firm estate,
When our sea-wallèd garden, the whole land,
Is full of weeds, her fairest flowers choked up,
Her fruit trees all unpruned, her hedges ruined,   45
Her knots° disordered, and her wholesome herbs
Swarming with caterpillars?
  GARD.   Hold thy peace.
He that hath suffered° this disordered spring
Hath now himself met with the fall of leaf.
The weeds which his broad-spreading leaves did
    shelter,   50
That seemed in eating him to hold him up,
Are plucked up root and all by Bolingbroke.
I mean the Earl of Wiltshire, Bushy, Green.
  SERV. What, are they dead?
  GARD.   They are, and Bolingbroke
Hath seized the wasteful King. Oh, what pity is it
That he had not so trimmed and dressed his land
As we this garden! We at time of year   57
Do wound the bark, the skin of our fruit trees,
Lest, being overproud° in sap and blood,
With too much riches it confound° itself.   60
Had he done so to great and growing men,
They might have lived to bear and he to taste
Their fruits of duty. Superfluous branches
We lop away, that bearing boughs may live.
Had he done so, himself had borne the crown   65
Which waste of idle hours hath quite thrown down.
  SERV. What, think you then the King shall be de-
    posed?
  GARD. Depressed° he is already, and deposed
'Tis doubt° he will be. Letters came last night
To a dear friend of the good Duke of York's   70
That tell black tidings.
  QUEEN. Oh, I am pressed to death° through want
    of speaking!   [*Coming forward.*]
Thou, old Adam's° likeness, set to dress this garden,
How dares thy harsh rude tongue sound this un-
    pleasing news?
What Eve, what serpent, hath suggested° thee   75
To make a second fall of cursèd man?
Why dost thou say King Richard is deposed?
Darest thou, thou little better thing than earth,
Divine° his downfall? Say where, when, and how
Camest thou by this ill tidings? Speak, thou wretch.
  GARD. Pardon me, madam. Little joy have I   81
To breathe this news, yet what I say is true.

Sc. iv: 3-5. bowls . . . rubs . . . bias: See App. 13. 7-8.
measure . . . measure: formal dance . . . limit. 14. remember:
remind. 18. boots: is of advantage. 26. My . . . pins: i.e., I'll
wager my misery against a trifle. 27. talk of state: discuss pol-
itics. 28. Against a change: in anticipation of revolution.
29. apricocks: apricots. 31. prodigal: extravagant. 34. sprays:
sprigs. 36. even: level, tidy.

40. compass . . . pale: limits of an enclosed park or garden.
46. knots: flowerbeds, often laid out in "knots" or fancy
shapes. See Pl. 16a. 48. suffered: allowed. 59. overproud: too
luxuriant. 60. confound: destroy. 68. Depressed: humbled.
69. 'Tis doubt: no doubt. 72. pressed to death: See Gen. Intro.
p. 27b. 73. old Adam: for Adam was the first gardener, as the
Gravedigger observed. See *Haml.*, V.i.33-44. 75. suggested:
prompted. 79. Divine: foretell by divination.

King Richard, he is in the mighty hold°
Of Bolingbroke. Their fortunes both are weighed.
In your lord's scale is nothing but himself,   85
And some few vanities that make him light;
But in the balance of great Bolingbroke,
Besides himself, are all the English peers,
And with that odds he weighs King Richard down.
Post you to London, and you will find it so.   90
I speak no more than everyone doth know.

    QUEEN. Nimble mischance, that art so light of
        foot,
Doth not thy embassage belong to me,°
And am I last that knows it? Oh, thou think'st
To serve me last, that I may longest keep   95
Thy sorrow in my breast. Come, ladies, go,
To meet at London London's King in woe.
What, was I born to this, that my sad look
Should grace the triumph of great Bolingbroke?
Gardener, for telling me these news of woe,   100
Pray God the plants thou graft'st may never grow.
                 [*Exeunt* QUEEN *and* LADIES.]

    GARD. Poor Queen! So that thy state might be no
       worse,
I would my skill were subject to thy curse.
Here did she fall° a tear; here in this place
I'll set a bank of rue,° sour herb of grace.   105
Rue, even for ruth,° here shortly shall be seen,
In the remembrance of a weeping Queen.
                      [*Exeunt.*]

Act IV

SCENE I. *Westminster Hall.*

[*Enter as to the Parliament,* BOLINGBROKE, AUMERLE,
NORTHUMBERLAND, PERCY, FITZWATER, SURREY, *the*
BISHOP OF CARLISLE, *the* ABBOT OF WESTMINSTER, *and
another* LORD, HERALD, OFFICERS, *and* BAGOT.]

    BOLING. Call forth Bagot.
Now, Bagot, freely speak thy mind. —
What thou dost know of noble Gloucester's death,
Who wrought it with° the King, and who per-
     formed
The bloody office of his timeless° end.   5
    BAGOT. Then set before my face the Lord Aumerle.
    BOLING. Cousin, stand forth, and look upon that
man.
    BAGOT. My Lord Aumerle, I know your daring
tongue

Scorns to unsay what once it hath delivered.
In that dead° time when Gloucester's death was
     plotted,   10
I heard you say, " Is not my arm of length,
That reacheth from the restful° English Court
As far as Calais, to mine uncle's head? "
Amongst much other talk, that very time,
I heard you say that you had rather refuse   15
The offer of a hundred thousand crowns
Than Bolingbroke's return° to England,
Adding withal, how blest this land would be
In this your cousin's death.
    AUM.   Princes and noble lords,
What answer shall I make to this base man?   20
Shall I so much dishonor my fair stars°
On equal terms to give him chastisement?
Either I must, or have mine honor soiled
With the attainder° of his slanderous lips.
There is my gage,° the manual seal° of death   25
That marks thee out for Hell. I say thou liest,
And will maintain what thou hast said is false
In thy heartblood, though being° all too base
To stain the temper° of my knightly sword.   29
    BOLING. Bagot, forbear. Thou shalt not take it up.
    AUM. Excepting one,° I would he were the best
In all this presence that hath moved me so.
    FITZ. If that thy valor stand on sympathy,°
There is my gage, Aumerle, in gage to thine.
By that fair sun which shows me where thou stand'st
I heard thee say, and vauntingly thou spakest it,   36
That thou wert cause of noble Gloucester's death.
If thou deny'st it twenty times, thou liest.
And I will turn thy falsehood to thy heart,
Where it was forgèd, with my rapier's point.   40
    AUM. Thou darest not, coward, live to see that day.
    FITZ. Now, by my soul, I would it were this hour.
    AUM. Fitzwater, thou art damned to Hell for this.
    H. PERCY. Aumerle, thou liest. His honor is as true
In this appeal as thou art all unjust.   45
And that thou art so, there I throw my gage,
To prove it on thee to the extremest point
Of mortal breathing.° Seize it, if thou darest.
    AUM. An if I do not, may my hands rot off
And never brandish more revengeful steel   50
Over the glittering helmet of my foe!
    LORD. I task the earth to the like,° forsworn
     Aumerle,
And spur thee on with full as many lies
As may be holloed in thy treacherous ear

---

83. **hold:** grasp.   93. **embassage . . . me:** should not your message have been delivered to me.   104. **fall:** let fall.   105. **rue:** called also "herb of grace," because *rue* means "repent." 106. **ruth:** pity.

    Act IV, Sc. i: 4. **wrought it with:** persuaded.   5. **timeless:** untimely.

10. **dead:** deadly.   12. **restful:** peaceful.   17. **Than . . . return:** than have Bolingbroke return.   21. **fair stars:** good fortune. 24. **attainder:** dishonorable accusation.   25. **gage:** pledge; i.e., glove. See I.i.67–74. **manual seal:** sealed warrant. 28. **though being:** although you are.   29. **temper:** lit., hardness.   31. **Excepting one:** with one exception; i.e., Bolingbroke. 33. **If . . . sympathy:** if you are so proud that you will only fight with an equal. **sympathy:** equality.   47–48. **to . . . breathing:** to your last breath.   52. **I . . . like:** I charge the earth to bear my gage too.

From sun to sun. There is my honor's pawn.°   55
Engage it° to the trial, if thou darest.
   AUM. Who sets° me else? By Heaven, I'll throw
  at all.
I have a thousand spirits in one breast,
To answer twenty thousand such as you.
   SURREY. My Lord Fitzwater, I do remember well
The very time Aumerle and you did talk.   61
   FITZ. 'Tis very true. You were in presence° then,
And you can witness with me this is true.
   SURREY. As false, by Heaven, as Heaven itself is
  true.
   FITZ. Surrey, thou liest.
   SURREY.   Dishonorable boy!   65
That lie shall lie so heavy on my sword
That it shall render vengeance and revenge
Till thou the lie-giver and that lie do lie
In earth as quiet as thy father's skull.
In proof whereof, there is my honor's pawn.   70
Engage it to the trial, if thou darest.
   FITZ. How fondly dost thou spur a forward horse!
If I dare eat, or drink, or breathe, or live,
I dare meet Surrey in a wilderness,°
And spit upon him whilst I say he lies,   75
And lies, and lies. There is my bond of faith,°
To tie thee to my strong correction.
As I intend to thrive in this new world,°
Aumerle is guilty of my true appeal.°
Besides, I heard the banished Norfolk say   80
That thou, Aumerle, didst send two of thy men
To execute the noble Duke at Calais.
   AUM. Some honest Christian trust me with a gage
That Norfolk lies. Here do I throw down this,
If he may be repealed,° to try his honor.   85
   BOLING. These differences shall all rest under gage
Till Norfolk be repealed. Repealed he shall be
And, though mine enemy, restored again
To all his lands and signories. When he's returned,
Against Aumerle we will enforce his trial.   90
   CAR. That honorable day shall ne'er be seen.
Many a time hath banished Norfolk fought
For Jesu Christ in glorious Christian field,
Streaming the ensign° of the Christian cross
Against black pagans, Turks, and Saracens;   95
And toiled° with works of war, retired himself
To Italy, and there at Venice gave
His body to that pleasant country's earth
And his pure soul unto his captain Christ,
Under whose colors he had fought so long.   100
   BOLING. Why, Bishop, is Norfolk dead?

   CAR. As surely as I live, my lord.
   BOLING. Sweet peace conduct his sweet soul to the
  bosom
Of good old Abraham!° Lords appellants,°
Your differences shall all rest under gage   105
Till we assign you to your days of trial.
            [Enter YORK, attended.]
   YORK. Great Duke of Lancaster, I come to thee
From plume-plucked° Richard, who with willing
  soul
Adopts thee heir, and his high scepter yields
To the possession of thy royal hand.   110
Ascend his throne, descending now from him,
And long live Henry, fourth of that name!
   BOLING. In God's name, I'll ascend the regal
  throne.
   CAR. Marry,° God forbid!
Worst in this royal presence may I speak,°   115
Yet best beseeming me to speak the truth.
Would God that any in this noble presence
Were enough noble to be upright judge
Of noble Richard! Then true noblesse would
Learn him forbearance from so foul a wrong.   120
What subject can give sentence on his king?
And who sits here that is not Richard's subject?
Thieves are not judged but they are by to hear,
Although apparent° guilt be seen in them.
And shall the figure of God's majesty,   125
His captain, steward, deputy elect,
Anointed, crowned, planted many years,
Be judged by subject and inferior breath,
And he himself not present? Oh, forfend° it, God,
That in a Christian climate souls refined   130
Should show so heinous, black, obscene a deed!
I speak to subjects, and a subject speaks,
Stirred up by God, thus boldly for his King.
My Lord of Hereford° here, whom you call King,
Is a foul traitor to proud Hereford's King.°   135
And if you crown him, let me prophesy,°
The blood of English shall manure the ground
And future ages groan for this foul act.
Peace shall go sleep with Turks and infidels,
And in this seat of peace tumultuous wars   140
Shall kin with kin and kind with kind° confound.

---

55. honor's pawn: pledge of my honor. 56. Engage it: make a
gage of it; i.e., accept it as a token of challenge. 57. sets: chal-
lenges. 62. in presence: in Court. See I.iii.289. 74. in a wil-
derness: i.e., a place where there is no escape. 76. bond of
faith: pledge. 78. new world: i.e., under Bolingbroke my
new King. 79. appeal: accusation. 85. repealed: called back
from banishment. 94. Streaming . . . ensign: flying the flag.
96. toiled: overwearied.

103-04. bosom . . . Abraham: i.e., Paradise. The phrase is from
the parable of Dives and Lazarus (Luke 16:22): "And it came to
pass that the beggar died, and was carried by the angels into
Abraham's bosom." 104. Lords appellants: accusing lords.
108. plume-plucked: crestfallen. 114. Marry: Mary, by the
Virgin. 115. Worst . . . speak: I am the worst speaker in this
royal assembly. 124. apparent: open. 129. forfend: forbid.
134. Hereford: i.e., Bolingbroke. 135. proud . . . King: i.e.,
Richard, the true King. 136. let me prophesy: Carlisle ex-
presses the theme of the whole series of Shakespeare's history
plays from Richard II to Richard III: that by wrongfully
seizing the throne of England the House of Lancaster caused
civil war in England for nearly a century. 141. kin . . . kind:
both words mean much the same, but puns on kin (of the same
family) and kind (nature) are common.

Disorder, horror, fear, and mutiny
Shall here inhabit, and this land be called
The field of Golgotha° and dead men's skulls.
Oh, if you raise this house against this house,   145
It will the woefulest division prove
That ever fell upon this cursèd earth.
Prevent it, resist it, let it not be so,
Lest child, child's children, cry against you " Woe "!
    NORTH. Well have you argued, sir, and, for your
        pains,   150
Of capital treason° we arrest you here.
My Lord of Westminster, be it your charge
To keep him safely till his day of trial.
May it please you, lords, to grant the commons' suit?
    BOLING. Fetch hither Richard, that in common
        view   155
He may surrender. So we shall proceed
Without suspicion.
    YORK.   I will be his conduct.   [*Exit.*]
    BOLING. Lords, you that here are under our arrest,
Procure your sureties° for your days of answer.
Little are we beholding to your love,   160
And little looked for at your helping hands.
[*Re-enter* YORK, *with* RICHARD, *and* OFFICERS *bearing
        the regalia.*]
    K. RICH. Alack, why am I sent for to a king
Before I have shook off the regal thoughts
Wherewith I reigned? I hardly yet have learned
To insinuate, flatter, bow, and bend my limbs.   165
Give sorrow leave awhile to tutor me
To this submission. Yet I well remember
The favors° of these men. Were they not mine?
Did they not sometime° cry " All hail! " to me?
So Judas did to Christ. But He in twelve   170
Found truth in all but one, I in twelve thousand,
        none.
God save the King! Will no man say amen?
Am I both priest and clerk?° Well then, amen.
God save the King! although I be not he,
And yet, amen if Heaven do think him me.   175
To do what service am I sent for hither?
    YORK. To do that office of thine own goodwill
Which tired majesty° did make thee offer,
The resignation of thy state and crown
To Henry Bolingbroke.   180
    K. RICH. Give me the crown. Here, Cousin, seize
        the crown.
Here, Cousin —
On this side my hand, and on that side yours.
Now is this golden crown like a deep well
That owes° two buckets, filling one another,   185

The emptier ever dancing in the air,
The other down, unseen and full of water.
That bucket down and full of tears am I,
Drinking my griefs whilst you mount up on high.
    BOLING. I thought you had been willing to resign.
    K. RICH. My crown I am, but still my griefs are
        mine.   191
You may my glories and my state depose.
But not my griefs. Still am I king of those.
    BOLING. Part of your cares you give me with your
        crown.
    K. RICH. Your cares° set up do not pluck my cares
        down.   195
My care is loss of care, by old care done.
Your care is gain of care, by new care won.
The cares I give I have, though given away.
They tend° the crown, yet still with me they stay.
    BOLING. Are you contented to resign the crown?
    K. RICH. Aye, no — no, aye, for I° must nothing
        be,   201
Therefore no no, for I resign to thee.
Now mark me how I will undo myself.
I give this heavy weight from off my head
And this unwieldy scepter from my hand,   205
The pride of kingly sway from out my heart.
With mine own tears I wash away my balm,
With mine own hands I give away my crown,
With mine own tongue deny my sacred state,
With mine own breath release all duty's rites.° 210
All pomp and majesty I do forswear,
My manors, rents, revénues I forgo,
My acts, decrees, and statutes I deny.
God pardon all oaths that are broke to me!
God keep all vows unbroke that swear to thee!   215
Make me, that nothing have, with nothing grieved,
And thou with all pleased, that hast all achieved!
Long mayst thou live in Richard's seat to sit,
And soon lie Richard in an earthy pit!
God save King Harry, unkinged Richard says,   220
And send him many years of sunshine days!
What more remains?
    NORTH. No more, but that you read
These accusations and these grievous crimes
Committed by your person and your followers
Against the state° and profit of this land,   225
That, by confessing them, the souls of men
May deem that you are worthily deposed.
    K. RICH. Must I do so? And must I ravel out°
My weaved-up folly? Gentle Northumberland,
If thy offenses were upon recórd,   230
Would it not shame thee in so fair a troop
To read a lecture of them? If thou wouldst,

---

144. **Golgotha:** the "Place of a Skull," the scene of the Cruci-
fixion. 151. **capital treason:** treason which carries a death pen-
alty. 159. **sureties:** bail. 168. **favors:** faces. 169. **sometime:**
once. 173. **priest . . . clerk:** In services in the Church of Eng-
land the priest read out the prayers and the clerk pronounced the
"Amen" at the end. 178. **tired majesty:** weariness of ruling.
185. **owes:** owns.

195–98. **cares . . . cares:** Richard plays on the various meanings
of *care* — responsibility, duty, sorrow, anxiety. 199. **tend:** at-
tend, wait on. 201. **Aye . . . I:** Puns on *aye* and *I* are common,
and more marked in the early texts, where both are spelt "I."
210. **duty's rites:** signs of respect to a King. 225. **state:** settled
order. 228. **ravel out:** unweave.

There shouldst thou find one heinous article,
Containing the deposing of a king
And cracking the strong warrant of an oath,　235
Marked with a blot, damned in the book of Heaven.
Nay, all of you that stand and look upon
Whilst that my wretchedness doth bait° myself,
Though some of you with Pilate wash your hands,°
Showing an outward pity, yet you Pilates　240
Have here delivered me to my sour cross,
And water cannot wash away your sin.

NORTH. My lord, dispatch.° Read o'er these ar-
　ticles.

K. RICH. Mine eyes are full of tears, I cannot see.
And yet salt water blinds them not so much　245
But they can see a sort° of traitors here.
Nay, if I turn mine eyes upon myself,
I find myself a traitor with the rest;
For I have given here my soul's consent
To undeck the pompous body of a king,　250
Made glory base and sovereignty a slave,
Proud majesty a subject, state a peasant.

NORTH. My lord——

K. RICH. No lord of thine, thou haught° insulting
　man,
Nor no man's lord. I have no name, no title,　255
No, not that name was given me at the font,
But 'tis usurped. Alack the heavy day,
That I have worn so many winters out
And know not now what name to call myself!
Oh, that I were a mockery king of snow,　260
Standing before the sun of Bolingbroke
To melt myself away in water drops!
Good King, great King, and yet not greatly good,
An if my word be sterling° yet in England,
Let it command a mirror hither straight,　265
That it may show me what a face I have,
Since it is bankrupt of his majesty.

BOLING. Go some of you and fetch a looking-glass.
　　　　　　　　　　[Exit an ATTENDANT.]

NORTH. Read o'er this paper while° the glass doth
　come.

K. RICH. Fiend, thou torment'st me ere I come to
　Hell!　　　　　　　　　　　　270

BOLING. Urge it no more, my Lord Northumber-
　land.

NORTH. The commons will not then be satisfied.

K. RICH. They shall be satisfied. I'll read enough
When I do see the very book indeed
Where all my sins are writ, and that's myself.　275
[Re-enter ATTENDANT, with a glass.] Give me the
　glass, and therein will I read.
No deeper wrinkles yet? Hath sorrow struck
So many blows upon this face of mine
And made no deeper wounds? O flattering glass,

Like to my followers in prosperity,　280
Thou dost beguile me! Was this face the face°
That every day under his household roof
Did keep ten thousand men? Was this the face
That, like the sun, did make beholders wink?
Was this the face that faced so many follies,　285
And was at last outfaced by Bolingbroke?
A brittle glory shineth in this face —
As brittle as the glory is the face.
　　　　　[Dashes the glass against the ground.]
For there it is, cracked in a hundred shivers.°
Mark, silent King, the moral of this sport,°　290
How soon my sorrow hath destroyed my face.

BOLING. The shadow° of your sorrow hath de-
　stroyed
The shadow of your face.

K. RICH.　　　　　　　　Say that again.
The shadow of my sorrow! Ha! Let's see.
'Tis very true, my grief lies all within.　295
And these external manners of laments
Are merely shadows to the unseen grief
That swells with silence in the tortured soul.
There lies the substance, and I thank thee, King,
For thy great bounty, that not only givest　300
Me cause to wail, but teachest me the way
How to lament the cause. I'll beg one boon,°
And then be gone and trouble you no more.
Shall I obtain it?

BOLING.　　　　　　Name it, fair Cousin.

K. RICH. "Fair Cousin"? I am greater than a
　king.　　　　　　　　　　　305
For when I was a king, my flatterers
Were then but subjects. Being now a subject,
I have a King here to my flatterer.
Being so great, I have no need to beg.

BOLING. Yet ask.　　　　　　　　310

K. RICH. And shall I have?

BOLING. You shall.

K. RICH. Then give me leave to go.

BOLING. Whither?

K. RICH. Whither you will, so I were from your
　sights.　　　　　　　　　　315

BOLING. Go, some of you convey° him to the
　Tower.

K. RICH. Oh, good! Convey? Conveyers are you all
That rise thus nimbly by a true king's fall.
　　[Exeunt KING RICHARD, some LORDS, and a GUARD.]

BOLING. On Wednesday next we solemnly set
　down
Our coronation. Lords, prepare yourselves.　320
　　　　　[Exeunt all except the BISHOP OF CARLISLE,
　　　　　the ABBOT OF WESTMINSTER, and AUMERLE.]

281. Was . . . face: imitated from the famous line in Marlowe's
Dr. Faustus, "Was this the face that launched a thousand ships?"
289. shivers: splinters. 290. moral . . . sport: inner meaning of
this byplay. 292. shadow: reflection. 302. boon: favor.
316. convey: escort; but Richard (l. 317) puns on the slang
meaning of *convey* — steal.

238. bait: worry. 239. with . . . hands: See Matthew 27:24–25.
243. dispatch: make haste. 246. sort: gang. 254. haught:
haughty. 264. sterling: current. 269. while: until.

ABBOT. A woeful pageant have we here beheld.

CAR. The woe's to come. The children yet unborn
Shall feel this day as sharp to them as thorn.

AUM. You holy clergymen, is there no plot
To rid the realm of this pernicious blot?   325

ABBOT. My lord,
Before I freely speak my mind herein,
You shall not only take the sacrament
To bury mine intents,° but also to effect
Whatever I shall happen to devise.   330
I see your brows are full of discontent,
Your hearts of sorrow and your eyes of tears.
Come home with me to supper, and I'll lay
A plot shall show us all a merry day.   [*Exeunt.*]

Act V

SCENE I. *London. A street leading to the Tower.*

[*Enter* QUEEN *and* LADIES.]

QUEEN. This way the King will come. This is the
     way
To Julius Caesar's ill-erected tower,°
To whose flint bosom my condemnèd lord
Is doomed a prisoner by proud Bolingbroke.
Here let us rest, if this rebellious earth   5
Have any resting for her true king's queen.

[*Enter* RICHARD *and* GUARD.]

But soft, but see, or rather do not see,
My fair rose° wither. Yet look up, behold,
That you in pity may dissolve to dew
And wash him fresh again with truelove tears.   10
Ah, thou the model where old Troy did stand,°
Thou map of honor, thou King Richard's tomb,
And not King Richard, thou most beauteous inn,
Why should hard-favored grief be lodged in thee
When triumph is become an alehouse° guest?   15

K. RICH. Join not with grief, fair woman, do not so,
To make my end too sudden. Learn, good soul,
To think our former state a happy dream,
From which awaked, the truth of what we are
Shows us but this. I am sworn brother,° sweet,   20
To grim Necessity, and he and I

329. bury . . . intents: conceal my intentions.
Act V, Sc. i: 2. Julius . . . tower: See *Rich III*, III.i.68,n;
Gen. Intro. p. 16a; and Pl. 3a. ill-erected: erected for evil.
8. rose: addressed to Richard. The rose is often used as an emblem of beauty. See *Haml*, III.i.160 and *I Hen IV*, I.iii.175.
11. model . . . stand: a ruin, like Troy after the sack. model: pattern. 13–15. beauteous . . . alehouse: In this extravagant parallel she means that Richard is like an expensive hotel which entertains Sorrow, while Bolingbroke, though a mere beer parlor, entertains Triumph. 20. sworn brother: Knights about to undertake some perilous enterprise often swore to share everything alike.

Will keep a league till death. Hie thee to France
And cloister° thee in some religious house.
Our holy lives must win a new world's° crown,
Which our profane° hours here have stricken down.

QUEEN. What, is my Richard both in shape and
     mind   26
Transformed and weakened? Hath Bolingbroke de-
     posed
Thine intellect? Hath he been in thy heart?
The lion dying thrusteth forth his paw
And wounds the earth, if nothing else, with rage
To be o'erpowered. And wilt thou, pupil-like,   31
Take thy correction mildly, kiss the rod,
And fawn on rage with base humility,
Which art a lion and a king of beasts?

K. RICH. A king of beasts, indeed. If aught but
     beasts,   35
I had been still a happy king of men.
Good sometime Queen, prepare thee hence for
     France.
Think I am dead, and that even here thou takest,
As from my deathbed, thy last living leave.
In winter's tedious nights sit by the fire   40
With good old folks, and let them tell thee tales
Of woeful ages long ago betid.°
And ere thou bid good night, to quit their griefs,°
Tell thou the lamentable tale of me,
And send the hearers weeping to their beds.   45
For why,° the senseless brands° will sympathize°
The heavy accent of thy moving tongue,
And in compassion weep the fire out;
And some will mourn in ashes, some coal-black,
For the deposing of a rightful king.   50

[*Enter* NORTHUMBERLAND *and others.*]

NORTH. My lord, the mind of Bolingbroke is
     changed.
You must to Pomfret,° not unto the Tower.
And, madam, there is order ta'en for you.
With all swift speed you must away to France.

K. RICH. Northumberland, thou ladder where-
     withal   55
The mounting Bolingbroke ascends my throne,
The time shall not be many hours of age
More than it is, ere foul sin gathering head°
Shall break into corruption. Thou shalt think,
Though he divide the realm and give thee half,   60
It is too little, helping him to all.
And he shall think that thou, which know'st the way
To plant unrightful kings, wilt know again,
Being ne'er so little urged,° another way
To pluck him headlong from the usurped throne.

23. cloister: become a nun. 24. new world's: i.e., heavenly.
25. profane: worldly. 42. betid: befallen. 43. to . . . griefs: to
recompense them for their sad tales. 46. For why: because.
senseless brands: logs that have no feeling. sympathize: feel for.
5. Pomfret: Pontefract Castle, near York. See *Rich III*, III.
iii 9–14. 58. gathering head: i.e., like a boil about to burst.
64. urged: encouraged.

The love of wicked men converts° to fear, 66
That fear to hate, and hate turns one or both
To worthy danger and deservèd death.
   NORTH. My guilt be on my head, and there an end.
Take leave and part, for you must part forthwith.
   K. RICH. Doubly divorced! Bad men, you violate
A twofold marriage — 'twixt my crown and me,
And then betwixt me and my married wife.
Let me unkiss the oath 'twixt thee and me.°
And yet not so, for with a kiss 'twas made. 75
Part us, Northumberland, I toward the north,
Where shivering cold and sickness pines the clime,
My wife to France, from whence, set forth in pomp,
She came adornèd hither like sweet May,
Sent back like Hallowmas° or short'st of day. 80
   QUEEN. And must we be divided? Must we part?
   K. RICH. Aye, hand from hand, my love, and heart
     from heart.
   QUEEN. Banish us both and send the King with
     me. 83
   NORTH. That were some love but little policy.°
   QUEEN. Then whither he goes, thither let me go.
   K. RICH. So two, together weeping, make one
     woe.
Weep thou for me in France, I for thee here.
Better far off than near, be ne'er the near.°
Go, count thy way with sighs, I mine with groans.
   QUEEN. So longest way shall have the longest
     moans. 90
   K. RICH. Twice for one step I'll groan, the way
     being short,
And piece the way out with a heavy heart.
Come, come, in wooing sorrow let's be brief,
Since, wedding it, there is such length in grief.
One kiss shall stop our mouths, and dumbly part.
Thus give I mine, and thus take I thy heart. 96
   QUEEN. Give me mine own again. 'Twere no good
     part
To take on me to keep and kill thy heart.
So, now I have mine own again, be gone,
That I may strive to kill it with a groan. 100
   K. RICH. We make woe wanton° with this fond
     delay.
Once more, adieu. The rest let sorrow say.
                           [Exeunt.]

SCENE II. *The* DUKE OF YORK'S *palace.*

[*Enter* YORK *and his* DUCHESS.]
   DUCH. My lord, you told me you would tell the
     rest,

When weeping made you break the story off
Of our two cousins coming into London.
   YORK. Where did I leave?
   DUCH.   At that sad stop, my lord,
Where rude misgoverned° hands from windows'
     tops 5
Threw dust and rubbish on King Richard's head.
   YORK. Then, as I said, the Duke, great Boling-
     broke,
Mounted upon a hot and fiery steed
Which his aspiring° rider seemed to know,
With slow but stately pace kept on his course 10
Whilst all tongues cried "God save thee, Boling-
     broke!"
You would have thought the very windows spake,
So many greedy looks of young and old
Through casements darted their desiring eyes
Upon his visage, and that all the walls 15
With painted imagery had said at once°
"Jesu preserve thee! Welcome, Bolingbroke!"
Whilst he, from the one side to the other turning,
Bareheaded, lower than his proud steed's neck,
Bespake them thus; "I thank you, countrymen."
And thus still doing, thus he passed along. 21
   DUCH. Alack, poor Richard! Where rode he the
     whilst?
   YORK. As in a theater the eyes of men
After a well-graced actor leaves the stage
Are idly bent on him that enters next, 25
Thinking his prattle to be tedious,
Even so, or with much more contempt, men's eyes
Did scowl on gentle Richard. No man cried "God
     save him!"
No joyful tongue gave him his welcome home.
But dust was thrown upon his sacred head, 30
Which with such gentle sorrow he shook off,
His face still combating with tears and smiles,
The badges° of his grief and patience,
That had not God, for some strong purpose,
     steeled
The hearts of men, they must perforce have melted,
And barbarism itself° have pitied him. 36
But Heaven hath a hand in these events,
To whose high will we bound our calm contents.°
To Bolingbroke are we sworn subjects now,
Whose state and honor I for aye allow. 40
   DUCH. Here comes my son Aumerle.
   YORK.   Aumerle that was,
But that is lost for being Richard's friend,
And, madam, you must call him Rutland now.
I am in Parliament pledge for his truth
And lasting fealty to the new-made King. 45

---

66. **converts:** changes.   **74. unkiss . . . me:** unmake our marriage vow.   **80. Hallowmas:** All Saints' Day, November 1.   **84. policy:** political wisdom.   **88. Better . . . near:** better be widely separated, if we cannot be nearer to each other.   **101. wanton:** frivolous. See III.iii.164.

Sc. ii: 5. misgoverned: ill-behaved.   **9. aspiring:** ambitious.   **15–16. all . . . once:** as if the walls had been covered with painted figures that cried out.   **33. badges:** tokens.   **36. barbarism itself:** even barbarians.   **38. bound . . . contents:** we force ourselves to be calmly contented.

[*Enter* AUMERLE.]

DUCH. Welcome, my son. Who are the violets° now
That strew the green lap of the new-come spring?

AUM. Madam, I know not, nor I greatly care not.
God knows I had as lief be none as one.

YORK. Well, bear you well in this new spring of time,   50
Lest you be cropped before you come to prime.
What news from Oxford? Hold those justs° and tri-umphs?

AUM. For aught I know, my lord, they do.

YORK. You will be there, I know.

AUM. If God prevent not, I purpose so.   55

YORK. What seal is that that hangs without thy bosom?
Yea, look'st thou pale? Let me see the writing.

AUM. My lord, 'tis nothing.

YORK.   No matter, then, who see it.
I will be satisfied. Let me see the writing.

AUM. I do beseech your Grace to pardon me.   60
It is a matter of small consequence,
Which for some reasons I would not have seen.

YORK. Which for some reasons, sir, I mean to see.
I fear, I fear ——

DUCH.   What should you fear?
'Tis nothing but some bond that he is entered into°
For gay apparel 'gainst° the triumph day.   66

YORK. Bound to himself! What doth he with a bond
That he is bound to? Wife, thou art a fool.
Boy, let me see the writing.

AUM. I do beseech you pardon me, I may not show it.   70

YORK. I will be satisfied. Let me see it, I say.

[*He plucks it out of his bosom and reads it.*]
Treason! Foul treason! Villain! Traitor! Slave!

DUCH. What is the matter, my lord?

YORK. Ho! Who is within there?

[*Enter a* SERVANT.] Saddle my horse.
God for His mercy, what treachery is here!   75

DUCH. Why, what is it, my lord?

YORK. Give me my boots, I say, saddle my horse.

[*Exit* SERVANT.]
Now, by mine honor, by my life, by my troth,
I will appeach° the villain.

DUCH.   What is the matter?

YORK. Peace, foolish woman.   80

DUCH. I will not peace. What is the matter, Au-merle?

AUM. Good Mother, be content. It is no more
Than my poor life must answer.

DUCH.   Thy life answer!

YORK. Bring me my boots. I will unto the King.

[*Re-enter* SERVANT *with boots.*]

DUCH. Strike him, Aumerle. Poor boy, thou art amazed.°   85
Hence, villain! Never more come in my sight.

YORK. Give me my boots, I say.

DUCH. Why, York, what wilt thou do?
Wilt thou not hide the trespass of thine own?°
Have we more sons? Or are we like to have?   90
Is not my teeming date° drunk up with time?
And wilt thou pluck my fair son from mine age
And rob me of a happy mother's name?
Is he not like thee? Is he not thine own?

YORK. Thou fond mad woman,   95
Wilt thou conceal this dark conspiracy?
A dozen of them here have ta'en the sacrament,
And interchangeably set down their hands,°
To kill the King at Oxford.

DUCH.   He shall be none.
We'll keep him here. Then what is that to him?

YORK. Away, fond woman! Were he twenty times my son,   101
I would appeach him.

DUCH.   Hadst thou groaned for him
As I have done, thou wouldst be more pitiful.°
But now I know thy mind. Thou dost suspect
That I have been disloyal to thy bed,   105
And that he is a bastard, not thy son.
Sweet York, sweet husband, be not of that mind.
He is as like thee as a man may be,
Not like to me, or any of my kin,
And yet I love him.

YORK. Make way, unruly woman!   [*Exit.*]   110

DUCH. After, Aumerle! Mount thee upon his horse,
Spur post,° and get before him to the King
And beg thy pardon ere he do accuse thee.
I'll not be long behind. Though I be old,
I doubt not but to ride as fast as York.   115
And never will I rise up from the ground
Till Bolingbroke have pardoned thee. Away, be gone!   [*Exeunt.*]

SCENE III. *Windsor Castle.*

[*Enter* BOLINGBROKE, HENRY PERCY, *and other* LORDS.]

BOLING. Can no man tell me of my unthrifty son?°
'Tis full three months since I did see him last.
If any plague hang over us, 'tis he.
I would to God, my lords, he might be found.
Inquire at London, 'mongst the taverns there,   5

---

46. violets: i.e., Court favorites.   52. justs: tournaments.
65. entered into: i.e., that he has signed to borrow money.
66. 'gainst: against, in anticipation of.   79. appeach: accuse.

85. amazed: bewildered.   89. trespass . . . own: sin committed by your own son.   91. teeming date: period of childbearing.
98. interchangeably . . . hands: i.e., each party of the conspiracy holds a document signed by all the others. See App. 6 and Pl. 11a.
103. pitiful: full of pity.   112. Spur post: ride fast. See App. 17.
   Sc. iii: 1. unthrifty son: prodigal son; i.e., Prince Henry, after-ward Henry V.

For there, they say, he daily doth frequent
With unrestrainèd loose companions,°
Even such, they say, as stand in narrow lanes
And beat our watch° and rob our passengers.°
Which he, young wanton and effeminate° boy, 10
Takes on the° point of honor to support
So dissolute a crew.
  H. PERCY. My lord, some two days since I saw the
    Prince
And told him of those triumphs held at Oxford.
  BOLING. And what said the gallant? 15
  H. PERCY. His answer was, he would unto the
    stews,°
And from the common'st creature pluck a glove
And wear it as a favor, and with that
He would unhorse the lustiest challenger.
  BOLING. As dissolute as desperate, yet through
    both 20
I see some sparks of better hope, which elder years
May happily bring forth. But who comes here?
                [*Enter* AUMERLE.]
  AUM. Where is the King?
  BOLING. What means our cousin, that he stares
    and looks
So wildly? 25
  AUM. God save your Grace! I do beseech your
    Majesty
To have some conference with your Grace alone.
  BOLING. Withdraw yourselves, and leave us here
    alone.   [*Exeunt* PERCY *and* LORDS.]
What is the matter with our cousin now?
  AUM. Forever may my knees grow to the earth,
My tongue cleave to my roof within my mouth, 31
Unless a pardon ere I rise or speak.
  BOLING. Intended or committed was this fault?
If on the first,° how heinous e'er it be,
To win thy after-love I pardon thee. 35
  AUM. Then give me leave that I may turn the key,
That no man enter till my tale be done.
  BOLING. Have thy desire.
  YORK. [*Within.*°] My liege, beware, look to thy-
    self.
Thou hast a traitor in thy presence there. 40
  BOLING. Villain, I'll make thee safe. [*Drawing.*]
  AUM. Stay thy revengeful hand. Thou hast no
    cause to fear.
  YORK. [*Within.*] Open the door, secure,° fool-
    hardy King.
Shall I for love speak treason° to thy face?
Open the door, or I will break it open. 45
                [*Enter* YORK.]
  BOLING. What is the matter, Uncle? Speak.
Recover breath, tell us how near is danger,

That we may arm us to encounter it.
  YORK. Peruse this writing here and thou shalt
    know
The treason that my haste forbids me show. 50
  AUM. Remember, as thou read'st, thy promise
    passed.
I do repent me. Read not my name there,
My heart is not confederate° with my hand.
  YORK. It was, villain, ere thy hand did set it down.
I tore it from the traitor's bosom, King. 55
Fear, and not love, begets his penitence.
Forget to pity him, lest thy pity prove
A serpent that will sting thee to the heart.
  BOLING. Oh, heinous, strong, and bold conspiracy!
Oh, loyal father of a treacherous son! 60
Thou sheer, immaculate, and silver fountain
From whence this stream through muddy passages
Hath held his current and defiled himself!
Thy overflow of good converts to bad,
And thy abundant goodness shall excuse 65
This deadly blot in thy digressing° son.
  YORK. So shall my virtue be his vice's bawd,
And he shall spend mine honor with his shame
As thriftless sons their scraping fathers' gold.
Mine honor lives when his dishonor dies, 70
Or my shamed life in his dishonor lies.
Thou kill'st me in his life. Giving him breath,
The traitor lives, the true man's put to death.
  DUCH. [*Within.*] What ho, my liege! For God's
    sake, let me in.
  BOLING. What shrill-voiced suppliant makes this
    eager cry? 75
  DUCH. A woman, and thy aunt, great King — 'tis
    I.
Speak with me, pity me, open the door.
A beggar begs that never begged before.
  BOLING. Our scene is altered from a serious thing,
And now changed to " The Beggar and the King."°
My dangerous cousin, let your mother in. 81
I know she is come to pray for your foul sin.
  YORK. If thou do pardon, whosoever pray,
More sins for this forgiveness prosper may.
This festered joint cut off, the rest rest sound, 85
This let alone will all the rest confound.
           [*Enter* DUCHESS OF YORK.]
  DUCH. O King, believe not this hardhearted man!
Love loving not itself none other can.°
  YORK. Thou frantic woman, what dost thou
    make° here?
Shall thy old dugs once more a traitor rear? 90
  DUCH. Sweet York, be patient. Hear me, gentle
    liege.   [*Kneels.*]

---

7. **loose companions:** low company. 9. **watch:** See Gen. Intro.
p. 18a. **passengers:** passers-by. 10. **effeminate:** self-indulgent.
11. **Takes on the:** regards it as a. 16. **stews:** brothels. 34. **If
. . . first:** i.e., intended. 39. **s.d., within:** off stage. 43. **secure:**
careless. 44. **speak treason:** i.e., by calling you a fool.

53. **confederate:** fellow conspirator with. 66. **digressing:** erring.
79–80. **Our . . . King:** the tragedy is now turning into comedy
and should be called *The Beggar and the King*. 88. **Love . . .
can:** a man who cannot love his own son cannot love anyone
else. 89. **make:** do.

BOLING. Rise up, good Aunt.

DUCH.   Not yet, I thee beseech.
Forever will I walk upon my knees,
And never see day that the happy sees
Till thou give joy — until thou bid me joy   95
By pardoning Rutland, my transgressing boy.

AUM. Unto my mother's prayers I bend my knee.
                                 [*Kneels.*]

YORK. Against them both my true joints bended
   be.   [*Kneels.*]
Ill mayst thou thrive if thou grant any grace!   99

DUCH. Pleads he in earnest? Look upon his face.
His eyes do drop no tears, his prayers are in jest,
His words come from his mouth, ours from our
   breast.
He prays but faintly and would be denied,
We pray with heart and soul and all beside.
His weary joints would gladly rise, I know,   105
Our knees shall kneel till to the ground they grow.
His prayers are full of false hypocrisy,
Ours of true zeal and deep integrity.
Our prayers do outpray his, then let them have
That mercy which true prayer ought to have.   110

BOLING. Good Aunt, stand up.

DUCH.   Nay, do not say " Stand up,"
Say " Pardon " first, and afterward " Stand up."
An if I were thy nurse, thy tongue to teach,
" Pardon " should be the first word of thy speech.
I never longed to hear a word till now.   115
Say " Pardon," King, let pity teach thee how.
The word is short, but not so short as sweet;
No word like " pardon " for kings' mouths so meet.

YORK. Speak it in French, king, say, " *Pardonne-
moi.*"°

DUCH. Dost thou teach pardon pardon to destroy?
Ah, my sour husband, my hardhearted lord,   121
That set'st the word itself against the word!
Speak " pardon " as 'tis current in our land,°
The chopping° French we do not understand.
Thine eye begins to speak, set thy tongue there.   125
Or in thy piteous heart plant thou thine ear,
That hearing how our plaints and prayers do pierce,
Pity may move thee " pardon " to rehearse.°

BOLING. Good Aunt, stand up.

DUCH.   I do not sue to stand.
Pardon is all the suit I have in hand.   130

BOLING. I pardon him, as God shall pardon me.

DUCH. Oh, happy vantage° of a kneeling knee!
Yet am I sick for fear. Speak it again.
Twice saying " pardon " doth not pardon twain,
But makes one pardon strong.

BOLING.   With all my heart   135
I pardon him.

---

119. **Pardonne-moi:** excuse me; *moi* was pronounced "moy."
123. **current . . . land:** i.e., with the English meaning. 124. **chop-
ping:** changing the meaning. 128. **rehearse:** repeat. 132. **van-
tage:** superior position, advantage.

DUCH.   A god on earth thou art.

BOLING. But for our trusty brother-in-law, and the
   Abbot,
With all the rest of that consorted crew,°
Destruction straight shall dog them at the heels.
Good Uncle, help to order several powers°   140
To Oxford, or where'er these traitors are.
They shall not live within this world, I swear,
But I will have them, if I once know where.
Uncle, farewell, and Cousin too, adieu.   144
Your mother well hath prayed, and prove you true.°

DUCH. Come, my old son. I pray God make thee
   new.   [*Exeunt.*]

SCENE IV. *The same.*

[*Enter* EXTON *and* SERVANT.]

EXTON. Didst thou not mark the King, what
   words he spake —
" Have I no friend will rid me of this living fear? "
Was it not so?

SERV.   These were his very words.

EXTON. " Have I no friend? " quoth he. He spake
   it twice,
And urged it twice together, did he not?   5

SERV. He did.

EXTON. And speaking it, he wistly° looked on me,
As who should say, " I would thou wert the man
That would divorce this terror from my heart,"
Meaning the King at Pomfret. Come, let's go.   10
I am the King's friend, and will rid his foe.
                                 [*Exeunt.*]

SCENE V. *Pomfret Castle.*

[*Enter* KING RICHARD.]

K. RICH. I have been studying how I may compare
This prison where I live unto the world.
And for because the world is populous,
And here is not a creature but myself,
I cannot do it, yet I'll hammer it out.   5
My brain I'll prove the female to my soul,
My soul the father, and these two beget
A generation of still breeding° thoughts,
And these same thoughts people this little world
In humors° like the people of this world,   10
For no thought is contented. The better sort,
As thoughts of things divine, are intermixed
With scruples,° and do set the word itself
Against the word.

---

138. **consorted crew:** crew of conspirators. 140. **powers:** forces.
145. **prove . . . true:** may you prove true.
   Sc. iv: 7. **wistly:** wistfully.
   Sc. v: 8. **still breeding:** ever breeding. 10. **humors:** varieties
of temperament. See App. 3. 13. **scruples:** religious doubts.

As thus, "Come, little ones," and then again,   15
"It is as hard to come as for a camel
To thread the postern° of a small needle's eye."
Thoughts tending to ambition, they do plot
Unlikely wonders — how these vain weak nails
May tear a passage through the flinty ribs   20
Of this hard world, my ragged° prison walls,
And, for they cannot, die in their own pride.
Thoughts tending to content flatter themselves
That they are not the first of fortune's slaves,°
Nor shall not be the last, like silly beggars   25
Who sitting in the stocks° refuge their shame,°
That many have and others must sit there.
And in this thought they find a kind of ease,
Bearing their own misfortunes on the back
Of such as have before endured the like.   30
Thus play I in one person many people,
And none contented. Sometimes am I King,
Then treasons make me wish myself a beggar,
And so I am. Then crushing penury
Persuades me I was better when a king.   35
Then am I kinged again. And by and by
Think that I am unkinged by Bolingbroke,
And straight am nothing. But whate'er I be,
Nor I nor any man that but man is
With nothing shall be pleased till he be eased   40
With being nothing. Music do I hear? [Music.]
Ha, ha! Keep time. How sour sweet music is
When time is broke and no proportion° kept!
So is it in the music of men's lives.
And here have I the daintiness of ear   45
To check time broke in a disordered string,°
But for the concord of my state and time
Had not an ear to hear my true time broke.
I wasted time, and now doth time waste me.   49
For now hath Time made me his numbering° clock.
My thoughts are minutes, and with sighs they jar°
Their watches on unto mine eyes, the outward
    watch,
Whereto my finger, like a dial's point,
Is pointing still, in cleansing them from tears.
Now, sir, the sound that tells what hour it is   55
Are clamorous groans, which strike upon my heart,
Which is the bell. So sighs and tears and groans
Show minutes, times, and hours. But my time
Runs posting on in Bolingbroke's proud joy
While I stand fooling here, his Jack-o'-the-clock.°
This music mads me, let it sound no more,   61
For though it have holp° madmen to their wits,°
In me it seems it will make wise men mad.

Yet blessing on his heart that gives it me!
For 'tis a sign of love, and love to Richard   65
Is a strange brooch° in this all-hating world.
            [Enter a GROOM OF THE STABLE.]
    GROOM. Hail, royal Prince!
    K. RICH.   Thanks, noble peer.°
The cheapest of us is ten groats too dear.°
What art thou? And how comest thou hither,
Where no man never comes but that sad dog   70
That brings me food to make misfortune live?
    GROOM. I was a poor groom of thy stable, King,
When thou wert king, who, traveling toward York,
With much ado at length have gotten leave
To look upon my sometimes royal master's face.   75
Oh, how it yearned° my heart when I beheld
In London streets, that coronation day,
When Bolingbroke rode on roan Barbary,
That horse that thou so often hast bestrid,
That horse that I so carefully have dressed!   80
    K. RICH. Rode he on Barbary? Tell me, gentle
        friend,
How went he under him?
    GROOM. So proudly as if he disdained the ground.
    K. RICH. So proud that Bolingbroke was on his
        back!
That jade° hath eat bread from my royal hand,   85
This hand hath made him proud with clapping
        him.
Would he not stumble? Would he not fall down,
Since pride must have a fall, and break the neck
Of that proud man that did usurp his back?
Forgiveness, horse! Why do I rail on thee,   90
Since thou, created to be awed by man,
Wast born to bear? I was not made a horse,
And yet I bear a burden like an ass,
Spurred, galled, and tired by jauncing° Bolingbroke.
            [Enter KEEPER, with a dish.]
    KEEP. Fellow, give place. Here is no longer stay.
    K. RICH. If thou love me, 'tis time thou wert away.
    GROOM. What my tongue dares not, that my heart
        shall say.   [Exit.]
    KEEP. My lord, will't please you to fall to?
    K. RICH. Taste of it first, as thou art wont to do.   99
    KEEP. My lord, I dare not. Sir Pierce of Exton,
who lately came from the King, commands the con-
trary.
    K. RICH. The Devil take Henry of Lancaster and
        thee!
Patience is stale, and I am weary of it.
            [Beats the KEEPER.]
    KEEP. Help, help, help!   105

17. postern: small door. 21. ragged: rough. 24. slaves: i.e., victims. 26. stocks: a form of punishment for minor offenses, the offender having his legs padlocked in the holes of a board. refuge . . . shame: excuse their disgrace. 43. proportion: harmony. 46. check . . . string: trouble about music played out of tune. 50. numbering: telling the time. 51. jar: tick. 60. Jack-o'-the-clock: See *Rich III*, IV.ii.117. 62. holp: helped. madmen . . . wits: The Greeks used music as a remedy for certain kinds of madness.

66. brooch: ornament; i.e., kindness. 67. noble peer: Richard replies ironically to "royal Prince" by calling the groom a noble peer (lit., equal). 68. ten . . . dear: a royal or rose noble was a gold coin of Edward II worth 10s; the noble was worth 6s 8d — less by ten groats (4d). 76. yearned: grieved. 85. jade: See III.iii.179. 94. jauncing: stirring up his horse to restless prancing.

[*Enter* EXTON *and* SERVANTS, *armed.*]

K. RICH. How now! What means death in this
    rude assault?
Villain, thy own hand yields thy death's instrument.
    [*Snatching an ax from a* SERVANT *and killing him.*]
Go thou, and fill another room in Hell.
    [*He kills another. Then* EXTON *strikes him down.*]
That hand shall burn in never-quenching fire
That staggers° thus my person. Exton, thy fierce
    hand   110
Hath with the King's blood stained the King's own
    land.
Mount, mount, my soul! Thy seat is up on high,
Whilst my gross flesh sinks downward, here to die.
                         [*Dies.*]

EXTON. As full of valor as of royal blood.
Both have I spilled — oh, would the deed were
    good!   115
For now the Devil, that told me I did well,
Says that this deed is chronicled in Hell.
This dead King to the living King I'll bear.
Take hence the rest, and give them burial here.
                     [*Exeunt.*]

SCENE VI. *Windsor Castle.*

[*Flourish. Enter* BOLINGBROKE, YORK, *with other*
LORDS, *and* ATTENDANTS.]

BOLING. Kind Uncle York, the latest news we hear
Is that the rebels have consumed with fire
Our town of Cicester° in Gloucestershire,
But whether they be ta'en or slain we hear not.
[*Enter* NORTHUMBERLAND.] Welcome, my lord.
    What is the news?   5
NORTH. First, to thy sacred state wish I all happi-
    ness.
The next news is, I have to London sent
The heads of Oxford, Salisbury, Blunt, and Kent.
The manner of their taking may appear
At large discoursèd in this paper here.   10
BOLING. We thank thee, gentle Percy, for thy
    pains,
And to thy worth will add right worthy gains.

110. staggers: makes stagger.
  Sc. vi: 3. Cicester: local pronunciation of Cirencester, an an-
cient town in Gloucestershire.

[*Enter* FITZWATER.]

FITZ. My lord, I have from Oxford sent to London
The heads of Brocas and Sir Bennet Seely,
Two of the dangerous consorted traitors   15
That sought at Oxford thy dire overthrow.
BOLING. Thy pains, Fitzwater, shall not be forgot,
Right noble is thy merit, well I wot.
[*Enter* HENRY PERCY, *and the* BISHOP OF CARLISLE.]
H. PERCY. The grand conspirator, Abbot of West-
    minster,
With clog° of conscience and sour melancholy   20
Hath yielded up his body to the grave.
But here is Carlisle living, to abide
Thy kingly doom and sentence of his pride.
BOLING. Carlisle, this is your doom.
Choose out some secret place, some reverend room,°
More than thou hast, and with it joy° thy life.   26
So as thou livest in peace, die free from strife.
For though mine enemy thou hast ever been,
High sparks of honor in thee have I seen.
    [*Enter* EXTON, *with persons bearing a coffin.*]
EXTON. Great King, within this coffin I present
Thy buried fear. Herein all breathless lies   31
The mightiest of thy greatest enemies,
Richard of Bordeaux, by me hither brought.
BOLING. Exton, I thank thee not, for thou hast
    wrought
A deed of slander with thy fatal hand   35
Upon my head and all this famous land.
EXTON. From your own mouth, my lord, did I this
    deed.
BOLING. They love not poison that do poison need,
Nor do I thee. Though I did wish him dead,
I hate the murderer, love him murderèd.   40
The guilt of conscience take thou for thy labor,
But neither my good word nor princely favor.
With Cain go wander thorough° shades of night,
And never show thy head by day nor light.
Lords, I protest, my soul is full of woe   45
That blood should sprinkle me to make me grow.
Come, mourn with me for that I do lament,
And put on sullen black incontinent.°
I'll make a voyage to the Holy Land
To wash this blood off from my guilty hand.   50
March sadly after, grace my mournings here
In weeping after this untimely bier.   [*Exeunt.*]

20. clog: weight. 25. reverend room: place respected. 26. joy:
enjoy. 43. thorough: through. 48. incontinent: forthwith.

Introduction

The Tragedy of Romeo and Juliet was probably written in 1594 or 1595. There is no precise evidence of date and nothing in the play which can be identified as a topical allusion except that the Nurse when trying to establish the time of Juliet's weaning says: "'Tis since the earthquake now eleven years" (I.iii.23). Earthquakes are so rare in England as to be notable, and there was an earthquake, well remembered, on April 6, 1580; but it would be rash to assume that the play was written in 1591; the reminiscences of this scatter-brained old woman are hardly good enough evidence for anything. The style, however, is unmistakably early, and the play was written when Shakespeare was still an admirer and an imitator of Marlowe. References to *Romeo and Juliet* begin early, the first occurring in 1595.

The story of Romeo and Juliet was well known, and had been told in Italian, French, and English; but the play was based on an English poem by Arthur Brooke called *The Tragical History of Romeus and Juliet,* printed in 1562. Brooke stated in his preface, "I saw the same argument lately set forth on stage with more commendation than I can look for," and it is probable that there were other stage versions between 1562 and 1595.

The story as told by Brooke ran to more than three thousand lines, but is much simpler than in Shakespeare's play. It begins by describing the feud between the Capilets and Montagues, and may be summarized as follows:

Romeus is a beautiful youth passionately in love with a lady who gives him no encouragement. Being reduced to utter misery, he is advised by one of his trustiest friends to choose another love. At Christmas time, Romeus and five friends go masked to the Capilets' banquet. He falls in love at first sight with Juliet, and she with him, and they declare their love. They then learn each other's names. Juliet is greatly disturbed, but resolves that she will serve him if he will make her his lawful wedded wife:

> For so perchance this new
> alliance may procure
> Unto our houses such a peace
> as ever shall endure.

Romeus constantly passes by Juliet's window, and at last on a moonlit night she leans out of the window and sees him. She promises to follow him if he will marry her. Romeus goes at once to Friar Lawrence, who is persuaded to marry them. Juliet sends her nurse to Romeus; the meeting is arranged and the lovers are married. Romeus gives the Nurse a ladder of cord and when night is come he climbs up to Juliet's bedroom. For the next month or two Romeus continues to visit her by night. On Easter Monday, Tybalt, Juliet's cousin, leads out a party to fight with the Montagues. Romeus tries to stop the fight, but is insulted by Tybalt. They fight and Tybalt is killed. The Capilets denounce Romeus, and the Prince condemns him to exile. Juliet is overwhelmed by distress, but the Nurse offers to go to Romeus, who is hiding in the Friar's cell. Meantime the Friar has learned of the sentence of banishment. Romeus becomes frantic with grief, but the Friar restores him to reason, and advises him to visit his lady. He goes, and they spend the night together. They part at dawn, and Romeus, having promised to keep her informed of his fortunes through the Friar, sets out for Mantua.

Juliet pines in his absence. Her mother perceives the change, and tells old Capilet that Juliet is pining because most of her friends are married, and she needs a husband. Suitors are encouraged and especially the County Paris. Juliet's mother commends the young man, but Juliet will have none of him. Lady Capilet tells her husband, who sends for Juliet. He threatens to cast her out if she disobeys. Juliet goes again to Friar Lawrence and declares that she will kill herself. The Friar tells Juliet of his skill in drugs and gives her a potion which will make her appear dead, promising that when she awakes in the tomb he and Romeus will take her away. Juliet goes back and tells her mother that she is ready to obey their command to marry Paris. Old Capilet is greatly pleased. Great preparations are made for the wedding, Juliet all the while deceiving her parents and the Nurse. The night before the wedding Juliet prepares the potion and drinks it. Next morning the Nurse finds her apparently dead. The family assemble and lament her untimely death. Meantime the Friar has sent Friar John to Mantua with a letter for Romeus, but Friar John, entering a religious house to find a companion for his journey, is detained because one of the brethren has died of the plague.

Peter, Romeus's servant, sees the funeral of Juliet, and hastens to Mantua to tell his master. Romeus buys poison of an apothecary. He writes a letter to his father, telling the whole story, and by night returns to Verona. With the aid of Peter he breaks open the tomb and laments over Juliet's body. Then he takes the poison and dies by her side. The Friar, alarmed that he has received no answer to his letter, goes to the tomb and finds Romeus dead. Juliet awakes, but when she sees Romeus, refuses to leave him. The Friar and Peter, alarmed by a noise, run away. Juliet stabs herself with Romeus's dagger. The watch, seeing lights in the tomb, raise the alarm and discover the bodies. They find the Friar and the servant and arrest them. Next day they inform the Prince. Everyone hurries to the tomb and the whole story is revealed. The Capilets and Montagues are reconciled and the two bodies are buried in a stately monument.

Brooke, though his verse was usually crude and very long-winded, had some sense of character, which Shakespeare found helpful and adapted closely. Three examples from Brooke will show what Shakespeare found and what he added for himself.

1. ROMEUS TELLS THE NURSE OF HIS PLAN TO MARRY JULIET (cf. I.iii.1–62; II.iv.180–232)

" On Saturday," quoth he,
    " if Juliet come to shrift,
She shall be shrived and married;
    how like you, Nurse, this drift? "
" Now, by my troth," quoth she,
    " God's blessing have your heart,
For yet in all my life I have
    not heard of such a part.
Lord, how you young men can
    such crafty wiles devise,
If that you love the daughter well,
    to blear the mother's eyes.
An easy thing it is,
    with cloak of holiness,
To mock the silly mother that
    suspecteth nothing less.
But that it pleasèd you
    to tell me of the case,
For all my many years perhaps
    I should have found it scarce.
Now for the rest let me
    and Juliet alone;
To get her leave, some feat [1] excuse
    I will devise anon:
For that her golden locks
    by sloth have been unkempt,
Or for unwares some wanton dream
    the youthful damsel dreamt,
Or for in thoughts of love
    her idle time she spent,

[1] neat.

Or otherwise within her heart
    deservèd to be shent.
I know her mother will
    in no case say her nay,
I warrant you she shall not fail
    to come on Saturday."
And then she swears to him,
    the mother loves her well;
And how she gave her suck in youth
    she leaveth not to tell.
" A pretty babe," quoth she,
    " it was when it was young;
Lord, how it could full prettily
    have prated with its tongue!
A thousand times and more
    I laid her on my lap,
And clapped her on the buttock soft,
    and kissed where I did clap.
And gladder then was I
    of such a kiss forsooth,
Than I had been to have a kiss
    of some old lecher's mouth."
And thus of Juliet's youth
    began this prating nurse,
And of her present state to make
    a tedious long discourse.
For though he pleasure took
    in hearing of his love,
The message answer seemed him
    to be of more behoove.
But when these beldams sit
    at ease upon their tale,
The day and eke the candlelight
    before their talk shall fail,
And part they say is true,
    and part they do devise,
Yet boldly do they that of both
    when no man checks their lies.
Then he six crowns of gold
    out of his pocket drew,
And gave them her, " A slight reward,"
    quoth he, " and so, adieu."

2. OLD CAPILET'S ANGER WITH JULIET (cf. III.iv.126–97)

The sire, whose swelling wrath
    her tears could not assuage,
With fiery eyes and scarlet cheeks
    thus spake her in his rage,
Whilst ruthfully stood by
    the maiden's mother mild.
" Listen," quoth he, " unthankful
    and thou disobedient child.
Hast thou so soon let slip
    out of thy mind the word
That thou so oftentimes hast heard
    rehearsèd at my board,

How much the Roman youth
  of parents stood in awe,
And eke what power upon their seed
  the fathers had by law?
Whom they not only might
  pledge, alienate, and sell,
(When so they stood in need) but more,
  if children did rebel,
The parents had the power
  of life and sudden death.
What if those goodmen should again
  receive the living breath,
In how straight bonds would they
  thy stubborn body bind?
What weapons would they seek for thee?
  What torments would they find
To chasten (if they saw)
  the lewdness of thy life,
Thy great unthankfulness to me,
  and shameful sturdy strife?
Such care thy mother had,
  so dear thou wert to me,
That I with long and earnest suit
  provided have for thee
One of the greatest lords,
  that wonnes [2] about this town,
And for his many virtues' sake
  a man of great renown.
Of whom both thou and I
  unworthy are too much,
So rich ere long he shall be left,
  his father's wealth is such,
Such is the nobleness
  and honour of the race
From whence his father came. And yet
  thou playest in this case
The dainty fool and stubborn girl;
  for want of skill
Thou dost refuse thy offered weal,
  and disobey my will.
Even by His strength I swear
  that first did give me life,
And gave me in my youth the strength
  to get thee on my wife,
Unless by Wednesday next
  thou bend as I am bent,
And at our castle called Freetown
  thou freely do assent
To County Paris' suit,
  and promise to agree
To whatsoever then shall pass
  'twixt him, my wife, and me,
Not only will I give
  all that I have away
From thee to those that shall me love,
  me honor and obey,

       [2] dwells.

But also to so close
  and to so hard a jail
I shall thee wed for all thy life
  that sure thou shalt not fail
A thousand times a day
  to wish for sudden death,
And curse the day and hour when first
  thy lungs did give thee breath.
Advise thee well and say
  that thou art warnèd now,
And think not that I speak in sport,
  or mind to break my vow.
For were it not that I
  to County Paris gave
My faith, which I must keep unfalsed,
  my honor so to save,
Ere thou go hence myself
  would see thee chastened so
That thou should'st once for all be taught
  thy duty how to know,
And what revenge of old
  these angry sires did find
Against their children that rebelled
  and showed themselves unkind."
These said, the old man straight
  is gone in haste away,
Ne for his daughter's answer would
  the testy father stay.

3. JULIET'S SOLILOQUY BEFORE TAKING THE POTION
  (cf. iv.iii.14–58)

  " What do I know," quoth she,
    " if that this powder shall
Sooner or later than it should
  or else not work at all?
And then, my craft descried
  as open as the day,
The peoples' tale and laughingstock
  shall I remain for aye.
And what know I," quoth she,
    " if serpents odious,
And other beasts and worms that are
  of nature venomous,
That wonted are to lurk
  in dark caves underground,
And commonly, as I have heard,
  in dead men's tombs are found,
Shall harm me yea or nay,
  where I shall lie as dead?
Or how shall I that always have
  in so fresh air been bred
Endure the loathsome stink
  of such a heapèd store
Of carcasses not yet consumed,
  and bones that long before
Entombèd were, where I
  my sleeping place shall have

Where all my ancestors do rest,
   my kindred's common grave?
Shall not the friar and my
   Romeus, when they come,
Find me, if I awake before,
   ystifled in the tomb? "
And whilst she in these thoughts
   doth dwell somewhat too long,
The force of her imagining
   anon did wax so strong
That she surmised she saw
   out of the hollow vault,
A grisly thing to look upon,
   the carcass of Tybalt,
Right in the selfsame sort
   that she few days before
Had seen him in his blood embrewed,
   to death eke wounded sore.
And then when she again
   within herself had weighed
That quick she should be buried there,
   and by his side be laid,
All comfortless, for she
   shall living fere [3] have none
But many a rotten carcass and
   full many a naked bone,
Her dainty tender parts
   'gan shiver all for dread,
Her golden hairs did stand upright
   upon her childish head.
Then, pressèd with the fear
   that she there livèd in,
A sweat as cold as mountain ice
   pierced through her tender skin,
That with the moisture hath
   wet every part of hers.
And more besides she vainly thinks
   whilst vainly thus she fears;
A thousand bodies dead
   have compassed her about,
And lest they will dismember her
   she greatly stands in doubt.
But when she felt her strength
   began to wear away
By little and little, and in her heart
   her fear increasèd aye,
Dreading that weakness might
   or foolish cowardice
Hinder the execution of
   the purposed enterprise,
As she had frantic been,
   in haste the glass she caught,
And up she drank the mixture quite,
   withouten farther thought.
Then on her breast she crossed
   her arms long and small,

And so, her senses failing her,
   into a trance did fall.

Romeo and Juliet was first published in 1597, when a quarto (Q1) appeared entitled: *An Excellent conceited Tragedie of Romeo and Iuliet. As it hath been often (with great applause) plaid publiquely, by the right Honourable the L. of Hunsdon* [4] *his Seruants.* A second quarto (Q2) was printed in 1599 with the title page: *The Most Excellent and lamentable Tragedie, of Romeo and Iuliet. Newly corrected, augmented, and amended, by the right Honourable the Lord Chamberlaine his Seruants.* There are great differences between the two quartos. Q1 is one of the pirated quartos of Shakespeare's plays, set up from a copy obtained by some underhand means, and giving a very corrupt version (see Gen. Intro. p. 66b). Q2 was set up either from Shakespeare's original manuscript or from the playhouse copy. It shows signs of revision and rewriting (see pp. 64b–65a), and in places the prompter's notes have crept in. Thus at IV.v.102, instead of *Enter Peter* Q2 reads *Enter Will Kempe* — the clown of the company.

Q1 is seven hundred lines shorter than Q2. In the early scenes it follows Q2 closely; in later scenes there are considerable differences. It is a far better production than the other pirated quartos, and was certainly used in printing Q2, as there are some striking similarities; the speeches of the Nurse in I.iii for some unexplained reason are printed in italics in both versions. At times its readings are so much better that mistakes in Q2 can be corrected by it.

A third quarto (Q3), printed in 1609, was ultimately used as copy for the first folio (F1) in 1623. There are two other quartos, one undated and the other printed in 1637. Editors usually base the text on Q2, but use readings from Q1 and F1 when thought preferable.

A comparison of Brooke's *Romeus and Juliet* with the play shows how skillfully Shakespeare wrote *Romeo and Juliet.* Brooke told the story of a love intrigue which lasted for nine months and then ended unhappily; Shakespeare compressed his play into five days' crescendo of passion and disaster. In the poem, Romeus and Juliet enjoyed their secret love for several weeks before the death of Tybalt caused Romeus to be banished; Shakespeare set the death of Tybalt and Romeo's

---

[3] companion.

[4] See Gen. Intro. p. 39b.

sentence of banishment between the morning of the marriage of Romeo and Juliet and their wedding night. The pace of the play throughout is quick and exciting.

The plot is superb. Each scene leads up naturally to the next to develop a theme which is stated in the Prologue:

A pair of star-crossed lovers take their life,
    Whose misadventured piteous overthrows
Doth with their death bury their parents' strife.

Romeo and Juliet is indeed a story of ill luck. Everything at first seems hopeful until some unforeseen mischance spoils the best-laid plans and the best intentions. By chance Romeo is present at the Capulets' feast and there sees Juliet and falls in love with her. To the Friar, who stands apart from the interminable feud of the Capulets and the Montagues, the marriage seems the luckiest of accidents:

For this alliance may so happy prove,
    To turn your households' rancor to pure love.

But the same chance which caused Romeo to meet Juliet also brought the quarrelsome Tybalt to oversee their meeting, to swear to kill Romeo, and to seek him on his return from his secret wedding. Chance again causes Mercutio to take on the quarrel, and, by sheer ill luck, in trying to part the combatants, Romeo causes Mercutio to miss his parry of Tybalt's thrust. The fatal duel between Romeo and Tybalt is the inevitable sequel, and one more death is added to the score of the family feud. Even so there might have been an ultimate reconciliation but for old Capulet's well-meaning plan to console Juliet by hastening on her wedding with Paris.

The final tragedy might still have been averted, for the Friar's desperate plan to save Juliet's honor by giving her the sleeping potion has every chance of success; but again chance interferes. The letter, which was to tell Romeo to rescue his wife, miscarries by unforeseeable accident, and the Friar reaches the vault just too late. The whole play is a succession of unlucky mischances, but Shakespeare has told his tale so well that at no time do any of the accidents seem in any way strained or unnatural. The actions of Tybalt, old Capulet, Romeo, and Juliet are entirely true to life and to their own individual natures; the characterization of the play is thus as skillful as its plotting.

Character in drama is shown in various ways: by a person's action; by his words, and not less by the way in which he expresses himself; and by what others say of him. All the characters in *Romeo and Juliet* are fully drawn. Thus in creating Romeo, Shakespeare before first bringing him onto the stage shows the anxiety of his parents at his moody behavior. Then Romeo himself appears and in his talk with Benvolio reveals his excess of emotion; in his love for the inaccessible Rosaline he is moody, distracted, and unbalanced. He continues in this mood until he has seen Juliet, and then his lethargy disappears; he rises to a lyric ecstasy and the old gay Romeo returns. Marriage makes him suddenly serious; he is even ready, contrary to his nature, to return fair words to the insolent Tybalt. But with the death of Mercutio he is forced into the duel with Tybalt, and his new happiness falls into ruin. In the Friar's cell he is reduced to a misery even more distracted than before, from which suicide seems the only way of escape. He revives at the prospect of being reunited to Juliet, but when the news reaches him that she is dead, self-slaughter is the natural answer and end to the turmoil of his emotions.

The other characters are as skillfully created. Juliet begins as a demure girl who is prepared to listen respectfully to the advice of her mother. When she has fallen in love, she becomes suddenly a woman of great courage and resource, who will face even death and fantastic horror to regain her husband.

It was perhaps less difficult for Shakespeare to create the older characters, such as the Nurse or old Capulet, but even these are fully shown; they are living people and not merely caricatures of testy elders. The old father is as quick-tempered as the rest of the family, whether toward a Montague or toward a daughter who is inclined to be a chop-logic; but in his own house at ease with his guests he will have no disorder, and he can even speak a word in praise of Romeo.

The most skillful, though not the most obvious, triumph of characterization is shown in the contrast between the five young men — Romeo, Benvolio, Paris, Mercutio, and Tybalt — for these are all young men of the same age and class, and yet each is distinct and individual.

Nevertheless, *Romeo and Juliet* was written when Shakespeare was still more of a poet than a dramatist. Again and again he holds up the action for a poetic speech or an exchange of word play. At its best, as in the love duet between Romeo and Juliet (II.ii) or in Juliet's soliloquy when waiting for Romeo (III.ii.1–31), the poetry is lyrical and lovely. At its worst, as in Lady Capulet's long description of Paris as a suitable "book" for Juliet (I.iii.81–94) or in Romeo's list of the bitter-sweetnesses of love (I.i.197–201), it verges on the absurd. The excessive wit, the puns, and the double and triple meanings with which the play abounds were pleasant enough to a generation nurtured on Lyly's *Euphues* or devoted to the conceits of the sonnet, but this style of writing soon went out of fashion as poets and dramatists became more interested in human beings and their problems and less fascinated by the game of playing with words.

With Shakespeare much wit is always a sign of an early play. *Romeo and Juliet* lacks the depth of the later tragedies, partly because Shakespeare's skill had not yet matured, partly because the theme itself is pathetic rather than essentially tragic. To effect that utter purging of the emotions which comes with the greatest tragedies there is needed a maturity in the victims and a magnitude in the theme. Neither Romeo nor Juliet has that greatness which is essential in the victim of deep tragedy; they suffer for the stupidity of their parents, and their fate is pathetic and accidental rather than truly tragic. Nevertheless *Romeo and Juliet* remains Shakespeare's first great play, which must have shown to the discerning playgoer that something was happening in the English theater.

Romeo and Juliet

DRAMATIS PERSONAE

ESCALUS, *Prince of Verona*

PARIS, *a young nobleman, kinsman to the Prince*

MONTAGUE } *heads of two houses at variance with*
CAPULET } *each other*

AN OLD MAN, *of the Capulet family*

ROMEO, *son to Montague*

MERCUTIO, *kinsman to the Prince, and friend to Romeo*

BENVOLIO, *nephew to Montague, and friend to Romeo*

TYBALT, *nephew to Lady Capulet*

FRIAR LAURENCE, *a Franciscan*

FRIAR JOHN, *of the same order*

BALTHASAR, *servant to Romeo*

SAMPSON } *servants to Capulet*
GREGORY }

PETER, *servant to Juliet's nurse*

ABRAHAM, *servant to Montague*

AN APOTHECARY

THREE MUSICIANS

PAGE *to Paris; another* PAGE; *an* OFFICER

LADY MONTAGUE, *wife to Montague*

LADY CAPULET, *wife to Capulet*

JULIET, *daughter to Capulet*

NURSE *to Juliet*

CITIZENS *of Verona:* KINSFOLK *of both houses;* MASKERS, GUARDS, WATCHMEN, *and* ATTENDANTS

CHORUS

SCENE — *Verona; Mantua.*

PROLOGUE

[*Enter* CHORUS.°]

CHOR. Two households, both alike in dignity,
In fair Verona, where we lay our scene,
From ancient grudge break to new mutiny,°
Where civil blood makes civil hands unclean.
From forth the fatal loins of these two foes   5
A pair of star-crossed° lovers take their life,
Whose misadventured piteous overthrows
Do with their death bury their parents' strife.
The fearful passage of their death-marked love,
And the continuance of their parents' rage,   10
Which, but their children's end, naught could remove,
Is now the two hours'° traffic° of our stage;
The which if you with patient ears attend,
What here shall miss, our toil shall strive to mend.°

For an analysis of the original staging of *R & J* see Gen. Intro. p. 56a–58b.
Prologue: Chorus. A Chorus or Prologue was seldom used by Shakespeare to introduce and explain the action of a play, but it was usual with the other dramatists. **3. mutiny:** quarrel. **6. star-crossed:** thwarted by evil stars. See App. 1. **12. two hours:** the normal time taken for a performance in the Elizabethan playhouse, where there was no scenery to change and the actors spoke rapidly. **traffic:** business. **14. What ... mend:** i.e., if you find shortcomings in our play, we will try to set them right.
Act I, Sc. i: s.d., swords and bucklers: See Pl. 22i, 22j.
1. carry coals: do dirty work, be put upon. **2. colliers:** coal-

Act I

SCENE I. *Verona. A public place.*

[*Enter* SAMPSON *and* GREGORY, *of the House of Capulet, with swords and bucklers.*°]

SAM. Gregory, on my word, we'll not carry coals.°

GRE. No, for then we should be colliers.°

SAM. I mean, an° we be in choler,° we'll draw.   5

GRE. Aye, while you live, draw your neck out o' the collar.°

SAM. I strike quickly, being moved.

GRE. But thou art not quickly moved to strike.

SAM. A dog of the house of Montague moves me.

GRE. To move is to stir, and to be valiant is to   11
stand. Therefore if thou art moved, thou runn'st away.

SAM. A dog of that house shall move me to stand. I will take the wall° of any man or maid of Montague's.   16

GRE. That shows thee a weak slave, for the weakest goes to the wall.°

SAM. 'Tis true, and therefore women, being the

dealers, notorious for their dirty tricks. **5. an:** if. **5–7. choler ... collar:** puns on "collier," "choler" (wrath), and "collar" (halter) are common. **15. take ... wall:** go on the inside of the sidewalk, where the ground was higher and less muddy, and so show superiority. **17–18. weakest ... wall:** Gregory retorts with another proverb.

weaker vessels, are ever thrust to the wall. Therefore
I will push Montague's men from the wall and thrust
his maids to the wall.   22

GRE. The quarrel is between our masters and us
their men.

SAM. 'Tis all one, I will show myself a tyrant.
When I have fought with the men, I will be cruel
with the maids. I will cut off their heads.   28

GRE. The heads of the maids?

SAM. Aye, the heads of the maids, or their maiden-
heads — take it in what sense thou wilt.

GRE. They must take it in sense that feel it.

SAM. Me they shall feel while I am able to stand.
And 'tis known I am a pretty piece of flesh.   35

GRE. 'Tis well thou art not fish. If thou hadst, thou
hadst been poor John.° Draw thy tool. Here comes
two of the house of Montagues.

[*Enter* ABRAHAM *and* BALTHASAR.]

SAM. My naked weapon is out. Quarrel — I will
back thee.

GRE. How! Turn thy back and run?   41

SAM. Fear me not.

GRE. No, marry,° I fear thee!

SAM. Let us take the law of our sides. Let them
begin.   45

GRE. I will frown as I pass by, and let them take it
as they list.

SAM. Nay, as they dare. I will bite my thumb° at
them, which is a disgrace to them, if they bear it.   50

ABR. Do you bite your thumb at us, sir?

SAM. I do bite my thumb, sir.

ABR. Do you bite your thumb at us, sir?

SAM. [*Aside to* GREGORY] Is the law of our side, if I
say aye?

GRE. No.   56

SAM. No, sir, I do not bite my thumb at you, sir;
but I bite my thumb, sir.

GRE. Do you quarrel, sir?

ABR. Quarrel, sir! No, sir.   60

SAM. But if you do, sir, I am for you. I serve as
good a man as you.

ABR. No better.

SAM. Well, sir.

[*Enter* BENVOLIO.]

GRE. [*Aside to* SAMPSON] Say "Better." Here
comes one of my master's kinsmen.   66

SAM. Yes, better, sir.

ABR. You lie.

SAM. Draw, if you be men. Gregory, remember
thy swashing° blow.   70

[*They fight.*]

BEN. Part, fools! [*Beating down their weapons.*]
Put up your swords. You know not what you do.

[*Enter* TYBALT.]

TYB. What, art thou drawn among these heartless
   hinds°?

Turn thee, Benvolio, look upon thy death.

BEN. I do but keep the peace. Put up thy sword,
Or manage it to part these men with me.   76

TYB. What, drawn, and talk of peace! I hate the
   word

As I hate Hell, all Montagues, and thee.

Have at thee, coward!   [*They fight.*]

[*Enter several of both houses, who join the fray; then
   enter* CITIZENS *and* PEACE OFFICERS, *with clubs.*]

1. OFF. Clubs, bills, and partisans°! Strike! Beat
   them down!   80

Down with the Capulets! Down with the Monta-
   gues!

[*Enter old* CAPULET *in his gown, and* LADY CAPULET.]

CAP. What noise is this? Give me my long sword,°
   ho!

LADY CAP. A crutch, a crutch! Why call you for a
   sword?

CAP. My sword, I say! Old Montague is come,
And flourishes his blade in spite of° me.   85

[*Enter old* MONTAGUE *and* LADY MONTAGUE.]

MON. Thou villain Capulet! — Hold me not, let
   me go.

LADY MON. Thou shalt not stir one foot to seek a
   foe.

[*Enter* PRINCE ESCALUS, *with his train.*]

PRIN. Rebellious subjects, enemies to peace,
Profaners of this neighbor-stainèd steel° —   89

Will they not hear? What ho! You men, you beasts,
That quench the fire of your pernicious rage
With purple fountains issuing from your veins,
On pain of torture, from those bloody hands
Throw your mistempered° weapons to the ground,
And hear the sentence of your movèd prince.   95

Three civil brawls, bred of an airy° word,
By thee, old Capulet and Montague,
Have thrice disturbed the quiet of our streets,
And made Verona's ancient citizens
Cast by their grave beseeming ornaments°   100

To wield old partisans, in hands as old,
Cankered with peace, to part your cankered° hate.
If ever you disturb our streets again,
Your lives shall pay the forfeit of the peace.

---

73. heartless hinds: a fourfold pun; *hind* means "servant" and
"female deer," and *heartless* "without feelings" and "without
harts" (male deer). This play is packed with phrases that carry
two or more meanings, often bawdy. **80. bills . . . partisans:**
See Pl. 21C, 21A. **82. long sword:** The old English long sword
was rapidly giving place to the rapier, introduced from the Con-
tinent. Capulet naturally calls for the old-fashioned weapon.
See Pl. 22i. **85. in . . . of:** to show his contempt for. **89. Pro-
faners . . . steel:** who profane (disgrace) your swords by staining
them with the blood of your neighbors. **94. mistempered:**
"wrathful" and "made for a bad purpose." **96. airy:** light as
air. **100. Cast . . . ornaments:** i.e., throw off the ornaments of
peace which are suitable to sober, aged citizens. **102. Cankered
. . . cankered:** corroded . . . malignant.

---

37. poor John: dried salted hake, a cheap food. **43. marry:**
Mary, by the Virgin Mary. **49. bite my thumb:** an insulting
gesture, made by snicking the thumbnail on the upper teeth.
70. swashing: smashing.

For this time, all the rest depart away.   105
You, Capulet, shall go along with me,
And, Montague, come you this afternoon,
To know our further pleasure in this case,
To old Freetown,° our common judgment place.
Once more, on pain° of death, all men depart.   110

[*Exeunt all but* MONTAGUE, LADY
MONTAGUE, *and* BENVOLIO.]

MON. Who set this ancient quarrel new abroach°?
Speak, Nephew, were you by when it began?
BEN. Here were the servants of your adversary
And yours close fighting ere I did approach.
I drew to part them. In the instant came   115
The fiery Tybalt, with his sword prepared,
Which as he breathed defiance to my ears,
He swung about his head and cut the winds,
Who, nothing hurt withal, hissed him in scorn.
While we were interchanging thrusts and blows,
Came more and more, and fought on part and part
Till the Prince came, who parted either part.   122
LADY MON. Oh, where is Romeo? Saw you him to-
day?
Right glad I am he was not at this fray.
BEN. Madam, an hour before the worshiped sun
Peered forth the golden window of the east,   126
A troubled mind drave me to walk abroad,
Where, underneath the grove of sycamore
That westward rooteth from the city's side,
So early walking did I see your son.   130
Towards him I made; but he was ware° of me,
And stole into the covert of the wood.
I, measuring his affections by my own,
That most are busied when they're most alone,
Being one too many by my weary self,
Pursued my humor,° not pursuing his,   135
And gladly shunned who gladly fled from me.
MON. Many a morning hath he there been seen,
With tears augmenting the fresh morning's dew,
Adding to clouds more clouds with his deep sighs.
But all so soon as the all-cheering sun   140
Should in the farthest east begin to draw
The shady curtains from Aurora's° bed,
Away from light steals home my heavy son,
And private in his chamber pens himself,
Shuts up his windows, locks fair daylight out,   145
And makes himself an artificial night.
Black and portentous must this humor prove
Unless good counsel may the cause remove.
BEN. My noble uncle, do you know the cause?
MON. I neither know it nor can learn of him.   150
BEN. Have you impórtuned° him by any means?
MON. Both by myself and many other friends.
But he, his own affections' counselor,
Is to himself — I will not say how true —

But to himself so secret and so close,   155
So far from sounding and discovery,
As is the bud bit with an envious° worm
Ere he can spread his sweet leaves to the air,
Or dedicate his beauty to the sun.
Could we but learn from whence his sorrows grow,
We would as willingly give cure as know.   161

[*Enter* ROMEO.]

BEN. See where he comes. So please you, step aside.
I'll know his grievance, or be much denied.
MON. I would thou wert so happy° by thy stay
To hear true shrift.° Come, madam, let's away.   165

[*Exeunt* MONTAGUE *and* LADY.]

BEN. Good morrow, Cousin.
ROM.   Is the day so young?
BEN. But new struck nine.
ROM.   Aye me, sad hours seem long!
Was that my father that went hence so fast?
BEN. It was. What sadness lengthens Romeo's
hours?
ROM. Not having that which, having, makes them
short.   170
BEN. In love?
ROM. Out——
BEN. Of love?
ROM. Out of her favor where I am in love.
BEN. Alas that love, so gentle in his view,°   175
Should be so tyrannous and rough in proof!°
ROM. Alas that love, whose view is muffled still,°
Should without eyes see pathways to his will!
Where shall we dine? Oh me! What fray was here?
Yet tell me not, for I have heard it all.   180
Here's much to do with hate, but more with love.
Why then, O brawling love! O loving hate!
O anything, of nothing first create!
O heavy lightness! Serious vanity!
Misshapen chaos of well-seeming forms!   185
Feather of lead, bright smoke, cold fire, sick health!
Still-waking° sleep, that is not what it is!
This love feel I, that feel no love in this.
Dost thou not laugh?
BEN.   No, Coz,° I rather weep.
ROM. Good heart, at what?
BEN.   At thy good heart's oppression. 190
ROM. Why, such is love's transgression.
Griefs of mine own lie heavy in my breast,
Which thou wilt propagate,° to have it pressed°
With more of thine. This love that thou hast shown
Doth add more grief to too much of mine own.   195
Love is a smoke raised with the fume° of sighs;
Being purged, a fire sparkling in lovers' eyes;
Being vexed, a sea nourished with lovers' tears.
What is it else? A madness most discreet,

109. Freetown: a misunderstanding of a line in *Romeus and Juliet*.
See *R & J* Intro. p. 228a.   110. pain: penalty.   111. abroach:
on foot.   131. ware: aware.   135. humor: mood.   142. Aurora's:
of the dawn.   151. importuned: asked repeatedly.

157. envious: hateful.   164. happy: fortunate.   165. shrift: con-
fession.   175. view: appearance.   176. in proof: i.e., when ex-
perienced.   177. view . . . still: sight is blindfolded always.
187. Still-waking: ever watchful.   189. Coz: cousin.   193. prop-
agate: increase. pressed: weighed down.   196. fume: mist.

A choking gall and a preserving sweet.   200
Farewell, my coz.
   BEN.   Soft! I will go along.
And if you leave me so, you do me wrong.
   ROM. Tut, I have lost myself, I am not here.
This is not Romeo, he's some other where.
   BEN. Tell me in sadness,° who is that you love?
   ROM. What, shall I groan and tell thee?   206
   BEN.   Groan! Why, no,
But sadly tell me who.
   ROM. Bid a sick man in sadness make his will.
Ah, word ill urged to one that is so ill!
In sadness, Cousin, I do love a woman.   210
   BEN. I aimed so near when I supposed you loved.
   ROM. A right good mark-man!° And she's fair I
love.
   BEN. A right fair mark, fair Coz, is soonest hit.
   ROM. Well, in that hit you miss. She'll not be hit
With Cupid's arrow. She hath Dian's° wit,   215
And in strong proof° of chastity well armed,
From love's weak childish bow she lives unharmed.
She will not stay the siege of loving terms,
Nor bide the encounter of assailing eyes,
Nor ope her lap to saint-seducing gold.   220
Oh, she is rich in beauty, only poor
That when she dies, with beauty dies her store.°
   BEN. Then she hath sworn that she will still live
chaste?
   ROM. She hath, and in that sparing makes huge
waste;
For beauty, starved with her severity,   225
Cuts beauty off from all posterity.
She is too fair, too wise, wisely too fair,
To merit bliss by making me despair.°
She hath forsworn° to love, and in that vow
Do I live dead, that live to tell it now.   230
   BEN. Be ruled by me, forget to think of her.
   ROM. Oh, teach me how I should forget to think.
   BEN. By giving liberty unto thine eyes.
Examine other beauties.
   ROM.   'Tis the way
To call hers exquisite, in question more.°   235
These happy masks° that kiss fair ladies' brows,
Being black, put us in mind they hide the fair.
He that is stricken blind cannot forget
The precious treasure of his eyesight lost.
Show me a mistress that is passing° fair,   240

What doth her beauty serve but as a note
Where I may read who passed° that passing fair?
Farewell. Thou canst not teach me to forget.
   BEN. I'll pay that doctrine,° or else die in debt.
                                  [*Exeunt.*]

SCENE II. *A street.*

[*Enter* CAPULET, PARIS, *and* SERVANT.]
   CAP. But Montague is bound° as well as I,
In penalty alike, and 'tis not hard, I think,
For men so old as we to keep the peace.
   PAR. Of honorable reckoning° are you both,
And pity 'tis you lived at odds so long.   5
But now, my lord, what say you to my suit?
   CAP. But saying o'er what I have said before.
My child is yet a stranger in the world —
She hath not seen the change of fourteen years.
Let two more summers wither in their pride   10
Ere we may think her ripe to be a bride.
   PAR. Younger than she are happy mothers made.
   CAP. And too soon marred are those so early made.
The earth hath swallowed all my hopes but she,
She is the hopeful lady of my earth.°   15
But woo her, gentle Paris, get her heart.
My will to her consent is but a part;
An she agree, within her scope of choice°
Lies my consent and fair according° voice.
This night I hold an old accustomed feast,   20
Whereto I have invited many a guest
Such as I love, and you among the store,
One more, most welcome, makes my number more
At my poor house look to behold this night
Earth-treading stars that make dark heaven light.   25
Such comfort as do lusty young men feel
When well-appareled April on the heel
Of limping winter treads, even such delight
Among fresh female buds shall you this night
Inherit at my house. Hear all, all see,   30
And like her most whose merit most shall be.
Which on more view, of many mine, being one,
May stand in number, though in reckoning none.°
Come, go with me. [*To* SERVANT, *giving a paper*]
     Go, sirrah,° trudge about
Through fair Verona. Find those persons out   35
Whose names are written there, and to them say

---

205. **in sadness**: seriously.   212. **mark-man**: marksman.
216. **Dian**: Diana, the Virgin huntress goddess, was not interested
in men.   217. **proof**: armor.   222. **with . . . store**: i.e., she will
leave no offspring to carry on her beauty. Cf. Sonnet 4.
228. **To . . . despair**: to make me desperate while she earns her
heavenly reward for keeping her vow of chastity.   229. **for-
sworn**: sworn that she will not.   234–35. **'Tis . . . more**: to ex-
amine their beauty is the way to realize her greater beauty.
235. **masks**: Elizabethan ladies, admiring an ivory complexion,
wore masks in the open air to preserve their faces from the
sun. These masks were usually black, but sometimes colored.
240. **passing**: exceedingly.

241–42. **note . . . passed**: the beauty of any other mistress re-
minds me of the surpassing beauty of my own.   244. **I'll . . .
doctrine**: I will pay for that teaching; i.e., I will have you con-
vinced that you are wrong.
    Sc. ii: 1. **bound**: i.e., to keep peace.   4. **Of . . . reckoning**:
reckoned honorable.   15. **hopeful . . . earth**: i.e., the only hope
left of my posterity. **earth**: body. See II.i.2.   18. **scope of choice**:
range of choice; i.e., if she chooses suitably.   19. **fair according**:
readily agreeing.   32–33. **Which . . . none**: i.e., my daughter will
be one amongst the beauties whom you will see, but none will
be worth more.   34. **sirrah**: spoken to his servant, a term used
for inferiors.

My house and welcome on their pleasure stay.

               [*Exeunt* CAPULET *and* PARIS.]

SERV. Find them out whose names are written here!
It is written that the shoemaker should meddle with
his yard° and the tailor with his last, the fisher   40
with his pencil and the painter with his nets; but I
am sent to find those persons whose names are here
writ, and can never find what names the writing per-
son hath here writ. I must to the learned. In good
time.°   45

       [*Enter* BENVOLIO *and* ROMEO.]

BEN. Tut, man, one fire burns out another's burn-
     ing,
   One pain is lessened by another's anguish.
Turn giddy, and be holp° by backward turning,
   One desperate grief cures with another's languish.
Take thou some new infection to thy eye,   50
And the rank poison of the old will die.
ROM. Your plantain° leaf is excellent for that.
BEN. For what, I pray thee?
ROM.   For your broken° shin.
BEN. Why, Romeo, art thou mad?
ROM. Not mad, but bound more than a madman
     is,   55
Shut up in prison, kept without my food,
Whipped and tormented° and —— Godden,° good
     fellow.
SERV. God gi' godden. I pray, sir, can you read?
ROM. Aye, mine own fortune in my misery.   60
SERV. Perhaps you have learned it without book,
but I pray, can you read anything you see?
ROM. Aye, if I know the letters and the language.
SERV. Ye say honestly. Rest you merry!°
ROM. Stay, fellow, I can read. [*Reads.*]   66
"Signior Martino and his wife and daughters;
County° Anselme and his beauteous sisters; the lady
widow of Vitruvio; Signior Placentio and his lovely
nieces; Mercutio and his brother Valentine; mine
uncle Capulet, his wife, and daughters; my fair niece
Rosaline; Livia; Signior Valentio and his cousin
Tybalt; Lucio and the lively Helena."   74
A fair assembly. Whither should they come?
SERV. Up.
ROM. Whither?
SERV. To supper, to our house.
ROM. Whose house?
SERV. My master's.   80
ROM. Indeed I should have asked you that before.
SERV. Now I'll tell you without asking. My master
is the great rich Capulet, and if you be not of the

House of Montagues, I pray come and crush° a cup
of wine. Rest you merry!   [*Exit.*]   86
BEN. At this same ancient feast of Capulet's
Sups the fair Rosaline whom thou so lovest,
With all the admirèd beauties of Verona.
Go thither, and with unattainted° eye   90
Compare her face with some that I shall show,
And I will make thee think thy swan a crow.
ROM. When the devout religion of mine eye
Maintains such falsehood, then turn tears to fires,
And these, who, often drowned, could never die,   95
   Transparent° heretics, be burned for liars!
One fairer than my love! The all-seeing sun
Ne'er saw her match since first the world begun.
BEN. Tut, you saw her fair, none else being by,
Herself poised° with herself in either eye.   100
But in that crystal scales let there be weighed
Your lady's love against some other maid
That I will show you shining at this feast,
And she shall scant° show well that now seems best.
ROM. I'll go along, no such sight to be shown,   105
But to rejoice in splendor of mine own.   [*Exeunt.*]

SCENE III. *A room in* CAPULET'S *house.*

       [*Enter* LADY CAPULET *and* NURSE.]

LADY CAP. Nurse, where's my daughter? Call her
     forth to me.
NURSE. Now, by my maidenhead at twelve year
     old,
I bade her come. What, lamb! What, ladybird!° —
God forbid! — Where's this girl? What, Juliet!

           [*Enter* JULIET.]

JUL. How now! Who calls?
NURSE. Your mother.
JUL. Madam, I am here. What is your will?   6
LADY CAP. This is the matter. Nurse, give leave
     awhile,
We must talk in secret. — Nurse, come back again.
I have remembered me, thou'st° hear our counsel.
Thou know'st my daughter's of a pretty age.   10
NURSE. Faith, I can tell her age unto an hour.
LADY CAP. She's not fourteen.
NURSE.   I'll lay fourteen of my teeth — .
And yet, to my teen° be it spoken, I have but four —.
She is not fourteen. How long is it now
To Lammastide?°
LADY CAP.   A fortnight and odd days.   15

39–40. shoemaker . . . yard: He mixes his metaphors, as is
common with servants in Shakespeare's plays. **yard:** measure.
44–45. In . . . time: what a lucky chance; i.e., the arrival of the
two gentlemen. **48. holp:** helped. **52. plantain:** a weed with
broad flat leaves, a popular remedy for bruises and nettle stings.
53. broken: with the skin broken. **55–57. bound . . . tor-
mented:** the usual treatment for lunatics. **Godden:** good eve-
ning, a form of greeting used in the afternoon. **65. Rest . . .
merry:** God keep you merry. **68. County:** Count

85. crush: quaff. **90. unattainted:** unbiased. **96. Transparent:**
bright. **100. poised:** balanced. **104. scant:** scarcely.

   Sc. iii: 3. ladybird: lit., a small round insect with bright red
spots; a pretty little thing. It also has a bad meaning, "tart."
The Nurse, realizing that she has used the wrong word, continues
abruptly: "God forbid!" **9. thou's:** thou shalt. **13. teen:**
sorrow. **15. Lammastide:** August 1. Shakespeare deliberately
sets the story in the hot season, when "the mad blood is stir-
ring." See III.i.3–4. In *Romeus and Juliet* the incident oc-
curred on Easter Sunday.

NURSE. Even or odd, of all days in the year,
Come Lammas Eve at night shall she be fourteen.
Susan and she — God rest all Christian souls! —
Were of an age. Well, Susan is with God.
She was too good for me. — But, as I said,   20
On Lammas Eve at night shall she be fourteen.
That shall she, marry, I remember it well.
'Tis since the earthquake now eleven years,°
And she was weaned — I never shall forget it —
Of all the days of the year, upon that day.   25
For I had then laid wormwood to my dug,
Sitting in the sun under the dovehouse wall;
My lord and you were then at Mantua. —
Nay, I do bear a brain.° — But, as I said,
When it did taste the wormwood on the nipple   30
Of my dug, and felt it bitter, pretty fool,
To see it tetchy,° and fall out with the dug!
Shake, quoth the dovehouse.° 'Twas no need, I
    trow,°
To bid me trudge.
And since that time it is eleven years;   35
For then she could stand high-lone° — nay, by the
    rood,°
She could have run and waddled all about,
For even the day before, she broke° her brow,
And then my husband — God be with his soul!
A'° was a merry man — took up the child.   40
"Yea," quoth he, "dost thou fall upon thy face?
Thou wilt fall backward when thou hast more wit,
Wilt thou not, Jule?" And, by my holidame,°
The pretty wretch left crying, and said "Aye."
To see now how a jest shall come about!   45
I warrant an I should live a thousand years,
I never should forget it. "Wilt thou not, Jule?"
    quoth he,
And, pretty fool, it stinted,° and said "Aye."
    LADY CAP. Enough of this. I pray thee hold thy
    peace.
    NURSE. Yes, madam, yet I cannot choose but laugh
To think it should leave crying, and say "Aye."   51
And yet, I warrant, it had upon its brow
A bump as big as a young cockerel's stone,°
A perilous° knock, and it cried bitterly.   54
"Yea," quoth my husband, "fall'st upon thy face?
Thou wilt fall backward when thou comest to age,
Wilt thou not, Jule?" It stinted, and said "Aye."
    JUL. And stint thou too, I pray thee, Nurse, say I.
    NURSE. Peace, I have done. God mark° thee to His
    grace!

Thou wast the prettiest babe that e'er I nursed.   60
An I might live to see thee married once,
I have my wish.
    LADY CAP. Marry, that "marry" is the very theme
I came to talk of. Tell me, daughter Juliet,
How stands your disposition to be married?   65
    JUL. It is an honor that I dream not of.
    NURSE. An honor! Were not I thine only nurse,
I would say thou hadst sucked wisdom from thy teat.
    LADY CAP. Well, think of marriage now. Younger
    than you
Here in Verona, ladies of esteem,   70
Are made already mothers. By my count,
I was your mother much upon these years
That you are now a maid. Thus then in brief —
The valiant Paris seeks you for his love.
    NURSE. A man, young lady! Lady, such a man   75
As all the world —— Why, he's a man of wax.°
    LADY CAP. Verona's summer hath not such a
    flower.
    NURSE. Nay, he's a flower, in faith, a very flower.
    LADY CAP. What say you? Can you love the gentle-
    man?
This night you shall behold him at our feast.   80
Read o'er the volume° of young Paris' face,
And find delight writ there with beauty's pen.
Examine every married lineament,°
And see how one another lends content,
And what obscured in this fair volume lies   85
Find written in the margent° of his eyes.
This precious book of love, this unbound lover,
To beautify him, only lacks a cover.
The fish lives in the sea, and 'tis much pride
For fair without the fair within to hide.°   90
That book in many's eyes doth share the glory
That in gold clasps locks in the golden story.
So shall you share all that he doth possess,
By having him making yourself no less.
    NURSE. No less! Nay, bigger. Women grow by
    men.   95
    LADY CAP. Speak briefly. Can you like of Paris'
    love?
    JUL. I'll look to like, if looking liking move.°
But no more deep will I endart mine eye   98
Than your consent° gives strength to make it fly.
                        [Enter a SERVINGMAN.]
    SERV. Madam, the guests are come, supper served
up, you called, my young lady asked for, the nurse
cursed in the pantry, and everything in extremity. I
must hence to wait. I beseech you, follow straight.°

23. 'Tis . . . years: See *R & J* Intro. p. 226a. 29. I . . . brain: I
have a head. 32. tetchy: peevish. 33. Shake . . . dovehouse:
This phrase has not been satisfactorily explained, but a dove-
house is a dovecote, where the lord of the manor bred pigeons
for his own table. trow: guess. 36. high-lone: quite alone.
rood: crucifix. 38. broke: broke the skin of. 40. A': he.
43. holidame: halidom, holy relic, upon which an oath was
sworn. 48. stinted: stopped. 53. stone: testicle. 54. peri-
lous: grievous. 59. mark: select.

76. man of wax: like a model in wax; i.e., perfect. 81–92. vol-
ume . . . story: The elaborate metaphor of Paris as a book is
continued throughout these lines. 83. married lineament: per-
fectly united part. 86. margent: margin. 90. For . . . hide: i.e.,
for a fair outside to cover a fair mind. 97. I'll . . . move: I'll
look at him if that will make me love him. 99. your consent:
This was the correct attitude of an Elizabethan maiden nicely
brought up. See Gen. Intro. p. 20a–b. 103. straight: at once,
straightway.

LADY CAP. We follow thee.   [*Exit* SERVINGMAN.]
  Juliet, the County stays.°   105
NURSE. Go, girl, seek happy nights to happy days.
                                                [*Exeunt.*]

SCENE IV. *A street.*

[*Enter* ROMEO, MERCUTIO, BENVOLIO, *with five or six*
    other MASKERS, *and* TORCHBEARERS]

ROM. What, shall this speech be spoke for our ex-
    cuse?
Or shall we on without apology?
BEN. The date is out of such prolixity.°
We'll have no Cupid hoodwinked° with a scarf,
Bearing a Tartar's painted bow of lath,°   5
Scaring the ladies like a crow-keeper;°
Nor no without-book prologue, faintly spoke
After the prompter, for our entrance.
But let them measure us by what they will,
We'll measure° them a measure, and be gone.   10
  ROM. Give me a torch. I am not for this am-
    bling.°
Being but heavy,° I will bear the light.
  MER. Nay, gentle Romeo, we must have you
    dance.
  ROM. Not I, believe me. You have dancing shoes
With nimble soles. I have a soul of lead   15
So stakes me to the ground I cannot move.
  MER. You are a lover. Borrow Cupid's wings,
And soar with them above a common bound.°
  ROM. I am too sore enpiercèd with his shaft
To soar with his light feathers, and so bound,   20
I cannot bound a pitch° above dull woe.
Under love's heavy burden do I sink.
  MER. And to sink in it, should you burden love,
Too great oppression for a tender thing.
  ROM. Is love a tender thing? It is too rough,   25
Too rude, too boisterous, and it pricks like thorn.
  MER. If love be rough with you, be rough with
    love.
Prick love for pricking, and you beat love down.
Give me a case to put my visage° in.
A visor for a visor!° What care I   30
What curious eye doth quote° deformities?

Here are the beetle° brows shall blush for me.
  BEN. Come, knock and enter, and no sooner in
But every man betake him to his legs.
  ROM. A torch for me. Let wantons light of heart
Tickle the senseless rushes° with their heels,   36
For I am proverbed with a grandsire phrase.°
I'll be a candleholder,° and look on.
The game was ne'er so fair, and I am done.°
  MER. Tut, dun's° the mouse, the constable's own
    word.°   40
If thou art dun, we'll draw thee from the mire
Of this sir-reverence° love wherein thou stick'st
Up to the ears. Come, we burn daylight,° ho.
  ROM. Nay, that's not so.
  MER.   I mean, sir, in delay
We waste our lights in vain, like lamps by day.   45
Take our good meaning, for our judgment sits
Five times in that ere once in our five wits.°
  ROM. And we mean well in going to this mask,
But 'tis no wit to go.
  MER.   Why, may one ask?
  ROM. I dreamed a dream tonight.
  MER.   And so did I. 50
  ROM. Well, what was yours?
  MER.   That dreamers often lie.
  ROM. In bed asleep, while they do dream things
    true.
  MER. Oh then, I see Queen Mab° hath been with
    you.
She is the fairies' midwife, and she comes
In shape no bigger than an agate stone°   55
On the forefinger of an alderman,
Drawn with a team of little atomies°
Athwart men's noses as they lie asleep —
Her wagon spokes made of long spinners'° legs;
The cover, of the wings of grasshoppers;   60
Her traces,° of the smallest spider's web;
Her collars, of the moonshine's watery beams;
Her whip, of cricket's bone; the lash, of film;°
Her wagoner, a small gray-coated gnat
Not half so big as a round little worm   65
Pricked from the lazy finger of a maid.°

105. **stays:** waits for you.

Sc. iv: 1–3. **What . . . prolixity:** Elizabethan entertainments were elaborate. When uninvited maskers wished to attend, it was customary for them to announce their coming by sending in a messenger, symbolically costumed, to make an appropriate speech. Benvolio says that such an elaborate device (*prolixity*) is out of date. His party will not provide someone dressed up as Cupid. 4. **hoodwinked:** blindfolded. 5. **Tartar's . . . lath:** imitation Tartar's bow. The Tartars were mounted archers; they therefore carried short curved bows, unlike the usual English longbow. 6. **crow-keeper:** scarecrow. 9–10. **measure . . . measure:** estimate . . . dance. See App. 24. 11. **ambling:** mincing. 12. **heavy:** sad. 18. **bound:** leap. 21. **pitch:** flight. See App. 26. 29. **visage:** face. Here the party put on grotesque masks. 30. **visor . . . visor:** mask for an ugly face. 31. **quote:** note.

32. **beetle:** overhanging. 36. **rushes:** Floors were commonly covered with rushes. 37. **am . . . phrase:** am provided with an old proverb. 38. **candleholder:** onlooker. See Pl. 17d. 39. **The . . . done:** be the game never so fair, I am too tired for it. 40–42. **dun's . . . love:** Mercutio cannot avoid a pun. He answers Romeo's "done" with "dun's the mouse" which apparently meant "still as a mouse." Mercutio then extends the meaning to "dun is in the mire," an old winter game in which the players hauled a heavy log representing a horse stuck in the mud. **dun:** gray-brown color. **constable's . . . word:** as the constable said. **sir-reverence:** a phrase used as substitute and apology for a filthy word. 43. **burn daylight:** waste time. 46–47. **Take . . . wits:** accept the best meaning of my words, for we are judged five times for our reputation before we are once judged for our intellect. 53. **Queen Mab:** the fairy queen. 55. **agate stone:** large seal ring. 57. **atomies:** tiny creatures; lit., motes in a sunbeam. 59. **spinners':** spiders'. 61. **traces:** harness. 63. **film:** spider's thread. 65–66. **worm . . . maid:** Lazy maids were said to grow maggots in their fingers.

Her chariot is an empty hazelnut,
Made by the joiner squirrel or old grub,
Time out o' mind the fairies' coachmakers.
And in this state she gallops night by night   70
Through lovers' brains, and then they dream of
    love;
O'er courtiers' knees, that dream on curtseys
    straight;
O'er lawyers' fingers, who straight dream on fees;
O'er ladies' lips, who straight on kisses dream,
Which oft the angry Mab with blisters plagues   75
Because their breaths with sweetmeats tainted are.
Sometime she gallops o'er a courtier's nose,
And then dreams he of smelling out a suit.°
And sometime comes she with a tithe pig's° tail
Tickling a parson's nose as a' lies asleep,   80
Then dreams he of another benefice.
Sometime she driveth o'er a soldier's neck,
And then dreams he of cutting foreign throats,
Of breaches, ambuscadoes, Spanish blades,
Of healths five fathom deep; and then anon   85
Drums in his ear, at which he starts and wakes,
And being thus frighted swears a prayer or two,
And sleeps again. This is that very Mab
That plaits the manes of horses in the night,
And bakes the elflocks° in foul sluttish hairs,   90
Which once untangled much misfortune bodes.
This is the hag,° when maids lie on their backs,
That presses them and learns them first to bear,
Making them women of good carriage.
This is she ——
    ROM.   Peace, peace, Mercutio, peace!   95
Thou talk'st of nothing.
    MER.   True, I talk of dreams,
Which are the children of an idle brain,
Begot of nothing but vain fantasy,°
Which is as thin of substance as the air
And more inconstant than the wind, who woos
Even now the frozen bosom of the North,   101
And, being angered, puffs away from thence,
Turning his face to the dew-dropping South.
    BEN. This wind you talk of blows us from our-
selves.
Supper is done, and we shall come too late.   105
    ROM. I fear, too early. For my mind misgives
Some consequence, yet hanging in the stars,
Shall bitterly begin his fearful date°
With this night's revels, and expire the term
Of a despisèd life° closed in my breast   110

By some vile forfeit of untimely death.
But He that hath the steerage of my course
Direct my sail! On, lusty gentlemen.
    BEN. Strike, drum.   [*Exeunt.*]

SCENE V. *A hall in* CAPULET's *house.*

[MUSICIANS *waiting. Enter* SERVINGMEN, *with
    napkins.*]

    1. SERV. Where's Potpan, that he helps not to take
away? He shift a trencher!° He scrape a trencher!
    2. SERV. When good manners shall lie all in one or
two men's hands, and they unwashed too, 'tis a foul
thing.   6
    1. SERV. Away with the joint stools,° remove the
court cupboard,° look to the plate.° Good thou,
save me a piece of marchpane.° And, as thou lovest
me, let the porter let in Susan Grindstone and Nell.
Antony, and Potpan!   11
    2. SERV. Aye, boy, ready.
    1. SERV. You are looked for and called for, asked
for and sought for, in the great chamber.°
    3. SERV. We cannot be here and there too. Cheerly,
boys. Be brisk a while, and the longer liver take all.°
                                [*They retire behind.*]
[*Enter* CAPULET, *with* JULIET *and others of his house,
    meeting the* GUESTS *and* MASKERS.]
    CAP. Welcome, gentlemen! Ladies that have their
    toes
Unplagued with corns will have a bout with you.
Ah ha, my mistresses! Which of you all   20
Will now deny to dance? She that makes dainty,°
She, I'll swear, hath corns — am I come near ye
now?°
Welcome, gentlemen! I have seen the day
That I have worn a visor,° and could tell
A whispering tale in a fair lady's ear   25
Such as would please. 'Tis gone, 'tis gone, 'tis gone.
You are welcome, gentlemen! Come, musicians,
    play.
A hall, a hall°! Give room! And foot it, girls.
                        [*Music plays, and they dance.*]
More light, you knaves, and turn the tables up,
And quench the fire, the room is grown too hot.   30
Ah, sirrah, this unlooked-for sport comes well.
Nay, sit, nay, sit, good Cousin Capulet,

78. **suit:** with the double meaning of "fine clothes" and "petition for favor," a common pun.   79. **tithe pig's:** The parson was entitled to a tithe or tenth of the produce of his parishioners, which he often took in kind. See Gen. Intro. p. 19a.   90. **elflocks:** The knots in the manes of horses and uncombed human hair were sometimes attributed to mischievous fairies.   92. **hag:** nightmare.   98. **fantasy:** fancy.   108. **date:** period.   109-10. **expire . . . life:** cause the lease of my life to come to an end.

Sc. v: 2. **trencher:** wooden platter.   7. **joint stools:** stools made of joiners' work. See Pl. 17a.   8. **court cupboard:** sideboard. See Pl. 20a. **plate:** silver plate.   9. **marchpane:** marzipan, a mixture made of almond paste, often in an elaborate shape.   14. **great chamber:** Elizabethan great houses had a great chamber used for dining and social occasions. After dinner the tables were pushed to one side, turned up (i.e., on their sides), and a space cleared for dancing.   16. **longer . . . all:** i.e., the last survivor takes all.   21. **makes dainty:** pretends to be shy.   22. **am . . . now:** i.e., do I touch a tender spot?   24. **worn a visor:** i.e., been a dancer.   28. **a hall, a hall!:** i.e., clear the hall for dancing.

For you and I are past our dancing days.
How long is 't now since last yourself and I
Were in a mask?

  2. CAP.   By 'r Lady, thirty years. 35
  CAP. What, man! 'Tis not so much, 'tis not so
  much.
'Tis since the nuptial of Lucentio,
Come Pentecost as quickly as it will,
Some five and twenty years, and then we masked.

  2. CAP. 'Tis more, 'tis more. His son is elder, sir,
His son is thirty.

  CAP.   Will you tell me that? 41
His son was but a ward° two years ago.

  ROM. [*To a* SERVINGMAN] What lady's that which
  doth enrich the hand
Of yonder knight?

  SERV. I know not, sir. 45

  ROM. Oh, she doth teach the torches to burn
  bright!
It seems she hangs upon the cheek of night
Like a rich jewel in an Ethiop's ear —
Beauty too rich for use, for earth too dear!
So shows a snowy dove trooping with crows 50
As yonder lady o'er her fellows shows.
The measure done, I'll watch her place of stand,
And, touching hers, make blessèd my rude hand.
Did my heart love till now? Forswear it, sight!
For I ne'er saw true beauty till this night. 55

  TYB. This, by his voice, should be a Montague.
Fetch me my rapier, boy. What dares the slave
Come hither, covered with an antic face,°
To fleer° and scorn at our solemnity?
Now, by the stock and honor of my kin, 60
To strike him dead I hold it not a sin.

  CAP. Why, how now, kinsman! Wherefore storm
  you so?

  TYB. Uncle, this is a Montague, our foe,
A villain, that is hither come in spite
To scorn at our solemnity this night. 65

  CAP. Young Romeo, is it?

  TYB.   'Tis he, that villain
  Romeo.

  CAP. Content thee, gentle Coz, let him alone,
He bears him like a portly° gentleman.
And, to say truth, Verona brags of him
To be a virtuous and well-governed youth. 70
I would not for the wealth of all this town
Here in my house do him disparagement.
Therefore be patient, take no note of him.
It is my will, the which if thou respect,
Show a fair presence and put off these frowns, 75
An ill-beseeming semblance° for a feast.

  TYB. It fits when such a villain is a guest.
I'll not endure him.

  CAP.   He shall be endured.
What, goodman boy° I say he shall. Go to, 80
Am I the master here, or you? Go to.
You'll not endure him! God shall mend my soul,
You'll make a mutiny among my guests!
You will set cock-a-hoop!° You'll be the man!

  TYB. Why, Uncle, 'tis a shame.

  CAP.   Go to, go to,
You are a saucy boy. Is't so, indeed? 85
This trick° may chance to scathe° you, I know what.
You must contrary me! Marry, 'tis time.
Well said, my hearts! You are a princox,° go.
Be quiet, or —— More light, more light! For shame!
I'll make you quiet. What, cheerly, my hearts! 90

  TYB. Patience perforce with willful choler meeting
Makes my flesh tremble in their different greeting.
I will withdraw. But this intrusion shall,
Now seeming sweet, convert to bitterest gall.
           [*Exit.*]

  ROM. [*To* JULIET] If I profane with my unworthi-
  est hand 95
This holy shrine, the gentle fine° is this,
My lips, two blushing pilgrims, ready stand
To smooth that rough touch with a tender kiss.

  JUL. Good° pilgrim, you do wrong your hand too
  much,
Which mannerly devotion° shows in this; 100
For saints have hands that pilgrims' hands do touch,
And palm to palm is holy palmers'° kiss.

  ROM. Have not saints lips, and holy palmers too?

  JUL. Aye, pilgrim, lips that they must use in
  prayer.

  ROM. Oh then, dear saint, let lips do what hands
  do. 105
They pray. Grant thou, lest faith turn to despair.

  JUL. Saints do not move, though grant for pray-
  ers' sake.

  ROM. Then move not while my prayer's effect I
  take.
Thus from my lips by thine my sin is purged.
         [*Kissing her.*]

  JUL. Then have my lips the sin that they have
  took. 110

  ROM. Sin from my lips? Oh, trespass sweetly
  urged!°

80. goodman boy: a contemptuous phrase. *Goodman* indicated a man under the rank of gentleman, but above that of a laborer; *boy*, a youngster, an insulting term. See III.i.69. **84. cock-a-hoop:** an ancient phrase of doubtful origin. In the sixteenth century it meant "to take the spigot out of the barrel, and so let the liquor flow without interruption," hence "be utterly reckless." Today it means "boastfully triumphant." Capulet means "You want to start a roughhouse." **86. trick:** habit, i.e., of quarreling. **scathe:** injure. **88. princox:** conceited boy. **96. fine:** punishment. **99–102. Good . . . kiss:** Juliet takes up Romeo's metaphor of "pilgrim," and for the next ten lines they follow it up with an elaborate play on religious imagery. **100. devotion:** the pilgrim's vow. **102. palmer:** a pilgrim who carried a palm leaf as a sign that he had made the journey to the Holy Land. **111. urged:** argued.

42. ward: a minor in charge of a guardian. **58. antic face:** grotesque mask. **59. fleer:** sneer. **68. portly:** dignified. **76. semblance:** appearance.

Give me my sin again.

JUL.   You kiss by the book.°

NURSE Madam, your mother craves a word with
     you.

ROM. What is her mother?

NURSE.   Marry, bachelor,

Her mother is the lady of the house,   115
And a good lady, and a wise and virtuous.
I nursed her daughter, that you talked withal.
I tell you, he that can lay hold of her
Shall have the chinks.°

ROM.   Is she a Capulet?

Oh, dear° account! My life is my foe's debt.°   120

BEN. Away, be gone. The sport is at the best.

ROM. Aye, so I fear. The more is my unrest.

CAP. Nay, gentlemen, prepare not to be gone,
We have a trifling foolish banquet° toward.
Is it e'en so? Why then, I thank you all,   125
I thank you, honest gentlemen. Good night.
More torches here! Come on, then, let's to bed.
Ah, sirrah, by my fay,° it waxes late.
I'll to my rest.   [*Exeunt all but* JULIET *and* NURSE.]

JUL. Come hither, Nurse. What is yond gentle-
     man?   130

NURSE. The son and heir of old Tiberio.

JUL. What's he that now is going out of door?

NURSE. Marry, that, I think, be young Petruchio.

JUL. What's he that follows there, that would not
     dance?

NURSE. I know not.   135

JUL. Go ask his name. If he be marrièd,
My grave is like to be my wedding bed.

NURSE. His name is Romeo, and a Montague,
The only son of your great enemy.   139

JUL. My only love sprung from my only hate!
Too early seen unknown, and known too late!
Prodigious° birth of love it is to me,
That I must love a loathèd enemy.

NURSE. What's this? What's this?

JUL.   A rhyme I learned even now
Of one I danced withal. [*One calls within,* "Juliet."]

NURSE.   Anon, anon!   145
Come, let's away, the strangers all are gone.

                                [*Exeunt.*]

112. by . . . book: according to the book of instructions; i.e.,
you are merely being gallant. 119. chinks: cash. 120. dear:
in the double meaning of "costly" and "beloved." foe's debt:
owed to my foe. 124. banquet: light refreshments. 128. fay:
faith. 142. Prodigious: monstrous, unnatural.

Act II

PROLOGUE

[*Enter* CHORUS]

CHOR. Now old desire° doth in his deathbed lie,
   And young affection gapes to be his heir.
That fair for which love groaned for and would die,
   With tender Juliet matched, is now not fair.
Now Romeo is beloved and loves again,   5
   Alike° bewitchèd by the charm of looks,
But to his foe supposed he must complain,
   And she steal love's sweet bait from fearful hooks.
Being held a foe, he may not have access
   To breathe such vows as lovers use to swear,   10
And she as much in love, her means much less
   To meet her new belovèd anywhere.
But passion lends them power, time means, to meet,
Tempering extremities° with extreme sweet. [*Exit.*]

SCENE I. *A lane by the wall of* CAPULET'S *orchard.*

[*Enter* ROMEO, *alone.*]

ROM. Can I go forward when my heart is here?
Turn back, dull earth,° and find thy center° out.
                                [*Exit.*]

[*Enter* BENVOLIO *with* MERCUTIO.]

BEN. Romeo! My cousin Romeo!

MER.   He is wise,
And, on my life, hath stol'n him home to bed.

BEN. He ran this way, and leaped this orchard
     wall.   5
Call, good Mercutio.

MER.   Nay, I'll conjure° too.
Romeo! Humors! Madman! Passion! Lover!
Appear thou in the likeness of a sigh.
Speak but one rhyme, and I am satisfied,
Cry but " aye me! " pronounce but " love " and
     "dove,"   10
Speak to my gossip° Venus one fair word,
One nickname for her purblind° son and heir,
Young Adam Cupid, he that shot so trim°
When King Cophetua° loved the beggar maid!
He heareth not, he stirreth not, he moveth not.   15

     Act II, Pro.: 1. old desire: i.e., Romeo's love for Rosaline.
6. Alike: equally. 14. Tempering extremities: moderating ex-
treme difficulties.

     Sc. i: 2. dull earth: i.e., my body. center: the absolute center
of the universe; i.e., Juliet. See App. 1. 6. conjure: call up a
spirit. 11. gossip: friend with whom one exchanges confidences
and scandal. 12. purblind: dim-sighted. 13. Young . . . trim:
This is a much disputed line; Q1 and Q2 read "Young Abra-
ham: Cupid he . . ." F1 reads: "Young Abraham Cupid." Most
editors emend to "Adam Cupid." Adam was a name given to
good archers, after Adam Bell, a famous one. See *M Ado*, I.i.261.
14. King Cophetua: the hero of a popular ballad; he fell in love
with a beggar maid, whom he married.

The ape is dead, and I must conjure him.
I conjure thee by Rosaline's bright eyes,
By her high forehead and her scarlet lip,
By her fine foot, straight leg, and quivering thigh,
And the demesnes° that there adjacent lie,   20
That in thy likeness thou appear to us!

BEN. An if he hear thee, thou wilt anger him.

MER. This cannot anger him. 'Twould anger him
To raise a spirit in his mistress' circle
Of some strange nature, letting it there stand   25
Till she had laid it and conjured it down.
That were some spite.° My invocation
Is fair and honest, and in his mistress' name
I conjure only but to raise up him.   29

BEN. Come, he hath hid himself among these trees,
To be consorted° with the humorous° night.
Blind is his love, and best befits the dark.

MER. If love be blind, love cannot hit the mark.
Now will he sit under a medlar° tree,
And wish his mistress were that kind of fruit   35
As maids call medlars when they laugh alone.
Oh, Romeo, that she were, Oh, that she were
An open et cetera,° thou a poperin° pear!
Romeo, good night. I'll to my truckle bed,°
This field bed is too cold for me to sleep.   40
Come, shall we go?

BEN.   Go then, for 'tis in vain
To seek him here that means not to be found.

[Exeunt.]

SCENE II.° CAPULET's orchard.

[Enter ROMEO.]

ROM. He jests at scars that never felt a wound.

[JULIET appears above at a window.]

But, soft! What light through yonder window
     breaks?
It is the east, and Juliet is the sun!
Arise, fair sun, and kill the envious moon,°
Who is already sick and pale with grief   5
That thou her maid art far more fair than she.
Be not her maid, since she is envious.
Her vestal° livery is but sick and green,
And none but fools do wear it. Cast it off.
It is my lady, oh, it is my love!   10

20. demesnes: domains.   27. spite: outrage.   31. consorted:
associated. humorous: moody.   34. medlar: a tree which pro-
duces a fruit like a small brown apple, only eaten when it has
grown soft; used here with a quibble on "meddler." See AYLI,
III.ii.124.   38. et cetera: often used (like "so-and-so") as a
nice substitute for a nasty word. poperin: lit., a pear from
Poperinghe in Flanders, but used obscenely for the male parts.
39. truckle bed: trundle bed, a bed on casters, pushed under the
great bed in the daytime.

Sc. ii: This division is not in the original play but has been
made by editors. See Gen. Intro. pp. 56b–57a.   4. envious
moon: the moon is also Diana, the virgin goddess.   8. vestal:
virgin.

Oh, that she knew she were!
She speaks, yet she says nothing. What of that?
Her eye discourses, I will answer it.
I am too bold, 'tis not to me she speaks.
Two of the fairest stars in all the heaven,   15
Having some business, do entreat her eyes
To twinkle in their spheres° till they return.
What if her eyes were there, they in her head?
The brightness of her cheek would shame those stars
As daylight doth a lamp; her eyes in heaven   20
Would through the airy region stream so bright
That birds would sing and think it were not night.
See how she leans her cheek upon her hand!
Oh, that I were a glove upon that hand,
That I might touch that cheek!

JUL.   Aye me!

ROM.   She speaks.
Oh, speak again, bright angel! For thou art   26
As glorious to this night, being o'er my head,
As is a wingèd messenger of Heaven
Unto the white-upturnèd wondering eyes
Of mortals that fall back to gaze on him   30
When he bestrides the lazy-pacing clouds
And sails upon the bosom of the air.

JUL. O Romeo, Romeo, wherefore art thou
     Romeo?
Deny thy father and refuse thy name,
Or, if thou wilt not, be but sworn my love   35
And I'll no longer be a Capulet.

ROM. [Aside] Shall I hear more, or shall I speak
     at this?

JUL. 'Tis but thy name that is my enemy.
Thou art thyself, though not a Montague.
What's Montague? It is nor hand, nor foot,   40
Nor arm, nor face, nor any other part
Belonging to a man. Oh, be some other name!
What's in a name? That which we call a rose
By any other name would smell as sweet.
So Romeo would, were he not Romeo called,   45
Retain that dear perfection which he owes°
Without that title. Romeo, doff thy name,
And for thy name, which is no part of thee,
Take all myself.

ROM.   I take thee at thy word.
Call me but love, and I'll be new baptized.   50
Henceforth I never will be Romeo.

JUL. What man art thou that, thus bescreened in
     night,
So stumblest on my counsel?

ROM.   By a name
I know not how to tell thee who I am.
My name, dear saint, is hateful to myself   55
Because it is an enemy to thee.
Had I it written, I would tear the word.

JUL. My ears have yet not drunk a hundred words
Of thy tongue's uttering, yet I know the sound.

17. spheres: See App. 1.   46. owes: owns.

Art thou not Romeo, and a Montague?   60
  ROM. Neither, fair saint, if either thee dislike.°
  JUL. How camest thou hither, tell me, and where-
    fore?
The orchard walls are high and hard to climb,
And the place death, considering who thou art,
If any of my kinsmen find thee here.   65
  ROM. With love's light wings did I o'erperch°
    these walls,
For stony limits cannot hold love out.
And what love can do, that dares love attempt,
Therefore thy kinsmen are no let° to me.
  JUL. If they do see thee, they will murder thee.   70
  ROM. Alack, there lies more peril in thine eye
Than twenty of their swords. Look thou but sweet,
And I am proof° against their enmity.
  JUL. I would not for the world they saw thee here.
  ROM. I have night's cloak to hide me from their
    eyes,   75
And but° thou love me, let them find me here.
My life were better ended by their hate
Than death prorogued,° wanting of thy love.
  JUL. By whose direction found'st thou out this
    place?
  ROM. By love, that first did prompt me to inquire.
He lent me counsel, and I lent him eyes.   81
I am no pilot, yet wert thou as far
As that vast shore washed with the farthest sea,
I would adventure for such merchandise.
  JUL. Thou know'st the mask of night is on my
    face,   85
Else would a maiden blush bepaint my cheek
For that which thou hast heard me speak tonight.
Fain would I dwell on form,° fain, fain deny
What I have spoke. But farewell compliment!°
Dost thou love me? I know thou wilt say "Aye,"   90
And I will take thy word. Yet if thou swear'st,
Thou mayst prove false. At lovers' perjuries
They say Jove laughs. O gentle Romeo,
If thou dost love, pronounce it faithfully.
Or if thou think'st I am too quickly won,   95
I'll frown and be perverse and say thee nay,
So thou wilt woo; but else, not for the world.
In truth, fair Montague, I am too fond,°
And therefore thou mayst think my 'havior light.
But trust me, gentleman, I'll prove more true   100
Than those that have more cunning to be strange.°
I should have been more strange, I must confess,
But that thou overheard'st, ere I was ware,
My true love's passion. Therefore pardon me,
And not impute this yielding to light love,   105
Which the dark night hath so discovered.
  ROM. Lady, by yonder blessed moon I swear,

That tips with silver all these fruit-tree tops ——
  JUL. Oh, swear not by the moon, th' inconstant
    moon,
That monthly changes in her circled orb,   110
Lest that thy love prove likewise variable.
  ROM. What shall I swear by?
  JUL.   Do not swear at all.
Or, if thou wilt, swear by thy gracious self,
Which is the god of my idolatry,
And I'll believe thee.
  ROM.   If my heart's dear love ——
  JUL. Well, do not swear. Although I joy in thee,
I have no joy of this contráct° tonight.   117
It is too rash, too unadvised, too sudden,
Too like the lightning, which doth cease to be
Ere one can say "It lightens." Sweet, good night!
This bud of love, by summer's ripening breath,   121
May prove a beauteous flower when next we meet.
Good night, good night! As sweet repose and rest
Come to thy heart as that within my breast!
  ROM. Oh, wilt thou leave me so unsatisfied?   125
  JUL. What satisfaction canst thou have tonight?
  ROM. The exchange of thy love's faithful vow for
    mine.
  JUL. I gave thee mine before thou didst request it,
And yet I would it were to give again.
  ROM. Wouldst thou withdraw it? For what pur-
    pose, love?   130
  JUL. But to be frank, and give it thee again.
And yet I wish but for the thing I have.
My bounty is as boundless as the sea,
My love as deep; the more I give to thee,
The more I have, for both are infinite.   135
I hear some noise within. Dear love, adieu!
              [NURSE *calls within.*°]
Anon,° good Nurse! Sweet Montague, be true.
Stay but a little, I will come again.   [*Exit.*]
  ROM. Oh, blessed, blessed night! I am afeard,
Being in night, all this is but a dream,   140
Too flattering-sweet to be substantial.
         [*Re-enter* JULIET, *above.*]
  JUL. Three words, dear Romeo, and good night
    indeed.
If that thy bent° of love be honorable,
Thy purpose marriage, send me word tomorrow
By one that I'll procure to come to thee,   145
Where and what time thou wilt perform the rite,
And all my fortunes at thy foot I'll lay,
And follow thee my lord throughout the world.
  NURSE. [*Within*] Madam!
  JUL. I come, anon. — But if thou mean'st not
    well, I do beseech thee ——   151
  NURSE. [*Within*] Madam!
  JUL.   By and by, I come —
To cease thy suit, and leave me to my grief.

---

61. dislike: displease.   66. o'erperch: fly over.   69. let: hin-
drance.   73. proof: armored.   76. And but: if only.   78. pro-
rogued: postponed.   88. dwell on form: behave according to
convention.   89. compliment: polite behavior.   98. fond: fool-
ishly affectionate.   101. strange: outwardly cold.

117. contract: betrothal.   136. s.d., within: off stage.   137. Anon:
by and by, in a moment.   143. bent: intention.

Tomorrow will I send.

ROM.   So thrive my soul ——

JUL. A thousand times good night!   [*Exit.*]

ROM. A thousand times the worse, to want thy
    light.   155

Love goes toward love as schoolboys from their
    books,

But love from love toward school with heavy looks.
                         [*Retiring slowly.*]

              [*Re-enter* JULIET, *above.*]

JUL. Hist! Romeo, hist! — Oh, for a falconer's°
    voice,

To lure this tassel-gentle° back again!   160

Bondage is hoarse,° and may not speak aloud,

Else would I tear the cave where Echo lies

And make her airy tongue more hoarse than mine

With repetition of my Romeo's name.

ROM. It is my soul that calls upon my name.   165

How silver-sweet sound lovers' tongues by night,

Like softest music to attending ears!

JUL. Romeo!

ROM.   My dear?°

JUL.   At what o'clock tomorrow

Shall I send to thee?

ROM.   At the hour of nine.

JUL. I will not fail. 'Tis twenty years till then.

I have forgot why I did call thee back.   171

ROM. Let me stand here till thou remember it.

JUL. I shall forget, to have thee still stand there,

Remembering how I love thy company.

ROM. And I'll still stay, to have thee still forget,

Forgetting any other home but this.   176

JUL. 'Tis almost morning. I would have thee
    gone,

And yet no farther than a wanton's° bird,

Who lets it hop a little from her hand,

Like a poor prisoner in his twisted gyves,°   180

And with a silk thread plucks it back again,

So loving-jealous of his liberty.

ROM. I would I were thy bird.

JUL.   Sweet, so would I.

Yet I should kill thee with much cherishing.

Good night, good night! Parting is such sweet sor-
    row   185

That I shall say good night till it be morrow.
                         [*Exit.*]

ROM. Sleep dwell upon thine eyes, peace in thy
    breast!

Would I were sleep and peace, so sweet to rest!

Hence will I to my ghostly° father's cell,   189

His help to crave and my dear hap° to tell.   [*Exit.*]

SCENE III. FRIAR LAURENCE'S *cell.*

[*Enter* FRIAR LAURENCE, *with a basket.*]

FRI. L. The gray-eyed morn smiles on the frown-
    ing night,

Checkering° the eastern clouds with streaks of light,

And fleckèd° darkness like a drunkard reels

From forth day's path and Titan's° fiery wheels.

Now, ere the sun advance his burning eye,   5

The day to cheer and night's dank dew to dry,

I must upfill° this osier cage° of ours

With baleful weeds and precious-juicèd flowers.

The earth that's Nature's mother is her tomb,

What is her burying grave, that is her womb.   10

And from her womb children of divers kind

We sucking on her natural bosom find,

Many for many virtues excellent,

None but for some, and yet all different.

Oh, mickle° is the powerful grace that lies   15

In herbs, plants, stones, and their true qualities.

For naught so vile that on the earth doth live,

But to the earth some special good doth give;

Nor aught so good but, strained from that fair use,

Revolts from true birth, stumbling on abuse.°   20

Virtue itself turns vice, being misapplied,

And vice sometime's by action dignified.

Within the infant rind of this small flower

Poison hath residence, and medicine power.

For this, being smelt, with that part cheers each
    part,   25

Being tasted, slays all senses with the heart.

Two such opposèd kings encamp them still°

In man as well as herbs, grace° and rude will°;

And where the worser is predominant,

Full soon the canker° death eats up that plant.   30

[*Enter* ROMEO.]

ROM. Good morrow, Father.

FRI. L.   Benedicite!

What early tongue so sweet saluteth me?

Young son, it argues a distempered° head

So soon to bid good morrow to thy bed.

Care keeps his watch in every old man's eye,   35

And where care lodges, sleep will never lie;

But where unbruisèd youth with unstuffed brain

Doth couch his limbs, there golden sleep doth reign.

Therefore thy earliness doth me assure

Thou art uproused by some distemperature.   40

Or if not so, then here I hit it right,

Our Romeo hath not been in bed tonight.

ROM. That last is true. The sweeter rest was mine.

FRI. L. God pardon sin! Wast thou with Rosaline?

ROM. With Rosaline, my ghostly father? No.   45

---

159. falconer: keeper of hawks.   160. tassel-gentle: male pere-
grine falcon.   161. Bondage is hoarse: i.e., being under the
control of my parents, I can only whisper.   168. My dear: In
Elizabethan times this was a phrase of tenderest affection.
178. wanton: spoiled child.   180. gyves: fetters   189. ghostly:
spiritual.   190. hap: luck.

Sc. iii: 2. Checkering: variegating.   3. flecked: dappled
4. Titan: the sun.   7. upfill: fill up. osier cage: wicker basket.
15. mickle: mighty.   20. abuse: misuse.   27. still: always.
28. grace: the power of goodness. rude will: man's natural desire
for evil.   30. canker: cankerworm.   33. distempered: disturbed.

I have forgot that name and that name's woe.

FRI. L. That's my good son. But where hast thou
    been, then?

ROM. I'll tell thee ere thou ask it me again.
I have been feasting with mine enemy,
Where on a sudden one hath wounded me   50
That's by me wounded. Both our remedies
Within thy help and holy physic° lies.
I bear no hatred, blessed man, for, lo,
My intercession likewise steads° my foe.

FRI. L. Be plain, good son, and homely° in thy
    drift.   55
Riddling confession finds but riddling shrift.°

ROM. Then plainly know my heart's dear love is
    set
On the fair daughter of rich Capulet.
As mine on hers, so hers is set on mine,
And all combined° save what thou must combine
By holy marriage. When, and where, and how,   61
We met, we wooed and made exchange of vow,
I'll tell thee as we pass; but this I pray,
That thou consent to marry us today.

FRI. L. Holy Saint Francis, what a change is here!
Is Rosaline, that thou didst love so dear,   66
So soon forsaken? Young men's love then lies
Not truly in their hearts, but in their eyes.
Jesu Maria, what a deal of brine
Hath washed thy sallow cheeks for Rosaline!   70
How much salt water thrown away in waste,
To season° love, that of it doth not taste!
The sun not yet thy sighs from heaven clears,
Thy old groans ring yet in mine ancient ears.
Lo, here upon thy cheek the stain doth sit   75
Of an old tear that is not washed off yet.
If e'er thou wast thyself and these woes thine,
Thou and these woes were all for Rosaline.
And art thou changed? Pronounce this sentence°
    then ——   79
Women may fall when there's no strength in men.

ROM. Thou chid'st me oft for loving Rosaline.

FRI. L. For doting, not for loving, pupil mine.

ROM. And bad'st me bury love.

FRI. L.   Not in a grave
To lay one in, another out to have.

ROM. I pray thee, chide not. She whom I love now
Doth grace for grace and love for love allow. 86
The other did not so.

FRI. L.   Oh, she knew well
Thy love did read by rote and could not spell.°
But come, young waverer, come, go with me,
In one respect I'll thy assistant be;   90
For this alliance may so happy prove,

To turn your households' rancor to pure love.

ROM. Oh, let us hence. I stand on sudden haste.°

FRI. L. Wisely and slow. They stumble that run
    fast.   [Exeunt.]

SCENE IV. *A street.*

[*Enter* BENVOLIO *and* MERCUTIO.]

MER. Where the devil should this Romeo be?
Came he not home tonight?

BEN. Not to his father's, I spoke with his man.

MER. Ah, that same pale hardhearted wench, that
    Rosaline,
Torments him so that he will sure run mad.   5

BEN. Tybalt, the kinsman of old Capulet,
Hath sent a letter to his father's house.

MER. A challenge, on my life.

BEN. Romeo will answer it.

MER. Any man that can write may answer a let-
ter.   10

BEN. Nay, he will answer the letter's master, how
he dares, being dared.

MER. Alas, poor Romeo, he is already dead!
Stabbed with a white wench's black eye, shot thor-
ough the ear with a love song, the very pin° of his
heart cleft with the blind bowboy's butt shaft.° And
is he a man to encounter Tybalt?   17

BEN. Why, what is Tybalt?

MER. More than Prince of Cats,° I can tell you.
Oh, he's the courageous captain of compliments.° He
fights as you sing prick song,° keeps time, distance,
and proportion; rests me his minim° rest, one,   22
two, and the third in your bosom. The very butcher
of a silk button, a duelist, a duelist, a gentleman of
the very first house,° of the first and second cause.°
Ah, the immortal passado! The punto reverso! The
hai!°

BEN. The what?   28

MER. The pox of such antic, lisping, affecting fan-
tasticoes,° these new tuners of accents! "By Jesu, a
very good blade! A very tall° man! A very good
whore! " Why, is not this a lamentable thing, Grand-

52. physic: remedy.   54. steads: benefits.   55. homely: simple.
56. shrift: absolution.   60. combined: united.   72. season: keep
fresh, as meat is kept wholesome by salt.   79. sentence:
proverb.   88. love . . . spell: your love was merely repeating
phrases by heart (by rote), like a child that pretends to read
because it knows the words.

93. Oh . . . haste: let us go quickly, for I am impatient.
  Sc. iv: 15. pin: center of the target.   16. butt shaft: un-
pointed arrow, used for target practice.   19. Prince of Cats: In
the tale of Reynard the Fox, Tibert (or Tybalt) is Prince of
Cats.   20. captain of compliments: expert in the niceties of
fashionable behavior.   21. prick song: melody accompanying a
song.   22. minim: the shortest note in music.   23–27. butcher
. . . hai: A professional fencer would undertake to touch his op-
ponent on any button of his doublet. Mercutio mocks Tybalt
because he is an expert with the new-fashioned rapier. See Pl.
22l. Dueling with the rapier had its own ritual and vocabulary,
such as passado, lunge; punto reverso, a backhanded stroke; and
hai, the cry as the fencer thrusts home.   25. first house: finest
school.   first . . . cause: the reasons which (according to the ex-
act rules of honor) caused a gentleman to issue a challenge.
See AYLI, V.iv.48–108.   30. fantasticoes: fantastical fellows.
31. tall: brave.

sire, that we should be thus afflicted with these strange flies, these fashionmongers, these perdona-mi's,° who stand so much on the new form that they cannot sit at ease on the old bench? Oh, their bones,° their bones!   37

[*Enter* ROMEO.]

BEN. Here comes Romeo, here comes Romeo.

MER. Without his roe, like a dried herring. Oh, flesh, flesh, how art thou fishified! Now is he for the numbers° that Petrarch flowed in. Laura° to his lady was but a kitchen wench — marry, she had a better love to berhyme her — Dido,° a dowdy;° Cleo- 43 patra, a gypsy;° Helen and Hero, hildings° and harlots; Thisbe, a gray eye or so, but not to the purpose. Signior Romeo, *bon jour!* — there's a French salutation to your French slop.° You gave us the counterfeit° fairly last night.

ROM. Good morrow to you both. What counterfeit did I give you?   50

MER. The slip, sir, the slip. Can you not conceive?

ROM. Pardon, good Mercutio, my business was great, and in such a case as mine a man may strain courtesy.   55

MER. That's as much as to say, Such a case as yours constrains a man to bow in the hams.

ROM. Meaning, to curtsy.

MER. Thou hast most kindly hit it.

ROM. A most courteous exposition.   60

MER. Nay, I am the very pink of courtesy.

ROM. Pink for flower.

MER. Right.

ROM. Why, then is my pump well flowered.°   64

MER. Well said. Follow me this jest now till thou hast worn out thy pump, that, when the single sole of it is worn, the jest may remain, after the wearing, solely singular.

ROM. Oh, single-soled jest, solely singular for the singleness!   70

MER. Come between us, good Benvolio. My wits faint.

ROM. Switch and spurs,° switch and spurs, or I'll cry a match.°   74

MER. Nay, if thy wits run the wild-goose chase,° I have done; for thou hast more of the wild goose in one of thy wits than, I am sure, I have in my whole five. Was I with you there for the goose?°   80

ROM. Thou wast never with me for anything when thou wast not there for the goose.

MER. I will bite thee by the ear for that jest.

ROM. Nay, good goose, bite not.

MER. Thy wit is a very bitter sweeting, it is a most sharp sauce.   85

ROM. And is it not well served in to a sweet goose?

MER. Oh, here's a wit of cheveril,° that stretches from an inch narrow to an ell broad!

ROM. I stretch it out for that word " broad," which, added to the goose, proves thee far and wide a broad goose.   91

MER. Why, is not this better now than groaning for love? Now art thou sociable,° now art thou Romeo; now art thou what thou art, by art as well as by nature. For this driveling love is like a great natural° that runs lolling up and down to hide his bauble° in a hole.   97

BEN. Stop there, stop there.

MER. Thou desirest me to stop in my tale against the hair.°

BEN. Thou wouldst else have made thy tale large.°   102

MER. Oh, thou art deceived — I would have made it short. For I was come to the whole depth of my tale, and meant indeed to occupy the argument no longer.   106

ROM. Here's goodly gear!°

[*Enter* NURSE *and* PETER.]

MER. A sail, a sail!

BEN. Two, two — a shirt and a smock.°

NURSE. Peter!   110

PET. Anon?

NURSE. My fan, Peter.

MER. Good Peter, to hide her face, for her fan's the fairer face.

NURSE. God ye good morrow, gentlemen.   115

MER. God ye good-den, fair gentlewoman.

NURSE. Is it good-den?°

MER. 'Tis no less, I tell you, for the bawdy hand of the dial is now upon the prick° of noon.

NURSE. Out upon you! What a man are you!   120

ROM. One, gentlewoman, that God hath made himself to mar.

NURSE. By my troth, it is well said. " For himself to mar," quoth a'? Gentlemen, can any of you tell me where I may find the young Romeo?   125

34–35. perdona-mi's: Italian for "pardon me." The man of fashion affected foreign languages. **36. bones:** with a pun on the French *bon.* **41. numbers:** verses. **Laura:** Petrarch's love, to whom he wrote his sonnets. **43–45. Dido . . . Thisbe:** all beautiful heroines of famous tragic stories. **dowdy:** slut. **gypsy:** Egyptian and so dusky. **hildings:** good-for-nothings. **47. slop:** baggy breeches. See Pl. 8c and p. 93a. **47–51. counterfeit . . . slip:** a counterfeit coin was called a slip. **64. pump . . . flowered:** my shoe is pinked (punched) with a pattern of flowers. See Pl. 8c. This kind of verbal wit, when every phrase has two or more meanings, was fashionable at this time, particularly among young gallants. **73. Switch . . . spurs:** at full gallop — urge your wit on. **74. match:** wager. Romeo means: If you can't keep up this wit contest, I claim the wager. **75. wild-goose chase:** a race where the second horseman must follow the first wherever he goes.

80. Was . . . goose: have I proved you to be a goose? **87. cheveril:** kid skin. **93. sociable:** i.e., Romeo, to Mercutio's delight, has now recovered his spirits. **96. natural:** fool. **97. bauble:** the fool's stick, ornamented with a doll's head. See Pl. 12f. **99–100. against . . . hair:** contrary to the natural life of the hair, as when one strokes a cat from the tail forward. **102. large:** licentious. **107. gear:** stuff. **109. shirt . . . smock:** man and a woman. **117. Is it good-den:** is it afternoon? **119. prick:** point.

ROM. I can tell you, but young Romeo will be older when you have found him than he was when you sought him. I am the youngest of that name, for fault of a worse.

NURSE. You say well.   130

MER. Yea, is the worst well? Very well took,° i' faith — wisely, wisely.

NURSE. If you be he, sir, I desire some confidence° with you.

BEN. She will indite° him to some supper.   135

MER. A bawd, a bawd, a bawd! So ho!°

ROM. What hast thou found?

MER. No° hare,° sir, unless a hare, sir, in a lenten pie, that is something stale and hoar° ere it be spent. [*Sings.*]   140

"An old hare hoar,
    And an old hare hoar,
Is very good meat in Lent.
    But a hare that is hoar,
    Is too much for a score   145
When it hoars ere it be spent."

Romeo, will you come to your father's? We'll to dinner thither.

ROM. I will follow you.

MER. Farewell, ancient lady, farewell [*Singing*], "lady, lady, lady."   151

[*Exeunt* MERCUTIO *and* BENVOLIO.]

NURSE. Marry, farewell! I pray you, sir, what saucy merchant was this, that was so full of his ropery?°

ROM. A gentleman, Nurse, that loves to hear himself talk, and will speak more in a minute than he will stand to in a month.   157

NURSE. An a' speak anything against me, I'll take him down, an a' were lustier than he is, and twenty such Jacks;° and if I cannot, I'll find those that shall. Scurvy knave! I am none of his flirt-gills,° I am none of his skainsmates.° [*Turning to* PETER] And thou must stand by too, and suffer every knave to use me at his pleasure?   164

PET. I saw no man use you at his pleasure. If I had, my weapon should quickly have been out, I warrant you. I dare draw as soon as another man, if I see occasion in a good quarrel and the law on my side.   169

NURSE. Now, afore God, I am so vexed that every part about me quivers. Scurvy knave! Pray you, sir, a word. And as I told you, my young lady bade me inquire you out — what she bade me say, I will keep to myself. But first let me tell ye, if ye should lead her into a fool's paradise, as they say, it were a 175 very gross kind of behavior, as they say. For the gentlewoman is young, and therefore if you should deal double with her, truly it were an ill thing to be offered to any gentlewoman, and very weak dealing.   181

ROM. Nurse, commend me to thy lady and mistress. I protest° unto thee ——

NURSE. Good heart, and, i' faith, I will tell her as much. Lord, Lord, she will be a joyful woman.   186

ROM. What wilt thou tell her, Nurse? Thou dost not mark° me.

NURSE. I will tell her, sir, that you do protest, which, as I take it, is a gentlemanlike offer.   190

ROM. Bid her devise
Some means to come to shrift this afternoon,
And there she shall at Friar Laurence' cell
Be shrived and married. Here is for thy pains.

NURSE. No, truly, sir, not a penny.   195

ROM. Go to, I say you shall.

NURSE. This afternoon, sir? Well, she shall be there.

ROM. And stay, good Nurse, behind the abbey wall.

Within this hour my man shall be with thee,   200
And bring thee cords made like a tackled stair,°
Which to the high topgallant° of my joy
Must be my convoy in the secret night.
Farewell. Be trusty, and I'll quit thy pains.°
Farewell, commend me to thy mistress.   205

NURSE. Now God in Heaven bless thee! Hark you, sir.

ROM. What say'st thou, my dear nurse?

NURSE. Is your man secret? Did you ne'er hear say Two may keep counsel, putting one away?°   209

ROM. I warrant thee, my man's as true as steel.

NURSE. Well, sir, my mistress is the sweetest lady — Lord, Lord, when 'twas a litle prating thing —— Oh, there is a nobleman in town, one Paris, that would fain lay knife aboard;° but she, good soul, had as lieve° see a toad, a very toad, as see him. I   215 anger her sometimes, and tell her that Paris is the properer° man. But I'll warrant you, when I say so, she looks as pale as any clout° in the versal world.° Doth not rosemary and Romeo begin both with a letter?   220

ROM. Aye, Nurse, what of that? Both with an R.

NURSE. Ah, mocker! That's the dog's name.° R is for the —— No, I know it begins with some other

---

131. took: understood.   133. confidence: for "conference." The old Nurse loves long words, but is not always sure of their meaning.   135. indite: for "invite."   136. So ho!: the hunter's cry signifying he has spied game.   138-51. No . . . lady: Mercutio, as usual, is mocking, to the great annoyance of the Nurse, who realizes that he is insulting her but cannot understand what he is saying.   138. hare: prostitute.   139. hoar: moldy.   153. ropery: for "roguery."   160. Jacks: knaves.   161. flirt-gills: loose women.   162. skainsmates: gangsters.

183. protest: declare.   188. mark: pay attention to.   201. tackled stair: rope ladder, as on a sailing ship.   202. topgallant: small mast fixed to the top of the mainmast.   204. quit . . . pains: reward your trouble.   209. putting . . . away: i.e., two can keep a secret only when but one of them knows it.   214. lay . . . aboard: get her for himself.   215. lieve: soon.   217. properer: more handsome.   218. clout: cloth.   versal world: universe.   222. dog's name: the letter R was called the dog's letter because it makes a growling sound.

letter — and she hath the prettiest sententious° of it,
of you and rosemary, that it would do you good to
hear it.   227

ROM. Commend me to thy lady.

NURSE. Aye, a thousand times. [*Exit* ROMEO.]
Peter!

PET. Anon?

NURSE. Peter, take my fan, and go before, and
apace.°   [*Exeunt.*] 232

SCENE V. CAPULET's *orchard*.

[*Enter* JULIET.]

JUL. The clock struck nine when I did send the
    nurse.
In half an hour she promised to return.
Perchance she cannot meet him. That's not so.
Oh, she is lame! Love's heralds should be thoughts,
Which ten times faster glide than the sun's beams,
Driving back shadows over lowering° hills.   6
Therefore do nimble-pinioned° doves draw love,
And therefore hath the wind-swift Cupid wings.
Now is the sun upon the highmost hill
Of this day's journey, and from nine till twelve   10
Is three long hours; yet she is not come.
Had she affections and warm youthful blood,
She would be as swift in motion as a ball,
My words would bandy° her to my sweet love,
And his to me.   15
But old folks, many feign as they were dead,
Unwieldy, slow, heavy and pale as lead.
[*Enter* NURSE, *with* PETER.] Oh, God, she comes! O
    honey Nurse, what news?
Hast thou met with him? Send thy man away.   19

NURSE. Peter, stay at the gate.   [*Exit* PETER.]

JUL. Now, good sweet Nurse —— Oh, Lord, why
look'st thou sad?
Though news be sad, yet tell them merrily;
If good, thou shamest the music of sweet news
By playing it to me with so sour a face.

NURSE. I am aweary, give me leave° a while.   25
Fie, how my bones ache! What a jaunce° have I had!

JUL. I would thou hadst my bones and I thy news.
Nay, come, I pray thee, speak, good, good Nurse,
    speak.

NURSE. Jesu, what haste? Can you not stay a
    while?
Do you not see that I am out of breath?   30

JUL. How art thou out of breath when thou hast
    breath
To say to me that thou art out of breath?
The excuse that thou dost make in this delay

Is longer than the tale thou dost excuse.
Is thy news good, or bad? Answer to that.   35
Say either, and I'll stay the circumstance.°
Let me be satisfied, is 't good or bad?

NURSE. Well, you have made a simple choice. You
know not how to choose a man. Romeo! No, not he,
though his face be better than any man's, yet his   40
leg excels all men's; and for a hand, and a foot, and a
body, though they be not to be talked on, yet they
are past compare. He is not the flower of courtesy,°
but, I'll warrant him, as gentle as a lamb. Go thy
ways, wench, serve God. What, have you dined at
home?   46

JUL. No, no. But all this did I know before.
What says he of our marriage? What of that?

NURSE. Lord, how my head aches! What a head
    have I!
It beats as it would fall in twenty pieces.   50
My back o' t' other side — ah, my back, my back!
Beshrew° your heart for sending me about
To catch my death with jauncing up and down!

JUL. I' faith, I am sorry that thou art not well.
Sweet, sweet, sweet Nurse, tell me, what says my
    love?   55

NURSE. Your love says, like an honest gentleman,
and a courteous, and a kind, and a handsome, and, I
warrant, a virtuous —— Where is your mother?

JUL. Where is my mother! Why, she is within,
Where should she be? How oddly thou repliest!   61
"Your love says, like an honest gentleman,
Where is your mother?"

NURSE.   Oh, God's Lady dear!°
Are you so hot°? Marry, come up,° I trow.
Is this the poultice for my aching bones?   65
Henceforward do your messages yourself.

JUL. Here's such a coil!° Come, what says
    Romeo?

NURSE. Have you got leave to go to shrift today?

JUL. I have.

NURSE. Then hie° you hence to Friar Laurence'
    cell,   70
There stays a husband to make you a wife.
Now comes the wanton blood up in your cheeks,
They'll be in scarlet straight at any news.
Hie you to church, I must another way,
To fetch a ladder by the which your love   75
Must climb a bird's nest soon when it is dark.
I am the drudge, and toil in your delight,
But you shall bear the burden soon at night.
Go, I'll to dinner, hie you to the cell.

JUL. Hie to high fortune! Honest Nurse, fare-
    well.   80

[*Exeunt.*]

---

225. **sententious:** for "sentence" — proverb.   232. **apace:**
quickly.

Sc. v: 6. **lowering:** frowning.   7. **nimble-pinioned:** swift-
winged.   14. **bandy:** hit back, as a tennis ball.   25. **give . . .
leave:** let me alone.   26. **jaunce:** running to and fro.

36. **stay . . . circumstance:** wait for details.   43. **flower of cour-
tesy:** perfect gentleman.   52. **Beshrew:** plague on.   63. **God's
. . . dear:** by God's dear Mother; i.e., the Virgin Mary.   64. **hot:**
eager.   **Marry . . . up:** An expression of angry impatience.
67. **coil:** fuss.   70. **hie:** hasten.

SCENE VI. FRIAR LAURENCE's *cell.*

[*Enter* FRIAR LAURENCE *and* ROMEO.]

FRI. L. So smile the Heavens upon this holy act
That afterhours with sorrow chide us not!

ROM. Amen, amen! But come what sorrow can,
It cannot countervail° the exchange of joy
That one short minute gives me in her sight.   5
Do thou but close our hands with holy words,
Then love-devouring death do what he dare,
It is enough I may but call her mine.

FRI. L. These violent delights have violent ends,
And in their triumph die, like fire and powder°   10
Which as they kiss consume. The sweetest honey
Is loathsome in his own deliciousness,
And in the taste confounds the appetite.
Therefore, love moderately, long love doth so,
Too swift arrives as tardy as too slow.   15
[*Enter* JULIET.] Here comes the lady. Oh, so light a
     foot
Will ne'er wear out the everlasting flint.
A lover may bestride the gossamer°
That idles in the wanton summer air,
And yet not fall, so light is vanity.°   20

JUL. Good even to my ghostly confessor.

FRI. L. Romeo shall thank thee, daughter, for us
     both.

JUL. As much to him, else is his thanks too much.°

ROM. Ah, Juliet, if the measure of thy joy
Be heaped like mine, and that thy skill be more   25
To blazon° it, then sweeten with thy breath
This neighbor air, and let rich music's tongue
Unfold the imagined happiness that both
Receive in either by this dear encounter.

JUL. Conceit,° more rich in matter than in words,
Brags of his substance, not of ornament.   31
They are but beggars that can count their worth,
But my true love is grown to such excess,
I cannot sum up sum of half my wealth.

FRI. L. Come, come with me, and we will make
     short work,   35
For, by your leaves, you shall not stay alone
Till Holy Church incorporate two in one. [*Exeunt.*]

Sc. vi: 4. **countervail:** counterbalance.   10. **fire . . . powder:** Elizabethan cannon were discharged by applying a lighted match to loose gunpowder. See Pl. 12a.   18. **gossamer:** a small spider's web that floats in the wind.   20. **vanity:** unreality. 23. **As . . . much:** may it be an evening good to him also, or else he has small cause for thanks.   26. **blazon:** describe, a herald's word for the technical description or painting of a coat of arms. 30. **Conceit:** understanding.

Act III

SCENE I. *A public place.*

[*Enter* MERCUTIO, BENVOLIO, PAGE, *and* SERVANTS.]

BEN. I pray thee, good Mercutio, let's retire.
The day is hot, the Capulets abroad,
And if we meet, we shall not 'scape a brawl;
For now these hot days is the mad blood stirring.   4

MER. Thou art like one of those fellows that when
he enters the confines of a tavern claps me his sword
upon the table and says, "God send me no need of
thee!" and by the operation of the second cup draws
it on the drawer,° when indeed there is no need.   10

BEN. Am I like such a fellow?

MER. Come, come, thou art as hot a Jack in thy
mood as any in Italy, and as soon moved to be
moody, and as soon moody to be moved.

BEN. And what to?   15

MER. Nay, an there were two such, we should have
none shortly, for one would kill the other. Thou!
Why, thou wilt quarrel with a man that hath a hair
more, or a hair less, in his beard than thou hast.
Thou wilt quarrel with a man for cracking nuts,   20
having no other reason but because thou hast hazel
eyes. What eye but such an eye would spy out such a
quarrel? Thy head is as full of quarrels as an egg is
full of meat, and yet thy head hath been beaten as
addle as an egg for quarreling. Thou hast quar-   25
reled with a man for coughing in the street, because
he hath wakened thy dog that hath lain asleep in the
sun. Didst thou not fall out with a tailor for wearing
his new doublet° before Easter? With another   30
for tying his new shoes with old ribbon? And yet
thou wilt tutor me from quarreling!°

BEN. An I were so apt to quarrel as thou art, any
man should buy the fee simple° of my life for an
hour and a quarter.   36

MER. The fee simple! Oh, simple!

[*Enter* TYBALT *and others.*]

BEN. By my head, here come the Capulets.

MER. By my heel, I care not.

TYB. Follow me close, for I will speak to them.
Gentlemen, good-den — a word with one of you.   41

MER. And but one word with one of us? Couple it
with something — make it a word and a blow.

TYB. You shall find me apt enough to that, sir, an
you will give me occasion.

MER. Could you not take some occasion without
giving?   47

TYB. Mercutio, thou consort'st° with Romeo ——

Act III, Sc. i: 10. **drawer:** potboy who fetches the drinks in a tavern.   30. **doublet:** See Pl. 8b and p. 93a.   32. **tutor . . . quarreling:** instruct me how to avoid quarreling.   35. **fee simple:** absolute possession, a legal phrase meaning "holding in perpetuity."   48. **consort'st:** you are a companion of. Mercutio takes up the other meaning of "consort"—a party of musicians playing different instruments.

MER. Consort! What, dost thou make us min-
strels? An thou make minstrels of us, look to hear
nothing but discords. Here's my fiddlestick,° here's
that shall make you dance. 'Zounds,° consort!   52

BEN. We talk here in the public haunt of men.
Either withdraw unto some private place,
And reason coldly of your grievances,   55
Or else depart. Here all eyes gaze on us.

MER. Men's eyes were made to look, and let them
    gaze.
I will not budge for no man's pleasure, I.

       [*Enter* ROMEO.]

TYB. Well, peace be with you, sir. Here comes my
    man.°   59

MER. But I'll be hanged, sir, if he wear your livery.
Marry, go before to field,° he'll be your follower.
Your worship in that sense may call him man.

TYB. Romeo, the hate I bear thee can afford
No better term than this — thou art a villain.   64

ROM. Tybalt, the reason that I have to love thee
Doth much excuse the appertaining rage
To such a greeting. Villain am I none,
Therefore farewell. I see thou know'st me not.°

TYB. Boy,° this shall not excuse the injuries   69
That thou hast done me, therefore turn and draw.

ROM. I do protest I never injured thee,
But love thee better than thou canst devise°
Till thou shalt know the reason of my love.
And so, good Capulet — which name I tender°
As dearly as mine own — be satisfied.   75

MER. Oh, calm, dishonorable, vile submission!
Alla stoccata° carries it away.   [*Draws.*]
Tybalt, you ratcatcher, will you walk?

TYB. What wouldst thou have with me?   79

MER. Good King of Cats,° nothing but one of
your nine lives, that I mean to make bold withal,
and, as you shall use me hereafter, dry-beat° the rest
of the eight. Will you pluck your sword out of his
pilcher° by the ears? Make haste, lest mine be about
your ears ere it be out.   85

TYB. I am for you.   [*Drawing.*]

ROM. Gentle Mercutio, put thy rapier up.

MER. Come, sir, your passado.°   [*They fight.*]

ROM. Draw, Benvolio, beat down their weapons.
Gentlemen, for shame, forbear this outrage!   90
Tybalt, Mercutio, the Prince expressly hath
Forbid this bandying° in Verona streets.

---

51. fiddlestick: i.e., rapier.   52. 'Zounds: by God's wounds, a
common oath.   59. my man: i.e., the man I want. Mercutio
chooses to interpret the word in the other sense of "my
servant."   61. field: a place convenient for a duel.   68. know'st
me not: i.e., that by my marriage with Juliet I am now your
kinsman.   69. Boy: See I.v.80,n.   72. devise: think.   74. ten-
der: regard.   77. Alla stoccata: a thrust. Mercutio thinks
that Tybalt with his newfangled skill with the rapier has ter-
rified Romeo into behaving like a coward.   80. King of Cats:
See II.iv.19,n.   82. dry-beat: bruise, beat without drawing
blood.   84. pilcher: scabbard; lit., leather coat.   88. passado:
See II.iv.27,n.   92. bandying: quarreling.

Hold, Tybalt, good Mercutio!
       [TYBALT *under* ROMEO's *arm stabs* MER-
       CUTIO *and flies with his followers.*]

MER.   I am hurt.
A plague o' both your houses! I am sped.°
Is he gone, and hath nothing?

BEN.   What, art thou hurt?

MER. Aye, aye, a scratch, a scratch — marry, 'tis
    enough.   96
Where is my page? Go, villain, fetch a surgeon.

       [*Exit* PAGE.]

ROM. Courage, man, the hurt cannot be much.

MER. No, 'tis not so deep as a well nor so wide as
a church door, but 'tis enough, 'twill serve. Ask for
me tomorrow and you shall find me a grave   101
man.° I am peppered, I warrant, for this world. A
plague o' both your houses! 'Zounds, a dog, a rat, a
mouse, a cat, to scratch a man to death! A braggart,
a rogue, a villain, that fights by the book of arith-
metic!° Why the devil came you between us! I was
hurt under your arm.   108

ROM. I thought all for the best.

MER. Help me into some house, Benvolio,
Or I shall faint. A plague o' both your houses!
They have made worms' meat of me. I have it,
And soundly too — your houses!   113

       [*Exeunt* MERCUTIO *and* BENVOLIO.]

ROM. This gentleman, the Prince's near ally,
My very friend, hath got his mortal hurt
In my behalf, my reputation stained
With Tybalt's slander — Tybalt, that an hour
Hath been my kinsman. O sweet Juliet,
Thy beauty hath made me effeminate,
And in my temper softened valor's steel!   120

       [*Re-enter* BENVOLIO.]

BEN. O Romeo, Romeo, brave Mercutio's dead!
That gallant spirit hath aspired° the clouds,
Which too untimely here did scorn the earth.

ROM. This day's black fate on more days doth de-
    pend,°
This but begins the woe others must end.   125

       [*Re-enter* TYBALT.]

BEN. Here comes the furious Tybalt back again.

ROM. Alive, in triumph! And Mercutio slain!
Away to Heaven, respective lenity,°
And fire-eyed fury be my conduct° now!
Now, Tybalt, take the "villain" back again   130
That late thou gavest me; for Mercutio's soul
Is but a little way above our heads,
Staying for thine to keep him company.
Either thou, or I, or both, must go with him.

---

94. sped: done for.   101–02. grave man: Mercutio's last pun.
106–07. book of arithmetic: exact rules of fencing.   122. as-
pired: soared to.   124. This . . . depend: i.e., this day is but
the beginning of many more fatal days.   128. respective lenity:
considerate mercy; i.e., I will no longer make allowances for
Tybalt as Juliet's kinsman.   129. conduct: guide.

TYB. Thou, wretched boy, that didst consort him
    here,   135
Shalt with him hence.
    ROM.   This shall determine that.
                        [*They fight;* TYBALT *falls.*]
    BEN. Romeo, away, be gone!
The citizens are up, and Tybalt slain.
Stand not amazed. The Prince will doom thee death
If thou art taken. Hence, be gone, away!   140
    ROM. Oh, I am fortune's fool!°
    BEN.   Why dost thou stay? [*Exit* ROMEO.]
                    [*Enter* CITIZENS, *etc.*]
    I. CIT. Which way ran he that killed Mercutio?
Tybalt, that murderer, which way ran he?
    BEN. There lies thy Tybalt.
    I. CIT.   Up, sir, go with me.
I charge thee in the Prince's name, obey.   145
[*Enter* PRINCE, *attended;* MONTAGUE, CAPULET, *their*
                WIVES, *and others.*]
    PRIN. Where are the vile beginners of this fray?
    BEN. O noble Prince, I can discover° all
The unlucky manage° of this fatal brawl.
There lies the man, slain by young Romeo,
That slew thy kinsman, brave Mercutio.   150
    LADY CAP. Tybalt, my cousin! Oh, my brother's
    child!
O Prince! O Cousin! Husband! Oh, the blood is spilt
Of my dear kinsman! Prince, as thou art true,
For blood of ours shed blood of Montague.
O Cousin, Cousin!   155
    PRIN. Benvolio, who began this bloody fray?
    BEN. Tybalt, here slain, whom Romeo's hand did
    slay —
Romeo that spoke him fair, bade him bethink
How nice° the quarrel was, and urged withal
Your high displeasure. All this uttered   160
With gentle breath, calm look, knees humbly bowed,
Could not take truce with the unruly spleen°
Of Tybalt deaf to peace, but that he tilts
With piercing steel at bold Mercutio's breast,
Who, all as hot, turns deadly point to point,   165
And, with a martial scorn, with one hand beats
Cold death aside and with the other sends
It back to Tybalt, whose dexterity
Retorts it. Romeo, he cries aloud,
" Hold, friends! Friends, part! " and, swifter than his
    tongue,   170
His agile arm beats down their fatal points,
And 'twixt them rushes. Underneath whose arm
An envious° thrust from Tybalt hit the life
Of stout Mercutio, and then Tybalt fled,
But by and by comes back to Romeo,   175
Who had but newly entertained revenge,
And to 't they go like lightning. For ere I

Could draw to part them was stout Tybalt slain,
And as he fell, did Romeo turn and fly.
This is the truth, or let Benvolio die.   180
    LADY CAP. He is a kinsman to the Montague,
Affection makes him false, he speaks not true.
Some twenty of them fought in this black strife,
And all those twenty could but kill one life.
I beg for justice, which thou, Prince, must give.   185
Romeo slew Tybalt, Romeo must not live.
    PRIN. Romeo slew him, he slew Mercutio.
Who now the price of his dear blood doth owe?
    MON. Not Romeo, Prince, he was Mercutio's
    friend.   189
His fault concludes but what the law should end,
The life of Tybalt.
    PRIN.   And for that offense
Immediately we do exile him hence.
I have an interest° in your hate's proceeding,
My blood for your rude brawls doth lie a-bleeding.
But I'll amerce° you with so strong a fine   195
That you shall all repent the loss of mine.
I will be deaf to pleading and excuses,
Nor tears nor prayers shall purchase out° abuses.
Therefore use none. Let Romeo hence in haste,
Else, when he's found, that hour is his last.   200
Bear hence this body, and attend our will.°
Mercy but murders, pardoning those that kill.
                                            ⌜*Exeunt.*⌝

SCENE II. CAPULET'S *orchard.*

                    [*Enter* JULIET.]
    JUL. Gallop apace, you fiery-footed steeds,
Toward Phoebus'° lodging. Such a wagoner
As Phaëton° would whip you to the west,
And bring in cloudy night immediately.
Spread thy close curtain, love-performing night,   5
That runaways' eyes° may wink, and Romeo
Leap to these arms, untalked of and unseen.
Lovers can see to do their amorous rites
By their own beauties; or, if love be blind,
It best agrees with night. Come, civil° night,   10
Thou sober-suited matron, all in black,
And learn me how to lose a winning match
Played for a pair of stainless maidenhoods.
Hood my unmanned blood bating° in my cheeks

---

141. fortune's fool: fooled by fortune.   147. discover: reveal.
148. manage: management, circumstances.   159. nice: trifling.
162. spleen: fiery temper.   173. envious: hateful.

193. an interest: i.e., Mercutio was my kinsman.   195. amerce:
punish.   198. purchase out: pay for.   201. attend . . . will: come
to receive my judgment.
    Sc. ii: 2. Phoebus: Phoebus, the sun, was daily drawn across
the sky in his chariot.   3. Phaëton: the sun god's son, who
tried to drive his father's chariot, but the horses bolted.
6. runaways' eyes: There has been much controversy about this
line, whether Phoebus or night is the runaway. Cf. *M of Ven,*
II.vi.47.   10. civil: respectable.   14. Hood . . . bating: images
from falconry. See App. 26. Hood: the hawk's head was covered
with a hood to keep it quiet. unmanned: untrained, and so
wild. bating: fluttering.

With thy black mantle, till strange love grown bold
Think true love acted simple modesty.   16
Come, night, come, Romeo, come, thou day in
    night,
For thou wilt lie upon the wings of night
Whiter than new snow on a raven's back.
Come, gentle night, come, loving, black-browed
    night,   20
Give me my Romeo; and when he shall die,
Take him and cut him out in little stars,
And he will make the face of heaven so fine
That all the world will be in love with night,
And pay no worship to the garish° sun.   25
Oh, I have bought the mansion of a love,
But not possessed it, and though I am sold,
Not yet enjoyed. So tedious is this day
As is the night before some festival
To an impatient child that hath new robes   30
And may not wear them. Oh, here comes my
    nurse,
And she brings news, and every tongue that speaks
But Romeo's name speaks heavenly eloquence.
[*Enter* NURSE, *with cords.*] Now, Nurse, what news?
    What hast thou there? The cords
That Romeo bid thee fetch?
    NURSE. Aye, aye, the cords. [*Throws them down.*]
    JUL. Aye me! What news? Why dost thou wring
    thy hands?
    NURSE. Ah, welladay! He's dead, he's dead, he's
    dead.
We are undone, lady, we are undone.
Alack the day! He's gone, he's killed, he's dead.
    JUL. Can Heaven be so envious?
    NURSE.   Romeo can,   40
Though Heaven cannot. O Romeo, Romeo!
Who ever would have thought it? Romeo!
    JUL. What devil art thou that dost torment me
    thus?
This torture should be roared in dismal Hell.
Hath Romeo slain himself? Say thou but "I,"°   45
And that bare vowel "I" shall poison more
Than the death-darting eye of cockatrice.°
I am not I, if there be such an I,
Or those eyes shut, that make thee answer "I."
If he be slain, say "I," or if not, no.   50
Brief sounds determine° of my weal or woe.
    NURSE. I saw the wound, I saw it with mine
    eyes —
God save the mark! — here on his manly breast.
A piteous corse,° a bloody piteous corse,
Pale, pale as ashes, all bedaubed in blood,   55
All in gore blood. I swounded at the sight.
    JUL. Oh, break, my heart! Poor bankrupt, break
    at once!

To prison, eyes, ne'er look on liberty!
Vile earth to earth resign, end motion here,
And thou and Romeo press one heavy bier!   60
    NURSE. O Tybalt, Tybalt, the best friend I had!
O courteous Tybalt! Honest gentleman!
That ever I should live to see thee dead!
    JUL. What storm is this that blows so contrary?
Is Romeo slaughtered, and is Tybalt dead?   65
My dear-loved cousin, and my dearer lord?
Then, dreadful trumpet, sound the general doom!°
For who is living if those two are gone?
    NURSE. Tybalt is gone, and Romeo banishèd —
Romeo that killed him, he is banishèd.   70
    JUL. Oh, God! Did Romeo's hand shed Tybalt's
    blood?
    NURSE. It did, it did. Alas the day, it did!
    JUL. Oh, serpent heart, hid with a flowering
    face!
Did ever dragon keep so fair a cave?
Beautiful tyrant! Fiend angelical!
Dove-feathered raven! Wolvish-ravening lamb!°   75
Despisèd substance of divinest show!
Just opposite to what thou justly seem'st,
A damnèd saint, an honorable villain!
O Nature, what hadst thou to do in Hell   80
When thou didst bower° the spirit of a fiend
In mortal paradise of such sweet flesh?
Was ever book containing such vile matter
So fairly bound? Oh, that deceit should dwell
In such a gorgeous palace!
    NURSE.   There's no trust,   85
No faith, no honesty in men — all perjured,
All forsworn, all naught, all dissemblers.°
Ah, where's my man? Give me some aqua vitae.°
These griefs, these woes, these sorrows, make me old.
Shame come to Romeo!
    JUL.   Blistered be thy tongue   90
For such a wish! He was not born to shame.
Upon his brow shame is ashamed to sit,
For 'tis a throne where honor may be crowned
Sole monarch of the universal earth.
Oh, what a beast was I to chide at him!   95
    NURSE. Will you speak well of him that killed
    your cousin?
    JUL. Shall I speak ill of him that is my husband?
Ah, poor my lord, what tongue shall smooth thy
    name
When I, thy three-hours wife, have mangled it?   99
But wherefore, villain, didst thou kill my cousin?
That villain cousin would have killed my husband.
Back, foolish tears, back to your native spring,
Your tributary drops belong to woe
Which you mistaking offer up to joy.   104

25. garish: gaudy.   45. Say ... "I": Puns on "aye" and "I"
are common.   47. cockatrice: a fabulous serpent so deadly that
it could slay by its mere glance.   51. determine: decide.
54. corse: corpse.

67. general doom: Day of Judgment.   73–76. Oh ... lamb:
This elaborate series of oxymoron (bitter-sweet) images is typical
of early Elizabethan dramatic poetry.   81. bower: embower.
87. dissemblers: hypocrites.   88. aqua vitae: spirits.

My husband lives, that Tybalt would have slain,
And Tybalt's dead, that would have slain my hus-
    band.
All this is comfort, wherefore weep I, then?
Some word there was, worser than Tybalt's death,
That murdered me. I would forget it fain,
But, oh, it presses to my memory   110
Like damnèd guilty deeds to sinners' minds.
"Tybalt is dead, and Romeo banishèd."
That "banishèd," that one word "banishèd,"
Hath slain ten thousand Tybalts. Tybalt's death
Was woe enough if it had ended there.   115
Or, if sour woe delights in fellowship,
And needly° will be ranked with other griefs,
Why followed not, when she said "Tybalt's dead,"
Thy father, or thy mother, nay, or both,
Which modern° lamentation might have moved?
But with a rearward following Tybalt's death,   121
"Romeo is banishèd." To speak that word
Is father, mother, Tybalt, Romeo, Juliet,
All slain, all dead. "Romeo is banishèd."
There is no end, no limit, measure, bound,   125
In that word's death; no words can that woe
    sound.
Where is my father, and my mother, Nurse?
  NURSE. Weeping and wailing over Tybalt's corse.
Will you go to them? I will bring you thither.
  JUL. Wash they his wounds with tears. Mine shall
    be spent,   130
When theirs are dry, for Romeo's banishment.
Take up those cords. Poor ropes, you are beguiled,
Both you and I, for Romeo is exiled.
He made you for a highway to my bed,
But I, a maid, die maiden-widowèd.   135
Come, cords, come, Nurse, I'll to my wedding bed,
And death, not Romeo, take my maidenhead!
  NURSE. Hie to your chamber. I'll find Romeo
To comfort you. I wot° well where he is.
Hark ye, your Romeo will be here at night.   140
I'll to him — he is hid at Laurence' cell.
  JUL. Oh, find him! Give this ring to my true
    knight,
And bid him come to take his last farewell.
                               [*Exeunt.*]

SCENE III. FRIAR LAURENCE'S *cell.*

[*Enter* FRIAR LAURENCE.]
  FRI. L. Romeo, come forth, come forth, thou fear-
    ful° man.
Affliction is enamored of thy parts,°
And thou art wedded to calamity.

[*Enter* ROMEO.]
  ROM. Father, what news? What is the Prince's
    doom?°
What sorrow craves acquaintance at my hand   5
That I yet know not?
  FRI. L.   Too familiar
Is my dear son with such sour company.
I bring thee tidings of the Prince's doom.
  ROM. What less than Doomsday is the Prince's
    doom?
  FRI. L. A gentler judgment vanished° from his
    lips,   10
Not body's death, but body's banishment.
  ROM. Ha, banishment! Be merciful, say "death,"
For exile hath more terror in his look,
Much more, than death. Do not say "banishment."
  FRI. L. Hence from Verona art thou banishèd.   15
Be patient, for the world is broad and wide.
  ROM. There is no world without° Verona walls,
But Purgatory, torture, Hell itself.
Hence banishèd is banished from the world,
And world's exile is death. Then "banishèd"   20
Is death mistermed. Calling death "banishèd,"
Thou cut'st my head off with a golden ax,
And smilest upon the stroke that murders me.
  FRI. L. Oh, deadly sin! Oh, rude unthankfulness!
Thy fault our law calls death, but the kind Prince,
Taking thy part, hath rushed° aside the law,   26
And turned that black word "death" to "banish-
    ment."
This is dear mercy, and thou seest it not.
  ROM. 'Tis torture, and not mercy. Heaven is
    here,
Where Juliet lives, and every cat and dog   30
And little mouse, every unworthy thing,
Live here in Heaven and may look on her,
But Romeo may not. More validity,
More honorable state, more courtship, lives
In carrion flies than Romeo. They may seize   35
On the white wonder of dear Juliet's hand,
And steal immortal blessing from her lips,
Who, even in pure and vestal modesty,
Still blush, as thinking their own kisses sin.
But Romeo may not, he is banishèd.   40
This may flies do, but I from this must fly.
They are free men, but I am banishèd.
And say'st thou yet that exile is not death?
Hadst thou no poison mixed, no sharp-ground knife,
No sudden mean of death, though ne'er so mean,
But "banishèd" to kill me? — "Banishèd"?   46
O Friar, the damnèd use that word in Hell,
Howling attends it. How hast thou the heart,
Being a divine, a ghostly confessor,
A sin-absolver, and my friend professed,   50
To mangle me with that word "banishèd"?

---

117. **needly:** necessarily. 120. **modern:** ordinary. 139. **wot:**
know.

  Sc. iii: 1. **fearful:** full of fear. 2. **Affliction . . . parts:** sorrow
has fallen in love with your good qualities.

4. **doom:** decree, punishment. 10. **vanished:** escaped from.
17. **without:** outside. 26. **rushed:** brushed.

FRI. L. Thou fond° madman, hear me but speak a
  word.
ROM. Oh, thou wilt speak again of banishment.
FRI. L. I'll give thee armor to keep off that word,
Adversity's sweet milk, philosophy,   55
To comfort thee, though thou art banishèd.
ROM. Yet " banishèd "? Hang up philosophy!
Unless philosophy can make a Juliet,
Displant° a town, reverse a Prince's doom,
It helps not, it prevails not. Talk no more.   60
FRI. L. Oh, then I see that madmen have no ears.
ROM. How should they when that wise men have
  no eyes?
FRI. L. Let me dispute° with thee of thy estate.°
ROM. Thou canst not speak of that thou dost not
  feel.
Wert thou as young as I, Juliet thy love,   65
An hour but married, Tybalt murderèd,
Doting like me, and like me banishèd,
Then mightst thou speak, then mightst thou tear thy
  hair
And fall upon the ground, as I do now,
Taking the measure of an unmade grave.   70
                    [Knocking within.]
FRI. L. Arise, one knocks. Good Romeo, hide thy-
  self.
ROM. Not I, unless the breath of heartsick groans
Mistlike enfold me from the search of eyes.
                    [Knocking.]
FRI. L. Hark how they knock! Who's there?
  Romeo, arise,
Thou wilt be taken. — Stay awhile! — Stand up,
                    [Knocking.]
Run to my study. — By and by!° — God's will,   76
What simpleness is this! — I come, I come!
                    [Knocking.]
Who knocks so hard? Whence come you? What's
  your will?
NURSE. [Within] Let me come in, and you shall
  know my errand.
I come from Lady Juliet.
FRI. L.   Welcome, then.   80
          [Enter NURSE.]
NURSE. O holy Friar, oh, tell me, holy Friar,
Where is my lady's lord, where's Romeo?
FRI. L. There on the ground, with his own tears
  made drunk.
NURSE. Oh, he is even in my mistress' case,
Just in her case!
FRI. L.   Oh, woeful sympathy!   85
Piteous predicament!
NURSE.   Even so lies she,
Blubbering and weeping, weeping and blubbering.
Stand up, stand up, stand, an you be a man.
For Juliet's sake, for her sake, rise and stand.

Why should you fall into so deep an O?°   90
ROM. Nurse!
NURSE. Ah sir, ah sir! Well, death's the end of all.
ROM. Spakest thou of Juliet? How is it with her?
Doth she not think me an old° murderer,
Now I have stained the childhood of our joy   95
With blood removed but little from her own?
Where is she? And how doth she? And what says
My concealed lady to our canceled love?
NURSE. Oh, she says nothing, sir, but weeps and
  weeps,
And now falls on her bed, and then starts up   100
And Tybalt calls, and then on Romeo cries,
And then down falls again.
ROM.   As if that name,
Shot from the deadly level° of a gun,
Did murder her, as that name's cursèd hand
Murdered her kinsman. Oh, tell me, Friar, tell me,
In what vile part of this anatomy°   106
Doth my name lodge? Tell me, that I may sack
The hateful mansion.   [Drawing his dagger.]
FRI. L.   Hold thy desperate hand.
Art thou a man? Thy form cries out thou art.
Thy tears are womanish, thy wild acts denote   110
The unreasonable fury of a beast.
Unseemly woman in a seeming man!
Or ill-beseeming beast in seeming both!°
Thou hast amazed me. By my holy order,
I thought thy disposition better tempered.°   115
Hast thou slain Tybalt? Wilt thou slay thyself?
And slay thy lady too that lives in thee,
By doing damnèd hate upon thyself?   118
Why rail'st thou on thy birth, the Heaven and earth?
Since birth and Heaven and earth all three do meet
In thee at once, which thou at once wouldst lose.
Fie, fie, thou shamest thy shape, thy love, thy wit,
Which, like a usurer,° abound'st in all,
And usest none in that true use indeed   124
Which should bedeck thy shape, thy love, thy wit.
Thy noble shape is but a form of wax,°
Digressing° from the valor of a man;
Thy dear love sworn, but hollow perjury,
Killing that love which thou hast vowed to cherish;
Thy wit, that ornament to shape and love,   130
Misshapen in the conduct of them both,
Like powder in a skill-less soldier's flask,
Is set afire by thine own ignorance,
And thou dismembered with thine own defense.°
What, rouse thee, man! Thy Juliet is alive,   135
For whose dear sake thou wast but lately dead.
There art thou happy. Tybalt would kill thee,
But thou slew'st Tybalt. There art thou happy too.

52. fond: foolish.   59. Displant: remove.   63. dispute: discuss.
estate: circumstances.   76. By . . . by: wait a moment.

90. an O: a great sigh.   94. old: veritable; lit., experienced·
103. level: aim.   106. anatomy: body.   113. Or . . . both: a
shameful beast, for you are neither man nor woman.   115. tem-
pered: mixed.   123. usurer: miser.   126. form of wax: i.e., a
mere dummy.   127. Digressing: differing.   134. dismembered
. . . defense: blown to pieces by your own weapon.

The law, that threatened death, becomes thy friend
And turns it to exile. There art thou happy.   140
A pack of blessings lights upon thy back,
Happiness courts thee in her best array;
But, like a misbehaved and sullen wench,
Thou pout'st upon thy fortune and thy love.
Take heed, take heed, for such die miserable.   145
Go, get thee to thy love, as was decreed,
Ascend her chamber — hence and comfort her.
But look thou stay not till the watch be set,°
For then thou canst not pass to Mantua,
Where thou shalt live till we can find a time   150
To blaze° your marriage, reconcile your friends,
Beg pardon of the Prince, and call thee back
With twenty hundred thousand times more joy
Than thou went'st forth in lamentation.
Go before, Nurse. Commend me to thy lady,   155
And bid her hasten all the house to bed,
Which heavy sorrow makes them apt unto.
Romeo is coming.

     NURSE. Oh Lord, I could have stayed here all the
        night
To hear good counsel. Oh, what learning is!   160
My lord, I'll tell my lady you will come.
     ROM. Do so, and bid my sweet prepare to chide.
     NURSE. Here, sir, a ring she bid me give you, sir.
Hie you, make haste, for it grows very late.   [*Exit.*]
     ROM. How well my comfort is revived by this!
     FRI. L. Go hence, good night, and here stands all
        your state.   166
Either be gone before the watch be set,
Or by the break of day disguised from hence.
Sojourn in Mantua. I'll find out your man,
And he shall signify from time to time   170
Every good hap to you that chances here.
Give me thy hand, 'tis late. Farewell, good night.
     ROM. But that a joy past joy calls out on me,
It were a grief so brief to part with thee.   174
Farewell.   [*Exeunt.*]

SCENE IV. *A room in* CAPULET'S *house.*

[*Enter* CAPULET, LADY CAPULET, *and* PARIS.]
     CAP. Things have fall'n out, sir, so unluckily,
That we have had no time to move° our daughter.
Look you, she loved her kinsman Tybalt dearly,
And so did I. Well, we were born to die.
'Tis very late, she'll not come down tonight.   5
I promise you, but for your company
I would have been abed an hour ago.
     PAR. These times of woe afford no time to woo.
Madam, good night. Commend me to your daugh-
        ter.

     LADY CAP. I will, and know her mind early tomor-
        row;   10
Tonight she's mewed° up to her heaviness.
     CAP. Sir Paris, I will make a desperate tender°
Of my child's love. I think she will be ruled
In all respects by me —— nay, more, I doubt it not
Wife, go you to her ere you go to bed,   15
Acquaint her here of my son° Paris' love,
And bid her, mark you me, on Wednesday next ——
But, soft! what day is this?
     PAR.   Monday, my lord.
     CAP. Monday! Ha, ha! Well, Wednesday is too
        soon.
O' Thursday let it be. O' Thursday, tell her,   20
She shall be married to this noble Earl.
Will you be ready? Do you like this haste?
We'll keep no great ado, a friend or two;
For, hark you, Tybalt being slain so late,
It may be thought we held him carelessly,   25
Being our kinsman, if we revel much.
Therefore we'll have some half a dozen friends,
And there an end. But what say you to Thursday?
     PAR. My lord, I would that Thursday were tomor-
        row.
     CAP. Well, get you gone. O' Thursday be it, then.
Go you to Juliet ere you go to bed,   31
Prepare her, wife, against° this wedding day.
Farewell, my lord. Light to my chamber, ho!
Afore me,° it is so very very late
That we may call it early by and by.   35
Good night.   [*Exeunt.*]

SCENE V. CAPULET's *orchard.*

[*Enter* ROMEO *and* JULIET, *above, at the window.*]
     JUL. Wilt thou be gone? It is not yet near day.
It was the nightingale, and not the lark,
That pierced the fearful hollow of thine ear.
Nightly she sings on yond pomegranate tree.
Believe me, love, it was the nightingale.   5
     ROM. It was the lark, the herald of the morn,
No nightingale. Look, love, what envious streaks
Do lace° the severing clouds in yonder east.
Night's candles are burnt out, and jocund day
Stands tiptoe on the misty mountaintops.   10
I must be gone and live, or stay and die.
     JUL. Yond light is not daylight, I know it, I.
It is some meteor that the sun exhales,°
To be to thee this night a torchbearer
And light thee on thy way to Mantua.   15
Therefore stay yet — thou need'st not to be gone.

---

148. **watch be set:** The watch go on duty at the gates for the night. See Gen. Intro. p. 18a.   151. **blaze:** make public.
     Sc. iv: 2. **move:** make the proposal to.

11. **mewed:** lit., caged like a hawk.   12. **desperate tender:** bold offer.   16. **son:** i.e., intended son-in-law.   32. **against:** in readiness for.   34. **Afore me:** an oath meaning "before God."
     Sc. v: 8. **lace:** cover with stripes.   13. **exhales:** draws out.
Cf. *I Hen IV*, V.i.19.

ROM. Let me be ta'en, let me be put to death,
I am content, so thou wilt have it so.
I'll say yon gray is not the morning's eye,
'Tis but the pale reflex° of Cynthia's° brow;   20
Nor that is not the lark whose notes do beat
The vaulty heaven so high above our heads.
I have more care to stay than will to go.
Come, death, and welcome! Juliet wills it so.
How is 't, my soul? Let's talk. It is not day.   25
    JUL. It is, it is. Hie hence, be gone, away!
It is the lark that sings so out of tune,
Straining harsh discords and unpleasing sharps.
Some say the lark makes sweet division.°
This doth not so, for she divideth us.   30
Some say the lark and loathèd toad change eyes.°
Oh, now I would they had changed voices too!
Since arm from arm that voice doth us affray,°
Hunting thee hence with hunt's-up° to the day.
Oh, now be gone, more light and light it grows.   35
    ROM. More light and light. More dark and dark
      our woes!

        [*Enter* NURSE, *to the chamber.*]

    NURSE. Madam!
    JUL. Nurse?
    NURSE. Your lady mother is coming to your cham-
      ber.   39
The day is broke, be wary, look about.   [*Exit.*]
    JUL. Then, window, let day in, and let life out.
    ROM. Farewell, farewell! One kiss, and I'll de-
      scend.   [*Descends.*]
    JUL. Art thou gone so? Love, lord, ay, husband,
      friend!
I must hear from thee every day in the hour,
For in a minute there are many days.   45
Oh, by this count I shall be much in years
Ere I again behold my Romeo!
    ROM. Farewell!
I will omit no opportunity
That may convey my greetings, love, to thee.   50
    JUL. Oh, think'st thou we shall ever meet again?
    ROM. I doubt it not, and all these woes shall serve
For sweet discourses in our time to come.
    JUL. Oh God! I have an ill-divining soul.
Methinks I see thee, now thou art below,   55
As one dead in the bottom of a tomb.
Either my eyesight fails or thou look'st pale.
    ROM. And trust me, love, in my eye so do you.
Dry sorrow drinks our blood.° Adieu, adieu!

                                            [*Exit.*]

    JUL. O Fortune, Fortune, all men call thee fickle.
If thou art fickle, what dost thou with him   61
That is renowned for faith? Be fickle, Fortune,

For then, I hope, thou wilt not keep him long,
But send him back.   64
    LADY CAP. [*Within*] Ho, daughter! Are you up?
    JUL. Who is 't that calls? It is my lady mother!
Is she not down so late, or up so early?
What unaccustomed cause procures her hither?

        [*Enter* LADY CAPULET.]

    LADY CAP. Why, how now, Juliet!
    JUL.   Madam, I am not well.
    LADY CAP. Evermore weeping for your cousin's
      death?   70
What, wilt thou wash him from his grave with
      tears?
And if thou couldst, thou couldst not make him live,
Therefore have done. Some grief shows much of
      love,
But much of grief shows still some want of wit.
    JUL. Yet let me weep for such a feeling° loss. 75
    LADY CAP. So shall you feel the loss, but not the
      friend
Which you weep for.
    JUL.   Feeling so the loss,
I cannot choose but ever weep the friend.
    LADY CAP. Well, girl, thou weep'st not so much for
      his death
As that the villain lives which slaughtered him.   80
    JUL. What villain, madam?
    LADY CAP.   That same villain, Romeo.
    JUL. [*Aside*] Villain and he be many miles
      asunder.
God pardon him! I do, with all my heart,
And yet no man like he doth grieve my heart.
    LADY CAP. That is because the traitor murderer
      lives.   85
    JUL. Aye, madam, from the reach of these my
      hands.
Would none but I might venge my cousin's death!
    LADY CAP. We will have vengeance for it, fear
      thou not.
Then weep no more. I'll send to one in Mantua,
Where that same banished runagate° doth live,   90
Shall give him such an unaccustomed dram°
That he shall soon keep Tybalt company.
And then I hope thou wilt be satisfied.
    JUL. Indeed I never shall be satisfied
With Romeo till I behold him — dead —   95
Is my poor heart so for a kinsman vexed.
Madam, if you could find out but a man
To bear a poison, I would temper° it,
That Romeo should, upon receipt thereof,
Soon sleep in quiet. Oh, how my heart abhors   100
To hear him named and cannot come to him,
To wreak° the love I bore my cousin
Upon his body that hath slaughtered him!

---

20. **reflex:** reflection. **Cynthia's:** the moon's.   29. **division:** mel-
ody.   31. **change eyes:** The toad has bright eyes and a harsh
croak, the lark dull eyes but a lovely voice.   33. **affray:** frighten.
34. **hunt's-up:** song played or sung in the early morning to arouse
the hunters.   59. **Dry . . . blood:** Sighing was supposed to con-
sume the heart's blood, hence Juliet's pallor.

75. **feeling:** deeply felt.   90. **runagate:** runaway.   91. **unaccus-
tomed dram:** unexpected dose.   98. **temper:** mix.   102. **wreak:**
revenge.

LADY CAP. Find thou the means, and I'll find such
      a man.
But now I'll tell thee joyful tidings, girl.   105
   JUL. And joy comes well in such a needy time.
What are they, I beseech your ladyship?
   LADY CAP. Well, well, thou hast a careful father,
      child,
One who, to put thee from thy heaviness,
Hath sorted° out a sudden day of joy,   110
That thou expect'st not, nor I looked not for.
   JUL. Madam, in happy time,° what day is that?
   LADY CAP. Marry, my child, early next Thursday
      morn,
The gallant, young, and noble gentleman,
The County Paris, at Saint Peter's Church,   115
Shall happily make thee there a joyful bride.
   JUL. Now, by Saint Peter's Church, and Peter
      too,
He shall not make me there a joyful bride.
I wonder at this haste, that I must wed
Ere he that should be husband comes to woo.   120
I pray you tell my lord and father, madam,
I will not marry yet. And when I do, I swear
It shall be Romeo, whom you know I hate,
Rather than Paris. These are news indeed!
   LADY CAP. Here comes your father, tell him so
      yourself   125
And see how he will take it at your hands.
            [*Enter* CAPULET *and* NURSE.]
   CAP. When the sun sets, the air doth drizzle dew,
But for the sunset of my brother's son
It rains downright.
How now! A conduit,° girl? What, still in tears?
Evermore showering? In one little body   131
Thou counterfeit'st° a bark,° a sea, a wind.
For still thy eyes, which I may call the sea,
Do ebb and flow with tears; the bark thy body is,
Sailing in this salt flood; the winds, thy sighs,   135
Who raging with thy tears, and they with them,
Without a sudden calm will overset
Thy tempest-tossed body. How now, wife!
Have you delivered to her our decree?
   LADY CAP. Aye, sir, but she will none, she gives
      you thanks.   140
I would the fool were married to her grave!
   CAP. Soft! Take me with you, take me with you,°
      wife.
How! Will she none? Doth she not give us thanks?
Is she not proud? Doth she not count her blest,
Unworthy as she is, that we have wrought   145
So worthy a gentleman to be her bridegroom?
   JUL. Not proud you have, but thankful that you
      have.
Proud can I never be of what I hate,
But thankful even for hate that is meant love.

   CAP. How, how! How, how! Chop-logic!° What
      is this?   150
"Proud," and "I thank you," and "I thank you
      not,"
And yet "not proud." Mistress minion,° you,
Thank me no thankings, nor proud me no prouds,
But fettle° your fine joints 'gainst Thursday next,
To go with Paris to Saint Peter's Church,   155
Or I will drag thee on a hurdle° thither.
Out, you green-sickness carrion!° Out, you baggage!
You tallow-face!
   LADY CAP.   Fie, fie! What, are you mad?
   JUL. Good Father, I beseech you on my knees,
Hear me with patience but to speak a word.   160
   CAP. Hang thee, young baggage! Disobedient
      wretch!
I tell thee what. Get thee to church o' Thursday
Or never after look me in the face.
Speak not, reply not, do not answer me.
My fingers itch. Wife, we scarce thought us blest
That God had lent us but this only child,   166
But now I see this one is one too much,
And that we have a curse in having her.
Out on her, hilding!
   NURSE.   God in Heaven bless her!
You are to blame, my lord, to rate° her so.   170
   CAP. And why, my lady wisdom? Hold your
      tongue,
Good prudence. Smatter° with your gossips, go.
   NURSE. I speak no treason.
   CAP.   Oh, God ye godden.
   NURSE. May not one speak?
   CAP.   Peace, you mumbling fool!
Utter your gravity o'er a gossip's bowl,   175
For here we need it not.
   LADY CAP.   You are too hot.
   CAP. God's bread! It makes me mad.
Day, night, hour, tide, time, work, play,
Alone, in company, still° my care hath been
To have her matched. And having now provided
A gentleman of noble parentage,   181
Of fair demesnes, youthful, and nobly trained,
Stuffed,° as they say, with honorable parts,°
Proportioned as one's thought would wish a man —
And then to have a wretched puling° fool,   185
A whining mammet,° in her fortune's tender,°
To answer "I'll not wed, I cannot love,
I am too young, I pray you, pardon me."
But an you will not wed, I'll pardon you.
Graze where you will, you shall not house with me.

110. sorted: chosen.   112. in . . . time: a vague phrase meaning
"indeed."   130. conduit: fountain.   132. counterfeit'st: imi-
tatest. bark: boat.   142. Take . . . you: let me understand you.

150. Chop-logic: one who splits hairs in an argument.   152. Mis-
tress minion: saucy miss.   154. fettle: make ready.   156. hurdle:
a wooden frame (like the hurdle used in foot races) on which
criminals were drawn to execution.   157. green-sickness carrion:
anemic lump of flesh.   170. rate: abuse.   172. Smatter: prattle.
179. still: always.   183. Stuffed: full. parts: qualities.   185. pul-
ing: whining.   186. mammet: doll. her . . tender: when good
fortune is offered her.

Look to 't, think on 't, I do not use to jest.   191
Thursday is near. Lay hand on heart, advise.°
An you be mine, I'll give you to my friend.
An you be not, hang, beg, starve, die in the streets,
For, by my soul, I'll ne'er acknowledge thee,   195
Nor what is mine shall never do thee good —
Trust to 't, bethink you, I'll not be forsworn.°
                                        [*Exit.*]
JUL. Is there no pity sitting in the clouds
That sees into the bottom of my grief?
O sweet my mother, cast me not away!   200
Delay this marriage for a month, a week;
Or, if you do not, make the bridal bed
In that dim monument where Tybalt lies.
    LADY CAP. Talk not to me, for I'll not speak a
        word.   204
Do as thou wilt, for I have done with thee. [*Exit.*]
    JUL. Oh, God! — O Nurse, how shall this be pre-
vented?
My husband is on earth, my faith in Heaven.
How shall that faith return again to earth
Unless that husband send it me from Heaven
By leaving earth? Comfort me, counsel me.   210
Alack, alack, that Heaven should practice strata-
        gems°
Upon so soft a subject as myself!
What say'st thou? Hast thou not a word of joy?
Some comfort, Nurse.
    NURSE.   Faith, here it is.   214
Romeo is banished, and all the world to nothing°
That he dares ne'er come back to challenge° you;
Or if he do, it needs must be by stealth.
Then, since the case so stands as now it doth,
I think it best you married with the County.
Oh, he's a lovely gentleman!   220
Romeo's a dishclout to him. An eagle, madam,
Hath not so green, so quick, so fair an eye
As Paris hath. Beshrew my very heart,
I think you are happy in this second match,
For it excels your first. Or if it did not,   225
Your first is dead, or 'twere as good he were
As living here and you no use of him.
    JUL. Speakest thou from thy heart?
    NURSE. And from my soul too, else beshrew them
        both.
    JUL. Amen!
    NURSE. What?
    JUL. Well, thou hast comforted me marvelous
        much.   230
Go in, and tell my lady I am gone,
Having displeased my father, to Laurence' cell,
To make confession and to be absolved.
    NURSE. Marry, I will, and this is wisely done.
                                        [*Exit.*]

JUL. Ancient damnation!° Oh, most wicked
        fiend!   235
Is it more sin to wish me thus forsworn,
Or to dispraise my lord with that same tongue
Which she hath praised him with above compare
So many thousand times? Go, counselor.
Thou and my bosom henceforth shall be twain.   240
I'll to the Friar, to know his remedy.
If all else fail, myself have power to die.   [*Exit.*]

Act IV

SCENE I. FRIAR LAURENCE'S *cell.*

[*Enter* FRIAR LAURENCE *and* PARIS.]
FRI. L. On Thursday, sir? The time is very short.
PAR. My father° Capulet will have it so,
And I am nothing slow to slack his haste.°
FRI. L. You say you do not know the lady's mind.
Uneven is the course,° I like it not.   5
PAR. Immoderately she weeps for Tybalt's death,
And therefore have I little talked of love,
For Venus smiles not in a house of tears.
Now, sir, her father counts it dangerous
That she doth give her sorrow so much sway,   10
And in his wisdom hastes our marriage,
To stop the inundation of her tears,
Which, too much minded by herself alone,
May be put from her by society.
Now do you know the reason of this haste.   15
    FRI. L. [*Aside*] I would I knew not why it should
        be slowed.
Look, sir, here comes the lady toward my cell.
                                [*Enter* JULIET.]
PAR. Happily met, my lady and my wife!
JUL. That may be, sir, when I may be a wife.
PAR. That may be must be, love, on Thursday
        next.   20
JUL. What must be shall be.
FRI. L.   That's a certain text.
PAR. Come you to make confession to this Father?
JUL. To answer that, I should confess to you.
PAR. Do not deny to him that you love me.
JUL. I will confess to you that I love him.   25
PAR. So will ye, I am sure, that you love me.
JUL. If I do so, it will be of more price
Being spoke behind your back than to your face.
PAR. Poor soul, thy face is much abused with tears.
JUL. The tears have got small victory by that,   30

---

235. Ancient damnation: damnable old woman.
    Act IV, Sc. i: 2. father: i.e., intended father-in-law. 3. And
... haste: I am as eager as he to push on the marriage.
5. Uneven ... course: a rough proceeding; i.e. to marry Juliet
before you have asked her consent.

192. advise: be advised. 197. be forsworn: break my oath.
211. stratagems: violent deeds. 215. all . . . nothing: there is
no chance. 216. challenge: claim.

For it was bad enough before their spite.°
  PAR. Thou wrong'st it more than tears with that
    report.
  JUL. That is no slander, sir, which is a truth,
And what I spake, I spake it to my face.
  PAR. Thy face is mine, and thou hast slandered it.
  JUL. It may be so, for it is not mine own.   36
Are you at leisure, holy Father, now,
Or shall I come to you at evening mass?
  FRI. L. My leisure serves me, pensive daughter,
    now.
My lord, we must entreat the time alone.   40
  PAR. God shield° I should disturb devotion!
Juliet, on Thursday early will I rouse ye.
Till then, adieu, and keep this holy kiss.   [*Exit.*]
  JUL. Oh, shut the door, and when thou hast done
    so,
Come weep with me — past hope, past cure, past
    help!   45
  FRI. L. Ah, Juliet, I already know thy grief,
It strains me past the compass° of my wits.
I hear thou must, and nothing may prorogue it,
On Thursday next be married to this County.
  JUL. Tell me not, Friar, that thou hear'st of
    this,   50
Unless thou tell me how I may prevent it.
If in thy wisdom thou canst give no help,
Do thou but call my resolution wise,
And with this knife I'll help it presently.°
God joined my heart and Romeo's, thou our hands,
And ere this hand, by thee to Romeo's sealed,   56
Shall be the label to another deed,°
Or my true heart with treacherous revolt
Turn to another, this shall slay them both.
Therefore, out of thy long-experienced time,   60
Give me some present counsel; or, behold,
'Twixt my extremes and me this bloody knife
Shall play the umpire, arbitrating that
Which the commission° of thy years and art
Could to no issue of true honor bring.   65
Be not so long to speak, I long to die
If what thou speak'st speak not of remedy.
  FRI. L. Hold, daughter. I do spy a kind of hope,
Which craves as desperate an execution
As that is desperate which we would prevent.   70
If, rather than to marry County Paris,
Thou hast the strength of will to slay thyself,
Then is it likely thou wilt undertake
A thing like death to chide away this shame,
That copest° with death himself to 'scape from it.
And, if thou darest, I'll give thee remedy.   76
  JUL. Oh, bid me leap, rather than marry Paris,
From off the battlements of yonder tower;

Or walk in thievish ways; or bid me lurk
Where serpents are; chain me with roaring bears;
Or shut me nightly in a charnel house,°   81
O'ercover'd quite with dead men's rattling bones,
With reeky° shanks and yellow chapless° skulls;
Or bid me go into a new-made grave,
And hide me with a dead man in his shroud —   85
Things that to hear them told have made me
    tremble —
And I will do it without fear or doubt,
To live an unstained wife to my sweet love.
  FRI. L. Hold, then, go home, be merry, give con-
    sent
To marry Paris. Wednesday is tomorrow.   90
Tomorrow night look that thou lie alone,
Let not thy nurse lie with thee in thy chamber.
Take thou this vial, being then in bed,
And this distillèd liquor drink thou off,
When presently through all thy veins shall run   95
A cold and drowsy humor;° for no pulse
Shall keep his native progress, but surcease.°
No warmth, no breath, shall testify thou livest.
The roses in thy lips and cheeks shall fade
To paly ashes, thy eyes' windows fall,   100
Like death when he shuts up the day of life.
Each part, deprived of supple government,
Shall, stiff and stark and cold, appear like death.
And in this borrowed likeness of shrunk death
Thou shalt continue two and forty hours,   105
And then awake as from a pleasant sleep.
Now, when the bridegroom in the morning comes
To rouse thee from thy bed, there art thou dead.
Then, as the manner of our country is,
In thy best robes uncovered on the bier   110
Thou shalt be borne to that same ancient vault
Where all the kindred of the Capulets lie.
In the meantime, against thou shalt awake,
Shall Romeo by my letters know our drift,°
And hither shall he come, and he and I   115
Will watch thy waking, and that very night
Shall Romeo bear thee hence to Mantua.
And this shall free thee from this present shame,
If no inconstant toy° nor womanish fear
Abate thy valor in the acting it.   120
  JUL. Give me, give me! Oh, tell not me of fear!
  FRI. L. Hold, get you gone, be strong and prosper-
    ous
In this resolve. I'll send a friar with speed
To Mantua, with my letters to thy lord.
  JUL. Love give me strength! And strength shal!
    help afford.   125
Farewell, dear Father!   [*Exeunt.*]

---

31. spite: injury.   **41. shield:** forbid.   **47. compass:** reach.
54. presently: immediately.   **56–57. ere . . . deed:** before my
hand consents to another contract. **label:** the strip of parchment
on which the seal is fixed. See Pl. 11a and App. 6.   **64. commis-
sion:** authority.   **75. copest:** encounterest.

81. charnel house: bone shed. In Shakespeare's time the church-
yard was used again and again; bones disinterred in making a
new grave were thrown into the charnel house. See App. 16.
83. reeky: stinking. **chapless:** without jaws.   **96. humor:** mois-
ture.   **97. surcease:** cease.   **114. drift:** intention.   **119. incon-
stant toy:** fickle fancy.

SCENE II. *Hall in* CAPULET'S *house.*

[*Enter* CAPULET, LADY CAPULET, NURSE, *and two*
SERVINGMEN.]

CAP. So many guests invite as here are writ.

[*Exit* FIRST SERVANT.]

Sirrah, go hire me twenty cunning cooks.

2. SERV. You shall have none ill, sir, for I'll try if
they can lick their fingers.

CAP. How canst thou try them so?   5

2. SERV. Marry, sir, 'tis an ill cook that cannot lick
his own fingers. Therefore he that cannot lick his
fingers goes not with me.

CAP. Go, be gone.   [*Exit* SECOND SERVANT.]
We shall be much unfurnished° for this time.   10
What, is my daughter gone to Friar Laurence?

NURSE. Aye, forsooth.

CAP. Well, he may chance to do some good on her.
A peevish self-willed harlotry° it is.

[*Enter* JULIET.]

NURSE. See where she comes from shrift with
    merry look.   15

CAP. How now, my headstrong! Where have you
    been gadding?

JUL. Where I have learned me to repent the sin
Of disobedient opposition
To you and your behests, and am enjoined
By holy Laurence to fall prostrate here,   20
To beg your pardon. Pardon, I beseech you!
Henceforward I am ever ruled by you.

CAP. Send for the County, go tell him of this.
I'll have this knot knit up tomorrow morning.

JUL. I met the youthful lord at Laurence' cell,   25
And gave him what becomèd° love I might,
Not stepping o'er the bounds of modesty.

CAP. Why, I am glad on 't, this is well. Stand up.
This is as 't should be. Let me see the County.
Aye, marry, go, I say, and fetch him hither.   30
Now, afore God, this reverend holy Friar,
All our whole city is much bound to him.

JUL. Nurse, will you go with me into my closet,
To help me sort° such needful ornaments
As you think fit to furnish me tomorrow?   35

LADY CAP. No, not till Thursday, there is time
    enough.

CAP. Go, Nurse, go with her. We'll to church to-
    morrow.   [*Exeunt* JULIET *and* NURSE.]

LADY CAP. We shall be short in our provision.
'Tis now near night.

CAP.   Tush, I will stir about,
And all things shall be well, I warrant thee, wife.
Go thou to Juliet, help to deck up her.   41
I'll not to bed tonight, let me alone,
I'll play the housewife for this once. What ho!
They are all forth. Well, I will walk myself

To County Paris, to prepare him up   45
Against tomorrow. My heart is wondrous light
Since this same wayward girl is so reclaimed.

[*Exeunt.*]

SCENE III. JULIET'S *chamber.*

[*Enter* JULIET *and* NURSE.]

JUL. Aye, those attires are best. But, gentle Nurse,
I pray thee leave me to myself tonight;
For I have need of many orisons°
To move the Heavens to smile upon my state,   4
Which, well thou know'st, is cross° and full of sin.

[*Enter* LADY CAPULET.]

LADY CAP. What, are you busy, ho? Need you my
    help?

JUL. No, madam, we have culled° such necessar-
    ies
As are behooveful° for our state° tomorrow.
So please you, let me now be left alone,
And let the nurse this night sit up with you,   10
For I am sure you have your hands full all
In this so sudden business.

LADY CAP.   Goodnight.
Get thee to bed and rest, for thou hast need.

[*Exeunt* LADY CAPULET *and* NURSE.]

JUL. Farewell! God knows when we shall meet
    again.
I have a faint cold fear thrills through my veins 15
That almost freezes up the heat of life.
I'll call them back again to comfort me.
Nurse! — What should she do here?
My dismal scene I needs must act alone.
Come, vial.   20
What if this mixture do not work at all?
Shall I be married then tomorrow morning?
No, no, this shall forbid it. Lie thou there.

[*Laying down a dagger.*]

What if it be a poison which the Friar
Subtly hath ministered° to have me dead,   25
Lest in this marriage he should be dishonored
Because he married me before to Romeo?
I fear it is. And yet methinks it should not,
For he hath still been tried° a holy man.
How if, when I am laid into the tomb,   30
I wake before the time that Romeo
Come to redeem me? There's a fearful point.
Shall I not then be stifled in the vault,
To whose foul mouth no healthsome air breathes in,
And there die strangled ere my Romeo comes?   35
Or if I live, is it not very like,
The horrible conceit° of death and night,

Sc. ii: **10. unfurnished:** unprovided.   **14. harlotry:** hussy.
26. becomed: suitable.   **34. sort:** select.

Sc. iii: **3. orisons:** prayers.   **5. cross:** thwarted.   **7. culled:**
selected.   **8. behooveful:** fit. **state:** position.   **25. ministered:**
administered, provided.   **29. still . . . tried:** always been proved.
37. conceit: idea.

Together with the terror of the place,
As in a vault, an ancient receptacle,
Where for this many hundred years the bones   40
Of all my buried ancestors are packed;
Where bloody Tybalt, yet but green in earth,
Lies festering in his shroud; where, as they say,
At some hours in the night spirits resort —
Alack, alack, is it not like that I   45
So early waking, what with loathsome smells
And shrieks like mandrakes'° torn out of the earth,
That living mortals hearing them run mad?
Oh, if I wake, shall I not be distraught,
Environèd with all these hideous fears,   50
And madly play with my forefathers' joints,
And pluck the mangled Tybalt from his shroud,
And in this rage, with some great kinsman's bone,
As with a club, dash out my desperate brains?
Oh, look! Methinks I see my cousin's ghost   55
Seeking out Romeo, that did spit his body
Upon a rapier's point. Stay, Tybalt, stay!
Romeo, I come! This do I drink to thee.
    [*She falls upon her bed, within the curtains.*]

SCENE IV. *Hall in* CAPULET'S *house.*

[*Enter* LADY CAPULET *and* NURSE.]

LADY CAP. Hold, take these keys, and fetch more
    spices, Nurse.
NURSE. They call for dates and quinces in the
    pastry.°

[*Enter* CAPULET.]

CAP. Come, stir, stir, stir! The second cock hath
    crowed,
The curfew bell hath rung, 'tis three o'clock.
Look to the baked meats, good Angelica.   5
Spare not for cost.
NURSE.   Go, you cotquean,° go,
Get you to bed. Faith, you'll be sick tomorrow
For this night's watching.
CAP.   No, not a whit. What! I have watched ere
    now
All night for lesser cause, and ne'er been sick.   10
LADY CAP. Aye, you have been a mousehunt° in
    your time,
But I will watch you from such watching now.
    [*Exeunt* LADY CAPULET *and* NURSE.]
CAP. A jealoushood,° a jealoushood!
[*Enter three or four* SERVINGMEN, *with spits, and
    logs, and baskets.*]   Now, fellow,
What's there?
  1. SERV. Things for the cook, sir, but I know not
    what.

CAP. Make haste, make haste. [*Exit* FIRST SERVING-
    MAN.] Sirrah, fetch drier logs.   15
Call Peter, he will show thee where they are.
  2. SERV. I have a head, sir, that will find out logs
And never trouble Peter for the matter.
CAP. Mass,° and well said, a merry whoreson,° ha!
Thou shalt be loggerhead. [*Exit* SECOND SERVING-
    MAN.] Good faith, 'tis day.   20
The County will be here with music straight,
For so he said he would. [*Music within.*] I hear him
    near.
Nurse! Wife! What ho! What, Nurse, I say!
[*Re-enter* NURSE.] Go waken Juliet, go and trim her
    up.
I'll go and chat with Paris. Hie, make haste,   25
Make haste. The bridegroom he is come already.°
Make haste, I say.   [*Exeunt.*]

SCENE V. JULIET'S *chamber.*

[*Enter* NURSE.]

NURSE. Mistress! What, mistress! Juliet! Fast, I
    warrant her, she.
Why, lamb! Why, lady! Fie, you slugabed!
Why, love, I say! Madam! Sweetheart! Why, bride!
What, not a word? You take your pennyworths
    now,
Sleep for a week; for the next night, I warrant,   5
The County Paris hath set up his rest°
That you shall rest but little. God forgive me,
Marry and amen, how sound is she asleep!
I needs must wake her. Madam, madam, madam!
Aye, let the County take you in your bed,   10
He'll fright you up, i' faith. Will it not be?
    [*Undraws the curtains.*]
What, dressed! And in your clothes! And down
    again!
I must needs wake you. Lady, lady, lady!
Alas, alas! Help, help! My lady's dead!
Oh, welladay that ever I was born!   15
Some aqua vitae, ho! My lord! My lady!
    [*Enter* LADY CAPULET.]
LADY CAP. What noise is here?
NURSE.   Oh, lamentable day!
LADY CAP. What is the matter?
NURSE.   Look, look! Oh, heavy day!
LADY CAP. Oh me, oh me! My child, my only life,
Revive, look up, or I will die with thee.   20
Help! help! Call help.
    [*Enter* CAPULET.]
CAP. For shame, bring Juliet forth, her lord is
    come.

---

47. **mandrakes:** mandragora, a narcotic root. See Pl. 12e.
    Sc. iv: 2. pastry: bakehouse.   **6. cotquean:** a man who med
dles with women's affairs.   **11. mousehunt:** one who follows
the girls; in today's slang "a wolf."   **13. jealoushood:** "Mrs.
Jealousy."

19. **Mass:** by the mass. **whoreson:** lit., bastard, but not used
seriously.   **26. The . . . already:** See App. 15.
    Sc. v: 6. set . . . rest: to hold one's hand, a metaphor from
primero, a card game; hence, "to be determined."

NURSE. She's dead, deceased, she's dead, alack the
day!

LADY CAP. Alack the day, she's dead, she's dead,
she's dead!

CAP. Ha! Let me see her. Out, alas! She's cold. 25
Her blood is settled and her joints are stiff.
Life and these lips have long been separated.
Death lies on her like an untimely frost
Upon the sweetest flower of all the field.

NURSE. Oh, lamentable day!

LADY CAP.   Oh, woeful time! 30

CAP. Death, that hath ta'en her hence to make me
wail,
Ties up my tongue and will not let me speak.

[*Enter* FRIAR LAURENCE *and* PARIS, *with* MUSICIANS.]

FRI. L. Come, is the bride ready to go to church?

CAP. Ready to go, but never to return.
O son, the night before thy wedding day 35
Hath death lain with thy wife. See, there she lies,
Flower as she was, deflowerèd by him.
Death is my son-in-law, Death is my heir,
My daughter he hath wedded. I will die,
And leave him all — life, living, all is Death's. 40

PAR. Have I thought long to see this morning's
face
And doth it give me such a sight as this?

LADY CAP. Accurst, unhappy, wretched, hateful
day!
Most miserable hour that e'er time saw
In lasting labor of his pilgrimage! 45
But one, poor one, one poor and loving child,
But one thing to rejoice and solace in,
And cruel death hath catched it from my sight!

NURSE. Oh, woe! Oh, woeful, woeful, woeful day!
Most lamentable day, most woeful day, 50
That ever, ever, I did yet behold!
Oh, day, oh, day, oh, day! Oh, hateful day!
Never was seen so black a day as this.
Oh, woeful day, oh, woeful day!

PAR. Beguiled, divorced, wronged, spited, slain!
Most detestable death, by thee beguiled, 56
By cruel cruel thee quite overthrown!
Oh, love! Oh, life! Not life, but love in death!

CAP. Despised, distressed, hated, martyred, killed!
Uncomfortable time, why camest thou now 60
To murder, murder our solemnity?
O child! O child! My soul, and not my child!
Dead art thou! Alack, my child is dead,
And with my child my joys are buried!

FRI. L. Peace ho, for shame! Confusion's cure lives
not 65
In these confusions. Heaven and yourself
Had part in this fair maid, now Heaven hath all,
And all the better is it for the maid.
Your part in her you could not keep from death,
But Heaven keeps his part in eternal life. 70
The most you sought was her promotion,

For 'twas your heaven she should be advanced.
And weep ye now, seeing she is advanced
Above the clouds, as high as Heaven itself?
Oh, in this love, you love your child so ill 75
That you run mad, seeing that she is well.
She's not well married that lives married long,
But she's best married that dies married young.
Dry up your tears, and stick your rosemary°
On this fair corse, and, as the custom is, 80
In all her best array bear her to church.
For though fond nature bids us all lament,
Yet nature's tears are reason's merriment.°

CAP. All things that we ordainèd festival
Turn from their office to black funeral. 85
Our instruments to melancholy bells,
Our wedding cheer to a sad burial feast,
Our solemn hymns to sullen dirges change,
Our bridal flowers serve for a buried corse,
And all things change them to the contrary. 90

FRI. L. Sir, go you in, and, madam, go with him.
And go, Sir Paris, everyone prepare
To follow this fair corse unto her grave.
The Heavens do lour upon you for some ill;
Move them no more by crossing their high will. 95

[*Exeunt* CAPULET, LADY CAPULET, PARIS, *and* FRIAR.]

1. MUS. Faith, we may put up our pipes, and be
gone.

NURSE. Honest good fellows, ah, put up, put up,
For well you know this is a pitiful case.   [*Exit.*]

2. MUS. Aye, by my troth, the case° may be
amended. 101

[*Enter* PETER.°]

PET. Musicians, oh, musicians, "Heart's ease °
heart's ease." Oh, an you will have me live, play
"Heart's ease."

1. MUS. Why "Heart's ease"? 105

PET. Oh, musicians, because my heart itself plays
"My heart is full of woe." Oh, play me some merry
dump,° to comfort me.

1. MUS. Not a dump we, 'tis no time to play
now. 110

PET. You will not, then?

1. MUS. No.

PET. I will then give it you soundly.

1. MUS. What will you give us?

PET. No money, on my faith, but the gleek.° I
will give you the minstrel.° 116

1. MUS. Then will I give you the serving creature.

PET. Then will I lay the serving creature's dagger

79. rosemary: rosemary was carried both for weddings and
funerals.   83. nature's . . . merriment: though it is natural to
weep, it is reasonable to rejoice because she has gone to a bet-
ter place.   100–01. case . . . case: a pun on *case* — "affair" and
case — "instrument box."   102. s.d., Enter Peter: Q2 has *Enter
Will Kempe,* the company's clown. See Gen. Intro. p. 60a. The
tedious foolery which follows is a specimen of one of his turns;
Kempe may perhaps have made it funny. **Heart's ease:** a pop-
ular song of the time.   108. dump: doleful ditty.   115. gleek:
mock.   116. I . . . minstrel: i.e., I'll beat you.

on your pate. I will carry no crotchets.° I'll re you,
I'll fa you, do you note me?   121

  1. MUS. An you re us and fa us, you note us.

  2. MUS. Pray you put up your dagger, and put out
your wit.

  PET. Then have at you with my wit! I will dry-
beat you with an iron wit, and put up my iron dag-
ger. Answer me like men: 127

    " When griping grief the heart doth wound
      And doleful dumps the mind oppress,
      Then music with her silver sound ——— "   130
Why " silver sound "? Why " music with her silver
sound "? — What say you, Simon Catling?°

  1. MUS. Marry, sir, because silver hath a sweet
sound.

  PET. Pretty! What say you, Hugh Rebeck?°   135

  2. MUS. I say " silver sound " because musicians
sound for silver.

  PET. Pretty too! What say you, James Sound-
post?°

  3. MUS. Faith, I know not what to say.   140

  PET. Oh, I cry you mercy, you are the singer.° I
will say for you. It is " music with her silver sound "
because musicians have no gold for sounding.

    " Then music with her silver sound   145
      With speedy help doth lend redress." [*Exit.*]

  1. MUS. What a pestilent knave is this same!

  2. MUS. Hang him, Jack! Come, we'll in here.
Tarry for the mourners, and stay° dinner.   150

                      [*Exeunt.*]

Act V

SCENE I. *Mantua. A street.*

        [*Enter* ROMEO.]

  ROM. If I may trust the flattering truth of sleep,°
My dreams presage some joyful news at hand.
My bosom's lord° sits lightly in his throne,
And all this day an unaccustomed spirit
Lifts me above the ground with cheerful thoughts.
I dreamed my lady came and found me dead —   6
Strange dream, that gives a dead man leave to
    think! —
And breathed such life with kisses in my lips
That I revived and was an emperor.
Ah me, how sweet is love itself possessed   10
When but love's shadows are so rich in joy!

[*Enter* BALTHASAR, *booted.*°] News from Verona!
    How now, Balthasar!
Dost thou not bring me letters from the Friar?
How doth my lady? Is my father well?
How fares my Juliet? That I ask again;   15
For nothing can be ill if she be well.

  BAL. Then she is well, and nothing can be ill.
Her body sleeps in Capels' monument,
And her immortal part with angels lives.
I saw her laid low in her kindred's vault,   20
And presently took post° to tell it you.
Oh, pardon me for bringing these ill news,
Since you did leave it for my office, sir.

  ROM. Is it e'en so? Then I defy you, stars!°
Thou know'st my lodging. Get me ink and paper,
And hire post horses.° I will hence tonight.   26

  BAL. I do beseech you, sir, have patience.
Your looks are pale and wild, and do import
Some misadventure.

  ROM.   Tush, thou art deceived.
Leave me, and do the thing I bid thee do.   30
Hast thou no letters to me from the Friar?

  BAL. No, my good lord.

  ROM.   No matter. Get thee gone,
And hire those horses. I'll be with thee straight.

                      [*Exit* BALTHASAR.]

Well, Juliet, I will lie with thee tonight.
Let's see for means.— O mischief, thou art swift   35
To enter in the thoughts of desperate men!
I do remember an apothecary,
And hereabouts he dwells, which late I noted
In tattered weeds,° with overwhelming° brows,
Culling of simples.° Meager were his looks,   40
Sharp misery had worn him to the bones.
And in his needy shop a tortoise hung,
An alligator stuffed and other skins
Of ill-shaped fishes; and about his shelves
A beggarly account° of empty boxes,   45
Green earthen pots, bladders, and musty seeds,
Remnants of packthread and old cakes of roses,°
Were thinly scattered, to make up a show.
Noting this penury, to myself I said,
" An if a man did need a poison now,   50
Whose sale is present death in Mantua,
Here lives a caitiff° wretch would sell it him."
Oh, this same thought did but forerun my need,
And this same needy man must sell it me.
As I remember, this should be the house.   55
Being holiday, the beggar's shop is shut.
What ho! Apothecary!

---

120. **carry no crotchets**: not put up with your whims.   133. **Cat-
ling**: catgut fiddle string.   135. **Rebeck**: a three-stringed fiddle.
See Pl. 19a.   139. **Soundpost**: part of a violin.   141. **I . . .
singer**: I ask your pardon, you're just a dumb singer.   150. **stay**:
wait for.

  Act V, Sc. i: 1. flattering . . . sleep: sleep that lies like truth.
3. **bosom'; lord**: heart.

12. **s.d., booted**: wearing riding boots, an indication that he has
ridden far.   21. **took post**: rode fast.   24. **defy . . . stars**:
Romeo throughout has been star-crossed by malignant fate.
Now he finally defies fate to do him any worse injury.   26. **post
horses**: See App. 17.   39. **weeds**: garments. **overwhelming**: over-
hanging.   40. **simples**: herbs.   45. **account**: number.   47. **cakes
of roses**: dried rose leaves compressed into a cake, used as a
perfume.   52. **caitiff**: miserable creature.

[*Enter* APOTHECARY.]

AP.   Who calls so loud?

ROM. Come hither, man. I see that thou art poor.
Hold, there is forty ducats. Let me have
A dram of poison, such soon-speeding gear°   60
As will disperse itself through all the veins,
That the life-weary taker may fall dead,
And that the trunk° may be discharged of breath
As violently as hasty powder fired
Doth hurry from the fatal cannon's womb.   65

AP. Such mortal drugs I have, but Mantua's law
Is death to any he that utters° them.

ROM. Art thou so bare and full of wretchedness,
And fear'st to die? Famine is in thy cheeks,
Need and oppression starveth in thy eyes,   70
Contempt and beggary hangs upon thy back,
The world is not thy friend, nor the world's law.
The world affords no law to make thee rich,
Then be not poor, but break it, and take this.

AP. My poverty, but not my will, consents.   75

ROM. I pay thy poverty and not thy will.

AP. Put this in any liquid thing you will,
And drink it off, and if you had the strength
Of twenty men, it would dispatch you straight.

ROM. There is thy gold, worse poison to men's
      souls,   80
Doing more murder in this loathsome world
Than these poor compounds that thou mayst not sell.
I sell thee poison, thou hast sold me none.
Farewell. Buy food, and get thyself in flesh.
Come, cordial and not poison, go with me   85
To Juliet's grave, for there must I use thee.

[*Exeunt.*]

SCENE II. FRIAR LAURENCE'S *cell.*

[*Enter* FRIAR JOHN.]

FRI. J. Holy Franciscan friar! Brother, ho!

[*Enter* FRIAR LAURENCE.]

FRI. L. This same should be the voice of Friar
John.
Welcome from Mantua. What says Romeo?
Or if his mind be writ, give me his letter.

FRI. J. Going to find a barefoot brother out,   5
One of our order, to associate° me
Here in this city visiting the sick,
And finding him, the searchers of the town,
Suspecting that we both were in a house
Where the infectious pestilence° did reign,   10
Sealed up the doors and would not let us forth,
So that my speed to Mantua there was stayed.

FRI. L. Who bare my letter, then, to Romeo?

FRI. J. I could not send it — here it is again —

---

60. gear: stuff.   63. trunk: body.   67. utters: sells.
   Sc. ii: 6. associate: accompany.   10. pestilence: the plague.
See Gen. Intro. p. 18a–b.

Nor get a messenger to bring it thee,   15
So fearful were they of infection.

FRI. L. Unhappy fortune! By my brotherhood,
The letter was not nice,° but full of charge°
Of dear import,° and the neglecting it
May do much danger. Friar John, go hence.   20
Get me an iron crow° and bring it straight
Unto my cell.

FRI. J. Brother, I'll go and bring it thee.   [*Exit.*]

FRI. L. Now must I to the monument alone.
Within this three hours will fair Juliet wake.   25
She will beshrew° me much that Romeo
Hath had no notice of these accidents.
But I will write again to Mantua,
And keep her at my cell till Romeo come.
Poor living corse, closed in a dead man's tomb!   30

[*Exit.*]

SCENE III. *A churchyard; in it a monument
belonging to the* CAPULETS.

[*Enter* PARIS *and his* PAGE, *bearing flowers and a
torch.*]

PAR. Give me thy torch, boy. Hence, and stand
      aloof.
Yet put it out, for I would not be seen.
Under yond yew trees lay thee all along,°
Holding thine ear close to the hollow ground.
So shall no foot upon the churchyard tread,   5
Being loose, unfirm, with digging up of graves,
But thou shalt hear it. Whistle then to me,
As signal that thou hear'st something approach.
Give me those flowers. Do as I bid thee, go.

PAGE. [*Aside*] I am almost afraid to stand alone
Here in the churchyard, yet I will adventure.   11

[*Retires.*]

PAR. Sweet flower, with flowers thy bridal bed I
      strew —
Oh, woe! Thy canopy is dust and stones —
Which with sweet water nightly I will dew,   14
Or, wanting that, with tears distilled by moans.
The obsequies° that I for thee will keep
Nightly shall be to strew thy grave and weep.

[*The* PAGE *whistles.*]

The boy gives warning something doth approach.
What cursèd foot wanders this way tonight,
To cross° my obsequies and true love's rite?   20
What, with a torch! Muffle° me, night, awhile.

[*Retires.*]

[*Enter* ROMEO *and* BALTHASAR, *with a torch,
mattock,° etc.*]

---

18. nice: trifling. full of charge: weighty.   19. dear import: great
importance.   21. crow: crowbar.   26. beshrew: blame.
   Sc. iii: 3. all along: at full length.   16. obsequies: funeral
rites.   20. cross: thwart.   21. Muffle: conceal.   22. s.d., mat-
tock: a tool like a pick, but with a broad end.

ROM. Give me that mattock and the wrenching
  iron.
Hold, take this letter. Early in the morning
See thou deliver it to my lord and father.
Give me the light. Upon thy life, I charge thee,   25
Whate'er thou hear'st or seest, stand all aloof,
And do not interrupt me in my course.
Why I descend into this bed of death
Is partly to behold my lady's face,
But chiefly to take thence from her dead finger   30
A precious ring, a ring that I must use
In dear employment. Therefore hence, be gone.
But if thou, jealous,° dost return to pry
In what I farther shall intend to do,
By Heaven, I will tear thee joint by joint   35
And strew this hungry churchyard with thy limbs.
The time and my intents are savage-wild,
More fierce and more inexorable far
Than empty° tigers or the roaring sea.
  BAL. I will be gone, sir, and not trouble you.   40
  ROM. So shalt thou show me friendship. Take
  thou that.
Live, and be prosperous, and farewell, good fellow.
  BAL. [*Aside*] For all this same, I'll hide me here-
  about.
His looks I fear, and his intents I doubt.   [*Retires.*]
  ROM. Thou detestable maw,° thou womb of death,
Gorged with the dearest morsel of the earth,   46
Thus I enforce thy rotten jaws to open,
And in despite° I'll cram thee with more food.
                              [*Opens the tomb.*]
  PAR. This is that banished haughty Montague
That murdered my love's cousin, with which grief
It is supposèd the fair creature died,   51
And here is come to do some villainous shame°
To the dead bodies. I will apprehend him.
                              [*Comes forward.*]
Stop thy unhallowed toil, vile Montague!
Can vengeance be pursued further than death?   55
Condemnèd villain, I do apprehend thee.
Obey, and go with me, for thou must die.
  ROM. I must indeed, and therefore came I hither.
Good gentle youth, tempt not a desperate man.
Fly hence and leave me. Think upon these gone,   60
Let them affright thee. I beseech thee, youth,
Put not another sin upon my head,
By urging me to fury. Oh, be gone!
By Heaven, I love thee better than myself,
For I come hither armed against myself.   65
Stay not, be gone. Live, and hereafter say
A madman's mercy bid thee run away.
  PAR. I do defy thy conjurations
And apprehend thee for a felon here.   69

ROM. Wilt thou provoke me? Then have at thee,
  boy!   [*They fight.*]
  PAGE. Oh, Lord, they fight! I will go call the
  watch.   [*Exit.*]
  PAR. Oh, I am slain! [*Falls.*] If thou be merciful,
Open the tomb, lay me with Juliet.   [*Dies.*]
  ROM. In faith, I will. Let me peruse this face.
Mercutio's kinsman, noble County Paris!   75
What said my man, when my betossèd soul
Did not attend° him as we rode? I think
He told me Paris should have married Juliet.
Said he not so? Or did I dream it so?
Or am I mad, hearing him talk of Juliet,   80
To think it was so? Oh, give me thy hand,
One writ with me in sour misfortune's book!
I'll bury thee in a triumphant grave —
A grave? Oh, no, a lantern,° slaughtered youth;
For here lies Juliet, and her beauty makes   85
This vault a feasting presence° full of light.
Death, lie thou there, by a dead man interred.
                 [*Laying* PARIS *in the monument.*]
How oft when men are at the point of death
Have they been merry! Which their keepers call
A lightning before death. Oh, how may I   90
Call this a lightning? O my love! My wife!
Death, that hath sucked the honey of thy breath,
Hath had no power yet upon thy beauty.
Thou art not conquered; beauty's ensign yet
Is crimson in thy lips and in thy cheeks,   95
And death's pale flag is not advancèd there.
Tybalt, liest thou there in thy bloody sheet?
Oh, what more favor can I do to thee
Than with that hand that cut thy youth in twain
To sunder his that was thine enemy?   100
Forgive me, Cousin! Ah, dear Juliet,
Why art thou yet so fair? Shall I believe
That unsubstantial death is amorous,
And that the lean abhorrèd monster keeps
Thee here in dark to be his paramour?   105
For fear of that, I still will stay with thee,
And never from this palace of dim night
Depart again. Here, here will I remain
With worms that are thy chambermaids. Oh, here
Will I set up my everlasting rest,°   110
And shake the yoke of inauspicious stars
From this world-wearied flesh. Eyes, look your last!
Arms, take your last embrace! And lips, O you
The doors of breath, seal with a righteous kiss
A dateless bargain to engrossing death!°   115
Come, bitter conduct,° come, unsavory guide!

77. attend: listen to.   **84. lantern:** dome or small turret with windows, set in the roof of a hall to give additional light. **86. presence:** Presence Chamber, where the Queen held public court.   **110. set . . . rest:** lit., stake all, with a pun on *rest* — death. A metaphor from primero, a card game in which a stake was reserved. When this was won, the game ended.   **115. dateless . . . death:** an everlasting agreement with death, which gains sole possession of everything.   **116. conduct:** guide.

33. jealous: curious.   **39. empty:** hungry.   **45. maw:** stomach.
48. despite: scorn.   **52. villainous shame:** Paris suspects that Romeo has come to steal some parts of the dead bodies from the tomb of the Capulets to work spells against them by necromancy.

Thou desperate pilot, now at once run on
The dashing rocks thy seasick weary bark.
Here's to my love! [*Drinks.*] O true apothecary!
Thy drugs are quick. Thus with a kiss I die. [*Dies.*]
[*Enter, at the other end of the churchyard,* FRIAR
     LAURENCE, *with a lantern, crow, and spade.*]
FRI. L. Saint Francis be my speed!° How oft to-
     night   121
Have my old feet stumbled° at graves! Who's there?
BAL. Here's one a friend, and one that knows you
     well.
FRI. L. Bliss be upon you! Tell me, good my
     friend,
What torch is yond that vainly lends his light   125
To grubs and eyeless skulls? As I discern,
It burneth in the Capel's monument.
BAL. It doth so, holy sir, and there's my master,
One that you love.
FRI. L.   Who is it?
BAL.   Romeo.
FRI. L. How long hath he been there?
BAL.   Full half an hour.   130
FRI. L. Go with me to the vault.
BAL.   I dare not, sir.
My master knows not but I am gone hence,
And fearfully did menace me with death
If I did stay to look on his intents.
FRI. L. Stay, then, I'll go alone. Fear comes upon
     me —   135
Oh, much I fear some ill unlucky thing.
BAL. As I did sleep under this yew tree here,
I dreamed my master and another fought,
And that my master slew him.
FRI. L.   Romeo! [*Advances.*]
Alack, alack, what blood is this which stains   140
The stony entrance of this sepulcher?
What mean these masterless and gory swords
To lie discolored by this place of peace?
[*Enters the tomb.*] Romeo! Oh, pale! Who else?
     What, Paris too?
And steeped in blood? Ah, what an unkind hour
Is guilty of this lamentable chance!   146
The lady stirs.   [JULIET *wakes.*]
JUL. O comfortable° Friar! Where is my lord?
I do remember well where I should be,
And there I am. Where is my Romeo?   150
                              [*Noise within.*]
FRI. L. I hear some noise. Lady, come from that
     nest
Of death, contagion, and unnatural sleep.
A greater power than we can contradict
Hath thwarted our intents. Come, come away.
Thy husband in thy bosom there lies dead,   155
And Paris too. Come, I'll dispose of thee
Among a sisterhood of holy nuns.

Stay not to question, for the watch is coming.
Come, go, good Juliet, I dare no longer stay.
JUL. Go, get thee hence, for I will not away.   160
                    [*Exit* FRIAR LAURENCE.]
What's here? A cup, closed in my true love's hand?
Poison, I see, hath been his timeless° end.
O churl! Drunk all, and left no friendly drop
To help me after? I will kiss thy lips —
Haply° some poison yet doth hang on them   165
To make me die with a restorative.   [*Kisses him.*]
Thy lips are warm.
I. WATCH. [*Within*] Lead, boy. Which way?
JUL. Yea, noise? Then I'll be brief. O happy dag-
     ger!   [*Snatching* ROMEO's *dagger.*]
This is thy sheath. [*Stabs herself.*] There rust, and
     let me die.   [*Falls on* ROMEO's *body, and dies.*]
     [*Enter* WATCH, *with the* PAGE *of* PARIS.]
PAGE. This is the place — there, where the torch
     doth burn.   171
I. WATCH. The ground is bloody. Search about
     the churchyard.
Go, some of you, whoe'er you find attach.°
Pitiful sight! Here lies the County slain,
And Juliet bleeding, warm, and newly dead,   175
Who here hath lain this two days burièd.
Go tell the Prince. Run to the Capulets,
Raise up the Montagues. Some others search.
We see the ground whereon these woes do lie,
But the true ground of all these piteous woes   180
We cannot without circumstance° descry.
     [*Re-enter some of the* WATCH, *with* BALTHASAR.]
2. WATCH. Here's Romeo's man. We found him in
     the churchyard.
I. WATCH. Hold him in safety till the Prince come
     hither.
[*Re-enter* FRIAR LAURENCE, *and another* WATCHMAN.]
3. WATCH. Here is a friar that trembles, sighs, and
     weeps.
We took this mattock and this spade from him   185
As he was coming from this churchyard's side.
I. WATCH. A great suspicion. Stay the friar too.
               [*Enter the* PRINCE *and* ATTENDANTS.]
PRIN. What misadventure is so early up
That calls our person from our morning rest?
     [*Enter* CAPULET, LADY CAPULET, *and others.*]
CAP. What should it be that they so shriek
     abroad?   190
LADY CAP. The people in the street cry Romeo,
Some Juliet, and some Paris, and all run
With open outcry toward our monument.
PRIN. What fear is this which startles in our ears?
I. WATCH. Sovereign, here lies the County Paris
     slain,   195
And Romeo dead, and Juliet, dead before,
Warm and new-killed.

---

121. speed: aid. 122. stumbled: Stumbling was regarded as an
evil omen. 148. comfortable: bringing comfort.

162. timeless: untimely. 165. Haply: perhaps. 173. attach:
arrest. 181. circumstance: knowledge of facts.

PRIN. Search, seek, and know how this foul mur-
der comes.

I. WATCH. Here is a friar, and slaughtered
Romeo's man,
With instruments upon them fit to open   200
These dead men's tombs.

CAP. Oh, heavens! O wife, look how our daughter
bleeds!
This dagger hath mista'en, for, lo, his house°
Is empty on the back of Montague,
And it missheathèd in my daughter's bosom!   205

LADY CAP. Oh me! This sight of death is as a bell°
That warns my old age to a sepulcher.

[*Enter* MONTAGUE *and others.*]

PRIN. Come, Montague, for thou art early up,
To see thy son and heir more early down.

MON. Alas, my liege, my wife is dead tonight,
Grief of my son's exile hath stopped her breath.   211
What further woe conspires against mine age?

PRIN. Look, and thou shalt see.

MON. O thou untaught! What manners is in this,
To press before thy father to a grave?   215

PRIN. Seal up the mouth of outrage° for a while
Till we can clear these ambiguities
And know their spring, their head, their true
scent.
And then will I be general of your woes,
And lead you even to death. Meantime forbear   220
And let mischance be slave to patience.
Bring forth the parties of suspicion.°

FRI. L. I am the greatest, able to do least,
Yet most suspected, as the time and place
Doth make against me, of this direful murder.   225
And here I stand, both to impeach° and purge°
Myself condemnèd and myself excused.

PRIN. Then say at once what thou dost know in
this.

FRI. L. I will be brief, for my short date of breath°
Is not so long as is a tedious tale.   230
Romeo, there dead, was husband to that Juliet,
And she, there dead, that Romeo's faithful wife.
I married them, and their stol'n marriage day
Was Tybalt's doomsday, whose untimely death
Banished the new-made bridegroom from this city,
For whom, and not for Tybalt, Juliet pined.   236
You, to remove that siege of grief from her,
Betrothed and would have married her perforce
To County Paris. Then comes she to me,
And with wild looks bid me devise some mean   240
To rid her from this second marriage,
Or in my cell there would she kill herself.
Then gave I her, so tutored by my art,

A sleeping potion, which so took effect
As I intended, for it wrought on her   245
The form of death. Meantime I writ to Romeo
That he should hither come as this dire night,
To help to take her from her borrowed grave,
Being the time the potion's force should cease.
But he which bore my letter, Friar John,   250
Was stayed by accident, and yesternight
Returned my letter back. Then all alone
At the prefixèd hour of her waking
Came I to take her from her kindred's vault,
Meaning to keep her closely° at my cell   255
Till I conveniently could send to Romeo.
But when I came, some minute ere the time
Of her awaking, here untimely lay
The noble Paris and true Romeo dead.
She wakes, and I entreated her come forth,   260
And bear this work of Heaven with patience.
But then a noise did scare me from the tomb,
And she too desperate would not go with me,
But, as it seems, did violence on herself.
All this I know, and to the marriage   265
Her nurse is privy.° And if aught in this
Miscarried by my fault, let my old life
Be sacrificed some hour before his time
Unto the rigor of severest law.   269

PRIN. We still° have known thee for a holy man.
Where's Romeo's man? What can he say in this?

BAL. I brought my master news of Juliet's death,
And then in post he came from Mantua
To this same place, to this same monument.
This letter he early bid me give his father,   275
And threatened me with death, going in the vault,
If I departed not and left him there.

PRIN. Give me the letter, I will look on it.
Where is the County's page, that raised the watch?
Sirrah, what made° your master in this place?   280

PAGE. He came with flowers to strew his lady's
grave,
And bid me stand aloof, and so I did.
Anon comes one with light to ope the tomb,
And by and by my master drew on him,
And then I ran away to call the watch.   285

PRIN. This letter doth make good the Friar's
words,
Their course of love, the tidings of her death.
And here he writes that he did buy a poison
Of a poor 'pothecary, and therewithal
Came to this vault to die and lie with Juliet. 290
Where be these enemies? Capulet! Montague!
See what a scourge is laid upon your hate
That Heaven finds means to kill your joys with love!
And I, for winking at your discords too,
Have lost a brace of kinsmen. All are punished. 295

CAP. O Brother Montague, give me thy hand.

---

203. **house:** i.e., scabbard.   206. **bell:** i.e., passing bell. See
App. 19.   216. **Seal . . . outrage:** At these words the curtains at
the back of the stage are closed to conceal the three bodies.
outrage: violent deeds.   222. **parties of suspicion:** suspected
parties.   226. **impeach:** accuse. **purge:** clear.   229. **short . . .
breath:** the little life still left to me.

255. **closely:** secretly.   266. **is privy:** shares the secret.   270. **still:**
always.   280. **made:** did.

This is my daughter's jointure,° for no more
Can I demand.

MON.   But I can give thee more.
For I will raise her statue in pure gold,
That whiles Verona by that name is known   300
There shall no figure at such rate° be set
As that of true and faithful Juliet.

297. jointure: dowry.   301. rate: value.

CAP. As rich shall Romeo's by his lady's lie,
Poor sacrifices of our enmity!

PRIN. A glooming peace this morning with it
          brings,   305
The sun for sorrow will not show his head.
Go hence, to have more talk of these sad things.
Some shall be pardoned and some punishèd.
For never was a story of more woe   309
Than this of Juliet and her Romeo.   [Exeunt.]

A MIDSUMMER NIGHT'S DREAM

Introduction

A Midsummer Night's Dream was probably written late in 1594 or early in 1595. There are a few topical allusions which can be identified.

1. Titania's speech (II.i.87–117) on the evil weather was presumably inspired by the excessively bad summer of 1594, which caused a failure of the harvest and much distress. There are several contemporary records of the disaster. Thus John Stow, in his *Annals:*

This year in the month of May, fell many great showers of rain, but in the months of June and July, much more; for it commonly rained every day, or night, till St. James's Day, and two days after together most extremely, all which, notwithstanding in the month of August there followed a fair harvest, but in the month of September fell great rains, which raised high waters, such as stayed the carriages, and bare down bridges, at Cambridge, Ware and elsewhere, in many places. Also the price of grain grew to be such as a strike or bushel of rye was sold for five shillings, a bushel of wheat for six, seven, or eight shillings, &c, for still it rose in price, which dearth happened (after the common opinion) more by means of overmuch transporting by our own merchants for their private gain, than through the unseasonableness of the weather passed.

2. In the rehearsal, Bottom warns his fellow actors (III.i.30):

Masters, you ought to consider with yourselves. To bring in — God shield us! — a lion among ladies is a most dreadful thing; for there is not a more fearful wildfowl than your lion living, and we ought to look to it.

On August 30, 1594, the infant son of King James VI of Scotland was baptized in Edinburgh. Queen Elizabeth was the godmother, and she sent a party of courtiers to Scotland to represent her at the ceremony. It is likely that those present, used to a far higher standard of courtly comforts and entertainments, brought back amusing accounts of the affair, especially of the grand dinner. The whole ceremony was described in a contemporary pamphlet which recorded that during the state banquet a chariot appeared, drawn by a blackamoor, wherein stood Ceres, Fecundity, Faith, Concord, Liberality, and Perseverance. " The chariot was to have been drawn in by a lion, but because his presence might have brought some fears to the nearest, or the sights of the lights and the torches might have commoved his tameness, it was thought meet that the Moor should supply that room."

There are other obviously topical allusions in the play, but as these have not been certainly identified, they do not throw much light on the date of writing. The most important is at V.i.52:

The thrice three Muses mourning for the death
Of Learning, late deceased in beggary.

That is some satire, keen and critical,
Not sorting with a nuptial ceremony.

If these words were written in 1594 or 1595, they would most probably refer to the death, in poverty, of Robert Greene on September 2, 1592 (see Gen. Intro. p. 39a). Greene's death was echoed for some years in pamphlets which could quite accurately be called " keen and critical." If the lines were written in 1599 for a revival of the play, then they may refer to the death of Edmund Spenser in January, 1599.

There is some evidence that the play has in parts been rewritten. Professor Dover Wilson in his edition notes that in the first 184 lines of Act V, the printer of the quarto has made several mistakes in dividing the lines of verse, and that these mistakes occur in passages where the rhythm of the verse is freer than in the rest of the play. For example, he printed the famous passage (ll. 11–18) thus:

The Poet's eye, in a fine frenzy, rolling, doth
  glance
From heaven to earth, from earth to heaven. And
  as
Imagination bodies forth the forms of things
Unknown: the Poet's pen turns them to shapes,
And gives too airy nothing, a local habitation,
And a name. Such tricks hath strong imagination.

Professor Dover Wilson guessed that these passages were later additions, written on the margin of the manuscript in such space as could be found, and that they baffled the compositor.

There is no record of early performance, but the play is so full of marriage preparations that most critics believe that it was composed for some particular wedding. Of the possible society weddings, that of William Stanley, Earl of Derby (and brother of a former patron of the Chamberlain's Men) with the Lady Elizabeth Vere, granddaughter of Lord Burghley, on January 26, 1595, best fits the probable date of writing; but there is no evidence, and the title page of the quarto definitely states that the play was "sundry times publicly acted."

A Midsummer Night's Dream was entered in the Stationers' Register on October 8, 1600, to Thomas Fisher. A first quarto appeared in 1600 with the title: *A Midsommer nights dreame. As it hath beene sundry times publickely acted, by the Right honourable, the Lord Chamberlaine his seruants. Written by William Shakespeare.* A second quarto, falsely dated 1600, was printed in 1619, and based on the first. The text printed in the first folio in 1623 was printed from a revised copy of the second quarto.

The plot of *A Midsummer Night's Dream* as a whole was Shakespeare's invention, but some of the details he took from Chaucer, Plutarch's "Life of Theseus," Ovid, folklore, and his own plays.

The situation at the opening of the play when "Duke" Theseus is about to wed the Amazon Queen Hippolyta may have been suggested by the opening lines of the *Knight's Tale* in the *Canterbury Tales.*

Whilom, as oldë stories tellen us,
There was a Duke that hightë Theseus;
Of Athenes he was lord and governour,
And in his timë such a conquerour,
That greater was there none under the sun.
Full many a richë country had he won;
That with his wisdom and his chivalry
He conquered all the regne of Femyny,
That whilom was y-cleped Scythia;
And weddedë the Queen Hippolita,
And brought her home with him in his country
With muchel glory and great solemnity.

The rest of the *Knight's Tale* has no connection with the play, but there are occasional phrases and suggestions, such as that Theseus was a mighty hunter.

This mean I now by mighty Theseus
That for to hunten is so desirous,
And namely the great hart in May,
That in his bed there daweth him no day,
That he nis [is not] clad, and ready for to ride
With hunt and horn, and houndës him beside.
For in his hunting hath he such delight,
That it is all his joy and appetite
To been himself the great hartë's bane,
For after Mars he serveth now Diane.

Shakespeare seems also to have read the "Life of Theseus" in *Plutarch's Lives,* from which he took an occcasional line or idea, including the name of Egeus.

The story of Pyramus and Thisbe was well known. It had been told by Ovid — Shakespeare's favorite Latin author — in the *Metamorphoses,* Book IV. Of this work an English translation by Arthur Golding, printed in 1567 in a long fourteen-syllable line, was almost as crude as Quince's version of the tragedy. The main parts of the story were thus Englished by Golding:

Within the town (of whose huge walls
  so monstrous high and thick
The fame is given Semiramis
  for making them of brick)
Dwelt hard together two young folk
  in houses joined so near
That under all one roof well nigh
  both two twain conveyèd were. . . .
The wall that parted house from house
  had riven therein a cranny
Which shrunk at making of the wall;
  this fault not marked of any
Of many hundred years before
  (what doth not love espy?)
These lovers first of all found out,
  and made a way whereby
To talk together secretly,
  and through the same did go
Their loving whisperings very light
  and safely to and fro.
Now as at one side Pyramus
  and Thisbe on the other
Stood often drawing one of them
  the pleasant breath from other,
"O thou envious wall," they said,
  "why let'st thou lovers thus?
What matter were it if that thou
  permitted both of us

In arms each other to embrace?
  Or if thou think that this
Were overmuch, yet mightest thou
  at least make room to kiss.
And yet thou shalt not find us churls:
  we think ourselves in debt
For this same piece of courtesy,
  in vouching safe to let
Our sayings to our friendly ears
  thus freely come and go."
Thus having where they stood in vain
  complainèd of their woe,
When night drew near, they bade adieu
  and each gave kisses sweet
Unto the parget [plaster] on their side,
  the which did never meet.
Next morning with her cheerful light
  had driven the stars aside
And Phoebus with his burning beams
  the dewy grass had dried.
These lovers at their wonted place
  by fore-appointment met.
Whereafter much complaint and moan
  they cov'nanted to get
Away from such as watchèd them,
  and in the evening late
To steal out of their fathers' house
  and eke the city gate.
And to th' intent that in the fields
  they strayed not up and down
They did agree at Ninus' tomb
  to meet without the town,
And tarry underneath a tree
  that by the same did grow
Which was a fair high mulberry
  with fruit as white as snow,
Hard by a cool and trickling spring.
  This bargain pleased them both
And so daylight (which to their thought
  away but slowly goeth)
Did in the ocean fall to rest,
  and night from thence doth rise.
As soon as darkness once was come,
  straight Thisbe did devise
A shift to wind her out of doors,
  that none that were within
Perceivèd her. And muffling her
  with clothes about her chin,
That no man might discern her face,
  to Ninus' tomb she came
Unto the tree, and sat her down
  there underneath the same.
Love made her bold. But see the chance,
  there comes besmeared with blood
About the chaps a lioness
  all foaming from the wood
From slaughter lately made of kine

to staunch [quench] her bloody thirst
  With water of the foresaid spring.
    Whom Thisbe spying first
Afar by moonlight, thereupon
  with fearful steps gan fly
And in a dark and irksome cave
  did hide herself thereby.
And as she fled away for haste
  she let her mantle fall
The which for fear she left behind,
  not looking back at all.
Now when the cruel lioness
  her thirst had staunchèd well,
In going to the wood she found
  the slender weed that fell
From Thisbe, which with bloody teeth
  in pieces she did tear.
The night was somewhat further spent
  ere Pyramus came there,
Who seeing in the subtle sand
  the print of lion's paw
Waxed pale for fear. But when also
  the bloody cloak he saw
All rent and torn, " One night," he said,
  " shall lovers two confound,
Of which long life deservèd she
  of all that live on ground.
My soul deserves of this mischance
  the peril for to bear.
I wretch have been the death of thee,
  which to this place of fear
Did cause thee in the night to come,
  and came not here before.
My wicked limbs and wretched guts
  with cruel teeth therefore
Devour ye, O ye lions all,
  that in this rock do dwell."
But cowards use to wish for death.
    The slender weed that fell
From Thisbe up he takes, and straight
  does bear it to the tree,
Which was appointed erst [formerly] the place
  of meeting for to be.
And when he had bewept and kissed
  the garment which he knew,
" Receive thou my blood too," quoth he,
  and therewithal he drew
His sword, the which among his guts
  he thrust, and by and by
Did draw it from the bleeding wound
  beginning for to die,
And cast himself upon his back.
    The blood did spin on high
As when a conduit pipe is cracked,
  the water bursting out
Does shoot itself a great way off
  and pierce the air about.

Then Thisbe comes out from her hiding place, sees her lover "beweltred in his blood," and laments at great length.

> This said, she took the sword yet warm
>   with slaughter of her love
> And setting it beneath her breast,
>   did to her heart it shove.

The Fairies came partly from folklore, partly from literature. Oberon, King of the Fairies, had appeared not long before in Greene's play *King James the Fourth*. Titania was a title of the goddess Diana, used by Ovid, but not by Golding in his translation. Belief in fairies, which had been fairly strong some generations before, was dying out except among the ignorant. This trend was thus summarized by King James VI of Scotland in his *Daemonology* (1597):

That fourth kind of spirits, which by the Gentiles was called Diana and her wandering Court, and amongst us was called the Phairy (as I told you), or our good neighbors, was one of the sorts of illusions that was rifest in the time of Papistry; for although it was holden odious to prophesy by the Devil, yet whom these kind of spirits carried away and informed, they were thought to be sonsiest and of best life. To speak of the many vain trattles [gossip] founded upon that illusion: how there was a King and Queen of Phairy, of such a jolly Court and train as they had, how they had a teind [tithe] and duty, as it were, of all goods; how they naturally rode and went, ate and drank, and did all other actions like natural men and women — I think it liker Virgil's *Campi Elysii* nor anything that ought to be believed by Christians, except in general, that as I spake sundry times before, the Devil illuded the senses of sundry simple creatures in making them believe that they saw and heard such things as were nothing so indeed.

Among educated men and women fairies had become a picturesque fancy, and a topic for pretty verse and Courtly entertainment.

Puck the mischief-maker was perhaps more credited than the King of the Fairies. He was known as Robin Goodfellow to country gossips. Thomas Nashe in *Terrors of the Night* (1593) had thus described him and his like:

In the time of infidelity, when spirits were so familiar with men that they called them *Dii Penates,* their household gods or their *lares,* they never sacrificed to them till sunsetting. The Robin Goodfellows, elves, fairies, hobgoblins of our latter age, which idolatrous former days and the fantastical world of Greece ycleped fawns, satyrs, dryads, and hamadryads, did most of their merry pranks in the night. Then ground they malt, and had hempen shirts for their labors, danced in rounds in green meadows, pinched maids in their sleep that swept not their houses clean, and led poor travelers out of their way notoriously.

Shakespeare was apparently the first to give the name of Puck (the pook or spirit) to Robin. The name may have been appropriately taken from Spenser's *Epithalamium* — the wedding song which he composed for his own wedding, and which appeared in the early weeks of 1595. In one of the later stanzas Spenser prayed that his wedding night might be free from alarms:

> Let no lamenting cries, nor doleful tears,
> Be heard all night, within nor yet without:
> Ne let false whispers, breeding hidden fears,
> Break gentle sleep with misconceivèd doubt.
> Let no deluding dreams, nor dreadful sights
> Make sudden sad affrights;
> Ne let house fires, nor lightnings' helpless harms,
> Ne let the Pook, nor other evil sprites,
> Ne let mischievous witches with their charms,
> Ne let hobgoblins, names whose sense we see not,
> Fray us with things that be not.

Other incidents Shakespeare took from his own plays. *Two Gentlemen of Verona* had told of the cross-wooing of two pairs of lovers whose affections had become mixed. In *Love's Labor's Lost* he had parodied the efforts of amateurs to produce a drama for a royal visitor. In *Romeo and Juliet,* Mercutio's outburst on Queen Mab (I.iv. 53–94) was the first sketch of fairy pranks.

A Midsummer Night's Dream aptly describes the play. Midsummer's Day was traditionally a general holiday and a time of merrymaking; Midsummer Night was the grand festival of witches and fairies. In a Midsummer Night's dream anything might happen. As is common in Elizabethan plays, there are three stories: the complex love affairs of Demetrius and Lysander, Hermia and Helena; the casting, rehearsal, and performance of the comical tragedy of Pyramus and Thisbe by the workingmen of Athens; and the troubles in fairyland between Oberon and Titania. Each plot is connected with the others, and all center in the wedding of Theseus and Hippolyta.

The play begins on solid earth. The final preparations for Theseus' wedding are being made when Egeus bursts in to demand his right as a father to bestow his daughter in marriage on the man of his choosing. The second scene introduces the Athenian workingmen and shows the casting of their play with Quince as director, Bottom as star performer, and the rest merely apprehensive amateurs. So long as daylight holds mortals are in control and the fairies lie hidden. But once the moon is up things of common day fade and the woods near Athens become the domain of the fairies, into which mortals trespass at their peril. In the third scene (II.i) we are introduced to Puck, the mischief-maker, Oberon, King of the Fairies, and Titania, his Queen. When Demetrius crashes into fairyland pursued by the clinging Helena, the dream begins and reality ends.

The characterization in the play is varied. The lovers are not very interesting if taken or played seriously, but if their speeches are regarded as a parody on romantic stories and the parts are played with a touch of burlesque, they become amusingly comic. Theseus and Hippolyta, so far as their small parts allow, are distinct. Theseus has already had considerable experience as a lover and a soldier, and he has ceased to be romantic. When Hippolyta tells him of the strange experiences of the lovers in the woods, he tolerantly answers that

> The lunatic, the lover, and the poet
> Are of imagination all compact.

This is hardly a gallant speech from a bridegroom on his wedding day, but the marriage itself was not a love match. Hippolyta too has character; she is an Amazon, a haughty, muscular lady with no patience for the crude efforts of Bottom and his fellow players. The contrast between Hippolyta and her husband is well shown during the play. The lady is bored and contemptuous, but Theseus remains gracious and encouraging to the least of his subjects.

All the workingmen are cunningly drawn.

Quince seems to be the oldest of the party, and there are hints that he is something of a poet — at least Bottom thinks he ought to write a ballad. Furthermore, Quince is a man of great tact; no one else, not even the Duke, can control Bottom. Snout and Starveling are the difficulty-makers who exist in every amateur dramatic society; "You can *never* bring in a wall," cries Snout triumphantly. But all are surpassed by Bottom, the weaver, who is magnificently stolid, unimaginative and imperturbable, yet a considerable wag in his own crude way. He alone remains calm before a jeering audience, and he subdues it to silence when lesser men such as the miserable Snout are put out of their parts and give up in despair. He keeps his head, even though it be an asshead, when the Fairy Queen falls demonstratively in love with him.

The third set of characters are the fairies. They are presented as little folk, and their size is constantly stressed. The cowslips are the bodyguard of the Fairy Queen, and a snake skin is

> Weed wide enough to wrap a fairy in,

yet their loves and passions are as intense as those of the humans.

The dream ends with dawn when everything has been restored: Demetrius has Helena, Lysander has Hermia, Bottom has his own natural face, and Oberon his Indian boy. When Theseus and Hippolyta come upon the sleeping lovers, the fairies have vanished and mortals are again in control. Then night returns; Bottom and his company present their play, a very human performance; the lovers go bedward; and the lights are put out in the great chamber. Once more the fairies swarm out, and in the end we are left doubting where reality began and dreaming ended.

Fantasy to be successful calls for a certain delicacy of imagination in the spectators. Shakespeare was lucky in the versatility of an audience which could pass from the bloody melodrama of *Richard III* and the tragedy of *Romeo and Juliet* to this delicate mixture of farce and fancy.

A Midsummer Night's Dream

DRAMATIS PERSONAE

THESEUS, *Duke of Athens*
EGEUS, *father to Hermia*
LYSANDER }
DEMETRIUS } *in love with Hermia*
PHILOSTRATE, *master of the revels to Theseus*
QUINCE, *a carpenter*
SNUG, *a joiner*
BOTTOM, *a weaver*
FLUTE, *a bellows-mender*
SNOUT, *a tinker*
STARVELING, *a tailor*

HIPPOLYTA, *queen of the Amazons, betrothed to Theseus*

HERMIA, *daughter to Egeus, in love with Lysander*
HELENA, *in love with Demetrius*

OBERON, *king of the fairies*
TITANIA, *queen of the fairies*
PUCK, *or Robin Goodfellow*
PEASEBLOSSOM }
COBWEB }
MOTH } *fairies*
MUSTARDSEED }
OTHER FAIRIES *attending their King and Queen.*
Attendants on Theseus and Hippolyta

SCENE — *Athens, and a wood near it.*

Act I

SCENE I. *Athens. The palace of Theseus.*

[*Enter* THESEUS, HIPPOLYTA, PHILOSTRATE, *and
Attendants.*]

THE. Now, fair Hippolyta,° our nuptial hour
Draws on apace;° four happy days bring in
Another moon. But oh, methinks, how slow
This old moon wanes! She lingers° my desires,
Like to a stepdame, or a dowager,   5
Long withering out a young man's revenue.°
HIP. Four days will quickly steep° themselves in
    night,
Four nights will quickly dream away the time,
And then the moon, like to a silver bow
New-bent in heaven, shall behold the night   10
Of our solemnities.
THE.   Go, Philostrate,
Stir up the Athenian youth to merriments,
Awake the pert° and nimble spirit of mirth.
Turn melancholy forth to funerals.
The pale companion° is not for our pomp.   15
          [*Exit* PHILOSTRATE.]
Hippolyta, I wooed thee with my sword,
And won thy love, doing thee injuries;
But I will wed thee in another key,
With pomp, with triumph, and with reveling.

[*Enter* EGEUS, HERMIA, LYSANDER, *and* DEMETRIUS.]
EGE. Happy be Theseus, our renownèd Duke!   20
THE. Thanks, good Egèus. What's the news with
    thee?
EGE. Full of vexation come I, with complaint
Against my child, my daughter Hermia.
Stand forth, Demetrius. My noble lord,
This man hath my consent to marry her.   25
Stand forth, Lysander. And, my gracious Duke,
This man hath bewitched the bosom of my child.
Thou, thou, Lysander, thou hast given her rhymes,
And interchanged love tokens with my child.
Thou hast by moonlight at her window sung,   30
With feigning° voice, verses of feigning love;
And stolen the impression of her fantasy°
With bracelets of thy hair, rings, gawds,° conceits,°
Knacks,° trifles, nosegays,° sweetmeats, messengers
Of strong prevailment in unhardened youth.   35
With cunning hast thou filched my daughter's heart,
Turned her obedience, which is due to me,
To stubborn harshness. And, my gracious Duke,
Be it so° she will not here before your Grace
Consent to marry with Demetrius,   40
I beg the ancient privilege of Athens,
As she is mine, I may dispose of her —
Which shall be either to this gentleman
Or to her death, according to our law
Immediately° provided in that case.   45
THE. What say you, Hermia? Be advised,° fair
    maid,

Act I, Sc. i: 1. **Hippolyta**: Queen of the Amazons, a legendary race of female warriors who lived in South Russia. Theseus had defeated them in battle. 2. **apace**: quickly. 4. **lingers**: delays. 5-6. **Like . . . revenue**: i.e., like a stepmother or a widowed mother (*dowager*) who has to be provided with an annuity. **withering out**: making to dwindle. 7. **steep**: turn into. 13. **pert**: lively. 15. **pale companion**: i.e., melancholy. **companion**: fellow.

31. **feigning**: deceptive. 32. **stolen . . . fantasy**: made a false impression on her imagination. 33. **gawds**: trifles. **conceits**: pretty compliments. 34. **Knacks**: knickknacks. **nosegays**: bunches of flowers. 39. **Be it so**: if. 45. **Immediately**: expressly. 46. **Be advised**: consider.

To you your father should be as a god,
One that composed° your beauties — yea, and one
To whom you are but as a form° in wax
By him imprinted and within his power   50
To leave the figure or disfigure it.
Demetrius is a worthy gentleman.

HER. So is Lysander.

THE.   In himself he is;
But in this kind,° wanting° your father's voice,
The other must be held the worthier.   55

HER. I would my father looked but with my eyes.

THE. Rather your eyes must with his judgment
   look.

HER. I do entreat your Grace to pardon me.
I know not by what power I am made bold,
Nor how it may concern my modesty,°   60
In such a presence here to plead my thoughts;
But I beseech your Grace that I may know
The worst that may befall me in this case
If I refuse to wed Demetrius.

THE. Either to die the death,° or to abjure   65
Forever the society of men.
Therefore, fair Hermia, question your desires.
Know of° your youth, examine well your blood,
Whether, if you yield not to your father's choice,
You can endure the livery of a nun —   70
For aye° to be in shady cloister mewed,°
To live a barren sister all your life,
Chanting faint hymns to the cold fruitless moon.°
Thrice blessèd they that master so their blood,
To undergo such maiden pilgrimage;   75
But earthlier happy° is the rose distilled,°
Than that which, withering on the virgin thorn,
Grows, lives, and dies in single blessedness.

HER. So will I grow, so live, so die, my lord,
Ere I will yield my virgin patent° up   80
Unto his lordship, whose unwishèd yoke
My soul consents not to give sovereignty.

THE. Take time to pause; and by the next new
   moon —
The sealing day betwixt my love and me,
For everlasting bond of fellowship° —   85
Upon that day either prepare to die
For disobedience to your father's will,
Or else to wed Demetrius, as he would,
Or on Diana's altar to protest°
For aye austerity and single life.   90

DEM. Relent, sweet Hermia. And, Lysander, yield

Thy crazèd title° to my certain right.

LYS. You have her father's love, Demetrius,
Let me have Hermia's. Do you marry him.

EGE. Scornful Lysander! True, he hath my love,
And what is mine my love shall render° him.   96
And she is mine, and all my right of her
I do estate° unto Demetrius.

LYS. I am, my lord, as well derived as he,
As well possessed;° my love is more than his;   100
My fortunes every way as fairly ranked,
If not with vantage,° as Demetrius'.
And, which is more than all these boasts can be,
I am beloved of beauteous Hermia.
Why should not I then prosecute my right?   105
Demetrius, I'll avouch it to his head,°
Made love to Nedar's daughter, Helena,
And won her soul, and she, sweet lady, dotes,
Devoutly dotes, dotes in idolatry,
Upon this spotted° and inconstant man.   110

THE. I must confess that I have heard so much,
And with Demetrius thought to have spoke thereof;
But, being overfull of self-affairs,
My mind did lose it. But, Demetrius, come,
And come, Egëus. You shall go with me.   115
I have some private schooling° for you both.
For you, fair Hermia, look you arm yourself
To fit your fancies° to your father's will,
Or else the law of Athens yields you up —
Which by no means we may extenuate —   120
To death, or to a vow of single life.
Come, my Hippolyta. What cheer, my love?
Demetrius and Egëus, go along.
I must employ you in some business
Against° our nuptial, and confer with you   125
Of something nearly° that concerns yourselves.

EGE. With duty and desire we follow you.

            [*Exeunt all but* LYSANDER *and* HERMIA.]

LYS. How now, my love! Why is your cheek so
   pale?
How chance the roses there do fade so fast?

HER. Belike for want of rain, which I could well
Beteem° them from the tempest of my eyes.   131

LYS. Aye me! for aught that I could ever read,
Could ever hear by tale or history,
The course of true love never did run smooth,
But either it was different in blood ——   135

HER. Oh, cross!° Too high to be enthralled° to
   low.°

LYS. Or else misgraffed° in respect of years ——

---

48. composed: formed.   49. form: shape.   54. in . . . kind: in
this case; i.e., the marriage. wanting: being without.   60. how
. . . modesty: whether it may make me appear immodest.
65. die . . . death: to be put to death by the law.   68. Know of:
remember.   71. aye: ever. mewed: caged.   73. moon: i.e.,
Diana, goddess of chastity and single life.   76. earthlier happy:
happier on earth. distilled: which sheds its essence on another.
80. virgin patent: privilege of my virginity.   84–85. sealing . . .
fellowship: the day when we conclude our marriage.   89. pro-
test: vow.

92. crazed title: flawed claim.   96. render: give up to.   98. es-
tate: transfer.   99–100. derived . . . possessed: of as good birth
and wealth.   102. vantage: advantage, superiority.   106. avouch
. . . head: declare it to his face.   110. spotted: stained.
116. schooling: advice.   118. fit . . . fancies: suit your ideas of
love.   125. Against: in anticipation of.   126. nearly: closely.
131. Beteem: bring forth.   136. cross: perversity. enthralled:
made servant to. low: one of low birth.   137. misgraffed: ill-
grafted.

HER. Oh, spite! Too old to be engaged to young.
LYS. Or else it stood upon the choice of
　　friends ——
HER. Oh, Hell! To choose love by another's eyes.
LYS. Or, if there were a sympathy in choice,　141
War, death, or sickness did lay siege to it,
Making it momentany° as a sound,
Swift as a shadow, short as any dream;
Brief as the lightning in the collied° night,　145
That, in a spleen,° unfolds both heaven and earth,
And ere a man hath power to say " Behold! "
The jaws of darkness do devour it up.
So quick bright things come to confusion.°
HER. If then true lovers have been ever crossed,°
It stands as an edíct in destiny.°　151
Then let us teach our trial patience,
Because it is a customary cross,
As due to love as thoughts and dreams and sighs,
Wishes and tears, poor fancy's° followers.　155
LYS. A good persuasion. Therefore hear me,
　　Hermia.
I have a widow aunt, a dowager
Of great revénue, and she hath no child.
From Athens is her house remote seven leagues;°
And she respects° me as her only son.　160
There, gentle Hermia, may I marry thee,
And to that place the sharp Athenian law
Cannot pursue us. If thou lovest me, then,
Steal forth thy father's house tomorrow night,
And in the wood, a league without the town,　165
Where I did meet thee once with Helena
To do observance to a morn of May,°
There will I stay for thee.
HER.　　　　　　　　My good Lysander!
I swear to thee, by Cupid's strongest bow,
By his best arrow with the golden head,°　170
By the simplicity of Venus' doves,°
By that which knitteth souls and prospers loves,
And by that fire which burned the Carthage Queen°
When the false Troyan under sail was seen ——
By all the vows that ever men have broke,　175
In number more than ever women spoke,
In that same place thou hast appointed me,
Tomorrow truly will I meet with thee.
LYS. Keep promise, love. Look, here comes Hel-
　　ena.

[*Enter* HELENA.]

HER. Godspeed, fair Helena! Whither away?
HEL. Call you me fair? That fair again unsay.
Demetrius loves your fair. O happy fair!　182
Your eyes are lodestars,° and your tongue's sweet air
More tunable than lark to shepherd's ear
When wheat is green, when hawthorn buds appear.
Sickness is catching. Oh, were favor° so,　186
Yours would I catch, fair Hermia, ere I go.
My ear should catch your voice, my eye your eye,
My tongue should catch your tongue's sweet melody.
Were the world mine, Demetrius being bated,°　190
The rest I'd give to be to you translated.°
Oh, teach me how you look, and with what art
You sway the motion° of Demetrius' heart!
HER. I frown upon him, yet he loves me still.
HEL. Oh, that your frowns would teach my smiles
　　such skill!　195
HER. I give him curses, yet he gives me love.
HEL. Oh, that my prayers could such affection
　　move!
HER. The more I hate, the more he follows me.
HEL. The more I love, the more he hateth me.
HER. His folly, Helena, is no fault of mine.　200
HEL. None but your beauty. Would that fault
　　were mine!
HER. Take comfort. He no more shall see my face.
Lysander and myself will fly this place.
Before the time I did Lysander see,
Seemed Athens as a paradise to me.　205
Oh then, what graces in my love do dwell,
That he hath turned a Heaven unto a Hell!
LYS. Helen, to you our minds we will unfold.
Tomorrow night, when Phoebe° doth behold
Her silver visage in the watery glass,°　210
Decking with liquid pearl the bladed grass,
A time that lovers' flights doth still° conceal,
Through Athens' gates have we devised to steal.
HER. And in the wood, where often you and I
Upon faint primrose beds were wont to lie,　215
Emptying our bosoms of their counsel sweet,
There my Lysander and myself shall meet,
And thence from Athens turn away our eyes,
To seek new friends and stranger companies.
Farewell, sweet playfellow. Pray thou for us,　220
And good luck grant thee thy Demetrius!
Keep word, Lysander. We must starve our sight
From lovers' food till morrow deep midnight.
LYS. I will, my Hermia. [*Exit* HERMIA.] Helena,
　　adieu.　224
As you on him, Demetrius dote on you!　[*Exit.*]
HEL. How happy some o'er other some° can be!

143. momentany: momentary.　**145. collied:** coal-black.
146. spleen: flash of wrath.　**149. confusion:** pronounced as four
syllables.　**150. crossed:** thwarted.　**151. edict in destiny:** decree
of fate.　**155. fancy:** love.　**159. league:** three miles.　**160. re-**
spects: regards.　　**167. do ... May:** observe May Day.
170. golden head: Cupid has two kinds of arrows, the leaden
causes dislike, the golden, love.　**171. Venus' doves:** Doves were
sacred to Venus, the goddess of love.　**173. Carthage Queen:**
Dido, Queen of Carthage, fell in love with Aeneas when he
visited her after his escape from Troy. Aeneas deserted her,
whereupon she mounted a funeral pyre and killed herself in
the flames.

183. lodestars: guiding stars.　**186. favor:** with double meaning,
"beauty" and "affection."　**190. bated:** excepted.　**191. trans-**
lated: transformed.　**193. motion:** inclination.　**209. Phoebe:**
Diana, the moon.　**210. watery glass:** i.e., reflected in the
water.　**212. still:** always.　**226. o'er ... some:** compared with
some others.

Through Athens I am thought as fair as she.
But what of that? Demetrius thinks not so,
He will not know what all but he do know.
And as he errs, doting on Hermia's eyes,   230
So I, admiring of his qualities.
Things base and vile, holding no quantity,°
Love can transpose to form and dignity.
Love looks not with the eyes, but with the mind;
And therefore is winged Cupid painted blind.   235
Nor hath Love's mind of any judgment taste;°
Wings, and no eyes, figure unheedy haste.
And therefore is Love said to be a child,
Because in choice he is so oft beguiled.
As waggish° boys in game themselves forswear,
So the boy Love is perjured everywhere: 241
For ere Demetrius looked on Hermia's eyne,°
He hailed down oaths that he was only mine;
And when this hail some heat from Hermia felt,
So he dissolved, and showers of oaths did melt.   245
I will go tell him of fair Hermia's flight.
Then to the wood will he tomorrow night
Pursue her; and for this intelligence°
If I have thanks, it is a dear expense.°
But herein mean I to enrich° my pain,   250
To have his sight thither and back again.   [*Exit.*]

SCENE II. *The same.* QUINCE'S *house.*

[*Enter* QUINCE, SNUG, BOTTOM, FLUTE, SNOUT,
and STARVELING.]

QUIN. Is all our company here?

BOT. You were best to call them generally,° man
by man, according to the scrip.°

QUIN. Here is the scroll of every man's name
which is thought fit, through all Athens, to play in
our interlude° before the Duke and the Duchess on
his wedding day at night.   7

BOT. First, good Peter Quince, say what the play
treats on. Then read the names of the actors, and so
grow to a point.°   10

QUIN. Marry,° our play is, *The most lamentable
comedy, and most cruel death of Pyramus and
Thisby.*

BOT. A very good piece of work, I assure you, and
a merry. Now, good Peter Quince, call forth   15
your actors by the scroll. Masters, spread yourselves.

QUIN. Answer as I call you. Nick Bottom, the
weaver.

BOT. Ready. Name what part I am for, and pro-
ceed.   21

QUIN. You, Nick Bottom, are set down for Pyra-
mus.

BOT. What is Pyramus? A lover, or a tyrant?

QUIN. A lover, that kills himself most gallant for
love.   26

BOT. That will ask some tears in the true perform-
ing of it. If I do it, let the audience look to their eyes,
I will move storms, I will condole° in some measure.
To the rest. Yet my chief humor° is for a tyrant. I
could play Ercles° rarely, or a part to tear a cat° in,
to make all split.   32

    " The raging rocks
        And shivering shocks
    Shall break the locks   35
        Of prison gates.
    And Phibbus'° car°
        Shall shine from far,
    And make and mar
        The foolish Fates."   40

This was lofty! Now name the rest of the players.
This is Ercles' vein, a tyrant's vein. A lover is more
condoling.

QUIN. Francis Flute, the bellows-mender.

FLU. Here, Peter Quince.   45

QUIN. Flute, you must take Thisby on you.

FLU. What is Thisby? A wandering knight?

QUIN. It is the lady that Pyramus must love.

FLU. Nay, faith, let not me play a woman. I have a
beard coming.   50

QUIN. That's all one. You shall play it in a mask,
and you may speak as small° as you will.

BOT. An° I may hide my face, let me play Thisby
too. I'll speak in a monstrous little voice, " Thisne,
Thisne." " Ah Pyramus, my lover dear! Thy Thisby
dear, and lady dear! "   56

QUIN. No, no. You must play Pyramus, and Flute,
you Thisby.

BOT. Well, proceed.

QUIN. Robin Starveling, the tailor.   60

STAR. Here, Peter Quince.

QUIN. Robin Starveling, you must play Thisby's
mother. Tom Snout, the tinker.

SNOUT. Here, Peter Quince.

QUIN. You, Pyramus' father. Myself, Thisby's   65
father. Snug, the joiner, you, the lion's part. And, I
hope, here is a play fitted.

SNUG. Have you the lion's part written? Pray you,
if it be, give it me, for I am slow of study.

QUIN. You may do it extempore, for it is nothing
but roaring.   71

BOT. Let me play the lion too. I will roar that I will

---

232. quantity: proportion.   236. Nor ... taste: i.e., Love has
no judgment.   240. waggish: frolicsome.   242. eyne: eyes.
248. intelligence: information.   249. dear expense: something
that costs one dear.   250. enrich: make rich — by the pleasure
of seeing him.
    Sc. ii: 2. generally: Bottom loves a long word, but usually
gets it wrong. Here he means "severally"; i.e., separately.
3. scrip: list.   6. interlude: play.   10. grow ... point: come to
a conclusion.   11. Marry: Mary, by the Virgin.

29. condole: lit., sympathize; Bottom means "lament."   30. hu-
mor: whim.   31. Ercles: Hercules, a roaring figure in the old
drama. tear a cat: proverbial expression for ham acting.
37. Phibbus: for "Phoebus." car: chariot.   52. small: shrilly.
53. An: if.

do any man's heart good to hear me; I will roar that
I will make the Duke say, "Let him roar again, let
him roar again."   75

QUIN. An you should do it too terribly, you would
fright the Duchess and the ladies, that they would
shriek; and that were enough to hang us all.

ALL. That would hang us, every mother's son.   80

BOT. I grant you, friends, if you should fright the
ladies out of their wits, they would have no more dis-
cretion but to hang us. But I will aggravate° my
voice so that I will roar you as gently as any sucking
dove, I will roar you an 'twere any nightingale.   85

QUIN. You can play no part but Pyramus; for
Pyramus is a sweet-faced man, a proper° man as one
shall see in a summer's day, a most lovely, gentle-
manlike man. Therefore you must needs play Pyra-
mus.   90

BOT. Well, I will undertake it. What beard were I
best to play it in?

QUIN. Why, what you will.

BOT. I will discharge it in either your straw-   95
color beard, your orange-tawny beard, your purple-
in-grain° beard, or your French-crown-color beard,
your perfect yellow.

QUIN. Some of your French crowns have no hair
at all,° and then you will play barefaced. But,   100
masters, here are your parts. And I am to entreat
you, request you, and desire you, to con° them by to-
morrow night; and meet me in the palace wood, a
mile without the town, by moonlight. There will we
rehearse, for if we meet in the city, we shall be
dogged with company, and our devices known.   106
In the meantime I will draw a bill of properties such
as our play wants. I pray you, fail me not.

BOT. We will meet, and there we may rehearse
most obscenely° and courageously. Take pains, be
perfect. Adieu.   111

QUIN. At the Duke's Oak we meet.

BOT. Enough. Hold or cut bowstrings.°

                              [*Exeunt.*]

Act II

SCENE I. *A wood near Athens.*

[*Enter, from opposite sides, a* FAIRY, *and* PUCK.]

PUCK. How now, spirit! Whither wander you?

FAI.   Over hill, over dale,

83. aggravate: for "moderate."   87. proper: handsome.
96–97. purple-in-grain: dyed purple.   99–100. French . . . all:
Loss of hair was one of the results of venereal or "French"
disease.   102. con: learn by heart.   110. obscenely: for "ob-
scurely."   113. Hold . . . bowstrings: a proverbial phrase, of
which the origin is not satisfactorily explained, meaning come
what may.

        Thorough° bush, thorough brier,
   Over park, over pale,°
        Thorough flood, thorough fire,   5
   I do wander everywhere,
   Swifter than the moon's sphere.
   And I serve the Fairy Queen,
   To dew her orbs° upon the green.
   The cowslips° tall her pensioners° be.   10
   In their gold coats spots you see;
   Those be rubies, fairy favors,
     In those freckles live their savors.
I must go seek some dewdrops here,
And hang a pearl in every cowslip's ear.   15
Farewell, thou lob° of spirits, I'll be gone.
Our Queen and all her elves come here anon.

PUCK. The King doth keep his revels here tonight.
Take heed the Queen come not within his sight;
For Oberon is passing° fell° and wrath,   20
Because that she as her attendant hath
A lovely boy, stolen from an Indian king.
She never had so sweet a changeling,°
And jealous Oberon would have the child
Knight of his train,° to trace° the forests wild;   25
But she perforce withholds the lovèd boy,
Crowns him with flowers, and makes him all her joy.
And now they never meet in grove or green,
By fountain clear or spangled starlight sheen,
But they do square,° that all their elves for fear   30
Creep into acorn cups and hide them there.

FAI. Either I mistake your shape and making
     quite,
Or else you are that shrewd and knavish sprite
Called Robin Goodfellow.° Are not you he
That frights the maidens of the villagery;   35
Skim milk, and sometimes labor in the quern,°
And bootless° make the breathless housewife churn;
And sometime make the drink to bear no barm;°
Mislead night wanderers, laughing at their harm?
Those that Hobgoblin call you, and sweet Puck,   40
You do their work, and they shall have good luck.
Are not you he?

PUCK.   Thou speak'st aright.
I am that merry wanderer of the night.
I jest to Oberon, and make him smile,
When I a fat and bean-fed horse beguile,   45

Act II, Sc. i: 3. Thorough: through.   4. pale: fence.   9. orbs:
fairy rings; circles of dark grass common in English meadows.
10. cowslips: a wild plant which grows in meadows, with clusters
of small yellow-orange flowers on a stem about eight to nine
inches tall. pensioners: the Queen's personal bodyguard, all
young men of fine physique and good family.   16. lob: lubber,
lout.   20. passing: exceedingly. fell: fierce.   23. changeling:
child exchanged by fairies. It was a country superstition that
the fairies sometimes stole a beautiful child and left an ugly one
in its place; here the changeling is the stolen child.   25. train:
following. trace: follow the tracks in.   30. square: quarrel.
34. Robin Goodfellow: See *MND* Intro. p. 272a–b.   36. quern:
handmill for grinding wheat.   37. bootless: vainly.   38. barm:
yeast.

Neighing in likeness of a filly foal.
And sometime lurk I in a gossip's° bowl,
In very likeness of a roasted crab;°
And when she drinks, against her lips I bob
And on her withered dewlap° pour the ale.   50
The wisest aunt, telling the saddest tale,
Sometime for three-foot stool mistaketh me;
Then slip I from her bum, down topples she,
And "tailor"° cries, and falls into a cough,
And then the whole quire° hold their hips and
        laugh,   55
And waxen in their mirth, and neeze,° and swear
A merrier hour was never wasted there.
But, room, fairy! Here comes Oberon.
FAI. And here my mistress. Would that he were
        gone!

[*Enter, from one side,* OBERON, *with his train; from
        the other,* TITANIA, *with hers.*]

OBE. Ill met by moonlight,° proud Titania.   60
TITA. What, jealous Oberon! Fairies, skip hence.
I have forsworn° his bed and company.
OBE. Tarry, rash wanton. Am not I thy lord?
TITA. Then I must be thy lady. But I know
When thou hast stolen away from fairyland,   65
And in the shape of Corin sat all day,
Playing on pipes of corn,° and versing love
To amorous Phillida.° Why art thou here,
Come from the farthest steppe of India
But that, forsooth, the bouncing Amazon,   70
Your buskined° mistress and your warrior love,
To Theseus must be wedded, and you come
To give their bed joy and prosperity?
OBE. How canst thou thus for shame, Titania,
Glance at my credit° with Hippolyta,   75
Knowing I know thy love to Theseus?
Didst thou not lead him through the glimmering
        night
From Perigenia, whom he ravishèd?
And make him with fair Aegle break his faith,
With Ariadne and Antiopa?°   80
TITA. These are the forgeries° of jealousy.
And never, since the middle summer's spring,
Met we on hill, in dale, forest, or mead,
By pavèd fountain or by rushy brook,

Or in the beachèd margent° of the sea,   85
To dance our ringlets° to the whistling wind,
But with thy brawls thou hast disturbed our sport.
Therefore° the winds, piping to us in vain,
As in revenge, have sucked up from the sea
Contagious fogs, which, falling in the land,   90
Have every pelting° river made so proud
That they have overborne their continents.°
The ox hath therefore stretched his yoke in vain,
The plowman lost his sweat, and the green corn°
Hath rotted ere his youth attained a beard.   95
The fold° stands empty in the drownèd field,
And crows are fatted with the murrion° flock.
The nine men's morris° is filled up with mud;
And the quaint° mazes° in the wanton° green,
For lack of tread, are undistinguishable.   100
The human mortals want° their winter here.
No night is now with hymn or carol blest.
Therefore the moon, the governess of floods,
Pale in her anger, washes all the air,
That rhéumatic diseases do abound.   105
And thorough this distemperature° we see
The seasons alter. Hoary-headed frosts
Fall in the fresh lap of the crimson rose,
And on old Hiems'° thin and icy crown
An odorous chaplet of sweet summer buds   110
Is, as in mockery, set. The spring, the summer,
The childing° autumn, angry winter, change
Their wonted liveries, and the mazed° world,
By their increase, now knows not which is which.
And this same progeny of evils comes   115
From our debate, from our dissension.
We are their parents and original.
OBE. Do you amend it, then. It lies in you.
Why should Titania cross her Oberon?
I do but beg a little changeling boy,   120
To be my henchman.°
TITA.   Set your heart at rest.
The fairyland buys not the child of me.

85. **margent**: margin. 86. **ringlets**: round dances. 88–114. Therefore . . . which: See *MND* Intro. p. 269a. 91. **pelting**: paltry.
92. **continents**: banks. 94. **corn**: wheat, oats, barley, rye, but
not maize. 96. **fold**: sheep-pen. 97. **murrion**: plague-stricken.
98. **nine . . . morris**: "Merels was a game for two players or
parties, each of whom had the same number of pebbles, disks,
pegs, or pins. It was also known as Nine Men's Morris, Five-
penny Morris, and Three Men's Morris, according to the number of 'men' used. The usual form of the diagram on which it is
played is a square with one or more squares inside it. The pegs
or stones placed at set points are moved by one side so as to take
up the men of the other." (*Shakespeare's England*, II.467.)
99. **quaint**: curious. **maze**: a set of elaborate and intricate paths
leading (or misleading) to a center. Those who know the secret
can find their way; those who do not are baffled at every turn.
To preserve the pattern in a village green, the paths must be
re-trod every year. At Hampton Court there is an ancient
maze with high yew hedges in which it is easy to be lost for
hours. **wanton**: luxuriant. 101. **want**: lack; i.e., are without the
usual winter feasting. 106. **distemperature**: disorder in nature. 109. **Hiems**: Winter. 112. **childing**: pregnant, fertile.
113. **mazed**: bewildered. 121. **henchman**: servant.

47. **gossip**: goodwife (by nature given to gossiping).   48. **crab**:
crab apple. Roasted apples were sometimes floated in drinks to
give flavor.   50. **dewlap**: loose skin under the chin.   54. **tailor**:
Nobody has as yet explained convincingly why we should cry
"tailor."   55. **quire**: company.   56. **neeze**: sneeze.   60. **moonlight**: The constant suggestion of moonlight throughout Acts
II, III, and IV is worth noting.   62. **forsworn**: sworn to avoid.
66–68. **shape . . . Phillida**: i.e., becoming an idle shepherd
making love to a shepherdess. Corin and Phillida are typical
names in pastoral verse.   67. **pipes of corn**: oaten straws, a favorite musical instrument of pastoral shepherds.   71. **buskined**:
wearing hunting boots. See Pl. 13a.   75. **credit**: reputation.
78–80. **Perigenia . . . Antiopa**: These details of Theseus's love
life Shakespeare found in Plutarch. See *MND* Intro. p. 270b.
81. **forgeries**: false inventions.

His mother was a votaress° of my order.
And in the spicèd Indian air, by night,
Full often hath she gossiped by my side;   125
And sat with me on Neptune's yellow sands,
Marking the embarkèd traders° on the flood,
When we have laughed to see the sails conceive
And grow big-bellied with the wanton wind,
Which she, with pretty and with swimming gait
Following — her womb then rich with my young
    squire —   131
Would imitate, and sail upon the land,
To fetch me trifles, and return again
As from a voyage, rich with merchandise.
But she, being mortal, of that boy did die,   135
And for her sake do I rear up her boy,
And for her sake I will not part with him.
    OBE. How long within this wood intend you stay?
    TITA. Perchance till after Theseus' wedding day.
If you will patiently dance in our round,   140
And see our moonlight revels, go with us;
If not, shun me, and I will spare° your haunts.
    OBE. Give me that boy, and I will go with thee.
    TITA. Not for thy fairy kingdom. Fairies, away!
We shall chide downright, if I longer stay.   145
                    [*Exit* TITANIA *with her train.*]
    OBE. Well, go thy way. Thou shalt not from this
    grove
Till I torment thee for this injury.
My gentle Puck, come hither. Thou rememberest
Since once I sat upon a promontory
And heard a mermaid,° on a dolphin's back,   150
Uttering such dulcet and harmonious breath
That the rude sea grew civil at her song,
And certain stars shot madly from their spheres°
To hear the sea maid's music.
    PUCK.   I remember.
    OBE. That very time I saw, but thou couldst not,
Flying between the cold moon and the earth,   156
Cupid all armed. A certain aim he took
At a fair° vestal thronèd by the west,
And loosed his love shaft smartly from his bow,
As it should pierce a hundred thousand hearts.   160
But I might see young Cupid's fiery shaft
Quenched in the chaste beams of the watery moon,
And the imperial votaress passed on,
In maiden meditation, fancy-free.
Yet marked I where the bolt° of Cupid fell.   165
It fell upon a little western flower,
Before milk-white, now purple with love's wound,

And maidens call it love-in-idleness.°
Fetch me that flower, the herb I showed thee
    once.
The juice of it on sleeping eyelids laid   170
Will make or man or woman madly dote
Upon the next live creature that it sees.
Fetch me this herb, and be thou here again
Ere the leviathan° can swim a league.
    PUCK. I'll put a girdle round about the earth°
In forty minutes.   [*Exit.*]
    OBE.   Having once this juice,   176
I'll watch Titania when she is asleep
And drop the liquor of it in her eyes.
The next thing then she waking looks upon,
Be it on lion, bear, or wolf, or bull,   180
On meddling monkey or on busy ape,
She shall pursue it with the soul of love.
And ere I take this charm from off her sight,
As I can take it with another herb,
I'll make her render up her page to me.   185
But who comes here? I am invisible,°
And I will overhear their conference.
        [*Enter* DEMETRIUS, HELENA *following him.*]
    DEM. I love thee not, therefore pursue me not.
Where is Lysander and fair Hermia?
The one I'll slay, the other slayeth me.   190
Thou told'st me they were stolen unto this wood,
And here am I, and wode° within this wood,
Because I cannot meet my Hermia.
Hence, get thee gone, and follow me no more.
    HEL. You draw me, you hardhearted adamant.°
But yet you draw not iron, for my heart   196
Is true as steel. Leave you° your power to draw,
And I shall have no power to follow you.
    DEM. Do I entice you? Do I speak you fair?
Or, rather, do I not in plainest truth   200
Tell you I do not nor I cannot love you?
    HEL. And even for that do I love you the more.
I am your spaniel, and, Demetrius,
The more you beat me, I will fawn on you.
Use me but as your spaniel, spurn me, strike me,
Neglect me, lose me — only give me leave,   206
Unworthy as I am, to follow you.
What worser place can I beg in your love —
And yet a place of high respect with me —
Than to be usèd as you use your dog?   210
    DEM. Tempt not too much the hatred of my spirit,
For I am sick when I do look on thee.
    HEL. And I am sick when I look not on you.
    DEM. You do impeach° your modesty too much,

---

123. votaress: devoted follower.   127. embarked traders: merchant ships.   142. spare: avoid.   150. heard a mermaid: probably an allusion to one of the elaborate entertainments prepared for Queen Elizabeth.   153. spheres: courses. See App. 1. 158–64. fair . . . fancy-free: a tactful and complimentary allusion to Queen Elizabeth, the Virgin Queen, whose bosom was impenetrable to Cupid's arrows. vestal: one vowed to virginity. votaress: one who has made a vow. fancy-free: not caught by love.   165. bolt: arrow.

168. love-in-idleness: wild pansy.   174. leviathan: whale. 175. I'll . . . earth: I'll fly round the earth.   186. I am invisible: Presumably Oberon here puts on a cloak to symbolize invisibility. Henslowe in his *Diary* noted that the Admiral's Men in 1598 bought "a robe for to go invisible."   192. wode: mad.   195. adamant: lodestone, a very hard magnetic stone. 197. Leave you: if you will leave off.   214. impeach: discredit.

To leave the city, and commit yourself 215
Into the hands of one that loves you not;
To trust the opportunity of night
And the ill counsel of a desert place
With the rich worth of your virginity.
 HEL. Your virtue is my privilege. For that 220
It is not night when I do see your face,
Therefore I think I am not in the night.
Nor doth this wood lack worlds of company,
For you in my respect° are all the world.
Then how can it be said I am alone 225
When all the world is here to look on me?
 DEM. I'll run from thee and hide me in the
  brakes,°
And leave thee to the mercy of wild beasts.
 HEL. The wildest hath not such a heart as you.
Run when you will, the story shall be changed. 230
Apollo flies, and Daphne holds the chase;°
The dove pursues the griffin;° the mild hind
Makes speed to catch the tiger — bootless° speed
When cowardice pursues, and valor flies.
 DEM. I will not stay thy questions, let me go. 235
Or, if thou follow me, do not believe
But I shall do thee mischief in the wood.
 HEL. Aye, in the temple, in the town, the field,
You do me mischief. Fie, Demetrius!
Your wrongs do set a scandal on my sex. 240
We cannot fight for love, as men may do;
We should be wooed, and were not made to woo.
       [Exit DEMETRIUS.*]*
I'll follow thee, and make a Heaven of Hell,
To die upon the hand I love so well. *[Exit.]*
 OBE. Fare thee well, nymph. Ere he do leave this
  grove, 245
Thou shalt fly him, and he shall seek thy love.
[Re-enter PUCK.*]* Hast thou the flower there?
 Welcome, wanderer.
 PUCK. Aye, there it is.
 OBE.   I pray thee, give it me.
I know a bank where the wild thyme blows,
Where oxlips° and the nodding violet grows; 250
Quite overcanopied with luscious woodbine,°
With sweet musk roses, and with eglantine.°
There sleeps Titania sometime of the night,
Lulled in these flowers with dances and delight.
And there the snake throws her enameled° skin,
Weed° wide enough to wrap a fairy in. 256
And with the juice of this I'll streak her eyes,
And make her full of hateful fantasies.
Take thou some of it, and seek through this grove.

A sweet Athenian lady is in love 260
With a disdainful youth. Anoint his eyes;
But do it when the next thing he espies
May be the lady. Thou shalt know the man
By the Athenian garments he hath on.
Effect it with some care, that he may prove 265
More fond° on her than she upon her love.
And look thou meet me ere the first cock crow.
 PUCK. Fear not, my lord, your servant shall do so.
          [Exeunt.]

SCENE II. *Another part of the wood.*

[Enter TITANIA, *with her train.]*
 TITA. Come, now a roundel° and a fairy song,
Then, for the third part of a minute, hence —
Some to kill cankers° in the musk-rose buds,
Some war with reremice° for their leathern wings,
To make my small elves coats, and some keep back
The clamorous owl that nightly hoots and wonders
At our quaint spirits. Sing me now asleep, 7
Then to your offices, and let me rest.
       [The fairies sing.]
 1. FAI. You spotted snakes with double tongue,
   Thorny hedgehogs, be not seen. 10
  Newts and blindworms,° do no wrong,
   Come not near our fairy Queen.
 CHORUS. Philomel,° with melody
   Sing in our sweet lullaby;
  Lulla, lulla, lullaby, lulla, lulla, lullaby. 15
    Never harm,
    Nor spell, nor charm,
   Come our lovely lady nigh.
   So, good night, with lullaby.

 1. FAI. Weaving spiders, come not here. 20
   Hence, you long-legged spinners, hence!
  Beetles black, approach not near.
   Worm nor snail, do no offense.
 CHORUS. Philomel, with melody
   Sing in our sweet lullaby; 25
  Lulla, lulla, lullaby, lulla, lulla, lullaby.
    Never harm,
    Nor spell, nor charm,
   Come our lovely lady nigh.
   So, good night, with lullaby.
 2. FAI. Hence, away! Now all is well.
   One aloof stand sentinel.
    [Exeunt FAIRIES. TITANIA *sleeps.]*
[Enter OBERON, *and squeezes the flower on*
    TITANIA's *eyelids.]*
 OBE. What thou seest when thou dost wake,

---

224. respect: estimation. 227. brakes: bushes. 231. Apollo . . .
chase: The natural order is reversed; the meek pursues the
strong. According to the legend, Apollo pursued Daphne,
who was turned into a laurel bush. 232. griffin: a fabulous
beast, eagle in front and lion behind. 233. bootless: vain.
250. oxlips: cross between the primrose and the cowslip.
251. woodbine: honeysuckle. 252. eglantine: sweetbrier.
255. enameled: shiny. 256. Weed: garment.

266. fond: foolishly doting.
 Sc. ii: 1. roundel: round dance. 3. cankers: cankerworms.
4. reremice: bats. 11. blindworm: slow worm, a small harmless
snakelike creature (actually a legless lizard), common in the
English countryside. 13. Philomel: the nightingale.

Do it for thy truelove take,
Love and languish for his sake.
Be it ounce,° or cat, or bear,   30
Pard,° or boar with bristled hair,
In thy eye that shall appear
When thou wakest, it is thy dear.
Wake when some vile thing is near.   [*Exit.*]

        [*Enter* LYSANDER *and* HERMIA.]

  LYS. Fair love, you faint with wandering in the
    wood,   35
And to speak troth,° I have forgot our way.
We'll rest us, Hermia, if you think it good,
   And tarry for the comfort of the day.
  HER. Be it so, Lysander. Find you out a bed,
For I upon this bank will rest my head.   40
  LYS. One turf shall serve as pillow for us both —
One heart, one bed, two bosoms, and one troth.
  HER. Nay, good Lysander, for my sake, my dear,
Lie further off yet, do not lie so near.
  LYS. Oh, take the sense, sweet, of my innocence!
Love takes the meaning in love's conference.   46
I mean that my heart unto yours is knit
So that but one heart we can make of it.
Two bosoms interchainèd with an oath,
So then two bosoms and a single troth.   50
Then by your side no bedroom me deny
For lying so, Hermia, I do not lie.
  HER. Lysander riddles very prettily.
Now much beshrew° my manners and my pride,
If Hermia meant to say Lysander lied.   55
But, gentle friend, for love and courtesy
Lie further off; in human modesty,
Such separation as may well be said
Becomes a virtuous bachelor and a maid,
So far be distant. And good night, sweet friend. 60
Thy love ne'er alter till thy sweet life end!
  LYS. Amen, amen, to that fair prayer say I,
And then end life when I end loyalty!
Here is my bed. Sleep give thee all his rest!   64
  HER. With half that wish the wisher's eye be
    pressed!   [*They sleep.*]

        [*Enter* PUCK.]

  PUCK. Through the forest have I gone,
But Athenian found I none
On whose eyes I might approve°
This flower's force in stirring love.
Night and silence. — Who is here?   70
Weeds of Athens he doth wear.
This is he, my master said,
Despisèd the Athenian maid,
And here the maiden, sleeping sound
On the dank and dirty ground.   75
Pretty soul! She durst not lie
Near this lacklove, this kill-courtesy.
Churl,° upon thy eyes I throw

All the power this charm doth owe.
When thou wakest, let love forbid   80
Sleep his seat on thy eyelid.
So awake when I am gone,
For I must now to Oberon.   [*Exit.*]

    [*Enter* DEMETRIUS *and* HELENA, *running.*]

  HEL. Stay, though thou kill me, sweet Demetrius.
  DEM. I charge thee, hence, and do not haunt me
    thus.   85
  HEL. Oh, wilt thou darkling° leave me? Do not so.
  DEM. Stay, on thy peril.° I alone will go. [*Exit.*]
  HEL. Oh, I am out of breath in this fond° chase!
The more my prayer, the lesser is my grace.
Happy is Hermia, wheresoe'er she lies,   90
For she hath blessèd and attractive eyes.
How came her eyes so bright? Not with salt tears;
If so, my eyes are oftener washed than hers.
No, no, I am as ugly as a bear,
For beasts that meet me run away for fear.   95
Therefore no marvel though Demetrius
Do, as a monster, fly my presence thus.
What wicked and dissembling° glass of mine
Made me compare with Hermia's sphery° eyne?
But who is here? Lysander! On the ground!   100
Dead? Or asleep? I see no blood, no wound.
Lysander, if you live, good sir, awake.
  LYS. [*Awaking*] And run through fire I will for
    thy sweet sake.
Transparent° Helena! Nature shows art,
That through thy bosom makes me see thy heart.
Where is Demetrius? Oh, how fit a word   106
Is that vile name to perish on my sword!
  HEL. Do not say so, Lysander, say not so.
What though he love your Hermia? Lord, what
    though?
Yet Hermia still loves you. Then be content.   110
  LYS. Content with Hermia! No, I do repent
The tedious minutes I with her have spent.
Not Hermia but Helena I love.
Who will not change a raven for a dove?
The will of man is by his reason swayed,   115
And reason says you are the worthier maid.
Things growing are not ripe until their season.
So I, being young, till now ripe not to reason;
And touching now the point° of human skill,
Reason becomes the marshal° to my will,°   120
And leads me to your eyes, where I o'erlook
Love's stories, written in love's richest book.
  HEL. Wherefore was I to this keen mockery born?
When at your hands did I deserve this scorn?
Is't not enough, is't not enough, young man,   125
That I did never, no, nor never can,
Deserve a sweet look from Demetrius' eye,

86. darkling: in the dark. **87. on . . . peril:** i.e., or harm will
come to you. **88. fond:** foolish. **98. dissembling:** deceiving.
99. sphery: starlike. **104. Transparent:** i.e., because her heart
is visible. **119. point:** high spot. **120. marshal:** director. **will:**
passion.

But you must flout my insufficiency?
Good troth, you do me wrong, good sooth,° you
   do,
In such disdainful manner me to woo.   130
But fare you well. Perforce I must confess
I thought you lord of more true gentleness.
Oh, that a lady, of one man refused,
Should of another therefore be abused!   [*Exit.*]
  LYS. She sees not Hermia. Hermia, sleep thou
   there.   135
And never mayst thou come Lysander near!
For as a surfeit of the sweetest things
The deepest loathing to the stomach brings,
Or as the heresies that men do leave
Are hated most of those they did deceive,   140
So thou, my surfeit and my heresy,
Of all be hated, but the most of me!
And, all my powers, address your love and might
To honor Helen and to be her knight!   [*Exit.*]
  HER. [*Awaking*] Help me, Lysander, help me! Do
   thy best   145
To pluck this crawling serpent from my breast!
Aye me, for pity! What a dream was here!
Lysander, look how I do quake with fear.
Methought a serpent eat my heart away,
And you sat smiling at his cruel prey.   150
Lysander! What, removed? Lysander! Lord!
What, out of hearing? Gone? No sound, no word?
Alack, where are you? Speak, an if you hear,
Speak, of all loves! I swoon almost with fear.
No? Then I well perceive you are not nigh.   155
Either death or you I'll find immediately.   [*Exit.*]

Act III

SCENE I. *The wood.* TITANIA *lying asleep.*

[*Enter* QUINCE, SNUG, BOTTOM, FLUTE, SNOUT, *and*
STARVELING.]
  BOT. Are we all met?
  QUIN. Pat, pat, and here's a marvelous convenient
place for our rehearsal. This green plot shall be our
stage, this hawthorn brake° our tiring-house;° and
we will do it in action as we will do it before the
Duke.   6
  BOT. Peter Quince——
  QUIN. What sayest thou, bully Bottom?
  BOT. There are things in this comedy of Pyramus
and Thisby that will never please. First, Pyra-   10
mus must draw a sword to kill himself, which the
ladies cannot abide. How answer you that?

129. **sooth:** truth.
Act III, Sc. i: 4. **brake:** thicket. **tiring-house:** dressing room.

  SNOUT. By'r lakin,° a parlous fear.
  STAR. I believe we must leave the killing out, when
all is done.   16
  BOT. Not a whit. I have a device to make all well.
Write me a prologue, and let the prologue seem to
say we will do no harm with our swords, and that
Pyramus is not killed indeed. And, for the more   20
better assurance, tell them that I Pyramus am not
Pyramus, but Bottom the weaver. This will put them
out of fear.
  QUIN. Well, we will have such a prologue, and it
shall be written in eight and six.°   25
  BOT. No, make it two more. Let it be written in
eight and eight.
  SNOUT. Will not the ladies be afeard of the lion?
  STAR. I fear it, I promise you.
  BOT. Masters, you ought to consider with   30
yourselves. To bring in — God shield us! — a lion
among ladies° is a most dreadful thing; for there is
not a more fearful wildfowl than your lion living,
and we ought to look to 't.
  SNOUT. Therefore another prologue must tell he is
not a lion.   36
  BOT. Nay, you must name his name, and half his
face must be seen through the lion's neck. And he
himself must speak through, saying thus, or to the
same defect° — "Ladies" — or "Fair ladies —   40
I would wish you" — or "I would request you" —
or "I would entreat you — not to fear, not to trem-
ble. My life for yours. If you think I come hither as a
lion, it were pity of my life. No, I am no such thing,
I am a man as other men are." And there indeed   45
let him name his name, and tell them plainly he is
Snug the joiner.
  QUIN. Well, it shall be so. But there is two hard
things: that is, to bring the moonlight into a cham-
ber, for you know Pyramus and Thisby meet by
moonlight.   51
  SNOUT. Doth the moon shine that night we play
our play?
  BOT. A calendar, a calendar! Look in the alma-
nac.° Find out moonshine, find out moonshine.
  QUIN. Yes, it doth shine that night.   56
  BOT. Why, then may you leave a casement° of the
great-chamber° window, where we play, open, and
the moon may shine in at the casement.
  QUIN. Aye, or else one must come in with a   60
bush of thorns and a lantern,° and say he comes to
disfigure,° or to present, the person of moonshine.
Then, there is another thing. We must have a wall in

14. **By'r lakin:** by our little lady; i.e., the Virgin Mary.
25. **eight . . . six:** the common ballad meter of alternate lines of
six and eight syllables.   31–32. **lion . . . ladies:** See *MND* Intro.
p. 269a–b.   40. **defect:** for "effect."   55. **almanac:** See App. 2.
57. **casement:** window opening on a hinge.   58. **great-chamber:**
hall of a great house. See Pl. 4b.   61. **bush . . . lantern:** sup-
posedly carried by the man in the moon.   62. **disfigure:** for
"prefigure."

the great chamber, for Pyramus and Thisby, says the story, did talk through the chink of a wall.   66

SNOUT. You can never bring in a wall. What say you, Bottom?

BOT. Some man or other must present wall. And let him have some plaster, or some loam,° or some roughcast° about him, to signify wall. And let   71 him hold his fingers thus, and through that cranny shall Pyramus and Thisby whisper.

QUIN. If that may be, then all is well. Come, sit down, every mother's son, and rehearse your   75 parts. Pyramus, you begin. When you have spoken your speech, enter into that brake. And so every one according to his cue.

[*Enter* PUCK *behind.*]

PUCK. What hempen homespuns° have we swaggering here,
So near the cradle of the Fairy Queen?   80
What, a play toward!° I'll be an auditor —
An actor too perhaps, if I see cause.

QUIN. Speak, Pyramus. Thisby, stand forth.

BOT. " Thisby, the flowers of odious savors
    sweet —— "

QUIN. Odors, odors.   85

BOT. " —— odors savors sweet.
So hath thy breath, my dearest Thisby dear.
But hark, a voice! Stay thou but here awhile,
    And by and by I will to thee appear."   [*Exit.*]

PUCK. A stranger Pyramus than e'er played here.
                                            [*Exit.*]

FLU. Must I speak now?   91

QUIN. Aye, marry must you, for you must understand he goes but to see a noise that he heard, and is to come again.

FLU. " Most radiant Pyramus, most lily-white of
    hue,   95
Of color like the red rose on triumphant brier,
Most briskly juvenal,° and eke° most lovely Jew,
As true as truest horse, that yet would never tire,
I'll meet thee, Pyramus, at Ninny's tomb."   99

QUIN. " Ninus' tomb," man. Why, you must not speak that yet. That you answer to Pyramus. You speak all your part at once, cues and all. Pyramus enter. Your cue is past. It is " never tire."   105

FLU. Oh — " As true as truest horse, that yet
    would never tire."

[*Re-enter* PUCK, *and* BOTTOM *with an ass's head.*]

BOT. " If I were fair, Thisby, I were only thine."

QUIN. Oh, monstrous! Oh, strange! We are haunted. Pray, masters! Fly, masters! Help!

[*Exeunt* QUINCE, SNUG, FLUTE, SNOUT, *and*
    STARVELING.]

PUCK. I'll follow you, I'll lead you about a round,°

Through bog, through bush, through brake,
    through brier.   110
Sometime a horse I'll be, sometime a hound,
    A hog, a headless bear, sometime a fire,
And neigh, and bark, and grunt, and roar, and
    burn,
Like horse, hound, hog, bear, fire, at every turn.
                                            [*Exit.*]

BOT. Why do they run away? This is a knavery of them to make me afeard.   116

[*Re-enter* SNOUT.]

SNOUT. O Bottom, thou art changed! What do I see on thee?

BOT. What do you see? You see an asshead of your own, do you?   120

[*Exit* SNOUT.]

[*Re-enter* QUINCE.]

QUIN. Bless thee, Bottom! Bless thee! Thou art translated.°   [*Exit.*]

BOT. I see their knavery. This is to make an ass of me, to fright me, if they could. But I will not stir from this place, do what they can. I will walk   125 up and down here, and I will sing, that they shall hear I am not afraid. [*Sings.*]
    " The ousel° cock so black of hue,
        With orange-tawny bill,
    The throstle° with his note so true,   130
        The wren° with little quill;° "

TITA. [*Awaking*] What angel wakes me from my flowery bed?

BOT. [*Sings.*]
    " The finch, the sparrow, and the lark,
        The plainsong° cuckoo gray,
    Whose note full many a man doth mark,   135
        And dares not answer nay° — "
for indeed who would set his wit to° so foolish a bird? Who would give a bird the lie, though he cry " cuckoo " never so?

TITA. I pray thee, gentle mortal, sing again.   140
Mine ear is much enamored of thy note,
So is mine eye enthrallèd° to thy shape.
And thy fair virtue's force perforce doth move me
On the first view to say, to swear, I love thee.

BOT. Methinks, mistress, you should have   145
little reason for that. And yet, to say the truth, reason and love keep little company together nowadays; the more the pity, that some honest neighbors will not make them friends. Nay, I can gleek° upon occasion.   150

TITA. Thou art as wise as thou art beautiful.

BOT. Not so, neither. But if I had wit enough to get out of this wood, I have enough to serve mine own turn.

---

70. loam: preparation of clay used for covering walls.   71. roughcast: rough plaster.   79. hempen homespuns: coarse clothing spun at home; i.e., country clowns.   81. toward: in hand.   97. juvenal: youth. eke: also.   109. about a round: roundabout.

122. translated: transformed.   128. ousel: blackbird.   130. throstle: thrush.   131. wren: the smallest of English birds. quill: feather.   134. plainsong: singing a simple melody.   135–36. Whose . . . nay: See App. II.   137. set . . . to: try to answer.   142. enthralled: enslaved.   149. gleek: wisecrack.

TITA. Out of this wood do not desire to go.   155
Thou shalt remain here, whether thou wilt or no.
I am a spirit of no common rate.
The summer still° doth tend° upon my state;
And I do love thee. Therefore go with me.
I'll give thee fairies to attend on thee,   160
And they shall fetch thee jewels from the deep,
And sing while thou on pressèd flowers dost sleep.
And I will purge thy mortal grossness so
That thou shalt like an airy spirit go.   164
Peaseblossom! Cobweb! Moth! And Mustardseed!

[*Enter* PEASEBLOSSOM, COBWEB, MOTH, *and*
MUSTARDSEED.]

1. FAI. Ready.
2. FAI.   And I.
3. FAI.   And I.
4. FAI.   And I.
ALL.   Where shall we go?
TITA. Be kind and courteous to this gentleman.
Hop in his walks, and gambol° in his eyes.
Feed him with apricocks° and dewberries,°
With purple grapes, green figs, and mulberries.   170
The honey bags steal from the humblebees,
And for night tapers crop their waxen thighs,
And light them at the fiery glowworm's eyes,
To have my love to bed and to arise.
And pluck the wings from painted butterflies,   175
To fan the moonbeams from his sleeping eyes.
Nod to him, elves, and do him courtesies.

1. FAI. Hail, mortal!
2. FAI. Hail!
3. FAI. Hail!   180
4. FAI. Hail!
BOT. I cry your Worship's mercy,° heartily. I be-
seech your Worship's name.
COB. Cobweb.
BOT. I shall desire you of more acquaintance,   185
good Master Cobweb. If I cut my finger, I shall make
bold with you.° Your name, honest gentleman?
PEAS. Peaseblossom.°
BOT. I pray you, commend me to Mistress   190
Squash,° your mother, and to Master Peascod,°
your father. Good Master Peaseblossom, I shall de-
sire you of more acquaintance too. Your name, I be-
seech you, sir?
MUS. Mustardseed.   195
BOT. Good Master Mustardseed, I know your pa-
tience well. That same cowardly, giantlike ox beef
hath devoured many a gentleman of your house. I
promise you your kindred hath made my eyes water
ere now. I desire your more acquaintance, good
Master Mustardseed.   201

TITA. Come, wait upon him; lead him to my
bower.
The moon methinks looks with a watery eye,
And when she weeps, weeps every little flower,
Lamenting some enforcèd chastity.   205
Tie up my love's tongue, bring him silently.

[*Exeunt.*]

SCENE II. *Another part of the wood.*

[*Enter* OBERON.]

OBE. I wonder if Titania be awaked,
Then, what it was that next came in her eye,
Which she must dote on in extremity.
[*Enter* PUCK.] Here comes my messenger.
                              How now, mad spirit!
What night rule° now about this haunted grove?   5
PUCK. My mistress with a monster is in love.
Near to her close and consecrated bower,
While she was in her dull and sleeping hour,
A crew of patches,° rude mechanicals,°
That work for bread upon Athenian stalls,°   10
Were met together to rehearse a play,
Intended for great Theseus' nuptial day.
The shallowest thickskin of that barren° sort,
Who Pyramus presented,° in their sport
Forsook his scene, and entered in a brake,   15
When I did him at this advantage take,
An ass's nole° I fixèd on his head.
Anon his Thisbe must be answerèd,
And forth my mimic° comes. When they him spy,
As wild geese that the creeping fowler eye,   20
Or russet-pated choughs,° many in sort,
Rising and cawing at the gun's report,
Sever themselves and madly sweep the sky,
So at his sight away his fellows fly.
And, at our stamp, here o'er and o'er one falls,   25
He murder cries, and help from Athens calls.
Their sense thus weak, lost with their fears thus
strong,
Made senseless things begin to do them wrong;
For briers and thorns at their apparel snatch,
Some sleeves, some hats, from yielders all things
catch.   30
I led them on in this distracted fear,
And left sweet Pyramus translated there,
When in that moment, so it came to pass,
Titania waked, and straightway loved an ass.
OBE. This falls out better than I could devise.   35
But hast thou yet latched° the Athenian's eyes
With the love juice, as I did bid thee do?

---

158. still: always. tend: attend.   168. gambol: caper.   169. ap-
ricocks: apricots. dewberries: blackberries.   182. I . . . mercy:
I beg your pardon.   186–87. Cobweb . . . you: an ancient means
of first aid for a cut finger.   189. Peaseblossom: the blossom
of a garden pea.   191. Squash: the unripe peapod. Peascod:
the full pod.

Sc. ii: 5. night rule: mischief.   9. patches: clowns. mechani-
cals: workingmen.   10. stalls: shops.   13. barren: empty-headed.
14. presented: represented.   17. nole: noddle, head.   19. mimic:
actor.   21. russet-pated choughs: gray-headed jackdaws.
36. latched: caught; i.e., charmed.

PUCK. I took him sleeping — that is finished too —
And the Athenian woman by his side,
That, when he waked, of force she must be eyed. 40
   [*Enter* HERMIA *and* DEMETRIUS.]
OBE. Stand close. This is the same Athenian.
PUCK. This is the woman, but not this the man.
DEM. Oh, why rebuke you him that loves you so?
Lay breath so bitter on your bitter foe.
HER. Now I but chide, but I should use thee worse,   45
For thou, I fear, hast given me cause to curse.
If thou hast slain Lysander in his sleep,
Being o'er shoes in blood, plunge in the deep,
And kill me too.
The sun was not so true unto the day   50
As he to me. Would he have stolen away
From sleeping Hermia? I'll believe as soon
This whole earth may be bored, and that the moon
May through the center° creep, and so displease
Her brother's noontide with the Antipodes.°   55
It cannot be but thou hast murdered him.
So should a murderer look, so dead,° so grim.
DEM. So should the murdered look, and so should I,
Pierced through the heart with your stern cruelty.
Yet you, the murderer, look as bright, as clear,   60
As yonder Venus° in her glimmering sphere.
HER. What's this to my Lysander? Where is he?
Ah, good Demetrius, wilt thou give him me?
DEM. I had rather give his carcass to my hounds.
HER. Out, dog! Out, cur! Thou drivest me past the bounds   65
Of maiden's patience. Hast thou slain him, then?
Henceforth be never numbered among men!
Oh, once tell true, tell true, even for my sake!
Durst thou have looked upon him being awake,
And hast thou killed him sleeping? Oh, brave touch.°   70
Could not a worm, an adder, do so much?
An adder did it, for with doubler tongue
Than thine, thou serpent, never adder stung.
DEM. You spend your passion on a misprised° mood.
I am not guilty of Lysander's blood,   75
Nor is he dead, for aught that I can tell.
HER. I pray thee, tell me then that he is well.
DEM. An if I could, what should I get therefore?
HER. A privilege never to see me more.
And from thy hated presence part I so.   80
See me no more, whether he be dead or no.   [*Exit.*]
DEM. There is no following her in this fierce vein.

Here therefore for a while I will remain.
So sorrow's heaviness doth heavier grow
For debt that bankrupt sleep doth sorrow owe,°   85
Which now in some slight measure it will pay
If for his tender° here I make some stay.
   [*Lies down and sleeps.*]
OBE. What hast thou done? Thou hast mistaken quite,
And laid the love juice on some truelove's sight.
Of thy misprision° must perforce ensue   90
Some true love turned, and not a false turned true.
PUCK. Then fate o'errules, that, one man holding troth,
A million fail, confounding oath on oath.°
OBE. About the wood go swifter than the wind,
And Helena of Athens look thou find.   95
All fancy-sick° she is and pale of cheer,°
With sighs of love that costs the fresh blood° dear.
By some illusion° see thou bring her here.
I'll charm his eyes against° she do appear.
PUCK. I go, I go, look how I go,   100
Swifter than arrow from the Tartar's° bow.   [*Exit.*]
OBE. Flower of this purple dye,
Hit with Cupid's archery,
Sink in apple of his eye.
When his love he doth espy,   105
Let her shine as gloriously
As the Venus of the sky.
When thou wakest, if she be by,
Beg of her for remedy.
   [*Re-enter* PUCK.]
PUCK. Captain of our fairy band,   110
Helena is here at hand,
And the youth, mistook by me,
Pleading for a lover's fee.
Shall we their fond pageant see?
Lord, what fools these mortals be!   115
OBE. Stand aside. The noise they make
Will cause Demetrius to awake.
PUCK. Then will two at once woo one,
That must needs be sport alone.
And those things do best please me   120
That befall preposterously.
   [*Enter* LYSANDER *and* HELENA.]
LYS. Why should you think that I should woo in scorn?
Scorn and derision never come in tears.
Look, when I vow, I weep, and vows so born
In their nativity all truth appears.   125

84–85. So . . . owe: a man in sorrow cannot sleep; sleep's debt to sorrow thus becomes heavier.   **87. tender:** offer; i.e., sleep.   **90. misprision:** mistake.   **92–93. Then . . . oath:** then fate overrules my efforts, for one man true in love, a million are false, breaking oath after oath.   **96. fancy-sick:** lovesick. **cheer:** face. **97. sighs . . . blood:** It was believed that sighs consumed the heart's blood.   **98. illusion:** deception.   **99. against:** by the time that.   **101. Tartar:** the Tartars, who live in Siberia, were famous bowmen.

---

54. center: i.e., of the earth. See App. 1.   **54–55. so . . . Antipodes:** i.e., the moon will pass through the earth and appear at the other side, to the annoyance of the sun who is shining there.   **57. dead:** deadly.   **61. Venus:** i.e., the star.   **70. touch:** feat.   **74. misprised:** mistaken.

How can these things in me seem scorn to you,
Bearing the badge of faith to prove them true?
   HEL. You do advance your cunning more and
     more.
  When truth kills truth, oh, devilish-holy fray!
These vows are Hermia's. Will you give her o'er?
  Weigh oath with oath, and you will nothing
    weigh.   131
Your vows to her and me, put in two scales,
Will even weigh — and both as light as tales.
   LYS. I had no judgment when to her I swore.
   HEL. Nor none, in my mind, now you give her
    o'er.   135
   LYS. Demetrius loves her, and he loves not you.
   DEM. [*Awaking.*] O Helen, goddess, nymph, per-
    fect, divine!
To what, my love, shall I compare thine eyne?
Crystal is muddy. Oh, how ripe in show   139
Thy lips, those kissing cherries, tempting grow!
That pure congealèd white, high Taurus'° snow,
Fanned with the eastern wind, turns to a crow
When thou hold'st up thy hand. Oh, let me kiss
This princess of pure white, this seal° of bliss!
   HEL. Oh, spite! Oh, Hell! I see you all are bent
To set against me for your merriment.   146
If you were civil and knew courtesy,
You would not do me thus much injury.
Can you not hate me, as I know you do,
But you must join in souls to mock me too?   150
If you were men, as men you are in show,
You would not use a gentle lady so —
To vow, and swear, and superpraise my parts,
When I am sure you hate me with your hearts.
You both are rivals, and love Hermia,   155
And now both rivals, to mock Helena.
A trim° exploit, a manly enterprise,
To conjure tears up in a poor maid's eyes
With your derision! None of noble sort
Would so offend a virgin, and extort   160
A poor soul's patience, all to make you sport.
   LYS. You are unkind, Demetrius. Be not so;
For you love Hermia — this you know I know.
And here, with all goodwill, with all my heart,
In Hermia's love I yield you up my part.   165
And yours of Helena to me bequeath,
Whom I do love, and will do till my death.
   HEL. Never did mockers waste more idle breath.
   DEM. Lysander, keep thy Hermia. I will none.
If e'er I loved her, all that love is gone.   170
My heart to her but as guest-wise sojourned,°
And now to Helen is it home returned,
There to remain.
   LYS.   Helen, it is not so.
   DEM. Disparage not the faith thou dost not know,

Lest, to thy peril, thou aby° it dear.   175
Look where thy love comes — yonder is thy dear.
          [*Re-enter* HERMIA.]
   HER. Dark night, that from the eye his function
    takes,
The ear more quick of apprehension makes.
Wherein it doth impair the seeing sense,
It pays the hearing double recompense.   180
Thou art not by mine eye, Lysander, found;
Mine ear, I thank it, brought me to thy sound.
But why unkindly didst thou leave me so?
   LYS. Why should he stay whom love doth press to
    go?
   HER. What love could press Lysander from my
    side?   185
   LYS. Lysander's love, that would not let him bide
Fair Helena, who more engilds the night
Than all yon fiery oes° and eyes of light.
Why seek'st thou me? Could not this make thee
    know,
The hate I bare thee made me leave thee so?   190
   HER. You speak not as you think. It cannot be.
   HEL. Lo, she is one of this confederacy!
Now I perceive they have conjoined all three
To fashion this false sport, in spite of me.°
Injurious Hermia! Most ungrateful maid!   195
Have you conspired, have you with these contrived°
To bait° me with this foul derision?
Is all the counsel that we two have shared,
The sister's vows, the hours that we have spent,
When we have chid the hasty-footed time   200
For parting us — Oh, is it all forgot?
All school days' friendship, childhood innocence?
We, Hermia, like two artificial° gods,
Have with our needles created both one flower,
Both on one sampler,° sitting on one cushion,   205
Both warbling of one song, both in one key —
As if our hands, our sides, voices, and minds
Had been incorporate.° So we grew together,
Like to a double cherry, seeming parted
But yet a union in partition —   210
Two lovely berries molded on one stem.
So, with two seeming bodies, but one heart,
Two of the first, like coats in heraldry,
Due but to one, and crownèd with one crest.°
And will you rent our ancient love asunder,   215
To join with men in scorning your poor friend?
It is not friendly, 'tis not maidenly.
Our sex, as well as I, may chide you for it,
Though I alone do feel the injury.

---

141. Taurus: a range of mountains in Asia Minor. 144. seal: guarantee. 157. trim: fine. 171. guest-wise sojourned: made a short stay.

175. aby: abide, pay for. 188. oes: circles; i.e., stars, with a pun on "o" and "i." 194. in . . . me: to spite me. 196. contrived: devised, plotted. 197. bait: taunt. 203. artificial: creative. 205. sampler: piece of embroidery. 208. incorporate: in one body. 213–14. Two . . . crest: i.e., two bodies with a single heart — an elaborate metaphor from heraldry. After marriage the coats of arms of husband and wife are united in one coat under one crest. See App. 9.

HER. I am amazèd at your passionate words.   220
I scorn you not. It seems that you scorn me.
    HEL. Have you not set Lysander, as in scorn,
To follow me and praise my eyes and face?
And made your other love, Demetrius,
Who even but now did spurn me with his foot,   225
To call me goddess, nymph, divine and rare,
Precious, celestial? Wherefore speaks he this
To her he hates? And wherefore doth Lysander
Deny your love, so rich within his soul,
And tender me, forsooth, affection,   230
But by your setting on, by your consent?
What though I be not so in grace as you,
So hung upon with love, so fortunate,
But miserable most, to love unloved?
This you should pity rather than despise.   235
    HER. I understand not what you mean by this.
    HEL. Aye, do, persever,° counterfeit sad looks,
Make mouths upon me when I turn my back,
Wink each at other, hold the sweet jest up.
This sport, well carried, shall be chronicled.°   240
If you have any pity, grace, or manners,
You would not make me such an argument.°
But fare ye well. 'Tis partly my own fault,
Which death or absence soon shall remedy.
    LYS. Stay, gentle Helena, hear my excuse.   245
My love, my life, my soul, fair Helena!
    HEL. Oh, excellent!
    HER.   Sweet, do not scorn her so.
    DEM. If she cannot entreat, I can compel.
    LYS. Thou canst compel no more than she entreat.
Thy threats have no more strength than her weak
    prayers.   250
Helen, I love thee, by my life, I do.
I swear by that which I will lose for thee,
To prove him false that says I love thee not.
    DEM. I say I love thee more than he can do.   254
    LYS. If thou say so, withdraw, and prove it too.
    DEM. Quick, come!
    HER.   Lysander, whereto tends all this?
    LYS. Away, you Ethiope!°
    DEM.   No, no, he'll ——
Seem to break loose,° take on as you would fol-
    low,
But yet come not. You are a tame man, go!
    LYS. Hang off, thou cat, thou bur! Vile thing, let
    loose,   260
Or I will shake thee from me like a serpent!

HER. Why are you grown so rude? What change is
    this?
Sweet love ——
    LYS.   Thy love! Out, tawny° Tartar, out!
Out, loathèd medicine! Hated potion, hence!   264
    HER. Do you not jest?
    HEL.   Yes, sooth, and so do you.
    LYS. Demetrius, I will keep my word with thee.
    DEM. I would I had your bond,° for I perceive
A weak bond° holds you. I'll not trust your word.
    LYS. What, should I hurt her, strike her, kill her
    dead?
Although I hate her, I'll not harm her so.   270
    HER. What, can you do me greater harm than
    hate?
Hate me! Wherefore? Oh, me! What news, my love!
Am not I Hermia? Are not you Lysander?
I am as fair now as I was erewhile.°
Since night you loved me, yet since night you left
    me.   275
Why, then you left me — Oh, the gods forbid! —
In earnest, shall I say?
    LYS.   Aye, by my life,
And never did desire to see thee more.
Therefore be out of hope, of question, of doubt;
Be certain, nothing truer. 'Tis no jest   280
That I do hate thee, and love Helena.
    HER. Oh, me! You juggler! You canker blossom!°
You thief of love! What, have you come by night
And stolen my love's heart from him?
    HEL.   Fine, i'faith!
Have you no modesty, no maiden shame,   285
No touch of bashfulness? What, will you tear
Impatient answers from my gentle tongue?
Fie, fie! You counterfeit, you puppet,° you!
    HER. Puppet? Why so? Aye, that way goes the
    game.
Now I perceive that she hath made compare   290
Between our statures, she hath urged her height.
And with her personage, her tall personage,
Her height, forsooth, she hath prevailed with him.
And are you grown so high in his esteem
Because I am so dwarfish and so low?   295
How low am I, thou painted maypole?° Speak —
How low am I? I am not yet so low
But that my nails can reach unto thine eyes.
    HEL. I pray you, though you mock me, gentlemen,
Let her not hurt me. I was never curst,°   300
I have no gift at all in shrewishness.
I am a right maid° for my cowardice.
Let her not strike me. You perhaps may think,
Because she is something lower than myself,

---

237. persever: keep it up.   240. chronicled: recorded in the history book.   242. argument: subject for a story.   257. Ethiope: Ethiopian. From the number of references to the dark complexion of different women in Shakespeare's plays it is evident that one of the boy actors was dark-skinned. See Gen. Intro. p. 58b.   257–58. No . . . loose: There is a difficulty of reading here. Q1 reads "No, no: heele, Seeme to breake loose." The Folio reads: "No, no, Sir, seem to breake loose." This makes sense. Hermia is clutching Lysander; Demetrius taunts him saying that he pretends to want a fight, but is in reality willing enough to be held back by a woman.

263. tawny: dark-skinned.   267. bond: written agreement.
268. weak bond: i.e., Hermia.   274. erewhile: a short while ago.
282. canker blossom: worm in the bud.   288. puppet: doll.
296. maypole: because compared to Hermia she is tall and thin.
300. curst: bad-tempered.   302. right maid: truly feminine.

That I can match her.

HER.   Lower! Hark again.   305

HEL. Good Hermia, do not be so bitter with me.
I evermore did love you, Hermia,
Did ever keep your counsels, never wronged you,
Save that, in love unto Demetrius,
I told him of your stealth unto this wood.   310
He followed you, for love I followed him;
But he hath chid° me hence, and threatened me
To strike me, spurn me, nay, to kill me too.
And now, so you will let me quiet go,
To Athens will I bear my folly back,   315
And follow you no further. Let me go.
You see how simple and how fond I am.

HER. Why, get you gone. Who is't that hinders
    you?

HEL. A foolish heart, that I leave here behind.

HER. What, with Lysander?

HEL.   With Demetrius.

LYS. Be not afraid. She shall not harm thee, Hel-
    ena.   321

DEM. No, sir, she shall not, though you take her
    part.

HEL. Oh, when she's angry, she is keen and
    shrewd!°
She was a vixen when she went to school,
And though she be but little, she is fierce.   325

HER. Little again! Nothing but low and little!
Why will you suffer her to flout me thus?
Let me come to her.

LYS.   Get you gone, you dwarf,
You minimus,° of hindering knotgrass° made,
You bead, you acorn.

DEM.   You are too officious   330
In her behalf that scorns your services.
Let her alone. Speak not of Helena,
Take not her part; for if thou dost intend
Never so little show of love to her,
Thou shalt aby it.

LYS.   Now she holds me not.   335
Now follow, if thou darest, to try whose right,
Of thine or mine, is most in Helena.

DEM. Follow! Nay, I'll go with thee, cheek by
    jole.°   [*Exeunt* LYSANDER *and* DEMETRIUS.]

HER. You, mistress, all this coil° is 'long of you.
Nay, go not back.

HEL.   I will not trust you, I,   340
Nor longer stay in your curst company.
Your hands than mine are quicker for a fray,
My legs are longer though, to run away.   [*Exit.*]

HER. I am amazed, and know not what to say.
                              [*Exit.*]

OBE. This is thy negligence. Still thou mistakest,

Or else committ'st thy knaveries willfully.   346

PUCK. Believe me, King of Shadows, I mistook.
Did not you tell me I should know the man
By the Athenian garments he had on?
And so far blameless proves my enterprise   350
That I have 'nointed an Athenian's eyes.
And so far am I glad it so did sort,
As this their jangling° I esteem a sport.

OBE. Thou see'st these lovers seek a place to fight.
Hie° therefore, Robin, overcast the night.   355
The starry welkin° cover thou anon°
With drooping fog, as black as Acheron,°
And lead these testy rivals so astray
As one come not within another's way.
Like to Lysander sometime frame thy tongue,   360
Then stir Demetrius up with bitter wrong.
And sometime rail thou like Demetrius,
And from each other look thou lead them thus
Till o'er their brows death-counterfeiting sleep
With leaden° legs and batty wings doth creep.   365
Then crush this herb into Lysander's eye,
Whose liquor hath this virtuous property,
To take from thence all error with his might,
And make his eyeballs roll with wonted sight.
When they next wake, all this derision°   370
Shall seem a dream and fruitless vision,
And back to Athens shall the lovers wend,
With league whose date till death shall never end.°
Whiles I in this affair do thee employ,
I'll to my Queen and beg her Indian boy.   375
And then I will her charmèd eye release
From monster's view, and all things shall be peace.

PUCK. My fairy lord, this must be done with haste,
For night's swift dragons° cut the clouds full fast,
And yonder shines Aurora's° harbinger,°   380
At whose approach, ghosts, wandering here and
    there,
Troop home to churchyards. Damnèd spirits all,
That in crossways° and floods have burial,
Already to their wormy beds are gone.
For fear lest day should look their shames upon,
They willfully themselves exíle from light,   386
And must for aye° consort with black-browed
    night.

OBE. But we are spirits of another sort.°
I with the morning's love have oft made sport,
And, like a forester, the groves may tread   390
Even till the eastern gate, all fiery-red,
Opening on Neptune with fair blessèd beams,
Turns into yellow gold his salt green streams.

---

353. jangling: wrangling.   355. Hie: hasten.   356. welkin:
sky. anon: at once.   357. Acheron: river of the underworld.
365. leaden: heavy.   370. derision: mockery.   373. With . . .
end: united everlastingly.   379. night's . . . dragons: the drag-
ons which draw the chariot of Night.   380. Aurora: the dawn.
harbinger: forerunner. See *Macb*, I.iv.44, and *Haml*, I.i.149–56.
383. crossways: suicides were buried at crossroads.   387. aye:
ever.   388. another sort: i.e., not damned or infernal, and so
able to endure daylight.

---

312. chid: scolded.   323. shrewd: a shrew.   329. minimus:
littlest thing. hindering knotgrass: believed to stunt growth; it
is a clinging weed.   338. cheek by jole: lit., cheek by jaw.
339. coil: tumult.

But, notwithstanding, haste. Make no delay.   394
We may effect this business yet ere day.   [*Exit.*]
  PUCK. Up and down, up and down,
I will lead them up and down.
I am feared in field and town.
Goblin, lead them up and down.
Here comes one.   400
       [*Re-enter* LYSANDER.]
  LYS. Where art thou, proud Demetrius? Speak
    thou now.
  PUCK. Here, villain, drawn° and ready. Where art
    thou?
  LYS. I will be with thee straight.
  PUCK.   Follow me, then,
To plainer° ground.
    [*Exit* LYSANDER, *as following the voice.*]
      [*Re-enter* DEMETRIUS.]
  DEM.   Lysander! Speak again.
Thou runaway, thou coward, art thou fled?   405
Speak! In some bush? Where dost thou hide thy
    head?
  PUCK. Thou coward, art thou bragging to the
    stars,
Telling the bushes that thou look'st for wars,
And wilt not come? Come, recreant.° Come, thou
    child,
I'll whip thee with a rod. He is defiled   410
That draws a sword on thee.
  DEM.   Yea, art thou there?
  PUCK. Follow my voice. We'll try no manhood
    here.°   [*Exeunt.*]
      [*Re-enter* LYSANDER.]
  LYS. He goes before me and still dares me on.
When I come where he calls, then he is gone.
The villain is much lighter-heeled than I,   415
I followed fast, but faster he did fly,
That fallen am I in dark uneven way,
And here will rest me. [*Lies down.*] Come, thou
    gentle day!
For if but once thou show me thy gray light,   419
I'll find Demetrius, and revenge this spite. [*Sleeps.*]
    [*Re-enter* PUCK *and* DEMETRIUS.]
  PUCK. Ho, ho, ho! Coward, why comest thou
    not?
  DEM. Abide° me, if thou darest, for well I wot°
Thou runn'st before me, shifting every place,
And darest not stand, nor look me in the face.
Where art thou now?
  PUCK.   Come hither. I am here.   425
  DEM. Nay, then, thou mock'st me. Thou shalt buy
    this dear
If ever I thy face by daylight see.
Now, go thy way. Faintness constraineth me
To measure out my length on this cold bed.

By day's approach look to be visited.   430
      [*Lies down and sleeps.*]
      [*Re-enter* HELENA.]
  HEL. O weary night, O long and tedious night,
Abate° thy hours! Shine comforts from the east,
That I may back to Athens by daylight,
From these that my poor company detest.
And sleep, that sometimes shuts up sorrow's eye,
Steal me awhile from mine own company.   436
      [*Lies down and sleeps.*]
  PUCK. Yet but three? Come one more,
Two of both kinds makes up four.
Here she comes, curst and sad.
Cupid is a knavish lad,   440
Thus to make poor females mad.
      [*Re-enter* HERMIA.]
  HER. Never so weary, never so in woe,
Bedabbled with the dew, and torn with briers,
I can no further crawl, no further go,
My legs can keep no pace with my desires.   445
Here will I rest me till the break of day.
Heavens shield Lysander, if they mean a fray!
      [*Lies down and sleeps.*]
  PUCK. On the ground
Sleep sound.
I'll apply   450
To your eye,
Gentle lover, remedy.
    [*Squeezing the juice on* LYSANDER'S *eye.*]
When thou wakest,
Thou takest
True delight   455
In the sight
Of thy former lady's eye.
And the country proverb known,
That every man should take his own,
In your waking shall be shown.   460
Jack shall have Jill,
Nought shall go ill,
The man shall have his mare again, and all shall be
    well.   [*Exit.*]

Act IV

SCENE I. *The same.* LYSANDER, DEMETRIUS,
HELENA, *and* HERMIA, *lying asleep.*

[*Enter* TITANIA *and* BOTTOM; PEASEBLOSSOM, COBWEB,
MOTH, MUSTARDSEED, *and other* FAIRIES *attending;*
OBERON *behind unseen.*]

  TITA. Come, sit thee down upon this flowery bed,
While I thy amiable cheeks do coy,°

---

402. **drawn**: with a sword drawn.   404. **plainer**: flatter.
409. **recreant**: traitor.   412. **We'll . . . here**: we will not make
trial of your courage here.   422. **Abide**: wait for. **wot**: know.

432. **Abate**: shorten.
Act IV, Sc. i: 2. **coy**: caress.

And stick musk roses in thy sleek smooth head,
  And kiss thy fair large ears, my gentle joy.
BOT. Where's Peaseblossom?   5
PEAS. Ready.
BOT. Scratch my head, Peaseblossom. Where's
Mounsieur Cobweb?
COB. Ready.
BOT. Mounsieur Cobweb, good mounsieur, get
you your weapons in your hand, and kill me a   11
red-hipped humblebee on the top of a thistle, and,
good mounsieur, bring me the honey bag. Do not
fret yourself too much in the action, mounsieur, and,
good mounsieur, have a care the honey bag break
not. I would be loath to have you overflown with   16
a honey bag, signior. Where's Mounsieur Mustard-
seed?
MUS. Ready.   19
BOT. Give me your neaf,° Mounsieur Mustard-
seed. Pray you, leave your courtesy,° good moun-
sieur.
MUS. What's your will?
BOT. Nothing, good mounsieur, but to help Caval-
ery° Cobweb to scratch. I must to the barber's,
mounsieur, for methinks I am marvelous hairy   25
about the face, and I am such a tender ass, if my hair
do but tickle me, I must scratch.
TITA. What, wilt thou hear some music, my sweet
  love?
BOT. I have a reasonable good ear in music.   30
Let's have the tongs and the bones.
TITA. Or say, sweet love, what thou desirest to eat.
BOT. Truly, a peck of provender. I could munch
your good dry oats. Methinks I have a great desire to
a bottle° of hay. Good hay, sweet hay, hath no   35
fellow.°
TITA. I have a venturous fairy that shall seek
The squirrel's hoard, and fetch thee new nuts.
BOT. I had rather have a handful or two of dried
peas. But I pray you let none of your people stir   40
me. I have an exposition° of sleep come upon me.
TITA. Sleep thou, and I will wind thee in my arms.
Fairies, be gone, and be all ways away.
                                    [Exeunt FAIRIES.]
So doth the woodbine the sweet honeysuckle   45
Gently entwist, the female ivy so
Enrings the barky fingers of the elm.
Oh, how I love thee! How I dote on thee!
                                    [They sleep.]
                [Enter PUCK.]
OBE. [Advancing] Welcome, good Robin. See'st
  thou this sweet sight?
Her dotage now I do begin to pity.   50
For, meeting her of late behind the wood,
Seeking sweet favors for this hateful fool,

I did upbraid her, and fall out with her;
For she his hairy temples then had rounded
With coronet of fresh and fragrant flowers,   55
And that same dew, which sometime on the buds
Was wont to swell, like round and orient pearls,
Stood now within the pretty flowerets' eyes
Like tears that did their own disgrace bewail.
When I had at my pleasure taunted her,   60
And she in mild terms begged my patience,
I then did ask of her her changeling child,
Which straight she gave me, and her fairy sent
To bear him to my bower in fairyland.
And now I have the boy, I will undo   65
This hateful imperfection of her eyes.
And, gentle Puck, take this transformèd scalp
From off the head of this Athenian swain,
That, he awaking when the other do,
May all to Athens back again repair,°   70
And think no more of this night's accidents
But as the fierce vexation of a dream.
But first I will release the Fairy Queen.
  Be as thou wast wont to be,
  See as thou wast wont to see.   75
  Dian's° bud o'er Cupid's flower
  Hath such force and blessèd power.
Now, my Titania, wake you, my sweet Queen.
TITA. My Oberon! What visions have I seen!
Methought I was enamored of an ass.   80
OBE. There lies your love.
TITA.   How came these things to pass?
Oh, how mine eyes do loathe his visage now!
OBE. Silence awhile. Robin, take off this head.
Titania, music call, and strike more dead
Than common sleep of all these five the sense.°   85
TITA. Music, ho! Music, such as charmeth sleep!
                                    [Music, still.]
PUCK. Now, when thou wakest, with thine own
  fool's eyes peep.
OBE. Sound, music! Come, my Queen, take hands
  with me,
And rock the ground whereon these sleepers be.   90
Now thou and I are new in amity,
And will tomorrow midnight solemnly
Dance in Duke Theseus' house triumphantly,
And bless it to all fair prosperity.
There shall the pairs of faithful lovers be   95
Wedded, with Theseus, all in jollity.
PUCK. Fairy King, attend, and mark.
I do hear the morning lark.
OBE. Then, my Queen, in silence sad,°
Trip we after night's shade.   100
We the globe can compass soon,
Swifter than the wandering moon.
TITA. Come, my lord, and in our flight,

---

20. neaf: fist.   21. leave . . . courtesy: i.e., there's no need to
bow.   23-24. Cavalery: cavaleiro, a gallant soldier.   35. bottle:
bundle.   36. fellow: equal.   41. exposition: for "disposition."

70. repair: return.   76. Dian: Diana. See I.i.73.   84-85. strike
. . . sense: make them more dead asleep than normal. these
five: i.e., Bottom, Demetrius, Lysander, Hermia, and Helena.
99. sad: serious.

Tell me how it came this night
That I sleeping here was found   105
With these mortals on the ground.   [*Exeunt.*]
    [*Horns winded° within. Enter* THESEUS,
      HIPPOLYTA, EGEUS, *and train.*]
  THE. Go, one of you, find out the forester,
For now our observation° is performed.
And since we have the vaward° of the day,
My love shall hear the music of my hounds.°   110
Uncouple in the western valley, let them go.
Dispatch, I say, and find the forester.
             [*Exit an* ATTENDANT.]
We will, fair Queen, up to the mountain's top,
And mark the musical confusion
Of hounds and echo in conjunction.   115
  HIP. I was with Hercules and Cadmus once
When in a wood of Crete they bayed° the bear
With hounds of Sparta. Never did I hear
Such gallant chiding;° for, besides the groves,
The skies, the fountains, every region near   120
Seemed all one mutual cry. I never heard
So musical a discord, such sweet thunder.
  THE. My hounds are bred out of the Spartan
    kind,
So flewed,° so sanded;° and their heads are hung
With ears that sweep away the morning dew;   125
Crook-kneed, and dewlapped° like Thessalian
    bulls;
Slow in pursuit, but matched in mouth like bells,°
Each under each.° A cry° more tunable
Was never holloed to, nor cheered with horn,
In Crete, in Sparta, nor in Thessaly.   130
Judge when you hear. But, soft! What nymphs are
    these?
  EGE. My lord, this is my daughter here asleep.
And this, Lysander. This Demetrius is,
This Helena, old Nedar's Helena.
I wonder of their being here together.   135
  THE. No doubt they rose up early to observe
The rite of May, and, hearing our intent,
Came here in grace of° our solemnity.°
But speak, Egëus, is not this the day   139
That Hermia should give answer of her choice?
  EGE. It is, my lord.
  THE. Go, bid the huntsmen wake them with their
    horns.
  [*Horns and shout within.°* LYSANDER, DEMETRIUS,
  HELENA, *and* HERMIA, *wake and start up.*]

Good morrow, friends. Saint Valentine° is past.
Begin these wood birds but to couple now?
  LYS. Pardon, my lord.
  THE.   I pray you all, stand up.
I know you two are rival enemies.   146
How comes this gentle concord in the world,
That hatred is so far from jealousy,
To sleep by hate, and fear no enmity?
  LYS. My lord, I shall reply amazedly,   150
Half sleep, half waking. But as yet, I swear,
I cannot truly say how I came here,
But, as I think — for truly would I speak,
And now I do bethink me, so it is —
I came with Hermia hither. Our intent   155
Was to be gone from Athens, where we might,
Without the peril° of the Athenian law —
  EGE. Enough, enough, my lord, you have enough.
I beg the law, the law, upon his head.
They would have stolen away. They would, Deme-
    trius,   160
Thereby to have defeated you and me,
You of your wife and me of my consent —
Of my consent that she should be your wife.
  DEM. My lord, fair Helen told me of their stealth,
Of this their purpose hither to this wood.   165
And I in fury hither followed them,
Fair Helena in fancy° following me.
But, my good lord, I wot not by what power —
But by some power it is — my love to Hermia,
Melted as the snow, seems to me now   170
As the remembrance of an idle gaud°
Which in my childhood I did dote upon.
And all the faith, the virtue of my heart,
The object and the pleasure of mine eye,
Is only Helena. To her, my lord,   175
Was I betrothed ere I saw Hermia.
But, like in sickness, did I loathe this food,
But, as in health, come to my natural taste,
Now I do wish it, love it, long for it,
And will forevermore be true to it.   180
  THE. Fair lovers, you are fortunately met.
Of this discourse we more will hear anon.
Egëus, I will overbear your will,
For in the temple, by and by, with us
These couples shall eternally be knit.   185
And, for° the morning now is something worn,
Our purposed hunting shall be set aside.
Away with us to Athens! Three and three,°
We'll hold a feast in great solemnity.
Come, Hippolyta.   190
    [*Exeunt* THESEUS, HIPPOLYTA, EGEUS, *and train.*]
  DEM. These things seem small and undistinguish-
    able,

---

106 s.d., winded: sounded. 108. observation: i.e., the rites of
May. See I.i.167. 109. vaward: forepart. 110. my hounds: See
MND Intro. p. 270b. 117. bayed: brought to bay. 119. chiding:
barking. 124. flewed: with hanging cheeks. sanded: sandy
colored. 126. dewlapped: the dewlap is a flap of loose skin hang-
ing down from the throats of cattle and certain kinds of dog and
hound. 127. matched . . . bells: In a perfect pack of hounds
each hound uttered a different note, the whole effect being a
harmony. 128. Each . . . each: one a note lower than the other.
cry: pack of hounds. 138. in . . . of: in compliment to. solem-
nity: celebration. 142 s.d., within: off stage

143. Saint Valentine: the day on which birds were supposed to
mate. 157. Without . . . peril: beyond danger. 167. fancy: love.
171. gaud: trifle. 186. for: since. 188. Three . . . three: i.e., a
triple wedding.

Like far-off mountains turnèd into clouds.

HER. Methinks I see these things with parted eye,
When everything seems double.

HEL.   So methinks.
And I have found Demetrius like a jewel,   195
Mine own, and not mine own.

DEM.   Are you sure
That we are awake? It seems to me
That yet we sleep, we dream. Do not you think
The Duke was here, and bid us follow him?

HER. Yea, and my father.

HEL.   And Hippolyta.   200

LYS. And he did bid us follow to the temple.

DEM. Why, then, we are awake. Let's follow him,
And by the way let us recount our dreams.

                                   [*Exeunt.*]

BOT. [*Awaking*] When my cue comes, call me,
and I will answer. My next is "Most fair Pyra-   205
mus." Heigh-ho! Peter Quince! Flute, the bellows-
mender! Snout, the tinker! Starveling! God's my life,
stolen hence, and left me asleep! I have had a most
rare vision. I have had a dream past the wit of man to
say what dream it was. Man is but an ass if he   211
go about to expound this dream. Methought I was —
there is no man can tell what. Methought I was —
and methought I had — but man is but a patched°
fool if he will offer to say what methought I   215
had. The eye of man hath not heard, the ear of man
hath not seen, man's hand is not able to taste, his
tongue to conceive, nor his heart to report, what my
dream was. I will get Peter Quince to write a ballad°
of this dream. It shall be called Bottom's Dream,   220
because it hath no bottom, and I will sing it in the
latter end of a play, before the Duke. Peradventure,°
to make it the more gracious, I shall sing it at her
death.°   [*Exit.*]

SCENE II. *Athens.* QUINCE'S *house.*

[*Enter* QUINCE, FLUTE, SNOUT, *and* STARVELING.]

QUIN. Have you sent to Bottom's house? Is he
come home yet?

STAR. He cannot be heard of. Out of doubt he is
transported.°

FLU. If he come not, then the play is marred. It
goes not forward, doth it?   6

QUIN. It is not possible. You have not a man in all
Athens able to discharge Pyramus but he.

FLU. No, he hath simply the best wit of any handi-
craft man in Athens.   10

QUIN. Yea, and the best person too, and he is a very
paramour for a sweet voice.

FLU. You must say "paragon." A paramour is,
God bless us, a thing of naught.°

                              [*Enter* SNUG.]

SNUG. Masters, the Duke is coming from the   15
temple, and there is two or three lords and ladies
more married. If our sport had gone forward, we
had all been made men.

FLU. Oh, sweet bully Bottom! Thus hath he lost
sixpence a day during his life;° he could not   20
have scaped sixpence a day. An the Duke had not
given him sixpence a day for playing Pyramus, I'll
be hanged. He would have deserved it. Sixpence a
day in Pyramus, or nothing.

                              [*Enter* BOTTOM.]

BOT. Where are these lads? Where are these
hearts?   26

QUIN. Bottom! Oh, most courageous day! Oh,
most happy hour!

BOT. Masters, I am to discourse wonders. But ask
me not what, for if I tell you I am no true Athe-   30
nian. I will tell you everything, right as it fell out.

QUIN. Let us hear, sweet Bottom.

BOT. Not a word of me. All that I will tell you is
that the Duke hath dined. Get your apparel to-   35
gether, good strings° to your beards, new ribbons to
your pumps.° Meet presently° at the palace. Every
man look o'er his part, for the short and the long is,
our play is preferred.° In any case, let Thisby have
clean linen, and let not him that plays the lion   40
pare his nails, for they shall hang out for the lion's
claws. And, most dear actors, eat no onions nor gar-
lic, for we are to utter sweet breath, and I do not
doubt but to hear them say it is a sweet comedy.   45
No more words. Away! Go, away!   [*Exeunt.*]

Act V

SCENE I. *Athens. The palace of* THESEUS.

[*Enter* THESEUS, HIPPOLYTA, PHILOSTRATE, LORDS,
                  and ATTENDANTS.]

HIP. 'Tis strange, my Theseus, that these lovers
   speak of.

THE. More strange than true. I never may believe
These antique fables, nor these fairy toys.°
Lovers and madmen have such seething brains,
Such shaping fantasies,° that apprehend   5
More than cool reason ever comprehends.
The lunatic, the lover, and the poet

214. patched: wearing a particolored coat, the regular costume
of a professional fool. 219. ballad: See App. 8. 222. Peradven-
ture: perchance. 224-25. at . . . death: i.e., Thisby's at the
end of the play.
Sc. ii: 4. transported: carried off.

14. naught: wickedness. 20. sixpence . . . life: i.e., a royal
pension of sixpence a day for life. 36. strings: i.e., for tying
them on. 37. pumps: shoes. presently: immediately. 39. pre-
ferred: accepted.
Act V, Sc. i: 3. fairy toys: trifling tales about fairies. 5. fanta-
sies: fancies.

Are of imagination all compact.°
One sees more devils than vast Hell can hold,
That is the madman. The lover, all as frantic,   10
Sees Helen's beauty in a brow of Egypt.°
The poet's eye, in a fine frenzy rolling,
Doth glance from heaven to earth, from earth to
     heaven,
And as imagination bodies forth
The forms of things unknown, the poet's pen   15
Turns them to shapes, and gives to airy nothing
A local habitation and a name.
Such tricks hath strong imagination
That if it would but apprehend some joy,
It comprehends some bringer of that joy;   20
Or in the night, imagining some fear,
How easy is a bush supposed a bear!

HIP. But all the story of the night told over,
And all their minds transfigured° so together,
More witnesseth than fancy's images,   25
And grows to something of great constancy,°
But, howsoever, strange and admirable.°

THE. Here come the lovers, full of joy and mirth.

[*Enter* LYSANDER, DEMETRIUS, HERMIA, *and* HELENA.]

Joy, gentle friends! Joy and fresh days of love
Accompany your hearts!

LYS.   More than to us   30
Wait in your royal walks, your board, your bed!

THE. Come now, what masques,° what dances
     shall we have
To wear away this long age of three hours
Between our after-supper and bedtime?
Where is our usual manager of mirth?   35
What revels are in hand? Is there no play
To ease the anguish of a torturing hour?
Call Philostrate.

PHILOST.   Here, mighty Theseus.

THE. Say, what abridgment° have you for this eve-
     ning?
What masque? What music? How shall we beguile
The lazy time, if not with some delight?   41

PHILOST. There is a brief° how many sports are
     ripe.°
Make choice of which your Highness will see first.

               [*Giving a paper.*]

THE. [*Reads.*]
   " The battle with the Centaurs,° to be sung
     By an Athenian eunuch to the harp."   45
We'll none of that. That have I told my love,
In glory of my kinsman Hercules.

" The riot of the tipsy Bacchanals,
   Tearing the Thracian singer in their rage."°
That is an old device, and it was played   50
When I from Thebes came last a conqueror.
" The thrice three Muses mourning for the death
   Of Learning,° late deceased in beggary."
That is some satire, keen and critical,
Not sorting with a nuptial ceremony.   55
" A tedious brief scene of young Pyramus
   And his love Thisbe, very tragical mirth."
Merry and tragical! Tedious and brief!
That is, hot ice and wondrous strange snow.
How shall we find the concord of this discord?   60

PHILOST. A play there is, my lord, some ten words
     long,
Which is as brief as I have known a play.
But by ten words, my lord, it is too long,
Which makes it tedious; for in all the play
There is not one word apt, one player fitted.   65
And tragical, my noble lord, it is,
For Pyramus therein doth kill himself.
Which, when I saw rehearsed, I must confess
Made mine eyes water, but more merry tears
The passion of loud laughter never shed.   70

THE. What are they that do play it?

PHILOST. Hardhanded men that work in Athens
     here,
Which never labored in their minds till now,
And now have toiled their unbreathed° memories
With this same play, against° your nuptial.   75

THE. And we will hear it.

PHILOST.   No, my noble lord,
It is not for you. I have heard it over,
And it is nothing, nothing in the world —
Unless you can find sport in their intents,°   79
Extremely stretched° and conned with cruel pain,°
To do you service.

THE.   I will hear that play,
For never anything can be amiss,
When simpleness and duty tender it.
Go, bring them in, and take your places, ladies.

               [*Exit* PHILOSTRATE.]

HIP. I love not to see wretchedness o'ercharged,°
And duty in his service perishing.°   86

THE. Why, gentle sweet, you shall see no such
     thing.

HIP. He says they can do nothing in this kind.°

THE. The kinder we, to give them thanks for
     nothing.
Our sport shall be to take what they mistake.   90

---

8. Are . . . compact: wholly composed of imagination — which in Shakespeare's time meant the "power of seeing things." 11. Sees . . . Egypt: i.e., to the lover a gypsy is as beautiful as Helen of Troy. Gypsies were supposed to be Egyptians. 24. transfigured: excited. 26. constancy: consistency; i.e., the fact that they are all excited shows that something strange has happened to them. 27. admirable: marvelous. 32. masques: courtly entertainments. 39. abridgment: pastime, entertainment. 42. brief: list. ripe: ready. 44. Centaurs: creatures half man, half horse.

48–49. riot . . . rage: the story of how Orpheus the singer was torn in pieces by the frenzied women worshippers of Bacchus. 52–53. death . . . Learning: See *MND* Intro. p. 269b. 74. unbreathed: unpracticed. 75. against: in anticipation of. 79. intents: intentions. 80. Extremely stretched: overreaching themselves. pain: labor. 85. wretchedness o'ercharged: poor men trying to do too much. 86. duty . . . perishing: a subject ruining himself through excess of zeal. 88. kind: i.e., acting.

And what poor duty cannot do, noble respect
Takes it in might, not merit.°
Where I have come, great clerks° have purposed
To greet me with premeditated welcomes,
Where I have seen them shiver and look pale,   95
Make periods in the midst of sentences,
Throttle their practiced accent in their fears,
And, in conclusion, dumbly have broke off,
Not paying me a welcome. Trust me, sweet,
Out of this silence yet I picked a welcome,   100
And in the modesty of fearful° duty
I read as much as from the rattling tongue
Of saucy and audacious eloquence.
Love, therefore, and tongue-tied simplicity
In least speak most, to my capacity.°   105

[*Re-enter* PHILOSTRATE.]

PHILOST. So please your Grace, the Prologue is ad-
dressed.°

THE. Let him approach.

[*Flourish of trumpets. Enter* QUINCE *for the*
PROLOGUE.]

PROL. If° we offend, it is with our goodwill.
That you should think, we come not to offend,
But with goodwill. To show our simple skill,   110
That is the true beginning of our end.
Consider, then, we come but in despite.°
We do not come, as minding to content you,
Our true intent is. All for your delight,
We are not here. That you should here repent you,
The actors are at hand, and, by their show,   116
You shall know all, that you are like to know.

THE. This fellow doth not stand upon points.°

LYS. He hath rid his prologue like a rough colt, he
knows not the stop. A good moral, my lord. It is not
enough to speak, but to speak true.   121

HIP. Indeed he hath played on his prologue like a
child on a recorder° — a sound, but not in govern-
ment.°

THE. His speech was like a tangled chain — 125
nothing impaired, but all disordered. Who is next?

[*Enter* PYRAMUS *and* THISBE, WALL, MOONSHINE, *and*
LION.]

PROL. Gentles, perchance you wonder at this show,
But wonder on, till truth make all things plain.
This man is Pyramus, if you would know.   130
This beauteous lady Thisby is certáin.
This man, with lime and roughcast, doth present
Wall, that vile Wall which did these lovers sunder,
And through Wall's chink, poor souls, they are con-
tent   134

To whisper. At the which let no man wonder.
This man, with lanthorn,° dog, and bush of thorn,
Presenteth Moonshine; for, if you will know,
By moonshine did these lovers think no scorn
To meet at Ninus' tomb, there, there to woo.
This grisly beast, which Lion hight° by name,   140
The trusty Thisby, coming first by night,
Did scare away, or rather did affright.
And, as she fled, her mantle she did fall,°
Which Lion vile with bloody mouth did stain.
Anon comes Pyramus, sweet youth and tall,   145
And finds his trusty Thisby's mantle slain.
Whereat, with blade, with bloody blameful blade,
He bravely broached his boiling bloody breast.
And Thisby, tarrying in mulberry shade,
His dagger drew, and died. For all the rest,   150
Let Lion, Moonshine, Wall, and lovers twain
At large discourse, while here they do remain.

[*Exeunt* PROLOGUE, PYRAMUS, THISBE, LION,
and MOONSHINE.]

THE. I wonder if the lion be to speak.

DEM. No wonder, my lord. One lion may when
many asses do.   155

WALL. In this same interlude it doth befall
That I, one Snout by name, present a wall,
And such a wall, as I would have you think,
That had in it a crannied° hole or chink,
Through which the lovers, Pyramus and Thisby,
Did whisper often very secretly.   161
This loam, this roughcast, and this stone doth show
That I am that same wall. The truth is so.
And this the cranny is, right and siníster,°   164
Through which the fearful lovers are to whisper.

THE. Would you desire lime and hair to speak
better?

DEM. It is the wittiest partition that ever I heard
discourse, my lord.

THE. Pyramus draws near the wall. Silence!   170

[*Re-enter* PYRAMUS.]

PYR. O grim-looked night! O night with hue so
black!
O night, which ever art when day is not!
O night, O night! alack, alack, alack,
I fear my Thisby's promise is forgot!
And thou, O wall, O sweet, O lovely wall,   175
That stand'st between her father's ground and
mine!
Thou wall, O wall, O sweet and lovely wall,
Show me thy chink, to blink through with mine
eyne!   [WALL *holds up his fingers.*]
Thanks, courteous wall. Jove shield thee well for
this!
But what see I? No Thisby do I see.   180
O wicked wall, through whom I see no bliss!
Cursed be thy stones for thus deceiving me!

91–92. noble . . . merit: i.e., a noble mind accepts the good in-
tention for the bad performance.   93. great clerks: learned
scholars.   101. fearful: full of fear.   105. capacity: understand-
ing.   106. addressed: ready.   108–17. If . . . know: Quince, by
mistaking his punctuation, makes woeful sense of his words.
112. despite: ill will.   118. stand . . . points: observe his punc-
tuation marks.   123. recorder: See Pl. 19b.   123–24. govern-
ment: control.

136. lanthorn: lantern with horn sides.   140. hight: called.
143. fall: let fall.   159. crannied: cracked.   164. sinister: left-
handed.

THE. The wall, methinks, being sensible,° should curse again. 184

PYR. No, in truth, sir, he should not. " Deceiving me " is Thisby's cue. She is to enter now, and I am to spy her through the wall. You shall see, it will fall pat as I told you. Yonder she comes.

[*Re-enter* THISBE.]

THIS. O wall, full often hast thou heard my moans,
For parting my fair Pyramus and me! 191
My cherry lips have often kissed thy stones,
Thy stones with lime and hair knit up in thee.

PYR. I see a voice. Now will I to the chink,
To spy an I can hear my Thisby's face. 195
Thisby!

THIS. My love thou art, my love I think.

PYR. Think what thou wilt, I am thy lover's grace;
And, like Limander,° am I trusty still. 199

THIS. And I like Helen,° till the Fates me kill.

PYR. Not Shafalus to Procrus° was so true.

THIS. As Shafalus to Procrus, I to you.

PYR. Oh, kiss me through the hole of this vile wall!

THIS. I kiss the wall's hole, not your lips at all.

PYR. Wilt thou at Ninny's tomb meet me straightway? 205

THIS. 'Tide life, 'tide death, I come without delay.

[*Exeunt* PYRAMUS *and* THISBE.]

WALL. Thus have I, wall, my part dischargèd so;
And, being done, thus wall away doth go. [*Exit.*]

THE. Now is the mural° down between the two neighbors.

DEM. No remedy, my lord, when walls are so willful to hear without warning. 212

HIP. This is the silliest stuff that ever I heard.

THE. The best in this kind are but shadows,° and the worst are no worse if imagination amend them.

HIP. It must be your imagination, then, and 216 not theirs.

THE. If we imagine no worse of them than they of themselves, they may pass for excellent men. Here come two noble beasts in, a man and a lion. 221

[*Re-enter* LION *and* MOONSHINE.]

LION. You, ladies, you, whose gentle hearts do fear

The smallest monstrous mouse that creeps on floor,
May now perchance both quake and tremble here,
When lion rough in wildest rage doth roar. 225
Then know that I, one Snug the joiner, am
A lion fell,° nor else no lion's dam;
For, if I should as lion come in strife
Into this place, 'twere pity on my life.°

THE. A very gentle beast, and of a good conscience. 231

DEM. The very best at a beast, my lord, that e'er I saw.

LYS. This lion is a very fox for his valor.

THE. True, and a goose for his discretion. 235

DEM. Not so, my lord, for his valor cannot carry his discretion, and the fox carries the goose.

THE. His discretion, I am sure, cannot carry his valor, for the goose carries not the fox. It is 240 well. Leave it to his discretion, and let us listen to the moon.

MOON. This lanthorn doth the hornèd moon present ——

DEM. He should have worn the horns on his head.

THE. He is no crescent, and his horns are invisible within the circumference. 247

MOON. This lanthorn doth the hornèd moon present,
Myself the man i' the moon do seem to be.

THE. This is the greatest error of all the rest. 250 The man should be put into the lantern. How is it else the man i' the moon?

DEM. He dares not come there for the candle, for you see it is already in snuff.° 254

HIP. I am aweary of this moon. Would he would change!

THE. It appears, by his small light of discretion, that he is in the wane. But yet, in courtesy, in all reason, we must stay the time.°

LYS. Proceed, Moon. 260

MOON. All that I have to say is, to tell you that the lanthorn is the moon; I, the man i' the moon; this thornbush, my thornbush; and this dog, my dog.

DEM. Why, all these should be in the lantern, 265 for all these are in the moon. But, silence! Here comes Thisbe.

[*Re-enter* THISBE.]

THIS. This is old Ninny's tomb. Where is my love?

LION. [*Roaring*] Oh —— [THISBE *runs off.*]

DEM. Well roared, Lion. 270

THE. Well run, Thisbe.

HIP. Well shone, Moon. Truly, the moon shines with a good grace.

[*The* LION *shakes* THISBE's *mantle, and exit.*]

THE. Well moused,° Lion.

LYS. And so the lion vanished. 275

DEM. And then came Pyramus.

[*Re-enter* PYRAMUS.]

PYR. Sweet Moon, I thank thee for thy sunny beams,
I thank thee, Moon, for shining now so bright.
For, by thy gracious, golden, glittering gleams,
I trust to take of truest Thisby sight. 280
But stay, oh, spite!
But mark, poor knight,

---

183. being sensible: having feeling. 199. Limander: for "Leander." 200. Helen: for "Hero," Leander's love. 201. Shafalus to Procrus: Cephalus to Procris. 209. mural: wall. 214. shadows: things of no substance. 227. fell: fierce. 229. pity . . . life: i.e., I should be hanged for it.

254. in snuff: smoking. Before self-consuming wicks were invented for candles, wicks had to be snuffed (cut) constantly or they would smoke foully. 259. stay . . . time: see it out. 273. moused: torn as a cat tears a mouse.

What dreadful dole° is here!
    Eyes, do you see?
    How can it be?   285
Oh, dainty duck! Oh, dear!
    Thy mantle good,
    What, stained with blood!
Approach, ye Furies fell!
    O Fates, come, come,   290
    Cut thread and thrum,°
Quail,° crush, conclude, and quell!°

THE. This passion, and the death of a dear friend,
would go near to make a man look sad.

HIP. Beshrew my heart, but I pity the man.   295

PYR. O wherefore, Nature, didst thou lions frame?
Since lion vile hath here deflowered my dear,
Which is — no, no — which was the fairest dame
That lived, that loved, that liked, that looked with
    cheer.
    Come, tears, confound.   300
    Out, sword, and wound
The pap of Pyramus.
    Aye, that left pap,
    Where heart doth hop.   [*Stabs himself.*]
Thus die I, thus, thus, thus.   305
    Now am I dead,
    Now am I fled,
My soul is in the sky.
    Tongue, lose thy light,   309
    Moon, take thy flight,   [*Exit* MOONSHINE.]
Now die, die, die, die, die.   [*Dies.*]

DEM. No die, but an ace, for him,° for he is but
one.

LYS. Less than an ace, man, for he is dead, he is
nothing.   315

THE. With the help of a surgeon he might yet
recover, and prove an ass.

HIP. How chance Moonshine is gone before
Thisbe comes back and finds her lover?

THE. She will find him by starlight. Here she
comes, and her passion ends the play.   321

[*Re-enter* THISBE.]

HIP. Methinks she should not use a long one for
such a Pyramus. I hope she will be brief.

DEM. A mote° will turn the balance, which Pyra-
mus, which Thisbe, is the better — he for a   325
man, God warrant us, she for a woman, God bless us.

LYS. She hath spied him already with those sweet
eyes.

DEM. And thus she means, videlicet:°   330

THIS. Asleep, my love?
    What, dead, my dove?
O Pyramus, arise!

Speak, speak. Quite dumb?
Dead, dead? A tomb   335
Must cover thy sweet eyes.
    These lily lips,
    This cherry nose,
These yellow cowslip cheeks,
    Are gone, are gone.   340
    Lovers, make moan.
His eyes were green as leeks.
    O Sisters Three,°
    Come, come to me,
With hands as pale as milk,   345
    Lay them in gore,
    Since you have shore
With shears his thread of silk.
    Tongue, not a word.
    Come, trusty sword,   350
Come, blade, my breast imbrue.°
        [*Stabs herself.*]
    And, farewell, friends.
    Thus Thisby ends.
    Adieu, adieu, adieu.   [*Dies.*]

THE. Moonshine and Lion are left to bury the
dead.   356

DEM. Aye, and Wall too.

BOT. [*Starting up*] No, I assure you the wall is
down that parted their fathers. Will it please you to
see the epilogue, or to hear a Bergomask° dance be-
tween two of our company?   361

THE. No epilogue, I pray you, for your play needs
no excuse. Never excuse, for when the players are all
dead, there need none to be blamed. Marry, if he
that writ it had played Pyramus and hanged   365
himself in Thisbe's garter, it would have been a fine
tragedy. And so it is, truly, and very notably dis-
charged. But, come, your Bergomask. Let your epi-
logue alone.   [*A dance.*]
The iron tongue of midnight hath told twelve.   370
Lovers, to bed, 'tis almost fairy time.
I fear we shall outsleep the coming morn
As much as we this night have overwatched.
This palpable-gross° play hath well beguiled
The heavy gait of night. Sweet friends, to bed.   375
A fortnight hold we this solemnity,
In nightly revels and new jollity.   [*Exeunt.*]

[*Enter* PUCK.]

PUCK. Now the hungry lion roars,
    And the wolf behowls the moon,
Whilst the heavy plowman snores,   380
    All with weary task fordone.°
Now the wasted brands° do glow,
    Whilst the screech owl, screeching loud,

---

283. dole: dolor, grief. 291. thrum: lit., the end of the thread
in a piece of weaving. So *cut thread and thrum* means "destroy
everything." 292. Quail: overwhelm. quell: slay. 312. No . . .
him: Demetrius makes a poor pun on *die* (perish) and *die* (sin-
gular of "dice"). ace: throw of one. 324. mote: speck of dust.
330. videlicet: namely, "viz."

343. Sisters Three: the three Fates who sit spinning man's des-
tiny. 351. imbrue: make bloody. 360. Bergomask: a rough
country-dance, named after the province of Bergamo in Italy,
whose people were noted for their rustic manners. 374. palpable-
gross: crudely gross. 381. fordone: overcome. 382. brands: fire-
brands.

Puts the wretch that lies in woe
  In remembrance of a shroud.   385
Now it is the time of night
  That the graves, all gaping wide,
Every one lets forth his sprite,
  In the churchway paths to glide.
And we fairies, that do run   390
  By the triple Hecate's° team,
From the presence of the sun,
  Following darkness like a dream,
Now are frolic. Not a mouse
Shall disturb this hallowed house.   395
I am sent with broom before,
To sweep the dust behind the door.

    [*Enter* OBERON *and* TITANIA *with their train.*]

OBE. Through the house give glimmering light,
By the dead and drowsy fire.
Every elf and fairy sprite   400
  Hop as light as bird from brier,
And this ditty, after me,
Sing, and dance it trippingly.
TITA. First, rehearse your song by rote,
To each word a warbling note.   405
Hand in hand, with fairy grace,
Will we sing, and bless this place.

    [*Song and dance.*]

OBE. Now, until the break of day,
Through this house each fairy stray.
To the best bridebed will we,   410
Which by us shall blessèd be,
And the issue there create
Ever shall be fortunate.

391. triple Hecate: The goddess Diana is sometimes referred to
as three-formed, because she was worshiped as Luna (or Cyn-
thia), the Moon, in Heaven; Diana on earth; and Proserpine (or
Hecate) in Hades.

So shall all the couples three
Ever true in loving be,   415
And the blots of Nature's hand
Shall not in their issue stand —
Never mole, harelip, nor scar,
Nor mark prodigious,° such as are
Despisèd in nativity,   420
Shall upon their children be.
With this field dew consecrate,
Every fairy take his gait,
And each several° chamber bless,
Through this palace, with sweet peace,   425
And the owner of it blest,
Ever shall in safety rest.
Trip away, make no stay,
Meet me all by break of day.

    [*Exeunt* OBERON, TITANIA, *and train.*]

PUCK. If we shadows have offended,   430
Think but this, and all is mended,
That you have but slumbered here
While these visions did appear,
And this weak and idle theme,
No more yielding but a dream,   435
Gentles, do not reprehend.
If you pardon, we will mend.
And, as I am an honest Puck,
If we have unearnèd luck
Now to scape the serpent's tongue,°   440
We will make amends ere long,
Else the Puck a liar call.
So, good night unto you all.
Give me your hands,° if we be friends,   444
And Robin shall restore amends.   [*Exit.*]

419. prodigious: unnatural. 424. several: separate. 440. ser-
pent's tongue: i.e., hissing. 444. Give . . . hands: clap.

THE MERCHANT OF VENICE

Introduction

The Merchant of Venice was probably written in 1595 or 1596, but there is no definite evidence of date. The style is maturer than that of *Romeo and Juliet* (c. 1594) and less mature than that of *II Henry IV* (c. 1598). The earliest recorded performance was in 1605, when the play was acted at Court before King James I on Shrove Sunday, February 10. It pleased the King so much that he ordered a second performance on the twelfth.

The play itself contains two possible topical allusions to events in 1594.

1.   . . . music is
Even as the flourish when true subjects bow
To a new-crowned monarch.

These lines (III.ii.48–50) may be a reflection of the coronation of Henry IV of France on February 27, 1594 — an event which caused considerable interest in England.

2. In the trial scene Gratiano says to Shylock:

Thou almost makest me waver in my faith,
To hold opinion with Pythagoras
That souls of animals infuse themselves
Into the trunks of men. Thy currish spirit
Governed a wolf who, hanged for human slaughter,
Even from the gallows did his fell soul fleet,
And whilst thou lay'st in thy unhallowed dam
Infused itself in thee, for thy desires
Are wolvish, bloody, starved, and ravenous.

This passage (IV.i.130–38) is a probable echo of the famous case of Dr. Roderigo Lopez, who was executed for high treason on June 7, 1594. Lopez was a Jewish physician who had come to England as a refugee from Portugal in 1559. In time he established a considerable practice at the Court and was appointed physician to the Queen. He also acted as an agent for the many spies who carried information between Spain and England. Early in 1594, the Earl of Essex, who had cause to dislike Lopez, thought that he had discovered a Spanish plot. Lopez, who was now an old man, was arrested, and while under examination told varying tales. He was accused of having taken bribes from the King of Spain to poison Queen Elizabeth. It seems likely that Lopez double-

crossed the King by taking the money without any intention of fulfilling the bargain. But with other alleged accomplices he was tried and found guilty. The Queen was at first unwilling to believe in his guilt, but after long delays he was hanged and quartered as a traitor. On the scaffold Lopez protested that he was innocent and declared that he " loved the Queen as well as he loved Jesus Christ." This remark coming from a known Jew "made no small laughter in the standers-by." As Lopez was sometimes called Lopus (or "wolf") by contemporaries, Gratiano's remark is probably topical.

There are two main stories in *The Merchant of Venice*. The first tells how Portia was to be wedded to the suitor who made the right choice of three caskets; the second shows how a cruel Jew agreed to lend a Christian a sum of money on the condition that if the debt was not repaid by a certain date the debtor should forfeit a pound of his flesh, and how when the case came to trial the Jew was outwitted.

There are many versions of both stories in different languages. The direct source of *The Merchant of Venice* was probably a play which has not survived. A play on the subject apparently existed in 1570.

One version of the story of the caskets, found in the medieval collection of tales known as the *Gesta Romanorum,* may be summarized as follows:

It was agreed that the daughter of the King of Ampluy should marry the son of the Emperor of Rome. The lady set out in a fair ship with a goodly company, but on the way the ship was wrecked and all were drowned but the lady; she was swallowed by a whale. When she found herself inside the whale's belly, she kindled a fire and used her knife so effectively that the whale, according to his nature, made for land, where a party which came down to take the whale rescued the lady. On her telling her story, she was conveyed to the Emperor, who had great compassion for her; but before giving her in marriage to his son he first desired to make proof that she was worthy. He therefore commanded three metal vessels to be brought forth. The first was made of gold set with precious stones, but within were

dead men's bones; it bore the words "Whoso choos-
eth me shall find what he deserveth." The second
vessel was made of fine silver, but filled with earth
and worms, and bore the words "Whoso chooseth
me shall find what his nature desireth." The third
vessel was made of lead, but within it was full of
precious stones, and it bore the words "Whoso choos-
eth me shall find that God hath disposed to him." So
the maiden, having prayed to God, looked first on
the vessel of gold; but when she saw the words she
said, "Though this vessel be full precious and made
of pure gold, nevertheless I know not what is within,
therefore, my dear Lord, this vessel will I not
choose." Then she looked at the vessel of silver and
having read the superscription, she said, "If I choose
this vessel, what is within I know not, but well I
wot there shall I find what my nature desireth, and
my nature desireth the lust of the flesh, therefore this
vessel will I not choose." Then she looked at the
third vessel, the vessel of lead, and she thought that
though the vessel was neither rich nor precious, yet
the words said "'Whoso chooseth me shall find that
God hath disposed,' and without doubt God never
disposeth any harm, therefore will I now choose this
vessel by the leave of God." So she chose the vessel
of lead and thus won both the precious jewels and
the son of the Emperor.

Of the various versions of the story of the
pound of flesh, the nearest is an Italian tale called
Il Pecorone, written by Ser Giovanni in 1378 and
printed in 1558. It was not printed in English in
Shakespeare's time. The outline of the story is as
follows:

Giannetto was the youngest son of a merchant of
Florence called Bindo. The merchant, being at point
of death, told his youngest son to go to Venice to
his godfather, Ansaldo, who was childless. Ansaldo
received his godson with great joy and encouraged
him to lead a pleasant life. After a while it seemed
good that Giannetto should see the world, so An-
saldo fitted out a ship full of rich merchandise to
voyage to Alexandria and trade there. Giannetto set
out, but on the way he came to a port called Bel-
monte, which was ruled by a rich and beautiful
widow who had ruined many gentlemen, for she
made a law that whosoever came to Belmonte should
be her wooer. If he could win her love, he should
become the lord of the country, but if he failed, then
he should lose all that he possessed. Giannetto de-
termined to try his luck. The lady received him most
courteously. They spent the day in feasting, and in
the evening when they were about to go to bed wine
and sweetmeats were offered to Giannetto, who ate
and drank; but the wine was drugged with a sleep-
ing potion and Giannetto fell asleep. The lady at

once took away his ship and all the merchandise,
and the next day sent him away.

When he returned to Venice Giannetto pretended
to his godfather that he had been shipwrecked. After
a while he became very downcast, and Ansaldo fitted
out a second ship, even richer than the first. Gian-
netto, however, had no thought of making good the
losses of Ansaldo; his one desire was again to try his
luck with the lady of Belmonte. As before, the lady
received him courteously and entertained him even
more lavishly; but again the wine and the sweet-
meats were brought, and Giannetto again fell asleep
before he could win the love of the lady. So once
more he returned penniless to Venice. Nevertheless
Ansaldo forgave him for the second time, and when
he saw that Giannetto could never be happy without
the lady who had already cost him so dear, he sold
most of his goods and even borrowed 10,000 ducats
from a Jew on the condition that if the ducats were
not repaid on the Feast of St. John, the Jew might
cut a pound of his flesh from any part of his body.

Thus newly equipped, Giannetto for the third
time returned to Belmonte. A great tournament was
held in his honor at which he distinguished himself
so greatly that the whole Court wished to have him
for their lord. When the time came for Giannetto
and the lady to go to bed, a damsel whispered to him
to beware of the wine. Giannetto therefore only
pretended to drink and feigned sleep, but when the
lady was about to rise and command that his ship
should be confiscated, he opened his eyes and cried
out that he had won the trial and now she must
marry him. So the wedding was lavishly celebrated,
and Giannetto ruled excellently, so engrossed in his
happiness that he forgot about his godfather. But
when at length the Feast of St. John came, Giannetto
suddenly remembered that on that very day An-
saldo's bond to the Jew would be forfeited. There-
upon he confessed all to his lady, who forthwith sent
him back to Venice to aid Ansaldo. The Jew had at
least shown so much mercy that he refrained from
demanding his forfeit until Ansaldo had been given
an opportunity of embracing his godson before he
died. Giannetto at once offered the Jew the payment
of his debt, and even as much as 100,000 ducats;
but the Jew was obdurate, and, though the whole
city of Venice was incensed against him, he would
accept no other payment than his pound of flesh.

Meanwhile the lady had herself come to Venice
in the guise of a Doctor of Law of Bologna, accom-
panied by two servants. Giannetto and the Jew went
to this Doctor, who first strongly urged the Jew to
have mercy, and to accept the 100,000 ducats; but
as the Jew still refused, they appealed to the tribunal
of Venice for judgment, which could only be that
the Jew should have his bond. All things were made
ready. The Jew ordered that Ansaldo should be

stripped naked. He took in his hand the razor which he had caused to be made especially for the purpose. But at this moment the Doctor interrupted him, saying: " Take heed what you do, for if you take more or less than one pound, your head will be struck off; and if you shed only one drop of blood, you shall die too." And further, the Doctor caused the executioner to bring the block and the ax. Then the Jew was bidden to proceed; but he thought better of it and replied that he would take the 100,000 ducats. But now the Doctor of Law in turn proved inflexible, and did not cease until the Jew in fury tore up the bond. Giannetto was overjoyed, and carried the ducats to the inn where the Doctor lodged to give them as a present; but the Doctor would not accept the money and asked only for the ring which Giannetto was wearing. Giannetto replied that this ring had been given him by his lady, whom he loved more than anything in this world; but at length he was moved by gratitude to part with his ring to the Doctor.

When Giannetto returned to Belmonte his lady had already reached home and resumed her woman's clothes, declaring that she had spent the time of her husband's absence at the baths. She received Ansaldo kindly, but to her husband she gave a cold welcome. He asked her why she was so cold to him. She answered that she did not want his kisses, which he must surely have been bestowing on his former mistresses in Venice. When he hotly denied the charge, she asked for her ring, and refused to believe his oath that he had given it to the Doctor. She swore moreover that he had given it to a woman. The tears began to rise in Giannetto's eyes, and then the lady could not keep up her pretense any longer. She embraced him, showed him the ring, and told him the whole story. So they came to love each other even more than before. As for Ansaldo, Giannetto called the damsel who had given him the good advice about the wine and married her to Ansaldo. So they all spent the rest of their lives in great felicity and contentment.

In writing or rewriting *The Merchant of Venice* Shakespeare had before him a recent and most successful play which also told of a Jew who hated all Christians. This was Marlowe's tragedy *The Jew of Malta,* which was one of Edward Alleyn's more successful parts and was still being played at the Rose playhouse. Barabas, the Jew of Malta, like Shylock had an only daughter and many ducats, but he was altogether a more monstrous and far less credible character than Shylock. In a few passages Shakespeare owed something to Marlowe in portraying Shylock as remorseless and vindictive; but Barabas was a monster of hate who did not hesitate to poison a whole nunnery because it contained the daughter who had offended him. In comparison Shylock is a mild-mannered simpleton.

The Merchant of Venice was entered in the Stationers' Register on July 22, 1598, to James Roberts as " a booke of the Marchaunt of Venyce, or otherwise called the Jewe of Venyce, Provided that yt bee not prynted by the said James Robertes or anye other whatsoever without lycence first had from the Right honorable the lord Chamberlen." This was apparently a blocking entry intended to prevent publication (see Gen. Intro. p. 66a). On October 28, 1600, Roberts transferred his rights in the play to Thomas Hayes, who shortly afterward produced a quarto (Q1) with the title: *The most excellent Historie of the Merchant of Venice. With the extreame crueltie of Shylocke the Jewe towards the sayd Merchant, in cutting a iust pound of his flesh: and the obtayning of Portia by the choyse of three chests. As it hath beene diuers times acted by the Lord Chamberlaine his Seruants. Written by William Shakespeare.* (See Pl. 14b).

The Merchant of Venice is the first play of Shakespeare's maturity. Hitherto he had been rather a poet using drama as a vessel for poetry, always ready to hold up the play so that a character might utter a poem or draw out the varieties of meaning of a phrase or a word for a dozen lines on end. Hereafter even the most lyrical of his speeches is an essential part of the action, so that in the later plays there are less fine writing and fewer ornate passages which can be extracted for an anthology; but withal he gained a greater power of statement and a deeper sense of human character. *The Merchant of Venice* is by far the most competent play that Shakespeare had yet written, in plot, situation, character, and dialogue.

Much of the success of the play is due to a well-knit plot which is worth studying in detail. It begins with Antonio the merchant, melancholy he knows not why, and unable to shake off the mood; and then, in the quiet that follows the departure of his noisy acquaintances, Bassanio, his young friend for whom he will sacrifice all, asks his help in the romantic gamble for Portia. The next scene gives a glimpse of Portia at home, bound by the strange condition of her father's will. With the third scene the play gains speed. It opens with mature ease. Bassanio enters in conversation with Shylock, and in thirty lines without preliminaries or explanation the whole situation and the characters of the two men are firmly shown: Bassanio overanxious for his loan, Shylock, the hardheaded businessman, coldly weighing the risk, and yet excited by the chance of a deal which may bring ruin on his old enemy Antonio. There are wrongs on both sides. Antonio may rightly hate Shylock's methods, but Shylock has every reason to resent Antonio's arrogant assumption of greater moral worth. The instinctive hatred of these two flares up and results in the monstrous proposal that Shylock lend the money gratis but that Antonio risk his life for the loan. The scene ends with Bassanio's foreboding that somehow the Jew will get his pound of flesh.

Shakespeare then quickens the excitement and shows the advance of the fortunes of the chief characters by a succession of ten short scenes: Belmont, where the Prince of Morocco has come to make his choice; Venice, with Launcelot Gobbo leaving the Jew to take service with Bassanio, Lorenzo eloping with Jessica, Shylock's worthless little daughter, and Bassanio setting out for Belmont; Belmont, where the Prince of Morocco reveals to himself the contents of the gold casket; Venice, where the news of Antonio's misfortunes is beginning to come through; Belmont, to see the Prince of Aragon open the silver casket and, as he departs crestfallen, the coming of Bassanio to try his luck; Venice, where Shylock's rage against Antonio has now ripened into implacable hate.

After these quick movements and the growing sense of doom, there follows the long, leisurely scene where Bassanio makes his choice of the caskets and wins the prize. The scene is deliberately drawn out, and the lyric moment enhanced by music until Portia with a free conscience can give herself to the man whom she would herself have chosen. Then, when everyone is still in the happy mood of congratulation, comes the sudden reversal for which the audience has been so well prepared: Antonio is bankrupt and the Jew will take his revenge. Two short scenes lead up to the

trial of the case of Shylock *versus* Antonio; it is still an exciting trial even to an audience long familiar with the old story. It is also a sign of Shakespeare's increasing skill as a dramatist that the great speech on the quality of mercy is not only entirely appropriate in its context, but is no longer than twenty-one lines.

In the final act Shakespeare returns to the mood of lyric love, and he creates by sheer poetry, and without any help from the electrician, the atmosphere of romantic moonlight on a warm summer's night passing gradually to dawn as the lovers all return to Belmont.

The characterization is as good as the plot; for the people are human, each with his faults and virtues. Antonio is an honest merchant, a friend to the death, but his treatment of Shylock is narrow-minded and self-righteous. Bassanio is a gay young spendthrift, but is forgiven much as an ardent lover. Portia is witty, attractive, courageous, intelligent, but nevertheless feline in her treatment of Shylock and of her husband over the ring. As for Shylock, opinion has changed during the centuries. In Shakespeare's time a Jew, especially on the stage, was a monster, capable of any cruelty toward a Christian; yet Shakespeare made him a man with real and bitter grievances enough to sour a saint. When the play was first acted there was little sympathy for him, and some surprise that he was let off so lightly. In more recent times, star actors who have taken the part have rather stressed the pathos in the Jew, so that in spite of his vindictiveness, Shylock often seems to stand out as the only man of worth in a worthless society.

The Merchant of Venice is not, however, one of Shakespeare's finest achievements. It should be compared rather with what had gone before than with the later plays. It lacks the sincerity and the depth of the greater comedies; at no time does Shakespeare tear the heart of the spectator, who is never seriously disturbed lest Bassanio choose the silver casket or Antonio bleed to death before his eyes. The play is a good tale admirably told, but no more.

The Merchant of Venice

DRAMATIS PERSONAE

THE DUKE OF VENICE
THE PRINCE OF MOROCCO ⎫
THE PRINCE OF ARAGON ⎬ *suitors to Portia*
ANTONIO, *a merchant of Venice*
BASSANIO, *his friend, suitor likewise to Portia*
SALANIO ⎫
SALARINO ⎬ *friends to Antonio and Bassanio*
GRATIANO ⎪
SALERIO ⎭
LORENZO, *in love with Jessica*
SHYLOCK, *a rich Jew*
TUBAL, *a Jew, his friend*
LAUNCELOT GOBBO, *the clown, servant to Shylock*
OLD GOBBO, *father to Launcelot*

LEONARDO, *servant to Bassanio*
BALTHASAR ⎫
STEPHANO ⎬ *servants to Portia*

PORTIA, *a rich heiress*
NERISSA, *her waiting-maid*
JESSICA, *daughter to Shylock*

MAGNIFICOES *of* Venice, OFFICERS *of the Court of Justice*, JAILER, SERVANTS *to Portia, and other* ATTENDANTS

SCENE — *Partly at Venice, and partly at Belmont, the seat of Portia, on the Continent.*

Act I

SCENE I. *Venice. A street.*

[*Enter* ANTONIO, SALARINO, *and* SALANIO.]
ANT. In sooth, I know not why I am so sad.
It wearies me, you say it wearies you;
But how I caught it, found it, or came by it,
What stuff 'tis made of, whereof it is born,
I am to° learn. 5
And such a want-wit sadness makes of me
That I have much ado to know myself.
SALAR. Your mind is tossing on the ocean —
There where your argosies° with portly° sail,
Like signiors and rich burghers° on the flood, 10
Or, as it were, the pageants° of the sea,
Do overpeer° the petty traffickers
That curtsy to them, do them reverence,
As they fly by them with their woven wings.°
SALAN. Believe me, sir, had I such venture forth,
The better part of my affections would 16
Be with my hopes abroad. I should be still°
Plucking the grass to know where sits the wind,
Peering in maps for ports, and piers, and roads.°
And every object that might make me fear 20
Misfortune to my ventures, out of doubt
Would make me sad.
SALAR.   My wind, cooling my broth,
Would blow me to an ague° when I thought

What harm a wind too great at sea might do.
I should not see the sandy hourglass run 25
But I should think of shallows and of flats,°
And see my wealthy *Andrew*° docked in sand
Vailing° her high top lower than her ribs
To kiss her burial. Should I go to church
And see the holy edifice of stone, 30
And not bethink me straight of dangerous rocks,
Which touching but my gentle vessel's side
Would scatter all her spices on the stream,
Enrobe the roaring waters with my silks —
And, in a word, but even now worth this, 35
And now worth nothing? Shall I have the thought
To think on this, and shall I lack the thought
That such a thing bechanced would make me sad?
But tell not me — I know Antonio
Is sad to think upon his merchandise. 40
ANT. Believe me, no. I thank my fortune for it,
My ventures are not in one bottom trusted,
Nor to one place, nor is my whole estate
Upon the fortune of this present year.
Therefore my merchandise makes me not sad. 45
SALAR. Why, then you are in love.
ANT.   Fie, fie!
SALAR. Not in love neither? Then let us say you are sad
Because you are not merry; and 'twere as easy
For you to laugh, and leap, and say you are merry
Because you are not sad. Now, by two-headed
    Janus,° 50

Act I, Sc. i: **5. am to:** have yet to. **9. argosies:** An argosy is a great merchant ship, sometimes called a carrack. **portly:** swelling. **10. burghers:** citizens, businessmen. **11. pageants:** elaborate spectacles, such as are shown on floats. **12. overpeer:** look down on. **14. woven wings:** i.e., sails. **17. still:** always. **19. roads:** anchorages. **23. ague:** fever.

26. flats: sandbanks. **27. Andrew:** the name of a ship. Probably Shakespeare has in mind the great carrack *St. Andrew* brought home to England after the capture of Cadiz in the summer of 1596. See Gen. Intro. p. 29b. **28. Vailing:** lowering. **50. Janus:** a Roman god with two faces, the one smiling, the other frowning.

Nature hath framed strange fellows in her time —
Some that will evermore peep through their eyes,
And laugh like parrots at a bagpiper,
And other of such vinegar aspéct
That they'll not show their teeth in way of smile   55
Though Nestor° swear the jest be laughable.

[*Enter* BASSANIO, LORENZO, *and* GRATIANO.]

SALAN. Here comes Bassanio, your most noble
    kinsman,
Gratiano, and Lorenzo. Fare ye well.
We leave you now with better company.

SALAR. I would have stayed till I had made you
    merry   60
If worthier friends had not prevented° me.

ANT. Your worth is very dear in my regard.
I take it, your own business calls on you,
And you embrace the occasion to depart.

SALAR. Good morrow, my good lords.   65

BASS. Good signiors both, when shall we laugh?
    Say, when?
You grow exceeding strange. Must it be so?

SALAR. We'll make our leisures to attend on yours.

[*Exeunt* SALARINO *and* SALANIO.]

LOR. My Lord Bassanio, since you have found An-
    tonio,
We two will leave you. But at dinnertime   70
I pray you have in mind where we must meet.

BASS. I will not fail you.

GRA. You look not well, Signior Antonio.
You have too much respect upon° the world.
They lose it that do buy it with much care.   75
Believe me, you are marvelously° changed.

ANT. I hold the world but as the world, Gra-
    tiano —
A stage where every man must play a part,
And mine a sad one.

GRA.   Let me play the fool.
With mirth and laughter let old wrinkles come,   80
And let my liver° rather heat with wine
Than my heart cool with mortifying° groans.
Why should a man whose blood is warm within
Sit like his grandsire cut in alabaster?°
Sleep when he wakes, and creep into the jaundice°
By being peevish? I tell thee what, Antonio —   86
I love thee, and it is my love that speaks —
There are a sort of men whose visages
Do cream and mantle° like a standing pond,
And do a willful stillness entertain,°   90

With purpose to be dressed in an opinion°
Of wisdom, gravity, profound conceit,°
As who should say, " I am Sir Oracle,
And when I ope my lips, let no dog bark! "
O my Antonio, I do know of these,   95
That therefore only are reputed wise
For saying nothing; when, I am very sure,
If they should speak, would almost damn those ears
Which, hearing them, would call their brothers
    fools.°
I'll tell thee more of this another time.   100
But fish not with this melancholy bait°
For this fool gudgeon,° this opinion.
Come, good Lorenzo. Fare ye well awhile.
I'll end my exhortation after dinner.

LOR. Well, we will leave you, then, till dinnertime.
I must be one of these same dumb wise men,   106
For Gratiano never lets me speak.

GRA. Well, keep me company but two years moe,°
Thou shalt not know the sound of thine own tongue.

ANT. Farewell. I'll grow a talker for this gear.°

GRA. Thanks, i'faith, for silence is only commend-
    able   111
In a neat's tongue° dried and a maid not vendible.°

[*Exeunt* GRATIANO *and* LORENZO.]

ANT. Is that anything now?

BASS. Gratiano speaks an infinite deal of nothing,
more than any man in all Venice. His reasons° are as
two grains of wheat hid in two bushels of chaff.   116
You shall seek all day ere you find them, and when
you have them, they are not worth the search.

ANT. Well, tell me now, what lady is the same
To whom you swore a secret pilgrimage   120
That you today promised to tell me of?

BASS. 'Tis not unknown to you, Antonio,
How much I have disabled mine estate
By something° showing a more swelling port°
Than my faint means would grant continuance.
Nor do I now make moan to be abridged°   126
From such a noble rate; but my chief care
Is to come fairly off from the great debts
Wherein my time, something too prodigal,
Hath left me gaged.° To you, Antonio,   130
I owe the most, in money and in love.
And from your love I have a warranty

---

91. dressed...opinion: get a reputation for. 92. conceit: thought. 98–99. If...fools: if they should say anything which would make their brothers fools and so be damned — a reminiscence of Matthew 5:22: "But I say unto you, that whosoever is angry with his brother without a cause shall be in danger of the judgment...but whosoever shall say, Thou fool, shall be in danger of hell fire." 101. melancholy bait: bait which causes melancholy, for *opinion* (reputation) is not worth having. 102. gudgeon: a small fish easily caught. 108. moe: more. 110. gear: stuff, chatter; *gear* is one of those words used vaguely like "case" or "lot." 112. neat's tongue: ox tongue. vendible: marketable. 115. reasons: intelligent remarks. 124. something: somewhat. swelling port: extravagant living; i.e., by being too much of a "playboy." 126. abridged: cut down. 130. gaged: pledged, in debt.

56. Nestor: the old veteran in the Greek army that went against Troy. Anything that Nestor guaranteed must be good. See *Tr & Cr.* 61. prevented: forestalled. 74. respect upon: respect for. 76. marvelously: exceedingly. 81. liver: regarded as the seat of the passions. 82. mortifying: deadly. 84. grandsire...alabaster: like the alabaster image of his grandfather. Alabaster was much used for monuments of the dead in English churches of the type shown in Pl. 2b. 85. jaundice: disorder in the bile, caused by, and causing, intense depression. 89. cream...mantle: cover with a thick motionless scum. 90. entertain: affect.

To unburden all my plots° and purposes
How to get clear of all the debts I owe.

   ANT. I pray you, good Bassanio, let me know it.
And if it stand, as you yourself still do,   136
Within the eye of honor,° be assured
My purse, my person, my extremest means,
Lie all unlocked to your occasions.°

   BASS. In my school days, when I had lost one
    shaft,°   140
I shot his fellow of the selfsame flight°
The selfsame way with more advisèd° watch,
To find the other forth, and by adventuring both,
I oft found both. I urge this childhood proof°
Because what follows is pure innocence.   145
I owe you much, and, like a willful youth,
That which I owe is lost. But if you please
To shoot another arrow that self way
Which you did shoot the first, I do not doubt,
As I will watch the aim, or° to find both   150
Or bring your latter hazard° back again,
And thankfully rest debtor for the first.

   ANT. You know me well, and herein spend but
    time
To wind about my love with circumstance.°
And out of doubt you do me now more wrong   155
In making question of my uttermost°
Than if you had made waste of all I have.
Then do but say to me what I should do
That in your knowledge may by me be done,
And I am prest° unto it. Therefore, speak.   160

   BASS. In Belmont is a lady richly left,°
And she is fair and, fairer than that word,
Of wondrous virtues. Sometimes from her eyes
I did receive fair speechless messages.
Her name is Portia, nothing undervalued   165
To Cato's daughter, Brutus' Portia.°
Nor is the wide world ignorant of her worth,
For the four winds blow in from every coast
Renownèd suitors. And her sunny locks
Hang on her temples like a golden fleece,   170
Which makes her seat of Belmont Colchos' strond,
And many Jasons come in quest of her.°
O my Antonio, had I but the means
To hold a rival place with one of them,
I have a mind presages° me such thrift°   175
That I should questionless be fortunate!

   ANT. Thou know'st that all my fortunes are at sea,
Neither have I money nor commodity

To raise a present° sum. Therefore go forth,
Try what my credit can in Venice do.   180
That shall be racked,° even to the uttermost,
To furnish thee to Belmont, to fair Portia.
Go, presently inquire, and so will I,
Where money is, and I no question make   184
To have it of my trust,° or for my sake.   [*Exeunt.*]

SCENE II. *Belmont. A room in* PORTIA's *house.*

[*Enter* PORTIA *and* NERISSA.]

   POR. By my troth,° Nerissa, my little body is
aweary of this great world.

   NER. You would be, sweet madam, if your mis-
eries were in the same abundance as your good for-
tunes are. And yet, for aught I see, they are as   5
sick that surfeit° with too much as they that starve
with nothing. It is no mean happiness, therefore, to
be seated in the mean. Superfluity comes sooner by
white hairs,° but competency° lives longer.   10

   POR. Good sentences,° and well pronounced.

   NER. They would be better if well followed.

   POR. If to do were as easy as to know what were
good to do, chapels had been churches and poor
men's cottages princes' palaces. It is a good di-   15
vine° that follows his own instructions. I can easier
teach twenty what were good to be done than be one
of the twenty to follow mine own teaching. The brain
may devise laws for the blood, but a hot temper leaps
o'er a cold decree. Such a hare is madness the   20
youth, to skip o'er the meshes° of good counsel the
cripple. But this reasoning° is not in the fashion° to
choose me a husband. Oh, me, the word "choose." I
may neither choose whom I would nor refuse whom
I dislike. So is the will of a living daughter   25
curbed by the will° of a dead father. Is it not hard,
Nerissa, that I cannot choose one, nor refuse none?

   NER. Your father was ever virtuous, and holy   30
men at their death have good inspirations. Therefore
the lottery° that he hath devised in these three chests
of gold, silver, and lead — whereof who chooses his
meaning chooses you — will, no doubt, never be
chosen by any rightly but one who shall rightly   35
love. But what warmth is there in your affection
toward any of these princely suitors that are already
come?

   POR. I pray thee, overname° them, and as thou

---

133. **plots:** plans. **136–37. stand . . . honor:** i.e., is honorable.
139. **occasions:** needs. 140. **shaft:** arrow. 141. **flight:** batch of
arrows. 142. **advised:** careful. 144. **proof:** experience. 150. **or:**
either. 151. **hazard:** risk, speculation. 153–54. **spend . . . cir-
cumstance:** you need not waste time by this indirect approach.
156. **In . . . uttermost:** in questioning whether I shall help you
to the uttermost. 160. **prest:** ready. 161. **richly left:** with a
rich legacy. 166. **Brutus' Portia:** See *Caesar,* II.i.233, etc.
171–72. **Colchos' . . . her:** Jason sailed to Colchos in the *Argo*
to fetch away the Golden Fleece. **strond:** strand, shore. 175. **pre-
sages:** foretells. **thrift:** profit.

179. **present:** immediate. 181. **racked:** stretched. 185. **trust:**
credit.
  Sc. ii: 1. **troth:** faith. 6. **surfeit:** gorge themselves.
9–10. **Superfluity . . . hairs:** a man who has too much ages
quickest. 10. **competency:** modest means. 11. **sentences:** prov-
erbs. 15–16. **divine:** preacher. 21. **meshes:** net. 22. **reason-
ing:** arguing. **fashion:** manner, way. 25–26. **will . . . will:** de-
sire . . . testament. 32. **lottery:** lucky draw. 39. **overname:**
repeat the names of.

namest them I will describe them, and according　40
to my description, level° at my affection.

NER. First, there is the Neapolitan Prince.

POR. Aye, that's a colt indeed, for he doth nothing
but talk of his horse, and he makes it a great　45
appropriation° to his own good parts that he can
shoe him himself. I am much afeard my lady his
mother played false with a smith.

NER. Then there is the County° Palatine.

POR. He doth nothing but frown, as who　50
should say, "If you will not have me, choose." He
hears merry tales and smiles not. I fear he will prove
the weeping philosopher° when he grows old, being
so full of unmannerly sadness in his youth. I had
rather be married to a death's-head° with a bone　55
in his mouth than to either of these. God defend me
from these two!

NER. How say you by the French lord, Monsieur
Le Bon?

POR. God made him, and therefore let him　60
pass for a man. In truth, I know it is a sin to be a
mocker, but he!—Why, he hath a horse better than
the Neapolitan's, a better bad habit of frowning than
the Count Palatine. He is every man in no man. If a
throstle° sing, he falls straight a-capering. He　65
will fence with his own shadow. If I should marry
him, I should marry twenty husbands. If he would
despise me, I would forgive him, for if he love me to
madness, I shall never requite him.　70

NER. What say you, then, to Falconbridge, the
young baron of England?

POR. You know I say nothing to him, for he
understands not me, nor I him. He hath neither
Latin, French, nor Italian, and you will come　75
into the court and swear that I have a poor penny-
worth in the English. He is a proper° man's picture,
but, alas! who can converse with a dumb show?°
How oddly he is suited! I think he bought his
doublet° in Italy, his round hose° in France,　80
his bonnet in Germany, and his behavior every-
where.°

NER. What think you of the Scottish lord, his
neighbor?

POR. That he hath a neighborly charity in　85
him, for he borrowed° a box of the ear of the Eng-
lishman and swore he would pay him again when he

was able. I think the Frenchman became his surety,
and sealed under° for another.

NER. How like you the young German, the Duke
of Saxony's nephew?　91

POR. Very vilely in the morning, when he is sober,
and most vilely in the afternoon, when he is drunk.
When he is best, he is a little worse than a man, and
when he is worst, he is little better than a beast.　95
An° the worst fall that ever fell, I hope I shall make
shift° to go without him.

NER. If he should offer to choose and choose
the right casket, you should refuse to perform
your father's will if you should refuse to accept
him.　102

POR. Therefore, for fear of the worst, I pray thee
set a deep glass of Rhenish° wine on the contrary°
casket, for if the Devil be within and that temptation
without, I know he will choose it. I will do　106
anything, Nerissa, ere I'll be married to a sponge.

NER. You need not fear, lady, the having any of
these lords. They have acquainted me with　110
their determinations, which is, indeed, to return to
their home and to trouble you with no more suit un-
less you may be won by some other sort° than your
father's imposition, depending on the caskets.　115

POR. If I live to be as old as Sibylla,° I will die as
chaste as Diana° unless I be obtained by the manner
of my father's will. I am glad this parcel of wooers
are so reasonable, for there is not one among them
but I dote on his very absence, and I pray God grant
them a fair departure.　121

NER. Do you not remember, lady, in your father's
time, a Venetian, a scholar and a soldier, that came
hither in company of the Marquis of Montferrat?

POR. Yes, yes, it was Bassanio, as I think he was so
called.

NER. True, madam. He of all the men that ever
my foolish eyes looked upon was the best deserving
a fair lady.　131

POR. I remember him well, and I remember him
worthy of thy praise. [*Enter a* SERVINGMAN.] How
now! What news?

SERV. The four strangers seek for you, madam, to
take their leave. And there is a forerunner　136
come from a fifth, the Prince of Morocco, who brings
word the Prince his master will be here tonight.

POR. If I could bid the fifth welcome with so good
a heart as I can bid the other four farewell, I should
be glad of his approach. If he have the condition of a

---

41. **level:** guess.　46. **appropriation:** special addition.　49. **County:**
Count.　53. **weeping philosopher:** Heraclitus, who wept over
the follies of mankind.　55. **death's-head:** skull.　65. **throstle:**
thrush.　77. **proper:** handsome.　78. **dumb show:** In some plays
the action is first symbolized by a pantomime in which the ac-
tors say nothing. For a specimen see *Haml,* III.ii.145.　80. **dou-**
blet: coat. **round hose:** short breeches. See Pl. 8b and comment
on p. 93a–b.　71–82. **What . . . everywhere:** These were common
criticisms of the English—that they knew no language but
their own and borrowed their fashions from every nation at once.
86. **borrowed:** received.

89. **sealed under:** agreed to be his surety. Before England and
Scotland were united in 1603, the French and the Scots were
close allies.　96. **An:** if.　96–97. **make shift:** contrive.
104. **Rhenish:** Rhine. **contrary:** opposite.　113. **sort:** manner.
116. **Sibylla:** the ancient prophetess to whom Apollo promised
that her years should be as many as the grains of sand which
she held in her hand.　117. **Diana:** virgin goddess of
chastity.

saint and the complexion of a devil,° I had rather he
should shrive° me than wive me.   145
Come, Nerissa. Sirrah,° go before.
Whiles we shut the gates upon one wooer, another
    knocks at the door.   [*Exeunt.*]

SCENE III. *Venice. A public place.*

[*Enter* BASSANIO *and* SHYLOCK.]

SHY. Three thousand ducats.° Well.
BASS. Aye, sir, for three months.
SHY. For three months. Well.
BASS. For the which, as I told you, Antonio shall
be bound.   5
SHY. Antonio shall become bound. Well.
BASS. May you stead° me? Will you pleasure me?
Shall I know your answer?
SHY. Three thousand ducats for three months, and
Antonio bound.   10
BASS. Your answer to that.
SHY. Antonio is a good man.
BASS. Have you heard any imputation to the con-
trary?
SHY. Oh, no, no, no, no. My meaning in say-   15
ing he is a good man is to have you understand me
that he is sufficient.° Yet his means are in supposi-
tion.° He hath an argosy bound to Tripolis, another
to the Indies. I understand, moreover, upon the
Rialto,° he hath a third at Mexico, a fourth for   20
England, and other ventures he hath, squandered
abroad. But ships are but boards, sailors but men.
There be land rats and water rats, water thieves and
land thieves — I mean pirates. And then there is the
peril of waters, winds, and rocks. The man is,   25
notwithstanding, sufficient. Three thousand ducats.
I think I may take his bond.
BASS. Be assured you may.
SHY. I will be assured I may, and that I may   30
be assured, I will bethink me. May I speak with
Antonio?
BASS. If it please you to dine with us.
SHY. Yes, to smell pork, to eat of the habitation
which your prophet the Nazarite conjured the   35
devil into.° I will buy with you, sell with you, talk
with you, walk with you, and so following; but I will
not eat with you, drink with you, nor pray with you.
What news on the Rialto? Who is he comes here?

[*Enter* ANTONIO.]

BASS. This is Signior Antonio.   41
SHY. [*Aside*] How like a fawning publican° he
    looks!
I hate him for he is a Christian,
But more for that in low simplicity
He lends out money gratis and brings down   45
The rate of usance° here with us in Venice.
If I can catch him once upon the hip,
I will feed fat the ancient grudge I bear him.
He hates our sacred nation, and he rails,
Even there where merchants most do congregate,
On me, my bargains, and my well-won thrift,°   51
Which he calls interest. Cursed be my tribe
If I forgive him!
BASS.   Shylock, do you hear?
SHY. I am debating of my present store,
And by the near guess of my memory,   55
I cannot instantly raise up the gross°
Of full three thousand ducats. What of that?
Tubal, a wealthy Hebrew of my tribe,
Will furnish me. But soft! How many months
Do you desire? [*To* ANTONIO] Rest you fair, good
    signior.   60
Your Worship was the last man in our mouths.
ANT. Shylock, although I neither lend nor borrow,
By taking nor by giving of excess,°
Yet to supply the ripe° wants of my friend
I'll break a custom. [*To* BASSANIO] Is he yet pos-
    sessed°   65
How much ye would?
SHY.   Aye, aye, three thousand ducats.
ANT. And for three months.
SHY. I had forgot — three months, you told me so.
Well, then, your bond, and let me see. But hear you,
Methought you said you neither lend nor borrow
Upon advantage.
ANT.   I do never use it.   71
SHY. When Jacob grazed his uncle Laban's°
    sheep —
This Jacob from our holy Abram was,
As his wise mother wrought in his behalf,
The third possessor — aye, he was the third° ——
ANT. And what of him? Did he take interest?   76

---

144. complexion . . . devil: the Devil was black.   145. shrive:
give me absolution.   146. Sirrah: form of address used to an
inferior.
Sc. iii: 1. ducat: worth about $2.   7. stead: help.   17. suffi-
cient: solvent. supposition: doubt.   20. Rialto: the Merchants'
Exchange, where businessmen met twice daily to make deals
and exchange news.   35–36. conjured . . . into: i.e., the swine
into which entered the devils cast out of the man of the
tombs in the country of the Gadarenes. See Mark 5:1–17.

42. fawning publican: The publicans were collectors of taxes for
the Romans. To a strict Jew *publican* was a term of bitter abuse,
as in the parable of the Pharisee and the publican, "The Pharisee
stood and prayed thus with himself, 'God, I thank thee,' that I
am not as other men are . . . or even as this publican.'" Luke
18:11.   46. usance: usury. Usury is the taking of excessive in-
terest, and so exploiting the needy; but in Shakespeare's time
even a moderate rate of interest was in theory regarded as
immoral, for Christians should help one another. In practice 10%
was allowed. Usury was one of the greatest abuses of the time.
See *M for Meas*, IV.iii.4–12.   51. thrift: profit.   56. gross: full
sum.   63. excess: interest; i.e., more than the original loan.
64. ripe: needing immediate help.   65. possessed: informed.
72. Jacob . . . Laban's: The story is told in Genesis 30:27–43.
74–75. wise . . . third: Jacob's mother by fraud persuaded Isaac
to bless his younger son. See Genesis 27.

SHY. No, not take interest, not, as you would say,
Directly interest. Mark what Jacob did.
When Laban and himself were compromised°
That all the eanlings° which were streaked and
    pied°   80
Should fall as Jacob's hire, the ewes, being rank,°
In the end of autumn turned to the rams.
And when the work of generation was
Between these woolly breeders in the act,
The skillful shepherd peeled me certain wands   85
And, in the doing of the deed of kind,°
He stuck them up before the fulsome° ewes,
Who, then conceiving, did in eaning time°
Fall° particolored lambs, and those were Jacob's.
This was a way to thrive, and he was blest.   90
And thrift is blessing, if men steal it not.
   ANT. This was a venture, sir, that Jacob served for,
A thing not in his power to bring to pass,
But swayed and fashioned by the hand of Heaven.
Was this inserted to make interest good?   95
Or is your gold and silver ewes and rams?
   SHY. I cannot tell. I make it breed as fast.
But note me, signior.
   ANT.   Mark you this, Bassanio,
The Devil can cite Scripture for his purpose.
An evil soul producing holy witness   100
Is like a villain with a smiling cheek,
A goodly apple rotten at the heart.
Oh, what a goodly outside falsehood hath!
   SHY. Three thousand ducats. 'Tis a good round
    sum.
Three months from twelve — then, let me see, the
    rate ——   105
   ANT. Well, Shylock, shall we be beholding to you?
   SHY. Signior Antonio, many a time and oft
In the Rialto you have rated° me
About my moneys and my usances.
Still have I borne it with a patient shrug,   110
For sufferance° is the badge of all our tribe.
You call me misbeliever, cutthroat dog,
And spit upon my Jewish gaberdine,°
And all for use of that which is mine own.
Well, then, it now appears you need my help.   115
Go to, then, you come to me and you say
"Shylock, we would have moneys." You say so,
You that did void your rheum° upon my beard
And foot me as you spurn a stranger cur
Over your threshold. Moneys is your suit.   120
What should I say to you? Should I not say,
"Hath a dog money? Is it possible
A cur can lend three thousand ducats?" Or
Shall I bend low and in a bondman's° key,

With bated breath and whispering humbleness,   125
Say this —
"Fair sir, you spit on me on Wednesday last,
You spurned me such a day, another time
You called me dog, and for these courtesies
I'll lend you thus much moneys"?   130
   ANT. I am as like to call thee so again,
To spit on thee again, to spurn thee too.
If thou wilt lend this money, lend it not
As to thy friends, for when did friendship take
A breed° for barren metal of his friend?   135
But lend it rather to thine enemy,
Who if he break,° thou mayst with better face
Exact the penalty.
   SHY.   Why, look you how you storm!
I would be friends with you, and have your love,
Forget the shames that you have stained me with,
Supply your present wants, and take no doit°   141
Of usance for my moneys, and you'll not hear me.
This is kind I offer.
   BASS. This were kindness.
   SHY.   This kindness will I show.
Go with me to a notary, seal me there   145
Your single bond.° And, in a merry sport,
If you repay me not on such a day,
In such a place, such sum or sums as are
Expressed in the condition, let the forfeit
Be nominated for an equal° pound   150
Of your fair flesh, to be cut off and taken
In what part of your body pleaseth me.
   ANT. Content, i' faith. I'll seal to such a bond,
And say there is much kindness in the Jew.
   BASS. You shall not seal to such a bond for me.
I'll rather dwell in my necessity.   156
   ANT. Why, fear not, man, I will not forfeit it.
Within these two months — that's a month before
This bond expires — I do expect return
Of thrice three times the value of this bond. 160
   SHY. O Father Abram, what these Christians are,
Whose own hard dealings teaches them suspect
The thoughts of others! Pray you, tell me this.
If he should break his day, what should I gain
By the exaction of the forfeiture?   165
A pound of man's flesh taken from a man
Is not so estimable, profitable neither,
As flesh of muttons, beefs, or goats. I say
To buy his favor I extend this friendship.
If he will take it, so; if not, adieu.   170
And, for my love, I pray you wrong me not.
   ANT. Yes, Shylock, I will seal unto this bond.
   SHY. Then meet me forthwith at the notary's.
Give him direction for this merry bond,
And I will go and purse the ducats straight,   175
See to my house, left in the fearful° guard

---

79. compromised: agreed. 80. eanlings: lambs. streaked . . .
pied: striped . . . particolored, or as in Genesis, "ringstraked and
spotted." 81. rank: in heat. 86. kind: nature. 87. fulsome:
fat. 88. eaning time: lambing season. 89. Fall: give birth to.
108. rated: abused. 111. sufferance: patience. 113. gaberdine:
cloak. 118. void . . . rheum: spit. 124. bondman: slave.

135. breed: increase. 137. break: go bankrupt. 141. doit: small
Dutch coin, "cent." 146. single bond: i.e., without any second
security. 150. equal: exact. 176. fearful: to be feared.

Of an unthrifty knave, and presently
I will be with you.
     ANT.   Hie thee, gentle Jew.   [*Exit* SHYLOCK.]
The Hebrew will turn Christian. He grows kind.
     BASS. I like not fair terms and a villain's mind.
     ANT. Come on. In this there can be no dismay.
My ships come home a month before the day.   182
                        [*Exeunt.*]

Act II

SCENE I. *Belmont. A room in* PORTIA'S *house.*

[*Flourish of cornets.*° *Enter the* PRINCE OF MOROCCO
and his train; PORTIA, NERISSA, *and others attending.*]

     MOR. Mislike me not for my complexion,
The shadowed° livery of the burnished sun,
To whom I am a neighbor and near bred.
Bring me the fairest creature northward born,
Where Phoebus'° fire scarce thaws the icicles,   5
And let us make incision for your love,
To prove whose blood is reddest,° his or mine.
I tell thee, lady, this aspéct° of mine
Hath feared° the valiant. By my love, I swear
The best-regarded virgins of our clime   10
Have loved it too. I would not change this hue,
Except to steal your thoughts, my gentle Queen.
     POR. In terms of choice I am not solely led
By nice direction of a maiden's eyes.°
Besides, the lottery of my destiny   15
Bars me the right of voluntary choosing.
But if my father had not scanted° me
And hedged me by his wit, to yield myself
His wife who wins me by that means I told you,
Yourself, renownèd Prince, then stood as fair   20
As any comer I have looked on yet
For my affection.
     MOR.   Even for that I thank you.
Therefore I pray you lead me to the caskets,
To try my fortune. By this scimitar°
That slew the Sophy° and a Persian prince   25
That won three fields° of Sultan Solyman,°
I would outstare the sternest eyes that look,
Outbrave the heart most daring on the earth,
Pluck the young sucking cubs from the she-bear,
Yea, mock the lion when he roars for prey,   30

To win thee, lady. But, alas the while!
If Hercules and Lichas° play at dice
Which is the better man, the greater throw
May turn by fortune from the weaker hand.
So is Alcides° beaten by his page,   35
And so may I, blind fortune leading me,
Miss that which one unworthier may attain,
And die with grieving.
     POR.   You must take your chance,
And either not attempt to choose at all
Or swear before you choose, if you choose wrong,
Never to speak to lady afterward   41
In way of marriage. Therefore be advised.
     MOR. Nor will not. Come, bring me unto my
chance.
     POR. First, forward to the temple. After dinner
Your hazard shall be made.
     MOR.   Good fortune, then!   45
To make me blest or cursed'st among men.
              [*Cornets, and exeunt.*]

SCENE II. *Venice. A street.*

[*Enter* LAUNCELOT GOBBO.]

     LAUN. Certainly my conscience will serve me to
run from this Jew my master. The fiend is at mine
elbow and tempts me, saying to me, "Gobbo,
Launcelot Gobbo, good Launcelot," or "good
Gobbo," or "good Launcelot Gobbo, use your legs,
take the start, run away." My conscience says,   5
"No, take heed, honest Launcelot, take heed, honest
Gobbo," or, as aforesaid, "honest Launcelot Gobbo,
do not run, scorn running with thy heels." Well, the
most courageous fiend bids me pack.° "Via!"° says
the fiend, "away!" says the fiend, "for the   10
heavens,° rouse up a brave mind," says the fiend,
"and run." Well, my conscience, hanging about the
neck of my heart, says very wisely to me, "My honest
friend Launcelot, being an honest man's son" — or
rather an honest woman's son, for indeed my   15
father did something smack, something grow to, he
had a kind of taste° — well, my conscience says,
"Launcelot, budge not." "Budge," says the fiend.
"Budge not," says my conscience. "Conscience,"
say I, "you counsel well." "Fiend," say I,   21
"you counsel well." To be ruled by my conscience,
I should stay with the Jew my master, who, God
bless the mark,° is a kind of devil; and to run away
from the Jew, I should be ruled by the fiend,   26

---

32. Lichas: the page of Hercules.   35. Alcides: Hercules.

     Sc. ii: 9. pack: get going. Via: get on.   10–11. for . . . heavens: for heavens' sake.   16–17. something . . . taste: my father was not too honest, there was a sort of burnt taste about him. Launcelot's remarks are at times more allusive than clear. smack: taste. grow to: a phrase used of milk burned in the pan. 23–24. God . . . mark: one of those meaningless phrases used as apology before an unpleasant remark.

Act II, Sc. i: s.d., Flourish of cornets: fanfare to announce the approach of a royal person. See Pl. 19c. 2. shadowed: black; my black skin shows that I am the servant of the sun. 5. Phoebus: the sun god. 7. reddest: i.e., bravest. 8. aspect: face. 9. feared: frightened. 13–14. In . . . eyes: I do not choose only by delicate ladylike distinctions of appearance. 17. scanted: restricted. 24. scimitar: curved sword. 25. Sophy: Shah of Persia. 26. fields: battles. Sultan Solyman: the Turkish Emperor.

who, saving your reverence,° is the Devil himself. Certainly the Jew is the very Devil incarnal,° and, in my conscience, my conscience is but a kind of hard conscience to offer to counsel me to stay with the Jew. The fiend gives the more friendly counsel. 31 I will run, fiend, my heels are at your command. I will run.

[*Enter* OLD GOBBO, *with a basket.*]

GOB. Master young man, you, I pray you which is the way to Master Jew's? 35

LAUN. [*Aside*] Oh heavens, this is my true-begotten father! Who, being more than sand-blind,° high-gravel blind, knows me not. I will try confusions° with him.

GOB. Master young gentleman, I pray you which is the way to Master Jew's? 41

LAUN. Turn up on your right hand at the next turning, but at the next turning of all, on your left; marry,° at the very next turning, turn of no hand, but turn down indirectly to the Jew's house. 46

GOB. By God's sonties,° 'twill be a hard way to hit. Can you tell me whether one Launcelot, that dwells with him, dwell with him or no?

LAUN. Talk you of young Master Launcelot? 50 [*Aside*] Mark me now, now will I raise the waters. Talk you of young Master Launcelot?°

GOB. No master, sir, but a poor man's son. His father, though I say it, is an honest exceeding° poor man, and, God be thanked, well to live.° 55

LAUN. Well, let his father be what 'a will, we talk of young Master Launcelot.

GOB. Your Worship's friend, and Launcelot,° sir.

LAUN. But I pray you, ergo,° old man, ergo, I beseech you, talk you of young Master Launcelot? 60

GOB. Of Launcelot, an't please your mastership.

LAUN. Ergo, Master Launcelot. Talk not of Master Launcelot, Father, for the young gentleman, according to Fates and Destinies and such odd 65 sayings, the Sisters Three° and such branches of learning, is indeed deceased, or as you would say in plain terms, gone to Heaven.

GOB. Marry, God forbid! The boy was the very staff of my age, my very prop. 70

LAUN. Do I look like a cudgel or a hovel post,° a staff or a prop? Do you know me, Father?

GOB. Alack the day, I know you not, young gentleman: but I pray you tell me, is my boy, God rest his soul, alive or dead? 75

LAUN. Do you not know me, Father?

GOB. Alack, sir, I am sand-blind. I know you not.

LAUN. Nay, indeed, if you had your eyes, you might fail of the knowing me. It is a wise father 80 that knows his own child. Well, old man, I will tell you news of your son. Give me your blessing. Truth will come to light, murder cannot be hid long, a man's son may, but at the length truth will out. 85

GOB. Pray you, sir, stand up. I am sure you are not Launcelot, my boy.

LAUN. Pray you let's have no more fooling about it, but give me your blessing. I am Launcelot, your boy that was, your son that is, your child that shall be.

GOB. I cannot think you are my son. 92

LAUN. I know not what I shall think of that, but I am Launcelot, the Jew's man, and I am sure Margery your wife is my mother. 95

GOB. Her name is Margery, indeed. I'll be sworn, if thou be Launcelot, thou art mine own flesh and blood. Lord worshiped might He be! What a beard hast thou got! Thou hast got more hair on thy chin than Dobbin my fill horse° has on his tail. 101

LAUN. It should seem, then, that Dobbin's tail grows backward. I am sure he had more hair of his tail than I have of my face when I last saw him. 105

GOB. Lord, how art thou changed! How dost thou and thy master agree? I have brought him a present. How 'gree you now?

LAUN. Well, well, but, for mine own part, as I have set up my rest° to run away, so I will not 110 rest till I have run some ground. My master's a very Jew. Give him a present! Give him a halter. I am famished in his service, you may tell every finger I have with my ribs. Father, I am glad you are come. Give me your present to one Master Bassanio, 115 who indeed gives rare new liveries. If I serve not him, I will run as far as God has any ground. Oh, rare fortune! Here comes the man. To him, Father, for I am a Jew if I serve the Jew any longer. 120

[*Enter* BASSANIO, *with* LEONARDO *and other followers.*]

BASS. You may do so, but let it be so hasted that supper be ready at the farthest by five of the clock. See these letters delivered, put the liveries to making, and desire Gratiano to come anon° to my lodging.

[*Exit a* SERVANT.]

LAUN. To him, Father.

GOB. God bless your Worship!

BASS. Gramercy!° Wouldst thou aught with me?

GOB. Here's my son, sir, a poor boy —— 129

---

27. saving . . . reverence: with apologies for the remark, used like "God save the mark"; see l. 23 above. 28. incarnal: for "incarnate." Launcelot loves big words, which he often gets wrong. 37. sand-blind: nearsighted; but as Old Gobbo is nearly blind, Launcelot infers that he has gravel, not sand, in his eyes. 39. confusions: for "conclusions." 43. marry: Mary, by the Virgin. 47. By . . . sonties: by God's saints. 52. Master Launcelot: *Master* was the proper title for a gentleman. Launcelot to fool his father pretends that he has gone up in the world. 54. exceeding: exceedingly. 55. well to live: who lives a good life; i.e., "poor but honest." 58. and Launcelot: i.e., plain Launcelot, not Master Launcelot. 59. ergo: therefore. 66. Sisters Three: the three Sisters of Destiny. Launcelot has picked up some literary jargon from his betters. 71. hovel post: post supporting a hovel.

101. fill horse: cart horse. 110. set . . . rest: determined to stake all; a metaphor from the card game of primero. See *R & J*, V.iii.110. 124. anon: at once. 128. Gramercy: God have mercy, a form of thanks.

LAUN. Not a poor boy, sir, but the rich Jew's man, that would, sir — as my father shall specify ——

GOB. He hath a great infection,° sir, as one would say, to serve ——   134

LAUN. Indeed, the short and the long is, I serve the Jew, and have a desire — as my father shall specify ——

GOB. His master and he, saving your Worship's reverence, are scarce cater-cousins° —— 139

LAUN. To be brief, the very truth is that the Jew, having done me wrong, doth cause me — as my father, being, I hope, an old man, shall frutify° unto you ——

GOB. I have here a dish of doves that I would bestow upon your Worship, and my suit is — 145

LAUN. In very brief, the suit is impertinent° to myself, as your Worship shall know by this honest old man, and though I say it, though old man, yet poor man, my father.

BASS. One speak for both. What would you? 150

LAUN. Serve you, sir.

GOB. That is the very defect° of the matter, sir.

BASS. I know thee well, thou hast obtained thy suit. Shylock thy master spoke with me this day, And hath preferred° thee, if it be preferment 155 To leave a rich Jew's service to become The follower of so poor a gentleman.

LAUN. The old proverb is very well parted° between my master Shylock and you, sir. You have the grace of God, sir, and he hath enough.° 160

BASS. Thou speak'st it well. Go, Father, with thy son. Take leave of thy old master and inquire My lodging out. Give him a livery More guarded° than his fellows'. See it done. 164

LAUN. Father, in. I cannot get a service, no, I have ne'er a tongue in my head. Well, if any man in Italy have a fairer table° which doth offer to swear upon a book, I shall have good fortune. Go to, here's a simple line of life. Here's a small trifle of wives — alas, fifteen wives is nothing! A'leven widows 170 and nine maids is a simple coming-in for one man. And then to 'scape drowning thrice, and to be in peril of my life with the edge of a feather bed° — here are simple scapes. Well, if Fortune be a woman, she's a good wench for this gear.° Father, 175 come. I'll take my leave of the Jew in the twinkling of an eye. [*Exeunt* LAUNCELOT *and* OLD GOBBO.]

BASS. I pray thee, good Leonardo, think on this.

These things being bought and orderly bestowed, Return in haste, for I do feast tonight 180 My best-esteemed acquaintance. Hie° thee, go.

LEON. My best endeavors shall be done herein.

[*Enter* GRATIANO.]

GRA. Where is your master?

LEON.   Yonder, sir, he walks. [*Exit.*]

GRA. Signior Bassanio ——

BASS. Gratiano!   185

GRA. I have a suit to you.

BASS.   You have obtained it.

GRA. You must not deny me. I must go with you to Belmont.

BASS. Why, then you must. But hear thee, Gratiano.

Thou art too wild, too rude, and bold of voice — Parts that become thee happily enough, 191 And in such eyes as ours appear not faults, But where thou art not known, why, there they show Something too liberal.° Pray thee, take pain To allay° with some cold drops of modesty 195 Thy skipping spirit, lest through thy wild behavior I be misconstrued° in the place I go to, And lose my hopes.

GRA.   Signior Bassanio, hear me. If I do not put on a sober habit, 199 Talk with respect,° and swear but now and then, Wear prayer books in my pocket, look demurely — Nay more, while grace is saying, hood mine eyes Thus with my hat, and sigh, and say "Amen" — Use all the observance of civility,° Like one well studied in a sad ostent° 205 To please his grandam, never trust me more.

BASS. Well, we shall see your bearing.

GRA. Nay, but I bar tonight. You shall not gauge° me By what we do tonight.

BASS.   No, that were pity. I would entreat you rather to put on 210 Your boldest suit of mirth, for we have friends That purpose merriment. But fare you well. I have some business.

GRA. And I must to Lorenzo and the rest, 214 But we will visit you at suppertime. [*Exeunt.*]

SCENE III. *The same. A room in* SHYLOCK'S *house.*

[*Enter* JESSICA *and* LAUNCELOT GOBBO.]

JES. I am sorry thou wilt leave my father so. Our house is hell, and thou, a merry devil, Didst rob it of some taste of tediousness.

---

133. infection: for "affection." 139. cater-cousins: good friends. 142. frutify: for "certify." 146. impertinent: for "pertinent." 152. defect: for "effect." 155. preferred: promoted, recommended. 158. parted: divided. 159-60. You . . . enough: the old proverb is "He that hath the grace of God hath enough." 164. guarded: ornamented with strips of braid. See Pl. 9n and comment on p. 94b. 167. table: palm of the hand. Here Launcelot indulges in some palmistry on his own hand. 173. with . . . bed: i.e., smothering. 175. gear: sort of thing. See I.i.110,n.

181. Hie: hasten. 194. liberal: free. 195. allay: dilute. 197. misconstrued: misinterpreted. 200. respect: respectability. 204. observance of civility: polite behavior. 205. sad ostent: solemn face. 208. gauge: measure.

But fare thee well. There is a ducat for thee.
And, Launcelot, soon at supper shalt thou see 5
Lorenzo, who is thy new master's guest.
Give him this letter, do it secretly,
And so farewell. I would not have my father
See me in talk with thee. 9

LAUN. Adieu! Tears exhibit° my tongue. Most
beautiful pagan, most sweet Jew! If a Christian did
not play the knave and get° thee, I am much de-
ceived. But, adieu. These foolish drops do something
drown my manly spirit. Adieu.

JES. Farewell, good Launcelot. 15

[_Exit_ LAUNCELOT GOBBO.]

Alack, what heinous sin is it in me
To be ashamed to be my father's child!
But though I am a daughter to his blood,
I am not to his manners. O Lorenzo,
If thou keep promise, I shall end this strife, 20
Become a Christian, and thy loving wife. [_Exit._]

SCENE IV. _The same. A street._

[_Enter_ GRATIANO, LORENZO, SALARINO, _and_ SALANIO.]

LOR. Nay, we will slink away in suppertime,
Disguise° us at my lodging, and return
All in an hour.

GRA. We have not made good preparation. 4

SALAR. We have not spoke us° yet of torchbearers.

SALAN. 'Tis vile unless it may be quaintly° or-
dered,
And better in my mind not undertook.

LOR. 'Tis now but four o'clock. We have two
hours
To furnish us.

[_Enter_ LAUNCELOT GOBBO, _with a letter._] Friend
Launcelot, what's the news?

LAUN. An it shall please you to break up° this, it
shall seem to signify. 11

LOR. I know the hand — in faith, 'tis a fair hand,
And whiter than the paper it writ on
Is the fair hand that writ.

GRA. Love news, in faith.

LAUN. By your leave, sir. 15

LOR. Whither goest thou?

LAUN. Marry, sir, to bid my old master the Jew to
sup tonight with my new master the Christian.

LOR. Hold here, take this. Tell gentle Jessica 20
I will not fail her — speak it privately.
Go, gentlemen, [_Exit_ LAUNCELOT GOBBO.]
Will you prepare you for this masque° tonight?
I am provided of a torchbearer. 24

SALAR. Aye, marry, I'll be gone about it straight.
SALAN. And so will I.

LOR. Meet me and Gratiano
At Gratiano's lodging some hour hence.

SALAR. 'Tis good we do so.

[_Exeunt_ SALARINO _and_ SALANIO.]

GRA. Was not that letter from fair Jessica?

LOR. I must needs tell thee all. She hath directed
How I shall take her from her father's house, 31
What gold and jewels she is furnished with,
What page's suit she hath in readiness.
If e'er the Jew her father come to Heaven,
It will be for his gentle daughter's sake. 35
And never dare misfortune cross her foot
Unless she do it under this excuse,
That she is issue to a faithless Jew.°
Come, go with me. Peruse this as thou goest. 39
Fair Jessica shall be my torchbearer. [_Exeunt._]

SCENE V. _The same. Before_ SHYLOCK's _house._

[_Enter_ SHYLOCK _and_ LAUNCELOT GOBBO.]

SHY. Well, thou shalt see, thy eyes shall be thy
judge,
The difference of old Shylock and Bassanio. —
What, Jessica! — Thou shalt not gormandize,
As thou hast done with me. — What, Jessica! —
And sleep and snore, and rend apparel out. — 5
Why, Jessica, I say!

LAUN. Why, Jessica!

SHY. Who bids thee call? I do not bid thee call.

LAUN. Your Worship was wont to tell me that I
could do nothing without bidding.

[_Enter_ JESSICA.]

JES. Call you? What is your will? 10

SHY. I am bid forth to supper, Jessica.
There are my keys. But wherefore should I go?
I am not bid for love, they flatter me.
But yet I'll go in hate, to feed upon
The prodigal Christian. Jessica, my girl, 15
Look to my house. I am right loath to go.
There is some ill abrewing toward my rest,
For I did dream of moneybags tonight.

LAUN. I beseech you, sir, go. My young master
doth expect your reproach.° 20

SHY. So do I his.

LAUN. And they have conspired together, I will
not say you shall see a masque; but if you do, then
it was not for nothing that my nose fell ableeding on
Black Monday° last at six o'clock i' the morn- 25

Sc. iii: 10. exhibit: for "inhibit" (forbid). See _M Ado_, IV.ii.5.
12. get: beget; i.e., Your true father must have been a Christian.
Sc. iv: Cf. this scene with _R & J_, I.iv. 2. Disguise:
put on masks. 5. spoke us: bespoke (ordered) for ourselves.
6. quaintly: elegantly. 11. break up: open by breaking the seal.
See App. 6. 23. masque: entertainment, at which the guests
wore masks.

36–38. And . . . Jew: the only excuse that Fortune could have for
harming her is that she is a Jew's daughter; i.e., in everything
else she is perfect. issue: child.
Sc. v: 20. reproach: for "approach." 25. Black Monday:
Easter Monday, so called because on Easter Monday 1360, when
Edward III was besieging Paris, it was so cold that many men
died on horseback.

ing, falling out that year on Ash Wednesday was
four year, in the afternoon.°

SHY. What, are there masques? Hear you me,
 Jessica.
Lock up my doors, and when you hear the drum
And the vile squealing of the wry-necked° fife,   30
Clamber not you up to the casements° then,
Nor thrust your head into the public street
To gaze on Christian fools with varnished° faces,
But stop my house's ears, I mean my casements.
Let not the sound of shallow foppery enter   35
My sober house. By Jacob's staff, I swear
I have no mind of feasting forth tonight,
But I will go. Go you before me, sirrah.
Say I will come.
 LAUN. I will go before, sir. Mistress, look out at
window, for all this.   41
There will come a Christian by
Will be worth a Jewess' eye.   [Exit.]
 SHY. What says that fool of Hagar's offspring,°
 ha?
 JES. His words were, "Farewell, mistress," noth-
ing else.   45
 SHY. The patch° is kind enough, but a huge
 feeder,
Snail-slow in profit, and he sleeps by day
More than the wildcat. Drones hive not with me,
Therefore I part with him, and part with him
To one that I would have him help to waste   50
His borrowed purse. Well, Jessica, go in.
Perhaps I will return immediately.
Do as I bid you, shut doors after you.
Fast bind, fast find,   54
A proverb never stale in thrifty mind.   [Exit.]
 JES. Farewell, and if my fortune be not crost,
I have a father, you a daughter, lost.   [Exit.]

SCENE VI. *The same.*

[*Enter* GRATIANO *and* SALARINO, *masked.*]
 GRA. This is the penthouse° under which Lorenzo
Desired us to make stand.
 SALAR.   His hour is almost past.
 GRA. And it is marvel he outdwells his hour,
For lovers ever run before the clock.
 SALAR. Oh, ten times faster Venus' pigeons fly   5
To seal love's bonds new-made than they are wont
To keep obligèd faith unforfeited!°

26–27. falling . . . afternoon: Launcelot is talking deliberate
nonsense, for Ash Wednesday is the first day of Lent. 30. wry-
necked: making the player twist his neck. 31. casements:
windows that open on hinges. 33. varnished: wearing painted
masks. 44. Hagar's offspring: Ishmaelite; i.e., vagabond. See
Genesis 15. 46. patch: fool.
 Sc. vi: 1. penthouse: projecting eaves. 5–7. Oh . . . unfor-
feited: i.e., a lover runs far quicker to win a new love than to
keep faith with an old. pigeons: doves which draw the chariot
of Venus, the goddess of love. obliged: already pledged.

 GRA. That ever holds. Who riseth from a feast
With that keen appetite that he sits down?
Where is the horse that doth untread° again   10
His tedious measures° with the unbated fire
That he did pace them first? All things that are,
Are with more spirit chasèd than enjoyed.
How like a younker° or a prodigal
The scarfèd° bark puts from her native bay,   15
Hugged and embracèd by the strumpet wind!
How like the prodigal doth she return,
With overweathered ribs and ragged sails,
Lean, rent, and beggared by the strumpet wind!
 SALAR. Here comes Lorenzo. More of this here-
 after.   20

[*Enter* LORENZO.]
 LOR. Sweet friends, your patience for my long
 abode.
Not I, but my affairs, have made you wait.
When you shall please to play the thieves for wives,
I'll watch as long for you then. Approach,
Here dwells my father Jew. Ho! Who's within?   25
[*Enter* JESSICA, *above, in boy's clothes.*]
 JES. Who are you? Tell me, for more certainty,
Albeit° I'll swear that I do know your tongue.
 LOR. Lorenzo, and thy love.
 JES. Lorenzo certain, and my love indeed,
For who love I so much? And now who knows   30
But you, Lorenzo, whether I am yours?
 LOR. Heaven and thy thoughts are witness that
 thou art.
 JES. Here, catch this casket, it is worth the pains.
I am glad 'tis night, you do not look on me,
For I am much ashamed of my exchange.°   35
But love is blind, and lovers cannot see
The pretty follies that themselves commit,
For if they could, Cupid himself would blush
To see me thus transformèd to a boy.   39
 LOR. Descend, for you must be my torchbearer.
 JES. What, must I hold a candle to my shames?
They in themselves, good sooth, are too too light.
Why, 'tis an office of discovery,° love,
And I should be obscured.
 LOR.   So are you, sweet,
Even in the lovely garnish° of a boy.   45
But come at once,
For the close night doth play the runaway,
And we are stayed° for at Bassanio's feast.   48
 JES. I will make fast the doors, and gild myself
With some more ducats, and be with you straight.
[*Exit above.*]
 GRA. Now, by my hood, a Gentile, and no Jew.
 LOR. Beshrew° me but I love her heartily,

10. untread: retrace. 11. measures: paces. 14. younker: gay
youth. 15. scarfed: decked out with flags. See Pl. 7b.
27. Albeit: although. 35. exchange: i.e., of boy's for girl's
clothes. 43. office of discovery: task which will reveal me.
45. garnish: ornament, dress. 48. stayed: waited. 52. Beshrew:
plague on.

For she is wise, if I can judge of her.
And fair she is, if that mine eyes be true.
And true she is, as she hath proved herself,   55
And therefore, like herself, wise, fair, and true,
Shall she be placèd in my constant soul.
[*Enter* JESSICA, *below.*] What, art thou come? On,
     gentlemen, away!
Our masquing mates by this time for us stay.
                    [*Exit with* JESSICA *and* SALARINO.]
                    [*Enter* ANTONIO.]
     ANT. Who's there?   60
     GRA. Signior Antonio!
     ANT. Fie, fie, Gratiano, where are all the rest?
'Tis nine o'clock. Our friends all stay for you.
No masque tonight. The wind is come about,
Bassanio presently° will go aboard.   65
I have sent twenty out to seek for you.
     GRA. I am glad on't. I desire no more delight
Than to be under sail and gone tonight.   [*Exeunt.*]

SCENE VII. *Belmont. A room in* PORTIA'S
                    house.

[*Flourish of cornets. Enter* PORTIA, *with the* PRINCE
     OF MOROCCO, *and their trains.*]
     POR. Go draw aside the curtains, and discover°
The several caskets to this noble Prince.
Now make your choice.
     MOR. The first, of gold, who this inscription bears,
"Who chooseth me shall gain what many men de-
     sire."   5
The second, silver, which this promise carries,
"Who chooseth me shall get as much as he de-
     serves."
This third, dull lead, with warning all as blunt,
"Who chooseth me must give and hazard all he
     hath."
How shall I know if I do choose the right?   10
     POR. The one of them contains my picture, Prince.
If you choose that, then I am yours withal.
     MOR. Some god direct my judgment! Let me see,
I will survey the inscriptions back again.
What says this leaden casket?   15
"Who chooseth me must give and hazard all he
     hath."
Must give — for what? For lead? Hazard for lead?
This casket threatens. Men that hazard all
Do it in hope of fair advantages.
A golden mind stoops not to shows of dross,°   20
I'll then nor give nor hazard aught for lead.
What says the silver with her virgin° hue?
"Who chooseth me shall get as much as he de-
     serves."

As much as he deserves! Pause there, Morocco,
And weigh thy value with an even hand.   25
If thou be'st rated by thy estimation,°
Thou dost deserve enough, and yet enough
May not extend so far as to the lady.
And yet to be afeard of my deserving
Were but a weak disabling of myself.   30
As much as I deserve! Why, that's the lady.
I do in birth deserve her, and in fortunes,
In graces and in qualities of breeding.
But more than these, in love I do deserve.
What if I strayed no further, but chose here?   35
Let's see once more this saying graved in gold:
"Who chooseth me shall gain what many men de-
     sire."
Why, that's the lady. All the world desires her.
From the four corners of the earth they come
To kiss this shrine, this mortal-breathing saint.   40
The Hyrcanian° deserts and the vasty wilds
Of wide Arabia are as throughfares° now
For princes to come view fair Portia.
The watery kingdom,° whose ambitious head
Spits in the face of heaven, is no bar   45
To stop the foreign spirits, but they come,
As o'er a brook, to see fair Portia.
One of these three contains her heavenly picture.
Is't like that lead contains her? 'Twere damnation
To think so base a thought. It were too gross   50
To rib her cerecloth° in the obscure grave.
Or shall I think in silver she's immured,°
Being ten times undervalued to tried gold?
Oh, sinful thought! Never so rich a gem
Was set in worse than gold. They have in England
A coin that bears the figure of an angel°   56
Stamped in gold, but that's insculped upon,
But here an angel in a golden bed
Lies all within. Deliver me the key.
Here do I choose, and thrive I as I may!   60
     POR. There, take it, Prince, and if my form lie
     there,
Then I am yours.   [*He unlocks the golden casket.*]
     MOR.   O Hell! What have we here?
A carrion Death,° within whose empty eye
There is a written scroll! I'll read the writing.
[*Reads.*] "All that glisters is not gold,   65
     Often have you heard this told.
     Many a man his life hath sold
     But my outside to behold.
     Gilded tombs do worms infold.
     Had you been as wise as bold,   70
     Young in limbs, in judgment old,

---

26. estimation: worth.   41. Hyrcanian: wild country south of
the Caspian Sea.   42. throughfares: thoroughfares.   44. watery
kingdom: ocean.   51. rib . . . cerecloth: enclose her shroud.
The *cerecloth* was a wax covering used in embalming the illus-
trious dead.   52. immured: walled in.   56. angel: gold coin
worth 10s. See Pl. 10c and App. 27.   63. Death: skull.
See Pl. 12f.

65. presently: immediately.

Sc. vii: 1. discover: reveal, disclose.   20. dross: scum thrown
off in smelting.   22. virgin: i.e., white.

Your answer had not been enscrolled.°
Fare you well. Your suit is cold."
Cold, indeed, and labor lost.
Then, farewell, heat, and welcome, frost!   75
Portia, adieu. I have too grieved a heart
To take a tedious leave. Thus losers part.

[*Exit with his train. Flourish of cornets.*]

POR. A gentle riddance. Draw the curtains, go.
Let all of his complexion choose me so.   [*Exeunt.*]

SCENE VIII. *Venice. A street.*

[*Enter* SALARINO *and* SALANIO.]

SALAR. Why, man, I saw Bassanio under sail.
With him is Gratiano gone along,
And in their ship I am sure Lorenzo is not.

SALAN. The villain Jew with outcries raised the
    Duke,
Who went with him to search Bassanio's ship.   5

SALAR. He came too late, the ship was under sail.
But there the Duke was given to understand
That in a gondola were seen together
Lorenzo and his amorous Jessica.
Besides, Antonio certified the Duke   10
They were not with Bassanio in his ship.

SALAN. I never heard a passion so confused,
So strange, outrageous, and so variable,
As the dog Jew did utter in the streets:
" My daughter! Oh, my ducats! Oh, my daughter!
Fled with a Christian! Oh, my Christian ducats!   16
Justice! The law! My ducats, and my daughter!
A sealed bag, two sealed bags of ducats,
Of double ducats, stolen from me by my daughter!
And jewels, two stones, two rich and precious stones,
Stolen by my daughter! Justice! Find the girl!   21
She hath the stones upon her, and the ducats! "

SALAR. Why, all the boys in Venice follow him
Crying his stones, his daughter, and his ducats.

SALAN. Let good Antonio look he keep his day,
Or he shall pay for this.

SALAR.   Marry, well remembered.   26
I reasoned° with a Frenchman yesterday
Who told me, in the narrow seas that part
The French and English, there miscarried
A vessel of our country richly fraught.°   30
I thought upon Antonio when he told me,
And wished in silence that it were not his.

SALAN. You were best to tell Antonio what you
    hear,
Yet do not suddenly, for it may grieve him.

SALAR. A kinder gentleman treads not the earth.
I saw Bassanio and Antonio part.   36
Bassanio told him he would make some speed
Of his return. He answered, " Do not so.

Slubber° not business for my sake, Bassanio,
But stay the very riping of the time.   40
And for the Jew's bond which he hath of me,
Let it not enter in your mind of love.
Be merry, and employ your chiefest thoughts
To courtship, and such fair ostents° of love
As shall conveniently become you there."   45
And even there, his eye being big with tears,
Turning his face, he put his hand behind him,
And with affection wondrous sensible°
He wrung Bassanio's hand, and so they parted.

SALAN. I think he only loves the world for him.
I pray thee, let us go and find him out   51
And quicken his embracèd heaviness
With some delight or other.

SALAR.   Do we so.   [*Exeunt.*]

SCENE IX. *Belmont. A room in* PORTIA'S *house.*

[*Enter* NERISSA *and a* SERVITOR.]

NER. Quick, quick, I pray thee. Draw the curtain
    straight.
The Prince of Aragon hath ta'en his oath,
And comes to his election° presently.

[*Flourish of cornets. Enter the* PRINCE OF ARAGON,
    PORTIA, *and their trains.*]

POR. Behold, there stand the caskets, noble Prince.
If you choose that wherein I am contained,   5
Straight shall our nuptial rites be solemnized.
But if you fail, without more speech, my lord,
You must be gone from hence immediately.

AR. I am enjoined by oath to observe three things.
First, never to unfold to anyone   10
Which casket 'twas I chose. Next, if I fail
Of the right casket, never in my life
To woo a maid in way of marriage.
Lastly,
If I do fail in fortune of my choice,   15
Immediately to leave you and be gone.

POR. To these injunctions everyone doth swear
That comes to hazard for my worthless self.

AR. And so have I addressed me.° Fortune now
To my heart's hope! Gold, silver, and base lead.   20
" Who chooseth me must give and hazard all he
    hath."
You shall look fairer ere I give or hazard.
What says the golden chest? Ha! Let me see:
" Who chooseth me shall gain what many men de-
    sire."
What many men desire! That " many " may be
    meant   25

---

72. enscrolled: inscribed, recorded.
Sc. viii: 27. reasoned: conversed. 30. fraught: laden.

39. Slubber: be slovenly with. 44. ostents: outward shows.
48. wondrous sensible: wonderfully full of feeling.
Sc. ix: 3. election: choice. 19. addressed me: prepared
myself.

By the fool multitude, that choose by show,
Not learning more than the fond° eye doth teach,
Which pries not to the interior but, like the martlet,°
Builds in the weather on the outward wall,
Even in the force and road of casualty.°   30
I will not choose what many men desire,
Because I will not jump° with common spirits
And rank me with the barbarous multitudes.
Why, then to thee, thou silver treasure house.
Tell me once more what title thou dost bear: 35
" Who chooseth me shall get as much as he de-
     serves."
And well said too, for who shall go about
To cozen° fortune, and be honorable
Without the stamp of merit?° Let none presume
To wear an undeservèd dignity.   40
Oh, that estates, degrees, and offices
Were not derived corruptly, and that clear honor
Were purchased by the merit of the wearer!
How many then should cover° that stand bare!
How many be commanded that command!   45
How much low peasantry would then be gleaned°
From the true seed of honor! And how much honor
Picked from the chaff and ruin of the times,
To be new-varnished!° Well, but to my choice.
" Who chooseth me shall get as much as he de-
     serves."   50
I will assume desert. Give me a key for this,
And instantly unlock my fortunes here.
              [He opens the silver casket.]
POR. *[Aside]* Too long a pause for that which you
     find there.
AR. What's here? The portrait of a blinking idiot,
Presenting me a schedule!° I will read it.   55
How much unlike art thou to Portia!
How much unlike my hopes and my deservings!
" Who chooseth me shall have as much as he de-
     serves."
Did I deserve no more than a fool's head?
Is that my prize? Are my deserts no better?   60
POR. To offend and judge are distinct offices,
And of opposèd natures.
AR.   What is here?
[Reads.] " The fire seven times trièd this.
     Seven times tried that judgment is
     That did never choose amiss.   65
     Some there be that shadows kiss.
     Such have but a shadow's bliss.
     There be fools alive, I wis,°
     Silvered o'er, and so was this.

Take what wife you will to bed,   70
     I will ever be your head.
     So be gone. You are sped."°
Still more fool I shall appear
By the time I linger here.
With one fool's head I came to woo,   75
But I go away with two.
Sweet, adieu. I'll keep my oath,
Patiently to bear my wroth.°
            [Exeunt ARAGON *and train.]*
POR. Thus hath the candle singed the moth.
Oh, these deliberate° fools! When they do choose,
They have the wisdom by their wit to lose.   81
NER. The ancient saying is no heresy,
Hanging and wiving goes by destiny.
POR. Come, draw the curtain, Nerissa.
              [Enter a SERVANT.*]*
SERV. Where is my lady?
POR.   Here. What would my lord?   85
SERV. Madam, there is alighted at your gate
A young Venetian, one that comes before
To signify the approaching of his lord,
From whom he bringeth sensible regreets,°
To wit, besides commends° and courteous breath,
Gifts of rich value. Yet I have not seen   91
So likely° an ambassador of love.
A day in April never came so sweet,
To show how costly summer was at hand,
As this forespurrer° comes before his lord.   95
POR. No more, I pray thee. I am half-afeard
Thou wilt say anon he is some kin to thee,
Thou spend'st such high-day wit° in praising him.
Come, come, Nerissa, for I long to see
Quick Cupid's post° that comes so mannerly.   100
NER. Bassanio, Lord Love, if thy will it be!
              [Exeunt.]

Act III

SCENE I. *Venice. A street.*

[Enter SALANIO *and* SALARINO.*]*
SALAN. Now, what news on the Rialto?
SALAR. Why, yet it lives there unchecked that An-
tonio hath a ship of rich lading wrecked on the nar-
row seas° — the Goodwins,° I think they call the
place, a very dangerous flat and fatal, where the car-
casses of many a tall ship lie buried, as they say,   5

---

27. fond: foolish.   28. martlet: martin, a bird of the swallow species.   30. casualty: mischance.   32. jump: agree.   38. cozen: cheat.   39. stamp of merit: seal certifying genuineness. 44. cover: wear their hats. See App. 7.   46. gleaned: plucked. 47–49. honor . . . new-varnished: how many men of noble family now ruined and living in poverty would be newly restored to their former glory. new-varnished: freshly painted. 55. schedule: writing.   68. I wis: assuredly.

72. sped: done for.   78. wroth: ruth, calamity.   80. deliberate: calculating.   89. sensible regreets: salutations full of feeling. 90. commends: salutations.   92. likely: handsome.   95. forespurrer: forerunner.   98. high-day wit: gay expressions. 100. post: messenger.
Act III, Sc. 1: 3. narrow seas: English Channel. Goodwins: Goodwin Sands, off the coast of Kent, a treacherous spot.

if my gossip Report be an honest woman of her word.

SALAN. I would she were as lying a gossip in that as ever knapped° ginger, or made her neighbors 10 believe she wept for the death of a third husband. But it is true, without any slips of prolixity,° or crossing the plain highway of talk,° that the good Antonio, the honest Antonio —— Oh, that I had a title good enough to keep his name company! — 16

SALAR. Come, the full stop.°

SALAN. Ha! What sayest thou? Why, the end is, he hath lost a ship.

SALAR. I would it might prove the end of his losses. 21

SALAN. Let me say "Amen" betimes, lest the Devil cross° my prayer, for here he comes in the likeness of a Jew. [*Enter* SHYLOCK.] How now, Shylock! What news among the merchants? 26

SHY. You knew, none so well, none so well as you, of my daughter's flight.

SALAR. That's certain. I, for my part, knew the tailor that made the wings she flew withal. 30

SALAN. And Shylock, for his own part, knew the bird was fledged,° and then it is the complexion° of them all to leave the dam.

SHY. She is damned for it.

SALAR. That's certain, if the Devil may be her judge. 36

SHY. My own flesh and blood to rebel!

SALAN. Out upon it, old carrion! Rebels it at these years?

SHY. I say, my daughter is my flesh and blood. 40

SALAR. There is more difference between thy flesh and hers than between jet and ivory, more between your bloods than there is between red wine and Rhenish.° But tell us, do you hear whether Antonio have had any loss at sea or no? 45

SHY. There I have another bad match° — a bankrupt, a prodigal, who dare scarce show his head on the Rialto, a beggar that was used to come so smug° upon the mart.° Let him look to his bond. He was wont to call me usurer — let him look to his 50 bond. He was wont to lend money for a Christian courtesy — let him look to his bond.

SALAR. Why, I am sure if he forfeit, thou wilt not take his flesh. What's that good for?

SHY. To bait fish withal. If it will feed noth- 55 ing else, it will feed my revenge. He hath disgraced me, and hindered° me half a million, laughed at my losses, mocked at my gains, scorned my nation, thwarted my bargains, cooled my friends, heated

mine enemies. And what's his reason? I am a 60 Jew. Hath not a Jew eyes? Hath not a Jew hands, organs, dimensions, senses, affections, passions? Fed with the same food, hurt with the same weapons, subject to the same diseases, healed by the same means, warmed and cooled by the same winter 65 and summer as a Christian is? If you prick us, do we not bleed? If you tickle us, do we not laugh? If you poison us, do we not die? And if you wrong us, shall we not revenge? If we are like you in the rest, we will resemble you in that. If a Jew wrong a 70 Christian, what is his humility?° Revenge. If a Christian wrong a Jew, what should his sufferance be by Christian example? Why, revenge. The villainy you teach me I will execute, and it shall go hard but° I will better the instruction. 76

[*Enter a* SERVANT.]

SERV. Gentlemen, my master Antonio is at his house, and desires to speak with you both.

SALAR. We have been up and down to seek him.

[*Enter* TUBAL.]

SALAN. Here comes another of the tribe. A 80 third cannot be matched, unless the Devil himself turn Jew.

[*Exeunt* SALANIO, SALARINO, *and* SERVANT.]

SHY. How now, Tubal! What news from Genoa? Hast thou found my daughter?

TUB. I often came where I did hear of her, but 85 cannot find her.

SHY. Why, there, there, there, there! A diamond gone, cost me two thousand ducats in Frankfort!° The curse never fell upon our nation till now, I never felt it till now. Two thousand ducats in 90 that, and other precious, precious jewels. I would my daughter were dead at my foot, and the jewels in her ear! Would she were hearsed° at my foot, and the ducats in her coffin! No news of them? Why, so. — And I know not what's spent in the search. 95 Why, thou loss upon loss! The thief gone with so much, and so much to find the thief, and no satisfaction, no revenge. Nor no ill luck stirring but what lights on my shoulders, no sighs but of my breathing, no tears but of my shedding. 101

TUB. Yes, other men have ill luck too. Antonio, as I heard in Genoa ——

SHY. What, what, what? Ill luck, ill luck?

TUB. Hath an argosy cast away, coming from Tripolis. 106

SHY. I thank God, I thank God! Is't true, is't true?

TUB. I spoke with some of the sailors that escaped the wreck. 110

SHY. I thank thee, good Tubal. Good news, good news! Ha, ha! Where? In Genoa?

---

10. knapped: chewed.   12. slips of prolixity: slipping into tedious talk.   12–13. crossing . . . talk: leaving plain speech.   17. full stop: i.e., cease this roundabout talk and come to the point.   23. cross: hinder.   32. fledged: ready to leave the nest.   complexion: nature.   43. Rhenish: Rhine (white wine).   46. match: bargain.   48. smug: neatly dressed.   49. mart: market place.   57. hindered: prevented me from making.

71. what . . . humility: in what way does he show Christian forbearance?   75–76. it . . . but: unless something prevents.   88. Frankfort: famous for its fairs, at which fine jewelry was sold.   93. hearsed: on her bier.

TUB. Your daughter spent in Genoa, as I heard, in one night fourscore ducats.

SHY. Thou stick'st a dagger in me. I shall 115 never see my gold again. Fourscore ducats at a sitting! Fourscore ducats!

TUB. There came divers° of Antonio's creditors in my company to Venice that swear he cannot choose but break.° 120

SHY. I am very glad of it. I'll plague him, I'll torture him. I am glad of it.

TUB. One of them showed me a ring that he had of your daughter for a monkey.

SHY. Out upon her! Thou torturest me, 125 Tubal. It was my turquoise, I had it of Leah when I was a bachelor. I would not have given it for a wilderness of monkeys.

TUB. But Antonio is certainly undone.

SHY. Nay, that's true, that's very true. Go, 130 Tubal, fee me° an officer.° Bespeak° him a fortnight before. I will have the heart of him if he forfeit, for were he out of Venice, I can make what merchandise° I will. Go, go, Tubal, and meet me at our synagogue. Go, good Tubal, at our synagogue, 135 Tubal. [*Exeunt.*]

SCENE II. *Belmont. A room in* PORTIA'S *house.*

[*Enter* BASSANIO, PORTIA, GRATIANO, NERISSA, *and* ATTENDANTS.]

POR. I pray you tarry. Pause a day or two
Before you hazard, for in choosing wrong
I lose your company. Therefore forbear awhile.
There's something tells me, but it is not love,
I would not lose you, and you know yourself, 5
Hate counsels not in such a quality.°
But lest you should not understand me well —
And yet a maiden hath no tongue but thought —
I would detain you here some month or two
Before you venture for me. I could teach you 10
How to choose right, but I am then forsworn.°
So will I never be. So may you miss me.
But if you do, you'll make me wish a sin —
That I had been forsworn. Beshrew your eyes,
They have o'erlooked° me, and divided me. 15
One half of me is yours, the other half yours,
Mine own, I would say, but if mine, then yours,
And so all yours! Oh, these naughty° times
Put bars between the owners and their rights!
And so, though yours, not yours. Prove it so, 20
Let fortune go to Hell for it, not I.

I speak too long, but 'tis to peize° the time,
To eke° it and to draw it out in length,
To stay you from election.
BASS.   Let me choose,
For as I am, I live upon the rack.° 25
POR. Upon the rack, Bassanio! Then confess
What treason° there is mingled with your love.
BASS. None but that ugly treason of mistrust
Which makes me fear the enjoying of my love.
There may as well be amity and life 30
'Tween snow and fire as treason and my love.
POR. Aye, but I fear you speak upon the rack,
Where men enforcèd do speak anything.
BASS. Promise me life, and I'll confess the truth.
POR. Well, then, confess and live.
BASS.   "Confess" and "love" 35
Had been the very sum of my confession.
Oh, happy torment when my torturer
Doth teach me answers for deliverance!
But let me to my fortune and the caskets.
POR. Away, then! I am locked in one of them. 40
If you do love me, you will find me out.
Nerissa and the rest, stand all aloof.
Let music sound while he doth make his choice,
Then, if he lose, he makes a swanlike end,°
Fading in music. That the comparison 45
May stand more proper, my eye shall be the stream
And watery deathbed for him. He may win,
And what is music then? Then music is
Even as the flourish° when true subjects bow
To a new-crowned monarch. Such it is 50
As are those dulcet sounds in break of day
That creep into the dreaming bridegroom's ear
And summon him to marriage. Now he goes,
With no less presence, but with much more love,
Than young Alcides° when he did redeem 55
The virgin tribute paid by howling Troy
To the sea monster. I stand for sacrifice.
The rest aloof are the Dardanian° wives,
With bleared visages,° come forth to view
The issue° of the exploit. Go, Hercules! 60
Live thou, I live. With much much more dismay
I view the fight than thou that makest the fray.
[*A song, whilst* BASSANIO *comments on the caskets to himself.*]
          "Tell me where is fancy° bred,
             Or in the heart or in the head?
                How begot, how nourishèd? 65
                   Reply, reply.
                It is engendered in the eyes,

---

118. divers: various. 120. break: go bankrupt. 131. fee me: hire. officer: sergeant of the law, who made arrests for debt. See *II Hen IV*, II.i for the officer at work. Bespeak: order, reserve. 133. merchandise: trade.

  Sc. ii: 6. quality: manner. 11. forsworn: perjured. 15. o'erlooked: bewitched. 18. naughty: wicked.

22. peize: retard. 23. eke: increase. 25. rack: in torment. See App. 10. 27. treason: Portia continues the image, for the rack was used only to extract confessions of treason. 44. swanlike end: Swans were supposed to sing once only, just before death. 49. flourish: fanfare of trumpets. 55. Alcides: Hercules, who rescued the daughter of the Trojan King from being sacrificed to a sea monster. 58. Dardanian: Trojan. 59. bleared visages: tear-stained faces. 60. issue: result. 63. fancy: love.

With gazing fed, and fancy dies
In the cradle where it lies.
     Let us all ring fancy's knell.   70
     I'll begin it. — Ding, dong, bell."
   ALL. "Ding, dong, bell."

BASS. So may the outward shows be least them-
selves.
The world is still° deceived with ornament.
In law, what plea so tainted and corrupt   75
But, being seasoned° with a gracious voice,
Obscures the show of evil? In religion,
What damnèd error but some sober brow
Will bless it, and approve° it with a text,
Hiding the grossness with fair ornament?   80
There is no vice so simple° but assumes
Some mark of virtue on his outward parts.
How many cowards whose hearts are all as false
As stairs of sand wear yet upon their chins
The beards of Hercules and frowning Mars,   85
Who, inward searched, have livers° white as milk.
And these assume but valor's excrement°
To render them redoubted!° Look on beauty
And you shall see 'tis purchased by the weight,
Which therein works a miracle in nature,   90
Making them lightest that wear most of it.
So are those crispèd snaky golden locks
Which make such wanton gambols with the wind
Upon supposèd fairness, often known
To be the dowry of a second head,   95
The skull that bred them in the sepulcher.°
Thus ornament is but the guilèd° shore
To a most dangerous sea, the beauteous scarf
Veiling an Indian° beauty — in a word,
The seeming truth which cunning times put on   100
To entrap the wisest. Therefore, thou gaudy gold,
Hard food for Midas,° I will none of thee.
Nor none of thee, thou pale and common drudge°
'Tween man and man. But thou, thou meager lead,
Which rather threatenest than dost promise aught,
Thy paleness moves me more than eloquence,   106
And here choose I. Joy be the consequence!

POR. [*Aside*] How all the other passions fleet to
air,
As doubtful thoughts, and rash-embraced despair,
And shuddering fear, and green-eyed jealousy!   110

O love, be moderate, allay thy ecstasy,
In measure rain thy joy, scant° this excess!
I feel too much thy blessing. Make it less,
For fear I surfeit!°

BASS.   What find I here?   115
[*Opening the leaden casket.*]
Fair Portia's counterfeit!° What demigod
Hath come so near creation? Move these eyes?
Or whether, riding on the balls of mine,
Seem they in motion? Here are severed lips,
Parted with sugar breath. So sweet a bar°   120
Should sunder such sweet friends. Here in her hairs
The painter plays the spider, and hath woven
A golden mesh to entrap the hearts of men
Faster than gnats in cobwebs. But her eyes —
How could he see to do them? Having made one,
Methinks it should have power to steal both his   126
And leave itself unfurnished.° Yet look how far
The substance of my praise doth wrong this shadow
In underprizing° it, so far this shadow
Doth limp behind the substance. Here's the scroll,
The continent° and summary of my fortune.   131
[*Reads.*] "You that choose not by the view,
     Chance as fair, and choose as true!
     Since this fortune falls to you,
     Be content and seek no new.   135
     If you be well pleased with this,
     And hold your fortune for your bliss,
     Turn you where your lady is
     And claim her with a loving kiss."
A gentle scroll. Fair lady, by your leave,   140
I come by note,° to give and to receive.
Like one of two contending in a prize
That thinks he hath done well in people's eyes,
Hearing applause and universal shout,
Giddy in spirit, still gazing in a doubt   145
Whether those peals of praise be his or no.
So, thrice-fair lady, stand I, even so,
As doubtful whether what I see be true,
Until confirmed, signed, ratified by you.

POR. You see me, Lord Bassanio, where I stand,
Such as I am. Though for myself alone   151
I would not be ambitious in my wish,
To wish myself much better; yet for you
I would be trebled twenty times myself —
A thousand times more fair, ten thousand times
More rich —   156
That only to stand high in your account,°
I might in virtues, beauties, livings,° friends,
Exceed account. But the full sum of me
Is sum of something which, to term in gross,   160
Is an unlessoned girl, unschooled, unpracticed,

---

74. still: always.   **75–76. tainted . . . seasoned:** as bad food is concealed by a strong sauce.   **79. approve:** prove.   **81. simple:** unmixed (with good).   **86. livers:** the liver was the seat of passion and emotion, and especially of courage; a coward's liver was therefore white and bloodless.   **87. excrement:** that which grows out of a man, such as hair or nails. Here *valor's excrement* is a fine manly beard.   **88. redoubted:** redoubtable, formidable.   **92–96. crisped . . . sepulcher:** i.e., curly golden hair is often borrowed, its true owner being a corpse.   **97. guiled:** beguiling.   **99. Indian:** dark, which was not considered beautiful. See Sonnet 127.   **102. Midas:** Midas, King of Phrygia, was granted his hasty wish that everything which he touched might be turned into gold. He forgot to except food.   **103. common drudge:** i.e., silver, because used for common trade.

112. scant: make less.   **115. surfeit:** sicken from excess.   **116. counterfeit:** portrait.   **120. So . . . bar:** i.e., sweet breath should naturally come between upper and lower lip.   **127. unfurnished:** without a companion.   **129. underprizing:** undervaluing.   **131. continent:** that which contains.   **141. by note:** as instructed.   **157. account:** estimation.   **158. livings:** possessions.

Happy in this, she is not yet so old
But she may learn. Happier than this,
She is not bred so dull but she can learn.
Happiest of all is that her gentle spirit   165
Commits itself to yours to be directed,
As from her lord, her governor, her king.
Myself and what is mine to you and yours
Is now converted.° But now I was the lord
Of this fair mansion, master of my servants,   170
Queen o'er myself. And even now, but now,
This house, these servants, and this same myself
Are yours, my lord. I give them with this ring,
Which when you part from, lose, or give away,
Let it presage the ruin of your love,   175
And be my vantage° to exclaim on° you.
    BASS. Madam, you have bereft me of all words.
Only my blood speaks to you in my veins,
And there is such confusion in my powers
As after some oration fairly spoke   180
By a belovèd prince, there doth appear
Among the buzzing pleasèd multitude,
Where every something, being blent together,
Turns to a wild of nothing, save of joy,   184
Expressed and not expressed. But when this ring
Parts from this finger, then parts life from hence.
Oh, then be bold to say Bassanio's dead!
    NER. My lord and lady, it is now our time
That have stood by and seen our wishes prosper
To cry, good joy. Good joy, my lord and lady!   190
    GRA. My Lord Bassanio and my gentle lady,
I wish you all the joy that you can wish,
For I am sure you can wish none from me.
And when your Honors mean to solemnize
The bargain of your faith, I do beseech you,   195
Even at that time I may be married too.
    BASS. With all my heart, so thou canst get a wife.
    GRA. I thank your lordship, you have got me
one.
My eyes, my lord, can look as swift as yours.
You saw the mistress, I beheld the maid,   200
You loved, I loved for intermission.°
No more pertains to me, my lord, than you.
Your fortune stood upon the casket there,
And so did mine too, as the matter falls;
For wooing here until I sweat again,   205
And swearing till my very roof° was dry
With oaths of love, at last, if promise last,
I got a promise of this fair one here
To have her love provided that your fortune
Achieved° her mistress.   210
    POR.   Is this true, Nerissa?
    NER. Madam, it is, so you stand pleased withal.
    BASS. And do you, Gratiano, mean good faith?
    GRA. Yes, faith, my lord.

    BASS. Our feast shall be much honored in your
marriage.   215
    GRA. We'll play with them the first boy for a thou-
sand ducats.
    NER. What, and stake down?°
    GRA. No. We shall ne'er win at that sport, and
stake down.   220
But who comes here? Lorenzo and his infidel?
What, and my old Venetian friend Salerio?
    [*Enter* LORENZO, JESSICA, *and* SALERIO, *a messenger
from Venice.*]
    BASS. Lorenzo and Salerio, welcome hither,
If that the youth of my new interest° here
Have power to bid you welcome. By your leave,
I bid my very friends and countrymen,   226
Sweet Portia, welcome.
    POR.   So do I, my lord.
They are entirely welcome.
    LOR. I thank your Honor. For my part, my lord,
My purpose was not to have seen you here,   230
But meeting with Salerio by the way,
He did entreat me, past all saying nay,
To come with him along.
    SALER.   I did, my lord,
And I have reason for it. Signior Antonio
Commends him to you.   [*Gives* BASSANIO *a letter.*]
    BASS.   Ere I ope his letter,   235
I pray you tell me how my good friend doth.
    SALER. Not sick, my lord, unless it be in mind,
Nor well, unless in mind. His letter there
Will show you his estate.
    GRA. Nerissa, cheer yon stranger, bid her wel-
come.   240
Your hand, Salerio. What's the news from Venice?
How doth that royal merchant, good Antonio?
I know he will be glad of our success.
We are the Jasons,° we have won the fleece.
    SALER. I would you had won the fleece that he hath
lost.   245
    POR. There are some shrewd° contents in yon
same paper
That steals the color from Bassanio's cheek.
Some dear friend dead, else nothing in the world
Could turn so much the constitution
Of any constant° man. What, worse and worse!   250
With leave, Bassanio, I am half yourself,
And I must freely have the half of anything
That this same paper brings you.
    BASS.   O sweet Portia,
Here are a few of the unpleasant'st words
That ever blotted paper! Gentle lady,   255
When I did first impart my love to you,
I freely told you all the wealth I had
Ran in my veins, I was a gentleman,

---

169. converted: transferred. 176. vantage: opportunity. exclaim
on: reproach. 201. intermission: to fill in the time. 206. roof:
i.e., of the mouth. 210. Achieved: won.

219. stake down: spot cash. 224. youth . . . interest: i.e., if
one so new to this house. 244. We . . . Jasons: See I.i.171,n
246. shrewd: bitter. 250. constant: well-balanced.

And then I told you true. And yet, dear lady,
Rating myself at nothing, you shall see   260
How much I was a braggart. When I told you
My state was nothing, I should then have told you
That I was worse than nothing; for, indeed,
I have engaged° myself to a dear friend,
Engaged my friend to his mere° enemy,   265
To feed my means. Here is a letter, lady,
The paper as the body of my friend
And every word in it a gaping wound,
Issuing lifeblood. But is it true, Salerio?
Have all his ventures failed? What, not one hit?
From Tripolis, from Mexico, and England,   271
From Lisbon, Barbary, and India?
And not one vessel scape the dreadful touch
Of merchant-marring rocks?
    SALER.   Not one, my lord.
Besides, it should appear that if he had   275
The present money to discharge the Jew,
He would not take it. Never did I know
A creature that did bear the shape of man
So keen and greedy to confound a man.
He plies the Duke at morning and at night,   280
And doth impeach° the freedom of the state
If they deny him justice. Twenty merchants,
The Duke himself, and the magnificoes°
Of greatest port° have all persuaded with him,
But none can drive him from the envious° plea   285
Of forfeiture, of justice, and his bond.
    JES. When I was with him I have heard him swear
To Tubal and to Chus, his countrymen,
That he would rather have Antonio's flesh
Than twenty times the value of the sum   290
That he did owe him. And I know, my lord,
If law, authority, and power deny not,
It will go hard with poor Antonio.
    POR. Is it your dear friend that is thus in trouble?
    BASS. The dearest friend to me, the kindest man,
The best-conditioned and unwearied spirit   296
In doing courtesies, and one in whom
The ancient Roman honor more appears
Than any that draws breath in Italy.
    POR. What sum owes he the Jew?   300
    BASS. For me, three thousand ducats.
    POR.   What, no more?
Pay him six thousand, and deface° the bond —
Double six thousand, and then treble that,
Before a friend of this description
Shall lose a hair through Bassanio's fault.   305
First go with me to church and call me wife,
And then away to Venice to your friend,
For never shall you lie by Portia's side
With an unquiet soul. You shall have gold
To pay the petty debt twenty times over.   310

When it is paid, bring your true friend along.
My maid Nerissa and myself meantime
Will live as maids and widows. Come, away!
For you shall hence upon your wedding day.
Bid your friends welcome, show a merry cheer.°
Since you are dear-bought, I will love you dear.   316
But let me hear the letter of your friend.
    BASS. [*Reads.*] " Sweet Bassanio, my ships have all
miscarried, my creditors grow cruel, my estate is very
low, my bond to the Jew is forfeit. And since in pay-
ing it it is impossible I should live, all debts are   321
cleared between you and I, if I might but see you at
my death. Notwithstanding, use your pleasure. If
your love do not persuade you to come, let not my
letter."   325
    POR. O love, dispatch all business, and be gone!
    BASS. Since I have your good leave to go away,
I will make haste. But till I come again
No bed shall e'er be guilty of my stay,   329
No rest be interposer 'twixt us twain. [*Exeunt.*]

SCENE III. *Venice. A street.*

[*Enter* SHYLOCK, SALARINO, ANTONIO, *and* JAILER.]
    SHY. Jailer, look to him. Tell not me of mercy.
This is the fool that lent out money gratis.
Jailer, look to him.
    ANT.   Hear me yet, good Shylock.
    SHY. I'll have my bond, speak not against my bond.
I have sworn an oath that I will have my bond.   5
Thou call'dst me dog before thou hadst a cause,
But since I am a dog, beware my fangs.
The Duke shall grant me justice. I do wonder,
Thou naughty jailer, that thou art so fond°
To come abroad with him at his request.   10
    ANT. I pray thee, hear me speak.
    SHY. I'll have my bond, I will not hear thee speak.
I'll have my bond, and therefore speak no more.
I'll not be made a soft and dull-eyed fool,
To shake the head, relent, and sigh, and yield   15
To Christian intercessors. Follow not,
I'll have no speaking. I will have my bond. [*Exit.*]
    SALAR. It is the most impenetrable cur
That ever kept° with men.
    ANT.   Let him alone.
I'll follow him no more with bootless° prayers.   20
He seeks my life — his reason well I know.
I oft delivered from his forfeitures
Many that have at times made moan to me,
Therefore he hates me.
    SALAR.   I am sure the Duke
Will never grant this forfeiture to hold.   25
    ANT. The Duke cannot deny the course of law.

---

264. engaged: pledged. 265. mere: sheer, entire. 281. impeach:
accuse. 283. magnificoes: chief men of Venice. 284. port: dig-
nity. 285. envious: spiteful. 302. deface: cancel.

315. merry cheer: cheerful face.
Sc. iii: 9. fond: foolish. 19. kept: lived. 20. bootless: vain

For the commodity° that strangers have
With us in Venice, if it be denied,
Will much impeach the justice of his state,
Since that the trade and profit of the city   30
Consisteth of all nations. Therefore go.
These griefs and losses have so bated° me
That I shall hardly spare a pound of flesh
Tomorrow to my bloody creditor.
Well, jailer, on. Pray God Bassanio come   35
To see me pay his debt, and then I care not!

[*Exeunt.*]

SCENE IV. *Belmont. A room in* PORTIA'S
house.

[*Enter* PORTIA, NERISSA, LORENZO, JESSICA, *and*
BALTHASAR.]

LOR. Madam, although I speak it in your presence,
You have a noble and a true conceit
Of godlike amity,° which appears most strongly
In bearing thus the absence of your lord.
But if you knew to whom you show this honor,   5
How true a gentleman you send relief,
How dear a lover of my lord your husband,
I know you would be prouder of the work
Than customary bounty° can enforce you.
POR. I never did repent for doing good,   10
Nor shall not now. For in companions
That do converse and waste the time together,
Whose souls do bear an equal yoke of love,
There must be needs a like proportion
Of lineaments, of manners, and of spirit.   15
Which makes me think that this Antonio,
Being the bosom lover of my lord,
Must needs be like my lord. If it be so,
How little is the cost I have bestowed
In purchasing the semblance° of my soul°   20
From out the state of hellish misery!
This comes too near the praising of myself,
Therefore no more of it. Hear other things.
Lorenzo, I commit into your hands
The husbandry° and manage of my house   25
Until my lord's return. For mine own part,
I have toward Heaven breathed a secret vow
To live in prayer and contemplation,
Only attended by Nerissa here,
Until her husband and my lord's return.   30
There is a monastery two miles off,
And there will we abide. I do desire you
Not to deny this imposition,°
The which my love and some necessity

Now lays upon you.
LOR.   Madam, with all my heart.   35
I shall obey you in all fair commands.
POR. My people do already know my mind,
And will acknowledge you and Jessica
In place of Lord Bassanio and myself.
And so farewell till we shall meet again.   40
LOR. Fair thoughts and happy hours attend on
you!
JES. I wish your ladyship all heart's content.
POR. I thank you for your wish, and am well
pleased
To wish it back on you. Fare you well, Jessica.

[*Exeunt* JESSICA *and* LORENZO.]

Now, Balthasar,   45
As I have ever found thee honest-true,
So let me find thee still. Take this same letter,
And use thou all the endeavor of a man
In speed to Padua. See thou render this
Into my cousin's hand, Doctor Bellario.   50
And look, what notes and garments he doth give
thee
Bring them, I pray thee, with imagined speed°
Unto the tranect,° to the common ferry
Which trades to Venice. Waste no time in words,
But get thee gone. I shall be there before thee.   55
BALTH. Madam, I go with all convenient speed.

[*Exit.*]

POR. Come on, Nerissa, I have work in hand
That you yet know not of. We'll see our husbands
Before they think of us.
NER.   Shall they see us?
POR. They shall, Nerissa, but in such a habit°   60
That they shall think we are accomplishèd°
With that we lack.° I'll hold thee any wager,
When we are both accoutered like young men,
I'll prove the prettier fellow of the two,
And wear my dagger with the braver grace,   65
And speak between the change of man and boy
With a reed° voice, and turn two mincing steps
Into a manly stride, and speak of frays
Like a fine bragging youth. And tell quaint lies,
How honorable ladies sought my love,   70
Which I denying, they fell sick and died,
I could not do withal.° Then I'll repent,
And wish, for all that, that I had not killed them.
And twenty of these puny lies I'll tell,
That men shall swear I have discontinued school
Above a twelvemonth. I have within my mind   76
A thousand raw° tricks of these bragging Jacks,°
Which I will practice.
NER.   Why, shall we turn to men?

27. commodity: privilege. 32. bated: made thin.

Sc. iv: 2–3. true . . . amity: you truly understand the meaning of great friendship. 9. customary bounty: ordinary kindness. 20. the semblance: i.e., a man like. my soul: my soul's mate. 25. husbandry: housekeeping. 33. imposition: task imposed.

52. imagined speed: quick as thought. 53. tranect: a word otherwise unknown, possibly the Italian *traghetto*, ferry. 60. habit: costume. 61. accomplished: equipped. 62. we lack: i.e., manhood. 67. reed: reedy, piping. 72. I . . . withal: I couldn't help it. 77. raw: adolescent, sophomoric. Jacks: knaves.

POR. Fie, what a question's that
If thou wert near a lewd interpreter!°   80
But come, I'll tell thee all my whole device
When I am in my coach, which stays for us
At the park gate, and therefore haste away,
For we must measure twenty miles today. [*Exeunt.*]

SCENE V. *The same. A garden.*

[*Enter* LAUNCELOT GOBBO *and* JESSICA.]

LAUN. Yes, truly, for, look you, the sins of the
father are to be laid upon the children. Therefore I
promise ye I fear you.° I was always plain with you,
and so now I speak my agitation° of the matter.
Therefore be of good cheer, for truly I think you   5
are damned. There is but one hope in it that can do
you any good, and that is but a kind of bastard hope
neither.

JES. And what hope is that, I pray thee?   10

LAUN. Marry, you may partly hope that your
father got you not, that you are not the Jew's daugh-
ter.

JES. That were a kind of bastard hope, indeed. So
the sins of my mother should be visited upon me.   16

LAUN. Truly, then, I fear you are damned both by
father and mother. Thus when I shun Scylla, your
father, I fall into Charybdis,° your mother. Well,
you are gone both ways.   20

JES. I shall be saved by my husband. He hath
made me a Christian.

LAUN. Truly, the more to blame he. We were
Christians enow° before, e'en as many as could well
live, one by another. This making of Christians   25
will raise the price of hogs. If we grow all to be pork-
eaters, we shall not shortly have a rasher on the coals
for money.

[*Enter* LORENZO.]

JES. I'll tell my husband, Launcelot, what you say.
Here he comes.   30

LOR. I shall grow jealous of you shortly, Launce-
lot, if you thus get my wife into corners.

JES. Nay, you need not fear us, Lorenzo. Launce-
lot and I are out.° He tells me flatly there is no mercy
for me in Heaven, because I am a Jew's daugh-   35
ter. And he says you are no good member of the
commonwealth, for in converting Jews to Christians
you raise the price of pork.   39

LOR. I shall answer that better to the common-
wealth than you can the getting-up of the Negro's
belly. The Moor° is with child by you, Launcelot.

LAUN. It is much that the Moor should be more
than reason, but if she be less than an honest woman,
she is indeed more than I took her for.   47

LOR. How every fool can play upon the word! I
think the best grace of wit will shortly turn into
silence, and discourse grow commendable in none
only but parrots. Go in, sirrah. Bid them prepare for
dinner.   52

LAUN. That is done, sir. They have all stomachs.

LOR. Goodly Lord, what a wit-snapper are you!
Then bid them prepare dinner.   56

LAUN. That is done too, sir, only "cover" is the
word.

LOR. Will you cover,° then, sir?

LAUN. Not so, sir, neither. I know my duty.   59

LOR. Yet more quarreling with occasion!° Wilt
thou show the whole wealth of thy wit in an instant?
I pray thee understand a plain man in his plain
meaning. Go to thy fellows, bid them cover the table,
serve in the meat, and we will come in to dinner.   65

LAUN. For the table, sir, it shall be served in. For
the meat, sir, it shall be covered. For your coming in
to dinner, sir, why, let it be as humors and conceits°
shall govern.   [*Exit.*]

LOR. Oh, dear discretion, how his words are
     suited!°   70
The fool hath planted in his memory
An army of good words, and I do know
A many fools that stand in better place
Garnished° like him, that for a tricksy° word
Defy the matter. How cheer'st thou, Jessica?   75
And now, good sweet, say thy opinion.
How dost thou like the Lord Bassanio's wife?

JES. Past all expressing. It is very meet
The Lord Bassanio live an upright life,
For having such a blessing in his lady,   80
He finds the joys of Heaven here on earth.
And if on earth he do not mean it,° then
In reason he should never come to Heaven.
Why, if two gods should play some heavenly match
And on the wager lay two earthly women,   85
And Portia one, there must be something else
Pawned° with the other, for the poor rude world
Hath not her fellow.

LOR.   Even such a husband
Hast thou of me as she is for a wife.

JES. Nay, but ask my opinion too of that.   90

LOR. I will anon. First, let us go to dinner.

JES. Nay, let me praise you while I have a stom-
ach.°

---

80. lewd interpreter: someone who saw a lewd meaning in your
words.
     Sc. v: 3. I . . . you: fear for you.   4. agitation: for "cogita-
tion."   18–19. Scylla . . . Charybdis: legendary sea monsters
who waited for mariners on either side of the Strait of Mes-
sina. Those who escaped the one were destroyed by the other.
24. enow: enough.   34. are out: have fallen out.   42. The Moor:
The scandal is obviously topical but cannot be explained.

57–58. cover . . . cover: lay the table . . . put on your hat (as in
the presence of an equal).   60. quarreling . . . occasion: quib-
bling at every opportunity.   68. humors . . . conceits: whims
and fancies.   70. suited: how he makes words suit his
purpose!   74. Garnished: furnished. tricksy: smart.   82. do
. . . it: i.e., to live an upright life.   87. Pawned: pledged; i.e.,
the other woman would need something extra to make her
equal the value of Portia.   92. stomach: appetite.

LOR. No, pray thee, let it serve for table talk.
Then, howsoe'er thou speak'st, 'mong other things
I shall digest it.   94
JES.   Well, I'll set you forth.   [*Exeunt.*]

Act IV

SCENE I. *Venice. A court of justice.*

[*Enter the* DUKE, *the* MAGNIFICOES, ANTONIO,
BASSANIO, GRATIANO, SALERIO, *and others.*]

DUKE. What, is Antonio here?
ANT. Ready, so please your Grace.
DUKE. I am sorry for thee. Thou art come to answer
A stony adversary, an inhuman wretch
Uncapable of pity, void and empty   5
From any dram of mercy.
ANT.   I have heard
Your Grace hath ta'en great pains to qualify°
His rigorous course. But since he stands obdúrate,
And that no lawful means can carry me
Out of his envy's reach, I do oppose   10
My patience to his fury, and am armed
To suffer, with a quietness of spirit,
The very tyranny and rage of his.
DUKE. Go one, and call the Jew into the court.
SALER. He is ready at the door. He comes, my
lord.   15
              [*Enter* SHYLOCK.]
DUKE. Make room, and let him stand before our
face.
Shylock, the world thinks, and I think so too,
That thou but lead'st this fashion° of thy malice
To the last hour of act. And then 'tis thought
Thou'lt show thy mercy and remorse° more strange
Than is thy strange apparent cruelty,   21
And where thou now exact'st the penalty,
Which is a pound of this poor merchant's flesh,
Thou wilt not only loose° the forfeiture,
But, touched with human gentleness and love,   25
Forgive a moiety° of the principal,
Glancing an eye of pity on his losses
That have of late so huddled on his back,
Enow to press a royal merchant down
And pluck commiseration of his state   30
From brassy bosoms and rough hearts of flint,
From stubborn Turks and Tartars, never trained
To offices° of tender courtesy.
We all expect a gentle answer, Jew.

SHY. I have possessed° your Grace of what I purpose,   35
And by our holy Sabbath have I sworn
To have the due and forfeit of my bond.
If you deny it, let the danger light
Upon your charter° and your city's freedom.
You'll ask me why I rather choose to have   40
A weight of carrion flesh than to receive
Three thousand ducats. I'll not answer that,
But say it is my humor° — is it answered?
What if my house be troubled with a rat,
And I be pleased to give ten thousand ducats   45
To have it baned?° What, are you answered yet?
Some men there are love not a gaping pig,°
Some that are mad if they behold a cat,
And others when the bagpipe sings i' the nose
Cannot contain their urine. For affection,°   50
Mistress of passion, sways it to the mood
Of what it likes or loathes. Now for your answer:
As there is no firm reason to be rendered
Why he cannot abide a gaping pig,
Why he, a harmless necessary cat,   55
Why he, a woolen bagpipe,° but of force
Must yield to such inevitable shame
As to offend, himself being offended,
So can I give no reason, nor I will not,
More than a lodgèd° hate and a certain loathing   60
I bear Antonio, that I follow thus
A losing° suit against him. Are you answered?
BASS. This is no answer, thou unfeeling man,
To excuse the current of thy cruelty.
SHY. I am not bound to please thee with my answers.   65
BASS. Do all men kill the things they do not love?
SHY. Hates any man the thing he would not kill?
BASS. Every offense is not a hate at first.
SHY. What, wouldst thou have a serpent sting thee
twice?
ANT. I pray you, think you question with the Jew.°
You may as well go stand upon the beach   71
And bid the main flood° bate° his usual height,
You may as well use question with the wolf
Why he hath made the ewe bleat for the lamb,
You may as well forbid the mountain pines   75
To wag their high tops and to make no noise
When they are fretten° with the gusts of heaven,
You may as well do anything most hard
As seek to soften that — than which what's
harder? —

---

35. **possessed:** informed.   39. **charter:** English cities were
granted royal charters by the sovereign which gave them
certain rights and privileges, but which could be revoked.
43. **humor:** whim.   46. **baned:** poisoned.   47. **gaping pig:** roasted
porker with a lemon in its mouth.   50. **affection:** natural disposition.   56. **woolen bagpipe:** bagpipe in a woolen cover. See Pl. 19c.
60. **lodged:** deep-seated.   62. **losing:** unprofitable.   70. **I . . .
Jew:** i.e., with one naturally hardhearted.   72. **main flood:**
ocean. **bate:** abate, lessen.   77. **fretten:** fretted, tormented.

Act IV. Sc. i: 7. **qualify:** moderate.   18. **fashion:** appearance.
20. **remorse:** pity.   24. **loose:** release.   26. **moiety:** part.
33. **offices:** actions.

His Jewish heart. Therefore, I do beseech you   80
Make no more offers, use no farther means,
But with all brief and plain conveniency
Let me have judgment and the Jew his will.

BASS. For thy three thousand ducats here is six.

SHY. If every ducat in six thousand ducats   85
Were in six parts and every part a ducat,
I would not draw° them. I would have my bond.

DUKE. How shalt thou hope for mercy, rendering
    none?

SHY. What judgment shall I dread, doing no
    wrong?
You have among you many a purchased slave   90
Which, like your asses and your dogs and mules,
You use in abject and in slavish parts°
Because you bought them. Shall I say to you,
Let them be free, marry them to your heirs?
Why sweat they under burdens? Let their beds   95
Be made as soft as yours, and let their palates
Be seasoned° with such viands? You will answer
" The slaves are ours." So do I answer you.
The pound of flesh which I demand of him
Is dearly bought. 'Tis mine, and I will have it.   100
If you deny me, fie upon your law!
There is no force in the decrees of Venice.
I stand for judgment. Answer — shall I have it?

DUKE. Upon my power I may dismiss this court
Unless Bellario, a learned Doctor   105
Whom I have sent for to determine this
Come here today.

SALER.   My lord, here stays without
A messenger with letters from the Doctor,
New-come from Padua.   109

DUKE. Bring us the letters. Call the messenger.

BASS. Good cheer, Antonio! What, man, courage
    yet!
The Jew shall have my flesh, blood, bones, and all
Ere thou shalt lose for me one drop of blood.

ANT. I am a tainted° wether of the flock,
Meetest for death. The weakest kind of fruit   115
Drops earliest to the ground, and so let me.
You cannot better be employed, Bassanio,
Than to live still and write mine epitaph.

[*Enter* NERISSA, *dressed like a lawyer's clerk.*]

DUKE. Came you from Padua, from Bellario?

NER. From both, my lord. Bellario greets your
    Grace.   [*Presenting a letter.*]

BASS. Why dost thou whet thy knife so earnestly?

SHY. To cut the forfeiture from that bankrupt
    there.   122

GRA. Not on thy sole,° but on thy soul, harsh Jew,
Thou makest thy knife keen. But no metal can —
No, not the hangman's ax — bear half the keenness
Of thy sharp envy. Can no prayers pierce thee?   126

SHY. No, none that thou hast wit enough to make.

GRA. Oh, be thou damned, inexecrable° dog!
And for thy life let justice be accused.°
Thou almost makest me waver in my faith,   130
To hold opinion with Pythagoras°
That souls of animals infuse themselves
Into the trunks of men. Thy currish spirit
Governed a wolf° who, hanged for human slaughter,
Even from the gallows did his fell° soul fleet,°   135
And whilst thou lay'st in thy unhallowed dam
Infused itself in thee, for thy desires
Are wolvish, bloody, starved, and ravenous.

SHY. Till thou canst rail the seal from off my bond,
Thou but offend'st° thy lungs to speak so loud.   140
Repair thy wit, good youth, or it will fall
To cureless ruin. I stand here for law.

DUKE. This letter from Bellario doth commend
A young and learnèd Doctor to our court.
Where is he?

NER.   He attendeth here hard by   145
To know your answer, whether you'll admit him.

DUKE. With all my heart. Some three or four of
    you
Go give him courteous conduct° to this place.
Meantime the court shall hear Bellario's letter.   149

CLERK. [*Reads.*] " Your Grace shall understand
that at the receipt of your letter I am very sick. But
in the instant that your messenger came, in loving
visitation was with me a young Doctor of Rome. His
name is Balthasar. I acquainted him with the cause
in controversy between the Jew and Antonio   155
the merchant. We turned o'er many books together.
He is furnished with my opinion, which, bettered
with his own learning — the greatness whereof I can-
not enough commend — comes with him, at my im-
portunity,° to fill up your Grace's request in   160
my stead. I beseech you let his lack of years be no
impediment to let him lack a reverend estimation,°
for I never knew so young a body with so old a head.
I leave him to your gracious acceptance, whose trial
shall better publish his commendation."°   166

DUKE. You hear the learned Bellario, what he
    writes.
And here, I take it, is the Doctor come.

[*Enter* PORTIA *for* BALTHASAR.] Give me your hand.
    Come you from old Bellario?   169

POR. I did, my lord.

DUKE.   You are welcome. Take your place.
Are you acquainted with the difference
That holds this present question in the court?

---

128. **inexecrable:** merciless.   129. **And . . . accused:** i.e., if you
are spared, justice itself commits a crime.   131. **Pythagoras:**
the Greek philosopher who taught the doctrine of the transmigra-
tion of souls.   134. **Governed a wolf:** See *M of Ven* Intro.
p. 299a–b.   135. **fell:** cruel. **fleet:** lose.   140. **offend'st:** dost
injure.   148. **conduct:** escort.   159–160. **importunity:** urgent
persuasion.   162. **reverend estimation:** respect due to one older.
165–66. **trial . . . commendation:** worth shall be demonstrated
when tested.

87. **draw:** receive.   92. **parts:** actions.   97. **seasoned:** pampered.
114. **tainted:** diseased.   123. **sole:** i.e., of your slipper.

POR. I am informèd throughly° of the cause.   173
Which is the merchant here, and which the Jew?
DUKE. Antonio and old Shylock, both stand forth.
POR. Is your name Shylock?
SHY.   Shylock is my name.
POR. Of a strange nature is the suit you follow,
Yet in such rule that the Venetian law
Cannot impugn° you as you do proceed.
[*To* ANTONIO.] You stand within his danger,° do you
    not?   180
ANT. Aye, so he says.
POR.   Do you confess the bond?
ANT. I do.
POR.   Then must the Jew be merciful.
SHY. On what compulsion must I? Tell me that.
POR. The quality° of mercy is not strained,°
It droppeth as the gentle rain from heaven   185
Upon the place beneath. It is twice blest;
It blesseth him that gives and him that takes.
'Tis mightiest in the mightiest. It becomes
The thronèd monarch better than his crown.
His scepter shows the force of temporal power,   190
The attribute to awe and majesty
Wherein doth sit the dread and fear of kings.
But mercy is above this sceptered sway,
It is enthronèd in the hearts of kings,
It is an attribute to God himself,   195
And earthly power doth then show likest God's
When mercy seasons° justice. Therefore, Jew,
Though justice be thy plea, consider this,
That in the course of justice none of us
Should see salvation. We do pray for mercy,   200
And that same prayer doth teach us all to render°
The deeds of mercy. I have spoke thus much
To mitigate the justice of thy plea,   203
Which if thou follow, this strict court of Venice
Must needs give sentence 'gainst the merchant there.
SHY. My deeds upon my head! I crave the law,
The penalty and forfeit of my bond.
POR. Is he not able to discharge the money?
BASS. Yes, here I tender° it for him in the court,
Yea, twice the sum. If that will not suffice,   210
I will be bound to pay it ten times o'er
On forfeit of my hands, my head, my heart.
If this will not suffice, it must appear
That malice bears down truth. And I beseech you
Wrest° once the law to your authority.   215
To do a great right, do a little wrong,
And curb this cruel devil of his will.
POR. It must not be. There is no power in Venice
Can alter a decree established.
'Twill be recorded for a precedent,   220
And many an error, by the same example,

Will rush into the state. It cannot be.
SHY. A Daniel° come to judgment! Yea, a Daniel!
O wise young judge, how I do honor thee!
POR. I pray you let me look upon the bond.   225
SHY. Here 'tis, most reverend Doctor, here it is.
POR. Shylock, there's thrice thy money offered
    thee.
SHY. An oath, an oath, I have an oath in Heaven.
Shall I lay perjury upon my soul?
No, not for Venice.
POR.   Why, this bond is forfeit,°   230
And lawfully by this the Jew may claim
A pound of flesh, to be by him cut off
Nearest the merchant's heart. Be merciful.
Take thrice thy money, bid me tear the bond.
SHY. When it is paid according to the tenor.°   235
It doth appear you are a worthy judge,
You know the law, your exposition
Hath been most sound. I charge you by the law,
Whereof you are a well-deserving pillar,
Proceed to judgment. By my soul I swear   240
There is no power in the tongue of man
To alter me. I stay here on my bond.
ANT. Most heartily I do beseech the court
To give the judgment.
POR.   Why then, thus it is.
You must prepare your bosom for his knife.   245
SHY. O noble judge! O excellent young man!
POR. For the intent and purpose of the law
Hath full relation° to the penalty
Which here appeareth due upon the bond.
SHY. 'Tis very true. O wise and upright judge!
How much more elder art thou than thy looks!   251
POR. Therefore lay bare your bosom.
SHY.   Aye, his breast.
So says the bond — doth it not, noble judge? —
"Nearest his heart." Those are the very words.
POR. It is so. Are there balance here to weigh   255
The flesh?
SHY.   I have them ready.
POR. Have by some surgeon, Shylock, on your
    charge,
To stop his wounds, lest he do bleed to death.
SHY. Is it so nominated in the bond?
POR. It is not so expressed, but what of that?   260
'Twere good you do so much for charity.
SHY. I cannot find it. 'Tis not in the bond.
POR. You, merchant, have you anything to say?
ANT. But little. I am armed and well prepared.
Give me your hand, Bassanio. Fare you well!   265
Grieve not that I am fallen to this for you,

---

173. throughly: thoroughly.   179. impugn: call in question.
180. within . . . danger: in his power to exact a penalty.
184. quality: nature. strained: forced; i.e., mercy must be given
freely.   197. seasons: is mixed with.   201. render: pay back.
209. tender: offer.   215. Wrest: wrench.

223. Daniel: In the History of Susanna in the Apocrypha,
Susanna was falsely accused of adultery by two elders, and
condemned to death; but Daniel, a wise young man, by ques-
tioning the elders separately revealed their false testimony.
230. bond is forfeit: i.e., the defendant must pay the forfeit
demanded.   235. tenor: intention.   248. Hath . . . relation: is
fully in accord with.

For herein Fortune shows herself more kind
Than is her custom. It is still° her use
To let the wretched man outlive his wealth,
To view with hollow eye and wrinkled brow   270
An age of poverty, from which lingering penance
Of such misery doth she cut me off.
Commend me to your honorable wife.
Tell her the process of Antonio's end,
Say how I loved you, speak me fair in death,   275
And when the tale is told, bid her be judge
Whether Bassanio had not once a love.
Repent but you that you shall lose your friend,
And he repents not that he pays your debt,
For if the Jew do cut but deep enough,   280
I'll pay it presently with all my heart.
    BASS. Antonio, I am married to a wife
Which is as dear to me as life itself,
But life itself, my wife, and all the world
Are not with me esteemed above thy life.   285
I would lose all, aye, sacrifice them all
Here to this devil, to deliver you.
    POR. Your wife would give you little thanks for
        that
If she were by to hear you make the offer.
    GRA. I have a wife whom, I protest, I love.   290
I would she were in Heaven so she could
Entreat some power to change this currish Jew.
    NER. 'Tis well you offer it behind her back.
The wish would make else an unquiet house.
    SHY. [*Aside*] These be the Christian husbands. I
        have a daughter.   295
Would any of the stock of Barrabas°
Had been her husband rather than a Christian!
[*To Portia.*] We trifle time. I pray thee, pursue
        sentence.
    POR. A pound of that same merchant's flesh is
        thine.
The court awards it, and the law doth give it.   300
    SHY. Most rightful judge!
    POR. And you must cut this flesh from off his
        breast.
The law allows it, and the court awards it.
    SHY. Most learned judge! A sentence! Come, pre-
        pare!
    POR. Tarry a little. There is something else.   305
This bond doth give thee here no jot of blood.
The words expressly are " a pound of flesh."
Take then thy bond, take thou thy pound of flesh,
But in the cutting it if thou dost shed
One drop of Christian blood, thy lands and goods
Are, by the laws of Venice, confiscate   311
Unto the state of Venice.
    GRA. O upright judge! Mark, Jew. O learnèd
        judge!

    SHY. Is that the law?
    POR.   Thyself shalt see the act.
For, as thou urgest justice, be assured   315
Thou shalt have justice, more than thou desirest.
    GRA. O learnèd judge! Mark, Jew, a learnèd judge!
    SHY. I take this offer, then. Pay the bond thrice
And let the Christian go.
    BASS.   Here is the money.
    POR. Soft!°   320
The Jew shall have all justice. Soft! No haste.
He shall have nothing but the penalty.
    GRA. O Jew! An upright judge, a learnèd judge!
    POR. Therefore prepare thee to cut off the flesh.
Shed thou no blood, nor cut thou less nor more   325
But just a pound of flesh. If thou cut'st more
Or less than a just° pound, be it but so much
As makes it light or heavy in the substance,
Or the division of the twentieth part
Of one poor scruple° — nay, if the scale do turn
But in the estimation of a hair —   331
Thou diest and all thy goods are confiscate.
    GRA. A second Daniel, a Daniel, Jew!
Now, infidel, I have you on the hip.°
    POR. Why doth the Jew pause? Take thy forfei-
        ture.   335
    SHY. Give me my principal and let me go.
    BASS. I have it ready for thee. Here it is.
    POR. He hath refused it in the open court.
He shall have merely justice and his bond.
    GRA. A Daniel, still say I, a second Daniel!   340
I thank thee, Jew, for teaching me that word.
    SHY. Shall I not have barely my principal?
    POR. Thou shalt have nothing but the forfeiture,
To be so taken at thy peril, Jew.
    SHY. Why, then the Devil give him good of it!
I'll stay no longer question.
    POR.   Tarry, Jew.   346
The law hath yet another hold on you.
It is enacted in the laws of Venice,
If it be proved against an alien
That by direct or indirect attempts   350
He seek the life of any citizen,
The party 'gainst the which he doth contrive°
Shall seize one half his goods. The other half
Comes to the privy coffer° of the state.
And the offender's life lies in the mercy   355
Of the Duke only, 'gainst all other voice.
In which predicament, I say, thou stand'st,
For it appears, by manifest proceeding,
That indirectly, and directly too,
Thou hast contrived against the very life   360
Of the defendant, and thou hast incurred

---

268. still: continually.   296. Barrabas: either Barabbas the
robber whom the Jews preferred to Jesus (see Luke 23:18–19)
or Barabas the Jew of Malta (see *M of Ven* Intro. p. 301a–b and
Gen. Intro. p. 37b), who was better known to playgoers.

320. Soft: pause a little.   327. just: exact.   330. scruple: minute
portion (actually, 20 grains).   334. on . . . hip: at a disadvantage.
352. contrive: plot.   354. privy coffer: privy purse. Shakespeare
is thinking rather of English finance at the time. Fines of this
kind were paid into the privy purse; i.e., the Sovereign's per-
sonal income.

The danger formerly by me rehearsed.
Down, therefore, and beg mercy of the Duke.

GRA. Beg that thou mayst have leave to hang thy-
self.

And yet, thy wealth being forfeit to the state,   365
Thou hast not left the value of a cord,
Therefore thou must be hanged at the state's charge.

DUKE. That thou shalt see the difference of our
spirits,
I pardon thee thy life before thou ask it.
For half thy wealth, it is Antonio's.   370
The other half comes to the general state,
Which humbleness may drive unto a fine.°

POR. Aye, for the state, not for Antonio.

SHY. Nay, take my life and all — pardon not that.
You take my house when you do take the prop   375
That doth sustain my house. You take my life
When you do take the means whereby I live.

POR. What mercy can you render him, Antonio?

GRA. A halter gratis. Nothing else, for God's sake.

ANT. So please my lord the Duke and all the
court,   380
To quit° the fine for one half of his goods,
I am content, so he will let me have
The other half in use, to render it,
Upon his death, unto the gentleman
That lately stole his daughter.   385
Two things provided more, that, for this favor,
He presently become a Christian.
The other, that he do record a gift,
Here in the court, of all he dies possessed
Unto his son Lorenzo and his daughter.   390

DUKE. He shall do this, or else I do recant
The pardon that I late pronouncèd here.

POR. Art thou contented, Jew? What dost thou
say?

SHY. I am content.

POR.   Clerk, draw a deed of gift.

SHY. I pray you give me leave to go from hence.
I am not well. Send the deed after me   396
And I will sign it.

DUKE.   Get thee gone, but do it.

GRA. In christening shalt thou have two god-
fathers.
Had I been judge, thou shouldst have had ten more,°
To bring thee to the gallows, not the font.   400

[Exit SHYLOCK.]

DUKE. Sir, I entreat you home with me to dinner.

POR. I humbly do desire your Grace of pardon.
I must away this night toward Padua,
And it is meet° I presently set forth.

DUKE. I am sorry that your leisure serves you not.
Antonio, gratify° this gentleman,   406
For, in my mind, you are much bound to him.

[Exeunt DUKE and his train.]

BASS. Most worthy gentleman, I and my friend
Have by your wisdom been this day acquitted
Of grievous penalties, in lieu whereof,   410
Three thousand ducats, due unto the Jew,
We freely cope° your courteous pains° withal.

ANT. And stand indebted, over and above,
In love and service to you evermore.

POR. He is well paid that is well satisfied,   415
And I, delivering you, am satisfied,
And therein do account myself well paid.
My mind was never yet more mercenary.
I pray you, know me when we meet again.°
I wish you well, and so I take my leave.   420

BASS. Dear sir, of force I must attempt you
further.
Take some remembrance of us — as a tribute,
Not as a fee. Grant me two things, I pray you —
Not to deny me, and to pardon me.   424

POR. You press me far, and therefore I will yield.
[To ANTONIO] Give me your gloves, I'll wear them
for your sake.
[To BASSANIO] And, for your love,° I'll take this ring
from you.
Do not draw back your hand. I'll take no more,
And you in love shall not deny me this.

BASS. This ring, good sir, alas! it is a trifle.   430
I will not shame myself to give you this.

POR. I will have nothing else but only this,
And now methinks I have a mind to it.

BASS. There's more depends on this than on the
value.
The dearest ring in Venice will I give you,   435
And find it out by proclamation.
Only for this, I pray you pardon me.

POR. I see, sir, you are liberal in offers.
You taught me first to beg, and now methinks   439
You teach me how a beggar should be answered.

BASS. Good sir, this ring was given me by my wife,
And when she put it on, she made me vow
That I should neither sell nor give nor lose it.

POR. That 'scuse serves many men to save their
gifts.
An° if your wife be not a madwoman,   445
And know how well I have deserved the ring,
She would not hold out enemy forever
For giving it to me. Well, peace be with you!

[Exeunt PORTIA and NERISSA.]

ANT. My Lord Bassanio, let him have the ring.
Let his deservings and my love withal   450
Be valued 'gainst your wife's commandment.

BASS. Go, Gratiano, run and overtake him.
Give him the ring, and bring him, if thou canst,
Unto Antonio's house. Away! Make haste.

[Exit GRATIANO.]

---

372. fine: a lesser penalty.   381. quit: remit.   399. ten more:
i.e., a jury of twelve to bring in a verdict of guilty.   404. meet: fit.
406. gratify: pay the fee of.

412. cope: meet, requite. pains: trouble.   419. know ... again:
a polite phrase meaning "I hope we shall see more of each
other"; but Portia uses it ironically.   427. for ... love: as a
keepsake.   445. An: if.

Come, you and I will thither presently,   455
And in the morning early will we both
Fly toward Belmont. Come, Antonio.   [*Exeunt.*]

SCENE II. *The same. A street.*

[*Enter* PORTIA *and* NERISSA.]

POR. Inquire the Jew's house out, give him this
    deed
And let him sign it. We'll away tonight
And be a day before our husbands home.
This deed will be well welcome to Lorenzo.

[*Enter* GRATIANO.]

GRA. Fair sir, you are well o'erta'en.   5
My Lord Bassanio upon more advice°
Hath sent you here this ring, and doth entreat
Your company at dinner.
POR.   That cannot be.
His ring I do accept most thankfully,
And so I pray you tell him. Furthermore,   10
I pray you show my youth old Shylock's house.
GRA. That will I do.
NER.   Sir, I would speak with you.
[*Aside to* PORTIA] I'll see if I can get my husband's
    ring,
Which I did make him swear to keep forever.
POR. [*Aside to* NERISSA] Thou mayst, I warrant.
    We shall have old° swearing   15
That they did give the rings away to men,
But we'll outface them, and outswear them too.
[*Aloud*] Away! Make haste. Thou know'st where I
    will tarry.
NER. Come, good sir, will you show me to this
    house?   [*Exeunt.*]

Act V

SCENE I. *Belmont. Avenue to* PORTIA'S *house.*

[*Enter* LORENZO *and* JESSICA.]

LOR. The moon shines bright. In such a night as
    this,
When the sweet wind did gently kiss the trees
And they did make no noise, in such a night
Troilus° methinks mounted the Troyan walls,
And sighed his soul towárd the Grecian tents,   5
Where Cressid lay that night.
JES.   In such a night

Did Thisbe° fearfully o'ertrip° the dew,
And saw the lion's shadow ere himself,°
And ran dismayed away.
LOR.   In such a night
Stood Dido° with a willow° in her hand   10
Upon the wild sea banks and waft° her love
To come again to Carthage.
JES.   In such a night
Medea° gathered the enchanted herbs
That did renew old Aeson.
LOR.   In such a night
Did Jessica steal from the wealthy Jew,   15
And with an unthrift° love did run from Venice
As far as Belmont.
JES.   In such a night
Did young Lorenzo swear he loved her well,
Stealing her soul with many vows of faith
And ne'er a true one.
LOR.   In such a night   20
Did pretty Jessica, like a little shrew,
Slander her love, and he forgave it her.
JES. I would outnight you did nobody come.
But hark, I hear the footing of a man.

[*Enter* STEPHANO.]

LOR. Who comes so fast in silence of the night?
STEPH. A friend.   26
LOR. A friend! What friend? Your name, I pray
    you, friend?
STEPH. Stephano is my name, and I bring word
My mistress will before the break of day
Be here at Belmont. She doth stray about   30
By holy crosses, where she kneels and prays
For happy wedlock hours.
LOR.   Who comes with her?
STEPH. None but a holy hermit° and her maid.
I pray you, is my master yet returned?
LOR. He is not, nor we have not heard from him.
But go we in, I pray thee, Jessica,   36
And ceremoniously let us prepare
Some welcome for the mistress of the house.

[*Enter* LAUNCELOT GOBBO.]

LAUN. Sola,° sola! Wo ha, ho! Sola, sola!
LOR. Who calls?   40
LAUN. Sola! Did you see Master Lorenzo? Master
Lorenzo, sola, sola!
LOR. Leave holloaing, man. Here.
LAUN. Sola! Where? Where?
LOR. Here.   45

---

7. **Thisbe:** For the sad story of Pyramus and Thisbe see *MND*,
V.i.108–354. **o'ertrip:** run trippingly over.   8. **himself:** i.e., Pyr-
amus.   10. **Dido:** the widowed queen of Carthage, whom Aeneas
loved and deserted. **willow:** the sign of a deserted lover.   11. **waft:**
waved to.   13. **Medea:** the sorceress who helped Jason to fetch
away the Golden Fleece and afterward refused to leave him.
Aeson was Jason's father.   16. **unthrift:** spendthrift.   33. **holy
hermit:** This good man does not appear for he has no existence
in fact. He is part of the feigned excuse for Portia's absence
from home. See III.iv.30.   39. **Sola:** Launcelot imitates the
sound of the postboy's horn. See App. 17.

Sc. ii: 6. **advice:** consideration.   15. **old:** any amount of.
Act V, Sc. i: 4. **Troilus:** Troilus the Trojan was deprived of
his love Cressida, who was taken away to the Greek camp.
See *Tr & Cr*, IV.ii. etc.

LAUN. Tell him there's a post come from my master, with his horn full of good news. My master will be here ere morning.   *[Exit.]*

LOR. Sweet soul, let's in, and there expect° their
    coming.
And yet no matter. Why should we go in?   50
My friend Stephano, signify, I pray you,
Within the house, your mistress is at hand,
And bring your music forth into the air.
                   [Exit STEPHANO.*]*
How sweet the moonlight sleeps upon this bank!
Here will we sit and let the sounds of music   55
Creep in our ears. Soft stillness and the night
Become the touches of sweet harmony.
Sit, Jessica. Look how the floor of heaven
Is thick inlaid with patines° of bright gold.
There's not the smallest orb which thou behold'st
But in his motion° like an angel sings,   61
Still quiring° to the young-eyed cherubins.
Such harmony is in immortal souls,
But whilst this muddy vesture of decay°
Doth grossly close it in, we cannot hear it.   65
[Enter MUSICIANS.*]* Come, ho! and wake Diana°
    with a hymn!
With sweetest touches pierce your mistress' ear,
And draw her home with music.   *[Music.]*
JES. I am never merry when I hear sweet music.
LOR. The reason is, your spirits are attentive.   70
For do but note a wild and wanton herd,
Or race of youthful and unhandled colts,
Fetching mad bounds, bellowing, and neighing loud,
Which is the hot condition of their blood.
If they but hear perchance a trumpet sound,   75
Or any air of music touch their ears,
You shall perceive them make a mutual stand,
Their savage eyes turned to a modest gaze
By the sweet power of music. Therefore the poet
Did feign that Orpheus° drew trees, stones, and
    floods,   80
Since naught so stockish,° hard, and full of rage
But music for the time doth change his nature.
The man that hath no music in himself,
Nor is not moved with concord of sweet sounds,
Is fit for treasons, stratagems,° and spoils.   85
The motions of his spirit are dull as night,
And his affections dark as Erebus.°
Let no such man be trusted. Mark the music.
        [Enter PORTIA *and* NERISSA.*]*
POR. That light we see is burning in my hall.
How far that little candle throws his beams!   90

So shines a good deed in a naughty world.
NER. When the moon shone, we did not see the
    candle.
POR. So doth the greater glory dim the less.
A substitute shines brightly as a king
Until a king be by, and then his state   95
Empties itself, as doth an inland brook
Into the main of waters. Music! Hark!
NER. It is your music, madam, of the house.
POR. Nothing is good, I see, without respect.°
Methinks it sounds much sweeter than by day.   100
NER. Silence bestows that virtue on it, madam.
POR. The crow doth sing as sweetly as the lark
When neither is attended,° and I think
The nightingale if she should sing by day,
When every goose is cackling, would be thought
No better a musician than the wren.   106
How many things by season seasoned are°
To their right praise and true perfection!
Peace, ho! The moon sleeps with Endymion,°
And would not be awaked.   *[Music ceases.]*
LOR.   That is the voice,   110
Or I am much deceived, of Portia.
POR. He knows me as the blind man knows the
    cuckoo,
By the bad voice.
LOR.   Dear lady, welcome home.
POR. We have been praying for our husbands'
    healths,   114
Which speed,° we hope, the better for our words.
Are they returned?
LOR.   Madam, they are not yet,
But there is come a messenger before
To signify their coming.
POR.   Go in, Nerissa.
Give order to my servants that they take
No note at all of our being absent hence —   120
Nor you, Lorenzo, Jessica, nor you.
                 [A tucket° sounds.]
LOR. Your husband is at hand, I hear his trumpet.
We are no telltales, madam, fear you not.
POR. This night methinks is but the daylight sick,
It looks a little paler. 'Tis a day   125
Such as the day is when the sun is hid.
    [Enter BASSANIO, ANTONIO, GRATIANO, *and their*
                  followers.]
BASS. We should hold day with the Antipodes
If you would walk in absence of the sun.°
POR. Let me give light, but let me not be light,
For a light wife doth make a heavy husband,   130

---

49. expect: await.   59. patines: plates.   61. in . . . motion: See App. 1.   62. quiring: singing.   64. muddy . . . decay: i.e., the mortal earthly body. So long as we are mortal we cannot hear immortal music.   66. wake Diana: the goddess Diana is also the moon; she loved a mortal shepherd called Endymion.   80. Orpheus: The musician of Thrace was so skillful that even the trees bent to listen to him.   81. stockish: like an unfeeling block.   85. stratagems: deeds of violence.   87. Erebus: Hell.

99. without respect: without reference to circumstances; i.e., in itself.   103. attended: listened to.   107. by . . . are: give a pleasant taste by appearing at the right time.   109. Endymion: See l. 66 above.   115. speed: prosper.   121. s.d., tucket: a short trumpet fanfare.   127-28. We . . . sun: if you always chose to walk in the dark it would be daylight with us at the same time as on the opposite side of the globe; i.e., your presence makes darkness light.

And never be Bassanio so for me.
But God sort° all! You are welcome home, my lord.
   BASS. I thank you, madam. Give welcome to my
     friend.
This is the man, this is Antonio,
To whom I am so infinitely bound.   135
   POR. You should in all sense be much bound to
     him,
For, as I hear, he was much bound for you.
   ANT. No more than I am well acquitted of.°
   POR. Sir, you are very welcome to our house.
It must appear in other ways than words,   140
Therefore I scant this breathing courtesy.°
   GRA. [*To* NERISSA] By yonder moon I swear you do
     me wrong.
In faith, I gave it to the judge's clerk.
Would he were gelt° that had it, for my part,
Since you do take it, love, so much at heart.   145
   POR. A quarrel, ho! Already! What's the matter?
   GRA. About a hoop of gold, a paltry ring
That she did give me, whose posy° was
For all the world like cutler's poetry
Upon a knife, "Love me, and leave me not."   150
   NER. What talk you of the posy or the value?
You swore to me when I did give it you
That you would wear it till your hour of death,
And that it should lie with you in your grave.   154
Though not for me, yet for your vehement oaths,
You should have been respective,° and have kept it.
Gave it a judge's clerk! No, God's my judge,
The clerk will ne'er wear hair on's face that had it.
   GRA. He will an if he live to be a man.
   NER. Aye, if a woman live to be a man.   160
   GRA. Now, by this hand, I gave it to a youth,
A kind of boy, a little scrubbèd° boy,
No higher than thyself, the judge's clerk,
A prating boy that begged it as a fee.
I could not for my heart deny it him.   165
   POR. You were to blame, I must be plain with you,
To part so slightly with your wife's first gift —
A thing stuck on with oaths upon your finger
And so riveted with faith unto your flesh.
I gave my love a ring and made him swear   170
Never to part with it, and here he stands.
I dare be sworn for him he would not leave it,
Nor pluck it from his finger, for the wealth
That the world masters. Now, in faith, Gratiano,
You give your wife too unkind a cause of grief.   175
An 'twere to me, I should be mad at it.
   BASS. [*Aside*] Why, I were best to cut my left
     hand off,
And swear I lost the ring defending it.
   GRA. My Lord Bassanio gave his ring away
Unto the judge that begged it, and indeed   180

Deserved it too. And then the boy, his clerk,
That took some pains in writing, he begged mine,
And neither man nor master would take aught
But the two rings.
   POR.   What ring gave you, my lord?
Not that, I hope, which you received of me.   185
   BASS. If I could add a lie unto a fault,
I would deny it, but you see my finger
Hath not the ring upon it. It is gone.
   POR. Even so void is your false heart of truth.
By Heaven, I will ne'er come in your bed   190
Until I see the ring.
   NER.   Nor I in yours
Till I again see mine.
   BASS.   Sweet Portia,
If you did know to whom I gave the ring,
If you did know for whom I gave the ring,
And would conceive° for what I gave the ring,
And how unwillingly I left the ring,   196
When naught would be accepted but the ring,
You would abate the strength of your displeasure.
   POR. If you had known the virtue of the ring,
Or half her worthiness that gave the ring,   200
Or your own honor to contain the ring,
You would not then have parted with the ring.
What man is there so much unreasonable,
If you had pleased to have defended it
With any terms of zeal, wanted the modesty   205
To urge the thing held as a ceremony?°
Nerissa teaches me what to believe.
I'll die for't but some woman had the ring.
   BASS. No, by my honor, madam, by my soul,
No woman had it, but a civil Doctor,°   210
Which did refuse three thousand ducats of me,
And begged the ring, the which I did deny him,
And suffered him to go displeased away,
Even he that did uphold the very life
Of my dear friend. What should I say, sweet lady?
I was enforced to send it after him,   216
I was beset with shame and courtesy,
My honor would not let ingratitude
So much besmear it. Pardon me, good lady,
For by these blessed candles of the night,   220
Had you been there, I think you would have begged
The ring of me to give the worthy Doctor.
   POR. Let not that Doctor e'er come near my house.
Since he hath got the jewel that I loved,
And that which you did swear to keep for me,   225
I will become as liberal as you.
I'll not deny him anything I have,
No, not my body nor my husband's bed.
Know him I shall, I am well sure of it.
Lie not a night from home, watch me like Argus.°
If you do not, if I be left alone,   231

---

132. sort: dispose of. 138. acquitted of: paid for. 141. scant
. . . courtesy: cut short this welcome of mere words. 144. gelt:
gelded. 148. posy: motto engraved inside a ring. 156. respec-
tive: careful. 162. scrubbed: scrubby.

195. conceive: imagine. 206. ceremony: something sacred.
210. civil Doctor: Doctor of Civil Law. 230. Argus: who had a
hundred eyes.

Now, by mine honor, which is yet mine own,
I'll have that Doctor for my bedfellow.
    NER. And I his clerk, therefore be well advised
How you do leave me to mine own protection.   235
    GRA. Well, do you so. Let not me take him, then,
For if I do, I'll mar the young clerk's pen.
    ANT. I am the unhappy subject of these quarrels.
    POR. Sir, grieve not you. You are welcome not-
    withstanding.
    BASS. Portia, forgive me this enforcèd wrong,
And in the hearing of these many friends   241
I swear to thee, even by thine own fair eyes,
Wherein I see myself——
    POR.   Mark you but that!
In both my eyes he doubly sees himself —
In each eye, one. Swear by your double self,   245
And there's an oath of credit.
    BASS.   Nay, but hear me.
Pardon this fault and by my soul I swear
I never more will break an oath with thee.
    ANT. I once did lend my body for his wealth,
Which, but for him that had your husband's ring,
Had quite miscarried. I dare be bound again,   251
My soul upon the forfeit, that your lord
Will never more break faith advisedly.°
    POR. Then you shall be his surety. Give him this,
And bid him keep it better than the other.   255
    ANT. Here, Lord Bassanio, swear to keep this ring.
    BASS. By Heaven, it is the same I gave the Doctor!
    POR. I had it of him. Pardon me, Bassanio,
For, by this ring, the Doctor lay with me.
    NER. And pardon me, my gentle Gratiano,   260
For that same scrubbèd boy, the Doctor's clerk,
In lieu of° this last night did lie with me.
    GRA. Why, this is like the mending of highways
In summer, where the ways are fair enough.   264
What, are we cuckolds° ere we have deserved it?
    POR. Speak not so grossly. You are all amazed.
Here is a letter, read it at your leisure.
It comes from Padua, from Bellario.
There you shall find that Portia was the Doctor,
Nerissa there her clerk. Lorenzo here   270
Shall witness I set forth as soon as you,

And even but now returned. I have not yet
Entered my house. Antonio, you are welcome,
And I have better news in store for you
Than you expect. Unseal this letter soon.   275
There you shall find three of your argosies
Are richly come to harbor suddenly.
You shall not know by what strange accident
I chancèd on this letter.
    ANT.   I am dumb.   279
    BASS. Were you the Doctor and I knew you not?
    GRA. Were you the clerk that is to make me cuck-
    old?
    NER. Aye, but the clerk that never means to do it
Unless he live until he be a man.
    BASS. Sweet Doctor, you shall be my bedfellow.
When I am absent, then lie with my wife.   285
    ANT. Sweet lady, you have given me life and liv-
    ing,
For here I read for certain that my ships
Are safely come to road.
    POR.   How now, Lorenzo!
My clerk hath some good comforts too for you.
    NER. Aye, and I'll give them him without a fee.
There do I give to you and Jessica,   291
From the rich Jew, a special deed of gift,
After his death, of all he dies possessed of.
    LOR. Fair ladies, you drop manna in the way
Of starvèd people.
    POR.   It is almost morning,   295
And yet I am sure you are not satisfied
Of these events at full. Let us go in.
And charge us there upon inter'gatories,°
And we will answer all things faithfully.
    GRA. Let it be so. The first inter'gatory   300
That my Nerissa shall be sworn on is
Whether till the next night she had rather stay,
Or go to bed now, being two hours to day.
But were the day come, I should wish it dark,
That I were couching with the Doctor's clerk.   305
Well, while I live I'll fear no other thing
So sore as keeping safe Nerissa's ring.   [Exeunt.]

---

253. advisedly: deliberately.   262. In lieu of: in return for.
265. cuckolds: deceived by our wives.

298. inter'gatories: interrogatories, a list of questions on oath
put to a suspected person or witness in the enquiry preliminary
to a trial.

The First Part of
KING HENRY THE FOURTH

Introduction[1]

The First Part of King Henry the Fourth was probably written in the autumn of 1597. The play is a sequel to *Richard II,* which had been published in the late summer of 1597 and was selling well, particularly because the followers of the Earl of Essex were finding certain parallels between that story and their own times (see *Rich II* Intro. p. 191a–b). In writing *I Henry IV* Shakespeare began the story at the point where *Richard II* ended, but his method of writing the sequel was quite different. Hitherto his history plays had been mostly serious; he certainly shaped historical facts and dates to suit his own purposes, but he seldom digressed. There was no clowning or laughter either in *Richard III* or in *Richard II.* In *Henry IV* half the play is occupied with the riotous and quite unhistorical low comedy of Sir John Falstaff and his gang. As a result there was less room for history, and Shakespeare reduced the historical plot to a series of simple scenes.

For his historical facts, Shakespeare went, as before, to Holinshed's *Chronicles,* from which he extracted and adapted ten episodes: 1. News is brought to the King that the Percies of Northumberland are growing troublesome (I.i). 2. The Percies come to Court and quarrel with the King (I.iii). 3. Hotspur, at home with his wife, prepares for his campaign against the King (II.ii). 4. Hotspur and Worcester, having joined with the Welsh Prince, Owen Glendower, agree on the terms of their alliance (III.i). 5. The King rebukes Prince Hal for his unprincely life (III.ii). 6. Hotspur, Worcester, and their friends prepare to give battle to the King's forces (IV.i). 7. The King's messenger proposes a parley (IV.iii). 8. Worcester and Vernon parley with the King, who offers terms (V.i). 9. Worcester falsely reports the King's offer and the battle begins (V.ii). 10. Hotspur is slain and the rebels are defeated at the Battle of Shrewsbury (V.iii, iv, v).

Some specimens will show how Shakespeare used his Holinshed:

1 See also App. 28.

1. THE QUARREL BETWEEN THE KING AND THE PERCIES (cf. I.i AND iii)

Henry Earl of Northumberland, with his brother Thomas Earl of Worcester, and his son the Lord Henry Percy, surnamed Hotspur, which were to King Henry in the beginning of his reign both faithful friends and earnest aiders, began now to envy his wealth and felicity; and especially they were grieved because the King demanded of the Earl and his son such Scottish prisoners as were taken at Holmedon and Nesbit; for of all the captives which were taken in the conflicts foughten in those two places, there was delivered to the King's possession only Mordake Earl of Fife, the Duke of Albany's son; though the King did divers and sundry times require deliverance of the residue, and that with great threatenings, wherewith the Percies being sore offended (for that they claimed them as their own proper prisoners, and their peculiar preys), by the counsel of the Lord Thomas Percy, Earl of Worcester, whose study was ever (as some write) to procure malice and set things in a broil, came to the King unto Windsor (upon a purpose to prove him), and there required of him that either by ransom or otherwise he would cause to be delivered out of prison Edmund Mortimer Earl of March, their cousin german, whom (as they reported) Owen Glendower kept in filthy prison, shackled with irons, only for that he took his part, and was to him faithful and true.

The King began not a little to muse at this request, and not without cause; for indeed it touched him somewhat near, sith this Edmund was son to Roger Earl of March, son to the Lady Philip, daughter of Lionel Duke of Clarence, the third son of King Edward the Third; which Edmund, at King Richard's going into Ireland, was proclaimed heir apparent to the crown and realm; whose aunt, called Eleanor, the Lord Henry Percy had married; and therefore King Henry could not well bear that any man should be earnest about the advancement of that lineage. The King, when he had studied on the matter, made answer that the Earl of March was not taken prisoner for his cause, nor in his service, but willingly suffered himself to be taken, because he would not withstand the attempts of Owen Glendower and his complices, and therefore he would neither ransom him nor relieve him.

The Percies with this answer and fraudulent excuse were not a little fumed, insomuch that Henry Hotspur said openly: " Behold, the heir of the realm is robbed of his right, and yet the robber with his own will not redeem him! " So in this fury the Percies departed, minding nothing more than to depose King Henry from the high type of his royalty, and to place in his seat their cousin Edmund Earl of March, whom they did not only deliver out of captivity, but also (to the high displeasure of King Henry) entered in league with the foresaid Glendower.

2. THE SUSPICIONS OF THE KING AGAINST PRINCE HENRY (cf. III.ii)

Lord Henry, Prince of Wales, eldest son to King Henry, got knowledge that certain of his father's servants were busy to give informations against him, whereby discord might arise betwixt him and his father; for they put into the King's head not only what evil rule (according to the course of youth) the Prince kept, to the offense of many, but also what great resort of people came to his house; so that the Court was nothing furnished with such a train as daily followed the Prince. These tales brought no small suspicion into the King's head, lest his son would presume to usurp the crown, he being yet alive; through which suspicious jealousy it was perceived that he favored not his son, as in times past he had done.

The Prince (sore offended with such persons as by slanderous reports sought not only to spot his good name abroad in the realm, but to sow discord also betwixt him and his father) wrote his letters into every part of the realm, to reprove all such slanderous devices of those that sought his discredit. And to clear himself the better (that the world might understand what wrong he had to be slandered in such wise), about the feast of Peter and Paul — to wit, the nine and twentieth day of June — he came to the Court with such a number of noblemen and other his friends that wished him well as the like train had been seldom seen repairing to the Court at any one time in those days. . . .

Thus were the father and the son reconciled, betwixt whom the said pickthanks had sown division, insomuch that the son, upon a vehement conceit of unkindness sprung in the father, was in the way to be worn out of favor. Which was the more likely to come to pass by their informations that privily charged him with riot and other uncivil demeanor unseemly for a Prince. Indeed he was youthfully given, grown to audacity, and had chosen him companions agreeable to his age, with whom he spent the time in such recreations, exercises, and delights as he fancied. But yet (it should seem by the report of some writers) that his behavior was not offensive or at least tending to the damage of anybody; sith he had a care to avoid doing of wrong, and to tether his affections within the tract of virtue, whereby he opened unto himself a ready passage of good liking among the prudent sort, and was beloved of such as could discern his disposition, which was in no degree so excessive as that he deserved in such vehement manner to be suspected.

The adventures of Sir John Falstaff and Prince Hal are wholly fictitious and mostly Shakespeare's own inventing, though the Prince's wild behavior had long become a stage tradition and had been shown in at least one play which still survives in print. This was a crude piece called *The famous victories of Henry the Fifth,* which crams into a succession of short scenes the more popular episodes of the King's life. This play had been acted by the now defunct company of the Queen's Men. It was entered for publication in 1594, though the earliest surviving copy is dated 1598. The main episodes in *The Famous Victories* are a robbery by the Prince and his companions on Gadshill, but the details differ from those of the incident in *I Henry IV;* a riot committed by the Prince and his followers, who are sent to prison; a courthouse scene where a thief is sentenced by the judge, whereupon the Prince gives the judge a box on the ear and is himself sent to prison; the sickness of King Henry IV; the reconciliation between father and son; a second scene of the King's sickness when the Prince, thinking that his father is dead, takes the crown but is recalled and again rebuked by the King, who dies directly after a further reconciliation; the new King Henry V on coming from his coronation dismisses his former companions, and immediately asks the Archbishop of Canterbury to expound his right to the French crown; the visit of the French King's ambassador, who presents a tun of tennis balls as a present from the Dauphin; the reconciliation of the King with the Lord Chief Justice; the enrollment of recruits; the news of the English advance received at the French Court; a scene in the French camp; Henry's orders for the battle; a brief battle scene (mostly indicated by noises behind the stage); the French offer of submission; the severe terms proposed by Henry; Henry's wooing of the French Princess Katharine; the French King's agreement to Henry's terms; and the final reconciliation. As well as the historical episodes, there are a number of passages of poor low comedy.

Shakespeare took little from this primitive drama. There is an occasional echo of a line, and while in *The Famous Victories* one of the Prince's wanton companions is called Sir John Oldcastle, alias Jockey, he not only has a very small part, appearing only twice, but he is undistinguished either for wit, bulk, or cowardice. In the first version of Shakespeare's *Henry IV*, the fat knight was called Oldcastle. The real Sir John Oldcastle was a very different person, of whom Holinshed wrote:

Also in this first year of this King's [Henry V's] reign Sir John Oldcastle, which by his wife was called Lord Cobham, a valiant captain and a hardy gentleman, was accused to the Archbishop of Canterbury of certain points of heresy, who, knowing him to be highly in the King's favor, declared to His Highness the whole accusation. The King first, having compassion of the nobleman, required the prelates that if he were a strayed sheep, rather by gentleness than by rigor to reduce him to the fold. And after this, he himself sent for him, and right earnestly exhorted him, and lovingly admonished him to reconcile himself to God and to His laws. The Lord Cobham not only thanked him for his most favorable clemency, but also declared first to him by word of mouth, and afterward by writing, the foundation of his faith and the ground of his belief, affirming His Grace to be his supreme head and competent judge, and none other person, offering a hundred knights and esquires to come to his purgation, or else to fight in open lists in defense of his just cause.

Oldcastle was nevertheless tried by a spiritual court, and found guilty of heresy. He was sent to the Tower to await the King's decision, but made his escape to Wales. For some years he lay in hiding, but was ultimately captured and brought to London, where he was condemned to death and burned as a heretic. He thus won a place in Fox's *Book of Martyrs* with others who suffered for their anti-Catholic opinions. Except for a somewhat profane habit of misquoting Scripture and parodying the Puritans, Shakespeare's fat knight has few of the marks of a Protestant martyr.

The name Oldcastle caused Shakespeare considerable trouble. In 1597 the title of Lord Cobham had recently passed to a nobleman called Henry Brooke, an unpleasant young man inclined to puritanism, and with a very good opinion of himself. He was so greatly offended that his predecessor should be presented on a public

stage in such a disreputable guise that Shakespeare was obliged to alter the name. The fat knight was therefore renamed Falstaff, after Sir John Fastolfe, who had already made a brief but discreditable appearance in *I Henry VI*. The real Falstolfe was a distinguished though unlucky commander in the French wars after Henry V's death. A few traces of the old name remain. The speech heading *Old.* (for *Fal.*) occurs once in the original quarto of the second part of *Henry IV*, and the epilogue refers to the scandal.

There was also some topicality in *I Henry IV*. The competition between the Chamberlain's and the Admiral's Men was growing acute, and in the scene where Falstaff plays the heavy father to Prince Hal (II.iv.311–527), Shakespeare parodied the pompous style of plays popular at the Rose playhouse and the tragic manner of Edward Alleyn (see Gen. Intro. pp. 36b–37b).

The play was printed very soon after its first performance. This was unusual, as the players, whenever possible, held back a popular play; they may however have been influenced by a desire to show the public that the change from Oldcastle to Falstaff had indeed been made. The play was entered for printing on February 26, 1598, to Andrew Wise as "The historye of Henry the iiiith with his battaile of Shrewsburye against Henry Hotspurre of the Northe with the conceipted mirthe of Sir John Falstoff." It appeared soon after with the title: *The History of Henrie the Fourth; With the battell at Shrewsburie, betweene the King and Lord Henry Percy, surnamed Henrie Hotspur of the North. With the humorous conceits of Sir John Falstalffe.* There is no suggestion in this title page that any second part had as yet been acted or planned. The quarto was reprinted in 1599 as "newly corrected by William Shakespeare," but this statement is untrue, as there are only minute differences between the first and second quartos. Other editions appeared in 1604, 1608, 1613, and 1622. The text printed in the first folio was set up from one of the quartos, from which the profane oaths have been carefully removed. Falstaff, it may be noted, was the most popular of all Shakespeare's characters and was more mentioned and quoted by contemporaries than any other.

In *I Henry IV* Shakespeare first reached complete maturity as a dramatist. In *Richard II* the characters lacked life. Richard himself was a picturesque and pathetic embodiment of sentimental poetry, but few of the others were interesting as individuals. The persons in *I Henry IV* are alive from the first; Shakespeare took elaborate care in creating his characters, especially Hotspur. In his first appearance (I.iii) Hotspur reveals his fiery and impatient mind, always darting away as a new thought appears, obsessed with a zeal for military honor which is not far from vanity, roused at a word, which makes him an easy victim for the King and his crafty uncle Worcester. Having drawn this side of his nature, Shakespeare next shows him (II.iii) in a charming little episode at home with his young wife; and to give added point to this episode has Prince Hal in the next scene briefly sum him up:

. . . the Hotspur of the North, he that kills me some six or seven dozen of Scots at a breakfast, washes his hands, and says to his wife, " Fie upon this quiet life! I want work." " O my sweet Harry," says she, " how many hast thou killed today? " " Give my roan horse a drench," says he, and answers, " Some fourteen," an hour after — " a trifle, a trifle."

It is cruel parody, but a sign that Shakespeare was now sure of himself, for only an artist who has complete self-confidence dares to make fun of his own serious efforts. Hotspur is next shown in conference with Glendower, Worcester, and Mortimer, and the contrast between these four very different characters is cleverly drawn. Hotspur has no patience with the Welshman's solemn claims to be extraordinary, is too impetuous to conceal his boredom, and mocks him beyond endurance; it is a tribute to Hotspur's personality, and a piece of subtle artistry, that such a man as Glendower should twice swallow his anger and give way. Hotspur is a blunt and practical young man with no use for poetry or art, natural or supernatural, insisting on his own way until it is given him and then yielding at once, and very fond of his wife in his own bluff way. He is a perfect specimen of the romantic soldier who filled Shakespeare with admiration and amusement, for he was careful to set Falstaff beside Hotspur. Falstaff's brief catechism on honor is a mocking echo of Hotspur's heroics. Hotspur dies at the hands of the Prince whom he had despised, lamenting not so much the loss of his hopes as of his honor as a soldier, and when he is dead his body is dishonorably prodded by the live Falstaff. Hotspur is the first of the full-length, elaborate studies of character which afterward abound in Shakespeare's plays.

Yet the most notable person in *I Henry IV* is Sir John Falstaff. In creating Falstaff Shakespeare used principally his own eyes and ears. Falstaff is the gross incarnation of a type of soldier found in any army, and there were many such — though on a lower level of greatness — swarming in London in the autumn of 1597, spending the profits of the campaign in taverns, brothels, and playhouses while they intrigued for a new command in the next season's campaign. Some of these captains were men of good family and education, younger sons who had no hope of an inheritance, and who preferred the excitements and loot of the wars to such a life as Justice Shallow lived in the country. Many were rogues who cheated the Government and their own men. Some ran to fat. Captain Nicholas Dawtrey, for instance, who was one of Edmund Spenser's acquaintances in Dublin, was so bulky that when he was wounded in battle it took eight men to shift him to the rear.[2] Moreover at all times military men have been noted for blustering ways and rich vocabularies.

There is no need to debate whether Falstaff was a coward. His philosophy — as is that of many a better man — was simple: " The better part of valor is discretion " (V.iv.120), and " Honor is a mere scutcheon " (V.i.142). " Give me life," he comments on the dead Blunt, " which if I can save, so; if not, honor comes unlooked for, and there's an end " (V.iii.63–65). He is quite out of place on any serious occasion, but for a rowdy evening a superb good companion. It is as well not to take Falstaff too seriously.

As for Prince Henry, he is shown as a young man who is deliberately posing as a waster so that when the time comes he may the more effectively confound the prophets and begin his reign by surprising his subjects. Herein he is as politic and crafty as his father. Henry IV had deliberately affected modesty, humility, and sobriety in contrast to his cousin, the shallow, pleasure-loving Richard II. The Prince purposely mixes with low company to contrast with his father; if his companions do not realize their part in this plan, the misfortune is theirs. In battle he shows himself the superior of Hotspur, not only as a soldier but in his complete understanding of men. This calculating self-control in all companies may not make him an amiable man, but it is preparing him to become a ruthlessly efficient ruler.

[2] See *The Falstaff Saga* by J. Dawtrey.

Henry IV, Part I

DRAMATIS PERSONAE

KING HENRY *the Fourth*
HENRY, *Prince of Wales*
JOHN *of Lancaster* } *sons to the King*
EARL OF WESTMORELAND
SIR WALTER BLUNT
THOMAS PERCY, *Earl of Worcester*
HENRY PERCY, *Earl of Northumberland*
HENRY PERCY, *surnamed* HOTSPUR, *his son*
EDMUND MORTIMER, *Earl of March*
RICHARD SCROOP, *Archbishop of York*
ARCHIBALD, *Earl of Douglas*
OWEN GLENDOWER
SIR RICHARD VERNON
SIR JOHN FALSTAFF
SIR MICHAEL, *a friend to the Archbishop of York*

POINS
GADSHILL
PETO
BARDOLPH

LADY PERCY, *wife to Hotspur and sister to Mortimer*
LADY MORTIMER, *daughter to Glendower and wife to Mortimer*
MISTRESS QUICKLY, *hostess of a tavern in Eastcheap*

LORDS, OFFICERS, SHERIFF, VINTNER, CHAMBERLAIN, DRAWERS, *two* CARRIERS, TRAVELERS, *and* ATTENDANTS

SCENE — *England and Wales.*

Act I

SCENE I. *London. The palace.*

[*Enter* KING HENRY, LORD JOHN OF LANCASTER, *the* EARL OF WESTMORELAND, SIR WALTER BLUNT, *and others.*]

KING. So shaken as we are, so wan with care,
Find we° a time for frighted peace to pant,
And breathe short-winded accents of new broils
To be commenced in stronds° afar remote.
No more the thirsty entrance of this soil   5
Shall daub her lips with her own children's blood.
No more shall trenching war° channel her fields,
Nor bruise her flowerets° with the armèd hoofs
Of hostile paces. Those opposèd eyes,
Which, like the meteors° of a troubled heaven,   10
All of one nature, of one substance bred,
Did lately meet in the intestine shock°
And furious close° of civil butchery,
Shall now, in mutual well-beseeming° ranks,
March all one way, and be no more opposed   15
Against acquaintance, kindred, and allies.
The edge of war, like an ill-sheathèd knife,
No more shall cut his master. Therefore, friends,
As far as to the sepulcher of Christ,
Whose soldier now, under whose blessèd cross   20
We are impressèd° and engaged to fight,

Forthwith a power of English shall we levy,
Whose arms were molded in their mothers' womb
To chase these pagans in those holy fields
Over whose acres walked those blessed feet   25
Which fourteen hundred years ago were nailed
For our advantage on the bitter cross.
But this our purpose now is twelvemonth old,
And bootless 'tis to tell you we will go.
Therefore we meet not now.° Then let me hear   30
Of you, my gentle cousin° Westmoreland,
What yesternight our Council did decree
In forwarding this dear expedience.°
WEST. My liege, this haste was hot in question,°
And many limits of the charge° set down   35
But yesternight, when all athwart° there came
A post° from Wales loaden° with heavy news,
Whose worst was that the noble Mortimer,°
Leading the men of Herefordshire to fight
Against the irregular° and wild Glendower,   40
Was by the rude hands of that Welshman taken,
A thousand of his people butchered.
Upon whose dead corpse there was such misuse,
Such beastly shameless transformation,
By those Welshwomen done as may not be   45
Without much shame retold or spoken of.
KING. It seems then that the tidings of this broil
Brake off our business for the Holy Land.

Act I, Sc. i: **2. Find we:** let us find. **4. stronds:** strands, shores. **7. trenching war:** trench warfare. **8. flowerets:** little flowers. **10. meteors:** comets or shooting stars, regarded as terrifying omens. **12. intestine shock:** clash of civil war. **13. close:** hand-to-hand battle. **14. well-beseeming:** seemly. **21. impressed:** enlisted.

29–30. bootless . . . now: i.e., there is no need to tell you of my decision, which has long been made. Our present meeting is to consider the details. **bootless:** vain. **31. cousin:** kinsman, used of any near relation. **33. dear expedience:** urgent enterprise, dear to me. **34. hot in question:** under eager discussion. **35. limits . . . charge:** estimates of the cost. **36. athwart:** cutting across. **37. post:** messenger. See App. 17. **loaden:** laden. **38. Mortimer:** See App. 28 and *I Hen IV* Intro. p. 333b. **40. irregular:** unruly.

WEST. This matched with other did, my gracious
    lord;
For more uneven° and unwelcome news   50
Came from the north and thus it did import:
On Holyrood Day,° the gallant Hotspur there,
Young Harry Percy, and brave Archibald,
That ever valiant and approvèd° Scot,
At Holmedon° met,   55
Where they did spend a sad and bloody hour,
As by discharge of their artillery,
And shape of likelihood,° the news was told.
For he that brought them, in the very heat
And pride of their contention° did take horse,   60
Uncertain of the issue° any way.
    KING. Here is a dear, a true industrious friend,
Sir Walter Blunt, new-lighted from his horse,
Stained with the variation of each soil
Betwixt that Holmedon and this seat of ours,   65
And he hath brought us smooth and welcome news.
The Earl of Douglas is discomfited.
Ten thousand bold Scots, two and twenty knights,
Balked° in their own blood did Sir Walter see
On Holmedon's plains. Of prisoners, Hotspur took
Mordake the Earl of Fife, and eldest son   71
To beaten Douglas; and the Earl of Athol,
Of Murray, Angus, and Menteith.
And is not this an honorable spoil?
A gallant prize? Ha, Cousin, is it not?   75
    WEST. In faith,
It is a conquest for a prince to boast of.
    KING. Yea, there thou makest me sad and makest
    me sin
In envy that my Lord Northumberland
Should be the father to so blest a son —   80
A son who is the theme of honor's tongue,
Amongst a grove, the very straightest plant,
Who is sweet Fortune's minion° and her pride —
Whilst I, by looking on the praise of him,
See riot and dishonor stain the brow   85
Of my young Harry. Oh, that it could be proved
That some night-tripping fairy° had exchanged
In cradle clothes our children where they lay,
And called mine Percy, his Plantagenet!
Then would I have his Harry, and he mine.   90
But let him from my thoughts. What think you,
    Coz,°
Of this young Percy's° pride? The prisoners
Which he in this adventure hath surprised

To his own use he keeps, and sends me word
I shall have none but Mordake Earl of Fife.   95
    WEST. This is his uncle's teaching. This is Wor-
    cester,
Malevolent° to you in all aspècts,
Which makes him prune° himself, and bristle up
The crest of youth against your dignity.
    KING. But I have sent for him to answer this, 100
And for this cause awhile we must neglect
Our holy purpose to Jerusalem.
Cousin, on Wednesday next our Council we
Will hold at Windsor. So inform the lords,
But come yourself with speed to us again,   105
For more is to be said and to be done
Than out of anger° can be uttered.
    WEST. I will, my liege.   [Exeunt.]

SCENE II. *London. An apartment of the
              Prince's.*

[*Enter the* PRINCE OF WALES *and* FALSTAFF.]
FAL. Now, Hal, what time of day is it, lad?
PRINCE. Thou art so fat-witted, with drinking of
old sack° and unbuttoning thee after supper and
sleeping upon benches after noon, that thou hast for-
gotten to demand that truly which thou wouldst   5
truly know. What a devil hast thou to do with the
time of the day? Unless hours were cups of sack, and
minutes capons, and clocks the tongues of bawds,
and dials the signs of leaping houses,° and the
blessed sun himself a fair hot wench in flame-colored
taffeta,° I see no reason why thou shouldst be so
superfluous to demand the time of the day.   13
    FAL. Indeed, you come near me now, Hal; for we
that take purses go by the moon and the seven stars,
and not by Phoebus,° he, " that wandering knight so
fair." And I prithee, sweet wag, when thou art King,
as, God save thy Grace — Majesty I should say, for
grace thou wilt have none ——   20
    PRINCE. What, none?
    FAL. No, by my troth,° not so much as will serve
to be prologue to an egg and butter.   24
    PRINCE. Well, how then? Come, roundly, roundly.
    FAL. Marry, then, sweet wag, when thou art King,
let not us that are squires of the night's body be
called thieves of the day's beauty.° Let us be Diana's

---

50. uneven: rough.   52. Holyrood Day: September 14.   54. ap-
proved: tried.   55. Holmedon: in Northumberland, near the
Scottish border.   58. shape of likelihood: what was likely to
happen.   60. pride . . . contention: height of battle.   61. issue:
result.   69. Balked: laid in ridges.   83. minion: darling.   87. night-
tripping fairy: a fairy coming by night. The fairies, so some
believed, used sometimes to steal a beautiful child and to leave
a changeling in its place.   91. Coz: cousin.   92. young Percy:
Shakespeare depicts Hotspur as a rash youth of about the same
age as Prince Hal. Actually at the battle of Shrewsbury (1403)
the Prince was barely 14 years old and Percy was 39.

97. Malevolent: boding evil, like a planet that brings disaster.
98. prune: preen, like a hawk in good condition trimming its
feathers.   107. out of anger: from an angry heart.
    Sc. ii: 3. sack: Spanish dry white wine.   10. leaping houses:
brothels.   11–12. flame-colored taffeta: bright red silk — the color
flaunted by harlots.   16. Phoebus: the sun, with a pun on the
Knight of the Sun, hero of a chivalric romance.   22. troth: truth.
27–28. let . . . beauty: i.e., do not let us who are gentlemen of the
dark (i.e., highwaymen) be called *thieves of the day's beauty* (i.e.
loafers) — with a pun on "beauty" and "booty."

foresters,° gentlemen of the shade, minions of the
moon. And let men say we be men of good govern-
ment,° being governed, as the sea is, by our noble
and chaste mistress the moon, under whose counte-
nance we steal.   33

PRINCE. Thou sayest well, and it holds well too;
for the fortune of us that are the moon's men doth
ebb and flow like the sea, being governed, as the sea
is, by the moon. As for proof, now — a purse of gold
most resolutely snatched on Monday night and   39
most dissolutely spent on Tuesday morning; got
with swearing "Lay by"° and spent with crying
"Bring in "° — now in as low an ebb as the foot of
the ladder,° and by and by in as high a flow as the
ridge of the gallows.

FAL. By the Lord, thou sayest true, lad. And is not
my hostess of the tavern a most sweet wench?   46

PRINCE. As the honey of Hybla,° my old lad of
the castle.° And is not a buff jerkin° a most sweet
robe of durance?°

FAL. How now, how now, mad wag! What, in thy
quips° and thy quiddities?° What a plague have I to
do with a buff jerkin?   52

PRINCE. Why, what a pox have I to do with my
hostess of the tavern?

FAL. Well, thou hast called her to a reckoning
many a time and oft.

PRINCE. Did I ever call for thee to pay thy part?

FAL. No. I'll give thee thy due, thou hast paid all
there.   60

PRINCE. Yea, and elsewhere, so far as my coin
would stretch. And where it would not, I have used
my credit.   63

FAL. Yea, and so used it that, were it not here
apparent that thou art heir° apparent —— But I
prithee, sweet wag, shall there be gallows standing
in England when thou art King? And resolution°
thus fobbed° as it is with the rusty curb of old
Father Antic° the law? Do not thou, when thou art
King, hang a thief.   70

PRINCE. No, thou shalt.

FAL. Shall I? Oh, rare! By the Lord, I'll be a
brave judge.

PRINCE. Thou judgest false already. I mean thou
shalt have the hanging of the thieves and so become
a rare hangman.   76

FAL. Well, Hal, well, and in some sort it jumps°
with my humor° as well as waiting in the court, I
can tell you.

PRINCE. For obtaining of suits?   80

FAL. Yea, for obtaining of suits,° whereof the
hangman° hath no lean wardrobe. 'Sblood,° I am as
melancholy as a gib-cat° or a lugged bear.°

PRINCE. Or an old lion, or a lover's lute.   84

FAL. Yea, or the drone of a Lincolnshire bagpipe.

PRINCE. What sayest thou to a hare,° or the melan-
choly of Moorditch?°   88

FAL. Thou hast the most unsavory similes, and art
indeed the most comparative,° rascaliest, sweet
young Prince. But, Hal, I prithee trouble me no more
with vanity. I would to God thou and I knew where
a commodity° of good names were to be bought. An
old lord of the Council rated° me the other day   94
in the street about you, sir, but I marked him not;
and yet he talked very wisely, but I regarded him
not; and yet he talked wisely, and in the street too.

PRINCE. Thou didst well, for wisdom cries out in
the streets, and no man regards it.°   100

FAL. Oh, thou hast damnable iteration,° and art
indeed able to corrupt a saint. Thou hast done much
harm upon me, Hal. God forgive thee for it! Before
I knew thee, Hal, I knew nothing; and now am I, if
a man should speak truly, little better than one   105
of the wicked. I must give over this life, and I will
give it over. By the Lord, an° I do not, I am a villain.
I'll be damned for never a king's son in Christen-
dom.

PRINCE. Where shall we take a purse tomorrow,
Jack?   111

FAL. 'Zounds,° where thou wilt, lad. I'll make one.
An I do not, call me villain and baffle° me.

PRINCE. I see a good amendment of life in thee —
from praying to purse-taking.

FAL. Why, Hal, 'tis my vocation, Hal. 'Tis no sin
for a man to labor in his vocation.   117
[*Enter* POINS.] Poins! Now shall we know if Gads-
hill have set a match.° Oh, if men were to be saved
by merit, what hole in Hell were hot enough for
him? This is the most omnipotent villain that ever
cried "Stand" to a true man.

PRINCE. Good morrow, Ned.   123

POINS. Good morrow, sweet Hal. What says Mon-

28–29. **Diana's foresters:** thieves who rob by night. *Diana:* the
moon.   30–31. **good government:** well-behaved.   41. **Lay by:**
i.e., "stick 'em up."   42. **Bring in:** i.e., the drink.   43. **ladder:**
from which a condemned man was thrust off the gallows in-
to space. See Gen. Intro. p. 27b.   47. **Hybla:** in Sicily, famous
for its honey.   47–48. **old . . . castle:** roisterer, with a pun on
Falstaff's original name of Oldcastle.   48. **buff jerkin:** leather
coat worn by the sheriff's sergeant.   49. **robe of durance:** coat
that endures (wears well) and that takes you to *durance* (pris-
on).   51. **quips:** wisecracks. **quiddities:** quibbles.   64–65. **here
. . . heir:** a pun, *heir* being pronounced as "hair."   67. **resolu-
tion:** a stout heart.   68. **fobbed:** fubbed, cheated.   69. **Father
Antic:** i.e., Daddy Buffoon.

77. **jumps:** agrees.   78. **humor:** whim.   81. **obtaining of suits:**
with a pun on *suit* — "petitions to the sovereign for favor" and
"clothes."   82. **hangman:** The clothes of the executed were the
hangman's perquisite. **'Sblood:** by God's blood.   83. **gib-cat:** tom-
cat. **lugged bear:** bear torn by the dogs. See App. 5.   87. **hare:**
regarded as a melancholy creature.   88. **melancholy of Moor-
ditch:** Moorditch was one of the open sewers of the City of
London, proverbial for its stink. See App. 4.   90. **comparative:**
quick at making comparisons.   93. **commodity:** parcel.   94. **rated:**
rebuked.   99–100. **wisdom . . . it:** quoted loosely from Prov-
erbs 1:20–24.   101. **iteration:** ability to quote.   107. **an:** if.
112. **'Zounds:** by God's Wounds.   113. **baffle:** disgrace. See *Rich
II*, I.i.170,n.   119. **set a match:** "framed a holdup."

sieur Remorse? What says Sir John Sack and Sugar? Jack! How agrees the Devil and thee about thy soul, that thou soldest him on Good Friday last for a cup of Madeira and a cold capon's leg?°   129

PRINCE. Sir John stands to his word, the Devil shall have his bargain, for he was never yet a breaker of proverbs.° He will give the Devil his due.

POINS. Then art thou damned for keeping thy word with the Devil.   135

PRINCE. Else he had been damned for cozening° the Devil.

POINS. But, my lads, my lads, tomorrow morning, by four o'clock, early at Gadshill!° There are pilgrims going to Canterbury with rich offer-   140 ings,° and traders riding to London with fat purses. I have vizards° for you all, you have horses for yourselves. Gadshill lies tonight in Rochester. I have bespoke° supper tomorrow night in Eastcheap. We may do it as secure as sleep. If you will go, I   145 will stuff your purses full of crowns. If you will not, tarry at home and be hanged.

FAL. Hear ye, Yedward,° if I tarry at home and go not, I'll hang you for going.   150

POINS. You will, chops?

FAL. Hal, wilt thou make one?

PRINCE. Who, I rob? I a thief? Not I, by my faith.

FAL. There's neither honesty, manhood, nor good fellowship in thee, nor thou camest not of the blood royal, if thou darest not stand for ten shillings.°

PRINCE. Well then, once in my days I'll be a madcap.   160

FAL. Why, that's well said.

PRINCE. Well, come what will, I'll tarry at home.

FAL. By the Lord, I'll be a traitor then, when thou art King.   165

PRINCE. I care not.

POINS. Sir John, I prithee, leave the Prince and me alone. I will lay him down such reasons for this adventure that he shall go.   169

FAL. Well, God give thee the spirit of persuasion and him the ears of profiting, that what thou speakest may move and what he hears may be believed,° that the true Prince may, for recreation sake, prove a false thief; for the poor abuses of the time want countenance.° Farewell. You shall find me in Eastcheap.   176

PRINCE. Farewell, thou latter spring!° Farewell, Allhallown summer!°   [Exit FALSTAFF.]

POINS. Now, my good sweet honey lord, ride with us tomorrow. I have a jest to execute that I can-   180 not manage alone. Falstaff, Bardolph, Peto, and Gadshill shall rob those men that we have already waylaid. Yourself and I will not be there, and when they have the booty, if you and I do not rob them, cut this head off from my shoulders.

PRINCE. How shall we part with them in setting forth?   188

POINS. Why, we will set forth before or after them, and appoint them a place of meeting, wherein it is at our pleasure to fail, and then will they adventure upon the exploit themselves; which they shall have no sooner achieved but we'll set upon them.   194

PRINCE. Yea, but 'tis like that they will know us by our horses, by our habits,° and by every other appointment,° to be ourselves.

POINS. Tut! Our horses they shall not see, I'll tie them in the wood. Our vizards we will change after we leave them. And, sirrah, I have cases of buckram° for the nonce,° to immask our noted outward garments.   202

PRINCE. Yea, but I doubt they will be too hard for us.

POINS. Well, for two of them, I know them to be as true-bred cowards as ever turned back; and for the third, if he fight longer than he sees rea-   207 son,° I'll forswear arms. The virtue of this jest will be the incomprehensible lies that this same fat rogue will tell us when we meet at supper — how thirty, at least, he fought with; what wards,° what blows, what extremities he endured. And in the reproof° of this lies the jest.   213

PRINCE. Well, I'll go with thee. Provide us all things necessary and meet me tomorrow night in Eastcheap. There I'll sup. Farewell.

POINS. Farewell, my lord.   [Exit.]

PRINCE. I know you all,° and will a while uphold° The unyoked humor° of your idleness.
Yet herein will I imitate the sun,   220
Who doth permit the base contagious° clouds
To smother up his beauty from the world,
That, when he please again to be himself,
Being wanted, he may be more wondered at
By breaking through the foul and ugly mists   225
Of vapors that did seem to strangle him.

128–29. Good . . . leg: Good Friday being the Church's most solemn fast day, to drink Madeira and eat chicken was a damnable sin.   131–32. breaker of proverbs: one to prove proverbs false.   136. cozening: cheating.   139. Gadshill: near Rochester in Kent. Some slight confusion is caused as the same name is used for one of the gang. See l. 118, and II.i. 36–106.   140–41. rich offerings: i.e., for the shrine of Saint Thomas à Becket at Canterbury.   142. vizards: masks.   144. bespoke: ordered.   149. Yedward: a form of Edward, Poins's first name.   157–58. blood . . . shillings: pun on royal, a coin worth 10s.   170–72. God . . . believed: Falstaff constantly drops into the pious jargon of professional preachers.   174–75. want countenance: need encouragement.

177. latter spring: late spring; i.e., green autumn.   178. Allhallown summer: Indian summer. Allhallown (All Saints' Day) is on November 1.   196. habits: clothes.   197. appointment: accouterment.   200–01. cases of buckram: overalls of coarse linen.   201. nonce: occasion.   207–08. fight . . . reason: This is Falstaff's avowed rule of life. See later V.iv.120.   211. wards: defense. See II.iv.215.   212. reproof: rebuttal.   218. I . . . all: This soliloquy is important for the understanding of the Prince's later treatment of Falstaff and the gang. uphold: tolerate.   219. unyoked humor: unrestrained behavior.   221. contagious: poisonous.

If all the year were playing holidays,
To sport would be as tedious as to work.
But when they seldom come, they wished-for come,
And nothing pleaseth but rare accidents.   230
So, when this loose behavior I throw off
And pay the debt I never promisèd,
By how much better than my word I am,
By so much shall I falsify men's hopes.
And like bright metal on a sullen° ground,   235
My reformation, glittering o'er my fault,
Shall show more goodly and attract more eyes
Than that which hath no foil° to set it off.
I'll so offend, to make offense a skill,°
Redeeming time° when men think least I will.   240
                              [*Exit.*]

SCENE III. *London. The palace.*

[*Enter the* KING, NORTHUMBERLAND, WORCESTER,
    HOTSPUR, SIR WALTER BLUNT, *with others.*]
KING. My blood hath been too cold and temperate,
Unapt to stir at these indignities,
And you have found me;° for accordingly
You tread upon my patience. But be sure
I will from henceforth rather be myself,°   5
Mighty and to be feared, than my condition,°
Which hath been smooth as oil, soft as young down,
And therefore lost that title of respect°
Which the proud soul ne'er pays but to the proud.
WOR. Our house, my sovereign liege, little de-
    serves   10
The scourge of greatness to be used on it,
And that same greatness too which our own hands
Have holp° to make so portly.°
NORTH. My lord——
KING. Worcester, get thee gone, for I do see   15
Danger and disobedience in thine eye.
O sir, your presence is too bold and peremptory,
And Majesty might never yet endure
The moody frontier of a servant brow.°
You have good leave to leave us.° When we need
Your use and counsel, we shall send for you.   21
                              [*Exit* WORCESTER.]
[*To* NORTHUMBERLAND] You were about to speak.
NORTH.   Yea, my good lord.
Those prisoners in your Highness' name demanded,°

Which Harry Percy here at Holmedon took,
Were, as he says, not with such strength denied   25
As is delivered to your Majesty.
Either envy,° therefore, or misprision°
Is guilty of this fault, and not my son.
    HOT. My liege, I did deny no prisoners.
But I remember, when the fight was done,   30
When I was dry with rage and éxtreme toil,
Breathless and faint, leaning upon my sword,
Came there a certain lord, neat, and trimly dressed,
Fresh as a bridegroom, and his chin new-reaped°
Showed like a stubble land at harvest home.   35
He was perfumèd like a milliner,
And 'twixt his finger and his thumb he held
A pouncet box,° which ever and anon
He gave his nose and took 't away again;
Who therewith angry, when it next came there,   40
Took it in snuff.° And still he smiled and talked,
And as the soldiers bore dead bodies by,
He called them untaught knaves, unmannerly,
To bring a slovenly unhandsome corse°
Betwixt the wind and his nobility.   45
With many holiday and lady terms°
He questioned me, amongst the rest, demanded
My prisoners in your Majesty's behalf.
I then, all smarting with my wounds being cold,
To be so pestered with a popinjay,°   50
Out of my grief° and my impatience
Answered neglectingly I know not what,
He should, or he should not; for he made me mad
To see him shine so brisk, and smell so sweet,
And talk so like a waiting gentlewoman°   55
Of guns and drums and wounds — God save the
    mark! —°
And telling me the sovereign'st° thing on earth
Was parmaceti° for an inward bruise;
And that it was great pity, so it was,
This villainous saltpeter should be digged   60
Out of the bowels of the harmless earth,
Which many a good tall° fellow had destroyed
So cowardly, and but for these vile guns,
He would himself have been a soldier.
This bald unjointed chat° of his, my lord,   65
I answered indirectly, as I said.
And I beseech you, let not his report
Come current° for an accusation

Betwixt my love and your high Majesty.

BLUNT. The circumstance considered, good my
    lord,   70
Whate'er Lord Harry Percy then had said
To such a person and in such a place,
At such a time, with all the rest retold,
May reasonably die and never rise
To do him wrong, or any way impeach°   75
What then he said, so he unsay it now.

KING. Why, yet° he doth deny his prisoners,
But with proviso° and exception,
That we at our own charge shall ransom straight
His brother-in-law, the foolish Mortimer,   80
Who, on my soul, hath willfully betrayed
The lives of those that he did lead to fight
Against that great magician,° damned Glendower,
Whose daughter, as we hear, the Earl of March
Hath lately married. Shall our coffers, then, 85
Be emptied to redeem a traitor home?
Shall we buy treason, and indent° with fears,
When they have lost and forfeited themselves?
No, on the barren mountains let him starve.
For I shall never hold that man my friend   90
Whose tongue shall ask me for one penny cost
To ransom home revolted Mortimer.

HOT. Revolted Mortimer!
He never did fall off,° my sovereign liege,
But by the chance of war. To prove that true   95
Needs no more but one tongue for all those wounds,
Those mouthèd° wounds, which valiantly he took
When on the gentle Severn's sedgy° bank,
In single opposition, hand to hand,
He did confound° the best part of an hour   100
In changing hardiment° with great Glendower.
Three times they breathed and three times did they
    drink,
Upon agreement, of swift Severn's flood;
Who then, affrighted with their bloody looks,
Ran fearfully among the trembling reeds,   105
And hid his crisp head in the hollow bank
Bloodstainèd with these valiant combatants.
Never did base and rotten policy°
Color her working° with such deadly wounds,
Nor never could the noble Mortimer   110
Receive so many, and all willingly.
Then let not him be slandered with revolt.

KING. Thou dost belie him,° Percy, thou dost belie
    him.
He never did encounter with Glendower.
I tell thee,   115
He durst as well have met the Devil alone

As Owen Glendower for an enemy.
Art thou not ashamed? But, sirrah,° henceforth
Let me not hear you speak of Mortimer.
Send me your prisoners with the speediest means,
Or you shall hear in such a kind from me   121
As will displease you. My Lord Northumberland,
We license your departure with your son.
Send us your prisoners, or you will hear of it.

        [*Exeunt* KING HENRY, BLUNT, *and train.*]

HOT. An if the Devil come and roar for them,
I will not send them. I will after straight   126
And tell him so, for I will ease my heart,
Albeit I make a hazard° of my head.

NORTH. What, drunk with choler?° Stay and
    pause awhile.
Here comes your uncle.

        [*Re-enter* WORCESTER.]

HOT.   Speak of Mortimer!   130
'Zounds, I will speak of him, and let my soul
Want mercy if I do not join with him.
Yea, on his part I'll empty all these veins,
And shed my dear blood drop by drop in the dust,
But I will lift the downtrod Mortimer   135
As high in the air as this unthankful King,
As this ingrate and cankered° Bolingbroke.

NORTH. Brother, the King hath made your nephew
    mad.

WOR. Who struck this heat up after I was gone?

HOT. He will, forsooth, have all my prisoners.
And when I urged the ransom once again   141
Of my wife's brother, then his cheek looked pale,
And on my face he turned an eye of death,
Trembling even at the name of Mortimer.

WOR. I cannot blame him. Was not he proclaimed
By Richard that dead is the next of blood?   146

NORTH. He was, I heard the proclamation.
And then it was when the unhappy King —
Whose wrongs in us God pardon!° — did set forth
Upon his Irish expedition,   150
From whence he intercepted° did return
To be deposed and shortly° murderèd.

WOR. And for whose death we in the world's wide
    mouth
Live scandalized and foully spoken of.

HOT. But, soft, I pray you. Did King Richard
    then   155
Proclaim my brother° Edmund Mortimer
Heir to the crown?

NORTH.   He did, myself did hear it.

HOT. Nay, then I cannot blame his cousin King,
That wished him on the barren mountains starve.
But shall it be that you, that set the crown   160

---

75. impeach: accuse, call in question.   77. yet: still, after all.
78. proviso: stipulation.   83. magician: See III.i.36–49.   87. in-
dent: make an agreement. See App. 6.   94. fall off: desert.
97. mouthed: looking like a mouth. 98. sedgy: reedy. 100. con-
found: consume.   101. changing hardiment: exchanging blows.
108. policy: cunning.   109. Color . . . working: disguise its real
intention.   113. belie him: lie about him.

118. sirrah: a form of address used to an inferior, here deliberately
insulting.   128. hazard: risk.   129. choler: wrath.   137. can-
kered: malignant.   149. Whose . . . pardon: may God forgive
the wrongs committed by us against him.   151. intercepted:
being hindered.   152. shortly: in a short time.   156. brother:
brother-in-law.

Upon the head of this forgetful man,
And for his sake wear the detested blot
Of murderous subornation,° shall it be
That you a world of curses undergo,
Being the agents, or base second means,°   165
The cords, the ladder, or the hangman rather?
Oh, pardon me that I descend so low,
To show the line° and the predicament°
Wherein you range° under this subtle King.
Shall it for shame be spoken in these days,   170
Or fill up chronicles in time to come,
That men of your nobility and power
Did gage° them both in an unjust behalf,
As both of you — God pardon it! — have done,
To put down Richard, that sweet lovely rose,   175
And plant this thorn, this canker,° Bolingbroke?
And shall it in more shame be further spoken,
That you are fooled, discarded, and shook off
By him for whom these shames ye underwent?
No, yet time serves wherein you may redeem   180
Your banished honors, and restore yourselves
Into the good thoughts of the world again,
Revenge the jeering and disdained° contempt
Of this proud King, who studies day and night
To answer all the debt he owes to you   185
Even with the bloody payment of your deaths.
Therefore, I say ——
    WOR.   Peace, Cousin, say no more.
And now I will unclasp a secret book,
And to your quick-conceiving° discontents
I'll read you matter deep and dangerous,   190
As full of peril and adventurous spirit
As to o'erwalk a current roaring loud
On the unsteadfast footing of a spear.°
    HOT. If he fall in, good night! Or sink or swim.
Send danger from the east unto the west,   195
So honor cross it from the north to south,
And let them grapple. Oh, the blood more stirs
To rouse a lion than to start a hare!
    NORTH. Imagination of some great exploit
Drives him beyond the bounds of patience.°   200
    HOT. By Heaven, methinks it were an easy leap,
To pluck bright honor from the pale-faced moon,
Or dive into the bottom of the deep,
Where fathom line could never touch the ground,
And pluck up drownèd honor by the locks,   205
So he that doth redeem her thence might wear
Without corrival° all her dignities.
But out upon this half-faced fellowship!°

    WOR. He apprehends a world of figures here,°
But not the form of what he should attend.   210
Good Cousin, give me audience for a while.
    HOT. I cry you mercy.
    WOR.   Those same noble Scots
That are your prisoners ——
    HOT.   I'll keep them all.
By God, he shall not have a Scot of them.
No, if a Scot would save his soul, he shall not. 215
I'll keep them, by this hand.
    WOR.   You start away
And lend no ear unto my purposes.
Those prisoners you shall keep.
    HOT.   Nay, I will, that's flat.
He said he would not ransom Mortimer.
Forbade my tongue to speak of Mortimer.   220
But I will find him when he lies asleep,
And in his ear I'll holloa "Mortimer!"
Nay,
I'll have a starling° shall be taught to speak
Nothing but "Mortimer," and give it him,   225
To keep his anger still in motion.
    WOR. Hear you, Cousin, a word.
    HOT. All studies here I solemnly defy,
Save how to gall° and pinch this Bolingbroke.
And that same sword-and-buckler° Prince of
    Wales,
But that I think his father loves him not   231
And would be glad he met with some mischance,
I would have him poisoned with a pot of ale.
    WOR. Farewell, kinsman. I'll talk to you
When you are better tempered to attend.   235
    NORTH. Why, what a wasp-stung and impatient
    fool
Art thou to break into this woman's mood,
Tying thine ear to no tongue but thine own!
    HOT. Why, look you, I am whipped and scourged
    with rods,
Nettled,° and stung with pismires,° when I hear
Of this vile politician,° Bolingbroke.   241
In Richard's time — what do you call the place? —
A plague upon it, it is in Gloucestershire,
'Twas where the madcap Duke his uncle kept,
His uncle York, where I first bowed my knee   245
Unto this king of smiles, this Bolingbroke —
'Sblood! —
When you and he came back from Ravenspurgh.
    NORTH. At Berkeley Castle.°
    HOT. You say true.   250
Why, what a candy deal° of courtesy

162–63. wear . . . subornation: wear the mark of shame as accessories to murder. subornation: procuring someone to commit a crime. 165. second means: assistants. 168. line: disgrace. predicament: class, category. 169. range: rank. 173. gage: pledge, engage. 176. canker: wild rose, contrasted with the garden rose. 183. disdained: disdainful. 189. quick-conceiving: quick-witted. 193. unsteadfast . . . spear: with a spear as unsteady bridge. 200. patience: self-control. 207. corrival: partner. 208. half-faced fellowship: starving partnership; i.e., sharing of honor which is insufficient for two to share.

209. apprehends . . . here: i.e., he is entirely carried away by his imagination. figures: shapes, fantasies. 224. starling: The starling, like the jackdaw and the parrot, can be taught to mimic sound. 229. gall: make sore. 230. sword-and-buckler: swashbuckler. 240. Nettled: whipped with nettles. pismires: ants. 241. politician: schemer. 249. Berkeley Castle: For this episode see *Rich II*, II.iii.41–50. 251. candy deal: deal of candy; i.e., hypocritical.

This fawning greyhound then did proffer me!
Look, " when his infant fortune came to age,"
And " gentle Harry Percy," and " kind Cousin."
Oh, the devil take such cozeners! God forgive me!
Good Uncle, tell your tale, I have done.   256
    WOR. Nay, if you have not, to it again.
We will stay° your leisure.
    HOT.   I have done, i' faith.
    WOR. Then once more to your Scottish prisoners.
Deliver them up without their ransom straight,   260
And make the Douglas' son your only mean°
For powers° in Scotland; which, for divers reasons
Which I shall send you written, be assured
Will easily be granted. [*To* NORTHUMBERLAND] You,
    my lord,
Your son in Scotland being thus employed,   265
Shall secretly into the bosom creep
Of that same noble prelate, well beloved,
The Archbishop.
    HOT. Of York, is it not?
    WOR. True, who bears hard°   270
His brother's death at Bristol, the Lord Scroop.
I speak not this in estimation,°
As what I think might be, but what I know
Is ruminated,° plotted, and set down,
And only stays but to behold the face   275
Of that occasion that shall bring it on.
    HOT. I smell it. Upon my life, it will do well.
    NORTH. Before the game is afoot, thou still° let'st
    slip.°
    HOT. Why, it cannot choose but be a noble plot.
And then the power of Scotland and of York,   280
To join with Mortimer, ha?
    WOR.   And so they shall.
    HOT. In faith, it is exceedingly well aimed.
    WOR. And 'tis no little reason bids us speed,
To save our heads by raising of a head;°
For, bear ourselves as even as we can,°   285
The King will always think him in our debt,
And think we think ourselves unsatisfied,
Till he hath found a time to pay us home.
And see already how he doth begin
To make us strangers to his looks of love.   290
    HOT. He does, he does. We'll be revenged on him.
    WOR. Cousin, farewell. No further go in this
Than I by letters shall direct your course.
When time is ripe, which will be suddenly,
I'll steal to Glendower and Lord Mortimer,   295
Where you and Douglas and our powers at once,
As I will fashion° it, shall happily meet,
To bear our fortunes in our own strong arms,

Which now we hold at much uncertainty.
    NORTH. Farewell, good Brother. We shall thrive,
    I trust.   300
    HOT. Uncle, adieu. Oh, let the hours be short
Till fields and blows and groans applaud our sport!
                                                                    [*Exeunt.*]

Act II

SCENE I. *Rochester. An innyard.*

[*Enter a* CARRIER *with a lantern in his hand.*]
    1. CAR. Heigh-ho! An it be not four by the day, I'll
be hanged. Charles's Wain° is over the new chim-
ney, and yet our horse not packed.° What, ostler!   4
    OSTLER. [*Within*] Anon, anon.
    1. CAR. I prithee, Tom, beat° Cut's° saddle, put a
few flocks° in the point.° Poor jade,° is wrung° in
the withers° out of all cess.°   8
                            [*Enter another* CARRIER.]
    2. CAR. Peas and beans are as dank here as a dog,
and that is the next way to give poor jades the bots.°
This house is turned upside down since Robin Ostler
died.
    1. CAR. Poor fellow, never joyed since the price of
oats rose. It was the death of him.   14
    2. CAR. I think this be the most villainous house in
all London road for fleas. I am stung like a tench.°
    1. CAR. Like a tench! By the mass, there is ne'er a
king Christen° could be better bit than I have been
since the first cock.   20
    2. CAR. Why, they will allow us ne'er a jordan,°
and then we leak in your chimney, and your cham-
ber lye° breeds fleas like a loach.
    1. CAR. What, ostler! Come away and be hanged!
Come away.   25
    2. CAR. I have a gammon of bacon° and two razes°
of ginger, to be delivered as far as Charing Cross.
    1. CAR. God's body! The turkeys in my pannier°
are quite starved. What, ostler! A plague on thee!
Hast thou never an eye in thy head? Canst not hear?
An 'twere not as good deed as drink to break the pate

---

258. **stay:** await.   261. **mean:** means.   262. **powers:** forces, ar-
mies.   270. **bears hard:** takes hardly.   272. **in estimation:**
as a guess.   274. **ruminated:** considered.   278. **still:** continu-
ously. **let'st slip:** let loose the greyhound.   284. **head:** armed
force.   285. **bear . . . can:** however discreetly we may behave.
297. **fashion:** contrive.

Act II, Sc. i: 2. **Charles's Wain:** Charles's Wagon, the con-
stellation of the Great Bear, called also the Great Dipper.
4. **horse . . . packed:** Carriers at this time used pack horses for
transport.   6. **beat:** i.e., to make the padding more even. **Cut:**
name of a horse with a docked tail.   7. **flocks:** tufts of wool. **point:**
pommel. **jade:** horse in poor condition. **wrung:** galled.   8. **withers:**
point of the shoulder. **out . . . cess:** excessively.   10. **bots:** worms.
16. **tench:** The tench and the loach (fresh-water fish) are some-
times infested with a form of louse.   19. **Christen:** Christian.
21. **jordan:** chamber pot.   23. **chamber lye:** urine. Elizabethan
sanitary arrangements and domestic habits were crude.   26. **gam-
mon of bacon:** cured ham. **razes:** roots.   28. **pannier:** basket.

on thee, I am a very villain. Come, and be hanged!
Hast no faith in thee?   35

[*Enter* GADSHILL.]

GADS. Good morrow, carriers. What's o'clock?

1. CAR. I think it be two o'clock.

GADS. I prithee lend me thy lantern, to see my geld-
ing in the stable.   39

1. CAR. Nay, by God, soft,° I know a trick worth
two of that, i' faith.

GADS. I pray thee, lend me thine.

2. CAR. Aye, when? Canst tell?° Lend me thy lan-
tern, quoth he? Marry, I'll see thee hanged first.

GADS. Sirrah carrier, what time do you mean to
come to London?   46

2. CAR. Time enough to go to bed with a candle, I
warrant thee. Come, Neighbor Mugs, we'll call up
the gentlemen. They will along with company, for
they have great charge.°   [*Exeunt* CARRIERS.]

GADS. What ho! Chamberlain!°   52

CHAM. [*Within*] At hand, quoth pickpurse.

GADS. That's even as fair as — at hand, quoth the
chamberlain; for thou variest no more from picking
of purses than giving direction doth from laboring.
Thou layest the plot° how.   57

[*Enter* CHAMBERLAIN.]

CHAM. Good morrow, Master Gadshill. It holds
current that I told you yesternight. There's a frank-
lin° in the wild° of Kent hath brought three hun-
dred marks° with him in gold. I heard him tell it to
one of his company last night at supper — a kind of
auditor, one that hath abundance of charge too, God
knows what. They are up already, and call for eggs
and butter. They will away presently.   66

GADS. Sirrah, if they meet not with Saint Nicholas'
clerks,° I'll give thee this neck.

CHAM. No, I'll none of it. I pray thee, keep that for
the hangman, for I know thou worshipest Saint
Nicholas as truly as a man of falsehood may.   72

GADS. What talkest thou to me of the hangman?
If I hang, I'll make a fat pair of gallows; for if I hang,
old Sir John hangs with me, and thou knowest he is
no starveling. Tut! There are other Trojans° that
thou dreamest not of, the which for sport sake   77
are content to do the profession some grace; that
would, if matters should be looked into, for their
own credit sake, make all whole. I am joined with no
foot landrakers,° no long-staff sixpenny strikers,°

none of these mad mustachio purple-hued malt-
worms;° but with nobility and tranquility, burgo-
masters and great oneyers,° such as can hold in,°
such as will strike sooner than speak, and speak   85
sooner than drink, and drink sooner than pray. And
yet, 'zounds, I lie; for they pray continually to their
saint, the commonwealth; or rather, not pray to her,
but prey on her, for they ride up and down on her
and make her their boots.°   91

CHAM. What, the commonwealth their boots? Will
she hold out water in foul way?

GADS. She will, she will — justice hath liquored°
her. We steal as in a castle, cocksure. We have the
receipt° of fern seed,° we walk invisible.   96

CHAM. Nay, by my faith, I think you are more
beholding to the night than to fern seed for your
walking invisible.

GADS. Give me thy hand. Thou shalt have a share
in our purchase,° as I am a true man.   101

CHAM. Nay, rather let me have it, as you are a
false thief.

GADS. Go to. "Homo" is a common name to all
men. Bid the ostler bring my gelding out of   105
the stable. Farewell, you muddy° knave. [*Exeunt.*]

SCENE II. *The highway, near* GADSHILL.

[*Enter* PRINCE HENRY *and* POINS.]

POINS. Come, shelter, shelter. I have removed Fal-
staff's horse, and he frets like a gummed velvet.°

PRINCE. Stand close.

[*Enter* FALSTAFF.]

FAL. Poins! Poins, and be hanged! Poins!   4

PRINCE. Peace, ye fat-kidneyed rascal! What a
brawling dost thou keep!

FAL. Where's Poins, Hal?

PRINCE. He is walked up to the top of the hill. I'll
go seek him.   9

FAL. I am accursed to rob in that thief's company.
The rascal hath removed my horse, and tied him I
know not where. If I travel but four foot by the
squier° further afoot, I shall break my wind. Well, I
doubt not but to die a fair death for all this, if I 'scape
hanging for killing that rogue. I have forsworn°   16
his company hourly any time this two and twenty
years, and yet I am bewitched with the rogue's

---

40. soft: go easy.   43. Canst tell: i.e., "says you!"   51. great
charge: much money.   52. Chamberlain: man in charge of the
bedrooms at an inn.   57. layest . . . plot: It was a common com-
plaint that the chamberlains of inns were in league with highway-
men.   60. franklin: rich farmer.   wild: weald; the hilly district
in Kent and adjoining counties.   61. mark: 13s 4d (⅔ of a
pound). See App. 27.   67–68. Saint Nicholas' clerks: thieves,
Saint Nicholas being their patron saint.   76. Trojans: good
lads.   81. foot landrakers: roving footpads; i.e., thieves so poor
that they go on foot.   long-staff . . . strikers: robbers who use a
long staff and will hold a man up for a pittance.

82–83. mustachio . . . maltworms: red-faced tipplers with great
mustaches.   84. oneyers: ones.   hold in: keep their mouths shut.
91. boots: booty. The chamberlain caps his remark with a pun
on leather boots.   94. liquored: greased.   96. receipt: directions
for using, recipe.   fern seed: The seed of the fern is so small that
it was said to be invisible, and if found on Saint John's Day, to
confer invisibility on the finder.   101. purchase: in thieves' lan-
guage, plunder.   106. muddy: muddleheaded.
     Sc. ii: 2. gummed velvet: Cheap velvet (as well as taf-
feta) was sometimes treated with gum to give it stiffening,
but it frayed sooner.   13. squier: square, rule.   16. forsworn:
sworn off.

company. If the rascal have not given me medicines°
to make me love him, I'll be hanged; it could not be
else, I have drunk medicines. Poins! Hal! A   21
plague upon you both! Bardolph! Peto! I'll starve ere
I'll rob a foot further. An 'twere not as good a deed
as drink, to turn true man and to leave these rogues,
I am the veriest varlet° that ever chewed with a   25
tooth. Eight yards of uneven ground is threescore
and ten miles afoot with me, and the stony-hearted
villains know it well enough. A plague upon it when
thieves cannot be true one to another! [*They*   30
whistle.] Whew! A plague upon you all! Give me
my horse, you rogues, give me my horse, and be
hanged!

PRINCE. Peace, ye fat-guts! Lie down, lay thine ear
close to the ground and list if thou canst hear the
tread of travelers.   35

FAL. Have you any levers to lift me up again,
being down? 'Sblood, I'll not bear mine own flesh so
far afoot again for all the coin in thy father's ex-
chequer. What a plague mean ye to colt° me thus?

PRINCE. Thou liest. Thou art not colted, thou art
uncolted.   42

FAL. I prithee, good Prince Hal, help me to my
horse, good king's son.

PRINCE. Out, ye rogue! Shall I be your ostler?   45

FAL. Go hang thyself in thine own heir-apparent
garters! If I be ta'en, I'll peach for this. An I have
not ballads° made on you all and sung to filthy tunes,
let a cup of sack be my poison. When a jest is so for-
ward, and afoot too! I hate it.   50

[*Enter* GADSHILL, BARDOLPH *and* PETO *with him.*]

GADS. Stand.

FAL. So I do, against my will.

POINS. Oh, 'tis our setter.° I know his voice. Bar-
dolph, what news?   54

BARD. Case° ye, case ye, on with your vizards.
There's money of the King's coming down the hill,
'tis going to the King's exchequer.

FAL. You lie, ye rogue, 'tis going to the King's
tavern.

GADS. There's enough to make us all.   60

FAL. To be hanged.

PRINCE. Sirs, you four shall front them in the nar-
row lane, Ned Poins and I will walk lower. If they
'scape from your encounter, then they light on us.

PETO. How many be there of them?   66

GADS. Some eight or ten.

FAL. 'Zounds, will they not rob us?

PRINCE. What, a coward, Sir John Paunch?

FAL. Indeed I am not John of Gaunt, your grand-
father, but yet no coward, Hal.   71

PRINCE. Well, we leave that to the proof.

POINS. Sirrah Jack, thy horse stands behind the

hedge. When thou needest him, there thou shalt find
him. Farewell, and stand fast.   75

FAL. Now cannot I strike him, if I should be
hanged.

PRINCE. Ned, where are our disguises?

POINS. Here, hard by. Stand close.

[*Exeunt* PRINCE *and* POINS.]

FAL. Now, my masters, happy man be his dole,°
say I. Every man to his business.   81

[*Enter the* TRAVELERS.]

1. TRAV. Come, neighbor. The boy shall lead our
horses down the hill. We'll walk afoot awhile, and
ease our legs.

THIEVES. Stand!

TRAVS. Jesus bless us!   86

FAL. Strike, down with them, cut the villains'
throats! Ah, whoreson° caterpillars,° bacon-fed
knaves! They hate us youth. Down with them, fleece
them.

TRAVS. Oh, we are undone, both we and ours for-
ever!   92

FAL. Hang ye, gorbellied° knaves, are ye undone?
No, ye fat chuffs,° I would your store were here!°
On, bacons,° on! What, ye knaves! Young men must
live. You are grand jurors,° are ye? We'll jure ye,
'faith.   97

[*Here they rob them and bind them. Exeunt.*]

[*Re-enter* PRINCE HENRY *and* POINS *disguised.*]

PRINCE. The thieves have bound the true men.
Now could thou and I rob the thieves and go mer-
rily to London, it would be argument° for a week,
laughter for a month, and a good jest forever.

POINS. Stand close. I hear them coming.   103

[*Enter the* THIEVES *again.*]

FAL. Come, my masters, let us share, and then to
horse before day. An the Prince and Poins be not
two arrant° cowards, there's no equity stirring.°
There's no more valor in that Poins than in a wild
duck.   108

PRINCE. Your money!

POINS. Villains! [*As they are sharing, the* PRINCE
and POINS *set upon them; they all run away; and* FAL-
STAFF, *after a blow or two, runs away too, leaving the
booty behind them.*]

PRINCE. Got with much ease. Now merrily to
horse.
The thieves are all scattered and possessed with fear
So strongly that they dare not meet each other.
Each takes his fellow for an officer.
Away, good Ned. Falstaff sweats to death,   115
And lards the lean earth as he walks along.

80. happy . . . dole: i.e., here's luck; lit., may the lucky man have
his reward.   88. whoreson: bastard. caterpillars: See *Rich II*,
II.iii.166,n.   93. gorbellied: big-bellied.   94. chuffs: mean
misers. were here: i.e., in your bellies.   95. bacons: fat pigs.
96. grand jurors: i.e., men of highest respectability.   101. argu-
ment: matter for talk.   106. arrant: complete. no . . . stirring:
no sound judgment in the world

19. medicines: love potions.   25. varlet: knave.   40. colt: trick.
48. ballads: See App. 8.   53. setter: the accomplice who brings
the victim in.   55. Case: mask

Were't not for laughing, I should pity him.

POINS. How the rogue roared!   [*Exeunt.*]

SCENE III. *Warkworth Castle.*

[*Enter* HOTSPUR *alone, reading a letter.*]

HOT. "But, for mine own part, my lord, I could
be well contented to be there, in respect of the love I
bear your house." He could be contented. Why is he
not, then? In respect of the love he bears our house.
He shows in this he loves his own barn better 5
than he loves our house. Let me see some more.
"The purpose you undertake is dangerous" — why,
that's certain. 'Tis dangerous to take a cold, to sleep,
to drink; but I tell you, my lord fool, out of this net-
tle danger we pluck this flower safety. "The purpose
you undertake is dangerous; the friends you 10
have named uncertain; the time itself unsorted;° and
your whole plot too light for the counterpoise of so
great an opposition." Say you so, say you so? I say
unto you again, you are a shallow cowardly 15
hind,° and you lie. What a lackbrain is this! By the
Lord, our plot is a good plot as ever was laid, our
friends true and constant — a good plot, good
friends, and full of expectation. An excellent plot,
very good friends. What a frosty-spirited rogue 20
is this! Why, my Lord of York° commends the plot
and the general course of the action. 'Zounds, an I
were now by this rascal, I could brain him with his
lady's fan. Is there not my father, my uncle, and
myself? Lord Edmund Mortimer, my Lord of 25
York, and Owen Glendower? Is there not besides
the Douglas? Have I not all their letters to meet me
in arms by the ninth of the next month? And are
they not some of them set forward already? What a
pagan rascal is this, an infidel! Ha! You shall see 30
now in very sincerity of fear and cold heart, will he
to the King, and lay open all our proceedings. Oh, I
could divide myself, and go to buffets,° for moving°
such a dish of skim milk with so honorable an 35
action! Hang him! Let him tell the King. We are
prepared. I will set forward tonight.

[*Enter* LADY PERCY.] How now, Kate! I must leave
you within these two hours.

LADY P. O my good lord, why are you thus alone?
For what offense have I this fortnight been 41
A banished woman from my Harry's bed?
Tell me, sweet lord, what is't that takes from thee
Thy stomach,° pleasure, and thy golden sleep?
Why dost thou bend thine eyes upon the earth, 45
And start so often when thou sit'st alone?
Why hast thou lost the fresh blood in thy cheeks,

And given my treasures° and my rights of thee
To thick-eyed° musing and cursed melancholy?
In thy faint slumbers I by thee have watched, 50
And heard thee murmur tales of iron wars,
Speak terms of manage° to thy bounding steed,
Cry "Courage! To the field!" And thou hast talked
Of sallies and retires,° of trenches, tents,
Of palisadoes,° frontiers,° parapets, 55
Of basilisks, of cannon, culverin,°
Of prisoners' ransom, and of soldiers slain,
And all the currents° of a heady° fight.
Thy spirit within thee hath been so at war
And thus hath so bestirred thee in thy sleep 60
That beads of sweat have stood upon thy brow,
Like bubbles in a late-disturbèd stream.
And in thy face strange motions have appeared,
Such as we see when men restrain their breath
On some great sudden hest.° Oh, what portènts are
these? 65
Some heavy business hath my lord in hand,
And I must know it, else he loves me not.

HOT. What ho! [*Enter* SERVANT.] Is Gilliams with
the packet gone?

SERV. He is, my lord, an hour ago.

HOT. Hath Butler brought those horses from the
sheriff? 70

SERV. One horse, my lord, he brought even now.

HOT. What horse? A roan, a crop-ear,° is it not?

SERV. It is, my lord.

HOT.   That roan shall be my throne.
Well, I will back him straight. Oh, Esperance!°
Bid Butler lead him forth into the park. 75

[*Exit* SERVANT.]

LADY P. But hear you, my lord.

HOT. What say'st thou, my lady?

LADY P. What is it carries you away?

HOT. Why, my horse, my love, my horse.

LADY P. Out, you mad-headed ape! 80
A weasel hath not such a deal of spleen°
As you are tossed with. In faith,
I'll know your business, Harry, that I will.
I fear my brother Mortimer doth stir
About his title, and hath sent for you 85
To line° his enterprise. But if you go ——

HOT. So far afoot, I shall be weary, love.

LADY P. Come, come, you paraquito,° answer me

Sc. iii: **11. unsorted:** ill-chosen. **16. hind:** female deer, the
essence of timidity. **21. Lord of York:** Richard Scroop, Arch-
bishop of York. **34. go to buffets:** come to blows. **moving:** trying
to move. **44. stomach:** appetite.

48. treasures: i.e., that ought to be mine. **49. thick-eyed:** dull-
sighted, because he sees nothing. **52. manage:** horsemanship.
54. sallies . . . retires: raids and retreats. **55 palisadoes:** defen-
sive protection of pointed stakes. See Pl. 12a. **frontiers:** barricades.
56. basilisks . . . culverin: the heavier pieces of artillery. The
basilisk was of 5-inch caliber and fired a shot of $15\frac{1}{2}$ lbs., the
cannon of 8-inch caliber with a 60-lb. shot, the culverin of $5\frac{1}{2}$-inch
caliber with a 17-lb. shot. Shakespeare is thinking of Elizabethan
ordnance rather than the cannon used in 1400. **58. currents:**
courses, rapid movement. **heady:** fierce. **65. hest:** command,
action. **72. crop-ear:** with short ears. **74. Esperance:** hope —
the battle cry of the Percies. **81. spleen:** anger, passion. **86. line:**
strengthen. **88. paraquito:** parrot.

Directly unto this question that I ask.
In faith, I'll break thy little finger, Harry,   90
An if thou wilt not tell me all things true.

HOT. Away,
Away, you trifler! Love! I love thee not,
I care not for thee, Kate. This is no world
To play with mammets° and to tilt with lips.°   95
We must have bloody noses and cracked crowns,
And pass them current° too. God's me, my horse!
What say'st thou, Kate? What wouldst thou have
        with me?

LADY P. Do you not love me? Do you not, indeed?
Well, do not, then, for since you love me not,   100
I will not love myself. Do you not love me?
Nay, tell me if you speak in jest or no.

HOT. Come, wilt thou see me ride?
And when I am o' horseback, I will swear
I love thee infinitely. But hark you, Kate,   105
I must not have you henceforth question me
Whither I go, nor reason whereabout.
Whither I must, I must. And, to conclude,
This evening must I leave you, gentle Kate.
I know you wise, but yet no farther wise   110
Than Harry Percy's wife. Constant you are,
But yet a woman. And for secrecy,
No lady closer, for I well believe
Thou wilt not utter what thou dost not know,
And so far will I trust thee, gentle Kate.   115

LADY P. How! So far?

HOT. Not an inch further. But hark you, Kate,
Whither I go, thither shall you go too;
Today will I set forth, tomorrow you.   119
Will this content you, Kate?

LADY P.   It must of force. [*Exeunt.*]

SCENE IV. *The Boar's Head Tavern in
Eastcheap.*

[*Enter the* PRINCE, *and* POINS.]

PRINCE. Ned, prithee come out of that fat° room,
and lend me thy hand to laugh a little.

POINS. Where hast been, Hal?

PRINCE. With three or four loggerheads° amongst
three or fourscore hogsheads.° I have sounded   5
the very base string of humility.° Sirrah, I am sworn
brother to a leash° of drawers, and can call them all
by their Christen names, as Tom, Dick, and Francis.
They take it already upon their salvation that though
I be but Prince of Wales, yet I am the king of   10
courtesy; and tell me flatly I am no proud Jack, like

Falstaff, but a Corinthian,° a lad of mettle, a good
boy, by the Lord, so they call me, and when I am
King of England, I shall command all the good lads
in Eastcheap. They call drinking deep, dyeing   15
scarlet, and when you breathe in your watering,°
they cry " hem!"° and bid you play it off.° To con-
clude, I am so good a proficient in one quarter of an
hour that I can drink with any tinker in his own   20
language during my life. I tell thee, Ned, thou hast
lost much honor that thou wert not with me in this
action. But, sweet Ned — to sweeten which name of
Ned, I give thee this pennyworth of sugar, clapped
even now into my hand by an underskinker,°   25
one that never spake other English in his life than
" Eight shillings and sixpence," and " You are wel-
come," with this shrill addition, " Anon,° anon, sir!
Score° a pint of bastard° in the Half-Moon,"° or so.
But, Ned, to drive away the time till Falstaff   30
come, I prithee do thou stand in some by-room while
I question my puny° drawer to what end he gave me
the sugar. And do thou never leave calling " Fran-
cis," that his tale to me may be nothing but   35
" Anon." Step aside, and I'll show thee a precedent.°

POINS. Francis!

PRINCE. Thou art perfect.

POINS. Francis!   [*Exit* POINS.]

[*Enter* FRANCIS.]

FRAN. Anon, anon, sir. Look down into the Pom-
garnet,° Ralph.

PRINCE. Come hither, Francis.

FRAN. My lord?   44

PRINCE. How long hast thou to serve, Francis?°

FRAN. Forsooth, five years, and as much as to ——

POINS. [*Within*] Francis!

FRAN. Anon, anon, sir.   49

PRINCE. Five year! By'r Lady, a long lease for the
clinking of pewter. But, Francis, darest thou be so
valiant as to play the coward with thy indenture°
and show it a fair pair of heels and run from it? 54

FRAN. Oh, Lord, sir, I'll be sworn upon all the
books in England I could find in my heart.°

POINS. [*Within*] Francis!

FRAN. Anon, sir.

PRINCE. How old art thou, Francis?

FRAN. Let me see — about Michaelmas next I shall
be ——   61

---

95. **mammets:** dolls. **tilt . . . lips:** kiss. **97. current:** with a pun
on *cracked crowns;* i.e., broken heads, and crown pieces, cracked
and so not current.

Sc. iv: 1. **fat:** stuffy. 4. **loggerheads:** blockheads. 5. **hogs-
heads:** casks. 5–6. **sounded . . . humility:** i.e., have sunk to
the lowest depth. 7. **leash:** set of three, properly used of a
leash of greyhounds.

12. **Corinthian:** a gay lad. 16. **watering:** drinking. 17. **cry
" hem ":** one of those exclamations made by topers, like "Here's
how." **play it off:** get it down. 25. **underskinker:** assistant bar-
tender. 28. **Anon:** at once or by and by, the drawer's cry,
"Coming, sir." 29. **Score:** chalk up, the method of recording
a debt for drink still used in English public houses. **bastard:**
a sweet white wine. **Half-Moon:** Each room in an inn or a tav-
ern had its own name. 32. **puny:** freshman. 36. **precedent:**
specimen.   42. **Pomgarnet:** Pomegranate — another room.
45. **How . . . Francis:** i.e., how many years of your apprentice-
ship still remain. As Francis has only served two of his seven
years, he is sixteen. 53. **indenture:** agreement of apprenticeship.
See App. 6. 56. **could . . . heart:** i.e., very willingly.

POINS. [*Within*] Francis!

FRAN. Anon, sir. Pray stay a little, my lord.

PRINCE. Nay, but hark you, Francis. For the sugar thou gavest me, 'twas a pennyworth, was't not? 66

FRAN. Oh, Lord, I would it had been two!

PRINCE. I will give thee for it a thousand pound. Ask me when thou wilt, and thou shalt have it. 70

POINS. [*Within*] Francis!

FRAN. Anon, anon.

PRINCE. Anon, Francis? No, Francis, but tomorrow, Francis; or, Francis, o' Thursday; or indeed, Francis, when thou wilt. But Francis!

FRAN. My lord?   76

PRINCE. Wilt thou rob this leathern-jerkin, crystal-button, not-pated, agate-ring, puke-stocking, caddis-garter, smooth-tongue, Spanish-pouch ——°   80

FRAN. Oh, Lord, sir, who do you mean?

PRINCE. Why, then, your brown bastard is your only drink, for look you, Francis, your white canvas doublet will sully. In Barbary,° sir, it cannot come to so much.

FRAN. What, sir?   86

POINS. [*Within*] Francis!

PRINCE. Away, you rogue! Dost thou not hear them call? [*Here they both call him; the* DRAWER *stands amazed, not knowing which way to go.*]

[*Enter* VINTNER.]

VINT. What, standest thou still, and hearest such a calling? Look to the guests within. [*Exit* FRANCIS.] My lord, old Sir John, with half-a-dozen more, are at the door. Shall I let them in?   94

PRINCE. Let them alone awhile, and then open the door. [*Exit* VINTNER.] Poins!

[*Re-enter* POINS.]

POINS. Anon, anon, sir.

PRINCE. Sirrah, Falstaff and the rest of the thieves are at the door. Shall we be merry?   99

POINS. As merry as crickets, my lad. But hark ye, what cunning match° have you made with this jest of the drawer? Come, what's the issue?°   103

PRINCE. I am now of all humors° that have showed themselves humors since the old days of Goodman Adam to the pupilage° of this present twelve o'clock at midnight.

[*Re-enter* FRANCIS.] What's o'clock, Francis? 108

FRAN. Anon, anon, sir.   [*Exit.*]

PRINCE. That ever this fellow should have fewer words than a parrot, and yet the son of a woman! His industry is upstairs and downstairs, his elo-

quence the parcel° of a reckoning. I am not yet of Percy's mind, the Hotspur of the North, he that kills me some six or seven dozen of Scots at a break- 115 fast, washes his hands, and says to his wife, "Fie upon this quiet life! I want work." "O my sweet Harry," says she, "how many hast thou killed to-day?" "Give my roan horse a drench,"° says he, and answers "Some fourteen" an hour after 120 — "a trifle, a trifle." I prithee call in Falstaff. I'll play Percy, and that damned brawn° shall play Dame Mortimer his wife. "Rivo!"° says the drunkard. Call in ribs, call in tallow.   125

[*Enter* FALSTAFF, GADSHILL, BARDOLPH, *and* PETO; FRANCIS *following with wine.*]

POINS. Welcome, Jack. Where hast thou been?

FAL. A plague of all cowards, I say, and a vengeance too! Marry, and amen! Give me a cup of sack, boy. Ere I lead this life long, I'll sew netherstocks° and mend them and foot them too. A plague of all cowards! Give me a cup of sack, rogue. Is there 131 no virtue extant?°   [*He drinks.*]

PRINCE. Didst thou never see Titan° kiss a dish of butter? Pitiful-hearted Titan, that melted° at the sweet tale of the sun's! If thou didst, then behold that compound.   136

FAL. You rogue, here's lime° in this sack too. There is nothing but roguery to be found in villainous man. Yet a coward is worse than a cup of sack with lime in it. A villainous coward! Go thy 140 ways, old Jack, die when thou wilt. If manhood, good manhood, be not forgot upon the face of the earth, then am I a shotten° herring. There live not three good men unhanged in England, and one of them is fat, and grows old. God help the while!° A bad world, I say. I would I were a weaver, I 146 could sing psalms° or anything. A plague of all cowards, I say still.

PRINCE. How now, woolsack! What mutter you?

FAL. A king's son! If I do not beat thee out of thy kingdom with a dagger of lath,° and drive all thy subjects afore thee like a flock of wild geese, I'll never wear hair on my face more. You Prince of Wales!   154

PRINCE. Why, you whoreson round man, what's the matter?

FAL. Are not you a coward? Answer me to that. And Poins there?

POINS. 'Zounds, ye fat paunch, an ye call me coward, by the Lord, I'll stab thee.   160

77–80. leathern-jerkin . . . Spanish-pouch: This list gives the outward characteristics of a prosperous innkeeper: leather coat (*jerkin*) with crystal buttons, close-cropped head (*not-pated*), large ring, gray (*puke*) stockings, worsted (*caddis*) garters, a *smooth tongue*, and a *pouch* of *Spanish* leather. 84. In Barbary: in North Africa — but the Prince's words have passed beyond location. 101. what . . . match: what is the game. 103. issue: result. 104. of . . . humors: i.e., will match my mood with any man's. 106. pupilage: boyhood.

113. parcel: items. 119. drench: purge. 122. brawn: fat pig. 124. Rivo: another drinkers' exclamation. See l. 17. 129. netherstocks: stockings, at this time cut out of material and sewed not knitted. See comment on p. 93b. 132. virtue extant: manhood in existence. 133. Titan: the sun. 134. that melted: i.e., the butter. 137. lime: used to adulterate wine by giving it a better color and taste. 143. shotten: without its roe. 145. God . . . while: God help these times. 146–47. weaver . . . psalms: See *T Night*, II.iii.61,n. 151. dagger of lath: wooden dagger.

FAL. I call thee coward! I'll see thee damned ere I call thee coward. But I would give a thousand pound I could run as fast as thou canst. You are straight enough in the shoulders, you care not who sees your back. Call you that backing of your friends? A plague upon such backing! Give me them that will face me. Give me a cup of sack. I am a rogue if I drunk today.   169

PRINCE. O villain! Thy lips are scarce wiped since thou drunkest last.

FAL. All's one for that. [*He drinks.*] A plague of all cowards, still say I.

PRINCE. What's the matter?   174

FAL. What's the matter! There be four of us here have ta'en a thousand pound this day morning.

PRINCE. Where is it, Jack? Where is it?

FAL. Where is it! Taken from us it is — a hundred upon poor four of us.   180

PRINCE. What, a hundred, man?

FAL. I am a rogue if I were not at half-sword° with a dozen of them two hours together. I have 'scaped by miracle. I am eight times thrust through the doublet,° four through the hose;° my buckler° 185 cut through and through; my sword hacked like a handsaw — *ecce signum!*° I never dealt° better since I was a man. All would not do. A plague of all cowards! Let them speak. If they speak more or less than truth, they are villains and the sons of darkness. 191

PRINCE. Speak, sirs, how was it?

GADS. We four set upon some dozen ——

FAL. Sixteen at least, my lord.

GADS. And bound them.   195

PETO. No, no, they were not bound.

FAL. You rogue, they were bound, every man of them, or I am a Jew else, an Ebrew° Jew.

GADS. As we were sharing, some six or seven fresh men set upon us ——   200

FAL. And unbound the rest, and then come in the other.

PRINCE. What, fought you with them all?   203

FAL. All! I know not what you call all, but if I fought not with fifty of them, I am a bunch of radish. If there were not two or three and fifty upon poor old Jack, then am I no two-legged creature.

PRINCE. Pray God you have not murdered some of them.   210

FAL. Nay, that's past praying for. I have peppered two of them — two I am sure I have paid,° two rogues in buckram suits. I tell thee what, Hal, if I tell thee a lie, spit in my face, call me horse.° Thou knowest my old ward.° Here I lay, and thus I bore

my point. Four rogues in buckram let drive at me ——   217

PRINCE. What, four? Thou saidst but two even now.

FAL. Four, Hal, I told thee four.

POINS. Aye, aye, he said four.   221

FAL. These four came all afront, and mainly° thrust at me. I made me no more ado, but took all their seven points in my target, thus.

PRINCE. Seven? Why, there were but four even now.   226

FAL. In buckram?

POINS. Aye, four, in buckram suits.

FAL. Seven, by these hilts,° or I am a villain else.

PRINCE. Prithee let him alone. We shall have more anon.

FAL. Dost thou hear me, Hal?

PRINCE. Aye, and mark thee too, Jack.   234

FAL. Do so, for it is worth the listening to. These nine in buckram that I told thee of ——

PRINCE. So, two more already.

FAL. Their points being broken ——

POINS. Down fell their hose.°   239

FAL. Began to give me ground. But I followed me close, came in foot and hand, and with a thought seven of the eleven I paid.

PRINCE. Oh, monstrous! Eleven buckram men grown out of two!   244

FAL. But, as the Devil would have it, three misbegotten knaves in Kendal green° came at my back and let drive at me; for it was so dark, Hal, that thou couldst not see thy hand.   248

PRINCE. These lies are like their father that begets them — gross as a mountain, open, palpable. Why, thou clay-brained guts, thou knotty-pated° fool, thou whoreson, obscene, greasy tallow catch ——°   253

FAL. What, art thou mad? Art thou mad? Is not the truth the truth?

PRINCE. Why, how couldst thou know these men in Kendal green when it was so dark thou couldst not see thy hand? Come, tell us your reason. What sayest thou to this?   259

POINS. Come, your reason, Jack, your reason.

FAL. What, upon compulsion? 'Zounds, an I were at the strappado, or all the racks° in the world, I would not tell you on compulsion. Give you a reason

---

222. mainly: violently. **229. hilts:** sword hilt. **238–39. Their . . . hose:** The Prince puns on the other meaning of *points*, laces tying the hose to the doublet. See p. 94a–b. **246. Kendal green:** cloth made (originally at Kendal in Westmoreland) of the poorest-quality wool, and used by woodmen and servants. **252. knotty-pated:** blockhead. **253. tallow catch:** the word is variously emended and interpreted. Johnson suggested "keech" — a lump of fat prepared by the butcher for the candlemaker. A *tallow catch* would naturally be "a thing for catching tallow"; i.e., the rim on the candlestick which, when piled up with the drippings of wax, is no bad image for Falstaff. **262. strappado . . . racks:** forms of torture. See App. 10.

182. at half-sword: within half a sword's length. A cautious fighter kept at greater distance. **185. doublet:** coat. **hose:** breeches. See Pl. 8b and comment on p. 93a–b. **buckler:** small shield. See Pls. 9 and 21i. **187. ecce signum:** behold the sign. **dealt:** fought. **198. Ebrew:** Hebrew. **212. paid:** paid home, done for. **214. horse:** Like the ass, the horse was regarded as stupid. **215. ward:** stance, position of guard. Here Falstaff reenacts his heroic exploit.

on compulsion! If reasons were as plentiful as   264
blackberries, I would give no man a reason upon
compulsion, I.

PRINCE. I'll be no longer guilty of this sin — this
sanguine° coward, this bed-presser, this horseback-
breaker, this huge hill of flesh ——   269

FAL. 'Sblood, you starveling,° you elf skin,° you
dried neat's tongue,° you bull's pizzle,° you stock-
fish!° Oh, for breath to utter what is like thee! You
tailor's yard, you sheath, you bow case, you vile
standing tuck ——°   274

PRINCE. Well, breathe a while, and then to it
again, and when thou hast tired thyself in base com-
parisons, hear me speak but this.

POINS. Mark, Jack.   278

PRINCE. We two saw you four set on four and
bound them, and were masters of their wealth. Mark
now, how a plain tale shall put you down. Then did
we two set on you four; and, with a word, outfaced
you from your prize, and have it, yea, and can show
it you here in the house. And, Falstaff, you carried
your guts away as nimbly, with as quick dex-   285
terity, and roared for mercy, and still run and roared,
as ever I heard bull calf. What a slave art thou, to
hack thy sword as thou hast done, and then say it
was in fight! What trick, what device, what starting
hole,° canst thou now find out to hide thee from this
open and apparent shame?   292

POINS. Come, let's hear, Jack. What trick hast thou
now?

FAL. By the Lord, I knew ye as well as he that
made ye. Why, hear you, my masters. Was it for me
to kill the heir apparent? Should I turn upon the true
Prince? Why, thou knowest I am as valiant as Her-
cules. But beware instinct, the lion will not touch the
true prince.° Instinct is a great matter, I was now a
coward on instinct. I shall think the better of   300
myself and thee during my life, I for a valiant lion,
and thou for a true Prince. But, by the Lord, lads, I
am glad you have the money. Hostess, clap to the
doors. Watch tonight, pray tomorrow. Gal-   305
lants, lads, boys, hearts of gold, all the titles of good
fellowship come to you! What, shall we be merry?
Shall we have a play extempore?

PRINCE. Content, and the argument° shall be thy
running away.   311

FAL. Ah, no more of that, Hal, an thou lovest me!

[*Enter* HOSTESS.]

HOSTESS. O Jesu, my lord the Prince!

PRINCE. How now, my lady the hostess! What say-
est thou to me?   316

HOSTESS. Marry, my lord, there is a nobleman of
the Court at door would speak with you. He says he
comes from your father.

PRINCE. Give him as much as will make him a
royal man,° and send him back again to my mother.

FAL. What manner of man is he?   323

HOSTESS. An old man.

FAL. What doth gravity out of his bed at mid-
night? Shall I give him his answer?   326

PRINCE. Prithee do, Jack.

FAL. Faith, and I'll send him packing.   [*Exit.*]

PRINCE. Now, sirs. By'r Lady, you fought fair; so
did you, Peto; so did you, Bardolph. You are lions
too, you ran away upon instinct, you will not touch
the true prince — no, fie!   332

BARD. Faith, I ran when I saw others run.

PRINCE. Faith, tell me now in earnest, how came
Falstaff's sword so hacked?

PETO. Why, he hacked it with his dagger, and said
he would swear truth out of England but he would
make you believe it was done in fight, and persuaded
us to do the like.   339

BARD. Yea, and to tickle our noses with speargrass
to make them bleed, and then to beslubber° our gar-
ments with it and swear it was the blood of true
men. I did that I did not this seven year before, I
blushed to hear his monstrous devices.   344

PRINCE. O villain, thou stolest a cup of sack eight-
een years ago, and wert taken with the manner,° and
ever since thou hast blushed° extempore. Thou hadst
fire and sword on thy side, and yet thou rannest
away. What instinct hadst thou for it?   350

BARD. My lord, do you see these meteors? Do you
behold these exhalations?°

PRINCE. I do.

BARD. What think you they portend?

PRINCE. Hot livers and cold purses.   355

BARD. Choler,° my lord, if rightly taken.

PRINCE. No, if rightly taken, halter.

[*Re-enter* FALSTAFF.] Here comes lean Jack, here
comes barebone. How now, my sweet creature of
bombast!° How long is't ago, Jack, since thou sawest
thine own knee?   361

---

268. sanguine: one suffering from an excess of the sanguine
humor. See App. 3.   270. you starveling: Falstaff, being
thoroughly roused, retorts with a string of images expressing
the thinness of the Prince. elf skin: sometimes emended to
eelskin, but probably it meant snakeskin, which, as Oberon ob-
served, was "Weed wide enough to wrap a fairy in." (*MND*,
II.i.256.)   271. neat's tongue: ox tongue. bull's pizzle: This
portion of the bull's anatomy was dried and used as a whip.
272. stockfish: dried codfish.   274. standing tuck: a rapier stuck
in the ground.   290–91. starting hole: a hole into which a rabbit
bolts for safety.   298–99. lion . . . prince: This was very gen-
erally believed.   310. argument: plot.

321–22. as . . . man: i.e., 3s 4d, which is the difference between
a *royal* (10s) and a noble (6s 8d). See App. 27. It is a sign of
Prince Hal's low behavior that he should make such jokes about
a nobleman of the Court.   341. beslubber: smear.   346. with
. . . manner: in the act.   347. blushed: For Bardolph's perma-
nent blush see III,iii.27–55 and *Hen V*, III.vi.108.   351–52. me-
teors . . . exhalations: Bardolph indicates his own fiery face
which, he claims, is proof that he is a man of wrath. exhala-
tions: meteors.   356. Choler: anger; pronounced in the same
way as "collar," and so puns on the two words are common.
See *T Night*, I.v.6,n.   360. bombast: cotton batting, used to
stuff garments to make them appear baggy.

FAL. My own knee! When I was about thy years, Hal, I was not an eagle's talon in the waist, I could have crept into any alderman's thumb ring.° A plague of sighing and grief! It blows a man up like a bladder. There's villainous news abroad. Here   366 was Sir John Bracy from your father; you must to the Court in the morning. That same mad fellow of the North, Percy, and he of Wales, that gave Amamon° the bastinado° and made Lucifer cuckold,° and swore the Devil his true liegeman° upon the cross of a Welsh hook — what a plague call you him?   372

POINS. O, Glendower.°

FAL. Owen, Owen, the same. And his son-in-law Mortimer, and old Northumberland, and that sprightly Scot of Scots, Douglas, that runs o' horseback up a hill perpendicular ——

PRINCE. He that rides at high speed and with his pistol kills a sparrow flying.   380

FAL. You have hit it.

PRINCE. So did he never the sparrow.

FAL. Well, that rascal hath good mettle° in him. He will not run.   384

PRINCE. Why, what a rascal art thou then, to praise him so for running!

FAL. O' horseback, ye cuckoo, but afoot he will not budge a foot.

PRINCE. Yes, Jack, upon instinct.   389

FAL. I grant ye, upon instinct. Well, he is there too, and one Mordake, and a thousand bluecaps° more. Worcester is stolen away tonight; thy father's beard is turned white with the news. You may buy land now as cheap as stinking mackerel.   395

PRINCE. Why, then, it is like, if there come a hot June and this civil buffeting hold, we shall buy maidenheads as they buy hobnails, by the hundreds.

FAL. By the mass, lad, thou sayest true; it is like we shall have good trading that way. But tell me, Hal, art not thou horrible afeard? Thou being heir apparent, could the world pick thee out three such enemies again as that fiend Douglas, that spirit Percy, and that devil Glendower? Art thou not horribly afraid? Doth not thy blood thrill at it?   407

PRINCE. Not a whit, i' faith. I lack some of thy instinct.

FAL. Well, thou wilt be horribly chid tomorrow when thou comest to thy father. If thou love me, practice an answer.   412

PRINCE. Do thou stand for° my father, and examine me upon the particulars of my life.

FAL. Shall I? Content. This chair shall be my state,° this dagger my scepter, and this cushion my crown.   417

PRINCE. Thy state is taken for a joined stool,° thy golden scepter for a leaden° dagger, and thy precious rich crown for a pitiful bald crown!   420

FAL. Well, an the fire of grace be not quite out of thee, now shalt thou be moved. Give me a cup of sack to make my eyes look red, that it may be thought I have wept; for I must speak in passion, and I will do it in King Cambyses'° vein.   426

PRINCE. Well, here is my leg.°

FAL. And here is my speech. Stand aside, nobility.

HOSTESS. Oh Jesu, this is excellent sport, i' faith!

FAL. Weep° not, sweet queen, for trickling tears are vain.   430

HOSTESS. Oh, the father,° how he holds his countenance!°

FAL. For God's sake, lords, convey my tristful° queen,
For tears do stop the floodgates of her eyes.   435

HOSTESS. Oh Jesu, he doth it as like one of these harlotry players° as ever I see!

FAL. Peace, good pint pot; peace, good ticklebrain. Harry, I do not only marvel where thou spendest thy time, but also how thou art accompanied.° For   440 though the camomile,° the more it is trodden on, the faster it grows, yet youth, the more it is wasted, the sooner it wears. That thou art my son, I have partly thy mother's word, partly my own opinion, but chiefly a villainous trick° of thine eye, and a   445 foolish hanging of thy nether° lip, that doth warrant° me. If then thou be son to me, here lies the point; why, being son to me, art thou so pointed at? Shall the blessed sun of heaven prove a micher°   450 and eat blackberries? A question not to be asked. Shall the son of England prove a thief and take purses? A question to be asked. There is a thing, Harry, which thou hast often heard of, and it is known to many in our land by the name of pitch. This pitch, as ancient writers do report, doth   455 defile; so doth the company thou keepest. For, Harry, now I do not speak to thee in drink but in tears, not in pleasure but in passion, not in words only, but in

---

416. state: throne.   418. joined stool: wooden stool made by a joiner. See Pl. 17a.   419. leaden: blunt.   426. King Cambyses': the chief character in an early drama which still survives; it is a marvelous specimen of ridiculous rant.   427. my leg: my curtsy. 430–35: Weep . . . eyes: Falstaff begins in the artificial style of earlier plays, of the kind still being acted by the rival company at the Rose. See Gen. Intro. p. 41b.   431. Oh . . . father: by God the Father.   holds . . . countenance: keeps a straight face. 434. tristful: sad, a poetical word.   437. harlotry players: worthless players. As the Admiral's Men were the only other company then playing in London, the parody of their heavy style was obvious.   440. how . . . accompanied: what company you keep. 441. For . . . camomile: The whole of this passage is a parody of the elaborate style of Lyly's Euphues. The camomile is a small creeping aromatic plant with a flower like a daisy.   445. trick: habit.   446. nether: lower.   447. warrant: guarantee.   450. micher: a truant.

---

364. thumb ring: large seal ring, especially common on the thumbs of businessmen.   369. Amamon: the name of a fiend. 370. bastinado: thrashing.   cuckold: a man deceived by his wife. See App. 11.   371. liegeman: subject.   373. O, Glendower: probably Shakespeare wrote O in his manuscript as abbreviation for Owen, which the printer mistook for an exclamation.   383. mettle: matter, material.   391. bluecaps: Scots.   413. stand for: represent,

woes also. And yet there is a virtuous man whom I have often noted in thy company, but I know not his name. 461

PRINCE. What manner of man, an it like your Majesty?

FAL. A goodly portly° man, i' faith, and a corpulent; of a cheerful look, a pleasing eye, and a 465 most noble carriage. And, as I think, his age some fifty, or, by'r Lady, inclining to threescore. And now I remember me, his name is Falstaff. If that man should be lewdly given, he deceiveth me, for, Harry, I see virtue in his looks. If then the tree may be 470 known by the fruit, as the fruit by the tree, then, peremptorily° I speak it, there is virtue in that Falstaff. Him keep with, the rest banish. And tell me now, thou naughty varlet, tell me, where hast thou been this month? 475

PRINCE. Dost thou speak like a king? Do thou stand for me, and I'll play my father.

FAL. Depose me? If thou dost it half so gravely, so majestically, both in word and matter, hang me up by the heels for a rabbit-sucker° or a poulter's° hare.

PRINCE. Well, here I am set. 482

FAL. And here I stand. Judge, my masters.

PRINCE. Now, Harry, whence come you?

FAL. My noble lord, from Eastcheap. 485

PRINCE. The complaints I hear of thee are grievous.

FAL. 'Sblood, my lord, they are false. Nay, I'll tickle ye° for a young Prince, i' faith. 489

PRINCE. Swearest thou, ungracious° boy? Henceforth ne'er look on me. Thou art violently carried away from grace. There is a devil haunts thee in the likeness of an old fat man, a tun° of man is thy companion. Why dost thou converse with that trunk of humors,° that bolting hutch° of beastliness, 495 that swollen parcel of dropsies, that huge bombard° of sack, that stuffed cloak bag° of guts, that roasted Manningtree° ox with the pudding in his belly, that reverend vice,° that gray iniquity, that father ruffian, that vanity in years? Wherein is he good, 500 but to taste sack and drink it? Wherein neat and cleanly,° but to carve a capon and eat it? Wherein cunning,° but in craft? Wherein crafty,° but in villainy? Wherein villainous, but in all things? Wherein worthy, but in nothing? 505

FAL. I would your Grace would take me with you.° Whom means your Grace?

PRINCE. That villainous abominable misleader of youth, Falstaff, that old white-bearded Satan.

FAL. My lord, the man I know. 510

PRINCE. I know thou dost.

FAL. But to say I know more harm in him than in myself were to say more than I know. That he is old, the more the pity, his white hairs do witness it; but that he is, saving your reverence, a whore- 515 master, that I utterly deny. If sack and sugar be a fault, God help the wicked! If to be old and merry be a sin, then many an old host that I know is damned. If to be fat be to be hated, then Pharaoh's lean kine are to be loved. No, my good lord. Banish Peto, 520 banish Bardolph, banish Poins. But for sweet Jack Falstaff, kind Jack Falstaff, true Jack Falstaff, valiant Jack Falstaff, and therefore more valiant, being, as he is, old Jack Falstaff, banish not him thy Harry's company, banish not him thy Harry's company. 525 Banish plump Jack, and banish all the world.

PRINCE. I do, I will. [*A knocking heard.*

Exeunt HOSTESS, FRANCIS, *and* BARDOLPH.]

[*Re-enter* BARDOLPH, *running.*]

BARD. Oh, my lord, my lord! The sheriff with a most monstrous watch° is at the door. 530

FAL. Out, ye rogue! Play out the play. I have much to say in the behalf of that Falstaff.

[*Re-enter the* HOSTESS.]

HOSTESS. Oh Jesu, my lord, my lord!—

PRINCE. Heigh, heigh! The Devil rides upon a fiddlestick.° What's the matter? 535

HOSTESS. The sheriff and all the watch are at the door. They are come to search the house. Shall I let them in?

FAL. Dost thou hear, Hal? Never call a true piece of gold a counterfeit. Thou art essentially mad, without seeming so. 541

PRINCE. And thou a natural coward, without instinct.

FAL. I deny your major.° If you will deny the sheriff, so; if not, let him enter. If I become not a cart° as well as another man, a plague on my bringing up! I hope I shall as soon be strangled with a halter as another. 548

PRINCE. Go, hide thee behind the arras,° the rest walk up above. Now, my masters, for a true face and good conscience.

FAL. Both which I have had; but their date is out,° and therefore I'll hide me. 553

PRINCE. Call in the sheriff.

[*Exeunt all except the* PRINCE *and* PETO.]

---

464. portly: dignified. 472. peremptorily: conclusively. 481. rabbit-sucker: young rabbit. poulter: poulterer. 489. I'll . . . ye: I'll show you how to do it. 490. ungracious: graceless. 493. tun: large barrel. 494–95. trunk of humors: great collection of diseases. 495. bolting hutch: round bin into which flour was sifted. 496. bombard: large leather jug. See Pl. 17f. 497. cloak bag: for carrying cloaks, "kit bag." 498. Manningtree: a town in Essex where there was a famous cattle market. At fairs it was often a custom to roast an ox whole. 499. vice: the Devil in the old Morality Plays. 502. cleanly: clever. 503. cunning: skillful. crafty: a craftsman. 506–07. take . . . you: explain yourself.

530. watch: See Gen. Intro. p. 18a. 534–35. Devil . . . fiddlestick: what's all the fuss about? 544. I . . . major: I deny your major premise, i.e., the main argument on which your conclusion is based; a phrase used in academic arguments. Falstaff puns also on "mayor." "Major" and "mayor" were pronounced alike. 546. cart: which will take him to execution. 549. arras: curtain. 552. date is out: time is expired.

[*Enter* SHERIFF *and the* CARRIER.]

Now, Master Sheriff, what is your will with me?

SHER. First, pardon me, my lord. A hue and
 cry°

Hath followed certain men unto this house.

PRINCE. What men?

SHER. One of them is well known, my gracious
 lord,

A gross fat man.

CAR.   As fat as butter.   560

PRINCE. The man, I do assure you, is not here,

For I myself at this time have employed him.

And, sheriff, I will engage my word to thee

That I will, by tomorrow dinnertime,

Send him to answer thee, or any man, 565

For anything he shall be charged withal.

And so let me entreat you leave the house.

SHER. I will, my lord. There are two gentlemen

Have in this robbery lost three hundred marks.

PRINCE. It may be so. If he have robbed these
 men,   570

He shall be answerable. And so farewell.

SHER. Good night, my noble lord.

PRINCE. I think it is good morrow, is it not?

SHER. Indeed, my lord, I think it be two o'clock.

     [*Exeunt* SHERIFF *and* CARRIER.]

PRINCE. This oily rascal is known as well as 575

Paul's.° Go, call him forth.

PETO. Falstaff! — Fast asleep behind the arras, and
snorting like a horse.

PRINCE. Hark how hard he fetches breath. Search
his pockets. [*He searcheth his pockets, and findeth
certain papers.*] What hast thou found? 582

PETO. Nothing but papers, my lord.

PRINCE. Let's see what they be. Read them.

PETO. [*Reads.*]

 "Item, A capon, ... 2s. 2d.

 Item, Sauce, ... 4d.

 Item, Sack, two gallons, ... 5s. 8d.

 Item, Anchovies and sack after supper, 2s. 6d.

 Item, Bread, ... ob.°"

PRINCE. Oh, monstrous! But one halfpenny- 591
worth of bread to this intolerable deal of sack! What
there is else, keep close, we'll read it at more advan-
tage. There let him sleep till day. I'll to the Court in
the morning. We must all to the wars, and thy 595
place shall be honorable. I'll procure this fat rogue a
charge of foot,° and I know his death will be a march
of twelvescore.° The money shall be paid back again
with advantage.° Be with me betimes in the morn-
ing. And so good morrow, Peto. 600

PETO. Good morrow, good my lord. [*Exeunt.*]

Act III

SCENE I. *Bangor. The* ARCHDEACON's *house.*

[*Enter* HOTSPUR, WORCESTER, MORTIMER, *and*
GLENDOWER.]

MORT. These promises are fair, the parties sure,

And our induction° full of prosperous hope.

HOT. Lord Mortimer, and Cousin Glendower,

Will you sit down?

And Uncle Worcester. A plague upon it! 5

I have forgot the map.

GLEND.   No, here it is.

Sit, Cousin Percy. Sit, good Cousin Hotspur,

For by that name as oft as Lancaster

Doth speak of you, his cheek looks pale, and with

A rising sigh he wisheth you in Heaven. 10

HOT. And you in Hell, as oft as he hears Owen
 Glendower spoke of.

GLEND. I cannot blame him. At my nativity°

The front° of heaven was full of fiery shapes,

Of burning cressets;° and at my birth 15

The frame and huge foundation of the earth

Shaked like a coward.

HOT. Why, so it would have done at the same sea-
son if your mother's cat had but kittened, though
yourself had never been born. 20

GLEND. I say the earth did shake when I was born.

HOT. And I say the earth was not of my mind

If you suppose as fearing you it shook.

GLEND. The heavens were all on fire, the earth did
tremble.

HOT. Oh, then the earth shook to see the heavens
 on fire,   25

And not in fear of your nativity.

Diseasèd nature oftentimes breaks forth

In strange eruptions; oft the teeming° earth

Is with a kind of colic pinched and vexed

By the imprisoning of unruly wind 30

Within her womb; which, for enlargement striving,

Shakes the old beldam° earth and topples down

Steeples and moss-grown towers. At your birth

Our grandam earth, having this distemperature,°

In passion° shook.

GLEND.   Cousin,° of many men 35

I do not bear these crossings.° Give me leave

To tell you once again that at my birth

The front of heaven was full of fiery shapes,

The goats ran from the mountains, and the herds

---

556. hue . . . cry: See Gen. Intro. p. 28a. 576. Paul's: St. Paul's
Church. See Gen. Intro. p. 17a and Pl. 2a. 590. ob: one half-
penny. 597. charge of foot: commission as commander of a
company of infantry. 598. twelvescore: i.e. paces. The pace
was 60 inches. 599. advantage: interest.

Act III, Sc. i: 2. induction: opening. 12. nativity: moment
of birth. See App. 1. 14. front: forehead. 15. burning cressets:
stars blazing like beacons. 28. teeming: pregnant. This theory
of earthquakes — that they were caused by the expulsion of
wind from within the earth — was generally believed. 32. bel-
dam: grandmother. 34. distemperature: disorder. 35. passion:
agitation. Cousin: kinsman; used of any relation. Hotspur
is remotely related to Glendower through Lady Percy. See
App. 28. 36. crossings: opposition.

Were strangely clamorous to the frighted fields.   40
These signs have marked me extraordinary,
And all the courses of my life do show
I am not in the roll of common men.
Where is he living, clipped in° with the sea
That chides° the banks of England, Scotland, Wales,
Which calls me pupil,° or hath read to me?°   46
And bring him out that is but woman's son
Can trace° me in the tedious ways of art,°
And hold me pace° in deep experiments.

HOT. I think there's no man speaks better Welsh.
I'll to dinner.   51

MORT. Peace, Cousin Percy, you will make him
    mad.

GLEND. I can call spirits from the vasty deep.

HOT. Why, so can I, or so can any man;
But will they come when you do call for them?   55

GLEND. Why, I can teach you, Cousin, to command
The Devil.

HOT. And I can teach thee, Coz, to shame the
    Devil°
By telling truth. Tell truth, and shame the Devil.   59
If thou have power to raise him, bring him hither,
And I'll be sworn I have power to shame him hence.
Oh, while you live, tell truth, and shame the Devil!

MORT. Come, come, no more of this unprofitable
    chat.

GLEND. Three times hath Henry Bolingbroke
    made head°
Against my power. Thrice from the banks of Wye
And sandy-bottomed Severn have I sent him   66
Bootless° home and weather-beaten back.

HOT. Home without boots, and in foul weather
    too!
How 'scapes he agues,° in the Devil's name?

GLEND. Come, here's the map. Shall we divide our
    right   70
According to our threefold order° ta'en?

MORT. The Archdeacon hath divided it
Into three limits° very equally.
England, from Trent and Severn hitherto,
By south and east is to my part assigned.   75
All westward, Wales beyond the Severn shore,
And all the fertile land within that bound,
To Owen Glendower. And, dear Coz, to you
The remnant northward, lying off from Trent.
And our indentures tripartite° are drawn;   80
Which being sealed interchangeably,°
A business that this night may execute,

Tomorrow, Cousin Percy, you and I
And my good Lord of Worcester will set forth
To meet your father and the Scottish power,   85
As is appointed us, at Shrewsbury.
My father° Glendower is not ready yet,
Nor shall we need his help these fourteen days.
Within that space you may have drawn together   89
Your tenants, friends, and neighboring gentlemen.

GLEND. A shorter time shall send me to you, lords.
And in my conduct shall your ladies come,
From whom you now must steal and take no leave;
For there will be a world of water shed
Upon the parting of your wives and you.   95

HOT. Methinks my moiety,° north from Burton
    here,
In quantity equals not one of yours.
See how this river comes me cranking in,°
And cuts me from the best of all my land
A huge half-moon, a monstrous cantle° out.   100
I'll have the current in this place dammed up,
And here the smug° and silver Trent shall run
In a new channel, fair and evenly.
It shall not wind with such a deep indent,°
To rob me of so rich a bottom° here.   105

GLEND. Not wind? It shall, it must. You see it
    doth.

MORT. Yea, but
Mark how he bears his course, and runs me up
With like advantage on the other side,
Gelding the opposèd continent° as much   110
As on the other side it takes from you.

WOR. Yea, but a little charge° will trench him
    here
And on this north side win this cape of land,
And then he runs straight and even.

HOT. I'll have it so. A little charge will do it.   115

GLEND. I'll not have it altered.

HOT.   Will not you?

GLEND. No, nor you shall not.

HOT.   Who shall say me nay?

GLEND. Why, that will I.

HOT. Let me not understand you, then. Speak it in
    Welsh.   120

GLEND. I can speak English, lord, as well as you;
For I was trained up in the English Court,
Where, being but young, I framèd to the harp
Many an English ditty lovely well,
And gave the tongue a helpful ornament,°   125
A virtue that was never seen in you.

HOT. Marry,°
And I am glad of it with all my heart.

I had rather be a kitten and cry mew
Than one of these same meter balladmongers.°   130
I had rather hear a brazen canstick turned,°
Or a dry wheel grate on the axletree;
And that would set my teeth nothing on edge,
Nothing so much as mincing poetry.
'Tis like the forced gait of a shuffling nag.   135

GLEND. Come, you shall have Trent turned.

HOT. I do not care. I'll give thrice so much
          land
To any well-deserving friend.
But in the way of bargain, mark ye me,
I'll cavil° on the ninth part of a hair.   140
Are the indentures drawn? Shall we be gone?

GLEND. The moon shines fair, you may away by
          night.
I'll haste the writer, and withal
Break with° your wives of your departure hence.
I am afraid my daughter will run mad,   145
So much she doteth on her Mortimer.   [Exit.]

MORT. Fie, Cousin Percy! How you cross my
          father!

HOT. I cannot choose. Sometime he angers me
With telling me of the moldwarp° and the ant,
Of the dreamer Merlin° and his prophecies,   150
And° of a dragon and a finless fish,
A clip-winged griffin° and a molten raven,
A couching lion and a ramping° cat,
And such a deal of skimble-skamble° stuff
As puts me from my faith. I tell you what —   155
He held me last night at least nine hours
In reckoning up the several° devils' names
That were his lackeys. I cried " hum," and " well, go
          to,"
But marked him not a word. Oh, he is as tedious
As a tired horse, a railing wife,   160
Worse than a smoky house. I had rather live
With cheese and garlic in a windmill, far,
Than feed on cates° and have him talk to me
In any summerhouse° in Christendom.

MORT. In faith, he is a worthy gentleman,   165
Exceedingly well read, and profited
In strange concealments;° valiant as a lion,
And wondrous affable, and as bountiful
As mines of India. Shall I tell you, Cousin?
He holds your temper° in a high respect,   170
And curbs himself even of his natural scope

When you come 'cross his humor; faith, he does.
I warrant you that man is not alive
Might so have tempted him as you have done
Without the taste of danger and reproof.   175
But do not use it oft, let me entreat you.

WOR. In faith, my lord, you are too willful-
          blame;°
And since your coming hither have done enough
To put him quite beside his patience.
You must needs learn, lord, to amend this fault.   180
Though sometimes it show greatness, courage,
          blood —
And that's the dearest° grace it renders you —
Yet oftentimes it doth present harsh rage,
Defect of manners, want of government,°
Pride, haughtiness, opinion,° and disdain;   185
The least of which haunting a nobleman
Loseth men's hearts, and leaves behind a stain
Upon the beauty of all parts besides,
Beguiling° them of commendation.

HOT. Well, I am schooled. Good manners be your
          speed!°   190
Here come our wives, and let us take our leave.

          [Re-enter GLENDOWER with the LADIES.]

MORT. This is the deadly spite° that angers me —
My wife can speak no English, I no Welsh.

GLEND. My daughter weeps. She will not part with
          you.
She'll be a soldier too, she'll to the wars.   195

MORT. Good Father, tell her that she and my aunt
          Percy
Shall follow in your conduct speedily.

          [GLENDOWER speaks to LADY MORTIMER in Welsh,
                    and she answers him in the same.]

GLEND. She is desperate here, a peevish self-willed
harlotry,° one that no persuasion can do good   199
upon.

          [LADY MORTIMER speaks in Welsh.]

MORT. I understand thy looks. That pretty Welsh°
Which thou pour'st down from these swelling
          heavens°
I am too perfect in; and but for shame,
In such a parley° should I answer thee.

          [LADY MORTIMER speaks again in Welsh.]

I understand thy kisses and thou mine,   205
And that's a feeling disputation.°
But I will never be a truant, love,
Till I have learned thy language; for thy tongue
Makes Welsh as sweet as ditties highly penned,
Sung by a fair queen in a summer's bower,   210

---

130. **meter balladmongers:** doggerel rhymesters. 131. **brazen . . .
turned:** brass candlestick being cut out on the lathe. 140. **cavil:**
raise objections. 144. **Break with:** break the news to. 149. **mold-
warp:** mole. 150. **Merlin:** the old magician at King Arthur's
Court. As the Welsh were (more or less) descendants of Arthur's
British countrymen, Merlin's prophecies would appeal to Glen-
dower. 151–53. **And . . . cat:** These beasts occur as symbols in
ancient prophecies. **griffin:** fabulous beast — half lion, half eagle.
153. **ramping:** on its hind legs. 154. **skimble-skamble:** rambling.
157. **several:** separate, different. 163. **cates:** delicacies. 164. **sum-
merhouse:** country house. 166–67. **profited . . . concealments:**
expert in strange mysteries. 170. **temper:** character.

177. **willful-blame:** to be blamed for willfulness. 182. **dearest:**
most valuable. 184. **government:** self-control. 185. **opinion:**
conceit. 189. **Beguiling:** causing to lose. 190. **Good . . . speed:**
may good manners bring you luck. 192. **spite:** vexation.
199. **harlotry:** silly girl. 201. **pretty Welsh:** i.e., tears.
202. **swelling heavens:** i.e., eyes full of tears. 204. **parley:**
manner of speech. 206. **feeling disputation:** conversation by
touch.

With ravishing division,° to her lute.

GLEND. Nay, if you melt, then will she run mad.

[LADY MORTIMER *speaks again in Welsh*.]

MORT. Oh, I am ignorance itself in this!

GLEND. She bids you on the wanton° rushes° lay
  you down

And rest your gentle head upon her lap,   215

And she will sing the song that pleaseth you

And on your eyelids crown the god of sleep,

Charming your blood with pleasing heaviness,°

Making such difference 'twixt wake and sleep

As is the difference betwixt day and night   220

The hour before the heavenly-harnessed team°

Begins his golden progress in the east.

MORT. With all my heart I'll sit and hear her sing.

By that time will our book,° I think, be drawn.

GLEND. Do so,   225

And those musicians that shall play to you

Hang in the air a thousand leagues from hence,

And straight they shall be here. Sit, and attend.

HOT. Come, Kate, thou art perfect in lying down.

Come, quick, quick, that I may lay my head in thy
  lap.   231

LADY P. Go, ye giddy goose.   [*The music plays*.]

HOT. Now I perceive the Devil understands
  Welsh,

And 'tis no marvel he is so humorous.°

By'r Lady, he is a good musician.   235

LADY P. Then should you be nothing but musical,
for you are altogether governed by humors. Lie still,
ye thief, and hear the lady sing in Welsh.

HOT. I had rather hear Lady, my brach,° howl in
Irish.   241

LADY P. Wouldst thou have thy head broken?

HOT. No.

LADY P. Then be still.

HOT. Neither — 'tis a woman's fault.   245

LADY P. Now God help thee!

HOT. To the Welsh lady's bed.

LADY P. What's that?

HOT. Peace! She sings.

[*Here* LADY MORTIMER *sings a Welsh song*.]

Come, Kate, I'll have your song too.   250

LADY P. Not mine, in good sooth.°

HOT. Not yours, in good sooth! Heart! You swear
like a comfit-maker's° wife. "Not you, in good
sooth," and "as true as I live," and "as God shall
mend me," and "as sure as day,"   255

And givest such sarcenet surety for thy oaths°

As if thou never walk'st further than Finsbury.°

Swear me, Kate, like a lady as thou art,

A good mouth-filling oath, and leave " in sooth,"

And such protest of pepper gingerbread°   260

To velvet guards° and Sunday citizens.°

Come, sing.

LADY P. I will not sing.

HOT. 'Tis the next way to turn tailor,° or be red-
breast teacher.° An the indentures be drawn,   265

I'll away within these two hours, and so come in

when ye will.   [*Exit*.]

GLEND. Come, come, Lord Mortimer, you are as
  slow

As hot Lord Percy is on fire to go.

By this our book is drawn. We'll but seal,   270

And then to horse immediately.

MORT.   With all my heart. [*Exeunt*.]

SCENE II. *London. The palace.*

[*Enter the* KING, PRINCE OF WALES, *and others*.]

KING. Lords, give us leave. The Prince of Wales
  and I

Must have some private conference. But be near at
  hand,

For we shall presently have need of you.

[*Exeunt* LORDS.]

I know not whether God will have it so,

For some displeasing service I have done,   5

That, in his secret doom,° out of my blood°

He'll breed revengement and a scourge for me;

But thou dost in thy passages of life

Make me believe that thou art only marked

For the hot vengeance and the rod of Heaven   10

To punish my mistreadings. Tell me else,

Could such inordinate° and low desires,

Such poor, such bare, such lewd,° such mean at-
  tempts,

Such barren pleasures, rude society,

As thou art matched withal and grafted to,   15

Accompany the greatness of thy blood,

And hold their level with thy princely heart?

PRINCE. So please your Majesty, I would I could

Quit° all offenses with as clear excuse

As well as I am doubtless I can purge   20

Myself of many I am charged withal.

Yet such extenuation let me beg

As, in reproof° of many tales devised,

Which oft the ear of greatness needs must hear,

260. pepper gingerbread: a very mild form of heat.   261. velvet
guards: literally bands of velvet used to ornament a gown (and
still used on the gown of a Ph.D.). See Pl. 9f and comment on
p. 94b. Sunday citizens: citizens in their Sunday best.   264. turn
tailor: Tailors (before the invention of the sewing machine) used
to sing at their work as they sat cross-legged.   265. redbreast
teacher: one who teaches caged birds to sing. The little English
robin was highly valued as a songbird.
  Sc. ii: 6. doom: judgment. out . . . blood: through one of my
children.   12. inordinate: intemperate.   13. lewd: low.   19. Quit:
acquit myself of.   23. reproof: rebuttal.

211. division: melody.   214. wanton: luxuriant. rushes: used to
cover floors.   218. heaviness: drowsiness.   221. team: i.e., the
horses of the sun.   224. book: agreement.   234. humorous: full
of whims.   240. brach: bitch.   251. sooth: truth.   253. comfit-
maker: candymaker.   256. sarcenet . . . oaths: you swear by
such soft things. sarcenet: fine silk.   257. Finsbury: Finsbury
fields, whither London citizens took their Sunday-afternoon walk.

By smiling pickthanks° and base newsmongers,   25
I may for some things true wherein my youth
Hath faulty wandered and irregular
Find pardon on my true submission.
    KING. God pardon thee! Yet let me wonder,
      Harry,
At thy affections, which do hold a wing   30
Quite from the flight° of all thy ancestors.
Thy place in Council thou hast rudely lost,
Which by thy younger brother is supplied,
And art almost an alien to the hearts
Of all the Court and princes of my blood.   35
The hope and expectation of thy time°
Is ruined, and the soul of every man
Prophetically doth forethink thy fall.
Had I so lavish of my presence been,
So common-hackneyed° in the eyes of men,   40
So stale and cheap to vulgar company,
Opinion,° that did help me to the crown,
Had still kept loyal to possession,°
And left me in reputeless banishment,
A fellow of no mark nor likelihood.   45
By being seldom seen, I could not stir
But like a comet I was wondered at,
That men would tell their children "This is he."
Others would say, "Where, which is Bolingbroke?"
And then I stole all courtesy from Heaven,   50
And dressed myself in such humility
That I did pluck allegiance from men's hearts,
Loud shouts and salutations from their mouths,
Even in the presence of the crownèd King.
Thus did I keep my person fresh and new,   55
My presence, like a robe pontifical,°
Ne'er seen but wondered at. And so my state,
Seldom but sumptuous, showed like a feast,
And won by rareness such solemnity.
The skipping° King, he ambled up and down,   60
With shallow jesters and rash bavin° wits,
Soon kindled and soon burnt; carded° his state,
Mingled his royalty with capering fools,
Had his great name profanèd with their scorns,
And gave his countenance, against his name,°   65
To laugh at gibing° boys and stand the push°
Of every beardless vain comparative,°
Grew a companion to the common streets,
Enfeoffed° himself to popularity,°

That, being daily swallowed by men's eyes,   70
They surfeited with honey and began
To loathe the taste of sweetness, whereof a little
More than a little is by much too much.
So when he had occasion to be seen,
He was but as the cuckoo is in June,°   75
Heard, not regarded; seen, but with such eyes
As, sick and blunted with community,°
Afford no extraordinary gaze,
Such as is bent on sunlike majesty
When it shines seldom in admiring eyes;   80
But rather drowsed and hung their eyelids down,
Slept in his face° and rendered such aspèct°
As cloudy° men use to their adversaries,
Being with his presence glutted, gorged, and full.
And in that very line,° Harry, standest thou;   85
For thou hast lost thy princely privilege
With vile participation.° Not an eye
But is aweary of thy common sight,
Save mine, which hath desired to see thee more,
Which now doth that I would not have it do —   90
Make blind itself with foolish tenderness.
    PRINCE. I shall hereafter, my thrice gracious
      lord,
Be more myself.
    KING.   For all the world
As thou art to this hour° was Richard then
When I from France set foot at Ravenspurgh,   95
And even as I was then is Percy now.
Now, by my scepter and my soul to boot,
He hath more worthy interest to the state
Than thou the shadow of succession;°
For of no right,° nor color like to right,   100
He doth fill fields with harness° in the realm,
Turns head against the lion's armèd jaws,
And being no more in debt to years than thou,°
Leads ancient lords and reverend bishops on
To bloody battles and to bruising arms.   105
What never-dying honor hath he got
Against renownèd Douglas! — whose high deeds,
Whose hot incursions° and great name in arms
Holds from all soldiers chief majority
And military title capital°   110
Through all the kingdoms that acknowledge Christ.
Thrice hath this Hotspur, Mars in swathling°
    clothes,
This infant warrior, in his enterprises
Discomfited great Douglas, ta'en him once,
Enlarged him, and made a friend of him,   115

25. pickthanks: men who curry favor by telling tales. 30-31. affections . . . flight: desires, natural inclinations . . . fly a different course. 36. time: lifetime. 40. common-hackneyed: at every man's call. A hackney is a hired horse. 42. Opinion: popular opinion. 43. loyal to possession: loyal to the possessor; i.e., Richard II. 56. robe pontifical: a bishop's robe. 60. skipping: frivolous. 61. bavin: brushwood for kindling, worthless and easily broken. 62. carded: adulterated. 65. against . . . name: contrary to the interest of his reputation. 66. gibing: mocking. stand . . . push: endure the sallies of. 67. beardless . . . comparative: every boy who cared to make jokes at his expense. 69. Enfeoffed: conveyed, made himself over to. popularity: low company, common people.

75. cuckoo . . . June: See App. 11. 77. community: that which is common. 82. in . . . face: in his presence — a gross insult. aspect: look. 83. cloudy: sullen. 85. line: class. 87. vile participation: mixing with low company. 94. to . . . hour: up to now. 99. shadow of succession: shadowy right of succession. 100. of no right: with no right. 101. harness: armor. 103. no . . . thou: See I.i.92,n. 108. incursions: raids. 109-10. Holds . . . capital: keeps from all other soldiers the claim to be considered the great est. 112. swathling: swaddling.

To fill the mouth of deep defiance up°
And shake the peace and safety of our throne.
And what say you to this? Percy, Northumberland,
The Archbishop's Grace of York, Douglas, Morti-
     mer,
Capitulate° against us and are up.   120
But wherefore do I tell these news to thee?
Why, Harry, do I tell thee of my foes,
Which art my near'st and dearest enemy?
Thou that art like enough through vassal° fear,
Base inclination, and the start of spleen°   125
To fight against me under Percy's pay,
To dog his heels and curtsy at his frowns,
To show how much thou art degenerate.

PRINCE. Do not think so, you shall not find it so.
And God forgive them that so much have swayed
Your Majesty's good thoughts away from me!   131
I will redeem all this on Percy's head,
And in the closing of some glorious day
Be bold to tell you that I am your son;
When I will wear a garment all of blood,   135
And stain my favors° in a bloody mask
Which, washed away, shall scour my shame with it.
And that shall be the day, whene'er it lights,
That this same child of honor and renown,
This gallant Hotspur, this all-praisèd knight,   140
And your unthought-of Harry chance to meet.
For every honor sitting on his helm,
Would they were multitudes, and on my head
My shames redoubled! For the time will come
That I shall make this Northern youth exchange
His glorious deeds for my indignities.   146
Percy is but my factor,° good my lord,
To engross° up glorious deeds on my behalf.
And I will call him to so strict account
That he shall render every glory up —   150
Yea, even the slightest worship° of his time —
Or I will tear the reckoning from his heart.
This, in the name of God, I promise here.
The which if He be pleased I shall perform,
I do beseech your Majesty may salve°   155
The long-grown wounds of my intemperance.
If not, the end of life cancels all bands,°
And I will die a hundred thousand deaths
Ere break the smallest parcel° of this vow.

KING. A hundred thousand rebels die in this.   160
Thou shalt have charge and sovereign trust herein.
[Enter BLUNT.] How now, good Blunt? Thy looks
     are full of speed.

BLUNT. So hath the business that I come to speak
     of.
Lord Mortimer of Scotland hath sent word

That Douglas and the English rebels met   165
The eleventh of this month at Shrewsbury.
A mighty and a fearful head° they are,
If promises be kept on every hand,
As ever offered foul play in a state.

KING. The Earl of Westmoreland set forth today,
With him my son, Lord John of Lancaster;   171
For this advértisement is five days old.
On Wednesday next, Harry, you shall set forward,
On Thursday we ourselves will march. Our meeting
Is Bridgenorth. And, Harry, you shall march   175
Through Gloucestershire, by which account,
Our business valued,° some twelve days hence
Our general forces at Bridgenorth shall meet.
Our hands are full of business. Let's away.
Advantage feeds him fat° while men delay.   180

[Exeunt.]

SCENE III. *Boar's Head Tavern in Eastcheap.*

[*Enter* FALSTAFF *and* BARDOLPH.]

FAL. Bardolph, am I not fallen away vilely since
this last action?° Do I not bate?° Do I not dwindle?
Why, my skin hangs about me like an old lady's
loose gown,° I am withered like an old applejohn.°
Well, I'll repent, and that suddenly, while I am in   5
some liking.° I shall be out of heart° shortly, and
then I shall have no strength to repent. An I have not
forgotten what the inside of a church is made of, I
am a peppercorn, a brewer's horse° — the inside of a
church! Company, villainous company, hath been
the spoil of me.   11

BARD. Sir John, you are so fretful you cannot live
long.

FAL. Why, there is it. Come sing me a bawdy song,
make me merry. I was as virtuously given as a gen-
tleman need to be — virtuous enough; swore little;
diced not above seven times a week; went to a
bawdyhouse not above once in a quarter — of an
hour; paid money that I borrowed, three or four   20
times; lived well, and in good compass.° And now I
live out of all order, out of all compass.

BARD. Why, you are so fat, Sir John, that you must
needs be out of all compass, out of all reasonable
compass, Sir John.   26

FAL. Do thou amend thy face, and I'll amend my
life. Thou art our admiral,° thou bearest the lantern

---

116. To . . . up: so that defiance may speak with a loud mouth.
120. Capitulate: make agreement. 124. vassal: slavish. 125. start
of spleen: impulse of bad temper. 136. favors: features, face.
147. factor: agent, buyer. 148. engross: buy up wholesale.
151. worship: honor. 155. salve: heal. 157. bands: bonds,
debts. 159. parcel: portion.

167. head: force. 177. Our . . . valued: considering how much
we have to do. 180. Advantage . . . fat: advantage makes the
most of his opportunities.
Sc. iii: 2. last action: i.e., the Gadshill affair. bate: grow thin.
4. loose gown: See Pl. 9m. applejohn: withered apple, long kept.
6. in . . . liking: in good condition. out of heart: have no heart
for it. 9. brewer's horse: i.e., old and decrepit. 21. compass:
(lit., circumference) limits, with a pun on Falstaff's girth. 28. ad-
miral: the admiral's ship, which led the way and carried a lighted
lantern by night so that the fleet should keep together.

in the poop,° but 'tis in the nose of thee. Thou art
the Knight of the Burning Lamp.   30

BARD. Why, Sir John, my face does you no harm.

FAL. No, I'll be sworn, I make as good use of it as
many a man doth of a death's-head° or a memento
mori.° I never see thy face but I think upon   35
Hell-fire and Dives° that lived in purple, for there he
is in his robes, burning, burning. If thou wert any-
way given to virtue, I would swear by thy face; my
oath should be " By this fire, that's God's angel."°
But thou art altogether given over, and wert in-   40
deed, but for the light in thy face, the son of utter
darkness. When thou rannest up Gadshill in the
night to catch my horse, if I did not think thou hadst
been an ignis fatuus° or a ball of wildfire,° there's no
purchase in money. Oh, thou art a perpetual tri-   45
umph,° an everlasting bonfire light! Thou hast
saved me a thousand marks in links° and torches,
walking with thee in the night betwixt tavern and
tavern. But the sack that thou hast drunk me would
have bought me lights as good cheap at the dear-   51
est chandler's° in Europe. I have maintained that
salamander° of yours with fire any time this two and
thirty years, God reward me for it!   55

BARD. 'Sblood, I would my face were in your
belly!

FAL. God-a-mercy! So should I be sure to be heart-
burned. [*Enter* HOSTESS.] How now, Dame Partlet
the hen!° Have you inquired yet who picked my
pocket?   61

HOSTESS. Why, Sir John, what do you think, Sir
John? Do you think I keep thieves in my house? I
have searched, I have inquired, so has my husband,
man by man, boy by boy, servant by servant.   65
The tithe° of a hair was never lost in my house
before.

FAL. Ye lie, hostess. Bardolph was shaved° and
lost many a hair, and I'll be sworn my pocket was
picked. Go to, you are a woman, go.   70

HOSTESS. Who, I? No, I defy thee. God's light, I
was never called so in mine own house before!

FAL. Go to, I know you well enough.

HOSTESS. No, Sir John, you do not know me, Sir
John. I know you, Sir John. You owe me money,   75
Sir John, and now you pick a quarrel to beguile me
of it. I bought you a dozen of shirts to your back.

FAL. Dowlas,° filthy dowlas. I have given them

away to bakers' wives, and they have made bolters°
of them.   81

HOSTESS. Now, as I am a true woman, holland° of
eight shillings an ell.° You owe money here besides,
Sir John, for your diet and by-drinkings,° and
money lent you, four and twenty pound.   86

FAL. He had his part of it. Let him pay.

HOSTESS. He? Alas, he is poor, he hath nothing.

FAL. How! Poor? Look upon his face — what call
you rich? Let them coin his nose, let them coin   90
his cheeks. I'll not pay a denier.° What, will you
make a younker° of me? Shall I not take mine ease
in mine inn but I shall have my pocket picked? I
have lost a seal ring of my grandfather's worth forty
mark.   95

HOSTESS. Oh Jesu, I have heard the Prince tell
him, I know not how oft, that that ring was cop-
per!°

FAL. How! The Prince is a Jack,° a sneak-cup.°
'Sblood, an he were here, I would cudgel him like a
dog if he would say so.   101

[*Enter the* PRINCE *and* PETO, *marching, and* FALSTAFF
meets them playing on his truncheon like a fife.]

How now, lad! Is the wind in that door, i' faith?
Must we all march?

BARD. Yea, two and two, Newgate fashion.°

HOSTESS. My lord, I pray you hear me.   105

PRINCE. What sayest thou, Mistress Quickly? How
doth thy husband? I love him well, he is an honest
man.

HOSTESS. Good my lord, hear me.

FAL. Prithee let her alone, and list to me.   110

PRINCE. What sayest thou, Jack?

FAL. The other night I fell asleep here behind the
arras, and had my pocket picked. This house is
turned bawdyhouse; they pick pockets.

PRINCE. What didst thou lose, Jack?   115

FAL. Wilt thou believe me, Hal? Three or four
bonds of forty pound apiece, and a seal ring of my
grandfather's.

PRINCE. A trifle, some eightpenny matter.

HOSTESS. So I told him, my lord, and I said I   120
heard your Grace say so. And, my lord, he speaks
most vilely of you, like a foul-mouthed man as he is,
and said he would cudgel° you.

PRINCE. What! He did not?

HOSTESS. There's neither faith, truth, nor woman-
hood in me else.   126

FAL. There's no more faith in thee than in a
stewed prune, nor no more truth in thee than in a

29. poop: stern.   34. death's-head: skull.   34–35. memento
mori: reminder of death.   36. Dives: the rich man in the par-
able of Dives and Lazarus. See Luke 16:19–31.   39. By . . .
angel: a parody of a line in Chapman's *Blind Beggar of
Alexandria*, a recent and popular play at the Rose Theater.
44. ignis fatuus: will-o'-the-wisp. wildfire: firework.   46. tri-
umph: rejoicing, celebrated with torches and bonfires.   47. links:
torches used to light the way on a dark night.   52. chandler:
seller of candles.   54. salamander: a kind of lizard, believed to
enjoy fire.   59–60. Dame . . . hen: the wife of Chanticleer the
cock in the story of Reynard the Fox.   66. tithe: tenth part.
68. shaved: caught venereal disease.   78. Dowlas: coarse linen.

80. bolters: sieves for sifting flour from bran.   82. holland: fine
linen.   83. ell: 45 inches.   85. by-drinkings: drinks between
meals.   91. denier: the smallest English coin, worth 1/10*d.*
92. younker: "sucker."   97. copper: copper-gilt was the cheap-
est kind of imitation gold.   99. Jack: knave. sneak-cup: one
who steals cups from taverns, the lowest kind of theft.
104. Newgate fashion: i.e., like the chain gang. Newgate: the
London prison for felons.   123. cudgel: beat.

drawn fox,° and for womanhood, Maid Marian may be the deputy's wife of the ward to thee.° Go, you thing, go.   131

HOSTESS. Say, what thing? What thing?

FAL. What thing! Why, a thing to thank God on.

HOSTESS. I am no thing to thank God on, I   135 would thou shouldst know it. I am an honest man's wife. And, setting thy knighthood aside, thou art a knave to call me so.

FAL. Setting thy womanhood aside, thou art a beast to say otherwise.   140

HOSTESS. Say, what beast, thou knave, thou?

FAL. What beast! Why, an otter.

PRINCE. An otter, Sir John! Why an otter?

FAL. Why, she's neither fish nor flesh. A man knows not where to have her.   145

HOSTESS. Thou art an unjust man in saying so. Thou or any man knows where to have me, thou knave, thou!

PRINCE. Thou sayest true, hostess, and he slanders thee most grossly.   150

HOSTESS. So he doth you, my lord, and said this other day you ought° him a thousand pound.

PRINCE. Sirrah, do I owe you a thousand pound?

FAL. A thousand pound, Hal! A million!   155 Thy love is worth a million. Thou owest me thy love.

HOSTESS. Nay, my lord, he called you Jack, and said he would cudgel you.

FAL. Did I, Bardolph?   160

BARD. Indeed, Sir John, you said so.

FAL. Yea, if he said° my ring was copper.

PRINCE. I say 'tis copper.° Darest thou be as good as thy word now?   164

FAL. Why, Hal, thou knowest, as thou art but man, I dare; but as thou art Prince, I fear thee as I fear the roaring of the lion's whelp.

PRINCE. And why not as the lion?

FAL. The King himself is to be feared as the lion. Dost thou think I'll fear thee as I fear thy   170 father? Nay, an I do, I pray God my girdle break.

PRINCE. Oh, if it should, how would thy guts fall about thy knees! But, sirrah, there's no room for faith, truth, nor honesty in this bosom of thine; it is all filled up with guts and midriff. Charge   175 an honest woman with picking thy pocket! Why, thou whoreson, impudent, embossed° rascal, if there were anything in thy pocket but tavern reckonings, memorandums of bawdyhouses, and one poor penny-

worth of sugar candy to make thee long-   180 winded, if thy pocket were enriched with any other injuries° but these, I am a villain. And yet you will stand to it, you will not pocket up wrong. Art thou not ashamed?   184

FAL. Dost thou hear, Hal? Thou knowest in the state of innocency Adam fell, and what should poor Jack Falstaff do in the days of villainy?° Thou seest I have more flesh than another man, and therefore more frailty. You confess, then, you picked my pocket?   190

PRINCE. It appears so by the story.

FAL. Hostess, I forgive thee. Go, make ready breakfast. Love thy husband, look to thy servants, cherish thy guests. Thou shalt find me tractable° to any honest reason. Thou seest I am pacified   195 still.° Nay, prithee be gone. [*Exit* HOSTESS.] Now, Hal, to the news at Court. For the robbery, lad, how is that answered?

PRINCE. Oh, my sweet beef,° I must still be good angel to thee. The money is paid back again.   200

FAL. Oh, I do not like that paying back. 'Tis a double labor.

PRINCE. I am good friends with my father, and may do anything.   204

FAL. Rob me the exchequer the first thing thou doest, and do it with unwashed hands° too.

BARD. Do, my lord.

PRINCE. I have procured thee, Jack, a charge of foot.   209

FAL. I would it had been of horse. Where shall I find one that can steal well? Oh for a fine thief, of the age of two and twenty or thereabouts! I am heinously° unprovided. Well, God be thanked for these rebels, they offend none but the virtuous. I laud them, I praise them.   215

PRINCE. Bardolph!

BARD. My lord?

PRINCE. Go bear this letter to Lord John of Lancaster, to my brother John; this to my Lord of Westmoreland. [*Exit* BARDOLPH.] Go, Peto, to horse,   220 to horse, for thou and I have thirty miles to ride yet ere dinnertime. [*Exit* PETO.] Jack, meet me tomorrow in the Temple Hall at two o'clock in the afternoon.

There shalt thou know thy charge, and there receive Money and order for their furniture.°   226

The land is burning, Percy stands on high,

And either we or they must lower lie: [*Exit.*]

FAL. Rare words! Brave world! Hostess, my breakfast, come!

Oh, I could wish this tavern were my drum! [*Exit.*]

---

129. drawn fox: fox driven out from cover, and so cunning. **129–30. Maid . . . thee:** Maid Marian, the woman in Robin Hood's gang, was a character in a morris dance (see App. 24). She was played by a man as lumpish and awkward. The wife of the deputy of the ward was likely to give herself airs of dignity. Falstaff means "you are more lumpish than Maid Marian compared with a most stately matron." **152. ought:** owed. **162. if he said:** See Touchstone on the virtue of "if" as a means of making a safe threat (*AYLI*, V.iv.100–08). **163. I . . . copper:** Here Falstaff gets the "lie direct." **177. embossed:** swollen.

181–82. pocket . . . injuries: a pun on the phrase "to pocket up injuries." **187. days of villainy:** these wicked times. **194. tractable:** agreeable. **196. still:** always. **199. beef:** ox. **206. unwashed hands:** without stopping to wash your hands. **212. heinously:** atrociously. **226. furniture:** equipment.

Act IV

SCENE I. *The rebel camp near Shrewsbury.*

[*Enter* HOTSPUR, WORCESTER, *and* DOUGLAS.]

HOT. Well said, my noble Scot. If speaking truth
In this fine age were not thought flattery,
Such attribution° should the Douglas have
As not a soldier of this season's stamp°
Should go so general current through the world.　5
By God, I cannot flatter, I do defy
The tongues of soothers;° but a braver place
In my heart's love hath no man than yourself.
Nay, task me to my word.° Approve° me, lord.
DOUG. Thou art the king of honor.　　　　　　10
No man so potent breathes upon the ground
But I will beard° him.
HOT.　　　　　　　　Do so, and 'tis well.
[*Enter a* MESSENGER *with letters.*]
What letters hast thou there? — I can but thank
　　you.
MESS. These letters come from your father.
HOT. Letters from him! Why comes he not him-
　　self?　　　　　　　　　　　　　　　　　15
MESS. He cannot come, my lord, he is grievous
　　sick.
HOT. 'Zounds! How has he the leisure to be sick
In such a justling° time? Who leads his power?
Under whose government come they along?
MESS. His letters bear his mind, not I, my lord.
WOR. I prithee tell me, doth he keep his bed?　21
MESS. He did, my lord, four days ere I set forth,
And at the time of my departure thence
He was much feared by his physicians.
WOR. I would the state of time had first been
　　whole°　　　　　　　　　　　　　　　25
Ere he by sickness had been visited.
His health was never better worth° than now.
HOT. Sick now! Droop now! This sickness doth
　　infect
The very lifeblood of our enterprise.
'Tis catching hither, even to our camp.　　　30
He writes me here that inward sickness —
And that his friends by deputation° could not
So soon be drawn,° nor did he think it meet
To lay so dangerous and dear° a trust
On any soul removed but on his own.　　　35

Yet doth he give us bold advértisement°
That with our small conjunction° we should on,
To see how fortune is disposed to us;
For, as he writes, there is no quailing now,
Because the King is certainly possessed°　　40
Of all our purposes. What say you to it?
WOR. Your father's sickness is a maim to us.
HOT. A perilous gash, a very limb lopped off.
And yet, in faith, it is not; his present want°
Seems more than we shall find it. Were it good　45
To set° the exact° wealth of all our states
All at one cast?° To set so rich a main°
On the nice hazard° of one doubtful hour?
It were not good, for therein should we read
The very bottom and the soul of hope,　　　50
The very list,° the very utmost bound°
Of all our fortunes.
DOUG.　　　　　　Faith, and so we should,
Where now remains a sweet reversion.°
We may boldly spend upon the hope of what
Is to come in.　　　　　　　　　　　　55
A comfort of retirement° lives in this.
HOT. A rendezvous, a home to fly unto,
If that the Devil and mischance look big°
Upon the maidenhead of our affairs.
WOR. But yet I would your father had been here.
The quality and hair° of our attempt　　　61
Brooks no division. It will be thought
By some, that know not why he is away,
That wisdom, loyalty, and mere dislike
Of our proceedings kept the Earl from hence.　65
And think how such an apprehension
May turn the tide of fearful faction,°
And breed a kind of question in our cause;
For well you know we of the offering° side
Must keep aloof from strict arbitrament,°　70
And stop all sight holes, every loop from whence
The eye of reason may pry in upon us.
This absence of your father's draws° a curtain
That shows the ignorant a kind of fear
Before not dreamed of.
HOT.　　　　　　　You strain too far.　75
I rather of his absence make this use.
It lends a luster and more great opinion,
A larger dare to our great enterprise,
Than if the Earl were here; for men must think
If we without his help can make a head°　　80
To push against a kingdom, with his help

---

36. advertisement: advice.　37. conjunction: forces that have joined.　40. possessed: informed.　44. his . . . want: the need of him at this present time.　46. set: hazard. exact: entire. 47. cast: throw of the dice. main: stake.　48. nice hazard: delicate chance.　51. list: limit. bound: boundary.　53. reversion: portion yet to come.　56. comfort of retirement: a place to which we can retire for comfort.　58. look big: threaten. 61. hair: nature.　67. fearful faction: timid rebellion.　69. offering: challenging.　70. strict arbitrament: exact judgment. 73. draws: draws back.　80. make a head: raise an army. See I.iii.284.

Act IV, Sc. i: 3. attribution: citation of merits.　4. season's stamp: of this year's minting. The idea is that Douglas is like a new coin, acceptable (*current*) everywhere as valuable. 7. soothers: flatterers.　9. task . . . word: cause me to make my word good. Approve: put to the proof.　12. beard: dare; lit., pull by the beard.　18. justling: jostling, disturbed.　25. I . . . whole: I wish the times themselves had first been healthy. 27. better worth: worth more.　32. deputation: deputy; i.e., he could not send anyone else.　33. drawn: drawn together. 34. dear: important.

We shall o'erturn it topsy-turvy down.
Yet all goes well, yet all our joints are whole.

DOUG. As heart can think. There is not such a word
Spoke of in Scotland as this term of fear.   85

[*Enter* SIR RICHARD VERNON.]

HOT. My cousin Vernon! Welcome, by my soul.

VER. Pray God my news be worth a welcome, lord.
The Earl of Westmoreland, seven thousand strong,
Is marching hitherward; with him Prince John.

HOT. No harm. What more?

VER.   And further, I have learned,   90
The King himself in person is set forth,
Or hitherward intended speedily,
With strong and mighty preparation.

HOT. He shall be welcome too. Where is his son,
The nimble-footed madcap Prince of Wales,   95
And his comrades, that daffed° the world aside
And bid it pass?°

VER.   All furnished,° all in arms;
All plumed like estridges that with the wind
Bated like eagles having lately bathed;°
Glittering in golden coats, like images;°   100
As full of spirit as the month of May,
And gorgeous as the sun at midsummer;
Wanton° as youthful goats, wild as young bulls.
I saw young Harry, with his beaver° on,
His cuisses° on his thighs, gallantly armed,   105
Rise from the ground like feathered Mercury,°
And vaulted with such ease into his seat
As if an angel dropped down from the clouds
To turn and wind a fiery Pegasus,°   109
And witch° the world with noble horsemanship.

HOT. No more, no more. Worse than the sun in
  March,
This praise doth nourish agues. Let them come.
They come like sacrifices in their trim,°
And to the fire-eyed maid of smoky war
All hot and bleeding will we offer them.   115
The mailèd Mars° shall on his altar sit
Up to the ears in blood. I am on fire
To hear this rich reprisal° is so nigh
And yet not ours. Come, let me taste my horse,
Who is to bear me like a thunderbolt   120
Against the bosom of the Prince of Wales.
Harry to Harry shall, hot horse to horse,

Meet and ne'er part till one drop down a corse.
Oh that Glendower were come!

VER.   There is more news.
I learned in Worcester, as I rode along,   125
He cannot draw his power this fourteen days.

DOUG. That's the worst tidings that I hear of yet.

WOR. Aye, by my faith, that bears a frosty sound.

HOT. What may the King's whole battle° reach
  unto?

VER. To thirty thousand.

HOT.   Forty let it be.   130
My father and Glendower being both away,
The powers of us may serve so great a day.
Come, let us take a muster speedily.
Doomsday is near. Die all, die merrily.

DOUG. Talk not of dying. I am out of° fear   135
Of death or death's hand for this one half-year.

[*Exeunt.*]

SCENE II. *A public road near Coventry.*

[*Enter* FALSTAFF *and* BARDOLPH.]

FAL. Bardolph, get thee before to Coventry, fill me
a bottle of sack. Our soldiers shall march through,
we'll to Sutton Co'fil'° tonight.

BARD. Will you give me money, Captain?

FAL. Lay out,° lay out.   5

BARD. This bottle makes an angel.°

FAL. An if it do, take it for thy labor. And if it
make twenty, take them all, I'll answer the coinage.°
Bid my Lieutenant Peto meet me at town's end.   10

BARD. I will, Captain. Farewell.   [*Exit.*]

FAL. If I be not ashamed of my soldiers,° I am a
soused gurnet.° I have misused the King's press°
damnably. I have got, in exchange of a hundred and
fifty soldiers, three hundred and odd pounds. I   15
press me none but good householders, yeomen's°
sons; inquire me out contracted bachelors,° such as
had been asked twice on the banns; such a commod-
ity° of warm slaves as had as lieve° hear the Devil as
a drum; such as fear the report of a caliver°   20
worse than a struck fowl or a hurt wild duck. I
pressed me none but such toasts-and-butter, with

---

129. battle: main army.   135. out of: free from.

Sc. ii: 3. Sutton Co'fil': Sutton Coldfield, a town in War-
wickshire.   5. Lay out: pay for it.   6. makes an angel: comes
to an angel (10s) which you owe me. See Pl. 10c.   7-9. take . . .
coinage: Falstaff deliberately misunderstands Bardolph's
"make" — "if the bottle will make angels, I'll guarantee the
coins."   12. If . . . soldiers: Falstaff (see following to l. 52) was
typical of many dishonest captains in the 1590's. His methods
of levying recruits are further shown in *II Hen IV*, III.ii. See
Gen. Intro. p. 30b–31a.   13. soused gurnet: pickled gurnet (sea
fish with a large head). King's press: the right to conscript
soldiers granted by the King's commission.   16. yeomen: wealthy
farmers.   17. contracted bachelors: bachelors engaged to be
married in a short time.   19. commodity: parcel. lieve: soon
20. caliver: lighter form of musket or harquebus, used by the
infantry. See Pl. 22f.

---

96. daffed: waved.   97. bid it pass: cried "let the world pass";
i.e., "who cares a damn?" furnished: in full armor.   97–99. All
. . . bathed: These lines are much annotated. As they stand they
mean: "All wearing plumes like ostriches that flap their wings
(*bate*) in the wind like eagles that have lately bathed." But the
comparison seems hardly apt. Either a line has been omitted
after *wind*, or *with* is a misprint of some such verb as
"wing."   100. images: i.e., of the saints in a Catholic church
103. Wanton: lusty.   104. beaver: visor of the helmet. See Pl. 8a.
105. cuisses: thigh pieces.   106. feathered Mercury: Mercury,
the messenger of the gods, wore winged sandals.   109. Pegasus:
Perseus's winged horse.   110. witch: bewitch.   113. in . . . trim:
dressed up.   116. mailèd Mars: the god of war in his armor.
118. reprisal: prize.

hearts in their bellies no bigger than pins' heads, and they have bought out their services. And now my whole charge consists of ancients, corporals, 25 lieutenants, gentlemen of companies,° slaves as ragged as Lazarus in the painted cloth° where the glutton's dogs licked his sores; and such as indeed were never soldiers, but discarded unjust serv- 30 ingmen,° younger sons to younger brothers,° revolted tapsters, and ostlers trade-fallen;° the cankers of a calm world and a long peace, ten times more dishonorable ragged than an old-faced ancient. And such have I to fill up the rooms of them that 35 have bought out their services that you would think that I had a hundred and fifty tattered prodigals lately come from swine-keeping, from eating draff and husks.° A mad fellow° met me on the way and told me I had unloaded all the gibbets° and 40 pressed the dead bodies. No eye hath seen such scarecrows. I'll not march through Coventry with them, that's flat. Nay, and the villains march wide betwixt the legs, as if they had gyves° on, for indeed I had the most of them out of prison. There's but a shirt and a half in all my company; and the half- 46 shirt is two napkins tacked together and thrown over the shoulders like a herald's coat° without sleeves; and the shirt, to say the truth, stolen from my host at St. Alban's, or the red-nose innkeeper of Daven- 50 try. But that's all one. They'll find linen enough on every hedge.°

[*Enter the* PRINCE *and* WESTMORELAND.]

PRINCE. How now, blown° Jack! How now, quilt! 54
FAL. What, Hal! How now, mad wag! What a devil dost thou in Warwickshire? My good Lord of Westmoreland, I cry you mercy. I thought your honor had already been at Shrewsbury. 59
WEST. Faith, Sir John, 'tis more than time that I were there, and you too; but my powers are there already. The King, I can tell you, looks for us all. We must away all night.
FAL. Tut, never fear me. I am as vigilant as a cat to steal cream. 65

25–26. charge . . . companies: Falstaff has picked up a selection of veterans of various ranks. ancients: ensigns, second lieutenants. gentlemen of companies: gentlemen of good family who served in the ranks of the companies of noblemen. 27. Lazarus . . . cloth: In taverns and less wealthy houses painted cloths showing scenes from Scripture and classical legend were hung on the walls instead of the more costly tapestry. See Pl. 6a. 31. servingmen: servants from some great household. See App. 14. younger . . . brothers: young gentlemen who had no hope of an allowance or a legacy. 32. ostlers trade-fallen: unemployed grooms. 39. draff . . . husks: offal and husks, like the Prodigal Son in the parable who "would fain have filled his belly with the husks that the swine did eat" (Luke, 15:11–32). mad fellow: wit. 40. unloaded . . . gibbets: The bodies of executed felons were often hung up in iron cages near the scene of the crime until they rotted. 44. gyves: fetters on the legs. 48. herald's coat: a sleeveless coat embroidered with the royal coat of arms. 51–52. linen . . . hedge: The washing was laid on the hedges to dry and air. See *W Tale*, IV.iii.23–24. 53. blown: inflated.

PRINCE. I think to steal cream indeed, for thy theft hath already made thee butter. But tell me, Jack, whose fellows are these that come after?
FAL. Mine, Hal, mine.
PRINCE. I did never see such pitiful rascals. 70
FAL. Tut, tut, good enough to toss,° food for powder, food for powder. They'll fill a pit as well as better. Tush, man, mortal men, mortal men.
WEST. Aye, but, Sir John, methinks they are exceeding poor and bare, too beggarly. 75
FAL. Faith, for their poverty, I know not where they had that; and for their bareness, I am sure they never learned that of me.
PRINCE. No, I'll be sworn, unless you call three fingers° on the ribs bare. But, sirrah, make haste. Percy is already in the field. 81
FAL. What, is the King encamped?
WEST. He is, Sir John. I fear we shall stay too long.
FAL. Well,
To the latter end of a fray and the beginning of a feast 85
Fits a dull fighter and a keen guest.   [*Exeunt.*]

SCENE III. *The rebel camp near Shrewsbury.*

[*Enter* HOTSPUR, WORCESTER, DOUGLAS, *and* VERNON.]

HOT. We'll fight with him tonight.
WOR.   It may not be.
DOUG. You give him then advantage.
VER.   Not a whit.
HOT. Why say you so? Looks he not for supply?°
VER. So do we.
HOT.   His is certain, ours is doubtful.
WOR. Good Cousin, be advised, stir not tonight. 5
VER. Do not, my lord.
DOUG.   You do not counsel well.
You speak it out of fear and cold heart.
VER. Do me no slander, Douglas. By my life,
And I dare well maintain it with my life,
If well-respected° honor bid me on, 10
I hold as little counsel with weak fear
As you, my lord, or any Scot that this day lives.
Let it be seen tomorrow in the battle
Which of us fears.
DOUG.   Yea, or tonight.
VER.   Content.
HOT. Tonight, say I. 15
VER. Come, come, it may not be. I wonder much,
Being men of such great leading° as you are,
That you foresee not what impediments
Drag back our expedition.° Certain horse°
Of my cousin Vernon's are not yet come up. 20

71. good . . . toss: i.e., on pikes; "good enough for cannon fodder." 79–80. three fingers: i.e., three fingers' thickness of fat.
Sc. iii: 3. supply: reinforcements. 10. well-respected: well-considered (not foolhardy). 17. leading: experience in leadership. 19. expedition: haste. horse: cavalry.

Your uncle Worcester's horse came but today,
And now their pride and mettle° is asleep,
Their courage with hard labor tame and dull,
That not a horse is half the half of himself.
HOT. So are the horses of the enemy   25
In general, journey-bated° and brought low.
The better part of ours are full of rest.
WOR. The number of the King exceedeth ours.
For God's sake, Cousin, stay till all come in.
                [*The trumpet sounds a parley.*]
                [*Enter* SIR WALTER BLUNT.]
BLUNT. I come with gracious offers from the King,
If you vouchsafe me hearing and respect.   31
HOT. Welcome, Sir Walter Blunt, and would to
    God
You were of our determination!°
Some of us love you well, and even those some
Envy your great deservings and good name   35
Because you are not of our quality,°
But stand against us like an enemy.
    BLUNT. And God defend° but still I should stand
    so
So long as out of limit and true rule
You stand against anointed Majesty.   40
But to my charge.° The King hath sent to know
The nature of your griefs, and whereupon
You conjure from the breast of civil peace
Such bold hostility, teaching his duteous land
Audacious cruelty. If that the King   45
Have any way your good deserts forgot,
Which he confesseth to be manifold,
He bids you name your griefs, and with all speed
You shall have your desires with interest,
And pardon absolute for yourself and these   50
Herein misled by your suggestion.°
    HOT. The King is kind, and well we know the
        King
Knows at what time to promise, when to pay.
My father and my uncle and myself
Did give him that same royalty he wears.   55
And when he was not six and twenty strong,
Sick in the world's regard,° wretched and low,
A poor unminded outlaw sneaking home,
My father gave him welcome to the shore.
And when he heard him swear and vow to God   60
He came but to be Duke of Lancaster,
To sue his livery° and beg his peace
With tears of innocency and terms of zeal,°
My father, in kind heart and pity moved,
Swore him assistance, and performed it too.   65
Now when the lords and barons of the realm

Perceived Northumberland did lean to him,
The more and less came in with cap and knee —
Met him in boroughs, cities, villages,
Attended him on bridges, stood in lanes,   70
Laid gifts before him, proffered him their oaths,
Gave him their heirs as pages, followed him
Even at the heels in golden° multitudes.
He presently, as greatness knows itself,
Steps me a little higher than his vow   75
Made to my father while his blood was poor,
Upon the naked shore at Ravenspurgh;
And now, forsooth, takes on him to reform
Some certain edicts and some strait° decrees
That lie too heavy on the commonwealth,   80
Cries out upon abuses, seems to weep
Over his country's wrongs. And by this face,
This seeming brow of justice, did he win
The hearts of all that he did angle for —
Proceeded further, cut me off the heads   85
Of all the favorites that the absent King
In deputation° left behind him here
When he was personal° in the Irish war.
    BLUNT. Tut, I came not to hear this.
    HOT.   Then to the point.
In short time after, he deposed the King,   90
Soon after that, deprived him of his life.
And in the neck° of that, tasked° the whole state.
To make that worse, suffered his kinsman March,
Who is, if every owner were well placed,
Indeed his king, to be engaged° in Wales,   95
There without ransom to lie forfeited;
Disgraced me in my happy victories,
Sought to entrap me by intelligence;°
Rated° mine uncle from the Council board,
In rage dismissed my father from the Court;   100
Broke oath on oath, committed wrong on wrong,
And in conclusion drove us to seek out
This head of safety,° and withal to pry
Into his title, the which we find
Too indirect° for long continuance.   105
    BLUNT. Shall I return this answer to the King?
    HOT. Not so, Sir Walter. We'll withdraw a
        while.
Go to the King, and let there be impawned°
Some surety for a safe return again,
And in the morning early shall mine uncle   110
Bring him our purposes. And so farewell.
    BLUNT. I would you would accept of grace and
        love.
    HOT. And maybe so we shall.
    BLUNT.   Pray God you do. [*Exeunt.*]

---

22. mettle: ardor.   26. journey-bated: tired by the journey.
33. determination: mind.   36. quality: fellowship, party.   38. de-
fend: forbid.   41. my charge: what I have been instructed
(*charged*) to say.   51. suggestion: temptation.   57. Sick . . .
regard: poorly regarded by the world.   62. sue . . . livery: claim
his inheritance. See *Rich II*, II.i.203; II.iii.129.   63. terms of
zeal: protestations of loyalty.

73. golden: wearing their richest clothes.   79. strait: strict.
87. In deputation: as his deputies.   88. was personal: went in
person.   92. in . . . neck: on top of. tasked: taxed.   95. engaged:
held as pledge, hostage.   98. intelligence: spies.   99. Rated:
dismissed with abuse.   103. head of safety: armed force to keep
us safe.   105. indirect: not in the straight line of descent.
108. impawned: kept as hostage.

SCENE IV. *York. The* ARCHBISHOP'S *palace.*

[*Enter the* ARCHBISHOP OF YORK *and* SIR MICHAEL.°]

ARCH. Hie, good Sir Michael, bear this sealèd
  brief°
With wingèd haste to the Lord Marshal,
This to my cousin Scroop, and all the rest
To whom they are directed. If you knew   4
How much they do import, you would make haste.
  SIR M.   My good lord,
I guess their tenor.°
  ARCH.   Like enough you do.
Tomorrow, good Sir Michael, is a day
Wherein the fortune of ten thousand men
Must bide the touch;° for, sir, at Shrewsbury,   10
As I am truly given to understand,
The King with mighty and quick-raisèd power
Meets with Lord Harry. And I fear, Sir Michael —
What with the sickness of Northumberland,
Whose power was in the first proportion,°   15
And what with Owen Glendower's absence thence,
Who with them was a rated sinew° too
And comes not in, o'er-ruled by prophecies —
I fear the power of Percy is too weak
To wage an instant° trial with the King.   20
  SIR M. Why, my good lord, you need not fear.
There is Douglas and Lord Mortimer.
  ARCH. No, Mortimer is not there.
  SIR M. But there is Mordake, Vernon, Lord Harry
  Percy,
And there is my Lord of Worcester and a head   25
Of gallant warriors, noble gentlemen.
  ARCH. And so there is. But yet the King hath
  drawn
The special head° of all the land together —
The Prince of Wales, Lord John of Lancaster,
The noble Westmoreland and warlike Blunt,   30
And many mo° corrivals° and dear men
Of estimation° and command in arms.
  SIR M. Doubt not, my lord, they shall be well op-
  posed.
  ARCH. I hope no less, yet needful 'tis to fear,
And, to prevent° the worst, Sir Michael, speed. 35
For if Lord Percy thrive not ere the King
Dismiss his power, he means to visit us,°
For he hath heard of our confederacy,°
And 'tis but wisdom to make strong against him.
Therefore make haste. I must go write again   40
To other friends. And so farewell, Sir Michael.
                                    [*Exeunt.*]

Act V

SCENE I. *The* KING'S *camp near Shrewsbury.*

[*Enter the* KING, PRINCE OF WALES, LORD JOHN OF
  LANCASTER, SIR WALTER BLUNT, *and* FALSTAFF.°]

KING. How bloodily the sun begins to peer
Above yon busky° hill! The day looks pale
At his distemperature.°
  PRINCE.   The southern wind
Doth play the trumpet° to his purposes,
And by his hollow whistling in the leaves   5
Foretells a tempest and a blustering day.
  KING. Then with the losers let it sympathize,
For nothing can seem foul to those that win.
    [*The trumpet sounds. Enter* WORCESTER
              and VERNON.]
How now, my Lord of Worcester! 'Tis not well
That you and I should meet upon such terms   10
As now we meet. You have deceived our trust,
And made us doff our easy robes of peace
To crush our old limbs in ungentle steel.
This is not well, my lord, this is not well.
What say you to it? Will you again unknit   15
This churlish knot° of all-abhorrèd war?
And move in that obedient orb° again
Where you did give a fair and natural light,
And be no more an exhaled meteor,°
A prodigy of fear,° and a portent   20
Of broachèd° mischief to the unborn times?
  WOR. Hear me, my liege.
For mine own part, I could be well content
To entertain the lag end of my life
With quiet hours, for I do protest   25
I have not sought the day of this dislike.
  KING. You have not sought it! How comes it,
  then?
  FAL. Rebellion lay in his way, and he found it.
  PRINCE. Peace, chewet,° peace!
  WOR. It pleased your Majesty to turn your looks
Of favor from myself and all our house.   31
And yet I must remember° you, my lord,
We were the first and dearest of your friends.
For you my staff of office° did I break
In Richard's time, and posted° day and night   35
To meet you on the way, and kiss your hand,
When yet you were in place and in account

Sc. iv: s.d., Sir Michael: He has not been identified, pre-
sumably a priest or knight in the Archbishop's service. 1. brief:
letter. 7. tenor: import. 10. bide . . . touch: be put to the
test. 15. in . . . proportion: the largest part. 17. rated sinew:
strength highly valued. 20. instant: immediate. 28. special
head: crack troops, "shock troops." 31. mo: more. corrivals:
supporters. 31–32. dear . . . estimation: men highly regarded.
35. prevent: forestall. 37. visit us: come our way. 38. confed-
eracy: conspiracy.

Act V, Sc. i: s.d., Falstaff: It is worth noting that Shakespeare
places Falstaff in immediate attendance on the King. 2. busky:
bushy. 3. distemperature: sickness. 4. play . . . trumpet: like
the trumpeter blowing an introductory flourish. 16. churlish
knot: knot which unites men for a brutal purpose. 17. obedient
orb: sphere of obedience, like a planet taking its natural course
See App. 1. 19. exhaled meteor: meteor created of vapor drawn
up by the sun. 20. prodigy of fear: a fearful sign of disaster.
21. broached: set loose; lit., tapped (like a cask). 29. chewet:
jackdaw. 32. remember: remind. 34. staff of office: See *Rich
II*, II.iii.26–28 and Pl. 8d. 35. posted: rode hastily.

Nothing so strong and fortunate as I.
It was myself, my brother, and his son
That brought you home, and boldly did outdare   40
The dangers of the time. You swore to us,
And you did swear that oath at Doncaster,
That you did nothing purpose 'gainst the state,
Nor claim no further than your new-fall'n right,°
The seat of Gaunt, Dukedom of Lancaster.   45
To this we swore our aid. But in short space
It rained down fortune showering on your head;
And such a flood of greatness fell on you,
What with our help, what with the absent King,
What with the injuries of a wanton° time,   50
The seeming sufferances° that you had borne,
And the contrarious winds that held the King
So long in his unlucky Irish wars
That all in England did repute him dead.
And from this swarm of fair advantages   55
You took occasion to be quickly wooed
To gripe° the general sway° into your hand;
Forgot your oath to us at Doncaster;
And being fed by us you used us so
As that ungentle gull,° the cuckoo's bird,°   60
Useth the sparrow — did oppress our nest;
Grew by our feeding to so great a bulk
That even our love durst not come near your sight
For fear of swallowing, but with nimble wing
We were enforced, for safety sake, to fly   65
Out of your sight and raise this present head.
Whereby we stand opposèd by such means
As you yourself have forged against yourself,
By unkind usage, dangerous countenance,°
And violation of all faith and troth°   70
Sworn to us in your younger enterprise.
    KING. These things indeed you have articulate,°
Proclaimed at market crosses, read in churches,
To face° the garment of rebellion
With some fine color that may please the eye   75
Of fickle changelings° and poor discontents,
Which gape and rub the elbow at the news
Of hurly-burly innovation.°
And never yet did insurrection want
Such water colors to impaint his cause,   80
Nor moody beggars, starving for a time
Of pell-mell havoc° and confusion.
    PRINCE. In both your armies there is many a soul
Shall pay full dearly for this encounter
If once they join in trial. Tell your nephew,   85
The Prince of Wales doth join with all the world
In praise of Henry Percy. By my hopes,

This present enterprise set off his head,°
I do not think a braver gentleman,
More active-valiant or more valiant-young,   90
More daring or more bold, is now alive
To grace this latter age with noble deeds.
For my part, I may speak it to my shame,
I have a truant been to chivalry,°
And so I hear he doth account me too.   95
Yet this before my father's majesty —
I am content that he shall take the odds°
Of his great name and estimation,
And will, to save the blood on either side,
Try fortune with him in a single fight.   100
    KING. And, Prince of Wales, so dare we venture
        thee,
Albeit considerations infinite
Do make against it. No, good Worcester, no,
We love our people well, even those we love
That are misled upon your cousin's part.   105
And, will they take the offer of our grace,
Both he and they and you — yea, every man —
Shall be my friend again and I'll be his.
So tell your cousin, and bring me word
What he will do. But if he will not yield,   110
Rebuke and dread correction wait on us°
And they shall do their office. So, be gone.
We will not now be troubled with reply.
We offer fair, take it advisedly.
                [Exeunt WORCESTER and VERNON.]
    PRINCE. It will not be accepted, on my life.   115
The Douglas and the Hotspur both together
Are confident against the world in arms.
    KING. Hence, therefore, every leader to his
        charge,°
For on their answer will we set on them.
And God befriend us as our cause is just!   120
[Exeunt all but the PRINCE OF WALES and FALSTAFF.]
    FAL. Hal, if thou see me down in the battle, and
bestride me so, 'tis a point of friendship.
    PRINCE. Nothing but a colossus° can do thee that
friendship. Say thy prayers, and farewell.   124
    FAL. I would 'twere bedtime, Hal, and all well.
    PRINCE. Why, thou owest God a death.   [Exit.]
    FAL. 'Tis not due yet, I would be loath to pay Him
before his day. What need I be so forward with him
that calls not on me? Well, 'tis no matter.   130
Honor pricks me on.° Yea, but how if honor prick
me off° when I come on? How then? Can honor set
to° a leg? No. Or an arm? No. Or take away the
grief of a wound? No. Honor hath no skill in sur-
gery, then? No. What is honor? A word. What   135
is in that word honor? What is that honor? Air. A

---

44. new-fall'n right: inheritance which had recently come.
50. wanton: wild.   51. sufferances: injuries.   57. gripe: grip.
general sway: rule of the whole state.   60. gull: nestling.
cuckoo's bird: See App. ii.   69. dangerous countenance:
threatening looks.   70. troth: truth.   72. articulate: drawn
up in schedules.   74. face: trim.   76. changelings: turncoats.
78. hurly-burly innovation: confusion and revolution.   82. havoc:
slaughter.

88. set . . . head: being excepted.   94. chivalry: knightly deeds.
97. take . . . odds: have the advantage.   111. wait on us: are
our servants.   118. charge: command.   123. colossus: See
Caesar, I.ii.135–38.   131. Honor . . . on: honor spurs me forward
to heroism.   131–32. prick me off: mark me down on the casu-
alty list.   132–33. set to: mend.

trim° reckoning! Who hath it? He that died o' Wed-
nesday. Doth he feel it? No. Doth he hear it? No.
'Tis insensible, then? Yea, to the dead. But will   140
it not live with the living? No. Why? Detraction°
will not suffer it. Therefore I'll none of it. Honor is
a mere scutcheon.° And so ends my catechism.

[Exit.]

SCENE II. *The rebel camp.*

[Enter WORCESTER and VERNON.]

WOR. Oh, no, my nephew must not know, Sir
  Richard,
The liberal and kind offer of the King.
VER. 'Twere best he did.
WOR.   Then are we all undone.
It is not possible, it cannot be
The King should keep his word in loving us.   5
He will suspect us still, and find a time
To punish this offense in other faults.
Suspicion all our lives shall be stuck full of eyes;
For treason is but trusted like the fox,
Who, ne'er so tame, so cherished and locked up,   10
Will have a wild trick° of his ancestors.
Look how we can, or° sad or merrily,
Interpretation will misquote° our looks,
And we shall feed like oxen at a stall,
The better cherished, still the nearer death.   15
My nephew's trespass may be well forgot.
It hath the excuse of youth and heat of blood,
And an adopted name of privilege,°
A harebrained Hotspur, governed by a spleen.°
All his offenses live upon my head   20
And on his father's. We did train° him on,
And, his corruption being ta'en from us,
We, as the spring of all, shall pay for all.
Therefore, good Cousin, let not Harry know,
In any case, the offer of the King.   25
VER. Deliver° what you will, I'll say 'tis so.
Here comes your cousin.

[Enter HOTSPUR and DOUGLAS.]

HOT. My uncle is returned.
Deliver up° my Lord of Westmoreland.
Uncle, what news?   30
WOR. The King will bid you battle presently.°
DOUG. Defy him by the Lord of Westmoreland.
HOT. Lord Douglas, go you and tell him so.
DOUG. Marry, and shall, and very willingly.

[Exit.]

WOR. There is no seeming mercy in the King.   35
HOT. Did you beg any? God forbid!
WOR. I told him gently of our grievances,
Of his oath-breaking, which he mended thus,
By now forswearing° that he is forsworn.
He calls us rebels, traitors, and will scourge   40
With haughty arms this hateful name in us.

[Re-enter DOUGLAS.]

DOUG. Arm, gentlemen, to arms! For I have
  thrown
A brave defiance in King Henry's teeth —
And Westmoreland, that was engaged,° did bear
  it —
Which cannot choose but bring him quickly on.   45
WOR. The Prince of Wales stepped forth before
  the King
And, Nephew, challenged you to single fight.
HOT. Oh, would the quarrel lay upon our heads,
And that no man might draw short breath° today
But I and Harry Monmouth! Tell me, tell me,   50
How showed his tasking?° Seem'd it in contempt?
VER. No, by my soul. I never in my life
Did hear a challenge urged° more modestly,
Unless a brother should a brother dare
To gentle exercise and proof of arms.   55
He gave you all the duties of° a man,
Trimmed up your praises with a princely tongue,
Spoke your deservings like a chronicle,
Making you ever better than his praise
By still dispraising praise valued with you.°   60
And, which became him like a prince indeed,
He made a blushing cital° of himself,
And chid his truant youth with such a grace
As if he mastered there a double spirit
Of teaching and of learning instantly.   65
There did he pause. But let me tell the world,
If he outlive the envy° of this day,
England did never owe° so sweet a hope,
So much miscónstrued in his wantonness.
HOT. Cousin, I think thou art enamored   70
On his follies. Never did I hear
Of any prince so wild a libertine.
But be he as he will, yet once ere night
I will embrace him with a soldier's arm,
That he shall shrink under my courtesy.   75
Arm, arm with speed. And, fellows, soldiers, friends,
Better consider what you have to do
Than I, that have not well the gift of tongue,
Can lift your blood up with persuasion.

[Enter a MESSENGER.]

MESS. My lord, here are letters for you.   80
HOT. I cannot read them now.
O gentlemen, the time of life is short!

---

137. trim: neat. 141. Detraction: slander. 143. scutcheon: coat
of arms, painted on boards or cloth, carried in the funeral of a
gentleman and afterward hung up in the church.
Sc. ii: 11. wild trick: wild habits. 12. or: either. 13. In-
terpretation . . . misquote: men will deliberately misinterpret.
18. adopted . . . privilege: his nickname Hotspur will be his
excuse. 19. spleen: impetuosity. 21. train: lure. 26. Deliver:
report. 29. Deliver up: release. Westmoreland had been hostage
for Worcester's safe return. 31. presently: immediately.

39. forswearing: falsely denying an oath. 44. engaged: pledged
as hostage. 49. draw . . . breath: i.e., in fighting. 51. tasking:
challenge. 53. urged: put forward. 56. duties of: respect due to.
60. By . . . you: by continuously saying that your praise was
undervalued. 62. cital: recital. 68. envy: malice. 69. owe: own.

To spend that shortness basely were too long
If life did ride upon a dial's point,°
Still° ending at the arrival of an hour.   85
An if we live, we live to tread on kings;
If die, brave death when princes die with us!
Now, for our consciences, the arms are fair
When the intent° of bearing them is just.

     [*Enter another* MESSENGER.]

MESS. My lord, prepare. The King comes on
     apace.   90
HOT. I thank him, that he cuts me from my tale,
For I profess not talking, only this —
Let each man do his best. And here draw I
A sword whose temper° I intend to stain
With the best blood that I can meet withal   95
In the adventure of this perilous day.
Now, Esperance! Percy! and set on.
Sound all the lofty instruments of war,
And by that music let us all embrace;
For, heaven to earth, some of us never shall   100
A second time do such a courtesy.

     [*The trumpets sound. They embrace, and exeunt.*]

SCENE III. *Plain between the camps.*

[*The* KING *enters with his power. Alarum to the battle.° Then enter* DOUGLAS *and* SIR WALTER BLUNT.]

BLUNT. What is thy name, that in the battle thus
Thou crossest me? What honor dost thou seek
Upon my head?
DOUG.   Know then, my name is Douglas,
And I do haunt thee in the battle thus
Because some tell me that thou art a King.   5
BLUNT. They tell thee true.
DOUG. The Lord of Stafford dear today hath
     bought
Thy likeness; for instead of thee, King Harry,°
This sword hath ended him. So shall it thee
Unless thou yield thee as my prisoner.   10
BLUNT. I was not born a yielder, thou proud Scot,
And thou shalt find a King that will revenge
Lord Stafford's death.

[*They fight.* DOUGLAS *kills* BLUNT. *Enter* HOTSPUR.]

HOT. O Douglas, hadst thou fought at Holmedon
     thus,   15
I never had triumphed upon a Scot.
DOUG. All's done, all's won. Here breathless lies
     the King.
HOT. Where?
DOUG. Here.
HOT. This, Douglas? No. I know this face full
     well.

A gallant knight he was, his name was Blunt,   20
Semblably furnished° like the King himself.
DOUG. A fool go with thy soul° whither it goes!
A borrowed title hast thou bought too dear.
Why didst thou tell me that thou wert a king?   24
HOT. The King hath many marching in his coats.°
DOUG. Now, by my sword, I will kill all his coats.
I'll murder all his wardrobe, piece by piece,
Until I meet the King.
HOT.   Up, and away!   28
Our soldiers stand full fairly for the day.° [*Exeunt.*]

[*Alarum. Enter* FALSTAFF, *alone.*]

FAL. Though I could 'scape shot-free° at London,
I fear the shot here. Here's no scoring but upon the
pate. Soft! Who are you? Sir Walter Blunt. There's
honor for you! Here's no vanity!° I am as hot as
molten lead, and as heavy too. God keep lead out of
me! I need no more weight than mine own   35
bowels. I have led my ragamuffins where they are
peppered.° There's not three of my hundred and
fifty left alive, and they are for the town's end, to beg
during life. But who comes here?   40

[*Enter the* PRINCE.]

PRINCE. What, stand'st thou idle here? Lend me
     thy sword.
Many a nobleman lies stark and stiff
Under the hoofs of vaunting enemies
Whose deaths are yet unrevenged. I prithee lend me
     thy sword.   44
FAL. O Hal, I prithee give me leave to breathe a
while. Turk Gregory° never did such deeds in arms
as I have done this day. I have paid Percy, I have
made him sure.
PRINCE. He is, indeed, and living to kill thee. I
prithee lend me thy sword.   50
FAL. Nay, before God, Hal, if Percy be alive, thou
get'st not my sword. But take my pistol, if thou wilt.
PRINCE. Give it me. What, is it in the case?
FAL. Aye, Hal, 'tis hot, 'tis hot. There's that will
sack a city.   56

[*The* PRINCE *draws it out, and finds it
to be a bottle of sack.*]

PRINCE. What, is it a time to jest and dally now?

[*He throws the bottle at him. Exit.*]

FAL. Well, if Percy be alive, I'll pierce° him. If he
do come in my way, so. If he do not, if I come in   60
his willingly, let him make a carbonado° of me. I

---

84. **dial's point:** hand of a clock.   85. **Still:** always.   89. **intent:** cause.   94. **temper:** lit., hardness, quality.

     Sc. iii: s.d., **Alarum . . . battle:** battle noises.   8. **thee . . . Harry:** Blunt is wearing the King's coat of arms and not his own, and so is mistaken by Douglas for the King.

21. **Semblably furnished:** wearing similar armor.   22. **A . . . soul:** a proverbial phrase, "you foolish soul."   25. **coats:** coats of arms.   29. **full . . . day:** i.e., are full of fight.   30. **shot-free:** without paying the *shot* (the tavern bill) which had been scored up against him.   33. **no vanity:** spoken ironically. "Who said honor was not a vain thing?"   36–37. **where . . . peppered:** Falstaff's heroism has a base motive. Until the army is remustered he will pocket the pay of his dead soldiers.   46. **Turk Gregory:** Pope Gregory VII, who had a reputation for ferocity. The Turk was proverbial for cruelty.   59. **pierce:** pronounced "perse," a pun on "Percy."   61. **carbonado:** piece of meat slashed for broiling.

like not such grinning honor as Sir Walter hath.
Give me life, which if I can save, so; if not, honor
comes unlooked-for, and there's an end.   [*Exit.*]

SCENE IV. *Another part of the field.*

[*Alarum. Excursions.*° *Enter the* KING, *the* PRINCE,
LORD JOHN OF LANCASTER, *and*
EARL OF WESTMORELAND.]

KING. I prithee
Harry, withdraw thyself, thou bleed'st too much.
Lord John of Lancaster, go you with him.
   LANC. Not I, my lord, unless I did bleed too.
   PRINCE. I beseech your Majesty, make up,°   5
Lest your retirement do amaze° your friends.
   KING. I will do so.
My Lord of Westmoreland, lead him to his tent.
   WEST. Come, my lord, I'll lead you to your tent.
   PRINCE. Lead me, my lord? I do not need your
     help.   10
And God forbid a shallow scratch should drive
The Prince of Wales from such a field as this,
Where stained° nobility lies trodden on
And rebels' arms triumph in massacres!
   LANC. We breathe° too long. Come, Cousin West-
     moreland,   15
Our duty this way lies. For God's sake, come.
         [*Exeunt* PRINCE JOHN *and* WESTMORELAND.]
   PRINCE. By God, thou hast deceived me, Lan-
     caster,
I did not think thee lord of such a spirit.
Before, I loved thee as a brother, John,
But now I do respect thee as my soul.   20
   KING. I saw him hold Lord Percy at the point
With lustier maintenance than I did look for
Of such an ungrown warrior.
   PRINCE.   Oh, this boy
Lends mettle° to us all!   [*Exit.*]
         [*Enter* DOUGLAS.]
   DOUG. Another King! They grow like Hydra's
     heads.°   25
I am the Douglas, fatal to all those
That wear those colors on them. What art thou,
That counterfeit'st the person of a king?
   KING. The King himself, who, Douglas, grieves at
     heart
So many of his shadows° thou hast met   30
And not the very King. I have two boys
Seek Percy and thyself about the field.
But, seeing thou fall'st on me so luckily,

I will assay° thee. So defend thyself.
   DOUG. I fear thou art another counterfeit,   35
And yet, in faith, thou bear'st thee like a king.
But mine I am sure thou art, whoe'er thou be,
And thus I win thee.
     [*They fight; the* KING *being in danger, re-enter*
     PRINCE OF WALES.]
   PRINCE. Hold up thy head, vile Scot, or thou art
     like
Never to hold it up again! The spirits   40
Of valiant Shirley, Stafford, Blunt,° are in my arms.
It is the Prince of Wales that threatens thee,
Who never promiseth but he means to pay.
            [*They fight:* DOUGLAS *flies.*]
Cheerly, my lord. How fares your Grace?
Sir Nicholas Gawsey hath for succor sent,   45
And so hath Clifton. I'll to Clifton straight.
   KING. Stay, and breathe a while.
Thou hast redeemed thy lost opinion,°
And showed thou makest some tender° of my life,
In this fair rescue thou hast brought to me.   50
   PRINCE. Oh God! They did me too much injury
That ever said I hearkened for° your death.
If it were so, I might have let alone
The insulting° hand of Douglas over you,
Which would have been as speedy in your end   55
As all the poisonous potions in the world,
And saved the treacherous labor of your son.
   KING. Make up to Clifton. I'll to Sir Nicholas
     Gawsey.   [*Exit.*]
         [*Enter* HOTSPUR.]
   HOT. If I mistake not, thou art Harry Monmouth.
   PRINCE. Thou speak'st as if I would deny my
     name.   60
   HOT. My name is Harry Percy.
   PRINCE.   Why, then I see
A very valiant rebel of the name.
I am the Prince of Wales. And think not, Percy,
To share with me in glory any more.
Two stars keep not their motion in one sphere,   65
Nor can one England brook a double reign
Of Harry Percy and the Prince of Wales.
   HOT. Nor shall it, Harry, for the hour is come
To end the one of us. And would to God
Thy name in arms were now as great as mine!   70
   PRINCE. I'll make it greater ere I part from thee,
And all the budding honors on thy crest
I'll crop, to make a garland for my head.
   HOT. I can no longer brook thy vanities.
         [*They fight.*]
         [*Enter* FALSTAFF.]
   FAL. Well said, Hal! To it, Hal! Nay, you shall
find no boy's play here, I can tell you.   76

Sc. iv: s.d., **Excursions:** noises to indicate rapid movements
in battle.   **5. make up:** go up to the front line.   **6. amaze:** fill
with dismay.   **13. stained:** bloodstained.   **15. breathe:** rest.
24. mettle: courage.   **25. Hydra's heads:** Hydra was a many-
headed monster slain by Hercules. As soon as one head was cut
off, two others grew in its place.   **30. shadows:** imitations.

34. assay: challenge.   **41. Shirley . . . Blunt:** who have all fallen
in the battle.   **48. opinion:** reputation.   **49. makest . . . tender:**
hast some regard for.   **52. hearkened for:** desired.   **54. insult-
ing:** triumphing.

[*Re-enter* DOUGLAS; *he fights with* FALSTAFF, *who falls down as if he were dead, and exit* DOUGLAS. HOTSPUR *is wounded, and falls.*]

HOT. O Harry, thou hast robbed me of my youth!
I better brook the loss of brittle life
Than those proud titles thou hast won of me.
They wound my thoughts worse than thy sword my
    flesh.   80
But thought's the slave of life, and life Time's fool,
And Time, that takes survèy of all the world,
Must have a stop.° Oh, I could prophesy,
But that the earthy and cold hand of death
Lies on my tongue. No, Percy, thou art dust,   85
And food for ——   [*Dies.*]
PRINCE. For worms, brave Percy. Fare thee well,
    great heart!
Ill-weaved ambition, how much art thou shrunk!
When that this body did contain a spirit,
A kingdom for it was too small a bound,°   90
But now two paces of the vilest earth
Is room enough. This earth that bears thee dead
Bears not alive so stout a gentleman.
If thou wert sensible° of courtesy,
I should not make so dear a show of zeal.°   95
But let my favors° hide thy mangled face,
And, even in thy behalf, I'll thank myself
For doing these fair rites of tenderness.
Adieu, and take thy praise with thee to Heaven!
Thy ignominy sleep with thee in the grave,   100
But not remembered in thy epitaph!

    [*He spieth* FALSTAFF *on the ground.*]

What, old acquaintance! Could not all this flesh
Keep in a little life? Poor Jack, farewell!
I could have better spared a better man.
Oh, I should have a heavy miss of thee   105
If I were much in love with vanity!°
Death hath not struck so fat a deer today,
Though many dearer, in this bloody fray.
Emboweled° will I see thee by and by.   109
Till then in blood by noble Percy lie.   [*Exit.*]

FAL. [*Rising up*] Emboweled! If thou embowel
me today, I'll give you leave to powder° me and eat
me too tomorrow. 'Sblood, 'twas time to counterfeit,
or that hot termagant° Scot had paid me scot and
lot° too. Counterfeit? I lie, I am no counterfeit.   115
To die is to be a counterfeit, for he is but the counter-
feit of a man who hath not the life of a man. But to
counterfeit dying when a man thereby liveth is to be

no counterfeit, but the true and perfect image of life
indeed. The better part of valor is discretion, in   120
the which better part I have saved my life. 'Zounds,
I am afraid of this gunpowder Percy, though he be
dead. How if he should counterfeit too, and rise? By
my faith, I am afraid he would prove the better   125
counterfeit. Therefore I'll make him sure. Yea, and
I'll swear I killed him. Why may he not rise as well
as I? Nothing confutes me but eyes, and nobody sees
me. Therefore, sirrah [*Stabbing him*], with a   130
new wound in your thigh, come you along with me.

    [*Takes up* HOTSPUR *on his back.*]

[*Re-enter the* PRINCE OF WALES *and* LORD JOHN
    OF LANCASTER.]

PRINCE. Come, Brother John, full bravely hast
    thou fleshed
Thy maiden sword.°
LANC.   But, soft! Whom have we here?
Did you not tell me this fat man was dead?   135
PRINCE. I did, I saw him dead,
Breathless and bleeding on the ground. Art thou
    alive?
Or is it fantasy° that plays upon our eyesight?
I prithee, speak, we will not trust our eyes   139
Without our ears. Thou art not what thou seem'st.
FAL. No, that's certain, I am not a double° man.
But if I be not Jack Falstaff, then am I a Jack. There
is Percy [*Throwing the body down*]. If your father
will do me any honor, so; if not, let him kill the next
Percy himself. I look to be either earl or duke, I can
assure you.   146
PRINCE. Why, Percy I killed myself, and saw thee
    dead.
FAL. Didst thou? Lord, Lord, how this world is
given to lying! I grant you I was down and out of
breath, and so was he. But we rose both at an   150
instant, and fought a long hour by Shrewsbury
clock. If I may be believed, so; if not, let them that
should reward valor bear the sin upon their own
heads. I'll take it upon my death, I gave him this
wound in the thigh. If the man were alive, and   155
would deny it, 'zounds, I would make him eat a
piece of my sword.
LANC. This is the strangest tale that ever I heard.
PRINCE. This is the strangest fellow, Brother John.
Come, bring your luggage nobly on your back.   160
For my part, if a lie may do thee grace,
I'll gild it with the happiest terms° I have.

    [*A retreat is sounded.*]

The trumpet sounds retreat,° the day is ours.
Come, Brother, let us to the highest° of the field,
To see what friends are living, who are dead.   165

    [*Exeunt* PRINCE OF WALES *and* LANCASTER.]

81–83. **thought's . . . stop:** thought can only exist while there is
life, but life is treated like a fool by Time, and Time itself will
end — a thought in one form or another constantly recurring in
Shakespeare's plays. **90. bound:** boundary. **94. sensible:** able
to feel. **95. show of zeal:** mark of respect. **96. favors:** scarf or
handkerchief given to a knight by his lady. **106. vanity:** folly.
109. Emboweled: disemboweled. He carries on the metaphor and
pun of deer (l. 107), for the last act in the hunt was the disem-
boweling of the slain deer. **112. powder:** pickle. **114. terma-
gant:** ferocious. **114–15. paid . . . lot:** paid all dues.

133–34. **fleshed . . . sword:** you have fought bravely in your
first action. **138. fantasy:** imagination, illusion. **141. double:**
i.e., a double of myself. **162. happiest terms:** best phrases.
163. trumpet . . . retreat: i.e., to recall the troops from the
pursuit. **164. highest:** i.e., ground.

FAL. I'll follow, as they say, for reward. He that
rewards me, God reward him! If I do grow great, I'll
grow less; for I'll purge, and leave sack, and live
cleanly as a nobleman should do.   [*Exit.*]

SCENE V. *Another part of the field.*

[*The trumpets sound. Enter the* KING, PRINCE
OF WALES, LORD JOHN OF LANCASTER, EARL
OF WESTMORELAND, *with* WORCESTER *and*
VERNON *prisoners.*]

KING. Thus ever did rebellion find rebuke.
Ill-spirited° Worcester! Did not we send grace,
Pardon, and terms of love to all of you?
And wouldst thou turn our offers contrary,
Misuse the tenor of thy kinsman's trust?   5
Three knights upon our party slain today,
A noble Earl and many a creature else
Had been alive this hour
If like a Christian thou hadst truly borne
Betwixt our armies true intelligence.   10
WOR. What I have done my safety urged me to.
And I embrace this fortune patiently,
Since not to be avoided it falls on me.
KING. Bear Worcester to the death, and Vernon
too.
Other offenders we will pause upon.   15
[*Exeunt* WORCESTER *and* VERNON, *guarded.*]
How goes the field?
PRINCE. The noble Scot, Lord Douglas, when he
saw

Sc. v: 2. Ill-spirited: evil-spirited.

The fortune of the day quite turned from him,
The noble Percy slain, and all his men
Upon the foot of fear, fled with the rest;   20
And falling from a hill, he was so bruised
That the pursuers took him. At my tent
The Douglas is, and I beseech your Grace
I may dispose of him.
KING.   With all my heart.
PRINCE. Then, Brother John of Lancaster, to you
This honorable bounty shall belong.   26
Go to the Douglas, and deliver him
Up to his pleasure, ransomless and free.
His valor shown upon our crests today
Hath taught us how to cherish such high deeds   30
Even in the bosom of our adversaries.
LANC. I thank your Grace for this high courtesy,
Which I shall give away immediately.
KING. Then this remains, that we divide our
power.
You, Son John, and my cousin Westmoreland   35
Toward York shall bend you with your dearest°
speed,
To meet Northumberland and the prelate Scroop,
Who, as we hear, are busily in arms.
Myself and you, Son Harry, will toward Wales,
To fight with Glendower and the Earl of March.   40
Rebellion in this land shall lose his sway,
Meeting the check° of such another day.
And since this business so fair is done,
Let us not leave till all our own be won. [*Exeunt.*]

36. dearest: best.   42. Meeting ... check: incurring such a
disaster.

The Second Part of
KING HENRY THE FOURTH

Introduction[1]

The *Second Part of King Henry the Fourth* was probably written in the spring of 1598, soon after the *First Part* was printed. It continues the story where the *First Part* ended.

The play was entered for publication to Andrew Wise and William Aspley on August 23, 1600, and a first quarto was published afterward with the title: *The Second part of Henrie the fourth, continuing to his death, and coronation of Henrie the fift. With the humours of sir Iohn Falstaffe, and swaggering Pistoll. As it hath been sundrie times publikely acted by the right honourable, the Lord Chamberlaine his seruants. Written by William Shakespeare. London. Printed by V. S. for Andrew Wise, and William Aspley. 1600.* The play was not again printed until the first folio of 1623.

The quarto of 1600 is a fairly good text, possibly set up from Shakespeare's own manuscript, but it omits several striking passages which first appeared in the folio. The more important of these are Morton's speech to Northumberland (I.i.166–79); Lord Bardolph's speech on plotting a rebellion (I.iii.35–55); the Archbishop's speech on the fickleness of the mob (I.iii.85–108); Lady Percy's speech in memory of her dead husband (II.iii.23–45); the Archbishop's speech on the grievances of his party (IV.i.55–79); and the passage between Mowbray and Westmoreland (IV.i. 103–39). The reason for these omissions is clear. At a time when readers and playgoers were oversensitive to possible political allusions, and especially after the troubles caused by Hayward's *Life of Henry the Fourth* (see Gen. Intro. p. 45a, and *Rich II* Intro. p. 191a–b), it was but common prudence to omit any lines which might arouse the suspicions of the Council. By August 1600 Essex was in disgrace, but he had many sympathizers, and it would not have been difficult for a zealous informer to have found some parallel between Essex and Hotspur or between Essex's grievances

[1] See also App. 28.

and those put out in the play by the party of the Archbishop of York.

The folio text was carefully revised and prepared for the press, but certain changes were made. In 1606 an Act of Parliament had been passed ordaining that anyone who in a stage play used the name of God, or of Christ Jesus, or of the Holy Ghost or the Trinity, should be fined £10 for each offense. As a result, the loose conversation of Falstaff and his friends was carefully purged; "Heaven" was substituted for "God," "in good earnest" for "God save me," "what" for "God's light"; even so mild a remark as "i' faith" was omitted.

In *II Henry IV* the Falstaff scenes were entirely Shakespeare's own invention, though some of the characters, such as Justice Shallow or Silence, may well have been portraits of worthies whom Shakespeare knew in his own home country. For his history, Shakespeare went as before to Holinshed's *Chronicle,* which gave him the necessary facts for the more serious scenes; but the events of the later part of the reign of Henry IV were not particularly dramatic, and Shakespeare contented himself with selecting a series of episodes to bridge the gap between the death of Hotspur at the Battle of Shrewsbury (which concluded Part I), and the accession of Prince Hal as King Henry V, which ends Part II. *II Henry IV* is thus rather a link between *I Henry IV* and *Henry V* than a drama complete and coherent in itself. Moreover, Holinshed's narrative was less colorful than usual, as some extracts will show:

I. THE REBELLION IN THE NORTH (cf. IV.i, ii, AND iii)

But at the same time, to his further disquieting, there was a conspiracy put in practice against him at home by the Earl of Northumberland, who had conspired with Richard Scroop, Archbishop of York, Thomas Mowbray, Earl Marshal, son to Thomas Duke of Norfolk (who for the quarrel betwixt him and King Henry had been banished, as ye have heard), the Lords Hastings, Faulconbridge, Bardolf, and divers others. It was appointed that they should meet all together with their whole power upon Yorkswold, at a day assigned, and that the Earl of Northumberland should be chieftain, promising to bring with him a great number of Scots. The Archbishop, accompanied with the Earl Marshal, devised certain articles of such matters as it was supposed that not only the commonalty of the realm, but also the nobility, found themselves grieved with; which articles they showed first unto such of their adherents as were near about them, and after sent them abroad to their friends further off; assuring them that for redress of such oppressions they would shed the last drop of blood in their bodies, if need were.

The Archbishop, not meaning to stay after he saw himself accompanied with a great number of men that came flocking to York to take his part in this quarrel, forthwith discovered his enterprise, causing the articles aforesaid to be set up in the public streets of the city of York, and upon the gates of the monasteries, that each man might understand the cause that moved him to rise in arms against the King, the reforming whereof did not yet appertain unto him. Hereupon, knights, esquires, gentlemen, yeomen, and other of the commons, as well as of the city, towns, and countries about, being allured either for desire of change or else for desire to see a reformation in such things as were mentioned in the articles, assembled together in great numbers; and the Archbishop, coming forth amongst them clad in armor, encouraged, exhorted, and (by all means he could) pricked them forth to take the enterprise in hand, and manfully to continue in their begun purpose, promising forgiveness of sins to all them whose hap it was to die in the quarrel. And thus not only all the citizens of York, but all other in the countries about, that were able to bear weapon came to the Archbishop and the Earl Marshal. Indeed, the respect that men had to the Archbishop caused them to like the better of the cause, since the gravity of his age, his integrity of life, and incomparable learning, with the reverend aspect of his amiable personage, moved all men to have him in no small estimation.

The King, advertised of these matters, meaning to prevent them, left his journey into Wales and marched with all speed toward the north parts. Also Ralph Neville, Earl of Westmoreland, that was not far off, together with the Lord John of Lancaster, the King's son, being informed of this rebellious attempt, assembled together such power as they might make, and, together with those which were appointed to attend on the said Lord John to defend the borders against the Scots (as the Lord Henry Fitzhugh, the Lord Ralph Ewers, the Lord Robert Umfreville, and others), made forward against the rebels and, coming into a plain within the forest of Gaultree, caused their standards to be pitched down in like sort as the Archbishop had pitched his over against them, being far stronger in number of people than the other; for (as some write) there were of the rebels at least twenty thousand men.

When the Earl of Westmoreland perceived the force of the adversaries, and that they lay still, and attempted not to come forward upon him, he subtly devised how to quail [quell] their purpose; and forthwith dispatched messengers unto the Archbishop to understand the cause as it were of that great assembly, and for what cause (contrary to the King's peace) they came so in armor. The Archbishop answered that he took nothing in hand against the King's peace, but that whatsoever he did tended rather to advance the peace and quiet of the commonwealth than otherwise; and where he and his company were in arms, it was for fear of the King, to whom he could have no free access by reason of such a multitude of flatterers as were about him; and therefore he maintained that his purpose to be good and profitable, as well for the King himself as for the realm, if men were willing to understand a truth. And herewith he showed forth a scroll, in which the articles were written whereof before ye have heard.

The messengers, returning to the Earl of Westmoreland, showed him what they had heard and brought from the Archbishop. When he had read the articles, he showed in word and countenance outwardly that he liked of the Archbishop's holy and virtuous intent and purpose, promising that he and his would prosecute the same in assisting the Archbishop, who, rejoicing hereat, gave credit to the Earl, and persuaded the Earl Marshal (against his will as it were) to go with him to a place appointed for them to commune together. Here, when they were met with like number on either part, the articles were read over, and without any more ado, the Earl of Westmoreland and those that were with him agreed to do their best to see that a reformation might be had according to the same.

The Earl of Westmoreland, using more policy than the rest, "Well," said he, "then our travail is come to the wished end; and where our people have been long in armor, let them depart home to their wonted trades and occupations. In the meantime let us drink together in sign of agreement, that the people on both sides may see it and know that it is true that we be light [agreed] at a point." They had no sooner shaken hands together but that a knight was sent straightway from the Archbishop to bring word to the people that there was peace concluded, commanding each man to lay aside his arms and to resort home to their houses. The people, beholding such tokens of peace as shaking of hands and drinking together of the Lords in loving manner, they being already wearied with the unaccustomed travail of war, brake up their field and returned homeward. But in the meantime whilst the people of the Archbishop's side withdrew away, the number on the contrary part increased according to order given by the Earl of Westmoreland; and yet the Archbishop perceived not that he was deceived until the Earl of Westmoreland arrested both him and the Earl Marshal, with divers other.

2. THE DEATH OF HENRY IV (cf. IV.iv; v)

The morrow after Candlemas Day began a Parliament which he [King Henry IV] had called at London, but he departed this life before the same Parliament was ended; for now that his provisions were ready, and that he was furnished with sufficient treasure, soldiers, captains, victuals, munitions, tall ships, strong galleys, and all things necessary for such a royal journey as he pretended [intended] to take into the Holy Land, he was eftsoons taken with a sore sickness, which was not a leprosy, stricken by the hand of God (saith Master Hall) as foolish friars imagined, but a very apoplexy of the which he languished till his appointed hour, and had none other grief nor malady. So that what man ordaineth, God altereth at His good will and pleasure, not giving place more to the Prince than to the poorest creature living when He seeeth his time to dispose of him this way or that, as to His omnipotent power and divine providence seemeth expedient. During this his last sickness he caused his crown (as some write) to be set on a pillow at his bed's head, and suddenly his pangs so sore troubled him that he lay as though all his vital spirits had been from him departed. Such as were about him, thinking verily that he had been departed, covered his face with a linen cloth.

The Prince his son, being hereof advertised, entered into the chamber, took away the crown, and departed. The father, being suddenly revived out of that trance, quickly perceived the lack of his crown, and having knowledge that the Prince his son had taken it away, caused him to come before his presence, requiring of him what he meant so to misuse himself. The Prince with a good audacity answered: "Sir, to mine and all men's judgment you seemed dead in this world, wherefore I, as your next heir apparent, took that as mine own, and not as yours." "Well, fair son," said the King with a great sigh, "what right I had to it, God knoweth." "Well," said the Prince, "if you die King, I will have the garland and trust to keep it with the sword against all mine enemies, as you have done." Then said the King, "I commit all to God, and remember you to do well." With that he turned himself in his bed, and shortly after departed to God in a chamber of the Abbots of Westminster called Jerusalem, the twentieth day of March, in the year 1413, and in the year of his age forty-six, when he had reigned thirteen years, five months, and odd days, in great perplexity and little pleasure (or fourteen years, as some have noted, who name not the disease whereof he died, but refer it to sickness absolutely, whereby his time of departure did approach and fetch him out of the world) . . .

3. THE REFORMATION OF THE NEW KING (cf. V.ii; v)

Such great hope and good expectation was had of this man's [Henry V's] fortunate success to follow that within three days after his father's decease divers noblemen and honorable personages did to him homage and swore to him due obedience, which had not been seen done to any of his predecessors Kings of this realm till they had been possessed of the crown. He was crowned the ninth of April, being Passion Sunday, which was a sore, ruggy, and tempestuous day with wind, snow, and sleet, that men greatly marveled thereat, making divers interpretations what the same might signify. But this King even at first appointing with himself to show that in his person princely honors should change public manners, he determined to put on him the shape of a new man. For whereas aforetime he had made himself a companion unto misruly mates of dissolute order and life, he now banished them all from his presence (but not unrewarded or else unpreferred), inhibiting them upon a great pain [penalty] not once to approach, lodge, or sojourn within ten miles of his Court or presence. And in their places he chose men of gravity, wit, and high policy, by whose wise counsel he might at all times rule to his honor and dignity, calling to mind how once to the high offense of the King his father he had with his fist stricken the Chief Justice for sending one of his minions (upon desert) to prison, when the Justice stoutly commanded himself also straight to ward, and he (then Prince) obeyed. The King after expelled him out of his Privy Council, banished him the Court, and made the Duke of Clarence (his younger brother) president of Council in his stead.

II Henry IV thus shows many signs of being an afterthought, a sequel written when the first part—especially the Falstaff scenes—had proved successful beyond all expectation. When the two parts are compared, it is clear that several of the persons and episodes in Part II are expansions of persons or ideas which were more slightly sketched in Part I. The Hostess, who made only a brief appearance in Part I, has developed into Mistress Quickly; the parodies of Alleyn's tragic style in the play scene (*I Hen IV*, II.iv) are embodied in a complete character in Ancient Pistol; Falstaff's account of how he had collected recruits for his company (*I Hen IV*, IV.ii.12–52) is expanded into a long scene with Justice Shallow (*II Hen IV*, III.ii). Indeed Falstaff, who began as the stooge of Prince Hal in Part I, in Part II has become the major and dominating character.

These developments are signs that to meet popular demand Shakespeare sacrificed history to fiction. In Part I 1,501 lines were given to the historical scenes, and 1,539 lines to the comic plot; in Part II 1,370 lines were given to history, but 1,991 lines to the Falstaff story. The historical plot of Part I is a coherent whole; in Part II it consists simply of nine scenes from history. Of these, three are given to the remnants of the Percy family, three to the dying King, two to the rebellion in the North, and one to the new King's first acts on succeeding his father. King Henry IV is indeed almost a minor character in his own play. He is shown paying the last of the debts for his usurpation of the throne. At his first appearance he is worn out with care and utters the finest of many Elizabethan apostrophes to sleep; in his last scene, after rebuking the prodigal son whom he still misunderstands, he supplements the account of his own methods of winning the crown (*I Hen IV*, III.ii) with cynical advice on how his son should keep it. Shakespeare indeed in his plays from time to time expressed the most devoted sentiments for the divinity of kingship, but he had no illusions about the frailty of kings. The play also shows the final development of Prince Hal from the wild playboy of Part I to the stern King who emerges at the end of Part II.

Nevertheless, in Part II far more even than in Part I, Falstaff and his gang are the main interest. They have also increased in stature. Mrs Quickly is now a voluble gossip, with a wonderful flow of chatter which gushes out in a continuous and illogical torrent. Her husband has disappeared, and she is completely dominated by Falstaff, who sponges on her shamelessly. Bardolph's nose is as red as ever, and there are three newcomers — Doll Tearsheet, a professional lady who includes Falstaff among her most distinguished customers; Falstaff's boy; and above all Ancient Pistol, who is a living parody of the rival

acting company, for he struts about the stage in Alleyn's best manner, Tamburlaine style, his vocabulary made up of scraps and misquotations of the wilder melodramas then in the repertory of the Rose playhouse.

Falstaff himself has gained in bulk and in wit; his scenes of low comedy with Mrs Quickly and Doll Tearsheet are wilder, funnier, and much lower than anything in Part I, and the scenes with Justice Shallow are perfect. Yet Falstaff steadily degenerates, and his fall is as tremendous as his bulk. It has been a fashion among critics to exalt Falstaff and to denounce Prince Hal for so ruthlessly rejecting him. There is little to commend this view. The truth is that Falstaff, although a lovable and infinitely witty rogue, has become repulsive by the end of the play. Falstaff is a perpetual joke, but a joke must never go stale or take itself too seriously. The friendship between royalty and a private man, even if wholly respectable, calls for infinite tact; between Falstaff and the Prince it can exist only so long as Prince Hal has no serious responsibilities. Immediately the position changes, Falstaff must gracefully retire to his tavern to tell tall stories of the gay days when he was the Prince's favorite. When Falstaff fails to realize the change, he loses that sense of humor which is his one redeeming quality. His comedy turns to tragedy, for he commits the unforgivable sin against friendship of forcing his old friend into an intolerable position when he must choose between the claims of friendship and of duty.

With Pistol and Justice Shallow, Falstaff has ridden from Gloucestershire, and arrives in London as King Henry V is coming from his coronation. At this most embarrassing and public moment the King is confronted by the sins of his youth incarnate in this gross bodily form. Everyone is watching to see what he will do; in that instant Henry must choose between his past and his future, and as Falstaff should have known long since, the King will not hesitate. So Falstaff's bubble is pricked and he shrinks away. His end is regrettable but inevitable, for Sir John — not Henry V — has been false to himself.

Henry IV, Part II

DRAMATIS PERSONAE

RUMOR, *the Presenter*
KING HENRY *the Fourth*
HENRY, PRINCE OF WALES, *after-*
  ward King Henry V ⎫
THOMAS, DUKE OF CLARENCE ⎬ *his sons*
PRINCE JOHN OF LANCASTER ⎪
PRINCE HUMPHREY OF GLOUCESTER ⎭
EARL OF WARWICK
EARL OF WESTMORELAND
EARL OF SURREY
GOWER
HARCOURT
BLUNT
LORD CHIEF JUSTICE *of the King's Bench*
A SERVANT *of the Chief Justice*
EARL OF NORTHUMBERLAND
SCROOP, *Archbishop of York*
LORD MOWBRAY
LORD HASTINGS
LORD BARDOLPH
SIR JOHN COLEVILE
TRAVERS and MORTON, *retainers of Northumberland*

SIR JOHN FALSTAFF
HIS PAGE
BARDOLPH
PISTOL
POINS
PETO
SHALLOW ⎫ *country justices*
SILENCE ⎬
DAVY, *servant to Shallow*
MOULDY, SHADOW, WART, FEEBLE, *and* BULLCALF, *re-cruits*
FANG *and* SNARE, *sheriff's officers*

LADY NORTHUMBERLAND
LADY PERCY
MISTRESS QUICKLY, *hostess of a tavern in Eastcheap*
DOLL TEARSHEET

LORDS *and* ATTENDANTS; PORTER, DRAWERS, BEADLES, GROOMS, &c. A DANCER, *speaker of the epilogue*

SCENE — *England.*

INDUCTION°

Warkworth.° Before the castle.

[*Enter* RUMOR, *painted full of tongues.*°]

RUM. Open your ears, for which of you will stop
The vent° of hearing when loud Rumor speaks?
I, from the Orient to the drooping West,
Making the wind my post horse,° still° unfold
The acts commencèd on this ball of earth.   5
Upon my tongues continual slanders ride,
The which in every language I pronounce,
Stuffing the ears of men with false reports.
I speak of peace while covert° enmity
Under the smile of safety wounds the world.   10
And who but Rumor, who but only I,
Make fearful musters° and prepared defense
Whiles the big year, swoln° with some other grief,

Is thought with child by the stern tyrant war,
And no such matter? Rumor is a pipe°   15
Blown by surmises, jealousies, conjectures,
And of so easy and so plain a stop°
That the blunt monster with uncounted heads,
The still-discordant° wavering multitude,
Can play upon it. But what need I thus   20
My well-known body to anatomize°
Among my household?° Why is Rumor here?
I run before King Harry's victory,
Who in a bloody field by Shrewsbury
Hath beaten down young Hotspur and his troops,
Quenching the flame of bold rebellion   26
Even with the rebels' blood. But what mean I
To speak so true at first? My office is
To noise abroad that Harry Monmouth fell
Under the wrath of noble Hotspur's sword,   30
And that the King before the Douglas' rage
Stooped his anointed head as low as death.
This have I rumored through the peasant towns
Between that royal field of Shrewsbury
And this worm-eaten hold° of ragged° stone,   35
Where Hotspur's father, old Northumberland,

Induction: introduction. Shakespeare seldom used any introduction, but with other dramatists it was common at this time for plays to be introduced by a short prologue spoken by a Chorus, o: Presenter. **s.d., Warkworth:** in Northumberland. **s.d., Rumor . . . tongues:** wearing a robe decorated with tongues. **2. vent:** passage. **4. post horse:** See App. **17. still:** always, continually. **9. covert:** secret. **12. Make . . . musters:** Shakespeare had in mind his own times. During the 1590's there were continual rumors of invasions and preparations. See Gen. Intro. pp. 28b–31a. **13. swoln:** swollen.

15. pipe: i.e., musical instrument. **17. plain a stop:** i.e., easy to play. **19. still-discordant:** always jarring; i.e., disagreeing. **21. anatomize:** analyze. **22. Among my household:** i.e., this crowded playhouse. **35. hold:** fortress. **ragged:** rough.

Lies crafty-sick.° The posts come tiring on,
And not a man of them brings other news
Than they have learned of me. From Rumor's
    tongues   39
They bring smooth comforts false, worse than true
    wrongs.   [*Exit.*]

Act I

SCENE I. *The same.*

[*Enter* LORD BARDOLPH.]

L. BARD. Who keeps the gate here, ho? [*The* POR-
TER *opens the gate.*] Where is the Earl?
POR. What shall I say you are?
L. BARD.   Tell thou the Earl
That the Lord Bardolph doth attend° him here.
POR. His lordship is walked forth into the orchard.
Please it your Honor, knock but at the gate   5
And he himself will answer.

[*Enter* NORTHUMBERLAND.]

L. BARD.   Here comes the Earl. [*Exit* PORTER.]
NORTH. What news, Lord Bardolph? Every min-
    ute now
Should be the father of some stratagem.°
The times are wild. Contention, like a horse
Full of high feeding, madly hath broke loose   10
And bears down all before him.
L. BARD.   Noble Earl,
I bring you certain° news from Shrewsbury.
NORTH. Good, an° God will!
L. BARD.   As good as heart can wish.
The King is almost wounded to the death,
And in the fortune° of my lord your son,   15
Prince Harry slain outright, and both the Blunts
Killed by the hand of Douglas. Young Prince John
And Westmoreland and Stafford fled the field,
And Harry Monmouth's brawn, the hulk Sir John,°
Is prisoner to your son. Oh, such a day,   20
So fought, so followed, and so fairly won,
Came not till now to dignify the times
Since Caesar's fortunes!
NORTH.   How is this derived?
Saw you the field? Came you from Shrewsbury?
L. BARD. I spake with one, my lord, that came from
    thence,   25
A gentleman well bred and of good name,

That freely rendered me these news for true.
    NORTH. Here comes my servant Travers, whom I
    sent
On Tuesday last to listen after news.

[*Enter* TRAVERS.]

    L. BARD. My lord, I overrode° him on the way,
And he is furnished with no certainties   31
More than he haply may retail from me.
    NORTH. Now, Travers, what good tidings comes
    with you?
    TRA. My lord, Sir John Umfrevile turned me back
With joyful tidings, and, being better horsed,   35
Outrode me. After him came spurring hard
A gentleman, almost forspent° with speed,
That stopped by me to breathe° his bloodied horse.
He asked the way to Chester, and of him
I did demand what news from Shrewsbury.   40
He told me that rebellion had bad luck,
And that young Harry Percy's spur was cold.
With that, he gave his able° horse the head,
And bending forward struck his armèd heels
Against the panting sides of his poor jade°   45
Up to the rowelhead,° and starting so
He seemed in running to devour the way,
Staying no longer question.
    NORTH.   Ha! Again.
Said he young Harry Percy's spur was cold?
Of Hotspur Coldspur? That rebellion   50
Had met ill luck?
    L. BARD.   My lord, I'll tell you what —
If my young lord your son have not the day,
Upon mine honor, for a silken point°
I'll give my barony. Never talk of it.
    NORTH. Why should that gentleman that rode by
    Travers   55
Give then such instances of loss?
    L. BARD.   Who, he?
He was some hilding° fellow that had stolen
The horse he rode on, and, upon my life,
Spoke at a venture. Look, here comes more news.

[*Enter* MORTON.]

    NORTH. Yea, this man's brow, like to a title leaf,
Foretells the nature of a tragic volume.°   61
So looks the strond° whereon the imperious flood
Hath left a witnessed usurpation.°
Say, Morton, didst thou come from Shrewsbury?
    MOR. I ran from Shrewsbury, my noble lord,   65
Where hateful death put on his ugliest mask
To fright our party.
    NORTH.   How doth my son and brother?

---

37. **crafty-sick:** pretending to be sick. See *I Hen IV*, IV.i.13–42.
   Act I, Sc. i: 3. attend: wait on. **8. stratagem:** deed of violence.
12. certain: sure. **13. an:** if. **15. in . . . fortune:** by the good
fortune. **19. brawn . . . John:** It is worth noting that Sir John
Falstaff is quite seriously regarded as one of the principal sup-
porters of the King. **brawn:** fat pig. **hulk:** large cargo ship, and
so a man of immense bulk.

30. **overrode:** overtook.   37. **forspent:** utterly exhausted.
38. **breathe:** rest.   43. **able:** strong.   45. **jade:** horse in poor con-
dition or vicious.   46. **rowelhead:** prick of the spur.   53. **silken
point:** silk lace for tying the doublet to the hose, so a thing of no
value; e.g., "shoestring."   57. **hilding:** worthless.   60–61. **title
. . . volume:** like the title page of a tragedy. For a specimen,
see Pl. 14a.   62. **strond:** shore.   62–63. **imperious . . . usur-
pation:** like the desolate wreckage left on the shore after a high
flood.

Thou tremblest, and the whiteness in thy cheek
Is apter than thy tongue to tell thy errand.
Even such a man, so faint, so spiritless,   70
So dull, so dead in look, so woebegone,
Drew Priam's° curtain in the dead of night
And would have told him half his Troy was burned.
But Priam found the fire ere he his tongue,
And I my Percy's death ere thou report'st it.   75
This thou wouldst say, " Your son did thus and thus,
Your brother thus. So fought the noble Douglas " —
Stopping my greedy ear with their bold deeds.
But in the end, to stop my ear indeed,
Thou hast a sigh to blow away this praise,   80
Ending with " Brother, son, and all are dead."
    MOR. Douglas is living, and your brother, yet,
But for my lord your son ——
    NORTH.   Why, he is dead.
See what a ready tongue suspicion hath!
He that but fears the thing he would not know   85
Hath by instinct knowledge from others' eyes
That what he feared is chanced.° Yet speak, Morton.
Tell thou an earl his divination° lies,
And I will take it as a sweet disgrace,
And make thee rich for doing me such wrong.   90
    MOR. You are too great to be by me gainsaid.°
Your spirit is too true, your fears too certain.
    NORTH. Yet, for all this, say not that Percy's dead.
I see a strange° confession in thine eye.
Thou shakest thy head, and hold'st it fear or sin   95
To speak a truth. If he be slain, say so.
The tongue offends not that reports his death.
And he doth sin that doth belie° the dead,
Not he which says the dead is not alive.
Yet the first bringer of unwelcome news   100
Hath but a losing office,° and his tongue
Sounds ever after as a sullen bell
Remembered tolling a departing friend.°
    L. BARD. I cannot think, my lord, your son is dead.
    MOR. I am sorry I should force you to believe   105
That which I would to God I had not seen.
But these mine eyes saw him in bloody state,
Rendering faint quittance,° wearied and out-
    breathed,
To Harry Monmouth, whose swift wrath beat down
The never-daunted Percy to the earth,   110
From whence with life he never more sprung up.
In few,° his death, whose spirit lent a fire
Even to the dullest peasant in his camp,
Being bruited° once, took fire and heat away
From the best-tempered° courage in his troops.   115

For from his metal was his party steeled,
Which once in him abated,° all the rest
Turned on themselves, like dull and heavy lead.
And as the thing that's heavy in itself
Upon enforcement° flies with greatest speed,   120
So did our men, heavy in Hotspur's loss,
Lend to this weight such lightness with their fear
That arrows fled not swifter toward their aim
Than did our soldiers, aiming at their safety,
Fly from the field. Then was that noble Worcester
Too soon ta'en prisoner. And that furious Scot,   126
The bloody Douglas, whose well-laboring sword
Had three times slain the appearance° of the King,
'Gan° vail his stomach° and did grace° the shame
Of those that turned their backs, and in his flight,
Stumbling in fear, was took. The sum of all   131
Is that the King hath won, and hath sent out
A speedy power° to encounter you, my lord,
Under the conduct° of young Lancaster
And Westmoreland. This is the news at full.   135
    NORTH. For this I shall have time enough to
      mourn.
In poison there is physic, and these news,
Having been well, that would have made me sick,
Being sick, have in some measure made me well.
And as the wretch whose fever-weakened joints,
Like strengthless hinges, buckle under life,   141
Impatient of his fit, breaks like a fire
Out of his keeper's° arms, even so my limbs,
Weakened with grief, being now enraged with
    grief,
Are thrice themselves. Hence, therefore, thou nice°
    crutch!   145
A scaly gauntlet° now with joints of steel
Must glove this hand. And hence, thou sickly quoif!°
Thou art a guard too wanton° for the head
Which princes, fleshed° with conquest, aim to hit.
Now bind my brows with iron, and approach   150
The ragged'st hour that time and spite dare bring
To frown upon the enraged Northumberland!
Let Heaven kiss earth! Now let not Nature's hand
Keep the wild flood confined! Let order die!
And let this world no longer be a stage   155
To feed contention in a lingering act,°
But let one spirit of the firstborn Cain°
Reign in all bosoms, that, each heart being set
On bloody courses, the rude scene may end,
And darkness be the burier of the dead!   160

117. **abated:** brought low.   120. **Upon enforcement:** when forced into motion.   128. **slain . . . appearance:** See *I Hen IV*, V.iii.8. 129. **'Gan:** began. **vail . . . stomach:** lower his courage. **grace:** do grace, justify.   133. **power:** force.   134. **conduct:** leadership.   143. **keeper:** nurse.   145. **nice:** delicate.   146. **scaly gauntlet:** steel glove. See Pl. 8a.   147. **quoif:** cap to keep the head warm.   148. **wanton:** frivolous.   149. **fleshed:** eager to taste blood.   156. **To . . . act:** to maintain strife in an act which seems never-ending; i.e., let the present strife be brought to a swift, bloody conclusion.   157. **firstborn Cain:** i.e., the first murderer.

72. **Priam:** King of Troy, which after ten years' siege was sacked by the Greeks. See *Haml*, II.ii.472–541.   87. **is chanced:** has happened.   88. **divination:** prophecy, intuition of disaster. 91. **gainsaid:** denied.   94. **strange:** uneasy.   98. **belie:** lie about. 101. **losing office:** duty which brings him loss.   103. **tolling . . . friend:** See App. 19.   108. **quittance:** payment, return of blows. 112. **few:** few words.   114. **bruited:** rumored.   115. **best-tempered:** of the finest quality of steel.

TRA. This strainèd° passion doth you wrong, my
    lord.
L. BARD. Sweet Earl, divorce not wisdom from
    your honor.
MOR. The lives of all your loving complices°
Lean on your health, the which if you give o'er
To stormy passion must perforce decay.   165
You cast the event° of war, my noble lord,
And summed the account of chance, before you said
" Let us make head."° It was your presurmise
That, in the dole° of blows, your son might drop.
You knew he walked o'er perils, on an edge,   170
More likely to fall in than to get o'er.
You were advised his flesh was capable
Of wounds and scars, and that his forward spirit
Would lift him where most trade° of danger ranged,
Yet did you say " Go forth." And none of this, 175
Though strongly apprehended, could restrain
The stiff-borne° action. What hath then befallen,
Or what hath this bold enterprise brought forth,
More than that being which was like to be?
L. BARD. We all that are engagèd to° this loss 180
Knew that we ventured on such dangerous seas
That if we wrought out° life 'twas ten to one.
And yet we ventured, for the gain proposed
Choked the respect° of likely peril feared.
And since we are o'erset, venture again.   185
Come, we will all put forth, body and goods.
MOR. 'Tis more than time. And, my most noble
    lord,
I hear for certain, and do speak the truth,
The gentle Archbishop of York is up°
With well-appointed powers. He is a man   190
Who with a double surety° binds his followers.
My lord your son had only but the corpse,
But shadows and the shows of men, to fight.
For that same word, " rebellion," did divide
The action of their bodies from their souls,   195
And they did fight with queasiness,° constrained,
As men drink potions, that their weapons only
Seemed on our side. But for their spirits and souls,
This word, " rebellion," it had froze them up
As fish are in a pond. But now the Bishop   200
Turns insurrection to religion.
Supposed sincere and holy in his thoughts,
He's followed both with body and with mind,
And doth enlarge his rising with the blood
Of fair King Richard,° scraped from Pomfret°
    stones;   205

Derives from heaven his quarrel and his cause;
Tells them he doth bestride a bleeding land,
Gasping for life under great Bolingbroke;
And more and less° do flock to follow him.   209
NORTH. I knew of this before, but, to speak truth,
This present grief had wiped it from my mind.
Go in with me, and counsel every man
The aptest° way for safety and revenge.   213
Get posts and letters, and make friends with speed.
Never so few, and never yet more need.   [Exeunt.]

SCENE II. *London. A street.*

[*Enter* FALSTAFF, *with his* PAGE *bearing his
    sword and buckler.*]
FAL. Sirrah, you giant,° what says the doctor to
my water?°
PAGE. He said, sir, the water itself was a good
healthy water, but for the party that owed° it, he
might have moe° diseases than he knew for.   6
FAL. Men of all sorts take a pride to gird° at me.
The brain of this foolish-compounded clay, man, is
not able to invent anything that tends to laughter
more than I invent or is invented on me. I am   10
not only witty in myself, but the cause that wit is in
other men. I do here walk before thee like a sow that
hath overwhelmed all her litter but one. If the Prince
put thee into my service for any other reason than
to set me off,° why, then I have no judgment.   15
Thou whoreson° mandrake,° thou art fitter to be
worn in my cap than to wait at my heels. I was never
manned° with an agate° till now. But I will inset
you neither in gold nor silver, but in vile ap- 20
parel, and send you back again to your master, for a
jewel — the juvenal,° the Prince your master, whose
chin is not yet fledged.° I will sooner have a beard
grow in the palm of my hand than he shall get one
on his cheek, and yet he will not stick to say his 25
face is a face royal.° God may finish it when He will,
'tis not a hair amiss yet. He may keep it still at a face
royal, for a barber shall never earn sixpence out of it,
and yet he'll be crowing as if he had writ man° ever
since his father was a bachelor.° He may keep   30

209. more . . . less: greatest and least, men of all classes.
213. aptest: fittest.
    Sc. ii: 1. you giant: It seems likely that about the beginning
of 1598 the Lord Chamberlain's Company acquired a small boy
actor who was a considerable success. See Gen. Intro. p. 59b. For
the boy carrying his master's sword and buckler, see Pl. 9a; also
Pl. 22i, j.   1–2. doctor . . . water: Inspection of the urine was
a common method of arriving at a diagnosis.   5. owed: owned.
6. moe: more.   7. gird: gibe.   15. set me off: be a contrast to
me.   17. whoreson: bastard. mandrake: a forked root resem-
bling a man in shape. See Pl. 12e.   19. manned: waited on.
agate: small figure cut in an agate.   22. juvenal: young man.
23. fledged: covered with down; lit., out of the nest.   26. face
royal: i.e., worth a royal — 10s. See App. 27.   29. writ man:
described himself as a man.   30. bachelor: young man.

161. strained: unnatural, excessive.   163. complices: accomplices.
166. cast . . . event: reckoned up the chances.   168. make head:
raise a force.   169. dole: distribution.   174. trade: traffic, resort.
177. stiff-borne: hard-fought.   180. engaged to: pledged to
endure.   182. wrought out: won through with.   184. respect:
consideration.   189. up: i.e., in arms.   191. double surety:
twofold pledge.   196. queasiness: nausea, sick hearts.   204–05. en-
large . . . Richard: make his rising more powerful by exhibiting
the blood of the murdered Richard.   205. Pomfret: Pontefract
Castle, where Richard II was murdered.

his own grace, but he's almost out of mine, I can as-
sure him. What said Master Dombledon about the
satin for my short cloak and my slops?°   34

PAGE. He said, sir, you should procure him better
assurance° than Bardolph. He would not take his
band° and yours, he liked not the security.   38

FAL. Let him be damned, like the glutton!° Pray
God his tongue be hotter! A whoreson Achitophel!°
A rascally yea-forsooth knave! To bear a gentleman
in hand,° and then stand upon security! The whore-
son smoothpates° do now wear nothing but high
shoes, and bunches of keys at their girdles. And if a
man is through with them in honest taking-up,°   45
then they must stand upon security. I had as lief they
would put ratsbane° in my mouth as offer to stop it
with security. I looked a'° should have sent me two
and twenty yards of satin, as I am a true knight, and
he sends me security. Well, he may sleep in se-   50
curity,° for he hath the horn of abundance, and the
lightness of his wife shines through it. And yet can-
not he see, though he have his own lantern to light
him.° Where's Bardolph?

PAGE. He's gone into Smithfield to buy your Wor-
ship a horse.   57

FAL. I bought him in Paul's,° and he'll buy me
a horse in Smithfield.° An I could get me but a
wife in the stews,° I were manned, horsed, and
wived.

[*Enter the* LORD CHIEF JUSTICE *and* SERVANT.]

PAGE. Sir, here comes the nobleman that com-
mitted° the Prince for striking him about Bardolph.

FAL. Wait close.° I will not see him.   65

CH. JUST. What's he that goes there?

SERV. Falstaff, an't please your lordship.

CH. JUST. He that was in question for the rob-
bery?   69

SERV. He, my lord. But he hath since done good
service at Shrewsbury, and, as I hear, is now going
with some charge° to the Lord John of Lancaster.

CH. JUST. What, to York? Call him back again.

SERV. Sir John Falstaff!   76

FAL. Boy, tell him I am deaf.

PAGE. You must speak louder. My master is deaf.

CH. JUST. I am sure he is, to the hearing of any-
thing good. Go, pluck him by the elbow. I must
speak with him.

SERV. Sir John!   83

FAL. What! A young knave, and begging! Is there
not wars? Is there not employment? Doth not the
King lack subjects? Do not the rebels need soldiers?
Though it be a shame to be on any side but one, it
is worse shame to beg than to be on the worst side,
were it worse than the name of rebellion can tell
how to make it.   90

SERV. You mistake me, sir.

FAL. Why, sir, did I say you were an honest man?
Setting my knighthood and my soldiership aside,° I
had lied in my throat if I had said so.   94

SERV. I pray you, sir, then set your knighthood and
your soldiership aside and give me leave to tell you
you lie in your throat° if you say I am any other than
an honest man.   98

FAL. I give thee leave to tell me so! I lay aside that
which grows to me!° If thou gettest any leave of me,
hang me. If thou takest leave, thou wert better be
hanged. You hunt counter.° Hence! Avaunt!°   103

SERV. Sir, my lord would speak with you.

CH. JUST. Sir John Falstaff, a word with you.

FAL. My good lord! God give your lordship good
time of day.° I am glad to see your lordship abroad.
I heard say your lordship was sick. I hope your   108
lordship goes abroad° by advice. Your lordship,
though not clean past your youth, hath yet some
smack° of age in you, some relish of the saltness° of
time, and I most humbly beseech your lordship to
have a reverend care of your health.   114

CH. JUST. Sir John, I sent for you before your ex-
pedition to Shrewsbury.

FAL. An 't please your lordship, I hear His Majesty
is returned with some discomfort° from Wales.   119

CH. JUST. I talk not of His Majesty. You would not
come when I sent for you.

FAL. And I hear, moreover, His Highness is fallen
into this same whoreson apoplexy.°

CH. JUST. Well, God mend him! I pray you let me
speak with you.   126

FAL. This apoplexy is, as I take it, a kind of leth-
argy, an 't please your lordship, a kind of sleeping in
the blood, a whoreson tingling.

CH. JUST. What tell you me of it? Be it as it is.

FAL. It hath its original from much grief, from
study and perturbation of the brain. I have read

---

34. **slops:** wide breeches. See Pl. 8c and comment on p. 93b.
37. **assurance:** guarantee.   38. **band:** bond.   39. **the glutton:**
i.e., Dives in the parable of Dives and Lazarus.   40. **Achitophel:**
the counselor who advised Absalom, King David's rebellious son.
See II Samuel 16. The parallel is not particularly apt.   41. **bear
... hand:** delude with false hope.   43. **smoothpates:** smooth-
headed citizens.   45. **taking-up:** obtaining on credit.   47. **rats-
bane:** rat poison.   48. **a':** he.   51. **security:** carelessness.
51–54. **horn ... him:** Falstaff puns on three meanings of horn:
(a) the cornucopia or horn of abundance, the mythological
symbol of a horn overflowing with fruits; (b) the cuckold's
horn, supposed to be worn by every husband deceived by his
wife; (c) the horn sides (horn being used before glass) of a lantern.
See App. 11.   58. **bought ... Paul's:** See Gen. Intro. p. 17a.
59. **Smithfield:** the London cattle market.   60. **stews:** brothels.
64. **committed:** sent to prison. See *I Hen IV,* Intro. p. 334b.
65. **Wait close:** stand close by me.   72. **charge:** command.

93. **Setting ... aside:** forgetting for a moment that I am a
knight and a soldier.   97. **lie ... throat:** the worst kind of lie; to
accuse a man of uttering it was a mortal offense.   100. **grows to
me:** is part of me.   103. **hunt counter:** i.e., off the scent.
Avaunt: be off.   106–07. **good ... day:** a form of polite saluta-
tion.   109. **abroad:** out of doors.   112. **smack:** taste. **saltness:**
probably the "saltness of age" as contrasted with the "freshness
of youth."   119. **discomfort:** indisposition.   124. **apoplexy:**
paralysis.

the cause of his effects in Galen.° It is a kind of deafness.   134

CH. JUST. I think you are fallen into the disease, for you hear not what I say to you.

FAL. Very well, my lord, very well. Rather, an 't please you, it is the disease of not listening, the malady of not marking, that I am troubled withal.   140

CH. JUST. To punish you by the heels° would amend the attention of your ears, and I care not if I do become your physician.   143

FAL. I am as poor as Job, my lord, but not so patient. Your lordship may minister the potion of imprisonment to me in respect of poverty, but how I should be your patient to follow your prescriptions, the wise may make some dram of a scruple,° or indeed a scruple itself.   149

CH. JUST. I sent for you when there were matters against you for your life, to come speak with me.

FAL. As I was then advised by my learnèd counsel in the laws of this land service,° I did not come.   155

CH. JUST. Well, the truth is, Sir John, you live in great infamy.

FAL. He that buckles him in my belt cannot live in less.

CH. JUST. Your means are very slender and your waste is great.   161

FAL. I would it were otherwise. I would my means were greater and my waist slenderer.

CH. JUST. You have misled the youthful Prince.

FAL. The young Prince hath misled me. I am the fellow with the great belly, and he my dog.   166

CH. JUST. Well, I am loath to gall° a new-healed wound. Your day's service at Shrewsbury hath a little gilded over your night's exploit on Gadshill. You may thank the unquiet time for your quiet o'erposting° that action.   171

FAL. My lord?

CH. JUST. But since all is well, keep it so. Wake not a sleeping wolf.

FAL. To wake a wolf is as bad as to smell a fox.

CH. JUST. What! You are as a candle, the better part burned out.

FAL. A wassail candle,° my lord, all tallow. If I did say of wax,° my growth would approve the truth.   181

CH. JUST. There is not a white hair on your face but should have his effect of gravity.

FAL. His effect of gravy, gravy, gravy.

CH. JUST. You follow the young Prince up and down like his ill angel.   186

FAL. Not so, my lord. Your ill angel is light,° but I hope he that looks upon me will take me without weighing. And yet, in some respects, I grant I cannot go. I cannot tell. Virtue is of so little regard   190 in these costermonger times° that true valor is turned bearherd.° Pregnancy° is made a tapster, and hath his quick wit wasted in giving reckonings. All the other gifts appertinent to man, as the malice of this age shapes them, are not worth a goose-   195 berry. You that are old consider not the capacities of us that are young, you do measure the heat of our livers with the bitterness of your galls. And we that are in the vaward° of our youth, I must confess, are wags° too.   200

CH. JUST. Do you set down your name in the scroll of youth, that are written down old with all the characters° of age? Have you not a moist eye? A dry hand? A yellow cheek? A white beard? A decreasing leg? An increasing belly? Is not your voice   205 broken? Your wind short? Your chin double? Your wit single?° And every part about you blasted with antiquity? And will you yet call yourself young? Fie, fie, fie, Sir John!   209

FAL. My lord, I was born about three of the clock in the afternoon, with a white head and something° a round belly. For my voice, I have lost it with hallooing and singing of anthems. To approve° my youth further, I will not. The truth is, I am only old in judgment and understanding. And he that   215 will caper with me for a thousand marks,° let him lend me the money, and have at him. For the box of the ear that the Prince gave you, he gave it like a rude prince, and you took it like a sensible lord. I have checked him for it, and the young lion repents — marry,° not in ashes and sackcloth, but in new silk and old sack.°   222

CH. JUST. Well, God send the Prince a better companion!

FAL. God send the companion a better Prince! I cannot rid my hands of him.   226

CH. JUST. Well, the King hath severed you and Prince Harry. I hear you are going with Lord John of Lancaster against the Archbishop and the Earl of Northumberland.   230

FAL. Yea, I thank your pretty sweet wit for it. But look you, pray, all you that kiss my lady Peace at home, that our armies join not in a hot day. For, by the Lord, I take but two shirts out with me, and I mean not to sweat extraordinarily. If it be a hot   235 day, and I brandish anything but a bottle, I would I

---

134. **Galen:** a Greek physician (died A.D. 201), and a writer of medical textbooks, still much studied in Shakespeare's time. 141. **by . . . heels:** by putting you in the stocks. 148. **dram . . . scruple:** a minute portion of a minute quantity. 155. **laws . . . service:** laws of military service. 167. **gall:** irritate. 170–71. **quiet o'erposting:** peaceful escape from. 179. **wassail candle:** a thick candle used at feasts. 180. **wax:** with a pun on *wax*, meaning grow greater.

187. **ill . . . light:** with the common pun on *angel* — a gold coin worth 6s.8d. See App. 27 and Pl. 10c. 191. **costermonger times:** i.e., when everything is reckoned by its cash value. 192. **bearherd:** leader of a tame bear. **Pregnancy:** quick wit. 199. **vaward:** vanguard. 200. **wags:** gay lads. 203. **characters:** signs. 207. **single:** feeble. 211. **something:** somewhat. 213. **approve:** demonstrate. 216. **marks:** 13s.4d. 221. **marry:** Mary, by the Virgin. 222. **sack:** Spanish wine. See IV.iii.102–35.

might never spit white° again. There is not a danger-
ous action can peep out his head but I am thrust
upon it. Well, I cannot last ever. But it was alway
yet the trick of our English nation, if they have 240
a good thing, to make it too common. If ye will needs
say I am an old man, you should give me rest. I
would to God my name were not so terrible to the
enemy as it is. I were better to be eaten to death with
a rust than to be scoured° to nothing with perpetual
motion. 247

CH. JUST. Well, be honest, be honest, and God
bless your expedition!

FAL. Will your lordship lend me a thousand pound
to furnish° me forth?

CH. JUST. Not a penny, not a penny. You are too
impatient to bear crosses.° Fare you well. Commend
me to my cousin Westmoreland. 254

[*Exeunt* CHIEF JUSTICE *and* SERVANT.]

FAL. If I do, fillip° me with a three-man beetle.° A
man can no more separate age and covetousness than
a' can part young limbs and lechery. But the gout
galls the one and the pox pinches the other, and so
both the degrees° prevent° my curses. Boy! 260

PAGE. Sir?

FAL. What money is in my purse?

PAGE. Seven groats° and twopence. 263

FAL. I can get no remedy against this consumption
of the purse. Borrowing only lingers and lingers it
out, but the disease is incurable. Go bear this letter to
my Lord of Lancaster, this to the Prince, this to the
Earl of Westmoreland. And this to old Mistress
Ursula, whom I have weekly sworn to marry since I
perceived the first white hair on my chin. [*Exit* PAGE] 270
About it. You know where to find me. [*Exit* PAGE]
A pox of this gout! Or a gout of this pox! For the one
or the other plays the rogue with my great toe. 'Tis
no matter if I do halt.° I have the wars for my
color,° and my pension shall seem the more reason-
able. A good wit will make use of anything. I 277
will turn diseases to commodity.° [*Exit.*]

SCENE III. *York. The* ARCHBISHOP's *palace.*

[*Enter the* ARCHBISHOP, *the* LORDS HASTINGS,
MOWBRAY, *and* BARDOLPH.]

ARCH. Thus have you heard our cause and known
our means.

And, my most noble friends, I pray you all
Speak plainly your opinions of our hopes.
And first, Lord Marshal, what say you to it?

MOWB. I well allow the occasion of° our arms, 5
But gladly would be better satisfied
How in° our means we should advance ourselves
To look with forehead bold and big enough
Upon the power and puissance° of the King.

HAST. Our present musters grow upon the file°
To five and twenty thousand men of choice,° 11
And our supplies° live largely in the hope
Of great Northumberland, whose bosom burns
With an incensèd fire of injuries.

L. BARD. The question then, Lord Hastings, stand-
eth thus: 15
Whether our present five and twenty thousand
May hold up head without Northumberland?

HAST. With him, we may.

L. BARD. Yea, marry, there's the point.
But if without him we be thought too feeble,
My judgment is, we should not step too far 20
Till we had his assistance by the hand.°
For in a theme° so bloody-faced as this
Conjecture, expectation, and surmise
Of aids incertain should not be admitted.

ARCH. 'Tis very true, Lord Bardolph, for indeed
It was young Hotspur's case at Shrewsbury. 26

L. BARD. It was, my lord, who lined° himself with
hope,
Eating the air on promise of supply,
Flattering himself in project of a power
Much smaller than the smallest of his thoughts.° 30
And so, with great imagination°
Proper to madmen, led his powers to death,
And winking° leaped into destruction.

HAST. But, by your leave, it never yet did hurt
To lay down likelihoods and forms of hope. 35

L. BARD. Yes, if this present quality of war,
Indeed the instant action,° a cause on foot,
Lives so in hope as in an early spring
We see the appearing buds, which to prove fruit,
Hope gives not so much warrant as despair 40
That frosts will bite them.° When we mean to build,
We first survey the plot,° then draw the model.°
And when we see the figure° of the house,
Then must we rate the cost of the erection,

Sc. iii: 5. occasion of: reason for. 7. in: with. 9. puissance:
might. 10. file: roster. 11. men of choice: picked men. 12. sup-
plies: reinforcements. 21. by . . . hand: at hand. 22. theme:
problem. 27. lined: strengthened. 29–30. in . . . thoughts: in
expectation of a force that turned out to be far less than he
had imagined. 31. imagination: i.e., lack of a sense of reality.
33. winking: with his eyes shut. 36–37. Yes . . . action: A
much-debated passage; possibly a line has been omitted. The
general meaning is that it is harmful to be optimistic when it
is a case of immediate war. 37–41. a . . . them: when a proj-
ect for war is set on foot, the promoter's hopes are like buds
in early spring. We may hope that they will become fruit, but
should fear that the frost will destroy them; i.e., "safety first."
42. plot: ground. model: plan. 43. figure: design.

237. spit white: not satisfactorily explained; perhaps a sign that
a man has drunk well, or "spit clean" — a sign of good health.
246. scoured: rubbed. 251. furnish: equip. 253. bear crosses:
a common pun. The phrase means (a) to endure disappointment,
and (b) to carry money — so called from the cross on the coin.
See Pl. 10a. 255. fillip: flip. three-man beetle: heavy ham-
mer wielded by three men, and used for pile-driving. 260. both
. . . degrees: i.e., youth and age. prevent: forestall; i.e., both
youth and age have their own curses already. 263. groats:
worth 4*d.* 275. halt: limp. 276. color: excuse. 278. com-
modity: advantage.

Which if we find outweighs ability,   45
What do we then but draw anew the model
In fewer offices,° or at last desist
To build at all? Much more, in this great work,
Which is almost to pluck a kingdom down
And set another up, should we survey   50
The plot of situation and the model,
Consent° upon a sure foundation,
Question surveyors, know our own estate,
How able such a work to undergo
To weigh against his opposite.° Or else   55
We fortify in paper° and in figures,
Using the names of men instead of men —
Like one that draws the model of a house
Beyond his power to build it, who, half through,
Gives o'er and leaves his part-created cost°   60
A naked subject to the weeping clouds,
And waste for churlish° winter's tyranny.

    HAST. Grant that our hopes, yet likely of fair birth,
Should be stillborn, and that we now possessed
The utmost man of expectation,°   65
I think we are a body strong enough,
Even as we are, to equal with the King.

    L. BARD. What, is the King but five and twenty
      thousand?

    HAST. To us° no more — nay, not so much, Lord
      Bardolph.
For his divisions, as the times do brawl,   70
Are in three heads: one power against the French,
And one against Glendower, perforce a third
Must take up us. So is the unfirm King
In three divided, and his coffers sound°
With hollow poverty and emptiness.   75

    ARCH. That he should draw his several° strengths
      together
And come against us in full puissance
Need not be dreaded.

    HAST.   If he should do so,
He leaves his back unarmed, the French and Welsh
Baying° him at the heels. Never fear that.   80

    L. BARD. Who is it like should lead his forces
      hither?

    HAST. The Duke of Lancaster and Westmoreland.
Against the Welsh, himself and Harry Monmouth.
But who is substituted° 'gainst the French,
I have no certain notice.

    ARCH.   Let us on,   85
And publish the occasion of our arms.
The commonwealth is sick of their own choice,
Their overgreedy love hath surfeited.°
A habitation giddy and unsure

Hath he that buildeth on the vulgar heart.°   90
O thou fond many,° with what loud applause
Didst thou beat Heaven with blessing Bolingbroke
Before he was what thou wouldst have him be!
And being now trimmed in thine own desires,°
Thou, beastly feeder, art so full of him   95
That thou provokest thyself to cast him up.
So, so, thou common dog, didst thou disgorge
Thy glutton bosom of the royal Richard.
And now thou wouldst eat thy dead vomit up,
And howl'st to find it.° What trust is in these
    times?   100
They that when Richard lived would have him die
Are now become enamored on his grave.
Thou° that threw'st dust° upon his goodly head
When through proud London he came sighing on
After the admirèd heels of Bolingbroke,   105
Criest now " O earth, yield us that king again,
And take thou this! " Oh, thoughts of men accursed!
Past and to come seems best, things present, worst.

    MOWB. Shall we go draw our numbers and set on?

    HAST. We are time's subjects, and time bids be
      gone.   [*Exeunt.*]

Act II

SCENE I. *London. A street.*°

[*Enter* HOSTESS, FANG *and his* BOY *with her, and*
      SNARE *following.*]

    HOST. Master Fang,° have you entered the ac-
tion?°

    FANG. It is entered.

    HOST. Where's your yeoman?° Is't a lusty yeo-
man? Will a' stand to 't?   5

    FANG. Sirrah, where's Snare?

    HOST. Oh Lord, aye! Good Master Snare.

    SNARE. Here, here.

    FANG. Snare, we must arrest Sir John Falstaff.

    HOST. Yea, good Master Snare. I have entered him
and all.   11

    SNARE. It may chance cost some of us our lives, for
he will stab.

    HOST. Alas the day! Take heed of him. He stabbed
me in mine own house, and that most beastly. In   15
good faith, he cares not what mischief he does, if his

---

47. **offices:** rooms.   52. **Consent:** agree.   55. **his opposite:** i.e.,
the cost.   56. **fortify in paper:** our plans are but paper.   60. **part-
created cost:** costly undertaking but half finished.   62. **churlish:**
rough.   65. **utmost ... expectation:** every man that we could
hope for.   69. **To us:** so far as we are concerned.   74. **sound:**
echo.   76. **several:** separate.   80. **Baying:** barking.   84. **sub-
stituted:** sent as deputy.   88. **surfeited:** overeaten.

90. **vulgar heart:** the love of the people.   91. **fond many:** foolish
multitude.   94. **trimmed ... desires:** decked out as you wished
him to be.   100. **howl'st ... it:** howl because you cannot find it.
103. **Thou:** i.e., the common people. **threw'st dust:** See *Rich II*,
V.ii.23–38.

    Act II, Sc. i: 1. **Master Fang:** the sheriff's sergeant. 1–2. **en-
tered ... action:** given notice of the action.   4. **yeoman:** the
sergeant's man.

weapon be out. He will foin° like any devil, he will
spare neither man, woman, nor child.   19

FANG. If I can close with him, I care not for his
thrust.

HOST. No, nor I neither. I'll be at your elbow.

FANG. An I but fist him once, an a' come but
within my vice° ——   24

HOST. I am undone by his going. I warrant you,
he's an infinitive° thing upon my score.° Good Mas-
ter Fang, hold him sure. Good Master Snare, let him
not 'scape. A' comes continuantly to Pie Corner —
saving your manhoods° — to buy a saddle, and he is
indited° to dinner to the Lubber's Head° in   30
Lumbert° Street, to Master Smooth's the silkman.
I pray ye, since my exion° is entered and my case so
openly known to the world, let him be brought in°
to his answer. A hundred mark is a long one for a
poor lone woman to bear. And I have borne, and   35
borne, and borne, and have been fubbed off,° and
fubbed off, and fubbed off, from this day to that day,
that it is a shame to be thought on. There is no
honesty in such dealing, unless a woman should   40
be made an ass and a beast, to bear every knave's
wrong. Yonder he comes, and that arrant° malmsey-
nose° knave Bardolph with him. Do your offices, do
your offices. Master Fang and Master Snare, do me,
do me, do me your offices.   45

[*Enter* FALSTAFF, PAGE, *and* BARDOLPH.]

FAL. How now! Whose mare's dead?° What's the
matter?

FANG. Sir John, I arrest you at the suit of Mistress
Quickly.

FAL. Away, varlets!° Draw, Bardolph. Cut me off
the villain's head. Throw the quean° in the chan-
nel.°   52

HOST. Throw me in the channel! I'll throw thee in
the channel. Wilt thou? Wilt thou? Thou bastardly
rogue! Murder, murder! Ah, thou honeysuckle° vil-
lain! Wilt thou kill God's officers and the King's?
Ah, thou honey-seed rogue! Thou art a honey-seed,
a man-queller,° and a woman-queller.   59

FAL. Keep them off, Bardolph.

FANG. A rescue!° A rescue!

HOST. Good people, bring a rescue or two. Thou
wo't, wo't thou? Thou wo't, wo't ta? Do, do, thou
rogue! Do, thou hempseed!°   64

PAGE. Away, you scullion!° You rampallian!° You
fustilarian!° I'll tickle your catastrophe.°

[*Enter the* LORD CHIEF JUSTICE, *and his men.*]

CH. JUST. What is the matter? Keep the peace
here, ho!

HOST. Good my lord, be good to me. I beseech you,
stand to me.   70

CH. JUST. How now, Sir John! What are you
brawling here?
Doth this become your place, your time and busi-
ness?
You should have been well on your way to York.
Stand from him, fellow. Wherefore hang'st upon
him?   74

HOST. O my most worshipful lord, an 't please
your Grace, I am a poor widow of Eastcheap, and he
is arrested at my suit.

CH. JUST. For what sum?   78

HOST. It is more than for some, my lord, it is for
all, all I have. He hath eaten me out of house and
home, he hath put all my substance into that fat belly
of his. But I will have some of it out again, or I will
ride thee o' nights like the mare.°   83

FAL. I think I am as like to ride the mare, if I
have any vantage of ground° to get up.

CH. JUST. How comes this, Sir John? Fie! What
man of good temper° would endure this tempest of
exclamation? Are you not ashamed to enforce a poor
widow to so rough a course to come by her own?   90

FAL. What is the gross sum that I owe thee?

HOST. Marry, if thou wert an honest man, thyself
and the money too. Thou didst swear to me upon a
parcel-gilt° goblet, sitting in my Dolphin Chamber,°
at the round table, by a sea-coal° fire, upon Wed-   95
nesday in Wheeson° week, when the Prince broke
thy head for liking° his father to a singing man° of
Windsor — thou didst swear to me then, as I was
washing thy wound, to marry me and make me my
lady thy wife. Canst thou deny it? Did not   100
goodwife Keech, the butcher's wife, come in then
and call me Gossip° Quickly? Coming in to borrow

---

18. foin: thrust.   **24. vice:** grip.   **26. infinitive:** Like many
other characters of her social standing in Shakespeare's plays,
Mrs. Quickly loves long words but does not always get them
right; she means "infinite." **score:** tavern account.   **29. saving
. . . manhoods:** a phrase of apology, usually for an improper
remark.   **30. indited:** for "invited." **Lubber's Head:** for Libbard's
(Leopard's) Head. See App. 12.   **32. ex-
ion:** for "action."   **33. brought in:** i.e., to court.   **36. fubbed
off:** put off.   **42. arrant:** out-and-out; lit., "errant" — vagabond.
43. malmsey-nose: For Bardolph's nose, see *I Hen IV*, III.iii.
27–55. **malmsey:** a sweet red wine.   **46. Whose . . . dead:** what's
all the fuss?   **50. varlets:** knaves.   **51. quean:** slut.   **52. channel:**
gutter.   **55. honeysuckle:** apparently for "homicidal," as "honey-
seed" (l. 58) is "homicide."   **59. man-queller:** man-killer.
61. A rescue: a call to passers-by to come to the help of the
officers (or their victim).

64. hempseed: gallows bird.   **65. scullion:** slavey, dishwasher.
rampallian: rascal.   **66. fustilarian:** stinker — from "fustilugs,"
a fat, frowsy woman. **catastrophe:** in modern slang, "fanny."
83. mare: nightmare, believed to be a spirit which bestrode those
who slept on their backs. See *R & J*, I.iv.92–94.   **85. vantage
of ground:** higher ground. Men of Falstaff's bulk need assistance
in getting their legs over the saddle.   **88. temper:** disposition.
94. parcel-gilt: partly gilt. **Dolphin Chamber:** Rooms in taverns
were named. See *I Hen IV*, II.iv.41.   **95. sea-coal:** coal from
mines transported by sea from Newcastle to London; *coal* usually
means "charcoal."   **96. Wheeson:** Whitsun, the seventh Sunday
after Easter; Pentecost.   **97. liking:** likening, comparing. **sing-
ing man:** singer in the choir. The insult was the suggestion that
the King and the chorister had the same father.   **102. Gossip:** a
name used by middle-class women in talking of each other.

a mess° of vinegar, telling us she had a good dish of
prawns, whereby thou didst desire to eat some,
whereby I told thee they were ill for a green°   105
wound? And didst thou not, when she was gone
downstairs, desire me to be no more so familiarity
with such poor people, saying that ere long they
should call me madam? And didst thou not kiss me
and bid me fetch thee thirty shillings? I put thee
now to thy book oath. Deny it, if thou canst.   112

FAL. My lord, this is a poor mad soul, and she says
up and down the town that her eldest son is like
you.° She hath been in good case,° and the truth is,
poverty hath distracted° her. But for these foolish
officers, I beseech you I may have redress against
them.   118

CH. JUST. Sir John, Sir John, I am well acquainted
with your manner of wrenching the true cause the
false way. It is not a confident brow, nor the throng
of words that come with such more than impudent
sauciness from you, can thrust me from a level°
consideration. You have, as it appears to me,   123
practiced upon° the easy-yielding spirit of this
woman, and made her serve your uses both in purse
and in person.

HOST. Yea, in truth, my lord.   128

CH. JUST. Pray thee, peace. Pay her the debt you
owe her, and unpay the villainy you have done her.
The one you may do with sterling money, and the
other with current° repentance.   132

FAL. My lord, I will not undergo this sneap° with-
out reply. You call honorable boldness impudent
sauciness. If a man will make courtesy° and say
nothing, he is virtuous. No, my lord, my humble
duty remembered,° I will not be your suitor.° I say
to you I do desire deliverance from these officers,
being upon hasty employment in the King's af-
fairs.   140

CH. JUST. You speak as having power to do wrong.
But answer in the effect of your reputation,° and
satisfy the poor woman.

FAL. Come hither, Hostess.   144

[Enter GOWER.]

CH. JUST. Now, Master Gower, what news?

GOW. The King, my lord, and Harry Prince of
    Wales
Are near at hand. The rest the paper tells.

FAL. As I am a gentleman.

HOST. Faith, you said so before.   149

FAL. As I am a gentleman. Come, no more words
of it.

HOST. By this heavenly ground I tread on, I must
be fain° to pawn both my plate and the tapestry of
my dining chambers.   155

FAL. Glasses, glasses, is the only drinking.° And
for thy walls, a pretty slight drollery,° or the story of
the Prodigal, or the German hunting° in water
work,° is worth a thousand of these bed hangings
and these fly-bitten tapestries.° Let it be ten pound,
if thou canst. Come, an 'twere not for thy hu-   161
mors,° there's not a better wench in England. Go,
wash thy face, and draw° the action. Come, thou
must not be in this humor with me, dost not know
me? Come, come, I know thou wast set onto this.

HOST. Pray thee, Sir John, let it be but twenty
nobles.° I' faith, I am loath to pawn my plate, so
God save me, la!

FAL. Let it alone, I'll make other shift.° You'll be
a fool still.   170

HOST. Well, you shall have it, though I pawn my
gown. I hope you'll come to supper. You'll pay me
all together?

FAL. Will I live? [*To* BARDOLPH] Go, with her,
with her. Hook on,° hook on.   175

HOST. Will you have Doll Tearsheet meet you at
supper?

FAL. No more words. Let's have her.

[*Exeunt* HOSTESS, BARDOLPH, OFFICERS, *and* BOY.]

CH. JUST. I have heard better news.

FAL. What's the news, my lord?   180

CH. JUST. Where lay the King last night?

GOW. At Basingstoke, my lord.

FAL. I hope, my lord, all's well. What is the news,
my lord?

CH. JUST. Come all his forces back?   185

GOW. No. Fifteen hundred foot, five hundred
    horse,
Are marched up to my Lord of Lancaster,
Against Northumberland and the Archbishop.

FAL. Comes the King back from Wales, my noble
    lord?

CH. JUST. You shall have letters of me presently.
Come, go along with me, good Master Gower.   191

FAL. My lord!

CH. JUST. What's the matter?

---

103. **mess:** quantity.   105. **green:** raw.   114–15. **eldest . . . you:**
i.e., that the Chief Justice is his father.   115. **in . . . case:** in
good circumstances.   116. **distracted:** made mad.   122. **level:**
unbiased.   124. **practiced upon:** tricked, taken advantage of.
131–32. **sterling . . . current:** sterling money (i.e., sound money)
is current (i.e., negotiable). Even the Chief Justice takes every
chance of making a pun, which moves Falstaff to answer him
with real irritation.   133. **sneap:** rebuke.   135. **make courtesy:**
curtsy, show signs of respect.   136–37. **my . . . remembered:**
with all due respects.   137. **be . . . suitor:** ask favors of you.
142. **in . . . reputation:** as becomes a man of your reputation.

154. **fain:** pleased, obliged.   156. **Glasses . . . drinking:** to be
in fashion one must have glasses, not metal cups.   157. **drollery:**
comic picture.   158. **German hunting:** a hunting scene painted
in Germany.   158–59. **water work:** distemper. For a specimen,
see Pl. 6a.   160. **tapestries:** Woven or embroidered tapestries
were expensive and high class, and Mrs. Quickly is naturally
proud of her furnishings. Falstaff proposes that she shall substi-
tute for them cheap new painted cloths.   162. **humors:** whims.
163. **draw:** withdraw.   167. **nobles:** coins worth 6s.8d. See App.
27.   169. **make . . . shift:** manage in some other way.   175. **Hook
on:** i.e., don't let her change her mind.

FAL. Master Gower, shall I entreat you with me to dinner? 195

GOW. I must wait upon my good lord here, I thank you, good Sir John.

CH. JUST. Sir John, you loiter here too long, being° you are to take soldiers up in counties as you go.

FAL. Will you sup with me, Master Gower? 201

CH. JUST. What foolish master taught you these manners, Sir John?

FAL. Master Gower, if they become me not, he was a fool that taught them me.° This is the right fencing grace, my lord — tap for tap, and so part fair.° 207

CH. JUST. Now the Lord lighten° thee! Thou art a great fool. [Exeunt.]

SCENE II. London. Another street.

[Enter PRINCE HENRY and POINS.]

PRINCE. Before God, I am exceeding weary.

POINS. Is 't come to that? I had thought weariness durst not have attached° one of so high blood. 3

PRINCE. Faith, it does me, though it discolors the complexion° of my greatness to acknowledge it. Doth it not show vilely in me to desire small° beer? 8

POINS. Why, a prince should not be so loosely studied° as to remember so weak a composition.°

PRINCE. Belike then my appetite was not princely got, for, by my troth, I do now remember the poor creature, small beer. But indeed these humble considerations make me out of love with my greatness. What a disgrace is it to me to remember thy 15 name! Or to know thy face tomorrow! Or to take note how many pair of silk stockings thou hast; viz., these, and those that were thy peach-colored ones! Or to bear the inventory of thy shirts, as one for superfluity° and another for use! But that the tennis-court keeper knows better than I. For it is a 20 low ebb of linen with thee when thou keepest not racket there,° as thou hast not done a great while be-

cause the rest of thy low countries have made a shift to eat up thy holland.° And God knows whether those that bawl out the ruins of thy linen shall 25 inherit His kingdom.° But the midwives say the children are not in the fault, whereupon the world increases, and kindreds are mightily strengthened.

POINS. How ill it follows, after you have la- 31 bored so hard, you should talk so idly! Tell me, how many good young princes would do so, their fathers being so sick as yours at this time is?

PRINCE. Shall I tell thee one thing, Poins? 35

POINS. Yes, faith, and let it be an excellent good thing.

PRINCE. It shall serve among wits of no higher breeding than thine.°

POINS. Go to. I stand the push° of your one thing that you will tell. 41

PRINCE. Marry, I tell thee it is not meet that I should be sad, now my father is sick. Albeit I could tell to thee, as to one it pleases me, for fault of a better, to call my friend, I could be sad, and sad indeed too.

POINS. Very hardly upon such a subject.° 47

PRINCE. By this hand, thou thinkest me as far in the Devil's book° as thou and Falstaff for obduracy° and persistency. Let the end try the man.° But I tell thee, my heart bleeds inwardly that my father is so sick. And keeping such vile company as thou art hath in reason taken from me all ostentation° of sorrow. 54

POINS. The reason?

PRINCE. What wouldst thou think of me if I should weep?

POINS. I would think thee a most princely hypocrite. 59

PRINCE. It would be every man's thought, and thou art a blessed fellow to think as every man thinks. Never a man's thought in the world keeps the roadway better than thine.° Every man would think me a hypocrite indeed. And what accites° your most worshipful thought to think so? 65

POINS. Why, because you have been so lewd,° and so much engraffed to° Falstaff.

PRINCE. And to thee. 68

---

199. being: since. 204–05. he . . . me: i.e., I am behaving as the Chief Justice taught me. If you don't like my manners, my master must have been a fool. 205–07. This . . . fair: This is good fencing, to give thrust for thrust, and so end all square on both sides. 208. lighten: enlighten.

Sc. ii: 3. attached: arrested, seized on. 4–5. discolors . . . complexion: makes me change color. 6. small: weak. 9–10. so . . . studied: such a slack student. 10. weak a composition: i.e., small beer. This enigmatic backchat is not easy to follow; like most specimens of wit, the more up to date it is at the moment of writing, the sooner it becomes outmoded and incomprehensible. Poins means that a prince with a proper sense of his duties and dignities would not condescend to remember small beer. The Prince continues the idea with a little lecture on the poor memories of great men, especially for names and faces. For a similar and more elaborate discourse, see King John, I.i.181–200. 19. for superfluity: to spare. 21–22. low . . . there: Tennis was much played by courtiers, who continuously changed their shirts as they sweated. Poins, being now reduced to one spare shirt, is ashamed to reveal his poverty on the tennis court.

23–24. rest . . . holland: an elaborate series of puns. low countries: tail end, and also the Netherlands. made a shift: contrived, with a pun on shift, meaning shirt. holland: the best linen. 24–26. God . . . kingdom: bawl is an emendation for "bal" of the quarto; the passage is omitted from the folio. If correct, the sentence apparently means "your crying bastards use your old shirts as diapers." 38–39. It . . . thine: it will be good enough for intelligences no better than yours. 40. push: attack. 47. Very . . . subject: Poins cynically comments that the Prince's grief at his father's death would hardly be very deep. 49. book: record. obduracy: impenitence. 50. Let . . . man: i.e., the outcome will show the man's worth — a hint of the serious purpose behind the Prince's behavior. 53. ostentation: outward show. 62–63. Never . . . thine: i.e., you are a perfect specimen of a commonplace mind. 64. accites: excites. 66. lewd: low. 67. engraffed to: grafted with, close to.

POINS. By this light, I am well spoke on, I can hear it with mine own ears. The worst that they can say of me is that I am a second brother° and that I am a proper fellow of my hands,° and those two things I confess I cannot help. By the mass, here comes Bardolph.   74

[*Enter* BARDOLPH *and* PAGE.]

PRINCE. And the boy that I gave Falstaff. A' had him from me Christian, and look if the fat villain have not transformed him ape.

BARD. God save your Grace!

PRINCE. And yours, most noble Bardolph!   79

BARD. Come, you virtuous ass, you bashful fool, must you be blushing? Wherefore blush you now? What a maidenly man-at-arms are you become! Is 't such a matter to get a pottle pot's° maidenhead?   84

PAGE. A' calls me e'en now, my lord, through a red lattice,° and I could discern no part of his face from the window.° At last I spied his eyes, and methought he had made two holes in the alewife's new petticoat and so peeped through.

PRINCE. Has not the boy profited?

BARD. Away, you whoreson upright rabbit, away!

PAGE. Away, you rascally Althaea's dream,° away!   94

PRINCE. Instruct us, boy. What dream, boy?

PAGE. Marry, my lord, Althaea dreamed she was delivered of a firebrand, and therefore I call him her dream.

PRINCE. A crown's worth of good interpretation. There 'tis, boy.   100

POINS. Oh, that this good blossom could be kept from cankers!° Well, there is sixpence to preserve thee.

BARD. An you do not make him hanged among you, the gallows shall have wrong.   105

PRINCE. And how doth thy master, Bardolph?

BARD. Well, my lord. He heard of your Grace's coming to town. There's a letter for you.

POINS. Delivered with good respect.° And how doth the martlemas,° your master?   110

BARD. In bodily health, sir.

POINS. Marry, the immortal part needs a physician, but that moves not him. Though that be sick, it dies not.   114

PRINCE. I do allow this wen° to be as familiar with me as my dog, and he holds his place, for look you how he writes.   117

POINS. [*Reads*] "John Falstaff, knight" — every man must know that, as oft as he has occasion to name himself. Even like those that are kin to the King, for they never prick their finger but they say "There's some of the King's blood spilt." "How comes that?" says he that takes upon him not to conceive.° The answer is as ready as a borrow-   125 er's cap, "I am the King's poor cousin, sir."

PRINCE. Nay, they will be kin to us or they will fetch it from Japhet.° But to the letter.   128

POINS. [*Reads*] "Sir John Falstaff, knight, to the son of the King, nearest his father, Harry Prince of Wales, greeting." Why, this is a certificate.°

PRINCE. Peace!   133

POINS. [*Reads*] "I will imitate the honorable Romans in brevity." He sure means brevity in breath, short-winded. "I commend me to thee, I commend thee, and I leave thee. Be not too familiar with Poins, for he misuses thy favors so much that he swears thou art to marry his sister Nell. Repent at idle times as thou mayest, and so farewell.   141

"Thine, by yea and no, which is as much as to say, as thou usest him, Jack Falstaff with my familiars, John with my brothers and sisters, and Sir John with all Europe."

My lord, I'll steep this letter in sack and make him eat it.

PRINCE. That's to make him eat twenty of his words. But do you use me thus, Ned? Must I marry your sister?   151

POINS. God send the wench no worse fortune! But I never said so.

PRINCE. Well, thus we play the fools with the time, and the spirits of the wise sit in the clouds and mock us. Is your master here in London?   157

BARD. Yea, my lord.

PRINCE. Where sups he? Doth the old boar feed in the old frank?°

BARD. At the old place, my lord, in Eastcheap.

PRINCE. What company?

PAGE. Ephesians,° my lord, of the old Church.

PRINCE. Sup any women with him?

PAGE. None, my lord, but old Mistress Quickly and Mistress Doll Tearsheet.   167

PRINCE. What pagan may that be?

PAGE. A proper gentlewoman, sir, and a kinswoman of my master's.

PRINCE. Even such kin as the parish heifers are to the town bull. Shall we steal upon them, Ned, at supper?

POINS. I am your shadow, my lord, I'll follow you.

---

71. **second brother:** i.e., without an inheritance.   72. **proper . . . hands:** fine fighter.   84. **pottle pot:** tankard holding two quarts. 85–86. **red lattice:** The lattice windows of taverns were painted red.   86–87. **discern . . . window:** because the red lattice was perfect camouflage for Bardolph's face.   93. **Althaea's dream:** i.e., that she had given birth to a firebrand. Actually, the boy was mistaken, for it was Hecuba's dream.   102. **cankers:** cankerworms.   109. **good respect:** nice manners — ironically said, for Bardolph is no courtier.   110. **martlemas:** Martinmas, "St. Martin's summer," a patch of fine weather that sometimes comes late in fall; Indian summer.   115. **wen:** tumor.

125. **conceive:** understand.   128. **fetch . . . Japhet:** i.e., if they cannot claim nearer kinship, they will go back to Noah. Japhet was the one of Noah's sons from whom the white races are supposed to be descended.   132. **certificate:** formal document, which often begins with a recital of the titles of the giver.   160. **frank:** sty.   164. **Ephesians:** like Trojans, Corinthians, etc., means gay lads, "the gang."

PRINCE. Sirrah,° you boy, and Bardolph, no word
to your master that I am yet come to town. There's
for your silence.   178

BARD. I have no tongue, sir.

PAGE. And for mine, sir, I will govern it.

PRINCE. Fare you well, go.

                              [*Exeunt* BARDOLPH *and* PAGE.]

This Doll Tearsheet should be some road.°   183

POINS. I warrant you as common as the way be-
tween St. Albans and London.

PRINCE. How might we see Falstaff bestow° him-
self tonight in his true colors and not ourselves be
seen?   188

POINS. Put on two leathern jerkins° and aprons,
and wait upon him at his table as drawers.°

PRINCE. From a god to a bull? A heavy descen-
sion!° It was Jove's case.° From a prince to a pren-
tice? A low transformation! That shall be mine, for
in everything the purpose must weigh with°   195
the folly. Follow me, Ned.   [*Exeunt.*]

SCENE III. *Warkworth. Before the castle.*

[*Enter* NORTHUMBERLAND, LADY NORTHUMBERLAND,
              and LADY PERCY.]

NORTH. I pray thee, loving wife and gentle daugh-
ter,
Give even way° unto my rough affairs.
Put not you on the visage of the times,
And be like them to Percy troublesome.

LADY N. I have given over, I will speak no more.
Do what you will, your wisdom be your guide.   6

NORTH. Alas, sweet wife, my honor is at pawn,
And, but my going,° nothing can redeem it.

LADY P. Oh, yet, for God's sake, go not to these
wars!   9
The time was, Father, that you broke your word
When you were more endeared to it° than now —
When your own Percy, when my heart's dear
Harry,
Threw many a northward look to see his father
Bring up his powers, but he did long in vain.
Who then persuaded you to stay at home?   15
There were two honors lost, yours and your son's.
For yours, the God of Heaven brighten it!
For his, it stuck upon him as the sun
In the gray° vault of heaven, and by his light
Did all the chivalry of England move   20

To do brave acts. He was indeed the glass
Wherein the noble youth did dress themselves.
He had no legs that practiced not his gait,
And speaking thick,° which nature made his blem-
ish,
Became the accents of the valiant,   25
For those that could speak low and tardily
Would turn their own perfection to abuse,
To seem like him. So that in speech, in gait,
In diet, in affections of delight,°
In military rules, humors of blood,°   30
He was the mark and glass, copy° and book,°
That fashioned others. And him — oh, wondrous
him!
Oh, miracle of men! — him did you leave,
Second to none, unseconded by you,
To look upon the hideous god of war   35
In disadvantage, to abide a field°
Where nothing but the sound of Hotspur's name
Did seem defensible.° So you left him.
Never, oh, never, do his ghost the wrong
To hold your honor more precise and nice°   40
With others than with him! Let them alone.
The Marshal and the Archbishop are strong.
Had my sweet Harry had but half their numbers,
Today might I, hanging on Hotspur's neck,
Have talked of Monmouth's° grave.

NORTH.   Beshrew° your heart, 45
Fair Daughter, you do draw my spirits from me
With new lamenting ancient oversights.
But I must go and meet with danger there,
Or it will seek me in another place
And find me worse provided.°

LADY N.   Oh, fly to Scotland,   50
Till that the nobles and the armèd commons
Have of their puissance° made a little taste.

LADY P. If they get ground and vantage of the
King,
Then join you with them, like a rib of steel,
To make strength stronger. But, for all our loves,
First let them try themselves. So did your son,   56
He was so suffered. So came I a widow,
And never shall have length of life enough
To rain upon remembrance with mine eyes,
That it may grow and sprout as high as heaven,   60
For recordation° to my noble husband.

NORTH. Come, come, go in with me. 'Tis with my
mind
As with the tide swelled up unto his height,
That makes a stillstand,° running neither way.

---

176 Sirrah: term of address used to inferiors.   183. road: i.e.,
available for all comers.   186. bestow: behave.   189. jerkins:
jackets.   190. drawers: waiters.   193. descension: descent in
the social scale.   Jove's case: in order to get the love of Europa,
Jupiter transformed himself into a bull.   195. weigh with: corre-
spond to.

Sc. iii: 2. Give . . . way: make the way smooth.   8. but my
going: unless I go.   11. more . . . it: had dearer reasons for keep-
ing it.   19. gray: Elizabethan writers did not always distinguish
between gray and sky-blue.

24. thick: fast.   29. affections of delight: in the things in which
he took pleasure.   30. humors of blood: natural inclination. See
App. 3.   31. copy: pattern.   book: book of manners.   36. abide
a field: fight a battle.   38. defensible: able to put up a defense.
40. precise . . . nice: exact and particular.   45. Monmouth: i.e.,
Prince Henry.   Beshrew: plague on.   50. provided: prepared.
52. puissance: might.   61. recordation: memorial.   64. still-
stand: standstill.

Fain would I go to meet the Archbishop,   65
But many thousand reasons hold me back.
I will resolve for Scotland. There am I
Till time and vantage° crave my company.
                                    [*Exeunt.*]

SCENE IV. *London. The Boar's Head Tavern
in Eastcheap.*

[*Enter two* DRAWERS.]

1. DRAW. What the devil hast thou brought there?
Applejohns?° Thou knowest Sir John cannot endure
an applejohn.   3

2. DRAW. Mass, thou sayest true. The Prince once
set a dish of applejohns before him, and told him
there were five more Sir Johns and, putting off his
hat, said " I will now take my leave of these six dry,
round, old, withered knights." It angered him to the
heart. But he hath forgot that.   10

1. DRAW. Why, then, cover, and set them down.°
And see if thou canst find out Sneak's noise,° Mis-
tress Tearsheet would fain hear some music. Dis-
patch. The room where they supped is too hot, they'll
come in straight.   15

2. DRAW. Sirrah, here will be the Prince and Mas-
ter Poins anon, and they will put on two of our
jerkins and aprons, and Sir John must not know of
it. Bardolph hath brought word.   20

1. DRAW. By the mass, here will be old utis.° It
will be an excellent stratagem.

2. DRAW. I'll see if I can find out Sneak. [*Exit.*]

[*Enter* HOSTESS *and* DOLL TEARSHEET.]

HOST. I' faith, sweetheart, methinks now you are
in an excellent good temperality.° Your pulsidge°
beats as extraordinarily as heart would desire, 26
and your color, I warrant you, is as red as any rose,
in good truth, la! But, i' faith, you have drunk too
much canaries,° and that's a marvelous searching°
wine, and it perfumes the blood ere one can say
" What's this? " How do you now?   32

DOLL. Better than I was. Hem!

HOST. Why, that's well said. A good heart's worth
gold. Lo, here comes Sir John.   35

[*Enter* FALSTAFF.]

FAL. [*Singing*] " When Arthur° first in court " —
Empty the jordan.° [*Exit* FIRST DRAWER.] — [*Sing-*

ing] " And was a worthy king." How now, Mistress
Doll!

HOST. Sick of a calm,° yea, good faith.   40

FAL. So is all her sect. An they be once in a calm,
they are sick.

DOLL. You muddy° rascal, is that all the comfort
you give me?

FAL. You make fat rascals,° Mistress Doll. 45

DOLL. I make them! Gluttony and diseases make
them, I make them not.

FAL. If the cook help to make the gluttony, you
help to make the diseases, Doll. We catch of you,
Doll, we catch of you. Grant that, my poor virtue,
grant that.   51

DOLL. Yea, joy, our chains and our jewels.°

FAL. " Your brooches, pearls, and ouches."° For
to serve bravely is to come halting off, you know; to
come off the breach with his pike bent bravely, and
to surgery bravely; to venture upon the charged
chambers° bravely ——   57

DOLL. Hang yourself, you muddy conger,° hang
yourself!

HOST. By my troth, this is the old fashion. You
two never meet but you fall to some discord. You are
both, i' good truth, as rheumatic° as two dry toasts.
You cannot one bear with another's confirmi- 62
ties.° What the goodyear!° One must bear, and that
must be you. You are the weaker vessel, as they say,
the emptier vessel.   66

DOLL. Can a weak empty vessel bear such a huge
full hogshead? There's a whole merchant's venture
of Bordeaux stuff° in him, you have not seen a
hulk° better stuffed in the hold. Come, I'll be friends
with thee, Jack. Thou art going to the wars, and
whether I shall ever see thee again or no, there is
nobody cares.   73

[*Re-enter* FIRST DRAWER.]

1. DRAW. Sir, Ancient° Pistol's below and would
speak with you.

DOLL. Hang him, swaggering rascal! Let him not
come hither. It is the foul-mouthedst rogue in Eng-
land.   78

HOST. If he swagger, let him not come here — no,
by my faith. I must live among my neighbors, I'll
no swaggerers. I am in good name and fame with
the very best. Shut the door, there comes no swag-

---

68. vantage: advantage.

Sc. iv: 2. Applejohns: a variety of apple which kept well, but
whose skin was liable to shrivel.   11. cover . . . down: put on
the cloth and lay the table.   12. noise: band of musicians.
21. old utis: rare fun.   25. temperality: Mrs. Quickly may mean
"temper" or may have mixed "temporal" with "spirits." pul-
sidge: pulse.   30. canaries: wine from the Canaries.   searching:
that reaches the spot quickly, intoxicating.   36. When Arthur:
the first lines of a popular ballad of Sir Lancelot.   37. jordan:
chamber pot. Elizabethan conveniences were primitive.

40. calm: qualm, feeling of queasiness.   43. muddy: dirty.
45. rascals: with a pun on *rascal*, meaning a deer in poor condi-
tion.   52. our . . . jewels: because old ruffians, like Falstaff,
wheedle the jewels out of Doll and her professional sisters.
53. Your . . ., ouches: another line from a ballad.   ouch: car-
buncle.   56–57. charged chambers: loaded cannon.   58. conger:
conger eel.   61. rheumatic: Mrs. Quickly mixes *rheumatic*, damp,
with "choleric," hot-tempered.   63. confirmities: for "infirm-
ities." What . . . goodyear: meaningless phrase, like "what
the deuce." Its origin is obscure.   68–69. merchant's . . .
stuff: whole cargo of Bordeaux wine.   70. hulk: trading ship.
74. Ancient: ensign, second lieutenant. The Ancient carried the
company ensign.

gerers here. I have not lived all this while to have swaggering now. Shut the door, I pray you.   85

FAL. Dost thou hear, Hostess?

HOST. Pray ye, pacify yourself, Sir John. There comes no swaggerers here.

FAL. Dost thou hear? It is mine Ancient.   89

HOST. Tilly-fally,° Sir John, ne'er tell me. Your ancient swaggerer comes not in my doors. I was before Master Tisick, the debuty,° t' other day, and as he said to me, 'twas no longer ago than Wednesday last, "I' good faith, Neighbor Quickly," says he — Master Dumbe, our minister, was by then —   95 "Neighbor Quickly," says he, "receive those that are civil, for," said he, "you are in an ill name." Now a' said so, I can tell whereupon. "For," says he, "you are an honest woman, and well thought on, therefore take heed what guests you receive.   100 Receive," says he, "no swaggering companions."° There comes none here. You would bless you to hear what he said. No, I'll no swaggerers.   104

FAL. He's no swaggerer, Hostess, a tame cheater,° i' faith. You may stroke him as gently as a puppy greyhound. He'll not swagger with a Barbary hen° if her feathers turn back in any show of resistance. Call him up, drawer.   [Exit FIRST DRAWER.]

HOST. Cheater, call you him? I will bar no honest man my house, nor no cheater. But I do not love swaggering, by my troth. I am the worse when one says swagger. Feel, masters, how I shake, look you, I warrant you.   114

DOLL. So you do, Hostess.

HOST. Do I? Yea, in very truth do I, an 'twere an aspen leaf. I cannot abide swaggerers.

[Enter PISTOL, BARDOLPH, and PAGE.]

PIST. God save you, Sir John!   119

FAL. Welcome, Ancient Pistol. Here, Pistol, I charge you° with a cup of sack. Do you discharge° upon mine hostess.

PIST. I will discharge upon her, Sir John, with two bullets.   124

FAL. She is pistolproof, sir, you shall hardly offend° her.

HOST. Come, I'll drink no proofs nor no bullets. I'll drink no more than will do me good, for no man's pleasure, I.   129

PIST. Then to you, Mistress Dorothy. I will charge you.

DOLL. Charge me! I scorn you, scurvy companion. What! You poor, base, rascally, cheating, lack-linen mate! Away, you moldy rogue, away! I am meat for your master.   135

PIST. I know you, Mistress Dorothy.

DOLL. Away, you cutpurse rascal! You filthy bung,° away! By this wine, I'll thrust my knife in your moldy chaps° an you play the saucy cuttle° with me. Away, you bottle-ale rascal! You baskethilt stale juggler,° you! Since when, I pray you, sir? God's light, with two points° on your shoulder? Much!   143

PIST. God let me not live but I will murder your ruff° for this.

FAL. No more, Pistol, I would not have you go off here. Discharge yourself of our company, Pistol.

HOST. No, good Captain Pistol, not here, sweet Captain.   150

DOLL. Captain! Thou abominable damned cheater, art thou not ashamed to be called captain? An captains were of my mind, they would truncheon° you out for taking their names upon you before you have earned them. You a captain! You slave,   155 for what? For tearing a poor whore's ruff in a bawdy house? He a captain! Hang him, rogue! He lives upon moldy stewed prunes and dried cakes. A captain! God's light, these villains will make the word as odious as the word "occupy,"° which   160 was an excellent good word before it was ill sorted,° therefore captains had need look to 't.

BARD. Pray thee go down, good Ancient.

FAL. Hark thee hither, Mistress Doll.   165

PIST. Not I. I tell thee what, Corporal Bardolph, I could tear her. I'll be revenged of her.

PAGE. Pray thee go down.

PIST. I'll see her damned first, to Pluto's damned lake,° by this hand, to the infernal deep, with Erebus° and tortures vile also. Hold hook and line, say I. Down, down, dogs! Down, faitors!° Have we not Hiren here?°   173

HOST. Good Captain Peesel, be quiet, 'tis very late, i' faith. I beseek you now, aggravate your choler.

PIST. These be good humors, indeed! Shall pack horses,
And hollow pampered jades of Asia,
Which cannot go but thirty mile a day,°   179

138. bung: purse (in thieves' language); but Doll is too angry to talk exact sense.   139. chaps: cheeks. cuttle: lit., the knife used by a cutpurse.   141. basket-hilt . . . juggler: one who shows off ancient tricks with an old sword.   142. points: laces (for fastening the breastplate to the shoulders).   145. ruff: See Pl. 13c and note on p. 95a.   153. truncheon: beat with their truncheons. A truncheon is a staff carried by officers and officials.   160. occupy: like "intercourse," the word had various meanings.   161. ill sorted: ill-used.   169-70. Pluto's . . . lake: Ancient Pistol loves to talk in a jargon collected from the more extravagant plays of the Admiral's Men at the Rose Theater. He was thus a living parody of the great actor Alleyn. See Gen. Intro. pp. 36b and 41b. Pluto: king of the underworld.   171. Erebus: Hell. 172-73. faitors: cheaters. Have . . . here: a much-parodied line from a play (now lost) by Peele.   177-79. Shall . . . day: misquotation of a famous line in Marlowe's Tamburlaine, Part II, where Tamburlaine enters in a chariot drawn by captive kings and cries: "Holla, ye pampered jades of Asia, What! Can you draw but twenty miles a day?"

90. Tilly-fally: an indignant exclamation.   92. debuty: deputy, the representative of the alderman, and responsible for order in his ward.   101. companions: ruffians.   105. cheater: the confidence man who brings the victim along, naturally smooth-tongued and nice-mannered.   107. Barbary hen: guinea fowl. 121. charge you: give you a toast. discharge: give a toast to. 126. offend: hurt.

Compare with Caesars, and with Cannibals,°
And Trojan Greeks? Nay, rather damn them with
King Cerberus,° and let the welkin° roar.
Shall we fall foul for toys?°

HOST. By my troth, Captain, these are very bitter
words.   185

BARD. Be gone, good Ancient. This will grow to
a brawl anon.

PIST. Die men like dogs! Give crowns like pins!
Have we not Hiren here?   189

HOST. O' my word, Captain, there's none such
here. What the goodyear! Do you think I would
deny her? For God's sake, be quiet.

PIST. Then feed, and be fat, my fair Calipolis.°
Come, give's some sack.   194
"Si fortune me tormente, sperato me contento."°
Fear we broadsides? No, let the fiend give fire.
Give me some sack. And, sweetheart, lie thou there.°
                  [Laying down his sword.]
Come we to full points° here, and are etceteras
    nothing?

FAL. Pistol, I would be quiet.   199

PIST. Sweet knight. I kiss thy neaf.° What! We
have seen the seven stars.°

DOLL. For God's sake, thrust him downstairs. I
cannot endure such a fustian° rascal.

PIST. Thrust him downstairs! Know we not Gallo-
way nags?°   205

FAL. Quoit° him down, Bardolph, like a shove-
groat shilling.° Nay, an a' do nothing but speak
nothing, a' shall be nothing here.

BARD. Come, get you downstairs.

PIST. What! Shall we have incision?° Shall we
imbrue?°   *[Snatching up his sword.]*   210
Then death rock me asleep, abridge° my doleful
    days!
Why then, let grievous, ghastly, gaping wounds
Untwine the Sisters Three!° Come, Atropos, I
    say!

HOST. Here's goodly stuff toward!°

FAL. Give me my rapier, boy.   215

DOLL. I pray thee, Jack, I pray thee do not draw.

FAL. Get you downstairs.
        [Drawing, and driving PISTOL out.]

HOST. Here's a goodly tumult! I'll forswear 219
keeping house afore I'll be in these tirrits° and
frights. So, murder, I warrant now. Alas, alas! Put
up your naked weapons, put up your naked 222
weapons.   *[Exeunt PISTOL and BARDOLPH.]*

DOLL. I pray thee, Jack, be quiet. The rascal's
gone. Ah, you whoreson little valiant villain you!

HOST. Are you not hurt i' the groin? Methought
a' made a shrewd thrust at your belly.   228
                [Re-enter BARDOLPH.]

FAL. Have you turned him out o' doors?

BARD. Yea, sir. The rascal's drunk. You have hurt
him, sir, i' the shoulder.

FAL. A rascal! To brave me!   232

DOLL. Ah, you sweet little rogue you! Alas, poor
ape, how thou sweatest! Come, let me wipe thy face,
come on, you whoreson chops. Ah, rogue! i' faith,
I love thee. Thou art as valorous as Hector of Troy,
worth five of Agamemnon, and ten times better than
the Nine Worthies.° Ah, villain!   239

FAL. A rascally slave! I will toss the rogue in a
blanket.

DOLL. Do, an thou darest for thy heart. An thou
dost, I'll canvass° thee between a pair of sheets. 244
                [Enter Music.°]

PAGE. The music is come, sir.

FAL. Let them play. Play, sirs. Sit on my knee,
Doll. A rascal bragging slave! The rogue fled from
me like quicksilver.   248

DOLL. I' faith, and thou followedst him like a
church. Thou whoreson little tidy Bartholomew
boar pig,° when wilt thou leave fighting o' days
and foining° o' nights, and begin to patch up thine
old body for Heaven?   253
*[Enter, behind, PRINCE HENRY and POINS, disguised
    as drawers.]*

FAL. Peace, good Doll! Do not speak like a death's-
head.° Do not bid me remember mine end.

DOLL. Sirrah, what humor's° the Prince of?

FAL. A good shallow young fellow. A' would have
made a good pantler,° a' would ha' chipped bread
well.°   259

DOLL. They say Poins has a good wit.

FAL. He a good wit? Hang him, baboon! His wit's

18o. Cannibals: for "Hannibals." **182. King Cerberus:** Cerberus was actually the three-headed dog which guarded the entrance to Hades. **welkin:** sky. **183. toys:** trifles. **193. Then . . . Calipolis:** a quotation from Peele's *Battle of Alcazar*, where the heroic Moor, Muly Mahomet, enters with a lump of the flesh of a lioness on his sword's point to sustain his starving wife Calipolis. **195. Si . . . contento:** Pistol's version of an Italian proverb meaning "If Fortune torments me, Hope contents me." **197. sweetheart . . . there:** To clap his sword noisily on the table was a common trick of the tavern bully. Cf. *R & J*, III.i. 5–10. **198. full points:** periods. Pistol has now strayed into metaphors from writing. **200. neaf:** fist. **201. have . . . stars:** i.e., made a night of it. **203. fustian:** ranting, lit., coarse cloth. **205. Galloway nags:** Irish horses of poor quality. **206. Quoit:** chuck. **207. shovegroat shilling:** *Shovegroat* (now called shovehalf-penny) is still played in English public houses. A smooth coin is slid along the table into a numbered space. **210. incision:** bloodletting. **imbrue:** dye our swords with blood. **211. abridge:** cut off. **213. Sisters Three:** The Three Sisters of Destiny who spin man's fate, of whom Atropos was one. **214. goodly . . . toward:** here's a fine to-do.

220. tirrits: twitters. **239. Nine Worthies:** the great heroes of legend. See *LLL*, V.i. 130–50; V.ii.536–722. **244. canvass:** Doll answers with a pun on canvass, meaning toss in a blanket, and encourage, have intercourse with. **s.d., Enter Music:** i.e., musicians. **250–51. Bartholomew . . . pig:** Roast pig was one of the special attractions at St. Bartholomew's Fair, held in London on August 24. **252. foining:** thrusting. **255. death's-head:** skull, carved on memorials and elsewhere to remind the beholder of his own end. See Pl. 12f. **256. humor:** character. See App. 3. **258. pantler:** pantryman. **258–59. chipped . . . well:** chipped off the crust, one of the pantryman's jobs.

as thick as Tewksbury mustard.° There's no more conceit° in him than is in a mallet.   263

DOLL. Why does the Prince love him so, then?

FAL. Because their legs are both of a bigness; and a' plays at quoits well; and eats conger and fennel;° and drinks off candles' ends for flapdragons;° and rides the wild mare° with the boys; and jumps upon joined stools;° and swears with a good grace; and wears his boots very smooth, like unto the sign   270 of the leg;° and breeds no bate with telling of discreet stories;° and such other gambol faculties a' has that show a weak mind and an able body, for the which the Prince admits him. For the Prince himself is such another, the weight of a hair will turn the scales between their avoirdupois.   277

PRINCE. Would not this nave of a wheel° have his ears cut off?

POINS. Let's beat him before his whore.

PRINCE. Look whether the withered elder hath not his poll clawed like a parrot.°   282

POINS. Is it not strange that desire should so many years outlive performance?

FAL. Kiss me, Doll.

PRINCE. Saturn° and Venus this year in conjunction! What says the almanac to that?   287

POINS. And look whether the fiery Trigon,° his man, be not lisping to his master's old tables,° his notebook, his counsel-keeper.

FAL. Thou dost give me flattering busses.°

DOLL. By my troth, I kiss thee with a most constant° heart.

FAL. I am old, I am old.   294

DOLL. I love thee better than I love e'er a scurvy young boy of them all.

FAL. What stuff wilt have a kirtle° of? I shall receive money o' Thursday. Shalt have a cap tomorrow. A merry song, come. It grows late, we'll to bed. Thou'lt forget me when I am gone.   300

DOLL. By my troth, thou'lt set me a-weeping an thou sayest so. Prove that ever I dress myself handsome till thy return. Well, hearken at the end.°

FAL. Some sack, Francis.   305

PRINCE & POINS. Anon, anon, sir.

[*Coming forward.*]

FAL. Ha! A bastard son of the King's? And art not thou Poins his brother?

PRINCE. Why, thou globe of sinful continents,° what a life dost thou lead!   310

FAL. A better than thou. I am a gentleman, thou art a drawer.

PRINCE. Very true, sir, and I come to draw you out by the ears.   314

HOST. Oh, the Lord preserve thy good Grace! By my troth, welcome to London. Now, the Lord bless that sweet face of thine! O Jesu, are you come from Wales?

FAL. Thou whoreson mad compound° of majesty, by this light flesh and corrupt blood, thou art welcome.   321

DOLL. How, you fat fool! I scorn you.

POINS. My lord, he will drive you out of your revenge and turn all to a merriment if you take not the heat.°   325

PRINCE. You whoreson candle mine° you, how vilely did you speak of me even now before this honest, virtuous, civil gentlewoman!

HOST. God's blessing of your good heart! And so she is, by my troth.   330

FAL. Didst thou hear me?

PRINCE. Yea, and you knew me, as you did when you ran away by Gadshill. You knew I was at your back, and spoke it on purpose to try my patience.

FAL. No, no, no, not so. I did not think thou wast within hearing.   337

PRINCE. I shall drive you then to confess the willful abuse, and then I know how to handle you.

FAL. No abuse, Hal, o' mine honor, no abuse.   340

PRINCE. Not to dispraise me, and call me pantler and bread-chipper and I know not what?

FAL. No abuse, Hal.

POINS. No abuse?   344

FAL. No abuse, Ned, i' the world. Honest Ned, none. I dispraised him before the wicked, that the wicked might not fall in love with him. In which doing, I have done the part of a careful friend and a true subject, and thy father is to give me thanks for it. No abuse, Hal. None, Ned, none. No, faith, boys, none.   351

PRINCE. See now whether pure fear and entire cowardice doth not make thee wrong this virtuous gentlewoman to close with° us. Is she of the wicked? Is thine hostess here of the wicked? Or is thy boy of the wicked? Or honest Bardolph, whose zeal burns in his nose, of the wicked?   357

---

262. **Tewksbury mustard:** Tewksbury is not far from Stratford-on-Avon, and its mustard balls were famous.   263. **conceit:** inventive wit.   266. **conger . . . fennel:** conger eel flavored with fennel sauce — the kind of dish eaten only by the young and hearty.   267. **flapdragons:** lighted candles floated in a glass of drink. The drinker must drink without burning himself.   268. **rides . . . mare:** plays wild games.   269. **joined stools:** See Pl. 17a.   270–71. **sign . . . leg:** picture of a perfect leg. See App. 12.   271–72. **breeds . . . stories:** causes no trouble by telling discreet tales; i.e., all his tales are indiscreet.   278. **nave . . . wheel:** i.e., the huge round center of the wheel of a country cart.   282. **poll . . . parrot:** Doll is on Falstaff's knee, ruffling his hair.   286. **Saturn:** the father of Jupiter, and so elderly. See App. 1 and 2.   288. **fiery Trigon:** The Zodiac was divided into four trigons; the fiery trigon consisted of the fiery signs, Aries, Leo, and Sagittarius.   289. **tables:** notebook; i.e., Mrs. Quickly.   291. **busses:** kisses.   293. **constant:** faithful.   297. **kirtle:** skirt. See Pl. 9i and k and comment on p. 94b.   304. **hearken . . . end:** a form of the proverb *respice finem:* look at the end; i.e., the end will show.

309. **sinful continents:** a triple pun on the five continents, on contents, and on continence.   319. **compound:** lump.   324–25. **if . . . heat:** if you don't strike while the iron is hot.   326. **candle mine:** mass of tallow.   354. **close with:** come to terms.

POINS. Answer, thou dead elm,° answer.

FAL. The Fiend hath pricked down Bardolph ir-recoverable, and his face is Lucifer's privy° kitchen, where he doth nothing but roast maltworms. For the boy, there is a good angel about him, but the Devil outbids him too.   363

PRINCE. For the women?

FAL. For one of them, she is in Hell already, and burns° poor souls. For the other, I owe her money, and whether she be damned for that I know not.

HOST. No, I warrant you.   369

FAL. No, I think thou art not, I think thou art quit° for that. Marry, there is another indictment upon thee, for suffering flesh to be eaten in thy house contrary to the law,° for the which I think thou wilt howl.   374

HOST. All victualers do so. What's a joint of mutton or two in a whole Lent?

PRINCE. You, gentlewoman ——

DOLL. What says your Grace?

FAL. His Grace° says that which his flesh rebels against.   [*Knocking within*]   380

HOST. Who knocks so loud at door? Look to the door there, Francis.

[*Enter* PETO.]

PRINCE. Peto, how now! What news?

PETO. The King your father is at Westminster, And there are twenty weak and wearied posts°   385 Come from the North. And as I came along, I met and overtook a dozen captains, Bareheaded, sweating, knocking at the taverns, And asking every one for Sir John Falstaff.

PRINCE. By Heaven, Poins, I feel me much to blame,   390 So idly to profane the precious time, When tempest of commotion, like the south° Borne with black vapor, doth begin to melt And drop upon our bare unarmèd heads.   394 Give me my sword and cloak. Falstaff, good night.

[*Exeunt* PRINCE HENRY, POINS, PETO, *and* BARDOLPH.]

FAL. Now comes in the sweetest morsel of the night, and we must hence and leave it unpicked. [*Knocking within*] More knocking at the door! [*Re-enter* BARDOLPH.] How now! What's the matter?

BARD. You must away to court, sir, presently.° A dozen captains stay at door for you.   402

FAL. [*To the* PAGE] Pay the musicians, sirrah. Farewell, hostess. Farewell, Doll. You see, my good wenches, how men of merit are sought after. The undeserver may sleep when the man of action is

called on. Farewell, good wenches. If I be not sent away post,° I will see you again ere I go.   408

DOLL. I cannot speak, if my heart be not ready to burst —— Well, sweet Jack, have a care of thyself.

FAL. Farewell, farewell.

[*Exeunt* FALSTAFF *and* BARDOLPH.]

HOST. Well, fare thee well. I have known thee these twenty-nine years come peascod time,° but an honester and truer-hearted man —— Well, fare thee well.   415

BARD. [*Within*] Mistress Tearsheet!

HOST. What's the matter?

BARD. [*Within*] Bid Mistress Tearsheet come to my master.   419

HOST. Oh, run, Doll, run. Run, good Doll. Come. [*She comes blubbered.°*] Yea, will you come, Doll?

[*Exeunt.*]

Act III

SCENE I. *Westminster. The palace.*

[*Enter* KING HENRY *in his nightgown,° with a* PAGE.]

K. HEN. Go call the Earls of Surrey and of War-wick. But ere they come bid them o'erread these letters, And well consider of them. Make good speed.

[*Exit* PAGE.]

How many thousand of my poorest subjects Are at this hour asleep! O Sleep, O gentle Sleep,   5 Nature's soft nurse, how have I frighted thee, That thou no more wilt weigh my eyelids down And steep my senses in forgetfulness? Why rather, Sleep, liest thou in smoky cribs,° Upon uneasy° pallets° stretching thee,   10 And hushed with buzzing night flies to thy slumber, Than in the perfumed chambers of the great, Under the canopies of costly state° And lulled with sound of sweetest melody? O thou dull god, why liest thou with the vile   15 In loathsome beds and leavest the kingly couch A watch case° or a common 'larum bell?° Wilt thou upon the high and giddy mast Seal up the ship boy's eyes, and rock his brains

---

358. **dead elm:** rotten dead tree. Next to the oak, the elm is the largest in girth of English trees.   360. **privy:** private.   367. **burns:** infects.   371. **quit:** forgiven.   372–73. **flesh . . . law:** See Gen. Intro. pp. 17b–18a.   379. **His Grace:** with a pun on "grace" in the theological sense of "state of grace."   385. **posts:** messengers. See App. 17.   392. **south:** Winds from the south brought rain.   401. **presently:** immediately.

408. **post:** posthaste.   413. **peascod time:** when the peas are in pod; early summer.   421. s.d., **blubbered:** weeping. The real emotion of the two women at Falstaff's departure is to be noted.

Act III, Sc. i: s.d., **nightgown:** dressing gown.   9. **cribs:** huts. 10. **uneasy:** uncomfortable. **pallets:** mattresses.   13. **state:** pomposity. See Pl. 17b.   17. **watch case:** interpreted as (a) sentry box or (b) case of a watch — a good image, as the sleepless King is like a watch which never stops working. **'larum bell:** either (a) a bell used for sounding alarms or (b) the bell of a clock or watch.

In cradle of the rude imperious surge   20
And in the visitation of the winds,
Who take the ruffian billows by the top,
Curling their monstrous heads and hanging them
With deafening clamor in the slippery clouds,
That, with the hurly,° death itself awakes?   25
Canst thou, O partial° Sleep, give thy repose
To the wet sea boy in an hour so rude,
And in the calmest and most stillest night,
With all appliances and means to boot,°
Deny it to a king? Then happy low,° lie down!   30
Uneasy lies the head that wears a crown.

       [*Enter* WARWICK *and* SURREY.]

  WAR. Many good morrows to your Majesty!
  K. HEN. Is it good morrow, lords?
  WAR. 'Tis one o'clock, and past.
  K. HEN. Why, then, good morrow to you all, my
    lords.   35
Have you read o'er the letters that I sent you?
  WAR. We have, my liege.
  K. HEN. Then you perceive the body of our king-
    dom
How foul it is, what rank diseases grow,
And with what danger, near the heart of it.   40
  WAR. It is but as a body yet distempered,°
Which to his former strength may be restored
With good advice and little medicine.
My Lord Northumberland will soon be cooled.
  K. HEN. Oh God! that one might read the book
    of fate,   45
And see the revolution of the times
Make mountains level, and the continent,°
Weary of solid firmness, melt itself
Into the sea! And other times to see
The beachy girdle of the ocean   50
Too wide for Neptune's hips, how chances mock,
And changes fill the cup of alteration
With divers liquors! Oh, if this were seen,
The happiest youth, viewing his progress through,
What perils past, what crosses° to ensue,   55
Would shut the book, and sit him down and die.
'Tis not ten years gone
Since Richard and Northumberland, great friends,
Did feast together, and in two years after
Were they at wars. It is but eight years since   60
This Percy was the man nearest my soul,
Who like a brother toiled in my affairs,
And laid his love and life under my foot —
Yea, for my sake, even to the eyes of Richard
Gave him defiance. But which of you was by —   65

[*To* WARWICK] You, Cousin Nevil,° as I may re-
    member —
When Richard, with his eye brimful of tears,
Then checked and rated° by Northumberland,
Did speak these words, now proved a prophecy?
"Northumberland, thou ladder by the which   70
My cousin Bolingbroke ascends my throne"° —
Though then, God knows, I had no such intent,
But that necessity so bowed the state°
That I and greatness were compelled to kiss —
"The time shall come," thus did he follow it,   75
"The time will come that foul sin, gathering
    head,
Shall break into corruption." So went on
Foretelling this same time's condition,
And the division of our amity.
  WAR. There° is a history in all men's lives,   80
Figuring the nature of the times deceased.°
The which observed, a man may prophesy,
With a near aim, of the main chance of things
As yet not come to life, which in their seeds
And weak beginnings lie intreasured.   85
Such things become the hatch and brood of time,
And by the necessary form of this
King Richard might create a perfect guess
That great Northumberland, then false to him,
Would of that seed grow to a greater falseness, 90
Which should not find a ground to root upon,
Unless on you.
  K. HEN.   Are these things then necessities?
Then let us meet them like necessities.
And that same word even now cries out on us.
They say the Bishop and Northumberland   95
Are fifty thousand strong.
  WAR.   It cannot be, my lord.
Rumor doth double, like the voice and echo,
The numbers of the feared. Please it your Grace
To go to bed. Upon my soul, my lord,
The powers that you already have sent forth   100
Shall bring this prize in very easily.
To comfort you the more, I have received
A certain instance° that Glendower is dead.
Your Majesty hath been this fortnight ill,   104
And these unseasoned° hours perforce must add
Unto your sickness.
  K. HEN.   I will take your counsel.
And were these inward° wars once out of hand,
We would, dear lords, unto the Holy Land.

                        [*Exeunt.*]

---

25. **hurly:** tumult. 26. **partial:** having favorites. 29. **means to boot:** means of helping sleep — as detailed in Sir Philip Sidney's famous sonnet. "Take thou of me smooth pillows, sweetest bed, /A chamber deaf to noise and blind to light,/A rosy garland and a weary head." In this soliloquy Shakespeare makes his contribution to the large collection of Elizabethan invocations to sleep. See also *Macb*, II.ii.35–43. 30. **low:** men of lowly rank. 41. **distempered:** sick, but not fatally. 47. **continent:** land, shore. 55. **crosses:** difficulties.

66. **Nevil:** This is an anachronism. The title of Earl of Warwick in Henry IV's time was held by the Beauchamp family. 68. **rated:** abused. 70–71. **Northumberland . . . throne:** See *Rich II*, V.i.55–68. 73. **bowed . . . state:** weighed down the nation. 80–92. **There . . . you:** i.e., a man's past shows what he will be in the future. Richard could guess that as Northumberland was false to him, so would he be to you. 81. **Figuring . . . deceased:** setting out the past. 103. **instance:** proof. 105. **unseasoned:** unseasonable, late. 107. **inward:** at home.

SCENE II. *Gloucestershire. Before* JUSTICE
SHALLOW's *house*

[*Enter* SHALLOW *and* SILENCE, *meeting;* MOULDY,
SHADOW, WART, FEEBLE, BULLCALF, *a* SERVANT *or two
with them.*]

SHAL. Come on, come on, come on, sir. Give me
your hand, sir, give me your hand, sir. An early
stirrer, by the rood!° And how doth my good cousin
Silence?

SIL. Good morrow, good Cousin Shallow.   5

SHAL. And how doth my cousin your bedfellow?
And your fairest daughter and mine, my goddaugh-
ter Ellen?

SIL. Alas, a black ousel,° Cousin Shallow!   9

SHAL. By yea and nay, sir, I dare say my cousin
William is become a good scholar. He is at Oxford
still, is he not?

SIL. Indeed, sir, to my cost.   13

SHAL. A' must, then, to the Inns o' Court° shortly.
I was once of Clement's Inn, where I think they will
talk of mad Shallow yet.   16

SIL. You were called "lusty Shallow" then,
Cousin.

SHAL. By the mass, I was called anything, and I
would have done anything indeed too, and roundly°
too. There was I, and little John Doit of Stafford-
shire, and black George Barnes, and Francis Pick-
bone, and Will Squele, a Cotswold man, — you had
not four such swingebucklers° in all Inns o' Court
again. And I may say to you we knew where   25
the bona robas° were, and had the best of them all
at commandment.° Then was Jack Falstaff, now
Sir John, a boy, and page to Thomas Mowbray,
Duke of Norfolk.

SIL. This Sir John, Cousin, that comes hither anon
about soldiers?   31

SHAL. The same Sir John, the very same. I see
him break Skogan's head at the court gate when a'
was a crack° not thus high. And the very same day
did I fight with one Sampson Stockfish, a fruiterer,
behind Gray's Inn. Jesu, Jesu, the mad days that I
have spent! And to see how many of my old ac-
quaintance are dead!   38

SIL. We shall all follow, Cousin.

SHAL. Certain, 'tis certain, very sure, very sure.
Death, as the Psalmist saith, is certain to all, all
shall die. How° a good yoke of bullocks at Stam-
ford° fair?   43

SIL. By my troth, I was not there.

SHAL. Death is certain. Is old Double of your town
living yet?

SIL. Dead, sir.   47

SHAL. Jesu, Jesu, dead! A' drew a good bow, and
dead! A' shot a fine shoot. John a Gaunt° loved him
well, and betted much money on his head. Dead!
A' would have clapped i' the clout° at twelvescore,°
and carried you a forehand shaft° a fourteen and
fourteen and a half, that it would have done a man's
heart good to see. How a score of ewes now?   55

SIL. Thereafter as they be. A score of good ewes
may be worth ten pounds.

SHAL. And is old Double dead?

SIL. Here come two of Sir John Falstaff's men, as
I think.   60

[*Enter* BARDOLPH, *and one with him.*]

BARD. Good morrow, honest gentlemen. I beseech
you, which is Justice Shallow?

SHAL. I am Robert Shallow, sir, a poor esquire°
of this county, and one of the King's Justices of the
Peace. What is your good pleasure with me?   65

BARD. My captain, sir, commends him to you, my
captain, Sir John Falstaff, a tall° gentleman, by
Heaven, and a most gallant leader.

SHAL. He greets me well, sir. I knew him a good
backsword man.° How doth the good knight? May
I ask how my lady his wife doth?   71

BARD. Sir, pardon, a soldier is better accommo-
dated° than with a wife.

SHAL. It is well said, in faith, sir, and it is well
said indeed too. Better accommodated! It is good,
yea, indeed is it. Good phrases are surely, and ever
were, very commendable. Accommodated! It comes
of *accommodo.*° Very good, a good phrase.

BARD. Pardon me, sir, I have heard the word.   80
Phrase call you it? By this good day, I know not the
phrase, but I will maintain the word with my sword
to be a soldierlike word, and a word of exceeding
good command,° by Heaven. Accommodated; that
is, when a man is, as they say, accommodated;   85
or when a man is, being, whereby a' may be thought
to be accommodated. Which is an excellent thing.

SHAL. It is very just.°

[*Enter* FALSTAFF.]

Look, here comes good Sir John. Give me your good
hand, give me your Worship's good hand. By   90
my troth, you like well° and bear your years very
well. Welcome, good Sir John.

FAL. I am glad to see you well, good Master Rob-
ert Shallow. Master Surecard, as I think?   95

Sc. ii: **3. rood:** crucifix. **9. ousel:** blackbird. **14. Inns o'
Court:** See Gen. Intro. p. 31b. **20. roundly:** "made a good job
of it." **24. swingebucklers:** swashbucklers. **26. bona robas:**
showy girls. **27. at commandment:** when we wanted. **34. crack:**
small boy. **42. How:** how much. **43. Stamford:** an ancient town
in Northamptonshire.

49. John a Gaunt: father of Henry IV. See *Rich II.* **52. clapped
. . . clout:** smacked it in the center of the target. **clout:** piece of
cloth used for the bull's-eye. **twelvescore:** i.e., 240 yards.
53. forehand shaft: heavy arrow for long-range shooting. **63. es-
quire:** gentleman of superior rank, rating immediately below a
knight. **67. tall:** valiant. **70. backsword man:** expert at single-
stick. A singlestick is a stick with a basketwork protection for
the hand. **73. accommodated:** provided — at this time regarded
as rather a precious word. **79. accommodo:** i.e., I provide.
83–84. word . . . command: an exceedingly good military term.
88. just: justly said. **91. like well:** look well, thrive.

SHAL. No, Sir John, it is my cousin Silence, in commission with me.°

FAL. Good Master Silence, it well befits you should be of the peace.

SIL. Your good Worship is welcome.   100

FAL. Fie! This is hot weather, gentlemen. Have you provided me here half a dozen sufficient° men?

SHAL. Marry, have we,° sir. Will you sit?

FAL. Let me see them, I beseech you.   105

SHAL. Where's the roll? Where's the roll? Where's the roll? Let me see, let me see, let me see. So, so, so,° so, so, so, so. Yea, marry, sir. Ralph Mouldy! Let them appear as I call, let them do so, let them do so. Let me see, where is Mouldy?   111

MOUL. Here, an 't please you.

SHAL. What think you, Sir John? A good-limbed fellow, young, strong, and of good friends.°

FAL. Is thy name Mouldy?   115

MOUL. Yea, an 't please you.

FAL. 'Tis the more time thou wert used.

SHAL. Ha, ha, ha! Most excellent, i' faith! Things that are moldy lack use. Very singular good! In faith, well said, Sir John, very well said.   120

FAL. Prick° him.

MOUL. I was pricked well enough before, an you could have let me alone. My old dame° will be undone now for one to do her husbandry° and her drudgery. You need not to have pricked me, there are other men fitter to go out than I.   126

FAL. Go to. Peace, Mouldy. You shall go. Mouldy, it is time you were spent.

MOUL. Spent!

SHAL. Peace, fellow, peace, stand aside. Know you where you are? For the other, Sir John. Let me see. Simon Shadow!°   132

FAL. Yea, marry, let me have him to sit under. He's like to be a cold° soldier.

SHAL. Where's Shadow?

SHAD. Here, sir.

FAL. Shadow, whose son art thou?   137

SHAD. My mother's son, sir.

FAL. Thy mother's son! Like enough, and thy father's shadow. So the son of the female is the shadow of the male. It is often so, indeed, but much° of the father's substance!   142

SHAL. Do you like him, Sir John?

FAL. Shadow will serve for summer. Prick him, for we have a number of shadows to fill up the muster book.°   146

SHAL. Thomas Wart!

FAL. Where's he?

WART. Here, sir.

FAL. Is thy name Wart?   150

WART. Yea, sir.

FAL. Thou art a very ragged wart.

SHAL. Shall I prick him down, Sir John?

FAL. It were superfluous, for his apparel is built upon his back, and the whole frame stands upon pins. Prick him no more.   156

SHAL. Ha, ha, ha! You can do it,° sir, you can do it. I commend you well. Francis Feeble!

FEE. Here, sir.

SHAL. What trade art thou, Feeble?   160

FEE. A woman's tailor,° sir.

SHAL. Shall I prick him, sir?

FAL. You may. But if he had been a man's tailor, he'd ha' pricked you. Wilt thou make as many holes in an enemy's battle as thou hast done in a woman's petticoat?   166

FEE. I will do my goodwill, sir. You can have no more.

FAL. Well said, good woman's tailor! Well said, courageous Feeble! Thou wilt be as valiant as the wrathful dove or most magnanimous mouse. Prick the woman's tailor. Well, Master Shallow, deep, Master Shallow.   173

FEE. I would Wart might have gone, sir.

FAL. I would thou wert a man's tailor, that thou mightst mend him and make him fit to go. I cannot put him to a private soldier that is the leader of so many thousands.° Let that suffice, most forcible Feeble.

FEE. It shall suffice, sir.   180

FAL. I am bound to thee, reverend Feeble. Who is next?

SHAL. Peter Bullcalf o' the green!

FAL. Yea, marry, let's see Bullcalf.

BULL. Here, sir.   185

FAL. 'Fore God, a likely fellow! Come, prick me Bullcalf till he roar again.

BULL. Oh Lord! Good my lord Captain ——

FAL. What, dost thou roar before thou art pricked?

BULL. Oh Lord, sir! I am a diseased man.   191

FAL. What disease hast thou?

BULL. A whoreson cold, sir, a cough, sir, which I caught with ringing in the King's affairs upon his coronation day,° sir.   195

FAL. Come, thou shalt go to the wars in a gown, we will have away thy cold, and I will take such order that thy friends shall ring for thee. Is here all?   199

SHAL. Here is two more called than your number.

---

97. in . . . me: he also holds a commission of the peace; i.e., is a magistrate.   102. sufficient: fit.   104. have we: we certainly have.   109. So . . . so: *So* used thus in dialogue usually indicates action or gesture. Shallow checks off the recruits from their names on the roll.   114. of . . . friends: i.e., comes of decent family.   121. Prick: mark him down on the list. The names of those selected from a list were actually pricked with a pin.   123. dame: mother.   124. husbandry: farm work.   132. Shadow: See Gen. Intro. p. 30b.   134. cold: with a pun on *cold*, meaning unwilling.   141. much: not much.   146. muster book: nominal roll.

157. You . . . it: you are a wit.   161. woman's tailor: Like modern male designers of women's wear, often a feeble specimen of manhood.   178. many thousands: i.e., lice.   195. coronation day: accession day, observed as an annual holiday. See App. 19.

You must have but four here, sir. And so I pray you go in with me to dinner.

FAL. Come, I will go drink with you, but I cannot tarry dinner. I am glad to see you, by my troth, Master Shallow.   205

SHAL. Oh, Sir John, do you remember since we lay all night in the windmill in Saint George's field?°

FAL. No more of that, good Master Shallow, no more of that.

SHAL. Ha! 'Twas a merry night. And is Jane Nightwork alive?   211

FAL. She lives, Master Shallow.

SHAL. She never could away with° me.

FAL. Never, never. She would always say she could not abide Master Shallow.   215

SHAL. By the mass, I could anger her to the heart. She was then a bona roba. Doth she hold her own well?

FAL. Old, old, Master Shallow.   219

SHAL. Nay, she must be old, she cannot choose but be old, certain she's old, and had Robin Nightwork by old Nightwork before I came to Clement's Inn.

SIL. That's fifty-five year ago.   224

SHAL. Ha, Cousin Silence, that thou hadst seen that that this knight and I have seen! Ha, Sir John, said I well?

FAL. We have heard the chimes at midnight, Master Shallow.   229

SHAL. That we have, that we have, that we have —in faith, Sir John, we have. Our watchword was "Hem boys!"° Come, let's to dinner, come, let's to dinner. Jesus, the days that we have seen! Come, come.   [Exeunt FALSTAFF and the JUSTICES.] 234

BULL. Good Master Corporate° Bardolph, stand my friend, and here's four Harry ten shillings in French crowns° for you. In very truth, sir, I had as lief° be hanged, sir, as go. And yet, for mine own 240 part, sir, I do not care, but rather because I am unwilling, and, for mine own part, have a desire to stay with my friends. Else, sir, I did not care, for mine own part, so much.

BARD. Go to, stand aside.   243

MOUL. And, good Master Corporal Captain, for my old dame's sake, stand my friend. She has nobody to do anything about her when I am gone, and she is old and cannot help herself. You shall have forty,° sir.

BARD. Go to, stand aside.   249

FEE. By my troth, I care not, a man can die but once. We owe God a death. I'll ne'er bear a base

mind. An 't° be my destiny, so; an 't be not, so. No man's too good to serve 's prince, and let it go which way it will, he that dies this year is quit° for the next.   255

BARD. Well said. Thou'rt a good fellow.

FEE. Faith, I'll bear no base mind.

[Re-enter FALSTAFF and the JUSTICES.]

FAL. Come, sir, which men shall I have?

SHAL. Four of which you please.

BARD. Sir, a word with you. I have three pound to free Mouldy and Bullcalf.   261

FAL. Go to. Well.

SHAL. Come, Sir John, which four will you have?

FAL. Do you choose for me.

SHAL. Marry, then, Mouldy, Bullcalf, Feeble, and Shadow.   267

FAL. Mouldy and Bullcalf. For you, Mouldy, stay at home till you are past service. And for your part, Bullcalf, grow till you come unto it. I will none of you.

SHAL. Sir John, Sir John, do not yourself wrong. They are your likeliest men, and I would have you served with the best.   274

FAL. Will you tell me, Master Shallow, how to choose a man? Care I for the limb, the thews,° the stature, bulk, and big assemblance° of a man! Give me the spirit, Master Shallow. Here's Wart. You see what a ragged appearance it is. A' shall charge you and discharge° you with the motion of a 280 pewterer's hammer,° come off and on swifter than he that gibbets on the brewer's bucket.° And this same half-faced° fellow, Shadow. Give me this man. He presents no mark to the enemy, the foeman may with as great aim level at the edge of a pen- 285 knife. And for a retreat, how swiftly will this Feeble the woman's tailor run off! Oh, give me the spare men, and spare me the great ones. Put me a caliver° into Wart's hand, Bardolph.   290

BARD. Hold, Wart, traverse.° Thus, thus, thus.

FAL. Come, manage me your caliver. So. Very well. Go to. Very good, exceeding good. Oh, give me always a little, lean, old, chapped,° bald shot. Well said, i' faith, Wart, thou'rt a good scab. Hold, there's a tester° for thee.   296

SHAL. He is not his craft's master, he doth not do it right. I remember at Mile End Green, when I lay at Clement's Inn — I was then Sir Dagonet in Ar-

252. An't: if it.   254. quit: exempt.   276. thews: sinews,
277. assemblance: composition, frame.   279–80. charge . . . dis-
charge: load and fire. See Pl. 22f, and p. 99a.   281. pewter-
er's hammer: when pewter is handwrought with a hammer,
the pewterer keeps up a quick, even beat.   282. gibbets . . .
bucket: The brewer's man was equipped with a wooden yoke
on his shoulder; at either end hung a chain and hook to which
he attached a bucket. gibbets: hangs.   283. half-faced: thin-
faced.   289. caliver: light musket used by the infantry. See Pl.
22f.   291. traverse: quick march. Here Wart is put through the
drill by Bardolph and Falstaff.   294. chapped: dry-skinned.
296. tester: sixpence.

207. Saint . . . field: an open district west of Southwark in
London — a low neighborhood.   213. could . . . with: could en-
dure.   232. Hem boys: one of those meaninglessly convivial cries,
like "Here's how."   235. Corporate: corporal.   236–37. Harry
. . . crowns: When Shakespeare wrote the play a Henry VII ten
shillings was worth 5s, and a French crown 4s. Bullcalf's con-
tribution was in all worth £1.   239. lief: soon.   247. forty: i.e.,
shillings.

thur's show° — there was a little quiver° fel-   300
low, and a' would manage you his piece thus, and a'
would about and about, and come you in and come
you in. " Rah, tah, tah,"° would a' say, " Bounce "°
would a' say, and away again would a' go, and again
would a' come. I shall ne'er see such a fellow.   306

FAL. These fellows will do well, Master Shallow.
God keep you, Master Silence. I will not use many
words with you. Fare you well, gentlemen both. I
thank you. I must a dozen mile tonight. Bardolph,
give the soldiers coats.   311

SHAL. Sir John, the Lord bless you! God prosper
your affairs! God send us peace! At your return visit
our house, let our old acquaintance be renewed.
Peradventure I will with ye to the court.   316

FAL. 'Fore God, I would you would, Master
Shallow.

SHAL. Go to, I have spoke at a word.° God keep
you.   320

FAL. Fare you well, gentle gentlemen. [*Exeunt*
JUSTICES.] On, Bardolph, lead the men away.
[*Exeunt* BARDOLPH, RECRUITS, *etc.*] As I return, I
will fetch off° these Justices. I do see the bottom of
Justice Shallow. Lord, Lord, how subject we   325
old men are to this vice of lying! This same starved
Justice hath done nothing but prate to me of the
wildness of his youth, and the feats he hath done
about Turnbull Street,° and every third word a lie,
duer° paid to the hearer than the Turk's trib-   330
ute.° I do remember him at Clement's Inn like a
man made after supper of a cheeseparing. When a'
was naked, he was for all the world like a forked
radish, with a head fantastically carved upon it with
a knife. A' was so forlorn that his dimensions   335
to any thick° sight were invisible. A' was the very
genius of famine, yet lecherous as a monkey, and
the whores called him mandrake.° A' came ever in
the rearward of the fashion, and sung those tunes
to the overscutched° huswives that he heard   340
the carmen whistle, and sware they were his fancies
or his good nights.° And now is this Vice's dagger°
become a squire, and talks as familiarly of John a
Gaunt as if he had been sworn brother to him, and

I'll be sworn a' ne'er saw him but once in the   345
tiltyard and then he burst his head for crowding
among the Marshal's men.° I saw it, and told John
a Gaunt he beat his own name, for you might have
thrust him and all his apparel into an eelskin, the
case of a treble hautboy° was a mansion for   350
him, a court. And now has he land and beefs. Well,
I'll be acquainted with him if I return, and it shall
go hard but I will make him a philosopher's two
stones° to me. If the young dace° be a bait for the
old pike, I see no reason in the law of nature   355
but I may snap at him. Let time shape, and there an
end.   [*Exit.*]

Act IV

SCENE I. *Yorkshire. Gaultree Forest.*

[*Enter the* ARCHBISHOP OF YORK, MOWBRAY,
HASTINGS, *and others.*]

ARCH. What is this forest called?

HAST. 'Tis Gaultree Forest, an 't shall please your
Grace.

ARCH. Here stand, my lords, and send discover-
ers° forth
To know the numbers of our enemies.

HAST. We have sent forth already.

ARCH.   'Tis well done.
My friends and brethren in these great affairs,   6
I must acquaint you that I have received
New-dated letters from Northumberland,
Their cold intent, tenor and substance, thus:
Here doth he wish his person, with such powers   10
As might hold sortance with his quality,°
The which he could not levy, whereupon
He is retired, to ripe° his growing fortunes,
To Scotland. And concludes in hearty prayers
That your attempts may overlive° the hazard   15
And fearful meeting of their opposite.°

MOWB. Thus do the hopes we have in him touch
ground
And dash themselves to pieces.

            [*Enter a* MESSENGER.]

HAST.   Now, what news?

---

300. Arthur's show: an archery club in which each of the members took the name of one of King Arthur's knights. Dagonet was Arthur's fool. quiver: nimble.   304. Rah . . . tah: imitation of drumbeats. The drum was used to give commands to the infantry. Bounce: bang! The description of the action of the shot is accurate. The front rank of marksmen came forward with their pieces loaded, fired, and then withdrew to the rear to reload. 319. spoke . . . word: mean what I say. 324. fetch off: get the better of. 329. Turnbull Street: a red-light district. 330. duer: more promptly when due. 330-31. Turk's tribute: The Turks were greatly feared by the peoples of the Mediterranean, and tribute demanded by the Turks was promptly paid. 336. thick: near. 338. mandrake: See I.ii.17n. 340. overscutched: often whipped — because they had played the whore. 342. fancies . . . nights: his love songs or his lullabies. Vice's dagger: wooden dagger — thin and harmless. See *T Night*, IV.ii. 134-41,n.

347. Marshal's men: The Knight Marshal was the Court official directly responsible for keeping order in the Court and its precincts. 350. hautboy: oboe, a long narrow wind instrument. 353-54. philosopher's . . . stones: i.e., the notions of transmuting base metal into gold and of compounding the elixir of life which would give perpetual youth. See App. 21. 354. dace: small fish used as live bait for pike.

Act IV, Sc. i: 3. discoverers: scouts. 11. hold . . . quality: be suitable to his rank. 13. ripe: make ripe. 15. overlive: survive. 16. opposite: opponent.

MESS. West of this forest, scarcely off a mile,
In goodly form° comes on the enemy,   20
And by the ground they hide I judge their number
Upon or near the rate of thirty thousand.

MOWB. The just proportion° that we gave them
    out.°
Let us sway° on and face them in the field.

ARCH. What well-appointed° leader fronts us
    here?   25

[*Enter* WESTMORELAND.]

MOWB. I think it is my Lord of Westmoreland.

WEST. Health and fair greeting from our general,
The Prince, Lord John and Duke of Lancaster.

ARCH. Say on, my Lord of Westmoreland, in
    peace.
What doth concern your coming?

WEST.   Then, my lord,   30
Unto your Grace do I in chief address
The substance of my speech. If that rebellion
Came like itself, in base and abject routs,°
Led on by bloody youth, guarded° with rags,
And countenanced° by boys and beggary —   35
I say if damned commotion° so appeared,
In his true, native, and most proper shape,
You, Reverend Father, and these noble lords
Had not been here, to dress the ugly form
Of base and bloody insurrection   40
With your fair honors. You, Lord Archbishop,
Whose see° is by a civil° peace maintained,
Whose beard the silver hand of peace hath touched,
Whose learning and good letters° peace hath tu-
    tored,
Whose white investments° figure innocence,   45
The dove and very blessed spirit of peace,
Wherefore do you so ill translate yourself
Out of the speech of peace that bears such grace
Into the harsh and boisterous tongue of war,
Turning your books to graves, your ink to blood,   50
Your pens to lances, and your tongue divine
To a loud trumpet and a point° of war?

ARCH. Wherefore do I this? So the question
    stands.
Briefly to this end: We are all diseased,
And with our surfeiting and wanton° hours   55
Have brought ourselves into a burning fever,
And we must bleed° for it. Of which disease
Our late King, Richard, being infected, died.
But,° my most noble Lord of Westmoreland,

I take not on me here as a physician,   60
Nor do I as an enemy to peace
Troop in the throngs of military men,
But rather show awhile like fearful war,
To diet rank° minds sick of happiness
And purge the obstructions which begin to stop   65
Our very veins of life. Hear me more plainly.
I have in equal° balance justly weighed
What wrongs our arms may do, what wrongs we
    suffer,
And find our griefs° heavier than our offenses.
We see which way the stream of time doth run,   70
And are enforced from our most quiet there
By the rough torrent of occasion,°
And have the summary of all our griefs,
When time shall serve, to show in articles,°
Which long ere this we offered to the King,   75
And might by no suit° gain our audience.°
When we are wronged and would unfold our
    griefs,
We are denied access unto his person
Even by those men that most have done us wrong.
The dangers of the days but newly gone,   80
Whose memory is written on the earth
With yet appearing blood, and the examples
Of every minute's instance,° present now,
Hath put us in these ill-beseeming° arms,
Not to break peace or any branch of it,   85
But to establish here a peace indeed,
Concurring both in name and quality.°

WEST. When ever yet was your appeal denied?
Wherein have you been gallèd° by the King?
What peer hath been suborned° to grate on° you,
That you should seal this lawless bloody book   91
Of forged rebellion with a seal divine,°
And consecrate commotion's bitter edge?°

ARCH. My brother general, the commonwealth,
To brother born a household cruelty,   95
I make my quarrel in particular.°

WEST. There is no need of any such redress,
Or if there were, it not belongs to you.

MOWB. Why not to him in part, and to us all
That feel the bruises of the days before,   100
And suffer the condition of these times

20. form: formation. 23. just proportion: exact estimate. gave
. . . out: reported. 24. sway: push. 25. well-appointed: well-
armed. 33. routs: mobs. 34. guarded: adorned, ornamented.
35. countenanced: supported. 36. commotion: riot. 42. see:
the ecclesiastical district controlled by the Archbishop. civil:
well-ordered. 44. good letters: wide reading. 45. investments:
vestments. 52. point: trumpet call. 55. surfeiting . . . wanton:
gluttonous and frivolous. 57. bleed: be let blood, a normal
treatment for fever. 59–66. But . . . life: i.e., but I do not intend
to be a physician and cure by bleeding, but rather by wholesome
diet and purges.

64. rank: a medical term meaning in a condition requiring blood-
letting. 67. equal: exact. 69. griefs: grievances. 72. occasion:
circumstances. 74. in articles: detailed in a schedule. 76. suit:
petition. audience: personal hearing. 82–83. examples . . . in-
stance: examples of which each minute gives fresh instances.
84. ill-beseeming: unseemly. 87. Concurring . . . quality: which
shall agree in name and nature; i.e., be a genuine peace.
89. galled: made sore. 90. suborned: procured. grate on: annoy.
91–92. you . . . divine: you should fix your divine seal as guaran-
teeing the forged deed of rebellion. book: deed, document.
93. edge: sword. 94–96. My . . . particular: These difficult lines
have been much annotated. As they stand, they are unintel-
ligible. Most commentators suspect that something has been left
out. Dr. Johnson, who amended *brother* in l. 94 to *quarrel*, ex-
plained *brother* in l. 95 as a reference to the Archbishop's own
brother put to death by the King. See *I Hen IV,* I.iii.270.

To lay a heavy and unequal° hand
Upon our honors?
    WEST.   Oh, my good Lord Mowbray,
Construe the times to their necessities,°
And you shall say indeed it is the time,   105
And not the King, that doth you injuries.
Yet for your part, it not appears to me
Either from the King or in the present time
That you should have an inch of any ground
To build a grief on. Were you not restored   110
To all the Duke of Norfolk's signories,°
Your noble and right well remembered father's?
    MOWB. What thing, in honor, had my father lost
That need to be revived and breathed in me?   114
The King that loved him, as the state stood then,
Was force perforce° compelled to banish him.
And then that Henry Bolingbroke° and he,
Being mounted and both rousèd in their seats,°
Their neighing coursers daring° of the spur,   119
Their armèd staves in charge,° their beavers° down,
Their eyes of fire sparkling through sights of
    steel
And the loud trumpet blowing them together —
Then, then, when there was nothing could have
    stayed
My father from the breast of Bolingbroke,
Oh, when the King did throw his warder° down,
His own life hung upon the staff he threw.   126
Then threw he down himself and all their lives
That by indictment° and by dint° of sword
Have since miscarried under Bolingbroke.
    WEST. You speak, Lord Mowbray, now you know
    not what.   130
The Earl of Hereford was reputed then
In England the most valiant gentleman.
Who knows on whom fortune would then have
    smiled?
But if your father had been victor there,
He ne'er had borne it out° of Coventry.   135
For all the country in a general voice
Cried hate upon him, and all their prayers and
    love
Were set on Hereford, whom they doted on
And blessed and graced° indeed, more than the
    King.
But this is mere digression from my purpose.   140
Here come I from our princely General
To know your griefs, to tell you from His Grace
That he will give you audience, and wherein

It shall appear that your demands are just,
You shall enjoy them, everything set off°   145
That might so much as think you enemies.
    MOWB. But he hath forced us to compel this offer,
And it proceeds from policy,° not love.
    WEST. Mowbray, you overween° to take it so.
This offer comes from mercy, not from fear.   150
For, lo! within a ken° our army lies,
Upon mine honor, all too confident
To give admittance to a thought of fear.
Our battle° is more full of names° than yours,
Our men more perfect in the use of arms,   155
Our armor all as strong, our cause the best.
Then reason will our hearts should be as good.
Say you not then our offer is compelled.
    MOWB. Well, by my will we shall admit no parley.
    WEST. That argues but the shame of your offense.
A rotten case abides no handling.   161
    HAST. Hath the Prince John a full commission,°
In very ample virtue° of his father,
To hear and absolutely to determine
Of what conditions we shall stand upon?   165
    WEST. That is intended in the General's name.°
I muse° you make so slight a question.
    ARCH. Then take, my Lord of Westmoreland, this
    schedule,
For this contains our general grievances.
Each° several article herein redressed,   170
All members of our cause, both here and hence,
That are insinewed to this action,
Acquitted by a true substantial form,
And present execution of our wills
To us and to our purposes confined,   175
We come within our awful banks again,
And knit our powers to the arm of peace.
    WEST. This will I show the General. Please you.
    lords,
In sight of both our battles we may meet,
And either end in peace — which God so frame!° —
Or to the place of difference° call the swords   181
Which must decide it.
    ARCH. My lord, we will do so.
                             [*Exit* WESTMORELAND.]
    MOWB. There is a thing within my bosom tells me

102. unequal: unjust. 104. Construe . . . necessities: remember that in these lawless times injustices must often be committed. construe: interpret. 111. signories: estates. 116. force perforce: forced by necessity, willy-nilly. 117. And . . . Bolingbroke: For this episode, see *Rich II*, I.iii. 100–18. 118. roused . . . seats: raised in their saddles. 119. daring: not afraid, eager for. 120. staves in charge: lances leveled in readiness. beaver: visor, face piece of the helmet. See Pl. 8a. 125. warder: staff. 128. indictment: legal accusation. dint: stroke. 135. ne'er . . . out: would not have got out alive. 139. graced: favored.

145. set off: laid aside, forgotten. 148. policy: cunning. 149. overween: presume. 151. ken: lit., the limit of sight, 20 miles. 154. battle: army drawn up for battle. names: distinguished leaders. 162. commission: written authority signed by the King. 163. virtue: power. 166. intended . . . name: naturally included as part of a general's powers. 167. muse: marvel. 170–77. Each . . . peace: when each separate (*several*) article of this schedule has been redressed, and when all the members who have made common cause with us, be they here or elsewhere (*hence*), that are joined by strong sinews (*insinewed*) to this action, and have been acquitted of any crime in proper legal form, and when our desires (*wills*) have been immediately satisfied (*executed*) but confined to what we intended, then will we return to the limits of due obedience (*awful banks*), and restore our army to peaceful labor. 180. frame: fashion, accomplish. 181. difference: dispute, battle.

That no conditions of our peace can stand.

HAST. Fear you not that. If we can make our
   peace   185
Upon such large terms and so absolute
As our conditions shall consist upon,
Our peace shall stand as firm as rocky mountains.

MOWB. Yea, but our valuation° shall be such
That every slight and false-derivèd cause —   190
Yea, every idle,° nice° and wanton° reason —
Shall to the King taste° of this action,
That, were our royal faiths martyrs in love,°
We shall be winnowed with so rough a wind
That even our corn shall seem as light as chaff   195
And good from bad find no partition.°

ARCH. No, no, my lord. Note this. The King is
   weary
Of dainty° and such picking° grievances.
For he hath found to end one doubt by death
Revives two greater in the heirs of life,°   200
And therefore will he wipe his tables° clean,
And keep no telltale to his memory
That may repeat and history his loss
To new remembrance. For full well he knows
He cannot so precisely weed this land   205
As his misdoubts present occasion.°
His foes are so enrooted with his friends
That, plucking to unfix an enemy,
He doth unfasten so and shake a friend.
So that this land, like an offensive wife   210
That hath enraged him on to offer strokes,
As he is striking, holds his infant up,
And hangs resolved correction° in the arm
That was upreared to execution.

HAST. Besides, the King hath wasted all his rods
On late offenders, that he now doth lack   216
The very instruments of chastisement.
So that his power, like to a fangless lion,
May offer,° but not hold.

ARCH.   'Tis very true.
And therefore be assured, my good Lord Marshal,
If we do now make our atonement° well,   221
Our peace will, like a broken limb united,
Grow stronger for the breaking.

MOWB.   Be it so.
Here is returned my Lord of Westmoreland.

   [*Re-enter* WESTMORELAND.]

WEST. The Prince is here at hand. Pleaseth your
   lordship   225

---

189. our valuation: the value set on us. 191. idle: slight.
nice: trivial. wanton: frivolous. 192. taste: seem to remind.
193. our . . . love: even if our faith in the King made us martyrs
to show our love; i.e., even if we suffered death to prove our
loyalty. 196. partition: separation. 198. dainty: precise. pick-
ing: petty, finicking. 199–200. end . . . life: i.e., for every man
put to death as a traitor, two others are born. 201. tables: note-
book. 206. misdoubts . . . occasion: suspicions give him cause.
213. hangs . . . correction: prevents his arm from making the in-
tended blow. 219. offer: threaten. 221. atonement: reconcili-
ation.

To meet His Grace just° distance 'tween our armies.

MOWB. Your Grace of York, in God's name, then,
   set forward.

ARCH. Before, and greet His Grace. My lord, we
   come.   [*Exeunt.*]

SCENE II. *Another part of the forest.*

[*Enter, from one side,* MOWBRAY, *attended; after-
ward, the* ARCHBISHOP, HASTINGS, *and others; from
the other side,* PRINCE JOHN OF LANCASTER, *and*
WESTMORELAND; OFFICERS, *and others with them.*]

LANC. You are well encountered here, my Cousin
   Mowbray.
Good day to you, gentle Lord Archbishop,
And so to you, Lord Hastings, and to all.
My Lord of York, it better showed with you
When that your flock, assembled by the bell,   5
Encircled you to hear with reverence
Your exposition on the holy text
Than now to see you here an iron man,°
Cheering a rout of rebels with your drum,
Turning the word to sword and life to death.   10
That man that sits within a monarch's heart,
And ripens in the sunshine of his favor,
Would he abuse the countenance of the King,
Alack, what mischiefs might he set abroach°
In shadow of such greatness! With you, Lord Bishop,
It is even so. Who hath not heard it spoken   16
How deep you were within the books of God?
To us the Speaker in His parliament,
To us the imagined voice of God Himself,
The very opener and intelligencer°   20
Between the grace, the sanctities of Heaven
And our dull workings.° Oh, who shall believe
But you misuse the reverence of your place,
Employ the countenance and grace of Heaven
As a false favorite doth his Prince's name,   25
In deeds dishonorable? You have ta'en up,
Under the counterfeited zeal of God,
The subjects of His substitute,° my father,
And both against the peace of Heaven and him
Have here upswarmed° them.

ARCH.   Good my Lord of Lancaster,   30
I am not here against your father's peace,
But, as I told my Lord of Westmoreland,
The time misordered doth, in common sense,
Crowd us and crush° us to this monstrous° form,
To hold our safety up.° I sent your Grace   35
The parcels° and particulars of our grief,

---

226. just: exact.
   Sc. ii: 8. iron man: man in armor. 14. set abroach: set going.
abroach: lit., tapped, like a cask. 20. intelligencer: agent.
22. workings: mental processes. 28. substitute: deputy. 30. up-
swarmed: raised up in swarms. 34. crush: compel. monstrous:
unnatural. 35. hold . . . up: support our own safety. 36. par-
cels: items.

The which hath been with scorn shoved from the
   Court,
Whereon this Hydra° son of war is born,
Whose dangerous eyes may well be charmed asleep
With grant of our most just and right desires,   40
And true obedience, of this madness cured,
Stoop tamely to the foot of majesty.
   MOWB. If not, we ready are to try our fortunes
To the last man.
   HAST.   And though we here fall down,
We have supplies° to second° our attempt.   45
If they miscarry, theirs shall second them,
And so success of mischief° shall be born,
And heir from heir shall hold this quarrel up
Whiles England shall have generation.
   LANC. You are too shallow, Hastings, much to
   shallow,   50
To sound° the bottom of the aftertimes.
   WEST. Pleaseth your Grace to answer them di-
   rectly
How far forth you do like their articles.
   LANC. I like them all, and do allow them well,
And swear here, by the honor of my blood,   55
My father's purposes have been mistook,
And some about him have too lavishly
Wrested° his meaning and authority.
My lord, these griefs shall be with speed redressed,
Upon my soul, they shall. If this may please you,   60
Discharge your powers unto their several counties,
As we will ours. And here between the armies
Let's drink together friendly and embrace,
That all their eyes may bear those tokens home°
Of our restorèd love and amity.   65
   ARCH. I take your princely word for these re-
   dresses.
   LANC. I give it you, and will maintain my word.
And thereupon I drink unto your Grace.
   HAST. Go, Captain, and deliver to the army   69
This news of peace. Let them have pay, and part.
I know it will well please them. Hie thee,° Captain.
                       [*Exit* OFFICER.]
   ARCH. To you, my noble Lord of Westmoreland.
   WEST. I pledge your Grace, and, if you knew what
   pains
I have bestowed to breed this present peace,
You would drink freely. But my love to ye   75
Shall show itself more openly hereafter.
   ARCH. I do not doubt you.
   WEST.   I am glad of it.
Health to my lord and gentle Cousin Mowbray.
   MOWB. You wish me health in very happy season,
For I am, on the sudden, something ill.   80

   ARCH. Against ill chances men are ever merry,
But heaviness foreruns the good event.°
   WEST. Therefore be merry, Coz, since sudden
   sorrow
Serves to say thus, "Some good thing comes to-
   morrow."   84
   ARCH. Believe me, I am passing° light in spirit.
   MOWB. So much the worse, if your own rule be
   true.   [*Shouts within*]
   LANC. The word of peace is rendered. Hark how
   they shout!
   MOWB. This had been cheerful after victory.
   ARCH. A peace is of the nature of a conquest,
For then both parties nobly are subdued,   90
And neither party loser.
   LANC.   Go, my lord,
And let our army be dischargèd too.
                   [*Exit* WESTMORELAND.]
And, good my lord, so please you, let our trains°
March by us, that we may peruse the men
We should have coped° withal.
   ARCH.   Go, good Lord Hastings,   95
And ere they be dismissed let them march by.
                      [*Exit* HASTINGS.]
   LANC. I trust, lords, we shall lie tonight together.
[*Re-enter* WESTMORELAND.] Now, Cousin, wherefore
   stands our army still?
   WEST. The leaders, having charge from you to
   stand,
Will not go off until they hear you speak.   100
   LANC. They know their duties.
                   [*Re-enter* HASTINGS.]
   HAST. My lord, our army is dispersed already.
Like youthful steers unyoked, they take their courses
East, west, north, south, or, like a school broke up,
Each hurries toward his home and sporting place.°
   WEST. Good tidings, my Lord Hastings, for the
   which   106
I do arrest thee, traitor, of high treason.
And you, Lord Archbishop, and you, Lord Mow-
   bray.
Of capital° treason I attach° you both.
   MOWB. Is this proceeding just and honorable?
   WEST. Is your assembly so?   111
   ARCH. Will you thus break your faith?
   LANC.   I pawned° thee none.
I promised you redress of these same grievances
Whereof you did complain, which, by mine honor,
I will perform with a most Christian care.   115
But for you, rebels, look to taste the due
Meet for rebellion and such acts as yours.
Most shallowly did you these arms commence,
Fondly° brought here, and foolishly sent hence.
Strike up our drums, pursue the scattered stray.°

38. Hydra: a many-headed monster slain by Hercules. 45. sup-
plies: reinforcements. second: support. 47. success of mischief:
succession of mischief; i.e., son following father. 51. sound: to
discover the depth by sounding. 58. Wrested: wrenched.
64. bear. . . home: carry home the report of our pledges (*tokens*)
of reconciliation. 71. Hie thee: hasten.

82. event: sequel. 85. passing: exceedingly. 93. trains: follow-
ers. 95. coped: encountered. 105. sporting place: playground.
109. capital: deserving death. attach: arrest. 112. pawned:
pledged. 119. Fondly: foolishly. 120. stray: stragglers.

God, and not we, hath safely fought today.   121
Some guard these traitors to the block of death,
Treason's true bed and yielder-up of breath.

[*Exeunt.*]

SCENE III. *Another part of the forest.*

[*Alarum. Excursions.° Enter* FALSTAFF *and*
COLEVILE, *meeting.*]

FAL. What's your name, sir? Of what condition°
are you, and of what place, I pray?

COLE. I am a knight, sir, and my name is Cole-
vile of the Dale.   4

FAL. Well, then, Colevile is your name, a knight
is your degree, and your place the dale. Colevile
shall be still your name, a traitor your degree, and
the dungeon your place, a place deep enough, so
shall you be still Colevile of the Dale.   10

COLE. Are not you Sir John Falstaff?

FAL. As good a man as he, sir, whoe'er I am. Do
ye yield, sir? Or shall I sweat for you? If I do sweat,
they are the drops° of thy lovers, and they weep for
thy death. Therefore rouse up fear and trembling,
and do observance to my mercy.   17

COLE. I think you are Sir John Falstaff, and in
that thought yield me.

FAL. I have a whole school° of tongues in this
belly of mine, and not a tongue of them all speaks
any other word but my name. An I had but a belly
of any indifferency,° I were simply the most   23
active fellow in Europe. My womb,° my womb, my
womb undoes me. Here comes our General.

[*Enter* PRINCE JOHN OF LANCASTER, WESTMORELAND,
BLUNT, *and others.*]

LANC. The heat° is past, follow no further now.
Call in the powers, good Cousin Westmoreland.   28

[*Exit* WESTMORELAND.]

Now, Falstaff, where have you been all this while?
When everything is ended, then you come.
These tardy tricks of yours will, on my life,
One time or other break some gallows' back.   32

FAL. I would be sorry, my lord, but it should be
thus. I never knew yet but rebuke and check was the
reward of valor. Do you think me a swallow, an ar-
row, or a bullet? Have I, in my poor and old   36
motion, the expedition° of thought? I have speeded
hither with the very extremest inch of possibility, I
have foundered ninescore and odd posts.° And here,
travel-tainted as I am, have, in my pure and im-
maculate valor, taken Sir John Colevile of the Dale,
a most furious knight and valorous enemy. But   42

what of that? He saw me, and yielded, that I may
justly say, with the hook-nosed fellow of Rome,°
" I came, saw, and overcame."

LANC. It was more of his courtesy than your de-
serving.   48

FAL. I know not. Here he is, and here I yield him.
And I beseech your Grace let it be booked with the
rest of this day's deeds, or, by the Lord, I will have
it in a particular ballad° else, with mine own picture
on the top on 't, Colevile kissing my foot. To the
which course if I be enforced, if you do not all show
like gilt twopences to me, and I in the clear sky   55
of fame o'ershine you as much as the full moon doth
the cinders of the element,° which show like pins'
heads to her, believe not the word of the noble.
Therefore let me have right, and let desert mount.

LANC. Thine's too heavy to mount.   62

FAL. Let it shine, then.

LANC. Thine's too thick to shine.

FAL. Let it do something, my good lord, that may
do me good, and call it what you will.   66

LANC. Is thy name Colevile?

COLE. It is, my lord.

LANC. A famous rebel art thou, Colevile.

FAL. And a famous true subject took him.   70

COLE. I am, my lord, but as my betters are
That led me hither. Had they been ruled by me,
You should have won them dearer than you have.

FAL. I know not how they sold themselves. But
thou, like a kind fellow, gavest thyself away gratis,
and I thank thee for thee.   76

[*Re-enter* WESTMORELAND.]

LANC. Now, have you left pursuit?

WEST. Retreat is made and execution° stayed.°

LANC. Send Colevile with his confederates
To York, to present° execution.   80
Blunt, lead him hence, and see you guard him
  sure.

[*Exeunt* BLUNT *and others with* COLEVILE.]

And now dispatch we toward the Court, my lords.
I hear the King my father is sore sick.
Our news shall go before us to His Majesty,
Which, Cousin, you shall bear to comfort him,   85
And we with sober speed will follow you.

FAL. My lord, I beseech you give me leave to go
Through Gloucestershire. And when you come to
  Court,
Stand my good lord, pray, in your good report.   89

LANC. Fare you well, Falstaff. I, in my condition,°
Shall better speak of you than you deserve.

[*Exeunt all except* FALSTAFF.]

FAL. I would you had but the wit. 'Twere better
than your dukedom. Good faith, this same young

Sc. iii: s.d., **Alarum. Excursions:** noises indicating the call
to arms and battle. **1. condition:** rank. **15. drops:** tears.
20. school: shoal. **23. indifferency:** normal size. **24. womb:**
belly. **27. heat:** i.e., of battle. **37. expedition:** speed. **39. posts:**
post horses.

44. hook-nosed . . . Rome: Julius Caesar, who reported his
victory over the King of Pontus in the words " *Veni, vidi, vici.*"
52. ballad: See App. 8. **57. cinders . . . element:** i.e., the stars.
78. execution: slaughter. **stayed:** stopped. **80. present:** im-
mediate. **90. condition:** i.e., as commander.

sober-blooded boy doth not love me, nor a man can-
not make him laugh — but that's no marvel,   95
he drinks no wine. There's never none of these de-
mure boys come to any proof,° for thin drink doth
so overcool their blood, and making many fish meals,
that they fall into a kind of male greensickness,°
and then when they marry, they get° wenches.   100
They are generally fools and cowards, which some
of us should be too but for inflammation.° A good
sherris sack° hath a twofold operation in it. It as-
cends me into the brain, dries me there all the fool-
ish and dull and crudy° vapors which environ   105
it, makes it apprehensive,° quick, forgetive,° full of
nimble, fiery, and delectable shapes — which, de-
livered o'er to the voice, the tongue, which is the
birth, becomes excellent wit. The second prop-   110
erty of your excellent sherris is the warming of the
blood, which, before cold and settled, left the liver°
white and pale, which is the badge of pusillanimity
and cowardice. But the sherris warms it and makes
it course from the inwards to the parts extreme.   115
It illumineth the face, which as a beacon° gives
warning to all the rest of this little kingdom, man,
to arm. And then the vital commoners and inland
petty spirits muster me all to their captain, the   120
heart, who, great and puffed up with this retinue,
doth any deed of courage, and this valor comes of
sherris. So that skill in the weapon is nothing with-
out sack, for that sets it awork, and learning a mere
hoard of gold kept by a devil till sack com-   125
mences° it and sets it in act and use. Hereof comes
it that Prince Harry is valiant, for the cold blood he
did naturally inherit of his father he hath, like lean
sterile and bare land, manured, husbanded,° and
tilled with excellent endeavor of drinking good   130
and good store of fertile sherris, that he is become
very hot and valiant. If I had a thousand sons, the
first humane principle I would teach them should be
to forswear thin potations, and to addict themselves
to sack.   135
[*Enter* BARDOLPH.] How now, Bardolph?

BARD. The army is discharged all and gone.

FAL. Let them go. I'll through Gloucestershire,
and there will I visit Master Robert Shallow, Es-

quire. I have him already tempering° between my
finger and my thumb, and shortly will I seal   141
with him. Come away.   [*Exeunt.*]

SCENE IV. *Westminster. The Jerusalem*
Chamber.

[*Enter* KING HENRY, *the* PRINCES THOMAS OF
CLARENCE *and* HUMPHREY OF GLOUCESTER,
WARWICK, *and others.*]

K. HEN. Now, lords, if God doth give successful
     end
To this debate° that bleedeth at our doors,
We will our youth lead on to higher fields
And draw no swords but what are sanctified.°
Our navy is addressed,° our power collected,   5
Our substitutes in absence° well invested,°
And everything lies level° to our wish.
Only, we want a little personal strength,
And pause us till these rebels, now afoot,
Come underneath the yoke of government.   10

WAR. Both which we doubt not but your Majesty
Shall soon enjoy.

K. HEN.   Humphrey, my son of Gloucester,
Where is the Prince your brother?

GLO. I think he's gone to hunt, my lord, at Wind-
     sor.

K. HEN. And how accompanied?

GLO.   I do not know, my lord.   15

K. HEN. Is not his brother, Thomas of Clarence,
     with him?

GLO. No, my good lord, he is in presence° here.

CLA. What would my lord and father?

K. HEN. Nothing but well to thee, Thomas of
     Clarence.
How chance thou art not with the Prince thy
     brother?   20
He loves thee, and thou dost neglect him, Thomas.
Thou hast a better place in his affection
Than all thy brothers. Cherish it, my boy,
And noble offices thou mayest effect
Of mediation, after I am dead,   25
Between his greatness and thy other brethren.
Therefore omit° him not, blunt not his love,
Nor lose the good advantage of his grace
By seeming cold or careless of his will.
For he is gracious if he be observed.°   30

---

97. come . . . proof: stand the test.   99. greensickness: a kind
of anemia from which unmarried girls suffered.   100. get: beget.
102. inflammation: the heating effects of liquor.   103. sherris
sack: a Spanish wine; sherry.   105. crudy: crude.   106. appre-
hensive: lively. forgetive: quick to invent.   112. liver: The liver
was regarded as the seat of the passions, and especially of courage.
See *T Night*, III.ii.65–67, for Sir Andrew Aguecheek's liver.
116. beacon: During the wars with Spain beacons were con-
tinually left ready on all high points and watched, so that warn-
ing of invasion could be immediately be given. The beacons were
lit several times, notably in 1588 to give warning of the
Spanish Armada.   126. commences: gives it its degree. "Com-
mencement" is the term used in the universities of Oxford and
Cambridge for permission to graduate.   129. husbanded: culti-
vated.

140. tempering: softening. The wax used for sealing documents
was made of beeswax and was softened, and not (like modern
shellac sealing wax) melted.

Sc. iv: 2. debate: dispute.   3–4. We . . . sanctified: The King
reverts to his old desire to lead a crusade to the Holy Land. See
I Hen IV, I.i.18–30.   5. addressed: ready.   6. substitutes in
absence: those who will be deputies in our absence. invested:
properly appointed.   7. level: ready.   17. in presence: in the
Court.   27. omit: neglect.   30. observed: humored.

He hath a tear for pity, and a hand
Open as day for melting charity.
Yet notwithstanding, being incensed, he's flint,
As humorous° as winter, and as sudden
As flaws congealèd° in the spring of day.　35
His temper, therefore, must be well observed.
Chide him for faults, and do it reverently,
When you perceive his blood inclined to mirth.
But, being moody, give him line and scope
Till that his passions, like a whale on ground,　40
Confound° themselves with working.° Learn this,
　　Thomas,
And thou shalt prove a shelter to thy friends,
A hoop of gold to bind thy brothers in,
That the united vessel of their blood,
Mingled with venom of suggestion —　45
As, force perforce, the age will pour it in —
Shall never leak,° though it do work as strong
As aconitum° or rash gunpowder.
　CLA. I shall observe him with all care and love.
　K. HEN. Why art thou not at Windsor with him,
　　Thomas?　50
　CLA. He is not there today. He dines in London.
　K. HEN. And how accompanied? Canst thou tell
　　that?
　CLA. With Poins, and other his continual fol-
　　lowers.
　K. HEN. Most subject is the fattest° soil to weeds,
And he, the noble image of my youth,　55
Is overspread with them. Therefore my grief
Stretches itself beyond the hour of death.
The blood weeps from my heart when I do shape,
In forms imaginary, the unguided days
And rotten times that you shall look upon　60
When I am sleeping with my ancestors.
For when his headstrong riot hath no curb,
When rage and hot blood are his councilors,
When means and lavish manners° meet together,
Oh, with what wings shall his affections fly　65
Toward fronting° peril and opposed decay!°
　WAR. My gracious lord, you look beyond° him
　　quite.
The Prince but studies his companions
Like a strange tongue, wherein, to gain the language,
'Tis needful that the most immodest word　70
Be looked upon and learned, which once attained,
Your Highness knows, comes to no further use
But to be known and hated. So, like gross terms,°

The Prince will in the perfectness of time
Cast off his followers, and their memory　75
Shall as a pattern° or a measure live,
By which His Grace must mete° the lives of others,
Turning past evils to advantages.
　K. HEN. 'Tis seldom when the bee doth leave her
　　comb
In the dead carrion.°
[Enter WESTMORELAND.] Who's here? Westmore-
　　land?　80
　WEST. Health to my sovereign, and new happiness
Added to that that I am to deliver!
Prince John your son doth kiss your Grace's hand.
Mowbray, the Bishop Scroop, Hastings, and all
Are brought to the correction of your law.　85
There is not now a rebel's sword unsheathed,
But Peace puts forth her olive everywhere.
The manner how this action hath been borne
Here at more leisure may your Highness read,
With every course° in his particular.　90
　K. HEN. O Westmoreland, thou art a summer bird
Which ever in the haunch of winter sings
The lifting-up of day.°
[Enter HARCOURT.]　　Look, here's more news.
　HAR. From enemies Heaven keep your Majesty,
And when they stand against you, may they fall　95
As those that I am come to tell you of!
The Earl Northumberland and the Lord Bardolph,
With a great power of English and of Scots,
Are by the Sheriff of Yorkshire overthrown.
The manner and true order of the fight,　100
This packet, please it you, contains at large.
　K. HEN. And wherefore should these good news
　　make me sick?
Will Fortune never come with both hands full,
But write her fair words still in foulest letters?
She either gives a stomach and no food —　105
Such are the poor, in health — or else a feast
And takes away the stomach — such are the rich
That have abundance and enjoy it not.
I should rejoice now at this happy news,
And now my sight fails, and my brain is giddy.　110
Oh me! Come near me. Now I am much ill.
　GLO. Comfort, your Majesty!
　CLA.　　　　　　　　　O my royal Father!
　WEST. My sovereign lord, cheer up yourself, look
　　up.
　WAR. Be patient, Princes. You do know these fits
Are with His Highness very ordinary.　115
Stand from him, give him air, he'll straight be well.
　CLA. No, no, he cannot long hold out these pangs.
The incessant care and labor of his mind
Hath wrought the mure° that should confine it in

---

34. **humorous:** capricious.　35. **flaws congealed:** snow flurries.
41. **Confound:** wear out. **working:** thrashing around.　43–47. **hoop
. . . leak:** The image is that of a cask, made of several staves
and held together by the hoops, which will hold any liquid,
no matter how penetrating. Thomas is the hoop, his brothers
the staves, and the cask will be tested by malicious tales.
48. **aconitum:** aconite, a poison extracted from the monkshood
(or wolfsbane).　54. **fattest:** richest.　64. **means . . . manners:**
opportunity and vicious ways.　66. **fronting:** opposing. **opposed
decay:** ruin which is standing ready like an enemy.　67. **look
beyond:** mistake.　73. **gross terms:** filthy words.

76. **pattern:** example.　77. **mete:** measure.　79–80. **'Tis . . . car-
rion:** the bees which have built in a dead carcass will seldom
leave it.　90. **course:** event.　92–93. **in . . . day:** at the latter
end (**haunch**) of winter sings to welcome the longer days.
119. **wrought . . . mure:** worn the wall thin.

So thin that life looks through and will break out.
GLO. The people fear me,° for they do observe
Unfathered° heirs and loathly° births of nature.
The seasons change their manners, as° the year   123
Had found some months asleep and leaped them
    over.
CLA. The river° hath thrice flowed,° no ebb be-
    tween,   125
And the old folk, time's doting chronicles,
Say it did so a little time before
That our great-grandsire, Edward, sicked and died.
    WAR. Speak lower, Princes, for the King recovers.
    GLO. This apoplexy will certain be his end.   130
    K. HEN. I pray you take me up and bear me hence
Into some other chamber. Softly, pray.   [*Exeunt.*]

SCENE V.° *Another chamber.*

[KING HENRY *lying on a bed:* CLARENCE, GLOUCESTER,
    WARWICK, *and others in attendance.*]
    K. HEN. Let there be no noise made, my gentle
        friends,
Unless some dull° and favorable° hand
Will whisper music to my weary spirit.
    WAR. Call for the music in the other room.
    K. HEN. Set me the crown upon my pillow here.   5
    CLA. His eye is hollow, and he changes much.
    WAR. Less noise, less noise!
            [*Enter* PRINCE HENRY.]
PRINCE.   Who saw the Duke of Clarence?
    CLA. I am here, Brother, full of heaviness.
    PRINCE. How now! Rain within doors,° and none
        abroad!
How doth the King?   10
    GLO. Exceeding ill.
    PRINCE.   Heard he the good news yet?
Tell it him.
    GLO. He altered much upon the hearing it.
    PRINCE. If he be sick with joy, he'll recover with-
        out physic.   15
    WAR. Not so much noise, my lords. Sweet Prince,
        speak low.
The King your father is disposed to sleep.
    CLA. Let us withdraw into the other room.

121. **fear me:** make me fearful.   122. **Unfathered:** i.e., unnatu-
ral. **loathly:** loathsome. Unnatural births, such as calves with
two heads, were regarded as portents of evil. 123. **as:** as if.
125. **river:** i.e., the Thames. **thrice flowed:** i.e., the tide rose
thrice without any intervening low tide. The Thames is a tidal
river. On very rare occasions the tide fails either to rise or to fall.
The phenomenon of no high tide occurred in Shakespeare's time
on September 6, 1592. The phenomenon was recorded by Holins-
hed as having also occurred on October 12, 1411.
    Sc. v: In the original texts no change of scene was marked or
intended. The King was carried either to the back of the stage
or to the chamber aloft (where the bed was already in position)
and the curtains were opened. See Gen. Intro. p. 55b and Pl. 5b.
2. **dull:** drowsy. **favorable:** kindly.   9. **Rain . . . doors:** i.e., why
do you all look so gloomy?

    WAR. Will 't please your Grace to go along with
        us?   19
    PRINCE. No, I will sit and watch here by the King.
                [*Exeunt all except the* PRINCE.]
Why doth the crown lie there upon his pillow,
Being so troublesome a bedfellow?
Oh, polished perturbation!° Golden care!
That keep'st the ports° of slumber open wide
To many a watchful night! Sleep with it now!   25
Yet not so sound and half so deeply sweet
As he whose brow with homely biggen° bound
Snores out the watch of night. O majesty!
When thou dost pinch thy bearer, thou dost sit
Like a rich armor worn in heat of day,   30
That scalds with safety.° By his gates of breath°
There lies a downy feather which stirs not.
Did he suspire,° that light and weightless down
Perforce must move. My gracious lord! My father!
This sleep is sound indeed, this is a sleep,   35
That from this golden rigol° hath divorced
So many English kings. Thy due from me
Is tears and heavy sorrows of the blood,°
Which nature, love, and filial tenderness
Shall, O dear Father, pay thee plenteously.   40
My due from thee is this imperial crown,
Which, as immediate from thy place and blood,
Derives° itself to me. Lo, here it sits,°
Which God shall guard. And put the world's whole
    strength°
Into one giant arm, it shall not force   45
This lineal° honor from me. This from thee
Will I to mine leave, as 'tis left to me.   [*Exit.*]
    K. HEN. Warwick! Gloucester! Clarence!
        [*Re-enter* WARWICK, GLOUCESTER, CLARENCE,
                and the rest.]
    CLA. Doth the King call?
    WAR. What would your Majesty? How fares your
        Grace?   50
    K. HEN. Why did you leave me here alone, my
        lords?
    CLA. We left the Prince my brother here, my
        liege,
Who undertook to sit and watch by you.
    K. HEN. The Prince of Wales! Where is he? Let
        me see him.
He is not here.   55
    WAR. This door is open, he is gone this way.
    GLO. He came not through the chamber where
        we stayed.
    K. HEN. Where is the crown? Who took it from
        my pillow?

23. **perturbation:** cause of anxiety.   24. **ports:** gates.   27. **biggen:**
coarse linen cloth tied round the head as a nightcap.   31. **scalds
. . . safety:** burns while it protects. **gates of breath:** nostrils.
33. **suspire:** breathe.   36. **rigol:** circle.   38. **blood:** heart.
43. **Derives:** comes by descent. **here it sits:** The Prince sets the
crown on his own head.   44. **And . . . strength:** even if the whole
strength of the world be put.   46. **lineal:** descending by right of
birth.

WAR. When we withdrew, my liege, we left it
  here.
K. HEN. The Prince hath ta'en it hence. Go, seek
  him out.   60
Is he so hasty that he doth suppose
My sleep my death?
Find him, my Lord of Warwick, chide him hither.
                                 [*Exit* WARWICK.]
This part° of his conjoins° with my disease,
And helps to end me. See, Sons, what things you
  are!   65
How quickly nature falls into revolt
When gold becomes her object!
For this the foolish overcareful fathers
Have broke their sleep with thoughts, their brains
  with care,
Their bones with industry.   70
For this they have engrossed° and pilèd up
The cankered° heaps of strange-achievèd° gold.
For this they have been thoughtful to invest°
Their sons with arts° and martial exercises.
When, like the bee, culling from every flower   75
The virtuous sweets,
Our thighs packed with wax, our mouths with
  honey,
We bring it to the hive, and, like the bees,
Are murdered for our pains. This bitter taste
Yield his engrossments° to the ending father.   80
[*Re-enter* WARWICK.] Now, where is he that will not
  stay so long
Till his friend sickness hath determined° me?
  WAR. My lord, I found the Prince in the next
  room,
Washing with kindly tears his gentle cheeks,
With such a deep demeanor° in great sorrow   85
That tyranny, which never quaffed but blood,°
Would, by beholding him, have washed his knife
With gentle eyedrops. He is coming hither.
  K. HEN. But wherefore did he take away the
  crown?
[*Re-enter* PRINCE HENRY.] Lo where he comes. Come
  hither to me, Harry.   90
Depart the chamber, leave us here alone.
                    [*Exeunt* WARWICK *and the rest.*]
  PRINCE. I never thought to hear you speak again.
  K. HEN. Thy wish was father, Harry, to that
  thought.
I stay too long by thee, I weary thee.
Dost thou so hunger for mine empty chair   95
That thou wilt needs invest thee with my honors
Before thy hour be ripe? O foolish youth!
Thou seek'st the greatness that will overwhelm thee.

Stay but a little, for my cloud of dignity
Is held from falling with so weak a wind   100
That it will quickly drop. My day is dim.
Thou hast stolen that which after some few hours
Were thine without offense, and at my death
Thou hast sealed up° my expectation.
Thy life did manifest thou lovedst me not,   105
And thou wilt have me die assured of it.
Thou hidest a thousand daggers in thy thoughts,
Which thou hast whetted on thy stony heart
To stab at half an hour of my life.
What! Canst thou not forbear me half an hour?
Then get thee gone and dig my grave thyself,   111
And bid the merry bells° ring to thine ear
That thou art crowned, not that I am dead.
Let all the tears that should bedew my hearse
Be drops of balm° to sanctify thy head.   115
Only compound° me with forgotten dust,
Give that which gave thee life unto the worms.
Pluck down my officers, break my decrees,
For now a time is come to mock at form.°
Harry the Fifth is crowned. Up, vanity!   120
Down, royal state!° All you sage counselors, hence!
And to the English Court assemble now,
From every region, apes of idleness!
Now, neighbor confines,° purge you of your scum.
Have you a ruffian that will swear, drink, dance,
Revel the night, rob, murder, and commit   126
The oldest sins the newest kind of ways?
Be happy, he will trouble you no more.
England shall double-gild his treble guilt,°
England shall give him office, honor, might.   130
For the fifth Harry from curbed license° plucks
The muzzle of restraint, and the wild dog
Shall flesh° his tooth on every innocent.
O my poor kingdom, sick with civil blows!°
When that my care could not withhold thy riots,
What wilt thou do when riot is thy care?°   136
Oh, thou wilt be a wilderness again,
Peopled with wolves, thy old inhabitants!
  PRINCE. Oh, pardon me, my liege! But for my
  tears,
The moist impediments unto my speech,   140
I had forestalled this dear and deep rebuke
Ere you with grief had spoke and I had heard
The course of it so far. There is your crown,
And He that wears the crown immortally
Long guard it yours! If I affect° it more   145
Than as your honor and as your renown,

---

64. **part:** action. **conjoins:** joins.   71. **engrossed:** bought up
wholesale.   72. **cankered:** rusted. **strange-achieved:** won in
strange ways.   73. **invest:** equip.   74. **arts:** learning.   79–80. This
. . . **engrossments:** his hoarding brings a bitter taste.   82. **deter-
mined:** ended.   85. **deep demeanor:** sad countenance.   86. **That
. . . blood:** that even a tyrant who drank nothing but blood.

104. **sealed up:** finally confirmed. See App. 6.   112. **bells:** See
App. 19.   115. **balm:** the sacred oil used in anointing a King.
116. **compound:** mix.   119. **form:** order.   121. **state:** dignity.
124. **confines:** countries. 129. **double-gild . . . guilt:** Shakespeare
repeated this pun in *Hen V*, II, Chorus, l. 26, and *Macb*, II.ii.55.
131. **curbed license:** restrained vice.   133. **flesh:** stain with
blood.   134. **civil blows:** the wounds of civil war.   135–36. **care
. . . care:** anxious watch . . . concern.   145 **affect:** desire.

Let me no more from this obedience° rise,
Which my most inward true and duteous spirit
Teacheth, this prostrate and exterior bending.
God witness with me, when I here came in   150
And found no course of breath within your Majesty,
How cold it struck my heart! If I do feign,
Oh, let me in my present wildness die,
And never live to show the incredulous world
The noble change that I have purposèd!   155
Coming to look on you, thinking you dead,
And dead almost, my liege, to think you were,
I spake unto this crown as having sense,
And thus upbraided it: " The care on thee depending
Hath fed upon the body of my father,   160
Therefore thou best of gold art worst of gold.
Other, less fine in carat, is more precious,
Preserving life in medicine potable.°
But thou, most fine, most honored, most renowned,
Hast eat thy bearer up." Thus, my most royal liege,
Accusing it, I put it on my head,   166
To try with it, as with an enemy
That had before my face murdered my father,
The quarrel of a true inheritor.
But if it did infect my blood with joy,   170
Or swell my thoughts to any strain of pride,
If any rebel or vain spirit of mine
Did with the least affection of a welcome
Give entertainment to the might of it,
Let God forever keep it from my head,   175
And make me as the poorest vassal° is
That doth with awe and terror kneel to it!
     K. HEN. O my son,
God put it in thy mind to take it hence,
That thou mightst win the more thy father's love
Pleading so wisely in excuse of it!   181
Come hither, Harry, sit thou by my bed,
And hear, I think, the very latest° counsel
That ever I shall breathe. God knows, my son,
By what bypaths and indirect° crooked ways   185
I met this crown, and I myself know well
How troublesome it sat upon my head.
To thee it shall descend with better quiet,
Better opinion,° better confirmation.°
For all the soil of the achievement° goes   190
With me into the earth. It seemed in me
But as an honor snatched with boisterous° hand,
And I had many living to upbraid
My gain of it by their assistances,
Which daily grew to quarrel and to bloodshed, 195
Wounding supposèd° peace. All these bold fears
Thou see'st with peril I have answered,

For all my reign hath been but as a scene
Acting that argument.° And now my death
Changes the mode,° for what in me was pur-
     chased°   200
Falls upon thee in a more fairer sort,
So° thou the garland° wear'st successively.°
Yet, though thou stand'st more sure than I could do,
Thou art not firm enough, since griefs are green.°
And all my friends, which thou must make thy
     friends,   205
Have but their stings and teeth newly ta'en out,
By whose fell working° I was first advanced
And by whose power I well might lodge a fear
To be again displaced. Which to avoid,
I cut them off, and had a purpose now   210
To lead out many to the Holy Land,
Lest rest and lying still might make them look
Too near unto my state.° Therefore, my Harry,
Be it thy course to busy giddy minds
With foreign quarrels, that action, hence borne
     out,°
May waste° the memory of the former days.   216
More would I, but my lungs are wasted so
That strength of speech is utterly denied me.
How I came by the crown, O God, forgive,
And grant it may with thee in true peace live! 220
     PRINCE. My gracious liege,
You won it, wore it, kept it, gave it me.
Then plain and right must my possession be,
Which I with more than with a common pain°
'Gainst all the world will rightfully maintain. 225
     [*Enter* LORD JOHN OF LANCASTER.]
     K. HEN. Look, look, here comes my John of Lan-
     caster.
     LANC. Health, peace, and happiness to my royal
     father!
     K. HEN. Thou bring'st me happiness and peace,
     Son John,
But health, alack, with youthful wings is flown
From this bare withered trunk. Upon thy sight 230
My worldly business makes a period.°
Where is my Lord of Warwick?
     PRINCE.   My Lord of Warwick!
     [*Re-enter* WARWICK, *and others.*]
     K. HEN. Doth any name particular belong
Unto the lodging where I first did swoon?
     WAR. 'Tis called Jerusalem, my noble lord.   235
     K. HEN. Laud° be to God! Even there my life must
     end.
It hath been prophesied to me many years

---

199. argument: plot (of a play).   200. mode: mood, musical
key, "tune." purchased: acquired.   202. So: since. garland:
crown. successively: by right of succession.   204. griefs . . .
green: grievances are fresh.   207. fell working: fierce labors.
212–13. look . . . state: examine my claims to the throne too
closely.   215. hence . . . out: i.e., in foreign lands.   216. waste:
wear away.   224. pain: labor.   231. period: full stop.
236. Laud: praise.

147. obedience: act of obedience; i.e., kneeling.   163. medicine
potable: gold in solution, called *aurum potabile* and regarded as
a medicine of great worth. See App. 21.   176. vassal: slave.
183. latest: last.   185. indirect: devious.   189. opinion: reputa-
tion. confirmation: approval.   190. soil . . . achievement: infamy
of the winning.   192. boisterous: violent.   196. supposed: unreal.

I should not die but in Jerusalem,
Which vainly I supposed the Holy Land.
But bear me to that chamber, there I'll lie,   240
In that Jerusalem shall Harry die.   [*Exeunt.*]

Act V

SCENE I. *Gloucestershire.* SHALLOW's *house.*

[*Enter* SHALLOW, FALSTAFF, BARDOLPH, *and* PAGE.]

SHAL. By cock and pie,° sir, you shall not away
tonight. What, Davy, I say!

FAL. You must excuse me, Master Robert Shallow.

SHAL. I will not excuse you, you shall not be ex-   5
cused, excuses shall not be admitted, there is no ex-
cuse shall serve, you shall not be excused. Why,
Davy!

[*Enter* DAVY.]

DAVY. Here, sir.

SHAL. Davy, Davy, Davy, Davy, let me see, Davy.
Let me see, Davy, let me see. Yea, marry, William
cook, bid him come hither. Sir John, you shall not
be excused.

DAVY. Marry, sir, thus, those precepts° cannot be
served. And, again, sir, shall we sow the headland
with wheat?   16

SHAL. With red wheat, Davy. But for William
cook — are there no young pigeons?

DAVY. Yes, sir. Here is now the smith's note for
shoeing and plow irons.   20

SHAL. Let it be cast° and paid. Sir John, you shall
not be excused.

DAVY. Now, sir, a new link to the bucket must
needs be had. And, sir, do you mean to stop any of
William's wages about the sack he lost the other day
at Hinckley fair?   26

SHAL. A' shall answer it. Some pigeons, Davy, a
couple of short-legged hens, a joint of mutton, and
any pretty little tiny kickshaws,° tell William cook.

DAVY. Doth the man of war stay all night, sir?   31

SHAL. Yea, Davy. I will use him well. A friend i'
the Court is better than a penny in purse. Use his
men well, Davy, for they are arrant knaves, and will
backbite.

DAVY. No worse than they are backbitten, sir, for
they have marvelous foul linen.

SHAL. Well conceited,° Davy. About thy business,
Davy.   40

DAVY. I beseech you, sir, to countenance° William
Visor of Woncot against Clement Perkes o' the hill.

SHAL. There is many complaints, Davy, against
that Visor. That Visor is an arrant knave, on my
knowledge.   46

DAVY. I grant your Worship that he is a knave,
sir. But yet, God forbid, sir, but a knave should have
some countenance at his friend's request. An honest
man, sir, is able to speak for himself when a knave is
not. I have served your Worship truly, sir, this   51
eight years, and if I cannot once or twice in a quarter
bear out° a knave against an honest man, I have but
a very little credit with your Worship. The knave is
mine honest friend, sir, therefore I beseech your
Worship let him be countenanced.   57

SHAL. Go to, I say he shall have no wrong. Look
about,° Davy. [*Exit* DAVY.] Where are you, Sir
John? Come, come, come, off with your boots. Give
me your hand, Master Bardolph.

BARD. I am glad to see your Worship.

SHAL. I thank thee with all my heart, kind Master
Bardolph. [*To the* PAGE] And welcome, my tall fel-
low. Come, Sir John.   66

FAL. I'll follow you, good Master Robert Shallow.
[*Exit* SHALLOW.] Bardolph, look to our horses.
[*Exeunt* BARDOLPH *and* PAGE.] If I were sawed into
quantities,° I should make four dozen of such   70
bearded hermits' staves° as Master Shallow. It is a
wonderful thing to see the semblable coherence° of
his men's spirits and his. They, by observing of him,
do bear themselves like foolish Justices; he, by con-
versing with them, is turned into a Justicelike   75
servingman. Their spirits are so married in conjunc-
tion with the participation of society° that they flock
together in consent,° like so many wild geese. If I
had a suit to Master Shallow, I would humor his
men with the imputation of being near° their   80
master. If to his men, I would curry with Master
Shallow that no man could better command his
servants. It is certain that either wise bearing or ig-
norant carriage° is caught, as men take diseases, one
of another. Therefore let men take heed of their   85
company. I will devise matter enough out of this
Shallow to keep Prince Harry in continual laughter
the wearing-out of six fashions, which is four terms,°
or two actions,° and a' shall laugh without inter-
vallums.° Oh, it is much that a lie with a slight   90

---

41. **countenance:** favor — when his case comes up for trial. There
is a good deal of local color in these Gloucestershire
scenes. *Woncot* (spelled Woodmancote) is a village in Gloucestershire,
and in Shakespeare's time there were Visors and Perkes living
thereabouts.   53. **bear out:** support.   58–59. **Look about:** get
moving.   70. **quantities:** lengths.   71. **staves:** staffs.   72. **sem-
blable coherence:** close likeness.   76–77. **so . . . society:** so
united by sharing the company of each other.   78. **in consent:**
by fellow feeling.   80. **near:** in the favor of.   84. **ignorant
carriage:** boorish behavior.   88. **four terms:** There were four
law terms in the year.   89. **actions:** lawsuits.   90. **intervallums:**
intermissions.

Act V, Sc. i: 1. **cock . . . pie:** an innocent rustic oath. Editors
dispute whether it means simply by cock and magpie, or is a
perversion of something stronger, as moderns use "Gee" and
"Jeez" for God and Jesus.   14. **precepts:** orders.   21. **cast:**
added up.   30. **kickshaws:** trifles, fancy dishes.   39. **Well
conceited:** very clever.

oath and a jest with a sad° brow will do with a fellow
that never had the ache in his shoulders!° Oh, you
shall see him laugh till his face be like a wet cloak
ill laid up!   95

SHAL. [*Within*] Sir John!

FAL. I come, Master Shallow, I come, Master Shal-
low.   [*Exit.*]

SCENE II. *Westminster. The palace.*

[*Enter* WARWICK *and the* LORD CHIEF JUSTICE,
meeting.]

WAR. How now, my Lord Chief Justice! Whither
away?

CH. JUST. How doth the King?

WAR. Exceeding well. His cares are now all ended.

CH. JUST. I hope, not dead.

WAR.   He's walked the way of nature,
And to our purposes he lives no more.   5

CH. JUST. I would His Majesty had called me with
him.
The service that I truly did his life
Hath left me open to all injuries.

WAR. Indeed I think the young King loves you
not.

CH. JUST. I know he doth not, and do arm myself
To welcome the condition of the time,   11
Which cannot look more hideously upon me
Than I have drawn it in my fantasy.°

[*Enter* LANCASTER, CLARENCE, GLOUCESTER,
WESTMORELAND, *and others.*]

WAR. Here come the heavy issue° of dead Harry.
Oh, that the living Harry had the temper   15
Of him, the worst of these three gentlemen!
How many nobles then should hold their places
That must strike sail° to spirits of vile sort!

CH. JUST. Oh God, I fear all will be overturned!

LANC. Good morrow, Cousin Warwick, good mor-
row.   20

GLO. & CLA. Good morrow, Cousin.

LANC. We meet like men that had forgot to speak.

WAR. We do remember, but our argument°
Is all too heavy to admit much talk.

LANC. Well, peace be with him that hath made
us heavy!   25

CH. JUST. Peace be with us, lest we be heavier!

GLO. Oh, good my lord, you have lost a friend
indeed,
And I dare swear you borrow not that face
Of seeming sorrow, it is sure your own.

LANC. Though no man be assured what grace to
find,°   30

You stand in coldest° expectation.
I am the sorrier. Would 'twere otherwise.

CLA. Well, you must now speak Sir John Falstaff
fair,
Which swims against your stream of quality.°

CH. JUST. Sweet Princes, what I did, I did in
honor,   35
Led by the impartial conduct of my soul,
And never shall you see that I will beg
A ragged and forestalled remission.°
If truth and upright innocency fail me,
I'll to the King my master that is dead,   40
And tell him who hath sent me after him.

WAR. Here comes the Prince.

[*Enter* KING HENRY *the Fifth, attended.*]

CH. JUST. Good morrow, and God save your Ma-
jesty!

K. HEN. V. This new and gorgeous garment, ma-
jesty,
Sits not so easy on me as you think.   45
Brothers, you mix your sadness with some fear.
This is the English, not the Turkish Court.
Not Amurath an Amurath succeeds,°
But Harry Harry. Yet be sad, good Brothers,
For, by my faith, it very well becomes you.   50
Sorrow so royally in you appears
That I will deeply put the fashion on,
And wear it in my heart. Why then, be sad,
But entertain no more of it, good Brothers,
Than a joint burden laid upon us all.   55
For me, by Heaven, I bid you be assured
I'll be your father and your brother too.
Let me but bear your love, I'll bear your cares.
Yet weep that Harry's dead, and so will I,
But Harry lives, that shall convert those tears   60
By number into hours of happiness.

PRINCES. We hope no other from your Majesty.

K. HEN. V. You all look strangely on me. And you
most.
You are, I think, assured I love you not.

CH. JUST. I am assured, if I be measured rightly,
Your Majesty hath no just cause to hate me.   66

K. HEN. V. No?
How might a prince of my great hopes forget
So great indignities you laid upon me?
What! Rate,° rebuke, and roughly send to prison
The immediate heir of England! Was this easy?   71
May this be washed in Lethe,° and forgotten?

CH. JUST. I then did use the person of your father,
The image of his power lay then in me.
And in the administration of his law,

91. sad: solemn. 92. ache . . . shoulders: i.e., rheumatism.
Sc. ii: 13. fantasy: imagination. 14. heavy issue: sad sons.
18. strike sail: i.e., as a ship lowers its sails in sign of submission.
23. argument: topic for conversation. 30. be . . . find: is sure
what treatment to expect from the new King.

31. coldest: least favorable. 34. swims . . . quality: which goes
against the inclination of a man of your quality. 38. ragged
. . . remission: beggarly pardon, asked for before an offense has
been committed. 48. Amurath . . . succeeds: In 1574 the
Sultan Amurath on succeeding to the throne had all his brothers
strangled, as also did his son in 1598. 70. Rate: scold.
72. Lethe: the river of forgetfulness.

Whiles I was busy for the commonwealth,
Your Highness pleasèd to forget my place,
The majesty and power of law and justice,
The image° of the King whom I presented,°
And struck me in my very seat of judgment.   80
Whereon, as an offender to your father,
I gave bold way to my authority,
And did commit you. If the deed were ill,
Be you contented, wearing now the garland,°
To have a son set your decrees at naught,   85
To pluck down justice from your awful bench,
To trip the course of law and blunt the sword
That guards the peace and safety of your person —
Nay, more, to spurn at your most royal image
And mock your workings in a second body.°   90
Question your royal thoughts, make the case yours.
Be now the father and propose a son,
Hear your own dignity so much profaned,
See your most dreadful laws so loosely slighted,
Behold yourself so by a son disdained.   95
And then imagine me taking your part,
And in your power soft-silencing your son.
After this cold considerance,° sentence me,
And, as you are a king, speak in your state°
What I have done that misbecame my place,   100
My person, or my liege's sovereignty.

K. HEN. V. You are right, Justice, and you weigh
   this well,
Therefore still bear the balance° and the sword.
And I do wish your honors may increase
Till you do live to see a son of mine   105
Offend you, and obey you, as I did.
So shall I live to speak my father's words:
"Happy am I that have a man so bold
That dares do justice on my proper° son,
And not less happy, having such a son,   110
That would deliver up his greatness so
Into the hands of justice." You did commit me.
For which, I do commit into your hand
The unstained sword that you have used° to bear —
With this remembrance, that you use the same   115
With the like bold, just, and impartial spirit
As you have done 'gainst me. There is my hand.
You shall be as a father to my youth.
My voice shall sound as you do prompt mine ear,
And I will stoop and humble my intents   120
To your well-practiced wise directions.
And, Princes all, believe me, I beseech you,
My father is gone wild° into his grave,
For in his tomb lie my affections.°
And with his spirit sadly I survive,   125

To mock the expectation of the world,
To frustrate prophecies, and to raze out
Rotten opinion,° who hath writ me down
After my seeming.° The tide of blood in me
Hath proudly flowed in vanity° till now.   130
Now doth it turn and ebb back to the sea,
Where it shall mingle with the state of floods
And flow henceforth in formal majesty.°
Now call we our high court of Parliament.
And let us choose such limbs of noble counsel   135
That the great body of our state may go
In equal rank with the best-governed nation,
That war, or peace, or both at once, may be
As things acquainted° and familiar to us.   139
In which you, Father, shall have foremost hand.
Our coronation done, we will accite,°
As I before remembered, all our state.°
And, God consigning° to my good intents,
No Prince nor peer shall have just cause to say,   144
God shorten Harry's happy life one day!   [Exeunt.]

SCENE III. *Gloucestershire.* SHALLOW's
   orchard.

[*Enter* FALSTAFF, SHALLOW, SILENCE, DAVY, BARDOLPH,
   and the PAGE.]

SHAL. Nay, you shall see my orchard, where in
an arbor we will eat a last year's pippin of my own
graffing,° with a dish of caraways,° and so forth.
Come, Cousin Silence. And then to bed.

FAL. 'Fore God, you have here a goodly dwelling
and a rich.

SHAL. Barren, barren, barren, beggars all, beggars
all, Sir John. Marry, good air. Spread, Davy, spread,
Davy. Well said, Davy.   10

FAL. This Davy serves you for good uses. He is
your servingman and your husband.°

SHAL. A good varlet,° a good varlet, a very good
varlet, Sir John. By the mass, I have drunk too much
sack at supper. A good varlet. Now sit down, now
sit down. Come, Cousin.   16

SIL. Ah, sirrah! quoth a',° we shall [*Singing*]
   "Do nothing but eat, and make good cheer,
      And praise God for the merry year,
      When flesh° is cheap and females dear,   20

---

79. **image:** likeness, representation. **presented:** represented.
84. **garland:** crown.   90. **second body:** deputy.   98. **cold considerance:** impartial consideration.   99. **your state:** i.e., as King and not as vengeful individual.   103. **balance:** the symbol of impartial justice.   109. **proper:** own.   114. **used:** been accustomed.   123. **gone wild:** because he takes the Prince's wildness with him.   124. **affections:** lusts.

128. **Rotten opinion:** the opinion that I was rotten.   129. **my seeming:** what I seemed to be.   130. **vanity:** frivolity.   133. **formal majesty:** kingly dignity.   139. **acquainted:** well known.   141. **accite:** summon.   142. **all . . . state:** i.e., the three estates of the realm — Lords, Bishops, Commons — which made up the Parliament.   143. **consigning:** agreeing.
Sc. iii: 3. **graffing:** grafting. **caraways:** caraway seeds, eaten with apples to counteract wind.   12. **husband:** husbandman; i.e., he looks after the farm.   13. **varlet:** servant.   17. **quoth a':** says he. Silence is another advertisement for the effects of sack; it moves him to song.   20. **flesh:** meat.

And lusty lads roam here and there
    So merrily,
And ever among so merrily."

FAL. There's a merry heart! Good Master Silence,
I'll give you a health° for that anon.   25

SHAL. Give Master Bardolph some wine, Davy.

DAVY. Sweet sir, sit, I'll be with you anon. Most
sweet sir, sit. Master Page, good Master Page, sit.
Proface!° What you want in meat we'll have in   30
drink. But you must bear,° the heart's° all. [*Exit.*]

SHAL. Be merry, Master Bardolph, and, my little
soldier there, be merry.

SIL. [*Singing*]
" Be merry, be merry, my wife has all,   35
    For women are shrews, both short and tall.
'Tis merry in hall when beards wag all,°
    And welcome merry Shrovetide.°
Be merry, be merry."   39

FAL. I did not think Master Silence had been a
man of this mettle.

SIL. Who, I? I have been merry twice and once
ere now.

[*Re-enter* DAVY.]

DAVY. [*To* BARDOLPH] There's a dish of leather-
coats° for you.

SHAL. Davy!   45

DAVY. Your Worship! [*To* BARDOLPH] I'll be with
you straight. A cup of wine, sir?

SIL. [*Singing*]
" A cup of wine that's brisk and fine,
    And drink unto the leman° mine,
        And a merry heart lives long-a."   50

FAL. Well said, Master Silence.

SIL. An we shall be merry, now comes in the
sweet o' the night.   54

FAL. Health and long life to you, Master Silence.

SIL. [*Singing.*]
" Fill the cup, and let it come.
    I'll pledge you a mile to the bottom."

SHAL. Honest Bardolph, welcome. If thou wantest
anything, and wilt not call, beshrew thy heart. Wel-
come, my little tiny thief [*To the* PAGE], and wel-
come indeed too. I'll drink to Master Bardolph, and
to all the cavaleros° about London.   63

DAVY. I hope to see London once ere I die.

BARD. An I might see you there, Davy——

SHAL. By the mass, you'll crack a quart together,
ha! Will you not, Master Bardolph?

BARD. Yea, sir, in a pottle pot.°   68

SHAL. By God's liggens,° I thank thee. The knave

will stick by thee, I can assure thee that. A' will not
out,° he is true-bred.

BARD. And I'll stick by him, sir.   72

SHAL. Why, there spoke a king. Lack nothing. Be
merry. [*Knocking within*] Look who's at door   74
there, ho! Who knocks?   [*Exit* DAVY.]

FAL. [*To* SILENCE, *seeing him take off a bumper*]
Why, now you have done me right.°

SIL. [*Singing*]
" Do me right,
    And dub me knight.
        Samingo."

Is 't not so?   80

FAL. 'Tis so.

SIL. Is 't so? Why then, say an old man can do
somewhat.

[*Re-enter* DAVY.]

DAVY. An 't please your Worship, there's one Pistol
come from the Court with news.   85

FAL. From the Court! Let him come in. [*Enter*
PISTOL.] How now, Pistol!

PIST. Sir John, God save you!

FAL. What wind blew you hither, Pistol?   89

PIST. Not the ill wind which blows no man to
good. Sweet knight, thou art now one of the great-
est men in this realm.

SIL. By 'r lady, I think a' be, but° Goodman° Puff
of Barson.

PIST. Puff!   95
Puff in thy teeth, most recreant° coward base!
Sir John, I am thy Pistol and thy friend,
And helter-skelter have I rode to thee,
And tidings do I bring and lucky joys
And golden times and happy news of price.   100

FAL. I pray thee, now, deliver them like a man of
this world.

PIST. A foutre° for the world and worldlings
base!
I speak of Africa and golden joys.

FAL. O base Assyrian knight, what is thy news?
Let King Cophetua° know the truth thereof.   106

SIL. [*Singing*] " And Robin Hood, Scarlet, and
John."

PIST. Shall dunghill curs confront the Helicons?°
And shall good news be baffled?°
Then, Pistol, lay thy head in Furies' lap.   110

SHAL. Honest gentleman, I know not your breed-
ing.°

PIST. Why then, lament therefore.

SHAL. Give me pardon, sir. If, sir, you come with
news from the Court, I take it there's but two ways,

either to utter them or to conceal them. I am, sir,
under the King, in some authority.   118

PIST. Under which King, Besonian?° Speak, or
die.

SHAL. Under King Harry.

PIST.   Harry the Fourth? Or Fifth? 120

SHAL. Harry the Fourth.

PIST.   A foutre for thine office!
Sir John, thy tender lambkin now is King,
Harry the Fifth's the man. I speak the truth.
When Pistol lies, do this,° and fig me,° like
The bragging Spaniard.

FAL. What, is the old King dead?   126

PIST. As nail in door. The things I speak are just.

FAL. Away, Bardolph! Saddle my horse. Master
Robert Shallow, choose what office thou wilt in the
land, 'tis thine. Pistol, I will double-charge thee with
dignities.   131

BARD. Oh joyful day! I would not take a knight-
hood for my fortune.

PIST. What! I do bring good news.   134

FAL. Carry Master Silence to bed. Master Shallow,
my Lord Shallow — be what thou wilt, I am for-
tune's steward° — get on thy boots.° We'll ride all
night. O sweet Pistol! Away, Bardolph! [Exit BAR-
DOLPH.] Come, Pistol, utter more to me, and withal
devise something to do thyself good. Boot, boot,
Master Shallow! I know the young King is sick 141
for me. Let us take any man's horses, the laws of
England are at my commandment. Blessed are they
that have been my friends, and woe to my Lord
Chief Justice!   145

PIST. Let vultures vile seize on his lungs also!
"Where is the life that late I led?" say they.
Why, here it is. Welcome these pleasant days!

          [Exeunt.]

SCENE IV. *London. A street.*

[*Enter* BEADLES, *dragging in* HOSTESS QUICKLY *and*
DOLL TEARSHEET.]

HOST. No, thou arrant knave, I would to God that
I might die, that I might have thee hanged. Thou
hast drawn my shoulder out of joint.

1. BEAD. The constables have delivered her over to
me, and she shall have whipping cheer° enough, I
warrant her. There hath been a man or two lately
killed about her.   7

DOLL. Nuthook,° nuthook, you lie. Come on, I'll

tell thee what, thou damned tripe-visaged° rascal,
an the child I now go with do miscarry, thou wert
better thou hadst struck thy mother, thou paper-
faced villain.   12

HOST. Oh the Lord, that Sir John were come! He
would make this a bloody day to somebody. But I
pray God the fruit of her womb miscarry!

1. BEAD. If it do, you shall have a dozen of cush-
ions again. You have but eleven now.° Come, I
charge you both go with me, for the man is dead that
you and Pistol beat amongst you.   19

DOLL. I'll tell you what, you thin man in a censer,°
I will have you as soundly swinged° for this — you
bluebottle° rogue, you filthy famished correctioner,°
if you be not swinged, I'll forswear half-kirtles.° 24

1. BEAD. Come, come, you she knight errant,°
come.

HOST. Oh God, that right should thus overcome
might! Well, of sufferance comes ease.

DOLL. Come, you rogue, come, bring me to a Jus-
tice.   30

HOST. Aye, come, you starved bloodhound.

DOLL. Goodman death, goodman bones!

HOST. Thou atomy° thou!

DOLL. Come, you thin thing, come, you rascal.

1. BEAD. Very well.   [*Exeunt.*]

SCENE V. *A public place near Westminster Abbey.*

[*Enter two* GROOMS, *strewing rushes.*°]

1. GROOM. More rushes, more rushes.

2. GROOM. The trumpets have sounded twice.

1. GROOM. 'Twill be two o'clock ere they come
from the coronation. Dispatch, dispatch. [*Exeunt.*]

[*Enter* FALSTAFF, SHALLOW, PISTOL, BARDOLPH, *and*
PAGE.]

FAL. Stand here by me, Master Robert Shallow, I
will make the King do you grace.° I will leer° upon
him as a' comes by, and do but mark the countenance
that he will give me.   8

PIST. God bless thy lungs, good knight.

FAL. Come here, Pistol, stand behind me. Oh, if I
had had time to have made new liveries, I would
have bestowed the thousand pound I borrowed of
you. But 'tis no matter, this poor show doth better.
This doth infer the zeal I had to see him.   15

9. **tripe-visaged:** with a pale pock-marked face, like tripe.
17. **eleven now:** i.e., to stuff herself out, as if pregnant. 20. **thin
. . . censer:** a *censer* is a pot with a lid in which perfume or
incense is burned, but the exact meaning of Doll's abuse has
not been found. 21. **swinged:** thrashed. 23. **bluebottle:**
because he wore a blue coat. **correctioner:** beadle, who admin-
istered correction. 24. **half-kirtles:** skirts. 25. **she . . . errant:**
female nightwalker. 33. **atomy:** for "anatomy," living skeleton.
Sc. v: s.d., **strewing rushes:** strewn as a mark of respect for
the occasion. 6. **grace:** favor. **leer:** look lovingly.

119. **Besonian:** recruit, "rookie." 124. **do this:** Here he makes
some expressive gesture. **fig me:** the sign of the fig (an insult of
immemorial antiquity) is made by thrusting the thumb between
the fore and middle fingers. 137. **steward:** and so able to be
generous with his mistress's goods. **boots:** large heavy boots used
by riders.
Sc. iv: 5. **whipping cheer:** a taste of the whip. Convicted
whores were publicly whipped. 8. **Nuthook:** lit., a hooked stick
for pulling down nuts, so one who grabs.

SHAL. It doth so.

FAL. It shows my earnestness of affection ——

SHAL. It doth so.

FAL. My devotion ——

SHAL. It doth, it doth, it doth.   20

FAL. As it were, to ride day and night, and not to
deliberate, not to remember, not to have patience to
shift me° ——

SHAL. It is best, certain.   24

FAL. But to stand stained with travel, and sweat-
ing with desire to see him, thinking of nothing else,
putting all affairs else in oblivion, as if there were
nothing else to be done but to see him.   29

PIST. 'Tis " *semper idem,*" for " *absque hoc nihil
est.*"° 'Tis all in every part.

SHAL. 'Tis so, indeed.

PIST. My knight, I will inflame thy noble liver,
And make thee rage.
Thy Doll, and Helen° of thy noble thoughts,   35
Is in base durance and contagious° prison,
Haled thither
By most mechanical° and dirty hand.
Rouse up revenge from ebon° den with fell Alecto's°
snake,
For Doll is in. Pistol speaks naught but truth.   40

FAL. I will deliver her.

     [*Shouts within, and the trumpets sound.*]

PIST. There roared the sea, and trumpet clangor
sounds.

[*Enter* KING HENRY V *and his train, the* LORD CHIEF
JUSTICE *among them.*]

FAL. God save thy Grace, King Hal! My royal
Hal!   44

PIST. The Heavens thee guard and keep, most
royal imp° of fame!

FAL. God save thee, my sweet boy!

K. HEN. V. My Lord Chief Justice, speak to that
vain man.

CH. JUST. Have you your wits? Know you what
'tis you speak?   49

FAL. My King! My Jove! I speak to thee, my heart!

K. HEN. V. I know thee not, old man. Fall to thy
prayers.
How ill white hairs become a fool and jester!
I have long dreamed of such a kind of man,
So surfeit-swelled,° so old, and so profane,
But, being awaked, I do despise my dream.   55
Make less thy body hence, and more thy grace.
Leave gormandizing. Know the grave doth gape
For thee thrice wider than for other men.
Reply not to me with a fool-born jest.

Presume not that I am the thing I was,   60
For God doth know, so shall the world perceive,
That I have turned away my former self,
So will I those that kept me company.
When thou dost hear I am as I have been,
Approach me, and thou shalt be as thou wast,   65
The tutor and the feeder of my riots.
Till then, I banish thee, on pain of death,
As I have done the rest of my misleaders,
Not to come near our person by ten mile.
For competence of life° I will allow you,   70
That lack of means enforce you not to evil.
And as we hear you do reform yourselves,
We will, according to your strength and qualities,
Give you advancement. Be it your charge, my
     lord,
To see performed the tenor° of our word.   75
Set on.   [*Exeunt* KING, *etc.*]

FAL. Master Shallow, I owe you a thousand pound.

SHAL. Yea, marry, Sir John, which I beseech you
to let me have home with me.   80

FAL. That can hardly be, Master Shallow. Do not
you grieve at this. I shall be sent for in private to
him. Look you, he must seem thus to the world.
Fear not your advancements, I will be the man yet
that shall make you great.   85

SHAL. I cannot well perceive how, unless you
should give me your doublet° and stuff me out with
straw. I beseech you, good Sir John, let me have five
hundred of my thousand.

FAL. Sir, I will be as good as my word. This that
you heard was but a color.°   91

SHAL. A color° that I fear you will die in, Sir John.

FAL. Fear no colors.° Go with me to dinner. Come,
Lieutenant Pistol, come, Bardolph. I shall be sent
for soon at night.°   96

[*Re-enter* PRINCE JOHN, *and the* LORD CHIEF JUSTICE;
OFFICERS *with them.*]

CH. JUST. Go, carry Sir John Falstaff to the Fleet.°
Take all his company along with him.

FAL. My lord, my lord ——

CH. JUST. I cannot now speak. I will hear you
soon.   100
Take them away.

PIST. *Si fortuna me tormenta, spero contenta.*°

[*Exeunt all but* PRINCE JOHN *and the* CHIEF JUSTICE.]

LANC. I like this fair proceeding of the King's.
He hath intent his wonted followers
Shall all be very well provided for,   105
But all are banished till their conversations
Appear more wise and modest to the world.

---

23. shift me: change my shirt.   **30–31. semper . . . est:** always
the same, for apart from this there is nothing.   **35. Helen:** the
ideal of all beautiful mistresses.   **36. contagious:** infectious.
London prisons were notoriously unsanitary.   **38. mechanical:**
workingman's.   **39. ebon:** black. **Alecto:** one of the Furies.
46. imp: little lad.   **54. surfeit-swelled:** swollen through over-
eating.

70. competence of life: means to live.   **75. tenor:** purpose.
87. doublet: jacket. See Pl. 8b and comment on p. 93a.   **91. color:**
pretense.   **92. color:** with a pun on "collar" — halter.   **93. Fear
no colors:** a proverbial phrase meaning "fear no one." See *T
Night,* I.v.6.   **96. at night:** i.e., for a private interview "after
office hours."   **97. Fleet:** a London prison.   **102. Si . . . contenta:**
See II.iv.195,n.

CH. JUST. And so they are.

LANC. The King hath called his Parliament, my
lord.

CH. JUST. He hath.   110

LANC. I will lay odds that ere this year expire
We bear our civil swords° and native fire
As far as France. I heard a bird so sing,   113
Whose music, to my thinking, pleased the King.
Come, will you hence?   [*Exeunt.*]

EPILOGUE°

[*Spoken by a* DANCER.]

First my fear,° then my curtsy, last my speech.
My fear is, your displeasure; my curtsy, my duty;
and my speech, to beg your pardons. If you look for
a good speech now, you undo me. For what I have
to say is of mine own making, and what indeed I   5
should say will, I doubt, prove mine own marring.
But to the purpose, and so to the venture. Be it
known to you, as it is very well, I was lately here in
the end of a displeasing play, to pray your patience
for it and to promise you a better. I meant in-   10

112. **civil swords:** the swords lately used in civil war.
    Epilogue: Epilogues are common in the plays of other drama-
tists but occur only in seven other Shakespearian plays. They
usually appeal for the approval or applause of the audience.
This Epilogue was evidently written for the first performance,
by way of apology for some play now unknown which had caused
displeasure, and for the scandal caused by the Oldcastle affair.
See *I Hen IV* Intro. p. 335a–b. 1. **fear:** lest you be displeased.

deed to pay you with this, which, if like an ill ven-
ture it come unluckily home, I break,° and you, my
gentle creditors, lose. Here I promised you I would
be, and here I commit my body to your mercies.   14
Bate me° some, and I will pay you some, and, as
most debtors do, promise you infinitely.

If my tongue cannot entreat you to acquit° me,
will you command me to use my legs? And yet that
were but light payment, to dance out of your debt.
But a good conscience will make any possible   20
satisfaction, and so would I. All the gentlewomen
here have forgiven me. If the gentlemen will not,
then the gentlemen do not agree with the gentle-
women, which was never seen before in such an as-
sembly.   26

One word more, I beseech you. If you be not too
much cloyed with fat meat, our humble author will
continue the story, with Sir John in it,° and make
you merry with fair Katharine of France. Where,
for anything I know, Falstaff shall die of a   31
sweat, unless already a' be killed with your hard
opinions, for Oldcastle died a martyr, and this is not
the man. My tongue is weary. When my legs are
too, I will bid you good night, and so kneel   35
down before you, but indeed to pray for the Queen.°

12. **break:** go bankrupt. 15. **Bate me:** let me off. 17. **acquit:**
release from a debt. 28–29. **will . . . it:** It is clear from this un-
fulfilled promise that Shakespeare had not yet started either to
plan or to write *Henry V.* 36. **pray . . . Queen:** This pious custom
still persists in the English theater, where a few bars of "God
Save the King" are played before or after the performance.

MUCH ADO ABOUT NOTHING

Introduction

Much Ado about Nothing was probably written in 1598. The first definite record of its existence occurs in the Stationers' Register, where there is a casual note, dated August 4, 1600, that four plays belonging to the Lord Chamberlain's Company are " to be staied " — that is, are not to be printed. The plays were: *As You Like It, Henry V*, Ben Jonson's *Every Man in His Humor*, and *Much Ado about Nothing*. Nevertheless, on August 23 the play was entered for printing in the normal way, together with *II Henry IV*, as the property of the printers Andrew Wise and William Aspley. Soon afterward a quarto appeared with the title page: *Much adoe about Nothing. As it hath been sundrie times publikely acted by the right honourable, the Lord Chamberlaine his seruants. Written by William Shakespeare. London. Printed by V.S. for Andrew Wise, and William Aspley. 1600.* This quarto is quite well printed and there are few serious difficulties in the text. There are, however, no divisions into acts and scenes; several notes of exit and entrance have been omitted; and the speakers' names are often confused. Thus Antonio, Leonato's brother, appears sometimes as " Old " (old man) or " Brother "; Don Pedro is " Pedro " and " Prince." The most interesting confusion is in the names of Dogberry and Verges, who in IV.ii become " Kempe " and " Cowley " — the actors who took the parts. These inconsistencies suggest that the printer was using the original manuscript of an author writing for his own company.

The plot is compounded of several incidents. The main story tells how Claudio, having fallen in love with Hero, is persuaded to believe that he has seen her talking with a lover at her bedroom window on the night before the wedding, and is thus led to repudiate her. This plot, in various forms, is not uncommon in tales of the sixteenth century; one version is told by Spenser in *The Faerie Queene*, Book II, Canto IV. The version nearest to that in *Much Ado* is to be found in a story by Matteo Bandello in an Italian novel published in 1554. The outline of Bandello's story is as follows:

In the year 1283, King Pedro of Aragon seized the Island of Sicily. While his Court was being held at Messina, one of his knights, Don Timbreo di Cardona, fell in love with a young lady called Fenicia, who was the daughter of Lionato de Lionati. The wedding day was appointed; but another knight, Signor Girondo Olerio Valentiano, had also fallen in love with Fenicia and wished to prevent the marriage. He therefore caused a young man to tell Don Timbreo that Fenicia had a lover who visited her secretly. So Don Timbreo hid in Lionato's garden, and there saw a young gentleman with two companions carrying a ladder. The ladder was placed against the wall, and one of the men climbed up and entered a window. Next morning Don Timbreo sent a messenger to Lionato to declare that with his own eyes he had perceived that Fenicia was disloyal to him and she could therefore find herself another husband. Fenicia was so dismayed by this unjust accusation that she fell into a deep swoon and even the physicians believed her to be dead. It was not until her mother began to prepare the body for burial that she opened her eyes. Thereupon Lionato was summoned, and they agreed that while the funeral ceremonies should proceed, Fenicia should meanwhile be sent away secretly into the country.

The report of Fenicia's death caused great sorrow in Messina, for when the case was examined the evidence on which she had been condemned appeared very slight. Don Timbreo was thus filled with remorse, as was Signor Girondo, who confessed his treacherous trick. The two men therefore came to Lionato, and Timbreo declared that he would recompense the injured father by obeying any command that might be laid on him. Lionato replied that since Don Timbreo wished to marry, he must take the lady whom he would offer, and to this Timbreo agreed.

A year had now passed. Fenicia was living under the name of Lucilla and her health had so greatly improved in the country that she was hardly recognizable. So Lionato arranged that Don Timbreo, accompanied by Signor Girondo and his friends, should attend mass at a village outside Messina, where he should meet the lady chosen for his bride. The mass being finished, Lucilla was brought out and the marriage was performed. At the marriage feast which followed all was revealed and the lovers were happily reconciled. Girondo humbly begged Fenicia's pardon, and the day's festivities were symmetrically completed by Girondo's betrothal to Fenicia's sister.

There is obviously some connection between this story and the play in the coincidence of the names Don Pedro, Lionato, and Messina, but the details vary considerably, and it is quite likely that the direct source of *Much Ado about Nothing* was some play that has now been lost.

There are indeed a few traces of apparent alteration in the play itself. In the quarto text, the opening stage direction reads: "*Enter Leonato, Governor of Messina, Innogen his wife, Hero his daughter, and Beatrice his niece, with a messenger.*" The wife reappears in a stage direction at the beginning of II.i, but she has no part in the play and is always omitted by modern editors.

There are other inconsistencies. The devices by which Borachio persuaded Margaret to impersonate Hero and Hero to sleep in another room are never satisfactorily explained in the play. It is possible, therefore, that *Much Ado about Nothing* is a play in two strata, the earlier being the Hero-Claudio story. When Shakespeare came to rewrite it, he expanded the story of Benedick and Beatrice, which is entirely his own invention, and in order to keep the play at the right length he was obliged to cut out much of the Hero-Claudio plot. As a result, some necessary explanations are missing. Moreover, it is noticeable that much of the Hero-Claudio story is written in the verse of Shakespeare's earlier style, while the Benedick-Beatrice story is mostly in prose.

There are other critical problems in *Much Ado about Nothing*. These are not noticeable on the stage, but they certainly obtrude when the play is read. The plot is complex, with three stories running parallel; these are the love affair of Hero and Claudio, which leads to disaster; the trap set to persuade Benedick and Beatrice to fall in love; and the plot of Don John, which is foiled by Dogberry and his Watch. The Hero-Claudio story again subdivides into three parts — the proxy wooing, the repudiation, and Hero's final restoration. This part of the play is on the whole weak, melodramatic, and to modern readers almost offensive, because after his outrageous conduct, Claudio's undeserved reward affronts the sense of justice.

The play begins with the return of Don Pedro, Prince of Aragon, with his officers from the wars, a scene which would have reminded Shakespeare's audience of a similar return from the wars after the successful expedition to Cadiz two years before (see Gen. Intro. p. 29b). Among the party are Claudio and Benedick. They are welcomed by Leonato, Governor of Messina, and by Hero his daughter and Beatrice his niece. Claudio, who had been attracted before the campaign, now falls in love with Hero and asks the Prince to negotiate the marriage for him. Then follows a masked dance. Don John, the Prince's bastard brother, a warped villain, persuades Claudio that the Prince is wooing Hero for himself. When Don Pedro, Leonato, Hero, and Claudio next meet, the Prince, to Claudio's amazement, explains that all is well. Leonato gladly consents to the wedding, Hero says nothing, and the two are betrothed. Thus ends the first scene of the second act. Shakespeare had therefore spent a whole act in tying up a tangle which falls apart at once. Why, ask the critics, these unnecessary complications? So far as the Hero and Claudio story is concerned, Shakespeare has now to go back and start again. Moreover, the modern reader is from this point alienated from Claudio. Since Don John had deceived him once, surely he might be more careful next time.

Nevertheless, against the objections of critics, it should be noted that *Much Ado about Nothing* is one of the best acting plays that Shakespeare ever wrote. Much of the success of this first act, and indeed of the whole Hero-Claudio story, depends on the actor taking the part of Don John. He is more important in person than in dialogue. He is a man of few words and therefore in the reading we are likely to overlook him. But when the play is adequately acted, with Don John malevolently brooding in the background, conspicuous and sinister in his silence, the story becomes far more effective.

Villainy has been foiled at the first attempt, but it is not vanquished. At this point Shakespeare begins to make the Benedick-Beatrice story move. Claudio and his friends plot to bring about the mating of Benedick and Beatrice by persuading each that the other is in love. A moment of high comedy is thus promised and foreshadowed. Immediately afterward another incident follows, which may be disastrous. Don John will try again. At the suggestion of one of his precious pair of villains, Borachio, he will endeavor to convince Claudio and Don Pedro that Hero is faithless. At this point we are told in detail what is about to happen. With the information firmly fixed in our minds, we are taken back to the other story. Both Benedick and Beatrice are to be deceived by overheard conversations. These developments are shown in two successive episodes, which, though divided into scenes by modern editors, are in fact one continuous scene.

The two episodes are carefully contrasted. First Benedick comes on alone, walks forward to the edge of the stage, and chats with the audience about love, and especially Claudio in love. He is thus much occupied with love thoughts, though not consciously for himself. Don Pedro and his fellow conspirators appear. Benedick hides and overhears the conversation that has been prepared for him. Benedick is then left alone to his own thoughts, and once more he soliloquizes. In the development of Shakespeare's dramatic art this is an interesting soliloquy, for it is the first of the more subtle, psychological revelations in which a mental process is laid bare before us. Benedick, like others before and since, has to make a complete reversal of his hitherto loudly proclaimed principles, and he must justify his inconsistency on the highest moral grounds. Then, as a man will, he immediately sees confirmation of his own happy thoughts in the plain and unfriendly words of Beatrice, who is still untouched. The whole of this scene is in prose. The next is a verse scene. Hero, accompanied by Margaret and Ursula, comes into the garden. Beatrice hides, and also overhears. Then the change is shown. The Beatrice whom we had hitherto seen was very much a speaker of bitter prose. Once she believes herself to be in love, she breaks out, almost spontaneously, into a sonnet. It may be, of course, that this rhymed passage is another outcrop of the old play, but if so why does Shakespeare leave this one speech and not the others? It is not an accident, but a most effective way of showing that Beatrice's mannishness, like armor, is the defense of a sensitive girl who is really afraid of losing control of her emotions.

The two avowed haters are now separately in love with each other, and the grand joke will be to see them meet for the first time. But at this point Shakespeare suspends the Benedick-Beatrice plot entirely; the joke will be the better for keeping. We are taken back to the story of Hero. Don John tells Claudio and Don Pedro of Hero's alleged behavior, but the window episode is not shown. Shakespeare was right to keep this in the background. If he had shown it, the deception would have been either so palpable that no excuse could be found for Claudio or so realistic that every excuse could be found for him. It is right, therefore, to keep it vague. To do this, and to surprise the audience and to show the passing of time, a new set of characters are now introduced — Dogberry, Verges, and the Watch. This admirable low comedy makes us for the moment entirely forget the others. Obviously it is nighttime, for the Watch come out only in the evening. Then Conrade and Borachio, Don John's agents in villainy, wander by. Borachio's plot has succeeded. He has received his reward, has spent some of it in the tavern, and is now confidentially drunk. Quite naturally, therefore, he tells Conrade what has happened. And quite naturally the Watch, who is standing by, overhears. From his words we realize that it was too dark to see, too far away to hear, and yet Claudio had believed. After this dramatic recital the villains are arrested by the Watch, and now the excitement begins. Will the truth come out before the wedding, or will Hero be falsely accused and vilely shamed?

This situation and its handling is a good illustration of a fundamental principle of Shakespeare's dramatic art.

There are two main ways of telling a story of misunderstanding. The first is to deceive the audience and the characters and then to spring a surprise and a reversal of the situation at the end. The second is to show the audience step by step what is happening, but to deceive the characters. Shakespeare prefers this method, whereby he achieves the effect of dramatic irony, which is always much deeper than surprise. Henceforward, in this part of the play every speech has two meanings. We are far more deeply moved by Hero's misfortunes when we can see them approaching than if they came suddenly and unexpectedly. Horror and the kindred feelings are always worse when the disaster can be foreseen as unavoidable.

The story now approaches tragedy. Hero dresses for her wedding. The bridegroom arrives. Then Dogberry enters. He has the news which will save everyone, if only he can tell it to Leonato; but both old men are pompous and foolish, each in his own way. Dogberry is too crass to tell his tale plainly, Leonato too fussy to realize that the constable has something important to say. Disaster is now inevitable, and we can only wait for it. The family assemble. Claudio carries out his threat and withdraws with his friends, leaving Hero apparently dead. Most of the party believe Hero to be guilty; only Beatrice instinctively, and the Friar by observation, believe in her innocence. Benedick at least will suspend judgment until he has heard the evidence more fully.

Throughout all this excitement we have forgotten the grand climax of the other plot — the moment when Benedick and Beatrice should next be alone together. Shakespeare has kept their declaration of love until there is no audience of tittering conspirators to jeer at their embarrassment. But once that moment is reached, the dialogue which follows is most moving — all the more because it is so genuine and so terse after the windy, theatrical rhetoric of Claudio and Leonato. Benedick, transformed for the moment into the " knight errant," must demand that his lady lay on him a task. He has asked for it; and the answer is right — " kill Claudio." Thus Benedick is presented with a knotty little problem in knight errantry: he must choose between love and friendship. The true knight would prefer his sworn brother before all others, man or woman; but the command of his newly won lady is also of great power, and Benedick, overcome rather than convinced by her torrential indignation, agrees and goes off to kill Claudio.

At this point the play is in some danger. Both plots have reached a moment of high tension; considerable adroitness will be needed to avoid either a flat conclusion or one of those interminable last acts which are all explanation. Shakespeare therefore cleans the slate and brings back Dogberry and Verges. One of the great advantages of the Elizabethan method of mixing clowns in more majestical matters is that it allowed a contrast and variety of emotions. The laughter which follows tears is heartier than the laughter of continuous farce. So the scene begins in low comedy with the pompous Dogberry examining the prisoners, which results in the Sexton's extracting the essential evidence to vindicate Hero.

We are now ready for the end, but Shakespeare raises the tension once more. Leonato and his old brother, vastly grieving, encounter Don Pedro and Claudio. Benedick accosts them and issues his challenge, but they refuse to take him seriously. Then comes the complete reversal. The prisoners are led in, Borachio confesses, and Claudio apologizes. Modern readers, however, find some difficulty in accepting what follows: Leonato's proposal that, since Hero is dead, Claudio shall marry another member of his family. After what has happened, it is hard to imagine that Leonato still regards this young man as a suitable husband for his only daughter. But to an Elizabethan the proposal would have seemed less astonishing. Marriage between great families was not an affair of love. Hero had moral and legal claims on Claudio; Claudio had promised to marry her and now rightly he must be made to fulfill his promise. As the favorite of his Prince, Claudio is such a very desirable match that much might be forgiven.

A few other matters have still to be disentangled. Benedick is shown briefly as a lover, and his halting efforts at love-making are much more agreeable than Claudio's more voluble protestations. And then, finally, the last surprise is disclosed when Hero is shown to be alive, and the whole story dissolves into merriment and dancing.

The play should not be taken too seriously. Shakespeare is providing entertainment for two hours, very varied and agreeable, but for all that, as it turns out, " much ado about nothing."

Much Ado about Nothing

DRAMATIS PERSONAE

DON PEDRO, *Prince of Aragon*
DON JOHN, *his bastard brother*
CLAUDIO, *a young lord of Florence*
BENEDICK, *a young lord of Padua*
LEONATO, *Governor of Messina*
ANTONIO, *his brother*
BALTHASAR, *attendant on Don Pedro*
CONRADE }
BORACHIO } *followers of Don John*
FRIAR FRANCIS
DOGBERRY, *a constable*

VERGES, *a headborough*
A SEXTON
A BOY

HERO, *daughter to Leonato*
BEATRICE, *niece to Leonato*
MARGARET }
URSULA } *gentlewomen attending on Hero*

MESSENGERS, WATCH, ATTENDANTS, ETC.

SCENE — *Messina.*

Act I

SCENE I. *Before* LEONATO's *house.*

[*Enter* LEONATO, HERO, *and* BEATRICE,
with a MESSENGER.]

LEON. I learn in this letter that Don Pedro of Aragon comes this night to Messina.

MESS. He is very near by this.° He was not three leagues off when I left him.

LEON. How many gentlemen have you lost in this action? 6

MESS. But few of any sort,° and none of name.°

LEON. A victory is twice itself when the achiever brings home full numbers. I find here that Don Pedro hath bestowed much honor on a young Florentine called Claudio. 11

MESS. Much deserved on his part, and equally remembered by Don Pedro. He hath borne himself beyond the promise of his age, doing in the figure of a lamb the feats of a lion. He hath indeed better bettered expectation than you must expect of me to tell you how. 17

LEON. He hath an uncle here in Messina will be very much glad of it.

MESS. I have already delivered him letters, and there appears much joy in him, even so much that joy could not show itself modest enough without a badge of bitterness.°

LEON. Did he break out into tears?

MESS. In great measure. 25

LEON. A kind° overflow of kindness.° There are no faces truer than those that are so washed. How much better is it to weep at joy than to joy at weeping!

BEAT. I pray you, is Signior Mountanto° returned from the wars, or no? 31

MESS. I know none of that name, lady. There was none such in the army of any sort.

LEON. What is he that you ask for, Niece?

HERO. My cousin means Signior Benedick of Padua. 36

MESS. Oh, he's returned, and as pleasant as ever he was.

BEAT. He° set up his bills° here in Messina and challenged Cupid at the flight;° and my uncle's 40 fool, reading the challenge, subscribed° for Cupid and challenged him at the bird bolt.° I pray you, how many hath he killed and eaten in these wars? But how many hath he killed? For indeed I promised to eat all of his killing. 45

LEON. Faith, Niece, you tax° Signior Benedick too much. But he'll be meet° with you, I doubt it not.

MESS. He hath done good service, lady, in these wars.

BEAT. You had musty victual, and he hath 50 holp° to eat it. He is a very valiant trencherman,° he hath an excellent stomach.

---

30. **Signior Mountanto:** "Signior Thruster." In fencing terms *montanto* was a thrust. **39–42. He ... bolt:** The point of Beatrice's elaborate jest is obscure. It may be paraphrased: Benedick challenged Cupid as an archer at the most difficult kind of shooting; my uncle's fool accepted, and challenged him to short-range competition with harmless arrows; i.e., Benedick is not the sort of man to cause a woman to fall in love. **39. set ... bills:** hung up a poster. **40. flight:** arrow used for long-range shooting. **41. subscribed:** signed underneath; i.e., accepted the challenge. **42. bird bolt:** short blunt arrow, used for shooting small birds — a harmless missile. See Pl. 22a. **46. tax:** censure, satirize. **47. meet:** even. **51. holp:** helped. **trencherman:** eater.

Act I, Sc. i: 3. by this: by this time. **7. sort:** rank. **name:** i.e., great family. **23. badge of bitterness:** a sign that joy is servant to sorrow; i.e. if he had not wept, his joy would have appeared immodest. **badge:** a metal plate bearing the master's coat of arms, worn by a servant. **26. kind:** natural. **kindness:** affection.

MESS. And a good soldier too, lady.

BEAT. And a good soldier to a lady, but what is he to a lord?   55

MESS. A lord to a lord, a man to a man, stuffed° with all honorable virtues.

BEAT. It is so indeed, he is no less than a stuffed man. But for the stuffing — well, we are all mortal.

LEON. You must not, sir, mistake my niece.   61 There is a kind of merry war betwixt Signior Benedick and her. They never meet but there's a skirmish of wit between them.   64

BEAT. Alas! he gets nothing by that. In our last conflict four of his five wits° went halting° off, and now is the whole man governed with one. So that if he have wit enough to keep himself warm, let him bear it for a difference° between himself and his horse; for it is all the wealth that he hath left,   70 to be known a reasonable creature.° Who is his companion now? He hath every month a new sworn brother.°

MESS. Is 't possible?   74

BEAT. Very easily possible. He wears his faith but as the fashion of his hat, it ever changes with the next block.°

MESS. I see, lady, the gentleman is not in your books.°

BEAT. No, an° he were, I would burn my   80 study. But I pray you who is his companion? Is there no young squarer° now that will make a voyage with him to the Devil?

MESS. He is most in the company of the right noble Claudio.   85

BEAT. Oh Lord, he will hang upon him like a disease. He is sooner caught than the pestilence, and the taker runs presently° mad. God help the noble Claudio! If he have caught the Benedick, it will cost him a thousand pound° ere a' be cured.   90

MESS. I will hold friends° with you, lady.

BEAT. Do, good friend.

LEON. You will never run mad,° Niece.

BEAT. No, not till a hot January.

MESS. Don Pedro is approached.   95

[*Enter* DON PEDRO, DON JOHN, CLAUDIO, BENEDICK, *and* BALTHASAR.]

D. PEDRO. Good Signior Leonato, you are come to

meet your trouble. The fashion of the world is to avoid cost, and you encounter it.

LEON. Never came trouble to my house in the likeness of your Grace; for trouble being gone,   100 comfort should remain, but when you depart from me, sorrow abides and happiness takes his leave.

D. PEDRO. You embrace your charge too willingly. I think this is your daughter.   104

LEON. Her mother hath many times told me so.

BENE. Were you in doubt, sir, that you asked her?

LEON. Signior Benedick, no, for then were you a child.   109

D. PEDRO. You have it full, Benedick. We may guess by this what you are, being a man.° Truly, the lady fathers herself.° Be happy, lady, for you are like an honorable father.

BENE. If Signior Leonato be her father, she would not have his head on her shoulders for all Messina, as like him as she is.   116

BEAT. I wonder that you will still be talking, Signior Benedick. Nobody marks you.

BENE. What, my dear Lady Disdain! Are you yet living?   120

BEAT. Is it possible Disdain should die while she hath such meet° food to feed it as Signior Benedick? Courtesy itself must convert to disdain if you come in her presence.   124

BENE. Then is courtesy a turncoat. But it is certain I am loved of all ladies, only you excepted. And I would I could find in my heart that I had not a hard heart, for truly I love none.

BEAT. A dear happiness° to women. They would else have been troubled with a pernicious suitor. I thank God and my cold blood I am of your hu-   131 mor° for that. I had rather hear my dog bark at a crow than a man swear he loves me.

BENE. God keep your ladyship still in that mind! So some gentleman or other shall 'scape a predestinate° scratched face.   136

BEAT. Scratching could not make it worse an 'twere such a face as yours were.

BENE. Well, you are a rare parrot-teacher.

BEAT. A bird of my tongue is better than a beast of yours.   141

BENE. I would my horse had the speed of your tongue, and so good a continuer. But keep your way, i' God's name. I have done.

BEAT. You always end with a jade's trick.° I know you of old.   146

D. PEDRO. That is the sum of all, Leonato. Signior Claudio and Signior Benedick, my dear friend Leonato hath invited you all. I tell him we shall stay here at the least a month, and he heartily prays   150

56. stuffed: The word is used with various meanings. The messenger means "crammed full"; Beatrice (l. 59) means "stuffed with straw." See III.iv.65.   66. five wits: i.e., common wit, imagination, fantasy, estimation, memory. halting: limping. 69. difference: an heraldic term — a slight difference in the coat of arms borne by different members of one family. See App. 9.   71. reasonable creature: man — and not quite a beast. 72-73. sworn brother: knights who had formed a romantic friendship for each other swore brotherhood that they would share good and evil fortune alike.   77. block: the wooden mold on which a felt hat is shaped.   78-79. in . . . books: in your good books; i.e., the list of your friends.   80. an: if.   82. squarer: quarreler.   88. presently: immediately.   90. thousand pound: See App. 27.   91. hold friends: be careful to keep friendly. 93. never . . . mad: i.e., "catch the Benedick." See l. 89 above.

111. being a man: i.e., you are known to be a dangerous man among the ladies.   112. fathers herself: is like her father. 122. meet: suitable.   129. dear happiness: rare good luck. 132. humor: mood.   136. predestinate: predestinated, fated. 145. jade's trick: dirty trick. A *jade* is a bad-tempered horse.

some occasion may detain us longer. I dare swear he is no hypocrite, but prays from his heart.

LEON. If you swear, my lord, you shall not be forsworn.° [*To* DON JOHN] Let me bid you 155 welcome, my lord. Being reconciled to the Prince your brother, I owe you all duty.

D. JOHN. I thank you. I am not of many words, but I thank you.

LEON. Please it your Grace lead on? 160

D. PEDRO. Your hand, Leonato. We will go together. [*Exeunt all except* BENEDICK *and* CLAUDIO.]

CLAUD. Benedick, didst thou note the daughter of Signior Leonato?

BENE. I noted her° not, but I looked on her. 165

CLAUD. Is she not a modest young lady?

BENE. Do you question me, as an honest man should do, for my simple true judgment? Or would you have me speak after my custom, as being a professed tyrant to their sex? 170

CLAUD. No, I pray thee speak in sober judgment.

BENE. Why, i' faith, methinks she's too low for a high praise, too brown for a fair praise, and too little for a great praise. Only this commendation I 175 can afford her, that were she other than she is, she were unhandsome; and being no other but as she is, I do not like her.

CLAUD. Thou thinkest I am in sport. I pray thee tell me truly how thou likest her. 180

BENE. Would you buy her, that you inquire after her?

CLAUD. Can the world buy such a jewel?

BENE. Yea, and a case to put it into. But speak you this with a sad brow?° Or do you play the 185 flouting Jack,° to tell us Cupid is a good hare-finder° and Vulcan° a rare° carpenter? Come, in what key shall a man take you, to go in the song?°

CLAUD. In mine eye she is the sweetest lady that ever I looked on. 190

BENE. I can see yet without spectacles, and I see no such matter. There's her cousin, an she were not possessed with a fury, exceeds her as much in beauty as the first of May doth the last of December. But I hope you have no intent to turn husband, have 196 you?

CLAUD. I would scarce trust myself, though I had sworn the contrary, if Hero would be my wife.

BENE. Is 't come to this? In faith, hath not the world one man but he will wear his cap with 200 suspicion?° Shall I never see a bachelor of threescore again? Go to, i' faith. An thou wilt needs thrust thy

neck into a yoke, wear the print° of it, and sigh away Sundays.° Look, Don Pedro is returned to seek you. 205

[*Re-enter* DON PEDRO.]

D. PEDRO. What secret hath held you here, that you followed not to Leonato's?

BENE. I would your Grace would constrain me to tell.

D. PEDRO. I charge thee on thy allegiance.° 210

BENE. You hear, Count Claudio. I can be secret as a dumb man, I would have you think so, but, on my allegiance, mark you this, on my allegiance. He is in love. With who? Now that is your Grace's part. Mark how short his answer is — with Hero, Leonato's short daughter. 216

CLAUD. If this were so, so were it uttered.

BENE. Like the old tale, my lord: "It is not so, nor 'twas not so, but, indeed, God forbid it should be so." 220

CLAUD. If my passion change not shortly, God forbid it should be otherwise.

D. PEDRO. Amen, if you love her, for the lady is very well worthy.

CLAUD. You speak this to fetch me in,° my lord.

D. PEDRO. By my troth, I speak my thought. 226

CLAUD. And in faith, my lord, I spoke mine.

BENE. And by my two faiths and troths, my lord, I spoke mine.

CLAUD. That I love her, I feel. 230

D. PEDRO. That she is worthy, I know.

BENE. That I neither feel how she should be loved, nor know how she should be worthy, is the opinion that fire cannot melt out of me. I will die in it at the stake. 235

D. PEDRO. Thou wast ever an obstinate heretic in the despite of° beauty.

CLAUD. And never could maintain his part but in the force of his will.° 239

BENE. That a woman conceived me, I thank her; that she brought me up, I likewise give her most humble thanks. But that I will have a recheat° winded° in my forehead, or hang my bugle in an invisible baldric,° all women shall pardon me. Because I will not do them the wrong to mistrust any, 245 I will do myself the right to trust none, and the fine° is, for the which I may go the finer, I will live a bachelor.

D. PEDRO. I shall see thee, ere I die, look pale with love. 250

BENE. With anger, with sickness, or with hunger,

155. be forsworn: break your oath. See *M Ado* Intro. p. 418b. 165. noted her: made careful notes on her. 185. sad brow: sober countenance. 186. flouting Jack: mocking knave. Cupid . . . hare-finder: Cupid, the blind god, is so keen-sighted that he can see a crouching hare. 187. Vulcan: the blacksmith god. rare: skillful. 187–88. Come . . . song: i.e., how shall I answer to fit your mood? 200–01. cap . . . suspicion: i.e., not suspect that he is a cuckold. See App. 11. | 203. print: impression. 203–04. sigh . . . Sundays: spend tedious weekends at home. 210. on . . . allegiance: the most solemn form of command, for to disobey was high treason. 225. fetch me in: make me give myself away. 236–37. in . . . of: in being spiteful about. 238–39. in . . . will: by sheer willfulness. 242. recheat: a call on the hunting horn, with the usual joke on the cuckold's horn. 243. winded: sounded. 244. baldric: the belt, slung across the chest, by which the hunter's horn was carried. 246. fine: conclusion.

my lord, not with love. Prove that ever I lose more blood with love than I will get again with drinking, pick out mine eyes with a ballad-maker's pen,° and hang me up at the door of a brothel house for the sign of blind Cupid.°   256

D. PEDRO. Well, if ever thou dost fall from this faith, thou wilt prove a notable argument.

BENE. If I do, hang me in a bottle like a cat° and shoot at me, and he that hits me, let him be clapped on the shoulder and called Adam.°   261

D. PEDRO. Well, as time shall try.° "In time the savage bull doth bear the yoke."°

BENE. The savage bull may, but if ever the sensible° Benedick bear it, pluck off the bull's   265 horns and set them in my forehead. And let me be vilely painted, and in such great letters as they write "Here is good horse to hire" let them signify under my sign "Here you may see Benedick the married man."   270

CLAUD. If this should ever happen, thou wouldst be horn-mad.°

D. PEDRO. Nay, if Cupid have not spent all his quiver in Venice,° thou wilt quake for this shortly.

BENE. I look for an earthquake too, then.   275

D. PEDRO. Well, you will temporize with the hours.° In the meantime, good Signior Benedick, repair to Leonato's. Commend me to him, and tell him I will not fail him at supper, for indeed he hath made great preparation.   280

BENE. I have almost matter enough in me for such an embassage, and so I commit you° ——

CLAUD. To the tuition of God. From my house, if I had it ——

D. PEDRO. The sixth of July. Your loving friend, Benedick.   286

BENE. Nay, mock not, mock not. The body of your discourse is sometime guarded° with fragments, and the guards° are but slightly basted° on neither. Ere you flout old ends° any further, examine your conscience. And so I leave you. [*Exit.*] 291

CLAUD. My liege, your Highness now may do me good.

D. PEDRO. My love is thine to teach. Teach it but how

And thou shalt see how apt it is to learn Any hard lesson that may do thee good.   295

CLAUD. Hath° Leonato any son, my lord?

D. PEDRO. No child but Hero, she's his only heir. Dost thou affect° her, Claudio?

CLAUD.   Oh, my lord, When you went onward on this ended action, I looked upon her with a soldier's eye,   300 That liked but had a rougher task in hand Than to drive liking to the name of love. But now I am returned and that war thoughts Have left their places vacant, in their rooms Come thronging soft and delicate desires,   305 All prompting me how fair young Hero is, Saying I liked her ere I went to wars.

D. PEDRO. Thou wilt be like a lover presently, And tire the hearer with a book of words. If thou dost love fair Hero, cherish it,   310 And I will break with her° and with her father, And thou shalt have her. Was 't not to this end That thou began'st to twist so fine a story?

CLAUD. How sweetly you do minister to love, That know love's grief by his complexion!°   315 But lest my liking might too sudden seem, I would have salved° it with a longer treatise.

D. PEDRO. What need the bridge much broader than the flood? The fairest grant is the necessity.° Look, what will serve is fit. 'Tis once° thou lovest, And I will fit thee with the remedy.   321 I know we shall have reveling tonight. I will assume thy part in some disguise, And tell fair Hero I am Claudio; And in her bosom I'll unclasp my heart,   325 And take her hearing prisoner with the force And strong encounter of my amorous tale. Then after to her father will I break, And the conclusion is, she shall be thine. In practice let us put it presently.   [*Exeunt.*]

SCENE II. *A room in* LEONATO'S *house.*

[*Enter* LEONATO *and* ANTONIO, *meeting.*]

LEON. How now, Brother! Where is my cousin,° your son? Hath he provided this music?

ANT. He is very busy about it. But, Brother, I can tell you strange news, that you yet dreamed not of.

LEON. Are they good?   6

ANT. As the event stamps them.° But they have a good cover,° they show well outward. The Prince° and Count Claudio, walking in a thick-pleached alley° in mine orchard, were thus much over- 10 heard by a man of mine. The Prince discovered° to Claudio that he loved my niece your daughter, and meant to acknowledge it this night in a dance; and if he found her accordant,° he meant to take the present time by the top,° and instantly break with you of it.   16

LEON. Hath the fellow any wit that told you this?

ANT. A good sharp fellow. I will send for him, and question him yourself.   20

LEON. No, no, we will hold it as a dream till it appear itself. But I will acquaint my daughter withal, that she may be the better prepared for an answer if peradventure this be true. Go you and tell her of it. [*Enter* ATTENDANTS.] Cousins, you know what you have to do. Oh, I cry you mercy,° friend 26 — go you with me, and I will use your skill. Good Cousin, have a care this busy time.   [*Exeunt.*]

SCENE III. *The same.*

[*Enter* DON JOHN *and* CONRADE.]

CON. What the goodyear,° my lord! Why are you thus out of measure sad?

D. JOHN. There is no measure in the occasion that breeds,° therefore the sadness is without limit.   5

CON. You should hear reason.

D. JOHN. And when I have heard it, what blessing brings it?

CON. If not a present remedy, at least a patient sufferance.°   10

D. JOHN. I wonder that thou, being (as thou sayest thou art) born under Saturn,° goest about to apply a moral medicine to a mortifying° mischief.° I cannot hide what I am.° I must be sad when I have cause, and smile at no man's jests; eat when I 15 have stomach, and wait for no man's leisure; sleep when I am drowsy, and tend on no man's business; laugh when I am merry, and claw° no man in his humor.   19

CON. Yea, but you must not make the full show of this till you may do it without controlment. You have of late stood out against your brother, and he hath ta'en you newly into his grace, where it is impossible you should take true root but by the fair weather that you make yourself. It is needful 25 that you frame the season° for your own harvest.

D. JOHN. I had rather be a canker° in a hedge than a rose in his grace, and it better fits my blood to be disdained of all than to fashion a carriage° 30 to rob love from any. In this, though I cannot be said to be a flattering honest man, it must not be denied but I am a plain-dealing villain. I am trusted with a muzzle, and enfranchised with a clog;° therefore I have decreed not to sing in my cage.° If I 35 had my mouth, I would bite; if I had my liberty, I would do my liking. In the meantime let me be that I am, and seek not to alter me.

CON. Can you make no use of your discontent?

D. JOHN. I make all use of it, for I use it only. 41 Who comes here? [*Enter* BORACHIO.] What news, Borachio?

BORA. I came yonder from a great supper. 43 The Prince your brother is royally entertained by Leonato, and I can give you intelligence° of an intended marriage.

D. JOHN. Will it serve for any model° to build mischief on? What is he for a fool that betroths himself to unquietness?   50

BORA. Marry, it is your brother's right hand.

D. JOHN. Who? The most exquisite Claudio?

BORA. Even he.

D. JOHN. A proper squire! And who, and who? Which way looks he?   55

BORA. Marry, on Hero, the daughter and heir of Leonato.

D. JOHN. A very forward March chick!° How came you to this?   59

BORA. Being entertained° for a perfumer, as I was smoking° a musty room comes me the Prince and Claudio, hand in hand, in sad° conference. I whipped me behind the arras,° and there heard it agreed upon that the Prince should woo Hero for himself, and having obtained her, give her to Count Claudio.   66

D. JOHN. Come, come, let us thither. This may prove food to my displeasure. That young start-up hath all the glory of my overthrow. If I can cross° him any way, I bless myself every way. You are both sure, and will assist me?   71

7. As . . . them: it depends on how things turn out. 8. cover: outward appearance. 8–16. The Prince . . . it: This is another of the misunderstandings which are never explained. See *M Ado* Intro. p. 418a–b. 9–10. thick-pleached alley: garden walk, sheltered by thick interlocked boughs, common in Old World gardens. See Pl. 16a. 11. discovered: revealed. 14. accordant: agreeable. 14–15. take . . . top: take time by the forelock. 26. cry . . . mercy: beg your pardon.

Sc. iii: 1. What . . . goodyear: a phrase whose origin has not been satisfactorily explained; probably something like "what the deuce." 4–5. no . . . breeds: the cause of my discontent is immeasurable. 10. sufferance: endurance. 12. born . . . Saturn: i.e., therefore grim and saturnine. See App. 2. 13. mortifying: killing. mischief: disease. 14. what I am: i.e., a royal bastard. 18 claw: stroke, flatter.

26. frame . . . season: contrive the proper occasion. 27. canker: wild rose. 30. fashion a carriage: force myself to behave politely. 34. enfranchised . . . clog: made free with a weight round my leg; i.e., I am treated like a fierce dog, trusted only when muzzled and chained. 35. decreed . . . cage: I will not sing like an imprisoned songbird. 45. intelligence: information. 48. model: ground plan. 58. forward . . . chick: i.e., precocious youngster. 60. entertained: employed. 61. smoking: burning perfume in. 62. sad: serious. 63. arras: tapestry hangings. 69. cross: thwart.

CON. To the death, my lord.

D. JOHN. Let us to the great supper. Their cheer is the greater that I am subdued. Would the cook were of my mind!° Shall we go prove° what's to be done?   76

BORA. We'll wait upon your lordship. [Exeunt.]

Act II

SCENE I. *A hall in* LEONATO'S *house.*

[*Enter* LEONATO, ANTONIO, HERO, BEATRICE, *and others.*]

LEON. Was not Count John here at supper?

ANT. I saw him not.

BEAT. How tartly that gentleman looks! I never can see him but I am heartburned° an hour after. 5

HERO. He is of a very melancholy disposition.

BEAT. He were an excellent man that were made just in the midway between him and Benedick. The one is too like an image and says nothing, and the other too like my lady's eldest son, evermore tattling.   11

LEON. Then half Signior Benedick's tongue in Count John's mouth, and half Count John's melancholy in Signior Benedick's face ——   14

BEAT. With a good leg and a good foot, Uncle, and money enough in his purse, such a man would win any woman in the world, if a'° could get her goodwill.

LEON. By my troth, Niece, thou wilt never get thee a husband if thou be so shrewd of° thy tongue.

ANT. In faith, she's too cursed.°   22

BEAT. Too cursed is more than cursed. I shall lessen God's sending that way, for it is said "God sends a cursed cow short horns,"° but to a cow too cursed he sends none.   26

LEON. So, by being too cursed, God will send you no horns.

BEAT. Just,° if he send me no husband, for the which blessing I am at him upon my knees 30 every morning and evening. Lord, I could not endure a husband with a beard on his face. I had rather lie in the woolen.°

LEON. You may light on a husband that hath no beard.   35

BEAT. What should I do with him? Dress him in my apparel and make him my waiting gentlewoman? He that hath a beard is more than a youth, and he that hath no beard is less than a man. And he 40 that is more than a youth is not for me, and he that is less than a man, I am not for him. Therefore I will even take sixpence in earnest° of the bearward,° and lead his apes into Hell.°

LEON. Well, then, go you into Hell?   44

BEAT. No, but to the gate, and there will the Devil meet me, like an old cuckold, with horns on his head, and say "Get you to Heaven, Beatrice, get you to Heaven. Here's no place for you maids." So deliver I up my apes, and away to Saint Peter for the Heavens. He shows me where the bachelors sit, and there live we as merry as the day is long.   52

ANT. [*To* HERO] Well, Niece, I trust you will be ruled by your father.

BEAT. Yes, faith, it is my cousin's duty to make curtsy and say, "Father, as it please you." But yet for all that, Cousin, let him be a handsome fellow, or else make another curtsy and say, "Father, as it please me."   59

LEON. Well, Niece, I hope to see you one day fitted with a husband.

BEAT. Not till God make men of some other metal° than earth. Would it not grieve a woman to be overmastered with a piece of valiant dust? To make an account of her life to a clod of way- 65 ward marl?° No, Uncle, I'll none. Adam's sons are my brethren, and truly, I hold it a sin to match in my kindred.°

LEON. Daughter, remember what I told you. If the Prince do solicit you in that kind, you know your answer.   71

BEAT. The fault will be in the music, Cousin, if you be not wooed in good time. If the Prince be too important,° tell him there is measure in everything, and so dance out the answer. For, hear me, 75 Hero. Wooing, wedding, and repenting is as a Scotch jig,° a measure,° and a cinquepace.° The first suit is hot and hasty, like a Scotch jig, and full as fantastical; the wedding, mannerly modest, as a measure full of state and ancientry;° and then 80 comes repentance, and, with his bad legs, falls into the cinquepace faster and faster till he sink into his grave.

LEON. Cousin, you apprehend passing° shrewdly.

BEAT. I have a good eye, Uncle, I can see a church by daylight.   86

74–75. Would . . . mind: i.e., he would then poison them all. 75. prove: see for ourselves.
  Act II, Sc. i: 5. am heartburned: suffer from indigestion. 17. a': he. 21. shrewd of: shrewish. 22. cursed: bitter. 24–25. God . . . horns: a common proverb, meaning that a bad-tempered cow has least power to hurt — with the inevitable joke on cuckold's horns. 29. Just: just so. 33. lie . . . woolen: i.e., without sheets, and so be tickled by the blankets.

42. in earnest: on account of service to be rendered. 43. bearward: keeper of bears and monkeys. See App. 5. lead . . . Hell: this was the proverbial fate of old maids who died unwed. 63. metal: material. 66. marl: clay. 67–68. match . . . kindred: marry a relative. 74. important: importunate. 77. Scotch jig: a lively, violent dance. measure: a stately formal dance. cinquepace: first five steps of the galliard, a quick, elaborate dance. See App. 24. 80. state . . . ancientry: formality and old-fashioned courtliness. 84. passing: exceedingly.

LEON. The revelers are entering, Brother. Make good room.   [*All put on their masks.*]
[*Enter* DON PEDRO, CLAUDIO, BENEDICK, BALTHASAR, DON JOHN, BORACHIO, MARGARET, URSULA, *and others, masked.*]

D. PEDRO. Lady, will you walk about° with your friend?   90

HERO. So you walk softly, and look sweetly, and say nothing, I am yours for the walk — and especially when I walk away.

D. PEDRO. With me in your company?

HERO. I may say so, when I please.   95

D. PEDRO. And when please you to say so?

HERO. When I like your favor,° for God defend° the lute should be like the case!°

D. PEDRO. My visor° is Philemon's roof.° Within the house is Jove.   100

HERO. Why, then, your visor should be thatched.

D. PEDRO. [*Drawing her aside*] Speak low, if you speak love.

BALTH. Well, I would you did like me.   104

MARG. So would not I, for your own sake, for I have many ill qualities.

BALTH. Which is one?

MARG. I say my prayers aloud.

BALTH. I love you the better. The hearers may cry "Amen."   110

MARG. God match me with a good dancer!

BALTH. Amen.

MARG. And God keep him out of my sight when the dance is done! Answer, clerk.°   114

BALTH. No more words. The clerk is answered.

URS. I know you well enough. You are Signior Antonio.

ANT. At a word, I am not.

URS. I know you by the waggling of your head.

ANT. To tell you true, I counterfeit him.   121

URS. You could never do him so ill-well unless you were the very man. Here's his dry hand up and down. You are he, you are he.

ANT. At a word, I am not.   125

URS. Come, come, do you think I do not know you by your excellent wit? Can virtue hide itself? Go to, mum, you are he. Graces will appear, and there's an end.

BEAT. Will you not tell me who told you so? 130

BENE. No, you shall pardon me.

BEAT. Nor will you not tell me who you are?

BENE. Not now.

BEAT. That I was disdainful, and that I had my good wit out of the *Hundred Merry Tales*° — well, this was Signior Benedick that said so.   136

BENE. What's he?

BEAT. I am sure you know him well enough.

BENE. Not I, believe me.

BEAT. Did he never make you laugh?   140

BENE. I pray you, what is he?

BEAT. Why, he is the Prince's jester — a very dull fool, only his gift is in devising impossible slanders. None but libertines delight in him, and the commendation is not in his wit, but in his villainy;   145 for he both pleases men and angers them, and then they laugh at him and beat him. I am sure he is in the fleet.° I would he had boarded me.

BENE. When I know the gentleman, I'll tell him what you say.   151

BEAT. Do, do. He'll but break a comparison or two on me, which, peradventure not marked or not laughed at, strikes him into melancholy — and then there's a partridge wing saved, for the fool will   155 eat no supper that night. [*Music*] We must follow the leaders.

BENE. In every good thing.

BEAT. Nay, if they lead to any ill, I will leave them at the next turning. [*Dance. Then exeunt all except* DON JOHN, BORACHIO, *and* CLAUDIO.]

D. JOHN. Sure my brother is amorous on Hero, and hath withdrawn her father to break with him about it. The ladies follow her, and but one visor remains.

BORA. And this is Claudio. I know him by his bearing.   166

D. JOHN. Are not you Signior Benedick?

CLAUD. You know me well. I am he.

D. JOHN. Signior, you are very near my brother in his love. He is enamored on Hero. I pray you, dissuade him from her. She is no equal for his   171 birth. You may do the part of an honest man in it.

CLAUD. How know you he loves her?

D. JOHN. I heard him swear his affection.   175

BORA. So did I too, and he swore he would marry her tonight.

D. JOHN. Come, let us to the banquet.°
                           [*Exeunt* DON JOHN *and* BORACHIO.]

CLAUD. Thus answer I in name of Benedick, But hear these ill news with the ears of Claudio. 'Tis certain so. The Prince woos for himself.   181 Friendship is constant in all other things Save in the office° and affairs of love; Therefore all hearts in love use their own tongues, Let every eye negotiate for itself,   185 And trust no agent, for beauty is a witch Against whose charms faith melteth into blood.°

---

89. walk about: dance a measure. See App. 24.   **97. favor:** face. **defend:** forbid.   **98. lute . . . case:** the instrument should be as ugly as its case, for Don Pedro is wearing a grotesque mask. **99. visor:** mask. **Philemon's roof:** Philemon and Baucis were a good old couple who unawares gave hospitality in their cottage to the gods Jupiter and Mercury.   **114. Answer, clerk:** In services in the Church of England the parson used to read the prayers and versicles, while the clerk led the congregation in the amens and responses.

135. *Hundred . . . Tales:* a popular book of jokes, first published in 1526.   **147–48. in . . . fleet:** i.e., among the returned soldiers. **178. banquet:** light refreshments given at an evening entertainment.   **183. office:** business.   **187. blood:** passion.

This is an accident of hourly proof,°
Which I mistrusted° not. Farewell, therefore, Hero!
[*Re-enter* BENEDICK.]
BENE. Count Claudio?   190
CLAUD. Yea, the same.
BENE. Come, will you go with me?
CLAUD. Whither?
BENE. Even to the next willow, about your own
business, County.° What fashion will you wear   195
the garland of? About your neck, like a usurer's
chain?° Or under your arm, like a lieutenant's
scarf? You must wear it one way, for the Prince
hath got your Hero.
CLAUD. I wish him joy of her.   200
BENE. Why, that's spoken like an honest drovier.°
So they sell bullocks. But did you think the Prince
would have served you thus?
CLAUD. I pray you, leave me.   204
BENE. Ho! Now you strike like the blind man.
'Twas the boy that stole your meat, and you'll beat
the post.
CLAUD. If it will not be, I'll leave you.   [*Exit.*]
BENE. Alas, poor hurt fowl! Now will he creep
into sedges.° But that my Lady Beatrice should   210
know me and not know me! The Prince's fool!
Ha? It may be I go under that title because I am
merry. Yea, but so I am apt to do myself wrong, I
am not so reputed. It is the base, though bitter, dis-
position of Beatrice that puts the world into her   215
person, and so gives me out.° Well, I'll be revenged
as I may.

[*Re-enter* DON PEDRO.]
D. PEDRO. Now, signior, where's the Count? Did
you see him?   219
BENE. Troth, my lord, I have played the part of
Lady Fame. I found him here as melancholy as a
lodge in a warren.° I told him, and I think I told
him true, that your Grace had got the goodwill of
this young lady. And I offered him my company to
a willow tree,° either to make him a garland,   225
as being forsaken, or to bind him up a rod, as being
worthy to be whipped.
D. PEDRO. To be whipped! What's his fault?
BENE. The flat transgression of a schoolboy who,
being overjoyed with finding a bird's nest, shows it
his companion, and he steals it.   231
D. PEDRO. Wilt thou make a trust a transgression?
The transgression is in the stealer.
BENE. Yet it had not been amiss the rod had been
made, and the garland too; for the garland he   235

might have worn himself, and the rod he might have
bestowed on you, who, as I take it, have stolen his
birds' nest.
D. PEDRO. I will but teach them to sing and restore
them to the owner.   240
BENE. If their singing answer your saying, by my
faith, you say honestly.
D. PEDRO. The Lady Beatrice hath a quarrel to
you. The gentleman that danced with her told her
she is much wronged by you.   245
BENE. Oh, she misused me past the endurance of
a block! An oak but with one green leaf on it would
have answered her. My very visor began to assume
life and scold with her. She told me, not thinking
I had been myself, that I was the Prince's jester, 250
that I was duller than a great thaw, huddling jest
upon jest with such impossible conveyance° upon
me that I stood like a man at a mark,° with a whole
army shooting at me. She speaks poniards,° and
every word stabs. If her breath were as terrible   255
as her terminations,° there were no living near her.
She would infect to the North Star. I would not
marry her though she were endowed with all that
Adam had left him before he transgressed. She
would have made Hercules have turned spit,°   260
yea, and have cleft his club to make the fire, too.
Come, talk not of her. You shall find her the infernal
Ate° in good apparel. I would to God some scholar
would conjure her;° for certainly while she is here
a man may live as quiet in Hell as in a sanctu-   265
ary, and people sin upon purpose because they would
go thither. So, indeed, all disquiet, horror, and per-
turbation follows her.
D. PEDRO. Look, here she comes.   270
[*Re-enter* CLAUDIO, BEATRICE, HERO,
and LEONATO.]
BENE. Will your Grace command me any service
to the world's end? I will go on the slightest errand
now to the Antipodes° that you can devise to send
me on. I will fetch you a toothpicker° now from the
furthest inch of Asia, bring you the length of   275
Prester John's° foot, fetch you a hair off the great
Cham's° beard, do you any embassage to the Pig-
mies,° rather than hold three words' conference
with this harpy. You have no employment for me?
D. PEDRO. None but to desire your good company.
BENE. Oh, God, sir, here's a dish I love not.   282
I cannot endure my Lady Tongue.   [*Exit.*]

---

188. accident . . . proof: common occurrence.   189. mistrusted:
suspected.   195. County: count.   196–97. usurer's chain: Men
of wealth used to advertise their importance by wearing long
gold chains — as a modern money lender often sports a large
diamond ring.   201. drovier: cattle-driver.   209. sedges: reeds.
215–16. puts . . . out: claims to know what everyone is saying
and describes me thus.   222. lodge . . . warren: a gamekeeper's
hut, a lonely, melancholy place.   225. willow tree: the emblem
of a forlorn lover.

252. conveyance: jugglery, trickery.   253. mark: target.   254. pon-
iards: daggers.   256. terminations: expressions.   260. turned spit:
Turning the spit on which meat was roasted was the most menial
of tasks in the kitchen.   263. Ate: the goddess of strife.
263–64. scholar . . . her: as evil spirits were exorcised in Latin,
a scholar was necessary. See *Haml.* I.i.42.   273. Antipodes: the
other end of the earth. Benedick will undertake any distant
voyage to get away from his tormentor.   274. toothpicker:
toothpick.   276. Prester John: fabled King of Abyssinia and
the strange parts beyond.   276–77. great Cham: the Mongol
Emperor.   278. Pigmies: another distant and romantic race.

D. PEDRO. Come, lady, come, you have lost the heart of Signior Benedick. 286

BEAT. Indeed, my lord, he lent it me awhile, and I gave him use for it, a double heart for his single one. Marry, once before he won it of me with false dice, therefore your Grace may well say I have lost it.° 291

D. PEDRO. You have put him down, lady, you have put him down.

BEAT. So I would not he should do me, my lord, lest I should prove the mother of fools. I have brought Count Claudio, whom you sent me to seek. 297

D. PEDRO. Why, how now, Count! Wherefore are you sad?

CLAUD. Not sad, my lord. 300

D. PEDRO. How then? Sick?

CLAUD. Neither, my lord.

BEAT. The Count is neither sad, nor sick, nor merry, nor well, but civil Count, civil as an 305 orange,° and something of that jealous complexion.

D. PEDRO. I' faith, lady, I think your blazon° to be true, though I'll be sworn, if he be so, his conceit° is false. Here, Claudio, I have wooed in thy name, and fair Hero is won. I have broke with her father, and his goodwill obtained. Name the day of marriage, and God give thee joy! 312

LEON. Count, take of me my daughter, and with her my fortunes. His Grace hath made the match, and all grace say "Amen" to it. 315

BEAT. Speak, Count, 'tis your cue.

CLAUD. Silence is the perfectest herald of joy. I were but little happy if I could say how much. Lady, as you are mine, I am yours. I give away myself for you, and dote upon the exchange. 320

BEAT. Speak, Cousin, or if you cannot, stop his mouth with a kiss, and let not him speak neither.

D. PEDRO. In faith, lady, you have a merry heart.

BEAT. Yea, my lord, I thank it, poor fool — it keeps on the windy side of care. My cousin tells him in his ear that he is in her heart.

CLAUD. And so she doth, Cousin. 329

BEAT. Good Lord, for alliance!° Thus goes everyone to the world but I, and I am sunburned,° I may sit in a corner and cry heigh-ho for a husband!

D. PEDRO. Lady Beatrice, I will get you one.

BEAT. I would rather have one of your father's getting.° Hath your Grace ne'er a brother like 335 you? Your father got excellent husbands, if a maid could come by them.

D. PEDRO. Will you have me, lady?

BEAT. No, my lord, unless I might have an- 340 other for working days. Your Grace is too costly to wear every day. But I beseech your Grace pardon me. I was born to speak all mirth and no matter. 344

D. PEDRO. Your silence most offends me, and to be merry best becomes you, for, out of question, you were born in a merry hour.

BEAT. No, sure, my lord, my mother cried; but then there was a star danced, and under that was I born. Cousins, God give you joy! 350

LEON. Niece, will you look to those things I told you of?

BEAT. I cry you mercy, Uncle. By your Grace's pardon. [*Exit.*]

D. PEDRO. By my troth, a pleasant-spirited lady.

LEON. There's little of the melancholy ele- 357 ment° in her, my lord. She is never sad but when she sleeps, and not ever sad then, for I have heard my daughter say she hath often dreamed of unhappiness and waked herself with laughing. 361

D. PEDRO. She cannot endure to hear tell of a husband.

LEON. Oh, by no means. She mocks all her wooers out of suit. 365

D. PEDRO. She were an excellent wife for Benedick.

LEON. Oh Lord, my lord, if they were but a week married they would talk themselves mad.

D. PEDRO. County Claudio, when mean you to go to church? 371

CLAUD. Tomorrow, my lord. Time goes on crutches till love have all his rites.

LEON. Not till Monday, my dear son, which is hence a just sevennight,° and a time too brief, too, to have all things answer my mind. 376

D. PEDRO. Come, you shake the head at so long a breathing.° But I warrant thee, Claudio, the time shall not go dully by us. I will, in the interim, undertake one of Hercules' labors, which is to bring 380 Signior Benedick and the Lady Beatrice into a mountain of affection the one with the other. I would fain have it a match, and I doubt not but to fashion it if you three will but minister such assistance as I shall give you direction. 386

LEON. My lord, I am for you, though it cost me ten nights' watchings.

CLAUD. And I, my lord.

D. PEDRO. And you too, gentle Hero?

HERO. I will do any modest office, my lord, to help my cousin to a good husband. 391

D. PEDRO. And Benedick is not the unhopefulest husband that I know. Thus far can I praise him. He is of a noble strain, of approved° valor and confirmed honesty. I will teach you how to humor 395

287–91. **Indeed . . . it:** This passage has not been satisfactorily explained, but when Beatrice is being sarcastic, she is liable to become cryptic.   305–06. **civil . . . orange:** with a pun on Seville oranges and their yellow color, which was the sign of jealousy.   307. **blazon:** description, originally a heraldic term.   308. **conceit:** imagination.   330. **Good . . . alliance:** Good Lord, what a thing this marrying is!   331. **sunburned:** no fine lady, for an ivory complexion was most admired.   335. **getting:** begetting.

357–58. **melancholy element:** See App. 3.   375. **a . . . sevennight:** exactly a week.   378. **breathing:** pause.   394. **approved:** proved

your cousin that she shall fall in love with Benedick.
And I, with your two helps, will so practice on
Benedick that, in despite of his quick wit and his
queasy° stomach, he shall fall in love with Beatrice.
If we can do this, Cupid is no longer an archer.   400
His glory shall be ours, for we are the only love
gods. Go in with me, and I will tell you my drift.°

[*Exeunt.*]

SCENE II. *The same.*

[*Enter* DON JOHN *and* BORACHIO.]

D. JOHN. It is so. The Count Claudio shall marry
the daughter of Leonato.

BORA. Yea, my lord, but I can cross it.   3

D. JOHN. Any bar, any cross,° any impediment
will be medicinable° to me. I am sick in displeasure
to him, and whatsoever comes athwart his affection°
ranges evenly° with mine. How canst thou cross
this marriage?   8

BORA. Not honestly, my lord, but so covertly that
no dishonesty shall appear in me.

D. JOHN. Show me briefly how.

BORA. I think I told your lordship, a year since,
how much I am in the favor of Margaret, the wait-
ing gentlewoman to Hero.

D. JOHN. I remember.   15

BORA. I can, at any unseasonable instant of the
night, appoint her to look out at her lady's chamber
window.

D. JOHN. What life is in that, to be the death of
this marriage?   20

BORA. The poison of that lies in you to temper.°
Go you to the Prince your brother. Spare not to tell
him that he hath wronged his honor in marrying the
renowned Claudio — whose estimation do you
mightily hold up — to a contaminated stale,° such
a one as Hero.   26

D. JOHN. What proof shall I make of° that?

BORA. Proof enough to misuse° the Prince, to vex
Claudio, to undo Hero, and kill Leonato. Look you
for any other issue?   30

D. JOHN. Only to despite° them I will endeavor
anything.

BORA. Go, then. Find me a meet° hour to draw
Don Pedro and the Count Claudio alone. Tell them
that you know that Hero loves me, intend a   35
kind of zeal both to the Prince and Claudio, as —
in love of your brother's honor, who hath made this
match, and his friend's reputation, who is thus like
to be cozened° with the semblance° of a maid —

that you have discovered thus. They will scarcely   40
believe this without trial. Offer them instances,°
which shall bear no less likelihood than to see me
at her chamber window, hear me call Margaret
Hero, hear Margaret term me Claudio,° and bring
them to see this the very night before the in-   45
tended wedding — for in the meantime I will so
fashion the matter that Hero shall be absent. And
there shall appear such seeming truth of Hero's dis-
loyalty that jealousy shall be called assurance° and
all the preparation overthrown.   51

D. JOHN. Grow this to what adverse issue it can,
I will put it in practice. Be cunning in the working
this and thy fee is a thousand ducats.°

BORA. Be you constant in the accusation and my
cunning shall not shame me.   56

D. JOHN. I will presently go learn their day of
marriage.   [*Exeunt.*]

SCENE III. LEONATO'S *orchard.*

[*Enter* BENEDICK.]

BENE. Boy!

[*Enter* BOY.]

BOY. Signior?

BENE. In my chamber window lies a book. Bring
it hither to me in the orchard.

BOY. I am here already, sir.   5

BENE. I know that, but I would have thee hence,
and here again. [*Exit* BOY.] I do much wonder that
one man, seeing how much another man is a fool
when he dedicates his behaviors to love, will, after
he hath laughed at such shallow follies in others,   10
become the argument of his own scorn by falling
in love — and such a man is Claudio. I have known
when there was no music with him but the drum
and the fife, and now had he rather hear the tabor
and the pipe.° I have known when he would   15
have walked ten mile afoot to see a good armor,°
and now will he lie ten nights awake carving the
fashion of a new doublet.° He was wont to speak
plain and to the purpose, like an honest man and a
soldier, and now is he turned orthography,° his   20
words are a very fantastical banquet — just so many
strange dishes. May I be so converted, and see with
these eyes? I cannot tell, I think not. I will not be
sworn but love may transform me to an oyster,   25

41. instances: proofs.   43–44. hear . . . Claudio: if Claudio had
heard the supposed Hero call someone else Claudio, he would
surely have guessed that there was a mistake. See *M Ado* Intro.
p. 418a.   50. assurance: certainty.   54. ducat: Italian coin
worth about $2.25.

Sc. iii: 14–15. tabor . . . pipe: the musical instruments of
shepherds and other men of peace. See Pl. 13d. tabor: small drum.
pipe: wind instrument made of a single pipe of wood.   16. armor:
suit of armor.   18. doublet: jacket, often elaborately cut and
embroidered. See Pl. 8b and p. 93a.   20. orthography: phrase-
maker.

399. queasy: delicate, particular.   402. drift: idea.
Sc. ii: 4. cross: obstacle. medicinable: healing medicine.
6. affection: liking.   7. ranges evenly: runs parallel.   21. temper:
mix.   25. stale: whore.   27. make of: offer for.   28. misuse:
deceive.   31. despite: spite.   33. meet: fit.   39. cozened:
cheated. semblance: appearance.

but I'll take my oath on it till he have made an
oyster of me he shall never make me such a fool.
One woman is fair, yet I am well; another is wise,
yet I am well; another virtuous, yet I am well. But
till all graces be in one woman, one woman 30
shall not come in my grace. Rich she shall be, that's
certain; wise, or I'll none; virtuous, or I'll never
cheapen° her; fair, or I'll never look on her; mild,
or come not near me; noble,° or not I for an angel;°
of good discourse, an excellent musician; and 35
her hair shall be of what color it please God. Ha!
The Prince and Monsieur Love! I will hide me in
the arbor.   [*Withdraws.*]

  [*Enter* DON PEDRO, CLAUDIO, LEONATO,
    and BALTHASAR.°]

 D. PEDRO. Come, shall we hear this music?

 CLAUD. Yea, my good lord. How still the evening
is,   40
As hushed on purpose to grace harmony!

 D. PEDRO. See you where Benedick hath hid him-
self?

 CLAUD. Oh, very well, my lord. The music ended,
We'll fit the kid fox with a pennyworth.°

 D. PEDRO. Come, Balthasar, we'll hear that song
again.   45

 BALTH. Oh, good my lord, tax° not so bad a voice
To slander music any more than once.

 D. PEDRO. It is the witness still° of excellency
To put a strange face° on his own perfection.
I pray thee, sing, and let me woo no more. 50

 BALTH. Because you talk of wooing, I will sing.
Since many a wooer doth commence his suit
To her he thinks not worthy, yet he woos,
Yet will he swear he loves.

 D. PEDRO.   Nay, pray thee, come.
Or if thou wilt hold longer argument, 55
Do it in notes.

 BALTH. Note this before my notes,
There's not a note of mine that's worth the noting.

 D. PEDRO. Why, these are very crotchets that he
speaks —
Note, notes, forsooth, and nothing.°

        [*Plays the tune.*]

 BENE. Now, divine air!° Now is his soul rav- 60
ished! Is it not strange that sheep's guts° should hale
souls out of men's bodies? Well, a horn for my
money, when all's done.

---

33. **cheapen:** bargain for. 34. **noble:** 6*s* 8*d*. **angel:** 10*s*. Puns
on these coins are common. See Pl. 10, and App. 27. 38. **s.d.,**
Balthasar: F1 prints "Jack Wilson," a singer who once took the
part. 44. **fit . . . pennyworth:** "we'll give him something for
his money." The *kid fox* is a reference to the fable of the Kid and
the Fox, told, for instance, in Spenser's *Shepherd's Calendar*, V.
The kid thought itself clever, but was carried off by the fox.
46. **tax:** censure. 48. **still:** always. 49. **strange face:** assumed
appearance. 59. **nothing:** a pun on noting. 60. **air:** tune.
61. **sheep's guts:** from which strings for musical instruments
were made. Benedick is no lover of chamber music.

BALTH. [*Sings.*]
 Sigh no more, ladies, sigh no more,
  Men were deceivers ever, 65
 One foot in sea and one on shore,
  To one thing constant never.
 Then sigh not so, but let them go,
  And be you blithe and bonny,
 Converting all your sounds of woe 70
  Into Hey nonny, nonny.

 Sing no more ditties, sing no moe°
  Of dumps° so dull and heavy.
 The fraud of men was ever so,
  Since summer first was leavy. 75
 Then sigh not so, but let them go,
  And be you blithe and bonny,
 Converting all your sounds of woe
  Into Hey nonny, nonny.

 D. PEDRO. By my troth, a good song.

 BALTH. And an ill singer, my lord.

 D. PEDRO. Ha, no, no, faith, thou singest well
enough for a shift.°   80

 BENE. An he had been a dog that should have
howled thus, they would have hanged him. And I
pray God his bad voice bode no mischief. I had as lief
have heard the night raven,° come what plague
could have come after it.   85

 D. PEDRO. Yea, marry, dost thou hear, Balthasar? I
pray thee get us some excellent music, for tomorrow
night we would have it at the Lady Hero's chamber
window.

 BALTH. The best I can, my lord. 90

 D. PEDRO. Do so. Farewell. [*Exit* BALTHASAR.]
Come hither, Leonato. What was it you told me of
today — that your niece Beatrice was in love with
Signior Benedick?

 CLAUD. Oh, aye. Stalk on, stalk on, the fowl sits.
I did never think that lady would have loved any
man.   97

 LEON. No, nor I neither. But most wonderful that
she should so dote on Signior Benedick, whom she
hath in all outward behaviors seemed ever to abhor.

 BENE. Is 't possible? Sits the wind in that corner?

 LEON. By my troth, my lord, I cannot tell 102
what to think of it but that she loves him with an
enraged° affection. It is past the infinite of thought.°

 D. PEDRO. Maybe she doth but counterfeit.

 CLAUD. Faith, like enough.

 LEON. Oh, God, counterfeit! There was never
counterfeit of passion came so near the life of pas-
sion as she discovers it.   111

 D. PEDRO. Why, what effects of passion shows she?

 CLAUD. Bait the hook well — this fish will bite.

 LEON. What effects, my lord? She will sit you,
you heard my daughter tell you how. 116

---

72. **moe:** more. 73. **dumps:** melancholy. 80. **shift:** makeshift
84. **night raven:** i.e., a bird of ill-omen. 104. **enraged:** furious
infinite of thought: i.e., unimaginable.

CLAUD. She did, indeed.

D. PEDRO. How, how, I pray you? You amaze me. I would have thought her spirit had been invincible against all assaults of affection.   120

LEON. I would have sworn it had, my lord, especially against Benedick.

BENE. I should think this a gull° but that the white-bearded fellow speaks it. Knavery cannot, sure, hide himself in such reverence.   125

CLAUD. He hath ta'en the infection. Hold it up.°

D. PEDRO. Hath she made her affection known to Benedick?

LEON. No, and swears she never will. That's her torment.   130

CLAUD. 'Tis true indeed, so your daughter says. "Shall I," says she, "that have so oft encountered him with scorn, write to him that I love him?"

LEON. This says she now when she is begin- 135 ning to write to him; for she'll be up twenty times a night, and there will she sit in her smock° till she have writ a sheet of paper. My daughter tells us all.

CLAUD. Now you talk of a sheet of paper, I remember a pretty jest your daughter told us of.

LEON. Oh, when she had writ it, and was reading it over, she found Benedick and Beatrice between the sheet?

CLAUD. That.   145

LEON. Oh, she tore the letter into a thousand halfpence, railed at herself that she should be so immodest to write to one that she knew would flout her. "I measure him," says she, "by my own spirit, for I should flout him if he writ to me — yea, though I love him, I should."   151

CLAUD. Then down upon her knees she falls, weeps, sobs, beats her heart, tears her hair, prays, curses. "O sweet Benedick! God give me patience!"

LEON. She doth indeed, my daughter says 156 so. And the ecstasy° hath so much overborne° her that my daughter is sometime afeard she will do a desperate outrage to herself. It is very true.

D. PEDRO. It were good that Benedick knew of it by some other, if she will not discover it.   161

CLAUD. To what end? He would make but a sport of it, and torment the poor lady worse.

D. PEDRO. An he should, it were an alms° to hang him. She's an excellent sweet lady, and out of all suspicion she is virtuous.   166

CLAUD. And she is exceeding wise.

D. PEDRO. In everything but in loving Benedick.

LEON. Oh, my lord, wisdom and blood combating in so tender a body, we have ten proofs to one that blood hath the victory. I am sorry for her, as I have just cause, being her uncle and her guardian.   174

D. PEDRO. I would she had bestowed this dotage on me. I would have daffed all other respects° and made her half myself. I pray you tell Benedick of it, and hear what a' will say.

LEON. Were it good, think you?   179

CLAUD. Hero thinks surely she will die; for she says she will die if he love her not, and she will die ere she make her love known, and she will die if he woo her rather than she will bate° one breath of her accustomed crossness.   184

D. PEDRO. She doth well. If she should make tender° of her love, 'tis very possible he'll scorn it, for the man, as you know all, hath a contemptible° spirit.

CLAUD. He is a very proper° man.

D. PEDRO. He hath indeed a good outward happiness.   191

CLAUD. Before God! And in my mind, very wise.

D. PEDRO. He doth indeed show some sparks that are like wit.

CLAUD. And I take him to be valiant.   195

D. PEDRO. As Hector, I assure you. And in the managing of quarrels you may say he is wise, for either he avoids them with great discretion or undertakes them with a most Christianlike fear.   200

LEON. If he do fear God, a' must necessarily keep peace. If he break the peace, he ought to enter into a quarrel with fear and trembling.

D. PEDRO. And so will he do, for the man doth fear God, howsoever it seems not in him by 205 some large jests he will make. Well, I am sorry for your niece. Shall we go seek Benedick, and tell him of her love?

CLAUD. Never tell him, my lord. Let her wear it out with good counsel.°   210

LEON. Nay, that's impossible. She may wear her heart out first.

D. PEDRO. Well, we will hear further of it by your daughter. Let it cool the while. I love Benedick well, and I could wish he would modestly ex- 215 amine himself to see how much he is unworthy so good a lady.

LEON. My lord, will you walk? Dinner is ready.

CLAUD. If he do not dote on her upon this, I will never trust my expectation.   220

D. PEDRO. Let there be the same net spread for her, and that must your daughter and her gentlewomen carry. The sport will be when they hold one an opinion of another's dotage, and no such matter. That's the scene that I would see, which will 225 be merely a dumb show.° Let us send her to call him in to dinner.

[*Exeunt* DON PEDRO, CLAUDIO, *and* LEONATO.]

BENE. [*Coming forward*] This can be no trick.

---

123. gull: trick.   126. Hold it up: keep the joke going.
137. smock: nightdress.   157. ecstasy: excess of emotion. overborne: overcome.   164. an alms: a good deed.   176. daffed . . . respects: pushed aside all other considerations.
183. bate: abate.   186. tender: offer.   187. contemptible: contemptuous.   189. proper: handsome.   209-10. wear counsel:
get over it by good advice.   226. dumb show: See *Haml*, III.ii.
146,n.

The conference was sadly borne.° They have the
truth of this from Hero. They seem to pity the   230
lady. It seems her affections have their full bent.°
Love me! Why, it must be requited. I hear how I am
censured.° They say I will bear myself proudly if I
perceive the love come from her. They say too   234
that she will rather die than give any sign of affec-
tion. I did never think to marry. I must not seem
proud. Happy are they that hear their detractions
and can put them to mending. They say the lady
is fair — 'tis a truth, I can bear them witness;   239
and virtuous — 'tis so, I cannot reprove° it; and wise,
but for loving me — by my troth, it is no addition
to her wit, nor no great argument of her folly, for
I will be horribly in love with her. I may chance
have some odd quirks° and remnants of wit   244
broken on me because I have railed so long against
marriage. But doth not the appetite alter? A man
loves the meat in his youth that he cannot endure in
his age. Shall quips° and sentences° and these
paper bullets° of the brain awe a man from the
career of his humor?° No, the world must be ·250
peopled. When I said I would die a bachelor, I did
not think I should live till I were married. Here
comes Beatrice. By this day, she's a fair lady! I do
spy some marks of love in her.   255

[*Enter* BEATRICE.]

BEAT. Against my will I am sent to bid you come
in to dinner.

BENE. Fair Beatrice, I thank you for your pains.

BEAT. I took no more pains for those thanks than
you take pains to thank me. If it had been painful, I
would not have come.   261

BENE. You take pleasure, then, in the message?

BEAT. Yea, just so much as you may take upon a
knife's point and choke a daw° withal. You   264
have no stomach, signior. Fare you well.   [*Exit.*]

BENE. Ha! "Against my will I am sent to bid you
come in to dinner." There's a double meaning in
that. "I took no more pains for those thanks than
you took pains to thank me." That's as much as to
say, "Any pains that I take for you is as easy   270
as thanks." If I do not take pity of her, I am a vil-
lain; if I do not love her, I am a Jew.° I will go get
her picture.   [*Exit.*]

229. **sadly borne:** seriously maintained. ▪ 231. **full bent:** are
tightly stretched, like a strung bow.   233. **censured:** judged.
240. **reprove:** disprove.   244. **quirks:** wisecracks.   248. **quips:**
jokes. **sentences:** proverbs, wise sayings.   249. **paper bullets:**
i.e., light and harmless.   250. **career . . . humor:** course of his
inclination. See V.i.135.   264. **daw:** jackdaw, a foolish bird.
272. **Jew:** i.e., an unbeliever.

Act III

SCENE I. LEONATO'S *orchard.*

[*Enter* HERO, MARGARET, *and* URSULA.]

HERO. Good Margaret, run thee to the parlor.
There shalt thou find my cousin Beatrice
Proposing° with the Prince and Claudio.
Whisper her ear and tell her I and Ursula
Walk in the orchard, and our whole discourse   5
Is all of her — say that thou overheard'st us.
And bid her steal into the plechèd° bower
Where honeysuckles, ripened by the sun,
Forbid the sun to enter, like favorites°
Made proud by princes, that advance their pride   10
Against that power that bred it. There will she hide
    her,
To listen our propose. This is thy office.°
Bear thee well in it, and leave us alone.

MARG. I'll make her come, I warrant you, pres-
    ently.°   [*Exit.*]

HERO. Now, Ursula, when Beatrice doth come,
As we do trace° this alley up and down   16
Our talk must only be of Benedick.
When I do name him, let it be thy part
To praise him more than ever man did merit.
My talk to thee must be how Benedick   20
Is sick in love with Beatrice. Of this matter
Is little Cupid's crafty arrow made,
That only wounds by hearsay.

[*Enter* BEATRICE, *behind.*]   Now begin,
For look where Beatrice, like a lapwing,° runs
Close by the ground to hear our conference.   25

URS. The pleasant'st angling is to see the fish
Cut with her golden oars° the silver stream,
And greedily devour the treacherous bait.
So angle we for Beatrice, who even now
Is couchèd in the woodbine coverture.°   30
Fear you not my part of the dialogue.

HERO. Then go we near her, that her ear lose
    nothing
Of the false sweet bait that we lay for it.

[*Approaching the bower*]

No, truly, Ursula, she is too disdainful.
I know her spirits are as coy and wild   35
As haggards° of the rock.

Act III, Sc. i: 3. **Proposing:** conversing.   7. **pleached:** covered
with branches. See I.ii.9.   9. **like favorites:** This sudden simile
could not have failed to remind original spectators of the Earl
of Essex, who had quarreled violently with Queen Elizabeth in
June 1598 and was in disgrace from September 1599 until his
execution on February 25, 1601. See Gen. Intro. p. 23b.   12. **office:**
duty.   14. **presently:** immediately.   16. **trace:** traverse.
24. **lapwing:** The lapwing, like the partridge, runs swiftly and
close to the ground.   27. **golden oars:** i.e., red fins. Some English
fresh-water fish, such as roach and perch, have conspicuously red
fins.   30. **woodbine coverture:** honeysuckle thicket, hiding place.
36. **haggards:** female wild hawks. See App. 26.

URS.   But are you sure
That Benedick loves Beatrice so entirely?
    HERO. So says the Prince and my new-trothèd°
        lord.
    URS. And did they bid you tell her of it, madam?
    HERO. They did entreat me to acquaint her of it.
But I persuaded them, if they loved Benedick,   41
To wish him wrestle with affection
And never to let Beatrice know of it.
    URS. Why did you so? Doth not the gentleman
Deserve as full as fortunate a bed   45
As ever Beatrice shall couch upon?
    HERO. Oh god of love! I know he doth deserve
As much as may be yielded to a man.
But Nature never framed a woman's heart
Of prouder stuff than that of Beatrice.   50
Disdain and scorn ride sparkling in her eyes,
Misprizing° what they look on, and her wit
Values itself so highly that to her
All matter else seems weak. She cannot love,
Nor take no shape nor project of affection,°   55
She is so self-endeared.°
    URS.   Sure, I think so,
And therefore certainly it were not good
She knew his love, lest she make sport at it.   58
    HERO. Why, you speak truth. I never yet saw man,
How wise, how noble, young, how rarely featured,
But she would spell him backward.° If fair-faced,
She would swear the gentleman should be her sister;
If black, why, Nature, drawing of an antique,°
Made a foul blot; if tall, a lance ill-headed,
If low, an agate° very vilely cut;   65
If speaking, why, a vane blown with all winds,
If silent, why, a block movèd with none.
So turns she every man the wrong side out,
And never gives to truth and virtue that
Which simpleness and merit purchaseth.   70
    URS. Sure, sure, such carping is not commendable.
    HERO. No, not to be so odd and from all fashions°
As Beatrice is cannot be commendable.
But who dare tell her so? If I should speak,
She would mock me into air. Oh, she would laugh
    me   75
Out of myself, press me to death° with wit!
Therefore let Benedick, like covered fire,
Consume away in sighs, waste inwardly.
It were a better death than die with mocks,
Which is as bad as die with tickling.   80
    URS. Yet tell her of it. Hear what she will say.
    HERO. No, rather I will go to Benedick
And counsel him to fight against his passion.

And truly I'll devise some honest slanders
To stain my cousin with. One doth not know   85
How much an ill word may empoison liking.
    URS. Oh, do not do your cousin such a wrong!
She cannot be so much without true judgment —
Having so swift and excellent a wit
As she is prized to have — as to refuse   90
So rare a gentleman as Signior Benedick.
    HERO. He is the only° man of Italy,
Always excepted my dear Claudio.
    URS. I pray you be not angry with me, madam,
Speaking my fancy. Signior Benedick,   95
For shape, for bearing, argument,° and valor,
Goes foremost in report through Italy.
    HERO. Indeed he hath an excellent good name.
    URS. His excellence did earn it ere he had it.
When are you married, madam?   100
    HERO. Why, every day, tomorrow. Come, go in.
I'll show thee some attires, and have thy counsel
Which is the best to furnish° me tomorrow.
    URS. She's limed,° I warrant you. We have caught
her, madam.
    HERO. If it prove so, then loving goes by haps.°
Some Cupid kills with arrows, some with traps.   106
                    [*Exeunt* HERO *and* URSULA.]
    BEAT. [*Coming forward*] What° fire is in mine
        ears? Can this be true?
Stand I condemned for pride and scorn so much?
Contempt, farewell, and maiden pride, adieu!
No glory lives behind the back of such.   110
And, Benedick, love on, I will requite thee,
    Taming my wild heart to thy loving hand.
If thou dost love, my kindness shall incite thee
    To bind our loves up in a holy band,
For others say thou dost deserve and I   115
Believe it better than reportingly.°   [*Exit.*]

SCENE II. *A room in* LEONATO'S *house.*

[*Enter* DON PEDRO, CLAUDIO, BENEDICK, *and* LEONATO.]
    D. PEDRO. I do but stay till your marriage be con-
summate, and then go I toward Aragon.
    CLAUD. I'll bring you thither, my lord, if you'll
vouchsafe me.   4
    D. PEDRO. Nay, that would be as great a soil in the
new gloss of your marriage as to show a child his
new coat and forbid him to wear it. I will only be
bold with° Benedick for his company, for from the
crown of his head to the sole of his foot he is all
mirth. He hath twice or thrice cut Cupid's bow-   10
string, and the little hangman° dare not shoot at
him. He hath a heart as sound as a bell, and his

38. new-trothed: newly betrothed. 52. Misprizing: despising.
55. take . . . affection: accept any form or idea of love for
another. 56. self-endeared: fond of herself. 61. spell . . .
backward: "turn him inside out." 63. antique: grotesque.
65. agate: a little figure cut in a seal ring. See *II Hen IV,*
I.ii.19. 72. from . . . fashions: so contrary. 76. press . . .
death: See Gen. Intro. p. 27b.

92. only: one and only, foremost. 96. argument: intelligent con-
versation. 103. furnish: dress. 104. limed: caught in birdlime.
105. haps: chance. 107–16. What . . . reportingly: See *M Ado*
Intro. p. 419a. reportingly: by the reports of others.
    Sc. ii: 7–8. be . . . with: be so bold as to ask. 11. hangman:
executioner.

tongue is the clapper, for what his heart thinks his
tongue speaks.

BENE. Gallants, I am not as I have been.   15

LEON. So say I. Methinks you are sadder.

CLAUD. I hope he be in love.

D. PEDRO. Hang him, truant! There's no true drop
of blood in him to be truly touched with love. If he
be sad, he wants money.   20

BENE. I have the toothache.

D. PEDRO. Draw it.

BENE. Hang it!

CLAUD. You must hang it first and draw it after-
ward.   25

D. PEDRO. What! Sigh for the toothache?

LEON. Where is but a humor or a worm.°

BENE. Well, everyone can master a grief° but he
that has it.

CLAUD. Yet say I he is in love.   30

D. PEDRO. There is no appearance of fancy° in him,
unless it be a fancy that he hath to strange disguises°
— as to be a Dutchman today, a Frenchman tomor-
row; or in the shape of two countries at once — as
a German from the waist downward, all slops,° and
a Spaniard from the hip upward, no doublet. Unless
he have a fancy to this foolery, as it appears he hath,
he is no fool for fancy, as you would have it appear
he is.   39

CLAUD. If he be not in love with some woman,
there is no believing old signs. A' brushes his hat o'
mornings. What should that bode?

D. PEDRO. Hath any man seen him at the barber's?

CLAUD. No, but the barber's man hath been   45
seen with him, and the old ornament of his cheek°
hath already stuffed tennis balls.°

LEON. Indeed, he looks younger than he did by
the loss of a beard.

D. PEDRO. Nay, a' rubs himself with civet.° Can
you smell him out by that?   51

CLAUD. That's as much as to say the sweet youth's
in love.

D. PEDRO. The greatest note of it is his melan-
choly.°

CLAUD. And when was he wont to wash his face?°

D. PEDRO. Yea, or to paint himself? For the which,
I hear what they say of him.   59

CLAUD. Nay, but his jesting spirit, which is now
crept into a lute string and now governed by stops.°

D. PEDRO. Indeed that tells a heavy tale for him.
Conclude, conclude he is in love.

CLAUD. Nay, but I know who loves him.   65

D. PEDRO. That would I know too. I warrant one
that knows him not.

CLAUD. Yes, and his ill conditions,° and, in de-
spite° of all, dies for him.

D. PEDRO. She shall be buried with her face up-
ward.°   71

BENE. Yet is this no charm for the toothache. Old
signior, walk aside with me. I have studied eight or
nine wise words to speak to you, which these hobby
horses° must not hear.

      [*Exeunt* BENEDICK *and* LEONATO.]

D. PEDRO. For my life, to break with him about
Beatrice.

CLAUD. 'Tis even so. Hero and Margaret have by
this played their parts with Beatrice, and then the
two bears will not bite one another when they meet.

      [*Enter* DON JOHN.]

D. JOHN. My lord and brother, God save you!   82

D. PEDRO. Good-den,° Brother.

D. JOHN. If your leisure served, I would speak with
you.   85

D. PEDRO. In private?

D. JOHN. If it please you. Yet Count Claudio may
hear, for what I would speak of concerns him.

D. PEDRO. What's the matter?   90

D. JOHN. [*To* CLAUDIO] Means your lordship to
be married tomorrow?

D. PEDRO. You know he does.

D. JOHN. I know not that, when he knows what I
know.   95

CLAUD. If there be any impediment, I pray you
discover it.

D. JOHN. You may think I love you not. Let that
appear hereafter, and aim better at me by that I now
will manifest. For my brother, I think he holds you
well, and in dearness of heart hath holp to effect your
ensuing marriage — surely suit ill spent and labor ill
bestowed.

D. PEDRO. Why, what's the matter?   104

D. JOHN. I came hither to tell you, and, circum-
stances shortened, for she has been too long a-talking
of, the lady is disloyal.

CLAUD. Who, Hero?

D. JOHN. Even she, Leonato's Hero, your Hero,
every man's Hero.   110

CLAUD. Disloyal?

D. JOHN. The word is too good to paint out her

---

27. humor ... worm: These were recognized causes of toothache.
humor: cold.   28. grief: pain.   31. fancy: love.   32. strange
disguises: It was a common criticism of Elizabethan gallants
that they wore a fantastical mixture of foreign fashions. See *M
of Ven*, II.ii.79.   35. slops: baggy breeches. See Pl. 8c and com-
ment on p. 93b.   46. old ... cheek: Benedick at his first en-
trance wore a large beard; now he is neatly trimmed and hides
the change by holding a handkerchief to his cheek.   47. tennis
balls: made of leather, stuffed with hair.   50. civet: a perfume,
much favored by gallants, made from a glandular secretion of
the civet cat.   55. melancholy: Benedick as the complete lover
is showing some of the outward signs. For Rosalind's description
of the symptoms see *AYLI*, III.ii.392–403. See App. 4.   56. wash
... face: i.e., with cosmetics. The fashionable gallant used
make-up.

61. crept ... stops: shrank to the size of a string on a lover's
lute, and is controlled by *stops* — the frets on the finger board by
which the tone is controlled. See Pl. 18d.   68. ill conditions: bad
qualities.   69. despite: spite.   70–71. buried ... upward: an-
other version of Margaret's remark at III.iv.26.   74–75. hobby-
horses: buffoons.   83. Good-den: good afternoon.

wickedness, I could say she were worse. Think you of a worse title and I will fit her to it. Wonder not till further warrant. Go but with me tonight, you shall see her chamber window entered, even the night before her wedding day. If you love her then, tomorrow wed her, but it would better fit your honor to change your mind.

CLAUD. May this be so? 120

D. PEDRO. I will not think it.

D. JOHN. If you dare not trust that you see, confess not that you know. If you will follow me, I will show you enough, and when you have seen more, and heard more, proceed accordingly. 125

CLAUD. If I see anything tonight why I should not marry her tomorrow, in the congregation where I should wed there will I shame her.

D. PEDRO. And as I wooed for thee to obtain her, I will join with thee to disgrace her. 130

D. JOHN. I will disparage her no farther till you are my witnesses. Bear it coldly° but till midnight, and let the issue show itself.

D. PEDRO. Oh, day untowardly turned!

CLAUD. Oh, mischief strangely thwarting! 135

D. JOHN. Oh, plague right well prevented! So will you say when you have seen the sequel. [*Exeunt.*]

SCENE III. *A street.*

[*Enter* DOGBERRY *and* VERGES *with the* WATCH.°]

DOGB. Are you good men and true?

VERG. Yea, or else it were pity but they should suffer salvation,° body and soul.

DOGB. Nay, there were a punishment too good for them, if they should have any allegiance° in them, being chosen for the Prince's watch. 6

VERG. Well, give them their charge,° Neighbor Dogberry.

DOGB. First, who think you the most desartless° man to be constable? 10

FIRST WATCH. Hugh Otecake, sir, or George Seacole, for they can write and read.

DOGB. Come hither, Neighbor Seacole. God hath blessed you with a good name. To be a well-favored° man is the gift of fortune, but to write and read comes by nature.° 16

SEC. WATCH. Both which, Master Constable ——

DOGB. You have. I knew it would be your answer.

Well, for your favor, sir, why, give God thanks and make no boast of it. And for your writing and 20 reading, let that appear when there is no need of such vanity. You are thought here to be the most senseless° and fit man for the constable of the watch, therefore bear you the lantern. This is your charge. You shall comprehend° all vagrom° men. You are to bid any man stand, in the Prince's name. 26

SEC. WATCH. How if a' will not stand?

DOGB. Why, then take no note of him, but let him go, and presently call the rest of the watch together and thank God you are rid of a knave. 31

VERG. If he will not stand when he is bidden, he is none of the Prince's subjects.

DOGB. True, and they are to meddle with none but the Prince's subjects. You shall also make no 35 noise in the streets, for for the watch to babble and to talk is most tolerable° and not to be endured.

WATCH. We will rather sleep than talk. We know what belongs to° a watch. 40

DOGB. Why, you speak like an ancient and most quiet watchman, for I cannot see how sleeping should offend. Only have a care that your bills° be not stolen. Well, you are to call at all the alehouses and bid those that are drunk get them to bed. 46

WATCH. How if they will not?

DOGB. Why, then let them alone till they are sober. If they make you not then the better answer, you may say they are not the men you took them for. 51

WATCH. Well, sir.

DOGB. If you meet a thief, you may suspect him, by virtue of your office, to be no true man. And for such kind of men, the less you meddle or make with them, why, the more is for your honesty. 56

WATCH. If we know him to be a thief, shall we not lay hands on him?

DOGB. Truly, by your office you may, but I think they that touch pitch will be defiled. The most 60 peaceable way for you, if you do take a thief, is to let him show himself what he is and steal out of your company.

VERG. You have been always called a merciful man, partner. 65

DOGB. Truly, I would not hang a dog by my will, much more a man who hath any honesty in him.

VERG. If you hear a child cry in the night, you must call to the nurse and bid her still it. 70

WATCH. How if the nurse be asleep and will not hear us?

DOGB. Why, then depart in peace and let the child wake her with crying; for the ewe that will not hear her lamb when it baas will never answer a calf when he bleats. 76

VERG. 'Tis very true.

132. coldly: patiently.
Sc. iii: s.d., with . . . Watch: See Gen. Intro. p. 18a.
3. salvation: for "damnation." Shakespeare's humbler characters often have an excessive love of long words which they misuse. 5. allegiance: loyalty, but Dogberry supposes it to mean "treachery." 7. charge: instructions. 9. desartless: for "deserving." 14. well-favored: handsome. 14–16. To . . . nature: Dogberry is mistaken. Beauty is a gift of Nature; Fortune gives such attainments as wealth and learning. For a discussion of this question on a higher plane, see *AYLI*, I.ii.34–57, and App. 18.

23. senseless: for "sensible." 25. comprehend: for "apprehend." vagrom: vagabond. See *M Ado* Intro. p. 419b. 37. tolerable: for "intolerable." 40. what . . . to: the duties of. 44. bills: the watchmen's weapon. See Pl. 21c.

DOGB. This is the end of the charge: You, Constable, are to present° the Prince's own person. If you meet the Prince in the night, you may stay him.   81

VERG. Nay, by 'r Lady, that I think a' cannot.

DOGB. Five shillings to one on 't, with any man that knows the statues,° he may stay him. Marry, not without the Prince be willing, for indeed the watch ought to offend no man, and it is an offense to stay a man against his will.

VERG. By 'r Lady, I think it be so.   89

DOGB. Ha, ah, ha! Well, masters, good night. An there be any matter of weight chances, call up me. Keep your fellows' counsels and your own, and good night. Come, neighbor.

WATCH. Well, masters, we hear our charge. Let us go sit here upon the church bench till two, and then all to bed.   96

DOGB. One word more, honest neighbors. I pray you watch about Signior Leonato's door, for the wedding being there tomorrow, there is a great coil° tonight. Adieu. Be vigitant,° I beseech you.

[*Exeunt* DOGBERRY *and* VERGES.]

[*Enter* BORACHIO *and* CONRADE.°]

BORA. What, Conrade!   102

WATCH. [*Aside*] Peace! Stir not.

BORA. Conrade, I say!

CON. Here, man, I am at thy elbow.

BORA. Mass,° and my elbow itched. I thought there would a scab° follow.

CON. I will owe thee an answer for that. And now forward with thy tale.   109

BORA. Stand thee close, then, under this penthouse,° for it drizzles rain, and I will, like a true drunkard, utter all to thee.

WATCH. [*Aside*] Some treason, masters. Yet stand close.

BORA. Therefore know I have earned of Don John a thousand ducats.   116

CON. Is it possible that any villainy should be so dear?

BORA. Thou shouldst rather ask if it were possible any villainy should be so rich, for when rich villains have need of poor ones, poor ones may make what price they will.   122

CON. I wonder at it.

BORA. That shows thou art unconfirmed.° Thou knowest that the fashion of a doublet, or a hat, or a cloak, is nothing to a man.°

CON. Yes, it is apparel.

BORA. I mean, the fashion.

CON. Yes, the fashion is the fashion.   129

BORA. Tush! I may as well say the fool's the fool. But seest thou not what a deformed thief this fashion is?

WATCH. [*Aside*] I know that Deformed, a' has been a vile thief this seven year, a' goes up and down like a gentleman. I remember his name.   136

BORA. Didst thou not hear somebody?

CON. No, 'twas the vane on the house.

BORA. Seest thou not, I say, what a deformed thief this fashion is? How giddily a' turns about all the hot bloods between fourteen and five and thirty? Sometimes fashioning them like Pharaoh's soldiers in the reechy° painting, sometime like god Bel's° priests in the old church window, sometime like the shaven Hercules in the smirched° worm-eaten 145 tapestry, where his codpiece° seems as massy as his club?

CON. All this I see, and I see that the fashion wears out more apparel than the man. But art not thou thyself giddy with the fashion too, that thou hast shifted out of thy tale into telling me of the fashion?   152

BORA. Not so, neither. But know that I° have tonight wooed Margaret, the Lady Hero's gentlewoman, by the name of Hero. She leans me out at her mistress' chamber window, bids me a thousand times good night. —I tell this tale vilely. I should first tell thee how the Prince, Claudio and my master, planted and placed and possessed° by my master Don John, saw afar off in the orchard this amiable encounter.   161

CON. And thought they Margaret was Hero?

BORA. Two of them did, the Prince and Claudio, but the Devil my master knew she was Mar- 165 garet. And partly by his oaths, which first possessed them, partly by the dark night, which did deceive them, but chiefly by my villainy, which did confirm any slander that Don John had made, away went Claudio enraged, swore he would meet her, as he was appointed, next morning at the temple and there before the whole congregation shame her with what he saw o'ernight, and send her home again without a husband.   175

FIRST WATCH. We charge you, in the Prince's name, stand!

SEC. WATCH. Call up the right master constable. We have here recovered° the most dangerous piece of lechery° that was known in the commonwealth.   181

---

80. present: represent.   84. statues: for "statutes."   99. coil: turmoil.   100. vigitant: for "vigilant."   101. s.d., Enter . . . Conrade: See *M Ado* Intro. p. 419b.   106. Mass: by the mass.
107. scab: with a pun on the two meanings of "blister" and "low fellow."   111. penthouse: overhanging roof of a shed or porch. See Gen. Intro. p. 56a.   124. unconfirmed: inexperienced.
126. is . . . man: is as nothing when compared to. Borachio (whose name means drunkard) is very fuddled. The thought at the back of his mind is that a man changes the fashion of his clothes, but that his character remains the same.

143. reechy: begrimed with smoke. Bel: from the story of *Bel and the Dragon* in the Apocrypha.   145. smirched: dirty.
146. codpiece: See Pl. 8c and comment on p. 93b.   153–75. I . . . husband: See *M Ado* Intro. p. 419b.   159. possessed: informed.   179. recovered: for 'discovered.'   180. lechery: for "treachery."

FIRST WATCH. And one Deformed is one of them. I know him, a' wears a lock.°

CON. Masters, masters ——

SEC. WATCH. You'll be made bring Deformed forth, I warrant you.　186

CON. Masters ——

FIRST WATCH. Never speak. We charge you let us obey° you to go with us.

BORA. We are like to prove a goodly commodity, being taken up of these men's bills.°　191

CON. A commodity in question, I warrant you. Come, we'll obey you.　[*Exeunt.*]

SCENE IV. HERO's *apartment.*

[*Enter* HERO, MARGARET, *and* URSULA.]

HERO. Good Ursula, wake my cousin Beatrice and desire her to rise.

URS. I will, lady.

HERO. And bid her come hither.　4

URS. Well.　[*Exit.*]

MARG. Troth, I think your other rebato° were better.

HERO. No, pray thee, good Meg, I'll wear this.

MARG. By my troth's not so good, and I warrant your cousin will say so.　10

HERO. My cousin's a fool, and thou art another. I'll wear none but this.

MARG. I like the new tire° within excellently, if the hair were a thought browner, and your gown's a most rare fashion, i' faith. I saw the Duchess of Milan's gown that they praise so.　16

HERO. Oh, that exceeds, they say.

MARG. By my troth 's but a nightgown° in respect of yours, — cloth o' gold, and cuts,° and laced with silver, set with pearls, down sleeves,° side　20 sleeves,° and skirts round underborne° with a bluish tinsel. But for a fine, quaint, graceful, and excellent fashion, yours is worth ten on't.

HERO. God give me joy to wear it! For my heart is exceeding heavy.　25

MARG. 'Twill be heavier soon by the weight of a man.

HERO. Fie upon thee! Art not ashamed?

MARG. Of what, lady? Of speaking honorably? Is not marriage honorable in a beggar? Is not　30 your lord honorable without marriage? I think you would have me say, "saving your reverence, a husband."° An bad thinking do not wrest true speaking, I'll offend nobody. Is there any harm in "the heavier for a husband"? None, I think, an it be the right husband and the right wife; otherwise 'tis light, and not heavy. Ask my Lady Beatrice else — here she comes.

[*Enter* BEATRICE.]

HERO. Good morrow, Coz.

BEAT. Good morrow, sweet Hero.　40

HERO. Why, how now? Do you speak in the sick tune?°

BEAT. I am out of all other tune, methinks.

MARG. Clap 's° into "Light-o'-love."° That goes without a burden.° Do you sing it, and I'll dance it.

BEAT. Ye light-o'-love, with your heels! Then,　47 if your husband have stables enough, you'll see he shall lack no barns.°

MARG. Oh, illegitimate construction! I scorn that with my heels.　51

BEAT. 'Tis almost five o'clock, Cousin, 'tis time you were ready. By my troth, I am exceeding ill. Heigh-ho!

MARG. For a hawk, a horse, or a husband?　55

BEAT. For the letter that begins them all, H.°

MARG. Well, an you be not turned Turk,° there's no more sailing by the star.

BEAT. What means the fool, trow?°

MARG. Nothing I, but God send everyone their heart's desire!　61

HERO. These gloves the Count sent me. They are an excellent perfume.

BEAT. I am stuffed,° Cousin, I cannot smell.

MARG. A maid, and stuffed! There's goodly catching of cold.　66

BEAT. Oh, God help me! God help me! How long have you professed apprehension?°

MARG. Ever since you left it. Doth not my wit become me rarely?　70

BEAT. It is not seen enough, you should wear it in your cap. By my troth, I am sick.

MARG. Get you some of this distilled Carduus Benedictus,° and lay it to your heart. It is the only thing for a qualm.°　75

HERO. There thou prickest her with a thistle.

183. lock: lovelock, a curl of hair hanging by the ear.　189. obey: for "command."　190-91. prove . . . bills: Borachio puns on the double meaning of bill, "weapon" and "acknowledgment of debt." commodity: goods. taken up: obtained on credit. bills: bonds guaranteeing payment on the terms agreed.

Sc. iv: 6. rebato: high collar or wire frame supporting the ruff. See Pl. 2b and comment on p. 95a.　13. tire: headdress. 18. nightgown: dressing gown, "house coat."　19. cuts: embroidered squares inserted in places where the material had been cut away.　20. down sleeves: long sleeves to the wrist. 20-21. side sleeves: hanging sleeves from the shoulder. See Pl. 7a and comment on p. 95a.　21. underborne: worn over or lined.

32-33. saving . . . husband: you seem to regard *husband* as an improper word. saving . . . reverence: often contracted to "sir-reverence," a phrase apologizing for an improper word or remark. 41-42. in . . . tune: i.e., as if you were unwell.　45. Clap: break into a song. Light-o'-love: a well-known ditty.　46. burden: chorus.　49. barns: with a pun on "bairns."　56. H: "H" and "ache" were pronounced alike.　57. turned Turk: become a heathen; i.e., have deserted your old faith.　59. trow: I wonder. 64. am stuffed: have a cold.　68. apprehension: sharp wit. 73-74. Carduus Benedictus: blessed thistle, a herb often and highly recommended as a cure for various complaints.　75. qualm: feeling of sickness.

BEAT. Benedictus! Why Benedictus? You have some moral° in this Benedictus.

MARG. Moral! No, by my troth, I have no moral meaning, I meant plain holy thistle. You may 80 think perchance that I think you are in love. Nay, by 'r Lady, I am not such a fool to think what I list; nor I list not to think what I can; nor, indeed, I cannot think, if I would think my heart out of thinking, that you are in love, or that you will be in love, 85 or that you can be in love. Yet Benedick was such another, and now is he become a man. He swore he would never marry, and yet now, in despite of his heart, he eats his meat without grudging. And how you may be converted, I know not, but methinks you look with your eyes as other women do.

BEAT. What pace is this that thy tongue keeps?

MARG. Not a false gallop.°   94

[*Re-enter* URSULA.]

URS. Madam, withdraw. The Prince, the Count, Signior Benedick, Don John, and all the gallants of the town, are come to fetch you to church.

HERO. Help to dress me, good Coz, good Meg, good Ursula.   [*Exeunt.*]

SCENE V. *Another room in* LEONATO's *house.*

[*Enter* LEONATO, *with* DOGBERRY *and* VERGES.]

LEON. What would you with me, honest neighbor?

DOGB. Marry, sir, I would have some confidence° with you that decerns° you nearly.

LEON. Brief, I pray you, for you see it is a busy time with me.   6

DOGB. Marry, this it is, sir.

VERG. Yes, in truth it is, sir.

LEON. What is it, my good friends?   9

DOGB. Goodman Verges, sir, speaks a little off the matter — an old man, sir, and his wits are not so blunt° as, God help, I would desire they were, but, in faith, honest as the skin between his brows.

VERG. Yes, I thank God I am as honest as any man living that is an old man and no honester than I.   17

DOGB. Comparisons are odorous° — *palabras,*° neighbor Verges.

LEON. Neighbors, you are tedious.   20

DOGB. It pleases your Worship to say so, but we are the poor Duke's officers.° But truly, for mine own part, if I were as tedious° as a king, I could find in my heart to bestow it all of your Worship.   25

LEON. All thy tediousness on me, ah?

DOGB. Yea, an 'twere a thousand pound more than 'tis, for I hear as good exclamation on your Worship

as of any man in the city, and though I be but a poor man, I am glad to hear it.   30

VERG. And so am I.

LEON. I would fain know what you have to say.

VERG. Marry, sir, our watch tonight, excepting your Worship's presence, ha' ta'en a couple of as arrant° knaves as any in Messina.   35

DOGB. A good old man, sir — he will be talking. As they say, "When the age is in, the wit is out." God help us! It is a world to see. Well said, i' faith, neighbor Verges. Well, God's a good man. An two men ride of a horse, one must ride behind. An 40 honest soul, i' faith, sir, by my troth he is, as ever broke bread. But God is to be worshiped, all men are not alike, alas, good neighbor!

LEON. Indeed, neighbor, he comes too short of you.   46

DOGB. Gifts that God gives.

LEON. I must leave you.

DOGB. One word, sir. Our watch, sir, have indeed comprehended° two aspicious° persons, and we would have them this morning examined before your Worship.   52

LEON. Take their examination yourself, and bring it me. I am now in great haste, as it may appear unto you.

DOGB. It shall be suffigance.°

LEON. Drink some wine ere you go. Fare you well.

[*Enter a* MESSENGER.]

MESS. My lord, they stay for you to give your daughter to her husband.   60

LEON. I'll wait upon them. I am ready.

[*Exeunt* LEONATO *and* MESSENGER.]

DOGB. Go, good partner, go, get you to Francis Seacole. Bid him bring his pen and inkhorn to the jail. We are now to examination these men.

VERG. And we must do it wisely.   65

DOGB. We will spare for no wit, I warrant you, here's that shall drive some of them to a noncome.° Only get the learned writer to set down our excommunication,° and meet me at the jail.   [*Exeunt.*]

Act IV

SCENE I. *A church.*

[*Enter* DON PEDRO, DON JOHN, LEONATO, FRIAR FRANCIS, CLAUDIO, BENEDICK, HERO, BEATRICE, *and attendants.*]

LEON. Come, Friar Francis, be brief — only to the plain form of marriage, and you shall recount their particular duties afterward.

78. moral: i.e., hidden meaning.   94. false gallop: canter.
Sc. v: 3. confidence: for "conference."   4. decerns: for "concerns."   12. blunt: for "sharp."   18. odorous: for "odious." palabras: for *pocas palabras*; i.e., few words.   22. poor . . . officers: the Duke's poor officers.   24. tedious: Dogberry supposes the word to be complimentary.

35. arrant: out-and-out.   50. comprehended: for "apprehended." aspicious: for "suspicious."   55. suffigance: for "sufficient." 67. noncome: for *non plus*, state of confusion.   69. excommunication: for "examination."

FRIAR. You come hither, my lord, to marry this
lady.   5

CLAUD. No.

LEON. To be married to her. Friar, you come to
marry her.

FRIAR. Lady, you come hither to be married to this
Count.   10

HERO. I do.

FRIAR. If either of you know any inward impedi-
ment why you should not be conjoined, I charge
you, on your souls, to utter it.

CLAUD. Know you any, Hero?   15

HERO. None, my lord.

FRIAR. Know you any, Count?

LEON. I dare make his answer, none.

CLAUD. Oh, what men dare do! What men may
do! What men daily do, not knowing what they do!

BENE. How now! Interjections? Why, then,   22
some be of laughing, as, ah, ha, he!

CLAUD. Stand thee by, Friar. Father, by your
leave,
Will you with free and unconstrainèd soul   25
Give me this maid, your daughter?

LEON. As freely, son, as God did give her me.

CLAUD. And what have I to give you back whose
worth
May counterpoise this rich and precious gift?

D. PEDRO. Nothing, unless you render her again.

CLAUD. Sweet Prince, you learn° me noble thank-
fulness.   31
There, Leonato, take her back again.
Give not this rotten orange to your friend,
She's but the sign and semblance of her honor.
Behold how like a maid she blushes here!   35
Oh, what authority and show of truth
Can cunning sin cover itself withal!
Comes not that blood as modest evidence
To witness simple virtue? Would you not swear,
All you that see her, that she were a maid,   40
By these exterior shows? But she is none.
She knows the heat of a luxurious° bed.
Her blush is guiltiness, not modesty.

LEON. What do you mean, my lord?

CLAUD.   Not to be married,
Not to knit my soul to an approved° wanton.   45

LEON. Dear my lord, if you, in your own proof,°
Have vanquished the resistance of her youth,
And made defeat of her virginity ——

CLAUD. I know what you would say. If I have
known her,
You will say she did embrace me as a husband,   50
And so extenuate the 'forehand sin.°
No, Leonato,

I never tempted her with word too large,°
But, as a brother to his sister, showed
Bashful sincerity and comely love.   55

HERO. And seemed I ever otherwise to you?

CLAUD. Out on thee! Seeming! I will write
against it.
You seem to me as Dian° in her orb,°
As chaste as is the bud ere it be blown,°
But you are more intemperate in your blood   60
Than Venus, or those pampered animals
That rage in savage sensuality.

HERO. Is my lord well, that he doth speak so
wide?°

LEON. Sweet Prince, why speak not you?

D. PEDRO.   What should I speak?
I stand dishonored, that have gone about   65
To link my dear friend to a common stale.

LEON. Are these things spoken, or do I but dream?

D. JOHN. Sir, they are spoken, and these things are
true.

BENE. This looks not like a nuptial.

HERO.   True! O God!

CLAUD. Leonato, stand I here?   70
Is this the Prince? Is this the Prince's brother?
Is this face Hero's? Are our eyes our own?

LEON. All this is so, but what of this, my lord?

CLAUD. Let me but move one question to your
daughter,
And by that fatherly and kindly power   75
That you have in her, bid her answer truly.

LEON. I charge thee do so, as thou art my child.

HERO. Oh, God defend me! How am I beset!°
What kind of catechizing call you this?

CLAUD. To make you answer truly to your name.

HERO. Is it not Hero? Who can blot that name   81
With any just reproach?

CLAUD.   Marry, that can Hero.
Hero itself can blot out Hero's virtue.
What man was he talked with you yesternight
Out at your window betwixt twelve and one?   85
Now, if you are a maid, answer to this.

HERO. I talked with no man at that hour, my lord.

D. PEDRO. Why, then are you no maiden. Leonato,
I am sorry you must hear. Upon mine honor,
Myself, my brother, and this grievèd Count   90
Did see her, hear her, at that hour last night
Talk with a ruffian at her chamber window,
Who hath indeed, most like a liberal° villain,
Confessed the vile encounters they have had
A thousand times in secret.   95

D. JOHN. Fie, fie! They are not to be named, my
lord,
Not to be spoke of,

Act IV, Sc. 1: 31. learn: teach.   42. luxurious: lustful.
45. approved: proved.   46. in . . . proof: by putting her resist-
ance to the test.   51. 'forehand sin: the sin of mating before
marriage, which could be partially excused since Claudio and
Hero were already betrothed. See Gen. Intro. p. 20a.

53. large: unrestrained.   58. Dian: Diana, goddess of chastity.
orb: sphere; i.e., the moon, for Diana was also Luna, the moon.
See *MND*, IV.i.76.   59. blown: fully opened.   63. so wide: i.e.,
so far from the truth.   78. beset: set upon.   93. liberal: gross.

There is not chastity enough in language
Without offense to utter them. Thus, pretty lady,
I am sorry for thy much misgovernment.°   100
    CLAUD. O Hero, what a Hero hadst thou been
If half thy outward graces had been placed
About thy thoughts and counsels of thy heart!
But fare thee well, most foul, most fair! Farewell,
Thou pure impiety and impious purity!   105
For thee I'll lock up all the gates of love,
And on my eyelids shall conjecture hang
To turn all beauty into thoughts of harm,°
And never shall it more be gracious.   109
    LEON. Hath no man's dagger here a point for me?
                      [HERO *swoons*.]
    BEAT. Why, how now, Cousin! Wherefore sink
    you down?
    D. JOHN. Come, let us go. These things, come thus
    to light,
Smother her spirits up.
    [*Exeunt* DON PEDRO, DON JOHN, *and* CLAUDIO.]
    BENE. How doth the lady?
    BEAT.   Dead, I think. Help, Uncle!
Hero! Why, Hero! Uncle! Signior Benedick! Friar!
    LEON. O Fate! Take not away thy heavy hand.
Death is the fairest cover for her shame   117
That may be wished for.
    BEAT.   How now, Cousin Hero!
    FRIAR. Have comfort, lady.
    LEON. Dost thou look up?   120
    FRIAR. Yea, wherefore should she not?
    LEON. Wherefore! Why, doth not every earthly
    thing
Cry shame upon her? Could she here deny
The story that is printed in her blood?°
Do not live, Hero, do not ope thine eyes.   125
For did I think thou wouldst not quickly die,
Thought I thy spirits were stronger than thy shames,
Myself would, on the rearward of reproaches,
Strike at thy life.° Grieved I, I had but one?
Chid I for that at frugal Nature's frame?   130
Oh, one too much by thee! Why had I one?
Why ever wast thou lovely in my eyes?
Why had I not with charitable hand
Took up a beggar's issue at my gates,
Who, smirchèd thus and mired with infamy,   135
I might have said, " No part of it is mine,
This shame derives itself from unknown loins "?
But mine, and mine I loved, and mine I praised,
And mine that I was proud on, mine so much
That I myself was to myself not mine,   140
Valuing of her — why, she, oh, she is fallen
Into a pit of ink, that the wide sea
Hath drops too few to wash her clean again,

And salt too little which may season° give
To her foul-tainted flesh!
    BENE.   Sir, sir, be patient.   145
For my part, I am so attired in wonder
I know not what to say.
    BEAT. Oh, on my soul, my cousin is belied!°
    BENE. Lady, were you her bedfellow last night?
    BEAT. No, truly not, although until last night   150
I have this twelvemonth been her bedfellow.
    LEON. Confirmed, confirmed! Oh, that is stronger
    made
Which was before barred up with ribs of iron!
Would the two Princes lie, and Claudio lie,   154
Who loved her so, that, speaking of her foulness,
Washed it with tears? Hence from her! Let her die.
    FRIAR. Hear me a little,
For I have only been silent so long
And given way unto this course of fortune
By noting of the lady.° I have marked   160
A thousand blushing apparitions
To start into her face, a thousand innocent shames
In angel whiteness beat away those blushes.
And in her eye there hath appeared a fire
To burn the errors that these Princes hold   165
Against her maiden truth. Call me a fool,
Trust not my reading nor my observations,
Which with experimental seal doth warrant
The tenor of my book° — trust not my age,
My reverence, calling, nor divinity —   170
If this sweet lady lie not guiltless here
Under some biting error.
    LEON.   Friar, it cannot be.
Thou seest that all the grace that she hath left
Is that she will not add to her damnation
A sin of perjury. She not denies it.   175
Why seek'st thou, then, to cover with excuse
That which appears in proper nakedness?
    FRIAR. Lady, what man is he you are accused of?
    HERO. They know that do accuse me, I know none.
If I know more of any man alive   180
Than that which maiden modesty doth warrant,
Let all my sins lack mercy! O my father,
Prove you that any man with me conversed
At hours unmeet, or that I yesternight
Maintained the change° of words with any creature,
Refuse me, hate me, torture me to death!   186
    FRIAR. There is some strange misprision° in the
    Princes.
    BENE. Two of them have the very bent° of honor,

---

100. misgovernment: evil conduct.   107–08. And . . . harm: hereafter whenever I see any beautiful woman I shall suspect her.   124. blood: blushes.   128–29. rearward . . . life: i.e., would kill you after this shame.

144. season: freshness.   148. belied: has had lies told about her.
157–60. Hear . . . lady: If the punctuation of these lines is correct, the Friar means that he has kept silence because he has been fully occupied in closely observing the lady.   167–69. observations . . . book: my observation of life, which sets the seal of practical experience on what I have learned from books. warrant: guarantee. tenor: purport.   185. Maintained . . . change: exchanged.   187. misprision: misunderstanding.   188. bent: natural inclination.

And if their wisdoms be misled in this,
The practice° of it lives in John the bastard, 190
Whose spirits toil in frame of° villainies.

LEON. I know not. If they speak but truth of her,
These hands shall tear her. If they wrong her honor,
The proudest of them shall well hear of it.
Time hath not yet so dried this blood of mine, 195
Nor age so eat up my invention,°
Nor fortune made such havoc of my means,
Nor my bad life reft me so much of friends,
But they shall find, awaked in such a kind,
Both strength of limb and policy of mind, 200
Ability in means and choice of friends,
To quit me° of them throughly.°

FRIAR.   Pause awhile,
And let my counsel sway you in this case.
Your daughter here the Princes left for dead.
Let her awhile be secretly kept in, 205
And publish it that she is dead indeed.
Maintain a mourning ostentation,°
And on your family's old monument
Hang mournful epitaphs,° and do all rites
That appertain unto a burial. 210

LEON. What shall become of this? What will this
do?

FRIAR. Marry, this, well carried,° shall on her be-
half
Change slander to remorse° — that is some good.
But not for that dream I on this strange course,
But on this travail look for greater birth. 215
She dying, as it must be so maintained,
Upon the instant that she was accused,
Shall be lamented, pitied, and excused
Of every hearer. For it so falls out,
That what we have we prize not to the worth 220
Whiles we enjoy it; but being lacked and lost,
Why, then we rack° the value, then we find
The virtue that possession would not show us
Whiles it was ours. So will it fare with Claudio.
When he shall hear she died upon his words, 225
The idea of her life shall sweetly creep
Into his study of imagination;°
And every lovely organ of her life
Shall come appareled in more precious habit,
More moving-delicate and full of life, 230
Into the eye and prospect of his soul
Than when she lived indeed. Then shall he mourn,
If ever love had interest in his liver,°
And wish he had not so accused her,

No, though he thought his accusation true. 235
Let this be so, and doubt not but success
Will fashion the event in better shape
Than I can lay it down in likelihood.
But if all aim but this be leveled false,
The supposition of the lady's death 240
Will quench the wonder of her infamy.°
And if it sort not° well, you may conceal her,
As best befits her wounded reputation,
In some reclusive° and religious life,
Out of all eyes, tongues, minds, and injuries. 245

BENE. Signior Leonato, let the Friar advise you.
And though you know my inwardness and love°
Is very much unto the Prince and Claudio,
Yet, by mine honor, I will deal in this
As secretly and justly as your soul 250
Should with your body.

LEON.   Being that° I flow in grief,
The smallest twine may lead me.

FRIAR. 'Tis well consented. Presently away,
For to strange sores strangely they strain the cure.
Come, lady, die to live. This wedding day 255
Perhaps is but prolonged. Have patience and en-
dure. [*Exeunt all but* BENEDICK *and* BEATRICE.°]

BENE. Lady Beatrice, have you wept all this while?

BEAT. Yea, and I will weep awhile longer.

BENE. I will not desire that.

BEAT. You have no reason, I do it freely.° 260

BENE. Surely I do believe your fair cousin is
wronged.

BEAT. Ah, how much might the man deserve of
me that would right her!

BENE. Is there any way to show such friendship?

BEAT. A very even° way, but no such friend. 265

BENE. May a man do it?

BEAT. It is a man's office, but not yours.

BENE. I do love nothing in the world so well as
you. Is not that strange? 270

BEAT. As strange as the thing I know not. It were
as possible for me to say I loved nothing so well as
you. But believe me not, and yet I lie not, I confess
nothing, nor I deny nothing. I am sorry for my
cousin. 275

BENE. By my sword, Beatrice, thou lovest me.

BEAT. Do not swear, and eat it.

BENE. I will swear by it that you love me, and I
will make him eat it that says I love not you.

BEAT. Will you not eat your word? 280

BENE. With no sauce that can be devised to it. I
protest I love thee.

BEAT. Why, then, God forgive me!

---

190. **practice**: plotting.   191. **toil . . . of**: labor to contrive.
196. **invention**: intellect.   202. **quit me**: pay back, avenge.
throughly: thoroughly.   207. **Maintain . . . ostentation**: perform
the outward shows of mourning, which in a noble family were
elaborate. See App. 9.   209. **epitaphs**: memorial verses.
212. **carried**: managed.   213. **remorse**: pity.   222. **rack**: stretch
out.   227. **study of imagination**: contemplation.   233. **liver**:
supposed to be the seat of the emotions, especially love.

236–41. **Let . . . infamy**: do this, and without doubt the result
will be even better than I can suggest; even if we fail in our aim,
her shame will be forgotten in her supposed death.   242. **sort
not**: does not turn out.   244. **reclusive**: retired.   247. **inwardness
. . . love**: intimate affection.   251. **Being that**: since.   256. **s.d.,
Benedick . . . Beatrice**: See *M Ado* Intro. p. 420a.   260. **freely**:
i.e., without your asking.   265. **even**: straight.

BENE. What offense, sweet Beatrice?

BEAT. You have stayed° me in a happy hour. I was about to protest I loved you.   286

BENE. And do it with all thy heart.

BEAT. I love you with so much of my heart that none is left to protest.

BENE. Come, bid me do anything for thee.   290

BEAT. Kill Claudio.

BENE. Ha! Not for the wide world.

BEAT. You kill me to deny it. Farewell.

BENE. Tarry, sweet Beatrice.

BEAT. I am gone, though I am here. There is no love in you. Nay, I pray you let me go.   296

BENE. Beatrice ——

BEAT. In faith, I will go.

BENE. We'll be friends first.

BEAT. You dare easier be friends with me than fight with mine enemy.   301

BENE. Is Claudio thine enemy?

BEAT. Is he not approved° in the height° a villain that hath slandered, scorned, dishonored my kins-woman? Oh, that I were a man! What, bear her in hand° until they come to take hands, and then, 306 with public accusation, uncovered slander, unmitigated rancor —— Oh, God, that I were a man! I would eat his heart in the market place.

BENE. Hear me, Beatrice ——   310

BEAT. Talk with a man out at a window! A proper saying!

BENE. Nay, but, Beatrice ——

BEAT. Sweet Hero! She is wronged, she is slandered, she is undone.   315

BENE. Beat ——

BEAT. Princes and Counties! Surely, a princely testimony, a goodly Count, Count Comfect,° a sweet gallant, surely! Oh, that I were a man for his sake! Or that I had any friend would be a man for   320 my sake! But manhood is melted into courtesies, valor into compliment, and men are only turned into tongue, and trim ones too. He is now as valiant as Hercules that only tells a lie, and swears it. I cannot be a man with wishing, therefore I will die a woman with grieving.   326

BENE. Tarry, good Beatrice. By this hand, I love thee.

BEAT. Use it for my love some other way than swearing by it.   330

BENE. Think you in your soul the Count Claudio hath wronged Hero?

BEAT. Yea, as sure as I have a thought or a soul.

BENE. Enough, I am engaged,° I will challenge him. I will kiss your hand, and so I leave you. By this hand, Claudio shall render me a dear account.°

As you hear of me, so think of me. Go, comfort your cousin. I must say she is dead. And so farewell.

                     [Exeunt.]   338

SCENE II.° *A prison.*

[Enter DOGBERRY, VERGES, *and* SEXTON, *in gowns; and the* WATCH, *with* CONRADE *and* BORACHIO.]

DOGB. Is our whole dissembly° appeared?

VERG. Oh, a stool and a cushion° for the sexton.

SEXTON. Which be the malefactors?

DOGB. Marry, that am I and my partner.

VERG. Nay, that's certain, we have the exhibition° to examine.   6

SEXTON. But which are the offenders that are to be examined? Let them come before Master Constable.

DOGB. Yea, marry, let them come before me. What is your name, friend?   11

BORA. Borachio.

DOGB. Pray write down Borachio. Yours, sirrah?

CON. I am a gentleman, sir, and my name is Conrade.   16

DOGB. Write down master gentleman Conrade. Masters, do you serve God?

CON. & BORA. Yea, sir, we hope.

DOGB. Write down that they hope they serve God. And write God first, for God defend° but God should go before such villains! Masters, it is proved already that you are little better than false knaves, and it will go near to be thought so shortly. How answer you for yourselves?   25

CON. Marry, sir, we say we are none.

DOGB. A marvelous witty fellow, I assure you, but I will go about with him.° Come you hither, sirrah, a word in your ear. Sir, I say to you, it is thought you are false knaves.   30

BORA. Sir, I say to you we are none.

DOGB. Well, stand aside. 'Fore God, they are both in a tale.° Have you writ down that they are none?

SEXTON. Master Constable, you go not the   35 way to examine. You must call forth the watch that are their accusers.

DOGB. Yea, marry, that's the eftest° way. Let the watch come forth. Masters, I charge you, in the Prince's name, accuse these men.   40

FIRST WATCH. This man said, sir, that Don John, the Prince's brother, was a villain.

Sc. ii: In the Q speech headings for this scene Dogberry's lines are marked "Kempe" and Verges' "Cowley" — the actors who first took the parts. For Kempe, see Gen. Intro. p. 44a–b. **1. dissembly:** for "assembly."   **2. cushion:** a mark of respect, due to one who can read and write.   **5. exhibition:** Verges gives the word a new meaning. Knowing that the legal word "inhibition" means "prohibition," he supposes that "instruction to proceed" should be "exhibition."   **21. defend:** forbid.   **28. go . . . him:** get around him.   **33–34. both . . . tale:** have agreed to tell the same story.   **38. eftest:** neatest; apparently the word was coined by Dogberry.

---

285. stayed: stopped.   **303. approved:** proved. **in . . . height:** in the highest degree.   **305–06. bear . . . hand:** delude her. **318. Count Comfect:** "Count Candy."   **334. engaged:** pledged. **336. render . . . account:** shall pay me dearly for it.

DOGB. Write down Prince John a villain. Why, this is flat perjury, to call a Prince's brother villain.

BORA. Master Constable —— 45

DOGB. Pray thee, fellow, peace. I do not like thy look, I promise thee.

SEXTON. What heard you him say else?

SEC. WATCH. Marry, that he had received a thousand ducats of Don John for accusing the Lady Hero wrongfully. 51

DOGB. Flat burglary as ever was committed.

VERG. Yea, by mass, that it is.

SEXTON. What else, fellow?

FIRST WATCH. And that Count Claudio did mean, upon his words, to disgrace Hero before the whole assembly and not marry her.

DOGB. O villain! Thou wilt be condemned into everlasting redemption° for this.

SEXTON. What else? 60

WATCH. This is all.

SEXTON. And this is more, masters, than you can deny. Prince John is this morning secretly stolen away. Hero was in this manner accused, in this very manner refused, and upon the grief of this sud- 65 denly died. Master Constable, let these men be bound and brought to Leonato's. I will go before and show him their examination. [*Exit.*]

DOGB. Come, let them be opinioned.°

VERG. Let them be in the hands —— 70

CON. Off, coxcomb!°

DOGB. God's my life, where's the sexton? Let him write down the Prince's officer, coxcomb. Come, bind them. Thou naughty varlet!°

CON. Away! You are an ass, you are an ass. 75

DOGB. Dost thou not suspect° my place? Dost thou not suspect my years? Oh, that he were here to write me down an ass! But, masters, remember that I am an ass, though it be not written down, yet forget not that I am an ass. No, thou villain, thou art full 80 of piety,°as shall be proved upon thee by good witness. I am a wise fellow, and, which is more, an officer; and, which is more, a householder; and, which is more, as pretty a piece of flesh° as any is in Messina; and one that knows the law, go to; and a rich fellow enough, go to; and a fellow that hath had losses;° and one that hath two gowns, and everything handsome about him. Bring him away. 89 Oh, that I had been writ down an ass! [*Exeunt.*]

---

59. redemption: for "damnation."   69. opinioned: pinioned.
71. coxcomb: fool, from the fool's cap. See *Lear*, I.iv.105–22, and Pl. 12f and 13c.   74. varlet: knave.   76. suspect: for "respect."   81. piety: for "impiety."   84. piece of flesh: creature.
87–88. hath . . . losses: i.e., been an even greater man than he is now.

Act V

SCENE I. *Before* LEONATO'S *house.*

[*Enter* LEONATO *and* ANTONIO.]

ANT. If you go on thus, you will kill yourself,
And 'tis not wisdom thus to second° grief
Against yourself.

LEON.   I pray thee, cease thy counsel,
Which falls into mine ears as profitless
As water in a sieve. Give not me counsel,   5
Nor let no comforter delight mine ear
But such a one whose wrongs do suit with° mine.
Bring me a father that so loved his child,
Whose joy of her is overwhelmed like mine,
And bid him speak of patience.   10
Measure his woe the length and breadth of mine,
And let it answer every strain° for strain,
As thus for thus, and such a grief for such,
In every lineament,° branch, shape, and form.
If such a one will smile and stroke his beard,   15
Bid sorrow wag, cry "hem!" when he should
     groan,
Patch° grief with proverbs, make misfortune drunk
With candlewasters,° bring him yet to me,
And I of him will gather patience.
But there is no such man. For, Brother, men   20
Can counsel and speak comfort to that grief
Which they themselves not feel; but, tasting it,
Their counsel turns to passion,° which before
Would give preceptial medicine to rage,°
Fetter strong madness in a silken thread,   25
Charm ache with air, and agony with words.
No, no, 'tis all men's office to speak patience
To those that wring° under the load of sorrow,
But no man's virtue nor sufficiency
To be so moral° when he shall endure   30
The like himself. Therefore give me no counsel.
My griefs cry louder than advértisement.°

ANT. Therein do men from children nothing
     differ.

LEON. I pray thee, peace. I will be flesh and blood.
For there was never yet philosopher   35
That could endure the toothache patiently,

Act V, Sc. i: 2. second: assist.   7. suit with: match with.
12. strain: used in the musical sense — let him match his song of woe with mine.   14. lineament: feature.   16. Bid . . . groan: This is a much-disputed line. As it stands in the Globe text it means: "Tell sorrow to be cheery when he should groan." wag: wag the beard in gay chatter, as in the song " 'Tis merry in hall when beards wag all." See *II Hen IV*, V.iii.37. hem: a drinker's exclamation, like "Here's how." Q and F read "And sorrow, wagge, crie hem." 17. Patch: cover. 18. candlewasters: those who sit up late. 23. Their . . . passion: their good advice becomes strong emotion. 24. preceptial . . . rage: would try to cure rage by healing advice. 28. wring: suffer torture. 30. moral: full of fine sentiment. 32. cry . . . advertisement: are too great to be consoled by good advice.

However they have writ the style of gods
And made a push° at chance° and sufferance.°
    ANT. Yet bend not all the harm upon yourself.
Make those that do offend you suffer too.   40
    LEON. There thou speak'st reason. Nay, I will do
    so.
My soul doth tell me Hero is belied,
And that shall Claudio know, so shall the Prince,
And all of them that thus dishonor her.   44
    ANT. Here comes the Prince and Claudio hastily.
          [*Enter* DON PEDRO *and* CLAUDIO.]
    D. PEDRO. Good-den, good-den.
    CLAUD.   Good day to both of you.
    LEON. Hear you, my lords——
    D. PEDRO. We have some haste, Leonato.
    LEON. Some haste, my lord! Well, fare you well,
    my lord.
Are you so hasty now? Well, all is one.
    D. PEDRO. Nay, do not quarrel with us, good old
    man.   50
    ANT. If he could right himself with quarreling,
Some of us would lie low.
    CLAUD.   Who wrongs him?
    LEON. Marry, thou dost wrong me, thou dissem-
    bler, thou.—
Nay, never lay thy hand upon thy sword.
I fear thee not.
    CLAUD.   Marry,° beshrew° my hand   55
If it should give your age such cause of fear.
In faith, my hand meant nothing to my sword.
    LEON. Tush, tush, man, never fleer° and jest at
    me.
I speak not like a dotard nor a fool,
As, under privilege of age, to brag   60
What I have done being young, or what would do
Were I not old. Know, Claudio, to thy head,
Thou hast so wronged mine innocent child and me
That I am forced to lay my reverence by,
And, with gray hairs and bruise of many days,   65
Do challenge thee to trial of a man.
I say thou hast belied mine innocent child.
Thy slander hath gone through and through her
    heart,
And she lies buried with her ancestors,
Oh, in a tomb where never scandal slept   70
Save this of hers, framed by thy villainy!
    CLAUD. My villainy?
    LEON.   Thine, Claudio, thine, I say.
    D. PEDRO. You say not right, old man.
    LEON.   My lord, my lord,
I'll prove it on his body, if he dare,
Despite his nice fence° and his active practice,   75

His May of youth° and bloom of lustihood.°
    CLAUD. Away! I will not have to do with you.
    LEON. Canst thou so daff° me? Thou hast killed
    my child.
If thou kill'st me, boy,° thou shalt kill a man.
    ANT. He shall kill two of us, and men indeed.   80
But that's no matter, let him kill one first,
Win me and wear me. Let him answer me.
Come, follow me, boy, come, sir boy, come, follow
    me.
Sir boy, I'll whip you from your foining° fence,
Nay, as I am a gentleman, I will.   85
    LEON. Brother——
    ANT. Content yourself. God knows I loved my
    niece,
And she is dead, slandered to death by villains
That dare as well answer a man indeed
As I dare take a serpent by the tongue.   90
Boys, apes, braggarts, Jacks,° milksops!
    LEON. Brother Antony——
    ANT. Hold you content. What, man! I know
    them, yea,
And what they weigh, even to the utmost scruple° —
Scambling,° outfacing,° fashion-monging° boys
That lie, and cog,° and flout, deprave° and slander,
Go antiquely° and show outward hideousness,   96
And speak off half a dozen dangerous words,
How they might hurt their enemies if they durst —
And this is all.
    LEON. But, Brother Antony——
    ANT.   Come, 'tis no matter.   100
Do not you meddle, let me deal in this.
    D. PEDRO. Gentlemen both, we will not wake° your
    patience.
My heart is sorry for your daughter's death.
But, on my honor, she was charged with nothing
But what was true, and very full of proof.   105
    LEON. My lord, my lord——
    D. PEDRO. I will not hear you.
    LEON. No? Come, Brother, away! I will be heard.
    ANT. And shall, or some of us will smart for it.
          [*Exeunt* LEONATO *and* ANTONIO.]
    D. PEDRO. See, see, here comes the man we went
    to seek.   110
          [*Enter* BENEDICK.]
    CLAUD. Now, signior, what news?
    BENE. Good day, my lord.
    D. PEDRO. Welcome, signior. You are almost come
to part almost a fray.   114
    CLAUD. We had like to have had our two noses
snapped off with two old men without teeth.

---

38. **made a push:** made a brave show against. **chance:** mis-
fortune. **sufferance:** pain.   55. **Marry:** Mary, by the Virgin
Mary. **beshrew:** plague on.   58. **fleer:** sneer.   75. **fence:**
fencing. Leonato as one of the older generation who used the
long sword despises the new-fashioned fencing with the rapier.
See Pl. 22j and comment.   76. **May of youth:** youth in full bloom. **lustihood:** manhood.
78. **daff:** put aside.   79. **boy:** a deliberate and deadly insult. Cf.
Cor, V.vi.101.   84. **foining:** thrusting.   91. **Jacks:** knaves.
93. **scruple:** minutest weight.   94. **Scambling:** pushing, quar-
relsome. **outfacing:** swaggering. **fashion-monging:** dressed in
the latest fashion.   95. **cog:** cheat. **deprave:** slander.   96. **an-
tiquely:** like buffoons.   102. **wake:** disturb

D. PEDRO. Leonato and his brother. What thinkest thou? Had we fought, I doubt we should have been too young for them.

BENE. In a false quarrel there is no true valor. I came to seek you both.   121

CLAUD. We have been up and down to seek thee, for we are high-proof° melancholy and would fain have it beaten away. Wilt thou use thy wit?

BENE. It is in my scabbard. Shall I draw it?   125

D. PEDRO. Dost thou wear thy wit by thy side?

CLAUD. Never any did so, though very many have been beside their wit. I will bid thee draw° as we do the minstrels, draw to pleasure us.

D. PEDRO. As I am an honest man, he looks pale. Art thou sick, or angry?   131

CLAUD. What, courage, man! What though care killed a cat, thou hast mettle enough in thee to kill care.

BENE. Sir, I shall meet your wit in the career.° an you charge it against me. I pray you choose another subject.   137

CLAUD. Nay, then, give him another staff.° This last was broke cross.°

D. PEDRO. By this light, he changes more and more. I think he be angry indeed.   141

CLAUD. If he be, he knows how to turn his girdle.°

BENE. Shall I speak a word in your ear?

CLAUD. God bless° me from a challenge!   144

BENE. [*Aside to* CLAUDIO] You are a villain. I jest not. I will make it good how you dare, with what you dare, and when you dare. Do me right, or I will protest° your cowardice. You have killed a sweet lady, and her death shall fall heavy on you. Let me hear from you.   151

CLAUD. Well, I will meet you, so I may have good cheer.°

D. PEDRO. What, a feast, a feast?

CLAUD. I' faith, I thank him. He hath bid me to a calf's head and a capon, the which if I do not carve most curiously,° say my knife's naught. Shall I not find a woodcock° too?

BENE. Sir, your wit ambles well, it goes easily.   159

D. PEDRO. I'll tell thee how Beatrice praised thy wit the other day. I said thou hadst a fine wit. "True," said she, "a fine little one." "No," said I, "a great wit." "Right," says she, "a great gross one." "Nay," said I, "a good wit." "Just," said she, "it hurts no-

body." "Nay," said I, "the gentleman is wise." "Certain," said she, "a wise gentleman." "Nay," said I, "he hath the tongues."° "That I be-   165 lieve," said she, "for he swore a thing to me on Monday night which he forswore on Tuesday morning. There's a double tongue, there's two tongues." Thus did she, an hour together, transshape° thy particular virtues. Yet at last she concluded, with a sigh, thou wast the properest man in Italy.   174

CLAUD. For the which she wept heartily, and said she cared not.

D. PEDRO. Yea, that she did, but yet, for all that, an if she did not hate him deadly, she would love him dearly. The old man's daughter told us all.   180

CLAUD. All, all, and, moreover, God saw him when he was hid in the garden.

D. PEDRO. But when shall we set the savage bull's horns° on the sensible Benedick's head?

CLAUD. Yea, and text underneath, "Here dwells Benedick the married man"?   186

BENE. Fare you well, boy. You know my mind. I will leave you now to your gossiplike° humor. You break jests as braggarts do their blades, which, God be thanked, hurt not. My lord, for your many   190 courtesies I thank you. I must discontinue your company. Your brother the bastard is fled from Messina. You have among you killed a sweet and innocent lady. For my Lord Lackbeard there, he and I shall meet, and till then peace be with him. [*Exit.*]

D. PEDRO. He is in earnest.   197

CLAUD. In most profound earnest, and I'll warrant you for the love of Beatrice.

D. PEDRO. And hath challenged thee.   200

CLAUD. Most sincerely.

D. PEDRO. What a pretty thing man is when he goes in his doublet and hose° and leaves off his wit!

CLAUD. He is then a giant to an ape, but then is an ape a doctor to such a man.°   206

D. PEDRO. But, soft you, let me be. Pluck up, my heart, and be sad.° Did he not say my brother was fled?

[*Enter* DOGBERRY, VERGES, *and the* WATCH, *with* CONRADE *and* BORACHIO.]

DOGB. Come, you, sir. If justice cannot tame you, she shall ne'er weigh more reasons in her balance. Nay, an you be a cursing hypocrite once, you must be looked to.

D. PEDRO. How now? Two of my brother's men bound! Borachio one!   215

CLAUD. Hearken after their offense, my lord.

---

123. high-proof: in the highest degree.   **128. draw:** start playing; i.e., draw the fiddle bow across the strings.   **135. career:** charge in a tilting match.   **138. staff:** tilting spear.   **139. broke cross:** In tilting the skillful rider broke his staff full on his opponent's shield. The novice who flinched from the impact broke his staff across it.   **142. turn . . . girdle:** a proverb used to describe an angry man; the origin and meaning are uncertain.   **144. bless:** preserve.   **149. protest:** proclaim.   **153. cheer:** entertainment.   **156–57. carve . . . curiously:** Carving was still part of a gentleman's education, as it had been in Chaucer's time. See the *Prologue* to the *Canterbury Tales*, l. 100.   **158. woodcock:** a foolish bird.

165. hath . . . tongues: can speak foreign languages.   **172. transshape:** transform.   **183–84. savage . . . horns:** See I.i.263–66.   **188. gossiplike:** tattling.   **202–03. goes . . . hose:** i.e., a man is a fine thing in his clothes (but without them, as Lear put it, he is no more than "a poor, bare, forked animal" — *Lear*, III.iv. 112).   **205–06. He . . . man:** clothed man is a much better thing than an ape, yet an ape is a learned man compared with such a fool.   **208. sad:** serious.

D. PEDRO. Officers, what offense have these men done?

DOGB. Marry, sir, they have committed false report; moreover, they have spoken untruths; secondarily, they are slanders; sixth and lastly, they have belied a lady; thirdly, they have verified unjust things; and, to conclude, they are lying knaves.   224

D. PEDRO. First, I ask thee what they have done; thirdly, I ask thee what's their offense; sixth and lastly, why they are committed; and, to conclude, what you lay to their charge.

CLAUD. Rightly reasoned, and in his own division,° and, by my troth, there's one meaning well suited.°   231

D. PEDRO. Who have you offended, masters, that you are thus bound to your answer? This learned constable is too cunning to be understood. What's your offense?   235

BORA. Sweet Prince, let me go no farther to mine answer. Do you hear me, and let this Count kill me. I have deceived even your very eyes. What your wisdoms could not discover, these shallow fools have brought to light, who in the night overheard   240 me confessing to this man how Don John your brother incensed me to slander the Lady Hero; how you were brought into the orchard and saw me court Margaret in Hero's garments; how you disgraced her, when you should marry her. My   245 villainy they have upon record, which I had rather seal with my death than repeat over to my shame. The lady is dead upon mine and my master's false accusation, and, briefly, I desire nothing but the reward of a villain.   251

D. PEDRO. Runs not this speech like iron through your blood?

CLAUD. I have drunk poison whiles he uttered it.

D. PEDRO. But did my brother set thee onto this?

BORA. Yea, and paid me richly for the practice of it.

D. PEDRO. He is composed and framed of treachery,
And fled he is upon this villainy.

CLAUD. Sweet Hero! Now thy image doth appear
In the rare semblance that I loved it first.   260

DOGB. Come, bring away the plaintiffs.° By this time our sexton hath reformed° Signior Leonato of the matter. And, masters, do not forget to specify, when time and place shall serve, that I am an ass.

VERG. Here, here comes Master Signior Leonato, and the sexton too.

[*Re-enter* LEONATO *and* ANTONIO, *with the* SEXTON.]

LEON. Which is the villain? Let me see his eyes,
That when I note another man like him,   270
I may avoid him. Which of these is he?

BORA. If you would know your wronger, look on me.

LEON. Art thou the slave that with thy breath hast killed
Mine innocent child?

BORA.   Yea, even I alone.

LEON. No, not so, villain, thou beliest thyself.
Here stand a pair of honorable men,   276
A third is fled that had a hand in it.
I thank you, Princes, for my daughter's death.
Record it with your high and worthy deeds.
'Twas bravely done, if you bethink you of it.   280

CLAUD. I know not how to pray your patience,
Yet I must speak. Choose your revenge yourself,
Impose me to what penance your invention°
Can lay upon my sin. Yet sinned I not
But in mistaking.

D. PEDRO.   By my soul, nor I.   285
And yet to satisfy this good old man
I would bend under any heavy weight
That he'll enjoin me to.

LEON. I cannot bid you bid my daughter live,
That were impossible. But I pray you both   290
Possess° the people in Messina here
How innocent she died, and if your love
Can labor aught in sad invention,°
Hang her an epitaph upon her tomb,
And sing it to her bones, sing it tonight.   295
Tomorrow morning come you to my house,
And since you could not be my son-in-law,
Be yet my nephew.° My brother hath a daughter,
Almost the copy of my child that's dead,
And she alone is heir to both of us.   300
Give her the right you should have given her cousin,
And so dies my revenge.

CLAUD.   O noble sir,
Your overkindness doth wring tears from me!
I do embrace your offer, and dispose
For henceforth of poor Claudio.   305

LEON. Tomorrow, then, I will expect your coming,
Tonight I take my leave. This naughty man
Shall face to face be brought to Margaret,
Who I believe was packed° in all this wrong,
Hired to it by your brother.

BORA.   No, by my soul, she was not,   310
Nor knew not what she did when she spoke to me,
But always hath been just and virtuous
In anything that I do know by her.

DOGB. Moreover, sir, which indeed is not under white and black, this plaintiff here, the of-   315 fender, did call me ass. I beseech you, let it be remembered in his punishment. And also, the watch heard them talk of one Deformed. They say he wears a key in his ear, and a lock hanging by it, and bor-

283. invention: imagination.   291. Possess: inform.   293. invention: work of imagination; i.e., funeral poem.   297-98. And ... nephew: See *M Ado* Intro. p. 420b.   309. packed: an accomplice, one of the pack.

230. division: categories.   230-31. one ... suited: one meaning dressed up in several different ways.   261. plaintiffs: for "defendants."   262. reformed: for "informed."

rows money in God's name, the which he hath　320
used so long and never paid that now men grow
hardhearted and will lend nothing for God's sake.
Pray you examine him upon that point.

LEON. I thank thee for thy care and honest pains.

DOGB. Your Worship speaks like a most thankful
and reverend youth, and I praise God for you.

LEON. There's for thy pains.　327

DOGB. God save the foundation!°

LEON. Go. I discharge thee of thy prisoner, and I
thank thee.　330

DOGB. I leave an arrant knave with your Worship,
which I beseech your Worship to correct yourself,
for the example of others. God keep your Worship!
I wish your Worship well. God restore you to health!
I humbly give you leave to depart, and if a merry
meeting may be wished, God prohibit° it!　336
Come, neighbor.　[*Exeunt* DOGBERRY *and* VERGES.]

LEON. Until tomorrow morning, lords, farewell.

ANT. Farewell, my lords. We look for you tomor-
row.

D. PEDRO. We will not fail.

CLAUD.　　　　　　　Tonight I'll mourn with Hero.

LEON. [*To the* WATCH] Bring you these fellows on.
We'll talk with Margaret,　341
How her acquaintance grew with this lewd° fellow.

[*Exeunt, severally.*]

SCENE II. LEONATO'S *garden.*

[*Enter* BENEDICK *and* MARGARET, *meeting.*]

BENE. Pray thee, sweet Mistress Margaret, de-
serve well at my hand by helping me to the speech
of Beatrice.

MARG. Will you, then, write me a sonnet in praise
of my beauty?　5

BENE. In so high a style, Margaret, that no man
living shall come over° it, for, in most comely truth,
thou deservest it.

MARG. To have no man come over me! Why, shall
I always keep belowstairs?°　10

BENE. Thy wit is as quick as the greyhound's
mouth. It catches.

MARG. And yours as blunt as the fencer's foils,
which hit but hurt not.　14

BENE. A most manly wit, Margaret. It will not
hurt a woman. And so, I pray thee call Beatrice. I
give thee the bucklers.°

MARG. Give us the swords, we have bucklers of our
own.　19

BENE. If you use them, Margaret, you must put in

the pikes° with a vice,° and they are dangerous
weapons for maids.

MARG. Well, I will call Beatrice to you, who I
think hath legs.　24

BENE. And therefore will come.

[*Exit* MARGARET.]

[*Sings.*]　　　　"The god of love,
　　　　　　　　That sits above,
　　　　　　And knows me, and knows me,
　　　　　　　　How pitiful I deserve ——"　29

I mean in singing, but in loving, Leander the good
swimmer, Troilus° the first employer of panders,
and a whole bookful of these quondam° carpetmon-
gers° whose names yet run smoothly in the even
road of a blank verse, why, they were never so truly
turned over and over as my poor self in love. Marry,
I cannot show it in rhyme. I have tried. I can　36
find out no rhyme to "lady" but "baby," an inno-
cent rhyme; for "scorn," "horn," a hard rhyme; for
"school," "fool," a babbling rhyme — very omi-
nous endings. No, I was not born under a rhyming
planet, nor I cannot woo in festival terms.　41

[*Enter* BEATRICE.] Sweet Beatrice, wouldst thou come
when I called thee?

BEAT. Yea, signior, and depart when you bid me.

BENE. Oh, stay but till then!　45

BEAT. "Then" is spoken, fare you well now. And
yet ere I go let me go with that I came, which is,
with knowing what hath passed between you and
Claudio.

BENE. Only foul words, and thereupon I will kiss
thee.　51

BEAT. Foul words is but foul wind, and foul wind
is but foul breath, and foul breath is noisome. There-
fore I will depart unkissed.

BENE. Thou hast frighted the word out of his right
sense, so forcible is thy wit. But I must tell thee
plainly, Claudio undergoes° my challenge, and
either I must shortly hear from him or I will sub-
scribe° him a coward. And I pray thee now, tell me
for which of my bad parts didst thou first fall in love
with me?　61

BEAT. For them all together, which maintained so
politic a state° of evil that they will not admit any
good part to intermingle with them. But for which
of my good parts did you first suffer love for me?　66

BENE. Suffer love — a good epithet! I do suffer
love indeed, for I love thee against my will.

---

328. foundation: i.e., this noble house.　336. prohibit: for
"grant."　342. lewd: wicked.

Sc. ii: 7. come over: overcome, with a pun on "stile."
10. belowstairs: i.e., with the servants.　17. give . . . bucklers:
yield you the victory. buckler: small shield. See Pl. 9 and 211.

21. pikes: spikes. The buckler was sometimes equipped with a
spike which could be pushed into the opponent's face. vice: screw.
30-31. Leander . . . Troilus: supreme specimens of lovesick
wooers. Marlowe's poem *Hero and Leander* had been published in
1598. For Troilus and his pander see *Tr & Cr.*　32. quondam:
former.　33. carpetmongers: "armchair generals," who have
distinguished themselves on the carpet and not on the field of
battle.　57. undergoes: endures; i.e., has received.　59. sub-
scribe: publicly proclaim. See I.i.41.　63. politic a state: well-
ordered community.

BEAT. In spite of your heart, I think — alas, poor heart! If you spite it for my sake, I will spite it for yours, for I will never love that which my friend hates.   72

BENE. Thou and I are too wise to woo peaceably.

BEAT. It appears not in this confession. There's not one wise man among twenty that will praise himself.   77

BENE. An old, an old instance, Beatrice, that lived in the time of good neighbors. If a man do not erect in this age his own tomb ere he dies, he shall live no longer in monument than the bell rings and the widow weeps.°   82

BEAT. And how long is that, think you?

BENE. Question. Why, an hour in clamor° and a quarter in rheum.° Therefore is it most expedient for the wise, if Don Worm, his conscience, find no impediment to the contrary, to be the trumpet of his own virtues, as I am to myself. So much for praising myself, who, I myself will bear witness, is praiseworthy. And now tell me, how doth your cousin?

BEAT. Very ill.   92

BENE. And how do you?

BEAT. Very ill too.

BENE. Serve God, love me, and mend. There will I leave you too, for here comes one in haste.   96

[*Enter* URSULA.]

URS. Madam, you must come to your uncle. Yonder's old coil° at home. It is proved my Lady Hero hath been falsely accused, the Prince and Claudio mightily abused. And Don John is the author of all, who is fled and gone. Will you come presently?   102

BEAT. Will you go hear this news, signior?

BENE. I will live in thy heart, die in thy lap, and be buried in thy eyes, and moreover I will go with thee to thy uncle's.   [*Exeunt.*]

SCENE III. *A church.*

[*Enter* DON PEDRO, CLAUDIO, *and three or four with tapers.*]

CLAUD. Is this the monument of Leonato?

A LORD. It is, my lord.

CLAUD. [*Reading out of a scroll.*]
    "Done to death by slanderous tongues
      Was the Hero that here lies.
    Death, in guerdon° of her wrongs,   5
      Gives her fame which never dies.
    So the life that died with shame
    Lives in death with glorious fame."

      Hang thou there upon the tomb,
      Praising her when I am dumb.   10
Now, music, sound, and sing your solemn hymn.

SONG

    Pardon, goddess of the night,°
    Those that slew thy virgin knight,°
    For the which, with songs of woe,
    Round about her tomb they go.
      Midnight, assist our moan,
      Help us to sigh and groan,
        Heavily, heavily.
      Graves, yawn, and yield your dead,
      Till death be utterèd,   20
        Heavily, heavily.°

CLAUD. Now, unto thy bones good night!
Yearly will I do this rite.

D. PEDRO. Good morrow, masters. Put your torches out.
The wolves have preyed, and look, the gentle day,
Before the wheels of Phoebus,° round about   26
Dapples the drowsy east with spots of gray.
Thanks to you all, and leave us. Fare you well.

CLAUD. Good morrow, masters. Each his several way.

D. PEDRO. Come, let us hence and put on other weeds,°   30
And then to Leonato's we will go.

CLAUD. And Hymen° now with luckier issue speed 's
Than this for whom we rendered up this woe.
           [*Exeunt.*]

SCENE IV. *A room in* LEONATO'S *house.*

[*Enter* LEONATO, ANTONIO, BENEDICK, BEATRICE, MARGARET, URSULA, FRIAR FRANCIS, *and* HERO.]

FRIAR. Did I not tell you she was innocent?

LEON. So are the Prince and Claudio, who accused her
Upon the error that you heard debated.
But Margaret was in some fault for this,
Although against her will,° as it appears   5
In the true course of all the question.°

ANT. Well, I am glad that all things sort° so well.

BENE. And so am I, being else by faith enforced
To call young Claudio to a reckoning for it.

LEON. Well, Daughter, and you gentlewomen all,
Withdraw into a chamber by yourselves,   11

79–82. If . . . weeps: The short memories of Elizabethan widows were notorious. For this reason most of the elaborate Elizabethan tombs were erected by the occupants for themselves. See Gen. Intro. p. 20a.   **84. clamor:** noisy grief.   **85. rheum:** moisture.   **98. old coil:** a great to-do.   **Sc. iii: 5. guerdon:** reward.

12. goddess . . . night: Diana, goddess of chastity.   **13. virgin knight:** i.e., Hero.   **19–21. Graves . . . heavily:** These lines do not make sense, unless the meaning is that the dead are to come up to listen to the dirge. The "sad inventions" of Claudio have indeed been "labored."   **26. wheels of Phoebus:** wheels of the sun god's chariot.   **30. weeds:** garments.   **32. Hymen:** god of marriage.   **Sc. iv: 5. will:** intention.   **6. question:** examination.   **7. sort:** turn out.

And when I send for you, come hither masked.
    [*Exeunt* LADIES.]
The Prince and Claudio promised by this hour
To visit me. You know your office, Brother.
You must be father to your brother's daughter,   15
And give her to young Claudio.
    ANT. Which I will do with confirmed counte-
    nance.°
    BENE. Friar, I must entreat your pains, I think.
    FRIAR. To do what, signior?
    BENE. To bind me, or undo me, one of them.   20
Signior Leonato, truth it is, good signior,
Your niece regards me with an eye of favor.
    LEON. That eye my daughter lent her — 'tis most
    true.
    BENE. And I do with an eye of love requite her.
    LEON. The sight whereof I think you had from
    me,   25
From Claudio, and the Prince. But what's your will?
    BENE. Your answer, sir, is enigmatical.
But, for my will, my will is, your goodwill
May stand with ours, this day to be conjoined
In the state of honorable marriage.   30
In which, good Friar, I shall desire your help.
    LEON. My heart is with your liking.
    FRIAR.   And my help.
Here comes the Prince and Claudio.
[*Enter* DON PEDRO *and* CLAUDIO, *and two or three
                others.*]
    D. PEDRO. Good morrow to this fair assembly.
    LEON. Good morrow, Prince. Good morrow,
    Claudio.   35
We here attend° you. Are you yet° determined
Today to marry with my brother's daughter?
    CLAUD. I'll hold my mind, were she an Ethiope.°
    LEON. Call her forth, Brother, here's the Friar
    ready.   [*Exit* ANTONIO.]
    D. PEDRO. Good morrow, Benedick. Why, what's
    the matter   40
That you have such a February face,
So full of frost, of storm, and cloudiness?
    CLAUD. I think he thinks upon the savage bull.°
Tush, fear not, man, we'll tip thy horns with gold,
And all Europa° shall rejoice at thee   45
As once Europa° did at lusty Jove
When he would play the noble beast in love.
    BENE. Bull Jove, sir, had an amiable low,
And some such strange bull leaped your father's cow
And got a calf in that same noble feat   50
Much like to you, for you have just his bleat.
    CLAUD. For this I owe you.° Here comes other
    reckonings.°

[*Re-enter* ANTONIO, *with the* LADIES *masked.*] Which
    is the lady I must seize upon?
    ANT. This same is she, and I do give you her.
    CLAUD. Why, then she's mine. Sweet, let me see
    your face.   55
    LEON. No, that you shall not till you take her hand
Before this Friar and swear to marry her.
    CLAUD. Give me your hand. Before this holy Friar,
I am your husband, if you like of me.   59
    HERO. And when I lived, I was your other wife,
    [*Unmasking*]
And when you loved, you were my other husband.
    CLAUD. Another Hero!
    HERO.   Nothing certainer.
One Hero died defiled, but I do live,
And surely as I live, I am a maid.   64
    D. PEDRO. The former Hero! Hero that is dead!
    LEON. She died, my lord, but whiles° her slander
    lived.
    FRIAR. All this amazement can I qualify.°
When after that the holy rites are ended,
I'll tell you largely° of fair Hero's death.
Meantime let wonder seem familiar,°   70
And to the chapel let us presently.
    BENE. Soft and fair, Friar. Which is Beatrice?
    BEAT. [*Unmasking*] I answer to that name. What
    is your will?
    BENE. Do not you love me?
    BEAT.   Why, no, no more than reason.
    BENE. Why, then your uncle, and the Prince, and
    Claudio   75
Have been deceived. They swore you did.
    BEAT. Do not you love me?
    BENE.   Troth, no, no more than reason.
    BEAT. Why, then my cousin, Margaret, and Ursula
Are much deceived, for they did swear you did.
    BENE. They swore that you were almost sick for me.
    BEAT. They swore that you were well-nigh dead
    for me.   81
    BENE. 'Tis no such matter. Then you do not love
    me?
    BEAT. No, truly, but in friendly recompense.
    LEON. Come, Cousin, I am sure you love the gen-
    tleman.
    CLAUD. And I'll be sworn upon 't that he loves her,
For here's a paper, written in his hand,   86
A halting° sonnet of his own pure brain,
Fashioned to Beatrice.
    HERO.   And here's another,
Writ in my cousin's hand, stolen from her pocket,
Containing her affection unto Benedick.   90
    BENE. A miracle! Here's our own hands against
our hearts. Come, I will have thee, but, by this light,
I take thee for pity.

---

17. confirmed countenance: straight face.   36. attend: wait
for. yet: still.   38. Ethiope: Ethiopian.   43. savage bull: See
I.i.263–66, and V.i.183.   45. Europa: Europe.   46. Europa: a
maiden loved by Jupiter, who transformed himself into a white
bull to get her.   52. owe you: i.e., will pay you back. reckon-
ings: matters.

66. but whiles: only so long as.   67. qualify: moderate.
69. largely: fully.   70. wonder . . . familiar: strange things seem
normal.   87. halting: lame.

BEAT. I would not deny you, but, by this good day,
I yield upon great persuasion, and partly to save 95
your life, for I was told you were in a consumption.

BENE. Peace! I will stop your mouth.

[Kissing her]

D. PEDRO. How dost thou, Benedick the married
man? 99

BENE. I'll tell thee what, Prince, a college of wit-
crackers cannot flout me out of my humor.° Dost
thou think I care for a satire or an epigram? No. If
a man will be beaten with brains, a' shall wear noth-
ing handsome about him.° In brief, since I do pur-
pose to marry, I will think nothing to any pur- 105
pose that the world can say against it; and therefore
never flout at me for what I have said against it, for
man is a giddy thing, and this is my conclusion. For
thy part, Claudio, I did think to have beaten 110
thee, but in that thou art like to be my kinsman, live
unbruised, and love my cousin.

CLAUD. I had well hoped thou wouldst have de-

___

101. humor: inclination.   102–04. If . . . him: a man who is
afraid of what others say will never be distinguished.

nied Beatrice, that I might have cudgeled thee out
of thy single life, to make thee a double-dealer, 116
which, out of question, thou wilt be if my cousin do
not look exceeding narrowly to thee.

BENE. Come, come, we are friends. Let's have a
dance ere we are married, that we may lighten our
own hearts and our wives' heels. 121

LEON. We'll have dancing afterward.

BENE. First, of my word, therefore play, music.
Prince, thou art sad. Get thee a wife, get thee a wife.
There is no staff° more reverend than one tipped
with horn.° 126

[Enter a MESSENGER.]

MESS. My lord, your brother John is ta'en in flight,
And brought with armed men back to Messina.

BENE. Think not on him till tomorrow. I'll devise
thee brave punishments for him. Strike up, 130
pipers!
[Dance. Exeunt.]

___

125. staff: walking stick used by the elderly and respectable.
125–6. tipped . . . horn: the usual joke about cuckolds. Benedick
thus gets the last word, for the Prince is at least half in love with
Beatrice.

THE LIFE OF KING HENRY THE FIFTH

Introduction[1]

The Life of King Henry the Fifth can be dated with some accuracy. In the Chorus before Act V (lines 28–34) there is an unmistakable reference to the Earl of Essex's triumphal departure for Ireland on March 29, 1599 (see Gen. Intro. p. 23b). By the early summer rumors were circulating in London that Essex had failed, and on September 28 he returned to London, and was thenceforward in disgrace. The complimentary lines in the Chorus would thus have been topical only for a few weeks in the spring of 1599.

Henry V is a continuation of *II Henry IV,* which had been produced about a year before. At the end of that play Shakespeare promised:

If you be not too much cloyed with fat meat, our humble author will continue the story, with Sir John in it, and make you merry with fair Katharine of France. Where, for anything I know, Falstaff shall die of a sweat, unless already a' be killed with your hard opinions, for Oldcastle died a martyr, and this is not the man.

The promise was not kept. Although the rest of the gang reappear, with a newcomer in Corporal Nym, Falstaff is not seen, though his death is reported in II.iii. It is not known why Falstaff thus vanished, but it would certainly have been difficult, after his devastating rejection (*II Hen IV,* V.v), for Shakespeare to bring him again into the presence of Henry V. It may be, as some critics maintain, that Shakespeare felt that Falstaff would overshadow the King and so spoil the play. It may be that Shakespeare himself had lost the knack of creating Falstaff; when Falstaff reappeared in *The Merry Wives of Windsor* only his bulk remained; his wit and his humor had woefully diminished. Or there may have been some quite practical reason, such as the departure of the actor who originally created the part. Whatever the explanation, the whole balance and structure of comedy and history in *Henry V* is different from that in *Henry IV.*

In writing the serious scenes Shakespeare, as in the other History Plays, again followed Holinshed's *Chronicle,* at times so closely that he did little more than turn Holinshed's prose into blank verse. The long lecture on the Salic law delivered by the Archbishop (I.ii.35–100) is a transcript, phrase for phrase, from the *Chronicle,* as is also the list of French casualties (IV.viii.81–110). Some extracts will show what Shakespeare owed to his source:

I. THE CHARACTER OF HENRY V

This Henry was a king of life without spot; a prince whom all men loved, and of none disdained; a captain against whom fortune never frowned, nor mischance once spurned; whose people him so severe a justicer both loved and obeyed, and so humane withal that he left no offense unpunished, nor friendship unrewarded; a terror to rebels, and suppressor of sedition; his virtues notable, his qualities most praiseworthy.

In strength and nimbleness of body from his youth few to him comparable; for in wrestling, leaping, and running, no man well able to compare. In casting of great iron bars and heavy stones he excelled commonly all men, never shrinking at cold, nor slothful for heat; and when he most labored, his head commonly uncovered; no more weary of harness [armor] than a light cloak; very valiantly abiding at needs both hunger and thirst; so manful of mind as never seen to quinch at a wound, or to smart at the pain; to turn his nose from evil savor, or to close his eyes from smoke or dust; no man more moderate in eating and drinking, with diet not delicate, but rather more meet for men of war than for princes or tender stomachs. Every honest person was permitted to come to him sitting at meal, where either secretly or openly to declare his mind. High and weighty causes, as well between men of war and other, he would gladly hear; and either determined them himself or else for end committed them to others. He slept very little, but that very soundly, insomuch that when his soldiers sang at night, or minstrels played, he then slept fastest; of courage invincible, of purpose unmutable; so wisehardy always as fear was banished from him; at every alarum he first in armor, and foremost in ordering. In time of war such was his providence, bounty, and hap as he had true intelligence not only what his enemies did, but what they said and intended. Of his devices and purposes, few, before the thing was at the point to be done, should be made privy.

[1] See also App. 28.

2. THE ARCHBISHOP'S ARGUMENT (cf. 1.ii.35–100)

[The Archbishop spoke] against the surmised and false feigned law Salic, which the Frenchmen allege ever against the Kings of England in bar of their just title to the crown of France. The very words of that supposed law are these: " *In terram Salicam mulieres ne succedant*"; that is to say, " Into the Salic land let not women succeed." Which the French glossers expound to be the realm of France, and that this law was made by King Pharamond; whereas yet their own authors affirm that the land Salic is in Germany, between the rivers of Elbe and Sala; and that when Charles the Great had overcome the Saxons, he placed there certain Frenchmen, which having in disdain the dishonest manners of the German women, made a law that the females should not succeed to any inheritance within that land, which at this day is called Meisen. So that, if this be true, this law was not made for the realm of France, nor the Frenchmen possessed the land Salic, till four hundred and one and twenty years after the death of Pharamond, the supposed maker of this Salic law; for this Pharamond deceased in the year 426 and Charles the Great subdued the Saxons, and placed the Frenchmen in those parts beyond the river of Sala, in the year 805.

Moreover, it appeareth by their own writers that King Pepin, which deposed Childeric, claimed the crown of France as heir general, for that he was descended of Blithild, daughter to King Clothair the First. Hugh Capet also (who usurped the crown upon Charles Duke of Loraine, the sole heir male of the line and stock of Charles the Great), to make his title seem true, and appear good (though indeed it was stark naught), conveyed himself as heir to the Lady Lingard, daughter to King Charlemagne, son to Lewis the Emperor, that was son to Charles the Great. King Lewis also, the Tenth (otherwise called Saint Lewis), being very heir to the said usurper Hugh Capet, could never be satisfied in his conscience how he might justly keep and possess the crown of France till he was persuaded and fully instructed that Queen Isabel his grandmother was lineally descended of the Lady Ermengard, daughter and heir to the above named Charles Duke of Loraine; by the which marriage, the blood and line of Charles the Great was again united and restored to the crown and scepter of France. So that more clear than the sun it openly appeareth that the title of King Pepin, the claim of Hugh Capet, the possession of Lewis — yea, and the French Kings to this day — are derived and conveyed from the heir female, though they would, under the color of such a feigned law, bar the Kings and Princes of this realm of England of their right and lawful inheritance.

The Archbishop further alleged out of the Book of Numbers this saying: " When a man dieth without a son, let the inheritance descend to his daughter."

3. THE KING'S WORDS BEFORE THE BATTLE (cf. iv.iii.21–67)

It is said that as he heard one of the host utter his wish to another thus: " I would to God there were with us now so many good soldiers as are at this hour within England!" the King answered: " I would not wish a man more here than I have. We are indeed in comparison to the enemies but a few, but if God of His clemency do favor us and our just cause (as I trust He will), we shall speed well enough. But let no man ascribe victory to our own strength and might, but only to God's assistance, to Whom I have no doubt we shall worthily have cause to give thanks therefore. And if so be that for our offenses' sakes we shall be delivered into the hands of our enemies, the less number we be, the less damage shall the realm of England sustain. But if we should fight in trust of multitude of men, and so get the victory (our minds being prone to pride), we should thereupon peradventure ascribe the victory not so much to the gift of God as to our own puissance, and thereby provoke His high indignation and displeasure against us. And if the enemy get the upper hand, then should our realm and country suffer more damage and stand in further danger. But be you of good comfort, and show yourselves valiant! God and our just quarrel shall defend us and deliver these our proud adversaries with all the multitude of them which you see (or at the least the most of them) into our hands."

Apart from the records in the *Chronicle,* several other dramatists had written plays about Henry V, who, like other national heroes, had become a legendary figure. A playgoer therefore expected some scenes showing the King's wild youth, his habit of passing disguised amongst common men, and his blunt wooing of French Kate. These were available to Shakespeare in the old play of *The Famous Victories of Henry the Fifth,* which had been printed in 1598 (see *I Hen IV* Intro. p. 334b).

The full version of *Henry V* was not printed until it appeared in the first folio in 1623. A casual note in the Stationers' Register, dated August 4, 1600, records that *Henry V, Much Ado about Nothing, As You Like It,* and Jonson's *Every Man out of His Humor* were to be " staied"; that is, not licensed for printing. Nevertheless in 1600 a pirated edition of *Henry V* appeared with the title: *The Chronicle History of Henry the fift, With his battel fought at Agin Court in*

France. Togither with Auncient Pistoll. As it hath bene sundry times playd by the Right honorable the Lord Chamberlaine his seruants. London. Printed by Thomas Creede, for Tho. Millington, and Iohn Busby. And are to be sold at his house in Carter Lane, next the Powle head. 1600. The text of this edition is incredibly bad and was reproduced from a version taken down by shorthand or else put together from memory. It is about a thousand lines shorter than the correct text, omits the Choruses and many speeches, and feebly paraphrases the rest. This quarto was reprinted in 1602 and in 1619. The text in the folio is fairly well printed, but the printer mistook a number of words and made woeful confusion of the passages in French.

An interval of about a year separated the writing of *Henry V* from the writing of *II Henry IV*. Much had happened in the London theaters during these months, particularly the success of Ben Jonson's *Every Man in His Humor*. In the rewritten version of that play, printed in 1616, there appears a prologue in which Jonson sneered at the usual methods of the actors who

> with three rusty swords,
> And help of some few foot and half-foot words,
> Fight over York and Lancaster's long jars,
> And in the tiring-house bring wounds to scars.

This prologue can hardly have been used at the original production of *Every Man in His Humor* by Shakespeare's company in 1598, but it certainly expressed the views of Jonson, and those who agreed with him, in demanding that the stage should present life realistically. Indeed Shakespeare seems to have been on the defensive in writing *Henry V,* for he prefaced the play with an apologetic Chorus to answer those critics who mocked at the absurdity of trying to show great events on a bare platform. A history play, Shakespeare claimed, did not attempt to be realistic; its aim was rather to stimulate the imagination of the spectator.

The feelings of critics toward *Henry V* differ according to the times. In moments of crisis or national peril, when patriotism is aglow, the play is a trumpet call to heroic action; in more pacific times it seems somewhat brassy for everyday enjoyment. In other ways *Henry V* is less satisfying than either part of *Henry IV*. There is not enough conflict or balance in the story. Henry himself is too perfect. And except for his one soliloquy and his prayer before Agincourt, he is seen only on the outside, as a king and not as a man. His enemies, the French, are too worthless, too obviously self-doomed, to be worthy opponents. The subplot also is uneven. The incidents, such as the moving account of the death of Falstaff, or Fluellen's beating of Pistol, are good in themselves, but they lack the coherence of the *Henry IV* plays. Shakespeare indeed relied rather on rhetoric than on a well-constructed plot; still, the rhetoric is magnificent, particularly in Henry's speeches to the conspirators (II.ii), or before Harfleur (III.i), his soliloquy in the night before the battle (IV.i.247–301), and his speech to Westmoreland (IV.iii.19–67).

Henry V is often spoken of as Shakespeare's ideal king. It may be so; but Shakespeare had no illusions about either Henry V or his father, Henry IV, who on his own confession was a scheming hypocrite and an unscrupulous liar, and whose last advice to his son was "to busy giddy minds With foreign quarrels." There is thus little glamor about the true motives for the French war; it is calculated policy. The clergy support it in the hope that it may distract attention from an embarrassing proposal to cut off their revenues. The nobles are eager for a fight, and the profits which may follow. Pistol expresses it most crudely and frankly:

> Yokefellows in arms,
> Let us to France, like horseleeches, my boys,
> To suck, to suck, the very blood to suck!

Yet even if Shakespeare may have felt little sentimentality about his hero, Henry V may still have been his ideal king, for Shakespeare realized that those qualities which make an ideal king are not the same as those which make a good companion. Henry is brutal and ruthless; he demands discipline in others and himself; he knows when to be stern and when to unbend; he can stir the hearts of his subjects; he has an overwhelming sense of his own responsibility. He is, above all things, efficient, and in practical matters the efficiency of Henry in his Council or on the battlefield is to be preferred to the humor of Falstaff in the tavern. Those critics who condemn Henry V for casting off his old companions are themselves guilty of a lack of humor.

Henry V

DRAMATIS PERSONAE

KING HENRY the *Fifth*
DUKE OF GLOUCESTER ⎫ *brothers to the King*
DUKE OF BEDFORD ⎭
DUKE OF EXETER, *uncle to the King*
DUKE OF YORK, *cousin to the King*
EARLS OF SALISBURY, WESTMORELAND, *and* WARWICK
ARCHBISHOP OF CANTERBURY
BISHOP OF ELY
EARL OF CAMBRIDGE
LORD SCROOP
SIR THOMAS GREY
SIR THOMAS ERPINGHAM, GOWER, FLUELLEN,
  MACMORRIS, JAMY, *officers in King Henry's army*
BATES, COURT, WILLIAMS, *soldiers in the same*
PISTOL, NYM, BARDOLPH
BOY
A HERALD
CHARLES *the Sixth, King of France*

LEWIS, *the Dauphin*
DUKES OF BURGUNDY, ORLEANS, *and* BOURBON
THE CONSTABLE *of France*
RAMBURES *and* GRANDPRÉ, *French lords*
GOVERNOR *of Harfleur*
MONTJOY, *a French herald*
AMBASSADORS *to the King of England*
ISABEL, *Queen of France*
KATHARINE, *daughter to Charles and Isabel*
ALICE, *a lady attending on her*
HOSTESS *of a tavern in Eastcheap, formerly Mistress
  Quickly, and now married to Pistol*
LORDS, LADIES, OFFICERS, SOLDIERS, CITIZENS,
  MESSENGERS, *and* ATTENDANTS

CHORUS

SCENE — *England; afterward France.*

PROLOGUE

[*Enter* CHORUS.°]

CHOR. O for a Muse of fire,° that would ascend
The brightest heaven of invention,°
A kingdom for a stage, princes to act
And monarchs to behold the swelling scene!
Then should the warlike Harry, like himself,   5
Assume the port° of Mars, and at his heels,
Leashed in like hounds, should famine, sword, and
      fire
Crouch° for employment. But pardon, gentles° all,
The flat unraisèd° spirits that have dared
On this unworthy scaffold to bring forth   10
So great an object. Can this cockpit° hold
The vasty fields of France? Or may we cram
Within this wooden O° the very casques°
That did affright the air at Agincourt?
Oh, pardon! Since a crooked figure may   15
Attest° in little place a million,
And let us, ciphers to this great accompt,°
On your imaginary forces° work.
Suppose within the girdle of these walls
Are now confined two mighty monarchies,   20
Whose high uprearèd and abutting° fronts
The perilous narrow ocean° parts asunder.
Piece out our imperfections with your thoughts.
Into a thousand parts divide one man,
And make imaginary puissance.°   25
Think when we talk of horses that you see them
Printing their proud hoofs i' the receiving earth.
For 'tis your thoughts that now must deck our kings,
Carry them here and there, jumping o'er times,
Turning the accomplishment of many years   30
Into an hourglass. For the which supply,
Admit me Chorus to this history,
Who prologue-like your humble patience pray
Gently to hear, kindly to judge, our play. [*Exit.*]

Act I

SCENE I. *London. An antechamber in the*
KING'S *palace.*

[*Enter the* ARCHBISHOP OF CANTERBURY, *and the*
BISHOP OF ELY.]

CANT. My lord, I'll tell you — that self° bill is
      urged
Which in the eleventh year of the last King's° reign

Prologue. Chorus: See *Hen V*, Intro. p. 454a. 1. Muse of fire: i.e., burning inspiration to kindle this audience.   1–2. that . . . invention: that would reach the topmost height of inspiration. invention: artistic invention.   6. port: bearing.   8. Crouch: be ready to spring. gentles: gentle spectators.   9. unraised: uninspired.   11. cockpit: i.e., playhouse.   13. wooden O: i.e., the Curtain Playhouse, which was a round frame building. See Gen. Intro. pp. 36a and 41b. very casques: even the actual helmets.   16. Attest: stand for.   17. accompt: reckoning.   18. imaginary forces: powers of imagination.

21. abutting: neighboring.   22. narrow ocean: i.e., English Channel.   25. puissance: might.
Act I, Sc. i: 1. self: same.   2. last King: i.e., Henry IV.

Was like° and had indeed against us passed
But that the scambling° and unquiet time
Did push it out of farther question.   5
  ELY. But how, my lord, shall we resist it now?
  CANT. It must be thought on. If it pass against
us,
We lose the better half of our possession.
For all the temporal° lands which men devout
By testament have given to the Church   10
Would they strip from us, being valued thus:
As much as would maintain, to the King's honor,
Full fifteen earls and fifteen hundred knights,
Six thousand and two hundred good esquires,
And, to relief of lazars° and weak age,   15
Of indigent faint souls past corporal toil,
A hundred almshouses right well supplied.
And to the coffers of the King beside,
A thousand pounds by the year. Thus runs the
    bill.
  ELY. This would drink deep.
  CANT.   'Twould drink the cup and all. 20
  ELY. But what prevention?
  CANT. The King is full of grace and fair regard.
  ELY. And a true lover of the Holy Church.
  CANT. The courses of his youth promised it not.
The breath no sooner left his father's body   25
But that his wildness, mortified° in him,
Seemed to die too. Yea, at that very moment,
Consideration° like an angel came
And whipped the offending Adam° out of him,
Leaving his body as a paradise   30
To envelop and contain celestial spirits.
Never was such a sudden scholar made,
Never came reformation in a flood
With such a heady currance,° scouring faults.
Nor never Hydra-headed° willfulness   35
So soon did lose his seat, and all at once,
As in this King.
  ELY.   We are blessed in the change.
  CANT. Hear him but reason° in divinity,
And all-admiring with an inward wish
You would desire the King were made a prelate. 40
Hear him debate of commonwealth affairs,
You would say it hath been all in all his study.
List° his discourse of war, and you shall hear
A fearful battle rendered you in music.
Turn him to any cause of policy,°   45

The Gordian knot° of it he will unloose,
Familiar as his garter — that, when he speaks,
The air, a chartered libertine,° is still,
And the mute wonder lurketh in men's ears,
To steal his sweet and honeyed sentences.°   50
So that the art and practic part of life
Must be the mistress° to this theoric.°
Which is a wonder how His Grace should glean it,
Since his addiction was to courses vain,
His companies° unlettered, rude, and shallow, 55
His hours filled up with riots, banquets, sports,
And never noted in him any study,
Any retirement, any sequestration°
From open haunts and popularity.
  ELY. The strawberry grows underneath the nettle,
And wholesome berries thrive and ripen best   61
Neighbored by fruit of baser quality.
And so the Prince obscured his contemplation
Under the veil of wildness, which no doubt
Grew like the summer grass, fastest by night,   65
Unseen, yet crescive in his faculty.°
  CANT. It must be so, for miracles are ceased,
And therefore we must needs admit the means°
How things are pérfected.
  ELY.   But, my good lord,
How now for mitigation° of this bill   70
Urged by the Commons? Doth His Majesty
Incline to it, or no?
  CANT.   He seems indifferent,°
Or rather swaying more upon our part
Than cherishing the exhibiters° against us.
For I have made an offer to His Majesty,   75
Upon° our spiritual convocation
And in regard of causes now in hand,
Which I have opened to His Grace at large,°
As touching France, to give a greater sum
Than ever at one time the clergy yet   80
Did to his predecessors part withal.
  ELY. How did this offer seem received, my lord?
  CANT. With good acceptance of His Majesty,
Save that there was not time enough to hear,
As I perceived His Grace would fain have done, 85
The severals and unhidden passages°
Of his true titles to some certain dukedoms,
And generally to the crown and seat of France,

3. **like:** likely.   4. **scambling:** contentious.   9. **temporal:** i.e.,
belonging to laymen. 15. **lazars:** beggars; lit., lepers. 26. **mor-
tified:** killed. 28. **Consideration:** serious thoughtfulness.
29. **whipped . . . Adam:** drove out the natural sinful spirit.
Lunatics were sometimes whipped to drive out the evil spirit
with which they were possessed. **Adam:** i.e., original sin.
34. **heady currance:** violent flood. The allusion is to Hercules'
method of cleansing the foul Augean stables, which he accom-
plished by turning a river through them. 35. **Hydra-headed:**
Hydra was a many-headed monster killed by Hercules.
38. **reason:** debate. 43. **List:** listen to. 45. **cause of policy:**
political problem.

46. **Gordian knot:** When Alexander the Great in his conquests
reached Gordium, he was told that the man who could untie the
knot which bound the pole to the yoke of the wagon of King
Gordius should be King of Asia. Alexander cut the knot with his
sword. 48. **chartered libertine:** privileged to be free. 50. **sen-
tences:** wise sayings. 51–52. **art . . . theoric:** his theories of life
must have been founded on his practical experience. **art:** crafts-
manship. **practic:** practical. 52. **mistress:** i.e., superior to.
55. **companies:** companions. 58. **sequestration:** separation.
66. **crescive . . . faculty:** growing by its own natural power.
68. **admit . . . means:** accept the natural cause. 70. **mitigation:**
moderating. 72. **indifferent:** impartial. 74. **exhibiters:** pro-
moters of the bill. 76. **Upon:** as a result of. 78. **opened . . .
large:** explained fully to His Majesty. 86. **severals . . . pas-
sages:** the particular and clear sources.

Derived from Edward,° his great-grandfather.

ELY. What was the impediment that broke this
off?   90

CANT. The French Ambassador upon that instant
Craved audience, and the hour I think is come
To give him hearing. Is it four o'clock?

ELY. It is.

CANT. Then go we in, to know his embassy,   95
Which I could with a ready guess declare
Before the Frenchman speak a word of it.

ELY. I'll wait upon you, and I long to hear it.
                                                        [*Exeunt.*]

SCENE II. *The same. The Presence Chamber.*°

[*Enter* KING HENRY, GLOUCESTER, BEDFORD, EXETER,
WARWICK, WESTMORELAND, *and* ATTENDANTS.]

K. HEN. Where is my gracious Lord of Canter-
bury?

EXE. Not here in presence.

K. HEN.   Send for him, good Uncle.

WEST. Shall we call in the Ambassador, my liege?

K. HEN. Not yet, my cousin. We° would be re-
solved,
Before we hear him, of some things of weight   5
That task° our thoughts, concerning us and France.

[*Enter the* ARCHBISHOP OF CANTERBURY
and the BISHOP OF ELY.]

CANT. God and His angels guard your sacred
throne,
And make you long become it!

K. HEN.   Sure we thank you.
My learnèd lord, we pray you to proceed
And justly and religiously unfold   10
Why the law Salic° that they have in France
Or° should, or should not, bar us in our claim.
And God forbid, my dear and faithful lord,
That you should fashion, wrest,° or bow° your
reading,
Or nicely° charge your understanding° soul   15
With opening titles miscreate,° whose right
Suits not in native colors with the truth.°
For God doth know how many now in health
Shall drop their blood in approbation°
Of what your Reverence shall incite us to.   20
Therefore take heed how you impawn° our person,
How you awake our sleeping sword of war.

89. Edward: i.e., Edward III.
    Sc. ii: s.d., Presence Chamber: the place where the King
gave public audiences.   4. We: the royal "we," used when a
King is speaking officially.   6. task: fully occupy.   11. law
Salic: the Salic law which forbade a woman's succeeding to the
throne, explained later, ll. 35–95.   12. Or: either.   14. wrest:
wrench. bow: bend.   15. nicely: unscrupulously. understanding:
i.e., that knows the truth to be otherwise.   16. opening . . .
miscreate: making claims falsely based.   17. Suits . . . truth:
does not match the natural color of truth.   19. approbation:
putting to the test.   21. impawn: pledge.

We charge you, in the name of God, take heed.
For never two such kingdoms did contend
Without much fall of blood, whose guiltless drops
Are every one a woe, a sore complaint   26
'Gainst him whose wrongs give edge unto the swords
That make such waste in brief mortality.°
Under this conjuration° speak, my lord,
For we will hear, note, and believe in heart   30
That what you speak is in your conscience washed
As pure as sin with baptism.

CANT. Then hear me, gracious Sovereign, and you
peers,
That owe yourselves, your lives and services,
To this imperial throne. There° is no bar   35
To make against your Highness' claim to France
But this, which they produce from Pharamond,
"*In terram Salicam mulieres ne succedant*" —
"No woman shall succeed in Salic land."
Which Salic land the French unjustly gloze°   40
To be the realm of France, and Pharamond
The founder of this law and female bar.
Yet their own authors faithfully affirm
That the land Salic is in Germany,
Between the floods° of Sala and of Elbe,   45
Where Charles the Great, having subdued the
Saxons,
There left behind and settled certain French.
Who, holding in disdain the German women
For some dishonest manners° of their life,
Established then this law: to wit, no female   50
Should be inheritrix in Salic land.
Which Salic, as I said, twixt Elbe and Sala,
Is at this day in Germany called Meisen.
Then doth it well appear the Salic law
Was not devisèd for the realm of France.   55
Nor did the French possess the Salic land
Until four hundred one and twenty years
After defunction° of King Pharamond,
Idly supposed the founder of this law,
Who died within the year of our redemption   60
Four hundred twenty-six. And Charles the Great
Subdued the Saxons, and did seat the French
Beyond the river Sala, in the year
Eight hundred five. Besides, their writers say,
King Pepin, which deposèd Childeric,   65
Did, as heir general, being descended
Of Blithild, which was daughter to King Clothair,
Make claim and title to the crown of France.
Hugh Capet also, who usurped the crown
Of Charles the Duke of Lorraine, sole heir male   70
Of the true line and stock of Charles the Great,
To find his title with some shows of truth —

28. waste . . . mortality: destruction of brief lives.   29. conjura-
tion: solemn appeal.   35–100. There . . . daughter: The whole
of this long speech is taken almost verbatim from Holinshed.
See *Hen V* Intro. p. 453a.   40. gloze: gloss; i.e., interpret.
45. floods: waters.   49. dishonest manners: loose conduct.
58. defunction: decease.

Though, in pure truth, it was corrupt and naught —
Conveyed° himself as heir to the Lady Lingare,
Daughter to Charlemagne, who was the son   75
To Lewis the Emperor, and Lewis the son
Of Charles the Great. Also King Lewis the Tenth,
Who was sole heir to the usurper Capet,
Could not keep quiet in his conscience,
Wearing the crown of France, till satisfied   80
That fair Queen Isabel, his grandmother,
Was lineal of° the Lady Ermengare,
Daughter to Charles the foresaid Duke of Lorraine.
By the which marriage the line of Charles the Great
Was reunited to the crown of France.   85
So that, as clear as is the summer's sun,
King Pepin's title and Hugh Capet's claim,
King Lewis his satisfaction, all appear
To hold in right and title of the female.
So do the Kings of France unto this day,   90
Howbeit they would hold up this Salic law
To bar your Highness claiming from the female,
And rather choose to hide them in a net°
Than amply to imbar° their crooked° titles
Usurped from you and your progenitors.   95
  K. HEN. May I with right and conscience make
    this claim?
  CANT. The sin upon my head, dread Sovereign!
For in the Book of Numbers° is it writ,
When the man dies, let the inheritance
Descend unto the daughter. Gracious lord,   100
Stand for your own, unwind your bloody flag,
Look back into your mighty ancestors.
Go, my dread lord, to your great-grandsire's tomb,
From whom you claim, invoke his warlike spirit,
And your great-uncle's, Edward the Black Prince,
Who on the French ground played a tragedy,°   106
Making defeat on the full power of France
Whiles his most mighty father on a hill
Stood smiling to behold his lion's whelp
Forage° in blood of French nobility.   110
Oh, noble English, that could entertain
With half their forces the full pride of France
And let another half stand laughing by,
All out of work and cold for action!
  ELY. Awake remembrance of these valiant dead,
And with your puissant° arm renew their feats.   116
You are their heir, you sit upon their throne.
The blood and courage that renownèd them
Runs in your veins, and my thrice-puissant liege
Is in the very May morn of his youth,   120
Ripe for exploits and mighty enterprises.

  EXE. Your brother kings and monarchs of the
    earth
Do all expect that you should rouse yourself,
As did the former lions of your blood.
  WEST. They know your Grace hath cause and
    means and might.   125
So hath your Highness. Never King of England
Had nobles richer and more loyal subjects,
Whose hearts have left their bodies here in England
And lie pavilioned° in the fields of France.   129
  CANT. Oh, let their bodies follow, my dear liege,
With blood and sword and fire to win your right.
In aid whereof we of the spiritualty
Will raise your Highness such a mighty sum
As never did the clergy at one time
Bring in to any of your ancestors.   135
  K. HEN. We must not only arm to invade the
    French,
But lay down our proportions° to defend
Against the Scot, who will make road° upon us
With all advantages.°
  CANT. They of those marches,° gracious sovereign,
Shall be a wall sufficient to defend   141
Our inland from the pilfering borderers.°
  K. HEN. We do not mean the coursing snatchers°
    only,
But fear the main intendment° of the Scot,
Who hath been still° a giddy° neighbor to us.   145
For you shall read that my great-grandfather
Never went with his forces into France
But that the Scot on his unfurnished kingdom
Came pouring, like the tide into a breach,
With ample and brim fullness of his force,   150
Galling the gleanèd land° with hot assays,°
Girding with grievous siege castles and towns,
That England, being empty of defense,
Hath shook and trembled at the ill neighborhood.
  CANT. She hath been then more feared° than
    harmed, my liege,   155
For hear her but exampled by herself.
When all her chivalry hath been in France,
And she a mourning widow of her nobles,
She hath herself not only well defended,
But taken and impounded° as a stray°   160
The King of Scots,° whom she did send to France,
To fill King Edward's fame with prisoner kings

---

74. Conveyed: falsely claimed.   82. lineal of: descended from.
93. net: i.e., a flimsy and ridiculous excuse.   94. imbar: secure.
crooked: false.   98. Book of Numbers: "If a man die, and
have no son, then shall ye cause his inheritance to pass to his
daughter." (27:8)   106. played a tragedy: i.e., the Battle of
Crécy (1346), when Edward III defeated the French. His son
Edward, the Black Prince, then a youth of sixteen, greatly dis-
tinguished himself.   110. Forage: seek his prey.   116. puissant:
mighty.

129. pavilioned: in their tents.   137. proportions: estimates of
the forces required.   138. make road: invade.   139. With . . .
advantages: explained in ll. 169–73.   140. marches: borders.
142. pilfering borderers: thieves living on the border. In the
fourteenth and fifteenth centuries there was a constant state of
war on the border between England and Scotland.   143. cours-
ing snatchers: raiding thieves.   144. intendment: design.
145. still: always. giddy: unreliable.   151. gleaned land: i.e.,
when the men of war were away. assays: attempts.   155. feared:
frightened.   160. impounded: shut up in the village pound.
stray: a stray beast.   161. King of Scots: David II, who was
taken while Edward III was absent on his Crécy campaign.
Actually he was sent to London, not to France.

And make her chronicle as rich with praise
As is the ooze and bottom of the sea
With sunken wreck and sumless° treasures.   165
   WEST. But there's a saying very old and true —
      "If that you will France win,
        Then with Scotland first begin."
For once the eagle England being in prey,°
To her unguarded nest the weasel Scot   170
Comes sneaking, and so sucks her princely eggs,
Playing the mouse in absence of the cat,
To tear and havoc° more than she can eat.
   EXE. It follows then the cat must stay at home.
Yet that is but a crushed° necessity,   175
Since we have locks to safeguard necessaries,
And pretty traps to catch the petty thieves,
While that the armèd hand doth fight abroad,
The advisèd° head defends itself at home.
For government, though high and low and lower,
Put into parts,° doth keep in one consent,°   181
Congreeing° in a full and natural close,°
Like music.
   CANT.   Therefore doth Heaven divide
The state of man in divers functions,
Setting endeavor in continual motion.   185
To which is fixèd, as an aim or butt,°
Obedience. For so work the honeybees,°
Creatures that by a rule in nature teach
The act of order to a peopled kingdom.
They have a King and officers of sorts,°   190
Where some, like magistrates, correct at home,
Others, like merchants, venture trade abroad,
Others, like soldiers, armèd in their stings,
Make boot° upon the summer's velvet buds,
Which pillage they with merry march bring home
To the tent royal of their Emperor.   196
Who, busied in his majesty, surveys
The singing masons building roofs of gold,
The civil citizens kneading up the honey,
The poor mechanic porters crowding in   200
Their heavy burdens at his narrow gate,
The sad-eyed Justice, with his surly hum,
Delivering o'er to executors° pale
The lazy yawning drone. I this infer,
That many things, having full reference   205
To one consent, may work contrariously.
As many arrows, loosed several ways,°
Come to one mark; as many ways meet in one town;

As many fresh streams meet in one salt sea;
As many lines close in the dial's center —   210
So may a thousand actions, once afoot,
End in one purpose, and be all well borne
Without defeat. Therefore to France, my liege.
Divide your happy England into four,
Whereof take you one quarter into France,   215
And you withal shall make all Gallia shake.
If we, with thrice such powers° left at home,
Cannot defend our own doors from the dog,
Let us be worried and our nation lose
The name of hardiness and policy.°   220
   K. HEN. Call in the messengers sent from the
     Dauphin.°   [Exeunt some ATTENDANTS.]
Now are we well resolved, and, by God's help,
And yours, the noble sinews° of our power,
France being ours, we'll bend it to our awe
Or break it all to pieces. Or there we'll sit,   225
Ruling in large and ample empery°
O'er France and all her almost kingly dukedoms,
Or lay these bones in an unworthy urn,
Tombless, with no remembrance over them.
Either our history shall with full mouth   230
Speak freely of our acts, or else our grave,
Like Turkish mute, shall have a tongueless mouth,
Not worshiped° with a waxen° epitaph.
[Enter AMBASSADORS of France.] Now are we well
    prepared to know the pleasure
Of our fair cousin° Dauphin, for we hear   235
Your greeting is from him, not from the King.
   I. AMB. May't please your Majesty to give us leave
Freely to render° what we have in charge,°
Or shall we sparingly show you far off
The Dauphin's meaning and our embassy?   240
   K. HEN. We are no tyrant, but a Christian king,
Unto whose grace our passion is as subject
As are our wretches fettered in our prisons.
Therefore with frank and with uncurbed plainness
Tell us the Dauphin's mind.
   I. AMB.   Thus, then, in few.°   245
Your Highness, lately sending into France,
Did claim some certain dukedoms, in the right
Of your great predecessor, King Edward the Third.
In answer of which claim, the Prince our master
Says that you savor too much of your youth,   250
And bids you be advised there's naught in France
That can be with a nimble galliard° won.
You cannot revel into dukedoms there.
He therefore sends you, meeter° for your spirit,
This tun° of treasure, and, in lieu of this,   255

165. sumless: countless.   169. in prey: seeking her prey. 173. havoc: rend in pieces.   175. crushed: forced.   179. advised: thoughtful.   181. Put . . . parts: i.e., divided among Ministers, as the various parts of music among the musicians. consent: harmony.   182. Congreeing: harmonizing.   close: cadence. 186. butt: target.   187–204. honeybees . . . drone: This elaborate parallel between a kingdom and a hive is found also in Lyly's *Euphues*, but it is fairly common. It was used before Queen Elizabeth by the Speaker in the Parliament of 1593. 190. of sorts: of different ranks.   194. boot: plunder.   203. executors: executioners.   207. loosed . . . ways: shot from different directions.

217. powers: forces.   220. policy: statesmanship.   221. Dauphin: The title given to the eldest son of the King of France; in Shakespeare's time (and in F1) called "Dolphin."   223. sinews: supports.   226. empery: rule.   233. worshiped: honored. waxen: i.e., not enduring.   235. cousin: used of any relation, but in Courtly etiquette all kings were related.   238. render: declare. have in charge: have been commanded to say.   245. in few: i.e., words.   252. galliard: a lively dance. See App. 24. 254. meeter: fitter.   255. tun: barrel.

Desires you let the dukedoms that you claim
Hear no more of you. This the Dauphin speaks.

K. HEN. What treasure, Uncle?

EXE.   Tennis balls,° my liege.

K. HEN. We are glad the Dauphin is so pleasant
    with us.
His present and your pains we thank you for. 260
When° we have matched our rackets to these balls,
We will in France, by God's grace, play a set
Shall strike his father's crown into the hazard.°
Tell him he hath made a match with such a wran-
    gler°
That all the courts of France will be disturbed 265
With chaces.° And we understand him well,
How he comes o'er us with° our wilder days,
Not measuring what use we made of them.
We never valued this poor seat of England,
And therefore, living hence, did give ourself 270
To barbarous license — as 'tis ever common
That men are merriest when they are from home.
But tell the Dauphin I will keep my state,°
Be like a king and show my sail of greatness,°
When I do rouse me in my throne of France. 275
For that I have laid by my majesty,
And plodded like a man for working days.
But I will rise there with so full a glory
That I will dazzle all the eyes of France —
Yea, strike the Dauphin blind to look on us. 280
And tell the pleasant Prince this mock of his
Hath turned his balls to gunstones,° and his soul
Shall stand sore chargèd for the wasteful vengeance
That shall fly with them. For many a thousand wid-
    ows 284
Shall this his mock mock out of their dear husbands,
Mock mothers from their sons, mock castles down;
And some are yet ungotten° and unborn
That shall have cause to curse the Dauphin's scorn.
But this lies all within the will of God,
To Whom I do appeal, and in Whose name 290
Tell you the Dauphin I am coming on,
To venge me° as I may and to put forth
My rightful hand in a well-hallowed cause.
So get you hence in peace, and tell the Dauphin
His jest will savor but of shallow wit 295
When thousands weep more than did laugh at it.
Convey them with safe conduct. Fare you well.

                  [Exeunt AMBASSADORS.*]*

EXE. This was a merry message.

K. HEN. We hope to make the sender blush at it.
Therefore, my lords, omit no happy° hour 300
That may give furtherance to our expedition.
For we have now no thought in us but France,
Save those to God, that run before our business.
Therefore let our proportions° for these wars
Be soon collected, and all things thought upon 305
That may with reasonable swiftness add
More feathers to our wings. For, God before,°
We'll chide this Dauphin at his father's door.
Therefore let every man now task his thought,°
That this fair action may on foot be brought. 310

                      [Exeunt. Flourish.]

Act II

PROLOGUE

               [Enter CHORUS.*]*

CHOR. Now all the youth of England are on fire,
And silken dalliance° in the wardrobe lies.
Now thrive the armorers, and honor's thought°
Reigns solely in the breast of every man.
They sell the pasture now to buy the horse, 5
Following the mirror° of all Christian kings
With wingèd heels, as English Mercuries.°
For now sits Expectation in the air,
And hides a sword from hilts unto the point
With crowns imperial, crowns and coronets, 10
Promised to Harry and his followers.
The French, advised by good intelligence
Of this most dreadful preparation,
Shake in their fear and with pale° policy°
Seek to divert the English purposes. 15
O England! Model to thy inward greatness,
Like little body with a mighty heart,
What mightst thou do that honor would thee do
Were all thy children kind° and natural!
But see thy fault! France hath in thee found out 20
A nest of hollow bosoms, which he fills
With treacherous crowns. And three corrupted men,
One, Richard Earl of Cambridge, and the second,
Henry Lord Scroop of Masham, and the third,
Sir Thomas Grey, knight, of Northumberland, 25
Have, for the gilt of France — oh, guilt° indeed! —

---

258. **Tennis balls:** made of leather stuffed with hair.
261–66. **When . . . chaces:** The King replies to the Ambassador
in a series of elaborate metaphors taken from tennis, which in
Shakespeare's time was played in a court surrounded on three
sides by walls. The game was a cross between the modern squash
rackets and lawn tennis, as both wall and floor were used.
263. **hazard:** a hole in the wall. If the ball is sent into the
hazard, the opponent cannot return it, and so loses his point.
264. **wrangler:** opponent. 266. **chaces:** second bounces, a missed
return. 267. **comes . . . with:** reminds us of. 273. **state:**
dignity. 274. **show . . . greatness:** will show full sail. 282. **gun-
stones:** cannon balls, originally made of stone. 287. **ungotten:**
unbegotten. 292. **venge me:** take my revenge.

300. **happy:** favorable. 304. **proportions:** forces. 307. **God be-
fore:** before God. 309. **task . . . thought:** take careful thought.
    Act II. Prologue: 2. **silken dalliance:** silk clothes suitable for
flirtations. 3. **honor's thought:** thoughts of honor to be won.
6. **mirror:** perfect pattern. 7. **winged . . . Mercuries:** Mercury,
the messenger of the gods, wore winged sandals. 14. **pale:**
frightened. **policy:** cunning. 19. **kind:** showing natural love.
26. **gilt . . . guilt:** The pun is common in Shakespeare.

Confirmed° conspiracy with fearful France.
And by their hands this grace of kings must die,
If Hell and treason hold their promises,
Ere he take ship for France, and in Southampton.
Linger your patience on, and we'll digest   31
The abuse of distance, force a play.°
The sum is paid, the traitors are agreed,
The King is set from London, and the scene
Is now transported, gentles, to Southampton.   35
There is the playhouse now, there must you sit.
And thence to France shall we convey you safe,
And bring you back, charming the narrow seas
To give you gentle pass. For, if we may,
We'll not offend one stomach° with our play.   40
But till the King come forth, and not till then,
Unto Southampton do we shift our scene.   [*Exit.*]

SCENE I. *London. A street.*

[*Enter* CORPORAL NYM *and* LIEUTENANT BARDOLPH.]

BARD. Well met, Corporal Nym.°

NYM. Good morrow, Lieutenant Bardolph.°

BARD. What, are Ancient° Pistol and you friends
yet?   4

NYM. For my part, I care not. I say little, but
when time shall serve, there shall be smiles — but
that shall be as it may. I dare not fight, but I will
wink° and hold out mine iron. It is a simple one,
but what though? It will toast cheese, and it will
endure cold as another man's sword will. And there's
an end.   11

BARD. I will bestow a breakfast to make you
friends, and we'll be all three sworn brothers° to
France. Let it be so, good Corporal Nym.

NYM. Faith, I will live so long as I may, that's the
certain of it. And when I cannot live any longer, I
will do as I may. That is my rest,° that is the rendez-
vous° of it.

BARD. It is certain, Corporal, that he is married to
Nell Quickly. And certainly she did you wrong, for
you were trothplight° to her.   21

NYM. I cannot tell. Things must be as they may.
Men may sleep, and they may have their throats

about them at that time, and some say knives have
edges. It must be as it may. Though patience be a
tired mare, yet she will plod. There must be con-
clusions. Well, I cannot tell.   27

[*Enter* PISTOL *and* HOSTESS.]

BARD. Here comes Ancient Pistol and his wife.
Good Corporal, be patient here. How now, mine
host Pistol!

PIST. Base tike,° call'st thou me host?°
Now, by this hand, I swear I scorn the term,
Nor shall my Nell keep lodgers.   33

HOST. No, by my troth, not long, for we cannot
lodge and board a dozen or fourteen gentlewomen
that live honestly by the prick of their needles but it
will be thought we keep a bawdy house straight.
[NYM *and* PISTOL *draw.*] Oh, welladay. Lady,° if
he be not drawn now! We shall see willful adultery
and murder committed.   40

BARD. Good Lieutenant! Good Corporal! Offer
nothing here.

NYM. Pish!

PIST. Pish for thee, Iceland dog! Thou prick-
eared° cur of Iceland!°

HOST. Good Corporal Nym, show thy valor, and
put up your sword.   46

NYM. Will you shog off?° I would have you
solus.°

PIST. "Solus," egregious dog? O viper vile!
The "solus" in thy most mervailous° face,   50
The "solus" in thy teeth, and in thy throat,
And in thy hateful lungs — yea, in thy maw,°
   perdy,°
And, which is worse, within thy nasty mouth!
I do retort the "solus" in thy bowels,
For I can take,° and Pistol's cock° is up,   55
And flashing fire will follow.

NYM. I am not Barbason,° you cannot conjure me.
I have a humor° to knock you indifferently well. If
you grow foul with me, Pistol, I will scour you with
my rapier, as I may, in fair terms. If you would walk
off, I would prick your guts a little, in good terms,
as I may. And that's the humor of it.   63

PIST. O braggart vile, and damnèd furious wight!°
The grave doth gape, and doting death is near,
Therefore exhale.°

BARD. Hear me, hear me what I say. He that
strikes the first stroke, I'll run him up to the hilts,
as I am a soldier.   [*Draws.*]

---

27. **Confirmed:** agreed to.   31–32. **digest . . . play:** i.e., we shall accept the difficulty of presenting different places on one stage, and by sheer imagination create our play. Some editors emend "we'll" to "well."   40. **one stomach:** anyone's critical taste.

Sc. i: 1. **Corporal Nym:** This worthy is a newcomer to the gang attached to Falstaff, who have already appeared in the two parts of *Hen IV*. His name means "steal." See *Hen V* Intro. p. 452a.   2. **Lieutenant Bardolph:** Bardolph has been promoted; he was only a corporal in *II Hen IV*.   3. **Ancient:** Ensign, Second Lieutenant.   8. **wink:** close an eye.   13. **sworn brothers:** Knights bent on heroic adventure sometimes swore brotherhood to each other, that they would share ill and good alike.   17. **rest:** last throw. See *R & J*, V.iii.110,n.   18. **rendez-vous:** meeting place, perhaps "last resort," but Nym uses words with meanings peculiar to himself.   21. **trothplight:** See Gen. Intro. p. 20a.

31. **tike:** cur. **host:** tavernkeeper. By marrying Mistress Quickly, Pistol takes over her business, but as a soldier he scorns to be considered a tradesman.   38. **Lady:** by Our Lady; i.e., the Virgin.   44. **prick-eared:** with straight erect ears. **cur of Iceland:** Iceland dogs were rough-haired and quarrelsome.   47. **shog off:** move off. A modern Nym would say "scram."   48. **solus:** alone.   50. **mervailous:** marvelous.   52. **maw:** stomach. **perdy:** by God.   55. **take:** catch fire, be offended. **cock:** see Pl. 22g.   57. **Barbason:** the name of a fiend, invented by Nym.   58. **humor:** See App. 3.   64. **wight:** man, a poetical word.   66. **exhale:** draw your last breath.

PIST. An oath of mickle° might, and fury shall
 abate.   70
Give me thy fist, thy forefoot to me give.
Thy spirits are most tall.°

NYM. I will cut thy throat, one time or other, in
fair terms. That is the humor of it.

PIST. "Couple a gorge!"°   75
That is the word. I thee defy again.
O hound of Crete, think'st thou my spouse to get?
No, to the spital° go,
And from the powdering tub° of infamy
Fetch forth the lazar kite of Cressid's kind,° 80
Doll Tearsheet° she by name, and her espouse.
I have, and I will hold, the quondam° Quickly
For the only she, and — pauca,° there's enough.
Go to.   84

[Enter the BOY.]

BOY. Mine host Pistol, you must come to my mas-
ter, and you, Hostess. He is very sick, and would
to bed. Good Bardolph, put thy face between his
sheets and do the office of a warming pan.° Faith,
he's very ill.

BARD. Away, you rogue!   90

HOST. By my troth, he'll yield the crow a pud-
ding° one of these days. The King has killed his
heart.° Good Husband, come home presently.°

[Exeunt HOSTESS and BOY.]

BARD. Come, shall I make you two friends? We
must to France together. Why the devil should we
keep knives to cut one another's throats? 96

PIST. Let floods o'erswell, and fiends for food
 howl on!

NYM. You'll pay me the eight shillings I won of
you at betting?

PIST. Base is the slave that pays.   100

NYM. That now I will have. That's the humor of it.

PIST. As manhood shall compound.° Push home.

[They draw.]

BARD. By this sword, he that makes the first thrust,
I'll kill him — by this sword, I will. 105

PIST. Sword is an oath, and oaths must have their
 course.

BARD. Corporal Nym, an° thou wilt be friends, be
friends. An thou wilt not, why, then be enemies with
me too. Prithee, put up.

NYM. I shall have my eight shillings I won of you
at betting?   111

PIST. A noble° shalt thou have, and present pay,
And liquor likewise will I give to thee,
And friendship shall combine, and brotherhood.
I'll live by Nym, and Nym shall live by me. 115
Is not this just? For I shall sutler° be
Unto the camp, and profits will accrue.
Give me thy hand.

NYM. I shall have my noble?

PIST. In cash most justly paid.   120

NYM. Well, then, that's the humor of 't.

[Re-enter HOSTESS.]

HOST. As ever you came of women, come in
quickly to Sir John. Ah, poor heart! He is so shaked
of a burning quotidian tertian° that it is most lam-
entable to behold. Sweet men, come to him. 126

NYM. The King hath run bad humors on the
knight. That's the even of it.

PIST. Nym, thou hast spoke the right,
His heart is fracted° and corroborate.° 130

NYM. The King is a good King. But it must be as
it may, he passes some humors and careers.°

PIST. Let us condole the knight, for, lambkins, we
 will live.

SCENE II. Southampton. A council chamber.

[Enter EXETER, BEDFORD, and WESTMORELAND.]

BED. 'Fore God, His Grace is bold, to trust these
 traitors.

EXE. They shall be apprehended by and by.

WEST. How smooth and even they do bear them-
 selves!
As if allegiance in their bosoms sat,
Crownèd with faith and constant loyalty. 5

BED. The King hath note of all that they intend,
By interception which they dream not of.

EXE. Nay, but the man that was his bedfellow,
Whom he hath dulled and cloyed° with gracious
 favors,
That he should, for a foreign purse, so sell 10
His sovereign's life to death and treachery.

[Trumpets sound. Enter KING HENRY, SCROOP,
 CAMBRIDGE, GREY, and ATTENDANTS.]

K. HEN. Now sits the wind fair, and we will
 aboard.
My Lord of Cambridge, and my kind Lord of Ma-
 sham,
And you, my gentle knight, give me your thoughts.

---

70. mickle: mighty. 72. tall: valiant. 75. Couple a gorge:
Elizabethan soldiers' French for "slit a throat." 78. spital:
hospital. 79. powdering tub: tub used for the cure of venereal
disease by sweating. 80. lazar . . . kind: Cressida, the pattern
of loose woman, ended her days in the hospital for venereal dis-
ease. lazar: beggar. kite: bird of prey. 81. Doll Tearsheet: See
II Hen IV. 82. quondam: former. She is now Mistress Pistol.
83. pauca: few words. 87–88. face . . . pan: for Bardolph's face
see I Hen IV, III.iii. 26–55. 91–92. yield . . . pudding: i.e., be
hanged and devoured by the crows. The Hostess is referring to
the boy. 92–93. his heart: i.e., Falstaff's. 93. presently: im-
mediately. 103. compound: come to terms. 107. an: if.

112. noble: 6s 8d — i.e., a reduction for cash payment.
116. sutler: canteen man. 125. quotidian tertian: The Hostess is
mixed in her medical terms; a quotidian is a fever which recurs
daily, a tertian recurs every third day. 130. fracted: cracked.
corroborate: the kind of high-sounding word which appeals
to Pistol, who apparently thinks that it means "split."
132. careers: lit., a short gallop at full speed, so headstrong whim.
 Sc. ii: 9. dulled . . . cloyed: made tired and overfull.

Think you not that the powers we bear with us   15
Will cut their passage through the force of France,
Doing the execution and the act
For which we have in head° assembled them?
   SCROOP. No doubt, my liege, if each man do his
    best.
   K. HEN. I doubt not that, since we are well per-
    suaded   20
We carry not a heart with us from hence
That grows not in a fair consent with ours,
Nor leave not one behind that doth not wish
Success and conquest to attend on us.   24
   CAM. Never was monarch better feared and loved
Than is your Majesty. There's not, I think, a subject
That sits in heartgrief and uneasiness
Under the sweet shade of your government.
   GREY. True. Those that were your father's enemies
Have steeped their galls° in honey, and do serve you
With hearts create° of duty and of zeal.   31
   K. HEN. We therefore have great cause of thank-
    fulness,
And shall forget the office° of our hand
Sooner than quittance° of desert and merit
According to the weight and worthiness.   35
   SCROOP. So service shall with steelèd sinews toil,
And labor shall refresh itself with hope,
To do your Grace incessant services.
   K. HEN. We judge no less. Uncle of Exeter,
Enlarge° the man committed yesterday   40
That railed against our person. We consider
It was excess of wine that set him on,
And on his more advice° we pardon him.
   SCROOP. That's mercy, but too much security.°
Let him be punished, Sovereign, lest example   45
Breed, by his sufferance,° more of such a kind.
   K. HEN. Oh, let us yet be merciful.
   CAM. So may your Highness, and yet punish too.
   GREY. Sir,
You show great mercy if you give him life,   50
After the taste of much correction.
   K. HEN. Alas, your too much love and care of me
Are heavy orisons° 'gainst this poor wretch!
If little faults, proceeding on distemper,°   54
Shall not be winked at, how shall we stretch our eye
When capital crimes, chewed, swallowed, and di-
   gested,
Appear before us? We'll yet enlarge that man,
Though Cambridge, Scroop, and Grey, in their dear
   care
And tender preservation of our person,
Would have him punished. And now to our French
   causes.   60

Who are the late commissioners?
   CAM. I one, my lord.
Your Highness bade me ask for it° today.
   SCROOP. So did you me, my liege.
   GREY. And I, my royal sovereign.   65
   K. HEN. Then, Richard Earl of Cambridge, there
   is yours,
There yours, Lord Scroop of Masham, and, sir
   knight,
Grey of Northumberland, this same is yours.
Read them, and know I know your worthiness.
My Lord of Westmoreland, and Uncle Exeter,   70
We will aboard tonight. Why, how now, gentlemen!
What see you in those papers that you lose
So much complexion? Look ye how they change!
Their cheeks are paper. Why, what read you there
That hath so cowarded° and chased your blood   75
Out of appearance?
   CAM.   I do confess my fault,
And do submit me to your Highness' mercy.
   GREY & SCROOP. To which we all appeal.
   K. HEN. The mercy that was quick° in us but late,
By your own counsel is suppressed and killed.   80
You must not dare, for shame, to talk of mercy,
For your own reasons° turn into your bosoms,
As dogs upon their masters, worrying you.
See you, my Princes and my noble peers,
These English monsters! My Lord of Cambridge
   here,   85
You know how apt our love was to accord
To furnish him with all appertinents°
Belonging to his honor. And this man
Hath, for a few light crowns, lightly conspired,
And sworn unto the practices° of France,   90
To kill us here in Hampton. To the which
This knight, no less for bounty bound to us
Than Cambridge is, hath likewise sworn. But, oh,
What shall I say to thee, Lord Scroop? Thou cruel,
Ingrateful, savage, and inhuman creature!   95
Thou that didst bear the key of all my counsels,
That knew'st the very bottom of my soul,
That almost mightst have coined me into gold
Wouldst thou have practiced on me for thy use,
May it be possible that foreign hire   100
Could out of thee extract one spark of evil
That might annoy° my finger? 'Tis so strange
That, though the truth of it stands off as gross°
As black and white, my eye will scarcely see it.
Treason° and murder ever kept together,   105
As two yoke devils sworn to either's purpose,
Working so grossly in a natural cause

---

18. in head: as an armed force. 30. galls: bitterness. 31. create: made of. 33. office: use. 34. quittance: payment. 40. Enlarge: set free. 43. on . . . advice: since he has a chance to reflect. 44. security: carelessness, lack of precaution. 46. his suffer-ance: by making allowance for him. 53. orisons: prayers. 54. distemper: drunkenness.

63. it: i.e., the document appointing him commissioner. 75. cow-arded: made a coward. 79. quick: living. 82. reasons: argu-ments. 87. appertinents: appurtenances, things pertaining to. 90. practices: plots. 102. annoy: hurt. 103. gross: plain, obvious. 105–08. Treason . . . them: usually treason and murder work to-gether and have some cause or excuse for their action which seems so natural that no one is surprised.

That admiration° did not hoop° at them.
But thou, 'gainst all proportion, didst bring in
Wonder to wait on treason and on murder.   110
And whatsoever cunning fiend it was
That wrought upon thee so preposterously
Hath got the voice° in Hell for excellence.
All other devils that suggest by treasons
Do botch and bungle up damnation   115
With patches, colors, and with forms being fetched
From glistering° semblances of piety.°
But he that tempered° thee bade thee stand up,°
Gave thee no instance° why thou shouldst do trea-
    son,
Unless to dub° thee with the name of traitor. 120
If that same demon that hath gulled° thee thus
Should with his lion gait° walk the whole world,
He might return to vasty Tartar° back,
And tell the legions " I can never win
A soul so easy as that Englishman's."   125
Oh, how hast thou with jealousy infected
The sweetness of affiance!° Show men dutiful?
Why, so didst thou. Seem they grave and learned?
Why, so didst thou. Come they of noble family?
Why, so didst thou. Seem they religious?   130
Why, so didst thou. Or are they spare in diet,
Free from gross passion or of mirth or anger,
Constant in spirit, not swerving with the blood,°
Garnished and decked in modest complement,°
Not working with the eye without the ear,   135
And but in purged° judgment trusting neither?
Such and so finely bolted° didst thou seem.
And thus thy fall hath left a kind of blot,
To mark the full-fraught° man and best indued°
With some suspicion. I will weep for thee,   140
For this revolt of thine, methinks, is like
Another fall of man. Their faults are open.
Arrest them to the answer of the law,
And God acquit them of their practices!

    EXE. I arrest thee of high treason, by the name of
        Richard Earl of Cambridge.   146
I arrest thee of high treason, by the name of Henry
    Lord Scroop of Masham.
I arrest thee of high treason, by the name of Thomas
    Grey, knight, of Northumberland.   150
    SCROOP. Our purposes God justly hath discovered,
And I repent my fault more than my death,
Which I beseech your Highness to forgive,
Although my body pay the price of it.

CAM. For me, the gold of France did not seduce,
Although I did admit it as a motive   156
The sooner to effect what I intended.
But God be thankèd for prevention,
Which I in sufferance heartily will rejoice,
Beseeching God and you to pardon me.   160
    GREY. Never did faithful subject more rejoice
At the discovery of most dangerous treason
Than I do at this hour joy o'er myself,
Prevented from a damnèd enterprise.
My fault, but not my body, pardon, Sovereign. 165
    K. HEN. God quit° you in his mercy! Hear your
        sentence.
You have conspired against our royal person,
Joined with an enemy proclaimed, and from his cof-
    fers
Received the golden earnest° of our death,
Wherein you would have sold your King to slaugh-
    ter,   170
His Princes and his peers to servitude,
His subjects to oppression and contempt,
And his whole kingdom into desolation.
Touching our person seek we no revenge,
But we our kingdom's safety must so tender,°   175
Whose ruin you have sought, that to her laws
We do deliver you. Get you therefore hence,
Poor miserable wretches, to your death.
The taste whereof, God of his mercy give
You patience to endure, and true repentance   180
Of all your dear offenses! Bear them hence.
    [Exeunt CAMBRIDGE, SCROOP, and GREY, guarded.]
Now, lords, for France, the enterprise whereof
Shall be to you, as us, like glorious.
We doubt not of a fair° and lucky war,
Since God so graciously hath brought to light 185
This dangerous treason lurking in our way
To hinder our beginnings. We doubt not now
But every rub° is smoothèd on our way.
Then forth, dear countrymen. Let us deliver
Our puissance into the hand of God,   190
Putting it straight in expedition.°
Cheerly to sea. The signs° of war advance.
No King of England if not King of France.
                                          [Exeunt.]

SCENE III. *London. Before a tavern.*

[*Enter* PISTOL, HOSTESS, NYM, BARDOLPH, *and* BOY.]
    HOST. Prithee, honeysweet Husband, let me bring
thee to Staines.°

---

108. admiration: wonder. hoop: whoop, cry out.   113. voice:
vote.   116–17. forms . . . piety: outward appearances of a re-
ligious motive.   117. glistering: falsely glittering.   118. tem-
pered: molded. stand up: i.e., as a finished work of art.
119. instance: reason.   120. dub: lit., confer the title of knight
on.   121. gulled: cheated.   122. lion gait: walking about like a
lion.   123. Tartar: Tartarus, Hell.   127. affiance: trust, loyalty.
133. blood: passion, lust.   134. complement: the outward signs
of a noble man.   136. purged: free from partiality.   137. bolted:
sifted, like fine flour sifted from the bran.   139. full-fraught:
lit., fully laden. indued: endowed.

166. quit: acquit, forgive.   169. earnest: money given on ac-
count of services to be rendered.   175. tender: care for.
184. fair: fortunate.   188. rub: impediment. See App. 13.
191. expedition: motion.   192. signs: standards.
    Sc. iii: 2. Staines: a town on the Thames, on the road to
Southampton.

PIST. No, for my manly heart doth yearn.° Bardolph, be blithe. Nym, rouse thy vaunting veins. Boy, bristle thy courage up, for Falstaff he is dead, And we must yearn therefore.   6

BARD. Would I were with him, wheresome'er he is, either in Heaven or in Hell!

HOST. Nay, sure he's not in Hell. He's in Arthur's bosom,° if ever man went to Arthur's bosom. A'° made a finer end and went away an it had been any christom child.° A' parted even just between twelve and one, even at the turning o' the tide. For after I saw him fumble with the sheets, and play with flow- ers, and smile upon his fingers' ends, I knew 16 there was but one way. For his nose was as sharp as a pen, and a' babbled° of green fields. "How now, Sir John!" quoth I. "What, man! Be o' good cheer." So a' cried out "God, God, God!" three or four 20 times. Now I, to comfort him, bid him a' should not think of God, I hoped there was no need to trouble himself with any such thoughts yet. So a' bade me lay more clothes on his feet. I put my hand into the bed and felt them, and they were as cold as any 25 stone. Then I felt to his knees, and they were as cold as any stone, and so upward and upward, and all was as cold as any stone.

NYM. They say he cried out of sack.°

HOST. Aye, that a' did.   30

BARD. And of women.

HOST. Nay, that a' did not.

BOY. Yes, that a' did, and said they were devils incarnate.

HOST. A' could never abide carnation.° 'Twas a color he never liked.   36

BOY. A' said once, the Devil would have him about women.

HOST. A' did in some sort, indeed, handle women, but then he was rheumatic, and talked of the whore of Babylon.   41

BOY. Do you not remember, a' saw a flea stick upon Bardolph's nose, and a' said it was a black soul burning in hell-fire?   44

BARD. Well, the fuel is gone that maintained that fire. That's all the riches I got in his service.

NYM. Shall we shog? The King will be gone from Southampton.

PIST. Come, let's away. My love, give me thy lips. Look to my chattels and my movables.   50

Let senses rule, the word is "Pitch and Pay."° Trust none, For oaths are straws, men's faiths are wafer cakes, And holdfast is the only dog, my duck. Therefore, Caveto° be thy counselor.   55 Go, clear thy crystals.° Yokefellows in arms, Let us to France, like horseleeches, my boys, To suck, to suck, the very blood to suck!

BOY. And that's but unwholesome food, they say.

PIST. Touch her soft mouth, and march.   61

BARD. Farewell, Hostess.   [*Kissing her.*]

NYM. I cannot kiss. That is the humor of it. But adieu.

PIST. Let housewifery° appear. Keep close, I thee command.   65

HOST. Farewell, adieu.   [*Exeunt.*]

SCENE IV. *France. The* KING'S *palace.*

[*Flourish.° Enter the* FRENCH KING, *the* DAUPHIN, DUKES OF BERRI *and* BRETAGNE, *the* CONSTABLE,° *and* OTHERS.]

FR. KING. Thus comes the English with full power upon us, And more than carefully it us concerns To answer royally in our defenses. Therefore the Dukes of Berri and of Bretagne, Of Brabant and of Orleans, shall make forth,   5 And you, Prince Dauphin, with all swift dispatch, To line and new-repair our towns of war With men of courage and with means defendant.° For England his approaches makes as fierce As waters to the sucking of a gulf.°   10 It fits us then to be as provident As fear may teach us out of late examples° Left by the fatal and neglected English Upon our fields.

DAU.   My most redoubted father, It is most meet we arm us 'gainst the foe,   15 For peace itself should not so dull a kingdom, Though war nor no known quarrel were in question, But that defenses, musters, preparations, Should be maintained, assembled, and collected As were a war in expectation.   20 Therefore I say 'tis meet we all go forth To view the sick and feeble parts of France. And let us do it with no show of fear — No, with no more than if we heard that England Were busied with a Whitsun morris dance.°   25

3. **yearn:** grieve. **9–10. Arthur's bosom:** the Hostess's version of "Abraham's bosom"; i.e., Heaven. **10. A':** he. **13. christom child:** a child in its christening robe, so a perfect innocent. **18. babbled:** The original folio reading is "and a Table of greene fields." The emendation "babbled" was suggested by Theobald in 1726 and is generally regarded as one of the most brilliant of all corrections. The likelier reading is "talk" (spelt "talke") — a misprint for "table" (and vice versa), which I have thrice met in my own proofs. The quarto reads "when I saw him fumble with the sheets and talk of floures." **29. sack:** Falstaff's favorite drink. See *II Hen IV*, IV.iii.103–35. **35. carnation:** flesh-color.

51. **Pitch . . . Pay:** cash down, no credit. 55. **Caveto:** caution. 56. **crystals:** eyes. 65. **housewifery:** good management. **Sc. iv: s.d., Flourish:** trumpet fanfare. **Constable:** a principal officer in the royal household. 8. **means defendant:** means of defense. 10. **gulf:** whirlpool. 12. **late examples:** See later ll. 53–64. 25. **Whitsun . . . dance:** i.e., innocent gaiety. Folk dancing in the open was a usual pastime in the Whitsun holidays, which fall in early summer. See App. 24.

For, my good liege, she is so idly kinged,°
Her scepter so fantastically borne
By a vain, giddy, shallow, humorous° youth,
That fear attends her not.

CON.   Oh, peace, Prince Dauphin!
You are too much mistaken in this King.   30
Question your Grace the late ambassadors,
With what great state he heard their embassy,
How well supplied with noble councilors,
How modest in exception,° and withal
How terrible in constant resolution,   35
And you shall find his vanities forespent°
Were but the outside of the Roman Brutus,°
Covering discretion with a coat of folly —
As gardeners do with ordure° hide those roots
That shall first spring and be most delicate.   40

DAU. Well, 'tis not so, my Lord High Constable,
But though we think it so, it is no matter.
In cases of defense 'tis best to weigh
The enemy more mighty than he seems.
So the proportions of defense are filled,°   45
Which of a weak and niggardly projection°
Doth, like a miser, spoil his coat with scanting
A little cloth.

FR. KING. Think we King Harry strong,
And, Princes, look you strongly arm to meet him.
The kindred of him hath been fleshed° upon us, 50
And he is bred out of that bloody strain
That haunted us in our familiar paths.
Witness our too much memorable shame
When Crécy battle fatally was struck,
And all our Princes captived by the hand   55
Of that black name, Edward, Black Prince of Wales,
Whiles that his mountain sire, on mountain stand-
     ing,
Up in the air, crowned with the golden sun,
Saw his heroical seed, and smiled to see him,
Mangle the work of nature and deface   60
The patterns that by God and by French fathers
Had twenty years been made. This is a stem
Of that victorious stock, and let us fear
The native mightiness and fate of him.

                [Enter a MESSENGER.]
MESS. Ambassadors from Harry King of England
Do crave admittance to your Majesty.   66

FR. KING. We'll give them present° audience. Go,
     and bring them.
        [Exeunt MESSENGER and certain LORDS.]
You see this chase is hotly followed, friends.

DAU. Turn head, and stop pursuit, for coward
     dogs

Most spend their mouths° when what they seem to
     threaten   70
Runs far before them. Good my sovereign,
Take up the English short, and let them know
Of what a monarchy you are the head.
Self-love, my liege, is not so vile a sin
As self-neglecting.

        [Re-enter LORDS, with EXETER and train.]
FR. KING.   From our brother England? 75
EXE. From him, and thus he greets your Majesty.
He wills you, in the name of God Almighty,
That you divest yourself, and lay apart
The borrowed glories that by gift of Heaven,
By law of nature and of nations, 'long°   80
To him and to his heirs; namely, the crown
And all wide-stretchèd honors that pertain
By custom and the ordinance of times
Unto the crown of France. That you may know
'Tis no siníster° nor no awkward claim,   85
Picked from the wormholes of long-vanished days,
Nor from the dust of old oblivion raked,
He sends you this most memorable line,°
In every branch truly demonstrative,
Willing you overlook this pedigree.   90
And when you find him evenly° derived
From his most famed of famous ancestors,
Edward the Third, he bids you then resign
Your crown and kingdom, indirectly° held
From him the native and true challenger.°   95

FR. KING. Or else what follows?
EXE. Bloody constraint,° for if you hide the crown
Even in your hearts, there will he rake for it.
Therefore in fierce tempest is he coming,
In thunder and in earthquake, like a Jove,   100
That, if requiring° fail, he will compel.
And bids you, in the bowels° of the Lord,
Deliver up the crown, and to take mercy
On the poor souls for whom this hungry war
Opens his vasty° jaws; and on your head   105
Turning the widows' tears, the orphans' cries,
The dead men's blood, the pining maidens' groans
For husbands, fathers, and betrothèd lovers
That shall be swallowed in this controversy.
This is his claim, his threatening, and my message —
Unless the Dauphin be in presence here,   111
To whom expressly I bring greeting too.

FR. KING. For us, we will consider of this further.
Tomorrow shall you bear our full intent
Back to our brother England.

DAU.   For the Dauphin, 115
I stand here for him. What to him from England?

EXE. Scorn and defiance, slight regard, contempt,
And anything that may not misbecome

26. idly kinged: has such a frivolous king.   28. humorous:
whimsical.   34. exception: disagreement.   36. forespent: former.
37. Roman Brutus: Lucius Junius Brutus (ancestor of Marcus
Brutus), who drove out Tarquin, pretended to be a simpleton.
39. ordure: manure.   45. So . . . filled: so long as the proper
measures of defense are taken.   46. of . . . projection: if too
meanly estimated.   50. fleshed: excited by the taste of first
blood.   67. present: immediate.

70. spend . . . mouths: bark.   80. 'long: belong.   85. sinister:
left-hand, irregular.   88. line: pedigree.   91. evenly: directly.
94. indirectly: not in the direct line of descent.   95. chal-
lenger: claimant.   97. constraint: force.   101. requiring: asking.
102. bowels: i.e., mercy.   105. vasty: vast.

The mighty sender, doth he prize you at.
Thus says my King. An if your father's Highness
Do not, in grant of all demands at large,   121
Sweeten the bitter mock you sent His Majesty,
He'll call you to so hot an answer of it
That caves and womby vaultages° of France
Shall chide your trespass, and return your mock
In second accent° of his ordnance.°   126
DAU. Say if my father render fair return,
It is against my will, for I desire
Nothing but odds° with England. To that end,
As matching to his youth and vanity,   130
I did present him with the Paris balls.°
EXE. He'll make your Paris Louvre° shake for it,
Were it the mistress Court of mighty Europe.
And be assured you'll find a difference,
As we his subjects have in wonder found,   135
Between the promise of his greener° days
And these he masters now. Now he weighs time°
Even to the utmost grain. That you shall read
In your own losses, if he stay in France.
FR. KING. Tomorrow shall you know our mind at
    full.   140
EXE. Dispatch us with all speed, lest that our King
Come here himself to question our delay,
For he is footed in this land already.
FR. KING. You shall be soon dispatched with fair
    conditions.
A night is but small breath and little pause   145
To answer matters of this consequence.
                              [Flourish. Exeunt.]

Act III

PROLOGUE

[Enter CHORUS.]
CHOR. Thus with imagined wing° our swift scene
    flies
In motion of no less celerity
Than that of thought. Suppose that you have seen
The well-appointed King at Hampton pier
Embark his royalty, and his brave° fleet   5
With silken streamers the young Phoebus° fan-
    ning.
Play with your fancies, and in them behold
Upon the hempen tackle ship boys climbing.
Hear the shrill whistle which doth order give

To sounds confused. Behold the threaden° sails, 10
Borne with the invisible and creeping wind,
Draw the huge bottoms through the furrowed sea,
Breasting the lofty surge. Oh, do but think
You stand upon the rivage° and behold
A city on the inconstant billows dancing,   15
For so appears this fleet majestical,
Holding due course to Harfleur.° Follow, follow.
Grapple your minds to sternage° of this navy,
And leave your England, as dead midnight still,
Guarded with grandsires, babies, and old women,
Either past or not arrived to pith° and puissance.
For who is he whose chin is but enriched   20
With one appearing hair that will not follow
These culled° and choice-drawn° cavaliers to
    France?
Work, work your thoughts, and therein see a siege.
Behold the ordnance on their carriages,   26
With fatal mouths gaping on girded° Harfleur.
Suppose the Ambassador from the French comes
    back,
Tells Harry that the King doth offer him
Katharine his daughter, and with her, to dowry, 30
Some petty and unprofitable dukedoms.
The offer likes° not. And the nimble gunner
With linstock° now the devilish cannon touches,
              [Alarum, and chambers go off.°]
And down goes all before them. Still be kind,   34
And eke out° our performance with your mind.
                                      [Exit.]

SCENE I. France. Before Harfleur.

[Alarum.° Enter KING HENRY, EXETER, BEDFORD,
GLOUCESTER, and SOLDIERS, with scaling ladders.°]
K. HEN. Once more unto the breach, dear friends,
    once more,
Or close the wall up with our English dead.
In peace there's nothing so becomes a man
As modest stillness and humility.
But when the blast of war blows in our ears,   5
Then imitate the action of the tiger,
Stiffen the sinews, summon up the blood,
Disguise fair nature with hard-favored° rage.
Then lend the eye a terrible aspéct,
Let it pry through the portage° of the head   10
Like the brass cannon. Let the brow o'erwhelm it
As fearfully as doth a gallèd° rock

---

124. vaultages: hollow places.   126. In . . . accent: i.e., to the echo. ordnance: cannon.   129. odds: disagreement.   131. Paris balls: i.e., the tennis balls from Paris.   132. Louvre: the royal palace in Paris.   136. greener: rawer, younger.   137. weighs time: i.e., no longer wastes it.

Act III. Prologue: 1. imagined wing: on the wing of imagination.   5. brave: splendid.   6. Phoebus: the sun.

10. threaden: linen.   14. rivage: shore.   17. Harfleur: opposite Le Havre at the mouth of the Seine.   18. sternage: the stern.   21. pith: strength.   24. culled: selected. choice-drawn: carefully chosen.   27. girded: surrounded.   32. likes: pleases.   33. linstock: the gunner's staff holding the match. See Pl. 12a. s.d., chambers go off: small cannon discharged. See Gen. Intro. p. 51b.   35. eke out: supplement.

Sc. i: s.d., Alarum: trumpet call to arms. scaling ladders: See Pl. 12a.   8. hard-favored: grim-faced.   10. portage: port-hole.   12. galled: worn by the sea.

O'erhang and jutty° his confounded° base,
Swilled with the wild and wasteful ocean.
Now set the teeth and stretch the nostril wide,　15
Hold hard the breath, and bend up every spirit
To his full height. On, on, you noblest English,
Whose blood is fet° from fathers of war proof!°
Fathers that, like so many Alexanders,
Have in these parts from morn till even fought,　20
And sheathed their swords for lack of argument.°
Dishonor not your mothers. Now attest
That those whom you called fathers did beget
　you.
Be copy now to men of grosser blood,
And teach them how to war. And you, good yeo-
　men,°　25
Whose limbs were made in England, show us here
The mettle of your pasture. Let us swear
That you are worth your breeding, which I doubt
　not,
For there is none of you so mean and base
That hath not noble luster in your eyes.　·　30
I see you stand like greyhounds in the slips,°
Straining upon the start. The game's afoot.
Follow your spirit, and upon this charge
Cry " God for Harry, England, and Saint George! "°
　　　　[*Exeunt. Alarum, and chambers go off.*]

SCENE II. *The same.*

[*Enter* NYM, BARDOLPH, PISTOL, *and* BOY.]

BARD. On, on, on, on, on! To the breach, to the
breach!

NYM. Pray thee, Corporal, stay. The knocks are
too hot, and, for mine own part, I have not a case°
of lives. The humor of it is too hot, that is the very
plainsong° of it.　6

PIST. The plainsong is most just, for humors do
abound:
" Knocks go and come, God's vassals drop and die,
　　And sword and shield,
　　In bloody field,　10
Doth win immortal fame."

BOY. Would I were in an alehouse in London! I
would give all my fame for a pot of ale and safety.

PIST. And I:　15
" If wishes would prevail with me,
　　My purpose should not fail with me,
　　But thither would I hie."°

BOY. " As duly, but not as truly,
　　As bird doth sing on bough."　20

13. jutty: jut over. confounded: worn. 18. fet: fetched. war-
proof: proved in war. 21. argument: matter for dispute.
25. yeomen: men from the country, who formed the bulk of the
archers. 31. slips: collar, quickly released, by which greyhounds
are held. 34. Saint George: patron saint of England.

Sc. ii: 4. case: set. 6. plainsong: simple tune. 18. hie:
hasten.

[*Enter* FLUELLEN.]

FLU. Up to the breach, you dogs! Avaunt,° you
cullions!°　　　　　　[*Driving them forward.*]

PIST. Be merciful, great Duke, to men of mold.°
Abate thy rage, abate thy manly rage,
Abate thy rage, great Duke!　25
Good bawcock,° bate thy rage. Use lenity, sweet
　chuck!°

NYM. These be good humors! Your Honor wins
bad humors.　　　　　　[*Exeunt all but* BOY.]

BOY. As young as I am, I have observed these three
swashers.° I am boy to them all three. But all　30
they three, though they would serve me, could not be
man to me, for indeed three such antics° do not
amount to a man. For Bardolph, he is white-livered°
and red-faced, by the means whereof a' faces it out
but fights not. For Pistol, he hath a killing　35
tongue and a quiet sword, by the means whereof a'
breaks words and keeps whole weapons. For Nym,
he hath heard that men of few words are the best
men, and therefore he scorns to say his prayers lest
a' should be thought a coward. But his few bad　40
words are matched with as few good deeds, for a'
never broke any man's head but his own, and that
was against a post when he was drunk. They will
steal anything and call it purchase.° Bardolph stole
a lute case, bore it twelve leagues, and sold it for　45
three halfpence. Nym and Bardolph are sworn broth-
ers in filching, and in Calais they stole a fire shovel.
I knew by that piece of service the men would carry
coals.° They would have me as familiar with men's
pockets as their gloves or their handkerchers.　50
Which makes much against my manhood, if I should
take from another's pocket to put into mine, for it is
plain pocketing-up° of wrongs. I must leave them,
and seek some better service. Their villainy goes　55
against my weak stomach, and therefore I must cast
it up.　　　　　　　　　　　　　　[*Exit.*]

[*Re-enter* FLUELLEN, GOWER *following.*]

GOW. Captain Fluellen, you must come presently
to the mines.° The Duke of Gloucester would speak
with you.　60

FLU. To the mines! Tell you the Duke it is not so
good to come to the mines. For look you, the mines
is not according to the disciplines of the war.° The
concavities of it is not sufficient. For look you, th'
athversary, you may discuss unto the Duke, look
you, is digt himself four yard under the counter-
mines. By Cheshu, I think a' will plow° up all if
there is not better directions.　68

21. Avaunt: be off. 22. cullions: base fellows. 23. mold: earth;
i.e., mortal men. 26. bawcock: fine cock. chuck: chick.
30. swashers: swaggerers. 32. antics: clowns, fantastics.
33. white-livered: i.e., cowardly. 44. purchase: thieves' word
for booty. 48–49. would . . . coals: do dirty work. 54. pocket-
ing-up: with a pun on the idiomatic meaning of *putting up with*.
59. mines: i.e., dug under the enemy's walls. 63. disciplines
. . . war: military science. 67. plow: blow. The Welshman when
talking English has some difficulty with the letters *b* and *v*.

GOW. The Duke of Gloucester, to whom the order of the siege is given, is altogether directed by an Irishman, a very valiant gentleman, i' faith.

FLU. It is Captain Macmorris, is it not?

GOW. I think it be.   73

FLU. By Cheshu, he is an ass, as in the world. I will verify as much in his beard. He has no more directions in the true disciplines of the wars, look you, of the Roman disciplines, than is a puppy dog.

[*Enter* MACMORRIS *and* CAPTAIN JAMY.°]

GOW. Here a' comes, and the Scots captain, Captain Jamy, with him.   80

FLU. Captain Jamy is a marvelous falorous gentleman, that is certain, and of great expedition and knowledge in th' aunchient wars, upon my particular knowledge of his directions. By Cheshu, he will maintain his argument as well as any military man in the world, in the disciplines of the pristine° wars of the Romans.   87

JAMY. I say gud day, Captain Fluellen.

FLU. Godden° to your Worship, good Captain James.

GOW. How now, Captain Macmorris! Have you quit the mines? Have the pioners° given o'er?   92

MAC. By Chrish, la! Tish ill done. The work ish give over, the trompet sound the retreat. By my hand, I swear, and my father's soul, the work ish ill done, it ish give over. I would have blowed up the town, so Chrish save me, la! in an hour. Oh, tish ill done, tish ill done, by my hand, tish ill done!   99

FLU. Captain Macmorris, I beseech you now will you vouchsafe me, look you, a few disputations with you, as partly touching or concerning the disciplines of the war, the Roman wars, in the way of argument, look you, and friendly communication — partly to satisfy my opinion, and partly for the satisfaction, look you, of my mind, as touching the direction of the military discipline. That is the point.   108

JAMY. It sall be vary gud, gud feith, gud Captains bath. And I sall quit° you with gud leve, as I may pick occasion. That sall I, marry.

MAC. It is no time to discourse, so Chrish save me. The day is hot, and the weather, and the wars, and the King, and the Dukes. It is no time to discourse. The town is beseeched,° and the trumpet call   115 us to the breach, and we talk and, be Chrish, do nothing. 'Tis shame for us all. So God sa' me, 'tis shame to stand still. It is shame, by my hand. And there is throats to be cut, and works to be done, and there ish nothing done, so Chrish sa' me, la!   121

JAMY. By the mess,° ere theise eyes of mine take

themselves to slomber, ay'll de gud service, or ay'll lig° i' the grund for it — aye, or go to death. And ay'll pay 't as valorously as I may, that sall I suerly do, that is the breff and the long. Marry, I wad full fain hear some question 'tween you tway.°   128

FLU. Captain Macmorris, I think, look you, under your correction, there is not many of your nation ——

MAC. Of my nation!° What ish my nation? Ish a villain, and a bastard, and a knave, and a rascal. What ish my nation? Who talks of my nation?   135

FLU. Look you, if you take the matter otherwise than is meant, Captain Macmorris, peradventure I shall think you do not use me with that affability as in discretion you ought to use me, look you, being as good a man as yourself, both in the disciplines of war and in the derivation of my birth and in other particularities.   142

MAC. I do not know you so good a man as myself. So Chrish save me, I will cut off your head.

GOW. Gentlemen both, you will mistake each other.

JAMY. A! That's a foul fault.

[*A parley° sounded.*]

GOW. The town sounds a parley.   149

FLU. Captain Macmorris, when there is more better opportunity to be required, look you, I will be so bold as to tell you I know the disciplines of war. And there is an end.   [*Exeunt.*]

SCENE III. *The Same. Before the Gates.*

[*The* GOVERNOR *and some* CITIZENS *on the walls; the English forces below. Enter* KING HENRY *and his train.*]

K. HEN. How yet resolves the governor of the town?
This is the latest parle° we will admit,
Therefore to our best mercy give yourselves,
Or like to men proud of destruction
Defy us to our worst. For, as I am a soldier —
A name that in my thoughts becomes me best —
If I begin the battery once again,
I will not leave the half-achieved° Harfleur
Till in her ashes she lie buried.
The gates of mercy shall be all shut up,   10
And the fleshed° soldier, rough and hard of heart,
In liberty of bloody hand shall range°
With conscience wide as Hell, mowing like grass

124. lig: lie.   128. tway: two.   133. Of my nation: Macmorris is spoiling for a fight, and ready to interpret any remark as an insult to Ireland.   148. s.d., parley: trumpet call, summoning to parley.
Sc. iii: 2. latest parle: last parley.   8. half-achieved: halfwon.   11. fleshed: See II.iv.50.   12. In . . . range: shall wander in search of plunder without restraint. If a city refused to yield and was afterward taken, the victorious soldiers were given free leave to ravage and plunder.

78. s.d., Macmorris . . . Jamy: There is no trace in the quarto of this passage between the Welshman, the Irishman, and the Scot, each speaking with his native accent.   86. pristine: ancient.
89. Godden: good afternoon.   92. pioners: pioneers, one of whose tasks was to construct mines (i.e., tunnels).   110. quit: requite; i.e., return your favors.   115. beseeched: besieged.
122. mess: mass.

Your fresh-fair virgins and your flowering infants.
What is it then to me if impious war,   15
Arrayed in flames like to the Prince of Fiends,
Do, with his smirched° complexion, all fell feats°
Enlinked to waste and desolation?
What is 't to me, when you yourselves are cause,
If your pure maidens fall into the hand   20
Of hot and forcing violation?
What rein can hold licentious wickedness
When down the hill he holds his fierce career?
We may as bootless° spend our vain command
Upon the enraged soldiers in their spoil   25
As send precepts to the leviathan°
To come ashore. Therefore, you men of Harfleur,
Take pity of your town and of your people
Whiles yet my soldiers are in my command,
Whiles yet the cool and temperate wind of grace   30
O'erblows the filthy and contagious clouds
Of heady° murder, spoil, and villainy.
If not, why, in a moment look to see
The blind and bloody soldier with foul hand
Defile the locks of your shrill-shrieking daughters,
Your fathers taken by the silver beards   36
And their most reverend heads dashed to the walls,
Your naked infants spitted upon pikes
Whiles the mad mothers with their howls confused
Do break the clouds, as did the wives of Jewry   40
At Herod's bloody-hunting slaughtermen.°
What say you? Will you yield, and this avoid,
Or, guilty in defense, be thus destroyed?
  GOV. Our expectation° hath this day an end.
The Dauphin, whom of succors we entreated,   45
Returns us that his powers are yet not ready
To raise so great a siege. Therefore, great King,
We yield our town and lives to thy soft mercy.
Enter our gates, dispose of us and ours,
For we no longer are defensible.   50
  K. HEN. Open your gates. Come, Uncle Exeter,
Go you and enter Harfleur. There remain,
And fortify it strongly 'gainst the French.
Use mercy to them all. For us, dear Uncle,
The winter coming on, and sickness growing   55
Upon our soldiers, we will retire to Calais.
Tonight in Harfleur will we be your guest,
Tomorrow for the march are we addressed.°
  [*Flourish. The* KING *and his train enter the town.*]

SCENE IV.° *The* FRENCH KING'S *palace.*

[*Enter* KATHARINE *and* ALICE.]
  KATH. Alice, tu as été en Angleterre, et tu parles
bien le langage.

---

17. smirched: stained with smoke. fell feats: terrible deeds.
24. bootless: vainly. 26. leviathan: whale. 32. heady: violent.
41. slaughtermen: i.e., at the Massacre of the Innocents. See
Matthew 2: 16–18. 44. expectation: hope. 58. addressed: ready.
  Sc. iv: The printer of the folio made sad havoc of the French
in this scene, which has been put right by editors. About 1602–04

ALICE. Un peu, madame.
  KATH. Je te prie, m'enseignez. Il faut que j'ap-
prenne à parler. Comment appelez-vous la main en
Anglais?   6
  ALICE. La main? Elle est appelée de hand.
  KATH. De hand. Et les doigts?
  ALICE. Les doigts? Ma foi, j'oublie les doigts, mais
je me souviendrai. Les doigts? Je pense qu'ils sont
appelés de fingres — oui, de fingres.   11
  KATH. La main, de hand, les doigts, de fingres. Je
pense que je suis le bon écolier. J'ai gagné deux mots
d'Anglais vîtement. Comment appelez-vous les
ongles?   15
  ALICE. Les ongles? Nous les appelons de nails.
  KATH. De nails. Ecoutez. Dites-moi si je parle
bien: de hand, de fingres, et de nails.
  ALICE. C'est bien dit, madame, il est fort bon   20
Anglais.
  KATH. Dites-moi l'Anglais pour le bras.
  ALICE. De arm, madame.
  KATH. Et le coude.
  ALICE. De elbow.   24
  KATH. De elbow. Je m'en fais la répétition de tous
les mots que vous m'avez appris dès à présent.
  ALICE. Il est trop difficile, madame, comme je
pense.
  KATH. Excusez-moi, Alice, écoutez: de hand, de
fingres, de nails, de arma, de bilbow.   31
  ALICE. De elbow, madame.
  KATH. Oh, Seigneur Dieu, je m'en oublie! De
elbow. Comment appelez-vous le col?
  ALICE. De neck, madame.   35
  KATH. De nick. Et le menton?
  ALICE. De chin.
  KATH. De sin. Le col, de nick, le menton, de sin.
  ALICE. Oui. Sauf votre honneur, en vérité, vous
prononcez les mots aussi droit que les natifs d'An-
gleterre.
  KATH. Je ne doute point d'apprendre, par la grace
de Dieu, et en peu de temps.   44
  ALICE. N'avez vous pas déjà oublié ce que je vous
ai enseigné?
  KATH. Non, je réciterai à vous promptement: de
hand, de fingres, de mails ——
  ALICE. De nails, madame.
  KATH. De nails, de arm, de ilbow.   50
  ALICE. Sauf votre honneur, de elbow.
  KATH. Ainsi dis-je: de elbow, de nick, et de sin.
Comment appelez-vous le pied et la robe?
  ALICE. De foot, madame, et de coun.   54

Shakespeare was lodging in London with a Huguenot family
called Mountjoy, and took some interest in the affairs of Mary
Mountjoy, the daughter of the house. (See Gen. Intro. p. 14b.)
Some commentators find pleasure in the thought that she may
have taught Shakespeare the French words for this play. Pre-
sumably they do not realize that the plain purpose of the scene
is to get some low amusement from the fact that certain words
which sound innocent in one language are indecent in the other.

KATH. De foot et de coun! Oh, Seigneur Dieu!
Ce sont mots de son mauvais, corruptible, gros, et
impudique, et non pour les dames d'honneur d'user.
Je ne voudrais prononcer ces mots devant les seig-
neurs de France pour tout le monde. Foh! Le foot et
le coun! Néanmoins, je réciterai une autre fois   60
ma leçon ensemble: de hand, de fingres, de nails, de
arm, de elbow, de nick, de sin, de foot, de coun.

ALICE. Excellent, madame!

KATH. C'est assez pour une fois. Allons-nous à   64
dîner.   [*Exeunt*]

SCENE V. *The same.*

[*Enter the* KING OF FRANCE, *the* DAUPHIN, *the* DUKE
OF BOURBON, *the* CONSTABLE OF FRANCE, *and others.*]

FR. KING. 'Tis certain he hath passed the river
    Somme.

CON. And if he be not fought withal, my lord,
Let us not live in France, let us quit all,
And give our vineyards to a barbarous people.

DAU. Oh, *Dieu vivant!* Shall a few sprays of us,   5
The emptying of our fathers' luxury,
Our scions, put in wild and savage stock,
Spurt up so suddenly into the clouds,
And overlook their grafters?°

BOUR. Normans, but bastard Normans, Norman
    bastards!   10
Mort de ma vie! If they march along
Unfought withal, but I will sell my dukedom
To buy a slobbery° and a dirty farm
In that nook-shotten° isle of Albion.

CON. *Dieu de batailles!* Where have they this
    mettle?°   15
Is not their climate foggy, raw, and dull,
On whom, as in despite,° the sun looks pale,
Killing their fruit with frowns? Can sodden water,°
A drench for surreined° jades,° their barley broth,
Decoct° their cold blood to such valiant heat?   20
And shall our quick blood, spirited with wine,
Seem frosty? Oh, for honor of our land,
Let us not hang like roping° icicles
Upon our houses' thatch whiles a more frosty people

Sweat drops of gallant youth in our rich fields! —
Poor we may call them in their native lords.°   26

DAU. By faith and honor,
Our madams mock at us, and plainly say
Our mettle is bred out, and they will give
Their bodies to the lust of English youth,   30
To new-store France with bastard warriors.

BOUR. They bid us to the English dancing schools,
And teach lavoltas° high and swift corantos,°
Saying our grace is only in our heels,
And that we are most lofty runaways.   35

FR. KING. Where is Montjoy the herald? Speed
    him hence.
Let him greet England with our sharp defiance.
Up, Princes! and, with spirit of honor edged
More sharper than your swords, hie to the field.
Charles Delabreth, High Constable of France,   40
You Dukes of Orleans, Bourbon, and of Berri,
Alençon, Brabant, Bar, and Burgundy,
Jaques Chatillon, Rambures, Vaudemont,
Beaumont, Grandpré, Roussi, and Fauconberg,
Foix, Lestrale, Bouciqualt, and Charolois° —   45
High Dukes, great Princes, barons, lords, and
    knights,
For your great seats° now quit you° of great
    shames.
Bar° Harry England, that sweeps through our land
With pennons painted in the blood of Harfleur.
Rush on his host as doth the melted snow   50
Upon the valleys whose low vassal seat
The Alps doth spit and void his rheum° upon.
Go down upon him; you have power enough,
And in a captive chariot into Rouen
Bring him our prisoner.

CON.   This becomes the great.   55
Sorry am I his numbers are so few,
His soldiers sick and famished in their march.
For I am sure when he shall see our army,
He'll drop his heart into the sink of fear
And for achievement° offer us his ransom.   60

FR. KING. Therefore, Lord Constable, haste on
    Montjoy,
And let him say to England that we send
To know what willing ransom he will give.
Prince Dauphin, you shall stay with us in Rouen.

DAU. Not so, I do beseech your Majesty.   65

FR. KING. Be patient, for you shall remain with us.
Now forth, Lord Constable and Princes all,
And quickly bring us word of England's fall.
                                         [*Exeunt.*]

Sc. v: 5–9. Shall . . . grafters: shall some sprigs (*sprays*) of
us French — bastards begotten by the lust (*luxury*) of our ances-
tors — be like slips for grafting (*scions*) which, when set in a wild
tree, grow great so suddenly and overtop the original tree from
which the slips were taken (*grafters*)? By this elaborate image
from the process of grafting cultivated slips onto a wild stock
(as is the custom of gardeners with fruit trees) the Dauphin is
reminding his party that many of the English nobility were
descended from the followers of William the Norman, who con-
quered Saxon England in 1066.   13. slobbery: muddy, sloppy.
14. nook-shotten: pushed in a corner; i.e., remote and barbarous.
15. mettle: material, courage.   17. despite: spite.   18. sodden
water: water boiled with slops.   19. surreined: overridden. jades:
horses in poor condition.   20. Decoct: warm up.   23. roping:
dangling.

26. Poor . . . lords: even their noblemen are a poor set.   33. la-
volta: a high jumping dance performed by two dancers with
arms intertwined. coranto: a quick sliding dance with unex-
pected movements. See App. 24.   40–45. Charles . . . Charolois:
this catalogue of names was taken direct from Holinshed.
47. seats: estates. quit you: rid yourselves.   48. Bar: stop.
52. void . . . rheum: spit.   60. for achievement: instead of
victory.

SCENE VI. *The English camp in Picardy.*

[*Enter* GOWER *and* FLUELLEN, *meeting.*]

GOW. How now, Captain Fluellen! Come you
from the bridge?

FLU. I assure you there is very excellent services
committed at the bridge.

GOW. Is the Duke of Exeter safe?   5

FLU. The Duke of Exeter is as magnanimous as
Agamemnon,° and a man that I love and honor with
my soul, and my heart, and my duty, and my life,
and my living, and my uttermost power. He is not
— God be praised and blessed! — any hurt in the
world, but keeps the bridge most valiantly, with ex-
cellent discipline. There is an Aunchient Lieutenant
there at the pridge, I think in my very conscience he
is as valiant a man as Mark Antony, and he is a man
of no estimation in the world, but I did see him do
as gallant service.   15

GOW. What do you call him?

FLU. He is called Aunchient Pistol.

GOW. I know him not.   20

[*Enter* PISTOL.]

FLU. Here is the man.

PIST. Captain, I thee beseech to do me favors.
The Duke of Exeter doth love thee well.

FLU. Aye, I praise God, and I have merited some
love at his hands.   25

PIST. Bardolph, a soldier, firm and sound of heart,
And of buxom° valor, hath, by cruel fate
And giddy Fortune's furious fickle wheel,
That goddess blind
That stands upon the rolling restless stone ——   30

FLU. By your patience, Aunchient Pistol. Fortune
is painted blind, with a muffler afore her eyes, to
signify to you that Fortune is blind. And she is
painted also with a wheel to signify to you, which
is the moral of it, that she is turning, and in-   35
constant, and mutability, and variation. And her
foot, look you, is fixed upon a spherical stone, which
rolls, and rolls, and rolls. In good truth, the poet
makes a most excellent description of it. Fortune is
an excellent moral.   40

PIST. Fortune is Bardolph's foe, and frowns on
     him,
For he hath stolen a pax,° and hanged must a' be.
A damnèd death!

Let gallows gape for dog, let man go free
And let not hemp his windpipe suffocate.   45
But Exeter hath given the doom of death
For pax of little price.
Therefore, go speak, the Duke will hear thy voice,
And let not Bardolph's vital thread be cut
With edge of penny cord and vile reproach.   50
Speak, Captain, for his life, and I will thee requite.

FLU. Aunchient Pistol, I do partly understand
your meaning.

PIST. Why then, rejoice therefore.

FLU. Certainly, Aunchient, it is not a thing to re-
joice at. For if, look you, he were my brother, I
would desire the Duke to use his good pleasure and
put him to execution, for discipline ought to be used.

PIST. Die and be damned! And figo° for thy
     friendship!   59

FLU. It is well.

PIST. The fig of Spain!   [*Exit.*]

FLU. Very good.

GOW. Why, this is an arrant° counterfeit rascal. I
remember him now — a bawd, a cutpurse.   65

FLU. I'll assure you a' uttered as prave words at
the pridge as you shall see in a summer's day. But it
is very well. What he has spoke to me, that is well,
I warrant you, when time is serve.   69

GOW. Why, 'tis a gull,° a fool, a rogue, that now
and then goes to the wars, to grace himself at his re-
turn into London under the form of a soldier. And
such fellows are perfect in the great commanders'
names. And they will learn you by rote where serv-
ices were done — at such and such a sconce,°   75
at such a breach, at such a convoy; who came off
bravely, who was shot, who disgraced, what terms
the enemy stood on. And this they con° perfectly in
the phrase of war, which they trick up with new-
tuned oaths. And what a beard of the general's cut°
and a horrid suit of the camp will do among foam-
ing bottles and ale-washed wits is wonderful to be
thought on. But you must learn to know such slan-
ders of the age,° or else you may be marvelously mis-
took.   85

FLU. I tell you what, Captain Gower, I do per-
ceive he is not the man that he would gladly make
show to the world he is. If I find a hole in his coat, I
will tell him my mind. [*Drum heard*] Hark you, the
King is coming, and I must speak with him   91
from the pridge. [*Drum and Colors.° Enter* KING
HENRY, GLOUCESTER, *and* SOLDIERS.] God pless your
Majesty!

Sc. vi: **7. Agamemnon:** general of the Greek forces that be-
sieged Troy. **27. buxom:** lively. **42. pax:** The actual incident
is from Holinshed: "Yet in this great necessity the poor people
of the country were not spoiled, nor anything taken of them
without payment, nor any outrage or offense done by the Eng-
lishmen, except one, which was that a soldier took a pyx out of a
church, for which he was apprehended, and the King not once re-
moved till the box was restored, and the offender strangled." A
pyx is the vessel in which the consecrated wafer is kept; a *pax* is
a plate stamped with the figure of a crucifix, kissed first by the
priest and then by the laity.

59. figo: fig, an insulting gesture made by thrusting the thumb
between the first and second fingers. **64. arrant:** out-and-out.
70. gull: simpleton. **75. sconce:** strong point, blockhouse.
78. con: learn by heart. **80. beard . . . cut:** After the Cádiz ex-
pedition Essex grew a great beard, which was much imitated
by his followers. **84. slanders . . . age:** abuses of our time.
92. s.d., Drum . . . colors: a drummer and a soldier carrying a
flag.

K. HEN. How now, Fluellen! Camest thou from the bridge?

FLU. Aye, so please your Majesty. The Duke of Exeter has very gallantly maintained the pridge. 95 The French is gone off, look you, and there is gallant and most prave passages. Marry, th' athversary was have possession of the pridge, but he is enforced to retire, and the Duke of Exeter is master of the pridge. I can tell your Majesty, the Duke is a prave man. 101

K. HEN. What men have you lost, Fluellen?

FLU. The perdition° of th' athversary hath been very great, reasonable great. Marry, for my part, I think the Duke hath lost never a man but one that is like to be executed for robbing a church, one Bardolph, if your Majesty know the man. His face is all bubukles,° and whelks,° and knobs, and flames o' fire. And his lips blows at his nose, and it is like a coal of fire, sometimes plue and sometimes red, but his nose is executed, and his fire's out. 112

K. HEN. We would have all such offenders so cut off. And we give express charge that in our marches through the country there be nothing compelled° from the villages, nothing taken but paid for, none of the French upbraided or abused in disdainful language. For when lenity and cruelty play for a kingdom, the gentler gamester is the soonest winner. 120

[*Tucket. Enter* MONTJOY.]

MONT. You know me by my habit.°

K. HEN. Well then, I know thee. What shall I know of thee?

MONT. My master's mind.

K. HEN. Unfold it. 124

MONT. Thus says my King: " Say thou to Harry of England: ' Though we seemed dead, we did but sleep. Advantage° is a better soldier than rashness.' Tell him we could have rebuked him at Harfleur, but that we thought not good to bruise an injury till it were full ripe.° Now we speak upon our 130 cue,° and our voice is imperial. England shall repent his folly, see his weakness, and admire° our sufferance.° Bid him therefore consider of his ransom, which must proportion the losses we have borne, the subjects we have lost, the disgrace we have digested; which in weight to reanswer, his pettiness 135 would bow under.° For our losses, his exchequer is too poor. For the effusion of our blood, the muster of his kingdom too faint a number. And for our disgrace, his own person, kneeling at our feet, but 140

a weak and worthless satisfaction. To this add defiance. And tell him, for conclusion, he hath betrayed his followers, whose condemnation is pronounced." So far my King and master, so much my office. 145

K. HEN. What is thy name? I know thy quality.°

MONT. Montjoy.

K. HEN. Thou dost thy office fairly. Turn thee back,
And tell thy King I do not seek him now,
But could be willing to march on to Calais 150
Without impeachment.° For to say the sooth,
Though 'tis no wisdom to confess so much
Unto an enemy of craft and vantage,°
My people are with sickness much enfeebled,
My numbers lessened, and those few I have 155
Almost no better than so many French.
Who when they were in health, I tell thee, herald,
I thought upon one pair of English legs
Did march three Frenchmen. Yet, forgive me, God,
That I do brag thus! This your air of France 160
Hath blown that vice in me. I must repent.
Go, therefore, tell thy master here I am.
My ransom is this frail and worthless trunk,
My army but a weak and sickly guard,
Yet, God before, tell him we will come on 165
Though France himself and such another neighbor
Stand in our way. There's for thy labor, Montjoy.
Go, bid thy master well advise himself.°
If we may pass, we will. If we be hindered,
We shall your tawny° ground with your red blood
Discolor. And so, Montjoy, fare you well. 171
The sum of all our answer is but this:
We would not seek a battle as we are,
Nor, as we are, we say we will not shun it.
So tell your master. 175

MONT. I shall deliver so. Thanks to your Highness.
[*Exit.*]

GLO. I hope they will not come upon us now.

K. HEN. We are in God's hand, Brother, not in theirs.
March to the bridge, it now draws toward night.
Beyond the river we'll encamp ourselves, 180
And on tomorrow bid them march away. [*Exeunt.*]

SCENE VII. *The French camp, near Agincourt.*

[*Enter the* CONSTABLE *of France, the* LORD RAMBURES, ORLEANS, DAUPHIN, *with others.*]

CON. Tut! I have the best armor° of the world. Would it were day!

ORL. You have an excellent armor, but let my horse have his due.

CON. It is the best horse of Europe. 5

ORL. Will it never be morning?

103. perdition: loss. 109. bubukles: large boils — a word coined by Fluellen from "bubo" and "carbuncles." whelks: pimples. 115. compelled: forced. 121. habit: garment; i.e., his herald's coat. 127. Advantage: profit; i.e., by waiting we win. 129–30. bruise . . . ripe: to burst the boil before it was ripe. 130–31. upon . . . cue: i.e., when it is the proper time. 132. admire: be astonished at. 133. sufferance: patience. 136–37. which . . . under: our injuries are so heavy that so slight a man must bend under the weight in attempting to repay them.

146. quality: profession; i.e., herald. 151. impeachment: prevention. 153. of . . . vantage: who is clever and has the advantage. 168. well . . . himself: think carefully. 170. tawny: yellow. Sc. vii: 1. armor: suit of armor.

DAU. My Lord of Orleans, and my Lord High Constable, you talk of horse and armor?

ORL. You are as well provided of both as any prince in the world.   10

DAU. What a long night is this! I will not change my horse with any that treads but on four pasterns.° Ca, ha! He bounds from the earth as if his entrails were hairs, *le cheval volant,* the Pegasus, *chez les narines de feu!*° When I bestride him, I soar, I am a hawk. He trots the air, the earth sings when he touches it, the basest horn of his hoof is more musical than the pipe of Hermes.   19

ORL. He's of the color of the nutmeg.

DAU. And of the heat of the ginger. It is a beast for Perseus. He is pure air and fire, and the dull elements of earth and water° never appear in him but only in patient stillness while his rider mounts him. He is indeed a horse, and all other jades you may call beasts.   26

CON. Indeed, my lord, it is a most absolute and excellent horse.

DAU. It is the prince of palfreys.° His neigh is like the bidding of a monarch, and his countenance enforces homage.   31

ORL. No more, Cousin.

DAU. Nay, the man hath no wit that cannot, from the rising of the lark to the lodging° of the lamb, vary deserved praise on my palfrey. It is a theme as fluent as the sea. Turn the sands into eloquent tongues and my horse is argument for them all. 'Tis a subject for a sovereign to reason on, and for a sovereign's sovereign to ride on, and for the world, familiar to us and unknown, to lay apart their   40 particular functions and wonder at him. I once writ a sonnet in his praise, and began thus: " Wonder of nature ―――― "

ORL. I have heard a sonnet begin so to one's mistress.   45

DAU. Then did they imitate that which I composed to my courser, for my horse is my mistress.

ORL. Your mistress bears well.

DAU. Me well, which is the prescript° praise and perfection of a good and particular mistress.   50

CON. Nay, for methought yesterday your mistress shrewdly shook your back.

DAU. So perhaps did yours.

CON. Mine was not bridled.

DAU. Oh, then belike she was old and gentle, and you rode like a kern° of Ireland, your French hose° off and in your strait strossers.°   57

CON. You have good judgment in horsemanship.

DAU. Be warned by me, then. They that ride so and ride not warily fall into foul bogs. I had rather have my horse to my mistress.

CON. I had as lief have my mistress a jade.

DAU. I tell thee, Constable, my mistress wears his own hair.   65

CON. I could make as true a boast as that if I had a sow to my mistress.

DAU. " *Le chien est retourné à son propre vomissement, et la truie lavée au bourbier.*"° Thou makest use of anything.   70

CON. Yet do I not use my horse for my mistress, or any such proverb so little kin to the purpose.

RAM. My Lord Constable, the armor that I saw in your tent tonight, are those stars or suns upon it?

CON. Stars, my lord.   76

DAU. Some of them will fall tomorrow, I hope.

CON. And yet my sky shall not want.

DAU. That may be, for you bear a many superfluously, and 'twere more honor some were away.   81

CON. Even as your horse bears your praises, who would trot as well were some of your brags dismounted.

DAU. Would I were able to load him with his desert! Will it never be day? I will trot tomorrow a mile, and my way shall be paved with English faces.

CON. I will not say so, for fear I should be   89 faced out of my way. But I would it were morning, for I would fain be about the ears of the English.

RAM. Who will go to hazard° with me for twenty prisoners?

CON. You must first go yourself to hazard ere you have them.   96

DAU. 'Tis midnight, I'll go arm myself.   [*Exit.*]

ORL. The Dauphin longs for morning.

RAM. He longs to eat the English.

CON. I think he will eat all he kills.   100

ORL. By the white hand of my lady, he's a gallant Prince.

CON. Swear by her foot, that she may tread out the oath.°

ORL. He is simply the most active gentleman of France.   106

CON. Doing his activity,° and he will still be doing.

ORL. He never did harm that I heard of.

CON. Nor will do none tomorrow. He will keep that good name still.   111

ORL. I know him to be valiant.

CON. I was told that by one that knows him better than you.

ORL. What's he?

---

12. **pastern:** the part of a horse's leg between hoof and fetlock. 14–15. **le . . . feu:** the flying horse, the Pegasus, with nostrils of fire. **Pegasus:** the winged horse of the Greek hero Perseus, who saved Andromache from the monster. 22–23. **air . . . water:** See App. 3. 29. **palfrey:** saddle horse. 34. **lodging:** lying down. 49. **prescript:** prescribed. 56. **kern:** Irish foot soldier. **French hose:** baggy breeches. See Pl. 8b and comment on p. 93a–b. 57. **strait strossers:** underpants.

68–69. **Le . . . bourbier:** the dog is turned to his own vomit again, and the sow that was washed to her wallowing in the mire. See II Peter 2 : 22. 92. **go to hazard:** play craps. 104. **tread . . oath:** fulfill his oath by dancing. 107. **Doing . . . activity:** i.e., playing the fool.

CON. Marry, he told me so himself, and he said he cared not who knew it.   118

ORL. He needs not. It is no hidden virtue in him.

CON. By my faith, sir, but it is. Never anybody saw it but his lackey. 'Tis a hooded valor, and when it appears, it will bate.°

ORL. Ill will never said well.

CON. I will cap that proverb with " There is flattery in friendship."   125

ORL. And I will take up that with " Give the Devil his due."

CON. Well placed. There stands your friend for the Devil. Have at the very eye of that proverb with " A pox of the Devil."   130

ORL. You are the better at proverbs, by how much " A fool's bolt° is soon shot."

CON. You have shot over.°

ORL. 'Tis not the first time you were overshot.°

[*Enter a* MESSENGER.]

MESS. My Lord High Constable, the English lie within fifteen hundred paces of your tents.   136

CON. Who hath measured the ground?

MESS. The Lord Grandpré.

CON. A valiant and most expert gentleman. Would it were day! Alas, poor Harry of England! He longs not for the dawning as we do.   141

ORL. What a wretched and peevish° fellow is this King of England, to mope with his fatbrained° followers so far out of his knowledge!°

CON. If the English had any apprehension,° they would run away.   146

ORL. That they lack, for if their heads had any intellectual armor, they could never wear such heavy headpieces.

RAM. That island of England breeds very valiant creatures. Their mastiffs° are of unmatchable courage.   152

ORL. Foolish curs, that run winking into the mouth of a Russian bear and have their heads crushed like rotten apples! You may as well say that's a valiant flea that dare eat his breakfast on the lip of a lion.   157

CON. Just, just, and the men do sympathize with the mastiffs in robustious° and rough coming-on, leaving their wits with their wives. And then give them great meals of beef, and iron and steel, they will eat like wolves, and fight like devils.   162

ORL. Aye, but these English are shrewdly out of beef.°

CON. Then shall we find tomorrow they have only stomachs to eat and none to fight. Now is it time to arm. Come, shall we about it?   167

ORL. It is now two o'clock. But let me see, by ten We shall have each a hundred Englishmen.

[*Exeunt.*]

Act IV

PROLOGUE

[*Enter* CHORUS.]

CHOR. Now entertain conjecture° of a time
When creeping murmur and the poring° dark
Fills the wide vessel of the universe.
From camp to camp through the foul womb of
        night
The hum of either army stilly° sounds,   5
That the fixed sentinels almost receive
The secret whispers of each other's watch.
Fire answers fire, and through their paly° flames
Each battle° sees the other's umbered° face.
Steed threatens steed, in high and boastful neighs
Piercing the night's dull ear. And from the tents   11
The armorers, accomplishing° the knights,
With busy hammers closing rivets up
Give dreadful note of preparation.
The country cocks do crow, the clocks do toll,   15
And the third hour of drowsy morning name.
Proud of their numbers and secure° in soul,
The confident and overlusty French
Do the low-rated° English play at dice,
And chide the cripple tardy-gaited° Night   20
Who, like a foul and ugly witch, doth limp
So tediously away. The poor condemnèd English,
Like sacrifices, by their watchful fires
Sit patiently and inly° ruminate
The morning's danger, and their gesture sad   25
Investing lank-lean cheeks and war-worn coats
Presenteth them unto the gazing moon
So many horrid ghosts. Oh, now who will behold
The royal captain of this ruined band
Walking from watch to watch, from tent to tent,   30
Let him cry " Praise and glory on his head! "
For forth he goes and visits all his host,
Bids them good morrow with a modest smile,
And calls them brothers, friends, and countrymen.

121–22. hooded . . . bate: a metaphor from hawking. See *R & J*, III.ii.14 and App. 26.   132. bolt: arrow.   133. shot over: i.e., missed the target.   134. overshot: outshot.   142. peevish: foolish.   143. fatbrained: fatheaded.   144. out . . . knowledge: in actions which he does not understand.   145. apprehension: intelligence, sense.   151. mastiffs: dogs bred particularly for baiting bears and bulls. See App. 5.   159. robustious: violent. 163–64. shrewdly . . . beef: The English were reputed to lose heart if deprived of beef. shrewdly: grievously.

Act IV. Prologue: 1. entertain conjecture: imagine.   2. poring: peering.   5. stilly: i.e., in the still night.   8. paly: pale. 9. battle: army. umbered: dark brown.   12. accomplishing: fixing on the equipment. A knight fully armored was actually riveted into his armor and could not get out of it without help. See Pl. 8a.   17. secure: careless, overconfident.   19. low-rated: valued at a low price.   20. tardy-gaited: slow-stepping.   24. inly: inwardly.

Upon his royal face there is no note   35
How dread an army hath enrounded him.
Nor doth he dedicate one jot of color
Unto the weary and all-watchèd night,
But freshly looks and overbears attaint°
With cheerful semblance and sweet majesty,   40
That every wretch, pining and pale before,
Beholding him, plucks comfort from his looks.
A largess° universal like the sun
His liberal eye doth give to every one,
Thawing cold fear, that mean and gentle° all   45
Behold, as may unworthiness define,°
A little touch° of Harry in the night.
And so our scene must to the battle fly,
Where — oh, for pity! — we shall much disgrace
With four or five most vile and ragged foils,°   50
Right ill-disposed in brawl ridiculous,
The name of Agincourt. Yet sit and see,
Minding° true things by what their mockeries° be.
                                        [Exit.]

SCENE I. *The English camp at Agincourt.*

[*Enter* KING HENRY, BEDFORD, *and* GLOUCESTER.]
    K. HEN. Gloucester, 'tis true that we are in great
        danger.
The greater therefore should our courage be.
Good morrow, Brother Bedford. God Almighty!
There is some soul of goodness in things evil,
Would men observingly° distill° it out.   5
For our bad neighbor makes us early stirrers,
Which is both healthful and good husbandry.°
Besides, they are our outward consciences,
And preachers to us all, admonishing
That we should dress us fairly for our end.   10
Thus may we gather honey from the weed,
And make a moral of° the Devil himself.
[*Enter* ERPINGHAM.] Good morrow, old Sir Thomas
        Erpingham.
A good soft pillow for that good white head
Were better than a churlish turf of France.   15
    ERP. Not so, my liege. This lodging likes° me
        better,
Since I may say "Now lie I like a king."
    K. HEN. 'Tis good for men to love their present
        pains
Upon example, so the spirit is eased.
And when the mind is quickened, out of doubt,   20

The organs, though defunct and dead before,
Break up their drowsy grave and newly move,
With casted slough° and fresh legerity.°
Lend me thy cloak, Sir Thomas. Brothers both,
Commend me to the Princes in our camp,   25
Do my good morrow to them, and anon
Desire them all to my pavilion.
    GLO. We shall, my liege.
    ERP. Shall I attend your Grace?
    K. HEN.   No, my good knight,
Go with my brothers to my lords of England.   30
I and my bosom must debate a while,
And then I would no other company.
    ERP. The Lord in Heaven bless thee, noble Harry!
                        [*Exeunt all but* KING.]
    K. HEN. God-a-mercy, old heart! Thou speak'st
        cheerfully.
                        [*Enter* PISTOL.]
    PIST. *Qui va là?*°   35
    K. HEN. A friend.
    PIST. Discuss unto me, art thou officer?
Or art thou base, common, and popular?°
    K. HEN. I am a gentleman of a company.°
    PIST. Trail'st thou the puissant° pike?°   40
    K. HEN. Even so. What are you?
    PIST. As good a gentleman as the Emperor.
    K. HEN. Then you are a better than the King.
    PIST. The King's a bawcock, and a heart of gold,
A lad of life, an imp° of fame,   45
Of parents good, of fist most valiant.
I kiss his dirty shoe, and from heartstring
I love the lovely bully. What is thy name?
    K. HEN. Harry le Roy.
    PIST. Le Roy! A Cornish name. Art thou of Cor-
        nish crew?   50
    K. HEN. No, I am a Welshman.
    PIST. Know'st thou Fluellen?
    K. HEN. Yes.
    PIST. Tell him I'll knock his leek° about his pate,
Upon Saint Davy's day.   55
    K. HEN. Do not you wear your dagger in your cap
that day, lest he knock that about yours.
    PIST. Art thou his friend?
    K. HEN. And his kinsman too.
    PIST. The figo for thee, then!   60
    K. HEN. I thank you. God be with you!
    PIST. My name is Pistol called.   [*Exit.*]
    K. HEN. It sorts well with your fierceness.
                    [*Enter* FLUELLEN *and* GOWER.]
    GOW. Captain Fluellen!   64
    FLU. So! In the name of Jesu Christ, speak lower.
It is the greatest admiration° in the universal world

---

39. overbears attaint: overcomes the stain of fear.   43. largess:
money freely given.   45. mean . . . gentle: poor men and gentle-
men.   46. as . . . define: so far as the author's poor ability can
show.   47. little touch: glimpse.   50. foils: rapiers. See *Hen V*
Intro. p. 454a.   53. Minding: bearing in mind. mockeries: poor
imitations.
    Sc. i: 5. observingly: by careful observation. distill: extract.
7. husbandry: economy.   12. make . . . of: find a moral lesson
in.   16. likes: pleases.

23. slough: skin. legerity: light spirits.   35. Qui va là: who goes
there?   38. popular: one who mixes in low company.   39. gentle-
man . . . company: gentleman volunteer. See Gen. Intro. p. 31a.
40. puissant: powerful. pike: See Pl. 21d.   45. imp: child.
54. leek: the national emblem of the Welsh.   66. admiration:
wonder.

when the true and aunchient prerogatifes° and laws of the wars is not kept. If you would take the pains but to examine the wars of Pompey the Great, you shall find, I warrant you, that there is no tiddle-   70 taddle nor pibble-pabble in Pompey's camp. I warrant you you shall find the ceremonies of the wars, and the cares of it, and the forms of it, and the sobriety of it, and the modesty of it, to be otherwise.   75

GOW. Why, the enemy is loud. You hear him all night.

FLU. If the enemy is an ass and a fool and a prating coxcomb, is it meet, think you, that we should also, look you, be an ass and a fool and a prating coxcomb? In your own conscience, now?   81

GOW. I will speak lower.

FLU. I pray you and beseech you that you will.

[*Exeunt* GOWER *and* FLUELLEN.]

K. HEN. Though it appear a little out of fashion, There is much care and valor in this Welshman.   86

[*Enter three soldiers,* JOHN BATES, ALEXANDER COURT, *and* MICHAEL WILLIAMS.]

COURT. Brother John Bates, is not that the morning which breaks yonder?

BATES. I think it be. But we have no great cause to desire the approach of day.   90

WILL. We see yonder the beginning of the day, but I think we shall never see the end of it. Who goes there?

K. HEN. A friend.

WILL. Under what captain serve you?   95

K. HEN. Under Sir Thomas Erpingham.

WILL. A good old commander and a most kind gentlemen. I pray you, what thinks he of our estate?

K. HEN. Even as men wrecked upon a sand, that look to be washed off the next tide.

BATES. He hath not told his thought to the King?

K. HEN. No, nor it is not meet° he should. For, though I speak it to you, I think the King is   105 but a man, as I am. The violet smells to him as it doth to me, the element° shows to him as it doth to me, all his senses have but human conditions. His ceremonies laid by, in his nakedness he appears but a man, and though his affections° are higher   110 mounted than ours, yet when they stoop,° they stoop with the like wing. Therefore when he sees reason of fears as we do, his fears, out of doubt, be of the same relish° as ours are. Yet, in reason, no man should possess him with any appearance of fear, lest he, by showing it, should dishearten his army.   117

BATES. He may show what outward courage he will, but I believe, as cold a night as 'tis, he could wish himself in Thames up to the neck. And so I

would he were, and I by him, at all adventures,° so we were quit° here.   122

K. HEN. By my troth, I will speak my conscience° of the King. I think he would not wish himself anywhere but where he is.

BATES. Then I would he were here alone. So should he be sure to be ransomed, and a many poor men's lives saved.   128

K. HEN. I dare say you love him not so ill, to wish him here alone, howsoever you speak this to feel other men's minds. Methinks I could not die anywhere so contented as in the King's company, his cause being just and his quarrel honorable.   134

WILL. That's more than we know.

BATES. Aye, or more than we should seek after. For we know enough if we know we are the King's subjects. If his cause be wrong, our obedience to the King wipes the crime of it out of us.   139

WILL. But if the cause be not good, the King himself hath a heavy reckoning to make when all those legs and arms and heads chopped off in a battle shall join together at the latter day and cry all "We died at such a place" — some swearing, some crying for a surgeon, some upon their wives left poor be-   145 hind them, some upon the debts they owe, some upon their children rawly° left. I am afeard there are few die well that die in a battle, for how can they charitably dispose of anything when blood is their argument? Now if these men do not die well, it will be a black matter for the King that led them to it, whom to disobey were against all proportion of subjection.°   153

K. HEN. So, if a son that is by his father sent about merchandise do sinfully miscarry° upon the sea, the imputation of his wickedness, by your rule, should be imposed upon his father that sent him. Or if a servant under his master's command transporting a sum of money be assailed by robbers and die in many irreconciled° iniquities, you may call the   160 business of the master the author of the servant's damnation. But this is not so. The King is not bound to answer the particular endings of his soldiers, the father of his son, nor the master of his servant. For they purpose not their death when they pur-   165 pose their services. Besides, there is no king, be his cause never so spotless, if it come to the arbiterment° of swords, can try it out with all unspotted soldiers. Some peradventure have on them the guilt of premeditated and contrived murder; some, of be-   170 guiling virgins with the broken seals of perjury; some, making the wars their bulwark, that have before gored the gentle bosom of peace with pillage and robbery. Now if these men have defeated the

67. prerogatifes: prerogatives, ordinances.   104. meet: fit.
107. element: sky.   110. affections: desires.   111. stoop: swoop
down.   114–15. of . . . relish: taste the same.

121. at . . . adventures: at all risks.   122. quit: rid of it.
123. conscience: innermost thought.   147. rawly: poorly provided.   152–53. proportion of subjection: proper behavior of a
subject.   155. sinfully miscarry: die in his sins.   160. irreconciled: not confessed and absolved.   167. arbiterment: decision.

law and outrun native punishment,° though 175
they can outstrip men, they have no wings to fly from
God. War is His beadle,° war is His vengeance, so
that here men are punished for before-breach of the
King's laws in now the King's quarrel. Where they
feared the death, they have borne life away, 180
and where they would be safe, they perish. Then if
they die unprovided, no more is the King guilty of
their damnation than he was before guilty of those
impieties for the which they are now visited. Every
subject's duty is the King's, but every subject's 185
soul is his own. Therefore should every soldier in the
wars do as every sick man in his bed, wash every
mote° out of his conscience. And dying so, death is
to him advantage, or not dying, the time was 190
blessedly lost wherein such preparation was gained.
And in him that escapes, it were not sin to think
that, making God so free an offer, He let him out-
live that day to see His greatness and to teach others
how they should prepare. 196

WILL. 'Tis certain every man that dies ill, the ill
upon his own head, the King is not to answer it.

BATES. I do not desire he should answer for me,
and yet I determine to fight lustily for him. 201

K. HEN. I myself heard the King say he would not
be ransomed.

WILL. Aye, he said so to make us fight cheerfully.
But when our throats are cut, he may be ransomed
and we ne'er the wiser.

K. HEN. If I live to see it, I will never trust his
word after. 208

WILL. You pay him, then. That's a perilous shot
out of an elder-gun, that a poor and a private dis-
pleasure can do against a monarch!° You may as
well go about to turn the sun to ice with fanning in
his face with a peacock's feather. You'll never trust
his word after! Come, 'tis a foolish saying. 215

K. HEN. Your reproof is something too round.° I
should be angry with you if the time were conven-
ient.

WILL. Let it be a quarrel between us if you live.

K. HEN. I embrace it. 221

WILL. How shall I know thee again?

K. HEN. Give me any gage° of thine, and I will
wear it in my bonnet. Then, if ever thou darest ac-
knowledge it, I will make it my quarrel. 225

WILL. Here's my glove. Give me another of thine.

K. HEN. There.

WILL. This will I also wear in my cap. If ever thou
come to me and say, after tomorrow, "This is my
glove," by this hand, I will take° thee a box on the
ear. 232

K. HEN. If ever I live to see it, I will challenge it.

WILL. Thou darest as well be hanged.

K. HEN. Well, I will do it, though I take thee in
the King's company. 237

WILL. Keep thy word. Fare thee well.

BATES. Be friends, you English fools, be friends.
We have French quarrels enow,° if you could tell
how to reckon. 241

K. HEN. Indeed, the French may lay twenty French
crowns to one they will beat us, for they bear them
on their shoulders. But it is no English treason to
cut French crowns, and tomorrow the King 245
himself will be a clipper.°   [Exeunt SOLDIERS.]
Upon° the King! Let us our lives, our souls,
Our debts, our careful° wives,
Our children, and our sins lay on the King!
We must bear all. Oh, hard condition, 250
Twin-born with greatness, subject to the breath
Of every fool, whose sense no more can feel
But his own wringing!° What infinite heartsease
Must kings neglect that private men enjoy!
And what have kings that privates have not too,
Save ceremony,° save general ceremony? 256
And what art thou, thou idol ceremony?
What kind of god art thou, that suffer'st more
Of mortal griefs than do thy worshipers?
What are thy rents?° What are thy comings-in?
O Ceremony, show me but thy worth! 261
What is thy soul of adoration?°
Art thou aught else but place, degree, and form,
Creating awe and fear in other men?
Wherein thou art less happy being feared 265
Than they in fearing.
What drink'st thou oft, instead of homage sweet,
But poisoned flattery? Oh, be sick, great greatness,
And bid thy ceremony give thee cure!
Think'st thou the fiery fever will go out 270
With titles blown from adulation?°
Will it give place to flexure° and low bending?
Canst thou, when thou command'st the beggar's
    knee,
Command the health of it? No, thou proud dream,
That play'st so subtly with a king's repose, 275
I am a king that find thee, and I know

240. enow: enough.   242–46. Indeed . . . clipper: The King puns
on double meanings of crown: "coin" and "head." "The French
may bet twenty to one they will beat us, for there are twenty
of them to our one; but it's no treason for an Englishman to
cut a French crown." As money at this time was stamped out
with an irregular rim, it was possible to clip pieces off. This
was a capital offense. See App. 27 and Pl. 10.   247–301. Upon
. . . advantages: This is the first time in the play that a glimpse
has been given of Henry's personal feelings. Hitherto he has
been the personification of official majesty.   248. careful: anx-
ious.   253. wringing: suffering.   256. ceremony: outward pomp,
here pronounced "seer'mony."   260. rents: profits.   262. soul
of adoration: the essential cause why you should be adored.
270–71. Think'st . . . adulation: can flattery with its empty
titles blow out the fire of a fever?   272. flexure: bending of the
knee.

175. outrun . . . punishment: escaped punishment at home.
177. beadle: the parish officer who administered punishment.
189. mote: speck.   209–11. That's . . . monarch: that's a silly
remark; what's the good of being annoyed with a king. elder-
gun: popgun.   216. round: direct.   223. gage: pledge, token.
231. take: give.

'Tis not the balm,° the scepter° and the ball,°
The sword, the mace,° the crown imperial,
The intertissued° robe of gold and pearl,
The farcèd° title running 'fore the king,   280
The throne he sits on, nor the tide of pomp
That beats upon the high shore of this world —
No, not all these, thrice-gorgeous ceremony,
Not all these, laid in bed majestical,
Can sleep so soundly as the wretched slave   285
Who with a body filled and vacant mind
Gets him to rest crammed with distressful bread,
Never sees horrid night, the child of Hell,
But, like a lackey, from the rise to set
Sweats in the eye of Phoebus° and all night   290
Sleeps in Elysium.° Next day after dawn,
Doth rise and help Hyperion° to his horse,
And follows so the ever-running year,
With profitable labor, to his grave.
And, but for ceremony, such a wretch,   295
Winding up° days with toil and nights with sleep,
Had the forehand and vantage of a king.
The slave, a member of the country's peace,°
Enjoys it, but in gross brain little wots°   299
What watch the King keeps to maintain the peace,
Whose hours the peasant best advantages.°
                  [*Re-enter* ERPINGHAM.]
ERP. My lord, your nobles, jealous of° your ab-
    sence,
Seek through your camp to find you.
    K. HEN.   Good old knight,
Collect them all together at my tent.   304
I'll be before thee.
    ERP.   I shall do 't, my lord.   [*Exit.*]
K. HEN. O God of battles, steel my soldiers'
    hearts!
Possess them not with fear, take from them now
The sense of reckoning if the opposèd numbers
Pluck their hearts from them. Not° today, O Lord,
Oh, not today, think not upon the fault   310
My father made in compassing the crown!
I Richard's body have interrèd new,
And on it have bestowed more contrite tears
Than from it issued forcèd drops of blood.
Five hundred poor I have in yearly pay,   315
Who twice a day their withered hands hold up
Toward Heaven, to pardon blood, and I have built

Two chantries° where the sad and solemn priests
Sing still° for Richard's soul. More will I do,
Though all that I can do is nothing worth,   320
Since that my penitence comes after all,
Imploring pardon.
                  [*Re-enter* GLOUCESTER.]
GLO. My liege!
K. HEN.   My brother Gloucester's voice? Aye,
I know thy errand, I will go with thee.   325
The day, my friends, and all things stay for me.
                                        [*Exeunt.*]

SCENE II. *The French camp.*

[*Enter the* DAUPHIN, ORLEANS, RAMBURES,
                and others.]
ORL. The sun doth gild our armor. Up, my lords!
DAU. *Montez à cheval!* My horse! Varlet!
    Laquais!° Ha!
ORL. O brave spirit!
DAU. *Via! Les eaux et la terre.*
ORL. *Rien puis? L'air et le feu.*   5
DAU. *Ciel,* Cousin Orleans.
                  [*Enter* CONSTABLE.]
Now, my Lord Constable!
    CON. Hark how our steeds for present° service
    neigh!
DAU. Mount them, and make incision in their
    hides,
That their hot blood may spin in English eyes   10
And dout° them with superfluous courage, ha!
RAM. What, will you have them weep our horses'
    blood?
How shall we then behold their natural tears?
                  [*Enter* MESSENGER.]
MESS. The English are embattled, you French
    peers.
CON. To horse, you gallant Princes! Straight to
    horse!   15
Do but behold yon poor and starvèd band
And your fair show shall suck away their souls,
Leaving them but the shales° and husks of men.
There is not work enough for all our hands,
Scarce blood enough in all their sickly veins   20
To give each naked curtal ax° a stain,
That our French gallants shall today draw out
And sheathe for lack of sport. Let us but blow on
    them,
The vapor of our valor will o'erturn them.
'Tis positive 'gainst all exceptions, lords,   25
That our superfluous lackeys and our peasants,

---

277. **balm:** holy oil with which a king is anointed. **scepter:** the golden rod held by a king. **ball:** a symbol of office. See Pl. 2b. 278. **mace:** a symbol of the power to strike down offenders. See Pl. 22h. 279. **intertissued:** interwoven. 280. **farced:** stuffed with pompous phrases. 290. **Phoebus:** the sun. 291. **Elysium:** Paradise. 292. **Hyperion:** the sun. 296. **Winding up:** completing. 298. **member . . . peace:** a citizen living in peace. 299. **wots:** knows. 301. **best advantages:** has the greatest advantage of; i.e., the days bring profit to the poor man but only anxiety to the King. 302. **jealous of:** suspicious — lest harm should have befallen. 309–22. **Not . . . pardon:** Henry never forgets that he and his father are usurpers on the English throne. See *II Hen IV*, IV.v.184–220.

318. **chantries:** chapels where priests sing Masses for the repose of the souls of the dead. 319. **still:** continuously.
Sc. ii: 2. **Laquais:** lackey, servant. 8. **present:** immediate. 11. **dout:** put out. 18. **shales:** shells. 21. **curtal ax:** cutlass, sword used by a horseman when the lance has been broken.

Who in unnecessary action swarm
About our squares of battle, were enow
To purge this field of such a hilding° foe,
Though we upon this mountain's basis by   30
Took stand for idle speculation.°
But that our honors must not. What's to say?
A very little little let us do,
And all is done. Then let the trumpets sound
The tucket sonance° and the note to mount,   35
For our approach shall so much dare° the field
That England shall couch down in fear and yield.

             [Enter GRANDPRÉ.]

  GRAND. Why do you stay so long, my lords of
    France?
Yon island carrions,° desperate of their bones,
Ill-favoredly° become the morning field.   40
Their ragged curtains° poorly are let loose,
And our air shakes them passing scornfully.
Big Mars seems bankrupt in their beggared host
And faintly through a rusty beaver° peeps.
The horsemen sit like fixèd candlesticks,°   45
With torch staves in their hand. And their poor
    jades
Lob down° their heads, dropping the hides and hips,
The gum down-roping° from their pale-dead eyes,
And in their pale dull mouths the gimmal° bit
Lies foul with chewed grass, still and motionless.
And their executors,° the knavish crows,   51
Fly o'er them, all impatient for their hour.
Description cannot suit itself in words
To demonstrate the life of such a battle
In life so lifeless as it shows itself.   55
  CON. They have said their prayers, and they stay
    for death.
  DAU. Shall we go send them dinners and fresh
    suits,
And give their fasting horses provender,
And after fight with them?
  CON. I stay but for my guidon.° To the field!   60
I will the banner from a trumpet take,
And use it for my haste. Come, come, away!
The sun is high, and we outwear° the day.

                  [Exeunt.]

SCENE III. *The English camp.*

[Enter GLOUCESTER, BEDFORD, EXETER, ERPINGHAM,
with all his host; SALISBURY and WESTMORELAND.]
  GLO. Where is the King?

---

29. **hilding:** worthless.   31. **speculation:** looking on.   35. **tucket
sonance:** trumpet call.   36. **dare:** dazzle, fascinate; the word
is used of catching larks.   39. **carrions:** carcasses.   40. **Ill-fa-
voredly:** leanly, uglily.   41. **curtains:** i.e., flags.   44. **beaver:** the
facepiece of the helmet. See Pl. 8a.   45. **fixed candlesticks:** like
ornamental figures on a candlestick.   47. **Lob down:** hang down.
48. **down-roping:** dangling down.   49. **gimmal:** jointed.   51. **ex-
ecutors:** i.e., those who will succeed to what is left of their bodies.
60. **guidon:** standard.   63. **outwear:** wear out, waste.

  BED. The King himself is rode to view their battle.
  WEST. Of fighting men they have full threescore
    thousand.
  EXE. There's five to one. Besides, they all are fresh.
  SAL. God's arm strike with us! 'Tis a fearful odds.
God be wi' you, Princes all. I'll to my charge.°   6
If we no more meet till we meet in Heaven,
Then, joyfully, my noble Lord of Bedford,
My dear Lord Gloucester, and my good Lord
    Exeter,
And my kind kinsman, warriors all, adieu!   10
  BED. Farewell, good Salisbury, and good luck go
    with thee!
  EXE. Farewell, kind lord. Fight valiantly today.
And yet I do thee wrong to mind° thee of it,
For thou art framed° of the firm truth of valor.

               [Exit SALISBURY.]

  BED. He is as full of valor as of kindness,   15
Princely in both.

             [Enter the KING.]

  WEST.   Oh, that we now had here
But one ten thousand of those men in England
That do no work today!
  K. HEN.   What's he that wishes so?
My cousin Westmoreland? No, my fair cousin.
If we are marked to die, we are enow   20
To do our country loss, and if to live,
The fewer men, the greater share of honor.
God's will! I pray thee wish not one man more.
By Jove, I am not covetous for gold,
Nor care I who doth feed upon° my cost.   25
It yearns° me not if men my garments wear,
Such outward things dwell not in my desires.
But if it be a sin to covet honor,
I am the most offending soul alive.
No, faith, my coz,° wish not a man from England.
God's peace! I would not lose so great an honor   31
As one man more, methinks, would share from me
For the best hope I have. Oh, do not wish one more!
Rather proclaim it, Westmoreland, through my
    host,
That he which hath no stomach to this fight,   35
Let him depart. His passport shall be made
And crowns for convoy put into his purse.
We would not die in that man's company
That fears his fellowship to die with us.°
This day is called the feast of Crispian.°   40
He that outlives this day and comes safe home
Will stand a-tiptoe when this day is named
And rouse him at the name of Crispian.
He that shall live this day and see old age
Will yearly on the vigil feast his neighbors   45

   Sc. iii: 6. charge: command.   13. **mind:** remind.   14. **framed:**
made.   25. **upon:** at.   26. **yearns:** grieves.   30. **coz:** cousin,
but used of any relation.   39. **fears . . . us:** is afraid to share
death with us.   40. **Crispian:** Crispin and Crispian were both
martyred at Soissons in A.D. 287. They became the patron saints
of shoemakers. Their day is October 25.

And say, "Tomorrow is Saint Crispian."
Then will he strip his sleeve and show his scars,
And say "These wounds I had on Crispin's Day."
Old men forget, yet all shall be forgot,
But he'll remember with advantages°   50
What feats he did that day. Then shall our names,
Familiar in his mouth as household words,
Harry the King, Bedford and Exeter,
Warwick and Talbot, Salisbury and Gloucester,
Be in their flowing cups freshly remembered.   55
This story shall the good man teach his son,
And Crispin Crispian shall ne'er go by,
From this day to the ending of the world,
But we in it shall be remembered —
We few, we happy few, we band of brothers.   60
For he today that sheds his blood with me
Shall be my brother. Be he ne'er so vile,
This day shall gentle his condition.°
And gentlemen in England now abed   64
Shall think themselves accursed they were not here,
And hold their manhoods cheap whiles any speaks
That fought with us upon Saint Crispin's Day.

        [Re-enter SALISBURY.*]*

SAL. My sovereign lord, bestow° yourself with
    speed.
The French are bravely in their battles° set,
And will with all expedience° charge on us.   70
  K. HEN. All things are ready, if our minds be so.
  WEST. Perish the man whose mind is backward
    now!
  K. HEN. Thou dost not wish more help from Eng-
    land, Coz?
  WEST. God's will! My liege, would you and I
    alone,
Without more help, could fight this royal battle!   75
  K. HEN. Why, now thou hast unwished five thou-
    sand men,
Which likes me better than to wish us one.
You know your places. God be with you all!
        [Tucket. Enter MONTJOY.*]*
  MONT. Once more I come to know of thee, King
    Harry,
If for thy ransom thou wilt now compound°   80
Before thy most assurèd overthrow.
For certainly thou art so near the gulf,°
Thou needs must be englutted.° Besides, in mercy,
The Constable desires thee thou wilt mind
Thy followers of repentance, that their souls   85
May make a peaceful and a sweet retire
From off these fields, where, wretches, their poor
    bodies
Must lie and fester.

  K. HEN.   Who hath sent thee now?
  MONT. The Constable of France.
  K. HEN. I pray thee, bear my former answer back.
Bid them achieve° me and then sell my bones.   91
Good God! Why should they mock poor fellows
    thus?
The man that once did sell the lion's skin
While the beast lived was killed with hunting him.
A many of our bodies shall no doubt   95
Find native° graves, upon the which, I trust,
Shall witness live in brass° of this day's work.
And those that leave their valiant bones in France,
Dying like men, though buried in your dunghills,
They shall be famed. For there the sun shall greet
    them   100
And draw their honors reeking° up to Heaven,
Leaving their earthly parts to choke your clime,
The smell whereof shall breed a plague in France.
Mark then abounding valor in our English,
That being dead, like to the bullet's grazing,   105
Break out into a second course of mischief,
Killing in relapse of mortality.°
Let me speak proudly. Tell the Constable
We are but warriors for the working day.°
Our gayness and our gilt are all besmirched   110
With rainy marching in the painful field.
There's not a piece of feather° in our host —
Good argument, I hope, we will not fly —
And time hath worn us into slovenry.
But, by the mass, our hearts are in the trim,   115
And my poor soldiers tell me yet ere night
They'll be in fresher robes, or they will pluck
The gay new coats o'er the French soldiers' heads
And turn them out of service.° If they do this —
As, if God please, they shall — my ransom then   120
Will soon be levied. Herald, save thou thy labor.
Come thou no more for ransom, gentle herald.
They shall have none, I swear, but these my joints,
Which if they have as I will leave 'em them,
Shall yield them little, tell the Constable.   125
  MONT. I shall, King Harry. And so fare thee well.
Thou never shalt hear herald any more.   *[Exit.]*
  K. HEN. I fear thou'lt once more come again for
    ransom.

        [Enter YORK.*]*

  YORK. My lord, most humbly on my knee I beg
The leading of the vaward.°   130

---

50. **with advantages**: i.e., the story will gain in telling.   63. **gentle . . . condition**: make him a gentleman.   68. **bestow**: move.   69. **battles**: order of battle.   70. **expedience**: haste.   80. **compound**: offer terms.   82. **gulf**: whirlpool.   83. **englutted**: swallowed.

91. **achieve**: win, kill.   96. **native**: i.e., in England.   97. **in brass**: i.e., a brass memorial tablet, of which there are many in English churches set up in the fifteenth, sixteenth, and seventeenth centuries.   101. **reeking**: rising up like mist.   107. **relapse of mortality**: deadly rebound, or renewed deadliness.   109. **working day**: in our working clothes; i.e., not much to look at.   112. **feather**: Knights and officers in Shakespeare's time used to deck their helmets with gay plumes. Henry's army is too bedraggled for any finery.   117–19. **they . . . service**: A servant on appointment was given a new livery; if dismissed, it was taken from him. See *M of Ven*, II.ii.161–64.   130. **vaward**: vanguard.

K. HEN. Take it, brave York. Now, soldiers, march
away.
And how Thou pleasest, God, dispose the day!

                                [*Exeunt.*]

SCENE IV.° *The field of battle.*

[*Alarum. Excursions. Enter* PISTOL, FRENCH SOLDIER,
and BOY.]

PIST. Yield, cur!
FR. SOL. *Je pense que vous êtes gentilhomme de
bonne qualité.*
PIST. Qualtitie calmie custure me!° Art thou a
gentleman? What is thy name? Discuss.   5
FR. SOL. *O Seigneur Dieu!*
PIST. O Signieur Dew should be a gentleman.
Perpend° my words, O Signieur Dew, and mark.
O Signieur Dew, thou diest on point of fox,°
Except, O signieur, thou do give to me   10
Egregious° ransom.
FR. SOL. *Oh, prenez miséricorde! Ayez pitié de
moi!°*
PIST. Moy shall not serve, I will have forty moys,
Or I will fetch thy rim° out at thy throat   15
In drops of crimson blood.
FR. SOL. *Est-il impossible d'échapper la force de
ton bras?*
PIST. Brass, cur!
Thou damned and luxurious° mountain goat,   20
Offer'st me brass?
FR. SOL. *Oh, pardonnez-moi!*
PIST. Say'st thou me so? Is that a ton of moys?
Come hither, boy. Ask me this slave in French
What is his name.   25
BOY. *Ecoutez. Comment êtes-vous appelé?*
FR. SOL. *Monsieur le Fer.*
BOY. He says his name is Master Fer.
PIST. Master Fer! I'll fer him, and firk° him, and
ferret° him. Discuss the same in French unto
him.
BOY. I do not know the French for fer, and ferret,
and firk.
PIST. Bid him prepare, for I will cut his throat.
FR. SOL. *Que dit-il, monsieur?*   35
BOY. *Il me commande de vous dire que vous faites
vous prêt, car ce soldat ici est disposé tout à cette
heure de couper votre gorge.*
PIST. Owy, cuppele gorge, permafoy.°

Sc. iv: As in III.iv, the French has been restored to sense by
editors. 4. Qualtitie . . . me: Pistol's attempt at a French
phrase, which has not been explained. 8. Perpend: observe.
9. fox: sword. 11. Egregious: enormous. 13. moi: pronounced
moy. 15. rim: lit., diaphragm, but Pistol is being picturesque.
20. luxurious: lustful. 29. firk: fetch. 30. ferret: worry.
39. cuppele . . . permafoy: Elizabethan soldiers who served in
France had their own versions of French phrases, of which these
are two. The "trays beans" and "mercy bowcups" of American
soldiers during World War II are comparable.

Peasant, unless thou give me crowns, brave crowns,
Or mangled shalt thou be by this my sword.   41
FR. SOL. *Oh, je vous supplie, pour l'amour de Dieu,
me pardonner! Je suis gentilhomme de bonne
maison. Gardez ma vie, et je vous donnerai deux
cents écus.*
PIST. What are his words?   46
BOY. He prays you to save his life. He is a gen-
tleman of a good house, and for his ransom he will
give you two hundred crowns.
PIST. Tell him my fury shall abate, and I   50
The crowns will take.
FR. SOL. *Petit monsieur, que dit-il?*
BOY. *Encore qu'il est contre son jurement de par-
donner aucun prisonnier; néanmoins, pour les écus
que vous l'avez promis, il est content de vous donner
la liberté, le franchisement.*   56
FR. SOL. *Sur mes genoux je vous donne mille re-
mercîmens, et je m'estime heureux que je suis tombé
entre les mains d'un chevalier, je pense, le plus brave,
vaillant, et très distingué seigneur d'Angleterre.* 61
PIST. Expound unto me, boy.
BOY. He gives you, upon his knees, a thousand
thanks, and he esteems himself happy that he hath
fallen into the hands of one, as he thinks, the most
brave, valorous, and thrice-worthy signieur of Eng-
land.
PIST. As I suck blood, I will some mercy show.
Follow me!   69
BOY. *Suivez-vous le grand capitaine.* [*Exeunt*
PISTOL, *and* FRENCH SOLDIER.] I did never know so
full a voice issue from so empty a heart. But the say-
ing is true, "The empty vessel makes the greatest
sound." Bardolph and Nym had ten times more
valor than this roaring devil i' the old play, that   75
everyone may pare his nails with a wooden dagger,°
and they are both hanged. And so would this be if
he durst steal anything adventurously. I must stay
with the lackeys, with the luggage of our camp. The
French might have a good prey of us if he knew
of it, for there is none to guard it but boys. [*Exit.*]

SCENE V. *Another part of the field.*

[*Enter* CONSTABLE, ORLEANS, BOURBON, DAUPHIN,
and RAMBURES.]

CON. *O diable!*
ORL. *O Seigneur! Le jour est perdu, tout est perdu!*
DAU. *Mort de ma vie!* All is confounded, all!
Reproach and everlasting shame
Sits mocking in our plumes. *O méchante fortune!* 5
Do not run away.   [*A short alarum.*]
CON.   Why, all our ranks are broke.

75–76. roaring . . . dagger: In the old miracle plays the Devil
was a popular character; he came in roaring and carried a wooden
sword. Cf. *T Night*, IV.ii.130–141.

DAU. Oh, perdurable° shame! Let's stab ourselves.
Be these the wretches that we played at dice for?
  ORL. Is this the King we sent to for his ransom?
  BOUR. Shame and eternal shame, nothing but
    shame!   10
Let us die in honor. Once more back again,
And he that will not follow Bourbon now,
Let him go hence, and with his cap in hand,
Like a base pander,° hold the chamber door
Whilst by a slave, no gentler than my dog,   15
His fairest daughter is contaminated.
  CON. Disorder, that hath spoiled us, friend° us
    now!
Let us on heaps go offer up our lives.
  ORL. We are enow yet living in the field
To smother up the English in our throngs,°   20
If any order might be thought upon.
  BOUR. The devil take order now! I'll to the throng.
Let life be short, else shame will be too long.
                                          [*Exeunt.*]

SCENE VI. *Another part of the field.*

[*Alarum. Enter* KING HENRY *and forces,* EXETER, *and
    others.*]

  K. HEN. Well have we done, thrice valiant coun-
    trymen.
But all's not done. Yet keep the French the field.
  EXE. The Duke of York commends him to your
    Majesty.
  K. HEN. Lives he, good Uncle? Thrice within this
    hour
I saw him down, thrice up again, and fighting.   5
From helmet to the spur all blood he was.
  EXE. In which array, brave soldier, doth he lie,
Larding° the plain, and by his bloody side,
Yokefellow to his honor-owing° wounds,
The noble Earl of Suffolk also lies.   10
Suffolk first died. And York, all haggled° over,
Comes to him, where in gore he lay insteeped,°
And takes him by the beard, kisses the gashes
That bloodily did yawn upon his face,
And cries aloud "Tarry, dear Cousin Suffolk!   15
My soul shall thine keep company to Heaven.
Tarry, sweet soul, for mine, then fly abreast,
As in this glorious and well-foughten field
We kept together in our chivalry!"
Upon these words I came and cheered him up.   20
He smiled me in the face, raught° me his hand,
And, with a feeble gripe,° says, "Dear my lord,
Commend my service to my sovereign."

So did he turn, and over Suffolk's neck
He threw his wounded arm and kissed his lips,   25
And so espoused to death, with blood he sealed
A testament° of noble-ending love.
The pretty and sweet manner of it forced
Those waters from me which I would have stopped.
But I had not so much of man in me,   30
And all my mother came into mine eyes
And gave me up to tears.
  K. HEN.   I blame you not,
For, hearing this, I must perforce compound°
With mistful eyes, or they will issue too.   [*Alarum.*]
But hark! What new alarum is this same?   35
The French have reinforced their scattered men.
Then every soldier kill his prisoners.°
Give the word through.   [*Exeunt.*]

SCENE VII. *Another part of the field.*

[*Enter* FLUELLEN *and* GOWER.]

  FLU. Kill the poys and the luggage! 'Tis expressly
against the law of arms. 'Tis as arrant a piece of
knavery, mark you now, as can be offer't. In your
conscience, now, is it not?   4
  GOW. 'Tis certain there's not a boy left alive, and
the cowardly rascals that ran from the battle ha'
done this slaughter. Besides, they have burned and
carried away all that was in the King's tent, where-
fore the King, most worthily, hath caused every
soldier to cut his prisoner's throat. Oh, 'tis a gallant
King!   11
  FLU. Aye, he was porn at Monmouth, Captain
Gower. What call you the town's name where
Alexander the Pig was born?
  GOW. Alexander the Great.   15
  FLU. Why, I pray you, is not pig great? The pig,
or the great, or the mighty, or the huge, or the
magnanimous, are all one reckonings, save the
phrase is a little variations.   19
  GOW. I think Alexander the Great was born in
Macedon. His father was called Philip of Macedon,
as I take it.
  FLU. I think it is in Macedon where Alexander is
porn. I tell you, Captain, if you look in the maps of
the 'orld, I warrant you sall find, in the com-   25
parisons between Macedon and Monmouth, that the
situations, look you, is both alike. There is a river
in Macedon, and there is also moreover a river at
Monmouth. It is called Wye at Monmouth, but it is
out of my prains what is the name of the other
river. But 'tis all one, 'tis alike as my fingers is   31
to my fingers, and there is salmons in both. If you
mark Alexander's life well, Harry of Monmouth's

Sc. v: 7. **perdurable:** enduring.   14. **pander:** one who in-
troduces the customer to a harlot.   17. **friend:** befriend.
20. **throngs:** numbers, crowd.
    Sc. vi: 8. **Larding:** making rich.   9. **honor-owing:** owning
honor, honorable.   11. **haggled:** hacked.   12. **insteeped:**
stained.   21. **raught:** reached.   22. **gripe:** grip.

27. **testament:** last will.   33. **compound:** come to terms.
37. **kill . . . prisoners:** i.e., lest the prisoners should turn on their
captors.

life is come after it indifferent° well, for there is
figures° in all things. Alexander, God knows, 35
and you know, in his rages, and his furies, and his
wraths, and his cholers, and his moods, and his dis-
pleasures, and his indignations, and also being a
little intoxicates in his prains, did, in his ales and
his angers, look you, kill his best friend, Cleitus. 41

GOW. Our King is not like him in that. He never
killed any of his friends.

FLU. It is not well done, mark you now, to take
the tales out of my mouth ere it is made and 45
finished. I speak but in the figures and comparisons
of it. As Alexander killed his friend Cleitus, being
in his ales and his cups, so also Harry Monmouth,
being in his right wits and his good judgments,
turned away the fat knight with the great-belly 50
doublet.° He was full of jests, and gipes,° and
knaveries, and mocks. I have forgot his name.

GOW. Sir John Falstaff.

FLU. That is he. I'll tell you there is good men
porn at Monmouth. 56

GOW. Here comes His Majesty.

[*Alarum. Enter* KING HENRY *and forces;* WARWICK,
GLOUCESTER, EXETER, *and others.*]

K. HEN. I was not angry since I came to France
Until this instant. Take a trumpet, herald.
Ride thou unto the horsemen on yon hill. 60
If they will fight with us, bid them come down,
Or void the field. They do offend our sight.
If they'll do neither, we will come to them,
And make them skirr° away as swift as stones
Enforcèd from the old Assyrian slings. 65
Besides, we'll cut the throats of those we have,
And not a man of them that we shall take
Shall taste our mercy. Go and tell them so.

[*Enter* MONTJOY.]

EXE. Here comes the herald of the French, my
liege. 69

GLO. His eyes are humbler than they used to be.

K. HEN. How now! What means this, herald?
Know'st thou not
That I have fined° these bones of mine for ransom?
Comest thou again for ransom?

MONT. No, great King.
I come to thee for charitable license,
That we may wander o'er this bloody field 75
To book° our dead, and then to bury them,
To sort our nobles from our common men.
For many of our Princes — woe the while! —
Lie drowned and soaked in mercenary blood.
So do our vulgar drench their peasant limbs 80
In blood of Princes, and their wounded steeds
Fret° fetlock-deep in gore, and with wild rage

Yerk° out their armèd heels at their dead masters,
Killing them twice. Oh, give us leave, great King,
To view the field in safety and dispose 85
Of their dead bodies!

K. HEN. I tell thee truly, herald,
I know not if the day be ours or no,
For yet a many of your horsemen peer°
And gallop o'er the field.

MONT. The days is yours.

K. HEN. Praisèd be God, and not our strength,
for it! 90
What is this castle called that stands hard by?

MONT. They call it Agincourt.

K. HEN. Then call we this the field of Agincourt,
Fought on the day of Crispin Crispianus.

FLU. Your grandfather of famous memory, 95
an 't please your Majesty, and your great-uncle
Edward the Plack Prince of Wales, as I have read
in the chronicles, fought a most prave pattle here
in France.

K. HEN. They did, Fluellen. 100

FLU. Your Majesty says very true. If your Majes-
ties is remembered of it, the Welshmen did good
service in a garden where leeks did grow, wearing
leeks in their Monmouth caps,° which, your
Majesty know, to this hour is an honorable badge of
the service. And I do believe your Majesty takes no
scorn to wear the leek upon Saint Tavy's Day.° 108

K. HEN. I wear it for a memorable honor,
For I am Welsh, you know, good countryman.

FLU. All the water in Wye cannot wash your
Majesty's Welsh plood out of your pody, I can tell
you that. God pless it and preserve it, as long as
it pleases His grace, and His majesty too!

K. HEN. Thanks, good my countryman. 115

FLU. By Jeshu, I am your Majesty's countryman,
I care not who know it, I will confess it to all the
'orld. I need not to be ashamed of your Majesty,
praised be God, so long as your Majesty is an honest
man. 120

K. HEN. God keep me so! Our heralds go with
him.
Bring me just° notice of the numbers dead
On both our parts. Call yonder fellow hither.

[*Points to* WILLIAMS. *Exeunt* HERALDS
with MONTJOY.]

EXE. Soldier, you must come to the King. 124

K. HEN. Soldier, why wearest thou that glove in
thy cap?

WILL. An 't please your Majesty, 'tis the gage of
one that I should fight withal, if he be alive.

K. HEN. An Englishman? 129

WILL. An 't please your Majesty, a rascal that

Sc. vii: **34. indifferent:** fairly. **35. figures:** significance.
50–51. great-belly doublet: In this form of doublet the front part
hung forward in the shape of a peapod. See Pl. 8d. **51. gipes:**
jibes. **64. skirr:** scurry. **72. fined:** reserved as a fine.
76. book: make a list of. **82. Fret:** plunge wildly.

83. Yerk: kick. **88. peer:** appear. **102–04. Welshmen . . .
caps:** This incident is otherwise unrecorded, nor is the origin
known of the Welsh custom of wearing leeks on St. David's Day.
108. Saint Tavy's Day: March 1. *Tavy* (David) was the patron
saint of Wales. **122. just:** exact.

swaggered with me last night, who, if alive and ever dare to challenge this glove, I have sworn to take him a box o' th' ear. Or if I can see my glove in his cap, which he swore as he was a soldier he would wear if alive, I will strike it out soundly.   136

K. HEN. What think you, Captain Fluellen? Is it fit this soldier keep his oath?

FLU. He is a craven and a villain else, an 't please your Majesty, in my conscience.   140

K. HEN. It may be his enemy is a gentleman of great sort, quite from the answer of his degree.°

FLU. Though he be as good a gentleman as the Devil is, as Lucifer and Belzebub himself, it is necessary, look your Grace, that he keep his vow and his oath. If he be perjured, see you now, his reputation is as arrant a villain and a Jacksauce° as ever his black shoe trod upon God's ground and his earth, in my conscience, la!   150

K. HEN. Then keep thy vow, sirrah, when thou meetest the fellow.

WILL. So I will, my liege, as I live.

K. HEN. Who servest thou under?

WILL. Under Captain Gower, my liege.   155

FLU. Gower is a good captain, and is good knowledge and literatured in the wars.

K. HEN. Call him hither to me, soldier.   158

WILL. I will, my liege.   [Exit.]

K. HEN. Here, Fluellen, wear thou this favor for me and stick it in thy cap. When Alençon and myself were down together,° I plucked this glove from his helm. If any man challenge this, he is a friend to Alençon and an enemy to our person. If thou encounter any such, apprehend him, an thou dost me love.   166

FLU. Your Grace doo's me as great honors as can be desired in the hearts of his subjects. I would fain see the man that has but two legs that shall find himself aggriefed at this glove, that is all, but I would fain see it once, an 't please God of His grace that I might see.   172

K. HEN. Knowest thou Gower?

FLU. He is my dear friend, an 't please you.

K. HEN. Pray thee, go seek him, and bring him to my tent.

FLU. I will fetch him.   [Exit.]

K. HEN. My Lord of Warwick, and my brother Gloucester,
Follow Fluellen closely at the heels.
The glove which I have given him for a favor   180
May haply purchase him a box o' th' ear.

It is the soldier's. I by bargain should
Wear it myself. Follow, good Cousin Warwick.
If that the soldier strike him, as I judge
By his blunt bearing he will keep his word,   185
Some sudden mischief may arise of it.
For I do know Fluellen valiant
And, touched with choler,° hot as gunpowder,
And quickly will return an injury.   189
Follow, and see there be no harm between them.
Go you with me, Uncle of Exeter.   [Exeunt.]

SCENE VIII. *Before* KING HENRY'S *pavilion.*

[*Enter* GOWER *and* WILLIAMS.]

WILL. I warrant it is to knight you, Captain.
[*Enter* FLUELLEN.]

FLU. God's will and His pleasure, Captain, I beseech you now, come apace° to the King. There is more good toward you peradventure than is in your knowledge to dream of.   5

WILL. Sir, know you this glove?

FLU. Know the glove! I know the glove is a glove.

WILL. I know this, and thus I challenge it.
[*Strikes him.*]

FLU. 'Sblood!° An arrant traitor as any is in the universal world, or in France, or in England!   11

GOW. How now, sir! You villain!

WILL. Do you think I'll be forsworn?°

FLU. Stand away, Captain Gower. I will give treason his payment into plows, I warrant you.   15

WILL. I am no traitor.

FLU. That's a lie in thy throat.° I charge you in His Majesty's name, apprehend him. He's a friend of the Duke Alençon's.   19
[*Enter* WARWICK *and* GLOUCESTER.]

WAR. How now, how now! What's the matter?

FLU. My Lord of Warwick, here is — praised be God for it! — a most contagious treason come to light, look you, as you shall desire in a summer's day. Here is His Majesty.
[*Enter* KING HENRY *and* EXETER.]

K. HEN. How now! What's the matter?   25

FLU. My liege, here is a villain and a traitor that, look your Grace, has struck the glove which your Majesty is take out of the helmet of Alençon.

WILL. My liege, this was my glove, here is the fellow of it. And he that I gave it to in change° promised to wear it in his cap. I promised to strike him if he did. I met this man with my glove in his cap, and I have been as good as my word.   34

FLU. Your Majesty hear now, saving your Maj-

142. quite . . . degree: far above his rank and therefore not required to answer.   148. Jacksauce: saucy knave. 161–62. Alençon . . . together: Holinshed records: "The King that day showed himself a valiant knight, albeit almost felled by the Duke of Alençon; yet with plain strength he slew two of the Duke's company, and felled the Duke himself, whom, when he would have yielded, the King's Guard, contrary to his mind, slew out of hand."

188. choler: temper.
    Sc. viii: 3. apace: quickly.   10. 'Sblood: by God's blood. 13. be forsworn: break my oath.   17. lie . . . throat: the most deadly insult, which could only be repaid by mortal combat. 31. change: exchange.

esty's manhood, what an arrant, rascally, beggarly, lousy knave it is. I hope your Majesty is pear me testimony and witness, and will avouchment,° that this is the glove of Alençon that your Majesty is give me. In your conscience, now.

K. HEN. Give me thy glove, soldier. Look, here is the fellow of it. 42
'Twas I, indeed, thou promised'st to strike,
And thou hast given me most bitter terms.°

FLU. An 't° please your Majesty, let his neck answer for it, if there is any martial law in the world.

K. HEN. How canst thou make me satisfaction?

WILL. All offenses, my lord, come from the heart. Never came any from mine that might offend your Majesty. 51

K. HEN. It was ourself thou didst abuse.

WILL. Your Majesty came not like yourself. You appeared to me but as a common man — witness the night, your garments, your lowliness. And 55 what your Highness suffered under that shape, I beseech you to take it for your own fault and not mine. For had you been as I took you for, I made no offense. Therefore I beseech your Highness pardon me. 60

K. HEN. Here, Uncle Exeter, fill this glove with crowns
And give it to this fellow. Keep it, fellow,
And wear it for an honor in thy cap
Till I do challenge it. Give him the crowns. 65
And, Captain, you must needs be friends with him.

FLU. By this day and this light, the fellow has mettle enough in his belly. Hold, there is twelvepence for you, and I pray you to serve God, and keep you out of prawls, and prabbles,° and quarrels, and dissensions, and I warrant you it is the better for you.

WILL. I will none of your money. 72

FLU. It is with a good will, I can tell you, it will serve you to mend your shoes. Come, wherefore should you be so pashful? Your shoes is not so good. 'Tis a good silling, I warrant you, or I will change it.

[*Enter an* ENGLISH HERALD.]

K. HEN. Now, herald, are the dead numbered?

HER. Here is the number of the slaughtered French.

K. HEN. What prisoners of good sort° are taken, Uncle? 80

EXE. Charles° Duke of Orleans, nephew to the King,
John Duke of Bourbon, and Lord Bouciqualt.
Of other lords and barons, knights and squires,
Full fifteen hundred, besides common men.

K. HEN. This note doth tell me of ten thousand French 85

That in the field lie slain. Of Princes in this number,
And nobles bearing banners,° there lie dead
One hundred twenty-six. Added to these,
Of knights, esquires, and gallant gentlemen,
Eight thousand and four hundred, of the which 90
Five hundred were but yesterday dubbed knights.
So that in these ten thousand they have lost
There are but sixteen hundred mercenaries.
The rest are Princes, barons, lords, knights, squires,
And gentlemen of blood and quality. 95
The names of those their nobles that lie dead:
Charles Delabreth, High Constable of France,
Jaques of Chatillon, Admiral of France,
The master of the crossbows, Lord Rambures,
Great Master of France, the brave Sir Guichard
    Dolphin, 100
John Duke of Alençon, Anthony Duke of Brabant,
The brother to the Duke of Burgundy,
And Edward Duke of Bar. Of lusty earls,
Grandpré and Roussi, Fauconberg and Foix, 104
Beaumont and Marle, Vaudemont and Lestrale.
Here was a royal fellowship° of death!
Where is the number of our English dead?

[HERALD *shows him another paper.*]

Edward the Duke of York, the Earl of Suffolk,
Sir Richard Ketly, Davy Gam, esquire.
None else of name, and of all other men 110
But five and twenty.° O God, Thy arm was here,
And not to us, but to Thy name alone,
Ascribe we all! When, without stratagem,
But in plain shock and even play of battle,
Was ever known so great and little loss 115
On one part and on th' other? Take it, God,
For it is none but Thine!

EXE.   'Tis wonderful!

K. HEN. Come, go we in procession to the village.
And be it death proclaimed through our host
To boast of this or take that praise from God 120
Which is His only.

FLU. Is it not lawful, an 't please your Majesty, to tell how many is killed?

K. HEN. Yes, Captain, but with this acknowledgment,
That God fought for us. 125

FLU. Yes, my conscience, He did us great good.

K. HEN. Do we all holy rites.
Let there be sung "*Non nobis*" and "*Te Deum*,"
The dead with charity enclosed in clay.
And then to Calais, and to England then, 130
Where ne'er from France arrived more happy men.

[*Exeunt.*]

---

38. avouchment: certify.   44. bitter terms: insults.   45. An 't: if it.   70. prabbles: brabbles, quarrels.   80. sort: rank. 81–111. Charles . . . twenty: This casualty list is taken directly from Holinshed.

87. bearing banners: i.e., displaying their coats of arms. 106. fellowship: partnership. 111. But . . . twenty: The English losses, though not so low as given by Shakespeare, have been variously estimated from 100 to 600 killed. The French lost over 10,000 killed through their insane tactics of charging in full armor through boggy ground against archers protected by a palisade of sharpened stakes.

Act V

PROLOGUE

[*Enter* CHORUS.]

CHOR. Vouchsafe to those that have not read the
story
That I may prompt them. And of such as have,
I humbly pray them to admit the excuse
Of time, of numbers, and due course of things
Which cannot in their huge and proper life   5
Be here presented. Now we bear the King
Toward Calais. Grant him there. There seen,
Heave him away upon your wingèd thoughts
Athwart the sea. Behold, the English beach
Pales in° the flood with men, with wives and boys,
Whose shouts and claps outvoice the deep-mouthed
sea,   11
Which like a mighty whiffler° 'fore the King
Seems to prepare his way. So let him land,
And solemnly see him set on to London.
So swift a pace hath thought that even now   15
You may imagine him upon Blackheath,°
Where that his lords desire him to have borne
His bruisèd helmet and his bended sword
Before him through the city. He forbids it,
Being free from vainness and self-glorious pride,
Giving full trophy,° signal,° and ostent°   21
Quite from himself to God. But now behold,
In the quick forge and working house° of thought,
How London doth pour out her citizens!
The mayor and all his brethren in best sort,°   25
Like to the Senators of the antique Rome,
With the plebeians swarming at their heels,
Go forth and fetch their conquering Caesar in.°
As, by a lower but loving likelihood,°
Were° now the General of our gracious Empress,
As in good time he may, from Ireland coming,   31
Bringing rebellion broachèd° on his sword,
How many would the peaceful city quit,
To welcome him! Much more, and much more
cause,
Did they this Harry. Now in London place him.
As yet the lamentation of the French   36
Invites the King of England's stay at home.
The Emperor's° coming in behalf of France,
To order peace between them. And omit
All the occurrences, whatever chanced,   40
Till Harry's back return again to France.
There must we bring him, and myself have played
The interim,° by remembering° you 'tis past.   43
Then brook abridgment,° and your eyes advance,
After your thoughts, straight back again to France.

[*Exit.*]

SCENE I. *France. The English camp.*

[*Enter* FLUELLEN *and* GOWER.]

GOW. Nay, that's right, but why wear you your
leek today? Saint Davy's Day is past.
FLU. There is occasions and causes why and
wherefore in all things. I will tell you, asse my
friend, Captain Gower. The rascally, scald,°   5
beggarly, lousy, pragging knave Pistol, which you
and yourself and all the world know to be no petter
than a fellow, look you now, of no merits, he is
come to me and prings me pread and salt yesterday,
look you, and bid me eat my leek. It was in a   10
place where I could not breed no contention° with
him, but I will be so bold as to wear it in my cap till
I see him once again, and then I will tell him a little
piece of my desires.

[*Enter* PISTOL.]

GOW. Why, here he comes, swelling like a turkey
cock.   16
FLU. 'Tis no matter for his swellings nor his
turkeycocks. God pless you, Aunchient Pistol! You
scurvy, lousy knave, God pless you.
PIST. Ha! Art thou bedlam?° Dost thou thirst,
base Trojan,°   20
To have me fold up Parca's fatal web?°
Hence! I am qualmish° at the smell of leek.
FLU. I peseech you heartily, scurvy, lousy knave,
at my desires, and my requests, and my petitions,
to eat, look you, this leek. Because, look you,   25
you do not love it, nor your affections and your
appetites and your digestions doo's not agree with
it, I would desire you to eat it.
PIST. Not for Cadwallader° and all his goats.
FLU. There is one goat for you. [*Strikes him.*]
Will you be so good, scald knave, as eat it?   31
PIST. Base Trojan, thou shalt die.
FLU. You say very true, scald knave, when God's
will is. I will desire you to live in the meantime, and
eat your victuals. Come, there is sauce for it.
[*Strikes him.*] You called me yesterday mountain

Act V. Prologue: 10. Pales in: encircles.   **12. whiffler:** an
officer who makes way for a royal procession.   **16. Blackheath:**
district south of London.   **21. trophy:** lit., pile of arms of the
defeated set up in triumph. **signal:** sign. **ostent:** display.
23. working house: workshop.   **25. in . . . sort:** in their best
clothes.   **27–28. With . . . in:** This incident forms the first two
scenes of *Julius Caesar*, which was first staged a few weeks after
the first performance of *Henry V*.   **29. loving likelihood:** much-
desired probability.   **30–34. Were . . . him:** See *Hen V* Intro.
p. 452a.   **32. broached:** stuck as on a spit, impaled.   **38. Em-
peror:** i.e., Sigismund, who came over to England in 1416 to
negotiate between Henry and the French King.

42–43. myself . . . interim: i.e., I have related all that is supposed
to have happened between Acts IV and V.   **43. remembering:**
reminding.   **44. brook abridgment:** endure the omission.
   Sc. i: 5. scald: scaly, scabby.   **11. breed no contention:** start
a quarrel.   **20. bedlam:** lunatic. **Trojan:** in Pistol's romantic
imagination a term of abuse.   **21. fold . . . web:** cut short the
thread of your fate (*Parca*).   **22. am qualmish:** feel sick.
29. Cadwallader: a Welsh Prince.

squire,° but I will make you today a squire of low
degree.° I pray you fall to. If you can mock a leek,
you can eat a leek.   39

GOW. Enough, Captain. You have astonished
him.

FLU. I say I will make him eat some part of my
leek or I will peat his pate four days. Bite, I pray
you. It is good for your green wound and your
ploody coxcomb.   45

PIST. Must I bite?

FLU. Yes, certainly, and out of doubt and out of
question too, and ambiguities.

PIST. By this leek, I will most horribly revenge.
I eat and eat, I swear ——   50

FLU. Eat, I pray you. Will you have some more
sauce to your leek? There is not enough leek to
swear by.

PIST. Quiet thy cudgel. Thou dost see I eat.   54

FLU. Much good do you, scald knave, heartily.
Nay, pray you throw none away, the skin is good
for your broken coxcomb. When you take occasions
to see leeks hereafter, I pray you mock at 'em. That
is all.

PIST. Good.   60

FLU. Aye, leeks is good. Hold you, there is a
groat° to heal your pate.

PIST. Me a groat!

FLU. Yes, verily and in truth you shall take it, or
I have another leek in my pocket which you shall
eat.   66

PIST. I take thy groat in earnest° of revenge.

FLU. If I owe you anything, I will pay you in
cudgels. You shall be a woodmonger,° and buy
nothing of me but cudgels. God b' wi' you, and   70
keep you, and heal your pate.   [Exit.]

PIST. All Hell shall stir for this.

GOW. Go, go. You are a counterfeit cowardly
knave. Will you mock at an ancient tradition, begun
upon an honorable respect and worn as a memora-
ble trophy of predeceased° valor, and dare not   75
avouch° in your deeds any of your words? I have
seen you gleeking° and galling° at this gentleman
twice or thrice. You thought because he could not
speak English in the native garb° he could not   80
therefore handle an English cudgel. You find it
otherwise, and henceforth let a Welsh correction
teach you a good English condition. Fare ye well.

[Exit.]

PIST. Doth Fortune play the huswife° with me
now?   85

News have I that my Doll° is dead i' the spital
Of malady of France,°
And there my rendezvous is quite cut off.
Old I do wax, and from my weary limbs
Honor is cudgeled. Well, bawd° I'll turn,   90
And something lean to cutpurse of quick hand.°
To England will I steal, and there I'll steal.
And patches will I get unto these cudgeled scars,
And swear I got them in the Gallia wars.   [Exit.]

SCENE II. France. A royal palace.

[Enter, at one door, KING HENRY, EXETER, BEDFORD,
GLOUCESTER, WARWICK, WESTMORELAND, and other
LORDS; at another, the FRENCH KING,° QUEEN ISABEL,
the PRINCESS KATHARINE, ALICE and other LADIES; the
DUKE OF BURGUNDY, and his train.]

K. HEN. Peace to this meeting, wherefore we are
met!
Unto our brother France, and to our sister,
Health and fair time of day. Joy and good wishes
To our most fair and princely cousin Katharine.
And, as a branch and member of this royalty°   5
By whom this great assembly is contrived,°
We do salute you, Duke of Burgundy.
And, Princes French, and peers, health to you all!

FR. KING. Right joyous are we to behold your face,
Most worthy Brother England, fairly met.   10
So are you, Princes English, every one.

Q. ISA. So happy be the issue, Brother England,
Of this good day and of this gracious meeting
As we are now glad to behold your eyes —
Your eyes, which hitherto have borne in them   15
Against the French, that met them in their bent,
The fatal balls of murdering basilisks.°
The venom of such looks, we fairly hope,
Have lost their quality, and that this day
Shall change all griefs and quarrels into love.   20

K. HEN. To cry amen to that, thus we appear.

Q. ISA. You English Princes all, I do salute you.

BUR. My duty to you both, on equal love,
Great Kings of France and England! That I have
labored,
With all my wits, my pains and strong endeavors,

86. Doll: She was called Nell in II.i.33, and many texts are
amended accordingly. It is possible that Shakespeare forgot that
Pistol had married the quondam Mrs. Quickly and not Doll
Tearsheet, who was last heard of as being treated in the hospital
(II.i.78-81). "Doll," however, is commonly used for any woman
of easy virtue.   87. malady of France: venereal disease.
90. bawd: brothel-keeper.   91. cutpurse . . . hand: See W Tale,
IV.iv.682-87, and Gen. Intro. p. 28a.
Sc. ii: s.d., French King: Actually the French King was in-
sane at this time and the Duke of Burgundy acted for him.
5. royalty: royal family.   6. contrived: arranged.   17. balls . . .
basilisks: a double pun, balls being eyeballs and cannon balls,
and basilisk large cannon and a fierce kind of serpent capable
of killing by its very look.

36-37. mountain squire: i.e., poor Welshman.   37-38. squire
. . . degree: as contrasted with a mountain squire. The Squire
of Low Degree was a popular romance.   62. groat: fourpence.
67. in earnest: as payment on account.   69. woodmonger:
dealer in wood.   75. predeceased: long since dead.   76. avouch:
certify.   77. gleeking: mocking. galling: annoying.   80. garb:
garment, fashion.   85. huswife: hussy.

To bring your most imperial Majesties   26
Unto this bar° and royal interview,
Your Mightiness on both parts best can witness.
Since then my office hath so far prevailed
That, face to face and royal eye to eye,   30
You have congreeted,° let it not disgrace me
If I demand, before this royal view,
What rub° or what impediment there is
Why that the naked, poor, and mangled Peace,
Dear nurse of arts, plenties, and joyful births,   35
Should not in this best garden of the world,
Our fertile France, put up her lovely visage?°
Alas, she hath from France too long been chased,
And all her husbandry° doth lie on heaps,
Corrupting in it° own fertility.   40
Her vine, the merry cheerer of the heart,
Unprunèd dies. Her hedges even-pleached,°
Like prisoners wildly overgrown with hair,
Put forth disordered twigs. Her fallow leas°
The darnel, hemlock, and rank fumitory°   45
Doth root upon while that the colter° rusts
That should deracinate° such savagery.
The even mead,° that erst brought sweetly forth
The freckled cowslip, burnet,° and green clover,
Wanting the scythe, all uncorrected, rank,   50
Conceives by idleness, and nothing teems
But hateful docks, rough thistles, kecksies,° burrs,
Losing both beauty and utility.
And as our vineyards, fallows, meads, and hedges,
Defective in their natures, grow to wildness,   55
Even so our houses and ourselves and children
Have lost, or do not learn for want of time,
The sciences that should become our country,
But grow like savages — as soldiers will
That nothing do but meditate on blood —   60
To swearing and stern looks, diffused° attire,
And everything that seems unnatural.
Which to reduce into our former favor
You are assembled. And my speech entreats
That I may know the let° why gentle Peace   65
Should not expel these inconveniences
And bless us with her former qualities.

K. HEN. If, Duke of Burgundy, you would the
      peace,
Whose want gives growth to the imperfections
Which you have cited, you must buy that peace   70
With full accord to all our just demands,
Whose tenors° and particular effects
You have enscheduled° briefly in your hands.

BUR. The King hath heard them, to the which as
      yet
There is no answer made.
K. HEN.   Well then, the peace,   75
Which you before so urged, lies in his answer.
FR. KING. I have but with a cursorary° eye
O'erglanced the articles. Pleaseth your Grace
To appoint some of your Council presently
To sit with us once more, with better heed   80
To resurvey them, we will suddenly
Pass our accept° and peremptory° answer.
K. HEN. Brother, we shall. Go, Uncle Exeter,
And Brother Clarence, and you, Brother Gloucester,
Warwick and Huntingdon, go with the King.   85
And take with you free power to ratify,
Augment, or alter, as your wisdoms best
Shall see advantageable for our dignity,
Anything in or out of our demands,
And we'll consign° thereto. Will you, fair Sister,   90
Go with the Princes, or stay here with us?
Q. ISA. Our gracious brother, I will go with them.
Haply a woman's voice may do some good
When articles too nicely° urged be stood on.
K. HEN. Yet leave our cousin Katharine here with
      us.   95
She is our capital° demand, comprised
Within the forerank of our articles.
Q. ISA. She hath good leave.

[*Exeunt all except* HENRY, KATHARINE, *and* ALICE.]

K. HEN.   Fair Katharine, and most fair,
Will you vouchsafe to teach a soldier terms°
Such as will enter at a lady's ear   100
And plead his love suit to her gentle heart?
KATH. Your Majesty shall mock at me. I cannot
speak your England.
K. HEN. O fair Katharine, if you will love me
soundly with your French heart, I will be glad to
hear you confess it brokenly with your English
tongue. Do you like me, Kate?   107
KATH. *Pardonnez-moi,* I cannot tell vat is " like
me."
K. HEN. An angel is like you, Kate, and you are
like an angel.   111
KATH. *Que dit-il? Que je suis semblable à les
anges?*
ALICE. *Oui, vraiment, sauf votre grace, ainsi dit-il.*
K. HEN. I said so, dear Katharine, and I must not
blush to affirm it.   117
KATH. *O bon Dieu! Les langues des hommes sont
pleines de tromperies.*
K. HEN. What says she, fair one? That the tongues
of men are full of deceits?
ALICE. Oui, dat de tongues of de mans is be full of
deceits. Dat is de Princess.   123

---

27. bar: court.   **31.** congreeted: met harmoniously.   **33.** rub: obstruction. See App. 13.   **37.** put . . . visage: raise her fair face. **39.** husbandry: agriculture.   **40.** it: its.   **42.** even-pleached: thick and even.   **44.** leas: open land.   **45.** darnel . . . fumitory: European weeds which grow in plowed fields.   **46.** colter: blade of the plowshare.   **47.** deracinate: uproot.   **48.** even mead: level meadow.   **49.** burnet: a weed with a brown flower.   **52.** docks . . . kecksies: weeds that grow in neglected meadows.   **61.** diffused: slovenly.   **65.** let: hindrance.   **72.** tenors: general intention.   **73.** enscheduled: listed.

77. cursorary: cursory, casual.   **82.** accept: acceptance. **peremptory**: final.   **90.** consign: agree.   **94.** nicely: precisely. **96.** capital: chief.   **99.** terms: phrases.

K. HEN. The Princess is the better Englishwoman. I' faith, Kate, my wooing is fit for thy understanding. I am glad thou canst speak no better English, for if thou couldst, thou wouldst find me such a plain king that thou wouldst think I had sold my farm to buy my crown. I know no ways to mince it° in love, but directly to say "I love you." 130 Then if you urge me farther than to say "Do you in faith?" I wear out my suit.° Give me your answer, i' faith, do. And so clap° hands and a bargain. How say you, lady? 135

KATH. Sauf votre honneur, me understand vell.

K. HEN. Marry, if you would put me to verses or to dance for your sake, Kate, why, you undid me. For the one, I have neither words nor measure,° and for the other, I have no strength in measure, 140 yet a reasonable measure in strength. If I could win a lady at leapfrog, or by vaulting into my saddle with my armor on my back, under the correction of° bragging be it spoken, I should quickly leap into a wife. Or if I might buffet for my love, or 145 bound° my horse for her favors, I could lay on like a butcher and sit like a jackanapes,° never off. But, before God, Kate, I cannot look greenly° nor gasp out my eloquence, nor I have no cunning in protestation — only downright oaths, which I never 150 use till urged, nor never break for urging. If thou canst love a fellow of this temper, Kate, whose face is not worth sunburning, that never looks in his glass for love of anything he sees there, let thine eye be thy cook.° I speak to thee plain soldier. If 155 thou canst love me for this, take me; if not, to say to thee that I shall die is true, but for thy love, by the Lord, no. Yet I love thee too. And while thou livest, dear Kate, take a fellow of plain and uncoined constancy,° for he perforce must do thee right, 160 because he hath not the gift to woo in other places. For these fellows of infinite tongue that can rhyme themselves into ladies' favors, they do always reason themselves out again. What! A speaker is but 165 a prater, a rhyme is but a ballad.° A good leg will fall, a straight back will stoop, a black beard will turn white, a curled pate will grow bald, a fair face will wither, a full eye will wax hollow. But a good heart, Kate, is the sun and the moon — or 170 rather the sun and not the moon, for it shines bright and never changes, but keeps his course truly. If thou would have such a one, take me. And take me, take a soldier. Take a soldier, take a king. And what

sayest thou then to my love? Speak, my fair, and fairly, I pray thee. 177

KATH. Is it possible dat I sould love de enemy of France?

K. HEN. No, it is not possible you should love the enemy of France, Kate. But in loving me you should love the friend of France, for I love France so well that I will not part with a village of it, I will have it all mine. And, Kate, when France is mine and I am yours, then yours is France and you are mine. 186

KATH. I cannot tell vat is dat.

K. HEN. No, Kate? I will tell thee in French, which I am sure will hang upon my tongue like a new-married wife about her husband's neck, 190 hardly to be shook off. Je quand sur le possession de France, et quand vous avez le possession de moi — let me see, what then? Saint Denis° ·be my speed! — donc votre est France et vous êtes mienne. It is as easy for me, Kate, to conquer the kingdom as 195 to speak so much more French. I shall never move thee in French, unless it be to laugh at me.

KATH. Sauf votre honneur, le Français que vous parlez, il est meilleur que l'Anglais lequel je parle.

K. HEN. No, faith, is 't not, Kate. But thy 202 speaking of my tongue, and I thine, most truly-falsely, must needs be granted to be much at one. But, Kate, dost thou understand thus much English — canst thou love me?

KATH. I cannot tell. 207

K. HEN. Can any of your neighbors tell, Kate? I'll ask them. Come, I know thou lovest me. And at night, when you come into your closet, you'll 210 question this gentlewoman about me. And I know, Kate, you will to her dispraise those parts in me that you love with your heart. But, good Kate, mock me mercifully, the rather, gentle Princess, because I love thee cruelly. If ever thou beest mine, Kate, as 215 I have a saving faith within me tells me thou shalt, I get thee with scambling,° and thou must therefore needs prove a good soldier-breeder. Shall not thou and I, between Saint Denis and Saint George, 220 compound a boy, half French, half English, that shall go to Constantinople and take the Turk by the beard?° Shall we not? What sayest thou, my fair flower-de-luce?°

KATH. I do not know dat. 225

K. HEN. No, 'tis hereafter to know, but now to promise. Do but now promise, Kate, you will endeavor for your French part of such a boy, and for my English moiety° take the word of a king and a bachelor. How answer you, la plus belle Katharine du monde, mon très cher et divine déesse? 232

129–30. mince it: talk in a fancy way.   132. wear . . . suit: i.e., go dumb, with a pun on the double meaning of suit — "petition" and "clothes."   134. clap: clasp.   139–41. measure . . . measure: meter . . . dancing . . . amount.   143. under . . . of: with apologies for.   146. bound: make prance.   147. jackanapes: monkey. See App. 5.   148. greenly: like an inexperienced youth. 154–55. let . . . cook: i.e., convert my plainness into something fancy and delectable.   159–60. uncoined constancy: genuine loyalty.   166. ballad: i.e., doggerel. See App. 8.

193. Saint Denis: patron saint of France.   217. scambling: scuffling.   222–23. Constantinople . . . beard: i.e., do romantic and heroic deeds. Actually the boy was Henry VI, a saintly innocent.   224. flower-de-luce: fleur-de-lis, wild iris, the emblem of the French kings.   230. moiety: share.

KATH. Your majestee ave *fausse* French enough to deceive de most *sage demoiselle* dat is *en France*.

K. HEN. Now, fie upon my false French! By mine honor, in true English, I love thee, Kate. By which honor I dare not swear thou lovest me, yet my blood begins to flatter me that thou dost, notwithstanding the poor and untempering° effect of my visage. 240 Now, beshrew° my father's ambition! He was thinking of civil wars when he got° me. Therefore was I created with a stubborn outside, with an aspect of iron, that when I come to woo ladies, I fright 245 them. But, in faith, Kate, the elder I wax, the better I shall appear. My comfort is that old age, that ill layer-up of beauty, can do no more spoil upon my face. Thou hast me, if thou hast me, at the worst, and thou shalt wear me, if thou wear me, bet- 250 ter and better. And therefore tell me, most fair Katharine, will you have me? Put off your maiden blushes, avouch the thoughts of your heart with the looks of an empress. Take me by the hand, and say "Harry of England, I am thine." Which word 255 thou shalt no sooner bless mine ear withal but I will tell thee aloud "England is thine, Ireland is thine, France is thine, and Henry Plantagenet is thine"— who, though I speak it before his face, if he be not fellow with the best king, thou shalt find the 260 best king of good fellows. Come, your answer in broken music,° for thy voice is music and thy English broken. Therefore, queen of all, Katharine, break thy mind to me in broken English — wilt thou have me? 266

KATH. Dat is as it sall please de *roi mon père*.

K. HEN. Nay, it will please him well, Kate, it shall please him, Kate.

KATH. Den it sall also content me. 270

K. HEN. Upon that I kiss your hand, and I call you my Queen.

KATH. *Laissez, mon seigneur, laissez, laissez. Ma foi, je ne veux point que vous abaissez votre grandeur en baisant la main d'une de votre seigneurie indigne serviteur. Excusez-moi, je vous supplie, mon très-puissant seigneur.* 277

K. HEN. Then I will kiss your lips, Kate.

KATH. *Les dames et demoiselles pour être baisées devant leur noces, il n'est pas la coutume de France.* 282

K. HEN. Madam my interpreter, what says she?

ALICE. Dat it is not be de fashion pour les ladies of France, — I cannot tell vat is *baiser* en Anglish.

K. HEN. To kiss. 287

ALICE. Your Majesty *entendre* bettre *que moi*.

K. HEN. It is not a fashion for the maids in France to kiss before they are married, would she say? 291

ALICE. *Oui, vraiment.*

K. HEN. O Kate, nice customs courtesy° to great kings. Dear Kate, you and I cannot be confined within the weak list° of a country's fashion. 295 We are the makers of manners, Kate, and the liberty that follows our places stops the mouth of all find-faults — as I will do yours, for upholding the nice° fashion of your country in denying me a kiss. Therefore, patiently and yielding. [*Kissing her*] You 300 have witchcraft in your lips, Kate. There is more eloquence in a sugar touch of them than in the tongues of the French Council, and they should sooner persuade Harry of England than a general petition of monarchs. Here comes your father. 306

[*Re-enter the* FRENCH KING *and his* QUEEN, BURGUNDY, *and other* LORDS.]

BUR. God save your Majesty! My royal cousin, teach you our Princess English?

K. HEN. I would have her learn, my fair cousin, how perfectly I love her, and that is good English.

BUR. Is she not apt? 312

K. HEN. Our tongue is rough, Coz, and my condition° is not smooth. So that, having neither the voice nor the heart of flattery about me, I cannot so conjure up the spirit of love in her that he will appear in his true likeness. 317

BUR. Pardon the frankness of my mirth if I answer you for that. If you would conjure in her, you must make a circle; if conjure up love in her in his true likeness, he must appear naked and blind. Can you blame her, then, being a maid yet rosed over with the virgin crimson of modesty, if she deny the appearance of a naked blind boy in her naked seeing self? It were, my lord, a hard condition for a maid to consign to. 326

K. HEN. Yet they do wink and yield, as love is blind and enforces.

BUR. They are then excused, my lord, when they see not what they do.

K. HEN. Then, good my lord, teach your cousin to consent winking. 332

BUR. I will wink on her to consent, my lord, if you will teach her to know my meaning. For maids well summered and warm kept are like flies at Bartholomewtide,° blind, though they have their eyes. And then they will endure handling, which before would not abide looking on. 338

K. HEN. This moral° ties me over to time and a hot summer, and so I shall catch the fly, your cousin, in the latter end, and she must be blind too.

BUR. As love is, my lord, before it loves. 342

K. HEN. It is so. And you may, some of you, thank love for my blindness, who cannot see many a fair

---

240. untempering: which cannot soften.   241. beshrew: plague on. 242. got: begot. 262. broken music: lit., music arranged for parts.

293. courtesy: bow.   295. list: boundary.   298. nice: prim. 314. condition: nature.   335–36. flies at Bartholomewtide: i.e., flies which grow torpid in late summer. St. Bartholomew's Day is August 24. 339. moral: symbol.

French city for one fair French maid that stands in
my way.

FR. KING. Yes, my lord, you see them perspec-
tively,° the cities turned into a maid, for they are
all girdled with maiden walls that war hath never
entered.   350

K. HEN. Shall Kate be my wife?

FR. KING. So please you.

K. HEN. I am content, so° the maiden cities you
talk of may wait on her. So the maid that stood in
the way for my wish shall show me the way to my
will.°   356

FR. KING. We have consented to all terms of rea-
son.

K. HEN. Is 't so, my lords of England?

WEST. The King hath granted every article.
His daughter first, and then in sequel all,
According to their firm proposèd natures.   362

EXE. Only he hath not yet subscribed this:
Where your Majesty demands that the King of
France, having any occasion to write for matter of
grant,° shall name your Highness in this form and
with this addition, in French, *Notre très-cher fils
Henri, Roi d'Angleterre, Héritier de France;* and
thus in Latin, *Praeclarissimus filius noster Henricus,
Rex Angliae, et Haeres Franciae.*   370

FR. KING. Nor this I have not, Brother, so denied,
But your request shall make me let it pass.

K. HEN. I pray you, then, in love and dear alli-
ance,
Let that one article rank with the rest,
And thereupon give me your daughter.   375

FR. KING. Take her, fair son, and from her blood
raise up
Issue to me, that the contending kingdoms
Of France and England, whose very shores look pale
With envy of each other's happiness,   379
May cease their hatred, and this dear conjunction°
Plant neighborhood and Christianlike accord
In their sweet bosoms, that never war advance
His bleeding sword 'twixt England and fair France.

ALL. Amen!

K. HEN. Now welcome, Kate. And bear me wit-
ness all,   385

That here I kiss her as my sovereign Queen.

                              [Flourish.]

Q. ISA. God, the best maker of all marriages,
Combine your hearts in one, your realms in one!
As man and wife, being two, are one in love,
So be there 'twixt your kingdoms such a spousal°
That never may ill office, or fell° jealousy,   391
Which troubles oft the bed of blessèd marriage,
Thrust in between the paction° of these kingdoms
To make divorce of their incorporate league —
That English may as French, French Englishmen,
Receive each other. God speak this Amen!   396

ALL. Amen!

K. HEN. Prepare we for our marriage. On which
day,
My Lord of Burgundy, we'll take your oath,
And all the peers', for surety° of our leagues.   400
Then shall I swear to Kate, and you to me.
And may our oaths well kept and prosperous be!

                        [Sennet. Exeunt.]

EPILOGUE

[Enter CHORUS.*]*

CHOR. Thus far, with rough and all-unable pen,
  Our bending° author hath pursued the story,
In little room confining mighty men,
  Mangling by starts° the full course of their glory.
Small time, but in that small most greatly lived   5
  This star of England. Fortune made his sword,
By which the world's best garden he achieved,°
  And of it left his son imperial lord.
Henry the Sixth, in infant bands° crowned King
  Of France and England, did this King succeed,
Whose state so many had the managing   11
  That they lost France and made his England
    bleed.
Which oft our stage hath shown,° and, for their sake
In your fair minds let this acceptance take.°   *[Exit.]*

390. **spousal:** marriage.   391. **fell:** fierce.   393. **paction:** agree-
ment.   400. **surety:** ratification.
 Epilogue: 2. **bending:** bowing.   4. **Mangling by starts:** mar-
ring the story by telling it in fragments.   7. **achieved:** won.
9. **infant bands:** swaddling clothes. **bands:** bonds.   13. **oft** . . .
shown, i.e., in the three parts of *Henry VI*.   14. **let** . . . **take:**
receive this.

348. **perspectively:** as through a "perspective" — a glass which
makes images distorted.   353. **so:** so long as.   356. **will:**
desire.   365–66. **to** . . . **grant:** i.e., in formal documents.
380. **conjunction:** union.

AS YOU LIKE IT

Introduction

As You Like It was first published in the first folio in 1623. The text is well printed and there are few misprints or difficulties of reading. The play was certainly written before August 1600, because there is a note in the Stationers' Register dated August 4, 1600, that *As You Like It* with three other plays was to be "staied," i.e., not printed (see Gen. Intro. pp. 65b–66a). Other evidence suggests that it was written after June 1599. Celia remarks (I.ii.94), ". . . since the little wit that fools have was silenced, the little foolery that wise men have makes a great show." This is probably a topical reference to the order of the Privy Council issued in June 1599, that certain of the more notorious books of satires should be collected and burned.

Jaques's famous speech on the seven ages of man beginning (II.vii.139),

> All the world's a stage
> And all the men and women merely players

was probably inspired by the motto of the new Globe Theater — *Totus mundus agit histrionem* (the whole world plays the actor). The Globe playhouse was completed and first occupied in the summer of 1599. There is also a direct quotation from Marlowe's *Hero and Leander* in the second of the lines (III.v.81):

> Dead shepherd, now I find thy saw of might —
> Whoever loved that loved not at first sight?

Hero and Leander was left unfinished at Marlowe's death on May 31, 1593. It was first published in 1598.

Shakespeare took the story of *As You Like It* from a novel called *Rosalynde* written by Thomas Lodge during a voyage to the Canaries and first published in 1590. *Rosalynde* was the most popular and one of the best of the pastoral romantic tales which were the fashion in the early 1590's. By 1598 the book was in its fourth edition. The story was thus likely to be well known to many in the original audience. Shakespeare followed his source fairly closely, though he added some characters of his own and changed most of the names. In *Rosalynde* the usurping Duke is called Torismond and the banished Duke

Gerismond; the hero is Rosader (Orlando) and the wicked brother Saladyne (Oliver); the two girls are Rosalynde and Alinda (Celia); the faithful servant is Adam Spencer, Phebe's swain is called Montanus (Sylvius), and the old shepherd Coridon (Corin).

Rosalynde was written in the elaborate leisurely style popularized by Lyly in *Euphues*. Indeed, to attract the reader Lodge gave his book the subtitle *Euphues' Golden Legacy. Found after his death in his cell at Silexedra. Bequeathed to Philautus's sons, nursed up with their father in England.* The outline of Lodge's tale runs as follows:

Old Sir John of Bordeaux lay dying. On his deathbed he bestowed legacies and much advice on his three sons Saladyne, the eldest, Fernandine, and Rosader, his youngest and favorite. As soon as his father was dead Saladyne began to meditate how he might rob his brothers, so he sent Fernandine away to study and made Rosader his footboy. As Rosader grew up he began to resent this treatment:

". . . why should I, that am a gentleman born, pass my time in such unnatural drudgery? Were it not better either in Paris to become a scholar, or in the Court a courtier, or in the field a soldier, than to live a footboy to my own brother? Nature hath lent me wit to conceive, but my brother denied me art to contemplate. I have strength to perform any honorable exploit, but no liberty to accomplish my virtuous endeavors. Those good parts that God hath bestowed upon me the envy of my brother doth smother in obscurity, the harder is my fortune, and the more his frowardness." (Cf. *AYLI*, I.i.1–26.)

At this moment Saladyne and his servants appeared and the brothers began to quarrel. Rosader seized a garden rake, dispersed the servants, and chased Saladyne into a loft. Saladyne promised redress, but learning that Torismond (who had banished the rightful king, Gerismond, and had usurped the throne of France) was holding a tournament at which a Norman wrestler was to challenge all comers, he persuaded Rosader to fight the wrestler and secretly bribed the wrestler to kill Rosader. So the latter appeared at the tournament, and there he began to cast eyes at Rosalynde, daughter of the banished King, as well he might,

". . . for upon her cheeks there seemed a battle between the graces, who should bestow most favors to make her excellent. The blush that gloried Luna when she kissed the shepherd on the hills of Latmos was not tainted with such a pleasant dye as the vermilion flourished on the silver hue of Rosalynde's countenance. Her eyes were like those lamps that make the wealthy covert of the heavens more gorgeous, sparkling favor and disdain, courteous and yet coy, as if in them Venus had placed all her amorets, and Diana all her chastity. The trammels of her hair, folded in a caul of gold, so far surpassed the burnished glister of the metal as the sun doth the meanest star in brightness. The tresses that folds in the brows of Apollo were not half so rich to the sight, for in her hairs it seemed Love had laid herself in ambush, to entrap the proudest eye that durst gaze upon their excellence. What should I need to decipher her particular beauties, when by the censure of all she was the paragon of all earthly perfection?"

Rosalynde was likewise attracted by Rosader and gave him such a loving look that he threw the wrestler and broke his neck. So Rosader, accompanied by a number of young gentlemen, returned home in triumph, to the surprise and disgust of Saladyne.

Soon afterward Torismond determined to banish Rosalynde in spite of the protests of her dear friend and cousin Alinda. So the two cousins decided to run away, though Alinda was fearful because there would be no man in their company. Rosalynde therefore disguised herself as a page and changed her name to Ganymede, Alinda changed hers to Aliena, and off they set. After a long journey they reached the Forest of Arden and there they came upon some verses which had been carved on the bark of a tree by a lovesick shepherd called Montanus. On they went, and by and by they encountered an old shepherd called Coridon. Aliena asked Coridon where they could find shelter, and he replied that his landlord was ready to sell both farm and stock. So Aliena agreed to buy the farm and to retain Coridon as her overseer.

Meanwhile Saladyne was again plotting to kill Rosader. Very early one morning with some of his servants he entered his brother's chamber, bound him, and chained him to a post in the hall, where he remained for three days without food, until Adam Spencer, a faithful old servant of Sir John, secretly released him. Rosader, however, pretended still to be bound until Saladyne and his guests were at dinner, when he ran among them with a poleax and put them to flight. Thereupon Saladyne and the survivors complained to the sheriff, who came to take Rosader. But Rosader and Adam broke through the sheriff's party and escaped to the Forest of Arden. The hard journey was almost too much for old Adam, who lay down ready to die. So Rosader went forth to seek food, and by chance lighted on the exiled King Gerismond, who with his outlaws was dining at a long table under the shade of some lemon trees. Rosader challenged any of the company to fight with him, but Gerismond courteously invited him to share the meal. Then Rosader went to fetch Adam, and as soon as he had revealed his name he was eagerly welcomed by the banished King.

Meanwhile Rosalynde in her disguise as Ganymede had encountered Rosader (who did not recognize the pretty youth) and learned of certain verses which he had made in honor of his love. So Ganymede pretended to rail at all women, but when she was alone she grew very sorry for herself. Next day the two girls again encountered Rosader, whose talk was still of the excellencies of his Rosalynde. Ganymede, to persuade him to stay longer, pretended to be Rosalynde and encouraged Rosader to woo her, and finally to carry the pretense still further Aliena said:

"'I'll play the priest. From this day forth Ganymede shall call thee husband, and thou shall call Ganymede wife, and so we'll have a marriage.'

"'Content,' quoth Rosader, and laughed.

"'Content,' quoth Ganymede, and changed as red as a rose. And so with a smile and a blush, they made up this jesting match, that after proved to a marriage in earnest, Rosader full little thinking he had wooed and won his Rosalynde."

In the meantime Torismond had begun to covet Saladyne's wealth, and first put him in prison, then banished him from the land. So Saladyne too made his way to the Forest of Arden, where in great weariness he lay down and fell asleep. While he was thus senseless a hungry lion came upon him and waited for him to move. At this moment Rosader passed by. He recognized his unkind brother, and after a struggle in his own mind whether or not he should leave him to his fate, he suddenly charged the lion with his boar spear and slew it. Saladyne woke up but at first did not recognize Rosader. When he realized how nobly Rosader had behaved, he begged his forgiveness and the two brothers were reconciled. Rosader thereupon took Saladyne and presented him to Gerismond.

All this while Rosader had neglected Ganymede, but by and by he returned to visit the two girls. As he was talking to Aliena certain rascals who prowled in the forest thought to kidnap her and carry her off to her father. Rosader fought valiantly, but was sorely wounded; Saladyne, attracted by the struggle, came to his rescue and together they drove off the enemy. As a result Aliena fell violently in love with Saladyne and he with her. Soon after this Coridon took the two girls to watch the behavior of Phoebe, the disdainful shepherdess loved by Montanus. Phoebe treated her swain with such bitter words that Ganymede started out from her hiding place and rebuked her hotly; but Phoebe was so greatly stirred by the beauty of Ganymede that she immediately fell in love. Saladyne now declared his love for Aliena and asked her to marry him:

"At the word 'marriage' Aliena stood in a maze what to answer, fearing that if she were too coy, to drive him away with her disdain, and if she were too courteous, to discover the heat of her desires."

So Aliena consented and Ganymede sent Saladyne to find Rosader.

Phoebe by this time was so much in love with Ganymede that she was almost dead. She therefore wrote Ganymede a letter, which she sent by Montanus. When Ganymede received the letter, she fell into a great laughter, but she went with Montanus to see Phoebe, and there she made Phoebe promise that if she could be persuaded to cease loving Ganymede she would marry Montanus, to which Phoebe agreed.

Then the preparations for the wedding of Saladyne and Aliena went forward with great joy. By and by Montanus came in dressed like a forsaken lover, and when King Gerismond heard his tale he sent for Phoebe and asked her why she was so disdainful of Montanus' love. She replied that she was in love with Ganymede. Gerismond then sent for Ganymede, whose face somehow reminded him of his daughter Rosalynde, but when he mentioned Rosalynde's name Rosader sighed deeply and told Gerismond that he loved her. Gerismond replied that if Rosalynde were there, he would give her to Rosader for his wife, at which Aliena was so amused that she could hardly keep countenance. Then Ganymede answered:

"'If I should affect the fair Phoebe, I should offer poor Montanus great wrong to win that from him in a moment that he hath labored for so many months. Yet have I promised to the beautiful shepherdess to wed myself never to woman except unto her — but with this promise, that if I can by reason suppress Phoebe's love toward me, she shall like of none but of Montanus.'

"'To that,' quoth Phoebe, 'I stand, for my love is so far beyond reason as will admit no persuasion of reason.'

"'For justice,' quoth he, 'I appeal to Gerismond.'

"'And to his censure will I stand,' quoth Phoebe.

"'And in your victory,' quoth Montanus, 'stands the hazard of my fortunes. For if Ganymede go away with conquest, Montanus is in conceit love's monarch. If Phoebe win, then am I in effect most miserable.'

"'We will see this controversy,' quoth Gerismond, 'and then we will to church. Therefore, Ganymede, let us hear your argument.'

"'Nay, pardon my absence a while,' quoth she, 'and you shall see one in store.'

"In went Ganymede and dressed herself in woman's attire, having on a gown of green, with kirtle of rich sendal, so quaint that she seemed Diana triumphing in the forest. Upon her head she wore a chaplet of roses, which gave her such a grace that she looked like Flora perked in the pride of all her flowers. Thus attired came Rosalynde in, and presented herself at her father's feet, with her eyes full of tears, craving **his** blessing and discoursing unto him all her fortunes, how she was banished by Torismond, and how ever since she lived in that country disguised."

So the weddings of all three pairs of lovers were celebrated, but hardly had they sat down to dinner when suddenly Fernandine (the second son of old Sir John) appeared in the forest and desired to speak with them. He told them that Torismond was approaching with an army to give battle with the twelve peers of France who had taken up arms to restore Gerismond to his kingdom. So Gerismond rose up, and Saladyne and Rosader seized their weapons, and thus leaving their brides they went off to do battle. Torismond's army was put to flight and he himself slain. Then Gerismond, the true King, returned to Paris, where he was received with great joy, and there he sent for Alinda and Rosalynde. He created Rosader heir to his kingdom, restored Saladyne to his lands, and suitably promoted the others.

Such was the story which Shakespeare turned into his comedy. He followed Lodge very closely for the major incidents, compressing a little and making some minor alterations. In the play, for instance, Orlando (Rosader) is wounded by the lioness and not by the kidnappers. *Rosalynde,* though a lighthearted tale, was for the most part seriously written; Shakespeare's *As You Like It* is full of little touches of parody and satire. And he added much of his own — in particular the genial Touchstone, fool by profession, cynic philosopher by nature; William and the underwashed Audrey, two real yokels to contrast with the pretty ladies and gentlemen playing at being foresters and shepherdesses; and above all Jaques, the melancholy intellectual.

When Shakespeare wrote this play, the vogue for satire was at its height, and Jonson's *Every Man in His Humor* (see Gen. Intro. p. 42a–b) was the success of the season with the Chamberlain's Men. It is therefore hardly likely that in 1599 Shakespeare could have seriously intended *As You Like It* to be nothing more than an old-fashioned pastoral romance. Moreover, though the play was far from being a comedy of humors, yet Shakespeare was to some extent influenced by the new fashion of elaborately depicting realistic characters. Indeed for the next few years his manner of writing plays changed. Hitherto he had balanced plot and character. Henceforward he was more interested in character, and he tended to pick out one or two persons in a play and to show their characters from every angle by bringing them into contact with a variety of persons and situations.

Jaques is the first notable example of this change. He exists simply as a study of character for its own sake. He has no essential part in the plot — indeed *As You Like It* could be acted without him — but he is nevertheless the most interesting and vivid of all the company in the Forest of Arden. We see more of him than of any of the other characters. He is not even allowed to appear until his entrance has been carefully prepared by an account of his moods and his moralizings. He is given the best speeches, even the speech on the seven ages of man. He is Shakespeare's picture — the first of several — of the melancholic humor (see App. 4.), but it is a special kind of melancholy " compounded of many simples, extracted from many objects, and indeed the sundry contemplation of my travels, in which my often rumination wraps me in a most humorous sadness."

As You Like It is also to some extent a satire on the pastoral ideals and conventions. The forest lovers behave according to their kind. Orlando woos his Rosalind in verses; but they are very poor verses, a very false gallop of verse. Ganymede (alias Rosalind) is moved momentarily to self-pity at the sorrows of the lovelorn Silvius; but Touchstone mocks her with his account of how he wooed Jane Smile and how he kissed her batlet and the cow's dugs that her pretty chapped hands had milked. Old Corin grows eloquent about the joys of the shepherd's life; but Touchstone overwhelms him with his courtly wit. The exiled courtiers hymn the pure joys of life under the greenwood tree; but Jaques caps their verses with some of his own —

> Here shall he see
> Gross fools as he,
> An if he will come to me.

But there is no need to take *As You Like It* too seriously. It is a lighthearted comedy which appeals to readers at all stages and in all lighter moods. It pleases some by its idyllic romance, others by its optimistic philosophy of simple goodness, and yet others by its cynical irony. Indeed, you can take this play just as you like it.

As You Like It

DRAMATIS PERSONAE

DUKE, *living in banishment*
FREDERICK, *his brother, and usurper of his dominions*
AMIENS ⎫
JAQUES ⎬ *lords attending on the banished Duke*
LE BEAU, *a courtier attending upon Frederick*
CHARLES, *wrestler to Frederick*
OLIVER ⎫
JAQUES ⎬ *sons of Sir Rowland de Boys*
ORLANDO ⎭
ADAM ⎫
DENNIS ⎬ *servants to Oliver*
TOUCHSTONE, *a clown*
SIR OLIVER MARTEXT, *a vicar*

CORIN ⎫
SILVIUS ⎬ *shepherds*
WILLIAM, *a country fellow, in love with Audrey*
A person representing Hymen

ROSALIND, *daughter to the banished Duke*
CELIA, *daughter to Frederick*
PHEBE, *a shepherdess*
AUDREY, *a country wench*

LORDS, PAGES, *and* ATTENDANTS, &c.

SCENE — *Oliver's house; Duke Frederick's court; and the Forest of Arden.*

Act I

SCENE I. *Orchard of* OLIVER'S *house.*

[*Enter* ORLANDO *and* ADAM.]

ORL. As I remember it, Adam, it was upon this fashion: Bequeathed° me by will but poor a° thousand crowns, and, as thou sayest, charged my brother, on his blessing,° to breed° me well — and there begins my sadness. My brother Jaques he 5 keeps at school, and report speaks goldenly of his profit; for my part, he keeps me rustically at home, or, to speak more properly, stays me° here at home unkept. For call you that keeping for a gentleman of my birth that differs not from the stalling of 10 an ox? His horses are bred better, for besides that they are fair with their feeding, they are taught their manage,° and to that end riders dearly° hired. But I, his brother, gain nothing under him but growth, for the which his animals on his dunghills are 15 as much bound to° him as I. Besides this nothing that he so plentifully gives me, the something that nature gave me his countenance seems to take from me.° He lets me feed with his hinds,° bars me° the place of a brother, and, as much as in him lies, 20 mines my gentility with my education.° This is it,

Adam, that grieves me, and the spirit of my father, which I think is within me, begins to mutiny against this servitude. I will no longer endure it, though yet I know no wise remedy how to avoid it.   26
ADAM. Yonder comes my master, your brother.
ORL. Go apart, Adam, and thou shalt hear how he will shake me up.°   30
[*Enter* OLIVER.]
OLI. Now, sir! What make you here?
ORL. Nothing. I am not taught to make anything.
OLI. What mar you then, sir?
ORL. Marry,° sir, I am helping you to mar that which God made, a poor unworthy brother of yours, with idleness.
OLI. Marry, sir, be better employed, and be naught awhile.°   39
ORL. Shall I keep your hogs and eat husks with them? What prodigal portion° have I spent that I should come to such penury?
OLI. Know you where you are, sir?
ORL. Oh, sir, very well, here in your orchard.
OLI. Know you before whom, sir?   45
ORL. Aye, better than him I am before knows me. I know you are my eldest brother, and, in the gentle condition of blood, you should so know me.° The courtesy of nations° allows you my better, in that you are the firstborn. But the same tradition 50 takes not away my blood, were there twenty brothers betwixt us. I have as much of my father in me as

you, albeit I confess your coming before me is nearer to his reverence.°

OLI. What, boy!°   55

ORL. Come, come, elder brother, you are too young in this.

OLI. Wilt thou lay hands on me, villain?

ORL. I am no villain. I am the youngest son of Sir Rowland de Boys; he was my father, and he is   60 thrice a villain that says such a father begot villains. Wert thou not my brother, I would not take this hand from thy throat till this other had pulled out thy tongue for saying so. Thou hast railed on° thyself.   65

ADAM. Sweet masters, be patient. For your father's remembrance, be at accord.

OLI. Let me go, I say.

ORL. I will not, till I please. You shall hear me. My father charged you in his will to give me   70 good education. You have trained me like a peasant, obscuring and hiding from me all gentlemanlike qualities. The spirit of my father grows strong in me, and I will no longer endure it. Therefore allow me such exercises° as may become a gentleman,   75 or give me the poor allottery° my father left me by testament. With that I will go buy my fortunes.

OLI. And what wilt thou do? Beg, when that is spent? Well, sir, get you in. I will not long be troubled with you, you shall have some part of your will.° I pray you leave me.   82

ORL. I will no further offend you than becomes me for my good.

OLI. Get you with him, you old dog.

ADAM. Is "old dog" my reward? Most true, I have lost my teeth in your service. God be with   88 my old master! He would not have spoke such a word.   [Exeunt ORLANDO and ADAM.]

OLI. Is it even so? Begin you to grow upon° me? I will physic your rankness,° and yet give no thousand crowns neither. Holla, Dennis!

[Enter DENNIS.]

DEN. Calls your Worship?

OLI. Was not Charles, the Duke's wrestler, here to speak with me?   95

DEN. So please you, he is here at the door and importunes access° to you.

OLI. Call him in. [Exit DENNIS.] 'Twill be a good way, and tomorrow the wrestling is.

[Enter CHARLES.]

CHA. Good morrow to your Worship.   100

OLI. Good Monsieur Charles, what's the new news at the new Court?

CHA. There's no news at the Court, sir, but the old news; that is, the old Duke is banished by his younger brother the new Duke, and three or   105 four loving lords have put themselves into voluntary exile with him, whose lands and revenues enrich the new Duke; therefore he gives them good leave to wander.

OLI. Can you tell if Rosalind, the Duke's daughter, be banished with her father?   111

CHA. Oh no, for the Duke's daughter, her cousin, so loves her, being ever from their cradles bred together, that she would have followed her exile or have died to stay behind her. She is at the Court and no less beloved of her uncle than his own daughter, and never two ladies loved as they do.

OLI. Where will the old Duke live?   119

CHA. They say he is already in the Forest of Arden,° and a many merry men with him, and there they live like the old Robin Hood° of England. They say many young gentlemen flock to him every day, and fleet° the time carelessly,° as they did in the golden world.°   125

OLI. What, you wrestle tomorrow before the new Duke?

CHA. Marry do I, sir, and I came to acquaint you with a matter. I am given, sir, secretly to understand that your younger brother, Orlando, hath a   130 disposition to come in disguised against me to try a fall.° Tomorrow, sir, I wrestle for my credit, and he that escapes me without some broken limb shall acquit° him well. Your brother is but young and tender, and, for your love, I would be loath to   135 foil° him, as I must for my own honor if he come in. Therefore, out of my love to you, I came hither to acquaint you withal, that either you might stay him from his intendment or brook° such disgrace well as he shall run into, in that it is a thing of his own search, and altogether against my will.   142

OLI. Charles, I thank thee for thy love to me, which thou shalt find I will most kindly requite. I had myself notice of my brother's purpose herein, and have by underhand means labored to dissuade him from it, but he is resolute. I'll tell thee, Charles — it is the stubbornest young fellow of France, full of ambition, an envious emulator° of every man's good parts, a secret and villainous contriver°   150 against me his natural brother. Therefore use thy discretion. I had as lief thou didst break his neck as his finger. And thou wert best look to 't, for if thou

53–54. is . . . reverence: gives you a greater claim to be highly regarded as he was.   55. What, boy: Here Oliver strikes Orlando. 64. railed on: abused.   75. exercises: training.   76. allottery: portion.   81–82. your will: your legacy, and what you desire. 91. grow upon: become troublesome to.   92. physic . . . rankness: cure your excess of blood. Rankness was a medical term for a condition requiring the letting of blood. See Caesar, III.i.152. 97. importunes access: asks for permission to see you on an urgent matter.

121. Arden: the Ardennes, in Belgium.   122. Robin Hood: the famous English outlaw of legend and ballad.   124. fleet: spend. carelessly: without a care.   125. golden world: the mythical good old days, before men learned to be wicked.   132. fall: i.e., in wrestling.   134. acquit: distinguish; lit., get a favorable verdict.   136. foil: overthrow.   140. brook: endure.   149. envious emulator: jealous hater.   150. contriver: plotter.

dost him any slight disgrace, or if he do not might-
ily grace himself on thee,° he will practice°   155
against thee by poison, entrap thee by some treacher-
ous device, and never leave thee till he hath ta'en thy
life by some indirect means or other. For I assure
thee, and almost with tears I speak it, there is not
one so young and so villainous this day living. I
speak but brotherly of him, but should I anatomize°
him to thee as he is, I must blush and weep, and
thou must look pale and wonder.   164

CHA. I am heartily glad I came hither to you. If
he come tomorrow, I'll give him his payment. If
ever he go alone° again, I'll never wrestle for prize
more. And so, God keep your Worship!   168

OLI. Farewell, good Charles. [*Exit* CHARLES.]
Now will I stir this gamester. I hope I shall see an
end of him, for my soul, yet I know not why, hates
nothing more than he. Yet he's gentle,° never
schooled, and yet learned, full of noble device,° of
all sorts enchantingly beloved, and indeed so much
in the heart of the world, and especially of my   175
own people, who best know him, that I am alto-
gether misprized.° But it shall not be so long, this
wrestler shall clear all. Nothing remains but that I
kindle° the boy thither, which now I'll go   179
about.   [*Exit.*]

SCENE II. *Lawn before the* DUKE's *palace.*

[*Enter* ROSALIND *and* CELIA.]

CEL. I pray thee, Rosalind, sweet my coz,° be
merry.

ROS. Dear Celia, I show more mirth than I am
mistress of, and would you yet I were merrier? Un-
less you could teach me to forget a banished   5
father, you must not learn° me how to remember
any extraordinary pleasure.

CEL. Herein I see thou lovest me not with the full
weight that I love thee. If my uncle, thy banished
father, had banished thy uncle, the Duke my   10
father, so thou hadst been still with me I could have
taught my love to take thy father for mine. So
wouldst thou if the truth of thy love to me were so
righteously tempered° as mine is to thee.   15

ROS. Well, I will forget the condition of my estate,
to rejoice in yours.

CEL. You know my father hath no child but I,
nor none is like to have. And truly, when he dies,
thou shalt be his heir, for what he hath taken away
from thy father perforce, I will render thee again in

affection. By mine honor, I will, and when I break
that oath, let me turn monster. Therefore, my sweet
Rose, my dear Rose, be merry.   25

ROS. From henceforth I will, Coz, and devise
sports. Let me see, what think you of falling in love?

CEL. Marry, I prithee do, to make sport withal.
But love no man in good earnest, nor no further in
sport neither than with safety of a pure blush thou
mayst in honor come off again.   32

ROS. What shall be our sport, then?

CEL. Let us sit and mock the good housewife For-
tune from her wheel,° that her gifts may henceforth
be bestowed equally.

ROS. I would we could do so, for her benefits are
mightily misplaced, and the bountiful blind woman
doth most mistake in her gifts to women.   39

CEL. 'Tis true, for those that she makes fair she
scarce° makes honest,° and those that she makes
honest she makes very ill-favoredly.°

ROS. Nay, now thou goest from Fortune's office to
Nature's. Fortune reigns in gifts of the world, not in
the lineaments° of Nature.   45

[*Enter* TOUCHSTONE.]

CEL. No? When Nature hath made a fair crea-
ture, may she not by Fortune fall into the fire?
Though Nature hath given us wit to flout° at For-
tune, hath not Fortune sent in this fool to cut off the
argument?   50

ROS. Indeed, there is Fortune too hard for Nature,
when Fortune makes Nature's natural° the cutter-
off of Nature's wit.

CEL. Peradventure this is not Fortune's work
neither, but Nature's, who perceiveth our natural
wits too dull to reason of such goddesses, and   55
hath sent this natural for our whetstone; for always
the dullness of the fool is the whetstone of the wits.
How now, wit! Whither wander you?°

TOUCH. Mistress, you must come away to your
father.   61

CEL. Were you made the messenger?

TOUCH. No, by mine honor, but I was bid to come
for you.

ROS. Where learned you that oath, fool?   65

TOUCH. Of a certain knight that swore by his
honor they were good pancakes, and swore by his
honor the mustard was naught.° Now I'll stand to
it the pancakes were naught and the mustard was
good, and yet was not the knight forsworn.°   71

---

155. grace . . . thee: distinguish himself at your expense. prac-
tice: plot.   162. anatomize: dissect, analyze.   167. alone: i.e.,
without support.   172. gentle: a natural gentleman.   173. noble
device: noble thoughts.   177. misprized: considered worthless,
despised.   179. kindle: incite.

Sc. ii: 1. coz: cousin.   6. learn: teach.   15. tempered: com-
pounded.

35. Fortune . . . wheel: Fortune was personified as a blind woman
spinning men's fortunes at a spinning wheel. For Fluellen's
learned discourse on this symbolism, see *Hen V*, III.vi.31–40.
See also App. 18.   41. scarce: seldom. honest: chaste.   42. ill-
favoredly: ugly.   45. lineaments: characteristics; i.e., features.
48. flout: mock.   52. natural: fool, one who is by nature an idiot.
Touchstone, however, hardly comes into this category of fools;
he is rather the professional jester.   59. wit . . . you: a variant
form of the saying "wit, whither wilt?" Cf. IV.i.168.   69. naught:
bad.   71. forsworn: false in his oath.

CEL. How prove you that, in the great heap of your knowledge?

ROS. Aye, marry, now unmuzzle your wisdom.

TOUCH. Stand you both forth now. Stroke your chins, and swear by your beards that I am a knave.

CEL. By our beards, if we had them, thou art.   79

TOUCH. By my knavery, if I had it, then I were. But if you swear by that that is not, you are not forsworn. No more was this knight swearing by his honor, for he never had any, or if he had, he had sworn it away before ever he saw those pancakes or that mustard.   85

CEL. Prithee who is 't that thou meanest?

TOUCH. One that old Frederick, your father, loves.

CEL. My father's love is enough to honor him. Enough! Speak no more of him, you'll be whipped for taxation° one of these days.   91

TOUCH. The more pity that fools may not speak wisely what wise men do foolishly.

CEL. By my troth, thou sayest true, for since the little wit that fools have was silenced, the little foolery that wise men have makes a great show.° Here comes Monsieur Le Beau.   97

ROS. With his mouth full of news.

CEL. Which he will put on us, as pigeons feed their young.°   100

ROS. Then shall we be news-crammed.

CEL. All the better. We shall be the more marketable. [*Enter* LE BEAU.] *Bon jour,* Monsieur Le Beau. What's the news?

LE BEAU. Fair Princess, you have lost much good sport.   106

CEL. Sport! Of what color?°

LE BEAU. What color, madam! How shall I answer you?

ROS. As wit and fortune will.   110

TOUCH. Or as the Destinies decree.

CEL. Well said. That was laid on with a trowel.°

TOUCH. Nay, if I keep not my rank ——

ROS. Thou losest thy old smell.°

LE BEAU. You amaze me, ladies. I would   115 have told you of good wrestling which you have lost the sight of.

ROS. Yet tell us the manner of the wrestling.

LE BEAU. I will tell you the beginning, and if it please your ladyships, you may see the end; for   120 the best is yet to do, and here where you are they are coming to perform it.

CEL. Well, the beginning, that is dead and buried.°

LE BEAU. There comes an old man and his three sons ——   126

CEL. I could match this beginning with an old tale.°

LE BEAU. Three proper° young men, of excellent growth and presence.°   130

ROS. With bills on their necks, "Be it known unto all men by these presents."°

LE BEAU. The eldest of the three wrestled with Charles, the Duke's wrestler, which Charles in a moment threw him, and broke three of his   135 ribs, that there is little hope of life in him. So he served the second, and so the third. Yonder they lie, the poor old man, their father, making such pitiful dole° over them that all the beholders take his part with weeping.   140

ROS. Alas!

TOUCH. But what is the sport, monsieur, that the ladies have lost?

LE BEAU. Why, this that I speak of.   144

TOUCH. Thus men may grow wiser every day. It is the first time that ever I heard breaking of ribs was sport for ladies.

CEL. Or I, I promise thee.

ROS. But is there any else longs to see this broken music° in his sides? Is there yet another dotes upon rib-breaking? Shall we see this wrestling, Cousin?   152

LE BEAU. You must if you stay here, for here is the place appointed for the wrestling, and they are ready to perform it.   155

CEL. Yonder, sure, they are coming. Let us now stay and see it.

[*Flourish.*° *Enter* DUKE FREDERICK, LORDS, ORLANDO, CHARLES, *and* ATTENDANTS.]

DUKE F. Come on. Since the youth will not be entreated, his own peril° on his forwardness.

ROS. Is yonder the man?   160

LE BEAU. Even he, madam.

CEL. Alas, he is too young! Yet he looks successfully.°

DUKE F. How now, Daughter and Cousin!° Are you crept hither to see the wrestling?   165

ROS. Aye, my liege, so please you give us leave.

DUKE F. You will take little delight in it, I can tell you, there is such odds in the man.° In pity of the challenger's youth I would fain° dissuade him,   170

---

91. taxation: satire.   94–96. since ... show: See *AYLI* Intro. p. 493a.   99–100. pigeons ... young: Pigeons thrust the food into the mouths of their young.   107. Sport ... color: Celia pretends that Le Beau had said "spot," the two words, in Shakespeare's time, being pronounced alike.   112. laid ... trowel: i.e., as a bricklayer slaps down the mortar.   113–14. rank ... smell: position as a professional fool; but Celia pretends that it means highly scented — like a fox.   123–24. the ... buried: i.e., tell the beginning that is now past history.

127–28. I ... tale: your words sound like the beginning of an old tale.   129. proper: handsome.   130. presence: appearance. 131–32. With ... presents: Rosalind makes a far-fetched pun. Le Beau's "presence" reminds her of "presents" as it occurs in the common formula at the beginning of many legal documents: "Know all men by these presents" — *noverint universi per praesentes.* bills: advertisements.   139. dole: lamentation. 149–50. broken music: lit., music performed by different kinds of instruments.   157. s.d., Flourish: fanfare of trumpets.   159. his ... peril: i.e., he does it at his own risk.   163. successfully: as if he would succeed.   164. Cousin: used of any near relation. 169. such ... man: the odds on Charles are so great.   170. fain: gladly.

but he will not be entreated. Speak to him, ladies, see if you can move him.

CEL. Call him hither, good Monsieur Le Beau.

DUKE F. Do so. I'll not be by.   174

LE BEAU. Monsieur the challenger, the Princess calls for you.

ORL. I attend° them with all respect and duty.

ROS. Young man, have you challenged Charles the wrestler?   179

ORL. No, fair Princess, he is the general challenger. I come but in, as others do, to try with him the strength of my youth.

CEL. Young gentleman, your spirits are too bold for your years. You have seen cruel proof of this man's strength. If you saw yourself with your   185 eyes, or knew yourself with your judgment, the fear of your adventure would counsel you to a more equal enterprise. We pray you, for your own sake, to embrace your own safety and give over this attempt.   190

ROS. Do, young sir, your reputation shall not therefore be misprized. We will make it our suit to the Duke that the wrestling might not go forward.

ORL. I beseech you punish me not with your hard thoughts, wherein I confess me much guilty, to deny so fair and excellent ladies anything. But let your fair eyes and gentle wishes go with me to my trial. Wherein if I be foiled, there is but one shamed that was never gracious; if killed, but one dead that   200 is willing to be so. I shall do my friends no wrong, for I have none to lament me; the world no injury, for in it I have nothing. Only in the world I fill up a place which may be better supplied when I have made it empty.   205

ROS. The little strength that I have, I would it were with you.

CEL. And mine, to eke out hers.

ROS. Fare you well. Pray Heaven I be deceived in you!   210

CEL. Your heart's desires be with you!

CHA. Come, where is this young gallant that is so desirous to lie with his mother earth?

ORL. Ready, sir, but his will hath in it a more modest working.°   215

DUKE F. You shall try but one fall.

CHA. No, I warrant your Grace, you shall not entreat him to a second, that have so mightily persuaded him from a first.   219

ORL. You mean to mock me after, you should not have mocked me before. But come your ways.°

ROS. Now Hercules be thy speed,° young man!

CEL. I would I were invisible, to catch the strong fellow by the leg.   [*They wrestle.*]

ROS. Oh, excellent young man!   225

CEL. If I had a thunderbolt in mine eye, I can tell who should down.   [*Shout.* CHARLES *is thrown.*]

DUKE F. No more, no more.

ORL. Yes, I beseech your Grace. I am not yet well breathed.°   230

DUKE F. How dost thou, Charles?

LE BEAU. He cannot speak, my lord.

DUKE F. Bear him away. What is thy name, young man?

ORL. Orlando, my liege, the youngest son of Sir Rowland de Boys.   235

DUKE F. I would thou hadst been son to some man else.
The world esteemed thy father honorable,
But I did find him still° mine enemy.
Thou shouldst have better pleased me with this deed
Hadst thou descended from another house.   240
But fare thee well, thou art a gallant youth.
I would thou hadst told me of another father.

[*Exeunt* DUKE FREDERICK, *train, and* LE BEAU.]

CEL. Were I my father, Coz, would I do this?

ORL. I am more proud to be Sir Rowland's son,
His youngest son, and would not change that calling°   245
To be adopted heir to Frederick.

ROS. My father loved Sir Rowland as his soul,
And all the world was of my father's mind.
Had I before known this young man his son,
I should have given him tears unto° entreaties   250
Ere he should thus have ventured.

CEL.   Gentle Cousin,
Let us go thank him and encourage him.
My father's rough and envious disposition
Sticks me at heart.° Sir, you have well deserved.
If you do keep your promises in love   255
But justly, as you have exceeded all promise,
Your mistress shall be happy.

ROS.   Gentleman,
[*Giving him a chain from her neck*]
Wear this for me, one out of suits° with Fortune,
That could° give more but that her hand lacks means.
Shall we go, Coz?

CEL.   Aye. Fare you well, fair gentleman.   260

ORL. Can I not say I thank you? My better parts
Are all thrown down,° and that which here stands up
Is but a quintain,° a mere lifeless block.

ROS. He calls us back. My pride fell with my fortunes,
I'll ask him what he would. Did you call, sir?   265
Sir, you have wrestled well and overthrown

230. breathed: exercised. 238. still: always. 245. calling: name.
250. unto: added to. 254. Sticks . . . heart: pierces me to the heart. 258. out of suits: not in the service of, not favored by.
259. could: would if she could. 261-62. My . . . down: i.e., I am behaving as if I had no manners. 263. quintain: a block, shaped like a man, used for tilting practice.

177. attend: wait on. 214-15. more . . . working: i.e., I do not intend to do anything so improper. 221. come . . . ways: i.e. come on. 222. speed: aid.

More than your enemies.°
CEL.   Will you go, Coz?
ROS. Have with you. Fare you well.

        [Exeunt ROSALIND *and* CELIA.*]*

ORL. What passion hangs these weights upon my
 tongue?   269
I cannot speak to her, yet she urged conference.°
O poor Orlando, thou art overthrown!
Or Charles or something weaker masters thee.

      [Re-enter LE BEAU.*]*

LE BEAU. Good sir, I do in friendship counsel you
To leave this place. Albeit you have deserved
High commendation, true applause, and love, 275
Yet such is now the Duke's condition
That he miscónstrues all that you have done.
The Duke is humorous.° What he is, indeed,
More suits you to conceive° than I to speak of.
ORL. I thank you, sir. And pray you tell me
 this: 280
Which of the two was daughter of the Duke
That here was at the wrestling?
LE BEAU. Neither his daughter, if we judge by
 manners;
But yet indeed the lesser° is his daughter.
The other is daughter to the banished Duke, 285
And here detained by her usurping uncle,
To keep his daughter company, whose loves
Are dearer than the natural bond of sisters.
But I can tell you that of late this Duke
Hath ta'en displeasure 'gainst his gentle niece, 290
Grounded upon no other argument
But that the people praise her for her virtues
And pity her for her good father's sake.
And, on my life, his malice 'gainst the lady
Will suddenly break forth. Sir, fare you well. 295
Hereafter, in a better world than this,
I shall desire more love and knowledge of you.
ORL. I rest much bounden to you. Fare you well.

         [Exit LE BEAU.*]*

Thus must I from the smoke into the smother,°
From tyrant Duke unto a tyrant brother. 300
But heavenly Rosalind!   *[Exit.]*

SCENE III. *A room in the palace.*

   [Enter CELIA *and* ROSALIND.*]*

CEL. Why, Cousin! Why, Rosalind! Cupid have
mercy! Not a word?
ROS. Not one to throw at a dog.
CEL. No, thy words are too precious to be cast

away upon curs, throw some of them at me. Come,
lame me with reasons.°   6
ROS. Then there were two cousins laid up, when
the one should be lamed with reasons and the other
mad without any.
CEL. But is all this for your father? 10
ROS. No, some of it is for my child's father. Oh,
how full of briers is this working-day world!
CEL. They are but burrs, Cousin, thrown upon
thee in holiday foolery. If we walk not in the trod-
den paths, our very petticoats will catch them. 15
ROS. I could shake them off my coat. These burrs
are in my heart.
CEL. Hem° them away.   19
ROS. I would try if I could cry hem and have him.
CEL. Come, come, wrestle with thy affections.
ROS. Oh, they take the part of a better wrestler
than myself!
CEL. Oh, a good wish upon you! You will try in
time, in despite° of a fall. But, turning these 25
jests out of service, let us talk in good earnest. Is it
possible, on such a sudden, you should fall into so
strong a liking with old Sir Rowland's youngest
son?   30
ROS. The Duke my father loved his father dearly.
CEL. Doth it therefore ensue that you should love
his son dearly? By this kind of chase,° I should hate
him, for my father hated his father dearly, yet I
hate not Orlando.   35
ROS. No, faith, hate him not, for my sake.
CEL. Why should I not? Doth he not deserve
well?
ROS. Let me love him for that, and do you love
him because I do. Look, here comes the Duke. 41
CEL. With his eyes full of anger.

   [Enter DUKE FREDERICK, *with* LORDS.*]*

DUKE F. Mistress, dispatch you with your safest
 haste°
And get you from our Court.
ROS.   Me, Uncle?
DUKE F.   You, Cousin.
Within these ten days if that thou be'st found 45
So near our public Court as twenty miles,
Thou diest for it.
ROS.   I do beseech your Grace,
Let me the knowledge of my fault bear with me.
If with myself I hold intelligence,°
Or have acquaintance with mine own desires, 50
If that I do not dream, or be not frantic° —
As I do trust I am not — then, dear Uncle,
Never so much as in a thought unborn
Did I offend your Highness.

---

267. More . . . enemies: i.e., my heart. 270. urged conference:
invited me to talk. 278. humorous: moody, touchy. 279. con-
ceive: imagine. 284. lesser: the F1 reads "taller," but later (IV.
iii.86–89) Rosalind is described as the taller. 299. smother: thick
smoke — a phrase like "out of the frying pan into the fire."

Sc. iii: 6. lame . . . reasons: make me lame by throwing
arguments at me. 19. Hem: i.e., cough them up. 25. despite:
spite. 33. By . . . chase: by chasing after that kind of argu-
ment. 43. safest haste: i.e., the quicker you go, the safer for
you. 49. If . . . intelligence: if I understood my own thoughts.
51. frantic: mad.

DUKE F.   Thus do all traitors.
If their purgation° did consist in words,   55
They are as innocent as grace° itself.
Let it suffice thee that I trust thee not.
    ROS. Yet your mistrust cannot make me a traitor.
Tell me whereon the likelihood depends.
    DUKE F. Thou art thy father's daughter, there's
        enough.   60
    ROS. So was I when your Highness took his duke-
        dom,
So was I when your Highness banished him.
Treason is not inherited, my lord,
Or if we did derive° it from our friends,°
What's that to me? My father was no traitor.   65
Then, good my liege, mistake me not so much
To think my poverty is treacherous.
    CEL. Dear sovereign, hear me speak.
    DUKE F. Aye, Celia, we stayed her for your sake,
Else had she with her father ranged along.°   70
    CEL. I did not then entreat to have her stay,
It was your pleasure and your own remorse.°
I was too young that time to value her,
But now I know her. If she be a traitor,
Why so am I. We still have slept together,   75
Rose at an instant, learned, played, eat together,
And wheresoe'er we went, like Juno's swans,°
Still we went coupled and inseparable.
    DUKE F. She is too subtle for thee, and her smooth-
        ness,
Her very silence and her patience,   80
Speak to the people, and they pity her.
Thou art a fool. She robs thee of thy name,
And thou wilt show more bright and seem more
        virtuous
When she is gone. Then open not thy lips.
Firm and irrevocable is my doom   85
Which I have passed upon her, she is banished.
    CEL. Pronounce that sentence then on me, my
        liege.
I cannot live out of her company.
    DUKE F. You are a fool. You, Niece, provide your-
        self.
If you outstay the time, upon mine honor,   90
And in the greatness of my word, you die.
        [*Exeunt* DUKE FREDERICK *and* LORDS.]
    CEL. O my poor Rosalind, whither wilt thou go?
Wilt thou change fathers? I will give thee mine.
I charge thee, be not thou more grieved than I am.
    ROS. I have more cause.
    CEL.   Thou hast not, Cousin. 95

Prithee, be cheerful. Know'st thou not the Duke
Hath banished me, his daughter?
    ROS.   That he hath not.
    CEL. No, hath not? Rosalind lacks then the love
Which teacheth thee that thou and I am one.   99
Shall we be sundered? Shall we part, sweet girl?
No. Let my father seek another heir.
Therefore devise with me how we may fly,
Whither to go and what to bear with us.
And do not seek to take your change upon you,°
To bear your griefs yourself and leave me out; 105
For, by this Heaven, now at our sorrows pale,
Say what thou canst, I'll go along with thee.
    ROS. Why, whither shall we go?
    CEL. To seek my uncle in the forest of Arden.
    ROS. Alas, what danger will it be to us,   110
Maids as we are, to travel forth so far!
Beauty provoketh thieves sooner than gold.
    CEL. I'll put myself in poor and mean attire
And with a kind of umber smirch my face.°
The like do you. So shall we pass along   115
And never stir assailants.
    ROS.   Were it not better,
Because that I am more than common tall,
That I did suit me° all points° like a man?
A gallant curtal ax° upon my thigh,
A boar spear° in my hand, and — in my heart   120
Lie there what hidden woman's fear there will —
We'll have a swashing° and a martial outside,
As many other mannish cowards have
That do outface it with their semblances.°   124
    CEL. What shall I call thee when thou art a man?
    ROS. I'll have no worse a name than Jove's own
        page,
And therefore look you call me Ganymede.
But what will you be called?
    CEL. Something that hath a reference to my state,
No longer Celia, but Aliena.°   130
    ROS. But, Cousin, what if we assayed° to steal
The clownish fool out of your father's Court?
Would he not be a comfort to our travel?
    CEL. He'll go along o'er the wide world with me,
Leave me alone to woo him. Let's away   135
And get our jewels and our wealth together,
Devise the fittest time and safest way
To hide us from pursuit that will be made
After my flight. Now go we in content   139
To liberty and not to banishment.   [*Exeunt.*]

104. take . . . you: bear your changed fortunes alone. 114. um-
ber . . . face: Elizabethan ladies regarded an ivory complexion
as beautiful. The pale complexions of the two girls would have
made them conspicuous among countryfolk. 118. suit me: dress
myself. all points: in every detail. 119. curtal ax: cutlass.
120. boar spear: See Pl. 7a. 122. swashing: swaggering.
124. semblances: outward appearances. 130. Aliena: i.e., the
alien, stranger. 131. assayed: attempted.

55. purgation: proof of innocence. 56. grace: i.e., divine grace.
64. derive: acquire by descent. friends: relations. 70. ranged
along: wandered in his company. 72. remorse: pity. 77. Juno's
swans: Editors have pointed out that Venus was the goddess
who possessed a chariot drawn by swans.

Act II

SCENE I. *The Forest of Arden.*

[*Enter* DUKE *Senior,* AMIENS, *and two or three* LORDS, *like foresters.*]

DUKE S. Now, my comates and brothers in exíle,
Hath not old custom° made this life more sweet
Than that of painted° pomp? Are not these woods
More free from peril than the envious Court?
Here feel we but the penalty of Adam,°   5
The seasons' difference, as the icy fang
And churlish chiding of the winter's wind,
Which, when it bites and blows upon my body,
Even till I shrink with cold, I smile and say
"This is no flattery. These are councilors   10
That feelingly° persuade me what I am."
Sweet are the uses° of adversity,
Which, like the toad, ugly and venomous,
Wears yet a precious jewel in his head.°
And this our life exempt from public haunt°   15
Finds tongues in trees, books in the running brooks,
Sermons in stones, and good in everything.°
I would not change it.

AMI.   Happy is your Grace,
That can translate the stubbornness of fortune
Into so quiet and so sweet a style.   20

DUKE S. Come, shall we go and kill us venison?
And yet it irks me the poor dappled fools,
Being native burghers° of this desert city,
Should in their own confines° with forkèd heads°
Have their round haunches gored.

1. LORD.   Indeed, my lord,
The melancholy Jaques grieves at that,   26
And, in that kind,° swears you do more usurp
Than doth your brother that hath banished you.
Today my Lord of Amiens and myself
Did steal behind him as he lay along°   30
Under an oak whose antique root peeps out
Upon the brook that brawls along this wood.
To the which place a poor sequestered° stag,
That from the hunter's aim had ta'en a hurt,
Did come to languish, and indeed, my lord,   35
The wretched animal heaved forth such groans
That their discharge did stretch his leathern coat
Almost to bursting, and the big round tears
Coursed one another down his innocent nose

In piteous chase. And thus the hairy fool,   40
Much markèd of the melancholy Jaques,
Stood on the extremest verge of the swift brook,
Augmenting it with tears.

DUKE S.   But what said Jaques?
Did he not moralize° this spectacle?

1. LORD. Oh yes, into a thousand similes.   45
First, for his weeping into the needless stream,
"Poor deer," quoth he, "thou makest a testament
As worldlings do, giving thy sum of more°
To that which had too much." Then, being there alone,
Left and abandoned of his velvet° friends,   50
"'Tis right," quoth he. "Thus misery doth part
The flux° of company." Anon a careless herd,
Full of the pasture, jumps along by him
And never stays to greet him. "Aye," quoth Jaques,
"Sweep on, you fat and greasy citizens,   55
'Tis just the fashion. Wherefore do you look
Upon that poor and broken bankrupt there?"
Thus most invectively° he pierceth through
The body of the country, city, Court,
Yea, and of this our life, swearing that we   60
Are mere usurpers, tyrants, and what's worse,
To fright the animals and to kill them up
In their assigned and native dwelling-place.

DUKE S. And did you leave him in this contemplation?

2. LORD. We did, my lord, weeping and commenting   65
Upon the sobbing deer.

DUKE S.   Show me the place.
I love to cope° him in these sullen° fits,
For then he's full of matter.°

1. LORD. I'll bring you to him straight. [*Exeunt.*]

SCENE II. *A room in the palace.*

[*Enter* DUKE FREDERICK, *with* LORDS.]

DUKE F. Can it be possible that no man saw them?
It cannot be. Some villains of my Court
Are of consent and sufferance° in this.

1. LORD. I cannot hear of any that did see her.
The ladies, her attendants of her chamber,   5
Saw her abed, and in the morning early
They found the bed untreasured of their mistress.

2. LORD. My lord, the roynish° clown at whom so oft
Your Grace was wont to laugh is also missing.
Hisperia, the Princess' gentlewoman,   10

Act II, Sc. i: **2. old custom**: long experience. **3. painted**: artificial. **5. but . . . Adam**: only the penalty laid on man; i.e., to feel the cold. "But" is an emendation for the F1 reading "not." **11. feelingly**: i.e., through my feelings. **12. uses**: advantages. **13–14. toad . . . head**: This was a common belief. **15. exempt . . . haunt**: free from crowds. **16–17. Finds . . . everything**: i.e., that there is everywhere a lesson in nature. **23. burghers**: citizens. **24. confines**: territories. **forked heads**: i.e., arrows. See Pl. 22a. **27. kind**: manner; i.e., hunting the deer. **30. lay along**: stretched at full length. **33. sequestered**: separated from the others.

44. moralize: make moral comments on. **48. sum of more**: i.e., adding your tears to the water. **50. velvet**: velvet-coated, sleek. **52. flux**: flow, crowd. **58. invectively**: with bitter satire. **67. cope**: encounter. **sullen**: moody. **68. matter**: good sense.
     Sc. ii: **3. of . . . sufferance**: willing accomplices. **8. roynish**: scurvy.

Confesses that she secretly o'erheard
Your daughter and her cousin much commend
The parts and graces of the wrestler
That did but lately foil the sinewy Charles,
And she believes, wherever they are gone,   15
That youth is surely in their company.

DUKE F. Send to his brother, fetch that gallant hither.
If he be absent, bring his brother to me.
I'll make him find him. Do this suddenly,
And let not search and inquisition° quail°   20
To bring again these foolish runaways.   [*Exeunt.*]

SCENE III. *Before* OLIVER'S *house.*

[*Enter* ORLANDO *and* ADAM, *meeting.*]

ORL. Who's there?

ADAM. What, my young master? O my gentle master!
O my sweet master! O you memory
Of old Sir Rowland! Why, what make° you here?
Why are you virtuous? Why do people love you?   5
And wherefore are you gentle, strong, and valiant?
Why would you be so fond° to overcome
The bonny prizer° of the humorous Duke?
Your praise is come too swiftly home before you.
Know you not, master, to some kind of men   10
Their graces serve them but as enemies?
No more do yours. Your virtues, gentle master,
Are sanctified and holy traitors° to you.
Oh, what a world is this when what is comely
Envenoms° him that bears it!   15

ORL. Why, what's the matter?

ADAM.   O unhappy youth!
Come not within these doors, within this roof
The enemy of all your graces lives.
Your brother — no, no brother, yet the son —
Yet not the son, I will not call him son   20
Of him I was about to call his father —
Hath heard your praises, and this night he means
To burn the lodging where you use to lie
And you within it. If he fail of that,
He will have other means to cut you off.   25
I overheard him and his practices.°
This is no place, this house is but a butchery.
Abhor it, fear it, do not enter it.

ORL. Why, whither, Adam, wouldst thou have me go?   29

ADAM. No matter whither so you come not here.

ORL. What, wouldst thou have me go and beg my food?
Or with a base and boisterous° sword enforce

A thievish living on the common road?
This I must do, or know not what to do.
Yet this I will not do, do how I can.   35
I rather will subject me° to the malice
Of a diverted blood° and bloody brother.

ADAM. But do not so. I have five hundred crowns,
The thrifty hire° I saved under your father,
Which I did store to be my foster nurse   40
When service should in my old limbs lie lame,
And unregarded age in corners thrown.
Take that, and He that doth the ravens feed,
Yea, providently caters for the sparrow,
Be comfort to my age! Here is the gold,   45
All this I give you. Let me be your servant.
Though I look old, yet I am strong and lusty,
For in my youth I never did apply
Hot and rebellious liquors in my blood,
Nor did not with unbashful forehead° woo   50
The means of° weakness and debility;
Therefore my age is as a lusty winter,
Frosty, but kindly. Let me go with you,
I'll do the service of a younger man
In all your business and necessities.   55

ORL. O good old man, how well in thee appears
The constant° service of the antique° world,
When service sweat for duty, not for meed!°
Thou art not for the fashion of these times,
Where none will sweat but for promotion,   60
And having that do choke their service up
Even with the having.° It is not so with thee.
But, poor old man, thou prunest a rotten tree
That cannot so much as a blossom yield
In lieu of all thy pains and husbandry.°   65
But come thy ways, we'll go along together,
And ere we have thy youthful wages spent
We'll light upon some settled low content.°

ADAM. Master, go on, and I will follow thee
To the last gasp, with truth and loyalty.   70
From seventeen years till now almost fourscore
Here livèd I, but now live here no more.
At seventeen years many their fortunes seek,
But at fourscore it is too late a week.°
Yet fortune cannot recompense me better   75
Than to die well and not my master's debtor.
          [*Exeunt.*]

---

36. subject me: submit.   37. diverted blood: i.e., one whose natural feelings have been turned aside.   39. thrifty hire: saved-up pay.   50. unbashful forehead: vicious boldness.   51. means of: i.e., pleasures that bring.   57. constant: faithful. antique: ancient, "good old."   58. meed: reward.   61–62. having . . . having: and as soon as they have their reward cease to give good service.   65. husbandry: economy.   68. settled . . . content: humble but contented way of living.   74. too . . . week: a week too late.

---

20. inquisition: inquiry. quail: slacken.
Sc. iii: 4. make: do.   7. fond: foolish.   8. prizer: prize fighter.
13. sanctified . . . traitors: traitors who appear pious and holy.
15. Envenoms: poisons.   26. practices: plots.   32. boisterous: threatening.

SCENE IV. *The* FOREST *of Arden.*

[*Enter* ROSALIND *disguised as* GANYMEDE, CELIA
disguised as ALIENA, *and* TOUCHSTONE.]

ROS. Oh, Jupiter, how weary are my spirits!

TOUCH. I care not for my spirits if my legs were not weary.

ROS. I could find in my heart to disgrace my man's apparel and to cry like a woman. But I must com- 5
fort the weaker vessel, as doublet and hose° ought to show itself courageous to petticoat, therefore, courage, good Aliena.

CEL. I pray you bear with me, I cannot go no further. 10

TOUCH. For my part, I had rather bear with you than bear you. Yet I should bear no cross° if I did bear you, for I think you have no money in your purse.

ROS. Well, this is the forest of Arden. 15

TOUCH. Aye, now am I in Arden, the more fool I. When I was at home, I was in a better place. But travelers must be content.

ROS. Aye, be so, good Touchstone.

[*Enter* CORIN *and* SILVIUS.] Look you who comes here, a young man and an old in solemn talk. 21

COR. That is the way to make her scorn you still.

SIL. Oh, Corin, that thou knew'st how I do love her!

COR. I partly guess, for I have loved ere now.

SIL. No, Corin, being old, thou canst not guess, 26
Though in thy youth thou wast as true a lover
As ever sighed upon a midnight pillow.
But if thy love were ever like to mine —
As sure I think did never man love so —
How many actions most ridiculous 30
Hast thou been drawn to by thy fantasy?°

COR. Into a thousand that I have forgotten.

SIL. Oh, thou didst then ne'er love so heartily!
If thou remember'st not the slightest folly
That ever love did make thee run into, 35
Thou hast not loved.
Or if thou hast not sat as I do now,
Wearing° thy hearer in° thy mistress' praise,
Thou hast not loved.
Or if thou hast not broke from company 40
Abruptly, as my passion now makes me,
Thou hast not loved.
Oh, Phebe, Phebe, Phebe! [*Exit.*]

ROS. Alas, poor shepherd! Searching of thy
wound,°
I have by hard adventure° found mine own. 45

TOUCH. And I mine. I remember when I was in love I broke my sword upon a stone and bid him take that for coming a-night to Jane Smile. And I remember the kissing of her batlet° and the cow's dugs that her pretty chopt° hands had milked. 50
And I remember the wooing of a peascod° instead of her, from whom I took two cods° and, giving her them again, said with weeping tears, "Wear these for my sake." We that are truelovers run into strange capers, but as all is mortal in nature, so is all nature in love mortal in folly.° 56

ROS. Thou speakest wiser than thou art ware of.

TOUCH. Nay, I shall ne'er be ware of mine own wit till I break my shins against it. 60

ROS.   Jove, Jove! This shepherd's passion
              Is much upon my fashion.

TOUCH. And mine, but it grows something stale with me.

CEL. I pray you, one of you question yon man
If he for gold will give us any food. 65
I faint almost to death.

TOUCH. Holloa, you clown!°

ROS. Peace, fool. He's not thy kinsman.

COR.   Who calls?

TOUCH. Your betters, sir.

COR.   Else are they very wretched.

ROS. Peace, I say. Good even to you, friend.

COR. And to you, gentle sir, and to you all. 70

ROS. I prithee, shepherd, if that love or gold
Can in this desert place buy entertainment,°
Bring us where we may rest ourselves and feed.
Here's a young maid with travel much oppressed
And faints for succor.

COR.   Fair sir, I pity her, 75
And wish, for her sake more than for mine own,
My fortunes were more able to relieve her.
But I am shepherd to another man
And do not shear the fleeces that I graze.°
My master is of churlish disposition 80
And little recks° to find the way to Heaven
By doing deeds of hospitality.
Besides, his cote,° his flocks and bounds of feed,°
Are now on sale, and at our sheepcote now,
By reason of his absence, there is nothing 85
That you will feed on. But what is, come see,
And in my voice most welcome shall you be.

ROS. What is he that shall buy his flock and pasture?

COR. That young swain° that you saw here but
erewhile,

Sc. iv: 6. doublet . . . hose: i.e., man's attire, for Rosalind is now dressed as Ganymede. See Pl. 8b and comment on p. 93a-b. 12. bear no cross: lit., endure no misfortune; but it also meant "have no money," as Elizabethan money had a cross on the reverse side. See Pl. 10a. 31. fantasy: fancy, love. 38. Wearing: wearing out. in: with. 44. Searching . . . wound: i.e., listening to you probing your wound. 45. hard adventure: painful chance.

49. batlet: bat used for beating clothes during washing. 50. chopt: chapped. 51. peascod: usually peapod, but here the whole plant. 52. cods: pods. 56. mortal in folly: deadly silly. 67. clown: rustic. 72. entertainment: accommodation. 79. do . . . graze: do not sell the wool of the sheep I feed — because he is a hired shepherd and not the owner. 81. recks: cares. 83. cote: cottage. bounds of feed: pastures. 89. swain: a poetic word, usually implying a young man in love.

That little cares for buying anything.   90

ROS. I pray thee, if it stand with honesty,
Buy thou the cottage, pasture, and the flock,
And thou shalt have to pay for it of us.

CEL. And we will mend° thy wages. I like this
place,
And willingly could waste my time in it.   95

COR. Assuredly the thing is to be sold.
Go with me. If you like upon report
The soil, the profit, and this kind of life,
I will your very faithful feeder be
And buy it with your gold right suddenly.   100

[Exeunt.]

SCENE V. *The forest.*

[Enter AMIENS, JAQUES, *and others.]*

AMI. *[Sings.]*

Under the greenwood tree
Who loves to lie with me,
And turn° his merry note
Unto the sweet bird's throat,
Come hither, come hither, come hither.   5
Here shall he see
No enemy
But winter and rough weather.

JAQ. More, more, I prithee, more.

AMI. It will make you melancholy, Monsieur
Jaques.   11

JAQ. I thank it. More, I prithee, more. I can suck
melancholy out of a song as a weasel sucks eggs.
More, I prithee, more.

AMI. My voice is ragged. I know I cannot please
you.   16

JAQ. I do not desire you to please me, I do desire
you to sing. Come, more, another stanzo.° Call you
'em stanzos?

AMI. What you will, Monsieur Jaques.

JAQ. Nay, I care not for their names, they owe me
nothing.° Will you sing?   23

AMI. More at your request than to please myself.

JAQ. Well then, if ever I thank any man, I'll
thank you. But that they call compliment is like the
encounter of two dog apes,° and when a man thanks
me heartily, methinks I have given him a penny and
he renders me the beggarly thanks.° Come, sing,
and you that will not, hold your tongues.   31

AMI. Well, I'll end the song. Sirs, cover° the
while.° The Duke will drink under this tree. He
hath been all this day to look you.

JAQ. And I have been all this day to avoid him.

94. **mend:** improve.
Sc. v: 3. **turn:** harmonize. Some editors read "tune."
18. **stanzo:** stanza; lit., a stand or set.   22–23. **owe me nothing:**
i.e., and so mean nothing to me.   28. **dog apes:** male baboons.
30. **beggarly thanks:** i.e., effusively like a beggar.   32. **cover:**
lay the table.   33. **the while:** in the meanwhile.

He is too disputable° for my company. I think of as
many matters as he, but I give Heaven thanks, and
make no boast of them. Come, warble, come.   38

SONG. *[All together here.]*

Who doth ambition shun,
And loves to live i' the sun,
Seeking the food he eats,
And pleased with what he gets,
Come hither, come hither, come hither.
Here shall he see   45
No enemy
But winter and rough weather.

JAQ. I'll give you a verse to this note,° that I made
yesterday in despite of my invention.°

AMI. And I'll sing it.   50

JAQ. Thus it goes:

If it do come to pass
That any man turn ass,
Leaving his wealth and ease
A stubborn will to please,
Ducdame,° ducdame, ducdame.   55
Here shall he see
Gross fools as he,
An if he will come to me.

AMI. What's that "ducdame?"   60

JAQ. 'Tis a Greek invocation to call fools into a
circle. I'll go sleep, if I can. If I cannot, I'll rail
against all the firstborn of Egypt.   63

AMI. And I'll go seek the Duke. His banquet is
prepared.   *[Exeunt. severally.°]*

SCENE VI. *The forest.*

[Enter ORLANDO *and* ADAM.]

ADAM. Dear master, I can go no further. Oh, I die
for food. Here lie I down, and measure out° my
grave. Farewell, kind master.

ORL. Why, how now, Adam! No greater heart in
thee? Live a little, comfort a little, cheer thyself   5
a little. If this uncouth forest yield anything savage,
I will either be food for it or bring it for food to thee.
Thy conceit° is nearer death than thy powers.° For
my sake be comfortable,° hold death awhile at the
arm's end. I will here be with thee presently,°   10
and if I bring thee not something to eat, I will give

36. **disputable:** argumentative.   48. **to . . . note:** to go with this
tune.   49. **despite . . . invention:** i.e., although I am no good
at this sort of thing. **in despite:** in spite of. **invention:** the
creative faculty.   56. **Ducdame:** a three-syllable word. Many
commentators have tried to trace the origin of this word. It is
most probably one of the many meaningless syllables—like
"hey nonny no"—so often used to fill out the line of a song.
Jaques' own explanation (l. 61) is that it is a Greek invocation
to call fools into a circle (i.e., set them gossiping). It has greatly
stimulated scholars to make learned guesses.   65. **s.d., severally:**
by different exits.
Sc. vi: 2. **measure out:** i.e., the length of.   8. **conceit:** imagi-
nation. **powers:** strength.   9. **comfortable:** comforted.   10. **pres-
ently:** immediately.

thee leave to die. But if thou diest before I come, thou
art a mocker of my labor. Well said! Thou lookest
cheerly, and I'll be with thee quickly. Yet thou liest
in the bleak air. Come, I will bear thee to some   15
shelter, and thou shalt not die for lack of a dinner
if there live anything in this desert. Cheerly, good
Adam!   [*Exeunt.*]

SCENE VII. *The forest.*

[*A table set out. Enter* DUKE *Senior,* AMIENS, *and*
LORDS *like outlaws.*]

DUKE S. I think he be transformed into a beast,
For I can nowhere find him like a° man.
    1. LORD. My lord, he is but even now gone hence.
Here was he merry, hearing of a song.
    DUKE S. If he, compact of jars,° grow musical,   5
We shall have shortly discord in the spheres.°
Go, seek him. Tell him I would speak with him.
                    [*Enter* JAQUES.]
    1. LORD. He saves my labor by his own approach.
    DUKE S. Why, how now, monsieur! What a life is
this
That your poor friends must woo your company?
What, you look merrily!   11
    JAQ. A fool, a fool! I met a fool i' the forest,
A motley fool,° a miserable world!
As I do live by food, I met a fool,
Who laid him down and basked him in the sun,   15
And railed on Lady Fortune in good terms,
In good set terms,° and yet a motley fool.
" Good morrow, fool," quoth I. " No, sir," quoth
he.
" Call me not fool till Heaven hath sent me fortune."
And then he drew a dial° from his poke,°   20
And looking on it with lackluster eye,
Says very wisely, " It is ten o'clock.
Thus we may see," quoth he, " how the world wags.
'Tis but an hour ago since it was nine,
And after one hour more 'twill be eleven,   25
And so, from hour to hour, we ripe and ripe,
And then, from hour to hour, we rot and rot,
And thereby hangs a tale." When I did hear
The motley fool thus moral on the time,
My lungs began to crow like chanticleer,°   30
That fools should be so deep-contemplative,°
And I did laugh sans° intermission
An hour by his dial. Oh, noble fool!
A worthy fool! Motley's the only wear.
    DUKE S. What fool is this?   35

    JAQ. Oh, worthy fool! One that hath been a cour-
tier,
And says if ladies be but young and fair,
They have the gift to know it. And in his brain,
Which is as dry as the remainder° biscuit
After a voyage, he hath strange places crammed   40
With observation, the which he vents°
In mangled forms.° Oh, that I were a fool!
I am ambitious for a motley coat.
    DUKE S. Thou shalt have one.
    JAQ.   It is my only suit,°
Provided that you weed your better judgments   45
Of all opinion that grows rank° in them
That I am wise. I must have liberty
Withal, as large a charter° as the wind
To blow on° whom I please. For so fools have,
And they that are most gallèd° with my folly,   50
They most must laugh. And why, sir, must they so?
The " why " is plain as way to parish church.
He that a fool doth very wisely, hit
Doth very foolishly, although he smart,
Not to seem senseless of the bob.° If not,   55
The wise man's folly is anatomized°
Even by the squandering° glances of the fool.
Invest° me in my motley, give me leave
To speak my mind, and I will through and through
Cleanse the foul body of the infected world,   60
If they will patiently receive my medicine.
    DUKE S. Fie on thee! I can tell what thou wouldst
do.
    JAQ. What, for a counter,° would I do but good?
    DUKE S. Most mischievous foul sin, in chiding sin.
For thou thyself hast been a libertine   65
As sensual as the brutish sting° itself,
And all the embossèd sores and headed evils
That thou with license of free foot° hast caught
Wouldst thou disgorge into the general world.
    JAQ. Why, who cries out on pride   70
That can therein tax any private party?°
Doth it not flow as hugely as the sea
Till that the weary very means do ebb?°
What woman in the city do I name
When that I say the city woman bears   75
The cost of princes on unworthy shoulders?
Who can come in and say that I mean her

Sc. vii: **2. like a:** in the shape of.   **5. compact of jars:** made
of discords.   **6. discord . . . spheres:** See App. 1.   **13. motley
fool:** i.e., a professional fool. *Motley* was the particolored dress
worn by court jesters. See Pl. 12f, 13c.   **17. set terms:** phrases
carefully composed.   **20. dial:** watch. **poke:** pocket.   **30. chan-
ticleer:** the cock.   **31. deep-contemplative:** profoundly thought-
ful.   **32. sans:** without.

39. remainder: leftover.   **41. vents:** utters.   **42. mangled
forms:** quaint phrases.   **44. suit:** with a pun on suit, meaning
petition and suit of clothes.   **46. rank:** abundantly, like weeds
in a garden.   **48. large a charter:** as free a privilege.   **49. blow
on:** censure.   **50. galled:** rubbed sore.   **55. Not . . . bob:** not
to pretend that he has not been hurt. **bob:** blow.   **56. anato-
mized:** dissected.   **57. squandering:** scattered far and wide.
58. Invest: robe.   **63. counter:** a valueless token.   **66. brutish
sting:** i.e., lust.   **67–68. embossed . . . foot:** carbuncles and boils
that result from licentious living.   **70–71. who . . . party:** who is
attacking any particular person when he denounces pride?
Satirists of the time, when rebuked for attacking individuals,
usually replied that they were denouncing the sin and not indi-
vidual sinners.   **73. weary . . . ebb:** i.e., until the means of pride
(i.e., wealth) grow tired and ebb away.

When such a one as she such is her neighbor?
Or what is he of basest function°
That says his bravery is not on my cost,°   80
Thinking that I mean him, but therein suits°
His folly to the mettle° of my speech?
There then, how then? What then? Let me see
    wherein
My tongue hath wronged him. If it do him right,°
Then he hath wronged himself. If he be free,°   85
Why then my taxing like a wild goose flies,
Unclaimed of any man. But who comes here?
    [*Enter* ORLANDO, *with his sword drawn.*]
  ORL. Forbear, and eat no more.
  JAQ.   Why, I have eat none yet.
  ORL. Nor shalt not, till necessity° be served.
  JAQ. Of what kind should this cock come of?   90
  DUKE S. Art thou thus boldened, man, by thy dis-
    tress?
Or else a rude despiser of good manners,
That in civility° thou seem'st so empty?
  ORL. You touched my vein at first.° The thorny
    point°
Of bare distress hath ta'en from me the show   95
Of smooth civility. Yet am I inland-bred°
And know some nurture. But forbear, I say.
He dies that touches any of this fruit
Till I and my affairs are answered.
  JAQ. An° you will not be answered with reason,
I must die.   101
  DUKE S. What would you have? Your gentleness
    shall force
More than your force move us to gentleness.
  ORL. I almost die for food, and let me have it.
  DUKE S. Sit down and feed, and welcome to our
    table.   105
  ORL. Speak you so gently? Pardon me, I pray you.
I thought that all things had been savage here,
And therefore put I on the countenance
Of stern commandment. But whate'er you are
That in this desert inaccessible,   110
Under the shade of melancholy boughs,
Lose and neglect the creeping hours of time,
If ever you have looked on better days,
If ever been where bells have knolled° to church,
If ever sat at any good man's feast,   115
If ever from your eyelids wiped a tear
And know what 'tis to pity and be pitied,
Let gentleness my strong enforcement° be.
In the which hope I blush, and hide my sword. 119

DUKE S. True is it that we have seen better days,
And have with holy bell been knolled to church,
And sat at good men's feasts, and wiped our eyes
Of drops that sacred pity hath engendered.
And therefore sit you down in gentleness
And take upon command° what help we have   125
That to your wanting may be ministered.
  ORL. Then but forbear your food a little while
Whiles, like a doe, I go to find my fawn
And give it food. There is an old poor man
Who after me hath many a weary step   130
Limped in pure love. Till he be first sufficed,°
Oppressed with two weak evils, age and hunger,
I will not touch a bit.
  DUKE S.   Go find him out,
And we will nothing waste till you return.   134
  ORL. I thank ye, and be blest for your good com-
    fort!   [*Exit.*]
  DUKE S. Thou seest we are not all alone unhappy.
This wide and universal theater
Presents more woeful pageants than the scene
Wherein we play in.
  JAQ.   All the world's a stage,°
And all the men and women merely players.   140
They have their exits and their entrances,
And one man in his time plays many parts,
His acts being seven ages. At first the infant,
Mewling° and puking in the nurse's arms.
Then the whining schoolboy, with his satchel   145
And shining morning face, creeping like snail
Unwillingly to school. And then the lover,
Sighing like furnace, with a woeful ballad°
Made to his mistress' eyebrow. Then a soldier,   149
Full of strange oaths and bearded like the pard,°
Jealous in honor,° sudden and quick in quarrel,
Seeking the bubble reputation°
Even in the cannon's mouth. And then the justice,
In fair round belly with good capon lined,°
With eyes severe and beard of formal cut,°   155
Full of wise saws° and modern instances,°
And so he plays his part. The sixth age shifts
Into the lean and slippered Pantaloon°
With spectacles on nose and pouch on side,   159
His youthful hose, well saved, a world too wide
For his shrunk shank, and his big manly voice,
Turning again toward childish treble, pipes
And whistles in his sound. Last scene of all,

---

79. **basest function:** most degraded kind of employment.
80. **bravery . . . cost:** his fine clothes have not cost me anything.
81. **suits:** fits.   82. **mettle:** material; i.e., his protest shows that my words have fitted him.   84. **do . . . right:** if my charges are just.   85. **free:** guiltless.   89. **necessity:** i.e., those who must have food.   93. **civility:** civilized behavior.   94. **touched . . . first:** i.e., your first guess is right; I am indeed desperate. **vein:** disposition. **thorny point:** acuteness.   96. **inland-bred:** one who knows civilization. See III.ii.363.   100. **An:** if.   114. **knolled:** tolled.   118. **enforcement:** means of forcing.

125. **upon command:** as you may choose to order.   131. **sufficed:** satisfied.   139. **All . . . stage:** See *AYLI* Intro. p. 493a.   144. **Mewling:** whimpering.   148. **ballad:** poem.   150. **pard:** leopard.   151. **Jealous in honor:** sensitive about his honor.   152. **bubble reputation:** fame as quickly burst as a bubble.   154. **good . . . lined:** bribed with the present of a fat chicken. It was a common complaint that those who wished for justice from country magistrates had to bring presents with them. Such magistrates were known as "basket justices."   155. **formal cut:** of severe pattern, trim.   156. **saws:** sayings. **modern instances:** commonplace illustrations.   158. **Pantaloon:** the foolish old man of Italian comedy.

That ends this strange eventful history,
Is second childishness and mere oblivion, 165
Sans teeth, sans eyes, sans taste, sans everything.
　　　[*Re-enter* ORLANDO, *with* ADAM.]
　DUKE S. Welcome. Set down your venerable bur-
　　then,
And let him feed.
　ORL. I thank you most for him.
　ADAM.　　　　　　　　So had you need.
I scarce can speak to thank you for myself. 170
　DUKE S. Welcome. Fall to. I will not trouble you
As yet, to question you about your fortunes.
Give us some music, and, good Cousin, sing.
　AMI. [*Sings.*]
　　Blow, blow, thou winter wind.
　　Thou art not so unkind 175
　　　As man's ingratitude.
　　Thy tooth is not so keen,
　　Because thou art not seen,
　　　Although thy breath be rude.
Heigh-ho! Sing, heigh-ho! unto the green holly. 180
Most friendship is feigning, most loving mere folly.
　　　Then, heigh-ho, the holly!
　　　This life is most jolly.

　　Freeze, freeze, thou bitter sky,
　　That dost not bite so nigh 185
　　　As benefits forgot.
　　Though thou the waters warp,°
　　Thy sting is not so sharp
　　　As friend remembered not.
Heigh-ho! Sing, heigh-ho! unto the green holly.
Most friendship is feigning, most loving mere folly.
　　　Then, heigh-ho, the holly!
　　　This life is most jolly.
　DUKE S. If that you were the good Sir Rowland's
　　son,
As you have whispered faithfully you were,
And as mine eye doth his effigies° witness
Most truly limned° and living in your face,
Be truly welcome hither. I am the Duke 195
That loved your father. The residue of your for-
　tune,°
Go to my cave and tell me. Good old man,
Thou art right welcome, as thy master is.
Support him by the arm. Give me your hand,
And let me all your fortunes understand. [*Exeunt.*]

187. warp: freeze.　193. effigies: image.　194. limned: painted.
96. residue . . . fortune: the rest of the story of your life.

Act III

SCENE I. *A room in the palace.*

[*Enter* DUKE FREDERICK, LORDS, *and* OLIVER.]
　DUKE F. Not see him since? Sir, sir, that cannot be.
But were I not the better part made mercy,
I should not seek an absent argument
Of my revenge, thou present.° But look to it.
Find out thy brother, wheresoe'er he is. 5
Seek him with candle, bring him dead or living
Within this twelvemonth, or turn thou no more
To seek a living in our territory.
Thy lands and all things that thou dost call thine
Worth seizure do we seize into our hands 10
Till thou canst quit° thee by thy brother's mouth
Of what we think against thee.
　OLI. Oh, that your Highness knew my heart in
　　this!
I never loved my brother in my life.
　DUKE F. More villain thou. Well, push him out of
　　doors, 15
And let my officers of such a nature
Make an extent upon° his house and lands.
Do this expediently° and turn him going.
　　　　　　　　　　　　　　　　　[*Exeunt.*]

SCENE II. *The forest.*

[*Enter* ORLANDO, *with a paper.*]
　ORL. "Hang there, my verse, in witness of my
　　love.
And thou, thrice-crownèd queen° of night, survey
With thy chaste eye, from thy pale sphere° above,
　Thy huntress' name that my full life doth sway.
O Rosalind! These trees shall be my books 5
　And in their barks my thoughts I'll character,°
That every eye which in this forest looks
　Shall see thy virtue witnessed° everywhere.
Run, run, Orlando, carve on every tree
The fair, the chaste, and unexpressive° she." 10
　　　　　　　　　　　　　　　　　[*Exit.*]
[*Enter* CORIN *and* TOUCHSTONE.]
　COR. And how like you this shepherd's life, Mas-
ter Touchstone?
　TOUCH. Truly, shepherd, in respect of itself, it is
a good life; but in respect that it is a shepherd's life,
it is naught.° In respect that it is solitary, I like 15

Act III, Sc. i: 3–4. I . . . present: I should not look for your
brother, but take vengeance on you.　11. quit: acquit.　17. Make
. . . upon: seize upon.　18. expediently: expeditiously.
　　Sc. ii: 2. thrice-crowned queen: the goddess Diana, so called
on earth; in Heaven she was Luna, the Moon, and in the under-
world, Persephone.　3. pale sphere: i.e., the moon.　6. character:
inscribe.　8. witnessed: borne witness to.　10. unexpressive: in-
expressible, beyond description.　15. naught: worthless.

it very well; but in respect that it is private,° it is a very vile life. Now, in respect it is in the fields, it pleaseth me well; but in respect it is not in the Court, it is tedious. As it is a spare° life, look you, it fits my humor well; but as there is no more plenty in it,   20 it goes much against my stomach. Hast any philosophy in thee, shepherd?

COR. No° more but that I know the more one sickens, the worse at ease he is; and that he that   25 wants money, means, and content is without three good friends; that the property of rain is to wet and fire to burn; that good pasture makes fat sheep, and that a great cause of the night is lack of the sun; that he that hath learned no wit by nature nor art°   30 may complain of good breeding or comes of a very dull kindred.

TOUCH. Such a one is a natural° philosopher. Wast ever in Court, shepherd?

COR. No, truly.   35

TOUCH. Then thou art damned.

COR. Nay, I hope.

TOUCH. Truly, thou art damned, like an ill-roasted egg all on one side.

COR. For not being at Court? Your reason.   40

TOUCH. Why, if thou never wast at Court, thou never sawest good manners.° If thou never sawest good manners, then thy manners must be wicked, and wickedness is sin, and sin is damnation. Thou art in a parlous° state, shepherd.   45

COR. Not a whit, Touchstone. Those that are good manners at the Court are as ridiculous in the country as the behavior of the country is most mockable at the Court. You told me you salute not at the Court, but you kiss your hands. That courtesy would be uncleanly if courtiers were shepherds.   52

TOUCH. Instance,° briefly, come, instance.

COR. Why, we are still handling our ewes, and their fells,° you know, are greasy.   55

TOUCH. Why, do not your courtier's hands sweat? And is not the grease of a mutton as wholesome as the sweat of a man? Shallow, shallow. A better instance, I say, come.

COR. Besides, our hands are hard.   60

TOUCH. Your lips will feel them the sooner. Shallow again. A more sounder instance, come.

COR. And they are often tarred over with the surgery of our sheep, and would you have us kiss tar? The courtier's hands are perfumed with civet.°   66

TOUCH. Most shallow man! Thou wormsmeat in

respect of a good piece of flesh indeed! Learn of the wise, and perpend.° Civet is of a baser birth than tar, the very uncleanly flux of a cat. Mend the instance, shepherd.   71

COR. You have too Courtly a wit for me. I'll rest.

TOUCH. Wilt thou rest damned? God help thee, shallow man! God make incision° in thee! Thou art raw.°   76

COR. Sir, I am a true laborer. I earn that I eat, get that I wear, owe no man hate, envy no man's happiness, glad of other men's good, content with my harm,° and the greatest of my pride is to see my ewes graze and my lambs suck.   81

TOUCH. That is another simple sin in you, to bring the ewes and the rams together and to offer to get your living by the copulation of cattle; to be bawd° to a bellwether, and to betray a she-lamb of a   85 twelvemonth to a crooked-pated, old, cuckoldy° ram, out of all reasonable match.° If thou beest not damned for this, the Devil himself will have no shepherds. I cannot see else how thou shouldst 'scape.   90

COR. Here comes young Master Ganymede, my new mistress's brother.

[*Enter* ROSALIND, *with a paper, reading.*]

ROS. "From the east to western Ind,°
    No jewel is like Rosalind.   94
    Her worth, being mounted on the wind,°
    Through all the world bears Rosalind.
    All the pictures fairest lined°
    Are but black to Rosalind.
    Let no face be kept in mind
    But the fair of Rosalind."   100

TOUCH. I'll rhyme you so eight years together, dinners and suppers and sleeping hours excepted. It is the right butterwomen's rank to market.°

ROS. Out, fool!   105

TOUCH. For a taste:
    If a hart do lack a hind,°
    Let him seek out Rosalind.
    If the cat will after kind,
    So be sure will Rosalind.   110
    Winter garments must be lined,
    So must slender Rosalind.
    They that reap must sheaf and bind,
    Then to cart with Rosalind.
    Sweetest nut hath sourest rind,   115
    Such a nut is Rosalind.
    He that sweetest rose will find
    Must find love's prick and Rosalind.

---

16. private: solitary. Touchstone as a frequenter of the court prefers a public kind of life.   **19. spare:** frugal.   **24–32. No . . . kindred:** Corin answers Touchstone's Court wit with a selection of rustic wisdom.   **30. nature . . . art:** See App. 18.   **33. natural:** with a pun on *natural*, meaning fool.   **42. good manners:** with double meaning — polite behavior and a moral life.   **45. parlous:** perilous.   **53. Instance:** give an example.   **55. fells:** fleeces.   **66. civet:** perfume obtained from glandular secretions of the civet cat.

69. perpend: consider.   **75. make incision:** cut to let blood — a common treatment for many complaints.   **76. raw:** unripe, "green."   **79–80. content . . . harm:** content to bear my own troubles.   **84. bawd:** go-between.   **86. cuckoldy:** lecherous.   **87. match:** mating.   **93. Ind:** India.   **95. mounted . . . wind:** blown about by the wind.   **97. lined:** drawn.   **104. right . . . market:** i.e., like a lot of old countrywomen ambling along to market.   **107. hart . . . hind:** male and female deer.

This is the very false gallop° of verses. Why do you infect yourself with them? 120

ROS. Peace, you dull fool! I found them on a tree.

TOUCH. Truly, the tree yields bad fruit.

ROS. I'll graff° it with you, and then I shall graff it with a medlar.° Then it will be the earliest fruit i' the country, for you'll be rotten ere you be half ripe, and that's the right virtue of the medlar.

TOUCH. You have said, but whether wisely or no, let the forest judge. 130

[*Enter* CELIA, *with a writing.*]

ROS. Peace!

Here comes my sister, reading. Stand aside.

CEL. [*Reads.*]

" Why should this a desert be?
   For it is unpeopled? No,
Tongues I'll hang on every tree, 135
   That shall civil° sayings show
Some, how brief the life of man
   Runs his erring° pilgrimage,
That the stretching of a span°
   Buckles in his sum of age; 140
Some, of violated vows
   'Twixt the souls of friend and friend.
But upon the fairest boughs,
   Or at every sentence end,
Will I Rosalinda write, 145
   Teaching all that read to know
The quintessence° of every sprite
   Heaven would in little show.
Therefore Heaven Nature charged
   That one body should be filled 150
With all graces wide-enlarged.
   Nature presently distilled
Helen's cheek, but not her heart,
   Cleopatra's majesty,
Atalanta's better part, 155
   Sad Lucretia's modesty.°
Thus Rosalind of many parts
   By heavenly synod° was devised,
Of many faces, eyes, and hearts,
   To have the touches dearest prized. 160
Heaven would that she these gifts should have,
And I to live and die her slave."

ROS. O most gentle pulpiter!° What tedious

homily° of love have you wearied your parishioners withal, and never cried " Have patience, good people! " 166

CEL. How now! Back, friends! Shepherd, go off a little. Go with him, sirrah.

TOUCH. Come, shepherd, let us make an honorable retreat, though not with bag and baggage, yet with scrip° and scrippage.° 171

[*Exeunt* CORIN *and* TOUCHSTONE.]

CEL. Didst thou hear these verses?

ROS. Oh, yes, I heard them all, and more too, for some of them had in them more feet than the verses would bear. 175

CEL. That's no matter. The feet might bear the verses.

ROS. Aye, but the feet were lame and could not bear themselves without the verse and therefore stood lamely in the verse. 180

CEL. But didst thou hear without wondering how thy name should be hanged and carved upon these trees?

ROS. I was seven of the nine days° out of the wonder before you came; for look here what I found on a palm tree. I was never so berhymed° since Pythagoras'° time, that I was an Irish rat, which I can hardly remember. 188

CEL. Trow° you who hath done this?

ROS. Is it a man?

CEL. And a chain that you once wore about his neck. Change you color?

ROS. I prithee — who?

CEL. Oh Lord, Lord! It is a hard matter for friends to meet, but mountains may be removed with earthquakes and so encounter. 196

ROS. Nay, but who is it?

CEL. Is it possible?

ROS. Nay, I prithee now with most petitionary vehemence,° tell me who it is. 200

CEL. Oh, wonderful, wonderful, and most wonderful wonderful! And yet again wonderful, and after that, out of all hooping!°

ROS. Good my complexion! Dost thou think though I am caparisoned° like a man, I have a 205 doublet and hose in my disposition?° One inch of delay more is a South Sea of discovery.° I prithee tell me who is it quickly, and speak apace. I would

---

119. **false gallop:** canter. The rolling motion of a canter is like the even stress of Orlando's bad verses.   123. **graff:** graft. 124. **medlar:** a fruit resembling a small brown apple, but not eaten until it has grown soft.   136. **civil:** civilized. 138. **erring:** wandering.   139. **span:** the distance between the thumb and forefinger of the stretched hand; about 9 inches.   147. **quintessence:** fifth essence, that which remains when the four elements have been taken away.   153–56. **Helen's . . . modesty:** Rosalind has the good parts of four famous women of story. Helen was divinely fair but unfaithful, Cleopatra, a Queen most royal but unchaste, Atalanta, a swift runner but led aside by cupidity, Lucretia, a model wife but betrayed.   158. **synod:** assembly. 163. **pulpiter:** preacher, an emendation for the F1 reading 'Jupiter.'

164. **homily:** sermon.   171. **scrip:** the shepherd's wallet. **scrippage:** a word invented by Touchstone to balance baggage.   184. **seven . . . days:** i.e., I have endured almost a nine days' wonder.   186. **berhymed:** rhymed to death. It was believed that in Ireland rats could be destroyed by incantation in rhyme.   187. **Pythagoras:** He taught the doctrine of the transmigration of souls — that the human soul after death passed into the body of an animal.   189. **Trow:** know. 199–200. **petitionary vehemence:** pleading emphasis.   203. **out . . . hooping:** beyond any cry of wonder.   205. **caparisoned:** decked out.   206. **disposition:** nature.   206–07. **One . . . discovery:** i.e., the slightest delay in telling me makes your story seem as endless as the South Sea to a voyager.

thou couldst stammer, that thou mightst pour this concealed man out of thy mouth as wine 210 comes out of a narrow-mouthed bottle, either too much at once or none at all. I prithee take the cork out of thy mouth that I may drink thy tidings.

CEL. So you may put a man in your belly. 215

ROS. Is he of God's making? What manner of man? Is his head worth a hat? Or his chin worth a beard?

CEL. Nay, he hath but a little beard.

ROS. Why, God will send more, if the man will be thankful. Let me stay the growth of his beard if thou delay me not the knowledge of his chin.° 222

CEL. It is young Orlando, that tripped up the wrestler's heels and your heart both in an instant.

ROS. Nay, but the devil take mocking. Speak, sad brow° and true maid.

CEL. I' faith, Coz, 'tis he.

ROS. Orlando?

CEL. Orlando. 230

ROS. Alas the day! What shall I do with my doublet and hose? What did he when thou sawest him? What said he? How looked he? Wherein went he? What makes he here? Did he ask for me? Where remains he? How parted he with thee? And 235 when shalt thou see him again? Answer me in one word.

CEL. You must borrow me Gargantua's° mouth first. 'Tis a word too great for any mouth of this age's size. To say aye and no to these particulars is more than to answer in a catechism. 241

ROS. But doth he know that I am in this forest and in man's apparel? Looks he as freshly as he did the day he wrestled? 244

CEL. It is as easy to count atomies° as to resolve the propositions of a lover,° but take a taste of my finding him,° and relish it with good observance. I found him under a tree, like a dropped acorn.

ROS. It may well be called Jove's tree when it drops forth such fruit. 250

CEL. Give me audience, good madam.

ROS. Proceed.

CEL. There lay he, stretched along° like a wounded knight.

ROS. Though it be pity to see such a sight, it well becomes the ground. 256

CEL. Cry "holloa"° to thy tongue, I prithee, it curvets° unseasonably. He was furnished° like a hunter.

ROS. Oh, ominous! He comes to kill my heart.

CEL. I would sing my song without a burden.° Thou bringest me out of tune. 263

ROS. Do you not know I am a woman? When I think, I must speak. Sweet, say on.

CEL. You bring me out. Soft! Comes he not here?

[*Enter* ORLANDO *and* JAQUES.]

ROS. 'Tis he. Slink by, and note him.

JAQ. I thank you for your company, but, good faith, I had as lief have been myself alone. 270

ORL. And so had I, but yet, for fashion sake, I thank you too for your society.

JAQ. God buy you.° Let's meet as little as we can.

ORL. I do desire we may be better strangers. 275

JAQ. I pray you mar no more trees with writing love songs in their barks.

ORL. I pray you mar no moe° of my verses with reading them ill-favoredly.°

JAQ. Rosalind is your love's name? 280

ORL. Yes, just.°

JAQ. I do not like her name.

ORL. There was no thought of pleasing you when she was christened.

JAQ. What stature is she of? 285

ORL. Just as high as my heart.

JAQ. You are full of pretty answers. Have you not been acquainted with goldsmiths' wives, and conned them out of rings?° 289

ORL. Not so, but I answer you right painted cloth,° from whence you have studied your questions.

JAQ. You have a nimble wit. I think 'twas made of Atalanta's° heels. Will you sit down with me? And we two will rail against our mistress the world, and all our misery. 296

ORL. I will chide no breather° in the world but myself, against whom I know most faults.

JAQ. The worst fault you have is to be in love.

ORL. 'Tis a fault I will not change for your best virtue. I am weary of you. 302

JAQ. By my troth, I was seeking for a fool when I found you.

ORL. He is drowned in the brook. Look but in and you shall see him. 306

JAQ. There I shall see mine own figure.

ORL. Which I take to be either a fool or a cipher.

JAQ. I'll tarry no longer with you. Farewell, good Signior Love. 310

ORL. I am glad of your departure. Adieu, good Monsieur Melancholy. [*Exit* JAQUES.]

221–22. **let . . . chin:** I can wait for his beard to grow, so long as you tell me whose chin it is.   225–26. **sad brow:** in sober earnest.   238. **Gargantua:** the enormous giant of Rabelais' satirical tale.   245. **atomies:** motes in a sunbeam.   245–46. **resolve . . . lover:** solve a lover's problems.   246–47. **taste . . . him:** i.e., to whet your appetite for my tale.   253. **along:** at full length.   257. **holloa:** hold up! whoa!   258. **curvets:** prances. **furnished:** equipped.

262. **burden:** refrain.   274. **God . . . you:** God be with you. 278. **moe:** more.   279. **ill-favoredly:** with a wry face.   281. **just:** exactly.   289. **out of rings:** Rings were often inscribed with "posies" — pretty little sentences or mottoes.   290–91. **painted cloth:** In taverns and other rooms for which genuine tapestry was too costly, coarse cloths painted with Scriptural or classical scenes were used to cover the walls. The figures were sometimes painted with texts or labels issuing from their mouths with suitable remarks. See Pl. 6a.   294. **Atalanta:** See l. 155,n. 297. **breather:** living creature.

ROS. [*Aside to* CELIA] I will speak to him like a saucy lackey,° and under that habit play the knave with him. Do you hear, forester? 315

ORL. Very well. What would you?

ROS. I pray you, what is 't o' clock?

ORL. You should ask me what time o' day. There's no clock in the forest. 319

ROS. Then there is no truelover in the forest, else sighing every minute and groaning every hour would detect the lazy foot of Time as well as a clock.°

ORL. And why not the swift foot of Time? Had not that been as proper? 325

ROS. By no means, sir. Time travels in divers° paces with divers persons. I'll tell you who Time ambles withal, who Time trots withal, who Time gallops withal, and who he stands still withal.

ORL. I prithee who doth he trot withal? 330

ROS. Marry, he trots hard with a young maid between the contract° of her marriage and the day it is solemnized. If the interim be but a sennight,° Time's pace is so hard that it seems the length of seven year. 335

ORL. Who ambles Time withal?

ROS. With a priest that lacks Latin and a rich man that hath not the gout; for the one sleeps easily because he cannot study, and the other lives merrily because he feels no pain, the one lacking the burden of lean and wasteful learning, the other knowing no burden of heavy tedious penury. These Time ambles withal.

ORL. Who doth he gallop withal? 344

ROS. With a thief to the gallows, for though he go as softly as foot can fall, he thinks himself too soon there.

ORL. Who stays it still withal?

ROS. With lawyers in the vacation, for they sleep between term and term and then they perceive not how Time moves. 351

ORL. Where dwell you, pretty youth?

ROS. With this shepherdess, my sister. Here in the skirts° of the forest, like fringe upon a petticoat.

ORL. Are you native of this place? 356

ROS. As the cony° that you see dwell where she is kindled.°

ORL. Your accent is something finer than you could purchase in so removed° a dwelling. 360

ROS. I have been told so of many. But indeed an old religious° uncle of mine taught me to speak, who was in his youth an inland man,° one that

knew courtship too well, for there he fell in love. I have heard him read many lectures against it, and I thank God I am not a woman, to be touched with so many giddy offenses as he hath generally taxed their whole sex withal. 368

ORL. Can you remember any of the principal evils that he laid to the charge of women?

ROS. There were none principal, they were all like one another as halfpence are, every one fault seeming monstrous till his fellow fault came to match it.

ORL. I prithee recount some of them. 375

ROS. No, I will not cast away my physic but on those that are sick. There is a man haunts the forest that abuses our young plants with carving "Rosalind" on their barks, hangs odes upon hawthorns and elegies on brambles — all, forsooth, deify- 380 ing the name of Rosalind. If I could meet that fancymonger,° I would give him some good counsel, for he seems to have the quotidian° of love upon him.

ORL. I am he that is so love-shaked. I pray you tell me your remedy. 386

ROS. There is none of my uncle's marks upon you. He taught me how to know a man in love, in which cage of rushes° I am sure you are not prisoner. 390

ORL. What were his marks?

ROS. A lean cheek, which you have not; a blue eye° and sunken, which you have not; an unquestionable° spirit, which you have not; a beard neglected, which you have not — but I pardon you 395 for that, for simply your having in beard is a younger brother's revenue.° Then your hose should be ungartered, your bonnet° unbanded,° your sleeve unbuttoned, your shoe untied, and everything about you demonstrating a careless desolation. But 400 you are no such man, you are rather point-device° in your accouterments,° as loving yourself than seeming the lover of any other.

ORL. Fair youth, I would I could make thee believe I love. 405

ROS. Me believe it! You may as soon make her that you love believe it, which, I warrant, she is apter to do than to confess she does. That is one of the points in the which women still give the lie to their consciences. But, in good sooth, are you he that hangs the verses on the trees wherein Rosalind is so admired? 412

ORL. I swear to thee, youth, by the white hand of Rosalind, I am that he, that unfortunate he.

ROS. But are you so much in love as your rhymes speak?

---

314. lackey: servant.　320–23. else . . . clock: by giving a sigh at each minute and a groan at each hour you would discover the slow passage of Time as clearly as if you had a clock. 326. divers: different.　332. contract: formal betrothal.　See Gen. Intro. p. 20a, and App. 15.　333. sennight: week. 355. skirts: outskirts.　357. cony: rabbit.　358. kindled: brought forth.　360. removed: remote.　362. religious: i.e., a hermit.　363. inland man: city dweller.

381–82. fancymonger: trader in love.　383. quotidian: fever which recurs daily.　390. cage of rushes: cage of reed made for little birds.　392–93. blue eye: with dark rings under the eye. See App. 4.　394. unquestionable: glum.　396–97. having . . . revenue: your beard anyhow is a poor thing like the income of a younger brother.　398. bonnet: hat. unbanded: without a band.　401. point-device: very neat.　402. accouterments: equipment

ORL. Neither rhyme nor reason can express how much.   419

ROS. Love is merely a madness, and I tell you deserves as well a dark house and a whip as madmen do.° And the reason why they are not so punished and cured is that the lunacy is so ordinary that the whippers are in love too. Yet I profess curing it by counsel.   425

ORL. Did you ever cure any so?

ROS. Yes, one, and in this manner. He was to imagine me his love, his mistress, and I set him every day to woo me. At which time would I, being but a moonish° youth, grieve, be effeminate,   430 changeable, longing and liking, proud, fantastical, apish, shallow, inconstant, full of tears, full of smiles, for every passion something and for no passion truly anything, as boys and women are for the most part cattle of this color. Would now like   435 him, now loathe him; then entertain him, then forswear° him; now weep for him, then spit at him; that I drave my suitor from his mad humor° of love to a living humor of madness, which was to forswear the full stream of the world° and to live in a   440 nook merely monastic.° And thus I cured him, and this way will I take upon me to wash your liver° as clean as a sound sheep's heart, that there shall not be one spot of love in 't.

ORL. I would not be cured, youth.   446

ROS. I would cure you if you would but call me Rosalind and come every day to my cote and woo me.

ORL. Now, by the faith of my love, I will. Tell me where it is.   451

ROS. Go with me to it and I'll show it you. And by the way you shall tell me where in the forest you live. Will you go?

ORL. With all my heart, good youth.   455

ROS. Nay, you must call me Rosalind. Come, Sister, will you go?   [*Exeunt.*]

SCENE III. *The forest.*

[*Enter* TOUCHSTONE *and* AUDREY; JAQUES *behind.*]

TOUCH. Come apace,° good Audrey. I will fetch up your goats, Audrey. And how, Audrey? Am I the man yet? Doth my simple feature content you?

AUD. Your features! Lord warrant us! What features?   6

TOUCH. I am here with thee and thy goats, as the most capricious° poet, honest Ovid, was among the Goths.°

JAQ. [*Aside*] Oh, knowledge ill-inhabited, worse than Jove in a thatched house!°   11

TOUCH. When° a man's verses cannot be understood, nor a man's good wit seconded° with the forward child understanding, it strikes a man more dead than a great reckoning in a little room.° Truly, I would the gods had made thee poetical.   16

AUD. I do not know what " poetical " is. Is it honest in deed and word? Is it a true thing?

TOUCH. No, truly, for the truest poetry is the most feigning, and lovers are given to poetry, and what they swear in poetry may be said as lovers they do feign.   22

AUD. Do you wish, then, that the gods had made me poetical?

TOUCH. I do, truly, for thou swearest to me thou art honest.° Now if thou wert a poet, I might have some hope thou didst feign.   27

AUD. Would you not have me honest?

TOUCH. No, truly, unless thou wert hard-favored,° for honesty coupled to beauty is to have honey a sauce to sugar.

JAQ. [*Aside*] A material° fool!

AUD. Well, I am not fair, and therefore I pray the gods make me honest.   34

TOUCH. Truly, and to cast away honesty upon a foul slut were to put good meat into an unclean dish.

AUD. I am not a slut, though I thank the gods I am foul.   39

TOUCH. Well, praised be the gods for thy foulness! Sluttishness may come hereafter. But be it as it may be, I will marry thee, and to that end I have been with Sir Oliver Martext,° the vicar of the next village, who hath promised to meet me in this place of the forest and to couple us.   45

JAQ. [*Aside*] I would fain see this meeting.

AUD. Well, the gods give us joy!

TOUCH. Amen. A man may, if he were of a fearful heart, stagger° in this attempt; for here we have no temple but the wood, no assembly but horn   50 beasts. But what though? Courage! As horns° are odious, they are necessary. It is said, " Many a man knows no end of his goods." Right, many a man has

8. **capricious:** with a pun on *caper:* a goat, a most lascivious beast.   **8–9. Ovid . . . Goths:** Ovid was banished from Rome for an intrigue with the daughter of the Emperor Augustus and forced to live with the Getae (*Goths*). There is a second pun on Goths and goats.   **11. Jove . . . house:** i.e., a god living in a cottage.   **12–15. When . . . room:** This cryptic remark is probably topical, but the allusion is lost. **seconded:** supported. **great . . . room:** i.e., a huge bill for a private dinner party.   **26. honest:** chaste.   **29. hard-favored:** plain-faced, homely.   **32. material:** full of matter.   **43. Sir . . . Martext:** A minister of the church was often a Bachelor of Arts, and so entitled "dominus," which was translated "sir." Oliver, however, is not a properly ordained minister but a local preacher who mars texts by his misinterpretations.   **49. stagger:** tremble.   **51. horns:** the inevitable joke about the cuckold's horn. See App. 11.

421–22. **dark . . . do:** This was the common treatment given to lunatics.   430. **moonish:** fickle, changeable as the moon.   437. **forswear:** deny with an oath.   438. **humor:** mood.   440. **full . . . world:** i.e., a full life.   441. **merely monastic:** an absolute monk.   442. **liver:** the seat of the passions.

Sc. iii: 1. **apace:** quickly.

good horns and knows no end of them. Well, that is the dowry of his wife, 'tis none of his own 55 getting. Horns? — Even so. — Poor men alone? No, no, the noblest deer hath them as huge as the rascal.° Is the single man therefore blessed? No. As a walled town is more worthier than a village, so is the forehead of a married man more honorable 60 than the bare brow of a bachelor; and by how much defense is better than no skill, by so much is a horn° more precious than to want. Here comes Sir Oliver. [Enter sir oliver martext.] Sir Oliver Martext, you are well met. Will you dispatch us here under this tree, or shall we go with you to your chapel? 67

sir oli. Is there none here to give the woman?

touch. I will not take her on gift of any man.

sir oli. Truly, she must be given° or the marriage is not lawful.

jaq. Proceed, proceed. I'll give her. 72

touch. Good even, good Master What-ye-call't. How do you, sir? You are very well met. God 'ild° you for your last company. I am very glad to see you. Even a toy° in hand here, sir. Nay, pray be covered.°

jaq. Will you be married, Motley? 79

touch. As the ox hath his bow,° sir, the horse his curb, and the falcon her bells, so man hath his desires; and as pigeons bill, so wedlock would be nibbling.°

jaq. And will you, being a man of your breeding, be married under a bush like a beggar? Get you 85 to church, and have a good priest that can tell you what marriage is. This fellow will but join you together as they join wainscot;° then one of you will prove a shrunk panel, and like green timber warp, warp. 90

touch. [Aside] I am not in the mind, but I were better to be married of him than of another. For he is not like to marry me well, and not being well married, it will be a good excuse for me hereafter to leave my wife. 95

jaq. Go thou with me, and let me counsel thee.

touch. Come, sweet Audrey.
We must be married or we must live in bawdry.
Farewell, good Master Oliver: not — 100
"O sweet Oliver,
O brave Oliver,
Leave me not behind thee — "
but —
"Wind° away, 105
Begone, I say,

I will not to wedding with thee."
[Exeunt jaques, touchstone and audrey.]

sir oli. 'Tis no matter. Ne'er a fantastical knave of them all shall flout° me out of my calling. 109
[Exit.]

scene iv. *The forest.*

[Enter rosalind and celia.]

ros. Never talk to me, I will weep.

cel. Do, I prithee, but yet have the grace to consider that tears do not become a man.

ros. But have I not cause to weep? 4

cel. As good cause as one would desire, therefore weep.

ros. His very hair is of the dissembling° color.

cel. Something browner than Judas's.° Marry, his kisses are Judas's own children. 10

ros. I'faith, his hair is of a good color.

cel. An excellent color. Your chestnut was ever the only color.

ros. And his kissing is as full of sanctity as the touch of holy bread. 15

cel. He hath bought a pair of cast° lips of Diana.° A nun of winter's sisterhood kisses not more religiously, the very ice of chastity is in them.

ros. But why did he swear he would come this morning and comes not? 21

cel. Nay, certainly there is no truth in him.

ros. Do you think so?

cel. Yes, I think he is not a pickpurse nor a horse-stealer; but for his verity in love, I do think him as concave as a covered goblet° or a worm-eaten nut.

ros. Not true in love? 29

cel. Yes, when he is in, but I think he is not in.

ros. You have heard him swear downright he was.

cel. "Was" is not "is." Besides, the oath of a lover is no stronger than the word of a tapster;° they are both the confirmer of false reckonings. He attends here in the forest on the Duke your father. 37

ros. I met the Duke yesterday and had much question° with him. He asked me of what parentage I was. I told him of as good as he, so he laughed and let me go. But what talk we of fathers when there is such a man as Orlando? 42

cel. Oh, that's a brave man! He writes brave verses, speaks brave words, swears brave oaths and breaks them bravely, quite traverse, athwart° the heart of his lover — as a puisny° tilter that spurs his

---

58. rascal: a young lean deer in poor condition.   62. horn: with a pun on the cornucopia or horn of plenty.   70. given: a woman was, in theory, the possession of her father until marriage, when he gave her away to her husband. This notion is still symbolized in the marriage service of the Church of England.   74. God 'ild: God reward.   77. toy: trifle.   77–78. be covered: put your hat on.   80. bow: yoke.   83. nibbling: i.e., getting at a man.   88. wainscot: wooden paneling. See Pl. 17.   105. Wind: turn.

109. flout: mock.
   Sc. iv: 8. dissembling: cheating.   9. browner ... Judas's: Judas Iscariot, the traitor, was portrayed with red hair.   16. cast: cast off. Some editors read "chaste."   17. Diana: the goddess of chastity.   28. concave ... goblet: as hollow as a drinking cup with a cover. See Pl. 20h.   35. tapster: the potboy in a tavern who brings the drinks.   39. question: conversation.   45. quite ... athwart: i.e., the glancing blow of one who is afraid to ride "full tilt" at his opponent.   46. puisny: inexperienced, paltry.

horse but on one side breaks his staff like a noble
goose. But all's brave that youth mounts and folly
guides. Who comes here?   49

[*Enter* CORIN.]

COR. Mistress and master, you have oft inquired
After the shepherd that complained of love
Who you saw sitting by me on the turf
Praising the proud disdainful shepherdess
That was his mistress.

CEL.   Well, and what of him?

COR. If you will see a pageant° truly played   55
Between the pale complexion of true love
And the red glow of scorn and proud disdain,
Go hence a little and I shall conduct you,
If you will mark it.

ROS.   Oh, come, let us remove.
The sight of lovers feedeth those in love.   60
Bring us to this sight and you shall say
I'll prove a busy actor in their play.   [*Exeunt.*]

SCENE V. *Another part of the forest.*

[*Enter* SILVIUS *and* PHEBE.]

SIL. Sweet Phebe, do not scorn me, do not, Phebe.
Say that you love me not, but say not so
In bitterness. The common executioner,
Whose heart the accustomed sight of death makes
    hard,
Falls° not the ax upon the humbled neck   5
But first begs pardon. Will you sterner be
Than he that dies and lives by bloody drops?

[*Enter* ROSALIND, CELIA, *and* CORIN, *behind.*]

PHE. I would not be thy executioner.
I fly thee, for I would not injure thee.
Thou tell'st me there is murder in mine eye.   10
'Tis pretty,° sure, and very probable,
That eyes, that are the frail'st and softest things,
Who shut their coward gates on atomies,°
Should be called tyrants, butchers, murderers!
Now I do frown on thee with all my heart,   15
And if mine eyes can wound, now let them kill thee.
Now counterfeit° to swoon, why, now fall down.
Or if thou canst not, oh, for shame, for shame,
Lie not, to say mine eyes are murderers!   19
Now show the wound mine eye hath made in thee.
Scratch thee but with a pin and there remains
Some scar of it. Lean but upon a rush,
The cicatrice° and capable impressure°
Thy palm some moment keeps. But now mine eyes,
Which I have darted at thee, hurt thee not,   25
Nor, I am sure, there is no force in eyes

That can do hurt.

SIL.   O dear Phebe,
If ever — as that ever may be near —
You meet in some fresh cheek the power of fancy,°
Then shall you know the wounds invisible   30
That love's keen arrows make.

PHE.   But till that time
Come not thou near me. And when that time comes,
Afflict me with thy mocks, pity me not,
As till that time I shall not pity thee.

ROS. And why, I pray you? Who might be your
    mother   35
That you insult, exult, and all at once
Over the wretched? What though you have no
    beauty —
As, by my faith, I see no more in you
Than without candle may go dark to bed° —
Must you be therefore proud and pitiless?   40
Why, what means this? Why do you look on me?
I see no more in you than in the ordinary
Of nature's salework.° 'Od's my little life,°
I think she means to tangle my eyes too!
No, faith, proud mistress, hope not after it. 45
'Tis not your inky brows, your black silk hair,°
Your bugle° eyeballs, nor your cheek of cream,
That can entame my spirits to your worship.
You foolish shepherd, wherefore do you follow her
Like foggy south,° puffing with wind and rain? 50
You are a thousand times a properer° man
Than she a woman. 'Tis such fools as you
That makes the world full of ill-favored children.
'Tis not her glass, but you, that flatters her,
And out of you she sees herself more proper   55
Than any of her lineaments° can show her.
But, mistress, know yourself. Down on your knees
And thank Heaven, fasting, for a good man's love.
For I must tell you friendly in your ear,
Sell when you can. You are not for all markets. 60
Cry the man mercy,° love him, take his offer.
Foul is most foul, being foul to be a scoffer.°
So take her to thee, shepherd. Fare you well.

PHE. Sweet youth, I pray you, chide a year to-
    gether.
I had rather hear you chide than this man woo. 65

ROS. He's fallen in love with your foulness and
she'll fall in love with my anger. If it be so, as fast as
she answers thee with frowning looks, I'll sauce her
with bitter words. Why look you so upon me?   70

PHE. For no ill will I bear you.

---

55. pageant: play.
Sc. v: 5. Falls: lets fall.   11. pretty: a pretty notion.
13. atomies: the smallest particles. See III.ii.245,n.   17. counter-
feit: pretend.   23. cicatrice: scar. capable impressure: imprint
retained.

29. fancy: love.   39. without . . . bed: i.e., you're not so brilliant
that you can go to bed by your own light.   42–43. ordinary . . .
salework: no extraordinary piece of goods.   43. 'Od's . . . life:
a mild oath, "bless us."   46. black . . . hair: Black was not con-
sidered beautiful. See Sonnet 130.   47. bugle: beady.   50. foggy
south: The south wind brought fogs and illness.   51. properer:
more handsome.   56. lineaments: features.   61. Cry . . . mercy:
ask his pardon.   62. Foul . . . scoffer: i.e., you are ugly anyway,
and uglier when you are disdainful.

ROS. I pray you do not fall in love with me,
For I am falser than vows made in wine.
Besides, I like you not. If you will know my house,
'Tis at the tuft° of olives here hard by.   75
Will you go, Sister? Shepherd, ply° her hard.
Come, Sister. Shepherdess, look on him better,
And be not proud. Though all the world could see,
None could be so abused in sight as he.
Come, to our flock.   80

     [*Exeunt* ROSALIND, CELIA *and* CORIN.]

PHE. Dead shepherd, now I find thy saw of
    might —
" Who ever loved that loved not at first sight? "°
SIL. Sweet Phebe ——
PHE.   Ha, what say'st thou, Silvius?
SIL. Sweet Phebe, pity me.
PHE. Why, I am sorry for thee, gentle Silvius.   85
SIL. Wherever sorrow is, relief would be.
If you do sorrow at my grief in love,
By giving love your sorrow and my grief
Were both extermined.   89
PHE. Thou hast my love. Is not that neighborly?
SIL. I would have you.
PHE.   Why, that were covetousness.
Silvius, the time was that I hated thee,
And yet it is not that I bear thee love.
But since that thou canst talk of love so well,
Thy company, which erst° was irksome to me,   95
I will endure, and I'll employ thee too.
But do not look for further recompense
Than thine own gladness that thou art employed.
SIL. So holy and so perfect is my love,
And I in such a poverty of grace,°   100
That I shall think it a most plenteous crop
To glean the broken ears after the man
That the main harvest reaps. Loose now and then
A scattered smile, and that I'll live upon.
PHE. Know'st thou the youth that spoke to me ere-
    while?°   105
SIL. Not very well, but I have met him oft,
And he hath bought the cottage and the bounds
That the old carlot° once was master of.
PHE. Think not I love him, though I ask for him.
'Tis but a peevish° boy, yet he talks well.   110
But what care I for words? Yet words do well
When he that speaks them pleases those that hear.
It is a pretty youth — not very pretty —
But, sure, he's proud, and yet his pride becomes him.
He'll make a proper man. The best thing in him
Is his complexion, and faster than his tongue   116
Did make offense his eye did heal it up.
He is not very tall, yet for his years he's tall.
His leg is but soso, and yet 'tis well.

There was a pretty redness in his lip,   120
A little riper and more lusty red
Than that mixed in his cheek, 'twas just the differ-
    ence
Betwixt the constant red and mingled damask.°
There be some women, Silvius, had they marked
    him
In parcels° as I did, would have gone near   125
To fall in love with him. But for my part,
I love him not nor hate him not, and yet
I have more cause to hate him than to love him.
For what had he to do to chide at me?   129
He said mine eyes were black and my hair black,
And, now I am remembered, scorned at me.
I marvel why I answered not again.
But that's all one, omittance is no quittance.°
I'll write to him a very taunting letter,
And thou shalt bear it. Wilt thou, Silvius?   135
SIL. Phebe, with all my heart.
PHE.   I'll write it straight,
The matter's in my head and in my heart.
I will be bitter with him and passing° short.
Go with me, Silvius.   [*Exeunt.*]

Act IV

SCENE I. *The forest.*

    [*Enter* ROSALIND, CELIA, *and* JAQUES.]

JAQ. I prithee, pretty youth, let me be better ac-
quainted with thee.
ROS. They say you are a melancholy fellow.
JAQ. I am so, I do love it better than laughing.   4
ROS. Those that are in extremity of either are
abominable fellows, and betray themselves to every
modern censure° worse than drunkards.
JAQ. Why, 'tis good to be sad and say nothing.
ROS. Why, then 'tis good to be a post.   9
JAQ. I have neither the scholar's melancholy,
which is emulation;° nor the musician's, which is
fantastical; nor the courtier's, which is proud; nor
the soldier's, which is ambitious; nor the lawyer's,
which is politic;° nor the lady's, which is nice; nor
the lover's, which is all these. But it is a melan-   15
choly of mine own, compounded of many simples,°
extracted from many objects, and indeed the sundry

---

75. tuft: clump.   76. ply: press, work at.   81–82. Dead . . .
sight: See *AYLI* Intro. p. 493a.   95. erst: erstwhile, formerly.
100. poverty of grace: poor favor.   105. erewhile: just now.
108. carlot: carl, peasant. See II.iv.75–87.   110. peevish: per-
verse, silly.

123. mingled damask: blended pink (the color of damask roses).
125. In parcels: in parts, each part separately.   133. omittance
. . . quittance: i.e., because I let him off now, that does not mean
that he will get off altogether.   138. passing: exceedingly.
    Act IV, Sc. i: 7. modern censure: trifling criticism.   11. emu-
lation: jealous rivalry.   14. politic: put on for crafty ends.
16. simples: drugs, ingredients.

contemplation of my travels, in which my often
rumination wraps me in a most humorous sad-
ness.° 20

ROS. A traveler!° By my faith, you have great
reason to be sad. I fear you have sold your own lands
to see other men's; then, to have seen much and to
have nothing is to have rich eyes and poor hands. 25

JAQ. Yes, I have gained my experience.

ROS. And your experience makes you sad. I had
rather have a fool to make me merry than experi-
ence to make me sad — and to travel for it too!

[*Enter* ORLANDO.]

ORL. Good day and happiness, dear Rosalind! 30

JAQ. Nay, then, God buy you° an you talk in
blank verse.   [*Exit.*]

ROS. Farewell, Monsieur Traveler. Look you lisp°
and wear strange suits. Disable° all the benefits of
your own country, be out of love with your 35
nativity° and almost chide God for making you that
countenance° you are, or I will scarce think you
have swam in a gondola.° Why, how now, Orlan-
do! Where have you been all this while? You a
lover! An you serve me such another trick, never
come in my sight more.   41

ORL. My fair Rosalind, I come within an hour of
my promise.

ROS. Break an hour's promise in love! He that
will divide a minute into a thousand parts and 45
break but a part of the thousandth part of a minute
in the affairs of love, it may be said of him that
Cupid hath clapped him o' the shoulder,° but I'll
warrant him heart-whole.

ORL. Pardon me, dear Rosalind.   50

ROS. Nay, an you be so tardy, come no more in my
sight. I had as lief be wooed of a snail.

ORL. Of a snail?

ROS. Aye, of a snail, for though he comes slowly,
he carries his house on his head — a better jointure,°
I think, than you make a woman. Besides, he brings
his destiny with him.   57

ORL. What's that?

ROS. Why, horns,° which such as you are fain to
be beholding to your wives for. But he comes armed
in his fortune and prevents the slander of his
wife.°

ORL. Virtue is no hornmaker, and my Rosalind is
virtuous.

ROS. And I am your Rosalind.   65

CEL. It pleases him to call you so, but he hath a
Rosalind of a better leer° than you.

ROS. Come, woo me, woo me, for now I am in a
holiday° humor and like enough to consent. What
would you say to me now an I were your very very
Rosalind?   71

ORL. I would kiss before I spoke.

ROS. Nay, you were better speak first, and when
you were graveled° for lack of matter, you might
take occasion to kiss. Very good orators, when 75
they are out, they will spit, and for lovers lacking —
God warn° us! — matter, the cleanliest shift° is to
kiss.

ORL. How if the kiss be denied?

ROS. Then she puts you to entreaty and there be-
gins new matter.   81

ORL. Who could be out, being before his beloved
mistress?

ROS. Marry, that should you if I were your mis-
tress, or I should think my honesty ranker° than my
wit.   86

ORL. What, of my suit?

ROS. Not out of your apparel, and yet out of your
suit.° Am not I your Rosalind?

ORL. I take some joy to say you are, because I
would be talking of her.   91

ROS. Well, in her person° I say I will not have
you.

ORL. Then in mine own person I die.

ROS. No, faith, die by attorney.° The poor world
is almost six thousand years old, and in all this time
there was not any man died in his own person, 96
videlicet,° in a love cause. Troilus had his brains
dashed out with a Grecian club, yet he did what he
could to die before, and he is one of the patterns of
love. Leander, he would have lived many a fair 100
year, though Hero had turned nun, if it had not
been for a hot midsummer night; for, good youth,
he went but forth to wash him in the Hellespont
and being taken with the cramp was drowned. And
the foolish chroniclers of that age found it was 105
"Hero of Sestos."° But these are all lies. Men have
died from time to time and worms have eaten them,
but not for love.

ORL. I would not have my right Rosalind of this
mind, for I protest her frown might kill me. 110

ROS. By this hand, it will not kill a fly. But come,

<hr />

18–20. my . . . sadness: by often ruminating on my experiences
I am filled with moody sadness.   21. A traveler: Jibes at English-
men who had traveled were common.   31. God . . . you: God
be with you.   33. lisp: affect a foreign accent.   34. Disable:
make slighting remarks about.   36. nativity: place and moment
of birth.   37. countenance: natural face.   38. swam . . . gon-
dola: i.e., visited Venice, which (like Paris for the modern
American) was the goal of all travelers.   48. clapped . . .
shoulder: arrested him, made him prisoner.   55. jointure: mar-
riage portion.   59. horns: See App. 11.   60–62. he . . . wife: i.e.,
the snail has his horns before marriage and so forestalls (*pre-
vents*) the slanders which his wife will bring him.

67. leer: look.   69. holiday: i.e., gay.   74. graveled: run aground.
77. warn: colloquial for "warrant." cleanliest shift: the cleanest
way of getting round the difficulty.   85. ranker: fouler.
89. suit: the same pun as in II.vii.44.   92. in . . . person: as her
representative.   94. by attorney: by proxy.   97. videlicet:
namely, "viz."   97–106. Troilus . . . Sestos: No one, says Rosa-
lind, has really died for love, not even the great lovers of legend,
such as Troilus, who was madly in love with Cressida, or
Leander who used to swim over the Hellespont to visit Hero of
Sestos and was drowned; historians in those days said that his
death was caused by Hero, but in truth it was the cramp.

now I will be your Rosalind in a more coming-on° disposition, and ask me what you will, I will grant it.

ORL. Then love me, Rosalind. 115

ROS. Yes, faith, will I, Fridays and Saturdays and all.

ORL. And wilt thou have me?

ROS. Aye, and twenty such.

ORL. What sayest thou? 120

ROS. Are you not good?

ORL. I hope so.

ROS. Why then, can one desire too much of a good thing? Come, Sister, you shall be the priest and marry us. Give me your hand, Orlando. What do you say, Sister? 126

ORL. Pray thee, marry us.

CEL. I cannot say the words.

ROS. You must begin, "Will you, Orlando ———"

CEL. Go to. Will you, Orlando, have to wife this Rosalind? 131

ORL. I will.

ROS. Aye, but when?

ORL. Why now, as fast as she can marry us. 134

ROS. Then you must say "I take thee, Rosalind, for wife."

ORL. I take thee, Rosalind, for wife.

ROS. I might ask you for your commission,° but I do take thee, Orlando, for my husband. There's a girl goes before the priest,° and certainly a woman's thought runs before her actions. 141

ORL. So do all thoughts, they are winged.

ROS. Now tell me how long you would have her after you have possessed her.

ORL. Forever and a day. 145

ROS. Say "a day," without the "ever." No, no, Orlando. Men are April when they woo, December when they wed. Maids are May when they are maids, but the sky changes when they are wives. I will be more jealous of thee than a Barbary cock pi- 150 geon over his hen, more clamorous than a parrot against° rain, more newfangled° than an ape, more giddy in my desires than a monkey. I will weep for nothing, like Diana in the fountain,° and I will do that when you are disposed to be merry. I will laugh like a hyen,° and that when thou art inclined to sleep. 157

ORL. But will my Rosalind do so?

ROS. By my life, she will do as I do.

ORL. Oh, but she is wise.

ROS. Or else she could not have the wit to do this. The wiser, the waywarder.° Make° the doors upon a woman's wit and it will out at the casement.° Shut

that and 'twill out at the keyhole. Stop that, 'twill fly with the smoke out at the chimney. 166

ORL. A man that had a wife with such a wit, he might say "Wit, whither wilt?" ° °

ROS. Nay, you might keep that check° for it till you met your wife's wit going to your neighbor's bed. 171

ORL. And what wit could wit have to excuse that?

ROS. Marry, to say she came to seek you there. You shall never take her without her answer, unless you take her without her tongue. Oh, that woman that cannot make her fault her husband's occasion,° let her never nurse her child herself, for she will breed it like a fool! 179

ORL. For these two hours, Rosalind, I will leave thee.

ROS. Alas, dear love, I cannot lack thee two hours!

ORL. I must attend the Duke at dinner. By two o'clock I will be with thee again. 185

ROS. Aye, go your ways, go your ways, I knew what you would prove. My friends told me as much, and I thought no less. That flattering tongue of yours won me. 'Tis but one cast away,° and so come, death! Two o'clock is your hour? 190

ORL. Aye, sweet Rosalind.

ROS. By my troth,° and in good earnest, and so God mend me, and by all pretty oaths that are not dangerous, if you break one jot of your promise or come one minute behind your hour, I will 195 think you the most pathetical break-promise, and the most hollow lover, and the most unworthy of her you call Rosalind, that may be chosen out of the gross band° of the unfaithful. Therefore beware my censure and keep your promise. 200

ORL. With no less religion than if thou wert indeed my Rosalind. So adieu.

ROS. Well, Time is the old justice that examines all such offenders, and let Time try. Adieu. 204

[*Exit* ORLANDO.]

CEL. You have simply misused our sex in your love prate. We must have your doublet and hose plucked over your head, and show the world what the bird hath done to her own nest.° 208

ROS. O Coz, Coz, Coz, my pretty little coz, that thou didst know how many fathom deep I am in love! But it cannot be sounded. My affection hath an unknown bottom,° like the bay of Portugal.

CEL. Or rather, bottomless, that as fast as you pour affection in, it runs out. 215

ROS. No, that same wicked bastard of Venus° that was begot of thought, conceived of spleen, and born

---

112. coming-on: encouraging. 138. commission: i.e., authority. 140. girl . . . priest: i.e., anticipates the priest's words, because she is so eager. 152. against: in anticipation of. newfangled: eager for novelties. 154. Diana . . . fountain: i.e., like a fountain with the figure of Diana, always dripping. 156. hyen: hyena. 163. waywarder: more capricious. Make: shut. 164. casement: window that opens on hinges.

168. Wit . . . wilt: a proverb—"Wit [*intelligence*], where are you going?" 169. check: rebuke. 176–77. that . . . occasion: that cannot blame her husband as the cause of her own faults. occasion: that which causes. 189. cast away: abandoned. 192. troth: truth. 199. gross band: vile company. 208. done . . . nest: i.e., fouled it. 213. unknown bottom: i.e., too deep to be measured. 216. bastard of Venus: i.e., Cupid.

of madness, that blind rascally boy that abuses every-
one's eyes because his own are out, let him be judge
how deep I am in love. I'll tell thee, Aliena, I can-
not be out of the sight of Orlando. I'll go find a
shadow and sigh till he come.   222

CEL. And I'll sleep.   [*Exeunt.*]

SCENE II. *The forest.*

[*Enter* JAQUES, LORDS, *and* FORESTERS.]

JAQ. Which is he that killed the deer?

A LORD. Sir, it was I.

JAQ. Let's present him to the Duke, like a Roman
conqueror, and it would do well to set the deer's
horns upon his head for a branch of victory. Have
you no song, forester, for this purpose?   7

FOR. Yes, sir.

JAQ. Sing it. 'Tis no matter how it be in tune so
it make noise enough.

FOR. [*Sings.*]
    What shall he have that killed the deer?
    His leather skin and horns to wear.
        Then sing him home.
            [*The rest shall bear this burden.*]
    Take thou no scorn to wear the horn,
    It was a crest ere thou wast born.   15
        Thy father's father wore it,
        And thy father bore it.
    The horn, the horn, the lusty horn
    Is not a thing to laugh to scorn.   [*Exeunt.*]

SCENE III. *The forest.*

[*Enter* ROSALIND *and* CELIA.]

ROS. How say you now? Is it not past two o'clock?
And here much° Orlando!

CEL. I warrant you with pure love and troubled
brain he hath ta'en his bow and arrows and is gone
forth to sleep. Look who comes here.   5

[*Enter* SILVIUS.]

SIL. My errand is to you, fair youth,
My gentle Phebe bid me give you this.
I know not the contents, but as I guess
By the stern brow and waspish action
Which she did use as she was writing of it,   10
It bears an angry tenor.° Pardon me,
I am but as a guiltless messenger.

ROS. Patience herself would startle at this letter
And play the swaggerer — bear this, bear all.°
She says I am not fair, that I lack manners,   15
She calls me proud, and that she could not love me
Were man as rare as phoenix.° 'Od's my will!

Her love is not the hare that I do hunt.
Why writes she so to me? Well, shepherd, well,
This is a letter of your own device.   20

SIL. No, I protest I know not the contents.
Phebe did write it.

ROS.   Come, come, you are a fool,
And turned into the extremity of love.
I saw her hand. She has a leathern° hand,
A freestone-colored° hand. I verily did think   25
That her old gloves were on, but 'twas her hands.
She has a huswife's hand, but that's no matter.
I say she never did invent this letter.
This is a man's invention and his hand.

SIL. Sure, it is hers.   30

ROS. Why, 'tis a boisterous° and a cruel style,
A style for challengers. Why, she defies me,
Like Turk to Christian. Women's gentle brain
Could not drop forth such giant-rude invention,
Such Ethiope° words, blacker in their effect°   35
Than in their countenance.° Will you hear the let-
    ter?

SIL. So please you, for I never heard it yet,
Yet heard too much of Phebe's cruelty.

ROS. She Phebes me. Mark how the tyrant writes.
[*Reads.*] "Art thou god to shepherd turned   40
        That a maiden's heart hath burned? "
Can a woman rail thus?

SIL. Call you this railing?

ROS. [*Reads.*]
    "Why, thy godhead laid apart,°
    Warr'st thou with a woman's heart? "   45
Did you ever hear such railing?
    "Whiles the eye of man did woo me,
    That could do no vengeance to me."
Meaning me a beast.
    "If the scorn of your bright eyne°   50
    Have power to raise such love in mine,
    Alack, in me what strange effect
    Would they work in mild aspéct!°
    Whiles you chid me, I did love,
    How then might your prayers move!   55
    He that brings this love to thee
    Little knows this love in me.
    And by him seal up thy mind,°
    Whether that thy youth and kind°
    Will the faithful offer take   60
    Of me and all that I can make,
    Or else by him my love deny,
    And then I'll study how to die."

SIL. Call you this chiding?

CEL. Alas, poor shepherd!   65

Sc. iii: 2. **here much:** i.e., a fine lot of. 11. **tenor:** intention.
14. **bear . . . all:** a person who could endure this would bear
anything. 17. **phoenix:** See *Temp*, III.iii.23,n.

24. **leathern:** i.e., the hand of a workingwoman, not of a lady.
25. **freestone-colored:** of the color of Bath brick; i.e., yellow-
brown. 31. **boisterous:** violent. 35. **Ethiope:** i.e., black. **effect:**
intention. 36. **countenance:** appearance. 44. **thy . . . apart:**
why do you, a god, become man? 50. **eyne:** eyes. 53. **mild
aspect:** gentle looks. 58. **seal . . . mind:** write your answer and
send it by him. 59. **kind:** nature.

ROS. Do you pity him? No, he deserves no pity.
Wilt thou love such a woman? What, to make thee
an instrument and play false strains upon thee!
Not to be endured! Well, go your way to her, for I
see love hath made thee a tame snake, and say   70
this to her: That if she loves me, I charge her to love
thee. If she will not, I will never have her unless
thou entreat for her. If you be a truelover, hence,
and not a word, for here comes more company.   75

                           [*Exit* SILVIUS.]

       [*Enter* OLIVER.]

OLI. Good morrow, fair ones. Pray you, if you
    know,
Where in the purlieus° of this forest stands
A sheepcote fenced about with olive trees?

    CEL. West of this place, down in the neighbor bot-
    tom.
The rank° of osiers° by the murmuring stream   80
Left on your right hand brings you to the place.
But at this hour the house doth keep itself,
There's none within.

    OLI. If that an eye may profit by a tongue,
Then should I know you by description,   85
Such garments and such years. " The boy is fair,
Of female favor,° and bestows himself°
Like a ripe sister,° the woman low,
And browner than her brother." Are not you
The owner of the house I did inquire for?   90

    CEL. It is no boast, being asked, to say we are.

    OLI. Orlando doth commend him to you both,
And to that youth he calls his Rosalind
He sends this bloody napkin. Are you he?

    ROS. I am. What must we understand by this?   95

    OLI. Some of my shame, if you will know of me
What man I am, and how, and why, and where
This handkercher was stained.

       CEL.   I pray you tell it.

    OLI. When last the young Orlando parted from
    you
He left a promise to return again   100
Within an hour, and pacing through the forest,
Chewing the food of sweet and bitter fancy,°
Lo, what befell! He threw his eye aside,
And mark what object did present itself.
Under an oak whose boughs were mossed with age
And high top bald with dry antiquity,   106
A wretched ragged man, o'ergrown with hair,
Lay sleeping on his back. About his neck
A green and gilded snake had wreathed itself,
Who with her head nimble in threats approached
The opening of his mouth. But suddenly,   111
Seeing Orlando, it unlinked itself
And with indented glides° did slip away

Into a bush, under which bush's shade
A lioness, with udders all drawn dry,°   115
Lay couching, head on ground, with catlike watch,
When that the sleeping man should stir. For 'tis
The royal disposition of that beast
To prey on nothing that doth seem as dead.
This seen, Orlando did approach the man   120
And found it was his brother, his elder brother.

    CEL. Oh, I have heard him speak of that same
    brother,
And he did render° him the most unnatural
That lived amongst men.

    OLI.   And well he might so do,
For well I know he was unnatural.   125

    ROS. But to Orlando. Did he leave him there,
Food to the sucked and hungry lioness?

    OLI. Twice did he turn his back and purposed so.
But kindness,° nobler ever than revenge,
And nature, stronger than his just occasion,°   130
Made him give battle to the lioness,
Who quickly fell before him. In which hurtling°
From miserable slumber I awaked.

    CEL. Are you his brother?

    ROS.   Was 't you he rescued?

    CEL. Was 't you that did so oft contrive to kill
    him?   135

    OLI. 'Twas I, but 'tis not I, I do not shame
To tell you what I was, since my conversion
So sweetly tastes, being the thing I am.

    ROS. But — for the bloody napkin?

    OLI.   By and by.
When from the first to last betwixt us two   140
Tears our recountments° had most kindly bathed,
As how I came into that desert place,
In brief, he led me to the gentle Duke,
Who gave me fresh array and entertainment,°
Committing me unto my brother's love.   145
Who led me instantly unto his cave,
There stripped himself, and here upon his arm
The lioness had torn some flesh away,
Which all this while had bled, and now he fainted
And cried, in fainting, upon Rosalind.   150
Brief, I recovered him, bound up his wound,
And after some small space, being strong at heart,
He sent me hither, stranger as I am,
To tell this story, that you might excuse
His broken promise, and to give this napkin,   155
Dyed in his blood, unto the shepherd youth
That he in sport doth call his Rosalind.

                 [ROSALIND *swoons*.]

    CEL. Why, how now, Ganymede! Sweet Gany-
    mede!

---

77. purlieus: boundaries.   80. rank: row. osiers: willows, of the
kind used for making baskets.   87. female favor: girlish face.
bestows himself: behaves.   88. Like . . . sister: like an elder
sister.   102. fancy: love.   113. indented glides: wavy motion.

115. udders . . . dry: i.e., hungry and fierce.   123. render: de-
scribe.   129. kindness: natural affection.   130. just occasion:
i.e., his opportunity for getting even with his wicked brother.
132. hurtling: noise of battle.   141. recountments: accounts of
our adventures.   144. entertainment: good treatment.

OLI. Many will swoon when they do look on blood.

CEL. There is more in it. Cousin Ganymede!   160

OLI. Look, he recovers.

ROS. I would I were at home.

CEL.   We'll lead you thither.
I pray you, will you take him by the arm?

OLI. Be of good cheer, youth. You a man! You
lack a man's heart.   165

ROS. I do so, I confess it. Ah, sirrah, a body would
think this was well counterfeited!° I pray you tell
your brother how well I counterfeited. Heigh-ho!

OLI. This was not counterfeit. There is too great
testimony in your complexion that it was a passion
of earnest.°   172

ROS. Counterfeit, I assure you.

OLI. Well then, take a good heart and counterfeit
to be a man.

ROS. So I do. But, i' faith, I should have been a
woman by right.

CEL. Come, you look paler and paler. Pray you
draw homeward. Good sir, go with us.

OLI. That will I, for I must bear answer back   180
How you excuse my brother, Rosalind.

ROS. I shall devise something. But I pray you com-
mend my counterfeiting to him. Will you go?

                                      [_Exeunt._]

Act V

SCENE I. _The forest._

[_Enter_ TOUCHSTONE _and_ AUDREY.]

TOUCH. We shall find a time, Audrey. Patience,
gentle Audrey.

AUD. Faith, the priest was good enough, for all the
old gentleman's saying.   4

TOUCH. A most wicked Sir Oliver, Audrey, a most
vile Martext. But, Audrey, there is a youth here in
the forest lays claim to you.

AUD. Aye, I know who 'tis. He hath no interest in
me in the world. Here comes the man you mean.   10

TOUCH. It is meat and drink to me to see a clown.
By my troth, we that have good wits have much to
answer for — we shall be flouting,° we cannot hold.

[_Enter_ WILLIAM.]

WILL. Good even, Audrey.   15

AUD. God ye good even, William.

WILL. And good even to you, sir.

TOUCH. Good even, gentle friend. Cover thy head,
cover thy head, nay, prithee be covered. How old
are you, friend?   20

WILL. Five and twenty, sir.

TOUCH. A ripe age. Is thy name William?

WILL. William, sir.

TOUCH. A fair name. Wast born i' the forest here?

WILL. Aye, sir, I thank God.   26

TOUCH. "Thank God," a good answer. Art rich?

WILL. Faith, sir, soso.

TOUCH. "Soso" is good, very good, very excellent
good. And yet it is not, it is but soso. Art thou wise?

WILL. Aye, sir, I have a pretty wit.   32

TOUCH. Why, thou sayest well. I do now remem-
ber a saying, "The fool doth think he is wise, but
the wise man knows himself to be a fool." The   35
heathen philosopher, when he had a desire to eat a
grape, would open his lips when he put it into his
mouth, meaning thereby that grapes were made to
eat and lips to open. You do love this maid?   40

WILL. I do, sir.

TOUCH. Give me your hand. Art thou learned?

WILL. No, sir.

TOUCH. Then learn this of me: To have is to have;
for it is a figure in rhetoric that drink, being   45
poured out of a cup into a glass, by filling the one
doth empty the other, for all your writers do consent
that _ipse_° is he. Now you are not _ipse,_ for I am he.

WILL. Which he, sir?   50

TOUCH. He, sir, that must marry this woman.
Therefore, you clown, abandon — which is in the
vulgar° leave, — the society — which in the boorish
is company — of this female — which in the com-
mon is woman. Which together is, abandon the   55
society of this female, or, clown, thou perishest; or,
to thy better understanding, diest; or, to wit, I kill
thee, make thee away, translate thy life into death,
thy liberty into bondage. I will deal in poison with
thee, or in bastinado,° or in steel, I will bandy   60
with thee in faction,° I will o'errun thee with pol-
icy,° I will kill thee a hundred and fifty ways. There-
fore tremble, and depart.

AUD. Do, good William.   64

WILL. God rest you merry sir.   [Exit.]

[_Enter_ CORIN.]

COR. Our master and mistress seek you. Come,
away, away!

TOUCH. Trip, Audrey! Trip, Audrey! I attend, I at-
tend.   [_Exeunt._]

SCENE II. _The forest._

[_Enter_ ORLANDO _and_ OLIVER.]

ORL. Is 't possible that on so little acquaintance you
should like her? That but seeing you should love
her? And, loving, woo? And, wooing, she should
grant? And will you persever to enjoy her?   5

49. ipse: himself.   53. vulgar: common tongue.   60. bastinado:
a thrashing.   60–61. bandy . . . faction: strive with you by in-
trigue.   61–62. o'errun . . . policy: overcome you by some crafty
device.

167. counterfeited: imitated, pretended.   171–72. passion of
earnest: genuine emotion.

Act V, Sc. i: 14. flouting: jesting.

OLI. Neither call the giddiness° of it in question, the poverty of her, the small acquaintance, my sudden wooing, nor her sudden consenting; but say with me, I love Aliena, say with her that she loves me, consent with both that we may enjoy each other. It shall be to your good, for my father's house and all the revenue that was old Sir Rowland's will I estate° upon you, and here live and die a shepherd.   14

ORL. You have my consent. Let your wedding be tomorrow. Thither will I invite the Duke and all 's contented followers. Go you and prepare Aliena, for look you, here comes my Rosalind.

[Enter ROSALIND.*]*

ROS. God save you, Brother.   20

OLI. And you, fair Sister.   *[Exit.]*

ROS. O my dear Orlando, how it grieves me to see thee wear thy heart in a scarf!

ORL. It is my arm.

ROS. I thought thy heart had been wounded with the claws of a lion.   26

ORL. Wounded it is, but with the eyes of a lady.

ROS. Did your brother tell you how I counterfeited to swoon when he showed me your handkercher?   30

ORL. Aye, and greater wonders than that.

ROS. Oh, I know where you are. Nay, 'tis true. There was never anything so sudden but the fight of two rams, and Caesar's thrasonical° brag of " I came, saw, and overcame."° For your brother and my sister no sooner met but they looked, no sooner looked   35 but they loved, no sooner loved but they sighed, no sooner sighed but they asked one another the reason, no sooner knew the reason but they sought the remedy. And in these degrees have they made a pair   40 of stairs to marriage which they will climb incontinent, or else be incontinent before marriage. They are in the very wrath° of love and they will together, clubs cannot part them.°   45

ORL. They shall be married tomorrow, and I will bid the Duke to the nuptial. But oh, how bitter a thing it is to look into happiness through another man's eyes! By so much the more shall I tomorrow be at the height of heart-heaviness, by how   50 much I shall think my brother happy in having what he wishes for.

ROS. Why then, tomorrow I cannot serve your turn for Rosalind?

ORL. I can live no longer by thinking.°   55

ROS. I will weary you then no longer with idle talking. Know of me then, for now I speak to some

purpose, that I know you are a gentleman of good conceit.° I speak not this that you should bear a good opinion of my knowledge, insomuch I say   60 I know you are. Neither do I labor for a greater esteem than may in some little measure draw a belief from you to do yourself good and not to grace me. Believe then, if you please, that I can do strange things. I have, since I was three year old, con-   65 versed with a magician most profound in his art and yet not damnable.° If you do love Rosalind so near the heart as your gesture cries it out, when your brother marries Aliena, shall you marry her. I know into what straits of fortune° she is driven, and   70 it is not impossible to me, if it appear not inconvenient to you, to set her before your eyes tomorrow human as she is and without any danger.

ORL. Speakest thou in sober meanings?   76

ROS. By my life, I do, which I tender° dearly, though I say I am a magician. Therefore put you in your best array, bid your friends, for if you will be married tomorrow, you shall, and to Rosalind if you will. *[Enter* SILVIUS *and* PHEBE.*]* Look, here   81 comes a lover of mine and a lover of hers.

PHE. Youth, you have done me much ungentleness°
To show the letter that I writ to you.

ROS. I care not if I have. It is my study°   85
To seem despiteful and ungentle to you.
You are there followed by a faithful shepherd.
Look upon him, love him, he worships you.

PHE. Good shepherd, tell this youth what 'tis to love.

SIL. It is to be all made of sighs and tears,   90
And so am I for Phebe.

PHE. And I for Ganymede.

ORL. And I for Rosalind.

ROS. And I for no woman.

SIL. It is to be all made of faith and service,   95
And so am I for Phebe.

PHE. And I for Ganymede.

ORL. And I for Rosalind.

ROS. And I for no woman.

SIL. It is to be all made of fantasy,°   100
All made of passion, and all made of wishes,
All adoration, duty, and observance,
All humbleness, all patience and impatience,
All purity, all trial,° all observance,°
And so am I for Phebe.   105

PHE. And so am I for Ganymede.

ORL. And so am I for Rosalind.

ROS. And so am I for no woman.   109

PHE. If this be so, why blame you me to love you?

Sc. ii: **6. giddiness:** rashness. **13. estate:** settle. **33. thrasonical:** boastful. **33–34. I . . . overcame:** Julius Caesar after his victory over the King of Pontus reported to the Senate in three words: *Veni, vidi, vici.* **44. wrath:** passion. **45. clubs . . . them:** When a brawl was started in London streets, there was a cry of "Clubs." Thereupon the apprentices in the shops seized their clubs and swarmed out to separate the parties. **55. thinking:** i.e., pretense.

59. conceit: intelligence. **67. not damnable:** i.e., his magic was used to good and not wicked ends. **70. straits of fortune:** difficult situation. **77. tender:** regard. **83. done . . . ungentleness:** you have not behaved like a gentleman toward me. **85. study:** deliberate purpose. **100. fantasy:** imagination. **104. all trial:** enduring any trial. **observance:** devotion.

SIL. If this be so, why blame you me to love you?

ORL. If this be so, why blame you me to love you?

ROS. Why do you speak too, " Why blame you me to love you? "   116

ORL. To her that is not here, nor doth not hear.

ROS. Pray you, no more of this, 'tis like the howling of Irish wolves against the moon. [*To* SILVIUS] I will help you if I can. [*To* PHEBE] I would   120
love you if I could. Tomorrow meet me all together. [*To* PHEBE] I will marry you if ever I marry woman, and I'll be married tomorrow. [*To* ORLANDO] I will satisfy you if ever I satisfied man, and you shall be married tomorrow. [*To* SILVIUS] I will content   125
you if what pleases you contents you, and you shall be married tomorrow. [*To* ORLANDO] As you love Rosalind, meet. [*To* SILVIUS] As you love Phebe, meet. And as I love no woman, I'll meet. So, fare you well. I have left you commands.   131

SIL. I'll not fail, if I live.

PHE. Nor I.

ORL. Nor I.   [*Exeunt.*]

SCENE III. *The forest.*

[*Enter* TOUCHSTONE *and* AUDREY.]

TOUCH. Tomorrow is the joyful day, Audrey, tomorrow will we be married.

AUD. I do desire it with all my heart, and I hope it is no dishonest° desire to desire to be a woman of the world. Here come two of the banished Duke's pages.   6

[*Enter two* PAGES.]

I. PAGE. Well met, honest gentleman.

TOUCH. By my troth, well met. Come, sit, sit, and a song.

2. PAGE. We are for you. Sit i' the middle.   10

I. PAGE. Shall we clap into 't° roundly, without hawking° or spitting or saying we are hoarse, which are the only prologues° to a bad voice?

2. PAGE. I' faith, i' faith, and both in a tune, like two gypsies on a horse.

SONG

It was a lover and his lass,
     With a hey, and a ho, and a hey nonino,
That o'er the green cornfield did pass
     In the springtime, the only pretty ringtime,°   20
When birds do sing, hey ding a ding, ding.
Sweet lovers love the spring.

Between the acres of the rye,
     With a hey, and a ho, and a hey nonino,
These pretty country folks would lie,   25

In the springtime, the only pretty ringtime,
When birds do sing, hey ding a ding, ding.
Sweet lovers love the spring.

This carol they began that hour,
     With a hey, and a ho, and a hey nonino,
How that a life was but a flower
     In the springtime, the only pretty ringtime,   30
When birds do sing, hey ding a ding, ding.
Sweet lovers love the spring.

And therefore take the present time,
     With a hey, and a ho, and a hey nonino,
For love is crownèd with the prime°
     In the springtime, the only pretty ringtime,   34
When birds do sing, hey ding a ding, ding.
Sweet lovers love the spring.

TOUCH. Truly, young gentlemen, though there was no great matter in the ditty, yet the note was very untunable.

I. PAGE. You are deceived, sir. We kept time, we lost not our time.   39

TOUCH. By my troth, yes. I count it but time lost to hear such a foolish song. God buy you, and God mend your voices! Come, Audrey.   [*Exeunt.*]

SCENE IV. *The forest.*

[*Enter* DUKE *Senior,* AMIENS, JAQUES, ORLANDO, OLIVER, *and* CELIA.]

DUKE S. Dost thou believe, Orlando, that the boy
Can do all this that he hath promised?

ORL. I sometimes do believe, and sometimes do not,
As those that fear they hope and know they fear.

[*Enter* ROSALIND, SILVIUS, *and* PHEBE.]

ROS. Patience once more, whiles our compact is urged.°   5
You say if I bring in your Rosalind,
You will bestow her on Orlando here?

DUKE S. That would I had I kingdoms to give with her.

ROS. And you say you will have her when I bring her?   9

ORL. That would I were I of all kingdoms king.

ROS. You say you'll marry me if I be willing?

PHE. That will I, should I die the hour after.

ROS. But if you do refuse to marry me,
You'll give yourself to this most faithful shepherd?

PHE. So is the bargain.   15

ROS. You say that you'll have Phebe if she will?

SIL. Though to have her and death were both one thing.

Sc. iii: 4. **dishonest:** unchaste.   11. **clap into 't:** get down to
it.   12. **hawking:** clearing the throat.   13. **only prologues:** usual
apologies.   20. **ringtime:** i.e., the time for wedding bells.

33. **prime:** perfection.
Sc. iv: 5. **compact is urged:** agreement is repeated.

ROS. I have promised to make all this matter
even,°
Keep you your word, O Duke, to give your daugh-
ter,
You yours, Orlando, to receive his daughter.   20
Keep your word, Phebe, that you'll marry me
Or else, refusing me, to wed this shepherd.
Keep your word, Silvius, that you'll marry her
If she refuse me. And from hence I go
To make these doubts all even.   25

[*Exeunt* ROSALIND *and* CELIA.]

DUKE S. I do remember in this shepherd boy
Some lively touches of my daughter's favor.°

ORL. My lord, the first time that I ever saw him
Methought he was a brother to your daughter.
But, my good lord, this boy is forest-born,   30
And hath been tutored in the rudiments
Of many desperate studies by his uncle,
Whom he reports to be a great magician
Obscurèd° in the circle of this forest.   34

[*Enter* TOUCHSTONE *and* AUDREY.]

JAQ. There is, sure, another flood toward, and
these couples are coming to the ark. Here comes a
pair of very strange beasts, which in all tongues are
called fools.

TOUCH. Salutation and greeting to you all!   39

JAQ. Good my lord, bid him welcome. This is the
motley-minded gentleman that I have so often met
in the forest. He hath been a courtier, he swears.

TOUCH. If any man doubt that, let him put me to
my purgation.° I have trod a measure.° I have   45
flattered a lady. I have been politic° with my friend,
smooth with mine enemy. I have undone three
tailors.° I have had four quarrels, and like to have
fought one.

JAQ. And how was that ta'en up?   50

TOUCH. Faith, we met, and found the quarrel was
upon the seventh cause.

JAQ. How seventh cause? Good my lord, like this
fellow.

DUKE S. I like him very well.   55

TOUCH. God 'ild° you, sir, I desire you of the like.
I press in here, sir, amongst the rest of the country
copulatives,° to swear and to forswear, according as
marriage binds and blood breaks. A poor virgin, sir,
an ill-favored thing, sir, but mine own. A poor hu-
mor of mine, sir, to take that that no man else will.
Rich honesty dwells like a miser, sir, in a poor house,
as your pearl in your foul oyster.   64

DUKE S. By my faith, he is very swift and senten-
tious.°

TOUCH. According to the fool's bolt,° sir, and such
dulcet diseases.°

JAQ. But for the seventh cause, how did you find
the quarrel on the seventh cause?   70

TOUCH. Upon a lie seven times removed — Bear
your body more seeming, Audrey — as thus, sir. I
did dislike the cut of a certain courtier's beard. He
sent me word if I said his beard was not cut well, he
was in the mind it was. This is called the Retort   75
Courteous. If I sent him word again " it was not
well cut," he would send me word he cut it to please
himself. This is called the Quip Modest. If again " it
was not well cut," he disabled my judgment.° This
is called the Reply Churlish. If again " it was   80
not well cut," he would answer I spake not true.
This is called the Reproof Valiant. If again " it was
not well cut," he would say I lie. This is called the
Countercheck Quarrelsome. And so to the Lie Cir-
cumstantial° and the Lie Direct.°   86

JAQ. And how oft did you say his beard was not
well cut?

TOUCH. I durst go no further than the Lie Cir-
cumstantial, nor he durst not give me the Lie Direct,
and so we measured swords and parted.

JAQ. Can you nominate in order now the degrees
of the lie?   94

TOUCH. Oh, sir, we quarrel in print,° by the book,
as you have books for good manners. I will name
you the degrees. The first, the Retort Courteous; the
second, the Quip Modest; the third, the Reply Churl-
ish; the fourth, the Reproof Valiant; the fifth, the
Counter check Quarrelsome; the sixth, the Lie with
Circumstance; the seventh, the Lie Direct. All   101
these you may avoid but the Lie Direct, and you may
avoid that too, with an " If." I knew when seven jus-
tices could not take up° a quarrel, but when the
parties were met themselves, one of them thought
but of an " If," as, " If you said so, then I said   106
so," and they shook hands and swore brothers. Your
" If " is the only peacemaker, much virtue in " If."

JAQ. Is not this a rare fellow, my lord? He's as
good at anything and yet a fool.   110

DUKE S. He uses his folly like a stalking-horse,°
and under the presentation of that he shoots his wit.

[*Enter* HYMEN,° ROSALIND, *and* CELIA. *Still*° *music*.]

HYM. Then is there mirth in Heaven
When earthly things made even   115
Atone° together.

18. make . . . even: straighten out.   27. favor: face.   34. Ob-
scured: living obscurely.   45. purgation: proving the truth of
my claim. trod a measure: danced a formal dance, a necessary
accomplishment of a courtier.   46. politic: crafty.   47–48. un-
done . . . tailors: i.e., by not paying their bills.   56. God 'ild:
God yield, a form of returning thanks.   58. copulatives: folk
desirous of being mated.   66. sententious: full of pithy sayings.

67. According . . . bolt: i.e., ready to let fly at anything, for
according to the proverb "A fool's bolt [arrow] is soon shot."
68. dulcet diseases: pleasant failings.   79. disabled my judg-
ment: said my judgment was weak.   86. Circumstantial: indirect.
Lie Direct: i.e., the direct accusation that the speaker is a liar
Any man who then refused to fight to redeem his honor showed
himself a coward.   95. quarrel . . . print: Processes quite as
fantastic are printed in some of the manuals of dueling.   104. take
up: make up.   111. stalking-horse: a real or imitation horse used
as cover to approach the game for a shot.   113. s.d., Hymen:
god of marriage. Still: soft.   116. Atone: agree.

Good Duke, receive thy daughter.
Hymen from Heaven brought her,
 Yea, brought her hither,
That thou mightst join her hand with his 120
Whose heart within his bosom is.
 ROS. [*To* DUKE S.] To you I give myself, for I am
  yours.
[*To* ORLANDO] To you I give myself, for I am yours.
 DUKE S. If there be truth in sight, you are my
  daughter.
 ORL. If there be truth in sight, you are my Rosa-
  lind. 125
 PHE. If sight and shape be true,
Why then, my love adieu!
 ROS. I'll have no father, if you be not he.
I'll have no husband, if you be not he.
Nor ne'er wed woman, if you be not she. 130
 HYM. Peace, ho! I bar confusion.
'Tis I must make conclusion
 Of these most strange events.
Here's eight that must take hands
To join in Hymen's bands 135
 If truth holds true contents.
You and you no cross° shall part.
You and you are heart in heart.
You to his love must accord
Or have a woman to your lord. 140
You and you are sure together,
As the winter to foul weather.
Whiles a wedlock hymn we sing
Feed yourselves with questioning,
That reason wonder may diminish, 145
How thus we met, and these things finish.
SONG
 Wedding is great Juno's crown.
  Oh, blessed bond of board and bed!
 'Tis Hymen peoples every town.
  High wedlock then be honorèd. 150
 Honor, high honor and renown,
 To Hymen, god of every town!
 DUKE S. O my dear niece, welcome thou art to me!
Even Daughter, welcome, in no less degree. 154
 PHE. I will not eat my word now thou art mine,
Thy faith my fancy to thee doth combine.
[*Enter* JAQUES DE BOYS.]
 JAQ. DE B. Let me have audience for a word or
  two.
I am the second son of old Sir Rowland
That bring these tidings to this fair assembly.
Duke Frederick, hearing how that every day 160
Men of great worth resorted to this forest,
Addressed° a mighty power,° which were on foot,
In his own conduct,° purposely to take
His brother here and put him to the sword.
And to the skirts of this wild wood he came, 165

---

137. **cross:** trouble. 162. **Addressed:** prepared. **power:** army.
163. **In . . . conduct:** under his own command.

Where meeting with an old religious man,°
After some question with him, was converted
Both from his enterprise and from the world,
His crown bequeathing to his banished brother,
And all their lands restored to them again 170
That were with him exiled. This to be true
I do engage° my life.
 DUKE S.   Welcome, young man,
Thou offer'st° fairly to thy brothers' wedding.
To one his lands withheld, and to the other
A land itself at large, a potent dukedom. 175
First, in this forest let us do those ends
That here were well begun and well begot.
And after, every of this happy number
That have endured shrewd° days and nights with us
Shall share the good of our returnèd fortune 180
According to the measure of their states.
Meantime, forget this new-fallen dignity,
And fall into our rustic revelry. 183
Play, music! And you, brides and bridegrooms all,
With measure heaped in joy, to the measures° fall.
 JAQ. Sir, by your patience. If I heard you rightly,
The Duke hath put on a religious life
And thrown into neglect the pompous Court?
 JAQ. DE B. He hath.
 JAQ. To him will I. Out of these convertites° 190
There is much matter to be heard and learned.
[*To* DUKE] You to your former honor I bequeath,
Your patience and your virtue well deserves it.
[*To* ORLANDO] You to a love that your true faith doth
  merit.
[*To* OLIVER] You to your land, and love, and great
  allies. 195
[*To* SILVIUS] You to a long and well-deservèd bed.
[*To* TOUCHSTONE] And you to wrangling, for thy
  loving voyage
Is but for two months victualed.° So, to your pleas-
  ures.
I am for other than for dancing measures.
 DUKE S. Stay, Jaques, stay. 200
 JAQ. To see no pastime I. What you would have
I'll stay to know at your abandoned cave. [*Exit.*]
 DUKE S. Proceed, proceed. We will begin these
  rites,
As we do trust they'll end, in true delights.
[*A dance.*]

EPILOGUE

 ROS. It is not the fashion to see the lady the epi-
logue, but it is no more unhandsome than to see the
lord the prologue. If it be true that good wine needs

---

166. **religious man:** hermit. 172. **engage:** pledge. 173. **Thou offer'st:** you make a good present. 179. **shrewd:** bitter. 185. **measures:** dances. 190. **convertites:** converts to the religious life. 198. **victualed:** provisioned.

no bush,° 'tis true that a good play needs no epi-
logue. Yet to good wine they do use good bushes,   5
and good plays prove the better by the help of good
epilogues. What a case am I in then, that am neither
a good epilogue nor cannot insinuate° with you in
the behalf of a good play! I am not furnished° like a
beggar, therefore to beg will not become me.   10
My way is to conjure° you, and I'll begin with the
women. I charge you, O women, for the love you

Epilogue: **3–4. good . . . bush:** good wine needs no advertise-
ment, an old proverb arising from the custom of vintners of
hanging up a bush as a sign of their trade.   **8. insinuate:**
ingratiate myself.   **9. furnished:** dressed.   **11. conjure:** win you
over by magic.

bear to men, to like as much of this play as please
you. And I charge you, O men, for the love you bear
to women — as I perceive by your simpering   15
none of you hates them — that between you and the
women the play may please. If I were a woman° I
would kiss as many of you as had beards that pleased
me, complexions that liked° me, and breaths that I
defied not. And I am sure as many as have good   20
beards or good faces or sweet breaths will, for my
kind offer, when I make curtsy bid me farewell.

[Exeunt.]

17. If . . . woman: In the play the part of Rosalind was acted
by a boy.   **19. liked:** pleased.

THE TRAGEDY OF JULIUS CAESAR

Introduction

The Tragedy of Julius Caesar was first printed in the first folio (F1) in 1623; the text is good and there are few difficulties. The play was written in 1599. There are several pieces of evidence for this date.

1. Thomas Platter, a German traveler, noted in his diary for the year 1599:

After dinner on the 21st of September, at about two o'clock, I went with my companions over the water, and in the strewn roof-house [the playhouse with a thatched roof] saw the tragedy of the first Emperor Julius with at least fifteen characters very well acted. At the end of the comedy they danced according to their custom with extreme elegance. Two men in men's clothes and two in women's gave this performance, in wonderful combination with each other.[1]

2. John Weever in The Mirror for Martyrs, or the Life and Death of Sir John Oldcastle, printed in 1601 but composed, as the author states, two years before, wrote:

The many-headed multitude were drawn
By Brutus' speech, that Caesar was ambitious.
When eloquent Mark Antony had shown
His virtues, who but Brutus then was vicious?

3. Ben Jonson in Every Man out of His Humour, printed in 1600, after Jonson had quarreled with the Chamberlain's Men, in a satirical passage made Clove begin a speech (III.i): "Then coming to the pretty animal, as reason long since is fled to animals, you know." This is a fairly clear sneer at Antony's words:

O judgment, thou art fled to brutish beasts,
And men have lost their reason! (III.ii.109)

Jonson commented unfavorably on Julius Caesar elsewhere. In the collection of jottings published posthumously in 1641 under the title Timber or Discoveries there appeared a critical note on Shakespeare, in which he wrote: "Many times he fell into those things which could not escape laughter, as when he said in the person of Caesar, one speaking to him: 'Caesar, thou dost me

[1] Quoted by E. K. Chambers, The Elizabethan Stage, Vol. II, pp. 364–65.

wrong.' He replied: 'Caesar never did wrong but with just cause,' and suchlike, which were ridiculous." The passage in Julius Caesar now reads:

Know, Caesar doth not wrong, nor without cause
Will he be satisfied. (III.i.47)

Presumably Shakespeare altered the offending line.

4. Shakespeare himself, when writing the Chorus to the last act of Henry the Fifth in the early months of 1599, had the theme of Julius Caesar in mind:

Like to the Senators of the antique Rome,
With the plebeians swarming at their heels,
Go forth and fetch their conquering Caesar in.

The story of Julius Caesar had often been retold in story, poem, and play before Shakespeare's time, but the direct sources of the play were the lives of Julius Caesar, Marcus Brutus, and Marcus Antonius in Sir Thomas North's translation of The Lives of the Noble Grecians and Romans by that eminent historiographer and philosopher, Plutarch of Chaeronea.

Plutarch was a Greek born in A.D. 46. He was educated at Athens, and became what would now be called a professor of philosophy. He lectured at Rome, and left a large collection of essays and learned articles called the Morals — once much read — as well as the famous Lives. These were a series of parallel biographies of eminent Greeks and Romans. Plutarch wrote forty-eight of these parallels, adding to most of them a brief comparison.

The Lives are not formal biographies, giving dates, places, and facts, but rather biographical and psychological studies of great men. Plutarch assumed that his readers were already familiar with the facts, and his intention was to portray character. He consulted the best authorities, and preferably those who could provide anecdotes and sayings, for, as he wrote, " the noblest deeds do not always show men's virtues and vices, but oftentimes a light occasion, a word, or some sport, makes men's natural dispositions and manners appear more plain than the famous battles wherein are slain ten thousand men or the great armies or cities won by siege or assault."

The *Lives* reached English readers in the translation made by Sir Thomas North and printed in 1579. North, however, went not to the Greek but to a French translation made from the Latin by Jacques Amyot and published in 1559 and 1565. A second edition of North's translation was printed in 1595 by Richard Field, who was also the printer of Shakespeare's *Venus and Adonis* and *The Rape of Lucrece.* "North's Plutarch" is a great book, a fine specimen of vigorous Elizabethan prose, for North himself was a man of very varied experience, with a lively mind and a superb mastery of words. There is no richer collection of historical material for a dramatist.

Nevertheless, to make a coherent play Shakespeare had to simplify vastly the history of events between Caesar's return to Rome in September 45 B.C. and the Second Battle of Philippi, two years later. Moreover, he did not choose to follow the common pattern of historical-biographical plays, which usually ended with the death of the hero in Act V. Instead he set the murder of Caesar in the third act, and in the last two acts showed how the murderers came to destruction. For this Plutarch was partly responsible, for *Julius Caesar* is based rather on his "Life of Brutus" than on that of Caesar.

Plutarch gave all the details of the story, and, equally important, some valuable indications of character. He summed up the difference between Brutus and Cassius thus:

And surely, in my opinion, I am persuaded that Brutus might indeed have come to have been the chiefest man of Rome if he could have contented himself for a time to have been next unto Caesar, and to have suffered his glory and authority, which he had gotten by his great victories, to consume with time. But Cassius being a choleric man, and hating Caesar privately more than he did the tyranny openly, he incensed Brutus against him. It was also reported that Brutus could evil away with the tyranny, and that Cassius hated the tyrant.

Shakespeare used his sources freely. His methods can best be seen by comparing a section of the play with Plutarch's narrative. In *Julius Caesar* the death and funeral of Caesar are shown in the third act. These events were thus described in the "Life of Brutus":

Now it was reported that Caesar was coming in his litter; for he determined not to stay in the Senate all that day (because he was afraid of the unlucky signs of the sacrifices), but to adjourn matters of importance unto the next session and council holden, feigning himself not to be well at ease. When Caesar came out of his litter, Popillius Laenas, that had talked before with Brutus and Cassius, and had prayed the gods they might bring this enterprise to pass, went unto Caesar, and kept him a long time with a talk. Caesar gave good ear unto him. Wherefore the conspirators (if so they should be called), not hearing what he said to Caesar, but conjecturing by that he had told them a little before that his talk was none other but the very discovery of their conspiracy, they were afraid every man of them, and one looking in another's face, it was easy to see that they all were of a mind that it was no tarrying for them till they were apprehended, but rather that they should kill themselves with their own hands.

And when Cassius and certain others clapped their hands on their swords under their gowns to draw them, Brutus marking the countenance and gesture of Laenas and considering that he did use himself rather like a humble and earnest suitor than like an accuser, he said nothing to his companions (because there were many among them that were not of the conspiracy), but with a pleasant countenance encouraged Cassius. And immediately after, Laenas went from Caesar and kissed his hand, which showed plainly that it was for some matter concerning himself that he had held him so long in talk. Now all the Senators being entered first into this place or chapter house where the council should be kept, all the other conspirators straight stood about Caesar's chair, as if they had something to have said to him. And some say that Cassius, casting his eyes upon Pompey's image, made his prayer unto it as if it had been alive. Trebonius, on the other side, drew Antonius aside as he came into the house where the Senate sat, and held him with a long talk without.

When Caesar was come into the house, all the Senate rose to honor him at his coming in. So when he was set, the conspirators flocked about him, and among them they presented one Tillius Cimber, who made humble suit for the calling-home again of his brother that was banished. They all made as though they were intercessors for him, and took him by the hands, and kissed his head and breast. Caesar at the first simply refused their kindness and entreaties; but afterward, perceiving they still pressed on him, he violently thrust them from him. Then Cimber with both his hands plucked Caesar's gown over his shoulders, and Casca that stood behind him drew his dagger first and struck Caesar upon the shoulder, but gave him no great wound. Caesar, feeling himself hurt, took him straight by the hand he held his dagger in, and cried out in Latin: O traitor Casca, what doest thou? Casca on the other side cried in Greek, and called his brother to help him.

So, divers running on a heap together to fly upon Caesar, he, looking about him to have fled, saw Brutus with a sword drawn in his hand ready to strike at him. Then he let Casca's hand go, and casting his gown over his face, suffered every man to strike at him that would. Then the conspirators, thronging one upon another because every man was desirous to have a cut at him, so many swords and daggers lighting upon one body, one of them hurt another, and among them Brutus caught a blow on his hand, because he would make one in murdering of him, and all the rest also were every man of them bloodied. Caesar being slain in this manner, Brutus, standing in the midst of the house, would have spoken and stayed the other Senators that were not of the conspiracy, to have told them the reason why they had done this fact. But they, as men both affrayed and amazed, fled one upon another's neck in haste to get out at the door, and no man followed them. For it was set down and agreed between them that they should kill no man but Caesar only, and should entreat all the rest to defend their liberty.

All the conspirators but Brutus, determining upon this matter, thought it good also to kill Antonius, because he was a wicked man, and that in nature favored tyranny; besides also, for that he was in great estimation with soldiers, having been conversant of long time amongst them, and specially having a mind bent to great enterprises, he was also of great authority at that time, being Consul with Caesar. But Brutus would not agree to it. First, for that he said it was not honest; secondly, because he told them there was hope of change in him. For he did not mistrust but that Antonius, being a noble-minded and courageous man, (when he should know that Caesar was dead) would willingly help his country to recover her liberty, having then an example unto him, to follow their courage and virtue. So Brutus by this means saved Antonius' life, who at that present time disguised himself, and stole away. But Brutus and his consorts, having their swords bloody in their hands, went straight to the Capitol, persuading the Romans as they went to take their liberty again.

Now at the first time when the murder was newly done, there were sudden outcries of people that ran up and down the city, the which indeed did the more increase the fear and tumult. But when they saw they slew no man, neither did spoil or make havoc of anything, then certain of the Senators, and many of the people, emboldening themselves, went to the Capitol unto them. There a great number of men being assembled together one after another, Brutus made an oration unto them to win the favor of the people, and to justify that they had done. All those that were by said they had done well, and cried unto them that they should boldly come down from the Capitol. Whereupon Brutus and his companions came boldly down into the market place. The rest followed in troop, but Brutus went foremost, very honorably compassed in round about with the noblest men of the city, which brought him from the Capitol, through the market place, to the pulpit for orations.

When the people saw him in the pulpit, although they were a multitude of rakehells of all sorts, and had a good will to make some stir, yet being ashamed to do it for the reverence they bore unto Brutus, they kept silence, to hear what he would say. When Brutus began to speak, they gave him quiet audience. Howbeit, immediately after they showed that they were not all contented with the murder. For when another called Cinna would have spoken and began to accuse Caesar, they fell into a great uproar among them, and marvelously reviled him. Insomuch that the conspirators again returned into the Capitol. There Brutus, being affrayed to be besieged, sent back again the noblemen that came hither with him, thinking it no reason that they which were no partakers of the murder should be partakers of the danger.

Then the next morning, the Senate being assembled and holden within the temple of the goddess Tellus — to wit, the Earth — and Antonius, Plancus, and Cicero having made a motion to the Senate in that assembly that they should take an order to pardon and forget all that was past, and to establish friendship and peace again, it was decreed that they should not only be pardoned, but also that the Consuls should refer it to the Senate what honors should be appointed unto them. This being agreed upon, the Senate broke up, and Antonius the Consul, to put them in heart that were in the Capitol, sent them his son for a pledge. Upon this assurance, Brutus and his companions came down from the Capitol, where every man saluted and embraced each other, among the which Antonius himself did bid Cassius to supper to him, and Lepidus also bade Brutus, and so one bade another as they had friendship and acquaintance together.

The next day following, the Senate, being called again to council, did first of all commend Antonius for that he had wisely stayed and quenched the beginning of a civil war. Then they also gave Brutus and his consorts great praises, and lastly they appointed them several governments of provinces. For unto Brutus they appointed Crete; Africa unto Cassius; Asia unto Trebonius; Bithynia unto Cimber; and unto the other Decius Brutus Albinus, Gaul on this side the Alps. When this was done, they came to talk of Caesar's will and testament, and of his funerals and tomb. Then Antonius, thinking good his testament should be read openly, and also that his body should be honorably buried, and not in hugger-mugger, lest the people might thereby take occasion to be worse offended if they did otherwise, Cassius stoutly spoke against it.

But Brutus went with the motion, and agreed unto it, wherein it seemeth he committed a second fault. For the first fault he did was when he would not consent to his fellow conspirators that Antonius should be slain. And therefore he was justly accused that thereby he had saved and strengthened a strong and grievous enemy of their conspiracy. The second fault was when he agreed that Caesar's funerals should be as Antonius would have them, the which indeed marred all. For first of all, when Caesar's testament was openly read among them, whereby it appeared that he bequeathed unto every citizen of Rome seventy-five drachmas a man, and that he left his gardens and arbors unto the people — which he had on this side of the river of Tiber in the place where now the Temple of Fortune is built — the people then loved him, and were marvelous sorry for him.

Afterward when Caesar's body was brought into the market place, Antonius making his funeral oration in praise of the dead, according to the ancient custom of Rome, and perceiving that his words moved the common people to compassion, he framed his eloquence to make their hearts yearn the more, and taking Caesar's gown all bloody in his hand, he laid it open to the sight of them all, showing what a number of cuts and holes it had upon it. Therewithal the people fell presently into such a rage and mutiny that there was no more order kept amongst the common people. For some of them cried out, " Kill the murderers! " Others plucked up forms, tables, and stalls about the market place, as they had done before at the funerals of Clodius, and having laid them all on a heap together, they set them on fire, and thereupon did put the body of Caesar, and burned it in the midst of the most holy places. And furthermore, when the fire was thoroughly kindled, some here, some there, took burning firebrands and ran with them to the murderers' houses that had killed him, to set them afire. Howbeit, the conspirators, foreseeing the danger before, had wisely provided for themselves, and fled.

The account given in the " Life of Antonius " differs very little, but there are a few additional details in the " Life of Caesar ":

So, Caesar coming into the [Senate] house, all the Senate stood up on their feet to do him honor. Then part of Brutus's company and confederates stood round about Caesar's chair, and part of them came also toward him, as though they made suit with Metellus Cimber, to call home his brother again from banishment. And thus, prosecuting still their suit, they followed Caesar till he was set in his chair. Who denying their petitions and being offended with them one after another, because the more they were denied, the more they pressed upon him and were the earnester with him, Metellus at length, taking the gown with both his hands, pulled it over his neck, which was the sign given the confederates to set upon him.

Then Casca behind him strake him in the neck with his sword. Howbeit, the wound was not great nor mortal, because, it seemed, the fear of such a devilish attempt did amaze him, and take his strength from him, that he killed him not at the first blow. But Caesar, turning straight unto him, caught hold of his sword and held it hard, and they both cried out, Caesar in Latin: " O vile traitor Casca, what doest thou? " And Casca in Greek to his brother, " Brother, help me." At the beginning of this stir, they that were present, not knowing of the conspiracy, were so amazed with the horrible sight they saw they had no power to fly, neither to help him, not so much as once to make any outcry. They on the other side that had conspired his death compassed him in on every side with their swords drawn in their hands, that Caesar turned him nowhere but he was stricken at by some, and still had naked swords in his face, and was hacked and mangled among them, as a wild beast taken of hunters. For it was agreed among them that every man should give him a wound, because all their parts should be in this murder. And then Brutus himself gave him one wound about his privities.

Men report also that Caesar did still defend himself against the rest, running every way with his body. But when he saw Brutus with his sword drawn in his hand, then he pulled his gown over his head and made no more resistance, and was driven, either casually, or purposely by the counsel of the conspirators, against the base whereupon Pompey's image stood, which ran all of a gore blood till he was slain. Thus it seemed that the image took just revenge of Pompey's enemy, being thrown down on the ground at his feet, and yielding up his ghost there, for the number of wounds he had upon him. For it is reported that he had three-and-twenty wounds upon his body. And divers of the conspirators did hurt themselves, striking one body with so many blows.

Shakespeare thus studied all three versions. He kept closely to the account of Caesar's death, but added the incident of the murderers bathing their hands in Caesar's blood. He omitted all suggestion of the events in the Senate House on the day after the murder, and moved the reconciliation of Antony with the conspirators back to the time of the murder. Brutus's speech to the crowd was actually given on the day of the murder; Shakespeare made it a prelude to Antony's speech at the funeral. Brutus's words were Shakespeare's own, but the clipped style was suggested by an earlier passage in the "Life of Brutus":

He was properly learned in the Latin tongue, and was able to make long discourse in it, besides that he could also plead very well in Latin. But for the Greek tongue, they do note in some of his epistles that he counterfeited that brief compendious manner of speech of the Lacedaemonians. As when the war was begun, he wrote unto the Pergamenians in this sort; "I understand you have given Dolabella money. If you have done it willingly, you confess you have offended me; if against your wills, show it then by giving me willingly." Another time again unto the Samians: "Your counsels be long, your doings be slow, consider the end." . . . These were Brutus's manner of letters, which were honored for their briefness.

Antony's magnificent speech, except for the bare hints given by Plutarch, was entirely Shakespeare's own devising. Much as he owed to Plutarch, the play was even more his own making.

The real Caesar had a curious career. In his early forties he was well known in Rome as a dangerously attractive vicious playboy. He owed more money than any Roman had ever owed before, and he was an expert racketeer, his particular line being elections; he controlled the toughest gangs who beat up the opposition voters. He then offered himself as a candidate for office, and as a result became military governor of Spain, which was one of the unruly provinces. This taste of political and military power seems to have excited him. Two years later, by a bargain with Crassus, the richest of the Roman capitalists, and Pompey, the most experienced of Roman generals, he became Consul; and then, to the surprise of all who knew him, he went off as commander of the Roman Army in Gaul on a five-year appointment, which was afterward extended by another five years. During this time he showed that he was a superb general, of the kind whose men will follow anywhere.

In 49 B.C. Caesar decided that politics in Rome were in such chaos that it was time for him to go back. So he set out, but with his army. The Senate was alarmed, it debated, it passed resolutions,

it adjourned. Still Caesar came on. Then the Senate ordered Pompey to go out and deal with him, but instead Caesar dealt with Pompey so effectively that he chased him out of Italy and over the Mediterranean to Egypt, where he was murdered. Caesar stayed in Egypt for a year. He was fascinated with the country and with its young Queen, Cleopatra. Then he came back to Rome in the autumn of 45 B.C. with his head full of schemes for the reorganization of the civilized world. For the next six months he put through many reforms, and then on the ides of March 44 B.C. he was murdered in the Senate House, and chaos came back.

In some ways *Julius Caesar* marks a change in Shakespeare's development as a dramatist. In the earlier tragedies he was concerned more with the interplay of events; in *Julius Caesar* he was interested rather in the motives of the protagonists, so that the theme of the play is not so much the life and death of a dictator as the mind and motives of Caesar's murderers. It seems clear that Shakespeare was more concerned with Brutus and Cassius than with Caesar. The portrait of Caesar is unsympathetic; he is a pompous tyrant, and though he commits no action that justifies murder, he has that insufferable sense of superiority which infuriates lesser men such as Cassius. This view of Caesar has been much criticized, but dramatically it is right. Had Caesar been shown as a noble and sympathetic patriot, there could have been no justification for the murder and no sympathy with Brutus and the rest.

In real life the events which are called history are very complex. In a play they must be shown in two or at most three hours. The dramatist must therefore compress, choosing one incident as typical of many and vastly simplifying the story. Shakespeare begins by showing how Caesar has made enemies of different kinds. First the tribunes of the people; they hate him because he has come back in triumph over Pompey, a Roman and their friend; they know that if Caesar remains dictator that will be the end of their power as leaders of the people. Then there is Cassius. He hates Caesar as a man. Caesar and he went to school together, and now Cassius must bow if Caesar even looks his way. Cassius is madly jealous of Caesar, and he first starts the conspiracy, but he knows that it will not sound convincing unless he can persuade others that there is some lofty motive behind it, or can find some better man than himself to lead and make the affair respectable. Brutus is his man.

In some ways the play is about Brutus rather than Caesar. Brutus is universally admired, for he is a genuine idealist. Five centuries before, his ancestor Lucius Junius Brutus led the revolt which drove out Tarquin, the last King of Rome. Once Brutus can be persuaded that Caesar is another Tarquin, Brutus will do anything. Brutus is thus faced with an insoluble problem: to live under the tyranny of Caesar is to allow a wrong; to kill Caesar is to commit a wrong. After a long struggle in his own mind he ultimately decides that the murder of Caesar is a holy duty. But a high-minded idealist is not the right man to lead a revolution which begins with murder. As soon as Cassius has made Brutus the leader of the movement, he has put himself into second place, and he must now obey his leader.

Up to the moment when Caesar is killed all goes well with the conspirators; but as soon as Caesar is dead fate turns against them. While the conspiracy was being planned, Cassius had warned Brutus against Antony, but Brutus despises Antony because he is not like himself, an austere, abstemious man. Thenceforward it becomes a contest between these two. At first the odds are against Antony; but by superior knowledge of human nature he overcomes Brutus and obtains leave to make the funeral speech over Caesar's body. Here is his chance. He understands crowds, and Brutus does not. Brutus thinks that it is only necessary to tell the crowd why he killed Caesar and they will at once fall into orderly democratic ways. Antony knows better, and by a magnificent piece of oratory he so turns the crowd against the conspirators that they flee for their lives. They had killed Caesar's body, but they had forgotten Caesar's spirit.

The story is resumed a few months later. Brutus and Cassius have fled to Greece, where they gather armies to meet Antony, who is now combined with Lepidus and young Octavius Caesar. Everything goes wrong, and the two leaders are openly squabbling. Both have degenerated, and there is little left now of the high ideals which began the business.

In the battle which follows their ill luck continues. Cassius kills himself through a misunderstanding, and Brutus is left alone with a few faithful followers, to surrender or to kill himself. Caesar's spirit has won.

Julius Caesar

DRAMATIS PERSONAE

JULIUS CAESAR

OCTAVIUS CAESAR ⎫
MARCUS ANTONIUS ⎬ *triumvirs after the death of*
M. AEMIL. LEPIDUS ⎭ *Julius Caesar*

CICERO ⎫
PUBLIUS ⎬ *Senators*
POPILIUS LENA ⎭

MARCUS BRUTUS ⎫
CASSIUS ⎪
CASCA ⎪
TREBONIUS ⎬ *conspirators against Julius*
LIGARIUS ⎪ *Caesar*
DECIUS BRUTUS ⎪
METELLUS CIMBER ⎪
CINNA ⎭

FLAVIUS *and* MARULLUS, *tribunes*
ARTEMIDORUS *of Cnidos, a teacher of rhetoric*
A SOOTHSAYER
CINNA, *a poet*
ANOTHER POET

LUCILIUS ⎫
TITINIUS ⎪
MESSALA ⎬ *friends to Brutus and Cassius*
YOUNG CATO ⎪
VOLUMNIUS ⎭

VARRO ⎫
CLITUS ⎪
CLAUDIUS ⎬ *servants to Brutus*
STRATO ⎪
LUCIUS ⎪
DARDANIUS ⎭

PINDARUS, *servant to Cassius*

CALPURNIA, *wife to Caesar*
PORTIA, *wife to Brutus*

SENATORS, CITIZENS, GUARDS, ATTENDANTS, &c.

SCENE — *Rome; the neighborhood of Sardis; the neighborhood of Philippi.*

Act I

SCENE I. *Rome. A street.*

[*Enter* FLAVIUS, MARULLUS, *and certain* COMMONERS.]

FLA. Hence! Home, you idle creatures, get you
home.
Is this a holiday? What! Know you not,
Being mechanical,° you ought not walk
Upon a laboring day without the sign°
Of your profession? Speak, what trade art thou?   5

1. COM. Why, sir, a carpenter.

MAR. Where is thy leather apron and thy rule?
What dost thou with thy best apparel on?
You, sir, what trade are you?

2. COM. Truly, sir, in respect of a fine workman,°
I am but, as you would say, a cobbler.   11

MAR. But what trade art thou? Answer me directly.°

2. COM. A trade, sir, that I hope I may use with
a safe conscience, which is indeed, sir, a mender of
bad soles.°   15

MAR. What trade, thou knave? Thou naughty
knave, what trade?

2. COM. Nay, I beseech you, sir, be not out° with
me. Yet if you be out, sir, I can mend you.

MAR. What mean'st thou by that? Mend me, thou
saucy fellow!   21

2. COM. Why, sir, cobble you.

FLA. Thou art a cobbler, art thou?

2. COM. Truly, sir, all that I live by is with the
awl. I meddle with no tradesman's matters, nor   25
women's matters, but with awl. I am indeed, sir, a
surgeon to old shoes. When they are in great danger, I re-cover them. As proper° men as ever trod
upon neat's leather° have gone upon my handiwork.

FLA. But wherefore art not in thy shop today?   31
Why dost thou lead these men about the streets?

2. COM. Truly, sir, to wear out their shoes, to get
myself into more work. But indeed, sir, we   35
make holiday, to see Caesar and to rejoice in his triumph.°

MAR. Wherefore rejoice? What conquest brings
he home?
What tributaries° follow him to Rome,
To grace in captive bonds his chariot wheels?
You blocks, you stones, you worse than senseless
things!   40
O you hard hearts, you cruel men of Rome,

Act I, Sc. i: 3. mechanical: workingmen.   **4. sign:** i.e., tools
and working clothes.   **10. in . . . workman:** so far as fine work
is concerned.   **12. directly:** without quibbling.   **15. soles:** puns
on "sole" and "soul" are inevitable. Cf. *M of Ven,* IV.i.123.

18. out: angry.   **28. proper:** handsome.   **29. neat's leather:**
oxhide.   **36. in his triumph:** Roman generals after a victorious
campaign entered Rome in a triumphal procession. Caesar's triumph, however, is over another Roman, Pompey.   **38. tributaries:** captives.

Knew you not Pompey? Many a time and oft
Have you climbed up to walls and battlements,
To towers and windows, yea, to chimney tops,°
Your infants in your arms, and there have sat   45
The livelong day with patient expectation
To see great Pompey pass the streets of Rome.
And when you saw his chariot but appear,
Have you not made a universal shout,
That Tiber trembled underneath her banks   50
To hear the replication° of your sounds
Made in her concave shores?
And do you now put on your best attire?
And do you now cull out° a holiday?
And do you now strew flowers in his way   55
That comes in triumph over Pompey's blood?
Be gone!
Run to your houses, fall upon your knees,
Pray to the gods to intermit° the plague
That needs must light on this ingratitude.   60
   FLA. Go, go, good countrymen, and for this fault
Assemble all the poor men of your sort.
Draw them to Tiber banks and weep your tears
Into the channel till the lowest stream
Do kiss the most exalted shores of all.   65
               [*Exeunt all the* COMMONERS.]
See whether their basest metal° be not moved.
They vanish tongue-tied in their guiltiness.
Go you down that way toward the Capitol,
This way will I. Disrobe the images°
If you do find them decked with ceremonies.°   70
   MAR. May we do so?
You know it is the feast of Lupercal.°
   FLA. It is no matter. Let no images
Be hung with Caesar's trophies. I'll about,
And drive away the vulgar from the streets.   75
So do you too, where you perceive them thick.
These growing feathers plucked from Caesar's wing
Will make him fly an ordinary pitch,°
Who else would soar above the view of men
And keep us all in servile fearfulness. [*Exeunt.*]   80

SCENE II. *A public place.*

[*Flourish. Enter* CAESAR; ANTONY, *for the course;*°
CALPURNIA, PORTIA, DECIUS, CICERO, BRUTUS, CASSIUS,
and CASCA; *a great crowd following, among them
a* SOOTHSAYER.]

44. chimney tops: Throughout the play Shakespeare has in
mind rather his own London than Rome. Such a sight as this was
familiar. Cf. the funeral of Queen Elizabeth, described in App. 16.
51. replication: echo.   54. cull out: choose to take.   59. inter-
mit: omit, leave out.   66. metal: material, stuff of which they
are made; "metal" and "mettle" were the same in Shakespeare's
time.   69. Disrobe . . . images: strip the statues.   70. cere-
monies: decorations.   72. Lupercal: Lupercalia, celebrated on
February 15. See I.ii.4,n.   78. pitch: flight. See App. 26.
   Sc. ii: s.d., for the course: stripped for running.

   CAE. Calpurnia!
   CASC.   Peace, ho! Caesar speaks.
   CAE.   [*Music ceases.*] Calpurnia!
   CAL. Here, my lord.
   CAE. Stand you directly in Antonius' way
When he doth run his course.° Antonius!
   ANT. Caesar, my lord?   5
   CAE. Forget not, in your speed, Antonius,
To touch Calpurnia, for our elders say
The barren, touchèd in this holy chase,
Shake off their sterile curse.
   ANT.   I shall remember:
When Caesar says " Do this," it is performed.   10
   CAE. Set on, and leave no ceremony out.
                   [*Flourish.*]
   SOOTH. Caesar!
   CAE. Ha! Who calls?
   CASC. Bid every noise be still — peace yet again!
   CAE. Who is it in the press° that calls on me?   15
I hear a tongue, shriller than all the music,
Cry " Caesar." Speak. Caesar is turned to hear.
   SOOTH. Beware the ides of March.°
   CAE.   What man is that?
   BRU. A soothsayer bids you beware the ides of
     March.°
   CAE. Set him before me. Let me see his face.   20
   CASS. Fellow, come from the throng. Look upon
     Caesar.
   CAE. What say'st thou to me now? Speak once
     again.
   SOOTH. Beware the ides of March.
   CAE. He is a dreamer. Let us leave him — pass.
     [*Sennet.° Exeunt all but* BRUTUS *and* CASSIUS.]
   CASS. Will you go see the order of the course?   25
   BRU. Not I.
   CASS. I pray you, do.
   BRU. I am not gamesome. I do lack some part
Of that quick spirit that is in Antony.
Let me not hinder, Cassius, your desires.   30
I'll leave you.
   CASS. Brutus, I do observe you now of late.
I have not from your eyes that gentleness
And show of love as I was wont to have.
You bear too stubborn and too strange a hand°   35
Over your friend that loves you.

4. run his course: At the feast of the Lupercalia "divers
noblemen's sons, young men (and some of them magistrates
themselves that govern them) . . . run naked through the city,
striking in sport them they meet in their way with leather
thongs, hair and all on, to make them give place. And many
noblewomen and gentlewomen also go of purpose to stand in
their way, and do put forth their hands to be stricken, as
scholars hold them out to their schoolmaster to be stricken, with
the ferula (rod), persuading themselves that, being with child,
they shall have good delivery, and so, being barren, that it will
make them conceive with child." (North's Plutarch.)   15. press:
crowd.   18. ides of March: March 15.   24. s.d., Sennet: trumpet
call.   35. bear . . . hand: your behavior toward your friend is too
rough and unkind.

BRU.   Cassius,
Be not deceived. If I have veiled my look,
I turn the trouble of my countenance
Merely upon myself. Vexèd I am
Of late with passions of some difference,°   40
Conceptions only proper to myself,
Which give some soil° perhaps to my behaviors.
But let not therefore my good friends be grieved —
Among which number, Cassius, be you one —
Nor cónstrue° any further my neglect   45
Than that poor Brutus, with himself at war,
Forgets the shows° of love to other men.
    CASS. Then, Brutus, I have much mistook your
passion,
By means whereof this breast of mine hath buried
Thoughts of great value, worthy cogitations.   50
Tell me, good Brutus, can you see your face?
    BRU. No, Cassius, for the eye sees not itself
But by reflection, by some other things.
    CASS. 'Tis just.
And it is very much lamented, Brutus,   55
That you have no such mirrors as will turn°
Your hidden worthiness into your eye,
That you might see your shadow.° I have heard
Where many of the best respect in Rome,
Except immortal Caesar,° speaking of Brutus,   60
And groaning underneath this age's yoke,°
Have wished that noble Brutus had his eyes.
    BRU. Into what dangers would you lead me, Cas-
sius,
That you would have me seek into myself
For that which is not in me?   65
    CASS. Therefore, good Brutus, be prepared to hear.
And since you know you cannot see yourself
So well as by reflection, I your glass
Will modestly discover to yourself
That of yourself which you yet know not of.   70
And be not jealous on° me, gentle Brutus.
Were I a common laugher,° or did use
To stale° with ordinary oaths my love
To every new protester;° if you know
That I do fawn on men and hug them hard,   75
And after scandal° them; or if you know
That I profess° myself in banqueting
To all the rout° — then hold me dangerous.
                          [*Flourish° and shout.*]
    BRU. What means this shouting? I do fear the
people
Choose Caesar for their king.

    CASS.   Aye, do you fear it?   80
Then must I think you would not have it so.
    BRU. I would not, Cassius, yet I love him well.
But wherefore do you hold me here so long?
What is it that you would impart to me?
If it be aught towárd the general good,   85
Set honor in one eye and death i' the other,
And I will look on both indifferently;°
For let the gods so speed° me as I love
The name of honor more than I fear death.
    CASS. I know that virtue to be in you, Brutus,   90
As well as I do know your outward favor.°
Well, honor is the subject of my story.
I cannot tell what you and other men
Think of this life, but for my single self
I had as lief° not be as live to be   95
In awe of such a thing as I myself.°
I was born free as Caesar; so were you.
We both have fed as well, and we can both
Endure the winter's cold as well as he.
For once, upon a raw and gusty day,   100
The troubled Tiber chafing with her shores,
Caesar said to me " Darest thou, Cassius, now
Leap in with me into this angry flood
And swim to yonder point? " Upon the word,
Accoutered° as I was, I plungèd in   105
And bade him follow. So indeed he did.
The torrent roared, and we did buffet it
With lusty sinews,° throwing it aside
And stemming it with hearts of controversy.°
But ere we could arrive the point proposed,   110
Caesar cried, " Help me, Cassius, or I sink! "
I, as Aeneas° our great ancestor
Did from the flames of Troy upon his shoulder
The old Anchises bear, so from the waves of Tiber
Did I the tired Caesar — and this man   115
Is now become a god, and Cassius is
A wretched creature, and must bend his body
If Caesar carelessly but nod on him.
He had a fever when he was in Spain,
And when the fit was on him, I did mark   120
How he did shake. 'Tis true, this god did shake.
His coward lips did from their color fly,°
And that same eye whose bend° doth awe the world
Did lose his° luster. I did hear him groan.   124
Aye, and that tongue of his that bade the Romans
Mark him and write his speeches in their books,
Alas, it cried, " Give me some drink, Titinius,"

---

40. passions . . . difference: conflicting emotions.   42. soil:
blemish.   45. construe: interpret.   47. shows: outward ap-
pearances.   56. turn: reflect.   58. shadow: reflection.   60. im-
mortal Caesar: spoken with great bitterness.   61. age's
yoke: burdens of these times.   71. jealous on: suspicious of.
72. laugher: jester.   73. stale: make common.   74. protester:
one who makes solemn protestations.   76. scandal: speak scan-
dal of.   77. profess: publicize.   78. rout: rabble.   78. s.d., Flour-
ish: a long trumpet call to announce the appearance of an
important person.

87. indifferently: unconcernedly.   88. speed: give good for-
tune to.   91. favor: face.   95. lief: soon.   96. In . . . myself:
afraid of a mere mortal like myself.   105. Accoutered: fully
armed.   108. sinews: muscles.   109. hearts . . . controversy:
eager rivalry.   112. Aeneas: Aeneas was one of the few Trojans
who escaped the sack of Troy. He carried off his old father
Anchises, and with his company sailed away to Italy, where, ac-
cording to legend, he became the founder of the Roman race.
Aeneas's adventures are the subject of Virgil's *Aeneid*.   122. His
. . . fly: the color fled from his cowardly lips.   123. bend: sway.
124. his: its.

As a sick girl. Ye gods! It doth amaze me
A man of such a feeble temper should
So get the start° of the majestic world   130
And bear the palm° alone.   [*Shout. Flourish.*]
  BRU. Another general shout!
I do believe that these applauses are
For some new honors that are heaped on Caesar.
  CASS. Why, man, he doth bestride the narrow
          world   135
Like a Colossus,° and we petty men
Walk under his huge legs and peep about
To find ourselves dishonorable graves.
Men at some time are masters of their fates.
The fault, dear Brutus, is not in our stars,°   140
But in ourselves, that we are underlings.°
Brutus, and Caesar. What should be in that Caesar?
Why should that name be sounded more than
          yours?
Write them together, yours is as fair a name.
Sound them, it doth become the mouth as well.   145
Weigh them, it is as heavy. Conjure° with 'em,
Brutus will start a spirit as soon as Caesar.
Now, in the names of all the gods at once,
Upon what meat doth this our Caesar feed   149
That he is grown so great? Age, thou art shamed!
Rome, thou hast lost the breed of noble bloods!
When went there by an age, since the great flood,
But it was famed with more than with one man?
When could they say till now that talked of Rome
That her wide walls encompassed but one man?
Now is it Rome indeed, and room° enough,   156
When there is in it but one only man.
Oh, you and I have heard our fathers say
There was a Brutus° once that would have brooked°
The eternal Devil to keep his state in Rome   160
As easily as a king.
  BRU. That you do love me, I am nothing jealous.
What you would work me to, I have some aim.
How I have thought of this and of these times,
I shall recount hereafter; for this present,   165
I would not, so with love I might entreat you,
Be any further moved. What you have said
I will consider. What you have to say
I will with patience hear, and find a time
Both meet° to hear and answer such high things.
Till then, my noble friend, chew upon this: 171
Brutus had rather be a villager

130. get the start: become the leader.   131. palm: prize, sign of
victory.   136. Colossus: the Colossus of Rhodes (an island in the
Aegean Sea) was one of the seven wonders of the ancient world.
It was a great bronze statue straddling the entrance to the
harbor, beneath which ships passed.   140. stars: many still
believed that a man's fate was governed by the stars. See App. 1.
141. underlings: inferior beings.   146. Conjure: use as an in-
cantation to summon up spirits.   156. Rome . . . room: both
words were pronounced and often spelled alike.   159. Brutus:
Lucius Junius Brutus was chiefly responsible for the expulsion
of Tarquin, the last King of Rome. Marcus Brutus claimed de-
scent from him. brooked: endured.   170. meet: fit.

Than to repute himself a son of Rome
Under these hard conditions as this time
Is like to lay upon us.   175
  CASS. I am glad that my weak words
Have struck but thus much show of fire from Bru-
    tus.
  BRU. The games are done, and Caesar is return-
    ing.
  CASS. As they pass by, pluck Casca by the sleeve,
And he will, after his sour fashion, tell you   180
What hath proceeded worthy note today.
          [*Re-enter* CAESAR *and his train.*]
  BRU. I will do so. But look you, Cassius,
The angry spot doth glow on Caesar's brow,
And all the rest look like a chidden train.°
Calpurnia's cheek is pale, and Cicero   185
Looks with such ferret° and such fiery eyes
As we have seen him in the Capitol,
Being crossed in conference° by some Senators.
  CASS. Casca will tell us what the matter is.
  CAE. Antonius!   190
  ANT. Caesar?
  CAE. Let me have men about me that are fat,
Sleek-headed men, and such as sleep o' nights.
Yond Cassius has a lean and hungry look.
He thinks too much, such men are dangerous.   195
  ANT. Fear him not, Caesar. He's not dangerous,
He is a noble Roman, and well given.°
  CAE. Would he were fatter! But I fear him not,
Yet if my name were liable to fear,
I do not know the man I should avoid   200
So soon as that spare Cassius. He reads much,
He is a great observer, and he looks
Quite through the deeds of men. He loves no plays
As thou dost, Antony; he hears no music.
Seldom he smiles, and smiles in such a sort   205
As if he mocked himself, and scorned his spirit
That could be moved to smile at anything.
Such men as he be never at heart's ease
While they behold a greater than themselves,
And therefore are they very dangerous.   210
I rather tell thee what is to be feared
Than what I fear, for always I am Caesar.
Come on my right hand, for this ear is deaf,
And tell me truly what thou think'st of him.
[*Sennet. Exeunt* CAESAR *and all his train but* CASCA.]
  CASC. You pulled me by the cloak. Would you
          speak with me?   215
  BRU. Aye, Casca. Tell us what hath chanced today
That Caesar looks so sad.
  CASC. Why, you were with him, were you not?
  BRU. I should not then ask Casca what had
    chanced.   219
  CASC. Why, there was a crown offered him; and

184. chidden train: scolded retinue.   186. ferret: ferrets have
little red eyes.   188. crossed . . . conference: opposed in debate.
197. well given: well disposed.

being offered him, he put it by with the back of his hand, thus. And then the people fell a-shouting.

BRU. What was the second noise for?

CASC. Why, for that too.   225

CASS. They shouted thrice. What was the last cry for?

CASC. Why, for that too.

BRU. Was the crown offered him thrice?

CASC. Aye, marry,° was 't, and he put it by thrice, every time gentler than other. And at every   230 putting-by mine honest neighbors shouted.

CASS. Who offered him the crown?

CASC. Why, Antony.

BRU. Tell us the manner of it, gentle Casca.

CASC. I can as well be hanged as tell the man-   235 ner of it.° It was mere foolery — I did not mark it. I saw Mark Antony offer him a crown, yet 'twas not a crown neither, 'twas one of these coronets;° and, as I told you, he put it by once. But for all that, to my thinking, he would fain° have had it. Then   240 he offered it to him again, then he put it by again. But, to my thinking, he was very loath to lay his fingers off it. And then he offered it the third time, he put it the third time by. And still as he refused it the rabblement hooted and clapped their chopped°   245 hands and threw up their sweaty nightcaps° and uttered such a deal of stinking breath because Caesar refused the crown that it had almost choked Caesar; for he swounded° and fell down at it. And for mine own part, I durst not laugh, for fear of opening my lips and receiving the bad air.   252

CASS. But, soft, I pray you. What, did Caesar swound?

CASC. He fell down in the market place and foamed at mouth and was speechless.   255

BRU. 'Tis very like — he hath the falling sickness.°

CASS. No, Caesar hath it not. But you, and I, And honest Casca, we have the falling sickness.

CASC. I know not what you mean by that,   260 but I am sure Caesar fell down. If the tagrag people did not clap him and hiss him according as he pleased and displeased them, as they use to do the players in the theater, I am no true man.

BRU. What said he when he came unto himself?

CASC. Marry, before he fell down, when he   265 perceived the common herd was glad he refused the crown, he plucked me ope° his doublet° and offered them his throat to cut. An° I had been a man of any occupation,° if I would not have taken him at a

word, I would I might go to Hell among the   270 rogues. And so he fell. When he came to himself again, he said if he had done or said anything amiss, he desired Their Worships to think it was his   273 infirmity. Three or four wenches where I stood cried, "Alas, good soul!" and forgave him with all their hearts; but there's no heed to be taken of them. If Caesar had stabbed their mothers, they would have done no less.

BRU. And after that, he came, thus sad, away?

CASC. Aye.   280

CASS. Did Cicero say anything?

CASC. Aye, he spoke Greek.

CASS. To what effect?   283

CASC. Nay, an I tell you that, I'll ne'er look you i' the face again. But those that understood him smiled at one another and shook their heads — but for mine own part, it was Greek to me. I could tell you more news too. Marullus and Flavius, for   288 pulling scarfs° off Caesar's images, are put to silence. Fare you well. There was more foolery yet, if I could remember it.

CASS. Will you sup with me tonight, Casca?

CASC. No, I am promised forth.

CASS. Will you dine with me tomorrow?

CASC. Aye, if I be alive, and your mind hold, and your dinner worth the eating.   295

CASS. Good. I will expect you.

CASC. Do so. Farewell, both.   [*Exit.*]

BRU. What a blunt fellow is this grown to be! He was quick mettle° when he went to school.   300

CASS. So is he now in execution
Of any bold or noble enterprise,
However he puts on this tardy° form.
This rudeness is a sauce to his good wit,
Which gives men stomach to digest his words   305
With better appetite.

BRU. And so it is. For this time I will leave you.
Tomorrow, if you please to speak with me,
I will come home to you, or, if you will,
Come home to me and I will wait for you.   310

CASS. I will do so. Till then, think of the world.
[*Exit* BRUTUS.]

Well, Brutus, thou art noble. Yet I see
Thy honorable mettle may be wrought
From that it is disposed.° Therefore it is meet
That noble minds keep ever with their likes,   315
For who so firm that cannot be seduced?
Caesar doth bear me hard,° but he loves Brutus.
If I were Brutus now and he were Cassius,
He should not humor° me. I will this night,
In several hands,° in at his windows throw,   320
As if they came from several citizens,

---

229. marry: Mary, by the Virgin.   235–36. I . . . it: I'll be hanged if I can tell.   238. coronets: little crowns worn by those of lesser rank than king.   240. fain: gladly.   245. chopped: chapped, toil-worn.   246. nightcaps: close-fitting caps. 250. swounded: swooned.   256. falling-sickness: epilepsy. 267. ope: open. doublet: short coat. See Pl. 8b and p. 93a. 268. An: if.   269. occupation: trade, and therefore provided with tools.

289. scarfs: decorations.   300. mettle: temperament, material. See I.i.66,n.   303. tardy: sluggish.   314. From . . . disposed: from its natural quality.   317. bear me hard: dislike me. 319. humor: influence.   320. several hands: different handwritings.

Writings, all tending to the great opinion
That Rome holds of his name, wherein obscurely
Caesar's ambition shall be glancèd at.
And after this let Caesar seat him° sure,　　　325
For we will shake him, or worse days endure.

　　　　　　　　　　　　　　　　　[*Exit.*]

SCENE III. *A street.*

[*Thunder and lightning. Enter, from opposite sides,*
CASCA, *with his sword drawn, and* CICERO.]

CIC. Good even, Casca. Brought you Caesar
　　home?
Why are you breathless? And why stare you so?
　　CASC. Are not you moved, when all the sway° of
　　　earth
Shakes like a thing unfirm? O Cicero,
I have seen tempests when the scolding winds　　5
Have rived° the knotty oaks, and I have seen
The ambitious ocean swell and rage and foam,
To be exalted° with the threatening clouds.
But never till tonight, never till now,
Did I go through a tempest dropping fire.　　10
Either there is a civil strife in Heaven,
Or else the world too saucy with the gods
Incenses them to send destruction.
　　CIC. Why, saw you anything more wonderful?
　　CASC. A common slave — you know him well by
　　　sight —　　　　　　　　　　　　　　15
Held up his left hand, which did flame and burn
Like twenty torches joined, and yet his hand,
Not sensible of° fire, remained unscorched.
Besides — I ha' not since put up my sword —
Against° the Capitol I met a lion,°　　　20
Who glazed° upon me and went surly by
Without annoying me. And there were drawn
Upon a heap a hundred ghastly women
Transformèd with their fear, who swore they saw
Men all in fire walk up and down the streets.　　25
And yesterday the bird of night° did sit
Even at noonday upon the market place,
Hooting and shrieking. When these prodigies
Do so conjointly meet, let not men say
" These are their reasons, they are natural."°　　30
For I believe they are portentous things
Unto the climate that they point upon.°
　　CIC. Indeed, it is a strange-disposèd time.
But men may cónstrue things after their fashion,

Clean from the purpose of the things themselves.
Comes Caesar to the Capitol tomorrow?　　36
　　CASC. He doth, for he did bid Antonius
Send word to you he would be there tomorrow.
　　CIC. Good night then, Casca. This disturbèd sky
Is not to walk in.
　　CASC.　　　　Farewell, Cicero. [*Exit* CICERO.] 40
　　　　　　　　　　[*Enter* CASSIUS.]
　　CASS. Who's there?
　　CASC.　　　　　A Roman.
　　CASS.　　　　　　　Casca, by your voice.
　　CASC. Your ear is good. Cassius, what night is
　　　this!
　　CASS. A very pleasing night to honest men.
　　CASC. Who ever knew the heavens menace so?
　　CASS. Those that have known the earth so full of
　　　faults.　　　　　　　　　　　　　　45
For my part, I have walked about the streets,
Submitting me unto the perilous night,
And thus unbraced,° Casca, as you see,
Have bared my bosom to the thunder stone.°
And when the cross° blue lightning seemed to open
The breast of Heaven, I did present myself　　51
Even in the aim and very flash of it.
　　CASC. But wherefore did you so much tempt the
　　　heavens?
It is the part of° men to fear and tremble
When the most mighty gods by tokens send　　55
Such dreadful heralds to astonish us.
　　CASS. You are dull, Casca, and those sparks of life
That should be in a Roman you do want,°
Or else you use not. You look pale and gaze
And put on fear and cast yourself in wonder,°　　60
To see the strange impatience of the heavens.
But if you would consider the true cause
Why all these fires, why all these gliding ghosts,
Why birds and beasts from quality and kind,°
Why old men fool and children calculate,°　　65
Why all these things change from their ordinance,°
Their natures and preformèd faculties,
To monstrous° quality, why, you shall find
That Heaven hath infused them with these spirits
To make them instruments of fear and warning　70
Unto some monstrous state.
Now could I, Casca, name to thee a man
Most like this dreadful night
That thunders, lightens, opens graves, and roars
As doth the lion in the Capitol° —　　　75
A man no mightier than thyself or me
In personal action, yet prodigious grown
And fearful,° as these strange eruptions are.

---

325. him: himself.

Sc. iii: 3. sway: settled order.　**6. rived:** split.　**8. exalted:** lifted high.　**18. sensible of:** sensitive to.　**20. Against:** beside. **Capitol . . . lion:** Shakespeare thought of the Capitol as if it were the Tower of London. Here were kept the lions which were among the sights of London. See Gen. Intro. p. 16a and Pl. 3a. **21. glazed:** glared.　**26. bird of night:** screech owl.　**30. These . . . natural:** this is the scientific explanation.　**31–32. portentous . . . upon:** they are omens of disaster toward the country which they threaten.

48. unbraced: with the doublet loose. See comment on p. 94a–b. **49. thunder stone:** thunderbolt.　**50. cross:** zigzag.　**54. part of:** natural to.　**58. want:** lack.　**60. cast . . . wonder:** are amazed. **64. from . . . kind:** contrary to their natural disposition.　**65. calculate:** prophesy.　**66. ordinance:** natural order.　**68. monstrous:** unnatural.　**75. lion . . . Capitol:** See note on l. 20. **78. fearful:** causing fear.

CASC. 'Tis Caesar that you mean, is it not, Cassius?

CASS. Let it be who it is. For Romans now   80
Have thews° and limbs like to their ancestors.
But, woe the while!° our fathers' minds are dead,
And we are governed with our mothers' spirits,
Our yoke and sufferance° show us womanish.

CASC. Indeed they say the Senators tomorrow   85
Mean to establish Caesar as a king,
And he shall wear his crown by sea and land
In every place save here in Italy.

CASS. I know where I will wear this dagger then.
Cassius from bondage will deliver Cassius.   90
Therein, ye gods, you make the weak most strong.
Therein, ye gods, you tyrants do defeat.
Nor stony tower, nor walls of beaten brass,
Nor airless dungeon, nor strong links of iron,
Can be retentive to the strength of spirit;   95
But life, being weary of these worldly bars,
Never lacks power to dismiss itself.
If I know this, know all the world besides,
That part of tyranny that I do bear
I can shake off at pleasure.   [*Thunder still.*]

CASC.   So can I.   100
So every bondman in his own hand bears
The power to cancel his captivity.

CASS. And why should Caesar be a tyrant, then?
Poor man! I know he would not be a wolf
But that he sees the Romans are but sheep.   105
He were no lion were not Romans hinds.°
Those that with haste will make a mighty fire
Begin it with weak straws. What trash° is Rome,
What rubbish and what offal, when it serves
For the base matter to illuminate°   110
So vile a thing as Caesar! But, O Grief,
Where hast thou led me? I perhaps speak this
Before a willing bondman; then I know
My answer must be made. But I am armed,
And dangers are to me indifferent.°   115

CASC. You speak to Casca, and to such a man
That is no fleering° telltale. Hold, my hand
Be factious° for redress of all these griefs,
And I will set this foot of mine as far
As who goes farthest.

CASS.   There's a bargain made.   120
Now know you, Casca, I have moved already
Some certain of the noblest-minded Romans
To undergo with me an enterprise

Of honorable-dangerous consequence.
And I do know, by this they stay° for me   125
In Pompey's porch;° for now, this fearful night,
There is no stir or walking in the streets,
And the complexion of the element°
In favor's° like the work we have in hand,
Most bloody, fiery, and most terrible.   130

[*Enter* CINNA.]

CASC. Stand close° awhile, for here comes one in
haste.

CASS. 'Tis Cinna, I do know him by his gait —
He is a friend. Cinna, where haste you so?

CIN. To find out you. Who's that? Metellus Cimber?

CASS. No, it is Casca, one incorporate   135
To our attempts.° Am I not stayed for, Cinna?

CIN. I am glad on 't. What a fearful night is this!
There's two or three of us have seen strange sights.

CASS. Am I not stayed for? Tell me.

CIN.   Yes, you are.
O Cassius, if you could   140
But win the noble Brutus to our party——

CASS. Be you content. Good Cinna, take this paper,
And look you lay it in the praetor's° chair,
Where Brutus may but find it, and throw this
In at his window; set this up with wax   145
Upon old Brutus'° statue. All this done,
Repair to Pompey's porch, where you shall find us.
Is Decius Brutus and Trebonius there?

CIN. All but Metellus Cimber, and he's gone
To seek you at your house. Well, I will hie,   150
And so bestow these papers as you bade me.

CASS. That done, repair to Pompey's theater.

[*Exit* CINNA.]

Come, Casca, you and I will yet ere day
See Brutus at his house. Three parts of him
Is ours already, and the man entire   155
Upon the next encounter yields him ours.

CASC. Oh, he sits high in all the people's hearts,
And that which would appear offense in us
His countenance, like richest alchemy,°
Will change to virtue and to worthiness.   160

CASS. Him and his worth and our great need of him
You have right well conceited.° Let us go,
For it is after midnight, and ere day
We will awake him and be sure of him.   [*Exeunt.*]

---

81. **thews:** sinews, strength.   82. **woe the while:** alas for the time.   84. **Our . . . sufferance:** our enduring this slavery.   106. **hinds:** female deer, the gentlest of creatures.   108. **trash:** twigs.   110. **base . . . illuminate:** the rubbish from which the light is kindled.   115. **indifferent:** a matter of indifference.   117. **fleering:** sneering.   118. **factious:** partisan.

125. **stay:** wait.   126. **Pompey's porch:** the portico, part of the theater Pompey had built.   128. **element:** sky.   129. **favor:** face, appearance.   131. **Stand close:** hide yourself.   135–36. **incorporate . . . attempts:** i.e., one of our conspiracy.   143. **praetor:** a Roman official next in rank to the consul, the highest official in Rome.   146. **old Brutus:** See I.ii.159,n.   159. **alchemy:** See App. 21.   162. **conceited:** perceived.

Act II

SCENE I. *Rome.* BRUTUS's *orchard.*

[*Enter* BRUTUS.]

BRU. What, Lucius, ho!
I cannot, by the progress of the stars,
Give guess how near to day. Lucius, I say!
I would it were my fault to sleep so soundly.   4
When, Lucius, when? Awake, I say! What, Lucius!

[*Enter* LUCIUS.]

LUC. Called you, my lord?
BRU. Get me a taper° in my study, Lucius.
When it is lighted, come and call me here.
LUC. I will, my lord.   [*Exit.*]
BRU. It must be by his death° and for my part   10
I know no personal cause to spurn at him,
But for the general.° He would be crowned.
How that might change his nature, there's the question.
It is the bright day that brings forth the adder,
And that craves° wary walking. Crown him? —
That —   15
And then, I grant, we put a sting in him,
That at his will he may do danger with.
The abuse of greatness is when it disjoins
Remorse° from power; and to speak truth of Caesar,
I have not known when his affections° swayed   20
More than his reason. But 'tis a common proof°
That lowliness is young ambition's ladder,
Whereto the climber-upward turns his face.
But when he once attains the upmost round,
He then unto the ladder turns his back,   25
Looks in the clouds, scorning the base degrees°
By which he did ascend. So Caesar may.
Then, lest he may, prevent.° And since the quarrel
Will bear no color° for the thing he is,
Fashion it thus:° that what he is, augmented,   30
Would run to these and these extremities.
And therefore think him as a serpent's egg
Which hatched would as his kind grow mischievous,
And kill him in the shell.

[*Re-enter* LUCIUS.]

LUC. The taper burneth in your closet,° sir.   35
Searching the window for a flint,° I found
This paper thus sealed up, and I am sure
It did not lie there when I went to bed.

[*Gives him the letter.*]

BRU. Get you to bed again. It is not day.
Is not tomorrow, boy, the ides of March?   40
LUC. I know not, sir.
BRU. Look in the calendar and bring me word.

LUC. I will, sir.   [*Exit.*]
BRU. The exhalations° whizzing in the air
Give so much light that I may read by them.   45

[*Opens the letter and reads.*]

" Brutus, thou sleep'st. Awake and see thyself.
Shall Rome, &c.° Speak, strike, redress."
" Brutus, thou sleep'st. Awake."
Such instigations have been often dropped
Where I have took them up.   50
" Shall Rome, &c." Thus must I piece it out —
Shall Rome stand under one man's awe? What,
Rome?
My ancestors did from the streets of Rome
The Tarquin drive, when he was called a king.
" Speak, strike, redress." Am I entreated   55
To speak and strike? O Rome, I make thee promise,
If the redress will follow, thou receivest
Thy full petition at the hand of Brutus!

[*Re-enter* LUCIUS.]

LUC. Sir, March is wasted fifteen days.   59

[*Knocking within.*]

BRU. 'Tis good. Go to the gate. Somebody knocks.

[*Exit* LUCIUS.]

Since Cassius first did whet me against Caesar
I have not slept.
Between the acting of a dreadful thing
And the first motion, all the interim is
Like a phantasma or a hideous dream.°   65
The Genius and the mortal instruments
Are then in council, and the state of man,
Like to a little kingdom, suffers then
The nature of an insurrection.°

[*Re-enter* LUCIUS.]

LUC. Sir, 'tis your brother° Cassius at the door,
Who doth desire to see you.
BRU.   Is he alone?   71
LUC. No, sir, there are moe° with him.
BRU.   Do you know them?
LUC. No, sir. Their hats° are plucked about their
ears,
And half their faces buried in their cloaks,
That by no means I may discover them   75
By any mark of favor.
BRU.   Let 'em enter. [*Exit* LUCIUS.]
They are the faction.° O Conspiracy,
Shamest thou to show thy dangerous brow by night,
When evils are most free? Oh, then by day

---

44. exhalations: meteors.   47. Rome, &c.: as the actor would be
supplied with the letter from which he reads, there was no need
for Shakespeare to include it in the manuscript.   63–65. Between
. . . dream: the interval between the first idea and the dreadful deed itself is like a hideous apparition or a nightmare.
66–69. Genius . . . insurrection: the mind (*genius*) and body
(*mortal instruments*), and a man's whole nature, are then like a
kingdom in a state of civil war.   70. brother: brother-in-law.
72. moe: more.   73. hats: Caesar's Romans in this play all
wear Elizabethan costumes — doublets, nightgowns, cloaks, and
wide-brimmed hats. This is one of several anachronisms in the
play.   77. the faction: of the party.

Act II, Sc. i: 7. taper: candle.   10. his death: i.e., Caesar's.
12. general: general good.   15. craves: demands.   19. Remorse:
pity.   20. affections: feelings.   21. proof: experience.   26. degrees: steps.   28. prevent: forestall.   29. bear . . . color: cannot be justified.   30. Fashion . . . thus: regard it in this way.
35. closet: small private room.   36. flint: used to make a light.

Where wilt thou find a cavern dark enough   80
To mask thy monstrous visage? Seek none, Con-
    spiracy —
Hide it in smiles and affability.
For if thou path, thy native semblance on,°
Not Erebus° itself were dim enough
To hide thee from prevention.°   85

[Enter the conspirators, CASSIUS, CASCA, DECIUS,
   CINNA, METELLUS CIMBER, *and* TREBONIUS.]

  CASS. I think we are too bold upon your rest.
Good morrow, Brutus. Do we trouble you?
  BRU. I have been up this hour, awake all night.
Know I these men that come along with you?
  CASS. Yes, every man of them, and no man here
But honors you, and every one doth wish   91
You had but that opinion of yourself
Which every noble Roman bears of you.
This is Trebonius.
  BRU.   He is welcome hither.
  CASS. This, Decius Brutus.
  BRU.   He is welcome too.   95
  CASS. This, Casca, this, Cinna, and this, Metellus
    Cimber.
  BRU. They are all welcome.
What watchful cares do interpose themselves
Betwixt your eyes and night?   99
  CASS. Shall I entreat a word?   *[They whisper.]*
  DEC. Here lies the east. Doth not the day break
    here?
  CASC. No.
  CIN. Oh, pardon, sir, it doth, and yon gray lines
That fret° the clouds are messengers of day.
  CASC. You shall confess that you are both de-
    ceived.
Here, as I point my sword, the sun arises,   106
Which is a great way growing on the south,
Weighing the youthful season of the year.°
Some two months hence up higher toward the north
He first presents his fire, and the high° east   110
Stands as the Capitol,° directly here.
  BRU. Give me your hands all over, one by one.
  CASS. And let us swear our resolution.
  BRU. No, not an oath. If not the face of men,
The sufferance° of our souls, the time's abuse —
If these be motives weak, break off betimes,°   116
And every man hence to his idle bed.
So let high-sighted° tyranny range on°
Till each man drop by lottery.° But if these,
As I am sure they do, bear fire enough   120
To kindle cowards and to steel with valor

The melting spirits of women, then, countrymen,
What need we any spur but our own cause
To prick° us to redress? What other bond
Than secret Romans that have spoke the word,   125
And will not palter?° And what other oath
Than honesty to honesty engaged°
That this shall be or we will fall for it?
Swear priests and cowards and men cautelous,°
Old feeble carrions° and such suffering souls   130
That welcome wrongs; unto bad causes swear
Such creatures as men doubt; but do not stain
The even° virtue of our enterprise,
Nor the insuppressive mettle of our spirits,
To think that or our cause or° our performance
Did need an oath when every drop of blood   136
That every Roman bears, and nobly bears,
Is guilty of a several bastardy
If he do break the smallest particle
Of any promise that hath passed from him.   140
  CASS. But what of Cicero? Shall we sound him?
I think he will stand very strong with us.
  CASC. Let us not leave him out.
  CIN.   No, by no means.
  MET. Oh, let us have him, for his silver hairs
Will purchase us a good opinion,   145
And buy men's voices to commend our deeds.
It shall be said his judgment ruled our hands.
Our youths and wildness shall no whit appear,
But all be buried in his gravity.
  BRU. Oh, name him not. Let us not break with
    him,°   150
For he will never follow anything
That other men begin.
  CASS.   Then leave him out.
  CASC. Indeed he is not fit.
  DEC. Shall no man else be touched but only Cae-
    sar?
  CASS. Decius, well urged.° I think it is not meet
Mark Antony, so well beloved of Caesar,   156
Should outlive Caesar. We shall find of him
A shrewd contriver;° and you know his means,
If he improve them, may well stretch so far
As to annoy° us all. Which to prevent,   160
Let Antony and Caesar fall together.
  BRU. Our course will seem too bloody, Caius Cas-
    sius,
To cut the head off and then hack the limbs,
Like wrath in death and envy° afterward.
For Antony is but a limb of Caesar.   165
Let us be sacrificers, but not butchers, Caius.
We all stand up against the spirit of Caesar,
And in the spirit of men there is no blood.

---

83. path . . . on: walk openly in your natural guise.   84. Erebus:
Hell.   85. prevention: premature discovery.   104. fret: orna-
ment.   107–08. great . . . year: in the first quarter of the year
the sun rises south of true east.   110. high: true.   111. Capitol:
See I.iii.20,n. The Tower of London also lay due east of the
city.   115. sufferance: suffering.   116. betimes: in good time.
118. high-sighted: with proud looks. range on: go in search of
prey.   119. lottery: turn.

124. prick: spur.   126. palter: play false.   127. engaged:
pledged.   129. cautelous: crafty.   130. carrions: carcasses.
133. even: steadfast.   135. or . . . or: either . . . or.   150. break
with him: disclose our plot to him.   155. urged: brought for-
ward.   158. shrewd contriver: cunning plotter.   160. annoy:
harm.   164. envy: hatred.

Oh, that we then could come by Caesar's spirit,
And not dismember Caesar! But, alas,   170
Caesar must bleed for it! And, gentle friends,
Let's kill him boldly, but not wrathfully.
Let's carve him as a dish fit for the gods,
Not hew him as a carcass fit for hounds.
And let our hearts, as subtle masters do,   175
Stir up their servants to an act of rage
And after seem to chide 'em.° This shall make
Our purpose necessary and not envious,
Which so appearing to the common eyes,
We shall be called purgers, not murderers.   180
And for Mark Antony, think not of him,
For he can do no more than Caesar's arm
When Caesar's head is off.
    CASS.   Yet I fear him,°
For in the ingrafted love he bears to Caesar ——
    BRU. Alas, good Cassius, do not think of him.
If he love Caesar, all that he can do   186
Is to himself, take thought and die for Caesar.
And that were much he should, for he is given
To sports, to wildness and much company.
    TRE. There is no fear° in him. Let him not die,
For he will live and laugh at this hereafter.   191
    [*Clock strikes.*]
    BRU. Peace! Count the clock.°
    CASS.   The clock hath stricken three.
    TRE. 'Tis time to part.
    CASS.   But it is doubtful yet
Whether Caesar will come forth today or no,
For he is superstitious grown of late,   195
Quite from the main° opinion he held once
Of fantasy, of dreams and ceremonies.
It may be these apparent prodigies,°
The unaccustomed terror of this night
And the persuasion of his augurers,°   200
May hold him from the Capitol today.
    DEC. Never fear that. If he be so resolved,
I can o'ersway him. For he loves to hear
That unicorns° may be betrayed with trees
And bears with glasses,° elephants with holes,°
Lions with toils° and men with flatterers ——   206
But when I tell him he hates flatterers,
He says he does, being then most flattered.
Let me work,

175–77. as . . . 'em: like some masters who first stir up their serv-
ants to commit some violence against an enemy and afterward
pretend to be angry.   183. Yet . . . him: It is part of the trag-
edy of Cassius that he always knows what should be done, but
allows himself to be overruled by Brutus.   190. fear: cause for
fear.   192. clock: There were in fact no striking clocks in
Caesar's time.   196. main: general.   198. apparent prodigies:
evident signs of disaster.   200. augurers: professional inter-
preters of omens.   204. unicorns: It was believed by some natu-
ral historians that the lion defeated the mythical unicorn by
guile. It would stand in front of a tree to provoke the unicorn
to charge, and then slip aside. The unicorn, impaled by his own
horn, thus became an easy prey.   205. glasses: mirrors; i.e.,
the bear, a vain creature, was led into a trap by its desire to look
at itself. holes: pits.   206. toils: nets.

For I can give his humor the true bent,°   210
And I will bring him to the Capitol.
    CASS. Nay, we will all of us be there to fetch him.
    BRU. By the eighth hour.° Is that the uttermost?
    CIN. Be that the uttermost, and fail not then.
    MET. Caius Ligarius doth bear Caesar hard,   215
Who rated° him for speaking well of Pompey.
I wonder none of you have thought of him.
    BRU. Now, good Metellus, go along by him.
He loves me well, and I have given him reasons.
Send him but hither and I'll fashion° him.   220
    CASS. The morning comes upon 's. We'll leave
    you, Brutus.
And friends, disperse yourselves, but all remember
What you have said, and show yourselves true Ro-
    mans.
    BRU. Good gentlemen, look fresh and merrily.
Let not our looks put on our purposes,   225
But bear it as our Roman actors do,
With untired spirits and formal constancy.°
And so, good morrow to you every one.
    [*Exeunt all but* BRUTUS.]
Boy! Lucius! Fast asleep! It is no matter.
Enjoy the honey-heavy dew of slumber.   230
Thou hast no figures° nor no fantasies
Which busy care draws in the brains of men,
Therefore thou sleep'st so sound.
    [*Enter* PORTIA.]
    POR.   Brutus, my lord!
    BRU. Portia, what mean you? Wherefore rise you
    now?
It is not for your health thus to commit   235
Your weak condition to the raw cold morning.
    POR. Nor for yours neither. You've ungently, Bru-
    tus,
Stole from my bed. And yesternight at supper
You suddenly arose and walked about,
Musing and sighing, with your arms across.   240
And when I asked you what the matter was,
You stared upon me with ungentle looks.
I urged you further, then you scratched your head,
And too impatiently stamped with your foot.
Yet I insisted, yet you answered not,   245
But with an angry wafture° of your hand
Gave sign for me to leave you. So I did,
Fearing to strengthen that impatience
Which seemed too much enkindled, and withal
Hoping it was but an effect of humor,°   250
Which sometime hath his hour with every man.
It will not let you eat, nor talk, nor sleep,
And, could it work so much upon your shape
As it hath much prevailed on your condition,

210. give . . . bent: bend his inclination in the right direction.
213. eighth hour: the normal time for starting business in
Shakespeare's London.   216. rated: rebuked.   220. fashion:
mold.   227. formal constancy: outward appearance of stead-
fastness.   231. figures: specters of the imagination.   246. waf-
ture: wave.   250. humor: moodiness.

I should not know you, Brutus. Dear my lord,   255
Make me acquainted with your cause of grief.
BRU. I am not well in health, and that is all.
POR. Brutus is wise, and were he not in health,
He would embrace the means to come by it.
BRU. Why, so I do. Good Portia, go to bed.   260
POR. Is Brutus sick, and is it physical°
To walk unbraced° and suck up the humors
Of the dank° morning? What, is Brutus sick,
And will he steal out of his wholesome bed
To dare the vile contagion of the night,   265
And tempt the rheumy° and unpurgèd air
To add unto his sickness? No, my Brutus;
You have some sick offense within your mind,
Which by the right and virtue of my place
I ought to know of. And, upon my knees,   270
I charm° you, by my once commended beauty,
By all your vows of love and that great vow
Which did incorporate and make us one,
That you unfold to me, yourself, your half,
Why you are heavy, and what men tonight   275
Have had resort to you; for here have been
Some six or seven who did hide their faces
Even from darkness.
            BRU.   Kneel not, gentle Portia.
POR. I should not need if you were gentle Brutus.
Within the bond of marriage, tell me, Brutus,   280
Is it excepted I should know no secrets
That appertain to you? Am I yourself
But, as it were, in sort or limitation,°
To keep with you at meals, comfort your bed,
And talk to you sometimes? Dwell I but in the sub-
      urbs°   285
Of your good pleasure? If it be no more,
Portia is Brutus' harlot,° not his wife.
BRU. You are my true and honorable wife,
As dear to me as are the ruddy drops°
That visit my sad heart.   290
POR. If this were true, then should I know this
      secret.
I grant I am a woman, but withal
A woman that Lord Brutus took to wife.
I grant I am a woman, but withal
A woman well reputed, Cato's° daughter.   295
Think you I am no stronger than my sex,
Being so fathered and so husbanded?
Tell me your counsels, I will not disclose 'em.
I have made strong proof of my constancy,°
Giving myself a voluntary wound   300

261. physical: good for your health.   262. unbraced: with
your coat open.   263. dank: damp air was believed to be a
cause of sickness.   266. rheumy: liable to cause rheumatism.
271. charm: adjure.   282–83. Am . . . limitation: am I your wife
only in a limited way?   285. suburbs: outskirts.   287. harlot:
the London brothels were situated in the suburbs.   289. ruddy
drops: blood.   295. Cato: Marcus Porcius Cato, a man of un-
usual political honesty, had consistently opposed Caesar. When
Caesar had finally defeated Pompey's armies, Cato killed himself
rather than live under a tyrant.   299. constancy: firmness.

Here in the thigh. Can I bear that with patience
And not my husband's secrets?
            BRU.   O ye gods,
Render me worthy of this noble wife!
                              [*Knocking within.*]
Hark, hark! One knocks. Portia, go in a while,
And by and by thy bosom shall partake   305
The secrets of my heart.
All my engagements I will construe to thee,
All the charáctery° of my sad brows.
Leave me with haste. [*Exit* PORTIA.] Lucius, who's
      that knocks?
            [*Re-enter* LUCIUS *with* LIGARIUS.]
LUC. Here is a sick man that would speak with
      you.   310
BRU. Caius Ligarius, that Metellus spake of.
Boy, stand aside. Caius Ligarius! How?
LIG. Vouchsafe good morrow from a feeble
      tongue.
BRU. Oh, what a time have you chose out, brave
      Caius,
To wear a kerchief!° Would you were not sick!   315
LIG. I am not sick if Brutus have in hand
Any exploit worthy the name of honor.
BRU. Such an exploit have I in hand, Ligarius,
Had you a healthful ear to hear of it.
LIG. By all the gods that Romans bow before,
I here discard my sickness! Soul of Rome!   321
Brave son, derived from honorable loins!
Thou, like an exorcist,° hast conjured up
My mortified° spirit. Now bid me run,
And I will strive with things impossible,   325
Yea, get the better of them. What's to do?
BRU. A piece of work that will make sick men
      whole.
LIG. But are not some whole that we must make
      sick?
BRU. That must we also. What it is, my Caius,
I shall unfold to thee as we are going   330
To whom it must be done.
LIG.   Set on your foot,
And with a heart new-fired I follow you,
To do I know not what, but it sufficeth
That Brutus leads me on.
BRU.   Follow me, then.   [*Exeunt.*]

SCENE II. CAESAR'S *house.*

[*Thunder and lightning. Enter* CAESAR, *in his night-
                        gown.°*]
CAE. Nor Heaven nor earth have been at peace to-
      night.
Thrice hath Calpurnia in her sleep cried out,

308. charactery: that which is written in my face.   315. ker-
chief: muffler, as worn by an invalid.   323. exorcist: one who
summons the spirits of the dead.   324. mortified: dead.
      Sc. ii: s.d., nightgown: dressing gown.

"Help, ho! They murder Caesar!" Who's within?
[*Enter a* SERVANT.]
SERV. My lord?
CAE. Go bid the priests do present° sacrifice,   5
And bring me their opinions of success.
SERV. I will, my lord.   [*Exit.*]
[*Enter* CALPURNIA.]
CAL. What mean you, Caesar? Think you to walk
forth?
You shall not stir out of your house today.
CAE. Caesar shall forth.° The things that threat-
ened me   10
Ne'er looked but on my back. When they shall see
The face of Caesar, they are vanishèd.
CAL. Caesar, I never stood on ceremonies,°
Yet now they fright me. There is one within,
Besides the things that we have heard and seen,   15
Recounts most horrid sights seen by the watch.°
A lioness hath whelpèd° in the streets.
And graves have yawned and yielded up their dead.
Fierce fiery warriors fight upon the clouds,
In ranks and squadrons and right form of war,   20
Which drizzled blood upon the Capitol.
The noise of battle hurtled in the air,
Horses did neigh and dying men did groan,
And ghosts did shriek and squeal about the streets.
O Caesar! these things are beyond all use,°   25
And I do fear them.
CAE.   What can be avoided
Whose end is purposed by the mighty gods?
Yet Caesar shall go forth, for these predictions
Are to the world in general as to Caesar.   29
CAL. When beggars die, there are no comets° seen.
The heavens themselves blaze forth the death of
princes.
CAE. Cowards die many times before their deaths,
The valiant never taste of death but once.
Of all the wonders that I yet have heard,
It seems to me most strange that men should fear,
Seeing that death, a necessary end,   36
Will come when it will come.
[*Re-enter* SERVANT.]
What say the augurers?
SERV. They would not have you to stir forth to-
day.
Plucking the entrails of an offering° forth,
They could not find a heart within the beast.   40
CAE. The gods do this in shame of cowardice.
Caesar should be a beast without a heart

If he should stay at home today for fear.
No, Caesar shall not. Danger knows full well
That Caesar is more dangerous than he.   45
We are two lions littered in one day,
And I the elder and more terrible.
And Caesar shall go forth.
CAL.   Alas, my lord,
Your wisdom is consumed in confidence.°
Do not go forth today. Call it my fear   50
That keeps you in the house, and not your own.
We'll send Mark Antony to the Senate House,
And he shall say you are not well today.
Let me, upon my knee, prevail in this.
CAE. Mark Antony shall say I am not well,   55
And, for thy humor,° I will stay at home.
[*Enter* DECIUS.]
Here's Decius Brutus. He shall tell them so.
DEC. Caesar, all hail! Good morrow, worthy Cae-
sar.
I come to fetch you to the Senate House.
CAE. And you are come in very happy time,   60
To bear my greeting to the Senators
And tell them that I will not come today.
Cannot is false, and that I dare not, falser —
I will not come today. Tell them so, Decius.
CAL. Say he is sick.
CAE.   Shall Caesar send a lie?   65
Have I in conquest stretched mine arm so far,
To be afeared to tell graybeards the truth?
Decius, go tell them Caesar will not come.
DEC. Most mighty Caesar, let me know some
cause,
Lest I be laughed at when I tell them so.   70
CAE. The cause is in my will — I will not come.
That is enough to satisfy the Senate.
But, for your private satisfaction,
Because I love you, I will let you know.
Calpurnia here, my wife, stays me at home.   75
She dreamt tonight she saw my statuë,°
Which like a fountain with a hundred spouts
Did run pure blood, and many lusty Romans
Came smiling and did bathe their hands in it.
And these does she apply for warnings and portents
And evils imminent, and on her knee   81
Hath begged that I will stay at home today.
DEC. This dream is all amiss interpreted.
It was a vision fair and fortunate.
Your statue spouting blood in many pipes,   85
In which so many smiling Romans bathed,
Signifies that from you great Rome shall suck
Reviving blood, and that great men shall press
For tinctures, stains, relics, and cognizance.°

5. present: immediate.   **10. Caesar . . . forth:** It was typical of
stage tyrants in Elizabethan drama to talk pompously of them-
selves in the third person.   **13. stood . . . ceremonies:** paid much
attention to omens.   **16. watch:** See Gen. Intro. p. 18a.
17. whelped: dropped its young.   **25. use:** custom.   **30. comets:**
comets were always regarded as portents of great disasters.
39. offering: sacrifice. Roman augurers had several methods of
divining the future. Any abnormality in the beast killed for sac-
rifice was regarded as highly significant.

49. confidence: overconfidence.   **56. humor:** whim.   **76. statue:**
here pronounced as three syllables.   **88–89. great . . . cogni-
zance:** Decius interprets the dream in a double sense. To Caesar
he implies that men shall seek honors from him in the form of
coats of arms and badges signifying that they are his personal
servants. To the audience the meaning of his speech is that men

This by Calpurnia's dream is signified.   90
CAE. And this way have you well expounded it.
DEC. I have, when you have heard what I can say.
And know it now — the Senate have concluded
To give this day a crown to mighty Caesar.
If you shall send them word you will not come,   95
Their minds may change. Besides, it were a mock
Apt to be rendered,° for someone to say
" Break up the Senate till another time,
When Caesar's wife shall meet with better dreams."
If Caesar hide himself, shall they not whisper   100
" Lo, Caesar is afraid "?
Pardon me, Caesar, for my dear dear love
To your proceeding bids me tell you this,
And reason to my love is liable.
CAE. How foolish do your fears seem now, Cal-
purnia!   105
I am ashamèd I did yield to them.
Give me my robe, for I will go.

[*Enter* PUBLIUS, BRUTUS, LIGARIUS, METELLUS, CASCA,
TREBONIUS, *and* CINNA.]

And look where Publius is come to fetch me.
PUB. Good morrow, Caesar.
CAE.   Welcome, Publius.
What, Brutus, are you stirred so early too?   110
Good morrow, Casca. Caius Ligarius,
Caesar was ne'er so much your enemy
As that same ague which hath made you lean.
What is 't o'clock?
BRU.   Caesar, 'tis strucken° eight.
CAE. I thank you for your pains and courtesy.

[*Enter* ANTONY.]

See! Antony, that revels long o' nights,   116
Is notwithstanding up. Good morrow, Antony.
ANT. So to most noble Caesar.
CAE.   Bid them prepare within.
I am to blame to be thus waited for.
Now, Cinna, now, Metellus. What, Trebonius!
I have an hour's talk in store for you.   121
Remember that you call on me today.
Be near me, that I may remember you.
TRE. Caesar, I will. [*Aside*] And so near will I be
That your best friends shall wish I had been fur-
ther.   125
CAE. Good friends, go in and taste some wine
with me,
And we like friends will straightway go together.
BRU. [*Aside*] That every like is not the same, O
Caesar,
The heart of Brutus yearns° to think upon!
[*Exeunt.*]

SCENE III. *A street near the Capitol.*

[*Enter* ARTEMIDORUS, *reading a paper.*]
ART. " Caesar, beware of Brutus; take heed of Cas-
sius; come not near Casca; have an eye to Cinna;
trust not Trebonius; mark well Metellus Cimber;
Decius Brutus loves thee not; thou hast wronged
Caius Ligarius. There is but one mind in all   5
these men, and it is bent against Caesar. If thou be-
est not immortal, look about you. Security° gives
way to conspiracy. The mighty gods defend thee!
                                " Thy lover, ARTEMIDORUS."
Here will I stand till Caesar pass along,   11
And as a suitor° will I give him this.
My heart laments that virtue cannot live
Out of the teeth of emulation.°
If thou read this, O Caesar, thou mayst live;   15
If not, the Fates with traitors do contrive.° [*Exit.*]

SCENE IV. *Another part of the same street,
before the house of* BRUTUS.

[*Enter* PORTIA *and* LUCIUS.]
POR. I prithee, boy, run to the Senate House.
Stay not to answer me, but get thee gone.
Why dost thou stay?
LUC.   To know my errand, madam.
POR. I would have had thee there, and here again,
Ere I can tell thee what thou shouldst do there.   5
O Constancy, be strong upon my side!
Set a huge mountain 'tween my heart and tongue!
I have a man's mind, but a woman's might.
How hard it is for women to keep counsel!
Art thou here yet?
LUC.   Madam, what should I do?   10
Run to the Capitol, and nothing else?
And so return to you, and nothing else?
POR. Yes, bring me word, boy, if thy lord look
well,
For he went sickly forth. And take good note
What Caesar doth, what suitors press to him.   15
Hark, boy! What noise is that?
LUC. I hear none, madam.
POR.   Prithee,° listen well.
I heard a bustling rumor° like a fray,
And the wind brings it from the Capitol.
LUC. Sooth, madam, I hear nothing.

[*Enter the* SOOTHSAYER.]

POR.   Come hither, fellow. 20
Which way hast thou been?
SOOTH.   At mine own house, good lady.

---

will preserve relics of his death. It was a custom to dip handker-
chiefs in the blood of those executed for their religious principles.
These relics were highly valued. **tincture**: stain, but in heraldic
language a coat of arms. **cognizance**: badge worn by a great
man's servant; also "token." **96–97. mock . . . rendered**: jibe
likely to be made. **114. strucken**: struck. **129. yearns**: grieves.

Sc. iii: **7. Security**: carelessness.   **12. suitor**: petitioner.
13–14. virtue . . . emulation: i.e., envy (*emulation*) always gets
its teeth into goodness.   **16. contrive**: plot.
     Sc. iv: **17. Prithee**: I pray thee.   **18. bustling rumor**: indis-
tinct noise.

POR. What is 't o'clock?

SOOTH.   About the ninth hour, lady.

POR. Is Caesar yet gone to the Capitol?

SOOTH. Madam, not yet. I go to take my stand   25
To see him pass on to the Capitol.

POR. Thou hast some suit to Caesar, hast thou
     not?

SOOTH. That I have, lady. If it will please Caesar
To be so good to Caesar as to hear me,
I shall beseech him to befriend himself.   30

POR. Why, know'st thou any harm's intended to-
     ward him?

SOOTH. None that I know will be, much that I
     fear may chance.
Good morrow to you. Here the street is narrow,
The throng that follows Caesar at the heels,
Of Senators, of praetors, common suitors,   35
Will crowd a feeble man almost to death.
I'll get me to a place more void,° and there
Speak to great Caesar as he comes along.   [*Exit.*]

POR. I must go in. Aye me, how weak a thing
The heart of women is! O Brutus,   40
The heavens speed° thee in thine enterprise!
Sure, the boy heard me. Brutus hath a suit
That Caesar will not grant. Oh, I grow faint.
Run, Lucius, and commend me to my lord.
Say I am merry. Come to me again,   45
And bring me word what he doth say to thee.
                      [*Exeunt severally.°*]

Act III

SCENE I. *Rome. Before the Capitol; the Sen-
ate sitting above.*

[*A crowd of people; among them* ARTEMIDORUS *and
the* SOOTHSAYER. *Flourish. Enter* CAESAR, BRUTUS, CAS-
SIUS, CASCA, DECIUS, METELLUS, TREBONIUS, CINNA;
ANTONY, LEPIDUS, POPILIUS, PUBLIUS, *and others.*]

CAE. The ides of March are come.

SOOTH. Aye, Caesar, but not gone.

ART. Hail, Caesar! Read this schedule.°

DEC. Trebonius doth desire you to o'erread,
At your best leisure, this his humble suit.   5

ART. O Caesar, read mine first, for mine's a suit
That touches Caesar nearer. Read it, great Caesar.

CAE. What touches us ourself shall be last served.

ART. Delay not, Caesar. Read it instantly.

CAE. What, is the fellow mad?

PUB.   Sirrah,° give place.   10

CASS. What, urge you your petitions in the street?
Come to the Capitol.

[*Caesar goes up to the Senate House, the rest fol-
lowing.*]

POP. I wish your enterprise today may thrive.

CASS. What enterprise, Popilius?

POP.   Fare you well. [*Advances to* CAESAR.]

BRU. What said Popilius Lena?   15

CASS. He wished today our enterprise might
     thrive.
I fear our purpose is discovered.

BRU. Look how he makes to° Caesar. Mark him.

CASS.   Casca,
Be sudden, for we fear prevention.
Brutus, what shall be done? If this be known,   20
Cassius or Caesar never shall turn back,
For I will slay myself.

BRU.   Cassius, be constant.
Popilius Lena speaks not of our purposes,
For look, he smiles and Caesar doth not change.

CASS. Trebonius knows his time, for look you,
     Brutus,   25
He draws Mark Antony out of the way.
           [*Exeunt* ANTONY *and* TREBONIUS.]

DEC. Where is Metellus Cimber? Let him go,
And presently prefer his suit to Caesar.

BRU. He is addressed.° Press near and second him.

CIN. Casca, you are the first that rears your hand.

CAE. Are we all ready? What is now amiss   31
That Caesar and his Senate must redress?

MET. Most high, most mighty, and most puissant
     Caesar,
Metellus Cimber throws before thy seat
A humble heart ——   [*Kneeling.*]

CAE.   I must prevent thee, Cimber.   35
These couchings° and these lowly° courtesies
Might fire the blood of ordinary men,
And turn preordinance and first decree
Into the law of children.° Be not fond,°
To think that Caesar bears such rebel blood   40
That will be thawed from the true quality
With that which melteth fools — I mean sweet
     words,
Low-crookèd° curtsies, and base spaniel fawning.
Thy brother by decree is banished.
If thou dost bend and pray and fawn for him,   45
I spurn thee like a cur out of my way.
Know, Caesar doth not wrong, nor without cause
Will he be satisfied.

MET. Is there no voice more worthy than my own,
To sound more sweetly in great Caesar's ear   50
For the repealing° of my banished brother?

BRU. I kiss thy hand, but not in flattery, Caesar,

---

37. **void:** empty.   41. **speed:** help.   46. s.d., **severally:** by
different exits.

     Act III, Sc. i: 3. **schedule:** paper.   10. **Sirrah:** term of address
used to an inferior.

18. **makes to:** goes toward.   36. **couchings:** low bowings. **lowly:**
humble.   38–39. **And . . . children:** i.e., my will has the force of
that which was ordained from the first, and does not change
capriciously, like the will of a child.   39. **fond:** foolish.
43. **Low-crooked:** bending low.   51. **repealing:** recalling.

Desiring thee that Publius Cimber may
Have an immediate freedom of repeal.
    CAE. What, Brutus!
    CASS.   Pardon, Caesar, Caesar, pardon.   55
As low as to thy foot doth Cassius fall,
To beg enfranchisement° for Publius Cimber.
    CAE. I could be well moved, if I were as you.
If I could pray to move, prayers would move me;
But I am constant as the Northern Star,   60
Of whose true-fixed and resting quality
There is no fellow° in the firmament.
The skies are painted with unnumbered° sparks,
They are all fire, and every one doth shine,
But there's but one in all doth hold his place.   65
So in the world. 'Tis furnished well with men,
And men are flesh and blood, and apprehensive;°
Yet in the number I do know but one
That unassailable holds on his rank,
Unshaked of motion. And that I am he,   70
Let me a little show it, even in this,
That I was constant Cimber should be banished,
And constant do remain to keep him so.
    CIN. O Caesar ——
    CAE.   Hence! Wilt thou lift up Olympus?
    DEC. Great Caesar ——
    CAE.   Doth not Brutus bootless° kneel?   75
    CASC. Speak, hands, for me!
        [CASCA *first, then the other Conspira-*
        tors and MARCUS BRUTUS *stab* CAESAR.]
    CAE. *Et tu, Brute?* Then fall, Caesar!   [*Dies.*]
    CIN. Liberty! Freedom! Tyranny is dead!
Run hence, proclaim, cry it about the streets.
    CASS. Some to the common pulpits, and cry out
" Liberty, freedom, and enfranchisement! "   81
    BRU. People, and Senators, be not affrighted.
Fly not, stand still. Ambition's debt is paid.
    CASC. Go to the pulpit, Brutus.
    DEC.   And Cassius too.
    BRU. Where's Publius?   85
    CIN. Here, quite confounded with this mutiny.
    MET. Stand fast together, lest some friend of Cae-
    sar's
Should chance ——
    BRU. Talk not of standing. Publius, good cheer.
There is no harm intended to your person,   90
Nor to no Roman else. So tell them, Publius.
    CASS. And leave us, Publius, lest that the people
Rushing on us should do your age some mischief.
    BRU. Do so, and let no man abide° this deed
But we the doers.
        [*Re-enter* TREBONIUS.]
    CASS.   Where is Antony?   95
    TRE. Fled to his house amazed.
Men, wives, and children stare, cry out, and run

As it were Doomsday.°
    BRU.   Fates, we will know your pleasures.
That we shall die, we know; 'tis but the time,
And drawing days out, that men stand upon.°   100
    CAS. Why, he that cuts off twenty years of life
Cuts off so many years of fearing death.
    BRU. Grant that, and then is death a benefit.
So are we Caesar's friends that have abridged
His time of fearing death. Stoop, Romans, stoop,
And let us bathe our hands in Caesar's blood   106
Up to the elbows, and besmear our swords.
Then walk we forth, even to the market place,
And waving our red weapons o'er our heads,
Let's all cry " Peace, freedom, and liberty! "   110
    CAS. Stoop then, and wash. How many ages hence
Shall this our lofty scene be acted over
In states unborn and accents yet unknown!
    BRU. How many times shall Caesar bleed in
    sport,°
That now on Pompey's basis° lies along°   115
No worthier than the dust!
    CASS.   So oft as that shall be,
So often shall the knot° of us be called
The men that gave their country liberty.
    DEC. What, shall we forth?
    CASS.   Aye, every man away.
Brutus shall lead, and we will grace his heels   120
With the most boldest and best hearts of Rome.
        [*Enter a* SERVANT.]
    BRU. Soft! Who comes here? A friend of An-
    tony's.
    SERV. Thus, Brutus, did my master bid me kneel,
Thus did Mark Antony bid me fall down,
And, being prostrate, thus he bade me say: 125
Brutus is noble, wise, valiant, and honest,
Caesar was mighty, bold, royal, and loving.
Say I love Brutus and I honor him,
Say I feared Caesar, honored him, and loved him.
If Brutus will vouchsafe that Antony   130
May safely come to him and be resolved°
How Caesar hath deserved to lie in death,
Mark Antony shall not love Caesar dead
So well as Brutus living, but will follow
The fortunes and affairs of noble Brutus   135
Thorough° the hazards of this untrod state°
With all true faith. So says my master Antony.
    BRU. Thy master is a wise and valiant Roman —
I never thought him worse.
Tell him, so please him come unto this place,   140
He shall be satisfied and, by my honor,
Depart untouched.
    SERV.   I'll fetch him presently.°   [*Exit.*]

98. Doomsday: the Day of Judgment. **100. stand upon:** trouble
themselves with. **114. in sport:** for entertainment, i.e., in
dramas. **115. Pompey's basis:** the base of Pompey's statue.
along: stretched out. **117. knot:** bunch, party. **131. resolved:**
freed from doubts. **136. Thorough:** through. **untrod state:**
uncertain future. **142. presently:** immediately.

57. enfranchisement: release. **62. fellow:** equal. **63. unnum-**
bered: innumerable. **67. apprehensive:** quick-witted. **75. boot-**
less: in vain. **94. abide:** pay the penalty for.

BRU. I know that we shall have him well to
   friend.°
CASS. I wish we may, but yet have I a mind
That fears him much, and my misgiving still   145
Falls shrewdly to the purpose.°

      [*Re-enter* ANTONY.]

BRU. But here comes Antony. Welcome, Mark
   Antony.
ANT. O mighty Caesar, dost thou lie so low?
Are all thy conquests, glories, triumphs, spoils,
Shrunk to this little measure? Fare thee well.   150
I know not, gentlemen, what you intend,
Who else must be let blood, who else is rank.°
If I myself, there is no hour so fit
As Caesar's death's hour, nor no instrument
Of half that worth as those your swords, made rich
With the most noble blood of all this world.   156
I do beseech ye, if you bear me hard,
Now, whilst your purpled hands do reek° and
   smoke,
Fulfill your pleasure. Live a thousand years,
I shall not find myself so apt to die.   160
No place will please me so, no mean° of death,
As here by Caesar, and by you cut off,
The choice and master spirits of this age.
BRU. O Antony, beg not your death of us.
Though now we must appear bloody and cruel,
As by our hands and this our present act   166
You see we do. Yet see you but our hands
And this the bleeding business they have done.
Our hearts you see not. They are pitiful,
And pity to the general wrong of Rome ——   170
As fire drives out fire, so pity pity ——
Hath done this deed on Caesar. For your part,
To you our swords have leaden° points, Mark An-
   tony.
Our arms in strength of malice,° and our hearts
Of brothers' temper, do receive you in   175
With all kind love, good thoughts, and reverence.
CASS. Your voice shall be as strong as any man's
In the disposing of new dignities.°
BRU. Only be patient till we have appeased
The multitude, beside themselves with fear,   180
And then we will deliver you the cause
Why I, that did love Caesar when I struck him,
Have thus proceeded.
ANT.   I doubt not of your wisdom.
Let each man render° me his bloody hand.
First, Marcus Brutus, will I shake with you.   185

Next, Caius Cassius, do I take your hand.
Now, Decius Brutus, yours, now yours, Metellus;
Yours, Cinna, and, my valiant Casca, yours ——
Though last, not least in love, yours, good Trebo-
   nius.
Gentlemen all — alas, what shall I say?   190
My credit now stands on such slippery ground
That one of two bad ways you must conceit° me,
Either a coward or a flatterer.
That I did love thee, Caesar, oh, 'tis true.
If then thy spirit look upon us now,   195
Shall it not grieve thee dearer than thy death
To see thy Antony making his peace,
Shaking the bloody fingers of thy foes,
Most noble! in the presence of thy corse?°
Had I as many eyes as thou hast wounds,   200
Weeping as fast as they stream forth thy blood,
It would become me better than to close
In terms of friendship with thine enemies.
Pardon me, Julius! Here wast thou bayed,° brave
   hart,   204
Here didst thou fall, and here thy hunters stand,
Signed in thy spoil° and crimsoned in thy lethe.°
O world, thou wast the forest to this hart,
And this, indeed, O world, the heart of thee.
How like a deer strucken by many princes
Dost thou here lie!   210
CASS. Mark Antony ——
ANT.   Pardon me, Caius Cassius.
The enemies of Caesar shall say this;
Then, in a friend, it is cold modesty.
CASS. I blame you not for praising Caesar so,
But what compact mean you to have with us?   215
Will you be pricked in number° of our friends,
Or shall we on, and not depend on you?
ANT. Therefore I took your hands, but was indeed
Swayed from the point by looking down on Caesar.
Friends am I with you all and love you all,   220
Upon this hope that you shall give me reasons
Why and wherein Caesar was dangerous.
BRU. Or else were this a savage spectacle.
Our reasons are so full of good regard
That were you, Antony, the son of Caesar,   225
You should be satisfied.
ANT.   That's all I seek.
And am moreover suitor that I may
Produce his body to the market place,
And in the pulpit, as becomes a friend,
Speak in the order of his funeral.   230
BRU. You shall, Mark Antony.
CASS.   Brutus, a word with you.
[*Aside to* BRUTUS] You know not what you do. Do
   not consent

---

143. well . . . friend: as a good friend.   146. Falls . . . purpose:
I am highly (*shrewdly*) disturbed at your proposal.   152. rank:
medical term, meaning in a state requiring bloodletting. Period-
ical bloodletting was considered good for the general health.
158. reek: steam.   161. mean: means.   173. leaden: blunt.
174. in . . . malice: having the power to do harm.   178. dispos-
ing . . . dignities: Brutus offers Antony fine sentiments. Cassius,
knowing his man better, proposes a share in the loot.   184. ren-
der: offer.

192. conceit: conceive, imagine.   199. corse: corpse.   204. bayed:
brought to bay; i.e., surrounded by baying hounds and unable
to escape. Antony uses the metaphors of hunting the deer.
206. Signed . . . spoil: stained with your slaughter (*spoil*). lethe:
blood.   216. pricked . . . number: marked in the list.

That Antony speak in his funeral.
Know you how much the people may be moved
By that which he will utter?

BRU.   By your pardon,   235
I will myself into the pulpit first,
And show the reason of our Caesar's death.
What Antony shall speak, I will protest
He speaks by leave and by permission,
And that we are contented Caesar shall   240
Have all true rites and lawful ceremonies.
It shall advantage more than do us wrong.

CASS. I know not what may fall. I like it not.

BRU. Mark Antony, here, take you Caesar's body.
You shall not in your funeral speech blame us,   245
But speak all good you can devise of Caesar,
And say you do 't by our permission.
Else shall you not have any hand at all
About his funeral. And you shall speak
In the same pulpit whereto I am going —   250
After my speech is ended.

ANT.   Be it so.
I do desire no more.

BRU. Prepare the body then, and follow us.

     [*Exeunt all but* ANTONY.]

ANT. O, pardon me, thou bleeding piece of earth,
That I am meek and gentle with these butchers!
Thou art the ruins of the noblest man   256
That ever livèd in the tide of times.
Woe to the hand that shed this costly blood!
Over thy wounds now do I prophesy,
Which like dumb mouths do ope° their ruby lips
To beg the voice and utterance of my tongue,   261
A curse shall light upon the limbs of men.
Domestic fury and fierce civil strife
Shall cumber all the parts of Italy.
Blood and destruction shall be so in use,   265
And dreadful objects so familiar,
That mothers shall but smile when they behold
Their infants quartered with° the hands of war,
All pity choked with custom of fell deeds.°
And Caesar's spirit ranging° for revenge,   270
With Até° by his side come hot from Hell,
Shall in these confines° with a monarch's voice
Cry " Havoc,"° and let slip the dogs of war,
That this foul deed shall smell above the earth
With carrion men, groaning for burial.   275

     [*Enter a* SERVANT.]

You serve Octavius Caesar,° do you not?

SERV. I do, Mark Antony.

ANT. Caesar did write for him to come to Rome.

SERV. He did receive his letters, and is coming,

And bid me say to you by word of mouth ——   280
[*Seeing the body*] O Caesar!

ANT. Thy heart is big.° Get thee apart and weep.
Passion,° I see, is catching, for mine eyes,
Seeing those beads of sorrow stand in thine,
Began to water. Is thy master coming?   285

SERV. He lies tonight within seven leagues of
Rome.

ANT. Post back with speed, and tell him what
hath chanced.
Here is a mourning Rome, a dangerous Rome,
No Rome of safety for Octavius yet.
Hie hence, and tell him so. Yet stay awhile.   290
Thou shalt not back till I have borne this corse
Into the market place. There shall I try,°
In my oration, how the people take
The cruel issue° of these bloody men,
According to the which, thou shalt discourse   295
To young Octavius of the state of things.
Lend me your hand.   [*Exeunt with* CAESAR'*s body.*]

SCENE II. *The Forum.*

[*Enter* BRUTUS *and* CASSIUS, *and a throng of*
CITIZENS.]

CITS. We will be satisfied. Let us be satisfied.

BRU. Then follow me, and give me audience,
friends.
Cassius, go you into the other street,
And part° the numbers.
Those that will hear me speak, let 'em stay here,   5
Those that will follow Cassius, go with him,
And public reasons shall be rendered
Of Caesar's death.

1. CIT.   I will hear Brutus speak.

2. CIT. I will hear Cassius, and compare their reasons
When severally we hear them rendered.   10

   [*Exit* CASSIUS, *with some of the* CITIZENS.]
   [BRUTUS *goes into the pulpit.*]

3. CIT. The noble Brutus is ascended. Silence!

BRU. Be patient till the last.
Romans, countrymen,° and lovers! Hear me for my
cause, and be silent, that you may hear. Believe me
for mine honor, and have respect to mine honor,   15
that you may believe. Censure° me in your wisdom,
and awake your senses, that you may the better
judge. If there be any in this assembly, any dear
friend of Caesar's, to him I say that Brutus' love to

---

260. ope: open.   268. quartered with: cut in pieces by.   269. All
. . . deeds: i.e., cruel (*fell*) deeds will be so common that men
will no longer feel pity.   270. ranging: roaming like a beast of
prey.   271. Até: goddess of mischief.   272. confines: bound-
aries; i.e., this country.   273. Cry "Havoc": no quarter! —no
prisoners will be taken.   276. Octavius Caesar: Octavius, who
ultimately became the Emperor Augustus, was the grandson of

Julius Caesar's sister Julia and was adopted by Caesar as his
heir.   282. big: swollen with emotion.   283. Passion: emotion.
292. try: test.   294. issue: action.
Sc. ii: 4. part: divide.   13. Romans, countrymen: See *Caesar*
Intro. p. 533a. Shakespeare uses prose for Brutus's speech to de-
note his "dry" style of speaking. Verse is the natural medium
for Antony's emotional outburst.   16. Censure: judge.

Caesar was no less than his. If then that friend　20
demand why Brutus rose against Caesar, this is my
answer — not that I loved Caesar less, but that I
loved Rome more. Had you rather Caesar were liv-
ing, and die all slaves, than that Caesar were dead,
to live all freemen? As Caesar loved me, I weep　25
for him; as he was fortunate, I rejoice at it; as he was
valiant, I honor him. But as he was ambitious, I slew
him. There is tears for his love, joy for his fortune,
honor for his valor, and death for his ambition. Who
is here so base that would be a bondman? If　31
any, speak, for him have I offended. Who is here so
rude° that would not be a Roman? If any, speak,
for him have I offended. Who is here so vile that
will not love his country? If any, speak, for him
have I offended. I pause for a reply.　37

ALL. None, Brutus, none.

BRU. Then none have I offended. I have done no
more to Caesar than you shall do to Brutus. The
question of his death is enrolled° in the Capitol, his
glory not extenuated, wherein he was worthy,　42
nor his offenses enforced,° for which he suffered
death.

[*Enter* ANTONY *and others, with* CAESAR'S *body.*]
Here comes his body, mourned by Mark Antony,
who, though he had no hand in his death, shall re-
ceive the benefit of his dying, a place in the　47
commonwealth — as which of you shall not? With
this I depart — that, as I slew my best lover for the
good of Rome, I have the same dagger for myself
when it shall please my country to need my death.

ALL. Live, Brutus! Live, live!　53

1. CIT. Bring him with triumph home unto his
house.

2. CIT. Give him a statue with his ancestors.

3. CIT. Let him be Caesar.

4. CIT.　　　　　　　　Caesar's better parts
Shall be crowned in Brutus.

1. CIT. We'll bring him to his house with shouts
and clamors.　58

BRU. My countrymen ——

2. CIT.　　　　　Peace! Silence! Brutus speaks.

1. CIT. Peace, ho!

BRU. Good countrymen, let me depart alone,
And, for my sake, stay here with Antony.　61
Do grace to Caesar's corpse, and grace his speech
Tending to Caesar's glories, which Mark Antony
By our permission is allowed to make.
I do entreat you, not a man depart,　65
Save I alone, till Antony have spoke.　　[*Exit.*]

1. CIT. Stay, ho, and let us hear Mark Antony!

3. CIT. Let him go up into the public chair.
We'll hear him. Noble Antony, go up.　69

ANT. For Brutus' sake, I am beholding to you.
[*Goes into the pulpit.*]

4. CIT. What does he say of Brutus?

3. CIT.　　　　　　　　He says, for Brutus' sake,
He finds himself beholding to us all.

4. CIT. 'Twere best he speak no harm of Brutus
here.

1. CIT. This Caesar was a tyrant.

3. CIT.　　　　　　　　　　Nay, that's certain.
We are blest that Rome is rid of him.　75

2. CIT. Peace! Let us hear what Antony can say.

ANT. You gentle Romans ——

ALL.　　　　　　Peace, ho! Let us hear him.

ANT. Friends, Romans, countrymen, lend me your
ears.
I come to bury Caesar, not to praise him.
The evil that men do lives after them,　80
The good is oft interrèd with their bones.
So let it be with Caesar. The noble Brutus
Hath told you Caesar was ambitious.
If it were so, it was a grievous fault,
And grievously hath Caesar answered it.　85
Here, under leave of Brutus and the rest —
For Brutus is an honorable man,
So are they all, all honorable men —
Come I to speak in Caesar's funeral.
He was my friend, faithful and just to me.　90
But Brutus says he was ambitious,
And Brutus is an honorable man.
He hath brought many captives home to Rome,
Whose ransoms did the general coffers° fill.
Did this in Caesar seem ambitious?　95
When that the poor have cried, Caesar hath wept —
Ambition should be made of sterner stuff.
Yet Brutus says he was ambitious,
And Brutus is an honorable man.
You all did see that on the Lupercal　100
I thrice presented him a kingly crown,
Which he did thrice refuse. Was this ambition?
Yet Brutus says he was ambitious,
And, sure, he is an honorable man.
I speak not to disprove what Brutus spoke,　105
But here I am to speak what I do know.
You all did love him once, not without cause.
What cause withholds you then to mourn for him?
O judgment, thou art fled to brutish beasts,
And men have lost their reason! Bear with me,°
My heart is in the coffin there with Caesar,　111
And I must pause till it come back to me.

1. CIT. Methinks there is much reason in his say-
ings.

2. CIT. If thou consider rightly of the matter,
Caesar has had great wrong.

3. CIT.　　　　　　　　　Has he, masters?　115
I fear there will a worse come in his place.

4. CIT. Marked ye his words? He would not take
the crown,

---

33. **rude:** barbarous.　41. **enrolled:** preserved among the records.
43. **enforced:** stressed.

94. **general coffers:** public treasury; lit., treasure chests.
110. **Bear with me:** be patient with me.

Therefore 'tis certain he was not ambitious.

1. CIT. If it be found so, some will dear abide° it.

2. CIT. Poor soul! His eyes are red as fire with
weeping.   120

3. CIT. There's not a nobler man in Rome than
Antony.

4. CIT. Now mark him, he begins again to speak.

ANT. But yesterday the word of Caesar might
Have stood against the world. Now lies he there,
And none so poor to do him reverence.   125
O masters, if I were disposed to stir
Your hearts and minds to mutiny and rage,
I should do Brutus wrong and Cassius wrong,
Who, you all know, are honorable men.
I will not do them wrong; I rather choose   130
To wrong the dead, to wrong myself and you,
Than I will wrong such honorable men.
But here's a parchment with the seal of Caesar —
I found it in his closet — 'tis his will.
Let but the commons° hear this testament —   135
Which, pardon me, I do not mean to read —
And they would go and kiss dead Caesar's wounds
And dip their napkins in his sacred blood,°
Yea, beg a hair of him for memory,
And, dying, mention it within their wills,   140
Bequeathing it as a rich legacy
Unto their issue.

4. CIT. We'll hear the will. Read it, Mark Antony.

ALL. The will, the will! We will hear Caesar's
will.

ANT. Have patience, gentle friends. I must not
read it.   145
It is not meet you know how Caesar loved you.
You are not wood, you are not stones, but men;
And, being men, hearing the will of Caesar,
It will inflame you, it will make you mad.
'Tis good you know not that you are his heirs,   150
For if you should, oh, what would come of it!

4. CIT. Read the will. We'll hear it, Antony.
You shall read us the will, Caesar's will.

ANT. Will you be patient? Will you stay awhile?
I have o'ershot myself to tell you of it.   155
I fear I wrong the honorable men
Whose daggers have stabbed Caesar. I do fear it.

4. CIT. They were traitors — honorable men!

ALL. The will! The testament!

2. CIT. They were villains, murderers. The will!
Read the will.   160

ANT. You will compel me then to read the will?
Then make a ring about the corpse of Caesar,
And let me show you him that made the will.
Shall I descend? And will you give me leave?

ALL. Come down.   165

2. CIT. Descend.

[*He comes down from the pulpit.*]

3. CIT. You shall have leave.

4. CIT. A ring. Stand round.

1. CIT. Stand from the hearse, stand from the
body.   169

2. CIT. Room for Antony, most noble Antony.

ANT. Nay, press not so upon me. Stand far off.

ALL. Stand back. Room! Bear back.

ANT. If you have tears, prepare to shed them now.
You all do know this mantle. I remember
The first time ever Caesar put it on.   175
'Twas on a summer's evening, in his tent,
That day he overcame the Nervii.
Look, in this place ran Cassius' dagger through.
See what a rent the envious Casca made.
Through this the well-belovèd Brutus stabbed,   180
And as he plucked his cursèd steel away,
Mark how the blood of Caesar followed it,
As rushing out of doors, to be resolved
If Brutus so unkindly knocked, or no.
For Brutus, as you know, was Caesar's angel.   185
Judge, O you gods, how dearly Caesar loved him!
This was the most unkindest cut of all,
For when the noble Caesar saw him stab,
Ingratitude, more strong than traitors' arms,
Quite vanquished him. Then burst his mighty heart,
And, in his mantle muffling up his face,   191
Even at the base of Pompey's statuë,
Which all the while ran blood, great Caesar fell.
Oh, what a fall was there, my countrymen!
Then I, and you, and all of us fell down,   195
Whilst bloody treason flourished over us.
Oh, now you weep, and I perceive you feel
The dint° of pity. These are gracious drops.   198
Kind souls, what weep you when you but behold
Our Caesar's vesture° wounded? Look you here —
Here is himself, marred, as you see, with traitors.

1. CIT. Oh, piteous spectacle!

2. CIT. Oh, noble Caesar!

3. CIT. Oh, woeful day!

4. CIT. Oh, traitors, villains!   205

1. CIT. Oh, most bloody sight!

2. CIT. We will be revenged.

ALL. Revenge! About! Seek! Burn! Fire! Kill!
Slay!
Let not a traitor live!

ANT. Stay, countrymen.   210

1. CIT. Peace there! Hear the noble Antony.

2. CIT. We'll hear him, we'll follow him, we'll die
with him.

ANT. Good friends, sweet friends, let me not stir
you up
To such a sudden flood of mutiny.   215
They that have done this deed are honorable.
What private griefs they have, alas, I know not,
That made them do it. They are wise and honorable,
And will, no doubt, with reasons answer you.

---

119. **dear abide:** See III.i.94.   135. **commons:** common people.
138. **dip . . . blood:** See II.ii.88–89,n.

198. **dint:** stroke.   200. **vesture:** clothing.

I come not, friends, to steal away your hearts.　220
I am no orator, as Brutus is,
But, as you know me all, a plain blunt man
That love my friend; and that they know full well
That gave me public leave to speak of him.
For I have neither wit, nor words, nor worth,　225
Action, nor utterance, nor the power of speech,
To stir men's blood. I only speak right on,
I tell you that which you yourselves do know,
Show you sweet Caesar's wounds, poor poor dumb
　　　mouths,
And bid them speak for me. But were I Brutus,　230
And Brutus Antony, there were an Antony
Would ruffle up your spirits, and put a tongue
In every wound of Caesar that should move
The stones of Rome to rise and mutiny.

ALL. We'll mutiny.　235

1. CIT. We'll burn the house of Brutus.

3. CIT. Away, then! Come, seek the conspirators.

ANT. Yet hear me, countrymen, yet hear me
　　speak.

ALL. Peace, ho! Hear Antony. Most noble An-
　　tony!

ANT. Why, friends, you go to do you know not
　　what.　240
Wherein hath Caesar thus deserved your loves?
Alas, you know not. I must tell you, then —
You have forgot the will I told you of.

ALL. Most true, the will! Let's stay and hear the
　　will.　244

ANT. Here is the will, and under Caesar's seal.
To every Roman citizen he gives,
To every several° man, seventy-five drachmas.

2. CIT. Most noble Caesar! We'll revenge his
　　death.

3. CIT. Oh, royal Caesar!

ANT. Hear me with patience.　250

ALL. Peace, ho!

ANT. Moreover, he hath left you all his walks,
His private arbors and new-planted orchards,
On this side Tiber. He hath left them you,
And to your heirs forever—common pleasures,　255
To walk abroad and recreate yourselves.
Here was a Caesar! When comes such another?

1. CIT. Never, never. Come, away, away!
We'll burn his body in the holy place,
And with the brands fire the traitors' houses.　260
Take up the body.

2. CIT. Go fetch fire.

3. CIT. Pluck down benches.

4. CIT. Pluck down forms,° windows, anything.

　　　　　[*Exeunt* CITIZENS *with the body*.]

ANT. Now let it work. Mischief, thou art afoot,
Take thou what course thou wilt.　266

[*Enter a* SERVANT.]　　　　　How now, fellow?

SERV. Sir, Octavius is already come to Rome.

247. **several:** individual.　264. **forms:** benches.

ANT. Where is he?

SERV. He and Lepidus° are at Caesar's house.

ANT. And thither will I straight to visit him.　270
He comes upon a wish.° Fortune is merry,
And in this mood will give us anything.

SERV. I heard him say Brutus and Cassius
Are rid like madmen through the gates of Rome.

ANT. Belike they had some notice of the people,
How I had moved them. Bring me to Octavius.

　　　　　　　　　　　　　　　　　[*Exeunt*.]

SCENE III. *A street.*

[*Enter* CINNA *the poet*.]

CIN. I dreamt tonight that I did feast with Caesar,
And things unluckily charge my fantasy.°
I have no will to wander forth of doors,
Yet something leads me forth.

　　　　　　　　　[*Enter* CITIZENS.]

1. CIT. What is your name?

2. CIT. Whither are you going?　　　　　　　5

3. CIT. Where do you dwell?

4. CIT. Are you a married man or a bachelor?

2. CIT. Answer every man directly.

1. CIT. Aye, and briefly.　　　　　　　　　10

4. CIT. Aye, and wisely.

3. CIT. Aye, and truly, you were best.

CIN. What is my name? Whither am I going?
Where do I dwell? Am I a married man or a bache-
lor? Then, to answer every man directly and　14
briefly, wisely and truly, wisely I say I am a bachelor.

2. CIT. That's as much as to say they are fools
that marry. You'll bear me a bang° for that, I fear.
Proceed, directly.

CIN. Directly, I am going to Caesar's funeral.　22

1. CIT. As a friend or an enemy?

CIN. As a friend.

2. CIT. That matter is answered directly.　25

4. CIT. For your dwelling, briefly.

CIN. Briefly, I dwell by the Capitol.

3. CIT. Your name, sir, truly.

CIN. Truly, my name is Cinna.

1. CIT. Tear him to pieces. He's a conspirator.　30

CIN. I am Cinna the poet, I am Cinna the poet.

4. CIT. Tear him for his bad verses, tear him for
his bad verses.　35

CIN. I am not Cinna the conspirator.

4. CIT. It is no matter, his name's Cinna. Pluck
but his name out of his heart, and turn him going.

3. CIT. Tear him, tear him! Come, brands.　40
Ho, firebrands — to Brutus', to Cassius'! Burn all.
Some to Decius' house, and some to Casca's, some
to Ligarius'. Away, go!　　　　　　[*Exeunt*.]

269. **Lepidus:** afterward one of the Big Three, with Antony and
Octavius. See IV.i.　271. **He . . . wish:** just when I wanted him.
　　Sc. iii: 2. **unluckily . . . fantasy:** my imagination is burdened
with thoughts of bad luck.　20. **bear . . . bang:** owe me a blow;
i.e., I'll strike you.

Act IV

SCENE I. *A house in Rome.*

[ANTONY, OCTAVIUS, *and* LEPIDUS, *seated at a table.*]

ANT. These many then shall die, their names are
    pricked.°
OCT. Your brother too must die. Consent you,
    Lepidus?
LEP. I do consent.
OCT.   Prick him down, Antony.
LEP. Upon condition Publius shall not live,
Who is your sister's son, Mark Antony.   5
ANT. He shall not live. Look, with a spot I damn°
    him.
But, Lepidus, go you to Caesar's house.
Fetch the will hither, and we shall determine
How to cut off some charge in legacies.°
LEP. What, shall I find you here?   10
OCT. Or here or at the Capitol.   [*Exit* LEPIDUS.]
ANT. This is a slight unmeritable° man,
Meet to be sent on errands. Is it fit,
The threefold world divided, he should stand
One of the three to share it?
OCT.   So you thought him,°   15
And took his voice who should be pricked to die
In our black sentence° and proscription.°
ANT. Octavius, I have seen more days than you.
And though we lay these honors on this man,
To ease ourselves of divers slanderous loads,°   20
He shall but bear them as the ass bears gold,
To groan and sweat under the business,
Either led or driven, as we point the way.
And having brought our treasure where we will,
Then take we down his load and turn him off,   25
Like to the empty ass, to shake his ears
And graze in commons.°
OCT.   You may do your will.
But he's a tried and valiant soldier.
ANT. So is my horse, Octavius, and for that
I do appoint him store of provender.°   30
It is a creature that I teach to fight,
To wind,° to stop, to run directly on,
His corporal motion° governed by my spirit.
And, in some taste,° is Lepidus but so.
He must be taught, and trained, and bid go forth,
A barren-spirited fellow, one that feeds   36

On abjects,° orts,° and imitations,
Which, out of use and staled by other men,
Begin his fashion.° Do not talk of him
But as a property.° And now, Octavius,   40
Listen great things. Brutus and Cassius
Are levying powers.° We must straight make
    head.°
Therefore let our alliance be combined,
Our best friends made, our means stretched,
And let us presently go sit in council   45
How covert matters° may be best disclosed,
And open perils surest answered.
OCT. Let us do so, for we are at the stake,°
And bayed about with many enemies.
And some that smile have in their hearts, I fear,   50
Millions of mischiefs.   [*Exeunt.*]

SCENE II. *Camp near Sardis.° Before* BRUTUS'S *tent.*

[*Drum. Enter* BRUTUS, LUCILIUS, LUCIUS, *and* SOL-
    DIERS; TITINIUS *and* PINDARUS *meet them.*]

BRU. Stand, ho!
LUCIL. Give the word, ho, and stand!
BRU. What now, Lucilius! Is Cassius near?
LUCIL. He is at hand, and Pindarus is come
To do you salutation from his master.   5
BRU. He greets me well. Your master, Pindarus,
In his own change,° or by ill officers,
Hath given me some worthy cause to wish
Things done undone. But if he be at hand,
I shall be satisfied.
PIN.   I do not doubt   10
But that my noble master will appear
Such as he is, full of regard° and honor.
BRU. He is not doubted. A word, Lucilius,
How he received you. Let me be resolved.
LUCIL. With courtesy and with respect enough,
But not with such familiar instances,°   16
Nor with such free and friendly conference,°
As he hath used of old.
BRU.   Thou hast described
A hot friend cooling. Ever note, Lucilius,
When love begins to sicken and decay,   20
It useth an enforcèd ceremony.°
There are no tricks in plain and simple faith.

Act IV, Sc. i: 1. pricked: See III.i.216,n.   6. damn: con-
demn.   9. cut . . . legacies: avoid paying some of the legacies.
12. unmeritable: without merit.   15. So . . . him: i.e., when you
made him a partner in our triumvirate (rule of three).   17. black
sentence: sentence of death. proscription: after a successful
revolution, lists were published of those "proscribed," who could
then be killed as public enemies.   20. slanderous loads: the
burden of slander.   27. graze . . . commons: in English villages
there was usually a common grazing ground where the villagers
turned out their beasts to feed.   30. provender: fodder.   32. wind:
turn.   33. corporal motion: bodily action.   34. in . . . taste: in
some measure.

37. abjects: worthless things. orts: scraps of food.   38–39. Which
. . . fashion: which he begins to use when they have ceased to
be fashionable with other men.   40. property: a thing to be
pushed around.   42. powers: armies. make head: gather forces.
46. covert matters: things hid.   48. at . . . stake: like a bear
surrounded by hounds. See App. 5.
  Sc. ii: s.d., Sardis: a city in Greece. Brutus and Cassius had
withdrawn to Greece, whither Antony and Octavius followed
them.   7. In . . . change: because he has changed his nature.
12. full . . . regard: worthy of respect.   16. familiar instances:
friendly behavior.   17. conference: talk.   21. enforced ceremony:
forced politeness.

But hollow men, like horses hot at hand,°
Make gallant show and promise of their mettle,
But when they should endure the bloody spur,   25
They fall their crests° and like deceitful jades°
Sink in the trial. Comes his army on?
    LUCIL. They mean this night in Sardis to be quartered.
The greater part, the horse in general,°
Are come with Cassius.   [*Low march within.*]
    BRU.   Hark! He is arrived   30
March gently on to meet him.
        [*Enter* CASSIUS *and his powers.*]
    CASS. Stand, ho!
    BRU. Stand, ho! Speak the word along.
    1. SOL. Stand!
    2. SOL. Stand!   35
    3. SOL. Stand!
    CASS. Most noble brother, you have done me wrong.
    BRU. Judge me, you gods! Wrong I mine enemies?
And if not so, how should I wrong a brother?
    CASS. Brutus, this sober° form of yours hides wrongs,   40
And when you do them ——
    BRU.   Cassius, be content,
Speak your griefs softly. I do know you well.
Before the eyes of both our armies here,
Which should perceive nothing but love from us,
Let us not wrangle. Bid them move away,   45
Then in my tent, Cassius, enlarge your griefs,°
And I will give you audience.
    CASS.   Pindarus,
Bid our commanders lead their charges° off
A little from this ground.   49
    BRU. Lucilius, do you the like, and let no man
Come to our tent till we have done our conference.
Let Lucius and Titinius guard our door. [*Exeunt.*]

SCENE III. BRUTUS's *tent.*

[*Enter* BRUTUS *and* CASSIUS.]
    CASS. That you have wronged me doth appear in this:
You have condemned and noted° Lucius Pella
For taking bribes here of the Sardians,
Wherein my letters, praying on his side,
Because I knew the man, were slighted off.°   5
    BRU. You wronged yourself to write in such a case.
    CASS. In such a time as this it is not meet

That every nice° offense should bear his comment.°
    BRU. Let me tell you, Cassius, you yourself
Are much condemned to have an itching palm,°
To sell and mart° your offices for gold   11
To undeservers.
    CASS.   I an itching palm!
You know that you are Brutus that speaks this,
Or, by the gods, this speech were else your last.
    BRU. The name of Cassius honors this corruption,
And chastisement doth therefore hide his head.   16
    CASS. Chastisement!
    BRU. Remember March, the ides of March remember.
Did not great Julius bleed for justice' sake?
What villain touched his body that did stab,   20
And not for justice? What, shall one of us,
That struck the foremost man of all this world
But for supporting robbers, shall we now
Contaminate our fingers with base bribes,
And sell the mighty space of our large honors   25
For so much trash as may be graspèd thus?
I had rather be a dog and bay the moon
Than such a Roman.
    CASS.   Brutus, bait not me,°
I'll not endure it. You forget yourself,
To hedge me in.° I am a soldier, I,   30
Older in practice, abler than yourself
To make conditions.°
    BRU.   Go to. You are not, Cassius.
    CASS. I am.
    BRU. I say you are not.
    CASS. Urge me no more, I shall forget myself.   35
Have mind upon your health,° tempt me no farther.
    BRU. Away, slight man!
    CASS. Is 't possible?
    BRU.   Hear me, for I will speak.
Must I give way and room to your rash choler?°
Shall I be frighted when a madman stares?   40
    CASS. O ye gods, ye gods! Must I endure all this?
    BRU. All this! Aye, more. Fret till your proud heart break.
Go show your slaves how choleric you are,
And make your bondmen° tremble. Must I budge?
Must I observe you? Must I stand and crouch   45
Under your testy humor?° By the gods,
You shall digest the venom of your spleen,
Though it do split you; for, from this day forth,
I'll use you for my mirth, yea, for my laughter,
When you are waspish.
    CASS.   Is it come to this?   50
    BRU. You say you are a better soldier.

---

23. **hot . . . hand:** restless when the rider wishes them to stand.
26. **fall . . . crests:** become crestfallen, spiritless. **jades:** poorspirited nags. 29. **horse . . . general:** all the cavalry. 40. **sober:** composed. 46. **griefs:** grievances. 48. **charges:** commands. Sc. iii: 2. **noted:** censured. 5. **slighted off:** treated slightingly.

8. **nice:** petty. **bear . . . comment:** be carefully noted. 10. **itching palm:** a hand always eager for bribes. 11. **mart:** trade. 28. **bait . . . me:** do not bark at me as though I were a bear. 30. **hedge . . . in:** control me. 32. **make conditions:** decide upon what conditions a man shall be appointed to office. 36. **health:** welfare. 39. **choler:** wrath. 44. **bondmen:** slaves. 46. **testy humor:** peevish temper.

Let it appear so, make your vaunting true
And it shall please me well. For mine own part,
I shall be glad to learn of noble men.

CASS. You wrong me every way, you wrong me,
　　Brutus.　　　　　　　　　　　　　　　　　　55
I said an elder soldier, not a better.
Did I say better?

BRU.　　　　　　　If you did, I care not.

CASS. When Caesar lived, he durst not thus have
　　moved me.

BRU. Peace, peace! You durst not so have tempted
　　him.

CASS. I durst not!　　　　　　　　　　　　60

BRU. No.

CASS. What, durst not tempt him!

BRU.　　　　　　　For your life you durst not.

CASS. Do not presume too much upon my love.
I may do that I shall be sorry for.

BRU. You have done that you should be sorry for.
There is no terror, Cassius, in your threats,　　66
For I am armed so strong in honesty
That they pass by me as the idle wind
Which I respect not. I did send to you
For certain sums of gold, which you denied me.　70
For I can raise no money by vile means —
By heaven, I had rather coin my heart,
And drop my blood for drachmas,° than to wring
From the hard hands of peasants their vile trash
By any indirection.° I did send　　　　　　75
To you for gold to pay my legions,
Which you denied me. Was that done like Cassius?
Should I have answered Caius Cassius so?
When Marcus Brutus grows so covetous,
To lock such rascal counters° from his friends,　80
Be ready, gods, with all your thunderbolts,
Dash him to pieces!

CASS.　　　　　　　I denied you not.

BRU. You did.

CASS.　　　　　　I did not. He was but a fool
That brought my answer back. Brutus hath rived°
　　my heart.　　　　　　　　　　　　　　　85
A friend should bear his friend's infirmities,
But Brutus makes mine greater than they are.

BRU. I do not, till you practice them on me.

CASS. You love me not.

BRU.　　　　　　　I do not like your faults.

CASS. A friendly eye could never see such faults.

BRU. A flatterer's would not, though they do ap-
　　pear　　　　　　　　　　　　　　　　　　91
As huge as high Olympus.°

CASS. Come, Antony, and young Octavius, come,
Revenge yourselves alone on Cassius,
For Cassius is aweary of the world —　　　　95
Hated by one he loves, braved° by his brother,

Checked° like a bondman, all his faults observed,
Set in a notebook, learned and conned by rote,°
To cast into my teeth. Oh, I could weep
My spirit from mine eyes! There is my dagger,　100
And here my naked breast; within, a heart
Dearer than Plutus'° mine, richer than gold.
If that thou be'st a Roman, take it forth,
I, that denied thee gold, will give my heart.
Strike, as thou didst at Caesar; for I know　　105
When thou didst hate him worst, thou lovedst him
　　better
Than ever thou lovedst Cassius.

BRU.　　　　　　　　　　　Sheathe your dagger.
Be angry when you will, it shall have scope;°
Do what you will, dishonor shall be humor.°
O Cassius, you are yokèd with a lamb　　　110
That carries anger as the flint bears fire,
Who, much enforcèd, shows a hasty spark
And straight is cold again.

CASS.　　　　　　　　　　Hath Cassius lived
To be but mirth and laughter to his Brutus,　　114
When grief and blood ill-tempered vexeth him?

BRU. When I spoke that, I was ill-tempered too.

CASS. Do you confess so much? Give me your
　　hand.

BRU. And my heart too.

CASS.　　　　　　　O Brutus!

BRU.　　　　　　　　　　　What's the matter?

CASS. Have not you love enough to bear with me
When that rash humor which my mother gave me
Makes me forgetful?

BRU.　　　　Yes, Cassius, and from henceforth,　121
When you are overearnest with your Brutus,
He'll think your mother chides, and leave you so.

POET. [*Within*] Let me go in to see the generals.
There is some grudge between 'em, 'tis not meet
They be alone.　　　　　　　　　　　　126

LUCIL. [*Within*] You shall not come to them.

POET. [*Within*] Nothing but death shall stay me.
[*Enter* POET, *followed by* LUCILIUS, TITINIUS, *and*
　　LUCIUS.]

CASS. How now! What's the matter?

POET. For shame, you generals! What do you
　　mean?　　　　　　　　　　　　　　　130
Love and be friends, as two such men should be,
For I have seen more years, I'm sure, than ye.

CASS. Ha, ha! How vilely doth this cynic° rhyme!

BRU. Get you hence, sirrah. Saucy fellow, hence!

CASS. Bear with him, Brutus. 'Tis his fashion.

BRU. I'll know his humor when he knows his
　　time.°　　　　　　　　　　　　　　　136

97. Checked: rebuked.　　**98. conned by rote:** learned by heart.
102. Plutus: for Pluto, the god of riches.　　**108. scope:** free play.
109. dishonor . . . humor: dishonorable conduct shall be regarded
as just your "humor." See App. 3.　　**133. cynic:** rude fellow.
Cynic philosophers, of whom Diogenes was the most memorable,
scorned easy living and polite manners.　　**136. I'll . . . time:** I will
be patient with his whims if he displays them at the proper time.

73. drachmas: Greek coins.　　**75. indirection:** crooked means.
80. rascal counters: wretched tokens.　　**85. rived:** split.
92. Olympus: the highest mountain in Thessaly and the home
of the gods.　　**96. braved:** taunted.

What should the wars do with these jigging fools?
Companion,° hence!
    CASS.   Away, away, be gone! [*Exit* POET.]
    BRU. Lucilius and Titinius, bid the commanders
Prepare to lodge their companies tonight.   140
    CASS. And come yourselves, and bring Messala
    with you
Immediately to us. [*Exeunt* LUCILIUS *and* TITINIUS.]
    BRU.   Lucius, a bowl of wine! [*Exit* LUCIUS.]
    CASS. I did not think you could have been so
    angry.
    BRU. O Cassius, I am sick of many griefs.
    CASS. Of your philosophy you make no use   145
If you give place to accidental evils.
    BRU. No man bears sorrow better. Portia is dead.
    CASS. Ha! Portia!
    BRU. She is dead.
    CASS. How 'scaped I killing when I crossed you
so?   150
Oh, insupportable and touching loss!
Upon what sickness?
    BRU.   Impatient of my absence,
And grief that young Octavius with Mark Antony
Have made themselves so strong — for with her
    death
That tidings came — with this she fell distract,°
And, her attendants absent, swallowed fire.   156
    CASS. And died so?
    BRU.   Even so.
    CASS.   O ye immortal gods!
[*Re-enter* LUCIUS, *with wine and taper.*]
    BRU. Speak no more of her. Give me a bowl of
wine.
In this I bury all unkindness, Cassius.   [*Drinks.*]
    CASS. My heart is thirsty for that noble pledge.
Fill, Lucius, till the wine o'erswell the cup.   161
I cannot drink too much of Brutus' love. [*Drinks.*]
    BRU. Come in, Titinius!   [*Exit* LUCIUS.]
[*Re-enter* TITINIUS, *with* MESSALA.]
    Welcome, good Messala.
Now sit we close about this taper here,
And call in question° our necessities.   165
    CASS. Portia, art thou gone?
    BRU.   No more, I pray you.
Messala, I have here receivèd letters
That young Octavius and Mark Antony
Come down upon us with a mighty power,
Bending their expedition toward Philippi.°   170
    MES. Myself have letters of the selfsame tenor.
    BRU. With what addition?
    MES. That by proscription and bills of outlawry
Octavius, Antony, and Lepidus
Have put to death a hundred Senators.   175
    BRU. Therein our letters do not well agree.

Mine speak of seventy Senators that died
By their proscriptions, Cicero being one.
    CASS. Cicero one!
    MES.   Cicero is dead,
And by that order of proscription.   180
Had you your letters from your wife, my lord?
    BRU. No, Messala.
    MES. Nor nothing in your letters writ of her?
    BRU. Nothing, Messala.
    MES.   That, methinks, is strange.
    BRU. Why ask you? Hear you aught of her in
yours?   185
    MES. No, my lord.
    BRU. Now, as you are a Roman, tell me true.
    MES. Then like a Roman bear the truth I tell —
For certain she is dead,° and by strange manner.
    BRU. Why, farewell, Portia. We must die, Mes-
sala.   190
With meditating that she must die once
I have the patience to endure it now.
    MES. Even so great men great losses should en-
dure.
    CASS. I have as much of this in art as you,
But yet my nature° could not bear it so.   195
    BRU. Well, to our work alive. What do you think
Of marching to Philippi presently?
    CASS. I do not think it good.
    BRU.   Your reason?
    CASS.   This it is:
'Tis better that the enemy seek us.
So shall he waste his means, weary his soldiers,   200
Doing himself offense,° whilst we lying still
Are full of rest, defense, and nimbleness.
    BRU. Good reasons must of force give place to
better.
The people 'twixt Philippi and this ground
Do stand but in a forced affection,   205
For they have grudged us contribution.
The enemy, marching along by them,
By them shall make a fuller number up,
Come on refreshed, new-added, and encouraged.
From which advantage shall we cut him off   210
If at Philippi we do face him there,
These people at our back.
    CASS.   Hear me, good brother ——
    BRU. Under your pardon. You must note beside
That we have tried the utmost of our friends,
Our legions are brimful, our cause is ripe.   215
The enemy increaseth every day,
We, at the height, are ready to decline.
There is a tide in the affairs of men

138. **Companion**: fellow, used as a word of contempt. 155. **dis-tract**: distraught. 165. **call . . . question**: consider. 170. **Phi-lippi**: a city in Macedon, where the decisive battles between the two forces were fought.

189. **certain . . . dead**: There seems to be a discrepancy in this passage, for Brutus has already told Cassius of Portia's death. Either the scene was rewritten and, as sometimes happened in the printing of Shakespeare's plays, both the original and the re-vised passage have been left, or else Shakespeare wished to exhibit Brutus displaying stoic calm. 194–95. **art . . . nature**: See App. 18. 201. **offense**: harm.

Which taken at the flood leads on to fortune;
Omitted, all the voyage of their life   220
Is bound in shallows and in miseries.
On such a full sea are we now afloat,
And we must take the current when it serves,
Or lose our ventures.
CASS.   Then, with your will, go on. 224
We'll along ourselves and meet them at Philippi.
BRU. The deep of night is crept upon our talk,
And nature must obey necessity,
Which we will niggard° with a little rest.
There is no more to say?
CASS.   No more. Good night.
Early tomorrow will we rise and hence.   230
BRU. Lucius! [*Re-enter* LUCIUS.] My gown.°
                                    [*Exit* LUCIUS.]
                    Farewell, good Messala.
Good night, Titinius. Noble, noble Cassius,
Good night, and good repose.
CASS.   O my dear brother!
This was an ill beginning of the night.
Never come such division 'tween our souls!   235
Let it not, Brutus.
BRU.   Everything is well.
CASS. Good night, my lord.
BRU.   Good night, good brother.
TIT. *and* MES. Good night, Lord Brutus.
BRU. Farewell, everyone. [*Exeunt all but* BRUTUS.]
          [*Re-enter* LUCIUS, *with the gown.*]
Give me the gown. Where is thy instrument?
LUC. Here in the tent.
BRU.   What, thou speak'st drowsily? 240
Poor knave, I blame thee not, thou art o'erwatched.°
Call Claudius and some other of my men.
I'll have them sleep on cushions in my tent.
LUC. Varro and Claudius!
          [*Enter* VARRO *and* CLAUDIUS.]
VAR. Calls my lord?   245
BRU. I pray you, sirs, lie in my tent and sleep.
It may be I shall raise you by and by
On business to my brother Cassius.
VAR. So please you, we will stand and watch your
          pleasure.
BRU. I will not have it so. Lie down, good sirs.
It may be I shall otherwise bethink me.   251
Look, Lucius, here's the book I sought for so,
I put it in the pocket of my gown.
               [VARRO *and* CLAUDIUS *lie down.*]
LUC. I was sure your lordship did not give it me.
BRU. Bear with me,° good boy, I am much forget-
          ful.   255
Canst thou hold up thy heavy eyes awhile,
And touch thy instrument a strain or two?
LUC. Aye, my lord, an 't please you.

228. niggard: satisfy grudgingly.   231. gown: nightgown, a gar-
ment like the modern dressing gown; another instance of Eliza-
bethan costume.   241. o'erwatched: weary with too much
watchfulness.   255. Bear . . . me: See III.ii.110,n.

BRU.   It does, my boy.
I trouble thee too much, but thou art willing.
LUC. It is my duty, sir.   260
BRU. I should not urge thy duty past thy might —
I know young bloods look for a time of rest.
LUC. I have slept, my lord, already.
BRU. It was well done, and thou shalt sleep again,
I will not hold thee long. If I do live,   265
I will be good to thee.   [*Music, and a song.*]
This is a sleepy tune. O murderous° slumber,
Lay'st thou thy leaden mace° upon my boy,
That plays thee music? Gentle knave, good night.
I will not do thee so much wrong to wake thee. 270
If thou dost nod, thou break'st thy instrument,
I'll take it from thee, and, good boy, good night.
Let me see, let me see, is not the leaf turned down
Where I left reading? Here it is, I think.
                                    [*Sits down.*]
          [*Enter the* GHOST OF CAESAR.]
How ill this taper burns! Ha! Who comes here?
I think it is the weakness of mine eyes   276
That shapes this monstrous apparition.
It comes upon me. Art thou anything?
Art thou some god, some angel, or some devil,
That makest my blood cold, and my hair to stare?
Speak to me what thou art.   281
GHOST. Thy evil spirit, Brutus.
BRU.   Why comest thou?
GHOST. To tell thee thou shalt see me at Philippi.
BRU. Well, then I shall see thee again?
GHOST. Ay, at Philippi.   285
BRU. Why, I will see thee at Philippi then.
                                    [*Exit* GHOST.]
Now I have taken heart, thou vanishest.
Ill spirit, I would hold more talk with thee.
Boy, Lucius! Varro! Claudius! Sirs, awake!
Claudius!   290
LUC. The strings, my lord, are false.
BRU. He thinks he still is at his instrument.
Lucius, awake!
LUC. My lord?   295
BRU. Didst thou dream, Lucius, that thou so
          criedst out?
LUC. My lord, I do not know that I did cry.
BRU. Yes, that thou didst. Didst thou see any-
          thing?
LUC. Nothing, my lord.
BRU. Sleep again, Lucius. Sirrah Claudius!   300
[*To* VARRO] Fellow thou, awake!
VAR. My lord?
CLAU. My lord?
BRU. Why did you so cry out, sirs, in your sleep?

267. murderous: i.e., because it deprives men of sense.   268. lead-
en mace: The metaphor is of the officer laying his mace upon a
prisoner whom he is arresting; "leaden" is often applied to sleep
because it is heavy and overwhelming. mace: See Pl. 22h. Officers
of the law carried a small mace as sign of office, as a modern
policeman wears the star badge.

VAR. *and* CLAU. Did we, my lord?

BRU.   Aye. Saw you anything?   305

VAR. No, my lord, I saw nothing.

CLAU.   Nor I, my lord.

BRU. Go and commend me to my brother Cassius.
Bid him set on his powers betimes before,°
And we will follow.

VAR. *and* CLAU. It shall be done, my lord. [*Exeunt.*]

Act V

SCENE I. *The plains of Philippi.*

[*Enter* OCTAVIUS, ANTONY, *and their* ARMY.]

OCT. Now, Antony, our hopes are answerèd.
You said the enemy would not come down,
But keep the hills and upper regions.
It proves not so, their battles° are at hand,
They mean to warn us at Philippi here,   5
Answering before we do demand of them.

ANT. Tut, I am in their bosoms,° and I know
Wherefore they do it. They could be content
To visit other places,° and come down
With fearful° bravery,° thinking by this face   10
To fasten in our thoughts that they have courage.
But 'tis not so.

[*Enter a* MESSENGER.]

MESS.   Prepare you, generals.
The enemy comes on in gallant show.
Their bloody sign of battle° is hung out,
And something to be done immediately.   15

ANT. Octavius, lead your battle softly on,
Upon the left hand of the even field.°

OCT. Upon the right hand I. Keep thou the left.

ANT. Why do you cross me in this exigent?°

OCT. I do not cross you, but I will do so.   20

[*March. Drum. Enter* BRUTUS, CASSIUS, *and their*
ARMY; LUCILIUS, TITINIUS, MESSALA, *and others.*]

BRU. They stand, and would have parley.

CASS. Stand fast, Titinius. We must out and talk.

OCT. Mark Antony, shall we give sign of battle?

ANT. No, Caesar, we will answer on their charge.
Make forth, the generals would have some words.

OCT. Stir not until the signal.   26

BRU. Words before blows. Is it so, countrymen?

OCT. Not that we love words better, as you do.

BRU. Good words are better than bad strokes, Octavius.

---

308. set . . . before: lead on his army ahead of ours in good time.
Act V, Sc. i: 4. battles: armies drawn up ready for battle.
7. in . . . bosoms: in the secrets of their hearts. 8–9. They . . .
places: i.e., they would prefer to be anywhere but here. 10. fearful: full of fear. bravery: brave show. 14. bloody . . . battle: red
flag of defiance. 17. even field: level ground. 19. exigent:
critical moment.

ANT. In your bad strokes, Brutus, you give good
words.   30
Witness the hole you made in Caesar's heart,
Crying " Long live! Hail, Caesar! "

CASS.   Antony,
The posture° of your blows are yet unknown,
But for your words, they rob the Hybla° bees,
And leave them honeyless.

ANT.   Not stingless too.   35

BRU. Oh, yes, and soundless too,
For you have stol'n their buzzing, Antony,
And very wisely threat before you sting.

ANT. Villains, you did not so when your vile daggers
Hacked one another in the sides of Caesar.   40
You showed your teeth like apes, and fawned like
hounds,
And bowed like bondmen, kissing Caesar's feet,
Whilst damnèd Casca, like a cur, behind
Struck Caesar on the neck. O you flatterers!

CASS. Flatterers! Now, Brutus, thank yourself.
This tongue had not offended so today   46
If Cassius might have ruled.

OCT. Come, come, the cause. If arguing make us
sweat,
The proof of it will turn to redder drops.
Look,   50
I draw a sword against conspirators.
When think you that the sword goes up° again?
Never, till Caesar's three and thirty wounds
Be well avenged, or till another Caesar
Have added slaughter to the sword of traitors.   55

BRU. Caesar, thou canst not die by traitors' hands,
Unless thou bring'st them with thee.

OCT.   So I hope.
I was not born to die on Brutus' sword.

BRU. Oh, if thou wert the noblest of thy strain,
Young man, thou couldst not die more honorable.

CASS. A peevish° schoolboy, worthless of such
honor,   61
Joined with a masker° and a reveler!

ANT. Old Cassius still!

OCT.   Come, Antony, away!
Defiance, traitors, hurl we in your teeth.
If you dare fight today, come to the field;   65
If not, when you have stomachs.°

[*Exeunt* OCTAVIUS, ANTONY, *and their* ARMY.]

CASS. Why, now, blow wind, swell billow, and
swim bark!°
The storm is up, and all is on the hazard.

BRU. Ho, Lucilius! Hark, a word with you.

LUCIL.   [*Standing forth*] My lord?

[BRUTUS *and* LUCILIUS *converse apart.*]

---

33. posture: quality. 34. Hybla: a mountain in Sicily famous
for the honey produced there. 52. goes up: returns to the scabbard. 61. peevish: silly. 62. masker: one who spends his time
in masques and night life. See I.ii.203–04; II.ii.116   66. stomachs: appetites. 67. bark: ship.

CASS. Messala!

MESS. [*Standing forth*] What says my general?

CASS. Messala,   71
This is my birthday, as° this very day
Was Cassius born. Give me thy hand, Messala.
Be thou my witness that, against my will,
As Pompey was, am I compelled to set   75
Upon one battle all our liberties.
You know that I held Epicurus strong,°
And his opinion. Now I change my mind,
And partly credit things that do presage.°
Coming from Sardis, on our former° ensign°   80
Two mighty eagles fell, and there they perched,
Gorging and feeding from our soldiers' hands,
Who to Philippi here consorted° us.
This morning are they fled away and gone,
And in their steads do ravens, crows, and kites   85
Fly o'er our heads and downward look on us,
As we were sickly prey. Their shadows seem
A canopy most fatal, under which
Our army lies, ready to give up the ghost.

MESS. Believe not so.

CASS.   I but believe it partly,   90
For I am fresh of spirit and resolved
To meet all perils very constantly.

BRU. Even so, Lucilius.

CASS.   Now, most noble Brutus,
The gods today stand friendly, that we may,
Lovers in peace, lead on our days to age!   95
But since the affairs of men rest still° incertain,
Let's reason with° the worst that may befall.
If we do lose this battle, then is this
The very last time we shall speak together.
What are you then determinèd to do?   100

BRU. Even by the rule of that philosophy
By which I did blame Cato for the death
Which he did give himself° — I know not how,
But I do find it cowardly and vile,
For fear of what might fall, so to prevent   105
The time of life° — arming myself with patience
To stay° the providence of some high powers
That govern us below.

CASS.   Then, if we lose this battle,
You are contented to be led in triumph
Thorough the streets of Rome?   110

BRU. No, Cassius, no. Think not, thou noble Ro-
man,
That ever Brutus will go bound to Rome.
He bears too great a mind. But this same day

Must end that work the ides of March begun,
And whether we shall meet again I know not.   115
Therefore our everlasting farewell take.
Forever and forever, farewell, Cassius!
If we do meet again, why, we shall smile;
If not, why then this parting was well made.

CASS. Forever and forever farewell, Brutus!   120
If we do meet again, we'll smile indeed;
If not, 'tis true this parting was well made.

BRU. Why then, lead on. Oh, that a man might
know
The end of this day's business ere it come!
But it sufficeth that the day will end,   125
And then the end is known. Come, ho! Away!

[*Exeunt.*]

SCENE II. *The field of battle.*

[*Alarum. Enter* BRUTUS *and* MESSALA.]

BRU. Ride, ride, Messala, ride, and give these bills°
Unto the legions on the other side. [*Loud alarum.*]
Let them set on at once, for I perceive
But cold demeanor° in Octavius' wing,
And sudden push gives them the overthrow.   5
Ride, ride, Messala. Let them all come down.

[*Exeunt.*]

SCENE III. *Another part of the field.*

[*Alarums. Enter* CASSIUS *and* TITINIUS.]

CASS. Oh, look, Titinius, look, the villains fly!
Myself have to mine own turned enemy.°
This ensign° here of mine was turning back.
I slew the coward, and did take it from him.

TIT. O Cassius, Brutus gave the word too early,
Who, having some advantage on Octavius,   6
Took it too eagerly. His soldiers fell to spoil
Whilst we by Antony are all enclosed.

[*Enter* PINDARUS.]

PIN. Fly further off, my lord, fly further off.
Mark Antony is in your tents, my lord.   10
Fly, therefore, noble Cassius, fly far off.

CASS. This hill is far enough. Look, look, Titinius,
Are those my tents where I perceive the fire?

TIT. They are, my lord.

CASS.   Titinius, if thou lovest me,
Mount thou my horse and hide thy spurs in him
Till he have brought thee up to yonder troops   16
And here again, that I may rest assured

---

72. as: on. 77. held . . . strong: was a firm believer in Epicurus, a Greek philosopher who taught his followers that the gods, if they existed, were not interested in man, and that they should therefore despise all superstition. 79. presage: foretell. 80. former: foremost. ensign: the colors carried by a company. 83. consorted: accompanied. 96. still: always. 97. reason with: consider. 101–03: Even . . . himself: i.e., according to my rule of life suicide is a cowardly way out of difficulties. Cato: See II. ii.295,n. 105–06. prevent . . . life: forestall the natural end of life. 107. stay: await.

Sc. ii: 1. bills: written messages. 4. cold demeanor: lack of offensive spirit.

Sc. iii: 2. Myself . . . enemy: i.e., I am now the enemy of my own men because they have become cowards. 3. ensign: used both for the company's colors and for the junior officer who carried them.

Whether yond troops are friend or enemy.
TIT. I will be here again, even with a thought.
                                        [Exit.]
CASS. Go, Pindarus, get higher on that hill —   20
My sight was ever thick.° Regard° Titinius,
And tell me what thou notest about the field.
                     [PINDARUS ascends the hill.]
This day I breathèd first. Time is come round,
And where I did begin, there shall I end,
My life is run his compass. Sirrah, what news?   25
PIN. *[Above]* O my lord!
CASS.   What news?
PIN. *[Above]* Titinius is enclosèd round about
With horsemen that make to him on the spur,
Yet he spurs on. Now they are almost on him.   30
Now, Titinius! Now some light.° Oh, he lights too.
He's ta'en. *[Shout.]* And, hark! They shout for joy.
CASS. Come down, behold no more.
Oh, coward that I am, to live so long,
To see my best friend ta'en before my face!   35
                     [PINDARUS descends.]
Come hither, sirrah.
In Parthia did I take thee prisoner,
And then I swore thee, saving of thy life,
That whatsoever I did bid thee do
Thou shouldst attempt it. Come now, keep thine
    oath.   40
Now be a free man, and with this good sword,
That ran through Caesar's bowels, search this
    bosom.
Stand not to answer. Here, take thou the hilts,
And when my face is covered, as 'tis now,
Guide thou the sword. *[PINDARUS stabs him]* Cae-
    sar, thou art revenged,   45
Even with the sword that killed thee.   *[Dies.]*
PIN. So, I am free, yet would not so have been,
Durst I have done my will. O Cassius!
Far from this country Pindarus shall run,
Where never Roman shall take note of him. *[Exit.]*
      [Re-enter TITINIUS with MESSALA.]
MES. It is but change,° Titinius, for Octavius   51
Is overthrown by noble Brutus' power,
As Cassius' legions are by Antony.
TIT. These tidings will well comfort Cassius.
MES. Where did you leave him?
TIT.   All disconsolate,   55
With Pindarus his bondman, on this hill.
MES. Is not that he that lies upon the ground?
TIT. He lies not like the living. Oh, my heart!
MES. Is not that he?
TIT.   No, this was he, Messala,
But Cassius is no more. O setting sun,   60
As in thy red rays thou dost sink to night,
So in his red blood Cassius' day is set,
The sun of Rome is set! Our day is gone,

Clouds, dews, and dangers come. Our deeds are
    done!
Mistrust of my success hath done this deed.   65
MES. Mistrust of good success hath done this
    deed.
O hateful error, melancholy's child,°
Why dost thou show to the apt° thoughts of men
The things that are not? O error, soon conceived,
Thou never comest unto a happy birth,   70
But kill'st the mother that engendered° thee!
TIT. What, Pindarus! Where art thou, Pindarus?
MES. Seek him, Titinius, whilst I go to meet
The noble Brutus, thrusting this report
Into his ears. I may say " thrusting " it,   75
For piercing steel and darts envenomèd
Shall be as welcome to the ears of Brutus
As tidings of this sight.
TIT.   Hie you, Messala,
And I will seek for Pindarus the while.
                     [Exit MESSALA.]
Why didst thou send me forth, brave Cassius?   80
Did I not meet thy friends? And did not they
Put on my brows this wreath of victory,
And bid me give it thee? Didst thou not hear their
    shouts?
Alas, thou hast miscónstrued everything!
But hold thee, take this garland on thy brow.   85
Thy Brutus bid me give it thee, and I
Will do his bidding. Brutus, come apace,
And see how I regarded Caius Cassius.
By your leave, gods, this is a Roman's part.
Come, Cassius' sword, and find Titinius' heart.   90
                     [Kills himself.]
*[Alarum. Re-enter MESSALA, with BRUTUS, young
    CATO, and others.]*
BRU. Where, where, Messala, doth his body lie?
MES. Lo, yonder, and Titinius mourning it.
BRU. Titinius' face is upward.
CATO.   He is slain.
BRU. O Julius Caesar, thou art mighty yet!
Thy spirit walks abroad, and turns our swords   95
In our own proper° entrails.   *[Low alarums.]*
CATO.   Brave Titinius!
Look whether he have not crowned dead Cassius!
BRU. Are yet two Romans living such as these?
The last of all the Romans, fare thee well!
It is impossible that ever Rome   100
Should breed thy fellow. Friends, I owe moe tears
To this dead man than you shall see me pay.
I shall find time, Cassius, I shall find time.
Come therefore, and to Thasos send his body.
His funerals shall not be in our camp,   105
Lest it discomfort us. Lucilius, come,
And come, young Cato. Let us to the field.
Labeo and Flavius, set our battles on.

---

21. thick: short. Regard: watch.   31. light: alight, descend.
51. change: exchange.

67. melancholy's child: See App. 4.   68. apt: ready to be
deceived.   71. engendered: conceived.   96. proper: own.

'Tis three o'clock, and, Romans' yet ere night   109
We shall try fortune in a second fight.°   [*Exeunt.*]

SCENE IV. *Another part of the field.*

[*Alarum. Enter, fighting,* SOLDIERS *of both armies;
then* BRUTUS, *young* CATO, LUCILIUS, *and others.*]

BRU. Yet, countrymen, oh, yet hold up your
heads!

CATO. What bastard doth not? Who will go with
me?
I will proclaim my name about the field.
I am the son of Marcus Cato, ho! —
A foe to tyrants, and my country's friend.   5
I am the son of Marcus Cato, ho!

BRU. And I am Brutus, Marcus Brutus, I —
Brutus, my country's friend. Know me for Brutus!
[*Exit.*]

LUCIL. O young and noble Cato, art thou down?
Why, now thou diest as bravely as Titinius,   10
And mayst be honored, being Cato's son.

1. SOL. Yield, or thou diest.

LUCIL.   Only I yield to die.
[*Offering money*] There is so much that thou wilt
kill me straight.
Kill Brutus, and be honored in his death.

1. SOL. We must not. A noble prisoner!   15

2. SOL. Room, ho! Tell Antony, Brutus is ta'en.

1. SOL. I'll tell the news. Here comes the general.
[*Enter* ANTONY.]
Brutus is ta'en, Brutus is ta'en, my lord.

ANT. Where is he?

LUCIL. Safe, Antony, Brutus is safe enough.   20
I dare assure thee that no enemy
Shall ever take alive the noble Brutus.
The gods defend him from so great a shame!
When you do find him, or alive or dead,
He will be found like Brutus, like himself.   25

ANT. This is not Brutus, friend, but, I assure you,
A prize no less in worth. Keep this man safe,
Give him all kindness. I had rather have
Such men my friends than enemies. Go on,
And see whether Brutus be alive or dead,   30
And bring us word unto Octavius' tent
How everything is chanced.   [*Exeunt.*]

SCENE V. *Another part of the field.*

[*Enter* BRUTUS, DARDANIUS, CLITUS, STRATO, *and*
VOLUMNIUS.]

BRU. Come, poor remains of friends, rest on this
rock.

110. **second fight:** There were two battles at Philippi; the second
actually occurred twenty days after the first and not (as in the
play) on the same day.

CLI. Statilius showed the torchlight, but, my lord,
He came not back. He is or ta'en or slain.

BRU. Sit thee down, Clitus. Slaying is the word,
It is a deed in fashion. Hark thee, Clitus.   5
[*Whispering.*]

CLI. What, I, my lord? No, not for all the world.

BRU. Peace then, no words.

CLI.   I'll rather kill myself.

BRU. Hark thee, Dardanius.   [*Whispering.*]

DAR.   Shall I do such a deed?

CLI. O Dardanius!

DAR. O Clitus!   10

CLI. What ill request did Brutus make to thee?

DAR. To kill him, Clitus. Look, he meditates.

CLI. Now is that noble vessel full of grief,
That it runs over even at his eyes.

BRU. Come hither, good Volumnius, list a word.

VOL. What says my lord?

BRU.   Why, this, Volumnius.   16
The ghost of Caesar hath appeared to me
Two several° times by night — at Sardis once,
And this last night here in Philippi fields.
I know my hour is come.

VOL.   Not so, my lord.   20

BRU. Nay, I am sure it is, Volumnius.
Thou seest the world, Volumnius, how it goes,
Our enemies have beat us to the pit. [*Low alarums.*]
It is more worthy to leap in ourselves
Than tarry till they push us. Good Volumnius,   25
Thou know'st that we two went to school together.
Even for that our love of old, I prithee
Hold thou my sword hilts whilst I run on it.

VOL. That's not an office for a friend, my lord.
[*Alarum still.*]

CLI. Fly, fly, my lord, there is no tarrying here.

BRU. Farewell to you, and you, and you, Volum-
nius.   31
Strato, thou hast been all this while asleep —
Farewell to thee too, Strato. Countrymen,
My heart doth joy that yet in all my life
I found no man but he was true to me.   35
I shall have glory by this losing day,
More than Octavius and Mark Antony
By this vile conquest shall attain unto.
So, fare you well at once, for Brutus' tongue
Hath almost ended his life's history.   40
Night hangs upon mine eyes, my bones would rest
That have but labored to attain this hour.
[*Alarum. Cry within,* "Fly, fly, fly!"]

CLI. Fly, my lord, fly!

BRU.   Hence! I will follow.
[*Exeunt* CLITUS, DARDANIUS, *and* VOLUMNIUS.]
I prithee, Strato, stay thou by thy lord.
Thou art a fellow of a good respect,°   45
Thy life hath had some smatch° of honor in it.

Sc. v: 18. **several:** separate.   45. **good respect:** worthy of re-
spect.   46. **smatch:** taste.

Hold then my sword, and turn away thy face
While I do run upon it. Wilt thou, Strato?
　　STRA. Give me your hand first. Fare you well, my
　　　lord.
　　BRU. Farewell, good Strato. [*Runs on his sword.*]
　　　Caesar, now be still.　　　　　　　　　　　　50
I killed not thee with half so good a will.　　[*Dies.*]
[*Alarum. Retreat. Enter* OCTAVIUS, ANTONY, MESSALA,
　　　　LUCILIUS, *and the* ARMY.]
　　OCT. What man is that?
　　MES. My master's man. Strato, where is thy mas-
　　　ter?
　　STRA. Free from the bondage you are in, Messala.
The conquerors can but make a fire of him,　　55
For Brutus only overcame himself,
And no man else hath honor by his death.
　　LUCIL. So Brutus should be found. I thank thee,
　　　Brutus,
That thou hast proved Lucilius' saying true.
　　OCT. All that served Brutus, I will entertain°
　　　them.　　　　　　　　　　　　　　　　　　60
Fellow, wilt thou bestow thy time with me?

60. entertain: take into service.

　　STRA. Aye, if Messala will prefer° me to you.
　　OCT. Do so, good Messala.
　　MES. How died my master, Strato?
　　STRA. I held the sword, and he did run on it.　　65
　　MES. Octavius, then take him to follow thee
That did the latest° service to my master.
　　ANT. This was the noblest Roman of them all.
All the conspirators, save only he,
Did that they did in envy of great Caesar.　　70
He only, in a general honest thought
And common good to all, made one of them.
His life was gentle,° and the elements
So mixed in him° that Nature might stand up
And say to all the world, "This was a man."　　75
　　OCT. According to his virtue let us use him,
With all respect and rites of burial.
Within my tent his bones tonight shall lie,
Most like a soldier, ordered honorably.
So call the field to rest, and let's away,　　80
To part° the glories of this happy day.　　[*Exeunt.*]

62. prefer: recommend.　　67. latest: last.　　73. gentle: noble.
73–74. elements . . . him: i.e., he was a man perfectly balanced.
See App. 3.　　81. part: share.

TWELFTH NIGHT
or What You Will

Introduction

Twelfth Night,[1] *or What You Will* was first printed in the folio of 1623; the text is good and presents few difficulties. The play was probably written in 1600 or 1601; there are a number of topical passages glancing at events in those years:

1. Maria says of Malvolio, " He does smile his face into more lines than is in the new map with the augmentation of the Indies " (III.ii.84). This map appeared in 1600. It was drawn by Edward Wright and was the first English map on the principle of Mercator's projection (see Pl. 1a).

2. " I will not give my part of this sport for a pension of thousands to be paid from the Sophy " (II.v.196). In 1597 Sir Anthony Shirley, a well-known adventurer and a close follower of the Earl of Essex, set out with his brother Robert and a party of Englishmen on a mission to the Sophy (Shah) of Persia. After many adventures they arrived safely, were kindly received, and handsomely rewarded. Some of the party returned by way of the Caspian Sea, Russia, and Archangel, and reached London in September 1600. Shirley himself was suspected of disloyalty and never came back to England. An account of the journey was quickly printed, but on October 2 it was suppressed by order of the Council, and all copies seized and burnt. A longer account was written by William Parry, one of the party, and entered for publication on November 11, 1601. Shirley's adventures caused much comment.

3. Viola comments on the fool (III.i.67):

This fellow is wise enough to play the fool,
And to do that well craves a kind of wit.
He must observe their mood on whom he jests,
The quality of persons, and the time,
And, like the haggard, check at every feather
That comes before his eye. This is a practice
As full of labor as a wise man's art.
For folly that he wisely shows is fit,
But wise men, folly fall'n, quite taint their wit.

Robert Armin, who in 1600 succeeded Will Kempe as the clown of the Lord Chamberlain's

Company, was expert at composing verses extempore. He would ask someone in the audience to suggest a topic and would then produce a poem out of his head. Late in 1600 or early in 1601 he printed a collection of these trifles called *Quips upon Questions*. One of the subjects was " He Plays the Fool," of which the first two of five stanzas run:

True it is, he plays the fool indeed,
But in the play, he plays it as he must;
Yet when the play is ended, then his speed
Is better than the pleasure of thy trust.
For he shall have what thou that time has spent,
Playing the fool, thy folly to content.

He plays the wise man then, and not the fool
That wisely for his living can do so.
So doth the carpenter with his sharp tool,
Cut his own finger oft, yet lives by 't too.
He is a fool to cut his limb, say I,
But not so with his tool to live thereby.

To this poem he added a " Quip ":

A merry man is often thought unwise,
Yet mirth in modesty's loved of the wise.
Then say, should he for a fool go
When he's a more fool that accounts him so?
Many men descant on another's wit
When they have less themselves in doing it.

Shakespeare at greater leisure rewrote this effort of the Company's new clown.

4. In a conversation between the Clown and Cesario (i.e., Viola in disguise) the Clown says (III.i.19):

CLO. I would, therefore, my sister had had no name, sir.
VIO. Why, man?
CLO. Why, sir, her name s a word, and to dally with that word might make my sister wanton. But indeed words are very rascals since bonds disgrace them.

The reference was probably to a scandalous case tried in the Star Chamber on June 12, 1600.

---

[1] January 6, the twelfth day after Christmas and the last and gayest night of the winter holidays. The title thus indicates a merry tale.

Mistress Mall Fowler, a woman of notoriously loose life, fell in love with one William Haynes. The two plotted to get rid of the woman's husband by accusing him of high treason, but the plot came to light after Fowler had been imprisoned in the Tower for some months. Haynes was condemned to pay a fine of £200, to stand in the pillory, and to have both his ears cut off; Mall Fowler was to be whipped and imprisoned perpetually; but the greatest disgust was expressed at the conduct of her brother, Henry Boughton, because he had been bawd and pander to his own sister. It is possible that in the passage quoted "bond" should read "bawd" (spelt "baud"); a similar misreading occurs in *Hamlet* I.iii.130.

5. In describing the shipwreck in *Twelfth Night* the Captain says (I.ii.10):

When you and those poor number saved with you
Hung on our driving boat, I saw your brother,
Most provident in peril, bind himself,
Courage and hope both teaching him the practice,
To a strong mast that lived upon the sea.

This passage was probably suggested to Shakespeare by an incident in a news pamphlet called *News from Ostend,* entered for publication on August 5, 1601. It records the miraculous escape in a sea fight of a man who " committed himself to the mercy of God and the merciless seas upon a piece of a mast rather than that he would fall into the hands of his bloody enemies. After he had so floated upon the waves of the sea an hour or two he was taken up by another ship which had spied the man driving on the water."

The earliest note of a performance of *Twelfth Night* occurs in the diary of John Manningham, a barrister of the Middle Temple, under the date February 2, 1602:

At our feast we had a play called *Twelve Night; or, What You Will,* much like *The Comedy of Errors,* or *Menaechmi* in Plautus, but most like and near to that in Italian called *Inganni.* A good practice in it to make the steward believe his lady widow was in love with him, by counterfeiting a letter as from his lady in general terms, telling him what she liked best in him, and prescribing his gesture in smiling, his apparel, etc., and then when he came to practice making him believe they took him to be mad.

As for the source of *Twelfth Night,* the resemblances noted by Manningham to *The Com-*edy *of Errors,* the *Menaechmi,* and two Italian plays called *Inganni* are not very close, though in each there are mistakes caused by the likeness of twins. Indeed about a dozen different stories could possibly have been used by Shakespeare. The nearest and likeliest is the tale of *Apolonius and Silla,* included by Barnabe Riche in a collection called *Riche His Farewell to the Military Profession* (1581). The outline of the story of *Apolonius and Silla* is as follows:

Apolonius, the young Duke of Constantinople, after a campaign against the Turks was driven by tempest to take refuge with his ships in Cyprus. Here he was entertained by Pontus the Governor, who had twin children, Silvio, a son, and Silla, a daughter. Silla fell in love with Apolonius and gave him every encouragement, but the young Duke was too much occupied with warlike thoughts to notice her, and after a time he sailed home. Silla decided to follow him. She persuaded her servant Pedro to pass her off as his sister, and together they took passage in a galley bound for Constantinople. At sea the captain of the ship began to make violent love to the girl; but a lucky storm arose, and the galley was driven ashore and broken to pieces. Most of the company were drowned, but Silla floated to shore on a chest which contained clothes and money belonging to the captain. She therefore dressed herself in man's clothes and, presenting herself at the Duke's palace under the name of "Silvio," was given employment by the Duke as a servingman.

By this time Apolonius himself had fallen in love with a young, beautiful, and wealthy widow named Julina. So "Silvio" was sent to carry his messages and love gifts, with the result that Julina fell violently in love with the supposed young gentleman. Meanwhile the real Silvio, suspecting that his sister had run off with Pedro, set out to pursue them, and in due course came to Constantinople. Here by chance the widow Julina met him, and calling him by name, asked him to supper the next night. Silvio was surprised but attracted. He accepted the invitation, and spent the night with his hostess. Next morning, realizing that some mistake had been made, he decided that it would be wisest to continue his travels.

Soon afterward, Julina went to the Duke to ask his permission to marry the man of her own choice, to which at first he consented; but when his servants told him that his own servingman had put his nose out of joint, he was so angry that he caused " Silvio " to be thrust into a dungeon. Julina, finding that " Silvio " no longer came to visit her, was much disturbed, and especially as she now realized that she was pregnant. So she came again to Apolonius, told her tale, and begged that " Silvio " might be released. Thereupon "Silvio" was brought before the Duke and Julina, but denied hotly being the father of Julina's child. This moved Julina to tears and protestations and the Duke to great wrath until "Silvio," seeing no other remedy, led Julina aside and revealed that she was indeed a woman. Thereupon the Duke, deeply touched by Silla's devotion to himself, married her with great solemnity. But Julina was now in a worse case than ever, for she did not know whom to claim as the father of her child. Such strange events, however, soon came to the ears of the true Silvio, who hastened back to Constantinople, married Julina, and was reunited with his sister.

If indeed Riche's story was the direct source of the main plot of *Twelfth Night*, Shakespeare took only the main outline and certain incidents. He made far less of the wooing of the Countess by the Duke, and he stressed the love of brother and sister. Moreover Olivia is not a widow, but —like Viola—a young woman mourning the loss of a brother. Shakespeare found nothing of the rescue of Sebastian or of the adventures of Antonio in *Apolonius and Silla,* nor any hint for the story of Toby, Maria, Andrew, and Malvolio.

In plotting the secondary scenes of lower comedy, Shakespeare borrowed some ideas from the new comedy of humors (see Gen. Intro. p. 42a). Andrew is a foolish gentleman of the same kindred as Ben Jonson's Matthew or Stephen, Maria is the witty servant who plots the mischief, Malvolio is the Puritan. But, as usual, Shakespeare refrained from elaborate and exact caricature of individuals or contemporary types. Though Malvolio is an essential killjoy, he neither sings psalms down the nose nor talks in a Scriptural jargon.

"Puritan" would have reminded Shakespeare of a notable case of a particular Puritan which had roused considerable controversy and inspired several pamphlets between 1596 and 1602. In 1596 John Darrell, a Puritan preacher, began to win a reputation as an exorcist who could drive out evil spirits from those possessed. His first case was that of Thomas Darling, the "Boy of Burton," who was taken with strange fits and hallucinations. Darrell was called in, and after a lengthy exercise of prayer the evil spirit was expelled. In 1597 Darrell and another preacher called George More were summoned to deal with seven persons in the house of Master Nicholas Starkey of Cleworth in Lancashire. Darrell was

again successful. After a bout of prayer wherein the preachers tried to pray down the crying of the spirits, which lasted continuously from seven in the morning till three in the afternoon, the possessed persons were at last relieved. In the following November Darrell was called to deal with the case of a boy called Somers at Nottingham. Unfortunately, soon afterward Somers confessed that he was a fraud, and a bitter controversy raged between the Puritans who believed in Darrell and the officials of the Church of England who were eager to see him discredited. Eventually Darrell and his fellow preacher were brought before the ecclesiastical commissioners for examination, and for several months they were kept in prison in London. Meanwhile the Bishop of London instructed his chaplain, the Reverend Samuel Harsnett, to write a book against Darrell. Darrell's friends retorted with pamphlets in his defense, which in their turn were counterattacked. Of the pro-Darrell pamphlets the most interesting was More's detailed account of the Starkey case, printed in 1600. More noted that soon after the arrival of the preachers, when they called for a Bible, the possessed children fell into laughter and cried out, "Reach them the bibble babble, bibble babble," which Sir Topas seems to echo (IV.ii.105). There was thus considerable topical significance for the original audience in the scenes of the Puritan Malvolio's supposed possession.

The general tone of *Twelfth Night* is musical-melancholy, and the play opens with a passage of music which creates the atmosphere for what is to follow. The first scene shows Orsino, Duke of Illyria. He is suffering from lover's melancholy in its milder form, and he is in love with love rather than with the Countess Olivia whom he is wooing. The second scene shows Viola newly rescued from shipwreck and about to drown her sorrows for her supposedly dead brother in adventure. The third scene, as is usual in Elizabethan drama, introduces the third set of characters — the household of Olivia, which includes Maria, her waiting gentlewoman; Sir Toby, her disreputable kinsman; Sir Andrew, the silly gentleman. All three scenes are in deliberate contrast of tone: the sentimental melancholy of the Duke, the practical energy of Viola, and the low comedy of Sir Toby and Sir Andrew.

Thus the three threads of the plot are displayed, and the play is ready to move. A short interval of time passes. Viola has now been transformed into "Cesario," the Duke's gentleman, and is already in high favor. "Cesario" is accordingly sent as the Duke's messenger to Olivia. The fifth scene will naturally show the delivery of this message. It begins with the entry of Maria and the Clown. At last Olivia herself appears, accompanied by her solemn steward Malvolio (see App. 14). The Clown comes forward to meet her. The Clown is an important person in the plot, for he connects the three threads of the story. He is moreover the direct cause of the downfall of Malvolio, for Malvolio's sneer that he is a barren rascal moves him to a spiteful revenge and begins the feud between them. Then "Cesario" enters as Orsino's messenger. The two women are here contrasted. Both are mourning the loss of a brother. "Cesario" is gay and excited in spite of her troubles, Olivia is listlessly enjoying her sorrow. She is always extravagant in her emotions, whether of sorrow or of love, and she would have made herself entirely ridiculous but for the tact of Viola — though Viola, being already in love with the Duke, is not a little jealous of her rival and is amused rather than sympathetic when she finds that she has roused a hopeless passion in Olivia. Olivia at the beginning of the interview is cold and dignified, but she soon unbends, and the ensuing conversation of these two is a good specimen of Elizabethan Court wit at its best. So "Cesario" departs, having fired the affections of Olivia, and the plot begins to gain speed.

The next scene (II.i) introduces the supposedly drowned Sebastian. As usual in planning a comedy of mistaken identities, Shakespeare lets the audience into the secret early, and thereby creates dramatic irony. We know that the real Sebastian is at hand, and that sooner or later brother and sister must meet. We see also from the close resemblance between them that some very pretty complications will arise. Moreover, brother and sister have that curious physiological and psychological affinity that sometimes occurs with identical twins. To underline the resemblance, in the next scene we have another look at "Cesario," when Malvolio gives her Olivia's ring.

Thus several events are pending: Olivia is in love with "Cesario," "Cesario" is in love with Orsino, and other complications are arising. Time, or rather the illusion of time, is now needed for their ripening. Shakespeare therefore inserts the drinking scene of Sir Toby, Sir Andrew, the Clown, and Maria, with its noisy revelry which brings down Malvolio, and thereby starts the plot for his downfall. The noise and low comedy in this scene (II.iii.) is in deliberate contrast to the quiet romantic beauty of the next, when directly after the Clown's song Viola in the safety of disguise discloses her love for Orsino.

In the next scene (II.v) we are taken back to Malvolio and to the finding and reading of the letter, an episode whose comic intensity is enhanced by its following hard upon the lyric mood of the preceding scene. After this "Cesario" comes again to Olivia, thereby provoking the peevishness of Sir Andrew. Then, both to separate Malvolio's love-making from the letter scene, and also to bring the reunion of brother and sister nearer, we have another brief glimpse of Sebastian and his adoring rescuer Antonio (III.iii).

The mood then changes again to low comedy when Malvolio makes his fantastic declaration of love to Olivia. She supposes that he is mad and gives him into Toby's charge to be confined as a lunatic. This is followed by Sir Andrew's saucy challenge and the mock duel between Sir Andrew and "Cesario," which again brings home to Viola the many inconveniences of disguise. The duel is interrupted by the quite natural appearance of Antonio, who is immediately arrested by the Duke's officers. At the end of this scene Viola, who is naturally quick-witted, realizes from Antonio's bitter words that Sebastian must be alive, and she goes off much excited. Sebastian himself then appears. At first he is mistaken by the Clown for "Cesario," and then set upon by two men who are complete strangers to him, so that in a moment he is involved in a fight with Toby. Hereupon, to complete the misunderstandings, the beautiful Countess comes out and invites him into her house.

After this — to give Sebastian time for his dinner, and to remind us of Malvolio — there follows a scene (IV.ii) where the Clown disguised as the curate comes to give spiritual consolation to Malvolio in his prison. This scene has the effect of bringing the sympathy back to Malvolio, for he has been overpunished. Sebastian now comes out of the house very bewildered, and the more so when a few moments later Olivia appears with a priest, and demands that he shall immediately plight troth with her. Sebastian's acquiescence is perhaps surprising, but he has endured such a series of shocks that he is not sure whether he is mad or dreaming, and anyhow Olivia is a very charming kind of delusion.

The plot is now ready for all the stories to be combined into one ending. Up to this point Shakespeare has given an air of unreality to Orsino's love by keeping him separate from Olivia, and of reality to Viola's love by setting her alongside Orsino. To unite all three threads of the story, Shakespeare now moves the Duke and his followers over to Olivia's house, thereby concentrating all the characters in one place. There for a moment the play becomes serious. " Cesario " is claimed as husband by Olivia and angrily discarded by Orsino, but before anything further can be said or done, Sir Toby and Sir Andrew — both much battered — wander in, thus distracting the attention from " Cesario." They are escorted away, and at this point, to everyone's astonishment, the real Sebastian enters.

Here is the true climax and high moment of the play — the recognition and the reunion of brother and sister. Viola knows that Sebastian is alive, Sebastian thinks that she is dead. His gradual realization that the impossible is true is exquisitely wrought. Here is the real ending, but Shakespeare never ends his plays at the height of emotion; he always slackens the tension before he dismisses his audience.

There are still two outstanding matters to be cleared up. First Orsino transfers his affections to Viola, who is incidentally the only person in the play who marries her original choice. Orsino's action is not so surprising as it might seem, for his real need has been not Olivia but a mate; from the first he has been attracted by Viola, and he is humbled by the realization that she could, while loving him, woo another for him. There is one other matter to be cleared up — Malvolio is still in prison. He is brought in and the trickery is explained, but when he realizes how he has been fooled, he rushes away in vengeful rage, and

finally forfeits all sympathy. So the lovers and the rest go into the house, leaving only the Clown. He brings the play to an end with an ironic, melancholy little ditty which gives that suggestion of pathos and questioning with which Shakespeare sometimes ends a comedy — the feeling that perhaps nothing very much matters after all.

Twelfth Night is deservedly the most popular of all Shakespeare's romantic comedies, and the most often acted. It is a perfect play for the stage; each player in turn has his moment and no one overshadows the rest. The plot is superbly planned, and each of the characters is completely formed.

The characterization is as good as the plot. Each person has enough character for his place in the play and no more. It is worth remembering that when Shakespeare wrote this play the vogue for the realistic comedy of humors was at its height (see Gen. Intro. p. 42a). The story of *Twelfth Night* is highly romantic; though it could not possibly have happened in real life, yet it remains alive long after more realistic comedies — actual transcripts from contemporary life — have faded into merely antiquarian curiosities. This is a paradox of literary art. Shakespeare realized, as Ben Jonson did not, that to hold the mirror up to nature a play needs to be something more than an exact reflection of contemporary manners. Shakespeare's scenes may be romantic and impossible, but his characters are human beings with the permanent characteristics of humanity, which survive long after passing fashions have been forgotten.

The design of *Twelfth Night* is beautifully proportioned and subtle. It is the most musical of all Shakespeare's plays. It not only begins with music, the whole play is an elaborate composition. Indeed, perhaps the best single word to describe *Twelfth Night* is " symphony," which according to the definition of the dictionary is " an elaborate orchestral composition of several contrasted but closely related movements."

Twelfth Night

DRAMATIS PERSONAE

ORSINO, *Duke of Illyria*
SEBASTIAN, *brother to Viola*
ANTONIO, *a sea captain, friend to Sebastian*
A SEA CAPTAIN, *friend to Viola*
VALENTINE ⎱ *gentlemen attending on the Duke*
CURIO ⎰
SIR TOBY BELCH, *uncle to Olivia*
SIR ANDREW AGUECHEEK
MALVOLIO, *steward to Olivia*

FABIAN ⎱ *servants to Olivia*
FESTE, *a clown* ⎰
OLIVIA
VIOLA
MARIA, *Olivia's woman*

LORDS, PRIESTS, SAILORS, OFFICERS, MUSICIANS,
  and other ATTENDANTS

SCENE — *A city in Illyria, and the seacoast near it.*

Act I

SCENE I. *An apartment in the* DUKE'S *palace.*

[*Enter* DUKE, CURIO, *and other* LORDS; MUSICIANS
    attending.]

DUKE. If music be the food of love, play on.
Give me excess of it, that, surfeiting,°
The appetite may sicken, and so die.
That strain again! It had a dying fall.°
Oh, it came o'er my ear like the sweet sound   5
That breathes upon a bank of violets,
Stealing and giving odor! Enough, no more.
'Tis not so sweet now as it was before.
O spirit of love, how quick and fresh art thou!
That, notwithstanding thy capacity   10
Receiveth as the sea, naught enters there,
Of what validity and pitch soe'er,
But falls into abatement and low price,
Even in a minute!° So full of shapes is fancy
That it alone is high fantastical.°   15
CUR. Will you go hunt, my lord?
DUKE.   What, Curio?
CUR. The hart.
DUKE. Why, so I do, the noblest that I have.
Oh, when mine eyes did see Olivia first,
Methought she purged the air of pestilence!°   20
That instant was I turned into a hart,
And my desires, like fell° and cruel hounds,
E'er since pursue me.
[*Enter* VALENTINE.] How now! What news from
    her?

VAL. So please my lord, I might not be admitted,
But from her handmaid do return this answer: 25
The element° itself, till seven years' heat,°
Shall not behold her face at ample view;°
But, like a cloistress,° she will veilèd walk
And water once a day her chamber round
With eye-offending brine — all this to season°   30
A brother's dead love, which she would keep fresh
And lasting in her sad remembrance.
DUKE. Oh, she that hath a heart of that fine frame
To pay this debt of love but to a brother,
How will she love when the rich golden shaft°   35
Hath killed the flock of all affections° else
That live in her; when liver, brain, and heart,°
These sovereign thrones, are all supplied, and filled
Her sweet perfections with one self king!°
Away before me to sweet beds of flowers.   40
Love thoughts lie rich when canopied with bowers.
                                    [*Exeunt.*]

SCENE II. *The seacoast.*

[*Enter* VIOLA, *a* CAPTAIN, *and* SAILORS.]

VIO. What country, friends, is this?
CAP. This is Illyria,° lady.
VIO. And what should I do in Illyria?
My brother he is in Elysium.°
Perchance he is not drowned. What think you, sail-
    ors?   5
CAP. It is perchance that you yourself were saved.
VIO. Oh, my poor brother! And so perchance may
    he be.

Act I, Sc. i: **2. surfeiting:** being overfull.   **4. dying fall:**
cadence which falls away.   **10–14. capacity ... minute:** i.e.,
though the spirit of love is as wide and deep as the sea, yet
whatever falls into it, no matter how valuable and lofty, be-
comes worthless in a moment. **pitch:** lit., the soaring flight of a
hawk.   **14–15. So ... fantastical:** love (*fancy*) is so full of im-
agination (*shapes*) that above all others (*alone*) it is overflow-
ing with fantasies (*high fantastical*). **20. purged ... pestilence:**
The plague was believed by many to be caused by foul air.
22. fell: fierce.

26. element: sky. **seven ... heat:** till seven years have passed.
27. ample view: fully. **28. cloistress:** nun in a cloister. **30. sea-
son:** keep fresh. **35. golden shaft:** Cupid has two arrows; the
golden causes love, the leaden dislike. **36. affections:** desires.
37. liver ... heart: These parts were believed to be the seat of
the passions, intelligence, and affection. **39. self king:** sole
object of adoration.
Sc. ii: **2. Illyria:** actually on the east coast of the Adriatic
sea, but Shakespeare has in fact chosen a picturesque name for
an imaginary kingdom. **4. Elysium:** Paradise.

CAP. True, madam. And to comfort you with
  chance,
Assure yourself, after our ship did split,   9
When you and those poor number saved with you
Hung on our driving° boat, I saw your brother,
Most provident in peril, bind himself,
Courage and hope both teaching him the practice,
To a strong mast that lived upon the sea;
Where, like Arion° on the dolphin's back,   15
I saw him hold acquaintance with the waves
So long as I could see.
  VIO. For saying so, there's gold.
Mine own escape unfoldeth to my hope,
Whereto thy speech serves for authority,   20
The like of him.° Know'st thou this country?
  CAP. Aye, madam, well, for I was bred and born
Not three hours' travel from this very place.
  VIO. Who governs here?
  CAP. A noble Duke, in nature as in name.   25
  VIO. What is his name?
  CAP. Orsino.
  VIO. Orsino! I have heard my father name him.
He was a bachelor then.
  CAP. And so is now, or was so very late.   30
For but a month ago I went from hence,
And then 'twas fresh in murmur — as, you know,
What great ones do the less will prattle of —
That he did seek the love of fair Olivia.
  VIO. What's she?   35
  CAP. A virtuous maid, the daughter of a Count
That died some twelvemonth since, then leaving her
In the protection of his son, her brother,
Who shortly also died. For whose dear love,
They say, she hath abjured the company   40
And sight of men.
  VIO.   Oh, that I served that lady,
And might not be delivered to the world
Till I had made mine own occasion mellow,
What my estate is!°
  CAP.   That were hard to compass,
Because she will admit no kind of suit,   45
No, not the Duke's.
  VIO. There is a fair behavior in thee, Captain.
And though that Nature with a beauteous wall
Doth oft close in pollution, yet of thee
I will believe thou hast a mind that suits   50
With this thy fair and outward character.°
I prithee, and I'll pay thee bounteously,
Conceal me what I am, and be my aid
For such disguise as haply shall become

The form of my intent. I'll serve this Duke.   55
Thou shalt present me as a eunuch° to him.
It may be worth thy pains, for I can sing,°
And speak to him in many sorts of music,
That will allow me very worth his service.°
What else may hap to time I will commit,   6e
Only shape thou thy silence to my wit.
  CAP. Be you his eunuch, and your mute I'll be.
When my tongue blabs, then let mine eyes not see.
  VIO. I thank thee. Lead me on.   [Exeunt.]

SCENE III. OLIVIA's *house*.

[*Enter* SIR TOBY BELCH *and* MARIA.]

SIR TO. What a plague means my niece, to take the
death of her brother thus? I am sure care's an enemy
to life.
  MAR. By my troth, Sir Toby, you must come in
earlier o' nights. Your cousin, my lady, takes great
exceptions to your ill hours.   5
  SIR TO. Why, let her except, before excepted.°
  MAR. Aye, but you must confine yourself within
the modest limits of order.   9
  SIR TO. Confine! I'll confine myself no finer than
I am. These clothes are good enough to drink in,
and so be these boots too. An° they be not, let them
hang themselves in their own straps.   13
  MAR. That quaffing and drinking will undo you.
I heard my lady talk of it yesterday, and of a foolish
knight that you brought in one night here to be her
wooer.
  SIR TO. Who, Sir Andrew Aguecheek?
  MAR. Aye, he.
  SIR TO. He's as tall° a man as any 's in Illyria. 20
  MAR. What's that to the purpose?
  SIR TO. Why, he has three thousand ducats a year.
  MAR. Aye, but he'll have but a year in all these
ducats. He's a very fool and a prodigal.   25
  SIR TO. Fie that you'll say so! He plays o' the viol
de gamboys,° and speaks three or four languages
word for word without book, and hath all the good
gifts of nature.   29
  MAR. He hath indeed, almost natural,° for besides
that he's a fool, he's a great quarreler. And but that
he hath the gift of a coward to allay the gust° he

11. driving: driven before the wind.   15. Arion: for the F1 read-
ing "Orion." Arion was a singer. He was captured by pirates
who were about to kill him. He asked to be allowed to sing for
the last time. Then he jumped into the sea, where a dolphin,
charmed by his song, carried him safe to land.   19-21. Mine
. . . him: i.e., my escape and your speech give me hope that he
is still alive.   43-44. mine . . . is: i.e., until the time is ripe for
me to reveal my own affairs.   51. character: face — an outward
indication of the nature within.

56. eunuch: boy singer.   57. I . . . sing: The part of Viola was
originally written for a boy with a good voice, but later small
alterations were made and the songs were given to the Clown.
59. allow . . . service: approve me as worth employing.
  Sc. iii: 6. except . . . excepted: Toby caps Maria's "excep-
tion" with a common legal phrase *exceptis excipiendis* (with the
exceptions already excepted).   12. An: if.   20. tall: Andrew is
tall and thin, but Toby implies that he is also "tall" in the
common meaning of "brave."   26-27. viol de gamboys: bass
viol, viola da gamba, so called because it was held between
the legs. See Pl. 18a.   30. natural: with a pun on "natural,"
meaning born fool.   33. allay . . . gust: water down the
taste.

hath in quarreling, 'tis thought among the prudent he would quickly have the gift of a grave.   35

SIR TO. By this hand, they are scoundrels and substractors° that say so of him. Who are they?

MAR. They that add, moreover, he's drunk nightly in your company.   39

SIR TO. With drinking healths to my niece. I'll drink to her as long as there is a passage in my throat and drink in Illyria. He's a coward and a coystrill° that will not drink to my niece till his brains turn o' the toe like a parish top.° What, wench! *Castiliano vulgo;*° for here comes Sir Andrew Agueface.   46

[*Enter* SIR ANDREW AGUECHEEK.]

SIR AND. Sir Toby Belch! How now, Sir Toby Belch!

SIR TO. Sweet Sir Andrew!

SIR AND. Bless you, fair shrew.   50

MAR. And you too, sir.

SIR TO. Accost, Sir Andrew, accost.°

SIR AND. What's that?

SIR TO. My niece's chambermaid.

SIR AND. Good Mistress Accost, I desire better acquaintance.   56

MAR. My name is Mary, sir.

SIR AND. Good Mistress Mary Accost ———

SIR TO. You mistake, knight. "Accost" is front her, board her, woo her, assail her.   60

SIR AND. By my troth, I would not undertake her in this company. Is that the meaning of "accost"?

MAR. Fare you well, gentlemen.

SIR TO. An thou let part so, Sir Andrew, would thou mightst never draw sword again.   66

SIR AND. An you part so, mistress, I would I might never draw sword again. Fair lady, do you think you have fools in hand?

MAR. Sir, I have not you by the hand.   70

SIR AND. Marry,° but you shall have, and here's my hand.

MAR. Now, sir, "thought is free." I pray you, bring your hand to the buttery bar° and let it drink.

SIR AND. Wherefore, sweetheart? What's your metaphor?   76

MAR. It's dry,° sir.

SIR AND. Why, I think so. I am not such an ass but I can keep my hand dry. But what's your jest?   80

MAR. A dry jest, sir.

SIR AND. Are you full of them?

MAR. Aye, sir, I have them at my fingers' ends. Marry, now I let go your hand, I am barren. [*Exit.*]

SIR TO. O knight, thou lackest a cup of canary.° When did I see thee so put down?   86

SIR AND. Never in your life, I think, unless you see canary put me down. Methinks sometimes I have no more wit than a Christian or an ordinary man has. But I am a great eater of beef° and I believe that does harm to my wit.   91

SIR TO. No question.

SIR AND. An I thought that, I'd forswear it. I'll ride home tomorrow, Sir Toby.

SIR TO. *Pourquoi,*° my dear knight?   95

SIR AND. What is "*pourquoi*"? Do or not do? I would I had bestowed that time in the tongues that I have in fencing, dancing and bearbaiting. Oh, had I but followed the arts!

SIR TO. Then hadst thou had an excellent head of hair.   101

SIR AND. Why, would that have mended my hair?

SIR TO. Past question, for thou seest it will not curl by nature.°   105

SIR AND. But it becomes me well enough, does 't not?

SIR TO. Excellent. It hangs like flax on a distaff,° and I hope to see a housewife take thee between her legs and spin it off.°   110

SIR AND. Faith, I'll home tomorrow, Sir Toby. Your niece will not be seen, or if she be, it's four to one she'll none of me. The Count himself here hard by woos her.   114

SIR TO. She'll none o' the Count. She'll not match above her degree,° neither in estate, years, nor wit. I have heard her swear 't. Tut, there's life in 't, man.

SIR AND. I'll stay a month longer. I am a fellow o' the strangest mind i' the world. I delight in masques and revels° sometimes altogether.   121

SIR TO. Art thou good at these kickshawses,° knight?

SIR AND. As any man in Illyria, whatsoever he be, under the degree of my betters. And yet I will not compare with an old man.°   126

SIR TO. What is thy excellence in a galliard,° knight?

SIR AND. Faith, I can cut a caper.°

SIR TO. And I can cut the mutton° to 't.   130

SIR AND. And I think I have the backtrick° simply as strong as any man in Illyria.

---

37. substractors: detractors. **43. coystrill:** knave. **44. parish top:** a large spinning top used by villagers on frosty days when it was too cold to work. **45. Castiliano vulgo:** i.e., keep a straight face; lit., a Castilian face. The origin of the phrase is disputed. **52. accost:** introduce yourself. **71. Marry:** Mary, by the Virgin. **74. buttery bar:** ledge on the half-door of the buttery on which tankards were rested. "Bar" is still used in this sense in "cocktail bar." The phrase "bring your hand to the buttery bar" is an invitation to a flirtation which Andrew is too simple to understand. **77. dry:** A dry hand denoted lack of generosity and desire.

85. canary: wine from the Canary Isles. **90. eater of beef:** Diet was believed to have considerable influence on bodily and mental health. **95. Pourquoi:** why. **104–05. curl by nature:** emendation for the F1 reading "cool my nature." **108. distaff:** used in spinning. **110. spin it off:** cause you to lose your hair as a result of venereal disease. **116. degree:** rank. **120–21. masques ... revels:** Courtly entertainments. See Gen. Intro. p. 32a. **122. kickshawses:** trifles. **126. old man:** expert. **127. galliard:** a quick, lively dance. See App. 24. **129. caper:** jump into the air. **130. cut ... mutton:** Mutton was often served with caper sauce. **131. backtrick:** a movement in dancing.

SIR TO. Wherefore are these things hid? Wherefore have these gifts a curtain before 'em? Are they like to take dust, like Mistress Mall's picture?°   135 Why dost thou not go to church in a galliard and come home in a coranto?° My very walk should be a jig,° I would not so much as make water but in a sinkapace.° What dost thou mean? Is it a world to hide virtues in? I did think, by the excellent constitution of thy leg, it was formed under the star   141 of a galliard.

SIR AND. Aye, 'tis strong, and it does indifferent well in a flame-colored stock. Shall we set about some revels?   145

SIR TO. What shall we do else? Were we not born under Taurus?°

SIR AND. Taurus! That's sides and heart.

SIR TO. No, sir, it is legs and thighs. Let me see thee caper. Ha! higher. Ha, ha! excellent!   150
[*Exeunt.*]

SCENE IV. *The* DUKE'S *palace.*

[*Enter* VALENTINE, *and* VIOLA *in man's attire.*]

VAL. If the Duke continue these favors toward you, Cesario, you are like to be much advanced. He hath known you but three days, and already you are no stranger.   4

VIO. You either fear his humor° or my negligence, that you call in question the continuance of his love. Is he inconstant, sir, in his favors?

VAL. No, believe me.

VIO. I thank you. Here comes the Count.

[*Enter* DUKE, CURIO, *and* ATTENDANTS.]

DUKE. Who saw Cesario, ho?   10

VIO. On your attendance, my lord. Here.

DUKE. Stand you a while aloof. Cesario, Thou know'st no less but all. I have unclasped To thee the book even of my secret soul.   14 Therefore, good youth, address thy gait unto her. Be not denied access, stand at her doors, And tell them there thy fixèd foot shall grow Till thou have audience.

VIO.   Sure, my noble lord, If she be so abandoned to her sorrow As it is spoke, she never will admit me.   20

DUKE. Be clamorous and leap all civil bounds° Rather than make unprofited return.

VIO. Say I do speak with her, my lord, what then?

DUKE. Oh, then unfold the passion of my love, Surprise her with discourse of my dear faith.   25 It shall become thee well to act my woes. She will attend it better in thy youth Than in a nuncio's° of more grave aspéct.°

VIO. I think not so, my lord.

DUKE.   Dear lad, believe it, For they shall yet belie thy happy years   30 That say thou art a man. Diana's lip Is not more smooth and rubious;° thy small pipe° Is as the maiden's organ, shrill and sound, And all is semblative° a woman's part. I know thy constellation is right apt°   35 For this affair. Some four or five attend him, All, if you will; for I myself am best When least in company. Prosper well in this, And thou shalt live as freely as thy lord, To call his fortunes thine.

VIO.   I'll do my best   40 To woo your lady. [*Aside*] Yet, a barful° strife! Whoe'er I woo, myself would be his wife. [*Exeunt.*]

SCENE V. OLIVIA'S *house.*

[*Enter* MARIA *and* CLOWN.]

MAR. Nay, either tell me where thou hast been, or I will not open my lips so wide as a bristle may enter in way of thy excuse. My lady will hang thee for thy absence.

CLO. Let her hang me. He that is well hanged in this world needs to fear no colors.°   6

MAR. Make that good.°

CLO. He shall see none to fear.

MAR. A good lenten° answer. I can tell thee where that saying was born, of "I fear no colors."   10

CLO. Where, good Mistress Mary?

MAR. In the wars, and that may you be bold to say in your foolery.   14

CLO. Well, God give them wisdom that have it, and those that are fools, let them use their talents.

MAR. Yet you will be hanged for being so long absent — or to be turned away, is not that as good as a hanging to you?

CLO. Many a good hanging prevents a bad   20 marriage, and for turning away, let summer bear it out.°

MAR. You are resolute, then?

---

135. Mistress . . . picture: a topical allusion now lost. Mall or Moll was a common nickname for a prostitute. This Mall may have been the notorious Mall Newberry. See *T Night* Intro. p. 566a.   **137. coranto:** a running dance.   **138. jig:** a lively dance.   **139. sinkapace:** "cinque pace," a dance of five steps. **146–47. born . . . Taurus:** The common penny almanac of the time printed the figure of a naked man surrounded by the signs of the zodiac with lines pointing to the parts of the body governed by each. Both Andrew and Toby are wrong, as Taurus governed the neck and throat.

Sc. iv: 5. humor: whim, inclination. See App. 3.   **21. civil bounds:** restraints of good manners.

28. nuncio: messenger. **grave aspect:** sober countenance.   **32. rubious:** ruby-red. **small pipe:** little throat.   **34. semblative:** resembling.   **35. constellation . . . apt:** you are born under a lucky star.   **41. barful:** full of bars, impediments.

Sc. v: 6. fear no colors: proverbial phrase meaning "I dare anyone." Since "collar," "color," and "choler" were pronounced alike, puns on these words were endless.   **7. Make . . . good:** prove it.   **9. lenten:** fasting, lean.   **21–22. let . . . out:** have the upper hand; i.e., if I have to go, I hope it's good weather.

CLO. Not so, neither, but I am resolved on two
points.° 25

MAR. That if one break, the other will hold, or if
both break, your gaskins° fall.

CLO. Apt, in good faith, very apt. Well, go thy
way. If Sir Toby would leave drinking, thou wert as
witty a piece of Eve's flesh° as any in Illyria. 31

MAR. Peace, you rogue, no more o' that. Here
comes my lady. Make your excuse wisely, you 33
were best. [Exit.]

CLO. Wit, an 't be thy will, put me into good fool-
ing! Those wits that think they have thee do very
oft prove fools, and I that am sure I lack thee may
pass for a wise man. For what says Quinapalus?°
"Better a witty fool than a foolish wit." 40
[Enter LADY OLIVIA with MALVOLIO.] God bless thee,
lady!

OLI. Take the fool away.

CLO. Do you not hear, fellows? Take away the
lady.

OLI. Go to, you're a dry fool, I'll no more of you.
Besides, you grow dishonest. 46

CLO. Two faults,° madonna, that drink and good
counsel will amend. For give the dry fool drink,
then is the fool not dry. Bid the dishonest man mend
himself; if he mend, he is no longer dishonest; 50
if he cannot, let the botcher° mend him. Anything
that's mended is but patched. Virtue that trans-
gresses is but patched with sin, and sin that amends
is but patched with virtue. If that this simple syllo-
gism° will serve, so. If it will not, what rem- 55
edy? As there is no true cuckold° but calamity,
so beauty's a flower. The lady bade take away the
fool, therefore I say again, take her away.

OLI. Sir, I bade them take away you. 60

CLO. Misprision° in the highest degree! Lady,
cucullus non facit monachum.° That's as much to
say as I wear not motley° in my brain. Good ma-
donna, give me leave to prove you a fool.

OLI. Can you do it? 65

CLO. Dexteriously, good madonna.

OLI. Make your proof.

CLO. I must catechize you for it, madonna. Good
my mouse° of virtue, answer me.

OLI. Well, sir, for want of other idleness, I'll bide
your proof. 71

CLO. Good madonna, why mournest thou?

OLI. Good fool, for my brother's death.

CLO. I think his soul is in Hell, madonna.

OLI. I know his soul is in Heaven, fool. 75

CLO. The more fool, madonna, to mourn for your
brother's soul being in Heaven. Take away the fool,
gentlemen.

OLI. What think you of this fool, Malvolio? Doth
he not mend? 80

MAL. Yes, and shall do till the pangs of death
shake him. Infirmity, that decays the wise, doth
ever make the better fool.

CLO. God send you, sir, a speedy infirmity, for the
better increasing your folly! Sir Toby will be sworn
that I am no fox, but he will not pass his word for
twopence that you are no fool. 86

OLI. How say you to that, Malvolio?

MAL. I marvel your ladyship takes delight in such
a barren rascal.° I saw him put down the other day
with an ordinary fool that has no more brain 90
than a stone. Look you now, he's out of his guard al-
ready. Unless you laugh and minister occasion° to
him, he is gagged. I protest, I take these wise men
that crow so at these set kind of fools no better than
the fools' zanies.° 96

OLI. Oh, you are sick of self-love, Malvolio, and
taste with a distempered appetite. To be generous,
guiltless, and of free° disposition is to take those
things for bird bolts° that you deem cannon 100
bullets. There is no slander in an allowed° fool,
though he do nothing but rail; nor no railing in a
known discreet man, though he do nothing but re-
prove.

CLO. Now Mercury° endue thee with leasing,°
for thou speakest well of fools! 106

[Re-enter MARIA.]

MAR. Madam, there is at the gate a young gentle-
man much desires to speak with you.

OLI. From the Count Orsino, is it?

MAR. I know not, madam. 'Tis a fair young man,
and well attended. 111

OLI. Who of my people hold him in delay?

MAR. Sir Toby, madam, your kinsman.

OLI. Fetch him off, I pray you. He speaks nothing
but madman, fie on him! [Exit MARIA.] Go you,
Malvolio. If it be a suit from the Count, I am 116
sick, or not at home — what you will, to dismiss it.
[Exit MALVOLIO.] Now you see, sir, how your fool-
ing grows old, and people dislike it. 119

CLO. Thou hast spoke for us, madonna, as if thy
eldest son should be a fool, whose skull Jove cram

25. points: laces used to attach the hose to the doublet.
27. gaskins: breeches. 31. Eve's flesh: erring woman — the
first hint that there is something between Toby and Maria.
39. Quinapalus: a character invented by Rabelais. The clown
specializes in mock learning. 47. Two faults: The fool is in dis-
grace and to cajole Olivia into good humor rattles out mock
learned nonsense. 51. botcher: an unskillful mender of old
garments. 55. syllogism: learned argument. 56. cuckold: hus-
band deceived by his wife. 61. Misprision: error. 62. cucullus
. . . monachum: a cowl does not make a monk. 63. motley: the
fool's particolored costume. See Pl. 12f, 13c. 69. mouse: a term
of endearment, like "duck."

89. barren rascal: By this remark Malvolio rouses the malice
of the fool, and so ultimately brings about his own downfall.
92. minister occasion: i.e., give him a lead. 96. zanies: stooges;
the zany was the clown's assistant who tried to copy his tricks.
99. free: innocent. 100. bird bolts: short, blunt headed arrows
used in a crossbow for killing small birds. See Pl. 22a. 101. al-
lowed: licensed. 105. Mercury: the god of thieves and rascals.
endue . . . leasing: endow you with lying.

with brains! for — here he comes° — one of thy kin
has a most weak pia mater.°

[*Enter* SIR TOBY.]

OLI. By mine honor, half-drunk. What is he at the
gate, Cousin?   125

SIR TO. A gentleman.

OLI. A gentleman! What gentleman?

SIR TO. 'Tis a gentleman here — a plague o' these
pickle-herring!° How now, sot!

CLO. Good Sir Toby!   130

OLI. Cousin, Cousin, how have you come so early
by this lethargy?°

SIR TO. Lechery! I defy lechery. There's one at the
gate.

OLI. Aye, marry, what is he?   135

SIR TO. Let him be the Devil an he will, I care not.
Give me faith, say I. Well, it's all one.   [*Exit.*]

OLI. What's a drunken man like, fool?

CLO. Like a drowned man, a fool, and a madman.
One draught above heat makes him a fool, the sec-
ond mads him, and a third drowns him.   141

OLI. Go thou and seek the crowner,° and let him
sit o' my coz,° for he's in the third degree of drink,
he's drowned. Go look after him.   144

CLO. He is but mad yet, madonna, and the fool
shall look to the madman.   [*Exit.*]

[*Re-enter* MALVOLIO.]

MAL. Madam, yond young fellow swears he will
speak with you. I told him you were sick; he takes
on him to understand so much, and therefore 150
comes to speak with you. I told him you were asleep;
he seems to have a foreknowledge of that too, and
therefore comes to speak with you. What is to be said
to him, lady? He's fortified against any denial.

OLI. Tell him he shall not speak with me.   155

MAL. Has been told so, and he says he'll stand at
your door like a sheriff's post,° and be the sup-
porter° to a bench, but he'll speak with you.

OLI. What kind o' man is he?

MAL. Why, of mankind.   160

OLI. What manner of man?

MAL. Of very ill manner. He'll speak with you,
will you or no.

OLI. Of what personage and years is he?   164

MAL. Not yet old enough for a man, nor young
enough for a boy, as a squash° is before 'tis a peas-
cod, or a codling when 'tis almost an apple. 'Tis
with him in standing water,° between boy and man.

He is very well-favored° and he speaks very shrew-
ishly.° One would think his mother's milk were
scarce out of him.   171

OLI. Let him approach. Call in my gentlewoman.

MAL. Gentlewoman, my lady calls.   [*Exit.*]

[*Re-enter* MARIA.]

OLI. Give me my veil. Come, throw it o'er 175
my face. We'll once more hear Orsino's embassy.

[*Enter* VIOLA *and* ATTENDANTS.]

VIO. The honorable lady of the house, which is
she?

OLI. Speak to me, I shall answer for her. Your
will?   180

VIO. Most radiant, exquisite, and unmatchable
beauty, I pray you tell me if this be the lady of the
house, for I never saw her. I would be loath to cast
away my speech, for besides that it is excellently
well penned, I have taken great pains to con° 185
it. Good beauties, let me sustain no scorn. I am very
comptible,° even to the least sinister° usage.

OLI. Whence came you, sir?

VIO. I can say little more than I have studied, and
that question's out of my part. Good gentle one, give
me modest assurance if you be the lady of the house,
that I may proceed in my speech.   192

OLI. Are you a comedian?°

VIO. No, my profound heart. And yet, by the very
fangs of malice I swear, I am not that I play.° Are
you the lady of the house?

OLI. If I do not usurp myself, I am.

VIO. Most certain, if you are she, you do usurp
yourself; for what is yours to bestow is not yours to
reserve. But this is from my commission.° I 200
will on with my speech in your praise, and then
show you the heart of my message.

OLI. Come to what is important in 't. I forgive
you the praise.   205

VIO. Alas, I took great pains to study it, and 'tis
poetical.

OLI. It is the more like to be feigned. I pray you
keep it in. I heard you were saucy at my gates, and
allowed your approach rather to wonder° at you than
to hear you. If you be not mad, be gone. If 211
you have reason, be brief. 'Tis not that time of
moon° with me to make one in so skipping° a dia-
logue.

MAR. Will you hoist sail, sir? Here lies your
way.

VIO. No, good swabber,° I am to hull° here a little

122. **here he comes:** i.e., Toby. This is the usual phrase to draw
attention to a character entering at the back of the stage. See
Gen. Intro. p. 56b.   123. **pia mater:** brain.   129. **pickle-herring:**
very salt and indigestible, and so causing thirst and wind.
132. **lethargy:** lack of sense.   142. **crowner:** coroner, whose
function is to hold an inquest on the bodies of those who die
unnaturally.   143. **coz:** cousin — used for any near relation.
157. **sheriff's post:** painted post set up before the house of the
sheriff as a sign of office.   158. **supporter:** support.   166. **squash:**
unripe peapod.   168. **standing water:** the moment at the change
of the tide when the water neither ebbs nor flows.

169. **well-favored:** good-looking.   170. **shrewishly:** like a shrew,
shrill.   185. **con:** learn by heart.   187. **comptible:** susceptible.
sinister: left-handed, unkind.   193. **comedian:** actor.   195. **that
I play:** i.e., the part I act, that of a man.   200. **from my com-
mission:** not included in my instructions.   210. **allowed . . .
wonder:** I allowed you to come in so that I might look at you —
not to listen to your prepared speeches.   212–13. **time of moon:**
lucky end of the month.   213. **skipping:** frivolous.   218. **swab-
ber:** one who swabs the decks. Viola retorts to Maria's "hoist
sail" with a series of nautical metaphors. **hull:** lie at anchor.

longer. Some mollification for your giant,° sweet
lady. Tell me your mind. I am a messenger.   220

OLI. Sure, you have some hideous matter to de-
liver when the courtesy of it is so fearful.° Speak
your office.

VIO. It alone concerns your ear. I bring no over-
ture° of war, no taxation of° homage. I hold   225
the olive in my hand, my words are as full of peace
as matter.

OLI. Yet you began rudely. What are you? What
would you?   229

VIO. The rudeness that hath appeared in me have
I learned from my entertainment. What I am, and
what I would, are as secret as maidenhead — to your
ears, divinity; to any other's, profanation.   234

OLI. Give us the place alone. We will hear this
divinity.° [Exeunt MARIA and ATTENDANTS.] Now,
sir, what is your text?

VIO. Most sweet lady——

OLI. A comfortable doctrine, and much may be
said of it. Where lies your text?   240

VIO. In Orsino's bosom.

OLI. In his bosom! In what chapter of his
bosom?

VIO. To answer by the method,° in the first of his
heart.   245

OLI. Oh, I have read it. It is heresy. Have you no
more to say?

VIO. Good madam, let me see your face.

OLI. Have you any commission from your lord to
negotiate with my face? You are now out of   250
your text. But we will draw the curtain and show
you the picture. Look you, sir, [Unveiling] such a
one I was this present° — is 't not well done?

VIO. Excellently done, if God did all.

OLI. 'Tis in grain,° sir, 'twill endure wind and
weather.   256

VIO. 'Tis beauty truly blent,° whose red and white
Nature's own sweet and cunning hand laid on.
Lady, you are the cruel'st she alive
If you will lead these graces to the grave   260
And leave the world no copy.°

OLI. Oh, sir, I will not be so hardhearted, I will
give out divers schedules of my beauty. It shall be
inventoried, and every particle and utensil labeled
to my will — as, item, two lips, indifferent red;   265

item, two gray eyes, with lids to them; item, one
neck, one chin, and so forth. Were you sent hither
to praise me?

VIO. I see what you are, you are too proud;
But if you were the Devil, you are fair.   270
My lord and master loves you. Oh, such love
Could be but recompensed, though you were
    crowned
The nonpareil° of beauty!

OLI.   How does he love me?

VIO. With adorations, fertile tears,   274
With groans that thunder love, with sighs of fire.

OLI. Your lord does know my mind. I cannot love
    him.
Yet I suppose him virtuous, know him noble,
Of great estate, of fresh and stainless youth;
In voices well divulged,° free, learned, and valiant;
And in dimension° and the shape of nature   280
A gracious person. But yet I cannot love him.
He might have took his answer long ago.

VIO. If I did love you in my master's flame,
With such a suffering, such a deadly life,
In your denial I would find no sense.   285
I would not understand it.

OLI.   Why, what would you?

VIO. Make me a willow cabin° at your gate,
And call upon my soul within the house;
Write loyal cantons° of contemnèd° love
And sing them loud even in the dead of night;   290
Halloo your name to the reverberate hills,
And make the babbling gossip of the air
Cry out "Olivia!" Oh, you should not rest
Between the elements of air and earth,
But you should pity me!

OLI.   You might do much.   295
What is your parentage?

VIO. Above my fortunes, yet my state is well.
I am a gentleman.

OLI.   Get you to your lord.
I cannot love him. Let him send no more,
Unless, perchance, you come to me again   300
To tell me how he takes it. Fare you well.
I thank you for your pains. Spend this for me.

VIO. I am no fee'd post,° lady, keep your purse.
My master, not myself, lacks recompense.
Love make his heart of flint that you shall love;   305
And let your fervor, like my master's, be
Placed in contempt! Farewell, fair cruelty. [Exit.]

OLI. "What is your parentage?"
"Above my fortunes, yet my state is well.
I am a gentleman." I'll be sworn thou art.   310
Thy tongue, thy face, thy limbs, actions, and spirit,

---

219. mollification . . . giant: Viola apologizes to Olivia for the
interruption — "I had to pacify your little lady." Maria's small-
ness is emphasized. See Gen. Intro. pp. 59b–60a. **222. courtesy
. . . fearful:** you must have some dreadful message to deliver if
it need such elaborate introduction.   **225. overture:** declara-
tion. **taxation of:** demand for.   **236. divinity:** Olivia takes up
Viola's *divinity*, and the two follow up the metaphor in their
conversation.   **244. To . . . method:** to keep up the metaphor.
252–53. such . . . present: This is the F1 reading, and has been
much emended. The general meaning is "This is what I really
am."   **255. in grain:** i.e., the colors are fast, they will not wash
out.   **257. blent:** blended.   **261. leave . . . copy:** die without
children to carry on the pattern. Cf. Sonnets 1–17.

273. nonpareil: without an equal.   **279. voices . . . divulged:**
spoken well of.   **280. dimension:** bodily form.   **287. willow
cabin:** an arbor of willow — the unhappy lover's tree.   **289. can-
tons:** songs. **contemned:** despised.   **303. fee'd post:** paid mes-
senger.

Do give thee fivefold blazon.° Not too fast. Soft,
   soft!
Unless the master were the man. How now!
Even so quickly may one catch the plague?
Methinks I feel this youth's perfections   315
With an invisible and subtle stealth
To creep in at mine eyes. Well, let it be.
What ho, Malvolio!

        [Re-enter MALVOLIO.*]*

  MAL.   Here, madam, at your service.
  OLI. Run after that same peevish messenger, 319
The County's° man. He left this ring behind him,
Would I or not. Tell him I'll none of it.
Desire him not to flatter with his lord,
Nor hold him up with hopes. I am not for him.
If that the youth will come this way tomorrow,
I'll give him reasons for 't. Hie thee,° Malvolio. 325
  MAL. Madam, I will.   *[Exit.]*
  OLI. I do I know not what, and fear to find
Mine eye too great a flatterer for my mind. 328
Fate, show thy force, ourselves we do not owe.°
What is decreed must be, and be this so.   *[Exit.]*

Act II

SCENE I. *The seacoast.*

[Enter ANTONIO *and* SEBASTIAN.*]*
  ANT. Will you stay no longer? Nor will you not
that I go with you?
  SEB. By your patience, no. My stars shine darkly
over me. The malignancy° of my fate might perhaps
distemper° yours, therefore I shall crave of you 5
your leave that I may bear my evils alone. It were
a bad recompense for your love to lay any of them
on you.
  ANT. Let me yet know of you whither you are
bound. 10
  SEB. No, sooth, sir. My determinate voyage is
mere extravagancy.° But I perceive in you so excel-
lent a touch of modesty that you will not extort from
me what I am willing to keep in; therefore it charges
me in manners the rather to express myself.° 15
You must know of me then, Antonio, my name is
Sebastian, which I called Roderigo.° My father was
that Sebastian of Messaline° whom I know you have

heard of. He left behind him myself and a sister,
both born in an hour. If the Heavens had been 20
pleased, would we had so ended! But you, sir, altered
that, for some hour before you took me from the
breach° of the sea was my sister drowned.
  ANT. Alas the day! 25
  SEB. A lady, sir, though it was said she much re-
sembled me, was yet of many accounted beautiful.
But though I could not with such estimable won-
der° overfar believe that, yet thus far I will boldly
publish° her — she bore a mind that envy could 30
not but call fair. She is drowned already, sir, with
salt water, though I seem to drown her remem-
brance again with more. 33
  ANT. Pardon me, sir, your bad entertainment.°
  SEB. O good Antonio, forgive me your trouble.
  ANT. If you will not murder me for my love, let
me be your servant.
  SEB. If you will not undo what you have done —
that is, kill him whom you have recovered — desire
it not. Fare ye well at once. My bosom is full of 40
kindness,° and I am yet so near the manners of my
mother that upon the least occasion more mine eyes
will tell tales of me. I am bound to the Count Or-
sino's Court. Farewell.   *[Exit.]*
  ANT. The gentleness of all the gods go with
    thee! 45
I have many enemies in Orsino's Court,
Else would I very shortly see thee there.
But, come what may, I do adore thee so
That danger shall seem sport, and I will go.
        [Exit.]

SCENE II. *A street.*

[Enter VIOLA, MALVOLIO *following.]*
  MAL. Were not you even now with the Countess
Olivia?
  VIO. Even now, sir. On a moderate pace I have
since arrived but hither. 4
  MAL. She returns this ring to you, sir. You might
have saved me my pains, to have taken it away your-
self. She adds, moreover, that you should put your
lord into a desperate assurance° she will none of
him. And one thing more, that you be never so
hardy to come again in his affairs, unless it be to re-
port your lord's taking of this. Receive it so. 12
  VIO. She took the ring of me. I'll none of it.
  MAL. Come, sir, you peevishly threw it to her; and
her will is, it should be so returned. If it be worth
stooping for, there it lies in your eye. If not, be it his
that finds it.   *[Exit.]*

---

312. **blazon:** coat of arms denoting a gentleman.   320. **County:** Count.   325. **Hie thee:** hasten.   329. **owe:** own.
  Act II, Sc. i: 4. malignancy: evil disposition. See App. 1. 5. **distemper:** disturb.   11–12. **determinate . . . extravagancy:** the journey I have determined is mere wandering. There is a touch of affectation in Sebastian's language.   14–15. **it . . . myself:** good manners demand that I tell you who I am.   17. **I . . . Roderigo:** hitherto I have pretended that my name was Roderigo.   18. **Messaline:** Messina in Sicily.

24. **breach:** where the waves break.   28–29. **estimable wonder:** admiring judgment.   30. **publish:** proclaim.   34. **your . . . entertainment:** looking after you so badly.   41. **kindness:** tender feeling.
  Sc. ii: 9. desperate assurance: certainty that there is no hope.

VIO. I left no ring with her. What means this
    lady?
Fortune forbid my outside have not charmed her!
She made good view of me;° indeed, so much   20
That sure methought her eyes had lost her tongue,
For she did speak in starts distractedly.
She loves me, sure, the cunning of her passion
Invites me in this churlish messenger.
None of my lord's ring! Why, he sent her none.   25
I am the man. If it be so, as 'tis,
Poor lady, she were better love a dream.
Disguise, I see thou art a wickedness,
Wherein the pregnant° enemy does much.
How easy is it for the proper-false°   30
In women's waxen hearts to set their forms!
Alas, our frailty is the cause, not we!
For such as we are made of, such we be.
How will this fadge?° My master loves her dearly;
And I, poor monster, fond as much on him,   35
And she, mistaken, seems to dote on me.
What will become of this? As I am man,
My state is desperate for my master's love;
As I am woman — now alas the day! —
What thriftless° sighs shall poor Olivia breathe!   40
O Time, thou must untangle this, not I!
It is too hard a knot for me to untie!   [Exit.]

SCENE III. OLIVIA's house.

[Enter SIR TOBY and SIR ANDREW.]

SIR TO. Approach, Sir Andrew. Not to be abed
after midnight is to be up betimes; and "diluculo
surgere,"° thou know'st ——
SIR AND. Nay, by my troth,° I know not. But I
know to be up late is to be up late.   5
SIR TO. A false conclusion. I hate it as an unfilled
can.° To be up after midnight, and to go to bed
then, is early, so that to go to bed after midnight is
to go to bed betimes. Does not our life consist of the
four elements?°   10
SIR AND. Faith, so they say, but I think it rather
consists of eating and drinking.
SIR TO. Thou 'rt a scholar. Let us therefore eat and
drink. Marian, I say, a stoup° of wine!

[Enter CLOWN.]

SIR AND. Here comes the fool, i' faith.   15
CLO. How now, my hearts! Did you never see the
picture of "we three"?°
SIR TO. Welcome, ass. Now let's have a catch.°

SIR AND. By my troth, the fool has an excellent
breast.° I had rather than forty shillings I had   20
such a leg, and so sweet a breath to sing, as the fool
has. In sooth, thou wast in very gracious fooling last
night, when thou spokest of Pigrogromitus, of the
Vapians passing the equinoctial of Queubus.° 'Twas
very good, i' faith. I sent thee sixpence for thy
leman.° Hadst it?   26
CLO. I did impeticos thy gratillity,° for Malvolio's
nose is no whipstock. My lady has a white hand, and
the Myrmidons are no bottle-ale houses.
SIR AND. Excellent! Why, this is the best fooling,
when all is done. Now, a song.   31
SIR TO. Come on, there is sixpence for you — let's
have a song.
SIR AND. There's a testril° of me too. If one knight
give a ——   35
CLO. Would you have a love song, or a song of
good life?
SIR TO. A love song, a love song.
SIR AND. Aye, aye. I care not for good life.
CLO. [Sings.]
   O mistress mine, where are you roaming?   40
   Oh, stay and hear, your truelove's coming,
      That can sing both high and low.
   Trip no further, pretty sweeting,
   Journeys end in lovers meeting,
      Every wise man's son doth know.   45
SIR AND. Excellent good, i' faith.
SIR TO. Good, good.
CLO. [Sings.]
   What is love? 'Tis not hereafter,
   Present mirth hath present laughter,
      What's to come is still unsure.   50
   In delay there lies no plenty,
   Then come kiss me, sweet and twenty,°
      Youth's a stuff will not endure.
SIR AND. A mellifluous° voice, as I am a true
knight.   55
SIR TO. A contagious breath.
SIR AND. Very sweet and contagious, i' faith.
SIR TO. To hear by the nose, it is dulcet in con-
tagion.° But shall we make the welkin° dance in-
deed? Shall we rouse the night owl in a catch°   60
that will draw three souls out of one weaver?° Shall
we do that?

---

20. made . . . me: took a good look at me. 29. pregnant: re-
sourceful. 30. proper-false: men who are handsome but deceit-
ful. 34. fadge: turn out. 40. thriftless: useless.

Sc. iii: 2–3. diluculo surgere: early to rise — a tag from the
schoolboy's Latin grammar. 4. troth: truth. 7. can: pot.
10. four elements: See App. 3. 14. stoup: large drinking pot.
See Pl. 20e and g. 17. we three: a picture of two asses, the
spectator being the third. 18. catch: rowdy song, where each
singer in turn catches up the song a few words after the others.

20. breast: voice. 23–24. Pigrogromitus . . . Queubus: more
mock learned foolery. 26. leman: sweetheart. 27. impeticos
. . . gratillity: pocket your tip. The rest of the fool's profundity
is unexplained; but as both knights are growing more and more
fuddled, it is not important. 34. testril: coin worth sixpence.
52. sweet . . . twenty: gay girl. 54. mellifluous: honey-sweet.
58–59. dulcet in contagion: sweetly catching. 59. welkin: sky.
60. catch: See l. 18, n. The words of the catch which they sing
at l. 75 are "Hold thy peace, thou knave." 61. three . . .
weaver: Weavers, mostly Puritan refugees from the Nether-
lands, were noted psalm singers. It will need a powerful song to
draw out three souls.

SIR AND. An you love me, let's do 't. I am dog at a
catch.   64

CLO. By 'r lady, sir, and some dogs will catch well.

SIR AND. Most certain. Let our catch be " Thou
knave."

CLO. " Hold thy peace, thou knave," knight?   69
I shall be constrained in 't to call thee knave, knight.

SIR AND. 'Tis not the first time I have constrained
one to call me knave. Begin, fool. It begins " Hold
thy peace."

CLO. I shall never begin if I hold my peace.

SIR AND. Good, i' faith. Come, begin.   75

[Catch sung.]

[Enter MARIA.]

MAR. What a caterwauling do you keep here! If
my lady have not called up her steward Malvolio and
bid him turn you out of doors, never trust me.   79

SIR TO. My lady's a Cataian,° we are politicians,°
Malvolio's a Peg-a-Ramsey,° and " Three merry
men be we." Am not I consanguineous?° Am I not
of her blood? Tillyvally.° Lady! [Sings.] " There
dwelt a man in Babylon, lady, lady! "   84

CLO. Beshrew me,° the knight's in admirable fool-
ing.

SIR AND. Aye, he does well enough if he be dis-
posed, and so do I too. He does it with a better grace,
but I do it more natural.   89

SIR TO. [Sings.] " Oh, the twelfth day of Decem-
ber "———

MAR. For the love o' God, peace!

[Enter MALVOLIO.]

MAL. My masters, are you mad? Or what are you?
Have you no wit, manners, nor honesty, but to gab-
ble like tinkers at this time of night? Do ye make
an alehouse of my lady's house, that ye squeak 95
out your coziers'° catches without any mitigation or
remorse of voice? Is there no respect of place, per-
sons, nor time in you?   99

SIR TO. We did keep time, sir, in our catches.
Sneck up!°

MAL. Sir Toby, I must be round° with you. My
lady bade me tell you that though she harbors you
as her kinsman, she's nothing allied to your dis-
orders. If you can separate yourself and your   105
misdemeanors, you are welcome to the house. If
not, an it would please you to take leave of her, she
is very willing to bid you farewell.

SIR TO. " Farewell,° dear heart, since I must needs
be gone."   110

MAR. Nay, good Sir Toby.

CLO. " His eyes do show his days are almost done."

MAL. Is't even so?

SIR TO. " But I will never die."   115

CLO. Sir Toby, there you lie.

MAL. This is much credit to you.

SIR TO. " Shall I bid him go? "

CLO. " What an if you do? "

SIR TO. " Shall I bid him go, and spare not? "   120

CLO. " Oh, no, no, no, no, you dare not."

SIR TO. Out o' tune, sir. Ye lie. Art any more than
a steward? Dost thou think because thou art virtu-
ous, there shall be no more cakes and ale?   125

CLO. Yes, by Saint Anne, and ginger shall be hot
i' the mouth too.

SIR TO. Thou 'rt i' the right. Go, sir, rub your
chain° with crumbs.° A stoup of wine, Maria!

MAL. Mistress Mary, if you prized my lady's   130
favor at anything more than contempt, you would
not give means for this uncivil rule.° She shall know
of it, by this hand.   [Exit.]

MAR. Go shake your ears.   134

SIR AND. 'Twere as good a deed as to drink when
a man's a-hungry, to challenge him the field, and
then to break promise with him and make a fool of
him.

SIR TO. Do 't, knight. I'll write thee a challenge, or
I'll deliver thy indignation to him by word of mouth.

MAR. Sweet Sir Toby, be patient for tonight. 142
Since the youth of the Count's was today with my
lady, she is much out of quiet. For Monsieur Mal-
volio, let me alone with him. If I do not gull   145
him into a nayword,° and make him a common
recreation,° do not think I have wit enough to lie
straight in my bed. I know I can do it.

SIR TO. Possess us, possess us. Tell us something
of him.   150

MAR. Marry, sir, sometimes he is a kind of Puri-
tan.

SIR AND. Oh, if I thought that, I'd beat him like a
dog!

SIR TO. What, for being a Puritan? Thy exquisite
reason, dear knight?   156

SIR AND. I have no exquisite reason for 't, but I
have reason good enough.

MAR. The devil a Puritan that he is, or anything
constantly, but a timepleaser;° an affectioned° 160
ass, that cons state° without book and utters it by
great swarths — the best persuaded of himself, so
crammed, as he thinks, with excellencies, that it is
his grounds of faith that all that look on him love
him. And on that vice in him will my revenge find
notable cause to work.   166

---

80. Catian: Chinaman. politicians: deep ones.   81. Peg-a-Ram-
sey: It is not known who this lady was or why Malvolio re-
sembled her.   82. consanguineous: related by blood. Toby's
mind has now strayed to Olivia.   83. Tillyvally: "hoity-toity."
85. Beshrew me: lit., ill luck take me.   96. coziers: cobblers.
101. Sneck up: be hanged.   102. round: direct.   109–21. Fare-
well . . . not: Toby and the Clown here indulge in an im-
promptu duet.

129. chain: i.e., of office as a steward. with crumbs: used for
polishing silver.   132. uncivil rule: disorderly conduct.   146. nay-
word: byword.   146–47. common recreation: general laughing-
stock.   160. timepleaser: one who suits his behavior to his own
advantage. affectioned: affected.   161. cons state: learns courtly
behavior by heart.

SIR TO. What wilt thou do?

MAR. I will drop in his way some obscure epistles of love, wherein, by the color of his beard, the shape of his leg, the manner of his gait, the expres- 170 sure of his eye, forehead, and complexion, he shall find himself most feelingly° personated. I can write very like my lady your niece. On a forgotten matter we can hardly make distinction of our hands. 175

SIR TO. Excellent! I smell a device.

SIR AND. I have 't in my nose too.

SIR TO. He shall think, by the letters that thou wilt drop, that they come from my niece, and that she's in love with him. 180

MAR. My purpose is indeed a horse of that color.

SIR AND. And your horse now would make him an ass.

MAR. Ass, I doubt not. 185

SIR AND. Oh, 'twill be admirable!

MAR. Sport royal, I warrant you. I know my physic will work with him. I will plant you two, and let the fool make a third, where he shall find the letter. Observe his construction of it. For 190 this night, to bed, and dream on the event. Farewell.
　　　　　　　　　　　　　　　　[Exit.]

SIR TO. Good night, Penthesilea.°

SIR AND. Before me, she's a good wench.

SIR TO. She's a beagle,° true-bred, and one that adores me. What o' that? 196

SIR AND. I was adored once too.

SIR TO. Let's to bed, knight. Thou hadst need send for more money.

SIR AND. If I cannot recover° your niece, I am a foul way out.° 201

SIR TO. Send for money, knight. If thou hast her not i' the end, call me cut.°

SIR AND. If I do not, never trust me, take it how you will. 205

SIR TO. Come, come, I'll go burn some sack.° 'Tis too late to go to bed now. Come, knight, come, knight.　　　　　　　　　　　　[Exeunt.]

SCENE IV. *The* DUKE's *palace.*

[*Enter* DUKE, VIOLA, CURIO, *and others.*]

DUKE. Give me some music. Now, good morrow, friends.
Now, good Cesario, but that piece of song,°

That old and antique song we heard last night.
Methought it did relieve my passion much,
More than light airs and recollected terms° 5
Of these most brisk and giddy-pacèd° times.
Come, but one verse.

CUR. He is not here, so please your lordship, that should sing it.

DUKE. Who was it? 10

CUR. Feste, the jester, my lord, a fool that the Lady Olivia's father took much delight in. He is about the house.

DUKE. Seek him out, and play the tune the while.
　　　　　　　[*Exit* CURIO. *Music plays.*]
Come hither, boy. If ever thou shalt love, 15
In the sweet pangs of it remember me;
For such as I am all truelovers are,
Unstaid and skittish in all motions else
Save in the constant image of the creature
That is beloved. How dost thou like this tune? 20

VIO. It gives a very echo to the seat
Where Love is throned.

DUKE. 　　　　　　　　　Thou dost speak masterly.
My life upon 't, young though thou art, thine eye
Hath stayed upon some favor° that it loves. 25
Hath it not, boy?

VIO. 　　　　　　　A little, by your favor.

DUKE. What kind of woman is 't?

VIO. 　　　　　　　　　　　　Of your complexion.

DUKE. She is not worth thee, then. What years, i' faith?

VIO. About your years, my lord.

DUKE. Too old, by Heaven. Let still° the woman take 30
An elder than herself, so wears she to him,
So sways she level in her husband's heart.
For, boy, however we do praise ourselves,
Our fancies are more giddy and unfirm,
More longing, wavering, sooner lost and worn, 35
Than women's are.

VIO. 　　　　　　　I think it well, my lord.

DUKE. Then let thy love be younger than thy-self,
Or thy affection cannot hold the bent.°
For women are as roses, whose fair flower
Being once displayed, doth fall that very hour. 40

VIO. And so they are. Alas, that they are so —
To die, even when they to perfection grow!
　　　　　　　　[*Re-enter* CURIO *and* CLOWN.]

DUKE. Oh, fellow, come, the song we had last night.
Mark it, Cesario, it is old and plain.
The spinsters and the knitters in the sun 45

---

172. feelingly: exactly. 192. Penthesilea: Queen of the Amazons, a large, muscular lady — an ironical description of the little gentlewoman. 195. beagle: a small hound. 200. recover: win. 201. foul . . . out: have wasted a lot of money. 203. cut: gelded. 206. burn . . . sack: warm some sack. Sack (Falstaff's favorite drink; see *II Hen IV*, IV.iii.103–35) was a Spanish wine. It was sometimes sweetened and drunk warm.

Sc. iv: 2. piece of song: another indication that Viola was originally intended to be the singer. See I.ii.57,n.

5. recollected terms: artificial phrases. 6. giddy-paced: frivolous. 25. favor: face. Viola (l. 26) in the safety of disguise takes up the word "by your favor," which Orsino interprets as "by your leave." 30. still: always. 38. hold . . . bent: keep the tension; the image is of a strung bow.

And the free maids that weave their thread with
  bones°
Do use to chant it. It is silly sooth,°
And dallies with the innocence of love,
Like the old age.
   CLO. Are you ready, sir?   50
   DUKE. Aye, prithee sing.   [*Music.*]
   CLO. [*Sings.*]
Come away, come away, death,
  And in sad cypress° let me be laid.
Fly away, fly away, breath,
  I am slain by a fair cruel maid.   55
My shroud° of white, stuck all with yew,
  Oh, prepare it!
My part of death, no one so true
  Did share it!

Not a flower, not a flower sweet,   60
  On my black coffin let there be strown.
Not a friend, not a friend greet
  My poor corpse, where my bones shall be thrown.
A thousand thousand sighs to save,
    Lay me, oh, where
Sad truelover never find my grave,
    To weep there!
   DUKE. There's for thy pains.   69
   CLO. No pains, sir. I take pleasure in singing, sir.
   DUKE. I'll pay thy pleasure then.
   CLO. Truly, sir, and pleasure will be paid, one
time or another.
   DUKE. Give me now leave to leave thee.   74
   CLO. Now, the melancholy god protect thee, and
the tailor make thy doublet° of changeable° taffeta,
for thy mind is a very opal. I would have men of
such constancy° put to sea, that their business might
be everything and their intent everywhere; for that's
it that always makes a good voyage of nothing. 80
Farewell.   [*Exit.*]
   DUKE. Let all the rest give place.
     [CURIO *and* ATTENDANTS *retire.*]
     Once more, Cesario,
Get thee to yond same sovereign cruelty.
Tell her my love, more noble than the world,
Prizes not quantity of dirty lands.   85
The parts° that fortune hath bestowed upon her,
Tell her I hold as giddily as fortune.°
But 'tis that miracle and queen of gems
That nature pranks° her in attracts my soul.
   VIO. But if she cannot love you, sir?   90
   DUKE. I cannot be so answered.
   VIO.   Sooth, but you must.

Say that some lady, as perhaps there is,
Hath for your love as great a pang of heart
As you have for Olivia. You cannot love her,
You tell her so. Must she not then be answered? 95
   DUKE. There is no woman's sides
Can bide the beating of so strong a passion
As love doth give my heart, no woman's heart
So big to hold so much. They lack retention.
Alas, their love may be called appetite —   100
No motion of the liver,° but the palate —
That suffer surfeit, cloyment, and revolt;
But mine is all as hungry as the sea,
And can digest as much. Make no compare
Between that love a woman can bear me   105
And that I owe Olivia.
   VIO.   Aye, but I know ——
   DUKE. What dost thou know?
   VIO. Too well what love women to men may owe.
In faith, they are as true of heart as we.
My father had a daughter loved a man,   110
As it might be, perhaps, were I a woman,
I should your lordship.
   DUKE.   And what's her history?
   VIO. A blank, my lord. She never told her love,
But let concealment, like a worm i' the bud,
Feed on her damask° cheek. She pined in thought,
And with a green and yellow melancholy   116
She sat like Patience on a monument,°
Smiling at grief. Was not this love indeed?
We men may say more, swear more, but indeed
Our shows are more than will,° for still we prove
Much in our vows, but little in our love.   121
   DUKE. But died thy sister of her love, my boy?
   VIO. I am all the daughters of my father's house,
And all the brothers too. And yet I know not.
Sir, shall I to this lady?
   DUKE.   Aye, that's the theme.   125
To her in haste. Give her this jewel. Say
My love can give no place, bide no denay.°
     [*Exeunt.*]

SCENE V. OLIVIA's *garden.*

[*Enter* SIR TOBY, SIR ANDREW, *and* FABIAN.]
   SIR TO. Come thy ways, Signior Fabian.
   FAB. Nay, I'll come. If I lose a scruple° of this
sport, let me be boiled to death with melancholy.
   SIR TO. Wouldst thou not be glad to have the nig-
gardly rascally sheepbiter° come by some notable
shame?   6
   FAB. I would exult, man. You know he brought

---

46. **weave . . . bones:** i.e., make lace with bone bobbins.
47. **silly sooth:** simple truth.   53. **cypress:** coffin of cypress
wood.   56. **shroud:** See App. 16.   76. **doublet:** jacket. See Pl.
8b and comment on p. 93a. **changeable:** changing its color as
the light falls.   78. **such constancy:** The fool is ironical, for
Orsino hitherto has been "to one thing constant never."
86. **parts:** wealth.   87. **giddily as fortune:** i.e., I am not inter-
ested in her wealth.   89. **pranks:** adorns.

101. **liver:** true passion, as in I.i.37.   115. **damask:** color of the
damask rose, pink and white.   117. **Patience . . . monument:** a
statue of Patience.   120. **Our . . . will:** our outward appearances
are greater than our feelings.   127. **denay:** denial.
   Sc. v: 2. **scruple:** minute part.   5. **sheepbiter:** sheepstealer.

me out o' favor with my lady about a bearbaiting° here. 10

SIR TO. To anger him we'll have the bear again, and we will fool him black and blue. Shall we not, Sir Andrew?

SIR AND. An we do not, it is pity of our lives. 15

SIR TO. Here comes the little villain. [*Enter* MARIA.] How now, my metal of India!°

MAR. Get ye all three into the box tree.° Malvolio's coming down this walk. He has been yonder i' the sun practicing behavior to his own shadow this 20 half-hour. Observe him, for the love of mockery, for I know this letter will make a contemplative idiot° of him. Close, in the name of jesting! Lie thou there, [*Throws down a letter*] for here comes the 25 trout that must be caught with tickling.° [*Exit.*]

[*Enter* MALVOLIO.]

MAL. 'Tis but fortune, all is fortune. Maria once told me she did affect me.° And I have heard herself come thus near, that, should she fancy, it should be one of my complexion. Besides, she uses me 30 with a more exalted respect than anyone else that follows her. What should I think on 't?

SIR TO. Here's an overweening rogue! 34

FAB. Oh, peace! Contemplation makes a rare turkeycock of him. How he jets under his advanced plumes!°

SIR AND. 'Slight,° I could so beat the rogue!

SIR TO. Peace, I say.

MAL. To be Count Malvolio! 40

SIR TO. Ah, rogue!

SIR AND. Pistol him, pistol him.

SIR TO. Peace, peace!

MAL. There is example for 't. The lady of the Strachy° married the yeoman of the wardrobe.° 45

SIR AND. Fie on him, Jezebel!°

FAB. Oh, peace! Now he's deeply in. Look how imagination blows him.

MAL. Having been three months married to her, sitting in my state° —— 50

SIR TO. Oh, for a stonebow,° to hit him in the eye!

MAL. Calling my officers about me, in my branched° velvet gown, having come from a day bed,° where I have left Olivia sleeping —— 55

SIR TO. Fire and brimstone!

FAB. Oh, peace, peace!

MAL. And then to have the humor of state.° And after a demure travel of regard,° telling them I know my place as I would they should do theirs, to ask for my kinsman Toby —— 61

SIR TO. Bolts and shackles!

FAB. Oh, peace, peace, peace! Now, now.

MAL. Seven of my people, with an obedient start, make out for him. I frown the while, and per- 65 chance wind up my watch, or play with my — some rich jewel.° Toby approaches, curtsies there to me ——

SIR TO. Shall this fellow live?

FAB. Though our silence be drawn from us with cars,° yet peace. 71

MAL. I extend my hand to him thus, quenching my familiar smile with an austere regard of control° ——

SIR TO. And does not Toby take you a blow o' the lips then? 76

MAL. Saying, "Cousin Toby, my fortunes having cast me on your niece, give me this prerogative° of speech ——"

SIR TO. What, what? 80

MAL. "You must amend your drunkenness."

SIR TO. Out, scab!

FAB. Nay, patience, or we break the sinews of our plot.

MAL. "Besides, you waste the treasure of your time with a foolish knight ——" 86

SIR AND. That's me, I warrant you.

MAL. "One Sir Andrew ——"

SIR AND. I knew 'twas I, for many do call me fool.

MAL. What employment have we here? 91

[*Taking up the letter.*]

FAB. Now is the woodcock° near the gin.°

SIR TO. Oh, peace! And the spirit of humors° intimate reading aloud to him! 94

MAL. By my life, this is my lady's hand. These be her very C's, her U's, and her T's; and thus makes she her great P's. It is, in contempt of question,° her hand.

SIR AND. Her C's, her U's and her T's. Why that? 100

MAL. [*Reads.*] "To the unknown beloved, this, and my good wishes: — " Her very phrases! By your leave, wax.° Soft, and the impressure her Lucrece,°

---

9. **bearbaiting:** a popular sport, detested by the Puritans. See App. 5. 17. **metal of India:** fine gold. 18. **box tree:** an evergreen shrub much used by Elizabethan gardeners for ornamental hedges. 22. **contemplative idiot:** pompous ass. 26. **caught . . . tickling:** a poacher's method of catching trout with the bare hand. 28. **she . . . me:** Olivia liked me. 36–37. **jets . . . plumes:** struts with his tail feathers up. 38. **'Slight:** by God's light. 44–45. **lady . . . Strachy:** She has not been identified. 45. **yeoman . . . wardrobe:** in a great household each department was under the control of a *yeoman*, or upper servant, and a "gentleman." See App. 14. 46. **Jezebel:** Andrew's knowledge of the Bible is weak, but at least he does know that Jezebel was a shameless person. 50. **state:** chair of state. 51. **stonebow:** crossbow for shooting stones. See Pl. 22c. 54. **branched:** embroidered with a pattern of leaves and branches. See Pl. 8b. 55. **day bed:** couch.

58. **humor of state:** dignified manner of some statesman. 59. **demure . . . regard:** glancing gravely from one to the other. 66–67. **my — some rich jewel:** Malvolio inadvertently touches his steward's chain. 70–71. **drawn . . . cars:** though we should be torn to pieces by chariots and wild horses. 73–74. **austere . . . control:** severe look of authority. 78. **prerogative:** privilege. 92. **woodcock:** regarded as a very simple bird. **gin:** trap. 93. **spirit of humors:** i.e., of mockery, as in a comedy of humors. See Gen. Intro. p. 42a and App. 3. 97. **contempt of question:** without any doubt. 103. **wax:** See App. 6. **her Lucrece:** the head of Lucrece, the device on her seal.

with which she uses to seal. 'Tis my lady. To whom
should this be?   105

FAB. This wins, him, liver and all.

MAL. [*Reads.*] " Jove knows I love.
         But who?
         Lips, do not move.
         No man must know."   110
"No man must know." What follows? The num-
bers° altered! "No man must know." If this should
be thee, Malvolio?

SIR TO. Marry, hang thee, brock!°

MAL. [*Reads.*]
" I may command where I adore,   115
         But silence, like a Lucrece knife,°
With bloodless stroke my heart doth gore.
         M, O, A, I, doth sway my life."

FAB. A fustian° riddle!

SIR TO. Excellent wench, say I.   120

MAL. " M, O, A, I, doth sway my life." Nay, but
first, let me see, let me see, let me see.

FAB. What dish o' poison has she dressed him!

SIR TO. And with what wing the staniel° checks
at it!   125

MAL. " I may command where I adore." Why, she
may command me. I serve her, she is my lady. Why,
this is evident to any formal capacity,° there is no ob-
struction in this. And the end — what should that
alphabetical position portend? If I could make   130
that resemble something in me —— Softly! M, O, A,
I ——

SIR TO. Oh, aye, make up that. He is now at a cold
scent.

FAB. Sowter° will cry upon 't for all this, though
it be as rank as a fox.°   136

MAL. M — Malvolio. M — why, that begins my
name.

FAB. Did not I say he would work it out? The cur
is excellent at faults.°   140

MAL. M — but then there is no consonancy° in
the sequel, that suffers under probation.° A should
follow, but O does.

FAB. And O shall end, I hope.

SIR TO. Aye, or I'll cudgel him and make him cry
O!   146

MAL. And then I comes behind.

FAB. Aye, an you had any eye behind you, you
might see more detraction at your heels than for-
tunes before you.   150

MAL. M, O, A, I. This simulation° is not as the

former. And yet, to crush° this a little, it would bow
to me,° for every one of these letters are in my name.
Soft! Here follows prose. [*Reads.*]   154

" If this fall into thy hand, revolve.° In my stars°
I am above thee; but be not afraid of greatness. Some
are born great, some achieve greatness, and some
have greatness thrust upon 'em. Thy Fates open
their hands. Let thy blood and spirit embrace them,
and to inure thyself to what thou art like to be,   160
cast thy humble slough° and appear fresh. Be oppo-
site with a kinsman, surly with servants, let thy
tongue tang° arguments of state, put thyself into the
trick of singularity.° She thus advises thee that sighs
for thee. Remember who commended thy yel-   165
low stockings, and wished to see thee ever cross-
gartered.° I say, remember. Go to, thou art made,
if thou desirest to be so. If not, let me see thee a
steward still, the fellow of servants, and not worthy
to touch Fortune's fingers. Farewell. She that   170
would alter services with thee,
            " THE FORTUNATE-UNHAPPY "

Daylight and champain° discovers not more. This is
open. I will be proud, I will read politic au-   175
thors,° I will baffle° Sir Toby, I will wash off gross
acquaintance, I will be point-device° the very man. I
do not now fool myself, to let imagination jade me,°
for every reason excites to this, that my lady loves
me. She did commend my yellow stockings of   180
late, she did praise my leg being cross-gartered; and
in this she manifests herself to my love, and with a
kind of injunction drives me to these habits of her
liking. I thank my stars I am happy. I will be
strange,° stout,° in yellow stockings, and cross-   185
gartered, even with the swiftness of putting on. Jove
and my stars be praised! Here is yet a postscript.
                              [*Reads.*]

" Thou canst not choose but know who I am. If
thou entertainest my love, let it appear in thy   190
smiling. Thy smiles become thee well, therefore in
my presence still smile, dear my sweet, i prithee."

Jove, I thank thee. I will smile, I will do every-   194
thing that thou wilt have me.   [*Exit.*]

FAB. I will not give my part of this sport for a
pension of thousands to be paid from the Sophy.°

SIR TO. I could marry this wench for this de-
vice ——   200

---

112. numbers: meter.   **114.** brock: badger.   **116.** Lucrece knife:
the knife with which Lucrece killed herself.   **119.** fustian: coarse
cloth, so "common."   **124.** staniel: kestrel, an inferior kind of
hawk. See App. 26.   **128.** formal capacity: normal intelligence.
135. Sowter: lit., cobbler, nickname for a clumsy hound.
135–36. cry . . . fox: he'll make a great cry, and follow it up, for
the scent is as strong as a fox's.   **140.** excellent at faults: will
follow the scent, however bad. fault: a break in a scent.   **141.** con-
sonancy: consistency.   **142.** suffers . . . probation: fails when
tested.   **151.** simulation: disguised meaning.

152. crush: force.   **152–53.** bow . . . me: incline my way.   **155.** re-
volve: ponder. stars: fate.   **161.** slough: snakeskin.   **163.** tang:
resound.   **164.** trick of singularity: unusual behavior.
166–67. cross-gartered: See Pl. 8c and comment on p. 93b.
174. champain: open country.   **175–76.** politic authors: books on
statecraft.   **176.** baffle: bring into disgrace. See *Rich II*, I.i.170,n.
177. point-device: exactly.   **178.** jade me: play me a dirty trick.
185. strange: distant. stout: haughty.   **198.** Sophy: Shah of
Persia. See *T Night* Intro. p. 565a.

SIR AND. So could I too.

SIR TO. And ask no other dowry with her but such another jest.

SIR AND. Nor I neither.

FAB. Here comes my noble gull-catcher.°   205

[*Re-enter* MARIA.]

SIR TO. Wilt thou set thy foot o' my neck?

SIR AND. Or o' mine either?

SIR TO. Shall I play my freedom at trey-trip,° and become thy bondslave?

SIR AND. I' faith, or I either?   210

SIR TO. Why, thou hast put him in such a dream that when the image of it leaves him he must run mad.

MAR. Nay, but say true. Does it work upon him?

SIR TO. Like aqua vitae° with a midwife.   216

MAR. If you will then see the fruits of the sport, mark his first approach before my lady. He will come to her in yellow stockings, and 'tis a color she abhors, and cross-gartered, a fashion she detests.   220 And he will smile upon her, which will now be so unsuitable to her disposition, being addicted to a melancholy as she is, that it cannot but turn him into a notable contempt. If you will see it, follow me.   225

SIR TO. To the gates of Tartar, thou most excellent devil of wit!

SIR AND. I'll make one too.   [*Exeunt.*]

Act III

SCENE I. OLIVIA's *garden.*

[*Enter* VIOLA, *and* CLOWN *with a tabor.*°]

VIO. Save thee, friend, and thy music. Dost thou live by thy tabor?

CLO. No, sir, I live by the church.

VIO. Art thou a churchman?°   4

CLO. No such matter, sir. I do live by the church, for I do live at my house, and my house doth stand by° the church.

VIO. So thou mayst say the King lies by a beggar, if a beggar dwell near him, or the church stands by thy tabor, if thy tabor stand by the church.   11

CLO. You have said, sir. To see this age! A sentence is but a cheveril° glove to a good wit. How quickly the wrong side may be turned outward!   15

VIO. Nay, that's certain. They that dally° nicely with words may quickly make them wanton.

CLO. I would, therefore, my sister had had no name, sir.   20

VIO. Why, man?

CLO. Why, sir, her name's a word, and to dally with that word might make my sister wanton. But indeed words are very rascals since bonds disgraced them.°   25

VIO. Thy reason, man?

CLO. Troth, sir, I can yield you none without words, and words are grown so false I am loath to prove reason with them.   29

VIO. I warrant thou art a merry fellow and carest for nothing.

CLO. Not so, sir. I do care for something, but in my conscience, sir, I do not care for you. If that be to care for nothing, sir, I would it would make you invisible.   35

VIO. Art not thou the Lady Olivia's fool?

CLO. No indeed, sir. The Lady Olivia has no folly. She will keep no fool, sir, till she be married, and fools are as like husbands as pilchards° are to herrings — the husband's the bigger. I am indeed not her fool, but her corrupter of words.   41

VIO. I saw thee late at the Count Orsino's.

CLO. Foolery, sir, does walk about the orb like the sun. It shines everywhere. I would be sorry, sir, but the fool should be as oft with your master as with my mistress. I think I saw your wisdom there.   47

VIO. Nay, an thou pass upon° me, I'll no more with thee. Hold, there's expenses for thee.

CLO. Now Jove, in his next commodity° of hair, send thee a beard!   51

VIO. By my troth, I'll tell thee, I am almost sick for one — [*Aside*] though I would not have it grow on my chin. Is thy lady within?

CLO. Would not a pair of these° have bred, sir?

VIO. Yes, being kept together and put to use.   56

CLO. I would play Lord Pandarus° of Phrygia,° sir, to bring a Cressida to this Troilus.

VIO. I understand you, sir. 'Tis well begged.   60

CLO. The matter, I hope, is not great, sir, begging but a beggar.° Cressida was a beggar. My lady is within, sir. I will construe to them whence you come, who you are and what you would are out of my welkin — I might say " element,"° but the word   65 is overworn.   [*Exit.*]

16. dally: play.   23–25. sister . . . them: See *T Night* Intro. p. 565b.   39. pilchard: a smaller variety of herring.   48. pass upon: make a thrust at.   50. commodity: consignment. 55. pair of these: i.e., wouldn't you like to give me another coin? 57. Pandarus: the go-between in the love affair of Cressida and Troilus. See *Tr & Cr.* Phrygia: the district of Asia Minor in which Troy stood.   61–62. The . . . beggar: the Clown is himself an incorrigible beggar. See V.i.31–42.   65. welkin . . . element: both words mean sky. *Element* is still overworn by writers of textbooks who cannot avoid the "supernatural element," the "pastoral element," etc.

205. gull-catcher: fool-catcher.   208. trey-trip: game played with cards and dice.   216. aqua vitae: spirits especially favored by old women such as Juliet's Nurse. See *R & J*, IV.v.16.
Act III, Sc. i: s.d., tabor: small drum. See Pl. 13d.
4. churchman: cleric.   7. by: near.   14. cheveril: kidskin.

vio. This fellow° is wise enough to play the fool,
And to do that well craves° a kind of wit.
He must observe their mood on whom he jests,
The quality of persons, and the time,   70
And, like the haggard,° check at° every feather
That comes before his eye. This is a practice
As full of labor as a wise man's art.
For folly that he wisely shows is fit,
But wise men, folly-fall'n, quite taint their wit.   75
          [*Enter* sir toby, *and* sir andrew.]
sir to. Save° you, gentleman.
vio. And you, sir.
sir and. *Dieu vous garde, monsieur.*
vio. *Et vous aussi. Votre serviteur.*
sir and. I hope, sir, you are, and I am yours.   81
sir to. Will you encounter° the house? My niece
is desirous you should enter, if your trade be to her.
vio. I am bound to your niece, sir. I mean she is
the list° of my voyage.   86
sir to. Taste your legs, sir, put them to motion.
vio. My legs do better understand me, sir, than I
understand what you mean by bidding me taste my
legs.   91
sir to. I mean to go, sir, to enter.
vio. I will answer you with gait and entrance. But
we are prevented.° [*Enter* olivia *and* maria.] Most
excellent accomplished lady, the heavens rain odors
on you!   96
sir and. That youth's a rare courtier. "Rain
odors," well.
vio. My matter hath no voice, lady, but to your
own most pregnant° and vouchsafed° ear.   100
sir and. "Odors," "pregnant," and "vouch-
safed." I'll get 'em all three all ready.
oli. Let the garden door be shut, and leave me to
my hearing. [*Exeunt* sir toby, sir andrew, *and*
maria.] Give me your hand, sir.   105
vio. My duty, madam, and most humble service.
oli. What is your name?
vio. Cesario is your servant's name, fair Princess.
oli. My servant, sir! 'Twas never merry world
Since lowly feigning was called compliment.   110
You're servant to the Count Orsino, youth.
vio. And he is yours, and his must needs be yours.
Your servant's servant is your servant, madam.
oli. For him, I think not on him. For his
          thoughts,
Would they were blanks rather than filled with me!
vio. Madam, I come to whet your gentle thoughts
On his behalf.   117

oli.   Oh, by your leave, I pray you,
I bade you never speak again of him.
But would you undertake another suit,
I had rather hear you to solicit that   120
Than music from the spheres.°
vio.   Dear lady ——
oli. Give me leave, beseech you. I did send,
After the last enchantment you did here,
A ring in chase of you. So did I abuse°
Myself, my servant, and, I fear me, you.   125
Under your hard construction° must I sit,
To force that on you, in a shameful cunning,
Which you knew none of yours. What might you
          think?
Have you not set mine honor at the stake
And baited it with all the unmuzzled thoughts°
That tyrannous heart can think? To one of your re-
          ceiving°   131
Enough is shown. A cypress,° not a bosom,
Hides my heart. So let me hear you speak.
vio. I pity you.
oli.   That's a degree to love.
vio. No, not a grize,° for 'tis a vulgar proof°
That very oft we pity enemies.   136
oli. Why, then, methinks 'tis time to smile again.
O world, how apt the poor are to be proud!
If one should be a prey, how much the better
To fall before the lion than the wolf!   140
          [*Clock strikes.*]
The clock upbraids me with the waste of time.
Be not afraid, good youth, I will not have you.
And yet, when wit and youth is come to harvest,
Your wife is like to reap a proper man.
There lies your way, due west.
vio.   Then westward ho!°   145
Grace and good disposition attend your ladyship!
You'll nothing, madam, to my lord by me?
oli. Stay.
I prithee tell me what thou think'st of me.   150
vio. That you do think you are not what you are.
oli. If I think so, I think the same of you.
vio. Then think you right. I am not what I am.
oli. I would you were as I would have you be!
vio. Would it be better, madam, than I am?   155
I wish it might, for now I am your fool.
oli. Oh, what a deal of scorn looks beautiful
In the contempt and anger of his lip!
A murderous guilt shows not itself more soon
Than love that would seem hid. Love's night is
          noon.   160
Cesario, by the roses of the spring,

---

67. **This fellow:** See *T Night* Intro. p. 565a–b. 68. **craves:** calls
for. 71. **haggard:** wild hawk. As this line seems to contra-
dict the preceding, some editors emend "And" to "But." **check
at:** go after. 76. **Save:** God save. 82. **encounter:** lit., go to
meet. Toby addresses this young courtier with the extravagant
terms fashionable at the time. 86. **list:** boundary, objective.
94. **prevented:** forestalled. 100. **pregnant:** receptive. **vouch-
safed:** condescending.

121. **music . . . spheres:** See App. 1, and *M of Ven*, V.i.60.
124. **abuse:** wrong. 126. **construction:** interpretation, judg-
ment. 129. **at . . . thoughts:** An image from bearbaiting. See
App. 5. 131. **receiving:** understanding. 132. **cypress:** a sheer
material. 135. **grize:** step. **vulgar proof:** common experience.
145. **westward ho:** the Thames waterman's cry. See Gen. Intro.
p. 16b.

By maidhood, honor, truth, and everything,
I love thee so, that, mauger° all thy pride,
Nor wit nor reason can my passion hide.
Do not extort thy reasons from this clause, 165
For that I woo, thou therefore hast no cause,
But rather reason thus with reason fetter,
Love sought is good, but given unsought is better.°
VIO. By innocence I swear, and by my youth,
I have one heart, one bosom, and one truth, 170
And that no woman has; nor never none
Shall mistress be of it, save I alone.
And so adieu, good madam. Nevermore
Will I my master's tears to you deplore.
OLI. Yet come again, for thou perhaps mayst
        move 175
That heart which now abhors to like his love.

[*Exeunt.*]

SCENE II. OLIVIA's *house.*

[*Enter* SIR TOBY, SIR ANDREW, *and* FABIAN.]
SIR AND. No, faith, I'll not stay a jot longer.
SIR TO. Thy reason, dear venom,° give thy reason.
FAB. You must needs yield your reason, Sir Andrew.   5
SIR AND. Marry, I saw your niece do more favors to the Count's servingman° than ever she bestowed upon me. I saw 't i' the orchard.
SIR TO. Did she see thee the while, old boy? Tell me that.   10
SIR AND. As plain as I see you now.
FAB. This was a great argument of love in her toward you.
SIR AND. 'Slight, will you make an ass o' me?
FAB. I will prove it legitimate, sir, upon the oaths of judgment and reason.   16
SIR TO. And they have been grand jurymen° since before Noah was a sailor.
FAB. She did show favor to the youth in your sight only to exasperate you, to awake your dormouse 20 valor, to put fire in your heart and brimstone in your liver. You should then have accosted her, and with some excellent jests, fire-new from the mint,° you should have banged the youth into dumbness. This was looked for at your hand, and this was 25 balked. The double gilt° of this opportunity you

let time wash off, and you are now sailed into the north of my lady's opinion, where you will hang like an icicle on a Dutchman's beard unless you do redeem it by some laudable attempt either of valor or policy.   31
SIR AND. An 't be any way, it must be with valor, for policy I hate. I had as lief be a Brownist° as a politician.   34
SIR TO. Why then, build me thy fortunes upon the basis of valor. Challenge me the Count's youth to fight with him. Hurt him in eleven places. My niece shall take note of it, and assure thyself there is no love broker° in the world can more prevail in man's commendation with woman than report of valor.   41
FAB. There is no way but this, Sir Andrew.
SIR AND. Will either of you bear me a challenge to him?
SIR TO. Go, write it in a martial hand. Be 45 curst° and brief. It is no matter how witty, so it be eloquent and full of invention.° Taunt him with the license of ink. If thou thou'st° him some thrice, it shall not be amiss. And as many lies as will lie 49 in thy sheet of paper, although the sheet were big enough for the bed of Ware° in England, set 'em down. Go, about it. Let there be gall° enough in thy ink, though thou write with a goose pen,° no matter. About it.
SIR AND. Where shall I find you?   55
SIR TO. We'll call thee at the cubiculo.° Go.

[*Exit* SIR ANDREW.]
FAB. This is a dear manikin to you, Sir Toby.
SIR TO. I have been dear to him, lad, some two thousand strong, or so.°
FAB. We shall have a rare letter from him. But you'll not deliver 't?   61
SIR TO. Never trust me, then, and by all means stir on the youth to an answer. I think oxen and wainropes° cannot hale them together. For Andrew, if he were opened and you find so much blood in his liver as will clog the foot of a flea, I'll eat the rest of the anatomy.   67
FAB. And his opposite, the youth, bears in his visage no great presage of cruelty.

163. mauger: in spite of. 165–68. Do . . . better: i.e., do not argue to yourself that because I (the woman) am the wooer, you should therefore have no reason to return my love; rather rebut that argument by this — it is good for a man to ask for a woman's love, but better still to receive it without asking. Sc. ii: 2. venom: poison, because Andrew is full of hate. 7. servingman: See App. 14. 17. grand juryman: The grand jury was chosen from the most respectable citizens. Fabian means "Judgment and Reason have been a most highly respected pair since the Flood." 23. fire-new . . . mint: i.e., as bright as new pennies. 26. double gilt: The best gold plate

was twice dipped. Fabian amuses himself and Toby by puzzling Andrew with this metaphorical talk. 33. Brownist: The Brownists were one of the most extreme sects of Puritans. 39. love broker: go-between in making a marriage, an important office when marriages were arranged. 46. curst: vicious. 47. invention: wit. 48. thou thou'st: to call a stranger "thou" was a considerable insult, as it implied that he was an inferior. 51. bed of Ware: a famous bed, made after the pattern of the bed illustrated in Pl. 17b. It could hold 7 couples at a time. It is now in the Victoria and Albert Museum in London. 52. gall: "oak apple," produced in the branches of an oak by a parasite, and used for making ink. Toby puns on "gall," meaning bitterness. 53. goose pen: the pen used at this time was made of a goose quill. 56. cubiculo: bedchamber. 58–59. I . . . so: I've cost him some 2,000 ducats. 64. wainropes: cart ropes.

[*Enter* MARIA.]

SIR TO. Look where the youngest wren of nine°
comes.　　　　　　　　　　　　　　　　　　71

MAR. If you desire the spleen, and will laugh your-
self into stitches, follow me. Yond gull Malvolio is
turned heathen, a very renegado,° for there is no
Christian that means to be saved by believing　75
rightly can ever believe such impossible passages of
grossness. He's in yellow stockings.

SIR TO. And cross-gartered?　　　　　　　79

MAR. Most villainously, like a pedant that keeps a
school i' the church. I have dogged him like his mur-
derer. He does obey every point of the letter that I
dropped to betray him. He does smile his face into
more lines than is in the new map° with the aug-
mentation of the Indies. You have not seen such　85
a thing as 'tis. I can hardly forbear hurling things
at him. I know my lady will strike him. If she do,
he'll smile and take 't for a great favor.

SIR TO. Come, bring us, bring us where he is.　90
　　　　　　　　　　　　　　　　　[*Exeunt.*]

SCENE III. *A street.*

[*Enter* SEBASTIAN *and* ANTONIO.]

SEB. I would not by my will have troubled you,
But since you make your pleasure of your pains,
I will no further chide you.

ANT.　　　I could not stay behind you. My desire,
More sharp than filèd steel, did spur me forth;　5
And not all love to see you, though so much
As might have drawn one to a longer voyage,
But jealousy what might befall your travel,
Being skill-less in these parts, which to a stranger,
Unguided and unfriended, often prove　　　10
Rough and unhospitable. My willing love,
The rather by these arguments of fear,
Set forth in your pursuit.

SEB.　　　　　　My kind Antonio,
I can no other answer make but thanks,
And thanks, and everoft° good turns　　　15
Are shuffled off with such uncurrent° pay.
But were my worth as is my conscience firm,
You should find better dealing. What's to do?
Shall we go see the reliques° of this town?

ANT. Tomorrow, sir. Best first go see your lodg-
ing.　　　　　　　　　　　　　　　　20

SEB. I am not weary, and 'tis long to night.
I pray you, let us satisfy our eyes
With the memorials and the things of fame
That do renown this city.

ANT.　　　　　　　　Would you'd pardon me.
I do not without danger walk these streets.　25
Once, in a sea fight, 'gainst the Count his galleys
I did some service, of such note indeed
That were I ta'en here it would scarce be answered.

SEB. Belike you slew great number of his people.

ANT. The offense is not of such a bloody nature,
Albeit the quality° of the time and quarrel　31
Might well have given us bloody argument.
It might have since been answered in repaying
What we took from them, which, for traffic's sake,°
Most of our city did. Only myself stood out,　35
For which, if I be lapsèd° in this place,
I shall pay dear.

SEB.　　　　Do not then walk too open.

ANT. It doth not fit me. Hold, sir, here's my purse.
In the south suburbs, at the Elephant,°
Is best to lodge. I will bespeak our diet°　40
While you beguile the time and feed your knowl-
　edge
With viewing of the town. There shall you have me.

SEB. Why I your purse?

ANT. Haply° your eye shall light upon some toy°
You have desire to purchase, and your store,　45
I think, is not for idle markets,° sir.

SEB. I'll be your purse bearer and leave you
For an hour.

ANT.　　　To the Elephant.

SEB. I do remember.　　　　　　　[*Exeunt.*]

SCENE IV. OLIVIA's *garden.*

[*Enter* OLIVIA *and* MARIA.]

OLI. I have sent after him. He says he'll come.
How shall I feast him? What bestow of him?°
For youth is bought more oft than begged or bor-
　rowed.
I speak too loud.
Where is Malvolio? He is sad and civil,°　　5
And suits well for a servant with my fortunes.
Where is Malvolio?

MAR. He's coming, madam, but in very strange
manner. He is sure possessed,° madam.

OLI. Why, what's the matter? Does he rave?　10

MAR. No, madam, he does nothing but smile.
Your ladyship were best to have some guard about
you if he come, for sure the man is tainted in 's wits.

OLI. Go call him hither. [*Exit* MARIA.] I am as
　mad as he,　　　　　　　　　　　　　15
If sad and merry madness equal be.

---

70. **youngest . . . nine:** the youngest of the brood, sometimes
called the "rickling," is often smaller than the rest. The wren is
the smallest of English birds.　　74. **renegado:** Christian turned
heathen.　　84. **new map:** See *T Night* Intro. p. 565a, and Pl. IA.
　　Sc. iii: 15. **and . . . oft:** Two words have apparently been
omitted in this line. Some editors read "ever *thanks, and* oft."
16. **uncurrent:** worthless.　　19. **reliques:** antiquities.

31. **quality:** nature.　　34. **traffic's sake:** for the sake of business.
36. **lapsed:** taken.　　39. **Elephant:** There was a famous London
Inn of this name on the south side of the Thames; it is now
known as the Elephant and Castle.　　40. **bespeak . . . diet:** order
our dinner.　　44. **Haply:** perchance. **toy:** trifle.　　46. **idle markets:**
unnecessary purchases.
　　Sc. iv: 2. **of him:** on him.　　5. **civil:** sober, serious.　　9. **pos-
sessed:** i.e., with an evil spirit. See *T Night* Intro. p. 567a-b.

[*Re-enter* MARIA, *with* MALVOLIO.] How now, Malvolio!

MAL. Sweet lady, ho, ho.

OLI. Smilest thou?
I sent for thee upon a sad occasion.   20

MAL. Sad, lady? I could be sad. This does make some obstruction in the blood, this cross-gartering, but what of that? If it please the eye of one, it is with me as the very true sonnet is, "Please one, and please all."°   25

OLI. Why, how dost thou, man? What is the matter with thee?

MAL. Not black in my mind, though yellow in my legs. It did come to his hands, and commands shall be executed. I think we do know the sweet Roman hand.°   31

OLI. Wilt thou go to bed, Malvolio?

MAL. To bed! Aye, sweetheart, and I'll come to thee.

OLI. God comfort thee! Why dost thou smile so and kiss thy hand so oft?   36

MAR. How do you, Malvolio?

MAL. At your request! Yes, nightingales answer daws.°

MAR. Why appear you with this ridiculous boldness before my lady?   41

MAL. "Be not afraid of greatness." 'Twas well writ.

OLI. What meanest thou by that, Malvolio?

MAL. "Some are born great——"   45

OLI. Ha!

MAL. "Some achieve greatness——"

OLI. What sayest thou?

MAL. "And some have greatness thrust upon them."   50

OLI. Heaven restore thee!

MAL. "Remember who commended thy yellow stockings."

OLI. Thy yellow stockings!

MAL. "And wished to see thee cross-gartered."

OLI. Cross-gartered!   56

MAL. "Go to, thou art made, if thou desirest to be so."

OLI. Am I made?   59

MAL. "If not, let me see thee a servant still."

OLI. Why, this is very midsummer madness.

[*Enter* SERVANT.]

SERV. Madam, the young gentleman of the Count Orsino's is returned. I could hardly entreat him back. He attends your ladyship's pleasure.   65

OLI. I'll come to him. [*Exit* SERVANT.] Good Maria, let this fellow be looked to. Where's my cousin Toby? Let some of my people have a special care of him. I would not have him miscarry° for the half of my dowry.   [*Exeunt* OLIVIA *and* MARIA.]   69

MAL. Oh, ho! Do you come near me now? No worse man than Sir Toby to look to me! This concurs directly with the letter. She sends him on purpose, that I may appear stubborn to him, for she incites me to that in the letter. "Cast thy humble slough," says she. "Be opposite with a kinsman, surly with servants, let thy tongue tang with arguments of state, put thyself into the trick of singularity"—and consequently sets down the manner how, as a sad face, a reverend carriage, a slow tongue, in the habit of some sir of note,° and so forth. I have limed° her, but it is Jove's doing, and Jove make me thankful! And when she went away now, "Let this fellow be looked to." Fellow! Not Malvolio, nor after my degree, but fellow.° Why, everything adheres together, that no dram of a scruple,° no scruple of a scruple, no obstacle, no incredulous or unsafe circumstance——What can be said? Nothing that can be can come between me and the full prospect of my hopes. Well, Jove, not I, is the doer of this, and he is to be thanked.   75 80 85 90

[*Re-enter* MARIA, *with* SIR TOBY *and* FABIAN.]

SIR TO. Which way is he, in the name of sanctity? If all the devils of Hell be drawn in little,° and Legion himself° possessed him, yet I'll speak to him.   96

FAB. Here he is, here he is. How is 't with you, sir? How is 't with you, man?

MAL. Go off, I discard you. Let me enjoy my private. Go off.   100

MAR. Lo, how hollow the fiend speaks within him! Did not I tell you? Sir Toby, my lady prays you to have a care of him.

MAL. Ah, ha! Does she so?   104

SIR TO. Go to, go to; peace, peace. We must deal gently with him. Let me alone. How do you, Malvolio? How is 't with you? What, man! defy the Devil. Consider, he's an enemy to mankind.

MAL. Do you know what you say?   110

MAR. La you, an you speak ill of the Devil, how he takes it at heart! Pray God he be not bewitched!

FAB. Carry his water° to the wise woman.   114

24–25. **Please . . . all:** The ditty is not a sonnet but a ballad, called "The crow sits upon the wall, Please one and please all." It was not at all the kind of song suitable for Malvolio. 31. **Roman hand:** The Italian handwriting (from which modern handwriting and *italic* type derives) was coming into fashion among aristocratic writers, and superseding the old English "Court" or "secretary" hand. 38–39. **nightingales . . . daws:** songbirds answer jackdaws.

69. **miscarry:** come to harm. 81. **sir of note:** great man. 82. **limed:** caught, as with birdlime. 86. **fellow:** the word has a double meaning. The fellow of a college or learned society is a man of dignity; the word is also used of an inferior. 87. **dram . . . scruple:** minutest part. 94. **in little:** into a small space. 95. **Legion himself:** the name given to the devils cast out of the man from the tombs (Mark 5: 1–19). Toby pretends that Malvolio is possessed and treats him accordingly. Witches (who could be of either sex) were often accused of causing possession. See *T Night* Intro. p. 567a–b. 114. **his water:** diagnosis of diseases by inspection of the urine was practiced by qualified doctors as well as by quacks. Cf. the gloomy report on Falstaff's health (*II Hen IV*, I.ii.1–6).

MAR. Marry, and it shall be done tomorrow morning, if I live. My lady would not lose him for more than I'll say.

MAL. How now, mistress!

MAR. Oh Lord!   119

SIR TO. Prithee, hold thy peace, this is not the way. Do you not see you move him? Let me alone with him.

FAB. No way but gentleness — gently, gently. The fiend is rough, and will not be roughly used.

SIR TO. Why, how now, my bawcock!° How dost thou, chuck?°   126

MAL. Sir!

SIR TO. Aye, biddy,° come with me. What, man! 'Tis not for gravity to play at cherry pit° with Satan. Hang him, foul collier!°   130

MAR. Get him to say his prayers, good Sir Toby, get him to pray.

MAL. My prayers, minx!

MAR. No, I warrant you, he will not hear of godliness.°   135

MAL. Go, hang yourselves all! You are idle shallow things. I am not of your element. You shall know more hereafter.   [Exit.]

SIR TO. Is 't possible?

FAB. If this were played upon a stage now, I could condemn it as an improbable fiction.   141

SIR TO. His very genius° hath taken the infection° of the device,° man.

MAR. Nay, pursue him now, lest the device take air and taint.°   145

FAB. Why, we shall make him mad indeed.

MAR. The house will be the quieter.

SIR TO. Come, we'll have him in a dark room and bound. My niece is already in the belief that he's mad. We may carry it thus, for our pleasure   150 and his penance, till our very pastime, tired out of breath, prompt us to have mercy on him, at which time we will bring the device to the bar° and crown thee for a finder of madmen. But see, but see.   155

[Enter SIR ANDREW.]

FAB. More matter for a May morning.°

SIR AND. Here's the challenge, read it. I warrant there's vinegar and pepper in 't.

FAB. Is 't so saucy?   159

SIR AND. Aye, is 't, I warrant him. Do but read.

SIR TO. Give me. [Reads.] "Youth, whatsoever thou art, thou art but a scurvy fellow."

FAB. Good, and valiant.   163

SIR TO. [Reads.] "Wonder not, nor admire° not in thy mind, why I do call thee so, for I will show thee no reason for 't."

FAB. A good note. That keeps you from the blow of the law.   169

SIR TO. [Reads.] "Thou comest to the Lady Olivia, and in my sight she uses thee kindly; but thou liest in thy throat.° That is not the matter I challenge thee for."

FAB. Very brief, and to exceeding good sense — less.   175

SIR TO. [Reads.] "I will waylay thee going home, where if it be thy chance to kill me ——"

FAB. Good.

SIR TO. [Reads.] "Thou killest me like a rogue and a villain."   180

FAB. Still you keep o' the windy side° of the law. Good.

SIR TO. [Reads.] "Fare thee well, and God have mercy upon one of our souls! He may have mercy upon mine, but my hope is better, and so look to thyself. Thy friend, as thou usest him, and thy sworn enemy,   ANDREW AGUECHEEK."
If this letter move him not, his legs cannot. I'll give 't him.   189

MAR. You may have very fit occasion for 't. He is now in some commerce with my lady, and will by and by depart.

SIR TO. Go, Sir Andrew. Scout me for him at the corner of the orchard like a bumbaily.° So   195 soon as ever thou seest him, draw, and, as thou drawest, swear horrible; for it comes to pass oft that a terrible oath, with a swaggering accent sharply twanged off, gives manhood more approbation than ever proof itself would have earned him. Away!

SIR AND. Nay, let me alone for swearing.°   [Exit.]

SIR TO. Now will not I deliver his letter, for the behavior of the young gentleman gives him out to be of good capacity and breeding. His employment between his lord and my niece confirms no   205 less. Therefore this letter, being so excellently ignorant, will breed no terror in the youth. He will find it comes from a clodpole.° But, sir, I will deliver his challenge by word of mouth, set upon Aguecheek a notable report of valor, and drive the gentle-   210 man, as I know his youth will aptly receive it, into a most hideous opinion of his rage, skill, fury, and impetuosity. This will so fright them both that they will kill one another by the look, like cockatrices.°   215

---

125. **bawcock:** fine fellow. Toby humors Malvolio by talking baby talk to him.   126. **chuck:** chick.   128. **biddy:** child's name for a chick.   129. **cherry pit:** a game of throwing cherry stones into a hole.   130. **foul collier:** The Devil is a collier (coalman) because he is black.   134-35. **will . . . godliness:** One of the tests usually applied to a witch was to ask him to say the Lord's Prayer. If he could not, or would not, it was a most suspicious sign of guilt.   142. **genius:** guardian angel. **taken . . . infection:** caught the plague.   143. **device:** plan.   144-45. **take . . . taint:** be spoiled and go bad.   154. **device . . . bar:** bring to public trial.   156. **May morning:** Mayday was a general holiday.

164. **admire:** be amazed.   171-72. **liest . . . throat:** This was the bitterest insult possible.   181. **windy side:** safe side.   195. **bumbaily:** sheriff's officer who made arrests for debt.   201. **let . . . swearing:** i.e., I'm an expert at swearing.   208. **clod·pole:** blockhead.   215. **cockatrice:** a fabulous serpent, able to kill by its mere look. See *Rich III*, I.ii.15n.

[*Re-enter* OLIVIA, *with* VIOLA.]

FAB. Here he comes with your niece. Give them way till he take leave, and presently after him.

SIR TO. I will meditate the while upon some horrid message for a challenge. 220

[*Exeunt* SIR TOBY, FABIAN, *and* MARIA.]

OLI. I have said too much unto a heart of stone,
And laid mine honor too unchary° out.
There's something in me that reproves my fault,
But such a headstrong potent fault it is
That it but mocks reproof. 225

VIO. With the same 'havior that your passion bears
Goes on my master's grief.

OLI. Here, wear this jewel for me, 'tis my picture.
Refuse it not, it hath no tongue to vex you.
And I beseech you come again tomorrow. 230
What shall you ask of me that I'll deny,
That honor saved may upon asking give?

VIO. Nothing but this — your true love for my master.

OLI. How with mine honor may I give him that
Which I have given to you?

VIO.   I will acquit° you. 235

OLI. Well, come again tomorrow. Fare thee well.
A fiend like thee might bear my soul to Hell. [*Exit.*]

[*Re-enter* SIR TOBY *and* FABIAN.]

SIR TO. Gentleman, God save thee.

VIO. And you, sir. 239

SIR TO. That defense thou hast, betake thee to 't. Of what nature the wrongs are thou hast done him, I know not, but thy interceptor, full of despite,° bloody as the hunter, attends thee at the orchard end. Dismount thy tuck,° be yare° in thy preparation, for thy assailant is quick, skillful, and deadly. 246

VIO. You mistake, sir. I am sure no man hath any quarrel to me. My remembrance is very free and clear from any image of offense done to any man. 250

SIR TO. You'll find it otherwise, I assure you. Therefore, if you hold your life at any price, betake you to your guard; for your opposite hath in him what youth, strength, skill, and wrath can furnish man withal. 255

VIO. I pray you, sir, what is he?

SIR TO. He is knight, dubbed° with unhatched° rapier and on carpet consideration,° but he is a devil in private brawl. Souls and bodies hath he divorced three, and his incensement at this moment is 260 so implacable that satisfaction can be none but by pangs of death and sepulcher. Hob, nob,° is his word, give 't or take 't.

VIO. I will return again into the house and desire some conduct of the lady. I am no fighter. I 265 have heard of some kind of men that put quarrels purposely on others, to taste their valor. Belike this is a man of that quirk.°

SIR TO. Sir, no, his indignation derives itself out of a very competent° injury. Therefore get you 270 on and give him his desire. Back you shall not to the house, unless you undertake that with me which with as much safety you might answer him. Therefore on, or strip your sword stark-naked, for meddle you must, that's certain, or forswear° to wear iron about you. 276

VIO. This is as uncivil as strange. I beseech you, do me this courteous office, as to know of the knight what my offense to him is. It is something of my negligence, nothing of my purpose. 280

SIR TO. I will do so. Signior Fabian, stay you by this gentleman till my return. [*Exit.*]

VIO. Pray you, sir, do you know of this matter?

FAB. I know the knight is incensed against 285 you, even to a mortal arbitrament,° but nothing of the circumstance more.

VIO. I beseech you, what manner of man is he?

FAB. Nothing of that wonderful promise, to 290 read him by his form, as you are like to find him in the proof of his valor. He is, indeed, sir, the most skillful, bloody, and fatal opposite that you could possibly have found in any part of Illyria. Will you walk toward him? I will make your peace with him if I can.

VIO. I shall be much bound to you for 't. I am one that had rather go with sir priest° than sir knight. I care not who knows so much of my 299 mettle. [*Exeunt.*]

[*Re-enter* SIR TOBY, *with* SIR ANDREW.]

SIR TO. Why, man, he's a very devil. I have not seen such a firago.° I had a pass with him, rapier, scabbard, and all, and he gives me the stuck-in° with such a mortal motion that it is inevitable; and on the answer, he pays you as surely as your feet 305 hit the ground they step on. They say he has been fencer to the Sophy.

SIR AND. Pox on 't, I'll not meddle with him.

SIR TO. Aye, but he will not now be pacified. Fabian can scarce hold him yonder. 310

SIR AND. Plague on 't, an I thought he had been valiant and so cunning in fence, I'd have seen him damned ere I'd have challenged him. Let him let the matter slip, and I'll give him my horse, gray Capilet. 315

---

222. unchary: heedlessly.   235. acquit: release from a payment. 243. despite: spite. 244. tuck: sword. yare: handy. 257. dubbed: knighted. unhatched: unhacked, not dented by use in battle. 258. carpet consideration: kneeling on a carpet, and not on the battlefield.   262. Hob, nob: hit or miss.

268. quirk: whim.   270. competent: considerable.   275. forswear: swear not to.   286. mortal arbitrament: decision by deadly combat.   298. sir priest: a Bachelor of Arts was termed "Dominus" (= Sir); in the class lists at Cambridge University the B.A.'s are still noted as "Ds." As most priests were graduates, they were called "Sir."   302. firago: for virago, a mannish woman.   303. stuck-in: thrust.

SIR TO. I'll make the motion. Stand here, make a good show on 't. This shall end without the perdition of souls. [*Aside*] Marry, I'll ride your horse as well as I ride you. 319

[*Re-enter* FABIAN *and* VIOLA.]

[*To* FABIAN] I have his horse to take up the quarrel. I have persuaded him the youth's a devil.

FAB. He is as horribly conceited° of him, and pants and looks pale, as if a bear were at his heels. 324

SIR TO. [*To* VIOLA] There's no remedy, sir, he will fight with you for 's oath sake. Marry, he hath better bethought him of his quarrel, and he finds that now scarce to be worth talking of. Therefore draw, for the supportance of his vow. He protests he will not hurt you. 330

VIO. [*Aside*] Pray God defend me! A little thing would make me tell them how much I lack of a man.

FAB. Give ground, if you see him furious. 334

SIR TO. Come, Sir Andrew, there's no remedy. The gentleman will, for his honor's sake, have one bout with you. He cannot by the duello° avoid it. But he has promised me, as he is a gentleman and a soldier, he will not hurt you. Come on — to 't. 340

SIR AND. Pray God he keep his oath!

VIO. I do assure you 'tis against my will.
[*They draw.*]

[*Enter* ANTONIO.]

ANT. Put up your sword. If this young gentleman Have done offense, I take the fault on me. If you offend him, I for him defy you. 345

SIR TO. You, sir! Why, what are you?

ANT. One, sir, that for his love dares yet do more Than you have heard him brag to you he will.

SIR TO. Nay, if you be an undertaker,° I am 349 for you. [*They draw.*]

[*Enter* OFFICERS.]

FAB. O good Sir Toby, hold! Here come the officers.

SIR TO. I'll be with you anon.

VIO. Pray, sir, put your sword up, if you please.

SIR AND. Marry will I, sir, and, for that I 356 promised you, I'll be as good as my word. He will bear you easily and reins well.

I. OFF. This is the man. Do thy office.

2. OFF. Antonio, I arrest thee at the suit of Count Orsino. 361

ANT. You do mistake me, sir.

I. OFF. No, sir, no jot. I know your favor° well, Though now you have no sea cap on your head. Take him away. He knows I know him well. 365

ANT. I must obey. [*To* VIOLA] This comes with seeking you.
But there's no remedy, I shall answer it.
What will you do, now my necessity

Makes me to ask you for my purse? It grieves me Much more for what I cannot do for you 370 Than what befalls myself. You stand amazed, But be of comfort.

2. OFF. Come, sir, away.

ANT. I must entreat of you some of that money.

VIO. What money, sir? 375
For the fair kindness you have showed me here, And, part, being prompted by your present trouble, Out of my lean and low ability° I'll lend you something. My having is not much; I'll make division of my present° with you. 380 Hold, there's half my coffer.°

ANT. Will you deny me now?
Is 't possible that my deserts to you Can lack persuasion? Do not tempt my misery, Lest that it make me so unsound a man As to upbraid you with those kindnesses 385 That I have done for you.

VIO. I know of none, Nor know I you by voice or any feature. I hate ingratitude more in a man Than lying vainness, babbling drunkenness, Or any taint of vice whose strong corruption 390 Inhabits our frail blood.

ANT. Oh, Heavens themselves!

2. OFF. Come, sir, I pray you, go.

ANT. Let me speak a little. This youth that you see here
I snatched one half out of the jaws of death, Relieved him with such sanctity of love, 395 And to his image, which methought did promise Most venerable worth, did I devotion.

I. OFF. What's that to us? The time goes by — away!

ANT. But oh, how vile an idol proves this god! Thou hast, Sebastian, done good feature shame. In nature there's no blemish but the mind; 401 None can be called deformed but the unkind. Virtue is beauty, but the beauteous evil Are empty trunks, o'erflourished by the Devil.°

I. OFF. The man grows mad. Away with him! Come, come, sir. 405

ANT. Lead me on. [*Exit with* OFFICERS.]

VIO. Methinks his words do from such passion fly
That he believes himself. So do not I. Prove true, imagination,° oh, prove true, That I, dear brother, be now ta'en for you! 410

SIR TO. Come hither, knight, come hither, Fabian. We'll whisper o'er a couplet or two of most sage saws.°

---

378. low ability: small means. 380. my present: what I have at present. 381. coffer: purse, lit., chest. 404. empty . . . Devil: over-elaborately carved chests which have nothing inside. See Pl. 17c. 409. Prove . . . imagination: Viola has never given up hope. Now she realizes from Antonio's words that Sebastian is not only alive but near. 413. saws: wise sayings.

323. as . . . conceited: has as horrible ideas of. 338. duello: the rules of duelling, a matter of great importance to a man of honor. 349. undertaker: meddler. 363. favor: face.

vio. He named Sebastian. I my brother know
Yet living in my glass, even such and so   415
In favor was my brother, and he went
Still in this fashion, color, ornament,
For him I imitate. Oh, if it prove,
Tempests are kind and salt waves fresh in love!°

                                 [*Exit.*]

sir to. A very dishonest paltry boy, and   420
more a coward than a hare. His dishonesty appears
in leaving his friend here in necessity and denying
him, and for his cowardship, ask Fabian.

fab. A coward, a most devout coward, religious
in it.   425

sir and. 'Slid,° I'll after him again and beat him.

sir to. Do. Cuff him soundly, but never draw thy
sword.

sir and. An I do not ———   [*Exit.*]

fab. Come, let's see the event.

sir to. I dare lay any money 'twill be nothing yet.
                                     [*Exeunt.*]

Act IV

SCENE I. *Before* olivia's *house.*

[*Enter* sebastian *and* clown.]

clo. Will you make me believe that I am not sent
for you?

seb. Go to, go to, thou art a foolish fellow. Let me
be clear of thee.

clo. Well held out, i' faith! No, I do not   5
know you; nor I am not sent to you by my lady, to
bid you come speak with her; nor your name is not
Master Cesario; nor this is not my nose neither.
Nothing that is so is so.

seb. I prithee, vent° thy folly somewhere else.
Thou know'st not me.   11

clo. Vent my folly! He has heard that word of
some great man and now applies it to a fool. Vent
my folly! I am afraid this great lubber, the world,
will prove a cockney.° I prithee now, ungird   15
thy strangeness and tell me what I shall vent to my
lady. Shall I vent to her that thou art coming?

seb. I prithee, foolish Greek,° depart from me.
There's money for thee. If you tarry longer, I   20
shall give worse payment.

---

419. salt . . . love: i.e., the sea has been kind, with a play of
words on "salt" and "fresh" = good, unsalted, and recent.
426. 'Slid: by God's eyelid.

     Act IV, Sc. i: 10. vent: utter.   14–15. lubber . . . cockney: a
much-disputed passage. The fool when posing as a philosopher
is not always very clear. As it stands, the passage means "this
great clumsy world will turn out to be a spoiled child (cockney)."
19. foolish Greek: foolish jester. The Greeks were considered
empty-headed and merry folk.

clo. By my troth, thou hast an open hand. These
wise men that give fools money get themselves a
good report — after fourteen years' purchase.°   25

[*Enter* sir andrew, sir toby, *and* fabian.]

sir and. Now, sir, have I met you again? There's
for you.

seb. Why, there's for thee, and there, and there.
Are all the people mad?   29

sir to. Hold, sir, or I'll throw your dagger o'er the
house.

clo. This will I tell my lady straight. I would not
be in some of your coats for twopence.   [*Exit.*]

sir to. Come on, sir, hold.   34

sir and. Nay, let him alone. I'll go another way to
work with him. I'll have an action of battery against
him, if there be any law in Illyria. Though I struck
him first, yet it's no matter for that.

seb. Let go thy hand.   39

sir to. Come, sir, I will not let you go. Come,
my young soldier, put up your iron. You are well
fleshed.° Come on.

seb. I will be free from thee. What wouldst thou
now?   44
If thou darest tempt me further, draw thy sword.

sir to. What, what? Nay, then I must have an
ounce or two of this malapert° blood from you.

[*Enter* olivia.]

oli. Hold, Toby. On thy life, I charge thee, hold!

sir to. Madam!   50

oli. Will it be ever thus? Ungracious wretch,
Fit for the mountains and the barbarous caves,
Where manners ne'er were preached! Out of my
     sight!
Be not offended, dear Cesario.
Rudesby,° be gone!

[*Exeunt* sir toby, sir andrew, *and* fabian.]
                     I prithee, gentle friend,   55
Let thy fair wisdom, not thy passion, sway
In this uncivil and unjust extent°
Against thy peace. Go with me to my house,
And hear thou there how many fruitless pranks   59
This ruffian hath botched° up, that thou thereby
Mayst smile at this. Thou shalt not choose but go.
Do not deny. Beshrew his soul for me,
He started one poor heart of mine in thee.

seb. What relish is in this? How runs the stream?
Or I am mad, or else this is a dream.   65
Let fancy still my sense in Lethe° steep.
If it be thus to dream, still let me sleep!

oli. Nay, come, I prithee. Would thou'dst be
     ruled by me!

---

25. fourteen . . . purchase: the value of land was reckoned to be
twelve times the annual rent, so this is a high rate.   42–43. well
fleshed: lit., you have shown courage in your first action; i.e.,
you've had enough fighting for the present. Cf. *I Hen IV,*
V.iv.133.   48. malapert: saucy.   55. Rudesby: ruffian.   57. ex-
tent: attack.   60. botched: patched.   66. Lethe: the river of
forgetfulness in the underworld.

SEB. Madam, I will.

OLI. Oh, say so, and so be!   [*Exeunt.*]

SCENE II. OLIVIA's *house.*

[*Enter* MARIA *and* CLOWN.]

MAR. Nay, I prithee put on this gown and this beard. Make him believe thou art Sir Topas° the curate. Do it quickly. I'll call Sir Toby the whilst.
          [*Exit.*]

CLO. Well, I'll put it on, and I will dissemble° myself in 't, and I would I were the first that ever   5
dissembled in such a gown. I am not tall enough to become the function well, nor lean enough to be thought a good student, but to be said an honest man and a good housekeeper goes as fairly as to say   10
a careful man and a great scholar. The competitors° enter.

[*Enter* SIR TOBY *and* MARIA.]

SIR TO. Jove bless thee, Master Parson.

CLO. *Bonos dies,* Sir Toby. For, as the old hermit of Prague, that never saw pen and ink, very   15
wittily said to a niece of King Gorboduc,° "That that is is," so I, being Master Parson, am Master Parson; for what is "that" but "that," and "is" but "is"?

SIR TO. To him, Sir Topas.   20

CLO. What ho,° I say! Peace in this prison!

SIR TO. The knave counterfeits well—a good knave.

MAL. [*Within*] Who calls there?

CLO. Sir Topas the curate, who comes to visit Malvolio the lunatic.   26

MAL. Sir Topas, Sir Topas, good Sir Topas, go to my lady.

CLO. Out, hyperbolical° fiend! How vexest thou this man! Talkest thou nothing but of ladies?   30

SIR TO. Well said, Master Parson.

MAL. Sir Topas, never was man thus wronged. Good Sir Topas, do not think I am mad. They have laid me here in hideous darkness.   34

CLO. Fie, thou dishonest Satan! I call thee by the most modest terms, for I am one of those gentle ones that will use the Devil himself with courtesy. Sayest thou that house is dark?

MAL. As Hell, Sir Topas.   39

CLO. Why, it hath bay windows transparent as barricadoes,° and the clerestories° toward the south-

north are as lustrous as ebony—and yet complainest thou of obstruction?

MAL. I am not mad, Sir Topas. I say to you, this house is dark.   45

CLO. Madman, thou errest. I say, there is no darkness but ignorance, in which thou art more puzzled than the Egyptians in their fog.°

MAL. I say, this house is as dark as ignorance, though ignorance were as dark as Hell. And I   50
say there was never man thus abused. I am no more mad than you are. Make the trial of it in any constant question.°

CLO. What is the opinion of Pythagoras° concerning wild fowl?   55

MAL. That the soul of our grandam might haply inhabit a bird.

CLO. What thinkest thou of his opinion?

MAL. I think nobly of the soul, and no way approve his opinion.   60

CLO. Fare thee well. Remain thou still in darkness. Thou shalt hold the opinion of Pythagoras ere I will allow of thy wits, and fear to kill a woodcock° lest thou dispossess the soul of thy grandam. Fare thee well.   65

MAL. Sir Topas, Sir Topas!

SIR TO. My most exquisite Sir Topas!

CLO. Nay, I am for all waters.°

MAR. Thou mightst have done this without thy beard and gown. He sees thee not.   70

SIR TO. To him in thine own voice, and bring me word how thou findest him. I would we were well rid of this knavery. If he may be conveniently delivered, I would he were, for I am now so far in offense with my niece that I cannot pursue with   75
any safety this sport to the upshot.° Come by and by to my chamber.   [*Exeunt* SIR TOBY *and* MARIA.]

CLO. [*Sings.*]
          Hey, Robin, jolly Robin,
          Tell me how thy lady does.   9

MAL. Fool——

CLO. "My lady is unkind, perdy."°

MAL. Fool——

CLO. "Alas, why is she so?"

MAL. Fool, I say——   84

CLO. "She loves another——" Who calls, ha?

MAL. Good fool, as ever thou wilt deserve well at my hand, help me to a candle, and pen, ink, and paper. As I am a gentleman, I will live to be thankful to thee for 't.

CLO. Master Malvolio!   90

MAL. Aye, good fool.

Sc. ii: 2. Sir Topas: See III.iv.298,n.   4. dissemble: disguise.
11. competitors: conspirators.   16. King Gorboduc: one of the legendary kings invented by early chroniclers to fill the gaps in English history before records began; but the Clown as usual introduces the name to give an air of learning to his nonsense.
21. What ho: Here the fool assumes a ministerial voice.
29. hyperbolical: extravagant.   41. barricadoes: barricades. clerestories: the upper part of the inner wall of a church above the arches, containing a row of windows.

48. fog: darkness; i.e., the ninth of the plagues of Egypt. See Exodus 10: 21–23.   52–53. constant question: coherent argument.   54. Pythagoras: Pythagoras held that the human soul after death could pass into a beast or a bird.   63. woodcock: regarded as a foolish bird.   68. for . . . waters: i.e., can turn my hand to anything.   76. upshot: conclusion.   81. perdy: by God.

CLO. Alas, sir, how fell you besides your five wits?°

MAL. Fool, there was never man so notoriously abused. I am as well in my wits, fool, as thou art.　96

CLO. But as well? Then you are mad indeed, if you be no better in your wits than a fool.

MAL. They have here propertied° me, keep me in darkness, send ministers to me, asses, and do all they can to face me out of my wits.　101

CLO. Advise you what you say. The minister is here. Malvolio, Malvolio, thy wits the Heavens restore! Endeavor thyself to sleep, and leave thy vain bibble-babble.　105

MAL. Sir Topas——

CLO. Maintain no words° with him, good fellow. Who, I, sir? Not I, sir. God be wi' you, good Sir Topas. Marry, amen. I will, sir, I will.

MAL. Fool, fool, fool, I say——　110

CLO. Alas, sir, be patient. What say you, sir? I am shent° for speaking to you.

MAL. Good fool, help me to some light and some paper. I tell thee I am as well in my wits as any man in Illyria.　115

CLO. Welladay° that you were, sir!

MAL. By this hand, I am. Good fool, some ink, paper, and light; and convey what I will set down to my lady. It shall advantage thee more than ever the bearing of letter did.　120

CLO. I will help you to 't. But tell me true, are you not mad indeed? Or do you but counterfeit?

MAL. Believe me, I am not, I tell thee true.

CLO. Nay, I'll ne'er believe a madman till I see his brains. I will fetch you light and paper and ink.　127

MAL. Fool, I'll requite it in the highest degree. I prithee be gone.

CLO. [Sings.]

　　　I am gone, sir,　　　　　　　130
　　　　And anon, sir,
　　　I'll be with you again,
　　　　In a trice,
　　　Like to the old vice,
　　　Your need to sustain,　　　　135
　　　Who, with dagger of lath,°
　　　In his rage and his wrath,
　　　　Cries, ah, ha! to the Devil,
　　　Like a mad lad,
　　　Pare thy nails, dad.　　　　　140
　　　Adieu, Goodman Devil.　　[Exit.]

SCENE III. OLIVIA's garden.

[Enter SEBASTIAN.]

SEB. This is the air, that is the glorious sun,
This pearl she gave me, I do feel 't and see 't.
And though 'tis wonder that enwraps me thus,
Yet 'tis not madness. Where's Antonio, then?
I could not find him at the Elephant.　　　　　5
Yet there he was, and there I found this credit,°
That he did range° the town to seek me out.
His counsel now might do me golden service.
For though my soul disputes well with my sense,
That this may be some error, but no madness,　10
Yet doth this accident and flood of fortune
So far exceed all instance,° all discourse,
That I am ready to distrust mine eyes
And wrangle with my reason, that persuades me
To any other trust but that I am mad,　　　　15
Or else the lady's mad — yet, if 'twere so,
She could not sway her house, command her followers,
Take and give back affairs and their dispatch
With such a smooth, discreet, and stable bearing
As I perceive she does. There's something in 't　20
That is deceivable.° But here the lady comes.

[Enter OLIVIA and PRIEST.]

OLI. Blame not this haste of mine. If you mean well,
Now go with me and with this holy man
Into the chantry° by. There, before him,
And underneath that consecrated roof,　　　　25
Plight° me the full assurance of your faith,
That my most jealous and too doubtful soul
May live at peace. He shall conceal it
While you are willing it shall come to note,
What time we will our celebration keep　　　　30
According to my birth. What do you say?

SEB. I'll follow this good man, and go with you,
And, having sworn truth, ever will be true.

OLI. Then lead the way, good Father, and
Heavens so shine,
That they may fairly note this act of mine!　35

[Exeunt.]

Act V

SCENE I. Before OLIVIA's house.

[Enter CLOWN and FABIAN.]

FAB. Now, as thou lovest me, let me see his letter.

CLO. Good Master Fabian, grant me another request.

92-93. five wits: i.e., full possession of your senses. The five were common wit, imagination, fantasy, estimation, and memory. 99. propertied: treated like a property; i.e., "thrust me into the attic." 107. Maintain no words: Here the fool resumes his assumed voice as he keeps up a dialogue with himself as Sir Topas addressing the Clown. 112. shent: rebuked. 116. Welladay: alas. 134-36. vice . . . lath: the clown's part in the old Morality plays. He was armed with a wooden dagger (dagger of lath), with which he attacked the Devil and tried to cut his nails.

Sc. iii: 6. credit: report. 7. range: traverse. 12. exceed . . . instance: go beyond anything recorded. 21. deceivable: deceptive. 24. chantry: chapel. 26. Plight: promise. Olivia is proposing not full marriage but formal betrothal, which will legally bind Sebastian. See Gen. Intro. p. 20a.

FAB. Anything.   5

CLO. Do not desire to see this letter.

FAB. This is to give a dog,° and in recompense desire my dog again.

[*Enter* DUKE, VIOLA, CURIO, *and* LORDS.]

DUKE. Belong you to the Lady Olivia, friends?

CLO. Aye, sir, we are some of her trappings.°   10

DUKE. I know thee well. How dost thou, my good fellow?

CLO. Truly, sir, the better for my foes and the worse for my friends.

DUKE. Just the contrary — the better for thy friends.   16

CLO. No, sir, the worse.

DUKE. How can that be?

CLO. Marry, sir, they praise me and make an ass of me. Now my foes tell me plainly I am an ass,   20 so that by my foes, sir, I profit in the knowledge of myself, and by my friends I am abused. So that, conclusions to be as kisses,° if your four negatives make your two affirmatives, why then, the worse for my friends, and the better for my foes.   26

DUKE. Why, this is excellent.

CLO. By my troth, sir, no, though it please you to be one of my friends.

DUKE. Thou shalt not be the worse for me. There's gold.   31

CLO. But that it would be double-dealing,° sir, I would you could make it another.

DUKE. Oh, you give me ill counsel.

CLO. Put your grace in your pocket,° sir, for this once, and let your flesh and blood obey it.   36

DUKE. Well, I will be so much a sinner, to be a double-dealer. There's another.

CLO. Primo, secundo, tertio, is a good play, and the old saying is, the third pays for all. The   40 triplex, sir, is a good tripping measure, or the bells of Saint Bennet,° sir, may put you in mind — one, two, three.

DUKE. You can fool no more money out of me at this throw. If you will let your lady know I am   45 here to speak with her, and bring her along with you, it may awake my bounty further.

CLO. Marry, sir, lullaby to your bounty till I come again. I go, sir, but I would not have you to think that my desire of having is the sin of covetous-   50

ness. But, as you say, sir, let your bounty take a nap. I will awake it anon.   [*Exit.*]

VIO. Here comes the man, sir, that did rescue me.

[*Enter* ANTONIO *and* OFFICERS.]

DUKE. That face of his I do remember well,
Yet when I saw it last it was besmeared   55
As black as Vulcan° in the smoke of war.
A bawbling° vessel was he captain of,
For shallow draught and bulk unprizable,°
With which such scathful grapple° did he make
With the most noble bottom° of our fleet   60
That very envy and the tongue of loss
Cried fame and honor on him. What's the matter?

1. OFF. Orsino, this is that Antonio
That took the *Phoenix* and her fraught° from
Candy,°   65
And this is he that did the *Tiger* board,   65
When your young nephew Titus lost his leg.
Here in the streets, desperate° of shame and state,°
In private brabble° did we apprehend him.

VIO. He did me kindness, sir, drew on my side,
But in conclusion put strange speech upon me.   70
I know not what 'twas but distraction.°

DUKE. Notable pirate! Thou salt-water thief!
What foolish boldness brought thee to their mercies
Whom thou, in terms so bloody and so dear,
Hast made thine enemies?

ANT.   Orsino, noble sir,   75
Be pleased that I shake off these names you give me.
Antonio never yet was thief or pirate,
Though I confess, on base and ground enough,
Orsino's enemy. A witchcraft drew me hither.
That most ingrateful boy there by your side   80
From the rude sea's enragèd and foamy mouth
Did I redeem — a wreck past hope he was.
His life I gave him and did thereto add
My love, without retention or restraint,
All his in dedication. For his sake   85
Did I expose myself, pure for his love,
Into the danger of this adverse° town,
Drew to defend him when he was beset,
Where being apprehended, his false cunning,
Not meaning to partake with me in danger,   90
Taught him to face me out of his acquaintance,
And grew a twenty years' removèd thing
While one would wink — denied me mine own purse,
Which I had recommended to his use
Not half an hour before.

VIO.   How can this be?   95

DUKE. When came he to this town?

Act V, Sc. i: 7. give a dog: This was a contemporary anecdote recorded in Manningham's diary: "Dr. Bullein, the Queen's kinsman, had a dog which he doted on, so much that the Queen understanding of it requested he would grant her one desire, and he should have whatsoever he should ask. She demanded his dog; he gave it, and, 'Now, Madam,' quoth he, 'you promised to give me my desire.' 'I will,' quoth she. 'Then I pray you give me my dog again.'" 10. trappings: ornamental accessories. 22–23. conclusions . . . kisses: as a kiss stops all lovers' arguments. 32. double-dealing: The Clown is trying to extract another coin from the Duke. 35. Put . . . pocket: forget your respectability. 42. Saint Bennet: St. Benedict, a London church.

56. Vulcan: the blacksmith god. 57. bawbling: trifling. 58. unprizable: not worth taking as a prize. 59. scathful grapple: destructive attack. 60. bottom: vessel. 64. fraught: cargo. Candy: Crete. 67. desperate: utterly regardless. state: civil behavior. 68. brabble: brawl. 71. distraction: madness. 87. adverse: hostile.

ANT. Today, my lord, and for three months be-
fore,
No interim, not a minute's vacancy,
Both day and night did we keep company.
        [*Enter* OLIVIA *and* ATTENDANTS.]
  DUKE. Here comes the Countess. Now Heaven
    walks on earth.   100
But for thee, fellow — fellow, thy words are mad-
ness.
Three months this youth hath tended upon me.
But more of that anon. Take him aside.
  OLI. What would my lord, but that he may not
    have,
Wherein Olivia may seem serviceable?   105
Cesario, you do not keep promise with me.
  VIO. Madam!
  DUKE. Gracious Olivia ——
  OLI. What do you say, Cesario? Good my
    lord ——
  VIO. My lord would speak, my duty hushes me.
  OLI. If it be aught to the old tune, my lord,   111
It is as fat° and fulsome° to mine ear
As howling after music.
  DUKE.   Still so cruel?
  OLI. Still so constant, lord.
  DUKE. What, to perverseness? You uncivil lady,
To whose ingrate° and unauspicious altars   116
My soul the faithful'st offerings hath breathed out
That e'er devotion tendered! What shall I do?
  OLI. Even what it please my lord that shall become
    him.
  DUKE. Why should I not, had I the heart to do it,
Like to the Egyptian thief° at point of death,   121
Kill what I love? — A savage jealousy
That sometime savors nobly. But hear me this.
Since you to nonregardance cast my faith,
And that I partly know the instrument   125
That screws° me from my true place in your favor,
Live you the marble-breasted tyrant still.
But this your minion,° whom I know you love,
And whom, by Heaven I swear, I tender dearly,
Him will I tear out of that cruel eye,   130
Where he sits crownèd in his master's spite.°
Come, boy, with me. My thoughts are ripe in mis-
chief.
I'll sacrifice the lamb that I do love,
To spite a raven's heart within a dove.
  VIO. And I, most jocund, apt, and willingly,   135
To do you rest, a thousand deaths would die.
  OLI. Where goes Cesario?
  VIO.   After him I love
More than I love these eyes, more than my life,

More, by all mores, than e'er I shall love wife.
If I do feign, you witnesses above   140
Punish my life for tainting of my love!
  OLI. Aye me, detested! How am I beguiled!
  VIO. Who does beguile you? Who does do you
    wrong?
  OLI. Hast thou forgot thyself? Is it so long?
Call forth the holy Father.
  DUKE.   Come, away!   145
  OLI. Whither, my lord? Cesario, husband, stay.
  DUKE. Husband!
  OLI.   Aye, husband. Can he that deny?
  DUKE. Her husband, sirrah!
  VIO.   No, my lord, not I.
  OLI. Alas, it is the baseness of thy fear
That makes thee strangle thy propriety.°   150
Fear not, Cesario. Take thy fortunes up.
Be that thou know'st thou art, and then thou art
As great as that thou fear'st.
  [*Enter* PRIEST.]   Oh, welcome, Father!
Father, I charge thee, by thy reverence,
Here to unfold, though lately we intended   155
To keep in darkness what occasion now
Reveals before 'tis ripe, what thou dost know
Hath newly passed between this youth and me.
  PRIEST. A contract of eternal bond of love,
Confirmed by mutual joinder of your hands,   160
Attested by the holy close of lips,
Strengthened by interchangement of your rings.
And all the ceremony of this compáct°
Sealed in my function, by my testimony.
Since when, my watch hath told me, toward my
    grave   165
I have traveled but two hours.
  DUKE. O thou dissembling cub! What wilt thou be
When time hath sowed a grizzle on thy case?°
Or will not else thy craft so quickly grow
That thine own trip shall be thine overthrow?°   170
Farewell, and take her, but direct thy feet
Where thou and I henceforth may never meet.
  VIO. My lord, I do protest ——
  OLI.   Oh, do not swear!
Hold little faith, though thou hast too much fear.
          [*Enter* SIR ANDREW.]
  SIR AND. For the love of God, a surgeon! Send one
presently° to Sir Toby.   176
  OLI. What's the matter?
  SIR AND. He has broke my head across and has
given Sir Toby a bloody coxcomb° too. For the love
of God, your help! I had rather than forty pound I
were at home.   181
  OLI. Who has done this, Sir Andrew?
  SIR AND. The Count's gentleman, one Cesario. We

---

112. **fat:** gross. **fulsome:** nauseous.   116. **ingrate:** ungrateful.
121. **Egyptian thief:** Thyamis, an Egyptian robber, captured
Chariclea and shut her in a cave. Being attacked by other rob-
bers, he rushed into the cave intending to slay her rather than
that she should fall into other hands.   125–26. **instrument . . .
screws:** a jack that forces.   128. **minion:** darling.   131. **in . . .
spite:** to the vexation of his master.

150. **strangle . . . propriety:** lit., choke your proper self; i.e., be-
have like a coward.   163. **compact:** agreement.   168. **hath . . .
case:** has brought you gray hairs.   170. **thine . . . overthrow:**
your trickery will overthrow you.   176. **presently:** immediately.
  179. **bloody coxcomb:** broken head.

took him for a coward, but he's the very Devil in-
cardinate.°   185

DUKE. My gentleman, Cesario?

SIR AND. 'Od's lifelings,° here he is! You broke
my head for nothing, and that that I did, I was set
on to do 't by Sir Toby.

VIO. Why do you speak to me? I never hurt you.
You drew your sword upon me without cause,   191
But I bespake you fair, and hurt you not.

SIR AND. If a bloody coxcomb be a hurt, you have
hurt me. I think you set nothing by a bloody cox-
comb. [Enter SIR TOBY and CLOWN.] Here comes
Sir Toby halting.° You shall hear more. But if   195
he had not been in drink, he would have tickled you
othergates° than he did.

DUKE. How now, gentleman! How is 't with
you?   200

SIR TO. That's all one. Has hurt me, and there's
the end on 't. Sot, didst see Dick surgeon, sot?

CLO. Oh, he's drunk, Sir Toby, an hour agone. His
eyes were set at eight i' the morning.°   205

SIR TO. Then he's a rogue, and a passy measures
pavin.° I hate a drunken rogue.

OLI. Away with him! Who hath made this havoc
with them?

SIR AND. I'll help you, Sir Toby, because we'll be
dressed together.   211

SIR TO. Will you help? An asshead and a coxcomb
and a knave, a thin-faced knave, a gull!

OLI. Get him to bed, and let his hurt be looked to.
[Exeunt CLOWN, FABIAN, SIR TOBY, and SIR ANDREW.]
            [Enter SEBASTIAN.]

SEB. I am sorry, madam, I have hurt your kins-
man,
But had it been the brother of my blood,
I must have done no less with wit and safety.
You throw a strange regard° upon me, and by that
I do perceive it hath offended you.   220
Pardon me, sweet one, even for the vows
We made each other but so late ago.

DUKE. One face, one voice, one habit, and two
persons,
A natural perspective,° that is and is not!

SEB. Antonio, O my dear Antonio!   225
How have the hours racked and tortured me
Since I have lost thee!

ANT. Sebastian are you?

SEB.   Fear'st thou that, Antonio?

ANT. How have you made division of yourself?
An apple, cleft in two, is not more twin   230
Than these two creatures. Which is Sebastian?

OLI. Most wonderful!

SEB. Do I stand there? I never had a brother,
Nor can there be that deity in my nature,
Of here and everywhere.° I had a sister,   235
Whom the blind waves and surges have devoured.
Of charity, what kin are you to me?
What countryman? What name? What parentage?

VIO. Of Messaline. Sebastian was my father.
Such a Sebastian was my brother too,   240
So went he suited° to his watery tomb.
If spirits can assume both form and suit,
You come to fright us.

SEB.   A spirit I am indeed,
But am in that dimension grossly clad°
Which from the womb I did participate.   245
Were you a woman, as the rest goes even,
I should my tears let fall upon your cheek,
And say "Thrice welcome, drownèd Viola!"

VIO. My father had a mole upon his brow.

SEB. And so had mine.   250

VIO. And died that day when Viola from her birth
Had numbered thirteen years.

SEB. Oh, that recórd is lively in my soul!
He finishèd indeed his mortal act
That day that made my sister thirteen years.   255

VIO. If nothing lets° to make us happy both
But this my masculine usurped attire,
Do not embrace me till each circumstance
Of place, time, fortune, do cohere and jump°
That I am Viola. Which to confirm,   260
I'll bring you to a captain in this town,
Where lie my maiden weeds,° by whose gentle help
I was preserved to serve this noble Count.
All the occurrence of my fortune since
Hath been between this lady and this lord.   265

SEB. [To OLIVIA] So comes it, lady, you have been
mistook.
But nature to her bias° drew in that.
You would have been contracted to a maid,
Nor are you therein, by my life, deceived,
You are betrothed both to a maid and man.   270

DUKE. Be not amazed. Right noble is his blood.
If this be so, as yet the glass° seems true,
I shall have share in this most happy wreck.
[To VIOLA] Boy, thou hast said to me a thousand
times
Thou never shouldst love woman like to me.   275

VIO. And all those sayings will I overswear,
And all those swearings keep as true in soul

---

185. incardinate: incarnate.   187. 'Od's lifelings: by God's little
life.   195. halting: limping.   196–97. othergates: otherwise.
205. Set . . . morning: dimmed by drink (set) since eight in the
morning.   206–07. passy . . . pavin: The folio reads "passy
measures panyn" (misprint for "pauyn"). Toby is very drunk.
The fool's words "set at eight" stir in his fuddled head the
memory that there were eight strains in the "passa measures
pavan," a slow, stately dance. See App. 24.   219. regard: look.
224. perspective: a picture which shows one image when seen in
front and another when viewed from an angle. See Rich II,
II.ii.18–20.

234–35. Nor . . . everywhere: I cannot be a god to be in two
places at once.   241. suited: clothed.   244. in . . . clad:
enclosed in bodily form.   256. lets: hinders.   259. jump:
agree.   262. weeds: garments.   267. bias: natural inclination.
272. glass: reflection.

As doth that orbèd continent the fire°
That severs day from night.

DUKE.   Give me thy hand,
And let me see thee in thy woman's weeds.   280

VIO. The captain that did bring me first on shore
Hath my maid's garments. He upon some action
Is now in durance,° at Malvolio's suit,
A gentleman, and follower of my lady's.

OLI. He shall enlarge him. Fetch Malvolio hither.
And yet, alas, now I remember me,   286
They say, poor gentleman, he's much distract.

[Re-enter CLOWN with a letter, and FABIAN.]
A most extracting frenzy° of mine own
From my remembrance clearly banished his.
How does he, sirrah?   290

CLO. Truly, madam, he holds Belzebub at the
stave's end° as well as a man in his case may do.
Has here writ a letter to you. I should have given 't
you today morning, but as a madman's epistles are
no gospels, so it skills° not much when they are de-
livered.   296

OLI. Open 't, and read it.

CLO. Look then to be well edified when the fool
delivers° the madman. [Reads.] "By the Lord,
madam "——   300

OLI. How now! Art thou mad?

CLO. No, madam, I do but read madness. An your
ladyship will have it as it ought to be, you must al-
low Vox.°

OLI. Prithee, read i' thy right wits.   305

CLO. So I do, madonna, but to read his right wits
is to read thus. Therefore perpend,° my Princess,
and give ear.

OLI. [To FABIAN] Read it you, sirrah.   309

FAB. [Reads.] "By the Lord, madam, you wrong
me, and the world shall know it. Though you have
put me into darkness and given your drunken
cousin rule over me, yet have I the benefit of my
senses as well as your ladyship. I have your own let-
ter that induced me to the semblance I put on, with
the which I doubt not but to do myself much right,
or you much shame. Think of me as you please. I
leave my duty a little unthought-of,° and speak out
of my injury.

      "THE MADLY USED MALVOLIO "

OLI. Did he write this?   320

CLO. Aye, madam.

DUKE. This savors not much of distraction.

OLI. See him delivered, Fabian. Bring him hither.
                     [Exit FABIAN.]

My lord, so please you, these things further thought
on,
To think me as well a sister as a wife,   325
One day shall crown the alliance on 't, so please you,
Here at my house and at my proper° cost.

DUKE. Madam, I am most apt to embrace your
offer.
[To VIOLA] Your master quits° you, and for your
service done him,
So much against the mettle° of your sex,   330
So far beneath your soft and tender breeding,
And since you called me master for so long,
Here is my hand. You shall from this time be
Your master's mistress.

OLI.   A sister! You are she.
       [Re-enter FABIAN, with MALVOLIO.]

DUKE. Is this the madman?   335

OLI.   Aye, my lord, this same.
How now, Malvolio!

MAL.   Madam, you have done me wrong,
Notorious wrong.

OLI.   Have I, Malvolio? No.

MAL. Lady, you have. Pray you peruse that letter.
You must not now deny it is your hand.
Write from° it, if you can, in hand or phrase,   340
Or say 'tis not your seal, not your invention.
You can say none of this. Well, grant it then
And tell me, in the modesty of honor,
Why you have given me such clear lights of favor,
Bade me come smiling and cross-gartered to you,
To put on yellow stockings and to frown   346
Upon Sir Toby and the lighter people.
And, acting this in an obedient hope,
Why have you suffered me to be imprisoned,
Kept in a dark house, visited by the priest,   350
And made the most notorious geck° and gull
That e'er invention played on? Tell me why.

OLI. Alas, Malvolio, this is not my writing,
Though, I confess, much like the character.°
But out of question 'tis Maria's hand.   355
And now I do bethink me it was she
First told me thou wast mad, then camest in smiling
And in such forms which here were presupposed
Upon thee in the letter. Prithee, be content.   359
This practice° hath most shrewdly passed upon thee,
But when we know the grounds and authors of it,
Thou shalt be both the plaintiff and the judge
Of thine own cause.

FAB.   Good madam, hear me speak,
And let no quarrel nor no brawl to come
Taint the condition° of this present hour,   365
Which I have wondered at. In hope it shall not,
Most freely I confess, myself and Toby

---

278. orbed . . . fire: the sun.   283. durance: confinement.
288. frenzy: madness.   291-92. holds . . . end: he keeps the
fiend at bay; i.e., he is putting up a fight against Belzebub, who
possesses him.   295. skills: makes little difference.   299. de-
livers: utters the words of.   304. allow Vox: the proper tone of
voice.   307. perpend: consider.   318. duty . . . unthought-of:
i.e., I do not write with the formal phrases that a steward
should use to his mistress.

327. proper: own.   329. quits: releases.   330. mettle: material
nature.   340. Write from: deny.   351. geck: fool.   354. Char-
acter: handwriting.   360. practice: plot.   365. Taint . . . con-
dition: spoil the harmony.

Set this device against Malvolio here,
Upon some stubborn and uncourteous parts
We had conceived° against him. Maria writ   370
The letter at Sir Toby's great importance,°
In recompense whereof he hath married her.
How with a sportful malice it was followed
May rather pluck on laughter than revenge,
If that the injuries be justly weighed   375
That have on both sides passed.

OLI. Alas, poor fool, how have they baffled° thee!

CLO. Why, "some are born great, some achieve
greatness, and some have greatness thrown upon
them." I was one, sir, in this interlude; one Sir   380
Topas, sir. But that's all one. "By the Lord, fool, I
am not mad." But do you remember? "Madam,
why laugh you at such a barren rascal? An you
smile not, he's gagged." And thus the whirligig of
time brings in his revenges.°   385

MAL. I'll be revenged on the whole pack of you.
[Exit.]

OLI. He hath been most notoriously abused.

DUKE. Pursue him, and entreat him to a peace.
He hath not told us of the captain yet.   390
When that is known, and golden time convents,°
A solemn combination shall be made
Of our dear souls. Meantime, sweet sister,
We will not part from hence. Cesario, come —
For so you shall be, while you are a man,   395

---

370. conceived: perceived.   371. importance: importunity, in-
sistence.   377. baffled: disgraced.   385. brings . . . revenges:
i.e., now I have my own back. See I.v.88.   391. golden . . .
convents: happy time summons.

But when in other habits you are seen,
Orsino's mistress and his fancy's Queen.
[Exeunt all, except CLOWN.]

CLO. [Sings.]
When that I was and a little tiny boy,
    With hey, ho, the wind and the rain,
A foolish thing was but a toy,   400
    For the rain it raineth every day.

But when I came to man's estate,
    With hey, ho, the wind and the rain,
'Gainst knaves and thieves men shut their gate,
    For the rain it raineth every day.   405

But when I came, alas! to wive,
    With hey, ho, the wind and the rain,
By swaggering could I never thrive,
    For the rain it raineth every day.

But when I came unto my beds,°   410
    With hey, ho, the wind and the rain,
With tosspots° still had drunken heads,
    For the rain it raineth every day.

A great while ago the world begun,
    With hey, ho, the wind and the rain,   415
But that's all one, our play is done,
    And we'll strive to please you every day.
[Exit.]

---

410. unto my beds: a difficult phrase, meaning probably "when
I came to the end of my life."   412. tosspots: drunkards.

The Tragedy of
HAMLET, PRINCE OF DENMARK

Introduction

Hamlet is in every way the most interesting play ever written. Apart from the fascination of Hamlet's character, it has a long and intricate history as a drama; the text is full of problems for the scholar; it teems with allusions for the antiquarian. For the last hundred and fifty years critics have competed in offering their key to the heart of Hamlet's mystery. It is the final ambition of every actor to give the part his own interpretation, and even the doctors, especially the psychiatrists, have taken Hamlet into the laboratory and examined his inhibitions.

The story of Hamlet in some form is at least seven hundred years old. Hamlet appears first as Amlethus in the *Historia Danica,* written by Saxo Grammaticus in the twelfth century. The original source of the English play is a French story told in the *Histoires tragiques* of François de Belleforest, published in Paris in 1576. The outline of Belleforest's story follows:

In pre-Christian times there was a Danish Prince called Horvendile, who was married to Queen Geruth. Their son was named Hamlet. Prince Horvendile was murdered by his brother Fengon, who thereupon married Queen Geruth. In order to escape from the tyranny of his uncle, Prince Hamlet pretended to be mad. Fengon was suspicious and tried to get at the truth by sending a harlot to tempt Hamlet, but Hamlet was forewarned. Then Fengon sent one of his councilors to hide secretly behind the arras in the Queen's chamber, so that he might overhear Hamlet's conversation with his mother. Hamlet came into the chamber, pretending in his madness to be a cock, and beating with his arms upon the arras he felt the eavesdropper. He slew him with his sword, cut the body in pieces, boiled them, and fed them to the hogs.

Fengon then sent Hamlet to the King of England, with sealed letters commanding that he should be put to death. On the voyage Hamlet read the letters and exchanged them for others in which it was ordered that the bearer should be hanged and he himself should be married to the daughter of the King of England. So Hamlet came back into Denmark, where he found that his supposed death was being celebrated in a mighty funeral feast. He waited until the guests were dead-drunk, and then set fire to the hall and burned them all. After this he went up to his uncle's bedchamber and, after delivering a speech on the duty of revenging his dead father, he cut off his uncle's head.

Hamlet now abandoned all pretense that he was mad. He summoned the Danes and made an oration in which he told the whole story, at which they were so moved that they proclaimed him King. After his coronation, he went back to England to fetch his wife. The King of England would have murdered him, but again he escaped. Then the Queen of Scots, whose name was Hermetrude, fell in love with him and insisted on marrying him. So Hamlet returned once more to Denmark with his two wives. But Hermetrude soon tired of him; she fell in love with Wiglerus, another of his uncles, and caused Hamlet to be murdered.

The Hamlet story appeared in England as a play at some time before 1589. In that year Thomas Nashe wrote a preface for Robert Greene's novel *Menaphon,* in which he satirized a number of contemporary writers. In this preface, Nashe wrote:

It is a common practice nowadays amongst a sort of shifting [1] companions, that run through every art and thrive by none, to leave the trade of *Noverint* [2] whereto they were born, and busy themselves with the endeavors of art, that could scarcely Latinize their neck verse [3] if they should have need. Yet English Seneca read by candlelight yields many good sentences as 'Blood is a beggar,' and so forth, and if you entreat him fair in a frosty morning, he will afford you whole Hamlets, I should say handfuls of tragical speeches.

Nashe was a very young man and loved clever obscure writing; but it seems likely that he was here referring to Thomas Kyd, the author of *The Spanish Tragedy,* which was then a fairly new play. *The Spanish Tragedy* told how old Hieronimo took vengeance on the murderers of his son

---

[1] shiftless. [2] scrivener; see Gen. Intro. p. 37a. [3] The verses read when a man pleaded "benefit of clergy." See Gen. Intro. p. 28a.

Horatio. If this passage indeed refers to Kyd, it seems likely that Kyd had followed up the success of *The Spanish Tragedy* with another story of revenge telling how the young Prince Hamlet took vengeance for his murdered father.

The first actual record of a play of *Hamlet* is in the summer of 1594. During the few days that the Lord Chamberlain's and the Lord Admiral's players acted together (see Gen. Intro. p. 39b), Henslowe noted that on June 11 they put on a play called *Hamlet*.

The next reference to *Hamlet* is in 1596, when Thomas Lodge wrote a book called *Wit's Misery*, in which he described allegorically various contemporary types. Among others was the Devil, Hate-Virtue, who could be known by this: " He walks for the most part in black under color of gravity, and looks as pale as the vizard of the ghost which cried so miserably at the Theater like an oyster wife, *Hamlet, revenge.*" As the Lord Chamberlain's Company was acting at the Theater at that time, Lodge's remarks show that *Hamlet* was one of the plays in their repertory. There was thus a *Hamlet* play in existence and popular between 1589 and 1596. It is not likely that this was Shakespeare's play as it is now known. The style is too mature for it to have been one of his early works, and in its printed version *Hamlet* includes a number of topical allusions which can certainly be referred to the years 1600 and 1601. These, however, may have been later additions.

The definite history of Shakespeare's *Hamlet* began in 1602. On July 26, James Roberts, the printer, entered in the Stationers' Register a " booke called the Revenge of Hamlett, Prince Denmarke, as yt was latelie Acted by the Lord Chamberleyne his servantes." This entry was probably intended to block publication (see Gen. Intro. p. 66a). Nevertheless, in 1603 there appeared the first version of Shakespeare's *Hamlet*, a quarto (Q1) with the title page: *The Tragicall Historie of Hamlet Prince of Denmarke. By William Shake-speare. As it hath beene diuerse times acted by his Highnesse seruants in the Cittie of London: as also in the two Vniuersities of Cambridge and Oxford, and else-where.* Since the Company are called " his Highnesse seruants," it is clear that Q1 was issued after May 19, when the Lord Chamberlain's Men ·became the King's Players. Q1 is a very garbled version of Shakespeare's play and obviously was a piracy. It is about seventeen hundred lines shorter than the

true play and differs in a number of details. The old councilor is called Corambis, not Polonius; the arrangement of the scenes is different; and there are important differences in the closet scene. More than two hundred and forty lines in Q1 did not appear in any form in the other versions, and much of the verse is in an early stiff style. Several different theories have been put forward to explain how Q1 was put together, but it is generally agreed that it was founded on the part of the actor who played Marcellus, for the scenes in which Marcellus appears are accurately reproduced. For the rest, it may either have been gathered by shorthand from an actual performance or vamped up by one of the minor actors who wrote down what he remembered of the play. Q1 has little value as a text, but some of the stage directions show what actually happened at a performance and are most interesting. It may indeed represent a version of the play in a transition stage before Shakespeare had completely rewritten the old *Hamlet*.

Among the interesting stage directions in Q1 the following are worth noting:

(a) *Enter in a Dumbe Shew, the King and the Queene, he sits downe in an Arbor, she leaues him: Then enters Lucianus with poyson in a Viall, and powres it in his ears, and goes away: Then the Queene commeth and findes him dead: and goes away with the other.* (III.ii.145)

(b) *Enter the ghost in his night gowne.* (III.iv.102)

(c) *Enter Ofelia playing on a Lute, and her haire downe singing.* (IV.v.20)

(d) *Enter King and Queene, Leartes, and other lordes, with a Priest after the coffin.* (V.i.240)

(e) *Enter a Bragart Gentleman.* (V.ii.80)

(f) *They catch one anothers Rapiers, and both are wounded, Leartes falles downe, the Queene falles downe and dies.* (V.ii.313)

Some of the differences between the first and second Quartos are shown in the General Introduction (pp. 61–2). Another illustration of the shortcomings of the compiler of Q1 occurs in his version of the famous " To be or not to be " speech (see III.i.56), which runs in Q1 thus:

To be, or not to be, I there's the point,
To Die, to sleepe, is that all? I all:
No, to sleepe, to dreame, I mary there it goes,
For in that dreame of death, when wee awake,
And borne before an euerlasting Judge,
From whence no passenger euer retur'nd,

The vndiscouered country, at whose sight
The happy smile, and the accursed damn'd.
But for this, the joyfull hope of this,
Whol'd beare the scornes and flattery of the world,
Scorned by the right rich, the rich curssed of the
   poore?
The widow being oppressed, the orphan wrong'd,
The taste of hunger, or a tirants raigne,
And thousand more calamities besides,
To grunt and sweate under this weary life,
When that he may his full *Quietus* make,
With a bare bodkin, who would this indure,
But for a hope of something after death?
Which pusles the braine, and doth confound the
   sence.
Which makes us rather beare those euilles we haue,
Than flie to others that we know not of.
I that, O this conscience makes cowardes of us all,
Lady in thy orizons, be all my sinnes remembred.

About a year later a new edition of the play
came out. This is known as the second quarto
(Q2). Its title page runs: *The Tragicall Historie
of Hamlet, Prince of Denmarke. By William
Shakespeare. Newly imprinted and enlarged to
almost as much againe as it was, according to the
true and perfect Coppie* (see Pl. 14d). Q2 gives
the fullest text of the play. It was probably set up
directly from Shakespeare's own manuscript, but
it is very carelessly printed and full of mistakes.
Q2 was reprinted in 1607 and 1611.

Hamlet was again printed in the first folio
(F1), in 1623. There are many differences be-
tween Q2 and F1. Some of the passages amount-
ing to more than two hundred lines in Q2 are
omitted, some new passages are added. The text
in F1 is much more carefully printed than in Q2
and many of the mistakes have been corrected.
On the other hand, F1 has many mistakes of its
own. In Q2 there is no division into acts or scenes;
in F1 the acts and scenes are marked down to the
beginning of Act II, Scene ii, but thereafter
omitted. The general opinion held by modern
scholars is that F1 was set up from a copy of the
play as later used in the playhouse. The problems
of the text of *Hamlet* are thus very complicated.
In modern texts, editors combine Q2 and F1 and
print all the passages. Where there is a difference
in reading, the editors either choose that which
seems to them best or else emend the text. The
study of the text of *Hamlet* indeed requires a
large volume to itself.

There has been so much critical interpretation
of *Hamlet* that a student should form his own im-
pression of the play before listening to any of the
arguments of the various sects of critics. It is as
well to remember an elementary fact, too often
forgotten — that *Hamlet* is an Elizabethan play
and not a Victorian treatise on philosophy or psy-
chology, and that it was written to be acted in the
Globe Theater about 1600. *Hamlet* belongs to a
well-known type of drama, the "revenge" play.
In such plays, there was a regular set of conven-
tions. Vengeance, at least on the stage, was a
pious duty laid on the next of kin. It was, in Ba-
con's words, "wild justice" — but something
more than justice, for a credit balance was neces-
sary. The Old Law claimed "an eye for an eye
and a tooth for a tooth"; vengeance required
both eyes, a jaw full of teeth, and above all that
its victim, after exquisite torment of body and
mind, should burn everlastingly in hell-fire. A
perfect vengeance, therefore, demanded great
artistry.

Most revenge plays were written according to a
common pattern. They required a crime, invaria-
bly murder, whereby the duty of vengeance was
laid on the next of kin; the discovery of the mur-
derer by the avenger, usually a matter of some
difficulty; the impediments to revenge; and fi-
nally, the triumphant conclusion in which the
murderer was appropriately destroyed. And,
since playgoers liked gore, the avenger and half
a dozen others must perish in one red ruin in
the last act, and it was usual to include at least
one ghost and a mad scene. The pattern had
been set in Kyd's *Spanish Tragedy*.

An example of satisfactory vengeance is to be
found in Thomas Nashe's novel *Jack Wilton, the
Unfortunate Traveller* (1594). Cutwolf, wishing
to exact vengeance on Esdras (who had mur-
dered his brother) corners his victim. Esdras in
despair promises to commit any desperate action
to save his own life, whereupon Cutwolf, who is
telling the story, demands:

First and foremost, he should renounce God and
His laws, and utterly disclaim the whole title or in-
terest he had in any covenant of salvation. Next, he
should curse Him to His face, as Job was willed by
his wife, and write an absolute firm obligation of
his soul to the Devil, without condition or exception.
Thirdly and lastly (having done this), he should
pray to God fervently never to have mercy upon him,
or pardon him. . . . These fearful ceremonies
brought to an end, I bade him ope his mouth and
gape wide. He did so (as what will not slaves do for

fear?); therewith made I no more ado, but shot him full into the throat with my pistol. No more spake he after, so did I shoot him that he might never speak after, or repent him. His body being dead looked as black as a toad. The Devil presently branded it for his own.

Revenges almost as extravagant occur in such plays as Kyd's *The Spanish Tragedy,* Marston's *Antonio's Revenge* (which is contemporary with *Hamlet*), and later in the tragedies of Webster and Tourneur. The reasons Hamlet gives for sparing his uncle (III.iii.74–95) would have been regarded as normal by any Elizabethan playgoer.

In writing *Hamlet,* Shakespeare began with one advantage. The audience knew the story. There was therefore no need to start with an explanation. Instead, in the first scene of the play Shakespeare set about creating atmosphere; and he put the playgoer in the right mood with a sense of foreboding that something indeed was "rotten in the state of Denmark." In the second scene, the plot begins to move. King Claudius is shown holding his first council. The King dispatches the various items of official business on the agenda, in the course of which the state of affairs in Denmark is fully revealed.

Hamlet is then left alone, and his first soliloquy reveals certain matters that are pressing on his mind. His mother, with indecent haste, has married the brother of her late husband. According to canon law, she has therefore committed incest, for in early Christian times the command that man and wife should be one flesh was taken so literally that all the wife's relations became the husband's and vice versa. Shakespeare next shows a scene of the Polonius family and the increasing difficulties of Ophelia's position. After this domestic scene of pure comedy, the action returns to the battlements. The ghost appears, leads Hamlet away, tells him the whole story of the murder in the orchard, and demands revenge. Thus ends the first part of the play, which shows how murder was revealed and the duty of vengeance laid on Prince Hamlet.

At this point, critics become indignant with Hamlet and ask why he did not at once kill his uncle; to which there is the common-sense answer that the word of a ghost seen alone at midnight is hardly good enough evidence to kill anyone. Moreover, according to contemporary theological notions, a Christian knew that the appearance of a spirit or wraith in the shade of a person

newly dead might be evil. As King James expressed it in his *Daemonology:*

Amongst the Gentiles, the Devil used that much to make them believe that it was some good spirit that appeared to them then, either to forewarn them of the death of their friend, or else to discover unto them the will of the defunct, or what was the way of his slaughter. . . . And this way he easily deceived the Gentiles, because they knew not God. And to that same effect is it that he now appears in that manner to some ignorant Christians. For he dare not so illude any that knoweth that neither can the spirit of the defunct return to his friend, or yet an angel use such forms.

The second part of the play starts some weeks later. In this part we are shown how Hamlet proved his uncle guilty. To indicate the passage of time, the play begins with Polonius sending his man Reynaldo to Paris with the next installment of Laertes' allowance. It shows also Hamlet's reaction to Ophelia's refusal to have anything more to do with him. For Hamlet the situation is even worse than at the beginning of the play, for he is now burdened with the horrible suspicion that as yet he can neither verify nor disprove. When Rosencrantz and Guildenstern tell him of the players, he sees his chance of proving once and for all the truth of the midnight revelation. His soliloquy at the end of Act II (ii.575–634) concludes with the words:

> The spirit that I have seen
> May be the Devil, and the Devil hath power
> To assume a pleasing shape. Yea, and perhaps
> Out of my weakness and my melancholy,
> As he is very potent with such spirits,
> Abuses me to damn me. I'll have grounds
> More relative than this. The play's the thing
> Wherein I'll catch the conscience of the King.

This emphasis on the Devil and on melancholy is a literal statement of scientific fact as it was believed by Shakespeare's contemporaries. Melancholy in its extremest forms was the cause of all kinds of mental aberration, including delusion and hallucination. Hamlet, therefore, anticipating modern scientists by some centuries, decides to apply an elementary form of lie detector to his uncle. In the play scene, Claudius reveals his guilt beyond any possible doubt. Now Hamlet knows for certain that it was a true ghost and not a figment of his melancholy imagination.

At this point the whole direction of the play changes. In the act of proving for certain the guilt of his uncle Hamlet has revealed to Claudius that he knows all. The initiative passes to Claudius, and he can take action against his nephew. As Claudius tries to pray, Hamlet passes by on his way to his mother. This is the only time in the play that Claudius is alone or that Claudius and Hamlet are alone together. But the opportunity for vengeance is unsuitable. Again the words of Hamlet's soliloquy (III.iii.74–95) should be taken literally. Revenge demanded hell-fire for the victim and at this moment Claudius was apparently in a state of grace. So Hamlet passes into his mother's chamber, and there he kills Polonius.

The third part of the play then begins. Hamlet himself has committed a murder, and the duty of vengeance is laid on Laertes. Soon afterward, Hamlet goes on his way to England and disappears for a long while. During his absence the second revenge story — the revenge of Laertes for his father Polonius — is set in motion. Ophelia meanwhile has gone mad. Laertes returns, leading a revolution, but the King overcomes him by superior will power and the two plot Hamlet's death. When Hamlet unexpectedly returns, destruction awaits him.

At this crisis Shakespeare deliberately holds back the final catastrophe. He introduces two new characters, the Gravediggers. The gravedigging scene has several dramatic purposes. It gives emotional relief, and it is a cynical contrast to Hamlet's lofty philosophy. Hamlet had brooded much over man and mortality; here in common life are the two who have the last word with man. Then comes the funeral of Ophelia, simple, almost sordid, and the sudden ferocity of the fight at the open grave. The excitement is growing, but once more Shakespeare holds us back. He introduces Osric, the fashionable courtier, with nothing to recommend him but his wealth, his clothes, and his pretty manners. He is, in fact, another of the " humor " types so common on the stage in these years. The audience is now ready for the final catastrophe, when both vengeances are consummated and all the guilty punished in one bloody ending.

When the play is viewed as a tragedy of the Elizabethan and not the Romantic era, many of its problems disappear. Nevertheless, there are other problems in *Hamlet*. Shakespeare took this old story of blood and revenge and made it modern — that is, modern to his generation. For some reason it seems to have been his favorite play. When he wrote it, he was, with all thinking men of his age, in a period of profound disillusionment and pessimism, and he made it the vessel into which he poured his thoughts on all kinds of problems: on fathers and children, on sex, on drunkenness, on suicide, on mortality and corruption, on ingratitude and loyalty, on acting, on handwriting even, on fate, on man and the universe. There is more of Shakespeare himself in this play than in any of his others.

Hamlet

DRAMATIS PERSONAE

CLAUDIUS, *King of Denmark*
HAMLET, *son to the late, and nephew to the present King*
POLONIUS, *Lord Chamberlain*
HORATIO, *friend to Hamlet*
LAERTES, *son to Polonius*
VOLTIMAND ⎫
CORNELIUS ⎪
ROSENCRANTZ ⎬ *courtiers*
GUILDENSTERN ⎪
OSRIC ⎪
A GENTLEMAN ⎭
A PRIEST
MARCELLUS ⎫ *officers*
BERNARDO ⎭
FRANCISCO, *a soldier*

REYNALDO, *servant to Polonius*
PLAYERS
TWO CLOWNS, *gravediggers*
FORTINBRAS, *Prince of Norway*
A CAPTAIN
ENGLISH AMBASSADORS

GERTRUDE, *Queen of Denmark, and mother to Hamlet*

OPHELIA, *daughter to Polonius*
LORDS, LADIES, OFFICERS, SOLDIERS, SAILORS, MESSENGERS, *and other* ATTENDANTS

GHOST *of Hamlet's father*

SCENE — *Denmark.*

Act I

SCENE I. *Elsinore. A platform° before the castle.*

[FRANCISCO *at his post. Enter to him* BERNARDO.]

BER. Who's there?

FRAN. Nay, answer me. Stand, and unfold yourself.°

BER. Long live the King!°

FRAN. Bernardo?

BER. He.   5

FRAN. You come most carefully upon your hour.

BER. 'Tis now struck twelve. Get thee to bed, Francisco.

FRAN. For this relief much thanks. 'Tis bitter cold,
And I am sick at heart.

BER. Have you had quiet guard?

FRAN.   Not a mouse stirring.   10

BER. Well, good night.
If you do meet Horatio and Marcellus,
The rivals° of my watch, bid them make haste.

FRAN. I think I hear them. Stand, ho! Who is there?

[*Enter* HORATIO *and* MARCELLUS.]

HOR. Friends to this ground.

MAR.   And liegemen° to the Dane.   15

FRAN. Give you good night.

MAR.   Oh, farewell, honest soldier.
Who hath relieved you?

FRAN.   Bernardo hath my place.
Give you good night.   [*Exit.*]

MAR.   Holloa! Bernardo!

BER.   Say,
What, is Horatio there?

HOR.   A piece of him.

BER. Welcome, Horatio. Welcome, good Marcellus.   20

MAR. What, has this thing appeared again tonight?

BER. I have seen nothing.

MAR. Horatio says 'tis but our fantasy,°
And will not let belief take hold of him
Touching this dreaded sight twice seen of us.   25
Therefore I have entreated him along
With us to watch the minutes of this night,
That if again this apparition come,
He may approve our eyes° and speak to it.

HOR. Tush, tush, 'twill not appear.

BER.   Sit down awhile,   30
And let us once again assail your ears,
That are so fortified against our story,
What we have two nights seen.

HOR.   Well, sit we down,
And let us hear Bernardo speak of this.

BER. Last night of all,   35
When yond same star that's westward from the pole°
Had made his course to illume° that part of heaven

Act I, Sc. i: s.d., **platform**: the level place on the ramparts where the cannon were mounted. **2. unfold yourself**: reveal who you are. **3. Long . . . King**: probably the password for the night. **13. rivals**: partners. **15. liegemen**: loyal subjects. **23. fantasy**: imagination. **29. approve our eyes**: verify what we have seen. **36. pole**: Polestar. **37. illume**: light.

Where now it burns, Marcellus and myself,
The bell then beating one ——
　　　　　　　[Enter GHOST.*]*

MAR. Peace, break thee off. Look where it comes
　　again! 40

BER. In the same figure, like the King that's
　　dead.

MAR. Thou art a scholar.° Speak to it, Horatio.

BER. Looks it not like the King? Mark it, Horatio.

HOR. Most like. It harrows° me with fear and
　　wonder.

BER. It would be spoke to.

MAR. 　　　　　　　Question it, Horatio. 45

HOR. What art thou that usurp'st this time of
　　night,
Together with° that fair and warlike form
In which the majesty of buried Denmark°
Did sometimes march? By Heaven I charge thee,
　　speak!

MAR. It is offended.

BER. 　　　　　　See, it stalks away! 50

HOR. Stay! Speak, speak! I charge thee, speak!
　　　　　　　　[Exit GHOST.*]*

MAR. 'Tis gone, and will not answer.

BER. How now, Horatio! You tremble and look
　　pale.
Is not this something more than fantasy?
What think you on 't? 55

HOR. Before my God, I might not this believe
Without the sensible and true avouch
Of mine own eyes.°

MAR. 　　　　Is it not like the King?

HOR. As thou art to thyself.
Such was the very armor he had on 60
When he the ambitious Norway combated.
So frowned he once when, in an angry parle,°
He smote the sledded Polacks° on the ice.
'Tis strange.

MAR. Thus twice before, and jump at this dead
　　hour,° 65
With martial stalk hath he gone by our watch.

HOR. In what particular thought to work I know
　　not,
But in the gross and scope° of my opinion
This bodes some strange eruption° to our state.

MAR. Good now, sit down and tell me, he that
　　knows, 70
Why this same strict and most observant watch
So nightly toils° the subject° of the land;
And why such daily cast of brazen cannon
And foreign mart° for implements of war;
Why° such impress° of shipwrights, whose sore
　　task 75
Does not divide the Sunday from the week;
What might be toward,° that this sweaty haste
Doth make the night joint laborer with the day.
Who is 't that can inform me?

HOR. 　　　　　　　That can I,
At least the whisper goes so. Our last King, 80
Whose image even but now appeared to us,
Was, as you know, by Fortinbras of Norway,
Thereto pricked° on by a most emulate° pride,
Dared to the combat, in which our valiant Ham-
　　let —
For so this side of our known world esteemed
　　him — 85
Did slay this Fortinbras. Who° by a sealed com-
　　pact,°
Well ratified by law and heraldry,°
Did forfeit, with his life, all those his lands
Which he stood seized of° to the conqueror.
Against the which, a moiety competent° 90
Was gagèd° by our King, which had returned
To the inheritance of Fortinbras
Had he been vanquisher, as by the same covenant
And carriage of the article designed°
His fell to Hamlet. Now, sir, young Fortinbras, 95
Of unimprovèd mettle° hot and full,
Hath in the skirts° of Norway here and there
Sharked° up a list of lawless resolutes,°
For food and diet,° to some enterprise 99
That hath a stomach° in 't. Which is no other —
As it doth well appear unto our state —
But to recover of us, by strong hand
And terms compulsatory,° those foresaid lands
So by his father lost. And this, I take it,
Is the main motive of our preparations, 105
The source of this our watch and the chief head°

Of this posthaste and romage° in the land.
  BER. I think it be no other but e'en so.
Well may it sort° that this portentous figure   109
Comes armèd through our watch, so like the King
That was and is the question of these wars.
  HOR. A mote° it is to trouble the mind's eye.
In the most high and palmy° state of Rome,
A little ere the mightiest Julius fell,   114
The graves stood tenantless, and the sheeted° dead
Did squeak and gibber° in the Roman streets.
As stars° with trains of fire and dews of blood,
Disasters° in the sun, and the moist star°
Upon whose influence Neptune's empire stands
Was sick almost to doomsday with eclipse.   120
And even the like precurse° of fierce events,
As harbingers° preceding still the fates
And prologue to the omen° coming on,
Have Heaven and earth together demonstrated
Unto our climatures° and countrymen.   125
[Re-enter GHOST.] But soft, behold! Lo where it
          comes again!
I'll cross it,° though it blast me. Stay, illusion!
If thou hast any sound, or use of voice,
Speak to me.
If° there be any good thing to be done   130
That may to thee do ease and grace to me,°
Speak to me.
If thou art privy to° thy country's fate,
Which, happily,° foreknowing may avoid,
Oh, speak!   135
Or if thou hast uphoarded in thy life
Extorted° treasure in the womb of earth,
For which, they say, you spirits oft walk in death,
Speak of it. Stay, and speak! [The cock crows.°]
          Stop it, Marcellus.
  MAR. Shall I strike at it with my partisan?°   140
  HOR. Do, if it will not stand.
  BER.   'Tis here!
  HOR.   'Tis here!
  MAR. 'Tis gone!   [Exit GHOST.]

107. posthaste . . . romage: urgency and bustle.   109. Well . . .
sort: it would be a natural reason.   112. mote: speck of dust.
113. palmy: flourishing.   115. sheeted: in their shrouds. See
App. 16.   116. gibber: utter strange sounds.   117. As stars:
The sense of the passage is here broken; possibly a line has been
omitted after l. 116.   118. Disasters: unlucky signs. moist star:
the moon, which influences the tides.   121. precurse: forewarn-
ing.   122. harbingers: forerunners. The harbinger was an offi-
cer of the Court who was sent ahead to make the arrangements
when the Court went on progress.   123. omen: disaster.
125. climatures: regions.   127. cross it: stand in its way.
130–39. If . . . speak: In popular belief there were four reasons
why the spirit of a dead man should walk: (a) to reveal a secret,
(b) to utter a warning, (c) to reveal concealed treasure, (d) to
reveal the manner of its death. Horatio thus adjures the ghost
by three potent reasons, but before he can utter the fourth the
cock crows.   131. grace to me: bring me into a state of spiritual
grace.   133. privy to: have secret knowledge of.   134. happily:
by good luck.   137. Extorted: evilly acquired.   139. s.d., cock
crows: i.e., a sign that dawn is at hand. See ll. 147–64.   140. par-
tisan: See Pl. 21a.

We do it wrong, being so majestical,
To offer it the show of violence,
For it is as the air invulnerable,   145
And our vain blows malicious mockery.
  BER. It was about to speak when the cock crew.
  HOR. And then it started like a guilty thing
Upon a fearful° summons. I have heard
The cock, that is the trumpet to the morn,   150
Doth with his lofty and shrill-sounding throat
Awake the god of day, and at his warning,
Whether in sea or fire, in earth or air,
The extravagant and erring° spirit hies
To his confine.° And of the truth herein   155
This present object made probation.°
  MAR. It faded on the crowing of the cock.
Some say that ever 'gainst° that season comes
Wherein Our Saviour's birth is celebrated,
The bird of dawning singeth all night long.   160
And then, they say, no spirit dare stir abroad,
The nights are wholesome, then no planets° strike,
No fairy takes° nor witch hath power to charm,
So hallowed and so gracious is the time.   164
  HOR. So have I heard and do in part believe it.
But look, the morn, in russet mantle clad,
Walks o'er the dew of yon high eastward hill.
Break we our watch up, and by my advice
Let us impart what we have seen tonight
Unto young Hamlet, for upon my life,   170
This spirit, dumb to us, will speak to him.
Do you consent we shall acquaint him with it,
As needful in our loves, fitting our duty?
  MAR. Let's do 't, I pray. And I this morning know
Where we shall find him most conveniently.   175
                                              [Exeunt.]

SCENE II. A room of state in the castle.

[Flourish.° Enter the KING, QUEEN, HAMLET,
    POLONIUS, LAERTES, VOLTIMAND, CORNELIUS,
          LORDS, and ATTENDANTS.]

  KING. Though yet of Hamlet our dear brother's
          death
The memory be green,° and that it us befitted
To bear our hearts in grief and our whole kingdom
To be contracted in one brow of woe,°
Yet so far hath discretion° fought with nature°   5
That we with wisest sorrow think on him,

149. fearful: causing fear.   154. extravagant . . . erring: both
words mean "wandering."   155. confine: place of confine-
ment.   156. probation: proof.   158. 'gainst: in anticipation of.
162. planets: Planets were supposed to bring disaster. See
App. 1.   163. takes: bewitches.
Sc. ii: s.d., Flourish: fanfare of trumpets.   2. green: fresh.
4. contracted . . . woe: i.e., every subject's forehead should be
puckered with grief.   5. discretion: common sense. nature:
natural sorrow.

Together with remembrance of ourselves.
Therefore our sometime sister,° now our Queen,
The imperial jointress° to this warlike state,
Have we, as 'twere with a defeated joy —   10
With an auspicious and a dropping eye,°
With mirth in funeral and with dirge in marriage,
In equal scale weighing delight and dole° —
Taken to wife. Nor have we herein barred
Your better wisdoms,° which have freely gone   15
With this affair along. For all, our thanks.
Now follows that you know. Young Fortinbras,
Holding a weak supposal° of our worth,
Or thinking by our late dear brother's death
Our state to be disjoint and out of frame,   20
Colleagued with the dream of his advantage,°
He hath not failed to pester us with message
Importing the surrender of those lands
Lost by his father, with all bonds of law,°
To our most valiant brother. So much for him. 25
Now for ourself, and for this time of meeting.
Thus much the business is: We have here writ
To Norway, uncle of young Fortinbras —
Who, impotent and bedrid, scarcely hears
Of this his nephew's purpose — to suppress   30
His further gait° herein, in that the levies,
The lists° and full proportions,° are all made
Out of his subject.° And we here dispatch
You, good Cornelius, and you, Voltimand,
For bearers of this greeting to old Norway,   35
Giving to you no further personal power
To business with the King more than the scope°
Of these delated articles° allow.
Farewell, and let your haste commend° your duty.
  COR. & VOLT. In that and all things will we show
  our duty.   40
  KING. We doubt it nothing. Heartily farewell.
        [*Exeunt* VOLTIMAND *and* CORNELIUS.]
And now, Laertes, what's the news with you?
You told us of some suit° — what is 't, Laertes?
You cannot speak of reason to the Dane
And lose your voice. What wouldst thou beg,
  Laertes,   45
That shall not be my offer, not thy asking?

The head is not more native° to the heart,
The hand more instrumental° to the mouth,
Than is the throne of Denmark to thy father.
What wouldst thou have, Laertes?
  LAER.   My dread° lord, 50
Your leave and favor to return to France,
From whence though willingly I came to Denmark
To show my duty in your coronation,
Yet now, I must confess, that duty done,   54
My thoughts and wishes bend again toward France
And bow them to your gracious leave and pardon.
  KING. Have you your father's leave? What says
  Polonius?
  POL. He hath, my lord, wrung from me my slow
  leave
By laborsome petition, and at last
Upon his will° I sealed my hard consent.°   60
I do beseech you give him leave to go.
  KING. Take thy fair hour, Laertes, time be thine,
And thy best graces spend° it at thy will!
But now, my cousin° Hamlet, and my son ——
  HAML. [*Aside*] A little more than kin and less
  than kind.°   65
  KING. How is it that the clouds still hang on you?
  HAML. Not so, my lord. I am too much i' the
  sun.
  QUEEN. Good Hamlet, cast thy nighted color° off,
And let thine eye look like a friend on Denmark.
Do not forever with thy vailèd lids°   70
Seek for thy noble father in the dust.
Thou know'st 'tis common — all that lives must die,
Passing through nature to eternity.
  HAML. Aye, madam, it is common.
  QUEEN.   If it be,
Why seems it so particular with thee?   75
  HAML. Seems, madam! Nay, it is. I know not
  "seems."
'Tis not alone my inky cloak, good Mother,
Nor customary suits of solemn black,
Nor windy suspiration of forced breath —
No, nor the fruitful river° in the eye,   80
Nor the dejected havior of the visage,°
Together with all forms, moods, shapes of grief —
That can denote me truly. These indeed seem,
For they are actions that a man might play.°
But I have that within which passeth show,   85
These but the trappings° and the suits of woe.

---

8. sister: sister-in-law. See *Haml* Intro. p. 603a.   9. jointress:
partner by marriage.   11. auspicious . . . eye: an eye at the same
time full of joy and of tears.   13. dole: grief.   14–15. barred
. . . wisdoms: i.e., in taking this step we have not shut out
your advice. As is obvious throughout the play, the Danes chose
their King by election and not by right of birth. See V.ii.65,
366.   18. weak supposal: poor opinion.   21. Colleagued . . .
advantage: uniting himself with this dream that here was a good
opportunity.   24. with . . . law: legally binding, as already ex-
plained in ll. 80–95, p. 606b, above.   31. gait: progress.   32. lists:
rosters. proportions: military establishments.   33. subject: sub-
jects.   37. scope: limit.   38. delated articles: detailed instruc-
tions. Claudius is following usual diplomatic procedure. Am-
bassadors sent on a special mission carried with them a letter
of introduction and greeting to the King of the foreign Court
and detailed instructions to guide them in the negotiations.
39. commend: display; lit., recommend.   43. suit: petition.

47. native: closely related.   48. instrumental: serviceable.
50. dread: dreaded, much respected.   60. will: desire. sealed
. . . consent: agreed to, but with great reluctance.   63. best . . .
spend: i.e., use your time well.   64. cousin: kinsman. The word
was used for any near relation.   65. A . . . kind: too near a re-
lation (uncle-father) and too little natural affection. kind: affec-
tionate.   68. nighted color: black. Hamlet alone is in deep
mourning; the rest of the Court wear gay clothes.   70. vailed
lids: lowered eyelids.   80. fruitful river: stream of tears.
81. dejected . . . visage: downcast countenance.   84. play:
act, as in a play.   86. trappings: ornaments.

KING. 'Tis sweet and commendable in your
    nature, Hamlet,
To give these mourning duties to your father.
But you must know your father lost a father,
That father lost, lost his, and the survivor bound   90
In filial obligation for some term
To do obsequious sorrow.° But to perséver
In obstinate condolement° is a course
Of impious stubbornness, 'tis unmanly grief.
It shows a will most incorrect to Heaven,   95
A heart unfortified,° a mind impatient,
An understanding simple and unschooled.
For what we know must be and is as common
As any the most vulgar° thing to sense,
Why should we in our peevish opposition   100
Take it to heart? Fie! 'Tis a fault to Heaven,
A fault against the dead, a fault to nature,
To reason most absurd, whose common theme
Is death of fathers, and who still hath cried,
From the first corse° till he that died today,   105
" This must be so." We pray you throw to earth
This unprevailing° woe, and think of us
As of a father. For let the world take note,
You are the most immediate° to our throne,
And with no less nobility of love   110
Than that which dearest father bears his son
Do I impart toward you. For your intent
In going back to school° in Wittenberg,
It is most retrograde° to our desire.
And we beseech you bend you° to remain   115
Here in the cheer and comfort of our eye,
Our chiefest courtier, cousin, and our son.
    QUEEN. Let not thy mother lose her prayers,
    Hamlet.
I pray thee, stay with us, go not to Wittenberg.   119
    HAML. I shall in all my best obey you, madam.
    KING. Why, 'tis a loving and a fair reply.
Be as ourself in Denmark. Madam, come,
This gentle and unforced accord of Hamlet
Sits smiling to my heart. In grace whereof,
No jocund health that Denmark drinks today   125
But the great cannon° to the clouds shall tell,
And the King's rouse° the Heaven shall bruit°
    again,
Respeaking earthly thunder. Come away.
          [*Flourish. Exeunt all but* HAMLET.]
    HAML. Oh, that this too too solid flesh would melt,
Thaw, and resolve itself into a dew!   130

Or that the Everlasting had not fixed
His canon° 'gainst self-slaughter! Oh, God! God!
How weary, stale, flat, and unprofitable
Seem to me all the uses° of this world!
Fie on 't, ah, fie! 'Tis an unweeded garden,   135
That grows to seed, things rank° and gross in
    nature
Possess it merely.° That it should come to this!
But two months dead! Nay, not so much, not two.
So excellent a King, that was, to this,
Hyperion° to a satyr.° So loving to my mother   140
That he might not beteem° the winds of heaven
Visit her face too roughly. Heaven and earth!
Must I remember? Why, she would hang on him
As if increase of appetite had grown   144
By what it fed on. And yet within a month ——
Let me not think on 't. — Frailty, thy name is
    woman! —
A little month, or ere those shoes were old
With which she followed my poor father's body,
Like Niobe° all tears. — Why she, even she —   149
Oh, God! A beast that wants discourse of reason°
Would have mourned longer — married with my
    uncle,
My father's brother, but no more like my father
Than I to Hercules. Within a month,
Ere yet the salt of most unrighteous tears
Had left the flushing in her gallèd° eyes,   155
She married. Oh, most wicked speed, to post°
With such dexterity° to incestuous sheets!
It is not, nor it cannot, come to good.
But break, my heart, for I must hold my tongue!
    [*Enter* HORATIO, MARCELLUS, *and* BERNARDO.]
    HOR. Hail to your lordship!
    HAML.   I am glad to see you well.   160
Horatio — or I do forget myself.
    HOR. The same, my lord, and your poor servant
    ever.
    HAML. Sir, my good friend — I'll change that
    name° with you.
And what make you from Wittenberg, Horatio?
Marcellus?   165
    MAR. My good lord?
    HAML. I am very glad to see you. [*To* BERNARDO]
    Good even, sir.
But what, in faith, make you from Wittenberg?
    HOR. A truant disposition, good my lord.
    HAML. I would not hear your enemy say so,   170
Nor shall you do my ear that violence

---

92. **obsequious sorrow:** the sorrow usual at funerals.   93. **obstinate condolement:** lamentation disregarding the will of God. 96. **unfortified:** not strengthened with the consolation of religion. 99. **vulgar:** common.   105. **corse:** corpse. There is unconscious irony in this remark, for the first corpse was that of Abel, also slain by his brother.   107. **unprevailing:** futile.   109. **most immediate:** next heir.   113. **school:** university.   114. **retrograde:** contrary.   115. **bend you:** incline.   126. **great cannon:** This Danish custom of discharging cannon when the King proposed a toast was much noted by Englishmen.   127. **rouse:** deep drink. **bruit:** sound loudly, echo.

132. **canon:** rule, law.   134. **uses:** ways.   136. **rank:** coarse. 137. **merely:** entirely.   140. **Hyperion:** the sun god. **satyr:** a creature half man, half goat — ugly and lecherous.   141. **beteem:** allow.   149. **Niobe:** She boasted of her children, to the annoyance of the goddess Artemis, who slew them all. Thereafter Niobe became so sorrowful that she changed into a rock everlastingly dripping water.   150. **wants . . . reason:** is without ability to reason.   155. **galled:** sore.   156. **post:** hasten.   157. **dexterity:** nimbleness.   164. **that name:** i.e., friend.

To make it truster of your own report
Against yourself. I know you are no truant.
But what is your affair in Elsinore?
We'll teach you to drink deep° ere you depart.   175
   HOR. My lord, I came to see your father's funeral.
   HAML. I pray thee do not mock me, fellow student.
I think it was to see my mother's wedding.
   HOR. Indeed, my lord, it followed hard upon.
   HAML. Thrift, thrift, Horatio! The funeral baked
     meats   180
Did coldly furnish forth the marriage tables.°
Would I had met my dearest° foe in Heaven
Or ever I had seen that day, Horatio!
My father! — Methinks I see my father.
   HOR. Oh, where, my lord?
   HAML.   In my mind's eye, Horatio. 185
   HOR. I saw him once. He was a goodly King.
   HAML. He was a man, take him for all in all.
I shall not look upon his like again.
   HOR. My lord, I think I saw him yesternight.
   HAML. Saw? Who?   190
   HOR. My lord, the King your father.
   HAML.   The King my father!
   HOR. Season your admiration° for a while
With an attent° ear till I may deliver,
Upon the witness of these gentlemen,
This marvel to you.
   HAML.   For God's love, let me hear. 195
   HOR. Two nights together had these gentlemen,
Marcellus and Bernardo, on their watch
In the dead vast and middle of the night,°
Been thus encountered. A figure like your father,
Armed at point exactly, cap-a-pie,°   200
Appears before them and with solemn march
Goes slow and stately by them. Thrice he walked
By their oppressed and fear-surprisèd eyes
Within his truncheon's° length, whilst they, dis-
    tilled°
Almost to jelly with the act of fear,   205
Stand dumb, and speak not to him. This to me
In dreadful secrecy impart they did,
And I with them the third night kept the watch,
Where, as they had delivered, both in time,   209
Form of the thing, each word made true and good,
The apparition comes. I knew your father.
These hands are not more like.
   HAML.   But where was this?
   MAR. My lord, upon the platform where we
    watched.
   HAML. Did you not speak to it?

   HOR.   My lord, I did,
But answer made it none. Yet once methought   215
It lifted up it° head and did address
Itself to motion, like as it would speak.
But even then the morning cock crew loud,
And at the sound it shrunk in haste away
And vanished from our sight.
   HAML.   'Tis very strange. 220
   HOR. As I do live, my honored lord, 'tis true,
And we did think it writ down in our duty
To let you know of it.
   HAML. Indeed, indeed, sirs, but this troubles me.
Hold you the watch tonight?
   MAR. & BER.   We do, my lord.   225
   HAML. Armed, say you?
   MAR. & BER.   Armed, my lord.
   HAML.   From top to toe?
   MAR. & BER. My lord, from head to foot.
   HAML. Then saw you not his face?
   HOR. Oh yes, my lord, he wore his beaver° up.
   HAML. What, looked he frowningly?   230
   HOR. A countenance more in sorrow than in an-
    ger.
   HAML. Pale, or red?
   HOR. Nay, very pale.
   HAML.   And fixed his eyes upon you?
   HOR. Most constantly.
   HAML.   I would I had been there.   235
   HOR. It would have much amazed you.
   HAML. Very like, very like. Stayed it long?
   HOR. While one with moderate haste might tell°
    a hundred.
   MAR. & BER. Longer, longer.
   HOR. Not when I saw 't.
   HAML.   His beard was grizzled?° No? 240
   HOR. It was as I have seen it in his life,
A sable silvered.°
   HAML.   I will watch tonight.
Perchance 'twill walk again.
   HOR.   I warrant it will.
   HAML. If it assume my noble father's person,
I'll speak to it though Hell itself should gape   245
And bid me hold my peace. I pray you all,
If you have hitherto concealed this sight,
Let it be tenable° in your silence still,
And whatsoever else shall hap tonight,
Give it an understanding, but no tongue.   250
I will requite° your loves. So fare you well.
Upon the platform, 'twixt eleven and twelve,
I'll visit you.
   ALL.   Our duty to your Honor.
   HAML. Your loves, as mine to you. Farewell.
               [Exeunt all but HAMLET.]
My father's spirit in arms! All is not well.   255

---

175. drink deep: For more on the drunken habits of the Danes, see I.iv.8–38. **180–81. Thrift . . . tables:** they hurried on the wedding for economy's sake, so that the remains of food served at the funeral might be used cold for the wedding. **baked meats:** feast. **182. dearest:** best-hated. **192. Season . . . admiration:** moderate your wonder. **193. attent:** attentive. **198. dead . . . night:** deep, silent midnight. **200. at . . . cap-a-pie:** complete in every detail, head to foot. See Pl. 8a. **204. truncheon:** a general's staff. **distilled:** melted.

216. it: its. **229. beaver:** front part of the helmet, which could be raised. **238. tell:** count. **240. grizzled:** gray. **242. sable silvered:** black mingled with white. **248. tenable:** held fast. **251. requite:** repay.

I doubt° some foul play. Would the night were
    come!
Till then sit still, my soul. Foul deeds will rise,
Though all the earth o'erwhelm them, to men's
    eyes.   [*Exit.*]

SCENE III. *A room in* POLONIUS's *house.*

[*Enter* LAERTES *and* OPHELIA.]
LAER. My necessaries° are embarked. Farewell.
And, Sister, as the winds give benefit
And convoy is assistant,° do not sleep,
But let me hear from you.
OPH.   Do you doubt that?
LAER. For Hamlet, and the trifling of his favor,°
Hold it a fashion and a toy in blood,°
A violet in the youth of primy° nature,
Forward, not permanent, sweet, not lasting,
The perfume and suppliance of a minute° —
No more.
OPH. No more but so?
LAER.   Think it no more.   10
For Nature crescent does not grow alone
In thews and bulk,° but as this temple° waxes
The inward service of the mind and soul
Grows wide withal. Perhaps he loves you now,
And now no soil nor cautel° doth besmirch   15
The virtue of his will.° But you must fear,
His greatness weighed,° his will is not his own,
For he himself is subject to his birth.
He may not, as unvalued persons do,
Carve° for himself, for on his choice depends   20
The safety and health of this whole state,
And therefore must his choice be circumscribed°
Unto the voice and yielding of that body
Whereof he is the head. Then if he says he loves you,
It fits your wisdom so far to believe it   25
As he in his particular act and place
May give his saying deed, which is no further
Than the main voice of Denmark goes withal.
Then weigh what loss your honor may sustain
If with too credent° ear you list his songs,   30
Or lose your heart, or your chaste treasure° open
To his unmastered importunity.
Fear it, Ophelia, fear it, my dear sister,
And keep you in the rear° of your affection,
Out of the shot and danger of desire.   35

The chariest maid is prodigal enough
If she unmask her beauty to the moon.
Virtue itself 'scapes not calumnious strokes.
The canker galls the infants° of the spring
Too oft before their buttons° be disclosed,   40
And in the morn and liquid dew of youth
Contagious blastments° are most imminent.
Be wary, then, best safety lies in fear.
Youth to itself rebels, though none else near.°
OPH. I shall the effect of this good lesson keep   45
As watchman to my heart. But, good my brother,
Do not, as some ungracious pastors do,
Show me the steep and thorny way to Heaven
Whilst, like a puffed° and reckless libertine,
Himself the primrose path of dalliance° treads   50
And recks not his own rede.°
LAER.   Oh, fear me not.
I stay too long. But here my father comes.
[*Enter* POLONIUS.] A double blessing is a double
    grace,
Occasion smiles° upon a second leave.
POL. Yet here, Laertes! Aboard, aboard, for
    shame!   55
The wind sits in the shoulder of your sail
And you are stayed° for. There, my blessing with
    thee!
And these few precepts in thy memory
Look thou cháracter.° Give thy thoughts no tongue,
Nor any unproportioned° thought his act.   60
Be thou familiar, but by no means vulgar.
Those friends thou hast, and their adoption tried,°
Grapple them to thy soul with hoops of steel,
But do not dull thy palm with entertainment°   64
Of each new-hatched unfledged° comrade. Beware
Of entrance to a quarrel, but being in,
Bear 't that the opposèd may beware of thee.
Give every man thy ear, but few thy voice.°
Take each man's censure,° but reserve thy judg-
    ment.
Costly thy habit° as thy purse can buy,   70
But not expressed in fancy° — rich, not gaudy.
For the apparel oft proclaims the man,
And they in France of the best rank and station
Are of a most select and generous chief in that.°

39. canker . . . infants: maggot harms the unopened buds.
40. buttons: buds.   42. Contagious blastments: infectious blasts.
44. though . . . near: without anyone else to encourage it.
49. puffed: panting.   50. primrose . . . dalliance: i.e., the pleas-
ant way of love-making.   51. recks . . . rede: takes no heed of
his own advice.   54. Occasion smiles: i.e., here is a happy
chance.   57. stayed: waited.   59. character: inscribe.   60. un-
proportioned: unsuitable.   62. adoption tried: friendship tested
by experience.   64. dull . . . entertainment: let your hand grow
callous with welcome.   65. unfledged: lit., newly out of the egg,
immature.   68. Give . . . voice: listen to everyone but commit
yourself to few.   69. censure: opinion.   70. habit: dress.
71. expressed in fancy: fantastic.   74. Are . . . that: A disputed
line; this is the F1 reading. Q2 reads "Or of the most select and
generous, chief in that"; i.e., the best noble and gentle families
are very particular in their dress. generous: of gentle birth,

256. doubt: suspect.
Sc. iii: 1. necessaries: baggage.   3. convoy . . . assistant:
means of conveyance is available.   5. favor: i.e., toward you.
6. toy in blood: trifling impulse.   7. primy: springtime; i.e.,
youthful.   8. perfume . . . minute: perfume which lasts only
for a minute.   11–12. For . . . bulk: for natural growth is not
only in bodily bulk.   12. temple: i.e., the body.   15. cautel:
deceit.   16. will: desire.   17. His . . . weighed: when you
consider his high position.   20. Carve: choose.   22. circum-
scribed: restricted.   30. credent: credulous.   31. chaste treas-
ure: the treasure of your chastity.   34. in . . . rear: i.e., far-
thest from danger.

Neither a borrower nor a lender be, 75
For loan oft loses both itself and friend
And borrowing dulls the edge of husbandry.°
This above all: To thine own self be true,
And it must follow, as the night the day,
Thou canst not then be false to any man. 80
Farewell. My blessing season° this in thee!

LAER. Most humbly do I take my leave, my lord.

POL. The time invites you. Go, your servants
tend.°

LAER. Farewell, Ophelia, and remember well
What I have said to you.

OPH. 'Tis in my memory locked, 85
And you yourself shall keep the key of it.

LAER. Farewell. [*Exit.*]

POL. What is 't, Ophelia, he hath said to you?

OPH. So please you, something touching the Lord
Hamlet.

POL. Marry,° well bethought.° 90
'Tis told me he hath very oft of late
Given private time to you, and you yourself
Have of your audience been most free and bounte-
ous.
If it be so — as so 'tis put on me,
And that in way of caution — I must tell you 95
You do not understand yourself so clearly
As it behooves° my daughter and your honor.
What is between you? Give me up the truth.

OPH. He hath, my lord, of late made many ten-
ders°
Of his affection to me. 100

POL. Affection! Pooh! You speak like a green girl,
Unsifted° in such perilous circumstance.
Do you believe his tenders, as you call them? 103

OPH. I do not know, my lord, what I should think.

POL. Marry, I'll teach you. Think yourself a baby
That you have ta'en these tenders° for true pay,
Which are not sterling.° Tender yourself more
dearly,
Or — not to crack the wind of° the poor phrase,
Running it thus — you'll tender me a fool. 109

OPH. My lord, he hath importuned me with love
In honorable fashion.

POL. Aye, fashion° you may call it. Go to, go to.

OPH. And hath given countenance to his speech,°
my lord,
With almost all the holy vows of Heaven.

POL. Aye, springes° to catch woodcocks.° I do
know, 115
When the blood burns, how prodigal° the soul

Lends the tongue vows. These blazes,° daughter,
Giving more light than heat, extinct in both,
Even in their promise as it is a-making,
You must not take for fire. From this time 120
Be something scanter of your maiden presence,
Set your entreatments at a higher rate
Than a command to parley.° For Lord Hamlet,
Believe so much in him, that he is young,
And with a larger tether° may he walk 125
Than may be given you. In few,° Ophelia,
Do not believe his vows, for they are brokers,°
Not of that dye which their investments° show,
But mere implorators° of unholy suits,
Breathing like sanctified and pious bawds° 130
The better to beguile. This is for all.
I would not, in plain terms, from this time forth
Have you so slander any moment leisure°
As to give words or talk with the Lord Hamlet.
Look to 't, I charge you. Come your ways. 135

OPH. I shall obey, my lord. [*Exeunt.*]

SCENE IV. *The platform*

[*Enter* HAMLET, HORATIO, *and* MARCELLUS.]

HAML. The air bites shrewdly.° It is very cold.

HOR. It is a nipping and an eager° air.

HAML. What hour now?

HOR. I thinks it lacks of twelve.

MAR. No, it is struck.

HOR. Indeed? I heard it not. It then draws near
the season 5
Wherein the spirit held his wont to walk.
[*A flourish of trumpets, and ordnance
shot off within.°*]
What doth this mean, my lord?

HAML. The King doth wake° tonight and takes
his rouse,°
Keeps wassail,° and the swaggering upspring reels.°
And as he drains his draughts of Rhenish° down,
The kettledrum and trumpet thus bray out 11
The triumph of his pledge.

HOR. Is it a custom?

HAML. Aye, marry, is 't.

---

117. blazes: flashes, quickly extinguished (*extinct*). **122–23. Set
. . . parley:** when you are asked to see him do not regard
it as a command to negotiate. **parley:** meeting to discuss
terms. **125. tether:** rope by which a grazing animal is fastened
to its peg. **126. In few:** in short. **127. brokers:** traveling
salesmen. **128. investments:** garments. **129. implorators:** men
who solicit. **130. bawds:** keepers of brothels. F1 and Q2 read
"bond," an easy misprint for "baud" — the Elizabethan spelling
of "bawd." **133. slander . . . leisure:** misuse any moment of
leisure.

Sc. iv: 1. shrewdly: bitterly. **2. eager:** sharp. **6. s.d.,
within:** off stage. **8. wake:** "makes a night of it." **rouse:** See
I.ii.127,n. **9. wassail:** revelry. **swaggering . . . reels:** reel in a
riotous dance. **10. Rhenish:** Rhine wine.

---

77. husbandry: economy. **81. season:** bring to fruit. **83. tend:**
attend. **90. Marry:** Mary, by the Virgin Mary. **well bethought:**
well remembered. **97. behooves:** is the duty of. **99. tenders:**
offers. **102. Unsifted:** untried. **106–09. tenders . . . tender:**
Polonius puns on "tenders," counters (used for money in games);
"tender," value; "tender," show. **107. sterling:** true currency.
108. crack . . . of: i.e., ride to death. **112. fashion:** mere show.
113. given . . . speech: confirmed his words. **115. springes:**
snares. **woodcocks:** foolish birds. **116. prodigal:** extravagantly.

But to my mind, though I am native here
And to the manner born, it is a custom   15
More honored in the breach than the observance.
This heavy-headed revel° east and west
Makes us traduced and taxed of° other nations.
They clepe° us drunkards, and with swinish phrase
Soil our addition,° and indeed it takes   20
From our achievements, though performed at
    height,°
The pith and marrow of our attribute.°
So oft it chances in particular men,
That for some vicious mole° of nature in them,
As in their birth — wherein they are not guilty,   25
Since nature cannot choose his origin —
By the o'ergrowth of some complexion,°
Oft breaking down the pales° and forts of reason,
Or by some habit that too much o'erleavens°   29
The form of plausive° manners, that these men —
Carrying, I say, the stamp of one defect,
Being Nature's livery,° or Fortune's star° —
Their virtues else — be they as pure as grace,
As infinite as man may undergo —
Shall in the general censure take corruption   35
From that particular fault. The dram of eale
Doth all the noble substance of a doubt
To his own scandal.°

> [*Enter* GHOST.]

HOR.   Look, my lord, it comes!
HAML. Angels and ministers of grace defend us!
Be thou a spirit of health or goblin damned,°   40
Bring with thee airs from Heaven or blasts from
    Hell,
Be thy intents wicked or charitable,
Thou comest in such a questionable° shape

---

17. **heavy-headed revel:** drinking which produces a thick head. 18. **traduced . . . of:** disgraced and censured by. 19. **clepe:** call. 20. **soil . . . addition:** smirch our honor. **addition:** lit., title of honor added to a man's name. 21. **though . . . height:** though of the highest merit. 22. **pith . . . attribute:** essential part of our honor; i.e., we lose the honor due to our achievements because of our reputation for drunkenness. 24. **mole:** blemish. 27. **o'ergrowth . . . complexion:** some quality allowed to overbalance the rest. See App. 3. 28. **pales:** defenses. 29. **o'er-leavens:** mixes with. 30. **plausive:** agreeable. 32. **Nature's livery:** i.e., inborn. **Fortune's star:** the result of ill luck. See App. 18. 36–38. **The . . . scandal:** This is the most famous of all disputed passages in Shakespeare's plays. The general meaning is clear: "a small portion of evil brings scandal on the whole substance, however noble." "Eale" is an Elizabethan spelling and pronunciation of "evil," as later in Q2 (II.ii.628); "deale" is the spelling and pronunciation of "Devil." The difficulty lies in "of a doubt," which is obviously a misprint for some such word as "corrupt"; but to be satisfactory it must fit the meter and be a plausible misprint. So far, although many guesses have been made, none is wholly convincing. The best is perhaps "often dout" — often put out. 40. **spirit . . . damned:** a holy spirit or damned fiend. Hamlet, until convinced at the end of the play scene (III.ii.298), is perpetually in doubt whether the ghost which he sees is a good spirit sent to warn him, or a devil sent to tempt him into some damnable action, or a hallucination created by his own diseased imagination. See II.ii.627–32. 43. **questionable:** inviting question.

That I will speak to thee. I'll call thee Hamlet,
King, Father, royal Dane. Oh, answer me!   45
Let me not burst in ignorance, but tell
Why thy canónized° bones, hearsèd° in death,
Have burst their cerements,° why the sepulcher
Wherein we saw thee quietly inurned°
Hath oped his ponderous and marble jaws   50
To cast thee up again. What may this mean,
That thou, dead corse, again, in complete steel,°
Revisit'st thus the glimpses of the moon,
Making night hideous, and we fools° of nature
So horridly to shake our disposition°   55
With thoughts beyond the reaches of our souls?
Say, why is this? Wherefore? What should we do?

> [GHOST *beckons* HAMLET.]

HOR. It beckons you to go away with it,
As if it some impartment° did desire
To you alone.
MAR.   Look with what courteous action   60
It waves you to a more removèd ground.
But do not go with it.
HOR.   No, by no means.
HAML. It will not speak. Then I will follow it.
HOR. Do not, my lord.
HAML.   Why, what should be the fear?
I do not set my life at a pin's fee,°   65
And for my soul, what can it do to that,
Being a thing immortal as itself?
It waves me forth again. I'll follow it.
HOR. What if it tempt you toward the flood, my
    lord,
Or to the dreadful summit of the cliff   70
That beetles o'er° his base into the sea,
And there assume some other horrible form
Which might deprive your sovereignty of reason°
And draw you into madness? Think of it.
The very place puts toys of desperation,°   75
Without more motive, into every brain
That looks so many fathoms to the sea
And hears it roar beneath.
HAML.   It waves me still.
Go on. I'll follow thee.
MAR. You shall not go, my lord.
HAML.   Hold off your hands. 80
HOR. Be ruled. You shall not go.
HAML.   My fate cries out,
And makes each petty artery in this body
As hardy as the Nemean lion's nerve.°
Still am I called. Unhand me, gentlemen.   84

---

47. **canonized:** buried with full rites according to the canon of the Church. **hearsed:** buried. 48. **cerements:** waxen shroud, used to wrap the bodies of the illustrious dead. 49. **inurned:** buried. 52. **complete steel:** full armor. 54. **fools:** dupes. 55. **disposition:** nature. 59. **impartment:** communication. 65. **fee:** value. 71. **beetles o'er:** juts out over. 73. **sovereignty of reason:** control of your reason over your actions. 75. **toys of desperation:** desperate fancies. 83. **Nemean . . . nerve:** sinew of a fierce beast slain by Hercules.

By Heaven, I'll make a ghost of him that lets° me!
I say, away! Go on. I'll follow thee.

                          [Exeunt GHOST *and* HAMLET.]

HOR. He waxes desperate with imagination.
MAR. Let's follow. 'Tis not fit thus to obey him.
HOR. Have after. To what issue will this come?
MAR. Something is rotten in the state of Den-
    mark.   90
HOR. Heaven will direct it.
MAR.   Nay, let's follow him.   *[Exeunt.]*

SCENE V. *Another part of the platform.*

              [Enter GHOST *and* HAMLET.]

HAML. Whither wilt thou lead me? Speak. I'll go
    no further.
GHOST. Mark me.
HAML.   I will.
GHOST.   My hour is almost come
When I to sulphurous and tormenting flames
Must render up myself.
HAML.   Alas, poor ghost!   4
GHOST. Pity me not, but lend thy serious hearing
To what I shall unfold.
HAML.   Speak. I am bound to hear.
GHOST. So art thou to revenge, when thou shalt
    hear.
HAML. What?
GHOST. I am thy father's spirit,
Doomed for a certain term to walk the night   10
And for the day confined to fast in fires
Till the foul crimes done in my days of nature
Are burnt and purged away. But that I am forbid
To tell the secrets of my prison house,
I could a tale unfold whose lightest word   15
Would harrow up thy soul, freeze thy young blood,
Make thy two eyes, like stars, start from their
    spheres,°
Thy knotted and combinèd° locks to part
And each particular° hair to stand an° end
Like quills upon the fretful porpentine.°   20
But this eternal blazon° must not be
To ears of flesh and blood. List, list, oh, list!
If thou didst ever thy dear father love ——
HAML. Oh, God!
GHOST. Revenge his foul and most unnatural mur-
    der.   25
HAML. Murder!
GHOST. Murder most foul, as in the best° it is,
But this most foul, strange, and unnatural.

HAML. Haste me to know 't, that I, with wings as
    swift
As meditation or the thoughts of love,   30
May sweep to my revenge.
GHOST.   I find thee apt,
And duller shouldst thou be than the fat° weed
That roots itself in ease° on Lethe wharf°
Wouldst thou not stir in this. Now, Hamlet, hear.
'Tis given out that, sleeping in my orchard,   35
A serpent stung me — so the whole ear of Denmark
Is by a forgèd process° of my death
Rankly abused. But know, thou noble youth,
The serpent that did sting thy father's life
Now wears his crown.
HAML.   Oh, my prophetic soul!   40
My uncle!
GHOST. Aye, that incestuous, that adulterate beast,
With witchcraft of his wit, with traitorous gifts —
O wicked wit and gifts, that have the power
So to seduce! — won to his shameful lust   45
The will of my most seeming-virtuous Queen.
O Hamlet, what a falling-off was there!
From me, whose love was of that dignity
That it went hand in hand even with the vow
I made to her in marriage, and to decline   50
Upon a wretch whose natural gifts were poor
To those of mine!
But virtue, as it never will be moved
Though lewdness court it in a shape of Heaven,°
So Lust, though to a radiant angel linked,   55
Will sate itself° in a celestial bed
And prey on garbage.
But soft! Methinks I scent the morning air.
Brief let me be. Sleeping within my orchard,
My custom always of the afternoon,   60
Upon my secure hour° thy uncle stole
With juice of cursèd hebenon° in a vial,
And in the porches° of my ears did pour
The leperous distillment,° whose effect
Holds such an enmity with blood of man   65
That swift as quicksilver it courses through
The natural gates and alleys of the body,
And with a sudden vigor it doth posset°
And curd, like eager° droppings into milk,
The thin and wholesome blood. So did it mine,   70
And a most instant tetter barked° about,
Most lazarlike,° with vile and loathsome crust,
All my smooth body.
Thus was I, sleeping, by a brother's hand

---

85. lets: hinders.
    Sc. v: 17. spheres: See App. 1.   18. knotted ... combined:
the hair that lies together in a mass.   19. particular: individual.
an: on.   20. porpentine: porcupine.   21. eternal blazon: de-
scription of eternity.   27. in ... best: i.e, murder is foul even
when there is a good excuse.

32. fat: thick, slimy, motionless.   33. in ease: undisturbed.
Lethe wharf: the bank of Lethe, the river of forgetfulness in the
underworld.   37. forged process: false account.   54. lewdness
... Heaven: though wooed by Lust disguised as an angel.
56. sate itself: gorge.   61. secure hour: time of relaxation.
62. hebenon: probably henbane, a poisonous plant.   63. porches:
entrances.   64. leperous distillment: distillation causing leprosy.
68. posset: curdle.   69. eager: acid.   71. tetter barked: erup-
tion formed a bark.   72. lazarlike: like leprosy.

Of life, of crown, of Queen, at once dispatched —
Cut off even in the blossoms of my sin,°   76
Unhouseled, disappointed, unaneled,°
No reckoning made, but sent to my account
With all my imperfections on my head.
Oh, horrible! Oh, horrible, most horrible!   80
If thou hast nature° in thee, bear it not.
Let not the royal bed of Denmark be
A couch for luxury° and damned incest.
But, howsoever thou pursuest this act,
Taint not thy mind, nor let thy soul contrive   85
Against thy mother aught. Leave her to Heaven
And to those thorns that in her bosom lodge
To prick and sting her. Fare thee well at once!
The glowworm shows the matin° to be near,
And 'gins to pale his uneffectual° fire.   90
Adieu, adieu, adieu! Remember me.   [*Exit.*]
HAML. O all you host of Heaven! O earth! What
    else?
And shall I couple Hell? Oh, fie! Hold, hold, my
    heart,
And you, my sinews, grow not instant old
But bear me stiffly up. Remember thee!   95
Aye, thou poor ghost, while memory holds a seat
In this distracted globe.° Remember thee!
Yea, from the table° of my memory
I'll wipe away all trivial fond° records,
All saws° of books, all forms,° all pressures° past,
That youth and observation copied there,   101
And thy commandment all alone shall live
Within the book and volume of my brain,
Unmixed with baser matter. Yes, by Heaven!
O most pernicious woman!   105
O villain, villain, smiling, damnèd villain!
My tables — meet it is I set it down
[*Writing*] That one may smile, and smile, and be a
    villain.
At least I'm sure it may be so in Denmark.
So, Uncle, there you are. Now to my word.°   110
It is " Adieu, adieu! Remember me."
I have sworn 't.
    HOR. & MAR. [*Within*] My lord, my lord!
        [*Enter* HORATIO *and* MARCELLUS.]
    MAR.   Lord Hamlet!
    HOR.   Heaven secure him!
HAML. So be it!
    MAR. Illo, ho, ho,° my lord!   115
    HAML. Hillo, ho, ho, boy! Come, bird, come.

76. Cut . . . sin: cut off in a state of sin and so in danger of
damnation. See III.iii.80–86.   77. Unhouseled . . . unaneled:
without receiving the sacrament, not properly prepared, unanoin-
ted — without extreme unction.   81. nature: natural feelings.
83. luxury: lust.   89. matin: morning.   90. uneffectual: made
ineffectual by daylight.   97. globe: i.e., head.   98. table: note-
book. Intellectual young men carried notebooks in which they
recorded good sayings and notable observations. See III.ii.42,n.
99. fond: trifling.   100. saws: wise sayings. forms: images in
the mind. pressures: impressions.   110. word: cue.   115. Illo
. . . ho: the falconer's cry to recall the hawk

    MAR. How is 't, my noble lord?
    HOR.   What news, my lord?
    HAML. Oh, wonderful!
    HOR. Good my lord, tell it.
    HAML.   No, you will reveal it.
    HOR. Not I, my lord, by Heaven.
    MAR.   Nor I, my lord.   120
    HAML. How say you, then, would heart of man
        once think it?
But you'll be secret?
    HOR. & MAR.   Aye, by Heaven, my lord.
    HAML. There's ne'er a villain dwelling in all Den-
        mark
But he's an arrant° knave.
    HOR. There needs no ghost, my lord, come from
        the grave   125
To tell us this.
    HAML.   Why, right, you are i' the right.
And so, without more circumstance° at all,
I hold it fit that we shake hands and part —
You as your business and desire shall point you,
For every man hath business and desire,   130
Such as it is. And for my own poor part,
Look you, I'll go pray.
    HOR. These are but wild and whirling° words, my
        lord.
    HAML. I'm sorry they offend you, heartily,
Yes, faith, heartily.
    HOR.   There's no offense, my lord.   135
    HAML. Yes, by Saint Patrick, but there is, Horatio,
And much offense too. Touching this vision here,
It is an honest° ghost, that let me tell you.
For your desire to know what is between us,
O'ermaster 't as you may. And now, good friends,
As you are friends, scholars, and soldiers,   141
Give me one poor request.
    HOR. What is 't, my lord? We will.
    HAML. Never make known what you have seen
        tonight.
    HOR. & MAR. My lord, we will not.
    HAML.   Nay, but swear 't.
    HOR.   In faith,   145
My lord, not I.
    MAR.   Nor I, my lord, in faith.
    HAML. Upon my sword.
    MAR.   We have sworn, my lord, already.
    HAML. Indeed, upon my sword,° indeed.
    GHOST. [*Beneath*] Swear.
    HAML. Ah, ha, boy! Say'st thou so? Art thou
        there, truepenny?°   150
Come on. You hear this fellow in the cellarage.
Consent to swear.

124. arrant: out-and-out.   127. circumstance: ceremony.
133. whirling: violent.   138. honest: true. See I.iv.40,n.
148. upon . . . sword: on the cross made by the hilt of the
sword; but for soldiers the sword itself was a sacred object.
150. truepenny: old boy.

HOR.   Propose the oath, my lord.

HAML. Never to speak of this that you have seen,
Swear by my sword.

GHOST. [*Beneath*] Swear.   155

HAML. *Hic et ubique?*° Then we'll shift our
ground.
Come hither, gentlemen,
And lay your hands again upon my sword.
Never to speak of this that you have heard,
Swear by my sword.   160

GHOST. [*Beneath*] Swear.

HAML. Well said, old mole! Canst work i' the
earth so fast?
A worthy pioner!° Once more remove,° good
friends.

HOR. Oh, day and night, but this is wondrous
strange!

HAML. And therefore as a stranger give it wel-
come.   165
There are more things in Heaven and earth, Hora-
tio,
Than are dreamt of in your philosophy.
But come,
Here, as before, never, so help you mercy,
How strange or odd soe'er I bear myself,   170
As I perchance hereafter shall think meet
To put an antic disposition° on,
That you, at such times seeing me, never shall,
With arms encumbered° thus, or this headshake,
Or by pronouncing of some doubtful phrase,   175
As "Well, well, we know," or "We could an if we
would,"
Or "If we list to speak," or "There be, an if they
might,"
Or such ambiguous giving out, to note
That you know aught of me. This not to do,
So grace and mercy at your most need help you, 180
Swear.

GHOST. [*Beneath*] Swear.

HAML. Rest, rest, perturbèd spirit! [*They swear.*]
So, gentlemen,
With all my love I do commend me to you.
And what so poor a man as Hamlet is   185
May do to express his love and friending° to you,
God willing, shall not lack. Let us go in together.
And still your fingers on your lips, I pray.
The time is out of joint. Oh, cursèd spite
That ever I was born to set it right!   190
Nay, come, let's go together.   [*Exeunt.*]

---

156. Hic et ubique: here and everywhere.   163. pioner: miner.
remove: move.   172. antic disposition: mad behavior.   174. en-
cumbered: folded.   186. friending: friendship.

Act II

SCENE I. *A room in* POLONIUS'S *house.*

[*Enter* POLONIUS *and* REYNALDO.]

POL. Give him this money and these notes, Rey-
naldo.

REY. I will, my lord.

POL. You shall do marvelous wisely, good Rey-
naldo,
Before you visit him, to make inquire
Of his behavior.

REY.   My lord, I did intend it.   5

POL. Marry, well said, very well said. Look you,
sir,
Inquire me first what Danskers° are in Paris,
And how, and who, what means,° and where they
keep,°
What company, at what expense, and finding
By this encompassment and drift of question°   10
That they do know my son, come you more nearer
Than your particular demands will touch it.°
Take you, as 'twere, some distant knowledge of him,
As thus, "I know his father and his friends,
And in part him." Do you mark this, Reynaldo?   15

REY. Aye, very well, my lord.

POL. "And in part him, but," you may say, "not
well.
But if 't be he I mean, he's very wild,
Addicted so and so "— and there put on him
What forgeries° you please. Marry, none so rank°
As may dishonor him, take heed of that,   21
But, sir, such wanton, wild, and usual slips
As are companions noted and most known
To youth and liberty.

REY.   As gaming, my lord.

POL. Aye, or drinking, fencing,° swearing, quar-
reling,   25
Drabbing.° You may go so far.

REY. My lord, that would dishonor him.

POL. Faith, no, as you may season° it in the charge.
You must not put another scandal on him,
That he is open to incontinency.°   30
That's not my meaning. But breathe his faults so
quaintly°
That they may seem the taints of liberty,
The flash and outbreak of a fiery mind,
A savageness in unreclaimèd° blood,

Act II, Sc. i: 7. Danskers: Danes.   8. what means: what their
income is.   keep: live.   10. encompassment . . . question:
roundabout method of questioning.   12. your . . . it: i.e., you
won't get at the truth by straight questions.   20. forgeries:
inventions.   rank: gross.   25. fencing: A young man who
haunted fencing schools would be regarded as quarrelsome and
likely to belong to the sporting set.   26. Drabbing: whoring.
28. season: qualify.   30. open . . . incontinency: So long as
Laertes does his drabbing inconspicuously Polonius would not
be disturbed.   31. quaintly: skillfully.   34. unreclaimed:
naturally wild.

Of general assault.°

REY.   But, my good lord ——   35

POL. Wherefore should you do this?

REY.   Aye, my lord,
I would know that.

POL.   Marry, sir, here's my drift,°
And I believe it is a fetch of warrant.°
You laying these slight sullies° on my son,
As 'twere a thing little soiled i' the working,   40
Mark you,
Your party in converse, him you would sound,
Having ever seen° in the prenominate° crimes
The youth you breathe of guilty, be assured
He closes with you in this consequence° ——   45
"Good sir," or so, or "friend," or "gentleman,"
According to the phrase or the addition°
Of man and country.

REY.   Very good, my lord.   49

POL. And then, sir, does he this — he does ——
What was I about to say? By the mass, I was about
to say something. Where did I leave?

REY. At "closes in the consequence," at "friend or
so," and "gentleman."

POL. At "closes in the consequence," aye, marry,
He closes with you thus: "I know the gentleman.
I saw him yesterday, or t'other day,   56
Or then, or then, with such, or such, and, as you
     say,
There was a' gaming, there o'ertook in 's rouse,
There falling out at tennis."° Or perchance,
"I saw him enter such a house of sale,"   60
Videlicet,° a brothel, or so forth.
See you now,
Your bait of falsehood takes this carp of truth.
And thus do we of wisdom and of reach,°
With windlasses° and with assays of bias,°   65
By indirections find directions out.°
So, by my former lecture and advice,
Shall you my son. You have me, have you not?

REY. My lord, I have.

POL.   God be wi' ye, fare ye well.

REY. Good my lord!   70

POL. Observe his inclination in° yourself.

REY. I shall, my lord.

POL. And let him ply his music.

REY.   Well, my lord.

POL. Farewell!   [*Exit* REYNALDO.]

[*Enter* OPHELIA.] How now, Ophelia! What's the
     matter?

OPH. Oh, my lord, my lord, I have been so af-
     frighted!   75

POL. With what, i' the name of God?

OPH. My lord, as I was sewing in my closet,°
Lord Hamlet, with his doublet° all unbraced,
No hat upon his head, his stockings fouled,
Ungartered and down-gyved° to his ankle,   80
Pale as his shirt, his knees knocking each other,
And with a look so piteous in purport
As if he had been loosèd out of Hell
To speak of horrors, he comes before me.

POL. Mad for thy love?

OPH.   My lord, I do not know,
But truly I do fear it.   86

POL.   What said he?

OPH. He took me by the wrist and held me hard.
Then goes he to the length of all his arm,
And with his other hand thus o'er his brow,
He falls to such perusal of my face   90
As he would draw it. Long stayed he so.
At last, a little shaking of mine arm,
And thrice his head thus waving up and down,
He raised a sigh so piteous and profound
As it did seem to shatter all his bulk   95
And end his being. That done, he lets me go.
And with his head over his shoulder turned,
He seemed to find his way without his eyes;
For out o' doors he went without their helps,
And to the last bended their light on me.   100

POL. Come, go with me. I will go seek the King.
This is the very ecstasy° of love,
Whose violent property fordoes° itself
And leads the will to desperate undertakings
As oft as any passion under heaven   105
That does afflict our natures. I am sorry.
What, have you given him any hard words of late?

OPH. No, my good lord, but, as you did command,
I did repel his letters and denied
His access to me.

POL.   That hath made him mad.   110
I am sorry that with better heed and judgment
I had not quoted° him. I feared he did but trifle
And meant to wreck thee, but beshrew° my jeal-
     ousy!
By Heaven, it is as proper° to our age
To cast beyond ourselves° in our opinions   115
As it is common for the younger sort
To lack discretion. Come, go we to the King.

---

35. Of . . . assault: common to all men.   37. drift: intention.
38. fetch . . . warrant: trick warranted to work.   39. sullies:
blemishes.   43. Having . . . seen: if ever he has seen. prenom-
inate: aforementioned.   45. closes . . . consequence: follows
up with this reply.   47. addition: title. See I.iv.20.   59. ten-
nis: Visitors to France were much impressed by the enthu-
siasm of all classes of Frenchmen for tennis, which in England
was mainly a courtier's game.   61. Videlicet: namely, "viz."
64. wisdom . . . reach: of far-reaching wisdom.   65. windlasses:
roundabout methods. assays of bias: making our bowl take a
curved course. See App. 13.   66. indirections . . . out: by in-
direct means come at the direct truth.   71. in: for.

77. closet: private room.   78. doublet: the short close-fitting
coat which was braced to the hose by laces. When a man was re-
laxing or careless of appearance, he *unbraced*, as a modern man
takes off his coat or unbuttons his waistcoat. See Pl. 8b and notes
on p. 93a.   80. down-gyved: hanging around his ankles like fet-
ters.   102. ecstasy: frenzy.   103. property fordoes: natural qual-
ity destroys.   112. quoted: observed carefully.   113. beshrew: a
plague on.   114. proper: natural.   115. cast . . . ourselves: be
too clever.

This must be known, which, being kept close, might
   move
More grief to hide than hate to utter love.°   119
Come.   [*Exeunt.*]

SCENE II. *A room in the castle.*

[*Flourish. Enter* KING, QUEEN, ROSENCRANTZ,
    GUILDENSTERN, *and* ATTENDANTS.]

KING. Welcome, dear Rosencrantz and Guilden-
   stern!
Moreover° that we much did long to see you,
The need we have to use you did provoke
Our hasty sending. Something have you heard
Of Hamlet's transformation — so call it,   5
Sith° nor the exterior nor the inward man
Resembles that it was. What it should be,
More than his father's death, that thus hath put him
So much from the understanding of himself
I cannot dream of. I entreat you both   10
That, being of so young days brought up with him
And sith so neighbored to his youth and havior°
That you vouchsafe your rest° here in our Court
Some little time, so by your companies
To draw him on to pleasures, and to gather   15
So much as from occasion you may glean,
Whether aught to us unknown afflicts him thus
That opened lies within our remedy.°
   QUEEN. Good gentlemen, he hath much talked of
   you,
And sure I am two men there art not living   20
To whom he more adheres.° If it will please you
To show us so much gentry° and goodwill
As to expend your time with us a while
For the supply and profit of our hope,°
Your visitation shall receive such thanks   25
As fits a king's remembrance.
   ROS.   Both your Majesties
Might, by the sovereign power you have of us,
Put your dread pleasures more into command
Than to entreaty.
   GUIL.   But we both obey,
And here give up ourselves, in the full bent°   30
To lay our service freely at your feet,
To be commanded.
   KING. Thanks, Rosencrantz and gentle Guilden-
   stern.

QUEEN. Thanks, Guildenstern and gentle Rosen-
   crantz.
And I beseech you instantly to visit   35
My too-much-changèd son. Go, some of you,
And bring these gentlemen where Hamlet is.
   GUIL. Heavens make our presence and our prac-
   tices
Pleasant and helpful to him!
   QUEEN.   Aye, amen! [*Exeunt* ROSENCRANTZ,
    GUILDENSTERN, *and some* ATTENDANTS.]
    [*Enter* POLONIUS.]
POL. The ambassadors from Norway, my good
   lord,   40
Are joyfully returned.
   KING. Thou still° hast been the father of good
   news.
   POL. Have I, my lord? I assure my good liege
I hold my duty as I hold my soul,
Both to my God and to my gracious King.   45
And I do think, or else this brain of mine
Hunts not the trail of policy so sure
As it hath used to do,° that I have found
The very cause of Hamlet's lunacy.   49
   KING. Oh, speak of that. That do I long to hear.
   POL. Give first admittance to the ambassadors.
My news shall be the fruit° to that great feast.
   KING. Thyself do grace° to them and bring them
   in.   [*Exit* POLONIUS.]
He tells me, my dear Gertrude, he hath found   54
The head and source of all your son's distemper.°
   QUEEN. I doubt it is no other but the main,°
His father's death and our o'erhasty marriage.
   KING. Well, we shall sift him.
    [*Re-enter* POLONIUS, *with* VOLTIMAND
             and CORNELIUS.]
            Welcome, my good friends!
Say, Voltimand, what from our brother Norway?
   VOLT. Most fair return of greetings and desires.
Upon our first,° he sent out to suppress   61
His nephew's levies, which to him appeared
To be a preparation 'gainst the Polack,
But better looked into, he truly found
It was against your Highness, whereat, grieved   65
That so his sickness, age, and impotence
Was falsely borne in hand,° sends out arrests
On Fortinbras; which he, in brief, obeys,
Receives rebuke from Norway, and in fine°
Makes vow before his uncle never more   70
To give the assay of arms° against your Majesty.
Whereon old Norway, overcome with joy,
Gives him three thousand crowns in annual fee

118–19. which . . . love: by being kept secret it may cause more
sorrow than it will cause anger by being revealed; i.e., the King
and Queen may be angry at the thought of the Prince's marrying
beneath his proper rank.

   Sc. ii: 2. Moreover: in addition to the fact that.   6. Sith:
since.   12. neighbored . . . havior: so near to his youthful
manner of living.   13. vouchsafe . . . rest: consent to stay.
18. opened . . . remedy: if revealed, might be put right by us.
21. To . . . adheres: whom he regards more highly.   22. gen-
try: courtesy.   24. supply . . . hope: to bring a profitable con-
clusion to our hope.   30. in . . . bent: stretched to our utter-
most.

   42. still: always.   47–48. Hunts . . . do: is not so good at fol-
lowing the scent of political events as it used to be.   52. fruit:
the dessert, which comes at the end of the feast.   53. do grace:
honor; i.e., by escorting them into the royal presence.   55. dis-
temper: mental disturbance.   56. main: principal cause.
61. first: i.e., audience.   67. borne in hand: imposed upon.
69. in fine: in the end.   71. give . . . arms: make an attack.

And his commission to employ those soldiers,
So levied as before, against the Polack.   75
With an entreaty, herein further shown,

                   [*Giving a paper*]

That it might please you to give quiet pass°
Through your dominions for this enterprise,
On such regards of safety and allowance°
As therein are set down.

KING.   It likes° us well,   80
And at our more considered time we'll read,
Answer, and think upon this business.
Meantime we thank you for your well-took labor.
Go to your rest. At night we'll feast together.
Most welcome home!

          [*Exeunt* VOLTIMAND *and* CORNELIUS.]

POL.   This business is well ended. 85
My liege, and madam, to expostulate°
What majesty should be, what duty is,
Why day is day, night night, and time is time,
Were nothing but to waste night, day, and time.
Therefore, since brevity is the soul of wit   90
And tediousness the limbs and outward flourishes,°
I will be brief. Your noble son is mad.
Mad call I it, for to define true madness,
What is 't but to be nothing else but mad?
But let that go.

QUEEN.   More matter, with less art.°
POL. Madam, I swear I use no art at all.
That he is mad, 'tis true. 'Tis true 'tis pity,
And pity 'tis 'tis true — a foolish figure,°
But farewell it, for I will use no art.
Mad let us grant him, then. And now remains 100
That we find out the cause of this effect,
Or rather say the cause of this defect,
For this effect defective comes by cause.
Thus it remains and the remainder thus.
Perpend.°   105
I have a daughter — have while she is mine —
Who in her duty and obedience, mark,
Hath given me this. Now gather and surmise.°
[*Reads.*]
" To the celestial, and my soul's idol, the most beau-
    tified° Ophelia — "
That's an ill phrase, a vile phrase, " beautified " is a
vile phrase. But you shall hear. Thus: [*Reads.*]
" In her excellent white bosom, these," and so forth.
QUEEN. Came this from Hamlet to her?   114
POL. Good madam, stay awhile, I will be faithful.
[*Reads.*] " Doubt thou the stars are fire,
         Doubt that the sun doth move,
         Doubt truth to be a liar,
         But never doubt I love.   119

" O dear Ophelia, I am ill at these numbers,° I
have not art to reckon my groans, but that I love thee
best, O most best, believe it. Adieu.
   " Thine evermore, most dear lady, whilst this
             machine° is to him, HAMLET."
This in obedience hath my daughter shown me,
And more above, hath his solicitings,   126
As they fell out by time, by means and place,
All given to mine ear.

KING.   But how hath she
Received his love?

POL.   What do you think of me?
KING. As of a man faithful and honorable.   130
POL. I would fain prove so. But what might you
    think,
When I had seen this hot love on the wing —
As I perceived it, I must tell you that,
Before my daughter told me — what might you
Or my dear Majesty your Queen here think   135
If I had played the desk or table book,°
Or given my heart awinking, mute and dumb,
Or looked upon this love with idle sight —
What might you think? No, I went round° to work,
And my young mistress thus I did bespeak:°   140
" Lord Hamlet is a Prince, out of thy star.°
This must not be." And then I prescripts° gave her
That she should lock herself from his resort,
Admit no messengers, receive no tokens.
Which done, she took the fruits of my advice.   145
And he, repulsèd, a short tale to make,
Fell into a sadness, then into a fast,
Thence to a watch, thence to a weakness,
Thence to a lightness,° and by this declension°
Into the madness wherein now he raves   150
And all we mourn for.

KING. Do you think this?
QUEEN.   It may be, very like.
POL. Hath there been such a time, I'd fain know
    that,
That I have positively said " 'Tis so "
When it proved otherwise?

KING.   Not that I know. 155
POL. [*Pointing to his head and shoulder.*] Take
    this from this, if this be otherwise.
If circumstances lead me, I will find
Where truth is hid, though it were hid indeed
Within the center.°

---

120. numbers: verses.   **124. machine:** i.e., body, an affected phrase.   **136. desk . . . book:** i.e., acted as silent go-between (desks and books being natural post offices for a love letter), or been a recipient of secrets but took no action (as desks and notebooks are the natural but inanimate places for keeping secrets).   **139. round:** straight.   **140. bespeak:** address.   **141. out . . . star:** above your destiny.   **142. prescripts:** instructions.   **147–49. Fell . . . lightness:** Hamlet's case history, according to Polonius, develops by stages — melancholy, loss of appetite, sleeplessness, physical weakness, mental instability, and finally madness.   **149. declension:** decline.   **159. center:** the very center of the earth. See App. 1.

---

77. quiet pass: unmolested passage.   **79. regards . . . allowance:** safeguard and conditions.   **80. likes:** pleases.   **86. expostulate:** indulge in an academic discussion.   **91. flourishes:** ornaments.   **95. art:** ornament.   **98. figure:** i.e., a figure of speech.   **105. Perpend:** note carefully.   **108. surmise:** guess the meaning.   **110. beautified:** beautiful.

KING.　　　　　　　How may we try it further?

POL. You know sometimes he walks four hours together　　　　　　　　　　　　　　160
Here in the lobby.

QUEEN.　　　　　So he does indeed.

POL. At such a time I'll loose° my daughter to him.
Be you and I behind an arras° then.
Mark the encounter. If he love her not,
And be not from his reason fall'n thereon,　　165
Let me be no assistant for a state,
But keep a farm and carters.°

KING.　　　　　　　　　　We will try it.

QUEEN. But look where sadly the poor wretch comes reading.

POL. Away, I do beseech you, both away.　　169
I'll board° him presently.　　　[*Exeunt* KING, QUEEN,
　　　　　　　　　　　　　　　　and ATTENDANTS.]
[*Enter* HAMLET, *reading*.] Oh, give me leave. How does my good Lord Hamlet?

HAML. Well, God-a-mercy.

POL. Do you know me, my lord?

HAML. Excellent well. You are a fishmonger.°

POL. Not I, my lord.　　　　　　　　　　175

HAML. Then I would you were so honest a man.

POL. Honest, my lord!

HAML. Aye, sir, to be honest, as this world goes, is to be one man picked out of ten thousand.

POL. That's very true, my lord.　　　　　180

HAML. For if the sun breed maggots° in a dead dog, being a god° kissing carrion° —— Have you a daughter?

POL. I have, my lord.　　　　　　　　184

HAML. Let her not walk i' the sun. Conception is a blessing, but not as your daughter may conceive — friend, look to 't.

POL. [*Aside*] How say you by that? Still harping on my daughter. Yet he knew me not at first, he said I was a fishmonger. He is far gone, far gone. And truly in my youth I suffered much extremity for love, very near this. I'll speak to him again. — What do you read, my lord?　　　　　　　　193

HAML. Words, words, words.

POL. What is the matter, my lord?

HAML. Between who?　　　　　　　　196

POL. I mean the matter that you read, my lord.

HAML. Slanders, sir. For the satirical rogue says here that old men have gray beards, that their faces are wrinkled, their eyes purging thick amber and plum-tree gum, and that they have a plentiful lack of wit, together with most weak hams.° All which,

sir, though I most powerfully and potently believe, yet I hold it not honesty to have it thus set down; for yourself, sir, should be old as I am if like a crab you could go backward.　　　　　　　　206

POL. [*Aside*] Though this be madness, yet there is method° in 't. — Will you walk out of the air, my lord?

HAML. Into my grave.　　　　　　　　210

POL. Indeed, that's out of the air. [*Aside*] How pregnant° sometimes his replies are! A happiness° that often madness hits on, which reason and sanity could not so prosperously be delivered of. I will leave him, and suddenly contrive the means of meeting between him and my daughter. — My honorable lord, I will most humbly take my leave of you.　　　　　　　　　　　　　　218

HAML. You cannot, sir, take from me anything that I will more willingly part withal — except my life, except my life, except my life.

POL. Fare you well, my lord.

HAML. These tedious old fools!

　　　[*Enter* ROSENCRANTZ *and* GUILDENSTERN.]

POL. You go to seek the Lord Hamlet. There he is.

ROS. [*To* POLONIUS] God save you, sir!　　225
　　　　　　　　　　　　　　　　[*Exit* POLONIUS.]

GUIL. My honored lord!

ROS. My most dear lord!

HAML. My excellent good friends!° How dost thou, Guildenstern? Ah, Rosencrantz! Good lads, how do you both?　　　　　　　　　　230

ROS. As the indifferent° children of the earth.

GUIL. Happy in that we are not overhappy.
On Fortune's cap we are not the very button.°

HAML. Nor the soles of her shoe?

ROS. Neither, my lord.　　　　　　　235

HAML. Then you live about her waist, or in the middle of her favors?

GUIL. Faith, her privates° we.

HAML. In the secret parts of Fortune? Oh, most true, she is a strumpet. What's the news?　　240

ROS. None, my lord, but that the world's grown honest.

HAML. Then is Doomsday near. But your news is not true. Let me question more in particular. What have you, my good friends, deserved at the hands of Fortune, that she sends you to prison hither?　　247

GUIL. Prison, my lord!

HAML. Denmark's a prison.

ROS. Then is the world one.

HAML. A goodly one, in which there are many

162. loose: turn loose. **163. arras:** tapestry hanging. **167. keep ... carters:** i.e., turn country squire — like Justice Shallow. See *II Hen IV*. **170. board:** accost. **174. fishmonger:** Hamlet is now in his "antic disposition," enjoying himself by fooling Polonius. **181. sun ... maggots:** a general belief. Cf. *Ant & Cleo*, II.vii.29–31. **182. god:** Q2 and F1 read "good." **carrion:** flesh. **202. hams:** knee joints.

208. method: order, sense. **212. pregnant:** apt, meaningful. **212. happiness:** good turn of phrase. **228. My ... friends:** As soon as Polonius has gone, Hamlet drops his assumed madness and greets Rosencrantz and Guildenstern naturally. **231. indifferent:** neither too great nor too little. **233. button:** i.e., at the top. **238. privates:** with a pun on "private parts" and "private," not concerned with politics.

confines,° wards,° and dungeons, Denmark being one o' the worst.

ROS. We think not so, my lord.   254

HAML. Why, then 'tis none to you, for there is nothing either good or bad but thinking makes it so. To me it is a prison.

ROS. Why, then your ambition° makes it one. 'Tis too narrow for your mind.   259

HAML. Oh, God, I could be bounded in a nutshell and count myself a king of infinite space were it not that I have bad dreams.

GUIL. Which dreams indeed are ambition, for the very substance of the ambitious° is merely the shadow of a dream.   265

HAML. A dream itself is but a shadow.

ROS. Truly, and I hold ambition of so airy and light a quality that it is but a shadow's shadow.

HAML. Then are our beggars bodies, and our monarchs and outstretched heroes the beggars' shadows.° Shall we to the Court? For, by my fay,° I cannot reason.°   272

ROS. & GUIL. We'll wait upon you.°

HAML. No such matter. I will not sort° you with the rest of my servants, for, to speak to you like an honest man, I am most dreadfully attended.° But in the beaten way of friendship, what make you at Elsinore?   278

ROS. To visit you, my lord, no other occasion.

HAML. Beggar that I am, I am even poor in thanks, but I thank you. And sure, dear friends, my thanks are too dear a halfpenny.° Were you not sent for? Is it your own inclining? Is it a free visitation?° Come, deal justly with me. Come, come. Nay, speak.   285

GUIL. What should we say, my lord?

HAML. Why, anything, but to the purpose.° You were sent for, and there is a kind of confession in your looks which your modesties have not craft enough to color.° I know the good King and Queen have sent for you.

ROS. To what end, my lord?   292

HAML. That you must teach me. But let me conjure° you, by the rights of our fellowship,° by the consonancy° of our youth, by the obligation of our ever preserved love, and by what more dear a better

proposer could charge you withal, be even° and direct with me, whether you were sent for, or no.   299

ROS. [*Aside to* GUILDENSTERN] What say you?

HAML. [*Aside*] Nay, then, I have an eye of you. — If you love me, hold not off.

GUIL. My lord, we were sent for.   303

HAML. I will tell you why. So shall my anticipation prevent your discovery, and your secrecy to the King and Queen molt no feather.° I have of late — but wherefore I know not — lost all my mirth, forgone all custom of exercises, and indeed it goes so heavily with my disposition that this goodly frame the earth seems to me a sterile promontory.   310 This most excellent canopy,° the air, look you, this brave o'erhanging firmament,° this majestical roof fretted° with golden fire — why, it appears no other thing to me than a foul and pestilent congregation of vapors. What a piece of work is a man!   315 How noble in reason! How infinite in faculty!° In form and moving° how express° and admirable! In action how like an angel! In apprehension how like a god! The beauty of the world! The paragon of animals! And yet, to me, what is this quintessence° of dust? Man delights not me — no, nor   320 woman neither, though by your smiling you seem to say so.

ROS. My lord, there was no such stuff in my thoughts.

HAML. Why did you laugh, then, when I said " Man delights not me "?

ROS. To think, my lord, if you delight not in man, what lenten entertainment° the players shall receive from you. We coted° them on the way, and hither are they coming to offer you service.   331

HAML. He that plays the King shall be welcome, His Majesty shall have tribute of me. The adventurous knight shall use his foil and target,° the lover shall not sigh gratis, the humorous man° shall end his part in peace, the clown shall make those laugh whose lungs are tickle o' the sere,° and the lady shall say her mind freely or the blank verse shall halt° for 't. What players are they?   340

ROS. Even those you were wont to take such delight in, the tragedians of the city.

HAML. How chances it they travel? Their resi-

---

252. **confines:** places of confinement. **wards:** cells.   258. **your ambition:** Rosencrantz is feeling after one possible cause of Hamlet's melancholy — thwarted ambition.   264. **substance . . . ambitious:** that on which an ambitious man feeds his fancies.   269–71. **Then . . . shadows:** i.e., by your reasoning beggars are the only men of substance, for kings and heroes are by nature ambitious and therefore "the shadows of a dream." **outstretched:** of exaggerated reputation.   271. **fay:** faith.   272. **reason:** argue.   273. **wait . . . you:** be your servants.   274. **sort:** class.   276. **dreadfully attended:** my attendants are a poor crowd.   282. **too . . . halfpenny:** not worth a halfpenny.   283. **free visitation:** voluntary visit.   287. **anything . . . purpose:** anything so long as it is not true.   290. **color:** conceal.   294. **conjure:** make solemn appeal to. **fellowship:** comradeship.   295. **consonancy:** concord.

298. **even:** straight.   304–06. **So . . . feather:** i.e., so by my telling you first you will not be obliged to betray the secrets of the King. **prevent:** forestall. **molt no feather:** be undisturbed.   311. **canopy:** covering.   312. **firmament:** sky.   313. **fretted:** ornamented.   316. **faculty:** power of the mind.   317. **moving:** movement. **express:** exact.   319. **quintessence:** perfection; the fifth essence, which would be left if the four elements were taken away.   329. **lenten entertainment:** meager welcome.   330. **coted:** overtook.   334. **foil . . . target:** rapier and small shield. See Pl. 22, l, i.   335. **humorous man:** the man who specializes in character parts; e.g., Jaques in *AYLI.* See App. 3.   338. **are . . . sere:** explode at a touch. The *sere* is part of the trigger mechanism of a gun which if "ticklish" will go off at a touch.   340. **halt:** limp.

dence, both in reputation and profit, was better both
ways.°   345

ROS. I° think their inhibition° comes by the
means of the late innovation.°

HAML. Do they hold the same estimation they did
when I was in the city? Are they so followed?

ROS. No, indeed are they not.   350

HAML. How comes it? Do they grow rusty?

ROS. Nay, their endeavor keeps in the wonted
pace.° But there is, sir, an eyrie° of children, little
eyases,° that cry out on the top of question° and
are most tyrannically° clapped for 't. These are   355
now the fashion, and so berattle° the common
stages° — so they call them — that many wearing
rapiers are afraid of goose quills° and dare scarce
come thither.   360

HAML. What, are they children? Who maintains
'em? How are they escoted?° Will they pursue the
quality° no longer than they can sing? Will they not
say afterward, if they should grow themselves to
common players — as it is most like if their means
are no better — their writers do them wrong to make
them exclaim against their own succession?°   368

ROS. Faith, there has been much to-do on both
sides, and the nation holds it no sin to tarre° them
to controversy. There was for a while no money bid
for argument° unless the poet and the player went
to cuffs° in the question.   373

HAML. Is 't possible?

GUIL. Oh, there has been much throwing-about of
brains.

HAML. Do the boys carry it away?

ROS. Aye, that they do, my lord, Hercules and his
load° too.   379

HAML. It is not very strange, for my uncle is King
of Denmark, and those that would make mows° at
him while my father lived give twenty, forty, fifty,
a hundred ducats apiece for his picture in little.
'Sblood,° there is something in this more than nat-
ural, if philosophy could find it out.   385

[Flourish of trumpets within.]

GUIL. There are the players.

HAML. Gentlemen, you are welcome to Elsinore.
Your hands. Come then. The appurtenance of wel-
come is fashion and ceremony.° Let me comply°
with you in this garb,° lest my extent° to the   390
players — which, I tell you, must show fairly out-
ward — should more appear like entertainment°
than yours. You are welcome. But my uncle-father
and aunt-mother are deceived.

GUIL. In what, my dear lord?   395

HAML. I am but mad north-northwest.° When
the wind is southerly,° I know a hawk from a hand-
saw.°

[Re-enter POLONIUS.]

POL. Well be with you, gentlemen!

HAML. Hark you, Guildenstern, and you too — at
each ear a hearer. That great baby you see there is
not yet out of his swaddling clouts.°   401

ROS. Happily he's the second time come to them,
for they say an old man is twice a child.

HAML. I will prophesy he comes to tell me of the
players, mark it. You say right, sir. O' Monday
morning, 'twas so indeed.   407

POL. My lord, I have news to tell you.

HAML. My lord, I have news to tell you. When
Roscius° was an actor in Rome ——

POL. The actors are come hither, my lord.

HAML. Buzz, buzz!°

POL. Upon my honor ——   413

HAML. Then came each actor on his ass ——

POL. The° best actors in the world, either for trag-
edy, comedy, history, pastoral, pastoral-comical,
historical-pastoral, tragical-historical, tragical-comi-
cal-historical-pastoral, scene individable° or poem
unlimited.° Seneca cannot be too heavy, nor Plau-
tus° too light. For the law of writ° and the liberty,°
these are the only men.   421

HAML. O Jephthah,° judge of Israel, what a treas-
ure hadst thou!

343–45. Their . . . ways: i.e., if they stayed in the city, it would
bring them more profit and fame.   346–79. I . . . too: This
is one of the several topical references in *Hamlet.* For de-
tails of the stage war between the Children's Companies,
see Gen. Intro. pp. 45a–46a.   346. inhibition: formal
prohibition.   347. innovation: riot.   352–53. endeavor . . .
pace: they try as hard as ever.   353. eyrie: nest.   354. eyases:
young hawks.   354. cry . . . question: either "cry in a shrill
voice" or perhaps "cry out the latest detail of the dis-
pute."   355. tyrannically: outrageously.   356. berattle: abuse.
357. common stages: the professional players. The boys acted
in "private" playhouses.   359. goose quills: pens; i.e., of such
as Ben Jonson.   362. escoted: paid.   363. quality: acting pro-
fession.   368. exclaim . . . succession: abuse the profession to
which they will afterward belong.   370. tarre: urge on to fight;
generally used of encouraging a dog.   372. argument: plot
of a play. See III.ii.242.   372–73. went to cuffs: boxed each
other's ears.   378–79. Hercules . . . load: Hercules carrying the
globe on his shoulders was the sign of the Globe Playhouse.
381. mows: grimaces.   384. 'Sblood: by God's blood.

388–89. appurtenance . . . ceremony: that which pertains to wel-
come is formal ceremony.   389. comply: use the formality of
welcome; i.e., shake hands with you.   390. garb: fashion. ex-
tent: outward behavior.   392. entertainment: welcome.
396. north-northwest: i.e., 327° (out of 360°) of the compass.
397. wind is southerly: the south wind was considered unhealthy.
396–97. hawk . . . handsaw: Either "handsaw" is a corruption
of "heronshaw," heron, or a hawk is a tool like a pickax. The
phrase means "I'm not so mad as you think."   401. clouts:
clothes.   410. Roscius: the most famous of Roman actors.
412. Buzz, buzz: slang for "stale news."   415–21. The . . .
men: Polonius reads out the accomplishments of the actors from
the license which they have presented him. For the wording of
the actual license granted to Shakespeare's company by King
James, see Gen. Intro. p. 13a.   418. scene individable: i.e., a
play preserving the unities. See Gen. Intro. p. 42a.   418–
19. poem unlimited: i.e., a play which disregards the rules.   419–
20. Seneca . . . Plautus: the Roman writers of tragedy and com-
edy with whose plays every educated man was familiar.   420. law
of writ: the critical rules; i.e., classical plays. liberty: plays
freely written; i.e., "modern" drama.   422. Jephthah: The story
of Jephthah is told in Judges, Chapter 11. He vowed that if suc-

POL. What a treasure had he, my lord?

HAML. Why,   425
   "One° fair daughter, and no more,
      The which he lovèd passing well."

POL. [*Aside*] Still° on my daughter.

HAML. Am I not i' the right, old Jephthah?

POL. If you call me Jephthah, my lord, I have a
daughter that I love passing well.   431

HAML. Nay, that follows not.

POL. What follows, then, my lord?

HAML. Why,
   "As by lot, God wot,"°   435
and then you know,
   "It came to pass, as most like it was —"
the first row° of the pious chanson° will show you
more, for look where my abridgement° comes.   439
[*Enter four or five* PLAYERS.] You are welcome, mas-
ters, welcome all. I am glad to see thee well. Wel-
come, good friends. Oh, my old friend!° Why, thy
face is valanced° since I saw thee last. Comest thou
to beard° me in Denmark? What, my young lady°
and mistress! By 'r Lady, your ladyship is nearer to
Heaven than when I saw you last, by the alti-   445
tude of a chopine.° Pray God your voice, like a piece
of uncurrent gold, be not cracked within the ring.°
Masters, you are all welcome. We'll e'en to 't like
French falconers,° fly at anything we see. We'll have
a speech straight. Come, give us a taste of your
quality° — come, a passionate speech.   452

I. PLAY. What speech, my good lord?

HAML. I heard thee speak me a speech once, but
it was never acted, or if it was, not above once; for
the play, I remember, pleased not the million, 'twas
caviar° to the general.° But it was — as I received
it, and others, whose judgments in such matters
cried in the top of mine° — an excellent play, well
digested° in the scenes, set down with as much   460
modesty° as cunning. I remember one said there
were no sallets° in the lines to make the matter
savory, nor no matter in the phrase that might in-
dict the author of affection,° but called it an honest

method, as wholesome as sweet, and by very   465
much more handsome than fine.° One speech in it
I chiefly loved. 'Twas Aeneas' tale to Dido,° and
thereabout of it especially where he speaks of
Priam's° slaughter. If it live in your memory, begin
at this line — let me see, let me see —   471
   "The rugged Pyrrhus,° like th' Hyrcanian
      beast,° —"
It is not so. It begins with "Pyrrhus."
"The° rugged Pyrrhus, he whose sable° arms,
   Black as his purpose, did the night resemble   475
When he lay couchèd in the ominous° horse,°
Hath now this dread and black complexion
      smeared
With heraldry° more dismal. Head to foot
Now is he total gules, horridly tricked   479
With blood of fathers, mothers, daughters, sons,
Baked and impasted° with the parching streets
That lend a tyrannous and a damnèd light
To their lord's murder. Roasted in wrath and
      fire,
And thus o'ersized with coagulate gore,°   484
With eyes like carbuncles, the hellish Pyrrhus
Old grandsire Priam seeks."
So, proceed you.

POL. 'Fore God, my lord, well spoken, with good
accent and good discretion.

I. PLAY.   "Anon he finds him   490
Striking too short at Greeks. His antique sword,
Rebellious to his arm, lies where it falls,
Repugnant to command.° Unequal matched,
Pyrrhus at Priam drives, in rage strikes wide,
But with the whiff and wind of his fell sword   495
The unnerved father falls. Then senseless Ilium,°
Seeming to feel this blow, with flaming top
Stoops to his base,° and with a hideous crash
Takes prisoner Pyrrhus' ear. For, lo! his sword,
Which was declining° on the milky° head   500
Of reverend Priam, seemed i' the air to stick.

nothing in the language which could charge the author with
affectation.   466. fine: subtle.   467. Aeneas' . . . Dido: the
story of the sack of Troy as told by Aeneas to Dido, Queen
of Carthage. The original is in Virgil's *Aeneid*. A similar
speech occurs in Marlowe's play *Dido, Queen of Carthage*.
469. Priam: the old King of Troy.   472. Pyrrhus: the son
of Achilles, one of the Greeks concealed in the Wooden
Horse.   472. Hyrcanian beast: the tiger.   474–541. The . . .
gods: The speech may be from some lost play of *Dido and
Aeneas*, but more likely it is Shakespeare's own invention. It is
written in the heavy elaborate style still popular in the dramas of
the Admiral's Men. The first player delivers it with excessive
gesture and emotion.   474. sable: black.   476. ominous: fate-
ful.   horse: the Wooden Horse by which a small Greek force
was enabled to make a secret entry into Troy.   478. heraldry:
painting. The image of heraldic painting is kept up in *gules* (the
heraldic term for red) and *tricked* (painted). See App. 9.
481. impasted: turned into a crust by the heat of the burning
city.   484. o'ersized . . . gore: covered over with congealed
blood.   493. Repugnant to command: refusing to be used.
496. Ilium: the citadel of Troy.   498. stoops . . . base: col-
lapses.   500. declining: bending toward.   milky: milk-white.

cessful against the Ammonites he would sacrifice the first crea-
ture to meet him on his return, which was his daughter.
426–37. One . . . was: Quotations from a ballad of Jephthah.
428. Still: always.   435. wot: knows.   438. row: line. pious
chanson: godly poem.   439. abridgement: entertainment. Cf.
MND, V.i.39.   441. old friend: i.e., the leading player.
442. valanced: bearded. A valance is a fringe hung round the
sides and bottom of a bed. See Pl. 17b.   443. beard: dare, with a
pun on "valanced." young lady: i.e., the boy who takes the
woman's parts.   446. chopine: lady's shoe with thick cork sole.
447. cracked . . . ring: Before coins were milled on the rim they
were liable to crack. When the crack reached the ring sur-
rounding the device, the coin was no longer valid. See Pl. 10.
450. French falconers: They were famous for their skill in hawk-
ing.   452. quality: skill as an actor.   457. caviar: sturgeon's
roe, a Russian delicacy not then appreciated (or known) by any
but gourmets. general: common herd.   459. cried . . . mine:
surpassed mine.   460. digested: composed.   461. modesty: mod-
eration.   462. sallets: tasty bits.   463–64. phrase . . . affection:

So as a painted tyrant° Pyrrhus stood,
And like a neutral to his will and matter,°
Did nothing.
But as we often see, against° some storm   505
A silence in the heavens, the rack° stand still,
The bold winds speechless and the orb° below
As hush as death, anon the dreadful thunder
Doth rend the region° — so after Pyrrhus' pause
Arousèd vengeance sets him new awork.   510
And never did the Cyclops'° hammers fall
On Mars's armor, forged for proof eterne,°
With less remorse° than Pyrrhus' bleeding sword
Now falls on Priam.   514
Out, out, thou strumpet, Fortune! All you gods,
In general synod° take away her power,
Break all the spokes and fellies° from her wheel,
And bowl the round nave° down the hill of Heaven
As low as to the fiends! "
    POL. This is too long.   520
    HAML. It shall to the barber's, with your beard.
Prithee, say on. He's for a jig° or a tale of bawdry,
or he sleeps. Say on. Come to Hecuba.
    1. PLAY. " But who, oh, who had seen the mobled°
      Queen — "
    HAML. " The mobled Queen "?
    POL. That's good, " mobled Queen " is good.
    1. PLAY. " Run barefoot up and down, threatening
      the flames
With bisson rheum,° a clout° upon that head
Where late the diadem stood, and for a robe,   530
About her lank and all o'erteemèd° loins
A blanket, in the alarm of fear caught up.
Who this had seen, with tongue in venom steeped
'Gainst Fortune's state would treason have pro-
    nounced.°
But if the gods themselves did see her then,   535
When she saw Pyrrhus make malicious sport
In mincing with his sword her husband's limbs,
The instant burst of clamor that she made,
Unless things mortal move them not at all,
Would have made milch° the burning eyes of
    Heaven
    540
And passion in the gods."

    POL. Look whether he has not turned his color
and has tears in 's eyes. Prithee, no more.
    HAML. 'Tis well; I'll have thee speak out the rest
of this soon. Good my lord, will you see the players
well bestowed?° Do you hear, let them be well used,
for they are the abstract and brief chronicles of the
time.° After your death you were better have a bad
epitaph than their ill report while you live.   551
    POL. My lord, I will use them according to their
desert.°
    HAML. God's bodykins,° man, much better. Use
every man after his desert and who shall 'scape
whipping? Use them after your own honor and dig-
nity. The less they deserve, the more merit is in your
bounty. Take them in.
    POL. Come, sirs.   559
    HAML. Follow him, friends. We'll hear a play to-
morrow. [*Exit* POLONIUS *with all the* PLAYERS *but the*
FIRST.] Dost thou hear me, old friend? Can you play
The Murder of Gonzago?
    1. PLAY. Aye, my lord.   564
    HAML. We'll ha 't tomorrow night. You could, for
a need, study a speech of some dozen or sixteen lines
which I would set down and insert in 't, could you
not?
    1. PLAY. Aye, my lord.   569
    HAML. Very well. Follow that lord, and look you
mock him not. [*Exit* FIRST PLAYER.] My good
friends, I'll leave you till night. You are welcome to
Elsinore.
    ROS. Good my lord!   574
    HAML. Aye, so, God be wi' ye! [*Exeunt* ROSEN-
    CRANTZ *and* GUILDENSTERN.] Now I am alone.
Oh, what a rogue and peasant slave am I!
Is it not monstrous that this player here,
But in a fiction, in a dream of passion,°
Could force his soul so to his own conceit°   579
That from her working° all his visage wanned,°
Tears in his eyes, distraction° in 's aspect,°
A broken voice, and his whole function° suiting
With forms to his conceit? And all for nothing!
For Hecuba!
What's Hecuba to him or he to Hecuba,   585
That he should weep for her? What would he do
Had he the motive and the cue for passion
That I have? He would drown the stage with tears
And cleave the general ear° with horrid speech,
Make mad the guilty and appal the free,°   590

---

502. painted tyrant: as in the painting of a tyrant.   503. neu-
tral . . . matter: one midway (*neutral*) between his desire (*will*)
and action (*matter*).   505. against: just before.   506. rack:
the clouds in the upper air. Cf. *Ant & Cleo,* IV.xiv.10.
507. orb: world.   509. region: the country round.   511. Cy-
clops': of Titans, giants who aided Vulcan, the blacksmith
god, to make armor for Mars, the war god.   512. proof
eterne: everlasting protection.   513. remorse: pity.   516. synod:
council.   517. fellies: the pieces forming the circumference
of a wooden wheel.   518. nave: center of the wheel.
522. jig: bawdy dance. See App. 24.   525. mobled:
muffled.   529. bisson rheum: blinding moisture. clout: rag.
531. o'erteemed: exhausted by bearing children; she had borne
fifty-two.   533–34. Who . . . pronounced: anyone who had seen
this sight would with bitter words have uttered treason against
the tyranny of Fortune.   540. milch: milky, i.e., dripping mois-
ture.

548. bestowed: housed.   549–50. abstract . . . time: they
summarize and record the events of our time. Elizabeth-
an players were often in trouble for too saucily comment-
ing on their betters in plays dealing with history or contem-
porary events and persons. See Gen. Intro. pp. 41a, 45a,
48a–b, 49a–b.   552. desert: rank.   553. God's bodykins: by
God's little body.   578. dream of passion: imaginary emotion.
579. conceit: imagination.   580. her working: i.e., the effect of
imagination. wanned: went pale.   581. distraction: frenzy.
aspect: countenance.   582. function: behavior.   589. general
ear: ears of the audience.   590. free: innocent.

Confound the ignorant, and amaze indeed
The very faculties of eyes and ears.
Yet I,
A dull and muddy-mettled° rascal, peak,°   594
Like John-a-dreams,° unpregnant of my cause,°
And can say nothing — no, not for a King
Upon whose property° and most dear life
A damned defeat° was made. Am I a coward?
Who° calls me villain? Breaks my pate across?
Plucks off my beard and blows it in my face?   600
Tweaks me by the nose? Gives me the lie i' the
    throat
As deep as to the lungs? Who does me this?
Ha!
'Swounds,° I should take it. For it cannot be
But I am pigeon-livered° and lack gall°   605
To make oppression bitter, or ere this
I should have fatted all the region kites
With this slave's offal.° Bloody, bawdy villain!
Remorseless, treacherous, lecherous, kindless° vil-
    lain!
Oh, vengeance!   610
Why, what an ass am I! This is most brave,
That I, the son of a dear father murdered,
Prompted to my revenge by Heaven and Hell,
Must, like a whore, unpack my heart with words
And fall a-cursing like a very drab,°   615
A scullion!°
Fie upon 't! Foh! About, my brain! Hum, I have
    heard
That guilty creatures sitting at a play
Have by the very cunning of the scene
Been struck so to the soul that presently°   620
They have proclaimed their malefactions;°
For murder, though it have no tongue, will speak
With most miraculous organ. I'll have these players
Play something like the murder of my father
Before mine uncle. I'll observe his looks,   625
I'll tent° him to the quick. If he but blench,°
I know my course. The° spirit that I have seen
May be the Devil, and the Devil hath power
To assume a pleasing shape. Yea, and perhaps
Out of my weakness and my melancholy,   630
As he is very potent with such spirits,
Abuses me to damn me.° I'll have grounds°

More relative than this.° The play's the thing
Wherein I'll catch the conscience of the King.

    [*Exit.*]

Act III

SCENE I. *A room in the castle.*

[*Enter* KING, QUEEN, POLONIUS, OPHELIA,
    ROSENCRANTZ, *and* GUILDENSTERN.]

KING. And can you, by no drift of circumstance,
Get from him why he puts on this confusion,
Grating° so harshly all his days of quiet
With turbulent and dangerous lunacy?   4
    ROS. He does confess he feels himself distracted,
But from what cause he will by no means speak.
    GUIL. Nor do we find him forward to be
        sounded,°
But, with a crafty madness, keeps aloof
When we would bring him on to some confession
Of his true state.
    QUEEN.   Did he receive you well?   10
    ROS. Most like a gentleman.
    GUIL. But with much forcing of his disposition.°
    ROS. Niggard of question,° but of our demands
Most free in his reply.
    QUEEN.   Did you assay him
To any pastime?°   15
    ROS. Madam, it so fell out that certain players
We o'erraught° on the way. Of these we told him,
And there did seem in him a kind of joy
To hear of it. They are about the Court,
And, as I think, they have already order   20
This night to play before him.
    POL.   'Tis most true.
And he beseeched me to entreat your Majesties
To hear and see the matter.
    KING. With all my heart, and it doth much con-
        tent me
To hear him so inclined.   25
Good gentlemen, give him a further edge,°
And drive his purpose on to these delights.
    ROS. We shall, my lord.
        [*Exeunt* ROSENCRANTZ *and* GUILDENSTERN.]
    KING.   Sweet Gertrude, leave us too,
For we have closely° sent for Hamlet hither,
That he, as 'twere by accident, may here   30

---

594. muddy-mettled: made of mud, not iron. peak: mope.
595. John-a-dreams: "Sleepy Sam." unpregnant ... cause:
barren of plans for vengeance.   597. property: personality, life.
598. defeat: ruin.   599–602. Who ... this: Hamlet runs through
all the insults which provoked a resolute man to mortal
combat. pate: head. lie ... throat: the bitterest of insults.
604. 'Swounds: by God's wounds.   605. pigeon-livered: "as
gentle as a dove." gall: spirit.   606–08. I ... offal: before this
I would have fed this slave's (i.e., the King's) guts to the kites.
fatted: made fat.   609. kindless: unnatural.   615. drab:
"moll."   616. scullion: the lowest of the kitchen servants.
620. presently: immediately.   621. proclaimed ... malefac-
tions: shouted out their crimes.   626. tent: probe. See *Cor*,
I.ix.31. blench: flinch.   627–32. The ... me: See *Haml*
Intro. p. 603a–b.   632. Abuses ... me: i.e., deceives me so that I

may commit the sin of murder which will bring me to damnation.
grounds: reasons for action.   633. relative ... this: i.e., more
convincing than the appearance of a ghost.

    Act III, Sc. i: 1. drift of circumstance: circumstantial evi-
dence, hint.   3. grating: disturbing.   7. forward ... sounded:
eager to be questioned.   12. much ... disposition: making a
great effort to be civil to us.   13. Niggard of question: not asking
many questions.   14–15. Did ... pastime: did you try to in-
terest him in any amusement.   17. o'erraught: overtook.
26. edge: encouragement.   29. closely: secretly.

Affront° Ophelia.
Her father and myself, lawful espials,°
Will so bestow ourselves that, seeing unseen,
We may of their encounter frankly judge
And gather by him, as he is behaved,°　　　　35
If 't be the affliction of his love or no
That thus he suffers for.

QUEEN.　　　　　　　　I shall obey you.
And for your part, Ophelia, I do wish
That your good beauties be the happy cause　　39
Of Hamlet's wildness. So shall I hope your virtues
Will bring him to his wonted way° again,
To both your honors.

OPH..　　　　　Madam, I wish it may. [Exit QUEEN.]
POL. Ophelia, walk you here. Gracious,° so please
　　you,
We will bestow ourselves. [To OPHELIA] Read on
　　this book,°
That show of such an exercise may color　　45
Your loneliness. We are oft to blame in this —
'Tis too much proved — that with devotion's
　　visage°
And pious action we do sugar o'er
The Devil himself.

KING. [Aside] Oh, 'tis too true!
How smart a lash that speech doth give my con-
　　science!　　　　　　　　　　　　　50
The harlot's cheek, beautied with plastering art,
Is not more ugly to the thing that helps it°
Than is my deed to my most painted° word.
Oh, heavy burden!　　　　　　　　54
POL. I hear him coming. Let's withdraw, my lord.
　　　　　　　　　　[Exeunt KING and POLONIUS.
　　　　　　　　[Enter HAMLET.°]
HAML. To be, or not to be — that is the question.
Whether 'tis nobler in the mind to suffer
The slings and arrows of outrageous° fortune,
Or to take arms against a sea° of troubles
And by opposing end them. To die, to sleep —　　60
No more, and by a sleep to say we end
The heartache and the thousand natural shocks
That flesh is heir to. 'Tis a consummation°
Devoutly to be wished. To die, to sleep,
To sleep — perchance to dream. Aye, there's the
　　rub,°　　　　　　　　　　　　65
For in that sleep of death what dreams may come
When we have shuffled off this mortal coil°

Must give us pause. There's the respect°
That makes calamity of so long life.°　　　69
For who would bear the whips and scorns of time,
The oppressor's wrong, the proud man's contumely°
The pangs of déspised love, the law's delay,
The insolence of office° and the spurns
That patient merit of the unworthy takes,°
When he himself might his quietus° make　　75
With a bare bodkin?° Who would fardels° bear,
To grunt and sweat under a weary life,
But that the dread of something after death,
The undiscovered country from whose bourn°
No traveler returns, puzzles the will,°　　80
And makes us rather bear those ills we have
Than fly to others that we know not of?
Thus° conscience does make cowards of us all,
And thus the native hue° of resolution
Is sicklied o'er with the pale cast° of thought,　　85
And enterprises of great pitch° and moment
With this regard their currents turn awry
And lose the name of action.° — Soft you now!
The fair Ophelia! Nymph, in thy orisons°
Be all my sins remembered.

OPH.　　　　　　　Good my lord,　　90
How does your Honor for this many a day?
HAML. I humbly thank you — well, well, well.
OPH. My lord, I have remembrances of yours
That I have longed long to redeliver.
I pray you now receive them.

HAML.　　　　　　No, not I.　　95
I never gave you aught.
OPH. My honored lord, you know right well you
　　did,
And with them words of so sweet breath composed
As made the things more rich. Their perfume lost,
Take these again, for to the noble mind　　100
Rich gifts wax poor when givers prove unkind.
There, my lord.
HAML. Ha, ha! Are you honest?°
OPH. My lord?
HAML. Are you fair?　　　　　　105
OPH. What means your lordship?
HAML. That if you be honest and fair, your hon-
esty should admit no discourse to your beauty.°

---

31. Affront: encounter.　32. lawful espials: who are justified in spying on him.　35. by . . . behaved: from him, from his behavior.　41. wonted way: normal state.　43. Gracious: your Majesty — addressed to the King.　44. book: i.e., of devotions.　47. devotion's visage: an outward appearance of religion.　52. ugly . . . it: i.e., lust, which is the cause of its artificial beauty.　53. painted: i.e., false.　55 s.d., Enter Hamlet: In Q1 the King draws attention to Hamlet's approach with the words "See where he comes poring upon a book." Hamlet is again reading, and is too much absorbed to notice Ophelia.　58. outrageous: cruel.　59. sea: i.e., an endless turmoil.　63. consummation: completion.　65. rub: impediment. See App. 13.　67. shuffled . . . coil: cast off this fuss of life.

68. respect: reason.　69. makes . . . life: makes it a calamity to have to live so long.　71. contumely: insulting behavior.　73. insolence of office: insolent behavior of government officials.　73–74. spurns . . . takes: insults which men of merit have patiently to endure from the unworthy.　75. quietus: discharge. See Sonnet 126.　76. bodkin: dagger. fardels: burdens, the coolie's pack.　79. bourn: boundary.　80. will: resolution, ability to act. 83–88. Thus . . . action: the religious fear that death may not be the end makes men shrink from heroic actions.　84. native hue: natural color.　85. cast: color.　86. pitch: height; used of the soaring flight of a hawk. See App. 26.　87–88. With . . . action: by brooding on this thought great enterprises are diverted from their course and fade away.　89. orisons: prayers.　103. honest: chaste.　107–08. That . . . beauty: if you are chaste and beautiful your chastity should have nothing to do with your beauty — because

OPH. Could beauty, my lord, have better commerce than with honesty?   110

HAML. Aye, truly, for the power of beauty will sooner transform honesty from what it is to a bawd° than the force of honesty can translate beauty into his likeness. This was sometime a paradox,° but now the time gives it proof. I did love you once.   116

OPH. Indeed, my lord, you made me believe so.

HAML. You should not have believed me, for virtue cannot so inoculate our old stock but we shall relish° of it. I loved you not.   120

OPH. I was the more deceived.

HAML. Get thee to a nunnery. Why wouldst thou be a breeder of sinners? I am myself indifferent honest,° but yet I could accuse me of such things that it were better my mother had not borne me. I am   125 very proud, revengeful, ambitious, with more offenses at my beck° than I have thoughts to put them in, imagination to give them shape, or time to act them in. What should such fellows as I do crawling between heaven and earth? We are arrant   130 knaves all. Believe none of us. Go thy ways to a nunnery.° Where's your father?

OPH. At home, my lord.

HAML. Let the doors be shut upon him, that he may play the fool nowhere but in 's own house. Farewell.   137

OPH. Oh, help him, you sweet Heavens!

HAML. If thou dost marry, I'll give thee this plague for thy dowry: Be thou as chaste as ice, as pure as snow — thou shalt not escape calumny.° Get thee to a nunnery, go. Farewell. Or if thou wilt needs marry, marry a fool, for wise men know well enough what monsters° you make of them. To a nunnery, go, and quickly too. Farewell.

OPH. O heavenly powers, restore him!   147

HAML. I have heard of your paintings° too, well enough. God hath given you one face and you make yourselves another. You jig,° you amble,° and you lisp,° and nickname God's creatures, and make your wantonness your ignorance.° Go to, I'll no more on 't — it hath made me mad. I say we will have no more marriages. Those that are married already, all but one, shall live; the rest shall keep as they   156 are. To a nunnery, go.   [Exit.]

OPH. Oh, what a noble mind is here o'erthrown! The courtier's, soldier's, scholar's, eye, tongue, sword —

The expectancy and rose° of the fair state,   160
The glass° of fashion and the mold of form,°
The observed of all observers — quite, quite down!
And I, of ladies most deject and wretched,
That sucked the honey of his music vows,
Now see that noble and most sovereign reason,   165
Like sweet bells jangled, out of tune and harsh,
That unmatched° form and feature of blown° youth
Blasted with ecstasy.° Oh, woe is me,
To have seen what I have seen, see what I see!   169
[Re-enter KING and POLONIUS.]

KING. Love! His affections° do not that way tend,
Nor what he spake, though it lacked form a little,
Was not like madness. There's something in his soul
O'er which his melancholy sits on brood,°
And I do doubt the hatch and the disclose°
Will be some danger. Which for to prevent,   175
I have in quick determination
Thus set it down: He shall with speed to England,
For the demand of our neglected tribute.
Haply° the seas and countries different
With variable objects° shall expel   180
This something-settled° matter in his heart
Whereon his brains still beating puts him thus
From fashion of himself.° What think you on 't?

POL. It shall do well. But yet do I believe
The origin and commencement of his grief   185
Sprung from neglected love. How now, Ophelia!
You need not tell us what Lord Hamlet said,
We heard it all. My lord, do as you please,
But, if you hold it fit, after the play
Let his Queen mother all alone entreat him   190
To show his grief. Let her be round° with him,
And I'll be placed, so please you, in the ear
Of all their conference. If she find him not,
To England send him, or confine him where
Your wisdom best shall think.

KING.   It shall be so.   195
Madness in great ones must not unwatched go.
[Exeunt.]

SCENE II. *A hall in the castle.*

[Enter HAMLET *and* PLAYERS.]

HAML. Speak the speech,° I pray you, as I pro-

(so Hamlet thinks in his bitterness) beautiful women are seldom chaste. 112. bawd: brothel-keeper. 115. paradox: statement contrary to accepted opinion. 120. relish: have some trace. 123–24. indifferent honest: moderately honorable. 127. at . . . beck: waiting to come when I beckon. 132. nunnery: i.e., a place where she will be removed from temptation. 141. calumny: slander. 145. monsters: horned beasts, cuckolds. See App. 11. 148. paintings: using make-up. 150. jig: dance lecherously. amble: walk artificially. 151. lisp: talk affectedly. 152–53. nickname . . . ignorance: give things indecent names and pretend to be too simple to understand their meanings.

160. expectancy . . . rose: bright hope. The rose is used as a symbol for beauty and perfection. Cf. *I Hen IV*, I.iii.175. 161. glass: mirror. mold of form: perfect pattern of manly beauty. 167. unmatched: unmatchable. blown: perfect, like an open flower at its best. 168. Blasted . . . ecstasy: ruined by madness. 170. affections: state of mind. 173. sits . . . brood: sits hatching. 174. doubt . . . disclose: suspect the brood which will result. 179. Haply: perhaps. 180. variable objects: novel sights. 181. something-settled: somewhat settled; i.e., not yet incurable. 182–83. puts . . . himself: i.e., separates him from his normal self. 191. round: direct.
Sc. ii: 1. the speech: which he has written. See ll. 266–67. The whole passage which follows is Shakespeare's own comment

nounced it to you, trippingly° on the tongue. But if
you mouth° it, as many of your players do, I had as
lief° the town crier spoke my lines. Nor do not saw
the air too much with your hand, thus, but use   5
all gently. For in the very torrent, tempest, and, as I
may say, whirlwind of passion, you must acquire and
beget a temperance that may give it smoothness. Oh,
it offends me to the soul to hear a robustious° peri-
wig-pated° fellow tear a passion to tatters, to   10
very rags, to split the ears of the groundlings,° who
for the most part are capable of nothing but inex-
plicable dumb shows° and noise. I would have such
a fellow whipped for o'erdoing Termagant° — it
out-Herods Herod. Pray you, avoid it.   16

1. PLAY. I warrant your Honor.

HAML. Be not too tame neither, but let your own
discretion be your tutor. Suit the action to the word,
the word to the action, with this special observ-   20
ance, that you o'erstep not the modesty of nature.
For anything so overdone is from° the purpose of
playing, whose end, both at the first and now, was
and is to hold as 'twere the mirror up to Nature —
to show Virtue her own feature, scorn her own   25
image, and the very age and body of the time his
form and pressure.° Now this overdone or come
tardy off, though it make the unskillful laugh, can-
not but make the judicious grieve, the censure of the
which one° must in your allowance o'erweigh a   30
whole theater of others. Oh, there be players° that I
have seen play, and heard others praise — and that
highly, not to speak it profanely — that neither hav-
ing the accent of Christians nor the gait of Christian,
pagan, nor man, have so strutted and bellowed   35
that I have thought some of Nature's journeymen°
had made men, and not made them well, they imi-
tated humanity so abominably.

1. PLAY. I hope we have reformed that indiffer-
ently° with us, sir.   41

HAML. Oh, reform it altogether. And let those that
play your clowns° speak no more than is set down

for them. For there be of them that will themselves
laugh, to set on some quantity of barren spec-   45
tators to laugh too, though in the meantime some
necessary question of the play be then to be consid-
ered. That's villainous, and shows a most pitiful°
ambition in the fool that uses it. Go, make you   50
ready. [*Exeunt* PLAYERS. *Enter* POLONIUS, ROSEN-
CRANTZ, *and* GUILDENSTERN.] How now, my lord!
Will the King hear this piece of work?

POL. And the Queen too, and that presently.

HAML. Bid the players make haste. [*Exit* POLO-
NIUS.] Will you two help to hasten them?   55

ROS. & GUIL. We will, my lord.

[*Exeunt* ROSENCRANTZ *and* GUILDENSTERN.]

HAML. What ho! Horatio!

[*Enter* HORATIO.]

HOR. Here, sweet lord, at your service.

HAML. Horatio, thou art e'en as just a man
As e'er my conversation coped° withal.   60

HOR. Oh, my dear lord ——

HAML.   Nay, do not think I flatter,
For what advancement° may I hope from thee,
That no revénue hast but thy good spirits
To feed and clothe thee? Why should the poor be
    flattered?
No, let the candied° tongue lick absurd pomp   65
And crook the pregnant hinges of the knee
Where thrift may follow fawning.° Dost thou
    hear?
Since my dear soul was mistress of her choice
And could of men distinguish, her election
Hath sealed° thee for herself. For thou hast been   70
As one in suffering all that suffers nothing,
A man that fortune's buffets and rewards
Hast ta'en with equal thanks. And blest are those
Whose blood and judgment are so well commingled
That they are not a pipe° for fortune's finger   75
To sound what stop she please. Give me that man
That is not passion's slave, and I will wear him
In my heart's core — aye, in my heart of heart,
As I do thee. Something too much of this.
There is a play tonight before the King.   80
One scene of it comes near the circumstance
Which I have told thee of my father's death.
I prithee when thou seest that act afoot,
Even with the very comment° of thy soul
Observe my uncle. If his occulted° guilt   85

on the actor's art and states the creed and practice of his
company as contrasted with the more violent methods of
Edward Alleyn and his fellows. See Gen. Intro. p. 41b.
2. trippingly: smoothly, easily.   **3. mouth:** "ham" it.   **4. lief:**
soon.   **9. robustious:** ranting.   **10. periwig-pated:** wearing
a wig.   **11. groundlings:** the poorer spectators, who stood in
the yard of the playhouse. See Gen. Intro. p. 53a.   **14. dumb
shows:** an old-fashioned dramatic device, still being used by the
Admiral's Men: before a tragedy, and sometimes before each act,
the characters mimed the action which was to follow. See later,
l. 145.   **15. Termagant:** God of the Saracens, who, like Herod,
was presented in early stage plays as a roaring tyrant.   **22. from:**
contrary to.   **26–27. very . . . pressure:** an exact reproduction of
the age. **form:** shape. **pressure:** imprint (of a seal).   **30. the
. . . one:** i.e., the judicious spectator.   **31. there . . . players:** An
obvious attack on Alleyn.   **36. journeymen:** hired workmen, not
masters of the trade.   **41. indifferently:** moderately.   **42–43. those
. . . clowns:** A hit at Will Kempe, the former clown of Shake-
speare's company. See Gen. Intro. p. 60a. Q1 adds the passage
"And then you have some again that keep one suit of jests, as a
man is known by one suit of apparel, and gentlemen quote his jests

down in their tables before they come to the play, as thus: 'Can-
not you stay till I eat my porridge?' and 'You owe me a quarter's
wages,' and 'My coat wants a cullison,' and 'Your beer is sour,'
and blabbering with his lips, and thus keeping in his cinquepace
of jests, when God knows the warm clown cannot make a jest un-
less by chance, as the blind man catcheth a hare. Masters tell
him of it."   **49. pitiful:** contemptible.   **60. coped:** met.   **62. ad-
vancement:** promotion.   **65. candied:** sugared over with hypoc-
risy.   **66–67. crook . . . fawning:** bend the ready knees whenever
gain will follow flattery.   **70. sealed:** set a mark on.   **75. pipe:** an
instrument that varies its notes.   **84. comment:** close observa-
tion.   **85. occulted:** concealed.

Do not itself unkennel° in one speech
It is a damnèd ghost° that we have seen
And my imaginations are as foul
As Vulcan's° stithy.° Give him heedful note,°
For I mine eyes will rivet to his face,   90
And after we will both our judgments join
In censure of his seeming.°

HOR.   Well, my lord.
If he steal aught the whilst this play is playing,
And 'scape detecting, I will pay the theft.

HAML. They are coming to the play. I must be
idle.°   95
Get you a place.
    [*Danish march. A flourish. Enter* KING, QUEEN,
POLONIUS, OPHELIA, ROSENCRANTZ, GUILDENSTERN,
    and other LORDS *attendant, with the* GUARD
                carrying torches.]

KING. How fares our cousin Hamlet?

HAML. Excellent, i' faith, of the chameleon's dish.
I eat the air, promise-crammed. You cannot feed ca-
pons so.°

KING. I have nothing with this answer,° Hamlet.
These words are not mine.

HAML. No, nor mine now.° [*To* POLONIUS] My
lord, you played once i' the university, you say?

POL. That did I, my lord, and was accounted a
good actor.   106

HAML. What did you enact?

POL. I did enact Julius Caesar. I was killed i' the
Capitol. Brutus killed me.

HAML. It was a brute part of him to kill so capital
a calf there. Be the players ready?   111

ROS. Aye, my lord, they stay upon your patience.°

QUEEN. Come hither, my dear Hamlet, sit by me.

HAML. No, good Mother, here's metal more attrac-
tive.   117

POL. [*To the* KING] Oh ho! Do you mark that?

HAML. Lady, shall I lie in your lap?
               [*Lying down at* OPHELIA's *feet*]

OPH. No, my lord.   120

HAML. I mean, my head upon your lap?

OPH. Aye, my lord.

HAML. Do you think I meant country matters?°

OPH. I think nothing, my lord.

HAML. That's a fair thought to lie between maids'
legs.   126

OPH. What is, my lord?

HAML. Nothing.

OPH. You are merry, my lord.

HAML. Who, I?   130

OPH. Aye, my lord.

HAML. Oh God, your only jig-maker.° What
should a man do but be merry? For look you how
cheerfully my mother looks, and my father died
within 's two hours.   135

OPH. Nay, 'tis twice two months, my lord.

HAML. So long? Nay, then, let the Devil wear
black, for I'll have a suit of sables.° Oh heavens! Die
two months ago, and not forgotten yet? Then there's
hope a great man's memory may outlive his   140
life half a year. But, by 'r Lady, he must build
churches then, or else shall he suffer not thinking on,
with the hobbyhorse,° whose epitaph is "For, oh,
for oh, the hobbyhorse is forgot."   145
[*Hautboys° play. The dumb show enters.° Enter a*
KING *and a* QUEEN *very lovingly, the* QUEEN *embrac-
ing him and he her. She kneels, and makes show of
protestation unto him. He takes her up, and declines
his head upon her neck, lays him down upon a bank
of flowers. She, seeing him asleep, leaves him. Anon
comes in a fellow, takes off his crown, kisses it, and
pours poison in the* KING's *ears, and exit. The* QUEEN
returns, finds the KING *dead, and makes passionate
action. The Poisoner, with some two or three Mutes,
comes in again, seeming to lament with her. The
dead body is carried away. The Poisoner woos the*
QUEEN *with gifts. She seems loath and unwilling
awhile, but in the end accepts his love.   Exeunt.*]

OPH. What means this, my lord?

HAML. Marry, this is miching mallecho.° It means
mischief.

OPH. Belike this show imports the argument° of
the play.   150
               [*Enter* PROLOGUE.]

HAML. We shall know by this fellow. The players
cannot keep counsel, they'll tell all.

OPH. Will he tell us what this show meant?

HAML. Aye, or any show that you'll show him. Be
not you ashamed to show, he'll not shame to tell you
what it means.   156

OPH. You are naught,° you are naught. I'll mark
the play.

---

86. **unkennel:** come to light; lit., force a fox from his hole.
87. **damned ghost:** See II.ii.627.   89. **Vulcan:** the black-
smith god. **stithy:** smithy. **heedful note:** careful observation.
92. **censure . . . seeming:** judgment on his looks.   95. **be idle:**
seem crazy.   98–100. **Excellent . . . so:** Hamlet takes "fare"
literally as "what food are you eating." The chameleon was sup-
posed to feed on air. **promise-crammed:** stuffed, like a fattened
chicken (*capon*) — but with empty promises.   101. **I . . . an-
swer:** I cannot make any sense of your answer.   103. **nor . . .
now:** i.e., once words have left the lips they cease to belong to
the speaker.   112. **stay . . . patience:** wait for you to be ready.
123. **country matters:** something indecent.

132. **jig-maker:** composer of jigs. See App. 24.   138. **suit of
sables:** a quibble on "sable," black, and "sable," gown
trimmed with sable fur, worn by wealthy old gentlemen.
See Pl. 9l.   144. **hobbyhorse:** imitation horse worn by perform-
ers in a morris dance, an amusement much disapproved of by the
godly. See App. 24.   145 s.d., **Hautboys:** oboes. **The dumb
show enters:** Critics have been disturbed because this dumb show
cannot be exactly paralleled in any other Elizabethan play, and
because the King is apparently not disturbed by it. Shakespeare's
intention, however, in presenting a play within a play is to pro-
duce something stagy and artificial compared with the play
proper. Moreover, as Hamlet has already complained, dumb
shows were often inexplicable.   147. **miching mallecho:** slinking
mischief.   149. **argument:** plot. She too is puzzled by the dumb
show.   157. **naught:** i.e., disgusting.

PRO.   For us, and for our tragedy,
Here stooping to your clemency,   160
We beg your hearing patiently.

HAML. Is this a prologue, or the posy of a ring?°

OPH. 'Tis brief, my lord.

HAML. As woman's love.

[*Enter two* PLAYERS, KING *and* QUEEN.]

P. KING. Full° thirty times hath Phoebus' cart°
gone round   165
Neptune's° salt wash and Tellus'° orbèd ground,
And thirty dozen moons with borrowed sheen°
About the world have times twelve thirties been,
Since love our hearts and Hymen° did our hands
Unite commutual° in most sacred bands.   170

P. QUEEN. So many journeys may the sun and
moon
Make us again count o'er ere love be done!
But, woe is me, you are so sick of late,
So far from cheer and from your former state,
That I distrust° you. Yet, though I distrust,   175
Discomfort you, my lord, it nothing must.
For women's fear and love holds quantity°
In neither aught or in extremity.°
Now what my love is, proof hath made you know,
And as my love is sized, my fear is so.   180
Where love is great, the littlest doubts are fear,
Where little fears grow great, great love grows there.

P. KING. Faith, I must leave thee,° love, and
shortly too,
My operant powers° their functions leave to do.
And thou shalt live in this fair world behind,   185
Honored, beloved, and haply one as kind
For husband shalt thou ——

P. QUEEN.   Oh, confound the rest!
Such love must needs be treason in my breast.
In second husband let me be accurst!
None wed the second but who killed the first.   190

HAML. [*Aside*] Wormwood,° wormwood.

P. QUEEN. The instances° that second marriage
move
Are base respects of thrift,° but none of love.
A second time I kill my husband dead
When second husband kisses me in bed.   195

P. KING. I do believe you think what now you
speak,
But what we do determine oft we break.
Purpose is but the slave to memory,

Of violent birth but poor validity,
Which now, like fruit unripe, sticks on the tree   200
But fall unshaken when they mellow be.
Most necessary 'tis that we forget
To pay ourselves what to ourselves is debt.
What to ourselves in passion we propose,
The passion ending, doth the purpose lose.   205
The violence of either grief or joy
Their own enactures° with themselves destroy.
Where joy most revels, grief doth most lament,
Grief joys, joy grieves, on slender accident.   209
This world is not for aye,° nor 'tis not strange
That even our loves should with our fortunes
change,
For 'tis a question left us yet to prove
Whether love lead fortune or else fortune love.
The great man down, you mark his favorite flies,
The poor advanced makes friends of enemies.   215
And hitherto doth love on fortune tend,
For who not needs shall never lack a friend,
And who in want a hollow friend doth try
Directly seasons° him his enemy.
But, orderly to end where I begun,   220
Our wills and fates do so contráry run
That our devices still are overthrown,
Our thoughts are ours, their ends none of our own.
So think thou wilt no second husband wed,   224
But die thy thoughts when thy first lord is dead.

P. QUEEN. Nor earth to me give food nor Heaven
light!
Sport and repose lock from me day and night!
To desperation turn my trust and hope!
An anchor's° cheer in prison be my scope!
Each opposite that blanks° the face of joy   230
Meet what I would have well and it destroy!
Both here and hence pursue me lasting strife
If, once a widow, ever I be wife!

HAML. If she should break it now!

P. KING. 'Tis deeply sworn. Sweet, leave me here
a while.   235
My spirits grow dull, and fain I would beguile
The tedious day with sleep.   [*Sleeps.*]

P. QUEEN.   Sleep rock thy brain,
And never come mischance between us twain!
                        [*Exit.*]

HAML. Madam, how like you this play?

QUEEN. The lady doth protest too much, methinks.

HAML. Oh, but she'll keep her word.   241

KING. Have you heard the argument?° Is there no
offense in 't?

HAML. No, no, they do but jest, poison in jest —
no offense i' the world.   245

KING. What do you call the play?

---

162. posy . . . ring: It was a pretty custom to inscribe rings with little mottoes or messages, which were necessarily brief. 165–238. Full . . . twain: The play is deliberately written in crude rhyming verse, full of ridiculous and bombastic phrases. 165. Phoebus' cart: the chariot of the sun. 166. Neptune: the sea god. Tellus: the earth goddess. 167. borrowed sheen: light borrowed from the sun. 169. Hymen: god of marriage. 170. commutual: mutually. 175. distrust: am anxious about. 177. quantity: proportion. 178. In . . . extremity: either nothing or too much. 183. leave thee: i.e., die. 184. operant powers: bodily strength. 191. Wormwood: bitterness. 192. instances: arguments. 193. respects of thrift: considerations of gain.

207. enactures: performances. 210. aye: ever. 219. seasons: ripens into. 229. anchor: anchorite, hermit. 230. blanks: makes pale. 242. argument: plot. When performances were given at Court it was sometimes customary to provide a written or printed synopsis of the story for the distinguished spectators.

HAML. *The Mousetrap.*° Marry, how? Tropically.° This play is the image of a murder done in Vienna. Gonzago is the Duke's name, his wife, Baptista. You shall see anon. 'Tis a knavish piece of   250
work, but what o' that? Your Majesty, and we that have free° souls, it touches us not. Let the galled jade wince, our withers are unwrung.°
[*Enter* LUCIANUS.] This is one Lucianus, nephew to the King.

OPH. You are as good as a chorus,° my lord.   255

HAML. I could interpret between you and your love, if I could see the puppets dallying.°

OPH. You are keen, my lord, you are keen.

HAML. It would cost you a groaning to take off my edge.   260

OPH. Still better, and worse.

HAML. So you must take your husbands.° Begin, murderer. Pox, leave thy damnable faces and begin. Come, the croaking raven doth bellow for revenge.

LUC. Thoughts black, hands apt, drugs fit, and
time agreeing,   266
Confederate season, else no creature° seeing,
Thou mixture rank of midnight weeds collected,
With Hecate's ban° thrice blasted, thrice infected,
Thy natural magic and dire property°   270
On wholesome life usurp immediately.

[*Pours the poison into the sleeper's ear.*]

HAML. He poisons him i' the garden for his estate.° His name's Gonzago. The story is extant, and written in very choice Italian. You shall see anon how the murderer gets the love of Gonzago's wife.

OPH. The King rises.   276

HAML. What, frighted with false fire!°

QUEEN. How fares my lord?

POL. Give o'er the play.

KING. Give me some light. Away!   280

POL. Lights, lights, lights!

[*Exeunt all but* HAMLET *and* HORATIO.]

HAML. "Why, let the stricken deer go weep,
The hart ungallèd play,
For some must watch while some must sleep.
Thus runs the world away."   285
Would not this, sir, and a forest of feathers° — if the rest of my fortunes turn Turk° with me — with two Provincial roses° on my razed° shoes, get me a fellowship° in a cry° of players, sir?

HOR. Half a share.   290

HAML. A whole one, I.
"For thou dost know, O Damon° dear,
This realm dismantled° was
Of Jove himself, and now reigns here
A very, very — pajock."°   295

HOR. You might have rhymed.

HAML. O good Horatio, I'll take the ghost's word for a thousand pound. Didst perceive?

HOR. Very well, my lord.

HAML. Upon the talk of the poisoning?   300

HOR. I did very well note him.

HAML. Ah, ha! Come, some music! Come, the recorders!°
"For if the King like not the comedy,
Why then, belike, he likes it not, perdy."°   305
Come, some music!

[*Re-enter* ROSENCRANTZ *and* GUILDENSTERN.]

GUIL. Good my lord, vouchsafe me a word with you.

HAML. Sir, a whole history.

GUIL. The King, sir ——   310

HAML. Aye, sir, what of him?

GUIL. Is in his retirement marvelous distempered.°

HAML. With drink, sir?

GUIL. No, my lord, rather with choler.°   315

HAML. Your wisdom should show itself more richer to signify this to the doctor, for for me to put him to his purgation° would perhaps plunge him into far more choler.   319

GUIL. Good my lord, put your discourse into some frame,° and start not so wildly from my affair.

HAML. I am tame, sir. Pronounce.

GUIL. The Queen your mother, in most great affliction of spirit, hath sent me to you.

HAML. You are welcome.   325

GUIL. Nay, good my lord, this courtesy is not of the right breed. If it shall please you to make me a wholesome answer, I will do your mother's commandment. If not, your pardon and my return shall be the end of my business.   330

HAML. Sir, I cannot.

GUIL. What, my lord?

HAML. Make you a wholesome answer, my wit's

---

247. Mousetrap: The phrase was used of a device to entice a person to his own destruction (OED).   **248. Tropically:** figuratively, with a pun on "trap."   **252. free:** innocent.   **252–53. galled . . . unwrung:** let a nag with a sore back flinch when the saddle is put on; our shoulders (being ungalled) feel no pain.   **255. chorus:** the chorus sometimes introduced the characters and commented on what was to follow. See, for instance, the Chorus in *Hen V.*   **257. puppets dallying:** Elizabethan puppets were crude marionettes, popular at fairs. While the figures were put through their motions, the puppet master explained what was happening.   **262. So . . . husbands:** i.e., as the marriage service expresses it, "for better, for worse."   **267. confederate . . . creature:** the opportunity conspiring with me, no other creature.   **269. Hecate's ban:** the curse of Hecate, goddess of witchcraft.   **270. property:** nature.   **273. estate:** kingdom.   **277. false fire:** a mere show.   **286. forest of feathers:** set of plumes, much worn by players.

287. turn Turk: turn heathen, and treat me cruelly.   **288. Provincial roses:** rosettes, worn on the shoes. **razed:** slashed, ornamented with cuts. See Pl. 8c.   **289. fellowship:** partnership. **cry:** pack.   **292. Damon:** Damon and Pythias were types of perfect friends.   **293. dismantled:** robbed.   **295. pajock:** peacock, a strutting, lecherous bird. These verses, and the lines above, may have come from some ballad, otherwise lost.   **303. recorders:** wooden pipes. See Pl. 19b.   **305. perdy:** by God.   **312. distempered:** disturbed; but Hamlet takes the word in its other sense of "drunk."   **315. choler:** anger, which Hamlet again pretends to understand as meaning "biliousness."   **317–18. put . . . purgation:** "give him a dose of salts."   **321. frame:** shape; i.e., "please talk sense."

diseased. But, sir, such answer as I can make you shall command, or rather, as you say, my mother. Therefore no more, but to the matter. My mother, you say —— 337

ROS. Then thus she says. Your behavior hath struck her into amazement and admiration.°

HAML. Oh, wonderful son that can so astonish a mother! But is there no sequel at the heels of this mother's admiration? Impart. 342

ROS. She desires to speak with you in her closet ere you go to bed.

HAML. We shall obey, were she ten times our mother. Have you any further trade with us?

ROS. My lord, you once did love me. 348

HAML. So I do still, by these pickers and stealers.°

ROS. Good my lord, what is your cause of distemper? You do surely bar the door upon your own liberty if you deny your griefs° to your friend.

HAML. Sir, I lack advancement.° 354

ROS. How can that be when you have the voice of the King himself for your succession in Denmark?

HAML. Aye, sir, but "While the grass grows"° — the proverb is something musty. [*Re-enter* 359 PLAYERS *with recorders.*] Oh, the recorders!° Let me see one. To withdraw° with you —— why do you go about to recover the wind° of me, as if you would drive me into a toil?°

GUIL. O my lord, if my duty be too bold, my love is too unmannerly.° 365

HAML. I do not well understand that. Will you play upon this pipe?

GUIL. My lord, I cannot.

HAML. I pray you.

GUIL. Believe me, I cannot.

HAML. I do beseech you. 371

GUIL. I know no touch of it, my lord.

HAML. It is as easy as lying. Govern these ventages° with your fingers and thumb, give it breath with your mouth, and it will discourse most eloquent music. Look you, these are the stops. 376

GUIL. But these cannot I command to any utterance of harmony, I have not the skill.

HAML. Why, look you now, how unworthy a thing you make of me! You would play upon me, 380 you would seem to know my stops, you would pluck out the heart of my mystery, you would sound me

from my lowest note to the top of my compass — and there is much music, excellent voice, in this little organ — yet cannot you make it speak. 'Sblood, do you think I am easier to be played on than a pipe? Call me what instrument you will, though you can fret° me, you cannot play upon me. [*Re-enter* POLONIUS.] God bless you, sir! 390

POL. My lord, the Queen would speak with you, and presently.

HAML. Do you see yonder cloud that's almost in shape of a camel?

POL. By the mass, and 'tis like a camel indeed.

HAML. Methinks it is like a weasel. 396

POL. It is backed like a weasel.

HAML. Or like a whale?

POL. Very like a whale.

HAML. Then I will come to my mother by 400 and by. They fool me to the top of my bent.° I will come by and by.

POL. I will say so. [*Exit* POLONIUS.]

HAML. "By and by" is easily said. Leave me, friends. [*Exeunt all but* HAMLET.] 'Tis now the very witching time° of night, 406 When churchyards yawn and Hell itself breathes out Contagion° to this world. Now could I drink hot blood, And do such bitter business as the day 409 Would quake to look on. Soft! Now to my mother. O heart, lose not thy nature, let not ever The soul of Nero° enter this firm bosom. Let me be cruel, not unnatural. I will speak daggers to her, but use none. My tongue and soul in this be hypocrites, 415 How in my words soever she be shent,° To give them seals° never, my soul, consent!

[*Exit.*]

SCENE III. *A room in the castle.*

[*Enter* KING, ROSENCRANTZ, *and* GUILDENSTERN.]

KING. I like him not, nor stands it safe with us To let his madness range.° Therefore prepare you. I your commission will forthwith dispatch, And he to England shall along with you. The terms of our estate° may not endure 5 Hazard so near us as doth hourly grow Out of his lunacies.

GUIL. We will ourselves provide.°

339. **admiration:** wonder. 349. **pickers . . . stealers:** i.e., hands — an echo from the Christian's duty in the catechism to keep his hands "from picking and stealing." 353. **deny . . . griefs:** refuse to tell your troubles. 354. **advancement:** promotion. Hamlet harks back to his previous interview with Rosencrantz and Guildenstern. See II.ii.258. 358. **While . . . grows:** the proverb ends "the steed starves." 360. **recorders:** See Pl. 19b. 361. **withdraw:** go aside. Hamlet leads Guildenstern to one side of the stage. 362. **recover . . . wind:** a hunting metaphor; approach me with the wind against you. 363. **toil:** net. 364–65. **if . . . unmannerly:** if I exceed my duty by asking these questions, then my affection for you shows lack of manners; i.e., forgive me if I have been impertinent. 374. **ventages:** holes, stops.

389. **fret:** annoy, with a pun on the frets or bars on stringed instruments by which the fingering is regulated. See Pl. 18b. 401. **top . . . bent:** See II.ii.30,n. 406. **witching time:** when witches perform their foul rites. 408. **Contagion:** infection. 412. **Nero:** Nero killed his own mother. Hamlet is afraid that in the interview to come he will lose all self-control. 416. **shent:** rebuked. 417. **give . . . seals:** ratify words by actions. See App. 6.

Sc. iii: 2. **range:** roam freely. 5. **terms . . . estate:** i.e., one in my position. 7. **ourselves provide:** make our preparations.

Most holy and religious fear° it is
To keep those many many bodies safe
That live and feed upon your Majesty.　　　　10
　　ROS. The single and peculiar° life is bound
With all the strength and armor of the mind
To keep itself from noyance,° but much more
That spirit upon whose weal° depends and rests
The lives of many. The cease of majesty°　　　15
Dies not alone, but like a gulf° doth draw
What's near it with it. It is a massy° wheel
Fixed on the summit of the highest mount,
To whose huge spokes ten thousand lesser things
Are mortised° and adjoined; which, when it falls,
Each small annexment, petty consequence,°　　21
Attends° the boisterous ruin. Never alone
Did the King sigh but with a general groan.
　　KING. Arm you, I pray you, to this speedy voyage,
For we will fetters put upon this fear,　　　25
Which now goes too free-footed.
　　ROS. & GUIL.　　　　　　We will haste us.
　　[Exeunt ROSENCRANTZ and GUILDENSTERN.]
　　　　　　　　[Enter POLONIUS.]
　　POL. My lord, he's going to his mother's closet.
Behind the arras I'll convey myself
To hear the process.° I'll warrant she'll tax° him
　　home.
And, as you said,° and wisely was it said,　　30
'Tis meet that some more audience than a mother,
Since nature makes them partial, should o'erhear
The speech, of vantage.° Fare you well, my liege.
I'll call upon you ere you go to bed
And tell you what I know.
　　KING.　　Thanks, dear my lord.　[Exit POLONIUS.]
Oh, my offense is rank,° it smells to Heaven.　36
It hath the primal eldest curse° upon 't,
A brother's murder. Pray can I not,
Though inclination be as sharp as will.°
My stronger guilt defeats my strong intent,　40
And like a man to double business bound,
I stand in pause where I shall first begin,
And both neglect. What if this cursèd hand
Were thicker than itself with brother's blood,
Is there not rain enough in the sweet heavens　45
To wash it white as snow? Whereto serves mercy
But to confront the visage of offense?°
And what's in prayer but this twofold force,
To be forestalled° ere we come to fall

Or pardoned being down? Then I'll look up,　50
My fault is past. But oh, what form of prayer
Can serve my turn? "Forgive me my foul mur-
　　der"?
That cannot be, since I am still possessed
Of those effects° for which I did the murder —
My crown, mine own ambition, and my Queen.　55
May one be pardoned and retain the offense?°
In the corrupted currents° of this world
Offense's gilded hand may shove by justice,
And oft 'tis seen the wicked prize° itself
Buys out the law. But 'tis not so above.　　60
There is no shuffling, there the action lies
In his true nature,° and we ourselves compelled
Even to the teeth and forehead° of our faults
To give in evidence. What then? What rests?
Try what repentance can. What can it not?　65
Yet what can it when one cannot repent?
Oh, wretched state! Oh, bosom black as death!
Oh, limèd° soul, that struggling to be free
Art more engaged!° Help, angels! Make assay!°
Bow, stubborn knees, and heart with strings of steel,
Be soft as sinews of the newborn babe!　　71
All may be well.　　　　　[Retires and kneels.]
　　　　　　　　[Enter HAMLET.]
　　HAML. Now might I do it pat, now he is praying,
And now I'll do 't. And so he goes to Heaven,°
And so am I revenged. That would be scanned:　75
A villain kills my father, and for that
I, his sole son, do this same villain send
To Heaven.
Oh, this is hire and salary,° not revenge.
He took my father grossly,° full of bread,　80
With all his crimes broad blown, as flush° as May,
And how his audit° stands who knows save
　　Heaven?
But in our circumstance and course of thought,°
'Tis heavy with him. And am I then revenged,
To take him in the purging of his soul,　　85
When he is fit and seasoned,° for his passage?
No.
Up, sword, and know thou a more horrid hent.°
When he is drunk asleep, or in his rage,
Or in the incestuous pleasure of his bed —　90
At gaming, swearing, or about some act
That has no relish of salvation in 't —
Then trip him, that his heels may kick at Heaven
And that his soul may be as damned and black

---

8. fear: anxiety.　11. peculiar: individual.　13. noyance:
injury.　14. weal: welfare.　15. cease of majesty: death of
a king.　16. gulf: whirlpool.　17. massy: massive.　20. mor-
tised: firmly fastened.　21. annexment . . . consequence:
attachment, smallest thing connected with it.　22. Attends:
waits on, is involved in.　29. process: proceeding. tax: cen-
sure.　30. as . . . said: Actually Polonius himself had said it
(III.i.189–93).　33. of vantage: from a place of vantage; i.e.,
concealment.　36. rank: foul.　37. primal . . . curse: the curse
laid upon Cain, the first murderer, who also slew his brother.
39. will: desire.　47. confront . . . offense: look crime in the
face.　49. forestalled: prevented.

54. effects: advantages.　56. offense: i.e., that for which he has
offended.　57. currents: courses, ways.　59. wicked prize: the
proceeds of the crime.　61–62. there . . . nature: in Heaven the
case is tried on its own merits.　63. teeth . . . forehead: i.e.,
face to face.　68. limed: caught as in birdlime.　69. engaged:
stuck fast. assay: attempt.　74. And . . . Heaven: See Haml
Intro. p. 604a.　79 hire . . . salary: i.e., a kind action deserving
pay.　80. grossly: i.e., when he was in a state of sin. See
I.v.74–80.　81. broad . . . flush: in full blossom, as luxuriant.
82. audit: account.　83. circumstance . . . thought: as it appears
to my mind.　86. seasoned: ripe.　88. hent: opportunity.

As Hell, whereto it goes. My mother stays.   95
This physic but prolongs thy sickly days.   [*Exit.*]
  KING. [*Rising*] My words fly up, my thoughts re-
    main below.
Words without thoughts never to Heaven go.
                                              [*Exit.*]

SCENE IV. *The* QUEEN's *closet.*

[*Enter* QUEEN *and* POLONIUS.]

  POL. He will come straight. Look you lay home
    to° him.
Tell him his pranks have been too broad° to bear
    with,
And that your grace hath screened and stood be-
    tween
Much heat and him. I'll sconce me° even here.
Pray you, be round with him.   5
  HAML. [*Within*] Mother, Mother, Mother!
  QUEEN.   I'll warrant you,
Fear me not. Withdraw, I hear him coming.
          [POLONIUS *hides behind the arras.*]
                [*Enter* HAML.]
  HAML. Now, Mother, what's the matter?
  QUEEN. Hamlet, thou hast thy father much of-
    fended.
  HAML. Mother, you have my father much of-
    fended.   10
  QUEEN. Come, come, you answer with an idle
    tongue.
  HAML. Go, go, you question with a wicked
    tongue.
  QUEEN. Why, how now, Hamlet!
  HAML.   What's the matter now?
  QUEEN. Have you forgot me?
  HAML.   No, by the rood,° not so.   14
You are the Queen, your husband's brother's wife,
And — would it were not so! — you are my mother.
  QUEEN. Nay, then, I'll set those to you that can
    speak.
  HAML. Come, come, and sit you down. You shall
    not budge,
You go not till I set you up a glass°
Where you may see the inmost part of you.   20
  QUEEN. What wilt thou do? Thou wilt not mur-
    der me?
Help, help, ho!
  POL. [*Behind*] What ho! Help, help, help!
  HAML. [*Drawing*] How now! A rat? Dead, for a
    ducat, dead! [*Makes a pass through the arras.*]
  POL. [*Behind*] Oh, I am slain! [*Falls and dies.*]
  QUEEN.   Oh me, what hast thou done?
  HAML. Nay, I know not. Is it the King?   26
  QUEEN. Oh, what a rash and bloody deed is this!

  HAML. A bloody deed! Almost as bad, good
    Mother,
As kill a king and marry with his brother.
  QUEEN. As kill a king!
  HAML.   Aye, lady, 'twas my word.   30
        [*Lifts up the arras and discovers* POLONIUS.]
Thou wretched, rash, intruding fool, farewell!
I took thee for thy better. Take thy fortune.
Thou find'st to be too busy is some danger.
Leave wringing of your hands. Peace! Sit you down,
And let me wring your heart. For so I shall   35
If it be made of penetrable stuff,
If damnèd custom have not brassed° it so
That it be proof and bulwark against sense.
  QUEEN. What have I done that thou darest wag
    thy tongue
In noise so rude against me?
  HAML.   Such an act   40
That blurs the grace and blush of modesty,
Calls virtue hypocrite, takes off the rose
From the fair forehead of an innocent love,
And sets a blister° there — makes marriage vows
As false as dicers' oaths. Oh, such a deed   45
As from the body of contraction° plucks
The very soul, and sweet religion makes
A rhapsody of words.° Heaven's face doth glow,
Yea, this solidity and compound mass,°
With tristful visage, as against the doom,°   50
Is thought-sick at the act.
  QUEEN.   Aye me, what act
That roars so loud and thunders in the index?°
  HAML. Look here upon this picture,° and on this,
The counterfeit presentment° of two brothers.
See what a grace was seated on this brow —   55
Hyperion's curls, the front° of Jove himself,
An eye like Mars, to threaten and command,
A station° like the herald Mercury°
New-lighted° on a heaven-kissing hill,
A combination° and a form indeed   60
Where every god did seem to set his seal°
To give the world assurance of a man.
This was your husband. Look you now what fol-
    lows.
Here is your husband, like a mildewed ear,
Blasting his wholesome brother. Have you eyes? 65
Could you on this fair mountain leave to feed

37. **brassed:** made brazen; i.e., impenetrable.   44. **sets a blis-
ter:** brands as a harlot.   46. **contraction:** the marriage contract.
48. **rhapsody of words:** string of meaningless words.   49. **solid-
ity . . . mass:** i.e., solid earth.   50. **tristful . . . doom:** sorrowful
face, as in anticipation of Doomsday.   52. **in . . . index:** i.e., if
the beginning (*index*, i.e., table of contents) is so noisy, what
will follow?   53. **picture:** Modern producers usually interpret
the pictures as miniatures, Hamlet wearing one of his father,
Gertrude one of Claudius. In the eighteenth century, wall por-
traits were used.   54. **counterfeit presentment:** portrait.
56. **front:** forehead.   58. **station:** figure; lit., standing. **Mercury:**
messenger of the gods, and one of the most beautiful.   59. **New-
lighted:** newly alighted.   60. **combination:** i.e., of physical
qualities.   61. **set . . . seal:** guarantee as a perfect man.

Sc. iv: 1. lay . . . to: be strict with.   **2. broad:** unrestrained.
Polonius is thinking of the obvious insolence of the remarks about
second marriage in the play scene.   **4. sconce me:** hide myself.
11. idle: foolish.   **14. rood:** crucifix.   **19. glass:** looking-glass.

And batten° on this moor? Ha! Have you eyes?
You cannot call it love, for at your age
The heyday° in the blood is tame, it's humble,   69
And waits upon the judgment. And what judgment
Would step from this to this? Sense° sure you have,
Else could you not have motion.° But sure that sense
Is apoplexed;° for madness would not err,
Nor sense to ecstasy° was ne'er so thralled°
But it reserved some quantity of choice   75
To serve in such a difference.° What devil was 't
That thus hath cozened° you at hoodman-blind?°
Eyes without feeling, feeling without sight,
Ears without hands or eyes, smelling sans° all,
Or but a sickly part of one true sense   80
Could not so mope.°
Oh, shame! Where is thy blush? Rebellious° Hell,
If thou canst mutine° in a matron's bones,
To flaming youth let virtue be as wax
And melt in her own fire. Proclaim no shame   85
When the compulsive ardor° gives the charge,
Since frost itself as actively doth burn,
And reason panders° will.

QUEEN.   O Hamlet, speak no more.
Thou turn'st mine eyes into my very soul,
And there I see such black and grainèd° spots   90
As will not leave their tinct.°

HAML.   Nay, but to live
In the rank sweat of an enseamèd° bed,
Stewed in corruption, honeying and making love
Over the nasty sty——

QUEEN.   Oh, speak to me no more,
These words like daggers enter in my ears.   95
No more, sweet Hamlet!

HAML.   A murderer and a villain,
A slave that is not twentieth part the tithe°
Of your precedent° lord, a vice of kings,°
A cutpurse° of the empire and the rule,
That from a shelf the precious diadem stole   100
And put it in his pocket!

QUEEN.   No more!

HAML. A king of shreds and patches——
[Enter GHOST] Save me, and hover o'er me with
your wings,
You heavenly guards! What would your gracious
figure?

QUEEN. Alas, he's mad!   105
HAML. Do you not come your tardy son to chide
That, lapsed in time and passion, lets go by
The important acting of your dread command?°
Oh, say!

GHOST. Do not forget. This visitation   110
Is but to whet thy almost blunted purpose.
But look, amazement on thy mother sits.
Oh, step between her and her fighting soul.
Conceit° in weakest bodies strongest works.
Speak to her, Hamlet.

HAML.   How is it with you, lady? 115
QUEEN. Alas, how is 't with you
That you do bend your eye on vacancy°
And with the incorporal° air do hold discourse?
Forth at your eyes your spirits wildly peep,
And as the sleeping soldiers in the alarm,   120
Your bedded° hairs, like life in excrements,°
Start up and stand an° end. O gentle son,
Upon the heat and flame of thy distemper°
Sprinkle cool patience. Whereon do you look?

HAML. On him, on him! Look you how pale he
glares!   125
His form and cause conjoined,° preaching to stones,
Would make them capable.° Do not look upon
me,
Lest with this piteous action you convert
My stern effects.° Then what I have to do   129
Will want true color — tears perchance for blood.

QUEEN. To whom do you speak this?

HAML.   Do you see nothing there?
QUEEN. Nothing at all, yet all that is I see.
HAML. Nor did you nothing hear?
QUEEN.   No, nothing but ourselves.
HAML. Why, look you there! Look how it steals
away!
My father, in his habit as he lived!   135
Look where he goes, even now, out at the portal!
                                    [Exit GHOST.]

QUEEN. This is the very coinage of your brain.
This bodiless creation ecstasy°
Is very cunning in.

HAML.   Ecstasy!   139
My pulse, as yours, doth temperately keep time,
And makes as healthful music. It is not madness
That I have uttered. Bring me to the test
And I the matter will reword, which madness
Would gambol° from. Mother, for love of grace,

---

67. **batten:** glut yourself. 69. **heyday:** excitement. 71. **Sense:**
feeling. 72. **motion:** desire. 73. **apoplexed:** paralyzed. 74. **ec-
stasy:** excitement, passion. See II.i.102. **thralled:** enslaved.
76. **serve . . . difference:** to enable you to see the difference be-
tween your former and your present husband. 77. **cozened:**
cheated. **hoodman-blind:** blind-man's-buff. 79. **sans:** without.
81. **mope:** be dull. 82–88. **Rebellious . . . will:** i.e., if the passion
(*Hell*) of a woman of your age is uncontrollable (*rebellious*), youth
can have no restraints; there is no shame in a young man's lust
when the elderly are just as eager and their reason (which should
control desire) encourages them. 83. **mutine:** mutiny. 86. **com-
pulsive ardor:** compelling lust. 88. **panders:** acts as go-between.
90. **grained:** dyed in the grain. 91. **tinct:** color. 92. **enseamed:**
greasy. 97. **tithe:** tenth part. 98. **precedent:** former. **vice of
kings:** caricature of a king. 99. **cutpurse:** thief.

107–08. **That . . . command:** who has allowed time to pass and
passion to cool, and neglects the urgent duty of obeying your
dread command. 114. **Conceit:** imagination. 117. **vacancy:**
empty space. 118. **incorporal:** bodiless. 121. **bedded:** evenly
laid. **excrements:** anything that grows out of the body, such as
hair or fingernails; here hair. 122. **an:** on. 123. **distemper:**
mental disturbance. 126. **form . . . conjoined:** his appearance
and the reason for his appearance joined. 127. **capable:** i.e., of
feeling. 128–29. **convert . . . effects:** change the stern action
which should follow. 138. **ecstasy:** madness. 144. **gambol:**
start away.

Lay not that flattering unction° to your soul,   145
That not your trespass but my madness speaks.
It will but skin and film the ulcerous place,
Whiles rank corruption, mining° all within,
Infects unseen. Confess yourself to Heaven,
Repent what's past, avoid what is to come,   150
And do not spread the compost° on the weeds
To make them ranker. Forgive me this my virtue,
For in the fatness° of these pursy° times
Virtue itself of vice must pardon beg —
Yea, curb° and woo for leave to do him good.   155
  QUEEN. O Hamlet, thou hast cleft my heart in
    twain.
  HAML. Oh, throw away the worser part of it,
And live the purer with the other half.
Good night. But go not to my uncle's bed.
Assume a virtue if you have it not.   160
That° monster, custom, who all sense doth eat,
Of habits devil,° is angel yet in this,
That to the use° of actions fair and good
He likewise gives a frock or livery
That aptly° is put on. Refrain tonight,   165
And that shall lend a kind of easiness
To the next abstinence, the next more easy.
For use almost can change the stamp° of nature,
And either the Devil,° or throw him out   169
With wondrous potency. Once more, good night.
And when you are desirous to be blest,
I'll blessing beg of you. For this same lord,
              [Pointing to POLONIUS]
I do repent; but Heaven hath pleased it so,
To punish me with this, and this with me,
That I must be their scourge and minister.   175
I will bestow° him, and will answer well
The death I gave him. So again good night.
I must be cruel only to be kind.
Thus bad begins, and worse remains behind.
One word more, good lady.
  QUEEN.   What shall I do?   180
  HAML. Not this, by no means, that I bid you do.
Let the bloat° king tempt you again to bed,
Pinch wanton° on your cheek, call you his mouse,
And let him, for a pair of reechy° kisses   184
Or paddling in your neck with his damned fingers,
Make you to ravel° all this matter out,
That I essentially am not in madness,

But mad in craft. 'Twere good you let him know.
For who that's but a Queen, fair, sober, wise,
Would from a paddock,° from a bat, a gib,°   190
Such dear concernings° hide? Who would do so?
No, in despite° of sense and secrecy,
Unpeg the basket on the house's top,
Let the birds fly, and like the famous ape,°
To try conclusions,° in the basket creep   195
And break your own neck down.
  QUEEN. Be thou assured if words be made of
    breath
And breath of life, I have no life to breathe
What thou hast said to me.
  HAML. I must to England. You know that?
  QUEEN.   Alack,   200
I had forgot. 'Tis so concluded on.
  HAML. There's letters sealed, and my two school-
    fellows,
Whom I will trust as I will adders fanged,
They bear the mandate.° They must sweep my way,
And marshal me to knavery. Let it work,   205
For 'tis the sport to have the enginer°
Hoist with his own petar.° And 't shall go hard
But I will delve one yard below their mines
And blow them at the moon: Oh, 'tis most sweet
When in one line two crafts° directly meet.   210
This man shall set me packing.
I'll lug the guts into the neighbor room.
Mother, good night. Indeed this counselor
Is now most still, most secret, and most grave
Who was in life a foolish prating knave.   215
Come, sir, to draw toward an end with you.
Good night, Mother.   [Exeunt severally,°
           HAMLET dragging in POLONIUS.]

Act IV

SCENE I. *A room in the castle.*

[*Enter* KING, QUEEN, ROSENCRANTZ, *and*
    GUILDENSTERN.]

  KING. There's matter° in these sighs, these pro-
    found heaves,
You must translate. 'Tis fit we understand them.
Where is your son?

---

145. unction: healing ointment.   **148. mining:** undermining.
151. compost: manure.   **153. fatness:** grossness. **pursy:** bloated.
155. curb: bow low.   **161–65. That . . . on:** i.e., custom (bad
habits) like an evil monster destroys all sense of good and evil, but
yet can become an angel (good habits) when it makes us perform
good actions as mechanically as we put on our clothes. **162. devil:**
This is the Q2 reading; the passage is omitted in F1. Probably the
word should be "evil." **163. use:** practice. **165. aptly:** readily.
168. stamp: impression. **169. either the Devil:** some verb such
as "shame" or "curb" has been omitted. **176. bestow:** get rid of.
182. bloat: bloated. **183. wanton:** lewdly. **184. reechy:** foul.
186. ravel: unravel, reveal.

190. paddock: toad. **gib:** tomcat. **191. dear concernings:**
important matters. **192. despite:** spite. **194. famous ape:**
The story is not known, but evidently told of an ape that
let the birds out of their cage and, seeing them fly, crept
into the cage himself and jumped out, breaking his own neck.
195. try conclusions: repeat the experiment. **204. mandate:**
command. **206. enginer:** engineer. **207. petar:** petard, land
mine. **210. crafts:** devices. **217 s.d., Exeunt severally:** i.e.,
by separate exits. In F1 there is no break here. The King en-
ters as soon as Hamlet has dragged the body away. Q2 marks the
break. The act division was first inserted in a quarto of 1676.
  Act IV. Sc. i: 1. matter: something serious.

QUEEN. Bestow this place° on us a little while.

[*Exeunt* ROSENCRANTZ *and* GUILDENSTERN.]

Ah, mine own lord, what have I seen tonight!   5

KING. What, Gertrude? How does Hamlet?

QUEEN. Mad as the sea and wind when both con-
tend
Which is the mightier. In his lawless fit,
Behind the arras hearing something stir,
Whips out his rapier, cries " A rat, a rat! "   10
And in this brainish apprehension° kills
The unseen good old man.

KING.   Oh, heavy deed!
It had been so with us had we been there.
His liberty is full of threats to all,
To you yourself, to us, to everyone.   15
Alas, how shall this bloody deed be answered?
It will be laid to us, whose providence°
Should have kept short,° restrained and out of
haunt,°
This mad young man. But so much was our love
We would not understand what was most fit,   20
But, like the owner of a foul disease,
To keep it from divulging° let it feed
Even on the pith° of life. Where is he gone?

QUEEN. To draw apart the body he hath killed,
O'er whom his very madness, like some ore   25
Among a mineral of metals base,
Shows itself pure. He weeps for what is done.

KING. O Gertrude, come away!
The sun no sooner shall the mountains touch
But we will ship him hence. And this vile deed   30
We must, with all our majesty and skill,
Both countenance° and excuse. Ho, Guildenstern!

[*Re-enter* ROSENCRANTZ *and* GUILDENSTERN.]

Friends both, go join you with some further aid.
Hamlet in madness hath Polonius slain,   34
And from his mother's closet hath he dragged him.
Go seek him out, speak fair, and bring the body
Into the chapel. I pray you, haste in this.

[*Exeunt* ROSENCRANTZ *and* GUILDENSTERN.]

Come, Gertrude, we'll call up our wisest friends,
And let them know both what we mean to do
And what's untimely done,°   40
Whose whisper o'er the world's diameter
As level as the cannon to his blank°
Transports his poisoned shot, may miss our name
And hit the woundless air. Oh, come away!
My soul is full of discord and dismay.   [*Exeunt.*]

---

4. Bestow . . . place: give place, leave us. 11. brainish ap-
prehension: mad imagination. 17. providence: foresight.
18. short: confined. out of haunt: away from others. 22. di-
vulging: becoming known. 23. pith: marrow. 32. counte-
nance: take responsibility for. 40. done: A half-line has been
omitted. Some editors fill the gap with "So, haply slander."
42. blank: target.

SCENE II. *Another room in the castle.*

[*Enter* HAMLET.]

HAML. Safely stowed.

ROS. & GUIL. [*Within*] Hamlet! Lord Hamlet!

HAML. But soft, what noise? Who calls on Ham-
let?
Oh, here they come.

[*Enter* ROSENCRANTZ *and* GUILDENSTERN.]

ROS. What have you done, my lord, with the dead
body?   5

HAML. Compounded it with dust, whereto 'tis kin.

ROS. Tell us where 'tis, that we may take it thence
And bear it to the chapel.

HAML. Do not believe it.

ROS. Believe what?   10

HAML. That I can keep your counsel and not mine
own. Besides, to be demanded of a sponge! What
replication° should be made by the son of a king?

ROS. Take you me for a sponge, my lord?   15

HAML. Aye, sir, that soaks up the King's counte-
nance,° his rewards, his authorities. But such officers
do the King best service in the end. He keeps them,
like an ape, in the corner of his jaw, first mouthed,
to be last swallowed. When he needs what you have
gleaned, it is but squeezing you and, sponge, you
shall be dry again.   23

ROS. I understand you not, my lord.

HAML. I am glad of it. A knavish speech sleeps in
a foolish ear.°

ROS. My lord, you must tell us where the body is,
and go with us to the King.   28

HAML. The body is with the King, but the King
is not with the body.° The King is a thing ——

GUIL. A thing, my lord?

HAML. Of nothing. Bring me to him. Hide   32
fox, and all after.°   [*Exeunt.*]

SCENE III. *Another room in the castle.*

[*Enter* KING, *attended.*]

KING. I have sent to seek him, and to find the
body.
How dangerous is it that this man goes loose!
Yet must not we put the strong law on him.
He's loved of the distracted° multitude,
Who like not in their judgment but their eyes;°   5
And where 'tis so, the offender's scourge° is
weighed,

Sc. ii: 14. replication: answer. 17. countenance: favor.
25-26. A . . . ear: a fool never understands the point of a sinister
speech. 29-30. The . . . body: Hamlet deliberately bewilders
his companions. 32-33. Hide . . . after: a form of the game of
hide-and-seek. With these words Hamlet runs away from them.

Sc. iii: 4. distracted: bewildered. 5. like . . . eyes: whose
likings are swayed not by judgment but by looks. 6. scourge:
punishment.

But never the offense. To bear° all smooth and
    even,
This sudden sending him away must seem
Deliberate pause.° Diseases desperate grown
By desperate appliance are relieved,   10
Or not at all.
[*Enter* ROSENCRANTZ.] How now! What hath be-
    fall'n?
ROS. Where the dead body is bestowed, my lord,
We cannot get from him.
    KING.   But where is he?
    ROS. Without, my lord, guarded, to know your
    pleasure.
    KING. Bring him before us.   15
    ROS. Ho, Guildenstern! Bring in my lord.
        [*Enter* HAMLET *and* GUILDENSTERN.]
    KING. Now, Hamlet, where's Polonius?
    HAML. At supper.
    KING. At supper! Where?   19
    HAML. Not where he eats, but where he is eaten.
A certain convocation of politic worms° are e'en at
him. Your worm is your only emperor for diet. We
fat all creatures else to fat us, and we fat ourselves
for maggots. Your fat king and your lean beggar is
but variable service,° two dishes, but to one table.
That's the end.   26
    KING. Alas, alas!
    HAML. A man may fish with the worm that hath
eat of a king, and eat of the fish that hath fed of that
worm.
    KING. What dost thou mean by this?
    HAML. Nothing but to show you how a king may
go a progress° through the guts of a beggar.
    KING. Where is Polonius?   34
    HAML. In Heaven — send thither to see. If your
messenger find him not there, seek him i' the other
place yourself. But indeed if you find him not with-
in this month, you shall nose him as you go up the
stairs into the lobby.   39
    KING. [*To some* ATTENDANTS] Go seek him there.
    HAML. He will stay till you come.
                 [*Exeunt* ATTENDANTS.]
    KING. Hamlet, this deed, for thine especial safety,
Which we do tender,° as we dearly grieve
For that which thou hast done, must send thee
    hence
With fiery quickness. Therefore prepare thyself.   45
The bark is ready and the wind at help,°
The associates tend,° and every thing is bent°
For England.
    HAML.   For England?
    KING.   Aye, Hamlet.

    HAML.   Good.
    KING. So is it if thou knew'st our purposes.
    HAML. I see a cherub that sees them. But, come,
for England! Farewell, dear Mother.   51
    KING. Thy loving father, Hamlet.
    HAML. My mother. Father and mother is man and
wife, man and wife is one flesh, and so, my mother.
Come, for England!   [*Exit.*]
    KING. Follow him at foot,° tempt° him with
    speed aboard.   56
Delay it not, I'll have him hence tonight.
Away! For everything is sealed and done
That else leans on the affair. Pray you make haste.
    [*Exeunt* ROSENCRANTZ *and* GUILDENSTERN.]
And, England, if my love thou hold'st at aught —
As my great power thereof may give thee sense,   61
Since yet thy cicatrice° looks raw and red
After the Danish sword, and thy free awe°
Pays homage to us — thou mayst not coldly set
Our sovereign process,° which imports at full,   65
By letters congruing° to that effect,
The present° death of Hamlet. Do it, England,
For like the hectic° in my blood he rages,
And thou must cure me. Till I know 'tis done,
Howe'er my haps,° my joys were ne'er begun.   70
                       [*Exit.*]

SCENE IV. *A plain in Denmark.*

[*Enter* FORTINBRAS, *a* CAPTAIN *and* SOLDIERS,
    marching.]
    FOR. Go, Captain, from me greet the Danish
    King.
Tell him that by his license Fortinbras
Craves the conveyance of a promised march°
Over his kingdom. You know the rendezvous.
If that His Majesty would aught with us,   5
We shall express our duty in his eye,°
And let him know so.
    CAP.   I will do 't, my lord.
    FOR. Go softly on.
              [*Exeunt* FORTINBRAS *and* SOLDIERS.]
[*Enter* HAMLET, ROSENCRANTZ, GUILDENSTERN, *and*
    others.]
    HAML. Good sir, whose powers° are these?
    CAP. They are of Norway, sir.   10
    HAML. How purposed, sir, I pray you?
    CAP. Against some part of Poland.

---

7. bear: make. 9. Deliberate pause: the result of careful
planning. 21. convocation . . . worms: an assembly of political-
minded worms. 25. variable service: choice of alternatives.
33. go a progress: make a state journey. 43. tender: regard
highly. 46. at help: favorable. 47. associates tend: your
companions are waiting. bent: ready.

56. at foot: at his heels. tempt: entice. 62. cicatrice: scar.
There is nothing in the play to explain this incident. 63. free
awe: voluntary submission. 64–65. coldly . . . process: hesi-
tate to carry out our royal command. 66. congruing: agreeing.
67. present: immediate. 68. hectic: fever. 70. Howe'er my
haps: whatever may happen to me.
Sc. iv: 3. Craves . . . march: asks for permission to transport
his army, as had already been promised. See II.ii.76–82. 6. in
. . . eye: before his eyes; i.e., in person. 9. powers: forces.

HAML. Who commands them, sir?

CAP. The nephew to old Norway, Fortinbras.   14

HAML. Goes it against the main° of Poland, sir,
Or for some frontier?

CAP. Truly to speak, and with no addition,°
We go to gain a little patch of ground
That hath in it no profit but the name.
To pay five ducats, five, I would not farm it,   20
Nor will it yield to Norway or the Pole
A ranker° rate should it be sold in fee.°

HAML. Why, then the Polack never will defend it.

CAP. Yes, it is already garrisoned.

HAML. Two thousand souls and twenty thousand
     ducats   25
Will not debate the question of this straw.
This is the imposthume of° much wealth and peace,
That inward breaks, and shows no cause without
Why the man dies. I humbly thank you, sir.

CAP. God be wi' you, sir.   [*Exit.*]

ROS.   Will 't please you go, my lord?   30

HAML. I'll be with you straight. Go a little before.
                [*Exeunt all but* HAMLET.]

How° all occasions do inform against° me
And spur my dull revenge! What is a man
If his chief good and market° of his time
Be but to sleep and feed? A beast, no more.   35
Sure, He that made us with such large discourse,
Looking before and after,° gave us not
That capability and godlike reason
To fust° in us unused. Now whether it be
Bestial oblivion, or some craven scruple   40
Of thinking too precisely on the event —
A thought which, quartered, hath but one part wis-
     dom
And ever three parts coward — I do not know
Why yet I live to say " This thing's to do,"   44
Sith I have cause, and will, and strength, and means
To do 't. Examples gross° as earth exhort me.
Witness this army, of such mass and charge,°
Led by a delicate and tender Prince
Whose spirit with divine ambition puffed
Makes mouths at the invisible event,°   50
Exposing what is mortal and unsure
To all that fortune, death, and danger dare,
Even for an eggshell.° Rightly to be great
Is not to stir without great argument,
But greatly to find quarrel in a straw   55
When honor's at the stake.° How stand I then,

That have a father killed, a mother stained,
Excitements of my reason and my blood,
And let all sleep while to my shame I see
The imminent death of twenty thousand men   60
That for a fantasy and trick° of fame
Go to their graves like beds, fight for a plot
Whereon the numbers cannot try the cause,°
Which is not tomb enough and continent°
To hide the slain? Oh, from this time forth,   65
My thoughts be bloody or be nothing worth!
                               [*Exit.*]

SCENE V. *Elsinore. A room in the castle.*

[*Enter* QUEEN, HORATIO, *and a* GENTLEMAN.]

QUEEN. I will not speak with her.

GEN. She is importunate, indeed distract.°
Her mood will needs be pitied.

QUEEN   What would she have?

GEN. She speaks much of her father, says she hears
There's tricks° i' the world, and hems° and beats
     her heart,   5
Spurns enviously° at straws, speaks things in doubt
That carry but half-sense. Her speech is nothing,
Yet the unshaped use° of it doth move
The hearers to collection.° They aim° at it,   9
And botch° the words up fit to their own thoughts,
Which, as her winks and nods and gestures yield
     them,
Indeed would make one think there might be
     thought,
Though nothing sure, yet much unhappily.

HOR. 'Twere good she were spoken with, for she
     may strew
Dangerous conjectures in ill-breeding minds.   15

QUEEN. Let her come in.   [*Exit* GENTLEMAN.]

[*Aside*] To my sick soul, as sin's true nature is,
Each toy° seems prologue to some great amiss.°
So full of artless jealousy° is guilt,
It spills itself in fearing to be spilt.°   20

[*Re-enter* GENTLEMAN, *with* OPHELIA.°]

OPH. Where is the beauteous Majesty of Den-
     mark?

QUEEN. How now, Ophelia!

OPH. [*Sings.*]
     " How should I your truelove know
           From another one?

---

15. main: mainland.   17. addition: exaggeration.   22. ranker:
richer. in fee: with possession as freehold.   27. imposthume
of: inward swelling caused by.   32–66. How . . . worth: The
soliloquy and all the dialogue after the exit of Fortinbras
are omitted in F1.   32. inform against: accuse.   34. market:
profit. 36–37. such . . . after: intelligence that enables us to con-
sider the future and the past.   39. fust: grow musty.   46. gross:
large.   47. charge: expense.   50. Makes . . . event: mocks at the
unseen risk.   53. eggshell: i.e., worthless trifle.   53–56. Rightly
. . . stake: true greatness is a matter of fighting not for a mighty
cause but for the merest trifle when honor is concerned.

61. fantasy . . . trick: illusion and whim.   63. Whereon . . .
cause: a piece of ground so small that it would not hold the
combatants.   64. continent: large enough to contain.

Sc. v: 2. distract: out of her mind.   5. tricks: trickery. hems:
makes significant noises.   6. Spurns enviously: kicks spitefully.
8. unshaped use: disorder.   9. collection: i.e., attempts to
find a sinister meaning. aim: guess.   10. botch: patch.   18. toy:
trifle. amiss: calamity.   19. artless jealousy: clumsy suspicion.
20. It . . . spilt: guilt reveals itself by its efforts at concealment.
20 s.d., Re-enter . . . Ophelia: Q1 notes "Enter Ophelia play-
ing on a lute, and her hair down, singing."

By his cockle hat° and staff   25
    And his sandal shoon."°
QUEEN. Alas, sweet lady, what imports this song?
OPH. Say you? nay, pray you, mark. [*Sings.*]
"He is dead and gone, lady,
    He is dead and gone,   30
At his head a grass-green turf,
    At his heels a stone."
Oh, oh!
QUEEN. Nay, but, Ophelia ——
OPH.   Pray you, mark. [*Sings.*]
"White his shroud as the mountain snow ——" 35
            [*Enter* KING.]
QUEEN. Alas, look here, my lord.
OPH. [*Sings.*]
        "Larded° with sweet flowers,
    Which bewept to the grave did go
        With truelove showers."°
KING. How do you, pretty lady?   40
OPH. Well, God 'ild° you! They say the owl was
a baker's daughter.° Lord, we know what we are
but know not what we may be. God be at your table!
KING. Conceit upon her father.   45
OPH. Pray you let's have no words of this, but
when they ask you what it means, say you this
[*Sings*]:
    "Tomorrow is Saint Valentine's day,°
        All in the morning betime,
    And I a maid at your window,   50
        To be your Valentine.

    "Then up he rose, and donned his clothes,
        And dupped° the chamber door,
    Let in the maid, that out a maid
        Never departed more."   55
KING. Pretty Ophelia!
OPH. Indeed, la, without an oath, I'll make an end
on 't. [*Sings.*]
    "By Gis° and by Saint Charity,
        Alack, and fie for shame!   60
    Young men will do 't, if they come to 't,
        By cock, they are to blame.
    Quoth she, before you tumbled me,
        You promised me to wed."
He answers:

"So would I ha' done, by yonder sun,   65
    An thou hadst not come to my bed."
KING. How long hath she been thus?
OPH. I hope all will be well. We must be patient.
But I cannot choose but weep to think they should
lay him i' the cold ground. My brother shall   70
know of it. And so I thank you for your good coun-
sel. Come, my coach! Good night, ladies, good night,
sweet ladies, good night, good night.   [*Exit.*]
KING. Follow her close,° give her good watch, I
pray you.   [*Exit* HORATIO.]
Oh, this is the poison of deep grief. It springs   76
All from her father's death. O Gertrude, Gertrude,
When sorrows come, they come not single spies,°
But in battalions! First, her father slain,
Next, your son gone, and he most violent author°
Of his own just remove. The people muddied,   81
Thick and unwholesome in their thoughts and
    whispers,
For good Polonius' death. And we have done but
    greenly°
In huggermugger° to inter him. Poor Ophelia
Divided from herself and her fair judgment,°   85
Without the which we are pictures,° or mere beasts.
Last, and as much containing as all these,
Her brother is in secret come from France,
Feeds on his wonder, keeps himself in clouds,
And wants not buzzers° to infect his ear   90
With pestilent speeches of his father's death,
Wherein necessity, of matter beggared,
Will nothing stick our person to arraign°
In ear and ear. O my dear Gertrude, this,
Like to a murdering piece,° in many places   95
Gives me superfluous death.   [*A noise within*]
    QUEEN.   Alack, what noise is this?
KING. Where are my Switzers?° Let them guard
    the door.
[*Enter another* GENTLEMAN.] What is the matter?
    GEN.   Save yourself, my lord.
The ocean, overpeering of his list,°
Eats not the flats° with more impetuous haste   100
Than young Laertes, in a riotous head,°
O'erbears your officers. The rabble call him lord,
And as the world were now but to begin,
Antiquity forgot, custom not known,
The ratifiers and props of every word,°   105

25. cockle hat: a hat adorned with a cockleshell worn by pil-
grims.   **26. sandal shoon:** sandals, the proper footwear of pil-
grims.   **37. Larded:** garnished.   **39. truelove showers:** the tears
of his faithful love.   **41. 'ild** (yield): reward.   **41–42. owl . . .
daughter:** An allusion to a legend that Christ once went into a
baker's shop and asked for bread. The baker's wife gave him a
piece but was rebuked by her daughter for giving him too much.
Thereupon the daughter was turned into an owl.   **48. Saint . . .
day:** February 14, the day when birds are supposed to mate.
According to the old belief the first single man then seen by a
maid is destined to be her husband.   **53. dupped:** opened.
59–62. Gis . . . cock: for "Jesus" and "God," both words being
used instead of the sacred names, like the modern "Jeez" and
"Ger."

74. close: closely.   **78. spies:** scouts.   **80. author:** cause.
83. done . . . greenly: shown immature judgment.   **84. hugger-
mugger:** secret haste, "any which way."   **85. Divided . . . judg-
ment:** no longer able to use her judgment.   **86. pictures:** lifeless
imitations.   **90. buzzers:** scandalmongers.   **92–93. Wherein . . .
arraign:** in which, knowing nothing of the true facts, he must
necessarily accuse us.   **95. murdering piece:** cannon loaded with
grapeshot.   **97. Switzers:** Swiss bodyguard.   **99. overpeering
. . . list:** looking over its boundary; i.e., flooding the mainland.
100. Eats . . . flats: floods not the flat country.   **101. in . . .
head:** with a force of rioters.   **104–05. Antiquity . . . word:** for-
getting ancient rule and ignoring old custom, by which all prom-
ises must be maintained.

They cry "Choose we — Laertes shall be King!"
Caps, hands, and tongues applaud it to the clouds —
"Laertes shall be King, Laertes King!"
QUEEN. How cheerfully on the false trail they cry!
Oh, this is counter,° you false Danish dogs!   110

[*Noise within*]

KING. The doors are broke.

[*Enter* LAERTES, *armed,* DANES *following.*]

LAER. Where is this King? Sirs, stand you all
without.
DANES. No, let's come in.
LAER.   I pray you, give me leave.
DANES. We will, we will.

[*They retire without the door.*]

LAER. I thank you. Keep the door. O thou vile
King,   115
Give me my father!
QUEEN.   Calmly, good Laertes.
LAER. That drop of blood that's calm proclaims
me bastard,
Cries cuckold° to my father, brands the harlot°
Even here, between the chaste unsmirchèd brows
Of my true mother.
KING.   What is the cause, Laertes,   120
That thy rebellion looks so giantlike?
Let him go, Gertrude. Do not fear° our person.
There's such divinity doth hedge a king°
That treason can but peep° to what it would,
Acts little of his will. Tell me, Laertes,   125
Why thou art thus incensed. Let him go, Gertrude.
Speak, man.
LAER. Where is my father?
KING.   Dead.
QUEEN.   But not by him.
KING. Let him demand his fill.
LAER. How came he dead? I'll not be juggled
with.   130
To Hell, allegiance! Vows, to the blackest devil!
Conscience and grace, to the profoundest pit!
I dare damnation. To this point I stand,
That both the worlds I give to negligence.°
Let come what comes, only I'll be revenged   135
Most throughly° for my father.
KING.   Who shall stay you?
LAER. My will, not all the world.
And for my means, I'll husband°·them so well
They shall go far with little.
KING.   Good Laertes,
If you desire to know the certainty   140
Of your dear father's death, is 't writ in your revenge

That, swoopstake,° you will draw both friend and
foe,
Winner and loser?
LAER. None but his enemies.
KING.   Will you know them, then?
LAER. To his good friends thus wide I'll ope my
arms,   145
And like the kind life-rendering pelican,°
Repast° them with my blood.
KING.   Why, now you speak
Like a good child and a true gentleman.
That I am guiltless of your father's death,
And am most sensibly° in grief for it,   150
It shall as level° to your judgment pierce
As day does to your eye.
DANES.   [*Within*] Let her come in.
LAER. How now! What noise is that?

[*Re-enter* OPHELIA.] O heat, dry up my brains! Tears
seven times salt
Burn out the sense and virtue of mine eye!   155
By Heaven, thy madness shall be paid with weight
Till our scale turn the beam.° O rose of May!°
Dear maid, kind sister, sweet Ophelia!
Oh heavens! Is 't possible a young maid's wits
Should be as mortal as an old man's life?   160
Nature is fine in love, and where 'tis fine
It sends some precious instance of itself
After the thing it loves.°
OPH. [*Sings.*]
    "They bore him barefaced on the bier,
        Hey non nonny, nonny, hey nonny,   165
        And in his grave rained many a tear ——"
Fare you well, my dove!
LAER. Hadst thou thy wits and didst persuade re
venge,
It could not move thus.
OPH. [*Sings.*]
    "You must sing down a-down   170
        An you call him a-down-a."
Oh, how the wheel° becomes it! It is the false stew-
ard, that stole his master's daughter.
LAER. This nothing's more than matter.°   174
OPH. There's° rosemary, that's for remembrance

---

110. **counter:** in the wrong direction of the scent. 118. **cuck-old:** a husband deceived by his wife. **brands . . . harlot:** Con-victed harlots were branded with a hot iron. Cf. III.iv.44. 122. **fear:** fear for. 123. **divinity . . . king:** divine protection surrounds a king as with a hedge. 124. **peep:** look over, not break through. 134. **That . . . negligence:** I do not care what happens to me in this world or the next. 136. **throughly:** thor-oughly. 138. **husband:** use economically.

142. **swoopstake:** "sweeping the board." 146. **life-rendering pelican:** The mother pelican was supposed to feed her young with blood from her own breast. 147. **Repast:** feed. 150. **sensi-bly:** feelingly. 151. **level:** clearly. 157. **turn . . . beam:** weigh down the beam of the scale. **rose of May:** perfection of young beauty. See III.i.160. 161–63. **Nature . . . loves:** i.e., her love for her father was so exquisite that she has sent her sanity after him. Laertes, especially in moments of emotion, is prone to use highly exaggerated speech. 172. **wheel:** explained variously as the spinning wheel, Fortune's wheel, or the refrain. The likeliest explanation is that she breaks into a little dance at the words "You must sing," and that the *wheel* is the turn as she circles round. 174. **This . . . matter:** this nonsense means more than sense. 175–85. **There's . . . died:** In the language of flowers, each has its peculiar meaning, and Ophelia distributes them appropriately: for her brother rosemary (remembrance) and pansies (thoughts); for the King fennel (flattery) and columbine

—pray you, love, remember. And there is pansies, that's for thoughts.

LAER. A document° in madness, thoughts and re-
membrance fitted. 179

OPH. There's fennel for you, and columbines. There's rue for you, and here's some for me — we may call it herb of grace o' Sundays. Oh, you must wear your rue with a difference. There's a daisy. I would give you some violets, but they withered all when my father died. They say a' made a good end. [*Sings.*] 186

"For bonny sweet Robin is all my joy."

LAER. Thought and affliction, passion, Hell itself, She turns to favor° and to prettiness.

OPH. [*Sings.*]

"And will a' not come again? 190
And will a' not come again?
No, no, he is dead,
Go to thy deathbed,
He never will come again.

"His beard was as white as snow, 195
All flaxen was his poll.°
He is gone, he is gone,
And we cast away moan.
God ha' mercy on his soul!"

And of all Christian souls, I pray God. God be wi'
you. [*Exit.*]

LAER. Do you see this, O God? 201

KING. Laertes, I must commune with your grief,
Or you deny me right. Go but apart,
Make choice of whom your wisest friends you will,
And they shall hear and judge 'twixt you and me.
If by direct or by collateral° hand 206
They find us touched,° we will our kingdom give,
Our crown, our life, and all that we call ours,
To you in satisfaction. But if not,
Be you content to lend your patience to us 210
And we shall jointly labor with your soul
To give it due content.

LAER. Let this be so.
His means of death, his obscure funeral,°
No trophy, sword, nor hatchment° o'er his bones,
No noble rite nor formal ostentation,° 215
Cry to be heard, as 'twere from Heaven to earth,
That I must call 't in question.

KING. So you shall,
And where the offense is let the great ax fall.
I pray you, go with me. [*Exeunt.*]

(thanklessness); for the Queen rue, called also herb o' grace (sorrow), and daisy (light of love). Neither is worthy of violets (faithfulness). **178. document:** instruction. **189. favor:** charm. **196. flaxen . . . poll:** white as flax was his head. **206. collateral:** i.e., as an accessory. **207. touched:** implicated. **213. obscure funeral:** Men of rank were buried with much ostentation. To bury Polonius "huggermugger" was thus an insult to his memory and to his family. See App. 9. **214. hatchment:** device of the coat of arms carried in a funeral and hung up over the tomb. **215. formal ostentation:** ceremony properly ordered.

SCENE VI. *Another room in the castle.*

[*Enter* HORATIO *and a* SERVANT.]

HOR. What are they that would speak with me?

SER. Seafaring men, sir. They say they have letters for you.

HOR. Let them come in. [*Exit* SERVANT.]
I do not know from what part of the world
I should be greeted, if not from Lord Hamlet. 5

[*Enter* SAILORS.]

1. SAIL. God bless you, sir.

HOR. Let Him bless thee too.

1. SAIL. He shall, sir, an 't please Him. There's a letter for you, sir. It comes from the ambassador that was bound for England — if your name be Horatio, as I am let to know it is. 11

HOR. [*Reads.*] "Horatio, when thou shalt have overlooked° this, give these fellows some means° to the King. They have letters for him. Ere we were two days old at sea, a pirate of very warlike ap- 15 pointment° gave us chase. Finding ourselves too slow of sail, we put on a compelled valor, and in the grapple I boarded them. On the instant they got clear of our ship, so I alone became their prisoner. They have dealt with me like thieves of mercy; 20 but they knew what they did — I am to do a good turn for them. Let the King have the letters I have sent, and repair thou to me with as much speed as thou wouldest fly death. I have words to speak in thine ear will make thee dumb, yet are they 25 much too light for the bore of the matter.° These good fellows will bring thee where I am. Rosen-crantz and Guildenstern hold their course for Eng-land. Of them I have much to tell thee. Farewell. 30

"He that thou knowest thine,
"HAMLET"

Come, I will make you way for these your letters,
And do 't the speedier that you may direct me
To him from whom you brought them. [*Exeunt.*]

SCENE VII. *Another room in the castle.*

[*Enter* KING *and* LAERTES.]

KING. Now must your conscience my acquittance
seal,°
And you must put me in your heart for friend,
Sith you have heard, and with a knowing ear,
That he which hath your noble father slain
Pursued my life.

LAER. It well appears. But tell me 5
Why you proceeded not against these feats,°
So crimeful and so capital° in nature,

Sc. vi: **13. overlooked:** read. **means:** access. **16. appoint-ment:** equipment. **26. too . . . matter:** i.e., words fall short, like a small shot fired from a cannon with too wide a bore.

Sc. vii: **1. my . . . seal:** acquit me. **6. feats:** acts. **7. capi-tal:** deserving death.

As by your safety, wisdom, all things else,
You mainly were stirred up.
  KING.   Oh, for two special reasons,
Which may to you perhaps seem much unsinewed,°
But yet to me they're strong. The Queen his mother
Lives almost by his looks, and for myself — 12
My virtue or my plague, be it either which —
She's so conjunctive° to my life and soul
That as the star moves not but° in his sphere, 15
I could not but by her. The other motive
Why to a public count° I might not go
Is the great love the general gender° bear him,
Who, dipping all his faults in their affection,°
Would, like the spring that turneth wood to stone,°
Convert his gyves to graces.° So that my arrows, 21
Too slightly timbered° for so loud a wind,
Would have reverted to my bow again
And not where I had aimed them.
  LAER. And so have I a noble father lost, 25
A sister driven into desperate terms,°
Whose worth, if praises may go back again,°
Stood challenger on mount of all the age
For her perfections.° But my revenge will come.
  KING. Break not your sleeps for that. You must
   not think
That we are made of stuff so flat and dull 31
That we can let our beard be shook with danger
And think it pastime. You shortly shall hear more.°
I loved your father, and we love ourself,
And that, I hope, will teach you to imagine —— 35
[Enter a MESSENGER, with letters.] How now! What
  news?
  MESS. Letters, my lord, from Hamlet.
This to your Majesty, this to the Queen.
  KING. From Hamlet! Who brought them?
  MESS. Sailors, my lord, they say — I saw them
  not.
They were given me by Claudio, he received them
Of him that brought them.   41
  KING. Laertes, you shall hear them.
Leave us.   [Exit MESSENGER.]
[Reads] "High and Mighty, you shall know I am
set naked° on your kingdom. Tomorrow shall I beg
leave to see your kingly eyes, when I shall, first ask-
ing your pardon thereunto, recount the occasion of
my sudden and more strange return.
               " HAMLET "
What should this mean? Are all the rest come
  back?
Or is it some abuse,° and no such thing? 50
  LAER. Know you the hand?
  KING. 'Tis Hamlet's character.° "Naked!"
And in a postscript here, he says "alone."
Can you advise me?
  LAER. I'm lost in it, my lord. But let him come.
It warms the very sickness in my heart 56
That I shall live and tell him to his teeth
"Thus didest thou."
  KING.   If it be so, Laertes —
As how should it be so, how otherwise? —
Will you be ruled by me?
  LAER.   Aye, my lord, 60
So you will not o'errule° me to a peace.
  KING. To thine own peace. If he be now returned,
As checking at° his voyage, and that he means
No more to undertake it, I will work him
To an exploit now ripe in my device, 65
Under the which he shall not choose but fall.
And for his death no wind of blame shall breathe,
But even his mother shall uncharge the practice°
And call it accident.
  LAER.   My lord, I will be ruled,
The rather if you could devise it so 70
That I might be the organ.°
  KING.   It falls right.
You have been talked of since your travel much,
And that in Hamlet's hearing, for a quality
Wherein they say you shine. Your sum of parts°
Did not together pluck such envy from him 75
As did that one, and that in my regard
Of the unworthiest siege.°
  LAER.   What part is that, my lord?
  KING. A very ribbon in the cap of youth,
Yet needful too; for youth no less becomes
The light and careless livery that it wears 80
Than settled age his sables and his weeds,°
Importing health and graveness. Two months since,
Here was a gentleman of Normandy.
I've seen myself, and served against, the French,
And they can well° on horseback; but this gallant
Had witchcraft in 't, he grew unto his seat, 86
And to such wondrous doing brought his horse
As had he been incorpsed and deminatured°
With the brave beast. So far he topped my thought°

---

10. unsinewed: weak, flabby. 14. conjunctive: joined insep-
arably. 15. moves . . . but: moves only in. See App. 1.
17. count: trial. 18. general gender: common people. 19. dip-
ping . . . affection: gilding his faults with their love. 20. like . . .
stone: In several places in England there are springs of water
so strongly impregnated with lime that they will quickly
cover with stone anything placed under them. 21. Convert
. . . graces: regard his fetters as honorable ornaments. 22. tim-
bered: shafted. A light arrow is caught by the wind and
blown back. 26. terms: condition. 27. if . . . again: if one may
praise her for what she used to be. 28–29. Stood . . . perfections:
i.e., her worth challenged the whole world to find one as perfect.
33. hear more: i.e., when news comes from England that Hamlet
is dead. 45. naked: destitute.

50. abuse: attempt to deceive. 52. character: handwriting.
61. o'errule: command. 63. checking at: swerving aside from,
like a hawk that leaves the pursuit of his prey. 68. uncharge
. . . practice: not suspect that his death was the result of the
plot. 71. organ: instrument. 74. sum of parts: accomplish-
ments as a whole. 77. siege: seat, place. 81. sables . . .
weeds: dignified robes. See III.ii.138. 85. can well: can do
well. 88. incorpsed . . . deminatured: of one body. 89. topped
my thought: surpassed what I could imagine.

That I, in forgery of shapes and tricks,°   90
Come short of what he did.
    LAER.   A Norman was 't?
    KING. A Norman.
    LAER. Upon my life, Lamond.
    KING.   The very same.
    LAER. I know him well. He is the brooch° indeed
And gem of all the nation.   95
    KING. He made confession° of you,
And gave you such a masterly report
For art and exercise in your defense,
And for your rapier most especial,
That he cried out 'twould be a sight indeed   100
If one could match you. The scrimers° of their na-
    tion,
He swore, had neither motion, guard, nor eye
If you opposed them. Sir, this report of his
Did Hamlet so envenom° with his envy
That he could nothing do but wish and beg   105
Your sudden coming o'er, to play with him.
Now, out of this ——
    LAER.   What out of this, my lord?
    KING. Laertes, was your father dear to you?
Or are you like the painting° of a sorrow,
A face without a heart?
    LAER.   Why ask you this?   110
    KING. Not that I think you did not love your
    father,
But that I know love is begun by time,
And that I see, in passages of proof,°
Time qualifies° the spark and fire of it.
There lives within the very flame of love   115
A kind of wick or snuff° that will abate it.
And nothing is at a like goodness still,°
For goodness, growing to a pleurisy,°
Dies in his own too much. That we would do
We should do when we would; for this "would"
    changes   120
And hath abatements and delays as many
As there are tongues, are hands, are accidents,
And then this "should" is like a spendthrift° sigh
That hurts by easing. But to the quick o' the ulcer.°
Hamlet comes back. What would you undertake
To show yourself your father's son in deed   126
More than in words?
    LAER.   To cut his throat i' the church.°

    KING. No place indeed should murder sanctuar-
    ize,°
Revenge should have no bounds. But, good Laertes,
Will you do this, keep close within your chamber.
Hamlet returned shall know you are come home.
We'll put on those° shall praise your excellence   132
And set a double varnish on the fame
The Frenchman gave you, bring you in fine° to-
    gether
And wager on your heads. He, being remiss,°   135
Most generous° and free from all contriving,°
Will not peruse the foils, so that with ease,
Or with a little shuffling, you may choose
A sword unbated,° and in a pass of practice°
Requite him for your father.
    LAER.   I will do 't,   140
And for that purpose I'll anoint my sword.
I bought an unction° of a mountebank°
So mortal that but dip a knife in it,
Where it draws blood no cataplasm° so rare,
Collected from all simples° that have virtue   145
Under the moon,° can save the thing from death
That is but scratched withal. I'll touch my point
With this contagion, that if I gall° him slightly,
It may be death.
    KING.   Let's further think of this,
Weigh what convenience both of time and means
May fit us to our shape.° If this should fail,   151
And that our drift look through our bad perform-
    ance,°
'Twere better not assayed. Therefore this project
Should have a back or second, that might hold
If this did blast in proof.° Soft! Let me see —   155
We'll make a solemn wager on your cunnings.
I ha 't.
When in your motion you are hot and dry —
As make your bouts° more violent to that end —
And that he calls for drink, I'll have prepared him
A chalice° for the nonce,° whereon but sipping,
If he by chance escape your venomed stuck,°   162
Our purpose may hold there. But stay, what noise?
[*Enter* QUEEN.] How now, sweet Queen!
    QUEEN. One woe doth tread upon another's heel,
So fast they follow. Your sister's drowned, Laertes.
    LAER. Drowned! Oh, where?   166

---

90. forgery . . . tricks: imagination of all kinds of fancy tricks.
shapes: fancies.   94. brooch: ornament.   96. confession:
report.   101. scrimers: fencers.   104. envenom: poison.
109. painting: i.e., imitation.   113. passages of proof: ex-
periences which prove.   114. qualifies: diminishes.   116. snuff:
Before the invention of self-consuming wicks for candles, the
wick smoldered and formed a ball of soot which dimmed the
light and gave out a foul smoke.   117. still: always.
118. pleurisy: fullness.   123. spendthrift: wasteful, because
sighing was supposed to be bad for the blood.   124. quick
. . . ulcer: i.e., to come to the real issue. quick: flesh, sensitive
part.   127. cut . . . church: i.e., to commit murder in a holy
place, which would bring Laertes in danger of everlasting damna-
tion; no crime could be worse.

128. sanctuarize: give sanctuary to.   132. put . . . those: set
on some.   134. fine: short.   135. remiss: careless.   136. gen-
erous: noble. contriving: plotting.   139. unbated: not blunt-
ed, with a sharp point. pass of practice: treacherous thrust.
142. unction: poison. mountebank: quack doctor.   144. cata-
plasm: poultice.   145. simples: herbs.   146. Under . . .
moon: herbs collected by moonlight were regarded as partic-
ularly potent.   148. gall: break the skin.   150–51. Weigh . . .
shape: consider the best time and method of carrying out our
plan.   152. drift . . . performance: intention be revealed through
bungling.   155. blast in proof: break in trial, like a cannon which
bursts when being tested.   159. bouts: attacks, in the fencing
match.   161. chalice: cup. nonce: occasion.   162. stuck:
thrust.

QUEEN. There is a willow grows aslant a brook
That shows his hoar° leaves in the glassy stream.
There with fantastic garlands did she come
Of crowflowers, nettles, daisies, and long purples
That liberal° shepherds give a grosser name,   171
But our cold maids do dead-men's-fingers call them.
There on the pendent° boughs her coronet weeds°
Clambering to hang, an envious sliver° broke,
When down her weedy trophies and herself   175
Fell in the weeping brook. Her clothes spread wide,
And mermaidlike awhile they bore her up—
Which time she chanted snatches of old tunes,
As one incapable° of her own distress,
Or like a creature native and indued°   180
Unto that element. But long it could not be
Till that her garments, heavy with their drink,
Pulled the poor wretch from her melodious lay°
To muddy death.
LAER.   Alas, then, she is drowned!
QUEEN. Drowned, drowned.   185
LAER. Too much of water hast thou, poor Ophelia,
And therefore I forbid my tears. But yet
It is our trick°— Nature her custom holds,
Let shame say what it will. When these° are gone,
The woman will be out.° Adieu, my lord.   190
I have a speech of fire that fain° would blaze
But that this folly douts° it.   [Exit.]
KING.   Let's follow, Gertrude.
How much I had to do to calm his rage!
Now fear I this will give it start again,
Therefore let's follow.   [Exeunt.]

Act V

SCENE I. *A churchyard.*

[*Enter two* CLOWNS,° *with spades, etc.*]
1. CLO. Is she to be buried in Christian burial°
that willfully seeks her own salvation?

---

168. hoar: gray. The underside of the leaves of the willow
are silver-gray.   171. liberal: coarse-mouthed.   173. pendent:
hanging over the water. coronet weeds: wild flowers woven
into a crown.   174. envious sliver: malicious branch.
179. incapable: not realizing.   180. indued: endowed; i.e.,
a creature whose natural home is the water (*element*).
183. lay: song.   187–88. But . . . trick: it is our habit; i.e., to
break into tears at great sorrow.   189. these: i.e., my tears.
190. woman . . . out: I shall be a man again.   191. fain:
willingly.   192. douts: puts out.
Act V, Sc. i: s.d., Clowns: countrymen. See Gen. Intro. p.
60a.   1. Christian burial: Suicides were not allowed burial in
consecrated ground, but were buried at crossroads. The grave-
diggers and the priest are professionally scandalized that Ophelia
should be allowed Christian burial solely because she is a
lady of the Court.

2. CLO. I tell thee she is, and therefore make her
grave straight.° The crowner° hath sat on her, and
finds it Christian burial.   5
1. CLO. How can that be, unless she drowned her-
self in her own defense?
2. CLO. Why, 'tis found so.
1. CLO. It must be "se offendendo,"° it cannot be
else. For here lies the point. If I drown myself   10
wittingly,° it argues an act, and an act hath three
branches — it is to act, to do, and to perform. Argal,°
she drowned herself wittingly.
2. CLO. Nay, but hear you, goodman delver.°   15
1. CLO. Give me leave. Here lies the water, good.
Here stands the man, good. If the man go to this
water and drown himself, it is will he, nill he° he
goes, mark you that; but if the water come to him
and drown him, he drowns not himself. Argal, he
that is not guilty of his own death shortens not his
own life.   22
2. CLO. But is this law?
1. CLO. Aye, marry, is 't, crowner's quest° law.
2. CLO. Will you ha' the truth on 't? If this had
not been a gentlewoman, she should have been
buried out o' Christian burial.   28
1. CLO. Why, there thou say'st. And the more pity
that great folks should have countenance° in this
world to drown or hang themselves more than their
even° Christian. Come, my spade. There is no an-
cient gentlemen but gardeners, ditchers, and   34
gravemakers. They hold up° Adam's profession.
2. CLO. Was he a gentleman?
1. CLO. A' was the first that ever bore arms.°
2. CLO. Why, he had none.   39
1. CLO. What, art a heathen? How dost thou un-
derstand the Scripture? The Scripture says Adam
digged. Could he dig without arms? I'll put another
question to thee. If thou answerest me not to the
purpose, confess thyself ——
2. CLO. Go to.   45
1. CLO. What is he that builds stronger than either
the mason, the shipwright, or the carpenter?
2. CLO. The gallows-maker, for that frame outlives
a thousand tenants.   50
1. CLO. I like thy wit well, in good faith. The gal-
lows does well, but how does it well? It does well to
those that do ill. Now thou dost ill to say the gallows
is built stronger than the church; argal, the gallows
may do well to thee. To 't again, come.   56
2. CLO. Who builds stronger than a mason, a ship-
wright, or a carpenter?

---

4. straight: straightway. crowner: coroner. See *T. Night*,
I.v.142n.   9. se offendendo: for *defendendo*, in self-defense.
11. wittingly: with full knowledge.   12. Argal: for the Latin
ergo, therefore.   15. delver: digger.   18. will he, nill he:
willy-nilly, whether he wishes or not.   24. quest: inquest.
30. countenance: favor.   33. even: fellow.   35. hold up: sup-
port.   38. bore arms: had a coat of arms — the outward sign of a
gentleman. See App. 9.

1. CLO. Aye, tell me that, and unyoke.°

2. CLO. Marry, now I can tell.   60

1. CLO. To 't.

2. CLO. Mass,° I cannot tell.

[*Enter* HAMLET *and* HORATIO, *afar off.*]

1. CLO. Cudgel thy brains no more about it, for your dull ass will not mend his pace with beating, and when you are asked this question next, say " A gravemaker." The houses that he makes last till Doomsday. Go, get thee to Yaughan,° fetch me   67 a stoup° of liquor.   [*Exit* SECOND CLOWN.]

[FIRST CLOWN *digs, and sings.*]

" In youth,° when I did love, did love,
    Methought it was very sweet,
To contract; oh, the time, for-a my behoove,°   71
    Oh, methought, there-a was nothing-a meet."

HAML. Has this fellow no feeling of his business, that he sings at grave-making?

HOR. Custom hath made it in him a property of easiness.°

HAML. 'Tis e'en so. The hand of little employment hath the daintier sense.°   78

1. CLO. [*Sings.*] " But age, with his stealing steps,
    Hath clawed me in his clutch,
And hath shipped me intil the land°
    As if I had never been such."   82

[*Throws up a skull.*]

HAML. That skull had a tongue in it, and could sing once. How the knave jowls° it to the ground, as if it were Cain's jawbone, that did the first murder! It might be the pate of a politician which this ass now o'erreaches°—one that would circumvent° God, might it not?

HOR. It might, my lord.   89

HAML. Or of a courtier, which could say " Good morrow, sweet lord! How dost thou, good lord? " This might be my lord Such-a-one that praised my lord Such-a-one's horse when he meant to beg it, might it not?

HOR. Aye, my lord.   95

HAML. Why, e'en so. And now my Lady Worm's chapless,° and knocked about the mazzard° with a sexton's spade. Here's fine revolution, an we had the trick to see 't. Did these bones cost no more the breeding but to play at loggats° with 'em? Mine ache to think on 't.   101

1. CLO. [*Sings.*] " A pickax and a spade, a spade,
    For and a shrouding sheet—
Oh, a pit of clay for to be made
    For such a guest is meet."   105

[*Throws up another skull.*]

HAML. There's another. Why may not that be the skull of a lawyer?° Where be his quiddities now, his quillets, his cases, his tenures, and his tricks? Why does he suffer this rude knave now to knock him about the sconce° with a dirty shovel, and will   110 not tell him of his action of battery? Hum! This fellow might be in 's time a great buyer of land, with his statutes, his recognizances, his fines, his double vouchers, his recoveries. Is this the fine° of his fines and the recovery of his recoveries, to have his   115 fine pate full of fine dirt? Will his vouchers vouch him no more of his purchases, and double ones too, than the length and breadth of a pair of indentures? The very conveyances of his lands will hardly lie in this box,° and must the inheritor himself have no more, ha?   121

HOR. Not a jot more, my lord.

HAML. Is not parchment made of sheepskins?

HOR. Aye, my lord, and of calfskins too.

HAML. They are sheep and calves which seek out assurance in that. I will speak to this fellow. Whose grave's this, sirrah?

1. CLO. Mine, sir. [*Sings.*]

" Oh, a pit of clay for to be made
    For such a guest is meet."   129

HAML. I think it be thine indeed, for thou liest in 't.

1. CLO. You lie out on 't, sir, and therefore 'tis not yours. For my part, I do not lie in 't, and yet it is mine.   135

HAML. Thou dost lie in 't, to be in 't and say it is thine. 'Tis for the dead, not for the quick, therefore thou liest.

1. CLO. 'Tis a quick lie, sir, 'twill away again, from me to you.   140

HAML. What man dost thou dig it for?

1. CLO. For no man, sir.

HAML. What woman, then?

1. CLO. For none, neither.

HAML. Who is to be buried in 't?   145

1. CLO. One that was a woman, sir, but, rest her soul, she's dead.

HAML. How absolute° the knave is! We must speak by the card,° or equivocation° will undo us.

---

59. **unyoke:** finish the job, unyoking the plow oxen being the end of the day's work.   62. **Mass:** by the mass. 67. **Yaughan:** apparently an innkeeper near the Globe Theatre. 68. **stoup:** large pot. See Pl. 20e.   69–105. **In youth . . . meet:** The song which the gravedigger sings without much care for accuracy or sense was first printed in *Tottel's Miscellany,* 1558. 71. **behoove:** benefit.   75–76. **property of easiness:** careless habit.   77–78. **hand . . . sense:** those who have little to do are the most sensitive.   81. **shipped . . . land:** shoved me into the ground.   84. **jowls:** dashes.   87. **o'erreaches:** gets the better of. **circumvent:** get around.   97. **chapless:** without jaws. **mazzard:** head, a slang word; lit., drinking-bowl.   100. **loggats:** a game in which billets of wood or bones were stuck in the ground and knocked over by throwing at them.

107–18. **lawyer . . . indentures:** Hamlet strings out a number of the legal phrases loved by lawyers: *quiddities:* subtle arguments; *quillets:* quibbles; *tenures:* titles to property; *tricks:* knavery; *statutes:* bonds; *recognizances:* obligations; *fines:* conveyances; *vouchers:* guarantors; *recoveries:* transfers; *indentures:* agreements. See App. 6 and Pl. 11a. 110. **sconce:** head; lit., blockhouse.   114. **fine:** ending. 120. **box:** coffin.   148. **absolute:** exact.   149. **by . . . card:** exactly. The card is the mariner's compass. **equivocation:** speak-

By the Lord, Horatio, this three years I have taken
note of it — the age is grown so picked° that the toe
of the peasant comes so near the heel of the courtier,
he galls his kibe.° How long hast thou been a grave-
maker?   154

1. CLO. Of all the days i' the year, I came to 't that
day that our last King Hamlet o'ercame Fortinbras.

HAML. How long is that since?

1. CLO. Cannot you tell that? Every fool can tell
that. It was that very day that young Hamlet was
born, he that is mad, and sent into England.   164

HAML. Aye, marry, why was he sent into England?

1. CLO. Why, because a' was mad. A' shall recover
his wits there, or, if a' do not, 'tis no great matter
there.

HAML. Why?

1. CLO. 'Twill not be seen in him there — there
the men are as mad as he.   170

HAML. How came he mad?

1. CLO. Very strangely, they say.

HAML. How " strangely "?

1. CLO. Faith, e'en with losing his wits.

HAML. Upon what ground?

1. CLO. Why, here in Denmark. I have been sexton
here, man and boy, thirty years.°

HAML. How long will a man lie i' the earth ere he
rot?   179

1. CLO. I' faith, if a' be not rotten before a' die —
as we have many pocky° corses nowadays that will
scarce hold the laying in — a' will last you some eight
year or nine year. A tanner will last you nine year.

HAML. Why he more than another?   185

1. CLO. Why, sir, his hide is so tanned with his
trade that a' will keep out water a great while, and
your water is a sore decayer of your whoreson° dead
body. Here's a skull now. This skull has lain in the
earth three and twenty years.   191

HAML. Whose was it?

1. CLO. A whoreson mad fellow's it was. Whose
do you think it was?

HAML. Nay, I know not.   195

1. CLO. A pestilence on him for a mad rogue! A'
poured a flagon of Rhenish on my head once. This
same skull, sir, was Yorick's skull, the King's jester.

HAML. This?

1. CLO. E'en that.

HAML. Let me see. [Takes the skull.] Alas, poor
Yorick! I knew him, Horatio — a fellow of infinite
jest, of most excellent fancy. He hath borne me on
his back a thousand times, and now how ab-   205
horred in my imagination it is! My gorge rises° at
it. Here hung those lips that I have kissed I know
not how oft. Where be your gibes now? Your gam-
bols? Your songs? Your flashes of merriment that
were wont to set the table on a roar? Not one 210
now, to mock your own grinning? Quite chop-
fallen?° Now get you to my lady's chamber and tell
her, let her paint an inch thick, to this favor° she
must come — make her laugh at that. Prithee, Hora-
tio, tell me one thing.

HOR. What's that, my lord?   217

HAML. Dost thou think Alexander looked o' this
fashion i' the earth?

HOR. E'en so.

HAML. And smelt so? Pah!

[Puts down the skull.]

HOR. E'en so, my lord.

HAML. To what base uses we may return, Horatio!
Why may not imagination trace the noble dust of
Alexander till he find it stopping a bunghole?°

HOR. 'Twere to consider too curiously° to consider
so.   228

HAML. No, faith, not a jot, but to follow him
thither with modesty° enough and likelihood to lead
it. As thus: Alexander died, Alexander was buried,
Alexander returneth into dust; the dust is earth; of
earth we make loam;° and why of that loam,
whereto he was converted, might they not stop a
beer barrel?   235

" Imperious Caesar, dead and turned to clay,
    Might stop a hole to keep the wind away.
  Oh, that that earth which kept the world in awe
    Should patch a wall to expel the winter's flaw!"°

But soft! But soft! Aside — here comes the King.

[Enter PRIESTS,° etc., in procession; the corpse of
    Ophelia, LAERTES and MOURNERS following;
        KING, QUEEN, their trains, etc.]

The Queen, the courtiers — who is this they follow?
And with such maimèd° rites? This doth betoken°
The corse they follow did with desperate hand   243
Fordo° its own life. 'Twas of some estate.°

206. My . . . rises: I feel sick. gorge: throat.   212. chop-
fallen: downcast, with a pun on "chapless," (see l. 97).
213. favor: appearance, especially in the face.   226. bunghole:
the hole in a beer barrel.   227. curiously: precisely.   230. with
modesty: without exaggeration.   233. loam: mixture of clay
and sand, used in plastering walls.   239. flaw: blast.   240. s.d.,
Enter Priests. The stage directions in early texts are less elaborate.
Q2 notes, curtly, Enter K.Q. Laertes and the corse. F1 has Enter
King, Queen, Laertes, and a coffin, with Lords attendant. Q1
prints Enter King and Queen, Laertes and other lords, with a
Priest after the coffin. This probably was how the scene was
originally staged. The modern directions ignore the whole signif-
icance of the "maimed rites" — Ophelia's funeral is insult-
ingly simple.   242. maimed: curtailed. betoken: indicate.
244. Fordo: destroy. estate: high rank.

ing with a double sense. The word was much discussed when
Hamlet was written. See App. 20.   151. picked: refined.
151–53. toe . . . kibe: i.e., the peasant follows the courtier so
closely that he rubs the courtier's heel into a blister. From
about 1598 onward, writers, especially dramatists, often sati-
rized the practice of yeoman farmers grown rich from war profits
in sending their awkward sons to London to learn gentlemanly
manners. Ben Jonson portrays two specimens in Stephen in
Every Man in His Humour and Sogliardo in Every Man out of
His Humour.   177. thirty years: The Clown's chronology has
puzzled critics, for the general impression is that Hamlet was
much younger.   181. pocky: suffering from the pox (venereal
disease).   189. whoreson: bastard, "son of a bitch."

Couch° we awhile, and mark.

                        [Retiring with HORATIO.]

LAER. What ceremony else?

HAML. That is Laertes, a very noble youth. Mark.

LAER. What ceremony else?   248

1. PRIEST. Her obsequies have been as far enlarged
As we have warranty.° Her death was doubtful,
And but that great command o'ersways the order,°
She should in ground unsanctified have lodged
Till the last trumpet; for° charitable prayers,
Shards,° flints, and pebbles should be thrown on her.
Yet here she is allowed her virgin crants,°   255
Her maiden strewments° and the bringing home
Of bell and burial.

LAER. Must there no more be done?

1. PRIEST.   No more be done.
We should profane the service of the dead
To sing a requiem and such rest to her   260
As to peace-parted souls.°

LAER.   Lay her i' the earth.
And from her fair and unpolluted flesh
May violets spring! I tell thee, churlish priest,
A ministering angel shall my sister be
When thou liest howling.

HAML.   What, the fair Ophelia! 265

QUEEN. *[Scattering flowers]* Sweets to the sweet.
Farewell!
I hoped thou shouldst have been my Hamlet's wife,
I thought thy bride bed to have decked, sweet maid,
And not have strewed thy grave.

LAER.   Oh, treble woe
Fall ten times treble on that cursèd head   270
Whose wicked deed thy most ingenious sense°
Deprived thee of! Hold off the earth a while
Till I have caught her once more in mine arms.

                       [Leaps into the grave.]
Now pile your dust upon the quick° and dead
Till of this flat a mountain you have made   275
To o'ertop old Pelion° or the skyish° head
Of blue Olympus.

HAML. *[Advancing]* What is he whose grief
Bears such an emphasis? Whose phrase of sorrow
Conjures the wandering stars and makes them
    stand°
Like wonder-wounded hearers? This is I,   280
Hamlet the Dane.   *[Leaps into the grave.]*

LAER. The Devil take thy soul!

                     [Grappling with him]

HAML.   Thou pray'st not well.
I prithee, take thy fingers from my throat,
For though I am not splenitive° and rash,
Yet have I in me something dangerous,   285
Which let thy wisdom fear. Hold off thy hand.

KING. Pluck them asunder.

QUEEN.   Hamlet, Hamlet!

ALL.   Gentlemen ——

HOR. Good my lord, be quiet.

             [The ATTENDANTS *part them,*
           and they come out of the grave.]

HAML. Why, I will fight with him upon this
    theme
Until my eyelids will no longer wag.   290

QUEEN. O my son, what theme?

HAML. I loved Ophelia. Forty thousand brothers
Could not, with all their quantity of love,
Make up my sum. What wilt thou do for her?

KING. Oh, he is mad, Laertes.   295

QUEEN. For love of God, forbear him.°

HAML. 'Swounds,° show me what thou'lt do.
Woo 't weep? Woo 't fight? Woo 't fast? Woo 't tear
    thyself?
Woo 't drink up eisel?° Eat a crocodile?
I'll do 't. Dost thou come here to whine?   300
To outface° me with leaping in her grave?
Be buried quick with her, and so will I.
And if thou prate of mountains, let them throw
Millions of acres on us, till our ground,
Singeing his pate against the burning zone,   305
Make Ossa° like a wart! Nay, an thou 'lt mouth,
I'll rant as well as thou.

QUEEN.   This is mere madness.
And thus awhile the fit will work on him.
Anon, as patient as the female dove
When that her golden couplets° are disclosed,° 310
His silence will sit drooping.

HAML.   Hear you, sir.
What is the reason that you use me thus?
I loved you ever. But it is no matter,
Let Hercules himself do what he may,   314
The cat will mew and dog will have his day.° *[Exit.]*

KING. I pray thee, good Horatio, wait upon him.

                    [Exit HORATIO.]

[To LAERTES] Strengthen your patience in our last
    night's speech.
We'll put the matter to the present push.°

---

245. **Couch:** lie down.   **249–50. Her ... warranty:** the funeral rites have been as complete as may be allowed.   **251. but ... order:** if the King's command had not overruled the proper procedure.   **253. for:** instead of.   **254. Shards:** pieces of broken crockery.   **255. crants:** wreaths of flowers — a sign that she had died unwed.   **256. maiden strewments:** the flowers strewn on the corpse of a maiden.   **261. peace-parted souls:** souls which departed in peace, fortified with the rites of the Church.   **271. most ... sense:** lively intelligence.   **274. quick:** living.   **276. Pelion:** When the giants fought against the gods in order to reach Heaven, they tried to pile Mount Pelion and Mount Ossa on Mount Olympus, the highest mountain in Greece. **skyish:** reaching the sky.   **279. stand:** stand still.

284. splenitive: hot-tempered.   **296. forbear him:** leave him alone.   **297–307. 'Swounds ... thou:** Hamlet in his excitement cries out that if Laertes wishes to make extravagant boasts of what he will do to show his sorrow, he will be even more extravagant.   **299. eisel:** vinegar.   **301. outface:** browbeat.   **306. Ossa:** See l. 276, n.   **310. couplets:** eggs, of which the dove lays two only. **disclosed:** hatched.   **314–15. Let ... day:** i.e., let this ranting hero have his turn; mine will come sometime.   **318. push:** test; lit., thrust of a pike.

Good Gertrude, set some watch over your son.
This grave shall have a living monument.°   320
An hour of quiet shortly shall we see,
Till then, in patience our proceeding be.   [*Exeunt.*]

SCENE II. *A hall in the castle.*

[*Enter* HAMLET *and* HORATIO.]

HAML. So much for this, sir. Now shall you see
    the other.
You do remember all the circumstance?

HOR. Remember it, my lord!

HAML. Sir, in my heart there was a kind of fight-
    ing
That would not let me sleep. Methought I lay   5
Worse than the mutines in the bilboes.° Rashly,
And praised be rashness for it, let us know,
Our indiscretion sometime serves us well
When our deep plots do pall.° And that should
    learn° us
There's a divinity that shapes our ends,   10
Roughhew them how we will.°

HOR.   That is most certain.

HAML. Up from my cabin,
My sea gown° scarfed° about me, in the dark
Groped I to find out them,° had my desire,
Fingered their packet, and in fine withdrew   15
To mine own room again, making so bold,
My fears forgetting manners, to unseal
Their grand commission where I found, Horatio —
Oh royal knavery! — an exact command,
Larded° with many several sorts of reasons,   20
Importing Denmark's health and England's too,
With, ho! such bugs° and goblins in my life°
That, on the supervise,° no leisure bated,°
No, not to stay the grinding of the ax,
My head should be struck off.

HOR.   Is 't possible?   25

HAML. Here's the commission. Read it at more
    leisure
But wilt thou hear me how I did proceed?

HOR. I beseech you.

HAML. Being thus benetted round with vil-
    lainies —
Ere I could make a prologue to my brains,   30
They had begun the play — I sat me down,
Devised a new commission, wrote it fair.
I once did hold it, as our statists° do,

A baseness to write fair, and labored much
How to forget that learning, but, sir, now   35
It did me yeoman's service.° Wilt thou know
The effect of what I wrote?

HOR.   Aye, good my lord.

HAML. An earnest conjuration from the King,
As England was his faithful tributary,
As love between them like the palm might flourish,
As peace should still her wheaten garland wear   41
And stand a comma 'tween their amities,°
And many suchlike "Ases"° of great charge,°
That, on the view and knowing of these contents,
Without debatement° further, more or less,   45
He should the bearers put to sudden death,
Not shriving time allowed.°

HOR.   How was this sealed?

HAML. Why, even in that was Heaven ordinant.°
I had my father's signet in my purse,
Which was the model° of that Danish seal —   50
Folded the writ° up in the form of the other,
Subscribed° it, gave 't the impression,° placed it
    safely,
The changeling° never known. Now the next day
Was our sea fight, and what to this was sequent°
Thou know'st already.   55

HOR. So Guildenstern and Rosencrantz go to 't.

HAML. Why, man, they did make love to this em-
    ployment.
They are not near my conscience, their defeat°
Does by their own insinuation° grow.
'Tis dangerous when the baser nature comes   60
Between the pass and fell incensèd points
Of mighty opposites.°

HOR.   Why, what a King is this!

HAML. Does it not, think'st thee, stand me now
    upon —
He that hath killed my King and whored my
    mother,
Popped in between the election and my hopes,°   65

read Elizabethan documents know, the more exalted the writer,
the worse his handwriting. As a girl Queen Elizabeth wrote a
beautiful script; as Queen her letters are as illegible as any. All
but the most confidential documents were copied out in a fair
hand by a secretary.   **36. yeoman's service:** faithful service.
The most reliable English soldiers were yeomen — farmers
and their men.   **42. stand . . . amities:** be a connecting
link of their friendship.   **43. "Ases":** Official documents
were written in flowery language full of metaphorical clauses
beginning with "As." Hamlet puns on "asses."   **great charge:**
"great weight" and "heavy burden."   **45. debatement:**
argument.   **47. Not . . . allowed:** without giving them time
even to confess their sins.   **48. ordinant:** directing, in con-
trol.   **50. model:** copy.   **51. writ:** writing.   **52. Subscribed:**
signed.   **impression:** of the seal.   **53. changeling:** lit., an ugly
child exchanged by the fairies for a fair one.   **54. sequent:** fol-
lowing.   **58. defeat:** destruction.   **59. by . . . insinuation:** be-
cause they insinuated themselves into this business.   **60-62. 'Tis
. . . opposites:** it is dangerous for inferior men to interfere in
a duel between mighty enemies.   **pass:** thrust.   **fell:** fierce.
65. Popped . . . hopes: As is from time to time shown in the play,
the Danes chose their King by election.

320. living monument: with the double meaning of "lifelike
memorial" and "the death of Hamlet."

   Sc. ii: 6. mutines . . . bilboes: mutineers in the shackles used
on board ship.   **9. pall:** fail.   **learn:** teach.   **10-11. There's . . .
will:** though we may make the rough beginning, God finishes our
designs.   **13. sea gown:** a thick coat with a high collar worn by
seamen.   **scarfed:** wrapped.   **14. them:** i.e., Rosencrantz and
Guildenstern.   **20. Larded:** garnished.   **22. bugs:** bugbears.
in my life: so long as I was alive.   **23. supervise:** reading.   **bated:**
allowed.   **33. statists:** statesmen. As scholars who have had to

Thrown out his angle° for my proper° life,
And with such cozenage° — is 't not perfect con-
  science,
To quit° him with this arm? And is 't not to be
  damned,
To let this canker° of our nature come
In further evil?   70

HOR. It must be shortly known to him from Eng-
land
What is the issue of the business there.

HAML. It will be short. The interim° is mine,
And a man's life's no more than to say "One."
But I am very sorry, good Horatio,   75
That to Laertes I forgot myself,
For by the image of my cause I see
The portraiture of his. I'll court his favors.
But, sure, the bravery° of his grief did put me
Into a towering passion.

HOR.   Peace! Who comes here?   80

[*Enter* OSRIC.°]

OSR. Your lordship is right welcome back to Den-
mark.

HAML. I humbly thank you, sir. Dost know this
water fly?°

HOR. No, my good lord.   84

HAML. Thy state is the more gracious,° for 'tis a
vice to know him. He hath much land, and fertile.
Let a beast be lord of beasts and his crib shall stand
at the King's mess.° 'Tis a chough,° but, as I say,
spacious° in the possession of dirt.   90

OSR. Sweet lord, if your lordship were at lei-
sure, I should impart a thing to you from His Maj-
esty.

HAML. I will receive it, sir, with all diligence of
spirit. Put your bonnet to his right use,° 'tis for the
head.

OSR. I thank your lordship, it is very hot.   97

HAML. No, believe me, 'tis very cold. The wind is
northerly.

OSR. It is indifferent° cold, my lord, indeed.   100

HAML. But yet methinks it is very sultry and hot,
for my complexion ——

OSR. Exceedingly, my lord. It is very sultry, as
'twere — I cannot tell how. But, my lord, His Majes-

ty bade me signify to you that he has laid a great
wager on your head. Sir, this is the matter ——

HAML. I beseech you, remember ——   108

[HAMLET *moves him to put on his hat.*]

OSR. Nay, good my lord, for mine ease, in good
faith. Sir, here is newly come to Court Laertes — be-
lieve me, an absolute° gentleman, full of most excel-
lent differences,° of very soft society° and great
showing.° Indeed, to speak feelingly° of him, he is
the card or calendar of gentry,° for you shall find in
him the continent of what part a gentleman would
see.°   116

HAML. Sir,° his definement suffers no perdition in
you, though I know to divide him inventorially
would dizzy the arithmetic of memory, and yet but
yaw neither, in respect of his quick sail. But in   120
the verity of extolment, I take him to be a soul of
great article, and his infusion of such dearth and
rareness as, to make true diction of him, his sem-
blable is his mirror, and who else would trace him,
his umbrage — nothing more.   125

OSR. Your lordship speaks most infallibly of
him.

HAML. The concernancy,° sir? Why do we wrap
the gentleman in our more rawer breath?°

OSR. Sir?°   129

HOR. Is 't not possible to understand in another
tongue? You will do 't, sir, really.

HAML. What imports the nomination° of this
gentleman?

OSR. Of Laertes?   135

HOR. His purse is empty already, all's golden
words are spent.

HAML. Of him, sir.

OSR. I know you are not ignorant ——   139

HAML. I would you did, sir. Yet, in faith, if you
did, it would not much approve° me. Well, sir?

---

66. **angle:** fishing rod and line. **proper:** own. 67. **cozenage:** cheat-
ing. 68. **quit:** pay back. 69. **canker:** maggot. See I.iii.39. 73. **in-
terim:** interval; between now and the news from England.
79. **bravery:** excessive show. 80 s.d., **Osric:** Osric is a specimen
of the fashionable, effeminate courtier. He dresses prettily and
talks the jargon of his class, which at this time affected elaborate
and allusive metaphors and at all costs avoided saying plain things
plainly. 83. **water fly:** a useless little creature that flits about.
85. **Thy . . . gracious:** you are in the better state. 88–89. **Let . . .
mess:** i.e., any man, however low, who has wealth enough will
find a good place at Court. **crib:** manger. **mess:** table.
89. **chough:** jackdaw. 90. **spacious:** wealthy. 95. **Put . . .
use:** i.e., put your hat on your head. Osric is so nice-mannered
that he cannot bring himself to wear his hat in the presence of
the Prince. See App. 7. 100. **indifferent:** moderately.

111. **absolute:** perfect. 112. **differences:** qualities peculiar to him-
self. **soft society:** gentle breeding. 112–13. **great showing:** distin-
guished appearance. 113. **feelingly:** with proper appreciation.
114. **card . . . gentry:** the very fashion plate of what a gentleman
should be. 115–16. **continent . . . see:** all the parts that should be
in a perfect gentleman. 117–25. **Sir . . . more:** Hamlet retorts in
similar but even more extravagant language. This is too much for
Osric (and for most modern readers). Hamlet's words may be par-
aphrased: "Sir, the description of this perfect gentleman loses
nothing in your account of him; though I realize that if one
were to try to enumerate his excellences, it would exhaust our
arithmetic, and yet" — here he changes the image to one of sail-
ing — "we should still lag behind him as he outsails us. But in
the true vocabulary of praise, I take him to be a soul of the
greatest worth, and his perfume" — i.e., his personal essence —
"so scarce and rare that to speak truly of him, the only thing
like him is his own reflection in his mirror, and everyone else
who tries to follow him merely his shadow." **yaw:** fall off from
the course laid. **verity . . . extolment:** in true praise. **infusion:**
essence. **semblable:** resemblance. **trace:** follow. **umbrage:** shadow.
127. **concernancy:** i.e., what is all this talk about? 127–28. **Why
. . . breath:** why do we discuss the gentleman with our inade-
quate voices? 129. **Sir:** Osric is completely baffled. 133. **nomi-
nation:** naming. 141. **approve:** commend.

OSR. You are not ignorant of what excellence Laertes is ——   144

HAML. I dare not confess that, lest I should compare with him in excellence, but to know a man well were to know himself.

OSR. I mean, sir, for his weapon,° but in the imputation° laid on him by them, in his meed° he's unfellowed.°   150

HAML. What's his weapon?

OSR. Rapier and dagger.

HAML. That's two of his weapons, but, well.

OSR. The King, sir, hath wagered with him six Barbary horses, against the which he has imponed,° as I take it, six French rapiers and poniards, with their assigns,° as girdle, hanger,° and so — three of the carriages, in faith, are very dear to fancy,° very responsive to° the hilts, most delicate carriages, and of very liberal conceit.°   160

HAML. What call you the carriages?

HOR. I knew you must be edified by the margent° ere you had done.

OSR. The carriages, sir, are the hangers.   164

HAML. The phrase would be more germane° to the matter if we could carry a cannon by our sides. I would it might be hangers till then. But, on — six Barbary horses against six French swords, their assigns, and three liberal-conceited carriages. That's the French bet against the Danish. Why is this " imponed," as you call it?   171

OSR. The King, sir, hath laid, sir, that in a dozen passes between yourself and him, he shall not exceed you three hits. He hath laid on twelve for nine,° and it would come to immediate trial if your lordship would vouchsafe the answer.

HAML. How if I answer no?   177

OSR. I mean, my lord, the opposition of your person in trial.

HAML. Sir, I will walk here in the hall. If it please His Majesty, it is the breathing-time of day with me.° Let the foils be brought, the gentleman willing, and the King hold his purpose, I will win for him an I can. If not, I will gain nothing but my shame and the odd hits.   185

OSR. Shall I redeliver you e'en so?

HAML. To this effect, sir, after what flourish° your nature will.

OSR. I commend my duty to your lordship.   189

HAML. Yours, yours. [*Exit* OSRIC.] He does well to commend it himself, there are no tongues else for 's turn.

HOR. This lapwing° runs away with the shell on his head.

HAML. He did comply with his dug° before he sucked it. Thus has he — and many more of the same breed that I know the drossy° age dotes on — only got the tune of the time and outward habit of encounter,° a kind of yesty collection° which carries them through and through the most fond° and   200 winnowed° opinions — and do but blow them to their trial, the bubbles are out.°

[*Enter a* LORD.]

LORD. My lord, His Majesty commended him to you by young Osric, who brings back to him that you attend him in the hall. He sends to know if your pleasure hold to play with Laertes, or that you will take longer time.   207

HAML. I am constant to my purposes, they follow the King's pleasure. If his fitness speaks, mine is ready, now or whensoever, provided I be so able as now.   211

LORD. The King and Queen and all are coming down.

HAML. In happy time.°

LORD. The Queen desires you to use some gentle entertainment° to Laertes before you fall to play.

HAML. She well instructs me.   [*Exit* LORD.]

HOR. You will lose this wager, my lord.   219

HAML. I do not think so. Since he went into France I have been in continual practice, I shall win at the odds. But thou wouldst not think how ill all's here about my heart — but it is no matter.

HOR. Nay, good my lord ——   224

HAML. It is but foolery, but it is such a kind of gaingiving° as would perhaps trouble a woman.

HOR. If your mind dislike anything, obey it. I will forestall their repair hither and say you are not fit.

HAML. Not a whit, we defy augury.° There's   230 special providence in the fall of a sparrow.° If it be now, 'tis not to come; if it be not to come, it will be now; if it be not now, yet it will come. The read-

iness is all. Since no man has aught of what he leaves,
what is 't to leave betimes? Let be.   235
[*Enter* KING, QUEEN, LAERTES, *and* LORDS, OSRIC *and
other* ATTENDANTS *with foils; a table and flagons of
wine on it.*]
KING. Come, Hamlet, come, and take this hand
from me.
            [*The* KING *puts* LAERTES' *hand into* HAMLET'S.]
HAML. Give me your pardon, sir. I've done you
wrong,
But pardon 't, as you are a gentleman.
This presence° knows,
And you must needs have heard, how I am pun-
ished   240
With sore distraction. What I have done
That might your nature, honor, and exception°
Roughly awake, I here proclaim was madness.
Was 't Hamlet wronged Laertes? Never Hamlet.
If Hamlet from himself be ta'en away,°   245
And when he's not himself does wrong Laertes,
Then Hamlet does it not, Hamlet denies it.
Who does it, then? His madness. If 't be so,
Hamlet is of the faction that is wronged,
His madness is poor Hamlet's enemy.   250
Sir, in this audience
Let my disclaiming from a purposed evil°
Free me so far in your most generous thoughts
That I have shot mine arrow o'er the house,
And hurt my brother.
LAER.   I am satisfied in nature,   255
Whose motive, in this case, should stir me most
To my revenge. But in my terms of honor
I stand aloof, and will no reconcilement
Till by some elder masters of known honor
I have a voice and precedent of peace   260
To keep my name ungored.° But till that time
I do receive your offered love like love
And will not wrong it.
HAML.   I embrace it freely,
And will this brother's wager frankly play.
Give us the foils. Come on.
LAER.   Come, one for me.   265
HAML. I'll be your foil,° Laertes. In mine ignor-
ance
Your skill shall, like a star i' the darkest night,
Stick° fiery off indeed.
LAER.   You mock me, sir.
HAML. No, by this hand.

KING. Give them the foils, young Osric. Cousin
Hamlet,   270
You know the wager?
HAML.   Very well, my lord.
Your Grace has laid the odds o' the weaker side.
KING. I do not fear it, I have seen you both.
But since he is bettered,° we have therefore odds.
LAER. This is too heavy, let me see another.   275
HAML. This likes° me well. These foils have all a
length?°   [*They prepare to play.*]
OSR. Aye, my good lord.
KING. Set me the stoups° of wine upon that table.
If Hamlet give the first or second hit,
Or quit° in answer of the third exchange,   280
Let all the battlements their ordnance fire.
The King shall drink to Hamlet's better breath,
And in the cup a union° shall he throw
Richer than that which four successive kings   284
In Denmark's crown have worn. Give me the cups,
And let the kettle° to the trumpet speak,
The trumpet to the cannoneer without,
The cannon to the Heavens, the Heaven to earth,
"Now the King drinks to Hamlet." Come, begin,
And you, the judges, bear a wary eye.   290
HAML. Come on, sir.
LAER.   Come, my lord.   [*They play.*]
HAML.   One.
LAER.   No.
HAML.   Judgment.
OSR. A hit, a very palpable° hit.
LAER.   Well, again.
KING. Stay, give me drink. Hamlet, this pearl is
thine° —
Here's to thy health.
            [*Trumpets sound, and cannon shot off within.*]
                        Give him the cup.   294
HAML. I'll play this bout first. Set it by a while.
Come. [*They play.*] Another hit, what say you?
LAER. A touch, a touch, I do confess.
KING. Our son shall win.
QUEEN.   He's fat° and scant of breath.
Here, Hamlet, take my napkin, rub thy brows.
The Queen carouses to thy fortune, Hamlet.   300
HAML. Good madam!
KING.   Gertrude, do not drink.
QUEEN. I will, my lord, I pray you pardon me.
                                    [*She drinks.*]
KING. [*Aside*] It is the poisoned cup, it is too late.
HAML. I dare not drink yet, madam — by and by.
QUEEN. Come, let me wipe thy face.   305
LAER. My lord, I'll hit him now.

239. presence: the whole Court.   242. exception: resentment.
245. If . . . away: i.e., Hamlet mad is not Hamlet.   252. Let . . .
evil: let my declaration that I did not intend any harm.
255–61. I . . . ungored: I bear you no grudge so far as concerns
my personal feelings, which would most readily move me to ven-
geance; but as this matter touches my honor, I cannot accept
your apology until I have been assured by those expert in matters
of honor that I may so do without loss of reputation.   266. foil:
Hamlet puns on the other meaning of foil — tin foil set behind
a gem to give it luster.   268. Stick . . . off: Shine out.

274. bettered: considered your superior.   276. likes: pleases.
have . . . length: are all of equal length.   278. stoups: drinking-
vessels.   280. quit: strike back.   283. union: a large pearl.
286. kettle: kettledrum.   292. palpable: clear.   293. this . . .
thine: With these words the King drops the poisoned pearl
into the cup intended for Hamlet.   298. fat: out of condition.

KING. I do not think 't.

LAER. [Aside] And yet 'tis almost against my
conscience.

HAML. Come, for the third, Laertes. You but
dally.°
I pray you pass with your best violence,
I am afeard you make a wanton of me.° 310

LAER. Say you so? Come on. [They play.]

OSR. Nothing, neither way.

LAER. Have at you now!

[LAERTES wounds HAMLET; then, in scuffling, they
change rapiers,° and HAMLET wounds LAERTES.]

KING. Part them, they are incensed.

HAML. Nay, come, again. [The QUEEN falls.]

OSR. Look to the Queen there, ho!

HOR. They bleed on both sides. How is it, my
lord? 315

OSR. How is 't, Laertes?

LAER. Why, as a woodcock to mine own springe,°
Osric,
I am justly killed with mine own treachery.

HAML. How does the Queen?

KING. She swounds to see them bleed.

QUEEN. No, no, the drink, the drink! — O my dear
Hamlet — 320
The drink, the drink! I am poisoned. [Dies.]

HAML. Oh, villainy! Ho! Let the door be locked.
Treachery! Seek it out. [LAERTES falls.]

LAER. It is here, Hamlet. Hamlet, thou art slain.
No medicine in the world can do thee good, 325
In thee there is not half an hour of life.
The treacherous instrument is in thy hand,
Unbated and envenomed. The foul practice
Hath turned itself on me. Lo, here I lie
Never to rise again. Thy mother's poisoned. 330
I can no more. The King, the King's to blame.

HAML. The point envenomed too!
Then, venom, to thy work. [Stabs the KING.]

ALL. Treason! Treason! 334

KING. Oh, yet defend me, friends, I am but hurt.

HAML. Here, thou incestuous, murderous,
damnèd Dane,
Drink off this potion. Is thy union° here?
Follow my mother. [KING dies.]

LAER. He is justly served.
It is a poison tempered° by himself.
Exchange forgiveness with me, noble Hamlet. 340
Mine and my father's death come not upon thee,°
Nor thine on me! [Dies.]

HAML. Heaven make thee free of it!° I follow
thee.
I am dead, Horatio. Wretched Queen, adieu!

You that look pale and tremble at this chance, 345
That are but mutes or audience to this act,
Had I but time — as this fell° sergeant,° Death,
Is strict in his arrest — oh, I could tell you ——
But let it be. Horatio, I am dead,
Thou livest. Report me and my cause aright 350
To the unsatisfied.°

HOR. Never believe it.
I am more an antique Roman° than a Dane.
Here's yet some liquor left.

HAML. As thou 'rt a man,
Give me the cup. Let go — by Heaven, I'll have 't.
O good Horatio, what a wounded name, 355
Things standing thus unknown, shall live behind
me!
If thou didst ever hold me in thy heart,
Absent thee from felicity a while,
And in this harsh world draw thy breath in pain
To tell my story. [March afar off, and shot within]
What warlike noise is this? 360

OSR. Young Fortinbras, with conquest come from
Poland,
To the ambassadors of England gives
This warlike volley.

HAML. Oh, I die, Horatio,
The potent poison quite o'ercrows° my spirit.
I cannot live to hear the news from England, 365
But I do prophesy the election° lights
On Fortinbras. He has my dying voice.°
So tell him, with the occurrents, more and less,
Which have solicited.° The rest is silence. [Dies.]

HOR. Now cracks a noble heart. Good night,
sweet Prince, 370
And flights of angels sing thee to thy rest!
[March within.]
Why does the drum come hither?

[Enter FORTINBRAS, and the ENGLISH AMBASSADORS,
with drum, colors, and ATTENDANTS.]

FOR. Where is this sight?

HOR. What is it you would see?
If aught of woe or wonder, cease your search. 374

FOR. This quarry cries on havoc.° O proud Death,
What feast is toward° in thine eternal cell
That thou so many princes at a shot
So bloodily hast struck?

I. AMB. The sight is dismal,
And our affairs from England come too late. 379
The ears are senseless that should give us hearing,

308. dally: play. 310. make . . . me: treat me like a child by
letting me win. 313. s.d., they . . . rapiers: See App. 25 and
Pl. 22l. 317. springe: snare. 337. union: pearl, as in l. 283.
339. tempered: mixed. 341. come . . . thee: are not on your
head. 343. Heaven . . . it: God forgive you.

347. fell: dread. sergeant: the officer of the Court who made
arrests. 351. unsatisfied: who do not know the truth.
352. antique Roman: like Cato and Brutus, who killed themselves
rather than survive in a world which was unpleasing to them.
364. o'ercrows: overpowers. 366. election: as King of Den-
mark. See l. 65 above. 367. voice: support. 368-69. occur-
rents . . . solicited: events great and small which have caused
me to act. 375. quarry . . . havoc: heap of slain denotes a
pitiless slaughter. See Caesar, III.i.273. 376. toward: being
prepared.

To tell him his commandment is fulfilled,
That Rosencrantz and Guildenstern are dead.
Where should we have our thanks?

HOR.   Not from his mouth
Had it the ability of life to thank you.
He never gave commandment for their death.   385
But since, so jump° upon this bloody question,°
You from the Polack wars, and you from England,
Are here arrived, give order that these bodies
High on a stage be placèd to the view,
And let me speak to the yet unknowing world   390
How these things came about. So shall you hear
Of carnal, bloody, and unnatural acts,
Of accidental judgments, casual slaughters,
Of deaths put on by cunning and forced cause,
And, in this upshot, purposes mistook   395
Fall'n on the inventors' heads.° All this can I
Truly deliver.

FOR.   Let us haste to hear it,
And call the noblest to the audience.
For me, with sorrow I embrace my fortune.   399

I have some rights of memory° in this kingdom,
Which now to claim my vantage° doth invite me.

HOR.   Of that I shall have also cause to speak,
And from his mouth whose voice will draw on
      more.°
But let this same be presently performed,
Even while men's minds are wild, lest more mis-
      chance   405
On plots and errors happen.

FOR.   Let four captains
Bear Hamlet, like a soldier, to the stage.
For he was likely, had he been put on,°
To have proved most royally. And for his passage
The soldiers' music and the rites of war   410
Speak loudly for him.
Take up the bodies. Such a sight as this
Becomes the field, but here shows much amiss.
Go, bid the soldiers shoot.

[*A dead march. Exeunt, bearing off the bodies;
      after which a peal of ordnance is shot off.*]

386. jump: exactly. See I.i.65. question: matter. 392–96. carnal
... heads: These lines sum up the whole tragedy: Claudius'
adultery with Gertrude, his murder of his brother, the death
of Ophelia due to an accident, that of Polonius by casual
chance, Hamlet's device which caused the deaths of Rosencrantz
and Guildenstern, the plan which went awry and caused the
deaths of Claudius and Laertes.

400. rights of memory: rights which will be remembered; i.e.,
with the disappearance of all the family of the original
King Hamlet the situation reverts to what it was before the
death of Fortinbras' father. See I.i.80–95.   401. vantage:
i.e., my advantage, there being none to dispute my claim.
403. voice ... more: i.e., Hamlet's dying voice will strengthen
your claim.   408. had ... on: had he become King.

The Tragedy of
TROILUS AND CRESSIDA

Introduction

The earliest record of Shakespeare's *Troilus and Cressida* is an entry in the Stationers' Register dated February 7, 1603, when it was assigned to James Roberts the printer with the note: " Entred for his copie in full Court holden this day to print when he hath gotten sufficient aucthority for yt, The booke of Troilus and Cresseda as yt is acted by my Lord Chamberlens Men." No copy of an edition of 1603 is known, and it is probable that this was a blocking entry (see Gen. Intro. p. 66a) made by Roberts at the request of the players to prevent any other printer from publishing the play. Roberts had similarly entered *As You Like It, Much Ado about Nothing,* and *Henry V* in 1600. On January 28, 1609, Richard Bonian and Henry Walley entered " a booke called the history of Troylus and Cressida," and during the year issued a quarto edition with the title *The Historie of Troylus and Cresseida. As it was acted by the Kings Maiesties seruants at the Globe. Written by William Shakespeare*. This quarto was reissued during the year with a new title page: *The Famous Historie of Troylus and Cresseid. Excellently expressing the beginning of their loues, with the conceited wooing of Pandarus Prince of Licia. Written by William Shakespeare.* To this second issue was also added a remarkable Epistle to the Reader:

A NEVER WRITER TO AN EVER READER. NEWS.

Eternal reader, you have here a new play, never staled with the stage, never clapper-clawed with the palms of the vulgar, and yet passing full of the palm comical; for it is a birth of your brain, that never undertook anything comical vainly: and were but the vain names of comedies changed for the titles of commodities, or of plays for pleas, you should see all those grand censors that now style them such vanities flock to them for the main grace of their gravities: especially this author's comedies, that are so framed to the life that they serve for the most common commentaries of all the actions of our lives showing such a dexterity, and power of wit that the most displeased with plays are pleased with his comedies. And all such dull and heavy-witted worldlings as were never capable of the wit of a comedy coming by report of them to his representations, have found that wit there that they never found in themselves, and have parted better-witted than they came, feeling an edge of wit set upon them more than ever they dreamed they had brain to grind it on. So much and such savored salt of wit is in his comedies that they seem (for their height of pleasure) to be born in that sea that brought forth Venus. Amongst all there is none more witty than this, and had I time I would comment upon it, though I know it needs not (for so much as will think your testern [sixpence] well bestowed) but for so much worth as even poor I know to be stuffed in it. It deserves such a labor as well as the best comedy in Terence or Plautus. And believe this, that when he is gone, and his comedies out of sale, you will scramble for them, and set up a new English Inquisition. Take this for a warning, and at the peril of your pleasure's loss, and judgments, refuse not, nor like this the less for not being sullied with the smoky breath of the multitude, but thank fortune for the 'scape it hath made amongst you. Since by the grand possessors' wills I believe you should have prayed for them rather than been prayed. And so I leave all such to be prayed for (for the states of their wit's healths) that will not praise it.

VALE

Troilus and Cressida was reprinted in the first folio of 1623, but there seem to have been difficulties. In two surviving copies of the folio, the first page only occurs immediately after *Romeo and Juliet;* in all other copies it was printed without pagination between *Henry VIII* (the last of the histories) and *Coriolanus* (the first of the tragedies). The likeliest explanation is that some dispute over the ownership of the play arose during the printing of the folio which was not settled until after the rest of the tragedies had been set up.

The plot of the play is twofold. The first story tells how Troilus obtained the love of Cressida with the aid of Pandarus, her uncle, and how she was taken to the Greek camp and there played the strumpet. The second story tells how the

Greeks, distressed by Achilles' withdrawal from the combat, arranged for Ajax to fight a friendly bout with Hector, and how thereafter Hector killed Achilles' young friend Patroclus, and was in turn treacherously slain by Achilles.

The tale of Troilus and Cressida was a later invention and not part of the original Greek cycle of the legends of Troy. It was so popular that "Cressida" and "Pandar" became the types of a wanton and a pimp. The best version in English was Chaucer's *Troylus and Cressyde*. The story of Achilles, Ajax, and Hector came originally from Homer's *Iliad*. In 1598 the first two of George Chapman's translations of the *Iliad* had appeared — *Seven Books of the Iliades* and *Achilles' Shield*. The books translated were I, II, VII, VIII, IX, X, XII and XVIII. From these books came Achilles' quarrel with Agamemnon and his withdrawal from the war, the character of Thersites, the combat of Ajax and Hector, the proposal to send Helen back, the embassy of Nestor and Odysseus (Ulysses) to Achilles, and the grief of Achilles for Patroclus. Shakespeare however owed little to his sources, medieval or Homeric, for anything more than the outline of the story and a few of the episodes. The plot of the play, most of the characterization, the speeches, and the situations were his own invention.

But Chapman gave an unexpected lead. He had dedicated his translation of the *Seven Books of the Iliades of Homer, Prince of Poets,* to "the most honored instance of the Achilleian virtues eternized by Divine Homer, the Earl of Essex, Earl Marshal, etc." Chapman further insisted on the parallel by addressing Essex as

Most true Achilles (whom by sacred prophecy Homer did but prefigure in his admirable object) and in whose unmatched virtues shine the dignities of the soul, and the whole excellence of royal humanity; let not the peasant-common politics of the world, that count all things servile and simple that pamper not their sensualities, burying quick in their filthy sepulchers the earth, the whole bodies and souls of honor, virtue and piety, stir your temper from perseverance in godlike pursuit of Eternity.

With this dedication before him, Shakespeare could hardly have failed to see certain remarkable likenesses between Essex and Achilles. Moreover events in the three years following the publication of Chapman's translation made the identifi-

cation more exact and significant (see Gen. Intro. p. 24a).

The parallel between the situation at Essex House in the winter of 1600–01, with Essex, Southampton, and Cuff snarling at the Queen and her Ministers, is so close to the situation in the play where Achilles, Patroclus, and Thersites sneer at Agamemnon, Nestor, Menelaus, Ajax, and the rest that no contemporary could have missed it. It is in fact far closer to the actual events of the time than to the original situation in the *Iliad*. Nevertheless *Troilus and Cressida* is not an allegory of the fortunes of the Earl of Essex. As elsewhere, Shakespeare saw a remarkable similarity and made the most of it.

The exact date of the writing of *Troilus and Cressida* cannot be fixed, but the probable conclusion is that it was written between the autumn of 1600 and the winter of 1602. It is not likely that the play was ever publicly acted. Indeed Bonian and Walley, after stating in their first edition that it was acted at the Globe, withdrew the statement and declared in the Epistle that it "was never staled with the stage, never clapper-clawed with the palms of the vulgar." It does however bear all the signs of a play prepared for a private and select audience. There are signs also that the Troilus section of the story is in part a rewriting of an old play. In the latter part of the play, in such scenes as III.v, there are patches of rhyme and rhythm very much in the early style of *Love's Labor's Lost*.

The quarto text issued in 1609 is fairly well printed, but differs in many small points from the text printed in the folio. Each version contains short passages omitted by the other. From certain similarities in the setting of the two texts, it seems either that the folio text was printed from a copy of the quarto carefully but not uniformly corrected from a playhouse copy, or that both texts derive from a common original.

Troilus and Cressida is one of the most puzzling of Shakespeare's plays, although at times one of the most powerful. It is distinctly an unpleasant play, and has therefore been ignored by those critics who prefer to avoid the dark corners in Shakespeare's mind. Here love is smirched and mocked with a filthy bitterness, and heroism is made ridiculous. Hector the brave, the one man of heroic stature in the play, is murdered in cold blood by Achilles, another classical "hero," who is shown as insubordinate, sulky, and lovesick.

There is no romance, no beauty, no heroism, and no nobility. *Troilus and Cressida* is the work of a man in the bitterest mood of disillusionment to whom the world has become " a foul and pestilent congregation of vapors."

The play opens with a sight of Troilus and Pandarus. Troilus is almost lust-mad with desire for Cressida. In the next scene Cressida is shown as Pandarus, her uncle, tries to win her sympathy for Troilus. Cressida answers him with cynical and equivocal jests; but when she is alone she utters her true thoughts (I.ii.308); she is as hot as Troilus, but more expert. She will take him when his passion has reached white heat, but not before.

The scene then passes to the Greek camp with the generals in council (I.iii). Everything is going wrong. Agamemnon as commander opens the debate. He is followed by old Nestor, the type of reminiscent ancient who complacently observes that ill fortune is the test of valor. Then Shakespeare puts into the mouth of Ulysses one of his greatest speeches (I.iii.75); all these troubles, says Ulysses, come because men refuse to conform to the pattern of the universe, and especially Achilles, who sulks and mocks them all. The argument is interrupted by the arrival of Aeneas from Troy to bring Hector's challenge to any Greek who will meet him in single combat.

The third set of characters — Ajax, Thersites, the bitter foul-mouthed commentator, Achilles, and his minion Patroclus — is now introduced (II.i) in a short patch of quick dialogue to contrast with the oratory of the previous scene. The debate of the Greek commanders is next paralleled by another debate in Priam's palace. The theme of the Greek debate was order and chaos; the theme of the Trojans is honor and reason. Reason and moral right demand that Helen shall be sent back to her lawful husband, " honor " that she shall remain. In the next scene the contrast and the comment on what has just been said is given by Thersites — " All the argument is a cuckold and a whore." The Greek generals come to Achilles, but he treats them insultingly and they agree to exalt Ajax, who is already almost bursting with his own pride.

The story then returns to Troilus. Pandarus fetches Cressida to him and in the presence of this greasy old man the lovers declare their passion. There is a cynical contrast here to the other great declarations of love which Shakespeare had created: Bassanio and Portia (*M of Ven*, III.ii), Benedict and Beatrice (*M Ado*, IV.i.257), Romeo and Juliet (II.ii). These lovers exchange not lyric passion but bawdy jests, though at the end they reach a height of emotion when — the most bitter touch of all — they swear constancy to each other, and Pandarus ushers them into a bedchamber.

The scene next passes to the Greek camp, where the Greeks promise to fetch Cressida from Troy and to restore her to her father Calchas, the Trojan traitor, in return for the Trojan Antenor whom they have captured. The Greek generals now turn the tables on Achilles. As he sits in the door of his tent they deliberately ignore him, and when he asks Ulysses for an explanation of this unexpected behavior, Shakespeare puts into the mouth of Ulysses the magnificent speech on Time's mutability (III.iii.145).

Early next morning Troilus must leave Cressida, but before he has time to bid her farewell Aeneas is at hand with the command that she must go to her father in the Greek camp with Diomedes as her escort. Cressida for the moment is wild with grief, but she goes calmly, somewhat resentful at Troilus' insistence that she be true to him. When she arrives in the Greek camp, she greets the warriors with easy familiarity. The indecisive combat between Hector and Ajax follows, and then the Greeks, like warriors of chivalrous romance, entertain their enemies for the night. After supper Diomedes slips away. Troilus and Ulysses follow and watch. Cressida comes out to Diomedes and dallies with her new love; she easily parts with the sleeve that was Troilus' gift, and invites Diomedes to come to her. Troilus is transfixed with horror and incredulity.

Next morning the war is renewed. There is confused and general fighting. Patroclus is slain and his body is carried to Achilles, who is at last roused to action. Meanwhile Hector, wearied with the fighting, lays aside his sword and helmet, and while he is still resting unarmed is attacked by Achilles and his Myrmidons and slain in cold blood. Troilus in horror goes back to tell the news in Troy.

Although the play itself is loosely constructed and the last scenes seem to have been hastily huddled together, Shakespeare took considerable care in creating his characters. Three in particular stand out: Thersites, Ulysses, and Cressida.

Thersites is a specimen of a type not uncommon in Shakespeare's times — the political malcontent (see App. 4), a man frustrated and thwarted in his ambitions who takes his revenge on the world by posing as a fearless, blistering critic of humanity too honest and clear-sighted to be deceived by humbug and romantic notions, and who always imputes the worst of motives to every action.

Ulysses is a very different kind of commentator. He is the farsighted realist, with a vast knowledge of human motives. His analysis of the causes of the Greek disasters (I.iii.75–210) is acute wisdom. He recognizes at once that the best means of bringing Achilles to his senses is to encourage the foolish Ajax (I.iii.367–86), and when the time comes he gives the best possible advice to Achilles, reminding him of the universal truth — the touch of nature that makes the whole world kin — that men always follow the newest fashion and soon forget the old (III.iii.95–215). He also at a glance recognizes Cressida for what she is (IV.v. 54–63).

Cressida is drawn with fascinated loathing. She is the born wanton, a creature wholly sensual, passing easily from one lover to the next. Troilus is her slave, but soon she finds his devoted passion tedious, especially when he demands loyalty. She meets her match in Diomedes, who quickly discovers how to reduce her from encouragement to pleading. It is not an attractive picture; but there is no romance in *Troilus and Cressida*.

In any other play Shakespeare would have ended on a note of tragedy, a quiet close, a eulogy dignified and noble for the dead Hector. But *Troilus and Cressida* is not the story of the death of a hero; its theme is lechery and incontinent varlets, and Shakespeare gave the last word to Pandarus, a rueful comment on his own disgusting trade: " O traitors and bawds, how earnestly are you set a-work, and how ill requited! "

Troilus and Cressida

DRAMATIS PERSONAE

PRIAM, *King of Troy*

HECTOR
TROILUS
PARIS } *his sons*
DEIPHOBUS
HELENUS

MARGARELON, *a bastard son of Priam*

AENEAS } *Trojan commanders*
ANTENOR

CALCHAS, *a Trojan priest, taking part with the Greeks*

PANDARUS, *uncle to Cressida*

AGAMEMNON, *the Grecian general*

MENELAUS, *his brother*

ACHILLES
AJAX } *Grecian commanders*
ULYSSES

NESTOR
DIOMEDES } *Grecian commanders*
PATROCLUS

THERSITES, *a deformed and scurrilous Grecian*

ALEXANDER, *servant to Cressida*

SERVANT *to Troilus*

SERVANT *to Paris*

SERVANT *to Diomedes*

HELEN, *wife to Menelaus*

ANDROMACHE, *wife to Hector*

CASSANDRA, *daughter to Priam; a prophetess*

CRESSIDA, *daughter to Calchas*

TROJAN *and* GREEK SOLDIERS, *and* ATTENDANTS

SCENE — *Troy, and the Grecian camp.*

PROLOGUE°

In Troy there lies the scene. From isles of Greece
The princes orgulous,° their high blood chafed,°
Have to the port of Athens sent their ships,
Fraught° with the ministers and instruments
Of cruel war. Sixty and nine that wore   5
Their crownets° regal from the Athenian bay
Put forth toward Phrygia,° and their vow is made
To ransack Troy, within whose strong immures°
The ravished Helen, Menelaus' Queen,   9
With wanton Paris sleeps, and that's the quarrel.
To Tenedos° they come,
And the deep-drawing barks do there disgorge
Their warlike fraughtage. Now on Dardan° plains
The fresh and yet unbruisèd Greeks do pitch
Their brave pavilions. Priam's six-gated city,   15
Dardan, and Timbria, Helias, Chetas, Troien,
And Antenorides,° with massy° staples,
And corresponsive and fulfilling bolts,
Sperr° up the sons of Troy.
Now expectation, tickling skittish spirits,   20

On one and other side, Trojan and Greek,
Sets all on hazard. And hither am I come
A Prologue armed, but not in confidence
Of author's pen or actor's voice, but suited
In like conditions as our argument,°   25
To tell you, fair beholders, that our play
Leaps o'er the vaunt and firstlings° of those broils,
Beginning in the middle, starting thence away
To what may be digested in a play.
Like, or find fault, do as your pleasures are.   30
Now good or bad, 'tis but the chance of war.

Act I

SCENE I. *Troy. Before* PRIAM'S *palace.*

[*Enter* PANDARUS *and* TROILUS.]

TRO. Call here my varlet,° I'll unarm again.
Why should I war without° the walls of Troy,
That find such cruel battle here within?
Each Trojan that is master of his heart,
Let him to field. Troilus, alas, hath none!   5
PAN. Will this gear° ne'er be mended?
   TRO. The Greeks are strong and skillful to their strength,

---

Prologue: Shakespeare, unlike other contemporary dramatists, seldom used a prologue to introduce a play. This **Prologue** is armed, in imitation of the armed Prologues used during the stage war by Marston in *Antonio and Mellida* and Jonson in *Poetaster* (see Gen. Intro. pp. 44a, 45a). 2. orgulous: proud. chafed: enraged. 4. Fraught: laden. 6. crownets: coronets, worn by petty kings. 7. Phrygia: Asia Minor. 8. immures: walls. 11. Tenedos: a Greek island in the Aegean Sea. 13. Dardan: Trojan. 16–17. Dardan . . . Antenorides: the names of the gates of Troy. 17. massy: massive. 19. Sperr: shut.

25. argument: plot, theme. 27. vaunt . . . firstlings: van and beginning.

   Act I, Sc. i: 1. varlet: servant, valet. 2. without: outside. 6. gear: business.

Fierce to their skill and to their fierceness valiant.
But I am weaker than a woman's tear,
Tamer than sleep, fonder° than ignorance, 10
Less valiant than the virgin in the night,
And skill-less as unpracticed infancy.

PAN. Well, I have told you enough of this. For my
part, I'll not meddle nor make no farther. He that
will have a cake out of the wheat must needs tarry
the grinding. 16

TRO. Have I not tarried?

PAN. Aye, the grinding. But you must tarry the
bolting.°

TRO. Have I not tarried?

PAN. Aye, the bolting. But you must tarry the
leavening. 20

TRO. Still have I tarried.

PAN. Aye, to the leavening. But here's yet in the
word "hereafter" the kneading, the making of the
cake, the heating of the oven, and the baking. Nay,
you must stay the cooling too, or you may chance to
burn your lips. 26

TRO. Patience herself, what goddess e'er she be,
Doth lesser blench° at sufferance° than I do.
At Priam's royal table do I sit,
And when fair Cressid comes into my thoughts —
So, traitor! — "When she comes!" — When is she
thence?

PAN. Well, she looked yesternight fairer than ever
I saw her look, or any woman else.

TRO. I was about to tell thee — when my heart,
As wedgèd with a sigh, would rive° in twain 35
Lest Hector or my father should perceive me,
I have, as when the sun doth light a storm,
Buried this sigh in wrinkle of a smile.
But sorrow that is couched in seeming gladness
Is like that mirth fate turns to sudden sadness. 40

PAN. An° her hair were not somewhat darker
than Helen's — well, go to — there were no more
comparison between the women. But for my part,
she is my kinswoman. I would not, as they term it,
praise her. But I would somebody had heard her talk
yesterday, as I did. I will not dispraise your sister
Cassandra's wit, but ——

TRO. O Pandarus! I tell thee, Pandarus —
When I do tell thee, there my hopes lie drowned,
Reply not in how many fathoms deep 50
They lie indrenched.° I tell thee I am mad
In Cressid's love. Thou answer'st "she is fair,"
Pour'st in the open ulcer of my heart
Her eyes, her hair, her cheek, her gait, her voice,
Handlest in thy discourse, oh, that her hand, 55
In whose comparison all whites are ink
Writing their own reproach, to whose soft seizure
The cygnet's down is harsh, and spirit of sense

Hard as the palm of plowman.° This thou tell'st me,
As true thou tell'st me, when I say I love her. 60
But, saying thus, instead of oil and balm,
Thou lay'st in every gash that love hath given me
The knife that made it.

PAN. I speak no more than truth.

TRO. Thou dost not speak so much. 65

PAN. Faith, I'll not meddle in 't. Let her be as she
is. If she be fair, 'tis the better for her. An she be not,
she has the mends in her own hands.°

TRO. Good Pandarus, how now, Pandarus!

PAN. I have had my labor for my travail, ill-
thought-on of her and ill-thought-on of you — gone
between and between, but small thanks for my labor.

TRO. What, art thou angry, Pandarus? What,
with me? 75

PAN. Because she's kin to me, therefore she's not
so fair as Helen. An she were not kin to me, she
would be as fair on Friday as Helen is on Sunday.°
But what care I? I care not an she were a blacka-
moor, 'tis all one to me. 80

TRO. Say I she is not fair?

PAN. I do not care whether you do or no. She's a
fool to stay behind her father.° Let her to the
Greeks, and so I'll tell her the next time I see her.
For my part, I'll meddle nor make no more i' the
matter.

TRO. Pandarus ——

PAN. Not I.

TRO. Sweet Pandarus ——

PAN. Pray you, speak no more to me. I will leave
all as I found it, and there an end. 91

[Exit. An alarum.]

TRO. Peace, you ungracious clamors! Peace, rude
sounds!
Fools on both sides! Helen must needs be fair
When with your blood you daily paint her thus.
I cannot fight upon this argument, 95
It is too starved a subject for my sword.
But Pandarus —— O gods, how do you plague me!
I cannot come to Cressid but by Pandar,
And he's as tetchy° to be wooed to woo
As she is stubborn-chaste against all suit. 100
Tell me, Apollo, for thy Daphne's° love,
What Cressid is, what Pandar, and what we.
Her bed is India,° there she lies, a pearl.
Between our Ilium and where she resides,
Let it be called the wild and wandering flood, 105
Ourself the merchant, and this sailing Pandar

57–59. to . . . plowman: compared with Cressida's gentle grasp,
swan's-down is hard, and the most sensitive of feeling as rough
as a plowman's hand. 68. has . . . hands: i.e., can make
herself up. 78. on Sunday: i.e., in her Sunday best.
82–83. She's . . . father: Cressida's father, Calchas, deserted to
the Greeks. 99. tetchy: touchy. 101. Daphne: one of Apollo's
unsuccessful loves. To avoid his approaches she was changed
into a laurel. 103. India: the symbol of distant, wealthy, and
romantic lands.

10. fonder: more foolish. 18. bolting: sifting of the flour.
28. blench: shy (like a horse). sufferance: pain. 35. rive:
split. 41. An: if. 51. indrenched: soaked.

Our doubtful hope, our convoy and our bark.°
[*Alarum. Enter* AENEAS.]

AENE. How now, Prince Troilus! Wherefore not
afield?

TRO. Because not there. This woman's answer
sorts,°

For womanish it is to be from thence.   110
What news, Aeneas, from the field today?

AENE. That Paris is returned home, and hurt.

TRO. By whom, Aeneas?

AENE.   Troilus, by Menelaus.

TRO. Let Paris bleed. 'Tis but a scar to scorn.   114
Paris is gored with Menelaus' horn.°   [*Alarum.*]

AENE. Hark, what good sport is out of town to-
day!

TRO. Better at home if " would I might " were
" may."

But to the sport abroad. Are you bound thither?

AENE. In all swift haste.

TRO.   Come, go we then together.   [*Exeunt.*]

SCENE II. *The same. A street.*

[*Enter* CRESSIDA *and* ALEXANDER *her man.*]

CRES. Who were those went by?

ALEX.   Queen Hecuba and Helen.

CRES. And whither go they?

ALEX.   Up to the eastern tower,
Whose height commands as subject all the vale,
To see the battle. Hector, whose patience
Is as a virtue fixed, today was moved.   5
He chid Andromache and struck his armorer,
And, like as there were husbandry° in war,
Before the sun rose he was harnessed° light,
And to the field goes he, where every flower
Did, as a prophet, weep what it foresaw   10
In Hector's wrath.

CRES.   What was his cause of anger?

ALEX. The noise goes, this: There is among the
Greeks
A lord of Trojan blood, nephew to Hector.
They call him Ajax.°

CRES.   Good, and what of him?

ALEX. They say he is a very man per se,°   15
And stands alone.

CRES. So do all men, unless they are drunk, sick,
or have no legs.

ALEX. This man, lady, hath robbed many beasts of
their particular additions.° He is as valiant as   20
the lion, churlish as the bear, slow as the elephant —

a man into whom Nature hath so crowded humors°
that his valor is crushed into folly, his folly sauced
with discretion. There is no man hath a virtue that
he hath not a glimpse of, nor any man an at-   25
taint° but he carries some stain of it. He is melan-
choly without cause and merry against the hair.° He
hath the joints of everything, but everything so out
of joint that he is a gouty Briareus,° many hands
and no use, or purblind Argus,° all eyes and no
sight.   31

CRES. But how should this man, that makes me
smile, make Hector angry?

ALEX. They say he yesterday coped° Hector in the
battle and struck him down, the disdain and shame
whereof hath ever since kept Hector fasting and
waking.   37

[*Enter* PANDARUS.]

CRES. Who comes here?

ALEX. Madam, your uncle Pandarus.

CRES. Hector's a gallant man.

ALEX. As may be in the world, lady.

PAN. What's that? What's that?

CRES. Good morrow, Uncle Pandarus.   43

PAN. Good morrow, Cousin° Cressid. What do
you talk of? Good morrow, Alexander. How do you,
Cousin? When were you at Ilium?°

CRES. This morning, Uncle.

PAN. What were you talking of when I came?
Was Hector armed and gone ere you came to Ilium?
Helen was not up, was she?   50

CRES. Hector was gone, but Helen was not up.

PAN. E'en so. Hector was stirring early.

CRES. That were we talking of, and of his anger.

PAN. Was he angry?

CRES. So he says here.

PAN. True, he was so. I know the cause too. He'll
lay about him today, I can tell them that. And there's
Troilus will not come far behind him. Let them take
heed of Troilus, I can tell them that too.   61

CRES. What, is he angry too?

PAN. Who, Troilus? Troilus is the better man of
the two.

CRES. Oh Jupiter! There's no comparison.   65

PAN. What, not between Troilus and Hector? Do
you know a man if you see him?

CRES. Aye, if I ever saw him before and knew him.

PAN. Well, I say Troilus is Troilus.   70

CRES. Then you say as I say, for I am sure he is not
Hector.

PAN. No, nor Hector is not Troilus in some de-
grees.°

---

107. bark: ship.   109. sorts: fits.   115. horn: i.e., because
Menelaus is a cuckold. See App. 11.

Sc. ii: 7. husbandry: economy; i.e., he got up early to make
the most of daylight.   8. harnessed: armored.   14. Ajax:
See App. 4.   15. per se: by himself, unique.   20. additions:
distinctive attributes.

22. humors: whims. See App. 3.   26. attaint: disgrace.
27. against . . . hair: i.e., the natural lie of the hair; "against the
grain."   29. Briareus: a monster with a hundred hands.
30. Argus: a monster with a hundred eyes.   34. coped: encoun-
tered.   44. Cousin: used for any near relation.   46. Ilium: the
citadel of Troy, the royal palace.   73–74. in . . . degrees: by
some distance.

CRES. 'Tis just to each of them, he is himself.

PAN. Himself! Alas, poor Troilus! I would he were.

CRES. So he is.   79

PAN. Condition, I had gone° barefoot to India.

CRES. He is not Hector.

PAN. Himself! No, he's not himself. Would a'° were himself! Well, the gods are above, time must friend or end. Well, Troilus, well, I would my heart were in her body! No, Hector is not a better man than Troilus.   86

CRES. Excuse me.

PAN. He is elder.

CRES. Pardon me, pardon me.

PAN. Th' other's not come to 't. You shall tell me another tale when th' other's come to 't. Hector shall not have his wit this year.

CRES. He shall not need it if he have his own.

PAN. Nor his qualities.

CRES. No matter.   95

PAN. Nor his beauty.

CRES. 'Twould not become him, his own's better.

PAN. You have no judgment, Niece. Helen herself swore th' other day that Troilus, for a brown favor° — for so 'tis, I must confess — not brown neither ——

CRES. No, but brown.   104

PAN. Faith, to say truth, brown and not brown.

CRES. To say the truth, true and not true.

PAN. She praised his complexion above Paris.

CRES. Why, Paris hath color enough.

PAN. So he has.

CRES. Then Troilus should have too much. If she praised him above, his complexion is higher than his. He having color enough, and the other higher, is too flaming a praise for a good complexion. I had as lief Helen's golden tongue had commended Troilus for a copper° nose.   115

PAN. I swear to you I think Helen loves him better than Paris.

CRES. Then she's a merry Greek° indeed.

PAN. Nay, I am sure she does. She came to him th' other day into the compassed° window — and you know he has not past three or four hairs on his chin ——   122

CRES. Indeed, a tapster's arithmetic° may soon bring his particulars therein to a total.

PAN. Why, he is very young. And yet will he, within three pound, lift as much as his brother Hector.   127

CRES. Is he so young a man and so old a lifter?°

PAN. But to prove to you that Helen loves him — she came and puts me her white hand to his cloven chin ——

CRES. Juno have mercy! How came it cloven?

PAN. Why you know 'tis dimpled. I think his smiling becomes him better than any man in all Phrygia.   136

CRES. Oh, he smiles valiantly.

PAN. Does he not?

CRES. Oh yes, an 'twere a cloud in autumn.

PAN. Why, go to, then. But to prove to you that Helen loves Troilus ——

CRES. Troilus will stand to the proof, if you'll prove it so.

PAN. Troilus! Why, he esteems her no more than I esteem an addle° egg.   145

CRES. If you love an addle egg as well as you love an idle head, you would eat chickens i' the shell.

PAN. I cannot choose but laugh to think how she tickled his chin. Indeed she has a marvelous white hand, I must needs confess ——   150

CRES. Without the rack.°

PAN. And she takes upon her to spy a white hair on his chin.

CRES. Alas, poor chin! Many a wart is richer.   155

PAN. But there was such laughing! Queen Hecuba laughed, that her eyes ran o'er.

CRES. With millstones.°

PAN. And Cassandra laughed.   159

CRES. But there was more temperate fire under the pot° of her eyes. Did her eyes run o'er too?

PAN. And Hector laughed.

CRES. At what was all this laughing?

PAN. Marry,° at the white hair that Helen spied on Troilus' chin.   165

CRES. An 't had been a green hair, I should have laughed too.

PAN. They laughed not so much at the hair as at his pretty answer.

CRES. What was his answer?

PAN. Quoth she, " Here's but two and fifty hairs on your chin, and one of them is white."

CRES. This is her question.   173

PAN. That's true, make no question of that. " Two and fifty hairs," quoth he, " and one white. That white hair is my father, and all the rest are his sons."° " Jupiter! " quoth she. " Which of these hairs is Paris my husband? " " The forked one,"° quoth he. " Pluck 't out, and give it him." But there was such laughing! And Helen so blushed, and Paris so chafed, and all the rest so laughed, that it passed.

---

80. Condition . . . gone: i.e., I wish Troilus was himself even if I had to go.   82. a': he.   100–01. brown favor: dark complexion.   115. copper: red.   118. merry Greek: The Greeks were considered gay folk, so *merry Greek* came to be a proverbial phrase for a lighthearted, frivolous person.   120. compassed: round.   123. tapster's arithmetic: such slight ability to add as a bartender (*tapster*) needs.   128. lifter: thief.

145. addle: addled, bad.   151. Without . . . rack: i.e., without being put to torture. See App. 10.   158. With millstones: "by the pailful."   161. pot: socket.   164. Marry: Mary, by the Virgin.   176–77. his sons: Priam had fifty sons.   178. forked one: i.e., the cuckold. See App. 11.

CRES. So let it° now, for it has been a great while going by. 184

PAN. Well, Cousin, I told you a thing yesterday. Think on 't.

CRES. So I do.

PAN. I'll be sworn 'tis true. He will weep you an 'twere° a man born in April.° 189

CRES. And I'll spring up in his tears an 'twere a nettle against May.   [*A retreat sounded.*]

PAN. Hark! They are coming from the field. Shall we stand up here and see them as they pass toward Ilium? Good Niece, do, sweet Niece Cressida. 195

CRES. At your pleasure.

PAN. Here, here, here's an excellent place, here we may see most bravely. I'll tell you them all by their names as they pass by, but mark Troilus above the rest. 200

[*AENEAS passes.*]

CRES. Speak not so loud.

PAN. That's Aeneas. Is not that a brave man? He's one of the flowers of Troy, I can tell you. But mark Troilus, you shall see anon.

CRES. Who's that? 205

[*ANTENOR passes.*]

PAN. That's Antenor. He has a shrewd wit, I can tell you, and he's a man good enough. He's one o' the soundest judgments in Troy, whosoever, and a proper man of person.° When comes Troilus? I'll show you Troilus anon. If he see me, you shall see him nod at me. 211

CRES. Will he give you the nod?°

PAN. You shall see.

CRES. If he do, the rich shall have more.°

[*HECTOR passes.*]

PAN. That's Hector, that, that, look you, that. There's a fellow! Go thy way, Hector! There's a brave man, Niece. Oh, brave Hector! Look how he looks! There's a countenance! Is 't not a brave man?

CRES. Oh, a brave man! 220

PAN. Is a' not? It does a man's heart good. Look you what hacks are on his helmet! Look you yonder, do you see? Look you there — there's no jesting, there's laying on, take 't off who will, as they say. There be hacks! 225

CRES. Be those with swords?

PAN. Swords! Anything, he cares not. An the Devil come to him, it's all one. By God's lid,° it does one's heart good. Yonder comes Paris, yonder comes Paris. [*PARIS passes.*] Look ye yonder, Niece. Is 't not a gallant man too, is 't not? Why, this is brave now. Who said he came hurt home today? He's not hurt. Why, this will do Helen's heart good now, ha!

Would I could see Troilus now! You shall see Troilus anon. 236

CRES. Who's that?

[*HELENUS passes.*]

PAN. That's Helenus. I marvel where Troilus is. That's Helenus. I think he went not forth today. That's Helenus. 240

CRES. Can Helenus fight, Uncle?

PAN. Helenus! No, yes, he'll fight indifferent° well. I marvel where Troilus is. Hark! Do you not hear the people cry "Troilus"? Helenus is a priest. 245

CRES. What sneaking fellow comes yonder?

[*TROILUS passes.*]

PAN. Where? Yonder? That's Deiphobus. 'Tis Troilus! There's a man, Niece! Hem! Brave Troilus! The prince of chivalry!

CRES. Peace, for shame, peace! 250

PAN. Mark him, note him. Oh, brave Troilus! Look well upon him, Niece. Look you how his sword is bloodied, and his helm more hacked than Hector's, and how he looks, and how he goes! Oh, admirable youth! He never saw° three-and-twenty. Go thy way, Troilus, go thy way! Had I a sister were a grace, or a daughter a goddess, he should take his choice. Oh, admirable man! Paris? Paris is dirt to him, and I warrant Helen, to change, would give an eye to boot.°

[*COMMON SOLDIERS pass.*]

CRES. Here come more. 261

PAN. Asses, fools, dolts! Chaff and bran, chaff and bran! Porridge after meat! I could live and die i' the eyes of° Troilus. Ne'er look, ne'er look, the eagles are gone — crows and daws,° crows and daws! I had rather be such a man as Troilus than Agamemnon and all Grece. 267

CRES. There is among the Greeks Achilles, a better man than Troilus.

PAN. Achilles! A drayman,° a porter, a very camel.

CRES. Well, well.

PAN. Well, well! Why, have you any discretion? Have you any eyes? Do you know what a man is? Is not birth, beauty, good shape, discourse, manhood, learning, gentleness, virtue, youth, liberality, and suchlike the spice and salt that season a man? 278

CRES. Aye, a minced° man. And then to be baked with no date in the pie, for then the man's date is out.°

PAN. You are such a woman! One knows not at what ward° you lie. 283

183. it: i.e., this interminable tale.   189. an 'twere: as if he was. born in April: the rainy month of Aquarius. See App. 2. 209. proper . . . person: a fine handsome man.   212. give . . . nod: i.e., recognize you.   214. rich . . . more: i.e., if he nods to you, you will be a greater noddy (simpleton) than ever. 228. lid: eyelid.
242. indifferent: fairly.   255. never saw: i.e., is not yet. 260. to boot: in addition; i.e., to get Troilus, Helen would give Paris and one of her eyes.   263–64. i' . . . of: gazing at. 265. daws: jackdaws.   270. drayman: man who drives a heavy cart.   279. minced: with a pun on mincing, affected. 280–81. date is out: time is up.   283. ward: position of defense.

CRES. Upon my back, to defend my belly; upon my wit, to defend my wiles; upon my secrecy, to defend mine honesty;° my mask,° to defend my beauty; and you, to defend all these. And at all these wards I lie, at a thousand watches.

PAN. Say one of your watches.   290

CRES. Nay, I'll watch you for that, and that's one of the chiefest of them too. If I cannot ward what I would not have hit, I can watch you for telling how I took the blow — unless it swell past hiding, and then it's past watching.°   295

PAN. You are such another!

[*Enter* TROILUS'S BOY.]

BOY. Sir, my lord would instantly speak with you.

PAN. Where?   299

BOY. At your own house. There he unarms him.

PAN. Good boy, tell him I come. [*Exit* BOY.] I doubt° he be hurt. Fare ye well, good Niece.

CRES. Adieu, Uncle.

PAN. I will be with you, Niece, by and by.

CRES. To bring, Uncle?   305

PAN. Aye, a token from Troilus.

CRES. By the same token, you are a bawd.°

[*Exit* PANDARUS.]

Words, vows, gifts, tears, and love's full sacrifice,
He offers in another's enterprise.
But more in Troilus thousandfold I see   310
Than in the glass° of Pandar's praise may be.
Yet hold I off. Women are angels, wooing.°
Things won are done, joy's soul lies in the doing.
That she beloved° knows naught that knows not
     this —
Men prize the thing ungained more than it is.   315
That she was never yet that ever knew°
Love got so sweet as when desire did sue.
Therefore this maxim out of love I teach:
Achievement is command; ungained, beseech.°
Then though my heart's content firm love doth bear,
Nothing of that shall from mine eyes appear.   321

[*Exeunt.*]

SCENE III. *The Grecian camp. Before*
AGAMEMNON'S *tent.*

[*Sennet.*° *Enter* AGAMEMNON, NESTOR, ULYSSES,
MENELAUS, *with others.*]

AGAM. Princes,
What grief hath set the jaundice on your cheeks?

The ample proposition that hope makes
In all designs begun on earth below
Fails in the promised largeness.° Checks and
     disasters   5
Grow in the veins of actions highest reared,°
As knots, by the conflux of meeting sap,
Infect the sound pine and divert his grain
Tortive° and errant from his course of growth.
Nor, Princes, is it matter new to us   10
That we come short of our suppose° so far
That after seven years' siege yet Troy walls stand;
Sith° every action that hath gone before,
Whereof we have recórd, trial did draw
Bias° and thwart,° not answering the aim   15
And that unbodied° figure of the thought
That gave 't surmised shape. Why then, you Princes,
Do you with cheeks abashed behold our works,
And call them shames? Which are indeed naught
     else
But the protractive° trials of great Jove   20
To find persistive constancy° in men.
The fineness of which metal is not found
In Fortune's love,° for then the bold and coward,
The wise and fool, the artist° and unread,
The hard and soft, seem all affined° and kin.   25
But in the wind and tempest of her frown,
Distinction with a broad and powerful fan,
Puffing at all, winnows the light away,
And what hath mass or matter, by itself
Lies rich in virtue and unmingled.°   30

NEST. With due observance of thy godlike seat,°
Great Agamemnon, Nestor shall apply
Thy latest words. In the reproof of chance°
Lies the true proof of men. The sea being smooth,
How many shallow bauble° boats dare sail   35
Upon her patient breast, making their way
With those of nobler bulk!
But let the ruffian Boreas° once enrage
The gentle Thetis,° and anon behold
The stronged-ribbed bark through liquid mountains
     cut,   40
Bounding between the two moist elements°
Like Perseus' horse.° Where's then the saucy boat,
Whose weak untimbered sides but even now
Corivaled° greatness? Either to harbor fled,

286. honesty: chastity. mask: Ladies wore masks to prevent sun tan.   295. watching: caring for.   302. doubt: am afraid. 307. bawd: one who introduces the customer to a prostitute. 311. glass: reflection.   312. wooing: while still being wooed. 314. That . . . beloved: i.e., any woman who has a lover. 316. That . . . knew: there was never a woman who did not know.   319. Achievement . . . beseech: when a woman is won, she is at her man's command; but before he has won her, he will beg.

Sc. iii: s.d., Sennet: trumpet call.

5. promised largeness: expected good results.   6. highest reared: undertaken on a large scale.   9. Tortive: twisting. 11. suppose: estimate.   13. Sith: since.   15. Bias: out of the direct course. See App. 13. thwart: awry.   16. unbodied: i.e., existing in the mind.   20. protractive: long-drawn-out. 21. persistive constancy: firmness to persist.   23. Fortune's love: i.e., when all goes well.   24. artist: scholar.   25. affined: related.   30. unmingled: i.e., with baser qualities.   31. seat: authority.   33. reproof of chance: defiance of fortune. 35. bauble: trifling.   38. Boreas: the north wind.   39. Thetis: a sea nymph, so the sea.   41. moist elements: i.e., air and water.   42. Perseus' horse: the Greek hero Perseus killed the sorceress Medea, and from her head came Pegasus, a winged horse, which Perseus rode.   44. Corivaled: competed with.

Or made a toast for Neptune. Even so   45
Doth valor's show° and valor's worth divide
In storms of Fortune. For in her ray and bright-
    ness
The herd hath more annoyance by the breese°
Than by the tiger. But when the splitting wind
Makes flexible the knees of knotted oaks,   50
And flies fled under shade, why then the thing of
    courage
As roused with rage with rage doth sympathize,
And with an accent tuned in selfsame key
Retorts to chiding Fortune.
    ULYSS.   Agamemnon,
Thou great commander, nerve° and bone of Greece,
Heart of our numbers, soul and only spirit   56
In whom the tempers and the minds of all
Should be shut up,° hear what Ulysses speaks.
Besides the applause and approbation
The which, [*To* AGAMEMNON] most mighty for thy
    place and sway,   60
[*To* NESTOR] And thou most reverend for thy
    stretched-out life,
I give to both your speeches, which were such
As Agamemnon and the hand of Greece
Should hold up high in brass,° and such again
As venerable Nestor, hatched in silver,°   65
Should with a bond of air, strong as the axletree
On which heaven rides, knit all the Greekish ears
To his experienced tongue, yet let it please both,
Thou great, and wise, to hear Ulysses speak.
    AGAM. Speak, Prince of Ithaca, and be 't of less
    expect   70
That matter needless, of importless burden,
Divide thy lips than we are confident
When rank Thersites opes his mastic jaws
We shall hear music, wit, and oracle.°   74
    ULYSS. Troy, yet upon his basis, had been down,
And the great Hector's sword had lacked a master,
But for these instances.°
The specialty of rule° hath been neglected.
And look how many Grecian tents do stand   79
Hollow upon this plain, so many hollow factions.
When that the general is not like the hive
To whom the foragers shall all repair,
What honey is expected? Degree° being vizarded,°

The unworthiest shows as fairly in the mask.°   84
The heavens themselves, the planets and this center,°
Observe degree, priority, and place,
Insisture,° course, proportion, season, form,
Office, and custom, in all line of order.
And therefore is the glorious planet Sol
In noble eminence enthroned and sphered   90
Amidst the other,° whose medicinable eye
Corrects the ill aspécts of planets evil,
And posts° like the commandment of a king,
Sans° check to good and bad. But when the planets
In evil mixture to disorder wander,   95
What plagues and what portents, what mutiny,
What raging of the sea, shaking of earth,
Commotion in the winds, frights, changes, horrors,
Divert and crack, rend and deracinate,°
The unity and married calm of states   100
Quite from their fixure!° Oh, when degree is
    shaked,
Which is the ladder to all high designs,
The enterprise is sick! How could communities,
Degrees in schools° and brotherhoods in cities,
Peaceful commerce from dividable° shores,   105
The primogenitive° and due of birth,
Prerogative° of age, crowns, scepters, laurels,
But by degree, stand in authentic place?
Take but degree away, untune that string,   109
And hark, what discord follows! Each thing meets
In mere oppugnancy.° The bounded° waters
Should lift their bosoms higher than the shores,
And make a sop of all this solid globe.
Strength should be lord of imbecility,°
And the rude son should strike his father dead. 115
Force should be right, or rather, right and wrong,
Between whose endless jar° justice resides,
Should lose their names, and so should justice too.
Then everything includes itself in power,
Power into will, will into appetite,   120
And appetite, a universal wolf,
So doubly seconded with° will and power,
Must make perforce a universal prey,
And last eat up himself. Great Agamemnon,
This chaos, when degree is suffocate,   125
Follows the choking.
And this neglection of degree it is
That by a pace goes backward, with a purpose
It hath to climb.° The general's disdained

---

46. **show**: i.e., outward show.   48. **breese**: gadfly.   55. **nerve**: sinew.   58. **shut up**: confined.   64. **hold . . . brass**: set up aloft inscribed in brass for all to read.   65. **hatched in silver**: lit., inlaid with silver, streaked with white.   70–74. **Speak . . . oracle**: This obscure speech may be paraphrased: "Speak, Prince of Ithaca, for we know that we shall hear nothing worthless from you, as we know that when Thersites opens his bitter mouth we shall hear neither harmony nor sense." **mastic**: lit., scourging, satirical; a word coined by Shakespeare from *mastix* (a scourge). The word had been much in use after Dekker's play *Satiromastix; or, The Whipping of the Satirist*, 1601. See Gen. Intro. pp. 45a–46a.   77. **instances**: reasons.   78. **specialty of rule**: special authority of the commander; i.e., discipline.   83. **Degree**: rank. **being vizarded**: wearing a mask. obscured.

84. **mask**: entertainment at which all the partakers are masked.   85. **center**: earth. See App. 1.   87. **Insisture**: regularity.   91. **other**: others.   93. **posts**: rides fast. See App. 17.   94. **Sans**: without.   99. **deracinate**: root out.   101. **fixure**: fixed place.   104. **Degrees in schools**: i.e., the three degrees in universities: Bachelor, Master, Doctor.   105. **dividable**: divided.   106. **primogenitive**: right of the firstborn.   107. **Prerogative**: privilege.   111. **mere oppugnancy**: utter conflict. **bounded**: confined.   114. **Strength . . . imbecility**: i.e., the strong young man should control his feeble father.   117. **jar**: conflict.   122. **seconded with**: supported by.   127–29. **And . . . climb**: this neglect of degree makes us go back when we seek to climb.

By him one step below, he by the next,   130
That next by him beneath. So every step,
Exampled by the first pace that is sick
Of his superior, grows to an envious fever
Of pale and bloodless emulation.°
And 'tis this fever that keeps Troy on foot,   135
Not her own sinews. To end a tale of length,
Troy in our weakness stands, not in her strength.
  NEST. Most wisely hath Ulysses here discovered°
The fever whereof all our power is sick.   139
  AGAM. The nature of the sickness found, Ulysses,
What is the remedy?
  ULYSS. The great Achilles, whom opinion crowns
The sinew and the forehand of our host,
Having his ear full of his airy fame,
Grows dainty of his worth, and in his tent   145
Lies mocking our designs. With him, Patroclus,
Upon a lazy bed, the livelong day
Breaks scurril° jests,
And with ridiculous and awkward action,
Which, slanderer, he imitation calls,   150
He pageants° us. Sometime, great Agamemnon,
Thy topless deputation° he puts on,
And like a strutting player whose conceit°
Lies in his hamstring,° and doth think it rich
To hear the wooden dialogue and sound   155
'Twixt his stretched footing° and the scaffoldage,°
Such to-be-pitied and o'erwrested° seeming
He acts thy greatness in. And when he speaks,
'Tis like a chime a-mending,° with terms un-
   squared,°
Which, from the tongue of roaring Typhon°
   dropped,   160
Would seem hyperboles. At this fusty stuff,
The large Achilles, on his pressed bed lolling,
From his deep chest laughs out a loud applause,
Cries "Excellent! 'Tis Agamemnon just.°   164
Now play me Nestor, hem, and stroke thy beard,
As he being dressed° to some oration."
That's done, as near as the extremest ends
Of parallels, as like as Vulcan and his wife.°
Yet god Achilles still cries "Excellent!
'Tis Nestor right. Now play him me, Patroclus,   170
Arming to answer in a night alarm."
And then, forsooth, the faint defects of age
Must be the scene of mirth, to cough and spit

And, with a palsy fumbling on his gorget,°
Shake in and out the rivet. And at this sport   175
Sir Valor dies, cries "Oh, enough, Patroclus,
Or give me ribs of steel! I shall split all
In pleasure of my spleen."° And in this fashion
All our abilities, gifts, natures, shapes,
Severals° and generals of grace exact,   180
Achievements, plots, orders, preventions,
Excitements to the field or speech for truce,
Success or loss, what is or is not, serves
As stuff for these two to make paradoxes.°
  NEST. And in the imitation of these twain,   185
Who, as Ulysses says, opinion crowns
With an imperial voice,° many are infect.
Ajax is grown self-willed, and bears his head
In such a rein, in full as proud a place
As broad Achilles; keeps his tent like him;   190
Makes factious feasts; rails on our state of war
Bold as an oracle; and sets Thersites,
A slave whose gall coins slanders like a mint,
To match us in comparisons with dirt,
To weaken and discredit our exposure,   195
How rank soever rounded in with danger.°
  ULYSS. They tax° our policy and call it cowardice,
Count wisdom as no member of the war,
Forestall prescience,° and esteem no act
But that of hand. The still and mental parts   200
That do contrive how many hands shall strike
When fitness calls them on, and know by measure
Of their observant toil the enemies' weight —
Why, this hath not a finger's dignity.   204
They call this bed work,° mappery,° closet war.
So that the ram° that batters down the wall,
For the great swing and rudeness of his poise,
They place before his hand that made the engine,
Or those that with the fineness of their souls
By reason guide his execution.   210
  NEST. Let this be granted, and Achilles' horse
Makes many Thetis' sons.°   [*Tucket.°*]
  AGAM. What trumpet? Look, Menelaus.
  MEN. From Troy.
                          [*Enter* AENEAS.]
  AGAM. What would you 'fore our tent?   215
  AENE. Is this great Agamemnon's tent, I pray you?
  AGAM. Even this.
  AENE. May one that is a herald and a prince
Do a fair message to his kingly ears?   219
  AGAM. With surety stronger than Achilles' arm

133–34. grows . . . emulation: becomes a feverish jealousy which makes our bravery (*emulation*) pale and bloodless. 138. discovered: revealed. 148. scurril: scurrilous. 151. pageants: mimics. 152. topless deputation: supreme authority. 153. conceit: intelligence. 154. hamstring: ridiculous posing; lit., the tendon behind the knee. 156. stretched footing: exaggerated stalking. scaffoldage: stage. 157. o'erwrested: overstrained. See III.iii.23,n. 159. chime a-mending: peal of bells out of tune. unsquared: inappropriate. 160. Typhon: a roaring monster buried beneath Mount Etna. 164. just: exactly. 166. dressed: about to begin. 168. Vulcan . . . wife: Vulcan was the blacksmith of the gods, unsuitably married to Venus.

174. gorget: armor for the throat. See Pl. 8a. 178. spleen: excessive laughter. 180. Severals: particular qualities. 184. paradoxes: absurdities. 186–87. opinion . . . voice: general opinion would wish to have commander. 195–96. exposure . . . danger: our exposure to danger however excessive. 197. tax: criticize. 199. Forestall prescience: condemn forethought. 205. bed work: armchair strategy. mappery: mere making of maps. 206. ram: battering-ram. 211–12. Achilles' . . . sons: Achilles' horse is worth many an Achilles (who was the son of Thetis). 212 s.d., Tucket: trumpet call.

'Fore all the Greekish heads, which with one voice
Call Agamemnon head and general.

AENE. Fair leave and large security. How may
A stranger to those most imperial looks
Know them from eyes of other mortals? 225

AGAM.   How!

AENE. Aye.
I ask that I might waken reverence,
And bid the cheek be ready with a blush
Modest as morning when she coldly eyes
The youthful Phoebus.° 230
Which is that god in office, guiding men?
Which is the high and mighty Agamemnon?

AGAM. This Trojan scorns us, or the men of Troy
Are ceremonious courtiers. 234

AENE. Courtiers as free, as debonair, unarmed,
As bending° angels, that's their fame in peace.
But when they would seem soldiers, they have
  galls,°
Good arms, strong joints, true swords, and, Jove's
  accord,°
Nothing so full of heart. But peace, Aeneas,
Peace, Trojan, lay thy finger on thy lips! 240
The worthiness of praise distains° his worth
If that the praised himself bring the praise forth.
But what the repining enemy commends,
That breath fame blows, that praise, sole pure,
  transcends. 244

AGAM. Sir, you of Troy, call you yourself Aeneas?

AENE. Aye, Greek, that is my name.

AGAM. What's your affair, I pray you?

AENE. Sir, pardon, 'tis for Agamemnon's ears.

AGAM. He hears naught privately that comes from
  Troy. 249

AENE. Nor I from Troy come not to whisper him.
I bring a trumpet to awake his ear,
To set his sense on the attentive bent,°
And then to speak.

AGAM.   Speak frankly as the wind.
It is not Agamemnon's sleeping hour.
That thou shalt know, Trojan, he is awake, 255
He tells thee so himself.

AENE.   Trumpet, blow loud,
Send thy brass voice through all these lazy tents,
And every Greek of mettle, let him know
What Troy means fairly shall be spoke aloud.

[*Trumpet sounds.*]

We have, great Agamemnon, here in Troy 260
A prince called Hector — Priam is his father —
Who in this dull and long-continued truce
Is rusty grown. He bade me take a trumpet,
And to this purpose speak: Kings, Princes, lords!
If there be one among the fair'st of Greece 265
That holds his honor higher than his ease,

That seeks his praise more than he fears his peril,
That knows his valor and knows not his fear,
That loves his mistress more than in confession
With truant° vows to her own lips he loves, 270
And dare avow° her beauty and her worth
In other arms than hers — to him this challenge.
Hector, in view of Trojans and of Greeks,
Shall make it good, or do his best to do it,
He hath a lady, wiser, fairer, truer, 275
Than ever Greek did compass in his arms,
And will tomorrow with his trumpet call
Midway between your tents and walls of Troy,
To rouse a Grecian that is true in love.
If any come, Hector shall honor him. 280
If none, he'll say in Troy, when he retires,
The Grecian dames are sunburnt° and not worth
The splinter of a lance. Even so much.

AGAM. This shall be told our lovers, Lord Aeneas.
If none of them have soul in such a kind, 285
We left them all at home. But we are soldiers,
And may that soldier a mere recreant° prove
That means not, hath not, or is not in love!
If then one is, or hath, or means to be,
That one meets Hector. If none else, I am he. 290

NEST. Tell him of Nestor, one that was a man
When Hector's grandsire sucked. He is old now,
But if there be not in our Grecian host
One noble man that hath one spark of fire,
To answer for his love, tell him from me 295
I'll hide my silver beard in a gold beaver,°
And in my vantbrace° put this withered brawn,
And meeting him will tell him that my lady
Was fairer than his grandam, and as chaste
As may be in the world. His youth in flood,° 300
I'll prove this truth with my three drops of blood.

AENE. Now Heavens forbid such scarcity of youth!

ULYSS. Amen.

AGAM. Fair Lord Aeneas, let me touch your hand.
To our pavilion shall I lead you, sir. 305
Achilles shall have word of this intent,
So shall each lord of Greece, from tent to tent.
Yourself shall feast with us before you go,
And find the welcome of a noble foe.

[*Exeunt all but* ULYSSES *and* NESTOR.]

ULYSS. Nestor! 310

NEST. What says Ulysses?

ULYSS. I have a young conception° in my brain.
Be you my time to bring it to some shape.

NEST. What is 't?

ULYSS. This 'tis: 315
Blunt wedges rive hard knots. The seeded pride
That hath to this maturity blown up

---

270. truant: runaway. 271. avow: declare. 282. sunburnt:
i.e., mere country wenches. 287. recreant: traitor. 296. beaver:
face piece of the helmet. See Pl. 8a. 297. vantbrace: armor
for the forearm. 300. His . . . flood: though his manhood be
in its prime. 312. young conception: fresh idea.

---

230. Phoebus: the sun. 236. bending: adoring. 237. galls:
bitterness. 238. Jove's accord: Jove is with them. 241. dis-
tains: sullies. 252. attentive bent: lit., stretched taut to hear.

In rank° Achilles must or° now be cropped,
Or, shedding,° breed a nursery of like evil,
To overbulk° us all.
   NEST.   Well, and how?   320
   ULYSS. This challenge that the gallant Hector
     sends,
However it is spread in general name,
Relates in purpose only to Achilles.
   NEST. The purpose is perspicuous even as sub-
     stance,
Whose grossness little characters sum up.°   325
And, in the publication, make no strain,
But that Achilles, were his brain as barren
As banks of Libya° — though Apollo knows,
'Tis dry enough — will, with great speed of judg-
     ment —
Aye, with celerity — find Hector's purpose   330
Pointing on him.
   ULYSS. And wake him to the answer, think you?
   NEST. Yes, 'tis most meet. Who may you else
     oppose
That can from Hector bring his honor off,°
If not Achilles? Though 't be a sportful combat,
Yet in this trial much opinion° dwells,   336
For here the Trojans taste our dear'st repute
With their finest palate. And trust to me, Ulysses,
Our imputation° shall be oddly poised°
In this wild action. For the success,   340
Although particular, shall give a scantling°
Of good or bad unto the general,°
And in such indexes, although small pricks°
To their subséquent volumes, there is seen
The baby figure of the giant mass   345
Of things to come at large. It is supposed
He that meets Hector issues from our choice.
And choice, being mutual act of all our souls,
Makes merit her election,° and doth boil
As 'twere from forth us all, a man distilled   350
Out of our virtues. Who miscarrying,
What heart from hence receives the conquering part,
To steel a strong opinion to themselves?°
Which entertained, limbs are his instruments,
In no less working than are swords and bows   355
Directive by the limbs.
   ULYSS. Give pardon to my speech.
Therefore 'tis meet Achilles meet not Hector.
Let us, like merchants, show our foulest wares,
And think perchance they'll sell. If not,   360

The luster of the better yet to show
Shall show the better. Do not consent
That ever Hector and Achilles meet,
For both our honor and our shame in this
Are dogged with two strange followers.   365
   NEST. I see them not with my old eyes. What are
     they?
   ULYSS. What glory our Achilles shares from Hec-
     tor,
Were he not proud, we all should share with him.
But he already is too insolent,
And we were better parch in Afric sun   370
Than in the pride and salt° scorn of his eyes,
Should he 'scape Hector fair. If he were foiled,°
Why then we did our main opinion crush
In taint of our best man.° No, make a lottery,
And by device° let blockish° Ajax draw   375
The sort° to fight with Hector. Among ourselves
Give him allowance for the better man;
For that will physic° the great Myrmidon°
Who broils in loud applause, and make him fall°
His crest that prouder than blue Iris° bends.   380
If the dull brainless Ajax comes safe off,
We'll dress him up in voices.° If he fail,
Yet go we under our opinion still
That we have better men. But, hit or miss,
Our project's life this shape of sense assumes,   385
Ajax employed plucks down Achilles' plumes.
   NEST. Ulysses,
Now I begin to relish thy advice,
And I will give a taste of it forthwith
To Agamemnon. Go we to him straight.   390
Two curs shall tame each other. Pride alone
Must tarre° the mastiffs on, as 'twere their bone.
                           [Exeunt.]

Act II

SCENE I. *The Grecian camp.*

[*Enter* AJAX *and* THERSITES.]
   AJAX. Thersites!
   THER. Agamemnon — how if he had boils — full,
all over, generally?
   AJAX. Thersites!
   THER. And those boils did run? — Say so — did
not the General run then? Were not that a botchy
core?°   7

---

318. rank: lit., overfull of blood, proud. or: either. 319. shedding:
i.e., its seeds. 320. overbulk: overwhelm. 325. grossness
. . . up: size is made up of little figures. 328. Libya: the
African desert. 334. bring . . . off: win honor. 336. opinion:
reputation. 339. imputation: good fame. oddly poised: unevenly
balanced. 341. scantling: sample. 342. general: army as a
whole. 343. small pricks: mere dots. 349. Makes . . . elec-
tion: chooses the best man. 351–53. Who . . . themselves: if he
fails, what an encouragement the winning side will gain to
strengthen (*steel*) their self-confidence (*opinion*).

371. salt: bitter. 372. foiled: defeated. 373–74. did . . . man:
lost our reputation (*opinion*) in the failure of our best man.
375. device: a trick. blockish: blockheaded. 376. sort: lot.
378. physic: give a dose to. Myrmidon: i.e., Achilles, who
was commander of the Myrmidons. 379. fall: lower. 380. Iris:
the rainbow. 382. dress . . . voices: congratulate him loudly.
392. tarre: urge on to fight.
   Act II, Sc. i: 6–7. botchy core: boil full of matter.

AJAX. Dog!

THER. Then would come some matter from him. I see none now.

AJAX. Thou bitch wolf's son, canst thou not hear? Feel, then.   [*Strikes him.*]

THER. The plague of Greece upon thee, thou mongrel beef-witted° lord!   14

AJAX. Speak then, thou vinewed'st° leaven, speak. I will beat thee into handsomeness.

THER. I shall sooner rail thee into wit and holiness. But I think thy horse will sooner con° an oration than thou learn a prayer without book. Thou canst strike, canst thou? A red murrain° o' thy jade's° tricks!   21

AJAX. Toadstool, learn° me the proclamation.

THER. Dost thou think I have no sense,° thou strikest me thus?

AJAX. The proclamation!   25

THER. Thou art proclaimed a fool, I think.

AJAX. Do not, porpentine,° do not. My fingers itch.

THER. I would thou didst itch from head to foot, and I had the scratching of thee. I would make thee the loathsomest scab in Greece. When thou art forth in the incursions,° thou strikest as slow as another.

AJAX. I say, the proclamation!   34

THER. Thou grumblest and railest every hour on Achilles, and thou art as full of envy at his greatness as Cerberus° is at Proserpina's° beauty — aye, that thou barkest at him.

AJAX. Mistress Thersites!

THER. Thou shouldst strike him.   40

AJAX. Cobloaf!°

THER. He would pun° thee into shivers with his fist, as a sailor breaks a biscuit.

AJAX. [*Beating him*] You whoreson° cur!

THER. Do, do.   45

AJAX. Thou stool° for a witch!

THER. Aye, do, do, thou sodden-witted lord! Thou hast no more brain than I have in mine elbows, an assinego° may tutor thee. Thou scurvy-valiant ass! Thou art here but to thrash Trojans, and thou art bought and sold among those of any wit, like a barbarian slave. If thou use to beat me, I will begin at thy heel and tell what thou art by inches, thou thing of no bowels° thou!

AJAX. You dog!   55

THER. You scurvy lord!

AJAX. [*Beating him*] You cur!

THER. Mars his idiot!° Do, rudeness, do, camel, do, do.

[*Enter* ACHILLES *and* PATROCLUS.]

ACHIL. Why, how now, Ajax! Wherefore do ye thus? How now, Thersites! What's the matter, man?

THER. You see him there, do you?

ACHIL. Aye. What's the matter?

THER. Nay, look upon him.   65

ACHIL. So I do. What's the matter?

THER. Nay, but regard him well.

ACHIL. Well! Why, so I do.

THER. But yet you look not well upon him, for whosoever you take him to be, he is Ajax.

ACHIL. I know that, fool.

THER. Aye, but that fool knows not himself.

AJAX. Therefore I beat thee.   73

THER. Lo, lo, lo, lo, what modicums of wit he utters! His evasions have ears thus long.° I have bobbed° his brain more than he has beat my bones. I will buy nine sparrows for a penny, and his pia mater° is not worth the ninth part of a sparrow. This lord, Achilles — Ajax, who wears his wit in his belly and his guts in his head — I'll tell you what I say of him.   81

ACHIL. What?

THER. I say, this Ajax ——

[AJAX *offers to strike him.*]

ACHIL. Nay, good Ajax.

THER. Has not so much wit ——   85

ACHIL. Nay, I must hold you.

THER. As will stop the eye of Helen's needle, for whom he comes to fight.

ACHIL. Peace, fool!

THER. I would have peace and quietness, but the fool will not. He there, that he. Look you there!

AJAX. O thou damned cur! I shall ——

ACHIL. Will you set your wit to a fool's?   94

THER. No, I warrant you, for a fool's will shame it.

PATR. Good words, Thersites.

ACHIL. What's the quarrel?

AJAX. I bade the vile owl go learn me the tenor of the proclamation, and he rails upon me.

THER. I serve thee not.

AJAX. Well, go to, go to.

THER. I serve here voluntary.°   104

ACHIL. Your last service was sufferance, 'twas not voluntary, no man is beaten voluntary. Ajax was here the voluntary, and you as under an impress.°

THER. E'en so, a great deal of your wit too   108 lies in your sinews, or else there be liars. Hector shall have a great catch if he knock out either of your

---

14. **beef-witted:** too much meat was believed to be bad for the wits. See *T Night*, I.iii.88.   15. **vinewed'st:** moldy, emendation for Q1 "unsalted" and F1 "whinid'st."   18. **con:** learn by heart.   20. **murrain:** plague. **jade:** bad-tempered horse.   22. **learn:** tell.   23. **sense:** feeling.   27. **porpentine:** porcupine.   33. **incursions:** raids.   37. **Cerberus:** the three-headed dog guarding the mouth of Hades. **Proserpina:** Queen of the underworld.   41. **Cobloaf:** little loaf with a round head.   42. **pun:** pound.   44. **whoreson:** bastard.   46. **stool:** closestool, privy.   49. **assinego:** little ass.   54. **bowels:** mercy.

brains. A' were as good crack a fusty nut with no
kernel.   112

ACHIL. What, with me too, Thersites?

THER. There's Ulysses and old Nestor, whose wit
was moldy ere your grandsires had nails on their
toes, yoke you° like draught oxen, and make you
plow up the wars.   117

ACHIL. What? What?

THER. Yes, good sooth. To, Achilles! To, Ajax!
To!

AJAX. I shall cut out your tongue.   121

THER. 'Tis no matter, I shall speak as much as
thou afterward.

PATR. No more words, Thersites, peace!   125

THER. I will hold my peace when Achilles'
brooch° bids me, shall I?

ACHIL. There's for you, Patroclus.

THER. I will see you hanged, like clotpoles,° ere I
come any more to your tents. I will keep where there
is wit stirring, and leave the faction of fools.   131

[Exit.]

PATR. A good riddance.

ACHIL. Marry, this, sir, is proclaimed through all
     our host:
That Hector, by the fifth hour of the sun,
Will with a trumpet 'twixt our tents and Troy   135
Tomorrow morning call some knight to arms
That hath a stomach,° and such a one that dare
Maintain — I know not what. 'Tis trash. Farewell.

AJAX. Farewell. Who shall answer him?

ACHIL. I know not. 'Tis put to lottery, otherwise
He knew his man.   141

AJAX. Oh, meaning you. I will go learn more of
it.   *[Exeunt.]*

SCENE II. *Troy. A room in* PRIAM's *palace.*

[Enter PRIAM, HECTOR, TROILUS, PARIS,
and HELENUS.]

PRI. After so many hours, lives, speeches spent,
Thus once again says Nestor from the Greeks:
"Deliver Helen, and all damage else,
As honor, loss of time, travail, expense,
Wounds, friends, and what else dear that is con-
     sumed   5
In hot digestion of this cormorant° war,
Shall be struck off." Hector, what say you to 't?

HECT. Though no man lesser fears the Greeks
     than I
As far as toucheth my particular,

116. **yoke you:** i.e., treat you two like beasts of burden.
127. **brooch:** an ornament that he hangs about him; i.e., Pa-
troclus. 129. **clotpoles:** blockheads. 137. **stomach:** i.e., for
a fight.

Sc. ii: 6. **cormorant:** devouring. The cormorant is a rapacious
sea bird.

Yet, dread Priam,   10
There is no lady of more softer bowels,
More spongy to suck in the sense of fear,
More ready to cry out " Who knows what follows? "
Than Hector is. The wound° of peace is surety,
Surety secure. But modest doubt is called   15
The beacon of the wise, the tent that searches
To the bottom of the worst. Let Helen go.
Since the first sword was drawn about this question
Every tithe soul, 'mongst many thousand dismes,°
Hath been as dear as Helen — I mean, of ours.   20
If we have lost so many tenths of ours
To guard a thing not ours, nor worth to us,
Had it our name, the value of one ten,
What merit's in that reason which denies
The yielding of her up?

TRO.   Fie, fie, my brother!   25
Weigh you the worth and honor of a king
So great as our dread father in a scale
Of common ounces? Will you with counters° sum°
The past proportion of his infinite?
And buckle in a waist most fathomless   30
With spans° and inches so diminutive
As fears and reasons? Fie, for godly shame!

HEL. No marvel, though you bite so sharp at rea-
     sons,
You are so empty of them. Should not our father
Bear the great sway of his affairs with reasons,   35
Because your speech hath none that tells him so?

TRO. You are for dreams and slumbers, brother
     priest.
You fur your gloves with reason.° Here are your
     reasons:
You know an enemy intends you harm,
You know a sword employed is perilous,   40
And reason flies the object of all harm.
Who marvels, then, when Helenus beholds
A Grecian and his sword, if he do set
The very wings of reason to his heels,
And fly like chidden Mercury from Jove,   45
Or like a star disorbed?° Nay, if we talk of reason,
Let's shut our gates, and sleep. Manhood and honor
Should have hare hearts, would they but fat their
     thoughts
With this crammed reason. Reason and respect°
Make livers° pale and lustihood deject.   50

14–17. **wound . . . worst:** peace is wounded by self-confidence
(*surety*), careless (*secure*) self-confidence; but a modest doubt of
success is like a guiding light (*beacon*) to the wise, or a probe (*tent*)
which cleans the wound to the bottom. **tent:** lit., a piece of lint
used to probe and clean out a wound. 19. **tithe . . . dismes:**
both mean tenth; i.e., since Helen came one man in ten of many
ten thousands. 28. **counters:** used in calculating large sums.
sum: reckon. 31 **spans:** little calculations; lit., the distance be-
tween thumb and little finger in the outstretched hand; i.e., 9
inches. 38. **fur . . . reason:** line your gloves with reasons; i.e.,
cowardly arguments. 46. **disorbed:** shot out of its course.
See App. 1. 49. **respect:** counting the consequences. 50. **livers:**
The liver was regarded as the seat of courage.

HECT. Brother, she is not worth what she doth
    cost
The holding.
    TRO.   What's aught but as 'tis valued?
    HECT. But value dwells not in particular will.°
It holds his estimate and dignity
As well wherein 'tis precious of itself   55
As in the prizer. 'Tis mad idolatry
To make the service greater than the god.
And the will dotes that is attributive
To what infectiously itself affects,
Without some image of the affected merit.°   60
    TRO. I take° today a wife, and my election°
Is led on in the conduct of my will,°
My will enkindled by mine eyes and ears,
Two traded° pilots 'twixt the dangerous shores
Of will and judgment. How may I avoid,   65
Although my will distaste what it elected,
The wife I chose? There can be no evasion
To blench° from this, and to stand firm by honor.
We turn not back the silks upon the merchant
When we have soiled them, nor the remainder
    viands   70
We do not throw in unrespective sieve°
Because we now are full. It was thought meet
Paris should do some vengeance on the Greeks.
Your breath of full consent bellied° his sails.
The seas and winds, old wranglers, took a truce,   75
And did him service. He touched the ports de-
    sired,
And for an old aunt whom the Greeks held captive
He brought a Grecian Queen, whose youth and
    freshness
Wrinkles Apollo's° and makes stale the morning.
Why keep we her? The Grecians keep our aunt.   80
Is she worth keeping? Why, she is a pearl,
Whose price hath launched above a thousand ships,°
And turned crowned kings to merchants.
If you'll avouch 'twas wisdom Paris went —   84
As you must needs, for you all cried "Go, go" —
If you'll confess he brought home noble prize —
As you must needs, for you all clapped your hands
And cried "Inestimable!" — why do you now
The issue° of your proper° wisdoms rate,°
And do a deed that Fortune never did,°   90
Beggar the estimation° which you prized

Richer than sea and land? Oh, theft most base,
That we have stol'n what we do fear to keep!
But thieves unworthy of a thing so stol'n,
That in their country did them that disgrace,   95
We fear to warrant in our native place!°
    CAS. [*Within*] Cry, Trojans, cry!
    PRI.   What noise? What shriek is this?
    TRO. 'Tis our mad sister, I do know her voice.
    CAS. [*Within*] Cry, Trojans!   100
    HECT. It is Cassandra.
[*Enter* CASSANDRA, *raving, with her hair about her
    ears.*]
    CAS. Cry, Trojans, cry! Lend me ten thousand
        eyes,
And I will fill them with prophetic tears.
    HECT. Peace, sister, peace!
    CAS. Virgins and boys, mid-age and wrinkled
        eld,°
Soft infancy, that nothing canst but cry,   105
Add to my clamors! Let us pay betimes
A moiety° of that mass of moan to come.
Cry, Trojans, cry! Practice your eyes with tears!
Troy must not be, nor goodly Ilion° stand,
Our firebrand brother, Paris, burns us all.   110
Cry, Trojans, cry! A Helen and a woe.
Cry, cry! Troy burns, or else let Helen go. [*Exit.*]
    HECT. Now, youthful Troilus, do not these high
        strains
Of divination in our sister work
Some touches of remorse?° Or is your blood   115
So madly hot that no discourse of reason,
Nor fear of bad success in a bad cause,
Can qualify° the same?
    TRO.   Why, Brother Hector,
We may not think the justness of each act
Such and no other than event° doth form it,   120
Nor once deject the courage of our minds,
Because Cassandra's mad. Her brainsick raptures
Cannot distaste° the goodness of a quarrel
Which hath our several honors all engaged   125
To make it gracious. For my private part,
I am no more touched than all Priam's sons.
And Jove forbid there should be done amongst us
Such things as might offend the weakest spleen°
To fight for and maintain!
    PAR. Else might the world convince° of levity
As well my undertakings as your counsels.   13⒈
But I attest° the gods your full consent

---

53. **particular will:** individual desire.   **58–60. And . . . merit:**
desire is mad when it inclines to what will cause it harm with-
out even the show of any advantage.   **61. I take:** suppose that I
choose. **election:** choice.   **62. will:** desire, lust.   **64. traded:** ex-
perienced.   **68. blench:** start aside, refuse.   **71. unrespective
sieve:** senseless garbage can.   **74. bellied:** blew out.   **79. Wrinkles
Apollo's:** i.e., makes the god Apollo look wrinkled.   **82. Whose
. . . ships:** a deliberate echo of Faustus' famous address to Helen
in Marlowe's *Dr. Faustus:* "Was this the face that launched a
thousand ships?"   **89. issue:** result. **proper:** own. **rate:** estimate
the value of.   **90. And . . . did:** i.e., show yourselves more fickle
even than Fortune.   **91. Beggar . . . estimation:** make worthless
the thing of value.

92–96. Oh . . . place: we are like thieves who have stolen
something too good for us, which disgraces us in our own coun-
try; we are afraid to admit the worth of (*fear to warrant*) Helen
in Troy; i.e., you were all enthusiastic when Paris brought
Helen back to Troy, but now you basely pretend that she is **not**
worth keeping.   **104. eld:** old age.   **107. moiety: part.**
109. Ilion: Ilium, the citadel of Troy.   **115. remorse:** pity.
118. qualify: moderate.   **120. event:** consequences.   **124. dis-
taste:** give a bad taste to.   **129. spleen:** temper.   **130. con-
vince:** convict.   **132. attest:** call to witness.

Gave wings to my propension,° and cut off
All fears attending on so dire a project.
For what, alas, can these my single arms?   135
What propugnation° is in one man's valor,
To stand the push and enmity of those
This quarrel would excite? Yet I protest
Were I alone to pass the difficulties,
And had as ample power as I have will,   140
Paris should ne'er retract what he hath done,
Nor faint in the pursuit.

PRI.   Paris, you speak
Like one besotted on your sweet delights.
You have the honey still, but these the gall,
So to be valiant is no praise at all.   145

PAR. Sir, I propose not merely to myself
The pleasures such a beauty brings with it,
But I would have the soil of her fair rape
Wiped off in honorable keeping her.
What treason were it to the ransacked Queen,   150
Disgrace to your great worths, and shame to me,
Now to deliver her possession up
On terms of base compulsion! Can it be
That so degenerate a strain as this
Should once set footing in your generous° bosoms?
There's not the meanest spirit on our party   156
Without a heart to dare, or sword to draw,
When Helen is defended, nor none so noble
Whose life were ill bestowed, or death unfamed,
Where Helen is the subject. Then, I say,   160
Well may we fight for her, whom, we know well,
The world's large spaces cannot parallel.

HECT. Paris and Troilus, you have both said well,
And on the cause and question now in hand
Have glozed,° but superficially, not much   165
Unlike young men, whom Aristotle° thought
Unfit to hear moral philosophy.
The reasons you allege do more conduce
To the hot passion of distempered° blood
Than to make up a free determination   170
'Twixt right and wrong; for pleasure and revenge
Have ears more deaf than adders to the voice
Of any true decision. Nature craves
All dues be rendered to their owners. Now,
What nearer debt in all humanity   175
Than wife is to the husband? If this law
Of nature be corrupted through affection,°
And that great minds, of partial indulgence
To their benumbèd wills, resist the same,
There is a law in each well-ordered nation   180
To curb those raging appetites that are
Most disobedient and refractory.
If Helen then be wife to Sparta's King,

As it is known she is, these moral laws
Of nature and of nations speak aloud   185
To have her back returned. Thus to persist
In doing wrong extenuates not wrong,
But makes it much more heavy. Hector's opinion
Is this in way of truth. Yet ne'ertheless,
My spritely brethren, I propend° to you   190
In resolution to keep Helen still,
For 'tis a cause that hath no mean dependence
Upon° our joint and several dignities.

TRO. Why, there you touched the life of our design.
Were it not glory that we more affected   195
Than the performance of our heaving spleens,
I would not wish a drop of Trojan blood
Spent more in her defense. But, worthy Hector,
She is a theme of honor and renown,
A spur to valiant and magnanimous deeds   200
Whose present courage may beat down our foes,
And fame in time to come canónize° us.
For I presume brave Hector would not lose
So rich advantage of a promised glory
As smiles upon the forehead of this action   205
For the wide world's revenue.

HECT.   I am yours,
You valiant offspring of great Priamus.
I have a roisting° challenge sent amongst
The dull and factious nobles of the Greeks
Will strike amazement to their drowsy spirits.   210
I was advértised° their great General slept
Whilst emulation° in the army crept.
This, I presume, will wake him.   [Exeunt.]

SCENE III. *The Grecian camp. Before the tent
of* ACHILLES.

[*Enter* THERSITES, *solus.*]

THER. How now, Thersites! What, lost in the
labyrinth of thy fury! Shall the elephant Ajax carry
it thus? He beats me, and I rail at him, oh, worthy
satisfaction! Would it were otherwise — that I could
beat him whilst he railed at me. 'Sfoot,° I'll learn   5
to conjure and raise devils, but I'll see some issue
of my spiteful execrations. Then there's Achilles, a
rare enginer.° If Troy be not taken till these two
undermine it, the walls will stand till they fall   10
of themselves. O thou great thunder-darter of Olym-
pus, forget that thou art Jove, the King of gods, and,
Mercury, lose all the serpentine craft of thy cadu-
ceus° if ye take not that little little less than little wit

---

133. propension: inclination.   136. propugnation: defense.
155. generous: noble.   165. glozed: commented.   166. Aristotle:
the Greek philosopher who died 322 B.C., — about ten cen-
turies after the siege of Troy.   169. distempered: drunken.
177. affection: lust.

190. propend: incline.   192–93. hath . . . Upon: does not lightly
concern.   202. canonize: set us in the calendar of the heroes.
208. roisting: blustering.   211. advertised: informed.   212. emu-
lation: jealous rivalry.
          Sc. iii: 5. 'Sfoot: by God's foot.   9. enginer: engineer.
14. caduceus: Mercury's snake-entwined wand.

from them that they have! Which short-armed 15
ignorance itself knows is so abundant scarce it will
not in circumvention° deliver a fly from a spider
without drawing their massy irons and cutting the
web. After this, the vengeance on the whole 20
camp! Or rather the Neapolitan boneache,° for that
methinks is the curse dependent on those that war
for a placket.° I have said my prayers, and devil
Envy say amen. What ho! My Lord Achilles!

[*Enter* PATROCLUS.]

PATR. Who's there? Thersites! Good Thersites,
come in and rail.   26

THER. If I could ha' remembered a gilt counter-
feit,° thou wouldst not have slipped out of my con-
templation. But it is no matter, thyself upon thy-
self! The common curse of mankind, folly and 30
ignorance, be thine in great revenue! Heaven bless
thee° from a tutor, and discipline come not near
thee! Let thy blood be thy direction° till thy death!
Then if she that lays thee out says thou art a fair
corse, I'll be sworn and sworn upon 't she never 35
shrouded any but lazars.° Amen. Where's Achilles?

PATR. What, art thou devout? Wast thou in
prayer?

THER. Aye, the Heavens hear me!

PATR. Amen.

[*Enter* ACHILLES.]

ACHIL. Who's there?

PATR. Thersites, my lord.

ACHIL. Where, where? Art thou come? Why, my
cheese, my digestion, why hast thou not served thy-
self in to my table so many meals? Come, what's
Agamemnon?   46

THER. Thy commander, Achilles. Then tell me,
Patroclus, what's Achilles?

PATR. Thy lord, Thersites. Then tell me, I pray
thee, what's thyself?   50

THER. Thy knower, Patroclus. Then tell me, Pa-
troclus, what art thou?

PATR. Thou mayst tell that knowest.

ACHIL. Oh, tell, tell.

THER. I'll decline° the whole question. Aga- 55
memnon commands Achilles, Achilles is my lord, I
am Patroclus' knower, and Patroclus is a fool.

PATR. You rascal!

THER. Peace, fool! I have not done.   60

ACHIL. He is a privileged man. Proceed, Thersites.

THER. Agamemnon is a fool, Achilles is a fool,
Thersites is a fool, and, as aforesaid, Patroclus is a
fool.   65

ACHIL. Derive this, come.

THER. Agamemnon is a fool to offer to command

Achilles, Achilles is a fool to be commanded of Aga-
memnon, Thersites is a fool to serve such a fool, and
Patroclus is a fool positive.   70

PATR. Why am I a fool?

THER. Make that demand of the prover. It suffices
me thou art. Look you, who comes here?

ACHIL. Patroclus, I'll speak with nobody. 74
Come in with me, Thersites.   [*Exit.*]

THER. Here is such patchery,° such juggling, and
such knavery! All the argument is a cuckold and a
whore, a good quarrel to draw emulous° factions
and bleed to death upon. Now, the dry serpigo° on
the subject!° And war and lechery confound all! 82

[*Exit.*]

[*Enter* AGAMEMNON, ULYSSES, NESTOR, DIOMEDES, *and*
AJAX.]

AGAM. Where is Achilles?

PATR. Within his tent, but ill-disposed, my lord.

AGAM. Let it be known to him that we are here.
He shent° our messengers, and we lay by
Our appertainments,° visiting of him.   87
Let him be told so, lest perchance he think
We dare not move° the question of our place,°
Or know not what we are.

PATR.   I shall say so to him. [*Exit.*]

ULYSS. We saw him at the opening of his tent.
He is not sick.

AJAX. Yes, lion-sick, sick of proud heart. You may
call it melancholy, if you will favor the man, 95
but, by my head, 'tis pride. But why, why? Let him
show us the cause. A word, my lord.

[*Takes* AGAMEMNON *aside*]

NEST. What moves Ajax thus to bay° at him?

ULYSS. Achilles hath inveigled his fool from him.

NEST. Who, Thersites?   100

ULYSS. He.

NEST. Then will Ajax lack matter, if he have lost
his argument.°

ULYSS. No, you see he is his argument that 104
has his argument, Achilles.

NEST. All the better. Their fraction° is more our
wish than their faction. But it was a strong compo-
sure° a fool could disunite.

ULYSS. The amity that wisdom knits not, folly may
easily untie. [*Re-enter* PATROCLUS.] Here comes
Patroclus.   111

NEST. No Achilles with him.

ULYSS. The elephant hath joints, but none for
courtesy. His legs are legs for necessity, not for flex-
ure.°   115

---

76. patchery: pretense.   **80. emulous:** jealous.   **81. dry ser-
pigo:** eruptions on the skin.   **82. the subject:** everyone.
86. shent: rebuked.   **87. appertainments:** privileges of rank.
89. We . . . move: we are afraid of asserting. **place:** i.e., as com-
mander.   **98. bay:** bark.   **103. argument:** topic of conversa-
tion; i.e., Thersites. **106. fraction:** division, quarrel. **108. compo-
sure:** unity.   **115. flexure:** bending. It was once believed that
the elephant had no leg joints.

17. circumvention: cunning.   **21. Neapolitan boneache:** vene-
real disease.   **23. placket:** opening in a petticoat; i.e., wench.
27–28. gilt counterfeit: false money, counter; called also a slip.
31–32. bless thee: preserve you.   **33. blood . . . direction:** de-
sires lead you.   **36. lazars:** lepers.   **55. decline:** go through.

PATR. Achilles bids me say he is much sorry
If anything more than your sport and pleasure
Did move your greatness and this noble state
To call upon him. He hopes it is no other
But for your health and your digestion sake,　120
An after-dinner's breath.°
　AGAM.　　　　　　　　Hear you, Patroclus.
We are too well acquainted with these answers.
But his evasion, winged thus swift with scorn,
Cannot outfly our apprehensions.°
Much attribute° he hath, and much the reason　125
Why we ascribe it to him. Yet all his virtues,
Not virtuously on his own part beheld,
Do in our eyes begin to lose their gloss —
Yea, like fair fruit in an unwholesome dish,
Are like to rot untasted. Go and tell him　130
We come to speak with him, and you shall not sin
If you do say we think him overproud
And underhonest; in self-assumption greater
Than in the note of judgment; and worthier than
　　himself
Here tend° the savage strangeness he puts on,　135
Disguise the holy strength of their command,
And underwrite in an observing kind
His humorous predominance° — yea, watch
His pettish lunes,° his ebbs, his flows, as if
The passage and whole carriage of this action　140
Rode on his tide. Go tell him this, and add
That if he overhold his price so much,
We'll none of him, but let him, like an engine°
Not portable,° lie under this report:
"Bring action hither, this cannot go to war.　145
A stirring dwarf we do allowance give
Before a sleeping giant." Tell him so.
　PATR. I shall, and bring his answer presently.°
　　　　　　　　　　　　　　　　[Exit.]
　AGAM. In second voice we'll not be satisfied,　149
We come to speak with him. Ulysses, enter you.
　　　　　　　　　　　　　　　[Exit ULYSSES.]
　AJAX. What is he more than another?
　AGAM. No more than what he thinks he is.
　AJAX. Is he so much? Do you not think he thinks
himself a better man than I am?
　AGAM. No question.　　　　　　155
　AJAX. Will you subscribe° his thought and say he
is?
　AGAM. No, noble Ajax. You are as strong, as val-
iant, as wise, no less noble, much more gentle, and
altogether more tractable.　　　160
　AJAX. Why should a man be proud? How doth
pride grow? I know not what pride is.

　AGAM. Your mind is the clearer, Ajax, and your
virtues the fairer. He that is proud eats up himself.
Pride is his own glass, his own trumpet, his own
chronicle, and whatever praises itself but in the deed
devours the deed in the praise.
　AJAX. I do hate a proud man as I hate the engen-
dering of toads.　　　　　170
　NEST. [Aside] Yet he loves himself. Is 't not
strange?
　　　　　　　[Re-enter ULYSSES.]
　ULYSS. Achilles will not to the field tomorrow.
　AGAM. What's his excuse?
　ULYSS.　　　　　　He doth rely on none,
But carries on the stream of his dispose
Without observance or respect of any,　175
In will peculiar and in self-admission.°
　AGAM. Why will he not, upon our fair request,
Untent his person, and share the air with us?
　ULYSS. Things small as nothing, for request's sake
　　only°
He makes important. Possessed he is with greatness,
And speaks not to himself but with a pride　181
That quarrels at self-breath. Imagined worth
Holds in his blood such swoln and hot discourse
That 'twixt his mental and his active parts
Kingdomed° Achilles in commotion rages　185
And batters down himself. What should I say?
He is so plaguy proud that the death tokens° of it
Cry "No recovery."
　AGAM.　　　　　　Let Ajax go to him.
Dear lord, go you and greet him in his tent.
'Tis said he holds you well, and will be led　190
At your request a little from himself.
　ULYSS. O Agamemnon, let it not be so!
We'll consecrate the steps that Ajax makes
When they go from Achilles. Shall the proud lord
That bastes his arrogance with his own seam,°　195
And never suffers matter of the world
Enter his thoughts, save such as do revolve
And ruminate himself, shall he be worshiped
Of that we hold an idol more than he?°
No, this thrice worthy and right valiant lord　200
Must not so stale his palm,° nobly acquired,
Nor, by my will, assubjugate° his merit,
As amply titled as Achilles is,
By going to Achilles.
That were to enlard his fat-already pride,　205
And add more coals to Cancer when he burns
With entertaining great Hyperion.°
This lord go to him! Jupiter forbid,

---

121. breath: exercise.　124. outfly . . . apprehensions: outdis-
tance our understanding.　125. attribute: honor.　135. tend:
wait upon.　137–38. underwrite . . . predominance: submit to
but observe his moody superiority.　139. lunes: freaks.　143. en-
gine: military machine, battering-ram.　144. Not portable: too
heavy to be moved.　148. presently: immediately.　156. sub-
scribe: agree with.

176. self-admission: admitting only his own judgment.　179. for
. . . only: only because they are asked for.　185. Kingdomed:
like a kingdom.　187. death tokens: plague spots indicating that
the disease has taken a fatal turn.　195. seam: grease.　199. Of
. . . he: a man whom we regard as more worshipful than he.
201. stale . . . palm: make his glory cheap.　202. assubju-
gate: lower.　206–07. add . . . Hyperion: make summer hotter:
The sun (Hyperion) enters the sign of Cancer in June. See App. 2.

And say in thunder " Achilles go to him."

NEST. [*Aside*] Oh, this is well. He rubs the vein
of him.°   210

DIO. [*Aside*] And how his silence drinks up this
applause!

AJAX. If I go to him, with my armèd fist
I'll pash° him o'er the face.

AGAM. Oh, no, you shall not go.

AJAX. An a' be proud with me, I'll pheeze° his
pride.   215
Let me go to him.

ULYSS. Not for the worth that hangs upon our
quarrel.

AJAX. A paltry, insolent fellow!

NEST. [*Aside*] How he describes himself!

AJAX. Can he not be sociable?   220

ULYSS. [*Aside*] The raven chides blackness.

AJAX. I'll let his humors blood.°

AGAM. [*Aside*] He will be the physician that
should be the patient.

AJAX. An all men were o' my mind ——   225

ULYSS. [*Aside*] Wit would be out of fashion.

AJAX. A'° should not bear it so, a' should eat
swords first. Shall pride carry it?

NEST. [*Aside*] An 'twould, you 'd carry half.

ULYSS. [*Aside*] A' would have ten shares.   230

AJAX. I will knead him, I'll make him supple.

NEST. [*Aside*] He's not yet through° warm.
Force° him with praises. Pour in, pour in, his am-
bition is dry.

ULYSS. [*To* AGAMEMNON] My lord, you feed too
much on this dislike.

NEST. Our noble General, do not do so.

DIO. You must prepare to fight without Achilles.

ULYSS. Why, 'tis this naming of him does him
harm.
Here is a man — but 'tis before his face,   240
I will be silent.

NEST.   Wherefore should you so?
He is not emulous,° as Achilles is.

ULYSS. Know the whole world, he is as valiant.

AJAX. A whoreson dog, that shall palter thus with
us!
Would he were a Trojan!   245

NEST. What a vice were it in Ajax now ——

ULYSS. If he were proud ——

DIO. Or covetous of praise ——

ULYSS. Aye, or surly borne ——

DIO. Or strange,° or self-affected!°   250

ULYSS. Thank the Heavens, lord, thou art of sweet
composure.
Praise him that got° thee, she that gave thee suck.

Famed be thy tutor, and thy parts of nature
Thrice-famed beyond, beyond all erudition.°
But he that disciplined thine arms to fight,   255
Let Mars divide eternity in twain
And give him half. And for thy vigor,
Bull-bearing Milo° his addition yield°
To sinewy Ajax. I will not praise thy wisdom,
Which, like a bourn,° a pale,° a shore, confines
Thy spacious and dilated° parts. Here's Nestor,
Instructed by the antiquary times,   262
He must, he is, he cannot but be wise.
But pardon, Father Nestor, were your days
As green° as Ajax', and your brain so tempered,
You should not have the eminence of him,   266
But be as Ajax.

AJAX.   Shall I call you father?

NEST. Aye, my good son.

DIO.   Be ruled by him, Lord Ajax.

ULYSS. There is no tarrying here. The hart
Achilles
Keeps thicket. Please it our great General   270
To call together all his state of war.°
Fresh kings are come to Troy. Tomorrow
We must with all our main of° power stand fast.
And here's a lord, come knights from east to west,
And cull their flower,° Ajax shall cope the best.   275

AGAM. Go we to council. Let Achilles sleep.
Light boats sail swift, though greater hulks draw
deep.   [*Exeunt.*]

Act III

SCENE I. *Troy. A room in* PRIAM'S *palace.*

[*Enter* PANDARUS *and a* SERVANT.]

PAN. Friend you, pray you, a word. Do you not
follow° the young Lord Paris?

SERV. Aye, sir, when he goes before me.

PAN. You depend upon him, I mean?

SERV. Sir, I do depend upon the Lord.   5

PAN. You depend upon a noble gentleman. I must
needs praise him.

SERV. The Lord be praised!

PAN. You know me, do you not?

SERV. Faith, sir, superficially.   10

PAN. Friend, know me better. I am the Lord
Pandarus.

210. rubs . . . him: flatters his disposition.   213. pash: smash.
215. pheeze: do for.   222. I'll . . . blood: I'll bleed his moodi-
ness. Bleeding was a recognized remedy for many complaints.
227. A': he.   232. through: thoroughly.   233. Force: stuff.
242. emulous: envious.   250. strange: standoffish, haughty. self-
affected: conceited.   252. got: begot.

254. erudition: learning.   258. Milo: a prodigiously strong
Greek athlete. addition yield: give up his claims to fame.
260. bourn: boundary. pale: fence.   261. dilated: spread far
and wide.   265. green: young.   271. state of war: chief com-
manders.   273. main of: full.   275. cull . . . flower: i.e., take
the pick of them.
Act III, Sc. i: 2. follow: serve.

SERV. I hope I shall know your Honor better.

PAN. I do desire it.

SERV. You are in the state of grace.°   15

PAN. Grace! Not so, friend. Honor and lordship are my titles.° [*Music within*] What music is this?

SERV. I do but partly know, sir. It is music in parts.°   20

PAN. Know you the musicians?

SERV. Wholly, sir.

PAN. Who play they to?

SERV. To the hearers, sir.

PAN. At whose pleasure, friend?   25

SERV. At mine, sir, and theirs that love music.

PAN. Command, I mean, friend.

SERV. Who shall I command, sir?

PAN. Friend, we understand not one another. I am too courtly, and thou art too cunning.° At   30 whose request do these men play?

SERV. That's to 't, indeed, sir. Marry, sir, at the request of Paris my lord, who is there in person; with him, the mortal Venus, the heartblood of beauty, love's invisible soul.   35

PAN. Who, my cousin Cressida?

SERV. No, sir, Helen. Could not you find out that by her attributes?

PAN. It should seem, fellow, that thou hast not seen the Lady Cressida. I come to speak with   40 Paris from the Prince Troilus. I will make a complimental assault° upon him, for my business seethes.°

SERV. Sodden business! There's a stewed phrase indeed!

[*Enter* PARIS *and* HELEN, *attended.*]

PAN. Fair be to you, my lord, and to all this fair company! Fair desires, in all fair measure, fairly guide them! Especially to you, fair Queen! Fair thoughts be your fair pillow!   49

HELEN. Dear lord, you are full of fair words.

PAN. You speak your fair pleasure, sweet Queen. Fair Prince, here is good broken music.°

PAR. You have broke it, Cousin. And, by my life, you shall make it whole again, you shall piece it out° with a piece of your performance. Nell, he is full of harmony.   56

PAN. Truly, lady, no.

HELEN. O sir ——   59

PAN. Rude,° in sooth, in good sooth,° very rude.

PAR. Well said, my lord! Well, you say so in fits.°

PAN. I have business to my lord, dear Queen. My lord, will you vouchsafe me a word?

HELEN. Nay, this shall not hedge us out.   65 We'll hear you sing, certainly.

PAN. Well, sweet Queen, you are pleasant with me. But, marry, thus, my lord. My dear lord, and most esteemed friend, your brother Troilus ——   70

HELEN. My Lord Pandarus, honey-sweet lord ——

PAN. Go to, sweet Queen, go to — commends himself most affectionately to you ——

HELEN. You shall not bob° us out of our melody. If you do, our melancholy upon your head!   75

PAN. Sweet Queen, sweet Queen, that's a sweet Queen, i' faith.

HELEN. And to make a sweet lady sad is a sour offense.   80

PAN. Nay, that shall not serve your turn, that shall it not, in truth, la. Nay, I care not for such words, no, no. And my lord, he desires you that if the King call for him at supper, you will make his excuse.   85

HELEN. My Lord Pandarus ——

PAN. What says my sweet Queen, my very very sweet Queen?

PAR. What exploit 's in hand? Where sups he tonight?   90

HELEN. Nay, but, my lord ——

PAN. What says my sweet Queen? My cousin will fall out with you. You must not know where he sups.

PAR. I'll lay my life, with my disposer° Cressida.

PAN. No, no, no such matter, you are wide. Come, your disposer is sick.

PAR. Well, I'll make excuse.

PAN. Aye, good my lord. Why should you say Cressida? No, your poor disposer's sick.   101

PAR. I spy.

PAN. You spy! What do you spy? Come, give me an instrument. Now, sweet Queen.

HELEN. Why, this is kindly done.   105

PAN. My niece is horribly in love with a thing you have, sweet Queen.

HELEN. She shall have it, my lord, if it be not my lord Paris.

PAN. He! No, she'll none of him, they two are twain.°   111

HELEN. Falling in, after falling out, may make them three.

PAN. Come, come, I'll hear no more of this. I'll sing you a song now.   115

HELEN. Aye, aye, prithee now. By my troth, sweet lord, thou hast a fine forehead.

PAN. Aye, you may,° you may.

HELEN. Let thy song be love. This love will undo us all. O Cupid, Cupid, Cupid!   120

PAN. Love! Aye, that it shall, i' faith.

---

15. **state of grace:** highly favored.   16–17. **Grace . . . titles:** Pandarus, who is not used to the literal-mindedness of the servant, replies that *Grace* (the courtesy title of a Duke) is not appropriate — he is merely entitled to be called "your honor" or "your lordship."   19–20. **music in parts:** i.e., with several instruments.   30. **cunning:** clever.   41–42. **make . . . assault:** attack him with compliments.   42. **seethes:** is urgent; lit., boils. 52. **broken music:** music performed by different kinds of instruments.   54. **piece it out:** fill it up.   60. **Rude:** i.e., my voice is rough. **sooth:** truth.   61. **in fits:** in starts, with a pun on it meaning the division of a song or tune.

74. **bob:** cheat.   94. **disposer:** either one disposed to merriment, gay friend, or controller.   111. **twain:** separated.   118. **you may:** i.e., jest at my expense.

PAR. Aye, good now, love, love, nothing but love.

PAN. In good troth, it begins so. [*Sings.*]

"Love, love, nothing but love, still more!　125
　　For, oh, love's bow
　　Shoots buck and doe.
　　The shaft confounds,
　　Not that it wounds,
But tickles still the sore.°　130
These lovers cry 'Oh! oh!' they die.
　Yet that which seems the wound to kill,
Doth turn oh! oh! to ha! ha! he!
　So dying love lives still.
Oh! oh! a while, but ha! ha! ha!　135
Oh! oh! groans out for ha! ha! ha!"
Heigh-ho!

HELEN. In love, i' faith, to the very tip of the nose.

PAR. He eats nothing but doves, love, and that breeds hot blood, and hot blood begets hot thoughts, and hot thoughts beget hot deeds, and hot deeds is love.　143

PAN. Is this the generation° of love? Hot blood, hot thoughts, and hot deeds? Why, they are vipers. Is love a generation of vipers? Sweet lord, who's afield today?

PAR. Hector, Deiphobus, Helenus, Antenor, and all the gallantry of Troy. I would fain have armed today, but my Nell would not have it so. How chance my brother Troilus went not?　151

HELEN. He hangs the lip at° something. You know all, Lord Pandarus.

PAN. Not I, honey-sweet Queen. I long to hear how they sped today. You'll remember your brother's excuse?

PAR. To a hair.

PAN. Farewell, sweet Queen.

HELEN. Commend me to your niece.　159

PAN. I will, sweet Queen.　[*Exit.*]

[*A retreat sounded*]

PAR. They're come from field. Let us to Priam's hall
To greet the warriors. Sweet Helen, I must woo you
To help unarm our Hector. His stubborn buckles,
With these your white enchanting fingers touched,
Shall more obey than to the edge of steel　165
Or force of Greekish sinews. You shall do more
Than all the island kings° — disarm great Hector.

HELEN. 'Twill make us proud to be his servant, Paris.
Yea, what he shall receive of us in duty
Gives us more palm° in beauty than we have —
Yea, overshines ourself.　171

PAR. Sweet, above thought I love thee. [*Exeunt.*]

SCENE II. *An orchard to* PANDARUS' *house.*

[*Enter* PANDARUS *and* TROILUS' BOY, *meeting.*]

PAN. How now! Where's thy master? At my cousin Cressida's?

BOY. No, sir, he stays for you to conduct him thither.

PAN. Oh, here he comes. [*Enter* TROILUS.] How now, how now!　5

TRO. Sirrah,° walk off.　[*Exit* BOY.]

PAN. Have you seen my cousin?

TRO. No, Pandarus. I stalk about her door
Like a strange soul upon the Stygian° banks　10
Staying for waftage.° Oh, be thou my Charon,
And give me swift transportance to those fields
Where I may wallow in the lily beds
Proposed for the deserver! O gentle Pandarus,
From Cupid's shoulder pluck his painted wings,　15
And fly with me to Cressid!

PAN. Walk here i' the orchard, I'll bring her straight.　[*Exit.*]

TRO. I am giddy, expectation whirls me round.
The imaginary relish is so sweet　20
That it enchants my sense. What will it be
When that the watery palates taste indeed
Love's thrice repurèd° nectar? Death, I fear me,
Swounding° destruction, or some joy too fine,
Too subtle-potent, tuned too sharp in sweetness,　25
For the capacity of my ruder powers.
I fear it much, and I do fear besides
That I shall lose distinction in my joys,
As doth a battle when they charge on heaps
The enemy flying.　30

[*Re-enter* PANDARUS.]

PAN. She's making her ready, she'll come straight.
You must be witty now. She does so blush, and
fetches her wind so short, as if she were frayed with
a sprite:° I'll fetch her. It is the prettiest villain. She
fetches her breath as short as a new-ta'en sparrow.
[*Exit.*]

TRO. Even such a passion doth embrace my bosom.
My heart beats thicker than a feverous pulse,
And all my powers do their bestowing lose,
Like vassalage° at unawares encountering　40
The eye of majesty.

[*Re-enter* PANDARUS *with* CRESSIDA.]

PAN. Come, come, what need you blush? Shame's
a baby. Here she is now. Swear the oaths now to her
that you have sworn to me. What, are you gone
again? You must be watched ere you be made tame,
must you? Come your ways, come your ways. An

---

130. **sore:** lit., a buck in its fourth year, with a pun on *sore*, meaning hurt. 144. **generation:** descent, breeding. 152. **hangs . . . at:** is troubled by. 167. **island kings:** kings of the Greek isles. 170. **palm:** reward.

Sc. ii: 6. **Sirrah:** term of address used to an inferior. 10. **Stygian:** the river Styx, which surrounded the underworld and across which souls were transported by Charon the ferryman. 11. **waftage:** passage. 23. **repured:** refined. 24. **Swounding:** swooning. 33-34. **frayed . . . sprite:** frightened by a ghost. 40. **vassalage:** a servant.

you draw backward, we'll put you i' the fills.° Why
do you not speak to her? Come, draw this curtain°
and let's see your picture. Alas the day, how　49
loath you are to offend daylight! An 'twere dark,
you'd close sooner. So, so, rub on, and kiss the
mistress.° How now! A kiss in fee farm!° Build
there, carpenter, the air is sweet. Nay, you shall fight
your hearts out ere I part you. The falcon as the
tercel,° for all the ducks i' the river. Go to, go to.　56

TRO. You have bereft me of all words, lady.

PAN. Words pay no debts, give her deeds. But
she'll bereave you o' the deeds too if she call your
activity in question. What, billing again? Here's "In
witness whereof the parties interchangeably"°　62
——Come in, come in. I'll go get a fire.

　　　　　　　　　　　　　　　　　[*Exit.*]

CRES. Will you walk in, my lord?

TRO. O Cressida, how often have I wished me
thus!

CRES. Wished, my lord? —The gods grant——
O my lord!

TRO. What should they grant? What makes this
pretty abruption?° What too curious dreg espies my
sweet lady in the fountain of our love?　71

CRES. More dregs than water, if my fears have
eyes.

TRO. Fears make devils of cherubins, they never
see truly.　75

CRES. Blind fear that seeing reason leads finds
safer footing than blind reason stumbling without
fear. To fear the worst oft cures the worse.　79

TRO. Oh, let my lady apprehend no fear. In all
Cupid's pageant there is presented no monster.

CRES. Nor nothing monstrous neither?

TRO. Nothing but our undertakings—when we
vow to weep seas, live in fire, eat rocks, tame tigers,
thinking it harder for our mistress to devise impo-
sition enough than for us to undergo any difficulty
imposed. This is the monstruosity in love, lady, that
the will is infinite and the execution confined, that
the desire is boundless and the act a slave to limit.°

CRES. They say all lovers swear more per-　91
formance than they are able, and yet reserve an abil-
ity that they never perform, vowing more than the
perfection of ten, and discharging less than the tenth
part of one. They that have the voice of lions and the
act of hares, are they not monsters?　96

TRO. Are there such? Such are not we. Praise us
as we are tasted, allow us as we prove, our head
shall go bare till merit crown it. No perfection in

reversion° shall have a praise in present. We will not
name desert° before his birth, and being born, his
addition° shall be humble. Few words to fair faith.
Troilus shall be such to Cressid as what envy can say
worst shall be a mock for his truth, and what truth
can speak truest, not truer than Troilus.°　106

CRES. Will you walk in, my lord?

　　　　　　　[*Re-enter* PANDARUS.]

PAN. What, blushing still? Have you not done
talking yet?

CRES. Well, Uncle, what folly I commit, I dedicate
to you.

PAN. I thank you for that. If my lord get a boy of
you, you'll give him me. Be true to my lord. If he
flinch, chide me for it.

TRO. You know now your hostages — your un-
cle's word and my firm faith.　116

PAN. Nay, I'll give my word for her too. Our kin-
dred, though they be long ere they are wooed, they
are constant being won. They are burrs, I can tell
you, they'll stick where they are thrown.　120

CRES. Boldness comes to me now, and brings me
heart.
Prince Troilus, I have loved you night and day
For many weary months.

TRO. Why was my Cressid then so hard to win?

CRES. Hard to seem won. But I was won, my lord,
With the first glance that ever — pardon me,　126
If I confess much, you will play the tyrant.
I love you now, but not, till now, so much
But I might master it. In faith, I lie.
My thoughts were like unbridled° children, grown
Too headstrong for their mother. See, we fools!　131
Why have I blabbed? Who shall be true to us
When we are so unsecret to ourselves?
But though I loved you well, I wooed you not.
And yet, good faith, I wished myself a man,　135
Or that we women had men's privilege
Of speaking first. Sweet, bid me hold my tongue,
For in this rapture° I shall surely speak
The thing I shall repent. See, see, your silence,
Cunning in dumbness, from my weakness draws
My very soul of counsel!° Stop my mouth.　141

TRO. And shall, albeit sweet music issues thence.

PAN. Pretty, i' faith.

CRES. My lord, I do beseech you pardon me,
'Twas not my purpose thus to beg a kiss.　145
I am ashamed. Oh heavens, what have I done?
For this time will I take my leave, my lord.

TRO. Your leave, sweet Cressid?

---

47. fills: shafts (of a cart).　48. curtain: veil.　51–52. rub
. . . mistress: a metaphor from bowls. *rub on:* roll on. *mistress:*
the "jack." See App. 13.　52. fee farm: perpetual possession.
56. tercel: male of a small species of hawk.　61–62. In . . .
interchangeably: a legal phrase in agreements, which continues
"set to their hands and seals."　70. abruption: breaking off.
90. slave to limit: only able to be performed to a limited
degree.

99–100. in reversion: a legal phrase meaning property which
will pass on the death of some other person; so "in the future."
101. desert: merit.　102. addition: title.　102–06. Few . . .
Troilus: good faith needs few words. Troilus will be so true to
Cressida that the worst that Envy can utter will be a mockery of
the truth, and when Truth is speaking its truest, it will not be
truer than Troilus.　130. unbridled: uncontrolled.　138. rapture:
ecstasy.　141. soul of counsel: secret of my heart.

PAN. Leave! An you take leave till tomorrow
morning ——   150
  CRES. Pray you content you.
  TRO. What offends you, lady?
  CRES. Sir, mine own company.
  TRO. You cannot shun yourself.
  CRES. Let me go and try.
I have a kind of self resides with you,   155
But an unkind self that itself will leave
To be another's fool. I would be gone.
Where is my wit? I know not what I speak.
  TRO. Well know they what they speak that speak
    so wisely.
  CRES. Perchance, my lord, I show more craft than
    love,   160
And fell so roundly° to a large° confession
To angle for your thoughts. But you are wise,
Or else you love not, for to be wise and love
Exceeds man's might, that dwells with gods above.
  TRO. Oh, that I thought it could be in a woman —
As, if it can, I will presume in you —   166
To feed for aye her lamp and flames of love,
To keep her constancy in plight° and youth,
Outliving beauty's outward, with a mind
That doth renew swifter than blood decays!   170
Or that persuasion could but thus convince me
That my integrity and truth to you
Might be affronted with the match and weight°
Of such a winnowed purity in love.
How were I then uplifted! But alas!   175
I am as true as truth's simplicity,
And simpler than the infancy of truth.
  CRES. In that I'll war with you.
  TRO.   Oh, virtuous fight
When right with right wars who shall be most right!
True swains° in love shall in the world to come   180
Approve° their truths by Troilus. When their
    rhymes,
Full of protest, of oath and big compare,
Want similes, truth tired with iteration° —
" As true as steel, as plantage to the moon,°
As sun to day, as turtle° to her mate,   185
As iron to adamant,° as earth to the center " —
Yet, after all comparisons of truth,
As truth's authentic author to be cited,
" As true as Troilus " shall crown up the verse
And sanctify the numbers.°
  CRES.   Prophet may you be! 190
If I be false, or swerve a hair from truth,
When time is old and hath forgot itself,
When waterdrops have worn the stones of Troy,

And blind oblivion swallowed cities up,
And mighty states characterless are grated°   195
To dusty nothing, yet let memory,
From false to false, among false maids in love,
Upbraid my falsehood! When they've said " as false
As air, as water, wind, or sandy earth,
As fox to lamb, or wolf to heifer's calf,   200
Pard° to the hind, or stepdame to her son,
" Yea," let them say, to stick the heart of falsehood,
" As false as Cressid."
  PAN. Go to, a bargain made. Seal it, seal it, I'll be
the witness. Here I hold your hand, here my cousin's.
If ever you prove false one to another, since I have
taken such pains to bring you together, let all pitiful
goers-between be called to the world's end after my
name — call them all Pandars, let all constant men
be Troiluses, all false women Cressids, and all brok-
ers-between Pandars! Say " Amen."
  TRO. Amen.
  CRES. Amen.   214
  PAN. Amen. Whereupon I will show you a cham-
ber with a bed, which bed, because it shall not speak
of your pretty encounters, press it to death.° Away!
              [*Exeunt* TROILUS *and* CRESSIDA.]
And Cupid grant all tongue-tied maidens here
Bed, chamber, Pandar to provide this gear! [*Exit.*]

SCENE III. *The Grecian camp.*

[*Flourish. Enter* AGAMEMNON, ULYSSES, DIOMEDES,
  NESTOR, AJAX, MENELAUS, *and* CALCHAS.]
  CAL. Now, Princes, for the service I have done
    you,
The advantage of the time prompts me aloud
To call for recompense. Appear it to your mind
That, through the sight I bear in things to love,
I have abandoned Troy, left my possession,   5
Incurred a traitor's name, exposed myself,
From certain and possessed conveniences,
To doubtful fortunes, sequestering° from me all
That time, acquaintance, custom, and condition
Made tame and most familiar to my nature,   10
And here, to do you service, am become
As new into the world, strange, unacquainted.
I do beseech you, as in way of taste,°
To give me now a little benefit
Out of those many registered in promise,   15
Which you say live to come in my behalf.
  AGAM. What wouldst thou of us, Trojan? Make
    demand.
  CAL. You have a Trojan prisoner called Antenor,
Yesterday took. Troy holds him very dear.
Oft have you — often have you thanks therefore —

---

161. roundly: directly. large: full.   168. plight: promise.
173. affronted . . . weight: met by equal truth.   180. swains:
lovers.   181. Approve: confirm.   183. iteration: simile.
184. plantage . . . moon: as plants are true to the moon. It is
still a very general belief that the growth of plants is controlled
by the moon.   185. turtle: dove.   186. adamant: the hardest
steel.   190. numbers: verses.

195. characterless . . . grated: are ground so small that not a
letter remains.   201. Pard: panther.   217. press . . . death: see
Gen. Intro. p. 27b.
    Sc. iii: 8. sequestering: separating.   13. taste: foretaste.

Desired my Cressid in right great exchange,   21
Whom Troy hath still° denied. But this Antenor
I know is such a wrest° in their affairs
That their negotiations all must slack
Wanting his manage, and they will almost   25
Give us a prince of blood, a son of Priam,
In change of him. Let him be sent, great Princes,
And he shall buy my daughter, and her presence
Shall quite strike off° all service I have done
In most accepted pain.°
    AGAM.   Let Diomedes bear him,   30
And bring us Cressid hither. Calchas shall have
What he requests of us. Good Diomed,
Furnish you° fairly for this interchange.
Withal, bring word if Hector will tomorrow
Be answered in his challenge. Ajax is ready.   35
    DIO. This shall I undertake, and 'tis a burden
Which I am proud to bear.
                [*Exeunt* DIOMEDES *and* CALCHAS.]
[*Enter* ACHILLES *and* PATROCLUS, *before their tent.*]
    ULYSS. Achilles stands i' the entrance of his tent.
Please it° our General pass strangely by him,
As if he were forgot, and, Princes all,   40
Lay negligent and loose regard° upon him.
I will come last. 'Tis like he'll question me
Why such unplausive° eyes are bent on him.
If so, I have derision medicinable
To use between your strangeness and his pride,   45
Which his own will shall have desire to drink.
It may do good. Pride hath no other glass
To show itself but pride, for supple knees
Feed arrogance and are the proud man's fees.
    AGAM. We'll execute your purpose and put on   50
A form of strangeness as we pass along.
So do each lord, and either greet him not
Or else disdainfully, which shall shake him more
Than if not looked on. I will lead the way.
    ACHIL. What, comes the General to speak with
      me?   55
You know my mind, I'll fight no more 'gainst Troy.
    AGAM. What says Achilles? Would he aught with
    us?
    NEST. Would you, my lord, aught with the General?
    ACHIL. No.
    NEST. Nothing, my lord.   60
    AGAM. The better.
             [*Exeunt* AGAMEMNON *and* NESTOR.]
    ACHIL. Good day, good day.
    MEN. How do you? How do you?   [*Exit.*]
    ACHIL. What, does the cuckold scorn me?
    AJAX. How now, Patroclus!   65

    ACHIL. Good morrow, Ajax.
    AJAX. Ha?
    ACHIL. Good morrow.
    AJAX. Aye, and good next day too.   [*Exit.*]
    ACHIL. What mean these fellows? Know they not
    Achilles?   70
    PATR. They pass by strangely. They were used to
    bend,
To send their smiles before them to Achilles,
To come as humbly as they used to creep
To holy altars.
    ACHIL.   What, am I poor of late?   74
'Tis certain greatness, once fall'n out with fortune,
Must fall out with men too. What the declined is,
He shall as soon read in the eyes of others
As feel in his own fall. For men, like butterflies,
Show not their mealy° wings but to the summer,
And not a man, for being simply man,   80
Hath any honor but honor for those honors
That are without him, as place, riches, and favor,
Prizes of accident as oft as merit.
Which when they fall, as being slippery standers,
The love that leaned on them as slippery too,   85
Do one pluck down another and together
Die in the fall. But 'tis not so with me.
Fortune and I are friends. I do enjoy
At ample point° all that I did possess,
Save these men's looks, who do methinks find out
Something not worth in me such rich beholding   91
As they have often given. Here is Ulysses.
I'll interrupt his reading.
How now, Ulysses!
    ULYSS.   Now, great Thetis' son!
    ACHIL. What are you reading?
    ULYSS.   A strange fellow here   95
Writes me: " That man, how dearly ever parted,°
How much in having, or without or in,
Cannot make boast to have that which he hath,
Nor feels not what he owes,° but by reflection,
As when his virtues shining upon others   100
Heat them, and they retort that heat again
To the first giver."
    ACHIL.   This is not strange, Ulysses.
The beauty that is borne here in the face
The bearer knows not, but commends itself
To others' eyes. Nor doth the eye itself,   105
That most pure spirit of sense, behold itself,
Not going from itself, but eye to eye opposed
Salutes each other with each other's form.
For speculation° turns not to itself
Till it hath traveled and is mirrored there   110

---

22. **still:** always.   23. **wrest:** controlling instrument; lit.,
the key which tightens the pegs in a musical instrument.
29. **strike off:** pay for.   30. **accepted pain:** agreeable labor.
33. **Furnish you:** equip yourself.   39. **Please it:** let it please
. . . to.   41. **regard:** look.   43. **unplausive:** disapproving.

79. **mealy:** powdery.   89. **At . . . point:** fully.   96. **how . . .
parted:** however richly endowed.   99. **owes:** owns.   109. **specu-
lation:** power of sight. It was thought that the eye shot out a
beam (like a searchlight) which caused the object to be visible
to the beholder. So in this image *speculation* cannot see itself
until the beam has passed out and been reflected back.

Where it may see itself. This is not strange at all.

ULYSS. I do not strain at the position —°
It is familiar — but at the author's drift,
Who in his circumstance expressly proves
That no man is the lord of anything,   115
Though in and of him there be much consisting,
Till he communicate his parts to others.
Nor doth he of himself know them for aught
Till he behold them formed in the applause
Where they're extended,° who, like an arch, rever-
     berates   120
The voice again, or like a gate of steel
Fronting the sun, receives and renders back
His figure and his heat. I was much rapt in° this,
And apprehended here immediately
The unknown Ajax.   125
Heavens, what a man is there! A very horse,
That has he knows not what. Nature, what things
     there are,
Most abject in regard and dear in use!°
What things again most dear in the esteem   129
And poor in worth! Now shall we see tomorrow —
An act that very chance doth throw upon him —
Ajax renowned. O heavens, what some men do
While some men leave to do!
How some men creep in skittish fortune's hall
Whiles others play the idiots in her eyes!   135
How one man eats into another's pride
While pride is fasting in his wantonness!
To see these Grecian lords! Why, even already
They clap the lubber° Ajax on the shoulder
As if his foot were on brave Hector's breast   140
And great Troy shrieking.

ACHIL. I do believe it, for they passed by me
As misers do by beggars, neither gave to me
Good word nor look. What, are my deeds forgot?

ULYSS. Time hath, my lord, a wallet at his back   146
Wherein he puts alms for oblivion,
A great-sized monster of ingratitudes.
Those scraps are good deeds past, which are de-
     voured
As fast as they are made, forgot as soon
As done. Perseverance, dear my lord,   150
Keeps honor bright. To have done is to hang
Quite out of fashion, like a rusty mail
In monumental mockery.° Take the instant way,
For honor travels in a strait° so narrow,
Where one but goes abreast. Keep then the path,
For emulation° hath a thousand sons   156
That one by one pursue. If you give way,
Or hedge aside from the direct forthright,°

Like to an entered tide they all rush by
And leave you hindmost.   160
Or like a gallant horse fall'n in first rank,
Lie there for pavement to the abject rear,
O'errun and trampled on. Then what they do in
     present,
Though less than yours in past, must o'ertop yours.
For time is like a fashionable host   165
That slightly shakes his parting guest by the hand,
And with his arms outstretched, as he would fly,
Grasps in the comer. Welcome ever smiles,
And farewell goes out sighing. Oh, let not virtue seek
Remuneration for the thing it was;   170
For beauty, wit,
High birth, vigor of bone, desert in service,
Love, friendship, charity, are subjects all
To envious and calumniating time.   174
One touch of nature makes the whole world kin,°
That all with one consent praise newborn gawds,°
Though they are made and molded of things past,
And give to dust that is a little gilt
More laud than gilt o'erdusted.
The present eye praises the present object.   180
Then marvel not, thou great and complete man,
That all the Greeks begin to worship Ajax,
Since things in motion sooner catch the eye
Than what not stirs. The cry went once on thee,
And still it might, and yet it may again,   185
If thou wouldst not entomb thyself alive
And case thy reputation in thy tent,
Whose glorious deeds, but in these fields of late,
Made emulous missions 'mongst the gods them-
     selves,
And drave great Mars to faction.°

ACHIL.   Of this my privacy   190
I have strong reasons.

ULYSS.   But 'gainst your privacy
The reasons are more potent and heroical.
'Tis known, Achilles, that you are in love
With one of Priam's daughters.°

ACHIL.   Ha! Known?

ULYSS. Is that a wonder?   195
The providence that's in a watchful state
Knows almost every grain of Plutus'° gold,
Finds bottom in the uncomprehensive° deeps,
Keeps place with thought, and almost like the gods
Does thoughts unveil in their dumb cradles.   200
There is a mystery, with whom relation
Durst never meddle,° in the soul of state,
Which hath an operation more divine

---

112. **position:** assertion.   120. **extended:** bestowed.   123. **rapt in:** taken by.   128. **abject . . . use:** despised but invaluable. 139. **lubber:** lout.   152–53. **rusty . . . mockery:** neglected suit of armor, which is a mocking memorial of the knight who once wore it.   154. **strait:** path.   156. **emulation:** jealousy.   158. **forthright:** straightforward path.

175. **One . . . kin:** one natural inclination (*touch*) unites everyone.   176. **gawds:** trifles.   189–90. **Made . . . faction:** caused the gods to grow jealous and take sides (*to faction*). In the *Iliad* each of the heroes was the favorite of one of the gods or goddesses, who were constantly squabbling.   194. **one . . . daughters:** i.e., Polyxena.   197. **Plutus:** god of wealth.   198. **uncomprehensive:** unplumbed.   201–02. **relation . . . meddle:** that which must never be pried into.

Than breath or pen can give expressure to.
All the commerce that you have had with **Troy**   205
As perfectly is ours as yours, my lord,
And better would it fit Achilles much
To throw down Hector than Polyxena.
But it must grieve young Pyrrhus° now at home
When fame shall in our islands sound her trump,
And all the Greekish girls shall tripping sing   211
"Great Hector's sister did Achilles win,
But our great Ajax bravely beat down him."
Farewell, my lord. I as your lover speak.
The fool slides o'er the ice that you should break.

                           [Exit.]

PATR. To this effect, Achilles, have I moved you.
A woman impudent and mannish grown
Is not more loathed than an effeminate man
In time of action. I stand condemned for this,
They think my little stomach° to the war   220
And your great love to me restrains you thus.
Sweet, rouse yourself, and the weak wanton Cupid
Shall from your neck unloose his amorous fold
And, like a dewdrop from the lion's mane,
Be shook to air.

ACHIL.   Shall Ajax fight with Hector?   225
PATR. Aye, and perhaps receive much honor by
    him.
ACHIL. I see my reputation is at stake,°
My fame is shrewdly gored.°
PATR.   Oh, then beware.
Those wounds heal ill that men do give themselves.
Omission to do what is necessary   230
Seals a commission to a blank of danger,°
And danger, like an ague, subtly taints
Even then when we sit idly in the sun.
ACHIL. Go call Thersites hither, sweet Patroclus.
I'll send the fool to Ajax, and desire him   235
To invite the Trojan lords after the combat
To see us here unarmed. I have a woman's longing,°
An appetite that I am sick withal,
To see great Hector in his weeds° of peace,
To talk with him, and to behold his visage,   240
Even to my full of view.

              [Enter THERSITES.*]*

           — A labor saved!

THER. A wonder!
ACHIL. What?
THER. Ajax goes up and down the field asking for
himself.   245
ACHIL. How so?
THER. He must fight singly tomorrow with Hec-
tor, and is so prophetically proud of a heroical cudg-
eling that he raves in saying nothing.

ACHIL. How can that be?   250
THER. Why, a' stalks up and down like a peacock
—a stride and a stand. Ruminates like a hostess°
that hath no arithmetic but her brain to set down her
reckoning. Bites his lip with a politic regard,° as
who should say " There were wit in this head, an
'twould out." And so there is, but it lies as coldly in
him as fire in a flint, which will not show without
knocking. The man's undone forever, for if Hector
break not his neck i' the combat, he'll break 't him-
self in vainglory. He knows not me. I said, " Good
morrow, Ajax," and he replies " Thanks, Agamem-
non." What think you of this man, that takes me for
the General? He's grown a very land fish,° lan-
guageless, a monster. A plague of opinion!° A man
may wear it on both sides, like a leather jerkin.   266
ACHIL. Thou must be my ambassador to him,
Thersites.
THER. Who, I? Why, he'll answer nobody, he pro-
fesses not answering. Speaking is for beggars, he
wears his tongue in 's arms. I will put on his pres-
ence.° Let Patroclus make demands to me, you shall
see the pageant° of Ajax.   273
ACHIL. To him, Patroclus. Tell him I humbly de-
sire the valiant Ajax to invite the most valorous Hec-
tor to come unarmed to my tent, and to procure safe-
conduct for his person of the magnanimous and
most illustrious six-or-seven-times-honored Captain
General of the Grecian army, Agamemnon, et cetera.
Do this.   280
PATR. Jove bless great Ajax!
THER. Hum!
PATR. I come from the worthy Achilles ——
THER. Ha!
PATR. Who most humbly desires you to invite
Hector to his tent ——
THER. Hum!
PATR. And to procure safe-conduct from Aga-
memnon.
THER. Agamemnon?   290
PATR. Aye, my lord.
THER. Ha!
PATR. What say you to 't?
THER. God be wi' you, with all my heart.
PATR. Your answer, sir.
THER. If tomorrow be a fair day, by eleven of the
clock it will go one way or other. Howsoever, he
shall pay for me ere he has me.
PATR. Your answer, sir.
THER. Fare you well, with all my heart.   300
ACHIL. Why, but he is not in this tune, is he?
THER. No, but he's out o' tune thus. What music
will be in him when Hector has knocked out his

---

209. **Pyrrhus:** Achilles' son.   220. **stomach:** appetite.   227. **at stake:** See App. 5.   228. **shrewdly gored:** grievously wounded. 231. **Seals . . . danger:** gives danger a blank check.   237. **woman's longing:** the insatiable longing of a pregnant woman. 239. **weeds:** garments.

252. **hostess:** tavernkeeper.   254. **politic regard:** the look of a politician.   264. **land fish:** freak of nature.   265. **opinion:** conceit.   271–72. **put . . . presence:** imitate his manner. 273. **pageant:** play.

brains I know not, but I am sure none unless the
fiddler Apollo get his sinews to make catlings° on.

ACHIL. Come, thou shalt bear a letter to him
straight.   308

THER. Let me bear another to his horse, for that's
the more capable° creature.

ACHIL. My mind is troubled like a fountain
stirred,
And I myself see not the bottom of it.

[*Exeunt* ACHILLES *and* PATROCLUS.]

THER. Would the fountain of your mind were
clear again, that I might water an ass at it! I had
rather be a tick in a sheep than such a valiant   315
ignorance.   [*Exit*]

Act IV

SCENE I. *Troy. A street.*

[*Enter, at one side,* AENEAS, *and* SERVANT *with a
torch; at the other,* PARIS, DEIPHOBUS, ANTENOR,
DIOMEDES, *and others, with torches.*]

PAR. See, ho! Who is that there?

DEI. It is the Lord Aeneas.

AENE. Is the Prince there in person?
Had I so good occasion to lie long
As you, Prince Paris, nothing but heavenly business
Should rob my bedmate of my company.   5

DIO. That's my mind too. Good morrow, Lord
Aeneas.

PAR. A valiant Greek, Aeneas — take his hand —
Witness the process° of your speech, wherein
You told how Diomed a whole week by days
Did haunt you in the field.

AENE. Health to you, valiant sir,   10
During all question° of the gentle truce.
But when I meet you armed, as black defiance
As heart can think or courage execute.

DIO. The one and other Diomed embraces.
Our bloods are now in calm, and, so long, health.
But when contention and occasion° meet,   16
By Jove, I'll play the hunter for thy life
With all my force, pursuit, and policy.°

AENE. And thou shalt hunt a lion that will fly
With his face backward. In humane gentleness, 20
Welcome to Troy! Now, by Anchises'° life,
Welcome indeed! By Venus' hand I swear
No man alive can love in such a sort
The thing he means to kill more excellently.

DIO. We sympathize.° Jove, let Aeneas live,   25

If to my sword his fate be not the glory,
A thousand complete courses of the sun!
But in mine emulous honor, let him die,
With every joint a wound, and that tomorrow.

AENE. We know each other well.   30

DIO. We do, and long to know each other worse.

PAR. This is the most despiteful° gentle greeting,
The noblest hateful love, that e'er I heard of.
What business, lord, so early?

AENE. I was sent for to the King, but why I know
not.   35

PAR. His purpose meets you. 'Twas to bring this
Greek
To Calchas' house, and there to render° him,
For the enfreed Antenor, the fair Cressid.
Let's have your company, or, if you please,
Haste there before us. I constantly do think,   40
Or rather, call my thought a certain knowledge,
My brother Troilus lodges there tonight.
Rouse him and give him note of our approach,
With the whole quality° wherefore. I fear
We shall be much unwelcome.

AENE.   That I assure you.   45
Troilus had rather Troy were borne to Greece
Than Cressid borne from Troy.

PAR.   There is no help,
The bitter disposition of the time
Will have it so. On, lord, we'll follow you.   49

AENE. Good morrow, all. [*Exit with* SERVANT.]

PAR. And tell me, noble Diomed, faith, tell me
true,
Even in the soul of sound good-fellowship,
Who, in your thoughts, deserves fair Helen best,
Myself or Menelaus?

DIO.   Both alike.
He merits well to have her that doth seek her   55
Not making any scruple of her soilure,°
With such a Hell of pain and world of charge.°
And you as well to keep her that defend her
Not palating° the taste of her dishonor
With such a costly loss of wealth and friends. 60
He, like a puling cuckold, would drink up
The lees and dregs of a flat tamed piece.°
You, like a lecher, out of whorish loins
Are pleased to breed out your inheritors.°
Both merits poised, each weighs nor less nor more,
But he as he, the heavier for a whore.°   66

PAR. You are too bitter to your countrywoman.

DIO. She's bitter to her country. Hear me, Paris.
For every false drop in her bawdy veins
A Grecian's life hath sunk; for every scruple°   70

---

306. catlings: catgut fiddle strings.   310. capable: intelligent.
Act IV, Sc. i: 8. process: gist.   11. question: converse.
16. occasion: opportunity.   18. policy: cunning.   21. Anchises:
father of Aeneas, whose mother was Venus.   25. sympathize:
have the same feeling.

32. despiteful: hateful.   37. render: restore.   44. quality:
nature of the business.   56. Not . . . soilure: regardless of her
dishonor.   57. charge: expense.   59. palating: relishing.
62. flat . . . piece: woman whose best has been enjoyed by oth-
ers.   64. inheritors: children.   65–66. each . . . whore: both
weigh alike, but you who have her are heavier for having a whore
as wife.   70. scruple: smallest part.

Of her contaminated carrion weight
A Trojan hath been slain. Since she could speak,
She hath not given so many good words breath
As for her Greeks and Trojans suffered death.

PAR. Fair Diomed, you do as chapmen° do,　75
Dispraise the thing that you desire to buy.
But we in silence hold this virtue well,
We'll not commend what we intend to sell.
Here lies our way.　　　　　　　　　[*Exeunt.*]

SCENE II. *Court of* PANDARUS' *house.*

[*Enter* TROILUS *and* CRESSIDA.]

TRO. Dear, trouble not yourself. The morn is cold.
CRES. Then, sweet my lord, I'll call mine uncle
　　down.
He shall unbolt the gates.
TRO.　　　　　　　　　　Trouble him not.
To bed, to bed. Sleep kill° those pretty eyes,
And give as soft attachment° to thy senses　5
As infants' empty of all thought!
CRES.　　　　　　　　　Good morrow, then.
TRO. I prithee now, to bed.
CRES.　　　　　　　　Are you aweary of me?
TRO. O Cressida! But that the busy day,
Waked by the lark, hath roused the ribald crows,
And dreaming night will hide our joys no longer,
I would not from thee.
CRES.　　　　　　　Night hath been too brief.
TRO. Beshrew° the witch! With venomous
　　wights° she stays　　　　　　　　12
As tediously as Hell, but flies the grasps of love
With wings more momentary-swift than thought.
You will catch cold, and curse me.
CRES.　　　　　　　　　Prithee tarry.　15
You men will never tarry.
O foolish Cressid! I might have still held off,
And then you would have tarried. Hark! There's
　　one up.
PAN. [*Within*] What, 's all the doors open here?
TRO. It is your uncle.　　　　　　　20
CRES. A pestilence on him! Now will he be mock-
　　ing.
I shall have such a life!

[*Enter* PANDARUS.]

PAN. How now, how now! How go° maiden-
heads? Here, you maid! Where's my cousin Cressid?
CRES. Go hang yourself, you naughty mocking
　　uncle!　　　　　　　　　　　26
You bring me to do — and then you flout me too.
PAN. To do what? To do what? Let her say what.
What have I brought you to do?

CRES. Come, come, beshrew your heart! You'll
　　ne'er be good,　　　　　　　　30
Nor suffer others.
PAN. Ha, ha! Alas, poor wretch! A poor capoc-
chia!° Hast not slept tonight? Would he not, a
naughty man, let it sleep? A bugbear take him!
CRES. Did not I tell you? Would he were knocked
　　i' the head!　　　　　　[*One knocks.*]　35
Who's that at door? Good Uncle, go and see.
My lord, come you again into my chamber.
You smile and mock me, as if I meant naughtily.
TRO. Ha, ha!
CRES. Come, you are deceived, I think of no such
　　thing.　　　　　　　　[*Knocking.*]　40
How earnestly they knock! Pray you come in.
I would not for half Troy have you seen here.
　　　　　[*Exeunt* TROILUS *and* CRESSIDA.]
PAN. Who's there? What's the matter? Will you
beat down the door? How now! What's the matter?

[*Enter* AENEAS.]

AENE. Good morrow, lord, good morrow.　46
PAN. Who's there? My Lord Aeneas! By my troth,
I knew you not. What news with you so early?
AENE. Is not Prince Troilus here?
PAN. Here! What should he do here?　　50
AENE. Come, he is here, my lord, do not deny
　　him.
It doth import him much° to speak with me.
PAN. Is he here, say you? 'Tis more than I know,
I'll be sworn. For my own part, I came in late. What
should he do here?　　　　　　　55
AENE. Who! Nay then, come, come, you'll do him
wrong ere you are ware. You'll be so true to him to
be false to him. Do not you know of him, but yet go
fetch him hither, go.

[*Re-enter* TROILUS.]

TRO. How now! What's the matter?　60
AENE. My lord, I scarce have leisure to salute you,
My matter is so rash.° There is at hand
Paris your brother and Deiphobus,
The Grecian Diomed, and our Antenor
Delivered to us, and for him forthwith,　65
Ere the first sacrifice, within this hour,
We must give up to Diomedes' hand
The Lady Cressida.
TRO.　　　　　　Is it so concluded?
AENE. By Priam and the general state° of Troy.
They are at hand and ready to effect it.　70
TRO. How my achievements° mock me!
I will go meet them. And, my Lord Aeneas,
We met by chance, you did not find me here.
AENE. Good, good, my lord. The secrets of nature
Have not more gift in taciturnity.　75
　　　　　[*Exeunt* TROILUS *and* AENEAS.]

---

75. chapmen: haggling traders.
Sc. ii: 4. kill: overcome.　5. attachment: seizure.　12. Be-
shrew: curse. wights: men.　23. How go: what's the price of.

33. capocchia: lit., knob of stick (used obscenely).　52. It . . .
much: it is of great importance for him.　62. rash: urgent.
69. state: assembly.　71. achievements: winnings, luck.

PAN. Is 't possible? No sooner got but lost? The devil take Antenor! The young Prince will go mad. A plague upon Antenor! I would they had broke 's neck!

[Re-enter CRESSIDA.]

CRES. How now! What's the matter? Who was here?   81

PAN. Ah, ah!

CRES. Why sigh you so profoundly? Where's my lord? Gone! Tell me, sweet Uncle, what's the matter?   85

PAN. Would I were as deep under the earth as I am above!

CRES. Oh, the gods! What's the matter?

PAN. Prithee get thee in. Would thou hadst ne'er been born! I knew thou wouldst be his death. Oh, poor gentleman! A plague upon Antenor!

CRES. Good Uncle, I beseech you, on my knees I beseech you, what's the matter?   94

PAN. Thou must be gone, wench, thou must be gone, thou art changed° for Antenor. Thou must to thy father, and be gone from Troilus. 'Twill be his death, 'twill be his bane,° he cannot bear it.   99

CRES. O you immortal gods! I will not go.

PAN. Thou must.

CRES. I will not, Uncle. I have forgot my father, I know no touch of consanguinity,°
No kin, no love, no blood, no soul, so near me
As the sweet Troilus. O you gods divine!   105
Make Cressid's name the very crown of falsehood
If ever she leave Troilus! Time, force, and death
Do to this body what extremes you can,
But the strong base and building of my love
Is as the very center of the earth,   110
Drawing all things to it. I'll go in and weep——

PAN. Do, do.

CRES. Tear my bright hair and scratch my praisèd cheeks,
Crack my clear voice with sobs, and break my heart   114
With sounding Troilus. I will not go from Troy.

[Exeunt.]

SCENE III. *Before PANDARUS' house.*

[Enter PARIS, TROILUS, AENEAS, DEIPHOBUS, ANTENOR, and DIOMEDES.]

PAR. It is great morning,° and the hour prefixed
For her delivery to this valiant Greek
Comes fast upon. Good my brother Troilus,
Tell you the lady what she is to do,
And haste her to the purpose.

TRO.   Walk into her house,   5

I'll bring her to the Grecian presently.
And to his hand when I deliver her,
Think it an altar, and thy brother Troilus
A priest, there offering to it his own heart.   *[Exit.]*

PAR. I know what 'tis to love,   10
And would, as I shall pity, I could help!
Please you walk in, my lords.   *[Exeunt.]*

SCENE IV. *A room in PANDARUS' house.*

[Enter PANDARUS and CRESSIDA.]

PAN. Be moderate, be moderate.

CRES. Why tell you me of moderation?
The grief is fine, full, perfect, that I taste,
And violenteth° in a sense as strong
As that which causeth it. How can I moderate it?   5
If I could temporize° with my affection,
Or brew it to a weak and colder palate,
The like allayment could I give my grief.
My love admits no qualifying dross,°
No more my grief, in such a precious loss.   10

PAN. Here, here, here he comes. *[Enter TROILUS.]*
Ah, sweet ducks!

CRES. O Troilus! Troilus!   *[Embracing him.]*

PAN. What a pair of spectacles is here! Let me embrace too. "O heart," as the goodly saying is,
     " O heart, heavy heart,
          Why sigh'st thou without breaking? "
where he answers again,
     " Because thou canst not ease thy smart   20
          By friendship nor by speaking."
There was never a truer rhyme. Let us cast away nothing, for we may live to have need of such a verse. We see it, we see it. How now, lambs!   25

TRO. Cressid, I love thee in so strained° a purity
That the blest gods, as angry with my fancy,°
More bright in zeal than the devotion which
Cold lips blow to their deities, take thee from me.

CRES. Have the gods envy?   30

PAN. Aye, aye, aye, aye, 'tis too plain a case.

CRES. And is it true that I must go from Troy?

TRO. A hateful truth.

CRES.   What, and from Troilus too?

TRO. From Troy and Troilus.

CRES.   Is it possible?

TRO. And suddenly, where injury of chance°   35
Puts back leave-taking, justles roughly by
All time of pause, rudely beguiles our lips
Of all rejoindure,° forcibly prevents
Our locked embrasures,° strangles our dear vows
Even in the birth of our own laboring breath.   40

96. **changed**: exchanged.   99. **bane**: destruction.   103. **consanguinity**: blood relationship.
Sc. iii: 1. great morning: broad daylight.

Sc. iv: 4. violenteth: is violent.   6. **temporize**: compromise.
9. **qualifying dross**: alloy to make it less than pure gold.
26. **strained**: i.e., of all impurities.   27. **fancy**: love.   35. **injury of chance**: the ill done us by Fortune.   38. **rejoindure**: reunion.   39. **embrasures**: embraces.

We two, that with so many thousand sighs
Did buy each other, must poorly sell ourselves
With the rude brevity and discharge of one.
Injurious time now with a robber's haste
Crams his rich thievery° up, he knows not how.   45
As many farewells as be stars in heaven,
With distinct breath and consigned kisses to them,°
He fumbles up into a loose adieu,
And scants us with a single famished kiss
Distasted° with the salt of broken tears.   50
    AENE. [*Within*] My Lord, is the lady ready?
    TRO. Hark! You are called. Some say the Genius°
      so
Cries " Come! " to him that instantly must die.
Bid them have patience, she shall come anon.   54
    PAN. Where are my tears? Rain, to lay this wind,
or my heart will be blown up by the root.   [*Exit.*]
    CRES. I must then to the Grecians?
    TRO.   No remedy.
    CRES. A woeful Cressid 'mongst the merry
      Greeks!°
When shall we see again?
    TRO. Hear me, my love. Be thou but true of heart.
    CRES. I true! How now! What wicked deem° is
      this?   61
    TRO. Nay, we must use expostulation° kindly,
For it is parting from us.°
I speak not " Be thou true " as fearing thee,
For I will throw my glove to° Death himself   65
That there's no maculation° in thy heart.
But " Be thou true " say I to fashion in
My sequent protestation.° Be thou true,
And I will see thee.
    CRES. Oh, you shall be exposed, my lord, to dan-
      gers   70
As infinite as imminent. But I'll be true.
    TRO. And I'll grow friend with danger. Wear this
      sleeve.°
    CRES. And you this glove. When shall I see you?
    TRO. I will corrupt the Grecian sentinels,
To give thee nightly visitation.   75
But yet, be true.
    CRES.   Oh heavens! " Be true " again!
    TRO. Hear why I speak it, love.
The Grecian youths are full of quality,°
They're loving, well composed with gifts of nature,
And flowing o'er with arts and exercise.°   80
How novelties may move and parts with person,°

45. thievery: plunder.   47. With . . . them: each farewell with
its own sigh and added kiss.   50. Distasted: distasteful.
52. Genius: guardian angel.   58. merry Greeks: See I.ii.118,n.
61. deem: thought.   62. expostulation: talk.   63. For . . . us:
for it is our last chance of talking.   65. throw . . . to: chal-
lenge to combat.   66. maculation: stain.   67–68. to . . . prot-
estation: to prepare for my vow which follows.   72. sleeve: often
richly embroidered and worn separately from the main garment.
See note on p. 95a.   78. quality: natural gifts.   80. exercise:
skill.   81. parts . . . person: accomplishments added to per-
sonal charm.

Alas, a kind of godly jealousy —
Which, I beseech you, call a virtuous sin —
Makes me afeard.
    CRES.   Oh heavens! You love me not.
    TRO. Die I a villain, then!   85
In this I do not call your faith in question,
So mainly as my merit. I cannot sing,
Nor heel the high lavolt,° nor sweeten talk,
Nor play at subtle games — fair virtues all,
To which the Grecians are most prompt and preg-
    nant.°   90
But I can tell that in each grace of these
There lurks a still and dumb-discoursive° devil
That tempts most cunningly. But be not tempted.
    CRES. Do you think I will?
    TRO. No.   95
But something may be done that we will not.
And sometimes we are devils to ourselves,
When we will tempt the frailty of our powers,
Presuming on their changeful potency.°
    AENE. [*Within*] Nay, good my lord!
    TRO.   Come, kiss, and let us part.   100
    PAR. [*Within*] Brother Troilus!
    TRO.   Good Brother, come you hither,
And bring Aeneas and the Grecian with you.
    CRES. My lord, will you be true?
    TRO. Who, I? Alas, it is my vice, my fault.
Whiles others fish with craft for great opinion,°
I with great truth catch mere simplicity.   106
Whilst some with cunning gild their copper
    crowns,°
With truth and plainness I do wear mine bare.
Fear not my truth. The moral of my wit
Is " plain and true," there's all the reach of it.   110
[*Enter* AENEAS, PARIS, ANTENOR, DEIPHOBUS, *and*
    DIOMEDES.]
Welcome, Sir Diomed! Here is the lady
Which for Antenor we deliver you.
At the port,° lord, I'll give her to thy hand,
And by the way possess° thee what she is.
Entreat her fair, and by my soul, fair Greek,   115
If e'er thou stand at mercy of my sword,
Name Cressid and thy life shall be as safe
As Priam is in Ilion.
    DIO.   Fair Lady Cressid,
So please you, save the thanks this Prince expects.
The luster in your eye, heaven in your cheek,   120
Pleads your fair usage, and to Diomed
You shall be mistress, and command him wholly.
    TRO. Grecian, thou dost not use me courteously,
To shame the zeal of my petition to thee
In praising her. I tell thee, lord of Greece,   125

88. lavolt: lavolta, a high stepping dance. See App. 24.   90. preg-
nant: apt.   92. dumb-discoursive: silently eloquent.   99. change-
ful potency: fickle power.   105. opinion: reputation.   107. gild
. . . crowns: Copper gilt was the poorest kind of imitation gold.
113. port: gate.   114. possess: tell.

She is as far high-soaring o'er thy praises
As thou unworthy to be called her servant.
I charge thee use her well, even for my charge,
For, by the dreadful Pluto,° if thou dost not,
Though the great bulk Achilles be thy guard,   130
I'll cut thy throat.

DIO.   Oh, be not moved, Prince Troilus.
Let me be privileged by my place and message
To be a speaker free. When I am hence,
I'll answer to my lust.° And know you, lord,
I'll nothing do on charge.° To her own worth   135
She shall be prized, but that° you say "Be 't so,"
I'll speak it in my spirit and honor "No!"

TRO. Come, to the port. I'll tell thee, Diomed,
This brave° shall oft make thee to hide thy head.
Lady, give me your hand, and as we walk   140
To our own selves bend we our needful talk.

[*Exeunt* TROILUS, CRESSIDA, *and* DIOMEDES.]

[*A trumpet sounds.*]

PAR. Hark! Hector's trumpet.

AENE.   How have we spent this morning!
The Prince must think me tardy and remiss,
That swore to ride before him to the field.

PAR. 'Tis Troilus' fault. Come, come, to field with
him.   145

DEI. Let us make ready straight.

AENE. Yea, with a bridegroom's fresh alacrity,
Let us address° to tend on Hector's heels.
The glory of our Troy doth this day lie   149
On his fair worth and single chivalry.°   [*Exeunt.*]

SCENE V. *The Grecian camp. Lists set out.*°

[*Enter* AJAX, *armed;* AGAMEMNON, ACHILLES,
PATROCLUS, MENELAUS, ULYSSES, NESTOR, *and others.*]

AGAM. Here art thou in appointment° fresh and
fair,
Anticipating time with starting courage.
Give with thy trumpet a loud note to Troy,
Thou dreadful Ajax, that the appallèd air
May pierce the head of the great combatant   5
And hale° him hither.

AJAX.   Thou, trumpet,° there's my purse.
Now crack thy lungs, and split thy brazen pipe.
Blow, villain, till thy spherèd bias cheek°
Outswell the colic of puffed Aquilon.°   9
Come, stretch thy chest, and let thy eyes spout blood.

129. Pluto: king of the underworld.   134. to my lust: as I
please.   135. on charge: because I am bidden.   136. that: if.
139. brave: boast.   148. address: make ready.   150. chivalry:
knightly combat.

Sc. v: s.d., Lists . . . out: place of combat prepared. Shake-
speare and his contemporaries, as well as earlier writers, imagined
the worthies of the Trojan war as medieval knights, fighting in
full armor, according to the rules of chivalry.   1. appoint-
ment: equipment.   6. hale: draw, haul. trumpet: trumpeter.
8. sphered . . . cheek: cheek blown out like a bowl.   9. Aquilon:
northwest wind.

Thow blow'st for Hector.   [*Trumpet sounds.*]

ULYSS. No trumpet answers.

ACHIL.   'Tis but early days.

AGAM. Is not yond Diomed, with Calchas' daugh-
ter?

ULYSS. 'Tis he, I ken° the manner of his gait,
He rises on the toe. That spirit of his   15
In aspiration lifts him from the earth.

[*Enter* DIOMEDES, *with* CRESSIDA.]

AGAM. Is this the Lady Cressid?

DIO.   Even she.

AGAM. Most dearly welcome to the Greeks, sweet
lady.

NEST. Our General doth salute you with a kiss.

ULYSS. Yet is the kindness but particular,   20
'Twere better she were kissed in general.

NEST. And very courtly counsel. I'll begin.
So much for Nestor.

ACHIL. I'll take that winter° from your lips, fair
lady.
Achilles bids you welcome.   25

MEN. I had good argument for kissing once.

PATR. But that's no argument for kissing now,
For thus popped Paris in his hardiment,°
And parted thus you and your argument.   29

ULYSS. O deadly gall, and theme of all our scorns!
For which we lose our heads to gild his horns.°

PATR. The first was Menelaus' kiss, this, mine.
Patroclus kisses you.

MEN.   Oh, this is trim!

PATR. Paris and I kiss evermore for him.

MEN. I'll° have my kiss, sir. Lady, by your leave.

CRES. In kissing, do you render or receive?   36

PATR. Both take and give.

CRES.   I'll make my match to live,
The kiss you take is better than you give,
Therefore no kiss.

MEN. I'll give you boot,° I'll give you three for
one.   40

CRES. You're an odd man. Give even, or give
none.

MEN. An odd man, lady! Every man is odd.

CRES. No, Paris is not, for you know 'tis true
That you are odd, and he is even with you.

MEN. You fillip° me o' the head.

CRES.   No, I'll be sworn.   45

ULYSS. It were no match, your nail against his
horn.
May I, sweet lady, beg a kiss of you?

CRES. You may.

ULYSS.   I do desire it.

14. ken: know.   24. winter: i.e., old Nestor's cold kiss.
28. hardiment: boldness.   31. gild . . . horns: i.e., to do honor
to our cuckold Menelaus.   35–52. I'll . . . you: This rhymed
passage is very similar to *LLL*, V.ii. 200–61 and 336–483.
If *Tr & Cr* is in part an old play, this passage is likely to be a
relic of the original stratum.   40. boot: advantage, extra pay-
ment.   45. fillip: flip.

CRES.　　　　　　　　　　　　Why, beg, then.
ULYSS. Why then, for Venus' sake, give me a kiss
When Helen is a maid again, and his.°　　　　　50
CRES. I am your debtor, claim it when 'tis due.
ULYSS. Never's my day, and then a kiss of you.
DIO. Lady, a word. I'll bring you to your father.
　　　　　　　　　　　　　[*Exit with* CRESSIDA.]
NEST. A woman of quick sense.°
ULYSS.　　　　　　　　　Fie, fie upon her!　54
There's language in her eye, her cheek, her lip —
Nay, her foot speaks, her wanton spirits look out
At every joint and motive° of her body.
Oh, these encounterers, so glib of tongue,
That give accosting° welcome ere it comes,
And wide unclasp° the tables° of their thoughts　60
To every ticklish° reader! Set them down
For sluttish spoils of opportunity,°
And daughters of the game.　　[*Trumpet within.*]
ALL. The Trojans' trumpet.
AGAM.　　　　　　　Yonder comes the troop.
[*Flourish. Enter* HECTOR, *armed;* AENEAS, TROILUS,
　　and other TROJANS, *with* ATTENDANTS.]
AENE. Hail, all the state of Greece! What shall be
　　done　　　　　　　　　　　　65
To him that victory commands? Or do you purpose
A victor shall be known?° Will you the knights
Shall to the edge of all extremity°
Pursue each other, or shall they be divided
By any voice or order of the field?　　　　70
Hector bade ask.
AGAM.　　　　Which way would Hector have it?
AENE. He cares not. He'll obey conditions.
ACHIL. 'Tis done like Hector, but securely° done,
A little proudly, and great deal misprizing°
The knight opposed.
AENE.　　　　　If not Achilles, sir,　　75
What is your name?
ACHIL.　　　　　If not Achilles, nothing.
AENE. Therefore Achilles. But whate'er, know
　　this.
In the extremity of great and little,
Valor and pride excel themselves in Hector,
The one almost as infinite as all,　　　　80
The other blank as nothing. Weigh him well,
And that which looks like pride is courtesy.
This Ajax is half made of Hector's blood.°
In love whereof, half Hector stays at home;
Half heart, half hand, half Hector comes to seek　85
This blended knight, half Trojan and half Greek.

ACHIL. A maiden° battle, then? Oh, I perceive
　　you.
　　　　　　　　　　　[*Re-enter* DIOMEDES.]
AGAM. Here is Sir Diomed. Go, gentle knight,
Stand by our Ajax. As you and Lord Aeneas
Consent upon the order of their fight,　　　90
So be it, either to the uttermost
Or else a breath. The combatants being kin
Half stints their strife before their strokes begin.
　　　　　　　[AJAX *and* HECTOR *enter the lists.*]
ULYSS. They are opposed already.
AGAM. What Trojan is that same that looks so
　　heavy?　　　　　　　　　　95
ULYSS. The youngest son of Priam, a true knight,
Not yet mature, yet matchless, firm of word,
Speaking in deeds and deedless in his tongue,
Not soon provoked nor being provoked soon
　　calmed;
His heart and hand both open and both free;　100
For what he has he gives, what thinks he shows,
Yet gives he not till judgment guide his bounty,
Nor dignifies an impair° thought with breath;
Manly as Hector, but more dangerous,
For Hector in his blaze of wrath subscribes　105
To tender objects,° but he in heat of action
Is more vindicative° than jealous love.
They call him Troilus, and on him erect
A second hope, as fairly built as Hector.
Thus says Aeneas, one that knows the youth　110
Even to his inches, and with private soul°
Did in great Ilion thus translate° him to me.
　　　　　　　[*Alarum.* HECTOR *and* AJAX *fight.*]
AGAM. They are in action.
NEST. Now, Ajax, hold thine own!
TRO.　　　　　　　　Hector, thou sleep'st.
Awake thee!　　　　　　　　　　115
AGAM. His blows are well disposed. There, Ajax!
DIO. You must no more.　　[*Trumpets cease.*]
AENE.　　　　　Princes, enough, so please you.
AJAX. I am not warm yet, let us fight again.
DIO. As Hector pleases.
HECT.　　　　　Why, then will I no more.
Thou art, great lord, my father's sister son,　120
A cousin-german° to great Priam's seed.
The obligation of our blood forbids
A gory emulation 'twixt us twain.
Were thy commixtion° Greek and Trojan so
That thou couldst say, "This hand is Grecian all,
And this is Trojan, the sinews of this leg　126
All Greek and this all Troy, my mother's blood
Runs on the dexter° cheek and this sinister°
Bounds in my father's," by Jove multipotent,

50. **his**: i.e., restored to Menelaus.　54. **sense**: feeling.　57. **motive**: limb.　59. **accosting**: Theobald's emendation for "coasting"; i.e., one who takes the initiative. Cf. *T Night*, I.iii. 52–64.　60. **unclasp**: open. **tables**: notebook.　61. **ticklish**: lecherous.　62. **sluttish . . . opportunity**: sluts to be picked up as desired.　67. **A . . . known**: i.e., a combat to a decisive end.　68. **edge . . . extremity**: to the death.　73. **securely**: foolhardily.　74. **misprizing**: disdaining.　83. **half . . . blood**: explained later at ll. 120–35.

87. **maiden**: bloodless.　103. **impair**: unfit.　105–06. **subscribes . . . objects**: i.e., shows mercy.　107. **vindicative**: vindictive.　111. **with . . . soul**: confidentially.　112. **translate**: interpret.　121. **cousin-german**: kinsman.　124. **commixtion**: mixture.　128. **dexter**: right. **sinister**: left.

Thou shouldst not bear from me a Greekish mem-
 ber°   130
Wherein my sword had not impressure made
Of our rank feud. But the just gods gainsay°
That any drop thou borrow'dst from thy mother,
My sacred aunt, should by my mortal sword
Be drained! Let me embrace thee, Ajax.   135
By him that thunders, thou hast lusty arms.
Hector would have them fall upon him thus.
Cousin, all honor to thee!

AJAX.   I thank thee, Hector.
Thou art too gentle and too free° a man.
I came to kill thee, Cousin, and bear hence   140
A great addition° earnèd in thy death.

HECT. Not Neoptolemus° so mirable,°
On whose bright crest Fame with her loud'st
 Oyes°
Cries, "This is he," could promise to himself
A thought of added honor torn from Hector.   145

AENE. There is expectance here from both the
 sides,
What further you will do.

HECT.   We'll answer it,
The issue° is embracement. Ajax, farewell.

AJAX. If I might in entreaties find success —
As seld I have the chance — I would desire   150
My famous cousin to our Grecian tents.

DIO. 'Tis Agamemnon's wish, and great Achilles
Doth long to see unarmed the valiant Hector.

HECT. Aeneas, call my brother Troilus to me.
And signify this loving interview   155
To the expecters° of our Trojan part,
Desire them home. Give me thy hand, my cousin.
I will go eat with thee, and see your knights.

AJAX. Great Agamemnon comes to meet us here.

HECT. The worthiest of them tell me name by
 name,   160
But for Achilles, my own searching eyes
Shall find him by his large and portly size.

AGAM. Worthy of arms! As welcome as to one
That would be rid of such an enemy,
But that's no welcome. Understand more clear   165
What's past and what's to come is strewed with
 husks
And formless ruin of oblivion.°
But in this extant° moment, faith and troth,
Strained purely from all hollow bias-drawing,°
Bids thee, with most divine integrity,   170
From heart of very heart, great Hector, welcome.

HECT. I thank thee, most imperious Agamemnon.

AGAM. [*To* TROILUS] My well-famed lord of Troy,
 no less to you.

MEN. Let me confirm my princely brother's greet-
 ing.
You brace of warlike brothers, welcome hither.   175

HECT. Who must we answer?

AENE.   The noble Menelaus.

HECT. Oh, you, my lord! By Mars his gauntlet,
 thanks!
Mock not that I affect the untraded° oath,
Your quondam° wife swears still by Venus' glove.
She's well, but bade me not commend her to you.

MEN. Name her not now, sir, she's a deadly theme.

HECT. Oh, pardon, I offend.   182

NEST. I have, thou gallant Trojan, seen thee oft,
Laboring for destiny,° make cruel way
Through ranks of Greekish youth. And I have seen
 thee,   185
As hot as Perseus,° spur thy Phrygian steed,
Despising many forfeits and subduements,°
When thou hast hung° thy advancèd sword i' the
 air,
Not letting it decline on the declined,
That I have said to some my standers-by   190
"Lo, Jupiter is yonder, dealing life!"
And I have seen thee pause and take thy breath
When that a ring of Greeks have hemmed thee in,
Like an Olympian° wrestling. This have I seen.
But this thy countenance, still locked in steel,° 195
I never saw till now. I knew thy grandsire,
And once fought with him. He was a soldier good,
But, by great Mars the captain of us all,
Never like thee. Let an old man embrace thee,
And, worthy warrior, welcome to our tents.   200

AENE. 'Tis the old Nestor.

HECT. Let me embrace thee, good old chronicle,°
That hast so long walked hand in hand with time.
Most reverend Nestor, I am glad to clasp thee.

NEST. I would my arms could match thee in con-
 tention,   205
As they contend with thee in courtesy.

HECT. I would they could.

NEST. Ha!   208
By his white beard, I'd fight with thee tomorrow.
Well, welcome, welcome! — I have seen the time.

ULYSS. I wonder now how yonder city stands,
When we have here her base and pillar by us.

HECT. I know your favor, Lord Ulysses, well.
Ah, sir, there's many a Greek and Trojan dead
Since first I saw yourself and Diomed   215
In Ilion, on your Greekish embassy.

---

130. member: limb.   **132.** gainsay: forbid.   **139.** free: gener-
ous.   **141.** addition: honor.   **142.** Neoptolemus: son of Achilles,
but presumably Achilles is meant. **mirable**: marvelous.
143. Oyes: Oyez (hear ye), the herald's warning to his hear-
ers.   **148. issue:** end.   **156. expecters:** supporters; lit., those
who wait for news. **166–67. husks . . . oblivion:** in time to
come nothing will be left but shapeless ruins. **168. extant:** pres-
ent.   **169. bias-drawing:** crooked dealing.

178. untraded: unusual.   **179. quondam:** former.   **184. La-
boring . . . destiny:** working for Fate.   **186. Perseus:** See I.iii.
42,n.   **187. forfeits . . . subduements:** men vanquished who
have forfeited their lives.   **188. hung:** i.e., refrained from strik-
ing.   **194. Olympian:** god.   **195. still . . . steel:** always enclosed
in armor. See IV.v.s.d.,n (p. 687a), and Pl. 8a.   **202. chronicle:**
i.e., record of the past.

ULYSS. Sir, I foretold you then what would ensue.
My prophecy is but half his journey yet,
For yonder walls that pertly front° your town,   219
Yond towers whose wanton tops do buss° the clouds,
Must kiss their own feet.

HECT.   I must not believe you.
There they stand yet, and modestly I think
The fall of every Phrygian stone will cost
A drop of Grecian blood. The end crowns all,
And that old common arbitrator, Time,   225
Will one day end it.

ULYSS.   So to him we leave it.
Most gentle and most valiant Hector, welcome.
After the General, I beseech you next
To feast with me and see me at my tent.

ACHIL. I shall forestall thee, Lord Ulysses, thou!
Now, Hector, I have fed mine eyes on thee,   231
I have with exact view perused thee, Hector,
And quoted° joint by joint.

HECT.   Is this Achilles?

ACHIL. I am Achilles.   234

HECT. Stand fair, I pray thee. Let me look on thee.

ACHIL. Behold thy fill.

HECT.   Nay, I have done already.

ACHIL. Thou art too brief. I will the second time,
As I would buy thee, view thee limb by limb.

HECT. Oh, like a book of sport thou'lt read me
    o'er,
But there's more in me than thou under-
    stand'st.   240
Why dost thou so oppress me with thine eye?

ACHIL. Tell me, you Heavens, in which part of his
    body
Shall I destroy him? Whether there, or there, or
    there?
That I may give the local wound a name,
And make distinct the very breach whereout   245
Hector's great spirit flew. Answer me, Heavens!

HECT. It would discredit the blest gods, proud
    man,
To answer such a question. Stand again.
Think'st thou to catch my life so pleasantly
As to prenominate° in nice conjecture   250
Where thou wilt hit me dead?

ACHIL.   I tell thee yea.

HECT. Wert thou an oracle to tell me so,
I'd not believe thee. Henceforth guard thee well,
For I'll not kill thee there, nor there, nor there,
But, by the forge that stithied° Mars his helm,   255
I'll kill thee everywhere — yea, o'er and o'er.
You wisest Grecians, pardon me this brag.
His insolence draws folly from my lips,
But I'll endeavor deeds to match these words,
Or may I never ——

AJAX.   Do not chafe thee, Cousin.   260

And you, Achilles, let these threats alone
Till accident or purpose bring you to 't.
You may have every day enough of Hector,
If you have stomach. The general state, I fear,
Can scarce entreat you to be odd with him.°   265

HECT. I pray you let us see you in the field.
We have had pelting° wars since you refused
The Grecians' cause.

ACHIL.   Dost thou entreat me, Hector?
Tomorrow do I meet thee, fell° as death,
Tonight all friends.

HECT.   Thy hand upon that match.   270

AGAM. First, all you peers of Greece, go to my tent,
There in the full convive we.° Afterward,
As Hector's leisure and your bounties shall
Concur together, severally° entreat him.   274
Beat loud the tabourines,° let the trumpets blow,
That this great soldier may his welcome know.

                      [*Exeunt all but* TROILUS *and* ULYSSES.]

TRO. My Lord Ulysses, tell me, I beseech you,
In what place of the field doth Calchas keep?°

ULYSS. At Menelaus' tent, most princely Troilus.
There Diomed doth feast with him tonight,   280
Who neither looks upon the heaven nor earth,
But gives all gaze and bent of amorous view
On the fair Cressid.

TRO. Shall I, sweet lord, be bound to you so much,
After we part from Agamemnon's tent,   285
To bring me thither?

ULYSS.   You shall command me, sir.
As gentle tell me, of what honor was
This Cressida in Troy? Had she no lover there
That wails her absence?

TRO. Oh, sir, to such as boasting show their scars,
A mock is due. Will you walk on, my lord?   291
She was beloved, she loved; she is, and doth.
But still sweet love is food for fortune's tooth.

                      [*Exeunt.*]

Act V

SCENE I. *The Grecian camp. Before* ACHILLES'
                      tent.

                      [*Enter* ACHILLES *and* PATROCLUS.]

ACHIL. I'll heat his blood with Greekish wine to-
    night,
Which with my scimitar I'll cool tomorrow.
Patroclus, let us feast him to the height.

PATR. Here comes Thersites.

263–65. You . . . him: i.e., you can fight Hector any day you
choose, but our army (*general state*) can hardly persuade you
to come out.   267. pelting: paltry.   269. fell: fearful.   272. con-
vive we: let us feast.   274. severally: individually.   275. tab-
ourines: drums.   278. keep: lodge.

219. front: stand in front of.   220. buss: kiss.   233. quoted:
noted.   250. prenominate: foretell.   255. stithied: forged.

[*Enter* THERSITES.]

ACHIL.   How now, thou core° of envy!
Thou crusty batch° of nature, what's the news? 5

THER. Why, thou picture of what thou seemest,
and idol of idiot-worshipers, here's a letter for thee.

ACHIL. From whence, fragment?

THER. Why, thou full dish of fool, from Troy. 10

PATR. Who keeps the tent now?°

THER. The surgeon's box, or the patient's wound.°

PATR. Well said, adversity! And what needs these
tricks?

THER. Prithee be silent, boy, I profit not by thy
talk. Thou art thought to be Achilles' male varlet.

PATR. Male varlet, you rogue! What's that? 19

THER. Why, his masculine whore. Now the rotten
diseases of the south,° the guts-griping, ruptures,
catarrhs, loads o' gravel i' the back, lethargies, cold
palsies, raw eyes, dirt-rotten livers, wheezing lungs,
bladders full of imposthume,° sciaticas, limekilns i'
the palm,° incurable boneache, and the riveled fee
simple of the tetter,° take and take again such pre-
posterous discoveries!°   28

PATR. Why, thou damnable box of envy thou,
what mean'st thou to curse thus?

THER. Do I curse thee?

PATR. Why, no, you ruinous butt,° you whoreson
indistinguishable° cur, no.   33

THER. No! Why art thou then exasperate, thou
idle immaterial skein of sleave silk, thou green sar-
cenet flap for a sore eye, thou tassel of a prodigal's
purse thou?° Ah, how the poor world is pestered
with such water flies,° diminutives of nature!

PATR. Out, gall!   40

THER. Finch-egg!°

ACHIL. My sweet Patroclus, I am thwarted quite
From my great purpose in tomorrow's battle.
Here is a letter from Queen Hecuba,
A token from her daughter, my fair love,   45
Both taxing° me and gaging° me to keep
An oath that I have sworn. I will not break it.
Fall Greeks, fail fame, honor or go or stay,
My major vow lies here, this I'll obey.
Come, come, Thersites, help to trim my tent.   50

This night in banqueting must all be spent.
Away, Patroclus!

[*Exeunt* ACHILLES *and* PATROCLUS.]

THER. With too much blood and too little brain,
these two may run mad, but if with too much brain
and too little blood they do, I'll be a curer 55
of madmen. Here's Agamemnon, an honest fellow
enough and one that loves quails,° but he has not so
much brain as earwax. And the goodly transforma-
tion of Jupiter there, his brother, the bull, the primi-
tive statue and oblique° memorial of cuckolds, 60
a thrifty shoeing horn in a chain hanging at his
brother's leg — to what form but that he is should
wit larded° with malice and malice forced° with
wit turn him to? To an ass were nothing, he is both
ass and ox. To an ox were nothing, he is both 65
ox and ass. To be a dog, a mule, a cat, a fitchew,° a
toad, a lizard, an owl, a puttock,° or a herring with-
out a rope, I would not care. But to be Menelaus! I
would conspire against destiny. Ask me not what I
would be if I were not Thersites, for I care not 70
to be the louse of a lazar,° so I were not Menelaus.
Hoy-day!° Spirits and fires!

[*Enter* HECTOR, TROILUS, AJAX, AGAMEMNON, ULYSSES,
NESTOR, MENELAUS, *and* DIOMEDES, *with lights.*]

AGAM. We go wrong, we go wrong.

AJAX.   No, yonder 'tis,
There, where we see the lights.

HECT.   I trouble you. 75

AJAX. No, not a whit.

[*Re-enter* ACHILLES.]

ULYSS.   Here comes himself to guide you.

ACHIL. Welcome, brave Hector, welcome, Princes
all.

AGAM. So now, fair Prince of Troy, I bid good
night.
Ajax commands the guard to tend on you.

HECT. Thanks and good night to the Greeks' Gen-
eral.   80

MEN. Good night, my lord.

HECT.   Good night, sweet Lord Menelaus.

THER. Sweet draught.° Sweet, quoth a'! Sweet
sink, sweet sewer.

ACHIL. Good night and welcome, both at once, to
those
That go or tarry.   85

AGAM. Good night.

[*Exeunt* AGAMEMNON *and* MENELAUS.]

ACHIL. Old Nestor tarries, and you too, Diomed,
Keep Hector company an hour or two.

DIO. I cannot, lord, I have important business
The tide° whereof is now. Good night, great Hector.

Act V, Sc. i: 4. **core**: center of a boil.   5. **crusty batch**:
overbaked loaf; i.e., black, hard, and bitter.   11. **Who ... now**:
i.e., the news that Thersites has a letter from Troy quickly
brings Achilles out of his tent.   12. **The ... wound**: Thersites
deliberately misunderstands tent as lint. See II.ii.16,n.   21. **south**:
regarded as an unhealthy quarter.   24. **imposthume**: abscess.
24–25. **limekilns ... palm**: arthritis.   26–27. **riveled ... tet-
ter**: permanent ownership (*fee simple*) of eruptions (*tetter*)
that pucker (*rivel*) the skin.   28. **discoveries**: revelations.
32. **ruinous butt**: broken-down barrel.   33. **indistinguishable**:
shapeless.   34–38. **thou ... thou**: Thersites now turns to curse
Patroclus's appearance. Patroclus is played as a dapper effemi-
nate youth, prettily dressed in green silk. **sleave silk**: skein
of raw silk. **sarcenet**: fine soft silk.   39. **water flies**: useless little
creatures that flit about. Cf. *Haml.*, V.ii.83.   41. **Finch-egg**:
i.e., little smooth thing.   46. **taxing**: blaming. **gaging**: pledg-
ing.

57. **quails**: courtesans.   60. **oblique**: indirect, symbolic
63. **larded**: basted. **forced**: stuffed.   66. **fitchew**: polecat.   67. **put-
tock**: kite.   71. **lazar**: leper.   72. **Hoy-day**: an exclamation
of surprise, as he sees lights approaching.   82. **draught**: privy
90. **tide**: decisive moment.

HECT. Give me your hand.   91

ULYSS. [*Aside to* TROILUS] Follow his torch, he
goes to Calchas' tent.

I'll keep you company.

TRO.   Sweet sir, you honor me.

HECT. And so good night.

[*Exit* DIOMEDES; ULYSSES *and* TROILUS *following.*]

ACHIL. Come, come, enter my tent.   94

[*Exeunt* ACHILLES, HECTOR, AJAX, *and* NESTOR.]

THER. That same Diomed's a false-hearted rogue,
a most unjust knave. I will no more trust him when
he leers than I will a serpent when he hisses. He will
spend his mouth° and promise, like Brabbler the
hound, but when he performs, astronomers   100
foretell it.° It is prodigious,° there will come some
change,° the sun borrows of the moon when Diomed
keeps his word. I will rather leave to see° Hector
than not to dog him. They say he keeps a Trojan
drab and uses the traitor Calchas' tent. I'll after.
Nothing but lechery! All incontinent varlets!   106

[*Exit.*]

SCENE II. *The same. Before* CALCHAS' *tent.*

[*Enter* DIOMEDES.]

DIO. What, are you up here, ho? Speak.

CAL. [*Within*] Who calls?

DIO. Diomed. Calchas, I think. Where's your
daughter?

CAL. [*Within*] She comes to you.

[*Enter* TROILUS *and* ULYSSES, *at a distance; after them,*
THERSITES.]

ULYSS. Stand where the torch may not discover us.

[*Enter* CRESSIDA.]

TRO. Cressid comes forth to him.   6

DIO.   How now, my charge!

CRES. Now, my sweet guardian! Hark, a word
with you.   [*Whispers.*]

TRO. Yea, so familiar!

ULYSS. She will sing any man at first sight.

THER. And any man may sing her, if he can take
her cliff.° She's noted.°   11

DIO. Will you remember?

CRES. Remember! Yes.

DIO. Nay, but do, then,

And let your mind be coupled with your words.   15

TRO. What should she remember?

ULYSS. List.

CRES. Sweet honey Greek, tempt me no more to
folly.

THER. Roguery!

DIO. Nay, then ——   20

CRES. I'll tell you what ——

DIO. Foh, foh! Come, tell a pin.° You are for-
sworn.

CRES. In faith, I cannot. What would you have me
do?

THER. A juggling trick — to be secretly open.

DIO. What did you swear you would bestow on
me?   25

CRES. I prithee do not hold me to mine oath.
Bid me do anything but that, sweet Greek.

DIO. Good night.

TRO. Hold, patience!

ULYSS. How now, Trojan!   30

CRES. Diomed ——

DIO. No, no, good night. I'll be your fool no more.

TRO. Thy better° must.

CRES. Hark, one word in your ear.

TRO. Oh, plague and madness!   35

ULYSS. You are moved, Prince. Let us depart, I
pray you,

Lest your displeasure should enlarge itself
To wrathful terms. This place is dangerous,
The time right deadly. I beseech you, go.

TRO. Behold, I pray you!

ULYSS.   Nay, good my lord, go off.   40
You flow to great distraction.° Come, my lord.

TRO. I pray thee stay.

ULYSS.   You have not patience, come.

TRO. I pray you stay. By Hell and all Hell's tor-
ments,

I will not speak a word.

DIO.   And so good night.

CRES. Nay, but you part in anger.

TRO.   Doth that grieve thee?   45
Oh, withered truth!

ULYSS.   Why, how now, lord!

TRO.   By Jove,
I will be patient.

CRES.   Guardian! — Why, Greek!

DIO. Foh, foh! Adieu, you palter.

CRES. In faith, I do not. Come hither once again.

ULYSS. You shake, my lord, at something. Will
you go?   50
You will break out.

TRO.   She strokes his cheek!

ULYSS.   Come, come.

TRO. Nay, stay, by Jove. I will not speak a word.
There is between my will and all offenses
A guard of patience. Stay a little while.   54

THER. How the devil luxury,° with his fat rump
and potato finger,° tickles these together! Fry, lech-
ery, fry!

DIO. But will you, then?

---

99. **spend . . . mouth:** bark.   100–01. **astronomers . . . it:** as-
trologers prophesy it. See App. 2.   101. **prodigious:** an omen.
102. **change:** revolution.   103. **leave to see:** lose seeing.

Sc. ii: 11. **cliff:** clef, a key in music. **noted:** observed, with
a pun on musical notes.

22. **pin:** trifle.   33. **better:** i.e., Troilus.   41. **distraction:**
agitation.   55. **luxury:** lechery.   56. **potato finger:** The sweet
potato was supposed to provoke lust.

CRES. In faith, I will, la. Never trust me else.
DIO. Give me some token for the surety of it.   60
CRES. I'll fetch you one.   [*Exit.*]
ULYSS. You have sworn patience.
TRO.   Fear me not, sweet lord.
I will not be myself, nor have cognition
Of what I feel. I am all patience.
[*Re-enter* CRESSIDA.] Now the pledge, now, now,
    now!   65
CRES. Here, Diomed, keep this sleeve.
TRO. O beauty! Where is thy faith?
ULYSS.   My lord——
TRO. I will be patient, outwardly I will.
CRES. You look upon that sleeve, behold it well.
He loved me. — O false wench! — Give 't me
    again.   70
DIO. Whose was 't?
CRES. It is no matter, now I have 't again.
I will not meet with you tomorrow night.
I prithee, Diomed, visit me no more.   74
THER. Now she sharpens. Well said, whetstone!
DIO. I shall have it.
CRES.   What, this?
DIO.   Aye, that.
CRES. Oh, all you gods! O pretty, pretty pledge!
Thy master now lies thinking in his bed
Of thee and me, and sighs, and takes my glove,
And gives memorial dainty kisses to it,   80
As I kiss thee. Nay, do not snatch it from me.
He that takes that doth take my heart withal.
DIO. I had your heart before, this follows it.
TRO. I did swear patience.
CRES. You shall not have it, Diomed, faith, you
    shall not.   85
I'll give you something else.
DIO. I will have this. Whose was it?
CRES.   It is no matter.
DIO. Come, tell me whose it was.
CRES. 'Twas one's that loved me better than you
    will.
But now you have it, take it.
DIO.   Whose was it?   90
CRES. By all Diana's waiting women° yond,
And by herself, I will not tell you whose.
DIO. Tomorrow will I wear it on my helm,
And grieve his spirit that dares not challenge it.
TRO. Wert thou the Devil, and worest it on thy
    horn,   95
It should be challenged.
CRES. Well, well, 'tis done, 'tis past. And yet it is
    not.
I will not keep my word.
DIO.   Why then, farewell.
Thou never shalt mock Diomed again.   99
CRES. You shall not go. One cannot speak a word
But it straight starts you.

91. waiting women: i.e., the stars. Diana being the moon.

DIO.   I do not like this fooling.
THER. Nor I, by Pluto. But that that likes° not
you pleases me best.
DIO.   What, shall I come? The hour?
CRES. Aye, come. O Jove! Do come. I shall be
    plagued.   105
DIO. Farewell till then.
CRES.   Good night. I prithee come.
                              [*Exit* DIOMEDES.]
Troilus, farewell! One eye yet looks on thee,
But with my heart the other eye doth see.
Ah, poor our sex! This fault in us I find,
The error of our eye directs our mind.   110
What error leads must err. Oh, then conclude
Minds swayed by eyes are full of turpitude. [*Exit.*]
THER. A proof of strength she could not publish
    more
Unless she said " My mind is now turned whore."
ULYSS. All's done, my lord.
TRO.   It is.
ULYSS.   Why stay we, then?
TRO. To make a recordation to° my soul   116
Of every syllable that here was spoke.
But if I tell how these two did coact,
Shall I not lie in publishing a truth?
Sith° yet there is a credence in my heart,   120
An esperance° so obstinately strong
That doth invert the attest° of eyes and ears,
As if those organs had deceptious functions,
Created only to calumniate.
Was Cressid here?
ULYSS.   I cannot conjure,° Trojan.   125
TRO. She was not, sure.
ULYSS.   Most sure she was.
TRO. Why, my negation hath no taste of madness.°
ULYSS. Nor mine, my lord. Cressid was here but
    now.
TRO. Let it not be believed for womanhood!
Think, we had mothers. Do not give advantage   130
To stubborn critics, apt without a theme
For depravation, to square° the general sex
By Cressid's rule.° Rather think this not Cressid.
ULYSS. What hath she done, Prince, that can soil
    our mothers?
TRO. Nothing at all, unless that this were she. 135
THER. Will a' swagger himself out on 's own eyes?
TRO. This she? No, this is Diomed's Cressida.
If beauty have a soul, this is not she.
If souls guide vows, if vows be sanctimonies,
If sanctimony be the gods' delight,   140
If there be rule in unity itself,
This is not she. Oh, madness of discourse

102. likes: pleases.   116. recordation to: remembrance in.
120. Sith: since.   121. esperance: hope.   122. invert ... at-
test: refuse to believe the evidence.   125. I ... conjure: i.e.,
these were not spirits.   127. negation ... madness: my
denial has no taint of madness; i.e., I am not mad to deny it.
132. square: measure.   133. rule: carpenter's rule.

That cause sets up with and against itself!
Bifold authority! Where reason can revolt
Without perdition, and loss assume all reason   145
Without revolt.° This is, and is not, Cressid!
Within my soul there doth conduce a fight
Of this strange nature, that a thing inseparate°
Divides more wider than the sky and earth,
And yet the spacious breadth of this division   150
Admits no orifex° for a point as subtle
As Ariachne's broken woof° to enter.
Instance,° oh instance, strong as Pluto's gates,
Cressid is mine, tied with the bonds of Heaven.
Instance, oh instance, strong as Heaven itself,   155
The bonds of Heaven are slipped, dissolved, and
    loosed,
And with another knot, five-finger-tied,
The fractions of her faith, orts° of her love,
The fragments, scraps, the bits and greasy relics
Of her o'ereaten° faith, are bound to Diomed.   160
   ULYSS. May worthy Troilus be half attached
With° that which here his passion doth express?
   TRO. Aye, Greek, and that shall be divulgèd well
In characters as red as Mars his heart
Inflamed with Venus. Never did young man fancy
With so eternal and so fixed a soul.   166
Hark, Greek. As much as I do Cressid love,
So much by weight hate I her Diomed.
That sleeve is mine that he'll bear on his helm.
Were it a casque° composed by Vulcan's skill,   170
My sword should bite it. Not the dreadful spout°
Which shipmen do the hurricane call,
Constringed in mass° by the almighty sun,
Shall dizzy with more clamor Neptune's ear
In his descent than shall my prompted sword   175
Falling on Diomed.
   THER. He'll tickle it for his concupy.°
   TRO. O Cressid! O false Cressid! False, false, false!
Let all untruths stand by thy stainèd name,
And they'll seem glorious.
   ULYSS.   Oh, contain yourself.   180
Your passion draws ears hither.

              [*Enter* AENEAS.]

   AENE. I have been seeking you this hour, my lord.
Hector by this is arming him in Troy,
Ajax your guard stays to conduct you home.
   TRO. Have with you, Prince. My courteous lord,
adieu.   185

142–46. Oh . . . revolt: a mad argument that is at the same time
for and against itself. Divided authority where reason can
turn against itself without becoming madness, and destruction
(*loss*) become reasonable; i.e., it is both reasonable and in-
sane to believe or to disbelieve what I have seen.   148. insepa-
rate: inseparable.   151. orifex: point of entry.   152. Ariachne's
. . . woof: the thread of a spider's web. Ariachne for Arachne,
who was turned into a spider.   153. Instance: proof.   158. orts:
scraps.   160. o'ereaten: overeaten, gorged.   161–62. attached
With: affected by.   170. casque: helmet.   171. spout: water-
spout.   173. Constringed in mass: drawn together.   177. He'll
. . . concupy: he'll be tickled for his lust.

Farewell, revolted fair! And, Diomed,
Stand fast, and wear a castle on thy head!°
   ULYSS. I'll bring you to the gates.
   TRO. Accept distracted thanks.   189

      [*Exeunt* TROILUS, AENEAS, *and* ULYSSES.]
   THER. Would I could meet that rogue Diomed! I
would croak like a raven, I would bode,° I would
bode. Patroclus will give me anything for the intel-
ligence of this whore. The parrot will not do more
for an almond° than he for a commodious° drab.
Lechery, lechery! Still wars and lechery! Nothing
else holds fashion. A burning devil take them!   197

                          [*Exit.*]

SCENE III. *Troy. Before* PRIAM'S *palace.*

     [*Enter* HECTOR *and* ANDROMACHE.]
   AND. When was my lord so much ungently tem-
     pered
To stop his ears against admonishment?
Unarm, unarm, and do not fight today.
   HECT. You train° me to offend you, get you in.
By all the everlasting gods, I'll go!   5
   AND. My dreams will sure prove ominous to the
     day.
   HECT. No more, I say.

               [*Enter* CASSANDRA.]
   CAS.   Where is my brother Hector?
   AND. Here, Sister, armed, and bloody in intent.
Consort with me in loud and dear petition,
Pursue we him on knees, for I have dreamed   10
Of bloody turbulence, and this whole night
Hath nothing been but shapes and forms of slaugh-
     ter.
   CAS. Oh, 'tis true.
   HECT.   Ho! Bid my trumpet sound!
   CAS. No notes of sally, for the Heavens, sweet
     Brother.
   HECT. Be gone, I say. The gods have heard me
     swear.   15
   CAS. The gods are deaf to hot and peevish° vows.
They are polluted offerings, more abhorred
Than spotted livers in the sacrifice.
   AND. Oh, be persuaded! Do not count it holy
To hurt by being just. It is as lawful,   20
For we would give much, to use violent thefts
And rob in the behalf of charity.
   CAS. It is the purpose that makes strong the vow,
But vows to every purpose must not hold.
Unarm, sweet Hector.
   HECT.   Hold you still, I say.   25

187. wear . . . head: i.e., nothing less than a castle will protect
you.   191. bode: prophesy disaster.   194–95. parrot . . . al-
mond: The love of parrots for almonds is proverbial.   195. com-
modious: accommodating.
Sc. iii: 4. train: encourage.   16. peevish: obstinate.

Mine honor keeps the weather of° my fate.
Life every man holds dear, but the dear man
Holds honor far more precious-dear than life.
[*Enter* TROILUS.] How now, young man! Mean'st
   thou to fight today?
   AND. Cassandra, call my father to persuade.   30
                  [*Exit* CASSANDRA.]
   HECT. No, faith, young Troilus. Doff thy harness,
   youth.
I am today i' the vein of chivalry.°
Let grow thy sinews till their knots be strong,
And tempt not yet the brushes of the war.
Unarm thee, go, and doubt thou not, brave boy,   35
I'll stand today for thee and me and Troy.
   TRO. Brother, you have a vice of mercy in you
Which better fits a lion than a man.
   HECT. What vice is that, good Troilus? Chide me
   for it.
   TRO. When many times the captive Grecian falls,
Even in the fan and wind of your fair sword,   41
You bid them rise and live.
   HECT. Oh, 'tis fair play.
   TRO.   Fool's play, by Heaven, Hector.
   HECT. How now! How now!
   TRO.   For the love of all the gods,
Let's leave the hermit pity with our mother,   45
And when we have our armors buckled on,
The venomed vengeance ride upon our swords,
Spur them to ruthful work,° rein them from ruth!
   HECT. Fie, savage, fie!
   TRO.   Hector, then 'tis wars.
   HECT. Troilus, I would not have you fight today.
   TRO. Who should withhold me?   51
Not fate, obedience, nor the hand of Mars
Beckoning with fiery truncheon my retire —
Not Priamus and Hecuba on knees,
Their eyes o'ergallèd° with recourse° of tears;   55
Nor you, my brother, with your true sword
   drawn —
Opposed to hinder me should stop my way
But by my ruin.
   [*Re-enter* CASSANDRA, *with* PRIAM.]
   CAS. Lay hold upon him, Priam, hold him fast.
He is thy crutch. Now if thou lose thy stay,   60
Thou on him leaning and all Troy on thee,
Fall all together.
   PRI.   Come, Hector, come, go back.
Thy wife hath dreamed, thy mother hath had vi-
   sions,
Cassandra doth foresee, and I myself
Am like a prophet suddenly enrapt,°   65
To tell thee that this day is ominous.
Therefore, come back.

   HECT.   Aeneas is afield,
And I do stand engaged° to many Greeks,
Even in the faith of valor, to appear
This morning to them.
   PRI.   Aye, but thou shalt not go.   70
   HECT. I must not break my faith.
You know me dutiful, therefore, dear sir,
Let me not shame respect, but give me leave
To take that course by your consent and voice
Which you do here forbid me, royal Priam.   75
   CAS. O Priam, yield not to him!
   AND.   Do not, dear Father.
   HECT. Andromache, I am offended with you.
Upon the love you bear me, get you in.
                [*Exit* ANDROMACHE.]
   TRO. This foolish, dreaming, superstitious girl
Makes all these bodements.°
   CAS.   Oh, farewell, dear Hector!   80
Look how thou diest! Look how thy eye turns pale!
Look how thy wounds do bleed at many vents!°
Hark how Troy roars, how Hecuba cries out!
How poor Andromache shrills her dolors forth!
Behold, distraction, frenzy, and amazement,   85
Like witless antics,° one another meet,
And all cry "Hector! Hector's dead! Oh, Hector!"
   TRO. Away! Away!
   CAS. Farewell. Yet, soft! Hector, I take my leave.
Thou dost thyself and all our Troy deceive.   [*Exit.*]
   HECT. You are amazed, my liege, at her exclaim.
Go in and cheer the town. We'll forth and fight,
Do deeds worth praise and tell you them at night.
   PRI. Farewell. The gods with safety stand about
   thee!
   [*Exeunt severally*° PRIAM *and* HECTOR.
                        Alarum.]
   TRO. They are at it, hark! Proud Diomed, believe,
I come to lose my arm or win my sleeve.   96
   [*Enter* PANDARUS.]
   PAN. Do you hear, my lord? Do you hear?
   TRO. What now?
   PAN. Here's a letter come from yond poor girl.
   TRO. Let me read.   100
   PAN. A whoreson tisick,° a whoreson rascally
tisick so troubles me, and the foolish fortune of this
girl; and what one thing, what another, that I shall
leave you one o' these days. And I have a rheum in
mine eyes too, and such an ache in my bones that,
unless a man were cursed, I cannot tell what to think
on 't. What says she there?   107
   TRO. Words, words, mere words, no matter from
   the heart.
The effect doth operate another way.
                [*Tearing the letter*]
Go, wind, to wind, there turn and change together.

---

26. keeps ... of: has the advantage of.   32. i' ... chivalry:
i.e., fighting for honor.   48. ruthful work: work that will rouse
pity; i.e., be ruthless.   55. o'ergalled: inflamed. recourse:
flowing.   65. enrapt: inspired.

68. engaged: pledged.   80. bodements: gloomy prophecies.
82. vents: openings.   86. antics: buffoons.   94 s.d., severally:
by different exits.   101. tisick: cough.

My love with words and errors still she feeds,   111
But edifies another with her deeds.

               [*Exeunt severally.*]

SCENE IV. *The field between Troy and the Grecian camp.*

[*Alarums. Excursions. Enter* THERSITES.]

THER. Now they are clapper-clawing° one another. I'll go look on. That dissembling abominable varlet Diomed has got that same scurvy doting foolish young knave's sleeve of Troy there in his helm. I would fain see them meet, that that same young   5 Trojan ass, that loves the whore there, might send that Greekish whoremasterly villain with the sleeve back to the dissembling luxurious drab, of a sleeveless° errand. O' the t'other side, the policy of those crafty swearing rascals, that stale old mouse-   10 eaten dry cheese Nestor, and that same dog fox Ulysses, is not proved worth a blackberry. They set me up in policy° that mongrel cur Ajax against that dog of as bad a kind, Achilles. And now is the cur Ajax prouder than the cur Achilles, and will   15 not arm today, whereupon the Grecians begin to proclaim barbarism,° and policy grows into an ill opinion.° Soft! Here comes sleeve, and t'other.

[*Enter* DIOMEDES *and* TROILUS.]

TRO. Fly not, for shouldst thou take the river Styx, I would swim after.

DIO.   Thou dost miscall retire.   21
I do not fly, but advantageous care
Withdrew me from the odds of multitude.
Have at thee!   24

THER. Hold thy whore, Grecian! Now for thy whore, Trojan! Now the sleeve, now the sleeve!

[*Exeunt* TROILUS *and* DIOMEDES, *fighting.*]

[*Enter* HECTOR.]

HECT. What art thou, Greek? Art thou for Hector's match?
Art thou of blood and honor?   29

THER. No, no, I am a rascal,° a scurvy railing knave, a very filthy rogue.

HECT. I do believe thee. Live.   [*Exit.*]

THER. God-a-mercy° that thou wilt believe me, but a plague break thy neck for frighting me! What's become of the wenching rogues? I think they have swallowed one another. I would laugh at that miracle — yet in a sort lechery eats itself. I'll seek   37 them.   [*Exit.*]

SCENE V. *Another part of the field.*

[*Enter* DIOMEDES *and* SERVANT.]

DIO. Go, go, my servant, take thou Troilus' horse,
Present the fair steed to my Lady Cressid.
Fellow, commend my service to her beauty.
Tell her I have chastised the amorous Trojan,
And am her knight by proof.

SERV.   I go, my lord.   [*Exit.*]   5

[*Enter* AGAMEMNON.]

AGAM. Renew, renew! The fierce Polydamas
Hath beat down Menon. Bastard Margarelon
Hath Doreus prisoner,
And stands colossus-wise,° waving his beam,°
Upon the pashed corses° of the kings   10
Epistrophus and Cedius. Polyxenes is slain,
Amphimachus and Thoas deadly hurt,
Patroclus ta'en or slain, and Palamedes
Sore hurt and bruised. The dreadful sagittary°
Appals our numbers. Haste we, Diomed,   15
To reinforcement, or we perish all.

[*Enter* NESTOR.]

NEST. Go, bear Patroclus' body to Achilles,
And bid the snail-paced Ajax arm for shame.
There is a thousand Hectors in the field.
Now here he fights on Galathe his horse,   20
And there lacks work. Anon he's there afoot,
And there they fly or die, like scalèd sculls°
Before the belching whale. Then is he yonder,
And there the strawy° Greeks, ripe for his edge,
Fall down before him like the mower's swath.   25
Here, there, and everywhere he leaves and takes,
Dexterity so obeying appetite
That what he will he does, and does so much
That proof is called impossibility.

[*Enter* ULYSSES.]

ULYSS. Oh, courage, courage, Princes! Great Achilles   30
Is arming, weeping, cursing, vowing vengeance.
Patroclus' wounds have roused his drowsy blood,
Together with his mangled Myrmidons,°
That noseless, handless, hacked and chipped, come to him,
Crying on Hector. Ajax hath lost a friend,   35
And foams at mouth, and he is armed, and at it,
Roaring for Troilus, who hath done today
Mad and fantastic execution,
Engaging and redeeming of himself
With such a careless force and forceless care   40
As if that luck, in very spite of cunning,
Bade him win all.

Sc. iv: 1. **clapper-clawing**: scratching and clawing. 9. **sleeveless**: futile. 12–13. **set ... policy**: thought it a clever plan to support. 17. **proclaim barbarism**: declare that ignorance is preferable. 17–18. **policy . . . opinion**: cleverness gets a bad name. 30. **rascal**: lit., a deer in poor condition. 33. **God-a-mercy**: thank God.

Sc. v: 9. **colossus-wise**: See *Caesar*, I.ii.135–38. **beam**: huge spear. 10. **pashed corses**: mangled corpses. 14. **sagittary**: a centaur, half man, half horse, who helped the Trojans. 22. **scaled sculls**: shoals of scaly fish. 24. **strawy**: weak as straw. 33. **Myrmidons**: Achilles' followers.

[*Enter* AJAX.]

AJAX. Troilus! Thou coward Troilus!   [*Exit.*]

DIO.   Aye, there, there.

NEST. So, so, we draw together.

[*Enter* ACHILLES.]

ACHIL.   Where is this Hector?

Come, come, thou boy-queller,° show thy face,   45

Know what it is to meet Achilles angry.

Hector! Where's Hector? I will none but Hector.

[*Exeunt.*]

SCENE VI. *Another part of the field.*

[*Enter* AJAX.]

AJAX. Troilus, thou coward Troilus, show thy
head!

[*Enter* DIOMEDES.]

DIO. Troilus, I say! Where's Troilus?

AJAX.   What wouldst thou?

DIO. I would correct him.

AJAX. Were I the General, thou shouldst have my
office

Ere that correction.° Troilus, I say! What, Troilus!   5

[*Enter* TROILUS.]

TRO. O traitor Diomed! Turn thy false face, thou
traitor,

And pay thy life thou owest me for my horse.

DIO. Ha, art thou there?

AJAX. I'll fight with him alone. Stand, Diomed.

DIO. He is my prize, I will not look upon.   10

TRO. Come both, you cogging° Greeks, have at
you both!   [*Exeunt, fighting.*]

[*Enter* HECTOR.]

HECT. Yea, Troilus? Oh, well fought, my young-
est brother!

[*Enter* ACHILLES.]

ACHIL. Now do I see thee, ha! Have at thee, Hec-
tor!

HECT. Pause, if thou wilt.

ACHIL. I do disdain thy courtesy, proud Trojan.

Be happy that my arms are out of use.   16

My rest and negligence befriends thee now,

But thou anon shalt hear of me again.

Till when, go seek thy fortune.   [*Exit.*]

HECT.   Fare thee well.

I would have been much more a fresher man   20

Had I expected thee.

[*Re-enter* TROILUS.] How now, my brother!

TRO. Ajax hath ta'en Aeneas. Shall it be?

No, by the flame of yonder glorious heaven,

He shall not carry him. I'll be ta'en too,

Or bring him off.° Fate, hear me what I say!   25

I reck not though I end my life today.   [*Exit.*]

[*Enter one in sumptuous armor.*]

HECT. Stand, stand, thou Greek, thou art a goodly
mark.

No? Wilt thou not? I like thy armor well.

I'll frush° it, and unlock the rivets all,   29

But I'll be master of it. Wilt thou not, beast, abide?

Why then, fly on, I'll hunt thee for thy hide.

[*Exeunt.*]

SCENE VII. *Another part of the field.*

[*Enter* ACHILLES, *with* MYRMIDONS.]

ACHIL. Come here about me, you my Myrmidons,

Mark what I say. Attend me where I wheel.

Strike not a stroke, but keep yourselves in breath.

And when I have the bloody Hector found,

Empale° him with your weapons round about,   5

In fellest manner execute your aims.

Follow me, sirs, and my proceedings eye.

It is decreed Hector the great must die.   [*Exeunt.*]

[*Enter* MENELAUS *and* PARIS, *fighting: then*
THERSITES.]

THER. The cuckold and the cuckold-maker are at
it. Now, bull! Now, dog! 'Loo,° Paris, 'loo! Now,
my double-henned sparrow! 'Loo, Paris, 'loo! The
bull has the game. Ware horns, ho!   12

[*Exeunt* PARIS *and* MENELAUS.]

[*Enter* MARGARELON.]

MAR. Turn, slave, and fight.

THER. What art thou?

MAR. A bastard son of Priam's.   15

THER. I am a bastard too, I love bastards. I am a
bastard begot, bastard instructed, bastard in mind,
bastard in valor, in everything illegitimate. One bear
will not bite another, and wherefore should one bas-
tard? Take heed, the quarrel's most ominous to us.
If the son of a whore fight for a whore, he tempts
judgment. Farewell, bastard.   [*Exit.*]

MAR. The Devil take thee, coward!   [*Exit.*]

SCENE VIII. *Another part of the field.*

[*Enter* HECTOR.]

HECT. Most putrefied core, so fair without,

Thy goodly armor thus hath cost thy life.

Now is my day's work done. I'll take good breath.

Rest, sword, thou hast thy fill of blood and death.

[*Puts off his helmet and hangs
his shield behind him.*]

---

45. **boy-queller:** boy-killer, because he has killed Patroclus.

   Sc. vi: 5. **Ere . . . correction:** before you should take from
me the privilege of correcting him.   11. **cogging:** cheating.
25. **bring . . . off:** rescue him.

29. **frush:** bruise.

   Sc. vii: 5. **Empale:** hedge in.   10. **Now . . . 'Loo:** Thersites
shouts encouragement as if a spectator in the bullring. See
App. 5.

[*Enter* ACHILLES *and* MYRMIDONS.]

ACHIL. Look, Hector, how the sun begins to set,
How ugly night comes breathing at his heels.   6
Even with the vail° and darking of the sun
To close the day up, Hector's life is done.
    HECT. I am unarmed, forgo this vantage, Greek.
    ACHIL. Strike, fellows, strike, this is the man I
        seek.   [HECTOR *falls.*]
So, Ilion, fall thou next! Now, Troy, sink down!
Here lies thy heart, thy sinews, and thy bone. 12
On, Myrmidons, and cry you all amain,
"Achilles hath the mighty Hector slain."
                              [*A retreat sounded*]
Hark! A retire upon our Grecian part.   15
    MYR. The Trojan trumpets sound the like, my
        lord.
    ACHIL. The dragon wing of night o'erspreads the
        earth,
And stickler-like° the armies separates.
My half-supped sword that frankly would have fed,
Pleased with this dainty bait, thus goes to bed. 20
                              [*Sheathes his sword.*]
Come, tie his body to my horse's tail.
Along the field I will the Trojan trail.
                       [*Exeunt. A retreat sounded.*]

SCENE IX. *Another part of the field.*

[*Enter* AGAMEMNON, AJAX, MENELAUS, NESTOR,
DIOMEDES, *and the rest, marching. Shouts within.*]

    AGAM. Hark! Hark! What shout is that?
    NEST. Peace, drums!
[*Within*] "Achilles! Achilles! Hector's slain!
        Achilles!"
    DIO. The bruit° is Hector's slain, and by Achilles.
    AJAX. If it be so, yet bragless let it be,   5
Great Hector was a man as good as he.
    AGAM. March patiently along. Let one be sent
To pray Achilles see us at our tent.
If in his death the gods have us befriended,   9
Great Troy is ours, and our sharp wars are ended.
                            [*Exeunt, marching.*]

SCENE X. *Another part of the field.*

[*Enter* AENEAS, PARIS, ANTENOR, *and* DEIPHOBUS.]

    AENE. Stand, ho! Yet are we masters of the field.
Never go home, here starve we out the night.

[*Enter* TROILUS.]

    TRO. Hector is slain.
    ALL.   Hector! The gods forbid!
    TRO. He's dead, and at the murderer's horse's tail
In beastly sort dragged through the shameful field.
Frown on, you Heavens, effect your rage with speed!
Sit, gods, upon your thrones, and smile at Troy! 7
I say, at once let your brief plagues be mercy,
And linger not our sure destructions on!
    AENE. My lord, you do discomfort all the host. 10
    TRO. You understand me not that tell me so.
I do not speak of flight, of fear, of death,
But dare all imminence° that gods and men
Address° their dangers in. Hector is gone.
Who shall tell Priam so, or Hecuba?   15
Let him that will a screech owl aye° be called
Go in to Troy, and say there "Hector's dead."
There is a word will Priam turn to stone,
Make wells and Niobes° of the maids and wives,
Cold statues of the youth, and, in a word,   20
Scare Troy out of itself. But march away.
Hector is dead, there is no more to say.
Stay yet. You vile abominable tents,
Thus proudly pight° upon our Phrygian plains,
Let Titan° rise as early as he dare,   25
I'll through and through you! And, thou great-sized
        coward,
No space of earth shall sunder our two hates.
I'll haunt thee like a wicked conscience still,°
That moldeth goblins swift as frenzy's thoughts.
Strike a free march to Troy! With comfort go.   30
Hope of revenge shall hide our inward woe.
                       [*Exeunt* AENEAS *and* TROJANS.]
[*As* TROILUS *is going out, enter, from the other side,*
        PANDARUS.]

    PAN. But hear you, hear you!
    TRO. Hence, broker lackey! Ignomy and shame
Pursue thy life, and live aye with thy name! [*Exit.*]
    PAN. A goodly medicine for my aching bones! O
world, world, world! Thus is the poor agent de-
spised! O traitors and bawds, how earnestly are you
set a-work, and how ill requited! Why should our
endeavor be so loved and the performance so
loathed? What verse for it? What instance for it?
Let me see: 41
    "Full merrily the humblebee doth sing
        Till he hath lost his honey and his sting,
        And being once subdued in armèd tail,
        Sweet honey and sweet notes together fail." 45
Good traders in the flesh, set this in your painted
cloths:°
    "As many as be here of Pandar's hall,

Sc. x: 13. imminence: impending evil.   14. Address: make
ready.   16. aye: always.   19. Niobe: She wept so grievously
for her dead children that she was turned into a stone fountain.
24. pight: pitched.   25. Titan: the sun.   28. still: always.
46–47. painted cloths: imitation tapestry, painted with Scrip-
tural or allegorical scenes. See Pl. 6a.

Sc. viii: 7. vail: lowering.   18. stickler-like: The *stickler*
was the umpire who intervened in a friendly combat.
    Sc. ix: 4. bruit: rumor.

Your eyes, half out, weep out at Pandar's fall.
Or if you cannot weep, yet give some groans,   50
Though not for me, yet for your aching bones.
Brethren and sisters of the hold-door trade,
Some two months hence my will shall here be
    made.
It should be now, but that my fear is this —

Some gallèd° goose of Winchester° would hiss.
Till then I'll sweat and seek about for eases,   56
And at that time bequeath you my diseases."

                      [*Exit.*]

55. galled: sore. **goose of Winchester:** prostitute. Prostitutes were called "Winchester geese" because they inhabited property in Southwark owned by the Bishop of Winchester.

The Tragedy of
OTHELLO, THE MOOR OF VENICE

Introduction

Othello was probably written in 1602. The earliest definite record of a performance occurs in the Court Accounts of King James I, which shows that it was played before the King on November 1, 1604. There are few certain indications of the date of writing, but some phrases were picked out of the play and embodied in the pirated version of *Hamlet* known as the first quarto (Q1), published in 1603. *Othello* probably followed either *Hamlet* or *Twelfth Night*.

The direct source of the play is not known. It is obviously derived from a story in the *Hecatomithi (Hundred Tales)* of Giraldi Cinthio, published in Venice in 1566, of which the outline runs as follows:

In Venice, there lived a Moor, valiant, handsome and highly regarded for his skill in war. A young lady named Disdemona fell in love with him, and he with her. In spite of objections from her parents, they married and lived happily in Venice. After a while the Moor was sent to command the garrison in Cyprus. Disdemona went with him and they safely reached the island. In their company were a captain, who was a favorite with the Moor, and an ensign; both were accompanied by their wives. The ensign fell desperately in love with Disdemona, but as she showed no interest in him, he supposed that she must be in love with the captain. So the ensign grew to hate them both. Soon afterward the captain was deprived of his rank for having attacked a soldier of the guard. Disdemona was greatly grieved, and endeavored to reconcile her husband to him. When the Moor told the ensign how his wife was asking him to restore the captain to favor, the ensign saw his chance and began to hint that the lady was in love with the captain. The Moor indignantly demanded proof, which the ensign found difficult to obtain; but at last he managed to steal the handkerchief embroidered in the Moorish fashion which her husband had given her. This handkerchief the ensign left on the captain's bed. The captain's wife was expert at embroidery, and she began to copy the work, and the ensign took care that the Moor should come on her while she was so engaged.

The Moor was now firmly convinced of his wife's guilt, and he bribed the ensign to kill the captain. One night as the captain was on his way to visit a courtesan, the ensign struck him such a blow in the right thigh that he cut off his leg. When the news reached Disdemona, she showed great grief, which confirmed the Moor's suspicions. So he plotted with the ensign to kill her. The ensign suggested that he should beat her with a stocking filled with sand, and when she was dead pull down part of the ceiling to make it appear an accident. This plan was carried out, and Disdemona was killed, to the great grief of everyone who knew her. But in a short while the Moor's feelings changed; he began to feel such sorrow at the death of his wife that he became almost mad, and realizing that the ensign was the cause of his loss, he hated him so bitterly that he would have slain him had he been able, but instead he turned him out of his company.

The ensign now began to plot against the Moor. He went to the captain, who had recovered from his wound, and told him that it was the Moor who had cut off his leg because of his jealous suspicions, and that Disdemona had in fact been murdered by her husband. Thereupon the captain accused the Moor, and the rulers of Venice commanded that the Moor should be brought back to the city. He was put to torture to persuade him to reveal the truth, but he denied everything. After some days in prison he was condemned to perpetual banishment. He was ultimately slain by the kinsfolk of Disdemona.

No English version of this tale is known, and it differs in many details from Shakespeare's play.

The text of *Othello* is difficult. There are three early versions: a quarto of 1622, the text of the first folio of 1623, and a later quarto of 1630. All three texts have many minor differences. That of F1 is the best, and has obviously been carefully prepared for the printer; it gives about 160 lines not found in the first quarto. On the other hand, the folio text has been most delicately refined, presumably to conform with an Act of Parliament of 1606 which forbade the use of the name of God in stage plays. It omits all the oaths which are found in the quarto; even such harmless remarks as "faith" and "pray" have been cut out or changed. On the whole the quarto is inferior to the folio; it adds a few lines of its own, but its readings are usually weaker. The quarto was probably printed from an earlier version of the playhouse manuscript, and the folio from a later copy revised and refined. The text used in modern editions is a compound of quarto and folio.

Othello is perhaps Shakespeare's greatest triumph as a stage play; it lacks the magnificent irrelevancies of *Hamlet* or the vastness of *Lear,* but it gains over both in concentration and design. There are, however, certain problems in *Othello* about which critics have argued endlessly. The first is the "time" problem, which is discussed in Appendix 22. The second is the problem of Iago's motives. Many different answers have been given by critics and actors.

Othello himself is a good example of the "tragic hero" as defined by Aristotle; he is a good man of great and simple virtues but with the fatal flaw of believing that men are what they seem. He is also a Moor, and so to Shakespeare and his audience a "black man." There was little color prejudice in Shakespeare's time, and on the stage the Moor was sometimes a heroic character. Indeed, the Moors in the sixteenth century were so powerful that they were greatly dreaded by all who had traffic in the Mediterranean.

Othello is a man of royal blood, proud of his descent. He has some characteristics of the savage, a hyperbolical utterance when roused and an unreasoning passion, but he is not portrayed as in any way an alien. He is "the noble Moor," a man "all-in-all sufficient."

He is also a professional soldier, a type common in literature and in life. In English literature there is a long line of distinguished military gentlemen with pleasant simple virtues and failings, beginning with Chaucer's Knight and coming down through Uncle Toby to Henry Esmond. Professional soldiers are inevitably molded by their profession. They are more exposed to physical danger than the civilian, but often sheltered from mental problems. They are faced with the duty of carrying out their orders in the most efficient way, but it is for the civilian to decide why the orders should first be given. Hence doubt and uncertainty are alien to the soldierly mind. "To be once in doubt," says Othello, "is once to be resolved." As soon as he has cleared up a situation, he acts quickly without further question. These qualities are admirable in the field, but by his marriage with a society lady of Venice, Othello finds himself involved in new problems in which his training and experience count for nothing. His love for Desdemona is not youthful passion, but a mature and mutual understanding, and this makes Iago's suggestion the more abhorrent to him. Othello is not a soldier of society who haunts Courts and capitals. He has lived all his life in camp and campaigns, and knows nothing of women.

Desdemona is the first woman who has ever come into Othello's life. She is a complete contrast, a lady moving in the best society of Venice, which was the most sophisticated and luxurious of all European cities, and particularly renowned for its ladies of pleasure. By convention Desdemona is often played as a perfect specimen of the Victorian young lady; but she is not so simple. Desdemona knew what she wanted and she won it in her own way, as is clear from Othello's account of their courtship. In public she has plenty of self-possession. Before the Duke she knows her own mind and states her case boldly. She takes the first opportunity of trying to prove that she can have her own way with her husband when she wishes; she easily persuades Othello to grant that Cassio may be allowed to plead his own cause. It is an unfortunate triumph, and brings about her destruction. When next she returns to Othello she is still in the same happy frame of mind, confident that he will do anything for her; but he has changed, for Iago has been working on him unceasingly. She cannot understand the alteration and she tries to win Othello back again by the same technique as before, which in the circumstances is disastrous. Desdemona has her weaknesses. She is soon thrown into panic by Othello's unexpected fury. In crises, she prefers to evade rather than face unpleasantness. She is, in short, a lively, vivacious, young woman moving in the best Venetian society. She wanted her man and she won him, but she knows very little of him and she realizes only too soon that he is utterly different from "the wealthy curlèd darlings of our nation." Her bewildered and pathetic simplicity at the end reveals that she was after all an inexperienced girl to whom the thought of disloyalty was so impossible that she could not even imagine jealousy in her husband.

Iago is one of Shakespeare's most subtle villains. He is an Italian, and therefore in Elizabethan eyes malignant by nature. There were many such in other plays, and indeed stories of real life in sixteenth-century Italy produce characters as ruthless and devilish. Iago loves mischief for its own sake and finds cruelty amusing. He believes that all women are false, and if Desdemona is true to Othello, it is because so far she has had no chance to be otherwise. Yet even so, given this character, why did he act as he did? Coleridge spoke of Iago's "motiveless malignity"; Hazlitt replied that Iago's motive was a perverted love of power. The fact is, however, that Iago's motives for the whole tragedy are laid bare in the first bitter outburst to Roderigo (I.i. 8–33). Shakespeare's audiences were well trained. No modern dramatist would dare to give such essential information in the first thirty-five lines.

Iago is a professional soldier. He has climbed up from the lowest rank until he is now within reach of the top. He naturally expects that Othello will select him as second in command, and his vanity is in part justified, for he is in many ways a greater man than Cassio. When he is rejected, he suffers the bitter blow which will come to everyone at some time or other when he sees himself passed over in favor of someone whom he despises. Injured vanity is a wrong to the essential self. This is the main cause of Iago's anger. It is not a dignified cause. Hence he refuses to face it out with his own conscience. He shies away from the sour truth that Othello considers Cassio to be a better soldier than himself. He begins to invent causes for Othello's choice — any excuse to get even with Othello. At any cost he will ease the writhing anguish of his hurt vanity by destroying those who have wronged him and all that they value most. These things are revealed in his soliloquies. Iago therefore begins with a lust to hurt both Othello and Cassio through Desdemona, but he soon becomes fascinated by his own cleverness and inextricably and fatally entangled in his own plot.

So Desdemona and Othello are brought to destruction. When Iago makes his foul suggestion, Othello feels, and how naturally, that he has been fooled. Who was he to know anything about the ways of a Venetian lady? "Honest" Iago, of course, knows everything:

This honest creature doubtless
Sees and knows more, much more, than he unfolds.

Not the least of Iago's subtlety is that he seems always to be keeping something back, to know more than he reveals. The incident which finally convinces Othello is the sight of the precious handkerchief in Cassio's hand. Had Desdemona been calmer, she would have remembered when she lost it; had Othello been less simple-minded, he would have asked Cassio how he came by it. But it is now too late. When he has seen Cassio giving Bianca the handkerchief, the situation is cleared up. There remains no doubt in Othello's mind; he must now do his duty, as he understands it.

The end is most moving. Othello is purged of all personal animosity. He sees Desdemona's death as a duty laid on him, and he does not consult his own heart when duty is concerned. In the last scene he approaches the bed not stealthily as a murderer, but as embodied vengeance, vindicating manhood wronged by the faithlessness of woman. Then, too late, he learns the truth, and his universe falls about him.

On the stage, *Othello* is the most often successfully acted of all Shakespeare's tragedies. The drama is perfectly constructed, and the theme is universal; jealousy in love is one of the commonest of human failings. Nevertheless there are certain changes in emphasis in the story of *Othello* as it affects modern spectators and readers, who are often inclined to regard Brabantio as a specimen of the heavy, slightly comic father. Like other fathers in Shakespeare's plays, such as old Capulet, Polonius, or Lear, he misunderstands his daughter and, to us at least, his anger that she should have chosen to wed Othello without first asking his leave is unseemly, unsympathetic, and crude. This was not the view in Shakespeare's day. Desdemona, as a lady of great family, was expected to make a suitable marriage with one of her own rank. The notion that anyone was free to marry at fancy was not generally held. It was utterly inconceivable that a girl of Desdemona's rank should run off in the night with a stranger, however distinguished. Brabantio is so dumfounded that he brings wild charges of witchcraft against Othello, for witchcraft is the only rational explanation of such an incredible breach of normal decent behavior. Brabantio was, therefore, a much-wronged man, and Desdemona was punished, albeit too brutally, for committing a sin against what at that time was regarded as fundamental decency.

Othello

DRAMATIS PERSONAE

DUKE OF VENICE

BRABANTIO, *a Senator*

OTHER SENATORS

GRATIANO, *brother to Brabantio*

LODOVICO, *kinsman to Brabantio*

OTHELLO, *a noble Moor in the service of the Venetian state*

CASSIO, *his lieutenant*

IAGO, *his ancient*

MONTANO, *Othello's predecessor in the government of Cyprus*

RODERIGO, *a Venetian gentleman*

CLOWN, *servant to Othello*

DESDEMONA, *daughter to Brabantio and wife to Othello*

EMILIA, *wife to Iago*

BIANCA, *mistress to Cassio*

SAILOR, MESSENGER, HERALD, OFFICERS, GENTLEMEN, MUSICIANS, *and* ATTENDANTS

SCENE — *Venice: a seaport in Cyprus.*

Act I

SCENE I. *Venice. A street.*

[*Enter* RODERIGO *and* IAGO.]

ROD. Tush, never tell me. I take it much unkindly
That thou, Iago, who hast had° my purse
As if the strings were thine, shouldst know of this.
IAGO. 'Sblood,° but you will not hear me.
If ever I did dream of such a matter,   5
Abhor me.
ROD. Thou told'st me thou didst hold him in thy
      hate.
IAGO. Despise me if I do not. Three great ones of
      the city,
In personal suit° to make me his Lieutenant,
Off-capped° to him. And, by the faith of man,   10
I know my price, I am worth no worse a place.
But he, as loving his own pride and purposes,
Evades them, with a bombast circumstance°
Horribly stuffed with epithets of war.°
And, in conclusion,   15
Nonsuits° my mediators, for, "Certes,"° says he,
"I have already chose my officer."
And what was he?
Forsooth, a great arithmetician,°
One Michael Cassio, a Florentine,   20
A fellow almost damned in a fair wife,°

That never set a squadron in the field,
Nor the division of a battle° knows
More than a spinster, unless the bookish theoric,°
Wherein the toged° Consuls° can propose   25
As masterly as he — mere prattle without practice
Is all his soldiership. But he, sir, had the election.
And I, of whom his eyes had seen the proof
At Rhodes, at Cyprus, and on other grounds   29
Christian and heathen, must be beleed° and calmed
By debitor and creditor. This countercaster,°
He, in good time,° must his Lieutenant be,
And I — God bless the mark!° — his Moorship's
      Ancient.°
ROD. By Heaven, I rather would have been his
      hangman.
IAGO. Why, there's no remedy. 'Tis the curse of
      service,   35
Preferment goes by letter and affection,
And not by old gradation,° where each second
Stood heir to the first. Now, sir, be judge yourself
Whether I in any just term am affined°
To love the Moor.
ROD.   I would not follow him, then. 40
IAGO. Oh, sir, content you,
I follow him to serve my turn upon him.
We cannot all be masters, nor all masters
Cannot be truly followed. You shall mark
Many a duteous and knee-crooking knave   45

Act I, Sc. i: 2. had: i.e., used. 4. 'Sblood: by God's blood.
9. In . . . suit: making this request in person. 10. Off-capped:
stood cap in hand. 13. bombast circumstance: bombastic
phrases. Bombast is cotton padding used to stuff out a gar-
ment. 14. stuffed . . . war: padded out with military terms.
16. Nonsuits: rejects the petition of. Certes: assuredly.
19. arithmetician: Contemporary books on military tactics are
full of elaborate diagrams and numerals to explain military for-
mations. Cassio is a student of such books. 21. almost . . . wife:
A much-disputed phrase. There is an Italian proverb, "You have
married a fair wife? You are damned." If Iago has this in mind,
he means by *almost* that Cassio is about to marry.

23. division . . . battle: organization of an army. 24. bookish
theoric: student of war; not a practical soldier. 25. toged:
wearing a toga. Consuls: councilors. Cf. I.ii.43. 30. beleed:
placed on the lee (or unfavorable) side. 31. countercaster:
calculator (repeating the idea of arithmetician). Counters were
used in making calculations. 32. in . . . time: A phrase express-
ing indignation. 33. God . . . mark: An exclamation of impa-
tience. Ancient: ensign, the third officer in the company of which
Othello is Captain and Cassio Lieutenant. 36–37. Preferment
. . . gradation: promotion comes through private recommenda-
tion and favoritism and not by order of seniority. 39. affined:
tied by affection.

That doting on his own obsequious bondage
Wears out his time, much like his master's ass,
For naught but provender, and when he's old,
    cashiered.°
Whip me such honest knaves. Others there are
Who, trimmed in forms and visages of duty,°   50
Keep yet their hearts attending on themselves,
And throwing but shows of service° on their lords
Do well thrive by them, and when they have lined
    their coats
Do themselves homage.° These fellows have some
    soul,
And such a one do I profess myself. For, sir,   55
It is as sure as you are Roderigo,
Were I the Moor, I would not be Iago.
In following him, I follow but myself.
Heaven is my judge, not I for love and duty,
But seeming so, for my peculiar° end.   60
For when my outward action doth demónstrate
The native act and figure of my heart°
In compliment extern,° 'tis not long after
But I will wear my heart upon my sleeve
For daws° to peck at. I am not what I am.°   65
   ROD. What a full fortune° does the thick-lips owe°
If he can carry 't thus!°
   IAGO.   Call up her father,
Rouse him. Make after him, poison his delight,
Proclaim him in the streets. Incense her kinsmen,
And though he in a fertile climate dwell,   70
Plague him with flies. Though that his joy be joy,
Yet throw such changes of vexation on 't
As it may lose some color.°
   ROD. Here is her father's house, I'll call aloud.
   IAGO. Do, with like timorous° accent and dire yell
As when, by night and negligence, the fire   76
Is spied in populous cities.
   ROD. What ho, Brabantio! Signior Brabantio, ho!
   IAGO. Awake! What ho, Brabantio! Thieves!
    Thieves! Thieves!
Look to your house, your daughter and your bags!°
Thieves! Thieves!   81

[BRABANTIO *appears above, at a window.*]

   BRA. What is the reason of this terrible summons?
What is the matter there?
   ROD. Signior, is all your family within?
   IAGO. Are your doors locked?
   BRA.   Why, wherefore ask you this?   85

   IAGO. 'Zounds,° sir, you're robbed. For shame,
    put on your gown,°
Your heart is burst, you have lost half your soul.
Even now, now, very now, an old black ram
Is tupping° your white ewe. Arise, arise,
Awake the snorting° citizens with the bell,   90
Or else the Devil° will make a grandsire of you.
Arise, I say.
   BRA.   What, have you lost your wits?
   ROD. Most reverend signior, do you know my
    voice?
   BRA. Not I. What are you?
   ROD. My name is Roderigo.   94
   BRA.   The worser welcome.
I have charged thee not to haunt about my doors.
In honest plainness thou hast heard me say
My daughter is not for thee, and now, in madness,
Being full of supper and distempering draughts,°
Upon malicious bravery° dost thou come   100
To start° my quiet.
   ROD. Sir, sir, sir ——
   BRA.   But thou must needs be sure
My spirit and my place have in them power
To make this bitter to thee.
   ROD.   Patience, good sir.
   BRA. What tell'st thou me of robbing? This is
    Venice,   105
My house is not a grange.°
   ROD.   Most grave Brabantio,
In simple and pure soul I come to you.
   IAGO. 'Zounds, sir, you are one of those that will
not serve God if the Devil bid you. Because we come
to do you service and you think we are ruffians,   110
you'll have your daughter covered with a Barbary°
horse, you'll have your nephews° neigh to you, you'll
have coursers for cousins,° and jennets° for ger-
mans.°
   BRA. What profane wretch art thou?   115
   IAGO. I am one, sir, that comes to tell you your
daughter and the Moor are now making the beast
with two backs.
   BRA. Thou art a villain.
   IAGO.   You are — a Senator.
   BRA. This thou shalt answer. I know thee, Roder-
    igo.   120
   ROD. Sir, I will answer anything. But I beseech you
If 't be your pleasure and most wise consent,
As partly I find it is, that your fair daughter,
At this odd-even° and dull° watch o' the night,
Transported with no worse nor better guard   125

---

48. cashiered: dismissed. The word at this time did not imply
dishonorable discharge.   **50. trimmed . . . duty:** decking them-
selves out with the outward forms of loyal service.   **52. throw-
ing . . . service:** serving merely in outward show.   **54. Do . . .
homage:** serve themselves. **homage:** an outward act signifying
obedience.   **60. peculiar:** particular, personal.   **62. native . . .
heart:** natural actions and shape of my secret designs.   **63. extern:**
outward.   **65. daws:** jackdaws; i.e., fools. **I . . . am:** i.e., I am in
secret a devil.   **66. full fortune:** overflowing good luck. **owe:**
own.   **67. carry't thus:** i.e., bring off this marriage. **72–73. throw
. . . color:** cause him some annoyance by way of variety to
tarnish his joy.   **75. timorous:** terrifying.   **80. bags:** moneybags.

86. 'Zounds: by God's wounds. **gown:** dressing gown.   **89. tup-
ping:** covering.   **90. snorting:** snoring.   **91. Devil:** The Devil in
old pictures and woodcuts was represented as black.   **99. dis-
tempering draughts:** liquor that makes senseless.   **100. bravery:**
defiance.   **101. start:** startle.   **106. grange:** lonely farm.
111. Barbary: Moorish.   **112. nephews:** grandsons.   **113. cousins:**
near relations. **jennets:** Moorish ponies.   **114. germans:** kins-
men.   **124. odd-even:** about midnight. **dull:** heavy, sleepy.

But with a knave of common hire, a gondolier,
To the gross clasps of a lascivious Moor —
If this be known to you, and your allowance,°
We then have done you bold and saucy wrongs.
But if you know not this, my manners tell me   130
We have your wrong rebuke. Do not believe
That from the sense of all civility°
I thus would play and trifle with your reverence.
Your daughter, if you have not given her leave,
I say again, hath made a gross revolt,°   135
Tying her duty, beauty, wit, and fortunes
In an extravagant° and wheeling° stranger
Of here and everywhere. Straight satisfy yourself.
If she be in her chamber or your house,
Let loose on me the justice of the state   140
For thus deluding you.
     BRA.   Strike on the tinder,° ho!
Give me a taper!° Call up all my people!
This accident is not unlike my dream.
Belief of it oppresses me already.
Light, I say! Light!   [*Exit above.*]
     IAGO.   Farewell, for I must leave you.   145
It seems not meet, nor wholesome to my place,°
To be produced — as if I stay I shall —
Against the Moor. For I do know the state,
However this may gall° him with some check,°
Cannot with safety cast° him. For he's embarked
With such loud reason to the Cyprus wars,   151
Which even now stand in act,° that, for their souls,
Another of his fathom° they have none
To lead their business. In which regard,
Though I do hate him as I do Hell pains,   155
Yet for necessity of present life
I must show out a flag° and sign of love,
Which is indeed but sign. That you shall surely find
     him,
Lead to the Sagittary° the raisèd search,   159
And there will I be with him. So farewell.   [*Exit.*]
     [*Enter, below,* BRABANTIO, *in his nightgown, and*
         SERVANTS *with torches.*]
     BRA. It is too true an evil. Gone she is,
And what's to come of my despisèd time°
Is naught but bitterness. Now, Roderigo,
Where didst thou see her? Oh, unhappy girl!
With the Moor, say'st thou? Who would be a
     father!   165

How didst thou know 'twas she? Oh, she deceives
     me
Past thought! What said she to you? Get more ta-
     pers.
Raise all my kindred. Are they married, think you?
     ROD. Truly, I think they are.
     BRA. Oh Heaven! How got she out? Oh, treason
     of the blood!°   170
Fathers, from hence trust not your daughters' minds
By what you see them act. Are there not charms°
By which the property° of youth and maidhood
May be abused?° Have you not read, Roderigo,
Of some such thing?
     ROD.   Yes, sir, I have indeed.   175
     BRA. Call up my brother. Oh, would you had had
     her!
Some one way, some another. Do you know
Where we may apprehend her and the Moor?
     ROD. I think I can discover him, if you please
To get good guard and go along with me.   180
     BRA. Pray you, lead on. At every house I'll call,
I may command° at most. Get weapons, ho!
And raise some special officers of night.
On, good Roderigo, I'll deserve your pains.°
                            [*Exeunt.*]

SCENE II. *Another street.*

     [*Enter* OTHELLO, IAGO, *and* ATTENDANTS
              with torches.]
     IAGO. Though in the trade of war I have slain
     men,
Yet do I hold it very stuff° o' the conscience
To do no contrivèd° murder. I lack iniquity
Sometimes to do me service. Nine or ten times
I had thought to have yerked° him here under the
     ribs.   5
     OTH. 'Tis better as it is.
     IAGO.   Nay, but he prated
And spoke such scurvy and provoking terms
Against your honor
That, with the little godliness I have,
I did full hard forbear him.° But I pray you, sir,   10
Are you fast° married? Be assured of this,
That the Magnifico° is much beloved,
And hath in his effect° a voice potential
As double as° the Duke's. He will divorce you,
Or put upon you what restraint and grievance   15

128. your allowance: by your permission.   132. from . . . civility: disregarding all sense of decent behavior.   135. gross revolt: indecent rebellion.   137. extravagant: vagabond. wheeling: wandering.   141. tinder: the primitive method of making fire, used before the invention of matches. A spark, made by striking flint on steel, fell on the tinder, some inflammable substance such as charred linen, which was blown into flame.   142. taper: candle. 146. place: i.e., as Othello's officer.   149. gall: make sore. check: rebuke.   150. cast: dismiss from service.   152. stand in act: are on the point of beginning.   153. fathom: depth. 157. flag: a sign of welcome.   159. Sagittary: presumably some building in Venice, not identified, used as a meeting place for the Council.   162. what's . . . time: the rest of my wretched life.

170. treason . . . blood: treachery of my own child.   172. charms: magic spells.   173. property: nature.   174. abused: deceived. 182. command: find supporters.   184. deserve . . . pains: reward your labor.

     Sc. ii: 2. stuff: material, nature.   3. contrived: deliberately planned.   5. yerked: jabbed.   10. full . . . him: had a hard job to keep my hands off him.   11. fast: securely.   12. Magnifico: the title of the chief men of Venice.   13. in . . . effect: what he can do.   13–14. potential . . . as: twice as powerful as.

The law, with all his might to enforce it on,
Will give him cable.°

OTH.   Let him do his spite.
My services which I have done the signiory°
Shall outtongue his complaints. 'Tis yet to know° —
Which, when I know that boasting is an honor,   20
I shall promulgate° — I fetch my life and being°
From men of royal siege,° and my demerits°
May speak unbonneted° to as proud a fortune
As this that I have reached. For know, Iago,
But that I love the gentle Desdemona,   25
I would not my unhousèd° free condition
Put into circumscription and confine°
For the sea's worth. But look! What lights come
    yond?

IAGO. Those are the raisèd father and his friends.
You were best go in.

OTH.   Not I, I must be found.   30
My parts,° my title, and my perfect° soul
Shall manifest me rightly. Is it they?

IAGO. By Janus,° I think no.

[*Enter* CASSIO, *and certain* OFFICERS *with torches.*]

OTH. The servants of the Duke, and my Lieuten-
    ant.
The goodness of the night upon you, friends!   35
What is the news?

CAS.   The Duke does greet you, General,
And he requires your haste-posthaste° appearance,
Even on the instant.

OTH.   What is the matter, think you?

CAS. Something from Cyprus, as I may divine.
It is a business of some heat. The galleys°   40
Have sent a dozen sequent° messengers
This very night at one another's heels,
And many of the consuls, raised and met,
Are at the Duke's already. You have been hotly
    called for
When, being not at your lodging to be found,   45
The Senate hath sent about three several° quests
To search you out.

OTH. 'Tis well I am found by you.
I will but spend a word here in the house
And go with you.   [*Exit.*]

CAS.   Ancient, what makes he here?

IAGO. Faith, he tonight hath boarded a land car-
    rack.°   50
If it prove lawful prize, he's made forever.

CAS. I do not understand.

IAGO.   He's married.

CAS.   To who?

[*Re-enter* OTHELLO.]

IAGO. Marry,° to —— Come, Captain, will you
    go?

OTH.   Have with you.

CAS. Here comes another troop to seek for you.

IAGO. It is Brabantio. General, be advised,°   55
He comes to bad intent.

[*Enter* BRABANTIO, RODERIGO, *and* OFFICERS *with torches and weapons.*]

OTH.   Holloa! Stand there!

ROD. Signior, it is the Moor.

BRA.   Down with him, thief!
                    [*They draw on both sides.*]

IAGO. You, Roderigo! Come, sir, I am for you.

OTH. Keep up° your bright swords, for the dew
    will rust them.
Good signior, you shall more command with years
Than with your weapons.   61

BRA. O thou foul thief, where hast thou stowed
    my daughter?
Damned as thou art, thou hast enchanted her.
For I'll refer me to all things of sense°
If she in chains of magic were not bound,   65
Whether a maid so tender, fair, and happy,
So opposite to marriage that she shunned
The wealthy curlèd darlings of our nation,
Would ever have, to incur a general mock,
Run from her guardage° to the sooty bosom   70
Of such a thing as thou, to fear, not to delight.
Judge me the world if 'tis not gross in sense°
That thou hast practiced on her with foul charms,
Abused her delicate youth with drugs or minerals
That weaken motion.° I'll have 't disputed on,°   75
'Tis probable, and palpable° to thinking.
I therefore apprehend and do attach° thee
For an abuser of the world, a practicer
Of arts inhibited and out of warrant.°
Lay hold upon him. If he do resist,   80
Subdue him at his peril.

OTH.   Hold your hands,
Both you of my inclining and the rest.
Were it my cue to fight, I should have known it
Without a prompter. Where will you that I go

---

17. cable: rope.   **18. signiory**: the state of Venice.   **19. 'Tis . . .
know**: it has still to be made known.   **21. promulgate**: proclaim.
fetch . . . being: am descended.   **22. royal siege**: throne. **de-
merits**: deserts.   **23. unbonneted**: A disputed phrase. Usually it
means "without a cap"; i.e., in sign that the wearer is standing
before a superior. But Othello means that his merits are such that
he need show deference to no man.   **26. unhoused**: unmarried.
27. confine: confinement.   **31. parts**: abilities. **perfect**: ready.
33. Janus: the two-faced God of the Romans, an appropriate
deity for Iago.   **37. haste-posthaste**: with the quickest possible
speed. When it was necessary to urge the postboy to greater
speed than usual, the letter or dispatch was inscribed "haste,
posthaste." The Earl of Essex once inscribed a letter "haste,
haste, haste posthaste, haste for life." See App. 17.   **40. galleys**:
Venetian ships manned and rowed by slaves; the fastest of
craft.   **41. sequent**: following one after another.   **46. several**:
separate.

50. carrack: the largest type of Spanish merchant ship.
53. Marry: Mary, by the Virgin — with a pun.   **55. advised**:
careful.   **59. Keep up**: sheathe.   **64. refer . . . sense**: i.e., by
every rational consideration.   **70. guardage**: guardianship.
72. gross in sense: i.e., plain to the perception.   **75. motion**
sense. disputed on: argued in the courts of law.   **76. palpable**:
clear.   **77. attach**: arrest.   **79. arts . . . warrant**: forbidden and
illegal acts; i.e., magic and witchcraft.

To answer this your charge?

BRA.   To prison, till fit time   85
Of law and course of direct session°
Call thee to answer.

OTH.   What if I do obey?
How may the Duke be therewith satisfied,
Whose messengers are here about my side
Upon some present° business of the state   90
To bring me to him?

1. OFF.   'Tis true, most worthy signior.
The Duke's in Council, and your noble self
I am sure is sent for.

BRA.   How! The Duke in Council!
In this time of the night! Bring him away.
Mine's not an idle° cause. The Duke himself,   95
Or any of my brothers of the state,
Cannot but feel this wrong as 'twere their own.
For if such actions may have passage free,°
Bondslaves and pagans shall our statesmen be.

                              [*Exeunt.*]

SCENE III. *A council chamber.*

[*The* DUKE *and* SENATORS *sitting at a table,* OFFICERS
attending.]

DUKE. There is no composition° in these news°
That gives them credit.

1. SEN.   Indeed they are disproportioned.
My letters say a hundred and seven galleys.

DUKE. And mine, a hundred and forty.

2. SEN.   And mine, two hundred.
But though they jump not on a just account° —   5
As in these cases, where the aim reports,°
'Tis oft with difference — yet do they all confirm
A Turkish fleet, and bearing up° to Cyprus.

DUKE. Nay, it is possible enough to judgment.
I do not so secure me in the error,°   10
But the main article° I do approve
In fearful° sense.

SAILOR. [*Within*] What ho! What ho! What ho!

1. OFF. A messenger from the galleys.

                    [*Enter* SAILOR.]

DUKE.   Now, what's the business?

SAIL. The Turkish preparation makes for Rhodes.
So was I bid report here to the state   15
By Signior Angelo.

DUKE. How say you by this change?

---

1. SEN.   This cannot be,
By no assay of reason.° 'Tis a pageant°
To keep us in false gaze.° When we consider
The importancy of Cyprus to the Turk,   20
And let ourselves again but understand
That as it more concerns the Turk than Rhodes,
So may he with more facile question bear° it,
For that it stands not in such warlike brace°
But altogether lacks the abilities   25
That Rhodes is dressed° in — if we make thought
    of this,
We must not think the Turk is so unskillful
To leave that latest which concerns him first,
Neglecting an attempt of ease and gain
To wake and wage° a danger profitless.   30

DUKE. Nay, in all confidence, he's not for Rhodes.

1. OFF. Here is more news.

                [*Enter a* MESSENGER.]

MESS. The Ottomites,° Reverend and Gracious,
Steering with due course toward the isle of Rhodes,
Have there injointed° them with an after-fleet.°   35

1. SEN. Aye, so I thought. How many, as you
    guess?

MESS. Of thirty sail. And now they do restem°
Their backward course, bearing with frank appear-
    ance°
Their purposes toward Cyprus. Signior Montano,
Your trusty and most valiant servitor,   40
With his free duty recommends you thus,°
And prays you to believe him.

DUKE. 'Tis certain then for Cyprus.
Marcus Luccicos, is not he in town?

1. SEN. He's now in Florence.   45

DUKE. Write from us to him, post-posthaste dis-
    patch.

1. SEN. Here comes Brabantio and the valiant
    Moor.

        [*Enter* BRABANTIO, OTHELLO, IAGO, RODERIGO,
                and OFFICERS.]

DUKE. Valiant Othello, we must straight employ
    you
Against the general enemy Ottoman.

[*To* BRABANTIO] I did not see you. Welcome, gentle
    signior,   50
We lacked your counsel and your help tonight.

BRA. So did I yours. Good your Grace, pardon
    me,
Neither my place nor aught I heard of business
Hath raised me from my bed, nor doth the general
    care
Take hold on me. For my particular° grief   55

---

86. course . . . session: trial in the ordinary courts, where witches
and other criminals are tried — and not by special commission as
a great man.   90. present: immediate.   95. idle: trivial.
98. have . . . free: be freely allowed.

Sc. iii: 1. composition: agreement. news: reports.   5. jump
. . . account: do not agree with an exact estimate.   6. aim re-
ports: i.e., intelligence reports of an enemy's intention often
differ in the details.   8. bearing up: making course for.   10. I
. . . error: I do not consider myself free from danger, because
the reports may not all be accurate.   11. main article: general
purport.   12. fearful: to be feared.

18. assay of reason: reasonable test. pageant: show.   19. false
gaze: looking the wrong way.   23. with . . . bear: take it more
easily.   24. brace: state of defense.   26. dressed: prepared.
30. wage: risk.   33. Ottomites: Turks.   35. injointed: joined.
after-fleet: following, second fleet.   37. restem: steer again.
38. frank appearance: no attempt at concealment.   41. With . . .
thus: with all due respect thus advises.   55. particular: personal.

Is of so floodgate° and o'erbearing nature
That it engluts° and swallows other sorrows,
And it is still itself.

DUKE.   Why, what's the matter?

BRA. My daughter! Oh, my daughter!

ALL.   Dead?

BRA.   Aye, to me.
She is abused, stol'n from me and corrupted   60
By spells and medicines bought of mountebanks.°
For nature so preposterously to err,
Being not deficient, blind, or lame of sense,
Sans° witchcraft could not.

DUKE. Whoe'er he be that in this foul proceeding
Hath thus beguiled your daughter of herself°   66
And you of her, the bloody book of law
You shall yourself read in the bitter letter
After your own sense — yea, though our proper° son
Stood in your action.

BRA.   Humbly I thank your Grace.   70
Here is the man, this Moor, whom now, it seems,
Your special mandate for the state affairs
Hath hither brought.

ALL.   We are very sorry for 't.

DUKE. [To OTHELLO] What in your own part can
     you say to this?

BRA. Nothing but this is so.   75

OTH. Most potent, grave, and reverend signiors,
My very noble and approved° good masters,
That I have ta'en away this old man's daughter,
It is most true — true, I have married her.
The very head and front° of my offending   80
Hath this extent, no more. Rude° am I in my speech,
And little blest with the soft phrase of peace.
For since these arms of mine had seven years' pith°
Till now some nine moons wasted, they have used
Their dearest° action in the tented field.   85
And little of this great world can I speak,
More than pertains to feats of broil and battle,
And therefore little shall I grace my cause
In speaking for myself. Yet, by your gracious pa-
     tience,
I will a round unvarnished tale° deliver   90
Of my whole course of love — what drugs, what
     charms,
What conjuration and what mighty magic —
For such proceeding I am charged withal —
I won his daughter.

BRA.   A maiden never bold,
Of spirit so still and quiet that her motion   95

Blushed at herself,° and she — in spite of nature,
Of years, of country, credit,° everything —
To fall in love with what she feared to look on!
It is a judgment maimed and most imperfect
That will confess° perfection so could err   100
Against all rules of nature, and must be driven
To find out practices° of cunning Hell
Why this should be. I therefore vouch° again
That with some mixtures° powerful o'er the blood,°
Or with some dram conjured° to this effect,   105
He wrought upon her.

DUKE.   To vouch this is no proof
Without more certain and more overt° test
Than these thin habits° and poor likelihoods°
Of modern seeming° do prefer° against him.

1. SEN. But, Othello, speak.   110
Did you by indirect and forcèd° courses
Subdue and poison this young maid's affections?
Or came it by request, and such fair question
As soul to soul affordeth?

OTH.   I do beseech you
Send for the lady to the Sagittary,   115
And let her speak of me before her father.
If you do find me foul in her report,
The trust, the office I do hold of you,
Not only take away, but let your sentence
Even fall upon my life.

DUKE.   Fetch Desdemona hither.   120

OTH. Ancient, conduct them, you best know the
     place.   [Exeunt IAGO and ATTENDANTS.]
And till she come, as truly as to Heaven
I do confess the vices of my blood,
So justly to your grave ears I'll present
How I did thrive in this fair lady's love   125
And she in mine.

DUKE.   Say it, Othello.

OTH. Her father loved me, oft invited me,
Still° questioned me the story of my life
From year to year, the battles, sieges, fortunes,   130
That I have passed.
I ran it through, even from my boyish days
To the very moment that he bade me tell it.
Wherein I spake of most disastrous chances,°
Of moving accidents° by flood and field,   135
Of hairbreadth 'scapes i' the imminent deadly
     breach,°
Of being taken by the insolent foe
And sold to slavery, of my redemption thence,

---

56. floodgate: i.e., like water rushing through an opened sluice.
57. engluts: swallows.   61. mountebanks: quack doctors, who
dealt in poisons and love potions. Cf. *Haml*, IV.vii.142.
64. Sans: without.   66. beguiled . . . herself: cheated your
daughter of herself; i.e., caused her to be "beside herself."
69. proper: own.   77. approved: tested; i.e., found good masters
by experience.   80. front: forehead.   81. Rude: rough, uncul-
tured.   83. pith: marrow.   85. dearest: most important.
90. round . . . tale: direct, unadorned account.

95–96. Of . . . herself: she was so shy that she blushed at the
slightest cause. motion: outward behavior.   97. credit: reputa-
tion.   100. will confess: would believe.   102. practices: plots.
103. vouch: declare.   104. mixtures: drugs. blood: passions.
105. conjured: mixed with spells.   107. overt: open.   108. thin
habits: slight evidence; lit., thin clothes. poor likelihoods: un-
convincing charges.   109. modern seeming: slight suspicion. pre-
fer: make a charge against.   111. forced: unnatural.   129. Still:
always, continually.   134. chances: accidents.   135. accidents:
occurrences.   136. breach: assault on a city. See Pl. 12a.

And portance° in my travels' history.
Wherein of antres° vast and deserts idle,°   140
Rough quarries, rocks, and hills whose heads touch
    heaven,
It was my hint° to speak — such was the process.°
And of the cannibals that each other eat,
The anthropophagi,° and men whose heads
Do grow beneath their shoulders.° This to hear
Would Desdemona seriously incline.   146
But still the house affairs would draw her thence,
Which ever as she could with haste dispatch,
She'd come again, and with a greedy ear
Devour up my discourse. Which I observing,   150
Took once a pliant° hour and found good means
To draw from her a prayer of earnest heart
That I would all my pilgrimage dilate,°
Whereof by parcels° she had something heard,
But not intentively.° I did consent,   155
And often did beguile her of° her tears
When I did speak of some distressful stroke
That my youth suffered. My story being done,
She gave me for my pains a world of sighs.
She swore, in faith, 'twas strange, 'twas passing
    strange,   160
'Twas pitiful, 'twas wondrous pitiful.
She wished she had not heard it, yet she wished
That Heaven had made her° such a man. She
    thanked me,
And bade me, if I had a friend that loved her,
I should but teach him how to tell my story   165
And that would woo her. Upon this hint I spake.
She loved me for the dangers I had passed,
And I loved her that she did pity them.
This only is the witchcraft I have used.
Here comes the lady, let her witness it.   170

[*Enter* DESDEMONA, IAGO, *and* ATTENDANTS.]

DUKE. I think this tale would win my daughter
    too.
Good Brabantio,
Take up this mangled matter at the best.°
Men do their broken weapons rather use
Than their bare hands.
    BRA.   I pray you hear her speak.   175
If she confess that she was half the wooer,
Destruction on my head if my bad blame
Light on the man! Come hither, gentle mistress.
Do you perceive in all this noble company
Where most you owe obedience?
    DES.   My noble Father,   180
I do perceive here a divided duty.

To you I am bound for life and education,
My life and education both do learn° me
How to respect you, you are the lord of duty,°
I am hitherto your daughter. But here's my hus-
    band,   185
And so much duty as my mother showed
To you, preferring you before her father
So much I challenge that I may profess
Due to the Moor my lord.
    BRA.   God be with you! I have done.
Please it your Grace, on to the state affairs.   190
I had rather to adopt a child than get° it.
Come hither, Moor.
I here do give thee that with all my heart
Which, but thou hast already, with all my heart
I would keep from thee. For your sake, jewel,   195
I am glad at soul I have no other child,
For thy escape would teach me tyranny,
To hang clogs on them. I have done, my lord.
    DUKE. Let me speak like yourself, and lay a sen-
    tence°
Which, as a grise° or step, may help these lovers
Into your favor.   201
When remedies are past, the griefs are ended
By seeing the worst, which late on hopes depended.°
To mourn a mischief that is past and gone
Is the next way to draw new mischief on.   205
What cannot be preserved when fortune takes,
Patience her injury a mockery makes.°
The robbed that smiles steals something from the
    thief.
He robs himself that spends a bootless° grief.
    BRA. So° let the Turk of Cyprus us beguile,   210
We lose it not so long as we can smile.
He bears the sentence well that nothing bears
But the free comfort which from thence he hears.
But he bears both the sentence and the sorrow
That, to pay grief, must of poor patience borrow.
These sentences, to sugar or to gall,   216
Being strong on both sides, are equivocal.
But words are words. I never yet did hear
That the bruisèd heart was piercèd through the ear.
I humbly beseech you, proceed to the affairs of
    state.   220
    DUKE. The Turk with a most mighty preparation
makes for Cyprus. Othello, the fortitude of the place

---

139. **portance:** bearing.   140. **antres:** caves. **idle:** worthless.
142. **hint:** occasion. **process:** proceeding, order.   144. **anthro-**
pophagi: cannibals.   144–45. **men ... shoulders:** See *Temp*,
III.iii.46–47,n.   151. **pliant:** suitable.   153. **dilate:** relate at
length.   154. **parcels:** portions.   155. **intentively:** intently.
156. **beguile ... of:** draw from her.   163. **her:** for her.   173. **Take**
... best: make the best settlement you can of this confused busi-
ness.

183. **learn:** teach.   184. **lord of duty:** the man to whom I owe
duty.   191. **get:** beget.   199. **sentence:** proverbial saying.
200. **grise:** degree, step.   202–03. **When ... depended:** our
anxieties end when the feared event happens.   207. **Patience ...**
makes: i.e., when we are not unduly disturbed by our misfor-
tunes, we mock Fortune.   209. **bootless:** vain.   210–19. **So ...**
ear: Brabantio retaliates sarcastically with a few "sentences"
of his own: Let the Turk take Cyprus; it is no loss if we smile at it.
It is easy enough to produce sententious consolation, it costs
nothing; but the man who has to endure both consolation and the
sorrow itself must needs be patient. These sentences work both
ways; mere words hurt no one. Cf. Leonato's similar outburst,
M Ado, V.i.3–38.

is best known to you, and though we have there a
substitute° of most allowed° sufficiency,° yet opin-
ion, a sovereign mistress of effects, throws a more
safer voice on you.° You must therefore be content
to slubber° the gloss of your new fortunes with this
more stubborn and boisterous expedition.   229

OTH. The tyrant custom, most grave Senators,
Hath made the flinty and steel couch of war
My thrice-driven° bed of down. I do agnize°
A natural and prompt alacrity
I find in hardness,° and do undertake
These present wars against the Ottomites.   235
Most humbly therefore bending to your state,
I crave fit disposition for my wife,
Due reference of place° and exhibition,°
With such accommodation and besort°
As levels with her breeding.°

DUKE.   If you please,   240
Be 't at her father's.

BRA.   I'll not have it so.

OTH. Nor I.

DES.   Nor I. I would not there reside,
To put my father in impatient thoughts
By being in his eye. Most gracious Duke,
To my unfolding° lend your prosperous° ear,   245
And let me find a charter° in your voice
To assist my simpleness.

DUKE. What would you, Desdemona?

DES. That I did love the Moor to live with him,
My downright violence and storm of fortunes   250
May trumpet to the world. My heart's subdued
Even to the very quality of my lord.°
I saw Othello's visage in his mind,
And to his honors and his valiant parts
Did I my soul and fortunes consecrate.   255
So that, dear lords, if I be left behind,
A moth of peace,° and he go to the war,
The rites for which I love him are bereft me,
And I a heavy interim° shall support
By his dear absence. Let me go with him.   260

OTH. Let her have your voices.
Vouch° with me, Heaven, I therefore beg it not
To please the palate of my appetite,
Nor to comply with heat — the young affects
In me defunct° — and proper satisfaction,   265

But to be free and bounteous° to her mind.°
And Heaven defend° your good souls, that you think
I will your serious and great business scant
For she is with me. No, when light-winged toys°
Of feathered Cupid seel° with wanton dullness   270
My speculative and officed instruments,°
That my disports° corrupt and taint my business,
Let housewives make a skillet° of my helm,
And all indign° and base adversities
Make head against° my estimation!°   275

DUKE. Be it as you shall privately determine,
Either for her stay or going. The affair cries haste,
And speed must answer 't. You must hence tonight.

DES. Tonight, my lord?

DUKE.   This night.

OTH.   With all my heart.

DUKE. At nine i' the morning here we'll meet
again.   280
Othello, leave some officer behind,
And he shall our commission° bring to you,
With such things else of quality and respect
As doth import you.°

OTH.   So please your Grace, my Ancient,
A man he is of honesty and trust.   285
To his conveyance I assign my wife,
With what else needful your good grace shall think
To be sent after me.

DUKE.   Let it be so.
Good night to everyone. [To BRABANTIO] And, noble
signior,
If virtue no delighted beauty lack,   290
Your son-in-law is far more fair than black.°

1. SEN. Adieu, brave Moor. Use Desdemona well.

BRA. Look to her, Moor, if thou hast eyes to see.
She has deceived her father, and may thee.°

[Exeunt DUKE, SENATORS, OFFICERS, etc.]

OTH. My life upon her faith! Honest Iago,   295
My Desdemona must I leave to thee.
I prithee, let thy wife attend on her,
And bring them after in the best advantage.°
Come, Desdemona, I have but an hour
Of love, of worldly matters and direction,   300
To spend with thee. We must obey the time.

[Exeunt OTHELLO and DESDEMONA.]

---

224. substitute: deputy commander. allowed: admitted. suffi-
ciency: efficiency.   224–27. yet ... you: yet public opinion,
which controls our actions, is such that we regard you as a safer
choice.   228. slubber: tarnish.   232. thrice-driven: three times
refined. agnize: confess.   234. hardness: hardship.   238. Due
... place: i.e., that she shall be treated as becomes my wife.
exhibition: allowance.   239. besort: attendants.   240. levels
... breeding: as suits her birth.   245. unfolding: plan; lit., re-
vealing. prosperous: favorable.   246. charter: privilege.
249–52. That ... lord: my love for the Moor is publicly shown by
the way in which I have violently taken my fortunes in my hands;
my heart has become a soldier like my husband. quality: profes-
sion.   257. moth of peace: a useless creature living in luxury.
259. interim: interval.   262. Vouch: certify.   264–65. young
... defunct: in me the passion of youth is dead.

266. bounteous: generous. to ... mind: Othello repeats Desde-
mona's claim that this is a marriage of minds.   267. defend: for-
bid.   269. toys: trifles.   270. seel: close up; a technical term
from falconry. See App. 26.   271. speculative ... instruments:
powers of sight and action; i.e., my efficiency as your general.
272. disports: amusements.   273. skillet: saucepan.   274. in-
dign: unworthy.   275. Make ... against: overcome. estima-
tion: reputation.   282. commission: formal document of appoint-
ment.   283–84. With ... you: with other matters that concern
your position and honor.   290–91. If ... black: if worthiness is a
beautiful thing in itself, your son-in-law, though black, has
beauty.   293–94. Look ... thee: Iago in the background takes
note of these words, and later reminds Othello of them with
deadly effect. See III.iii.206.   298. in ... advantage: at the best
opportunity.

ROD. Iago!

IAGO. What say'st thou, noble heart?

ROD. What will I do, thinkest thou?

IAGO. Why, go to bed and sleep.   305

ROD. I will incontinently° drown myself.

IAGO. If thou dost, I shall never love thee after. Why, thou silly gentleman!

ROD. It is silliness to live when to live is torment, and then have we a prescription to die when death is our physician.   311

IAGO. Oh, villainous! I have looked upon the world for four times seven years, and since I could distinguish betwixt a benefit and an injury I never found man that knew how to love himself. Ere I would say I would drown myself for the love of a guinea hen, I would change my humanity with a baboon.   318

ROD. What should I do? I confess it is my shame to be so fond,° but it is not in my virtue° to amend it.

IAGO. Virtue! A fig! 'Tis in ourselves that we are thus or thus. Our bodies are gardens, to the which our wills° are gardeners. So that if we will plant nettles or sow lettuce, set hyssop and weed up   325 thyme, supply it with one gender° of herbs or distract it with many, either to have it sterile with idleness or manured with industry — why, the power and corrigible° authority of this lies in our wills. If the balance of our lives had not one scale of   330 reason to poise° another of sensuality, the blood and baseness of our natures would conduct us to most preposterous conclusions. But we have reason to cool our raging motions, our carnal stings,° our unbitted° lusts, whereof I take this that you call love to be a sect or scion.°   337

ROD. It cannot be.

IAGO. It is merely a lust of the blood and a permission of the will. Come, be a man. Drown thyself! Drown cats and blind puppies. I have professed me thy friend, and I confess me knit to thy deserving with cables of perdurable° toughness. I could never better stead° thee than now. Put money in thy purse, follow thou the wars, defeat thy favor with an   345 usurped beard° — I say put money in thy purse. It cannot be that Desdemona should long continue her love to the Moor — put money in thy purse — nor he his to her. It was a violent commencement,   350 and thou shalt see an answerable sequestration° — put but money in thy purse. These Moors are changeable in their wills. — Fill thy purse with money. The food that to him now is as luscious as locusts° shall be to him shortly as bitter as coloquintida.°   355 She must change for youth. When she is sated with his body, she will find the error of her choice. She must have change, she must — therefore put money in thy purse. If thou wilt needs damn thyself, do it a more delicate way than drowning. Make all   360 the money thou canst.° If sanctimony and a frail vow betwixt an erring° barbarian and a supersubtle Venetian be not too hard for my wits and all the tribe of Hell, thou shalt enjoy her — therefore make money. A pox of drowning thyself! It is clean out of the way. Seek thou rather to be hanged in   366 compassing° thy joy than to be drowned and go without her.

ROD. Wilt thou be fast to my hopes if I depend on the issue?   370

IAGO. Thou art sure of me. Go, make money. I have told thee often, and I retell thee again and again, I hate the Moor. My cause is hearted,° thine hath no less reason. Let us be conjunctive° in our revenge against him. If thou canst cuckold° him,   375 thou dost thyself a pleasure, me a sport. There are many events in the womb of time, which will be delivered. Traverse,° go, provide thy money. We will have more of this tomorrow. Adieu.   380

ROD. Where shall we meet i' the morning?

IAGO. At my lodging.

ROD. I'll be with thee betimes.°

IAGO. Go to, farewell. Do you hear, Roderigo?

ROD. What say you?   386

IAGO. No more of drowning, do you hear?

ROD. I am changed. I'll go sell all my land. [*Exit.*]

IAGO. Thus do I ever make my fool my purse,
For I mine own gained knowledge should profane
If I would time expend with such a snipe   391
But for my sport and profit. I hate the Moor,
And it is thought abroad that 'twixt my sheets
He has done my office. I know not if 't be true,
But I for mere suspicion in that kind   395
Will do as if for surety. He holds me well,
The better shall my purpose work on him.
Cassio's a proper° man. Let me see now,
To get his place, and to plume up° my will
In double knavery —— How, how? — Let's see. —
After some time, to abuse Othello's ear   401
That he is too familiar with his wife.
He hath a person and a smooth dispose
To be suspected,° framed to make women false.

---

306. **incontinently:** immediately.   320. **fond:** foolishly in love. virtue: manhood.   324. **wills:** desires.   326. **gender:** kind. 329. **corrigible:** correcting, directing.   331. **poise:** weigh. 335. **carnal stings:** fleshly desires.   336. **unbitted:** uncontrolled. 337. **sect or scion:** Both words mean a slip taken from a tree and planted to produce a new growth.   343. **perdurable:** very hard.   344. **stead:** help.   345–46. **defeat . . . beard:** disguise your face by growing a beard.   351. **answerable sequestration:** corresponding separation; i.e., reaction.

354. **locusts:** It is not known what fruit was called a locust. 355. **coloquintida:** known as "bitter apple," a form of gherkin from which a purge was made.   360–61. **Make . . . canst:** turn all you can into ready cash.   362. **erring:** vagabond.   367. **compassing:** achieving.   373. **hearted:** heartfelt.   374. **conjunctive:** united.   375. **cuckold:** make him a cuckold. See App. 11. 379. **Traverse:** quickstep.   384. **betimes:** in good time, early. 398. **proper:** handsome.   399. **plume up:** glorify.   403–04. **He . . . suspected:** an easy way with him that is naturally suspected.

The Moor is of a free and open nature   405
That thinks men honest that but seem to be so,
And will as tenderly be led by the nose
As asses are.
I have 't. It is engendered.° Hell and night   409
Must bring this monstrous birth to the world's light.
                                                          [*Exit.*]

Act II

SCENE I. *A seaport in Cyprus. An open place
              near the wharf.*

[*Enter* MONTANO *and two* GENTLEMEN.]

MON. What from the cape can you discern at sea?
1. GENT. Nothing at all. It is a high-wrought
        flood.°
I cannot 'twixt the heaven and the main°
Descry a sail.
MON. Methinks the wind hath spoke aloud at
        land,   5
A fuller blast ne'er shook our battlements.
If it hath ruffianed° so upon the sea,
What ribs of oak, when mountains melt on them,
Can hold the mortise?° What shall we hear of this?
2. GENT. A segregation° of the Turkish fleet.   10
For do but stand upon the foaming shore,
The chidden billow seems to pelt the clouds,
The wind-shaked surge, with high and monstrous
        mane,
Seems to cast water on the burning Bear,°
And quench the guards of the ever-fixèd Pole.°   15
I never did like molestation° view
On the enchafèd° flood.
MON.   If that the Turkish fleet
Be not ensheltered and embayed,° they are
        drowned.
It is impossible to bear it out.
              [*Enter a* THIRD GENTLEMAN.]
3. GENT. News, lads! Our wars are done.   20
The desperate tempest hath so banged the Turks
That their designment halts.° A noble ship of Venice
Hath seen a grievous wreck and sufferance°
On most part of their fleet.

MON. How! Is this true?
3. GENT.   The ship is here put in,   25
A Veronesa. Michael Cassio,
Lieutenant to the warlike Moor Othello,
Is come on shore, the Moor himself at sea,
And is in full commission° here for Cyprus.
MON. I am glad on 't. 'Tis a worthy governor.   30
3. GENT. But this same Cassio, though he speak of
        comfort
Touching the Turkish loss, yet he looks sadly
And prays the Moor be safe, for they were parted
With foul and violent tempest.
MON.   Pray Heavens he be,
For I have served him, and the man commands   35
Like a full° soldier. Let's to the seaside, ho!
As well to see the vessel that's come in
As to throw out our eyes for brave Othello,
Even till we make the main and the aerial blue
An indistinct regard.°
3. GENT.   Come, let's do so.   40
For every minute is expectancy
Of more arrivance.°
                              [*Enter* CASSIO.]
CAS. Thanks, you the valiant of this warlike isle
That so approve the Moor! Oh, let the heavens
Give him defense against the elements,   45
For I have lost him on a dangerous sea.
MON. Is he well shipped?°
CAS. His bark is stoutly timbered, and his pilot
Of very expert and approved allowance.°
Therefore my hopes, not surfeited° to death,   50
Stand in bold cure.°   [*A cry within:*
                                        "*A sail, a sail, a sail!*"]
              [*Enter a* FOURTH GENTLEMAN.]
CAS. What noise?
4. GENT. The town is empty. On the brow o' the
        sea
Stand ranks of people, and they cry " A sail! "
CAS. My hopes do shape° him for the governor.   54
                                        [*Guns heard*]
2. GENT. They do discharge their shot of courtesy.
Our friends, at least.
CAS.   I pray you, sir, go forth,
And give us truth who 'tis that is arrived.
2. GENT. I shall.   [*Exit.*]
MON. But, good Lieutenant, is your General
        wived?   60
CAS. Most fortunately. He hath achieved° a maid
That paragons° description and wild fame,
One that excels the quirks of blazoning pens
And in the essential vesture of creation

---

409. engendered: conceived.

Act II, Sc. i: 2. high-wrought flood: heavy sea.   3. main:
sea.   7. ruffianed: played the ruffian.   9. hold . . . mortise:
remain fast joined.   10. segregation: separation.   14. Bear:
the Great Bear.   15. guards . . . Pole: stars in the "tail" of the
Little Bear constellation.   16. molestation: disturbance.
17. enchafed: angry.   18. embayed: anchored in some bay.
22. designment halts: plan is made lame.   23. sufferance:
damage.

29. in . . . commission: with full powers. See I.iii.281–82.
36. full: perfect.   39–40. Even . . . regard: until we can no longer
distinguish between sea and sky.   41–42. For . . . arrivance:
every minute more arrivals are expected.   47. well shipped: in a
good ship.   49. approved allowance: proved skill.   50. sur-
feited: sickened.   51. Stand . . . cure: have every hope of cure.
55. shape: imagine.   61. achieved: won.   62. paragons: surpasses.

Does tire the ingener.°
[*Re-enter* SECOND GENTLEMAN.] How now! Who has
   put in?   65
   2. GENT. 'Tis one Iago, Ancient to the General.
   CAS. He has had most favorable and happy speed.
Tempests themselves, high seas, and howling
   winds,
The guttered° rocks, and congregated sands,
Traitors ensteeped° to clog the guiltless keel,   70
As having sense of beauty, do omit
Their mortal natures,° letting go safely by
The divine Desdemona.
   MON.   What is she?
   CAS. She that I spake of, our great Captain's cap-
   tain,
Left in the conduct° of the bold Iago,   75
Whose footing° here anticipates our thoughts
A sennight's° speed. Great Jove, Othello guard,
And swell his sail with thine own powerful breath,
That he may bless this bay with his tall ship,
Make love's quick pants in Desdemona's arms,   80
Give renewed fire to our extincted° spirits,
And bring all Cyprus comfort.
⌜*Enter* DESDEMONA, EMILIA, IAGO, RODERIGO,
   and ATTENDANTS.⌝
                         Oh, behold,
The riches of the ship is come on shore!
Ye men of Cyprus, let her have your knees.
Hail to thee, lady! And the grace of Heaven,   85
Before, behind thee, and on every hand,
Enwheel° thee round!
   DES.   I thank you, valiant Cassio.
What tidings can you tell me of my lord?
   CAS. He is not yet arrived, nor know I aught
But that he's well and will be shortly here.   90
   DES. Oh, but I fear—— How lost you company?
   CAS. The great contention of the sea and skies
Parted our fellowship.° — But, hark! A sail.
   [*A cry within:* "A sail, a sail!" *Guns heard.*]
   2. GENT. They give their greeting to the citadel.
This likewise is a friend.
   CAS.   See for the news. [*Exit* GENTLEMAN.]
Good Ancient, you are welcome. [*To* EMILIA] Wel-
   come, mistress.
Let it not gall your patience, good Iago,
That I extend my manners.° 'Tis my breeding°
That gives me this bold show of courtesy.°   100
   [*Kissing her.*]

   IAGO. Sir, would she give you so much of her lips
As of her tongue she oft bestows on me,
You'd have enough.
   DES.   Alas, she has no speech.
   IAGO. In faith, too much,
I find it still° when I have list° to sleep.   105
Marry, before your ladyship, I grant,
She puts her tongue a little in her heart
And chides with thinking.
   EMIL. You have little cause to say so.
   IAGO. Come on, come on. You are pictures° out of
   doors,   110
Bells° in your parlors, wildcats in your kitchens,
Saints in your injuries,° devils being offended,
Players in your housewifery, and housewives in your
   beds.
   DES. Oh, fie upon thee, slanderer!
   IAGO. Nay, it is true, or else I am a Turk.°   115
You rise to play, and go to bed to work.
   EMIL. You shall not write my praise.
   IAGO.   No, let me not.
   DES. What wouldst thou write of me if thou
   shouldst praise me?
   IAGO. O gentle lady, do not put me to 't,
For I am nothing if not critical.°   120
   DES. Come on, assay.° — There's one gone to the
   harbor?
   IAGO. Aye, madam.
   DES. I am not merry, but I do beguile
The thing I am by seeming otherwise.
Come, how wouldst thou praise me?   125
   IAGO. I am about it, but indeed my invention
Comes from my pate as birdlime does from
   frieze° —
It plucks out brains and all. But my Muse labors,
And thus she is delivered.
If she be fair and wise, fairness and wit,   130
The one's for use, the other useth it.
   DES. Well praised! How if she be black and witty?
   IAGO. If she be black, and thereto have a wit,
She'll find a white° that shall her blackness fit.
   DES. Worse and worse.   135
   EMIL. How if fair and foolish?
   IAGO. She never yet was foolish that was fair,
For even her folly helped her to an heir.
   DES. These are old fond paradoxes° to make fools
laugh i' the alehouse. What miserable praise hast
thou for her that's foul and foolish?   141

63–65. One . . . ingener: one that is too good for the fancy
phrases (*quirks*) of painting pens (i.e., poets) and in her absolute
perfection wearies the artist (i.e., the painter). (Cassio is full of
gallant phrases and behavior, in contrast to Iago's bluntness.) in-
gener: inventor.   69. guttered: worn into channels.   70. en-
steeped: submerged.   71–72. omit . . . natures: forbear their
deadly nature.   75. conduct: escort.   76. footing: arrival.
77. sennight: week.   81. extincted: extinguished.   87. En-
wheel: encompass.   93. fellowship: company.   99. extend my
manners: i.e., salute your wife. breeding: bringing-up.   100. bold
. . . courtesy: i.e., of saluting your wife with a kiss — a piece of

presumptuous behavior which indicates that Cassio regards him-
self as Iago's social superior.   105. still: continuously. list: desire.
110. pictures: i.e., painted and dumb.   111. Bells: i.e., ever
clacking.   112. Saints . . . injuries: saints when you hurt anyone
else.   115. Turk: heathen.   120. critical: bitter.   121. assay:
try.   126–27. my . . . frieze: my literary effort (*invention*) is as
hard to pull out of my head as frieze (cloth with a nap) stuck to
birdlime.   134. white: with a pun on *wight* (l. 159), man, person.
139. fond paradoxes: foolish remarks, contrary to general
opinion.

IAGO. There's none so foul, and foolish thereunto,
But does foul pranks which fair and wise ones do.

DES. Oh, heavy ignorance! Thou praisest the worst
best. But what praise couldst thou bestow on a de-
serving woman indeed, one that in the authority of
her merit did justly put on the vouch of very malice
itself?°   148

IAGO. She that was ever fair and never proud,
Had tongue at will° and yet was never loud,
Never lacked gold and yet went never gay,
Fled from her wish and yet said " Now I may."
She that, being angered, her revenge being nigh,
Bade her wrong stay and her displeasure fly.
She that in wisdom never was so frail   155
To change the cod's head for the salmon's tail.°
She that could think and ne'er disclose her mind,
See suitors following and not look behind.
She was a wight, if ever such wight were——

DES. To do what?   160

IAGO. To suckle fools and chronicle small beer.°

DES. Oh, most lame and impotent conclusion! Do
not learn of him, Emilia, though he be thy husband.
How say you, Cassio? Is he not a most profane and
liberal° counselor?   165

CAS. He speaks home,° madam. You may relish°
him more in the soldier than in the scholar.

IAGO. [Aside] He° takes her by the palm. Aye,
well said, whisper. With as little a web as this will I
ensnare as great a fly as Cassio. Aye, smile upon   170
her, do, I will gyve° thee in thine own courtship.
You say true, 'tis so indeed. If such tricks as these
strip you out of your Lieutenantry, it had been better
you had not kissed your three fingers° so oft, which
now again you are most apt to play the sir° in.   175
Very good, well kissed! An excellent courtesy! 'Tis
so indeed. Yet again your fingers to your lips? Would
they were clyster pipes° for your sake! [Trumpet
within.] The Moor! I know his trumpet.   180

CAS. 'Tis truly so.

DES. Let's meet him and receive him.

CAS. Lo where he comes!

[Enter OTHELLO and ATTENDANTS.]

OTH. O my fair warrior!°

DES.   My dear Othello!

OTH. It gives me wonder great as my content   185
To see you here before me. O my soul's joy!
If after every tempest come such calms,

May the winds blow till they have wakened death!
And let the laboring bark climb hills of seas
Olympus-high,° and duck again as low   190
As Hell's from Heaven! If it were now to die,
'Twere now to be most happy, for I fear
My soul hath her content so absolute
That not another comfort like to this
Succeeds in unknown fate.   194

DES.   The Heavens forbid
But that our loves and comforts should increase,
Even as our days do grow!

OTH.   Amen to that, sweet powers!
I cannot speak enough of this content.
It stops me here,° it is too much of joy.
And this, and this, the greatest discords be   200

[Kissing her]

That e'er our hearts shall make!

IAGO. [Aside]   Oh, you are well tuned now,
But I'll set down the pegs° that make this music,
As honest as I am.

OTH.   Come, let us to the castle.
News, friends. Our wars are done, the Turks are
     drowned.
How does my old acquaintance of this isle?   205
Honey, you shall be well desired in Cyprus,
I have found great love amongst them. O my sweet,
I prattle out of fashion,° and I dote
In mine own comforts. I prithee, good Iago,
Go to the bay and disembark my coffers.°   210
Bring thou the master° to the citadel.
He is a good one, and his worthiness
Does challenge° much respect. Come, Desdemona,
Once more well met at Cyprus.   214

[Exeunt all but IAGO and RODERIGO.]

IAGO. Do thou meet me presently° at the harbor.
Come hither. If thou beest valiant — as they say base
men being in love have then a nobility in their na-
tures more than is native to them — list me. The
Lieutenant tonight watches on the court of guard.°
First, I must tell thee this. Desdemona is directly in
love with him.   221

ROD. With him! Why, 'tis not possible.

IAGO. Lay thy finger thus,° and let thy soul be in-
structed. Mark me with what violence she first loved
the Moor, but for° bragging and telling her   225
fantastical lies. And will she love him still for prat-
ing? Let not thy discreet heart think it. Her eye must
be fed, and what delight shall she have to look on the
Devil?° When the blood is made dull with the act

146–48. one . . . itself: one so deserving that even malice would
declare her good.   150. tongue . . . will: a ready flow of words.
156. To . . . tail: to prefer the tail end of a good thing to the
head of a poor thing.   161. chronicle . . . beer: write a whole
history about trifles (small beer: thin drink).   165. liberal:
gross. 166. home: to the point. relish: appreciate. 168–79. He
. . . sake: As so often, Shakespeare without using elaborate stage
directions exactly indicates the action in the dialogue. Cf. W Tale,
I.ii.111–18.   171. gyve: fetter.   174. kissed . . . fingers: a
gesture of gallantry. 175. play . . . sir: act the fine gentle-
man. 179. clyster pipes: an enema syringe. 184. warrior:
because she is a soldier's wife. See I.iii.249.

190. Olympus-high: high as Olympus, the highest mountain in
Greece.   199. here: i.e., in the heart.   202. set . . . pegs: i.e.,
make you sing in a different key. A stringed instrument was
tuned by the pegs.   208. prattle . . . fashion: talk idly.
210. coffers: trunks. 211. master: captain of the ship. 213. chal-
lenge: claim. 215. presently: immediately. 219. watches . . .
guard: is on duty with the guard. The court of guard meant
both the guard itself and the guardroom. 223. finger thus: i.e.,
on the lips. 225. but for: only for. 229. Devil: See I.i.91,n.

of sport, there should be, again to inflame it 230
and to give satiety a fresh appetite, loveliness in fa-
vor,° sympathy in years, manners, and beauties, all
which the Moor is defective in. Now, for want of
these required conveniences, her delicate tenderness
will find itself abused, begin to heave the 235
gorge,° disrelish and abhor the Moor. Very nature
will instruct her in it and compel her to some second
choice. Now, sir, this granted — as it is a most preg-
nant and unforced position° — who stands so emi-
nently in the degree of this fortune as Cassio 240
does? A knave very voluble, no further conscion-
able° than in putting on the mere form of civil and
humane seeming° for the better compassing of his
salt° and most hidden loose affection? Why, none,
why, none. A slipper° and subtle knave, a finder-
out of occasions, that has an eye can stamp 246
and counterfeit advantages,° though true advantage
never present itself. A devilish knave! Besides, the
knave is handsome, young, and hath all those requi-
sites in him that folly and green° minds look 250
after. A pestilent complete knave, and the woman
hath found him already.

    ROD. I cannot believe that in her. She's full of
most blest condition.° 255

    IAGO. Blest fig's-end!° The wine she drinks is
made of grapes. If she had been blest, she would
never have loved the Moor. Blest pudding! Didst
thou not see her paddle° with the palm of his hand?
Didst not mark that? 260

    ROD. Yes, that I did, but that was but courtesy.

    IAGO. Lechery, by this hand, an index° and ob-
scure prologue to the history of lust and foul
thoughts. They met so near with their lips that
their breaths embraced together. Villainous 265
thoughts, Roderigo! When these mutualities° so
marshal the way, hard at hand comes the master and
main exercise, the incorporate° conclusion. Pish!
But, sir, be you ruled by me. I have brought you
from Venice. Watch you tonight. For the com- 270
mand, I'll lay 't upon you. Cassio knows you not.
I'll not be far from you. Do you find some occasion
to anger Cassio, either by speaking too loud, or taint-
ing° his discipline, or from what other course you
please which the time shall more favorably 275
minister.°

    ROD. Well.

    IAGO. Sir, he is rash and very sudden in choler,°
and haply° may strike at you. Provoke him, that he
may, for even out of that will I cause these of 280
Cyprus to mutiny, whose qualification° shall come
into no true taste again but by the displanting° of
Cassio. So shall you have a shorter journey to your
desires by the means I shall then have to pre- 285
fer° them, and the impediment most profitably re-
moved without the which there were no expectation
of our prosperity.

    ROD. I will do this, if I can bring it to any oppor-
tunity. 290

    IAGO. I warrant thee. Meet me by and by at the
citadel. I must fetch his necessaries ashore. Farewell.

    ROD. Adieu.   [*Exit.*]

    IAGO. That Cassio loves her, I do well believe it.
That she loves him, 'tis apt and of great credit.° 296
The Moor, howbeit that I endure him not,
Is of a constant, loving, noble nature,
And I dare think he'll prove to Desdemona
A most dear husband. Now, I do love her too, 300
Not out of absolute lust, though peradventure
I stand accountant for as great a sin,
But partly led to diet° my revenge
For that I do suspect the lusty Moor 304
Hath leaped into my seat. The thought whereof
Doth like a poisonous mineral° gnaw my inwards.
And nothing can or shall content my soul
Till I am evened with him, wife for wife.
Or failing so, yet that I put the Moor
At least into a jealousy so strong 310
That judgment° cannot cure. Which thing to do,
If this poor trash of Venice, whom I trash°
For his quick hunting,° stand the putting-on,°
I'll have our Michael Cassio on the hip,
Abuse him to the Moor in the rank garb° — 315
For I fear Cassio with my nightcap too —
Make the Moor thank me, love me, and reward me
For making him egregiously° an ass
And practicing upon° his peace and quiet
Even to madness. 'Tis here, but yet confused. 320
Knavery's plain face is never seen till used.   [*Exit.*]

278. choler: anger.   279. haply: perhaps.   281. qualification:
appeasement.   282. displanting: removal.   286. prefer: pro-
mote.   296. apt . . . credit: likely and very credible.   303. diet:
feed.   306. poisonous mineral: corrosive poison. See I.ii.74.
311. judgment: reason.   312. trash . . . trash: rubbish . . . dis-
card.   312–13. trash . . . hunting: F1 reads "trace" and Q1
"crush." If the emendation "trash" is correct, it means "hold
back from outrunning the pack." Cf. *Temp.* I.ii.81,n.   313. put-
ting-on: encouraging.   315. rank garb: gross manner; i.e., by
accusing him of being Desdemona's lover.   318. egregiously:
notably.   319. practicing upon: plotting against.

232. favor: face.   235–36. heave . . . gorge: retch. gorge: throat.
238–39. pregnant . . . position: very significant and probable ar-
gument.   241–42. no . . . conscionable: who has no more con-
science.   243. humane seeming: courteous appearance.   244. salt:
lecherous.   245. slipper: slippery.   246–47. stamp . . . advan-
tages: forge false opportunities.   250. green: inexperienced,
foolish.   255. condition: disposition.   256. Blest fig's-end:
blest nonsense, a phrase used as a substitute in contempt for a
phrase just used, as is also *blest pudding* (l.258).   259. paddle:
play.   262. index: table of contents.   266. mutualities: mutual
exchanges.   268. incorporate: bodily.   274. tainting: disparag-
ing.   276. minister: provide.

SCENE II. *A street.*

[*Enter a* HERALD *with a proclamation,* PEOPLE *following.*]

HER. It is Othello's pleasure, our noble and valiant General, that upon certain tidings now arrived, importing the mere perdition° of the Turkish fleet, every man put himself into triumph° — some to dance, some to make bonfires, each man to what 5 sport and revels his addiction° leads him. For, besides these beneficial news, it is the celebration of his nuptial. So much was his pleasure should be proclaimed. All offices° are open, and there is full liberty of feasting from this present hour of five till 10 the bell have told eleven. Heaven bless the isle of Cyprus and our noble General Othello!   [*Exeunt.*]

SCENE III. *A hall in the castle.*

[*Enter* OTHELLO, DESDEMONA, CASSIO, *and* ATTENDANTS.]

OTH. Good Michael, look you to the guard tonight. Let's teach ourselves that honorable stop, Not to outsport discretion.°

CAS.   Iago hath direction what to do, But notwithstanding with my personal eye 5 Will I look to 't.

OTH.   Iago is most honest. Michael, good night. Tomorrow with your earliest° Let me have speech with you. Come, my dear love, The purchase made, the fruits are to ensue — That profit's yet to come 'tween me and you. 10 Good night.

[*Exeunt* OTHELLO, DESDEMONA, *and* ATTENDANTS.]
[*Enter* IAGO.]

CAS. Welcome, Iago. We must to the watch.

IAGO. Not this hour, Lieutenant, 'tis not yet ten o' the clock. Our General cast° us thus early for the love of his Desdemona, who let us not therefore blame. He hath not yet made wanton the night with her, and she is sport for Jove. 17

CAS. She's a most exquisite lady.

IAGO. And, I'll warrant her, full of game.

CAS. Indeed she's a most fresh and delicate creature. 21

IAGO. What an eye she has! Methinks it sounds a parley to provocation.°

CAS. An inviting eye, and yet methinks right modest.

IAGO. And when she speaks, is it not an alarum° to love? 27

CAS. She is indeed perfection.

IAGO. Well, happiness to their sheets! Come, Lieutenant, I have a stoup° of wine, and here without are a brace of Cyprus gallants that would fain° have a measure to the health of black Othello. 33

CAS. Not tonight, good Iago. I have very poor and unhappy brains for drinking. I could well wish courtesy would invent some other custom of entertainment.

IAGO. Oh, they are our friends. But one cup — I'll drink for you. 39

CAS. I have drunk but one cup tonight, and that was craftily qualified° too, and behold what innovation° it makes here. I am unfortunate in the infirmity, and dare not task° my weakness with any more. 44

IAGO. What, man! 'Tis a night of revels. The gallants desire it.

CAS. Where are they?

IAGO. Here at the door. I pray you call them in.

CAS. I'll do 't, but it dislikes° me.   [*Exit.*]

IAGO. If I can fasten but one cup upon him, 50 With that which he hath drunk tonight already He'll be as full of quarrel and offense As my young mistress' dog. Now my sick fool Roderigo, Whom love hath turned almost the wrong side out, To Desdemona hath tonight caroused° 55 Potations pottle-deep,° and he's to watch. Three lads of Cyprus, noble swelling° spirits That hold their honors in a wary distance,° The very elements° of this warlike isle, Have I tonight flustered with flowing cups, 60 And they watch too. Now, 'mongst this flock of drunkards, Am I to put our Cassio in some action That may offend the isle. But here they come. If consequence do but approve my dream,° My boat sails freely, both with wind and stream. 65

[*Re-enter* CASSIO, *with him* MONTANO *and* GENTLEMEN, SERVANTS *following with wine.*]

CAS. 'Fore God, they have given me a rouse° already.

MON. Good faith, a little one — not past a pint, as I am a soldier.

IAGO. Some wine, ho! [*Sings.*] 70

26. **alarum:** call to arms.   31. **stoup:** large drinking vessel. See Pl. 20e.   32. **fain:** gladly.   41. **craftily qualified:** cunningly mixed.   42. **innovation:** revolution, disturbance.   43. **task:** burden.   49. **dislikes:** displeases.   55. **caroused:** drunk healths. 56. **pottle-deep:** "bottoms up"; a pottle held two quarts. 57. **swelling:** bursting with pride.   58. **hold . . . distance:** "have a chip on their shoulders."   59. **very elements:** typical specimens.   64. **If . . . dream:** if what follows proves my dream true.   66. **rouse:** a deep drink.

Sc. ii: 3. **mere perdition:** absolute destruction.   4. **put . . . triumph:** celebrate.   6. **addiction:** inclination.   9. **offices:** the kitchen and buttery — i.e., free food and drink for all.

Sc. iii: 3. **outsport discretion:** let the fun go too far.   7. **with . . . earliest:** very early.   14. **cast:** dismissed.   22–23. **sounds . . . provocation:** invites to a love talk.

" And let me the cannikin° clink, clink,
    And let me the cannikin clink.
      A soldier's a man,
      A life's but a span.°
    Why, then let a soldier drink."   75
Some wine, boys!

CAS. 'Fore God, an excellent song.

IAGO. I learned it in England, where indeed they
are most potent in potting.° Your Dane, your Ger-
man, and your swag-bellied° Hollander — Drink,
ho! — are nothing to your English.   81

CAS. Is your Englishman so expert in his drink-
ing?

IAGO. Why, he drinks you with facility your Dane
dead drunk, he sweats not° to overthrow your Al-
main,° he gives your Hollander a vomit° ere the
next pottle can be filled.   87

CAS. To the health of our General!

MON. I am for it, Lieutenant, and I'll do you jus-
tice.   90

IAGO. O sweet England! [*Sings.*]
" King Stephen was a worthy peer,
    His breeches cost him but a crown.
    He held them sixpence all too dear,°   95
      With what he called the tailor lown.°

"He was a wight of high renown,
    And thou art but of low degree.
'Tis pride that pulls the country down.
    Then take thine auld cloak about thee."
Some wine, ho!   100

CAS. Why, this is a more exquisite song than the
other.

IAGO. Will you hear 't again?

CAS. No, for I hold him to be unworthy of his
place that does those things. Well, God's above all,
and there be souls must be saved and there be souls
must not be saved.   107

IAGO. It's true, good Lieutenant.

CAS. For mine own part — no offense to the Gen-
eral, nor any man of quality° — I hope to be saved.

IAGO. And so do I too, Lieutenant.   112

CAS. Aye, but, by your leave, not before me. The
Lieutenant is to be saved before the Ancient. Let's
have no more of this, let's to our affairs. God   115
forgive us our sins! Gentlemen, let's look to our busi-
ness. Do not think, gentlemen, I am drunk. This is
my Ancient, this is my right hand and this is my

left. I am not drunk now, I can stand well enough
and speak well enough.   120

ALL. Excellent well.

CAS. Why, very well, then, you must not think
then that I am drunk.   [*Exit.*]

MON. To the platform,° masters. Come, let's set
the watch.°   125

IAGO. You see this fellow that is gone before.
He is a soldier fit to stand by Caesar
And give direction. And do but see his vice.
'Tis to his virtue a just equinox,°
The one as long as the other. 'Tis pity of him.   130
I fear the trust Othello puts him in
On some odd time° of his infirmity
Will shake this island.

MON.   But is he often thus?

IAGO. 'Tis evermore the prologue to his sleep.
He'll watch the horologe a double set,°   135
If drink rock not his cradle.

MON.   It were well
The General were put in mind of it.
Perhaps he sees it not, or his good nature
Prizes the virtue that appears in Cassio
And looks not on his evils. Is not this true?   140
            [*Enter* RODERIGO.]

IAGO. [*Aside to him*] How now, Roderigo! I pray
you, after the Lieutenant. Go.   [*Exit* RODERIGO.]

MON. And 'tis great pity that the noble Moor
Should hazard such a place as his own second
With one of an ingraft° infirmity.   145
It were an honest action to say
So to the Moor.

IAGO.   Not I, for this fair island.
I do love Cassio well, and would do much
To cure him of this evil — But, hark! What noise?
      [*A cry within:* " Help! help! "]
      [*Re-enter* CASSIO, *driving in* RODERIGO.]

CAS. 'Zounds! You rogue! You rascal!

MON.   What's the matter, Lieutenant?   150

CAS. A knave teach me my duty!
But I'll beat the knave into a wicker bottle.°

ROD. Beat me!

CAS. Dost thou prate, rogue? [*Striking* RODERIGO.]

MON.   Nay, good Lieutenant, [*Staying him.*]
I pray you, sir, hold your hand.

CAS.   Let me go, sir,
Or I'll knock you o'er the mazzard.°

MON.   Come, come, you're drunk.   155

CAS. Drunk!   [*They fight.*]

---

71. **cannikin**: drinking pot. See Pl. 20e.   74. **span**: lit., the meas-
ure between the thumb and little finger of the outstretched hand;
about 9 inches.   79. **potent in potting**: desperate drinkers.
For the Danes' potency in potting see *Haml.*, I.iv.8–38.
80. **swag-bellied**: with loose bellies. Germans and Dutchmen
were almost as famous for drinking as the Danes.   85. **sweats
not**: has no need to labor excessively.   86. **Almain**: German.
86. **gives . . . vomit**: drinks as much as will make a Dutchman
throw up.   94. **sixpence . . . dear**: too dear by sixpence.
95. **lown**: lout.   111. **quality**: rank.

124. **platform**: the level place on the ramparts where the cannon
were mounted.   124–25. **set . . . watch**: mount guard.   129. **just
equinox**: exact equal.   132. **some . . . time**: some time or other.
135. **watch . . . set**: stay awake the clock twice round.   145. **in-
graft**: engrafted, firmly fixed.   152. **But . . . bottle**: One of those
bad-tempered threatening phrases which have no very exact
meaning, like "I'll knock him into a cocked hat." **wicker bottle**:
large bottle covered with wicker, demijohn.   154. **mazzard**:
head, a slang word.

IAGO. [*Aside to* RODERIGO] Away, I say. Go out
and cry a mutiny.°   [*Exit* RODERIGO.]
Nay, good Lieutenant! God's will, gentlemen!
Help, ho! — Lieutenant — sir — Montano — sir —
Help, masters! — Here's a goodly watch indeed!
          [*A bell rings.*]
Who's that that rings the bell? — Diablo,° ho!   160
The town will rise. God's will, Lieutenant, hold —
You will be shamed forever.
          [*Re-enter* OTHELLO *and* ATTENDANTS.]
OTH.   What is the matter here?
MON. 'Zounds, I bleed still, I am hurt to the death.
          [*Faints.*]
OTH. Hold, for your lives!   165
IAGO. Hold, ho! Lieutenant — sir — Montano —
gentlemen —
Have you forgot all sense of place and duty?
Hold! The General speaks to you. Hold, hold, for
shame!
OTH. Why, how now, ho! From whence ariseth
this?
Are we turned Turks, and to ourselves do that   170
Which Heaven hath forbid the Ottomites?
For Christian shame, put by this barbarous brawl.
He that stirs next to carve for his own rage°
Holds his soul light, he dies upon his motion.°
Silence that dreadful bell. It frights the isle   175
From her propriety.° What is the matter, masters?
Honest Iago, that look'st dead with grieving,
Speak, who began this? On thy love, I charge
thee.
IAGO. I do not know. Friends all but now, even
now,
In quarter and in terms like bride and groom   180
Devesting° them for bed. And then, but now,
As if some planet had unwitted men,°
Swords out, and tilting° one at other's breast
In opposition bloody. I cannot speak
Any beginning to this peevish odds,°   185
And would in action glorious I had lost
Those legs that brought me to a part of it!
OTH. How comes it, Michael, you are thus for-
got?°
CAS. I pray you, pardon me, I cannot speak.
OTH. Worthy Montano, you were wont be civil.°
The gravity and stillness° of your youth   191
The world hath noted, and your name is great
In mouths of wisest censure.° What's the matter
That you unlace° your reputation thus,

And spend your rich opinion° for the name   195
Of a night brawler? Give me answer to it.
  MON. Worthy Othello, I am hurt to danger.
Your officer, Iago, can inform you —
While I spare speech, which something now offends
me —
Of all that I do know. Nor know I aught   200
By me that's said or done amiss this night,
Unless self-charity° be sometimes a vice,
And to defend ourselves it be a sin
When violence assails us.
  OTH.   Now, by Heaven,
My blood begins my safer guides to rule,   205
And passion, having my best judgment collied,°
Assays to lead the way. If I once stir,
Or do but lift this arm, the best of you
Shall sink in my rebuke. Give me to know
How this foul rout° began, who set it on,   210
And he that is approved° in this offense,
Though he had twinned with me, both at a birth,
Shall lose me. What! In a town of war,
Yet wild, the people's hearts brimful of fear,
To manage° private and domestic quarrel,   215
In night, and on the court and guard of safety!
'Tis monstrous. Iago, who began 't?
  MON. If partially affined, or leagued in office,
Thou dost deliver° more or less than truth,
Thou art no soldier.
  IAGO.   Touch me not so near.   220
I had rather have this tongue cut from my mouth
Than it should do offense to Michael Cassio.
Yet I persuade myself to speak the truth
Shall nothing wrong him. Thus it is, General.
Montano and myself being in speech,   225
There comes a fellow crying out for help,
And Cassio following him with determined sword
To execute upon him. Sir, this gentleman
Steps in to Cassio and entreats his pause.°
Myself the crying fellow did pursue,   230
Lest by his clamor — as it so fell out —
The town might fall in fright. He, swift of foot,
Outran my purpose, and I returned the rather
For that I heard the clink and fall of swords,
And Cassio high in oath, which till tonight   235
I ne'er might say before. When I came back —
For this was brief — I found them close together,
At blow and thrust, even as again they were
When you yourself did part them.
More of this matter cannot I report.   240
But men are men, the best sometimes forget.
Though Cassio did some little wrong to him,
As men in rage strike those that wish them best,

---

157. cry . . . mutiny: cry that a mutiny has broken out; i.e., raise
a riot.   160. Diablo: the Devil.   173. carve . . . rage: to satisfy
his hunger for rage.   174. upon . . . motion: at his first move-
ment.   176. propriety: natural behavior.   181. Devesting: tak-
ing off their clothes.   182. planet . . . men: as if some evil star
had made men mad. See App. 1.   183. tilting: thrusting.
185. peevish odds: silly disagreement.   188. are . . . forgot:
have so forgotten yourself.   190. civil: well behaved.   191. still-
ness: staid behavior.   193. censure: judgment.   194. unlace:
undo.

195. spend . . . opinion: lose your good reputation.   202. self-
charity: love for oneself.   206. collied: darkened.   210. rout:
riot, uproar.   211. approved: proved guilty.   215. manage: be
concerned with.   218-19. If . . . deliver: if, because you are in-
fluenced by partiality or because he is your fellow officer, you re-
port. affined: bound.   229. entreats . . . pause: begs him to stop.

Yet surely Cassio, I believe, received
From him that fled some strange indignity,   245
Which patience could not pass.

OTH.   I know, Iago,
Thy honesty and love doth mince this matter,
Making it light to Cassio. Cassio, I love thee,
But never more be officer of mine.

[*Re-enter* DESDEMONA, *attended.*] Look, if my gentle
     love be not raised up!   250
I'll make thee an example.

DES.   What's the matter?

OTH. All's well now, sweeting.° Come away to
     bed. [*To* MONTANO, *who is led off*]
Sir, for your hurts, myself will be your surgeon.
Lead him off.
Iago, look with care about the town,   255
And silence those whom this vile brawl distracted.
Come, Desdemona. 'Tis the soldiers' life
To have their balmy slumbers waked with strife.

            [*Exeunt all but* IAGO *and* CASSIO.]

IAGO. What, are you hurt, Lieutenant?

CAS. Aye, past all surgery.   260

IAGO. Marry, Heaven forbid!

CAS. Reputation, reputation, reputation! Oh, I
have lost my reputation! I have lost the immortal
part of myself, and what remains is bestial. My repu-
tation, Iago, my reputation!   265

IAGO. As I am an honest man, I thought you had
received some bodily wound. There is more sense
in that than in reputation. Reputation is an idle and
most false imposition,° oft got without merit and
lost without deserving. You have lost no repu-   270
tation at all unless you repute yourself such a loser.
What, man! There are ways to recover the General
again. You are but now cast in his mood,° a punish-
ment more in policy° than in malice — even so as
one would beat his offenseless dog to affright an im-
perious lion.° Sue to him again and he's yours.   277

CAS. I will rather sue to be despised than to de-
ceive so good a commander with so slight, so
drunken, and so indiscreet an officer. Drunk? And
speak parrot?° And squabble? Swagger? Swear?
And discourse fustian° with one's own shadow? O
thou invisible spirit of wine, if thou hast no name to
be known by, let us call thee devil!   284

IAGO. What was he that you followed with your
sword? What had he done to you?

CAS. I know not.

IAGO. Is 't possible?   288

CAS. I remember a mass of things, but nothing
distinctly — a quarrel, but nothing wherefore. Oh

God, that men should put an enemy in their mouths
to steal away their brains! That we should, with joy,
pleasance,° revel, and applause, transform ourselves
into beasts!   294

IAGO. Why, but you are now well enough. How
came you thus recovered?

CAS. It hath pleased the devil drunkenness to give
place to the devil wrath. One unperfectness shows
me another, to make me frankly despise my-
self.   300

IAGO. Come, you are too severe a moraler.° As the
time, the place, and the condition of this country
stands, I could heartily wish this had not befall-
en. But since it is as it is, mend it for your own
good.   305

CAS. I will ask him for my place again, he shall
tell me I am a drunkard! Had I as many mouths as
Hydra,° such an answer would stop them all. To be
now a sensible man, by and by a fool, and pres-
ently a beast! Oh, strange! Every inordinate° cup is
unblest, and the ingredient is a devil.   312

IAGO. Come, come, good wine is a good familiar
creature, if it be well used. Exclaim no more against
it. And, good Lieutenant, I think you think I love
you.

CAS. I have well approved it, sir. I drunk!   317

IAGO. You or any man living may be drunk at
some time, man. I'll tell you what you shall do. Our
General's wife is now the General. I may say so in
this respect, for that he hath devoted and given up
himself to the contemplation, mark, and denote-
ment° of her parts and graces. Confess yourself
freely to her, importune her help to put you in your
place again. She is of so free, so kind, so apt,° so   325
blessed a disposition, she holds it a vice in her
goodness not to do more than she is requested. This
broken joint between you and her husband entreat
her to splinter° and, my fortunes against any lay°
worth naming, this crack of your love shall grow
stronger than it was before.   331

CAS. You advise me well.

IAGO. I protest, in the sincerity of love and honest
kindness.

CAS. I think it freely, and betimes in the morning
I will beseech the virtuous Desdemona to undertake
for me. I am desperate of my fortunes if they check
me here.°

IAGO. You are in the right. Good night, Lieuten-
ant, I must to the watch.   340

CAS. Good night, honest Iago.   [*Exit.*]

IAGO. And what's he then that says I play the vil-
lain?

---

252. **sweeting:** sweetheart.   269. **imposition:** a quality laid on
a man by others.   273. **cast . . . mood:** dismissed because he is in
a bad mood.   275. **in policy:** i.e., because he must appear to be
angry before the Cypriots.   275-77. **even . . . lion:** a proverb
meaning that when the lion sees the dog beaten, he will know
what is coming to him.   281. **speak parrot:** babble.   282. **fustian:**
nonsense; lit., cheap cloth.

293. **pleasance:** a gay time.   301. **moraler:** moralizer.   307. **Hy-
dra:** a hundred-headed beast slain by Hercules.   311. **inordinate:**
excessive.   322. **denotement:** careful observation.   324. **apt:**
ready.   329. **splinter:** put in splints.   329. **lay:** bet.   337-38. **I
. . . here:** I despair of my future if my career is stopped short
here.

When this advice is free I give and honest,
Probal° to thinking, and indeed the course
To win the Moor again? For 'tis most easy   345
The inclining Desdemona to subdue
In any honest suit. She's framed° as fruitful
As the free elements.° And then for her
To win the Moor, were 't to renounce his baptism,
All seals and symbols of redeemèd sin,   350
His soul is so enfettered to her love
That she may make, unmake, do what she list,
Even as her appetite shall play the god
With his weak function.° How am I then a villain
To counsel Cassio to this parallel course,   355
Directly to his good? Divinity of Hell!
When devils will the blackest sins put on,
They do suggest° at first with heavenly shows,
As I do now. For whiles this honest fool
Plies° Desdemona to repair his fortunes,   360
And she for him pleads strongly to the Moor,
I'll pour this pestilence into his ear,
That she repeals° him for her body's lust.
And by how much she strives to do him good,
She shall undo her credit with the Moor.   365
So will I turn her virtue into pitch,
And out of her own goodness make the net
That shall enmesh them all.
[*Enter* RODERIGO.] How now, Roderigo!

ROD. I do follow here in the chase, not like a hound
that hunts but one that fills up the cry.° My   370
money is almost spent, I have been tonight exceed-
ingly well cudgeled, and I think the issue will be I
shall have so much experience for my pains and so,
with no money at all and a little more wit, return
again to Venice.   375

IAGO. How poor are they that have not patience!
What wound did ever heal but by degrees?
Thou know'st we work by wit and not by witch-
craft,
And wit depends on dilatory Time.°
Does 't not go well? Cassio hath beaten thee,   380
And thou by that small hurt hast cashiered Cassio.
Though other things grow fair against the sun,
Yet fruits that blossom first will first be ripe.°
Content thyself awhile. By the mass, 'tis morning.
Pleasure and action make the hours seem short.   385
Retire thee, go where thou art billeted.
Away, I say. Thou shalt know more hereafter.
Nay, get thee gone. [*Exit* RODERIGO.] Two things are
to be done:

My wife must move for° Cassio to her mistress,
I'll set her on,   390
Myself the while to draw the Moor apart
And bring him jump° when he may Cassio find
Soliciting his wife. Aye, that's the way.
Dull not device° by coldness and delay.   [*Exit.*]

Act III

SCENE I. *Before the castle.*

[*Enter* CASSIO *and some* MUSICIANS.]
CAS. Masters, play here, I will content your
  pains° —
Something that's brief, and bid " Good morrow,
  General."°   [*Music.*]
      [*Enter* CLOWN.]
CLO. Why, masters, have your instruments been
in Naples,° that they speak i' the nose thus?
1. MUS. How, sir, how?   5
CLO. Are these, I pray you, wind instruments?
1. MUS. Aye, marry are they, sir.
CLO. Oh, thereby hangs a tail.
1. MUS. Whereby hangs a tale, sir?   9
CLO. Marry, sir, by many a wind instrument that
I know. But, masters, here's money for you. And the
General so likes your music that he desires you, for
love's sake, to make no more noise with it.
1. MUS. Well, sir, we will not.   15
CLO. If you have any music that may not be heard,
to 't again. But, as they say, to hear music the Gen-
eral does not greatly care.
1. MUS. We have none such, sir.
CLO. Then put up your pipes in your bag, for I'll
away. Go, vanish into air, away!   21
                           [*Exeunt* MUSICIANS.]
CAS. Dost thou hear, my honest friend?
CLO. No, I hear not your honest friend, I hear you.
CAS. Prithee keep up thy quillets.° There's a poor
piece of gold for thee. If the gentlewoman that at-
tends the General's wife be stirring, tell her there's
one Cassio entreats her a little favor of speech. Wilt
thou do this?   28
CLO. She is stirring, sir. If she will stir hither, I
shall seem to notify unto her.
CAS. Do, good my friend.   [*Exit* CLOWN.]

---

344. Probal: probable.   **347. framed:** made.   **348. free ele-**
ments: i.e., the air.   **354. function:** intelligence.   **358. suggest:**
seduce.   **360. Plies:** vigorously urges.   **363. repeals:** calls
back.   **370. one . . . cry:** See *MND*, IV.i.127–28,n.   **379. And**
. . . Time: and cleverness must wait for Time, who is in no hurry.
382–83. Though . . . ripe: though the fruit ripens in the sun, yet
the first fruit to ripen will come from the earliest blossoms;
i.e., our first plan — to get Cassio cashiered — has succeeded,
the rest will soon follow.

389. move for: petition for.   **392. jump:** at the moment, just.
394. Dull . . . device: do not spoil the plan.
  Act III, Sc. i: 1. content . . . pains: reward your labor.   **2. bid**
. . . General: It was a common custom to play or sing a song be-
neath the bedroom window of a distinguished guest or of a newly
wedded couple on the morning after their wedding night.   **4. in**
Naples: a reference to the Neapolitan (i.e., venereal) disease.
24. keep . . . quillets: put away your wisecracks.

[*Enter* IAGO.] In happy time,° Iago.

IAGO. You have not been abed, then?

CAS. Why, no, the day had broke
Before we parted. I have made bold, Iago,   35
To send in to your wife. My suit to her
Is that she will to virtuous Desdemona
Procure me some access.

IAGO.   I'll send her to you presently,
And I'll devise a mean to draw the Moor
Out of the way, that your convérse and business   40
May be more free.

CAS. I humbly thank you for 't. [*Exit* IAGO.] I
     never knew
A Florentine more kind° and honest.

       [*Enter* EMILIA.]

EMIL. Good morrow, good Lieutenant. I am sorry
For your displeasure,° but all will sure be well.   45
The General and his wife are talking of it,
And she speaks for you stoutly. The Moor replies
That he you hurt is of great fame in Cyprus
And great affinity,° and that in wholesome wisdom
He might not but° refuse you. But he protests he
     loves you,   50
And needs no other suitor but his likings°
To take the safest occasion by the front
To bring you in° again.

CAS.   Yet I beseech you
If you think fit, or that it may be done,
Give me advantage of some brief discourse   55
With Desdemona alone.

EMIL.   Pray you, come in.
I will bestow you where you shall have time.
To speak your bosom freely.°

CAS.   I am much bound to you. [*Exeunt.*]

SCENE II. *A room in the castle.*

[*Enter* OTHELLO, IAGO, *and* GENTLEMEN.]

OTH. These letters give, Iago, to the pilot,
And by him do my duties° to the Senate.
That done, I will be walking on the works.°
Repair there to me.

IAGO.   Well, my good lord, I'll do 't.

OTH. This fortification, gentlemen, shall we
     see 't?   5

GENT. We'll wait upon your lordship. [*Exeunt.*]

SCENE III. *The garden of the castle.*

[*Enter* DESDEMONA, CASSIO, *and* EMILIA.]

DES. Be thou assured, good Cassio, I will do
All my abilities in thy behalf.

EMIL. Good madam, do. I warrant it grieves my
     husband
As if the case were his.

DES. Oh, that's an honest fellow. Do not doubt,
     Cassio,   5
But I will have my lord and you again
As friendly as you were.

CAS.   Bounteous madam,
Whatever shall become of Michael Cassio,
He's never anything but your true servant.   9

DES. I know 't. I thank you. You do love my lord.
You have known him long, and be you well as-
     sured
He shall in strangeness stand no farther off
Than in a politic distance.°

CAS.   Aye, but, lady,
That policy may either last so long,
Or feed upon such nice and waterish diet,°   15
Or breed itself so out of circumstance,°
That, I being absent and my place supplied,°
My General will forget my love and service.

DES. Do not doubt° that. Before Emilia here
I give thee warrant of thy place.° Assure thee,   20
If I do vow a friendship, I'll perform it
To the last article. My lord shall never rest.
I'll watch him tame° and talk him out of patience,
His bed shall seem a school, his board a shrift.°
I'll intermingle every thing he does   25
With Cassio's suit. Therefore be merry, Cassio,
For thy solicitor shall rather die
Than give thy cause away.

[*Enter* OTHELLO *and* IAGO, *at a distance.*]

EMIL. Madam, here comes my lord.

CAS. Madam, I'll take my leave.   30

DES. Nay, stay and hear me speak.

CAS. Madam, I am very ill at ease,
Unfit for mine own purposes.°

DES. Well, do your discretion.   [*Exit* CASSIO.]

IAGO. Ha! I like not that.

OTH. What dost thou say?

IAGO. Nothing, my lord. Or if — I know not
     what.   35

OTH. Was not that Cassio parted from my wife?

---

32. In . . . time: i.e., I am glad to see you.   43. Florentine . . . kind: Iago is a Venetian. Cassio means: even one of my own people could not have been kinder.   45. your displeasure: i.e., that Othello is displeased with you.   49. affinity: kindred. 50. might . . . but: i.e., he must.   51. likings: affections. 52–53. safest . . . in: to take the first opportunity to restore you to your position. front: forehead; i.e., to take Time by the forelock.   58. speak . . . freely: declare what is on your mind.   Sc. ii: 2. do . . . duties: express my loyalty.   3. works: fortifications.

Sc. iii: 12–13. He . . . distance: i.e., his apparent coldness to you shall only be so much as his official position demands for reasons of policy.   15. nice . . . diet: have such weak encouragement.   16. breed . . . circumstance: become so used to the situation.   17. supplied: filled by another.   19. doubt: fear. 20. give . . . place: guarantee that you will be restored to your position.   23. watch . . . tame: as wild hawks are made tame by keeping them from sleep. See App. 26.   24. shrift: place of confession and absolution.   33. Unfit . . . purposes: in no condition to plead my own cause.

IAGO. Cassio, my lord! No, sure, I cannot think it,
That he would steal away so guilty-like,
Seeing you coming.
    OTH.   I do believe 'twas he.   40
    DES. How now, my lord!
I have been talking with a suitor here,
A man that languishes in your displeasure.
    OTH. Who is 't you mean?
    DES. Why, your Lieutenant, Cassio. Good my
    lord,   45
If I have any grace or power to move you,
His present reconciliation take.°
For if he be not one that truly loves you,
That errs in ignorance and not in cunning,°
I have no judgment in an honest face.   50
I prithee call him back.
    OTH.   Went he hence now?
    DES. Aye, sooth, so humbled
That he hath left part of his grief with me,
To suffer with him. Good love, call him back.
    OTH. Not now, sweet Desdemona, some other
    time.   55
    DES. But shall 't be shortly?
    OTH.   The sooner, sweet, for you.
    DES. Shall 't be tonight at supper?
    OTH.   No, not tonight.
    DES. Tomorrow dinner then?
    OTH.   I shall not dine at home.
I meet the captains at the citadel.
    DES. Why, then tomorrow night or Tuesday
    morn,   60
On Tuesday noon, or night, on Wednesday morn.
I prithee name the time, but let it not
Exceed three days. In faith, he's penitent,
And yet his trespass, in our common reason°   64
Save that, they say, the wars must make examples
Out of their best — is not almost° a fault
To incur a private check.° When shall he come?
Tell me, Othello. I wonder in my soul
What you would ask me that I should deny,   69
Or stand so mammering° on. What! Michael Cassio,
That came a-wooing with you, and so many a
    time
When I have spoke of you dispraisingly
Hath ta'en your part — to have so much to do
To bring him in! Trust me, I could do much ——
    OTH. Prithee, no more. Let him come when he
    will.   75
I will deny thee nothing.
    DES.   Why, this is not a boon.°
'Tis as I should entreat you wear your gloves,
Or feed on nourishing dishes, or keep you warm,
Or sue to you to do a peculiar° profit

To your own person. Nay, when I have a suit   80
Wherein I mean to touch your love indeed,
It shall be full of poise° and difficult weight,°
And fearful to be granted.°
    OTH.   I will deny thee nothing.
Whereon I do beseech thee grant me this,
To leave me but a little to myself.   85
    DES. Shall I deny you? No. Farewell, my lord.
    OTH. Farewell, my Desdemona. I'll come to thee
    straight.
    DES. Emilia, come. Be as your fancies teach you.°
Whate'er you be, I am obedient.

              [*Exeunt* DESDEMONA *and* EMILIA.]
    OTH. Excellent wretch! Perdition catch my soul
But I do love thee! And when I love thee not,   91
Chaos° is come again.
    IAGO. My noble lord ——
    OTH.   What dost thou say, Iago?
    IAGO. Did Michael Cassio,° when you wooed my
    lady,
Know of your love?   95
    OTH. He did, from first to last. Why dost thou
ask?
    IAGO. But for a satisfaction of my thought,
No further harm.
    OTH.   Why of thy thought, Iago?
    IAGO. I did not think he had been acquainted with
    her.
    OTH. Oh yes, and went between us very oft.   100
    IAGO. Indeed!
    OTH. Indeed! Aye, indeed. Discern'st thou aught
    in that?
Is he not honest?
    IAGO. Honest, my lord!
    OTH. Honest! Aye, honest.
    IAGO. My lord, for aught I know.
    OTH. What dost thou think?
    IAGO. Think, my lord!   105
    OTH. Think, my lord! By Heaven, he echoes me
As if there were some monster in his thought
Too hideous to be shown. Thou dost mean some-
    thing.
I heard thee say even now thou likedst not that
When Cassio left my wife. What didst not like?
And when I told thee he was of my counsel   111
In my whole course of wooing, thou criedst "In-
    deed!"
And didst contract and purse thy brow together
As if thou then hadst shut up in thy brain
Some horrible conceit.° If thou dost love me,   115
Show me thy thought

---

82. poise: weight in the scales. **difficult weight:** hard to estimate.   **83. fearful . . . granted:** only granted with a sense of fear.   **88. Be . . . you:** please yourself.   **92. Chaos:** the utter confusion that existed before order was established in the universe. The idea of order and chaos is worked out elaborately in *Tr & Cr,* I.iii.83–124.   **94. Did . . . Cassio:** See App. 22.   **115. conceit:** conception, notion.

---

47. His . . . take: accept his immediate apology and forgive him. **49. in cunning:** knowingly.   **64. common reason:** common sense. **66. not almost:** hardly.   **67. check:** rebuke.   **70. mammering:** hesitating.   **76. boon:** great favor.   **79. peculiar:** particular.

IAGO. My lord, you know I love you.

OTH.   I think thou dost,
And for° I know thou'rt full of love and honesty
And weigh'st thy words before thou givest them
          breath,
Therefore these stops of thine fright me the more.
For such things in a false disloyal knave   121
Are tricks of custom, but in a man that's just
They're close delations,° working from the heart,
That passion cannot rule.

IAGO.   For Michael Cassio,
I dare be sworn I think that he is honest.   125

OTH. I think so too.

IAGO.   Men should be what they seem,
Or those that be not, would they might seem none!°

OTH. Certain, men should be what they seem.

IAGO. Why, then I think Cassio's an honest man.

OTH. Nay, yet there's more in this.   130
I prithee speak to me as to thy thinkings,
As thou dost ruminate, and give thy worst of
          thoughts
The worst of words.

IAGO.   Good my lord, pardon me.
Though I am bound to every act of duty,
I am not bound to that all slaves are free to.   135
Utter my thoughts? Why, say they are vile and false,
As where's that palace whereinto foul things
Sometimes intrude not? Who has a breast so pure
But some uncleanly apprehensions
Keep leets and law days, and in session sit   140
With meditations lawful?°

OTH. Thou dost conspire against thy friend, Iago,
If thou but think'st him wronged and makest his
          ear
A stranger to thy thoughts.

IAGO.   I do beseech you —
Though I perchance am vicious in my guess,   145
As, I confess, it is my nature's plague
To spy into abuses, and oft my jealousy°
Shapes faults that are not — that your wisdom yet,
From one that so imperfectly conceits,°
Would take no notice, nor build yourself a trouble
Out of his scattering° and unsure observance.°   151
It were not for your quiet nor your good,
Nor for my manhood, honesty, or wisdom,
To let you know my thoughts.

OTH.   What dost thou mean?

IAGO. Good name in man and woman, dear my
          lord,   155

Is the immediate° jewel of their souls.
Who steals my purse steals trash — 'tis something,
          nothing,
'Twas mine, 'tis his, and has been slave to thou-
          sands —
But he that filches from me my good name
Robs me of that which not enriches him   160
And makes me poor indeed.

OTH. By Heaven, I'll know thy thoughts.

IAGO. You cannot if my heart were in your hand,
Nor shall not whilst 'tis in my custody.

OTH. Ha!

IAGO.   Oh, beware, my lord, of jealousy.   165
It is the green-eyed monster which doth mock°
The meat° it feeds on. That cuckold lives in bliss
Who, certain of his fate, loves not his wronger.°
But, oh, what damnèd minutes tells he o'er   169
Who dotes, yet doubts, suspects, yet strongly loves!

OTH. Oh, misery!

IAGO. Poor and content is rich, and rich enough,
But riches fineless° is as poor as winter
To him that ever fears he shall be poor.
Good Heaven, the souls of all my tribe defend   175
From jealousy!

OTH.   Why, why is this?
Think'st thou I'd make a life of jealousy,
To follow still the changes of the moon
With fresh suspicions? No, to be once in doubt
Is once to be resolved.° Exchange me for a goat   180
When I shall turn the business of my soul
To such exsufflicate and blown surmises,
Matching thy inference.° 'Tis not to make me jeal-
          ous
To say my wife is fair, feeds well, loves company,
Is free of speech, sings, plays, and dances well.   185
Where virtue is, these are more virtuous.
Nor from mine own weak merits will I draw
The smallest fear or doubt of her revolt,°
For she had eyes, and chose me. No, Iago,
I'll see before I doubt, when I doubt, prove,   190
And on the proof, there is no more but this —
Away at once with love or jealousy!

IAGO. I am glad of it, for now I shall have reason
To show the love and duty that I bear you
With franker spirit. Therefore, as I am bound,   195
Receive it from me. I speak not yet of proof.
Look to your wife. Observe her well with Cassio.
Wear your eye thus, not jealous nor secure.°

---

118. **for:** since.   123. **close delations:** concealed accusations.   127. **seem none:** i.e., not seem to be honest men.   138–41. **Who . . . lawful:** whose heart is so pure but that some foul suggestion will sit on the bench alongside lawful thoughts; i.e., foul thoughts will rise even on the most respectable occasions. **leet:** court held by the lord of the manor. **law days:** days when courts sit. **session:** sitting of the court.   147. **jealousy:** suspicion.   149. **conceits:** conceives, imagines.   151. **scattering:** scattered, casual. **observance:** observation.

156. **immediate:** most valuable.   166. **doth mock:** makes a mockery of.   167. **meat:** i.e., victim.   167–68. **That . . . wronger:** i.e., the cuckold who hates his wife and knows her falseness is not tormented by suspicious jealousy. See App. 11.   173. **fineless:** limitless.   179–80. **to . . . resolved:** whenever I find myself in doubt I at once seek out the truth.   181–83. **When . . . inference:** when I shall allow that which concerns me most dearly to be influenced by such trifling suggestions as yours. **exsufflicate:** blown up, like a bubble.   188. **revolt:** faithlessness.   198. **secure:** overconfident.

I would not have your free and noble nature
Out of self-bounty° be abused, look to 't.   200
I know our country disposition well.
In Venice° they do let Heaven see the pranks
They dare not show their husbands. Their best con-
          science
Is not to leave 't undone, but keep 't unknown.

OTH. Dost thou say so?   205

IAGO. She did deceive her father,° marrying you,
And when she seemed to shake and fear your looks,
She loved them most.

OTH.   And so she did.

IAGO.   Why, go to, then.
She that so young could give out such a seeming
To seel° her father's eyes up close as oak ——   210
He thought 'twas witchcraft — but I am much to
          blame.
I humbly do beseech you of your pardon
For too much loving you.

OTH.   I am bound to thee forever.

IAGO. I see this hath a little dashed your spirits.

OTH. Not a jot, not a jot.

IAGO.   I' faith, I fear it has.   215
I hope you will consider what is spoke
Comes from my love, but I do see you're moved.
I am to pray you not to strain my speech
To grosser issues° nor to larger reach°
Than to suspicion.   220

OTH. I will not.

IAGO.   Should you do so, my lord,
My speech should fall into such vile success°
As my thoughts aim not at. Cassio's my worthy
          friend. —
My lord, I see you're moved.

OTH.   No, not much moved.
I do not think but Desdemona's honest.°   225

IAGO. Long live she so! And long live you to think
          so!

OTH. And yet, how nature erring from itself ——

IAGO. Aye, there's the point. As — to be bold with
          you —
Not to affect° many proposed matches°
Of her own clime, complexion, and degree,   230
Whereto we see in all things nature tends° ——
Foh! One may smell in such a will most rank,°
Foul disproportion, thoughts unnatural.

But pardon me. I do not in position
Distinctly speak of her, though I may fear   235
Her will, recoiling to her better judgment,
May fall to match° you with her country forms,°
And happily° repent.

OTH.   Farewell, farewell.
If more thou dost perceive, let me know more.
Set on thy wife to observe. Leave me, Iago.   240

IAGO. [*Going*] My lord, I take my leave.

OTH. Why did I marry? This honest creature
          doubtless
Sees and knows more, much more, than he unfolds.

IAGO. [*Returning*] My lord, I would I might en-
          treat your honor
To scan this thing no further. Leave it to time.   245
Though it be fit that Cassio have his place,
For sure he fills it up with great ability,
Yet if you please to hold him off awhile,
You shall by that perceive him and his means.
Note if your lady strain his entertainment°   250
With any strong or vehement importunity —
Much will be seen in that. In the meantime,
Let me be thought too busy in my fears —
As worthy cause I have to fear I am —
And hold her free, I do beseech your Honor.   255

OTH. Fear not my government.°

IAGO. I once more take my leave.   [*Exit.*]

OTH. This fellow's of exceeding honesty,
And knows all qualities,° with a learned spirit,   259
Of human dealings.° If I do prove her haggard,
Though that her jesses were my dear heartstrings,
I'd whistle her off and let her down the wind
To prey at fortune.° Haply, for I am black
And have not those soft parts of conversation
That chamberers° have, or for I am declined   265
Into the vale of years — yet that's not much —
She's gone, I am abused, and my relief
Must be to loathe her. Oh, curse of marriage,
That we can call these delicate creatures ours,
And not their appetites! I had rather be a toad   270
And live upon the vapor of a dungeon
Than keep a corner in the thing I love
For others' uses. Yet, 'tis the plague of great ones,
Prerogatived° are they less than the base.
'Tis destiny unshunnable, like death.   275
Even then this forkèd plague° is fated to us
When we do quicken.° Desdemona comes.

---

200. **self-bounty:** natural goodness.   202. **In Venice:** Venice was notorious for its loose women; the Venetian courtesans were among the sights of Europe and were much commented upon by travelers.   206. **She . . . father:** Iago deliberately echoes Brabantio's parting words. See I.iii.293–94.   210. **seel:** blind. See I.iii.270,n.   219. **grosser issues:** worse conclusions. **larger reach:** i.e., more widely.   222. **success:** result.   225. **honest:** When applied to Desdemona, "honest" means "chaste," but applied to Iago it has the modern meaning of "open and sincere."   229. **affect:** be inclined to. **proposed matches:** offers of marriage.   231. **in . . . tends:** i.e., a woman naturally marries a man of her own country, color, and rank.   232. **will . . . rank:** desire most lustful.

237. **match:** compare. **country forms:** the appearance of her countrymen; i.e., white men.   238. **happily:** haply, by chance.   250. **strain . . . entertainment:** urge you to receive him.   256. **government:** self-control.   259. **qualities:** different kinds.   259–60. **with . . . dealings:** with wide experience of human nature.   260–63. **If . . . fortune:** Othello keeps up the imagery of falconry throughout. He means: If I find that she is wild, I'll whistle her off the game and let her go where she will, for she's not worth keeping. See App. 26. **haggard:** a wild hawk. **jesses:** the straps attached to a hawk's legs.   265. **chamberers:** playboys.   274. **Prerogatived:** privileged.   276. **forked plague:** i.e., to be a cuckold.   277. **quicken:** stir in our mother's womb.

[*Re-enter* DESDEMONA *and* EMILIA.] If she be false, oh,
  then Heaven mocks itself!
I'll not believe 't.
  DES.   How now, my dear Othello!
Your dinner, and the generous° islanders   280
By you invited, do attend your presence.
  OTH. I am to blame.
  DES.   Why do you speak so faintly?
Are you not well?
  OTH. I have a pain upon my forehead here.
  DES. Faith, that's with watching,° 'twill away
    again.   285
Let me but bind it hard, within this hour
It will be well.
  OTH.   Your napkin° is too little.
      [*He puts the handkerchief from him,*
                        and she drops it.]
Let it alone. Come, I'll go in with you.
  DES. I am very sorry that you are not well.
            [*Exeunt* OTHELLO *and* DESDEMONA.]
  EMIL. I am glad I have found this napkin.   290
This was her first remembrance from the Moor.
My wayward° husband hath a hundred times
Wooed me to steal it, but she so loves the token,
For he conjured° her she should ever keep it,
That she reserves it evermore about her   295
To kiss and talk to. I'll have the work ta'en out,°
And give 't Iago. What he will do with it
Heaven knows, not I.
I nothing but to please his fantasy.°
            [*Re-enter* IAGO.]
  IAGO. How now! What do you here alone?   300
  EMIL. Do not you chide, I have a thing for you.
  IAGO. A thing for me? It is a common thing——
  EMIL. Ha!
  IAGO. To have a foolish wife.   304
  EMIL. Oh, is that all? What will you give me now
For that same handkerchief?
  IAGO.   What handkerchief?
  EMIL. What handkerchief!
Why, that the Moor first gave to Desdemona,
That which so often you did bid me steal.
  IAGO. Hast stol'n it from her?   310
  EMIL. No, faith, she let it drop by negligence,
And, to the advantage,° I being here took 't up.
Look, here it is.
  IAGO.   A good wench. Give it me.
  EMIL. What will you do with 't, that you have
    been so earnest
To have me filch it?   314
  IAGO. [*Snatching it*] Why, what's that to you?
  EMIL. If 't be not for some purpose of import,

Give 't me again. Poor lady, she'll run mad
When she shall lack it.
  IAGO. Be not acknown on 't,° I have use for it.
Go, leave me.   [*Exit* EMILIA.]
I will in Cassio's lodging lose this napkin,   321
And let him find it. Trifles light as air
Are to the jealous confirmations strong
As proofs of Holy Writ. This may do something.
The Moor already changes with my poison.   325
Dangerous conceits are in their natures poisons,
Which at the first are scarce found to distaste,°
But with a little° act upon the blood
Burn like the mines of sulphur. I did say so.°
Look where he comes!
[*Re-enter* OTHELLO.] Not poppy,° nor mandragora,°
Nor all the drowsy syrups of the world,   331
Shall ever medicine thee to that sweet sleep
Which thou owedst° yesterday.
  OTH.   Ha! Ha! False to me?
  IAGO. Why, how now, General! No more of that.
  OTH. Avaunt!° Be gone! Thou hast set me on the
    rack.°   335
I swear 'tis better to be much abused
Than but to know 't a little.
  IAGO.   How now, my lord!
  OTH. What sense had I of her stol'n hours of lust?
I saw 't not, thought it not, it harmed not me.
I slept the next night well, was free and merry. 340
I found not Cassio's kisses on her lips.
He that is robbed, not wanting° what is stol'n,
Let him not know 't and he's not robbed at all.
  IAGO. I am sorry to hear this.
  OTH. I had been happy if the general camp,   345
Pioners° and all, had tasted her sweet body,
So I had nothing known. Oh, now forever
Farewell the tranquil mind! Farewell content!
Farewell the plumèd° troop and the big wars
That make ambition virtue! Oh, farewell,   350
Farewell the neighing steed and the shrill trump,
The spirit-stirring drum, the ear-piercing fife,
The royal banner and all quality,°
Pride, pomp, and circumstance of glorious war!
And, O you mortal engines,° whose rude throats
The immortal Jove's dread clamors counterfeit,°
Farewell! Othello's occupation's gone!   357
  IAGO. Is 't possible, my lord?
  OTH. Villain, be sure thou prove my love a whore,
Be sure of it, give me the ocular proof.   360

319. Be . . . on't: know nothing about it.   **327. distaste:** taste
unpleasantly.   **328. with a little:** in a little while.   **329. I . . .
so:** As Iago says this, Othello is seen approaching, with all the
signs of his agitation outwardly visible.   **330. poppy:** opium.
mandragora: called also mandrake, a root used as a drug to bring
sleep. See Pl. 12e.   **333. owedst:** owned, possessed.   **335. Avaunt:**
be off! **on . . . rack:** i.e., in torment. See App. 10.   **342. wanting:**
missing.   **346. Pioners:** pioneers, the lowest type of soldier.
349. plumed: wearing plumes in the helmet.   **353. quality:** mili-
tary rank.   **355. mortal engines:** deadly cannon.   **356. counter-
feit:** imitate.

280. generous: noble, of gentle blood.   **285. watching:** lack of
sleep.   **287. napkin:** handkerchief.   **292. wayward:** unaccount-
able.   **294. conjured:** begged with an oath.   **296. work . . . out:**
pattern copied.   **299. fantasy:** whim.   **312. to . . . advantage:**
thereby giving me the opportunity.

Or by the worth of man's eternal soul,
Thou hadst been better have been born a dog
Than answer my waked wrath!

IAGO.   Is 't come to this?

OTH. Make me to see 't, or at the least so prove it
That the probation° bear no hinge nor loop   365
To hang a doubt on, or woe upon thy life!

IAGO. My noble lord——

OTH. If thou dost slander her and torture me,
Never pray more, abandon all remorse.°
On horror's head horrors accumulate,   370
Do deeds to make Heaven weep, all earth amazed,
For nothing canst thou to damnation add
Greater than that.

IAGO.   Oh, grace! Oh, Heaven defend me!
Are you a man? Have you a soul or sense?   374
God be wi' you, take mine office. O wretched fool,
That livest to make thine honesty a vice!
O monstrous world! Take note, take note, O world,
To be direct and honest is not safe.
I thank you for this profit,° and from hence   379
I'll love no friend, sith° love breeds such offense.

OTH. Nay, stay. Thou shouldst be honest.

IAGO. I should be wise, for honesty's a fool,
And loses that it works for.

OTH.   By the world,
I think my wife be honest, and think she is not.
I think that thou art just, and think thou art not.
I'll have some proof. Her name, that was as fresh
As Dian's° visage, is now begrimed and black   387
As mine own face. If there be cords, or knives,
Poison, or fire, or suffocating streams,
I'll not endure it. Would I were satisfied!   390

IAGO. I see, sir, you are eaten up with passion.
I do repent me that I put it to you.
You would be satisfied?

OTH.   Would! Nay, I will.

IAGO. And may, but, how? How satisfied, my
lord?
Would you, the supervisor,° grossly gape on?   395
Behold her topped?

OTH.   Death and damnation! Oh!

IAGO. It were a tedious difficulty, I think,
To bring them to that prospect.° Damn them then,
If ever mortal eyes do see them bolster°
More than their own! What then? How then?   400
What shall I say? Where's satisfaction?
It is impossible you should see this,
Were they as prime° as goats, as hot as monkeys,
As salt° as wolves in pride,° and fools as gross
As ignorance made drunk. But yet I say   405
If imputation° and strong circumstances,

Which lead directly to the door of truth,
Will give you satisfaction, you may have 't.

OTH. Give me a living° reason she's disloyal.

IAGO. I do not like the office.   410
But sith I am entered in this cause so far,
Pricked° to 't by foolish honesty and love,
I will go on. I lay with Cassio lately,
And being troubled with a raging tooth,
I could not sleep.   415
There are a kind of men so loose of soul
That in their sleeps will mutter their affairs.
One of this kind is Cassio.
In sleep I heard him say "Sweet Desdemona,
Let us be wary, let us hide our loves."   420
And then, sir, would he gripe° and wring my
hand,
Cry "O sweet creature!" and then kiss me hard,
As if he plucked up kisses by the roots
That grew upon my lips. Then laid his leg   424
Over my thigh, and sighed and kissed, and then
Cried "Cursed fate that gave thee to the Moor!"

OTH. Oh, monstrous! Monstrous!

IAGO.   Nay, this was but his dream.

OTH. But this denoted a foregone conclusion.
'Tis a shrewd doubt,° though it be but a dream.

IAGO. And this may help to thicken other proofs
That do demónstrate thinly.

OTH.   I'll tear her all to pieces.   431

IAGO. Nay, but be wise. Yet we see nothing done.
She may be honest yet. Tell me but this:
Have you not sometimes seen a handkerchief   434
Spotted with strawberries° in your wife's hand?

OTH. I gave her such a one, 'twas my first gift.

IAGO. I know not that. But such a handkerchief—
I am sure it was your wife's—did I today
See Cassio wipe his beard with.

OTH.   If it be that——

IAGO. If it be that, or any that was hers,   440
It speaks against her with the other proofs.

OTH. Oh, that the slave had forty thousand lives!
One is too poor, too weak, for my revenge.
Now do I see 'tis true. Look here, Iago,
All my fond love thus do I blow to Heaven—   445
'Tis gone.
Arise, black Vengeance, from thy hollow cell!
Yield up, O Love, thy crown and hearted° throne
To tyrannous hate! Swell, bosom, with thy fraught,°
For 'tis of aspics'° tongues!

IAGO.   Yet be content.   450

OTH. Oh, blood, blood, blood!

IAGO. Patience, I say. Your mind perhaps may
change.

---

365. probation: proof.   369. remorse: pity.   379. profit: profitable lesson.   380. sith: since.   387. Dian: Diana, goddess of chastity.   395. supervisor: looker-on.   398. prospect: sight. 399. bolster: sleep together.   403. prime: lustful.   404. salt: eager. in pride: in heat.   406. imputation: probability.

409. living: tangible.   412. Pricked: spurred on.   421. gripe: grip.   429. shrewd doubt: bitter suspicion.   435. with strawberries: with a pattern of strawberries.   448. hearted: in my heart.   449. fraught: freight, load.   450. aspic: asp, a small poisonous snake. See *Ant & Cleo,* V.ii.351–56.

OTH. Never, Iago. Like to the Pontic Sea,
Whose icy current and compulsive course
Ne'er feels retiring ebb but keeps due on   455
To the Propontic and the Hellespont;°
Even so my bloody thoughts, with violent pace,
Shall ne'er look back, ne'er ebb to humble love,
Till that capable° and wide revenge   459
Swallow them up. Now, by yond marble Heaven,
In the due reverence of a sacred vow   [*Kneels.*]
I here engage° my words.
    IAGO.   Do not rise yet.   [*Kneels.*]
Witness, you ever burning lights above,
You elements that clip° us round about,
Witness that here Iago doth give up   465
The execution of his wit, hands, heart,
To wronged Othello's service! Let him command,
And to obey shall be in me remorse,°
What bloody business ever.   [*They rise.*]
    OTH.   I greet thy love,
Not with vain thanks, but with acceptance bounte-
    ous,   470
And will upon the instant put thee to 't.°
Within these three days let me hear thee say
That Cassio's not alive.
    IAGO. My friend is dead. 'Tis done at your request.
But let her live.
    OTH. Damn her, lewd minx! Oh, damn her!   475
Come, go with me apart. I will withdraw,
To furnish me with some swift means of death
For the fair devil. Now art thou my Lieutenant.
    IAGO. I am your own forever.   [*Exeunt.*]

SCENE IV. *Before the castle.*

[*Enter* DESDEMONA, EMILIA, *and* CLOWN.]
    DES. Do you know, sirrah, where Lieutenant Cas-
sio lies?
    CLO. I dare not say he lies anywhere.
    DES. Why, man?
    CLO. He's a soldier, and for one to say a soldier
lies is stabbing.   6
    DES. Go to. Where lodges he?
    CLO. To tell you where he lodges is to tell you
where I lie.
    DES. Can anything be made of this?   10
    CLO. I know not where he lodges, and for me to
devise a lodging, and say he lies here or he lies there,
were to lie in mine own throat.

DES. Can you inquire him out and be edified by
report?°   15
    CLO. I will catechize the world for him; that is,
make questions and by them answer.
    DES. Seek him, bid him come hither. Tell him I
have moved my lord on his behalf and hope all will
be well.   20
    CLO. To do this is within the compass of man's
wit, and therefore I will attempt the doing it.
                                                 [*Exit.*]
    DES. Where should I lose that handkerchief,
    Emilia?
    EMIL. I know not, madam.
    DES. Believe me, I had rather have lost my purse
Full of crusados.° And, but my noble Moor   26
Is true of mind and made of no such baseness
As jealous creatures are, it were enough
To put him to ill thinking.
    EMIL.   Is he not jealous?   29
    DES. Who, he? I think the sun where he was born
Drew all such humors° from him.
    EMIL.   Look where he comes.
    DES. I will not leave him now till Cassio
Be called to him.
[*Enter* OTHELLO.] How is 't with you, my lord?
    OTH. Well, my good lady. [*Aside*] Oh, hardness to
    dissemble!
How do you, Desdemona?
    DES.   Well, my good lord.   35
    OTH. Give me your hand. This hand is moist,°
    my lady.
    DES. It yet has felt no age nor known no sorrow.
    OTH. This argues fruitfulness and liberal heart.
Hot, hot, and moist — this hand of yours requires
A sequester° from liberty, fasting and prayer,   40
Much castigation, exercise devout.
For here's a young and sweating devil here,
That commonly rebels. 'Tis a good hand,
A frank one.
    DES.   You may indeed say so,
For 'twas that hand that gave away my heart.   45
    OTH. A liberal° hand. The hearts of old gave
    hands,
But our new heraldry is hands, not hearts.°
    DES. I cannot speak of this. Come now, your prom-
    ise.

Sc. iv: 14–15. **edified by report:** enlightened by the informa-
tion. Desdemona speaks with mock pomposity.   26. **crusados:**
small gold Portuguese coins.   31. **humors:** moods; lit., damp-
nesses.   36. **moist:** a hot moist palm was believed to show desire.
40. **sequester:** separation.   46. **liberal:** overgenerous.   46–47. **The
. . . hearts:** once love and deeds went together, but now it is all
deeds (i.e., faithlessness) and no love. This phrase has been taken
as a reference to the order of baronets created by James I in 1611,
who bore on their heraldic coats of arms the device of the "bloody
hand of Ulster." If so, the lines are a later addition; but the
reference is very doubtful. The contrast between hearts (true
love and faith) and hands (actions) is natural (see *Lear* I.ii. 72–
73). As Othello's passions rise, he ceases to be entirely coherent.

453–56. **Like . . . Hellespont:** In Pliny's *Natural History*, trans-
lated by Philemon Holland in 1601, it was noted that "the sea
Pontus (Black Sea) evermore floweth and runneth out into Pro-
pontis (Sea of Marmora) but the sea never returneth back again
within Pontus." **Hellespont:** the Dardanelles.   459. **capable:**
comprehensive, complete.   462. **engage:** pledge.   464. **ele-
ments . . . clip:** skies that embrace, surround.   468. **remorse:**
solemn obligation.   471. **put . . . to't:** put you to the proof.

OTH. What promise, chuck?°

DES. I have sent to bid Cassio come speak with
    you.   50

OTH. I have a salt and sorry rheum° offends me.
Lend me thy handkerchief.

DES. Here, my lord.

OTH. That which I gave you.

DES. I have it not about me.

OTH. Not?

DES. No indeed, my lord.

OTH. That's a fault. That handkerchief   55
Did an Egyptian° to my mother give.
She was a charmer, and could almost read
The thoughts of people. She told her while she kept
    it
'Twould make her amiable and subdue my father
Entirely to her love, but if she lost it   60
Or made a gift of it, my father's eye
Should hold her loathed and his spirits should hunt
After new fancies. She dying gave it me,
And bid me, when my fate would have me wive,
To give it her. I did so. And take heed on 't,   65
Make it a darling like your precious eye.
To lose 't or give 't away were such perdition
As nothing else could match.

DES.   Is 't possible?

OTH. 'Tis true. There's magic in the web of it.
A sibyl° that had numbered in the world   70
The sun to course two hundred compasses
In her prophetic fury° sewed the work.
The worms were hallowed that did breed the silk,
And it was dyed in mummy° which the skillful
Conserved° of maidens' hearts.

DES.   Indeed! Is 't true? 75

OTH. Most veritable, therefore look to 't well.

DES. Then would to God that I had never seen 't.

OTH. Ha! Wherefore?

DES. Why do you speak so startlingly and rash?

OTH. Is 't lost? Is 't gone? Speak, is it out o' the
    way?   80

DES. Heaven bless us!

OTH. Say you?

DES. It is not lost, but what an if it were?

OTH. How!

DES. I say it is not lost.

OTH. Fetch 't, let me see it.   85

DES. Why, so I can, sir, but I will not now.
This is a trick to put me from my suit.
Pray you let Cassio be received again.

OTH. Fetch me the handkerchief. My mind mis-
    gives.

DES. Come, come,   90
You'll never meet a more sufficient man.

OTH. The handkerchief!

DES.   I pray talk me of Cassio.

OTH. The handkerchief!

DES.   A man that all his time
Hath founded his good fortunes on your love,
Shared dangers with you ——   95

OTH. The handkerchief!

DES. In sooth, you are to blame.

OTH. Away!   [Exit.]

EMIL. Is not this man jealous?

DES. I ne'er saw this before.   100
Sure there's some wonder in this handkerchief.
I am most unhappy in the loss of it.

EMIL. 'Tis not a year or two shows us a man.°
They are all but stomachs and we all but food.
They eat us hungerly, and when they are full 105
They belch us. Look you, Cassio and my husband.

[Enter CASSIO and IAGO.]

IAGO. There is no other way, 'tis she must do 't.
And, lo, the happiness!° Go and impórtune her.

DES. How now, good Cassio! What's the news
    with you?

CAS. Madam, my former suit. I do beseech you
That by your virtuous means I may again   111
Exist, and be a member of his love
Whom I with all the office of my heart
Entire honor. I would not be delayed.
If my offense be of such mortal kind   115
That nor my service past nor present sorrows
Nor purposed merit in futurity°
Can ransom me into his love again,
But to know so must be my benefit.
So shall I clothe me in a forced content   120
And shut myself up in some other course
To Fortune's alms.°

DES.   Alas, thrice-gentle Cassio!
My advocation° is not now in tune.
My lord is not my lord, nor should I know him
Were he in favor as in humor altered.°   125
So help me every spirit sanctified,
As I have spoken for you all my best
And stood within the blank° of his displeasure
For my free speech! You must awhile be patient.
What I can do I will, and more I will   130
Than for myself I dare. Let that suffice you.

IAGO. Is my lord angry?

---

103. 'Tis . . . man: it does not take a couple of years for us to
discover the nature of a man; i.e., he soon shows his real na-
ture.   108. And . . . happiness: what good luck, here she is.
117. Nor . . . futurity: nor my good resolutions for the future.
119–22. But . . . alms: if I know that Othello will not restore me
to my position, it will have this benefit: I shall force myself
to be contented and try my luck elsewhere. Fortune's alms: what
Fortune may give me.   123. advocation: advocacy, pleading.
125. favor . . . altered: as changed in face as in mood.
128. blank: aim. The blank is the bull's-eye of a target.

---

49. chuck: a term of affection, but not the kind of word with
which a person of Othello's dignity would normally address his
wife. He is beginning to treat her with contemptuous familiarity.
See IV.ii.24.   51. rheum: common cold.   56. Egyptian: gypsy.
70. sibyl: prophetess.   72. fury: inspiration.   74. mummy: a
concoction made from Egyptian mummies.   75. Conserved:
prepared.

EMIL.   He went hence but now,
And certainly in strange unquietness.

IAGO. Can he be angry? I have seen the cannon
When it hath blown his ranks into the air,   135
And, like the Devil, from his very arm
Puffed his own brother, and can he be angry?
Something of moment then. I will go meet him.
There's matter in 't indeed if he be angry.

DES. I prithee do so. [*Exit* IAGO.] Something sure
    of state,   140
Either from Venice, or some unhatched practice
Made demonstrable° here in Cyprus to him,
Hath puddled° his clear spirit. And in such cases
Men's natures wrangle with inferior things,
Though great ones are their object.° 'Tis even so,
For let our finger ache and it indues°   146
Our other healthful members even to that sense
Of pain. Nay, we must think men are not gods,
Nor of them look for such observancy
As fits the bridal.° Beshrew me° much, Emilia,   150
I was, unhandsome warrior° as I am,
Arraigning his unkindness with my soul,
But now I find I had suborned the witness,°
And he's indicted falsely.

EMIL. Pray Heaven it be state matters, as you
    think,   155
And no conception nor no jealous toy°
Concerning you.

DES. Alas the day, I never gave him cause!

EMIL. But jealous souls will not be answered so.
They are not ever jealous for the cause,   160
But jealous for they are jealous. 'Tis a monster
Begot upon itself, born on itself.

DES. Heaven keep that monster from Othello's
    mind!

EMIL. Lady, amen.

DES. I will go seek him. Cassio, walk hereabout.
If I do find him fit, I'll move your suit,   166
And seek to effect it to my uttermost.

CAS. I humbly thank your ladyship.

    [*Exeunt* DESDEMONA *and* EMILIA.]
    [*Enter* BIANCA.]

BIAN. Save you, friend Cassio!

CAS.   What make you from° home?
How is it with you, my most fair Bianca?   170
I' faith, sweet love, I was coming to your house.

BIAN. And I was going to your lodging, Cassio.
What, keep a week away? Seven days and nights?

Eightscore eight hours? And lovers' absent hours,
More tedious than the dial eightscore times?°   175
Oh, weary reckoning!

CAS.   Pardon me, Bianca.
I have this while with leaden thoughts been pressed,
But I shall in a more continuate time°
Strike off this score of absence. Sweet Bianca,

    [*Giving her* DESDEMONA'*s* *handkerchief*]
Take me this work out.°

BIAN.   O Cassio, whence came this?   180
This is some token from a newer friend.
To the felt absence now I feel a cause.
Is 't come to this? Well, well.

CAS.   Go to, woman!
Throw your vile guesses in the Devil's teeth,   184
From whence you have them. You are jealous now
That this is from some mistress, some remembrance.
No, by my faith, Bianca.

BIAN.   Why, whose is it?

CAS. I know not, sweet. I found it in my chamber.
I like the work well. Ere it be demanded —
As like enough it will — I'd have it copied.   190
Take it, and do 't, and leave me for this time.

BIAN. Leave you! Wherefore?

CAS. I do attend here on the General,
And think it no addition,° nor my wish,
To have him see me womaned.°

BIAN.   Why, I pray you?   195

CAS. Not that I love you not.

BIAN.   But that you do not love me.
I pray you bring me on the way a little,
And say if I shall see you soon at night.

CAS. 'Tis but a little way that I can bring you,
For I attend here. But I'll see you soon.   200

BIAN. 'Tis very good, I must be circumstanced.°
                  [*Exeunt.*]

Act IV

SCENE I. *Cyprus. Before the castle.*

    [*Enter* OTHELLO *and* IAGO.]

IAGO. Will you think so?

OTH.   Think so, Iago!

IAGO.   What,
To kiss in private?

OTH.   An unauthorized kiss.

IAGO. Or to be naked with her friend in bed

141–42. unhatched . . . demonstrable: some plot, not yet matured, which has been revealed.   143. puddled: muddied, stirred up.   143–45. in . . . object: when men are disturbed by great matters, they show their temper in small things.   146. indues: endows, pervades.   150. bridal: honeymoon. Beshrew me: plague on me.   151. unhandsome warrior: clumsy soldier. Desdemona continually thinks of herself as Othello's companion in arms. Cf. I.iii.249ff.   153. suborned . . . witness: corrupted the evidence; i.e., it is my fault, not his.   156. jealous toy: silly suspicion.   169. make . . . from: are you doing away from.

174–75. And . . . times: when one's lover is absent for a week does it not seem far longer than a hundred and sixty clock hours?   178. continuate time: i.e., when my time is not continually being interrupted.   180. Take . . . out: copy this pattern.   194. addition: honor.   195. womaned: with a girl.   201. circumstanced: put off.

An hour or more, not meaning any harm?

OTH. Naked in bed, Iago, and not mean harm!   5
It is hypocrisy against the Devil.°
They that mean virtuously and yet do so,
The Devil their virtue tempts and they tempt
    Heaven.°

IAGO. So° they do nothing, 'tis a venial° slip.
But if I give my wife a handkerchief——   10

OTH. What then?

IAGO. Why, then, 'tis hers, my lord, and being
    hers,
She may, I think, bestow 't on any man.

OTH. She is protectress of her honor too.
May she give that?   15

IAGO. Her honor is an essence that's not seen.
They have it very oft that have it not.°
But for the handkerchief——

OTH. By Heaven, I would most gladly have forgot
    it.
Thou said'st—oh, it comes o'er my memory,   20
As doth the raven o'er the infected house,°
Boding° to all—he had my handkerchief.

IAGO. Aye, what of that?

OTH.   That's not so good now.

IAGO.   What,
If I had said I had seen him do you wrong?
Or heard him say—as knaves be such abroad,   25
Who having, by their own importunate suit,
Or voluntary dotage° of some mistress,
Convincèd or supplied° them, cannot choose
But they must blab——

OTH.   Hath he said anything?

IAGO. He hath, my lord, but be you well assured,
No more than he'll unswear.

OTH.   What hath he said?   31

IAGO. Faith, that he did——I know not what he
    did.

OTH. What? What?

IAGO. Lie——

OTH.   With her?

IAGO.   With her, on her, what you will.   34

OTH. Lie° with her! Lie on her!—We say lie
on her when they belie her.—Lie with her!
'Zounds, that's fulsome!° Handkerchief—confes-
sions—handkerchief!—To confess, and be hanged
for his labor. First to be hanged, and then to confess.
I tremble at it. Nature would not invest herself in
such shadowing passion without some instruc-   41

tion.° It is not words that shake me thus. Pish!
Noses, ears, and lips. Is 't possible?—Confess?—
Handkerchief?—Oh, devil!   [Falls in a trance.]

IAGO. Work on,   45
My medicine, work! Thus credulous fools are
    caught,
And many worthy and chaste dames even thus,
All guiltless, meet reproach. What ho! My lord!
My lord, I say! Othello! [Enter CASSIO.] How now,
    Cassio!

CAS. What's the matter?   50

IAGO. My lord is fall'n into an epilepsy.
This is his second fit, he had one yesterday.

CAS. Rub him about the temples.

IAGO.   No, forbear,
The lethargy° must have his quiet course.
If not, he foams at mouth and by and by   55
Breaks out to savage madness. Look, he stirs.
Do you withdraw yourself a little while,
He will recover straight. When he is gone,
I would on great occasion speak with you.

    [Exit CASSIO.]
How is it, General? Have you not hurt your head?°

OTH. Dost thou mock me?   61

IAGO.   I mock you! No, by Heaven.
Would you would bear your fortune like a man!

OTH. A hornèd man's a monster and a beast.

IAGO. There's many a beast, then, in a populous
    city,
And many a civil° monster.   65

OTH. Did he confess it?

IAGO.   Good sir, be a man.
Think every bearded fellow that's but yoked°
May draw with you.° There's millions now alive
That nightly lie in those unproper beds
Which they dare swear peculiar.° Your case is bet-
    ter.   70
Oh, 'tis the spite of Hell, the Fiend's archmock,
To lip° a wanton in a secure couch°
And to suppose her chaste! No, let me know,
And knowing what I am, I know what she shall be.

OTH. Oh, thou art wise, 'tis certain.

IAGO.   Stand you awhile apart,   75
Confine yourself but in a patient list.°
Whilst you were here o'erwhelmèd with your
    grief—
A passion most unsuiting such a man—
Cassio came hither. I shifted him away,

Act IV, Sc. i: 6. hypocrisy . . . Devil: "double-crossing the
Devil"; i.e., they are behaving in a most suspicious way.
7–8. They . . . Heaven: i.e., those who go to bed together and
mean no harm are asking the Devil to tempt them, and they make
God suspect their innocence.   9. So: so long as. venial: pardon-
able.   17. They . . . not: i.e., many are honored who have no
honor.   21. As . . . house: i.e., as a bird of prey waits for its vic-
tim to die.   22. Boding: foretelling evil.   27. dotage: infatuation.
28. Convinced or supplied: overcome or satisfied their desires.
35–44. Lie . . . devil: Othello breaks into incoherent muttering
before he falls down in a fit.   37. fulsome: disgusting.

40–42. Nature . . . instruction: nature would not fill me with such
overwhelming emotion unless there was some cause.   54. leth-
argy: epileptic fit. Cf. II Hen IV, I.i.127–29.   60. Have . . .
head: With brutal cynicism Iago asks whether Othello is suffering
from cuckold's headache.   65. civil: sober, well-behaved citizen.
67. yolked: married.   68. draw . . . you: lit., be your yoke fel-
low, share your fate.   69–70. That . . . peculiar: that lie nightly
in beds which they believe are their own but which others have
shared.   72. lip: kiss. secure couch: lit., a carefree bed; i.e., a
bed which has been used by the wife's lover, but secretly
76. patient list: confines of patience.

And laid good 'scuse upon your ecstasy,°   80
Bade him anon return and here speak with me,
The which he promisèd. Do but encave° yourself,
And mark the fleers,° the gibes, and notable scorns,
That dwell in every region of his face.
For I will make him tell the tale anew,   85
Where, how, how oft, how long ago, and when
He hath and is again to cope° your wife.
I say but mark his gesture. Marry, patience,
Or I shall say you are all in all in spleen,°
And nothing of a man.

OTH.   Dost thou hear, Iago?   90
I will be found most cunning in my patience,
But — dost thou hear? — most bloody.

     IAGO.   That's not amiss,
But yet keep time in all. Will you withdraw?

                    [OTHELLO *retires*.]

Now will I question Cassio of Bianca,
A housewife° that by selling her desires   95
Buys herself bread and clothes. It is a creature
That dotes on Cassio, as 'tis the strumpet's plague
To beguile many and be beguiled by one.
He, when he hears of her, cannot refrain
From the excess of laughter. Here he comes.   100

[*Re-enter* CASSIO.] As he shall smile, Othello shall go mad,
And his unbookish° jealousy must construe°
Poor Cassio's smiles, gestures, and light behavior
Quite in the wrong. How do you now, Lieutenant?

     CAS. The worser that you give me the addition°
Whose want even kills me.   106

     IAGO. Ply° Desdemona well, and you are sure
on 't.
Now, if this suit lay in Bianca's power,
How quickly should you speed!

     CAS.   Alas, poor caitiff!°

     OTH. Look how he laughs already!   110

     IAGO. I never knew a woman love man so.

     CAS. Alas, poor rogue! I think, i' faith, she loves
me.

     OTH. Now he denies it faintly and laughs it out.

     IAGO. Do you hear, Cassio?

     OTH.   Now he impórtunes him   115
To tell it o'er. Go to. Well said, well said.

     IAGO. She gives it out that you shall marry her.
Do you intend it?

     CAS. Ha, ha, ha!   120

     OTH. Do you triumph, Roman?° Do you triumph?

     CAS. I marry her! What, a customer!° I prithee

bear some charity to my wit. Do not think it so unwholesome. Ha, ha, ha!   125

     OTH. So, so, so, so. They laugh that win.°

     IAGO. Faith, the cry goes that you shall marry her.

     CAS. Prithee say true.

     IAGO. I am a very villain else.

     OTH. Have you scored° me? Well.   130

     CAS. This is the monkey's own giving out. She is persuaded I will marry her out of her own love and flattery, not out of my promise.

     OTH. Iago beckons me, now he begins the story.

     CAS. She was here even now. She haunts me in every place. I was the other day talking on the sea bank with certain Venetians, and thither comes the bauble,° and, by this hand, she falls me thus about my neck ——   140

     OTH. Crying " O dear Cassio! " as it were. His gesture imports it.

     CAS. So hangs and lolls and weeps upon me, so hales° and pulls me. Ha, ha, ha!   144

     OTH. Now he tells how she plucked him to my chamber. Oh, I see that nose of yours, but not that dog I shall throw it to.

     CAS. Well, I must leave her company.

     IAGO. Before me!° Look where she comes.   149

     CAS. 'Tis such another fitchew!° Marry, a perfumed one. [*Enter* BIANCA.] What do you mean by this haunting of me?

     BIAN. Let the Devil and his dam° haunt you! What did you mean by that same handkerchief you gave me even now? I was a fine fool to take it.   155
I must take out the work? A likely piece of work, that you should find it in your chamber and not know who left it there! This is some minx's token, and I must take out the work? There, give it your hobbyhorse.° Wheresoever you had it, I'll take out no work on 't.   161

     CAS. How now, my sweet Bianca! How now! How now!

     OTH. By Heaven, that should be my handkerchief!   165

     BIAN. An° you'll come to supper tonight, you may. An you will not, come when you are next prepared for.   [*Exit.*]

     IAGO. After her, after her.

     CAS. Faith, I must, she'll rail i' the street else.   171

     IAGO. Will you sup there?

     CAS. Faith, I intend so.

     IAGO. Well, I may chance to see you, for I would very fain° speak with you.   175

     CAS. Prithee, come, will you?

     IAGO. Go to. Say no more.   [*Exit* CASSIO.]

---

80. ecstasy: fit.   82. encave: hide.   83. fleers: scornful grins. 87. cope: encounter.   89. spleen: hot temper. Cf. *I Hen IV*, V.ii.19.   95. housewife: hussy.   102. unbookish: unlearned, simple. construe: interpret.   105. addition: title (Lieutenant) which he has lost.   107. Ply: urge.   109. caitiff: wretch. 121. triumph, Roman: The word "triumph" suggests "Roman" because the Romans celebrated their victories with triumphs, elaborate shows, and processions. Cf. *Caesar*, I.i.56.   123. customer: harlot.   126. They . . . win: a proverbial saying. See *Temp*, II.i.33. 130. scored: marked, as with a blow from a whip.   139. bauble: toy, plaything.   144. hales: hauls, drags.   149. Before me: by my soul, a mild oath.   150. fitchew: polecat, a creature most demonstrative in the mating season.   153. dam: mother. 160. hobbyhorse: harlot.   166. An: if.   175. fain: gladly.

OTH. [*Advancing*] How shall I murder him, Iago?

IAGO. Did you perceive how he laughed at his vice?   181

OTH. Oh, Iago!

IAGO. And did you see the handkerchief?

OTH. Was that mine?

IAGO. Yours, by this hand. And to see how he prizes the foolish woman your wife! She gave it him, and he hath given it his whore.   187

OTH. I would have him nine years a-killing. A fine woman! A fair woman! A sweet woman!

IAGO. Nay, you must forget that.

OTH. Aye, let her rot, and perish, and be damned tonight, for she shall not live. No, my heart is turned to stone, I strike it and it hurts my hand. Oh, the world hath not a sweeter creature. She might lie by an emperor's side, and command him tasks.   196

IAGO. Nay, that's not your way.°

OTH. Hang her! I do but say what she is, so delicate with her needle, an admirable musician — oh, she will sing the savageness out of a bear — of so high and plenteous wit and invention ——   201

IAGO. She's the worse for all this.

OTH. Oh, a thousand thousand times. And then, of so gentle a condition!°

IAGO. Aye, too gentle.   205

OTH. Nay, that's certain. But yet the pity of it, Iago! O Iago, the pity of it, Iago!

IAGO. If you are so fond° over her iniquity, give her patent° to offend, for if it touch not you, it comes near nobody.   210

OTH. I will chop her into messes.° Cuckold me!

IAGO. Oh, 'tis foul in her.

OTH. With mine officer!

IAGO. That's fouler.   215

OTH. Get me some poison, Iago, this night. I'll not expostulate° with her, lest her body and beauty unprovide° my mind again. This night, Iago.   218

IAGO. Do it not with poison, strangle her in her bed, even the bed she hath contaminated.

OTH. Good, good. The justice of it pleases. Very good.

IAGO. And for Cassio, let me be his undertaker.° You shall hear more by midnight.   225

OTH. Excellent good. [*A trumpet within.*] What trumpet is that same?

IAGO. Something from Venice, sure. 'Tis Lodovico

Come from the Duke. And see, your wife is with him.

[*Enter* LODOVICO, DESDEMONA, *and* ATTENDANTS.]

LOD. God save the worthy General!

OTH.   With all my heart, sir.   229

LOD. The Duke and Senators of Venice greet you.

[*Gives him a letter.*]

OTH. I kiss the instrument° of their pleasures.

[*Opens the letter, and reads.*]

DES. And what's the news, good Cousin Lodovico?

IAGO. I am very glad to see you, signior. Welcome to Cyprus.

LOD. I thank you. How does Lieutenant Cassio?

IAGO. Lives, sir.   236

DES. Cousin, there's fall'n between him and my lord

An unkind breach, but you shall make all well.

OTH. Are you sure of that?

DES. My lord?

OTH. [*Reads.*] "This fail you not to do, as you will ——"   240

LOD. He did not call, he's busy in the paper. Is there division 'twixt my lord and Cassio?

DES. A most unhappy one. I would do much To atone° them, for the love I bear to Cassio.

OTH. Fire and brimstone!

DES.   My lord?

OTH.   Are you wise?°   245

DES. What, is he angry?

LOD.   Maybe the letter moved him, For, as I think, they do command him home, Deputing Cassio in his government.°

DES. By my troth,° I am glad on 't.

OTH.   Indeed!

DES.   My lord?

OTH. I am glad to see you mad.

DES.   Why, sweet Othello?   250

OTH. Devil!   [*Striking her.*]

DES. I have not deserved this.

LOD. My lord, this would not be believed in Venice

Though I should swear I saw 't. 'Tis very much.° Make her amends, she weeps.

OTH.   O devil, devil!   255

If that the earth could teem with a woman's tears, Each drop she falls would prove a crocodile.° Out of my sight!

DES.   I will not stay to offend you. [*Going.*]

LOD. Truly, an obedient lady.

I do beseech your lordship, call her back.   260

OTH. Mistress!

DES. My lord?

---

197. **Nay . . . way**: i.e., don't get soft thoughts about her. 204. **condition**: nature. 208. **fond**: foolish. 209. **patent**: a grant by the King of some special privilege. 211. **messes**: little pieces. 217. **expostulate**: argue. 218. **unprovide**: weaken. 224. **be . . . undertaker**: undertake to manage his business. In Shakespeare's plays the word does *not* mean "mortician."

231. **instrument**: i.e., the official letter which he has just received. 244. **atone**: reconcile. 245. **Are . . . wise**: i.e., in saying you bear love to Cassio. 248. **in . . . government**: in his place as governor. 249. **troth**: truth. 254. **'Tis . . . much**: this is too much. 256–57. **If . . . crocodile**: if the earth could breed from woman's tears, each tear that she lets fall would become a crocodile. It was believed that the crocodile would cry and sob to attract the sympathetic passer-by, who was then snapped up.

OTH. What would you with her, sir?

LOD.   Who, I, my lord?

OTH. Aye, you did wish that I would make her
turn.

Sir, she can turn and turn, and yet go on
And turn again. And she can weep, sir, weep.   265
And she's obedient, as you say, obedient,
Very obedient. Proceed you in your tears.
Concerning this, sir — oh, well-painted passion!° —
I am commanded home. Get you away.
I'll send for you anon. Sir, I obey the mandate,   270
And will return to Venice. Hence, avaunt!

[*Exit* DESDEMONA.]

Cassio shall have my place. And, sir, tonight,
I do entreat that we may sup together.
You are welcome, sir, to Cyprus. Goats and mon-
keys!   [*Exit.*]

LOD. Is this the noble Moor whom our full Senate
Call all-in-all sufficient? This the nature   276
Whom passion could not shake? Whose solid vir-
tue
The shot of accident nor dart of chance
Could neither graze nor pierce?

IAGO.   He is much changed.

LOD. Are his wits safe? Is he not light of brain?

IAGO. He's that he is. I may not breathe my cen-
sure°   281
What he might be. If what he might he is not,
I would to Heaven he were!°

LOD.   What, strike his wife!

IAGO. Faith, that was not so well, yet would I knew
That stroke would prove the worst!

LOD.   Is it his use?°   285
Or did the letters work upon his blood,
And new-create this fault?

IAGO.   Alas, alas!
It is not honesty in me to speak
What I have seen and known. You shall observe
him,
And his own courses° will denote him so   290
That I may save my speech. Do but go after,
And mark how he continues.

LOD. I am sorry that I am deceived in him.

[*Exeunt.*]

SCENE II. *A room in the castle.*

[*Enter* OTHELLO *and* EMILIA.]

OTH. You have seen nothing, then?

EMIL. Nor ever heard, nor ever did suspect.

OTH. Yes, you have seen Cassio and she together.

EMIL. But then I saw no harm, and then I heard
Each syllable that breath made up between them.   5

OTH. What, did they never whisper?

EMIL.   Never, my lord.

OTH. Nor send you out o' the way?

EMIL. Never.

OTH. To fetch her fan, her gloves, her mask, nor
nothing?

EMIL. Never, my lord.   10

OTH. That's strange.

EMIL. I durst, my lord, to wager she is honest,
Lay down my soul at stake.° If you think other,
Remove your thought, it doth abuse your bosom.
If any wretch have put this in your head,   15
Let Heaven requite it with the serpent's curse!°
For if she be not honest, chaste, and true,
There's no man happy, the purest of their wives
Is foul as slander.

OTH. Bid her come hither. Go.   [*Exit* EMILIA.]
She says enough. Yet she's a simple bawd°   20
That cannot say as much. This is a subtle whore,
A closet° lock and key of villainous secrets.
And yet she'll kneel and pray, I have seen her do 't.

[*Enter* DESDEMONA *with* EMILIA.]

DES. My lord, what is your will?

OTH.   Pray, chuck,° come hither.

DES. What is your pleasure?

OTH.   Let me see your eyes.   25
Look in my face.

DES.   What horrible fancy's this?

OTH. [*To* EMILIA] Some of your function,° mis-
tress.
Leave procreants alone and shut the door,
Cough, or cry hem, if anybody come.
Your mystery,° your mystery. Nay, dispatch.°   30

[*Exit* EMILIA.]

DES. Upon my knees, what doth your speech im-
port?
I understand a fury in your words,
But not the words.

OTH. Why, what art thou?

DES. Your wife, my lord, your true and loyal wife.

OTH. Come, swear it, damn thyself,   35
Lest, being like one of Heaven,° the devils them-
selves
Should fear to seize thee. Therefore be double-
damned.
Swear thou art honest.

DES.   Heaven doth truly know it.

Sc. ii: 13. at stake: as the stake, the bet.   16. serpent's
curse: i.e., the curse laid on the serpent in the Garden of Eden.
20. bawd: keeper of a brothel.   22. closet: box in which secret
papers are kept.   24. chuck: See III.iv.49,n.   27. Some . . .
function: get about your business; i.e., prostitution. Othello pre-
tends that Emilia is keeper of a brothel and Desdemona one of
the women.   30. mystery: profession. dispatch: be quick.
36. being . . . Heaven: because you look like an angel.

268. well-painted passion: cleverly imitated emotion; *passion* is
any violent emotion.   281. censure: opinion, judgment.   283. I
. . . were: I wish he were the man he ought to be. Once more
Iago hints that he is holding back some unpleasant fact.   285. Is
. . . use: does he always behave like this?   290. courses: ways,
behavior.

OTH. Heaven truly knows that thou art false as
Hell.
DES. To whom, my lord? With whom? How am
I false?   40
OTH. O Desdemona! Away! Away! Away!
DES. Alas the heavy day! Why do you weep?
Am I the motive of these tears, my lord?
If haply you my father do suspect
An instrument of this your calling-back,   45
Lay not your blame on me. If you have lost him,
Why, I have lost him too.
OTH.   Had it pleased Heaven
To try me with affliction, had they rained
All kinds of sores and shames on my bare head,
Steeped me in poverty to the very lips,   50
Given to captivity me and my utmost hopes,
I should have found in some place of my soul
A drop of patience. But, alas, to make me
A fixèd figure for the time of scorn
To point his slow unmoving finger at!°   55
Yet could I bear that too, well, very well.
But there where I have garnered up my heart,°
Where either I must live or bear no life,
The fountain from the which my current runs
Or else dries up — to be discarded thence!   60
Or keep it as a cistern for foul toads
To knot and gender° in! Turn thy complexion there,
Patience, thou young and rose-lipped cherubin —
Aye, there, look grim as Hell!
DES. I hope my noble lord esteems me honest.   65
OTH. Oh, aye, as summer flies are in the sham-
bles,°
That quicken even with blowing.° O thou weed,
Who art so lovely fair and smell'st so sweet
That the sense aches at thee, would thou hadst ne'er
been born!   69
DES. Alas, what ignorant sin have I committed?
OTH. Was this fair paper,° this most goodly book,
Made to write "whore" upon? What committed!
Committed! O thou public commoner!°
I should make very forges of my cheeks°
That would to cinders burn up modesty   75
Did I but speak thy deeds. What committed!
Heaven stops the nose at it, and the moon winks.
The bawdy wind, that kisses all it meets,
Is hushed within the hollow mine° of earth
And will not hear it. What committed!   80
Impudent strumpet!

DES.   By Heaven, you do me wrong.
OTH. Are not you a strumpet?
DES.   No, as I am a Christian.
If to preserve this vessel for my lord
From any other foul unlawful touch
Be not to be a strumpet, I am none.   85
OTH. What, not a whore?
DES.   No, as I shall be saved.
OTH. Is 't possible?
DES. Oh, Heaven forgive us!
OTH.   I cry you mercy, then.
I took you for that cunning whore of Venice
That married with Othello. [Raising his voice.]
You, mistress,   90
That have the office opposite to Saint Peter,°
And keep the gate of Hell!
[Re-enter EMILIA.] You, you, aye, you!
We have done our course, there's money for your
pains.   93
I pray you turn the key, and keep our counsel.°
                                                    [Exit.]
EMIL. Alas, what does this gentleman conceive?°
How do you, madam? How do you, my good lady?
DES. Faith, half-asleep.
EMIL. Good madam, what's the matter with my
lord?
DES. With who?
EMIL. Why, with my lord, madam.   100
DES. Who is thy lord?
EMIL.   He that is yours, sweet lady.
DES. I have none. Do not talk to me, Emilia.
I cannot weep, nor answer have I none
But what should go by water.° Prithee tonight
Lay on my bed my wedding sheets. Remember,   105
And call thy husband hither.
EMIL.   Here's a change indeed!   [Exit.]
DES. 'Tis meet I should be used so, very meet.
How have I been behaved that he might stick
The small'st opinion on my least misuse?°
                                    [Re-enter EMILIA with IAGO.]
IAGO. What is your pleasure, madam? How is 't
with you?   110
DES. I cannot tell. Those that do teach young babes
Do it with gentle means and easy tasks.
He might have chid me so, for, in good faith,
I am a child to chiding.
IAGO.   What's the matter, lady?   114
EMIL. Alas, Iago, my lord hath so bewhored her,
Thrown such despite and heavy terms upon her,
As true hearts cannot bear.
DES. Am I that name, Iago?
IAGO.   What name, fair lady?

54–55. A . . . at: A difficult image, much discussed. F1 reads
"slow and moving finger"; Q1 reads "slow unmoving." Probably
it means "a perpetual mark for scorn to point at with motion-
less finger." time of scorn: (perhaps) scorn for all time. 57. gar-
nered . . . heart: stored the harvest of my love. 62. gender:
mate. 66. shambles: slaughterhouse. 67. quicken . . . blow-
ing: come to life as soon as the eggs are laid. 71. fair paper: i.e.,
her white body. 73. public commoner: one who offers herself to
all comers. 74. I . . . cheeks: i.e., my cheeks would be as hot as
a forge if I told the truth. 79. hollow mine: i.e., the cave where
the winds were supposed to be kept.

91. office . . . Peter: St. Peter kept the keys to Heaven.
94. counsel: i.e., secret. 95. conceive: imagine. 104. should
. . . water: be expressed in tears. 108–09. How . . . misuse:
what have I done that he could find the smallest reason to find
fault with my least mistake?

DES. Such as she says my lord did say I was.   119
EMIL. He called her whore. A beggar in his drink
Could not have laid such terms upon his callet.°
   IAGO. Why did he so?
   DES. I do not know. I am sure I am none such.
   IAGO. Do not weep, do not weep. Alas the day!
   EMIL. Hath she forsook so many noble matches,
Her father and her country and her friends,   126
To be called whore? Would it not make one weep?
   DES. It is my wretched fortune.
   IAGO.   Beshrew him for 't!
How comes this trick upon him?
   DES.   Nay, Heaven doth know.
   EMIL. I will be hanged if some eternal villain,
Some busy and insinuating rogue,   131
Some cogging, cozening° slave, to get some office,
Have not devised this slander. I'll be hanged else.
   IAGO. Fie, there is no such man, it is impossible.
   DES. If any such there be, Heaven pardon him!
   EMIL. A halter pardon him! And Hell gnaw his
     bones!   136
Why should he call her whore? Who keeps her com-
   pany?
What place? What time? What form? What likeli-
   hood?
The Moor's abused by some most villainous knave,
Some base notorious knave, some scurvy fellow.
O Heaven, that such companions° Thou'dst unfold,°
And put in every honest hand a whip   142
To lash the rascals naked through the world
Even from the east to the west!
   IAGO.   Speak withindoor.°
   EMIL. Oh, fie upon them! Some such squire° he
   was   145
That turned your wit the seamy side without,
And made you to suspect me with the Moor.
   IAGO. You are a fool. Go to.°
   DES.   O good Iago,
What shall I do to win my lord again?   149
Good friend, go to him, for, by this light of Heaven,
I know not how I lost him. Here I kneel.
If e'er my will did trespass 'gainst his love
Either in discourse of thought or actual deed,
Or that mine eyes, mine ears, or any sense
Delighted them in any other form,   155
Or that I do not yet, and ever did,
And ever will, though he do shake me off
To beggarly divorcement, love him dearly,
Comfort forswear° me! Unkindness may do much,
And his unkindness may defeat° my life,   160
But never taint my love. I cannot say "whore,"
It doth abhor me now I speak the word.

To do the act that might the addition° earn
Not the world's mass of vanity° could make me.
   IAGO. I pray you be content, 'tis but his humor.
The business of the state does him offense,   166
And he does chide with you.
   DES. If 'twere no other——
   IAGO. 'Tis but so, I warrant. [*Trumpets within.*]
Hark how these instruments summon to supper!
The messengers of Venice stay the meat.°   170
Go in, and weep not, all things shall be well.
         [*Exeunt* DESDEMONA *and* EMILIA.]
[*Enter* RODERIGO.] How now, Roderigo!
   ROD. I do not find that thou dealest justly with me.
   IAGO. What in the contrary?   175
   ROD. Every day thou daffest° me with some de-
vice, Iago, and rather, as it seems to me now, keep-
est from me all conveniency° than suppliest me with
the least advantage of hope. I will indeed no longer
endure it, nor am I yet persuaded to put up in peace
what already I have foolishly suffered.   182
   IAGO. Will you hear me, Roderigo?
   ROD. Faith, I have heard too much, for your words
and performances are no kin together.
   IAGO. You charge me most unjustly.   186
   ROD. With naught but truth. I have wasted myself
out of my means. The jewels you have had from me
to deliver to Desdemona would half have corrupted
a votarist.° You have told me she hath received
them, and returned me expectations and comforts of
sudden respect and acquaintance, but I find none.
   IAGO. Well, go to, very well.   194
   ROD. Very well! Go to! I cannot go to, man, nor
'tis not very well. By this hand, I say 'tis very scurvy,
and begin to find myself fopped° in it.
   IAGO. Very well.   198
   ROD. I tell you 'tis not very well. I will make my-
self known to Desdemona. If she will return me my
jewels, I will give over my suit and repent my un-
lawful solicitation. If not, assure yourself I will seek
satisfaction of you.
   IAGO. You have said now.°
   ROD. Aye, and said nothing but what I protest in-
tendment of doing.   206
   IAGO. Why, now I see there's mettle° in thee, and
even from this instant do build on thee a better opin-
ion than ever before. Give me thy hand, Roderigo.
Thou hast taken against me a most just exception,°
but yet I protest I have dealt most directly in thy
affair.   211
   ROD. It hath not appeared.
   IAGO. I grant indeed it hath not appeared, and

---

121. laid . . . callet: used such words about his moll.   132. cog-
ging, cozening: deceiving, cheating.   141. companions: low crea-
tures. unfold: bring to light.   144. Speak withindoor: don't
shout so loud that all the street will hear you.   145. squire:
fine fellow.   148. Go to: An expression of derision.   159. for-
swear: repudiate.   160. defeat: destroy.

163. addition: title. Cf. IV.i.105.   164. vanity: i.e., riches.
170. meat: serving of supper.   176. thou daffest: you put me
aside. Cf. *I Hen IV*, IV.i.96.   178. conveniency: opportunity.
190. votarist: one who has taken a vow, here a nun.   197. fopped:
fooled.   204. You . . . now: or in modern slang, "Oh yeah."
207. mettle: metal, good stuff.   209. just exception: reason-
able grievance.

your suspicion is not without wit° and judgment.
But, Roderigo, if thou hast that in thee indeed   216
which I have greater reason to believe now than ever
— I mean purpose, courage, and valor — this night
show it. If thou the next night following enjoy not
Desdemona, take me from this world with treachery
and devise engines° for my life.   222

ROD. Well, what is it? Is it within reason and compass?

IAGO. Sir, there is especial commission come from
Venice to depute Cassio in Othello's place.

ROD. Is that true? Why, then Othello and Desdemona return again to Venice.   228

IAGO. Oh, no. He goes into Mauritania, and takes
away with him the fair Desdemona, unless his abode
be lingered here by some accident. Wherein none can
be so determinate° as the removing of Cassio.   233

ROD. How do you mean, "removing of" him?

IAGO. Why, by making him uncapable° of Othello's place, knocking out his brains.

ROD. And that you would have me to do?   237

IAGO. Aye, if you dare do yourself a profit and a
right. He sups tonight with a harlotry,° and thither
will I go to him. He knows not yet of his honorable
fortune. If you will watch his going thence, which I
will fashion to fall out between twelve and one, you
may take him at your pleasure. I will be near to
second your attempt, and he shall fall between us.
Come, stand not amazed at it, but go along   245
with me. I will show you such a necessity in his
death that you shall think yourself bound to put it
on him. It is now high suppertime, and the night
grows to waste. About it.   250

ROD. I will hear further reason for this.

IAGO. And you shall be satisfied.   [*Exeunt.*]

SCENE III. *Another room in the castle.*

[*Enter* OTHELLO, LODOVICO, DESDEMONA, EMILIA, *and*
ATTENDANTS.]

LOD. I do beseech you, sir, trouble yourself no
further.

OTH. Oh, pardon me, 'twill do me good to walk.

LOD. Madam, good night. I humbly thank your
ladyship.

DES Your Honor is most welcome.

OTH.   Will you walk, sir?
Oh — Desdemona ——   5

DES. My lord?

OTH. Get you to bed on the instant, I will be returned forthwith. Dismiss your attendant there.
Look it be done.

DES. I will, my lord.   10

[*Exeunt* OTHELLO, LODOVICO, *and* ATTENDANTS.]

EMIL. How goes it now? He looks gentler than
he did.

DES. He says he will return incontinent.°
He hath commanded me to go to bed,
And bade me to dismiss you.

EMIL.   Dismiss me!   14

DES. It was his bidding, therefore, good Emilia,
Give me my nightly wearing,° and adieu.
We must not now displease him.

EMIL. I would you had never seen him!

DES. So would not I. My love doth so approve°
him   19
That even his stubbornness, his checks, his frowns —
Prithee, unpin me — have grace and favor in them.

EMIL. I have laid those sheets you bade me on the
bed.

DES. All's one. Good faith, how foolish are our
minds!
If I do die before thee, prithee shroud me
In one of those same sheets.

EMIL.   Come, come, you talk.   25

DES. My mother had a maid called Barbara.
She was in love, and he she loved proved mad
And did forsake her. She had a song of "willow"° —
An old thing 'twas, but it expressed her fortune,
And she died singing it. That song tonight   30
Will not go from my mind. I have much to do
But to go hang my head all at one side
And sing it like poor Barbara. Prithee, dispatch.

EMIL. Shall I go fetch your nightgown?

DES.   No, unpin me here.
This Lodovico is a proper man.   35

EMIL. A very handsome man.

DES. He speaks well.

EMIL. I know a lady in Venice would have walked
barefoot to Palestine for a touch of his nether°
lip.   40

DES. [*Singing*]
"The poor soul sat sighing by a sycamore tree,
     Sing all a green willow.
Her hand on her bosom, her head on her knee,
     Sing willow, willow, willow.
The fresh streams ran by her, and murmured her
         moans,   45
     Sing willow, willow, willow.
Her salt tears fell from her, and softened the
         stones — "
Lay by these — [*Singing*]
     "Sing willow, willow, willow."
Prithee, hie thee, he'll come anon.° — [*Singing*]   50
"Sing all a green willow must be my garland.

---

215. wit: wisdom.   222. engines: instruments of torture.
233. determinate: decisive.   235. uncapable: unable to take.
239. harlotry: harlot.

Sc. iii: 12. incontinent: immediately.   16. nightly wearing:
nightgown.   19. approve: commend.   28. willow: the emblem
of the forlorn lover.   39. nether: lower.   50. anon: soon.

Let nobody blame him, his scorn I approve —— "
Nay, that's not next. Hark! Who is 't that knocks?
EMIL. It's the wind.
DES. [*Singing*]
" I called my love false love, but what said he then?
 Sing willow, willow, willow.   56
If I court moe° women, you'll couch with moe
  men."
So get thee gone, good night. Mine eyes do itch.
Doth that bode weeping?
EMIL.   'Tis neither here nor there.
DES. I have heard it said so. Oh, these men, these
 men!   60
Dost thou in conscience think — tell me, Emilia —
That there be women do abuse their husbands
In such gross kind?
EMIL.   There be some such, no question.
DES. Wouldst thou do such a deed for all the
 world?
EMIL. Why, would not you?
DES.   No, by this heavenly light! 65
EMIL. Nor I neither by this heavenly light. I might
do 't as well i' the dark.
DES. Wouldst thou do such a deed for all the
 world?
EMIL. The world's a huge thing. It is a great price
For a small vice.
DES.   In troth, I think thou wouldst not. 70
EMIL. In troth, I think I should, and undo 't when
I had done. Marry, I would not do such a thing for
a joint ring,° nor for measures of lawn,° nor for
gowns, petticoats, nor caps, nor any petty exhibi-
tion;° but for the whole world — why, who would
not make her husband a cuckold to make him a
monarch? I should venture Purgatory for 't. 77
DES. Beshrew me if I would do such a wrong
For the whole world.
EMIL. Why, the wrong is but a wrong i' the
world, and having the world for your labor, 'tis a
wrong in your own world and you might quickly
make it right.
DES. I do not think there is any such woman. 84
EMIL. Yes, a dozen, and as many to the vantage°
as would store° the world they played for.
But I do think it is their husbands' faults
If wives do fall. Say that they slack their duties
And pour our treasures into foreign laps,
Or else break out in peevish jealousies, 90
Throwing restraint° upon us, or say they strike us,
Or scant our former having in despite,°

Why, we have galls,° and though we have some
 grace,
Yet have we some revenge. Let husbands know
Their wives have sense like them. They see and smell
And have their palates both for sweet and sour, 96
As husbands have. What is it that they do
When they change us for others? Is it sport?
I think it is. And doth affection breed it?
I think it doth. Is 't frailty that thus errs? 100
It is so too. And have not we affections,
Desires for sport, and frailty, as men have?
Then let them use us well. Else let them know
The ills we do, their ills instruct us so.
DES. Good night, good night. Heaven me such
 uses° send,   105
Not to pick bad from bad, but by bad mend!
          [*Exeunt.*]

Act V

SCENE I. *Cyprus. A street.*

[*Enter* IAGO *and* RODERIGO.]
IAGO. Here, stand behind this bulk,° straight° will
 he come.
Wear thy good rapier bare, and put it home.
Quick, quick, fear nothing, I'll be at thy elbow.
It makes us, or it mars us. Think on that,
And fix most firm thy resolution.   5
ROD. Be near at hand, I may miscarry in 't.
IAGO. Here, at thy hand. Be bold, and take thy
 stand.   [*Retires.*]
ROD. I have no great devotion to the deed,
And yet he hath given me satisfying reasons.
'Tis but a man gone. Forth, my sword. He dies. 10
IAGO. I have rubbed this young quat° almost to the
 sense,°
And he grows angry. Now, whether he kill Cassio,
Or Cassio him, or each do kill the other,
Every way makes my gain. Live Roderigo,
He calls me to a restitution large°   15
Of gold and jewels that I bobbed° from him
As gifts to Desdemona.
It must not be. If Cassio do remain,
He hath a daily beauty in his life
That makes me ugly,° and besides, the Moor 20
May unfold° me to him. There stand I in much
 peril.

---

57. moe: more. 73. joint ring: ring made in two pieces, a lover's
gift. measures of lawn: lengths of finest lawn, or as a modern
woman would say, "sheer nylon." 74–75. petty exhibition:
small allowance of money. 85. as . . . vantage: and more too;
vantage is that added to the exact weight to give generous meas-
ure. 86. store: stock, fill up. 91. Throwing restraint: putting
restraints. 92. scant . . . despite: for spite cut down our allow-
ance.

93. galls: bile, the cause of bitterness. 105. uses: practices.
 Act V, Sc. i: 1. bulk: stall outside a shop. straight: straight-
way. 11. quat: pimple. to . . . sense: to the quick, to the raw.
15. large: full. 16. bobbed: cheated. 19–20. He . . . ugly:
by comparison with him I am a poor thing. Iago is conscious of
his lack of social graces. 21. unfold: expose.

No, he must die. Be 't so. I hear him coming.

[*Enter* CASSIO.]

ROD. I know his gait, 'tis he. Villain, thou diest!

[*Makes a pass at* CASSIO.]

CAS. That thrust had been mine enemy indeed
But that my coat is better than thou know'st.° 25
I will make proof of thine.

[*Draws, and wounds* RODERIGO.]

ROD. Oh, I am slain!

[IAGO *from behind wounds* CASSIO
in the leg, and exit.]

CAS. I am maimed for ever. Help, ho! Murder!
Murder! [*Falls.*]

[*Enter* OTHELLO.]

OTH. The voice of Cassio. Iago keeps his word.
ROD. Oh, villain that I am!
OTH. It is even so.
CAS. Oh, help, ho! Light! A surgeon! 30
OTH. 'Tis he. O brave Iago, honest and just,
That hast such noble sense of thy friend's wrong!
Thou teachest me. Minion,° your dear lies dead,
And your unblest fate hies.° Strumpet, I come!
Forth of my heart those charms, thine eyes, are
blotted. 35
Thy bed lust-stained shall with lust's blood be
spotted. [*Exit.*]

[*Enter* LODOVICO *and* GRATIANO.]

CAS. What ho! No watch?° No passage?° Mur-
der! Murder!
GRA. 'Tis some mischance, the cry is very dire-
ful.
CAS. Oh, help!
LOD. Hark!
ROD. Oh, wretched villain! 40
LOD. Two or three groan. It is a heavy° night.
These may be counterfeits.° Let's think 't unsafe
To come in to the cry without more help.
ROD. Nobody come? Then shall I bleed to death.
LOD. Hark!

[*Re-enter* IAGO, *with a light.*]

GRA. Here's one comes in his shirt, with light and
weapons. 46
IAGO. Who's there? Whose noise is this that cries
on° murder?
LOD. We do not know.
IAGO. Did not you hear a cry?
CAS. Here, here! For Heaven's sake, help me!
IAGO. What's the matter? 50
GRA. This is Othello's Ancient, as I take it.
LOD. The same indeed, a very valiant fellow.
IAGO. What are you here that cry so grievously?
CAS. Iago? Oh, I am spoiled, undone by villains!
Give me some help. 55

IAGO. Oh me, Lieutenant! What villains have done
this?
CAS. I think that one of them is hereabout,
And cannot make away.
IAGO. Oh, treacherous villains!
[*To* LODOVICO *and* GRATIANO.] What are you there?
Come in and give some help.
ROD. Oh, help me here! 60
CAS. That's one of them.
IAGO. Oh, murderous slave! Oh, villain!

[*Stabs* RODERIGO.]

ROD. Oh, damned Iago! Oh, inhuman dog!
IAGO. Kill men i' the dark! Where be these bloody
thieves?
How silent is this town! Ho! Murder! Murder!
What may you be? Are you of good or evil? 65
LOD. As you shall prove us, praise us.
IAGO. Signior Lodovico?
LOD. He, sir.
IAGO. I cry you mercy. Here's Cassio hurt by vil-
lains.
GRA. Cassio! 70
IAGO. How is 't, brother?
CAS. My leg is cut in two.
IAGO. Marry, Heaven forbid!
Light, gentlemen. I'll bind it with my shirt.

[*Enter* BIANCA.]

BIAN. What is the matter, ho? Who is 't that
cried?
IAGO. Who is 't that cried! 75
BIAN. Oh, my dear Cassio! My sweet Cassio! Oh,
Cassio, Cassio, Cassio!
IAGO. Oh, notable strumpet! Cassio, may you sus-
pect
Who they should be that have thus mangled you?
CAS. No. 80
GRA. I am sorry to find you thus. I have been to
seek you.
IAGO. Lend me a garter. So. Oh, for a chair,
To bear him easily hence!
BIAN. Alas, he faints! Oh, Cassio, Cassio, Cassio!
IAGO. Gentlemen all, I do suspect this trash 85
To be a party in this injury.
Patience awhile, good Cassio. Come, come,
Lend me a light. Know we this face or no?
Alas, my friend and my dear countryman
Roderigo? No — yes, sure. Oh Heaven! Roderigo.
GRA. What, of Venice? 91
IAGO. Even he, sir. Did you know him?
GRA. Know him! Aye.
IAGO. Signior Gratiano? I cry you gentle pardon.°
These bloody accidents must excuse my manners,
That so neglected you.
GRA. I am glad to see you. 95
IAGO. How do you, Cassio? Oh, a chair, a chair!
GRA. Roderigo!

---

25. coat . . . know'st: i.e., I wear mail under my coat. 33. Min-
ion: darling, in a bad sense. 34. hies: comes on quickly.
37. watch: police. See Gen. Intro. p. 18a. No passage: nobody
passing. 42. heavy: thick. 43. counterfeits: fakes. 47. cries
on: cries out.

93. I . . . pardon: I beg you kindly pardon me.

IAGO. He, he, 'tis he. [*A chair brought in*] Oh,
    that's well said, the chair.
Some good man bear him carefully from hence.
I'll fetch the General's surgeon. [*To* BIANCA] For
    you, mistress,   100
Save you your labor. He that lies slain here, Cassio,
Was my dear friend. What malice was between you?
  CAS. None in the world, nor do I know the man.
  IAGO. [*To* BIANCA] What, look you pale? Oh, bear
    him out o' the air.

        [CASSIO *and* RODERIGO *are borne off.*]

Stay you, good gentlemen. Look you pale, mistress?
Do you perceive the gastness° of her eye?   106
Nay, if you stare, we shall hear more anon.
Behold her well, I pray you look upon her.
Do you see, gentlemen? Nay, guiltiness will speak,
Though tongues were out of use.   110

        [*Enter* EMILIA.]

  EMIL. 'Las, what's the matter? What's the matter,
    husband?
  IAGO. Cassio hath here been set on in the dark
By Roderigo, and fellows that are 'scaped.
He's almost slain, and Roderigo dead.   114
  EMIL. Alas, good gentlemen! Alas, good Cassio!
  IAGO. This is the fruit of whoring. Prithee, Emilia,
Go know of Cassio where he supped tonight.
What, do you shake at that?
  BIAN. He supped at my house, but I therefore
    shake not.
  IAGO. Oh, did he so? I charge you, go with me.
  EMIL. Fie, fie upon thee, strumpet!   121
  BIAN. I am no strumpet, but of life as honest
As you that thus abuse me.
  EMIL.   As I! Foh! Fie upon thee!
  IAGO. Kind gentlemen, let's go see poor Cassio
    dressed.°
Come, mistress, you must tell 's another tale.   125
Emilia, run you to the citadel,
And tell my lord and lady what hath happed!
Will you go on? I pray. [*Aside*] This is the night
That either makes me or fordoes° me quite.

                      [*Exeunt.*]

SCENE II. *A bedchamber in the castle.* DESDE-
MONA *in bed asleep, a light burning.*

        [*Enter* OTHELLO.]

OTH. It is the cause,° it is the cause, my soul.
Let me not name it to you, you chaste stars!
It is the cause. Yet I'll not shed her blood,

Nor scar that whiter skin of hers than snow
And smooth as monumental alabaster.°   5
Yet she must die, else she'll betray more men.
Put out the light, and then put out the light.
If I quench thee, thou flaming minister,°
I can again thy former light restore,
Should I repent me. But once put out thy light,   10
Thou cunning'st° pattern of excelling nature,
I know not where is that Promethean heat°
That can thy light relume.° When I have plucked
    the rose,
I cannot give it vital growth again,
It needs must wither. I'll smell it on the tree.   15

                  [*Kissing her*]

Ah, balmy breath, that dost almost persuade
Justice to break her sword! One more, one more.
Be thus when thou art dead, and I will kill thee,
And love thee after. One more, and this the last.
So sweet was ne'er so fatal. I must weep,   20
But they are cruel tears. This sorrow's heavenly,
It strikes where it doth love. She wakes.
  DES. Who's there? Othello?
  OTH.   Aye, Desdemona.
  DES. Will you come to bed, my lord?
  OTH. Have you prayed tonight, Desdemona?   25
  DES. Aye, my lord.
  OTH. If you bethink yourself of any crime
Unreconciled as yet to Heaven and grace,
Solicit for it straight.
  DES. Alas, my lord, what may you mean by that?
  OTH. Well, do it, and be brief. I will walk by.   30
I would not kill thy unpreparèd spirit.
No, Heaven forfend! I would not kill thy soul.°
  DES. Talk you of killing?
  OTH. Aye, I do.
  DES. Then Heaven have mercy on me!
  OTH. Amen, with all my heart!
  DES. If you say so, I hope you will not kill me.   35
  OTH. Hum!
  DES. And yet I fear you, for you are fatal° then
When your eyes roll so. Why I should fear I know
    not,
Since guiltiness I know not, but yet I feel I fear.
  OTH. Think on thy sins.
  DES.   They are loves I bear to you.   40
  OTH. Aye, and for that thou diest.
  DES. That death's unnatural that kills for loving.
Alas, why gnaw you so your nether lip?
Some bloody passion shakes your very frame.
These are portents,° but yet I hope, I hope,   45

---

106. gastness: ghastly look.   124. dressed: i.e., his wound
dressed.   129. fordoes: ruins.

    Sc. ii: 1. It . . . cause: The meaning of the opening lines of
this speech has been much discussed. The *cause* is Desdemona's
supposed faithlessness; Othello, at this moment, sees himself as
embodied vengeance, the venger of man betrayed by woman.

5. monumental alabaster: Alabaster is white translucent stone,
much used for memorial effigies on Elizabethan tombs.   8. minis-
ter: servant.   11. cunning'st: most skillfully made.   12. Pro-
methean heat: fire from Heaven. Prometheus stole fire from
Heaven and first gave it to man.   13. relume: relight.   27-32. If
. . . soul: Othello will be a merciful murderer. Cf. *Haml.*, I.v.76-
80. forfend: forbid.   37 fatal: deadly.   45. portents: signs
foretelling disaster.

They do not point on me.

OTH.   Peace, and be still!

DES. I will so. What's the matter?

OTH. That handkerchief which I so loved and gave
  thee

Thou gavest to Cassio.

DES.   No, by my life and soul!

Send for the man, and ask him.

OTH.   Sweet soul, take heed, 50

Take heed of perjury, thou art on thy deathbed.

DES. Aye, but not yet to die.

OTH.   Yes, presently.°

Therefore confess thee freely of thy sin,

For to deny each article with oath

Cannot remove nor choke the strong conception°

That I do groan withal. Thou art to die.   56

DES. Then Lord have mercy on me!

OTH.   I say amen.

DES. And have you mercy too! I never did

Offend you in my life, never loved Cassio

But with such general warranty° of Heaven   60

As I might love. I never gave him token.

OTH. By Heaven, I saw my handkerchief in 's
  hand.

O perjured woman! Thou dost stone° my heart,

And makest me call what I intend to do

A murder, which I thought a sacrifice.   65

I saw the handkerchief.

DES.   He found it, then,

I never gave it him. Send for him hither.

Let him confess a truth.

OTH.   He hath confessed.

DES. What, my lord?

OTH. That he hath used thee.

DES.   How? Unlawfully?   70

OTH. Aye.

DES. He will not say so.

OTH.   No, his mouth is stopped.

Honest Iago hath ta'en order for 't.

DES. Oh, my fear interprets! What, is he dead?

OTH. Had all his hairs been lives, my great revenge

Had stomach for them all.   75

DES. Alas, he is betrayed, and I undone!

OTH. Out, strumpet! Weep'st thou for him to my
  face?

DES. Oh, banish me, my lord, but kill me not!

OTH. Down, strumpet!

DES. Kill me tomorrow, let me live tonight!   80

OTH. Nay, if you strive ——

DES. But half an hour!

OTH.   Being done, there is no pause.

DES. But while I say one prayer!

OTH.   It is too late.

                                   [*He stifles her.*]

EMIL. [*Within*] My lord, my lord! What ho! My
  lord, my lord!

OTH. What noise is this? Not dead? Not yet quite
  dead?   85

I that am cruel am yet merciful,

I would not have thee linger in thy pain.

So, so.

EMIL. [*Within*] What ho! My lord, my lord!

OTH.   Who's there?

EMIL. [*Within*] Oh, good my lord, I would speak
  a word with you!   90

OTH. Yes, 'tis Emilia. By and by. She's dead.

'Tis like she comes to speak of Cassio's death.

The noise was here. Ha! No more moving?

Still as the grave. Shall she come in? Were 't
  good?

I think she stirs again. No. What's best to do? 95

If she come in, she'll sure speak to my wife.

My wife! My wife! What wife? I have no wife.

Oh, insupportable! Oh, heavy hour!

Methinks it should be now a huge eclipse

Of sun and moon, and that the affrighted globe 100

Should yawn at alteration.°

EMIL.   [*Within*] I do beseech you

That I may speak with you, O good my lord!

OTH. I had forgot thee. Oh, come in, Emilia.

Soft, by and by. Let me the curtains° draw.   104

Where art thou?   [*Unlocks the door.*]

[*Enter* EMILIA.] What's the matter with thee now?

EMIL. Oh, my good lord, yonder 's foul murders
  done!

OTH. What, now?

EMIL. But now, my lord.

OTH. It is the very error° of the moon.

She comes more nearer earth than she was wont

And makes men mad.   111

EMIL. Cassio, my lord, hath killed a young Vene-
  tian

Called Roderigo.

OTH.   Roderigo killed!

And Cassio killed!

EMIL.   No, Cassio is not killed.

OTH. Not Cassio killed! Then murder's out of
  tune,   115

And sweet revenge grows harsh.

DES. Oh, falsely, falsely murdered!

EMIL.   Alas, what cry is that?

OTH. That! What?

EMIL. Out and alas! That was my lady's voice.

Help! Help, ho! Help! O lady, speak again!   120

Sweet Desdemona! O sweet mistress, speak!

DES. A guiltless death I die.

EMIL. Oh, who hath done this deed?

DES. Nobody, I myself. Farewell.

---

52. **presently:** at once.   55. **conception:** thought.   60. **warranty:**
permission.   63. **stone:** turn to stone.

101. **yawn at alteration:** gape with wonder at some monstrous
change.   104. **curtains:** i.e., of the bed. See Pl. 17b.   109. **error:**
wandering out of her proper course.

Commend me to my kind lord. Oh, farewell!   125
                                    [*Dies.*]

OTH. Why, how should she be murdered?

EMIL. Alas, who knows?

OTH. You heard her say herself it was not I.

EMIL. She said so. I must needs report the truth.

OTH. She's like a liar gone to burning Hell.
'Twas I that killed her.

EMIL.   Oh, the more angel she,   130
And you the blacker devil!

OTH. She turned to folly,° and she was a whore.

EMIL. Thou dost belie her, and thou art a devil.

OTH. She was false as water.

EMIL.   Thou art rash as fire to say
That she was false. Oh, she was heavenly true!   135

OTH. Cassio did top her, ask thy husband else.
Oh, I were damned beneath all depth in Hell
But that I did proceed upon just grounds
To this extremity. Thy husband knew it all.

EMIL. My husband!   140

OTH. Thy husband.

EMIL. That she was false to wedlock?

OTH. Aye, with Cassio. Nay, had she been true,
If Heaven would make me such another world
Of one entire and perfect chrysolite,°   145
I'd not have sold her for it.

EMIL. My husband!

OTH.   Aye, 'twas he that told me first.
An honest man he is, and hates the slime
That sticks on filthy deeds.

EMIL.   My husband!

OTH. What needs this iteration,° woman? I say
thy husband.   150

EMIL. Oh, mistress, villainy hath made mocks with
love!
My husband say that she was false!

OTH.   He, woman.
I say thy husband. Dost understand the word?
My friend, thy husband, honest, honest Iago.

EMIL. If he say so, may his pernicious soul   155
Rot half a grain a day! He lies to the heart.
She was too fond of her most filthy bargain.

OTH. Ha!

EMIL. Do thy worst.
This deed of thine is no more worthy Heaven   160
Than thou wast worthy her.

OTH.   Peace, you were best.

EMIL. Thou hast not half that power to do me
harm
As I have to be hurt. O gull!° O dolt!°
As ignorant as dirt! Thou hast done a deed ——
I care not for thy sword, I'll make thee known,   165
Though I lost twenty lives. Help! Help, ho! Help!
The Moor hath killed my mistress! Murder! Murder!

[*Enter* MONTANO, GRATIANO, IAGO, *and others.*]

MON. What is the matter? How now, General!

EMIL. Oh, are you come, Iago? You have done
well,
That men must lay their murders on your neck.   170

GRA. What is the matter?

EMIL. Disprove this villain, if thou be'st a man.
He says thou told'st him that his wife was false.
I know thou didst not, thou'rt not such a villain.
Speak, for my heart is full.   175

IAGO. I told him what I thought, and told no more
Than what he found himself was apt° and true.

EMIL. But did you ever tell him she was false?

IAGO. I did.

EMIL. You told a lie, an odious, damnèd lie,   180
Upon my soul, a lie, a wicked lie!
She false with Cassio! Did you say with Cassio?

IAGO. With Cassio, mistress. Go to, charm your
tongue.°

EMIL. I will not charm my tongue, I am bound to
speak.
My mistress here lies murdered in her bed.   185

ALL. Oh, Heavens forfend!

EMIL. And your reports have set the murder on.

OTH. Nay, stare not, masters. It is true indeed.

GRA. 'Tis a strange truth.

MON. Oh, monstrous act!

EMIL.   Villainy, villainy, villainy!   190
I think upon 't. I think I smell 't. Oh, villainy!
I thought so then.° I'll kill myself for grief.
Oh, villainy, villainy!

IAGO. What, are you mad? I charge you, get you
home.

EMIL. Good gentlemen, let me have leave to
speak.   195
'Tis proper I obey him, but not now.
Perchance, Iago, I will ne'er go home.

OTH. Oh! Oh! Oh!   [*Falling on the bed.*]

EMIL.   Nay, lay thee down and roar,
For thou hast killed the sweetest innocent
That e'er did lift up eye.

OTH.   [*Rising*] Oh, she was foul!   200
I scarce did know you, Uncle. There lies your niece,
Whose breath indeed these hands have newly
stopped.
I know this act shows horrible and grim.

GRA. Poor Desdemona! I am glad thy father's
dead.
Thy match was mortal° to him, and pure grief   205
Shore his old thread in twain.° Did he live now,
This sight would make him do a desperate turn —
Yea, curse his better angel from his side,

---

132. folly: lewdness.   145. chrysolite: a semiprecious stone,
usually green in color.   150. iteration: repetition.   163. gull:
dupe. dolt: dull-witted ass.

177. apt: likely.   183. charm . . . tongue: be silent.   192. I . . .
then: i.e., I suspected this earlier — as for example when Iago
took the handkerchief. See III.iii.313.   205. match . . . mortal:
i.e., grief at this marriage killed him.   206. Shore . . . twain:
cut his thread of life in two.

And fall to reprobation.°

OTH. 'Tis pitiful, but yet Iago knows 210
That she with Cassio hath the act of shame
A thousand times committed. Cassio confessed it.
And she did gratify his amorous works
With that recognizance° and pledge of love
Which I first gave her, I saw it in his hand. 215
It was a handkerchief, an antique token
My father gave my mother.

EMIL. Oh, Heaven! Oh, heavenly powers!

IAGO. 'Zounds! Hold your peace.

EMIL.   'Twill out, 'twill out. I peace!
No, I will speak as liberal as the north.° 220
Let Heaven and men and devils, let them all,
All, all, cry shame against me, yet I'll speak.

IAGO. Be wise, and get you home.

EMIL.   I will not. [IAGO *offers to stab* EMILIA.]

GRA.   Fie!
Your sword upon a woman!

EMIL. O thou dull Moor! That handkerchief thou
 speak'st of 225
I found by fortune and did give my husband,
For often with a solemn earnestness,
More than indeed belonged to such a trifle,
He begged of me to steal it.

IAGO.   Villainous whore!

EMIL. She give it Cassio! No, alas, I found it, 230
And I did give 't my husband.

IAGO.   Filth, thou liest!

EMIL. By Heaven, I do not, I do not, gentlemen.
Oh, murderous coxcomb!° What should such a fool
Do with so good a wife?

OTH.   Are there no stones° in Heaven
But what serve for the thunder? Precious villain!

[*He runs at* IAGO. IAGO, *from behind,*
    stabs EMILIA, *and exit.*]

GRA. The woman falls. Sure, he hath killed his
 wife. 236

EMIL. Aye, aye. Oh, lay me by my mistress' side.

GRA. He's gone, but his wife's killed.

MON. 'Tis a notorious villain. Take you this
 weapon,
Which I have here recovered from the Moor. 240
Come, guard the door without, let him not pass,
But kill him rather. I'll after that same villain,
For 'tis a damnèd slave.

[*Exeunt all but* OTHELLO *and* EMILIA.]

OTH.   I am not valiant neither.
But every puny whipster° gets my sword.
But why should honor outlive honesty? 245
Let it go all.

EMIL. What did thy song bode, lady?
Hark, canst thou hear me? I will play the swan,

And die in music.° [*Singing*]
  "Willow, willow, willow."
Moor, she was chaste. She loved thee, cruel Moor,
So come my soul to bliss as I speak true. 250
So speaking as I think, I die, I die. [*Dies.*]

OTH. I have another weapon in this chamber.
It is a sword of Spain,° the ice brook's temper.° —
Oh, here it is. Uncle, I must come forth.

GRA. [*Within*] If thou attempt it, it will cost thee
 dear. 255
Thou hast no weapon, and perforce must suffer.

OTH. Look in upon me then, and speak with me,
Or, naked° as I am, I will assault thee.

[*Re-enter* GRATIANO.]

GRA. What is the matter?

OTH.   Behold, I have a weapon,
A better never did itself sustain 260
Upon a soldier's thigh. I have seen the day
That with this little arm and this good sword
I have made my way through more impediments
Than twenty times your stop. But, oh, vain boast!
Who can control his fate? 'Tis not so now. 265
Be not afraid, though you do see me weaponed.
Here is my journey's end, here is my butt°
And very sea mark of my utmost sail.°
Do you go back dismayed? 'Tis a lost fear.
Man but a rush° against Othello's breast, 270
And he retires. Where should Othello go?
Now, how dost thou look now? O ill-starred wench!
Pale as thy smock! When we shall meet at compt,°
This look of thine will hurl my soul from Heaven
And fiends will snatch at it. Cold, cold, my girl!
Even like thy chastity. Oh, cursèd slave! 276
Whip me, ye devils,
From the possession of this heavenly sight!
Blow me about in winds! Roast me in sulphur!
Wash me in steep-down gulfs° of liquid fire! 280
O Desdemona! Desdemona! Dead!
Oh! Oh! Oh!

[*Enter* LODOVICO, MONTANO, CASSIO *carried in a chair,
 and* OFFICERS *with* IAGO, *prisoner.*]

LOD. Where is this rash and most unfortunate
 man?

OTH. That's he that was Othello. Here I am.

LOD. Where is that viper? Bring the villain forth.

OTH. I look down toward his feet,° but that's a
 fable. 286

247–48. play . . . music: i.e., I will sing at my death. It was believed that swans sang once only, just before they died. 253. sword of Spain: Spanish swords and rapiers, from Toledo or Bilbao, were famous. ice . . . temper: hardened in ice-cold water. 258. naked: unarmed. 267. butt: aim. 268. And . . . sail: the mark that I have reached the end of my voyage. sea mark: a conspicuous object by which the mariner checks his course. 270. Man . . . rush: attack with only a reed. 273. compt: account; i.e., the Day of Judgment. 280. steep-down gulfs: sheer whirlpools. 286. toward . . . feet: i.e., to see if he has the cloven hoof of a devil.

209. reprobation: damnation; i.e., by self-murder. 214. recognizance: badge, token. 220. liberal . . . north: as freely as the north wind, which is loud and bitter. 233. coxcomb: conceited fool. 234. stones: thunderbolts. 244. whipster: whippersnapper.

If that thou be'st a devil,° I cannot kill thee.
                              [*Wounds* IAGO.]
  LOD. Wrench his sword from him.
  IAGO.   I bleed, sir, but not killed.
  OTH. I am not sorry neither. I'd have thee live,
For, in my sense, 'tis happiness to die.   290
  LOD. O thou Othello, that wert once so good,
Fall'n in the practice° of a damnèd slave,
What shall be said to thee?
  OTH.   Why, anything.
An honorable murderer, if you will,
For naught did I in hate, but all in honor.   295
  LOD. This wretch hath part confessed his villainy.
Did you and he consent in Cassio's death?
  OTH. Aye.
  CAS. Dear General, I never gave you cause.
  OTH. I do believe it, and I ask your pardon. 300
Will you, I pray, demand that demidevil
Why he hath thus ensnared my soul and body?
  IAGO. Demand me nothing. What you know, you
    know.
From this time forth I never will speak word.
  LOD. What, not to pray?
  GRA.   Torments will ope your lips. 305
  OTH. Well, thou dost best.
  LOD. Sir, you shall understand what hath befall'n,
Which, as I think, you know not. Here is a letter
Found in the pocket of the slain Roderigo,
And here another. The one of them imports 310
The death of Cassio to be undertook
By Roderigo.
  OTH. Oh, villain!
  CAS.   Most heathenish and most gross!
  LOD. Now here's another discontented paper,
Found in his pocket too. And this, it seems, 315
Roderigo meant to have sent this damnèd villain
But that, belike, Iago in the interim
Came in and satisfied him.
  OTH.   Oh, the pernicious caitiff!
How came you, Cassio, by that handkerchief
That was my wife's?
  CAS.   I found it in my chamber. 320
And he himself confessed but even now
That there he dropped it for a special purpose
Which wrought to his desire.
  OTH.   O fool! Fool! Fool!
  CAS. There is besides in Roderigo's letter
How he upbraids Iago, that he made him 325
Brave° me upon the watch, whereon it came
That I was cast.° And even but now he spake
After long seeming dead, Iago hurt him,
Iago set him on.
  LOD. You must forsake this room, and go with us.
Your power and your command is taken off, 331

287. **If . . . devil:** if you are an evil spirit and no man. 292. **Fall'n . . . practice:** destroyed by the plotting. 326. **Brave:** dare, insult. 327. **cast:** dismissed.

And Cassio rules in Cyprus. For this slave,
If there be any cunning cruelty
That can torment him much and hold him long,°
It shall be his. You shall close prisoner rest 335
Till that the nature of your fault be known
To the Venetian state. Come, bring away.
  OTH. Soft you,° a word or two before you go.
I have done the state some service, and they know 't.
No more of that. I pray you, in your letters, 340
When you shall these unlucky deeds relate,
Speak of me as I am, nothing extenuate,
Nor set down aught in malice. Then must you speak
Of one that loved not wisely but too well,
Of one not easily jealous, but, being wrought, 345
Perplexed in the extreme, of one whose hand,
Like the base Indian, threw a pearl away
Richer than all his tribe° — of one whose subdued
    eyes,
Albeit unusèd to the melting mood,
Drop tears as fast as the Arabian trees 350
Their medicinal gum. Set you down this,
And say besides that in Aleppo once,
Where a malignant and a turbaned Turk
Beat a Venetian and traduced° the state,
I took by the throat the circumcisèd dog 355
And smote him, thus.   [*Stabs himself.*]
  LOD. Oh, bloody period!
  GRA.   All that's spoke is marred.°
  OTH. I kissed thee ere I killed thee. No way but
    this,
Killing myself, to die upon a kiss.
      [*Falls on the bed, and dies.*]
  CAS. This did I fear, but thought he had no
    weapon. 360
For he was great of heart.
  LOD.   [*To* IAGO] O Spartan° dog,
More fell° than anguish, hunger, or the sea!
Look on the tragic loading° of this bed,
This is thy work. The object poisons sight,
Let it be hid.° Gratiano, keep the house, 365
And seize upon the fortunes of the Moor,
For they succeed on you. To you, Lord Governor,
Remains the censure of this hellish villain,
The time, the place, the torture.
Oh, enforce it!
Myself will straight aboard, and to the state 370
This heavy act with heavy heart relate. [*Exeunt.*]

334. **hold . . . long:** i.e., in dying. 338. **Soft you:** pause awhile.
347-48. **base . . . tribe:** A much discussed passage. F1 reads
"Iudean" (Judean), and if correct it would refer to Judas Iscariot, who betrayed Jesus. Shakespeare does not elsewhere use
the word "Judean," and he does associate India with pearls, as
in *Tr & Cr*, I.i.105: "Her bed is India, There she lies a pearl."
354. **traduced:** insulted. 357. **marred:** spoiled. 361. **Spartan:**
i.e., hardhearted. 362. **fell:** cruel. 363. **loading:** burden — the
bodies of Desdemona and Othello. 365. **Let . . . hid:** At these
words the curtains are closed across the inner stage (or chamber, if
this scene was acted aloft), concealing all three bodies. See Pl. 5b.

MEASURE FOR MEASURE

Introduction

Measure for Measure was played before the Court of King James I on December 26, 1604. Apart from this one fact recorded in the Revels Accounts [1] nothing is known of the play, but the style suggests that it was then fairly new. It was first printed in the first folio (F1) in 1623, where the text omits some essential stage direction and contains many corrupt lines and wrong line divisions. There are also a number of passages of indifferent writing which may be the work of a second hand.

The nearest parallel to the story of the play in Elizabethan times occurs in a dramatic piece called *Promos and Cassandra* written by George Whetstone and published in 1578. Four years later Whetstone published a prose version of the story in a collection called *The Heptameron of Civil Discourses*. The outline of the story is as follows:

In Julio in Hungary, Lord Promos revived an old law by which incontinence was punished by the death of the man and the perpetual shame of the woman. As a result a young gentleman called Andrugio was condemned to death. His sister, Cassandra, thereupon petitioned Lord Promos to pardon her brother. Promos was so much delighted with her beauty and conversation that he reprieved Andrugio, but after a while his liking changed to lust and he demanded that she should ransom her brother by sacrificing her honor. Cassandra, won over by her brother's pleading, reluctantly agreed on the condition that Promos should then pardon her brother and marry her. Promos promised to abide by these conditions, but as soon as he had satisfied his will he commanded the jailer to present Cassandra with her brother's head. The jailer, however, befriended Andrugio and instead brought to Cassandra the head of a newly executed felon, and then set Andrugio free. Cassandra thereupon complained to the King, who hastened to do justice on Promos. He commanded that Promos should marry Cassandra and forthwith be beheaded, but no sooner had the marriage been solemnized than Cassandra begged the King to spare her new husband. When the King refused, Andrugio, perceiving the grief of his sister, came forward and at the risk of his own life begged the King to be merciful. The King was so greatly moved that he pardoned Andrugio and Promos.

Although the story in its general details resembles the story of the play, it is likely that some other version, possibly one of the many Elizabethan plays now lost, was the actual source of *Measure for Measure*. But even if Shakespeare took his outline from Whetstone, he added Lucio and the affairs of Pompey from his own imagination, and very considerably altered the details and the motivation of the plot.

Measure for Measure is one of Shakespeare's unpleasant plays, and has, on the whole, been roughly treated by the earlier critics, though some modern writers have praised it as a highly moral play on the theme of " judge not that ye be not judged." It is not surprising that critics should disagree, for the play presents a stark problem in human conduct: When a woman is offered the choice of saving a condemned man — her brother, as it happens — at the cost of her own chastity, what should she do? As Shakespeare states the problem there is no simple answer.

The play opens quickly. Vincentio, Duke of Vienna, declares that he is about to travel incognito to Poland. He appoints Angelo to be his Deputy with full powers of life and death, and he disappears. It is not necessarily ironical that the Deputy should be named Angelo, for he is by most recognized standards a good man; he is austere, conscientious, and efficient, and he alone can be trusted to cleanse the morals of Vienna without fear of unpopularity. Angelo immediately begins a long overdue reformation. Brothels are pulled down, and an old fierce law whereby incontinence is punished by death is put into force. One of the offenders against this law is a young gentleman named Claudio who finds himself in prison awaiting execution. Claudio's friends are horrified, especially Lucio. Claudio sees that his only possible chance of reprieve lies in an appeal for mercy. So he sends Lucio to fetch his sister Isabella to plead with Deputy Angelo.

Isabella is a proper match for Angelo. She too is austere and cold-blooded. Indeed, when Lucio

[1] I.e., the sums expended on entertainment for the Court.

calls upon her she is about to take her vows as a nun and is complaining that the rules of the order are not strict enough. Nevertheless, she consents to plead for her brother and with Lucio she goes to the Deputy. Her appeal is so eloquent and moving that it has the most unexpected and devastating result. Suddenly the old restraint snaps, and Angelo in a moment is mad to commit that very offense which he has spent his life in suppressing. He becomes raging with desire for Isabella. So he tells her to come again. When she returns he makes her the monstrous proposal that he will pardon Claudio at the price of her yielding to his will. Naturally Isabella is shocked, but she is not frightened, for, as she reflects, her brother, being an honorable young man, will naturally prefer to die to save her honor.

All this, with the comic business of the disreputable but ever cheerful Pompey, takes up the first two acts. Meanwhile the Duke, instead of going to Poland, has disguised himself as a friar and is watching events. In this guise he is allowed to enter the jail to minister to the prisoners. The third act opens in the prison with the supposed friar exhorting Claudio not to be afraid of death, with the result that Claudio is in the right frame of mind to die cheerfully when Isabella enters to tell him of her conversation with the Deputy. At first she says that there is no hope of reprieve, but when she goes on to repeat Angelo's offer and to say complacently that she would gladly give her life for her brother, there comes over the wretched Claudio an appalling horror of death, and he pleads with his sister to save his life at Angelo's price. Thus twice disillusioned by the faithlessness of man, Isabella turns from him with fury and loathing. Here is the problem fairly and freely stated — since Angelo will grant mercy on no other terms, which is to be sacrificed, Claudio's life or Isabella's honor?

Much of the irritation which critics feel with *Measure for Measure* is caused by Shakespeare's refusal either to give an answer to the question or to present the case sentimentally. There is no clear line between black and white. Angelo is neither ruffian nor seducer, but a man caught by the wildest, fiercest, most irrational, and most irresistible passion. In his sane moments he is the man of the highest principles. Nor is Isabella a warmhearted, generous, self-sacrificing heroine; she is hard, cold, and self-righteous, for it requires no exalted nobility to preserve her own honor at the cost of her brother's life. Nor is Claudio, from what we see of him, particularly worth saving. The trouble is that Shakespeare has made his characters human beings and not idealized types.

At this point in the play Angelo, Isabella, and Claudio are in such a tangle that for each of them disaster seems inevitable; but thereafter instead of making his story a tragedy of human frailties, Shakespeare changes the whole direction of the play and converts it into a thriller of the conventional type. The problem ceases to be one of ethics and becomes one of plot: how to save Claudio, reward Isabella, cheat Angelo, and bring a happy ending to all.

The disguised Duke now takes charge. As it happened, there was another lady in the case. Five years earlier Angelo had been betrothed to Mariana of the moated grange, but her dowry was lost in a shipwreck, and he in a most ungentlemanly manner repudiated the bargain. Yet in spite of all she still loves him. So the Duke proposes that Isabella shall pretend to agree to Angelo's condition, but that they shall meet in some dark spot where Mariana shall take her place. And this is done. To most moderns the solution is distasteful and hardly creditable to the two women or the supposed friar. It would not, however, have shocked Shakespeare's audience. According to accepted notions, Mariana had a moral if not a legal claim on Angelo as her husband (see Gen. Intro. p. 20a). Moreover, marriage included certain obligations on each party which Shakespeare elsewhere calls "bedright." If Angelo refused Mariana her rights as a wife, she was justified in obtaining them by trickery.

Once Angelo has, as he thinks, seduced Isabella, he suffers the natural and inevitable reaction, which is itself as fierce as the original passion. He now loathes himself and loathes Isabella so bitterly that instead of pardoning Claudio as he had promised, he sends an order that Claudio shall instantly be beheaded, and further, that there may be no doubt in his own mind, he commands the head to be sent to him. All this the disguised Duke learns during his visit to the prison.

Here is an unexpected turn. The Duke first suggests that the head of Barnardine, who is awaiting execution, shall be shaved and otherwise disguised and substituted for Claudio's. But Barnardine thwarts this plan by refusing to be beheaded. However, by good luck another prisoner has just died, and by further good luck his head is not unlike Claudio's. So the head is dispatched to Angelo and passes the inspection. The play must now be wound up.

The Duke sends a message announcing his return to Vienna and commands that all petitioners with a grievance shall attend him. He appears without his disguise and is greeted by Angelo and the rest. The two women come forward and accuse Angelo, who replies that either they are mad or else are the tools of some plotter. Thereupon the Duke leaves Angelo to try the case and withdraws to return a few moments later in his friar's disguise. The " friar " is closely questioned and ordered to be sent to prison, but in the scuffle his cowl is pulled off and he is revealed as Angelo's Prince. Angelo thus stands convicted and can only confess his guilt. There remains the passing of judgments. The Duke declares that Angelo must legally marry Mariana forthwith and after due penitence be forgiven. Lucio, who has made some very slanderous observations on the Duke, is condemned to whipping and to marrying a prostitute. Claudio is forgiven and told to marry his mistress. And as for Isabella, the Duke decides to make her his own wife. The ending, to say the least, is more symmetrical than convincing.

It is not, however, necessarily a blemish in a play, especially an Elizabethan play, that the story should be improbable. Few of Shakespeare's comedies could possibly have happened in real life, but usually no one takes the stories too seriously, because they never touch the deeper levels of emotion. This play in its earlier and middle scenes has been too powerful. Emotions have been so painfully stirred by the central problem that the critical instincts demand an answer. A profound moral issue has been stated, and we are not to be satisfied by a series of plots and stratagems, no matter how ingenious.

Measure for Measure indeed is marred by a certain confusion of purpose. Shakespeare the working playwright wished to provide his company with a new play on an old theme. It was a familiar story, with the commonest tricks of the theater: disguises, surprises, distressed virgins, thwarted seducers, and a happy ending. But Shakespeare the expert in humanity took charge. He treated his puppets seriously, and he made them human, with the result that the soul of the play became too great for its body.

Measure for Measure

DRAMATIS PERSONAE

VINCENTIO, *the Duke*
ANGELO, *Deputy*
ESCALUS, *an ancient lord*
CLAUDIO, *a young gentleman*
LUCIO, *a fantastic*
TWO OTHER GENTLEMEN
PROVOST
THOMAS ⎱ *two friars*
PETER ⎰
A JUSTICE
VARRIUS
ELBOW, *a simple constable*
FROTH, *a foolish gentleman*

POMPEY, *servant to Mistress Overdone*
ABHORSON, *an executioner*
BARNARDINE, *a dissolute prisoner*

ISABELLA, *sister to Claudio*
MARIANA, *betrothed to Angelo*
JULIET, *beloved of Claudio*
FRANCISCA, *a nun*
MISTRESS OVERDONE, *a bawd*

LORDS, OFFICERS, CITIZENS, BOY, *and* ATTENDANTS

SCENE — *Vienna.*

Act I

SCENE I. *An apartment in the* DUKE'S *palace.*

[*Enter* DUKE, ESCALUS, LORDS *and* ATTENDANTS.]

DUKE. Escalus.
ESCAL. My lord.
DUKE. Of government the properties to unfold
Would seem in me to affect speech and discourse,°
Since I am put° to know that your own science° 5
Exceeds, in that, the lists° of all advice
My strength can give you. Then no more remains,
But that to your sufficiency, as your worth is able,°
And let them work. The nature of our people, 10
Our city's institutions, and the terms°
For common justice, you're as pregnant° in
As art and practice hath enriched any
That we remember. There is our commission,°
From which we would not have you warp.° Call
   hither, 15
I say, bid come before us Angelo.

[*Exit an* ATTENDANT.]

What figure° of us think you he will bear?
For you must know, we have with special soul
Elected him our absence to supply,°
Lent him our terror, dressed him with our love, 20
And given his deputation° all the organs°
Of our own power. What think you of it?

ESCAL. If any in Vienna be of worth
To undergo such ample grace and honor,
It is Lord Angelo.
DUKE.   Look where he comes. 25

[*Enter* ANGELO.]

ANG. Always obedient to your Grace's will,
I come to know your pleasure.
DUKE.   Angelo,
There is a kind of character° in thy life,
That to th' observer doth thy history
Fully unfold. Thyself and thy belongings 30
Are not thine own so proper as to waste
Thyself upon thy virtues, they on thee.°
Heaven doth with us as we with torches do,
Not light them for themselves; for if our virtues
Did not go forth of us, 'twere all alike 35
As if we had them not. Spirits are not finely
   touched°
But to fine issues, nor Nature never lends
The smallest scruple° of her excellence
But, like a thrifty goddess, she determines
Herself the glory of a creditor, 40
Both thanks and use. But I do bend my speech
To one that can my part in him advértise.°
Hold° therefore, Angelo. —
In our remove° be thou at full ourself.
Mortality° and mercy in Vienna 45
Live in thy tongue and heart. Old Escalus,
Though first in question, is thy secondary.°
Take thy commission.
ANG.   Now, good my lord,

Act I, Sc. i: 3–4. Of . . . discourse: i.e., for me to tell you about the principles (*properties*) of governing would seem to be mere desire to make a speech. 5. put: made. science: expert knowledge. 6. lists: limits. 9. But . . . able: A sentence seems to have been omitted between "sufficiency" and "able." 11. terms: periods when the courts sit. 12. pregnant: expert. 14. commission: formal document setting out in detail the duties of his appointment. 15. warp: deviate. 17. figure: likeness. 19. our . . . supply: to fill up our place when absent. 21. deputation: appointment to act as my deputy. organs: instruments.

28. character: stamp, impression. 30–32. Thyself . . . thee: i.e., your good qualities are not your own private property to be wasted on yourself. 36. touched: tested. 38. scruple: minute part. 42. my . . . advertise: teach me how to govern. 43. Hold: observe, remember. 44. remove: absence. 45. Mortality: power to condemn to death. 47. Though . . . secondary: though first summoned, is your subordinate.

Let there be some more test made of my metal°
Before so noble and so great a figure   50
Be stamped upon it.

DUKE.   No more evasion.
We have with a leavened° and preparèd choice
Proceeded to you, therefore take your honors.
Our haste from hence is of so quick condition
That it prefers itself,° and leaves unquestioned°   55
Matters of needful value. We shall write to you,
As time and our concernings shall impórtune,
How it goes with us, and do look to know
What doth befall you here. So fare you well.
To the hopeful execution do I leave you   60
Of your commissions.

ANG.   Yet give leave, my lord,
That we may bring you something on the way.

DUKE. My haste may not admit it,
Nor need you, on mine honor, have to do
With any scruple.° Your scope is as mine own,   65
So to enforce or qualify the laws
As to your soul seems good. Give me your hand.
I'll privily away. I love the people,
But do not like to stage me to their eyes.
Though it do well, I do not relish well   70
Their loud applause and Aves vehement,°
Nor do I think the man of safe discretion
That does affect° it. Once more, fare you well.

ANG. The Heavens give safety to your purposes!

ESCAL. Lead forth and bring you back in happi-
    ness!   75

DUKE. I thank you. Fare you well.   [*Exit.*]

ESCAL. I shall desire you, sir, to give me leave
To look into the bottom of° my place.
A power I have, but of what strength and nature   80
I am not yet instructed.

ANG. 'Tis so with me. Let us withdraw together,
And we may soon our satisfaction have
Touching that point.

ESCAL.   I'll wait upon your Honor.

[*Exeunt.*]

SCENE II. *A street.*

[*Enter* LUCIO *and two* GENTLEMEN.]

LUCIO. If the Duke, with the other dukes, come
not to composition° with the King of Hungary, why
then all the dukes fall upon the King.

1. GENT. Heaven grant us its peace, but not the
King of Hungary's!   5

2. GENT. Amen.

LUCIO. Thou concludest like the sanctimonious pi-
rate that went to sea with the Ten Commandments,
but scraped one out of the table.

2. GENT. "Thou shalt not steal?"   10

LUCIO. Aye, that he razed.

1. GENT. Why, 'twas a commandment to command
the captain and all the rest from their functions.°
They put forth to steal. There's not a soldier of us
all that in the thanksgiving before meat do relish
the petition well that prays for peace.

2. GENT. I never heard any soldier dislike it.

LUCIO. I believe thee, for I think thou never wast
where grace was said.   20

2. GENT. No? A dozen times at least.

1. GENT. What, in meter?

LUCIO. In any proportion° or in any language.

1. GENT. I think or in any religion.

LUCIO. Aye, why not? Grace is grace,° despite   25
of all controversy. As, for example, thou thyself art
a wicked villain, despite of all grace.

1. GENT. Well, there went but a pair of shears be-
tween us.°

LUCIO. I grant, as there may between the lists°
and the velvet. Thou art the list.   31

1. GENT. And thou the velvet. Thou art good vel-
vet, thou're a three-piled° piece, I warrant thee. I had
as lief be a list of an English kersey° as be piled as
thou art piled, for a French velvet. Do I speak feel-
ingly° now?   36

LUCIO. I think thou dost, and indeed with most
painful feeling of thy speech I will, out of thine
own confession, learn to begin thy health, but whilst
I live forget to drink after thee.   40

1. GENT. I think I have done myself wrong, have
I not?

2. GENT. Yes, that thou hast, whether thou art
tainted or free.

[*Enter* MISTRESS OVERDONE.]

LUCIO. Behold, behold, where Madam Mitigation
comes! I have purchased as many diseases under   46
her roof as come to——

2. GENT. To what, I pray?

LUCIO. Judge.

2. GENT. To three thousand dolors° a year.   50

1. GENT. Aye, and more.

LUCIO. A French crown° more.

---

49. **metal:** mettle; i.e., material, worth. "Mettle" and "metal"
were the same word in Shakespeare's time.   52. **leavened:** al-
lowed to work like leaven; i.e., mature consideration.   55. **prefers
itself:** takes precedence. **unquestioned:** undiscussed.   64–65. **have
. . . scruple:** i.e., hesitate to use your power to the full.   68–71. **I
. . . vehement:** a tactful compliment to King James I, who
(unlike Queen Elizabeth) disliked cheering crowds. **Aves:** salu-
tations.   73. **affect:** desire.   79. **look . . . of:** examine care-
fully.

Sc. ii: 2. **composition:** agreement.

13. **from . . . functions:** to forbid them to fulfill their tasks.
23. **proportion:** meter.   25. **Grace is grace:** with a pun on grace,
meaning holy life.   28–29. **there . . . us:** i.e., we were cut from
the same piece.   30. **lists:** the outer edge or selvage, which
is made of plain material.   33. **three-piled:** i.e., thick velvet
of the best quality, with a pun on piled, meaning made bald as a
result of the French (venereal) disease.   34. **kersey:** thick
woolen cloth.   36. **feelingly:** i.e., to make you feel pain.
50. **dolors:** with a pun on dollars.   52. **French crown:** the same
joke as in ll. 32–34 above.

1. GENT. Thou art always figuring° diseases in me,
but thou art full of error. I am sound.

LUCIO. Nay, not as one would say healthy, 55
but so sound as things that are hollow. Thy bones
are hollow, impiety has made a feast of thee.

1. GENT. How now! Which of your hips has the
most profound sciatica? 60

MRS. OV. Well, well, there's one yonder arrested
and carried to prison was worth five thousand of
you all.

2. GENT. Who's that, I pray thee?

MRS. OV. Marry,° sir, that's Claudio, Signior
Claudio. 66

1. GENT. Claudio to prison? 'Tis not so.

MRS. OV. Nay, but I know 'tis so. I saw him ar-
rested, saw him carried away, and, which is more,
within these three days his head to be chopped off.

LUCIO. But after all this fooling, I would not have
it so. Art thou sure of this? 72

MRS. OV. I am too sure of it. And it is for getting
Madam Julietta with child.

LUCIO. Believe me, this may be. He promised 75
to meet me two hours since, and he was ever precise
in promise-keeping.

2. GENT. Besides, you know, it draws something
near to the speech we had to such a purpose. 79

1. GENT. But most of all, agreeing with the procla-
mation.

LUCIO. Away! Let's go learn the truth of it.

[*Exeunt* LUCIO *and* GENTLEMEN.]

MRS. OV. Thus, what with the war, what with the
sweat,° what with the gallows, and what with pov-
erty, I am custom-shrunk.° [*Enter* POMPEY.] 85
How now! What's the news with you?

POM. Yonder man is carried to prison.

MRS. OV. Well, what has he done?

POM. A woman.

MRS. OV. But what's his offense? 90

POM. Groping for trouts in a peculiar° river.

MRS. OV. What, is there a maid with child by him?

POM. No, but there's a woman with maid by him.
You have not heard of the proclamation, have you?

MRS. OV. What proclamation, man? 95

POM. All houses° in the suburbs° of Vienna must
be plucked down.

MRS. OV. And what shall become of those in the
city?

POM. They shall stand for seed. They had 100
gone down too but that a wise burgher put in for
them.°

MRS. OV. But shall all our houses of resort in the
suburbs be pulled down? 105

POM. To the ground, mistress.

MRS. OV. Why, here's a change indeed in the com-
monwealth! What shall become of me?

POM. Come, fear not you. Good counselors 110
lack no clients. Though you change your place, you
need not change your trade, I'll be your tapster° still.
Courage! There will be pity taken on you. You that
have worn your eyes almost out in the service, you
will be considered. 115

MRS. OV. What's to do here, Thomas Tapster?
Let's withdraw.

POM. Here comes Signior Claudio, led by the Pro-
vost° to prison, and there's Madam Juliet.

[*Exeunt.*]

[*Enter* PROVOST, CLAUDIO, JULIET, *and* OFFICERS.°]

CLAUD. Fellow, why dost thou show me thus to
the world?
Bear me to prison, where I am committed.

PROV. I do it not in evil disposition,
But from Lord Angelo by special charge.

CLAUD. Thus can the demigod Authority
Make us pay down for our offense by weight° 125
The words of Heaven° — on whom it will, it will;
On whom it will not, so; yet still 'tis just.

[*Re-enter* LUCIO *and two* GENTLEMEN.]

LUCIO. Why, how now, Claudio! Whence comes
this restraint?°

CLAUD. From too much liberty, my Lucio, liberty.
As surfeit° is the father of much fast, 130
So every scope° by the immoderate use
Turns to restraint. Our natures do pursue,
Like rats that ravin° down their proper bane,°
A thirsty evil, and when we drink we die.

LUCIO. If I could speak so wisely under an 135
arrest, I would send for certain of my creditors. And
yet, to say the truth, I had as lief have the foppery°
of freedom as the morality of imprisonment. What's
thy offense, Claudio?

CLAUD. What but to speak of would offend again.

LUCIO. What, is 't murder? 141

CLAUD. No.

LUCIO. Lechery?

CLAUD. Call it so.

PROV. Away, sir! You must go. 145

CLAUD. One word, good friend. Lucio, a word
with you.

LUCIO. A hundred, if they'll do you any good.
Is lechery so looked after?°

---

53. **figuring:** calculating, imagining.   65. **Marry:** Mary, by the
Virgin.   84. **sweat:** sweating sickness, a form of the plague.
85. **I . . . custom-shrunk:** my trade is failing.   91. **peculiar:**
private.   96. **houses:** brothels. **suburbs:** The most notorious
London brothels were located in the suburbs.   101–102. **put . . .
them:** made a bid for them.

112. **tapster:** bartender, the waiter who brings the drinks; i.e.
pimp.   119. **Provost:** officer of the law.   120 s.d.: At this point
the folio marks a new scene.   125. **pay . . . weight:** pay heavily
for.   126. **words of Heaven:** possibly a reference to Romans 9:
15–18. "I will have mercy on whom I will have mercy . . . there-
fore hath He mercy on whom He will have mercy, and whom He
will He hardeneth." Here also there seems to be some omission
in the text.   128. **restraint:** arrest.   130. **surfeit:** excess
131. **scope:** liberty.   133. **ravin:** devour greedily. **bane:** poison
137. **foppery:** folly.   148. **looked after:** seriously regarded.

CLAUD. Thus stands it with me. Upon a true con-
tráct°
I got possession of Julietta's bed.   150
You know the lady. She is fast my wife,
Save that we do the denunciation lack
Of outward order.° This we came not to,
Only for propagation° of a dower
Remaining in the coffer° of her friends,   155
From whom we thought it meet° to hide our love
Till time had made them° for us. But it chances
The stealth of our most mutual entertainment
With character° too gross is writ on Juliet.
    LUCIO. With child, perhaps?
    CLAUD.   Unhappily, even so.   160
And the new Deputy now for the Duke —
Whether it be the fault and glimpse° of newness,
Or whether that the body public be
A horse whereon the governor doth ride,
Who, newly in the seat, that it may know   165
He can command, lets it straight feel the spur —
Whether the tyranny be in his place,
Or in his eminence that fills it up,
I stagger in.° But this new governor
Awakes me all the enrollèd penalties   170
Which have, like unscoured° armor, hung by the
    wall
So long that nineteen zodiacs° have gone round
And none of them been worn; and, for a name,°
Now puts° the drowsy and neglected act
Freshly on me. 'Tis surely for a name.   175
    LUCIO. I warrant it is. And thy head stands so
tickle° on thy shoulders that a milkmaid, if she be
in love, may sigh it off. Send after the Duke, and ap-
peal to him.
    CLAUD. I have done so, but he's not to be found. I
    prithee,   180
Lucio, do me this kind service.
This day my sister should the cloister enter
And there receive her approbation.°
Acquaint her with the danger of my state,
Implore her, in my voice, that she make friends   185
To the strict Deputy, bid herself assay° him.
I have great hope in that, for in her youth
There is a prone° and speechless dialect
Such as move men. Beside, she hath prosperous art
When she will play with reason and discourse,   190
And well she can persuade.
    LUCIO. I pray she may, as well for the encourage-

ment of the like, which else would stand under griev-
ous imposition, as for the enjoying of thy life, who
I would be sorry should be thus foolishly lost at a
game of ticktack.° I'll to her.   196
    CLAUD. I thank you, good friend Lucio.
    LUCIO. Within two hours.
    CLAUD.   Come, officer, away! [*Exeunt.*]

SCENE III. *A monastery.*

[*Enter* DUKE *and* FRIAR THOMAS.]
    DUKE. No, holy Father, throw away that thought,
Believe not that the dribbling dart° of love
Can pierce a complete° bosom. Why I desire thee
To give me secret harbor hath a purpose
More grave and wrinkled° than the aims and ends
Of burning youth.
    FRI. T.   May your Grace speak of it?   6
    DUKE. My holy sir, none better knows than you
How I have ever loved the life removed,°
And held in idle price° to haunt assemblies
Where youth, and cost° and witless bravery° keeps.
I have delivered to Lord Angelo,   11
A man of stricture° and firm abstinence,
My absolute power and place here in Vienna,
And he supposes me traveled to Poland,
For so I have strewed it in the common ear,   15
And so it is received. Now, pious sir,
You will demand of me why I do this.
    FRI. T. Gladly, my lord.
    DUKE. We have strict statutes and most biting
    laws,
The needful bits and curbs to headstrong weeds,°
Which for this fourteen years we have let slip,   21
Even like an o'ergrown lion in a cave,
That goes not out to prey. Now, as fond° fathers,
Having bound up the threatening twigs of birch
Only to stick it in their children's sight   25
For terror, not to use, in time the rod
Becomes more mocked than feared, so our decrees,
Dead to infliction,° to themselves are dead,
And liberty° plucks justice by the nose,
The baby beats the nurse, and quite athwart°   30
Goes all decorum.
    FRI. T.   It rested in° your Grace
To unloose this tied-up justice when you pleased.

---

149. **true contract:** betrothal. See Gen. Intro. p. 20a.   152–53. **de-
nunciation . . . order:** lack formal pronouncement of the mar-
riage ceremony.   154. **propagation:** increase.   155. **coffer:** safe-
keeping; lit., strongbox.   156. **meet:** fit.   157. **made them:** i.e.,
our friends, and so approving our marriage.   159. **character:**
handwriting.   162. **fault . . . glimpse:** mistaken glamor.
169. **stagger in:** am uncertain.   171. **unscoured:** rusty.   172. **zo-
diacs:** years. See App. 1.   173. **name:** notable example.
174. **puts:** applies.   177. **tickle:** unsteadily.   183. **approbation:**
novitiate, period of trial.   186. **assay:** attempt, i.e., to persuade
him.   188. **prone:** effective.

196. **ticktack:** lit., a game played on a board with pegs fitted
into holes.

    Sc. iii: 2. dribbling dart: arrow feebly shot.   3. **complete:**
fully protected.   5. **wrinkled:** i.e., suitable for an experi-
enced man.   8. **removed:** private.   9. **in . . . price:** as worth-
less.   10. **cost:** extravagance. **bravery:** ostentation.   12. **stric-
ture:** strict life.   20. **weeds:** Theobald's emendation of "steeds"
is preferable.   23. **fond:** foolish.   28. **Dead to infliction:** i.e.,
never carried into effect.   29. **liberty:** license.   30. **athwart:**
awry, in the wrong direction.   31. **rested in:** was in the power
of.

And it in you more dreadful would have seemed
Than in Lord Angelo.

DUKE.   I do fear too dreadful.
Sith° 'twas my fault to give the people scope,   35
'Twould be my tyranny to strike and gall them
For what I bid them do. For we bid this be done
When evil deeds have their permissive pass,°
And not the punishment. Therefore indeed, my
    father,
I have on Angelo imposed the office,   40
Who may, in the ambush° of my name, strike
    home,
And yet my nature never in the fight
To do in slander.° And to behold his sway,
I will, as 'twere a brother of your order,
Visit both prince and people, therefore I prithee 45
Supply me with the habit,° and instruct me
How I may formally in person bear me
Like a true friar.° Moe° reasons for this action
At our more leisure shall I render you,
Only, this one: Lord Angelo is precise,   50
Stands at a guard with envy,° scarce confesses
That his blood flows or that his appetite
Is more to bread than stone. Hence shall we see,
If power change purpose, what our seemers be.°
                                    [*Exeunt.*]

SCENE IV. *A nunnery.*

[*Enter* ISABELLA *and* FRANCISCA.]

ISAB. And have you nuns no farther privileges?
FRAN. Are not these large enough?
ISAB. Yes, truly. I speak not as desiring more,
But rather wishing a more strict restraint   4
Upon the sisterhood, the votarists° of Saint Clare.°
LUCIO. [*Within*] Ho! Peace be in this place!
ISAB.   Who's that which calls?
PRAN. It is a man's voice. Gentle Isabella,
Turn you the key,° and know his business of him.
You may, I may not, you are yet unsworn.
When you have vowed, you must not speak with
    men   10
But in the presence of the prioress.
Then, if you speak, you must not show your face,
Of if you show your face, you must not speak.
He calls again. I pray you answer him.   [*Exit.*]

ISAB. Peace and prosperity! Who is 't that calls?
                                [*Enter* LUCIO.]
LUCIO. Hail, virgin, if you be, as those cheek roses
Proclaim you are no less! Can you so stead° me   17
As bring me to the sight of Isabella,
A novice of this place, and the fair sister
To her unhappy brother Claudio?   20
ISAB. Why " her unhappy brother "? Let me ask
The rather, for I now must make you know
I am that Isabella and his sister.
LUCIO. Gentle and fair, your brother kindly greets
    you.
Not to be weary° with you, he's in prison.   25
ISAB. Woe me! For what?
LUCIO. For that which, if myself might be his
    judge,
He should receive his punishment in thanks.
He hath got his friend° with child.
ISAB. Sir, make me not your story.°
LUCIO.   It is true.   30
I would not — though 'tis my familiar sin
With maids to seem the lapwing,° and to jest,
Tongue far from heart — play with all virgins so.
I hold you as a thing enskied° and sainted,
By your renouncement, an immortal spirit,   35
And to be talked with in sincerity,
As with a saint.
ISAB. You do blaspheme the good in mocking
    me.
LUCIO. Do not believe it. Fewness° and truth, 'tis
    thus:
Your brother and his lover have embraced.   40
As those that feed grow full — as blossoming time,
That from the seedness° the bare fallow brings
To teeming foison° — even so her plenteous womb
Expresseth his full tilth and husbandry.
ISAB. Someone with child by him? — My cousin
    Juliet?   45
LUCIO. Is she your cousin?
ISAB. Adoptedly, as school maids change their
    names
By vain, though apt, affection.
LUCIO.   She it is.
ISAB. Oh, let him marry her.
LUCIO.   This is the point.
The Duke is very strangely gone from hence,   50
Bore many gentlemen, myself being one,
In hand, and hope of action.° But we do learn
By those that know the very nerves° of state,
His givings-out were of an infinite distance

From his true-meant design.° Upon his place,   55
And with full line of his authority,
Governs Lord Angelo, a man whose blood
Is very snow broth, one who never feels
The wanton stings and motions of the sense,
But doth rebate° and blunt his natural edge   60
With profits of the mind, study and fast.
He — to give fear to use and liberty,°
Which have for long run by° the hideous law,
As mice by lions — hath picked out an act
Under whose heavy sense° your brother's life   65
Falls into forfeit. He arrests him on it,
And follows close the rigor of the statute,
To make him an example. All hope is gone
Unless you have the grace by your fair prayer
To soften Angelo. And that's my pith of° business
'Twixt you and your poor brother.   71

ISAB. Doth he so seek his life?

LUCIO.   Has censured° him
Already, and, as I hear, the Provost hath
A warrant for his execution.

ISAB. Alas! What poor ability's in me   75
To do him good?

LUCIO.   Assay the power you have.

ISAB. My power? Alas, I doubt ——

LUCIO.   Our doubts are traitors,
And make us lose the good we oft might win
By fearing to attempt. Go to Lord Angelo,
And let him learn to know when maidens sue,   80
Men give like gods, but when they weep and kneel,
All their petitions are as freely theirs
As they themselves would owe them.°

ISAB. I'll see what I can do.

LUCIO.   But speedily.

ISAB. I will about it straight,   85
No longer staying but to give the Mother
Notice of my affair. I humbly thank you.
Commend me to my brother. Soon at night
I'll send him certain word of my success.

LUCIO. I take my leave of you.   89

ISAB.   Good sir, adieu. [*Exeunt.*]

Act II

SCENE I. *A hall in* ANGELO'S *house.*

[*Enter* ANGELO, ESCALUS, *and a* JUSTICE, PROVOST,
OFFICERS, *and other* ATTENDANTS, *behind.*]

ANG. We must not make a scarecrow of the law,
Setting it up to fear° the birds of prey,

And let it keep one shape till custom make it
Their perch, and not their terror.

ESCAL.   Aye, but yet
Let us be keen, and rather cut a little   5
Than fall,° and bruise to death. Alas, this gentle-
man,
Whom I would save, had a most noble father!
Let but your Honor know,
Whom I believe to be most strait in virtue,
That in the working of your own affections,   10
Had time cohered° with place or place with wish-
ing,
Or that the resolute acting of your blood
Could have attained the effect of your own purpose,
Whether you had not sometime in your life
Erred in this point which now you censure him,   15
And pulled the law upon you.

ANG. 'Tis one thing to be tempted, Escalus,
Another thing to fall. I not deny,
The jury, passing on the prisoner's life,
May in the sworn twelve have a thief or two   20
Guiltier than him they try. What's open made to
justice,
That justice seizes. What know the laws
That thieves do pass on° thieves? 'Tis very preg-
nant,°
The jewel that we find, we stoop and take't,
Because we see it, but what we do not see   25
We tread upon, and never think of it.
You may not so extenuate his offense
For° I have had such faults, but rather tell me
When I that censure him do so offend,
Let mine own judgment pattern out my death,   30
And nothing come in partial.° Sir, he must die.

ESCAL. Be it as your wisdom will.

ANG.   Where is the Provost?

PROV. Here, if it like° your Honor.

ANG.   See that Claudio
Be executed by nine tomorrow morning.
Bring him his confessor, let him be prepared,   35
For that's the utmost of his pilgrimage.°
                      [*Exit* PROVOST.]

ESCAL. [*Aside*] Well, Heaven forgive him, and
forgive us all!
Some rise by sin, and some by virtue fall.
Some run from brakes of ice,° and answer none,°
And some condemnèd for a fault alone.°   40
[*Enter* ELBOW, *and* OFFICERS *with* FROTH
and POMPEY.]

ELB. Come, bring them away. If these be good
people in a commonweal that do nothing but use

54–55. His . . . design: his declared intentions were very differ-
ent from his true plan.   60. rebate: abate, dull.   62. use . . .
liberty: customary licentiousness.   63. run by: ignored.
65. sense: meaning, intention.   70. my . . . of: the main pur-
pose of my.   72. censured: passed sentence on.   83. As . . .
them: as if they themselves possessed them; i.e., had the granting.
     Act II, Sc. i: 2. fear: frighten.

6. fall: let fall, strike.   11. cohered: agreed.   23. pass on:
i.e., pass judgment on. pregnant: obvious.   28. For: because.
31. nothing . . . partial: no partiality be shown to me.   33. like:
please.   36. utmost . . . pilgrimage: limit of his life on earth.
39. brakes of ice: a curious phrase, probably corrupt; *brakes:*
lit., thickets. answer none: are never called to account.   40. fault
alone: i.e., a single lapse which is no crime.

their abuses° in common houses, I know no law. Bring them away.

ANG. How now, sir! What's your name? And 45 what's the matter?

ELB. If it please your Honor, I am the poor Duke's constable, and my name is Elbow. I do lean upon justice, sir, and do bring in here before your good Honor two notorious benefactors. 50

ANG. Benefactors? Well, what benefactors are they? Are they not malefactors?

ELB. If it please your Honor, I know not well what they are. But precise° villains they are, that I am 55 sure of, and void of° all profanation in the world that good Christians ought to have.

ESCAL. This comes off well. Here's a wise officer.

ANG. Go to.° What quality are they of? Elbow is your name? Why dost thou not speak, Elbow? 60

POM. He cannot, sir, he's out at elbow.

ANG. What are you, sir?

ELB. He, sir! A tapster, sir, parcel-bawd,° one that serves a bad woman, whose house, sir, was, as 65 they say, plucked down in the suburbs. And now she professes a hothouse,° which I think is a very ill house too.

ESCAL. How know you that?

ELB. My wife, sir, whom I detest° before Heaven and your Honor —— 70

ESCAL. How? Thy wife?

ELB. Aye, sir — whom, I thank Heaven, is an honest woman ——

ESCAL. Dost thou detest her therefore?

ELB. I say, sir, I will detest myself also, as 75 well as she, that this house, if it be not a bawd's house, it is pity of her life, for it is a naughty house.

ESCAL. How dost thou know that, constable?

ELB. Marry, sir, by my wife, who if she had 80 been a woman cardinally° given, might have been accused in fornication, adultery, and all uncleanliness there.

ESCAL. By the woman's means?

ELB. Aye, sir, by Mistress Overdone's means. 85 But as she spit in his face, so she defied him.

POM. Sir, if it please your Honor, this is not so.

ELB. Prove it before these varlets° here, thou honorable man, prove it.

ESCAL. Do you hear how he misplaces?° 90

POM. Sir, she came in great with child, and longing, saving your Honor's reverence,° for stewed prunes. Sir, we had but two in the house, which at

that very distant time stood, as it were, in a fruit dish, a dish of some threepence — your Honors 95 have seen such dishes, they are not China dishes, but very good dishes ——

ESCAL. Go to, go to. No matter for the dish, sir.

POM. No indeed, sir, not of a pin, you are therein in the right. But to the point. As I say, this 100 Mistress Elbow, being, as I say, with child, and being great-bellied, and longing, as I said, for prunes, and having but two in the dish, as I said, Master Froth here, this very man, having eaten the rest, as I said, and, as I say, paying for them very honestly — for, as you know, Master Froth, I could not give you threepence again. 107

FROTH. No indeed.

POM. Very well — you being then, if you be remembered, cracking the stones of the foresaid prunes ——

FROTH. Aye, so I did indeed.

POM. Why, very well. I telling you then, if 110 you be remembered, that such a one and such a one were past cure of the thing you wot° of, unless they kept very good diet, as I told you —— 116

FROTH. All this is true.

POM. Why, very well, then ——

ESCAL. Come, you are a tedious fool. To the purpose. What was done to Elbow's wife that he 120 hath cause to complain of? Come me to what was done to her.

POM. Sir, your Honor cannot come to that yet.

ESCAL. No, sir, nor I mean it not.

POM. Sir, but you shall come to it, by your 125 Honor's leave. And I beseech you, look into Master Froth here, sir, a man of fourscore pound a year, whose father died at Hallowmas° — was't not at Hallowmas, Master Froth?

FROTH. Allhallond Eve.° 130

POM. Why, very well, I hope here be truths. He, sir, sitting, as I say, in a lower chair, sir — 'twas in the Bunch of Grapes,° where, indeed, you have a delight to sit, have you not? 135

FROTH. I have so, because it is an open room, and good for winter.

POM. Why, very well, then, I hope here be truths.

ANG. This will last out a night in Russia When nights are longest there. I'll take my leave, And leave you to the hearing of the cause, 141 Hoping you'll find good cause to whip them all.

ESCAL. I think no less. Good morrow to your lordship. [*Exit* ANGELO.]

Now, sir, come on. What was done to Elbow's wife, once more? 145

POM. Once, sir? There was nothing done to her once.

---

43. abuses: improper behavior.   55. precise: puritanical. 56. void of: free from.   59. Go to: get on.   64. parcel-bawd: partly bawd (i.e., pimp), — and partly tapster.   67. professes a hothouse: her business is a brothel.   69. detest: for "protest." 81. cardinally: for "carnally."   88. varlets: knaves.   90. misplaces: mistakes the meanings of his words.   92. saving . . . reverence: begging your Honor's pardon — a phrase used to apologize for an improper remark.

115. wot: know.   128. Hallowmas: All Saints' Day, November 1. 130. Allhallond Eve: Halloween, October 31.   134. Bunch of Grapes: the name of a room.

ELB. I beseech you, sir, ask him what this man did to my wife.

POM. I beseech your Honor, ask me.   150

ESCAL. Well, sir, what did this gentleman to her?

POM. I beseech you, sir, look in this gentleman's face. Good Master Froth, look upon his Honor, 'tis for a good purpose. Doth your Honor mark his face?

ESCAL. Aye, sir, very well.   156

POM. Nay, I beseech you mark it well.

ESCAL. Well, I do so.

POM. Doth your Honor see any harm in his face?

ESCAL. Why, no.

POM. I'll be supposed° upon a book, his face is the worst thing about him. Good, then. If his face be the worst thing about him, how could Mas-   165 ter Froth do the constable's wife any harm? I would know that of your Honor.

ESCAL. He's in the right. Constable, what say you to it?

ELB. First, an it like you,° the house is a re-   170 spected house. Next, this is a respected fellow, and his mistress is a respected woman.

POM. By this hand, sir, his wife is a more re- spected person than any of us all.

ELB. Varlet, thou liest, thou liest, wicked varlet! The time is yet to come that she was ever respected° with man, woman, or child.   177

POM. Sir, she was respected with him before he married with her.

ESCAL. Which is the wiser here? Justice or In- iquity? Is this true?

ELB. O thou caitiff!° O thou varlet! O thou wicked Hannibal!° I respected with her before I was mar- ried to her! If ever I was respected with her, or   185 she with me, let not your Worship think me the poor Duke's officer. Prove this, thou wicked Hanni- bal, or I'll have mine action of battery° on thee.

ESCAL. If he took you a box o' th' ear, you might have your action of slander too.   190

ELB. Marry, I thank your good Worship for it. What is't your Worship's pleasure I shall do with this wicked caitiff?

ESCAL. Truly, officer, because he hath some of- fenses in him that thou wouldst discover if thou   195 couldst, let him continue in his courses till thou knowest what they are.

ELB. Marry, I thank your Worship for it. Thou seest, thou wicked varlet, now, what's come   200 upon thee. Thou art to continue now, thou varlet, thou art to continue.

ESCAL. Where were you born, friend?

FROTH. Here in Vienna, sir.

ESCAL. Are you of fourscore pounds a year?

FROTH. Yes, an 't please you, sir.   205

ESCAL. So. What trade are you of, sir?

POM. A tapster, a poor widow's tapster.

ESCAL. Your mistress' name?

POM. Mistress Overdone.

ESCAL. Hath she had any more than one husband?

POM. Nine, sir, Overdone by the last.

ESCAL. Nine! Come hither to me, Master Froth. Master Froth, I would not have you acquainted with tapsters. They will draw you,° Master Froth,   215 and you will hang them. Get you gone, and let me hear no more of you.

FROTH. I thank your Worship. For mine own part, I never come into any room in a taphouse but I am drawn in.   220

ESCAL. Well, no more of it, Master Froth. Fare- well. [*Exit* FROTH.] Come you hither to me, Master Tapster. What's your name, Master Tapster?

POM. Pompey.

ESCAL. What else?   225

POM. Bum, sir.

ESCAL. Troth,° and your bum is the greatest thing about you, so that, in the beastliest sense, you   229 are Pompey the Great. Pompey, you are partly a bawd, Pompey, howsoever you color° it in being a tapster, are you not? Come, tell me true. It shall be the better for you.

POM. Truly, sir, I am a poor fellow that would live.   235

ESCAL. How would you live, Pompey? By being a bawd? What do you think of the trade, Pompey? Is it a lawful trade?

POM. If the law would allow it, sir.

ESCAL. But the law will not allow it, Pompey, nor it shall not be allowed in Vienna.   240

POM. Does your Worship mean to geld and splay° all the youth of the city?

ESCAL. No, Pompey.

POM. Truly, sir, in my poor opinion, they will to't, then. If your Worship will take order for the   245 drabs° and the knaves, you need not to fear the bawds.

ESCAL. There are pretty orders beginning. I can tell you. It is but heading° and hanging.   250

POM. If you head and hang all that offend that way but° for ten year together, you'll be glad to give out a commission for more heads. If this law hold in Vienna ten year, I'll rent the fairest house in it after° threepence a bay.° If you live to see this come   255 to pass, say Pompey told you so.

ESCAL. Thank you, good Pompey, and in requital

---

163. **supposed:** for "deposed"; i.e., sworn as a witness.   170. **an . . . you:** if it please you.   176. **respected:** Elbow thinks it means "suspected."   183. **caitiff:** rogue.   184. **Hannibal:** for "Cannibal."   188. **battery:** Elbow, as Escalus points out, is mixed in his legal terms.

215. **draw you:** draw drink for you, with a pun on hang, draw, and quarter.   228. **Troth:** in truth.   231. **color:** conceal.   241. **splay:** castrate.   246. **drabs:** whores.   250. **heading:** beheading.   252. **but:** only.   254. **after:** at the rate of.   255. **bay:** bay window.

of your prophecy, hark you. I advise you, let me not
find you before me again upon any complaint what-
soever — no, not for dwelling where you do.°   260
If I do, Pompey, I shall beat you to your tent, and
prove a shrewd Caesar° to you. In plain dealing,
Pompey, I shall have you whipped. So for this time,
Pompey, fare you well.   265

POM. I thank your Worship for your good counsel.
[*Aside*] But I shall follow it as the flesh and fortune
shall better determine.
Whip me? No, no, let carman whip his jade.°   269
The valiant heart's not whipped out of his trade.
                                          [*Exit.*]

ESCAL. Come hither to me, Master Elbow, come
hither, Master Constable. How long have you been
in this place of constable?

ELB. Seven year and a half, sir.

ESCAL. I thought by your readiness in the of-   275
fice you had continued in it sometime. You say seven
years together?

ELB. And a half, sir.

ESCAL. Alas, it hath been great pains to you. They
do you wrong to put you so oft upon 't.° Are   280
there not men in your ward sufficient to serve it?

ELB. Faith, sir, few of any wit in such matters. As
they are chosen, they are glad to choose me for
them. I do it for some piece of money, and go
through with all.   285

ESCAL. Look you bring me in the names of some
six or seven, the most sufficient of your parish.

ELB. To your Worship's house, sir?

ESCAL. To my house. Fare you well. [*Exit* ELBOW.]
What's o'clock, think you?   290

JUST. Eleven, sir.

ESCAL. I pray you home to dinner with me.

JUST. I humbly thank you.

ESCAL. It grieves me for the death of Claudio,
But there's no remedy.   295

JUST. Lord Angelo is severe.

ESCAL.   It is but needful.
Mercy is not itself that oft looks so,
Pardon is still° the nurse of second woe.
But yet — poor Claudio! There is no remedy.   299
Come, sir.   [*Exeunt.*]

SCENE II. *Another room in the same.*

[*Enter* PROVOST *and a* SERVANT.]

SERV. He's hearing of a cause. He will come
    straight.
I'll tell him of you.

260. dwelling . . . do: i.e., in a brothel.   262. shrewd Caesar:
Julius Caesar defeated Pompey and pursued him to Egypt, where
he was murdered.   269. jade: poor-spirited nag.   280. put . . .
upon 't: lay the burden on you. The constable was chosen by the
parish, but could pay a deputy to take his place.   298. still: al-
ways.

PROV.   Pray you, do. [*Exit* SERVANT.] I'll know
His pleasure, maybe he will relent. Alas,
He hath but as offended in a dream!°
All sects, all ages smack of this vice, and he   5
To die for 't!

[*Enter* ANGELO.]

ANG.   Now what's the matter, Provost?

PROV. Is it your will Claudio shall die tomorrow?

ANG. Did not I tell thee yea? Hadst thou not
    order?
Why dost thou ask again?

PROV.   Lest I might be too rash.
Under your good correction,° I have seen   10
When, after execution, Judgment hath
Repented o'er his doom.

ANG.   Go to. Let that be mine.
Do you your office, or give up your place,
And you shall well be spared.

PROV.   I crave your Honor's pardon.
What shall be done, sir, with the groaning Juliet?
She's very near her hour.   16

ANG.   Dispose of her
To some more fitter place, and that with speed.

[*Re-enter* SERVANT.]

SERV. Here is the sister of the man condemned
Desires access to you.

ANG.   Hath he a sister?

PROV. Aye, my good lord, a very virtuous maid
And to be shortly of a sisterhood,   21
If not already.

ANG. Well, let her be admitted.   [*Exit* SERVANT.]
See you the fornicatress be removed.
Let her have needful, but not lavish, means,
There shall be order for 't.

[*Enter* ISABELLA *and* LUCIO.]

PROV.   God save your Honor!   25

ANG. Stay a little while. [*To* ISABELLA] You're
    welcome.
What's your will?

ISAB. I am a woeful suitor to your Honor,
Please but your Honor hear me.

ANG.   Well, what's your suit?

ISAB. There is a vice that most I do abhor,
And most desire should meet the blow of justice, 30
For which I would not plead but that I must,
For which I must not plead but that I am
At war 'twixt will and will not.

ANG.   Well, the matter?

ISAB. I have a brother is condemned to die,
I do beseech you, let it be his fault,°   35
And not my brother.

PROV. [*Aside*] Heaven give thee moving graces!

ANG. Condemn the fault, and not the actor of it?
Why, every fault's condemned ere it be done.

Sc. ii: 4. offended . . . dream: his offense is imaginary.
10. Under . . . correction: i.e., if you will pardon me.   35. let . . .
fault: i.e., let his fault be condemned.

Mine were the very cipher of a function,°
To fine the faults whose fine stands in recórd°   40
And let go by the actor.

ISAB.   Oh, just but severe law!
I had a brother,° then. — Heaven keep your Honor!

LUCIO. [*Aside to* ISABELLA] Give 't not o'er so. To
    him again, entreat him,
Kneel down before him, hang upon his gown.
You are too cold. If you should need a pin,°   45
You could not with more tame a tongue desire it.
To him, I say!

ISAB. Must he needs die?

ANG.   Maiden, no remedy.

ISAB. Yes, I do think that you might pardon him,
And neither Heaven nor man grieve at the mercy.

ANG. I will not do 't.

ISAB.   But can you, if you would?

ANG. Look, what I will not, that I cannot do. 52

ISAB. But might you do 't, and do the world no
    wrong,
If so your heart were touched with that remorse°
As mine is to him?

ANG.   He's sentenced, 'tis too late. 55

LUCIO. [*Aside to* ISABELLA] You are too cold.

ISAB. Too late? Why, no. I, that do speak a word,
May call it back again. Well, believe this,
No ceremony° that to great ones 'longs° —
Not the king's crown, nor the deputed sword,°   60
The marshal's truncheon,° nor the judge's robe —
Become them with one half so good a grace
As mercy does.
If he had been as you, and you as he,
You would have slipped like him, but he, like you,
Would not have been so stern.

ANG.   Pray you be gone. 66

ISAB. I would to Heaven I had your potency°
And you were Isabel! Should it then be thus?
No, I would tell what 'twere to be a judge,
And what a prisoner.

LUCIO. [*Aside to* ISABELLA] Aye, touch him,
    there's the vein.

ANG. Your brother is a forfeit of the law,
And you but waste your words.

ISAB.   Alas, alas!
Why, all the souls that were were forfeit once,
And He that might the vantage° best have took
Found out the remedy. How would you be   75
If He, which is the top of judgment,° should
But judge you as you are? Oh, think on that,

And mercy then will breathe within your lips,
Like man new-made.

ANG.   Be you content, fair maid.
It is the law, not I, condemn your brother.   80
Were he my kinsman, brother, or my son,
It should be thus with him. He must die tomor-
    row.

ISAB. Tomorrow! Oh, that's sudden! Spare him,
    spare him!
He's not prepared for death. Even for our kitchens
We kill the fowl of season.° Shall we serve Heaven
With less respect than we do minister   86
To our gross selves? Good, good my lord, bethink
    you,
Who is it that hath died for this offense?
There's many have committed it.

LUCIO. [*Aside to* ISABELLA] Aye, well said.

ANG. The law hath not been dead, though it hath
    slept.   90
Those many had not dared to do that evil
If the first that did the edíct infringe
Had answered° for his deed. Now 'tis awake,
Takes note of what is done, and, like a prophet,
Looks in a glass° that shows what future evils,   95
Either now, or by remissness new-conceived,
And so in progress to be hatched and born,
Are now to have no súccessive degrees,°
But, ere they live, to end.

ISAB.   Yet show some pity.

ANG. I show it most of all when I show justice,
For then I pity those I do not know,   101
Which a dismissed offense would after gall,
And do him right that, answering one foul wrong,
Lives not to act another. Be satisfied,
Your brother dies tomorrow, be content.   105

ISAB. So you must be the first that gives his sen-
    tence,
And he, that suffers. Oh, it is excellent
To have a giant's strength, but it is tyrannous
To use it like a giant.

LUCIO. [*Aside to* ISABELLA] That's well said.

ISAB. Could great men thunder   110
As Jove himself does, Jove would ne'er be quiet,
For every pelting,° petty officer
Would use his Heaven for thunder.
Nothing but thunder! Merciful Heaven,
Thou rather with thy sharp and sulphurous bolt
Split'st the unwedgeable and gnarlèd oak   116
Than the soft myrtle. But man, proud man,
Dressed in a little brief authority,
Most ignorant of what he's most assured,
His glassy essence,° like an angry ape,   120
Plays such fantastic tricks before high Heaven

---

39. cipher . . . function: an office worth nothing.   **40. fine . . .
record:** punish faults that are already condemned.   **42. had a
brother:** i.e., he is as good as dead.   **45. pin:** worthless trifle.
54. remorse: pity.   **59. ceremony:** symbol of greatness. Cf. *Hen
V*, IV.i.253–301. **'longs:** belongs.   **60. deputed sword:** the sword
of Justice, carried before the Deputy, and symbolizing his power.
61. truncheon: staff of office.   **67. potency:** power.   **74. van-
tage:** advantage; i.e., to punish mankind.   **76. top of judgment:**
Supreme Judge.

85. of season: at the proper time of year.   **93. answered:** been
condemned.   **95. glass:** i.e., a magic glass which shows the fu-
ture.   **98. successive degrees:** successors.   **112. pelting:** pal-
try.   **120. glassy essence:** fragile nature.

As make the angels weep — who, with our spleens,°
Would all themselves laugh mortal.°

LUCIO. [*Aside to* ISABELLA] Oh, to him, to him,
    wench! He will relent,
He's coming, I perceive 't.

PROV. [*Aside*] Pray Heaven she win him!   125

ISAB. We cannot weigh our brother with ourself.
Great men may jest with saints, 'tis wit in them,
But in the less foul profanation.

LUCIO. Thou'rt i' the right, girl, more o' that.

ISAB. That in the captain's but a choleric° word
Which in the soldier is flat blasphemy.   131

LUCIO. [*Aside to* ISABELLA] Art avised° o' that?
    More on't.

ANG. Why do you put these sayings upon me?

ISAB. Because authority, though it err like others,
Hath yet a kind of medicine in itself   135
That skins the vice o' the top.° Go to your bosom,
Knock there, and ask your heart what it doth know
That's like my brother's fault. If it confess
A natural guiltiness such as is his,
Let it not sound a thought upon your tongue   140
Against my brother's life.

ANG.   [*Aside*] She speaks, and 'tis
Such sense that my sense breeds° with it. Fare you
    well.

ISAB. Gentle my lord, turn back.

ANG. I will bethink me. Come again tomorrow.

ISAB. Hark how I'll bribe you. Good my lord, turn
    back.   145

ANG. How? Bribe me?

ISAB. Aye, with such gifts that Heaven shall share
    with you.

LUCIO. [*Aside to* ISABELLA] You had marred all
    else.

ISAB. Not with fond sicles° of the tested gold,
Or stones whose rates are either rich or poor   150
As fancy values them, but with true prayers
That shall be up at Heaven and enter there
Ere sunrise, prayers from preservèd souls,
From fasting maids whose minds are dedicate
To nothing temporal.

ANG.   Well, come to me tomorrow.   155

LUCIO. [*Aside to* ISABELLA] Go to, 'tis well. Away!

ISAB. Heaven keep your Honor safe!

ANG. [*Aside*] Amen.
For I am that way going to temptation,
Where prayers cross.°

ISAB.   At what hour tomorrow
Shall I attend your lordship?

ANG.   At any time 'fore noon.   160

ISAB. 'Save° your Honor!

[*Exeunt* ISABELLA, LUCIO, *and* PROVOST.]

ANG.   From thee — even from thy virtue!
What's this, what's this? Is this her fault or mine?
The tempter or the tempted, who sins most?
Ha!
Not she, nor doth she tempt. But it is I   165
That, lying by the violet in the sun,
Do as the carrion does, not as the flower,
Corrupt with virtuous season.° Can it be
That modesty may more betray our sense
Than woman's lightness? Having waste ground
    enough,   170
Shall we desire to raze the sanctuary,
And pitch our evils there? Oh, fie, fie, fie!
What dost thou, or what art thou, Angelo?
Dost thou desire her foully for those things
That make her good? Oh, let her brother live.   175
Thieves for their robbery have authority
When judges steal themselves. What, do I love her,
That I desire to hear her speak again
And feast upon her eyes? What is't I dream on?
O cunning enemy, that to catch a saint   180
With saints dost bait thy hook! Most dangerous
Is that temptation that doth goad us on
To sin in loving virtue. Never could the strumpet,
With all her double vigor, art and nature,°
Once stir my temper, but this virtuous maid   185
Subdues me quite. Ever till now,
When men were fond,° I smiled, and wondered
    how.   [*Exit.*]

SCENE III. *A room in a prison.*

[*Enter, severally,*° DUKE *disguised as a friar,
    and* PROVOST.]

DUKE. Hail to you, Provost! So I think you are.

PROV. I am the Provost. What's your will, good
    Friar?

DUKE. Bound by my charity and my blest order,
I come to visit the afflicted spirits
Here in the prison. Do me the common right   5
To let me see them, and to make me know
The nature of their crimes, that I may minister
To them accordingly.

PROV. I would do more than that, if more were
    needful.

[*Enter* JULIET.] Look, here comes one — a gentle-
    woman of mine   10

---

122. **with . . . spleens:** if they had our spleens. The spleen was regarded as the seat of laughter.   123. **laugh mortal:** laugh themselves to death.   130. **choleric:** hot-tempered.   132. **avised:** advised, aware.   136. **skins . . . top:** covers the sore, but does not heal it.   142. **breeds:** quickens, stirs.   149. **sicles:** shekels.   159. **cross:** are at cross-purposes.

161. **'Save:** God save.   165–68. **But . . . season:** i.e., the same sun brings the violet to its full sweetness and causes the carrion to stink. **Corrupt:** decay. **virtuous:** giving strength. **season:** summer sun.   184. **art . . . nature:** See App. 18.   187. **fond:** doting, foolish.
    Sc. iii: **s.d. severally:** by separate entrances.

Who, falling in the flaws° of her own youth,
Hath blistered° her report.° She is with child,
And he that got it, sentenced, a young man
More fit to do another such offense
Than die for this.   15
    DUKE. When must he die?
    PROV.   As I do think, tomorrow.
[*To* JULIET] I have provided for you. Stay awhile,
And you shall be conducted.
    DUKE. Repent you, fair one, of the sin you carry?
    JUL. I do, and bear the shame most patiently.   20
    DUKE. I'll teach you how you shall arraign your
        conscience,
And try your penitence, if it be sound
Or hollowly put on.
    JUL.   I'll gladly learn.
    DUKE. Love you the man that wronged you?   24
    JUL. Yes, as I love the woman that wronged him.
    DUKE. So, then, it seems your most offenseful act
Was mutually committed?
    JUL.   Mutually.
    DUKE. Then was your sin of heavier kind than his.
    JUL. I do confess it, and repent it, Father.
    DUKE. 'Tis meet so, Daughter. But lest you do re-
        pent   30
As that° the sin hath brought you to this shame,
Which sorrow is always toward ourselves, not
    Heaven,
Showing we would not spare Heaven° as we love it,
But as we stand in fear ——
    JUL. I do repent me as it is an evil,   35
And take the shame with joy.
    DUKE.   There rest.
Your partner, as I hear, must die tomorrow,
And I am going with instruction° to him.
Grace go with you. *Benedicite!*   [*Exit.*]
    JUL. Must die tomorrow! Oh, injurious love,   40
That respites me a life whose very comfort
Is still a dying horror!°
    PROV.   'Tis pity of him.   [*Exeunt.*]

SCENE IV. *A room in* ANGELO'S *house.*

[*Enter* ANGELO.]

    ANG. When I would pray and think, I think and
      pray
To several subjects.° Heaven hath my empty words,
Whilst my invention,° hearing not my tongue,
Anchors on Isabel. Heaven in my mouth,

As if I did but only chew His name,   5
And in my heart the strong and swelling evil
Of my conception.° The state, whereon I studied,
Is like a good thing, being often read,
Grown feared° and tedious. Yea, my gravity,
Wherein — let no man hear me — I take pride,   10
Could I with boot° change for an idle plume°
Which the air beats for vain.° O place, O form,
How often dost thou with thy case,° thy habit,°
Wrench awe from fools, and tie the wiser souls
To thy false seeming! Blood, thou art blood.   15
Let's write good angel on the Devil's horn;
'Tis not the Devil's crest.°
[*Enter a* SERVANT.] How now! Who's there?
    SERV. One Isabel, a sister, desires access to you.
    ANG. Teach her the way. Oh heavens!
Why does my blood thus muster to my heart,   20
Making both it unable for itself,
And dispossessing all my other parts
Of necessary fitness?
So play the foolish throngs with one that swoons,
Come all to help him, and so stop the air   25
By which he should revive. And even so
The general subject° to a well-wished king
Quit their own part, and in obsequious fondness
Crowd to his presence, where their untaught love
Must needs appear offense.°
[*Enter* ISABELLA.] How now, fair maid?   30
    ISAB. I am come to know your pleasure.
    ANG. That you might know° it would much better
      please me
Than to demand what 'tis. Your brother cannot live.
    ISAB. Even so. — Heaven keep your Honor!
    ANG. Yet may he live awhile, and, it may be,   35
As long as you or I. Yet he must die.
    ISAB. Under your sentence?
    ANG. Yea.
    ISAB. When, I beseech you? That in his reprieve,
Longer or shorter, he may be so fitted°   40
That his soul sicken not.
    ANG. Ha! Fie, these filthy vices! It were as good
To pardon him that hath from nature stolen
A man already made, as to remit°
Their saucy sweetness that do coin Heaven's image
In stamps° that are forbid. 'Tis all as easy   46

---

7. **conception:** thought.   9. **feared:** the F1 reading. Some edi-
tors emend to "seared": withered.   11. **boot:** advantage. **plume:**
feather, the mark of the brainless gallant.   12. **the . . . vain:**
vainly fans the air.   13. **case:** outside. **habit:** garment.
16–17. **Let's . . . crest:** If the reading is correct, the passage
probably means "since desire (*blood*) is natural, let us call the
Devil a good angel, and then his horn is the badge of an angel
and not a devil"; i.e., Angelo is saying, "To hell with my re-
spectability. Evil, be thou my good."   27. **general subject:**
common crowd.   27–30. **The . . . offense:** See I.i.68,n.   32. **know:**
Angelo cynically sees a double meaning in "pleasure" and
"know" — i.e., have carnal knowledge.   40. **fitted:** prepared
for death.   44. **remit:** forgive.   46. **stamps:** lit., the dies by
which coins were stamped.

11. **flaws:** gusts of passion.   12. **blistered:** blemished. **report:**
reputation.   31. **As that:** because.   33. **spare Heaven:** i.e.,
avoid grieving God.   38. **instruction:** religious counsel.   40–42. **Oh
. . . horror:** oh, destroying love that spares my life everlast-
ingly (*still*) deprived by horrible death of my true love.
    Sc. iv: 2. **several subjects:** i.e., contrary purposes.   3. **in-
vention:** imagination, power of expression.

Falsely to take away a life true made
As to put metal in restrainèd means
To make a false one.°
    ISAB. 'Tis set down so in Heaven, but not in
        earth.   50
    ANG. Say you so? Then I shall pose you° quickly.
Which had you rather — that the most just law
Now took your brother's life, or, to redeem him,
Give up your body to such sweet uncleanness
As she that he hath stained?
    ISAB.   Sir, believe this,   55
I had rather give my body than my soul.
    ANG. I talk not of your soul. Our compelled sins
Stand more for number than for accompt.°
    ISAB.   How say you?°
    ANG. Nay, I'll not warrant that, for I can speak
Against the thing I say. Answer to this: 60
I, now the voice of the recorded law,
Pronounce a sentence on your brother's life.
Might there not be a charity in sin
To save this brother's life?
    ISAB.   Please you to do't,
I'll take it as a peril to my soul,   65
It is no sin at all, but charity.
    ANG. Pleased you° to do't at peril of your soul,
Were equal poise° of sin and charity.
    ISAB. That I do beg his life, if it be sin,
Heaven let me bear it! You granting of my suit,   70
If that be sin, I'll make it my morn prayer
To have it added to the faults of mine,
And nothing of your answer.
    ANG.   Nay, but hear me.
Your sense pursues not mine.° Either you are ig-
      norant,   74
Or seem so, craftily, and that's not good.
    ISAB. Let me be ignorant, and in nothing good,
But graciously to know I am no better.
    ANG. Thus wisdom wishes to appear most bright
When it doth tax° itself, as these black masks
Proclaim an enshield° beauty ten times louder   80
Than beauty could, displayed. But mark me,
To be receivèd plain, I'll speak more gross:
Your brother is to die.
    ISAB. So.
    ANG. And his offense is so, as it appears,   85
Accountant° to the law upon that pain.°
    ISAB. True.
    ANG. Admit no other way to save his life —
As I subscribe not that, nor any other,

But in the loss of question° — that you, his sister,
Finding yourself desired of such a person   91
Whose credit with the judge, or own great place,
Could fetch your brother from the manacles
Of the all-building° law; and that there were
No earthly mean to save him, but that either   95
You must lay down the treasures of your body
To this supposed, or else to let him suffer —
What would you do?
    ISAB. As much for my poor brother as myself.
That is, were I under the terms of death,   100
The impression of keen whips I'd wear as rubies,
And strip myself to death, as to a bed
That longing have been sick for, ere I'd yield
My body up to shame.
    ANG.   Then must your brother die.
    ISAB. And 'twere the cheaper way.   105
Better it were a brother died at once
Than that a sister, by redeeming him,
Should die forever.
    ANG. Were not you, then, as cruel as the sentence
That you have slandered so?   110
    ISAB. Ignomy in ransom° and free pardon
Are of two houses.° Lawful mercy
Is nothing kin to foul redemption.
    ANG. You seemed of late to make the law a tyrant,
And rather proved the sliding of your brother   115
A merriment than a vice.
    ISAB. Oh, pardon me, my lord. It oft falls out,
To have what we would have, we speak not what
      we mean.
I something do excuse the thing I hate
For his advantage that I dearly love.   120
    ANG. We are all frail.
    ISAB.   Else° let my brother die,
If not a feodary,° but only he
Owe° and succeed thy weakness.
    ANG. Nay, women are frail too.
    ISAB. Aye, as the glasses where they view them-
      selves,   125
Which are as easy broke as they make forms.°
Women! — Help Heaven! Men their creation mar
In profiting by° them. Nay, call us ten times frail,
For we are soft as our complexions are,
And credulous to° false prints.°
    ANG.   I think it well.   130
And from this testimony of your own sex —
Since, I suppose, we are made to be no stronger
Than faults may shake our frames — let me be
    bold —

46–49. 'tis . . . one: i.e., it is much the same to take away the life of a man lawfully begotten as to create an illegitimate child (lit., to make a false coin by using metal in a forbidden way). 51. pose you: put a difficult question to you. 58. Stand . . . accompt: are counted but not charged up against us. How . . . you: i.e., do you really mean it? 67. Pleased you: if you agreed. 68. poise: weight. 74. Your . . . mine: You do not mean the same as I. 79. tax: censure. 80. enshield: concealed. 86. Accountant: forfeit. pain: penalty.

89–90. As . . . question: as I do not admit this, or anything else, but for the sake of argument; "loss" is probably a corrupt reading. 94. all-building: this is the F1 reading; Theobald's emendation "all-binding" is preferable. 111. Ignomy in ransom: an ignominious payment for release. 112. two houses: i.e., different families. 121–23. Else . . . weakness: Another corrupt passage. 122. feodary: confederate. 123. Owe: own. 126. forms: appearances, reflections. 128. profiting by: taking advantage of. 130. credulous to: deceived by. prints: impressions.

I do arrest your words.° Be that you are,
That is, a woman. If you be more, you're none. 135
If you be one — as you are well expressed
By all external warrants — show it now,
By putting on the destined livery.°

ISAB. I have no tongue but one. Gentle my lord,
Let me entreat you speak the former language.°

ANG. Plainly conceive, I love you. 141

ISAB. My brother did love Juliet,
And you tell me that he shall die for it.

ANG. He shall not, Isabel, if you give me love.

ISAB. I know your virtue hath a license in 't, 145
Which seems a little fouler than it is,
To pluck on others.

ANG.   Believe me, on mine honor,
My words express my purpose.

ISAB. Ha! Little honor to be much believed,
And most pernicious purpose! — Seeming, seem-
    ing! — 150
I will proclaim thee, Angelo, look for 't.
Sign me a present° pardon for my brother,
Or with an outstretched throat I'll tell the world
    aloud
What man thou art.

ANG.   Who will believe thee, Isabel?
My unsoiled name, the austereness of my life, 155
My vouch° against you, and my place i' the state,
Will so your accusation overweigh
That you shall stifle in your own report,
And smell of calumny. I have begun,
And now I give my sensual race the rein. 160
Fit thy consent to my sharp appetite,
Lay by all nicety and prolixious° blushes
That banish what they sue for. Redeem thy brother
By yielding up thy body to my will,
Or else he must not only die the death, 165
But thy unkindness shall his death draw out
To lingering sufferance.° Answer me tomorrow,
Or, by the affection° that now guides me most,
I'll prove a tyrant to him. As for you, 169
Say what you can, my false o'erweighs your
    true.   [*Exit.*]

ISAB. To whom should I complain? Did I tell this,
Who would believe me? Oh, perilous mouths,
That bear in them one and the selfsame tongue,
Either of condemnation or approof,°
Bidding the law make curtsy to their will, 175
Hooking both right and wrong to the appetite,
To follow as it draws! I'll to my brother.
Though he hath fall'n by prompture° of the blood,
Yet hath he in him such a mind of honor

That had he twenty heads to tender° down 180
On twenty bloody blocks, he'd yield them up
Before his sister should her body stoop
To such abhorred pollution.
Then, Isabel, live chaste, and, Brother, die.
More than our brother is our chastity. 185
I'll tell him yet of Angelo's request,
And fit his mind to death, for his soul's rest.   [*Exit.*]

Act III

SCENE I. *A room in the prison.*

[*Enter* DUKE *disguised as before,* CLAUDIO, *and*
PROVOST.]

DUKE. So then, you hope of pardon from Lord
    Angelo?

CLAUD. The miserable have no other medicine
But only hope.
I've hope to live, and am prepared to die. 4

DUKE. Be absolute for° death. Either death or life
Shall thereby be the sweeter. Reason thus with life:
If I do lose thee, I do lose a thing
That none but fools would keep. A breath thou art,
Servile to all the skyey° influences
That dost this habitation where thou keep'st 10
Hourly afflict. Merely,° thou art death's fool,
For him thou labor'st by thy flight to shun,
And yet runn'st toward him still. Thou art not noble,
For all the accommodations° that thou bear'st
Are nursed by baseness.° Thou'rt by no means val-
    iant, 15
For thou dost fear the soft and tender fork°
Of a poor worm.° Thy best of rest is sleep,
And that thou oft provokest, yet grossly fear'st
Thy death, which is no more. Thou art not thyself,
For thou exist'st on many a thousand grains 20
That issue out of dust. Happy thou art not,
For what thou hast not, still thou strivest to get,
And what thou hast, forget'st. Thou art not certain,
For thy complexion shifts to strange effects,°
After° the moon. If thou art rich, thou'rt poor, 25
For, like an ass whose back with ingots bows,
Thou bear'st thy heavy riches but a journey,
And death unloads thee. Friend hast thou none,
For thine own bowels,° which do call thee sire,

---

134. **arrest ... words:** take you at your word.   138. **destined
livery:** i.e., the frailty of your sex.   140. **former language:** i.e.,
before you began to make these proposals.   152. **present:** imme-
diate.   156. **vouch:** declaration.   162. **prolixious:** superfluous.
167. **sufferance:** suffering.   168. **affection:** lust.   174. **approof:**
approval.   178. **prompture:** inciting.

180. **tender:** offer.
    Act III, Sc. i: 5. absolute for: certain of.   9. **skyey:** i.e.,
of the stars. See App. 1.   11. **Merely:** entirely.   14. **accommo-
dations:** comforts.   15. **nursed by baseness:** supplied by
base means.   16. **fork:** forked tongue, which was believed to con-
tain the sting.   17. **worm:** snake.   24. **complexion:** constitution
(varying as the balance of the humors changes). See App. 3.
shifts ... effects: constantly changes.   25. **After:** like.   29. **bow-
els:** offspring.

The mere effusion of thy proper° loins,   30
Do curse the gout, serpigo,° and the rheum°
For ending thee no sooner. Thou hast nor youth nor
    age,
But, as it were, an after-dinner's sleep,
Dreaming on both; for all thy blessed youth
Becomes as agèd, and doth beg the alms   35
Of palsied eld.° And when thou art old and rich,
Thou hast neither heat, affection, limb, nor beauty,
To make thy riches pleasant. What's yet in this
That bears the name of life? Yet in this life   39
Lie hid moe thousand deaths. Yet death we fear,
That makes these odds all even.

CLAUD.   I humbly thank you.
To sue to live, I find I seek to die,
And, seeking death, find life. Let it come on.

ISAB. [*Within*] What ho! Peace here, grace and
    good company!

PROV. Who's there? Come in. The wish deserves a
    welcome.   45

DUKE. Dear sir, ere long I'll visit you again.

CLAUD. Most holy sir, I thank you.

            [*Enter* ISABELLA.]

ISAB. My business is a word or two with Claudio.

PROV. And very welcome. Look, signior, here's
    your sister.

DUKE. Provost, a word with you.   50

PROV. As many as you please.

DUKE. Bring me to hear them speak where I may
be concealed.

       [*Exeunt* DUKE *and* PROVOST.]

CLAUD. Now, Sister, what's the comfort?

ISAB. Why,   55
As all comforts are, most good, most good indeed.
Lord Angelo, having affairs to Heaven,
Intends you for his swift ambassador,
Where you shall be an everlasting leiger.°
Therefore your best appointment° make with speed,
Tomorrow you set on.

CLAUD.   Is there no remedy?   61

ISAB. None but such remedy as, to save a head,
To cleave a heart in twain.

CLAUD.   But is there any?

ISAB. Yes, Brother, you may live.
There is a devilish mercy in the judge,   65
If you'll implore it, that will free your life,
But fetter you till death.

CLAUD.   Perpetual durance?°

ISAB. Aye, just, perpetual durance, a restraint,
Though all the world's vastidity° you had,
To a determined scope.°

CLAUD.   But in what nature?   70

ISAB. In such a one as, you consenting to't,
Would bark your honor from that trunk you bear,
And leave you naked.

CLAUD.   Let me know the point.°

ISAB. Oh, I do fear thee, Claudio, and I quake
Lest thou a feverous life shouldst entertain,   75
And six or seven winters more respect
Than a perpetual honor. Darest thou die?
The sense of death is most in apprehension,°
And the poor beetle that we tread upon
In corporal sufferance° finds a pang as great   80
As when a giant dies.

CLAUD.   Why give you me this shame?
Think you I can a resolution fetch
From° flowery tenderness? If I must die,
I will encounter darkness° as a bride,
And hug it in mine arms.   85

ISAB. There spake my brother, there my father's
    grave
Did utter forth a voice. Yes, thou must die.
Thou art too noble to conserve a life
In base appliances.° This outward-sainted Deputy,
Whose settled° visage and deliberate° word   90
Nips youth i' the head, and follies doth emmew°
As falcon doth the fowl,° is yet a devil.
His filth within being cast,° he would appear
A pond as deep as Hell.

CLAUD.   The prenzie° Angelo!

ISAB. Oh, 'tis the cunning livery° of Hell,   95
The damned'st body to invest° and cover
In prenzie guards!° Dost thou think,° Claudio? —
If I would yield him my virginity,
Thou mightst be freed.

CLAUD.   Oh, Heavens, it cannot be!

ISAB. Yes, he would give 't thee, from this rank of-
    fense,   100
So to offend him still. This night's the time
That I should do what I abhor to name,
Or else thou diest tomorrow.

CLAUD.   Thou shalt not do't.

ISAB. Oh, were it but my life,
I'd throw it down for your deliverance   105
As frankly° as a pin.

CLAUD.   Thanks, dear Isabel.

ISAB. Be ready, Claudio, for your death tomorrow.

CLAUD. Yes. Has he affections° in him

---

73. point: i.e., truth.   **78.** The . . . apprehension: the physical feeling of death is mostly imagination.   **80.** corporal sufferance: bodily suffering.   **82–83.** resolution . . . From: find courage in. **84.** darkness: death.   **89.** In . . . appliances: by low means. **90.** settled: firm, solemn. deliberate: severe.   **91.** emmew: keep in the coop.   **92.** As . . . fowl: because the hen fears to come out when the hawk is overhead.   **93.** cast: vomited.   **94.** prenzie: a doubtful word which does not appear elsewhere and is probably a misprint; by the context it should mean "prim," "respectable." **95.** livery: uniform.   **96.** invest: clothe.   **97.** guards: braid sewn on as ornament to a livery. Dost . . . think: would you be-lieve it.   **106.** frankly: freely.   **108.** affections: feelings.

---

30. proper: own.   **31.** serpigo: a skin disease. rheum: excessive moisture, supposed to cause catarrh and rheumatism. **35–36.** alms . . . eld: charity for a paralyzed old man.   **59.** leiger: a resident ambassador, as distinguished from an ambassador extraor-dinary sent on a special mission.   **60.** appointment: prepara-tion.   **67.** durance: imprisonment.   **69.** vastidity: immensity. **70.** determined scope: fixed limit.

That thus can make him bite the law by the nose,
When he would force° it? Sure, it is no sin,   110
Or of the deadly seven it is the least.

ISAB. Which is the least?

CLAUD. If it were damnable, he being so wise,
Why would he for the momentary trick
Be perdurably fined?° — O Isabel!   115

ISAB. What says my brother?

CLAUD.   Death is a fearful thing.

ISAB. And shamèd life a hateful.

CLAUD. Aye, but to die, and go we know not
    where,
To lie in cold obstruction° and to rot,
This sensible° warm motion° to become   120
A kneaded clod° and the delighted spirit
To bathe in fiery floods, or to reside
In thrilling° region of thick-ribbèd ice —
To be imprisoned in the viewless° winds,
And blown with restless violence round about   125
The pendent world, or to be worse than worst
Of those that lawless and incertain thought
Imagine howling — 'tis too horrible!
The weariest and most loathèd worldly life
That age, ache, penury, and imprisonment   130
Can lay on nature is a paradise
To what we fear of death.

ISAB. Alas, alas!

CLAUD.   Sweet sister, let me live.
What sin you do to save a brother's life,
Nature dispenses with° the deed so far   135
That it becomes a virtue.

ISAB.   O you beast!
O faithless coward! O dishonest wretch!
Wilt thou be made a man out of my vice?
Is't not a kind of incest, to take life
From thine own sister's shame? What should I
    think?   140
Heaven shield my mother played my father fair!
For such a warpèd slip of wilderness°
Ne'er issued from his blood. Take my defiance!
Die, perish! Might but my bending down
Reprieve thee from thy fate, it should proceed.   145
I'll pray a thousand prayers for thy death,
No word to save thee.

CLAUD. Nay, hear me, Isabel.

ISAB.   Oh, fie, fie, fie!
Thy sin's not accidental, but a trade.
Mercy to thee would prove itself a bawd.   150
'Tis best that thou diest quickly.

CLAUD.   Oh, hear me, Isabella!

[*Re-enter* DUKE.]

DUKE. Vouchsafe a word, young sister, but one
    word.

ISAB. What is your will?

DUKE. Might you dispense with your leisure, I
would by and by° have some speech with you.   155
The satisfaction I would require is likewise your
own benefit.

ISAB. I have no superfluous leisure. My stay must
be stolen out of other affairs, but I will attend you
awhile.   [*Walks apart.*]

DUKE. Son, I have overheard what hath passed be-
tween you and your sister. Angelo had never the
purpose to corrupt her, only he hath made an assay
of her virtue to practice his judgment° with   165
the disposition of natures. She, having the truth of
honor in her, hath made him that gracious denial
which he is most glad to receive. I am confessor to
Angelo, and I know this to be true. Therefore pre-
pare yourself to death. Do not satisfy your   170
resolution° with hopes that are fallible.° Tomorrow
you must die, go to your knees, and make ready.

CLAUD. Let me ask my sister pardon. I am so out
of love with life that I will sue to be rid of it.

DUKE. Hold you there. Farewell. [*Exit* CLAUDIO.]
Provost, a word with you!   176

[*Re-enter* PROVOST.]

PROV. What's your will, Father?

DUKE. That now you are come, you will be gone.
Leave me awhile with the maid. My mind   180
promises with my habit no loss° shall touch her by
my company.

PROV. In good time.

[*Exit* PROVOST. ISABELLA *comes forward.*]

DUKE. The hand that hath made you fair hath
made you good. The goodness that is cheap in beauty
makes beauty brief in goodness, but grace, be-   185
ing the soul of your complexion, shall keep the body
of it ever fair. The assault that Angelo hath made to
you fortune hath conveyed to my understanding, and
but that frailty hath examples for his falling, I   190
should wonder at Angelo. How will you do to con-
tent this substitute,° and to save your brother?

ISAB. I am now going to resolve him.° I had rather
my brother die by the law than my son should   195
be unlawfully born. But oh, how much is the good
Duke deceived in Angelo! If ever he return and I
can speak to him, I will open my lips in vain, or dis-
cover his government.°

DUKE. That shall not be much amiss.° Yet,   200
as the matter now stands, he will avoid your accu-

---

sation, he made trial of you only. Therefore fasten your ear on my advisings. To the love I have in doing good a remedy presents itself. I do make myself believe that you may most uprighteously 205 do a poor wronged lady a merited benefit, redeem your brother from the angry law, do no stain to your own gracious person, and much please the absent Duke, if peradventure he shall ever return to 210 have hearing of this business.

ISAB. Let me hear you speak farther. I have spirit to do anything that appears not foul in the truth of my spirit.

DUKE. Virtue is bold, and goodness never 215 fearful. Have you not heard speak of Mariana, the sister of Frederick the great soldier who miscarried at sea?

ISAB. I have heard of the lady, and good words went with her name. 220

DUKE. She should this Angelo have married, was affianced° to her by oath, and the nuptial appointed. Between which time of the contract and limit° of the solemnity, her brother Frederick was 225 wrecked at sea, having in that perished vessel the dowry of his sister. But mark how heavily this befell to the poor gentlewoman. There she lost a noble and renowned brother, in his love toward her ever most kind and natural, with him the portion and sinew of her fortune, her marriage dowry, with 230 both her combinate° husband, this well-seeming° Angelo.

ISAB. Can this be so? Did Angelo so leave her?

DUKE. Left her in her tears, and dried not one of them with his comfort, swallowed his vows 235 whole, pretending in her discoveries of dishonor. In few,° bestowed her on° her own lamentation, which she yet wears for his sake, and he, a marble° to her tears, is washed with them, but relents not.

ISAB. What a merit were it in death to take 240 this poor maid from the world! What corruption in this life, that it will let this man live! But how out of this can she avail?

DUKE. It is a rupture that you may easily heal. And the cure of it not only saves your brother, but keeps you from dishonor in doing it. 245

ISAB. Show me how, good Father.

DUKE. This forenamed maid hath yet in her the continuance of her first affection. His unjust unkindness, that in all reason should have quenched 250 her love, hath, like an impediment in the current, made it more violent and unruly. Go you to Angelo, answer his requiring with a plausible obedience, agree with his demands to the point. Only refer yourself to this advantage:° first, that your stay 255

with him may not be long, that the time may have all shadow and silence in it, and the place answer to convenience. This being granted in course—and now follows all—we shall advise this wronged maid to stead up your appointment,° go in your 260 place. If the encounter acknowledge itself hereafter, it may compel him to her recompense. And here, by this, is your brother saved, your honor untainted, the poor Mariana advantaged, and the corrupt 265 Deputy scaled.° The maid will I frame° and make fit for his attempt. If you think well to carry this as you may, the doubleness of the benefit defends the deceit from reproof. What think you of it?

ISAB. The image° of it gives me content al- 270 ready, and I trust it will grow to a most prosperous perfection.

DUKE. It lies much in your holding up.° Haste you speedily to Angelo. If for this night he entreat you to his bed, give him promise of satisfaction. 275 I will presently to Saint Luke's. There, at the moated grange,° resides this dejected Mariana. At that place call upon me, and dispatch with Angelo, that it may be quickly.

ISAB. I thank you for this comfort. Fare you 280 well, good Father. [*Exeunt severally.*]

SCENE II. *The street before the prison.*

[*Enter, on one side,* DUKE *disguised as before; on the other,* ELBOW, *and* OFFICERS *with* POMPEY.]

ELB. Nay, if there be no remedy for it but that you will needs buy and sell men and women like beasts, we shall have all the world drink brown and white bastard.°

DUKE. Oh heavens! what stuff is here? 5

POM. 'Twas never merry world since, of two usuries,° the merriest was put down, and the worser allowed by order of law a furred gown° to keep him warm, and furred with fox and lambskins too, to signify that craft, being richer than innocency, 10 stands for the facing.°

ELB. Come your way, sir. 'Bless you, good Father Friar.

DUKE. And you, good Brother Father. What offense hath this man made you, sir? 15

ELB. Marry, sir, he hath offended the law. And, sir, we take him to be a thief too, sir, for we have found upon him, sir, a strange picklock,° which we have sent to the Deputy.

---

222. affianced: betrothed: See Gen. Intro. p. 20a.   224. limit: appointed date.   231. combinate: affianced. well-seeming: hypocritical.   237. In few: briefly. bestowed . . . on: i.e., left her to. 238. marble: i.e., coldhearted.   254–55. Only . . . advantage: only demand for yourself this condition.

260. stead . . . appointment: keep the appointment in your stead. 266. scaled: weighed. frame: prepare.   270. image: thought. 273. It . . . up: i.e., the success of the plan depends on your support. 276–77. moated grange: a large farm surrounded by a moat.

Sc. ii: 4. bastard: lit., a sweet Spanish wine.   6–7. two usuries: i.e., prostitution and moneylending.   8. furred gown: gown trimmed with fox fur, the outward sign of wealth. See Pl. 9l. 10–11. craft . . . facing: cunning is represented by the trimming (*facing*).   18. picklock: skeleton key. See Pl. 13c.

DUKE. Fie, sirrah! A bawd, a wicked bawd!   20
The evil that thou causest to be done,
That is thy means to live. Do thou but think
What 'tis to cram a maw° or clothe a back
From such a filthy vice. Say to thyself,
"From their abominable and beastly touches   25
I drink, I eat, array myself, and live."
Canst thou believe thy living is a life,
So stinkingly depending?° Go mend, go mend.

POM. Indeed, it does stink in some sort, sir, but
yet, sir, I would prove ——   30

DUKE. Nay, if the Devil have given thee proofs
for sin,
Thou wilt prove his. Take him to prison, officer.
Correction and instruction must both work
Ere this rude beast will profit.

ELB. He must before the Deputy, sir, he has   35
given him warning. The Deputy cannot abide a
whoremaster. If he be a whoremonger, and comes
before him, he were as good go a mile on his er-
rand.°

DUKE. That we were all, as some would seem to
be,   40
From our faults, as faults from seeming, free!

ELB. His neck will come to your waist — a cord,°
sir.

POM. I spy comfort, I cry bail. Here's a gentleman
and a friend of mine.

[*Enter* LUCIO.]

LUCIO. How now, noble Pompey! What, at   45
the wheels° of Caesar? Art thou led in triumph?
What, is there none of Pygmalion's images,° newly
made woman, to be had now, for putting the hand
in the pocket and extracting it clutched?° What   49
reply, ha? What sayest thou to this tune, matter and
method? Is't not drowned i' the last rain, ha? What
sayest thou, Trot?° Is the world as it was, man?
Which is the way? Is it sad, and few words? Or
how? The trick of it?

DUKE. Still thus, and thus, still worse!   55

LUCIO. How doth my dear morsel, thy mistress?
Procures she still, ha?

POM. Troth, sir, she hath eaten up all her beef,
and she is herself in the tub.°

LUCIO. Why, 'tis good, it is the right of it, it   60
must be so. Ever your fresh whore and your pow-

dered° bawd — an unshunned° consequence, it must
be so. Art going to prison, Pompey?

POM. Yes, faith, sir.

LUCIO. Why, 'tis not amiss, Pompey. Fare-   65
well. Go say I sent thee thither. For debt, Pompey?
Or how?

ELB. For being a bawd, for being a bawd.

LUCIO. Well then, imprison him. If imprisonment
be the due of a bawd, why, 'tis his right. Bawd   70
is he doubtless, and of antiquity too, bawd-born.
Farewell, good Pompey. Commend me to the prison,
Pompey. You will turn good husband° now, Pom-
pey, you will keep the house.   74

POM. I hope, sir, your good Worship will be my
bail.

LUCIO. No, indeed will I not, Pompey. It is not the
wear.° I will pray, Pompey, to increase your bond-
age. If you take it not patiently, why, your mettle°
is the more. Adieu, trusty Pompey. 'Bless you,
Friar.   81

DUKE. And you.

LUCIO. Does Bridget paint° still, Pompey, ha?

ELB. Come your ways, sir, come.

POM. You will not bail me, then, sir?   85

LUCIO. Then, Pompey, nor now. What news
abroad, Friar? What news?

ELB. Come your ways, sir, come.

LUCIO. Go to kennel, Pompey, go. [*Exeunt* ELBOW,
POMPEY, *and* OFFICERS.] What news, Friar, of the
Duke?

DUKE. I know none. Can you tell me of any?

LUCIO. Some say he is with the Emperor of Rus-
sia, other some,° he is in Rome. But where is he,
think you?   95

DUKE. I know not where, but wheresoever, I wish
him well.

LUCIO. It was a mad fantastical trick of him to
steal from the state, and usurp° the beggary he was
never born to. Lord Angelo dukes it well in his ab-
sence, he puts transgression to't.   101

DUKE. He does well in't.

LUCIO. A little more lenity to lechery would do no
harm in him. Something too crabbed that way,
Friar.   105

DUKE. It is too general a vice, and severity must
cure it.

LUCIO. Yes, in good sooth, the vice is of a great
kindred, it is well allied. But it is impossible to ex-
tirp° it quite, Friar, till eating and drinking be put   111
down. They say this Angelo was not made by
man and woman after this downright way of crea-
tion. Is it true, think you?

DUKE. How should he be made, then?

LUCIO. Some report a sea maid° spawned him;
some, that he was begot between two stockfishes.°
But it is certain that when he makes water, his   117
urine is congealed ice. That I know to be true, and
he is a motion generative,° that's infallible.

DUKE. You are pleasant, sir, and speak apace.°

LUCIO. Why, what a ruthless thing is this in   121
him, for the rebellion of a codpiece° to take away
the life of a man! Would the Duke that is absent
have done this? Ere he would have hanged a man
for the getting a hundred bastards, he would   125
have paid for the nursing a thousand. He had some
feeling of the sport, he knew the service, and that
instructed him to mercy.

DUKE. I never heard the absent Duke much de-
tected for° women. He was not inclined that way.

LUCIO. Oh, sir, you are deceived.   131

DUKE. 'Tis not possible.

LUCIO. Who, not the Duke? Yes, your beggar of
fifty,° and his use was to put a ducat in her   134
clackdish.° The Duke had crotchets° in him. He
would be drunk too, that let me inform you.

DUKE. You do him wrong, surely.

LUCIO. Sir, I was an inward of his. A shy fellow
was the Duke. And I believe I know the cause of his
withdrawing.   140

DUKE. What, I prithee, might be the cause?

LUCIO. No, pardon, 'tis a secret must be locked
within the teeth and the lips. But this I can let you
understand, the greater file° of the subject° held the
Duke to be wise.   145

DUKE. Wise! Why, no question but he was.

LUCIO. A very superficial, ignorant, unweighing
fellow.

DUKE. Either this is envy in you, folly, or mistak-
ing. The very stream of his life and the busi-   150
ness he hath helmed° must, upon a warranted need,°
give him a better proclamation.° Let him be but
testimonied in his own bringings-forth,° and he shall
appear to the envious a scholar, a statesman, and a
soldier. Therefore you speak unskillfully, or if   155
your knowledge be more, it is much darkened in
your malice.

LUCIO. Sir, I know him, and I love him.

DUKE. Love talks with better knowledge, and
knowledge with dearer love.   160

LUCIO. Come, sir, I know what I know.

DUKE. I can hardly believe that, since you know
not what you speak. But if ever the Duke return, as
our prayers are he may, let me desire you to make
your answer before him. If it be honest you   165
have spoke, you have courage to maintain it. I am
bound to call upon you, and, I pray you, your name?

LUCIO. Sir, my name is Lucio, well known to the
Duke.   170

DUKE. He shall know you better, sir, if I may live
to report you.

LUCIO. I fear you not.

DUKE. Oh, you hope the Duke will return no
more, or you imagine me too unhurtful an op-   175
posite. But indeed I can do you little harm. You'll
forswear this again.

LUCIO. I'll be hanged first. Thou art deceived in
me, Friar. But no more of this. Canst thou tell if
Claudio die tomorrow or no?   180

DUKE. Why should he die, sir?

LUCIO. Why? For filling a bottle with a tundish.°
I would the Duke we talk of were returned again.
This ungenitured° agent will unpeople the province
with continency; sparrows must not build in   185
his house eaves, because they are lecherous. The
Duke yet would have dark deeds darkly answered,
he would never bring them to light. Would he were
returned! Marry, this Claudio is condemned   189
for untrussing.° Farewell, good Friar. I prithee pray
for me. The Duke, I say to thee again, would eat
mutton on Fridays.° He's not past it yet, and I say
to thee he would mouth° with a beggar though she
smelt brown bread and garlic. Say that I said   194
so. Farewell.   [*Exit.*]

DUKE. No might nor greatness in mortality°
Can censure 'scape; back-wounding calumny
The whitest virtue strikes. What king so strong
Can tie the gall up in the slanderous tongue?
But who comes here?   200

[*Enter* ESCALUS, PROVOST, *and* OFFICERS *with*
MISTRESS OVERDONE.]

ESCAL. Go, away with her to prison!

MRS. OV. Good my lord, be good to me. Your
Honor is accounted a merciful man, good my lord.

ESCAL. Double and treble admonition, and still
forfeit° in the same kind! This would make   205
mercy swear and play the tyrant.

PROV. A bawd of eleven years' continuance, may
it please your Honor.

MRS. OV. My lord, this is one Lucio's infor-   210
mation against me. Mistress Kate Keepdown was
with child by him in the Duke's time, he promised
her marriage. His child is a year and a quarter old.
come Philip and Jacob.° I have kept it myself, and
see how he goes about to abuse me!   215

115. sea maid: mermaid.   **116.** stockfishes: dried codfish.
119. motion generative: a masculine puppet.   **120.** apace:
excessively.   **122.** rebellion . . . codpiece: i.e., because his lust
got the better of him. codpiece: See Pl. 8c and comment on p. 93b.
130. detected for: suspected of.   **133–34.** your . . . fifty: i.e.,
he had an affair with an old beggarwoman.   **135.** clackdish:
wooden bowl carried by beggars. crotchets: odd ways.   **144.** file:
lit., list, quantity. subject: people.   **151.** helmed: steered. **upon
. . . need:** if assurance is needed.   **152.** proclamation: report.
153. bringings-forth: actions.

182. tundish: funnel.   **184.** ungenitured: impotent.   **190.** un-
trussing: taking down his breeches.   **191–92.** eat . . . Fri-
days: lit., be no fasting man; *mutton* also means a prostitute.
193. mouth: kiss.   **196.** mortality: human life.   **205.** forfeit:
offending.   **214.** Philip . . . Jacob: St. Philip and St. James
Day (May 1).

ESCAL. That fellow is a fellow of much license. Let him be called before us. Away with her to prison! Go to, no more words. [*Exeunt* OFFICERS *with* MISTRESS OVERDONE.] Provost, my brother Angelo will not be altered, Claudio must die tomorrow. Let him be furnished with divines, and have all chari- 221 table preparation. If my brother wrought by my pity,° it should not be so with him.

PROV. So please you, this friar hath been 224 with him, and advised him for the entertainment of death.

ESCAL. Good even, good Father.

DUKE. Bliss and goodness on you!

ESCAL. Of whence are you?

DUKE. Not of this country, though my chance is now 230
To use it for my time. I am a brother
Of gracious order, late come from the See°
In special business from His Holiness.

ESCAL. What news abroad i' the world?

DUKE. None but that there is so great a fever 235 on goodness that the dissolution° of it must cure it. Novelty is only in request, and it is as dangerous to be aged in any kind of course as it is virtuous to be constant in any undertaking. There is scarce truth enough alive to make societies secure, but se- 240 curity enough to make fellowships accurst° — much upon this riddle runs the wisdom of the world. This news is old enough, yet it is every day's news. I pray you, sir, of what disposition was the Duke? 244

ESCAL. One that, above all other strifes, contended especially to know himself.

DUKE. What pleasure was he given to?

ESCAL. Rather rejoicing to see another merry than merry at anything which professed to make 249 him rejoice — a gentleman of all temperance. But leave we him to his events,° with a prayer they may prove prosperous, and let me desire to know how you find Claudio prepared. I am made to understand that you have lent him visitation. 254

DUKE. He professes to have received no sinister measure° from his judge, but most willingly humbles himself to the determination of justice. Yet had he framed to himself, by the instruction° of his 258 frailty, many deceiving promises of life, which I, by my good leisure, have discredited to him, and now is he resolved to die.

ESCAL. You have paid the Heavens your function,° and the prisoner the very debt of your calling.° 263 I have labored for the poor gentleman to the extrem-

est shore° of my modesty. But my brother 265 Justice have I found so severe that he hath forced me to tell him he is indeed Justice.°

DUKE. If his own life answer the straitness of his proceeding, it shall become him well, wherein if he chance to fail, he hath sentenced himself. 270

ESCAL. I am going to visit the prisoner. Fare you well.

DUKE. Peace be with you!

            [*Exeunt* ESCALUS *and* PROVOST.]

He° who the sword of Heaven will bear 275
Should be as holy as severe,
Pattern in himself to know,
Grace to stand and virtue go,
More nor less to others paying
Than by self-offenses weighing. 280
Shame to him whose cruel striking
Kills for faults of his own liking!
Twice treble shame on Angelo,
To weed my vice and let his grow!
Oh, what may man within him hide, 285
Though angel on the outward side!
How may likeness made in crimes,
Making practice on the times,
To draw with idle spiders' strings
Most ponderous and substantial things!° 290
Craft against vice I must apply.
With Angelo tonight shall lie
His old betrothèd but despisèd,
So disguise shall, by the disguisèd,
Pay with falsehood false exacting, 295
And perform an old contracting.   [*Exit.*]

Act IV

SCENE I. *The moated grange at* ST. LUKE'S.

[*Enter* MARIANA *and a* BOY.]

BOY. [*Sings.*]
Take, O, take those lips away
    That so sweetly were forsworn,
And those eyes, the break of day,°
    Lights that do mislead the morn.
But my kisses bring again, bring again,   5
Seals of love, but sealed in vain, sealed in vain.

MARI. Break off thy song, and haste thee quick away.
Here comes a man of comfort, whose advice

222–23. **wrought . . . pity:** acted as mercifully as I would. 232. **See:** i.e., Rome. 236. **dissolution:** death. 240–41. **security accurst:** i.e., since everyone nowadays demands security there is no true friendship. 251. **events:** own affairs. 255–56. **sinister measure:** unjust sentence. 258. **instruction:** prompting. 262. **You . . . function:** you have done your duty toward God. 263. **debt . . . calling:** what your holy office demands.

265. **shore:** limit. 267. **indeed Justice:** i.e., Justice without mercy. 275–96. **He . . . contracting:** Most critics believe this passage in rhymed octosyllabic verse was not written by Shakespeare. 287–90. **How . . . things:** an obscure passage which has not been satisfactorily explained.
     Act IV, Sc. i: 3. break of day: i.e., like the dawn.

Hath often stilled my brawling° discontent.

[*Exit* BOY.]

[*Enter* DUKE *disguised as before.*] I cry you mercy,°
   sir, and well could wish   10
You had not found me here so musical.
Let me excuse me, and believe me so,
My mirth it much displeased, but pleased my woe.

DUKE. 'Tis good, though music oft hath such a
   charm
To make bad good, and good provoke to harm. 15
I pray you tell me, hath anybody inquired for me
here today? Much upon this time have I promised
here to meet.

MARI. You have not been inquired after. I have
sat here all day.   20

[*Enter* ISABELLA.]

DUKE. I do constantly believe you. The time is
come even now. I shall crave your forbearance a
little. Maybe I will call upon you anon, for some ad-
vantage to yourself.

MARI. I am always bound to you.   [*Exit.*]

DUKE. Very well met, and well come.   26
What is the news from this good Deputy?

ISAB. He hath a garden circummured° with brick
Whose western side is with a vineyard backed,
And to that vineyard is a planchèd° gate 30
That makes his opening with this bigger key.
This other doth command a little door
Which from the vineyard to the garden leads.
There have I made my promise
Upon the heavy middle of the night 35
To call upon him.

DUKE. But shall you on your knowledge find this
   way?

ISAB. I have ta'en a due and wary° note upon 't.
With whispering and most guilty diligence,
In action all of precept,° he did show me 40
The way twice o'er.

DUKE.   Are there no other tokens
Between you 'greed concerning her observance?°

ISAB. No, none, but only a repair i' the dark,
And that I have possessed him my most stay
Can be but brief. For I have made him know 45
I have a servant comes with me along
That stays upon° me, whose persuasion is°
I come about my brother.

DUKE.   'Tis well borne up.°
I have not yet made known to Mariana
A word of this. What ho! Within! Come forth! 50

[*Re-enter* MARIANA.] I pray you be acquainted with
   this maid,
She comes to do you good.

ISAB.   I do desire the like.

DUKE. Do you persuade yourself that I respect
   you?°

MARI. Good Friar, I know you do, and have found
it.

DUKE. Take, then, this your companion by the
   hand, 55
Who hath a story ready for your ear.
I shall attend your leisure. But make haste,
The vaporous night approaches.

MARI. Will't please you walk aside?

[*Exeunt* MARIANA *and* ISABELLA.]

DUKE. O place and greatness, millions of false eyes
Are stuck upon thee! Volumes of report 61
Run with these false and most contrarious quests°
Upon thy doings! Thousand escapes of wit
Make thee the father of their idle dreams,
And rack° thee in their fancies!

[*Re-enter* MARIANA *and* ISABELLA.] Welcome, how
   agreed? 65

ISAB. She'll take the enterprise upon her, Father,
If you advise it.

DUKE.   It is not my consent
But my entreaty too.

ISAB.   Little have you to say
When you depart from him, but, soft and low,
"Remember now my brother."

MARI.   Fear me not. 70

DUKE. Nor, gentle Daughter, fear you not at all.
He is your husband on a precontract.
To bring you thus together, 'tis no sin,
Sith° that the justice of your title to him
Doth flourish° the deceit. Come, let us go. 75
Our corn's to reap, for yet our tithe's° to sow.

[*Exeunt.*]

SCENE II. *A room in the prison.*

[*Enter* PROVOST *and* POMPEY.]

PROV. Come hither, sirrah. Can you cut off a man's
head?

POM. If the man be a bachelor, sir, I can. But if he
be a married man, he's his wife's head, and I can
never cut off a woman's head. 5

PROV. Come, sir, leave me your snatches° and
yield me a direct answer. Tomorrow morning are
to die Claudio and Barnardine. Here is in our prison
a common executioner, who in his office lacks 10
a helper. If you will take it on you to assist him, it
shall redeem you from your gyves.° If not, you shall

9. **brawling:** noisy.   **10. cry . . . mercy:** beg your pardon.
28. circummured: walled round. See Pl. 16a.   **30. planched:**
planked.   **38. wary:** careful.   **40. In . . . precept:** instructing
me by his gestures.   **42. her observance:** what she must observe.
47. stays upon: waits for. **whose . . . is:** who has been told.
48. borne up: planned.

53. **respect you:** esteem.   62. **quests:** following of the scent.
65. **rack:** stretch, pull to pieces.   74. **Sith:** since.   75. **flour-
ish:** embellish.   76. **tithe's:** the F1 reading. Some editions
emend to "tilth," plowing.
Sc. ii: 6. **snatches:** wisecracks.   12. **gyves:** fetters.

have your full time of imprisonment, and your deliverance with an unpitied whipping, for you have been a notorious bawd.   15

POM. Sir, I have been an unlawful bawd time out of mind, but yet I will be content to be a lawful hangman. I would be glad to receive some instruction from my fellow partner.

PROV. What ho! Abhorson! Where's Abhorson, there?   20

[*Enter* ABHORSON.]

ABHOR. Do you call, sir?

PROV. Sirrah, here's a fellow will help you tomorrow in your execution. If you think it meet, compound° with him by the year, and let him abide   25 here with you. If not, use him for the present, and dismiss him. He cannot plead his estimation° with you, he hath been a bawd.

ABHOR. A bawd, sir? Fie upon him! He will discredit our mystery.°   30

PROV. Go to, sir, you weigh equally.° A feather will turn the scale.   [*Exit.*]

POM. Pray, sir, by your good favor — for surely, sir, a good favor° you have, but that you have a hanging look — do you call, sir, your occupation° a mystery?   36

ABHOR. Aye, sir, a mystery.

POM. Painting, sir, I have heard say, is a mystery, and your whores, sir, being members of my occupation, using painting, do prove my occupation   40 a mystery. But what mystery there should be in hanging, if I should be hanged, I cannot imagine.

ABHOR. Sir, it is a mystery.

POM. Proof?   45

ABHOR. Every true man's apparel fits your thief. If it be too little for your thief, your true man thinks it big enough; if it be too big for your thief, your thief thinks it little enough. So every true man's apparel fits your thief.°   50

[*Re-enter* PROVOST.]

PROV. Are you agreed?

POM. Sir, I will serve him, for I do find your hangman is a more penitent trade than your bawd. He doth oftener ask forgiveness.°   55

PROV. You, sirrah, provide your block and your ax tomorrow four o'clock.

ABHOR. Come on, bawd, I will instruct thee in my trade. Follow.

POM. I do desire to learn, sir. And I hope, if you have occasion to use me for your own turn, you   60

shall find me yare;° for truly, sir, for your kindness I owe you a good turn.

PROV. Call hither Barnardine and Claudio.

[*Exeunt* POMPEY *and* ABHORSON.]

The one has my pity, not a jot the other,
Being a murderer, though he were my brother.   65

[*Enter* CLAUDIO.] Look, here's the warrant, Claudio,
   for thy death.
'Tis now dead midnight, and by eight tomorrow
Thou must be made immortal. Where's Barnardine?

CLAUD. As fast locked up in sleep as guiltless labor
When it lies starkly in the traveler's bones.°   70
He will not wake.

PROV.   Who can do good on him?
Well, go, prepare yourself. [*Knocking within.*] But
   hark, what noise? —
Heaven give your spirits comfort! [*Exit* CLAUDIO.]
   By and by.° —
I hope it is some pardon or reprieve
For the most gentle Claudio.

[*Enter* DUKE *disguised as before.*] Welcome, Father.

DUKE. The best and wholesomest spirits of the
   night   76
Envelop you, good Provost! Who called here of late?

PROV. None, since the curfew rung.

DUKE. Not Isabel?

PROV.   No.

DUKE.   They will, then, ere't be long.

PROV. What comfort is for Claudio?   80

DUKE. There's some in hope.

PROV.   It is a bitter Deputy.

DUKE. Not so, not so, his life is paralleled
Even with the stroke and line of his great justice.°
He doth with holy abstinence subdue
That in himself which he spurs on his power   85
To qualify° in others. Were he mealed° with that
Which he corrects, then were he tyrannous,
But this being so, he's just.   [*Knocking within.*]
                    Now are they come? [*Exit* PROVOST.]
This is a gentle Provost. Seldom when°
The steelèd° jailer is the friend of men.   90
                    [*Knocking within.*]
How now! What noise? That spirit's possessed with
   haste
That wounds the unsisting° postern with these
   strokes.

[*Re-enter* PROVOST.]

PROV. There he must stay until the officer
Arise to let him in. He is called up.

DUKE. Have you no countermand for Claudio yet,

25. compound: contract.   27. estimation: worth.   30. mystery: trade practiced by skilled craftsmen.   31. weigh equally: i.e., you both follow a despised occupation.   34. favor: with double meaning of "kindness" and "face."   35. occupation: trade, work performed with the hands. Cf. *Caesar*, I.ii.269.   46–50. Every . . . thief: i.e., an honest man's clothes suit the thief who steals them.   55. ask forgiveness: It was part of the etiquette of an execution for the hangman to ask for the forgiveness of his victim.

61. yare: handy.   69–70. As . . . bones: i.e., like the innocent sleep that comes to the weary traveler. starkly: stiffly.   73. By . . . by: in a moment — in answer to the knocking.   82–83. his . . . justice: i.e., his good life and his sense of justice seem parallel like the lines in a diagram.   86. qualify: moderate. mealed: spotted.   89. Seldom when: it is seldom that.   90. steeled: hardhearted.   92. unsisting: The word is not otherwise known, and is variously emended; e.g., unresisting, unassisting.

But he must die tomorrow?

PROV.   None, sir, none.   96

DUKE. As near the dawning, Provost, as it is,
You shall hear more ere morning.

PROV.   Happily°
You something know, yet I believe there comes
No countermand — no such example have we.   100
Besides, upon the very siege° of justice
Lord Angelo hath to the public ear
Professed the contrary.

[*Enter a* MESSENGER.] This is his lordship's man.

DUKE. And here comes Claudio's pardon.

MESS. [*Giving a paper*] My lord hath sent   105
you this note, and by me this further charge, that
you swerve not from the smallest article of it, neither
in time, matter, or other circumstance. Good mor-
row, for, as I take it, it is almost day.

PROV. I shall obey him.   [*Exit* MESSENGER.]

DUKE. [*Aside*] This is his pardon, purchased by
    such sin   111
For which the pardoner himself is in.
Hence hath offense his quick celerity
When it is borne in high authority.
When vice makes mercy, mercy's so extended   115
That for the fault's love is the offender friended.
Now, sir, what news?

PROV. I told you. Lord Angelo, belike thinking
me remiss in mine office, awakens me with this un-
wonted putting-on° — methinks strangely, for   120
he hath not used it before.

DUKE. Pray you, let's hear.

PROV. [*Reads.*] " Whatsoever you may hear to the
contrary, let Claudio be executed by four of the
clock, and in the afternoon Barnardine. For   125
my better satisfaction, let me have Claudio's head
sent me by five. Let this be duly performed, with a
thought that more depends on it than we must yet
deliver. Thus fail not to do your office, as you will
answer it at your peril." What say you to this,   130
sir?

DUKE. What is that Barnardine who is to be exe-
cuted in the afternoon?

PROV. A Bohemian born, but here nursed up and
bred, one that is a prisoner nine years old.   135

DUKE. How came it that the absent Duke had not
either delivered him to his liberty or executed him?
I have heard it was ever his manner to do so.

PROV. His friends still wrought reprieves for him.
And indeed his fact,° till now in the govern-   140
ment of Lord Angelo, came not to an undoubtful°
proof.

DUKE. It is now apparent?   144

PROV. Most manifest, and not denied by himself.

DUKE. Hath he borne himself penitently in prison?
How seems he to be touched?

PROV. A man that apprehends death no more
dreadfully but as a drunken sleep — careless,   149
reckless, and fearless of what's past, present, or to
come, insensible of mortality and desperately mor-
tal.°

DUKE. He wants advice.°

PROV. He will hear none. He hath evermore had
the liberty of the prison. Give him leave to es-   155
cape hence, he would not. Drunk many times a day,
if not many days entirely drunk. We have very oft
awaked him as if to carry him to execution, and
showed him a seeming warrant for it. It hath   160
not moved him at all.

DUKE. More of him anon. There is written in your
brow, Provost, honesty and constancy. If I read it
not truly, my ancient skill beguiles me, but in the
boldness of my cunning° I will lay myself in   165
hazard. Claudio, whom here you have warrant to
execute, is no greater forfeit to the law than Angelo
who hath sentenced him. To make you understand
this in a manifested effect, I crave but four   170
days' respite, for the which you are to do me both a
present and a dangerous courtesy.

PROV. Pray, sir, in what?

DUKE. In the delaying death.

PROV. Alack, how may I do it, having the   175
hour limited,° and an express command, under pen-
alty, to deliver his head in the view of Angelo? I
may make my case as Claudio's, to cross° this in the
smallest.

DUKE. By the vow of mine Order I warrant   180
you, if my instructions may be your guide. Let this
Barnardine be this morning executed, and his head
borne to Angelo.

PROV. Angelo hath seen them both, and will dis-
cover the favor.°   185

DUKE. Oh, death's a great disguiser, and you may
add to it. Shave the head, and tie° the beard, and
say it was the desire of the penitent to be so bared
before his death. You know the course is com-   190
mon. If anything fall to you upon this more than
thanks and good fortune, by the saint whom I pro-
fess, I will plead against it with my life.

PROV. Pardon me, good Father, it is against my
oath.

DUKE. Were you sworn to the Duke, or to the
Deputy?   195

PROV. To him, and to his substitutes.

DUKE. You will think you have made no offense
if the Duke avouch the justice of your dealing?   200

PROV. But what likelihood is in that?

DUKE. Not a resemblance, but a certainty. Yet
since I see you fearful, that neither my coat, integ-

151–52. insensible . . . mortal: having no thought of death and in
a desperate state of deadly sin.   153. advice: spiritual coun-
sel.   165. cunning: skill.   176. limited: appointed.   178. cross:
thwart.   185. favor: face.   188. tie: trim short.

98. Happily: perhaps.   101. siege: seat.   120. putting-on: urg-
ing.   140. fact: deed, crime.   141. undoubtful: certain.

rity, nor persuasion can with ease attempt you, I will go further than I meant, to pluck all fears 205 out of you. [*Producing a letter*] Look you, sir, here is the hand and seal of the Duke. You know the character,° I doubt not, and the signet is not strange to you.

PROV. I know them both.   210

DUKE. The contents of this is the return of the Duke. You shall anon overread it at your pleasure, where you shall find within these two days he will be here. This is a thing that Angelo knows not, for he this very day receives letters of strange tenor 215 — perchance of the Duke's death, perchance entering into some monastery — but, by chance, nothing of what is writ. Look, the unfolding star° calls up the shepherd. Put not yourself into amazement 220 how these things should be. All difficulties are but easy when they are known. Call your executioner, and off with Barnardine's head. I will give him a present shrift° and advise him for a better place. Yet you are amazed, but this shall absolutely re- 225 solve you. Come away, it is almost clear dawn.

[*Exeunt.*]

SCENE III. *Another room in the same.*

[*Enter* POMPEY.]

POM. I am as well acquainted° here as I was in our house of profession. One would think it were Mistress Overdone's own house, for here be many of her old customers. First, here's young Master 5 Rash. He's in for a commodity of brown paper and old ginger, ninescore and seventeen pounds, of which he made five marks, ready money. Marry, then ginger was not much in request, for the old women were all dead.° Then is there here one Master 10 Caper, at the suit of Master Threepile the mercer, for some four suits of peach-colored satin, which now peaches° him a beggar. Then have we here young Dizy, and young Master Deep-vow, and Master 15 Copper-spur, and Master Starve-lackey the rapier and dagger man,° and young Drop-heir that killed lusty Pudding, and Master Forthlight the tilter,° and brave Master Shooty° the great traveler, and wild Half-can that stabbed Pots, and I think forty 20

more — all great doers in our trade, and are now " for the Lord's sake."°

[*Enter* ABHORSON.]

ABHOR. Sirrah, bring Barnardine hither.

POM. Master Barnardine! You must rise and be hanged, Master Barnardine!

ABHOR. What ho, Barnardine!   25

BARNAR. [*Within*] A pox o' your throats! Who makes that noise there? What are you?

POM. Your friends, sir, the hangman. You must be so good, sir, to rise and be put to death.

BARNAR. [*Within*] Away, you rogue, away! I am sleepy.   30

ABHOR. Tell him he must awake, and that quickly too.

POM. Pray, Master Barnardine, awake till you are executed, and sleep afterward.   35

ABHOR. Go in to him and fetch him out.

POM. He is coming, sir, he is coming, I hear his straw rustle.

ABHOR. Is the ax upon the block, sirrah?

POM. Very ready, sir.   40

[*Enter* BARNARDINE.]

BARNAR. How now, Abhorson? What's the news with you?

ABHOR. Truly, sir, I would desire you to clap into° your prayers, for look you, the warrant's come.   45

BARNAR. You rogue, I have been drinking all night, I am not fitted for 't.

POM. Oh, the better, sir, for he that drinks all night and is hanged betimes in the morning may sleep the sounder all the next day.   50

ABHOR. Look you, sir, here comes your ghostly° Father. Do we jest now, think you?

[*Enter* DUKE *disguised as before.*]

DUKE. Sir, induced by my charity, and hearing how hastily you are to depart, I am come to advise you, comfort you, and pray with you.   55

BARNAR. Friar, not I. I have been drinking hard all night, I will have more time to prepare me, or they shall beat out my brains with billets.° I will not consent to die this day, that's certain.

DUKE. O sir, you must, and therefore I beseech you   60 Look forward on the journey you shall go.

BARNAR. I swear I will not die today for any man's persuasion.

DUKE. But hear you.

BARNAR. Not a word. If you have anything to 65 say to me, come to my ward,° for thence will not I today.   [*Exit.*]

DUKE. Unfit to live or die. O gravel° heart!

---

208. **character:** handwriting.   219. **unfolding star:** the morning star which summons the shepherd to lead his sheep from the fold.   224. **present shrift:** immediate absolution.

Sc. iii: 1. **well acquainted:** have as many acquaintances. 6–10. **commodity . . . dead:** Interest on loans had been fixed by Act of Parliament at 10%, but moneylenders evaded the statute by the legal device of "commodities." In return for a loan of cash the borrower also purchased a parcel (*commodity*) of worthless goods, such as lutestrings, for which he promised to pay back a much higher sum. Master Rash's "commodity" consisted of brown paper and ginger. **marks:** 13*s*.4*d*.   14. **peaches:** denounces.   16–17. **rapier . . . man:** bully.   18. **tilter:** fencer. 19. **Shooty:** i.e., shoe tie.

22. **for . . . sake:** Prisoners were obliged to pay for their own food in prisons. Those who had no money were allowed to appeal to the charity of passers by to give them alms "for the Lord's sake."   44. **clap into:** get going with.   51. **ghostly:** spiritual.   58. **billet:** a thick stick.   66. **ward:** cell.   68. **gravel:** hard as stone.

After him, fellows, bring him to the block.
      [*Exeunt* ABHORSON *and* POMPEY.]
      [*Enter* PROVOST.]

PROV. Now, sir, how do you find the prisoner? 70
DUKE. A creature unprepared, unmeet for death,
And to transport him in the mind he is
Were damnable.
PROV.   Here in the prison, Father,
There died this morning of a cruel fever
One Ragozine, a most notorious pirate, 75
A man of Claudio's years, his beard and head
Just of his color. What if we do omit
This reprobate till he were well inclined,
And satisfy the Deputy with the visage
Of Ragozine, more like to Claudio? 80
DUKE. Oh, 'tis an accident that Heaven provides!
Dispatch it presently,° the hour draws on
Prefixed by Angelo. See this be done,
And sent according to command, whiles I
Persuade this rude wretch willingly to die. 85
PROV. This shall be done, good Father, presently.
But Barnardine must die this afternoon.
And how shall we continue Claudio,
To save me from the danger that might come
If he were known alive?
DUKE.   Let this be done. 90
Put them in secret holds, both Barnardine and
    Claudio.
Ere twice the sun hath made his journal° greeting
To the under generation,° you shall find
Your safety manifested.
PROV. I am your free dependant.° 95
DUKE. Quick, dispatch, and send the head to
    Angelo.   [*Exit* PROVOST.]
Now will I write letters to Angelo —
The Provost, he shall bear them — whose contents
Shall witness to him I am near at home,
And that, by great injunctions, I am bound 100
To enter publicly. Him I'll desire
To meet me at the consecrated fount,
A league below the city, and from thence,
By cold gradation° and well-balanced form,
We shall proceed with Angelo. 105
      [*Re-enter* PROVOST.]
PROV. Here is the head, I'll carry it myself.
DUKE. Convenient is it. Make a swift return,
For I would commune with you of such things
That want no ear but yours.
PROV.   I'll make all speed. [*Exit.*]
ISAB. [*Within*] Peace ho, be here! 110
DUKE. The tongue of Isabel. She's come to know
If yet her brother's pardon be come hither.
But I will keep her ignorant of her good,
To make her heavenly comforts of despair

When it is least expected.
      [*Enter* ISABELLA.]
ISAB.   Ho, by your leave! 115
DUKE. Good morning to you, fair and gracious
    daughter.
ISAB. The better, given me by so holy a man.
Hath yet the Deputy sent my brother's pardon?
DUKE. He hath released him, Isabel, from the
    world.
His head is off, and sent to Angelo. 120
ISAB. Nay, but it is not so.
DUKE. It is no other. Show your wisdom, Daugh-
    ter,
In your close° patience.
ISAB. Oh, I will to him and pluck out his eyes!
DUKE. You shall not be admitted to his sight. 125
ISAB. Unhappy Claudio! Wretched Isabel!
Injurious world! Most damnèd Angelo!
DUKE. This nor hurts him nor profits you a jot.
Forbear it therefore, give your cause to Heaven.
Mark what I say, which you shall find 130
By every syllable a faithful verity.
The Duke comes home tomorrow — nay, dry your
    eyes,
One of our covent,° and his confessor,
Gives me this instance.° Already he hath carried
Notice to Escalus and Angelo, 135
Who do prepare to meet him at the gates,
There to give up their power. If you can, pace° your
    wisdom
In that good path that I would wish it go,
And you shall have your bosom° on this wretch,
Grace of the Duke, revenges to your heart, 140
And general honor.
ISAB.   I am directed by you.
DUKE. This letter, then, to Friar Peter give.
'Tis that he sent me of the Duke's return.
Say, by this token, I desire his company
At Mariana's house tonight. Her cause and yours
I'll perfect° him withal, and he shall bring you 146
Before the Duke, and to the head° of Angelo
Accuse him home and home. For my poor self,
I am combinèd° by a sacred vow,
And shall be absent. Wend you with this letter. 150
Command these fretting waters from your eyes
With a light heart. Trust not my holy Order
If I pervert your course. — Who's here?
      [*Enter* LUCIO.]
LUCIO. Good even. Friar, where's the Provost?
DUKE. Not within, sir. 155
LUCIO. O pretty Isabella, I am pale at mine heart
to see thine eyes so red. Thou must be patient. I am
fain to dine and sup with water and bran, I dare not

---

82. **presently:** immediately.   92. **journal:** daily.   93. **under generation:** i.e., the Antipodes.   95. **your . . . dependant:** entirely your servant.   104. **cold gradation:** deliberate steps.

123. **close:** secret.   133. **covent:** convent, monastery.   134. **instance:** news.   137. **pace:** direct.   139. **your bosom:** what your heart desires.   146. **perfect:** fully inform.   147. **head:** face.   149. **combined:** bound.

for my head fill my belly, one fruitful meal   160
would set me to't. But they say the Duke will be
here tomorrow. By my troth, Isabel, I loved thy
brother. If the old fantastical Duke of dark corners°
had been at home, he had lived.   [*Exit* ISABELLA.]

DUKE. Sir, the Duke is marvelous little be-   166
holding to your reports, but the best is, he lives not
in them.°

LUCIO. Friar, thou knowest not the Duke so well
as I do. He's a better woodman° than thou takest
him for.   170

DUKE. Well, you'll answer this one day. Fare ye
well.

LUCIO. Nay, tarry, I'll go along with thee. I can
tell thee pretty tales of the Duke.   175

DUKE. You have told me too many of him already,
sir, if they be true. If not true, none were enough.

LUCIO. I was once before him for getting a wench
with child.   180

DUKE. Did you such a thing?

LUCIO. Yes, marry did I. But I was fain to for-
swear it, they would else have married me to the
rotten medlar.°

DUKE. Sir, your company is fairer than hon-   185
est. Rest you well.°

LUCIO. By my troth, I'll go with thee to the lane's
end. If bawdy talk offend you, we'll have very little
of it. Nay, Friar, I am a kind of burr, I shall   189
stick.   [*Exeunt.*]

SCENE IV. *A room in* ANGELO's *house.*

[*Enter* ANGELO *and* ESCALUS.]

ESCAL. Every letter he hath writ hath disvouched°
other.

ANG. In most uneven and distracted manner. His
actions show much like to madness. Pray Heaven his
wisdom be not tainted! And why meet him at   5
the gates, and redeliver our authorities there?

ESCAL. I guess not.

ANG. And why should we proclaim it in an   8
hour before his entering that if any crave redress of
injustice, they should exhibit their petitions in the
street?

ESCAL. He shows his reason for that. To have a
dispatch of complaints, and to deliver us from   13
devices° hereafter, which shall then have no power
to stand against us.

ANG. Well, I beseech you let it be proclaimed be-
times i' the morn. I'll call you at your house. Give

notice to such men of sort° and suit° as are to meet
him.   20

ESCAL. I shall, sir. Fare you well.

ANG. Good night.   [*Exit* ESCALUS.]
This deed unshapes° me quite, makes me unpreg-
nant,°
And dull to all proceedings. A deflowered maid!
And by an eminent body that enforced   25
The law against it! But that her tender shame
Will not proclaim against her maiden loss,°
How might she tongue me! Yet reason dares her
no,°
For my authority bears of a credent bulk°
That no particular scandal once can touch   30
But it confounds the breather. He should have lived,
Save that his riotous youth, with dangerous sense,°
Might in the times to come have ta'en revenge
By so receiving a dishonored life
With ransom of such shame. Would yet he had
lived!   35
Alack, when once our grace we have forgot,
Nothing goes right. We would, and we would not.
                          [*Exit.*]

SCENE V. *Fields without the town.*

[*Enter* DUKE *in his own habit, and* FRIAR PETER.]

DUKE. These letters at fit time deliver me.°
                    [*Giving letters*]
The Provost knows our purpose and our plot.
The matter being afoot, keep your instruction,
And hold you ever to our special drift,°
Though sometimes you do blench° from this to
that,   5
As cause doth minister. Go call at Flavius' house,
And tell him where I stay. Give the like notice
To Valentius, Rowland, and to Crassus,
And bid them bring the trumpets to the gate.   9
But send me Flavius first.

FRI. P.   It shall be speeded well. [*Exit.*]
               [*Enter* VARRIUS.]

DUKE. I thank thee, Varrius, thou hast made good
haste.
Come, we will walk. There's other of our friends
Will greet us here anon, my gentle Varrius.
                       [*Exeunt.*]

---

19. **sort:** high rank. **suit:** with petitions.   23. **unshapes:** upsets.
unpregnant: unapt.   27. **maiden loss:** loss of virginity.   28. **dares
. . . no:** tells her not to.   29. **credent bulk:** my authority is so
great that I will be believed.   32. **sense:** feeling.
    Sc. v: 1. **me:** for me.   4. **drift:** purpose.   5. **blench:** start
aside.

---

164. **dark corners:** always meeting women in the dark.
167–68. **lives . . . them:** i.e., they are lies.   169. **woodman:** hun-
ter; i.e., of women.   184. **medlar:** fruit of the apple kind, eaten
only when it has gone soft.   186. **Rest . . . well:** I bid you fare-
well.
    Sc. iv: 1. **disvouched:** contradicted.   14. **devices:** plots.

SCENE VI. *Street near the city gate.*

[*Enter* ISABELLA *and* MARIANA.]

ISAB. To speak so indirectly I am loath.
I would say the truth, but to accuse him so,
That is your part. Yet I am advised to do it —
He says, to veil full purpose.°

MARI.   Be ruled by him.

ISAB. Besides, he tells me that if peradventure   5
He speak against me on the adverse side,
I should not think it strange, for 'tis a physic
That's bitter to sweet end.

MARI. I would Friar Peter ——

ISAB.   Oh, peace! The Friar is come.

[*Enter* FRIAR PETER.]

FRI. P. Come, I have found you out a stand° most
fit,   10
Where you may have such vantage° on the Duke,
He shall not pass you. Twice have the trumpets
sounded,
The generous° and gravest citizens
Have hent° the gates, and very near upon
The Duke is entering.Therefore hence, away!   15
[*Exeunt.*]

Act V

SCENE I. *The city gate.*

[MARIANA *veiled,* ISABELLA, *and* FRIAR PETER, *at their
stand. Enter* DUKE, VARRIUS, LORDS, ANGELO, ESCALUS,
LUCIO, PROVOST, OFFICERS, *and* CITIZENS,
at several doors.]

DUKE. My very worthy cousin,° fairly met!
Our old and faithful friend, we are glad to see you.

ANG. & ESCAL. Happy return be to your royal
Grace!

DUKE. Many and hearty thankings to you both.
We have made inquiry of you, and we hear   5
Such goodness of your justice that our soul
Cannot but yield you forth to public thanks,
Forerunning more requital.°

ANG.   You make my bonds° still greater.

DUKE. Oh, your desert speaks loud, and I should
wrong it
To lock it in the wards of covert bosom°   10
When it deserves, with characters° of brass,

A forted° residence 'gainst the tooth of time
And razure of oblivion. Give me your hand,
And let the subject° see, to make them know
That outward courtesies would fain proclaim   15
Favors that keep within. Come, Escalus,
You must walk by us on our other hand.
And good supporters are you.

[FRIAR PETER *and* ISABELLA *come forward.*]

FRI. P. Now is your time. Speak loud, and kneel
before him.   19

ISAB. Justice, O royal Duke! Vail your regard°
Upon a wronged, I would fain have said, a maid!
O worthy prince, dishonor not your eye
By throwing it on any other object
Till you have heard me in my true complaint,
And given me justice, justice, justice, justice!   25

DUKE. Relate your wrongs. In what? By whom?
Be brief.
Here is Lord Angelo shall give you justice.
Reveal yourself to him.

ISAB.   O worthy Duke,
You bid me seek redemption of the Devil.
Hear me yourself, for that which I must speak   30
Must either punish me, not being believed,
Or wring redress from you. Hear me, O hear me,
here!

ANG. My lord, her wits, I fear me, are not firm.
She hath been a suitor to me for her brother
Cut off by course of justice ——

ISAB.   By course of justice!   35

ANG. And she will speak most bitterly and strange.

ISAB. Most strange, but yet most truly, will I speak.
That Angelo's forsworn, is it not strange?
That Angelo's a murderer, is't not strange?
That Angelo is an adulterous thief,   40
A hypocrite, a virgin-violator,
Is it not strange and strange?

DUKE.   Nay, it is ten times strange.

ISAB. It is not truer he is Angelo
Than this is all as true as it is strange.
Nay, it is ten times true, for truth is truth   45
To the end of reckoning.

DUKE.   Away with her! — Poor soul,
She speaks this in the infirmity of sense.

ISAB. O Prince, I conjure thee, as thou believest
There is another comfort than this world,
That thou neglect me not, with that opinion   50
That I am touched with madness! Make not impos-
sible
That which but seems unlike. 'Tis not impossible
But one, the wicked'st caitiff° on the ground,
May seem as shy, as grave, as just, as absolute°
As Angelo. Even so may Angelo,   55
In all his dressings,° characts,° titles, forms,

Sc. vi: 4. veil . . . purpose: not to reveal our full plan.
10. stand: place.   11. vantage: advantageous position.   13. gen-
erous: well-born.   14. hent: occupied.

Act V, Sc. i: 1. cousin: kinsman.   8. Forerunning . . . re-
quital: preceding other forms of reward. bonds: debts.   10. cov-
ert bosom: i.e., the secrecy of my heart.   11. characters: letters.

12. forted: fortified.   14. the subject: my subjects.   20. Vail
. . . regard: lower your glance.   53. caitiff: wretch.   54. abso-
lute: perfect.   56. dressings: outward shows. characts: marks
of distinction.

Be an archvillain — believe it, royal Prince.
If he be less, he's nothing, but he's more
Had I more name for badness.

DUKE.   By mine honesty,
If she be mad — as I believe no other —   60
Her madness hath the oddest frame of sense,
Such a dependency of thing on thing,
As e'er I heard in madness.

ISAB.   O gracious Duke,
Harp not on that, nor do not banish reason
For inequality,° but let your reason serve   65
To make the truth appear where it seems hid,
And hide the false seems true.

DUKE.   Many that are not mad
Have, sure, more lack of reason. What would you
    say?

ISAB. I am the sister of one Claudio,
Condemned upon the act of fornication   70
To lose his head, condemned by Angelo.
I, in probation° of a sisterhood,
Was sent to by my brother, one Lucio
As then the messenger ——

LUCIO.   That's I, an't like° your Grace.
I came to her from Claudio, and desired her   75
To try her gracious fortune with Lord Angelo
For her poor brother's pardon.

ISAB.   That's he indeed.

DUKE. You were not bid to speak.

LUCIO.   No, my good lord,
Nor wished to hold my peace.

DUKE.   I wish you now, then.
Pray you take note of it. And when you have   80
A business for yourself, pray Heaven you then
Be perfect.

LUCIO.   I warrant your Honor.

DUKE. The warrant's for yourself, take heed to't.

ISAB. This gentleman told somewhat of my
    tale ——

LUCIO. Right.   85

DUKE. It may be right, but you are i' the wrong
To speak before your time. Proceed.

ISAB.   I went
To this pernicious caitiff Deputy ——

DUKE. That's somewhat madly spoken.

ISAB.   Pardon it,
The phrase is to the matter.°   90

DUKE. Mended again. The matter — proceed.

ISAB. In brief — to set the needless process by,
How I persuaded, how I prayed, and kneeled,
How he refelled° me, and how I replied —
For this was of much length — the vile conclu-
    sion
I now begin with grief and shame to utter.   96
He would not, but by gift of my chaste body

To his concupiscible° intemperate lust,
Release my brother, and, after much debatement,
My sisterly remorse° confutes mine honor,   100
And I did yield to him. But the next morn betimes,
His purpose surfeiting,° he sends a warrant
For my poor brother's head.

DUKE.   This is most likely!

ISAB. Oh, that it were as like° as it is true!

DUKE. By Heaven, fond° wretch, thou know'st
    not what thou speak'st,   105
Or else thou art suborned° against his honor
In hateful practice.° First, his integrity
Stands without blemish. Next, it imports no reason
That with such vehemency he should pursue   109
Faults proper° to himself. If he had so offended,
He would have weighed thy brother by himself,
And not have cut him off. Someone hath set you on.
Confess the truth, and say by whose advice
Thou camest here to complain.

ISAB.   And is this all?
Then, O you blessed ministers above,   115
Keep me in patience, and with ripened time
Unfold the evil which is here wrapped up
In countenance!° — Heaven shield your Grace from
    woe,
As I, thus wronged, hence unbelievèd go!   119

DUKE. I know you'd fain be gone. — An officer!
To prison with her! — Shall we thus permit
A blasting and a scandalous breath to fall
On him so near us? This needs must be a practice.
Who knew of your intent and coming hither?   124

ISAB. One that I would were here, Friar Lodo-
    wick.

DUKE. A ghostly Father, belike. Who knows that
    Lodowick?

LUCIO. My lord, I know him, 'tis a meddling friar,
I do not like the man. Had he been lay,° my lord,
For certain words he spake against your Grace   129
In your retirement, I had swinged° him soundly.

DUKE. Words against me! This's a good friar, be-
    like!
And to set on this wretched woman here
Against our substitute! Let this friar be found.

LUCIO. But yesternight, my lord, she and that
    friar,
I saw them at the prison. A saucy friar,   135
A very scurvy fellow.

FRI. P. Blessed be your royal Grace!
I have stood by, my lord, and I have heard
Your royal ear abused. First, hath this woman
Most wrongfully accused your substitute,   140
Who is as free from touch or soil with her

---

65. **inequality:** injustice.   72. **probation:** novitiate.   74. **an't like:** if it please.   90. **to . . . matter:** fitting.   94. **refelled:** refused.

98. **concupiscible:** lecherous.   100. **remorse:** pity.   102. **surfeiting:** sickening after excess.   104. **like:** likely.   105. **fond:** foolish.   106. **suborned:** bribed to make a false accusation.   107. **practice:** plot.   110. **proper:** belonging.   118. **countenance:** favoritism.   128. **lay:** a layman.   130. **swinged:** thrashed.

As she from one ungot.°
DUKE.   We did believe no less.
Know you that Friar Lodowick that she speaks
of?
FRI. P. I know him for a man divine and holy,
Not scurvy, nor a temporary° meddler   145
As he's reported by this gentleman,
And, on my trust, a man that never yet
Did, as he vouches, misreport your Grace.
LUCIO. My lord, most villainously, believe it.
FRI. P. Well, he in time may come to clear him-
self,   150
But at this instant he is sick, my lord,
Of a strange fever. Upon his mere request —
Being come to knowledge that there was complaint
Intended 'gainst Lord Angelo — came I hither,
To speak, as from his mouth, what he doth know
Is true and false, and what he with his oath   156
And all probation° will make up full clear,
Whensoever he's convented.° First, for this woman,
To justify this worthy nobleman,
So vulgarly and personally accused,   160
Her shall you hear disprovèd to her eyes
Till she herself confess it.
DUKE.   Good Friar, let's hear it.
[ISABELLA *is carried off guarded;*
and MARIANA *comes forward.*]
Do you not smile at this, Lord Angelo? —
O Heaven, the vanity of wretched fools! —
Give us some seats. Come, Cousin Angelo,   165
In this I'll be impartial,° be you judge
Of your own cause. Is this the witness, Friar?
First, let her show her face, and after speak.
MARI. Pardon, my lord, I will not show my face
Until my husband bid me.   170
DUKE. What, are you married?
MARI. No, my lord.
DUKE. Are you a maid?
MARI. No, my lord.
DUKE. A widow, then?   175
MARI. Neither, my lord.
DUKE. Why, you are nothing, then — neither
maid, widow, nor wife?
LUCIO. My lord, she may be a punk,° for many of
them are neither maid, widow, nor wife.   180
DUKE. Silence that fellow. I would he had some
cause
To prattle for himself.
LUCIO. Well, my lord.
MARI. My lord, I do confess I ne'er was married,
And I confess, besides, I am no maid.   185
I have known° my husband, yet my husband
Knows not that ever he knew me.

LUCIO. He was drunk, then, my lord. It can be no
better.   190
DUKE. For the benefit of silence, would thou wert
so too!
LUCIO. Well, my lord.
DUKE. This is no witness for Lord Angelo.
MARI. Now I come to't, my lord.
She that accuses him of fornication   195
In selfsame manner doth accuse my husband,
And charges him, my lord, with such a time
When I'll depose° I had him in mine arms
With all the effect of love.
ANG. Charges she moe° than me?
MARI.   Not that I know. 200
DUKE. No? You say your husband.
MARI. Why, just, my lord, and that is Angelo,
Who thinks he knows that he ne'er knew my body,
But knows he thinks that he knows Isabel's.   204
ANG. This is a strange abuse. Let's see thy face.
MARI. My husband bids me, now I will unmask.
[*Unveiling.*]
This is that face, thou cruel Angelo,
Which once thou sworest was worth the looking on.
This is the hand which, with a vowed contráct,
Was fast belocked in thine. This is the body   210
That took away the match° from Isabel,
And did supply thee at thy garden house
In her imagined person.
DUKE.   Know you this woman?
LUCIO. Carnally, she says.
DUKE.   Sirrah, no more!
LUCIO. Enough, my lord.   215
ANG. My lord, I must confess I know this woman.
And five years since there was some speech of mar-
riage
Betwixt myself and her, which was broke off,
Partly for that her promisèd proportions°
Came short of composition,° but in chief   220
For that her reputation was disvalued
In levity.° Since which time of five years
I never spake her with, saw her, nor heard from her,
Upon my faith and honor.
MARI.   Noble Prince,
As there comes light from Heaven and words from
breath,   225
As there is sense in truth and truth in virtue,
I am affianced° this man's wife as strongly
As words could make up vows. And, my good lord,
But Tuesday night last gone in's garden house
He knew me as a wife. As this is true,   230
Let me in safety raise me from my knees,
Or else for ever be confixèd° here,
A marble monument!

ANG.　　　　　　　I did but smile till now.
Now, good my lord, give me the scope of justice,
My patience here is touched. I do perceive　235
These poor informal° women are no more
But instruments of some more mightier member
That sets them on. Let me have way, my lord,
To find this practice out.
DUKE.　　　　　　　Aye, with my heart,
And punish them to your height of pleasure.　240
Thou foolish friar, and thou pernicious woman,
Compact° with her that's gone, think'st thou thy
　　oaths,
Though they would swear down each particular
　　saint,
Were testimonies against his worth and credit　244
That's sealed in approbation?° You, Lord Escalus,
Sit with my cousin, lend him your kind pains°
To find out this abuse, whence 'tis derived.
There is another friar that set them on.
Let him be sent for.
FRI. P.　Would he were here, my lord! For he in-
　　deed　250
Hath set the women on to this complaint.
Your Provost knows the place where he abides,
And he may fetch him.
DUKE.　　　　　Go, do it instantly. [*Exit* PROVOST.]
And you, my noble and well-warranted cousin,
Whom it concerns to hear this matter forth,　255
Do with your injuries as seems you best,
In any chastisement. I for a while will leave you,
But stir not you till you have well determined°
Upon these slanderers.　259
ESCAL.　My lord, we'll do it throughly.° [*Exit*
DUKE.] Signior Lucio, did not you say you knew
that Friar Lodowick to be a dishonest person?
LUCIO.　" *Cucullus non facit monachum.*"° Hon-
est in nothing but in his clothes, and one that hath
spoke most villainous speeches of the Duke.　265
ESCAL.　We shall entreat you to abide here till he
come, and enforce° them against him. We shall find
this friar a notable fellow.
LUCIO.　As any in Vienna, on my word.　269
ESCAL.　Call that same Isabel here once again. I
would speak with her. [*Exit an* ATTENDANT.] Pray
you, my lord, give me leave to question, you shall
see how I'll handle her.
LUCIO.　Not better than he, by her own report.
ESCAL.　Say you?　275
LUCIO.　Marry, sir, I think if you handled her pri-
vately, she would sooner confess. Perchance publicly
she'll be ashamed.
ESCAL.　I will go darkly° to work with her.

LUCIO.　That's the way, for women are light at
midnight.　281
[*Re-enter* OFFICERS *with* ISABELLA; *and* PROVOST *with
the* DUKE *in his friar's habit.*]
ESCAL.　Come on, mistress. Here's a gentlewoman
denies all that you have said.
LUCIO.　My lord, here comes the rascal I spoke of,
here with the Provost.　285
ESCAL.　In very good time. Speak not you to him
till we call upon you.
LUCIO.　Mum.
ESCAL.　Come, sir, did you set these women on
to slander Lord Angelo? They have confessed you
did.
DUKE.　'Tis false.　291
ESCAL.　How! Know you where you are?
DUKE.　Respect to your great place! And let the
　　Devil
Be sometime honored for his burning throne!　295
Where is the Duke? 'Tis he should hear me speak.
ESCAL.　The Duke's in us,° and we will hear you
　　speak.
Look you speak justly.
DUKE.　Boldly, at least. But, oh, poor souls,
Come you to seek the lamb here of the fox?　300
Good night to your redress! Is the Duke gone?
Then is your cause gone too. The Duke's unjust.
Thus to retort° your manifest appeal,
And put your trial in the villain's mouth
Which here you come to accuse.　305
LUCIO.　This is the rascal, this is he I spoke of.
ESCAL.　Why, thou unreverend and unhallowed
　　friar,
Is't not enough thou hast suborned these women
To accuse this worthy man, but, in foul mouth,
And in the witness of his proper° ear,　310
To call him villain? And then to glance from him
To the Duke himself, to tax° him with injustice?
Take him hence, to the rack with him! We'll touse°
　　you
Joint by joint, but we will know his purpose.
What, " unjust "!
DUKE.　　　　　　　Be not so hot. The Duke　315
Dare no more stretch this finger of mine than he
Dare rack his own. His subject am I not,
Nor here provincial.° My business in this state
Made me a looker-on here in Vienna,
Where I have seen corruption boil and bubble　320
Till it o'errun the stew° — laws for all faults,
But faults so countenanced that the strong statutes
Stand like the forfeits° in a barber's shop,
As much in mock as mark.°

236. informal: crazy.　242. Compact: confederate.　245. sealed
in approbation: warranted as true.　246. pains: trouble.　258. de-
termined: decided.　260. throughly: thoroughly.　263. Cucullus
. . . monachum: a cowl does not make a monk.　267. enforce:
bring home, declare.　279. darkly: subtly.

297. in us: represented by us.　303. retort: reject.　310. proper:
own.　312. tax: charge.　313. touse: tear.　318. provincial:
a member of this ecclesiastical province.　321. stew: caldron.
323. forfeits: teeth extracted by barbers (who were also sur-
geons and dentists) strung up as trophies of their trade.　324. As
. . . mark: to be mocked at as much as observed.

ESCAL. Slander to the state! Away with him to
prison!   325
ANG. What can you vouch against him, Signior
Lucio?
Is this the man that you did tell us of?
LUCIO. 'Tis he, my lord. Come hither, goodman
baldpate. Do you know me?   330
DUKE. I remember you, sir, by the sound of your
voice. I met you at the prison, in the absence of the
Duke.
LUCIO. Oh, did you so? And do you remember
what you said of the Duke?
DUKE. Most notedly, sir.   335
LUCIO. Do you so, sir? And was the Duke a flesh-
monger, a fool, and a coward, as you then reported
him to be?
DUKE. You must, sir, change persons with me ere
you make that report. You indeed spoke so of
him, and much more, much worse.   340
LUCIO. O thou damnable fellow! Did not I pluck
thee by the nose for thy speeches?
DUKE. I protest I love the Duke as I love myself.
ANG. Hark how the villain would close° now,
after his treasonable abuses!   345
ESCAL. Such a fellow is not to be talked withal.
Away with him to prison! Where is the Provost?
Away with him to prison! Lay bolts enough upon
him. Let him speak no more. Away with those gig-
lets° too, and with the other confederate companion!
DUKE. [To the PROVOST] Stay, sir, stay awhile.
ANG. What, resists he? Help him, Lucio.
LUCIO. Come, sir, come, sir, come, sir. Foh,   355
sir! Why, you bald-pated, lying rascal, you must be
hooded, must you? Show your knave's visage, with
a pox to you! Show your sheepbiting° face, and be
hanged an hour! Will't not off?   360
[Pulls off the friar's hood, and discovers the Duke.]
DUKE. Thou art the first knave that e'er madest a
Duke.
First, Provost, let me bail these gentle three.
[To LUCIO] Sneak not away, sir, for the Friar and
you
Must have a word anon. Lay hold on him.
LUCIO. This may prove worse than hanging.   365
DUKE. [To ESCALUS] What you have spoke I par-
don. Sit you down.
We'll borrow place of him. [To ANGELO] Sir, by
your leave.
Hast thou or word, or wit, or impudence,
That yet can do thee office? If thou hast,
Rely upon it till my tale be heard,   370
And hold no longer out.
ANG.   O my dread lord,
I should be guiltier than my guiltiness
To think I can be undiscernible°

When I perceive your Grace, like power divine,
Hath looked upon my passes.° Then, good Prince,
No longer session° hold upon my shame,   376
But let my trial be mine own confession.
Immediate sentence then, and sequent° death,
Is all the grace I beg.
DUKE.   Come hither, Mariana.
Say, wast thou e'er contracted to this woman?   380
ANG. I was, my lord.
DUKE. Go take her hence, and marry her in-
stantly.
Do you the office, Friar, which consummate,
Return him here again. Go with him, Provost.
[Exeunt ANGELO, MARIANA, FRIAR PETER,
and PROVOST.]
ESCAL. My lord, I am more amazed at his dis-
honor   385
Than at the strangeness of it.
DUKE.   Come hither, Isabel.
Your friar is now your Prince. As I was then
Advértising° and holy to your business,
Not changing heart with habit, I am still
Attorneyed° at your service.
ISAB.   Oh, give me pardon   390
That I, your vassal,° have employed and pained
Your unknown sovereignty!
DUKE.   You are pardoned, Isabel.
And now, dear maid, be you as free to us.
Your brother's death, I know, sits at your heart,
And you may marvel why I obscured myself,   395
Laboring to save his life, and would not rather
Make rash remonstrance° of my hidden power
Than let him so be lost. O most kind maid,
It was the swift celerity of his death,
Which I did think with slower foot came on,   400
That brained my purpose. But peace be with him!
That life is better life, past fearing death,
Than that which lives to fear. Make it your comfort,
So happy is your brother.
ISAB.   I do, my lord.
[Re-enter ANGELO, MARIANA, FRIAR PETER,
and PROVOST.]
DUKE. For this new-married man approaching
here,   405
Whose salt° imagination yet hath wronged
Your well-defended honor, you must pardon
For Mariana's sake. But as he adjudged your
brother —
Being criminal, in double violation
Of sacred chastity, and of promise breach   410
Thereon dependent, for your brother's life —
The very mercy of the law cries out
Most audible, even from his proper tongue,

344. close: "climb down."   349. giglets: wantons.   359. sheep-
biting: sheepstealing.   373. undiscernible: not revealed.

375. passes: acts, trespasses. 376. session: trial.   378. se-
quent: following. 388. Advertising: attentive.   390. Attor-
neyed: employed as your pleader. 391. vassal: slave. 397. rash
remonstrance: hasty demonstration. 406. salt: lustful.

" An Angelo for Claudio, death for death! "   414
Haste still pays haste, and leisure answers leisure,
Like doth quit° like, and measure still for measure.
Then, Angelo, thy fault's thus manifested,
Which, though thou wouldst deny, denies thee van-
    tage.
We do condemn thee to the very block   419
Where Claudio stooped to death, and with like haste.
Away with him!

    MARI.   O my most gracious lord,
I hope you will not mock me with a husband.

    DUKE. It is your husband mocked you with a hus-
    band.
Consenting to the safeguard of your honor,
I thought your marriage fit, else imputation,°   425
For that he knew you, might reproach your life
And choke your good to come. For his possessions,
Although by confiscation they are ours,
We do instate and widow you withal,°
To buy you a better husband.

    MARI.   O my dear lord,   430
I crave no other, nor no better man.

    DUKE. Never crave him, we are definitive.°

    MARI. Gentle my liege——   [*Kneeling.*]

    DUKE.   You do but lose your labor.
Away with him to death! [*To* LUCIO] Now, sir, to
    you.

    MARI. O my good lord! Sweet Isabel, take my
    part,   435
Lend me your knees, and all my life to come
I'll lend you all my life to do you service.

    DUKE. Against all sense you do impórtune her.
Should she kneel down in mercy of this fact,
Her brother's ghost his pavèd° bed would break,
And take her hence in horror.   441

    MARI.   Isabel,
Sweet Isabel, do yet but kneel by me,
Hold up your hands, say nothing, I'll speak all.
They say best men are molded out of faults,
And, for the most, become much more the better
For being a little bad. So may my husband.   446
O Isabel, will you not lend a knee?

    DUKE. He dies for Claudio's death.

    ISAB.   Most bounteous sir, [*Kneeling.*]
Look, if it please you, on this man condemned
As if my brother lived. I partly think   450
A due sincerity governed his deeds,
Till he did look on me. Since it is so,
Let him not die. My brother had but justice,
In that he did the thing for which he died.
For Angelo,   455
His act did not o'ertake his bad intent,°
And must be buried but as an intent

That perished by the way. Thoughts are no subjects,°
Intents but merely thoughts.

    MARI.   Merely, my lord.

    DUKE. Your suit's unprofitable. Stand up, I say.
I have bethought me of another fault.   461
Provost, how came it Claudio was beheaded
At an unusual hour?

    PROV.   It was commanded so.

    DUKE. Had you a special warrant for the deed?

    PROV. No, my good lord, it was by private mes-
    sage.   465

    DUKE. For which I do discharge you of your office.
Give up your keys.

    PROV.   Pardon me, noble lord,
I thought it was a fault, but knew it not,
Yet did repent me, after more advice.°
For testimony whereof, one in the prison   470
That should by private order else have died
I have reserved alive.

    DUKE.   What's he?

    PROV.   His name is Barnardine.

    DUKE. I would thou hadst done so by Claudio.
Go fetch him hither, let me look upon him.

                    [*Exit* PROVOST.]

    ESCAL. I am sorry one so learned and so wise   475
As you, Lord Angelo, have still° appeared
Should slip so grossly, both in the heat of blood
And lack of tempered judgment afterward.

    ANG. I am sorry that such sorrow I procure,
And so deep sticks it in my penitent heart   480
That I crave death more willingly than mercy.
'Tis my deserving, and I do entreat it.

    [*Re-enter* PROVOST, *with* BARNARDINE, CLAUDIO
          muffled,° *and* JULIET.]

    DUKE. Which is that Barnardine?

    PROV.   This, my lord.

    DUKE. There was a friar told me of this man.
Sirrah, thou art said to have a stubborn soul   485
That apprehends no further than this world,
And squarest° thy life according. Thou'rt con-
    demned.
But, for those earthly faults, I quit° them all,
And pray thee take this mercy to provide
For better times to come. Friar, advise him,   490
I leave him to your hand. What muffled fellow's
    that?

    PROV. This is another prisoner that I saved,
Who should have died when Claudio lost his head,
As like almost to Claudio as himself.

                [*Unmuffles* CLAUDIO.]

    DUKE. [*To* ISABELLA] If he be like your brother,
    for his sake   495
Is he pardoned, and, for your lovely sake,

---

416. quit: pay for.   425. imputation: slander.   429. instate . . .
withal: bestow on you as his widow.   432. definitive: resolute.
440. paved: Persons of rank were buried inside the church be-
neath the pavement.   456. His . . . intent: he did not commit
the act which he intended.

458. no subjects: not subject to punishment.   469. advice: con-
sideration.   476. still: always.   482 s.d., muffled: i.e., his
face concealed in a muffler.   487. squarest: measurest.
488. quit: forgive.

Give me your hand and say you will be mine,
He is my brother too. But fitter time for that.
By this Lord Angelo perceives he's safe,
Methinks I see a quickening in his eye.   500
Well, Angelo, your evil quits° you well.
Look that you love your wife, her worth worth
    yours.
I find an apt remission° in myself,
And yet here's one in place I cannot pardon.
[*To* LUCIO] You, sirrah, that knew me for a fool, a
    coward,   505
One all of luxury,° an ass, a madman,
Wherein have I so deserved of you
That you extol me thus?
    LUCIO. 'Faith, my lord, I spoke it but according to
the trick. If you will hang me for it, you may, but I
had rather it would please you I might be whipped.
    DUKE. Whipped first, sir, and hanged after.
Proclaim it, Provost, round about the city,
If any woman wronged by this lewd fellow —   515
As I have heard him swear himself there's one
Whom he begot with child — let her appear
And he shall marry her. The nuptial finished,
Let him be whipped and hanged.
    LUCIO. I beseech your Highness, do not marry me
to a whore. Your Highness said even now I made
you a Duke. Good my lord, do not recompense me
in making me a cuckold.

501. quits: pays back.   503. remission: readiness to forgive.
506. luxury: lust.

    DUKE. Upon mine honor, thou shalt marry her.
Thy slanders I forgive, and therewithal   525
Remit thy other forfeits.° — Take him to prison,
And see our pleasure herein executed.
    LUCIO. Marrying a punk, my lord, is pressing to
death° whipping, and hanging.
    DUKE. Slandering a prince deserves it.   530
        [*Exeunt* OFFICERS *with* LUCIO.]
She, Claudio, that you wronged, look you restore.
Joy to you, Mariana! Love her, Angelo.
I have confessed her,° and I know her virtue.
Thanks, good friend Escalus, for thy much goodness,
There's more behind° that is more gratulate.°   535
Thanks, Provost, for thy care and secrecy.
We shall employ thee in a worthier place.
Forgive him, Angelo, that brought you home
The head of Ragozine for Claudio's.
The offense pardons itself. Dear Isabel,   540
I have a motion° much imports your good,
Whereto if you'll a willing ear incline,
What's mine is yours, and what is yours is mine.
So bring us to our palace, where we'll show
What's yet behind, that's meet you all should know.
        [*Exeunt.*]

526. forfeits: punishments.   528-29. pressing to death: See
Gen. Intro. p. 27b.   533. confessed her: heard her confession;
i.e., when he was posing as a friar.   535. behind: to come.
gratulate: gratifying.   541. motion: proposal.

THE TRAGEDY OF KING LEAR

Introduction

The Tragedy of King Lear is usually regarded by critics as Shakespeare's greatest play, but it is not his most popular, for there is something terrifying in the grandeur of the tragedy and its immense pessimism. Nor is the play often acted on the stage, for the part of Lear requires an actor of exceptional range of emotional expression. Indifferently produced, *Lear* is tedious, but when greatly acted it is almost too intolerably moving.

King Lear can be more precisely dated than most of Shakespeare's plays. On November 26, 1607, Nathaniel Butter and John Busby entered in the Register of the Stationers' Company and so claimed their right to print " A booke called Master William Shakespeare his historye of King Lear, as yt was played before the Kinges maiestie at Whitehall vppon Sainct Stephens night (December 26) at Christmas Last, by his maiesties servantes playinge vsually at the Globe on the Bankysde."

Lear was thus acted before King James and his Court in the Christmas holidays of 1606. The earliest quarto of the play (Q1) is dated 1608. There are also some evidences in the play itself which show that Shakespeare wrote it between February and December 1606. Gloucester's observations on " these late eclipses in the sun and moon " probably refer to notable eclipses that occurred on September 27 and October 2, 1605. To the superstitious, an eclipse was always an alarming event. Shakespeare, however, took these speeches from a pamphlet called *Strange, fearful and true news which happened at Carlstadt in the Kingdom of Croatia*. It was translated from the High Dutch and told of fearful signs and portents, which according to the editor, one Edward Gresham, an almanac-writer, were divine warnings of threatening disasters:

The Earth's and Moon's late and horrible obscurations, the frequent eclipsations of the fixed bodies; by the wandering, the fixed stars, I mean the planets, within these few years more than ordinary, shall without doubt (salved divine inhibition) have their effects no less admirable than the positions unusual. Which PEUCER with many more too long to rehearse out of continual observation and the consent of all

authors noted to be new leagues, traitorous designments, catching at kingdoms, translation of empire, downfall of men in authority, emulations, ambition, innovations, factious sects, schisms and much disturbance and troubles in religion and matters of the Church, with many other things infallible in sequent such orbical positions and phenomenes.

The preface to this astonishing work was dated February 11, 1606. The similarity of phrase, rhythm, and sentiment is too close to have been accidental. Shakespeare also took a few details from *A declaration of egregious popish impostures to withdraw the hearts of her Majesty's subjects from their allegiance, and from the truth of the Christian religion, professed in England, under the pretense of casting out devils*. This book was written in 1602–03 by the Reverend Samuel Harsnett, chaplain to the Bishop of London. Harsnett had taken considerable part in the controversies which raged around John Darrell the exorcist (see *T. Night* Intro. p. 567a-b), and was the author of the official exposure of Darrell's claims. After the Darrell controversy had died down, Harsnett turned to attack the Jesuit exorcists in *A Declaration*. From this book Shakespeare took also the names of Edgar's fiends — Frateretto, Flibbertigibbet, Hopdidance, Modo and Mahu.

The text of *King Lear* is difficult. Q1 is very badly printed and full of errors. Many verse lines are printed as prose, the punctuation is chaotic, and misprints and meaningless phrases are common. There has been considerable controversy among scholars about the origin of this text but so far no wholly convincing explanation has been put forward to account for all its peculiarities. The version of the play printed in the first folio in 1623 was based on a copy of Q1 which had been very carefully corrected and much revised; it omits about three hundred lines and adds a few new passages. Editors in preparing a modern text usually make an amalgamation of Q1 and F1, adapting those readings which seem best.

The story of King Lear and his three daughters was well known. It was one of the many fables which old chroniclers had inserted into the history of England to bridge the gap between Biblical history and the time when records of fact begin. In Holinshed's *Chronicles,* for instance, it is stated that:

Leir the son of Baldud was admitted ruler over the Britons, in the year of the world 3105, at what time Joash reigned in Judah. This Leir was a prince of right noble demeanor, governing his land and subjects in great wealth. He made the town of Caerleir now called Leicester, which standeth upon the river of Sore. It is written that he had by his wife three daughters without other issue, whose names were Gonorilla, Regan, and Cordeilla, which daughters he greatly loved, but especially Cordeilla, the youngest, far above the two elder. When this Leir therefore was come to great years, and began to wax unwieldy through age, he thought to understand the affections of his daughters toward him, and prefer her whom he best loved to the succession over the kingdom. Whereupon he first asked Gonorilla, the eldest, how well she loved him: who calling her gods to record, protested that she loved him more than her own life, which by right and reason should be most dear unto her. With which answer the father being well pleased, turned to the second, and demanded of her how well she loved him: who answered (confirming her sayings with great oaths) that she loved him more than tongue could express, and far above all other creatures of the world.

Then called he his youngest daughter Cordeilla before him, and asked of her what account she made of him, unto whom she made this answer as followeth: " Knowing the great love and fatherly zeal that you have always born toward me (for the which I may not answer you otherwise than I think, and as my conscience leadeth me) I protest unto you that I have loved you ever, and will continually (while I live) love you as my natural father. And if you would more understand of the love that I bear you, ascertain yourself that so much as you have, so much you are worth, and so much I love you, and no more." The father, being nothing content with this answer, married his two eldest daughters, the one unto Henninus the Duke of Cornwall, and the other unto Maglanus the Duke of Albania, betwixt whom he willed and ordained that his land should be divided after his death, and the one half thereof immediately should be assigned to them in hand: but for the third daughter Cordeilla he reserved nothing.

There are various versions of the rest of the story, but all agree in the general outline: that after Lear had foolishly disinherited his youngest daughter, he was driven out by his two elder daughters and at last made his way to France.

Here his youngest daughter received him kindly and raised an army to restore him to his kingdom. In the war which followed, the two wicked sisters and their husbands were destroyed. The story is related in Spenser's *Fairie Queene,* Book 2, Canto X, Stanza 32, and concludes thus:

So to his crown she him restored again,
  In which he died, made ripe for death by eld,
  And after willed it should to her remain.
Who peaceably the same long time did weld,
And all men's hearts in due obedience held,
Till that her sisters' children, woxen strong,
Through proud ambition, against her rebelled,
And overcommen kept in prison long,
Till weary of that wretched life, herself she hong.

Spenser was the first to call the youngest daughter Cordelia. In the other versions she is Cordeil, Cordeilla, or Cordella. Shakespeare took the name from Spenser, but he was the first to give the plot an unhappy ending. He thus transmuted an old tale in which evil is punished and good restored into a tremendous and pessimistic drama, of which Gloucester's words form the most fitting motto:

As flies to wanton boys are we to the gods.
They kill us for their sport.

The whole conception of the play is Shakespeare's own; he owed nothing to his sources for the madness of Lear, Kent's devotion, the storm, the fool, Oswald, and above all the ending with Cordelia hanged and Lear dying of old age and a broken heart.

Shakespeare's play has a double plot. Parallel with the sufferings of Lear at the hands of his daughters runs the story of Gloucester, who is destroyed by his own base son. This story was apparently suggested by a brief tale in Sir Philip Sidney's romance *Arcadia* of an old Prince of Paphlagonia who was similarly served by a bastard son.

Shakespeare, however, was not the first to write a play on the theme. In Henslowe's *Diary* there are two mentions of performances of a " King Lear " at the Rose theater in 1594. This play, or yet another on the theme was published in 1605 as *The True Chronicle History of King Leir and his three daughters, Gonorill, Ragan and Cordella.* The play of *King Leir* is very crude. It begins with Leir proclaiming that, since he has lost his wife, his daughters lack a mother's care and must marry. The first scenes follow the familiar story. Ragan and Gonorill are bestowed on Cornwall and Cambria, and Cordella is cast out, but she finds a protector in the Gallian King, who follows her in disguise, falls in love, and takes her back with him to France. Gonorill soon tires of Leir and ill-treats him. Leir is deserted by all except Perillus, who remains as his faithful but rather ineffective councilor. Perillus advises him to go to Ragan, but she likewise ill-treats him. The two old men then wander away. A murderer is sent in pursuit to kill them, but he relents because whenever he is about to commit the deed a clap of thunder warns him to desist. At last Leir and Perillus reach the coast of Britain and pass over to France, where they land. There, as it happens, the Gallian King and Cordella, having disguised themselves as country-folk, are spending a day by the seashore. They come on the two old men, half-starving. Leir at first does not recognize his wronged daughter. When Cordella reveals herself, he kneels to her for forgiveness, but she insists that it is her duty to kneel, and the two indulge in a competition of kneeling for about sixty lines. Thereafter, the Gallian King invades Britain. There is a short battle in which the wicked daughters are defeated and Leir and his party are victorious. In this play, as in all other versions except Shakespeare's, Leir is restored to his kingdom.

In writing *King Lear,* Shakespeare thus had the advantage that the story was quite familiar to his audience. He could therefore begin where he wished without elaborate explanation. Shakespeare's *Lear* opens at the moment when the old King has already decided in council that he will divide his kingdom and is about to ratify the decision in a public ceremony at which his daughters are expected to play their parts. It is the last time when the old King is ever to appear in his full majesty, and he expects his vanity to be humored to the full. Goneril and Regan easily fall in with this mood, but Cordelia, bitterly resentful of the order to " heave her heart into her mouth," suffers from a kind of paralysis of the will. Whatever she might have wished to say on any other occasion, all that she can utter is " Nothing." To Lear it is the worst public affront that he has ever suffered and, coming so unexpectedly from his best-loved daughter, it arouses in him the spirit of wrath. His plans are upset, Kent, his one faithful follower, is cast out, and Lear is alone. The play thus reaches its decisive moment in the very first scene. Thereafter we are shown how this tyrannical old man is goaded beyond endurance until his spirit breaks and he is purged of his wrath.

Lear dominates the first scene. He is still King, but as soon as he has resigned his crown, he ceases to be the master and becomes the subject of his daughters. He refuses to realize the change, and in Goneril's house he behaves in complete disregard of her wishes or convenience. When she protests at the ill behavior of his followers, her words are sneering and unkind, but not unreasonable. Lear's terrible curse is not justified (I.iv.297–312). Sending Kent before him, he rushes away to find Regan, his second daughter. When he reaches Gloucester's castle, whither Regan and Cornwall, her husband, have removed, the first person to greet him is Kent, his messenger, locked in the stocks as if he were no better than a common vagabond. When Regan treats him more coldly even than Goneril, and later, when Goneril herself arrives, Lear is left no choice but abject submission. This is too much for the proud old man and in his ungovernable rage he dashes out into the storm, followed by Kent and the Fool.

Lear's madness can be traced step by step. As events develop it becomes inevitable. A man of such violent temper must never be checked, or disaster will follow; he has no reserve of emotion or restraint. Cordelia angers him and she is cursed. Goneril offends him and she is cursed to the limits of malediction. Regan and Goneril both offend him and Lear's language fails, for he has exhausted the power of relieving emotion by words, and he cannot and will not allow anger the relief of tears. The only other relief possible is madness. The tragedy of Lear is that he brings his suffering on his own head by a grievous stupidity.

Linked to the story of Lear and his three daughters is the story of Gloucester and his two sons. Edmund, the bastard, is the most interesting and unscrupulous villain created by Shakespeare. He has every quality which makes for material success. He has a clear head; he is an opportunist; he has no scruples or conscience and is therefore unhampered by those restraints which check normal men; he is indeed the perfect egoist. In the play Edmund is shown climbing step by step to the highest rung. First he ousts his brother from his father's favor. Next he betrays his father to Cornwall and so becomes Earl of Gloucester. Then complications arise as both sisters fall in love with him. He plays with them both, waiting to see which of them will give him the greater advantage. After the battle, when Lear and Cordelia are his prisoners, he orders them to be murdered, for he now sees the final step. With the old King dead and both daughters in his power, there is nothing to prevent him from winning the crown.

Lear is a difficult play for modern readers. Shakespeare was always experimenting; in this play he experimented with the possibilities of a concentrated poetic imagery that is most elaborate and at times exceedingly difficult to comprehend.

The use of a particular kind of symbolic imagery is especially remarkable and well worth detailed study. The play abounds in animal images. In *Hamlet* man was "the paragon of animals." In *Lear* he is "hog in sloth, fox in stealth, wolf in greediness, dog in madness, lion in prey." It is as if Shakespeare wished to portray a world in which most men and women are beasts, and only

the exceptional few redeem "Nature from the general curse." Apart from this use of images which constantly recur, Shakespeare effected a grim irony by the use of two words which sound throughout the play like the tolling of a knell: "nature" and "nothing."

Lear, Gloucester, and Edmund each in turn call on Nature. To the old fathers Nature is the goddess of natural affection by whose law children are naturally loyal to their parents. To Edmund — the "natural" son — Nature is the goddess of the wild; he is "natural" man because he is by nature a beast. "Nature," "natural," and "unnatural" recur again and again with every shade of meaning and misunderstanding.

There is also a devastating irony in the word "nothing." Cordelia at the critical moment can only utter "Nothing," and Lear replies "Nothing will come of nothing." He is wrong — from this one word "nothing" begins the whole devastating tragedy.

King Lear

DRAMATIS PERSONAE

LEAR, *King of Britain*
KING OF FRANCE
DUKE OF BURGUNDY
DUKE OF CORNWALL
DUKE OF ALBANY
EARL OF KENT
EARL OF GLOUCESTER
EDGAR, *son to Gloucester*
EDMUND, *bastard son to Gloucester*
CURAN, *a courtier*
OLD MAN, *tenant to Gloucester*
DOCTOR
FOOL

OSWALD, *steward to Goneril*
A CAPTAIN *employed by Edmund*
GENTLEMAN *attendant on Cordelia*
HERALD
SERVANTS *to Cornwall*

GONERIL
REGAN } *daughters to Lear*
CORDELIA

KNIGHTS *of Lear's train*, CAPTAINS, MESSENGERS, SOLDIERS, *and* ATTENDANTS

SCENE — *Britain.*

Act I

SCENE I.° KING LEAR'S *palace.*

[*Enter* KENT, GLOUCESTER, *and* EDMUND.]

KENT. I thought the King had more affected° the Duke of Albany than Cornwall.

GLO. It did always seem so to us. But now, in the division of the kingdom, it appears not which of the Dukes he values most, for equalities are so weighed that curiosity in neither can make choice of either's moiety.° 7

KENT. Is not this your son, my lord?

GLO. His breeding, sir, hath been at my charge. I have so often blushed to acknowledge him that now I am brazed° to it. 11

KENT. I cannot conceive° you.

GLO. Sir, this young fellow's mother could. Whereupon she grew round-wombed, and had indeed, sir, a son for her cradle ere she had a husband for her bed. Do you smell a fault?

KENT. I cannot wish the fault undone, the issue° of it being so proper.° 18

GLO. But I have, sir, a son by order of law, some year elder than this, who yet is no dearer in my account. Though this knave came something saucily into the world before he was sent for, yet was his mother fair, there was good sport at his making,

and the whoreson° must be acknowledged. Do you know this noble gentleman, Edmund? 25

EDM. No, my lord.

GLO. My Lord of Kent. Remember him hereafter as my honorable friend.

EDM. My services to your lordship.

KENT. I must love you, and sue to know you better. 31

EDM. Sir, I shall study deserving.°

GLO. He hath been out nine years, and away he shall again. The King is coming.

[*Sennet.*° *Enter one bearing a coronet,*° KING LEAR, CORNWALL, ALBANY, GONERIL, REGAN, CORDELIA, *and* ATTENDANTS.]

LEAR. Attend° the lords of France and Burgundy, Gloucester. 35

GLO. I shall, my liege.

[*Exeunt* GLOUCESTER *and* EDMUND.]

LEAR. Meantime we shall express our darker purpose.°
Give me the map there. Know that we have divided
In three our kingdom. And 'tis our fast intent
To shake all cares and business from our age, 40
Conferring them on younger strengths while we
Unburdened crawl toward death. Our son° of Cornwall,
And you, our no less loving son of Albany,
We have this hour a constant will° to publish 44
Our daughters' several° dowers, that future strife

Act I, Sc. i: As the opening words of this scene show, Lear has already decided on the division of the kingdom. There remains only the public and ceremonious announcement of his abdication. **1. more affected:** had more affection for. **5–7. equalities . . . moiety:** for their shares are so equal that a close examination (*curiosity*) cannot decide which share (*moiety*) is to be preferred. **11. brazed:** become brazen; lit., brass-plated. **12. conceive:** understand. **17. issue:** result; i.e., child. **18. proper:** handsome.

24. whoreson: rogue; lit., son of a whore. **32. I . . . deserving:** I shall do my best to deserve your favor. **34 s.d., Sennet:** trumpet call used to announce the approach of a procession. **coronet:** a small crown worn by those of lesser rank than King. **35. Attend:** wait on. **37. we . . . purpose:** we will explain what we have hitherto kept dark. Lear, speaking officially as King, uses the royal "we." **42. son:** son-in-law. **44. constant will:** firm intention. **45. several:** separate.

May be prevented° now. The Princes, France and
 Burgundy,
Great rivals in our youngest daughter's love,
Long in our Court have made their amorous so-
 journ,
And here are to be answered. Tell me, my daugh-
 ters,
Since now we will divest us both of rule,   50
Interest of territory, cares of state,
Which of you shall we say doth love us most?
That we our largest bounty may extend
Where nature doth with merit challenge.° Goneril,
Our eldest-born, speak first.   55
 GON. Sir, I love you more than words can wield°
  the matter,
Dearer than eyesight, space, and liberty,
Beyond what can be valued, rich or rare,
No less than life, with grace, health, beauty, honor,
As much as child e'er loved or father found —   60
A love that makes breath poor and speech unable —
Beyond all manner of so much° I love you.
 COR. [*Aside*] What shall Cordelia do? Love, and
  be silent.
 LEAR. Of all these bounds, even from this line to
  this,   64
With shadowy forests and with champains riched,°
With plenteous rivers and wide-skirted meads,°
We make thee lady. To thine and Albany's issue
Be this perpetual. What says our second daughter,
Our dearest Regan, wife to Cornwall? Speak.   70
 REG. I am made of that self metal° as my sister,
And prize me at her worth.° In my true heart
I find she names my very deed of love,
Only she comes too short. That I profess
Myself an enemy to all other joys   75
Which the most precious square of sense possesses,°
And find I am alone felicitate°
In your dear Highness' love.
 COR.   [*Aside*] Then poor Cordelia!
And yet not so, since I am sure my love's
More ponderous than my tongue.°   80
 LEAR. To thee and thine hereditary ever
Remain this ample third of our fair kingdom,
No less in space, validity° and pleasure
Than that conferred on Goneril. Now, our joy,
Although the last, not least, to whose young love 85
The vines of France and milk of Burgundy
Strive to be interested,° what can you say to draw

A third more opulent than your sisters? Speak.
 COR. Nothing, my lord.°
 LEAR. Nothing!   90
 COR. Nothing.
 LEAR. Nothing will come of nothing.° Speak
  again.
 COR. Unhappy that I am, I cannot heave
My heart into my mouth. I love your Majesty
According to my bond,° nor more nor less.   95
 LEAR. How, how, Cordelia! Mend your speech a
  little,
Lest it may mar your fortunes.
 COR.   Good my lord,
You have begot me, bred me, loved me. I
Return those duties back as are right fit,
Obey you, love you, and most honor you.   100
Why have my sisters husbands if they say
They love you all? Haply,° when I shall wed,
That lord whose hand must take my plight° shall
  carry
Half my love with him, half my care and duty.
Sure, I shall never marry like my sisters,   105
To love my father all.
 LEAR. But goes thy heart with this?
 COR.   Aye, good my lord.
 LEAR. So young, and so untender?
 COR. So young, my lord, and true.
 LEAR. Let it be so. Thy truth then be thy dower.
For, by the sacred radiance of the sun,   111
The mysteries of Hecate,° and the night,
By all the operation of the orbs°
From whom we do exist and cease to be,
Here I disclaim° all my paternal care,   115
Propinquity,° and property of blood,°
And as a stranger to my heart and me
Hold thee from this forever. The barbarous Scyth-
  ian,°
Or he that makes his generation messes
To gorge his appetite° shall to my bosom   120
Be as well neighbored, pitied, and relieved°
As thou my sometime daughter.
 KENT.   Good my liege ——
 LEAR. Peace, Kent!
Come not between the dragon° and his wrath.
I loved her most, and thought to set my rest° 125

89. **Nothing, my lord:** See Intro. *Lear*, p. 782a.   92. **Nothing
. . . nothing:** the old maxim *Ex nihilo nihil fit.*   95. **bond:** i.e.,
the tie of natural affection and duty which binds daughter to
father.   102. **Haply:** it may happen.   103. **plight:** promise made
at betrothal.   112. **Hecate:** goddess of witchcraft. Cf. *Macb.*
II.i.52; III.ii.41–43.   113. **orbs:** stars.   115. **disclaim:** renounce.
116. **Propinquity:** relationship. **property of blood:** claim which
you have as being of my blood.   118. **Scythian:** inhabitant of
South Russia, regarded as the worst kind of savage.   119–20. **Or
. . . appetite:** or he that feeds gluttonously on his own children.
121. **relieved:** helped in distress.   124. **dragon:** the Dragon of
Britain was Lear's heraldic device and also a symbol of his feroc-
ity.   125. **set . . . my rest:** lit., to risk all — a term in the card
game called primero. Lear uses it with the double meaning of
"find rest."

46. **prevented:** forestalled.   54. **Where . . . challenge:** where
natural affection and desert have an equal claim on my bounty.
56. **wield:** declare.   62. **Beyond . . . much:** i.e., beyond all these
things.   65. **champains riched:** enriched with fertile fields.
66. **wide-skirted meads:** extensive pasture lands.   71. **self metal:**
same material.   72. **prize . . . worth:** value me at the same price.
76. **most . . . possesses:** feeling in the highest degree pos-
sesses. **square:** the carpenter's rule; i.e., measurement.   77. **fe-
licitate:** made happy.   79–80. **love's . . . tongue:** love is heavier
than my words.   83. **validity:** value.   87. **interested:** have a
share in.

On her kind nursery.° Hence, and avoid° my sight!
So be my grave my peace, as here I give
Her father's heart from her! Call France. Who stirs?
Call Burgundy. Cornwall and Albany,   129
With my two daughters' dowers digest° this third.
Let pride, which she calls plainness,° marry her.
I do invest you jointly with my power,
Pre-eminence,° and all the large effects
That troop with majesty.° Ourself, by monthly
    course,°
With reservation of a hundred knights   135
By you to be sustained, shall our abode
Make with you by due turns. Only we still retain
The name and all the additions° to a king.
The sway, revenue, execution of the rest,
Belovèd Sons, be yours, which to confirm,   140
This coronet° part betwixt you.

KENT.   Royal Lear,
Whom I have ever honored as my King,
Loved as my father, as my master followed,
As my great patron thought on in my prayers ——

LEAR. The bow is bent and drawn, make from the
    shaft.°   145

KENT. Let it fall rather, though the fork° invade
The region of my heart. Be Kent unmannerly
When Lear is mad. What wouldst thou do, old
    man?°
Think'st thou that duty shall have dread to speak
When power to flattery bows? To plainness honor's
    bound   150
When majesty stoops to folly.° Reverse thy doom,°
And in thy best consideration check
This hideous rashness. Answer my life my judgment,
Thy youngest daughter does not love thee least,
Nor are those empty-hearted whose low sound   155
Reverbs° no hollowness.

LEAR.   Kent, on thy life, no more.

KENT. My life I never held but as a pawn°
To wage against thy enemies, nor fear to lose it,
Thy safety being the motive.

LEAR.   Out of my sight!

KENT. See better, Lear, and let me still remain
The true blank° of thine eye.   161

LEAR. Now, by Apollo ——

KENT.   Now, by Apollo, King.
Thou swear'st thy gods in vain.

LEAR.   O vassal!° Miscreant!°
        [*Laying his hand on his sword.*]

ALB. & CORN. Dear sir, forbear.

KENT. Do.
Kill thy physician, and the fee bestow   166
Upon the foul disease. Revoke thy doom,
Or whilst I can vent clamor° from my throat
I'll tell thee thou dost evil.

LEAR.   Hear me, recreant!°
On thy allegiance,° hear me!   170
Since thou hast sought to make us break our vow,
Which we durst never yet, and with strained° pride
To come between our sentence and our power° ——
Which nor our nature nor our place can bear,
Our potency made good° — take thy reward.   175
Five days we do allot thee, for provision°
To shield thee from diseases of the world,
And on the sixth to turn thy hated back
Upon our kingdom. If on the tenth day following
Thy banished trunk° be found in our dominions,
The moment is thy death. Away! By Jupiter,   181
This shall not be revoked.

KENT. Fare° thee well, King. Sith° thus thou wilt
    appear,
Freedom lives hence, and banishment is here.
[*To* CORDELIA] The gods to their dear shelter take
    thee, maid,   185
That justly think'st and hast most rightly said!
[*To* REGAN *and* GONERIL] And your large° speeches
    may your deeds approve,°
That good effects° may spring from words of love.
Thus Kent, O Princes, bids you all adieu.   189
He'll shape his old course in a country new.   [*Exit.*]
[*Flourish.° Re-enter* GLOUCESTER, *with* FRANCE,
    BURGUNDY, *and* ATTENDANTS.]

GLO. Here's France and Burgundy, my noble lord.

LEAR. My lord of Burgundy,
We first address toward you, who with this King
Hath rivaled for our daughter. What, in the least,
Will you require° in present° dower with her,   195
Or cease your quest of love?

BUR.   Most royal Majesty,

---

126. **nursery:** care. **avoid:** depart from.   130. **digest:** absorb.
131. **plainness:** honest plain speech.   133. **Pre-eminence:** authority.   133–34. **large . . . majesty:** the outward show of power
that goes with rule.   134. **course:** turn.   138. **additions:** titles
of honor.   141. **coronet:** i.e., the coronet which was to have been
the symbol of Cordelia's kingdom.   145. **shaft:** arrow.   146. **fork:**
point of a forked arrow. See Pl. 22a.   148. **old man:** Kent, who
is as quick-tempered as Lear, has lost control of his tongue. The
phrase to a still ruling king is grossly insulting.   149–51. **Think'st
. . . folly:** This is one of many passages in *Lear* where the abstract
is strikingly and effectively used for the person. It means: "Do
you think that a man who keeps his sense of duty will be afraid
to speak when he sees a king yielding to his flatterers? An
honorable man is forced to speak plainly when a king becomes
a fool."   151. **doom:** sentence.   156. **Reverbs:** re-echoes.
157. **pawn:** a pledge to be sacrificed.   161. **blank:** aim; i.e.,
something which you look at. The blank is the center of the target.

163. **vassal:** wretch. **Miscreant:** lit., misbeliever.   168. **vent
clamor:** utter a cry.   169. **recreant:** traitor.   170. **On . . .
allegiance:** The most solemn form of command that can be laid
upon a subject, for to disobey it is to commit high treason.
172. **strained:** excessive.   173. **To . . . power:** to interpose yourself between my decree and my royal will; i.e., to make me revoke an order.   175. **Our . . . good:** my power being now asserted.   176. **for provision:** for making your preparations.
180. **trunk:** body.   183–90. **Fare . . . new:** The rhyme in this
passage and elsewhere in the play is used for the particular purpose of stiffening the speech and giving it a special prophetic or
moral significance; cf. III.vi.109–20.   183. **Sith:** since.
187. **large:** fine-sounding. **approve:** i.e., be shown in deeds.
188. **effects:** results.   190 s.d., **Flourish:** trumpet fanfare.
195. **require:** request. **present:** immediate.

I crave no more than what your Highness offered,
Nor will you tender° less.

LEAR.   Right noble Burgundy,
When she was dear° to us, we did hold her so,
But now her price is fall'n. Sir, there she stands.   200
If aught within that little seeming substance,°
Or all of it, with our displeasure pieced°
And nothing more, may fitly like° your Grace,
She's there, and she is yours.

BUR.   I know no answer.

LEAR. Will you, with those infirmities she owes,°
Unfriended, new-adopted to our hate,   206
Dowered with our curse and strangered with our
     oath,°
Take her, or leave her?

BUR.   Pardon me, royal sir,
Election makes not up on such conditions.°

LEAR. Then leave her, sir. For, by the power that
     made me,   210
I tell you all her wealth. [*To* FRANCE] For you, great
     King,
I would not from your love make such a stray,°
To match you where I hate. Therefore beseech you
To avert your liking° a more worthier way
Than on a wretch whom Nature° is ashamed   215
Almost to acknowledge hers.

FRANCE.   This is most strange,
That she that even but now was your best object,
The argument° of your praise, balm of your age,
Most best, most dearest, should in this trice of time
Commit a thing so monstrous, to dismantle°   220
So many folds of favor. Sure, her offense
Must be of such unnatural degree
That monsters it,° or your forevouched° affection
Fall'n into taint.° Which to believe of her
Must be a faith that reason without miracle   225
Could never plant in me.°

COR.   I yet beseech your Majesty —
If for I want that glib and oily art,
To speak and purpose not,° since what I well intend
I'll do 't before I speak — that you make known
It is no vicious blot,° murder, or foulness,   230
No unchaste action or dishonored step,
That hath deprived me of your grace and favor,

198. tender: offer.   199. dear: in the double sense of "beloved"
and "valuable."   201. little . . . substance: creature that seems
so small. Part of Lear's anger with Cordelia is that so small a
body seems to hold so proud a heart.   202. pieced: added to
it.   203. fitly like: suitably please.   205. owes: possesses.
207. strangered . . . oath: made a stranger to me by my oath.
209. Election . . . conditions: i.e., one does not choose one's wife
on such conditions.   212. from . . . stray: remove myself so far
from showing love to you.   214. avert . . . liking: turn your
affection.   215. Nature: See *Lear* Intro. p. 783b.   218. argument:
topic.   220. dismantle: lit., take off (as a cloak).   223. monsters
it: makes it a monster. forevouched: previously declared.
224. Fall'n . . . taint: become bad.   224–26. Which . . . me: that
is so contrary to reason that only a miracle could make me be-
lieve it.   228. and . . . not: and not mean it.   230. vicious blot:
vicious act which blots my honor.

But even for want of that for which I am richer,
A still-soliciting° eye, and such a tongue
As I am glad I have not, though not to have it   235
Hath lost me in° your liking.

LEAR.   Better thou
Hadst not been born than not to have pleased me
     better.

FRANCE. Is it but this? A tardiness in nature°
Which often leaves the history unspoke
That it intends to do? My Lord of Burgundy,   240
What say you to the lady? Love's not love
When it is mingled with regards that stand
Aloof from the entire point.° Will you have her?
She is herself a dowry.

BUR.   Royal Lear,
Give but that portion which yourself proposed,   245
And here I take Cordelia by the hand,
Duchess of Burgundy.

LEAR. Nothing. I have sworn, I am firm.

BUR. I am sorry then you have so lost a father
That you must lose a husband.

COR.   Peace be with Burgundy!   250
Since that respects of fortune° are his love,
I shall not be his wife.

FRANCE. Fairest Cordelia, that art most rich being
     poor,
Most choice forsaken, and most loved despised,
Thee and thy virtues here I seize upon,   255
Be it lawful I take up what's cast away.
Gods, gods! 'Tis strange that from their cold'st
     neglect
My love should kindle to inflamed respect.°
Thy dowerless daughter, King, thrown to my
     chance,
Is Queen of us, of ours, and our fair France.   260
Not all the dukes of waterish° Burgundy
Can buy this unprized precious maid of me.
Bid them farewell, Cordelia, though unkind.
Thou losest here, a better where to find.

LEAR. Thou hast her, France. Let her be thine,
     for we   265
Have no such daughter, nor shall ever see
That face of hers again. Therefore be gone
Without our grace, our love, our benison.°
Come, noble Burgundy.   [*Flourish. Exeunt all but*
     FRANCE, GONERIL, REGAN, *and* CORDELIA.]

FRANCE. Bid farewell to your sisters.   270

COR. The jewels of our father,° with washed° eyes
Cordelia leaves you. I know you what you are,

234. still-soliciting: always begging favors.   236. lost me in: de-
prived me of.   238. tardiness in nature: natural slowness.
242–43. When . . . point: when it is mixed with other motives
(the amount of the dowry) which have nothing to do with the
thing itself (love).   251. respects of fortune: considerations
of my dowry.   258. inflamed respect: warmer affection.
261. waterish: with the double meaning of "with many rivers"
and "feeble."   268. benison: blessing.   271. The . . . father:
i.e., creatures whom my father values so highly. washed: weeping,
but also made clearsighted by tears.

And, like a sister, am most loath to call
Your faults as they are named. Use well our father.
To your professèd° bosoms I commit him.   275
But yet, alas, stood I within his grace,°
I would prefer° him to a better place.
So farewell to you both.

REG. Prescribe not us our duties.

GON.   Let your study
Be to content your lord, who hath received you   280
At Fortune's alms.° You have obedience scanted,°
And well are worth the want that you have wanted.°

COR. Time shall unfold what plaited° cunning
    hides.
Who cover faults, at last shame them derides.
Well may you prosper!

FRANCE.   Come, my fair Cordelia. 285
[Exeunt FRANCE *and* CORDELIA.]

GON. Sister,° it is not a little I have to say of what
most nearly appertains to us both. I think our father
will hence tonight.

REG. That's most certain, and with you, next
month with us.   290

GON. You see how full of changes his age is, the
observation we have made of it hath not been little.
He always loved our sister most, and with what poor
judgment he hath now cast her off appears too
grossly.

REG. 'Tis the infirmity of his age. Yet he hath ever
but slenderly known himself.   297

GON. The best and soundest of his time hath been
but rash. Then must we look to receive from his age
not alone the imperfections of long-ingrafted con-
dition,° but therewithal the unruly waywardness
that infirm and choleric years bring with them.   303

REG. Such unconstant starts° are we like to have
from him as this of Kent's banishment.

GON. There is further compliment° of leave-tak-
ing between France and him. Pray you, let's hit° to-
gether. If our father carry authority with such dis-
positions° as he bears, this last surrender of his will
but offend us.   310

REG. We shall further think on 't.

GON. We must do something, and i' the heat.°
[Exeunt.]

---

275. **professed**: which profess such love. 276. **within . . . grace**:
in his favor. 277. **prefer**: promote. 281. **At . . . alms**: as an
act of charity from Fortune. **scanted**: neglected. 282. **And
. . . wanted**: and well deserve the same lack of love which you
have shown. 283. **plaited**: pleated, enfolded. Cf. ll. 220–21.
286–312. **Sister . . . heat**: The abrupt change from rhyme to
prose marks the change from the emotion of the previous episodes
to the cynical frankness of the two sisters. 301–02. **long-in-
grafted condition**: temper which has long been part of his nature.
304. **unconstant starts**: sudden outbursts. 306. **compliment**:
formality. 307. **hit**: agree. 309. **dispositions**: frame of mind.
312. **i' the heat**: while the iron is hot.

SCENE II. *The* EARL OF GLOUCESTER'S *castle.*

[Enter EDMUND, *with a letter.*]

EDM. Thou, Nature,° art my goddess, to thy law
My services are bound. Wherefore should I
Stand in the plague of custom, and permit
The curiosity of nations to deprive me,   4
For that I am some twelve or fourteen moonshines
Lag of a brother?° Why bastard? Wherefore
    base?
When my dimensions are as well compact,°
My mind as generous° and my shape as true,
As honest madam's issue? Why brand they us
With base? With baseness? Bastardy? Base, base?
Who in the lusty stealth of nature take   11
More composition and fierce quality°
Than doth, within a dull, stale, tired bed,
Go to the creating a whole tribe of fops°
Got° 'tween asleep and wake? Well then,   15
Legitimate Edgar, I must have your land.
Our father's love is to the bastard Edmund
As to the legitimate — fine word, "legitimate"!
Well, my legitimate, if this letter speed°
And my invention° thrive, Edmund the base   20
Shall top the legitimate. I grow, I prosper.
Now, gods, stand up for bastards!

[Enter GLOUCESTER.]

GLO. Kent banished thus! And France in choler
    parted!
And the King gone tonight! Subscribed° his power!
Confined to exhibition!° All this done   25
Upon the gad!° Edmund, how now! What news?

EDM. So please your lordship, none.
[Putting up the letter.]

GLO. Why so earnestly seek you to put up that let-
    ter?

EDM. I know no news, my lord.

GLO. What paper were you reading?   30

EDM. Nothing, my lord.°

GLO. No? What needed then that terrible dis-
patch° of it into your pocket? The quality of noth-
ing hath not such need to hide itself. Let's see. Come,
if it be nothing, I shall not need spectacles.   36

EDM. I beseech you, sir, pardon me. It is a letter
from my brother that I have not all o'erread, and for

Sc. ii: 1. **Thou, Nature**: Edmund, the "natural" son of his
father, appeals to Nature, whose doctrine is every man ruth-
lessly for himself. 2–6. **Wherefore . . . brother**: Why should I
allow myself to be plagued by custom and nice distinctions
(*curiosity*) which deprive me of my natural rights, because I am a
year younger (*lag*: lagging behind) than my legitimate brother?
7. **compact**: put together, framed. 8. **generous**: noble. 12. **More
. . . quality**: more fiber and ferocity. 14. **fops**: fools. 15. **Got**:
begotten. 19. **speed**: prosper. 20. **invention**: plan. 24. **Sub-
scribed**: signed away. 25. **Confined to exhibition**: reduced to
a pension. 26. **gad**: prick of a goad; i.e., the spur of the
moment. 31. **Nothing, my lord**: Gloucester's tragedy also be-
gins with the word "nothing." See I i.89. 32–33. **terrible dis-
patch**: i.e., hasty thrusting.

so much as I have perused, I find it not fit for your o'erlooking.° 40

GLO. Give me the letter, sir.

EDM. I shall offend, either to detain or give it. The contents, as in part I understand them, are to blame.

GLO. Let's see, let's see. 44

EDM. I hope, for my brother's justification, he wrote this but as an essay° or taste of my virtue.

GLO. [Reads.] "This policy and reverence of age° makes the world bitter to the best of our times,° keeps our fortunes from us till our oldness cannot relish them. I begin to find an idle and fond° 50 bondage in the oppression of aged tyranny, who sways not as it hath power, but as it is suffered.° Come to me, that of this I may speak more. If our father would sleep till I waked him, you should enjoy half his revenue forever, and live the beloved 55 of your brother,   EDGAR."
Hum! Conspiracy! — "Sleep till I waked him, you should enjoy half his revenue!" — My son Edgar! Had he a hand to write this? A heart and brain to breed it in? When came this to you? Who brought it?

EDM. It was not brought me, my lord, there's the cunning of it. I found it thrown in at the casement° of my closet.° 65

GLO. You know the character° to be your brother's?

EDM. If the matter were good, my lord, I durst swear it were his, but in respect of that, I would fain think it were not.

GLO. It is his.

EDM. It is his hand, my lord, but I hope his heart is not in the contents. 73

GLO. Hath he never heretofore sounded you in this business?

EDM. Never, my lord. But I have heard him oft maintain it to be fit that, sons at perfect age and fathers declining, the father should be as ward to the son, and the son manage his revenue. 79

GLO. Oh, villain, villain! His very opinion in the letter! Abhorred villain! Unnatural, detested, brutish villain! Worse than brutish! Go, sirrah, seek him — aye, apprehend him. Abominable villain! Where is he? 84

EDM. I do not well know, my lord. If it shall please you to suspend your indignation against my brother till you can derive from him better testimony of his intent, you should run a certain course.° Where, if you violently proceed against him, mistaking his purpose, it would make a great gap° in your own 90

honor and shake in pieces the heart of his obedience.° I dare pawn down my life for him that he hath wrote this to feel° my affection to your honor and to no further pretense of danger. 95

GLO. Think you so?

EDM. If your honor judge it meet, I will place you where you shall hear us confer of this, and by an auricular assurance° have your satisfaction, and that without any further delay than this very evening.

GLO. He cannot be such a monster — 102

EDM. Nor is not, sure.

GLO. — to his father, that so tenderly and entirely loves him. Heaven and earth! Edmund, seek 105 him out, wind me into him,° I pray you. Frame the business after your own wisdom. I would unstate myself, to be in a due resolution.°

EDM. I will seek him, sir, presently,° convey° the business as I shall find means, and acquaint you withal. 111

GLO. These late eclipses° in the sun and moon portend no good to us. Though the wisdom of nature° can reason° it thus and thus, yet nature finds itself scourged by the sequent° effects. Love cools, 115 friendship falls off, brothers divide. In cities, mutinies; in countries, discord; in palaces, treason; and the bond cracked 'twixt son and father. This villain of mine comes under the prediction, there's son against father. The King falls from bias of na- 120 ture,° there's father against child. We have seen the best of our time. Machinations, hollowness, treachery, and all ruinous disorders follow us disquietly to our graves. Find out this villain, Edmund, it shall lose thee nothing. Do it carefully. And the noble and true-hearted Kent banished! His offense, honesty! 'Tis strange.   [Exit.] 127

EDM. This is the excellent foppery° of the world, that when we are sick in fortune — often the surfeit° of our own behavior — we make guilty of our 130 disasters the sun, the moon, and the stars, as if we were villains by necessity, fools by heavenly compulsion; knaves, thieves, and treachers by spherical predominance;° drunkards, liars, and adulterers by an enforced obedience of planetary influence;° 135 and all that we are evil in, by a divine thrusting on

40. o'erlooking: reading. 46. essay: trial. 47. policy . . . age: this custom of respecting old men. 48. best . . . times: i.e., when we are still young. 50. fond: foolish. 52. suffered: allowed. 64. casement: window. 65. closet: room. 66. character: handwriting. 88. certain course: i.e., know where you are going. 90. gap: hole.

91. shake . . . obedience: cause him no longer to obey you loyally. 94. feel: test. 100. auricular assurance: proof heard with your own ears. 106. wind . . . him: worm your way into his confidence for me. 107–08. I . . . resolution: I would lose my earldom to learn the truth. This is one of many touches of bitter irony in this tragedy, for it is not until he has "unstated himself" that Gloucester does indeed learn the truth about his two sons. 109. presently: at once. convey: manage. 112. These . . . eclipses: See Intro. Lear, p. 780a and App. 2. 113. wisdom of nature: i.e., a rational explanation. 114. reason: explain. 115. sequent: subsequent. 120–21. bias of nature: natural inclination. See App. 13. 128. foppery: folly. 129. surfeit: lit., eating to excess and its results. 133–34. treachers . . . predominance: traitors because the stars so decreed when we were born. 135. enforced . . . influence: because we were forced to be so in obeying the influence of the stars.

— an admirable evasion of whoremaster° man, to
lay his goatish disposition to the charge of a star!°
My father compounded with my mother under the
dragon's tail, and my nativity° was under Ursa   140
Major,° so that it follows I am rough and lecherous.
Tut, I should have been that I am had the maiden-
liest star in the firmament twinkled on my bas-   144
tardizing. Edgar—— [Enter EDGAR.] And pat he
comes like the catastrophe° of the old comedy. My
cue is villainous melancholy, with a sigh like Tom
o' Bedlam.° Oh, these eclipses do portend these di-
visions! Fa, sol, la, mi.°

EDG. How now, Brother Edmund! What serious
contemplation are you in?   151

EDM. I am thinking, Brother, of a prediction I
read this other day, what should follow these eclipses.

EDG. Do you busy yourself about that?   155

EDM. I promise you the effects he writes of suc-
ceed° unhappily, as of unnaturalness between the
child and the parent; death, dearth, dissolutions of
ancient amities;° divisions in state, menaces and
maledictions against King and nobles; needless diffi-
dences,° banishment of friends, dissipation of co-
horts,° nuptial breaches, and I know not what.   163

EDG. How long have you been a sectary astro-
nomical?°

EDM. Come, come, when saw you my father last?

EDG. Why, the night gone by.   168

EDM. Spake you with him?

EDG. Aye, two hours together.

EDM. Parted you in good terms? Found you no
displeasure in him by word or countenance?

EDG. None at all.   173

EDM. Bethink yourself wherein you may have of-
fended him. And at my entreaty forbear his presence
till some little time hath qualified° the heat of his
displeasure, which at this instant so rageth in him
that with the mischief of your person it would
scarcely allay.°

EDG. Some villain hath done me wrong.   180

EDM. That's my fear. I pray you have a continent
forbearance° till the speed of his rage goes slower,
and, as I say, retire with me to my lodging, from
whence I will fitly bring you to hear my lord speak.

Pray ye, go, there's my key. If you do stir abroad,
go armed.   186

EDG. Armed, Brother!

EDM. Brother, I advise you to the best — go armed.
I am no honest man if there be any good meaning
toward you. I have told you what I have seen and
heard, but faintly, nothing like the image and horror
of it. Pray you, away.   192

EDG. Shall I hear from you anon?

EDM. I do serve you in this business.

[Exit EDGAR.]

A credulous father, and a brother noble,   195
Whose nature is so far from doing harms
That he suspects none, on whose foolish honesty
My practices° ride easy. I see the business.
Let me, if not by birth, have lands by wit.   199
All with me's meet° that I can fashion fit.°   [Exit.]

SCENE III. The DUKE OF ALBANY's palace.

[Enter GONERIL and OSWALD, her steward.]

GON. Did my father strike my gentleman for
    chiding of his fool?°

OSW. Yes, madam.

GON. By day and night he wrongs me. Every hour
He flashes into one gross crime or other
That sets us all at odds. I'll not endure it.   5
His knights grow riotous, and himself upbraids us
On every trifle. When he returns from hunting,
I will not speak with him. Say I am sick.
If you come slack of former services,°
You shall do well, the fault of it I'll answer.   10

OSW. He's coming, madam, I hear him.

[Horns within.]

GON. Put on what weary negligence you please,
You and your fellows, I'd have it come to question.°
If he distaste it, let him to our sister,
Whose mind and mine, I know, in that are one,   15
Not to be overruled. Idle old man,
That still would manage those authorities
That he hath given away! Now, by my life,
Old fools are babes again, and must be used
With checks as flatteries when they are seen abused.°
Remember what I tell you.

OSW.   Very well, madam.   21

GON. And let his knights have colder looks among
    you.
What grows of it, no matter, advise your fellows so.
I would breed from hence occasions,° and I shall,

---

137. whoremaster: lecherous.   137–38. to . . . star: to say that
some star caused him to have the morals of a goat.   140. na-
tivity: moment of birth.   140–41. Ursa Major: the Great Bear.
146. catastrophe: the final episode.   146–48. my . . . Bedlam:
I must now pretend to be a melancholic and sigh like a lunatic
beggar. Tom o' Bedlam was a lunatic discharged from Bedlam
(Bethlehem Hospital for lunatics). See II.iii.14.   149. Fa . . .
mi: Edmund hums to himself.   156. succeed: follow.   159. ami-
ties: friendships.   162. diffidences: distrusts.   162–63. dissi-
pation of cohorts: breaking-up of established friendships (lit.,
of troops of soldiers).   164. sectary astronomical: a follower of
the sect of astrologers.   176. qualified: lessened.   178–79. with
. . . allay: it would scarcely be lessened even if he did you some
bodily injury.   181–82. continent forbearance: self-control
which will keep you from any rash action.

198. practices: plots.   200. meet: suitable. fashion fit: make fit
my purposes.
'Sc. iii: 1. fool: professional jester. See Pl. 12j, 13c.   9. come
. . . services: do not wait on him as efficiently as you used to.
13. to question: or in modern slang, to a showdown.   19–20. Old
. . . abused: old men must be treated like babies, and scolded,
not flattered, when they are naughty.   24. breed . . . occasions:
find excuses for taking action.

That I may speak. I'll write straight to my sister   25
To hold my very course. Prepare for dinner.
                                        [*Exeunt.*]

SCENE IV. *A hall in the same.*

[*Enter* KENT, *disguised.*]

KENT. If but as well I other accents borrow
That can my speech defuse,° my good intent
May carry through itself to that full issue
For which I razed° my likeness. Now, banished
    Kent,
If thou canst serve where thou dost stand con-
    demned,   5
So may it come, thy master whom thou lovest
Shall find thee full of labors.
    [*Horns within.*° *Enter* LEAR, KNIGHTS, *and*
        ATTENDANTS.]
LEAR. Let me not stay a jot for dinner. Go get it
ready. [*Exit an* ATTENDANT.] How now! What art
thou?   10
KENT. A man, sir.
LEAR. What dost thou profess?° What wouldst
thou with us?   13
KENT. I do profess to be no less than I seem — to
serve him truly that will put me in trust, to love him
that is honest, to converse with him that is wise and
says little, to fear judgment,° to fight when I cannot
choose, and to eat no fish.°   18
LEAR. What art thou?
KENT. A very honest-hearted fellow, and as poor
as the King.
LEAR. If thou be as poor for a subject as he is for
a king, thou art poor enough. What wouldst thou?
KENT. Service.   25
LEAR. Who wouldst thou serve?
KENT. You.
LEAR. Dost thou know me, fellow?
KENT. No, sir, but you have that in your counte-
nance° which I would fain call master.   30
LEAR. What's that?
KENT. Authority.
LEAR. What services canst thou do?   33
KENT. I can keep honest counsel, ride, run, mar a
curious tale in telling it,° and deliver a plain message
bluntly. That which ordinary men are fit for, I am
qualified in, and the best of me is diligence.
LEAR. How old art thou?
KENT. Not so young, sir, to love a woman for

singing, nor so old to dote on her for anything. I
have years on my back forty-eight.   42
LEAR. Follow me, thou shalt serve me. If I like
thee no worse after dinner, I will not part from thee
yet. Dinner, ho, dinner! Where's my knave? My
fool? Go you, and call my fool hither. [*Exit an* AT-
TENDANT. *Enter* OSWALD.] You, you, sirrah, where's
my daughter?
OSW. So please you ——   [*Exit.*]
LEAR. What says the fellow there? Call the clot-
poll° back. [*Exit a* KNIGHT.] Where's my fool, ho? I
think the world's asleep. [*Re-enter* KNIGHT.]   52
How now! Where's that mongrel?
KNIGHT. He says, my lord, your daughter is not
well.   55
LEAR. Why came not the slave back to me when I
called him?
KNIGHT. Sir, he answered me, in the roundest°
manner, he would not.
LEAR. He would not!   60
KNIGHT. My lord, I know not what the matter is,
but, to my judgment, your Highness is not enter-
tained° with that ceremonious affection° as you
were wont. There's a great abatement of kindness
appears as well in the general dependents° as in the
Duke himself also and your daughter.   67
LEAR. Ha! Sayest thou so?
KNIGHT. I beseech you pardon me, my lord, if I be
mistaken, for my duty cannot be silent when I think
your Highness wronged.   71
LEAR. Thou but rememberest° me of mine own
conception. I have perceived a most faint neglect°
of late, which I have rather blamed as mine own
jealous curiosity° than as a very pretense° and pur-
pose of unkindness. I will look further into 't. But
where's my fool? I have not seen him this two
days.   78
KNIGHT. Since my young lady's going into France,
sir, the fool hath much pined away.
LEAR. No more of that, I have noted it well. Go
you, and tell my daughter I would speak with her.
[*Exit an* ATTENDANT.] Go you, call hither my   84
fool. [*Exit an* ATTENDANT. *Re-enter* OSWALD.] Oh, you
sir, you, come you hither, sir. Who am I, sir?
OSW. My lady's father.
LEAR. My lady's father! My lord's knave. You
whoreson dog! You slave! You cur!   89
OSW. I am none of these, my lord, I beseech your
pardon.

Sc. iv: 2. **defuse:** make indistinct, disguise.   4. **razed:** lit.,
shaved off, disguised.   7 **s.d., within:** off stage.   12. **What . . .
profess:** what is your profession?   17. **judgment:** The Day of
Judgment; i.e., I have a conscience.   18. **eat no fish:** I don't
observe fast days, and am therefore no Catholic.   30. **coun-
tenance:** bearing.   34–35. **mar . . . it:** I'm not one to delight in
overelaborate (*curious*) phrases when telling my tale; i.e., he
will have none of the fantastic talk of the typical courtier — such
as Shakespeare mocks in the character of Osric (see *Haml,*
V.ii.81–201). Kent himself mimics this fashion later (II.ii.111–14).

51. **clotpoll:** clodpole, blockhead.   58. **roundest:** plainest.
63. **entertained:** treated. **ceremonious affection:** affection
which shows itself in ceremony. Manners even between children
and parents were very formal. Neglect of courtesies to the ex-
King shows deliberate disrespect.   66. **dependents:** servants of
the house.   72. **rememberest:** remind.   73. **faint neglect:** i.e.,
the "weary negligence" commanded by Goneril (I.iii.12).
75. **jealous curiosity:** excessive suspicion. **pretense:** deliberate
intention.

LEAR. Do you bandy° looks with me, you rascal?
                                              [*Striking him.*]
OSW. I'll not be struck, my lord.   94
KENT. Nor tripped neither, you base football
player.   [*Tripping up his heels.*]
LEAR. I thank thee, fellow. Thou servest me, and
I'll love thee.   98
KENT. Come, sir, arise, away! I'll teach you differ-
ences.° Away, away! If you will measure your lub-
ber's length again, tarry. But away! Go to, have you
wisdom? So.   [*Pushes* OSWALD *out.*]
LEAR. Now, my friendly knave, I thank thee.
There's earnest° of thy service.   104
                                    [*Giving* KENT *money.*]
                                          [*Enter* FOOL.]
FOOL. Let me hire him too. Here's my coxcomb.°
                                [*Offering* KENT *his cap.*]
LEAR. How now, my pretty knave! How dost
thou?
FOOL. Sirrah, you were best take my coxcomb.
KENT. Why, fool?   110
FOOL. Why, for taking one's part that's out of
favor. Nay, an thou canst not smile as the wind sits,°
thou'lt catch cold shortly. There, take my coxcomb.
Why, this fellow hath banished two on 's daughters,
and done the third a blessing against his will. If thou
follow him, thou must needs wear my coxcomb.
How now, Nuncle!° Would I had two coxcombs and
two daughters!   118
LEAR. Why, my boy?
FOOL. If I gave them all my living, I'd keep my
coxcombs myself. There's mine, beg another of thy
daughters.
LEAR. Take heed, sirrah, the whip.°   123
FOOL. Truth's a dog must to kennel. He must be
whipped out, when Lady the brach° may stand by
the fire and stink.
LEAR. A pestilent gall to me!°
FOOL. Sirrah, I'll teach thee a speech.
LEAR. Do.
FOOL. Mark it, Nuncle: 130
    "Have more than thou showest,
     Speak less than thou knowest,
     Lend less than thou owest,°
     Ride more than thou goest,°

Learn more than thou trowest,°   135
Set less than thou throwest.°
Leave thy drink and thy whore,
And keep in-a-door,
And thou shalt have more
Than two tens to a score."°   140
KENT. This is nothing, fool.
FOOL. Then 'tis like the breath of an unfeed law-
yer. You gave me nothing for 't. Can you make no
use of nothing, Nuncle?
LEAR. Why, no, boy, nothing can be made out of
nothing.°   146
FOOL. [*To* KENT] Prithee tell him so much the
rent of his land comes to. He will not believe a fool.
LEAR. A bitter fool!   150
FOOL. Dost thou know the difference, my boy, be-
tween a bitter fool and a sweet fool?
LEAR. No, lad, teach me.
FOOL.   "That lord that counseled thee
          To give away thy land,   155
          Come place him here by me,
          Do thou for him stand.
        The sweet and bitter fool
          Will presently appear —
          The one in motley° here,   160
          The other found out there."
LEAR. Dost thou call me fool, boy?
FOOL. All thy other titles thou hast given away.
That thou wast born with.
KENT. This is not altogether fool, my lord.   165
FOOL. No, faith, lords and great men will not let
me.° If I had a monopoly° out, they would have part
on 't. And ladies too, they will not let me have all the
fool to myself, they'll be snatching. Give me an egg,
Nuncle, and I'll give thee two crowns.
LEAR. What two crowns shall they be?   172
FOOL. Why, after I have cut the egg in the middle
and eat up the meat, the two crowns of the egg.
When thou clovest thy crown i' the middle and gav-
est away both parts, thou borest thine ass on thy
back o'er the dirt.° Thou hadst little wit in thy bald
crown when thou gavest thy golden one away. If I
speak like myself° in this, let him be whipped that
first finds it so. [*Singing*]   180
    "Fools had ne'er less wit in a year,
     For wise men are grown foppish,
     And know not how their wits to wear,
     Their manners are so apish."°

---

92. **bandy:** lit., hit the ball to and fro as in tennis.   100. **dif-
ferences:** of rank.   104. **earnest:** money given on account of
services to be rendered. Lear thus formally engages Kent as his
servant.   105. **coxcomb:** the cap shaped like a cock's comb
(crest) worn by the professional fool.   112. **an . . . sits:** i.e.,
if you can't curry favor with those in power.   117. **Nuncle:**
Uncle.   123. **the whip:** The fool's profession was precarious,
and in real life too smart a joke brought its painful reward.
In March 1605 Stone, a professional fool, was whipped for com-
menting on the diplomatic mission about to sail for Spain that
"there went sixty fools into Spain, besides my Lord Admiral
and his two sons."   125. **Lady . . . brach:** Lady the pet bitch.
127. **A . . . me:** this pestilent fool rubs me on a sore spot.
133. **owest:** possess.   134. **goest:** walk.

135. **trowest:** know.   136. **Set . . . throwest:** don't bet a larger
stake than you can afford to lose.   139-40. **And . . . score:**
and then your money will increase.   145-46. **nothing . . . noth-
ing:** Lear unconsciously repeats himself. See I.i.92.   160. **motley:**
the particolored uniform worn by a fool.   166-67. **will . . . me:**
i.e., keep all my folly to myself.   167. **monopoly:** a royal patent
giving the holders the sole right to deal in some commodity. The
granting of such monopolies to courtiers was one of the crying
scandals of the time.   176-77. **thine . . . dirt:** an old tale of the
typical simple-minded countryman.   179. **like myself:** i.e., like
a fool.   181-84. **Fools . . . apish:** there's no job left for fools

LEAR. When were you wont to be so full of songs,
sirrah?   186

FOOL. I have used it, Nuncle, ever since thou mad-
est thy daughters thy mother. For when thou gav-
est them the rod and puttest down thine own
breeches, [*Singing*]   190
  " Then they for sudden joy did weep,
    And I for sorrow sung,
  That such a king should play bopeep,
    And go the fools among."   194
Prithee, Nuncle, keep a schoolmaster that can teach
thy fool to lie. I would fain learn to lie.

LEAR. An° you lie, sirrah, we'll have you whipped.

FOOL. I marvel what kin thou and thy daugh-   199
ters are. They'll have me whipped for speaking true,
thou'lt have me whipped for lying, and sometimes I
am whipped for holding my peace. I had rather be
any kind o' thing than a fool. And yet I would not
be thee, Nuncle. Thou hast pared thy wit o' both
sides and left nothing i' the middle. Here comes one
o' the parings.   206

[*Enter* GONERIL.]

LEAR. How now, Daughter! What makes that
frontlet° on? Methinks you are too much of late i'
the frown.   209

FOOL. Thou wast a pretty fellow when thou hadst
no need to care for her frowning. Now thou art an
O without a figure.° I am better than thou art now.
I am a fool, thou art nothing. [*To* GONERIL] Yes,
forsooth, I will hold my tongue, so your face bids me,
though you say nothing.   215
  " Mum, mum.
    He that keeps nor crust nor crumb,°
    Weary of all, shall want some."
[*Pointing to* LEAR] That's a shealed peascod.°

GON. Not only, sir, this your all-licensed° fool,
But other of your insolent retinue   221
Do hourly carp° and quarrel, breaking forth
In rank and not to be endurèd riots. Sir,
I had thought, by making this well known unto you,
To have found a safe redress, but now grow fearful
By what yourself too late have spoke and done   226
That you protect this course and put it on°
By your allowance.° Which if you should, the fault
Would not 'scape censure, nor the redresses sleep,
Which, in the tender of a wholesome weal,   230
Might in their working do you that offense
Which else were shame, that then necessity
Will call discreet proceeding.°

FOOL. For, you know, Nuncle,
" The hedge sparrow fed the cuckoo° so long   235
  That it had it head bit off by it young."
So out went the candle, and we were left darkling.°

LEAR. Are you our daughter?

GON. Come, sir,   239
I would you would make use of that good wisdom
Whereof I know you are fraught,° and put away
These dispositions° that of late transform you
From what you rightly are.

FOOL. May not an ass know when the cart draws
the horse? Whoop, Jug! I love thee.°   245

LEAR. Doth any here know me? This is not Lear.
Doth Lear walk thus? Speak thus? Where are his
eyes?
Either his notion° weakens, his discernings
Are lethargied°——Ha! Waking? 'Tis not so.
Who is it that can tell me who I am?   250

FOOL. Lear's shadow.

LEAR. I would learn that, for, by the marks of
sovereignty,° knowledge, and reason, I should be
false persuaded I had daughters.   255

FOOL. Which they will make an obedient father.

LEAR. Your name, fair gentlewoman?

GON. This admiration,° sir, is much o' the savor
Of° other your new pranks. I do beseech you
To understand my purposes aright.   260
As you are old and reverend, you should be wise.
Here do you keep a hundred knights and squires,
Men so disordered,° so deboshed° and bold,
That this our Court, infected with their manners,
Shows like a riotous inn. Epicurism° and lust   265
Make it more like a tavern or a brothel
Than a graced° palace. The same itself doth speak
For instant remedy. Be then desired
By her that else will take the thing she begs
A little to disquantity your train,°   270
And the remainder that shall still depend,°
To be such men as may besort° your age,
Which know themselves and you.

LEAR.   Darkness and devils!
Saddle my horses, call my train together.
Degenerate bastard! I'll not trouble thee.   275
Yet have I left a daughter.

GON. You strike my people, and your disordered
  rabble

be shameful toward a father, but would be justified as mere dis-
cretion.   235. cuckoo: for the habits of the cuckoo see App. 11.
237. darkling: in the dark.   241. fraught: stored, endowed.
242. dispositions: moods.   245. Whoop ... thee: one of the
meaningless cries made by the fool to distract attention.   248. no-
tion: understanding.   249. lethargied: paralyzed.   253–54. marks
of sovereignty: the outward signs which show that I am King.
258. admiration: pretended astonishment.   258–59. much ...
Of: tastes much the same as.   263. disordered: disorderly.
deboshed: debauched.   265. Epicurism: self-indulgence, riotous
living.   267. graced: gracious.   270. disquantity ... train:
diminish the number of your followers.   271. depend: be your
dependents.   272. besort: be suitable for.

nowadays, because the wise men are so like them. apish: like
apes, who always imitate.   198. An: if.   208. frontlet: frown;
lit., a band worn on the forehead.   211–12. an ... figure: a ci-
pher.   217. crumb: inside of the loaf.   219. shealed peascod:
a shelled peapod.   220. all-licensed: allowed to take all liberties.
222. carp: find fault.   227. put it on: encourage it.   228. allow-
ance: approval.   230–33. Which ... proceeding: if you continue
to be a nuisance I shall be forced to keep my state peaceful by
taking measures which will annoy you and would at other times

Make servants of their betters.

[*Enter* ALBANY.]

LEAR. Woe, that too late repents. — [*To* ALBANY]
  Oh, sir, are you come?
Is it your will? Speak, sir. Prepare my horses. 280
Ingratitude, thou marble-hearted fiend,
More hideous when thou show'st thee in a child
Than the sea monster!

ALB.   Pray, sir, be patient.

LEAR. [*To* GONERIL] Detested kite!° Thou liest.
My train are men of choice and rarest parts,° 285
That all particulars of duty know,
And in the most exact regard support
The worships of their name.° O most small fault,
How ugly didst thou in Cordelia show! 289
That, like an engine, wrenched my frame of nature
From the fixed place,° drew from my heart all love
And added to the gall.° O Lear, Lear, Lear!
Beat at this gate, that let thy folly in

[*Striking his head*]

And thy dear judgment out!° Go, go, my people.

ALB. My lord, I am guiltless, as I am ignorant
Of what hath moved you.

LEAR.   It may be so, my lord. 296
Hear, Nature, hear,° dear goddess, hear!
Suspend thy purpose if thou didst intend
To make this creature fruitful.
Into her womb convey sterility. 300
Dry up in her the organs of increase,°
And from her derogate° body never spring
A babe to honor her! If she must teem,°
Create her child of spleen,° that it may live
And be a thwart disnatured° torment to her. 305
Let it stamp wrinkles in her brow of youth,
With cadent° tears fret° channels in her cheeks,
Turn all her mother's pains and benefits
To laughter and contempt, that she may feel
How sharper than a serpent's tooth it is 310
To have a thankless child! Away, away!   [*Exit*.]

ALB. Now, gods that we adore, whereof comes this?

GON. Never afflict yourself to know the cause,
But let his disposition have that scope
That dotage gives it. 315

[*Re-enter* LEAR.]

LEAR. What, fifty of my followers at a clap!°
Within a fortnight!°

ALB.   What's the matter, sir?

LEAR. I'll tell thee. [*To* GONERIL] Life and death!
  I am ashamed
That thou hast power to shake my manhood° thus,
That these hot tears, which break from me perforce,
Should make thee worth them. Blasts and fogs upon
  thee! 321
The untented woundings° of a father's curse
Pierce every sense about thee! Old fond° eyes,
Beweep this cause again, I'll pluck ye out
And cast you with the waters that you lose 325
To temper° clay. Yea, is it come to this?
Let it be so. Yet have I left a daughter
Who I am sure is kind and comfortable.°
When she shall hear this of thee, with her nails
She'll flay thy wolvish visage. Thou shalt find 330
That I'll resume the shape which thou dost think
I have cast off forever. Thou shalt, I warrant thee.

[*Exeunt* LEAR, KENT, *and* ATTENDANTS.]

GON. Do you mark that, my lord?

ALB. I° cannot be so partial, Goneril,
To the great love I bear you —— 335

GON. Pray you, content. What, Oswald, ho!
[*To the* FOOL] You, sir, more knave than fool, after
  your master.

FOOL. Nuncle Lear, Nuncle Lear, tarry, take the
fool with thee.°
     "A fox, when one has caught her, 340
       And such a daughter,
       Should sure to the slaughter,
       If my cap would buy a halter.
       So the fool follows after."   [*Exit*.]

GON. This man hath had good counsel. A hundred
  knights! 345
'Tis politic° and safe to let him keep
At point° a hundred knights. Yes, that on every
  dream,
Each buzz,° each fancy, each complaint, dislike,
He may enguard his dotage with their powers
And hold our lives in mercy. Oswald, I say! 350

ALB. Well, you may fear too far.

GON.   Safer than trust too far.
Let me still take away the harms I fear,
Not fear still to be taken.° I know his heart.
What he hath uttered I have writ my sister.
If she sustain him and his hundred knights 355
When I have showed the unfitness ——

---

284. kite: the lowest of the birds of prey, an eater of offal.
285. parts: accomplishments. 287–88. in . . . name: and in
every minute detail uphold their honorable names. 290–91. like
. . . place: like a little instrument (e.g., a lever) dislodged my
firm nature. 292. gall: bitterness. 293–94. Beat . . . out: the
first signs of madness in Lear. 297. Hear . . . hear: In making
this terrible curse, Lear also calls on Nature, but as goddess
of natural affection. Cf. I.ii.1–22. 301. increase: childbearing.
302. derogate: debased. 303. teem: conceive. 304. spleen:
malice. 305. thwart disnatured: perverse and unnatural.
307. cadent: falling. fret: wear away. 316. at a clap: at one
blow 316–17. What . . . fortnight: As Lear goes out he learns

that Goneril has herself already begun to take steps "a little to
disquantity his train" by ordering that fifty of them shall depart
within a fortnight. To a man who regards his own dignity so
highly, this fresh blow is devastating. 319. shake my man-
hood: i.e., with sobs. 322. untented woundings: raw wounds.
A tent was a small roll of lint used to clean out a wound
before it was bound up. 323. fond: foolish. 326. temper: mix.
328. comfortable: full of comfort. 334–35. I . . . you: i.e., al-
though my love makes me partial to you, yet I must protest.
338–39. take . . . thee: i.e., take your fool and your own folly.
346. politic: good policy. 347. At point: fully armed. 348. buzz:
rumor. 352–53. Let . . . taken: let me always remove what I
fear will harm me rather than live in perpetual fear.

[*Re-enter* OSWALD.] How now, Oswald!
What, have you writ that letter to my sister?

OSW. Yes, madam.

GON. Take you some company, and away to horse.
Inform her full of my particular fear,   360
And thereto add such reasons of your own
As may compact it more.° Get you gone,
And hasten your return. [*Exit* OSWALD.] No, no, my
    lord,
This milky gentleness and course° of yours
Though I condemn not, yet, under pardon,   365
You are much more attasked° for want of wisdom
Than praised for harmful mildness.°

ALB. How far your eyes may pierce I cannot tell.
Striving to better, oft we mar what's well.

GON. Nay, then ———   370

ALB. Well, well, the event.°   [*Exeunt.*]

SCENE V. *Court before the same.*

[*Enter* LEAR, KENT, *and* FOOL.]

LEAR. Go you before to Gloucester with these let-
ters. Acquaint my daughter no further with any-
thing you know than comes from her demand out
of the letter. If your diligence be not speedy, I shall
be there afore you.   5

KENT. I will not sleep, my lord, till I have delivered
your letter.   [*Exit.*]

FOOL. If a man's brains were in 's heels, were 't
not in danger of kibes?°

LEAR. Aye, boy.   10

FOOL. Then I prithee be merry. Thy wit shall ne'er
go slipshod.°

LEAR. Ha, ha, ha!

FOOL. Shalt see thy other daughter will use thee
kindly,° for though she's as like this as a crab's° like
an apple, yet I can tell what I can tell.   16

LEAR. Why, what canst thou tell, my boy?

FOOL. She will taste as like this as a crab does to
a crab. Thou canst tell why one's nose stands i' the
middle on 's face?   20

LEAR. No.

FOOL. Why, to keep one's eyes of either side 's
nose, that what a man cannot smell out he may spy
into.

LEAR. I did her wrong ———   25

FOOL. Canst tell how an oyster makes his shell?

LEAR. No.

FOOL. Nor I neither, but I can tell why a snail has
a house.   30

362. compact it more: make my argument more convincing.
364. milky . . . course: this milksop behavior.   366. attasked:
blamed.   367. harmful mildness: a mildness which may prove
harmful.   371. the event: i.e., we must see what will happen.
    Sc. v: 9. kibes: chilblains.   11–12. Thy . . . slipshod: i.e.,
you don't need slippers, for you have no brains to be protected
from chilblains.   15. kindly: after her kind; i.e., nature.
crab: crab apple.

LEAR. Why?

FOOL. Why, to put 's head in, not to give it away
to his daughters and leave his horns without a case.

LEAR. I will forget my nature. — So kind a father!
— Be my horses ready?   36

FOOL. Thy asses are gone about 'em. The reason
why the seven stars are no more than seven is a
pretty reason.

LEAR. Because they are not eight?   40

FOOL. Yes, indeed. Thou wouldst make a good
fool.

LEAR. To take 't again perforce!° Monster ingrati-
tude!

FOOL. If thou wert my fool, Nuncle, I'd have thee
beaten for being old before thy time.   46

LEAR. How's that?

FOOL. Thou shouldst not have been old till thou
hadst been wise.

LEAR. Oh, let me not be mad, not mad, sweet
    Heaven!   50
Keep me in temper.° I would not be mad!
[*Enter* GENTLEMAN.] How now! Are the horses
    ready?

GENT. Ready, my lord.

LEAR. Come, boy.

FOOL. She that's a maid now and laughs at my de-
parture   55
Shall not be a maid long, unless things be cut shorter.
                                                   [*Exeunt.*]

Act II

SCENE I. *The* EARL OF GLOUCESTER'S *castle.*

[*Enter* EDMUND *and* CURAN, *meeting.*]

EDM. Save thee,° Curan.

CUR. And you, sir. I have been with your father,
and given him notice that the Duke of Cornwall and
Regan his Duchess will be here with him this night.

EDM. How comes that?   6

CUR. Nay, I know not. You have heard of the
news abroad — I mean the whispered ones, for they
are yet but ear-kissing° arguments?

EDM. Not I. Pray you what are they?   10

CUR. Have you heard of no likely wars toward
'twixt the Dukes of Cornwall and Albany?

EDM. Not a word.   14

CUR. You may do, then, in time. Fare you well,
sir.   [*Exit.*]

43. To . . . perforce: I will take back my kingdom by force.
51. temper: sanity.
    Act II, Sc. i: 1. Save thee: God save thee.   9. ear-kissing:
whispered close in the ear.

EDM. The Duke be here tonight? The better! Best!
This weaves itself perforce into my business.
My father hath set guard to take my brother,
And I have one thing, of a queasy question,°
Which I must act. Briefness and fortune, work!   20
Brother, a word, descend.° Brother, I say!
[*Enter* EDGAR.] My father watches. O sir, fly this
    place.
Intelligence° is given where you are hid.
You have now the good advantage of the night.   24
Have you not spoken 'gainst the Duke of Cornwall?
He's coming hither, now, i' the night, i' the haste,
And Regan with him. Have you nothing said
Upon his party 'gainst the Duke of Albany?
Advise yourself.
EDG.   I am sure on 't, not a word.
EDM. I hear my father coming. Pardon me,   30
In cunning° I must draw my sword upon you.
Draw. Seem to defend yourself. Now quit you well.°
Yield. Come before my father. Light, ho, here!
Fly, Brother. Torches, torches! So farewell.
                                    [*Exit* EDGAR.]
Some blood drawn on me would beget opinion°   35
                              [*Wounds his arm.*]
Of my more fierce endeavor. I have seen drunkards
Do more than this in sport. Father, Father!
Stop, stop! No help?
[*Enter* GLOUCESTER *and* SERVANTS *with torches.*]
GLO. Now, Edmund, where's the villain?
EDM. Here stood he in the dark, his sharp sword
    out,   40
Mumbling° of wicked charms, conjuring the moon°
To stand 's auspicious° mistress.
GLO.   But where is he?
EDM. Look, sir, I bleed.
GLO.   Where is the villain, Edmund?
EDM. Fled this way, sir. When by no means he
    could ——
GLO. Pursue him, ho! — Go after.
                          [*Exeunt some* SERVANTS.]
                    " By no means " what?   45
EDM. Persuade me to the murder of your lordship,
But that I told him the revenging gods
'Gainst parricides did all their thunders bend,
Spoke with how manifold and strong a bond
The child was bound to the father. Sir, in fine,°   50
Seeing how loathly opposite I stood°
To his unnatural purpose, in fell° motion

With his preparèd° sword he charges home
My unprovided° body, lanced mine arm.
But when he saw my best alarumed spirits°   55
Bold in the quarrel's right, roused to the encounter,
Or whether gasted° by the noise I made,
Full suddenly he fled.
GLO.   Let him fly far.
Not in this land shall he remain uncaught,
And found — dispatch.° The noble Duke my mas-
    ter,   60
My worthy arch and patron,° comes tonight.
By his authority I will proclaim it,
That he which finds him shall deserve our thanks,
Bringing the murderous caitiff° to the stake.°
He that conceals him, death.   65
EDM. When I dissuaded him from his intent
And found him pight° to do it, with curst° speech
I threatened to discover him. He replied,
" Thou unpossessing bastard! Dost thou think,
If I would stand against thee, could the reposal   70
Of any trust, virtue, or worth in thee
Make thy words faithed?° No. What I should
    deny —
As this I would, aye, though thou didst produce
My very character° — I'd turn it all°
To thy suggestion,° plot, and damnèd practice.°   75
And thou must make° a dullard of the world
If they not thought the profits of my death
Were very pregnant and potential spurs°
To make thee seek it."
GLO.   Strong and fastened° villain!
Would he deny his letter? I never got° him.   80
                              [*Tucket° within*]
Hark, the Duke's trumpets! I know not why he
    comes.
All ports I'll bar,° the villain shall not 'scape,
The Duke must grant me that. Besides, his pic-
    ture
I will send far and near, that all the kingdom
May have due note of him, and of my land,   85
Loyal and natural° boy, I'll work the means
To make thee capable.°

19. **queasy question**: which needs delicate handling; *queasy* means on the point of vomiting.   21. **descend**: i.e., from the chamber where he has been hiding.   23. **Intelligence**: information.   31. **In cunning**: as a pretense.   32. **quit . . . well**: defend yourself well. Here they clash their swords together.   35. **beget opinion**: give the impression.   41–42. **Mumbling . . . mistress**: This is the kind of story which would especially appeal to Gloucester. Cf. I.ii.112.   41. **conjuring . . . moon**: calling on Hecate, goddess of witchcraft.   42. **auspicious**: favorable.   50. **in fine**: in short.   51. **how . . . stood**: with what loathing I opposed.   52. **fell**: fearful.

53. **prepared**: drawn.   54. **unprovided**: unguarded.   55. **my . . . spirits**: my stoutest spirits called out by the alarm.   57. **gasted**: terrified.   60. **And . . . dispatch**: and when he's found, kill him.   61. **arch . . . patron**: chief support and protector.   64. **caitiff**: wretch; lit., captive. **to . . . stake**: i.e., place of execution.   67. **pight**: determined. **curst**: bitter.   72. **faithed**: believed.   74. **character**: handwriting. Cf. I.ii.66. **turn it all**: make it appear to be.   75. **suggestion**: idea. **practice**: plot.   76–79. **make . . . it**: you would have to make people dull indeed before they would disbelieve that your chief motive was to benefit by my death.   78. **pregnant . . . spurs**: obvious and powerful encouragements.   79. **fastened**: confirmed.   80. **got**: begot. **s.d., Tucket**: trumpet call.   82. **ports . . . bar**: I'll have the seaports watched to prevent his escape.   86. **natural**: i.e., one who has the proper feelings of son to father. Gloucester does not as yet realize what "nature" means to Edmund. See I.ii.1.   87. **capable**: i.e., legitimate; lit., capable of succeeding as my heir.

[*Enter* CORNWALL, REGAN, *and* ATTENDANTS.]

CORN. How now, my noble friend! Since I came
  hither,
Which I can call but now, I have heard strange
  news.
REG. If it be true, all vengeance comes too short
Which can pursue the offender. How dost, my lord?
GLO. Oh, madam, my old heart is cracked, is
  cracked!   92
REG. What, did my father's godson seek your life?
He whom my father named? Your Edgar?
GLO. Oh, lady, lady, shame would have it hid!   95
REG. Was he not companion with the riotous
  knights
That tend upon my father?
GLO. I know not, madam. 'Tis too bad, too bad.
EDM. Yes, madam, he was of that consort.°   99
REG. No marvel then, though he were ill affected.°
'Tis they have put him on° the old man's death,
To have the waste and spoil of his revènues.
I have this present evening from my sister
Been well informed of them, and with such cautions
That if they come to sojourn at my house,   105
I'll not be there.
CORN.   Nor I, assure thee, Regan.
Edmund, I hear that you have shown your father
A childlike office.°
EDM.   'Twas my duty, sir.
GLO. He did bewray° his practice, and received
This hurt you see, striving to apprehend him.   110
CORN. Is he pursued?
GLO.   Aye, my good lord.
CORN. If he be taken, he shall never more
Be feared of doing° harm. Make your own purpose,
How in my strength you please.° For you, Edmund,
Whose virtue and obedience doth this instant   115
So much commend itself, you shall be ours.
Natures of such deep trust we shall much need.
You we first seize on.
EDM.   I shall serve you, sir,
Truly, however else.
GLO.   For him I thank your Grace.
CORN. You know not why we came to visit
  you ——   120
REG. Thus out of season, threading dark-eyed
  night.°
Occasions, noble Gloucester, of some poise,°
Wherein we must have use of your advice.
Our father he hath writ, so hath our sister,
Of differences, which I least thought it fit   125
To answer from° our home. The several messengers

From hence attend dispatch.° Our good old friend,
Lay comforts to your bosom, and bestow
Your needful counsel to our business,
Which craves the instant use.°
GLO.   I serve you, madam.   130
Your Graces are right welcome. [*Flourish. Exeunt.*]

SCENE II. *Before* GLOUCESTER'S *castle.*

[*Enter* KENT *and* OSWALD, *severally.*°]

OSW. Good dawning to thee, friend. Art of this
house?
KENT. Aye.
OSW. Where may we set our horses?
KENT. I' the mire.   5
OSW. Prithee, if thou lovest me, tell me.
KENT. I love thee not.
OSW. Why, then I care not for thee.
KENT. If I had thee in Lipsbury pinfold,° I would
make thee care for me.   10
OSW. Why dost thou use me thus? I know thee
not.
KENT. Fellow, I know thee.
OSW. What dost thou know me for?   14
KENT. A° knave, a rascal, an eater of broken
meats; a base, proud, shallow, beggarly, three-suited,
hundred-pound, filthy, worsted-stocking knave; a
lily-livered, action-taking knave; a whoreson, glass-
gazing, superserviceable, finical rogue; one-trunk-
inheriting slave; one that wouldst be a bawd in   20
way of good service, and art nothing but the compo-
sition of a knave, beggar, coward, pander, and the
son and heir of a mongrel bitch — one whom I will
beat into clamorous whining if thou deniest the least
syllable of thy addition.   26
OSW. Why, what a monstrous fellow art thou,
thus to rail on one that is neither known of thee nor
knows thee!   29
KENT. What a brazen-faced varlet art thou, to

127. **attend dispatch:** are waiting to be sent back.   130. **craves
. . . use:** requires immediate action.
  Sc. ii: s.d., **severally:** by different entrances.   9. **Lipsbury
pinfold:** This phrase has not been convincingly explained.
A pinfold is a village pound, a small enclosure in which strayed
beasts are kept until reclaimed by their owners; a pinfold was a
good place for a fight whence neither side could escape.   15–26. **A
. . . addition:** Kent here sums up the characteristics of the more
unpleasant kind of gentleman servingman of whom Oswald is a
fair specimen (see App. 14). **broken meats:** remains of food
sent down from the high table. **three-suited:** allowed three suits
a year. **hundred-pound:** i.e., the extent of his wealth. **worsted-
stocking:** no gentleman, or he would have worn silk. **lily-livered:**
cowardly. **action-taking knave:** one who goes to law instead of
risking a fight. **glass-gazing:** always looking at himself in a
mirror. **superserviceable:** too eager to do what his master
wishes. **finical:** finicky. **one-trunk-inheriting:** whose whole
inheritance from his father will go into one trunk. **bawd . . .
service:** ready to serve his master's lusts if it will please him.
composition: mixture. **pander:** pimp. **addition:** lit., title of
honor added to a man's name.

99. **consort:** party.   100. **though . . . affected:** if he had traitor-
ous thoughts.   101. **put . . . on:** persuaded him to cause.
108. **childlike office:** filial service.   109. **bewray:** reveal.
113. **of doing:** because he might do.   113–14. **Make . . . please:**
use my authority for any action you care to take.   121. **thread-
ing . . . night:** making our way through the darkness.   122. **poise:**
weight.   126. **from:** away from.

deny thou knowest me! Is it two days ago since I tripped up thy heels and beat thee before the King? Draw, you rogue. For though it be night, yet the moon shines. I'll make a sop o' the moonshine of you.° Draw, you whoreson cullionly° barber- 35
monger,° draw.   [*Drawing his sword.*]

OSW. Away! I have nothing to do with thee.

KENT. Draw, you rascal. You come with letters against the King, and take vanity the puppet's part° against the royalty of her father. Draw, you rogue, or I'll so carbonado° your shanks. Draw, you rascal, come your ways. 42

OSW. Help, ho! Murder! Help!

KENT. Strike, you slave. Stand, rogue, stand, you neat slave, strike.   [*Beating him.*]

OSW. Help, ho! Murder! Murder! 46

[*Enter* EDMUND, *with his rapier drawn,* CORNWALL, REGAN, GLOUCESTER, *and* SERVANTS.]

EDM. How now! What's the matter?

                    [*Parting them.*]

KENT. With you, goodman boy,° an you please. Come, I'll flesh you,° come on, young master.

GLO. Weapons! Arms! What's the matter here?

CORN. Keep peace, upon your lives. 52
He dies that strikes again. What is the matter?

REG. The messengers from our sister and the King. 55

CORN. What is your difference?° Speak.

OSW. I am scarce in breath, my lord.

KENT. No marvel, you have so bestirred your valor. You cowardly rascal, Nature disclaims in thee. A tailor made thee.° 60

CORN. Thou art a strange fellow — a tailor make a man?

KENT. Aye, a tailor, sir. A stonecutter or a painter could not have made him so ill, though he had been but two hours at the trade. 65

CORN. Speak yet, how grew your quarrel?

OSW. This ancient ruffian, sir, whose life I have spared at suit of his gray beard—— 68

KENT. Thou whoreson zed! Thou unnecessary letter!° My lord, if you will give me leave, I will

tread this unbolted° villain into mortar, and daub the walls of a jakes° with him. Spare my gray beard, you wagtail?°

CORN. Peace, sirrah!

You beastly knave, know you no reverence?° 75

KENT. Yes, sir, but anger hath a privilege.°

CORN. Why art thou angry?

KENT. That such a slave as this should wear a sword,
Who wears no honesty. Such smiling rogues as these,
Like rats, oft bite the holy cords a-twain 80
Which are too intrinse to unloose;° smooth° every passion
That in the natures of their lords rebel;
Bring oil to fire, snow to their colder moods;
Renege, affirm,° and turn their halcyon° beaks
With every gale and vary of their masters, 85
Knowing naught, like dogs, but following.
A plague upon your epileptic visage!
Smile you my speeches, as I were a fool?
Goose,° if I had you upon Sarum° plain,
I'd drive ye cackling home to Camelot.° 90

CORN. What, art thou mad, old fellow?

GLO. How fell you out? Say that.

KENT. No contraries hold more antipathy
Than I and such a knave.

CORN. Why dost thou call him knave? What is his fault? 95

KENT. His countenance likes me not.°

CORN. No more perchance does mine, nor his, nor hers.

KENT. Sir, 'tis my occupation to be plain.
I have seen better faces in my time
Than stands on any shoulder that I see 100
Before me at this instant.

CORN.   This° is some fellow
Who, having been praised for bluntness, doth affect
A saucy roughness,° and constrains the garb
Quite from his nature.° He cannot flatter, he——
An honest mind and plain — he must speak truth!
An they will take it, so. If not, he's plain. 106
These kind of knaves I know, which in this plainness

Harbor more craft and more corrupter ends
Than twenty silly ducking observants
That stretch their duties nicely.°   110
    KENT. Sir,° in good faith, in sincere verity,
Under the allowance of your great aspéct,
Whose influence, like the wreath of radiant fire
On flickering Phoebus'° front ——
    CORN.   What mean'st by this?   114
    KENT. To go out of my dialect, which you discom-
mend so much. I know, sir, I am no flatterer. He that
beguiled you in a plain accent was a plain knave,
which, for my part, I will not be, though I should
win your displeasure to entreat me to 't.°   120
    CORN. What was the offense you gave him?
    OSW. I never gave him any.
It pleased the King his master very late
To strike at me, upon his misconstruction,°   124
When he, conjunct,° and flattering his displeasure,
Tripped me behind; being down, insulted, railed,
And put upon him such a deal of man
That worthied him,° got praises of the King
For him attempting° who was self-subdued,°
And in the fleshment° of this dread exploit   130
Drew on me here again.
    KENT.   None of these rogues and cowards
But Ajax is their fool.°
    CORN.   Fetch forth the stocks!
You stubborn° ancient knave, you reverend° brag-
    gart,
We'll teach you ——
    KENT.   Sir, I am too old to learn.
Call not your stocks for me. I serve the King,   135
On whose employment I was sent to you.
You shall do small respect, show too bold malice
Against the grace and person of my master,
Stocking his messenger.°
    CORN. Fetch forth the stocks! As I have life and
    honor,   140

109–10. silly . . . nicely: silly servants who are always bowing to
their masters as they strain to carry out their orders.
111–14. Sir . . . front: Kent now changes his tone from the honest
blunt man to the affected courtier. See I.iv.34. Phoebus:
the sun god.   116–20. He . . . to't: the man who posed as blunt
and honest and deceived you was simply a knave. I shall never
be a knave, even if you ask me and are angry because I refuse.
124. upon . . . misconstruction: because he deliberately misinter-
preted my words.   125. conjunct: i.e., joining with the King.
128. worthied him: got him favor.   129. attempting: attacking.
self-subdued: made no resistance.   130. fleshment: excitement.
131–32. None . . . fool: This cryptic but devastating remark
rouses Cornwall to fury, for he realizes from Kent's insolent tone,
manner, and gesture that by "Ajax" he is himself intended. Ajax
was the ridiculous braggart of the Greek army whom Shakespeare
had already dramatized in *Tr & Cr*. The name Ajax had further
unsavory significances for the original audience, for "Ajax"
was a common synonym for a jakes — a very evil-smelling place.
Kent thus implies "All these knaves and cowards are fooling this
stinking braggart." See App. 4.   133. stubborn: rude. rever-
end: old.   137–39. You . . . messenger: As the King's repre-
sentative, Kent is entitled to respectful treatment; to put him in
the stocks is to offer an intolerable insult to the King. See ll.
147–54 below and II.iv.22–24.

There shall he sit till noon.
    REG. Till noon! Till night, my lord, and all night
too.
    KENT. Why, madam, if I were your father's dog,
You should not use me so.
    REG.   Sir, being his knave, I will.
    CORN. This is a fellow of the selfsame color   145
Our sister speaks of. Come, bring away° the stocks!
                              [*Stocks brought out*]
    GLO. Let me beseech your Grace not to do so.
His fault is much, and the good King his master
Will check° him for 't. Your purposed low correc-
    tion°
Is such as basest and contemnèd'st° wretches   150
For pilferings and most common trespasses
Are punished with. The King must take it ill
That he, so slightly valued in his messenger,
Should have him thus restrained.
    CORN.   I'll answer that.
    REG. My sister may receive it much more worse
To have her gentleman abused, assaulted,   156
For following her affairs. Put in his legs.
                              [KENT *is put in the stocks.*]
Come, my good lord, away.
                              [*Exeunt all but* GLOUCESTER *and* KENT.]
    GLO. I am sorry for thee, friend. 'Tis the Duke's
    pleasure,
Whose disposition all the world well knows   160
Will not be rubbed° nor stopped. I'll entreat for thee.
    KENT. Pray do not, sir. I have watched and trav-
    eled hard,
Some time I shall sleep out, the rest I'll whistle.
A good man's fortune may grow out at heels.°   165
Give you good morrow!°
    GLO. The Duke's to blame in this, 'twill be ill-
    taken.   [*Exit.*]
    KENT. Good King, that must approve the common
    saw,°
Thou out of Heaven's benediction comest
To the warm sun!°
Approach, thou beacon to this underglobe,°   170
That by thy comfortable beams I may
Peruse this letter! Nothing almost sees miracles
But misery.° I know 'tis from Cordelia,
Who hath most fortunately been informed
Of my obscurèd course,° and shall find time   175
From this enormous state,° seeking to give

146. bring away: fetch out.   149. check: rebuke, punish.
purposed . . . correction: the degrading punishment which you
propose.   150. contemnèd'st: most despised.   161. rubbed:
turned aside, a metaphor from the game of bowls.   164. A . . .
heels: even a good man may suffer a shabby fate.   165. Give . . .
morrow: a good morning to you.   167. approve . . . saw: stress
the truth of the common proverb.   168–69. Thou . . . sun: you
are coming out of the shade into the heat.   170. beacon . . .
underglobe: the rising sun.   172–73. Nothing . . . misery: only
those who are wretched appreciate miracles.   175. obscurèd
course: i.e., my actions in disguise.   176. this . . . state: these
wicked times.

Losses their remedies. All weary and o'erwatched,
Take vantage, heavy eyes, not to behold
This shameful lodging. 179
Fortune, good night. Smile once more, turn thy
wheel! [*Sleeps.*]

SCENE III. *A wood.*

[*Enter* EDGAR.]

EDG. I heard myself proclaimed,°
And by the happy° hollow of a tree
Escaped the hunt. No port is free, no place,
That guard and most unusual vigilance
Does not attend my taking.° Whiles I may 'scape 5
I will preserve myself, and am bethought°
To take the basest and most poorest shape
That ever penury in contempt of man
Brought near to beast.° My face I'll grime with filth,
Blanket° my loins, elf° all my hair in knots, 10
And with presented nakedness° outface
The winds and persecutions of the sky.
The country gives me proof and precedent°
Of Bedlam beggars,° who with roaring voices
Strike in their numbed and mortified° bare
arms 15
Pins, wooden pricks, nails, sprigs of rosemary,
And with this horrible object, from low° farms,
Poor pelting° villages, sheepcotes and mills,
Sometime with lunatic bans,° sometime with pray-
ers, 19
Enforce their charity. Poor Turlygod! Poor Tom!°
That's something yet. Edgar I nothing am.° [*Exit.*]

SCENE IV. *Before* GLOUCESTER'S *castle.* KENT *in the stocks.*

[*Enter* LEAR, FOOL, *and* GENTLEMAN.]

LEAR. 'Tis strange that they should so depart from
home
And not send back my messenger.
GENT. As I learned,

Sc. iii: 1. proclaimed: See II.i.82–85. 2. happy: lucky.
5. attend my taking: watch to take me. 6. am bethought: have
decided. 8–9. penury . . . beast: poverty, to show that man
is a contemptible creature, reduced to the level of a beast.
10. Blanket: cover with only a blanket. elf: mat. Matted hair
was believed to be caused by elves. Cf. *R & J*, I.iv.88–91.
11. with . . . nakedness: bold in my nakedness. 13. proof . . .
precedent: examples. 14. Bedlam beggars: lunatics discharged
from Bedlam (or Bethlehem) Hospital, the London madhouse.
These sturdy beggars were the terror of the countryside. See
I.ii.148. 15. mortified: numbed. 17. low: humble. 18. pelt-
ing: paltry. 19. bans: curses. 20. Poor . . . Tom: Edgar re-
hearses the names which a bedlam calls himself. 21. That's . . .
am: there's still a chance for me; as Edgar I am a dead man.

The night before there was no purpose° in them
Of this remove.
KENT. Hail to thee, noble master!
LEAR. Ha! 5
Makest thou this shame thy pastime?°
KENT. No, my lord.
FOOL. Ha, ha! He wears cruel° garters. Horses are
tied by the heads, dogs and bears by the neck, mon-
keys by the loins, and men by the legs. When a man's
overlusty at legs,° then he wears wooden nether-
stocks.° 11
LEAR. What's he that hath so much thy place mis-
took
To set thee here?
KENT. It is both he and she,
Your son and daughter.
LEAR. No. 15
KENT. Yes.
LEAR. No, I say.
KENT. I say yea.
LEAR. No, no, they would not.
KENT. Yes, they have. 20
LEAR. By Jupiter, I swear no.
KENT. By Juno, I swear aye.
LEAR. They durst not do 't,
They could not, would not do 't. 'Tis worse than
murder
To do upon respect° such violent outrage.
Resolve° me with all modest haste which way 25
Thou mightest deserve, or they impose, this usage,
Coming from us.°
KENT. My lord, when at their home
I did commend your Highness' letters to them,
Ere I was risen from the place that showed
My duty kneeling, came there a reeking post,° 30
Stewed in his haste, half-breathless, panting forth
From Goneril his mistress salutations,
Delivered letters, spite of intermission,°
Which presently° they read. On whose contents
They summoned up their meiny,° straight took
horse, 35
Commanded me to follow and attend
The leisure of their answer, gave me cold looks.
And meeting here the other messenger,
Whose welcome, I perceived, had poisoned mine—
Being the very fellow that of late 40
Displayed so saucily° against your Highness—
Having more man than wit about me, drew.
He raised the house with loud and coward cries.

Sc. iv: 3. purpose: intention. 6. Makest . . . pastime: are
you sitting there for amusement? 7. cruel: with a pun on
"crewel" — worsted. 10. overlusty at legs: i.e., a vagabond.
11. netherstocks: stockings. 24. upon respect: the respect due
to me, their King and father. 25. Resolve: inform. 27. Com-
ing . . . us: Lear uses the royal "we" — "from us, the King."
30. reeking post: sweating messenger. 33. spite of intermission:
in spite of the delay in reading my letter (which should have come
first). 34. presently: immediately. 35. meiny: followers.
41. Displayed so saucily: behaved so insolently.

Your son and daughter found this trespass worth°
The shame which here it suffers.   45
    FOOL. Winter's not gone yet° if the wild geese fly
that way.

        "Fathers that wear rags
            Do make their children blind,
        But fathers that bear bags°   50
            Shall see their children kind.
        Fortune, that arrant whore,
            Ne'er turns the key° to the poor."

But for all this, thou shalt have as many dolors° for
thy daughters as thou canst tell° in a year.   55
    LEAR. Oh,° how this mother swells up toward my
        heart!
Hysterica passio, down, thou climbing sorrow,
Thy element's° below! Where is this daughter?
    KENT. With the Earl, sir, here within.   59
    LEAR. Follow me not, stay here.   [*Exit.*]
    GENT. Made you no more offense but what you
speak of?
    KENT. None.
How chance the King comes with so small a train?
    FOOL. An thou hadst been set i' the stocks for that
question, thou hadst well deserved it.   66
    KENT. Why, fool?
    FOOL. We'll° set thee to school to an ant, to teach
thee there's no laboring i' the winter. All that follow
their noses° are led by their eyes but blind men, 70
and there's not a nose among twenty but can smell
him that's stinking. Let go thy hold when a great
wheel runs down a hill, lest it break thy neck with
following it, but the great one that goes up the hill,
let him draw thee after. When a wise man gives 75
thee better counsel, give me mine again. I would
have none but knaves follow it, since a fool gives it.

        "That sir which serves and seeks for gain,
            And follows but for form,°   80
        Will pack° when it begins to rain,
            And leave thee in the storm.

        "But I will tarry, the fool will stay,
            And let the wise man fly.
        The knave turns fool that runs away,   85
            The fool no knave, perdy."°

    KENT. Where learned you this, fool?

44. worth: deserving.   46. Winter's . . . yet: there's more
trouble to come.   50. bear bags: have money.   53. turns . . .
key: opens the door.   54. dolors: with a pun on "dollars."
55. tell: count.   56–58. Oh . . . below: The *mother*, called also
hysterica passio, was an overwhelming feeling of physical distress
and suffocation. Lear's mental suffering is now beginning to cause
a physical breakdown. This sensation, and the violent throbbing
of his heart until finally it ceases, can be traced in Lear's speeches.
See ll. 122, 138, 200–01; III.iv.14.   58. element: natural place.
68–77. We'll . . . it: The fool is so much amused at Kent's
discomfiture that he strings off a series of wise sayings to
show his own clearer understanding of Lear's state.   69–70. fol-
low . . . noses: go straight ahead.   80. but . . . form: merely
for show.   81. pack: clear out.   86. perdy: by God.

    FOOL. Not i' the stocks, fool.
        [*Re-enter* LEAR, *with* GLOUCESTER.]
    LEAR. Deny to speak with me? They are sick?
        They are weary?
They have traveled all the night? Mere fetches,°   90
The images° of revolt and flying off.
Fetch me a better answer.
    GLO.   My dear lord,
You know the fiery quality° of the Duke,
How unremovable and fixed he is
In his own course.   95
    LEAR. Vengeance! Plague! Death! Confusion!
Fiery? What quality? Why, Gloucester, Gloucester,
I'd speak with the Duke of Cornwall and his wife.
    GLO. Well, my good lord, I have informed them
        so.
    LEAR. Informed them! Dost thou understand me,
        man?   100
    GLO. Aye, my good lord.
    LEAR. The King would speak with Cornwall, the
        dear father
Would with his daughter speak, commands her
        service.
Are they informed of this? My breath and blood!
"Fiery"? "The fiery Duke"? Tell the hot Duke
        that——   105
No, but not yet. Maybe he is not well.
Infirmity doth still neglect all office
Whereto our health is bound.° We are not our-
        selves
When nature being oppressed commands the mind
To suffer with the body. I'll forbear,   110
And am fall'n out with my more headier will,°
To take the indisposed and sickly fit
For the sound man. [*Looking on* KENT] Death on
        my state! Wherefore
Should he sit here? This act persuades me
That this remotion° of the Duke and her   115
Is practice° only. Give me my servant forth.°
Go tell the Duke and 's wife I'd speak with them,
Now, presently. Bid them come forth and hear me,
Or at their chamber door I'll beat the drum
Till it cry sleep to death.°   120
    GLO. I would have all well betwixt you. [*Exit.*]
    LEAR. Oh, me, my heart, my rising heart! But
        down!°   122
    FOOL. Cry to it, Nuncle, as the cockney° did to
the eels when she put 'em i' the paste alive. She
knapped° 'em o' the coxcombs with a stick, and
cried "Down, wantons, down!" 'Twas her brother
that, in pure kindness to his horse, buttered his hay.

90. fetches: excuses.   91. images: exact likenesses.   93. qual-
ity: nature.   107–08. Infirmity . . . bound: when a man is sick,
he neglects his proper duty.   111. am . . . will: regret my hasti-
ness.   115. remotion: removal.   116. practice: pretense. Give
. . . forth: release my servant at once.   120. cry . . . death: kill
sleep by its noise.   122. Oh . . . down: See ll. 56–58.   123. cock-
ney: Londoner.   125. knapped: cracked.

[*Re-enter* GLOUCESTER, *with* CORNWALL, REGAN, *and*
          SERVANTS.]

LEAR. Good morrow to you both.

CORN.   Hail to your Grace! [KENT *is set at liberty.*]

REG. I am glad to see your Highness.   130

LEAR. Regan, I think you are, I know what reason
I have to think so. If thou shouldst not be glad,
I would divorce me from thy mother's tomb,
Sepúlchring an adultress.° [*To* KENT] Oh, are you
          free?
Some other time for that. Belovèd Regan,   135
Thy sister's naught.° O Regan, she hath tied
Sharp-toothed unkindness, like a vulture, here.
                              [*Points to his heart.*]
I can scarce speak to thee, thou'lt not believe
With how depraved a quality —— O Regan!   139

REG. I pray you, sir, take patience. I have hope
You less know how to value her desert
Than she to scant her duty.

LEAR.   Say, how is that?

REG. I cannot think my sister in the least
Would fail her obligation. If, sir, perchance
She have restrained the riots of your followers,   145
'Tis on such ground and to such wholesome end
As clears her from all blame.

LEAR. My curses on her!

REG.   Oh, sir, you are old,
Nature in you stands on the very verge
Of her confine.° You should be ruled and led   150
By some discretion that discerns your state
Better than you yourself. Therefore I pray you
That to our sister you do make return.
Say you have wronged her, sir.

LEAR.   Ask her forgiveness?   154
Do you but mark how this becomes the house.° ——
[*Kneeling*] "Dear daughter, I confess that I am old,
Age is unnecessary. On my knees I beg
That you'll vouchsafe me raiment, bed, and food."

REG. Good sir, no more, these are unsightly tricks.
Return you to my sister.

LEAR.   [*Rising*] Never, Regan.   160
She hath abated me of half my train,
Looked black upon me, struck me with her tongue,
Most serpentlike, upon the very heart.
All the stored vengeances of Heaven fall
On her ingrateful top!° Strike her young bones,
You taking airs, with lameness.

CORN.   Fie, sir, fie!   166

LEAR. You nimble lightnings, dart your blinding
          flames
Into her scornful eyes. Infect her beauty,
You fen-sucked fogs,° drawn by the powerful sun
To fall° and blast her pride.   170

REG. Oh, the blest gods! So will you wish on me
When the rash mood is on.

LEAR. No, Regan, thou shalt never have my curse.
Thy tender-hefted° nature shall not give
Thee o'er to harshness. Her eyes are fierce, but thine
Do comfort and not burn. 'Tis not in thee   176
To grudge my pleasures, to cut off my train,
To bandy hasty words, to scant my sizes,°
And in conclusion to oppose the bolt°
Against my coming in. Thou better know'st   180
The offices of nature, bond of childhood,
Effects of courtesy, dues of gratitude.
Thy half o' the kingdom hast thou not forgot,
Wherein I thee endowed.

REG.   Good sir, to the purpose.°

LEAR. Who put my man i' the stocks?
                              [*Tucket within.*]

CORN.   What trumpet's that?   185

REG. I know 't, my sister's. This approves° her
          letter,
That she would soon be here.
          [*Enter* OSWALD.]   Is your lady come?

LEAR. This is a slave whose easy-borrowed pride
Dwells in the fickle grace of her he follows.°
Out, varlet,° from my sight!

CORN.   What means your Grace?   190

LEAR. Who stocked my servant? Regan, I have
          good hope
Thou didst not know on 't. Who comes here?
[*Enter* GONERIL.]   O Heavens,
If you do love old men, if your sweet sway
Allow° obedience, if yourselves are old,
Make it your cause. Send down, and take my part!
[*To* GONERIL] Art not ashamed to look upon this
          beard?   196
O Regan, wilt thou take her by the hand?

GON. Why not by the hand, sir? How have I of-
          fended?
All's not offense that indiscretion finds
And dotage terms so.°

LEAR.   O sides, you are too tough,   200
Will you yet hold?° How came my man i' the
          stocks?

CORN. I set him there, sir. But his own disorders
Deserved much less advancement.°

LEAR.   You! Did you?

REG. I pray you, Father, being weak, seem so.°
If till the expiration of your month   205
You will return and sojourn with my sister,

---

174. **tender-hefted**: gently framed.   178. **scant my sizes**: reduce
my allowances.   179. **oppose . . . bolt**: bar the door.   184. **Good
. . . purpose**: and in good time to; or, please talk sense.
186. **approves**: confirms.   188–89. **whose . . . follows**: who soon
puts on airs because his fickle mistress favors him.   190. **varlet**:
knave.   194. **Allow**: approve of.   199–200. **that . . . so**: be-
cause a silly old man says so. See I.i.149–51,n.   200–01. **O
. . . hold**: See II.iv.56–58,n, above.   203. **advancement**: pro-
motion.   204. **seem so**: i.e., behave suitably.

133–34. **divorce . . . adultress**: i.e., I would suspect that your
dead mother had been false to me.   136. **naught**: wicked.
150. **confine**: boundary, edge.   155. **becomes . . . house**: i.e.,
suits my dignity.   165. **top**: head.   169. **fen-sucked fogs**: Cf.
I.iv.321.   170. **fall**: fall upon.

Dismissing half your train, come then to me.
I am now from home and out of that provision
Which shall be needful for your entertainment.°
   LEAR. Return to her, and fifty men dismissed?
No, rather I abjure° all roofs, and choose   211
To wage against the enmity o' the air,
To be a comrade with the wolf and owl —
Necessity's sharp pinch! Return with her?   214
Why, the hot-blooded France, that dowerless took
Our youngest-born — I could as well be brought
To knee his throne and, squirelike,° pension beg
To keep base life afoot. Return with her?
Persuade me rather to be slave and sumpter°
To this detested groom.   [*Pointing at* OSWALD.]
   GON.   At your choice, sir.   220
   LEAR. I prithee, Daughter, do not make me mad.
I will not trouble thee, my child. Farewell.
We'll no more meet, no more see one another.
But yet thou art my flesh, my blood, my daughter,
Or rather a disease that's in my flesh   225
Which I must needs call mine. Thou art a boil,
A plague sore, an embossed carbuncle,°
In my corrupted blood. But I'll not chide thee.
Let shame come when it will, I do not call it.
I do not bid the thunderbearer° shoot,   230
Nor tell tales of thee to high-judging Jove.
Mend when thou canst, be better at thy leisure.
I can be patient, I can stay with Regan,
I and my hundred knights.
   REG.   Not altogether so.
I looked not for you yet, nor am provided   235
For your fit welcome. Give ear, sir, to my sister,
For those that mingle reason with your passion
Must be content to think you old,° and so ——
But she knows what she does.
   LEAR.   Is this well spoken?
   REG. I dare avouch° it, sir. What, fifty followers?
Is it not well? What should you need of more?   241
Yea, or so many, sith° that both charge and danger°
Speak 'gainst so great a number? How in one house
Should many people under two commands
Hold amity? 'Tis hard, almost impossible.   245
   GON. Why might not you, my lord, receive attendance
From those that she calls servants or from mine?
   REG. Why not, my lord? If then they chanced to
   slack° you,
We could control them. If you will come to me,
For now I spy a danger, I entreat you   250
To bring but five and twenty. To no more

Will I give place or notice.
   LEAR. I gave you all ——
   REG.   And in good time you gave it.
   LEAR. Made you my guardians, my depositaries,°
But kept a reservation° to be followed   255
With such a number. What, must I come to you
With five and twenty, Regan? Said you so?
   REG. And speak 't again, my lord, no more with
   me.
   LEAR. Those wicked creatures yet do look well-
   favored,°
When others are more wicked. Not being the worst
Stands in some rank of praise.° [*To* GONERIL] I'll go
   with thee.   261
Thy fifty yet doth double five and twenty,
And thou art twice her love.
   GON.   Hear me, my lord.
What need you five and twenty, ten, or five,
To follow in a house where twice so many   265
Have a command to tend you?
   REG.   What need one?
   LEAR. Oh,° reason not the need. Our basest beg-
   gars
Are in the poorest thing superfluous.°
Allow not nature more than nature needs,
Man's life's as cheap as beast's. Thou art a lady.   270
If only to go warm were gorgeous,
Why, nature needs not what thou gorgeous wear'st,
Which scarcely keeps thee warm. But for true
   need ——
You Heavens, give me that patience, patience I need!
You see me here, you gods, a poor old man,   275
As full of grief as age, wretched in both.
If it be you that stirs these daughters' hearts
Against their father, fool me not so much
To bear it tamely.° Touch me with noble anger,
And let not women's weapons, water drops,   280
Stain my man's cheeks! No, you unnatural hags,
I will have such revenges on you both
That all the world shall —— I will do such
   things —
What they are, yet I know not, but they shall be
The terrors of the earth. You think I'll weep.   285
No, I'll not weep.°
I have full cause of° weeping, but this heart
Shall break into a hundred thousand flaws°
Or ere I'll weep. O fool, I shall go mad!
                 [*Exeunt* LEAR, GLOUCESTER, KENT, *and* FOOL.]

---

209. entertainment: maintenance.   211. abjure: refuse with an oath.   217. squirelike: like a servant.   219. sumpter: pack horse, beast of burden.   227. embossed carbuncle: swollen boil.   230. thunderbearer: Jupiter.   237–38. those . . . old: those who consider your passion with reason realize that you are old — and should be wise.   240. avouch: guarantee.   242. sith: since.   charge . . . danger: expense and risk of maintaining.   248. slack: neglect.

254. depositaries: trustees.   255. reservation: condition. See I.i.134–41.   259. well-favored: handsome.   260–61. Not . . . praise: i.e., since Goneril is not so bad as Regan, that is one thing in her favor.   267–74. Oh . . . need: the needs of a beggar are very different from the needs of a king — but above all Lear needs not dignity but patience.   267–68. Our . . . superfluous: even the few possessions of a beggar are not absolutely necessary.   278–79. fool . . . tamely: do not degrade me so much that I just tamely endure it.   286. No . . . weep: See *Lear* Intro. p. 782b.   287. of: for.   288. flaws: broken pieces.

CORN. Let us withdraw, 'twill be a storm.   290

              [Storm and tempest.]

REG. This house is little. The old man and his people

Cannot be well bestowed.

GON.   'Tis his own blame. Hath put himself from rest,

And must needs taste his folly.

REG. For his particular,° I'll receive him gladly,

But not one follower.

GON.   So am I purposed.   296

Where is my Lord of Gloucester?

CORN. Followed the old man forth. He is returned.

          [Re-enter GLOUCESTER.]

GLO. The King is in high rage.

CORN.   Whither is he going?   299

GLO. He calls to horse, but will I know not whither.

CORN. 'Tis best to give him way, he leads himself.

GON. My lord, entreat him by no means to stay.

GLO. Alack, the night comes on, and the bleak winds

Do sorely ruffle. For many miles about

There's scarce a bush.

REG.   Oh, sir, to willful men   305

The injuries that they themselves procure

Must be their schoolmasters. Shut up your doors.

He is attended with a desperate train,

And what they may incense° him to, being apt°

To have his ear abused,° wisdom bids fear.   310

CORN. Shut up your doors, my lord, 'tis a wild night.

My Regan counsels well. Come out o' the storm.

                   [Exeunt.]

Act III

SCENE I. *A heath.*

[Storm still.° Enter KENT and a GENTLEMAN, meeting.]

KENT. Who's there, besides foul weather?

GENT. One minded like the weather, most unquietly.

KENT. I know you. Where's the King?

GENT. Contending with the fretful elements.

Bids the wind blow the earth into the sea,   5

Or swell the curlèd waters 'bove the main,°

That things might change or cease; tears his white hair,

Which the impetuous blasts, with eyeless° rage,

Catch in their fury, and make nothing of;

Strives in his little world of man° to outscorn   10

The to-and-fro-conflicting wind and rain.

This night, wherein the cub-drawn bear° would couch,°

The lion and the belly-pinchèd° wolf

Keep their fur dry, unbonneted° he runs,

And bids what will take all.

KENT.   But who is with him?   15

GENT. None but the fool, who labors to outjest

His heart-struck injuries.

KENT.   Sir, I do know you,

And dare, upon the warrant of my note,°

Commend a dear° thing to you. There is division,

Although as yet the face of it be covered   20

With mutual cunning, 'twixt Albany and Cornwall,

Who have — as who have not that their great stars

Throned and set high?° — servants, who seem no less,

Which are to France the spies and speculations°

Intelligent of our state° — what hath been seen,

Either in snuffs and packings° of the Dukes,   26

Or the hard rein which both of them have borne

Against the old kind King, or something deeper,

Whereof perchance these are but furnishings° ——

But true it is, from France there comes a power°   30

Into this scattered kingdom, who already,

Wise in our negligence, have secret feet

In some of our best ports and are at point°

To show their open banner. Now to you.

If on my credit° you dare build so far   35

To make your speed to Dover, you shall find

Some that will thank you, making just report

Of how unnatural and bemadding sorrow

The King hath cause to plain.°

I am a gentleman of blood° and breeding,   40

And from some knowledge and assurance° offer

This office° to you.

GENT. I will talk further with you.

KENT.   No, do not.

For confirmation that I am much more

Than my outwall,° open this purse and take   45

What it contains. If you shall see Cordelia —

---

8. eyeless: blind.   10. little . . . man: It was a common Elizabethan idea, sometimes elaborately worked out, that individual man was a little world (microcosm) and reproduced in himself the universe (macrocosm).   12. cub-drawn bear: she-bear sucked dry, and therefore hungry. couch: take shelter.   13. belly-pinched: ravenous.   14. unbonneted: without a hat.   18. upon . . . note: guaranteed by my observation of you.   19. dear: precious.   22–23. that . . . high: whom Fate has set in a great position.   24. speculations: informers.   25. Intelligent . . . state: report on the state of our affairs.   26. snuffs . . . packings: resentment and plotting against each other.   29. furnishings: excuses. The sentence is not finished.   30. power: army.   33. at point: on the point of, about to.   35. credit: trustworthiness.   39. plain: complain.   40. blood: noble family.   41. knowledge . . . assurance: sure knowledge.   42. office: undertaking.   45. outwall: outside.

295. his particular: himself personally.   309. incense: incite. apt: ready.   310. abused: deceived.

Act III, Sc. i: s.d., still: continuing.   6. main: mainland.

As fear not but you shall — show her this ring,
And she will tell you who your fellow° is
That yet you do not know. Fie on this storm!
I will go seek the King.

GENT.   Give me your hand.   50
Have you no more to say?

KENT. Few words, but, to effect, more than all
    yet —
That when we have found the King — in which your
    pain°
That way, I'll this — he that first lights on him   54
Holloa the other.   [*Exeunt severally.*]

SCENE II. *Another part of the heath.*
Storm still.

[*Enter* LEAR *and* FOOL.]

LEAR. Blow, winds, and crack your cheeks! Rage!
    Blow!
You cataracts and hurricanoes,° spout
Till you have drenched our steeples, drowned the
    cocks!°
You sulphurous and thought-executing° fires,
Vaunt-couriers° to oak-cleaving thunderbolts,   5
Singe my white head! And thou, all-shaking thun-
    der,
Smite flat the thick rotundity o' the world!
Crack nature's molds,° all germens° spill at once
That make ingrateful man!   9

FOOL. O Nuncle, Court holy water° in a dry
house is better than this rain water out o' door. Good
Nuncle, in, and ask thy daughters' blessing. Here's
a night pities neither wise man nor fool.

LEAR. Rumble thy bellyful! Spit, fire! Spout, rain!
Nor rain, wind, thunder, fire, are my daughters.   15
I tax° not you, you elements, with unkindness.
I never gave you kingdom, called you children,
You owe me no subscription.° Then let fall
Your horrible pleasure. Here I stand, your slave,
A poor, infirm, weak, and despised old man.   20
But yet I call you servile ministers°
That have with two pernicious daughters joined
Your high-engendered battles° 'gainst a head
So old and white as this. Oh, oh! 'Tis foul!

FOOL. He that has a house to put 's head in has a
good headpiece.   26

"The° codpiece° that will house
    Before the head has any,
The head and he shall louse
    So beggars marry many.   30
The man that makes his toe
    What he his heart should make
Shall of a corn cry woe,
    And turn his sleep to wake."

For there was never yet fair woman but she made
mouths in a glass.°   36

LEAR. No, I will be the pattern of all patience,
I will say nothing.

[*Enter* KENT.]

KENT. Who's there?

FOOL. Marry,° here's grace and a codpiece — that's
a wise man and a fool.   41

KENT. Alas, sir, are you here? Things that love
    night
Love not such nights as these. The wrathful skies
Gallow° the very wanderers of the dark   44
And make them keep their caves. Since I was man,
Such sheets of fire, such bursts of horrid thunder,
Such groans of roaring wind and rain, I never
Remember to have heard. Man's nature cannot
    carry°
The affliction nor the fear.

LEAR.   Let the great gods,
That keep this dreadful pother° o'er our heads,   50
Find out their enemies now. Tremble, thou wretch,
That hast within thee undivulgèd crimes
Unwhipped of justice. Hide thee, thou bloody hand,
Thou perjured, and thou simular man of virtue°
That art incestuous. Caitiff, to pieces shake,   55
That under covert and convenient seeming°
Hast practiced on man's life. Close pent-up guilts,
Rive your concealing continents° and cry
These dreadful summoners grace.° I am a man
More sinned against than sinning.

KENT.   Alack, bareheaded! 60
Gracious my lord, hard by here is a hovel.
Some friendship will it lend you 'gainst the tempest.
Repose you there while I to this hard house —
More harder than the stones whereof 'tis raised,

27–34. The . . . wake: the man who goes wenching before he has
a roof over his head will become a lousy beggar. The man who is
kinder to his toe than to his heart will be kept awake by his
corns — i.e., Lear has been kinder to his feet (his daughters)
than to his heart (himself). The Fool's remarks, especially
when cryptic and indecent, are not easy to paraphrase.
27. codpiece: lit., the opening in the hose. See Pl. 8c and comment
on p. 93b.   35–36. made . . . glass: made faces in a mirror.
40. Marry: Mary, by the Virgin.   44. Gallow: terrify.
48. carry: endure.   50. pother: turmoil.   54. simular . . . vir-
tue: a man who pretends to be virtuous.   56. under . . . seem-
ing: under a false appearance of propriety.   57. Rive . . . con-
tinents: split open that which covers and conceals you.
58–59. cry . . . grace: ask for mercy from these dreadful sum-
moners. The summoner was the officer of the ecclesiastical court
who summoned a man to appear to answer a charge of im-
morality. See Gen. Intro. p. 26a.

48. fellow: companion.   53. pain: labor.

Sc. ii: 2. hurricanoes: waterspouts.   3. cocks: weathercocks
on top of the steeples.   4. thought-executing: killing as quick
as thought.   5. Vaunt-couriers: forerunners.   8. nature's molds:
the molds in which men are made. germens: seeds of life.
10. Court . . . water: flattery of great ones.   16. tax: accuse.
18. subscription: submission.   21. servile ministers: servants
who slavishly obey your masters.   23. high-engendered battles:
armies begotten on high.

Which even but now, demanding after you,   65
Denied me to come in — return, and force
Their scanted courtesy.

LEAR.   My wits begin to turn.
Come on, my boy. How dost, my boy? Art cold?
I am cold myself. Where is this straw, my fellow?
The art of our necessities is strange,   70
That can make vile things precious.° Come, your
     hovel.
Poor fool and knave, I have one part in my heart
That's sorry yet for thee.

FOOL. [Singing]
     " He° that has and a little tiny wit —
        With hey, ho, the wind and the rain —   75
        Must make content with his fortunes fit,°
     For the rain it raineth every day."

LEAR. True, my good boy. Come, bring us to this
     hovel.   [Exeunt LEAR and KENT.]

FOOL. This is a brave night to cool a courtesan.
I'll speak a prophecy° ere I go: 80
" When priests are more in word than matter,
When brewers mar their malt with water,
When nobles are their tailors' tutors,°
No heretics burned, but wenches' suitors,
When every case in law is right,   85
No squire in debt, nor no poor knight,
When slanders do not live in tongues,
Nor cutpurses come not to throngs,
When usurers tell their gold i' the field,
And bawds and whores do churches build —   90
Then shall the realm of Albion°
Come to great confusion.
Then comes the time, who lives to see 't,
That going shall be used with feet."°   94
This prophecy Merlin shall make, for I live before
     his time.°   [Exit.]

SCENE III. GLOUCESTER's castle.

[Enter GLOUCESTER and EDMUND.]

GLO. Alack, alack, Edmund, I like not this unnatu-
ral dealing. When I desired their leave that I might
pity him,° they took from me the use of mine own

70–71. art . . . precious: our needs are like the art of the alche-
mist (who was forever experimenting to try to transmute base
metal into gold). See App. 21.   74–77. He . . . day: another
stanza of the song which the Fool in Twelfth Night sings at the
end of the play.   76. Must . . . fit: i.e., must be content with a
fortune as slim as his wit.   80–94. prophecy . . . feet: The fool
gives a list of common events, pretending that they are never
likely to happen. The prophecy is a parody of riddling prophe-
cies popular at this time which were attributed to Merlin, the old
magician of King Arthur's Court.   83. nobles . . . tutors: Young
noblemen and gallants were very particular about the fashion and
cut of their clothes.   91. Albion: England.   94. going . . . feet:
feet will be used for walking.   95. This . . . time: A piece of
mock pedantry, for — according to Holinshed's Chronicles —
King Lear died some generations before King Arthur.
Sc. iii: 3. him: Lear.

---

house, charged me, on pain of their perpetual dis-
pleasure, neither to speak of him, entreat for him,
nor any way sustain° him.   6

EDM. Most savage and unnatural!

GLO. Go to, say you nothing. There's a division be-
twixt the Dukes, and a worse matter than that. I
have received a letter this night, 'tis dangerous   10
to be spoken. — I have locked the letter in my closet.
These injuries the King now bears will be revenged
home.° There is part of a power already footed.° We
must incline to the King. I will seek him and privily°
relieve him. Go you, and maintain talk with   15
the Duke, that my charity be not of him perceived.
If he ask for me, I am ill and gone to bed. Though I
die for it, as no less is threatened me, the King my
old master must be relieved. There is some   20
strange thing toward, Edmund. Pray you be careful.
                                    [Exit.]

EDM. This courtesy, forbid thee,° shall the Duke
Instantly know, and of that letter too.
This seems a fair deserving,° and must draw me
That which my father loses, no less than all.   25
The younger rises when the old doth fall.   [Exit.]

SCENE IV. The heath. Before a hovel.

[Enter LEAR, KENT, and FOOL.]

KENT. Here is the place, my lord. Good my lord,
     enter.
The tyranny° of the open night's too rough
For nature to endure.   [Storm still.]

LEAR.   Let me alone.

KENT. Good my lord, enter here.

LEAR.   Wilt break my heart?

KENT. I had rather break mine own. Good my
     lord, enter.   5

LEAR. Thou think'st 'tis much that this conten-
     tious° storm
Invades us to the skin. So 'tis to thee,
But where the greater malady is fixed°
The lesser is scarce felt. Thou'dst shun a bear,
But if thy flight lay toward the raging sea   10
Thou'dst meet the bear i' the mouth. When the
     mind's free°
The body's delicate. The tempest in my mind
Doth from my senses take all feeling else
Save what beats there.° Filial ingratitude!
Is it not as this mouth should tear this hand   15

---

6. sustain: relieve.   13. home: to the utmost. footed: landed.
14. privily: secretly.   22. forbid thee: forbidden to thee.   24. This
. . . deserving: i.e., by betraying my father, I shall deserve
much of (be rewarded by) the Duke.
Sc. iv: 2. tyranny: cruelty.   6. contentious: striving against
us.   8. the . . . fixed: i.e., in the mind.   11. free: i.e., from
cares.   14. what . . . there: i.e., the mental anguish which
is increased by the thumping of Lear's overtaxed heart.

For lifting food to 't? But I will punish home.
No, I will weep no more. In such a night
To shut me out! Pour on, I will endure.
In such a night as this! O Regan, Goneril!
Your old kind father, whose frank heart gave
     all —— 20
Oh, that way madness lies, let me shun that,
No more of that.

    KENT.   Good my lord, enter here.

    LEAR. Prithee, go in thyself, seek thine own ease.
This tempest will not give me leave to ponder
On things would hurt me more. But I'll go in. 25
[*To the* FOOL] In, boy, go first. You houseless pov-
     erty° ——
Nay, get thee in. I'll pray, and then I'll sleep.

                         [FOOL *goes in.*]

Poor naked wretches, wheresoe'er you are,
That bide° the pelting of this pitiless storm,
How shall your houseless heads and unfed sides, 30
Your looped and windowed° raggedness, defend you
From seasons such as these? Oh, I have ta'en
Too little care of this! Take physic, pomp.°
Expose thyself to feel what wretches feel,
That thou mayst shake the superflux° to them 35
And show the Heavens more just.

    EDG. [*Within*] Fathom and half, fathom and half!
Poor Tom!

       [*The* FOOL *runs out from the hovel.*]

    FOOL. Come not in here, Nuncle, here's a spirit.
Help me, help me! 40

    KENT. Give me thy hand. Who's there?

    FOOL. A spirit, a spirit. He says his name's Poor
Tom.

    KENT. What art thou that dost grumble there i'
     the straw?
Come forth. 45

       [*Enter* EDGAR *disguised as a madman.*]

    EDG. Away! The foul fiend follows me!
" Through the sharp hawthorn blows the cold
     wind."
Hum! Go to thy cold bed and warm thee.

    LEAR. Hast thou given all to thy two daughters?
And art thou come to this?° 50

    EDG. Who gives anything to Poor Tom? Whom
the foul fiend hath led through fire and through
flame, through ford and whirlpool, o'er bog and
quagmire, that hath laid knives under his pillow
and halters in his pew,° set ratsbane° by his 55
porridge, made him proud of heart to ride on a bay
trotting horse over four-inched° bridges, to course°

his own shadow for a traitor. Bless thy five wits!°
Tom's a-cold. Oh, do de, do de, do de. Bless thee from
whirlwinds, star-blasting,° and taking!° Do Poor
Tom some charity, whom the foul fiend vexes. There
could I have him now, and there, and there 62
again, and there.°   [*Storm still.*]

    LEAR. What, have his daughters brought him to
     this pass?
Couldst thou save nothing? Didst thou give them
     all?

    FOOL. Nay, he reserved a blanket,° else we had
been all shamed. 67

    LEAR. Now, all the plagues that in the pendulous°
     air
Hang fated o'er men's faults light on thy daugh-
     ters!

    KENT. He hath no daughters, sir. 71

    LEAR. Death, traitor! Nothing could have subdued
     nature
To such a lowness but his unkind daughters.
Is it the fashion that discarded fathers
Should have thus little mercy on their flesh? 75
Judicious punishment! 'Twas this flesh begot
Those pelican° daughters.

    EDG.   "Pillicock sat on Pillicock Hill.
           Halloo, halloo, loo, loo!"°

    FOOL. This cold night will turn us all to fools and
madmen. 81

    EDG. Take heed o' the foul fiend. Obey thy par-
ents, keep thy word justly, swear not, commit not
with man's sworn spouse, set not thy sweet heart on
proud array. Tom's a-cold.

    LEAR. What hast thou been? 86

    EDG. A servingman,° proud in heart and mind,
that curled my hair, wore gloves in my cap, served
the lust of my mistress's heart and did the act of dark-
ness with her, swore as many oaths as I spake 90
words and broke them in the sweet face of Heaven.
One that slept in the contriving of lust and waked
to do it. Wine loved I deeply, dice dearly, and in
woman outparamoured° the Turk.° False of heart,
light of ear, bloody of hand, hog in sloth,° fox in 95
stealth, wolf in greediness, dog in madness, lion in
prey. Let not the creaking of shoes nor the rustling
of silks betray thy poor heart to woman. Keep thy
foot out of brothels, thy hand out of plackets,°

---

58. **five wits:** i.e., common wit, imagination, fantasy, estima-
tion, and memory.   60. **star-blasting:** evil caused by a
planet. **taking:** malignant influence of fairies. Cf. *Haml.* I.i.163.
61–63. **There . . . there:** Poor Tom is chasing his own vermin.
66. **blanket:** i.e., his only covering. See II.iii.10.   68. **pendulous:**
overhanging.   77. **pelican:** The pelican was the pattern of
devoted motherhood because it fed its young on its own blood;
but when the young grew strong, they turned on their parents.
78–79. **Pillicock . . . loo:** an old rhyme.   87–97. **A servingman
. . . prey:** This is another description of the gentleman serving-
man. See II.ii.15–26.   94. **outparamoured:** had more mistresses
than. **the Turk:** the Turkish Emperor.   95. **hog in sloth:** See
Lear Intro. p. 783a.   99. **plackets:** openings in a petticoat.

---

26. **houseless poverty:** poor homeless people.   29. **bide:** endure.
31. **looped . . . windowed:** full of holes and gaps.   33. **Take . . .
pomp:** i.e., cure yourselves, you great men.   35. **superflux:**
superfluity, what you do not need.   49–50. **Hast . . . this:** At
the sight of the supposed lunatic Lear goes quite mad. Such utter
destitution, he says, can only have been caused by daughters as
unkind as his own.   55. **pew:** seat. **ratsbane:** rat poison.
57. **four-inched:** i.e., narrow. **course:** hunt after.

thy pen from lenders' books,° and defy the foul
fiend.   101
" Still through the hawthorn blows the cold wind.
Says suum, mun, ha, no, nonny.
Dolphin my boy, my boy, sessa! Let him trot by."
                                        [*Storm still.*]
LEAR. Why, thou wert better in thy grave 104
than to answer with thy uncovered body this ex-
tremity of the skies. Is man no more than this? Con-
sider him well. Thou° owest the worm no silk, the
beast no hide, the sheep no wool, the cat no per-
fume.° Ha! Here's three on 's are sophisticated.
Thou art the thing itself. Unaccommodated 110
man is no more but such a poor, bare, forked animal
as thou art. Off, off, you lendings!° Come, unbutton
here.   [*Tearing off his clothes.*] 113
FOOL. Prithee, Nuncle, be contented, 'tis a naughty
night to swim in. Now a little fire in a wild field
were like an old lecher's heart, a small spark, all the
rest on 's body cold. Look, here comes a walking
fire.   119

        [*Enter* GLOUCESTER, *with a torch.*]

EDG. This is the foul fiend Flibbertigibbet. He be-
gins at curfew° and walks till the first cock, he gives
the web and the pin,° squints the eye and makes the
harelip, mildews the white wheat and hurts the poor
creature of earth.
" Saint° Withold footed thrice the 'old,° 125
    He met the nightmare° and her ninefold.°
        Bid her alight,
        And her troth plight,
    And aroint thee, witch, aroint° thee! "
KENT. How fares your Grace?   130
LEAR. What's he?
KENT. Who's there? What is 't you seek?
GLO. What are you there? Your names?
EDG. Poor Tom, that eats the swimming frog, the
toad, the tadpole, the wall newt, and the water; 135
that in the fury of his heart, when the foul fiend
rages, eats cow dung for sallets;° swallows the old
rat and the ditch dog;° drinks the green mantle of

100. pen . . . books: The debtor often acknowledged the debt by
signing in the lender's account book. There are many such
acknowledgments in Henslowe's *Diary* (see Gen. Intro. p. 65a).
107-13. Thou . . . here: There is usually an underlying sense in
Lear's ravings. The bedlam, he says, has not borrowed silk from
the silkworm, or furs from the beast, or wool from the sheep to
cover himself. Kent, the Fool, and he himself are therefore
sophisticated — adulterated, wearing coverings not their own.
Natural man, *unaccommodated* (i.e., not provided with such
conveniences), is just a naked animal. Lear will therefore
strip himself naked and cease to be artificial. 108-09. cat . . .
perfume: a perfume taken from the civet cat, which has glands
that function in the same manner as the skunk's. 112. lendings:
things borrowed. 121. curfew: sounded at 9 P.M. 122. web . . .
pin: eye diseases, cataract. 125-29. Saint . . . thee: a charm to
keep horses from suffering from nightmare. 125. 'old: wold,
uncultivated downland. 126. nightmare: nightmare was be-
lieved to be caused by a fiend. ninefold: nine young. 129. a-
roint: be gone. 137. sallets: salads. 138. ditch dog: dog
drowned in a ditch.

the standing pool; who is whipped from tithing to
tithing,° and stock-punished, and imprisoned; 140
who hath had three suits° to his back, six shirts to
his body, horse to ride, and weapon to wear.
" But mice and rats and such small deer
    Have been Tom's food for seven long year."
Beware my follower. Peace, Smulkin,° peace, thou
    fiend!   146
GLO. What, hath your Grace no better company?
EDG. The Prince of Darkness is a gentleman.
Modo he's called, and Mahu.
GLO. Our flesh and blood is grown so vile, my
    lord,   150
That it doth hate what gets° it.
EDG. Poor Tom's a-cold.
GLO. Go in with me. My duty cannot suffer
To obey in all your daughters' hard commands.
Though their injunction be to bar my doors 155
And let this tyrannous night take hold upon you,
Yet have I ventured to come seek you out
And bring you where both fire and food is ready.
LEAR. First let me talk with this philosopher.
What is the cause of thunder?°   160
KENT. Good my lord, take his offer, go into the
    house.
LEAR. I'll talk a word with this same learnèd
    Theban.°
What is your study?°
EDG. How to prevent the fiend and to kill vermin.
LEAR. Let me ask you one word in private. 165
KENT. Impórtune him once more to go, my lord.
His wits begin to unsettle.
GLO. Canst thou blame him?   [*Storm still.*]
His daughters seek his death. Ah, that good Kent!
He said it would be thus, poor banished man!
Thou say'st the King grows mad. I'll tell thee,
    friend,   170
I am almost mad myself. I had a son,
Now outlawed from my blood. He sought my life
But lately, very late. I loved him, friend,
No father his son dearer. Truth to tell thee, 174
The grief hath crazed my wits. What a night's this!
I do beseech your Grace —
LEAR.   Oh, cry you mercy, sir.
Noble philosopher, your company.
EDG. Tom's a-cold.
GLO. In, fellow, there, into the hovel. Keep thee
    warm.
LEAR. Come, let's in all.
KENT.   This way, my lord.
LEAR.   With him, 180
I will keep still with my philosopher.

140. tithing: district, parish. 141. three suits: See II.ii.16.
145-49. Smulkin . . . Mahu: familiar spirits. See *Lear* Intro.
p. 780b. 151. gets: begets. 160. cause of thunder: This was
much disputed by philosophers of the time. 162. Theban: i.e.,
Greek philosopher. 163. study: particular interest, or in
modern academic jargon, "special field."

KENT. Good my lord, soothe him, let him take the
fellow.

GLO. Take him you on.

KENT. Sirrah, come on, go along with us.

LEAR. Come, good Athenian.°   185

GLO. No words, no words. Hush.

EDG. "Child° Rowland to the dark tower came.
His word was still 'Fie, foh, and fum,
I smell the blood of a British man.'"

[Exeunt.]

SCENE V. GLOUCESTER'S *castle.*

[Enter CORNWALL *and* EDMUND.]

CORN. I will have my revenge ere I depart his
house.

EDM. How, my lord, I may be censured,° that na-
ture° thus gives way to loyalty, something fears me
to think of.   5

CORN. I now perceive it was not altogether your
brother's evil disposition made him seek his death,
but a provoking merit, set a-work by a reprovable
badness in himself.°   9

EDM. How malicious is my fortune, that I must
repent to be just!° This is the letter he spoke of,
which approves° him an intelligent party° to the
advantages of France. Oh heavens, that this treason
were not, or not I the detector!   14

CORN. Go with me to the Duchess.

EDM. If the matter of this paper be certain, you
have mighty business in hand.

CORN. True or false, it hath made thee Earl of
Gloucester. Seek out where thy father is, that he
may be ready for our apprehension.°   20

EDM. *[Aside]* If I find him comforting the King,
it will stuff his suspicion more fully.—I will per-
sever° in my course of loyalty, though the conflict be
sore between that and my blood.   24

CORN. I will lay trust upon thee, and thou shalt
find a dearer father in my love.   *[Exeunt.]*

185. Athenian: like "Theban," l. 162. 187–89. Child . . . man:
jumbled snatches of old ballads. *Child* in old ballads is used
of young warriors who have not yet been knighted.
Sc. v: 3. censured: judged. 4. nature: i.e., natural affection
toward my father yielding to loyalty to my Duke. For Edmund's
real sentiments on nature see I.ii.1–2. 8–9. but . . . himself: i.e.,
but a good quality in Edgar that provoked him to commit murder
because of the reprehensible badness in Gloucester. 11. re-
pent . . . just: be sorry because I have acted rightly (in betray-
ing my father). 12. approves: proves. intelligent party: spy,
one with secret information. 20. apprehension: arrest. 23. per-
sever: persevere.

SCENE VI.° *A chamber in a farmhouse
adjoining the castle.*

[Enter GLOUCESTER, LEAR, KENT, FOOL, *and* EDGAR.]

GLO. Here is better than the open air, take it
thankfully. I will piece out the comfort with what
addition I can. I will not be long from you.

KENT. All the power of his wits has given way to
his impatience.° The gods reward your kindness!   6

[Exit GLOUCESTER.]

EDG. Fraterretto° calls me, and tells me Nero° is
an angler in the lake of darkness. Pray, innocent,°
and beware the foul fiend.

FOOL. Prithee, Nuncle, tell me whether a madman
be a gentleman or a yeoman.°   11

LEAR. A king, a king!

FOOL. No, he's a yeoman that has a gentleman to
his son, for he's a mad yeoman that sees his son a
gentleman before him.°   15

LEAR. To have a thousand with red burning spits°
Come hissing in upon 'em ——

EDG. The foul fiend bites my back.

FOOL. He's mad that trusts in the tameness of a
wolf, a horse's health, a boy's love, or a whore's
oath.

LEAR. It shall be done, I will arraign them
straight.°   22

[To EDGAR] Come, sit thou here, most learned jus-
ticer.°

[To the FOOL] Thou, sapient° sir, sit here. Now, you
she-foxes!

EDG. Look where he stands and glares! Wantest
thou eyes at trial,° madam?   26

"Come o'er the bourn, Bessy, to me."

FOOL. "Her boat hath a leak,
    And she must not speak
Why she dares not come over to thee."   30

EDG. The foul fiend haunts poor Tom in the voice
of a nightingale. Hopdance° cries in Tom's belly for

Sc. vi: In this scene Lear is completely mad, the Fool is
half-witted, and Edgar is pretending to be a lunatic. 6. impa-
tience: suffering. 7. Fraterretto: another fiend's name from
Harsnett's book. See *Lear* Intro. p. 780b. Nero: the debauched
Roman Emperor who fiddled while Rome burned. 8. innocent:
fool. 10–11. whether . . . yeoman: The fool is much interested
in the social status of a madman and proceeds to discuss the
problem. yeoman: farmer, a notoriously wealthy class at this
time. 13–15. No . . . him: Many yeomen farmers who had be-
come wealthy by profiteering from the wars and dearths sent
their sons to London to learn to become gentlemen, as fifty years
ago Chicago meat packers sent their sons to Harvard and their
daughters to England, to be presented at Court. This social
change was much commented on, and is illustrated in Jonson's
comedy *Every Man out of His Humour*. 16. spits: thin iron rods
thrust through meat on which the meat was turned before the fire
in roasting; very useful weapons in emergency. 22. straight:
straightway. 23. justicer: judge. 24. sapient: wise.
25–26. Wantest . . . trial: can you not see who is at your trial
(i.e., this fiend)? But Edgar is deliberately talking madly.
32. Hopdance: another name from Harsnett.

two white herring. Croak not,° black angel, I have
no food for thee.

KENT. How do you, sir? Stand you not so
    amazed.°   35
Will you lie down and rest upon the cushions?

LEAR. I'll see their trial first. Bring in the evidence.
[To EDGAR] Thou robèd man of justice,° take thy
    place.
[To the FOOL] And thou, his yokefellow of equity,°
Bench° by his side. [To KENT] You are o' the com-
    mission,°   40
Sit you too.

EDG. Let us deal justly.
"Sleepest or wakest thou, jolly shepherd?
    Thy sheep be in the corn,
And for one blast of thy minikin° mouth,   45
    Thy sheep shall take no harm."
Purr! The cat is gray.

LEAR. Arraign her first. 'Tis Goneril. I here take
my oath before this honorable assembly, she kicked
the poor King her father.   50

FOOL. Come hither, mistress. Is your name Gon-
eril?

LEAR. She cannot deny it.

FOOL. Cry you mercy,° I took you for a joint
stool.°   55

LEAR. And here's another, whose warped° looks
    proclaim
What store° her heart is made on. Stop her there!
Arms, arms, sword, fire! Corruption° in the place!
False justicer, why hast thou let her 'scape?

EDG. Bless thy five wits!   60

KENT. Oh, pity! Sir, where is the patience now,
That you so oft have boasted to retain?

EDG. [Aside] My tears begin to take his part so
    much
They'll mar my counterfeiting.°

LEAR. The little dogs and all,   65
Tray, Blanch, and Sweetheart, see, they bark at me.

EDG. Tom will throw his head at them. Avaunt,
you curs!
    Be thy mouth or black or white,
    Tooth that poisons if it bite,   70
    Mastiff, greyhound, mongrel grim,
    Hound or spaniel, brach° or lym,°
    Or bobtail tike or trundletail,°

Tom will make them weep and wail.
    For, with throwing thus my head,   75
    Dogs leap the hatch, and all are fled.
Do de, de, de. Sessa! Come, march to wakes° and
fairs and market towns. Poor Tom, thy horn° is
dry.   79

LEAR. Then let them anatomize° Regan, see what
breeds about her heart. Is there any cause in nature
that makes these hard hearts? [To EDGAR] You, sir, I
entertain° for one of my hundred, only I do not like
the fashion of your garments. You will say they are
Persian attire,° but let them be changed.   86

KENT. Now, good my lord, lie here and rest
awhile.

LEAR. Make no noise, make no noise. Draw the
curtains. So, so, so.° We'll go to supper i' the morn-
ing. So, so, so.   91

FOOL. And I'll go to bed at noon.°
    [Re-enter GLOUCESTER.]

GLO. Come hither, friend. Where is the King my
master?

KENT. Here, sir, but trouble him not. His wits are
gone.

GLO. Good friend, I prithee take him in thy arms.
I have o'erheard a plot of death upon him.   96
There is a litter° ready, lay him in 't,
And drive toward Dover, friend, where thou shalt
    meet
Both welcome and protection. Take up thy master.
If thou shouldst dally° half an hour, his life,   100
With thine and all that offer to defend him,
Stand in assurèd loss. Take up, take up,
And follow me, that will to some provision
Give thee quick conduct.

KENT.   Oppressèd nature sleeps.
This rest might yet have balmed° thy broken sin-
ews,   105
Which, if convenience will not allow,
Stand in hard cure.° [To the FOOL] Come, help to
    bear thy master.
Thou must not stay behind.

GLO.   Come, come, away.
    [Exeunt all but EDGAR.]

EDG. When we our betters see bearing our woes,
We scarcely think our miseries our foes.   110

---

33. **Croak not:** don't rumble in my empty belly. The correct
Elizabethan word for this embarrassing manifestation is "wam-
ble."   35. **amazed:** astonished — a strong word.   38. **robed
. . . justice:** another glance at Edgar's blanket.   39. **yokefellow
of equity:** partner in the law.   40. **Bench:** sit on the judge's
bench. **commission:** Persons of high rank or those accused of
extraordinary crimes were not tried before the ordinary courts,
but by a commission specially appointed.   45. **minikin:** dainty.
55. **Cry . . . mercy:** I beg your pardon. **joint stool:** wooden
stool of joiner's work. See Pl. 17a.   56. **warped:** malignant.
57. **store:** material.   58. **Corruption:** bribery.   63–64. **My . . .
counterfeiting:** i.e., I am so sorry for the King that I can hardly
keep up this pretense.   72. **brach:** bitch. **lym:** bloodhound.
73. **trundletail:** curly tail.

77. **wakes:** merrymakings.   78. **horn:** a horn bottle carried by
beggars in which they stored the drink given by the charitable.
80. **anatomize:** dissect.   84. **entertain:** engage.   86. **Persian
attire:** i.e., of a magnificent and foreign fashion. There had
been considerable interest in Persia for some years, especially
after the return of some of the followers of Sir Anthony Shirley
from his famous expedition. See *T. Night* Intro. p. 565a.   90. **So
. . . so:** In dialogue "so, so" usually indicates action. Here
Lear imagines the bed curtains are being drawn.   92. **And . . .
noon:** i.e., if it's suppertime in the morning, it will be bedtime at
noon. The fool disappears after this scene.   97. **litter:** a form
of bed or stretcher enclosed by curtains used for carrying the
sick or the wealthy.   100. **dally:** hesitate.   105. **balmed:**
soothed.   107. **Stand . . . cure:** will hardly be cured.

Who alone suffers suffers most i' the mind,
Leaving free things and happy shows behind.
But then the mind much sufferance doth o'erskip
When grief hath mates, and bearing fellowship.°
How light and portable my pain seems now   115
When that which makes me bend makes the King
     bow,
He childed as I fathered! Tom, away!
Mark the high noises,° and thyself° bewray
When false opinion, whose wrong thought defiles
     thee,
In thy just proof repeals° and reconciles thee.   120
What will hap more tonight, safe 'scape the King!
Lurk,° lurk.   [*Exit.*]

SCENE VII. GLOUCESTER's *castle.*

[*Enter* CORNWALL, REGAN, GONERIL, EDMUND, *and*
         SERVANTS.]

   CORN. Post speedily to my lord your husband.°
Show him this letter. The army of France is landed.
Seek out the traitor Gloucester.
             [*Exeunt some of the* SERVANTS.]
   REG. Hang him instantly.
   GON. Pluck out his eyes.   5
   CORN. Leave him to my displeasure. Edmund,
keep you our sister company. The revenges we are
bound to take upon your traitorous father are not fit
for your beholding. Advise the Duke, where you are
going, to a most festinate° preparation. We are
bound to the like. Our posts° shall be swift and in-
telligent° betwixt us. Farewell, dear Sister. Fare-
well, my Lord of Gloucester.°   13
[*Enter* OSWALD.] How now! Where's the King?
   OSW. My Lord of Gloucester° hath conveyed him
     hence.   15
Some five or six and thirty of his knights,
Hot questrists° after him, met him at gate,
Who, with some other of the lords dependents,°
Are gone with him toward Dover, where they boast
To have well-armèd friends.

109–14. **When . . . fellowship:** when we see better men than our-
selves suffering as we do, our sufferings seem slight. The man
who suffers endures most in his mind because he contrasts his
present misery with his happy past; but when he has companions
in misery (*bearing fellowship*), his mind suffers less.   118. **high
noises:** i.e., the "hue and cry" of the pursuers. See Gen. Intro.
p. 28a.   118–20. **thyself . . . thee:** do not reveal yourself until
the belief in your guilt is proved wrong and you are called back.
120. **repeals:** calls back from banishment.   122. **Lurk:** lie hid.
   Sc. vii: 1. **Post . . . husband:** These words are addressed to
Goneril. **Post:** ride fast.   10. **festinate:** hasty.   11. **posts:**
messengers. See App. 17.   12. **intelligent:** full of information.
13. **Lord of Gloucester:** i.e., Edmund, who has been promoted for
his treachery.   15. **Lord of Gloucester:** i.e., the old Earl.
17. **questrists:** seekers.   18. **lords dependents:** lords of his
party.

   CORN.   Get horses for your mistress.   20
   GON. Farewell, sweet lord, and Sister.
   CORN. Edmund, farewell.
          [*Exeunt* GONERIL, EDMUND, *and* OSWALD.]
             Go seek the traitor Gloucester.
Pinion him like a thief, bring him before us.
                  [*Exeunt other* SERVANTS.]
Though well we may not pass° upon his life
Without the form of justice, yet our power   25
Shall do a courtesy to our wrath,° which men
May blame but not control. Who's there? The
     traitor?
[*Enter* GLOUCESTER, *brought in by two or three.*]
   REG. Ungrateful fox! 'Tis he.
   CORN. Bind fast his corky° arms.
   GLO. What mean your Graces? Good my friends,
     consider   30
You are my guests. Do me no foul play, friends.
   CORN. Bind him, I say.   [SERVANTS *bind him.*]
   REG.   Hard, hard. O filthy traitor!
   GLO. Unmerciful lady as you are, I'm none.
   CORN. To this chair bind him. Villain, thou shalt
     find ——   [REGAN *plucks his beard.*]
   GLO. By the kind gods, 'tis most ignobly done
To pluck me by the beard.°   36
   REG. So white, and such a traitor!
   GLO.   Naughty lady,
These hairs which thou dost ravish° from my
     chin
Will quicken° and accuse thee. I am your host.
With robbers' hands my hospitable favors°   40
You should not ruffle thus. What will you do?
   CORN. Come, sir, what letters had you late from
     France?
   REG. Be simple answerer, for we know the truth.
   CORN. And what confederacy° have you with the
     traitors
Late footed in the kingdom?   45
   REG. To whose hands have you sent the lunatic
     King?
Speak.
   GLO. I have a letter guessingly set down,
Which came from one that's of a neutral heart,
And not from one opposed.
   CORN.   Cunning.
   REG.   And false
   CORN. Where hast thou sent the King?
   GLO.   To Dover.   50
   REG. Wherefore to Dover? Wast thou not charged
     at peril° ——
   CORN. Wherefore to Dover? Let him first answer
     that.

---

24. **pass:** pass judgment on.   25–26. **yet . . . wrath:** yet because
we are all-powerful we will give way to our wrath.   29. **corky:**
dry and withered.   36. **pluck . . . beard:** the greatest indignity
that could be offered.   38. **ravish:** seize.   39. **quicken:** come
to life.   40. **hospitable favors:** the face of your host.   44. **con-
federacy:** alliance, understanding.   51. **at peril:** under penalty.

GLO. I am tied to the stake, and I must stand the course.°

REG. Wherefore to Dover, sir?   55

GLO. Because I would not see thy cruel nails
Pluck out his poor old eyes, nor thy fierce sister
In his anointed° flesh stick boarish fangs.
The sea, with such a storm as his bare head
In hell-black night endured, would have buoyed up,°
And quenched the stellèd fires.°   61
Yet, poor old heart, he holp° the heavens to rain.
If wolves had at thy gate howled that stern time,
Thou shouldst have said, "Good porter, turn the key,"°
All cruels else subscribed.° But I shall see   65
The wingèd vengeance overtake such children.

CORN. See 't shalt thou never. Fellows, hold the chair.
Upon these eyes of thine I'll set my foot.

GLO. He that will think to live till he be old,
Give me some help! Oh, cruel! Oh, you gods!   70

[GLOUCESTER'S *eye is put out*.]

REG. One side will mock another, the other too.

CORN. If you see vengeance ——

1. SERV.   Hold your hand, my lord.
I have served you ever since I was a child,
But better service have I never done you
Than now to bid you hold.

REG.   How now, you dog!   75

1. SERV. If you did wear a beard upon your chin,
I'd shake it on this quarrel. What do you mean?

CORN. My villain!

[*They draw and fight.* CORNWALL *is wounded.*]

1. SERV. Nay, then, come on, and take the chance of anger.

REG. Give me thy sword. A peasant stand up thus!

[*Takes a sword and runs at him behind.*]

1. SERV. Oh, I am slain! My lord, you have one eye left
To see some mischief on him. Oh!   [*Dies.*]

CORN. Lest it see more, prevent it. Out, vile jelly!
Where is thy luster now?

[*Puts out* GLOUCESTER'S *other eye.*]

GLO. All dark and comfortless. Where's my son Edmund?   85
Edmund, enkindle all the sparks° of nature,
To quit° this horrid act.

REG.   Out, treacherous villain!
Thou call'st on him that hates thee. It was he
That made the overture° of thy treasons to us,
Who is too good to pity thee.   90

GLO. Oh, my follies! Then Edgar was abused.
Kind gods, forgive me that, and prosper him!

REG. Go thrust him out at gates, and let him smell
His way to Dover.   [*Exit one with* GLOUCESTER.]
                    How is 't, my lord? How look you?

CORN. I have received a hurt. Follow me, lady.
Turn out that eyeless villain. Throw this slave   96
Upon the dunghill. Regan, I bleed apace.°
Untimely comes this hurt. Give me your arm.

[*Exit* CORNWALL, *led by* REGAN.]

2. SERV. I'll never care what wickedness I do
If this man come to good.

3. SERV.   If she live long,   100
And in the end meet the old course of death,°
Women will all turn monsters.

2. SERV. Let's follow the old Earl, and get the bedlam°
To lead him where he would. His roguish madness
Allows itself to anything.   105

3. SERV. Go thou. I'll fetch some flax and whites of eggs
To apply to his bleeding face. Now, Heaven help
him!   [*Exeunt severally.*]

Act IV

SCENE I. *The heath.*

[*Enter* EDGAR.]

EDG. Yet better thus, and known to be contemned,°
Than still° contemned and flattered. To° be worst,
The lowest and most dejected thing of fortune,
Stands still in esperance, lives not in fear.
The lamentable change is from the best,   5
The worst returns to laughter. Welcome then,
Thou unsubstantial air that I embrace!
The wretch that thou hast blown unto the worst
Owes nothing to thy blasts. — But who comes here?

[*Enter* GLOUCESTER, *led by an* OLD MAN.]

My father, poorly led?° World, world, O world!
But that thy strange mutations make us hate thee,

Life would not yield to age.   12

OLD MAN. Oh, my good lord, I have been your ten-
ant, and your father's tenant, these fourscore years.

GLO. Away, get thee away. Good friend, be gone.
Thy comforts can do me no good at all,   17
Thee they may hurt.

OLD MAN. Alack, sir, you cannot see your way.

GLO. I have no way and therefore want no eyes.
I stumbled when I saw. Full oft 'tis seen,   21
Our means secure us, and our mere defects
Prove our commodities.° Ah, dear Son Edgar,
The food° of thy abusèd father's wrath,
Might I but live to see thee in my touch,   25
I'd say I had eyes again!

OLD MAN.   How now! Who's there?

EDG. [*Aside*] Oh gods! Who is 't can say "I am
at the worst"?
I am worse than e'er I was.

OLD MAN.   'Tis poor mad Tom.

EDG. [*Aside*] And worse I may be yet. The worst
is not
So long as we can say "This is the worst."°   30

OLD MAN. Fellow, where goest?

GLO.   Is it a beggarman?

OLD MAN. Madman and beggar too.

GLO. He has some reason, else he could not beg.
I' the last night's storm I such a fellow saw,
Which made me think a man a worm. My son   35
Came then into my mind, and yet my mind
Was then scarce friends with him. I have heard more
since.
As flies to wanton boys are we to the gods,
They kill us for their sport.

EDG.   [*Aside*] How should this be?
Bad is the trade that must play fool to sorrow,   40
Angering itself and others.° Bless thee, master!

GLO. Is that the naked fellow?

OLD MAN.   Aye, my lord.

GLO. Then, prithee get thee gone. If for my sake
Thou wilt o'ertake us hence a mile or twain
I' the way toward Dover, do it for ancient love,   45
And bring some covering for this naked soul,
Who I'll entreat to lead me.

OLD MAN.   Alack, sir, he is mad.

GLO. 'Tis the times' plague° when madmen lead
the blind.
Do as I bid thee, or rather do thy pleasure.
Above the rest, be gone.   50

OLD MAN. I'll bring him the best 'parel° that I
have,
Come on 't what will.   [*Exit.*]

GLO. Sirrah, naked fellow ——

EDG. Poor Tom's a-cold. [*Aside*] I cannot daub°
it further.

GLO. Come hither, fellow.   55

EDG. [*Aside*] And yet I must. — Bless thy sweet
eyes, they bleed.

GLO. Know'st thou the way to Dover?

EDG. Both stile and gate, horseway and footpath.
Poor Tom hath been scared out of his good wits.
Bless thee, good man's son, from the foul fiend!   60
Five fiends have been in Poor Tom at once — of lust,
as Obidicut; Hobbididence, prince of dumbness;
Mahu, of stealing; Modo, of murder; Flibbertigib-
bet,° of mopping and mowing,° who since possesses
chambermaids and waiting-women. So, bless thee,
master!   66

GLO. Here, take this purse, thou whom the Heav-
ens' plagues
Have humbled to all strokes.° That I am wretched
Makes thee the happier. Heavens, deal so still!
Let the superfluous and lust-dieted man,   70
That slaves your ordinance, that will not see
Because he doth not feel, feel your power quickly.°
So distribution should undo excess°
And each man have enough. Dost thou know
Dover?

EDG. Aye, master.   75

GLO. There is a cliff whose high and bending°
head
Looks fearfully in the confinèd deep.
Bring me but to the very brim of it,
And I'll repair the misery thou dost bear
With something rich about me. From that place   80
I shall no leading need.

EDG.   Give me thy arm.
Poor Tom shall lead thee.   [*Exeunt.*]

SCENE II. *Before the* DUKE OF ALBANY's *palace.*

[*Enter* GONERIL *and* EDMUND.]

GON. Welcome, my lord. I marvel our mild hus-
band
Not met us on the way.

[*Enter* OSWALD.] Now, where's your master?

OSW. Madam, within, but never man so changed.
I told him of the army that was landed.

22–23. Our . . . commodities: when we are well off we grow care-
less, and then our misfortunes prove blessings.   24. food: object.
29–30. The . . . worst: so long as a man is alive, he may yet
reach a lower depth of misery.   40–41. Bad . . . others: this
business of pretending to be mad and fooling a man in such dis-
tress as Gloucester is now hateful.   48. times' plague: a sign of
these diseased times.   51. 'parel: apparel

54. daub: plaster it over, pretend.   62–64. Obidicut . . .
Flibbertigibbet: these names also come from Harsnett. See *Lear*
Intro. p. 780b.   64. mopping . . . mowing: making faces and
grimaces. Cf. *Temp.*, IV.i.47.   68. humbled . . . strokes: made
so humble that you can endure anything.   69–72. Heavens . . .
quickly: you gods, deal with others as you have dealt with me; let
the man who has too much and pampers his own lusts, who re-
gards your commands as contemptuously as he regards his
slaves, that will not understand until he is hurt, feel your power
quickly. This passage echoes Lear's words (III.iv.33–36).
73. So . . . excess: then the man with too much would distribute
his excessive wealth.   76. bending: overhanging.

He smiled at it. I told him you were coming.   5
His answer was "The worse." Of Gloucester's
      treachery
And of the loyal service of his son
When I informed him, then he called me sot
And told me I had turned the wrong side out.   9
What most he should dislike seems pleasant to him,
What like, offensive.

GON. [To EDMUND] Then shall you go no further.
It is the cowish° terror of his spirit,
That dares not undertake.° He'll not feel wrongs
Which tie° him to an answer. Our wishes on the way
May prove effects.° Back, Edmund, to my brother.
Hasten his musters° and conduct his powers.°   16
I° must change arms at home and give the distaff°
Into my husband's hands. This trusty servant
Shall pass between us. Ere long you are like to hear,
If you dare venture in your own behalf,   20
A mistress's° command. Wear this. Spare speech.
                              [Giving a favor.]
Decline your head. This kiss, if it durst speak,
Would stretch thy spirits up into the air.
Conceive,° and fare thee well.

EDM.   Yours in the ranks of death.
GON. My most dear Gloucester! [Exit EDMUND.]
Oh, the difference of man and man!   26
To thee a woman's services are due,
My fool° usurps my body.

OSW.   Madam, here comes my lord. [Exit.]
                      [Enter ALBANY.]
GON. I have been worth the whistle.°
ALB.   O Goneril!
You are not worth the dust which the rude wind   30
Blows in your face. I fear your disposition.
That° nature which contemns it origin
Cannot be bordered certain in itself.
She that herself will sliver° and disbranch
From her material sap,° perforce must wither   35
And come to deadly use.

GON. No more, the text is foolish.°
ALB. Wisdom and goodness to the vile seem vile.

Filths savor but themselves.° What have you done?
Tigers, not daughters, what have you performed?
A father, and a gracious agèd man   41
Whose reverence even the head-lugged bear° would
      lick,
Most barbarous, most degenerate, have you madded!
Could my good brother° suffer you to do it?
A man, a prince, by him so benefited!   45
If that the Heavens do not their visible spirits°
Send quickly down to tame these vile offenses,
It will come.
Humanity must perforce prey on itself,
Like monsters of the deep.°

GON.   Milk-livered° man!   50
That bear'st a cheek for blows, a head for wrongs,
Who hast not in thy brows an eye discerning
Thine honor from thy suffering;° that not know'st
Fools do those villains pity who are punished
Ere they have done their mischief.° Where's thy
      drum?   55
France spreads his banners in our noiseless land,
With plumèd helm thy state begins to threat,
Whiles thou, a moral° fool, sit'st still and criest
"Alack, why does he so?"

ALB.   See thyself, devil!
Proper deformity° seems not in the fiend   60
So horrid as in woman.

GON.   O vain fool!
ALB. Thou changèd and self-covered° thing, for
      shame,
Bemonster not thy feature.° Were 't my fitness
To let these hands obey my blood,°
They are apt enough to dislocate and tear   65
Thy flesh and bones. Howe'er° thou art a fiend,
A woman's shape doth shield thee.

GON. Marry, your manhood!° Mew!°
                      [Enter a MESSENGER.]
ALB. What news?
MESS. O my good lord, the Duke of Cornwall's
      dead,   70
Slain by his servant, going to put out
The other eye of Gloucester.

Sc. ii: **12. cowish:** cowardly. **13. undertake:** show initia-
tive, venture. **14. tie:** force. **14–15. Our . . . effects:** our
hopes (of love) as we rode together may be fulfilled. **16. musters:**
troops which have been collected. **powers:** forces. **17–18. I
. . . hands:** I must become the soldier and leave my husband to do
the spinning. **17. distaff:** stick used in spinning, essentially the
work of the housewife. **21. mistress's:** in the double sense of
lady and lover. Edmund, having disposed of his brother and
father, now looks higher; he will through Goneril become pos-
sessed of her half of the kingdom of Lear. **24. Conceive:** use
your imagination. **28. My fool:** i.e., my husband is no more
than a fool to me. **29. worth . . . whistle:** There is a proverb
"'Tis a poor dog that is not worth the whistle." Goneril means:
I was once worth being regarded as your dog. **32–36. That . . .
use:** that creature which despises its father (*origin*) cannot be
kept within bounds; she that cuts herself off from her family tree
will perish and like a dead branch come to the burning. **34. sliver:**
slice off. **35. material sap:** that sap which is part of herself.
37. text is foolish: i.e., this is a silly sermon.

39. Filths . . . themselves: the filthy like the taste only of
filth. **42. head-lugged bear:** a bear with its head torn by the
hounds. See App. 5. **44. good brother:** Cornwall. **46. visible
spirits:** avenging spirits in visible form. **49–50. Humanity . . .
deep:** A thought more than once expressed by Shakespeare —
that when natural law is broken, men will degenerate into beasts
and prey on each other. Cf. *Tr & Cr*, I.iii.101–24; Gen. Intro.
p. 7b–8a. **50. Milk-livered:** cowardly; the liver was regarded as
the seat of courage. **52–53. Who . . . suffering:** who cannot
see when the insults which you endure are dishonorable to you.
54–55. Fools . . . mischief: only a fool pities a villain when he
is punished to prevent his committing a crime. **58. moral:**
moralizing. **60. Proper deformity:** deformity natural to a fiend.
62. self-covered: hiding your true self (i.e., devil) under the
guise of a woman. **63. Bemonster . . . feature:** do not change
your shape into a fiend. **64. blood:** anger. **66. Howe'er:** al-
though. **68. Marry . . . manhood:** you're a fine specimen of a
man! **Mew:** a catcall.

ALB.   Gloucester's eyes!

MESS. A servant that he bred, thrilled with re-
morse,°
Opposed against the act, bending his sword
To his great master, who thereat enraged   75
Flew on him and amongst them felled him dead,
But not without that harmful stroke which since
Hath plucked him after.

ALB.   This shows you are above,
You justicers, that these our nether crimes°
So speedily can venge. But, oh, poor Gloucester! 80
Lost he his other eye?

MESS.   Both, both, my lord.
This letter, madam, craves a speedy answer.
'Tis from your sister.

GON.   [*Aside*] One way I like this well,
But being widow, and my Gloucester° with her, 85
May all the building in my fancy pluck°
Upon my hateful life. Another way,
The news is not so tart. — I'll read, and answer.
                              [*Exit.*]

ALB. Where was his son when they did take his
eyes?

MESS. Come with my lady hither.

ALB.   He is not here. 90

MESS. No, my good lord, I met him back again.°

ALB. Knows he the wickedness?

MESS. Aye, my good lord, 'twas he informed
against him,
And quit the house on purpose, that their punish-
ment
Might have the freer course.

ALB.   Gloucester, I live 95
To thank thee for the love thou show'dst the King,
And to revenge thine eyes. Come hither, friend.
Tell me what more thou know'st.   [*Exeunt.*]

SCENE III. *The French camp near Dover.*

[*Enter* KENT *and a* GENTLEMAN.]

KENT. Why the King of France is so suddenly
gone back know you the reason?

GENT. Something he left imperfect in the state
which since his coming-forth is thought of, which
imports to the kingdom so much fear and danger
that his personal return was most required and nec-
essary.   7

KENT. Who hath he left behind him general?

GENT. The Marshal of France, Monsieur La Far.

KENT. Did your letters pierce the Queen to any
demonstration of grief?   12

GENT. Aye, sir. She took them, read them in my
presence,
And now and then an ample tear trilled down
Her delicate cheek. It seemed she was a queen 15
Over her passion,° who most rebel-like
Sought to be king o'er her.

KENT.   Oh, then it moved her.

GENT. Not to a rage. Patience and Sorrow strove
Who should express her goodliest.° You have
seen
Sunshine and rain at once. Her smiles and tears 20
Were like a better way.° Those happy smilets°
That played on her ripe lip seemed not to know
What guests were in her eyes, which parted thence
As pearls from diamonds dropped. In brief,
Sorrow would be a rarity most beloved 25
If all could so become it.°

KENT.   Made she no verbal question?

GENT. Faith, once or twice she heaved the name of
"Father"
Pantingly forth, as if it pressed her heart,
Cried "Sisters! Sisters! Shame of ladies! Sisters!
Kent! Father! Sisters! What, i' the storm? i' the
night?   30
Let pity not be believed!" There she shook
The holy water from her heavenly eyes,
And clamor-moistened.° Then away she started
To deal with grief alone.

KENT.   It is the stars,
The stars above us, govern our conditions, 35
Else one self° mate and mate could not beget
Such different issues.° You spoke not with her
since?

GENT. No.

KENT. Was this before the King returned?

GENT.   No, since.

KENT. Well, sir, the poor distressèd Lear's i' the
town,   40
Who sometime in his better tune remembers
What we are come about, and by no means
Will yield to see his daughter.

GENT.   Why, good sir?

KENT. A sovereign° shame so elbows° him. His
own unkindness
That stripped her from his benediction, turned her
To foreign casualties,° gave her dear rights 46
To his doghearted daughters. These things sting
His mind so venomously that burning shame
Detains him from Cordelia.

GENT.   Alack, poor gentleman!

---

73. **thrilled ... remorse:** trembling with pity. **79. nether
crimes:** crimes committed on earth below. **85. my Gloucester:**
i.e., Edmund. **86. May ... pluck:** may pull down my castle
in the air (i.e., her desire to marry Edmund). **91. met ...
again:** met him as he was on his way back.

Sc. iii: **16. passion:** emotion. **19. express ... goodliest:**
make her seem more beautiful. **21. like ... way:** even more
lovely. **smilets:** little smiles. **25-26. Sorrow ... it:** if every-
one looked so beautiful in sorrow, it would be a quality much
sought after. **33. clamor-moistened:** wet her cries of grief with
tears. **36. self:** same. **37. issues:** children. **44. sovereign:**
overpowering. **elbows:** plucks him by the elbow, reminding
him of the past. **46. casualties:** chances, accidents.

KENT. Of Albany's and Cornwall's powers you
    heard not?   50
    GENT. 'Tis so, they are afoot.
    KENT. Well, sir, I'll bring you to our master Lear,
And leave you to attend him. Some dear cause°
Will in concealment wrap me up awhile.
When I am known aright, you shall not grieve   55
Lending° me this acquaintance. I pray you, go
Along with me.   [*Exeunt.*]

SCENE IV. *The same. A tent.*

[*Enter, with drum and colors,*° CORDELIA, DOCTOR,
and SOLDIERS.]

    COR. Alack, 'tis he. Why, he was met even now
As mad as the vexed sea, singing aloud,
Crowned with rank fumiter and furrow weeds,
With burdocks, hemlock, nettles, cuckoo flowers,
Darnel,° and all the idle weeds that grow   5
In our sustaining° corn. A century° send forth.
Search every acre in the high-grown° field,
And bring him to our eye. [*Exit an* OFFICER.] What
    can man's wisdom
In the restoring his bereavèd sense?
He that helps him take all my outward worth.°   10
    DOCT. There is means, madam.
Our foster nurse° of nature is repose,
The which he lacks. That to provoke in him
Are many simples operative,° whose power
Will close the eye of anguish.
    COR.   All blest secrets,   15
All you unpublished virtues° of the earth,
Spring with my tears! Be aidant and remediate°
In the good man's distress! Seek, seek for him,
Lest his ungoverned rage dissolve the life
That wants the means to lead it.°

[*Enter a* MESSENGER.]

    MESS.   News, madam.   20
The British powers are marching hitherward.
    COR. 'Tis known before, our preparation stands
In expectation of them.° O dear Father,
It is thy business that I go about,
Therefore great France   25
My mourning and important° tears hath pitied.
No blown° ambition doth our arms incite,

But love, dear love, and our aged father's right.
Soon may I hear and see him!   [*Exeunt.*]

SCENE V. GLOUCESTER'S *castle.*

[*Enter* REGAN *and* OSWALD.]

    REG. But are my brother's powers set forth?
    OSW.   Aye, madam.
    REG. Himself in person there?
    OSW.   Madam, with much ado.
Your sister is the better soldier.
    REG. Lord Edmund spake not with your lord at
    home?
    OSW. No, madam.   5
    REG. What might import my sister's letter to him?
    OSW. I know not, lady.
    REG. Faith, he is posted° hence on serious matter.
It was great ignorance, Gloucester's eyes being out,
To let him live. Where he arrives he moves   10
All hearts against us. Edmund, I think, is gone,
In pity of his misery, to dispatch
His nighted° life, moreover to descry
The strength o' the enemy.   14
    OSW. I must needs after him, madam, with my
    letter.
    REG. Our troops set forth tomorrow. Stay with us,
The ways are dangerous.
    OSW.   I may not, madam.
My lady charged my duty° in this business.
    REG. Why should she write to Edmund? Might
    not you
Transport her purposes by word? Belike,   20
Something — I know not what — I'll love thee
    much,
Let me unseal the letter.
    OSW.   Madam, I had rather ——
    REG. I know your lady does not love her husband,
I am sure of that. And at her late being here   24
She gave strange œillades° and most speaking looks
To noble Edmund. I know you are of her bosom.°
    OSW. I, madam?
    REG. I speak in understanding. You are, I know 't.
Therefore I do advise you, take this note.°
My lord is dead, Edmund and I have talked,   30
And more convenient is he for my hand
Than for your lady's. You may gather more.
If you do find him, pray you give him this,
And when your mistress hears thus much from you,
I pray desire her call her wisdom to her.   35
So, fare you well.
If you do chance to hear of that blind traitor,

---

53. **dear cause:** important reason.   56. **Lending:** bestowing on.
    Sc. iv: **s.d., drum . . . colors:** a drummer and a soldier carry-
ing a flag.   3–5. **fumiter . . . Darnel:** These are all English wild
flowers and weeds.   6. **sustaining:** which maintains life.   **cen-
tury:** company of a hundred soldiers.   7. **high-grown:** The
season is therefore late summer.   10. **outward worth:** visible
wealth.   12. **foster nurse:** the nurse who feeds.   14. **simples
operative:** efficacious herbs.   16. **unpublished virtues:** secret
remedies.   17. **aidant . . . remediate:** helpful and remedial.
20. **wants . . . it:** that has no sense to guide it.   22–23. **our . . .
them:** our army is ready to meet them.   26. **important:** im-
portunate, pleading.   27. **blown:** puffed up.

     Sc. v: 8. **is posted:** has ridden fast.   13. **nighted:** blinded.
18. **charged my duty:** entrusted it to me as a solemn duty.
25. **œillades:** loving looks.   26. **of . . . bosom:** in her confidence.
29. **take . . . note:** observe this.

Preferment° falls on him that cuts him off.
osw. Would I could meet him, madam! I should show   39
What party I do follow.
REG.   Fare thee well.   [*Exeunt.*]

SCENE VI. *Fields near Dover.*

[*Enter* GLOUCESTER, *and* EDGAR *dressed like a peasant.*]

GLO. When shall we come to the top of that same hill?
EDG. You do climb up it now. Look how we labor.
GLO. Methinks the ground is even.
EDG.   Horrible steep.
Hark, do you hear the sea?
GLO.   No, truly.
EDG. Why then your other senses grow imperfect
By your eyes' anguish.
GLO.   So may it be, indeed.   6
Methinks thy voice is altered, and thou speak'st
In better phrase and matter than thou didst.
EDG. You're much deceived. In nothing am I changed
But in my garments.
GLO.   Methinks you're better-spoken.   10
EDG. Come on, sir, here's the place. Stand still.
     How° fearful
And dizzy 'tis to cast one's eyes so low!
The crows and choughs° that wing the midway air
Show scarce so gross as beetles. Halfway down
Hangs one that gathers samphire,° dreadful trade!
Methinks he seems no bigger than his head.   16
The fishermen that walk upon the beach
Appear like mice, and yond tall anchoring bark°
Diminished to her cock° — her cock, a buoy
Almost too small for sight. The murmuring surge
That on the unnumbered idle pebbles chafes   21
Cannot be heard so high. I'll look no more,
Lest my brain turn and the deficient sight
Topple down headlong.°
GLO.   Set me where you stand.
EDG. Give me your hand. You are now within a foot   25
Of the extreme verge. For all beneath the moon
Would I not leap upright.
GLO.   Let go my hand.
Here, friend, 's another purse, in it a jewel

Well worth a poor man's taking. Fairies and gods°
Prosper it with thee! Go thou further off.   30
Bid me farewell, and let me hear thee going.
EDG. Now fare you well, good sir.
GLO.   With all my heart.
EDG. Why I do trifle thus with his despair
Is done to cure it.°
GLO. [*Kneeling*] O you mighty gods!
This world I do renounce, and in your sights   35
Shake patiently my great affliction off.
If° I could bear it longer and not fall
To quarrel with your great opposeless wills,
My snuff° and loathèd part of nature should
Burn itself out. If Edgar live, oh, bless him!   40
Now, fellow, fare thee well. [*He falls forward.°*]
EDG.   Gone, sir. Farewell.
And yet I know not how conceit° may rob
The treasury of life when life itself
Yields to the theft.° Had he been where he thought,
By this had thought been past. Alive or dead?   45
Ho, you sir! Friend! Hear you, sir! Speak!
Thus might he pass° indeed. Yet he revives.
What are you, sir?
GLO.   Away, and let me die.
EDG. Hadst thou been aught but gossamer,° feathers, air,
So many fathom down precipitating,   50
Thou'dst shivered like an egg. But thou dost breathe,
Hast heavy substance, bleed'st not, speak'st, art sound.
Ten masts at each° make not the altitude
Which thou hast perpendicularly fell.
Thy life's a miracle. Speak yet again.   55
GLO. But have I fall'n, or no?
EDG. From the dread summit of this chalky bourn.°
Look up a-height, the shrill-gorged° lark so far
Cannot be seen or heard. Do but look up.
GLO. Alack, I have no eyes.   60

38. Preferment: promotion.
    Sc. vi: 11–24. How . . . headlong: This vivid description of the cliffs at Dover seems to have been written from direct observation. The King's Players visited Dover in September 1606. 13. choughs: jackdaws. 15. samphire: a strongly perfumed plant which grows on the chalk cliffs of Dover. 18. bark: ship. 19. cock: cockboat, the small ship's boat, usually towed behind. 23–24. deficient . . . headlong: my sight failing, cause me to topple headlong.

29. Fairies . . . gods: As this tale is pre-Christian, it is natural for the characters to call on the gods of the "elder world." 33–34. Why . . . it: Edgar's purpose is to persuade his blinded father to go on living by the thought that he has been miraculously preserved after falling from a great height. When Gloucester begins to recover from the shock, Edgar has dropped his pretense of being a bedlam and speaks in a natural (but still disguised) voice. 37–40. If . . . out: if I could endure my misery longer without quarreling with the wish of Heaven, I would wait for the rest of my hateful life to burn itself out. 39. snuff: lit., smoking end of a burnt out candle. 41 s.d., falls forward. To be effective this episode needs an actor who is not afraid of hurting himself, for unless Gloucester's fall is heavy it is quite unconvincing. After his fall, he lies stunned for a few moments. 42. conceit: imagination. 44. Yields . . . theft: i.e., is willing to die. 47. pass: pass away, die. 49. gossamer: the parachute-like web made by a species of small spider by which it floats through the air. 53. Ten . . . each: ten masts, one on top of the other. 57. bourn: boundary. 58. shrill-gorged: shrill-throated. The lark is a small brown bird which flies to a great height and there remains fluttering and singing a shrill but beautiful song.

Is wretchedness deprived that benefit,
To end itself by death? 'Twas yet some comfort
When misery could beguile° the tyrant's rage
And frustrate his proud will.

EDG.   Give me your arm.
Up, so. How is 't? Feel you your legs? You stand.

GLO. Too well, too well.

EDG.   This is above all strangeness.   66
Upon the crown o' the cliff, what thing was that
Which parted from you?

GLO.   A poor unfortunate beggar.

EDG. As I stood here below, methought his eyes
Were two full moons, he had a thousand noses,   70
Horns whelked° and waved like the enridgèd° sea.
It was some fiend, therefore, thou happy father,
Think that the clearest° gods, who make them honors
Of men's impossibilities,° have preserved thee.

GLO. I do remember now. Henceforth I'll bear   75
Affliction till it do cry out itself
"Enough, enough," and die. That thing you speak of,
I took it for a man. Often 'twould say
"The fiend, the fiend." He led me to that place.

EDG. Bear free° and patient thoughts. But who
comes here?   80

[*Enter* LEAR, *fantastically dressed with wild flowers.*]

The safer sense will n'er accommodate
His master thus.°

LEAR. No,° they cannot touch me for coining, I
am the King himself.

EDG. O thou side-piercing sight!   85

LEAR. Nature's above art° in that respect. There's
your press money. That fellow handles his bow like
a crowkeeper,° draw me a clothier's yard.° Look,
look, a mouse! Peace, peace, this piece of toasted
cheese will do 't. There's my gauntlet,° I'll prove it
on a° giant. Bring up the brown bills.° Oh, well-

flown, bird! I' the clout,° i' the clout. Hewgh!° Give
the word.°   93

EDG. Sweet marjoram.°

LEAR. Pass.

GLO. I know that voice.   96

LEAR. Ha! Goneril, with a white beard! They
flattered me like a dog, and told me I had white
hairs in my beard ere the black ones were there. To
say "aye" and "no" to everything that I said!
"Aye" and "no" too was no good divinity.°   101
When the rain came to wet me once and the wind to
make me chatter, when the thunder would not peace
at my bidding, there I found 'em, there I smelt 'em
out. Go to, they are not men o' their words. They
told me I was everything. 'Tis a lie, I am not ague-
proof.   107

GLO. The trick° of that voice I do well remember.
Is 't not the King?

LEAR.   Aye, every inch a king.
When I do stare, see how the subject quakes.   110
I pardon that man's life. What was thy cause?
Adultery?
Thou shalt not die. Die for adultery! No.
The wren goes to 't, and the small gilded fly
Does lecher in my sight.   115
Let copulation thrive, for Gloucester's bastard son
Was kinder to his father than my daughters
Got 'tween the lawful sheets.
To 't, luxury,° pell-mell! For I lack soldiers.
Behold yond simpering dame,   120
Whose face between her forks° presages snow,
That minces virtue° and does shake the head
To hear of pleasure's name.
The fitchew,° nor the soilèd° horse, goes to 't
With a more riotous appetite.   125
Down from the waist they are Centaurs,°
Though women all above.
But to° the girdle do the gods inherit,
Beneath is all the fiends'.
There's Hell, there's darkness, there's the sulphurous pit,   130
Burning, scalding, stench, consumption, fie, fie, fie!
Pah, pah! Give me an ounce of civet,° good apothecary, to sweeten my imagination. There's money for thee.

GLO. Oh, let me kiss that hand!   135

LEAR. Let me wipe it first, it smells of mortality.

GLO. O ruined piece of nature! This great world
Shall so wear out to naught.° Dost thou know me?

---

63. beguile: cheat (by death).   71. whelked: with spiral twists. enridged: wavy.   73. clearest: most glorious.   73–74. who ... impossibilities: who cause themselves to be honored by performing miracles impossible to men.   80. free: innocent. 81–82. The ... thus: a man in his right senses would never adorn himself thus. Edgar with unconscious irony repeats Lear's "accommodated." See III.iv.110.   83–93. No ... word: Lear's madness has a sort of logical coherence. He begins by saying that he cannot be charged with coining, because it was his right as king to issue the coin, a natural right. From coin his mind goes to the use of coin as *press money* for soldiers (money given to a conscripted recruit as token that he has been engaged), thence to the recruits at archery practice. Then his mind is distracted by a mouse, but comes back to his quarrel with his sons-in-law. He will throw down his gauntlet as a challenge to single combat against any odds. He comes back to the archery range, and a good shot right in the bull's-eye.   86. Nature's ... art: See App. 18.   88. crowkeeper: a man hired to scare away crows from the crop. clothier's yard: The expert archer drew his arrow back a full yard to the ear.   90. gauntlet: glove, token of challenge. 90–91. prove ... a: i.e., fight even a.   91. brown bills: i.e., the infantry. See Pl. 21c. brown: varnished to keep from rusting.

92. clout: the canvas target. Hewgh: imitation of the whizz of the arrow.   93. word: password.   94. marjoram: a savory herb.   101. no ... divinity: i.e., false doctrine.   108. trick: peculiar, individual quality of the voice.   119. luxury: lust.   121. forks: legs.   122. minces virtue: walks with a great air of virtue.   124. fitchew: polecat, a creature demonstratively oversexed. soiled: fed on spring grass.   126. Centaurs: creatures half man and half stallion. 128. But to: only down to.   132. civet: perfume. See III.iv. 108–09,n.   137–38. O ... naught: O ruined masterpiece of nature, the universe likewise will come to nothing.

LEAR. I remember thine eyes well enough. Dost
thou squiny° at me? No, do thy worst, blind Cu-
pid,° I'll not love. Read thou this challenge, mark
but the penning on 't.　　　　　　　　　　142

GLO. Were all the letters suns, I could not see one.

EDG. I would not take this from report. It is,
And my heart breaks at it.

LEAR. Read.　　　　　　　　　　　　146

GLO. What, with the case of eyes?

LEAR. Oh ho, are you there with me?° No eyes
in your head, nor no money in your purse? Your
eyes are in a heavy case, your purse in a light. Yet
you see how this world goes.　　　　　　　151

GLO. I see it feelingly.

LEAR. What, art mad? A man may see how this
world goes with no eyes. Look with thine ears. See
how yond Justice rails upon yond simple thief. Hark,
in thine ear. Change places and, handy-dandy,°
which is the Justice, which is the thief? Thou hast
seen a farmer's dog bark at a beggar?　　　159

GLO. Aye, sir.

LEAR. And the creature run from the cur? There
thou mightst behold the great image of authority.°
A dog's obeyed in office.
Thou rascal beadle,° hold thy bloody hand!
Why dost thou lash that whore? Strip thine own
　　back.　　　　　　　　　　　　　165
Thou hotly lust'st to use her in that kind°
For which thou whip'st her. The usurer hangs the
　　cozener.°
Through tattered clothes small vices do appear,
Robes and furred gowns hide all. Plate sin with gold
And the strong lance of justice hurtless breaks.　170
Arm it in rags, a pigmy's straw does pierce it.
None does offend, none, I say, none, I'll able° 'em.
Take that of me, my friend, who have the power
To seal the accuser's lips. Get thee glass eyes°
And, like a scurvy° politician, seem　　　175
To see the things thou dost not.
Now, now, now, now. Pull off my boots. Harder,
　　harder. So.

EDG. Oh, matter and impertinency° mixed!
Reason in madness!　　　　　　　　　179

LEAR. If thou wilt weep my fortunes, take my eyes.
I know thee well enough. Thy name is Gloucester.
Thou must be patient, we came crying hither.
Thou know'st the first time that we smell the air,
We wawl and cry. I will preach to thee. Mark.

GLO. Alack, alack the day!　　　　　　185

LEAR. When we are born, we cry that we are come
To this great stage of fools. This 's a good block.°
It were a delicate stratagem to shoe
A troop of horse with felt. I'll put 't in proof,°
And when I have stol'n upon these sons-in-law,
Then, kill, kill, kill, kill, kill, kill!　　　191

[*Enter a* GENTLEMAN, *with* ATTENDANTS.]

GENT. Oh, here he is. Lay hand upon him. Sir,
Your most dear daughter ——

LEAR. No rescue? What, a prisoner? I am even
The natural fool of Fortune.° Use me well,　195
You shall have ransom.° Let me have a surgeon,
I am cut to the brains.

GENT.　　　　　　　　You shall have anything.

LEAR. No seconds?° All myself?
Why, this would make a man a man of salt,°
To use his eyes for garden waterpots,　　200
Aye, and laying autumn's dust.

GENT. Good sir ——

LEAR. I will die bravely, like a smug bridegroom.°
　　What!
I will be jovial. Come, come, I am a king,
My masters, know you that.

GENT. You are a royal one, and we obey you.　205

LEAR. Then there's life in 't. Nay, an you get it,
you shall get it by running. Sa, sa, sa, sa.°

[*Exit running.* ATTENDANTS *follow.*]

GENT. A sight most pitiful in the meanest wretch,
Past speaking of in a king! Thou hast one daughter
Who redeems nature from the general curse　210
Which twain have brought her to.°

EDG. Hail, gentle sir.

GENT.　　　　　　Sir, speed you. What's your will?

EDG. Do you hear aught, sir, of a battle toward?°

GENT. Most sure and vulgar.° Everyone hears that
Which can distinguish sound.

EDG.　　　　　　But, by your favor,　215
How near's the other army?

GENT. Near and on speedy foot, the main descry
Stands on the hourly thought.°

EDG.　　　　　　I thank you, sir. That's all.

GENT. Though that the Queen on special cause is
　　here,
Her army is moved on.

---

140. squiny: look sideways, like a prostitute.　140–41. blind
Cupid: the usual sign hung over a brothel.　148. are . . . me:
do you agree with me?　157. handy-dandy: the nursery game of
"Handy-pandy, sugar candy, which hand will you have?"
162. image of authority: figure showing the true meaning of au-
thority.　164. beadle: parish officer.　166. kind: manner.
167. usurer . . . cozener: the swindler hangs the crook.
172. able: give power to.　174. glass eyes: spectacles.
175. scurvy: lit., with skin disease, "lousy."　178. matter . . .
impertinency: sense and nonsense.

187. block: hat; lit., the block on which a felt hat is molded.
From hat Lear's mind turns to *felt*.　189. put . . . proof: try it
out.　195. natural . . . Fortune: born to be fooled by Fortune.
196. ransom: Prisoners of good family could buy their free-
dom from their captors. Cf. *Hen V*, IV.iii.79–125.　198. No
seconds: no one to help me.　199. man of salt: because tears
are salt.　202. like . . . bridegroom: It was said of Lord Grey
of Wilton, who was led out as if to be executed on December 9,
1603, that he "had such gaiety and cheer in his countenance that
he seemed a dapper young bridegroom."　207. Sa . . . sa: a cry
used sometimes in sudden action.　210–11. Who . . . to: See
Lear Intro. p. 783b.　213. toward: at hand.　214. vulgar:
common, in everyone's mouth.　217–18. the . . . thought: the
main body is expected to come into sight at any time now.

EDG.   I thank you, sir.   [*Exit* GENTLEMAN.]

GLO. You ever-gentle gods, take my breath from
me.   221
Let not my worser spirit tempt me again
To die before you please!

EDG.   Well pray you, Father.

GLO. Now, good sir, what are you?

EDG. A most poor man, made tame to fortune's
blows,   225
Who, by the art° of known and feeling sorrows,
Am pregnant to° good pity. Give me your hand.
I'll lead you to some biding.°

GLO.   Hearty thanks.
The bounty and the benison° of Heaven
To boot, and boot!°

[*Enter* OSWALD.]

OSW.   A proclaimed° prize! Most happy!   230
That eyeless head of thine was first framed flesh
To raise my fortunes. Thou old unhappy traitor,
Briefly thyself remember.° The sword is out
That must destroy thee.

GLO.   Now let thy friendly hand
Put strength enough to 't.   [EDGAR *interposes*.]

OSW.   Wherefore, bold peasant,   235
Darest thou support a published° traitor? Hence,
Lest that the infection of his fortune take
Like hold on thee! Let go his arm.

EDG. Chill° not let go, zir, without vurther 'ca-
sion.°

OSW. Let go, slave, or thou diest!   241

EDG. Good gentleman, go your gait,° and let poor
volk pass. An chud° ha' been zwaggered out of my
life, 'twould not ha' been zo long as 'tis by a vort-
night. Nay, come not near th' old man, keep out,
che vor ye,° or I'se try whether your costard° or my
ballow° be the harder. Chill be plain with you.   247

OSW. Out, dunghill!   [*They fight*.]

EDG. Chill pick your teeth, zir. Come, no matter
vor your foins.°   [OSWALD *falls*.]

OSW. Slave, thou hast slain me. Villain, take my
purse.
If ever thou wilt thrive, bury my body,
And give the letters which thou find'st about me
To Edmund Earl of Gloucester. Seek him out   254
Upon the British party. Oh, untimely death!
Death!   [*Dies*.]

EDG. I know thee well — a serviceable° villain,
As duteous to the vices of thy mistress

As badness would desire.

GLO.   What, is he dead?

EDG. Sit you down, Father, rest you.   260
Let's see these pockets. The letters that he speaks of
May be my friends. He's dead. I am only sorry
He had no other deathsman. Let us see.
Leave, gentle wax,° and, manners, blame us not.
To know our enemies' minds, we'd rip their hearts,
Their papers is more lawful. [*Reads*.]   266
"Let our reciprocal vows be remembered. You
have many opportunities to cut him off. If your will
want not,° time and place will be fruitfully offered.
There is nothing done if he return the conqueror.
Then am I the prisoner, and his bed my jail, from
the loathed warmth whereof deliver me, and supply
the place for your labor.   274
"Your — wife, so I would say — affectionate
servant,   GONERIL."
Oh, undistinguished space° of woman's will!
A plot upon her virtuous husband's life,
And the exchange my brother! Here, in the sands,
Thee I'll rake up,° the post unsanctified°   281
Of murderous lechers, and in the mature time
With this ungracious paper strike the sight
Of the death-practiced° Duke. For him 'tis well
That of thy death and business I can tell.   285

GLO. The King is mad. How° stiff° is my vile
sense,°
That I stand up, and have ingenious° feeling
Of my huge sorrows! Better I were distract.°
So should my thoughts be severed from my griefs,
And woes by wrong imaginations lose   290
The knowledge of themselves.   [*Drum afar off*]

EDG.   Give me your hand.
Far off methinks I hear the beaten drum.
Come, Father, I'll bestow you with a friend.
[*Exeunt*.]

SCENE VII. *A tent in the French camp.* LEAR
on a bed asleep, soft music playing,
GENTLEMAN, *and others attending.*

[*Enter* CORDELIA, KENT, *and* DOCTOR.]

COR. ● thou good Kent, how shall I live and
work,
To match thy goodness? My life will be too short,
And every measure fail me.

KENT. To be acknowledged, madam, is o'erpaid.
All my reports go with the modest truth,   5

---

226. art: long experience.   227. pregnant to: able to conceive.
228. biding: resting-place.   229. benison: blessing.   230. To
. . . boot: in the highest degree. proclaimed: Cf. IV.v.37–8.
233. thyself remember: prepare for death — by confessing your
sins.   236. published: publicly proclaimed.   239–48. Chill . . .
you: Edgar speaks stage rustic dialect.   240. Chill: I'll. vur-
ther 'casion: further occasion, reason.   242. go . . . gait: go
your own way.   243. chud: should.   246. che . . . ye: I warn
yer. costard: head; lit., apple.   247. ballow: cudgel.   250. foins:
thrusts.   257. serviceable: diligent.

264. Leave . . . wax: Here he breaks the seal. See App. 6.
268–69. will . . . not: desire is not lacking. *Will* means both
willingness and lust.   278. undistinguished space: limitless,
extending beyond the range of sight.   281. rake up: hide in the
dust. post unsanctified: unholy messenger.   284. death-prac-
ticed: whose death is plotted.   286–88. How . . . sorrows: i.e.,
if only I could go mad and forget my sorrows. stiff: strong.
sense: sanity. ingenious: sensitive. distract: mad.

Nor more nor clipped, but so.°
    COR.   Be better suited.°
These weeds° are memories of those worser hours.
I prithee put them off.
    KENT.   Pardon me, dear madam,
Yet to be known shortens my made intent.°
My boon° I make it that you know me not   10
Till time and I think meet.
    COR. Then be 't so, my good lord. [*To the* DOCTOR]
        How does the King?
    DOCT. Madam, sleeps still.
    COR. O you kind gods,
Cure this great breach in his abusèd nature!   15
The untuned and jarring senses, oh, wind up°
Of this child-changèd° father!
    DOCT.   So please your Majesty
That we may wake the King. He hath slept long.
    COR. Be governed by your knowledge, and pro-
    ceed
I' the sway° of your own will. Is he arrayed?   20
    GENT. Aye, madam. In the heaviness of his sleep
We put fresh garments on him.
    DOCT. Be by, good madam, when we do awake
    him.
I doubt not of his temperance.°
    COR.   Very well.
    DOCT. Please you, draw near. Louder the music
    there!   25
    COR. O my dear Father! Restoration hang
Thy medicine on my lips, and let this kiss
Repair those violent harms that my two sisters
Have in thy reverence made!
    KENT.   Kind and dear Princess!
    COR. Had you not been their father, these white
    flakes   30
Had challenged pity of them. Was this a face
To be opposed against the warring winds?
To stand against the deep dread-bolted thunder?
In the most terrible and nimble stroke
Of quick, cross lightning?° To watch — poor
    perdu!° —   35
With this thin helm? Mine enemy's dog,
Though he had bit me, should have stood that night
Against my fire, and wast thou fain, poor Father,
To hovel thee with swine and rogues forlorn
In short and musty straw? Alack, alack!   40
'Tis wonder that thy life and wits at once
Had not concluded all. He wakes. Speak to him.
    DOCT. Madam, do you, 'tis fittest.

Sc. vii: 6. Nor . . . so: neither exaggerated nor curtailed, but
exact. suited: garbed.   7. weeds: garments; i.e., his livery
as Lear's servant.   9. Yet . . . intent: my plan will be frustrated
if I am revealed now.   10. boon: request for a favor.   16. wind
up: i.e., as the loose string of a musical instrument is tightened.
17. child-changed: transformed by the treatment of his
children.   20. sway: direction.   24. temperance: sanity.
35. cross lightning: forked lightning. perdu: sentry in an ex-
posed position.

    COR. How does my royal lord? How fares your
    Majesty?
    LEAR. You do me wrong to take me out o' the
    grave.   45
Thou art a soul in bliss,° but I am bound
Upon a wheel of fire that mine own tears
Do scald like molten lead.
    COR.   Sir, do you know me?
    LEAR. You are a spirit, I know. When did you
    die?
    COR. Still, still far wide!   50
    DOCT. He's scarce awake. Let him alone awhile.
    LEAR. Where have I been? Where am I? Fair day-
    light?
I am mightily abused. I should e'en die with pity
To see another thus. I know not what to say.
I will not swear these are my hands. Let's see,   55
I feel this pin prick. Would I were assured
Of my condition!
    COR.   Oh, look upon me, sir,
And hold your hands in benediction o'er me.
No, sir, you must not kneel.
    LEAR.   Pray do not mock me.
I am a very foolish fond old man,   60
Fourscore and upward, not an hour more nor less,
And, to deal plainly,
I fear I am not in my perfect mind.
Methinks I should know you and know this man,
Yet I am doubtful, for I am mainly ignorant   65
What place this is, and all the skill I have
Remembers not these garments, nor I know not
Where I did lodge last night. Do not laugh at me,
For, as I am a man, I think this lady
To be my child Cordelia.
    COR.   And so I am, I am.   70
    LEAR. Be your tears wet? Yes, faith. I pray weep
    not.
If you have poison for me, I will drink it.
I know you do not love me, for your sisters
Have, as I do remember, done me wrong.
You have some cause, they have not.
    COR.   No cause, no cause.   75
    LEAR. Am I in France?
    KENT.   In your own kingdom, sir.
    LEAR. Do not abuse me.
    DOCT. Be comforted, good madam. The great
    rage,
You see, is killed in him. And yet it is danger
To make him even o'er° the time he has lost.   80
Desire him to go in, trouble him no more
Till further settling.
    COR. Will 't please your Highness walk?
    LEAR.   You must bear with me.
Pray you now, forget and forgive. I am old and
    foolish.
         [*Exeunt all but* KENT *and* GENTLEMAN.]
    46. bliss: Heaven.   80. even o'er: go over.

GENT. Holds it true, sir, that the Duke of Corn-
wall was so slain?   86

KENT. Most certain, sir.

GENT. Who is conductor of his people?

KENT. As 'tis said, the bastard son of Gloucester.

GENT. They say Edgar, his banished son, is with
the Earl of Kent in Germany.   91

KENT. Report is changeable.° 'Tis time to look
about. The powers of the kingdom approach apace.

GENT. The arbiterment° is like to be bloody. Fare
you well, sir.   [Exit.]

KENT. My point and period° will be throughly°
        wrought,   97
Or well or ill, as this day's battle's fought. [Exit.]

Act V

SCENE I. *The British camp near Dover.*

[*Enter, with drum and colors,* EDMUND, REGAN,
        GENTLEMEN, *and* SOLDIERS.]

EDM. Know° of the Duke if his last purpose hold,
Or whether since he is advised by aught
To change the course. He's full of alteration
And self-reproving. Bring his constant° pleasure.
                [*To a* GENTLEMAN, *who goes out.*]

REG. Our sister's man is certainly miscarried.   5

EDM. 'Tis to be doubted,° madam.

REG.   Now, sweet lord,
You know the goodness I intend upon you.
Tell me, but truly, but then speak the truth,
Do you not love my sister?

EDM.   In honored love.   9

REG. But have you never found my brother's way
To the forfended° place?

EDM.   That thought abuses° you.

REG. I am doubtful that you have been conjunct
And bosomed with her, as far as we call hers.°

EDM. No, by mine honor, madam.

REG. I never shall endure her. Dear my lord,   15
Be not familiar with her.

EDM.   Fear me not.—
She and the Duke her husband!

[*Enter, with drum and colors,* ALBANY, GONERIL, *and*
                SOLDIERS.]

GON. [*Aside*] I had rather lose the battle than that
        sister
Should loosen him and me.

ALB. Our very loving sister, well bemet.   20
Sir, this I hear: The King is come to his daughter,
With others whom the rigor of our state°
Forced to cry out.° Where I could not be honest,
I never yet was valiant. For this business,
It toucheth us, as France invades our land,   25
Not bolds the King, with others, whom I fear
Most just and heavy causes make oppose.°

EDM. Sir, you speak nobly.

REG.   Why is this reasoned?°

GON. Combine together 'gainst the enemy,
For these domestic and particular broils   30
Are not the question here.

ALB.   Let's then determine
With the ancient of war° on our proceedings.

EDM. I shall attend you presently at your tent.

REG. Sister, you'll go with us?

GON. No.   35

REG. 'Tis most convenient. Pray you go with us.

GON. [*Aside*] Oh ho, I know the riddle.° —I
        will go.

[*As they are going out, enter* EDGAR *disguised.*]

EDG. If e'er your Grace had speech with man so
        poor,
Hear me one word.

ALB.   I'll overtake you. Speak.
                [*Exeunt all but* ALBANY *and* EDGAR.]

EDG. Before you fight the battle, ope this letter.
If you have victory, let the trumpet sound   41
For him that brought it. Wretched though I seem,
I can produce a champion that will prove
What is avouchèd° there. If you miscarry,
Your business of the world hath so an end,   45
And machination ceases. Fortune love you!

ALB. Stay till I have read the letter.

EDG.   I was forbid it.
When time shall serve, let but the herald cry
And I'll appear again.   49

ALB. Why, fare thee well. I will o'erlook° thy
        paper.   [*Exit* EDGAR.]

        [*Re-enter* EDMUND.]

EDM. The enemy's in view. Draw up your powers.
Here is the guess° of their true strength and forces
By diligent discovery, but your haste
Is now urged on you.

ALB.   We will greet the time.° [*Exit.*]

EDM. To° both these sisters have I sworn my love,

<hr>

92. **Report . . . changeable:** rumors are not reliable.   94. **arbi-
terment:** decision.   97. **point . . . period:** lit., full stop; the end
of my chapter. **throughly:** thoroughly.

Act V, Sc. i: 1. **Know:** learn.   4. **constant:** firm; i.e., final
decision.   6. **doubted:** feared.   11. **forfended:** forbidden.
abuses: wrongs; i.e., you should not have such a thought.
12–13. **I . . . hers:** I am afraid that you have been united in in-
timacy with her in every way.

22. **rigor . . . state:** our harsh government.   23. **cry out:** protest.
24–27. **For . . . oppose:** this business concerns us particularly,
not because France is encouraging Lear and others who rightly
oppose us, but because he is invading our country.   28. **reasoned:**
argued.   32. **ancient of war:** experienced commanders.   37. **Oh
. . . riddle:** i.e., you are afraid to leave me alone with Edmund.
44. **avouched:** declared.   50. **o'erlook:** read.   52. **guess:**
estimate.   54. **greet . . . time:** i.e., go to meet our enemy.
55–69. **To . . . debate:** Edmund has now reached the crisis in his
fortunes. Both sisters are in love with him, he can have either.
Or he can aim higher and, with Lear and Cordelia out of the way,
achieve the whole kingdom for himself.

Each jealous of the other, as the stung   56
Are of the adder. Which of them shall I take?
Both? One? Or neither? Neither can be enjoyed
If both remain alive. To take the widow
Exasperates, makes mad her sister Goneril,   60
And hardly shall I carry out my side,°
Her husband being alive. Now then we'll use
His countenance° for the battle, which being done,
Let her who would be rid of him devise
His speedy taking-off. As for the mercy   65
Which he intends to Lear and to Cordelia,
The battle done, and they within our power,
Shall never see his pardon, for my state
Stands on me to defend, not to debate.°   [*Exit.*]

SCENE II. *A field between the two camps.*

[*Alarum within. Enter, with drum and colors,* LEAR,
CORDELIA, *and* SOLDIERS, *over the stage; and exeunt.
Enter* EDGAR *and* GLOUCESTER.]
EDG. Here, Father, take the shadow of this tree
For your good host. Pray that the right may thrive.
If ever I return to you again,
I'll bring you comfort.
GLO.   Grace go with you, sir!   [*Exit* EDGAR.]
[*Alarum and retreat within. Re-enter* EDGAR.]
EDG. Away, old man. Give me thy hand, away!
King Lear hath lost, he and his daughter ta'en.°
Give me thy hand, come on.   7
GLO. No farther, sir. A man may rot even here.
EDG. What, in ill thoughts again? Men° must
    endure
Their going hence, even as their coming hither.   10
Ripeness° is all. Come on.
GLO.   And that's true too.   [*Exeunt.*]

SCENE III. *The British camp near Dover.*

[*Enter, in conquest, with drum and colors,* EDMUND,
LEAR *and* CORDELIA, *as prisoners,* CAPTAIN, SOLDIERS,
etc.]
EDM. Some officers take them away. Good guard,
Until their greater pleasures° first be known
That are to censure them.
COR.   We are not the first
Who with best meaning have incurred the worst.
For thee, oppressèd King, am I cast down.   5
Myself could else outfrown false fortune's frown.°

Shall we not see these daughters and these sisters?
LEAR. No, no, no, no! Come, let's away to prison.
We two alone will sing like birds i' the cage.
When thou dost ask me blessing, I'll kneel down   10
And ask of thee forgiveness. So we'll live,
And pray, and sing, and tell old tales, and laugh
At gilded butterflies,° and hear poor rogues
Talk of Court news. And we'll talk with them too,
Who loses and who wins, who's in, who's out,   15
And take upon 's the mystery of things°
As if we were God's spies. And we'll wear out,
In a walled prison, packs and sects of great ones
That ebb and flow by the moon.°
EDM.   Take them away.
LEAR. Upon such sacrifices, my Cordelia,   20
The gods themselves throw incense. Have I caught
    thee?
He that parts us shall bring a brand° from Heaven,
And fire us° hence like foxes. Wipe thine eyes.
The goodyears° shall devour them, flesh and fell,°
Ere they shall make us weep. We'll see 'em starve
    first.   25
Come.   [*Exeunt* LEAR *and* CORDELIA, *guarded.*]
EDM. Come hither, Captain, hark.
Take thou this note. Go follow them to prison.
One step I have advanced thee. If thou dost
As this instructs thee, thou dost make thy way
To noble fortunes. Know thou this, that men   30
Are as the time is.° To be tender-minded
Does not become a sword.° Thy great employment
Will not bear question.° Either say thou'lt do 't,
Or thrive by other means.
CAPT.   I'll do 't, my lord.
EDM. About it, and write happy° when thou hast
    done.   35
Mark, I say, instantly, and carry it so
As I have set it down.
CAPT. I cannot draw a cart, nor eat dried oats.
If it be man's work, I'll do 't.   [*Exit.*]
[*Flourish. Enter* ALBANY, GONERIL, REGAN, *another*
CAPTAIN, *and* SOLDIERS.]
ALB. Sir, you have shown today your valiant
    strain,°   40
And fortune led you well. You have the captives
That were the opposites° of this day's strife.
We do require them of you, so to use them
As we shall find their merits and our safety
May equally determine.

13. **gilded butterflies:** i.e., Court folk.   16. **take . . . things:**
pretend to understand deep secrets.   18–19. **packs . . . moon:**
parties at Court whose fortunes change monthly.   22. **a brand:**
fire.   23. **fire us:** drive us out by fire.   24. **goodyears:** The
phrase "what the goodyear" meant "what the deuce"; hence
"goodyear" means something vaguely evil. Lear is talking
baby talk — "The bogeymen shall have them." **fell:** skin.
30–31. **men . . . is:** i.e., in brutal times men must be brutes.
32. **sword:** soldier.   32–33. **Thy . . . question:** the duty now laid on
you is too important and brutal to be argued about.   35. **happy:**
fortunate.   40. **strain:** blood, courage.   42. **opposites:** opponents.

---

61. **my side:** i.e., of the bargain.   63. **countenance:** authority.
68–69. **for . . . debate:** my fortune is now in such a state that I
must act, not argue.

Sc. ii: 6. **ta'en:** taken.   9–11. **Men . . . all:** Shakespeare had
already expressed this stoical view of life in *Haml.*, V.ii.231.
11. **Ripeness:** perfect readiness.

Sc. iii: 2. **their . . . pleasures:** the will of my superiors.
3–6. **We . . . frown:** See I.i.183–90,n.

EDM.   Sir, I thought it fit   45
To send the old and miserable King
To some retention and appointed guard,°
Whose age has charms in it, whose title more,
To pluck the common bosom° on his side
And turn our impressed lances° in our eyes   50
Which do command them. With him I sent the
    Queen,
My reason all the same, and they are ready
Tomorrow or at further space to appear
Where you shall hold your session.° At this time
We sweat and bleed. The friend hath lost his friend,
And the best quarrels, in the heat, are cursed   56
By those that feel their sharpness.°
The question of Cordelia and her father
Requires a fitter place.
    ALB.   Sir, by your patience,
I hold you but a subject° of this war,   60
Not as a brother.
    REG.   That's as we list to grace him.
Methinks our pleasure might have been demanded
Ere you had spoke so far. He led our powers,
Bore the commission of my place and person,°
The which immediacy may well stand up   65
And call itself your brother.°
    GON.   Not so hot.
In his own grace he doth exalt himself
More than in your addition.°
    REG.   In my rights,
By me invested, he compeers° the best.
    GON. That were the most, if he should husband
    you.   70
    REG. Jesters do oft prove prophets.
    GON.   Holloa, holloa!
That eye that told you so looked but a-squint.
    REG. Lady, I am not well, else I should answer
From a full-flowing stomach.° General,
Take thou my soldiers, prisoners, patrimony,   75
Dispose of them, of me, the walls are thine.°
Witness the world that I create thee here
My lord and master.
    GON.   Mean you to enjoy him?
    ALB. The let-alone° lies not in your goodwill.
    EDM. Nor in thine, lord.
    ALB.   Half-blooded fellow, yes.   80
    REG. [*To* EDMUND] Let the drum strike, and prove
    my title thine.

ALB. Stay yet, hear reason. Edmund, I arrest thee
On capital treason,° and in thine attaint°
This gilded serpent. [*Pointing to* GONERIL] For
    your claim, fair Sister,
I bar it in the interest of my wife.   85
'Tis she is subcontracted° to this lord,
And I, her husband, contradict your bans.°
If you will marry, make your loves to me.
My lady is bespoke.°
    GON.   An interlude!°
    ALB. Thou art armed, Gloucester. Let the trumpet
    sound.   90
If none appear to prove upon thy person
Thy heinous,° manifest, and many treasons,
There is my pledge. [*Throwing down a glove*] I'll
    prove it on thy heart
Ere I taste bread, thou art in nothing less
Than I have here proclaimed thee.
    REG.   Sick, oh, sick!   95
    GON. [*Aside*] If not, I'll ne'er trust medicine.°
    EDM. [*Throwing down a glove*] There's my ex-
    change. What in the world he is
That names me traitor, villainlike he lies.°
Call by thy trumpet. He that dares approach,
On him, on you — who not? — I will maintain
My truth and honor firmly.   101
    ALB. A herald, ho!
    EDM.   A herald, ho, a herald!
    ALB. Trust to thy single° virtue, for thy soldiers,
All levied in my name, have in my name
Took their discharge.
    REG.   My sickness grows upon me.   105
    ALB. She is not well. Convey her to my tent.
                    [*Exit* REGAN, *led.*]
[*Enter a* HERALD.] Come hither, herald. — Let the
    trumpet sound. —
And read out this.   108
    CAPT. Sound, trumpet!   [*A trumpet sounds.*]
    HER. [*Reads.*] "If any man of quality or degree°
within the lists° of the army will maintain upon Ed-
mund, supposed Earl of Gloucester, that he is a
manifold traitor, let him appear by the third sound
of the trumpet. He is bold in his defense."   114
    EDM. Sound!   [*First trumpet.*]
    HER. Again!   [*Second trumpet.*]
Again!   [*Third trumpet.*]
                    [*Trumpet answers within.*]
[*Enter* EDGAR *at the third sound, armed, with a
    trumpet before him.*]

---

47. **retention . . . guard:** where he can be kept and properly
guarded.   49. **common bosom:** the sympathies of our soldiers.
50. **impressed lances:** the soldiers we have conscripted.   54. **ses-
sion:** trial.   56–57. **And . . . sharpness:** i.e., with the battle
hardly over we are in no condition to judge this matter calmly.
60. **subject:** i.e., not one who gives orders.   64. **commission . . .
person:** commission appointing him commander as my deputy.
65–66. **The . . . brother:** since he is my general, he is fit to be con-
sidered your equal.   68. **your addition:** the title which you have
given him. See I.i.138.   69. **compeers:** equals.   74. **full-flowing
stomach:** in full wrath.   76. **walls . . . thine:** i.e., you have won
the outer defenses.   79. **let-alone:** power to prevent.

83. **capital treason:** treason deserving death. **and . . . attaint:** and
accused with you (*attaint:* impeachment).   86. **subcontracted:**
already betrothed.   87. **bans:** notice of intention to marry,
read out in church for three Sundays previous to the marriage.
89. **bespoke:** already reserved. **An interlude:** i.e., this is mere
play-acting.   92. **heinous:** odious.   96. **medicine:** poison.
98. **villainlike . . . lies:** he lies like a villain. This is the lie direct,
which was a direct challenge to mortal combat. Cf. *AYLI*,
V.iv.69–108.   103. **single:** solitary, unaided.   110. **quality or
degree:** rank or high position.   111. **lists:** roll call, roster.

ALB. Ask him his purposes, why he appears
Upon this call o' the trumpet.°
    HER.   What are you? 119
Your name, your quality? And why you answer
This present summons?
    EDG.   Know my name is lost,
By treason's tooth bare-gnawn and canker-bit.°
Yet am I noble as the adversary
I come to cope.°
    ALB.   Which is that adversary?
    EDG. What's he that speaks for Edmund, Earl of
        Gloucester?   125
    EDM. Himself. What say'st thou to him?
    EDG.   Draw thy sword,
That if my speech offend a noble heart,
Thy arm may do thee justice. Here is mine.
Behold, it is the privilege of mine honors,
My oath, and my profession.° I protest,   130
Mauger° thy strength, youth, place, and eminence,
Despite thy victor sword and fire-new° fortune,
Thy valor and thy heart, thou art a traitor,
False to thy gods, thy brother, and thy father,
Conspirant° 'gainst this high illustrious Prince, 135
And from the extremest upward of thy head
To the descent and dust below thy foot
A most toad-spotted° traitor. Say thou " No,"
This sword, this arm, and my best spirits are bent
To prove upon thy heart, whereto I speak,   140
Thou liest.
    EDM. In wisdom I should ask thy name,
But since thy outside looks so fair and warlike
And that thy tongue some say of breeding° breathes,
What safe and nicely° I might well delay
By rule of knighthood I disdain and spurn.   145
Back do I toss these treasons to thy head,
With the hell-hated lie o'erwhelm thy heart,
Which for they yet glance by and scarcely bruise,
This sword of mine shall give them instant way   149
Where they shall rest forever. Trumpets, speak!

        [Alarums. They fight. EDMUND falls.]
    ALB. Save him, save him!
    GON.   This is practice,° Gloucester.
By the law of arms thou wast not bound to answer
An unknown opposite. Thou art not vanquished,
But cozened° and beguiled.
    ALB.   Shut your mouth, dame,
Or with this paper° shall I stop it. Hold, sir, 155

Thou worse than any name, read thine own evil.
No tearing, lady. I perceive you know it.
    GON. Say if I do, the laws are mine, not thine.
Who can arraign me for 't?
    ALB.   Most monstrous! 159
Know'st thou this paper?
    GON.   Ask me not what I know. [Exit.]
    ALB. Go after her. She's desperate, govern° her.
    EDM. What you have charged me with, that have
        I done,
And more, much more. The time will bring it out.
'Tis past, and so am I. But what art thou
That hast this fortune on me? If thou 'rt noble,
I do forgive thee.
    EDG.   Let's exchange charity.   166
I am no less in blood than thou art, Edmund.
If more, the more thou hast wronged me.
My name is Edgar, and thy father's son.
The gods are just, and of our pleasant vices   170
Make instruments to plague us.°
The dark and vicious place where thee he got°
Cost him his eyes.
    EDM.   Thou hast spoken right, 'tis true.
The wheel is come full circle,° I am here.
    ALB. Methought thy very gait did prophesy   175
A royal nobleness. I must embrace thee.
Let sorrow split my heart if ever I
Did hate thee or thy father!
    EDG.   Worthy Prince, I know 't.
    ALB. Where have you hid yourself?   179
How have you known the miseries of your father?
    EDG. By nursing them, my lord. List a brief tale,
And when 'tis told, oh, that my heart would
        burst!
The bloody proclamation to escape°
That followed me so near — Oh, our lives' sweet-
        ness!
That we the pain of death would hourly die   185
Rather than die at once!° — taught me to shift
Into a madman's rags, to assume a semblance
That very dogs disdained. And in this habit
Met I my father with his bleeding rings,   189
Their precious stones new-lost, became his guide,
Led him, begged for him, saved him from despair,
Never — oh, fault! — revealed myself unto him
Until some half-hour past, when I was armed.
Not sure, though hoping, of this good success,
I asked his blessing, and from first to last   195
Told him my pilgrimage. But his flawed heart —
Alack, too weak the conflict to support! —
'Twixt two extremes of passion, joy and grief,

118-19. Ask . . . trumpet: The combat follows the normal pro-
cedure of chivalry. Cf. *Rich II*, I.iii. Edgar is wearing full
armor, his face concealed by his closed helmet. See Pl. 8a.
122. canker-bit: corrupted by maggots.   124. cope: meet, en-
counter.   130. profession: i.e., as a knight.   131. Mauger:
in spite of.   132. fire-new: brand-new — like a new coin.
135. Conspirant: conspiring.   138. toad-spotted: i.e., venomous
as a toad. Cf. *AYLI*, II.i.13.   143. say of breeding: accent
of a gentleman.   144. nicely: i.e., if I stood on niceties of
procedure.   151. practice: treachery.   154. cozened: cheated.
155. this paper: her love letter to Edmund, which Edgar had
taken from Oswald's corpse. See IV.vi.267–76.

161. govern: control.   170–71. of . . . us: This is the answer to
Gloucester's lighthearted words at the opening of the play — "Do
you smell a fault?" (I.i.16)   172. got: begot.   174. The . . .
circle: i.e., I end as I began — an outcast of fortune.   183. The
. . . escape: in order to escape after the proclamation for my ar-
rest. See II.iii.1.   184–86. Oh . . . once: life is so sweet to us that
we will endure the pains of death hourly if only we can live.

Burst smilingly.°

EDM.   This speech of yours hath moved me,
And shall perchance do good. But speak you on.
You look as you had something more to say.   201

ALB. If there be more, more woeful, hold it in,
For I am almost ready to dissolve,
Hearing of this.

EDG.   This would have seemed a period°
To such as love not sorrow, but another,   205
To amplify too much, would make much more,
And top extremity.°
Whilst I was big in clamor,° came there in a man
Who, having seen me in my worst estate,   209
Shunned my abhorred society. But then, finding
Who 'twas that so endured, with his strong arms
He fastened on my neck, and bellowed out
As he'd burst heaven, threw him on my father,
Told the most piteous tale of Lear and him
That ever ear received. Which in recounting   215
His grief grew puissant,° and the strings of life°
Began to crack. Twice then the trumpets sounded,
And there I left him tranced.°

ALB.   But who was this?

EDG. Kent, sir, the banished Kent, who in disguise
Followed his enemy King,° and did him service
Improper for a slave.   221

[Enter a GENTLEMAN, with a bloody knife.]

GENT. Help, help, oh, help!

EDG.   What kind of help?

ALB.   Speak, man.

EDG. What means this bloody knife?

GENT.   'Tis hot, it smokes.
It came even from the heart of — oh, she's dead!

ALB. Who dead? Speak, man.   225

GENT. Your lady, sir, your lady. And her sister
By her is poisoned. She hath confessed it.

EDM. I was contracted° to them both. All three
Now marry in an instant.

EDG.   Here comes Kent.   229

ALB. Produce the bodies, be they alive or dead.

[Exit GENTLEMAN.]

This judgment of the Heavens, that makes us tremble,
Touches us not with pity.

[Enter KENT.] Oh, is this he?
The time will not allow the compliment
Which very manners urges.

KENT.   I am come
To bid my King and master aye good night.   235
Is he not here?

ALB.   Great thing of us forgot!

Speak, Edmund, where's the King? And where's
      Cordelia?
See's thou this object, Kent?

[The bodies of GONERIL and REGAN are brought in.]

KENT. Alack, why thus?

EDM.   Yet Edmund was beloved.°
The one the other poisoned for my sake,   240
And after slew herself.

ALB. Even so. Cover their faces.

EDM. I pant for life. Some good I mean to do,
Despite of mine own nature. Quickly send —
Be brief in it — to the castle, for my writ   245
Is on the life of Lear and on Cordelia.
Nay, send in time.

ALB.   Run, run, oh, run!

EDG. To who, my lord? Who hath the office? Send
Thy token of reprieve.°

EDM. Well thought on. Take my sword.   250
Give it the Captain.

ALB.   Haste thee, for thy life.   [Exit EDGAR.]

EDM. He hath commission from thy wife and me
To hang Cordelia in the prison and
To lay the blame upon her own despair,
That she fordid° herself.   255

ALB. The gods defend her! Bear him hence
      awhile.   [EDMUND is borne off.]

[Re-enter LEAR, with CORDELIA dead in his arms,
      EDGAR, CAPTAIN, and others following.]

LEAR. Howl, howl, howl, howl! Oh, you are men
      of stones.
Had I your tongues and eyes, I'd use them so
That heaven's vault should crack. She's gone forever!
I know when one is dead and when one lives.   260
She's dead as earth. Lend me a looking-glass.
If that her breath will mist or stain the stone,°
Why, then she lives.

KENT.   Is this the promised end?°

EDG. Or image of that horror?

ALB.   Fall and cease.°

LEAR. This feather stirs, she lives. If it be so,   265
It is a chance which does redeem all sorrows
That ever I have felt.

KENT. [Kneeling] Oh, my good master!

LEAR. Prithee, away.

EDG.   'Tis noble Kent, your friend.

LEAR. A plague upon you, murderers, traitors all!
I might have saved her. Now she's gone forever!
Cordelia, Cordelia! Stay a little. Ha!   271
What is 't thou say'st? Her voice was ever soft,
Gentle and low, an excellent thing in woman.
I killed the slave that was a-hanging thee.

CAPT. 'Tis true, my lords, he did.

196–99. But ... smilingly: In the performance the significance
of Edgar's speech can easily be missed. Gloucester has died
from excessive emotion (passion), and Kent is near his end.
204. period: end.   207. top extremity: exceed the extreme limit
of what could be endured.   208. clamor: grief.   216. puissant:
powerful, overwhelming.   strings of life: heartstrings.
218. tranced: in a faint.   220. enemy King: the King who had
declared him an enemy.   228. contracted: betrothed.

239. Yet ... beloved: The bastard's last grim triumph — two
women died for his love.   249. token of reprieve: sign that they
are reprieved.   255. fordid: destroyed.   262. stone: glass.
263. the ... end: i.e., Doomsday.   264. Fall ... cease: i.e.,
let Doomsday come and the world end.

LEAR.   Did I not, fellow? 275
I have seen the day with my good biting falchion°
I would have made them skip. I am old now,
And these same crosses° spoil me. Who are you?
Mine eyes are not o' the best, I'll tell you straight.

KENT. If fortune brag of two she loved and hated,
One of them we behold.   281

LEAR. This is a dull sight. Are you not Kent?

KENT.   The same,
Your servant Kent. Where is your servant Caius?

LEAR. He's a good fellow, I can tell you that. 284
He'll strike, and quickly too. He's dead and rotten.

KENT. No, my good lord, I am the very man° ——

LEAR. I'll see that straight.

KENT. That from your first of difference° and de-
cay
Have followed your sad steps.

LEAR.   You are welcome hither.

KENT. Nor no man else. All's cheerless, dark, and
deadly.   290
Your eldest daughters have fordone themselves,
And desperately are dead.

LEAR.   Aye, so I think.

ALB. He knows not what he says, and vain is it
That we present us to him.

EDG.   Very bootless.°

[*Enter a* CAPTAIN.]

CAPT. Edmund is dead, my lord.

ALB.   That's but a trifle here. 295
You lords and noble friends, know our intent.
What comfort to this great decay° may come
Shall be applied. For us, we will resign,
During the life of this old Majesty,
To him our absolute power.

[*To* EDGAR *and* KENT] You, to your rights, 300
With boot,° and such addition as your honors
Have more than merited. All friends shall taste
The wages of their virtue, and all foes
The cup of their deservings. Oh, see, see!°

LEAR. And my poor fool° is hanged! No, no, no
life!   305
Why should a dog, a horse, a rat, have life
And thou no breath at all? Thou'lt come no more,
Never, never, never, never, never!
Pray you, undo this button.° Thank you, sir.
Do you see this? Look on her, look, her lips, 310
Look there, look there!   [*Dies.*]

EDG.   He faints. My lord, my lord!

KENT. Break, heart, I prithee break!

EDG.   Look up, my lord.

KENT. Vex not his ghost. Oh, let him pass! He
hates him
That would upon the rack° of this tough world
Stretch him out longer.

EDG.   He is gone indeed. 315

KENT. The wonder is he hath endured so long.
He but usurped his life.

ALB. Bear them from hence. Our present business
Is general woe. [*To* KENT *and* EDGAR] Friends of my
soul, you twain
Rule in this realm and the gored state sustain. 320

KENT. I have a journey, sir, shortly to go.
My master calls me,° I must not say no.

ALB. The weight of this sad time we must obey,
Speak what we feel, not what we ought to say. 324
The oldest hath borne most. We that are young
Shall never see so much, nor live so long.

[*Exeunt, with a dead march.*]

---

276. falchion: curved sword. **278. crosses:** troubles. **283–86. Your
. . . man:** This is the first and only mention of a Caius, which
was apparently the name assumed by Kent in his disguise.
288. difference: changed state.   **294. bootless:** useless.
297. decay: i.e., Lear.

301. boot: advantage.   **304. Oh . . . see:** There is a sudden
change in Lear.   **305. fool:** Cordelia; *fool* is often used as a
term of affection.   **309. Pray . . . button:** For the last time Lear
is oppressed by the violent beating of his heart before it is stilled
forever.   **314. rack:** See App. 10.   **322. calls me:** i.e., to follow
him into the darkness.

THE TRAGEDY OF MACBETH

Introduction

In some ways *The Tragedy of Macbeth* is the least satisfactory of the four great tragedies, though the great scenes — the murder of Duncan, the banquet scene, the sleepwalking scene — are as powerful as anything Shakespeare ever wrote. Apart from Macbeth and his wife, the characterization — especially of the minor persons — is far less detailed than in *Lear* or *Hamlet*. Indeed there is a general agreement amongst scholars that *Macbeth* has not been finished with the same care as the others and that other hands than Shakespeare's have contributed to the play. The speech of the bleeding captain, if not the whole of I.ii, and the operatic episode between Hecate and the witches (III.v and IV.i) are not in Shakespeare's manner. Thomas Middleton, who wrote a play called *The Witch* about 1612, is often considered the author of these passages, especially as the songs to which reference is made in the stage directions of IV.i are given in full in *The Witch*.

There are other indications in the text itself, either that Shakespeare was himself revising or rewriting an old play, or that he had a collaborator. These are most noticeable in the last Act, where the rhymes and diction are often feeble or forced, and the rhythm unlike Shakespeare's. The differences can best be seen by comparing two small link scenes. These are II.iv and III.vi. The conversation in the first scene between Ross and the old man is not in Shakespeare's usual style, while the speech of Lennox is by contrast full of the subtlest tones and hints of meaning.

Macbeth was probably written in 1606. The remarks of the Porter about equivocation — "Faith here's an equivocator, that could swear in both the scales against either scale, who committed treason enough for God's sake, yet could not equivocate to Heaven" — are a likely reference to the notorious trial and execution of Father Garnet for being an accessory to the Gunpowder Plot. Garnet admitted that he had deliberately deceived his accusers, and justified himself by the doctrine of equivocation (see Gen. Intro. p. 17a and App. 20).

If, as is likely, the inconsistencies of style are due to hasty writing, then it is possible that the play was written by command as one of the plays to be given before King James I and the King of Denmark during the latter's notable visit to England in the summer of 1606. Shakespeare's company were the King's Players, and it would be natural for them to be commanded to produce a story of Scottish history touching on the ancestry of their patron. In the previous summer, when King James made a visit in state to the University of Oxford, three little boys, dressed as nymphs, greeted him with a short Latin speech, reminding him of the ancient legend of the Three Sisters who had prophesied future glory to Banquo's descendants.

Macbeth was being played in London in 1611, and was one of several plays visited by Dr. Simon Forman, a well-known astrologer of the time, who wrote as follows:[1]

In *Macbeth* at the Globe, 1610 (1611), the 20 of April (Saturday), there was to be observed, first, how Macbeth and Banquo, two noblemen of Scotland, riding through a wood; there stood before them three women fairies or nymphs, and saluted Macbeth, saying three times unto him, " Hail Macbeth, King of Codon [Cawdor]; for thou shalt be a king, but shalt beget no kings, etc." Then said Banquo, " What, all to Macbeth and nothing to me? " " Yes," said the nymphs, " hail to thee Banquo, thou shalt beget kings, yet be no king." And so they departed and came to the court of Scotland, to Duncan, King of Scots, and it was in the days of Edward the Confessor. And Duncan bade them both kindly welcome, and made Macbeth forthwith Prince of Northumberland, and sent him home to his own castle; and appointed Macbeth to provide for him, for he would sup with him the next day at night; and did so. And Macbeth contrived to kill Duncan and through the persuasion of his wife did that night murder the king in his own castle, being his guest. And there were many prodigies seen that night and the day before. And when Macbeth had murdered the king, the blood on his hands could not be washed off by any means, nor from his wife's hands, which handled the bloody daggers in hiding them; by which

[1] E. K. Chambers, *William Shakespeare*, II, 337. The original manuscript is in the Bodleian Library at Oxford; its genuineness was at one time suspected but has now been established.

means they became both much amazed and affronted. The murder being known, Duncan's two sons fled, the one to England, the [other to] Wales, to save themselves. They being fled, they were supposed guilty of the murder of their father, which was nothing so. Then was Macbeth crowned king; and then he for fear of Banquo, his old companion, that he should beget kings but be no king himself, he contrived the death of Banquo, and caused him to be murdered on the way as he rode. The next night, being at supper with his noblemen whom he had bid to a feast, to the which also Banquo should have come, he began to speak of noble Banquo, and to wish that he were there. And as he thus did, standing up to drink a carouse to him, the ghost of Banquo came and sat down in his chair behind him. And he, turning about to sit down again, saw the ghost of Banquo, which fronted him so, that he fell into a great passion of fear and fury, uttering many words about his murder; by which, when they heard that Banquo was murdered they suspected Macbeth.

Then Macduff fled to England to the king's son; and so they raised an army, and came into Scotland. And at Dunston Anyse [Dunsinane] overthrew Macbeth. In the meantime while Macduff was in England, Macbeth slew Macduff's wife and children, and after in the battle Macduff slew Macbeth.

Observe also how Macbeth's queen did rise in the night in her sleep and walk, and talked and confessed all, and the doctor noted her words.

Macbeth was first printed in F1 in 1623, where the text is not very satisfactory and shows some signs of cutting and alteration. The main story of the play was derived from two episodes in Holinshed's *Chronicles*. The first is the history of Macbeth, from which the main outline of the plot was taken. The second, which provided the details of the murder of Duncan, is the story of the murder of King Duff by Donwald, who also was encouraged by an ambitious wife. The story of Macbeth was followed fairly closely. In Holinshed, the incident of the three witches is thus told:

Shortly after happened a strange and uncouth wonder, which afterward was the cause of much trouble in the realm of Scotland, as ye shall after hear. It fortuned as Macbeth and Banquo journeyed toward Forres, where the King then lay, they went sporting by the way together without other company, save only themselves, passing through the woods and fields, when suddenly in the midst of a laund [lawn, open place] there met them three women in strange and wild apparel, resembling creatures of elder world, whom when they atten-

tively beheld, wondering much at the sight, the first of them spake and said: "All hail, Macbeth, Thane of Glammis!" (for he had lately entered into that dignity and office by the death of his father Sinell). The second of them said: "Hail, Macbeth, Thane of Cawder!" But the third said: "All hail, Macbeth, that hereafter shalt be King of Scotland!"

Then Banquo: "What manner of women" (saith he) "are you, that seem so little favorable unto me, whereas to my fellow here, besides high offices, ye assign also the kingdom, appointing forth nothing for me at all?" "Yes," (saith the first of them) "we promise greater benefits unto thee than unto him, for he shall reign indeed, but with an unlucky end; neither shall he leave any issue behind him to succeed in his place, where contrarily thou indeed shalt not reign at all, but of thee those shall be born which shall govern the Scottish kingdom by long order of continual descent." Herewith the foresaid women vanished immediately out of their sight. This was reputed at the first but some vain fantastical illusion by Macbeth and Banquo, insomuch that Banquo would call Macbeth, in jest, King of Scotland, and Macbeth again would call him in sport likewise the father of many kings. But afterward the common opinion was that these women were either the weird sisters, that is (as ye would say) the goddesses of destiny, or else some nymphs or fairies, imbued with knowledge of prophecy by their necromantical science, because everything came to pass as they had spoken. For shortly after, the Thane of Cawder being condemned at Forres of treason against the King committed, his lands, livings, and offices were given of the King's liberality to Macbeth.

The same night after, at supper, Banquo jested with him and said: "Now, Macbeth, thou hast obtained those things which the two former sisters prophesied, there remaineth only for thee to purchase that which the third said should come to pass." Whereupon Macbeth revolving the thing in his mind, began even then to devise how he might attain to the kingdom; but yet he thought with himself that he must tarry a time, which should advance him thereto (by the divine Providence) as it had come to pass in his former preferment. But shortly after it chanced that King Duncan, having two sons by his wife which was the daughter of Siward, Earl of Northumberland, he made the elder of them, called Malcolm, Prince of Cumberland, as it were thereby to appoint him his successor in the kingdom, immediately after his decease. Macbeth, sore troubled herewith, for that he saw by this means his hope sore hindered (where, by the old laws of the realm, the ordinance was that if he that should succeed were not of able age to take the charge upon himself, he that was next of blood unto him should be admitted), he began to take counsel how he might usurp the kingdom by force, having a just quarrel so to do (as he took the matter) for that Duncan did what in him lay to defraud him of all manner of title and claim which he might in time to come pretend unto the crown.

The words of the three weird sisters also (of whom before you have heard) greatly encouraged him hereunto, but specially his wife lay sore upon him to attempt the thing, as she that was very ambitious, burning in unquenchable desire to bear the name of a Queen. At length therefore, communicating his purposed intent with his trusty friends, amongst whom Banquo was the chiefest, upon confidence of their promised aid, he slew the King at Enverns [Inverness], or (as some say) at Botgosvane, in the sixth year of his reign. Then having a company about him of such as he had made privy to his enterprise, he caused himself to be proclaimed King, and forthwith went unto Scone, where (by common consent) he received the investure of the kingdom according to the accustomed manner. The body of Duncan was first conveyed unto Elgin, and there buried in kingly wise; but afterward it was removed and conveyed unto Colmekill, and there laid in a sepulcher amongst his predecessors, in the year after the birth of our Saviour, 1046.

The murder of King Duff by Donwald was thus described:

Donwald thus being the more kindled in wrath by the words of his wife, determined to follow her advice in the execution of so heinous an act. Whereupon devising with himself for a while, which way he might best accomplish his cursed intent, at length gat opportunity, and sped his purpose as followeth. It chanced that the King, upon the day before he purposed to depart forth of the castle, was long in his oratory at his prayers, and there continued till it was late in the night. At the last, coming forth, he called such afore him as had faithfully served him in pursuit and apprehension of the rebels, and giving them hearty thanks, he bestowed sundry honorable gifts amongst them, of the which number Donwald was one, as he that had been ever accounted a most faithful servant to the King.

At length, having talked with them a long time, he got him into his privy chamber, only with two of his chamberlains, who having brought him to bed, came forth again, and then fell to banqueting with Donwald and his wife, who had prepared divers delicate dishes, and sundry sorts of drinks for their rear supper or collation, whereat they sat up so long till they had charged their stomachs with such full gorges that their heads were no sooner got to the pillow but asleep they were so fast that a man might have removed the chamber over them sooner than to have awakened them out of their drunken sleep.

Then Donwald, though he abhorred the act greatly in heart, yet through instigation of his wife he called four of his servants unto him (whom he had made privy to his wicked intent before, and framed to his purpose with large gifts) and now declaring unto them after what sort they should work the feat, they gladly obeyed his instructions, and speedily going about the murder they enter the chamber (in which the King lay) a little before cock's crow, where they secretly cut his throat as he lay sleeping, without any buskling [bustling, noise] at all; and immediately by a postern gate they carried forth the dead body into the fields, and throwing it upon an horse there provided ready for that purpose, they convey it unto a place about two miles distant from the castle, where they stayed, and gat certain laborers to help them to turn the course of a little river running through the fields there, and digging a deep hole in the channel, they bury the body in the same, ramming it up with stones and gravel so closely that setting the water in the right course again, no man could perceive that anything had been newly digged there. This they did by order appointed them by Donwald as is reported, for that the body should not be found and by bleeding (when Donwald should be present) declare him to be guilty of the murder. For such an opinion men have, that the dead corpse of any man being slain will bleed abundantly if the murderer be present. But for what consideration soever they buried him there, they had no sooner finished the work but that they slew them whose help they used herein, and straightwise thereupon fled into Orkney.

Donwald, about the time that the murder was in doing, got him amongst them that kept the watch, and so continued in company with them all the residue of the night. But in the morning when the noise was raised in the King's chamber how the King was slain, his body conveyed away, and the bed all berayed with blood, he with the watch ran thither, as though he had known nothing of the matter, and breaking into the chamber and finding cakes of blood in the bed and on the floor about the sides of it, he forthwith slew the chamberlains, as guilty of that heinous murder, and then like a mad man running to and fro, he ransacked every corner within the castle as though it had been to have seen if he might have found either the body or any of the murderers hid in any privy place. But at length coming to the postern gate and finding it open, he burdened [accused] the chamberlains, whom he had slain, with all the fault, they having the keys of the gates committed to their keeping all the night, and therefore it could not be otherwise (said he) but that they were of counsel in committing of that most detestable murder.

Finally, such was his own earnest diligence in the

severe inquisition and trial of the offenders herein, that some of the lords began to mislike the matter, and to smell forth shrewd tokens that he should not be altogether clear himself. But for so much as they were in that country, where he had the whole rule, what by reason of his friends and authority together, they doubted to utter what they thought, till time and place should better serve thereunto, and hereupon they got them away every man to his home.

According to the *Chronicles,* Macbeth reigned well for some years, until he began to brood on the words of the three weird sisters that the kingdom should come to Banquo's posterity. He therefore planned to have Banquo slain, but Fleance, Banquo's son, escaped. Hereafter Macbeth's character degenerated until " he found such sweetness by putting his nobles thus to death that his earnest thirst for blood in his own behalf might in no wise be satisfied." He was warned by a prophecy against Macduff:

And surely hereupon had he put Macduff to death, but that a certain witch, whom he had in great trust, had told that he should never be slain with man born of any woman, nor vanquished till the wood of Bernane came to the castle of Dunsinane. By this prophecy Macbeth put all fear out of his heart, supposing he might do what he would, without any fear to be punished for the same, for by the one prophecy he believed it was impossible for any man to vanquish him, and by the other impossible to slay him. This vain hope caused him to do many outrageous things, to the grievous oppression of his subjects. At length Macduff, to avoid peril of life, purposed with himself to pass into England, to procure Malcolm Cammore to claim the crown of Scotland. But this was not so secretly devised by Macduff but that Macbeth had knowledge given him thereof; for kings (as is said) have sharp sight like unto lynx, and long ears like unto Midas. For Macbeth had, in every nobleman's house, one sly fellow or other in fee with him, to reveal all that was said or done within the same, by which sight he oppressed the most part of the nobles of his realm."

The long passage between Malcolm and Macduff (IV.iii) follows the *Chronicles* closely, for Holinshed recorded the conversation at some length; but the final battle in which Macbeth was killed took place not in Dunsinane castle but on the open field; Macduff pursued Macbeth on horseback and overtook him. Then:

Macbeth, perceiving that Macduff was hard at his back, leapt beside his horse, saying: " Thou traitor, what meaneth it that thou shouldest thus in vain follow me that am not appointed to be slain by any creature that is born of a woman? Come on therefore, and receive thy reward which thou has deserved for thy pains! " and therewithal he lifted up his sword, thinking to have slain him.

But Macduff, quickly avoiding from his horse, ere he came at him, answered (with his naked sword in his hand) saying: " It is true, Macbeth, and now shall thine insatiable cruelty have an end, for I am even he that thy wizards have told thee of, who was never born of my mother, but ripped out of her womb." Therewithal he stepped unto him, and slew him in the place. Then cutting his head from his shoulders, he set it upon a pole, and brought it unto Malcolm. This was the end of Macbeth, after he had reigned seventeen years over the Scottishmen.

To a greater extent than the other great tragedies *Macbeth* is a tragedy of fate. All the tragedies illustrate the idea that there's a divinity that shapes our ends. It may simply be a comet which foretells the death of princes, or the darker feeling that

As flies to wanton boys are we to the gods.
They kill us for their sport.

Yet, until the end, some way of escape seems possible. But Macbeth from the beginning is the plaything of that evil power which uses the witches as his ministers. When Macbeth first appears with Banquo, he has been brooding on treason, and the prophecy that he shall be " Thane of Cawdor " and " King hereafter " comes pat on his thoughts. The first prophecy is fulfilled at once. Thereafter Macbeth is caught by fate.

Macbeth's character is a mixture of good and evil qualities. He has bravery and nobility counterbalanced by ambition. Above all he is controlled by an overpowering imagination which makes him see not only what the results of an action will be, but also its essential meaning. The third scene ends with the tragic foreboding that the prophecy will be fulfilled; Macbeth has already foreseen the manner of its fulfilling and he is horrified by the sight. Nevertheless his loyalty and his ambition are evenly balanced until he comes into the presence of his wife. Lady Macbeth is at the same time greater and lesser than her husband. She has a hardness which he lacks, but she has none of his subtlety and perception. She knows her husband well and despises him a little, but to satisfy her ambition, which is the crude desire to have her man King, she will devote herself soul and body to evil.

So the murder is accomplished, although Macbeth realizes that this deed is not only evil in itself, but will bring inevitable retribution. When Duncan is dead, the contrast between man and wife becomes more vivid. Macbeth is overwhelmed with the significance of his filthy deed. His wife is concerned only with the details of what must be done next — with facts. She has no imagination. This passage between Macbeth and Lady Macbeth after the murder is one of the finest examples of " atmosphere " ever created in drama.

The imagery used in this scene, and indeed throughout the whole play, is notable. Three ideas are predominant; blood, water, and darkness. From this point onward, the tragedy is splashed with blood. Once the murder has been committed, the blood of Duncan drips down the stairs after Macbeth until it pervades his whole universe, and he stands alone in a universal sea of blood. Lady Macbeth still thinks that a little water will clear them of this deed; Macbeth knows that all great Neptune's ocean will never make them clean.

Upon this intensity of horror breaks in the knocking. Coleridge objected to this vulgar porter, but he is dramatically essential. After the intensity of what has just gone before, some change or explosion is necessary to release the emotional tension, and crude laughter is the most effective. It brings us back to earth. The murder is discovered, Malcolm and Donalbain escape, and Fate begins to turn her wheel.

This ends the first part of the play. The second part begins with Act III. Macbeth is King, and the third prophecy has been fulfilled; but there were other prophecies made to Banquo. Macbeth is beginning to realize that it has all been in vain. One murder begets another. Macbeth's degeneration is swift and terrible. Banquo is murdered,

and inevitably Fleance escapes. The second part of the play ends with the murder of Banquo.

Macbeth again seeks the witches; having no earthly friends, he will put his trust in them. As before, he is given three prophecies.

The last act brings the tragedy to its close. It begins with the sleepwalking scene, which sums up and concentrates the full horror of the whole business. The resistance of this hard, practical woman has broken down. She was the real cause and the agent of the tragedy. In the words which she utters in her sleep, she gives her own answer to the casual remark that " a little water clears us of this deed." This is the true dramatic irony, tragic and terrible, where the easiest remarks have the most ghastly significance and are echoed by a kind of devilish chuckle.

Macbeth now has only the prophecies left to defend and comfort him as the avengers gather round. Lady Macbeth is dying, and when he learns that she has gone the full realization of his own tragedy comes to him:

> Life's but a walking shadow, a poor player
> That struts and frets his hour upon the stage
> And then is heard no more. It is a tale
> Told by an idiot, full of sound and fury,
> Signifying nothing.

So everything was futile, the murder of Duncan and all the blood, for life itself has no meaning.

Two things are particularly worth noting about this play. The first is that *Macbeth* is a chronicle play and, as with Shakespeare's other plays of British history, Holinshed was its source. Yet Shakespeare has moved a long way from his last chronicle play of *Henry V*. The second is that Macbeth is a play with a villain as hero. It was twelve years since Shakespeare last wrote a chronicle with the villain as hero — *Richard III*. These two plays have much in common — ghosts, prophecies, spirits, ambitious villains, soliloquies, and the idea of a brooding fate; but a comparison of the two will show how Shakespeare had grown.

Macbeth

DRAMATIS PERSONAE

DUNCAN, *King of Scotland*
MALCOLM } *his sons*
DONALBAIN }
MACBETH } *generals of the King's army*
BANQUO }
MACDUFF }
LENNOX }
ROSS } *noblemen of Scotland*
MENTEITH }
ANGUS }
CAITHNESS }
FLEANCE, *son to Banquo*
SIWARD, *Earl of Northumberland, general of the English forces*
YOUNG SIWARD, *his son*
SEYTON, *an officer attending on Macbeth*
BOY, *son to Macduff*

AN ENGLISH DOCTOR
A SCOTCH DOCTOR
A SERGEANT
A PORTER
AN OLD MAN

LADY MACBETH
LADY MACDUFF
GENTLEWOMAN *attending on Lady Macbeth*

HECATE
THREE WITCHES
APPARITIONS
LORDS, GENTLEMEN, OFFICERS, SOLDIERS, MURDERERS, ATTENDANTS, AND MESSENGERS

SCENE — *Scotland; England.*

Act I

SCENE I. *A desert place.*

[*Thunder and lightning. Enter* THREE WITCHES.°]

1. WITCH. When shall we three meet again
In thunder, lightning, or in rain?
2. WITCH. When the hurly-burly's° done,
When the battle's lost and won.
3. WITCH. That will be ere the set of sun. 5
1. WITCH. Where the place?
2. WITCH.   Upon the heath.
3. WITCH. There to meet with Macbeth.
1. WITCH. I come, Graymalkin.°
ALL. Paddock° calls. — Anon!° 10
Fair is foul, and foul is fair.
Hover through the fog and filthy air. [*Exeunt.*]

SCENE II. *A camp near Forres.*

[*Alarum within.*° *Enter* DUNCAN, MALCOLM,
DONALBAIN, LENNOX, *with* ATTENDANTS,
meeting a bleeding SERGEANT.]

DUN. What bloody man is that? He can report,
As seemeth by his plight, of the revolt
The newest state.
MAL.   This is the sergeant

Act I, Sc. i: s.d., Enter . . . witches: See App. 23.   3. hurly-burly: commotion.   9. Graymalkin: a common name for a gray cat; it is the First Witch's familiar spirit.   10. Paddock: toad. Anon: at once, "I am coming."

Sc. ii: s.d., Alarum within: trumpet call to arms, off stage.

Who like a good and hardy soldier fought
'Gainst my captivity. Hail, brave friend! 5
Say to the King the knowledge of the broil
As thou didst leave it.
SERG.   Doubtful it stood,
As two spent swimmers that do cling together
And choke their art.° The merciless Macdonwald —
Worthy to be a rebel, for to that 10
The multiplying villainies of nature
Do swarm upon him — from the western isles
Of kerns and gallowglasses° is supplied.°
And fortune, on his damnèd quarrel smiling,
Showed° like a rebel's whore. But all's too weak. 15
For brave Macbeth — well he deserves that name —
Disdaining fortune, with his brandished steel,
Which smoked with bloody execution,
Like valor's minion° carvèd out his passage
Till he faced the slave, 20
Which ne'er shook hands, nor bade farewell to him,
Till he unseamed him° from the nave to the chaps,°
And fixed his head upon our battlements.
DUN. Oh, valiant Cousin! Worthy gentleman!
SERG. As whence the sun 'gins his reflection° 25
Shipwrecking storms and direful thunders break,
So from that spring whence comfort seemed to come

9. choke . . . art: i.e., prevent each other from swimming. art: skill.   13. kerns . . . gallowglasses: types of wild Irish soldiers. The kern fought on foot, the gallowglass was armed with an ax and fought on horseback. supplied: aided.   15. Showed: appeared.   19. minion: darling.   22. unseamed him: ripped Macdonwald open. nave . . . chaps: from navel to cheeks. 25. whence . . . reflection: from that quarter where the sun first appears; i.e., the east.

Discomfort swells. Mark, King of Scotland, mark.
No sooner justice had, with valor armed,
Compelled these skipping kerns to trust their heels,
But the Norweyan° lord, surveying vantage,°　31
With furbished° arms and new supplies of men,
Began a fresh assault.

DUN.　　　　　　　Dismayed not this
Our captains, Macbeth and Banquo?

SERG.　　　　　　　　　Yes,
As sparrows eagles, or the hare the lion.　35
If I say sooth,° I must report they were
As cannons overcharged with double cracks,°
So they
Doubly redoubled strokes upon the foe.
Except they meant to bathe in reeking° wounds,
Or memorize another Golgotha,°　　　　40
I cannot tell ——
But I am faint, my gashes cry for help.

DUN.　So well thy words become thee as thy
　　wounds.
They smack of honor both. Go get him surgeons.
　　　　　　　　　　[Exit SERGEANT, *attended.]*
Who comes here?

　　　　　　[Enter ROSS.]
MAL.　　　　The worthy Thane° of Ross.　45
LEN. What a haste looks through his eyes! So
　　should he look
That seems to speak things strange.

ROSS.　　　　　　　　　God save the King!
DUN. Whence camest thou, worthy Thane?

ROSS.　　　　　　　From Fife, great King,
Where the Norweyan banners flout° the sky
And fan our people cold.　　　　　　50
Norway himself, with terrible numbers,
Assisted by that most disloyal traitor
The Thane of Cawdor, began a dismal conflict,
Till that Bellona's bridegroom,° lapped in proof,°
Confronted him with self-comparisons,°　55
Point against point rebellious, arm 'gainst arm,
Curbing his lavish° spirit. And, to conclude,
The victory fell on us.

DUN.　　　　　　Great happiness!
ROSS. That now
Sweno, the Norways' king, craves composition.°
Nor would we deign him burial of his men　60
Till he disbursèd, at Saint Colme's inch,°

31. Norweyan: from Norway. surveying vantage: seeing his
chance.　32. furbished: polished; i.e., not yet stained with
battle.　36. sooth: truth.　37. overcharged . . . cracks: loaded
with two cannon balls.　39. reeking: steaming.　40. memorize
. . . Golgotha: cause a slaughter which would make the place as
memorable as Golgotha; i.e., the "Place of a Skull" where
Christ was crucified.　45. Thane: a Scottish title, almost equiv-
alent to the English "Earl." See V.viii.62–64.　49. flout: defy.
54. Bellona's bridegroom: the mate of the goddess of war; i.e.,
Macbeth. lapped in proof: clad in armor of proof; i.e., tested.
55. Confronted . . . self-comparisons: showed him a man as
good as himself.　57. lavish: insolent.　59. craves composition:
asks for terms of peace.　61. Saint . . . inch: the Island of St.
Columba in the Firth of Forth.

Ten thousand dollars to our general use.

DUN. No more that Thane of Cawdor shall de-
　　ceive
Our bosom interest.° Go pronounce his present°
　　death,
And with his former title greet Macbeth.　65
ROSS. I'll see it done.
DUN. What he hath lost noble Macbeth hath won.
　　　　　　　　　　　　　　[Exeunt.]

SCENE III. *A heath.*

[Thunder. Enter the THREE WITCHES.]
1. WITCH. Where hast thou been, Sister?
2. WITCH. Killing swine.°
3. WITCH. Sister, where thou?
1. WITCH. A sailor's wife had chestnuts in her lap,
And mounched, and mounched, and mounched.
　"Give me," quoth I.　　　　　　5
"Aroint thee,° witch!" the rump-fed° ronyon°
　cries.
Her husband's to Aleppo gone, master o' the *Tiger.*
But in a sieve I'll thither sail
And, like a rat without a tail,
I'll do, I'll do, and I'll do.　　　　　10
2. WITCH. I'll give thee a wind.
1. WITCH. Thou'rt kind.
3. WITCH. And I another.
1. WITCH. I myself have all the other,
And the very ports they blow,°　　　15
All the quarters that they know
I' the shipman's card.°
I will drain him dry as hay.
Sleep shall neither night nor day
Hang upon his penthouse lid.°　　　20
He shall live a man forbid.°
Weary sennights° nine times nine
Shall he dwindle, peak,° and pine.
Though his bark° cannot be lost,
Yet it shall be tempest-tost.　　　25
Look what I have.
2. WITCH. Show me, show me.
1. WITCH. Here I have a pilot's thumb,
Wrecked as homeward he did come.
　　　　　　　　　　[Drum within.]
3. WITCH. A drum, a drum!　　　　30
Macbeth doth come.

64. bosom interest: that which concerns me most dearly. present:
immediate.
Sc. iii: 2. Killing swine: witches were commonly accused of
killing the pigs of their neighbors.　6. Aroint thee: be off.
rump-fed: Editors are not agreed whether it means "fed on the
best rumpsteak," "fed on the scraps," or "large-bottomed."
ronyon: scabby creature.　15. they blow: i.e., toward which the
winds blow.　17. shipman's card: mariner's compass.　20. pent-
house lid: eyelid; lit., roof of a shed.　21. forbid: under a curse.
22. sennights: weeks.　23. peak: grow thin.　24. bark: ship.

ALL. The weird° sisters, hand in hand,
Posters° of the sea and land,
Thus do go about, about.
Thrice to thine, and thrice to mine,   35
And thrice again, to make up nine.
Peace! The charm's wound up.°

[*Enter* MACBETH *and* BANQUO.]

MACB. So foul and fair a day I have not seen.
BAN. How far is 't called to Forres?° What are
    these
So withered, and so wild in their attire,   40
That look not like the inhabitants o' the earth
And yet are on 't? Live you? Or are you aught
That man may question? You seem to understand
    me,
By each at once her choppy° finger laying
Upon her skinny lips. You should be women,   45
And yet your beards° forbid me to interpret
That you are so.
    MACB.   Speak, if you can. What are you?
1. WITCH. All hail, Macbeth! Hail to thee, Thane
    of Glamis!
2. WITCH. All hail, Macbeth! Hail to thee, Thane
    of Cawdor!
3. WITCH. All hail, Macbeth, that shalt be King
    hereafter!   50
BAN. Good sir, why do you start, and seem to fear
Things that do sound so fair? I' the name of truth,
Are ye fantastical,° or that indeed
Which outwardly ye show? My noble partner
You greet with present grace and great prediction
Of noble having° and of royal hope,   56
That he seems rapt° withal. To me you speak not.
If you can look into the seeds of time
And say which grain will grow and which will not,
Speak then to me, who neither beg nor fear   60
Your favors nor your hate.
1. WITCH. Hail!
2. WITCH. Hail!
3. WITCH. Hail!
1. WITCH. Lesser than Macbeth, and greater.   65
2. WITCH. Not so happy,° yet much happier.
3. WITCH. Thou shalt get° kings, though thou be
    none.
So all hail, Macbeth and Banquo!
1. WITCH. Banquo and Macbeth, all hail!   69
MACB. Stay, you imperfect speakers, tell me more.
By Sinel's° death I know I am Thane of Glamis,
But how of Cawdor? The Thane of Cawdor lives,

A prosperous gentleman, and to be King
Stands not within the prospect of belief,
No more than to be Cawdor. Say from whence   75
You owe° this strange intelligence?° Or why
Upon this blasted heath you stop our way
With such prophetic greeting? Speak, I charge you.

[WITCHES *vanish.*]

BAN. The earth hath bubbles as the water has,   79
And these are of them. Whither are they vanished?
MACB. Into the air, and what seemed corporal°
    melted
As breath into the wind. Would they had stayed!
    BAN. Were such things here as we do speak
    about?
Or have we eaten on the insane root°
That takes the reason prisoner?   85
MACB. Your children shall be kings.
    BAN.   You shall be King.
MACB. And Thane of Cawdor too. Went it not so?
BAN. To the selfsame tune and words. Who's
    here?

[*Enter* ROSS *and* ANGUS.]

ROSS. The King hath happily received, Macbeth,
The news of thy success. And when he reads   90
Thy personal venture in the rebels' fight,
His wonders and his praises do contend
Which should be thine or his.° Silenced° with that,
In viewing o'er the rest o' the selfsame day,
He finds thee in the stout Norweyan ranks,   95
Nothing afeard of what thyself didst make,
Strange images of death.° As thick as hail
Came post with post,° and every one did bear
Thy praises in his kingdom's great defense,
And poured them down before him.
    ANG.   We are sent   100
To give thee, from our royal master, thanks,
Only to herald thee° into his sight,
Not pay thee.
    ROSS. And for an earnest° of a greater honor,
He bade me, from him, call thee Thane of Cawdor.
In which addition,° hail, most worthy Thane!   106
For it is thine.
    BAN.   What, can the Devil speak true?
MACB. The Thane of Cawdor lives. Why do you
    dress me
In borrowed robes?
    ANG.   Who was the Thane lives yet,
But under heavy judgment bears that life   110
Which he deserves to lose. Whether he was com-
    bined

---

32. **weird:** having to do with destiny, spelt "weyard" and "wey-
ward" in F1.   33. **Posters:** quick riders.   37. **wound up:** i.e.,
completed.   39. **Forres:** a town about 25 miles from Inverness.
44. **choppy:** chapped.   46. **your beards:** For a woman to have a
beard was sinister. When Falstaff escapes disguised as a witch,
Parson Evans remarks, "By yea and no, I think the 'oman is a
witch indeed. I like not when a 'oman has a great peard."
(*Merry Wives*, I.v.202)   53. **fantastical:** creatures of the imagi-
nation.   56. **having:** possessions.   57. **rapt:** in a trance.
66. **happy:** lucky.   67. **get:** beget.   71. **Sinel:** Macbeth's father.

76. **owe:** own, possess. **intelligence:** knowledge.   81. **corporal:**
corporeal, of bodily substance.   84. **insane root:** henbane or
hemlock, supposed to cause madness.   93. **thine or his:** whether
he should wonder or praise you. **Silenced:** speechless with ad-
miration.   97. **Strange . . . death:** i.e., Macbeth was threatened
with death, and caused death.   98. **post . . . post:** See App. 17.
102. **herald thee:** act as the herald bringing you into the King's
presence.   104. **earnest:** lit., money given on account of the
main payment.   106. **addition:** title of honor.

With those of Norway, or did line° the rebel
With hidden help and vantage,° or that with both
He labored in his country's wreck, I know not.
But treasons capital,° confessed and proved,   115
Have overthrown him.

MACB.   [*Aside*] Glamis, and Thane of Cawdor.
The greatest is behind.° — Thanks for your
     pains. —
Do you not hope your children shall be kings,
When those that gave the Thane of Cawdor to me
Promised no less to them?

BAN.   That, trusted home,°   120
Might yet enkindle° you unto the crown,
Besides the Thane of Cawdor. But 'tis strange.
And oftentimes, to win us to our harm,
The instruments of darkness tell us truths,
Win us with honest trifles, to betray 's   125
In deepest consequence.°
Cousins, a word, I pray you.

MACB.   [*Aside*] Two truths are told
As happy prologues to the swelling act
Of the imperial theme.° — I thank you, gentle-
     men. —
[*Aside*] This supernatural soliciting°   130
Cannot be ill, cannot be good. If ill,
Why hath it given me earnest of success,
Commencing in a truth? I am Thane of Cawdor.
If good, why do I yield to that suggestion
Whose horrid image doth unfix my hair   135
And make my seated° heart knock at my ribs,
Against the use of nature?° Present fears
Are less than horrible imaginings.
My thought, whose murder yet is but fantastical,°
Shakes so my single state of man° that function
Is smothered in surmise,° and nothing is   141
But what is not.

BAN.   Look how our partner's rapt.

MACB. [*Aside*] If chance will have me King, why,
     chance may crown me,
Without my stir.

BAN.   New honors come upon him,
Like our strange garments,° cleave not to their mold
But with the aid of use.

MACB.   [*Aside*] Come what come may,   146
Time and the hour runs through° the roughest day.

BAN. Worthy Macbeth, we stay upon your leisure.

---

112. **line:** support.   113. **vantage:** assistance.   115. **capital:** deserving death.   117. **behind:** yet to come.   120. **home:** fully. 121. **enkindle:** set you on fire to get.   126. **In . . . consequence:** in matters of the greatest importance.   128–29. **prologues . . . theme:** the first two truths are like the prologue to a powerful scene which will lead me to the crown.   130. **soliciting:** incitement.   136. **seated:** embedded.   137. **Against . . . nature:** in an unnatural way, as if it had broken loose.   139. **whose . . . fantastical:** in which murder is as yet only imagined.   140. **single . . . man:** Man was often regarded as a "microcosm," or universe in miniature, with all the functions of a kingdom existing in himself. **state:** kingdom.   140–41. **function . . . surmise:** action is choked by imagination.   145. **Like . . . garments:** like a new suit of clothes.   147. **runs through:** comes to the end of.

MAC. Give me your favor. My dull brain was
     wrought
With things forgotten. Kind gentlemen, your pains°
Are registered° where every day I turn   151
The leaf to read them. Let us toward the King.
Think upon what hath chanced, and at more time,
The interim having weighed it,° let us speak
Our free hearts each to other.

BAN.   Very gladly.   155

MACB. Till then, enough. Come, friends.

                               [*Exeunt.*]

SCENE IV. *Forres. The palace.*

[*Flourish.*° *Enter* DUNCAN, MALCOLM, DONALBAIN,
LENNOX, *and* ATTENDANTS.]

DUN. Is execution done on Cawdor? Are not
Those in commission° yet returned?

MAL.   My liege,
They are not yet come back. But I have spoke
With one that saw him die, who did report
That very frankly he confessed his treasons,   5
Implored your Highness' pardon, and set forth
A deep repentance. Nothing in his life
Became him like the leaving it. He died
As one that had been studied in his death
To throw away the dearest thing he owed   10
As 'twere a careless trifle.°

DUN.   There's no art
To find the mind's construction in the face.°
He was a gentleman on whom I built
An absolute trust.

[*Enter* MACBETH, BANQUO, ROSS, *and* ANGUS.]

             O worthiest Cousin!
The sin of my ingratitude even now   15
Was heavy on me. Thou art so far before
That swiftest wing of recompense is slow
To overtake thee. Would thou hadst less deserved,
That the proportion both of thanks and payment
Might have been mine! Only I have left to say,   20
More is thy due than more than all can pay.

MACB. The service and the loyalty I owe,
In doing it, pays itself. Your Highness' part
Is to receive our duties. And our duties
Are to your throne and state children and servants,°
Which do but what they should, by doing every-
     thing   26

---

150. **pains:** troubles.   151. **registered:** recorded; i.e., in my heart.   154. **The . . . it:** having considered it meanwhile.   **Sc. iv: s.d., Flourish:** trumpet fanfare.   2. **in commission:** For important state trials the accused was tried not by the ordinary courts but by a body of great persons summoned by a special commission.   9–11. **studied . . . trifle:** made it his study to throw away his life as a mere trifle.   11–12. **There's . . . face:** i.e., there is no method of discovering a man's character from his face.   24–25. **our . . . servants:** i.e., we owe duty to you as our King as if we were your children or servants.

Safe toward° your love and honor.

DUN.   Welcome hither.
I have begun to plant thee, and will labor
To make thee full of growing. Noble Banquo,
That hast no less deserved, nor must be known   30
No less to have done so, let me infold thee
And hold thee to my heart.

BAN.   There if I grow,
The harvest is your own.

DUN.   My plenteous joys,
Wanton° in fullness, seek to hide themselves
In drops of sorrow. Sons, kinsmen, thanes,   35
And you whose places are the nearest, know,
We will establish our estate° upon
Our eldest, Malcolm, whom we name hereafter
The Prince of Cumberland. Which honor must
Not unaccompanied invest him only,   40
But signs of nobleness, like stars, shall shine
On all deservers. From hence to Inverness,
And bind us further to you.

MACB. The rest is labor, which is not used for
you.°
I'll be myself the harbinger,° and make joyful   45
The hearing of my wife with your approach,
So humbly take my leave.

DUN.   My worthy Cawdor!

MACB. [Aside] The Prince of Cumberland! That
is a step
On which I must fall down or else o'erleap,
For in my way it lies. Stars, hide your fires,   50
Let not light see my black and deep desires.
The eye wink° at the hand, yet let that be
Which the eye fears, when it is done, to see.   [Exit.]

DUN. True, worthy Banquo, he is full so° valiant,
And in his commendations I am fed,   55
It is a banquet to me. Let's after him,
Whose care is gone before to bid us welcome.
It is a peerless kinsman.   [Flourish. Exeunt.]

SCENE V. *Inverness.* MACBETH'S *castle.*

[*Enter* LADY MACBETH, *reading a letter.*]

LADY M. " They met me in the day of success, and
I have learned by the perfectest report they have more
in them than mortal knowledge. When I burned in
desire to question them further, they made them-
selves air, into which they vanished. Whiles° I stood
rapt in the wonder of it, came missives° from the   6
King, who all-hailed me 'Thane of Cawdor,' by

which title, before, these weird sisters saluted me,
and referred me to the coming-on of time, with
' Hail, King that shalt be! ' This have I thought   10
good to deliver thee, my dearest partner of greatness,
that thou mightst not lose the dues of rejoicing° by
being ignorant of what greatness is promised thee.
Lay it to thy heart, and farewell."
Glamis thou art, and Cawdor, and shalt be
What thou art promised. Yet do I fear thy nature.
It is too full o' the milk of human kindness
To catch the nearest way. Thou wouldst be great,
Art not without ambition, but without   20
The illness° should attend it. What thou wouldst
highly,
That wouldst thou holily — wouldst not play false,
And yet wouldst wrongly win. Thou'dst have, great
Glamis,
That which cries " Thus thou must do, if thou have
it,
And that which rather thou dost fear to do   25
Than wishest should be undone." Hie° thee hither,
That I may pour my spirits in thine ear,
And chastise with the valor of my tongue
All that impedes thee from the golden round°
Which fate and metaphysical° aid doth seem   30
To have thee crowned withal.

        [*Enter a* MESSENGER.] What is your tidings?

MESS. The King comes here tonight.

LADY M.   Thou'rt mad to say it.
Is not thy master with him? Who, were 't so,
Would have informed for preparation.°

MESS. So please you, it is true. Our Thane is com-
ing.   35
One of my fellows had the speed of° him,
Who, almost dead for breath, had scarcely more
Than would make up his message.

LADY M.   Give him tending,°
He brings great news.   [*Exit* MESSENGER.]
                The raven himself is hoarse
That croaks the fatal entrance of Duncan   40
Under my battlements. Come, you spirits
That tend on mortal thoughts, unsex me here,
And fill me, from the crown to the toe, topfull
Of direst cruelty! Make thick my blood,
Stop up the access and passage to remorse,°   45
That no compunctious visitings of nature°
Shake my fell purpose, nor keep peace between
The effect and it!° Come to my woman's breasts,
And take my milk for gall,° you murdering minis-
ters,°

---

27. Safe toward: with sure regard for.   **34. Wanton:** grow wild.
37. establish . . . estate: settle our kingdom on; i.e., by declar-
ing him to be our heir.   **44. The . . . you:** i.e., anything done
for you is pleasure, everything else is tedious.   **45. harbinger:** an
official of the Court who made preparations for lodging when the
King went on progress.   **52. wink:** shut; i.e., be blind to what
I do.   **54. full so:** as fully — as you say.

    Sc. v: 5. Whiles: while.   **6. missives:** messengers.

12. dues of rejoicing: what is due to rejoicing, joy.   **21. ill-
ness:** wickedness.   **26. Hie:** hasten.   **29. golden round:** the
crown.   **30. metaphysical:** supernatural.   **34. informed . . .
preparation:** informed me so that I might be prepared.   **36. had
. . . of:** overtook.   **38. tending:** attention.   **45. remorse:** pity.
46. compunctious . . . nature: natural feelings of pity. **compunc-
tious:** remorseful   **48. The . . . it:** i.e., pity and the effecting
of my dreadful (*fell*) purpose.   **49. take . . . gall:** turn my milk
to gall (i.e., bitterness). **murdering ministers:** spirits of murder.

Wherever in your sightless° substances   50
You wait on nature's mischief! Come, thick night,
And pall° thee in the dunnest° smoke of Hell,
That my keen knife see not the wound it makes,
Nor Heaven peep through the blanket of the dark°
To cry "Hold, hold!"
[*Enter* MACBETH.] Great Glamis! Worthy Cawdor!
Greater than both, by the all-hail hereafter!   56
Thy letters have transported me beyond
This ignorant present, and I feel now
The future in the instant.

MACB.   My dearest love,
Duncan comes here tonight.

LADY M.   And when goes hence?   60

MACB. Tomorrow, as he purposes.

LADY M.   Oh, never
Shall sun that morrow see!
Your face, my Thane, is as a book where men
May read strange matters. To beguile° the time,
Look like the time, bear welcome in your eye,   65
Your hand, your tongue. Look like the innocent
     flower
But be the serpent under 't. He that's coming
Must be provided for. And you shall put
This night's great business into my dispatch,
Which shall to all our nights and days to come   70
Give solely sovereign sway° and masterdom.

MACB. We will speak further.

LADY M.   Only look up clear.°
To alter favor° ever is to fear.
Leave all the rest to me.   [*Exeunt.*]

SCENE VI. *Before* MACBETH'S *castle.*

[*Hautboys*° *and torches. Enter* DUNCAN, MALCOLM,
     DONALBAIN, BANQUO, LENNOX, MACDUFF, ROSS,
     ANGUS, *and* ATTENDANTS.]

DUN. This castle hath a pleasant seat,° the air
Nimbly° and sweetly recommends itself
Unto our gentle senses.

BAN.   This guest of summer,
The temple-haunting martlet,° does approve°
By his loved mansionry° that the heaven's breath   5
Smells wooingly here. No jutty,° frieze,°
Buttress, nor coign of vantage° but this bird

Hath made his pendent bed and procreant cradle.°
Where they most breed and haunt, I have observed
The air is delicate.

[*Enter* LADY MACBETH.]

DUN.   See, see, our honored hostess!   10
The love that follows us sometime is our trouble,
Which still we thank as love. Herein I teach you
How you shall bid God 'ild° us for your pains,
And thank us for your trouble.

LADY M.   All our service
In every point twice done, and then done double,   15
Were poor and single business to contend°
Against those honors deep and broad wherewith
Your Majesty loads our house. For those of old,
And the late dignities heaped up to them,
We rest your hermits.°

DUN.   Where's the Thane of Cawdor?   20
We coursed° him at the heels, and had a purpose
To be his purveyor.° But he rides well,
And his great love, sharp as his spur, hath holp° him
To his home before us. Fair and noble hostess,
We are your guest tonight.

LADY M.   Your servants ever   25
Have theirs, themselves, and what is theirs, in
     compt,°
To make their audit at your Highness' pleasure,
Still to return your own.°

DUN.   Give me your hand,
Conduct me to mine host. We love him highly,
And shall continue our graces toward him.   30
By your leave, hostess.   [*Exeunt.*]

SCENE VII. MACBETH'S *castle.*

[*Hautboys and torches. Enter a* SEWER,° *and divers*
     SERVANTS *with dishes and service, and pass over*
     the stage. Then enter MACBETH.]

MACB. If it were done when 'tis done, then 'twere
     well
It were done quickly. If the assassination
Could trammel up the consequence, and catch,
With his surcease, success,° that but this blow
Might be the be-all and the end-all here,   5
But° here, upon this bank and shoal of time,

8. **procreant cradle:** cradle where the young are hatched.
13. **God 'ild:** God reward.   16. **poor . . . contend:** poor and
weak in comparison.   20. **rest . . . hermits:** remain bound to
pray for you. **hermit:** beadsman, one who prays for the soul of a
benefactor. Cf. *Rich II*, III.ii.116.   21. **coursed:** chased.
22. **purveyor:** an officer who went ahead to make preparation for
the provisions when the Court went on progress. See *harbinger*
(I.iv.45,n).   23. **holp:** helped.   26. **compt:** account.   28. Still
. . . **own:** always to give you back your own; i.e., all that we
have is yours, and we must make an account of it when you
demand it.
Sc. vii: s.d., **sewer:** server.   2–4. If . . . **success:** i.e., if
only the murder could have no ·aftereffects but be final and
successful at Duncan's death (*surcease*). **trammel:** to entangle
in a net.   6. **But:** even.

50. **sightless:** unseen.   52. **pall:** cover as with a pall. **dun-
nest:** darkest.   54. **Nor . . . dark:** nor Heaven (i.e., some good
spirit) peer through the darkness which covers as with a blanket.
64. **beguile:** deceive.   71. **sovereign sway:** royal, absolute
power.   72. **clear:** i.e., with a look of innocence.   73. **alter
favor:** change countenance; i.e., to look as if you were afraid.
Sc. vi: s.d., **Hautboys:** oboes.   1. **seat:** situation.   2. **Nim-
bly:** briskly.   4. **martlet:** a species of swallow which builds for
her nest a little round mud cell under the eaves of the roof. **ap-
prove:** demonstrate.   5. **mansionry:** building.   6. **jutty:** part
of a building which juts out. **frieze:** horizontal band of masonry.
7. **coign of vantage:** convenient corner.

We'd jump° the life to come. But in these cases
We still have judgment here, that we but teach
Bloody instructions, which being taught return   9
To plague the inventor. This even-handed justice
Commends the ingredients of our poisoned chalice°
To our own lips. He's here in double trust.
First, as I am his kinsman and his subject,
Strong both against the deed. Then, as his host,
Who should against his murderer shut the door,   15
Not bear the knife myself. Besides, this Duncan
Hath borne his faculties° so meek, hath been
So clear° in his great office, that his virtues
Will plead like angels trumpet-tongued against
The deep damnation of his taking-off.   20
And pity, like a naked newborn babe,°
Striding the blast, or Heaven's cherubin horsed
Upon the sightless couriers° of the air,
Shall blow the horrid deed in every eye,
That tears shall drown the wind. I have no spur   25
To prick the sides of my intent, but only
Vaulting ambition, which o'erleaps itself
And falls on the other.°
[*Enter* LADY MACBETH.] How now! What news?
    LADY M. He has almost supped. Why have you
        left the chamber?
    MACB. Hath he asked for me?
    LADY M.   Know you not he has?   30
    MACB. We will proceed no further in this business.
He hath honored me of late, and I have bought
Golden opinions from all sorts of people,
Which would be worn now in their newest gloss,
Not cast aside so soon.
    LADY M.   Was the hope drunk   35
Wherein you dressed yourself? Hath it slept since?
And wakes it now, to look so green and pale
At what it did so freely?° From this time
Such I account thy love. Art thou afeard°
To be the same in thine own act and valor   40
As thou art in desire? Wouldst thou have that
Which thou esteem'st the ornament of life°
And live a coward in thine own esteem,
Letting "I dare not" wait upon "I would,"
Like the poor cat i' the adage?°
    MACB.   Prithee, peace.   45
I dare do all that may become a man.

Who dares do more is none.
    LADY M.   What beast was 't then
That made you break° this enterprise to me?
When you durst do it, then you were a man,
And to be more than what you were, you would   50
Be so much more the man. Nor time nor place
Did then adhere,° and yet you would make both.
They have made themselves, and that their fitness
        now
Does unmake you. I have given suck, and know
How tender 'tis to love the babe that milks me.   55
I would, while it was smiling in my face,
Have plucked my nipple from his boneless gums
And dashed the brains out, had I so sworn as you
Have done to this.
    MACB.   If we should fail?
    LADY M.   We fail!
But screw your courage to the sticking-place   60
And we'll not fail. When Duncan is asleep —
Whereto the rather shall his day's hard journey
Soundly invite him — his two chamberlains
Will I with wine and wassail° so convince°
That memory, the warder of the brain,   65
Shall be a fume, and the receipt of reason
A limbec only.° When in swinish sleep
Their drenchèd natures lie as in a death,
What cannot you and I perform upon
The unguarded Duncan? What not put upon   70
His spongy° officers, who shall bear the guilt
Of our great quell?°
    MACB.   Bring forth men-children only,
For thy undaunted mettle° should compose
Nothing but males. Will it not be received,   74
When we have marked with blood those sleepy two
Of his own chamber, and used their very daggers,
That they have done 't?
    LADY M.   Who dares receive it other,
As we shall make our griefs and clamor roar
Upon his death?
    MACB.   I am settled, and bend up°
Each corporal agent to this terrible feat.   80
Away, and mock the time with fairest show.
False face must hide what the false heart doth know.
                                    [*Exeunt.*]

---

7. **jump:** risk.   11. **chalice:** cup.   17. **faculties:** powers.   18. **clear:** innocent.   21. **naked . . . babe:** i.e., an object which moves the hardest-hearted to pity.   23. **sightless couriers:** unseen messengers.   28. **other:** i.e., side.   38. **freely:** without compulsion.   39. **afeard:** afraid, scared.   42. **ornament of life:** i.e., the crown.   45. **adage:** proverb. The proverb is common and runs "The cat would eat fish but would not wet her feet."

48. **break:** reveal.   51-52. **Nor . . . adhere:** there was then no suitable time or place for the murder.   64. **wassail:** carousing. **convince:** overcome.   65-67. **memory . . . only:** memory, which keeps watch in the brain, will be confused by the fumes of drink and the reason become like a still (*limbec*) distilling only confused thoughts. Cf. *Temp*, V.i.64-68. **receipt:** receptacle; i.e., that part of the brain which contains the reason.   71. **spongy:** that soak up drink like a sponge.   72. **quell:** murder.   73. **mettle:** material.   79. **bend up:** stretch tight (as a strung bow).

Act II

SCENE I.° *Inverness. Court of* MACBETH's
castle.

[*Enter* BANQUO, *and* FLEANCE *bearing a torch before
him.*]

BAN. How goes the night, boy?

FLE. The moon is down, I have not heard the
clock.

BAN. And she goes down at twelve.

FLE.   I take 't 'tis later, sir.

BAN. Hold, take my sword. There's husbandry°
in Heaven,

Their candles are all out. Take thee that too.°   5

A heavy summons° lies like lead upon me,

And yet I would not sleep. Merciful powers,

Restrain in me the cursèd thoughts that nature

Gives way to in repose!

[*Enter* MACBETH, *and a* SERVANT *with a torch.*]

            Give me my sword.

Who's there?   10

MACB. A friend.

BAN. What, sir, not yet at rest? The King's abed.

He hath been in unusual pleasure, and

Sent forth great largess° to your offices.°

This diamond he greets your wife withal,   15

By the name of most kind hostess, and shut up

In measureless content.°

MACB.   Being unprepared,

Our will became the servant to defect,

Which else should free have wrought.°

BAN.   All's well.

I dreamed last night of the three weird sisters.   20

To you they have showed some truth.

MACB.   I think not of them.

Yet when we can entreat an hour to serve,

We would spend it in some words upon that busi-
ness,

If you would grant the time.

BAN.   At your kind'st leisure.

MACB. If you shall cleave to my consent, when
'tis,°   25

It shall make honor for you.

BAN.   So° I lose none

In seeking to augment it, but still keep

My bosom franchised and allegiance clear,

I shall be counseled.

MACB.   Good repose the while!

BAN. Thanks, sir. The like to you!   30

[*Exeunt* BANQUO *and* FLEANCE.]

MACB. Go bid thy mistress, when my drink is
ready,

She strike upon the bell. Get thee to bed.

[*Exit* SERVANT.]

Is this a dagger which I see before me,

The handle toward my hand? Come, let me clutch
thee.

I have thee not, and yet I see thee still.   35

Art thou not, fatal vision, sensible°

To feeling as to sight? Or art thou but

A dagger of the mind, a false creation,

Proceeding from the heat-oppressèd brain?

I see thee yet, in form as palpable°   40

As this which now I draw.

Thou marshal'st° me the way that I was going,

And such an instrument I was to use.

Mine eyes are made the fools o' the other senses,

Or else worth all the rest. I see thee still,   45

And on thy blade and dudgeon° gouts° of blood,

Which was not so before. There's no such thing.

It is the bloody business which informs°

Thus to mine eyes. Now o'er the one half-world

Nature seems dead, and wicked dreams abuse   50

The curtained° sleep. Witchcraft celebrates

Pale Hecate's° offerings, and withered murder,

Alarumed by his sentinel, the wolf,

Whose howl 's his watch,° thus with his stealthy
pace,

With Tarquin's ravishing strides,° toward his de-
sign   55

Moves like a ghost. Thou sure and firm-set earth,

Hear not my steps, which way they walk, for fear

Thy very stones prate of my whereabout,

And take the present horror° from the time,   59

Which now suits° with it. Whiles I threat, he lives.

Words to the heat of deeds too cold breath gives.

[*A bell rings.*]

I go, and it is done. The bell invites me.

Hear it not, Duncan, for it is a knell

That summons thee to Heaven, or to Hell.   [*Exit.*]

Act II, Sc. i: The divisions into acts and scenes, though
made in F1, are not always apt. There is no pause in the ac-
tion from I.vii to the end of II.iii.   **4. husbandry:** economy.
5. that too: i.e., his buckler.   **6. heavy summons:** i.e., I am
very weary. Cf. *Caesar,* IV.iii.267–69.   **14. largess:** gifts of
money. **offices:** servants' quarters.   **16–17. shut . . . content:**
he has ended the day in the greatest content.   **17–19. Being . . .
wrought:** i.e., as we were not properly prepared, our entertain-
ment was not so good as we would have wished; it would other-
wise have been more lavish.   **25. If . . . 'tis:** if you will be one
of my party, when it is formed.   **26–29. So . . . counseled:** so
long as I do not lose my honor in seeking to increase it, but keep
my faith free (*franchised*) and my loyalty unstained, I will be
on your side. In the *Chronicle* Banquo was said to have been a
fellow conspirator against Duncan. Since, however, Banquo was
the ancestor of King James I, Shakespeare was careful to acquit
him of such treachery.   **36. sensible:** able to be felt.   **40. palpable:**
obvious, clear.   **42. marshal'st:** conductest.   **46. dudgeon:**
handle. **gouts:** drops.   **48. informs:** creates forms.   **51. curtained:**
with the bed curtains drawn.   **52. Hecate:** goddess of witchcraft.
See later III.v.   **54. howl's . . . watch:** who tells the time by
howling.   **55. Tarquin's . . . strides:** Tarquin, the last King of
Rome, was so overcome by his lust for Lucrece that he ravished
her. The story is told in Shakespeare's *Rape of Lucrece.*   **59. present
horror:** i.e., the silence of midnight.   **60. suits:** matches.

SCENE II. *The same.*

[*Enter* LADY MACBETH.]

LADY M. That which hath made them drunk hath
    made me bold,
What hath quenched them hath given me fire.
    Hark! Peace!
It was the owl that shrieked, the fatal bellman,
Which gives the stern'st good night.° He is about it.
The doors are open, and the surfeited° grooms°   5
Do mock their charge° with snores. I have drugged
    their possets,°
That death and nature do contend about them,
Whether they live or die.

MACB.   [*Within*] Who's there? What ho!

LADY M. Alack, I am afraid they have awaked   10
And 'tis not done. The attempt and not the deed
Confounds us. Hark! I laid their daggers ready,
He could not miss 'em. Had he not resembled
My father as he slept, I had done 't.
[*Enter* MACBETH.]   My husband!

MACB. I have done the deed. Didst thou not hear
    a noise?   15

LADY M. I heard the owl scream and the crickets
    cry.
Did not you speak?

MACB.   When?

LADY M.   Now.

MACB.   As I descended?

LADY M. Aye.

MACB. Hark!
Who lies i' the second chamber?

LADY M.   Donalbain.   20

MACB. This is a sorry sight.
                    [*Looking on his hands.*]

LADY M. A foolish thought, to say a sorry sight.

MACB. There's one did laugh in 's sleep, and one
    cried "Murder!"
That they did wake each other. I stood and heard
    them.   24
But they did say their prayers, and addressed them
Again to sleep.

LADY M.   There are two lodged together.

MACB. One cried "God bless us!" and "Amen"
    the other,
As they had seen me with these hangman's hands.°

Sc. ii: 3–4. fatal . . . night: On the night before an execu-
tion in London the bell of St. Sepulcher's Church (near Newgate
prison) was tolled, and at midnight the bellman rang a hand-bell
outside the cell of the condemned, bidding him think on his
sins. This custom had been established by Robert Dow, merchant
tailor, in 1604. 5. surfeited: overfed. groom: servant of the
chamber, who slept at the foot of the King's bed. 6. charge:
him whom they are responsible for watching. possets: warm drink
of milk and ale, taken as a nightcap. 28. hangman's hands:
To Shakespeare's audience, fresh from the excitements of the
execution of the plotters in the Gunpowder Treason, this image
would be full of ghastly significance. It was the hangman's busi-
ness to tear the vitals out of his victim before hacking him into
pieces. See Gen. Intro. 17a, 27b.

Listening their fear, I could not say "Amen"
When they did say "God bless us!"

LADY M.   Consider it not so deeply.   30

MACB. But wherefore could not I pronounce
    "Amen"?
I had most need of blessing, and "Amen"
Stuck in my throat.

LADY M.   These deeds must not be thought
After these ways. So, it will make us mad.

MACB. Methought I heard a voice cry "Sleep no
    more!   35
Macbeth does murder sleep"— the innocent sleep,
Sleep that knits up the raveled sleave° of care,
The death of each day's life, sore labor's bath,
Balm of hurt minds, great nature's second course,°
Chief nourisher in life's feast——

LADY M.   What do you mean?   40

MACB. Still° it cried "Sleep no more!" to all the
    house.
"Glamis hath murdered sleep, and therefore Caw-
    dor
Shall sleep no more. Macbeth shall sleep no
    more."

LADY M. Who was it that thus cried? Why, worthy
    Thane,
You do unbend° your noble strength to think   45
So brainsickly of things. Go get some water
And wash this filthy witness from your hand.
Why did you bring these daggers from the place?
They must lie there. Go carry them, and smear
The sleepy grooms with blood.

MACB.   I'll go no more.   50
I am afraid to think what I have done,
Look on 't again I dare not.

LADY M.   Infirm of purpose!
Give me the daggers. The sleeping and the dead
Are but as pictures. 'Tis the eye of childhood
That fears a painted devil. If he do bleed,   55
I'll gild° the faces of the grooms withal,
For it must seem their guilt.   [*Exit.*]
                    [*Knocking within.*]

MACB.   Whence is that knocking?
How is 't with me when every noise appals me?
What hands are here? Ha! They pluck out mine
    eyes!
Will all great Neptune's ocean wash this blood   60
Clean from my hand? No, this my hand will
    rather
The multitudinous seas incarnadine,°
Making the green one red.
                [*Re-enter* LADY MACBETH.]

LADY M. My hands are of your color, but I shame

37. raveled sleave: tangled skein. 39. second course: i.e.,
the main part of a feast. 41. Still: continuously. 45. unbend:
relax. 56. gild: a grim pun. Shakespeare's contemporaries
were however not very exact in their names for colors, and they
often confused "red" and "gold." Cf. II.iii.118 and *Temp,*
V.i. 279–80. 62. incarnadine: make red.

To wear a heart so white. [*Knocking within.*] I hear
a knocking   65
At the south entry. Retire we to our chamber.
A little water clears us of this deed.°
How easy is it then! Your constancy
Hath left you unattended. [*Knocking within.*]
Hark! More knocking.
Get on your nightgown,° lest occasion call us   70
And show us to be watchers.° Be not lost
So poorly in your thoughts.
     MACB. To know my deed, 'twere best not know
     myself.   [*Knocking within.*]
Wake Duncan with thy knocking! I would thou
couldst!   [*Exeunt.*]

SCENE III. *The same.*

[*Enter a* PORTER.° *Knocking within.*]

PORT. Here's a knocking indeed! If a man were
porter of Hell gate, he should have old° turning the
key.° [*Knocking within.*] Knock, knock, knock!
Who's there, i' the name of Beelzebub? Here's a
farmer that hanged himself on th' expectation of   5
plenty.° Come in time, have napkins° enow° about
you, here you'll sweat for 't. [*Knocking within.*]
Knock, knock! Who's there, in th' other devil's
name? Faith, here's an equivocator,° that could
swear in both the scales against either scale, who   10
committed treason enough for God's sake, yet could
not equivocate to Heaven. Oh, come in, equivocator.
[*Knocking within.*] Knock, knock, knock! Who's
there? Faith, here's an English tailor come hither,
for stealing out of a French hose.° Come in, tailor,
here you may roast your goose.° [*Knocking* 16
within.] Knock, knock, never at quiet! What are
you? But this place is too cold for Hell. I'll devil-
porter it no further. I had thought to have let in
some of all professions that go the primrose   20

---

67. A . . . deed: See V.i.48 and *Macb* Intro. p. 832a.   70. night-
gown: dressing gown.   70–71. lest . . . watchers: lest something
should cause us to be summoned, and we should be found still
out of bed.
   Sc. iii: s.d., Enter a porter: See *Macb* Intro. p. 832a.
2. old: slang for "any amount of."   2–3. turning . . . key:
opening the door.   5–6. farmer . . . plenty: Farmers who hoarded
corn in the hope of high prices in a time of dearth were often the
subject for jest and satire. In Jonson's *Every Man out of His
Humor* Sordido the farmer believes from the weather forecast in
his almanac that the harvest will fail. When his hopes of profi-
teering are disappointed he hangs himself, but is cut down by
his neighbors. When he revives, he abuses them for cutting and
not untying the rope.   6. napkins: towels. enow: enough.
9. equivocator: See *Macb* Intro. p. 828a and App. 20.   14–15. Eng-
lish . . . hose: It was double theft; he not only stole the fashion
but helped himself to some of the cloth, for French hose at
this time were very full and baggy. See Pl. 8b and comment
on p. 93b.   16. goose: with a pun on goose, the tailor's pressing
iron.

---

way° to the everlasting bonfire. [*Knocking within.*]
Anon, anon! I pray you remember the porter.
                                  [*Opens the gate.*]
           [*Enter* MACDUFF *and* LENNOX.]
   MACD. Was it so late, friend, ere you went to bed
That you do lie so late?   25
   PORT. Faith, sir, we were carousing till the second
cock.° And drink, sir, is a great provoker of three
things.
   MACD. What three things does drink especially
provoke?   30
   PORT. Marry, sir, nose-painting, sleep, and urine.
Lechery, sir, it provokes and unprovokes. It pro-
vokes the desire, but it takes away the performance.
Therefore much drink may be said to be an equivo-
cator with lechery. It makes him and it mars   35
him, it sets him on and it takes him off, it persuades
him and disheartens him, makes him stand to and
not stand to; in conclusion, equivocates him in a
sleep and giving him the lie, leaves him.   40
   MACD. I believe drink gave thee the lie last night.
   PORT. That it did, sir, i' the very throat on me.
But I requited° him for his lie, and I think being
too strong for him, though he took up my legs some-
time, yet I made a shift° to cast° him.   46
   MACD. Is thy master stirring?
[*Enter* MACBETH]. Our knocking has awaked him.
      Here he comes.
   LEN. Good morrow, noble sir.
   MACB.   Good morrow, both.
   MACD. Is the King stirring, worthy Thane?
   MACB.   Not yet.   50
   MACD. He did command me to call timely on him.
I have almost slipped the hour.
   MACB.   I'll bring you to him.
   MACD. I know this is a joyful trouble to you,
But yet 'tis one.
   MACB. The labor we delight in physics° pain.   55
This is the door.
   MACD.   I'll make so bold to call,
For 'tis my limited service.°   [*Exit.*]
   LEN. Goes the King hence today?
   MACB.   He does. He did appoint so.
   LEN. The night has been unruly. Where we lay,
Our chimneys were blown down, and, as they say,
Lamentings heard i' the air, strange screams of
      death,   61
And prophesying with accents terrible
Of dire combustion° and confused events
New-hatched to the woeful time. The obscure bird°
Clamored the livelong night. Some say the earth 65

20–21. primrose way: the broad and pleasant path that leads to
Hell.   26–27. second cock: 3 A.M. First cock was midnight and
third cock an hour before dawn. Cf. *R & J*, IV.iv.3–4.   44. re-
quited: paid him back.   46. made a shift: managed. cast: throw
up.   55. physics: cures.   57. limited service: duty assigned me.
63. dire combustion: some terrific event about to blaze out.
64. obscure bird: owl.

Was feverous and did shake.

MACB.   'Twas a rough night.

LEN. My young remembrance cannot parallel
A fellow to it.

[*Re-enter* MACDUFF.]

MACD. O horror, horror, horror! Tongue nor heart
Cannot conceive nor name thee.

MACB. & LEN.   What's the matter?   70

MACD. Confusion now hath made his masterpiece.
Most sacrilegious murder hath broke ope
The Lord's anointed temple, and stole thence
The life o' the building.

MACB.   What is 't you say? The life?

LEN. Mean you His Majesty?   75

MACD. Approach the chamber, and destroy your
   sight
With a new Gorgon.° Do not bid me speak.
See, and then speak yourselves.

[*Exeunt* MACBETH *and* LENNOX.]
                               Awake, awake!
Ring the alarum bell. Murder and treason!
Banquo and Donalbain! Malcolm! Awake!   80
Shake off this downy sleep, death's counterfeit,
And look on death itself! Up, up, and see
The great doom's image!° Malcolm! Banquo!
As from your graves rise up, and walk like sprites,
To countenance° this horror. Ring the bell.   85

[*Bell rings.*]

[*Enter* LADY MACBETH.]

LADY M. What's the business,
That such a hideous trumpet calls to parley°
The sleepers of the house? Speak, speak!

MACD.   O gentle lady,
'Tis not for you to hear what I can speak.
The repetition, in a woman's ear,   90
Would murder as it fell.

[*Enter* BANQUO.] O Banquo, Banquo!
Our royal master's murdered.

LADY M.   Woe, alas!
What, in our house?

BAN.   Too cruel anywhere.
Dear Duff, I prithee, contradict thyself,
And say it is not so.   95

[*Re-enter* MACBETH *and* LENNOX, *with* ROSS.]

MACB. Had I but died an hour before this chance,
I had lived a blessèd time, for from this instant
There's nothing serious in mortality.°
All is but toys.° Renown and grace is dead,
The wine of life is drawn, and the mere lees   100
Is left this vault° to brag of.

[*Enter* MALCOLM *and* DONALBAIN.]

DON. What is amiss?

MACB.   You are, and do not know 't.

The spring, the head, the fountain of your blood
Is stopped, the very source of it is stopped.

MACD. Your royal father's murdered.

MAL.   Oh, by whom?   105

LEN. Those of his chamber, as it seemed, had
   done 't.
Their hands and faces were all badged° with blood,
So were their daggers, which unwiped we found
Upon their pillows.
They stared, and were distracted, no man's life   110
Was to be trusted with them.

MACB. Oh, yet I do repent me of my fury,
That I did kill them.

MACD.   Wherefore did you so?

MACB. Who can be wise, amazed, temperate and
   furious,
Loyal and neutral, in a moment? No man.   115
The expedition° of my violent love
Outrun the pauser reason.° Here lay Duncan,
His silver skin laced with his golden blood,°
And his gashed stabs looked like a breach in nature
For ruin's wasteful entrance. There, the murderers,
Steeped in the colors of their trade, their daggers
Unmannerly breeched° with gore. Who could re-
   frain   122
That had a heart to love, and in that heart
Courage to make 's love known?

LADY M.   Help me hence, ho!

MACD. Look to the lady.

MAL. [*Aside to* DONALBAIN] Why do we hold our
   tongues,   125
That most may claim this argument for ours?°

DON. [*Aside to* MALCOLM] What should be spoken
   here, where our fate,
Hid in an auger hole,° may rush and seize us?
Let's away,   129
Our tears are not yet brewed.°

MAL. [*Aside to* DONALBAIN] Nor our strong sorrow
Upon the foot of motion.°

BAN. Look to the lady.

[LADY MACBETH *is carried out.*]

And when we have our naked frailties hid,
That suffer in exposure,° let us meet,
And question this most bloody piece of work,
To know it further. Fears and scruples shake us.
In the great hand of God I stand, and thence   136

107. **badged:** marked; lit., wearing a badge as a servant of mur-
der.   116. **expedition:** hasty action.   117. **pauser reason:**
reason which causes a man to pause before acting.   118. **laced
. . . blood:** overlaid with blood as a garment is ornamented with
gold. Macbeth in his attempt to conceal his guilt uses highflown
and exaggerated language. **golden:** red. See II.ii.56.   122. **Un-
mannerly breeched:** covered as with breeches in an unbecoming
way.   126. **That . . . ours:** i.e., who are most concerned with
this business.   128. **auger hole:** a small hole made by an auger;
i.e., destruction may come on us from the smallest circumstance.
130. **Our . . . brewed:** we have not yet had time for weeping.
131. **Upon . . . motion:** is not yet moving.   132-33. **our . . . ex-
posure:** i.e., when we have put on our clothes. All but Macduff
have come straight from their beds.

77. **Gorgon:** the snake-headed monster Medusa, so terrible to
look upon that it turned those who saw it to stone.   83. **great
. . . image:** the picture of the Day of Doom.   85. **countenance:**
to be in keeping with.   87. **parley:** conference of war.   98. **mor-
tality:** human life.   99. **toys:** trifles.   101. **vault:** universe.

Against the undivulged pretense° I fight
Of treasonous malice.

MACD.   And so do I.

ALL.   So all.

MACB. Let's briefly put on manly readiness,
And meet i' the hall together.

ALL.   Well contented.   140

[*Exeunt all but* MALCOLM *and* DONALBAIN.]

MAL. What will you do? Let's not consort° with
them.
To show an unfelt sorrow is an office
Which the false man does easy. I'll to England.

DON. To Ireland, I. Our separated fortune
Shall keep us both the safer. Where we are   145
There's daggers in men's smiles. The near in blood,
The nearer bloody.°

MAL.   This murderous shaft° that's shot
Hath not yet lighted,° and our safest way
Is to avoid the aim. Therefore to horse,
And let us not be dainty° of leave-taking,   150
But shift away. There's warrant in that theft
Which steals itself when there's no mercy left.°

[*Exeunt.*]

SCENE IV. *Outside* MACBETH'S *castle.*

[*Enter* ROSS *with an* OLD MAN.]

OLD MAN. Threescore and ten I can remember
well.
Within the volume of which time I have seen
Hours dreadful and things strange, but this sore
night
Hath trifled former knowings.°

ROSS.   Ah, good Father,
Thou seest the heavens, as troubled with man's act,
Threaten his bloody stage. By the clock 'tis day,   6
And yet dark night strangles the traveling lamp.°
Is 't night's predominance,° or the day's shame,°
That darkness does the face of earth entomb
When living light should kiss it?

OLD MAN.   'Tis unnatural,   10
Even like the deed that's done. On Tuesday last
A falcon towering in her pride of place°
Was by a mousing owl hawked at and killed.

137. undivulged pretense: the intention of the crime which has
not yet been revealed. Cf. *W Tale*, III.ii.17–18.   141. consort:
associate with.   146–47. The . . . bloody: the nearer we are by
blood relationship to the King, the more likely to be murdered.
147. shaft: arrow.   148. lighted: come to earth.   150. dainty:
particular.   151–52. There's . . . left: i.e., we are justified in
stealing away in these merciless times.

Sc. iv: 4. trifled . . . knowings: everything I have known be-
fore is a trifle compared with this.   7. strangles . . . lamp:
blots out the sun. traveling: either moving in its course or
struggling. In Shakespeare's time "travel" and "travail"
(strive) were the same word. F1 spells "travailing."   8. pre-
dominance: supremacy. day's shame: i.e., is the day ashamed
of this dreadful deed and so unwilling to show its face.
12. towering . . . place: towering proudly aloft.

ROSS. And Duncan's horses — a thing most
strange and certain —
Beauteous and swift, the minions of their race,   15
Turned wild in nature, broke their stalls, flung out,
Contending 'gainst obedience, as they would make
War with mankind.

OLD MAN.   'Tis said they eat each other.

ROSS. They did so, to the amazement of mine eyes,
That looked upon 't.

[*Enter* MACDUFF.] Here comes the good Macduff.
How goes the world, sir, now?

MACD.   Why, see you not?   21

ROSS. Is 't known who did this more than bloody
deed?

MACD. Those that Macbeth hath slain.

ROSS.   Alas the day!
What good could they pretend?°

MACD.   They were suborned.°
Malcolm and Donalbain, the King's two sons,   25
Are stol'n away and fled, which puts upon them
Suspicion of the deed.

ROSS.   'Gainst nature still.
Thriftless ambition, that wilt ravin up°
Thine own life's means!° Then 'tis most like
The sovereignty will fall upon Macbeth.   30

MACD. He is already named,° and gone to Scone
To be invested.

ROSS.   Where is Duncan's body?

MACD. Carried to Colmekill,°
The sacred storehouse of his predecessors
And guardian of their bones.

ROSS.   Will you to Scone?   35

MACD. No, Cousin, I'll to Fife.

ROSS.   Well, I will thither.

MACD. Well, may you see things well done there.
Adieu!
Lest our old robes sit easier than our new!

ROSS. Farewell, Father.

OLD MAN. God's benison° go with you, and with
those   40
That would make good of bad and friends of foes!

[*Exeunt.*]

Act III

SCENE I. *Forres. The palace.*

[*Enter* BANQUO.]

BAN. Thou hast it now. King, Cawdor, Glamis,
all,
As the weird women promised, and I fear

24. pretend: allege. suborned: bribed.   28. ravin up: devour
greedily.   29. own . . . means: i.e., parent.   31. named:
elected.   33. Colmekill: Iona, the ancient burying place of the
Kings of Scotland.   40. benison: blessing.

Thou play'dst most foully for 't. Yet it was said
It should not stand in thy posterity,
But that myself should be the root and father   5
Of many kings. If there come truth from them —
As upon thee, Macbeth, their speeches shine —
Why, by the verities on thee made good,
May they not be my oracles as well
And set me up in hope? But hush, no more.   10
[*Sennet*° *sounded. Enter* MACBETH, *as King;* LADY
  MACBETH, *as Queen;* LENNOX, ROSS, LORDS, LADIES,
    and ATTENDANTS.]

MACB. Here's our chief guest.

LADY M.   If he had been forgotten,
It had been as a gap in our great feast,
And all-thing° unbecoming.

MACB. Tonight we hold a solemn° supper, sir,
And I'll request your presence.

BAN.   Let your Highness   15
Command upon me, to the which my duties
Are with a most indissoluble tie
Forever knit.

MACB. Ride you this afternoon?

BAN.   Aye, my good lord.   20

MACB. We should have else desired your good ad-
    vice,
Which still° hath been both grave and prosperous,
In this day's council, but we'll take tomorrow.
Is 't far you ride?

BAN. As far, my lord, as will fill up the time   25
'Twixt this and supper. Go not my horse the better,
I must become a borrower of the night
For a dark hour or twain.

MACB.   Fail not our feast.

BAN. My lord, I will not.

MACB. We hear our bloody cousins are bestowed
In England and in Ireland, not confessing   31
Their cruel parricide, filling their hearers
With strange invention. But of that tomorrow,
When therewithal we shall have cause of state
Craving us jointly.° Hie° you to horse. Adieu,   35
Till you return at night. Goes Fleance with you?

BAN. Aye, my good lord. Our time does call
    upon 's.°

MACB. I wish your horses swift and sure of foot,
And so I do commend you to their backs.   39
Farewell.   [*Exit* BANQUO.]
Let every man be master of his time
Till seven at night. To make society
The sweeter welcome, we will keep ourself
Till suppertime alone. While° then, God be with
    you!

                  [*Exeunt all but* MACBETH
                     and an ATTENDANT.]

Sirrah, a word with you. Attend° those men   45
Our pleasure?

ATT. They are, my lord, without° the palace gate.

MACB. Bring them before us. [*Exit* ATTENDANT.]
                     To be thus is nothing,
But to be safely thus. Our fears in Banquo
Stick deep, and in his royalty of nature°   50
Reigns that which would be feared. 'Tis much he
    dares,
And to° that dauntless temper of his mind,
He hath a wisdom that doth guide his valor
To act in safety. There is none but he
Whose being I do fear. And under him   55
My Genius is rebuked, as it is said
Mark Antony's was by Caesar.° He chid the sisters
When first they put the name of King upon me,
And bade them speak to him. Then prophetlike
They hailed him father to a line of kings.   60
Upon my head they placed a fruitless crown
And put a barren scepter in my gripe,°
Thence to be wrenched with an unlineal° hand,
No son of mine succeeding. If 't be so,
For Banquo's issue have I filed° my mind,   65
For them the gracious Duncan have I murdered,
Put rancors° in the vessel of my peace
Only for them, and mine eternal jewel°
Given to the common enemy of man°
To make them kings — the seed of Banquo kings!
Rather than so, come, Fate, into the list,°   71
And champion° me to the utterance!° Who's there?

    [*Re-enter* ATTENDANT, *with* TWO MURDERERS.]

Now go to the door, and stay there till we call.
                     [*Exit* ATTENDANT.]
Was it not yesterday we spoke together?

1. MUR. It was, so please your Highness.

MACB.   Well then, now   75
Have you considered of my speeches? Know
That it was he in the times past which held you
So under fortune,° which you thought had been
Our innocent self. This I made good° to you
In our last conference, passed in probation° with
    you,   80
How you were borne in hand,° how crossed, the in-
    struments,
Who wrought with them, and all things else that
    might
To half a soul and to a notion crazed°

---

45. **Attend:** wait.   47. **without:** outside.   50. **royalty of na-**
ture: kingly nature.   52. **to:** added to.   56–57. **My . . . Caesar:**
See *Ant & Cleo,* II.iii.18–29, and *Caesar,* II.i.66.   62. **gripe:**
grip.   63. **unlineal:** not descended from me.   65. **filed:** defiled.
67. **rancors:** bitterness.   68. **eternal jewel:** i.e., immortal
soul.   69. **common . . . man:** the Devil.   71. **list:** place of com-
bat.   72. **champion:** fight against in single combat. **to . . .**
utterance: *à l'outrance,* to the uttermost, a term in chivalry for a
combat to the death.   77–78. **held . . . fortune:** was the cause
of your bad fortune.   79. **made good:** demonstrated.
80. **passed in probation:** proved.   81. **borne in hand:** deceived.
83. **notion crazed:** even to a half-wit.

Act III, Sc. i: 10 s.d., **Sennet:** a trumpet call.   13. **all-**
thing: every way.   14. **solemn:** ceremonious. See III.iv.1.
22. **still:** always.   35. **Craving us jointly:** demanding the at-
tention of both of us. **Hie:** hasten.   37. **Our . . . upon 's:** our
business is urgent.   44. **While:** till.

Say " Thus did Banquo."

1. MUR.   You made it known to us.

MACB. I did so, and went further, which is now
Our point of second meeting. Do you find   86
Your patience so predominant in your nature
That you can let this go? Are you so gospeled,°
To pray for this good man and for his issue,
Whose heavy hand hath bowed° you to the grave
And beggared yours forever?

1. MUR.   We are men, my liege.   91

MACB. Aye, in the catalogue ye go for men,
As hounds and greyhounds, mongrels, spaniels, curs,
Shoughs,° water rugs° and demiwolves,° are clept°
All by the name of dogs. The valued file°   95
Distinguishes the swift, the slow, the subtle,
The housekeeper, the hunter, every one
According to the gift which bounteous Nature
Hath in him closed,° whereby he does receive
Particular addition from the bill   100
That writes them all alike.° And so of men.
Now if you have a station in the file,°
Not i' the worst rank of manhood, say it,
And I will put that business in your bosoms
Whose execution takes your enemy off,   105
Grapples you to the heart and love of us,
Who wear our health but sickly in his life°
Which in his death were perfect.

2. MUR.   I am one, my liege,
Whom the vile blows and buffets of the world
Have so incensed that I am reckless what   110
I do to spite the world.

1. MUR.   And I another
So weary with disasters, tugged with° fortune,
That I would set my life on any chance
To mend it or be rid on 't.

MACB.   Both of you
Know Banquo was your enemy.

BOTH MURS.   True, my lord.   115

MACB. So is he mine, and in such bloody distance°
That every minute of his being thrusts
Against my near'st of life.° And though I could
With barefaced power sweep him from my sight
And bid my will avouch° it, yet I must not,   120
For certain friends that are both his and mine,
Whose loves I may not drop, but wail his fall°
Who I myself struck down. And thence it is
That I to your assistance do make love,

Masking° the business from the common eye   125
For sundry weighty reasons.

2. MUR.   We shall, my lord,
Perform what you command us.

1. MUR.   Though our lives ——

MACB. Your spirits shine through you. Within this
    hour at most
I will advise you where to plant yourselves,
Acquaint you with the perfect spy o' the time,°   130
The moment on 't. For 't must be done tonight,
And something° from the palace, always thought
That I require a clearness.° And with him —
To leave no rubs° nor botches in the work —
Fleance his son, that keeps him company,   135
Whose absence is no less material to me
Than is his father's, must embrace the fate
Of that dark hour. Resolve yourselves apart.°
I'll come to you anon.

BOTH MURS.   We are resolved, my lord.

MACB. I'll call upon you straight. Abide within.
                    [*Exeunt* MURDERERS.]

It is concluded. Banquo, thy soul's flight,   141
If it find Heaven, must find it out tonight. [*Exit.*]

SCENE II. *The palace.*

[*Enter* LADY MACBETH *and a* SERVANT.]

LADY M. Is Banquo gone from Court?

SERV. Aye, madam, but returns again tonight.

LADY M. Say to the King I would attend his leisure
For a few words.

SERV.   Madam, I will.   [*Exit.*]

LADY M.   Naught's had, all's spent,
Where our desire is got without content.   5
'Tis safer to be that which we destroy
Than by destruction dwell in doubtful joy.
[*Enter* MACBETH.] How now, my lord! Why do you
    keep alone,
Of sorriest fancies your companions making,
Using those thoughts which should indeed have
    died   10
With them they think on? Things without all
    remedy
Should be without regard. What's done is done.

MACB. We have scotched° the snake, not killed it.
She'll close° and be herself, whilst our poor malice
Remains in danger of her former tooth.°   15

---

88. **so gospeled**: such a good Christian.   90. **bowed**: bent down
double.   94. **Shoughs**: shaggy-haired dogs. **water rugs**: dogs
used to the water. **demiwolves**: dogs which are half wolf. **clept**:
called.   95. **valued file**: list of those considered first class.
99. **in . . . closed**: enclosed in him.   99–101. **whereby . . . alike**:
i.e., from his special quality, each kind of dog has his particular
distinction (*addition*) which makes him more than a mere
"dog."   102. **station . . . file**: place.   107. **in . . . life**: so long
as he is alive.   112. **tugged with**: pulled about by.   116. **dis-
tance**: disagreement, quarrel.   118. **near'st of life**: inmost being,
myself.   120. **avouch**: justify.   122. **wail . . . fall**: pretend to
lament his death.

125. **Masking**: hiding.   130. **Acquaint . . . time**: send someone
to tell you the exact moment.   132. **something**: some distance.
133. **clearness**: i.e., that no suspicion falls on me.   134. **rubs**:
impediments. See App. 13.   138. **Resolve . . . apart**: make up
your minds by yourselves.

Sc. ii: 13. **scotched**: wounded slightly. F1 reads "scorched."
14. **close**: heal.   14–15. **whilst . . . tooth**: while we for all our
hatred are in as great danger from her as before.

But let the frame of things disjoint, both the worlds
    suffer,°
Ere we will eat our meal in fear and sleep
In the affliction of these terrible dreams
That shake us nightly. Better be with the dead,
Whom we, to gain our peace, have sent to peace,   20
Than on the torture of the mind to lie
In restless ecstasy.° Duncan is in his grave,
After life's fitful fever he sleeps well.
Treason has done his worst. Nor steel, nor poison,
Malice domestic, foreign levy, nothing,   25
Can touch him further.

LADY M.   Come on,
Gentle my lord, sleek o'er your rugged looks,°
Be bright and jovial among your guests tonight.

MACB. So shall I, love, and so, I pray, be you.
Let your remembrance apply to Banquo,   30
Present him eminence,° both with eye and tongue,
Unsafe the while,° that we
Must lave° our honors in these flattering streams
And make our faces vizards° to our hearts,
Disguising what they are.

LADY M.   You must leave this.   35

MACB. Oh, full of scorpions is my mind, dear wife!
Thou know'st that Banquo, and his Fleance, lives.

LADY M. But in them Nature's copy's not eterne.°

MACB. There's comfort yet, they are assailable.
Then be thou jocund. Ere the bat hath flown   40
His cloistered flight,° ere to black Hecate's summons
The shard-borne° beetle with his drowsy hums
Hath rung night's yawning peal, there shall be done
A deed of dreadful note.

LADY M.   What's to be done?

MACB. Be innocent of the knowledge, dearest
    chuck,°   45
Till thou applaud the deed. Come, seeling night,°
Scarf° up the tender eye of pitiful day,
And with thy bloody and invisible hand
Cancel and tear to pieces that great bond°
Which keeps me pale! Light thickens, and the crow
Makes wing to the rooky° wood.   51
Good things of day begin to droop and drowse
Whiles night's black agents to their preys do rouse.
Thou marvel'st at my words. But hold thee still,
Things bad begun make strong themselves by ill.
So prithee go with me.   [*Exeunt.*]

16. let . . . suffer: let the universe fall to pieces, let heaven and
earth perish. 22. ecstasy: madness. 27. sleek . . . looks: make
smooth your wild looks. 31. Present . . . eminence: make much
of him. 32. Unsafe . . . while: we are unsafe so long as. 33. lave:
bathe. 34. vizards: masks. 38. Nature's . . . eterne: i.e., man
holds his life only on a temporary lease (*copy*) — not perpetual
freehold — from Nature. 41. cloistered flight: flight in cloisters.
42. shard-borne: borne aloft by its horny wings. 45. chuck:
chick. 46. seeling night: an image from the taming of hawks.
See App. 26. 47. Scarf: blindfold. 49. great bond: lit., that
which binds me; i.e., Banquo's life. 51. rooky: murky.

SCENE III. *A park near the palace.*

[*Enter three* MURDERERS.°]

1. MUR. But who did bid thee join with us?

3. MUR.   Macbeth.

2. MUR. He needs not our mistrust, since he de-
    livers
Our offices,° and what we have to do,
To the direction just.°

1. MUR.   Then stand with us.
The west yet glimmers with some streaks of day.   5
Now spurs the lated° traveler apace
To gain the timely inn, and near approaches
The subject of our watch.

3. MUR.   Hark! I hear horses.

BAN. [*Within*] Give us a light there, ho!

2. MUR.   Then 'tis he. The rest
That are within the note of expectation°   10
Already are i' the Court.

1. MUR.   His horses go about.

3. MUR. Almost a mile. But he does usually —
So all men do — from hence to the palace gate
Make it their walk.

2. MUR.   A light, a light!

[*Enter* BANQUO, *and* FLEANCE *with a torch.*]

3. MUR.   'Tis he.

1. MUR. Stand to 't.   15

BAN. It will be rain tonight.

1. MUR.   Let it come down.

[*They set upon* BANQUO.]

BAN. Oh, treachery! Fly, good Fleance, fly, fly, fly!
Thou mayst revenge. O slave!

[*Dies.* FLEANCE *escapes.*]

3. MUR. Who did strike out the light?

1. MUR.   Was 't not the way?

3. MUR. There's but one down, the son is fled.

2. MUR.   We have lost   20
Best half of our affair.

1. MUR. Well, let's away and say how much is
    done.   [*Exeunt.*]

SCENE IV. *Hall in the palace.*

[*A banquet prepared. Enter* MACBETH, LADY
MACBETH, ROSS, LENNOX, LORDS, *and* ATTENDANTS.]

MACB. You know your own degrees,° sit down.
    At first
And last the hearty welcome.

LORDS.   Thanks to your Majesty.

Sc. iii: s.d., three Murderers: The presence of the third
murderer is not explained, but he is presumably the "perfect
spy o' the time." See III.i.130. 3. offices: duty. 4. To . . .
just: in exact detail. 6. lated: belated. 10. within . . . ex-
pectation: noted as expected at the feast.

Sc. iv: 1. degrees: ranks. This is a state banquet at which
each guest sits according to his rank.

MACB. Ourself will mingle with society
And play the humble host.
Our hostess keeps her state,° but in best time   5
We will require her welcome.

LADY M. Pronounce it for me, sir, to all our friends,
For my heart speaks they are welcome.

[*Enter* FIRST MURDERER, *to the door.*]

MACB. See, they encounter thee with their hearts'
thanks.
Both sides are even.° Here I'll sit i' the midst.   10
Be large in mirth,° anon we'll drink a measure°
The table round. [*Approaching the door.*] There's
blood upon thy face.

MUR. 'Tis Banquo's then.

MACB. 'Tis better thee without than he within.
Is he dispatched?   15

MUR. My lord, his throat is cut. That I did for
him.

MACB. Thou art the best o' the cutthroats. Yet he's
good
That did the like for Fleance. If thou didst it,
Thou art the nonpareil.°

MUR.   Most royal sir.
Fleance is 'scaped.   20

MACB. [*Aside*] Then comes my fit again. I had
else been perfect,
Whole as the marble, founded as the rock,
As broad and general as the casing° air.   23
But now I am cabined, cribbed,° confined, bound in
To saucy° doubts and fears. — But Banquo's safe?

MUR. Aye, my good lord. Safe in a ditch he bides,
With twenty trenchèd gashes on his head,
The least a death to nature.°

MACB.   Thanks for that.   28
[*Aside*] There the grown serpent lies. The worm°
that's fled
Hath nature that in time will venom breed,
No teeth for the present. Get thee gone. Tomorrow
We'll hear ourselves again.   [*Exit* MURDERER.]

LADY M.   My royal lord,
You do not give the cheer. The feast° is sold
That is not often vouched, while 'tis a-making,
'Tis given with welcome. To feed were best at home,
From thence the sauce to meat is ceremony,   36
Meeting were bare without it.

MACB.   Sweet remembrancer!
Now good digestion wait on appetite,
And health on both!

LEN.   May 't please your Highness sit.

[*The* GHOST OF BANQUO *enters, and sits in* MACBETH'S
place.]

MACB. Here had we now our country's honor
roofed°   40
Were the graced° person of our Banquo present,
Who may I rather challenge for unkindness
Than pity for mischance!

ROSS.   His absence, sir,
Lays blame upon his promise. Please 't your High-
ness
To grace us with your royal company.   45

MACB. The table's full.

LEN.   Here is a place reserved, sir.

MACB. Where?

LEN. Here, my good lord. What is 't that moves
your Highness?

MACB. Which of you have done this?

LORDS.   What, my good lord?

MACB. Thou canst not say I did it. Never shake
Thy gory locks at me.   51

ROSS. Gentlemen, rise. His Highness is not well.

LADY M. Sit, worthy friends. My lord is often thus,
And hath been from his youth. Pray you keep seat,
The fit is momentary, upon a thought°   55
He will again be well. If much you note him,
You shall offend him and extend his passion.°
Feed, and regard him not. Are you a man?

MACB. Aye, and a bold one, that dare look on that
Which might appall the Devil.

LADY M.   Oh, proper stuff! 60
This is the very painting of your fear.
This is the air-drawn dagger which you said
Led you to Duncan. Oh, these flaws° and starts,
Impostors to true fear, would well become
A woman's story at a winter's fire,   65
Authorized by her grandam.° Shame itself!
Why do you make such faces? When all's done,
You look but on a stool.°

MACB. Prithee see there! Behold! Look! Lo! How
say you?
Why, what care I? If thou canst nod, speak too.   70
If charnel houses° and our graves must send
Those that we bury back, our monuments
Shall be the maws of kites.°   [*Exit* GHOST.]

LADY M.   What, quite unmanned in folly?

MACB. If I stand here, I saw him.

LADY M.   Fie, for shame!

40. our . . . roofed: all the most honorable men in the country
under our roof.   41. graced: honored.   55. upon a thought: as
quick as thought.   57. extend . . . passion: increase his fit.
63. flaws: lit., gusts of wind.   66. Authorized . . . grandam:
vouched for by her grandmother.   68. You . . . stool: Unlike the
ghost which appeared on the battlements to Hamlet and his
friends, Banquo's ghost is a hallucination, visible only to Mac-
beth. It has, however, almost always been the custom on the
stage to have it visible. See s.d. at l. 39. stool: joined stool. See
Pl. 17a. Only those of highest rank sat on chairs.   71. charnel
houses: See App. 16.   72–73. our . . . kites: our graves shall be
in the bellies of birds of prey.

5. keeps . . . state: i.e., sits on her throne apart.   10. even:
equal.   11. large in mirth: unrestrained in your enjoyment.
measure: toast; lit., a quantity of drink.   19. nonpareil: with-
out an equal.   23. casing: enclosing.   24. cribbed: hampered.
25. saucy: insolent.   28. nature: natural life.   29. worm: a
little snake. Cf. *Ant & Cleo*, V.ii.243.   33–36. feast . . . cere-
mony: i.e., there is no hospitality at a feast where the guests
are not made welcome; without welcome, it is a mere bought
dinner — one can feed better at home; when one is away from
home, ceremony should accompany the feast.

MACB. Blood hath been shed ere now, i' the olden time,   75
Ere humane statute purged the gentle weal° —
Aye, and since too, murders have been performed
Too terrible for the ear. The time has been
That when the brains were out, the man would die,
And there an end. But now they rise again,   80
With twenty mortal murders on their crowns,°
And push us from our stools. This is more strange
Than such a murder is.

LADY M.   My worthy lord,
Your noble friends do lack you.

MACB.   I do forget.
Do not muse at me, my most worthy friends.   85
I have a strange infirmity, which is nothing
To those that know me. Come, love and health to all,
Then I'll sit down. Give me some wine, fill full.
I drink to the general joy o' the whole table,
And to our dear friend Banquo, whom we miss.   90
Would he were here! To all and him we thirst,
And all to all.

LORDS.   Our duties, and the pledge.

[*Re-enter* GHOST.]

MACB. Avaunt!° And quit my sight! Let the earth
hide thee!
Thy bones are marrowless, thy blood is cold,
Thou hast no speculation° in those eyes   95
Which thou dost glare with.

LADY M.   Think of this, good peers,
But as a thing of custom.° 'Tis no other,
Only it spoils the pleasure of the time.

MACB. What man dare, I dare.
Approach thou like the rugged Russian bear,   100
The armed rhinoceros, or the Hyrcan° tiger.
Take any shape but that° and my firm nerves
Shall never tremble. Or be alive again,
And dare me to the desert° with thy sword.
If trembling I inhabit then, protest me   105
The baby of a girl.° Hence, horrible shadow!
Unreal mockery, hence!   [*Exit* GHOST.]
                Why, so. Being gone,
I am a man again. Pray you sit still.

LADY M. You have displaced° the mirth, broke the
good meeting,
With most admired° disorder.

MACB.   Can such things be,   110
And overcome° us like a summer's cloud,

Without our special wonder? You make me strange
Even to the disposition that I owe°
When now I think you can behold such sights
And keep the natural ruby of your cheeks   115
When mine is blanched with fear.

ROSS.   What sights, my lord?

LADY M. I pray you speak not, he grows worse and
worse.
Question enrages him. At once, good night.
Stand not upon the order of your going,°
But go at once.

LEN.   Good night, and better health   120
Attend His Majesty!

LADY M.   A kind good night to all!

[*Exeunt all but* MACBETH
and LADY MACBETH.]

MACB. It will have blood. They say blood will have
blood.
Stones have been known to move and trees to speak.
Augurs° and understood relations° have
By maggot pies and choughs° and rooks brought
forth   125
The secret'st man of blood. What is the night?

LADY M. Almost at odds° with morning, which is
which.

MACB. How say'st thou that Macduff denies his
person
At our great bidding?

LADY M.   Did you send to him, sir?

MACB. I hear it by the way, but I will send.   130
There's not a one of them but in his house
I keep a servant feed.° I will tomorrow,
And betimes° I will, to the weird sisters.
More shall they speak, for now I am bent° to know,
By the worst means, the worst. For mine own good
All causes shall give way. I am in blood   136
Stepped in so far that should I wade no more,
Returning were as tedious as go o'er.
Strange things I have in head that will to hand,
Which must be acted ere they may be scanned.°

LADY M. You lack the season of all natures, sleep.°

MACB. Come, we'll to sleep. My strange and self-
abuse°   142
Is the initiate fear° that wants hard use.
We are yet but young in deed.   [*Exeunt.*]

---

112. **special wonder:** universal astonishment. Macbeth cannot understand why the others are seemingly so calm. 113. **owe:** own, possess. 119. **Stand . . . going:** do not wait to take leave in order of rank. The disorderly end to the banquet contrasts with its formal beginning (l. 1). 124. **Augurs:** auguries, omens. **understood relations:** the relation between the omen and what it signifies. 125. **maggot pies . . . choughs:** magpies and jackdaws, birds which were regarded as having mystic qualities. 127. **at odds:** striving. 132. **feed:** in my pay as a spy. 133. **betimes:** in good time. 134. **bent:** eager — like a taut bowstring. 140. **scanned:** examined. 141. **the . . . sleep:** sleep, which (like salt) gives seasoning to keep nature fresh. 142. **self-abuse:** self-deception. 143. **initiate fear:** a novice's fear; i.e., when I have more experience in murder I shall not be troubled with apparitions.

---

76. **Ere . . . weal:** before humane laws made the state civilized. 81. **twenty . . . crowns:** with twenty deadly wounds on their heads. 93. **Avaunt:** be gone. 95. **speculation:** power of sight. 97. **custom:** common occurrence. 101. **Hyrcan:** from Hyrcania, south of the Caspian Sea, where according to Pliny's *Natural History* tigers roamed. 102. **that:** i.e., the specter of Banquo. 104. **desert:** i.e., a place where neither of us could escape. 105–06. **If . . . girl:** i.e., if then I live trembling (show myself a coward), proclaim that I am the baby of a young girl. 109. **displaced:** upset. 110. **admired:** to be wondered at. 111. **overcome:** come over, overshadow.

SCENE V. *A heath*.

[*Thunder. Enter the* THREE WITCHES, *meeting*
HECATE.°]

1. WITCH. Why, how now, Hecate! You look
angerly.°
HEC. Have I not reason, beldams° as you are,
Saucy and overbold? How did you dare
To trade and traffic with Macbeth
In riddles and affairs of death,　　　　　　　5
And I, the mistress of your charms,
The close contriver° of all harms,
Was never called to bear my part,
Or show the glory of our art?
And, which is worse, all you have done　　　10
Hath been but for a wayward° son,
Spiteful and wrathful, who, as others do,
Loves for his own ends, not for you.
But make amends now. Get you gone,
And at the pit of Acheron°　　　　　　　　15
Meet me i' the morning. Thither he
Will come to know his destiny.
Your vessels and your spells provide,
Your charms and everything beside.
I am for the air, this night I'll spend　　　20
Unto a dismal and a fatal end.
Great business must be wrought ere noon.
Upon the corner of the moon
There hangs a vaporous drop profound.
I'll catch it ere it come to ground,　　　　25
And that distilled by magic sleights°
Shall raise such artificial sprites°
As by the strength of their illusion
Shall draw him on to his confusion.°
He shall spurn fate, scorn death, and bear　30
His hopes 'bove wisdom, grace, and fear.
And you all know security°
Is mortals' chiefest enemy.
　　　　　[*Music and a song within:* " Come away,°
　　　　　　　　　　　come away " etc.]
Hark! I am called. My little spirit, see,　　34
Sits in a foggy cloud and stays for me.　[*Exit.*]
1. WITCH. Come, let's make haste, she'll soon be
back again.　　　　　　　　　　[*Exeunt.*]

SCENE VI. *Forres. The palace*.

[*Enter* LENNOX *and another* LORD.]
LEN. My former speeches have but hit your
thoughts,

Which can interpret farther.° Only I say
Things have been strangely borne.° The gracious
　　Duncan
Was pitied of° Macbeth. Marry,° he was dead.
And the right-valiant Banquo walked too late,　5
Whom, you may say, if 't please you, Fleance killed,
For Fleance fled. Men must not walk too late.
Who cannot want° the thought how monstrous
It was for Malcolm and for Donalbain
To kill their gracious father? Damnèd fact!　10
How it did grieve Macbeth! Did he not straight,
In pious rage, the two delinquents tear
That were the slaves of drink and thralls° of sleep?
Was not that nobly done? Aye, and wisely too,
For 'twould have angered any heart alive　15
To hear the men deny 't. So that I say
He has borne all things well. And I do think
That had he Duncan's sons under his key —
As, an 't° please Heaven, he shall not — they should
　　find
What 'twere to kill a father. So should Fleance.　20
But, peace! For from broad° words, and 'cause he
　　failed
His presence° at the tyrant's feast, I hear
Macduff lives in disgrace. Sir, can you tell
Where he bestows himself?
　　LORD.　　　　　　　　The son of Duncan,
From whom this tyrant holds the due of birth,　25
Lives in the English Court, and is received
Of the most pious Edward° with such grace
That the malevolence of fortune nothing
Takes from his high respect.° Thither Macduff
Is gone to pray the holy King, upon his aid　30
To wake Northumberland and warlike Siward,
That by the help of these, with Him above
To ratify the work, we may again
Give to our tables meat, sleep to our nights,
Free from our feasts and banquets bloody knives,
Do faithful homage and receive free honors° —　36
All which we pine for now. And this report
Hath so exasperate the King that he
Prepares for some attempt of war.
　　LEN.　　　　　　　　　Sent he to Macduff?
　　LORD. He did. And with an absolute " Sir, not I,"
The cloudy° messenger turns me his back,　41
And hums, as who should say " You'll rue the time
That clogs° me with this answer."
　　LEN.　　　　　　　And that well might
Advise him to a caution, to hold what distance

Sc. v: s.d., Hecate: goddess of witchcraft. See *Macb* Intro.
p. 828a.　1. angerly: angrily.　2. beldams: hags.　7. close con-
triver: secret inventor.　11. wayward: perverse.　15. Acheron:
Hell.　26. sleights: devices.　27. artificial sprites: spirits
created by magic art.　29. confusion: destruction.　32. se-
curity: false sense of safety.　33. s.d., Come away: The words
of this song and of "Black Spirits" (IV.i.43) occur in a play
called *The Witch* by Thomas Middleton.

Sc. vi: 1–2. hit . . . farther: given you matter from which to
draw conclusions.　3. borne: managed.　4. of: by. Marry:
Mary, by the Virgin.　8. want: be without.　13. thralls: slaves.
19. an't: if it.　21. broad: too free.　21–22. failed . . . presence:
failed to appear.　27. most . . . Edward: King Edward the
Confessor (died 1066), regarded as a most saintly person.
28–29. malevolence . . . respect: in spite of his misfortunes he is
regarded with the highest respect.　36. free honors: honors be-
stowed on free men, and not as a reward for crimes.　41. cloudy:
surly.　43. clogs: obstructs.

His wisdom can provide. Some holy angel   45
Fly to the Court of England and unfold
His message ere he come, that a swift blessing
May soon return to this our suffering country
Under a hand accursed!

LORD.   I'll send my prayers with him.   [*Exeunt.*]

Act IV

SCENE I.° *A cavern. In the middle, a boiling
caldron.*

[*Thunder. Enter the* THREE WITCHES.]

1. WITCH. Thrice the brinded° cat hath mewed.
2. WITCH. Thrice and once the hedgepig° whined.
3. WITCH. Harpier° cries " 'Tis time, 'tis time."
1. WITCH. Round about the caldron go.
In the poisoned entrails throw.   5
Toad, that under cold stone
Days and nights has thirty-one
Sweltered° venom sleeping got,
Boil thou first i' the charmèd pot.

ALL.   Double, double toil and trouble,   10
Fire burn and caldron bubble.

2. WITCH. Fillet of a fenny° snake,
In the caldron boil and bake.
Eye of newt and toe of frog,
Wool of bat and tongue of dog,   15
Adder's fork° and blindworm's sting,°
Lizard's leg and howlet's° wing,
For a charm of powerful trouble,
Like a Hell broth boil and bubble.

ALL.   Double, double toil and trouble,   20
Fire burn and caldron bubble.

3. WITCH. Scale of dragon, tooth of wolf,
Witches' mummy,° maw and gulf°
Of the ravined° salt-sea shark,
Root of hemlock digged i' the dark,   25
Liver of blaspheming Jew,
Gall of goat and slips of yew
Slivered° in the moon's eclipse,
Nose of Turk and Tartar's lips,
Finger of birth-strangled babe   30
Ditch-delivered° by a drab,

Make the gruel thick and slab.°
Add thereto a tiger's chaudron,°
For the ingredients of our caldron.

ALL.   Double, double toil and trouble,   35
Fire burn and caldron bubble.

2. WITCH. Cool it with a baboon's blood,
Then the charm is firm and good.

[*Enter* HECATE *to the other* THREE WITCHES.]

HEC.   Oh, well done! I commend your pains,
And everyone shall share i' the gains.   40
And now about the caldron sing
Like elves and fairies in a ring,
Enchanting all that you put in.

[*Music and a song:* " Black Spirits,"° etc.
HECATE *retires.*]

2. WITCH. By the pricking of my thumbs,
Something wicked this way comes.   45
Open, locks,
Whoever knocks!

[*Enter* MACBETH.]

MACB.   How now, you secret, black, and midnight
hags!
What is 't you do?

ALL.   A deed without a name.

MACB.   I conjure you, by that which you profess,°
Howe'er you come to know it, answer me.   51
Though you untie the winds° and let them fight
Against the churches; though the yesty° waves
Confound and swallow navigation up;
Though bladed° corn be lodged° and trees blown
down;   55
Though castles topple on their warders' heads;
Though palaces and pyramids do slope
Their heads to their foundations; though the treas-
ure
Of nature's germens° tumble all together,
Even till destruction sicken — answer me   60
To what I ask you.

1. WITCH.   Speak.

2. WITCH.   Demand.

3. WITCH.   We'll answer.

1. WITCH. Say, if thou'dst rather hear it from our
mouths,
Or from our masters?

MACB.   Call 'em, let me see 'em.

1. WITCH. Pour in sow's blood that hath eaten
Her nine farrow,° grease that's sweaten   65
From the murderer's gibbet° throw
Into the flame.

ALL.   Come, high or low,

Act IV, Sc. i: See *Macb* Intro. p. 828a.   **1. brinded:** brin-
dled, striped.   **2. hedgepig:** hedgehog.   **3. Harpier:** the name
of a familiar spirit.   **8. Sweltered:** sweated out.   **12. fenny:**
from a fen.   **16. fork:** tongue. **blindworm's sting:** the blindworm
is a small snakelike legless lizard; it does not, in fact, have
a sting.   **17. howlet:** small owl.   **23. mummy:** dried corpse.
Mummy from Egypt was formerly considered a potent drug, and
regularly stocked by old-time druggists. **maw . . . gulf:** belly
and gullet.   **24. ravined:** ravenous.   **28. Slivered:** sliced.
31. Ditch-delivered: born in a ditch.

32. slab: like thick mud.   **33. chaudron:** entrails.   **43. s.d.,
Black Spirits:** See III.v.33,n.   **50. profess:** i.e., the art of witch-
craft.   **52. untie . . . winds:** Witches were reputed to be
able to control the winds.   **53. yesty:** foaming.   **55. bladed:** in
the ear. **lodged:** laid flat.   **59. nature's germens:** the seeds
of matter, all living things.   **65. farrow:** young.   **66. gibbet:**
gallows on which the bodies of executed criminals were hung as a
warning.

Thyself and office deftly show!

[*Thunder.* FIRST APPARITION: *an armed Head.*]

MACB. Tell me, thou unknown power——

1. WITCH.   He knows thy thought.
Hear his speech, but say thou naught.   70

1. APP. Macbeth! Macbeth! Macbeth! Beware Macduff,
Beware the Thane of Fife. Dismiss me. Enough.

[*Descends.*]

MACB. Whate'er thou art, for thy good caution thanks.
Thou hast harped° my fear aright. But one word more——

1. WITCH. He will not be commanded. Here's another,   75
More potent than the first.

[*Thunder.* SECOND APPARITION: *a bloody Child.*]

2. APP. Macbeth! Macbeth! Macbeth!

MACB. Had I three ears, I'd hear thee.

2. APP. Be bloody, bold, and resolute, laugh to scorn
'The power of man, for none of woman born   80
Shall harm Macbeth.   [*Descends.*]

MACB. Then live, Macduff. What need I fear of thee?
But yet I'll make assurance double sure,
And take a bond of fate.° Thou shalt not live,
That I may tell pale-hearted fear it lies,   85
And sleep in spite of thunder.

[*Thunder.* THIRD APPARITION: *a Child crowned, with a tree in his hand.*]

What is this
That rises like the issue of a king,
And wears upon his baby brow the round
And top of sovereignty?°

ALL.   Listen, but speak not to 't.

3. APP. Be lion-mettled, proud, and take no care
Who chafes, who frets, or where conspirers are.   91
Macbeth shall never vanquished be until
Great Birnam Wood to high Dunsinane Hill
Shall come against him.   [*Descends.*]

MACB.   That will never be.
Who can impress° the forest, bid the tree   95
Unfix his earthbound root? Sweet bodements!°
Good!
Rebellion's head, rise never till the wood
Of Birnam rise, and our high-placed Macbeth
Shall live the lease of nature,° pay his breath
To time and mortal custom. Yet my heart   100
Throbs to know one thing. Tell me, if your art
Can tell so much. Shall Banquo's issue ever
Reign in this kingdom?

ALL.   Seek to know no more.

---

74. harped: hit upon.   84. bond of fate: i.e., to force fate to keep the agreement, he will kill Macduff.   88–89. round . . . sovereignty: a crown.   95. impress: conscript.   96. bodements: prophecies.   99. lease of nature: the natural length of life. Cf. III.ii.38.

MACB. I will be satisfied. Deny me this,
And an eternal curse fall on you! Let me know.   105
Why sinks that caldron? And what noise is this?

[*Hautboys.*]

1. WITCH. Show!
2. WITCH. Show!
3. WITCH. Show!
ALL. Show his eyes, and grieve his heart.   110
Come like shadows, so depart!

[*A show of eight* KINGS,° *the last with a glass*° *in his hand,* BANQUO'S GHOST *following.*]

MACB. Thou art too like the spirit of Banquo. Down!
Thy crown does sear mine eyeballs. And thy hair,
Thou other gold-bound brow, is like the first.
A third is like the former. Filthy hags!   115
Why do you show me this? A fourth! Start, eyes!
What, will the line stretch out to the crack of doom?
Another yet! A seventh! I'll see no more.
And yet the eighth appears, who bears a glass
Which shows me many more, and some I see   120
That twofold balls and treble scepters° carry.
Horrible sight! Now I see 'tis true,
For the blood-boltered° Banquo smiles upon me,
And points at them for his. What, is this so?

1. WITCH. Aye, sir, all this is so. But why   125
Stands Macbeth thus amazedly?
Come, Sisters, cheer we up his sprites,°
And show the best of our delights.
I'll charm the air to give a sound
While you perform your antic round,°   130
That this great King may kindly say
Our duties did his welcome pay.

[*Music. The* WITCHES *dance, and then vanish, with* HECATE.]

MACB. Where are they? Gone? Let this pernicious hour
Stand aye accursèd in the calendar!
Come in, without there!

[*Enter* LENNOX.]

LEN.   What's your Grace's will?   135

MACB. Saw you the weird sisters?

LEN.   No, my lord.

MACB. Came they not by you?

LEN.   No indeed, my lord.

MACB. Infected be the air whereon they ride,
And damned all those that trust them! I did hear
The galloping of horse. Who was 't came by?   140

LEN. 'Tis two or three, my lord, that bring you word
Macduff is fled to England.

---

111. s.d., A . . . kings: a dumb show, figures passing across the back of the stage in silent action. glass: mirror.   121. twofold . . . scepters: i.e., the insignia of the Kingdoms of England, Scotland, and Ireland united in 1603 when King James VI of Scotland (Banquo's descendant) became also James I of England.   123. blood-boltered: with his hair matted with blood.   127. sprites: spirits.   130. antic round: fantastic dance.

MACB.   Fled to England!
LEN. Aye, my good lord.
MACB. [*Aside*] Time, thou anticipatest my dread
   exploits.
The flighty purpose never is o'ertook   145
Unless the deed go with it.° From this moment
The very firstlings° of my heart shall be
The firstlings of my hand. And even now,
To crown my thoughts with acts, be it thought and
   done.
The castle of Macduff I will surprise,   150
Seize upon Fife, give to the edge o' the sword
His wife, his babes, and all unfortunate souls
That trace him in his line.° No boasting like a fool,
This deed I'll do before this purpose cool.   154
But no more sights! — Where are these gentlemen?
Come, bring me where they are.   [*Exeunt.*]

SCENE II. *Fife*. MACDUFF S *castle*.

[*Enter* LADY MACDUFF, *her* SON, *and* ROSS.]
L. MACD. What had he done, to make him fly the
   land?
ROSS. You must have patience, madam.
L. MACD.   He had none.
His flight was madness. When our actions do not,
Our fears do make us traitors.
ROSS.   You know not
Whether it was his wisdom or his fear.   5
L. MACD. Wisdom! To leave his wife, to leave his
   babes,
His mansion and his titles,° in a place
From whence himself does fly? He loves us not,
He wants the natural touch. For the poor wren,
The most diminutive of birds, will fight,   10
Her young ones in her nest, against the owl.
All is the fear and nothing is the love,
As little is the wisdom, where the flight
So runs against all reason.
ROSS.   My dearest coz,°
I pray you school° yourself. But, for your husband,
He is noble, wise, judicious, and best knows   16
The fits o' the season.° I dare not speak much fur-
   ther.
But cruel are the times, when we are traitors
And do not know ourselves, when we hold rumor
From what we fear, yet know not what we fear,   20
But float upon a wild and violent sea
Each way and move.° I take my leave of you.

Shall not be long but I'll be here again.
Things at the worst will cease, or else climb upward
To what they were before. My pretty cousin,   25
Blessing upon you!
L. MACD. Fathered he is, and yet he's fatherless.
ROSS. I am so much a fool, should I stay longer,
It would be my disgrace and your discomfort.
I take my leave at once.   [*Exit.*]
L. MACD.   Sirrah, your father's dead.   30
And what will you do now? How will you live?
SON. As birds do, Mother.
L. MACD.   What, with worms and flies?
SON. With what I get, I mean, and so do they.
L. MACD. Poor bird! Thou'dst never fear the net
   nor lime,°
The pitfall nor the gin.°   35
SON. Why should I, Mother? Poor birds they are
   not set for.°
My father is not dead, for all your saying.
L. MACD. Yes, he is dead. How wilt thou do for a
   father?
SON. Nay, how will you do for a husband?
L. MACD. Why, I can buy me twenty at any
   market.
SON. Then you'll buy 'em to sell again.   40
L. MACD. Thou speak'st with all thy wit, and yet,
   i' faith,
With wit enough for thee.
SON. Was my father a traitor, Mother?
L. MACD. Aye, that he was.
SON. What is a traitor?   45
L. MACD. Why, one that swears and lies.
SON. And be all traitors that do so?
L. MACD. Every one that does so is a traitor, and
   must be hanged.   50
SON. And must they all be hanged that swear and
   lie?
L. MACD. Every one.
SON. Who must hang them?
L. MACD. Why, the honest men.   55
SON. Then the liars and swearers are fools, for
there are liars and swearers enow to beat the honest
men and hang up them.
L. MACD. Now, God help thee, poor monkey! But
how wilt thou do for a father?   60
SON. If he were dead, you'd weep for him. If you
would not, it were a good sign that I should quickly
have a new father.
L. MACD. Poor prattler, how thou talk'st!
     [*Enter a* MESSENGER.]
MESS. Bless you, fair dame! I am not to you
   known,   65
Though in your state of honor I am perfect.°
I doubt° some danger does approach you nearly.

145–46. The . . . it: the plan is never fulfilled unless carried
out at once.   147. firstlings: lit., first fruits.   153. trace . . .
line: i.e., are related to him.
   Sc. ii: 7. titles: possessions; lit., that to which he has a
title.   14. coz: cousin.   15. school: discipline.   17. fits . . .
season: sudden changes of the times.   21–22. But . . . move:
like a ship, powerless in a tempest, carried hither and thither.

34. lime: birdlime.   35. gin: snare.   36. Poor . . . for: no one
sets a trap for a poor bird.   66. state . . . perfect: I well know
you to be an honorable person.   67. doubt: suspect.

If you will take a homely° man's advice,
Be not found here. Hence, with your little ones.
To fright you thus, methinks I am too savage,   70
To do worse to you were fell° cruelty,
Which is too nigh your person. Heaven preserve
   you!
I dare abide no longer.   [*Exit.*]
  L. MACD.   Whither should I fly?
I have done no harm. But I remember now
I am in this earthly world, where to do harm   75
Is often laudable, to do good sometime
Accounted dangerous folly. Why, then, alas,
Do I put up that womanly defense,
To say I have done no harm? — What are these
   faces?
           [*Enter* MURDERERS.]
  1. MUR. Where is your husband?   80
  L. MACD. I hope, in no place so unsanctified
Where such as thou mayst find him.
  1. MUR.   He's a traitor.
  SON. Thou liest, thou shag-eared° villain!
  1. MUR.   What, you egg!° [*Stabbing him.*]
Young fry° of treachery!
  SON.   He has killed me, Mother. 84
Run away, I pray you!   [*Dies.*]
      [*Exit* LADY MACDUFF, *crying* " Murder! "
        Exeunt MURDERERS, *following her.*]

SCENE III.° *England. Before the* KING's
          palace.

      [*Enter* MALCOLM *and* MACDUFF.]
  MAL. Let us seek out some desolate shade, and
   there
Weep our sad bosoms empty.
  MACD.   Let us rather
Hold fast the mortal° sword, and like good men
Bestride our downfall'n birthdom.° Each new morn
New widows howl, new orphans cry, new sorrows
Strike Heaven on the face, that it resounds   6
As if it felt with Scotland and yelled out
Like syllable of dolor.°
  MAL.   What I believe, I'll wail,
What know, believe. And what I can redress,
As I shall find the time to friend,° I will.   10
What you have spoke, it may be so perchance.
This tyrant, whose sole name° blisters our tongues,
Was once thought honest. You have loved him well,

He hath not touched you yet. I am young, but
  something
You may deserve of him through me, and wisdom
To offer up a weak, poor, innocent lamb   16
To appease an angry god.
  MACD. I am not treacherous.
  MAL.   But Macbeth is.
A good and virtuous nature may recoil
In an imperial charge.° But I shall crave your par-
  don.   20
That which you are, my thoughts cannot transpose.°
Angels are bright still, though the brightest fell.
Though all things foul would wear the brows of
  grace,
Yet grace must still look so.°
  MACD.   I have lost my hopes.
  MAL. Perchance even there where I did find my
  doubts.   25
Why in that rawness° left you wife and child,
Those precious motives, those strong knots of love,
Without leave-taking? I pray you
Let not my jealousies be your dishonors,   29
But mine own safeties.° You may be rightly just,
Whatever I shall think.
  MACD.   Bleed, bleed, poor country.
Great tyranny, lay thou thy basis sure,
For goodness dare not check thee. Wear thou thy
  wrongs,
The title is affeered.° Fare thee well, lord.
I would not be the villain that thou think'st   35
For the whole space that's in the tyrant's grasp
And the rich East to boot.
  MAL.   Be not offended.
I speak not as in absolute fear of you.
I think our country sinks beneath the yoke.
It weeps, it bleeds, and each new day a gash   40
Is added to her wounds. I think withal
There would be hands uplifted in my right,
And here from gracious England have I offer
Of goodly thousands. But for all this,
When I shall tread upon the tyrant's head,   45
Or wear it on my sword, yet my poor country
Shall have more vices than it had before,
More suffer and more sundry ways than ever,
By him that shall succeed.
  MACD.   What should he be?
  MAL. It is myself I mean, in whom I know   50
All the particulars of vice so grafted°
That when they shall be opened, black Macbeth
Will seem as pure as snow, and the poor state
Esteem him as a lamb, being compared

---

68. homely: simple, plain.   71. fell: fierce.   83. shag-eared:
hairy-eared. egg: i.e., unhatched traitor.   84. fry: spawn.
  Sc. iii: The conversation between Malcolm and Macduff
comes from the *Chronicle.*   3. mortal: deadly.   4. birthdom:
native land.   6–8. that . . . dolor: that even the heavens re-
sound as if they echoed the lamentations of Scotland.   10. time
to friend: the time to be friendly.   12. sole name: very name
by itself.

19–20. A . . . charge: even a good man may degenerate and do a
wicked deed if ordered by a king.   21. transpose: alter.   24. look
so: i.e., like itself, gracious.   26. rawness: unprotected state.
29–30. Let . . . safeties: i.e., I am suspicious not because I
would dishonor you but would look after my own safety.   34. title
is affeered: legal right is confirmed.   51. grafted: engrafted, in-
grown.

With my confineless harms.°

MACD.   Not in the legions   55
Of horrid Hell can come a devil more damned
In evils to top Macbeth.

MAL.   I grant him bloody,
Luxurious,° avaricious, false, deceitful,
Sudden, malicious, smacking of every sin
That has a name. But there's no bottom, none,   60
In my voluptuousness.° Your wives, your daughters,
Your matrons and your maids, could not fill up
The cistern of my lust, and my desire
All continent impediments would o'erbear°
That did oppose my will. Better Macbeth   65
Than such a one to reign.

MACD.   Boundless intemperance
In nature is a tyranny. It hath been
The untimely emptying of the happy throne,
And fall of many kings. But fear not yet
To take upon you what is yours. You may   70
Convey your pleasures in a spacious plenty,°
And yet seem cold,° the time° you may so hood-
     wink.
We have willing dames enough. There cannot be
That vulture in you to devour so many
As will to greatness dedicate themselves,   75
Finding it so inclined.°

MAL.   With this there grows
In my most ill-composed affection such
A stanchless° avarice that, were I King,
I should cut off the nobles for their lands,
Desire his jewels and this other's house.   80
And my more-having would be as a sauce
To make me hunger more, that I should forge
Quarrels unjust against the good and loyal,
Destroying them for wealth.

MACD.   This avarice
Sticks deeper, grows with more pernicious root   85
Than summer-seeming° lust, and it hath been
The sword of° our slain kings. Yet do not fear.
Scotland hath foisons° to fill up your will
Of your mere own.° All these are portable,°
With other graces weighed.°   90

MAL. But I have none. The king-becoming
     graces —
As justice, verity, temperance, stableness,°
Bounty, perseverance, mercy, lowliness,

Devotion, patience, courage, fortitude —
I have no relish of° them, but abound   95
In the division of each several crime,°
Acting it many ways. Nay, had I power, I should
Pour the sweet milk of concord into Hell,
Uproar the universal peace, confound
All unity on earth.

MACD.   Oh, Scotland, Scotland!   100

MAL. If such a one be fit to govern, speak.
I am as I have spoken.

MACD.   Fit to govern!
No, not to live. O nation miserable!
With an untitled° tyrant bloody-sceptered,
When shalt thou see thy wholesome days again,
Since that the truest issue of thy throne°   106
By his own interdiction° stands accursed,
And does blaspheme his breed? Thy royal father
Was a most sainted King. The Queen that bore thee,
Oftener upon her knees than on her feet,   110
Died every day she lived.° Fare thee well!
These evils thou repeat'st upon thyself
Have banished me from Scotland. O my breast,
Thy hope ends here!

MAL.   Macduff, this noble passion,°
Child of integrity, hath from my soul   115
Wiped the black scruples, reconciled my thoughts
To thy good truth and honor. Devilish Macbeth
By many of these trains° hath sought to win me
Into his power, and modest wisdom plucks me
From overcredulous haste. But God above   120
Deal between thee and me! For even now
I put myself to thy direction, and
Unspeak mine own detraction, here abjure
The taints and blames I laid upon myself,
For strangers to my nature. I am yet   125
Unknown to woman, never was forsworn,°
Scarcely have coveted what was mine own,
At no time broke my faith, would not betray
The Devil to his fellow, and delight
No less in truth than life. My first false speaking
Was this upon myself. What I am truly   131
Is thine and my poor country's to command,
Whither indeed, before thy here-approach,
Old Siward, with ten thousand warlike men,
Already at a point,° was setting forth.   135
Now we'll together, and the chance of goodness
Be like our warranted quarrel! Why are you silent?

MACD. Such welcome and unwelcome things at
     once

55. confineless harms: the uncontrollable evil which I shall commit.   58. Luxurious: lustful.   61. voluptuousness: lust.   64. All . . . o'erbear: would overcome all restraining barriers.   71. Convey . . . plenty: find plenty of room in which to indulge your pleasures secretly.   72. cold: chaste. time: i.e., the world.   73–76. There . . . inclined: however greedy you are, there will be as many women eager to satisfy one in your great position.   78. stanchless: insatiable.   86. summer-seeming: which lasts like summer; i.e., only for a season.   87. sword of: which has killed.   88. foisons: plenty.   89. mere own: absolute property. portable: endurable.   90. With . . . weighed: so long as there are good qualities to counterbalance them.   92. stableness: constancy.

95. relish of: taste for.   96. division . . . crime: in every part of each particular kind of crime.   104. untitled: having no legal right to be King.   106. issue . . . throne: child of your King.   107. interdiction: exclusion.   111. Died . . . lived: i.e., lived continually in a state of grace. The phrase comes from I Corinthians 15:31: "I protest by your rejoicing which I have in Christ Jesus our Lord, I die daily."   114. Passion: emotion.   118. trains: enticements.   126. was forsworn: broke my oath.   135. at a point: ready for action.

'Tis hard to reconcile.

[*Enter a* DOCTOR.]

MAL. Well, more anon. Comes the King forth, I
pray you?   140

DOCT. Aye, sir, there are a crew of wretched souls
That stay his cure.° Their malady convinces
The great assay of art,° but at his touch,
Such sanctity hath Heaven given his hand,   144
They presently° amend.

MAL.   I thank you, Doctor. [*Exit* DOCTOR.]

MACD. What's the disease he means?

MAL.   'Tis called the Evil.°
A most miraculous work in this good King,
Which often, since my here-remain in England,
I have seen him do. How he solicits Heaven,
Himself best knows. But strangely visited people,
All swoln° and ulcerous, pitiful to the eye,   151
The mere° despair of surgery, he cures,
Hanging a golden stamp° about their necks,
Put on with holy prayers. And 'tis spoken,
To the succeeding royalty he leaves   155
The healing benediction. With this strange virtue
He hath a heavenly gift of prophecy,
And sundry blessings hang about his throne
That speak him full of grace.

[*Enter* ROSS.]

MACD.   See, who comes here?   159

MAL. My countryman, but yet I know him not.

MACD. My ever gentle° cousin, welcome hither.

MAL. I know him now. Good God, betimes° re-
move
The means that makes us strangers!

ROSS.   Sir, amen.

MACD. Stands Scotland where it did?

ROSS.   Alas, poor country!
Almost afraid to know itself! It cannot   165
Be called our mother, but our grave. Where nothing
But who knows nothing is once seen to smile;
Where sighs and groans and shrieks that rend the
air
Are made, not marked; where violent sorrow seems
A modern ecstasy.° The dead man's knell   170
Is there scarce asked for who, and good men's lives
Expire before the flowers in their caps,
Dying or ere they sicken.

MACD.   Oh, relation
Too nice,° and yet too true!

MAL.   What's the newest grief?

ROSS. That of an hour's age doth hiss the speaker.°
Each minute teems° a new one.

MACD.   How does my wife?   176

ROSS. Why, well.

MACD.   And all my children?

ROSS.   Well too.

MACD. The tyrant has not battered at their peace?

ROSS. No, they were well at peace when I did
leave 'em.

MACD. Be not a niggard° of your speech. How
goes 't?   180

ROSS. When I came hither to transport the tidings,
Which I have heavily borne, there ran a rumor
Of many worthy fellows that were out,°
Which was to my belief witnessed° the rather,
For that I saw the tyrant's power° afoot.   185
Now is the time of help, your eye in Scotland
Would create soldiers, make our women fight,
To doff° their dire distresses.

MAL.   Be 't their comfort
We are coming thither. Gracious England hath
Lent us good Siward and ten thousand men —   190
An older and a better soldier none
That Christendom gives out.

ROSS.   Would I could answer
This comfort with the like! But I have words
That would be howled out in the desert air,
Where hearing should not latch° them.

MACD.   What concern they?   195
The general cause? Or is it a fee grief
Due to some single breast?°

ROSS.   No mind that's honest
But in it shares some woe, though the main part
Pertains to you alone.

MACD.   If it be mine,
Keep it not from me, quickly let me have it.   200

ROSS. Let not your ears despise my tongue forever,
Which shall possess them with the heaviest sound
That ever yet they heard.

MACD.   Hum! I guess at it.

ROSS. Your castle is surprised, your wife and babes
Savagely slaughtered. To relate the manner   205
Were, on the quarry° of these murdered deer,
To add the death of you.

MAL.   Merciful Heaven!
What, man! Ne'er pull your hat upon your brows.°
Give sorrow words. The grief that does not speak
Whispers the o'erfraught° heart and bids it break.

---

142. stay . . . cure: wait for him to heal them.   142–43. con-
vinces . . . art: defeats the attempts of the medical art.
145. presently: immediately.   146. the Evil: scrofula, a skin
disease. Holinshed notes that King Edward the Confessor "used
to help those that were vexed with the disease commonly called
the King's Evil and left that virtue as it was a portion of in-
heritance unto his successors." The reference here is dragged in as
a compliment to King James I who was at first unwilling to con-
tinue the practice of touching sufferers until urged by his Eng-
lish Ministers.   151. swoln: swollen.   152. mere: utter, sheer.
153. stamp: medal.   161. gentle: noble.   162. betimes: soon.
170. modern ecstasy: slight mental disturbance.   174. nice: exact.

175. That . . . speaker: i.e., there are so many sorrows that a
report only one hour old is hissed as stale news.   176. teems:
gives birth to.   180. niggard: sparing.   183. out: i.e., in re-
bellion.   184. witnessed: confirmed.   185. power: army.
188. doff: put off.   195. latch: catch.   196–97. fee . . . breast:
a grief which belongs to a single owner.   206. quarry: heap of
slain deer after a hunt. Cf. *Haml.*, V.ii.375.   208. What . . .
brows: one of many instances when the action is described in the
dialogue.   210. o'erfraught: overladen.

MACD. My children too?

ROSS.   Wife, children, servants, all 211
That could be found.

MACD.   And I must be from thence!
My wife killed too?

ROSS.   I have said.

MAL.   Be comforted.
Let's make us medicines of our great revenge,
To cure this deadly grief.   215

MACD. He has no children.° All my pretty ones?
Did you say all? O Hellkite! All?
What, all my pretty chickens and their dam
At one fell swoop?

MAL. Dispute° it like a man.

MACD.   I shall do so, 220
But I must also feel it as a man.
I cannot but remember such things were,
That were most precious to me. Did Heaven look on
And would not take their part? Sinful Macduff,
They were all struck for thee! Naught° that I am,
Not for their own demerits, but for mine, 226
Fell slaughter on their souls. Heaven rest them now!

MAL. Be this the whetstone of your sword. Let
    grief
Convert to anger, blunt not the heart, enrage it.

MACD. Oh, I could play the woman with mine
    eyes,   230
And braggart with my tongue! But, gentle Heavens,
Cut short all intermission.° Front to front°
Bring thou this fiend of Scotland and myself,
Within my sword's length set him. If he 'scape,
Heaven forgive him too!

MAL.   This tune goes manly. 235
Come, go we to the King. Our power is ready,
Our lack is nothing but our leave.° Macbeth
Is ripe for shaking, and the powers above
Put on their instruments. Receive what cheer you
    may.
The night is long that never finds the day. 240
                    [*Exeunt.*]

Act V

SCENE I. *Dunsinane. Anteroom in the castle.*

[*Enter a* DOCTOR OF PHYSIC *and a*
WAITING GENTLEWOMAN.]

DOCT. I have two nights watched with you, but
can perceive no truth in your report. When was it
she last walked?   3

GEN. Since His Majesty went into the field,° I
have seen her rise from her bed, throw her night-
gown upon her, unlock her closet,° take forth paper,
fold it, write upon 't, read it, afterward seal it, and
again return to bed, yet all this while in a most fast
sleep.   9

DOCT. A great perturbation in nature, to receive at
once the benefit of sleep and do the effects of watch-
ing! In this slumbery agitation, besides her walking
and other actual performances, what, at any time,
have you heard her say?   15

GEN. That, sir, which I will not report after her.

DOCT. You may to me, and 'tis most meet you
should.

GEN. Neither to you nor anyone, having no wit-
ness to confirm my speech. [*Enter* LADY MAC- 21
BETH, *with a taper.*°] Lo you, here she comes! This
is her very guise,° and, upon my life, fast asleep.
Observe her. Stand close.°

DOCT. How came she by that light? 25

GEN. Why, it stood by her. She has light by her
continually, 'tis her command.

DOCT. You see, her eyes are open.

GEN. Aye, but their sense is shut.

DOCT. What is it she does now? Look how she
rubs her hands.   31

GEN. It is an accustomed action with her to seem
thus washing her hands. I have known her continue
in this a quarter of an hour.

LADY M. Yet here's a spot.   35

DOCT. Hark! She speaks. I will set down what
comes from her, to satisfy my remembrance the more
strongly.

LADY M. Out, damned spot! Out, I say! One, two
— why, then 'tis time to do 't. Hell is murky. 40
Fie, my lord, fie! A soldier, and afeard? What need
we fear who knows it, when none can call our power
to account? Yet who would have thought the old
man to have had so much blood in him? 45

DOCT. Do you mark that?

LADY M. The Thane of Fife had a wife. Where is
she now? What, will these hands ne'er be clean?°
No more o' that, my lord, no more o' that. You mar
all with this starting.   50

DOCT. Go to, go to. You have known what you
should not.

GEN. She has spoke what she should not, I am
sure of that. Heaven knows what she has known.

LADY M. Here's the smell of the blood still. All the
perfumes of Arabia will not sweeten this little hand.
Oh, oh, oh!

DOCT. What a sigh is there! The heart is sorely
charged.°   60

216. He . . . children: either Malcolm has no children and so can-
not truly sympathize; or — more probably — Macbeth has no
children and so Macduff can never exact a full vengeance.
220. Dispute: strive against. 225. Naught: worthless. 232. in-
termission: interval between actions. Front to front: face to face.
237. leave: permission to go.

Act V, Sc. i: 4. went . . . field: set out with his army.
6. closet: chest containing private papers. 22. s.d., taper:
candle. 23. guise: custom — as described in ll. 4–9. 24. close:
hidden. 48. these . . . clean: Cf. II.ii.67. 60. charged:
burdened.

GEN. I would not have such a heart in my bosom
for the dignity of the whole body.

DOCT. Well, well, well ——

GEN. Pray God it be, sir.   64

DOCT. This disease is beyond my practice. Yet I
have known those which have walked in their sleep
who have died holily in their beds.

LADY M. Wash your hands, put on your night-
gown, look not so pale. I tell you yet again, Banquo's
buried, he cannot come out on 's grave.   71

DOCT. Even so?

LADY M. To bed, to bed, there's knocking at the
gate. Come, come, come, come, give me your hand.
What's done cannot be undone. To bed, to bed,   75
to bed.   [*Exit.*]

DOCT. Will she go now to bed?

GEN. Directly.

DOCT. Foul whisperings are abroad. Unnatural
    deeds

Do breed unnatural troubles. Infected minds   80
To their deaf pillows will discharge their secrets.
More needs she the divine than the physician.
God, God forgive us all! Look after her,
Remove from her the means of all annoyance,°
And still° keep eyes upon her. So good night.   85
My mind she has mated° and amazed my sight.
I think, but dare not speak.

GEN.   Good night, good Doctor.   [*Exeunt.*]

SCENE II. *The country near Dunsinane.*

[*Drum and colors.° Enter* MENTEITH, CAITHNESS,
    ANGUS, LENNOX, *and* SOLDIERS.]

MENT. The English power is near, led on by Mal-
    colm,
His uncle Siward, and the good Macduff.
Revenges burn in them, for their dear° causes
Would to the bleeding and the grim alarm°
Excite the mortified° man.

ANG.   Near Birnam Wood   5
Shall we well meet them. That way are they coming.

CAITH. Who knows if Donalbain be with his
    brother?

LEN. For certain, sir, he is not. I have a file°
Of all the gentry. There is Siward's son,
And many unrough° youths that even now   10
Protest their first of manhood.°

MENT.   What does the tyrant?

CAITH. Great Dunsinane he strongly fortifies.
Some say he's mad. Others, that lesser hate him,

Do call it valiant fury. But for certain
He cannot buckle his distempered cause   15
Within the belt of rule.°

ANG.   Now does he feel
His secret murders sticking on his hands,
Now minutely revolts upbraid his faith breach.°
Those he commands move only in command,
Nothing in love. Now does he feel his title   20
Hang loose about him, like a giant's robe
Upon a dwarfish thief.

MENT.   Who then shall blame
His pestered° senses to recoil and start,
When all that is within him does condemn
Itself for being there?

CAITH.   Well, march we on,   25
To give obedience where 'tis truly owed.
Meet we the medicine of the sickly weal,°
And with him pour we, in our country's purge,
Each drop of us.

LEN.   Or so much as it needs
To dew° the sovereign flower° and drown the
    weeds.   30
Make we our march toward Birnam.

                  [*Exeunt, marching.*]

SCENE III. *Dunsinane. A room in the castle.*

[*Enter* MACBETH, DOCTOR, *and* ATTENDANTS.]

MACB. Bring me no more reports, let them fly all.
Till Birnam Wood remove to Dunsinane   2
I cannot taint° with fear. What's the boy Malcolm?
Was he not born of woman? The spirits that know
All mortal consequences° have pronounced me thus·
"Fear not, Macbeth, no man that's born of woman
Shall e'er have power upon thee." Then fly, false
    thanes,   7
And mingle with the English epicures.°
The mind I sway by and the heart I bear
Shall never sag with doubt nor shake with fear.   10

[*Enter a* SERVANT.] The Devil damn thee black,°
    thou cream-faced loon!°
Where got'st thou that goose look?

SERV. There is ten thousand ——

MACB.   Geese, villain?

SERV.   Soldiers, sir.

MACB. Go prick thy face and overred° thy fear,

15–16. buckle . . . rule: keep his evil cause under control.
18. Now . . . breach: his disloyalty is blamed every minute by
those who rebel against him.   23. pestered: troubled.
27. medicine . . . weal: that which will heal the commonwealth;
i.e., Malcolm and his party.   30. dew: water. sovereign flower:
in the double meaning of "all-powerful healing herb" and "true
King."

    Sc. iii: 3. taint: be infected.   5. mortal consequences:
human fate.   8. epicures: gluttons; i.e., no soldiers.   11. Devil
. . . black: Black was the Devil's own color, and it was believed
that, when the Devil had claimed a soul as his own, the body
turned black. Cf. *Haml* Intro. p. 603a. loon: fool.   14. overred:
make red.

---

84. annoyance: harm.   85. still: continuously.   86. mated:
confounded.
    Sc. ii: s.d., Drum and colors: a drummer and a soldier carry-
ing a flag.   3. dear: heartfelt.   4. alarm: call to arms.
5. mortified: half-dead.   8. file: list. Cf. III.i.95.   10. un-
rough: smooth-chinned.   11. Protest . . . manhood: show that
they have hardly reached manhood.

Thou lily-livered° boy. What soldiers, patch?°   15
Death of thy soul! Those linen° cheeks of thine
Are counselors to fear. What soldiers, wheyface?
    SERV. The English force, so please you.
    MACB. Take thy face hence.   [*Exit* SERVANT.]
                            Seyton! — I am sick at heart,
When I behold —— Seyton, I say! — This push°
Will cheer me ever or disseat° me now.   21
I have lived long enough. My way° of life
Is fall'n into the sear,° the yellow leaf,
And that which should accompany old age,
As honor, love, obedience, troops of friends,   25
I must not look to have, but in their stead
Curses, not loud but deep, mouth-honor, breath,
Which the poor heart would fain deny, and dare not.
Seyton!

                [*Enter* SEYTON.]

    SEY. What's your gracious pleasure?
    MACB.   What news more?   30
    SEY. All is confirmed, my lord, which was re-
        ported.
    MACB. I'll fight till from my bones my flesh be
        hacked.
Give me my armor.
    SEY.   'Tis not needed yet.
    MACB. I'll put it on.
Send out moe° horses, skirr° the country round,   35
Hang those that talk of fear. Give me mine armor.
How does your patient, Doctor?
    DOCT.   Not so sick, my lord,
As she is troubled with thick-coming fancies
That keep her from her rest.
    MACB.   Cure her of that.
Canst thou not minister to a mind diseased,   40
Pluck from the memory a rooted sorrow,
Raze out the written troubles of the brain,
And with some sweet oblivious antidote
Cleanse the stuffed° bosom of that perilous stuff
Which weighs upon the heart?
    DOCT.   Therein the patient   45
Must minister to himself.
    MACB. Throw physic to the dogs, I'll none of it.
Come, put mine armor on, give me my staff.
Seyton, send out. Doctor, the thanes fly from me.
Come, sir, dispatch.° If thou couldst, Doctor, cast
The water° of my land, find her disease   51
And purge it to a sound and pristine° health,

I would applaud thee to the very echo,
That should applaud again. Pull 't off, I say.
What rhubarb, senna,° or what purgative drug   55
Would scour these English hence? Hear'st thou of
    them?
    DOCT. Aye, my good lord, your royal preparation
Makes us hear something.
    MACB.   Bring it after me.
I will not be afraid of death and bane
Till Birnam Forest come to Dunsinane.   60
    DOCT. [*Aside*] Were I from Dunsinane away and
    clear,
Profit again should hardly draw me here.
                                [*Exeunt.*]

SCENE IV. *Country near Birnam Wood.*

[*Drum and colors. Enter* MALCOLM, *old* SIWARD *and
    his* SON, MACDUFF, MENTEITH, CAITHNESS, ANGUS,
        LENNOX, ROSS, *and* SOLDIERS, *marching.*]
    MAL. Cousins, I hope the days are near at hand
That chambers will be safe.°
    MENT.   We doubt it nothing.
    SIW. What wood is this before us?
    MENT.   The wood of Birnam.
    MAL. Let every soldier hew him down a bough,
And bear 't before him. Thereby shall we shadow°
The numbers of our host, and make discovery   6
Err in report of us.
    SOLDS.   It shall be done.
    SIW. We learn no other but the confident tyrant
Keeps still in Dunsinane, and will endure
Our setting down before 't.°
    MAL.   'Tis his main hope.   10
For where there is advantage to be given,
Both more and less° have given him the revolt,
And none serve with him but constrainèd° things
Whose hearts are absent too.
    MACD.   Let our just censures
Attend the true event,° and put we on   15
Industrious soldiership.
    SIW.   The time approaches
That will with due decision make us know
What we shall say we have and what we owe.°
Thoughts speculative their unsure hopes relate,
But certain issue strokes must arbitrate.°   20
Toward which advance the war.
                        [*Exeunt, marching.*]

---

15. **lily-livered:** white-livered, cowardly. **patch:** fool. 16. **linen:**
i.e., pale as linen. 20. **push:** attack; lit., push of pike, decisive
assault. 21. **disseat:** unseat. 22. **way:** Dr. Johnson conjec-
tured that the correct reading was "May" (i.e., springtime).
This is very likely, as the image of May for youth at its prime is
common. Cf. Sonnet 73.1. 23. **sear:** dry and withered.
35. **moe:** more. **skirr:** scour. 44. **stuffed:** overfull. 50. **dis-**
patch: be quick — addressed to the servant who is buckling on
the armor. 50-51. **cast . . . water:** Inspection or "casting" of
the urine (called uroscopy) as an aid to diagnosis was the com-
mon practice of contemporary physicians. Cf. *II Hen IV*,
I.ii.1-6. 52. **pristine:** former.

55. **senna:** purgative herb.
    Sc. iv: 2. **chambers . . . safe:** i.e., a man will have nothing
to fear in his own home. 5. **shadow:** conceal. 10. **setting . . .**
before 't: siege. 12. **more . . . less:** i.e., men of all ranks.
13. **constrained:** forced. 14-15. **Let . . . event:** let us wait until
after the battle before passing judgment on that. 18. **owe:** own.
19-20. **Thoughts . . . arbitrate:** these guesses are mere hopes;
we shall only find out for certain by strokes. **arbitrate:** decide.

SCENE V. *Dunsinane. Within the castle.*

[*Enter* MACBETH, SEYTON, *and* SOLDIERS, *with drum and colors.*]

MACB. Hang out our banners on the outward
  walls.
The cry is still " They come." Our castle's strength
Will laugh a siege to scorn. Here let them lie
Till famine and the ague° eat them up.
Were they not forced° with those that should be
  ours,   5
We might have met them dareful, beard to beard,
And beat them backward home.
  [*A cry of women within.*] What is that noise?
SEY. It is the cry of women, my good lord. [*Exit.*]
MACB. I have almost forgot the taste of fears.
The time has been my senses would have cooled   10
To hear a night shriek, and my fell of hair°
Would at a dismal treatise° rouse and stir
As life were in 't. I have supped full with horrors.
Direness, familiar to my slaughterous thoughts,
Cannot once start me.°
  [*Re-enter* SEYTON.] Wherefore was that cry?   15
SEY. The Queen, my lord, is dead.
MACB. She should have died hereafter,°
There would have been a time for such a word.
Tomorrow, and tomorrow, and tomorrow
Creeps in this petty pace from day to day,   20
To the last syllable of recorded time,
And all our yesterdays have lighted fools
The way to dusty death. Out, out, brief candle!
Life's but a walking shadow, a poor player
That struts and frets his hour upon the stage   25
And then is heard no more. It is a tale
Told by an idiot, full of sound and fury,
Signifying nothing.
  [*Enter a* MESSENGER.] Thou comest to use thy tongue,
  thy story quickly.
MESS. Gracious my lord,   30
I should report that which I say I saw,
But know not how to do it.
MACB.   Well, say, sir.
MESS. As I did stand my watch upon the hill,
I looked toward Birnam, and anon methought
The wood began to move.
MACB.   Liar and slave!   35
MESS. Let me endure your wrath if 't be not so.
Within this three mile may you see it coming,
I say, a moving grove.
MACB.   If thou speak'st false,
Upon the next tree shalt thou hang alive
Till famine cling° thee. If thy speech be sooth,° 40
I care not if thou dost for me as much.

I pull in° resolution,° and begin
To doubt the equivocation° of the fiend
That lies like truth. " Fear not, till Birnam Wood
Do come to Dunsinane." And now a wood   45
Comes toward Dunsinane. Arm, arm, and out!
If this which he avouches does appear,
There is nor flying hence nor tarrying here.
I 'gin to be aweary of the sun,   49
And wish the estate o' the world were now undone.
Ring the alarum bell! Blow, wind! Come, wrack!°
At least we'll die with harness° on our back.
                                       [*Exeunt.*]

SCENE VI. *Dunsinane. Before the castle.*

[*Drum and colors. Enter* MALCOLM, *old* SIWARD,
  MACDUFF, *and their* ARMY, *with boughs.*]

MAL. Now near enough. Your leavy° screens
  throw down,
And show like those you are. You, worthy Uncle,
Shall, with my cousin, your right noble son,
Lead our first battle.° Worthy Macduff and we
Shall take upon 's what else remains to do,   5
According to our order.
SIW.   Fare you well.
Do we but find the tyrant's power tonight,
Let us be beaten if we cannot fight.
MACD. Make all our trumpets speak, give them all
  breath,   9
Those clamorous harbingers° of blood and death.
                                       [*Exeunt.*]

SCENE VII. *Another part of the field.*

[*Alarums. Enter* MACBETH.]

MACB. They have tied me to a stake, I cannot fly,
But bearlike I must fight the course.° What's he
That was not born of woman? Such a one
Am I to fear, or none.
  [*Enter* YOUNG SIWARD.]
YOUNG SIW. What is thy name?
MACB.   Thou'lt be afraid to hear it. 5
YOUNG SIW. No, though thou call'st thyself a hot-
  ter name
Than any is in Hell.
MACB.   My name's Macbeth.
YOUNG SIW. The Devil himself could not pro-
  nounce a title
More hateful to mine ear.

Sc. v: 4. ague: fever.   5. forced: reinforced.   11. fell of
hair: the hair on my scalp.   12. treatise: discourse.   15. start
me: make me start.   17. She . . . hereafter: she would have
died at some time or other.   40. cling: wither. sooth: truth.

42. pull in: rein in, check. resolution: courage.   43. equivo-
cation: quibbling. See II.iii.9, and App. 20.   51. wrack: wreck.
52. harness: armor.
  Sc. vi: 1. leavy: leafy.   4. battle: division.   10. harbinger:
See I.iv.45,n.
  Sc. vii: 1–2. They . . . course: See App. 5.

MACB.　　　　　　　No, nor more fearful.

YOUNG SIW. Thou liest, abhorrèd tyrant. With my
　　sword　　　　　　　　　　　　　　　　　　　10
I'll prove the lie thou speak'st.
　　　　[*They fight, and* YOUNG SIWARD *is slain.*]

MACB. Thou wast born of woman.
But swords I smile at, weapons laugh to scorn,
Brandished by man that's of a woman born. [*Exit.*]
　　　　[*Alarums. Enter* MACDUFF.]

MACD. That way the noise is. Tyrant, show thy
　　face!
If thou be'st slain and with no stroke of mine,　　15
My wife and children's ghosts will haunt me still.
I cannot strike at wretched kerns° whose arms
Are hired to bear their staves.° Either thou, Mac-
　　beth,
Or else my sword, with an unbattered edge,
I sheathe again undeeded. There thou shouldst be,
By this great clatter, one of greatest note　　21
Seems bruited.° Let me find him, Fortune!
And more I beg not.　　　　　[*Exit. Alarums.*]
　　　　[*Enter* MALCOLM *and old* SIWARD.]

SIW. This way, my lord, the castle's gently ren-
　　dered.°
The tyrant's people on both sides do fight,　　25
The noble thanes do bravely in the war,
The day almost itself professes yours,
And little is to do.

MAL.　　　　　We have met with foes
That strike beside us.°

SIW.　　Enter, sir, the castle.　[*Exeunt. Alarum.*]

SCENE VIII. *Another part of the field.*

[*Enter* MACBETH.]

MACB. Why should I play the Roman fool and die
On mine own sword?° Whiles I see lives, the gashes
Do better upon them.
　　　　　　[*Enter* MACDUFF.]

MACD.　　　　　Turn, hellhound, turn!

MACB. Of all men else I have avoided thee.
But get thee back, my soul is too much charged　　5
With blood of thine already.

MACD.　　　　　I have no words.
My voice is in my sword, thou bloodier villain
Than terms can give thee out!　　　[*They fight.*]

MACB.　　　　　Thou losest labor.
As easy mayst thou the intrenchant° air
With thy keen sword impress° as make me bleed.

Let fall thy blade on vulnerable crests.°　　11
I bear a charmèd life, which must not yield
To one of woman born.

MACD.　　　　　Despair thy charm,
And let the angel whom thou still° hast served
Tell thee Macduff was from his mother's womb　　15
Untimely ripped.

MACB. Accursèd be that tongue that tells me so,
For it hath cowed my better part of man!
And be these juggling fiends no more believed
That palter° with us in a double sense,　　20
That keep the word of promise to our ear
And break it to our hope. I'll not fight with thee.

MACD.　　Then yield thee, coward,
And live to be the show and gaze o' the time.
We'll have thee, as our rarer monsters are,　　25
Painted upon a pole,° and underwrit,
"Here may you see the tyrant."

MACB.　　　　　　I will not yield,
To kiss the ground before young Malcolm's feet,
And to be baited° with the rabble's curse.
Though Birnam Wood be come to Dunsinane,　　30
And thou opposed, being of no woman born,
Yet I will try the last. Before my body
I throw my warlike shield. Lay on, Macduff,
And damned be him that first cries "Hold,
　　enough!"　　　[*Exeunt, fighting. Alarums.*]
[*Retreat. Flourish. Enter, with drum and colors,*
　　MALCOLM, *old* SIWARD, ROSS, *the other* THANES,
　　　　　and SOLDIERS.]

MAL. I would the friends we miss were safe ar-
　　rived.　　　　　　　　　　　　　　　　35

SIW. Some must go off.° And yet, by these I see,
So great a day as this is cheaply bought.

MAL. Macduff is missing, and your noble son.

ROSS. Your son, my lord, has paid a soldier's debt.
He only lived but till he was a man,　　40
The which no sooner had his prowess confirmed
In the unshrinking station° where he fought
But like a man he died.

SIW.　　　　　Then he is dead?

ROSS. Aye, and brought off the field. Your cause
　　of sorrow
Must not be measured by his worth, for then　　45
It hath no end.

SIW.　　Had he his hurts before?

ROSS. Aye, on the front.

SIW.　　　　Why then, God's soldier be he!
Had I as many sons as I have hairs,
I would not wish them to a fairer death.
And so his knell is knolled.

MAL.　　　　　He's worth more sorrow,　　50
And that I'll spend for him.

---

17. kerns: See I.ii.13.　　**18. staves:** i.e., spears.　　**22. bruited:**
revealed by the noise.　　**24. gently rendered:** easily surrendered.
29. beside us: on our side.

　　Sc. viii: 1–2. play . . . sword: For instances of *Roman fools,*
who killed themselves in the moment of defeat, see *Caesar,*
V.iii.23–46; V.v.44–51.　　**9. intrenchant:** that cannot be cut.
10. impress: make an impression on.

11. vulnerable crests: heads that can be wounded.　　**14. still:**
always.　　**20. palter:** juggle.　　**26. Painted . . . pole:** i.e., on a
placard stuck on a pole.　　**29. baited:** worried, as a bear by
hounds.　　**36. go off:** die.　　**42. unshrinking station:** i.e., by
standing firm and undismayed when he fought with Macbeth.

SIW.   He's worth no more.
They say he parted well and paid his score.°
And so God be with him! Here comes newer com-
    fort.
    [*Re-enter* MACDUFF, *with* MACBETH's *head.*]
MACD. Hail, King! For so thou art. Behold where
    stands
The usurper's cursèd head. The time is free.°   55
I see thee compassed with thy kingdom's pearl,°
That speak my salutation in their minds,
Whose voices I desire aloud with mine:
Hail, King of Scotland!
ALL.   Hail, King of Scotland!   [*Flourish.*]
MAL. We shall not spend a large expense of time
Before we reckon with your several° loves,   61

And make us even with you.° My thanes and kins-
    men,
Henceforth be Earls, the first that ever Scotland
In such an honor named. What's more to do,   65
Which would be planted newly with the time,
As calling home our exiled friends abroad
That fled the snares of watchful tyranny,
Producing forth the cruel ministers
Of this dead butcher and his fiendlike Queen,
Who, as 'tis thought, by self and violent hands   70
Took off her life — this, and what needful else
That calls upon us, by the grace of Grace
We will perform in measure,° time, and place.
So thanks to all at once and to each one,
Whom we invite to see us crowned at Scone.   75
                                        [*Flourish. Exeunt.*]

---

52. score: debt.   **55. time is free:** i.e., liberty is restored.
56. compassed . . . pearl: surrounded by the pearl (or as we now
say, flower) of the kingdom.   **61. several:** separate, individual.

62. even . . . you: i.e., by paying what we owe.   **73. measure:**
i.e., full measure.

The Tragedy of
ANTONY AND CLEOPATRA

Introduction

The Tragedy of Antony and Cleopatra was probably written in 1607 or 1608. On May 20, 1608, Edward Blount, the stationer, entered in the Stationers' Register two books, the first being " A book called The book of Pericles Prince of Tyre," and the second " A book called Antony and Cleopatra." *Pericles* was printed separately in a quarto in 1609. No quarto of *Antony and Cleopatra* is known, and the play first appeared in the folio (F1) in 1623. The play may have been written a year or two before the entry, for in 1607 Samuel Daniel, who in 1594 had already written a tragedy called *Cleopatra* in the manner of Seneca, produced a new edition with alterations that have some resemblance to passages in Shakespeare's play. Shakespeare may, of course, have followed Daniel. From the evidence of style, it seems likely that *Antony and Cleopatra* came after *Macbeth* and *Lear*. The style is easier, and the imagery less concentrated.

Antony and Cleopatra is the sequel to *Julius Caesar*. As before, Shakespeare took his story from North's Plutarch (see *Caesar* Intro. p. 529b) but he had fewer difficulties. North's translation of the " Life of Marcus Antonius " gave him all the facts and the matter for many of the finest speeches. The drama begins four years after the murder of Julius Caesar. The Triumvirs — the " Big Three " — have overcome the party of Brutus and Cassius and now the Roman world has been divided between them, Antony's share being the rich East. When the play begins Antony is at the height of his passion for Cleopatra, before his fortunes have begun to decline. The story as given in Plutarch's " Life of Marcus Antonius " is full, and Shakespeare, as usual, selected and rearranged those incidents which he needed to make a good play. At times, indeed, he followed Plutarch so closely that he did little more than turn North's fine prose into finer blank verse. Thus the gorgeous description of Antony's first meeting with Cleopatra (II.ii. 190–245) appeared in North's prose as follows:

Antonius being thus inclined, the last and extremest mischiefs of all other (to wit, the love of Cleopatra) lighted on him, who did waken and stir up many vices yet hidden in him, and were never seen to any. And if any spark of goodness or hope of rising were left him, Cleopatra quenched it straight, and made it worse than before. The manner how he fell in love with her was this. Antonius, going to make war with the Parthians, sent to command Cleopatra to appear personally before him when he came into Cilicia, to answer unto such accusations as were laid against her, being this: that she had aided Cassius and Brutus in their war against him. The messenger sent unto Cleopatra to make his summons unto her was called Dellius, who when he had thoroughly considered her beauty, the excellent grace and sweetness of her tongue, he nothing mistrusted that Antonius would do any hurt to so noble a lady, but rather assured himself that within a few days she should be in great favor with him. Thereupon he did her great honor, and persuaded her to come into Cilicia as honorably furnished as she could possible; and bade her not to be afraid at all of Antonius, for he was a more courteous lord than any that she had ever seen. Cleopatra, on the other side, believing Dellius' words, and guessing by the former access and credit she had with Julius Caesar and Cnaeus Pompey (the son of Pompey the Great) only for her beauty, she began to have good hope that she might more easily win Antonius. For Caesar and Pompey knew her when she was but a young thing, and knew not then what the world meant; but now she went to Antonius at the age when a woman's beauty is at the prime, and she also of best judgment. So she furnished herself with a world of gifts, store of gold and silver and of riches and other sumptuous ornaments, as is credible enough she might bring from so great a house and from so wealthy and rich a realm as Egypt was. But yet she carried nothing with her wherein she trusted more than in herself, and in the charms and enchantment of her passing beauty and grace. Therefore when she was sent unto by divers letters, both from Antonius himself and also from his friends, she made so light of it and mocked Antonius so much that she disdained to set forward otherwise but to take her barge in the river of Cydnus, the poop whereof was of gold, the sails of purple, and the oars of silver, which kept stroke in rowing after the sound of the music of flutes, hautboys, cithers, viols, and such other instruments as they played upon in the barge. And now for the person of herself: She was laid under a pavilion of cloth-of-gold of tissue, appareled and attired like the goddess Venus commonly drawn in picture; and hard by her, on either hand of her, pretty fair boys, appareled as painters do set forth god Cupid, with little fans in their hands with the which they fanned wind upon her. Her ladies and gentlewomen also, the fairest of them, were appareled like the nymphs Nereides (which are the mermaids of the waters) and like the Graces, some steering the helm, others tending the tackle and ropes of the barge, out of the which there came a wonderful passing sweet savor of perfumes that perfumed the wharf's side, pestered with innumerable multitudes of people. Some of them followed the barge all along the river's side, others also ran out of the city to see her coming in, so that in the end there ran such multitudes of people one after another to see her that Antonius was left post-alone in the market place in his imperial seat to give audience. And there went a rumor in the people's mouths that the goddess Venus was come to play with the god Bacchus for the general good of all Asia.

Another passage which Shakespeare took over and adapted was the conversation between the soothsayer and Antonius (II.iii.10–30):

But in all other manner of sports and exercises, wherein they passed the time away the one with the other, Antonius was ever inferior unto Caesar, and always lost, which grieved him much. With Antonius there was a soothsayer or astronomer of Egypt that could cast a figure and judge of men's nativities to tell them what should happen to them. He, either to please Cleopatra or else for that he found it so by his art, told Antonius plainly that his fortune (which of itself was excellent good, and very great) was altogether blemished and obscured by Caesar's fortune; and therefore he counseled him utterly to leave his company and to get him as far from him as he could. "For thy demon," said he, "(that is to say, the good angel and spirit that keepeth thee) is afraid of his, and being courageous and high when he is alone becometh fearful and timorous when he cometh near unto the other." Howsoever it was, the events ensuing proved the Egyptian's words true.

The final scene of Cleopatra's death (V.ii) was also described in some detail by Plutarch:

There was a young gentleman, Cornelius Dolabella, that was one of Caesar's very great familiars and besides did bear no ill will unto Cleopatra. He sent her word secretly, as she had requested him, that Caesar determined to take his journey through Syria and that within three days he would send her away before with her children. When this was told Cleopatra, she requested Caesar that it would please him to suffer her to offer the last oblations of the dead unto the soul of Antonius. . . .

Then having ended these doleful plaints, [she] crowned the tomb with garlands and sundry nosegays and marvelous lovingly embraced the same, she commanded they should prepare her bath, and when she had bathed and washed herself she fell to her meat and was sumptuously served. Now whilst she was at dinner there came a countryman and brought her a basket. The soldiers that warded at the gates asked him straight what he had in his basket. He opened his basket and took out the leaves that covered the figs and showed them that they were figs he brought. They all of them marveled to see so goodly figs. The countryman laughed to hear them, and bade them take some if they would. They believed he told them truly, and so bade him carry them in. After Cleopatra had dined, she sent a certain table [tablet] written and sealed unto Caesar and commanded them all to go out of the tomb where she was, except for the two women; then she shut the doors to her. Caesar when he had received this table, and began to read her lamentation and petition requesting him that he would let her be buried with Antonius, found straight what she meant and thought to have gone thither himself. Howbeit, he sent one before in all haste that might be to see what it was.

Her death was very sudden. For those whom Caesar sent unto her ran thither in all haste possible, and found the soldiers standing at the gate, mistrusting nothing, nor understanding of her death. But when they had opened the doors, they found Cleopatra stark-dead, laid upon a bed of gold attired and arrayed in her royal robes, and one of her two women, which was called Iras, dead at her feet, and her other woman called Charmian half-dead and trembling, trimming the diadem which Cleopatra wore upon her head. One of the soldiers, seeing her, angrily said unto her: "Is that well done, Charmian?" "Very well," said she again, " and meet for a Princess descended from the race of so many noble Kings." She said no more, but fell down dead hard by the bed.

Some report that this aspic was brought unto her in the basket with figs and that she had commanded them to hide it under the fig leaves, so that when she should think to take out the figs the aspic should bite her before she should see her; howbeit, that when she would have taken away the leaves for the figs she perceived it and said: " Art thou here then?" And so, her arm being naked, she put it to the aspic to be bitten. Others say again that she kept it in a box and that she did prick and thrust it with a spindle of gold, so that the aspic being angered withal, leaped out with great fury, and bit her in the arm. Howbeit, few can tell the truth. For they report also that she had hidden poison in a hollow razor which she carried in the hair of her head. And yet was there no mark seen on her body or any sign discerned that she was poisoned, neither also did they find this serpent in her tomb. But it was reported only that there were seen certain fresh steps or tracks where it had gone, on the tomb side toward the sea, and specially by the door side. Some say also that they found two little pretty bitings in her arm, scant to be discerned, the which it seemed Caesar himself gave credit unto, because in his triumph he carried Cleopatra's image with an asp biting her arm. And thus goeth the report of her death.

Here Shakespeare took his incidents from Plutarch, but the dialogue is almost all his own.

The reputation of *Antony and Cleopatra* as a play has suffered unjustly because of changes in the convention of the stage. As printed in a modern edition, the play has an impossible multiplicity of scenes. In Act IV alone fifteen are marked, each with its appropriate locality. But Shakespeare did not think of these little episodes in terms of place; neither in F1 nor in the original production was there division into acts and scenes. Shakespeare indeed was stretching to the utmost the possibilities of the Globe stage. Episode succeeds episode in different parts of the stage,[1] giving an illusion of the rush of events as each of the chief persons nears the climax of his fortune. The direction of this play must have needed careful and elaborate timing. Only when *Antony and Cleopatra* is acted with speed on a bare stage in the Elizabethan convention are its magnificent planning and superb poetry fully revealed. Such an effect is quite impossible on any stage where scenery must be changed or where there is any attempt to give a realistic background.

Nevertheless, *Antony and Cleopatra* does demand of spectator and reader a closer attention than is usual. By 1608 Shakespeare had so

[1] The student will find it interesting to work out the Elizabethan staging of *Antony and Cleopatra;* but he should use the original stage directions of the folio and not those of a modern text. See Gen. Intro. pp. 56a–58b.

trained his audience that from the first flourish of the trumpets they were intent to follow every word.

The play is remarkable for its characterization and for the peculiar quality of its poetry. As before, in *Julius Caesar,* Shakespeare reduces the complex events of history to the simple clash of personality. The protagonists are Octavius Caesar (nephew and heir of Julius Caesar), Antony, and Cleopatra. Antony has already appeared in *Julius Caesar.* He is a full character, a man who enjoys pleasures of every kind, but who can also endure the extremes of hardship. He has subtlety of intellect, which does not, however, prevent him from deceiving himself, and great personal charm. In the earlier play, he outwitted Brutus and Cassius by his greater knowledge of man and by sheer personality; and it was his generalship and leading which ultimately gave the victory to Caesar's party. In *Antony and Cleopatra* he is shown in his decadence. Though the others still recognize his good qualities, he becomes besotted with passion and degenerates into a fool; and before his death he is little better than an " old ruffian."

Character can be developed in a drama in many ways, by the actions and words of the character himself and by what others say of him. The great dramatist combines every method, subtly and imperceptibly building up the impression in the mind of the spectator. Antony is spoken of by everyone. Caesar brings out his worst, Lepidus with his tactful apologies reveals his greatest weaknesses. In this play, Shakespeare invented a character to be the commentator on the action. Enobarbus stands for sanity, common sense, and cynicism. Enobarbus himself is a " character." A blunt, cynical soldier, he is the absolutely honest man, the kind of person that Iago pretended to be. He is thus a natural commentator and, significantly, he is Shakespeare's own invention, for the name alone occurs in Plutarch. The contrast between Enobarbus and his master is brought out in the very beginning. Whenever Antony becomes at all sentimental, Enobarbus brings him back to his senses. Enobarbus follows Antony's fortunes until nearly the end, and then he deserts him not because Antony is beaten but because Antony has degenerated into a fool; and then when Antony sends his treasure after him, Enobarbus realizes that after all he was wrong and that Antony for all his faults was a divine master, and this treachery breaks his heart. It is through Enobarbus that the divine streak in Antony is finally displayed.

Octavius, Antony's opponent, is shown as a very young man, and the contrast between their ages becomes more marked toward the end of the play. In fact Antony was thirty-nine at the time of Julius Caesar's death, Octavius twenty years younger. Octavius is a cold-blooded young man who moves unemotionally to gain his own ends. He sacrifices his sister in his game with Antony; he remains sober during the drunken party on Pompey's galley; he alone can look Cleopatra straight in the face without any quickening of the pulse. He is in fact Fortune's prudent darling.

Nevertheless the whole story and success of the play must turn on Cleopatra. Many have told the story of this woman who fascinated two Emperors, and their estimates differ widely. Shakespeare, however, followed Plutarch; to him Cleopatra is a magnificent courtesan, a creature of gaiety, instinct, and passion with few, if any, higher feelings than the enjoyment of the moment; but yet she is unique among women and can therefore defy all normal rules of propriety and morality. The part, incidentally, was played by a boy, but this was not necessarily a disadvantage. A good boy actor, well trained, is capable of a great range of emotion, and had his boy not been up to the part, Shakespeare would never have written it.

It needs vast skill to create such a character so convincingly that we can sympathize with Antony's passion for her. She is shown in her infinite variety as a woman of amazing charm and personality, quite apart from her physical beauty. She gives a lesson to Charmian on how to keep her man (I.iii) and at all times, except at the very end, she can control and fascinate Antony. She is, nevertheless, a quick-tempered beauty, as the unfortunate messenger discovers (II.v), but her anger is soon allayed, and the contrast is seen in her self-satisfied analysis of Antony's new wife. Cleopatra knows that she has nothing to fear from a widow of thirty with a round face, brown hair, a low forehead, and no majesty in her movement.

Shakespeare must also show how she appeals to others. This is more difficult. He achieves it in the gorgeous description of her first meeting with Antony (II.ii.190–231), which is pronounced not by Antony or by one of her adorers but by the cynic Enobarbus. If Cleopatra can produce this effect on Enobarbus, she must indeed have been a charmer. The other side of her nature is brought out as clearly. Toward the end, when Antony's fortunes are hopeless, Thyreus comes from Octavius. Cleopatra, who is thinking of changing sides, sets about fascinating Caesar's messenger. Antony overhears her. He has heard that tone before, and he rounds on her with a flow of abuse as vile as Enobarbus' speech was lyrical.

Her death is magnificent. She must live in brightness or she will wither, and when she knows that there remains only for her to be carried to Rome to be displayed as Caesar's most interesting captive, she realizes that the time has come for the dark. She dies as spectacularly as she lives, and Charmian pronounces her epitaph:

Now boast thee, Death, in thy possession lies
A lass unparalleled. Downy windows, close,
And golden Phoebus, never be beheld
Of eyes again so royal!

Antony and Cleopatra

DRAMATIS PERSONAE

ANTONY ⎫
OCTAVIUS CAESAR ⎬ *triumvirs*
LEPIDUS ⎭
SEXTUS POMPEIUS

DOMITIUS ENOBARBUS ⎫
VENTIDIUS
EROS
SCARUS ⎬ *friends to Antony*
DERCETAS
DEMETRIUS
PHILO ⎭

MECAENAS ⎫
AGRIPPA
DOLABELLA ⎬ *friends to Caesar*
PROCULEIUS
THYREUS
GALLUS ⎭

MENAS ⎫
MENECRATES ⎬ *friends to Sextus Pompeius*
VARRIUS ⎭

TAURUS, *lieutenant general to Caesar*
CANIDIUS, *lieutenant general to Antony*
SILIUS, *an officer in Ventidius's army*
EUPHRONIUS, *an ambassador from Antony to Caesar*
ALEXAS
MARDIAN, *a eunuch* ⎫
SELEUCUS ⎬ *attendants on Cleopatra*
DIOMEDES ⎭
A SOOTHSAYER
A CLOWN

CLEOPATRA, *Queen of Egypt*
OCTAVIA, *sister to Caesar, and wife to Antony*
CHARMIAN ⎫ *attendants on Cleopatra*
IRAS ⎭

OFFICERS, SOLDIERS, MESSENGERS, *and other*
ATTENDANTS

SCENE — *In several parts of the Roman Empire.*

Act I

SCENE I. *Alexandria. A room in* CLEOPATRA'S *palace.*

[*Enter* DEMETRIUS *and* PHILO.]

PHI. Nay, but this dotage of our General's
O'erflows the measure.° Those his goodly eyes,
That o'er the files° and musters of the war
Have glowed like plated° Mars, now bend, now turn
The office and devotion of their view°   5
Upon a tawny° front.° His captain's heart,
Which in the scuffles of great fights hath burst
The buckles on his breast, reneges all temper,°
And is become the bellows and the fan°
To cool a gypsy's° lust.
[*Flourish.*° *Enter* ANTONY, CLEOPATRA, *her* LADIES,
the train, with EUNUCHS *fanning her.*]
                Look where they come.   10
Take but good note, and you shall see in him

Act I, Sc. i: **2. O'erflows . . . measure:** exceeds all calcula-
tion. **3. files:** ranks. **4. plated:** in armor. **4–5. now . . .
view:** gaze with devoted service. **6. tawny:** dusky; lit., yellow-
ish-brown. **front:** forehead. **8. reneges . . . temper:** refuses all
self-restraint. **9. bellows . . . fan:** i.e., alternately rousing and
allaying. **10. gypsy:** Gypsies were supposed to have come from
Egypt, hence their name. Shakespeare thought of Cleopatra as a
dusky Queen; actually she was descended from one of the Mace-
donian generals of Alexander the Great. **s.d., Flourish:** fanfare
of trumpets.

The triple pillar° of the world transformed
Into a strumpet's fool. Behold and see.
  CLEO. If it be love indeed, tell me how much.
  ANT. There's beggary in the love that can be reck-
    oned.   15
  CLEO. I'll set a bourn° how far to be beloved.
  ANT. Then must thou needs find out new Heaven,
    new earth.
             [*Enter an* ATTENDANT.]
  ATT. News, my good lord, from Rome ——
  ANT.   Grates° me. The sum.°
  CLEO. Nay, hear them,° Antony.
Fulvia° perchance is angry, or who knows   20
If the scarce-bearded Caesar have not sent
His powerful mandate° to you, " Do this, or this.
Take in that kingdom, and enfranchise° that.
Perform 't, or else we damn° thee."
  ANT.   How, my love!
  CLEO. Perchance! Nay, and most like.   25
You must not stay here longer, your dismission°
Is come from Caesar, therefore hear it, Antony.
Where's Fulvia's process?° Caesar's, I would say?
  Both?

12. triple pillar: one of the three pillars; i.e., the Triumvirate
(Big Three). See *Ant & Cleo* Intro. p. 863a. **16. bourn:**
boundary. **18. Grates:** bores; lit., jars. **The sum:** give me a
summary. **19. them:** i.e., the news. **20. Fulvia:** Antony's
legal wife, a managing and shrewish lady. **22. mandate:** com-
mand. **23. enfranchise:** set free. **24. damn:** condemn. **26. dis-
mission:** dismissal. **28. process:** summons to appear before
a court of law.

Call in the messengers. As I am Egypt's Queen,
Thou blushest, Antony, and that blood of thine   30
Is Caesar's homager.° Else so° thy cheek pays shame
When shrill-tongued Fulvia scolds. The messengers!

ANT. Let Rome in Tiber melt, and the wide arch
Of the ranged empire° fall! Here is my space.
Kingdoms are clay. Our dungy° earth alike   35
Feeds beast as man. The nobleness of life
Is to do thus, when such a mutual pair
               [*Embracing.*]
And such a twain can do 't, in which I bind,
On pain of punishment, the world to weet
We stand up peerless.°

CLEO.   Excellent falsehood!   40
Why did he marry Fulvia and not love her?
I'll seem the fool I am not, Antony
Will be himself.°

ANT.   But stirred by Cleopatra.
Now, for the love of Love and her soft hours,
Let's not confound° the time with conference
    harsh.°
                            45
There's not a minute of our lives should stretch
Without some pleasure now. What sport tonight?
CLEO. Hear the ambassadors.
ANT.   Fie, wrangling Queen!
Whom everything becomes, to chide, to laugh,
To weep, whose every passion fully strives   50
To make itself, in thee, fair and admired!
No messenger but thine, and all alone
Tonight we'll wander through the streets and note
The qualities° of people. Come, my Queen.
Last night you did desire it. Speak not to us.   55
   [*Exeunt* ANTONY *and* CLEOPATRA *with their train.*]
DEM. Is Caesar with Antonius prized so slight?
PHI. Sir, sometimes, when he is not Antony,
He comes too short of that great property°
Which still° should go with Antony.
DEM.   I am full sorry
That he approves the common liar,° who   60
Thus speaks of him at Rome. But I will hope
Of better deeds tomorrow. Rest you happy!
                       [*Exeunt.*]

---

31. **Caesar's homager:** one who pays homage to Caesar; i.e., recognizes him as a superior. **Else so:** or else.   33–34. **wide ... empire:** This is one of the many concentrated phrases in *Ant & Cleo* which convey their meaning emotionally and are so difficult to paraphrase. The image is of the sweep of a great arch, stone supporting stone. **ranged:** set in order.   35. **dungy:** manured.   36–40. **The ... peerless:** i.e., love is the noblest thing in life; when such a pair as we are in each other's arms, I force the world to know that our love is without a rival. **weet:** know.   42–43. **I'll ... himself:** i.e., even if I fool myself that Antony loves me, Antony won't pretend.   45. **confound:** waste. **conference harsh:** rough talk.   54. **qualities:** characteristics. **58. property:** personal quality.   59. **still:** always.   60. **approves ... liar:** proves that the lies commonly told about him are true.

SCENE II. *The same. Another room.*

[*Enter* CHARMIAN, IRAS, ALEXAS, *and a* SOOTHSAYER.]
CHAR. Lord Alexas, sweet Alexas, most anything
Alexas, almost most absolute° Alexas, where's the
soothsayer that you praised so to the Queen? Oh,
that I knew this husband which you say must charge
his horns with garlands!°   5
ALEX. Soothsayer!
SOOTH. Your will?
CHAR. Is this the man? Is 't you, sir, that know
    things?
SOOTH. In nature's infinite book of secrecy
A little I can read.
ALEX.   Show him your hand.   10
            [*Enter* ENOBARBUS.]
ENO. Bring in the banquet° quickly, wine enough
Cleopatra's health to drink.
CHAR. Good sir, give me good fortune.
SOOTH. I make not, but foresee.
CHAR. Pray then, foresee me one.   15
SOOTH. You shall be yet far fairer than you are.
CHAR. He means in flesh.
IRAS. No, you shall paint when you are old.
CHAR. Wrinkles forbid!
ALEX. Vex not his prescience.° Be attentive.   20
CHAR. Hush!
SOOTH. You shall be more beloving than beloved.
CHAR. I had rather heat my liver with drinking.
ALEX. Nay, hear him.   24
CHAR. Good now,° some excellent fortune! Let me
be married to three Kings in a forenoon, and widow
them all. Let me have a child at fifty, to whom Herod
of Jewry may do homage.° Find me to marry me
with Octavius Caesar, and companion me with my
mistress.   30
SOOTH. You shall outlive the lady whom you serve.
CHAR. Oh, excellent! I love long life better than
    figs.
SOOTH. You have seen and proved° a fairer for-
    mer fortune
Than that which is to approach.   34
CHAR. Then belike my children shall have no
names.° Prithee, how many boys and wenches° must
I have?
SOOTH. If every of your wishes had a womb,
And fertile every wish, a million.
CHAR. Out, fool! I forgive thee for a witch.°   40

Sc. ii: 2. absolute: perfect.   4–5. **charge ... garlands:** wear a wreath on his horns like an ox going to be sacrificed; i.e., when I shall make him a cuckold. See App. 11.   11. **banquet:** wine and light refreshments, not the main feast.   20. **prescience:** power of foresight.   25. **Good now:** now, my good man. 27–28. **Herod ... homage:** Herod was always represented as a ferocious tyrant. A child to whom he would do homage would thus have considerable character.   33. **proved:** experienced. 35–36. **have ... names:** i.e., be bastards.   36. **wenches:** girls. 40. **I ... witch:** you are a wizard, so I forgive you your plain speaking.

ALEX. You think none but your sheets are privy to° your wishes.

CHAR. Nay, come, tell Iras hers.

ALEX. We'll know all our fortunes.

ENO. Mine and most of our fortunes tonight shall be — drunk to bed. 46

IRAS. There's a palm presages° chastity, if nothing else.

CHAR. E'en as the o'erflowing Nilus presageth famine! 50

IRAS. Go, you wild bedfellow, you cannot sooth-say.

CHAR. Nay, if an oily palm be not a fruitful prognostication,° I cannot scratch mine ear. Prithee, tell her but a workaday fortune. 55

SOOTH. Your fortunes are alike.

IRAS. But how, but how? Give me particulars.

SOOTH. I have said. 59

IRAS. Am I not an inch of fortune better than she?

CHAR. Well, if you were but an inch of fortune better than I, where would you choose it?

IRAS. Not in my husband's nose.

CHAR. Our worser thoughts Heavens mend! Alexas — come, his fortune, his fortune! Oh, let 65 him marry a woman that cannot go,° sweet Isis,° I beseech thee! And let her die too, and give him a worse! And let worse follow worse, till the worst of all follow him laughing to his grave, fiftyfold a cuckold! Good Isis, hear me this prayer, though thou deny me a matter of more weight. Good Isis, I beseech thee! 72

IRAS. Amen. Dear goddess, hear that prayer of the people! For as it is a heartbreaking to see a handsome man loose-wived, so it is a deadly sorrow to behold a foul knave uncuckolded. Therefore, dear Isis, keep decorum,° and fortune him accordingly! 78

CHAR. Amen.

ALEX. Lo, now, if it lay in their hands to make me a cuckold, they would make themselves whores but they'd do 't!

ENO. Hush! Here comes Antony.

CHAR. Not he, the Queen.

[Enter CLEOPATRA.]

CLEO. Saw you my lord?

ENO. No, lady.

CLEO. Was he not here?

CHAR. No, madam. 85

CLEO. He was disposed to mirth, but on the sudden A Roman° thought hath struck him. Enobarbus!

ENO. Madam?

CLEO. Seek him, and bring him hither. Where's Alexas? 89

ALEX. Here, at your service. My lord approaches.

CLEO. We will not look upon him. Go with us.

[Exeunt.]

[Enter ANTONY with a MESSENGER and ATTENDANTS.]

MESS. Fulvia thy wife first came into the field.

ANT. Against my brother Lucius?

MESS. Aye. But soon that war had end, and the time's state° 95 Made friends of them, jointing their force 'gainst Caesar, Whose better issue° in the war from Italy Upon the first encounter drave them.

ANT. Well, what worst?

MESS. The nature of bad news infects° the teller.

ANT. When it concerns the fool or coward. On. Things that are past are done with me. 'Tis thus — Who tells me true, though in his tale lie death, 102 I hear him as he flattered.°

MESS. Labienus — This is stiff news — hath with his Parthian force Extended° Asia from Euphrates, 105 His conquering banner shook from Syria To Lydia and to Ionia, Whilst ——

ANT. Antony, thou wouldst say ——

MESS. Oh, my lord!

ANT. Speak to me home,° mince not the general tongue.° Name Cleopatra as she is called in Rome. 110 Rail thou in Fulvia's phrase, and taunt my faults With such full license as both truth and malice Have power to utter. Oh, then we bring forth weeds When our quick minds lie still, and our ills told us Is as our earing.° Fare thee well awhile. 115

MESS. At your noble pleasure. [Exit.]

ANT. From Sicyon,° ho, the news! Speak there!

1. ATT. The man from Sicyon, is there such a one?

2. ATT. He stays upon your will.

ANT. Let him appear. These strong Egyptian fetters I must break, 120 Or lose myself in dotage.

[Enter another MESSENGER.] What are you?

2. MESS. Fulvia thy wife is dead.

ANT. Where died she?

2. MESS. In Sicyon. 123 Her length of sickness, with what else more serious

95. time's state: state of the times. 97. better issue: greater success. 99. infects: brings disaster on. 103. as . . . flattered: as if he brought me good news. 105. Extended: seized on. 109. home: plainly. general tongue: what everyone is saying. 113-15. Oh . . . earing: i.e., when we do not use our minds to consider what should be done, we suffer from the evils which follow idleness, but to have our misfortunes told us produces good results. still: fallow, unused. earing: plowing. 117. Sicyon: a town in Greece where Antony had parted from Fulvia.

41-42. privy to: know the secrets of. 47. presages: foretells. 53-54. oily . . . prognostication: A moist palm was believed to be a sign of an amorous disposition. fruitful prognostication: indication of wantonness. 66. cannot go: is no use. Isis: Egyptian goddess of the moon. 78. decorum: a sense of what is appropriate. 87. Roman: i.e., solemn.

Importeth thee to know, this bears. [*Gives a letter.*]

ANT.   Forbear° me. [*Exit* SECOND MESSENGER.]
There's a great spirit gone! Thus did I desire it.
What our contempts do often hurl from us,
We wish it ours again. The present pleasure,
By revolution lowering,° does become
The opposite of itself. She's good, being gone, 130
The hand could° pluck her back that shoved her on.
I must from this enchanting Queen break off.
Ten thousand harms, more than the ills I know,
My idleness doth hatch. How now! Enobarbus!

[*Re-enter* ENOBARBUS.]

ENO. What's your pleasure, sir? 135

ANT. I must with haste from hence.

ENO. Why, then we kill all our women. We see
how mortal an unkindness is to them. If they suffer
our departure, death's the word.°

ANT. I must be gone. 140

ENO. Under a compelling occasion° let women die.
It were pity to cast them away for nothing, though
between them and a great cause they should be es-
teemed nothing. Cleopatra, catching but the least
noise of this, dies instantly. I have seen her die twenty
times upon far poorer moment.° I do think there is
mettle° in death which commits some loving act
upon her, she hath such a celerity in dying.°

ANT. She is cunning past man's thought. 150

ENO. Alack, sir, no, her passions° are made of
nothing but the finest part of pure love. We cannot
call her winds and waters sighs and tears, they are
greater storms and tempests than almanacs° can re-
port. This cannot be cunning in her. If it be, she
makes a shower of rain as well as Jove. 157

ANT. Would I had never seen her!

ENO. Oh, sir, you had then left unseen a wonder-
ful piece of work, which not to have been blest
withal would have discredited your travel.°

ANT. Fulvia is dead. 162

ENO. Sir?

ANT. Fulvia is dead.

ENO. Fulvia!

ANT. Dead. 166

ENO. Why, sir, give the gods a thankful sacrifice.
When it pleaseth their deities to take the wife of a
man from him, it shows to man the tailors of the
earth, comforting therein, that when old robes are
worn out there are members to make new.° If 171

there were no more women but Fulvia, then had you
indeed a cut,° and the case to be lamented. This grief
is crowned with consolation. Your old smock brings
forth a new petticoat. And indeed the tears live in an
onion° that should water this sorrow. 177

ANT. The business she hath broachèd° in the state
Cannot endure my absence.

ENO. And the business you have broached here
cannot be without you, especially that of Cleopatra's,
which wholly depends on your abode. 182

ANT. No more light answers. Let our° officers
Have notice what we purpose. I shall break
The cause of our expedience° to the Queen 185
And get her leave to part. For not alone
The death of Fulvia, with more urgent touches,°
Do strongly speak to us, but the letters too
Of many our contriving friends° in Rome
Petition us at home. Sextus Pompeius 190
Hath given the dare to Caesar, and commands
The empire of the sea. Our slippery people,
Whose love is never linked to the deserver
Till his deserts are past, begin to throw
Pompey the Great and all his dignities 195
Upon his son,° who, high in name and power,
Higher than both in blood and life, stands up
For the main soldier.° Whose quality,° going on,
The sides o' the world may danger. Much is breed-
ing
Which, like the courser's hair, hath yet but life 200
And not a serpent's poison.° Say our pleasure,
To such whose place is under us, requires
Our quick remove from hence.

ENO. I shall do 't.   [*Exeunt.*]

SCENE III. *The same. Another room.*

[*Enter* CLEOPATRA, CHARMIAN, IRAS, *and* ALEXAS.]

CLEO. Where is he?

CHAR.   I did not see him since.

CLEO. See where he is, who's with him, what he
does.
I did not send you. If you find him sad,
Say I am dancing; if in mirth, report
That I am sudden sick. Quick, and return. 5

[*Exit* ALEXAS.]

CHAR. Madam, methinks if you did love him
dearly,

125. Forbear: leave. 129. By . . . lowering: changed to the opposite by a turn of the wheel. 131. could: would if it could.
138–39. If . . . word: if they have to endure our departing, they swear they'll die. 141. Under . . . occasion: if it's really necessary. 147. moment: occasion. 148. mettle: material, good stuff. 149. celerity in dying: speed at dying; i.e., death is like one of her lovers, to whom she yields very willingly.
151. passions: emotions. 155. almanacs: See App. 2. 161. dis-credited . . . travel: i.e., you would have missed one of the most interesting sights in the world. 168–71. When . . . new: i.e., the gods are like tailors; when one suit is worn out they can make a new one. members: people.

173. cut: loss. 176–77. tears . . . onion: i.e., you'll have to use an onion if you want to shed tears for Fulvia. 178. broached: caused. To broach is to open a cask. 183. our: Antony assumes the tone of a commander asserting himself. 185. expedience: hasty departure. 187. touches: matters which touch us.
189. contriving friends: friends who plot for us. 194–96. be-gin . . . son: begin to think young Pompey as worthy a man as his father. 197–98. stands . . . soldier: intends to become the supreme soldier. 198. quality: position, success. 200–01. cours-er's . . . poison: It was commonly believed that a horse's hair left in water would turn into a living creature.

You do not hold the method to enforce
The like from him.

CLEO.   What should I do I do not?

CHAR. In each thing give him way, cross him in
   nothing.

CLEO. Thou teachest like a fool the way to lose
   him.   10

CHAR. Tempt him not so too far, I wish, forbear.°
In time we hate that which we often fear.°
But here comes Antony.

   [*Enter* ANTONY.]

CLEO.   I am sick and sullen.

ANT. I am sorry to give breathing° to my pur-
   pose ——   14

CLEO. Help me away, dear Charmian, I shall fall.
It cannot be thus long, the sides of nature
Will not sustain it.

ANT.   Now, my dearest Queen ——

CLEO. Pray you stand farther from me.

ANT.   What's the matter?

CLEO. I know, by that same eye, there's some good
   news.
What says the married woman? You may go.   20
Would she had never given you leave to come!
Let her not say 'tis I that keep you here.
I have no power upon you, hers you are.

ANT. The gods best know ——

CLEO.   Oh, never was there queen
So mightily betrayed! Yet at the first   25
I saw the treasons planted.

ANT.   Cleopatra ——

CLEO. Why should I think you can be mine and
   true,
Though you in swearing shake the thrònèd gods,
Who have been false to Fulvia? Riotous madness,
To be entangled with those mouth-made vows   30
Which break themselves in swearing!

ANT.   Most sweet Queen ——

CLEO. Nay, pray you seek no color° for your
   going,
But bid farewell and go. When you sued staying,°
Then was the time for words. No going then.
Eternity was in our lips and eyes,   35
Bliss in our brows' bent, none our parts so poor
But was a race of Heaven.° They are so still,
Or thou, the greatest soldier of the world,
Art turned the greatest liar.

ANT.   How now, lady!

CLEO. I would I had thy inches, thou shouldst
   know   40
There were a heart in Egypt.

ANT.   Hear me, Queen.

The strong necessity of time commands
Our services awhile, but my full heart
Remains in use with you. Our Italy
Shines o'er with civil swords.° Sextus Pompeius   45
Makes his approaches to the port of Rome.
Equality of two domestic powers
Breed scrupulous faction.° The hated, grown to
   strength,
Are newly grown to love. The condemned Pompey,
Rich in his father's honor, creeps apace   50
Into the hearts of such as have not thrived
Upon the present state, whose numbers threaten,
And quietness grown sick of rest would purge
By any desperate change. My more particular,
And that which most with you should safe° my go-
   ing,   55
Is Fulvia's death.

CLEO. Though age from folly could not give me
   freedom,
It does from childishness. Can Fulvia die?°

ANT. She's dead, my Queen.
Look here, and at thy sovereign leisure read   60
The garboils° she awaked. At the last, best.
See when and where she died.

CLEO.   Oh, most false love!
Where be the sacred vials° thou shouldst fill
With sorrowful water? Now I see, I see,
In Fulvia's death, how mine received shall be.   65

ANT. Quarrel no more, but be prepared to know
The purposes I bear, which are, or cease,°
As you shall give the advice. By the fire
That quickens Nilus' slime,° I go from hence
Thy soldier, servant, making peace or war   70
As thou affect'st.°

CLEO.   Cut my lace,° Charmian, come,
But let it be. I am quickly ill and well,
So° Antony loves.

ANT.   My precious Queen, forbear,
And give true evidence to his love, which stands
An honorable trial.

CLEO.   So Fulvia told me.   75
I prithee, turn aside and weep for her,
Then bid adieu to me, and say the tears
Belong to Egypt. Good now, play one scene
Of excellent dissembling,° and let it look
Like perfect honor.

ANT.   You'll heat my blood. No more. 80

CLEO. You can do better yet, but this is meetly.°

45. civil swords: swords drawn in civil war.   47–48. Equality . . .
faction: when parties are equally balanced, each side is cautious
in taking action.   55. safe: make safe; i.e., you need not
fear that I am returning to my wife.   58. Can . . . die: the
mistress's bitter sneer that the legal wife lives forever.   61. gar-
boils: commotions.   63. vials: tear bottles.   67. which . . .
cease: which shall be carried out or canceled.   68–69. By . . .
slime: by the sun which makes fertile the mud of the Nile.
71. affect'st: desire. Cut . . . lace: See *Rich III*, IV.i.34,n.
73. So: so long as.   79. dissembling: hypocrisy.   81. meetly:
good.

   Sc. iii: 11. I . . . forbear: please forbear to torment him.
12. fear: frighten.   14. breathing: breath, words.   32. color:
excuse.   33. sued staying: begged to be allowed to stay.
37. race of Heaven: belonged to some heavenly creatures. She is
reminding Antony of his own words (I.i.36–40).

ANT. Now, by my sword——

CLEO.　　　　　　　　　And target.° Still he mends,
But this is not the best. Look, prithee, Charmian,
How this Herculean° Roman does become
The carriage of his chafe.°　　　　　　　　　　85

ANT. I'll leave you, lady.

CLEO.　　　　　　Courteous lord, one word.
Sir, you and I must part, but that's not it.
Sir, you and I have loved, but there's not it —
That you know well. Something it is I would——
Oh, my oblivion is a very Antony,　　　　　　90
And I am all forgotten.°

ANT.　　　　　　But that your royalty
Holds idleness your subject, I should take you
For idleness itself.°

CLEO.　　　　　　'Tis sweating labor
To bear such idleness so near the heart
As Cleopatra this. But, sir, forgive me,　　　　95
Since my becomings° kill me when they do not
Eye well° to you. Your honor calls you hence,
Therefore be deaf to my unpitied folly,
And all the gods go with you! Upon your sword
Sit laurel victory! And smooth success　　　　100
Be strewed before your feet!

ANT.　　　　　　Let us go. Come,
Our separation so abides and flies
That thou residing here go'st yet with me,
And I hence fleeting here remain with thee.°　104
Away!　　　　　　　　　　　　[*Exeunt.*]

SCENE IV. *Rome.* CAESAR'S *house.*

[*Enter* OCTAVIUS CAESAR, *reading a letter,* LEPIDUS,
and their train.]

CAES. You may see, Lepidus, and henceforth
　　　know,
It is not Caesar's natural vice to hate
Our great competitor.° From Alexandria
This is the news. He fishes, drinks, and wastes
The lamps of night in revel, is not more manlike　5
Than Cleopatra, nor the Queen of Ptolemy
More womanly than he. Hardly gave audience, or
Vouchsafed° to think he had partners. You shall find
　　　there
A man who is the abstract of all faults
That all men follow.°

LEP.　　　　　　I must not think there are　10
Evils enow° to darken all his goodness.
His faults in him seem as the spots of Heaven,
More fiery by night's blackness,° hereditary
Rather than purchased,° what he cannot change
Than what he chooses.　　　　　　　15

CAES. You are too indulgent. Let us grant it is not
Amiss to tumble on the bed of Ptolemy,
To give a kingdom for a mirth,° to sit
And keep the turn of tippling with a slave,
To reel the streets at noon and stand the buffet°　20
With knaves that smell of sweat. Say this becomes
　　　him —
As his composure° must be rare indeed
Whom these things cannot blemish — yet must
　　　Antony
No way excuse his soils° when we do bear
So great weight in his lightness.° If he filled　25
His vacancy° with his voluptuousness,
Full surfeits° and the dryness of his bones°
Call on him for 't.° But to confound such time
That drums him from his sport and speaks as loud
As his own state and ours,° 'tis to be chid　30
As we rate boys who, being mature in knowledge,
Pawn their experience to their present pleasure,
And so rebel to judgment.°

[*Enter a* MESSENGER.]

LEP.　　　　　　　Here's more news.

MESS. Thy biddings have been done, and every
　　　hour,
Most noble Caesar, shalt thou have report　　35
How 'tis abroad. Pompey is strong at sea,
And it appears he is beloved of those
That only have feared Caesar. To the ports
The discontents° repair, and men's reports
Give him° much wronged.

CAES.　　　　I should have known no less.　40
It hath been taught us from the primal state°
That he which is was wished until he were,°
And the ebbed man, ne'er loved till ne'er worth love,
Comes deared by being lacked.° This common body,

11. enow: enough.　12–13. His . . . blackness: i.e., as the black night shows up the stars, so Antony's good qualities make the bad more conspicuous.　Lepidus is always anxious to avoid trouble and tries to prevent the differences between Caesar and Antony from coming to a head.　13–14. hereditary . . . purchased: born in him rather than acquired.　18. mirth: jest.　20. stand . . . buffet: exchange blows.　22. composure: nature.　24. soils: blemishes.　25. weight . . . lightness: trouble because of his frivolity.　26. vacancy: leisure hours.　27. surfeits: excesses of eating and drinking. dryness . . . bones: the results of loose living.　28. Call . . . for't: call him to a reckoning.　28–30. confound . . . ours: but to waste that time which summons him from sport to his duty and demands that he attend to his business and ours.　30–33. 'tis . . . judgment: is to be worthy of blame, as we rebuke boys who indulge in pleasures which by experience and judgment they know to be harmfu'.　39. discontents: discontented.　40. Give him: give him out to be.　41. primal state: the very beginning.　42. That . . . were: i.e., the "coming man" is desired until he has "arrived" — and then everyone hates him.　43–44. And . . . lacked: the man

82. target: shield. See Pl. 9d.　84. Herculean: Antony claimed to be descended from Hercules.　84–85. does . . . chafe: how fine he looks when he is angry. chafe: annoyance.　90–91. Oh . . . forgotten: A cry of pathos, another of Shakespeare's untranslatable phrases; "even when I forget everything I remember only Antony, though he utterly forgets me."　91–93. But . . . itself: I would regard you as idleness personified were it not that idleness is one of your subjects.　96. becomings: graces.　97. Eye well: seem good.　102–04. Our . . . thee: or, as Sidney put it, "My true love hath my heart, and I have his." fleeting: sailing.

Sc. iv: 3. competitor: partner.　8. Vouchsafed: condescended.
9–10. abstract . . . follow: is a summary of all human faults.

Like to a vagabond flag upon the stream,   45
Goes to and back, lackeying the varying tide,
To rot itself with motion.°
    MESS.   Caesar, I bring thee word,
Menecrates and Menas, famous pirates,
Make the sea serve them, which they ear and wound
With keels of every kind. Many hot inroads   50
They make in Italy. The borders maritime
Lack blood° to think on 't, and flush° youth revolt.
No vessel can peep forth but 'tis as soon
Taken as seen, for Pompey's name strikes more
Than could his war resisted.
    CAES.   Antony,   55
Leave thy lascivious wassails.° When thou once
Wast beaten from Modena, where thou slew'st
Hirtius and Pansa, consuls, at thy heel
Did famine follow, whom thou fought'st against,
Though daintily brought up, with patience more
Than savages could suffer. Thou didst drink   61
The stale° of horses and the gilded° puddle
Which beasts would cough at. Thy palate then did
    deign
The roughest berry on the rudest hedge —
Yea, like the stag when snow the pasture sheets,   65
The barks of trees thou browsedst. On the Alps
It is reported thou didst eat strange flesh
Which some did die to look on. And all this —
It wounds thine honor that I speak it now —
Was borne so like a soldier that thy cheek   70
So much as lanked not.°
    LEP.   'Tis pity of him.
    CAES. Let his shames quickly
Drive him to Rome. 'Tis time we twain
Did show ourselves i' the field, and to that end
Assemble we immediate council. Pompey   75
Thrives in our idleness.
    LEP.   Tomorrow, Caesar,
I shall be furnished to inform you rightly
Both what by sea and land I can be able
To front° this present time.
    CAES.   Till which encounter,
It is my business too. Farewell.   80
    LEP. Farewell, my lord. What you shall know
    meantime
Of stirs abroad, I shall beseech you, sir,

To let me be partaker.
    CAES.   Doubt not, sir.
I knew it for my bond.°   [*Exeunt.*]

SCENE V. *Alexandria.* CLEOPATRA's *palace.*

[*Enter* CLEOPATRA, CHARMIAN, IRAS, *and* MARDIAN.]
    CLEO. Charmian!
    CHAR. Madam?
    CLEO. Ha, ha!
Give me to drink mandragora.°
    CHAR.   Why, madam?
    CLEO. That I might sleep out this great gap of
    time   5
My Antony is away.
    CHAR.   You think of him too much.
    CLEO. Oh, 'tis treason!
    CHAR.   Madam, I trust not so.
    CLEO. Thou, eunuch Mardian!
    MAR.   What's your Highness' pleasure?
    CLEO. Not now to hear thee sing, I take no
    pleasure
In aught a eunuch has. 'Tis well for thee   10
That, being unseminared,° thy freer thoughts
May not fly forth of Egypt. Hast thou affections?
    MAR. Yes, gracious madam.
    CLEO. Indeed!
    MAR. Not in deed, madam, for I can do nothing
But what indeed is honest to be done.   16
Yet have I fierce affections, and think
What Venus did with Mars.
    CLEO.   O Charmian,
Where think'st thou he is now? Stands he, or sits
    he?
Or does he walk? Or is he on his horse?   20
O happy horse, to bear the weight of Antony!
Do bravely, horse! For wot'st thou° whom thou
    movest?
The demi-Atlas° of this earth, the arm
And burgonet° of men. He's speaking now,
Or murmuring, " Where's my serpent of old Nile? "
For so he calls me. Now I feed myself   26
With most delicious poison. Think on me,
That am with Phoebus'° amorous pinches black
And wrinkled deep in time?° Broad-fronted°
    Caesar,
When thou wast here above the ground, I was   30
A morsel for a monarch. And great Pompey
Would stand and make his eyes grow in my brow.
There would he anchor his aspect° and die

whose power has slipped away is never loved till he is not worth
loving and becomes precious because of his absence. **44–47. This
. . . motion:** the common herd are like a flag floating this way
and that on the water, as the tide ebbs and flows, till it
rots by the constant movement. "Flag" is usually interpreted
as water iris; if so, this is the only time that Shakespeare uses
the word in this sense. More probably he had noticed some ac-
tual flag trailing in the waters of the Thames and carried up
and down by the tide till it rotted away. **lackeying:** following
like a servant; Theobald's emendation for F1 "lacking." Shake-
speare does elsewhere use "lackey" as a verb. **52. Lack
blood:** go pale. **flush:** in full vigor. **56. wassails:** revels.
stale: urine. **gilded:** covered with a yellow film. **71. lanked not:**
did not grow thin. **79. front:** confront.

83. I . . . bond: it is part of my agreement with you.
    Sc. v: 4. mandragora: mandrake, a sleep-inducing drug. Cf.
Oth, III.iii.330. **11. unseminared:** gelded. **22. wot'st thou:**
do you know. **23. demi-Atlas:** i.e., upholding half the world.
Atlas bore the Earth upon his shoulders. **24. burgonet:** helmet.
See Pl. 22d. **28. Phoebus:** the sun god. **29. in time:** by time.
Broad-fronted: with wide forehead. **33. aspect:** look.

With looking on his life.

[*Enter* ALEXAS.]

ALEX.   Sovereign of Egypt, hail!

CLEO. How much unlike art thou Mark Antony!
Yet, coming from him, that great medicine hath   36
With his tinct gilded thee.°
How goes it with my brave Mark Antony?

ALEX. Last thing he did, dear Queen,
He kissed — the last of many doubled kisses —   40
This Orient pearl. His speech sticks in my heart.

CLEO. Mine ear must pluck it thence.

ALEX.   "Good friend," quoth he,
"Say the firm Roman to great Egypt sends
This treasure of an oyster. At whose foot,
To mend the petty present, I will piece°   45
Her opulent throne with kingdoms. All the East,
Say thou, shall call her mistress." So he nodded,
And soberly did mount an arm-gaunt° steed,
Who neighed so high that what I would have spoke
Was beastly dumbed by him.

CLEO.   What, was he sad or merry?   50

ALEX. Like to the time o' the year between the ex-
tremes
Of hot and cold, he was nor sad nor merry.

CLEO. Oh, well-divided disposition! Note him,
Note him, good Charmian, 'tis the man, but note
him.
He was not sad, for he would shine on those   55
That make their looks by his; he was not merry,
Which seemed to tell them his remembrance lay
In Egypt with his joy; but between both.
Oh, heavenly mingle! Be'st thou sad or merry,
The violence of either thee becomes   60
So does it no man else. Met'st thou my posts?°

ALEX. Aye, madam, twenty several messengers.
Why do you send so thick?

CLEO.   Who's born that day
When I forget to send to Antony
Shall die a beggar. Ink and paper, Charmian.   65
Welcome, my good Alexas. Did I, Charmian,
Ever love Caesar so?

CHAR.   Oh, that brave Caesar!

CLEO. Be choked with such another emphasis!
Say the brave Antony.

CHAR.   The valiant Caesar!

CLEO. By Isis, I will give thee bloody teeth   70
If thou with Caesar paragon° again
My man of men.

CHAR.   By your most gracious pardon,
I sing but after you.

CLEO.   My salad days,°

When I was green in judgment, cold in blood,
To say as I said then! But come, away,   75
Get me ink and paper.
He shall have every day a several° greeting,
Or I'll unpeople Egypt.   [*Exeunt.*]

Act II

SCENE I. *Messina.* POMPEY'S *house.*

[*Enter* POMPEY, MENECRATES, *and* MENAS, *in warlike manner.*]

POM. If the great gods be just, they shall assist
The deeds of justest men.

MENE.   Know, worthy Pompey,
That what they do delay, they not deny.

POM. Whiles we are suitors to their throne, decays
The thing we sue for.

MENE.   We, ignorant of ourselves,   5
Beg often our own harms, which the wise powers
Deny us for our good. So find we profit
By losing of our prayers.

POM.   I shall do well.
The people love me, and the sea is mine.
My powers are crescent,° and my auguring° hope
Says it will come to the full. Mark Antony   11
In Egypt sits at dinner, and will make
No wars withoutdoors. Caesar gets money where
He loses hearts. Lepidus flatters both,
Of both is flattered, but he neither loves   15
Nor either cares for him.

MEN.   Caesar and Lepidus
Are in the field. A mighty strength they carry.

POM. Where have you this? 'Tis false.

MEN.   From Silvius, sir.

POM. He dreams. I know they are in Rome to-
gether,
Looking for Antony. But all the charms of love,   20
Salt° Cleopatra, soften thy waned° lip!
Let witchcraft join with beauty, lust with both!
Tie up the libertine in a field of feasts,
Keep his brain fuming. Epicurean cooks
Sharpen with cloyless° sauce his appetite,   25
That sleep and feeding may prorogue° his honor
Even till a Lethed dullness!°

[*Enter* VARRIUS.]   How now, Varrius!

VAR. This is most certain that I shall deliver.
Mark Antony is every hour in Rome

36–37. medicine . . . thee: i.e., the very sight of Antony has been
like a dose of tincture of gold. See App. 21.   45. piece: en-
large.   48. arm-gaunt: a much-disputed word not satisfactorily
explained, unless, perhaps, lean and hard from bearing armor.
61. posts: messengers. See App. 17.   71. paragon: make equal.
73. salad days: i.e., when I was green and inexperienced.

78. several: separate.

Act II, Sc. i: 10. crescent: growing. auguring: prophesying
good.   21. Salt: lustful. waned: withered.   25. cloyless: of
which he never has too much.   26. prorogue: suspend.   27. Lethed
dullness: dull forgetfulness. Lethe was the river of forget-
fulness in the underworld.

Expected. Since he went from Egypt 'tis   30
A space° for farther travel.

POM.   I could have given less matter
A better ear. Menas, I did not think
This amorous surfeiter would have donned his helm
For such a petty war. His soldiership
Is twice the other twain. But let us rear   35
The higher our opinion,° that our stirring
Can from the lap of Egypt's widow pluck
The ne'er-lust-wearied Antony.

MEN.   I cannot hope
Caesar and Antony shall well greet together.
His wife that's dead did trespasses to Caesar,   40
His brother warred upon him — although I think
Not moved by Antony.

POM.   I know not, Menas,
How lesser enmities may give way to greater.
Were 't not that we stand up against them all,
'Twere pregnant° they should square° between
     themselves,   45
For they have entertainèd° cause enough
To draw their swords. But how the fear of us
May cément their divisions and bind up
The petty difference, we yet not know.
Be 't as our gods will have 't! It only stands   50
Our lives upon to use our strongest hands.°
Come, Menas.   [*Exeunt.*]

SCENE II. *Rome. The house of* LEPIDUS.

[*Enter* ENOBARBUS *and* LEPIDUS.]

LEP. Good Enobarbus, 'tis a worthy deed,
And shall become you well, to entreat your Captain
To soft and gentle speech.

ENO.   I shall entreat him
To answer like himself. If Caesar move him,
Let Antony look over Caesar's head   5
And speak as loud as Mars. By Jupiter,
Were I the wearer of Antonius' beard,
I would not shave 't today.°

LEP.   'Tis not a time
For private stomaching.°

ENO.   Every time
Serves for the matter that is then born in 't.   10

LEP. But small to greater matters must give way.

ENO. Not if the small come first.

LEP.   Your speech is passion.
But pray you stir no embers up. Here comes
The noble Antony.

[*Enter* ANTONY *and* VENTIDIUS.]

ENO.   And yonder, Caesar.

[*Enter* CAESAR, MECAENAS, *and* AGRIPPA.]

ANT. If we compose° well here, to Parthia.   15
Hark, Ventidius.

CAES.   I do not know,
Mecaenas. Ask Agrippa.

LEP.   Noble friends,
That which combined us was most great, and let not
A leaner action rend us. What's amiss,
May it be gently heard. When we debate   20
Our trivial difference loud, we do commit
Murder in healing wounds. Then, noble partners,
The rather for I earnestly beseech,
Touch you the sourest points with sweetest terms,
Nor curstness° grow to the matter.

ANT.   'Tis spoken well.   25
Were we before our armies and to fight,
I should do thus.   [*Flourish.*]

CAES. Welcome to Rome.

ANT. Thank you.

CAES. Sit.

ANT. Sit, sir.

CAES. Nay, then.

ANT. I learn you take things ill which are not so,
Or being, concern you not.

CAES.   I must be laughed at   30
If, or for° nothing or a little, I
Should say myself offended, and with you
Chiefly i' the world — more laughed at that I should
Once name you derogately° when to sound your
     name
It not concerned me.

ANT.   My being in Egypt, Caesar,   35
What was 't to you?

CAES. No more than my residing here at Rome
Might be to you in Egypt. Yet if you there
Did practice on° my state, your being in Egypt
Might be my question.°

ANT.   How intend° you "practiced"?   40

CAES. You may be pleased to catch at mine intent
By what did here befall me. Your wife and brother
Made wars upon me, and their contestation
Was theme for you,° you were the word° of war.

ANT. You do mistake your business. My brother
     never   45
Did urge me in his act. I did inquire it,
And have my learning° from some true reports°
That drew their swords with you. Did he not rather
Discredit my authority with yours,

31. A space: i.e., time.   35–36. rear . . . opinion: have a better opinion of ourselves.   45. pregnant: likely. square: quarrel. 46. entertained: received.   50–51. It . . . hands: our lives depend on our using our hands strongly.

Sc. ii: 7–8. Were . . . today: i.e., I would dare Caesar to insult me. To pluck at a man's beard was a deadly insult. Cf. *Lear*, III.vii.35–36, 76–77.   9. private stomaching: squabbling over personal grievances.

15. compose: come to terms.   25. curstness: bitterness.   31. or for: either for.   34. derogately: disparagingly.   39. practice on: plot against.   40. question: affair. intend: mean. 43–44. contestation . . . you: fighting with me a subject which concerned you.   44. word: watchword; i.e., they claimed that they were fighting for you.   47. learning: information. reports: reporters. As often, Shakespeare uses the abstract for the concrete word.

And make the wars alike against my stomach,°   50
Having alike your cause?° Of this my letters
Before did satisfy you. If you'll patch a quarrel,°
As matter whole you have not to make it with,
It must not be with this.

CAES.   You praise yourself
By laying defects of judgment to me, but   55
You patched up your excuses.

ANT.   Not so, not so.
I know you could not lack, I am certain on 't,
Very necessity of this thought, that I,
Your partner in the cause 'gainst which he fought,
Could not with graceful eyes attend° those wars   60
Which fronted° mine own peace. As for my wife,
I would you had her spirit in such another.
The third o' the world is yours, which with a snaffle°
You may pace° easy, but not such a wife.

ENO. Would we had all such wives, that the   65
men might go to wars with the women!

ANT. So much uncurbable, her garboils, Caesar,
Made out of her impatience, which not wanted
Shrewdness of policy too, I grieving grant
Did you too much disquiet.° For that you must   70
But say I could not help it.

CAES.   I wrote to you
When rioting in Alexandria. You
Did pocket up my letters, and with taunts
Did gibe my missive° out of audience.

ANT.   Sir,
He fell upon me ere admitted.° Then   75
Three Kings I had newly feasted and did want
Of what I was i' the morning. But next day
I told him of myself, which was as much
As to have asked him pardon. Let this fellow
Be nothing of our strife. If we contend,   80
Out of our question wipe him.

CAES.   You have broken
The article of your oath, which you shall never
Have tongue to charge me with.

LEP.   Soft, Caesar!

ANT. No, Lepidus, let him speak.
The honor is sacred which he talks on now,   85
Supposing that I lacked it. But on, Caesar,
The article of my oath.

CAES. To lend me arms and aid when I required
    them,

The which you both denied.

ANT.   Neglected rather,
And then when poisoned hours had bound me up
From mine own knowledge. As nearly as I may,   91
I'll play the penitent to you, but mine honesty
Shall not make poor my greatness, nor my power
Work without it.° Truth is that Fulvia,
To have me out of Egypt, made wars here,   95
For which myself, the ignorant motive, do
So far ask pardon as befits mine honor
To stoop in such a case.

LEP.   'Tis noble-spoken.

MEC. If it might please you to enforce no further
The griefs between ye, to forget them quite   100
Were to remember that the present need
Speaks to atone° you.

LEP.   Worthily spoken, Mecaenas.

ENO. Or if you borrow one another's love for the
instant, you may, when you hear no more words of
Pompey, return it again. You shall have time to
wrangle in when you have nothing else to do.   107

ANT. Thou art a soldier only. Speak no more.

ENO. That truth should be silent I had almost
    forgot.   110

ANT. You wrong this presence,° therefore speak
    no more.

ENO. Go to, then, your considerate stone.°

CAES. I do not much dislike the matter, but
The manner, of his speech. For 't cannot be
We shall remain in friendship, our conditions°   115
So differing in their acts. Yet if I knew
What hoop° should hold us stanch,° from edge to
    edge
O' the world I would pursue it.

AGR.   Give me leave, Caesar.

CAES. Speak, Agrippa.

AGR. Thou hast a sister by the mother's side,
Admired Octavia. Great Mark Antony   121
Is now a widower.

CAES.   Say not so, Agrippa.
If Cleopatra heard you, your reproof
Were well deserved of rashness.

ANT. I am not married, Caesar. Let me hear   125
Agrippa further speak.

AGR. To hold you in perpetual amity,
To make you brothers and to knit your hearts
With an unslipping knot, take Antony°
Octavia to his wife, whose beauty claims   130
No worse a husband than the best of men,
Whose virtue and whose general graces speak

---

50. stomach: inclination.   **51. Having . . . cause:** i.e., those who fought against you were fighting against me.   **52. patch a quarrel:** make a quarrel out of patches.   **60. with . . . attend:** could not pay favorable attention to.   **61. fronted:** opposed. **63. snaffle:** a bit without a curb, used only with a horse easy to manage.   **64. pace:** ride.   **67–70. So . . . disquiet:** I regretfully admit that her brawls (*garboils*), caused by an impatience which was not indeed without deliberate shrewdness, caused you too much anxiety (*disquiet*). Antony is finding it difficult to keep his end up against Caesar's direct accusations, and the logical sequence of his thought suffers.   **74. gibe my missive:** mock my messenger.   **75. ere admitted:** before he was given permission to come in.

92–94. but . . . it: i.e., but even if I am honest, I am not going to be too humble, nor will I use my power dishonestly.   **102. atone:** make one, reconcile.   **111. presence:** noble company; lit., presence chamber, the room in Court where Caesar gave formal audiences.   **112. your . . . stone:** i.e., I'll say nothing but think quite a bit.   **115. conditions:** natures.   **117. hoop:** i.e., like that of a barrel. **stanch:** free from leaks.   **129. take Antony:** let Antony take.

That which none else can utter. By this marriage
All little jealousies which now seem great,
And all great fears which now import° their dan-
    gers,   135
Would then be nothing. Truths would be tales°
Where now half-tales be truths. Her love to both
Would each to other and all loves to both
Draw after her. Pardon what I have spoke,
For 'tis a studied,° not a present, thought,°   140
By duty ruminated.

ANT.   Will Caesar speak?

CAES. Not till he hears how Antony is touched
With what is spoke already.

ANT.   What power is in Agrippa
If I would say, " Agrippa, be it so,"
To make this good?

CAES.   The power of Caesar, and   145
His power unto Octavia.

ANT.   May I never
To this good purpose, that so fairly shows,
Dream of impediment! Let me have thy hand.
Further this act of grace, and from this hour
The heart of brothers govern in our loves   150
And sway our great designs!

CAES.   There is my hand.
A sister I bequeath you whom no brother
Did ever love so dearly. Let her live
To join our kingdoms and our hearts, and never
Fly off our loves again!

LEP.   Happily, amen!   155

ANT. I did not think to draw my sword 'gainst
    Pompey,
For he hath laid strange courtesies and great
Of late upon me. I must thank him only,
Lest my remembrance suffer ill report,
At heel of that, defy him.

LEP.   Time calls upon 's.   160
Of us must Pompey presently° be sought,
Or else he seeks out us.

ANT.   Where lies he?

CAES. About the Mount Misenum.

ANT.   What's his strength
By land?

CAES. Great and increasing. But by sea   165
He is an absolute master.

ANT.   So is the fame.°
Would we had spoke together! Haste we for it.
Yet ere we put ourselves in arms, dispatch we
The business we have talked of.

CAES.   With most gladness,
And do invite you to my sister's view,°   170
Whither straight I'll lead you.

ANT.   Let us, Lepidus,

Not lack your company.

LEP.   Noble Antony,
Not sickness should detain me.

[*Flourish. Exeunt* CAESAR, ANTONY, *and* LEPIDUS.]

MEC. Welcome from Egypt, sir.   174

ENO. Half the heart of Caesar, worthy Mecaenas!
My honorable friend Agrippa!

AGR. Good Enobarbus!

MEC. We have cause to be glad that matters are so
well digested. You stayed well by 't° in Egypt.   180

ENO. Aye, sir, we did sleep day out of counte-
nance, and made the night light with drinking.

MEC. Eight wild boars roasted whole at a break-
fast and but twelve persons there. Is this true?   185

ENO. This was but as a fly by an eagle. We had
much more monstrous matter of feast which wor-
thily deserved noting.

MEC. She's a most triumphant lady, if report be
square to° her.   190

ENO. When she first met Mark Antony, she pursed
up° his heart, upon the river of Cydnus.°

AGR. There she appeared indeed,° or my reporter
devised well for her.°

ENO. I° will tell you.   195
The barge she sat in, like a burnished throne,
Burned on the water. The poop° was beaten gold,
Purple the sails, and so perfumèd that
The winds were lovesick with them. The oars were
    silver,
Which to the tune of flutes kept stroke and made
The water which they beat to follow faster,   201
As amorous of their strokes. For her own person,
It beggared all description. She did lie
In her pavilion, cloth of gold of tissue,°
O'er picturing that Venus where we see   205
The fancy outwork nature.° On each side her
Stood pretty dimpled boys, like smiling Cupids,
With divers-colored° fans, whose wind did seem
To glow° the delicate cheeks which they did cool,
And what they undid did.

AGR.   Oh, rare for Antony!   210

ENO. Her gentlewomen, like the Nereides,°
So many mermaids, tended her i' the eyes,
And made their bends adornings.° At the helm
A seeming mermaid steers. The silken tackle°

---

135. **import:** bring with them.   136. **tales:** i.e., not regarded seriously.   140. **studied:** carefully considered. **present thought:** a thought that has just occurred to me.   161. **presently:** immediately.   166. **fame:** report.   170. **sister's view:** to visit my sister.

180. **stayed . . . by't:** had a good time.   190. **square to:** accurate about.   191–92. **pursed up:** put in the bag.   192. **Cydnus:** a river in Asia Minor.   193. **appeared indeed:** made a good show.   194. **devised . . . her:** wrote her up well.   195–245. **I . . . rig- gish:** For the original of this famous description see *Ant & Cleo* Intro. pp. 863b–864a. It is superb artistry to give this rapturous and lyrical account of Cleopatra to the cynical Enobarbus.   197. **poop:** stern.   204. **cloth . . . tissue:** "sheer" cloth of gold.   206. **fancy . . . nature:** the imagination of the artist surpasses nature. See Pl. 7a.   208. **divers-colored:** different-colored.   209. **glow:** make blush.   211. **Nereides:** sea nymphs.   212–13. **tended . . . adornings:** a much-discussed phrase; proba- bly meaning "they watched her slightest glance as they prettily bent to fulfill her pleasure."   214. **tackle:** rigging.

Swell with the touches of those flower-soft hands
That yarely frame the office.° From the barge   216
A strange invisible perfume hits the sense
Of the adjacent wharfs. The city cast
Her people out upon her. And Antony,
Enthronèd i' the market place, did sit alone,   220
Whistling to the air, which, but for vacancy,°
Had gone to gaze on Cleopatra too,
And made a gap in nature.

AGR.   Rare Egyptian!

ENO. Upon her landing, Antony sent to her,
Invited her to supper. She replied   225
It should be better he became her guest,
Which she entreated. Our courteous Antony,
Whom ne'er the word of "No" woman heard
     speak,
Being barbered ten times o'er, goes to the feast,
And, for his ordinary,° pays his heart   230
For what his eyes eat only.

AGR.   Royal wench!
She made great Caesar lay his sword to bed.
He plowed her, and she cropped.

ENO.   I saw her once
Hop forty paces through the public street.
And having lost her breath, she spoke, and panted,
That she did make defect perfection,   236
And breathless, power breathe forth.

MEC. Now Antony must leave her utterly.

ENO. Never. He will not.
Age cannot wither her, nor custom stale   240
Her infinite variety. Other women cloy
The appetites they feed, but she makes hungry
Where most she satisfies. For vilest things
Become themselves in her, that the holy priests
Bless her when she is riggish.°   245

MEC. If beauty, wisdom, modesty, can settle
The heart of Antony, Octavia is
A blessèd lottery° to him.

AGR.   Let us go.
Good Enobarbus, make yourself my guest   249
Whilst you abide here.

ENO.   Humbly, sir, I thank you. [Exeunt.]

SCENE III. *The same.* CAESAR'S *house.*

[*Enter* ANTONY, CAESAR, OCTAVIA *between them, and*
     ATTENDANTS.]

ANT. The world and my great office will some-
     times
Divide me from your bosom.

OCT.   All which time
Before the gods my knee shall bow my prayers
To them for you.

ANT.   Good night, sir. My Octavia,
Read not my blemishes in the world's report.   5
I have not kept my square,° but that to come
Shall all be done by the rule. Good night, dear lady.
Good night, sir.

CAES. Good night.   [*Exeunt all but* ANTONY.]
                    [*Enter* SOOTHSAYER.]

ANT. Now, sirrah,° you do wish yourself in
     Egypt?   10

SOOTH. Would I had never come from thence, nor
     you
Thither!

ANT. If you can, your reason?

SOOTH.   I see it in
My motion,° have it not in my tongue. But yet
Hie you° to Egypt again.

ANT.   Say to me   15
Whose fortunes shall rise higher, Caesar's or mine?

SOOTH. Caesar's.
Therefore, O Antony, stay not by his side.
Thy demon,° that thy spirit which keeps thee, is
Noble, courageous, high, unmatchable,   20
Where Caesar's is not. But near him thy angel
Becomes a fear,° as being o'erpowered. Therefore
Make space enough between you.

ANT.   Speak this no more.

SOOTH. To none but thee, no more but when to
     thee.
If thou dost play with him at any game,   25
Thou art sure to lose, and, of that natural luck,
He beats thee 'gainst the odds. Thy luster thickens°
When he shines by. I say again, thy spirit
Is all afraid to govern thee near him,
But he away, 'tis noble.

ANT.   Get thee gone.   30
Say to Ventidius I would speak with him.
                    [*Exit* SOOTHSAYER.]
He shall to Parthia. Be it art or hap,
He hath spoken true. The very dice obey him,
And in our sports my better cunning faints°
Under his chance.° If we draw lots, he speeds.°   35
His cocks do win the battle still° of mine
When it is all to naught, and his quails° ever
Beat mine, inhooped, at odds. I will to Egypt.
And though I make this marriage for my peace,
I' the East my pleasure lies.
          [*Enter* VENTIDIUS.] Oh, come, Ventidius,   40
You must to Parthia. Your commission's° ready.
Follow me, and receive 't.   [*Exeunt.*]

216. yarely ... office: carry out their task like good sailors. Cf. *Temp,* I.i.4–7.   221. but ... vacancy: but that it would have caused a vacuum.   230. ordinary: dinner.   245. riggish: wanton.   248. lottery: prize in a lottery.

Sc. iii: 6. kept my square: kept straight; lit., within the boundary.   10. sirrah: my man, a term used to an inferior.   12–13. in My motion: by intuition.   14. Hie you: hasten.   19. demon: the spirit which watches over you; guardian angel.   21–22. angel ... fear: your guardian angel is afraid.   27. luster thickens: brightness grows dim.   34. cunning faints: knowledge fails.   35. chance: luck. speeds: wins.   36. still: always.   37. quails: Quail-fighting was a popular sport in Egypt. The two birds were set down within a hoop and fought till one was driven out.   41. commission: document of appointment.

SCENE IV. *The same. A street.*

[*Enter* LEPIDUS, MECAENAS, *and* AGRIPPA.]

LEP. Trouble yourselves no further. Pray you
hasten
Your generals after.

AGR.   Sir, Mark Antony
Will e'en but kiss Octavia, and we'll follow.

LEP. Till I shall see you in your soldier's dress,
Which will become you both, farewell.

MEC.   We shall,   5
As I conceive° the journey, be at the Mount
Before you, Lepidus.

LEP.   Your way is shorter.
My purposes do draw me much about.°
You'll win two days upon me.

MEC. & AGR.   Sir, good success!   9

LEP. Farewell.   [*Exeunt.*]

SCENE V. *Alexandria.* CLEOPATRA's *palace.*

[*Enter* CLEOPATRA, CHARMIAN, IRAS, *and* ALEXAS.]

CLEO. Give me some music — music, moody food
Of us that trade in love.

ALL.   The music, ho!

[*Enter* MARDIAN *the eunuch.*]

CLEO. Let it alone, let's to billiards. Come, Char-
mian.

CHAR. My arm is sore. Best play with Mardian.

CLEO. As well a woman with a eunuch played   5
As with a woman. Come, you'll play with me, sir?

MAR. As well as I can, madam.

CLEO. And when goodwill is showed, though 't
come too short,
The actor may plead pardon. I'll none now.
Give me mine angle,° we'll to the river. There,   10
My music playing far off, I will betray
Tawny-finned fishes. My bended hook shall pierce
Their slimy jaws, and as I draw them up,
I'll think them every one an Antony,
And say " Ah, ha! You're caught."

CHAR.   'Twas merry when   15
You wagered on your angling, when your diver
Did hang a salt fish on his hook, which he
With fervency drew up.

CLEO.   That time — oh, times! —
I laughed him out of patience, and that night
I laughed him into patience. And next morn,   20
Ere the ninth hour, I drunk him to his bed,
Then put my tires° and mantles on him whilst
I wore his sword Philippan.°

[*Enter a* MESSENGER.]   Oh, from Italy!

Ram thou thy fruitful tidings in mine ears,
That long time have been barren.

MESS.   Madam, madam ——   25

CLEO. Antonius dead! If thou say so, villain,
Thou kill'st thy mistress. But well and free,
If thou so yield him, there is gold, and here
My bluest veins to kiss — a hand that Kings
Have lipped, and trembled kissing.   30

MESS. First, madam, he is well.

CLEO.   Why, there's more gold.
But, sirrah, mark, we use
To say the dead are well. Bring it to that,
The gold I give thee will I melt and pour
Down thy ill-uttering throat.   35

MESS. Good madam, hear me.

CLEO.   Well, go to,° I will.
But there's no goodness in thy face. If Antony
Be free and healthful — so tart a favor°
To trumpet such good tidings! If not well,
Thou shouldst come like a Fury° crowned with
snakes,   40
Not like a formal man.°

MESS.   Will 't please you hear me?

CLEO. I have a mind to strike thee ere thou
speak'st.
Yet if thou say Antony lives, is well,
Or friends with Caesar or not captive to him,
I'll set thee in a shower of gold and hail°   45
Rich pearls upon thee.

MESS.   Madam, he's well.

CLEO.   Well said.

MESS. And friends with Caesar.

CLEO.   Thou'rt an honest man.

MESS. Caesar and he are greater friends than ever.

CLEO. Make thee a fortune from me.

MESS.   But yet, madam ——

CLEO. I do not like " But yet." It does allay   50
The good precedence.° Fie upon " But yet "!
" But yet " is as a jailer to bring forth
Some monstrous malefactor. Prithee, friend,
Pour out the pack of matter° to mine ear,
The good and bad together. He's friends with
Caesar,   55
In state of health, thou say'st, and thou say'st free.

MESS. Free, madam! No, I made no such report.
He's bound unto Octavia.

CLEO.   For what good turn?

MESS. For the best turn i' the bed.

CLEO.   I am pale, Charmian.

MESS. Madam, he's married to Octavia.   60

CLEO. The most infectious pestilence upon thee!

[*Strikes him down.*]

Sc. iv: 6. conceive: understand.   8. draw . . . about: make
me take a much longer way.
Sc. v: 10. angle: fishing rod.   22. tires: headdresses.
23. sword Philippan: the sword he wore at the Battle of Philippi.

36. go to: get on.   38. so . . . favor: such a sour expression.
40. Fury: fiend.   41. formal man: man of normal shape.
45. hail: rain down like hail.   50-51. allay . . . precedence: mix
something base with the goodness that has gone before.   54. pack
of matter: all the contents of the bag at once.

MESS. Good madam, patience.

CLEO. What say you? Hence, [*Strikes him again.*]
Horrible villain! Or I'll spurn thine eyes
Like balls before me, I'll unhair thy head.

        [*She hales him up and down.*]

Thou shalt be whipped with wire, and stewed in
    brine,   65
Smarting in lingering pickle.

MESS.   Gracious madam,
I that do bring the news made not the match.

CLEO. Say 'tis not so, a province I will give thee
And make thy fortunes proud. The blow thou hadst
Shall make thy peace for moving me to rage,   70
And I will boot° thee with what gift beside
Thy modesty can beg.

MESS.   He's married, madam.

CLEO. Rogue, thou hast lived too long.

                [*Draws a knife.*]

MESS.   Nay, then I'll run.
What mean you, madam? I have made no fault.

                  [*Exit.*]

CHAR. Good madam, keep yourself within your-
    self.   75
The man is innocent.

CLEO. Some innocents 'scape not the thunderbolt.
Melt Egypt into Nile! And kindly creatures
Turn all to serpents! Call the slave again.
Though I am mad, I will not bite him. Call.   80

CHAR. He is afeard to come.

CLEO.   I will not hurt him. [*Exit* CHARMIAN.]
These hands do lack nobility, that they strike
A meaner than myself, since I myself
Have given myself the cause.

[*Re-enter* CHARMIAN *and* MESSENGER.] Come hither,
    sir.
Though it be honest, it is never good   85
To bring bad news. Give to a gracious message
A host of tongues, but let ill tidings tell
Themselves when they be felt.

MESS.   I have done my duty.

CLEO. Is he married?
I cannot hate thee worser than I do   90
If thou again say " Yes."

MESS.   He's married, madam.

CLEO. The gods confound thee! Dost thou hold
    there still?

MESS. Should I lie, madam?

CLEO.   Oh, I would thou didst,
So half my Egypt were submerged and made
A cistern for scaléd snakes! Go get thee hence.   95
Hadst thou Narcissus° in thy face, to me
Thou wouldst appear most ugly. He is married?

MESS. I crave your Highness' pardon.

CLEO.   He is married?

MESS. Take no offense that I would not offend you.
To punish me for what you make me do   100
Seems much unequal.° He's married to Octavia.

CLEO. Oh, that his fault should make a knave of
    thee,
That art not what thou'rt sure of! Get thee hence.
The merchandise which thou hast brought from
    Rome   104
Are all too dear for me. Lie they upon thy hand,
And be undone by 'em!   [*Exit* MESSENGER.]

CHAR.   Good your Highness, patience.

CLEO. In praising Antony, I have dispraised
    Caesar.

CHAR. Many times, madam.

CLEO.   I am paid for 't now.
Lead me from hence,
I faint. O Iras, Charmian! 'Tis no matter.   110
Go to the fellow, good Alexas. Bid him
Report the feature of Octavia, her years,
Her inclination,° let him not leave out
The color of her hair. Bring me word quickly.

              [*Exit* ALEXAS.]

Let him forever go, let him not —— Charmian,   115
Though he be painted one way like a Gorgon,°
The other way's a Mars. [*To* MARDIAN] Bid you
    Alexas
Bring me word how tall she is. Pity me, Charmian,
But do not speak to me. Lead me to my chamber.

                [*Exeunt.*]

SCENE VI. *Near Misenum.*

[*Flourish. Enter* POMPEY *and* MENAS *from one side,
with drum and trumpet; at another,* CAESAR, ANTONY,
LEPIDUS, ENOBARBUS, MECAENAS, *with* SOLDIERS
marching.]

POM. Your hostages I have, so have you mine,
And we shall talk before we fight.

CAES.   Most meet
That first we come to words, and therefore have we
Our written purposes before us sent.
Which if thou hast considered, let us know   5
If 'twill tie up thy discontented sword
And carry back to Sicily much tall° youth
That else must perish here.

POM.   To you all three,
The Senators° alone of this great world,
Chief factors° for the gods, I do not know   10
Wherefore my father should revengers want,
Having a son and friends, since Julius Caesar,
Who at Philippi the good Brutus ghosted,°

71. **boot:** benefit. **96. Narcissus:** a youth so beautiful that
he fell in love with his own reflection in the water and perished
seeking it.

101. **unequal:** unfair. 113. **inclination:** what she likes and dis-
likes. 116. **Gorgon:** a creature so terrible to look on that all
who saw her turned to stone.

Sc. vi: 7. **tall:** brave. 9. **Senators:** councilors, governors.
10. **factors:** agents. 13. **ghosted:** haunted. See *Caesar,* IV.iii.
275–87.

There saw you laboring for him. What was 't
That moved pale Cassius to conspire, and what　15
Made the all-honored honest Roman, Brutus,
With the armèd rest, courtiers of beauteous freedom,
To drench° the Capitol, but that they would
Have one man but a man? And that is it
Hath made me rig my navy, at whose burden　20
The angered ocean foams, with which I meant
To scourge the ingratitude that despiteful° Rome
Cast on my noble father.

CAES.　　　　　　　　　　Take your time

ANT. Thou canst not fear° us, Pompey, with thy
　　sails,　　　　　　　　　　　　　　　24
We'll speak with thee at sea. At land, thou know'st
How much we do o'ercount thee.

POM.　　　　　　　　　　At land indeed
Thou dost o'ercount° me of my father's house.
But since the cuckoo° builds not for himself,
Remain in 't as thou mayst.

LEP.　　　　　　　　　Be pleased to tell us —
For this is from the present° — how you take　30
The offers we have sent you.

CAES.　　　　　　　　　There's the point.

ANT. Which do not be entreated to, but weigh
What it is worth embraced.

CAES.　　　　　　　　And what may follow,
To try a larger fortune.

POM.　　　　　　You have made me offer
Of Sicily, Sardinia, and I must　　　　　　35
Rid all the sea of pirates. Then, to send
Measures of wheat to Rome. This 'greed upon,
To part with unhacked edges° and bear back
Our targes undinted.°

CAES., ANT., & LEP.　That's our offer.

POM.　　　　　　　　　Know, then,
I came before you here a man prepared　　41
To take this offer. But Mark Antony
Put me to some impatience. Though I lose
The praise of it by telling, you must know
When Caesar and your brother were at blows,　45
Your mother came to Sicily and did find
Her welcome friendly.

ANT.　　　　　I have heard it, Pompey,
And am well studied° for a liberal thanks
Which I do owe you.

POM.　　　　　Let me have your hand.
I did not think, sir, to have met you here.　50

ANT. The beds i' the East are soft, and thanks to
　　you,
That called me timelier than my purpose hither,
For I have gained by 't.

18. drench: i.e., with blood.　22. despiteful: hateful, cruel.
24. fear: frighten.　27. o'ercount: outbid. Antony had bought
the house of the elder Pompey and refused to pay for it.
28. cuckoo: See App. 11.　30. For . . . present: i.e., this wran-
gling is off the point.　38. unhacked edges: i.e., without fighting.
39. targes undinted: shields undented.　48. am . . . studied:
have long thought. Cf. II.ii.156–60.

CAES.　　　　　　　　Since I saw you last
There is a change upon you.

POM.　　　　　　　　Well, I know not
What counts° harsh Fortune casts upon my face,　55
But in my bosom shall she never come
To make my heart her vassal.°

LEP.　　　　　　　　Well met here.

POM. I hope so, Lepidus. Thus we are agreed.
I crave our composition° may be written
And sealed between us.

CAES.　　　　　　　That's the next to do.　60

POM. We'll feast each other ere we part, and let's
Draw lots who shall begin.

ANT.　　　　　　　That will I, Pompey.

POM. No, Antony, take the lot.
But, first or last, your fine Egyptian cookery　64
Shall have the fame. I have heard that Julius Caesar
Grew fat with feasting there.

ANT.　　　　　　　You have heard much.

POM. I have fair meanings, sir.

ANT.　　　　　　　And fair words to them.

POM. Then so much have I heard.
And I have heard, Apollodorus carried ——

ENO. No more of that. He did so.

POM.　　　　　　　What, I pray you?　70

ENO. A certain Queen to Caesar in a mattress.

POM. I know thee now. How farest thou, soldier?

ENO.　　　　　　　　　　Well,
And well am like to do, for I perceive
Four feasts are toward.

POM.　　　　　　Let me shake thy hand.
I never hated thee. I have seen thee fight　75
When I have envied thy behavior.

ENO.　　　　　　　　　　Sir,
I never loved you much, but I ha' praised ye
When you have well deserved ten times as much
As I have said you did.

POM.　　　　　　Enjoy thy plainness,
It nothing ill becomes thee.　　　　　　80
Aboard my galley I invite you all.
Will you lead, lords?

CAES., ANT., & LEP.　Show us the way, sir.

POM.　　　　　　　　　　Come.

[Exeunt all but MENAS and ENOBARBUS.]

MEN. [Aside] Thy father, Pompey, would ne'er
have made this treaty. — You and I have known,°
sir.　　　　　　　　　　　　　　86

ENO. At sea, I think.

MEN. We have, sir.

ENO. You have done well by water.

MEN. And you by land.　　　　　　90

ENO. I will praise any man that will praise me,
though it cannot be denied what I have done by land.

MEN. Nor what I have done by water.　94

55. counts: accounts; i.e., whether my debts to Fortune are
recorded in my face.　57. vassal: slave.　59. composition:
agreement.　85. known: met before.

ENO. Yes, something you can deny for your own safety. You have been a great thief by sea.

MEN. And you by land.

ENO. There I deny my land service. But give me your hand, Menas. If our eyes had authority, here they might take two thieves kissing.   101

MEN. All men's faces are true, whatsome'er their hands are.

ENO. But there is never a fair woman has a true face.   105

MEN. No slander, they steal hearts.

ENO. We came hither to fight with you.

MEN. For my part, I am sorry it is turned to a drinking. Pompey doth this day laugh away his fortune.   110

ENO. If he do, sure he cannot weep 't back again.

MEN. You've said, sir. We looked not for Mark Antony here. Pray you, is he married to Cleopatra?

ENO. Caesar's sister is called Octavia.   116

MEN. True, sir, she was the wife of Caius Marcellus.

ENO. But she is now the wife of Marcus Antonius.

MEN. Pray ye, sir?   120

ENO. 'Tis true.

MEN. Then is Caesar and he forever knit together.

ENO. If I were bound to divine° of this unity, I would not prophesy so.   125

MEN. I think the policy of that purpose made more° in the marriage than the love of the parties.

ENO. I think so too. But you shall find the band that seems to tie their friendship together will be the very strangler of their amity. Octavia is of a holy, cold, and still conversation.°   131

MEN. Who would not have his wife so?

ENO. Not he that himself is not so, which is Mark Antony. He will to his Egyptian dish again. Then shall the sighs of Octavia blow the fire up in Caesar, and, as I said before, that which is the strength of their amity shall prove the immediate author° of their variance. Antony will use his affection where it is. He married but his occasion here.°   140

MEN. And thus it may be. Come, sir, will you aboard? I have a health for you.

ENO. I shall take it, sir. We have used our throats in Egypt.   144

MEN. Come, let's away.   [Exeunt.]

124. divine: prophesy. 126–27. policy ... more: political advantage of that arrangement had more to do with. 131. still conversation: "dumb" behavior. 138. author: cause. 140. married ... here: married to suit his immediate need.

SCENE VII. *On board* POMPEY's *galley, off Misenum.*

[*Music plays. Enter two or three* SERVANTS, *with a banquet.*°]

1. SERV. Here they'll be, man. Some o' their plants° are ill-rooted already, the least wind i' the world will blow them down.

2. SERV. Lepidus is high-colored.   5

1. SERV. They have made him drink alms drink.°

2. SERV. As they pinch° one another by the disposition,° he cries out "No more," reconciles them to his entreaty and himself to the drink.

1. SERV. But it raises the greater war between him and his discretion.   11

2. SERV. Why, this it is to have a name in great men's fellowship. I had as lief have a reed that will do me no service as a partisan° I could not heave.

1. SERV. To be called into a huge sphere, and   16 not to be seen to move in 't, are the holes where eyes should be, which pitifully disaster the cheeks.°

[*A sennet*° *sounded. Enter* CAESAR, ANTONY, LEPIDUS, POMPEY, AGRIPPA, MECAENAS, ENOBARBUS, MENAS, *with other* CAPTAINS.]

ANT. [*To* CAESAR] Thus do they, sir. They take the flow o' the Nile   20
By certain scales i' the pyramid. They know
By the height, the lowness, or the mean if dearth
Or foison° follow. The higher Nilus swells,
The more it promises. As it ebbs, the seedsman
Upon the slime and ooze scatters his grain,   25
And shortly comes to harvest.

LEP. You've strange serpents there.

ANT. Aye, Lepidus.

LEP. Your serpent of Egypt is bred now of your mud by the operation of your sun. So is your crocodile.°   31

ANT. They are so.

POM. Sit — and some wine! A health to Lepidus!

LEP. I am not so well as I should be, but I'll ne'er out.°   36

ENO. Not till you have slept. I fear me you'll be in till then.

LEP. Nay, certainly I have heard the Ptolemies' pyramises° are very goodly things — without contradiction, I have heard that.   41

Sc. vii: s.d., banquet: dessert and wine. 2. plants: soles of the feet, with a pun on growing plants. 6. alms drink: dregs given to the beggars. 7. pinch: irritate. 7–8. by ... disposition: according to each man's nature. 15. partisan: a heavy weapon. See Pl. 21a. 16–18. To ... cheeks: a complex image; it may be paraphrased "to be summoned to occupy a great and conspicuous place, like a planet in the sky, and then to be a failure, is to be like eyeless sockets which pitifully scar the face." 19 s.d., sennet: trumpet call. 23. foison: plenty. 29–31. Your ... crocodile: This was very generally believed. 35–36. I'll ... out: I'll never refuse a drink. Lepidus is by this time very fuddled. 40. pyramises: the nearest Lepidus can get to "pyramides," the Elizabethan form of pyramids. See V.ii.61.

MEN. [*Aside to* POMPEY] Pompey, a word.

POM. [*Aside to* MENAS] Say in mine ear. What
　is 't?

MEN. [*Aside to* POMPEY] Forsake thy seat, I do
　beseech thee, Captain,
And hear me speak a word.

POM. [*Aside to* MENAS] Forbear me till anon.° —
This wine for Lepidus!　　　　　　　　　　45

LEP. What manner o' thing is your crocodile?

ANT. It is shaped, sir, like itself, and it is as broad
as it hath breadth. It is just so high as it is, and
moves with it own organs. It lives by that which
nourisheth it, and the elements° once out of it, it
transmigrates.

LEP. What color is it of?　　　　　　　　52

ANT. Of it° own color too.

LEP. 'Tis a strange serpent.

ANT. 'Tis so. And the tears of it are wet.

CAES. Will this description satisfy him?

ANT. With the health that Pompey gives him, else
he is a very epicure.°　　　　　　　　　58

POM. [*Aside to* MENAS] Go hang, sir, hang! Tell
　me of that? Away!
Do as I bid you. — Where's this cup I called for?

MEN. [*Aside to* POMPEY] If for the sake of merit
　thou wilt hear me,　　　　　　　　　61
Rise from thy stool.

POM. [*Aside to* MENAS] I think thou'rt mad. The
　matter?　　　　　　　[*Rises, and walks aside.*]

MEN. I have ever held my cap off to thy fortunes.°

POM. Thou hast served me with much faith.
　What's else to say?
Be jolly, lords.

ANT.　　　　These quicksands, Lepidus —　65
Keep off them, for you sink.°

MEN. Wilt thou be lord of all the world?

POM.　　　　　　　　What say'st thou?

MEN. Wilt thou be lord of the whole world?
　That's twice.

POM. How should that be?

MEN.　　　　　　　　But entertain it,
And though thou think me poor, I am the man　70
Will give thee all the world.

POM.　　　　　　　　Hast thou drunk well?

MEN. No, Pompey, I have kept me from the cup.
Thou art, if thou darest be, the earthly Jove.
Whate'er the ocean pales° or sky inclips°
Is thine if thou wilt ha 't.

POM.　　　　　　　Show me which way.　75

MEN. These three world-sharers, these com-
　petitors,
Are in thy vessel. Let me cut the cable,

And when we are put off, fall to their throats.
All there is thine.

POM.　　　　　Ah, this thou shouldst have done,
And not have spoke on 't! In me 'tis villainy,　80
In thee 't had been good service. Thou must know
'Tis not my profit that does lead mine honor,
Mine honor, it. Repent that e'er thy tongue
Hath so betrayed thine act. Being done unknown,
I should have found it afterward well done,　85
But must condemn it now. Desist, and drink.

MEN. [*Aside*] For this
I'll never follow thy palled° fortunes more.
Who seeks and will not take when once 'tis offered
Shall never find it more.

POM.　　　　　　This health to Lepidus!　90

ANT. Bear him ashore. I'll pledge it for him,
　Pompey.

ENO. Here's to thee, Menas!

MEN.　　　　　　Enobarbus, welcome!

POM. Fill till the cup be hid.

ENO. There's a strong fellow, Menas.

[*Pointing to the* ATTENDANT *who carries off* LEPIDUS.]

MEN. Why?　　　　　　　　　　　　95

ENO. A' bears the third part of the world, man,
see'st not?

MEN. The third part then is drunk. Would it were
　all,
That it might go on wheels!°

ENO. Drink thou, increase the reels.°　　100

MEN. Come.

POM. This is not yet an Alexandrian feast.°

ANT. It ripens toward it. Strike the vessels,° ho!
Here's to Caesar!

CAES.　　　　　I could well forbear 't.
It's monstrous labor when I wash my brain　105
And it grows fouler.

ANT.　　　　　Be a child o' the time.

CAES. Possess it,° I'll make answer.
But I had rather fast from all four days
Than drink so much in one.

ENO. [*To* ANTONY] Ha, my brave Emperor!　110
Shall we dance now the Egyptian Bacchanals,°
And celebrate our drink?

POM.　　　　　　Let's ha 't, good soldier.

ANT. Come, let's all take hands
Till that the conquering wine hath steeped our sense
In soft and delicate Lethe.

ENO.　　　　　　All take hands.　115
Make battery to our ears with the loud music,
The while I'll place you. Then the boy shall sing,
The holding° every man shall bear as loud
As his strong sides can volley.

44. anon: by and by.　50. elements: The word is used with a large range of meanings. Antony here means "life."　53. it: its.　58. epicure: i.e., expert drinker.　63. held . . . fortunes: i.e., have been your faithful servant.　65–66. These . . . sink: Lepidus here lapses into a coma.　74. pales: fences in. inclips: embraces.

88. palled: decayed.　99. on wheels: fast; from the proverb "The world goes on wheels."　100. reels: revelry.　102. Alexandrian feast: i.e., as rowdy as those given by Cleopatra.　103. Strike . . . vessels: either "tap fresh casks" or "bang the cups on the tables."　107. Possess it: have it your own way.　111. Bacchanals: dances to Bacchus, the god of wine.　118. holding: refrain.

[*Music plays.* ENOBARBUS *places them hand in hand.*]
THE SONG

Come, thou monarch of the vine,   120
Plumpy Bacchus with pink eyne!°
In thy fats° our cares be drowned,
With thy grapes our hairs be crowned.
Cup us, till the world go round,
Cup us, till the world go round!   125

CAES. What would you more? Pompey, good
    night. Good brother,
Let me request you off.° Our graver business
Frowns at this levity. Gentle lords, let's part,
You see we have burnt our cheeks. Strong Enobarb
Is weaker than the wine, and mine own tongue   130
Splits what it speaks. The wild disguise hath almost
Anticked us all.° What needs more words? Good
    night.
Good Antony, your hand.

POM.   I'll try you on the shore.

ANT. And shall, sir. Give 's your hand.

POM.   O Antony,
You have my father's house. — But what? We are
    friends.   135
Come, down into the boat.

ENO.   Take heed you fall not.
       [*Exeunt all but* ENOBARBUS *and* MENAS.]
Menas, I'll not on shore.

MEN.   No, to my cabin.
These drums! These trumpets, flutes! What!
Let Neptune° hear we bid a loud farewell   139
To these great fellows. Sound and be hanged, sound
    out!   [*Sound a flourish, with drums.*]

ENO. Hoo! says a'. There's my cap.

MEN. Hoo! Noble Captain, come.   [*Exeunt.*]

Act III

SCENE I. *A plain in Syria.*

[*Enter* VENTIDIUS *as it were in triumph,°* with SILIUS,
and other ROMANS, OFFICERS, *and* SOLDIERS, *the dead
body of* PACORUS *borne before him.*]

VEN. Now, darting Parthia,° art thou struck, and
    now
Pleased fortune does of Marcus Crassus' death

---

121. eyne: eyes.   122. fats: vats, casks.   127. request . . . off:
beg you to come away.   132. Anticked us all: turned us all into
clowns.   139. Neptune: the god of the sea.
    Act III, Sc. i: s.d., Ventidius . . . triumph: Ventidius had
been sent to Parthia by Antony (II.iii.40–45) to avenge the
death of the Roman leader Crassus, defeated and killed by the
Parthians under King Orodes in Mesopotamia in 53 B.C.
1. darting Parthia: The Parthians had defeated the heavy-armed
and slow-moving Roman legions by their method of fighting.
They rode light-armed on horses from which they shot arrows into
the close ranks, and were away before the Romans could catch
them.

Make me revenger. Bear the King's son's body
Before our army. Thy Pacorus, Orodes,
Pays this for Marcus Crassus.

SIL.   Noble Ventidius,   5
Whilst yet with Parthian blood thy sword is warm,
The fugitive Parthians follow. Spur through Media,
Mesopotamia, and the shelters whither
The routed fly. So thy grand° Captain Antony
Shall set thee on triumphant chariots and   10
Put garlands on thy head.

VEN.   O Silius, Silius,
I have done enough. A lower place, note well,
May make too great an act.° For learn this, Silius —
Better to leave undone than by our deed
Acquire too high a fame when him we serve's away.
Caesar and Antony have ever won   16
More in their officer than person. Sossius,
One of my place in Syria, his lieutenant,
For quick accumulation of renown,
Which he achievèd by the minute, lost his favor.   20
Who does i' the wars more than his Captain can
Becomes his Captain's Captain. And ambition,
The soldier's virtue, rather makes choice of loss
Than gain which darkens him.
I could do more to do Antonius good,   25
But 'twould offend him, and in his offense
Should my performance perish.

SIL.   Thou hast, Ventidius, that
Without the which a soldier and his sword
Grants scarce distinction. Thou wilt write to
    Antony?

VEN. I'll humbly signify what in his name,   30
That magical word of war, we have effected,
How with his banners and his well-paid ranks
The ne'er-yet-beaten horse of Parthia
We have jaded° out o' the field.

SIL.   Where is he now?

VEN. He purposeth to Athens. Whither, with what
    haste   35
The weight° we must convey with 's will permit,
We shall appear before him. On, there, pass along!
                    [*Exeunt.*]

SCENE II. *Rome. An antechamber in* CAESAR'S
house.

[*Enter* AGRIPPA *at one door and* ENOBARBUS *at
another.*]

AGR. What, are the brothers parted?

ENO. They have dispatched° with Pompey. He is
    gone,

---

9. grand: great.   12–13. A . . . act: i.e., a subordinate com-
mander can do too well.   34. jaded: reduced to jades; i.e., poor-
spirited nags.   36. The weight: i.e., the body of Pacorus and
the loot.
    Sc. ii: 2. dispatched: finished their business.

The other three are sealing.° Octavia weeps
To part from Rome, Caesar is sad, and Lepidus
Since Pompey's feast, as Menas says, is troubled   5
With the greensickness.°

AGR.   'Tis° a noble Lepidus.

ENO. A very fine one. Oh, how he loves Caesar!

AGR. Nay, but how dearly he adores Mark
     Antony!

ENO. Caesar? Why, he's the Jupiter of men.

AGR. What's Antony? The god of Jupiter.   10

ENO. Spake you of Caesar? How! The nonpareil!°

AGR. O Antony! O thou Arabian bird!°

ENO. Would you praise Caesar, say " Caesar." Go
     no further.

AGR. Indeed he plied them both with excellent
     praises.

ENO. But he loves Caesar best, yet he loves
     Antony.   15

Ho! Hearts, tongues, figures, scribes, bards, poets,
     cannot
Think, speak, cast,° write, sing, number° — ho! —
His love to Antony. But as for Caesar,
Kneel down, kneel down, and wonder.

AGR.   Both he loves.

ENO. They are his shards,° and he their beetle.
     [*Trumpet within.*] So,   20
This is to horse. Adieu, noble Agrippa.

AGR. Good fortune, worthy soldier, and farewell.
     [*Enter* CAESAR, ANTONY, LEPIDUS, *and* OCTAVIA.]

ANT. No further, sir.

CAES. You take from me a great part of myself.
Use me well in 't. Sister, prove such a wife   25
As my thoughts make thee, and as my farthest band
Shall pass on thy approof.° Most noble Antony,
Let not the piece of virtue which is set
Betwixt us as the cément of our love,
To keep it builded, be the ram° to batter   30
The fortress of it. For better might we
Have loved without this mean° if on both parts
This be not cherished.

ANT.   Make me not offended
In your distrust.

CAES.   I have said.

ANT.   You shall not find,
Though you be therein curious,° the least cause   35
For what you seem to fear. So the gods keep you,
And make the hearts of Romans serve your ends!
We will here part.

CAES. Farewell, my dearest Sister, fare thee well.
The elements° be kind to thee, and make   40
Thy spirits all of comfort! Fare thee well.

OCT. My noble brother!

ANT. The April's in her eyes. It is love's spring,
And these the showers to bring it on. Be cheerful.

OCT. Sir, look well to my husband's house,
     and ——

CAES.   What,   45
Octavia?

OCT.   I'll tell you in your ear.

ANT. Her tongue will not obey her heart, nor can
Her heart inform her tongue,° the swan's-down
     feather,
That stands upon the swell at full of tide
And neither way inclines.   50

ENO. [*Aside to* AGRIPPA] Will Caesar weep?

AGR. [*Aside to* ENOBARBUS] He has a cloud in 's
     face.°

ENO. [*Aside to* AGRIPPA] He were the worse for
     that were he a horse.°
So is he, being a man.

AGR. [*Aside to* ENOBARBUS] Why, Enobarbus,
When Antony found Julius Caesar dead,
He cried almost to roaring, and he wept   55
When at Philippi he found Brutus slain.

ENO. [*Aside to* AGRIPPA] That year indeed he was
     troubled with a rheum.°
What willingly he did confound° he wailed,°
Believe 't, till I wept too.

CAES.   No, sweet Octavia,
You shall hear from me still. The time shall not   60
Outgo my thinking on you.

ANT.   Come, sir; come,
I'll wrestle° with you in my strength of love.
Look, here I have you, thus I let you go,
And give you to the gods.

CAES.   Adieu. Be happy!   64

LEP. Let all the number of the stars give light
To thy fair way!

CAES. Farewell, farewell! [*Kisses* OCTAVIA.]

ANT.   Farewell!
     [*Trumpets sound. Exeunt.*]

SCENE III. *Alexandria.* CLEOPATRA'S *palace.*

[*Enter* CLEOPATRA, CHARMIAN, IRAS, *and* ALEXAS.]

CLEO. Where is the fellow?

ALEX.   Half afeard to come.

CLEO. Go to, go to.

---

3. sealing: See App. 6.   6. greensickness: a form of anemia
common to teen-age girls.   6–20. 'Tis . . . beetle: Agrippa and
Enobarbus mimic Lepidus's tactful efforts to keep his partners
from quarreling.   11. nonpareil: unparalleled.   12. Arabian
bird: phoenix; i.e., unique creature. See *Temp*, III.iii.21–23,n.
17. cast: reckon. number: make verses.   20. shards: the horny
wings of the beetle.   26–27. as . . . approof: as my most ex-
travagant bond (*band*) shall guarantee. approof: proof of your
behavior.   30. ram: battering ram.   32. mean: means.
35. be . . . curious: make most careful inquiry.

40. elements: i.e., sea and sky.   47–48. Her . . . tongue: she is
so full of emotion that she can neither speak nor be silent.
51. cloud . . . face: i.e., looks as if he would weep.   52. were . . .
horse: a "cloud in the face" is also a dark patch between a
horse's eyes, believed to denote bad temper.   57. rheum: cold.
58. confound: overthrow. wailed: wept over.   62. wrestle:
i.e., they embrace at parting.

[*Enter* MESSENGER.]   Come hither, sir.

ALEX.   Good Majesty,
Herod of Jewry dare not look upon you
But when° you are well pleased.

CLEO.   That Herod's head
I'll have. But how, when Antony is gone   5
Through whom I might command it? Come thou
    near.

MESS. Most gracious Majesty——

CLEO. Didst thou behold Octavia?

MESS. Aye, dread Queen.

CLEO. Where?   10

MESS. Madam, in Rome
I looked her in the face, and saw her led
Between her brother and Mark Antony.

CLEO. Is she as tall as me?

MESS.   She is not, madam.

CLEO. Didst hear her speak? Is she shrill-tongued
    or low?   15

MESS. Madam, I heard her speak. She is low-
    voiced.

CLEO. That's not so good. He cannot like her long.

CHAR. Like her! Oh, Isis! 'Tis impossible.

CLEO. I think so, Charmian. Dull of tongue and
    dwarfish.
What majesty is in her gait? Remember,   20
If e'er thou look'dst on majesty.

MESS.   She creeps.
Her motion and her station are as one.
She shows a body rather than a life,
A statue than a breather.°

CLEO.   Is this certain?

MESS. Or I have no observance.

CHAR.   Three in Egypt   25
Cannot make better note.

CLEO.   He's very knowing,
I do perceive 't. There's nothing in her yet.
The fellow has good judgment.

CHAR.   Excellent.

CLEO. Guess at her years, I prithee.

MESS.   Madam,
She was a widow——

CLEO.   Widow! Charmian, hark.   30

MESS. And I do think she's thirty.

CLEO. Bear'st thou her face in mind? Is 't long or
    round?

MESS. Round even to faultiness.

CLEO. For the most part, too, they are foolish that
    are so.
Her hair, what color?   35

MESS. Brown, madam, and her forehead
As low° as she would wish it.

CLEO.   There's gold for thee.

Thou must not take my former sharpness ill.
I will employ thee back again, I find thee
Most fit for business. Go make thee ready,   40
Our letters are prepared.   [*Exit* MESSENGER.]

CHAR.   A proper° man.

CLEO. Indeed he is so. I repent me much
That so I harried him. Why, methinks, by him,
This creature's no such thing.°

CHAR.   Nothing, madam.

CLEO. The man hath seen some majesty, and
    should know.   45

CHAR. Hath he seen majesty? Isis else defend,°
And serving you so long!

CLEO. I have one thing more to ask him yet, good
    Charmian.
But 'tis no matter, thou shalt bring him to me
Where I will write. All may be well enough.   50

CHAR. I warrant you, madam.

    [*Exeunt.*]

SCENE IV. *Athens. A room in* ANTONY'S *house.*

[*Enter* ANTONY *and* OCTAVIA.]

ANT. Nay, nay, Octavia, not only that——
That were excusable, that and thousands more
Of semblable° import — but he hath waged
New wars 'gainst Pompey, made his will, and read
    it
To public ear,   5
Spoke scantly° of me. When perforce he could not
But pay me terms of honor,° cold and sickly
He vented° them, most narrow measure lent me.
When the best hint° was given him, he not took 't,
Or did it from his teeth.°

OCT.   O my good lord,   10
Believe not all. Or if you must believe,
Stomach° not all. A more unhappy lady,
If this division chance, ne'er stood between,
Praying for both parts.
The good gods will mock me presently   15
When I shall pray, " Oh, bless my lord and hus-
    band! "
Undo that prayer, by crying out as loud,
" Oh, bless my brother! " Husband win, win brother,
Prays, and destroys the prayer — no midway
'Twixt these extremes at all.

ANT.   Gentle Octavia,   20
Let your best love draw to that point° which seeks
Best to preserve it. If I lose mine honor,
I lose myself. Better I were not yours

41. proper: fine.   44. This . . . thing: i.e., nothing to worry about.
46. defend: forbid.
    Sc. iv: 3. semblable: like.   6. scantly: disrespectfully.
6–7. could . . . honor: was obliged to say honorable things about
me.   8. vented: uttered.   9. hint: opportunity.   10. from . . .
teeth: i.e., gave me lip service only.   12. Stomach: be angry
at.   21. draw . . . point: i.e., be bestowed on me.

Sc. iii: 4. But when: except when.   21–24. She . . . breather:
i.e., Octavia is insignificant and demure; moving or standing,
she is a dummy.   36. low: A low forehead showed lack of in-
telligence.

Than yours so branchless.° But, as you requested,
Yourself shall go between 's. The meantime, lady,
I'll raise the preparation of a war   26
Shall stain° your brother. Make your soonest haste,
So your desires are yours.

OCT.   Thanks to my lord.
The Jove of power make me most weak, most weak,
Your reconciler! Wars 'twixt you twain would be
As if the world should cleave, and that slain men
Should solder up the rift.   32

ANT. When it appears to you where this begins,
Turn your displeasure that way, for our faults
Can never be so equal that your love   35
Can equally move with them. Provide your going,
Choose your own company, and command what
        cost
Your heart has mind to.   [*Exeunt.*]

SCENE V. *The same. Another room.*

[*Enter* ENOBARBUS *and* EROS, *meeting.*]

ENO. How now, friend Eros!

EROS. There's strange news come, sir.

ENO. What, man?

EROS. Caesar and Lepidus have made wars upon
Pompey.

ENO. This is old. What is the success?°   6

EROS. Caesar, having made use of him in the wars
'gainst Pompey, presently denied him rivality,°
would not let him partake in the glory of the action.
And not resting here, accuses him of letters he had
formerly wrote to Pompey, upon his own appeal,°
seizes him. So the poor third is up,° till death en-
large his confine.°   13

ENO. Then, world, thou hast a pair of chaps,° no
        more,
And throw between them all the food thou hast,
They'll grind the one the other. Where's Antony?

EROS. He's walking in the garden—thus, and
        spurns°   17
The rush° that lies before him, cries "Fool
        Lepidus!"
And threats the throat of that his officer
That murdered Pompey.

ENO.   Our great navy's rigged.   20

EROS. For Italy and Caesar. More, Domitius.
My lord desires you presently. My news
I might have told hereafter.

ENO.   'Twill be naught.

24. branchless: without branches; i.e., lopped of honors.
27. stain: discredit.
Sc. v: 6 success: result.   8. rivality: partnership.   11. ap-
peal: accusation.   12. poor . . . up: i.e., so No. 3 of the Big
Three is in jail.   13. enlarge . . . confine: make wider his
place of confinement.   14. pair of chaps: an upper and a lower
jaw; i.e., Antony and Octavius.   17. spurns: kicks at.   18. rush:
i.e., one of the rushes with which the floor was strewn.

But let it be. Bring me to Antony.   24

EROS. Come, sir.   [*Exeunt.*]

SCENE VI. *Rome.* CAESAR'S *house.*

[*Enter* CAESAR, AGRIPPA, *and* MECAENAS.]

CAES. Contemning° Rome, he has done all this,
        and more,
In Alexandria. Here's the manner of 't.
I' the market place, on a tribunal° silvered
Cleopatra and himself in chairs of gold
Were publicly enthroned. At the feet sat   5
Caesarion,° whom they call my father's° son,
And all the unlawful issue° that their lust
Since then hath made between them. Unto her
He gave the stablishment° of Egypt, made her
Of lower Syria, Cyprus, Lydia,   10
Absolute Queen.

MEC.   This in the public eye?

CAES. I' the common show place, where they
        exercise.
His sons he there proclaimed the Kings of Kings.
Great Media, Parthia, and Armenia
He gave to Alexander. To Ptolemy he assigned   15
Syria, Cilicia, and Phoenicia. She
In the habiliments° of the goddess Isis
That day appeared, and oft before gave audience,
As 'tis reported, so.

MEC.   Let Rome be thus
Informed.

AGR.   Who, queasy with his insolence   20
Already, will their good thoughts call from him.

CAES. The people know it, and have now received
His accusations.

AGR.   Who does he accuse?

CAES. Caesar. And that, having in Sicily
Sextus Pompeius spoiled, we had not rated him°   25
His part o' the isle. Then does he say he lent me
Some shipping unrestored. Lastly, he frets
That Lepidus of the Triumvirate
Should be deposed, and, being that we detain
All his revenue.

AGR.   Sir, this should be answered.   30

CAES. 'Tis done already, and the messenger gone.
I have told him Lepidus was grown too cruel,
That he his high authority abused
And did deserve his change.° For what I have con-
        quered,
I grant him part, but then in his Armenia   35
And other of his conquered kingdoms I
Demand the like.

Sc. vi: 1. Contemning: despising.   3. tribunal: high throne.
6. Caesarion: the son of Cleopatra by Julius Caesar. father's:
Octavius was the adopted son of Julius Caesar.   7. unlawful
issue: bastard children.   9. stablishment: rule.   17. habili-
ments: robes.   25. rated him: given as his share.   34. change:
i.e., of fortune.

MEC. He'll never yield to that.

CAES. Nor must not then be yielded to in this.

[*Enter* OCTAVIA, *with her train.*]

OCT. Hail, Caesar, and my lord! Hail, most dear
Caesar!

CAES. That ever I should call thee castaway! 40

OCT. You have not called me so, nor have you
cause.

CAES. Why have you stol'n upon us thus? You
come not
Like Caesar's sister. The wife of Antony
Should have an army for an usher,° and
The neighs of horse to tell of her approach 45
Long ere she did appear. The trees by the way
Should have borne men, and expectation fainted,°
Longing for what it had not. Nay, the dust
Should have ascended to the roof of Heaven,
Raised by your populous troops. But you are come
A market maid to Rome, and have prevented° 51
The ostentation° of our love, which left unshown
Is often left unloved. We should have met you
By sea and land, supplying every stage
With an augmented greeting.

OCT. Good my lord, 55
To come thus was I not constrained,° but did it
On my free will. My lord, Mark Antony,
Hearing that you prepared for war, acquainted
My grieved ear withal, whereon I begged
His pardon for return.

CAES. Which soon he granted, 60
Being an obstruct° 'tween his lust and him.

OCT. Do not say so, my lord.

CAES. I have eyes upon him,
And his affairs come to me on the wind.
Where is he now?

OCT. My lord, in Athens.

CAES. No, my most wronged sister, Cleopatra 65
Hath nodded him to her. He hath given his empire
Up to a whore, who now are levying
The Kings o' the earth for war. He hath assembled
Bocchus, the King of Libya; Archelaus,
Of Cappadocia; Philadelphos, King 70
Of Paphlagonia; the Thracian King, Adallas;
King Malchus of Arabia; King of Pont;
Herod of Jewry; Mithridates, King
Of Comagene; Polemon and Amyntas,
The Kings of Mede and Lycaonia, 75
With a more larger list of scepters.

OCT. Aye, me, most wretched,
That have my heart parted betwixt two friends
That do afflict each other!

CAES. Welcome hither.
Your letters did withhold° our breaking-forth

Till we perceived both how you were wrong led 80
And we in negligent danger.° Cheer your heart.
Be you not troubled with the time,° which drives
O'er your content these strong necessities,
But let determined things to destiny
Hold unbewailed their way.° Welcome to Rome,
Nothing more dear to me. You are abused 86
Beyond the mark° of thought. And the high gods,
To do you justice, make them ministers
Of us and those that love you. Best of comfort,
And ever welcome to us.

AGR. Welcome, lady. 90

MEC. Welcome, dear madam.
Each heart in Rome does love and pity you.
Only the adulterous Antony, most large
In his abominations, turns you off,
And gives his potent regiment° to a trull° 95
That noises it° against us.

OCT. Is it so, sir?

CAES. Most certain. Sister, welcome. Pray you,
Be ever known to patience. My dear'st sister!

[*Exeunt.*]

SCENE VII. *Near Actium.* ANTONY'S *camp.*

[*Enter* CLEOPATRA *and* ENOBARBUS.]

CLEO. I will be even with thee, doubt it not.

ENO. But why, why, why?°

CLEO. Thou hast forspoke° my being in these
wars,
And say'st it is not fit.

ENO. Well, is it, is it?

CLEO. If not denounced against us, why should
not we 5
Be there in person?°

ENO. [*Aside*] Well, I could reply.
If we should serve with horse and mares together,
The horse were merely° lost, the mares would bear
A soldier and his horse.

CLEO. What is 't you say? 10

ENO. Your presence needs must puzzle Antony,
Take from his heart, take from his brain, from 's
time,
What should not then be spared. He is already
Traduced° for levity, and 'tis said in Rome
That Photinus, a eunuch, and your maids 15
Manage this war.

---

44. **usher**: gentleman in attendance. 47. **expectation fainted**: people in the crowd should have fainted in their eagerness to see you. 51. **prevented**: forestalled. 52. **ostentation**: ceremonious show. 56. **constrained**: forced. 61. **obstruct**: obstruction. 79. **withhold**: keep back.

81. **negligent danger**: danger through our own neglect. 82. **time**: these difficult days. 84–85. **But . . . way**: Caesar, as the soothsayer had warned Antony (II.iii.15–30), was a man of destiny. **determined . . . destiny**: that which is decided by Fate. 87. **mark**: limit. 95. **potent regiment**: great authority. **trull**: whore. 96. **noises it**: is clamorous.

Sc. vii: 2. **But . . . why**: Enobarbus has no respect for Cleopatra, whom he treats not as a queen but as Antony's mistress and plaything. 3. **forspoke**: spoken against. 5–6. **If . . . person**: even if war has not been declared against me, why should I not be there? 8. **merely**: utterly. 14. **Traduced**: criticized.

CLEO.   Sink Rome, and their tongues rot
That speak against us! A charge we bear i' the war,
And as the president of my kingdom will
Appear there for a man. Speak not against it,
I will not stay behind.
ENO.   Nay, I have done.   20
Here comes the Emperor.
                [*Enter* ANTONY *and* CANIDIUS.]
    ANT.   Is it not strange, Canidius,
That from Tarentum and Brundusium
He could so quickly cut° the Ionian sea,
And take in° Toryne? You have heard on 't, sweet?
    CLEO. Celerity is never more admired   25
Than by the negligent.
    ANT.   A good rebuke,
Which might have well becomed the best of men,
To taunt at slackness. Canidius, we
Will fight with him by sea.
    CLEO.   By sea. What else?
    CAN. Why will my lord do so?
    ANT.   For that he dares us to 't.   30
    ENO. So hath my lord dared him to single fight.
    CAN. Aye, and to wage this battle at Pharsalia,
Where Caesar fought with Pompey. But these offers,
Which serve not for his vantage, he shakes off,
And so should you.
    ENO.   Your ships are not well manned,   35
Your mariners are muleters,° reapers, people
Ingrossed by swift impress.° In Caesar's fleet
Are those that often have 'gainst Pompey fought.
Their ships are yare,° yours heavy. No disgrace
Shall fall you for refusing him at sea,   40
Being prepared for land.
    ANT.   By sea, by sea.
    ENO. Most worthy sir, you therein throw away
The absolute soldiership° you have by land,
Distract° your army, which doth most consist
Of war-marked° footmen, leave unexecuted   45
Your own renownèd knowledge,° quite forgo
The way which promises assurance, and
Give up yourself merely° to chance and hazard
From firm security.
    ANT.   I'll fight at sea.
    CLEO. I have sixty sails, Caesar none better.   50
    ANT. Our overplus of shipping will we burn,
And with the rest full-manned, from the head of
    Actium
Beat the approaching Caesar. But if we fail,
We then can do 't at land.
[*Enter a* MESSENGER.]   Thy business?   54
    MESS. The news is true, my lord, he is descried.°

Caesar has taken Toryne.
    ANT. Can he be there in person? 'Tis impossible.
Strange that his power° should be. Canidius,
Our nineteen legions thou shalt hold by land,   59
And our twelve thousand horse. We'll to our ship.
Away, my Thetis!°
[*Enter a* SOLDIER.]   How now, worthy soldier?
    SOLD. O noble Emperor, do not fight by sea,
Trust not to rotten planks. Do you misdoubt
This sword and these my wounds? Let the Egyptians
And the Phoenicians go a-ducking.° We   65
Have used to conquer standing on the earth
And fighting foot to foot.
    ANT.   Well, well. Away!
    [*Exeunt* ANTONY, CLEOPATRA, *and* ENOBARBUS.]
    SOLD. By Hercules, I think I am i' the right.
    CAN. Soldier, thou art. But his whole action grows
Not in the power on 't.° So our leader's led,   70
And we are women's men.
    SOLD.   You keep by land
The legions and the horse whole, do you not?
    CAN. Marcus Octavius, Marcus Justeius,
Publicola, and Caelius are for sea.   74
But we keep whole by land. This speed of Caesar's
Carries beyond belief.
    SOLD.   While he was yet in Rome,
His power went out in such distractions° as
Beguiled all spies.
    CAN.   Who's his lieutenant, hear you?
    SOLD. They say one Taurus.
    CAN.   Well I know the man.
                [*Enter a* MESSENGER.]
    MESS. The Emperor calls Canidius.   80
    CAN. With news the time's with labor,° and
    throes° forth
Each minute some.   [*Exeunt.*]

SCENE VIII.° *A plain near Actium.*

[*Enter* CAESAR, *and* TAURUS, *with his army,*
            marching.]
    CAES. Taurus!
    TAUR. My lord?
    CAES. Strike not by land, keep whole. Provoke not
    battle
Till we have done at sea. Do not exceed
The prescript of this scroll.° Our fortune lies   5
Upon this jump.°   [*Exeunt.*]

23. **cut:** cut across.   24. **take in:** occupy.   36. **muleters:** mule-teers, mule-drivers.   37. **Ingrossed . . . impress:** hurriedly conscripted.   3? **yare:** easily handled.   43. **absolute soldiership:** overwhelming superiority.   44. **Distract:** confuse.   45. **war-marked:** veteran.   45–46. **leave . . . knowledge:** i.e., make no use of your superior generalship.   48. **merely:** utterly.   55. **descried:** observed.

58. **power:** army.   61. **Thetis:** sea nymph.   65. **go a-ducking:** take to the water.   69–70. **his . . . on 't:** he is not wholly guided by military reasons.   77. **distractions:** small parties.   81. **with labor:** in childbirth. **throes:** i.e., produces news.
    Sc. viii: There are no scene divisions in F1. This division into little scenes, each with its different locality, was made by editors in the eighteenth century. See *Ant & Cleo* Intro., p. 865a.   5. **prescript . . . scroll:** what is laid down in these written orders.   6. **jump:** hazard.

SCENE IX. *Another part of the plain.*

[*Enter* ANTONY *and* ENOBARBUS.]

ANT. Set we our squadrons on yond side o' the hill,
In eye of Caesar's battle, from which place
We may the number of the ships behold,
And so proceed accordingly.   [*Exeunt.*]

SCENE X. *Another part of the plain.*

[*Enter* CANIDIUS, *marching with his land army one
way; and* TAURUS, *the lieutenant of* CAESAR, *with his
army, the other way. After their going-in is heard
the noise of a sea fight.*]
[*Alarum. Enter* ENOBARBUS.]

ENO. Naught, naught, all naught! I can behold no
    longer!
The *Antoniad*, the Egyptian Admiral,°
With all their sixty, fly and turn the rudder.
To see 't mine eyes are blasted.
          [*Enter* SCARUS.]

SCAR.   Gods and goddesses,
All the whole synod° of them!
   ENO.   What's thy passion? 5
SCAR. The greater cantle° of the world is lost
With very ignorance. We have kissed away
Kingdoms and provinces.
   ENO.   How appears the fight?
SCAR. On our side like the tokened pestilence,°
Where death is sure. Yon ribaudrèd nag° of
    Egypt —   10
Whom leprosy o'ertake! — i' the midst o' the fight,
When vantage like a pair of twins appeared,
Both as the same or rather ours the elder° —
The breese upon her, like a cow in June!° —
Hoists sails and flies.   15
   ENO. That I beheld.
Mine eyes did sicken at the sight, and could not
Endure a further view.
   SCAR.   She once being loofed,°
The noble ruin of her magic, Antony,
Claps on his sea wing, and like a doting mallard,°
Leaving the fight in height,° flies after her. 21
I never saw an action of such shame.
Experience, manhood, honor, ne'er before
Did violate so itself.
   ENO.   Alack, alack!
          [*Enter* CANIDIUS.]

CAN. Our fortune on the sea is out of breath, 25

And sinks most lamentably. Had our General
Been what he knew himself, it had gone well.
Oh, he has given example for our flight
Most grossly by his own!
   ENO.   Aye, are you thereabouts?
Why then, good night indeed.   30
   CAN. Toward Peloponnesus are they fled.
   SCAR. 'Tis easy to 't, and there I will attend°
What further comes.
   CAN.   To Caesar will I render
My legions and my horse. Six Kings already
Show me the way of yielding.
   ENO.   I'll yet follow 35
The wounded chance° of Antony, though my reason
Sits in the wind against me.°   [*Exeunt.*]

SCENE XI. *Alexandria.* CLEOPATRA'S *palace.*

[*Enter* ANTONY *with* ATTENDANTS.]

ANT. Hark! The land bids me tread no more
    upon 't,
It is ashamed to bear me. Friends, come hither.
I am so lated° in the world that I
Have lost my way forever. I have a ship
Laden with gold. Take that, divide it. Fly, 5
And make your peace with Caesar.
   ALL.   Fly! Not we.
ANT. I have fled myself, and have instructed
    cowards
To run and show their shoulders.° Friends, be gone.
I have myself resolved upon a course
Which has no need of you. Be gone.   10
My treasure's in the harbor, take it. Oh,
I followed that I blush to look upon.
My very hairs do mutiny, for the white
Reprove the brown for rashness, and they them
For fear and doting. Friends, be gone. You shall 15
Have letters from me to some friends that will
Sweep your way for you. Pray you, look not sad,
Nor make replies of loathness. Take the hint
Which my despair proclaims, let that be left
Which leaves itself. To the seaside straightway. 20
I will possess you of that ship and treasure.
Leave me, I pray, a little. Pray you now.
Nay, do so, for indeed I have lost command,
Therefore I pray you. I'll see you by and by.
                  [*Sits down.*]
[*Enter* CLEOPATRA *led by* CHARMIAN *and* IRAS, EROS
following.]

EROS. Nay, gentle madam, to him, comfort him.
IRAS. Do, most dear Queen.   26
CHAR. Do! Why, what else?

Sc. x: 2. Admiral: the Egyptian flagship. 5. synod: assembly. 6. cantle: slice. 9. tokened pestilence: plague when the red spots appear which denote death. 10. ribaudred nag: foul mare. 12–13. vantage . . . elder: victory seemed to favor both sides, and ours rather than theirs. 14. breese . . . June: like a cow stung by a gadfly in the summer. 18. loofed: luffed, her ship turned into the wind. 20. doting mallard: lovesick wild drake. 21. in height: at its fiercest.

32. attend: await. 36. wounded chance: damaged fortune. 36–37 reason . . . me: good sense is against me. Sc. xi: 3. lated: belated; i.e., lost in the dark. 8. show . . . shoulders: i.e., their backs in flight.

CLEO. Let me sit down. Oh, Juno!

ANT. No, no, no, no, no.

EROS. See you here, sir?   30

ANT. Oh, fie, fie, fie!

CHAR. Madam!

IRAS. Madam, O good Empress!

EROS. Sir, sir!

ANT. Yes, my lord, yes. He° at Philippi kept   35
His sword e'en like a dancer,° while I struck
The lean and wrinkled Cassius. And 'twas I
That the mad Brutus ended.° He alone
Dealt on lieutenantry° and no practice° had
In the brave squares° of war. Yet now —— No
     matter.   40

CLEO. Ah! Stand by.

EROS. The Queen, my lord, the Queen.

IRAS. Go to him, madam, speak to him.
He is unqualitied° with very shame.

CLEO. Well then, sustain me.° Oh!   45

EROS. Most noble sir, arise, the Queen approaches.
Her head's declined, and death will seize her but°
Your comfort makes the rescue.

ANT. I have offended reputation,°
A most unnoble swerving.

EROS.   Sir, the Queen.   50

ANT. Oh, whither hast thou led me, Egypt? See
How I convey my shame out of thine eyes
By looking back what I have left behind
Stroyed° in dishonor.

CLEO.   O my lord, my lord,
Forgive my fearful sails! I little thought   55
You would have followed.

ANT.   Egypt, thou knew'st too well
My heart was to thy rudder tied by the strings,
And thou shouldst tow me after. O'er my spirit
Thy full supremacy thou knew'st, and that
Thy beck might from the bidding of the gods   60
Command me.

CLEO.   Oh, my pardon!

ANT.   Now I must
To the young man send humble treaties,° dodge
And palter in the shifts of lowness,° who
With half the bulk o' the world played as I pleased,
Making and marring fortunes. You did know   65
How much you were my conqueror, and that
My sword, made weak by my affection, would
Obey it on all cause.

CLEO.   Pardon, pardon!

---

35. He: Octavius Caesar.   36. Sword . . . dancer: i.e., for show
not use.   36–38. while . . . ended: Antony is lying. For the
deaths of Cassius and Brutus see *Caesar*, V.iii.45–46; V.v.50–51.
39. Dealt on lieutenantry: let his subordinates do the fighting.
practice: experience.   40. squares: squadrons.   44. unqualitied:
unmanned, having lost his natural quality.   45. sustain
me: As before, Cleopatra faints to attract his sympathy. See
I.iii.71.   47. but: unless.   49. reputation: honor.   54. Stroyed:
destroyed.   62. treaties: proposals for an armistice.
62–63. dodge . . . lowness: make shifty excuses in my reduced
state.

ANT. Fall° not a tear, I say. One of them rates°
All that is won and lost. Give me a kiss,   70
Even this repays me. We sent our schoolmaster.
Is he come back? Love, I am full of lead.
Some wine, within there, and our viands! Fortune
     knows
We scorn her most when most she offers blows.
     [*Exeunt.*]

SCENE XII. *Egypt.* CAESAR'S *camp.*

[*Enter* CAESAR, DOLABELLA, THYREUS, *with others.*]

CAES. Let him appear that's come from Antony.
Know you him?

DOL.   Caesar, 'tis his schoolmaster.
An argument that he is plucked when hither
He sends so poor a pinion° of his wing,
Which had superfluous Kings for messengers   5
Not many moons gone by.

[*Enter* EUPHRONIUS, *ambassador from* ANTONY.]

CAES.   Approach, and speak.

EUPH. Such as I am, I come from Antony.
I was of late as petty to his ends°
As is the morn dew on the myrtle leaf
To his grand sea.

CAES.   Be 't so. Declare thine office.   10

EUPH. Lord of his fortunes he salutes thee, and
Requires° to live in Egypt. Which not granted,
He lessens his requests, and to thee sues
To let him breathe between the heavens and earth,
A private man in Athens. This for him.   15
Next, Cleopatra does confess thy greatness,
Submits her to thy might, and of thee craves
The circle° of the Ptolemies for her heirs,
Now hazarded to thy grace.°

CAES.   For Antony,
I have no ears to his request. The Queen   20
Of audience nor desire shall fail, so° she
From Egypt drive her all-disgracèd friend,
Or take his life there. This if she perform,
She shall not sue unheard. So to them both.

EUPH. Fortune pursue thee!

CAES.   Bring him through the bands.°   25
     [*Exit* EUPHRONIUS.]

[*To* THYREUS] To try thy eloquence, now 'tis time.
     Dispatch.
From Antony win Cleopatra. Promise,
And in our name, what she requires. Add more,
From thine invention,° offers. Women are not
In their best fortunes strong, but want will per-
     jure   30

---

69. Fall: let fall. rates: is worth.
     Sc. xii: 4. pinion: feather.   8. petty . . . ends: insignificant
to his intentions.   12. Requires: requests.   18. circle: crown.
19. hazarded . . . grace: yours to dispose of as you will.   21. so:
so long as.   25. bands: companies, army.   29. From . . . in-
vention: as it occurs to you.

The ne'er-touched vestal. Try thy cunning, Thyreus.
Make thine own edict for thy pains,° which we
Will answer as a law.
    THYR.   Caesar, I go.
    CAES. Observe how Antony becomes his flaw,°
And what thou think'st his very action speaks   35
In every power that moves.°
    THYR.   Caesar, I shall. [*Exeunt.*]

SCENE XIII. *Alexandria.* CLEOPATRA'S *palace.*

[*Enter* CLEOPATRA, ENOBARBUS, CHARMIAN, *and* IRAS.]
    CLEO. What shall we do, Enobarbus?
    ENO.   Think, and die.
    CLEO. Is Antony or we in fault for this?
    ENO. Antony only, that would make his will°
Lord of his reason. What though you fled
From that great face of war, whose several ranges°
Frighted each other, why should he follow?   6
The itch of his affection should not then
Have nicked° his captainship, at such a point,
When half to half the world opposed, he being
The merèd question.° 'Twas a shame no less   10
Than was his loss to course° your flying flags
And leave his navy gazing.
    CLEO.   Prithee, peace.
[*Enter* ANTONY, *with* EUPHRONIUS *the Ambassador.*]
    ANT. Is that his answer?
    EUPH.   Aye, my lord.
    ANT. The Queen shall then have courtesy so she
Will yield us up.
    EUPH.   He says so.
    ANT.   Let her know 't.   16
To the boy Caesar send this grizzled head,
And he will fill thy wishes to the brim
With principalities.°
    CLEO.   That head, my lord?
    ANT. To him again. Tell him he wears the rose
Of youth upon him, from which the world should
    note   21
Something particular. His coin, ships, legions,
May be a coward's, whose ministers would prevail
Under the service of a child as soon
As i' the command of Caesar. I dare him therefore
To lay his gay comparisons° apart   26
And answer me declinéd,° sword against sword,
Ourselves alone. I'll write it. Follow me.
              [*Exeunt* ANTONY *and* EUPHRONIUS.]

    ENO. [*Aside*] Yes, like enough, high-battled°
    Caesar will
Unstate his happiness° and be staged to the show
Against a sworder!° I see men's judgments are   31
A parcel of their fortunes,° and things outward
Do draw the inward quality after them,
To suffer all alike. That he should dream,
Knowing all measures,° the full Caesar will   35
Answer his emptiness! Caesar, thou hast subdued
His judgment too.
            [*Enter an* ATTENDANT.]
    ATT.   A messenger from Caesar.
    CLEO. What, no more ceremony? See, my women,
Against the blown rose° may they stop their nose
That kneeled unto the buds. Admit him, sir.   40
            [*Exit* ATTENDANT.]
    ENO. [*Aside*] Mine honesty and I begin to
    square.°
The loyalty well held to fools does make
Our faith mere folly. Yet he that can endure
To follow with allegiance a fall'n lord
Does conquer him that did his master conquer,   45
And earns a place i' the story.
            [*Enter* THYREUS.]
    CLEO.   Caesar's will?
    THYR. Hear it apart.
    CLEO.   None but friends. Say boldly.
    THYR. So, haply,° are they friends to Antony.
    ENO. He needs as many, sir, as Caesar has,
Or needs not us. If Caesar please, our master   50
Will leap to be his friend. For us, you know
Whose he is we are, and that is Caesar's.
    THYR.   So.
Thus then, thou most renowned. Caesar entreats
Not to consider in what case thou stand'st
Further than he is Caesar.°
    CLEO.   Go on. Right royal.   55
    THYR. He knows that you embrace not Antony
As you did love but as you feared him.
    CLEO.   Oh!
    THYR. The scars upon your honor therefore he
Does pity as constrainèd° blemishes
Not as deserved.
    CLEO.   He is a god and knows   60
What is most right. Mine honor was not yielded,
But conquered merely.
    ENO.   [*Aside*] To be sure of that,

---

29. **high-battled:** with his great army.   30. **Unstate . . . happiness:** lay aside his superiority.   30–31. **staged . . . sworder:** make a public exhibition of himself by fighting a professional swordsman.   31–32. **men's . . . fortunes:** men's judgments are part (*parcel*) of their fortunes; i.e., a defeated man becomes a fool.   35. **Knowing . . . measures:** having had experience of all kinds of fortune.   39. **blown rose:** rose that has shed its petals.   41. **square:** quarrel   48. **haply:** perhaps.   53–55. **Caesar . . . Caesar:** Caesar begs you to forget that you have been defeated by him and to remember only that he is Caesar; i.e., a generous victor.   59. **constrained:** forced.

---

32. **Make . . . pains:** make your own terms for your labors.
34. **how . . . flaw:** how Antony behaves now he is a broken man.
35–36. **And . . . moves:** and how his actions reveal his state of mind.
    Sc. xiii: 3. **will:** lust.   5. **ranges:** ranks.   8. **nicked:** snipped, cut short.   10. **mered question:** sole matter in dispute.
11. **course:** chase after.   19. **principalities:** kingdoms.   26. **gay comparisons:** the gay signs that he is a young man.   27. **declined:** in my decline.

I will ask Antony. Sir, sir, thou art so leaky
That we must leave thee to thy sinking, for
Thy dearest quit thee.   [*Exit.*]

THYR.   Shall I say to Caesar   65
What you require of him? For he partly begs
To be desired to give. It much would please him
That of his fortunes you should make a staff
To lean upon. But it would warm his spirits
To hear from me you had left Antony,   70
And put yourself under his shroud,°
The universal landlord.

CLEO.   What's your name?

THYR. My name is Thyreus.

CLEO.   Most kind messenger,
Say to great Caesar this: In deputation°
I kiss his conquering hand. Tell him I am prompt
To lay my crown at 's feet, and there to kneel.   76
Tell him from his all-obeying° breath I hear
The doom of Egypt.

THYR.   'Tis your noblest course.
Wisdom and fortune combating together,
If that the former dare but what it can,   80
No chance may shake it. Give me grace° to lay
My duty on your hand.°

CLEO.   Your Caesar's father oft,
When he hath mused of taking kingdoms in,
Bestowed his lips on that unworthy place
As it rained kisses.

[*Re-enter* ANTONY *and* ENOBARBUS.]

ANT.   Favors, by Jove that thunders!   85
What art thou, fellow?

THYR.   One that but performs
The bidding of the fullest man and worthiest
To have command obeyed.

ENO.   [*Aside*] You will be whipped.

ANT. Approach, there! Ah, you kite!° Now, gods
and devils!
Authority melts from me. Of late, when I cried
    " Ho! "   90
Like boys unto a muss,° Kings would start forth
And cry " Your will? " Have you no ears?
I am Antony yet.
[*Enter* ATTENDANTS.] Take hence this Jack,° and
whip him.

ENO.   [*Aside*] 'Tis better playing with a lion's
    whelp
Than with an old one dying.

ANT.   Moon and stars!   95
Whip him. Were 't twenty of the greatest tributaries
That do acknowledge Caesar, should I find them
So saucy with the hand of she here — what's her
    name

Since she was Cleopatra?° Whip him, fellows,
Till, like a boy, you see him cringe his face   100
And whine aloud for mercy. Take him hence.

THYR. Mark Antony ——

ANT.   Tug him away. Being whipped,
Bring him again. This Jack of Caesar's shall
Bear us an errand to him.

[*Exeunt* ATTENDANTS, *with* THYREUS.]
You were half-blasted ere I knew you. Ha!   105
Have I my pillow left unpressed in Rome,
Forborne the getting° of a lawful race,
And by a gem of women, to be abused°
By one that looks on feeders?°

CLEO.   Good my lord ——

ANT. You have been a boggler° ever.   110
But when we in our viciousness grow hard —
Oh, misery on 't! — the wise gods seel° our eyes,
In our own filth drop our clear judgments, make us
Adore our errors, laugh at 's while we strut
To our confusion.°

CLEO.   Oh, is 't come to this?   115

ANT. I found you as a morsel cold upon
Dead Caesar's trencher. Nay, you were a fragment
Of Cneius Pompey's, besides what hotter hours,
Unregistered in vulgar fame, you have
Luxuriously° picked out. For I am sure,   120
Though you can guess what temperance should be,
You know not what it is.

CLEO.   Wherefore is this?

ANT. To let a fellow that will take rewards
And say " God quit you! "° be familiar with
My playfellow, your hand, this kingly seal   125
And plighter of high hearts! Oh, that I were
Upon the hill of Basan,° to outroar
The hornèd herd! For I have savage cause,
And to proclaim it civilly were like
A haltered neck which does the hangman thank
For being yare about him.

[*Re-enter* ATTENDANTS, *with* THYREUS.]
                        Is he whipped?   131

1. ATT. Soundly, my lord.

ANT.   Cried he? And begged he pardon?

1. ATT. He did ask favor.

ANT. If that thy father live, let him repent
Thou wast not made his daughter. And be thou
    sorry   135
To follow Caesar in his triumph, since
Thou hast been whipped for following him. Hence-
forth

---

71. **shroud:** covering, protection.   74. **In deputation:** by means
of you his deputy.   77. **all-obeying:** which all obey.   81. **grace:**
favor.   81–82. **to . . . hand:** to kiss your hand.   89. **kite:** the
lowest of the birds of prey, an offal-eater.   91. **muss:** a game
in which something is scrambled for.   93. **Jack:** knave.

99. **Since . . . Cleopatra:** now that she is no longer Cleopatra.
107. **getting:** begetting.   108. **abused:** shamed.   109. **feeders:**
beggars who whine for food.   110. **boggler:** shifty thing.
112. **seel:** close up. See App. 26.   115. **confusion:** destruction.
120. **Luxuriously:** lustfully.   124. **God . . . you:** God reward
you, — the beggar's thanks.   127. **hill of Basan:** a reminiscence
of Psalm 68 (in the Prayer Book version): "as the hill of Basan,
so is God's hill; even a high hill as the hill of Basan . . . fat bulls
of Basan close me in on every side."

The white hand of a lady fever thee,°
Shake thou to look on 't. Get thee back to Caesar,
Tell him thy entertainment. Look thou say   140
He makes me angry with him, for he seems
Proud and disdainful, harping on what I am,
Not what he knew I was. He makes me angry,
And at this time most easy 'tis to do 't,
When my good stars that were my former guides
Have empty left their orbs° and shot their fires 146
Into the abysm of Hell. If he mislike
My speech and what is done, tell him he has
Hipparchus, my enfranchèd° bondman, whom
He may at pleasure whip, or hang, or torture, 150
As he shall like, to quit me.° Urge it thou.
Hence with thy stripes, begone! [*Exit* THYREUS.]
    CLEO. Have you done yet?
    ANT.   Alack, our terrene° moon
Is now eclipsed, and it portends alone
The fall of Antony.
    CLEO.   I must stay his time.°   155
    ANT. To flatter Caesar, would you mingle eyes
With one that ties his points?°
    CLEO.   Not know me yet?
    ANT. Coldhearted toward me?
    CLEO.   Ah, dear, if I be so,
From my cold heart let Heaven engender hail
And poison it in the source, and the first stone 160
Drop in my neck. As it determines,° so
Dissolve my life! The next Caesarion smite!
Till by degrees the memory of my womb,
Together with my brave Egyptians all,
By the discandying° of this pelleted° storm 165
Lie graveless, till the flies and gnats of Nile
Have buried them for prey!
    ANT.   I am satisfied.
Caesar sits down in Alexandria, where
I will oppose his fate. Our force by land
Hath nobly held. Our severed navy too 170
Have knit again, and fleet,° threatening most sealike.
Where hast thou been, my heart? Dost thou hear,
    lady?
If from the field I shall return once more
To kiss these lips, I will appear in blood.
I and my sword will earn our chronicle.° 175
There's hope in 't yet.
    CLEO. That's my brave lord!
    ANT. I will be treble-sinewed, hearted, breathed,°
And fight maliciously.° For when mine hours
Were nice° and lucky, men did ransom lives 180

Of me for jests, but now I'll set my teeth
And send to darkness all that stop me. Come,
Let's have one other gaudy° night. Call to me
All my sad captains, fill our bowls once more.
Let's mock the midnight bell.
    CLEO.   It is my birthday. 185
I had thought to have held it poor, but since my lord
Is Antony again, I will be Cleopatra.
    ANT. We will yet do well.
    CLEO. Call all his noble captains to my lord.
    ANT. Do so, we'll speak to them. And tonight I'll
    force 190
The wine peep through their scars. Come on, my
    Queen,
There's sap in 't yet. The next time I do fight
I'll make death love me, for I will contend
Even with his pestilent scythe.
                [*Exeunt all but* ENOBARBUS.]
    ENO. Now he'll outstare the lightning. To be
    furious 195
Is to be frighted out of fear, and in that mood
The dove will peck the estridge.° And I see still,
A diminution in our Captain's brain
Restores his heart. When valor preys on reason,
It eats the sword it fights with. I will seek 200
Some way to leave him.   [*Exit.*]

Act IV

SCENE I. *Before Alexandria.* CAESAR'S *camp.*

[*Enter* CAESAR, AGRIPPA, *and* MECAENAS, *with his
army;* CAESAR *reading a letter.*]
    CAES. He calls me boy,° and chides as° he had
    power
To beat me out of Egypt. My messenger
He hath whipped with rods, dares me to personal
    combat,
Caesar to Antony. Let the old ruffian know
I have many other ways to die, meantime 5
Laugh at his challenge.
    MEC.   Caesar must think,
When one so great begins to rage, he's hunted
Even to falling. Give him no breath, but now
Make boot° of his distraction. Never anger
Made good guard for itself.
    CAES.   Let our best heads 10
Know that tomorrow the last of many battles
We mean to fight. Within our files there are
Of those that served Mark Antony but late

---

138. fever thee: give you fever.   146. orbs: spheres. See App. 1.
149. enfranched: freed.   151. quit me: get even with me.
153. terrene: earthly.   155. stay . . . time: i.e., wait till his
rage has blown itself out.   157. ties . . . points: i.e., acts as
his valet. See *I Hen IV*, II.iv.238–39.   161. determines: comes to
an end, melts.   165. discandying: dissolving. pelleted: i.e., hail.
171. fleet: float.   175. our chronicle: our place in history.
178. breathed: have my breath again.   179. maliciously:
furiously.   180. nice: delicate, particular.

183. gaudy: rowdy.   197. estridge: hawk.
    Act IV, Sc. i: 1. boy: a bitter insult. See *Cor*, V.vi.101–13.
as: as if.   9. Make boot: take advantage.

Enough to fetch him in. See it done.
And feast the army, we have store to do 't,   15
And they have earned the waste. Poor Antony!
                                        [*Exeunt.*]

SCENE II. *Alexandria.* CLEOPATRA'S *palace.*

[*Enter* ANTONY, CLEOPATRA, ENOBARBUS, CHARMIAN,
      IRAS, ALEXAS, *with others.*]

ANT. He will not fight with me, Domitius?
ENO.   No.
ANT. Why should he not?
ENO. He thinks, being twenty times of better for-
   tune,
He is twenty men to one.
ANT.   Tomorrow, soldier,
By sea and land I'll fight. Or I will live   5
Or bathe my dying honor in the blood
Shall° make it live again. Woo 't° thou fight well?
ENO. I'll strike, and cry " Take all."°
ANT.   Well said. Come on.
Call forth my household servants. Let's tonight
Be bounteous at our meal.
[*Enter three or four* SERVITORS.] Give me thy hand,
Thou hast been rightly honest — so hast thou —   11
Thou — and thou — and thou. You have served me
   well,
And Kings have been your fellows.
CLEO. [*Aside to* ENOBARBUS] What means this?
ENO. [*Aside to* CLEOPATRA] 'Tis one of those odd
   tricks which sorrow shoots
Out of the mind.
ANT.   And thou art honest too.   15
I wish I could be made so many men,
And all of you clapped up° together in
An Antony, that I might do you service
So good as you have done.
SERV.   The gods forbid!
ANT. Well, my good fellows, wait on me tonight.
Scant not my cups, and make as much of me   21
As when mine empire was your fellow too
And suffered my command.
CLEO. [*Aside to* ENOBARBUS] What does he mean?
ENO. [*Aside to* CLEOPATRA] To make his followers
   weep.
ANT.   Tend me tonight.
Maybe it is the period° of your duty.   25
Haply you shall not see me more, or if,
A mangled shadow, perchance tomorrow
You'll serve another master. I look on you
As one that takes his leave. Mine honest friends,
I turn you not away, but like a master   30
Married to your good service, stay till death.

Tend me tonight two hours, I ask no more,
And the gods yield° you for 't!
ENO.   What mean you, sir,
To give them this discomfort? Look, they weep,
And I, an ass, am onion-eyed.° For shame,   35
Transform us not to women.
ANT.   Ho, ho, ho!
Now the witch take me° if I meant it thus!
Grace grow where those drops fall! My hearty
   friends,
You take me in too dolorous a sense.   39
For I spake to you for your comfort, did desire you
To burn this night with torches. Know, my hearts,
I hope well of tomorrow, and will lead you
Where rather I'll expect victorious life
Than death and honor. Let's to supper, come,   44
And drown consideration.°   [*Exeunt.*]

SCENE III. *The same. Before the palace.*

[*Enter two* SOLDIERS *to their guard.*]

1. SOLD. Brother, good night. Tomorrow is the
   day.
2. SOLD. It will determine one way. Fare you well.
Heard you of nothing strange about the streets?
1. SOLD. Nothing. What news?
2. SOLD. Belike 'tis but a rumor. Good night to
   you.   5
1. SOLD. Well, sir, good night.
              [*Enter two other* SOLDIERS.]
2. SOLD. Soldiers, have careful watch.
3. SOLD. And you. Good night, good night.
[*They place themselves in every corner of the stage.*]
4. SOLD. Here we. And if tomorrow
Our navy thrive, I have an absolute hope   10
Our landmen will stand up.
3. SOLD.   'Tis a brave army,
And full of purpose.
      [*Music of hautboys° as under the stage.*]
4. SOL.   Peace! What noise?
1. SOLD.   List, list!
2. SOLD. Hark!
1. SOLD.   Music i' the air.
3. SOLD.   Under the earth.
4. SOLD. It signs well,° does it not?
3. SOLD.   No.
1. SOLD.   Peace, I say!
What should this mean?   15
2. SOLD. 'Tis the god Hercules, whom Antony
   loved,
Now leaves him.

33. yield: reward.   35. am onion-eyed: can't help weeping.
37. witch . . . me: may I be bewitched.   45. consideration:
worry.
   Sc. iii: 12 s.d., hautboys: oboes   14. It . . . well: it is a good
sign.

Sc. ii: 7. Shall: which shall. Woo 't: wilt.   8. Take all:
i.e., no mercy, the winner takes all.   17. clapped up: fastened.
25. period: end.

1. SOLD. Walk. Let's see if other watchmen
Do hear what we do.

2. SOLD.   How now, masters!

ALL. [*Speaking together*] How now! How now!
Do you hear this?

1. SOLD. Aye, is 't not strange?   20

3. SOLD. Do you hear, masters? Do you hear?

1. SOLD. Follow the noise so far as we have
quarter.°

Let's see how it will give off.°

ALL. Content. 'Tis strange.   [*Exeunt.*]

SCENE IV. *The same. A room in the palace.*

[*Enter* ANTONY *and* CLEOPATRA, CHARMIAN *and others
attending.*]

ANT. Eros! Mine armor, Eros!

CLEO.   Sleep a little.

ANT. No, my chuck.° Eros, come. Mine armor,
Eros!

[*Enter* EROS *with armor.*]

Come, good fellow, put mine iron on.
If fortune be not ours today, it is
Because we brave her. Come.

CLEO.   Nay, I'll help too   5
What's this for?

ANT.   Ah, let be, let be! Thou art
The armorer of my heart. False, false. This, this.

CLEO. Sooth, la, I'll help. Thus it must be.

ANT.   Well, well,
We shall thrive now. Seest thou, my good fellow?
Go put on thy defenses.

EROS.   Briefly, sir.   10

CLEO. Is not this buckled well?

ANT.   Rarely, rarely.
He that unbuckles this till we do please
To daff 't° for our repose shall hear a storm.
Thou fumblest, Eros, and my Queen's a squire°
More tight° at this than thou. Dispatch. O love,   15
That thou couldst see my wars today, and knew'st
The royal occupation!° Thou shouldst see
A workman in 't.

[*Enter an armed* SOLDIER.] Good morrow to thee,
welcome.
Thou look'st like him that knows a warlike charge.
To business that we love we rise betime,   20
And go to 't with delight.

SOLD.   A thousand, sir,
Early though 't be, have on their riveted trim,°
And at the port° expect you.

[*Shout. Trumpets flourish.*]

[*Enter* CAPTAINS *and* SOLDIERS.]

CAPT. The morn is fair. Good morrow, General.

ALL. Good morrow, General.

ANT.   'Tis well blown,° lads.   25
This morning, like the spirit of a youth
That means to be of note, begins betimes.
So, so, come, give me that. This way, well said.
Fare thee well, dame, whate'er becomes of me.
This is a soldier's kiss.° Rebukable   30
And worthy shameful check it were to stand
On more mechanic compliment.° I'll leave thee
Now like a man of steel. You that will fight,
Follow me close, I'll bring you to 't. Adieu.

[*Exeunt* ANTONY, EROS, CAPTAINS, *and* SOLDIERS.]

CHAR. Please you, retire to your chamber.

CLEO.   Lead me.   35
He goes forth gallantly. That he and Caesar might
Determine this great war in single fight!
Then Antony —— But now —— Well, on.

[*Exeunt.*]

SCENE V. *Alexandria.* ANTONY'S *camp.*

[*Trumpets sound. Enter* ANTONY *and* EROS, *a* SOLDIER
meeting them.]

SOLD. The gods make this a happy day to Antony!

ANT. Would thou and those thy scars had once
prevailed
To make me fight at land!

SOLD.   Hadst thou done so,
The Kings that have revolted and the soldier
That has this morning left thee would have still   5
Followed thy heels.

ANT.   Who's gone this morning?

SOLD.   Who!
One ever near thee. Call for Enobarbus,
He shall not hear thee, or from Caesar's camp
Say "I am none of thine."

ANT.   What say'st thou?

SOLD.   Sir,
He is with Caesar.

EROS.   Sir, his chests and treasure   10
He has not with him.

ANT.   Is he gone?

SOLD.   Most certain.

ANT. Go, Eros, send his treasure after. Do it,
Detain no jot, I charge thee. Write to him ——
I will subscribe° —— gentle adieus and greetings.
Say that I wish he never find more cause   15
To change a master. Oh, my fortunes have
Corrupted honest men! Dispatch. Enobarbus!

[*Exeunt.*]

---

22. **quarter:** the limit of the sentry's beat.   23. **give off:** end.
   Sc. iv: 2. **chuck:** chick.   13. **daff 't:** doff it, put it off.
14. **squire:** the duty of the squire was to arm his knight.
15. **tight:** handy.   17. **royal occupation:** i.e., war, the work
for kings.   22. **riveted trim:** riveted finery; i.e., armor.
23. **port:** gate.

25. **blown:** i.e., the "flourish."   30. **soldier's kiss:** i.e., a
quick one.   32. **mechanic compliment:** the long leave-taking of a
civilian.
   Sc. v: 14. **subscribe:** sign.

SCENE VI. *Alexandria.* CAESAR'S *camp.*

[*Flourish. Enter* CAESAR *with* AGRIPPA, ENOBARBUS,
and others.]

CAES. Go forth, Agrippa, and begin the fight.
Our will is Antony be took alive.
Make it so known.

AGR. Caesar, I shall. [*Exit.*]

CAES. The time of universal peace is near. 5
Prove this a prosperous day, the three-nooked°
world
Shall bear the olive freely.

[*Enter a* MESSENGER.]

MESS. Antony
Is come into the field.

CAES. Go charge Agrippa
Plant those that have revolted in the van,
That Antony may seem to spend his fury 10
Upon himself. [*Exeunt all but* ENOBARBUS.]

ENO. Alexas did revolt, and went to Jewry
On affairs of Antony, there did persuade
Great Herod to incline himself to Caesar
And leave his master Antony. For this pains 15
Caesar hath hanged him. Canidius and the rest
That fell away have entertainment,° but
No honorable trust. I have done ill,
Of which I do accuse myself so sorely
That I will joy no more.

[*Enter a* SOLDIER *of* CAESAR'S.]

SOLD. Enobarbus, Antony 20
Hath after thee sent all thy treasure, with
His bounty overplus.° The messenger
Came on my guard, and at thy tent is now
Unloading of his mules.

ENO. I give it you.

SOLD. Mock not, Enobarbus. 25
I tell you true. Best you safed° the bringer
Out of the host. I must attend mine office,
Or would have done 't myself. Your Emperor
Continues still a Jove. [*Exit.*]

ENO. I am alone the villain of the earth, 30
And feel I am so most. O Antony,
Thou mine of bounty, how wouldst thou have paid
My better service when my turpitude
Thou dost so crown with gold! This blows° my
heart.
If swift thought break it not, a swifter mean 35
Shall outstrike thought. But thought will do 't, I feel.
I fight against thee! No. I will go seek
Some ditch wherein to die, the foul'st best fits
My latter part of life. [*Exit.*]

Sc. vi: **6. three-nooked:** three-cornered. **17. entertainment:**
employment. **22. overplus:** in addition. **26. safed:** conducted
safely. **34. blows:** swells to bursting.

SCENE VII. *Field of battle between the camps.*

[*Alarum. Drums and trumpets. Enter* AGRIPPA *and
others.*]

AGR. Retire, we have engaged ourselves too far.
Caesar himself has work, and our oppression°
Exceeds what we expected. [*Exeunt.*]
[*Alarums. Enter* ANTONY, *and* SCARUS *wounded.*]

SCAR. O my brave Emperor, this is fought indeed!
Had we done so at first, we had droven them home
With clouts° about their heads.

ANT. Thou bleed'st apace. 6

SCAR. I had a wound here that was like a T,
But now 'tis made an H.° [*Retreat afar off.*]

ANT. They do retire.

SCAR. We'll beat 'em into bench holes.° I have yet
Room for six scotches° more. 10

[*Enter* EROS.]

EROS. They are beaten, sir, and our advantage
serves
For a fair victory.

SCAR. Let us score their backs
And snatch 'em up, as we take hares, behind.
'Tis sport to maul a runner.

ANT. I will reward thee
Once for thy spritely comfort, and tenfold 15
For thy good valor. Come thee on.

SCAR. I'll halt° after. [*Exeunt.*]

SCENE VIII. *Under the walls of Alexandria.*

[*Alarum. Enter* ANTONY, *in a march;* SCARUS, *with
others.*]

ANT. We have beat him to his camp. Run one
before
And let the Queen know of our gests.° Tomorrow,
Before the sun shall see 's, we'll spill the blood
That has today escaped. I thank you all,
For doughty-handed° are you, and have fought 5
Not as you served the cause, but as 't had been
Each man's like mine. You have shown all Hectors.°
Enter the city, clip° your wives, your friends,
Tell them your feats whilst they with joyful tears
Wash the congealment from your wounds and kiss
The honored gashes whole. [*To* SCARUS] Give me
thy hand. 11

Sc. vii: **2. oppression:** opposition. **6. clouts:** rags; i.e.,
bandages. **7–8. like . . . H:** The "T" has not been satisfactorily
explained. "H" and "ache" were pronounced alike, and the pun
is common. **9. bench holes:** the seats of privies. **10. scotches:**
gashes; i.e., I have room for a few more wounds on my body.
16. halt: limp.
Sc. viii: **2. gests:** deeds. **5. doughty-handed:** stalwart.
7. Hectors: Hector was the heroic champion of the Trojans in
the war against the Greeks. See *Tr & Cr.* **8. clip:** embrace.

[*Enter* CLEOPATRA, *attended.*] To this great fairy° I'll
    commend thy acts,
Make her thanks bless thee. O thou day o' the world,°
Chain mine armed neck. Leap thou, attire and all,
Through proof of harness° to my heart, and there
Ride on the pants triumphing!
    CLEO.   Lord of lords!   16
O infinite virtue,° comest thou smiling from
The world's great snare° uncaught?
    ANT.   My nightingale,
We have beat them to their beds. What, girl! though
    gray
Do something mingle with our younger brown, yet
    ha' we   20
A brain that nourishes our nerves° and can
Get goal for goal of youth. Behold this man.
Commend unto his lips thy favoring hand.
Kiss it, my warrior. He hath fought today
As if a god in hate of mankind had   25
Destroyed in such a shape.
    CLEO.   I'll give thee, friend,
An armor all of gold. It was a King's.
    ANT. He has deserved it, were it carbuncled°
Like holy Phoebus' car.° Give me thy hand.
Through Alexandria make a jolly march,   30
Bear our hacked targets like the men that owe°
    them.
Had our great palace the capacity
To camp this host, we all would sup together
And drink carouses° to the next day's fate,
Which promises royal peril. Trumpeters,   35
With brazen din blast you the city's ear.
Make mingle with our rattling tabourines,°
That Heaven and earth may strike their sounds to-
    gether,
Applauding our approach.   [*Exeunt.*]

SCENE IX. CAESAR'S *camp.*

[SENTINELS *at their post.*]

1. SOLD. If we be not relieved within this hour,
We must return to the court of guard.° The night
Is shiny, and they say we shall embattle
By the second hour i' the morn.
    2. SOLD.   This last day was
A shrewd° one to 's.
             [*Enter* ENOBARBUS.]
    ENO.   Oh, bear me witness, night —— 5
    3. SOLD. What man is this?

2. SOLD.   Stand close, and list him.
    ENO. Be witness to me, O thou blessèd moon,
When men revolted shall upon recòrd
Bear hateful memory, poor Enobarbus did
Before thy face repent!
    1. SOLD.   Enobarbus!
    3. SOLD.   Peace!   10
Hark further.
    ENO. O sovereign mistress of true melancholy,°
The poisonous damp of night disponge° upon me,
That life, a very rebel to my will,
May hang no longer on me. Throw my heart   15
Against the flint and hardness of my fault,
Which, being dried with grief, will break to powder
And finish all foul thoughts. O Antony,
Nobler than my revolt is infamous,
Forgive me in thine own particular,°   20
But let the world rank me in register
A master leaver and a fugitive.
O Antony! O Antony!   [*Dies.*]
    2. SOLD.   Let's speak to him.
    1. SOLD. Let's hear him, for the things he speaks
May concern Caesar.
    3. SOLD.   Let's do so. But he sleeps. 25
    1. SOLD. Swoons rather, for so bad a prayer as his
Was never yet for sleep.
    2. SOLD.   Go we to him.
    3. SOLD. Awake, sir, awake. Speak to us.
    2. SOLD.   Hear you, sir?
    1. SOLD. The hand of death hath raught° him.
          [*Drums afar off.*] Hark! The drums   30
Demurely wake the sleepers. Let us bear him
To the court of guard, he is of note. Our hour
Is fully out.
    3. SOLD. Come on, then, he may recover yet.
                [*Exeunt with the body.*]

SCENE X. *Between the two camps.*

[*Enter* ANTONY *and* SCARUS, *with their army.*]

    ANT. Their preparation is today by sea.
We please them not by land.
    SCAR.   For both, my lord.
    ANT. I would they'd fight i' the fire or i' the air.°
We'd fight there too. But this it is. Our foot
Upon the hills adjoining to the city   5
Shall stay with us. Order for sea is given,
They have put forth the haven,
Where their appointment° we may best discover
And look on their endeavor.   [*Exeunt.*]

---

12. fairy: charmer.   13. day . . . world: brightest creature in the world.   15. proof of harness: armor of proof.   17. virtue: valor. 18. world's . . . snare: i.e., the uncertain risk of war. 21. nerves: sinews.   28. carbuncled: set with gems.   29. car: chariot. 31. owe: own.   34. carouses: healths drunk to the bottom of the cup.   37. tabourines: drums.
    Sc. ix: 2. court of guard: guardroom.   5. shrewd: bitter.

12. O . . . melancholy: the moon.   13. disponge: squeeze out as from a sponge.   20. in . . . particular: as far as t concerns you.   30. raught: laid hold on.
    Sc. x: 3. i' . . . air: i.e., in the other two elements. See App. 3.
8. appointment: purpose.

SCENE XI. *Another part of the same.*

[*Enter* CAESAR, *and his army.*]

CAES. But being charged,° we will be still by land,
Which, as I take 't, we shall, for his best force
Is forth° to man his galleys.° To the vales,
And hold our best advantage.   [*Exeunt.*]

SCENE XII. *Hills adjoining to Alexandria.*

[*Enter* ANTONY *and* SCARUS.]

ANT. Yet they are not joined. Where yond pine
     does stand
I shall discover all. I'll bring thee word
Straight how 'tis like to go.   [*Exit.*]
SCAR.   Swallows have built
In Cleopatra's sails their nests. The augurers°
Say they know not, they cannot tell, look grimly,   5
And dare not speak their knowledge. Antony
Is valiant, and dejected, and by starts
His fretted° fortunes give him hope, and fear,
Of what he has, and has not.

[*Alarum afar off, as at a seafight.*]
[*Re-enter* ANTONY.]

ANT.   All is lost.
This foul Egyptian hath betrayed me.   10
My fleet hath yielded to the foe, and yonder
They cast their caps up and carouse together
Like friends long lost. Triple-turned whore!° 'Tis
     thou
Hast sold me to this novice, and my heart
Makes only wars on thee. Bid them all fly,   15
For when I am revenged upon my charm,
I have done all. Bid them all fly. Begone.

[*Exit* SCARUS.]

O sun, thy uprise shall I see no more.
Fortune and Antony part here, even here
Do we shake hands. All come to this? The hearts
That spanieled° me at heels, to whom I gave   21
Their wishes, do discandy, melt their sweets
On blossoming Caesar, and this pine is barked,°
That overtopped them all. Betrayed I am.
O this false soul of Egypt! This grave charm,°
Whose eye becked° forth my wars and called them
     home,   26
Whose bosom was my crownet,° my chief end,
Like a right gypsy° hath at fast and loose°

Beguiled me to the very heart of loss.°
What, Eros, Eros!

[*Enter* CLEOPATRA.] Ah, thou spell! Avaunt!   30
CLEO. Why is my lord enraged against his love?
ANT. Vanish, or I shall give thee thy deserving,
And blemish° Caesar's triumph. Let him take thee,
And hoist thee up to the shouting plebeians.
Follow his chariot, like the greatest spot   35
Of all thy sex. Most monsterlike, be shown
For poor'st diminutives, for doits.° And let
Patient Octavia plow thy visage up
With her preparèd nails.   [*Exit* CLEOPATRA.]
                              'Tis well thou'rt gone,
If it be well to live. But better 'twere   40
Thou fell'st into my fury, for one death
Might have prevented many. Eros, ho!
The shirt of Nessus° is upon me. Teach me,
Alcides,° thou mine ancestor, thy rage.
Let me lodge Lichas on the horns o' the moon,   45
And with those hands that grasped the heaviest club
Subdue my worthiest self. The witch shall die.
To the young Roman boy she hath sold me, and I
     fall
Under this plot. She dies for 't. Eros, ho!   [*Exit.*]

SCENE XIII. *Alexandria.* CLEOPATRA'S *palace.*

[*Enter* CLEOPATRA, CHARMIAN, IRAS, *and* MARDIAN.]

CLEO. Help me, my women! Oh, he is more mad
Than Telamon° for his shield. The boar of Thes-
     saly°
Was never so embossed.°
CHAR.   To the monument!
There lock yourself, and send him word you are
     dead.
The soul and body rive° not more in parting   5
Than greatness going off.
CLEO.   To the monument!
Mardian, go tell him I have slain myself.
Say that the last I spoke was "Antony,"
And word it, prithee, piteously. Hence, Mardian,   9
And bring me how he takes my death. To the monu-
     ment!   [*Exeunt.*]

29. very . . . loss: center of loss, utter loss.   **33. blemish:**
spoil, because it would make Cleopatra lack.   **36-37. monsterlike . . .
doits:** like a rare freak be shown to the commonest of the people
for pennies.   **43. shirt of Nessus:** The centaur Nessus, when
fatally wounded by Hercules, told Deianira (Hercules' bride) to
dip a shirt in the blood. The shirt was brought to Hercules by
Lichas, his page, but when he put it on, it stuck to his flesh
and began to consume him. In his agony Hercules threw Lichas
into the sea and killed himself.   **44. Alcides:** Hercules.
    Sc. xiii: 2. Telamon: Ajax, who went mad when the shield of
the dead hero Achilles was awarded to Ulysses instead of himself.
boar of Thessaly: a boar sent by the goddess Diana into the
kingdom of Calydon and slain by Meleager.   **3. embossed:**
foaming at the mouth, hard-driven.   **5. rive:** split.

Sc. xi: 1. But . . . charged: unless we are charged.   **3. forth:**
gone forth. **galleys:** ships propelled by oars.
    Sc. xii: 4. augurers: officials who foretold the future by
observing omens of various kinds.   **8. fretted:** frayed.
13. Triple-turned whore: whore who has double-crossed three
men, i.e., Pompey, Julius Caesar, and himself.   **21. spanieled:**
fawned on like spaniels.   **23. pine is barked:** i.e., I am like a pine
stripped of its bark.   **25. grave charm:** great sorceress.
26. becked: beckoned.   **27. crownet:** coronet.   **28. gypsy:** See
I.i.10. **fast . . . loose:** a trickster's game.

SCENE XIV. *The same. Another room.*

[*Enter* ANTONY *and* EROS.]

ANT. Eros, thou yet behold'st me?

EROS.   Aye, noble lord.

ANT. Sometime we see a cloud that's dragonish,°
A vapor sometime like a bear or lion,
A towered citadel, a pendent° rock,
A forkèd mountain, or blue promontory   5
With trees upon 't that nod unto the world
And mock our eyes with air. Thou hast seen these
          signs,
They are black vesper's pageants.°

EROS.   Aye, my lord.

ANT. That which is now a horse, even with a
          thought
The rack dislimns° and makes it indistinct   10
As water is in water.

EROS.   It does, my lord.

ANT. My good knave Eros, now thy Captain is
Even such a body. Here I am Antony,
Yet cannot hold this visible shape, my knave.
I made these wars for Egypt, and the Queen —   15
Whose heart I thought I had, for she had mine,
Which, whilst it was mine, had annexed unto 't
A million moe,° now lost — she, Eros, has
Packed cards° with Caesar, and false-played my
          glory
Unto an enemy's triumph.   20
Nay, weep not, gentle Eros, there is left us
Ourselves to end ourselves.

[*Enter* MARDIAN.]   Oh, thy vile lady!
She has robbed me of my sword.

MAR.   No, Antony.
My mistress loved thee, and her fortunes mingled
With thine entirely.

ANT.   Hence, saucy eunuch, peace! 25
She hath betrayed me, and shall die the death.

MAR. Death of one person can be paid but once,
And that she has discharged. What thou wouldst do
Is done unto thy hand. The last she spake
Was "Antony! Most noble Antony!"   30
Then in the midst a tearing groan did break
The name of Antony. It was divided
Between her heart and lips. She rendered° life,
Thy name so buried in her.

ANT.   Dead, then?

MAR.   Dead.

ANT. Unarm, Eros. The long day's task is done,
And we must sleep. [*To* MARDIAN] That thou de-
          part'st hence safe   36
Does pay thy labor richly. Go.   [*Exit* MARDIAN.]

Off, pluck off.
The sevenfold shield of Ajax cannot keep
The battery from my heart.° Oh, cleave, my sides!
Heart, once be stronger than thy continent,°   40
Crack thy frail case! Apace, Eros, apace!
No more a soldier. Bruisèd pieces,° go,
You have been nobly borne. From me° awhile.

[*Exit* EROS.]

I will o'ertake thee, Cleopatra, and
Weep for my pardon. So it must be, for now   45
All length° is torture. Since the torch is out,
Lie down and stray no farther. Now all labor
Mars what it does. Yea, very force entangles
Itself with strength. Seal° then, and all is done.
Eros! — I come, my Queen. Eros! — Stay for me.
Where souls do couch on flowers, we'll hand in
          hand,   51
And with our sprightly port° make the ghosts gaze.
Dido and her Aeneas° shall want troops,°
And all the haunt be ours. Come, Eros, Eros!

[*Re-enter* EROS.]

EROS. What would my lord?

ANT.   Since Cleopatra died   55
I have lived in such dishonor that the gods
Detest my baseness. I, that with my sword
Quartered the world, and o'er green Neptune's back
With ships made cities, condemn myself to lack
The courage of a woman — less noble mind   60
Than she which by her death our Caesar tells
" I am conqueror of myself." Thou art sworn, Eros,
That when the exigent° should come — which now
Is come indeed — when I should see behind me
The inevitable prosecution° of   65
Disgrace and horror, that, on my command,
Thou then wouldst kill me. Do 't, the time is come.
Thou strikest not me, 'tis Caesar thou defeat'st.
Put color in thy cheek.

EROS.   The gods withhold me!
Shall I do that which all the Parthian darts,   70
Though enemy, lost aim and could not?

ANT.   Eros,
Wouldst thou be windowed° in great Rome and
          see
Thy master thus with pleached° arms, bending
          down
His corrigible° neck, his face subdued
To penetrative° shame, whilst the wheeled seat 75
Of fortunate Caesar, drawn before him, branded

Sc. xiv: 2. **dragonish:** shaped like a serpent.   4. **pendent:**
hanging in the air.   8. **black . . . pageants:** sights seen in the
evening.   10. **rack dislimns:** drifting cloud paints out.   18. **moe:**
more.   19. **Packed cards:** i.e., cheated in the deal.   33. **ren-**
dered: gave up.

38–39. **sevenfold . . . heart:** even the seven thicknesses of hide
of Ajax's shield cannot keep off the troubles which assault my
heart.   40. **continent:** that which contains it.   42. **pieces:**
i.e., of armor.   43. **From me:** leave me.   46. **length:** prolonging
of life.   49. **Seal:** complete the business. See App. 6.
52. **sprightly port:** lively bearing.   53. **Dido . . . Aeneas:** typical
lovers-till-death in classical story. See *Temp*, II.i.76. **troops:**
admiring followers.   63. **exigent:** emergency.   65. **prosecution:**
pursuit.   72. **windowed:** standing at a window.   73. **pleached:**
folded.   74. **corrigible:** submissive.   75. **penetrative:** pene-
trating.

His baseness that ensued?°

EROS.   I would not see 't.

ANT. Come, then, for with a wound I must be
cured.
Draw that thy honest sword, which thou hast worn
Most useful for thy country.

EROS.   O sir, pardon me!   80

ANT. When I did make thee free, sworest thou not
then
To do this when I bade thee? Do it at once,
Or thy precédent services are all
But accidents unpurposed. Draw, and come.

EROS. Turn from me then that noble countenance,
Wherein the worship of the whole world lies.   86

ANT. Lo thee!   [*Turning from him.*]

EROS. My sword is drawn.

ANT.   Then let it do at once
The thing why thou hast drawn it.

EROS.   My dear master,
My Captain, and my Emperor, let me say,   90
Before I strike this bloody stroke, farewell.

ANT. 'Tis said, man, and farewell.

EROS. Farewell, great chief. Shall I strike now?

ANT.   Now, Eros.

EROS. Why, there then. Thus I do escape the
sorrow
Of Antony's death.   [*Kills himself.*]

ANT.   Thrice nobler than myself!   95
Thou teachest me, O valiant Eros, what
I should and thou couldst not. My Queen and Eros
Have by their brave instruction got upon° me
A nobleness in record. But I will be
A bridegroom in my death,° and run into 't   100
As to a lover's bed. Come then, and, Eros,
Thy master dies thy scholar. To do thus
                         [*Falling on his sword.*]
I learned of thee. How! Not dead? Not dead?
The guard, ho! Oh, dispatch me!

        [*Enter* DERCETAS *and* GUARD.]

1. GUARD.   What's the noise?

ANT. I have done my work ill, friends. Oh, make
an end   105
Of what I have begun.

2. GUARD.   The star is fallen.

1. GUARD. And time is at his period.°

ALL.   Alas, and woe!

ANT. Let him that loves me strike me dead.

1. GUARD.   Not I.

2. GUARD. Nor I.   109

3. GUARD. Nor anyone.   [*Exeunt* GUARD.]

DER. Thy death and fortunes bid thy followers fly.
This sword but shown to Caesar, with this tidings,
Shall enter me with him.°

        [*Enter* DIOMEDES.]

DIO. Where's Antony?

DER.   There, Diomed, there.

DIO.   Lives he?   114
Wilt thou not answer, man?   [*Exit* DERCETAS.]

ANT. Art thou there, Diomed? Draw thy sword,
and give me
Sufficing strokes for death.

DIO.   Most absolute lord,
My mistress Cleopatra sent me to thee.

ANT. When did she send thee?

DIO.   Now, my lord.

ANT.   Where is she?

DIO. Locked in her monument. She had a prophe-
sying fear   120
Of what hath come to pass. For when she saw —
Which never shall be found — you did suspect
She had disposed° with Caesar, and that your rage
Would not be purged, she sent you word she was
dead;
But fearing since how it might work, hath sent   125
Me to proclaim the truth, and I am come,
I dread too late.

ANT. Too late, good Diomed. Call my guard, I
prithee.

DIO. What ho, the Emperor's guard! The guard,
what ho!
Come, your lord calls.   130

   [*Enter four or five of the* GUARD *of* ANTONY.]

ANT. Bear me, good friends, where Cleopatra
bides.
'Tis the last service that I shall command you.

1. GUARD. Woe, woe are we, sir, you may not live
to wear
All your true followers out.

ALL.   Most heavy day!

ANT. Nay, good my fellows, do not please sharp
Fate   135
To grace it with your sorrows.° Bid that welcome
Which comes to punish us, and we punish it
Seeming to bear it lightly. Take me up.
I have led you oft. Carry me now, good friends,
And have my thanks for all.   140
                     [*Exeunt, bearing* ANTONY.]

SCENE XV. *The same. A monument.*

[*Enter* CLEOPATRA, *and her maids aloft, with*
             CHARMIAN, *and* IRAS.]

CLEO. O Charmian, I will never go from hence.

CHAR. Be comforted, dear madam.

CLEO.   No, I will not.
All strange and terrible events are welcome,
But comforts we despise. Our size of sorrow,

76–77. branded . . . ensued: marked as with a brand the baseness
of the man who followed.   98. instruction . . . upon: example
won over.   100. bridegroom . . . death: Cf. *Lear*, IV.vi.202.
107. period: end.   113. enter . . . him: get me into his favor.
123. disposed: come to terms.   135–36. please . . . sorrows: i.e.
do not let cruel Fate rejoice because it has made you sad.

Proportioned to our cause, must be as great   5
As that which makes it.

[*Enter, below,* DIOMEDES.] How now! Is he dead?

DIO. His death's upon him, but not dead.

Look out o' the other side your monument.

His guard have brought him thither.

[*Enter, below,* ANTONY, *borne by the* GUARD.]

CLEO.   O sun,

Burn the great sphere° thou movest in! Darkling°
     stand   10

The varying shore o' the world. O Antony,

Antony, Antony! Help, Charmian, help. Iras, help.

Help, friends below. Let's draw him hither.

ANT.   Peace!

Not Caesar's valor hath o'erthrown Antony,

But Antony's hath triumphed on itself.   15

CLEO. So it should be, that none but Antony

Should conquer Antony, but woe 'tis so!

ANT. I am dying, Egypt, dying, only

I here impórtune death awhile° until

Of many thousand kisses the poor last   20

I lay upon thy lips.

CLEO.   I dare not, dear,

Dear my lord, pardon, I dare not,

Lest I be taken. Not the imperious show

Of the full-fortuned Caesar ever shall

Be brooched with me.° If knife, drugs, serpents,
     have   25

Edge, sting, or operation, I am safe.

Your wife Octavia, with her modest eyes

And still conclusion,° shall acquire no honor

Demuring° upon me. But come, come, Antony —

Help me, my women — we must draw thee up.   30

Assist, good friends.

ANT.   Oh, quick, or I am gone.

CLEO. Here's sport indeed! How heavy weighs my
     lord!

Our strength is all gone into heaviness.°

That makes the weight. Had I great Juno's power,

The strong-winged Mercury° should fetch thee up

And set thee by Jove's side. Yet come a little —   36

Wishers were ever fools — oh, come, come, come,

[*They heave* ANTONY *aloft to* CLEOPATRA.]

And welcome, welcome! Die where thou hast lived.

Quicken° with kissing. Had my lips that power,

Thus would I wear them out.

ALL.   A heavy sight!   40

ANT. I am dying, Egypt, dying.

Give me some wine, and let me speak a little.

CLEO. No, let me speak, and let me rail so high

That the false housewife° Fortune break her wheel,

Provoked by my offense.

ANT.   One word, sweet Queen.   45

Of Caesar seek your honor, with your safety. Oh!

CLEO. They do not go together.

ANT.   Gentle, hear me.

None about Caesar trust but Proculeius.

CLEO. My resolution and my hands I'll trust,

None about Caesar.   50

ANT. The miserable change now at my end

Lament nor sorrow at, but please your thoughts

In feeding them with those my former fortunes

Wherein I lived the greatest Prince o' the world,

The noblest, and do now not basely die,   55

Not cowardly put off my helmet to

My countryman, a Roman by a Roman

Valiantly vanquished. Now my spirit is going,

I can no more.

CLEO.   Noblest of men, woo 't die?

Hast thou no care of me? Shall I abide   60

In this dull world, which in thy absence is

No better than a sty? Oh, see, my women,

[ANTONY *dies.*]

The crown o' the earth doth melt. My lord!

Oh, withered is the garland° of the war,

The soldier's pole° is fall'n. Young boys and girls

Are level now with men. The odds° is gone,   66

And there is nothing left remarkable

Beneath the visiting moon.   [*Faints.*]

CHAR.   Oh, quietness, lady!

IRAS. She's dead too, our sovereign.

CHAR.   Lady!

IRAS.   Madam!

CHAR. O madam, madam, madam!

IRAS.   Royal Egypt,   70

Empress!

CHAR. Peace, peace, Iras!

CLEO. No more, but e'en a woman, and com-
     manded

By such poor passion as the maid that milks

And does the meanest chares.° It were for me   75

To throw my scepter at the injurious° gods,

To tell them that this world did equal theirs

Till they had stol'n our jewel. All's but naught.

Patience is sottish,° and impatience does

Become a dog that's mad. Then is it sin   80

To rush into the secret house of death

Ere death dare come to us? How do you, women?

What, what! Good cheer! Why, how now, Char-
     mian!

My noble girls! Ah, women, women, look,

Our lamp is spent, it's out! Good sirs, take heart.   85

We'll bury him, and then, what's brave,° what's
     noble,

Sc. xv: **10. sphere:** course. See App. 1. **Darkling:** in the dark.   **19. importune . . . awhile:** beg death to forbear for a while.   **23–25. Not . . . me:** the triumphal procession of the all-fortunate Caesar shall never be ornamented with me. **brooched:** worn like a brooch.   **28. still conclusion:** quiet disapproval. **29. Demuring:** looking primly.   **33. heaviness:** grief.   **35. Mercury:** the messenger of the gods, who wore winged sandals. **39. Quicken:** make live.

44. housewife: hussy.   **64. garland:** ornament, glory.   **65. pole:** the guiding star.   **66. odds:** superiority.   **75. chares:** chores. **76. injurious:** who injure us.   **79. sottish:** stupid.   **86. brave:** fine.

Let's do it after the high Roman fashion,
And make death proud to take us. Come, away.
This case° of that huge spirit now is cold.
Ah, women, women! Come, we have no friend 90
But resolution° and the briefest end.

[*Exeunt, those above bearing off* ANTONY's *body.*]

Act V

SCENE I. *Alexandria.* CAESAR's *camp.*

[*Enter* CAESAR, AGRIPPA, DOLABELLA, MECAENAS,
GALLUS, PROCULEIUS, *and others, his council of war.*]

CAES. Go to him, Dolabella, bid him yield.
Being so frustrate,° tell him he mocks
The pauses that he makes.°

DOL.   Caesar, I shall. [*Exit.*]
[*Enter* DERCETAS, *with the sword of* ANTONY.]

CAES. Wherefore is that? And what art thou that
    darest
Appear thus to us?

DER.   I am called Dercetas.   5
Mark Antony I served, who best was worthy
Best to be served. Whilst he stood up and spoke,
He was my master, and I wore my life
To spend upon his haters. If thou please
To take me to thee, as I was to him   10
I'll be to Caesar. If thou pleasest not,
I yield thee up my life.

CAES.   What is 't thou say'st?

DER. I say, O Caesar, Antony is dead.

CAES. The breaking of so great a thing should
    make
A greater crack. The round world   15
Should have shook lions into civil streets,
And citizens to their dens.° The death of Antony
Is not a single doom.° In the name lay
A moiety° of the world.

DER.   He is dead, Caesar.
Not by a public minister of justice,   20
Nor by a hired knife, but that self hand
Which writ his honor in the acts it did
Hath, with the courage which the heart did lend it,
Splitted the heart. This is his sword.
I robbed his wound of it. Behold it stained   25
With his most noble blood.

CAES.   Look you sad, friends?
The gods rebuke me, but it is tidings

To wash the eyes of Kings.

AGR.   And strange it is
That nature must compel us to lament
Our most persisted deeds.

MEC.   His taints and honors 30
Waged equal° with him.

AGR.   A rarer spirit never
Did steer humanity. But you, gods, will give us
Some faults to make us men. Caesar is touched.

MEC. When such a spacious mirror's set before
    him,°
He needs must see himself.

CAES.   O Antony!   35
I have followed thee to this. But we do lance
Diseases in our bodies. I must perforce
Have shown to thee such a declining day,
Or look on thine. We could not stall° together
In the whole world. But yet let me lament,   40
With tears as sovereign° as the blood of hearts,
That thou, my brother, my competitor
In top of all design,° my mate in empire,
Friend and companion in the front of war,
The arm of mine own body and the heart   45
Where mine his thoughts did kindle, that our stars
Unreconciliable° should divide
Our equalness to this. Hear me, good friends——
But I will tell you at some meeter° season.
[*Enter an* EGYPTIAN.] The business of this man looks
    out of him,   50
We'll hear him what he says. Whence are you?

EGYP. A poor Egyptian yet.° The Queen my mis-
    tress,
Confined in all she has, her monument,
Of thy intents desires instruction,
That she preparedly may frame herself   55
To the way she's forced to.

CAES.   Bid her have good heart.
She soon shall know of us, by some of ours,
How honorable and how kindly we
Determine for her, for Caesar cannot live   59
To be ungentle.°

EGYP.   So the gods preserve thee! [*Exit.*]

CAES. Come hither, Proculeius. Go and say
We purpose her no shame. Give her what comforts
The quality of her passion° shall require,
Lest in her greatness by some mortal° stroke
She do defeat us, for her life in Rome   65
Would be eternal in our triumph.° Go,

---

89. **case:** i.e., body. 91. **resolution:** courage.
    Act V, Sc. i: 2. **frustrate:** thwarted. 2–3. **mocks . . . makes:**
delays are a mockery. 15–17. **The . . . dens:** i.e., at Antony's
death there should have been omens such as accompanied the end
of Julius Caesar. See *Caesar,* I.iii–II.ii. 18. **single doom:** the
death of one man. 19. **moiety:** half, large part.

31. **Waged equal:** were an equal match. 34. **a . . . him:** i.e., in
Antony's fortune he saw a reflection of his own. 39. **stall:**
lit., share the same stall. 41. **sovereign:** powerful. 42–43. **com-
petitor . . . design:** partner in the greatest achievements.
46–47. **stars Unreconciliable:** fate which would not allow
us to agree. 49. **meeter:** fitter. 52. **yet:** still; i.e., until
you tell us our fate. 60. **ungentle:** ungenerous. 63. **quality
. . . passion:** nature of her emotion. 64. **mortal:** fatal.
65–66. **for . . . triumph:** the fame of our triumphant return to
Rome would be everlasting if we could carry her alive in the
procession.

And with your speediest bring us what she says
And how you find of her.

PRO.   Caesar, I shall.   [*Exit.*]

CAES. Gallus, go you along.   [*Exit* GALLUS.]
        Where's Dolabella,
To second Proculeius?

ALL.   Dolabella!   70

CAES. Let him alone, for I remember now
How he's employed. He shall in time be ready.
Go with me to my tent, where you shall see
How hardly I was drawn into this war,
How calm and gentle I proceeded still ·   75
In all my writings. Go with me, and see
What I can show in this.   [*Exeunt.*]

SCENE II. *Alexandria. The monument.*

[*Enter* CLEOPATRA, CHARMIAN, *and* IRAS.]

CLEO. My desolation does begin to make
A better life. 'Tis paltry to be Caesar.
Not being Fortune, he's but Fortune's knave,°
A minister° of her will. And it is great
To do that thing that ends all other deeds,   5
Which shackles accidents and bolts up change,°
Which sleeps, and never palates more the dug,
The beggar's nurse and Caesar's.°

[*Enter, to the gates of the monument,* PROCULEIUS,
        GALLUS, *and* SOLDIERS.]

PRO. Caesar sends greeting to the Queen of Egypt,
And bids thee study on what fair demands   10
Thou mean'st to have him grant thee.

CLEO.   What's thy name?

PRO. My name is Proculeius.

CLEO.   Antony
Did tell me of you, bade me trust you, but
I do not greatly care to be deceived,
That have no use for trusting. If your master   15
Would have a Queen his beggar, you must tell him
That majesty, to keep decorum,° must
No less beg than a kingdom. If he please
To give me conquered Egypt for my son,
He gives me so much of mine own as I   20
Will kneel to him with thanks.

PRO.   Be of good cheer.
You're fall'n into a princely hand, fear nothing.
Make your full reference° freely to my lord,

Sc. ii: 3. knave: attendant.   4. minister: servant.   6. Which
. . . change: lit., which fetters chance and locks up misfortune;
i.e., which puts an end to the uncertainties of life.   7–8. Which
. . . Caesar's: F1 reads "dung." There is no need to alter it.
The passage then means, "death makes us sleep and never more
eat the dung (i.e., food grown out of manure), which nourishes
alike a beggar and Caesar." It is an echo of Antony's "our dungy
earth alike feeds beast and man" (I.i.35–36). These morbid
broodings on the various transmutations of matter are common in
the early seventeenth century.   17. keep decorum: i.e., the only
request which a Queen can rightly ask is a kingdom.   23. refer-
ence: request.

Who is so full of grace that it flows over
On all that need. Let me report to him   25
Your sweet dependency,° and you shall find
A conqueror that will pray in aid for kindness°
Where he for grace is kneeled to.

CLEO.   Pray you tell him
I am his fortune's vassal° and I send him
The greatness he has got.° I hourly learn   30
A doctrine of obedience, and would gladly
Look him i' the face.

PRO.   This I'll report, dear lady.
Have comfort, for I know your plight is pitied
Of him that caused it.

GAL. You see how easily she may be surprised.   35
[*Here* PROCULEIUS *and two of the* GUARD *ascend the
monument by a ladder placed against a window, and,
having descended, come behind* CLEOPATRA. *Some of
        the* GUARD *unbar and open the gates.°*]
Guard her till Caesar come.   [*Exit.*]

IRAS. Royal Queen!

CHAR. O Cleopatra! Thou art taken, Queen!

CLEO. Quick, quick, good hands.
                    [*Drawing a dagger.*]

PRO.   Hold, worthy lady, hold.
                    [*Seizes and disarms her.*]
Do not yourself such wrong, who are in this   40
Relieved,° but not betrayed.

CLEO.   What, of death too,
That rids our dogs of languish?°

PRO.   Cleopatra,
Do not abuse my master's bounty by
The undoing of yourself. Let the world see
His nobleness well acted, which your death   45
Will never let come forth.

CLEO.   Where art thou, Death?
Come hither, come! Come, come, and take a Queen
Worth many babes and beggars!

PRO.   Oh, temperance, lady!

CLEO. Sir, I will eat no meat, I'll not drink, sir.
If idle talk will once be necessary,   50
I'll not sleep neither. This mortal house° I'll ruin,
Do Caesar what he can. Know, sir, that I
Will not wait pinioned° at your master's Court,
Nor once be chastised with the sober eye
Of dull Octavia. Shall they hoist me up   55
And show me to the shouting varletry°
Of censuring Rome? Rather a ditch in Egypt

---

26. sweet dependency: willing dependence.   27. pray . . . kind-
ness: petition to be allowed to do you kindness.   29. vassal:
slave.   29–30. I . . . got: i.e., I admit that he is in every way
superior.   35. s.d., Here . . . gates: There is no stage direction
in F1, which however prints *Pro* before l. 33, "This, I'll report,"
and again before l. 35, "You see how easily . . ." The stage direc-
tion in the text was devised by Malone from the passage in Plu-
tarch, but editors do not explain how the action could have been
carried out on the stage of the Globe.   41. Relieved: aided.
42. languish: wasting-away.   51. mortal house: i.e., body.
53. pinioned: bound like a criminal.   56. shouting varletry:
mob of yelling slaves.

Be gentle grave unto me! Rather on Nilus' mud
Lay me stark-naked, and let the water flies
Blow me into abhorring!° Rather make   60
My country's high pyramides my gibbet,
And hang me up in chains!

PRO.   You do extend
These thoughts of horror further than you shall
Find cause in Caesar.

                    [*Enter* DOLABELLA.]

DOL.   Proculeius,
What thou hast done thy master Caesar knows,   65
And he hath sent for thee. For the Queen,
I'll take her to my guard.

PRO.   So, Dolabella,
It shall content me best. Be gentle to her.
[*To* CLEOPATRA] To Caesar I will speak what you
          shall please,
If you'll employ me to him.

CLEO.   Say I would die.   70

          [*Exeunt* PROCULEIUS *and* SOLDIERS.]

DOL. Most noble Empress, you have heard of me?
CLEO. I cannot tell.
DOL.   Assuredly you know me.
CLEO. No matter, sir, what I have heard or known.
You laugh when boys or women tell their dreams —
Is 't not your trick?

DOL.   I understand not, madam.   75
CLEO. I dreamed there was an Emperor Antony.
Oh, such another sleep, that I might see
But such another man!

DOL.   If it might please ye ——
CLEO. His face was as the heavens, and therein
          stuck
A sun and moon, which kept their course and
          lighted   80
The little O, the earth.

DOL.   Most sovereign creature ——
CLEO. His legs bestrid the ocean. His reared arm
Crested° the world. His voice was propertied
As all the tunèd spheres,° and that to friends.
But when he meant to quail° and shake the orb,   85
He was as rattling thunder. For his bounty,
There was no winter in 't, an autumn 'twas
That grew the more by reaping. His delights
Were dolphinlike, they showed his back above
The element they lived in.° In his livery   90
Walked crowns and crownets,° realms and islands
          were
As plates° dropped from his pocket.

DOL.   Cleopatra ——

60. Blow . . . abhorring: lay their eggs in me until I become
loathsome.   83. Crested: surmounted, as a crest does a coat of
arms.   83–84. propertied . . . spheres: had the quality of music
like the perfect harmony of the spheres. See App. 1.   85. quail:
make quail.   88–90. His . . . in: as a dolphin shows his back
above the water, so Antony in his pleasures showed himself
above ordinary men.   90–91. In . . . crownets: Kings and Princes
wore his livery (i.e., were his servants).   92. plates: silver coins.

CLEO. Think you there was, or might be, such a
          man
As this I dreamed of?

DOL.   Gentle madam, no.
CLEO. You lie, up to the hearing of the gods.   95
But if there be, or ever were, one such,
It's past the size of dreaming. Nature wants stuff
To vie strange forms with fancy, yet to imagine
An Antony were nature's piece 'gainst fancy,
Condemning shadows quite.°

DOL.   Hear me, good madam.   100
Your loss is as yourself, great, and you bear it
As answering to the weight. Would I might never
O'ertake pursued success but I do feel,
By the rebound of yours, a grief that smites
My very heart at root.

CLEO.   I thank you, sir.   105
Know you what Caesar means to do with me?
DOL. I am loath to tell you what I would you
          knew.
CLEO. Nay, pray you, sir ——
DOL.   Though he be honorable ——
CLEO. He'll lead me then in triumph?
DOL. Madam, he will, I know 't.   110

          [*Flourish and shout within:* " Make way there.
                                        Caesar! "]

[*Enter* CAESAR, GALLUS, PROCULEIUS, MECAENAS,
          SELEUCUS, *and others of his train.*]

CAES. Which is the Queen of Egypt?
DOL. It is the Emperor, madam.

                              [CLEOPATRA *kneels.*]

CAES. Arise, you shall not kneel.
I pray you, rise, rise, Egypt.

CLEO.   Sir, the gods   115
Will have it thus. My master and my lord
I must obey.

CAES.   Take to you no hard thoughts.
The record of what injuries you did us,
Though written in our flesh, we shall remember
As things but done by chance.

CLEO.   Sole sir o' the world,   120
I cannot project° mine own cause so well
To make it clear, but do confess I have
Been laden with like frailties which before
Have often shamed our sex.

CAES.   Cleopatra, know
We will extenuate° rather than enforce.°   125
If you apply yourself to our intents,°
Which toward you are most gentle, you shall find
A benefit in this change. But if you seek
To lay on me a cruelty by taking

97–100. Nature . . . quite: Nature cannot invent such strange
creatures as we can imagine, but to create the form of Antony was
Nature's masterpiece, better than any unreal thing created by
imagination; i.e., the real Antony was finer than anything that
could be imagined.   121. project: set forth.   125. extenuate:
excuse. enforce: emphasize.   126. If . . . intents: if you carry
out our wishes.

Antony's course, you shall bereave yourself   130
Of my good purposes and put your children
To that destruction which I'll guard them from
If thereon you rely. I'll take my leave.

CLEO. And may, through all the world. 'Tis
    yours, and we,   134
Your scutcheons° and your signs of conquest, shall
Hang in what place you please. Here, my good
    lord.

CAES. You shall advise me in all for Cleopatra.

CLEO. This is the brief° of money, plate, and
    jewels
I am possessed of. 'Tis exactly valued,
Not petty things admitted.° Where's Seleucus?   140

SEL. Here, madam.

CLEO. This is my treasurer. Let him speak, my
    lord,
Upon his peril, that I have reserved
To myself nothing. Speak the truth, Seleucus.

SEL. Madam,   145
I had rather seal my lips than to my peril
Speak that which is not.

CLEO.   What have I kept back?

SEL. Enough to purchase what you have made
    known.

CAES. Nay, blush not, Cleopatra. I approve
Your wisdom in the deed.

CLEO.   See, Caesar! Oh, behold   150
How pomp° is followed! Mine will now be yours,
And should we shift estates,° yours would be mine.
The ingratitude of this Seleucus does
Even make me wild. O slave, of no more trust
Than love that's hired! What, goest thou back?
    Thou shalt   155
Go back, I warrant thee, but I'll catch thine eyes,
Though they had wings. Slave, soulless villain, dog!
O rarely base!

CAES.   Good Queen, let us entreat you.

CLEO. O Caesar, what a wounding shame is this,
That thou vouchsafing here to visit me,   160
Doing the honor of thy lordliness
To one so meek, that mine own servant should
Parcel° the sum of my disgraces by
Addition of his envy!° Say, good Caesar,
That I some lady° trifles have reserved,   165
Immoment toys,° things of such dignity
As we greet modern° friends withal. And say
Some nobler token I have kept apart
For Livia and Octavia, to induce
Their mediation. Must I be unfolded   170
With° one that I have bred? The gods! It smites me

---

135. **scutcheons:** painted coats of arms displayed at funerals and other ceremonial occasions.   138. **brief:** inventory. 140. **Not . . . admitted:** not even the trifles omitted.   151. **pomp:** greatness.   152. **shift estates:** change places.   163. **Parcel:** add to.   164. **envy:** malice.   165. **lady:** feminine.   166. **Immoment toys:** valueless trifles.   167. **modern:** slight.   170-71. **unfolded With:** exposed by.

Beneath the fall I have. [*To* SELEUCUS] Prithee go
    hence,
Or I shall show the cinders° of my spirits
Through the ashes of my chance.° Wert thou a man,
Thou wouldst have mercy on me.

CAES.   Forbear, Seleucus. [*Exit* SELEUCUS.]

CLEO. Be it known that we, the greatest, are mis-
    thought°   176
For things that others do, and when we fall,
We answer others' merits in our name,°
Are therefore to be pitied.

CAES.   Cleopatra,
Not what you have reserved, nor what acknowl-
    edged,   180
Put we i' the roll of conquest.° Still be 't yours.
Bestow it at your pleasure, and believe
Caesar's no merchant, to make prize° with you
Of things that merchants sold. Therefore be cheered.
Make not your thoughts your prisons. No, dear
    Queen,   185
For we intend so to dispose you as
Yourself shall give us counsel. Feed, and sleep.
Our care and pity is so much upon you
That we remain your friend. And so adieu.

CLEO. My master, and my lord!

CAES.   Not so. Adieu.   190
    [*Flourish. Exeunt* CAESAR *and his train.*]

CLEO. He words me, girls, he words me, that I
    should not
Be noble to myself. But, hark thee, Charmian.
    [*Whispers to* CHARMIAN.]

IRAS. Finish, good lady. The bright day is done,
And we are for the dark.

CLEO.   Hie° thee again.
I have spoke already, and it is provided.   195
Go put it to the haste.

CHAR.   Madam, I will.
    [*Re-enter* DOLABELLA.]

DOL. Where is the Queen?

CHAR.   Behold, sir. [*Exit.*]

CLEO.   Dolabella!

DOL. Madam, as thereto sworn by your command,
Which my love makes religion to obey,
I tell you this. Caesar through Syria   200
Intends his journey, and within three days
You with your children will he send before.
Make your best use of this. I have performed
Your pleasure and my promise.

CLEO.   Dolabella,
I shall remain your debtor.

DOL.   I your servant.   205
Adieu, good Queen, I must attend on Caesar.

CLEO. Farewell, and thanks.   [*Exit* DOLABELLA.]

---

173. **cinders:** hot coals.   174. **chance:** misfortune.   176. **misthought:** misjudged.   178. **We . . . name:** we are responsible for the deeds of others done in our name.   181. **Put . . . conquest:** we shall record in the inventory of the victory.   183. **make prize:** estimate the value.   194. **Hie:** hasten.

Now, Iras, what think'st thou?
Thou, an Egyptian puppet,° shalt be shown
In Rome, as well as I. Mechanic° slaves   210
With greasy aprons, rules and hammers, shall
Uplift us to the view. In their thick breaths,
Rank of gross diet, shall we be enclouded
And forced to drink their vapor.

IRAS.   The gods forbid!
CLEO. Nay, 'tis most certain, Iras. Saucy lictors°
Will catch at us like strumpets, and scald rhymers°
Ballad us out o' tune. The quick comedians°   216
Extemporally° will stage us and present
Our Alexandrian revels. Antony
Shall be brought drunken forth, and I shall see
Some squeaking Cleopatra boy° my greatness   220
I' the posture of a whore.

IRAS.   Oh, the good gods!
CLEO. Nay, that's certain.
IRAS. I'll never see 't, for I am sure my nails
Are stronger than mine eyes.

CLEO.   Why, that's the way
To fool their preparation, and to conquer   225
Their most absurd intents.

[*Re-enter* CHARMIAN.]   Now, Charmian!
Show me, my women, like a Queen. Go fetch
My best attires. I am again for Cydnus,°
To meet Mark Antony. Sirrah° Iras, go.
Now, noble Charmian, we'll dispatch indeed,   230
And when thou hast done this chare I'll give thee
     leave
To play till Doomsday. Bring our crown and all.
                         [*Exit* IRAS. *A noise within.*]
Wherefore's this noise?

     [*Enter a* GUARDSMAN.]
GUARD.   Here is a rural fellow
That will not be denied your Highness' presence.
He brings you figs.   235
CLEO. Let him come in.   [*Exit* GUARDSMAN.]
                    What poor an instrument
May do a noble deed! He brings me liberty.
My resolution's placed, and I have nothing
Of woman in me. Now from head to foot
I am marble-constant,° now the fleeting moon   240
No planet is of mine.

[*Re-enter* GUARDSMAN, *with* CLOWN° *bringing
     in a basket.*]
GUARD.   This is the man.
CLEO. Avoid, and leave him.   [*Exit* GUARDSMAN.]
Hast thou the pretty worm° of Nilus there

That kills and pains not?   244
CLO. Truly, I have him. But I would not be the
party that should desire you to touch him, for his
biting is immortal.° Those that do die of it do sel-
dom or never recover.   248
CLEO. Rememberest thou any that have died on 't?
CLO. Very many, men and women too. I heard of
one of them no longer than yesterday — a very hon-
est woman, but something given to lie, as a woman
should not do but in the way of honesty — how she
died of the biting of it, what pain she felt. Truly, she
makes a very good report o' the worm. But he that
will believe all that they say shall never be saved
by half that they do. But this is most fallible,° the
worm's an odd worm.
CLEO. Get thee hence. Farewell.   260
CLO. I wish you all joy of the worm.

               [*Setting down his basket.*]
CLEO. Farewell.
CLO. You must think this, look you, that the worm
will do his kind.°
CLEO. Aye, aye. Farewell.   265
CLO. Look you, the worm is not to be trusted but
in the keeping of wise people, for indeed there is no
goodness in the worm.
CLEO. Take thou no care, it shall be heeded.
CLO. Very good. Give it nothing, I pray you, for it
is not worth the feeding.   271
CLEO. Will it eat me?
CLO. You must not think I am so simple but I
know the Devil himself will not eat a woman. I
know that a woman is a dish for the gods, if the
Devil dress° her not. But truly these same whoreson°
devils do the gods great harm in their women, for in
every ten that they make, the devils mar five.
CLEO. Well, get thee gone. Farewell.   280
CLO. Yes, forsooth. I wish you joy o' the worm.
                                          [*Exit.*]

[*Re-enter* IRAS *with a robe, crown, etc.*]
CLEO. Give me my robe, put on my crown. I have
Immortal longings° in me. Now no more
The juice of Egypt's grape shall moist this lip.   285
Yare,° yare, good Iras, quick. Methinks I hear
Antony call. I see him rouse himself
To praise my noble act, I hear him mock
The luck of Caesar, which the gods give men
To excuse their afterwrath.° Husband, I come.   290
Now to that name my courage prove my title!
I am fire and air. My other elements
I give to baser life. So, have you done?

---

208. puppet: i.e., we shall become characters in puppet shows. 209. Mechanic: slave laborers. 214. lictors: officers of the law. 215. scald rhymers: scabby poets. See App. 8. 216. quick comedians: quick-witted players. 217. Extemporally: impromptu. 220. squeaking . . . boy: some boy player with a squeaky voice act Cleopatra. 228. Cyndus: Cleopatra's thoughts turn back to her first meeting with Antony. See II.ii.191–231. 229. Sirrah: The word was sometimes addressed to women. 240. marble-constant: as firm and coldhearted as marble in my resolve. 241. s.d., Clown: countryman. 243. worm: snake.

247. immortal: for "mortal." As is usual with Shakespeare's humbler characters, this clown loves long words without being too sure of their meanings. 258. fallible: for "infallible." 264. will . . . kind: will act according to his nature. 276. dress: make ready. whoreson: bastard, son of a bitch. 284. Immortal longings: longings for immortality. 286. Yare: quick. 289–90. which . . . afterwrath: the gods give men excessive good luck which afterward brings down on them Divine wrath.

Come, then, and take the last warmth of my lips.
Farewell, kind Charmian. Iras, long farewell. 295
    [Kisses them. IRAS *falls and dies.]*
Have I the aspic° in my lips? Dost fall?
If thou and nature can so gently part,
The stroke of death is as a lover's pinch,
Which hurts, and is desired. Dost thou lie still?
If thus thou vanishest, thou tell'st the world 300
It is not worth leave-taking.
    CHAR. Dissolve, thick cloud, and rain, that I may say
The gods themselves do weep!
    CLEO.   This proves me base.
If she first meet the curlèd Antony,
He'll make demand of her, and spend that kiss 305
Which is my Heaven to have. Come, thou mortal°
    wretch,
    [To an asp, which she applies to her breast]
With thy sharp teeth this knot intrinsicate°
Of life at once untie. Poor venomous fool,
Be angry, and dispatch. Oh, couldst thou speak,
That I might hear thee call great Caesar ass 310
Unpolicied!°
    CHAR.   Oh, Eastern star!
    CLEO.   Peace, peace!
Dost thou not see my baby at my breast,
That sucks the nurse asleep?
    CHAR.   Oh, break! Oh, break!
    CLEO. As sweet as balm, as soft as air, as gentle —
O Antony! — Nay, I will take thee too. 315
    [Applying another asp to her arm.]
What should I stay ——   *[Dies.]*
    CHAR. In this vile world? So, fare thee well.
Now boast thee, Death, in thy possession lies
A lass unparalleled. Downy windows,° close,
And golden Phoebus, never be beheld 320
Of eyes again so royal! Your crown's awry.
I'll mend it,° and then play.
    [Enter the GUARD, *rushing in.]*
    1. GUARD. Where is the Queen?
    CHAR.   Speak softly, wake her not.
    1. GUARD. Caesar hath sent ——
    CHAR.   Too slow a messenger. *[Applies an asp.]*
Oh, come apace,° dispatch. I partly feel thee. 325
    1. GUARD. Approach, ho! All's not well. Caesar's
    beguiled.
    2. GUARD. There's Dolabella sent from Caesar. Call
    him.
    1. GUARD. What work is here! Charmian, is this
    well done?
    CHAR. It is well done, and fitting for a Princess
Descended of so many royal Kings. 330

Ah, soldier.   *[Dies.]*
    [Re-enter DOLABELLA.]*
    DOL. How goes it here?
    2. GUARD.   All dead.
    DOL.   Caesar, thy thoughts
Touch their effects° in this. Thyself art coming
To see performed the dreaded act which thou
So sought'st to hinder. 335
    [Within. "A way there, a way for Caesar!"]
    [Re-enter CAESAR *and his train.]*
    DOL. O sir, you are too sure an augurer.
That you did fear is done.
    CAES.   Bravest° at the last,
She leveled at° our purposes, and being royal,
Took her own way. The manner of their deaths?
I do not see them bleed.
    DOL.   Who was last with them? 341
    1. GUARD. A simple countryman that brought her
    figs.
This was his basket.
    CAES.   Poisoned, then.
    1. GUARD.   O Caesar,
This Charmian lived but now, she stood and spake.
I found her trimming up the diadem 345
On her dead mistress. Tremblingly she stood,
And on the sudden dropped.
    CAES.   O noble weakness!
If they had swallowed poison, 'twould appear
By external swelling. But she looks like sleep,
As she would catch another Antony 350
In her strong toil of grace.°
    DOL.   Here, on her breast,
There is a vent° of blood, and something blown.°
The like is on her arm.
    1. GUARD. This is an aspic's trail. And these fig
    leaves
Have slime upon them, such as the aspic leaves 355
Upon the caves of Nile.
    CAES.   Most probable
That so she died, for her physician tells me
She hath pursued conclusions° infinite
Of easy ways to die. Take up her bed,
And bear her women from the monument. 360
She shall be buried by her Antony.
No grave upon the earth shall clip° in it
A pair so famous. High events as these
Strike those that make them, and their story is
No less in pity than his glory which 365
Brought them to be lamented. Our army shall
In solemn show attend this funeral,
And then to Rome. Come, Dolabella, see
High order in this great solemnity.   *[Exeunt.]*

---

296. aspic: asp, a small poisonous snake.   306. mortal: deadly.
307. intrinsicate: intricate.   310–11. ass Unpolicied: cheated
in his politic tricks.   319. Downy windows: eyelids soft as down.
322. mend it: put it straight.   325. apace: quickly.

333. Touch . . . effects: are fulfilled.   337. Bravest: finest.
338. leveled at: aimed at, guessed.   351. toil of grace: snare
of her beauty.   352. vent: discharge. blown: swollen.   358. con-
clusions: experiments.   362. clip: embrace.

THE TRAGEDY OF CORIOLANUS

Introduction

Very little is known of the date or the circumstances of the writing or the production of *The Tragedy of Coriolanus*. There are no contemporary references to the play, which was first published in the first folio (F1) in 1623. On the evidence of style alone, *Coriolanus* is usually dated 1607–09. There are a few passages in the play itself which would have been topically significant during these years, but they are not sufficiently definite to be indisputable evidence of date.

1. From mid-May to the end of July 1607 there was very serious rioting in England, particularly in the counties of Northamptonshire, Warwick, and Leicester. Considerable grievance was felt when rich men began to enclose the common lands and to convert tillage into pasture. The rioters tore down the hedges and filled up the ditches. In the country district there was very general sympathy for them. These disturbances were hotly discussed and were attributed to various causes. According to Howe's *Annals,* the rioters themselves declared that they wished

the prevention of further depopulation, the increase and continuance of tillage to relieve their wives and children, and chiefly because it had been credibly reported unto them by many that of very late years there were three hundred and forty towns decayed and depopulated, and that they supposed by this insurrection and casting down of enclosures to cause reformation.

As the rioters did not yield to persuasion and did not obey proclamations, some of the leaders were arrested and executed for high treason. This was the most serious civil disturbance in England for forty years. A play in which the chief motive is the clash of interests between the "rich" and the "poor" would therefore have had some special significance at this time.

2.   You are no surer, no,
Than is the coal of fire upon the ice. (I.i.176–77)

In the winter of 1607–08 occurred the worst frost for fifty-three years, to which there are many references. The following is from Howe's *Annals:*

The eighth of December began the hard frost which continued seven days and then thawed gently five days' space. And the two and twentieth the same month the frost began again very violently so as within four days many persons did walk halfway over the Thames upon the ice, and by the thirtieth of December the multitude at every ebb and half-flood passed over the Thames in divers places. And although the violence of the frost abated now and then, yet it held from the third of January until the fifteenth of the same, so as many set up booths and stands of sundry things to sell upon the ice, and some shot at pricks and played at bowls and other exercises of pleasure upon the ice.

On January 8, John Chamberlain wrote:

Above Westminster the Thames is quite frosted over and the Archbishop came from Lambeth on Twelfth Day over the ice to the Court. Many fantastical experiments are daily put in practice, as certain youths burned a gallon of wine upon the ice and made all the passengers partakers.[1]

3.
And in the brunt of seventeen battles since,
He lurched all swords of the garland.

This rare phrase (II.ii.104–05) is echoed in Ben Jonson's *Epicoene; or, The Silent Woman.*

You have lurched your friends of the better half of the garland, by concealing this part of the plot.

Epicoene was produced in 1609 or 1610.

4.   wants not spirit
To say he'll turn your current in a ditch
And make your channel his? (III.i.95–97)

This poetic image is an echo of the gossip caused by a sensational and much-discussed project when Hugh Middleton, goldsmith, obtained permission to bring clean water into London by channels from streams in Hertfordshire. His project was begun on February 20, 1609, and finished on Michaelmas Day 1613, during which time, according to Howe's *Annals,* Master Middleton "spent much money, endured despite and derisions of the vulgar and envious, answered many

---

[1] *Letters Written by John Chamberlain,* ed. by N. E. McClure, 2 vols., American Philosophical Society, 1936, Vol. I, p. 253.

causeless hindrances and complaints of sundry persons through whose ground he was to cut his water passage."

The source of *Coriolanus* is the life of Caius Martius Coriolanus in North's translation of Plutarch's *Lives* (see *Caesar* Intro. p. 529a). Shakespeare followed his source closely, although for his own purposes he compressed the story and somewhat altered the incidents. In Plutarch there were two insurrections, both occurring after the capture of Corioli, when the plebeians withdrew in a body from Rome. The enemies of Rome, hearing of this trouble, began to invade Roman territory, which caused the Senate to appeal to the people, but they would not yield. Accordingly:

The Senate, being afraid of their departure, did send unto them certain of the pleasantest old men, and the most acceptable to the people among them. Of those Menenius Agrippa was he who was sent for chief man of the message from the Senate. He, after many good persuasions and gentle requests made to the people on the behalf of the Senate, knit up his oration in the end with a notable tale, in this manner: That on a time all the members of man's body did rebel against the belly, complaining of it that it only remained in the midst of the body without doing anything, neither did bear any labor to the maintenance of the rest; whereas all other parts and members did labor painfully, and were very careful to satisfy the appetites and desires of the body. And so the belly, all this notwithstanding, laughed at their folly, and said: "It is true I first receive all meats that nourish man's body; but afterward I send it again to the nourishment of other parts of the same. Even so (quoth he) O you, my masters, and citizens of Rome, the reason is alike between the Senate and you. For matters being well digested, and their counsels thoroughly examined, touching the benefit of the commonwealth, the Senators are cause of the common commodity that cometh unto every one of you."

The people were persuaded by this appeal and by the promise that tribunes should be appointed:

So Junius Brutus and Sicinius Vellutus were the first tribunes of the people that were chosen, who had only been the causers and procurers of this sedition. Hereupon, the city being grown again to good quiet and unity, the people immediately went to the wars, showing that they had a good will to do better than ever they did, and to be very willing to obey the magistrates in that they would command concerning the wars.

North's Plutarch served Shakespeare well, for the narrative is clear and full of vivid description of events and persons. Martius himself is thus described:

This man also is a good proof to confirm some men's opinions, that a rare and excellent wit untaught doth bring forth many good and evil things together, as a fat soil that lieth unmanured bringeth forth both herbs and weeds. For this Martius' natural wit and great heart did marvelously stir up his courage, to do and attempt notable acts. But on the other side, for lack of education he was so choleric and impatient that he would yield to no living creature, which made him churlish, uncivil, and altogether unfit for any man's conversation. Yet men marveling much at his constancy, that he was never overcome with pleasure, nor money, and how he would endure easily all manner of pains and travails, thereupon they well liked and commended his stoutness and temperancy. But for all that, they could not be acquainted with him, as one citizen useth to be with another in the city.

Many of the incidents and speeches in the play were followed very closely. Thus the episode in Act IV, scene iv, where Coriolanus enters the house of Aufidius, was based on the following passage by Plutarch:

It was even twilight when he entered the city of Antium, and many people met him in the streets, but no man knew him. So he went directly to Tullus Aufidius' house, and when he came thither, he got him up straight to the chimney hearth and sat him down, and spake not a word to any man, his face all muffled over. They of the house, spying him, wondered what he should be, and yet they durst not bid him rise. For ill-favoredly muffled and disguised as he was, yet there appeared a certain majesty in his countenance and in his silence. Whereupon they went to Tullus, who was at supper, to tell him of the strange disguising of this man. Tullus rose presently from the board, and coming toward him, asked him what he was, and wherefore he came. Then Martius unmuffled himself, and after he had paused awhile, making no answer, he said unto him:

"If thou knowest me not yet, Tullus, and seeing me, dost not perhaps believe me to be the man I am indeed, I must of necessity bewray myself to be that I am. I am Caius Martius, who hath done to thyself particularly, and to all the Volsces generally, great hurt and mischief, which I cannot deny for my surname of Coriolanus that I bear. For I never had other benefit nor recompense of the true and painful service I have done, and the extreme dangers I have been in, but this only surname — a good memory and witness of the malice and displeasure thou shouldest bear me. Indeed the name only remaineth with me. For the rest the envy and cruelty of the people of Rome have taken from me, by the sufferance of the dastardly nobility and magistrates, who have forsaken me, and let me be banished by the people. This extremity hath now driven me to come as a poor suitor, to take thy chimney hearth, not of any hope I have to save my life thereby; for if I had feared death, I would not have come hither to have put myself in hazard, but pricked forward with desire to be revenged of them that thus have banished me; which now I do begin, in putting my person into the hands of their enemies.

"Wherefore, if thou hast any heart to be wreaked [revenged] of the injuries thy enemies have done thee, speed thee now, and let my misery serve thy turn, and so use it as my service may be a benefit to the Volsces, promising thee that I will fight with better goodwill for all you than I did when I was against you, knowing that they fight more valiantly who know the force of the enemy than such as have never proved it. And if it be so that thou dare not, and that thou art weary to prove fortune any more, then am I also weary to live any longer. And it were no wisdom in thee to save the life of him who hath been heretofore thy mortal enemy, and whose service now can nothing help nor pleasure thee."

Tullus, hearing what he said, was a marvelous glad man, and taking him by the hand, he said unto him: "Stand up, O Martius, and be of good cheer, for in proffering thyself unto us thou doest us great honor, and by this means thou mayest hope also of greater things at all the Volsces' hands." So he feasted him for that time, and entertained him in the honorablest manner he could, talking with him of no other matter at that present. But within few days after they fell to consultation together, in what sort they should begin their wars.

The scene (V.iii) where the ladies of Rome make their final and successful plea to Coriolanus also follows the original very closely:

Now was Martius set then in his chair of state, with all the honors of a general, and when he had spied the women coming afar off, he marveled what the matter meant. But afterward, knowing his wife which came foremost, he determined at the first to persist in his obstinate and inflexible rancor. But overcome in the end with natural affection, and being altogether altered to see them, his heart would not serve him to tarry their coming to his chair, but, coming down in haste, he went to meet them, and first he kissed his mother, and embraced her a pretty while, then his wife and little children. And Nature so wrought with him that the tears fell from his eyes, and he could not keep himself from making much of them, but yielded to the affection of his blood, as if he had been violently carried with the fury of a most swift-running stream. After he had thus lovingly received them, and perceiving that his mother Volumnia would begin to speak to him, he called the chiefest of the council of the Volsces to hear what she would say. Then she spake in this sort:

"If we held our peace, my son, and determined not to speak, the state of our poor bodies, and present sight of our raiment, would easily bewray to thee what life we have led at home since thy exile and abode abroad. But think now with thyself how much more unfortunate than all the women living we are come hither, considering that the sight which should be most pleasant to all other to behold, spiteful Fortune had made most fearful to us — making myself to see my son, and my daughter here her husband, besieging the walls of his native country; so as that which is the only comfort to all other in their adversity and misery, to pray unto the gods and to call to them for aid, is the only thing which plungeth us into most deep perplexity. For we cannot, alas! together pray both for victory to our country and for safety of thy life also; but a world of grievous curses — yea, more than any mortal enemy can heap upon us — are forcibly wrapped up in our prayers. For the bitter sop of most hard choice is offered thy wife and children, to forgo one of the two: either to lose the person of thyself or the nurse of their native country.

"For myself, my son, I am determined not to tarry till Fortune, in my lifetime, do make an end of this war. For if I cannot persuade thee rather to do good unto both parties than to overthrow and destroy the one, preferring love and nature before the malice and calamity of wars, thou shalt see, my son, and trust unto it, thou shalt no sooner march forward to assault thy country but thy foot shall tread upon thy mother's womb that brought thee first into this world. And I may not defer to see the day, either that my son be led prisoner in triumph by his natural countrymen or that he himself do triumph of them, and of his natural country. For if it were so that my request tended to save thy country in destroying the Volsces, I must confess thou wouldest hardly and doubtfully resolve on that. For as to destroy thy natural country, it is altogether unmeet and unlawful, so were it not just, and less honorable, to betray those that put their trust in thee.

"But my only demand consisteth to make a jail delivery of all evils, which delivereth equal benefit and safety both to the one and the other, but most honorable for the Volsces. For it shall appear that, having victory in their hands, they have of special favor granted us singular graces, peace and amity, albeit themselves have no less part of both than we. Of which good, if so it came to pass, thyself is the only author, and so hast thou the only honor. But if it fail and fall out contrary, thyself alone deservedly shalt carry the shameful reproach and burden of either party. So, though the end of war be uncertain, yet this notwithstanding is most certain, that if it be thy chance to conquer, this benefit shalt thou reap of thy goodly conquest, to be chronicled the plague and destroyer of thy country. And if Fortune overthrow thee, then the world will say that through desire to revenge thy private injuries thou hast forever undone thy good friends, who did most lovingly and courteously receive thee."

Martius gave good ear unto his mother's words, without interrupting her speech at all, and after she had said what she would, he held his peace a pretty while, and answered not a word. Hereupon she began again to speak unto him, and said: " My son, why dost thou not answer me? Dost thou think it good altogether to give place unto thy choler and desire of revenge, and thinkest thou it not honesty for thee to grant thy mother's request in so weighty a cause? Dost thou take it honorable for a noble man to remember the wrongs and injuries done him, and dost not in like case think it an honest noble man's part to be thankful for the goodness that parents do show to their children, acknowledging the duty and reverence they ought to bear unto them? No man living is more bound to show himself thankful in all parts and respects than thyself, who so unnaturally showest all ingratitude. Moreover (my son) thou hast sorely taken of thy country, exacting grievous payments upon them in revenge of the injuries offered thee. Besides, thou hast not hitherto showed thy poor mother any courtesy. And therefore it is not only honest, but due unto me, that without compulsion I should obtain my so just and reasonable request of thee. But since by reason I cannot persuade thee to it, to what purpose do I defer my last hope? " And with these words, herself, his wife and children, fell down upon their knees before him.

Martius, seeing that, could refrain no longer, but went straight and lift her up, crying out, " Oh, Mother, what have you done to me? " And holding her hard by the right hand, " Oh, Mother," said he, " you have won a happy victory for your country, but mortal and unhappy for your son; for I see myself vanquished by you alone." These words being spoken openly, he spake a little apart with his mother and wife, and then let them return again to Rome, for so they did request him. And so remain-ing in camp that night, the next morning he dis-lodged and marched homeward into the Volsces' country again, who were not all of one mind, nor all alike contented. For some misliked him and that he had done. Other, being well pleased that peace should be made, said that neither the one nor the other deserved blame nor reproach. Other, though they misliked that was done, did not think him an ill man for that he did, but said he was not to be blamed, though he yielded to such a forcible extremity. Howbeit no man contraried his depar-ture, but all obeyed his commandment, more for respect of his worthiness and valiancy than for fear of his authority.

Coriolanus has never been a general favorite. In 1934 it was played in Paris at a time of politi-cal tension and caused riots between extremists of both right and left. The play, nevertheless, is admirably written and Shakespeare preserves a unity of tone throughout. There is no digression, secondary plot, or clowning. Indeed the strength of *Coriolanus* is also its undoing; Shakespeare has shown up the weaknesses of all shades of political parties so clearly that few readers feel themselves untouched.

Shakespeare indeed seems to have had no great affection for any of his characters except Vir-gilia. This is unusual, for even Edmund and Iago, his greatest studies of evil, have qualities which appeal, if not to our affection, at least to our admiration. The character of Caius Marcius Coriolanus is a full-length and remorseless study of a man of limited mentality. Coriolanus is a professional soldier. He judges everyone by his military value; if the Roman citizens cannot fight, let them starve. He has all the assurance of the ignorant man who can get his own way by force because no one dares resist him. In war he is invaluable, in peace an impossible member of the state. His good qualities are simple. He has immense physical courage and a surprising tenderness for his wife; for Virgilia has all the womanly weaknesses so conspicuously wanting in Volumnia.

Virgilia cares nothing for decorations or mili-tary honors so long as her man comes back to her; she brings out his tenderest qualities. His ferocity he owes to his mother Volumnia, who is a portrait of the old-fashioned Roman matron, a type which Shakespeare seems not to have ad-mired. In some ways the play is as much a trag-edy of Volumnia as of Coriolanus. He is his mother's creation, and in the end she has the bitterness of destroying him. When he returns as leader of the Volscians, it is her appeal which saves Rome. She overcomes him and molds him to her will, as she has always done; but she saves the city at the cost of her son's life.

Coriolanus is one of Shakespeare's few political plays, and much critical comment has been expended on the supposed antidemocratic feeling exhibited in the crowd scenes. Two charges are made against the crowds in *Coriolanus* and in *Julius Caesar:* they are fickle, and their breath stinks. The second fact was indeed obvious to any Londoner who attended the Globe Theater. The first accusation is more serious.

At the beginning of the play, the crowd is shown as hungry and starving. They suspect the patricians, and from what is seen of Coriolanus and his friends, their suspicions are not unreasonable. All crowds, and even quite intelligent persons, at times of economic disturbance lay the blame for scarcities or the black market on the obviously prosperous. The plebeians of Rome have no reason to love Caius Marcius at any time, yet after his achievements at Corioli they are willing in a moment of generosity to forgive him the past and to elect him Consul. But when

the Tribunes work on their feelings, a natural reaction follows and the citizens agree that they have made a mistake: Coriolanus has not deserved their love.

In the eyes of the patricians the Tribunes are villainous demagogues, yet they have a case. They are in the difficult position of all labor leaders who have to decide whether they should secure the immediate advantage of their own people or continue to endure intolerable conditions for the sake of the larger unit, the state. At all times Caius Marcius is the enemy of the people, and when he is driven out, the state for a while benefits; but the Tribunes in solving one problem have created a greater, for Coriolanus was the only man who could keep Aufidius in check. Now both Coriolanus and Aufidius are at the gates of Rome. So the Tribunes are made to learn the first political lesson, which is that a crowd will follow a successful leader but will desert him as soon as he seems to be failing. There is however no need to regard the Roman crowds as exceptionally fickle. Humanity in the mass respects only success. Even in modern democracies an educated electorate has been known to desert its leader.

Coriolanus

DRAMATIS PERSONAE

CAIUS MARCIUS, *afterward* CAIUS MARCIUS CORIOLANUS
TITUS LARTIUS }
COMINIUS } *generals against the Volscians*
MENENIUS AGRIPPA, *friend to Coriolanus*
SICINIUS VELUTUS }
JUNIUS BRUTUS } *tribunes of the people*
YOUNG MARCIUS, *son of Coriolanus*
A ROMAN HERALD
TULLUS AUFIDIUS, *general of the Volscians*
LIEUTENANT *to Aufidius*
CONSPIRATORS *with Aufidius*
A CITIZEN *of Antium*

TWO VOLSCIAN GUARDS
VOLUMNIA, *mother to Coriolanus*
VIRGILIA, *wife to Coriolanus*
VALERIA, *friend to Virgilia*
GENTLEWOMAN *attending on Virgilia*

ROMAN *and* VOLSCIAN SENATORS, PATRICIANS, AEDILES,
  LICTORS, SOLDIERS, CITIZENS, MESSENGERS, SERVANTS
  to Aufidius, and other ATTENDANTS

SCENE — *Rome and the neighborhood; Corioli and
  the neighborhood; Antium.*

Act I

SCENE I. *Rome. A street.*

[*Enter a company of mutinous* CITIZENS, *with staves,
clubs, and other weapons.*]

1. CIT. Before we proceed any further, hear me speak.

ALL. Speak, speak.

1. CIT. You are all resolved rather to die than to famish? 5

ALL. Resolved, resolved.

1. CIT. First, you know Caius Marcius is chief enemy to the people.

ALL. We know 't, we know 't. 9

1. CIT. Let us kill him, and we'll have corn° at our own price. Is 't a verdict?

ALL. No more talking on 't. Let it be done — away, away!

2. CIT. One word, good citizens. 14

1. CIT. We are accounted poor citizens, the patricians, good. What authority surfeits° on would relieve us. If they would yield us but the superfluity° while it were wholesome, we might guess they relieved us humanely, but they think we are too 19 dear.° The leanness that afflicts us, the object of our misery, is as an inventory to particularize their abundance,° our sufferance is a gain to them. Let us revenge this with our pikes,° ere we become rakes.°

For the gods know I speak this in hunger for bread, not in thirst for revenge. 25

2. CIT. Would you proceed especially against Caius Marcius?

ALL. Against him first. He's a very dog to the commonalty. 29

2. CIT. Consider you what services he has done for his country?

1. CIT. Very well, and could be content to give him good report for 't but that he pays himself with being proud.

2. CIT. Nay, but speak not maliciously. 35

1. CIT. I say unto you, what he hath done famously, he did it to that end. Though soft-conscienced men can be content to say it was for his country, he did it to please his mother and to be partly proud,° which he is, even to the altitude of his virtue.° 41

2. CIT. What he cannot help in his nature you account a vice in him. You must in no way say he is covetous.

1. CIT. If I must not, I need not be barren of accusations. He hath faults, with surplus, to tire in repetition. [*Shouts within.*] What shouts are these? The other side o' the city is risen. Why stay we prating here? To the Capitol!

ALL. Come, come. 50

1. CIT. Soft! Who comes here?

[*Enter* MENENIUS AGRIPPA.]

2. CIT. Worthy Menenius Agrippa, one that hath always loved the people.

1. CIT. He's one honest enough. Would all the rest were so! 55

MEN. What work's, my countrymen, in hand? Where go you

Act I, Sc. i: **10. corn:** wheat, barley, oats, rye, but *not* our "corn," which was not known in Shakespeare's time and in England today is called maize or Indian corn. **16. surfeits:** feeds to excess. **17. superfluity:** what they do not need. **20. dear:** expensive. **20–21. The . . . abundance:** our leanness, which is the reason why we are miserable, is an indication of their prosperity; i.e., the poorer we are, the richer they become. **23. pikes:** pitchforks. **rakes:** i.e., as lean as rakes.

39–40. to . . . proud: partly to be proud. **40–41. altitude . . . virtue:** i.e., his pride is as high as his courage.

With bats° and clubs? The matter? Speak, I pray
 you.
 1. CIT. Our business is not unknown to the Sen-
ate. They have had inkling, this fortnight, what we
intend to do, which now we'll show 'em in deeds.
They say poor suitors have strong breaths. They
shall know we have strong arms too.   62
 MEN. Why, masters, my good friends, mine hon-
 est neighbors,
Will you undo yourselves?
 1. CIT. We cannot, sir, we are undone already.
 MEN. I tell you, friends, most charitable care
Have the patricians of you. For your wants,
Your suffering in this dearth, you may as well
Strike at the Heaven with your staves as lift them
Against the Roman state, whose course will on 71
The way it takes, cracking ten thousand curbs
Of more strong link asunder than can ever
Appear in your impediment.° For the dearth,
The gods, not the patricians, make it, and 75
Your knees to them, not arms, must help. Alack,
You are transported by calamity°
Thither where more attends you, and you slander
The helms° o' the state, who care for you like
 fathers,
When you curse them as enemies. 80
 1. CIT. Care for us! True, indeed! They ne'er
cared for us yet. Suffer us to famish, and their store-
houses crammed with grain; make edicts for usury,
to support usurers; repeal daily any wholesome act
established against the rich, and provide more
piercing° statutes daily to chain up and restrain the
poor. If the wars eat us not up, they will, and there's
all the love they bear us. 89
 MEN. Either you must
Confess yourselves wondrous malicious
Or be accused of folly. I shall tell you
A pretty tale. It may be you have heard it,
But since it serves my purpose, I will venture
To stale 't° a little more. 95
 1. CIT. Well, I'll hear it, sir. Yet you must not
think to fob off° our disgrace with a tale. But, an 't
please you, deliver.°
 MEN. There° was a time when all the body's mem-
 bers
Rebelled against the belly, thus accused it: 100
That only like a gulf° it did remain
I' the midst o' the body, idle and unactive,
Still cupboarding the viand,° never bearing

Like labor with the rest, where the other instru-
 ments 104
Did see and hear, devise, instruct, walk, feel,
And, mutually participate,° did minister
Unto the appetite and affection° common
Of the whole body. The belly answered —— 109
 1. CIT. Well, sir, what answer made the belly?
 MEN. Sir, I shall tell you. With a kind of smile,
Which ne'er came from the lungs, but even thus —
For, look you, I may make the belly smile
As well as speak — it tauntingly replied
To the discontented members, the mutinous parts
That envied his receipt° — even so most fitly 116
As you malign our Senators for that
They are not such as you.
 1. CIT. Your belly's answer? What!
The kingly crowned head, the vigilant eye,
The counselor heart, the arm our soldier, 120
Our steed the leg, the tongue our trumpeter,
With other muniments and petty helps°
In this our fabric, if that they ——
 MEN. What then?
'Fore me,° this fellow speaks! What then? What
 then?
 1. CIT. Should by the cormorant° belly be re-
 strained, 125
Who is the sink o' the body ——
 MEN. Well, what then?
 1. CIT. The former agents, if they did complain,
What could the belly answer?
 MEN. I will tell you.
If you'll bestow a small — of what you have little —
Patience awhile, you'st hear the belly's answer.
 1. CIT. You're long about it.
 MEN. Note me this, good friend. 131
Your most grave belly was deliberate,
Not rash like his accusers, and thus answered:
" True is it, my incorporate° friends," quoth he,
" That I receive the general food at first, 135
Which you do live upon, and fit it is,
Because I am the storehouse and the shop
Of the whole body. But, if you do remember,
I send it through the rivers of your blood,
Even to the Court, the heart, to the seat o' the brain.
And through the cranks° and offices° of man, 141
The strongest nerves° and small inferior veins
From me receive that natural competency
Whereby they live. And though that all at once,
You, my good friends " — this says the belly, mark
 me —— 145

---

57. bats: cudgels. **71–74. whose . . . impediment:** i.e., which
will continue on its course, overcoming far stronger impediments
than you can offer. **curbs:** restraints; lit., the chain of the bit
which passes round the lower jaw of the horse. **in . . . impedi-
ment:** in anything you can do to hinder. **77. transported by
calamity:** carried away by the storm of ill fortune. **79. helms:**
steersmen. **87. piercing:** oppressive. **95. stale 't:** make staler by
repeating. F1 reads "scale't." **97. fob off:** put off with a trick.
98. deliver: hand it out, tell your tale. **99–150. There . . . to 't:**
See *Cor* Intro. p. 910a. **101. gulf:** whirlpool. **103. viand:** food.

106. mutually participate: in mutual partnership. **108. affec-
tion:** desire. **116. his receipt:** what he received. **122. muni-
ments . . . helps:** fortifications and minor defenses. **124. 'Fore
me:** a mild oath, substituted for "before God." **125. cormorant:**
a sea bird noted for its greed. **134. incorporate:** united in one
body. **141. cranks:** winding passages. **offices:** parts of the house
where the work is done; e.g., kitchen and pantry. **142. nerves:**
sinews.

1. CIT. Aye, sir, well, well.

MEN.   " Though all at once cannot
See what I do deliver out to each,
Yet I can make my audit up, that all
From me do back receive the flour of all,   149
And leave me but the bran." What say you to 't?

1. CIT. It was an answer. How apply you this?

MEN. The Senators of Rome are this good belly,
And you the mutinous members. For examine
Their counsels and their cares, digest things rightly
Touching the weal o' the common,° you shall find
No public benefit which you receive   156
But it proceeds or comes from them to you
And no way from yourselves. What do you think,
You, the great toe of this assembly?

1. CIT. I the great toe! Why the great toe?   160

MEN. For that being one o' the lowest, basest,
     poorest,
Of this most wise rebellion, thou go'st foremost.
Thou rascal,° that art worst in blood to run,°
Lead'st first to win some vantage.
But make you ready your stiff bats and clubs.   165
Rome and her rats are at the point of battle,
The one side must have bale.°

     [*Enter* CAIUS MARCIUS.] Hail, noble Marcius!

MAR. Thanks. What's the matter, you dissentious°
     rogues,
That, rubbing the poor itch of your opinion,°
Make yourselves scabs?

1. CIT.   We have ever your good word.   170

MAR. He that will give good words to thee will
     flatter
Beneath abhorring.° What would you have, you
     curs,
That like nor peace nor war? The one affrights you,
The other makes you proud. He that trusts to you,
Where he should find you lions, finds you hares,
Where foxes, geese. You are no surer, no,   176
Than is the coal of fire upon the ice,
Or hailstone in the sun. Your virtue° is
To make him worthy whose offense subdues him°
And curse that justice did it. Who deserves greatness
Deserves your hate. And your affections are   181
A sick man's appetite, who desires most that
Which would increase his evil. He that depends
Upon your favors swims with fins of lead
And hews down oaks with rushes.° Hang ye! Trust
     ye?   185
With every minute you do change a mind,
And call him noble that was now your hate,

Him vile that was your garland. What's the matter,
That in these several places of the city
You cry against the noble Senate, who,   190
Under the gods, keep you in awe,° which else
Would feed on one another? What's their seeking?

MEN. For corn at their own rates, whereof, they
     say,
The city is well stored.

MAR.   Hang 'em! They say!
They'll sit by the fire and presume to know   195
What's done i' the Capitol; who's like to rise,
Who thrives and who declines; side factions° and
     give out
Conjectural marriages; making parties strong
And feebling such as stand not in their liking
Below their cobbled shoes. They say there's grain
     enough!   200
Would the nobility lay aside their ruth°
And let me use my sword, I'd make a quarry°
With thousands of these quartered° slaves, as high
As I could pick° my lance.

MEN. Nay, these are almost thoroughly persuaded,
For though abundantly they lack discretion,   206
Yet are they passing° cowardly. But I beseech you,
What says the other troop?

MAR.   They are dissolved. Hang 'em!
They said they were a-hungry; sighed forth prov-
     erbs,
That hunger broke stone walls, that dogs must eat,
That meat was made for mouths, that the gods sent
     not   211
Corn for the rich men only. With these shreds
They vented their complainings, which being an-
     swered,
And a petition granted them, a strange one —
To break the heart of generosity°   215
And make bold power look pale — they threw their
     caps
As they would hang them on the horns o' the moon,
Shouting their emulation.°

MEN.   What is granted them?

MAR. Five Tribunes to defend their vulgar wis-
     doms,
Of their own choice. One's Junius Brutus,   220
Sicinius Velutus, and I know not —— 'Sdeath!°
The rabble should have first unroofed the city
Ere so prevailed with me. It will in time
Win upon power° and throw forth greater themes
For insurrection's arguing.

MEN.   This is strange.   225

---

155. weal . . . common: welfare of the common people. 163. ras-
cal: lean deer, not worth hunting. worst . . . run: in the poorest
condition for running.   167. bale: injury.   168. dissentious:
seditious.   169. opinion: self-esteem.   172. Beneath abhorring:
i.e., "disgusting" would be too weak a word for flattery given to
this crowd.   178. virtue: i.e., your idea of manhood.   179. whose
. . . him: who is brought low by his own wrongdoing.
185. rushes: The rush is often used as a symbol for weakness, as
in the phrase "a broken reed."

191. awe: obedience.   197. side factions: take sides with parties.
201. ruth: pity.   202. quarry: heap of slaughtered deer after the
hunt. Cf. *Haml*, V.ii.375; *Macb*, IV.iii.206.   203. quartered:
cut in quarters.   204. pick: throw.   207. passing: exceedingly.
215. heart of generosity: the heart of the gentry.   218. emula-
tion: rivalry; i.e., vying with each other in shouting.
221. 'Sdeath: by God's death.   224. Win . . . power: overcome
authority.

MAR. Go get you home, you fragments!

[*Enter a* MESSENGER, *hastily.*]

MESS. Where's Caius Marcius?

MAR.   Here. What's the matter?

MESS. The news is, sir, the Volsces are in arms.

MAR. I am glad on 't. Then we shall ha' means to
vent

Our musty superfluity.° See, our best elders.   230

[*Enter* COMINIUS, TITUS LARTIUS, *and other* SENATORS;
    JUNIUS BRUTUS *and* SICINIUS VELUTUS.]

1. SEN. Marcius, 'tis true that you have lately told
us —

The Volsces are in arms.

MAR.   They have a leader,

Tullus Aufidius, that will put you to 't.°

I sin in envying his nobility,

And were I anything but what I am,   235

I would wish me only he.

COM.   You have fought together?

MAR. Were half to half the world by the ears,°
and he

Upon my party, I'd revolt, to make

Only my wars with him. He is a lion

That I am proud to hunt.

1. SEN.   Then, worthy Marcius,   240

Attend upon Cominius to these wars.

COM. It is your former promise.

MAR.   Sir, it is,

And I am constant.° Titus Lartius, thou

Shalt see me once more strike at Tullus' face.

What, art thou stiff?° Stand'st out?°

LART.   No, Caius Marcius.   245

I'll lean upon one crutch and fight with t'other,

Ere stay behind this business.

MEN.   Oh, true-bred!

1. SEN. Your company to the Capitol, where, I
know,

Our greatest friends attend us.

LART.   [*To* COMINIUS] Lead you on.

[*To* MARCIUS] Follow Cominius. We must follow
you,   250

Right worthy you priority.°

COM.   Noble Marcius!

1. SEN. [*To the* CITIZENS] Hence to your homes,
be gone!

MAR. Nay, let them follow.

The Volsces have much corn. Take these rats thither

To gnaw their garners.° Worshipful mutiners,°

Your valor puts well forth.° Pray follow.   255

[CITIZENS *steal away. Exeunt all
but* SICINIUS *and* BRUTUS.]

SIC. Was ever man so proud as is this Marcius?

BRU. He has no equal.

SIC. When we were chosen Tribunes for the peo-
ple ——

BRU. Marked you his lip and eyes?

SIC.   Nay, but his taunts.

BRU. Being moved, he will not spare to gird° the
gods.   260

SIC. Bemock the modest moon.

BRU. The present wars devour him! He is grown

Too proud to be so° valiant.

SIC.   Such a nature,

Tickled with good success, disdains the shadow

Which he treads on at noon. But I do wonder   265

His insolence can brook to be commanded

Under Cominius.

BRU.   Fame, at the which he aims,

In whom already he's well graced, cannot

Better be held, nor more attained, than by

A place below the first. For what miscarries   270

Shall be the general's fault, though he perform

To the utmost of a man, and giddy censure°

Will then cry out of Marcius " Oh, if he

Had borne° the business! "

SIC.   Besides, if things go well,

Opinion, that so sticks on Marcius, shall   275

Of his demerits° rob Cominius.

BRU.   Come.

Half all Cominius' honors are to Marcius,

Though Marcius earned them not. And all his faults

To Marcius shall be honors, though indeed

In aught he merit not.

SIC.   Let's hence, and hear   280

How the dispatch is made,° and in what fashion,

More than his singularity,° he goes

Upon this present action.

BRU.   Let's along.   [*Exeunt.*]

SCENE II. *Corioli. The Senate House.*

[*Enter* TULLUS AUFIDIUS, *with* SENATORS *of Corioli.*]

1. SEN. So your opinion is, Aufidius,

That they of Rome are entered in° our counsels,

And know how we proceed.

AUF.   Is it not yours?

What ever have been thought on in this state

That could be brought to bodily act ere Rome   5

Had circumvention?° 'Tis not four days gone

Since I heard thence. These are the words — I think

I have the letter here — yes, here it is.

229–30. vent . . . superfluity: dispose of our stale excess; i.e.,
some of these unnecessary rogues will be killed.   233. put . . .
to 't: keep you busy.   237. by . . . ears: i.e., quarreling.   243. con-
stant: firm to my promise.   245. stiff: obstinate. Stand'st out:
i.e., will you oppose?   251. Right . . . priority: it is right that
you should go first.   254. garners: granaries. mutiners: mu-
tineers.   255. puts . . . forth: makes a good show.

260. gird: taunt.   263. to be so: i.e., because he is so.
272. giddy censure: fickle opinion.   274. borne: been in charge
of.   276. demerits: deserts.   281. dispatch is made: business
is settled.   282. singularity: own peculiar behavior.
Sc. ii: 2. are . . . in: have access to.   6. circumvention:
means of circumventing it.

[*Reads.*] " They have pressed a power,° but it is not
　　　known
Whether for east or west. The dearth is great,　　10
The people mutinous. And it is rumored,
Cominius, Marcius your old enemy,
Who is of Rome worse hated than of° you,
And Titus Lartius, a most valiant Roman,
These three lead on this preparation　　　　　15
Whither 'tis bent.° Most likely 'tis for you.
Consider of it."

1. SEN.　　　　　Our army's in the field.
We never yet made doubt but Rome was ready
To answer us.

AUF.　　　　　Nor did you think it folly
To keep your great pretenses veiled till when　　20
They needs must show themselves, which in the
　　　hatching,°
It seemed, appeared to Rome. By the discovery
We shall be shortened in our aim,° which was
To take in many towns ere almost Rome
Should know we were afoot.

2. SEN.　　　　　Noble Aufidius,　　25
Take your commission,° hie° you to your bands.°
Let us alone to guard Corioli.
If they set down before 's,° for the remove°
Bring up your army, but I think you'll find
They've not prepared for us.

AUF.　　　　　Oh, doubt not that,　　30
I speak from certainties. Nay, more,
Some parcels° of their power are forth already,
And only hitherward. I leave your Honors.
If we and Caius Marcius chance to meet,
'Tis sworn between us, we shall ever strike　　35
Till one can do no more.

ALL.　　　　　The gods assist you!
AUF. And keep your Honors safe!
1. SEN.　　　　　Farewell.
2. SEN.　　　　　Farewell.
ALL. Farewell.　　　　　[*Exeunt.*]

SCENE III. *Rome. A room in* MARCIUS' *house.*

[*Enter* VOLUMNIA *and* VIRGILIA. *They set them down
　　on two low stools, and sew.*]

VOL. I pray you, Daughter, sing, or express your-
self in a more comfortable sort. If my son were my
husband, I should freelier rejoice in that absence
wherein he won honor than in the embracements of
his bed where he would show most love. When　　5
yet he was but tender-bodied, and the only son of
my womb; when youth with comeliness plucked all

gaze his way;° when, for a day of kings' entreaties,
a mother should not sell him an hour from her be-
holding — I, considering how honor would be-　　10
come such a person, that it was no better than pic-
turelike to hang by the wall° if renown made it not
stir, was pleased to let him seek danger where he was
like to find fame. To a cruel war I sent him, from
whence he returned, his brows bound with　　15
oak.° I tell thee, Daughter, I sprang not more in
joy at first hearing he was a man-child than now in
first seeing he had proved himself a man.

VIR. But had he died in the business, madam, how
then?

VOL. Then his good report° should have been　　20
my son, I therein would have found issue.° Hear me
profess sincerely. Had I a dozen sons, each in my
love alike and none less dear than thine and　　25
my good Marcius, I had rather had eleven die nobly
for their country than one voluptuously° surfeit out
of action.

[*Enter a* GENTLEWOMAN.]

GEN. Madam, the Lady Valeria is come to visit
　　you.

VIR. Beseech you, give me leave to retire myself.
VOL. Indeed you shall not.　　　　　31
Methinks I hear hither your husband's drum,
See him pluck Aufidius down by the hair,
As children from a bear, the Volsces shunning him.
Methinks I see him stamp thus, and call thus:　　35
" Come on, you cowards! You were got° in fear,
Though you were born in Rome." His bloody brow
With his mailed hand then wiping, forth he goes,
Like to a harvestman that's tasked to° mow
Or all, or° lose his hire.　　　　　40

VIR. His bloody brow! Oh, Jupiter, no blood!
VOL. Away, you fool! It more becomes a man
Than gilt his trophy.° The breasts of Hecuba,
When she did suckle Hector, looked not lovelier
Than Hector's forehead when it spit forth blood　45
At Grecian sword, contemning.° Tell Valeria
We are fit to bid her welcome.

[*Exit* GENTLEWOMAN.]

VIR. Heavens bless° my lord from fell° Aufidius!
VOL. He'll beat Aufidius' head below his knee,
And tread upon his neck.　　　　　50
[*Enter* VALERIA, *with an* USHER° *and* GENTLEWOMAN.]

VAL. My ladies both, good day to you.

Sc. iii: **7–8. when . . . way:** when he was so attractive a youth
that everyone stared at him.　**12. hang . . . wall:** i.e., in idle-
ness.　**15–16. bound . . . oak:** wearing a garland of oak leaves,
the Roman equivalent of the Congressional Medal.　**20. good
report:** fame.　**21. issue:** children.　**27. voluptuously:** luxuri-
ously.　**36. got:** begotten.　**39. tasked to:** given the task of.
40. Or . . . or: either . . . or.　**43. Than . . . trophy:** than gilt is
appropriate on his memorial. In Shakespeare's time much gilt
was used on the memorials and monuments in English churches.
46. contemning: disdaining.　**48. bless:** protect. **fell:** fierce.
50 s.d., usher: gentleman acting as escort.

9. pressed a power: drafted an army.　**13. of:** by.　**16. bent:**
intended.　**21. hatching:** disclosing.　**23. be . . . aim:** fall short
of our aim.　**26. commission:** document formally appointing him
as commander. **hie:** hasten. **bands:** companies.　**27. set . . . be-
fore 's:** besiege us. **remove:** relief.　**32. parcels:** detachments.

vol. Sweet madam.

vir. I am glad to see your ladyship.

val. How do you both? You are manifest house-keepers.° What are you sewing here? A fine spot,° in good faith. How does your little son?   57

vir. I thank your ladyship, well, good madam.

vol. He had rather see the swords and hear a drum than look upon his schoolmaster.   61

val. O' my word, the father's son. I'll swear 'tis a very pretty boy. O' my troth,° I looked upon him o' Wednesday half an hour together, has such a confirmed° countenance. I saw him run after a gilded butterfly, and when he caught it, he let it go   66 again; and after it again, and over and over he comes, and up again; catched it again. Or whether his fall enraged him, or how 'twas, he did so set his teeth and tear it — oh, I warrant, how he mammocked° it!

vol. One on 's father's moods.   72

val. Indeed, la, 'tis a noble child.

vir. A crack,° madam.

val. Come, lay aside your stitchery. I must have you play the idle huswife with me this afternoon.

vir. No, good madam, I will not out of doors.

val. Not out of doors!

vol. She shall, she shall.   80

vir. Indeed, no, by your patience. I'll not over the threshold till my lord return from the wars.

val. Fie, you confine yourself most unreasonably. Come, you must go visit the good lady that lies in.°

vir. I will wish her speedy strength, and visit   87 her with my prayers, but I cannot go thither.

vol. Why, I pray you?   90

vir. 'Tis not to save labor, nor that I want love.

val. You would be another Penelope.° Yet they say all the yarn she spun in Ulysses' absence did but fill Ithaca full of moths. Come, I would your cambric° were sensible° as your finger, that you might leave pricking it for pity. Come, you shall go with us.   97

vir. No, good madam, pardon me. Indeed I will not forth.

val. In truth, la, go with me, and I'll tell you excellent news of your husband.

vir. Oh, good madam, there can be none yet.

val. Verily, I do not jest with you. There came news from him last night.

vir. Indeed, madam?   105

val. In earnest, it's true, I heard a Senator speak it. Thus it is. The Volsces have an army forth, against

whom Cominius the general is gone, with one part of our Roman power. Your lord and Titus Lartius are set down before their city Corioli. They nothing doubt prevailing,° and to make it brief wars. This is true, on mine honor. And so I pray go with us.

vir. Give me excuse, good madam, I will obey you in everything hereafter.   115

vol. Let her alone, lady. As she is now, she will but disease our better mirth.

val. In troth, I think she would. Fare you well, then. Come, good sweet lady. Prithee, Virgilia, turn thy solemnness out o' door and go along with us.

vir. No, at° a word, madam. Indeed, I must   122 not. I wish you much mirth.

val. Well then, farewell.   [*Exeunt.*]

SCENE IV. *Before Corioli.*

[*Enter, with drum and colors,* MARCIUS, TITUS LARTIUS, CAPTAINS *and* SOLDIERS. *To them a* MESSENGER.]

mar. Yonder comes news. A wager they have met.

lart. My horse to yours, no.

mar.   'Tis done.

lart.   Agreed.

mar. Say, has our general met the enemy?

mess. They lie in view, but have not spoke as yet.

lart. So, the good horse is mine.

mar.   I'll buy him of you.   5

lart. No, I'll nor sell nor give him. Lend you him I will
For half a hundred years. Summon the town.

mar. How far off lie these armies?

mess.   Within this mile and half,

mar. Then shall we hear their larum,° and they ours.
Now, Mars, I prithee, make us quick in work,   10
That we with smoking swords may march from hence
To help our fielded° friends! Come, blow thy blast.

[*They sound a parley.° Enter two* SENATORS *with others, on the walls.*]

Tullus Aufidius, is he within your walls?

1. sen. No, nor a man that fears you less than he —
That's lesser than a little. Hark, our drums   15
                                           [*Drum afar off.*]
Are bringing forth our youth! We'll break our walls
Rather than they shall pound° us up. Our gates,

55–56. **manifest housekeepers:** obviously being good housewives. 56. **spot:** pattern.   63. **O' my troth:** by my truth.   65. **confirmed:** determined.   71. **mammocked:** tore it to pieces. 74. **crack:** imp.   86. **lies in:** has had a baby.   92. **Penelope:** the wife of Ulysses. After the siege of Troy she waited for ten years for her husband to return to their home in Ithaca. To put off the persistent wooers who wished to marry her, she said she must first complete a piece of weaving, which she unraveled each night.   95. **cambric:** fine linen. **sensible:** sensitive.

111–12. **They . . . prevailing:** they have every confidence that they will win.   122. **at:** in.
Sc. iv: 9. **larum:** alarum, call to arms.   12. **fielded:** in the field. **s.d., sound a parley:** i.e., trumpet call summoning to a conference.   17. **pound:** shut up as in a pound.

Which yet seem shut, we have but pinned with
    rushes,°
They'll open of themselves. Hark you, far off!
                        [*Alarum*° *far off.*]
There is Aufidius. List what work he makes   20
Amongst your cloven° army.
MAR.   Oh, they are at it!
LART. Their noise be our instruction. Ladders, ho!
    [*Enter the army of the Volsces.*]
MAR. They fear us not, but issue forth their city.
Now put your shields before your hearts and fight
With hearts more proof° than shields. Advance,
    brave Titus.   25
They do disdain us much beyond our thoughts,°
Which makes me sweat with wrath. Come on, my
    fellows.
He that retires, I'll take him for a Volsce,
And he shall feel mine edge.
    [*Alarum. The* ROMANS *are beaten back to their
        trenches. Re-enter* MARCIUS, *cursing.*]
MAR. All the contagion of the south° light on you,
You shames of Rome! You herd of —— Boils and
    plagues   31
Plaster you o'er, that you may be abhorred
Farther than seen, and one infect another
Against the wind a mile!° You souls of geese,
That bear the shapes of men, how have you run 35
From slaves that apes would beat! Pluto° and Hell!
All hurt behind, backs red, and faces pale
With flight and agued° fear! Mend,° and charge
    home,
Or, by the fires of Heaven,° I'll leave the foe   39
And make my wars on you. Look to 't. Come on.
If you'll stand fast, we'll beat them to their wives,
As they us to our trenches followed.
    [*Another alarum. The Volsces fly, and
           MARCIUS follows them to the gates.*]
So, now the gates are ope. Now prove good seconds.°
'Tis for the followers Fortune widens them,
Not for the flyers. Mark me, and do the like.   45
                            [*Enters the gates.*]
1. SOL. Foolhardiness — not I.
2. SOL.   Nor I. [MARCUS *is shut in.*]
1. SOL. See, they have shut him in.
ALL.   To the pot,° I warrant him.
                    [*Alarum continues.*]
    [*Re-enter* TITUS LARTIUS.]
LART. What is become of Marcius?

ALL.   Slain, sir, doubtless.
1. SOL. Following the flyers at the very heels,
With them he enters, who, upon the sudden,   50
Clapped to their gates. He is himself alone,
To answer° all the city.
LART.   O noble fellow!
Who sensibly° outdares his senseless sword,
And, when it bows, stands up! Thou art left,
    Marcius.
A carbuncle° entire, as big as thou art,   55
Were not so rich a jewel. Thou wast a soldier
Even to Cato's° wish, not fierce and terrible
Only in strokes; but, with thy grim looks and
The thunderlike percussion of thy sounds,
Thou madest thine enemies shake as if the world 60
Were feverous and did tremble.
    [*Re-enter* MARCIUS, *bleeding, assaulted by the
             enemy.*]
1. SOL.   Look, sir.
LART.   Oh, 'tis Marcius!
Let's fetch him off,° or make remain alike.°
    [*They fight, and all enter the city.*]

SCENE V. *Within Corioli. A street.*

    [*Enter certain* ROMANS, *with spoils.*]
1. ROM. This will I carry to Rome.
2. ROM. And I this.
3. ROM. A murrain° on 't! I took this for silver.
    [*Alarum contines still afar off.*]
[*Enter* MARCIUS *and* TITUS LARTIUS *with a trumpet.*]
MAR. See here these movers° that do prize their
    hours   5
At a cracked° drachma!° Cushions, leaden spoons,
Irons of a doit,° doublets that hangmen would
Bury with those that wore them,° these base slaves,
Ere yet the fight be done, pack up. Down with them!
And hark what noise the General makes! To him!
There is the man of my soul's hate, Aufidius,   11
Piercing our Romans. Then, valiant Titus, take
Convenient numbers to make good the city,
Whilst I, with those that have the spirit, will haste
To help Cominius.
LART.   Worthy sir, thou bleed'st.   15
Thy exercise hath been too violent
For a second course° of fight.
MAR.   Sir, praise me not,

---

18. pinned . . . rushes: fastened only with rushes.   19 s.d.,
alarum: see l. 9.   21. cloven: cleft, cut-up.   25. proof: tough,
tested like the best armor.   26. They . . . thoughts: they despise
us more than we can think.   30. south: A wind from the south
was believed to bring fog, sickness, and bad luck.   34. Against
. . . mile: even when you are a mile off and the wind is blowing
against you.   36. Pluto: god and ruler of the underworld.
38. agued: shivering. Mend: pull yourselves together.   39. fires
of Heaven: stars.   43. seconds: supports.   47. To . . . pot: lit.,
melting-pot; i.e., it's all up with him.

52. answer: oppose.   53. sensibly: endowed with feeling.
55. carbuncle: The term was used for any precious stone of a
transparent red.   57. Cato's: Cato the Censor was famous for
his austere views on life and conduct.   62. fetch . . . off:
rescue him. alike: i.e., bloody.
    Sc. v: 3. murrain: plague.   5. movers: creatures, human only
because they move.   6. cracked: worthless. drachma: a Greek
coin.   7. Irons . . . doit: ironmongery not worth half a cent.
7–8. doublets . . . them: The clothes of the executed were the
hangman's perquisite. For doublets, see Pl. 8b and comment on
p. 93a.   17. course: round. See App. 5.

My work hath yet not warmed me.° Fare you well.
The blood I drop is rather physical°
Than dangerous to me. To Aufidius thus   20
I will appear, and fight.

LART.   Now the fair goddess Fortune
Fall deep in love with thee, and her great charms
Misguide thy opposers' swords! Bold gentleman,
Prosperity be thy page!°

MAR.   Thy friend no less
Than those she placeth highest! So farewell.   25

LART. Thou worthiest Marcius! [*Exit* MARCIUS.]
Go sound thy trumpet in the market place,
Call thither all the officers o' the town,
Where they shall know our mind. Away!

                               [*Exeunt.*]

SCENE VI. *Near the camp of* COMINIUS.

[*Enter* COMINIUS, *as it were in retire, with* SOLDIERS.]
   COM. Breathe you,° my friends. Well fought. We
     are come off°
Like Romans, neither foolish in our stands
Nor cowardly in retire. Believe me, sirs,
We shall be charged again. Whiles we have struck,
By interims and conveying gusts° we have heard   5
The charges of our friends. Ye Roman gods,
Lead their successes as we wish our own,
That both our powers, with smiling fronts encoun-
     tering,
May give you thankful sacrifice!
[*Enter a* MESSENGER.]   Thy news?
   MESS. The citizens of Corioli have issued,   10
And given to Lartius and to Marcius battle.
I saw our party to their trenches driven,
And then I came away.

COM.   Though thou speak'st truth,
Methinks thou speak'st not well. How long is 't
     since?
   MESS. Above an hour, my lord.   15
   COM. 'Tis not a mile, briefly° we heard their
     drums.
How couldst thou in a mile confound° an hour
And bring thy news so late?
   MESS.   Spies of the Volsces
Held me in chase, that I was forced to wheel°
Three or four miles about. Else had I, sir,   20
Half an hour since brought my report.
              [*Enter* MARCIUS.]
COM.   Who's yonder,

That does appear as he were flayed? Oh, gods!
He has the stamp° of Marcius, and I have
Beforetime seen him thus.

MAR.   Come I too late?

COM. The shepherd knows not thunder from a
     tabor°   25
More than I know the sound of Marcius' tongue
From every meaner man.

MAR.   Come I too late?

COM. Aye, if you come not in the blood of others,
But mantled in your own.

MAR.   Oh, let me clip° ye
In arms as sound as when I wooed, in heart   30
As merry as when our nuptial day was done,
And tapers° burned to bedward!°

COM.   Flower of warriors,
How is 't with Titus Lartius?

MAR. As with a man busied about decrees —
Condemning some to death, and some to exile;   35
Ransoming him or pitying, threatening the other;
Holding Corioli in the name of Rome,
Even like a fawning greyhound in the leash,
To let him slip at will.

COM.   Where is that slave
Which told me they had beat you to your trenches?
Where is he? Call him hither.

MAR.   Let him alone,   41
He did inform the truth. But for our gentlemen,
The common file° — a plague! Tribunes for
     them! —
The mouse ne'er shunned the cat as they did budge°
From rascals worse than they.

COM.   But how prevailed you?   45

MAR. Will the time serve to tell? I do not think.
Where is the enemy? Are you lords o' the field?
If not, why cease you till you are so?

COM.   Marcius,
We have at disadvantage fought, and did
Retire to win our purpose.   50

MAR. How lies their battle?° Know you on which
     side
They have placed their men of trust?

COM.   As I guess, Marcius,
Their bands i' the vaward° are the Antiates,
Of their best trust, o'er them Aufidius,
Their very heart of hope.°

MAR.   I do beseech you,   55
By all the battles wherein we have fought,
By the blood we have shed together, by the vows

---

18. My . . . me: I have not yet warmed up to any work worth
praising.   19. physical: salutary, healthful. Bloodletting was a
cure in many complaints.   24. Prosperity . . . page: may good
fortune be your page (i.e., servant) to attend on you.

    Sc. vi: 1. Breathe you: take breath, pause. are . . . off: have
left the fight.   5. By . . . gusts: at intervals borne to us by the
wind.   16. briefly: a short while since.   17. confound: waste.
19. wheel: make a detour.

23. stamp: impression, appearance.   25. tabor: small drum, an
instrument of peace. See Pl. 13d.   29. clip: embrace.   32. tapers:
candles. bedward: toward bed.   42–43. gentlemen . . . file: the
gentlemen who served as volunteers, usually in the commander's
own company, were the pick of the army. The *common file* — the
ordinary soldiers — were usually unwilling conscripts. See Gen.
Intro. p. 31a. file: list, roster. Cf. *Macb*, III.i.95.   44. budge:
shrink.   51. battle: army.   53. vaward: vanguard.   55. heart
of hope: greatest hope.

We have made to endure friends, that you directly
Set me against Aufidius and his Antiates.
And that you not delay the present but,   60
Filling the air with swords advanced° and darts,
We prove° this very hour.
   COM.   Though I could wish
You were conducted to a gentle bath,
And balms applied to you, yet dare I never
Deny your asking. Take your choice of those   65
That best can aid your action.
   MAR.   Those are they
That most are willing. If any such be here —
As it were sin to doubt — that love this painting°
Wherein you see me smeared, if any fear
Lesser his person than an ill report,   70
If any think brave death outweighs bad life
And that his country's dearer than himself,
Let him alone, or so many so minded,
Wave thus, to express his disposition,
And follow Marcius.   75
   [They all shout, and wave their swords, take him
        up in their arms, and cast up their caps.]
Oh, me alone! Make you a sword of me?°
If these shows be not outward, which of you
But is four Volsces? None of you but is
Able to bear against the great Aufidius
A shield as hard as his. A certain number,   80
Though thanks to all, must I select from all. The rest
Shall bear the business in some other fight,
As cause will be obeyed.° Please you to march,
And four shall quickly draw out my command,°
Which men are best inclined.
   COM.   March on, my fellows.   85
Make good this ostentation° and you shall
Divide° in all with us   [Exeunt.]

SCENE VII. *The gates of Corioli.*

[TITUS LARTIUS, *having set a guard upon Corioli,
going with drum and trumpet toward* COMINIUS
and CAIUS MARCIUS, *enters with a* LIEUTENANT,
other SOLDIERS, *and a* SCOUT.]
   LART. So, let the ports° be guarded. Keep your
        duties

As I have set them down. If I do send, dispatch
Those centuries° to our aid. The rest will serve
For a short holding. If we lose the field,
We cannot keep the town.
   LIEU.   Fear not our care, sir.   5
   LART. Hence, and shut your gates upon 's.
Our guider, come, to the Roman camp conduct us.
                                                    [Exeunt.]

SCENE VIII. *A field of battle between the
Roman and the Volscian camps.*

[*Alarum as in battle. Enter, from opposite sides,*
MARCIUS *and* AUFIDIUS.]
   MAR. I'll fight with none but thee, for I do hate
        thee
Worse than a promise-breaker.
   AUF.   We hate alike.
Not Afric owns a serpent I abhor
More than thy fame and envy. Fix thy foot.
   MAR. Let the first budger° die the other's slave,   5
And the gods doom him after!
   AUF.   If I fly, Marcius,
Holloa° me like a hare.
   MAR.   Within these three hours, Tullus,
Alone I fought in your Corioli walls
And made what work I pleased. 'Tis not my blood
Wherein thou seest me masked. For thy revenge   10
Wrench up° thy power to the highest.
   AUF.   Wert thou the Hector
That was the whip of your bragged progeny,°
Thou shouldst not 'scape me here.
[*They fight, and certain Volsces come in the aid of*
AUFIDIUS. MARCIUS *fights till they be driven in
breathless.*]
Officious, and not valiant, you have shamed me   14
In your condemnèd seconds.°   [Exeunt.]

SCENE IX. *The Roman camp.*

[*Flourish.° Alarum. A retreat is sounded. Enter
from one side,* COMINIUS *with the* ROMANS; *from the
other side,* MARCIUS, *with his arm in a scarf.*]
   COM. If I should tell thee o'er° this thy day's work,
Thou'lt not believe thy deeds. But I'll report it
Where Senators shall mingle tears with smiles;
Where great patricians shall attend,° and shrug,°

---

61. advanced: raised.   62. prove: try our luck.   68. painting:
i.e., blood.   76. Oh . . . me: do you wave me aloft as if I were a
sword? There has been much dispute about this line. It is to
be noted that the main difficulties in this play occur in the
speeches of Marcius when he is under emotional stress. It was
presumably Shakespeare's intention to show him as a man who
became incoherent at moments of excitement; the difficulties,
therefore, are not due to any corruption of the text but to
Marcius' emotion. See later III.i.102; III.iii.68.   83. As . . .
obeyed: as occasion demands.   84. And . . . command: and four
officers shall quickly select the volunteers who are to go with me.
86. Make . . . ostentation: let this show of eagerness be made
good in battle.   87. Divide: i.e., the loot.
   Sc. vii: 1. ports: gates.

3. centuries: companies of a hundred men each.
   Sc. viii: 5. budger: one who gives way.   7. Holloa: shout at,
to make me run faster.   11. Wrench up: as with a lever or a jack.
11-12. Hector . . . progeny: that Hector who scourged your
ancestors, about whom you boasted so much. (Either Shake-
speare or Aufidius is in error, for Hector was the champion of the
Trojans from whom the Romans claimed to be descended.)
15. condemned seconds: "damned help."
   Sc. ix: s.d., Flourish: trumpet fanfare.   1. tell . . . o'er: re-
peat to you.   4. attend: listen. shrug: i.e., doubt.

I' the end admire;° where ladies shall be frighted   5
And, gladly quaked,° hear more; where the dull
    Tribunes
That, with the fusty plebeians, hate thine honors
Shall say against their hearts° "We thank the gods
Our Rome hath such a soldier."
Yet camest thou to a morsel of this feast,   10
Having fully dined before.

[*Enter* TITUS LARTIUS, *with his power, from the
                    pursuit.*]

LART.   O General,
Here is the steed, we the caparison.°
Hadst thou beheld ——

MAR.   Pray now, no more. My mother,
Who has a charter to extol her blood,°
When she does praise me grieves me. I have done
As you have done, that's what I can — induced   16
As you have been, that's for my country.
He that has but effected his goodwill°
Hath overta'en mine act.

COM.   You shall not be
The grave of your deserving,° Rome must know   20
The value of her own. 'Twere a concealment
Worse than a theft, no less than a traducement,°
To hide your doings and to silence that
Which, to the spire and top of praises vouched,°
Would seem but modest. Therefore I beseech you ——
In sign of what you are, not to reward   26
What you have done — before our army hear me.

MAR. I have some wounds upon me, and they
    smart
To hear themselves remembered.

COM.   Should they not,
Well might they fester 'gainst ingratitude,   30
And tent° themselves with death. Of all the horses,
Whereof we have ta'en good and good store, of all
The treasure in this field achieved and city,
We render you the tenth, to be ta'en forth
Before the common distribution, at   35
Your only° choice.

MAR.   I thank you, General,
But cannot make my heart consent to take
A bribe to pay my sword. I do refuse it,
And stand upon my common part with those
That have beheld the doing.°   40

[*A long flourish. They all cry* "Marcius! Marcius!"
cast up their caps and lances. COMINIUS *and* LARTIUS
                                stand bare.°]

MAR. May° these same instruments, which you
    profane,
Never sound more! When drums and trumpets shall
I' the field prove flatterers, let Courts and cities be
Made all of false-faced soothing!°
When steel grows soft as the parasite's silk,   45
Let him be made a coverture for the wars!
No more, I say! For that I have not washed
My nose that bled, or foiled° some debile° wretch,
Which without note here's many else have done,
You shout me forth   50
In acclamations hyperbolical,
As if I loved my little should be dieted
In praises sauced with lies.°

COM.   Too modest are you,
More cruel to your good report than grateful
To us that give you truly. By your patience,   55
If 'gainst yourself you be incensed, we'll put you,
Like one that means his proper° harm, in manacles,
Then reason safely with you. Therefore be it known,
As to us, to all the world, that Caius Marcius   5〈
Wears this war's garland.° In token of the which,
My noble steed, known to the camp, I give him,
With all his trim belonging.° And from this time,
For what he did before Corioli, call him,
With all the applause and clamor of the host,
CAIUS MARCIUS CORIOLANUS. Bear   6〈
The addition° nobly ever!

[*Flourish. Trumpets sound, and drums.*]

my share with everyone else who was in the action.   40 s.d., bare:
bareheaded, as a mark of honor. See App. 7.   41–46. May
. . . wars: a difficult and much disputed passage, much
emended by editors. F1 reads: "May these same Instruments,
which you prophane,/Never sound more: when Drums and
Trumpets shall/I' th' field prove flatterers, let Courts and
Cities be/Made all of false-fac'd soothing:/When Steele grows
soft, as the Parasites Silke,/Let him be made an Overture
for th' Warres." The main difficulty is in the word "over-
ture," which elsewhere in Shakespeare means discovery, ex-
posure, or proposal (see *Lear*, III.vii.89; *W Tale*, II.i.172; *T
Night*, I.v.224). Editors have therefore substituted "coverture,"
which means "covering" (Cf. *M Ado*, III.i.30), but it does not
greatly help the sense. The F1 reading can however be interpreted
as it stands, for the word "overture" in Elizabethan speech
sometimes means "overthrower." Coriolanus is weak from his
wounds and, as often when in a state of high emotion, he becomes
incoherent (see I.vi.76; III.iii.68). He means "when drums and
trumpets are debased by being used for flattery (and not to
sound charges), then Courts and cities (where peaceful parasites
live) will naturally be full of smooth falsehood. When steel (the
soldiers' covering) grows as soft as the courtier's silk, then the
courtier overthrows the honor of war." More briefly, his meaning
is: "When soldiers turn flatterers, they behave like civilians and
bring dishonor on war."   44. false-faced soothing: deceitful
flattery.   48. foiled: overthrown. debile: feeble.   52–53. my
. . . lies: my small accomplishment should be given a fancy diet
of lies.   57. proper: own.   60. Wears . . . garland: i.e., carries
the chief honor of this war.   62. trim belonging: equipment and
harness in fine condition.   66. addition: title of honor added to a
man's name, and so honor.

5. admire: be overwhelmed with astonishment.   6. quaked:
made to tremble.   8. against . . . hearts: although they dislike
you.   12. Here . . . caparison: Coriolanus is the horse himself,
the rest of us merely its coverings. caparison: a long saddlecloth
used on ceremonial occasions.   14. charter . . . blood: special
privilege to praise her own child.   18. effected . . . will: done his
best.   20. charge . . . deserving: your deserts shall not be buried
with you for lack of recognition.   22. traducement: slander.
24. spire . . . vouched: publicly declared as high as the tops of
church spires.   31. tent: A tent was a roll of linen inserted into
a wound to cleanse it; "to tent" is thus to cleanse. So, Cominius
says, Marcius' wounds might be expected to fester and bring
death if his fellow soldiers should neglect to give him the praises
due to him.   36. only: sole.   39–40. stand . . . doing: I will take

ALL. Caius Marcius Coriolanus!

COR. I will go wash,
And when my face is fair,° you shall perceive
Whether I blush or no. Howbeit, I thank you.   70
I mean to stride your steed, and at all times
To undercrest your good addition
To the fairness of my power.°

COM.   So, to our tent,
Where ere we do repose us we will write
To Rome of our success. You, Titus Lartius,   75
Must to Corioli back. Send us to Rome
The best,° with whom we may articulate°
For their own good and ours.

LART.   I shall, my lord.

COR. The gods begin to mock me. I, that now
Refused most princely gifts, am bound to beg   80
Of my lord General.

COM.   Take 't, 'tis yours. What is 't?

COR. I sometime lay° here in Corioli
At a poor man's house, he used me kindly.
He cried to me, I saw him prisoner,
But then Aufidius was within my view   85
And wrath o'erwhelmed my pity. I request you
To give my poor host freedom.

COM.   Oh, well begged!
Were he the butcher of my son, he should
Be free as is the wind. Deliver him, Titus.

LART. Marcius, his name?

COR.   By Jupiter, forgot.   90
I am weary, yea, my memory is tired.
Have we no wine here?

COM.   Go we to our tent.
The blood upon your visage dries, 'tis time
It should be looked to. Come.   [*Exeunt.*]

SCENE X. *The camp of the Volsces.*

[*A flourish. Cornets. Enter* TULLUS AUFIDIUS, *bloody,
with two or three* SOLDIERS.]

AUF. The town is ta'en!

I. SOL. 'Twill be delivered back on good condi-
tion.°

AUF. Condition!
I would I were a Roman, for I cannot,
Being a Volsce, be that I am. Condition!   5
What good condition can a treaty find
I' the part that is at mercy?° Five times, Marcius,
I have fought with thee, so often hast thou beat me,
And wouldst do so, I think, should we encounter
As often as we eat. By the elements,°   10

If e'er again I meet him beard to beard,
He's mine, or I am his. Mine emulation°
Hath not that honor in 't it had, for where
I thought to crush him in an equal force,
True sword to sword, I'll potch° at him some way,
Or wrath or craft may get him.

I. SOL.   He's the Devil.   16

AUF. Bolder, though not so subtle. My valor's
poisoned
With only suffering stain by him, for him
Shall fly out of itself. Nor sleep nor sanctuary,
Being naked, sick, nor fane° nor Capitol,   20
The prayers of priests nor times of sacrifice,
Embarquements° all of fury, shall lift up
Their rotten privilege and custom 'gainst
My hate to Marcius. Where I find him, were it
At home, upon my brother's guard,° even there,   25
Against the hospitable canon,° would I
Wash my fierce hand in 's heart. Go you to the city.
Learn how 'tis held, and what they are that must
Be hostages for Rome.

I. SOL.   Will not you go?

AUF. I am attended° at the cypress grove. I pray
you —   30
'Tis south the city mills — bring me word thither
How the world goes, that to the pace of it
I may spur on my journey.

I. SOL.   I shall, sir.   [*Exeunt.*]

Act II

SCENE I. *Rome. A public place.*

[*Enter* MENENIUS, *with the two* TRIBUNES *of the
people,* SICINIUS *and* BRUTUS.]

MEN. The augurer° tells me we shall have news
tonight.

BRU. Good or bad?

MEN. Not according to the prayer of the people,
for they love not Marcius.   5

SIC. Nature teaches beasts to know their friends.

MEN. Pray you, who does the wolf love?

SIC. The lamb.

MEN. Aye, to devour him, as the hungry plebe-
ians would the noble Marcius.   11

BRU. He's a lamb indeed, that baas like a bear.

MEN. He's a bear indeed, that lives like a lamb.

---

69. **fair:** clean.   72–73. **undercrest . . . power:** I will wear this
good honor as a crest as far as I possibly can.   77. **best:** i.e.,
chief men of Corioli. **articulate:** draw up articles of peace.
82. **lay:** lodged.
  Sc. x: 2. **condition:** terms.   7. **I' . . . mercy:** on the beaten
side.   10. **elements:** sky and sea.

12. **emulation:** jealousy.   15. **potch:** poke at.   20. **fane:**
temple.   22. **Embarquements:** things that hinder.   25. **upon
. . . guard:** with my brother guarding him.   26. **hospitable
canon:** law of hospitality.   30. **attended:** waited for.
  Act II, Sc. i: 1. **augurer:** official who foretold future events
from various omens. Cf. *Caesar,* II.ii.37–40.

You two are old men. Tell me one thing that I shall ask you.

BOTH. Well, sir.   17

MEN. In what enormity is Marcius poor in, that you two have not in abundance?

BRU. He's poor in no one fault, but stored with all.

SIC. Especially in pride.   22

BRU. And topping all others in boasting.

MEN. This is strange now. Do you two know how you are censured° here in the city, I mean of us o' the right-hand file?° Do you?   26

BOTH. Why, how are we censured?

MEN. Because you talk of pride now — will you not be angry?

BOTH. Well, well, sir, well.   30

MEN. Why, 'tis no great matter, for a very little thief of occasion° will rob you of a great deal of patience. Give your dispositions the reins,° and be angry at your pleasures — at the least, if you take it as a pleasure to you in being so. You blame Marcius for being proud?

BRU. We do it not alone, sir.   37

MEN. I know you can do very little alone, for your helps are many,° or else your actions would grow wondrous single.° Your abilities are too infantlike for doing much alone. You talk of pride. Oh, that you could turn your eyes toward the napes of your necks and make but an interior survey of your good selves! Oh, that you could!   44

BOTH. What then, sir?

MEN. Why, then you should discover a brace of unmeriting,° proud, violent, testy magistrates, alias fools, as any in Rome.   49

SIC. Menenius, you are known well enough too.

MEN. I am known to be a humorous° patrician, and one that loves a cup of hot wine with not a drop of allaying Tiber° in 't; said to be something imperfect in favoring the first complaint,° hasty and tinderlike° upon too trivial motion;° one that 55 converses more with the buttock of the night than with the forehead of the morning. What I think I utter, and spend my malice in my breath. Meeting two such wealsmen° as you are — I cannot call you Lycurguses° — if the drink you give me touch my 60 palate adversely, I make a crooked face at it. I can't say your Worships have delivered the matter well when I find the ass in compound with the major part

of your syllables.° And though I must be content to bear with those that say you are reverend grave 66 men, yet they lie deadly that tell you you have good faces. If you see this in the map of my microcosm,° follows it that I am known well enough too? What harm can your bisson conspectuities° glean out of this character, if I be known well enough too?   72

BRU. Come, sir, come, we know you well enough.

MEN. You know neither me, yourselves, nor anything. You are ambitious for poor knaves' caps and legs.° You wear out a good wholesome forenoon in hearing a cause between an orange wife and a fossetseller,° and then rejourn° the controversy of threepence to a second day of audience. When you 80 are hearing a matter between party and party, if you chance to be pinched with the colic, you make faces like mummers;° set up the bloody flag against° all patience; and in roaring for a chamber pot, dismiss the controversy bleeding,° the more entangled by your hearing. All the peace you make in their cause is calling both the parties knaves. You are a pair of strange ones.   89

BRU. Come, come, you are well understood to be a perfecter giber° for the table than a necessary bencher° in the Capitol.

MEN. Our very priests must become mockers if they shall encounter such ridiculous subjects as 94 you are. When you speak best unto the purpose, it is not worth the wagging of your beards, and your beards deserve not so honorable a grave as to stuff a botcher's° cushion or to be entombed in an ass's packsaddle. Yet you must be saying Marcius is proud, who, in a cheap estimation,° is worth all 101 your predecessors since Deucalion,° though peradventure some of the best of 'em were hereditary hangmen. Godden° to your Worships. More of your conversation would infect my brain, being the herdsmen of the beastly plebeians. I will be bold to take my leave of you.   [BRUTUS *and* SICINIUS *go aside.*] [*Enter* VOLUMNIA, VIRGILIA, *and* VALERIA.] How now, my as fair as noble ladies — and the moon, were she

---

64–65. ass . . . syllables: there is "ass" (stupidity) in everything you say.   68. map . . . microcosm: i.e., face. Man was often regarded as a little universe (*microcosm*) which reproduces all the qualities of the great universe (macrocosm). The idea has already been elaborately worked out by Menenius in the fable of the belly. See I.i.99. Cf. *II Hen IV*, IV.iii.116.   71. bisson conspectuities: blear-eyed visions.   75–76. poor . . . legs: i.e., outward marks of respect. See App. 7.   78–79. orange . . . seller: a woman who sells oranges and a seller of wooden faucets for barrels, whose disputes are not of great importance.   79. rejourn: adjourn.   83. mummers: dancers in mumming dances, where the dancers disguised themselves and performed various rowdy antics. set . . . against: declared war on — a red flag being a sign of defiance.   86. bleeding: unhealed.   91. perfecter giber: better at making jokes.   92. bencher: Senator.   99. botcher: a mender of torn clothes.   101. cheap estimation: at a low valuation.   102. Deucalion: in classical legend Deucalion (like Noah in Genesis) survived the great flood that wiped out mankind.   104. Godden: good evening.

---

25. censured: judged, estimated.   26. right-hand file: i.e., by those of the Right, the patricians.   31–32. very . . . occasion: a very slight cause, like a thief.   33. Give . . . reins: let your feelings take control.   39. helps . . . many: i.e., you have your crowd to back you up.   40. single: feeble.   48. unmeriting: undeserving.   51. humorous: whimsical.   53. allaying Tiber: Tiber water to dilute it.   53–54. something . . . complaint: rather too prone not to listen to both sides of the case.   55. tinderlike: i.e., catching fire easily. motion: impulse.   59. wealsmen: statesmen.   60. Lycurguses: Lycurgus, who drew up the constitution and laws of Sparta, was regarded as a man of godlike wisdom.

earthly, no nobler — whither do you follow your
eyes so fast?   109

VOL. Honorable Menenius, my boy Marcius ap-
proaches. For the love of Juno, let's go.

MEN. Ha! Marcius coming home!

VOL. Aye, worthy Menenius, and with most pros-
perous approbation.°

MEN. Take my cap, Jupiter,° and I thank thee.
Hoo! Marcius coming home?   116

VIR. & VAL. Nay, 'tis true.

VOL. Look, here's a letter from him. The state°
hath another, his wife another, and I think there's
one at home for you.   120

MEN. I will make my very house reel tonight. A
letter for me?

VIR. Yes, certain — there's a letter for you, I
saw 't.   124

MEN. A letter for me! It gives me an estate of
seven years' health, in which time I will make a lip°
at the physician. The most sovereign prescription in
Galen° is but empiricutic,° and, to this preserva-
tive,° of no better report than a horse drench.°
Is he not wounded? He was wont to come home
wounded.   131

VIR. Oh, no, no, no.

VOL. Oh, he is wounded, I thank the gods for 't.

MEN. So do I too, if it be not too much. Brings a'°
victory in his pocket? The wounds become him.

VOL. On 's brows. Menenius, he comes the   137
third time home with the oaken garland.

MEN. Has he disciplined° Aufidius soundly?

VOL. Titus Lartius writes they fought together,
but Aufidius got off.   141

MEN. And 'twas time for him too, I'll warrant him
that. An° he had stayed by him, I would not have
been so fidiused° for all the chests in Corioli and the
gold that's in them. Is the Senate possessed° of
this?   146

VOL. Good ladies, let's go. Yes, yes, yes, the Senate
has letters from the General, wherein he gives my
son the whole name° of the war. He hath in this
action outdone his former deeds doubly.   151

VAL. In troth, there's wondrous things spoke of
him.

MEN. Wondrous! Aye, I warrant you, and not
without his true purchasing.°   155

VIR. The gods grant them true!

VOL. True! Pow, wow.°

MEN. True! I'll be sworn they are true. Where is
he wounded? [*To the* TRIBUNES] God save your
good Worships! Marcius is coming home. He has
more cause to be proud. Where is he wounded?   162

VOL. I' the shoulder and i' the left arm. There will
be large cicatrices° to show the people when he shall
stand for his place.° He received in the repulse of
Tarquin seven hurts i' the body.   166

MEN. One i' the neck, and two i' the thigh —
there's nine that I know.

VOL. He had, before this last expedition, twenty-
five wounds upon him.

MEN. Now it's twenty-seven. Every gash was an
enemy's grave. [*A shout and flourish.*] Hark! The
trumpets.   173

VOL. These are the ushers° of Marcius. Before
him he carries noise, and behind him he leaves tears.
Death, that dark spirit, in 's nervy° arm doth lie,
Which, being advanced,° declines,° and then men
die.   178

[*A sennet.° Trumpets sound. Enter* COMINIUS *and*
TITUS LARTIUS; *between them,* CORIOLANUS, *crowned
with an oaken garland; with* CAPTAINS *and* SOLDIERS,
and a HERALD.]

HER. Know, Rome, that all alone Marcius did fight
Within Corioli gates, where he hath won,   180
With fame, a name to Caius Marcius — these
In honor follows Coriolanus.°
Welcome to Rome, renowned Coriolanus!
                                            [*Flourish.*]

ALL. Welcome to Rome, renownèd Coriolanus!

COR. No more of this, it does offend my heart.
Pray now, no more.

COM.   Look, sir, your mother!

COR.   Oh,
You have, I know, petitioned all the gods   187
For my prosperity!   [*Kneels.*]

VOL.   Nay, my good soldier, up.
My gentle Marcius, worthy Caius, and
By deed-achieving honor° newly named —   190
What is it? — Coriolanus must I call thee? ——
But, oh, thy wife!

COR.   My gracious silence, hail!
Wouldst thou have laughed had I come coffined
home,
That weep'st to see me triumph? Ah, my dear,°
Such eyes the widows in Corioli wear,   195
And mothers that lack sons.

---

114. prosperous approbation: highest fame.   115. Take . . .
Jupiter: i.e., he throws his cap into the air. Jupiter is the god of
the sky. The characters in Shakespeare's *Coriolanus* were dressed
in Elizabethan and not Roman costumes.   118. state: the
Government; i.e., the Senate.   126. lip: face.   128. Galen: a
Roman writer on medical matters who in Shakespeare's time was
regarded as the supreme authority. He lived in the second cen-
tury A.D., several centuries after Coriolanus' time. empiricutic:
empirical, mere quackery.   128-29. to . . . preservative: com-
pared with this cordial.   129. horse drench: purge given to a
horse, a crude form of medicine.   135. a': he.   139. disciplined:
beaten.   143. An: if.   144. fidiused: i.e., given the treatment
which Aufidius received.   145. possessed: informed.   150. name:
glory.   155. true purchasing: honest acquisition.

157. Pow, wow: a phrase of strong contempt.   164. cicatrices:
scars.   165. stand . . . place: be a candidate for election.
174. ushers: escorts.   177. nervy: sinewy.   178. advanced:
raised. declines: falls.   s.d., sennet: a few notes on the trumpet.
181-82. these . . . Coriolanus: *Coriolanus* is added as an honor-
able addition to *Caius Marcius.*   190. deed-achieving honor:
honor which comes from heroic achievement.   194. my dear:
In Shakespeare's time this was a very strong term of affection.

MEN.　　　　　　　　Now the gods crown thee!
COR. And live you yet? [*To* VALERIA] O my sweet
　　lady, pardon.
VOL. I know not where to turn. Oh, welcome
　　home.
And welcome, General. And ye're welcome all.
　　MEN. A hundred thousand welcomes. I could
　　　weep,　　　　　　　　　　　　　　　　　　　200
And I could laugh, I am light and heavy. Welcome.
A curse begin at very root on 's heart
That is not glad to see thee! You are three
That Rome should dote on. Yet, by the faith of men,
We have some old crab trees° here at home that will
　　not　　　　　　　　　　　　　　　　　　　　　205
Be grafted to your relish.° Yet welcome, warriors.
We call a nettle but a nettle, and
The faults of fools but folly.
COM.　　　　　　　　　Ever right.
COR. Menenius, ever, ever.
HER. Give way there, and go on.
COR. [*To* VOLUMNIA *and* VIRGILIA] Your hand, and
　　yours.　　　　　　　　　　　　　　　　　　　210
Ere in our own house I do shade my head,
The good patricians must be visited,
From whom I have received not only greetings,
But with them change° of honors.
VOL.　　　　　　　　　I have lived
To see inherited my very wishes　　　　　　　215
And the buildings of my fancy.° Only
There's one thing wanting, which I doubt not but
Our Rome will cast upon thee.
COR.　　　　　　　　　Know, good Mother,
I had rather be their servant in my way
Than sway° with them in theirs.
COM.　　　　　　　On, to the Capitol!　　　220
[*Flourish. Cornets. Exeunt in state, as before.*]
[BRUTUS *and* SICINIUS *come forward.*]
BRU. All tongues speak of him, and the bleared
　　sights
Are spectacled° to see him. Your prattling nurse
Into a rapture° lets her baby cry
While she chats° him. The kitchen malkin° pins
Her richest lockram° 'bout her reechy° neck,　　225
Clambering the walls to eye him. Stalls, bulks,° win-
　　dows,
Are smothered up, leads° filled and ridges horsed
With variable complexions,° all agreeing
In earnestness to see him. Seld-shown flamens°

Do press among the popular throngs, and puff　230
To win a vulgar station.° Our veiled dames
Commit the war of white and damask in
Their nicely gawded cheeks to the wanton spoil
Of Phoebus' burning kisses.° Such a pother,
As if that whatsoever god who leads him　　　235
Were slyly crept into his human powers,
And gave him graceful posture.
SIC.　　　　　　　　　On the sudden
I warrant him Consul.
BRU.　　　　　　　Then our office may,
During his power, go sleep.
SIC. He cannot temperately transport his honors
From where he should begin and end, but will　241
Lose those he hath won.
BRU.　　　　　　　In that there's comfort.
SIC.　　　　　　　　　　　Doubt not
The commoners, for whom we stand, but they
Upon their ancient malice will forget°
With the least cause these his new honors, which
That he will give them make I as little question　246
As he is proud to do 't.
BRU.　　　　　　　I heard him swear,
Were he to stand for Consul, never would he
Appear i' the market place, nor on him put
The napless vesture of humility,°　　　　　　250
Nor showing, as the manner is, his wounds
To the people, beg their stinking breaths.
SIC.　　　　　　　　　　　'Tis right.
BRU. It was his word. Oh, he would miss it rather
Than carry it but by the suit of the gentry° to him,
And the desire of the nobles.
SIC.　　　　　　　　I wish no better　　255
Than have him hold that purpose and to put it
In execution.
BRU.　　　　　　　'Tis most like he will.
SIC. It shall be to him then, as our good wills,°
A sure destruction.
BRU.　　　　　　　So it must fall out
To him or our authorities. For an end,°　　　260
We must suggest° the people in what hatred

205. **crab trees**: crab-apple trees.　206. **to . . . relish**: to suit your
taste.　214. **change**: addition, variety.　216. **buildings . . .
fancy**: my castles in the air.　220. **sway**: rule.　221–22. **bleared
. . . spectacled**: the shortsighted put on spectacles.　223. **rap-
ture**: fit.　224. **chats**: chatters about. **malkin**: slut.　225. **lock-
ram**: linen collar.　**reechy**: dirty.　226. **bulks**: wooden pro-
jections in front of a shop.　227. **leads**: i.e., rooftops covered
with lead.　227–28. **ridges . . . complexions**: the ridges of the
roofs thronged with crowds of all sorts sitting astride. Cf. the ac-
count of the crowd at Queen Elizabeth's funeral in App. 16.
229. **Seld-shown flamens**: priests seldom seen in public.

231. **vulgar station**: place in the crowd.　231–34. **Our . . . kisses**:
our veiled ladies of fashion risk their dainty pink and white
cheeks in the hot sunshine. Cf. *AYLI*, I.iii.114,n. **nicely gawded**:
carefully colored. **Phoebus**: the sun god.　242–44. **Doubt . . .
forget**: without doubt the common people, whom we represent,
because of their ancient hatred for him will forget.　250. **nap-
less . . . humility**: the threadbare toga which shows humility.
According to North's *Plutarch* "the custom of Rome was at that
time that such as did sue for any office should for certain days be-
fore be in the market place only with a poor gown on their backs,
and without any coat underneath, to pray the citizens to remem-
ber them at the day of election; which was thus devised either to
move the people the more by requesting them in such humble ap-
parel, or else because they might show them their wounds they
had gotten in the wars in the service of the commonwealth, as
manifest marks and testimonies of their valiantness."　254. **bu**
. . . gentry: otherwise than at the request of the gentlemen
258. **good wills**: best efforts.　260. **For an end**: to bring matter
to a head.　261. **suggest**: prompt.

He still° hath held them; that to 's power he would
Have made them mules,° silenced their pleaders and
Dispropertied° their freedoms, holding them,
In human action and capacity,   265
Of no more soul nor fitness for the world
Than camels in the war, who have their provand°
Only for bearing burdens, and sore blows
For sinking under them.
    SIC.   This, as you say, suggested
At some time when his soaring insolence   270
Shall touch the people — which time shall not want,
If he be put upon 't,° and that's as easy
As to set dogs on sheep — will be his fire
To kindle their dry stubble, and their blaze
Shall darken him forever.
                    [*Enter a* MESSENGER.]
    BRU.   What's the matter?   275
    MESS. You are sent for to the Capitol. 'Tis thought
That Marcius shall be Consul.
I have seen the dumb men throng to see him and
The blind to hear him speak. Matrons flung gloves,
Ladies and maids their scarfs and handkerchers,
Upon him as he passed. The nobles bended,   281
As to Jove's statue, and the commons made
A shower and thunder with their caps and shouts.
I never saw the like.
    BRU.   Let's to the Capitol,
And carry with us ears and eyes for the time,°   285
But hearts for the event.°
    SIC.   Have with you.°   [*Exeunt.*]

SCENE II. *The same. The Capitol.*

[*Enter two* OFFICERS, *to lay cushions.*]
    1. OFF. Come, come, they are almost here. How
many stand for consulships?
    2. OFF. Three, they say. But 'tis thought of every-
one Coriolanus will carry it.   4
    1. OFF. That's a brave fellow, but he's vengeance°
proud, and loves not the common people.
    2. OFF. Faith, there have been many great men
that have flattered the people who ne'er loved them,
and there be many that they have loved they   10
know not wherefore. So that if they love they know
not why, they hate upon no better a ground. There-
fore for Coriolanus neither to care whether they love
or hate him manifests the true knowledge he has in
their disposition, and out of his noble carelessness
lets them plainly see 't.   17
    1. OFF. If he did not care whether he had their
love or no, he waved indifferently° 'twixt doing

them neither good nor harm. But he seeks their hate
with greater devotion than they can render it him,
and leaves nothing undone that may fully discover
him their opposite.° Now, to seem to affect° the
malice and displeasure of the people is as bad as that
which he dislikes, to flatter them for their love.   26
    2. OFF. He hath deserved worthily of his country.
And his ascent is not by such easy degrees as those
who, having been supple° and courteous to the peo-
ple, bonneted,° without any further deed to have
them° at all into their estimation and report.   31
But he hath so planted his honors in their eyes and
his actions in their hearts that for their tongues to be
silent and not confess so much were a kind of un-
grateful injury. To report otherwise were a malice
that, giving itself the lie, would pluck reproof and
rebuke from every ear that heard it.   38
    1. OFF. No more of him, he's a worthy man. Make
way, they are coming.
[*A sennet. Enter, with* LICTORS *before them,* COMIN-
    IUS *the Consul,* MENENIUS, CORIOLANUS, SENATORS,
        SICINIUS *and* BRUTUS. *The* SENATORS *take
        their places; the* TRIBUNES *take their
        places by themselves.* CORIOLANUS
                    stands.]
    MEN. Having determined of° the Volsces and
To send for Titus Lartius, it remains,
As the main point of this our after-meeting,
To gratify° his noble service that
Hath thus stood for his country. Therefore please
        you,   45
Most reverend and grave elders, to desire
The present Consul, and last General
In our well-found° successes, to report
A little of that worthy work performed
By Caius Marcius Coriolanus, whom   50
We met here both to thank and to remember
With honors like himself.
    1. SEN.   Speak, good Cominius.
Leave nothing out for length, and make us think
Rather our state's defective for requital
Than we to stretch it out.° [*To the* TRIBUNES] Mas-
        ters o' the people,   55
We do request your kindest ears, and after,
Your loving motion toward the common body,
To yield what passes here.°
    SIC.   We are convented
Upon a pleasing treaty,° and have hearts

23–24. discover . . . opposite: reveal him as their enemy. 24. af-
fect: desire. 29. supple: obsequious. 30. bonneted: with their
hats in their hands. See App. 7. 30–31. have them: got them-
selves. 41. determined of: made our decisions concerning.
44. gratify: give a token of gratitude to, reward. 48. well-
found: fortunate. 53–55. make . . . out: rather make us think
that Rome lacks the means to reward him properly than that we
should be unwilling to be generous. 57–58. Your . . . here: your
friendly influence with the common body to agree to what is
passed here. 58–59. We . . . treaty: we have met to discuss a
pleasant motion.

262. still: always. 263. mules: beasts of burden. 264. Dis-
propertied: dispossessed them of. 267. provand: fodder.
272. put upon 't: moved to do it. 285. for . . . time: for the
present. 286. for . . . event: for the future. Have . . . you:
agreed.
    Sc. ii: 5. vengeance: with a vengeance, 19. waved indiffer-
ently: wavered impartially.

Inclinable to honor and advance   60
The theme of our assembly.
  BRU.   Which the rather
We shall be blessed° to do if he remember
A kinder value of the people than
He hath hereto prized them at.
  MEN.   That's off,° that's off,
I would you rather had been silent. Please you   65
To hear Cominius speak?
  BRU.   Most willingly.
But yet my caution was more pertinent
Than the rebuke you give it.
  MEN.   He loves your people,
But tie him not to be their bedfellow.
Worthy Cominius, speak. [CORIOLANUS *offers to go
away*.] Nay, keep your place.   70
  I. SEN. Sit, Coriolanus, never shame to hear
What you have nobly done.
  COR.   Your Honors' pardon.
I had rather have my wounds to heal again
Than hear say how I got them.
  BRU.   Sir, I hope
My words disbenched° you not.
  COR.   No, sir. Yet oft   75
When blows have made me stay, I fled from words.
You soothed not,° therefore hurt not. But your
    people,
I love them as they weigh.°
  MEN.   Pray now, sit down.
  COR. I had rather have one scratch my head i' the
    sun
When the alarum were struck than idly sit   80
To hear my nothings monstered.°   [*Exit.*]
  MEN.   Masters of the people,
Your multiplying spawn how can he flatter —
That's thousand to one good one° — when you now
    see
He had rather venture all his limbs for honor   84
Than one on 's° ears to hear it? Proceed, Cominius.
  COM. I shall lack voice. The deeds of Coriolanus
Should not be uttered feebly. It is held
That valor is the chiefest virtue and
Most dignifies the haver. If it be,
The man I speak of cannot in the world   90
Be singly counterpoised.° At sixteen years,
When Tarquin made a head for° Rome, he fought
Beyond the mark of others.° Our then dictator,
Whom with all praise I point at, saw him fight
When with his Amazonian chin° he drove   95

The bristled lips before him. He bestrid
An o'erpress'd Roman, and i' the Consul's view
Slew three opposers. Tarquin's self he met,
And struck him on his knee. In that day's feats,
When he might act the woman in the scene,°   100
He proved the best man i' the field, and for his meed°
Was brow-bound with the oak. His pupil age
Man-entered thus,° he waxed like a sea,
And in the brunt of seventeen battles since,   104
He lurched all swords of the garland.° For this last,
Before and in Corioli, let me say,
I cannot speak him home.° He stopped the flyers,
And by his rare example made the coward
Turn terror into sport. As weeds before
A vessel under sail, so men obeyed,   110
And fell below his stem.° His sword, death's stamp,°
Where it did mark, it took. From face to foot
He was a thing of blood, whose every motion
Was timed with dying cries. Alone he entered
The mortal° gate of the city, which he painted   115
With shunless destiny;° aidless came off,°
And with a sudden reinforcement struck
Corioli like a planet.° Now all's his.
When, by and by, the din of war gan° pierce
His ready sense, then straight his doubled spirit   120
Requickened what in flesh was fatigate,°
And to the battle came he, where he did
Run reeking° o'er the lives of men as if
'Twere a perpetual spoil.° And till we called
Both field and city ours, he never stood   125
To ease his breast with panting.
  MEN.   Worthy man!
  I. SEN. He cannot but with measure fit° the
    honors
Which we devise him.
  COM.   Our spoils he kicked at,
And looked upon things precious as they were
The common muck of the world. He covets less   130
Than misery itself would give,° rewards
His deeds with doing them, and is content
To spend the time to end it.°

100. act . . . scene: Coriolanus was more fitted to take the part of a woman than that of a hero. At this time women's parts in plays were taken by boys. See Gen. Intro. p. 59b. The number of images taken from the stage in this play is notable. See II.ii.149; III.ii.105–06; V.iii.40–42.   101. meed: reward.   102–03. His . . . thus: his boyhood being thus turned into manhood.   105. lurched . . . garland: he won all the honors himself. lurched: lit., won a love set (won all the points in the game).   107. speak . . . home: speak of him adequately.   111. stem: prow. stamp: lit., that which makes an impression, particularly the mold used for stamping coins.   115. mortal: deadly.   115–16. painted . . . destiny: made red with death that could not be avoided.   116. came off: withdrew as victor.   118. planet: thunderbolt.   119. gan: began.   121. fatigate: wearied.   123. Run reeking: i.e., wherever he went, there was a reek (hot steam) of blood.   124. spoil: slaughter. Cf. *Caesar*, III.i.206.   127. He . . . fit: he will be a very fit man for.   130–31. He . . . give: his desires are less than what belongs to the most wretched creature.   132–33. is . . . it: i.e., the action is its own reward.

62. blessed: happy.   64. That's off: leave that out.   75. disbenched: caused you to leave your seat.   77. soothed not: did not flatter.   78. as . . . weigh: i.e., very lightly.   81. monstered: exaggerated.   83. That's . . . one: in which only one in a thousand is any good.   85. one on 's: one of his.   91. singly counterpoised: counterbalanced by any single man.   92. made . . . for: raised an army against.   93. Beyond . . . others: beyond anything that others effected.   95. Amazonian chin: beardless like an Amazon. The Amazons were the women soldiers of Scythia (South Russia).

MEN.   He's right noble.
Let him be called for.

1. SEN.   Call Coriolanus.

OFF. He doth appear.   135

[*Re-enter* CORIOLANUS.]

MEN. The Senate, Coriolanus, are well pleased
To make thee Consul.

COR.   I do owe them still°
My life and services.

MEN.   It then remains
That you do speak to the people.

COR.   I do beseech you
Let me o'erleap° that custom, for I cannot   140
Put on the gown,° stand naked, and entreat them,
For my wounds' sake, to give their suffrage.° Please
      you
That I may pass this doing.

SIC.   Sir, the people
Must have their voices, neither will they bate°
One jot of ceremony.

MEN.   Put° them not to 't.   145
Pray you, go fit you to the custom, and
Take to you, as your predecessors have,
Your honor with your form.°

COR.   It is a part
That I shall blush in acting, and might well
Be taken from the people.

BRU.   Mark you that?   150

COR. To brag unto them thus I did, and thus,
Show them the unaching scars which I should hide,
As if I had received them for the hire
Of their breath only!

MEN.   Do not stand upon 't.°
We recommend to you, Tribunes of the people,   155
Our purpose to them. And to our noble Consul
Wish we all joy and honor.

SENS. To Coriolanus come all joy and honor!

[*Flourish of cornets. Exeunt all but* SICINIUS *and*
                    BRUTUS.]

BRU. You see how he intends to use the people.

SIC. May they perceive 's intent! He will require
      them°   160
As if he did contemn° what he requested
Should be in them to give.

BRU.   Come, we'll inform them
Of our proceedings here. On the market place,
I know, they do attend us.   [*Exeunt.*]

---

137. still: always.   **140. o'erleap:** omit.   **141. Put . . . gown:** See
II.i.250; II.iii.44.   **142. suffrage:** vote.   **144. bate:** omit.
145. Put: force.   **147–48. Take . . . form:** before you assume
your honorable office you must, as have all who have gone before
you, observe the formalities of election.   **154. Do . . . upon 't:** do
not insist upon it.   **160. require them:** ask their votes.   **161. con-
temn:** despise.

SCENE III. *The same. The Forum.*

[*Enter seven or eight* CITIZENS.]

1. CIT. Once,° if he do require our voices, we
ought not to deny him.

2. CIT. We may, sir, if we will.

3. CIT. We have power in ourselves to do it, but it
is a power that we have no power to do. For if he   5
show us his wounds and tell us his deeds, we are to
put our tongues into those wounds and speak for
them. So, if he tell us his noble deeds, we must also
tell him our noble acceptance of them. Ingratitude
is monstrous. And for the multitude to be ingrateful
were to make a monster of the multitude, of the
which we being members, should bring ourselves to
be monstrous members.   14

1. CIT. And to make us no better thought of, a
little help will serve, for once we stood up about
the corn, he himself stuck not° to call us the many-
headed multitude.   18

3. CIT. We have been called so of many, not that
our heads are some brown, some black, some auburn,
some bald, but that our wits are so diversely colored.
And truly I think if all our wits were to issue out of
one skull, they would fly east, west, north, south,
and their consent of one direct way° should be at
once to all the points o' the compass.   26

2. CIT. Think you so? Which way do you judge
my wit would fly?

3. CIT. Nay, your wit will not so soon out as an-
other man's will, 'tis strongly wedged up in a block-
head. But if it were at liberty, 'twould, sure, south-
ward.°   32

2. CIT. Why that way?

3. CIT. To lose itself in a fog, where being three
parts melted away with rotten dews, the fourth
would return for conscience' sake, to help to get thee
a wife.   37

2. CIT. You are never without your tricks.° You
may, you may.

3. CIT. Are you all resolved to give your voices?
But that's no matter, the greater part carries it. I
say, if he would incline to the people, there was never
a worthier man.   43

[*Enter* CORIOLANUS *in a gown of humility,°*
                    with MENENIUS.]

Here he comes, and in the gown of humility. Mark
his behavior. We are not to stay all together, but to
come by him where he stands, by ones, by twos, and
by threes. He's to make his requests by particu-   47
lars,° wherein every one of us has a single honor, in
giving him our own voices with our own tongues.

Sc. iii: 1. Once: in a word.   **17. stuck not:** did not hesitate.
25. consent . . . way: the nearest they would get to agreeing to.
32. southward: See I.iv.30,n.   **38. tricks:** jokes.   **43 s.d.,
gown . . . humility:** See II.i.250.   **48. by particulars:** one by one.

Therefore follow me, and I'll direct you how you
shall go by him.   52

ALL. Content, content.   [*Exeunt* CITIZENS.]

MEN. O sir, you are not right. Have you not
known

The worthiest men have done 't?

COR.   What must I say? —   55
"I pray, sir "——— Plague upon 't! I cannot bring
My tongue to such a pace. "Look, sir, my wounds!
I got them in my country's service when
Some certain of your brethren roared, and ran
From the noise of our own drums."

MEN.   Oh me, the gods!   60
You must not speak of that. You must desire them
To think upon you.

COR.   Think upon me! Hang 'em!
I would they would forget me, like the virtues
Which our divines lose by 'em.°

MEN.   You'll mar all.
I'll leave you. Pray you, speak to 'em, I pray you,   65
In wholesome° manner.   [*Exit.*]

COR.   Bid them wash their faces,
And keep their teeth clean. [*Re-enter two of the* CITI-
ZENS.] So, here comes a brace.

[*Re-enter a third* CITIZEN.] You know the cause, sir,
of my standing here.

3. CIT. We do, sir. Tell us what hath brought you
to 't.   70

COR. Mine own desert.

2. CIT. Your own desert!

COR. Aye, but not mine own desire.

3. CIT. How! Not your own desire!

COR. No, sir, 'twas never my desire yet to trouble
the poor with begging.   76

3. CIT. You must think if we give you anything,
we hope to gain by you.

COR. Well then, I pray your price o' the consul-
ship?   80

1. CIT. The price is to ask it kindly.

COR. Kindly! Sir, I pray, let me ha 't. I have
wounds to show you, which shall be yours in private.
— Your good voice, sir, what say you?

2. CIT. You shall ha 't, worthy sir.   85

COR. A match,° sir. There's in all two worthy
voices begged. I have your alms. Adieu.

3. CIT. But this is something odd.

2. CIT. An 'twere to give again — but 'tis no
matter.   [*Exeunt the three* CITIZENS.]

[*Re-enter two other* CITIZENS.]

COR. Pray you now, if it may stand with the tune
of your voices that I may be Consul, I have here the
customary gown.

4. CIT. You have deserved nobly of your country,
and you have not deserved nobly.   95

COR. Your enigma?

4. CIT. You have been a scourge to her enemies,
you have been a rod to her friends.° You have not
indeed loved the common people.   99

COR. You should account me the more virtuous
that I have not been common in my love. I will, sir,
flatter my sworn brother,° the people, to earn a
dearer° estimation of them. 'Tis a condition° they
account gentle.° And since the wisdom of their
choice is rather to have my hat than my heart,   105
I will practice the insinuating° nod, and be off to
them most counterfeitly;° that is, sir, I will counter-
feit the bewitchment° of some popular man, and
give it bountiful to the desirers. Therefore, beseech
you, I may be Consul.   110

5. CIT. We hope to find you our friend, and there-
fore give you our voices heartily.

4. CIT. You have received many wounds for your
country.

COR. I will not seal° your knowledge with   114
showing them. I will make much of your voices, and
so trouble you no farther.

BOTH CITS. The gods give you joy, sir heartily!
          [*Exeunt.*]

COR. Most sweet voices!
Better° it is to die, better to starve,   120
Than crave the hire which first we do deserve.°
Why in this woolvish toge° should I stand here,
To beg of Hob and Dick° that do appear
Their needless vouches?° Custom calls me to 't.
What custom wills, in all things should we do 't,
The dust on ántique time would lie unswept,   126
And mountainous error be too highly heaped
For truth to o'erpeer.° Rather than fool it so,
Let the high office and the honor go
To one that would do thus. I am half-through.   130
The one part suffered, the other will I do.

[*Re-enter three* CITIZENS *more.*] Here come moe°
voices.

Your voices. For your voices I have fought,
Watched° for your voices, for your voices bear
Of wounds two dozen odd. Battles thrice six   135
I have seen, and heard of, for your voices have

97–98. You . . . friends: though you have scourged our enemies
with a cat-o'-nine-tails, you have also beaten our friends with a
rod.   102. sworn brother: brother in arms. Two knights some-
time swore to each other to share all dangers and prosperity alike.
103. dearer: more valuable. condition: manner of behavior.
104. gentle: the mark of a gentleman.   106. insinuating:
flattering.   106–07. be . . . counterfeitly: take off my hat in a
most deceptive way.   108. bewitchment: winning behavior. For
an example, see *Rich II*, I.iv.23–36.   114. seal: complete. See
App. 6.   120–31. Better . . . do: for a similar use of rhyme see
Lear, I.i.183,n.   121. crave . . . deserve: beg for pay which we
have already earned.   122. woolvish toge: i.e., like a wolf in
sheep's clothing. The toga (*toge*) was the gown worn by upper
class Romans.   123. Hob . . . Dick: "Tom, Dick, and Harry."
124. vouches: guarantees.   128. o'erpeer: look over the top.
132. moe: more.   134. Watched: kept guard.

63–64. like . . . 'em: like the virtues which our preachers recom-
mend and they lose by neglecting to follow.   66. wholesome:
reasonable.   86. A match: a bargain made.

Done many things, some less, some more. Your voices.
Indeed, I would be Consul.

6. CIT. He has done nobly, and cannot go without
any honest man's voice.   140

7. CIT. Therefore let him be Consul. The gods give
him joy, and make him good friend to the people!

ALL. Amen, amen. God save thee, noble Consul!
            [*Exeunt.*]

COR. Worthy voices!   145

[*Re-enter* MENENIUS, *with* BRUTUS *and* SICINIUS.]

MEN. You have stood your limitation,° and the
  Tribunes
Endue you with the people's voice.° Remains
That in the official marks° invested you
Anon do meet the Senate.

COR.   Is this done?

SIC. The custom of request° you have discharged.
The people do admit you, and are summoned 151
To meet anon upon your approbation.°

COR. Where? At the Senate House?

SIC.   There, Coriolanus.

COR. May I change these garments?

SIC.   You may, sir.

COR. That I'll straight do and, knowing myself
again,   155
Repair to the Senate House.

MEN. I'll keep you company. Will you along?

BRU. We stay here for the people.

SIC.   Fare you well.
  [*Exeunt* CORIOLANUS *and* MENENIUS.]
He has it now, and, by his looks, methinks
'Tis warm at 's heart.   160

BRU. With a proud heart he wore his humble
  weeds.°
Will you dismiss the people?
     [*Re-enter* CITIZENS.]

SIC. How now, my masters! Have you chose this
  man?

1. CIT. He has our voices, sir.   164

BRU. We pray the gods he may deserve your loves.

2. CIT. Amen, sir. To my poor unworthy notice,
He mocked us when he begged our voices.

3. CIT.   Certainly
He flouted° us downright.

1. CIT. No, 'tis his kind of speech, he did not mock
  us.   169

2. CIT. Not one amongst us save yourself but says
He used us scornfully. He should have showed us
His marks of merit, wounds received for 's country.

SIC. Why, so he did, I am sure.

CITIZENS. No, no, no man saw 'em.

3. CIT. He said he had wounds which he could
  show in private,

And with his hat, thus waving it in scorn, 175
"I would be Consul," says he. "Aged custom,
But by your voices,° will not so permit me.
Your voices therefore." When we granted that,
Here was "I thank you for your voices. Thank you.
Your most sweet voices. Now you have left your
  voices,   180
I have no further° with you." Was not this mockery?

SIC. Why, either were you ignorant to see 't,°
Or, seeing it, of such childish friendliness
To yield your voices?

BRU.   Could you not have told him,
As you were lessoned,° when he had no power, 185
But was a petty servant to the state,
He was your enemy, ever spake against
Your liberties and the charters° that you bear
I' the body of the weal?° And now, arriving
A place of potency and sway o' the state,° 190
If he should still malignantly remain
Fast foe to the plebeii,° your voices might
Be curses to yourselves? You should have said
That as his worthy deeds did claim no less
Than what he stood for, so his gracious nature 195
Would think upon you for your voices, and
Translate° his malice toward you into love,
Standing your friendly lord.

SIC.   Thus to have said,
As you were foreadvised, had touched° his spirit
And tried his inclination, from him plucked 200
Either his gracious promise, which you might,
As cause had called you up, have held him to;°
Or else it would have galled° his surly nature,
Which easily endures not article°
Tying him to aught. So, putting him to rage, 205
You should have ta'en the advantage of his choler,°
And passed him unelected.

BRU.   Did you perceive
He did solicit you in free° contempt
When he did need your loves, and do you think
That his contempt shall not be bruising to you 210
When he hath power to crush? Why, had your
  bodies
No heart among you? Or had you tongues to cry
Against the rectorship of judgment?°

SIC.   Have you
Ere now denied the asker? And now again,
Of him that did not ask but mock, bestow 215

177. **But . . . voices:** unless you give me your approval. 181. **no
further:** no more business. 182. **were . . . see 't:** were you too
ignorant to notice it? 185. **lessoned:** taught. 188. **charters:**
privileges. 189. **weal:** state. 190. **A . . . state:** a position of
power where he can direct the affairs of state. 192. **plebeii:**
plebeians, common people. 197. **Translate:** transform.
199. **touched:** tested. 200–02. **from . . . to:** extracted from him
some kindly promise which on some later occasion you might have
made him keep. 203. **galled:** rubbed sore. 204. **article:** condi-
tion. 206. **choler:** anger. 208. **free:** openly expressed.
213. **Against . . . judgment:** contrary to the rule of reason; i.e.,
why did you agree to a decision so contrary to common sense?

146. **limitation:** appointed time. 147. **Endue . . . voice:** con-
firm (lit., clothe) you as duly chosen by the people. 148. **official
marks:** insignia of office. 150. **custom of request:** the customary
request for the people's approval. 152. **approbation:** formal con-
firmation. 161. **weeds:** garments. 168. **flouted:** mocked.

Your sued-for tongues?°

3. CIT. He's not confirmed, we may deny him yet.

2. CIT. And will deny him.

I'll have five hundred voices of that sound.

  1. CIT. I twice five hundred, and their friends to
    piece 'em.°   220

  BRU. Get you hence instantly, and tell those
    friends

They have chose a Consul that will from them take

Their liberties, make them of no more voice

Than dogs that are as often beat for barking

As therefore kept to do so.

  SIC.   Let them assemble,   225

And, on a safer judgment, all revoke

Your ignorant election. Enforce° his pride

And his old hate unto you. Besides, forget not

With what contempt he wore the humble weed,

How in his suit° he scorned you. But your loves,

Thinking upon his services, took from you   231

The apprehension of his present portance,°

Which most gibingly, ungravely,° he did fashion°

After° the inveterate hate he bears you.

  BRU.   Lay

A fault on us, your Tribunes, that we labored,   235

No impediment between, but that° you must

Cast your election on him.

  SIC.   Say you chose him

More after our commandment than as guided

By your own true affections, and that your minds,

Preoccupied with what you rather must do   240

Than what you should, made you against the grain°

To voice him Consul. Lay the fault on us.

  BRU. Aye, spare us not. Say we read lectures to
  you,

How youngly he began to serve his country,   244

How long continued. And what stock he springs of,

The noble house o' the Marcians, from whence came

That Ancus Marcius, Numa's daughter's son,

Who, after great Hostilius, here was King.

Of the same house Publius and Quintus were,

That our best water brought by conduits hither,

And Censorinus, nobly named so,   251

Twice being by the people chosen censor,

Was his great ancestor.°

SIC.   One thus descended,

That hath beside well in his person wrought°

To be set high in place, we did commend   255

To your remembrances. But you have found,

Scaling° his present bearing with his past,

That he's your fixed enemy, and revoke

Your sudden approbation.

  BRU.   Say you ne'er had done 't —

Harp on that still — but by our putting on.   260

And presently, when you have drawn your number,

Repair to the Capitol.

  CITS.   We will so. Almost all

Repent in their election.   [*Exeunt* CITIZENS.]

  BRU.   Let them go on.

This mutiny were better put in hazard

Than stay, past doubt, for greater.°   265

If, as his nature is, he fall in rage

With their refusal, both observe and answer

The vantage of his anger.°

  SIC.   To the Capitol, come.

We will be there before the stream o' the people,

And this shall seem, as partly 'tis, their own   270

Which we have goaded onward.   [*Exeunt.*]

Act III

SCENE I. *Rome. A street.*

[*Cornets. Enter* CORIOLANUS, MENENIUS, *all the*
GENTRY, COMINIUS, TITUS LARTIUS, *and other*
SENATORS.]

  COR. Tullus Aufidius then had made new head?°

  LART. He had, my lord, and that it was which
    caused

Our swifter composition.°

  COR. So then the Volsces stand but as at first,

Ready, when time shall prompt them, to make road

Upon 's° again.

  COM.   They are worn, Lord Consul, so   6

That we shall hardly in our ages see

Their banners wave again.

  COR.   Saw you Aufidius?

  LART. On safeguard° he came to me, and did curse

Against the Volsces, for they had so vilely   10

Yielded the town. He is retired to Antium.

COR. Spoke he of me?

LART.   He did, my lord.

COR.   How? What?

LART. How often he had met you, sword to sword;
That of all things upon the earth he hated
Your person most; that he would pawn his fortunes
To hopeless restitution° so he might   16
Be called your vanquisher.

COR.   At Antium lives he?

LART. At Antium.

COR. I wish I had a cause to seek him there,
To oppose his hatred fully. Welcome home.   20
[*Enter* SICINIUS *and* BRUTUS.] Behold, these are the
    Tribunes of the people,
The tongues o' the common mouth. I do despise
    them,
For they do prank them° in authority
Against all noble sufferance.°

SIC.   Pass no further.

COR. Ha! What is that?   25

BRU. It will be dangerous to go on. No further.

COR. What makes this change?

MEN. The matter?

COM. Hath he not passed the noble and the com-
    mon?

BRU. Cominius, no.

COR.   Have I had children's voices?   30

I. SEN. Tribunes, give way, he shall to the market
    place.

BRU. The people are incensed against him.

SIC.   Stop,
Or all will fall in broil.

COR.   Are these your herd?
Must these have voices, that can yield them now
And straight disclaim their tongues? What are your
    offices?°   35
You being their mouths, why rule you not their
    teeth?
Have you not set them on?

MEN.   Be calm, be calm.

COR. It is a purposed thing,° and grows by plot,
To curb the will of the nobility.
Suffer 't, and live with° such as cannot rule,   40
Nor ever will be ruled.

BRU.   Call 't not a plot.
The people cry you mocked them, and of late,
When corn was given them gratis, you repined,°
Scandaled° the suppliants for the people, called
    them
Time-pleasers, flatterers, foes to nobleness.   45

COR. Why, this was known before.

BRU.   Not to them all.

COR. Have you informed them sithence?°

BRU.   How! I inform them!

COM. You are like to do such business.

BRU.   Not unlike,
Each way, to better yours.°

COR. Why then should I be Consul? By yond
    clouds,   50
Let me deserve so ill as you, and make me
Your fellow Tribune.

SIC.   You show too much of that
For which the people stir. If you will pass
To where you are bound,° you must inquire your
    way,
Which you are out of, with a gentler spirit,   55
Or never be so noble as a Consul,
Nor yoke with° him for Tribune.

MEN.   Let's be calm.

COM. The people are abused,° set on. This
    paltering°
Becomes not Rome, nor has Coriolanus
Deserved this so dishonored rub,° laid falsely   60
I' the plain way of his merit.

COR.   Tell me of corn!
This was my speech, and I will speak 't again ——

MEN. Not now, not now.

I. SEN.   Not in this heat, sir, now.

COR. Now, as I live, I will. My nobler friends,
I crave their pardons.   65
For the mutable, rank-scented many,° let them
Regard me as I do not flatter, and
Therein behold themselves. I say again,
In soothing them, we nourish 'gainst our Senate
The cockle° of rebellion, insolence, sedition,   70
Which we ourselves have plowed for, sowed and
    scattered,
By mingling them with us, the honored number,
Who lack not virtue, no, nor power, but that
Which they have given to beggars.°

MEN.   Well, no more.

I. SEN. No more words, we beseech you.

COR.   How! No more!   75
As for my country I have shed my blood,
Not fearing outward force, so shall my lungs
Coin words till their decay against those measles°
Which we disdain should tetter° us, yet sought
The very way to catch them.

BRU.   You speak o' the people   80
As if you were a god to punish, not
A man of their infirmity.

---

16. **hopeless restitution:** beyond all hope of recovery. **23. prank them:** make themselves fine fellows. **24. Against . . . sufferance:** beyond the endurance of the nobles. **35. offices:** duties. **38. purposed thing:** "frame-up." **40. live with:** you will have to live with. **43. repined:** were dissatisfied. **44. Scandaled:** spoke harshly about.

47. sithence: since then. **48–49. Not . . . yours:** I certainly am likely to do what I can to get the better of you. **53–54. pass . . . bound:** reach the consulship which you aim at. **57. yoke with:** serve with. **58. abused:** deceived. **paltering:** trickery. **60. rub:** obstacle. See App. 13. **66. rank-scented many:** stinking multitude. **70. cockle:** a weed that grows in the wheat. **73–74. Who . . . beggars:** who still have plenty of valor and power, except for what we have given away to beggars. **78. measles:** plague spots. **79. tetter:** break out on our skins. Cf. *Haml.* I.v.71.

SIC.   'Twere well
We let the people know 't.
  MEN.   What, what? His choler?
  COR. Choler!
Were I as patient as the midnight sleep,   85
By Jove, 'twould be my mind!
  SIC.   It is a mind
That shall remain a poison where it is,
Not poison any further.
  COR.   Shall remain!
Hear you this Triton° of the minnows? Mark you
His absolute " shall "?
  COM.   'Twas from the canon.°
  COR.   " Shall "!   90
O good but most unwise patricians! Why,
You grave but reckless Senators, have you thus
Given Hydra° here to choose an officer
That with his peremptory " shall," being but
The horn and noise o' the monster's, wants not
     spirit   95
To say he'll turn your current in a ditch
And make your channel his?° If he have power,
Then vail your ignorance;° if none, awake
Your dangerous lenity. If you are learned,
Be not as common fools; if you are not,   100
Let them have cushions by you.° You are plebeians
If they be Senators. And they are no less
When, both your voices blended, the great'st taste
Most palates theirs.° They choose their magistrate,
And such a one as he, who puts his " shall,"   105
His popular " shall," against a graver bench
Than ever frowned in Greece. By Jove himself,
It makes the Consuls base! And my soul aches
To know, when two authorities are up,
Neither supreme, how soon confusion°   110
May enter 'twixt the gap of both and take
The one by the other.
  COM.   Well, on to the market place.
  COR. Whoever gave that counsel, to give forth
The corn o' the storehouse gratis, as 'twas used
Sometime in Greece ——
  MEN.   Well, well, no more of that.   115
  COR. Though there the people had more absolute
     power,
I say they nourished disobedience, fed
The ruin of the state.
  BRU.   Why, shall the people give
One that speaks thus their voice?

  COR.   I'll give my reasons,
More worthier than their voices. They know the
     corn   120
Was not our recompense,° resting well assured
They ne'er did service for 't. Being pressed to the
     war,
Even when the navel° of the state was touched,
They would not thread the gates.° This kind of
     service
Did not deserve corn gratis. Being i' the war,   125
Their mutinies and revolts, wherein they showed
Most valor, spoke not for them. The accusation
Which they have often made against the Senate,
All cause unborn,° could never be the native
Of our so frank donation.° Well, what then?   130
How shall this bosom multiplied° digest
The Senate's courtesy? Let deeds express
What's like to be their words: " We did request it,
We are the greater poll,° and in true fear
They gave us our demands." Thus we debase   135
The nature of our seats, and make the rabble
Call our cares fears, which will in time
Break ope the locks o' the Senate and bring in
The crows to peck the eagles.
  MEN.   Come, enough.
  BRU. Enough, with overmeasure.
  COR.   No, take more.   140
What may be sworn by, both divine and human,
Seal what I end withal! This double worship,
Where one part does disdain with cause, the other
Insult without all reason; where gentry, title, wis-
     dom,°
Cannot conclude° but by the yea and no   145
Of general ignorance — it must omit
Real necessities, and give way the while
To unstable slightness. Purpose so barred, it follows
Nothing is done to purpose. Therefore, beseech
     you —
You that will be less fearful than discreet,°   150
That love the fundamental part of state
More than you doubt the change on 't,° that prefer
A noble life before a long, and wish
To jump° a body with a dangerous physic
That's sure of death without it — at once pluck out
The multitudinous tongue. Let them not lick   156
The sweet which is their poison. Your dishonor°

---

89. Triton: the trumpeter of Neptune, the sea god.   90. from . . .
canon: contrary to law.   93. Hydra: a many-headed beast slain
by Hercules.   96–97. turn . . . his: he will direct your stream
into a ditch and use your watercourse for his own. See *Cor* Intro.
p. 909b. 98. vail . . . ignorance: lower your ignorance; i.e., have
more sense.   101. have . . . you: i.e., share equally in the govern-
ment with you.   102–04. And . . . theirs: Once more Coriolanus,
in his excitement, grows incoherent. He means that they are no
less than Senators if when you vote together you must submit to
eating what the more numerous plebeians like best. Cf. I.vi.76;
III.iii.68.   110. confusion: utter ruin.

121. our recompense: given by us as a reward for service.
123. navel: very center.   124. thread . . . gates: pass through
the gates in single file — on the way to war.   129. All . . . un-
born: without any cause.   129–30. native . . . donation: true
reason for our generous gift.   131. bosom multiplied: i.e., bosom
of the "rank-scented many," the mob.   134. We . . . poll: we
have more votes.   144. gentry . . . wisdom: the gentlemen, the
nobles, and the wise men; another instance of Shakespeare's
frequent use of abstract words for the concrete.   145. conclude:
reach a decision.   150. less . . . discreet: i.e., wise men rather
than cowards.   152. doubt . . . on 't: fear a revolution.   154. jump:
risk.   157. Your dishonor: i.e., the dishonorable condition to
which you have now sunk.

Mangles true judgment and bereaves the state
Of that integrity which should become 't,
Not having the power to do the good it would   160
For the ill which doth control 't.

BRU.   Has said enough.

SIC. Has spoken like a traitor, and shall answer
As traitors do.

COR.   Thou wretch, despite° o'erwhelm thee!
What should the people do with these bald Trib-
unes?   165
On whom depending, their obedience fails
To the greater bench.° In a rebellion,
When what's not meet, but what must be, was law,
Then were they chosen. In a better hour,
Let what is meet be said it must be meet,   170
And throw their power i' the dust.

BRU. Manifest treason!

SIC.   This a Consul? No.

BRU. The Aediles,° ho!
[*Enter an* AEDILE.] Let him be apprehended.

SIC. Go, call the people [*Exit* AEDILE.], in whose
    name myself
Attach° thee as a traitorous innovator,°   175
A foe to the public weal. Obey, I charge thee,
And follow to thine answer.°

COR.   Hence, old goat!

SENS., ETC. We'll surety° him.

COM.   Aged sir, hands off.

COR. Hence, rotten thing! Or I shall shake thy
    bones
Out of thy garments.

SIC.   Help, ye citizens!   180
[*Enter a rabble of* CITIZENS, *with the* AEDILES.]

MEN. On both sides, more respect.

SIC. Here's he that would take from you all your
    power.

BRU. Seize him, Aediles!

CITS. Down with him! Down with him!

SENS., ETC. Weapons, weapons, weapons!   185
          [*They all bustle about* CORIOLANUS.]

ALL THE PEOPLE. Tribunes! — Patricians! — Citi-
zens! — What ho!
Sicinius! — Brutus! — Coriolanus! — Citizens! —
Peace, peace, peace! — Stay! Hold! Peace!

MEN. What is about to be? I am out of breath.
Confusion's° near. I cannot speak. You, Tribunes
To the people! Coriolanus, patience!   191
Speak, good Sicinius.

SIC.   Hear me, people. Peace!

CITS. Let's hear our Tribune. Peace! — Speak,
speak, speak.

SIC. You are at point to lose your liberties.

Marcius would have all from you, Marcius,   195
Whom late you have named for Consul.

MEN.   Fie, fie, fie!
This is the way to kindle, not to quench.

I. SEN. To unbuild the city, and to lay all flat.

SIC. What is the city but the people?

CITS.   True,
The people are the city.   200

BRU. By the consent of all, we were established
The people's magistrates.

CITS.   You so remain.

MEN. And so are like to do.

COM. That is the way to lay the city flat,
To bring the roof to the foundation,   205
And bury all which yet distinctly ranges°
In heaps and piles of ruin.

SIC.   This deserves death.

BRU. Or let us stand to our authority,
Or let us lose it. We do here pronounce,
Upon the part o'° the people, in whose power   210
We were elected theirs, Marcius is worthy
Of present death.

SIC.   Therefore lay hold of him,
Bear him to the rock Tarpeian,° and from thence
Into destruction cast him.

BRU.   Aediles, seize him!

CITS. Yield, Marcius, yield!

MEN.   Hear me one word.
Beseech you, Tribunes, hear me but a word.   216

AEDI. Peace, peace!

MEN. [*To* BRUTUS] Be that you seem, truly your
    country's friend,
And temperately proceed to what you would
Thus violently redress.

BRU.   Sir, those cold ways,   220
That seem like prudent helps, are very poisonous
Where the disease is violent. Lay hands upon him,
And bear him to the rock.

COR.   No, I'll die here. [*Drawing his sword.*]
There's some among you have beheld me fighting.
Come, try upon yourselves what you have seen me.

MEN. Down with that sword! Tribunes, with-
draw awhile.   226

BRU. Lay hands upon him.

MEN.   Help Marcius, help,
You that be noble, help him, young and old!

CITS. Down with him, down with him!
    [*In this mutiny, the* TRIBUNES, *the* AEDILES,
                  and the PEOPLE, *are beat in.*]

MEN. Go, get you to your house, be gone, away!
All will be naught° else.

2. SEN.   Get you gone.

COM.   Stand fast.   231

---

164. despite: contempt.   167. greater bench: the more honor-
able assembly; i.e., the Senate.   173. Aediles: officers of the law.
175. Attach: arrest. innovator: revolutionary.   177. to . . . an-
swer: to answer the charge against you.   178. surety: go bail for.
190. Confusion: See l. 110.

206. ranges: stands orderly.   210. Upon . . . o': on behalf of.
213. rock Tarpeian: a precipitous rock on the Capitoline Hill in
Rome. Traitors were executed by being thrown from this rock.
231. naught: ruined.

We have as many friends as enemies.
  MEN. Shall it be put to that?
  I. SEN.   The gods forbid!
I prithee, noble friend, home to thy house.
Leave us to cure this cause.
  MEN.   For 'tis a sore upon us   235
You cannot tent° yourself. Be gone, beseech you.
  COM. Come, sir, along with us.
  COR. I would they were barbarians — as they are,
Though in Rome littered — not Romans — as they
     are not,
Though calved i' the porch o' the Capitol ——
  MEN.   Be gone.   240
Put not your worthy rage into your tongue.
One time will owe another.°
  COR.   On fair ground
I could beat forty of them.
  MEN.   I could myself
Take up a brace o' the best of them — yea, the two
     Tribunes.
  COM. But now 'tis odds beyond arithmetic,   245
And manhood is called foolery when it stands
Against a falling fabric.° Will you hence
Before the tag° return? Whose rage doth rend
Like interrupted waters,° and o'erbear
What they are used to bear.
  MEN.   Pray you be gone.   250
I'll try whether my old wit be in request
With those that have but little. This must be
     patched
With cloth of any color.
  COM.   Nay, come away.
     [*Exeunt* CORIOLANUS, COMINIUS, *and others.*]
  I. PAT. This man has marred his fortune.
  MEN. His nature is too noble for the world.   255
He would not flatter Neptune for his trident,
Or Jove for 's power to thunder. His heart's his
     mouth —
What his breast forges, that his tongue must vent,
And, being angry, does forget that ever
He heard the name of death.   [*A noise within.*]
Here's goodly work!
  2. PAT.   I would they were abed!   261
  MEN. I would they were in Tiber! What the
     vengeance!
Could he not speak 'em fair?
     [*Re-enter* BRUTUS *and* SICINIUS, *with the rabble.*]
  SIC.   Where is this viper
That would depopulate the city and
Be every man himself?
  MEN.   You worthy Tribunes ——   265
  SIC. He shall be thrown down the Tarpeian rock
With rigorous hands. He hath resisted law,

And therefore law shall scorn him further trial
Than the severity of the public power,
Which he so sets at naught.
  I. CIT.   He shall well know   270
The noble Tribunes are the people's mouths,
And we their hands.
  CITS. He shall, sure on 't.
  MEN.   Sir, sir ——
  SIC. Peace!
  MEN. Do not cry havoc° where you should but
     hunt   275
With modest warrant.
  SIC.   Sir, how comes 't that you
Have holp° to make this rescue?
  MEN.   Hear me speak.
As I do know the Consul's worthiness,
So can I name his faults ——
  SIC.   Consul! What Consul?
  MEN. The Consul Coriolanus.
  BRU.   He Consul!   280
  CITS. No, no, no, no, no.
  MEN. If, by the Tribunes' leave, and yours, good
     people,
I may be heard, I would crave a word or two,
The which shall turn° you to no further harm
Than so much loss of time.
  SIC.   Speak briefly then,   285
For we are peremptory° to dispatch
This viperous traitor. To eject him hence
Were but one danger, and to keep him here
Our certain death. Therefore it is decreed
He dies tonight.
  MEN.   Now the good gods forbid   290
That our renownèd Rome, whose gratitude
Toward her deservèd children is enrolled
In Jove's own book, like an unnatural dam
Should now eat up her own!
  SIC. He's a disease that must be cut away.   295
  MEN. Oh, he's a limb that has but a disease —
Mortal to cut it off, to cure it easy.
What has he done to Rome that's worthy death?
Killing our enemies, the blood he hath lost —
Which, I dare vouch, is more than that he hath   300
By many an ounce — he dropped it for his country.
And what is left, to lose it by his country
Were to us all that do 't and suffer it
A brand° to the end o' the world
  SIC.   This is clean kam.°
  BRU. Merely° awry. When he did love his coun-
     try,   305
It honored him.
  MEN.   The service of the foot

---

236. **tent:** cleanse. Cf. I.ix.31.   242. **One . . . another:** i.e., our turn will come.   247. **falling fabric:** falling house.   248. **tag:** rabble.   249. **interrupted waters:** waters that have burst their banks.

275. **havoc:** the cry of "no quarter." See *Caesar*, III.i.270-75. 277. **holp:** helped.   284. **turn:** put.   286. **peremptory:** firmly determined.   304. **brand:** dishonorable mark. For certain offenses, the guilty were branded with red-hot irons. **clean kam:** quite wrong.   305. **Merely:** entirely.

Being once gangrened, is not then respected
For what before it was.

BRU.　　　　　　　　We'll hear no more.
Pursue him to his house and pluck him thence,
Lest his infection, being of catching nature,　　310
Spread further.

MEN.　　　　　　One word more, one word.
This tiger-footed rage, when it shall find
The harm of unscanned swiftness,° will, too late,
Tie leaden pounds° to 's heels. Proceed by process,°
Lest parties,° as he is beloved, break out,　　315
And sack great Rome with Romans.

BRU.　　　　　　　　　If it were so ——
SIC. What do ye talk?
Have we not had a taste of his obedience?
Our Aediles smote? Ourselves resisted? Come.

MEN. Consider this. He has been bred i' the wars
Since he could draw a sword, and is ill schooled　321
In bolted° language — meal and bran together
He throws without distinction. Give me leave,
I'll go to him and undertake to bring him
Where he shall answer, by a lawful form,　　325
In peace, to his utmost peril.°

I. SEN.　　　　　　　Noble Tribunes,
It is the humane way. The other course
Will prove too bloody, and the end of it
Unknown to the beginning.

SIC.　　　　　　　Noble Menenius,
Be you then as the people's officer.　　330
Masters, lay down your weapons.

BRU.　　　　　　　　Go not home.
SIC. Meet on the market place. We'll attend you
there,
Where, if you bring not Marcius, we'll proceed
In our first way.

MEN.　　　　　I'll bring him to you.
[*To the* SENATORS] Let me desire your company. He
must come,　　335
Or what is worst will follow.

I. SEN.　　　　Pray you, let's to him. [*Exeunt.*]

SCENE II. *A room in* CORIOLANUS'S *house.*

[*Enter* CORIOLANUS, *with* PATRICIANS.]
COR. Let them pull all about mine ears, present me
Death on the wheel,° or at wild horses' heels,°
Or pile ten hills on the Tarpeian rock,
That the precipitation might downstretch
Below the beam° of sight, yet will I still　　5
Be thus to them.

I. PAT.　　　　　You do the nobler.
COR. I muse° my mother
Does not approve me further,° who was wont
To call them woolen vassals,° things created
To buy and sell with groats,° to show bare heads　10
In congregations, to yawn, be still, and wonder
When one but of my ordinance° stood up
To speak of peace or war.
[*Enter* VOLUMNIA.]　　　I talk of you.
Why did you wish me milder? Would you have me
False to my nature? Rather say I play　　15
The man I am.

VOL.　　　　　O sir, sir, sir,
I would have had you put your power well on
Before you had worn it out.

COR.　　　　　　Let go.
VOL. You might have been enough the man you
are
With striving less to be so. Lesser had been　20
The thwartings of your dispositions if
You had not showed them how ye were disposed
Ere they lacked power to cross you.

COR.　　　　　　　Let them hang.
VOL. Aye, and burn too.
[*Enter* MENENIUS *with the* SENATORS.]
MEN. Come, come, you have been too rough,
something too rough.　　25
You must return and mend it.

I. SEN.　　　　　　There's no remedy,
Unless, by not so doing, our good city
Cleave in the midst, and perish.

VOL.　　　　　　Pray be counseled.
I have a heart as little apt° as yours,
But yet a brain that leads my use of anger　30
To better vantage.

MEN.　　　　Well said, noble woman!
Before he should thus stoop to the herd, but that
The violent fit o' the time° craves it as physic
For the whole state, I would put mine armor on,
Which I can scarcely bear.

COR.　　　　　　What must I do?　35
MEN. Return to the Tribunes.

COR.　　　　　Well, what then? What then?
MEN. Repent what you have spoke.

COR. For them! I cannot do it to the gods.
Must I then do 't to them?

VOL.　　　　　You are too absolute,°
Though therein you can never be too noble　40
But when extremities speak.° I have heard you say
Honor and policy,° like unsevered° friends,

---

313. **unscanned swiftness:** ill-considered haste.　314. **pounds:** weights. **process:** legal proceeding.　315. **parties:** rival parties. 322. **bolted:** lit., sifted, carefully chosen.　326. **to . . . peril:** i.e., under penalty of death.
　Sc. ii: 2. **Death . . . wheel:** i.e., break me on the wheel — a lingering death. **wild . . . heels:** torn to pieces by wild horses. 5. **beam:** range.

7. **muse:** wonder.　8. **approve . . . further:** show more approval of my actions.　9. **woolen vassals:** slaves that wear wool; i.e., cheap clothes.　10. **To . . . groats:** whose business is only with "dimes." **groat:** fourpence.　12. **ordinance:** rank.　29. **apt:** ready; i.e., to yield to the plebeians.　33. **violent . . . time:** i.e., the present riots.　39. **absolute:** unbending.　41. **But . . . speak:** except when extreme dangers demand.　42. **policy:** craftiness. **unsevered:** inseparable.

I' the war do grow together. Grant that, and tell me,
In peace what each of them by the other lose,
That they combine not there.
    COR.   Tush, tush!
    MEN.   A good demand.   45
    VOL. If it be honor in your wars to seem
The same you are not, which, for your best ends,
You adopt your policy, how is it less or worse
That it shall hold companionship in peace
With honor, as in war, since that to both   50
It stands in like request?°
    COR.   Why force you this?°
    VOL. Because that now it lies you on° to speak
To the people — not by your own instruction,
Nor by the matter which your heart prompts you,
But with such words that are but roted in°   55
Your tongue, though but bastards and syllables
Of no allowance° to your bosom's truth.
Now this no more dishonors you at all
Than to take in a town with gentle words,
Which else would put you to your fortune° and   60
The hazard of much blood.
I would dissemble° with my nature where
My fortunes and my friends at stake required
I should do so in honor. I am in this,°
Your wife, your son, these Senators, the nobles,   65
And you will rather show our general louts°
How you can frown than spend a fawn upon 'em
For the inheritance° of their loves and safeguard
Of what that want might ruin.
    MEN.   Noble lady!
Come, go with us, speak fair. You may salve° so   70
Not what is dangerous present, but the loss
Of what is past.
    VOL.   I prithee now, my son,
Go° to them, with this bonnet in thy hand,
And thus far having stretched it, here be with them,
Thy knee bussing° the stones — for in such business
Action is eloquence, and the eyes of the ignorant   76
More learnèd than the ears — waving thy head,
Which often thus, correcting thy stout heart,
Now humble as the ripest mulberry
That will not hold° the handling. Or say to them
Thou art their soldier, and being bred in broils°   81
Hast not the soft way which, thou dost confess,
Were fit for thee to use, as they to claim,
In asking their good loves. But thou wilt frame°

Thyself, forsooth, hereafter theirs, so far   85
As thou hast power and person.
    MEN.   This but done,
Even as she speaks, why, their hearts were yours.
For they have pardons, being asked, as free
As words to little purpose.
    VOL.   Prithee now,
Go, and be ruled.° Although I know thou hadst
    rather   90
Follow thine enemy in a fiery gulf°
Than flatter him in a bower.°
[*Enter* COMINIUS.]   Here is Cominius.
    COM. I have been i' the market place, and, sir, 'tis fit
You make strong party,° or defend yourself
By calmness or by absence. All's in anger.   95
    MEN. Only fair speech.
    COM.   I think 'twill serve, if he
Can thereto frame his spirit.
    VOL.   He must, and will.
Prithee now, say you will, and go about it.
    COR. Must I go show them my unbarbed sconce?°
    Must I,
With my base tongue, give to my noble heart   100
A lie that it must bear? Well, I will do 't.
Yet, were there but this single plot° to lose,
This mold of Marcius, they to dust should grind it,
And throw 't against the wind. To the market
    place!
You have put me now to such a part° which never
I shall discharge to the life.°
    COM.   Come, come, we'll prompt you.   106
    VOL. I prithee now, sweet son, as thou hast said
My praises made thee first a soldier, so,
To have my praise for this, perform a part
Thou hast not done before.
    COR.   Well, I must do 't.   110
Away, my disposition, and possess me
Some harlot's spirit! My throat of war be turned,
Which quired with° my drum, into a pipe
Small as an eunuch, or the virgin voice
That babies lulls asleep! The smiles of knaves   115
Tent° in my cheeks, and schoolboys' tears take up
The glasses of my sight!° A beggar's tongue
Make motion through my lips, and my armed knees,
Who bowed but in my stirrup, bend like his
That hath received an alms! I will not do 't,   120
Lest I surcease° to honor mine own truth,
And by my body's action teach my mind
A most inherent baseness.
    VOL.   At thy choice, then.

---

51. **in . . . request:** is equally required; i.e., "policy" is as necessary in peace as in war. **force . . . this:** urge this argument. 52. **lies . . . on:** is your duty to. 55. **roted in:** learned by heart. 57. **Of . . . allowance:** not acknowledged. 60. **put . . . fortune:** cause you to risk all. 62. **dissemble:** play the hypocrite. 64. **in this:** in this matter. 66. **general louts:** those louts that make up the populace. 68. **inheritance:** possession. 70. **salve:** heal. 73–86. **Go . . . person:** Here, as often, Shakespeare uses the dialogue for stage direction. Volumnia plucks the hat off his head and shows him by her own actions how he should act his part. 75. **bussing:** kissing. 80. **hold:** endure. 81. **broils:** fights. 84. **frame:** make.

90. **ruled:** obedient. 91. **gulf:** whirlpool. 92. **bower:** i.e., a place for love-making. 94. **You . . . party:** have a large party with you. 99. **unbarbed sconce:** unarmed head. **sconce:** lit., blockhouse. 102. **plot:** plot of earth; i.e., his own body, a common poetic image. 105. **part:** actor's part. 106. **discharge . . . life:** act realistically. See II.ii.100,n. 113. **quired with:** sang to the tune of. 116. **Tent:** encamp. 117. **glasses . . . sight:** eyeballs. 121. **surcease:** cease.

To beg of thee, it is my more dishonor
Than thou of them. Come all to ruin, let   125
Thy mother rather feel thy pride than fear
Thy dangerous stoutness, for I mock at death
With as big heart as thou. Do as thou list.°
Thy valiantness was mine, thou suck'dst it from me,
But owe° thy pride thyself.
    COR.   Pray be content.   130
Mother, I am going to the market place,
Chide me no more. I'll mountebank° their loves,
Cog° their hearts from them, and come home be-
    loved
Of all the trades in Rome. Look, I am going.
Commend me to my wife. I'll return Consul,   135
Or never trust to what my tongue can do
I' the way of flattery further.
    VOL.   Do your will. [*Exit.*]
    COM. Away! The tribunes do attend you. Arm
    yourself°
To answer mildly, for they are prepared
With accusations, as I hear, more strong   140
Than are upon you yet.
    COR. The word° is "mildly." Pray you let us go.
Let them accuse me by invention,° I
Will answer in mine honor.
    MEN.   Aye, but mildly.   144
    COR. Well, mildly be it then. Mildly!   [*Exeunt.*]

SCENE III. *The same. The Forum.*

    [*Enter* SICINIUS *and* BRUTUS.]
    BRU. In this point charge him home,° that he
    affects°
Tyrannical power. If he evade us there,
Enforce him with° his envy to° the people,
And that the spoil got on° the Antiates
Was ne'er distributed.
    [*Enter an* AEDILE.]   What, will he come?   5
    AED. He's coming.
    BRU.   How accompanied?
    AED. With old Menenius and those Senators
That always favored him.
    SIC.   Have you a catalogue
Of all the voices that we have procured,
Set down by the poll?°
    AED.   I have, 'tis ready.   10
    SIC. Have you collected them by tribes?
    AED.   I have.
    SIC. Assemble presently° the people hither.

And when they hear me say "It shall be so
I' the right and strength o' the commons," be it
    either
For death, for fine, or banishment, then let them,
If I say fine, cry "Fine," if death, cry "Death,"   16
Insisting on the old prerogative°
And power i' the truth° o' the cause.
    AED.   I shall inform them.
    BRU. And when such time they have begun to cry,
Let them not cease, but with a din confused   20
Enforce the present execution
Of what we chance to sentence.
    AED.   Very well.
    SIC. Make them be strong, and ready for this hint°
When we shall hap to give 't them.
    BRU.   Go about it.   [*Exit* AEDILE.]
Put him to choler straight.° He hath been used   25
Ever to conquer and to have his worth
Of contradiction.° Being once chafed,° he cannot
Be reined again to temperance. Then he speaks
What's in his heart, and that is there which looks
With us to break his neck.
    SIC.   Well, here he comes.   30
    [*Enter* CORIOLANUS, MENENIUS, *and* COMINIUS, *with*
          SENATORS *and* PATRICIANS.]
    MEN. Calmly, I do beseech you.
    COR. Aye, as an ostler,° that for the poorest piece
Will bear the knave by the volume.° The honored
    gods
Keep Rome in safety, and the chairs of justice
Supplied with worthy men! Plant love among 's!   35
Throng our large temples with the shows° of
    peace,
And not our streets with war!
    1. SEN.   Amen, amen.
    MEN. A noble wish.
    [*Re-enter* AEDILE, *with* CITIZENS.]
    SIC. Draw near, ye people.
    AED. List to your Tribunes, audience. Peace, I say!
    COR. First, hear me speak.
    BOTH TRIBUNES.   Well, say. Peace, ho!   41
    COR. Shall I be charged no further than this pres-
    ent?
Must all determine here?°
    SIC.   I do demand,
If you submit you° to the people's voices,
Allow their officers, and are content   45
To suffer lawful censure° for such faults
As shall be proved upon you.
    COR.   I am content.

---

128. **as . . . list:** as you please.   130. **owe:** own.   132. **mounte-
bank:** win them over like a cheap trickster at a fair.   133. **Cog:**
cheat.   138. **Arm yourself:** be prepared.   142. **word:** password.
143. **Let . . . invention:** let them invent accusations.
    Sc. iii: 1. **charge . . . home:** press your accusation. **affects:**
seeks.   3. **Enforce . . . with:** stress. **envy to:** hatred of.   4. **got
on:** won from.   10. **by . . . poll:** man by man.   12. **presently:**
immediately.

17. **prerogative:** sovereign right.   18. **truth:** justice.   23. **hint:**
occasion.   25. **Put . . . straight:** make him lose his temper at
once.   26–27. **his . . . contradiction:** full allowance to contra-
dict.   27. **chafed:** rubbed, made angry.   32. **ostler:** man who
tends horses.   32–33. **for . . . volume:** i.e., for a penny will
submit to be called knave by the bookful.   36. **shows:** pageants.
43. **determine here:** be concluded here.   44. **you:** yourself.
46. **censure:** judgment.

MEN. Lo, citizens, he says he is content.
The warlike service he has done, consider. Think
Upon the wounds his body bears, which show   50
Like graves i' the holy churchyard.
      COR.   Scratches with briers,
Scars to move laughter only.
      MEN.   Consider further
That when he speaks not like a citizen,
You find him like a soldier. Do not take
His rougher accents for malicious sounds,   55
But, as I say, such as become a soldier
Rather than envy you.°
      COM.   Well, well, no more.
      COR. What is the matter
That being passed for Consul with full voice,
I am so dishonored that the very hour   60
You take it off again?
      SIC.   Answer to us.
      COR. Say, then. 'Tis true, I ought so.
      SIC. We charge you that you have contrived° to
      take
From Rome all seasoned office,° and to wind°
Yourself into a power tyrannical,   65
For which you are a traitor to the people.
      COR. How! Traitor!
      MEN.   Nay, temperately — your promise.
      COR. The° fires i' the lowest Hell fold in° the
      people!
Call me their traitor! Thou injurious° Tribune!
Within thine eyes sat twenty thousand deaths,°   70
In thy hands clutched as many millions, in
Thy lying tongue both numbers, I would say
" Thou liest " unto thee with a voice as free
As I do pray the gods.
      SIC.   Mark you this, people?
      CITS. To the rock, to the rock with him!
      SIC.   Peace!   75
We need not put new matter to his charge.
What you have seen him do and heard him speak,
Beating your officers, cursing yourselves,
Opposing laws with strokes, and here defying
Those whose great power must try him. Even this,
So criminal and in such capital kind,°   81
Deserves the extremest death.
      BRU.   But since he hath
Served well for Rome ——
      COR.   What do you prate of service?
      BRU. I talk of that that know it.
      COR. You?   85
      MEN. Is this the promise that you made your
      mother?

COM. Know, I pray you ——
      COR.   I'll know no further.
Let them pronounce the steep Tarpeian death,
Vagabond exile, flaying, pent° to linger
But with a grain a day, I would not buy   90
Their mercy at the price of one fair word,
Nor check my courage for what they can give,
To have 't with saying " Good morrow."
      SIC.   For that he has,
As much as in him lies, from time to time
Envied against° the people, seeking means   95
To pluck away their power, as now at last
Given hostile strokes, and that not in the presence
Of dreaded justice but on the ministers
That do distribute it — in the name o' the people,
And in the power of us the Tribunes, we,   100
Even from this instant, banish him our city,
In peril of precipitation
From off the rock Tarpeian, never more
To enter our Rome gates. I' the people's name
I say it shall be so.   105
      CITS. It shall be so, it shall be so, let him away.
He's banished, and it shall be so.
      COM. Hear me, my masters, and my common
      friends ——
      SIC. He's sentenced, no more hearing.
      COM.   Let me speak.
I have been Consul, and can show for Rome   110
Her enemies' marks upon me. I do love
My country's good with a respect more tender,
More holy and profound, than mine own life,
My dear wife's estimate,° her womb's increase
And treasure of my loins. Then if I would   115
Speak that ——
      SIC.   We know your drift. — Speak what?
      BRU. There's no more to be said but he is banished,
As enemy to the people and his country.
It shall be so.
      CITS.   It shall be so, it shall be so.
      COR. You common cry° of curs! Whose breath I
      hate   120
As reek o' the rotten fens, whose loves I prize
As the dead carcasses of unburied men
That do corrupt my air, I banish you,
And here remain with your uncertainty!°
Let every feeble rumor shake your hearts,   125
Your enemies, with nodding of their plumes,°
Fan you into despair! Have the power still
To banish your defenders, till at length
Your ignorance, which finds not till it feels,
Making not reservation of yourselves,   130
Still your own foes, deliver you as most
Abated captives to some nation

---

57. **envy you:** express hatred for you.   63. **contrived:** plotted.
64. **seasoned office:** long-established offices. **wind:** insinuate.
68–74. **The . . . gods:** Once again Coriolanus becomes incoherent
with rage. Cf. I.vi.76; III.i.102.   68. **fold in:** enclose.   69. **injurious:** insulting.   70. **Within . . . deaths:** even if you had
twenty thousand deaths in your glance.   81. **capital kind:**
deserving death.

89. **pent:** shut in.   95. **Envied against:** shown hatred for.
114. **estimate:** honor.   120. **cry:** pack.   124. **And . . . uncertainty:** may you remain here in a state of confusion.   126. **plumes,**
i.e., on their helmets.

That won you without blows!° Despising,
For you, the city, thus I turn my back.
There is a world elsewhere.   135

          [*Exeunt* CORIOLANUS, COMINIUS,
          MENENIUS, SENATORS *and* PATRICIANS.]

AED. The people's enemy is gone, is gone!
CITS. Our enemy is banished! He is gone! Hoo!
Hoo!

       [*They all shout, and throw up their caps.*]

SIC. Go, see him out at gates, and follow him,
As he hath followed you, with all despite.°
Give him deserved vexation.° Let a guard   140
Attend us through the city.

CITS. Come, come, let's see him out at gates, come.
The gods preserve our noble Tribunes! Come.

                          [*Exeunt.*]

Act IV

SCENE I. *Rome. Before a gate of the city.*

[*Enter* CORIOLANUS, VOLUMNIA, VIRGILIA, MENENIUS,
COMINIUS, *with the young nobility of Rome.*]

COR. Come, leave your tears, a brief farewell. The
    beast
With many heads butts me away. Nay, Mother,
Where is your ancient courage? You were used
To say extremity° was the trier of spirits,
That common chances common men could bear,   5
That when the sea was calm all boats alike
Showed mastership in floating. Fortune's blows,
When most struck home, being gentle wounded,
    craves
A noble cunning.° You were used to load me
With precepts that would make invincible   10
The heart that conned° them.

VIR.   Oh, heavens! Oh, heavens!

COR.   Nay, I prithee, woman ——

VOL. Now the red pestilence° strike all trades in
    Rome,
And occupations° perish!

COR.   What, what, what!   14
I shall be loved when I am lacked.° Nay, Mother,
Resume that spirit when you were wont to say

If you had been the wife of Hercules,
Six of his labors you'd have done, and saved
Your husband so much sweat. Cominius,
Droop not, adieu. Farewell, my wife, my mother.
I'll do well yet. Thou old and true Menenius,   21
Thy tears are salter than a younger man's,
And venomous to thine eyes. My sometime General,
I have seen thee stern, and thou hast oft beheld
Heart-hardening spectacles. Tell these sad women
'Tis fond° to wail inevitable strokes,   26
As 'tis to laugh at 'em. My mother, you wot° well
My hazards still° have been your solace. And
Believe 't not lightly — though I go alone,
Like to a lonely dragon that his fen   30
Makes feared and talked of more than seen — your
    son
Will or exceed the common, or be caught
With cautelous° baits and practice.°

VOL.   My first son,
Whither wilt thou go? Take good Cominius
With thee awhile. Determine on some course   35
More than a wild exposture° to each chance
That starts i' the way before thee.

COR.   Oh, the gods!

COM. I'll follow thee a month, devise with thee
Where thou shalt rest, that thou mayst hear of us
And we of thee. So, if the time thrust forth   40
A cause for thy repeal,° we shall not send
O'er the vast world to seek a single man
And lose advantage,° which doth ever cool
I' the absence of the needer.

COR.   Fare ye well.
Thou hast years upon thee, and thou art too full   45
Of the wars' surfeits° to go rove with one
That's yet unbruised. Bring me but out at gate.
Come, my sweet wife, my dearest mother, and
My friends of noble touch,° when I am forth,
Bid me farewell, and smile. I pray you come.   50
While I remain above the ground you shall
Hear from me still, and never of me aught
But what is like me formerly.

MEN.   That's worthily
As any ear can hear. Come, let's not weep.
If I could shake off but one seven years   55
From these old arms and legs, by the good gods,
I'd with thee every foot.

COR.   Give me thy hand.
Come.   [*Exeunt.*]

128–33. till ... blows: till at last your ignorance (which will not
be revealed till you suffer for it and which makes you always your
own worst enemies) shall deliver you as most humiliated (*abated*)
captives to some nation that wins you without blows.   139. de-
spite: spite.   140. vexation: torment.
    Act IV, Sc. i: 4. extremity: misfortune.   7–9. Fortune's ...
cunning: when Fortune's blows strike home, to remain true to
one's birth (*gentle*) under the wound demands a noble knowledge;
i.e., only the noble heart can endure the blows of Fortune bravely.
Cf. *Tr & Cr*, I.iii.33–37.   9. cunning: skill.   11. conned:
learned by heart.   13. red pestilence: one of the forms of the
dreaded plague.   14. occupations: tradesmen.   15. lacked:
missed.

26. fond: foolish.   27. wot: know.   28. still: always.   33. cau-
telous: crafty. practice: plotting.   36. exposture: exposure.
41. repeal: recall from banishment.   43. advantage: the oppor-
tunity.   45–46. thou ... surfeits: you are sick of too much war.
surfeits: state of overfullness.   49. noble touch: proved nobility.
touch: tested by the touchstone. See *Rich III*, IV.ii.8,n.

SCENE II. *The same. A street near the gate.*

[*Enter the two* TRIBUNES, SICINIUS *and* BRUTUS, *with the* AEDILE.]

SIC. Bid them all home, he's gone, and we'll no
further.
The nobility are vexed, whom we see have sided°
In his behalf.

BRU.   Now we have shown our power,
Let us seem humbler after it is done
Than when it was a-doing.

SIC.   Bid them home.   5
Say their great enemy is gone, and they
Stand in their ancient strength.

BRU.   Dismiss them home.   [*Exit* AEDILE.]
Here comes his mother.

[*Enter* VOLUMNIA, VIRGILIA, *and* MENENIUS.]

SIC.   Let's not meet her.

BRU.   Why?

SIC. They say she's mad.

BRU. They have ta'en note of° us. Keep on your
way.   10

VOL. Oh, ye're well met. The hoarded plague°
o' the gods
Requite your love!

MEN.   Peace, peace, be not so loud.

VOL. If that I could for weeping, you should
hear ——
Nay, and you shall hear some. [*To* BRUTUS] Will you
be gone?

VIR. [*To* SICINIUS] You shall stay too. I would I
had the power   15
To say so to my husband.

SIC.   Are you mankind?°

VOL. Aye, fool, is that a shame? Note but this fool.
Was not a man my father? Hadst thou foxship°
To banish him that struck more blows for Rome
Than thou hast spoken words?

SIC.   Oh, blessed Heavens!   20

VOL. Moe noble blows than ever thou wise words,
And for Rome's good. I'll tell thee what, yet go.
Nay, but thou shalt stay too. I would my son
Were in Arabia,° and thy tribe before him,
His good sword in his hand.

SIC.   What then?

VIR.   What then!   25
He'd make an end of thy posterity.°

VOL. Bastards and all.
Good man, the wounds that he does bear for Rome!

MEN. Come, come, peace.

SIC. I would he had continued to his country   30
As he began, and not unknit himself

The noble knot° he made.

BRU.   I would he had.

VOL. "I would he had!" 'Twas you incensed the
rabble,
Cats, that can judge as fitly of his worth
As I can of those mysteries which Heaven   35
Will not have earth to know.

BRU.   Pray let us go.

VOL. Now pray, sir, get you gone.
You have done a brave deed. Ere you go, hear this:
As far as doth the Capitol exceed
The meanest house in Rome, so far my son —   40
This lady's husband here, this, do you see? —
Whom you have banished, does exceed you all.

BRU. Well, well, we'll leave you.

SIC.   Why stay we to be baited°
With one that wants her wits?

VOL.   Take my prayers with you.

[*Exeunt* TRIBUNES.]

I would the gods had nothing else to do   45
But to confirm my curses! Could I meet 'em
But once a day, it would unclog° my heart
Of what lies heavy to 't.

MEN.   You have told them home,
And, by my troth, you have cause. You'll sup with
me?

VOL. Anger's my meat. I sup upon myself,   50
And so shall starve with feeding. Come, let's go.
Leave this faint puling,° and lament as I do,
In anger, Juno-like.° Come, come, come.

[*Exeunt* VOLUMNIA *and* VIRGINIA.]

MEN. Fie, fie, fie!   [*Exit.*]

SCENE III. *A highway between Rome and Antium.*

[*Enter a* ROMAN *and a* VOLSCE, *meeting.*]

ROM. I know you well, sir, and you know me.
Your name, I think, is Adrian.

VOLS. It is so, sir. Truly, I have forgot you.

ROM. I am a Roman, and my services are, as you
are, against 'em. Know you me yet?   5

VOLS. Nicanor? No.

ROM. The same, sir.

VOLS. You had more beard when I last saw you,
but your favor is well appeared by your tongue.°
What's the news in Rome? I have a note from the
Volscian state, to find you out there. You have well
saved me a day's journey.   12

ROM. There hath been in Rome strange insurrec-

Sc. ii: 2. **sided:** taken sides.   10. **ta'en . . . of:** noticed.
11. **hoarded plague:** plague kept in store for a special punishment.   16. **mankind:** a mannish woman.   18. **foxship:** low cunning.   24. **Arabia:** i.e., the desert, where there is no escaping.
26. **posterity:** descendants, tribe.

32. **noble knot:** i.e., that which bound Rome to him.   43. **baited:** worried, like a bear by the hounds.   47. **unclog:** take the weight from.   52. **puling:** whining.   53. **Juno-like:** Juno was Queen of Heaven; her anger therefore was thunderous.
Sc. iii: 9. **favor . . . tongue:** face is seen in your speech; i.e., your Latin accent shows that you are a Roman.

tions, the people against the Senators, patricians, and nobles.

VOLS. Hath been! Is it ended, then? Our state think not so. They are in a most warlike preparation, and hope to come upon them in the heat of their division.   19

ROM. The main blaze of it is past, but a small thing would make it flame again. For the nobles receive so to heart the banishment of that worthy Coriolanus that they are in a ripe aptness° to take all power from the people, and to pluck from them their Tribunes forever. This lies glowing, I can tell you, and is almost mature for the violent breaking-out.   27

VOLS. Coriolanus banished!

ROM. Banished, sir.

VOLS. You will be welcome with this intelligence,° Nicanor.   31

ROM. The day serves well for them now. I have heard it said the fittest time to corrupt a man's wife is when she's fallen out with her husband. Your noble Tullus Aufidius will appear well in these wars, his great opposer, Coriolanus, being now in no request of° his country.   38

VOLS. He cannot choose. I am most fortunate thus accidentally to encounter you. You have ended my business, and I will merrily accompany you home.

ROM. I shall, between this and supper, tell you most strange things from Rome, all tending to the good of their adversaries. Have you an army ready, say you?   46

VOLS. A most royal one, the centurions and their charges,° distinctly° billeted, already in the entertainment,° and to be on foot at an hour's warning.   50

ROM. I am joyful to hear of their readiness, and am the man, I think, that shall set them in present° action. So, sir, heartily well met, and most glad of your company.   54

VOLS. You take my part from me, sir. I have the most cause to be glad of yours.

ROM. Well, let us go together.   [Exeunt.]

SCENE IV. *Antium. Before* AUFIDIUS's *house.*

[*Enter* CORIOLANUS *in mean apparel, disguised and muffled.*]

COR. A goodly city is this Antium. City,
'Tis I that made thy widows. Many an heir
Of these fair edifices 'fore° my wars
Have I heard groan and drop. Then know me not,

Lest that thy wives with spits,° and boys with stones,
In puny battle slay me.
[*Enter a* CITIZEN.]   Save you,° sir.   6

CIT. And you.

COR.   Direct me, if it be your will,
Where great Aufidius lies. Is he in Antium?

CIT. He is, and feasts the nobles of the state
At his house this night.

COR.   Which is his house, beseech you? 10

CIT. This, here before you.

COR.   Thank you, sir. Farewell. [*Exit* CITIZEN.]
O world, thy slippery turns! Friends now fast sworn,
Whose double bosoms seem to wear one heart,
Whose hours, whose bed, whose meal and exercise
Are still together, who twin, as 'twere, in love 15
Unseparable, shall within this hour,
On a dissension of a doit,° break out
To bitterest enmity. So fellest° foes,
Whose passions and whose plots have broke their sleep
To take the one the other, by some chance,   20
Some trick not worth an egg, shall grow dear friends
And interjoin their issues.° So with me.
My birthplace hate I, and my love's upon
This enemy town. I'll enter. If he slay me,
He does fair justice. If he give me way,   25
I'll do his country service.   [*Exit.*]

SCENE V. *The same. A hall in* AUFIDIUS's *house.*

[*Music within. Enter a* SERVINGMAN.]

1. SERV. Wine, wine, wine!—What service is here! I think our fellows are asleep.   [*Exit.*]

[*Enter another* SERVINGMAN.]

2. SERV. Where's Cotus? My master calls for him. Cotus!   [*Exit.*]

[*Enter* CORIOLANUS.]

COR. A goodly house. The feast smells well, but I Appear not like a guest.   6

[*Re-enter the* FIRST SERVINGMAN.]

1. SERV. What would you have, friend? Whence are you? Here's no place for you. Pray go to the door.   [*Exit.*]

COR. I have deserved no better entertainment,°
In being Coriolanus.   11

[*Re-enter* SECOND SERVINGMAN.]

2. SERV. Whence are you, sir? Has the porter° his

---

23. **ripe aptness:** ready and eager.   31. **intelligence:** news. 37–38. **in ... of:** not required by.   48. **charges:** men in their command. **distinctly:** individually.   48–49. **in ... entertainment:** hired.   52. **present:** immediate.
Sc. iv: 3. **'fore:** before.

5. **spits:** iron rods on which meat was roasted, useful domestic weapons.   6. **Save you:** God bless you.   17. **dissension ... doit:** quarrel not worth half a cent. **doit:** half a farthing.   18. **fellest:** fiercest.   22. **interjoin ... issues:** arrange for their children to intermarry.
Sc. v: 10. **entertainment:** reception.   12. **porter:** keeper of the outer gate.

eyes in his head that he gives entrance to such companions?° Pray get you out.

COR. Away!   15

2. SERV. Away! Get you away.

COR. Now thou'rt troublesome.

2. SERV. Are you so brave?° I'll have you talked with anon.°

[*Enter a* THIRD SERVINGMAN. *The first meets him.*]

3. SERV. What fellow's this?   20

1. SERV. A strange one as ever I looked on. I cannot get him out o' the house. Prithee call my master to him.   [*Retires.*]

3. SERV. What have you to do here, fellow? Pray you avoid° the house.   25

COR. Let me but stand, I will not hurt your hearth.

3. SERV. What are you?

COR. A gentleman.

3. SERV. A marvelous poor one.   30

COR. True, so I am.

3. SERV. Pray you, poor gentleman, take up some other station,° here's no place for you. Pray you avoid. Come.   34

COR. Follow your function,° go and batten on cold bits.°   [*Pushes him away from him.*]

3. SERV. What, you will not? Prithee tell my master what a strange guest he has here.

2. SERV. And I shall.   [*Exit.*]

3. SERV. Where dwell'st thou?   40

COR. Under the canopy.°

3. SERV. Under the canopy!

COR. Aye.

3. SERV. Where's that?

COR. I' the city of kites and crows.   45

3. SERV. I' the city of kites and crows! What an ass it is! Then thou dwell'st with daws° too?

COR. No, I serve not thy master.

3. SERV. How, sir! Do you meddle with my master?   51

COR. Aye, 'tis an honester service than to meddle with thy mistress. Thou pratest, and pratest. Serve with thy trencher,° hence!   [*Beats him away.*

Exit THIRD SERVINGMAN.]

[*Enter* AUFIDIUS *with the* SECOND SERVINGMAN.]

AUF. Where is this fellow?   55

2. SERV. Here, sir. I'd have beaten him like a dog but for disturbing the lords within.   [*Retires.*]

AUF. Whence comest thou? What wouldst thou? Thy name?

Why speak'st not? Speak, man. What's thy name?

COR. [*Unmuffling.*]   If, Tullus,   60

Not yet thou knowest me and, seeing me, dost not

Think me for the man I am, necessity

Commands me name myself.

AUF.   What is thy name?

COR. A name unmusical to the Volscians' ears,

And harsh in sound to thine.

AUF.   Say, what's thy name?   65

Thou hast a grim appearance, and thy face

Bears a command in 't. Though thy tackle's° torn,

Thou show'st a noble vessel. What's thy name?

COR. Prepare thy brow to frown. — Know'st thou me yet?

AUF. I know thee not. — Thy name?   70

COR. My name is Caius Marcius, who hath done

To thee particularly, and to all the Volsces,

Great hurt and mischief — thereto witness may

My surname, Coriolanus. The painful° service,

The extreme dangers, and the drops of blood   75

Shed for my thankless country are requited

But with that surname, a good memory,°

And witness of the malice and displeasure

Which thou shouldst bear me. Only that name remains.

The cruelty and envy of the people,   80

Permitted by our dastard° nobles, who

Have all forsook me, hath devoured the rest,

And suffered me by the voice of slaves to be

Whooped° out of Rome. Now this extremity

Hath brought me to thy hearth. Not out of hope —

Mistake me not — to save my life, for if   86

I had feared death, of all the men i' the world

I would have 'voided thee, but in mere spite,

To be full quit of° those my banishers,

Stand I before thee here. Then if thou hast   90

A heart of wreak° in thee that wilt revenge

Thine own particular wrongs, and stop those maims

Of shame° seen through thy country, speed thee straight,

And make my misery serve thy turn. So use it

That my revengeful services may prove   95

As benefits to thee, for I will fight

Against my cankered° country with the spleen°

Of all the underfiends.° But if so be

Thou darest not this and that to prove more fortunes°

Thou'rt tired, then, in a word, I also am   100

Longer to live most weary, and present

My throat to thee and to thy ancient malice,

Which not to cut would show thee but a fool,

Since I have ever followed thee with hate,

Drawn tuns° of blood out of thy country's breast,

---

14. **companions:** low fellows.   18. **brave:** insolent.   19. **anon:** at once.   25. **avoid:** get out of.   33. **station:** standing place. 35. **Follow . . . function:** do your job.   35–36. **batten . . . bits:** feed on the scraps.   41. **canopy:** the heavens.   47. **daws:** jackdaws.   54. **trencher:** wooden plate.

67. **tackle:** rigging.   74. **painful:** laborious.   77. **memory:** memorial.   81. **dastard:** cowardly.   84. **Whooped:** pursued with shouts of derision.   89. **full . . . of:** fully revenged on. 91. **wreak:** vengeance.   92–93. **maims . . . shame:** shameful injuries.   97. **cankered:** eaten up by the maggots of ingratitude. **spleen:** anger.   98. **underfiends:** the fiends below.   99. **prove . . . . fortunes:** risk the fortune of war again.   105. **tuns:** barrels. A *tun* is a large cask, used especially for wine.

And cannot live but to thy shame° unless   106
It be to do thee service.

AUF.   O Marcius, Marcius!
Each word thou hast spoke hath weeded from my
    heart
A root of ancient envy.° If Jupiter
Should from yond cloud speak divine things,   110
And say " 'Tis true," I'd not believe them more
Than thee, all-noble Marcius. Let me twine
Mine arms about that body where-against
My grainèd ash° a hundred times hath broke,
And scarred the moon with splinters. Here I clip°
The anvil of my sword, and do contest   116
As hotly and as nobly with thy love
As ever in ambitious strength I did
Contend against thy valor. Know thou first,
I loved the maid I married, never man   120
Sighed truer breath, but that I see thee here,
Thou noble thing! more dances my rapt° heart
Than when I first my wedded mistress saw
Bestride my threshold. Why, thou Mars! I tell thee
We have a power on foot, and I had purpose   125
Once more to hew thy target° from thy brawn,°
Or lose mine arm for 't. Thou hast beat me out
Twelve several times, and I have nightly since
Dreamed of encounters 'twixt thyself and me.
We have been down together in my sleep,   130
Unbuckling helms,° fisting each other's throat,
And waked half-dead with nothing. Worthy Mar-
    cius,
Had we no quarrel else to Rome but that
Thou art thence banished, we would muster all
From twelve to seventy, and pouring war   135
Into the bowels of ungrateful Rome,
Like a bold flood o'erbear. Oh, come, go in,
And take our friendly Senators by the hands,
Who now are here taking their leaves of me,
Who am prepared against your territories,   140
Though not for Rome itself.

COR.   You bless me, gods!

AUF. Therefore, most absolute° sir, if thou wilt
    have
The leading of thine own revenges, take
The one half of my commission, and set down —
As best thou art experienced, since thou know'st
Thy country's strength and weakness — thine own
    ways,   146
Whether to knock against the gates of Rome,
Or rudely visit them in parts remote,
To fright them, ere destroy. But come in.
Let me commend° thee first to those that shall   150
Say yea to thy desires. A thousand welcomes!

106. cannot . . . shame: i.e., while I live I am a record of your
shame.   109. envy: hatred.   114. grained ash: the stout ash
shaft of my spear.   115. clip: embrace.   122. rapt: enraptured.
126. target: small shield. See Pl. 9d. brawn: the muscles of the
arm.   131. helms: helmets.   142. absolute: perfect.   150. com-
mend: introduce.

And more a friend than e'er an enemy;
Yet, Marcius, that was much. Your hand. Most wel-
    come! [*Exeunt* CORIOLANUS *and* AUFIDIUS. *The
    two* SERVINGMEN *come forward.*]

1. SERV. Here's a strange alteration!   154
2. SERV. By my hand, I had thought to have
strucken° him with a cudgel, and yet my mind gave
me° his clothes made a false report of him.

1. SERV. What an arm he has! He turned me about
with his finger and his thumb as one would set up
a top.   161
2. SERV. Nay, I knew by his face that there was
something in him. He had, sir, a kind of face, me-
thought —— I cannot tell how to term it.

1. SERV. He had so, looking as it were —— Would
I were hanged, but I thought there was more in him
than I could think.   167
2. SERV. So did I, I'll be sworn. He is simply° the
rarest man i' the world.

1. SERV. I think he is. But a greater soldier than
he, you wot one.   171
2. SERV. Who? My master?
1. SERV. Nay, it's no matter for that.
2. SERV. Worth six on him.
1. SERV. Nay, not so neither. But I take him to be
the greater soldier.   176
2. SERV. Faith, look you, one cannot tell how to say
that. For the defense of a town, our General is ex-
cellent.

1. SERV. Aye, and for an assault too.   180
    [*Re-enter* THIRD SERVINGMAN.]

3. SERV. O slaves, I can tell you news, news, you
rascals!

1. & 2. SERV. What, what, what? Let's partake.
3. SERV. I would not be a Roman, of all nations. I
had as lieve° be a condemned man.   186

1. & 2. SERV. Wherefore? Wherefore?
3. SERV. Why, here's he that was wont to thwack°
our General — Caius Marcius.

1. SERV. Why do you say thwack our General?
3. SERV. I do not say thwack our General,   192
but he was always good enough for him.

2. SERV. Come, we are fellows and friends. He was
ever too hard for him, I have heard him say so him-
self.   196

1. SERV. He was too hard for him directly, to say
the troth on 't. Before Corioli he scotched° him and
notched him like a carbonado.°

2. SERV. An he had been cannibally given, he
might have broiled and eaten him too.   201

1. SERV. But more of thy news?
3. SERV. Why, he is so made on here within as if
he were son and heir to Mars — set at upper end o'

156. strucken: hit.   156–57. gave me: told me, misgave me.
168. simply: without other description.   186. lieve: soon.
189. thwack: wallop.   198. scotched: slashed.   199. car-
bonado: steak scored for grilling.

the table, no question asked him by any of the Senators, but they stand bald° before him. Our General himself makes a mistress of him, sanctifies himself with 's hand,° and turns up the white o' the eye to his discourse. But the bottom of the news is, our General is cut i' the middle, and but one half of 210 what he was yesterday, for the other has half, by the entreaty and grant of the whole table. He'll go, he says, and sowl° the porter of Rome gates by the ears. He will mow all down before him, and leave his passage polled.° 215

2. SERV. And he's as like to do 't as any man I can imagine.

3. SERV. Do 't! He will do 't, for look you, sir, he has as many friends as enemies, which friends, sir, as it were, durst not, look you, sir, show themselves, as we term it, his friends whilst he's in directitude.°

1. SERV. Directitude! What's that? 222

3. SERV. But when they shall see, sir, his crest up again and the man in blood, they will out of their burrows, like conies° after rain, and revel all with him. 227

1. SERV. But when goes this forward?

3. SERV. Tomorrow, today, presently. You shall have the drum struck up this afternoon. 'Tis, as it were, a parcel° of their feast, and to be executed ere they wipe their lips. 232

2. SERV. Why, then we shall have a stirring world again. This peace is nothing° but to rust iron, increase tailors, and breed ballad-makers.°

1. SERV. Let me have war, say I. It exceeds peace as far as day does night, it's spritely,° waking, audible,° and full of vent.° Peace is a very apoplexy,° lethargy, mulled,° deaf, sleepy, insensible, a getter of more bastard children than war's a destroyer of men. 241

2. SERV. 'Tis so. And as war, in some sort, may be said to be a ravisher, so it cannot be denied but peace is a great maker of cuckolds.°

1. SERV. Aye, and it makes men hate one another.

3. SERV. Reason,° because they then less need 247 one another. The wars for my money. I hope to see Romans as cheap° as Volscians. They are rising,° they are rising. 250

1. & 2. SERV. In, in, in, in! [*Exeunt.*]

---

206. bald: bareheaded, as a sign of respect. 207–08. sanctifies . . . hand: touches him with his hand as if he were something holy. 213. sowl: pull out. 215. polled: shorn. 221. directitude: Servants in Shakespeare's plays often use big words without knowing their meanings; possibly he intended "discredit." 226. conies: rabbits. 231. parcel: part. 234. This . . . nothing: When *Coriolanus* was written many of Shakespeare's contemporaries, especially unemployed ex-captains, openly lamented the end of the Spanish wars. 235. ballad-makers: See App. 8. 237. spritely: full of spirit. 238. audible: quick to hear. full of vent: full of excited talk. apoplexy: lethargy. See *I! Hen IV,* I.ii.122–28. 239. mulled: warm and drowsy. 245. cuckolds: deceived husbands. 247. Reason: with good reason. 249. cheap: poor things. ᴀre rising: i.e., have finished dinner.

SCENE VI. *Rome. A public place.*

[*Enter the two* TRIBUNES, SICINIUS *and* BRUTUS.]

SIC. We hear not of him, neither need we fear him.
His remedies are tame° i' the present peace
And quietness of the people, which before
Were in wild hurry. Here do we make his friends
Blush that the world goes well, who rather had, 5
Though they themselves did suffer by 't, behold
Dissentious numbers pestering° streets than see
Our tradesmen singing in their shops and going
About their functions friendly.

BRU. We stood to 't in good time.
     [*Enter* MENENIUS.] Is this Menenius? 10

SIC. 'Tis he, 'tis he. Oh, he is grown most kind
Of late. Hail, sir!

MEN.   Hail to you both!

SIC. Your Coriolanus is not much missed
But with° his friends. The commonwealth doth stand,
And so would do were he more angry at it. 15

MEN. All's well, and might have been much better if
He could have temporized.°

SIC.   Where is he, hear you?

MEN. Nay, I hear nothing. His mother and his wife
Hear nothing from him.

     [*Enter three or four* CITIZENS.]

CITS. The gods preserve you both!

SIC.   Godden, our neighbors. 20

BRU. Godden to you all, godden to you all.

1. CIT. Ourselves, our wives, and children, on our knees,
Are bound to pray for you° both.

SIC.   Live, and thrive!

BRU. Farewell, kind neighbors. We wished Coriolanus
Had loved you as we did.

CITS.   Now the gods keep you! 25

BOTH TRIBS. Farewell, farewell.
     [*Exeunt* CITIZENS.]

SIC. This is a happier and more comely time
Than when these fellows ran about the streets
Crying confusion.

BRU.   Caius Marcius was
A worthy officer i' the war, but insolent, 30
O'ercome with pride, ambitious past all thinking,
Self-loving——

SIC.   And affecting one sole throne,
Without assistance.°

MEN.   I think not so.

Sc. vi: 2. remedies . . . tame: the actions he would have taken (had he been Consul) are no longer dangerous. 7. pestering: crowding. 14. But with: except by. 17. temporized: compromised. 23. Are . . . you: i.e., as our benefactors and patrons. 32–33. affecting . . . assistance: aiming to be King by himself.

SIC. We should by this, to all our lamentation,°
If he had gone forth° Consul, found it so.   35
BRU. The gods have well prevented it, and Rome
Sits safe and still without him.

[*Enter an* AEDILE.]

AED.   Worthy Tribunes,
There is a slave, whom we have put in prison,
Reports the Volsces with two several powers°
Are entered in the Roman territories,   40
And with the deepest malice of the war
Destroy what lies before 'em.
MEN.   'Tis Aufidius,
Who, hearing of our Marcius' banishment,
Thrusts forth his horns° again into the world,
Which were inshelled when Marcius stood for
          Rome,   45
And durst not once peep out.
SIC.   Come, what talk you
Of Marcius?
BRU. Go see this rumorer whipped. It cannot be
The Volsces dare break with us.
MEN.   Cannot be!
We have record that very well it can,
And three examples of the like have been   50
Within my age.° But reason with the fellow
Before you punish him, where he heard this,
Lest you shall chance to whip your information°
And beat the messenger who bids beware
Of what is to be dreaded.
SIC.   Tell not me.   55
I know this cannot be.
BRU.   Not possible.

[*Enter a* MESSENGER.]

MESS. The nobles in great earnestness are going
All to the Senate House. Some news is come
That turns their countenances.°
SIC.   'Tis this slave.
Go whip him 'fore the people's eyes. His raising,   60
Nothing but his report.
MESS.   Yes, worthy sir,
The slave's report is seconded,° and more,
More fearful, is delivered.°
SIC.   What more fearful?
MESS. It is spoke freely out of many mouths —
How probable I do not know — that Marcius,   65
Joined with Aufidius, leads a power 'gainst Rome,
And vows revenge as spacious as between
The young'st and oldest thing.°
SIC.   This is most likely!
BRU. Raised only that the weaker sort may wish
Good Marcius home again.

SIC.   The very trick° on 't.   70
MEN. This is unlikely.
He and Aufidius can no more atone°
Than violentest contrariety.

[*Enter a* SECOND MESSENGER.]

2. MESS. You are sent for to the Senate.
A fearful army, led by Caius Marcius   75
Associated with Aufidius, rages
Upon our territories, and have already
O'erborne° their way, consumed with fire, and took
What lay before them.

[*Enter* COMINIUS.]

COM. Oh, you have made good work!
MEN.   What news? What news?   80
COM. You have holp to ravish your own daugh-
          ters, and
To melt the city leads° upon your pates,
To see your wives dishonored to your noses ——
MEN. What's the news? What's the news?
COM. Your temples burned in their cement, and
Your franchises,° whereon you stood,° confined   86
Into an auger's bore.°
MEN.   Pray now, your news? —
You have made fair work, I fear me. — Pray, your
          news? —
If Marcius should be joined with Volscians ——
COM.   If!
He is their god. He leads them like a thing   90
Made by some other deity than nature,
That shapes man better. And they follow him,
Against us brats, with no less confidence
Than boys pursuing summer butterflies,
Or butchers killing flies.
MEN.   You have made good work,   95
You and your apron men,° you that stood so much
Upon the voice of occupation° and
The breath of garlic-eaters!
COM. He'll shake your Rome about your ears.
MEN.   As Hercules
Did shake down mellow fruit. You have made fair
          work!   100
BRU. But is this true, sir?
COM.   Aye, and you'll look pale
Before you find it other. All the regions
Do smilingly revolt, and who resist
Are mocked for valiant ignorance°
And perish constant° fools. Who is 't can blame
          him?   105

34. to . . . lamentation: to the sorrow of us all.   35. gone forth:
been elected.   39. several powers: separate armies.   44. Thrusts
. . . horns: i.e., like a snail.   51. age: lifetime.   53. informa-
tion: teacher.   59. turns . . . countenances: makes them look
pale.   62. seconded: supported.   63. delivered: related, told.
67–68. as . . . thing: i.e., that he will spare neither young nor
old

70. trick: device.   72. atone: be friends.   78. O'erborne: i.e.,
like a river in flood.   82. melt . . . leads: the roofs of build-
ings were often covered with lead. When a building caught fire
the molten lead was a considerable danger to the fire-fighters.
86. franchises: privileges; e.g., of being able to refuse to con-
firm the election of a Consul. stood: insisted.   87. auger's
bore: a tiny hole such as is made by an auger.   96. apron men:
artisans. Cf. *Caesar,* I.i.7.   97. voice of occupation: vote of
the workingman.   104. valiant ignorance: being brave fools.
105. constant: loyal.

Your enemies and his find something in him.
  MEN. We are all undone unless
The noble man have mercy.
  COM.   Who shall ask it?
The Tribunes cannot do 't for shame, the people
Deserve such pity of him as the wolf   110
Does of the shepherds. For his best friends, if they
Should say " Be good to Rome," they charged° him
   even
As those should do that had deserved his hate,
And therein showed like enemies.
  MEN.   'Tis true.
If he were putting to my house the brand°   115
That should consume it, I have not the face
To say " Beseech you, cease." You have made fair
   hands,°
You and your crafts!° You have crafted fair!
  COM.   You have brought
A trembling upon Rome such as was never
So incapable of help.
  BOTH TRIBS.   Say not we brought it.   120
  MEN. How! Was it we? We loved him, but, like
   beasts
And cowardly nobles, gave way unto your clusters,°
Who did hoot him out o' the city.
  COM.   But I fear
They'll roar him in again. Tullus Aufidius,
The second name of men,° obeys his points° 125
As if he were his officer.° Desperation
Is all the policy, strength, and defense
That Rome can make against them.
         [*Enter a troop of* CITIZENS.]
  MEN.   Here come the clusters.
And is Aufidius with him? You are they
That made the air unwholesome when you cast 130
Your stinking greasy caps in hooting at
Coriolanus' exile. Now he's coming,
And not a hair upon a soldier's head
Which will not prove a whip. As many coxcombs°
As you threw caps up will he tumble down, 135
And pay you for your voices. 'Tis no matter,
If he could burn us all into one coal,
We have deserved it.
  CITS. Faith, we hear fearful news.
  I. CIT.   For mine own part,
When I said banish him, I said 'twas pity. 140
  2. CIT. And so did I.
  3. CIT. And so did I, and, to say the truth, so did
very many of us. That we did, we did for the best,
and though we willingly consented to his banish-
ment, yet it was against our will.   146

  COM. Ye're goodly things, you voices!
  MEN.   You have made
Good work, you and your cry!° Shall 's to the Capi-
tol?
  COM. Oh, aye, what else?
         [*Exeunt* COMINIUS *and* MENENIUS.]
  SIC. Go, masters, get you home, be not dismayed.
These are a side that would be glad to have 151
This true which they so seem to fear. Go home,
And show no sign of fear.
  I. CIT. The gods be good to us! Come, masters,
let's home. I ever said we were i' the wrong when
we banished him.   156
  2. CIT. So did we all. But come, let's home.
                [*Exeunt* CITIZENS.]
  BRU. I do not like this news.
  SIC. Nor I.   159
  BRU. Let's to the Capitol. Would half my wealth
Would buy this for a lie!
  SIC.   Pray let us go. [*Exeunt.*]

SCENE VII. *A camp, at a small distance from Rome.*

    [*Enter* AUFIDIUS, *with his* LIEUTENANT.]
  AUF. Do they still fly to the Roman?
  LIEU. I do not know what witchcraft's in him, but
Your soldiers use him as the grace 'fore meat,
Their talk at table, and their thanks at end,
And you are darkened in this action, sir, 5
Even by your own.°
  AUF.   I cannot help it now,
Unless, by using means, I lame the foot
Of our design. He bears himself more proudlier,
Even to my person, than I thought he would
When first I did embrace him. Yet his nature 10
In that's no changeling,° and I must excuse
What cannot be amended.
  LIEU.   Yet I wish, sir —
I mean for your particular° — you had not
Joined in commission with him, but either
Had borne the action of yourself or else 15
To him had left it solely.
  AUF. I understand thee well, and be thou sure,
When he shall come to his account, he knows not
What I can urge against him. Although it seems,
And so he thinks, and is no less apparent 20
To the vulgar eye, that he bears all things fairly,
And shows good husbandry° for the Volscian state,
Fights dragonlike, and does achieve° as soon
As draw his sword, yet he hath left undone

---

112. **charged:** accused. 115. **brand:** firebrand. 117. **have . . .
hands:** have done a fine job. 118. **crafts:** trade-unions.
122. **clusters:** mobs. 125. **second . . . men:** the most famous
after Coriolanus. **points:** trumpet calls, by which a commander
issued his orders. 126. **officer:** lieutenant. 134. **coxcombs:**
heads, lit., the fool's cap. See Pl. 13c.

148. **cry:** See III.iii.120,n.
  Sc. vii: 6. **own:** i.e., soldiers. 11. **no changeling:** i.e., is
true to his nature. A changeling was a child substituted by
the fairies for one they had stolen. 13. **your particular:** as
far as concerns yourself. 22. **husbandry:** management.
23. **achieve:** win.

That which shall break his neck or hazard mine   25
Whene'er we come to our account.
    LIEU. Sir, I beseech you, think you he'll carry
      Rome?
    AUF. All places yield to him ere he sits down,°
And the nobility of Rome are his.
The Senators and patricians love him too.   30
The Tribunes are no soldiers, and their people
Will be as rash in the repeal° as hasty
To expel him thence. I think he'll be to Rome
As is the osprey to the fish,° who takes it
By sovereignty of nature.° First he was   35
A noble servant to them, but he could not
Carry his honors even.° Whether 'twas pride,
Which out of° daily fortune ever taints°
The happy° man, whether defect of judgment,
To fail in the disposing of those chances   40
Which he was lord of, or whether nature,
Not to be other than one thing, not moving
From the casque to the cushion,° but commanding
    peace
Even with the same austerity and garb°
As he controlled the war, but one of these —   45
As he hath spices° of them all, not all,
For I dare so far free him — made him feared,
So hated, and so banished. But he has a merit,
To choke it in the utterance.° So our virtues
Lie in the interpretation of the time,   50
And power, unto itself most commendable,
Hath not a tomb so evident as a chair
To extol what it hath done.°
One fire drives out one fire — one nail, one nail.
Rights by rights fouler, strengths by strengths do
    fail.   55
Come, let's away. When, Caius, Rome is thine,
Thou art poor'st of all, then shortly art thou mine.
                  [Exeunt.]

28. **sits down:** lays siege.   32. **rash . . . repeal:** hasty to call him
back.   34. **osprey . . . fish:** The osprey is a species of fish-eating
hawk.   It was believed that it so fascinated fishes that they
turned up their bellies to be more easily caught.   35. **sover-
eignty of nature:** natural superiority.   37. **even:** well balanced.
38. **out of:** in the course of. **taints:** infects.   39. **happy:** lucky.
42–43. **not . . . cushion:** not able to adjust himself from war to
peace. **casque:** helmet.   44. **austerity . . . garb:** severe behavior.
46. **spices:** flavors.   48–49. **But . . . utterance:** his merit should
have caused the sentence of banishment to be suppressed.
49–53. **So . . . done:** a difficult sentence. If the reading is correct,
the meaning appears to be: "Our good qualities depend on the
value which our contemporaries give them; and a man of power,
however worthy he may consider himself, is brought to destruc-
tion when he praises himself from his own chair of office"; i.e.,
a proud man brings ruin on himself by his pride.

Act V

SCENE I. *Rome. A public place.*

[*Enter* MENENIUS, COMINIUS, SICINIUS *and* BRUTUS,
the two TRIBUNES, *with others.*]
    MEN. No, I'll not go. You hear what he hath said
Which was sometime° his General, who loved him
In a most dear particular.° He called me father,
But what o' that? Go, you that banished him,
A mile before his tent fall down, and knee   5
The way into his mercy. Nay, if he coyed°
To hear Cominius speak, I'll keep at home.
    COM. He would not seem to know me.
    MEN.   Do you hear?
    COM. Yet one time he did call me by my name.
I urged our old acquaintance, and the drops   10
That we have bled together. Coriolanus
He would not answer to, forbade all names.
He was a kind of nothing, titleless,
Till he had forged himself a name o' the fire
Of burning Rome.
    MEN.   Why, so. You have made good work!   15
A pair of Tribunes that have racked° for Rome,
To make coals cheap. A noble memory!
    COM. I minded him how royal 'twas to pardon
When it was less expected. He replied
It was a bare petition° of a state   20
To one whom they had punished.
    MEN.   Very well.
Could he say less?
    COM. I offered° to awaken his regard
For 's private friends. His answer to me was
He could not stay to pick them in a pile   25
Of noisome musty chaff. He said 'twas folly,
For one poor grain or two, to leave unburned,
And still to nose° the offense.
    MEN.   For one poor grain or two!
I am one of those. His mother, wife, his child,
And this brave fellow too, we are the grains.   30
You are the musty chaff, and you are smelt
Above the moon. We must be burned for you.
    SIC. Nay, pray be patient. If you refuse your aid
In this so never-needed° help, yet do not
Upbraid 's with our distress. But sure, if you   35
Would be your country's pleader, your good tongue,
More than the instant army we can make,°
Might stop our countryman.
    MEN.   No, I'll not meddle.
    SIC. Pray you, go to him.
    MEN.   What should I do?

    Act V, Sc. i: 2. sometime: at one time.   3. **In . . . particular:**
in a most personal manner.   6. **coyed:** disdained.   16. **racked:**
strained, made great efforts.   20. **bare petition:** paltry request.
23. **offered:** attempted.   28. **nose:** smell.   34. **so never-needed:**
never so much needed as now.   37. **the . . . make:** the army we
can raise at short notice.

BRU. Only make trial what your love can do   40
For Rome, toward Marcius.

MEN.   Well, and say that Marcius
Return me, as Cominius is returned,
Unheard — what then?
But as a discontented friend, grief-shot°
With his unkindness? Say 't be so?

SIC.   Yet your goodwill   45
Must have that thanks from Rome after the
     measure
As you intended well.°

MEN.   I'll undertake 't.
I think he'll hear me. Yet, to bite his lip
And hum at good Cominius much unhearts° me.
He was not taken well,° he had not dined.   50
The veins unfilled, our blood is cold, and then
We pout upon the morning, are unapt
To give or to forgive. But when we have stuffed
These pipes and these conveyances of our blood
With wine and feeding, we have suppler souls   55
Than in our priestlike fasts. Therefore I'll watch
     him
Till he be dieted to my request,°
And then I'll set upon him.

BRU. You know the very road into his kindness,
And cannot lose your way.

MEN.   Good faith, I'll prove him,   60
Speed how it will.° I shall ere long have knowledge
Of my success.   [*Exit.*]

COM.   He'll never hear him.

SIC.   Not?

COM. I tell you, he does sit in gold,° his eye
Red as 'twould burn Rome, and his injury
The jailer to his pity.° I kneeled before him.   65
'Twas very faintly he said "Rise," dismissed me
Thus, with his speechless hand. What he would do,
He sent in writing after me, what he would not,
Bound with an oath to yield to his conditions.°
So that all hope is vain   70
Unless his noble mother, and his wife,
Who, as I hear, mean to solicit him
For mercy to his country. Therefore let's hence,
And with our fair entreaties haste them on.
                                          [*Exeunt.*]

---

44. grief-shot: struck by grief.   46–47. after . . . well: in pro-
portion to your efforts.   49. unhearts: disheartens.   50. not . . .
well: not approached at a good moment.   57. dieted . . . re-
quest: till his stomach be in a fit state for me to ask.   61. Speed
. . . will: whatever the result may be.   63. sit in gold: i.e., on a
gold throne like a conqueror.   64–65. his . . . pity: his sense of
anger locking up his sense of pity.   69. Bound . . . conditions: he
is bound by an oath to observe the conditions of his appointment
as General.

SCENE II. *Entrance to the Volscian camp be-
fore Rome. Two* SENTINELS *on guard.*

[*Enter to them* MENENIUS.]

1. SEN. Stay. Whence are you?

2. SEN.   Stand, and go back.

MEN. You guard like men, 'tis well. But, by your
     leave,
I am an officer of state, and come
To speak with Coriolanus.

1. SEN.   From whence?

MEN.   From Rome.

1. SEN. You may not pass, you must return. Our
     General   5
Will no more hear from thence.

2. SEN. You'll see your Rome embraced with fire
     before
You'll speak with Coriolanus.

MEN.   Good my friends,
If you have heard your General talk of Rome,
And of his friends there, it is lots to blanks°   10
My name hath touched your ears. It is Menenius.

1. SEN. Be it so, go back. The virtue° of your
     name
Is not here passable.°

MEN.   I tell thee, fellow,
Thy General is my lover. I have been
The book° of his good acts, whence men have
     read   15
His fame unparalleled haply amplified.°
For I have ever verified° my friends,
Of whom he's chief, with all the size that verity
Would without lapsing suffer. Nay, sometimes,
Like to a bowl upon a subtle° ground,   20
I have tumbled past° the throw, and in his praise
Have almost stamped the leasing.° Therefore,
     fellow,
I must have leave to pass.

1. SEN. Faith, sir, if you had told as many lies in
his behalf as you have uttered words in your own,
you should not pass here — no, though it were as
virtuous to lie as to live chastely. Therefore go
back.   28

MEN. Prithee, fellow, remember my name is
Menenius, always factionary on° the party of your
General.

2. SEN. Howsoever° you have been his liar, as you
say you have, I am one that, telling true under him,
must say you cannot pass. Therefore go back.   35

Sc. ii: 10. lots to blanks: i.e., winning tickets in a lottery
to blank tickets. In an Elizabethan lottery the chances of a
prize were about one in forty.   12. virtue: power.   13. passable:
valid to let you pass.   15. book: the record.   16. haply ampli-
fied: perchance exaggerated.   17. verified: borne witness to.
20. subtle: tricky. See App. 13.   21. tumbled past: overshot.
22. stamped . . . leasing: given the lie (*leasing*) the impression
(*stamp*) of truth.   30. factionary on: a keen supporter of.
33. Howsoever: even if you have.

MEN. Has he dined, canst thou tell? For I would not speak with him till after dinner.

1. SEN. You are a Roman, are you?

MEN. I am, as thy General is.   39

1. SEN. Then you should hate Rome, as he does. Can you, when you have pushed out your gates the very defender of them and, in a violent popular ignorance, given your enemy your shield, think to front° his revenges with the easy groans of old women, the virginal palms of your daughters,   45 or with the palsied° intercession of such a decayed dotant° as you seem to be? Can you think to blow out the intended fire your city is ready to flame in with such weak breath as this? No, you are deceived. Therefore back to Rome, and prepare for your execution. You are condemned. Our General has sworn you out° of reprieve and pardon.   54

MEN. Sirrah, if thy captain knew I were here, he would use me with estimation.°

1. SEN. Come, my captain knows you not.

MEN. I mean, thy General.   58

1. SEN. My General cares not for you. Back, I say, go, lest I let forth your half-pint of blood. — Back — that's the utmost of your having — back.

MEN. Nay, but, fellow, fellow ——

[*Enter* CORIOLANUS *and* AUFIDIUS.]

COR. What's the matter?   64

MEN. Now, you companion, I'll say an errand for° you. You shall know now that I am in estimation, you shall perceive that a Jack guardant cannot office° me from my son Coriolanus. Guess but by my entertainment with him if thou standest not i' the state of° hanging, or of some death more long in   70 spectatorship° and crueler in suffering. Behold now presently, and swoon for what's to come upon thee. The glorious gods sit in hourly synod° about thy particular° prosperity, and love thee no worse than thy old father Menenius does! O my son, my   75 son! Thou art preparing fire for us. Look thee, here's water to quench it. I was hardly° moved to come to thee, but being assured none but myself could move thee, I have been blown out of your gates with   80 sighs, and conjure thee to pardon Rome and thy petitionary° countrymen. The good gods assuage thy wrath, and turn the dregs of it upon this varlet here — this, who, like a block,° hath denied my access to thee.   85

COR. Away!

MEN. How! Away!

COR. Wife, mother, child, I know not. My affairs

Are servanted to° others. Though I owe° My revenge properly,° my remission° lies   90 In Volscian breasts. That we have been familiar, Ingrate° forgetfulness shall poison rather Than pity note how much. Therefore be gone. Mine ears against your suits are stronger than Your gates against my force. Yet, for I loved thee, Take this along — I writ it for thy sake,   96 And would have sent it. [*Gives him a letter.*] Another word, Menenius, I will not hear thee speak. This man, Aufidius, Was my beloved in Rome. Yet thou behold'st.

AUF. You keep a constant temper.   100

[*Exeunt* CORIOLANUS *and* AUFIDIUS.]

1. SEN. Now, sir, is your name Menenius?

2. SEN. 'Tis a spell, you see, of much power. You know the way home again.

1. SEN. Do you hear how we are shent° for keeping your greatness back?   105

2. SEN. What cause do you think I have to swoon?

MEN. I neither care for the world nor your General. For such things as you, I can scarce think there's any, ye're so slight.° He that hath a will to die   110 by himself fears it not from another. Let your General do his worst. For you, be that you are, long, and your misery increase with your age! I say to you, as I was said to, Away!   [*Exit.*]

1. SEN. A noble fellow, I warrant him.   115

2. SEN. The worthy fellow is our General. He's the rock, the oak not to be wind-shaken.   [*Exeunt.*]

SCENE III. *The tent of* CORIOLANUS.

[*Enter* CORIOLANUS, AUFIDIUS, *and others.*]

COR. We will before the walls of Rome tomorrow Set down our host.° My partner in this action, You must report to the Volscian lords how plainly° I have borne this business.

AUF.   Only their ends You have respected, stopped your ears against   5 The general suit° of Rome, never admitted A private whisper — no, not with such friends That thought them sure of you.

COR.   This last old man, Whom with a cracked heart I have sent to Rome, Loved me above the measure of a father —   10 Nay, godded° me indeed. Their latest refuge° Was to send him, for whose old love I have, Though I showed sourly to him, once more offered The first conditions, which they did refuse

---

44. front: confront.   46. palsied: paralyzed.   47. dotant: dodderer.   53–54. sworn . . . out: sworn not to.   56. estimation: respect.   65. say . . . for: tell a tale of.   67. Jack . . . office: Jack-in-office cannot keep.   69–70. i' . . . of: in danger of. 70–71. more . . . spectatorship: which gives the spectators a longer show.   73. synod: council.   74. particular: very own. 77. hardly: with difficulty.   82. petitionary: pleading.   84. block: block of wood, blockhead.

89. servanted to: under the orders of. owe: own.   90. properly: as my own. remission: power to forgive.   92. Ingrate: ungrateful.   104. shent: rebuked.   110. slight: hardly noticeable.   Sc. iii: 2. Set . . . host: i.e., begin the siege. Cf. I.ii.28. 3. plainly: honestly.   6. suit: petition.   11. godded: treated as a god. latest refuge: last resort.

And cannot now accept. To grace him only   15
That thought he could do more, a very little
I have yielded to. Fresh embassies and suits,
Nor from the state nor private friends, hereafter
Will I lend ear to. [*Shout within.*] Ha! What shout
     is this?
Shall I be tempted to infringe my vow   20
In the same time 'tis made? I will not.
    [*Enter, in mourning habits,* VIRGILIA, VOLUMNIA,
leading young MARCIUS, VALERIA, *and* ATTENDANTS.]
My wife comes foremost, then the honored mold
Wherein this trunk° was framed, and in her hand
The grandchild to her blood. But out, affection!
All bond and privilege of nature, break!°   25
Let it be virtuous to be obstinate.
What is that curtsy worth? Or those doves' eyes,
Which can make gods forsworn? I melt, and am not
Of stronger earth than others. My mother bows,
As if Olympus to a molehill should   30
In supplication nod. And my young boy
Hath an aspéct of intercession° which
Great Nature cries " Deny not." Let the Volsces
Plow Rome and harrow Italy. I'll never
Be such a gosling to obey instinct, but stand   35
As if a man were author° of himself
And knew no other kin.
    VIR.   My lord and husband!
    COR. These eyes are not the same I wore in Rome.
    VIR. The sorrow that delivers us thus changed
Makes you think so.
    COR.   Like a dull actor° now   40
I have forgot my part and I am out,
Even to a full disgrace. Best of my flesh,
Forgive my tyranny, but do not say,
For that "Forgive our Romans." Oh, a kiss
Long as my exile, sweet as my revenge!   45
Now, by the jealous Queen of Heaven,° that kiss
I carried from thee, dear, and my true lip
Hath virgined it° e'er since. You gods! I prate,
And the most noble mother of the world
Leave unsaluted. Sink, my knee, i' the earth,   50
                      [*Kneels.*]
Of thy deep duty more impression show
Than that of common sons.
    VOL.   Oh, stand up blest
Whilst, with no softer cushion than the flint,
I kneel before thee and unproperly
Show duty, as mistaken all this while   55
Between the child and parent.   [*Kneels.*]
    COR.   What is this?
Your knees to me? To your corrected son?
Then let the pebbles on the hungry beach

Fillip° the stars, then let the mutinous winds
Strike the proud cedars 'gainst the fiery sun,   60
Murdering impossibility,° to make
What cannot be, slight work.
    VOL.   Thou art my warrior,
I holp to frame thee. Do you know this lady?
    COR. The noble sister of Publicola,
The moon of Rome,° chaste as the icicle   65
That's curdied° by the frost from purest snow
And hangs on Dian's temple — dear Valeria!
    VOL. This is a poor epitome° of yours,
Which by the interpretation of full time°
May show like all yourself.
    COR.   The god° of soldiers,   70
With the consent of supreme Jove, inform°
Thy thoughts with nobleness, that thou mayst prove
To shame unvulnerable, and stick i' the wars
Like a great sea mark,° standing every flaw°
And saving those that eye thee!
    VOL.   Your knee, sirrah.   75
    COR. That's my brave boy!
    VOL. Even he, your wife, this lady, and myself
Are suitors to you.
    COR.   I beseech you, peace.
Or if you'd ask, remember this before.
The thing I have forsworn to° grant may never   80
Be held by you denials. Do not bid me
Dismiss my soldiers, or capitulate°
Again with Rome's mechanics. Tell me not
Wherein I seem unnatural. Desire not
To allay my rages and revenges with   85
Your colder reasons.
    VOL.   Oh, no more, no more!
You have said you will not grant us anything,
For we have nothing else to ask but that
Which you deny already. Yet we will ask,
That, if you fail in our request, the blame   90
May hang upon your hardness. Therefore hear us.
    COR. Aufidius, and you Volsces, mark, for we'll
Hear naught from Rome in private. Your request?
    VOL. Should° we be silent and not speak, our
     raiment
And state of bodies would bewray° what life   95
We have led since thy exile. Think with thyself
How more unfortunate than all living women

23. trunk: body.   25. All . . . break: break every tie and claim of my natural love for mother, wife, and son.   32. aspect of intercession: pleading look.   36. author: maker.   40. dull actor: another image taken from the playhouse. Cf. II.ii.100, and Sonnet 23, 1–2.   46. Queen of Heaven: Juno.   48. virgined it: kept it chaste.   59. Fillip: flip, dash against.   61. Murdering impossibility: i.e., make impossible events happen; no disaster can seem impossible when his mother, whom he had worshiped, kneels to him. 65. moon of Rome: i.e., the very goddess of chastity, for Diana was worshiped as the moon.   66. curdied: curdled.   68. epitome: shorter edition. Here Volumnia takes Coriolanus' son by the hand.   69. interpretation . . . time: when time shall have fully interpreted him, keeping up the image of "epitome."   70. The god: i.e., may the god.   71. inform: form, make.   74. sea mark: a conspicuous landmark seen from the sea which enables a navigator to check his position. flaw: gust of wind.   80. forsworn to: sworn not to.   82. capitulate: agree to conditions of surrender. 94–191. Should . . . peace: See *Cor* Intro. p. 911b for the original of this speech.   95. bewray: betray, reveal.

Are we come hither. Since that thy sight, which
    should
Make our eyes flow with joy, hearts dance with
    comforts,
Constrains them weep and shake with fear and sor-
    row,   100
Making the mother, wife, and child to see
The son, the husband, and the father tearing
His country's bowels out. And to poor we
Thine enmity's most capital.° Thou barr'st us
Our prayers to the gods, which is a comfort   105
That all but we enjoy. For how can we,
Alas! how can we for our country pray,
Whereto we are bound, together with thy victory,
Whereto we are bound? Alack, or we must lose
The country, our dear nurse, or else thy person, 110
Our comfort in the country. We must find
An evident° calamity, though we had
Our wish, which side should win. For either thou
Must, as a foreign recreant,° be led
With manacles thorough our streets, or else   115
Triumphantly tread on thy country's ruin,
And bear the palm° for having bravely shed
Thy wife and children's blood. For myself, son,
I purpose not to wait on fortune till
These wars determine.° If I cannot persuade thee
Rather to show a noble grace to both parts°   121
Than seek the end of one, thou shalt no sooner
March to assault thy country than to tread —
Trust to 't, thou shalt not — on thy mother's womb
That brought thee to this world.

    VIR.   Aye, and mine, 125
That brought you forth this boy, to keep your name
Living to time.

    BOY.   A' shall not tread on me.
I'll run away till I am bigger, but then I'll fight.

    COR. Not of a woman's tenderness to be
Requires nor child nor woman's face to see.° 130
I have sat too long.   [*Rising.*]

    VOL.   Nay, go not from us thus.
If it were so that our request did tend
To save the Romans, thereby to destroy
The Volsces whom you serve, you might condemn
    us
As poisonous of your honor. No, our suit   135
Is that you reconcile them. While the Volsces
May say " This mercy we have showed," the Ro-
    mans,
" This we received," and each in either side
Give the all-hail° to thee, and cry " Be blest
For making up this peace! " Thou know'st, great
    son,   140

The end of war's uncertain, but this certain,
That if thou conquer Rome, the benefit
Which thou shalt thereby reap is such a name
Whose repetition will be dogged with curses,
Whose chronicle thus writ: " The man was noble,
But with his last attempt he wiped it out,   146
Destroyed his country, and his name remains
To the ensuing age abhorred." Speak to me, son.
Thou hast affected° the fine strains° of honor,
To imitate the graces of the gods,   150
To tear with thunder the wide cheeks o' the air,
And yet to charge thy sulphur with a bolt
That should but rive an oak.° Why dost not speak?
Think'st thou it honorable for a noble man   154
Still to remember wrongs? Daughter, speak you.
He cares not for your weeping. Speak thou, boy.
Perhaps thy childishness will move him more
Than can our reasons. There's no man in the world
More bound to 's mother, yet here he lets me prate
Like one i' the stocks.° Thou hast never in thy life
Showed thy dear mother any courtesy,   161
When she, poor hen, fond of no second brood,
Has clucked thee to the wars and safely home,
Loaden° with honor. Say my request's unjust,
And spurn me back. But if it be not so,   165
Thou art not honest, and the gods will plague thee,
That thou restrain'st from me the duty which
To a mother's part belongs. He turns away.
Down, ladies, let us shame him with our knees.
To his surname Coriolanus 'longs° more pride 170
Than pity to our prayers. Down — an end,
This is the last. So we will home to Rome,
And die among our neighbors. Nay, behold 's.
This boy, that cannot tell what he would have,
But kneels and holds up hands for fellowship,° 175
Does reason° our petition with more strength
Than thou hast to deny 't. Come, let us go.
This fellow had a Volscian to his mother,
His wife is in Corioli, and his child
Like him by chance. Yet give us our dispatch.° 180
I am hushed until our city be afire,
And then I'll speak a little.

    COR. [*After holding her by the hand, silent*] O
        Mother, Mother!
What have you done? Behold, the Heavens do ope,
The gods look down, and this unnatural scene
They laugh at. O my mother, Mother! Oh!   185
You have won a happy victory to Rome,
But, for your son, believe it, oh, believe it,
Most dangerously you have with him prevailed,
If not most mortal° to him. But let it come.

---

104. **capital:** deadly.   112. **evident:** manifest.   114. **recreant:**
traitor.   117. **bear ... palm:** receive the palm of victory.
120. **determine:** end.   121. **parts:** sides.   129–30. **Not ... see:**
unless a man is to become as tender as a woman, he must not look
at his child or his wife.   139. **all-hail:** the salutation given to
kings. Cf. *Rich II*, IV.i.167–69; *Macb*, I.v.56.

149. **affected:** loved. **strains:** instincts.   151–53. **To ... oak:** to
make a noise that would split the air and yet to load your gun-
powder with a cannon ball which would only split an oak.
160. **one ... stocks:** i.e., a railing vagabond. See App. 10.
164. **Loaden:** laden.   170. **'longs:** belongs.   175. **fellowship:**
partnership, friendship.   176. **reason:** argue.   180. **dispatch:**
dismissal.   189. **mortal:** mortally.

Aufidius, though I cannot make true wars,   190
I'll frame convenient° peace. Now, good Aufidius,
Were you in my stead, would you have heard
A mother less? Or granted less, Aufidius?

AUF. I was moved withal.

COR.   I dare be sworn you were.
And, sir, it is no little thing to make   195
Mine eyes to sweat compassion. But, good sir,
What peace you'll make, advise me. For my part,
I'll not to Rome, I'll back with you, and pray you,
Stand to me° in this cause. O Mother! Wife!

AUF. [*Aside*] I am glad thou hast set thy mercy
     and thy honor   200
At difference in thee. Out of that I'll work
Myself a former fortune.°

       [*The* LADIES *make signs to* CORIOLANUS.]

COR. [*To* VOLUMNIA, VIRGILIA, *etc.*] Aye, by and
by —
But we will drink together, and you shall bear
A better witness back than words, which we
On like conditions will have countersealed.°   205
Come, enter with us. Ladies, you deserve
To have a temple built you. All the swords
In Italy, and her confederate arms,
Could not have made this peace.   [*Exeunt.*]

SCENE IV. *Rome. A public place.*

[*Enter* MENENIUS *and* SICINIUS.]

MEN. See you yond coign° o' the Capitol, yond
cornerstone?

SIC. Why, what of that?

MEN. If it be possible for you to displace it with
your little finger, there is some hope the ladies of   5
Rome, especially his mother, may prevail with him.
But I say there is no hope in 't. Our throats are sen-
tenced, and stay upon° execution.

SIC. Is 't possible that so short a time can alter the
condition of a man?   10

MEN. There is differency between a grub and a
butterfly, yet your butterfly was a grub. This Marcius
is grown from man to dragon. He has wings, he's
more than a creeping thing.

SIC. He loved his mother dearly.   15

MEN. So did he me. And he no more remembers
his mother now than an eight-year-old horse. The
tartness of his face sours ripe grapes. When he
walks, he moves like an engine,° and the ground
shrinks before his treading. He is able to pierce a

corslet° with his eye, talks like a knell, and his hum°
is a battery. He sits in his state° as a thing made for
Alexander.° What he bids be done is finished with
his bidding.° He wants nothing of a god but eternity
and a Heaven to throne in.   26

SIC. Yes, mercy, if you report him truly.

MEN. I paint him in the character.° Mark what
mercy his mother shall bring from him. There is no
more mercy in him than there is milk in a male tiger
— that shall our poor city find. And all this is long
of° you.   32

SIC. The gods be good unto us!

MEN. No, in such a case the gods will not be good
unto us. When we banished him, we respected not
them, and he returning to break our necks, they re-
spect not us.   37

[*Enter a* MESSENGER.]

MESS. Sir, if you'd save your life, fly to your house.
The plebeians have got your fellow Tribune
And hale° him up and down, all swearing if   40
The Roman ladies bring not comfort home,
They'll give him death by inches.

[*Enter another* MESSENGER.]

SIC.   What's the news?

2. MESS. Good news, good news. The ladies have
     prevailed,
The Volscians are dislodged,° and Marcius gone.
A merrier day did never yet greet Rome —   45
No, not the expulsion of the Tarquins.

SIC.   Friend,
Art thou certain this is true? Is it most certain?

2. MESS. As certain as I know the sun is fire.
Where have you lurked° that you make doubt of it?
Ne'er through an arch so hurried the blown tide°
As the recomforted through the gates. Why, hark
     you!   51

[*Trumpets, hautboys, drums beat, all together.*]
The trumpets, sackbuts,° psalteries,° and fifes,
Tabors° and cymbals and the shouting Romans,
Make the sun dance. Hark you!   [*A shout within.*]

MEN.   This is good news.
I will go meet the ladies. This Volumnia   55
Is worth of Consuls, Senators, patricians,
A cityful, of Tribunes, such as you,
A sea and land full. You have prayed well today.
This morning for ten thousand of your throats
I'd not have given a doit. Hark how they joy!   60

[*Music still, with shouts.*]

191. convenient: suitable.   199. Stand to me: support me.
201–02. I'll . . . fortune: I will restore my own fortunes to what
they were.   203–05. you . . . countersealed: you shall take back
not only an oral promise but a written and sealed agreement.

Sc. iv: 1. coign: corner.   8. stay upon: wait for.   19. engine:
battering-ram, a heavy, lumbering machine.

21. corslet: breastplate. hum: grunt.   22. state: chair of state.
22–23. thing . . . Alexander: like a statue of Alexander the Great.
24–25. What . . . bidding: his orders are carried out by the time
he has finished giving them.   28. in . . . character: in his true
character.   31–32. long of: because of.   40. hale: haul.   44. are
dislodged: have abandoned the siege.   49. lurked: been hiding.
50. Ne'er . . . tide: This image is taken from the rush of waters
between the arches of London Bridge. See Gen. Intro. p. 16b.
52. sackbut: a form of trombone. psalteries: stringed instru-
ments played with both hands.   53. Tabors: drums.

SIC. First, the gods bless you for your tidings.
    Next,
Accept my thankfulness.
    2. MESS.   Sir, we have all
Great cause to give great thanks.
    SIC.   They are near the city?
    2. MESS. Almost at point to enter.
    SIC.   We will meet them,   64
And help the joy.   [*Exeunt.*]

SCENE V. *The same. A street near the gate.*

[*Enter two* SENATORS *with* VOLUMNIA, VIRGILIA,
VALERIA, *etc., passing over the stage, followed
by* PATRICIANS *and others.*]

    1. SEN. Behold our patroness, the life of Rome!
Call all your tribes together, praise the gods,
And make triumphant fires,° strew flowers before
    them.
Unshout the noise° that banished Marcius,
Repeal him with the welcome of his mother,   5
Cry " Welcome, ladies, welcome! "
    ALL.   Welcome, ladies,
Welcome!
    [*A flourish with drums and trumpets. Exeunt.*]

SCENE VI. *Corioli. A public place.*

[*Enter* TULLUS AUFIDIUS, *with* ATTENDANTS.]

    AUF. Go tell the lords o' the city I am here.
Deliver them this paper. Having read it,
Bid them repair to the market place, where I,
Even in theirs and in the commons' ears,
Will vouch the truth of it. Him I accuse   5
The city ports° by this hath entered, and
Intends to appear before the people, hoping
To purge° himself with words. Dispatch.
                          [*Exeunt* ATTENDANTS.]
[*Enter three or four* CONSPIRATORS *of* AUFIDIUS'
                    faction.]
Most welcome!
    1. CON.   How is it with our General?
    AUF.   Even so   10
As with a man by his own alms empoisoned,
And with his charity slain.
    2. CON.   Most noble sir,
If you do hold the same intent wherein
You wished us parties, we'll deliver you
Of your great danger.
    AUF.   Sir, I cannot tell.   15
We must proceed as we do find the people.

    3. CON. The people will remain uncertain whilst
'Twixt you there's difference, but the fall of either
Makes the survivor heir of all.
    AUF.   I know it,
And my pretext to strike at him admits   20
A good construction. I raised him, and I pawned
Mine honor for his truth. Who being so heightened,
He watered his new plants with dews of flattery,
Seducing so my friends. And, to this end,
He bowed° his nature, never known before   25
But to be rough, unswayable, and free.
    3. CON. Sir, his stoutness
When he did stand for Consul, which he lost
By lacking of stooping ——
    AUF.   That I would have spoke of.
Being banished for 't, he came unto my hearth,   30
Presented to my knife his throat. I took him,
Made him joint servant with me, gave him way
In all his own desires — nay, let him choose
Out of my files,° his projects to accomplish,
My best and freshest men, served his designments°
In mine own person, holp to reap the fame   36
Which he did end all his,° and took some pride
To do myself this wrong. Till at the last
I seemed his follower, not partner, and
He waged me with his countenance, as if   40
I had been mercenary.°
    1. CON.   So he did, my lord.
The army marveled at it, and in the last,
When he had carried Rome and that we looked
For no less spoil than glory ——
    AUF.   There was it
For which my sinews° shall be stretched upon him.
At a few drops of women's rheum,° which are   46
As cheap as lies, he sold the blood and labor
Of our great action. Therefore shall he die,
And I'll renew me in his fall. But hark!
[*Drums and trumpets sound, with great shouts of
                the people.*]
    1. CON. Your native town you entered like a post,°
And had no welcomes home, but he returns,   51
Splitting the air with noise.
    2. CON.   And patient fools,
Whose children he hath slain, their base throats tear
With giving him glory.
    3. CON.   Therefore, at your vantage,°
Ere he express himself, or move the people   55
With what he would say, let him feel your sword,
Which we will second. When he lies along,°
After your way his tale pronounced shall bury
His reasons with his body.

---

25. **bowed:** forced.   34. **files:** ranks.   35. **designments:** de-
signs.   36–37. **holp . . . his:** helped to reap the crop of his fame,
which he gathered up as all his own.   40–41. **waged . . . mer-
cenary:** gave me patronizing looks, as if I had been his hired man.
45. **sinews:** strength.   46. **rheum:** moisture, tears.   50. **post:**
a postboy, whom no one notices.   54. **at . . . vantage:** take your
opportunity.   57. **along:** stretched out.

Sc. v: 3. **triumphant fires:** bonfires of joy.   4. **Unshout . . .
noise:** i.e., reverse your decision.
    Sc. vi: 6. **ports:** gates.   8. **purge:** clear.

AUF.   Say no more.
Here come the lords.   60
        [*Enter the* LORDS *of the city.*]
LORDS. You are most welcome home.
    AUF.   I have not deserved it.
But, worthy lords, have you with heed perused
What I have written to you?
    LORDS.   We have.
    I. LORD.   And grieve to hear 't.
What faults he made before the last, I think
Might have found easy fines.° But there to end   65
Where he was to begin, and give away
The benefit of our levies, answering us
With our own charge,° making a treaty where
There was a yielding — this admits no excuse.
    AUF. He approaches. You shall hear him.   70
[*Enter* CORIOLANUS, *marching with drum and colors,
        the commoners being with him.*]
    COR. Hail, lords! I am returned your soldier,
No more infected with my country's love
Than when I parted hence, but still subsisting°
Under your great command. You are to know
That prosperously I have attempted, and   75
With bloody passage led your wars even to
The gates of Rome. Our spoils we have brought
        home
Do more than counterpoise° a full third part
The charges of the action. We have made peace,
With no less honor to the Antiates   80
Than shame to the Romans. And we here deliver,
Subscribed° by the Consuls and patricians,
Together with the seal o' the Senate, what
We have compounded° on.
    AUF.   Read it not, noble lords,
But tell the traitor,° in the highest degree   85
He hath abused your powers.
    COR. Traitor! How now!
    AUF.   Aye, traitor, Marcius!
    COR.   Marcius!
    AUF. Aye, Marcius, Caius Marcius. Dost thou
        think
I'll grace thee with that robbery, thy stol'n name
Coriolanus, in Corioli?   90
You lords and heads o' the state, perfidiously
He has betrayed your business, and given up,
For certain drops of salt, your city Rome —
I say " your city " — to his wife and mother,

Breaking his oath and resolution like   95
A twist° of rotten silk, never admitting
Council o' the war,° but at his nurse's tears
He whined and roared away your victory,
That pages blushed at him, and men of heart
Looked wondering each at other.
    COR.   Hear'st thou, Mars?   100
    AUF. Name not the god, thou boy of tears!°
    COR.   Ha!
    AUF. No more.
    COR. Measureless liar, thou hast made my heart
Too great for what contains it. " Boy! " O slave!
Pardon me, lords, 'tis the first time that ever   105
I was forced to scold. Your judgments, my grave
        lords,
Must give this cur the lie. And his own notion° —
Who wears my stripes impressed upon him, that
Must bear my beating to his grave — shall join
To thrust the lie unto him.   110
    I. LORD. Peace, both, and hear me speak.
    COR. Cut me to pieces, Volsces, men and lads,
Stain all your edges° on me. " Boy! " False hound!
If you have writ your annals true,° 'tis there
That, like an eagle in a dovecote, I   115
Fluttered your Volscians in Corioli.
Alone I did it. " Boy! "
    AUF.   Why, noble lords,
Will you be put in mind of his blind fortune,°
Which was your shame, by this unholy braggart
'Fore your own eyes and ears?
    ALL CONS.   Let him die for 't.   120
    ALL THE PEOPLE. Tear him to pieces. — Do it pres-
ently. — He killed my son. — My daughter. — He
killed my cousin Marcus. — He killed my father.
    2. LORD. Peace, ho! No outrage. Peace!   125
The man is noble, and his fame folds in
This orb o' the earth.° His last offenses to us
Shall have judicious° hearing. Stand, Aufidius,
And trouble not the peace.
    COR.   Oh, that I had him,
With six Aufidiuses, or more, his tribe,   130
To use my lawful sword!
    AUF.   Insolent villain!
    ALL CONS. Kill, kill, kill, kill, kill him!
        [*The* CONSPIRATORS *draw, and kill* CORIOLANUS.
                AUFIDIUS *stands on his body.*]
    LORDS.   Hold, hold, hold, hold!
    AUF. My noble masters, hear me speak.

---

65. fines: penalties.   66–68. give . . . charge: give away the
profitable spoils which should have been taken, and leave us to
pay for the wars ourselves. In Shakespeare's time, when the doc-
trine of total war had not yet been established, the winning side
expected to make a profit out of the plunder brought home.
Coriolanus admits (ll. 76–78) that the spoils have only paid for
about a third of the expenses.   73. subsisting: continuing.
78. counterpoise: counterbalance.   82. Subscribed: signed.
84. compounded: agreed.   85. traitor: As before, the accusation
that he is a traitor moves Coriolanus to ungovernable fury. Cf.
III.iii.66.

96. twist: skein.   96–97. never . . . war: never asking the ad-
vice of his council of war. (It was normal for a commander's
commission to include a clause that in all major decisions he
should consult his council of war, composed of senior commanders.)
101. boy of tears: crybaby. To call a man a "boy" was a gross
and deliberate insult. Cf. *R & J*, III.i.69; *M Ado*, V.i.83–85.
107. notion: sense.   113. edges: i.e., swords.   114. If . . . true:
if your history books tell the truth.   118. blind fortune: lucky
success.   126–27. folds . . . earth: is universal.   128. judi-
cious: judicial; i.e., in a court of law.

1. LORD.   O Tullus——
2. LORD. Thou hast done a deed whereat valor will
weep.
3. LORD. Tread not upon him. Masters all, be
quiet.   135
Put up your swords.
AUF. My lords, when you shall know — as in this
rage
Provoked by him, you cannot — the great danger
Which this man's life did owe you,° you'll rejoice
That he is thus cut off. Please it your Honors   140
To call me to your Senate, I'll deliver°
Myself your loyal servant, or endure
Your heaviest censure.°
1. LORD.   Bear from hence his body,
And mourn you for him. Let him be regarded

138–39. the . . . you: the great danger you were in so long as this
man was alive.   141. deliver: submit.   143. censure: condem-
nation.

As the most noble corse° that ever herald°   145
Did follow to his urn.°
2. LORD.   His own impatience
Takes from Aufidius a great part of blame.
Let's make the best of it.
AUF.   My rage is gone,
And I am struck with sorrow. Take him up.
Help, three o' the chiefest soldiers, I'll be one.   150
Beat thou the drum, that it speak mournfully.
Trail your steel pikes.° Though in this city he
Hath widowed and unchilded many a one
Which to this hour bewail the injury,
Yet he shall have a noble memory.   155
Assist.   [*Exeunt, bearing the body of* CORIOLANUS.
                    A dead march sounded.]

145. corse: corpse. herald: See App. 9.   146. urn: tomb.
152. Trail . . . pikes: At military funerals the pikemen marched
in the procession with pikes trailed and reversed. See Pl. 9a.

THE WINTER'S TALE

Introduction

The Winter's Tale is one of the last of Shake-speare's plays. It was probably written in 1610 or 1611. Dr. Simon Forman, a well-known astrologer of the time, described a performance which he had seen at the Globe on May 15, 1611.[1] Forman's note runs as follows:

In *The Winter's Tale* at the Globe, 1611, the 15 of May (Wednesday),

Observe there how Leontes, the King of Sicilia, was overcome with jealousy of his wife with the King of Bohemia, his friend, that came to see him; and how he contrived his death and would have had his cup bearer to have poisoned; who gave the King of Bohemia warning thereof and fled with him to Bohemia.

Remember also how he sent to the Oracle of Apollo and the answer of Apollo, that she was guiltless and that the king was jealous etc.; and how except the child was found again that was lost, the king should die without issue; for the child was carried into Bohemia and there laid in a forest and brought up by a shepherd; and the King of Bohemia's son married that wench; and how they fled into Sicilia to Leontes; and the shepherd having showed the letter of the nobleman by whom Leontes sent away that child and the jewels found about her, she was known to be Leontes' daughter, and was then sixteen years old.

Remember also the rogue that came in all tattered like coll pixie [a mischievous fairy], and how he feigned him sick and to have been robbed of all that he had; and how he cozened the poor man of all his money; and after came to the sheep shear with a peddler's pack and there cozened them again of all their money; and how he changed apparel with the King of Bohemia's son; and then how he turned courtier etc. Beware of trusting feigned beggars or fawning fellows.

There are records in the Revels Accounts that the play was acted at Court by the King's Players on November 5, 1611, and again in February 1613 during the festivities to celebrate the marriage of Princess Elizabeth, daughter of King James I, to the Elector Palatine.

The play was first printed in the first folio (F1) in 1623. The original text was probably set up from a copy of the play made by a profes-sional scribe. There are few difficulties except that in the F1 text the characters who are to appear are gathered at the head of each scene, in imitation of the manner used in printing classical plays, and most of the entrances and exits have been omitted.

The source of the play is one of Robert Greene's most popular novels, *Pandosto: The Triumph of Time* (see Gen. Intro. p. 37b). It was published in 1588 and reprinted in 1592, 1595, and 1607. Shakespeare took most of his incidents from the novel, but he used his material freely. The outline of the story runs as follows:

Pandosto, King of Bohemia, is happily married to Bellaria. They have one child, a boy called Garinter. Egistus, King of Sicilia, who had been brought up with Pandosto, comes to visit them with a great train of followers. He is treated with great courtesy and hospitality, and Bellaria especially is so attentive to her husband's old friend that they frequently walk together in the garden " where they two in private and pleasant devices would pass away the time to both their contents."

After a while Pandosto begins to suffer from melancholy. He grows suspicious of his wife and at length so insanely jealous that he orders Franion, his cupbearer, to poison Egistus. Franion reveals the command to Egistus, and the two, together with Egistus' followers, sail away to Sicilia. Pandosto is so angry at being thus outwitted that he causes his wife to be imprisoned and issues a public proclamation that she has committed adultery with Egistus and has plotted to murder him. In prison Bellaria gives birth to a daughter. Pandosto's first inclination is to cause both wife and daughter to be burned, but his nobles protest and he yields so far as to grant that the babe shall be abandoned in a cockboat in the open sea.

Pandosto next assembles his courtiers and accuses Bellaria in open court. She answers his accusation boldly and demands that evidence shall be produced. This increases Pandosto's anger, but he yields to her plea to send to the Isle of Delphos to inquire of the Oracle of Apollo. When the sealed answer of the god has been brought back, the Queen is publicly indicted. Then the oracle is opened and read out:

SUSPICION IS NO PROOF: JEALOUSY IS AN UNEQUAL JUDGE: BELLARIA IS CHASTE: EGISTUS BLAMELESS:

---

[1] E. K. Chambers, *William Shakespeare*, ii, 340.

FRANION A TRUE SUBJECT: PANDOSTO JEALOUS: HIS
BABE AN INNOCENT: AND THE KING SHALL LIVE WITH-
OUT AN HEIR IF THAT WHICH IS LOST BE NOT FOUND.

The King is immediately convinced of his error,
and so overcome by remorse that he begs his nobles
to ask Bellaria to forgive him; but at that moment
news comes that the boy Garinter has died sud-
denly. At this shock, Bellaria falls down dead
and Pandosto can hardly be prevented from kill-
ing himself. He orders that the bodies of his wife
and son be buried in a rich sepulcher, whither
once a day he will repair to bewail his misfor-
tune.

Meanwhile the boat carrying Pandosto's daugh-
ter has drifted ashore on the coast of Sicilia. The
babe, who is almost dead from hunger and cold, is
discovered by a poor shepherd called Porrus; she is
wrapped in a mantle of scarlet richly embroidered
with gold, with a gold chain about her neck. Porrus
takes her home to his wife, and since they are child-
less, they decide to bring her up as their own. The
child is named Fawnia and grows up to be a girl
of surpassing beauty and excellent intelligence.
Meanwhile Egistus' only son, Prince Dorastus, has
grown into manhood, but he refuses his father's ur-
gent command that he should take a wife. Soon
afterward, while out hawking, he comes upon
Fawnia, and immediately they fall in love with
each other. They meet again, but Fawnia, who has
realized that her lover is the Prince, declares that
she will receive him only as a shepherd. So Doras-
tus disguises himself as a shepherd and comes to
woo her. They plight troth, but as Dorastus knows
that his father will never consent to the marriage,
he collects money and jewels so that they may run
away and live in Italy until the King is either dead
or reconciled.

The love of Fawnia for Dorastus is observed by
the old shepherd and his wife, who are greatly
troubled. Porrus decides to go to Court, taking the
mantle with him that he may show the King how
Fawnia was found. Meanwhile, Dorastus confides
in his old servant Capnio, and then on the ap-
pointed day he fetches Fawnia and they board a
ship bound for Italy. Meanwhile Capnio has en-
countered Porrus on his way to the palace. Realiz-
ing that if Porrus is allowed to tell his tale all will
be revealed, Capnio causes the old shepherd to be
taken forcibly on board.

The ship puts out to sea, but is turned out of her
course by a violent storm and enters a harbor in
Bohemia. By Capnio's advice, Dorastus changes his
name to Meleagrus, and conceals his identity. The
report of Fawnia's beauty is soon carried to the
Court, whither the lovers are summoned. King
Pandosto immediately falls in love with the beauti-
ful girl, and that he may woo her for himself, he

sends Dorastus and Capnio to prison. Fawnia re-
jects his advances with scorn.

By this time Egistus has heard the story and has
guessed the identity of "Meleagrus." He sails to
Bohemia, where he and his old friend King Pan-
dosto are reconciled. Then he asks that Prince Do-
rastus be released and that Capnio, Porrus, and
Fawnia be executed. When the offenders are
brought forth, old Porrus is at last able to tell his
story. Pandosto recognizes his daughter, and the
young lovers are married; but soon afterward Pan-
dosto again falls into melancholy and is so over-
come with remorse at his conduct toward his wife
and daughter that he kills himself.

In writing *The Winter's Tale* Shakespeare
took over the main details of the story, but he
invented many situations and all the dialogue,
except for an occasional phrase. He changed the
names of the characters and he added Paulina,
Antigonus, and the young shepherd. The most
important change, however, was in the ending.
He brings Hermione back to life after sixteen
years and he spares Leontes. Shakespeare also
invented Autolycus, though he adopted some of
the rascal's tricks from the *Conny-catching* pam-
phlets in which Greene had described the ways
of the professional rogues about London. The
incident where Autolycus picks the pocket of
the Clown (IV.iv) had already been described
in the *Second and Last Part of Conny-catching*
as "A kind conceit of a foist [pickpocket] per-
formed in Paul's."

There walked in the middle walk a plain country
farmer, a man of good wealth, who had a well-lined
purse only barely thrust up in a round slop; which
a crew of foists having perceived, their hearts were
set on fire to have it, and everyone had a fling at
him, but all in vain, for he kept his hand close in
his pocket, and his purse fast in his fist like a subtle
churl that either had been forewarned of Paul's, or
else had aforetime smoked some of that faculty.
Well, howsoever, it was impossible to do any good
with him, he was so wary. The foists, spying this,
strained their wits to the highest string how to
compass this bung; yet could not all their politic
conceits fetch the farmer over, for jostle him, chat
with him, offer to shake him by the hand — all
would not serve to get his hand out of his pocket.

At last one of the crew that for his skill might
have been doctorate in his mystery amongst them
all chose out a good foist, one of a nimble hand and
great agility, and said to the rest thus: "Masters,
it shall not be said such a base peasant shall slip
away from such a crew of gentlemen foists as we

are and not have his purse drawn; and therefore this time I'll play the stall myself, and if I hit him not home, count me for a bungler forever." And so left them, and went to the farmer and walked directly before him and next him three or four turns. At last, standing still, he cried out, " Alas, honest man, help me, I am not well." And with that sunk down suddenly in a sown [swoon]. The poor farmer, seeing a proper young gentleman (as he thought) fall dead afore him, stepped to him, held him in his arms, rubbed him and chafed him. At this there gathered a great multitude of people about him, and the whilst the foist drew the farmer's purse and away. By that the other thought the feat was done, he began to come something to himself again, and so, half-staggering, stumbled out of Paul's and went after the crew where they had appointed to meet, and there boasted of his wit and experience.

The Winter's Tale is a better play to see on the stage than to read. It is full of good theater, though critics have from time to time found blemishes in its construction. As with *Pericles, Cymbeline,* and *The Tempest,* the theme of the play is reconciliation. Wrongs committed by one generation are reconciled in the children. Such a theme requires the passage of many years. Shakespeare therefore divided the play into two parts, the first showing how Leontes unjustly accused his wife Hermione, the second how the daughter whom he supposed to have been lost was miraculously restored, and how Hermione came back to life.

The story is frankly " a winter's tale " — and " A sad tale's best for winter " — in which no one expects any probability. Nevertheless, to make the story plausible, the original motives for Leontes' jealousy must be credible. Shakespeare is sometimes criticized because Leontes' jealousy bursts forth without any apparent cause. Nevertheless, there are some warning signs before the explosion. Leontes is an obstinate man. He will not listen to Polixenes' very reasonable desire to go home. He is piqued by Polixenes' refusal to stay, and is ready to think unreasonably of him. When Hermione succeeds almost at once in making Polixenes change his mind, the sudden thought comes to Leontes that there must be something between them, and in a moment he is on the verge of what Elizabethans called " horn madness." The jealous husband is a common butt in comedies and farces, in which exact truth to life is not to be expected. In *The*

Winter's Tale Shakespeare treats jealousy tragically, and to be satisfactory it must also be convincing. To appreciate Leontes' outburst, we must look not only at Leontes, but at what Leontes sees, and with his distorted vision (I.i. 108). The success of this scene depends therefore on the acting of Hermione, whose natural and innocent friendliness must be so presented that it might conceivably give some cause for suspicion to a diseased mind.

The curse of jealousy is that it breeds from suspicion. Once started, any little incident becomes strong proof. Moreover, in drama there must always be contraction of time. In a novel, or in reality, jealousy may be fed by a succession of incidents gradually accumulating day after day. In a play, all these must be compressed within a few scenes.

Leontes' character is well brought out in the opening scene. He is an obstinate and immature person, and therefore the more opposition he meets, the stronger his obstinacy becomes. He has also an inordinate fear of ridicule and gossip. Leontes thus works himself into an unreasoning passion of jealousy, and the moment he has revealed his fantastic suspicion to Camillo, he is caught in his own foolishness. He knows that there is neither proof nor evidence, though his mind is so unbalanced that he would not listen if there were. When he cannot persuade any of his followers to believe his accusations, he gambles wildly and appeals to the oracle of the god.

The oracle of Apollo is the axle on which this play turns. Here too stage presentation is needed, for in the acting the oracle must be treated with all the marks of reverence and religious awe. When the sealed judgment of the oracle has been brought back, Hermione is indicted. It is an excellent trial scene, and full of excitement. Once Hermione is allowed to defend herself, she answers the charge with such impressive dignity that Leontes quickly becomes the defendant in his own action. She too appeals to the oracle. The judgment of the oracle is opened, and Hermione is decisively vindicated. Leontes has appealed to Divine judgment. Now he spurns the verdict, and is at once the victim of Divine wrath. The sudden contrasts of this scene, the noise of Leontes' fury, the horrified silence of his Court, broken by the hurried footsteps of the distressed messenger, are magnificently dramatic. The scene ends with Leontes contrite, and Hermione apparently dead.

When the play is dissected in the study, it becomes a little difficult to explain, or to believe in, Paulina's action. How or why did she keep Hermione concealed for sixteen years? "How" is not easily explained, but after all this is a "winter's tale." "Why" is clear. Paulina and all have seen that the god Apollo is now controlling the fate of Sicilia. He has vindicated Hermione, but he has also said that the King shall live without an heir until that which is lost is found. Leontes must therefore be kept away from Hermione at all costs. Paulina acts for the best as she sees it.

The third scene in Act III is a link scene between the two parts of the play. There Shakespeare shows us that the babe Perdita is saved. This is his normal method of telling a story; [2] he does not keep back such essential information in order that he may end his play with a surprise in the last scene. He does, however, deliberately try to persuade us that Hermione is dead.

The interval between the two parts of the play is bridged by the appearance of Time to announce the passing of sixteen years. The story then continues at the sheepshearing feast, when young Prince Florizel and Perdita, the natural

² See *M. Ado* Intro. p. 419b.

Queen of the shepherds, fall in love. Florizel is a young man of considerable personality, who will brave his father and sacrifice a kingdom for his love. The plot now moves very quickly. On Camillo's advice, Florizel and Perdita run away to Sicilia, where they are received by Leontes; but almost at once Polixenes arrives in hot pursuit, and at last the truth is revealed.

Shakespeare has been much criticized because he did not present in the action either the meeting between Polixenes and Leontes, or the scene where the old shepherd produces the proof of Perdita's birth, or the recognition of Perdita by her father. In this matter Shakespeare's judgment was better than that of his critics. Had these three powerful and emotional episodes been shown, the final squaring-up would inevitably have been prolonged, and the emotions of the audience would have been exhausted before the end. The ending of the play is not Leontes' discovery of his daughter, nor his reconciliation with his wife, nor the vindication of Hermione, but the reunion of mother and daughter. Hermione has been wronged. The last scene is hers. Her existence has been carefully concealed from everyone until suddenly she comes to life. This scene also needs the living actor. In the reading it is fantastic. When well acted on the stage, it is most pathetic and moving.

The Winter's Tale

DRAMATIS PERSONAE

LEONTES, *King of Sicilia*
MAMILLIUS, *young Prince of Sicilia*
CAMILLO
ANTIGONUS
CLEOMENES } *four lords of Sicilia*
DION
POLIXENES, *King of Bohemia*
FLORIZEL, *Prince of Bohemia*
ARCHIDAMUS, *a lord of Bohemia*
OLD SHEPHERD, *reputed father of Perdita*
CLOWN, *his son*
AUTOLYCUS, *a rogue*
A MARINER

A JAILER
HERMIONE, *Queen to Leontes*
PERDITA, *daughter to Leontes and Hermione*
PAULINA, *wife to Antigonus*
EMILIA, *a lady attending on Hermione*
MOPSA
DORCAS } *shepherdesses*

Other LORDS *and* GENTLEMEN, LADIES, OFFICERS *and* SERVANTS, SHEPHERDS, *and* SHEPHERDESSES.

TIME, *as Chorus*

SCENE — *Partly in Sicilia, and partly in Bohemia.*

Act I

SCENE I. *Antechamber in* LEONTES' *palace.*

[*Enter* CAMILLO *and* ARCHIDAMUS.]

ARC. If you shall chance, Camillo, to visit Bohemia on the like occasion whereon my services are now on foot,° you shall see, as I have said, great difference betwixt our Bohemia and your Sicilia.   5

CAM. I think this coming summer the King of Sicilia means to pay Bohemia the visitation which he justly owes him.

ARC. Wherein our entertainment shall shame us we will be justified in our loves,° for indeed ——

CAM. Beseech you ——   11

ARC. Verily, I speak it in the freedom of my knowledge. We cannot with such magnificence — in so rare —— I know not what to say. We will give you sleepy drinks, that your senses, unintelligent of our insufficience,° may, though they cannot praise us, as little accuse us.   17

CAM. You pay a great deal too dear for what's given freely.

ARC. Believe me, I speak as my understanding instructs me, and as mine honesty puts it to utterance.

CAM. Sicilia cannot show himself overkind to   23 Bohemia.° They were trained together in their childhoods, and there rooted betwixt them then such an affection, which cannot choose but branch° now.

Since their more mature dignities and royal necessities made separation of their society,° their en-   28 counters, though not personal, have been royally attorneyed° with interchange of gifts, letters, loving embassies, that they have seemed to be together, though absent; shook hands, as over a vast;° and embraced, as it were, from the ends of opposed winds.° The Heavens continue their loves!   35

ARC. I think there is not in the world either malice or matter to alter it. You have an unspeakable comfort of your young Prince Mamillius. It is a gentleman of the greatest promise that ever came into my note.   40

CAM. I very well agree with you in the hopes of him. It is a gallant child, one that indeed physics the subject,° makes old hearts fresh. They that went on crutches ere he was born desire yet their life to see him a man.   45

ARC. Would they else be content to die?

CAM. Yes, if there were no other excuse why they should desire to live.

ARC. If the King had no son, they would de-   49 sire to live on crutches till he had one.   [*Exeunt.*]

SCENE II. *A room of state in the same.*

[*Enter* LEONTES, HERMIONE, MAMILLIUS, POLIXENES, CAMILLO, *and* ATTENDANTS.]

POL. Nine changes of the watery star hath been The shepherd's note° since we have left our throne

---

Act I, Sc. i: 2–3. on . . . foot: i.e., as attendant on your King. Both lords use somewhat exaggerated speech as they pay polite compliments to each other.   9–10. Wherein . . . loves: although we shall not be able to entertain you so lavishly, yet our love will be as genuine.   15–16. unintelligent . . . insufficience: not be able to realize our shortcomings.   23–24. Sicilia . . . Bohemia: Leontes, King of Sicilia . . . and Polixenes, King of Bohemia.
26. branch: put out branches as it grows to maturity.

28. society: companionship.   28–30. encounters . . . attorneyed: their meetings have been made through deputies.   33. vast: great distance.   34–35. opposed winds: the opposite ends of the earth. 42–43. physics . . . subject: is good medicine for the whole nation.
Sc. ii: 1–2. Nine . . . note: i.e., it is now nine months. watery star: the moon. Polixenes also in making his formal farewell speaks in the elaborate vocabulary of compliment.

Without a burden.° Time as long again
Would be filled up, my brother, with our thanks,
And yet we should, for perpetuity,   5
Go hence in debt. And therefore, like a cipher,°
Yet standing in rich place, I multiply
With one "We thank you" many thousands moe°
That go before it.

LEON.   Stay your thanks a while,
And pay them when you part.

POL.   Sir, that's tomorrow.   10
I° am questioned by my fears of what may chance
Or breed upon our absence, that may blow
No sneaping° winds at home to make us say
"This is put forth too truly." Besides, I have
    stayed
To tire your royalty.°

LEON.   We are tougher, brother,   15
Than you can put us to 't.

POL.   No longer stay.

LEON. One sevennight° longer.

POL.   Very sooth,° tomorrow.

LEON. We'll part the time between 's,° then, and
    in that
I'll no gainsaying.°

POL.   Press me not, beseech you, so.
There is no tongue that moves — none, none i' the
    world —   20
So soon as yours could win me. So it should now
Were there necessity in your request, although
'Twere needful I denied it. My affairs
Do even drag me homeward, which to hinder
Were in your love a whip to me,° my stay   25
To you a charge and trouble. To save both,
Farewell, our brother.

LEON.   Tongue-tied our Queen? Speak you.

HER. I had thought, sir, to have held my peace
    until
You had drawn oaths from him not to stay. You, sir,
Charge° him too coldly. Tell him you are sure   30
All in Bohemia's well, this satisfaction
The bygone day proclaimed. Say this to him,
He's beat from his best ward.°

LEON.   Well said, Hermione.

HER. To tell he longs to see his son were strong.
But let him say so then, and let him go.   35
But let him swear so and he shall not stay,
We'll thwack him hence with distaffs.°

Yet your royal presence I'll adventure
The borrow of a week. When at Bohemia
You take my lord, I'll give him my commission°
To let him there a month behind the gest   41
Prefixed° for's parting. Yet, good deed, Leontes,
I love thee not a jar° o' the clock behind
What lady she her lord. You'll stay?

POL.   No, madam.

HER. Nay, but you will?

POL.   I may not, verily.   45

HER. Verily!
You put me off with limber vows,° but I,
Though you would seek to unsphere the stars° with
    oaths,
Should yet say "Sir, no going." Verily,
You shall not go. A lady's "verily" 's   50
As potent as a lord's. Will you go yet?
Force me to keep you as a prisoner,
Not like a guest; so you shall pay your fees°
When you depart, and save your thanks. How say
    you?   54
My prisoner? Or my guest? By your dread "verily,"
One of them you shall be.

POL.   Your guest, then, madam.
To be your prisoner should import offending,
Which is for me less easy to commit
Than you to punish.

HER.   Not your jailer, then,
But your kind hostess. Come, I'll question you   60
Of my lord's tricks and yours when you were
    boys.
You were pretty lordings° then?

POL.   We were, fair Queen,
Two lads that thought there was no more behind°
But such a day tomorrow as today,
And to be boy eternal.

HER.   Was not my lord   65
The verier wag° o' the two?

POL. We were as twinned lambs that did frisk i'
    the sun,
And bleat the one at the other. What we changed°
Was innocence for innocence, we knew not
The doctrine of ill-doing, nor dreamed   70
That any did. Had we pursued that life,
And our weak spirits ne'er been higher reared
With stronger blood,° we should have answered
    Heaven

3. **burden:** occupant.   6. **cipher:** the figure o, which means noth-
ing in itself, but much in 10,000.   8. **moe:** more.   11–14. **I . . .
truly:** i.e., my fears make me ask myself what evil may be hap-
pening in my absence, lest some ill wind at home may cause me to
say they were only too true. **sneaping:** withering.   15. **royalty:**
your royal behavior.   17. **sevennight:** week. **sooth:** truth.
18. **part . . . between 's:** split the difference between us.   19. **gain-
saying:** refusal.   24–25. **which . . . me:** it would be a punishment to
keep me from home, even though in your love you wish me to stay.
30. **Charge:** make demand of.   32–33. **Say . . . ward:** if you tell him
that all is well in Bohemia, he is driven from his best defense.
ward: position of defense in sword play.   36–37. **But . . . distaffs:**

i.e., if he swears that he wants to go home to see his son, we
women will understand that plea and send him packing. **thwack:**
beat. **distaff:** the wooden rod used in spinning, a woman's occupa-
tion.   40. **commission:** permission.   41–42. **gest Prefixed:** time
allotted.   43. **jar:** tick.   47. **limber vows:** slender protestations;
something stronger than "verily" is needed to prove that he is
forced to go.   48. **unsphere . . . stars:** pull the stars out of their
courses. See App. 1.   53. **pay . . . fees:** a prisoner had to pay
the fees due to his jailer before he could be released.   62. **lord-
ings:** little lords.   63. **behind:** to come.   66. **verier wag:**
naughtier boy.   68. **changed:** exchanged.   72–73. **And . . . blood:**
if we had never grown more passionate as we grew stronger.

Boldly " Not guilty," the imposition cleared
Hereditary ours.°

HER.   By this we gather   75
You have tripped since.

POL.   O my most sacred lady!
Temptations have since then been born to 's. For
In those unfledged° days was my wife a girl,
Your precious self had then not crossed the eyes
Of my young playfellow.

HER.   Grace to boot!°   80
Of this make no conclusion,° lest you say
Your Queen and I are devils. Yet go on.
The offenses we have made you do we'll answer
If you first sinned with us, and that with us
You did continue fault, and that you slipped not   85
With any but with us.

LEON.   Is he won yet?

HER. He'll stay, my lord.

LEON.   At my request he would not.
Hermione, my dearest, thou never spokest
To better purpose.

HER.   Never?

LEON.   Never but once.

HER. What! Have I twice said well? When was 't
    before?   90
I prithee tell me, cram 's with praise, and make 's
As fat as tame things.° One good deed dying tongue-
    less
Slaughters a thousand waiting upon that.°
Our praises are our wages. You may ride 's
With one soft kiss a thousand furlongs ere   95
With spur we heat an acre. But to the goal.
My last good deed was to entreat his stay.
What was my first? It has an elder sister,
Or I mistake you. Oh, would her name were Grace!
But once before I spoke to the purpose — when?
Nay, let me have 't, I long.

LEON.   Why, that was when   101
Three crabbèd° months had soured themselves to
    death
Ere I could make thee open thy white hand
And clap° thyself my love. Then didst thou utter
" I am yours forever."

HER.   'Tis grace indeed.   105
Why, lo you now,° I have spoke to the purpose twice.
The one forever earned a royal husband,
The other for some while a friend.°

LEON.   [Aside] Too hot, too hot!
To mingle friendship far is mingling bloods.
I have tremor cordis° on me. My heart dances,   110
But not for joy, not joy. This entertainment°
May a free face° put on, derive a liberty
From heartiness, from bounty, fertile bosom,°
And well become the agent. 'T may, I grant,
But to be paddling palms° and pinching fingers,
As now they are, and making practiced smiles,   116
As in a looking-glass, and then to sigh, as 'twere
The mort° o' the deer — oh, that is entertainment
My bosom likes not, nor my brows!° Mamillius,
Art thou my boy?

MAM.   Aye, my good lord.

LEON.   I' fecks!°   120
Why, that's my bawcock.° What, hast smutched°
    thy nose?
They say it is a copy out of mine. Come, captain,
We must be neat — not neat,° but cleanly, captain.
And yet the steer, the heifer, and the calf
Are all called neat. — Still virginaling°   125
Upon his palm! — How now, you wanton calf!
Art thou my calf?

MAM.   Yes, if you will, my lord.

LEON. Thou want'st a rough pash,° and the
    shoots° that I have,
To be full like me. Yet they say we are
Almost as like as eggs. Women say so,   130
That will say anything. But were they false
As o'erdyed blacks,° as wind, as waters, false
As dice are to be wished by one that fixes
No bourn 'twixt his and mine,° yet were it true
To say this boy were like me. Come, Sir Page,   135
Look on me with your welkin° eye. Sweet villain!
Most dear'st! My collop!° Can thy dam° ———? May 't
    be? —
Affection,° thy intention stabs the center!
Thou dost make possible things not so held,
Communicatest with dreams — how can this be? —
With what's unreal thou coactive art,°   141

 enes is something more than a friend to his wife. "Friend" in
Shakespeare's day sometimes meant "lover." See M for Meas,
I.iv.29.   110. tremor cordis: palpitation of the heart.   111. en-
tertainment: kindly treatment.   112. free face: innocent appear-
ance.   113. fertile bosom: natural kindliness.   115. paddling
palms: playing with each other's hands.   118. mort: the blast on
the horn denoting the death of the deer and the end of the hunt.
119. brows: Leontes hereafter becomes obsessed by the thought
that he is a cuckold. See App. 11.   120. I' fecks: faith.   121. baw-
cock: fine cock.   smutched: smudged.   123. not neat: he shies
away from neat (calf), as it implies another horned beast.
125. virginaling: playing as on the virginals. See Pl. 19f.
128. pash: head. shoots: growth; i.e., hair.   132. o'erdyed blacks:
black material so often dyed that it has become rotten.   132-
34. false . . . mine: as false as a dishonest gambler would wish the
dice to be who observes no boundary (bourn) between his and
mine.   136. welkin: blue as the sky.   137. collop: lit., a slice, so
slice of me. dam: mother.   138. Affection: is it affection that
she shows? Her intention (i.e., lust) stabs me to the heart. The
whole passage is deliberately incoherent as Leontes' monstrous
thoughts take shape.   141. thou . . . art: you join with.

74–75. the . . . ours: i.e., we were such innocents then that even
the original sin (which all men inherit from Adam) should have
been forgiven.   78. unfledged: when we were still in the nest.
80. Grace to boot: Heaven help me!   81. make no conclusion: do
not carry the argument to a further conclusion.   92. tame things:
beasts fattened for eating.   92–93. One . . . that: if one good
deed is not rewarded by praise, a thousand others which might
have followed are killed off.   102. crabbed: wretched.   104. clap:
clasp hands on the bargain.   106. lo . . . now: well now!   108. a
friend: With these words, Hermione leads Polixenes aside, holding
his hand, and chattering to him gaily. As Leontes watches them,
he is suddenly overcome by the devastating thought that Polix-

And fellow'st° nothing. Then 'tis very credent
Thou mayst cojoin with something; and thou dost,
And that beyond commission,° and I find it,
And that to the infection of my brains   145
And hardening of my brows.

POL.   What means Sicilia?

HER. He something seems unsettled.

POL.   How, my lord!
What cheer? How is 't with you, best Brother?

HER.   You look
As if you held a brow of much distraction.°
Are you moved, my lord?

LEON.   No, in good earnest. 150
How sometimes nature° will betray its folly,
Its tenderness, and make itself a pastime
To harder bosoms!° Looking on the lines
Of my boy's face, methought I did recoil
Twenty-three years, and saw myself unbreeched,°
In my green velvet coat, my dagger muzzled° 156
Lest it should bite its master, and so prove,
As ornaments oft do, too dangerous.
How like, methought, I then was to this kernel,
This squash,° this gentleman. Mine honest friend,
Will you take eggs for money?°   161

MAM. No, my lord, I'll fight.

LEON. You will! Why, happy man be 's dole!° My
brother,
Are you so fond of your young Prince as we
Do seem to be of ours?

POL.   If at home, sir,   165
He's all my exercise, my mirth, my matter —
Now my sworn friend, and then mine enemy,
My parasite,° my soldier, statesman, all.
He makes a July's day short as December,
And with his varying childness° cures in me   170
Thoughts that would thick my blood.

LEON.   So stands this squire
Officed with me.° We two will walk, my lord,
And leave you to your graver steps. Hermione,
How thou lovest us show in our brother's wel-
come.
Let what is dear in Sicily be cheap.   175
Next to thyself and my young rover, he's
Apparent° to my heart.

HER.   If you would seek us,
We are yours i' the garden. Shall 's attend you there?

LEON. To your own bents° dispose you. You'll be
found,
Be you beneath the sky. [Aside] I am angling now,
Though you perceive me not how I give line.   181
Go to, go to!
How she holds up the neb,° the bill, to him!
And arms her with the boldness of a wife
To her allowing° husband!

[Exeunt POLIXENES, HERMIONE, and ATTENDANTS.]

                        Gone already!   185
Inch-thick, knee-deep, o'er head and ears a forked
one!°
Go, play, boy, play. Thy mother plays, and I
Play too, but so disgraced a part whose issue
Will hiss me to my grave. Contempt and clamor
Will be my knell. Go, play, boy, play. There have
been,   190
Or I am much deceived, cuckolds ere now.
And many a man there is, even at this present,
Now, while I speak this, holds his wife by the arm,
That little thinks she has been sluiced in 's absence
And his pond fished by his next neighbor, by   195
Sir Smile, his neighbor. Nay, there's comfort in 't
Whiles other men have gates and those gates opened,
As mine, against their will. Should all despair
That have revolted wives, the tenth of mankind
Would hang themselves. Physic for 't there is none.
It is a bawdy planet, that will strike   201
Where 'tis predominant,° and 'tis powerful, think it,
From east, west, north, and south. Be it concluded,
No barricado° for a belly, know 't,
It will let in and out the enemy   205
With bag and baggage. Many thousand on 's
Have the disease and feel 't not. How now, boy!

MAM. I am like you, they say.

LEON.   Why, that's some comfort.
What, Camillo there?

CAM. Aye, my good lord.   210

LEON. Go play, Mamillius. Thou'rt an honest man.

[Exit MAMILLIUS.]

Camillo, this great sir will yet stay longer.

CAM. You had much ado to make his anchor hold.
When you cast out, it still came home.

LEON.   Didst note it?

CAM. He would not stay at your petitions, made
His business more material.°

LEON.   Didst perceive it?   216

[Aside] They're here° with me already, whispering,
rounding°
"Sicilia is a so-forth." 'Tis far gone

---

142. fellow'st: are companion to.   144. commission: i.e., what is lawful.   148–49. You . . . distraction: from the wrinkles in your brow you appear to be much worried.   151. nature: natural feelings.   152–53. pastime . . . bosoms: a joke to coarser minds.   155. unbreeched: as a small boy, not yet old enough to wear breeches.   156. muzzled: fastened in its sheath.   160. squash: the peapod before it is ripe. Cf. T Night, I.v.166.   161. eggs . . . money: a proverb meaning to accept worthless trifles for good money; i.e., be imposed upon.   163. happy . . . dole: a common proverb meaning "May it be his luck to be happy."   168. parasite: hanger-on.   170. varying childness: the varying moods of a child.   171–72. So . . . me: this young man stands in the same relation to me.   177. Apparent: heir apparent, next in succession.

179. bents: inclinations.   183. neb: beak.   185. allowing: approving.   186. forked one: cuckold.   201–02. bawdy . . . predominant: we live under the influence of a planet that makes us bawdy. See App. 1. Cf. Lear, I.ii.128–41.   204. barricado: defense to keep the enemy out.   215–16. made . . . material: i.e., he said his business was too important.   217. here: i.e., they make the V sign at me — which in Shakespeare's time meant "You are a cuckold." rounding: murmuring.

When I shall gust° it last. — How came 't, Camillo,
That he did stay?

LEON.   At the good Queen's entreaty.   220

LEON. At the Queen's be 't. " Good " should be
pertinent,°
But, so it is, it is not. Was this taken°
By any understanding pate but thine?
For thy conceit is soaking,° will draw in
More than the common blocks.° Not noted, is 't,
But of the finer natures? By some severals   226
Of headpiece extraordinary?° Lower messes°
Perchance are to this business purblind? Say.

CAM. Business, my lord! I think most understand
Bohemia stays here longer.

LEON.   Ha!

CAM.   Stays here longer.   230

LEON. Aye, but why?

CAM. To satisfy your Highness, and the entreaties
Of our most gracious mistress.

LEON.   Satisfy!°
The entreaties of your mistress! Satisfy!
Let that suffice. I have trusted thee, Camillo,   235
With all the nearest things to my heart, as well
My chamber councils.° Wherein, priestlike, thou
Hast cleansed my bosom, I from thee departed
Thy penitent reformed. But we have been
Deceived in thy integrity, deceived   240
In that which seems so.

CAM.   Be it forbid, my lord!

LEON. To bide upon 't,° thou art not honest, or
If thou inclinest that way, thou art a coward
Which hoxes° honesty behind, restraining
From course required. Or else thou must be counted
A servant grafted° in my serious trust   246
And therein negligent; or else a fool
That seest a game played home, the rich stake
drawn,°
And takest it all for jest.

CAM.   My gracious lord,
I may be negligent, foolish, and fearful.   250
In every one of these no man is free
But that his negligence, his folly, fear,
Among the infinite doings of the world,
Sometime puts forth.° In your affairs, my lord,
If ever I were willful-negligent,   255
It was my folly. If industriously

I played the fool, it was my negligence,
Not weighing well the end. If° ever fearful
To do a thing where I the issue doubted,
Whereof the execution did cry out   260
Against the nonperformance, 'twas a fear
Which oft infects the wisest. These, my lord,
Are such allowed° infirmities that honesty
Is never free of. But, beseech your Grace,
Be plainer with me, let me know my trespass   265
By its own visage. If I then deny it,
'Tis none of mine.

LEON.   Ha' not you seen, Camillo —
But that's past doubt, you have, or your eyeglass°
Is thicker than a cuckold's horn — or heard,
For to a vision so apparent rumor   270
Cannot be mute° — or thought, for cogitation°
Resides not in that man that does not think —
My wife is slippery? If thou wilt confess,
Or else be impudently negative,
To have nor eyes nor ears nor thought, then say
My wife's a hobbyhorse,° deserves a name   276
As rank° as any flax wench that puts to
Before her trothplight.° Say 't and justify 't.

CAM. I would not be a stander-by to hear
My sovereign mistress clouded so without   280
My present° vengeance taken. 'Shrew my heart,
You never spoke what did become you less
Than this, which to reiterate were sin
As deep as that, though true.

LEON.   Is whispering nothing?
Is leaning cheek to cheek? Is meeting noses?   285
Kissing with inside lip? Stopping the career
Of laughter with a sigh — a note infallible
Of breaking honesty?° — Horsing° foot on foot?
Skulking in corners? Wishing clocks more swift?
Hours, minutes? Noon, midnight? And all eyes
Blind with the pin and web° but theirs, theirs only,
That would unseen be wicked? Is this nothing?   292
Why, then the world and all that's in 't is nothing,
The covering sky is nothing, Bohemia nothing,
My wife is nothing, nor nothing have these nothings
If this be nothing.

CAM.   Good my lord, be cured   296
Of this diseased opinion, and betimes,
For 'tis most dangerous.

LEON.   Say it be, 'tis true.

CAM. No, no, my lord.

LEON.   It is. You lie, you lie.

---

219. **gust:** taste, get to hear of.   221. **pertinent:** i.e., *good* should be (but is not) the right word for her.   222. **taken:** observed. 224. **conceit is soaking:** understanding quickly absorbs the truth. 225. **blocks:** blockheads.   226–27. **severals . . . extraordinary:** individuals of unusual intelligence.   227. **messes:** those who sit at the lower tables in the hall.   233. **Satisfy:** Leontes, who is in the mood to see a double meaning in everything, takes *satisfy* to mean "satisfy her lust."   237. **chamber councils:** state secrets. 242. **To . . . upon 't:** to insist on it.   244. **hoxes:** cripples; lit., hamstrings, cuts the tendon behind the knee.   246. **grafted:** planted.   248. **played . . . drawn:** in grim earnest, great winnings made.   254. **puts forth:** grows leaves and flowers like a plant.

258–62. **If . . . wisest:** if I ever feared to do a thing which ought to have been done rather then left undone because I was doubtful of the consequences, it was a fear that often afflicts the wisest. 263. **allowed:** excusable.   268. **eyeglass:** the lens of the eye. 270–71. **to . . . mute:** for in a matter so clear to sight gossip cannot be silent.   271. **cogitation:** power of thought.   276. **hobbyhorse:** loose woman.   277. **rank:** foul.   277–78. **flax wench . . . trothplight:** any common creature that anticipates her marriage. **flax wench:** lit., a woman who spins flax, "factory hand." 281. **present:** immediate.   288. **breaking honesty:** virtue giving way. **Horsing:** setting.   291. **pin . . . web:** cataract of the eye.

I say thou liest, Camillo, and I hate thee, 300
Pronounce thee a gross lout, a mindless slave,
Or else a hovering temporizer° that
Canst with thine eyes at once see good and evil,
Inclining to them both. Were my wife's liver
Infected as her life, she would not live 305
The running of one glass.°

CAM.   Who does infect her?

LEON. Why, he that wears her like her medal,
   hanging
About his neck, Bohemia. Who if I
Had servants true about me, that bare eyes
To see alike mine honor as their profits, 310
Their own particular thrifts,° they would do that
Which should undo more doing. Aye, and thou,
His cupbearer — whom I from meaner form
Have benched and reared to worship,° who mayst
   see
Plainly as Heaven sees earth and earth sees Heaven,
How I am galled° — mightst bespice° a cup, 316
To give mine enemy a lasting wink,
Which draught to me were cordial.°

CAM.   Sir, my lord,
I could do this, and that with no rash potion,
But with a lingering dram° that should not work
Maliciously like poison. But I cannot 321
Believe this crack° to be in my dread mistress,
So sovereignly being honorable.°
I have loved thee ——

LEON.   Make that thy question,° and go rot!
Dost think I am so muddy, so unsettled, 325
To appoint myself in this vexation;° sully
The purity and whiteness of my sheets,
Which to preserve is sleep, which being spotted
Is goads, thorns, nettles, tails of wasps;
Give scandal to the blood o' the Prince my son, 330
Who I do think is mine and love as mine,
Without ripe moving° to 't? Would I do this?
Could man so blench?°

CAM.   I must believe you, sir.
I do, and will fetch off° Bohemia for 't,
Provided that when he's removed, your Highness
Will take again your Queen as yours at first, 336
Even for your son's sake, and thereby for sealing
The injury of tongues° in Courts and kingdoms

Known and allied to yours.

LEON.   Thou dost advise me
Even so as I mine own course have set down. 340
I'll give no blemish to her honor, none.

CAM. My lord,
Go then, and with a countenance as clear
As friendship wears at feasts, keep with° Bohemia
And with your Queen. I am his cupbearer. 345
If from me he have wholesome beverage,
Account me not your servant.

LEON.   This is all.
Do 't and thou hast the one half of my heart,
Do 't not, thou splitt'st thine own.

CAM.   I'll do 't, my lord.

LEON. I will seem friendly, as thou hast advised
me.   [Exit.]

CAM. O miserable lady! But for me, 351
What case stand I in? I must be the poisoner
Of good Polixenes. And my ground° to do 't
Is the obedience to a master, one
Who, in rebellion with himself, will have 355
All that are his so too. To do this deed,
Promotion follows. If I could find example
Of thousands that had struck anointed kings
And flourished after, I 'd not do 't. But since
Nor brass nor stone nor parchment° bears not one,
Let villainy itself forswear 't.° I must 361
Forsake the Court. To do 't, or no, is certain
To me a breakneck. Happy star reign now!°
Here comes Bohemia.

              [Re-enter POLIXENES.]

POL.   This is strange. Methinks
My favor here begins to warp.° Not speak? 365
Good day, Camillo.

CAM.   Hail, most royal sir!

POL. What is the news i' the Court?

CAM.   None rare, my lord.

POL. The King hath on him such a countenance
As° he had lost some province, and a region
Loved as he loves himself. Even now I met him
With customary compliment,° when he, 371
Wafting his eyes to the contrary and falling
A lip of much contempt,° speeds from me, and
So leaves me to consider what is breeding°
That changes thus his manners. 375

CAM. I dare not know, my lord.

POL. How! Dare not! Do not. Do you know, and
   dare not!
Be intelligent° to me. 'Tis thereabouts,°

302. hovering temporizer: a man of no principles. 306. running
... glass: one turn of the hourglass. 311. particular thrifts:
special advantages. 313–14. meaner ... worship: from sitting
at the bottom end of the bench have promoted to sit amongst the
nobility. 316. galled: rubbed sore. bespice: add spice to; i.e.,
poison. 318. cordial: a tonic. 320. lingering dram: a dose that
would work slowly. 322. crack: flaw. 323. sovereignly ...
honorable: so supremely honorable. 324. Make ... question:
i.e., if you doubt my words. 326. appoint ... vexation: to cause
myself this grief deliberately. appoint: lit., dress myself in.
332. ripe moving: good reason to move me. 333. blench: lit.,
shy like a horse at imaginary fears. 334. fetch off: remove, make
way with. 337–38. sealing ... tongues: stopping malicious
gossip.

344. keep with: keep company with. 353. ground: reason.
360. Nor ... parchment: i.e., every kind of record. 361. for-
swear 't: swear not to do it. 363. Happy ... now: may some
lucky star direct us. 365. warp: shrink. 369. As: as if. 371. cus-
tomary compliment: usual salutation. 372–73. Wafting ...
contempt: turning his eyes away from me and making a con-
temptuous movement with his lower lip. falling: letting fall.
374. breeding: hatching. 378. Be intelligent: tell me. 'Tis
thereabouts: i.e., you are hinting at something.

For, to yourself, what you do know, you must,
And cannot say, you dare not. Good Camillo,   380
Your changed complexions are to me a mirror
Which shows me mine changed too, for I must be
A party in this alteration, finding
Myself thus altered with 't.

CAM.   There is a sickness
Which puts some of us in distemper,° but   385
I cannot name the disease. And it is caught
Of you that yet are well.

POL.   How! Caught of me!
Make me not sighted like the basilisk.°
I have looked on thousands who have sped° the
    better
By my regard, but killed none so. Camillo —   390
As you are certainly a gentleman, thereto
Clerklike experienced,° which no less adorns
Our gentry than our parents' noble names,
In whose success we are gentle° — I beseech you
If you know aught which does behoove my knowl-
    edge,   395
Thereof to be informed, imprison 't not
In ignorant concealment.

CAM.   I may not answer.
POL. A sickness caught of me, and yet I well!
I must be answered. Dost thou hear, Camillo?
I conjure° thee, by all the parts° of man   400
Which honor does acknowledge, whereof the least
Is not this suit of mine, that thou declare
What incidency° thou dost guess of harm
Is creeping toward me — how far off, how near,
Which way to be prevented if to be,   405
If not, how best to bear it.

CAM.   Sir, I will tell you,
Since I am charged in honor° and by him
That I think honorable. Therefore mark my coun-
    sel,
Which must be ev'n as swiftly followed as
I mean to utter it, or both yourself and me   410
Cry lost, and so good night!

POL.   On, good Camillo.
CAM. I am appointed him° to murder you.
POL. By whom, Camillo?

CAM.   By the King.
POL.   For what?
CAM. He thinks — nay, with all confidence he
    swears,
As he had seen 't, or been an instrument   415
To vice° you to 't — that you have touched his
    Queen
Forbiddenly.

POL.   Oh then, my best blood turn
To an infected jelly, and my name
Be yoked with his that did betray the Best!°
Turn then my freshest reputation to   420
A savor° that may strike the dullest nostril
Where I arrive, and my approach be shunned —
Nay, hated too, worse than the great'st infection
That e'er was heard or read!

CAM.   Swear his thought over
By each particular star in Heaven and   425
By all their influences, you may as well
Forbid the sea for to obey the moon
As or by oath° remove or counsel shake
The fabric of his folly, whose foundation
Is piled upon his faith, and will continue   430
The standing of his body.°

POL.   How should this grow?
CAM. I know not. But I am sure 'tis safer to
Avoid what's grown than question how 'tis born.
If therefore you dare trust my honesty,
That lies enclosèd in this trunk° which you   435
Shall bear along impawned,° away tonight!
Your followers I will whisper to the business,
And will by twos and threes at several posterns°
Clear them o' the city. For myself, I'll put
My fortunes to your service, which are here   440
By this discovery lost. Be not uncertain,
For, by the honor of my parents, I
Have uttered truth. Which if you seek to prove,
I dare not stand by, nor shall you be safer
Than one condemned by the King's own mouth,
    thereon   445
His execution sworn.

POL.   I do believe thee.
I saw his heart in 's face. Give me thy hand.
Be pilot to me and thy places shall
Still neighbor mine. My ships are ready, and
My people did expect my hence departure   450
Two days ago. This jealousy
Is for a precious creature. As she's rare,
Must it be great. And as his person's mighty,
Must it be violent. And as he does conceive
He is dishonored by a man which ever   455
Professed° to him, why, his revenges must
In that be made more bitter. Fear o'ershades me.
Good expedition be my friend, and comfort
The gracious Queen, part of his theme, but nothing
Of his ill-ta'en suspicion!° Come, Camillo,   460
I will respect thee as a father if

385. distemper: mental sickness.   388. basilisk: a fabulous ser-
pent able to kill by its glance. See *Rich III*, I.ii.151,n.   389. sped:
fared.   392. Clerklike experienced: with the experience of a man
of education.   394. In . . . gentle: from whom by descent we are
called gentlemen.   400. conjure: solemnly demand. parts: qual-
ities.   403. incidency: likelihood.   407. charged in honor: bound
by my honor.   412. him: by him.   416. vice: screw, force.

419. that . . . Best: i.e., Judas Iscariot, who betrayed Jesus.
421. savor: stink.   428. oath: i.e., even if you swear that you are
innocent he will not believe you.   431. standing . . . body: so
long as he can stand.   435. trunk: body.   436. impawned: as a
pledge of my faith.   438. several posterns: different gates.
456. Professed: i.e., that he was a true friend.   458-60. Good . . .
suspicion: may my speedy departure help me to escape and bring
comfort to the gracious Queen who is partly the cause of his
anger, but not a true cause for suspicion.

Thou bear'st my life off hence. Let us avoid.°

CAM. It is in mine authority to command
The keys of all the posterns. Please your Highness
To take the urgent hour.° Come, sir, away. 465
         [*Exeunt.*]

Act II

SCENE I. *A room in* LEONTES' *palace.*

[*Enter* HERMIONE, MAMILLIUS, *and* LADIES.]

HER. Take the boy to you. He so troubles me
'Tis past enduring.

1. LADY.   Come, my gracious lord,
Shall I be your playfellow?

MAM.   No, I'll none of you.

1. LADY. Why, my sweet lord?

MAM. You'll kiss me hard, and speak to me as if
I were a baby still. I love you better. 6

2. LADY. And why so, my lord?

MAM.   Not for because
Your brows are blacker — yet black brows, they say,
Become some women best, so that there be not
Too much hair there, but in a semicircle, 10
Or a half-moon made with a pen.

2. LADY.   Who taught you this?

MAM. I learned it out of women's faces. Pray now,
What color are your eyebrows?

1. LADY.   Blue, my lord.

MAM. Nay, that's a mock. I have seen a lady's nose
That has been blue, but not her eyebrows.

1. LADY.   Hark ye, 15
The Queen your mother rounds apace. We shall
Present our services to a fine new Prince
One of these days, and then you'd wanton° with us,
If we would have you.

2. LADY.   She is spread of late
Into a goodly bulk. Good time encounter her!° 20

HER. What wisdom stirs amongst you? Come, sir,
 now
I am for you again. Pray you, sit by us
And tell 's a tale.

MAM.   Merry or sad shall 't be?

HER. As merry as you will.

MAM. A sad tale's best for winter. I have one 25
Of sprites and goblins.

HER.   Let's have that, good sir.
Come on, sit down. Come on, and do your best
To fright me with your sprites, you're powerful at it.

MAM. There was a man ——

Nay, come, sit down, then on.

MAM. Dwelt by a churchyard — I will tell it
softly. 30
Yon crickets° shall not hear it.

HER.   Come on, then,
And give 't me in mine ear.

[*Enter* LEONTES, *with* ANTIGONUS, LORDS, *and*
OTHERS.]

LEON. Was he met there? His train? Camillo
with him?

1. LORD. Behind the tuft of pines I met them.
 Never
Saw I men scour° so on their way. I eyed them 35
Even to their ships.

LEON.   How blest am I
In my just censure,° in my true opinion!
Alack, for lesser knowledge, how accursed
In being so blest! There may be in the cup
A spider° steeped and one may drink, depart, 40
And yet partake° no venom, for his knowledge
Is not infected. But if one present
The abhorred ingredient to his eye, make known
How he hath drunk, he cracks his gorge,° his sides,
With violent hefts.° I have drunk, and seen the
 spider. 45
Camillo was his help in this, his pander.°
There is a plot against my life, my crown,
All's true that is mistrusted.° That false villain
Whom I employed was pre-employed by him.
He has discovered° my design, and I 50
Remain a pinched° thing — yea, a very trick
For them to play at will. How came the posterns
So easily open?

1. LORD.   By his great authority,
Which often hath no less prevailed than so
On your command.

LEON.   I know 't too well. 55
Give me the boy. I am glad you did not nurse him.
Though he does bear some signs of me, yet you
Have too much blood in him.

HER.   What is this? Sport?

LEON. Bear the boy hence, he shall not come about
her.
Away with him! And let her sport herself 60
With that she's big with, for 'tis Polixenes
Has made thee swell thus.

HER.   But I'd say he had not,
And I'll be sworn you would believe my saying,
Howe'er you lean to the nayward.°

LEON.   You, my lords,
Look on her, mark her well. Be but about 65

---

462. avoid: be gone. 465. take . . . hour: take our opportunity
quickly while we can.
 Act II, Sc. i: 18. wanton: play the fool. 20. Good . . . her:
may she have an easy confinement.

31. Yon crickets: i.e., the chattering ladies. 35. scour: scurry.
37. censure: judgment. 40. spider: The spider was regarded as
poisonous. 41. partake: suffer from. 44. cracks . . . gorge:
bursts his throat. 45. hefts: heavings. 46. pander: one who
acts as go-between for a man and a harlot. 48. mistrusted:
suspected. 50. discovered: revealed. 51. pinched: tormented.
64. nayward: denial.

To say " She is a goodly lady " and
The justice of your hearts will thereto add
" 'Tis pity she's not honest, honorable."
Praise her but for this her withoutdoor form,°
Which on my faith deserves high speech, and
    straight   70
The shrug, the hum or ha, these petty brands
That calumny doth use. Oh, I am out,°
That mercy does, for calumny will sear°   73
Virtue itself. These shrugs, these hums and ha's,
When you have said " She's goodly," come between
Ere you can say " She's honest." But be 't known,
From him that has most cause to grieve it should be,
She's an adulteress.

    HER.   Should a villain say so,
The most replenished° villain in the world,
He were as much more villain. You, my lord,   80
Do but mistake.

    LEON.   You have mistook, my lady,
Polixenes for Leontes. O thou thing!
Which I'll not call a creature of thy place,°
Lest barbarism,° making me the precedent,
Should a like language use to all degrees,   85
And mannerly distinguishment leave out
Betwixt the prince and beggar.° I have said
She's an adulteress, I have said with whom.
More, she's a traitor, and Camillo is
A federary° with her; and one that knows,   90
What she should shame to know herself
But with her most vile principal, that she's
A bedswerver,° even as bad as those
That vulgars° give bold'st titles — aye, and privy°
To this their late escape.

    HER.   No, by my life,   95
Privy to none of this. How will this grieve you
When you shall come to clearer knowledge, that
You thus have published° me! Gentle my lord,
You scarce can right me throughly° then to say
You did mistake.

    LEON.   No. If I mistake   100
In those foundations which I build upon,
The center° is not big enough to bear
A schoolboy's top. Away with her, to prison!
He who shall speak for her is afar-off guilty
But that he speaks.°

    HER.   There's some ill planet° reigns.   105

I must be patient till the Heavens look
With an aspéct° more favorable. Good my lords,
I am not prone to weeping, as our sex
Commonly are, the want of which vain dew
Perchance shall dry your pities. But I have   110
That honorable grief lodged here which burns
Worse than tears drown. Beseech you all, my lords,
With thoughts so qualified° as your charities
Shall best instruct you, measure° me. And so
The King's will be performed!

    LEON.   Shall I be heard?   115
    HER. Who is 't that goes with me? Beseech your
      Highness,
My women may be with me, for you see
My plight requires it. Do not weep, good fools,°
There is no cause. When you shall know your mis-
    tress
Has deserved prison, then abound in tears   120
As I come out. This action I now go on
Is for my better grace. Adieu, my lord.
I never wished to see you sorry, now
I trust I shall. My women, come, you have leave.
    LEON. Go, do our bidding. Hence!   125
      [*Exit* QUEEN, *guarded, with* LADIES.]
    1. LORD. Beseech your Highness, call the Queen
      again.
    ANT. Be certain what you do, sir, lest your justice
Prove violence, in the which three great ones suffer,
Yourself, your Queen, your son.
    1. LORD.   For her, my lord,
I dare my life lay down and will do 't, sir,   130
Please you to accept it, that the Queen is spotless
I' the eyes of Heaven and to you. I mean
In this which you accuse her.
    ANT.   If it prove
She's otherwise, I'll keep my stables where
I lodge my wife, I'll go in couples° with her,   135
Than when I feel and see her no farther trust her.
For every inch of woman in the world,
Aye, every dram° of woman's flesh, is false
If she be.
    LEON. Hold your peaces.
    1. LORD.   Good my lord ——   139
    ANT. It is for you we speak, not for ourselves.
You are abused, and by some putter-on°
That will be damned for 't. Would I knew the vil-
    lain,
I would land-damn° him. Be she honor-flawed,
I have three daughters — the eldest is eleven,   144
The second and the third, nine, and some five —
If this prove true, they'll pay for 't. By mine honor,

---

69. withoutdoor form: outward shape.   72. out: wrong.   73. sear: brand.   79. replenished: complete.   83. creature ... place: one in your royal position.   84. barbarism: the ignorant multitude.   85–87. Should ... beggar: should use the same low word to women of every rank, and omit the distinction which showed the difference between a queen and beggarwoman.   90. federary: confederate.   93. bedswerver: false to the marriage bed. 94. vulgars: the lowest creatures. privy: sharing the secret of. 98. published: publicly proclaimed.   99. throughly: thoroughly. 102. center: the center of the Earth, what was regarded as the pivot of the universe.   104–05. afar-off ... speaks: is partially guilty even for speaking well of her. 105. ill planet: See I.ii.201,n. The notion of the evil influence of the stars runs through this part of the play.

107. aspect: See App. I.   113. qualified: mixed with kindness; to "qualify" is lit. to mix water with strong drink.   114. measure: judge.   118. fools: The word is sometimes used as a term of endearment.   135. go in couples: tied together like a pair of greyhounds.   138. dram: minute portion.   141. putter-on: suggesting knave.   143. land-damn: a much-disputed word, otherwise unknown. It obviously means something unpleasant.

I'll geld 'em all, fourteen they shall not see,
To bring false generations.° They are coheirs,
And I had rather glib° myself than they
Should not produce fair issue.

LEON.   Cease, no more. 150
You smell this business with a sense as cold
As is a dead man's nose. But I do see 't and feel 't
As you feel doing thus,° and see withal
The instruments° that feel.

ANT.   If it be so,
We need no grave to bury honesty. 155
There's not a grain of it the face to sweeten
Of the whole dungy earth.

LEON.   What! Lack I credit?°
I. LORD. I had rather you did lack than I, my lord,
Upon this ground.° And more it would content me
To have her honor true than your suspicion, 160
Be blamed for 't how you might.

LEON.   Why, what need we°
Commune with you of this, but rather follow
Our forceful instigation?° Our prerogative
Calls not your counsels,° but our natural goodness
Imparts this. Which if you, or stupefied 165
Or seeming so in skill,° cannot or will not
Relish a truth like us, inform yourselves
We need no more of your advice. The matter,
The loss, the gain, the ordering on 't, is all
Properly ours.

ANT.   And I wish, my liege, 170
You had only in your silent judgment tried it,
Without more overture.°

LEON.   How could that be?
Either thou art most ignorant by age,
Or thou wert born a fool. Camillo's flight,
Added to their familiarity — 175
Which was as gross° as ever touched conjecture,°
That lacked sight only, naught for approbation°
But only seeing, all other circumstances
Made up to the deed — doth push on this proceeding.
Yet, for a greater confirmation, 180
For in an act of this importance 'twere
Most piteous to be wild,° I have dispatched in post°
To sacred Delphos,° to Apollo's temple,
Cleomenes and Dion, whom you know
Of stuffed sufficiency.° Now from the oracle 185

They will bring all, whose spiritual counsel had,
Shall stop or spur me. Have I done well?

I. LORD. Well done, my lord.

LEON. Though I am satisfied and need no more
Than what I know, yet shall the oracle 190
Give rest to the minds of others, such as he
Whose ignorant credulity will not
Come up to the truth. So have we thought it good
From our free° person she should be confined,
Lest that the treachery of the two fled hence 195
Be left her to perform. Come, follow us.
We are to speak in public, for this business
Will raise us all.

ANT.   [*Aside*] To laughter, as I take it, 199
If the good truth were known.   [*Exeunt.*]

SCENE II. *A prison.*

[*Enter* PAULINA, *a* GENTLEMAN, *and* ATTENDANTS.]
PAUL. The keeper of the prison, call to him.
Let him have knowledge who I am.
                      [*Exit* GENTLEMAN.]
                      Good lady,
No Court in Europe is too good for thee.
What dost thou, then, in prison?
[*Re-enter* GENTLEMAN, *with the* JAILER.] Now, good
    sir,
You know me, do you not?

JAIL.   For a worthy lady, 5
And one who much I honor.

PAUL.   Pray you, then,
Conduct me to the Queen.

JAIL.   I may not, madam.
To the contrary I have express commandment.

PAUL. Here's ado,
To lock up honesty and honor from 10
The access of gentle visitors! Is 't lawful, pray you,
To see her women? Any of them? Emilia?

JAIL. So please you, madam,
To put apart these your attendants, I
Shall bring Emilia forth.

PAUL.   I pray now, call her. 15
Withdraw yourselves.
          [*Exeunt* GENTLEMAN *and* ATTENDANTS.]

JAIL.   And, madam,
I must be present at your conference.

PAUL. Well, be 't so, prithee.   [*Exit* JAILER.]
Here's such ado to make no stain a stain 19
As passes coloring.°
[*Re-enter* JAILER, *with* EMILIA.] Dear gentlewoman,
How fares our gracious lady?

EMIL. As well as one so great and so forlorn
May hold together. On her frights and griefs,
Which never tender lady hath borne greater,

148. To . . . generations: to produce bastards. 149. glib: geld. 153. doing thus: He makes some gesture, probably clenching his own fists. 154. instruments: i.e., the fingers. 157. Lack I credit: am I not believed? 159. ground: foundation. 161. Why . . . we: Leontes, being unable to persuade his nobles by argument, falls back on his dignity and speaks to them with the royal "we." 163. forceful instigation: powerful incentive. 163–64. Our . . . counsels: as your King I am under no obligation to ask your advice. 166. skill: cunning. 172. overture: disclosure. 176. gross: obvious. touched conjecture: caused suspicion. 177. approbation: proof. 182. wild: rash. in post: hastily. See App. 17. 183. Delphos: See *W. Tale* Intro. p. 959b. 185. Of . . . sufficiency: fully competent.

194. free: guiltless.
Sc. ii: 20. passes coloring: outdoes any painting.

She is something° before her time delivered.   25
  PAUL. A boy?
  EMIL.   A daughter, and a goodly babe,
Lusty and like to live. The Queen receives
Much comfort in 't, says " My poor prisoner,
I am innocent as you."
  PAUL.   I dare be sworn.
These dangerous unsafe lunes° i' the King, be-
    shrew° them!   30
He must be told on 't, and he shall. The office
Becomes a woman best, I'll take 't upon me.
If I prove honey-mouthed,° let my tongue blister
And never to my red-looked° anger be
The trumpet any more. Pray you, Emilia,   35
Commend my best obedience° to the Queen.
If she dares trust me with her little babe,
I'll show 't the King and undertake to be
Her advocate to the loud'st. We do not know
How he may soften at the sight o' the child.   40
The silence often of pure innocence
Persuades when speaking fails.
  EMIL.   Most worthy madam,
Your honor and your goodness is so evident
That your free° undertaking cannot miss
A thriving issue.° There is no lady living   45
So meet° for this great errand. Please your ladyship
To visit the next room, I'll presently°
Acquaint the Queen of your most noble offer,
Who but today hammered of° this design,
But durst not tempt° a minister of honor,°   50
Lest she should be denied.
  PAUL.   Tell her, Emilia,
I'll use that tongue I have. If wit flow from 't
As boldness from my bosom, let 't not be doubted
I shall do good.
  EMIL.   Now be you blest for it!   54
I'll to the Queen. Please you, come something nearer.
  JAIL. Madam, if 't please the Queen to send the
    babe,
I know not what I shall incur to pass it,°
Having no warrant.°
  PAUL.   You need not fear it, sir.
This child was prisoner to the womb, and is
By law and process of great nature thence   60
Freed and enfranchised° — not a party to
The anger of the King, nor guilty of,
If any be, the trespass of the Queen.
  JAIL. I do believe it.
  PAUL. Do not you fear. Upon mine honor, I   65
Will stand betwixt you and danger.   [*Exeunt.*]

SCENE III. *A room in* LEONTES' *palace.*

[*Enter* LEONTES, ANTIGONUS, LORDS, *and* SERVANTS.]
  LEON. Nor night nor day no rest. It is but weak-
    ness
To bear the matter thus, mere weakness. If
The cause were not in being° — part o' the cause,
She the adulteress, for the harlot King
Is quite beyond mine arm, out of the blank°   5
And level° of my brain, plotproof.° But she
I can hook to me. Say that she were gone,
Given to the fire, a moiety° of my rest
Might come to me again. Who's there?
  1. SERV.   My lord?
  LEON. How does the boy?
  1. SERV.   He took good rest tonight,   10
'Tis hoped his sickness is discharged.°
  LEON. To see his nobleness!
Conceiving the dishonor of his mother,
He straight declined, drooped, took it deeply,
Fastened and fixed the shame on 't in himself,   15
Threw off his spirit,° his appetite, his sleep,
And downright languished. Leave me solely.° Go,
See how he fares. [*Exit* SERVANT.] Fie, fie! No
    thought of him.°
The very thought of my revenges that way
Recoil upon me. In himself too mighty,   20
And in his parties, his alliance,° let him be
Until a time may serve. For present vengeance,
Take it on her. Camillo and Polixenes
Laugh at me, make their pastime at my sorrow.
They should not laugh if I could reach them, nor
Shall she within my power.
          [*Enter* PAULINA, *with a* CHILD.]
  1. LORD.   You must not enter.   26
  PAUL. Nay, rather, good my lords, be second° to
    me.
Fear you his tyrannous passion more, alas,
Than the Queen's life? A gracious innocent soul,
More free° than he is jealous.
  ANT.   That's enough.   30
  2. SERV. Madam, he hath not slept tonight, com-
    manded
None should come at him.
  PAUL.   Not so hot, good sir.
I come to bring him sleep. 'Tis such as you,
That creep like shadows by him and do sigh
At each his needless heavings, such as you   35
Nourish the cause of his awaking. I
Do come with words as medicinal° as true,

25. something: somewhat.   30. lunes: mad fits. beshrew: plague
on.   33. honey-mouthed: sweet in words.   34. red-looked: red-
faced.   36. best obedience: a formal phrase of respectful compli-
ment.   44. free: voluntary.   45. thriving issue: successful re-
sult.   46. meet: fitting.   47. presently: immediately.   49. ham-
mered of: kept on thinking about.   50. tempt: try, approach.
minister of honor: one of the chief ministers.   57. what . . . it:
what risks I run if I let it pass out of the prison.   58. warrant:
written order.   61. enfranchised: set at liberty.

Sc. iii: 3. were . . . being: was not real. Leontes in his agita-
tion speaks in half-formed sentences.   5. blank: lit., the center
of the target.   6. level: aim. plotproof: proof against my plots.
8. moiety: part.   11. discharged: gone from him.   16. Threw
. . . spirit: became dispirited.   17. solely: alone.   18. him: i.e.,
Polixenes.   21. his . . . alliance: those who side with him, his
allies.   27. second: support.   30. free: innocent.   37. medic-
inal: healing.

Honest as either, to purge him of that humor°
That presses° him from sleep.

LEON.   What noise there, ho?

PAUL. No noise, my lord, but needful conference°
About some gossips° for your Highness.

LEON.   How!   41
Away with that audacious lady! Antigonus,
I charged thee that she should not come about me.
I knew she would.

ANT.   I told her so, my lord,
On your displeasure's peril and on mine,   45
She should not visit you.

LEON.   What, canst not rule her?

PAUL. From all dishonesty he can. In this,
Unless he take the course that you have done,
Commit me for committing honor, trust it,
He shall not rule me.

ANT.   La you now,° you hear.   50
When she will take the rein I let her run,
But she'll not stumble.

PAUL.   Good my liege, I come —
And I beseech you hear me, who professes
Myself your loyal servant, your physician,
Your most obedient counselor, yet that dares   55
Less appear so in comforting° your evils
Than such as most seem yours — I say I come
From your good Queen.

LEON.   Good Queen!

PAUL.   Good Queen, my lord.
Good Queen, I say good Queen,
And would by combat make her good, so were I   60
A man, the worst about you.

LEON.   Force her hence.

PAUL. Let him that makes but trifles of his eyes
First hand me. On mine own accord I'll off,
But first I'll do my errand. The good Queen,
For she is good, hath brought you forth a daugh-
ter —   65
Here 'tis — commends it to your blessing.

                     [*Laying down the* CHILD.]

LEON.   Out!
A mankind° witch! Hence with her, out o' door!
A most intelligencing° bawd!

PAUL.   Not so.
I am as ignorant in that as you
In so entitling me, and no less honest
Than you are mad — which is enough, I'll warrant,   70
As this world goes, to pass for honest.

LEON.   Traitors!
Will you not push her out? Give her the bastard.
Thou dotard! Thou art woman-tired,° unroosted°

By thy Dame Partlet° here. Take up the bastard,   75
Take 't up, I say. Give 't to thy crone.°

PAUL.   Forever°
Unvenerable be thy hands if thou
Takest up the Princess by that forced baseness°
Which he has put upon 't!

LEON.   He dreads his wife.

PAUL. So I would you did. Then 'twere past all
doubt   80
You'd call your children yours.

LEON.   A nest of traitors!

ANT. I am none, by this good light.

PAUL.   Nor I, nor any
But one that's here, and that's himself. For he
The sacred honor of himself, his Queen's,
His hopeful son's, his babe's, betrays to slander,   85
Whose sting is sharper than the sword's, and will
not —
For as the case now stands, it is a curse
He cannot be compelled to 't — once remove
The root of his opinion, which is rotten
As ever oak or stone was sound.

LEON.   A callat°   90
Of boundless tongue, who late hath beat her husband
And now baits° me! This brat is none of mine,
It is the issue of Polixenes.
Hence with it, and together with the dam
Commit them to the fire!

PAUL.   It is yours,   95
And, might we lay the old proverb to your charge,
So like you 'tis the worse. Behold, my lords,
Although the print° be little, the whole matter
And copy of the father — eye, nose, lip,   99
The trick of 's frown, his forehead, nay, the valley,°
The pretty dimples of his chin and cheek,
His smiles,
The very mold and frame of hand, nail, finger.
And thou, good goddess Nature, which hast made it
So like to him that got° it, if thou hast   105
The ordering° of the mind too, 'mongst all colors
No yellow° in 't, lest she suspect, as he does,
Her children not her husband's!

LEON.   A gross hag!
And, lozel,° thou art worthy to be hanged
That wilt not stay her tongue.

ANT.   Hang all the husbands   110
That cannot do that feat, you'll leave yourself
Hardly one subject.

LEON.   Once more, take her hence.

---

75. **Dame Partlet:** the nagging hen in the story of *Reynard the Fox.*   76. **crone:** withered old woman.   76–79. **Forever . . . upon 't:** i.e., he tells you to pick up the "bastard"; if you obey his command and thereby admit that this child is not a true Princess, may your hands be despised forever.   78. **forced baseness:** the base birth which he forces on her.   90. **callat:** drab.   92. **baits:** worries.   98. **print:** type.   100. **valley:** little cleft in the chin.   105. **got:** begot.   106. **ordering:** regulation.   107. **yellow:** the color of jealousy.   109. **lozel:** low fellow.

38. **humor:** mental illness. See App. 3.   39. **presses:** keeps. 40. **needful conference:** necessary consideration.   41. **gossips:** godparents.   50. **La . . . now:** there now.   56. **comforting:** bringing true comfort to.   67. **mankind:** mannish woman.   68. **intelligencing:** cunning and full of secrets.   74. **woman-tired:** henpecked. **unroosted:** driven off the perch.

PAUL. A most unworthy and unnatural lord
Can do no more.
LEON.   I'll ha' thee burned.
PAUL.   I care not.
It is a heretic that makes the fire,   115
Not she which burns in 't. I'll not call you tyrant,
But this most cruel usage of your Queen —
Not able to produce more accusation
Than your own weak-hinged fancy — something
      savors
Of tyranny, and will ignoble make you —   120
Yea, scandalous to the world.
LEON.   On your allegiance,°
Out of the chamber with her! Were I a tyrant,
Where were her life? She durst not call me so
If she did know me one. Away with her!   124
PAUL. I pray you, do not push me, I'll be gone.
Look to your babe, my lord, 'tis yours. Jove send her
A better guiding spirit! What needs these hands?°
You, that are thus so tender o'er his follies,
Will never do him good, not one of you.   129
So, so. Farewell, we are gone.   [Exit.]
LEON. Thou, traitor, hast set on thy wife to this.
My child? Away with 't! Even thou, that hast
A heart so tender o'er it, take it hence
And see it instantly consumed with fire,
Even thou and none but thou. Take it up straight.
Within this hour bring me word 'tis done,   136
And by good testimony° or I'll seize thy life,
With what thou else call'st thine. If thou refuse
And wilt encounter with my wrath, say so.
The bastard brains with these my proper° hands
Shall I dash out. Go, take it to the fire,   141
For thou set'st on thy wife.
ANT.   I did not, sir.
These lords, my noble fellows, if they please,
Can clear me in 't.
LORDS.   We can. My royal liege,
He is not guilty of her coming hither.   145
LEON. You're liars all.
I. LORD. Beseech your Highness, give us better
      credit.
We have always truly served you, and beseech you
So to esteem of us. And on our knees we beg,
As recompense of our dear services   150
Past and to come, that you do change this purpose,
Which being so horrible, so bloody, must
Lead on to some foul issue. We all kneel.
LEON. I am a feather for each wind that blows.
Shall I live on to see this bastard kneel   155
And call me father? Better burn it now
Than curse it then. But be it, let it live.
It shall not, neither. You, sir, come you hither,

You that have been so tenderly officious
With Lady Margery, your midwife there,   160
To save this bastard's life — for 'tis a bastard,
So sure as this beard's gray° — what will you adven-
      ture
To save this brat's life?
ANT.   Anything, my lord,
That my ability may undergo,
And nobleness impose. At least thus much: 165
I'll pawn° the little blood which I have left
To save the innocent — anything possible.
LEON. It shall be possible. Swear by this sword
Thou wilt perform my bidding.
ANT.   I will, my lord.
LEON. Mark and perform it. Seest thou? For the
      fail   170
Of any point in 't shall not only be
Death to thyself but to thy lewd-tongued° wife,
Whom for this time we pardon. We enjoin° thee,
As thou art liegeman° to us, that thou carry
This female bastard hence, and that thou bear it
To some remote and desert place quite out   176
Of our dominions, and that there thou leave it,
Without more mercy, to it° own protection
And favor of the climate. As by strange fortune
It came to us, I do in justice charge thee,   180
On thy soul's peril and thy body's torture,
That thou commend it strangely° to some place
Where chance may nurse or end it. Take it up.
ANT. I swear to do this, though a present death
Had been more merciful. Come on, poor babe.   185
Some powerful spirit instruct the kites and ravens
To be thy nurses! Wolves and bears, they say,
Casting their savageness aside, have done
Like offices of pity. Sir, be prosperous
In more than this deed does require!° And blessing
Against this cruelty fight on thy side,   191
Poor thing, condemned to loss!
                          [Exit with the CHILD.]
LEON.   No, I'll not rear
Another's issue.
                          [Enter a SERVANT.]
SERV.   Please your Highness, posts
From those you sent to the oracle are come
An hour since. Cleomenes and Dion,   195
Being well° arrived from Delphos, are both landed,
Hasting to the Court.
I. LORD.   So please you, sir, their speed
Hath been beyond account.
LEON.   Twenty-three days
They have been absent. 'Tis good speed, foretells
The great Apollo suddenly° will have   200

162. beard's gray: i.e., Antigonus' beard, which Leontes seizes.
166. pawn: pledge.   172. lewd-tongued: foul-mouthed.   173. en-
join: command.   174. liegeman: true subject.   178. it: its.
182. commend it strangely: commit it as a stranger.   190. re-
quire: deserve.   196. well: safely.   200. suddenly: quickly.

121. On . . . allegiance: the most solemn command that can be
laid by a sovereign on his subject; to disobey is to commit high
treason.   127. What . . . hands: i.e., you need not push me.
137. testimony: proof.   140. proper: own.

The truth of this appear. Prepare you, lords,
Summon a session,° that we may arraign°
Our most disloyal lady. For as she hath
Been publicly accused, so shall she have
A just and open trial. While she lives   205
My heart will be a burden to me. Leave me,
And think upon my bidding.   [*Exeunt.*]

Act III

SCENE I.° *A seaport in Sicilia.*

[*Enter* CLEOMENES *and* DION.]

CLE. The climate's delicate, the air most sweet,
Fertile the isle, the temple much surpassing
The common praise it bears.
     DION.   I shall report,
For most it caught me, the celestial habits° —
Methinks I so should term them — and the reverence
Of the grave wearers. Oh, the sacrifice!   6
How ceremonious, solemn, and unearthly
It was i' the offering!
     CLE.   But of all, the burst
And the ear-deafening voice o' the oracle,
Kin to Jove's thunder, so surprised my sense   10
That I was nothing.
     DION.   If the event° o' the journey
Prove as successful to the Queen — oh, be 't so! —
As it hath been to us rare, pleasant, speedy,
The time is worth the use on 't.
     CLE.   Great Apollo
Turn all to the best! These proclamations,   15
So forcing faults upon Hermione,
I little like.
     DION.   The violent carriage° of it
Will clear or end the business. When the oracle,
Thus by Apollo's great divine sealed up,
Shall the contents discover, something rare°   20
Even then will rush to knowledge. Go. Fresh horses!
And gracious be the issue!   [*Exeunt.*]

SCENE II. *A court of justice.*

[*Enter* LEONTES, LORDS, *and* OFFICERS.]

LEON. This sessions, to our great grief we pro-
     nounce,
Even pushes° 'gainst our heart. The party tried

The daughter of a King, our wife, and one
Of us too much beloved. Let us be cleared°
Of being tyrannous, since we so openly   5
Proceed in justice, which shall have due course,
Even to the guilt or the purgation.°
Produce the prisoner.
     OFF. It is His Highness' pleasure that the Queen
Appear in person here in court. Silence!   10
[*Enter* HERMIONE, *guarded,* PAULINA, *and* LADIES
attending.]
     LEON. Read the indictment.
     OFF. [*Reads.*] " Hermione, Queen to the worthy
Leontes, King of Sicilia, thou art here accused and
arraigned of high treason, in committing adultery
with Polixenes, King of Bohemia, and conspir-   15
ing with Camillo to take away the life of our Sover-
eign Lord the King, thy royal husband. The pre-
tense° whereof being by circumstances partly laid
open, thou, Hermione, contrary to the faith and al-
legiance of a true subject, didst counsel and aid them,
for their better safety, to fly away by night."   22
     HER. Since what I am to say must be but that
Which contradicts my accusation, and
The testimony on my part no other   25
But what comes from myself, it shall scarce boot°
     me
To say " Not guilty." Mine integrity,°
Being counted falsehood, shall, as I express it,°
Be so received. But thus, if Powers Divine
Behold our human actions, as they do,   30
I doubt not then but innocence shall make
False accusation blush and tyranny
Tremble at patience. You, my lord, best know,
Who least will seem to do so, my past life
Hath been as continent, as chaste, as true,   35
As I am now unhappy — which is more
Than history can pattern, though devised
And played to take spectators.° For behold me
A fellow of the royal bed, which owe°
A moiety° of the throne, a great King's daughter,
The mother to a hopeful Prince, here standing   41
To prate and talk for life and honor 'fore
Who please to come and hear. For life, I prize it
As I weigh grief, which I would spare. For honor,
'Tis a derivative from me to mine,°   45
And only that I stand for. I appeal
To your own conscience, sir, before Polixenes
Came to your Court, how I was in your grace,
How merited to be so; since he came,
With what encounter so uncurrent I   50

---

202. session: court of law. arraign: formally accuse.
     Act III, Sc. i: The purpose of this short scene is to stress the
importance of the oracle on which the plot now turns.   4. celes-
tial habits: heavenly robes.   11. event: result.   17. violent
carriage: headstrong manner of proceeding.   20. rare: unex-
pected.
     Sc. ii: 2. pushes: thrusts.

4. cleared: shown innocent.   7. purgation: acquittal.   18. pre-
tense: intention.   26. boot: be of advantage to.   27. integrity:
truthfulness.   28. as . . . it: even as I say it.   37–38. history
. . . spectators: can be paralleled in history, even though turned
into a play specially written to move an audience.   39. owe:
possess.   40. moiety: share.   45. derivative . . . mine: passes
as an inheritance to my son.

Have strained, to appear thus.° If one jot beyond
The bound of honor, or in act or will
That way inclining, hardened be the hearts
Of all that hear me, and my near'st of kin
Cry fie° upon my grave!

LEON.   I ne'er heard yet   55
That any of these bolder vices wanted
Less impudence to gainsay° what they did
Than to perform it first.

HER.   That's true enough,
Though 'tis a saying, sir, not due to me.

LEON. You will not own it.

HER.   More than mistress of   60
Which comes to me in name of fault I must not
At all acknowledge.° For Polixenes,
With whom I am accused, I do confess
I loved him as in honor he required,
With such a kind of love as might become   65
A lady like me, with a love even such,
So and no other, as yourself commanded.
Which not to have done I think had been in me
Both disobedience and ingratitude
To you and toward your friend, whose love had
    spoke   70
Even since it could speak, from an infant, freely
That it was yours. Now, for conspiracy,
I know not how it tastes, though it be dished
For me to try how. All I know of it
Is that Camillo was an honest man,   75
And why he left your Court, the gods themselves,
Wotting° no more than I, are ignorant.

LEON. You knew of his departure, as you know
What you have underta'en to do in 's absence.

HER. Sir,   80
You speak a language that I understand not.
My life stands in the level° of your dreams,
Which I'll lay down.

LEON.   Your actions are my dreams.
You had a bastard by Polixenes,
And I but dreamed it. As you were past all shame —
Those of your fact° are so — so past all truth. 86
Which to deny concerns more than avails;° for as
Thy brat hath been cast out, like to itself,
No father owning it — which is, indeed,
More criminal in thee than it — so thou   90
Shalt feel our justice, in whose easiest passage
Look for no less than death.

HER.   Sir, spare your threats.
The bug° which you would fright me with I seek.

To me can life be no commodity.°
The crown and comfort of my life, your favor,   95
I do give lost, for I do feel it gone,
But know not how it went. My second joy
And first-fruits of my body, from his presence
I am barred like one infectious. My third comfort,
Starred° most unluckily, is from my breast,   100
The innocent milk in it most innocent mouth,
Haled° out to murder. Myself on every post
Proclaimed a strumpet, with immodest hatred
The childbed privilege° denied which 'longs°
To women of all fashion; lastly, hurried   105
Here to this place i' the open air before
I have got strength of limit.° Now, my liege,
Tell me what blessings I have here alive,
That I should fear to die? Therefore proceed.
But yet hear this, mistake me not, no life —   110
I prize it not a straw — but for mine honor,
Which I would free, if I shall be condemned
Upon surmises, all proofs sleeping else°
But what your jealousies awake, I tell you
'Tis rigor and not law. Your Honors all,   115
I do refer me° to the oracle.
Apollo be my judge!

I. LORD.   This your request
Is altogether just. Therefore bring forth,
And in Apollo's name, his oracle.

[*Exeunt certain* OFFICERS.]

HER. The emperor of Russia was my father.   120
Oh, that he were alive, and here beholding
His daughter's trial! That he did but see
The flatness° of my misery, yet with eyes
Of pity, not revenge!

[*Re-enter* OFFICERS, *with* CLEOMENES *and* DION.]

OFF. You here shall swear upon this sword of jus-
    tice   125
That you, Cleomenes and Dion, have
Been both at Delphos, and from thence have brought
This sealed-up oracle by the hand delivered
Of great Apollo's priest, and that since then
You have not dared to break the holy seal   130
Nor read the secrets in 't.

CLE. & DION.   All this we swear.

LEON. Break up the seals° and read.

OFF. [*Reads.*] "Hermione is chaste: Polixenes
blameless: Camillo a true subject: Leontes a jealous
tyrant: his innocent babe truly begotten: and the
King shall live without an heir if that which is lost
be not found."   137

LORDS. Now blessed be the great Apollo!

HER.   Praised!

49–51. since . . . thus: I charge you to say since Polixenes came to
Court what intercourse I have had with him that was unlawful,
which causes me to appear as a prisoner. 55. fie: a word express-
ing strong contempt. 57. gainsay: deny. 60–62. More . . .
acknowledge: I must not acknowledge more faults than are
naturally mine. 77. Wotting: if they know. 82. level: range,
so in danger of being hit by. 86. your fact: who act as you have
done. 87. Which . . . avails: you may choose to deny it, but
it will have no effect. 93. bug: bogey.

94. commodity: advantage. 100. Starred: fated. 102. Haled:
hauled. 104. childbed privilege: the privilege of lying-in after
confinement. 'longs: belongs. 107. strength of limit: strength to
endure it. 113. all . . . else: all other proof being neglected.
116. refer me: appeal. 123. flatness: abjectness. 132. Break
. . . seals: open. See App. 6.

LEON. Hast thou read truth?

OFF.   Aye, my lord, even so
As it is here set down.   140

LEON. There is no truth at all i' the oracle.
The sessions shall proceed. This is mere falsehood.

[*Enter* SERVANT.]

SERV. My lord the King, the King!

LEON.   What is the business?

SERV. O sir, I shall be hated to report it!
The Prince your son, with mere conceit° and fear
Of the Queen's speed,° is gone.

LEON.   How! Gone!

SERV.   Is dead. 146

LEON. Apollo's angry, and the Heavens them-
selves
Do strike at my injustice. [HERMIONE *faints*.] How
now there!

PAUL. This news is mortal° to the Queen. Look
down
And see what death is doing.

LEON.   Take her hence. 150
Her heart is but o'ercharged,° she will recover.
I have too much believed mine own suspicion.
Beseech you, tenderly apply to her
Some remedies for life.

[*Exeunt* PAULINA *and* LADIES, *with* HERMIONE.]
                              Apollo, pardon
My great profaneness 'gainst thine oracle! 155
I'll reconcile me to Polixenes,
New-woo my Queen, recall the good Camillo,
Whom I proclaim a man of truth, of mercy.
For, being transported by my jealousies
To bloody thoughts and to revenge, I chose 160
Camillo for the minister to poison
My friend Polixenes, which had been done
But that the good mind of Camillo tardied°
My swift command, though I with death and with
Reward did threaten and encourage him. 165
Not doing it and being done, he, most humane
And filled with honor, to my kingly guest
Unclasped my practice,° quit his fortunes here,
Which you knew great, and to the hazard
Of all incertainties himself commended, 170
No richer than his honor.° How he glisters°
Thorough° my rust! And how his piety°
Does my deeds make the blacker!

[*Re-enter* PAULINA.]

PAUL.   Woe the while!°
Oh, cut my lace,° lest my heart, cracking it,
Break too!

I. LORD. What fit° is this, good lady? 175

145. conceit: thought. 146. speed: misfortune, plight. 149. mor-
tal: deadly, fatal. 151. o'ercharged: overfull of emotion.
163. tardied: delayed in obeying. 168. Unclasped my practice:
revealed my plot. 171. No . . . honor: having nothing else but
his honor. glisters: glitters, shines bright. 172. Thorough:
through. piety: goodness. 173. Woe . . . while: woe on this
time. 174. cut my lace: See *Rich III*, IV.i.34,n. 175. fit: mad fit.

PAUL. What studied° torments, tyrant, hast for
me?
What wheels? Racks? Fires? What flaying? Boiling
In leads or oils?° What old or newer torture
Must I receive, whose every word deserves
To taste of thy most worst? Thy tyranny, 180
Together working with thy jealousies,
Fancies too weak for boys, too green and idle
For girls of nine, oh, think what they have done,
And then run mad indeed, stark-mad! For all
Thy bygone fooleries were but spices° of it. 185
That thou betray'dst Polixenes, 'twas nothing.
That did but show thee, of a fool, inconstant
And damnable ingrateful. Nor was 't much
Thou wouldst have poisoned good Camillo's honor
To have him kill a King — poor trespasses, 190
More monstrous standing by.° Whereof I reckon
The casting-forth to crows thy baby daughter
To be or none or little, though a devil
Would have shed water out of fire ere done 't.
Nor is 't directly laid to thee, the death 195
Of the young Prince, whose honorable thoughts,
Thoughts high for one so tender, cleft the heart
That could conceive° a gross and foolish sire
Blemished° his gracious dam. This is not, no,
Laid to thy answer. But the last — O lords, 200
When I have said, cry "Woe!" — The Queen, the
Queen,
The sweet'st, dear'st creature's dead,° and venge-
ance for 't
Not dropped down yet.

I. LORD.   The higher powers forbid!

PAUL. I say she's dead, I'll swear 't. If word nor
oath
Prevail not, go and see. If you can bring 205
Tincture or luster° in her lip, her eye,
Heat outwardly or breath within, I'll serve you
As I would do the gods. But, O thou tyrant!
Do not repent these things, for they are heavier
Than all thy woes can stir. Therefore betake thee
To nothing but despair. A thousand knees 211
Ten thousand years together,° naked, fasting,
Upon a barren mountain, and still winter
In storm perpetual, could not move the gods
To look that way thou wert.

176. studied: carefully thought-out. 177–78. What . . . oils:
See App. 10. 185. spices: slight tastes. 190–91. poor . . . by:
slight offenses compared with your monstrous crimes. 198. con-
ceive: imagine. 199. Blemished: defiled. 201–02. Queen . . .
dead: The author of a "winter's tale" must not be pressed too in-
sistently for details which he has omitted. It is clear from this
speech, and from Leontes' words at the end (V.iii.130–40), that
Paulina at this moment and Leontes a little later both believed
Hermione to be dead indeed. It is never disclosed how Hermione
was later found to be alive. nor is there any hint to the audience.
This is the one important occasion in all Shakespeare's plays
where he introduces a major surprise in the last scene. 206. Tinc-
ture or luster: color or brightness. 211–12. A . . . together: if
you were to kneel on a thousand knees for ten thousand years.

LEON.   Go on, go on,   215
Thou canst not speak too much. I have deserved
All tongues to talk their bitterest.
  1. LORD.   Say no more.
Howe'er the business goes, you have made fault
I' the boldness of your speech.
  PAUL.   I am sorry for 't.
All faults I make, when I shall come to know them,
I do repent. Alas! I have showed too much   221
The rashness of a woman. He is touched
To the noble heart. What's gone and what's past
    help
Should be past grief. Do not receive affliction
At my petition. I beseech you, rather   225
Let me be punished that have minded° you
Of what you should forget. Now, good my liege,
Sir, royal sir, forgive a foolish woman.
The love I bore your Queen — lo, fool again!
I'll speak of her no more, nor of your children,   230
I'll not remember you of° my own lord,
Who is lost too. Take your patience to you,°
And I'll say nothing.
  LEON.   Thou didst speak but well
When most the truth, which I receive much better
Than to be pitied of thee. Prithee bring me   235
To the dead bodies of my Queen and son.
One grave shall be for both, upon them shall
The causes of their death appear, unto
Our shame perpetual. Once a day I'll visit
The chapel where they lie, and tears shed there   240
Shall be my recreation. So long as nature
Will bear up with this exercise,° so long
I daily vow to use it. Come and lead me
To these sorrows.   [Exeunt.]

SCENE III. *Bohemia. A desert country near the sea.*

[*Enter* ANTIGONUS, *with a* CHILD, *and a* MARINER.]
  ANT. Thou art perfect,° then, our ship hath
    touched upon
The deserts of Bohemia?°
  MAR.   Aye, my lord, and fear
We have landed in ill time. The skies look grimly
And threaten present blusters. In my conscience,
The Heavens with that we have in hand are angry
And frown upon 's.   6
  ANT. Their sacred wills be done! Go, get aboard,
Look to thy bark. I'll not be long before

I call upon thee.
  MAR. Make your best haste, and go not   10
Too far i' the land. 'Tis like to be loud weather.
Besides, this place is famous for the creatures
Of prey that keep° upon 't.
  ANT.   Go thou away.
I'll follow instantly.
  MAR.   I am glad at heart
To be so rid o' the business.   [Exit.]
  ANT.   Come, poor babe.   15
I have heard, but not believed, the spirits o' the dead
May walk again. If such thing be, thy mother
Appeared to me last night, for ne'er was dream
So like a waking. To me comes a creature,
Sometimes her head on one side, some another.   20
I never saw a vessel of like sorrow,
So filled and so becoming. In pure white robes,
Like very sanctity,° she did approach
My cabin where I lay, thrice bowed before me,
And, gasping to begin some speech, her eyes   25
Became two spouts. The fury spent, anon
Did this break from her: " Good Antigonus,
Since fate, against thy better disposition,
Hath made thy person for the thrower-out
Of my poor babe, according to thine oath,   30
Places remote° enough are in Bohemia.
There weep and leave it crying, and for the babe
Is counted lost forever, Perdita°
I prithee call't. For this ungentle business,
Put on thee by my lord, thou ne'er shalt see   35
Thy wife Paulina more." And so, with shrieks,
She melted into air. Affrighted much,
I did in time collect myself, and thought
This was so, and no slumber.° Dreams are toys,°
Yet for this once — yea, superstitiously —   40
I will be squared° by this. I do believe
Hermione hath suffered death, and that
Apollo would, this being indeed the issue
Of King Polixenes, it should here be laid,
Either for life or death, upon the earth   45
Of its right father. Blossom,° speed thee well!
There lie, and there thy character.° There these,°
Which may, if fortune please, both breed° thee,
    pretty,
And still rest thine. The storm begins. Poor wretch,
That for thy mother's fault art thus exposed   50
To loss and what may follow! Weep I cannot,
But my heart bleeds, and most accursed am I
To be by oath enjoined to this. Farewell!
The day frowns more and more. Thou'rt like to have
A lullaby too rough. I never saw   55

---

226. minded: reminded.   231. remember . . . of: make you remember.   232. Take . . . you: be patient.   241–42. nature . . . exercise: nature permits me to continue this devotion.

Sc. iii: 1. perfect: certain.   2. deserts of Bohemia: Bohemia, as Ben Jonson and other wiseacres have pointed out, has no sea-coast. Shakespeare, however, took his geography from Greene. See *W Tale* Intro. p. 960a.

13. keep: live.   23. very sanctity: holiness itself.   31. remote: deserted.   33. Perdita: i.e., the lost one.   39. This . . . slumber: this was real and not a dream. toys: trifles.   41. squared: ruled.   46. Blossom: little flower.   47. character: writing; i.e., the account of Perdita's birth which Antigonus has prepared and which later reveals her origin. these: i.e., the box of gold and jewels.   48. breed: pay for your bringing up.

The heavens so dim by day. A savage clamor!°
Well may I get aboard! This is the chase.°
I am gone forever.   [*Exit, pursued by a bear.*°]
                    [*Enter a* SHEPHERD.]

SHEP. I would there were no age between ten and
three and twenty, or that youth would sleep out   60
the rest. For there is nothing in the between but get-
ting wenches with child, wronging the ancientry,°
stealing, fighting. — Hark you now! Would any but
these boiled brains° of nineteen and two and twenty
hunt this weather? They have scared away two of
my best sheep, which I fear the wolf will sooner find
than the master. If anywhere I have them, 'tis by
the seaside, browsing of ivy. Good luck, an 't be thy
will! What have we here? Mercy on 's, a barne,° a
very pretty barne! A boy or a child,° I wonder?   70
A pretty one, a very pretty one. Sure, some scape.°
Though I am not bookish, yet I can read waiting
gentlewoman in the scape. This has been some stair-
work, some trunkwork,° some behind-door work.
They were warmer that got this than the poor thing
is here. I'll take it up for pity. Yet I'll tarry till my
son come, he hallooed but even now. Whoa, ho,
hoa!

                    [*Enter* CLOWN.°]

CLO. Hilloa, loa!   80
SHEP. What, art so near? If thou'lt see a thing to
talk on when thou art dead and rotten, come hither.
What ailest thou, man?
CLO. I have seen two such sights, by sea and by
land! But I am not to say it is a sea, for it is now the
sky. Betwixt the firmament° and it you cannot thrust
a bodkin's° point.
SHEP. Why, boy, how is it?   88
CLO. I would you did but see how it chafes, how it
rages, how it takes up° the shore! But that's not to
the point. Oh, the most piteous cry of the poor souls!
Sometimes to see 'em, and not to see 'em — now the
ship boring the moon with her mainmast, and anon
swallowed with yest° and froth, as you'd thrust a
cork into a hogshead. And then for the land   95
service,° to see how the bear tore out his shoulder
bone, how he cried to me for help and said his name

was Antigonus, a nobleman. But to make an end of
the ship, to see how the sea flapdragoned° it. But
first, how the poor souls roared, and the sea mocked
them, and how the poor gentleman roared and the
bear mocked him, both roaring louder than the sea
or weather.   104
SHEP. Name of mercy, when was this, boy?
CLO. Now, now. I have not winked since I saw
these sights. The men are not yet cold under water,
nor the bear half dined on the gentleman. He's at it
now.   109
SHEP. Would I had been by, to have helped the
old man!
CLO. I would you had been by the ship side, to
have helped her. There your charity would have
lacked footing.°   114
SHEP. Heavy matters! Heavy matters! But look
thee here, boy. Now bless thyself. Thou mettest with
things dying, I with things newborn. Here's a sight
for thee, look thee, a bearing cloth° for a squire's°
child! Look thee here, take up, take up, boy, open 't.
So, let's see. It was told me I should be rich by the
fairies.° This is some changeling.° Open 't. What's
within, boy?   123
CLO. You're a made old man. If the sins of your
youth are forgiven you, you're well to live. Gold! All
gold!
SHEP. This is fairy gold, boy, and 'twill prove so.
Up with 't, keep it close. Home, home, the next°
way. We are lucky, boy, and to be so still requires
nothing but secrecy. Let my sheep go. Come, good
boy, the next way home.   131
CLO. Go you the next way with your findings. I'll
go see if the bear be gone from the gentleman, and
how much he hath eaten. They are never curst° but
when they are hungry. If there be any of him left,
I'll bury it.   136
SHEP. That's a good deed. If thou mayest discern
by that which is left of him what he is, fetch me to
the sight of him.
CLO. Marry° will I, and you shall help to put him
i' the ground.   141
SHEP. 'Tis a lucky day, boy, and we'll do good
deeds on 't.   [*Exeunt.*]

56. savage clamor: i.e., the noise of the hunt.   57. chase: the
beast being hunted.   58 s.d., Exit . . . bear: this famous stage
direction comes from F1. It is often claimed that a real bear was
used. Bears appear in other plays of the time, and tame bears
were not unknown; but a bear on its hind legs is of all beasts the
most easily personated by a man.   62. ancientry: the elderly
and respectable.   64. boiled brains: lunatics.   69. barne: bairn,
child.   70. child: baby girl.   71. scape: fun.   74. trunkwork:
hiding in chests.   79 s.d., Clown: rustic.   86. firmament: vault
of heaven.   87. bodkin: pin.   90. takes up: rushes up.   94. yest:
yeast, foam.   95–96. land service: what was done on land.

99. flapdragoned: swallowed it up. Swallowing flapdragons
(lighted raisins floating on liquor) was a winter amusement.
114. footing: a chance of helping.   118. bearing-cloth: christen-
ing robe. squire: gentleman of wealth.   121–22. rich . . . fairies:
made rich by the fairies. The simple-minded believed that the
fairies could bring gold to bestow on those whom they favored;
but fairy gold was liable to disappear as mysteriously as it
came.   122. changeling: a child taken or left by the fairies in
exchange for another.   128. next: nearest.   134. curst: savage.
140. Marry: Mary, by the Virgin.

Act IV

SCENE I.

[*Enter* TIME, *the Chorus.*°]

TIME. I, that please some, try all, both joy and
    terror
Of good and bad, that makes and unfolds error,
Now take upon me, in the name of Time,
To use my wings.° Impute it not a crime
To me or my swift passage that I slide   5
O'er sixteen years and leave the growth untried°
Of that wide gap, since it is in my power
To o'erthrow law and in one self-born hour
To plant and o'erwhelm custom. Let me pass
The same I am, ere ancient'st order was   10
Or what is now received. I witness to
The times that brought them in. So shall I do
To the freshest things now reigning, and make stale
The glistering of this present, as my tale
Now seems to it. Your patience this allowing,   15
I turn my glass° and give my scene such growing
As° you had slept between. Leontes leaving,°
The effects of his fond° jealousies so grieving
That he shuts up himself, imagine me,
Gentle spectators, that I now may be   20
In fair Bohemia. And remember well,
I mentioned a son o' the King's, which Florizel
I now name to you, and with speed so pace°
To speak of Perdita, now grown in grace
Equal with wondering. What of her ensues   25
I list not° prophesy, but let Time's news
Be known when 'tis brought forth. A shepherd's
    daughter,
And what to her adheres,° which follows after,
Is the argument° of Time. Of this allow
If ever you have spent time worse ere now.   30
If never, yet that Time himself doth say
He wishes earnestly you never may.   [*Exit.*]

SCENE II. *Bohemia. The palace of* POLIXENES.

[*Enter* POLIXENES *and* CAMILLO.]

POL. I pray thee, good Camillo, be no more im-
portunate. 'Tis a sickness denying thee anything, a
death to grant this.   3
CAM. It is fifteen years since I saw my country.

Though I have for the most part been aired abroad,°
I desire to lay my bones there. Besides, the penitent
King, my master, hath sent for me, to whose feeling
sorrows I might be some allay° — or I o'erween° to
think so, which is another spur to my departure.   10
POL. As thou lovest me, Camillo, wipe not out the
rest of thy services by leaving me now. The need I
have of thee thine own goodness hath made. Better
not to have had thee than thus to want° thee. Thou,
having made me businesses which none without thee
can sufficiently manage, must either stay to execute
them thyself or take away with thee the very serv-
ices thou hast done — which if I have not enough
considered, as too much I cannot, to be more thank-
ful to thee shall be my study, and my profit   20
therein, the heaping friendships.° Of that fatal coun-
try Sicilia prithee speak no more, whose very nam-
ing punishes me with the remembrance of that
penitent, as thou callest him, and reconciled King,
my brother, whose loss of his most precious Queen
and children are even now to be afresh lamented.
Say to me, when sawest thou the Prince Florizel, my
son? Kings are no less unhappy, their issue not being
gracious,° than they are in losing them when they
have approved° their virtues.   32
CAM. Sir, it is three days since I saw the Prince.
What his happier affairs may be are to me unknown.
But I have missingly noted° he is of late much re-
tired from Court and is less frequent to° his princely
exercises than formerly he hath appeared.   38
POL. I have considered so much, Camillo, and
with some care. So far that I have eyes under my
service which look upon his removedness,° from
whom I have this intelligence, that he is seldom
from° the house of a most homely shepherd, a man,
they say, that from very nothing, and beyond the
imagination of his neighbors, is grown into an un-
speakable estate.   46
CAM. I have heard, sir, of such a man, who hath
a daughter of most rare note. The report of her is
extended more than can be thought to begin from
such a cottage.   50
POL. That's likewise part of my intelligence, but
I fear the angle° that plucks our son thither. Thou
shalt accompany us to the place, where we will,
not appearing what we are, have some question with
the shepherd, from whose simplicity I think it not
uneasy° to get the cause of my son's resort thither.
Prithee be my present partner in this business, and
lay aside the thoughts of Sicilia.   58

Act IV, Sc. i: s.d., Time, the Chorus: Shakespeare seldom
uses a symbolic character to introduce an act. Here *Time*, with
his hourglass, symbolizes the passage of sixteen years. In the
modern theater a note on the program is sufficient.   4. use my
wings: fly over a great space.   6. untried: unexperienced, not
shown.   16. glass: hourglass.   17. As: as if. Leontes leaving:
i.e., shifting the action away from Sicilia to Bohemia.   18. fond:
foolish.   23. pace: go on.   26. list not: do not care to.   28. ad-
heres: belongs.   29. argument: plot of the play.

Sc. ii: 5. aired abroad: lived in the air of a foreign country.
9. allay: alleviation. o'erween: presume.   14. want: be without.
21. heaping friendships: acts of friendship which you heap on me.
31. gracious: full of grace.   32. approved: proved.   36. miss-
ingly noted: noticed because I missed him.   37. frequent to:
frequently at.   41. look . . . removedness: spy on his absence.
43. from: out of.   52. angle: fishhook.   56. uneasy: difficult.

CAM. I willingly obey your command.

POL. My best Camillo! We must disguise our-
selves.   [*Exeunt.*]

SCENE III. *A road near the* SHEPHERD'S *cottage.*

[*Enter* AUTOLYCUS,° *singing.*]

AUT.
" When daffodils begin to peer,°
    With heigh! the doxy° over the dale,
Why, then comes in the sweet o' the year,
    For the red blood reigns in the winter's pale.°

" The white sheet bleaching on the hedge,   5
    With heigh! the sweet birds, oh, how they sing!
Doth set my pugging° tooth on edge,
    For a quart of ale is a dish for a king.

" The lark, that tirra-lyra chants,
    With heigh! with heigh! the thrush and the jay,
Are summer songs for me and my aunts,°   11
    While we lie tumbling in the hay."

I have served Prince Florizel and in my time wore
three-pile,° but now I am out of service:

" But shall I go mourn for that, my dear?   15
    The pale moon shines by night.
And when I wander here and there,
    I then do most go right.

" If tinkers may have leave to live,
    And bear the sow-skin budget,°   20
Then my account I well may give,
    And in the stocks avouch it."°

My traffic is sheets. When the kite builds, look to
lesser linen.° My father named me Autolycus, who
being, as I am, littered under Mercury,° was like-
wise a snapper-up of unconsidered trifles. With   26
die and drab I purchased this caparison,° and my
revenue is the silly cheat.° Gallows and knock are
too powerful on the highway.° Beating and hanging

are terrors to me. For the life to come, I sleep out the
thought of it. A prize! A prize!   32

[*Enter* CLOWN.]

CLO. Let me see, every 'leven wether tods,° every
tod yields pound and odd shilling, fifteen hundred
shorn, what comes the wool to?

AUT. [*Aside*] If the springe° hold, the cock's°
mine.   37

CLO. I cannot do't without counters.° Let me see,
what am I to buy for our sheepshearing feast? Three
pound of sugar, five pound of currants, rice — what
will this sister of mine do with rice? But my father
hath made her mistress of the feast, and she lays it
on. She hath made me four and twenty nosegays for
the shearers, three-man songmen° all, and very good
ones. But they are most of them means° and bases,
but one puritan amongst them, and he sings   47
psalms to hornpipes. I must have saffron to color
the warden pies,° mace,° dates — none, that's out of
my note° — nutmegs, seven, a race° or two of gin-
ger, but that I may beg, four pound of prunes, and
as many of raisins o' the sun.°   52

AUT. Oh, that ever I was born!

[*Groveling on the ground.*]

CLO. I' the name of me ——

AUT. Oh, help me, help me! Pluck but off these
rags, and then death, death!   56

CLO. Alack, poor soul! Thou hast need of more
rags to lay on thee rather than have these off.

AUT. O sir, the loathsomeness of them offends me
more than the stripes I have received, which are
mighty ones and millions.   61

CLO. Alas, poor man! A million of beating may
come to a great matter.

AUT. I am robbed, sir, and beaten, my money and
apparel ta'en from me, and these detestable things
put upon me.   66

CLO. What, by a horseman or a footman?

AUT. A footman, sweet sir, a footman.

CLO. Indeed, he should be a footman by the gar-
ments he has left with thee. If this be a horseman's
coat, it hath seen very hot service. Lend me thy
hand, I'll help thee. Come, lend me thy hand.   73

[*Helping him up.*]

AUT. O good sir, tenderly. Oh!

CLO. Alas, poor soul!

AUT. O good sir, softly, good sir! I fear, sir, my
shoulder blade is out.   77

CLO. How now! Canst stand?

AUT. Softly, dear sir [*Picks his pocket.*], good sir,
softly. You ha' done me a charitable office.

Sc. iii: s.d., Autolycus: See *W Tale* Intro. p. 960b.   1. When
. . . peer: i.e., in early spring.   2. doxy: tramp's moll.   4. in
. . . pale: in place of winter's pale blood.   7. pugging: thieving.
11. aunts: women.   14. three-pile: the thickest and costliest
kind of velvet.   20. budget: tool bag.   22. stocks . . . it: ac-
knowledge my trade (i.e., vagabondage) in the stocks.   23–24. My
. . . linen: my line is stealing the sheets that are drying and
bleaching on the hedges, just as a kite snatches up small pieces
when it is building its nest.   25. littered . . . Mercury: born
when the planet Mercury is in the ascendant. In classical legend
Autolycus was the son of the god Mercury, and a most skillful thief.
26–27. With . . . caparison: dicing and drabbing have brought me
this outfit (i.e., rags).   28. cheat: in thieves' language, the
"sucker."   28–29. Gallows . . . highway: I am too scared of the
gallows and hard knocks to become a highwayman.

33. 'leven . . . tods: eleven sheep make a tod of wool (about 28
lbs.).   36. springe: snare. cock: woodcock; i.e., victim.   38. count-
ers: used for calculating large sums.   45. three-man songmen:
singers of three-part songs.   46. means: tenors.   49. warden
pies: pies made of warden pears. mace: a spice used for flavoring.
49–50. out . . . note: not in my note of what must be bought.
50. race: root.   52. raisins . . . sun: sun-dried raisins.

CLO. Dost lack any money? I have a little money for thee. 83

AUT. No, good sweet sir. No, I beseech you, sir. I have a kinsman not past three-quarters of a mile hence, unto whom I was going. I shall there have money, or anything I want. Offer me no money, I pray you, that kills my heart.°

CLO. What manner of fellow was he that robbed you? 90

AUT. A fellow, sir, that I have known to go about with troll-my-dames.° I knew him once a servant of the Prince. I cannot tell, good sir, for which of his virtues it was, but he was certainly whipped out of the Court. 95

CLO. His vices, you would say, there's no virtue whipped out of the Court. They cherish it° to make it stay there, and yet it will no more but abide.° 99

AUT. "Vices" I would say, sir. I know this man well. He hath been since an ape-bearer,° then a process-server,° a bailiff. Then he compassed a motion of the Prodigal Son,° and married a tinker's wife within a mile where my land and living lies, and, having flown over° many knavish professions, he settled only in rogue.° Some call him Autolycus.

CLO. Out upon him! Prig,° for my life, prig. 108 He haunts wakes, fairs, and bearbaitings.

AUT. Very true, sir — he, sir, he. That's the rogue that put me into this apparel. 111

CLO. Not a more cowardly rogue in all Bohemia. If you had but looked big and spit at him, he'd have run.

AUT. I must confess to you, sir, I am no fighter. I am false of heart that way, and that he knew, I warrant him.

CLO. How do you now? 118

AUT. Sweet sir, much better than I was. I can stand and walk. I will even take my leave of you, and pace softly toward my kinsman's. 121

CLO. Shall I bring thee on the way?

AUT. No, good-faced sir. No, sweet sir.

CLO. Then fare thee well. I must go buy spices for our sheepshearing. 125

AUT. Prosper you, sweet sir! [Exit CLOWN.] Your purse is not hot enough to purchase your spice. I'll be with you at your sheepshearing, too. If I make not this cheat bring out another and the shearers prove sheep, let me be unrolled° and my name put in the book of virtue! [Sings.] 131

"Jog on, jog on, the footpath way,
    And merrily hent° the stile-a.
A merry heart goes all the day,   134
    Your sad tires in a mile-a."   [Exit.]

SCENE IV. *The* SHEPHERD'S *cottage*.

[*Enter* FLORIZEL *and* PERDITA.]

FLO. These your unusual weeds° to each part of you
Do give a life. No shepherdess, but Flora
Peering in April's front.° This your sheepshearing
Is as a meeting of the petty gods,
And you the queen on't.

PER.   Sir, my gracious lord,   5
To chide at your extremes° it not becomes me.
Oh, pardon, that I name them! Your high self,
The gracious mark o' the land,° you have obscured
With a swain's° wearing, and me, poor lowly maid,
Most goddesslike pranked up.° But that our feasts
In every mess have folly and the feeders   11
Digest it with a custom, I should blush
To see you so attired, sworn, I think,
To show myself a glass.°

FLO.   I bless the time
When my good falcon made her flight across   15
Thy father's ground.°

PER.   Now Jove afford you cause!°
To me the difference forges dread,° your greatness
Hath not been used to fear. Even now I tremble
To think your father, by some accident,
Should pass this way as you did. Oh, the Fates!   20
How would he look, to see his work, so noble,
Vilely bound up?° What would he say? Or how
Should I, in these my borrowed flaunts,° behold
The sternness of his presence?

FLO.   Apprehend°
Nothing but jollity. The gods themselves,   25
Humbling their deities to love, have taken

---

133. hent: leap.

Sc. iv: 1. weeds: garments. Perdita is dressed like the goddess Flora in a costume provided by Prince Florizel (ll. 9–10). Florizel is dressed in a matching costume as her lover (ll. 8–9). 2–3. Flora . . . front: Flora, the goddess of flowers, appearing early in April. 6. extremes: exaggerations. 8. gracious . . . land: the "observed of all observers." 9. swain: young countryman, a word much used by pastoral poets. 10. pranked up: dressed up. 10–14. But . . . glass: if it were not that in our feasts someone plays the fool in every party and the rest excuse it as part of the fun, I should blush to see you dressed as my companion, and I would swear you did it to make me see myself reflected in you (i.e., too gay for a humble shepherdess). sworn: This is the F1 reading. Many editors emend to "swoon" or "swound," which makes better sense. 15–16. When . . . ground: In *Pandosto*, the young Prince first encountered his love while hawking. See *W Tale* Intro. p. 960a. 16. afford . . . cause: give you good reason for "blessing the time." 17. the . . . dread: the difference in rank between us makes me afraid. 21–22. his . . . up: to see the work of which he was the author bound in so poor a cover. 23. flaunts: finery. 24. Apprehend: think.

---

88. kills my heart: breaks my heart. 92. troll-my-dames: a game in which balls were rolled through hoops on a board. 98. cherish it: treat it lovingly. 99. abide: make a short stay. Cynical remarks about Court life are common at this date. 101. ape-bearer: owner of a tame monkey. 102. process-server: sheriff's officer — a despised occupation. 102–03. compassed . . . Son: acquired a puppet show of the story of the Prodigal Son. 106. flown over: tried his hand at. 107. settled . . . rogue: settled down to become a rogue. 108. Prig: thief. 130. unrolled: struck off the roll of thieves.

The shapes of beasts upon them. Jupiter
Became a bull, and bellowed; the green Neptune
A ram, and bleated; and the fire-robed god,
Golden Apollo,° a poor humble swain,   30
As I seem now. Their transformations
Were never for a piece of beauty rarer,
Nor in a way so chaste, since my desires
Run not before mine honor, nor my lusts
Burn hotter than my faith.

PER.   Oh, but, sir,   35
Your resolution cannot hold when 'tis
Opposed, as it must be, by the power of the King.
One of these two must be necessities,
Which then will speak, that you must change this
        purpose,
Or I my life.°

FLO.   Thou dearest Perdita,   40
With these forced° thoughts I prithee darken not
The mirth o' the feast. Or° I'll be thine, my fair,
Or not my father's. For I cannot be
Mine own, nor anything to any, if
I be not thine. To this I am most constant,   45
Though destiny say no. Be merry, gentle.
Strangle such thoughts as these with anything
That you behold the while. Your guests are coming.
Lift up your countenance,° as it were the day
Of celebration of that nuptial which   50
We two have sworn shall come.

PER.   O Lady Fortune,
Stand you auspicious!

FLO.   See, your guests approach.
Address yourself to entertain them sprightly,°
And let's be red with mirth.

[Enter SHEPHERD, CLOWN, MOPSA, DORCAS, and others,
    with POLIXENES and CAMILLO disguised.]

SHEP. Fie, Daughter! When my old wife lived,
        upon   55
This day she was both pantler,° butler, cook,
Both dame and servant — welcomed all, served all;
Would sing her song and dance her turn, now here,
At upper end o' the table, now i' the middle,
On his shoulder, and his. Her face o' fire   60
With labor and the thing she took to quench it
She would to each one sip. You are retired,°
As if you were a feasted one and not
The hostess of the meeting. Pray you, bid
These unknown friends to 's welcome, for it is   65
A way to make us better friends, more known.
Come, quench your blushes and present yourself
That which you are, mistress o' the feast. Come on,
And bid us welcome to your sheepshearing,

As your° good flock shall prosper.

PER.   [To POLIXENES] Sir, welcome.   70
It is my father's will I should take on me
The hostessship o' the day. [To CAMILLO] You're
        welcome, sir.
Give me those flowers there, Dorcas. Reverend sirs,
For you there's rosemary and rue,° these keep
Seeming and savor° all the winter long.   75
Grace and remembrance be to you both,
And welcome to our shearing!

POL.   Shepherdess,
A fair one are you. Well you fit our ages
With flowers of winter.

PER.   Sir, the year growing ancient,
Not yet on summer's death nor on the birth   80
Of trembling winter, the fairest flowers o' the sea-
        son°
Are our carnations and streaked gillyvors,°
Which some call nature's bastards. Of that kind
Our rustic garden's barren, and I care not
To get slips of them.

POL.   Wherefore, gentle maiden,   85
Do you neglect them?

PER.   For I have heard it said
There is an art which in their piedness shares
With great creating Nature.°

POL.   Say there be,
Yet Nature is made better by no mean°
But Nature makes that mean. So, over that art   90
Which you say adds to Nature, is an art
That Nature makes. You see, sweet maid, we marry
A gentler scion° to the wildest stock,
And make conceive a bark of baser kind
By bud of nobler race.° This is an art   95
Which does mend Nature — change it rather, but
The art itself is Nature.

PER.   So it is.

POL. Then make your garden rich in gillyvors,
And do not call them bastards.

PER.   I'll not put
The dibble° in earth to set one slip of them,   100
No more than were I painted° I would wish
This youth should say 'twere well, and only there-
        fore
Desire to breed by me. Here's flowers for you,
Hot lavender, mints, savory, marjoram,
The marigold that goes to bed wi' the sun   105

29–30. fire-robed . . . Apollo: Apollo was god of the sun.
38–40. One . . . life: when the King opposes our marriage, either
you must leave me or I must die.   41. forced: far-fetched, un-
natural.   42. Or: either.   49. Lift . . . countenance: look up
cheerfully.   53. sprightly: with gay spirits.   56. pantler: keeper
of the pantry.   62. are retired: withdraw yourself.

70. As your: as you hope that your.   74. rosemary . . . rue:
These in the language of flowers mean "remembrance" and
"grace."   75. Seeming . . . savor: appearance and fragrance.
81. season: i.e., summer.   82. streaked gillyvors: probably the
streaked variety of clove pink.   88. There . . . nature: their
streaks are caused by artificial crossing and not by natural
growth. Perdita finds something distastefully unnatural in the
process.   89. mean: method.   93. scion: slip for grafting.
94–95. And . . . race: make the baser stock bring forth the culti-
vated.   100. dibble: tool used for making holes in the ground for
planting.   101. painted: made up to look more beautiful than I am.

And with him rises weeping.° These are flowers
Of middle summer, and I think they are given
To men of middle age. You're very welcome.

CAM. I should leave grazing were I of your flock,
And only live by gazing.

PER.   Out, alas!   110
You'd be so lean that blasts of January
Would blow you through and through. Now, my
     fair'st friend,
I would I had some flowers o' the spring that might
Become your time of day, and yours, and yours,
That wear upon your virgin branches yet   115
Your maidenheads growing. O° Proserpina,
For the flowers now that frighted thou let'st fall
From Dis's wagon! — daffodils,
That come before the swallow dares, and take
The winds of March with beauty; violets dim,   120
But sweeter than the lids of Juno's eyes
Or Cytherea's° breath; pale primroses,
That die unmarried, ere they can behold
Bright Phoebus in his strength, a malady
Most incident to maids; bold oxlips° and   125
The crown imperial;° lilies of all kinds,
The flower-de-luce° being one! — oh, these I lack
To make you garlands of, and my sweet friend,
To strew him o'er and o'er!

FLO.   What, like a corse?°
PER. No, like a bank for love to lie and play on,
Not like a corse; or if, not to be buried,   131
But quick and in mine arms. Come, take your
     flowers.
Methinks I play as I have seen them do
In Whitsun pastorals.° Sure this robe of mine
Does change my disposition.

FLO.   What you do   135
Still betters what is done. When you speak, sweet,
I'd have you do it ever. When you sing,
I'd have you buy and sell so, so give alms,
Pray so, and, for the ordering your affairs,
To sing them too. When you do dance, I wish you
A wave o' the sea, that you might ever do   141
Nothing but that, move still, still so,
And own no other function. Each your doing,
So singular° in each particular,
Crowns what you are doing in the present deeds,°
That all your acts are queens.

PER. O Doricles,°   146
Your praises are too large.° But that your youth,
And the true blood which peeps fairly through 't,
Do plainly give you out an unstained° shepherd,
With wisdom I might fear, my Doricles,   150
You wooed me the false way.

FLO.   I think you have
As little skill° to fear as I have purpose
To put you to 't. But come, our dance, I pray.
Your hand, my Perdita. So turtles° pair
That never mean to part.

PER.   I'll swear for 'em.   155
POL. This is the prettiest lowborn lass that ever
Ran on the greensward. Nothing she does or seems
But smacks° of something greater than herself,
Too noble for this place.

CAM.   He tells her something
That makes her blood look out. Good sooth, she is
The queen of curds and cream.

CLO.   Come on, strike up!°   161
DOR. Mopsa must be your mistress. Marry, garlic,
To mend her kissing with!°

MOP.   Now, in good time!°
CLO. Not a word, a word, we stand upon our
     manners.°
Come, strike up!

[Music. Here a dance of
SHEPHERDS and SHEPHERDESSES.]

POL. Pray, good shepherd, what fair swain is this
Which dances with your daughter?

SHEP. They call him Doricles, and boasts himself
To have a worthy feeding.° But I have it
Upon his own report and I believe it,   170
He looks like sooth.° He says he loves my daughter.
I think so too, for never gazed the moon
Upon the water as he'll stand and read
As 'twere my daughter's eyes. And, to be plain,
I think there is not half a kiss to choose   175
Who loves another best.

POL.   She dances featly.°
SHEP. So she does anything, though I report it
That should be silent. If young Doricles
Do light upon her, she shall bring him that
Which he not dreams of.   180

[Enter SERVANT.]

SERV. O master, if you did but hear the peddler
at the door, you would never dance again after a
tabor° and pipe — no, the bagpipe could not move
you. He sings several tunes faster than you'll tell°

105–06. goes . . . weeping: closes at sunset and opens in the
morning wet with dew.   116–27. O . . . one: Proserpina, accord-
ing to the myth, was gathering flowers in her garden when Pluto
(or Dis) carried her off in a chariot to his kingdom of the under-
world. The flowers are all early spring flowers which bloom in
March or April.   122. Cytherea: Venus.   125. oxlips: a cross
between cowslip and primrose.   126. crown imperial: a form of
lily with a cluster of yellow pendant flowers.   127. flower-de-
luce: wild iris.   129. corse: corpse.   134. Whitsun pastorals:
country morris dances performed at Whitsuntide. Whitsun
(Pentecost) is a feast which falls seven weeks after Easter. See
App. 24.   144. singular: unique.   145. in . . . deeds: what you
are doing at present.

146. Doricles: the name which Florizel has assumed when dis-
guised as a shepherd.   147. large: exaggerated.   149. unstained:
pure.   152. skill: cause.   154. turtles: turtledoves.   158. smacks:
tastes.   161. strike up: i.e., the music.   162–63. garlic . . . with:
you'll need to eat garlic to avoid smelling her breath.   163. in
. . . time: "I like that!"   164. we . . . manners: we are on our
best behavior.   169. feeding: pasture.   171. sooth: truth.
176. featly: neatly.   183. tabor: small drum, a shepherd's in-
strument. See Pl. 13d.   184. tell: count.

money, he utters them as he had eaten ballads° and all men's ears grew to° his tunes. 186

CLO. He could never come better,° he shall come in. I love a ballad but even too well, if it be doleful matter merrily set down, or a very pleasant thing indeed and sung lamentably. 190

SERV. He hath songs for man or woman, of all sizes, no milliner can so fit his customers with gloves. He has the prettiest love songs for maids, so without bawdry, which is strange, with such delicate burdens of dildos and fadings,° "jump her 195 and thump her." And where some stretch-mouthed° rascal would, as it were, mean mischief and break a foul gap° into the matter, he makes the maid to answer "Whoop, do me no harm, good man," puts him off, slights him, with "Whoop, do me no harm, good man." 201

POL. This is a brave fellow.

CLO. Believe me, thou talkest of an admirable conceited° fellow. Has he any unbraided wares?° 204

SERV. He hath ribbons of all the colors i' the rainbow, points° more than all the lawyers in Bohemia can learnedly handle, though they come to him by the gross — inkles,° caddises,° cambrics, 208 lawns.° Why, he sings 'em over as they were gods or goddesses, you would think a smock° were a she-angel, he so chants to the sleeve hand° and the work about the square° on 't. 212

CLO. Prithee bring him in, and let him approach singing.

PER. Forewarn him that he use no scurrilous 215 words in 's tunes. [*Exit* SERVANT.]

CLO. You have of° these peddlers that have more in them than you'd think, Sister.

PER. Aye, good brother, or go about to think.
[*Enter* AUTOLYCUS, *singing.*]

AUT.

　"Lawn as white as driven snow, 220
　　Cypress° black as e'er was crow,
　　Gloves as sweet as damask roses,°
　　Masks° for faces and for noses,
　　Bugle° bracelet, necklace amber,
　　Perfume for a lady's chamber, 225
　　Golden quoifs° and stomachers°
　　For my lads to give their dears,

Pins and poking sticks° of steel,
What maids lack from head to heel.
Come buy of me, come, come buy, come buy,
Buy, lads, or else your lasses cry. 231
Come buy."

CLO. If I were not in love with Mopsa, thou shouldst take no money of me, but being enthralled° as I am, it will also be the bondage of° certain ribbons and gloves. 236

MOP. I was promised them against° the feast, but they come not too late now.

DOR. He hath promised you more than that, or there be liars.

MOP. He hath paid you all he promised you. Maybe he has paid you more which will shame you to give him again. 243

CLO. Is there no manners left among maids? Will they wear their plackets° where they should bear their faces? Is there not milking time, when you are going to bed, or kiln hole,° to whistle off these secrets, but you must be tittletattling before all our guests? 'Tis well they are whispering. Clamor° your tongues, and not a word more. 251

MOP. I have done. Come, you promised me a tawdry lace° and a pair of sweet gloves.

CLO. Have I not told thee how I was cozened° by the way and lost all my money? 255

AUT. And indeed, sir, there are cozeners abroad, therefore it behooves men to be wary.

CLO. Fear not thou, man, thou shalt lose nothing here.

AUT. I hope so, sir, for I have about me many parcels of charge.° 261

CLO. What hast here? Ballads?

MOP. Pray now, buy some. I love a ballad in print o' life, for then we are sure they are true.

AUT. Here's one to a very doleful tune, how a usurer's wife was brought to bed of twenty money-bags at a burden, and how she longed to eat adders' heads and toads carbonadoed.° 268

MOP. Is it true, think you?

AUT. Very true, and but a month old.

DOR. Bless me° from marrying a usurer! 271

AUT. Here's the midwife's name to 't, one Mistress Taleporter, and five or six honest wives that were present. Why should I carry lies abroad?

MOP. Pray you now, buy it.

CLO. Come on, lay it by. And let's first see moe ballads. We'll buy the other things anon. 278

AUT. Here's another ballad of a fish that appeared

---

185. ballads: See App. 8.　186. grew to: were stuck fast to.
187. better: more welcome.　195. burdens . . . fadings: with refrains of *dildo* and *fading* in the songs.　196. stretch-mouthed: wide-mouthed.　198. foul gap: dirty crack.　204. conceited: intelligent. unbraided wares: untarnished, not shop-soiled.
206. points: laces for fastening doublet and hose together. See Notes on Contemporary Costume, pp. 93a–95b.　208. inkles: tapes. caddises: worsted tape for garters.　209. lawns: fine linens.　210. smock: nightdress.　211. sleeve hand: cuff.
212. square: embroidered neck square.　217. You . . . of: some of.　221. Cypress: crape.　222. Gloves . . . roses: perfumed gloves.　223. Masks: Fashionable ladies wore masks to protect their faces from the sun.　224. Bugle: long bead.　226. quoif: headdress. stomachers: embroidered fronts for women's dresses.

228. poking sticks: metal rods used for ironing the pleats in a ruff.
234. enthralled: enslaved.　235. be . . . of: I shall take into servitude.　237. against: in time for.　245. plackets: petticoats.　247. kiln hole: the fireplace where malt is made, a convenient place for gossip.　250. Clamor: silence.　253. tawdry lace: silk necktie.　254. cozened: cheated.　261. parcels of charge: goods of value.　268. carbonadoed: grilled.　271. Bless me: save me.

upon the coast on Wednesday the fourscore of April,
forty thousand fathom above water, and sung this
ballad against the hard hearts of maids. It was
thought she was a woman, and was turned into a
cold fish for she would not exchange flesh with one
that loved her. The ballad is very pitiful and as
true.

DOR. Is it true too, think you?   287

AUT. Five Justices' hands at it, and witnesses more
than my pack will hold.

CLO. Lay it by too. Another.

AUT. This is a merry ballad, but a very pretty one.

MOP. Let's have some merry ones.   293

AUT. Why, this is a passing° merry one and goes
to the tune of " Two maids wooing a man." There's
scarce a maid westward° but she sings it. 'Tis in re-
quest, I can tell you.

MOP. We can both sing it. If thou'lt bear a part,
thou shalt hear. 'Tis in three parts.

DOR. We had the tune on 't a month ago.   300

AUT. I can bear my part, you must know 'tis my
occupation.° Have at it with you.

AUT., DOR., & MOP.

A. " Get you hence, for I must go
          Where it fits not you to know.
               D. Whither? *M.* Oh, whither? *D.* Whither?
M.   It becomes thy oath full well,   306
          Thou to me thy secrets tell.
               D. Me too, let me go thither.

M. " Or thou goest to the grange° or mill.
D.   If to either, thou dost ill.   310
               A. Neither. *D.* What, neither? *A.* Neither.
D.   Thou hast sworn my love to be.
M.   Thou hast sworn it more to me.
               Then whither goest? Say, whither? "   314

CLO. We'll have this song out anon by ourselves.
My father and the gentlemen are in sad° talk, and
we'll not trouble them. Come, bring away thy pack
after me. Wenches, I'll buy for you both. Peddler,
let's have the first choice. Follow me, girls.   320

          [*Exit with* DORCAS *and* MOPSA.]

AUT. And you shall pay well for 'em.

          [*Follows singing.*]

" Will you buy any tape,
          Or lace for your cape,
My dainty duck, my dear-a?
          Any silk, any thread,
          Any toys° for your head,   325
Of the new'st, and finest, finest wear-a?
          Come to the peddler,
          Money's a meddler
That doth utter° all men's ware-a." [*Exit.*]   329

294. passing: exceedingly.   296. westward: in the west country.
302. occupation: business. The ballad-seller used to sing his bal-
lads before selling them.   309. grange: large farmhouse.
316. sad: serious.   326. toys: trifles, ornaments.   330. utter: sell.

[*Re-enter* SERVANT.]

SERV. Master, there is three carters, three shep-
herds, three neatherds,° three swineherds, that have
made themselves all men of hair. They call them-
selves saltiers,° and they have a dance which   334
the wenches say is a gallimaufry° of gambols, be-
cause they are not in 't. But they themselves are o'
the mind, if it be not too rough for some that know
little but bowling,° it will please plentifully.   339

SHEP. Away! We'll none on 't. Here has been too
much homely foolery already. I know, sir, we weary
you.

POL. You weary those that refresh us. Pray let's
see these four threes of herdsmen.   344

SERV. One three of them, by their own report, sir,
hath danced before the King, and not the worst of
the three but jumps twelve foot and a half by the
squier.°

SHEP. Leave your prating. Since these good men
are pleased, let them come in, but quickly now.   351

SERV. Why, they stay at door, sir.   [*Exit.*]

          [*Here a dance of twelve* SATYRS.]

POL. O Father, you'll know more of that here-
after.

[*To* CAMILLO] Is it not too far gone? 'Tis time to
part them.

He's simple and tells much. How now, fair shep-
herd!   355
Your heart is full of something that does take
Your mind from feasting. Sooth,° when I was young
And handed° love as you do, I was wont
To load my she with knacks.° I would have ran-
          sacked
The peddler's silken treasury and have poured it
To her acceptance. You have let him go   361
And nothing marted° with him. If your lass
Interpretation should abuse° and call this
Your lack of love or bounty, you were straited°
For a reply — at least if you make a care   365
Of happy holding her.

FLO.   Old sir, I know
She prizes not such trifles as these are.
The gifts she looks from me are packed and locked
Up in my heart, which I have given already,
But not delivered. Oh, hear me breathe my life   370
Before this ancient sir, who, it should seem,
Hath sometime loved! I take thy hand, this hand,
As soft as dove's down and as white as it,
Or Ethiopian's tooth, or the fanned° snow that's
          bolted°   374
By the Northern blasts twice o'er.

332. neatherds: cowmen.   334. saltiers: satyrs.   335. galli-
maufry: mix-up, medley.   339. bowling: bowls, a quiet game.
349. squier: carpenter's rule.   357. Sooth: in truth.   358. handed:
handled.   359. knacks: trifles, little gifts.   362. marted: traded.
363. Interpretation . . . abuse: should misinterpret your mean-
ness.   364. straited: in a difficulty.   374. fanned: blown.
bolted: sifted, like fine flour.

POL.   What follows this?
How prettily the young swain seems to wash
The hand was fair before! I have put you out.
But to your protestation, let me hear
What you profess.
FLO.   Do, and be witness to 't.
POL. And this my neighbor too?
FLO.   And he, and more   380
Than he, and men, the earth, the Heavens, and all.
That were I crowned the most imperial monarch,
Thereof most worthy, were I the fairest youth
That ever made eye swerve,° had force and knowl-
     edge
More than was ever man's, I would not prize them
Without her love, for her employ them all,   386
Commend them and condemn them to her service
Or to their own perdition.
POL.   Fairly offered.
CAM. This shows a sound affection.
SHEP.   But, my daughter,
Say you the like to him?
PER.   I cannot speak   390
So well, nothing so well — no, nor mean better.
By the pattern of mine own thoughts I cut out
The purity of his.
SHEP.   Take hands, a bargain!
And, friends unknown, you shall bear witness to 't.
I give my daughter to him, and will make   395
Her portion equal his.
FLO.   Oh, that must be
I' the virtue of your daughter.° One being dead,°
I shall have more than you can dream of yet,
Enough then for your wonder. But come on,
Contract us 'fore these witnesses.°
SHEP.   Come, your hand,   400
And, Daughter, yours.
POL.   Soft, swain, awhile, beseech you.
Have you a father?
FLO.   I have, but what of him?
POL. Knows he of this?
FLO.   He neither does nor shall.
POL. Methinks a father
Is at the nuptial of his son a guest   405
That best becomes the table. Pray you once more,
Is not your father grown incapable
Of reasonable affairs?° Is he not stupid
With age and altering rheums?° Can he speak?
     Hear?   409
Know man from man? Dispute his own estate?°

Lies he not bedrid? And again does nothing
But what he did being childish?
FLO.   No, good sir,
He has his health and ampler strength indeed
Than most have of his age.
POL.   By my white beard,
You offer him, if this be so, a wrong   415
Something unfilial. Reason° my son
Should choose himself a wife, but as good reason
The father, all whose joy is nothing else
But fair posterity,° should hold some counsel°
In such a business.
FLO.   I yield all this,   420
But for some other reasons, my grave sir,
Which 'tis not fit you know, I not acquaint
My father of this business.
POL.   Let him know 't.
FLO. He shall not.
POL.   Prithee let him.
FLO.   No, he must not.
SHEP. Let him, my son. He shall not need to
     grieve   425
At knowing of thy choice.
FLO.   Come, come, he must not.
Mark our contract.
POL.   Mark your divorce, young sir,
                    [Discovering° himself.]
Whom son I dare not call, thou art too base
To be acknowledged. Thou a scepter's heir,
That thus affects a sheep hook!° Thou old traitor,
I am sorry that by hanging thee I can   431
But shorten thy life one week. And thou, fresh piece
Of excellent witchcraft, who of force° must know
The royal fool thou copest° with —
SHEP.   Oh, my heart!
POL. I'll have thy beauty scratched with briers, and
     made   435
More homely than thy state. For thee, fond° boy,
If I may ever know thou dost but sigh
That thou no more shalt see this knack° — as never
I mean thou shalt — we'll bar thee from succession,
Not hold thee of our blood — no, not our kin —
Far than Deucalion off.° Mark thou my words.   441
Follow us to the Court. Thou churl,° for this time,
Though full of our displeasure, yet we free thee
From the dead blow° of it. And you, enchantment —
Worthy enough a herdsman, yea, him too,   445

384. made . . . swerve: made women look at him.   396-97. Oh . . . daughter: only in the worth of your daughter can you equal my wealth.   397. One . . . dead: i.e., when the King my father is dead.   400. Contract . . . witnesses: In Shakespeare's time a contract made before witnesses was legally binding. Hence Polixenes' hasty interruption before the lovers join hands. See Gen. Intro. p. 20a.   407-08. incapable . . . affairs: not capable of looking after his own affairs rationally.   409. altering rheums: diseases which change his nature.   410. Dispute . . . estate: discuss his own business.

416. Reason: it is reasonable that.   418-19. joy . . . posterity: joy lies solely in his son being father of worthy children. In this speech Polixenes explains the normal Elizabethan theory of marriage: a man must choose a wife acceptable in rank to his parents because by her he will breed children to prolong the family.   419. hold . . . counsel: give some advice.   427 s.d., Discovering: revealing.   430. sheep hook: shepherd's crook; i.e., a shepherdess.   433. of force: necessarily.   434. copest: hast to do with.   436. fond: foolish.   438. knack: trifle.   441. Far . . . off: as far back as Deucalion, who in classical myth was, like Noah in Genesis, the survivor of the great flood.   442. churl: boor.   444. dead blow: blow which will strike you dead.

That makes himself, but for our honor therein,
Unworthy thee° — if ever henceforth thou
These rural latches to his entrance open,
Or hoop his body more with thy embraces,
I will devise a death as cruel for thee   450
As thou art tender to 't.°   [*Exit.*]

PER.   Even here undone!
I was not much afeard, for once or twice
I was about to speak and tell him plainly
The selfsame sun that shines upon his Court
Hides not his visage from our cottage but   455
Looks on alike. Will 't please you, sir, be gone?
I told you what would come of this. Beseech you,
Of your own state take care. This dream of mine —
Being now awake, I'll queen it no inch farther,
But milk my ewes and weep.

CAM.   Why, how now, Father!   460
Speak ere thou diest.

SHEP.   I cannot speak, nor think,
Nor dare to know that which I know. O sir!
You have undone a man of fourscore three,
That thought to fill his grave in quiet — yea,
To die upon the bed my father died,   465
To lie close by his honest bones. But now
Some hangman must put on my shroud and lay me
Where no priest shovels in dust. O cursèd wretch,
That knew'st this was the Prince, and wouldst adventure
To mingle faith with him! Undone! Undone!   470
If I might die within this hour, I have lived
To die when I desire.   [*Exit.*]

FLO.   Why look you so upon me?
I am but sorry, not afeard, delayed,
But nothing altered. What I was, I am,
More straining on for plucking back, not following
My leash unwillingly.°

CAM.   Gracious my lord,   476
You know your father's temper. At this time
He will allow no speech, which I do guess
You do not purpose to him, and as hardly
Will he endure your sight as yet, I fear.   480
Then, till the fury of His Highness settle,
Come not before him.

FLO.   I not purpose it.
I think, Camillo?°

CAM.   Even he, my lord.

PER. How often have I told you 'twould be thus!
How often said, my dignity would last   485
But till 'twere known!

FLO.   It cannot fail but by
The violation of my faith, and then

Let Nature crush the sides o' the earth together
And mar° the seeds within! Lift up thy looks.
From my succession wipe me, Father, I   490
Am heir to my affection.°

CAM.   Be advised.

FLO. I am, and by my fancy.° If my reason
Will thereto be obedient, I have reason.
If not, my senses, better pleased with madness,
Do bid it welcome.

CAM.   This is desperate, sir.   495

FLO. So call it. But it does fulfill my vow,
I needs must think it honesty. Camillo,
Not for Bohemia, nor the pomp that may
Be thereat° gleaned — for all the sun sees, or
The close earth wombs,° or the profound seas hide
In unknown fathoms — will I break my oath   501
To this my fair beloved. Therefore I pray you,
As you have ever been my father's honored friend,
When he shall miss me — as, in faith, I mean not
To see him any more — cast your good counsels
Upon his passion. Let myself and fortune   506
Tug° for the time to come. This you may know
And so deliver, I am put to sea
With her whom here I cannot hold onshore.
And most oppórtune° to our need I have   510
A vessel rides° fast by, but not prepared
For this design. What course I mean to hold
Shall nothing benefit your knowledge, nor
Concern me the reporting.°

CAM.   O my lord!
I would your spirit were easier for advice,   515
Or stronger for your need.

FLO.   Hark, Perdita. [*Drawing her aside.*]
I'll hear you by and by.

CAM.   He's irremovable,
Resolved for flight. Now were I happy if
His going I could frame to serve my turn,
Save him from danger, do him love and honor,   520
Purchase the sight again of dear Sicilia
And that unhappy King, my master, whom
I so much thirst to see.

FLO.   Now, good Camillo,
I am so fraught° with curious° business that
I leave out ceremony.

CAM.   Sir, I think   525
You have heard of my poor services, i' the love
That I have borne your father?

FLO.   Very nobly
Have you deserved. It is my father's music
To speak your deeds, not little of his care
To have them recompensed as thought on.

445–47. yea . . . thee: yes, and also good enough for my son, who would not be good enough for you if the honor of my family was not concerned. 451. As . . . to 't: as you are too gentle to endure it. 475–76. More . . . unwillingly: like a greyhound, held back by the leash, I strain to be let loose. 483. I . . . Camillo: Here Florizel recognizes Camillo through his disguise.

489. mar: destroy. 491. heir . . . affection: my love is my inheritance. 492. fancy: love. 499. thereat: i.e., in the Court of my father. 500. wombs: hides within itself. 507. Tug: pull against each other. 510. opportune: fortunate. 511. rides: is at anchor. 512–14. What . . . reporting: it will be better for you not to know, and I do not intend to tell you, where I mean to go. 524. fraught: burdened. curious: that requires all my attention.

CAM.   Well, my lord,   530
If you may please to think I love the King,
And through him what is nearest to him, which is
Your gracious self, embrace but my direction,°
If your more ponderous° and settled° project
May suffer alteration. On mine honor   535
I'll point you where you shall have such receiving
As shall become your highness° — where you may
Enjoy your mistress — from the whom, I see,
There's no disjunction° to be made but by
As Heavens forefend! your ruin — marry her,   540
And with my best endeavors in your absence
Your discontenting father strive to qualify°
And bring him up to liking.

FLO.   How, Camillo,
May this, almost a miracle, be done?   544
That I may call thee something more than man
And after that trust to thee.

CAM.   Have you thought on
A place whereto you'll go?

FLO.   Not any yet.
But as the unthought-on accident is guilty
To what we wildly do,° so we profess
Ourselves to be the slaves of chance, and flies   550
Of every wind that blows.

CAM.   Then list° to me.
This follows, if you will not change your purpose
But undergo this flight — make for Sicilia,
And there present yourself and your fair Princess,
For so I see she must be, 'fore Leontes.   555
She shall be habited° as it becomes
The partner of your bed. Methinks I see
Leontes opening his free arms and weeping   558
His welcomes forth; asks thee the son forgiveness,
As 'twere i' the father's person;° kisses the hands
Of your fresh Princess; o'er and o'er divides him
'Twixt his unkindness and his kindness;° the one
He chides to Hell and bids the other grow
Faster than thought or time.

FLO.   Worthy Camillo,
What color for my visitation° shall I   565
Hold up before him?

CAM.   Sent by the King your father
To greet him and to give him comforts. Sir,
The manner of your bearing toward him, with
What you as from your father shall deliver,   569
Things known betwixt us three, I'll write you down.
The which shall point you forth at every sitting°
What you must say, that he shall not perceive

But that you have your father's bosom° there
And speak his very heart.

FLO.   I am bound to you.
There is some sap° in this.

CAM.   A course more promising   575
Than a wild dedication of yourselves
To unpathed waters, undreamed shores, most
   certain
To miseries enough, no hope to help you
But as you shake off one to take another —
Nothing so certain as your anchors, who   580
Do their best office if they can but stay you
Where you'll be loath to be.° Besides, you know
Prosperity's the very bond of love,
Whose fresh complexion and whose heart together
Affliction alters.

PER.   One of these is true.   585
I think affliction may subdue the cheek,
But not take in° the mind.

CAM.   Yea, say you so?
There shall not at your father's house these seven
   years
Be born another such.

FLO.   My good Camillo,
She is as forward of her breeding as   590
She is i' the rear o' her birth.°

CAM.   I cannot say 'tis pity
She lacks instructions,° for she seems a mistress
To most that teach.

PER.   Your pardon, sir, for this
I'll blush you thanks.

FLO.   My prettiest Perdita!
But oh, the thorns we stand upon! Camillo,   595
Preserver of my father, now of me,
The medicine of° our house, how shall we do?
We are not furnished° like Bohemia's son,
Nor shall appear in Sicilia.

CAM.   My lord,   599
Fear none of this. I think you know my fortunes
Do all lie there. It shall be so my care
To have you royally appointed° as if
The scene you play were mine. For instance, sir,
That you may know you shall not want, one
     word.   [They talk aside.]   604
     [Re-enter AUTOLYCUS.]
AUT. Ha, ha! What a fool Honesty is! And Trust,
his sworn brother,° a very simple gentleman! I have
sold all my trumpery, not a counterfeit stone, not a

---

533. embrace . . . direction: follow my advice.   534. ponderous:
weighty. settled: fixed.   537. highness: high rank.   539. dis-
junction: separation.   542. qualify: mollify.   548–49. un-
thought-on . . . do: unexpected accident is the cause of our act-
ing in this wild way.   551. list: listen.   556. habited: clothed.
560. As . . . person: as if you were your father.   561–62. o'er . . .
kindness: he is divided between his unkind behavior to your
father and his welcome to you.   565. color . . . visitation: excuse
for my visit.   571. point . . . sitting: give you exact instructions
for each conference.

573. bosom: heart, approval.   575. sap: life.   580–82. Nothing
. . . be: i.e., the most sure thing about such a voyage is that wher-
ever you anchor you will be miserable, but more miserable if you
sail on.   587. take in: capture.   590–91. She . . . birth: she is
in her nature as high above what one would expect in a shepherd's
daughter as she is beneath me in her humble birth.   592. lacks
instructions: has had no schooling.   597. medicine of: that
which keeps healthy.   598. furnished: provided for.   602. roy-
ally appointed: equipped like a prince.   606. sworn brother:
See M Ado, I.i.72–73,n.

ribbon, glass, pomander,° brooch, table book,° bal-
lad, knife, tape, glove, shoe tie, bracelet, horn ring,
to keep my pack from fasting.° They throng   610
who should buy first as if my trinkets had been hal-
lowed° and brought a benediction to the buyer. By
which means I saw whose purse was best in picture,°
and what I saw to my good use I remembered. My
clown, who wants but something° to be a reason-
able man, grew so in love with the wenches' song
that he would not stir his pettitoes° till he had both
tune and words, which so drew the rest of the herd
to me that all their other senses stuck in ears.   620
You might have pinched a placket, it was senseless.
'Twas nothing to geld a codpiece° of a purse. I
would have filed keys off that hung in chains. No
hearing, no feeling, but my sir's song and admiring
the nothing of it. So that in this time of lethargy°
I picked and cut most of their festival purses, and
had not the old man come in with a whoobub°
against his daughter and the King's son and scared
my choughs° from the chaff, I had not left a purse
alive in the whole army.   630

[CAMILLO, FLORIZEL, *and* PERDITA *come forward.*]
CAM. Nay, but my letters, by this means being
    there
So soon as you arrive, shall clear that doubt.
FLO. And those that you'll procure from King
    Leontes ——
CAM. Shall satisfy your father.
PER.   Happy be you!
All that you speak shows fair.
CAM.   Who have we here? [*Seeing* AUTOLYCUS]
We'll make an instrument of this, omit   636
Nothing may give us aid.
AUT. If they have overheard me now, why, hang-
ing.
CAM. How now, good fellow! Why shakest thou
so? Fear not, man, here's no harm intended to thee.
AUT. I am a poor fellow, sir.   643
CAM. Why, be so still, here's nobody will steal
that° from thee. Yet for the outside of thy property
we must make an exchange. Therefore disease° thee
instantly, — thou must think there's a necessity in 't
— and change garments with this gentleman.
Though the pennyworth on his side be the worst,
yet hold thee, there's some boot.°   650
AUT. I am a poor fellow, sir. [*Aside*] I know ye
well enough.

CAM. Nay, prithee dispatch.° The gentleman is
half flayed° already.   654
AUT. Are you in earnest, sir? [*Aside*] I smell the
trick on 't.
FLO. Dispatch, I prithee.
AUT. Indeed, I have had earnest,° but I cannot
with conscience take it.   659
CAM. Unbuckle, unbuckle.

[FLORIZEL *and* AUTOLYCUS *exchange garments.*]
Fortunate mistress — let my prophecy
Come home to ye!° — you must retire yourself
Into some covert.° Take your sweetheart's hat
And pluck it o'er your brows, muffle your face,
Dismantle you,° and, as you can, disliken°   665
The truth of your own seeming,° that you may —
For I do fear eyes over — to shipboard
Get undescried.°
PER.   I see the play so lies
That I must bear a part.
CAM.   No remedy.
Have you done there?
FLO.   Should I now meet my father,   670
He would not call me son.
CAM. Nay, you shall have no hat.

                                   [*Giving it to* PERDITA.]
Come, lady, come. Farewell, my friend.
AUT.   Adieu, sir.
FLO. O Perdita, what have we twain forgot!
Pray you, a word.
CAM. [*Aside*] What I do next shall be to tell the
    King   675
Of this escape and whither they are bound,
Wherein my hope is I shall so prevail
To force him after. In whose company
I shall review° Sicilia, for whose sight
I have a woman's longing.°
FLO.   Fortune speed° us!   680
Thus we set on, Camillo, to the seaside.
CAM. The swifter speed, the better.

        [*Exeunt* FLORIZEL, PERDITA, *and* CAMILLO.]
AUT. I understand the business, I hear it. To° have
an open ear, a quick eye, and a nimble hand is nec-
essary for a cutpurse. A good nose is requisite also,
to smell out work for the other senses. I see this is
the time that the unjust man doth thrive. What an
exchange had this been without boot! What a boot is
here with this exchange! Sure the gods do this year
connive° at us, and we may do anything ex-   690
tempore.° The Prince himself is about a piece of

608. pomander: ball of perfume. table book: notebook.   610. to
. . . fasting: i.e., the pack is quite empty.   612. hallowed: blessed
by the Pope.   613. best . . . picture: had most faces; i.e., coins
with the King's head.   616. wants . . . something: just lacks
something; i.e., wits.   618. pettitoes: trotters.   622. codpiece:
See Pl. 8c and comment on p. 93b.   625. lethargy: lack of feeling.
627. whoobub: hubbub.   629. choughs: jackdaws, simpletons.
645. that: i.e., your poverty.   646. disease: take off your "case";
i.e., coat.   649–50. Though . . . boot: though the value of the ex-
change is worse for him, yet here is something extra for you —
whereupon Camillo gives him money. boot: advantage.

653. dispatch: be quick.   654. flayed: skinned.   658. earnest:
money on account.   661–62. let . . . ye: may my prophecy — that
you shall be a "fortunate mistress" — come true.   663. covert:
thicket.   665. Dismantle you: take off your cloak. disliken: dis-
guise.   666. The . . . seeming: your true appearance.   668. un-
descried: undiscovered.   679. review: see again.   680. woman's
longing: as keen a desire as pregnant women have for certain
foods. speed: be lucky to.   683–702. To . . . work: See *W Tale*
Intro. p. 960b.   690. connive: wink.   691. extempore: without
preparation.

iniquity, stealing away from his father with his clog° at his heels. If I thought it were a piece of honesty to acquaint the King withal, I would not do 't. I hold it the more knavery to conceal it, and therein am I constant° to my profession.   698

[*Re-enter* CLOWN *and* SHEPHERD.] Aside, aside, here is more matter for a hot° brain. Every lane's end, every shop, church, session, hanging, yields a careful man work.

CLO. See, see, what a man you are now! There is no other way but to tell the King she's a changeling° and none of your flesh and blood.   705

SHEP. Nay, but hear me.

CLO. Nay, but hear me.

SHEP. Go to,° then.

CLO. She being none of your flesh and blood, your flesh and blood has not offended the King, and   710 so your flesh and blood is not to be punished by him. Show those things you found about her, those secret things, all but what she has with her. This being done, let the law go whistle, I warrant you.   715

SHEP. I will tell the King all, every word — yea, and his son's pranks too, who I may say is no honest man, neither to his father nor to me, to go about to make me the King's brother-in-law.   720

CLO. Indeed, brother-in-law was the farthest off you could have been to him, and then your blood had been the dearer° by I know how much an ounce.

AUT. [*Aside*] Very wisely, puppies!   725

SHEP. Well, let us to the King. There is that in this fardel° will make him scratch his beard.

AUT. [*Aside*] I know not what impediment this complaint may be to the flight of my master.

CLO. Pray heartily he be at palace.   731

AUT. [*Aside*] Though I am not naturally honest, I am so sometimes by chance. Let me pocket up my peddler's excrement.° [*Takes off his false beard.*] How now, rustics! Whither are you bound?   735

SHEP. To the palace, an it like° your Worship.

AUT. Your affairs there — what, with whom, the condition of that fardel, the place of your dwelling, your names, your ages, of what having,° breeding, and anything that is fitting to be known, discover.°

CLO. We are but plain fellows, sir.   742

AUT. A lie, you are rough and hairy. Let° me have no lying. It becomes none but tradesmen, and they often give us soldiers the lie. But we pay them for

it with stamped coin, not stabbing steel, therefore they do not give us the lie.   748

CLO. Your Worship had like to have given us one if you had not taken yourself with the manner.°

SHEP. Are you a courtier, an 't like° you, sir?

AUT. Whether it like me or no, I am a courtier. Seest thou not the air of the Court in these enfoldings?° Hath not my gait in it the measure of   755 the Court? Receives not thy nose Court odor from me? Reflect I not on thy baseness Court contempt? Thinkest thou, for that I insinuate,° or toaze° from thee thy business, I am therefore no courtier? I am courtier cap-à-pie,° and one that will either push on or pluck back thy business there. Whereupon I command thee to open° thy affair.   763

SHEP. My business, sir, is to the King.

AUT. What advocate hast thou to him?

SHEP. I know not, an 't like you.

CLO. Advocate's the court word for a pheasant.° Say you have none.

SHEP. None, sir, I have no pheasant, cock nor hen.   770

AUT. How blessed are we that are not simple men! Yet nature might have made me as these are, Therefore I will not disdain.°

CLO. This cannot be but° a great courtier.

SHEP. His garments are rich, but he wears them not handsomely.   776

CLO. He seems to be the more noble in being fantastical. A great man, I'll warrant. I know by the picking on 's teeth.°

AUT. The fardel there? What's i' the fardel? Wherefore that box?   781

SHEP. Sir, there lies such secrets in this fardel and box which none must know but the King, and which he shall know within this hour if I may come to the speech of him.   785

AUT. Age,° thou hast lost thy labor.

SHEP. Why, sir?

AUT. The King is not at the palace. He is gone aboard a new ship to purge melancholy° and air himself. For if thou beest capable of things serious, thou must know the King is full of grief.   791

SHEP. So 'tis said, sir, about his son, that should have married a shepherd's daughter.

AUT. If that shepherd be not in handfast,° let him fly. The curses he shall have, the tortures he shall feel, will break the back of man, the heart of monster.

---

693. clog: a weight fastened to his leg; i.e., Perdita.   **698. constant:** true.   **700. hot:** quick.   **704. changeling:** See III.iii.122,n. **708. Go to:** go on.   **724. dearer:** more valuable.   **727. fardel:** bundle.   **734. excrement:** beard; lit., that which grows out of a man. Autolycus now assumes the superior manners and affected speech of a courtier toward a countryman.   **736. as . . . like:** if it pleases.   **740. having:** wealth.   **741. discover:** reveal to me. **743–48. Let . . . lie:** "To give the lie" is to call a man a liar — a deadly insult to a soldier, which was answered with a stab. But when tradesmen give the lie by selling false goods, they make their customers pay for it.

750. if . . . manner: if you had not caught yourself in the act (of lying).   **751. an 't like:** if it please.   **755. enfoldings:** coverings.   **758. insinuate:** wind myself into. **toaze:** comb; lit., to card wool ready for spinning.   **761. cap-à-pie:** head to foot. **763. open:** explain.   **768. Advocate's . . . pheasant:** *advocate* is the word they use at Court for the bribe of a pheasant.   **773. disdain:** be proud.   **774. cannot . . . but:** must be.   **779. picking . . . teeth:** Toothpicks were a foreign fashion; to possess one showed that the owner had traveled.   **786. Age:** old man. **789. purge melancholy:** A drastic purge was one of the remedies for melancholy.   **794. in handfast:** locked up.

CLO. Think you so, sir?   798

AUT. Not he alone shall suffer what wit can make heavy and vengeance bitter; but those that are germane° to him, though removed fifty times, shall all come under the hangman. Which though it be great pity, yet it is necessary. An old sheep-whistling rogue, a ram-tender, to offer to have his daughter come into grace!° Some say he shall be stoned, but that death is too soft for him say I. Draw our throne into a sheepcote!° All deaths are too few, the sharpest too easy.   808

CLO. Has the old man e'er a son, sir, do you hear, an 't like you, sir?

AUT. He has a son, who shall be flayed alive; then, 'nointed° over with honey, set on the head of a wasp's nest; then stand till he be three-quarters and a dram° dead; then recovered again with aqua vitae° or some other hot infusion; then, raw as he is, 815 and in the hottest day prognostication° proclaims, shall he be set against a brick wall, the sun looking with a southward eye upon him, where he is to behold him with flies blown° to death. But what talk we of these traitorly rascals, whose miseries are 820 to be smiled at, their offenses being so capital?° Tell me, for you seem to be honest plain men, what you have to the King. Being something gently considered,° I'll bring you where he is aboard, tender° your persons to his presence, whisper him in your behalfs. And if it be in man besides the King to effect your suits, here is man shall do it.   827

CLO. He seems to be of great authority. Close with him, give him gold, and though authority be a stubborn bear, yet he is oft led by the nose with gold. Show the inside of your purse to the outside of his hand, and no more ado. Remember "stoned," and "flayed alive."   834

SHEP. An 't please you, sir, to undertake the business for us, here is that gold I have. I'll make it as much more and leave this young man in pawn till I bring it you.

AUT. After I have done what I promised?

SHEP. Aye, sir.   840

AUT. Well, give me the moiety.° Are you a party in this business?

CLO. In some sort, sir. But though my case° be a pitiful one, I hope I shall not be flayed out of it.

AUT. Oh, that's the case of the shepherd's son. Hang him, he'll be made an example.   846

CLO. Comfort, good comfort! We must to the

King and show our strange sights. He must know 'tis none of your daughter nor my sister, we are gone else. Sir, I will give you as much as this old man does when the business is performed, and remain, as he says, your pawn till it be brought you.   853

AUT. I will trust you. Walk before toward the seaside. Go on the right hand. I will but look upon the hedge and follow you.

CLO. We are blest in this man, as I may say, even blest.

SHEP. Let's before as he bids us. He was provided° to do us good.   860

[Exeunt SHEPHERD and CLOWN.]

AUT. If I had a mind to be honest, I see Fortune would not suffer me. She drops booties in my mouth. I am courted now with a double occasion,° gold and a means to do the Prince my master good, which who knows how that may turn back to my advancement? I will bring these two moles, these blind ones, aboard him. If he think it fit to shore them° again and that the complaint they have to the King concerns him nothing, let him call me rogue for being so far officious, for I am proof against that title and what shame else belongs to 't. To him will I   872 present them. There may be matter in it.   [Exit.]

Act V

SCENE I. A room in LEONTES' palace.

[Enter LEONTES, CLEOMENES, DION, PAULINA, and SERVANTS.]

CLE. Sir, you have done enough, and have performed
A saintlike sorrow. No fault could you make
Which you have not redeemed, indeed paid down
More penitence than done trespass. At the last,
Do as the Heavens have done, forget your evil,   5
With them forgive yourself.

LEON.   Whilst I remember
Her and her virtues, I cannot forget
My blemishes in them,° and so still think of
The wrong I did myself. Which was so much
That heirless it hath made my kingdom, and   10
Destroyed the sweet'st companion that e'er man
Bred his hopes out of.

PAUL.   True, too true, my lord.
If, one by one, you wedded all the world,
Or from the all that are took something good
To make a perfect woman, she you killed   15
Would be unparalleled.

801. germane: related.   805. grace: favor.   806-07. Draw . . . sheepcote: make our King a relative of a shepherd.   812. 'nointed: anointed.   814. dram: a very small weight. aqua vitae: spirits.   816. prognostication: The common penny Almanack and Prognostication, published annually, gave confident forecasts of the weather. See App. 2.   819. blown: made to swell.   821. capital: deserving death.   823-24. gently considered: on the considerations proper to a gentleman; i.e., cash in advance.   824. tender: introduce.   841. moiety: half.   843. case: with the double meaning of "affair" and "outer covering."

859. provided: sent by Providence.   863. double occasion: twofold benefit.   868. shore them: put them ashore.
Act V, Sc. i: 8. My . . . them: my faults toward them.

LEON.   I think so. Killed!
She I killed! I did so, but thou strikest me
Sorely to say I did. It is as bitter
Upon thy tongue as in my thought. Now, good
     now,°
Say so but seldom.
CLE.   Not at all, good lady.   20
You might have spoken a thousand things that
     would
Have done the time more benefit and graced
Your kindness better.°
PAUL.   You are one of those
Would have him wed again.
DION.   If you would not so,
You pity not the state, nor the remembrance   25
Of his most sovereign name,° consider little
What dangers, by His Highness' fail of issue,°
May drop upon his kingdom and devour
Incertain lookers-on.° What were more holy
Than to rejoice the former Queen is well?°   30
What holier than, for royalty's repair,°
For present comfort and for future good,
To bless the bed of majesty again
With a sweet fellow° to 't?
PAUL.   There is none worthy,
Respecting° her that's gone. Besides, the gods   35
Will have fulfilled their secret purposes.
For has not the divine Apollo said,
Is 't not the tenor° of his oracle,
That King Leontes shall not have an heir
Till his lost child be found? Which that it shall   40
Is all as monstrous to our human reason°
As my Antigonus to break his grave
And come again to me, who, on my life,
Did perish with the infant. 'Tis your counsel
My lord should to the Heavens be contrary,   45
Oppose against their wills. [*To* LEONTES] Care not
     for issue,
The crown will find an heir. Great Alexander
Left his to the worthiest, so his successor
Was like to be the best.
LEON.   Good Paulina,
Who hast the memory of Hermione,   50
I know, in honor, oh, that ever I
Had squared me to° thy counsel! — Then, even now
I might have looked upon my Queen's full eyes,
Have taken treasure from her lips ——
PAUL.   And left them
More rich for what they yielded.

LEON.   Thou speak'st truth.   55
No more such wives, therefore, no wife. One worse,
And better used, would make her sainted spirit
Again possess her corpse, and on this stage,
Where we offenders now appear soul-vexed,
And begin, "Why to me?"°
PAUL.   Had she such power,   60
She had just cause.
LEON.   She had, and would incense me
To murder her I married.
PAUL.   I should so.
Were I the ghost that walked, I'd bid you mark
Her eye, and tell me for what dull part in 't
You chose her. Then I'd shriek that even your ears
Should rift° to hear me, and the words that fol-
     lowed   66
Should be "Remember mine."
LEON.   Stars, stars,
And all eyes else dead coals! Fear thou no wife.
I'll have no wife, Paulina.
PAUL.   Will you swear
Never to marry but by my free leave?   70
LEON. Never, Paulina, so be blest my spirit!
PAUL. Then, good my lords, bear witness to his
     oath.
CLE. You tempt him overmuch.
PAUL.   Unless another,
As like Hermione as is her picture,
Affront his eye.
CLE.   Good madam ——
PAUL.   I have done.   75
Yet, if my lord will marry — if you will, sir,
No remedy but you will — give me the office
To choose you a Queen. She shall not be so young
As was your former, but she shall be such
As, walked your first Queen's ghost,° it should take
     joy   80
To see her in your arms.
LEON.   My true Paulina,
We shall not marry till thou bid'st us.
PAUL.   That
Shall be when your first Queen's again in breath,
Never till then.
                    [*Enter a* GENTLEMAN.]
GEN. One that gives out himself Prince Florizel,
Son of Polixenes, with his Princess, she   86
The fairest I have yet beheld, desires access
To your high presence.
LEON.   What with him? He comes not
Like to his father's greatness. His approach,
So out of circumstance° and sudden, tells us   90
'Tis not a visitation framed,° but forced
By need and accident. What train?

19. **good now:** my good lady.   22–23. **graced . . . better:** shown
your kindness to better advantage.   25–26. **remembrance . . .
name:** nor the perpetuation of the King's name in his child.
27. **fail of issue:** lack of an heir.   29. **Incertain lookers-on:** the
troubled beholders.   30. **well:** dead. Cf. *Ant & Cleo*, II.v.33–34.
31. **royalty's repair:** the restoring of the King.   34. **fellow:** com-
panion.   35. **Respecting:** compared with.   38. **tenor:** purpose.
41. **as . . . reason:** as wildly impossible to believe.   52. **squared
. . . to:** ruled myself by.

60. **Why to me:** why have you done this wrong to me?   66. **rift:**
split.   80. **As . . . ghost:** if your first Queen's ghost walked
again.   90. **out of circumstance:** without the ceremony which
should accompany him.   91. **framed:** planned.

GEN.   But few,
And those but mean.

LEON.   His Princess, say you, with him?

GEN. Aye, the most peerless piece of earth,° I
     think,
That e'er the sun shone bright on.

PAUL.   O Hermione, 95
As every present time doth boast itself
Above a better gone, so must thy grave
Give way to what's seen now! Sir,° you yourself
Have said and writ so, but your writing now
Is colder than that theme. " She had not been, 100
Nor was not to be equaled " — thus your verse
Flowed with her beauty once. 'Tis shrewdly ebbed°
To say you have seen a better.

GEN.   Pardon, madam.
The one I have almost forgot — your pardon —
The other, when she has obtained your eye, 105
Will have your tongue too. This is a creature,
Would she begin a sect, might quench the zeal
Of all professors° else, make proselytes
Of who she but bid follow.

PAUL.   How! Not women?

GEN. Women will love her that she is a woman
More worth than any man, men that she is 111
The rarest of all women.

LEON.   Go, Cleomenes,
Yourself, assisted with your honored friends,
Bring them to our embracement.°

          [*Exeunt* CLEOMENES *and others.*]
                         Still, 'tis strange
He thus should steal upon us.

PAUL.   Had our Prince, 115
Jewel of children, seen this hour, he had paired
Well with this lord. There was not full a month
Between their births.

LEON. Prithee, no more, cease. Thou know'st
He dies to me again when talked of. Sure, 120
When I shall see this gentleman, thy speeches
Will bring me to consider that which may
Unfurnish° me of reason. They are come.

[*Re-enter* CLEOMENES *and others, with* FLORIZEL *and*
          PERDITA.]

Your mother was most true to wedlock, Prince,
For she did print your royal father off,° 125
Conceiving you. Were I but twenty-one,
Your father's image is so hit in you,°
His very air, that I should call you Brother,
As I did him, and speak of something wildly
By us performed before. Most dearly welcome! 130

And your fair Princess — goddess! — oh, alas!
I lost a couple that 'twixt heaven and earth
Might thus have stood begetting wonder as
You, gracious couple, do. And then I lost —
All mine own folly — the society, 135
Amity° too, of your brave father, whom,
Though bearing misery,° I desire my life
Once more to look on him.

FLO.   By his command
Have I here touched Sicilia, and from him
Give you all greetings that a king at friend° 140
Can send his brother. And but infirmity,
Which waits upon worn times,° hath something
     seized
His wished ability, he had himself
The lands and waters 'twixt your throne and his
Measured to look upon you, whom he loves — 145
He bade me say so — more than all the scepters
And those that bear them living.

LEON.   O my brother,
Good gentleman! The wrongs I have done thee stir
Afresh within me, and these thy offices,°
So rarely kind, are as interpreters 150
Of my behindhand slackness!° Welcome hither,
As is the spring to the earth. And hath he too
Exposed this paragon° to the fearful usage,
At least ungentle, of the dreadful Neptune,
To greet a man not worth her pains, much less 155
The adventure of her person?

FLO.   Good my lord,
She came from Libya.°

LEON.   Where the warlike Smalus,
That noble honored lord, is feared and loved?

FLO. Most royal sir, from thence, from him whose
     daughter 159
His tears proclaimed his, parting with her. Thence,
A prosperous south wind friendly, we have crossed,
To execute the charge° my father gave me
For visiting your Highness. My best train°
I have from your Sicilian shores dismissed,
Who for Bohemia bend, to signify 165
Not only my success in Libya, sir,
But my arrival, and my wife's, in safety
Here where we are.

LEON.   The blessèd gods
Purge all infection from our air whilst you
Do climate° here! You have a holy father, 170
A graceful gentleman, against whose person,
So sacred as it is, I have done sin.

---

94. **earth:** i.e., flesh.   98–103. **Sir . . . better:** Paulina turns on
the gentleman-poet for his insincerity in forgetting the former
extravagance of his praises of Hermione.   102. **shrewdly ebbed:**
has, like the tide, bitterly begun to decline.   108. **professors:**
those who profess a zeal for religion, particularly the Puritans.
114. **to . . . embracement:** that we may welcome them.   123. **Un-
furnish:** deprive.   125. **print . . . off:** strike off an exact copy
of your father.   127. **hit in you:** exactly reproduced in you.

136. **Amity:** friendship.   137. **Though . . . misery:** though bear-
ing my burden of sorrow.   140. **at friend:** being in a state of
friendship.   141–42. **but . . . times:** but that weakness which
comes with old age has somewhat prevented him from being able
to do as he desired.   149. **offices:** acts of courtesy.   151. **my . . .
slackness:** my slackness in not sending to greet him before this.
153. **paragon:** perfect creature.   156–57. **Good . . . Libya:** Flori-
zel here tells the tale prepared for him by Camillo.   162. **charge:**
command.   163. **My . . . train:** most of my followers.   170. **cli-
mate:** remain in our country.

For which the Heavens, taking angry note,
Have left me issueless, and your father's blest,
As he from Heaven merits it, with you   175
Worthy his goodness. What might I have been,
Might I a son and daughter now have looked on,
Such goodly things as you!

            [*Enter a* LORD.]

LORD.   Most noble sir,
That which I shall report will bear no credit
Were not the proof so nigh. Please you, great sir,
Bohemia greets you from himself by me,   181
Desires you to attach° his son, who has —
His dignity and duty both cast off —
Fled from his father, from his hopes, and with
A shepherd's daughter.

LEON.   Where's Bohemia? Speak.   185
LORD. Here in your city, I now came from him.
I speak amazedly,° and it becomes
My marvel and my message. To your Court
Whiles he was hastening, in the chase, it seems,
Of this fair couple, meets he on the way   190
The father of this seeming lady and
Her brother, having both their country quitted
With this young Prince.

FLO.   Camillo has betrayed me,
Whose honor and whose honesty till now
Endured all weathers.

LORD.   Lay 't so to his charge.   195
He's with the King your father.

LEON.   Who? Camillo?
LORD. Camillo, sir, I spake with him, who now
Has these poor men in question. Never saw I
Wretches so quake. They kneel, they kiss the earth,
Forswear° themselves as often as they speak.   200
Bohemia stops his ears, and threatens them
With divers deaths° in death.

PER.   O my poor father!
The Heaven sets spies upon us, will not have
Our contract celebrated.

LEON.   You are married?
FLO. We are not, sir, nor are we like to be,   205
The stars, I see, will kiss the valleys first.
The odds for high and low's alike.°

LEON.   My lord,
Is this the daughter of a king?

FLO.   She is
When once she is my wife.

LEON. That " once " I see by your good father's
   speed   210
Will come on very slowly. I am sorry,
Most sorry, you have broken from his liking
Where you were tied in duty, and as sorry
Your choice is not so rich in worth as beauty,
That you might well enjoy her.

FLO.   Dear, look up.   215

Though Fortune, visible an enemy,°
Should chase us with my father, power no jot
Hath she to change our loves. Beseech you, sir,
Remember since you owed no more to time
Than I do now.° With thought of such affections,
Step forth mine advocate. At your request   221
My father will grant precious things as trifles.

LEON. Would he do so, I'd beg your precious mis-
   tress,
Which he counts but a trifle.

PAUL.   Sir, my liege,
Your eye hath too much youth in 't.° Not a month
'Fore your Queen died she was more worth such
   gazes   226
Than what you look on now.

LEON.   I thought of her,
Even in these looks I made. [*To* FLORIZEL] But your
   petition
Is yet unanswered. I will to your father.
Your honor not o'erthrown by your desires,°   230
I am friend to them and you. Upon which errand
I now go toward him, therefore follow me
And mark what way I make.° Come, good my lord.

                    [*Exeunt.*]

SCENE II.° *Before* LEONTES' *palace.*

     [*Enter* AUTOLYCUS *and a* GENTLEMAN.]

AUT. Beseech you, sir, were you present at this re-
lation?

1. GEN. I was by at the opening of the fardel, heard
the old shepherd deliver the manner° how he found
it. Whereupon, after a little amazedness,° we were
all commanded out of the chamber. Only this me-
thought I heard the shepherd say — he found the
child.   8

AUT. I would most gladly know the issue of it.

1. GEN. I make a broken delivery° of the business,
but the changes I perceived in the King and Camillo
were very notes of admiration.° They seemed al-
most, with staring on one another, to tear the cases°
of their eyes. There was speech in their dumbness,
language in their very gesture, they looked as   15
they had heard of a world ransomed or one de-
stroyed. A notable passion° of wonder appeared in
them, but the wisest beholder that knew no more
but seeing could not say if the importance° were joy

---

216. visible an enemy: who is clearly our enemy.   219-20. Re-
member . . . now: remember when you were as young as I am.
225. Your . . . in 't: i.e., you are too much attracted by this lady.
Paulina is alarmed by Leontes' obvious interest in Perdita.
230. Your . . . desires: provided that you have not behaved dis-
honorably toward her.   233. mark . . . make: see what success
I have.

   Sc. ii: See *W Tale* Intro. p. 962b.   4. deliver . . . manner: re-
late the circumstances.   5. amazedness: confused wonder.
10. broken delivery: disjointed account.   12. admiration: great
wonder.   13. cases: sockets.   17. passion: emotion.   19. im-
portance: import.

---

182. attach: arrest.   187. amazedly: confusedly.   200. For-
swear: deny on oath.   202. divers deaths: different kinds of
death.   207. odds . . . alike: bad luck comes to high and low alike.

or sorrow. But in the extremity of the one, it must
needs be.   21
[*Enter another* GENTLEMAN.] Here comes a gentle-
man that haply knows more. The news, Rogero?

2. GEN. Nothing but bonfires. The oracle is ful-
filled, the King's daughter is found. Such a deal of
wonder is broken out within this hour that ballad-
makers° cannot be able to express it.   27
[*Enter a third* GENTLEMAN.] Here comes the Lady
Paulina's steward. He can deliver you more. How
goes it now, sir? This news which is called true is so
like an old tale that the verity of it is in strong sus-
picion. Has the King found his heir?   32

3. GEN. Most true, if ever truth were pregnant by
circumstance.° That which you hear you'll swear
you see, there is such unity in the proofs. The mantle
of Queen Hermione's, her jewel about the neck of it,
the letters of Antigonus found with it, which they
know to be his character,° the majesty of the crea-
ture° in resemblance of the mother, the affection
of nobleness° which Nature shows above her   40
breeding,° and many other evidences proclaim her
with all certainty to be the King's daughter. Did you
see the meeting of the two Kings?

2. GEN. No.   45

3. GEN. Then have you lost a sight which was to
be seen, cannot be spoken of. There might you have
beheld one joy crown another, so and in such man-
ner that it seemed sorrow wept to take leave of them,
for their joy waded in tears. There was casting- 50
up of eyes, holding-up of hands, with countenance
of such distraction that they were to be known by
garment, not by favor.° Our King, being ready to
leap out of himself for joy of his found daughter, as
if that joy were now become a loss, cries " Oh,   55
thy mother, thy mother! " then asks Bohemia for-
giveness, then embraces his son-in-law, then again
worries he his daughter with clipping° her. Now he
thanks the old shepherd, which stands by like a
weather-bitten conduit of many kings' reigns.°   60
I never heard of such another encounter, which
lames report to follow it and undoes description to
do it.°

2. GEN. What, pray you, became of Antigonus,
that carried hence the child?   65

3. GEN. Like an old tale still, which will have mat-
ter to rehearse, though credit be asleep and not an
ear open.° He was torn to pieces with a bear. This

avouches° the shepherd's son, who has not only his
innocence, which seems much, to justify him, but a
handkerchief and rings of his that Paulina knows.

1. GEN. What became of his bark and his follow-
ers?   73

3. GEN. Wrecked the same instant of their master's
death and in the view of the shepherd. So that all the
instruments which aided to expose the child were
even then lost when it was found. But oh, the noble
combat that 'twixt joy and sorrow was fought in
Paulina! She had one eye declined for the loss of 80
her husband, another elevated that the oracle was ful-
filled. She lifted the Princess from the earth, and so
locks her in embracing as if she would pin her to her
heart that she might no more be in danger of los-
ing.   85

1. GEN. The dignity of this act was worth the audi-
ence of kings and princes, for by such was it acted.

3. GEN. One of the prettiest touches of all, and that
which angled for mine eyes, caught the water 90
though not the fish, was when, at the relation of the
Queen's death, with the manner how she came to 't
bravely confessed and lamented by the King, how
attentiveness wounded his daughter till, from one
sign of dolor° to another, she did, with an " Alas,"
I would fain° say bleed tears, for I am sure my heart
wept blood. Who was most marble° there changed
color, some swooned, all sorrowed. If all the world
could have seen 't, the woe had been universal.   100

1. GEN. Are they returned to the Court?

3. GEN. No. The Princess, hearing of her mother's
statue, which is in the keeping of Paulina — a piece
many years in doing and now newly performed by
that rare Italian master, Julio Romano,° who,   105
had he himself eternity° and could put breath into
his work, would beguile Nature of her custom,° so
perfectly he is her ape.° He so near to Hermione hath
done Hermione that they say one would speak to her
and stand in hope of answer. — Thither with all
greediness of affection are they gone, and there they
intend to sup.   112

2. GEN. I thought she had some great matter there
in hand, for she hath privately twice or thrice a day,
ever since the death of Hermione, visited that re-
moved house. Shall we thither, and with our com-
pany piece° the rejoicing?   117

1. GEN. Who would be thence that has the benefit
of access? Every wink of an eye, some new grace
will be born. Our absence makes us unthrifty to our
knowledge.° Let's along.   [*Exeunt* GENTLEMEN.]

AUT. Now had I not the dash of my former   122

---

27. ballad-makers: See App. 8.   33–34. pregnant . . . circum-
stance: probable by the evidence.   38. character: handwriting.
39. creature: child; i.e., Perdita.   39–40. affection . . . noble-
ness: natural nobility.   41. breeding: upbringing.   51–53. with
. . . favor: i.e., their faces were so changed by their emotions
that they could only be recognized by their garments, not by
their looks.   58. clipping: embracing.   60. weather-bitten . . .
reigns: like a weather-worn fountain that has stood for many
years.   62–63. lames . . . it: makes any tale seem lame and is be-
yond description.   66–68. which . . . open: which the teller in-
sists on telling though no one will believe it or listen.

69. avouches: corroborates.   95. dolor: grief.   96. fain: gladly.
98. marble: firm.   105. Julio Romano: a famous Italian artist
who died in 1546.   106. eternity: i.e., unlimited time for his
work.   107. beguile . . . custom: cheat Nature of her power to
create living things.   108. ape: imitator.   117. piece: complete;
lit., add a piece to.   120–21. unthrifty . . . knowledge: careless in
acquiring knowledge; i.e., we shall miss the latest news.

life in me, would preferment drop on my head. I
brought the old man and his son aboard the Prince,
told him I heard them talk of a fardel and I　125
know not what. But he at that time, overfond of the
shepherd's daughter — so he then took her to be —
who began to be much seasick, and himself little
better, extremity of weather continuing, this mystery
remained undiscovered. But 'tis all one to me, for
had I been the finder-out of this secret, it would not
have relished° among my other discredits.　133
[Enter SHEPHERD and CLOWN.] Here come those I
have done good to against my will, and already ap-
pearing in the blossoms of their fortune.°

SHEP. Come, boy, I am past moe children, but thy
sons and daughters will be all gentlemen born.　138

CLO. You are well met, sir. You denied° to fight
with me this other day because I was no gentleman
born. See you these clothes? Say you see them not
and think me still no gentleman born. You were
best say these robes are not gentlemen born. Give
me the lie,° do, and try whether I am not now a
gentleman born.　145

AUT. I know you are now, sir, a gentleman born.

CLO. Aye, and have been so any time these four
hours.

SHEP. And so have I, boy.　149

CLO. So you have. But I was a gentleman born be-
fore my father, for the King's son took me by the
hand and called me Brother, and then the two Kings
called my father Brother, and then the Prince my
brother and the Princess my sister called my father
Father. And so we wept, and there was the first gen-
tlemanlike tears that ever we shed.　156

SHEP. We may live, son, to shed many more.

CLO. Aye, or else 'twere hard luck, being in so pre-
posterous° estate as we are.　159

AUT. I humbly beseech you, sir, to pardon me all
the faults I have committed to your Worship, and
to give me your good report to the Prince my master.

SHEP. Prithee, son, do, for we must be gentle now
we are gentlemen.　165

CLO. Thou wilt amend thy life?

AUT. Aye, an it like your good Worship.

CLO. Give me thy hand. I will swear to the Prince
thou art as honest a true fellow as any is in Bohemia.

SHEP. You may say it, but not swear it.　171

CLO. Not swear it, now I am a gentleman? Let
boors and franklins° say it, I'll swear it.

SHEP. How if it be false, son?　175

CLO. If it be ne'er so false, a true gentleman may
swear it in the behalf of his friend. And I'll swear to
the Prince thou art a tall fellow of thy hands° and

that thou wilt not be drunk; but I know thou art no
tall fellow of thy hands and that thou wilt be drunk.
But I'll swear it, and I would thou wouldst be a tall
fellow of thy hands.　182

AUT. I will prove so, sir, to my power.

CLO. Aye, by any means prove a tall fellow. If I
do not wonder how thou darest venture to be drunk,
not being a tall fellow, trust me not. Hark! The
Kings and the Princes, our kindred, are going to see
the Queen's picture. Come, follow us. We'll be thy
good masters.　[Exeunt.]

SCENE III. A chapel in PAULINA's house.

[Enter LEONTES, POLIXENES, FLORIZEL, PERDITA,
CAMILLO, PAULINA, LORDS, and ATTENDANTS.]

LEON. O grave and good Paulina, the great com-
fort
That I have had of thee!

PAUL.　　　　　　　What, sovereign sir,
I did not well, I meant well. All my services
You have paid home.° But that you have vouch-
safed
With your crowned brother and these your con-
tracted　　　　　　　　　　　　　　　　　5
Heirs of your kingdoms my poor house to visit,
It is a surplus of your grace,° which never
My life may last to answer.

LEON.　　　　　　　　　O Paulina,
We honor you with trouble. But we came
To see the statue of our Queen. Your gallery　10
Have we passed through, not without much content
In many singularities,° but we saw not
That which my daughter came to look upon,
The statue of her mother.

PAUL.　　　　　　　As she lived peerless,
So her dead likeness, I do well believe,　15
Excels whatever yet you looked upon
Or hand of man hath done. Therefore I keep it
Lonely, apart. But here it is. Prepare
To see the life as lively mocked° as ever　19
Still sleep mocked death. Behold, and say 'tis well.

[PAULINA draws a curtain, and discovers
HERMIONE standing like a statue.]

I like your silence, it the more shows off
Your wonder. But yet speak. First you, my liege.
Comes it not something near?

LEON.　　　　　　　Her natural posture!
Chide me, dear stone, that I may say indeed
Thou art Hermione. Or rather thou art she　25
In thy not chiding, for she was as tender
As infancy and grace. But yet, Paulina,

133. relished: found favor.　136. blossoms . . . fortune: showing
in their new finery their good fortune. See ll. 141–45.　139. de-
nied: refused.　143–44. Give . . . lie: Cf. IV.iv.743–51.　159. pre-
posterous: for "prosperous."　174. boors . . . franklins: peasants
and farmers.　178. tall . . . hands: brave man of action.

Sc. iii: 4. paid home: fully rewarded.　7. surplus . . . grace:
addition to your favor.　12. singularities: rare works of art.
19. lively mocked: exactly mimicked.

Hermione was not so much wrinkled, nothing
So agèd as this seems.

POL.   Oh, not by much.   29

PAUL. So much the more our carver's excellence,
Which lets go by some sixteen years and makes her
As° she lived now.

LEON.   As now she might have done,
So much to my good comfort as it is
Now piercing to my soul. Oh, thus she stood,
Even with such life of° majesty, warm life,   35
As now it coldly stands, when first I wooed her!
I am ashamed. Does not the stone rebuke me
For being more stone than it? O royal piece,
There's magic in thy majesty, which has
My evils conjured to remembrance and   40
From thy admiring daughter took the spirits,
Standing like stone with thee.

PER.   And give me leave,
And do not say 'tis superstition, that
I kneel and then implore her blessing. Lady,
Dear Queen, that ended when I but began,   45
Give me that hand of yours to kiss.

PAUL.   Oh, patience!
The statue is but newly fixed,° the color's
Not dry.

CAM. My lord, your sorrow was too sore laid on,
Which sixteen winters cannot blow away,   50
So many summers dry. Scarce any joy
Did ever so long live, no sorrow
But killed itself much sooner.

POL.   Dear my brother,
Let him that was the cause of this have power
To take off so much grief from you as he   55
Will piece up° in himself.

PAUL.   Indeed, my lord,
If I had thought the sight of my poor image
Would thus have wrought° you — for the stone is
        mine —
I'd not have showed it.

LEON.   Do not draw the curtain.

PAUL. No longer shall you gaze on 't, lest your
        fancy°   60
May think anon it moves.

LEON.   Let be, let be.
Would I were dead, but that, methinks, already ——
What was he that did make it? See, my lord,
Would you not deem it breathed? And that those
        veins
Did verily bear blood?

POL.   Masterly done.   65
The very life seems warm upon her lip.

LEON. The fixture of her eye has motion in 't,°
As we are mocked with art.

32. As: as if.   35. life of: living.   47. fixed: painted. It was
customary in England to paint statues in lifelike colors.
56. piece up: make up.   58. wrought: affected.   60. fancy:
imagination.   67. The . . . in 't: even the fixed look in the eye
seems to have life.

PAUL.   I'll draw the curtain.
My lord's almost so far transported° that
He'll think anon it lives.

LEON.   O sweet Paulina,   70
Make me to think so twenty years together!
No settled° senses of the world can match
The pleasure of that madness. Let 't alone.

PAUL. I am sorry, sir, I have thus far stirred you,
        but
I could afflict you farther.

LEON.   Do, Paulina,   75
For this affliction has a taste as sweet
As any cordial° comfort. Still, methinks
There is an air comes from her. What fine chisel
Could ever yet cut breath? Let no man mock me,
For I will kiss her.

PAUL.   Good my lord, forbear.   80
The ruddiness upon her lip is wet,
You'll mar it if you kiss it, stain your own
With oily painting. Shall I draw the curtain?

LEON. No, not these twenty years.

PER.   So long could I
Stand by, a looker-on.

PAUL.   Either forbear,   85
Quit presently the chapel, or resolve you
For more amazement. If you can behold it,
I'll make the statue move indeed, descend
And take you by the hand. But then you'll think,
Which I protest against, I am assisted   90
By wicked powers.

LEON.   What you can make her do
I am content to look on, what to speak
I am content to hear, for 'tis as easy
To make her speak as move.

PAUL.   It is required
You do awake your faith. Then all stand still.   95
On — those that think it is unlawful business°
I am about, let them depart.

LEON.   Proceed.
No foot shall stir.

PAUL.   Music, awake her, strike! [Music.]
'Tis time, descend, be stone no more, approach.
Strike all that look upon with marvel. Come,   100
I'll fill your grave up. Stir — nay, come away,
Bequeath to death your numbness, for from him
Dear life redeems you. You perceive she stirs.

                [HERMIONE comes down.]
Start not, her actions shall be holy as
You hear my spell is lawful. Do not shun her   105
Until you see her die again, for then
You kill her double. Nay, present your hand.
When she was young you wooed her, now in age
Is she become the suitor?

LEON.   Oh, she's warm!

69. transported: taken out of himself, excited.   72. settled:
sane.   77. cordial: heartwarming.   96. unlawful business: i.e.,
black magic.

If this be magic, let it be an art   110
Lawful as eating.

POL.   She embraces him.

CAM. She hangs about his neck.
If she pertain to life, let her speak too.

POL. Aye, and make 't manifest where she has
    lived,
Or how stolen from the dead.

PAUL.   That she is living,   115
Were it but told you, should be hooted at
Like an old tale. But it appears she lives,
Though yet she speak not. Mark a little while.
Please you to interpose, fair madam. Kneel
And pray your mother's blessing. Turn, good lady,
Our Perdita is found.

HER.   You gods, look down,   121
And from your sacred vials pour your graces
Upon my daughter's head! Tell me, mine own,
Where hast thou been preserved? Where lived?
    How found
Thy father's Court? For thou shalt hear that I,   125
Knowing by Paulina that the oracle
Gave hope thou wast in being,° have preserved
Myself to see the issue.°

PAUL.   There's time enough for that,
Lest they desire upon this push° to trouble
Your joys with like relation. Go together,   130
You precious winners all. Your exultation

127. in being: still living.   128. issue: sequel.   129. push: excitement.

Partake to° everyone. I, an old turtle,°
Will wing me to some withered bough and there
My mate, that's never to be found again,
Lament till I am lost.

LEON.   Oh, peace, Paulina!   135
Thou shouldst a husband take by my consent,
As I by thine a wife. This is a match,
And made between 's by vows. Thou hast found
    mine,
But how is to be questioned. For I saw her,
As I thought, dead, and have in vain said many   140
A prayer upon her grave. I'll not seek far —
For him, I partly know his mind — to find thee
An honorable husband. Come, Camillo,
And take her by the hand, whose worth and honesty
Is richly noted and here justified°   145
By us, a pair of kings. Let's from this place.
What! Look upon my brother.° Both your pardons,
That e'er I put between your holy looks
My ill suspicion. This your son-in-law,   149
And son unto the King, whom, Heavens directing,
Is trothplight to your daughter. Good Paulina,
Lead us from hence, where we may leisurely
Each one demand and answer to his part
Performed in this wide gap of time since first   154
We were dissevered.° Hastily lead away. [Exeunt.]

132. Partake to: share with. turtle: turtledove.   145. justified: proved true.   147. brother: i.e., Polixenes.   155. dissevered: separated.

THE TEMPEST

Introduction

So far as is known or guessed, *The Tempest* is Shakespeare's last comedy. It is natural, therefore, even if dangerous, to regard it with some sentiment and to identify Prospero, the old magician bidding farewell to his art, with Shakespeare making his final appearance as a playwright. Whether we indulge this fancy — and it is no more than a fancy — or not, *The Tempest* certainly contains some of Shakespeare's finest and maturest poetry, and reveals his supreme mastery over English blank verse.

The Tempest was written about 1611. There is a record in the Revels Accounts which shows that the play was acted by the King's Players in Whitehall before King James, on Hallowmas Night (November 1) in 1611. It was again played at Court as one of the fourteen plays acted by the same company in February 1613 during the wedding festivities of the Princess Elizabeth and the Elector Palatine.

The Tempest was first published in the first folio (F1) in 1623. The text is interesting, for it was unusually well prepared for the press. It is divided into acts and scenes, and the stage directions are full and elaborate.

No complete source for *The Tempest* has been found. A German play called the *Comedy of the Beautiful Sidea,* written by Jacob Ayrer of Nuremberg sometime before 1605, has some resemblances. There is a magician Prince with a spirit attendant and an only daughter who falls in love with the son of her father's enemy. There may be some connection between this play and *The Tempest,* for Ayrer wrote other plays which were adapted from plays taken over to Germany by English players; but stories of a magician with an only daughter who falls in love are common in all fairy tales. There are, however, pieces and fragments from other sources which Shakespeare obviously found useful. The story of the shipwreck and of the mysterious island owes a good deal to an event which was recent and sensational and of which there are several contemporary comments. It is thus described in Howe's *Annals:*

In the year 1609 the Adventurers and Company of Virginia sent from London a fleet of eight ships with people to supply and make strong the Colony in Virginia, Sir Thomas Gates being General in a ship of 300 ton. In this ship was also Sir George Somers, who was Admiral, and Captain Newport Vice-Admiral, and with them about 160 persons. This ship was Admiral, and kept company with the rest of the fleet to the height of 30 degrees, and being then assembled to consult touching divers matters, they were surprised with a most extreme violent storm which scattered the whole fleet; yet all the rest of the fleet bent their course for Virginia, where by God's special favor they arrived safely, but this great ship, though new, and far stronger than any of the rest, fell into a great leak, so as mariners and passengers were forced for three days' space to do their utmost to save themselves from sudden sinking. But notwithstanding their incessant pumping, and casting out of water by buckets, and all other means, yet the water covered all the goods within the hold, and all men were utterly tired and spent in strength, and overcome with labor, and hopeless of any succor. Most of them were gone to sleep, yielding themselves to the mercy of the sea, being all very desirous to die upon any shore wheresoever. Sir George Somers, sitting at the stern, seeing the ship desperate of relief, looking every minute when the ship would sink, he espied land, which according to his and Captain Newport's opinion they judged it should be that dreadful coast of the Bermodes, which islands were of all nations said and supposed to be enchanted and inhabited with witches and devils, which grew by reason of accustomed monstrous thunder, storm, and tempest, near unto those islands. Also for that the whole coast is so wondrous dangerous of rocks that few can approach them but with unspeakable hazard of shipwreck. Sir George Somers, Sir Thomas Gates, Captain Newport, and the rest suddenly agreed of two evils to choose the least, and so in a kind of desperate resolution directed the ship mainly for these islands, which by God's divine providence at a high water ran right between two strong rocks, where it stuck fast without breaking. Which gave leisure and good opportunity for them to hoist out their boat, and to land all their people as well sailors, as soldiers, and others in good safety, and being come ashore, they were soon refreshed and cheered, the soil and air being most sweet and delicate. The salt water did great spoil to most of the ship's lading and victual, yet some meal was well recovered, with many particular things for their common use, and they all humbly thanked

God for His great mercy in so preserving them from destruction.

Then presently they sought farther into the island for food, which being never yet inhabited by any people, was overgrown with woods, and the woods replenished with wild swine, which swine as it is very probable swam thither out of some shipwreck. They found also great multitude of fowl of sundry kinds, being then in a manner very tame. They found some fruit, as mulberries, pears, and palmytoes [palmettos], with stately cedar trees. And in the sea, and in the rocks, great plenty of most pleasant and wholesome fish.

Here of necessity they were constrained to stay almost ten months, in which space by the special mercy and Divine Providence of Almighty God to make good the discovery of the islands unto them, that they by diligence and industry saved so much of the timber, tackling, and other things out of their great ship which lay wrecked and stuck fast between two rocks as therewithal, and with such supply of stuff as they found in those islands, they builded their two vessels, the lesser whereof so soon as it was finished, it was manned, and sent to go to the Colony in Virginia, to signify unto them how all things had happened with their commanders and their company, and that they would shortly set sail for Virginia. And when the bigger vessel was finished, and victualed with swine's flesh, and with what else that place would afford them, these Commanders, with all their company, embarked themselves, and by God's great mercy arrived safely at Virginia, when all Englishmen deemed them to be utterly cast away.

News of these events reached England in the early autumn of 1610, and two pamphlets were printed — *A Discovery of the Barmudas* and *A Declaration of the Estate of the Colony in Virginia.* About a year later, William Strachey, who was one of those cast ashore on Bermuda, wrote *A True Reportory of the Wreck and Redemption of Sir Thomas Gates upon and from the Islands of the Bermudas.* This was not printed until 1625, but as a number of phrases in Strachey's report seem to have been caught up into *The Tempest,* it is possible that Shakespeare saw it in manuscript.

Prospero's island is not, however, situated in the West Indies, but in the Mediterranean, somewhere off the direct course between Tunis and Naples. Shakespeare's idea of the magic island may also have been first suggested by a passage in William Parry's *New and Large Discourse of the Travels of Sir Anthony Shirley,*

Knight, describing Shirley's astonishing journeyings in Persia and Russia. This book came out in 1601, and Shakespeare seems to have read it, for he refers more than once to Shirley's Persian adventure. Parry describes how

within two days' passage of Candia [Crete], as we came toward Ciprus (which I had almost omitted) there is also a Greekish isle (whose name — I am ashamed therefore — I have quite forgotten), whereupon we touched and watered, which is some half-mile over, having one religious house therein and alone, with about some twenty Greek friggots [friars] inhabiting the same, which is (as we thought) another Eden, and the most pleasant place that ever our eyes beheld for the exercise of a solitary and contemplative life; for it is furnished with the foison of all God's good blessings. All kind of fruits (as apples, pears, plums, oranges, lemons, pomegranates, and the like) in great abundance groweth there; with most pleasant gardens, replenished with all manner of odoriferous flowers and wholesome herbs for sallets and medicines; wherein breaketh forth many fresh and crystal-clear springs of water; having therewithal cattle (as beeves and muttons there naturally bred) more than sufficient to serve that house. In our travels many times, falling into dangers and unpleasant places, this only island would be the place where we would wish ourselves to end our lives.

Another book which Shakespeare obviously read when writing *The Tempest* was John Florios' translation of Montaigne's *Essays,* published in 1603, for a passage from the Essay " Of the Cannibals " (No. XXX) is followed very closely in Gonzalo's little discourse of his ideal commonwealth (II.i). Montaigne notes how one of his servants told him of a tribe of savages which followed the rule of nature:

. . . it is a nation, would I answer Plato, that hath no kind of traffic, no knowledge of letters, no intelligence of numbers, no name of magistrate, nor of politic superiority; no use of service, of riches or of poverty; no contracts, no successions, no partitions, no occupation but idle; no respect of kindred, but common; no apparel but natural; no manuring of lands, no use of wine, corn, or metal. The very words that import lying, falsehood, treason, dissimulations, covetousness, envy, detraction, and pardon were never heard of amongst them. How dissonant would he find his imaginary commonwealth from this perfection.

The Tempest was thus a play written for the Court of King James I, a play performed at a memorable Court wedding, and a fairy tale. Any working dramatist writes his play to suit his actors and his audience. For the last seven or eight years, the English Court had taken particular delight in masques (see Gen. Intro. p. 47b). *The Tempest* is not a masque, though there is inserted a little device which is a masque in miniature in honor of the betrothal of Ferdinand and Miranda. A masque was essentially an amateur affair, and not suited to the rougher audience of the Elizabethan playhouse, nor did the professional companies have the capital to invest in such costly devices. But when acting at Court for a special occasion, they had the use of stage machinery and scenery for such episodes as the storm at sea or the banquet which vanishes " by a quaint device." The King's Players had also extras for dancing and, if necessary, singing.

The Tempest has all the familiar incidents of the fairy tale: the magician with the familiar spirit and a beautiful daughter. But even a fairy tale may be used for a serious theme. The theme of *The Tempest,* as of *The Winter's Tale,* is reconciliation. This theme had interested Shakespeare not a little. In his early tragedy *Romeo and Juliet* he treated it tragically; the eternal feud between the families of Capulet and Montague is ended only when two young lovers have died as a sacrifice to the stupidity of their parents. A story of reconciliation telling of two generations must necessarily cover a long stretch of time. In *The Winter's Tale,* Shakespeare divided his play into two parts, with an interval of sixteen years symbolically indicated by Time as a Chorus. In *The Tempest,* he evolved a plot which not only brings the two generations together, but does actually preserve the unity of time, for the whole action on the stage occurs within the time of real events and almost in the same place.

If a dramatist is to construct his play of two generations and at the same time keep the unity of time, he must either choose a story so well known to the audience that they need only be told at what point the play begins, or if the story is new, quite early some explanation of past events must be given. Such explanations can be very tedious and artificial. Shakespeare begins with a stirring, noisy scene, a ship at sea in great peril. The ship runs aground. Then, in the quiet that follows, there enter an elderly man and his daughter. Here begins the glimpse

into past history which is necessary before the story can move further. Critics differ in their opinions about the interpretation of this scene. To some, Prospero is yet another specimen of Shakespeare's somewhat overbearing, tyrannical fathers, like Capulet or Polonius. To others, he is a shy, gentle, melancholy student. The impression which the character will make on an audience depends on the interpretation of this scene. The common view is that, though technically excellent, the scene is inclined to be difficult. Prospero, as he tells his story, keeps interjecting: " Thou attend'st not. — Dost thou hear? " as if he were an incompetent schoolteacher trying to keep the attention of an undisciplined class. Miranda, too, seems a little lacking in politeness when she cannot at least pretend to be listening.

There is another and likelier interpretation. Hitherto, Miranda has known nothing of her father's past; now she must learn. As a Duke Prospero has been a failure; he must now tell his daughter and be judged by her. It is a humiliating moment — a trial which at some time or other comes to all parents when for the first time their children look at them frankly and critically. When Prospero comes to tell his story, he lives again in the past and speaks musingly to himself more than to her. His ejaculations are in fact pleas to Miranda because he is so desperately anxious that she shall judge his case favorably and pass a merciful verdict. It is also necessary, as a matter of mere stage technique, that a long speech shall be broken up, or it becomes tedious. Miranda says little not because she is inattentive or unsympathetic, but because she is amazed at this strange tale, not knowing what will come next.

The play is now ready to move. Miranda is asleep when Ariel — a spirit of the air — appears. Except to Prospero and to the audience, Ariel, unless assuming a disguise, is always invisible to the other characters.

We are next introduced to Caliban, who in contrast with Ariel is a creature all earth. He is Shakespeare's portrait of the horrid savage. Caliban was greatly admired by critics of the eighteenth century as a marvelous effort of the imagination. Shakespeare seemed not to have shared the views of his contemporary Montaigne that savages are naturally gentle creatures, though it is perhaps unfair to judge by this specimen, whose mother was a witch and father a devil. With such heredity one hardly expects refinement. Yet Shakespeare is always fair to Caliban. He has his case and is allowed to state it. It is not surprising that he should be fascinated by Stephano and Trinculo, with their divine liquor.

The plot is now on the move, and hereafter Prospero makes his victims dance to his music. Ferdinand comes in, and at first glance, he and Miranda "change eyes." This to the Elizabethans was the ideal form of true love:

Who ever loved that loved not at first sight?

But Prospero, so that things may not be too easy for Ferdinand, pretends to be rough and terrifying, and from that moment Ferdinand becomes Miranda's slave.

After this idyllic scene, a very different and less ideal set of people are introduced. They are Prospero's wrongers, Alonso, the father of Ferdinand, and the wicked pair Sebastian and Antonio. Also in this party is Gonzalo, the old councilor, who is a sort of refined version of Polonius. The bold, bad men Sebastian and Antonio plot Alonso's murder so nicely and so grimly. Their conversation is admirably invented — neither of them quite likes to give plain words to a plain, dirty action. But this is a fairy tale, and no blood is to be shed; besides, Prospero and Ariel always have the situation well in hand. So Alonso is saved and the party wander away to their predestined meeting place with Prospero.

Next, to clean the palate of the unpleasant taste of this scene, follows a passage of first-class low comedy. Trinculo, the jester, encounters the cowering Caliban. There is a kind of parody here of Miranda's first sight of a human being. Then comes Stephano, the drunken butler, and finds Trinculo covered by Caliban's cloak, and all three go off inspired by liquor.

Shakespeare then repeats the pattern. Ferdinand and Miranda pass from love to courtship and a pledging of troth. To high romance the natural contrast is low comedy when Stephano, Trinculo, and Caliban re-enter, with Caliban the only man among them with a plan. He will murder Prospero. It is part of Caliban's simplicity that he mistakes the nature of Stephano, who has not the stuff in him to make a murderer.

Now Prospero has everything ready for the conversion of Alonso, and to crown Alonso's sorrow there comes the sudden, unexpected, overwhelming denunciation of Ariel. Thereafter Prospero, knowing that all is as he would have it, relents toward Ferdinand and accepts him, and in honor of the lovers presents a little wedding masque, which is suddenly broken off as he remembers the plot. It is the excuse for one of the most famous, oft-quoted, and finest of Shakespeare's speeches.

The play is now working toward an end. The three plotters, Caliban, Stephano, and Trinculo, are punished; they were poor plotters after all. A few gay cloths on a line easily turned them aside. Finally, all Prospero's enemies are brought before him and forgiven. To Alonso, his son is restored, and both old men are reconciled in the happiness of their children. *The Tempest* is a very simple story.

In *The Tempest,* Shakespeare has finally achieved complete mastery over words in the blank-verse form. This power is shown throughout the play, but particularly in some of Prospero's greatest speeches, such as "Our revels now are ended" (IV.i.148), or in his farewell to his art (V.i.33). There is in these speeches a kind of organ note not hitherto heard. Shakespeare's thought was as deep as in his tragedies, but now he was able to express each thought with perfect meaning and its own proper harmony. Of his comedies, certainly *The Tempest* is Shakespeare's greatest dramatic poem. Unlike some of his other plays, it is better in the reading than on the stage.

The Tempest

DRAMATIS PERSONAE

ALONSO, *King of Naples*
SEBASTIAN, *his brother*
PROSPERO, *the right Duke of Milan*
ANTONIO, *his brother, the usurping Duke of Milan*
FERDINAND, *son to the King of Naples*
GONZALO, *an honest old councilor*
ADRIAN }
FRANCISCO } *lords*
CALIBAN. *a savage and deformed slave*
TRINCULO, *a jester*
STEPHANO, *a drunken butler*
MASTER *of a ship*
BOATSWAIN

MARINERS
MIRANDA, *daughter to Prospero*
ARIEL, *an airy spirit*

IRIS }
CERES }
JUNO } *presented by spirits*
NYMPHS }
REAPERS }

OTHER SPIRITS, *attending on Prospero*

SCENE — *A ship at sea: an uninhabited island.*

Act I

SCENE I. *On a ship at sea. A tempestuous noise of thunder and lightning heard.*°

[*Enter a* SHIPMASTER *and a* BOATSWAIN.]
MAST. Boatswain!
BOATS. Here, master. What cheer?
MAST. Good,° speak to the mariners. Fall to't yarely,° or we run ourselves aground. Bestir, bestir. [*Exit.*]

[*Enter* MARINERS.]
BOATS. Heigh, my hearts! Cheerly, cheerly, my 6 hearts! Yare, yare! Take in the topsail.° Tend° to the master's whistle. Blow till thou burst thy wind, if room° enough!

[*Enter* ALONSO, SEBASTIAN, ANTONIO, FERDINAND, GONZALO, *and others.*]
ALON. Good boatswain, have care. Where's the master? Play the men.° 11
BOATS. I pray now, keep below.
ANT. Where is the master, boatswain?
BOATS. Do you not hear him? You mar our labor. Keep your cabins. You do assist the storm. 15
GON. Nay, good, be patient.
BOATS. When the sea is. Hence! What cares these roarers for the name of King? To cabin. Silence! Trouble us not.
GON. Good, yet remember whom thou hast aboard. 21

BOATS. None that I more love than myself. You are a councilor. If you can command these elements to silence, and work the peace of the present,° we will not hand a rope more. Use your authority. If you cannot, give thanks you have lived so long, and make yourself ready in your cabin for the mischance of the hour, if it so hap. Cheerly, good hearts! 29 Out of our way, I say. [*Exit.*]
GON. I have great comfort from this fellow. Methinks he hath no drowning mark upon him, his complexion is perfect gallows.° Stand fast, good Fate, to his hanging. Make the rope of his destiny our cable, for our own doth little advantage. If 35 he be not born to be hanged, our case is miserable. [*Exeunt.*]

[*Re-enter* BOATSWAIN.]
BOATS. Down with the topmast! Yare! Lower, lower! Bring her to try with main course.° [*A cry within.*] A plague upon this howling! They are louder than the weather or our office.° 40
[*Re-enter* SEBASTIAN, ANTONIO, *and* GONZALO.] Yet again! What do you here? Shall we give o'er, and drown? Have you a mind to sink?
SEB. A pox o' your throat, you bawling, blasphemous, incharitable dog!
BOATS. Work you, then. 45
ANT. Hang, cur! Hang, you whoreson,° insolent noisemaker. We are less afraid to be drowned than thou art.
GON. I'll warrant him for drowning,° though the

Act I, Sc. i: s.d.. On . . . heard: The ship is in great danger. The wind is blowing hard from the sea; on the other side lies the rocky island, and between there is too little sea room for her to sail past without being driven ashore by the drift. For the type of ship, see Pl. 7b. 3. Good: my good man. 4. yarely: quickly, smartly. 7. Take . . . topsail: i.e., to lessen the drift. Tend: attend. 9. room: sea room. 11. Play . . . men: act like men.

24. work . . . present: bring us peace at once. 32–33. hath . . . gallows: Gonzalo remembers the proverb "He that is born to be hanged will never be drowned," and the boatswain looks like a gallows bird. 38. try . . . course: i.e., use only the mainsail to heave her to. course: sail. 40. office: business. 46. whoreson: bastard. 49. warrant . . . drowning: guarantee him against drowning.

ship were no stronger than a nutshell and as leaky as
an unstanched wench.   51
   BOATS. Lay her ahold,° ahold! Set her two
courses.° Off to sea again, lay her off.

                     [*Enter* MARINERS *wet.*]

   MAR. All lost! To prayers, to prayers! All lost!   55
   BOATS. What, must our mouths be cold?°
   GON. The King and Prince at prayers! Let's assist
them,
For our case is as theirs.
   SEB.   I'm out of patience.
   ANT. We are merely cheated of our lives by
drunkards.
This wide-chapped° rascal — would thou mightst lie
drowning
The washing of ten tides!°
   GON.   He'll be hanged yet,   61
Though every drop of water swear against it
And gape at widest to glut° him.

      [*A confused noise within:* "Mercy on us!"
      — "We split, we split!" — "Farewell my
      wife and children!" — "Farewell, brother!"
      — "We split, we split, we split!"]

   ANT. Let's all sink with the King.
   SEB. Let's take leave of him.   68

         [*Exeunt* ANTONIO *and* SEBASTIAN.]

   GON. Now would I give a thousand furlongs of
sea for an acre of barren ground, long heath,° brown
furze,° anything. The wills above be done! But   72
I would fain die a dry death.   [*Exeunt.*]

SCENE II. *The island. Before* PROSPERO's *cell.*

         [*Enter* PROSPERO *and* MIRANDA.]

   MIRA. If by your art, my dearest father, you have
Put the wild waters in this roar, allay° them.
The sky, it seems, would pour down stinking pitch
But that the sea, mounting to the welkin's° cheek,
Dashes the fire out. Oh, I have suffered   5
With those that I saw suffer! A brave vessel,
Who had no doubt some noble creature in her,
Dashed all to pieces. Oh, the cry did knock
Against my very heart! Poor souls, they perished!
Had I been any god of power, I would   10
Have sunk the sea within the earth or ere
It should the good ship so have swallowed and
The fraughting° souls within her.
   PRO.   Be collected.°

No more amazement. Tell your piteous heart
There's no harm done.
   MIRA.   Oh, woe the day!
   PRO.   No harm.   15
I have done nothing but in care of thee,
Of thee, my dear one, thee, my daughter, who
Art ignorant of what thou art, naught knowing
Of whence I am, nor that I am more better
Than Prospero, master of a full° poor cell,   20
And thy no greater father.
   MIRA.   More to know
Did never meddle° with my thoughts.
   PRO.   'Tis time
I should inform thee farther. Lend thy hand,
And pluck my magic garment from me. — So.

              [*Lays down his mantle.*]

Lie there, my art. Wipe thou thine eyes, have com-
   fort.   25
The direful spectacle of the wreck, which touched
The very virtue of compassion in thee,
I have with such provision° in mine art
So safely ordered that there is no soul,
No, not so much perdition° as a hair,   30
Betid° to any creature in the vessel
Which thou heard'st cry, which thou saw'st sink. Sit
   down,
For thou must now know farther.
   MIRA.   You have often
Begun to tell me what I am, but stopped,
And left me to a bootless inquisition,°   35
Concluding "Stay, not yet."
   PRO.   The hour's now come,
The very minute bids thee ope thine ear.
Obey, and be attentive. Canst thou remember
A time before we came unto this cell?
I do not think thou canst, for then thou wast not   40
Out° three years old.
   MIRA.   Certainly, sir, I can.
   PRO. By what? By any other house or person?
Of anything the image tell me that
Hath kept with thy remembrance.
   MIRA.   'Tis far off,
And rather like a dream than an assurance   45
That my remembrance warrants. Had I not
Four or five women once that tended me?
   PRO. Thou hadst, and more, Miranda. But how
   is it
That this lives in thy mind? What seest thou else
In the dark backward and abysm of time?°   50
If thou remember'st aught ere thou camest here,
How thou camest here thou mayst.
   MIRA.   But that I do not.

---

52. **ahold:** close to the wind. **52–53. two courses:** two sails; i.e.,
set the foresail as well. The maneuver of heaving-to has failed;
the boatswain now hopes to get the ship moving into the wind
enough to pass the island. **56. mouths be cold:** Here the boat-
swain abandons hope and falls to drinking. **60. wide-chapped:**
large-cheeked, because full of liquor. **61. washing . . . tides:**
Pirates were hanged on the seashore and left until three high
tides had passed over them. **63. glut:** swallow. **71. long
heath:** rough grass. **72. furze:** a prickly bushy shrub.
Sc. ii: 2. allay: abate. **4. welkin:** sky. **13. fraughting:** lit.,
who were her freight. **collected:** calm.

20. **full:** exceedingly. **22. meddle:** interfere; i.e., cause to be
curious. **28. provision:** foresight. **30. perdition:** loss.
31. Betid: befallen. **35. bootless inquisition:** vain inquiry.
41. Out: more than. **50. abysm of time:** i.e., the past, which is
like a dark abyss.

PRO. Twelve year since, Miranda, twelve year
since,
Thy father was the Duke of Milan, and
A prince of power.

MIRA.   Sir, are not you my father?   55

PRO. Thy mother was a piece of virtue, and
She said thou wast my daughter, and thy father
Was Duke of Milan, and his only heir
A Princess, no worse issued.

MIRA.   Oh, the Heavens!
What foul play had we that we came from thence?
Or blessèd was't we did?

PRO.   Both, both, my girl.   61
By foul play, as thou say'st, were we heaved thence,
But blessedly holp° hither.

MIRA.   Oh, my heart bleeds
To think o' the teen° that I have turned you to,
Which is from my remembrance! Please you, far-
ther.   65

PRO. My brother, and thy uncle, called Antonio —
I pray thee mark me — that a brother should
Be so perfidious! — he whom, next thyself,
Of all the world I loved, and to him put
The manage° of my state — as at that time   70
Through all the signories° it was the first,
And Prospero the prime° Duke, being so reputed
In dignity, and for the liberal arts°
Without a parallel, those being all my study
The government I cast upon my brother,   75
And to my state grew stranger, being transported
And rapt in secret studies. Thy false uncle —
Dost thou attend me?

MIRA.   Sir, most heedfully.

PRO. Being once perfected° how to grant suits,
How to deny them, who to advance, and who   80
To trash for overtopping,° new-created°
The creatures that were mine, I say, or changed 'em,
Or else new-formed 'em — having both the key°
Of officer and office, set all hearts i' the state
To what tune pleased his ear, that now he was   85
The ivy which had hid my princely trunk,
And sucked my verdure out on't. Thou attend'st
not.°

MIRA. Oh, good sir, I do.

PRO.   I pray thee, mark me.
I, thus neglecting worldly ends, all dedicated
To closeness° and the bettering of my mind   90
With that which, but by being so retired,°
O'erprized all popular rate,° in my false brother

Awaked an evil nature. And my trust,
Like a good parent, did beget of him
A falsehood in its contrary as great   95
As my trust was, which had indeed no limit,
A confidence sans° bound. He being thus lorded,
Not only with what my revenue yielded,
But what my power might else exact, like one
Who having into truth, by telling of it,   100
Made such a sinner of his memory,
To credit his own lie, he did believe
He was indeed the Duke° — out o' the substitution,
And executing the outward face of royalty,
With all prerogative.° — Hence his ambition grow-
ing —   105
Dost thou hear?

MIRA.   Your tale, sir, would cure deafness.

PRO. To have no screen between this part he
played
And him he played it for, he needs will be
Absolute Milan.° Me, poor man, my library
Was dukedom large enough. Of temporal royalties°
He thinks me now incapable; confederates,°   111
So dry° he was for sway, wi' the King of Naples
To give him annual tribute, do him homage,
Subject his coronet to his crown,° and bend
The dukedom, yet unbowed — alas, poor Milan! —
To most ignoble stooping.

MIRA.   Oh, the Heavens!   116

PRO. Mark his condition, and the event,° then tell
me
If this might be a brother.

MIRA.   I should sin
To think but nobly of my grandmother.
Good wombs have borne bad sons.

PRO.   Now the condition.   120
This King of Naples, being an enemy
To me inveterate, hearkens my brother's suit.
Which was that he, in lieu o' the premises,°
Of homage, and I know not how much tribute,
Should presently° extirpate° me and mine   125
Out of the dukedom, and confer fair Milan,
With all the honors, on my brother. Whereon,
A treacherous army levied, one midnight
Fated to the purpose did Antonio open
The gates of Milan, and, i' the dead of darkness   130
The ministers for the purpose hurried thence
Me and thy crying self.

---

63. **holp:** helped. 64. **teen:** sorrow. 70. **manage:** management.
71. **signories:** lordships. 72. **prime:** leading. 73. **liberal arts:**
academic learning. 79. **perfected:** become perfect by practice.
81. **trash . . . overtopping:** check for running ahead, a metaphor
from training a pack of hounds. **new-created:** made them new
creatures — by altering their minds. 83. **key:** tool used for
tuning a stringed instrument. 87. **Thou . . . not:** See *Temp*
Intro. p. 1003a. 90. **closeness:** privacy. 91. **but . . . retired:**
except that it kept me away from state affairs. 92. **O'erprized
. . . rate:** was worth more than it is commonly regarded.

97. **sans:** without. 97–103. **He . . . Duke:** he, getting such
greatness not only from my wealth but also by abusing my power,
began to believe as he had hitherto pretended, that he was in
truth the Duke. 103–05. **out . . . prerogative:** from being my
substitute and acting outwardly as Duke with all the rights of a
ruler. 109. **Absolute Milan:** Duke of Milan in fact. 110. **tem-
poral royalties:** worldly power. 111. **confederates:** conspires.
112. **dry:** thirsty. 114. **Subject . . . crown:** i.e., pay homage as
to his overlord. The coronet was worn as a symbol by rulers of
lower rank than that of King. 117. **event:** sequel. 123. **in . . .
premises:** in return for these conditions. 125. **presently:** im-
mediately. **extirpate:** root out.

MIRA.   Alack, for pity!
I, not remembering how I cried out then.
Will cry it o'er again. It is a hint°
That wrings mine eyes to't.
PRO.   Hear a little further,   135
And then I'll bring thee to the present business
Which now's upon 's, without the which this story
Were most impertinent.
MIRA.   Wherefore did they not
That hour destroy us?
PRO.   Well demanded, wench.   139
My tale provokes that question. Dear, they durst not,
So dear the love my people bore me, nor set
A mark so bloody on the business, but
With colors fairer painted their foul ends.
In few,° they hurried us aboard a bark,   144
Bore us some leagues to sea, where they prepared
A rotten carcass of a butt,° not rigged,
Nor tackle, sail, nor mast. The very rats
Instinctively have quit it. There they hoist us,
To cry to the sea that roared to us, to sigh
To the winds, whose pity, sighing back again,   150
Did us but loving wrong.
MIRA.   Alack, what trouble
Was I then to you!
PRO.   Oh, a cherubin
Thou wast that did preserve me. Thou didst smile,
Infusèd with a fortitude from Heaven,   154
When I have decked the sea with drops full salt.
Under my burden groaned, which raised in me
An undergoing stomach° to bear up
Against what should ensue.
MIRA.   How came we ashore?
PRO. By Providence divine.
Some food we had, and some fresh water, that   160
A noble Neapolitan, Gonzalo,
Out of his charity, who being then appointed
Master of this design, did give us, with
Rich garments, linens, stuffs, and necessaries,
Which since have steaded much.° So, of his gentle-
ness,   165
Knowing I loved my books, he furnished me
From mine own library with volumes that
I prize above my dukedom.
MIRA.   Would I might
But ever see that man!
PRO.   Now I arise. [*Resumes his mantle.*]
Sit still, and hear the last of our sea sorrow.   170
Here in this island we arrived, and here
Have I, thy schoolmaster, made thee more profit
Than other princes can that have more time
For vainer hours, and tutors not so careful.
MIRA. Heavens thank you for't! And now I pray
you, sir,   175

For still 'tis beating° in my mind, your reason
For raising this sea storm?
PRO.   Know thus far forth.°
By accident most strange, bountiful Fortune,
Now my dear lady,° hath mine enemies
Brought to this shore. And by my prescience°   180
I find my zenith° doth depend upon
A most auspicious star, whose influence
If now I court not,° but omit, my fortunes
Will ever after droop. Here cease more questions.
Thou art inclined to sleep, 'tis a good dullness,   185
And give it way. I know thou canst not choose.
[MIRANDA *sleeps.*]
Come away, servant, come. I am ready now.
Approach, my Ariel, come.
[*Enter* ARIEL.]
ARI. All hail, great master! Grave sir, hail! I come
To answer thy best pleasure, be 't to fly,   190
To swim, to dive into the fire, to ride
On the curled clouds, to thy strong bidding task°
Ariel and all his quality.°
PRO.   Hast thou, spirit,
Performed to point° the tempest that I bade thee?
ARI. To every article.   195
I boarded the King's ship. Now on the beak,
Now in the waist,° the deck, in every cabin,
I flamed amazement.° Sometime I'd divide,
And burn in many places; on the topmast,   199
The yards and bowsprit, would I flame distinctly,
Then meet and join. Jove's lightnings, the precur-
sors°
O' the dreadful thunderclaps, more momentary
And sight-outrunning were not. The fire and cracks
Of sulphurous roaring the most mighty Neptune
Seem to besiege, and make his bold waves tremble —
Yea, his dread trident shake.
PRO.   My brave spirit!   206
Who was so firm, so constant, that this coil°
Would not infect his reason?
ARI.   Not a soul
But felt a fever of the mad° and played
Some tricks of desperation.° All but mariners   210
Plunged in the foaming brine, and quit the vessel,
Then all afire with me. The King's son, Ferdinand,
With hair upstaring — then like reeds, not hair —
Was the first man that leaped, cried, " Hell is empty,

---

134. hint: occasion.   144. In few: in a few words.   146. butt: tub.   157. undergoing stomach: courage to endure, the stomach being regarded as the seat of valor.   165. have ... much: have been of great benefit.

176. beating: throbbing.   177. Know ... forth: i.e., I will now tell you more.   179. Now ... lady: Fortune (once my foe) is now kind to me.   180. prescience: foreknowledge.   181. zenith: the highest point of my fortunes.   183. court not: do not seek to win.   192. task: impose a task on.   193. quality: ability.   194. to point: in all points, exactly.   197. waist: that part of the ship which lies between forecastle and poop. See Pl. 7a and 6a.   198. flamed amazement: appeared in the form of fire which caused amazement. This phenomenon, known as Saint Elmo's fire or a corposant, is sometimes seen on ships during a storm.   201. precursors: forerunners.   207. coil: confusion.   209. fever ... mad: fever of madness.   210. tricks of desperation: desperate tricks.

And all the devils are here."
PRO.   Why, that's my spirit! 215
But was not this nigh shore?
ARI.   Close by, my master.
PRO. But are they, Ariel, safe?
ARI.   Not a hair perished,
On their sustaining° garments not a blemish,
But fresher than before. And, as thou badest me,
In troops I have dispersed them 'bout the isle.   220
The King's son have I landed by himself,
Whom I left cooling of the air with sighs
In an odd angle° of the isle, and sitting
His arms in this sad knot.°
PRO.   Of the King's ship,
The mariners, say how thou hast disposed,   225
And all the rest o' the fleet.
ARI.   Safely in harbor
Is the King's ship — in the deep nook where once
Thou call'dst me up at midnight to fetch dew
From the still-vexed Bermoothes,° there she's hid.
The mariners all under hatches stowed,   230
Who, with a charm joined to their suffered labor,°
I have left asleep. And for the rest o' the fleet,
Which I dispersed, they all have met again,
And are upon the Mediterranean flote,°
Bound sadly home for Naples,   235
Supposing that they saw the King's ship wrecked
And his great person perish.
PRO.   Ariel, thy charge
Exactly is performed. But there's more work.
What is the time o' the day?
ARI.   Past the midseason.
PRO. At least two glasses.° The time 'twixt six and
now   240
Must by us both be spent most preciously.
ARI. Is there more toil? Since thou dost give me
pains,°
Let me remember° thee what thou hast promisèd,
Which is not yet performed me.
PRO.   How now? Moody?
What is't thou canst demand?
ARI.   My liberty.   245
PRO. Before the time be out? No more!
ARI.   I prithee
Remember I have done thee worthy service,
Told thee no lies, made thee no mistakings, served
Without or grudge or grumblings. Thou didst
promise
To bate° me a full year.
PRO.   Dost thou forget   250
From what a torment I did free thee?
ARI.   No.

PRO. Thou dost, and think'st it much to tread the
ooze
Of the salt deep,
To run upon the sharp wind of the North,
To do me business in the veins o' the earth   255
When it is baked with frost.
ARI.   I do not, sir.
PRO. Thou liest, malignant thing! Hast thou forgot
The foul witch Sycorax, who with age and envy
Was grown into a hoop?° Hast thou forgot her?
ARI. No, sir.
PRO.   Thou hast. Where was she born?
Speak, tell me.   260
ARI. Sir, in Argier.°
PRO.   Oh, was she so? I must
Once in a month recount what thou hast been,
Which thou forget'st. This damned witch Sycorax,
For mischiefs manifold and sorceries terrible
To enter human hearing,° from Argier,   265
Thou know'st, was banished. For one thing she did°
They would not take her life. Is not this true?
ARI. Aye, sir.
PRO. This blue-eyed° hag was hither brought
with child,
And here was left by the sailors. Thou, my slave,
As thou report'st thyself, wast then her servant.   271
And, for thou wast a spirit too delicate
To act her earthy and abhorred commands,
Refusing her grand hests,° she did confine thee,
By help of her more potent ministers   275
And in her most unmitigable° rage,
Into a cloven pine. Within which rift
Imprisoned thou didst painfully remain
A dozen years. Within which space she died,
And left thee there, where thou didst vent thy
groans   280
As fast as mill wheels strike.° Then was this is-
land —
Save for the son that she did litter here,
A freckled whelp hag-born° — not honored with
A human shape.
ARI.   Yes, Caliban her son.
PRO. Dull thing, I say so, he, that Caliban   285
Whom now I keep in service. Thou best know'st
What torment I did find thee in. Thy groans
Did make wolves howl and penetrate the breasts
Of ever-angry bears. It was a torment
To lay upon the damned, which Sycorax   290
Could not again undo. It was mine art,
When I arrived and heard thee, that made gape
The pine and let thee out.
ARI.   I thank thee, master.

218. sustaining: which bore them up.   223. angle: corner.
224. in . . . knot: sadly folded. Ariel imitates the posture.
229. still-vexed Bermoothes: ever stormy Bermudas. 231. joined
. . . labor: as well as the labor they had endured.   234. flote:
sea. 240. glasses: i.e., hours; turns of the hourglass. 242. pains:
toil. 243. remember: remind. 250. bate: abate, lessen.

259. grown . . . hoop: bent double. 261. Argier: Algiers. 265. To
. . . hearing: for a human being to hear.   266. one . . . did: This
good action is not recalled. 269. blue-eyed: with dark rings
under the eyes.   274. hests: commands.   276. unmitigable:
absolute.   281. mill . . . strike: i.e., the continuous clack of a
water mill.   283. hag-born: child of a hag.

PRO. If thou more murmur'st, I will rend an oak°
And peg thee in his knotty entrails till   295
Thou hast howled away twelve winters.

ARI.   Pardon, master.
I will be correspondent° to command,
And do my spiriting° gently.

PRO.   Do so, and after two days
I will discharge thee.

ARI.   That's my noble master!
What shall I do? Say what. What shall I do?   300

PRO. Go make thyself like a nymph o' the sea.
Be subject to no sight but thine and mine, invisible
To every eyeball else. Go take this shape,
And hither come in't. Go, hence with diligence!
                              [*Exit* ARIEL.]
Awake, dear heart, awake! Thou hast slept well.
Awake!

MIRA. The strangeness of your story put   306
Heaviness in me.

PRO.   Shake it off. Come on,
We'll visit Caliban my slave, who never
Yields us kind answer.

MIRA.   'Tis a villain, sir,
I do not love to look on.

PRO.   But, as 'tis,   310
We cannot miss° him. He does make our fire,
Fetch in our wood, and serves in offices
That profit us. What ho! Slave! Caliban!
Thou earth,° thou! Speak.

CAL. [*Within*]   There's wood enough within.

PRO. Come forth, I say! There's other business for
    thee.   315
Come, thou tortoise! When?
[*Re-enter* ARIEL *like a water nymph.*] Fine appari-
    tion! My quaint° Ariel,
Hark in thine ear.

ARI.   My lord, it shall be done.   [*Exit.*]

PRO. Thou poisonous slave, got° by the Devil him-
    self
Upon thy wicked dam,° come forth!   320
                    [*Enter* CALIBAN.]

CAL. As wicked dew as e'er my mother brushed
With raven's feather from unwholesome fen
Drop on you both! A southwest° blow on ye
And blister you all o'er!

PRO. For this, be sure, tonight thou shalt have
    cramps,   325
Side stitches that shall pen thy breath up. Urchins°
Shall, for that vast° of night that they may work,
All exercise on thee. Thou shalt be pinched
As thick as honeycomb, each pinch more stinging

Than bees that made 'em.

CAL.   I must eat my dinner.   330
This island's mine, by Sycorax my mother,
Which thou takest from me. When thou camest first,
Thou strokedst me, and madest much of me, wouldst
    give me
Water with berries in't.° And teach me how
To name the bigger light, and how the less,   335
That burn by day and night. And then I loved thee,
And showed thee all the qualities° o' th' isle,
The fresh springs, brine pits, barren place and fer-
    tile.
Cursèd be I that did so! All the charms
Of Sycorax, toads, beetles, bats, light on you!   340
For I am all the subjects that you have,
Which first was mine own king. And here you sty°
    me
In this hard rock whiles you do keep from me
The rest o' th' island.

PRO.   Thou most lying slave,
Whom stripes° may move, not kindness! I have used
    thee,   345
Filth as thou art, with human care, and lodged thee
In mine own cell till thou didst seek to violate
The honor of my child.

CAL. Oh ho, oh ho! Would 't had been done!
Thou didst prevent me. I had peopled else   350
This isle with Calibans.

PRO.   Abhorrèd slave,
Which any print° of goodness wilt not take,
Being capable of all ill! I pitied thee,
Took pains to make thee speak, taught thee each
    hour   354
One thing or other. When thou didst not, savage,
Know thine own meaning, but wouldst gabble like
A thing most brutish, I endowed thy purposes
With words that made them known. But thy vile
    race,
Though thou didst learn, had that in't which good
    natures
Could not abide to be with. Therefore wast thou
Deservedly confined into this rock,   361
Who hadst deserved more than a prison.

CAL. You taught me language, and my profit on't
Is I know how to curse. The red plague° rid° you
For learning° me your language!

PRO.   Hagseed,° hence!   365
Fetch us in fuel, and be quick, thou'rt best,
To answer other business. Shrug'st thou, malice?
If thou neglect'st, or dost unwillingly
What I command, I'll rack thee with old° cramps,

---

294. rend an oak: i.e., a far worse torment than imprisonment in a
pine.   297. correspondent: agreeable, submissive.   298. spirit-
ing: my work as a spirit.   311. miss: do without.   314. earth:
lump of dirt.   317. quaint: elegant.   319. got: begotten.
320. dam: mother.   323. southwest: regarded as an unhealthy
wind.   326. Urchins: goblins, or hedgehogs.   327. vast: deso-
late period.

334. Water . . . in't: Shakespeare apparently took this from
Strachey's account, which records that the castaways made a
pleasant drink from cedar berries. See *Temp.* Intro. p. 1002a.
337. qualities: good spots.   342. sty: pen.   345. stripes: blows.
352. print: impression.   364. red plague: bubonic plague. rid:
destroy.   365. learning: teaching. Hagseed: son of a hag.
369. old: abundant.

Fill all thy bones with aches,° make thee roar   370
That beasts shall tremble at thy din.
    CAL.   No, pray thee.
[*Aside*] I must obey. His art is of such power
It would control my dam's god, Setebos,   373
And make a vassal° of him.
    PRO.   So, slave. Hence!
                       [*Exit* CALIBAN.]
[*Re-enter* ARIEL, *invisible, playing and singing;*
      FERDINAND *following.*]
    ARI. [*Sings.*]
    "Come unto these yellow sands,
      And then take hands.
    Curtsied when you have and kissed
      The wild waves whist,°
    Foot it featly° here and there,   380
    And, sweet sprites, the burden° bear."
BURDEN. [*Dispersedly*]° "Hark, hark!"
                    "Bowwow."
ARI. "The watchdogs bark."
BURDEN. [*Dispersedly*]   "Bowwow."
ARI. "Hark, hark! I hear
    The strain of strutting chanticleer   385
    Cry Cock-a-diddle-dow."
FER. Where should this music be? I' th' air or th'
earth?
It sounds no more, and, sure, it waits upon
Some god o' th' island. Sitting on a bank,
Weeping again the King my father's wreck,   390
This music crept by me upon the waters,
Allaying both their fury and my passion°
With its sweet air. Thence I have followed it,
Or it hath drawn me rather. But 'tis gone.   395
No, it begins again.
    ARI. [*Sings.*]
    "Full fathom five thy father lies,
      Of his bones are coral made,
    Those are pearls that were his eyes.
      Nothing of him that doth fade   400
    But doth suffer a sea change
    Into something rich and strange.
    Sea nymphs hourly ring his knell."
BURDEN.   "Dingdong."
ARI. "Hark! Now I hear them. — Dingdong,
    bell."   404
FER. The ditty does remember my drowned father.
This is no mortal business, nor no sound
That the earth owes.° — I hear it now above me.
PRO. The fringèd curtains of thine eye advance,°
And say what thou seest yond.
    MIRA.   What is't? A spirit?
Lord, how it looks about! Believe me, sir,   410

It carries a brave form.° But 'tis a spirit.
    PRO. No, wench, it eats and sleeps and hath such
    senses
As we have, such. This gallant which thou seest
Was in the wreck, and but he's something stained
With grief, that's beauty's canker,° thou mightst
    call him   415
A goodly person. He hath lost his fellows,
And strays about to find 'em.
    MIRA.   I might call him
A thing divine, for nothing natural
I ever saw so noble.
    PRO.   [*Aside*] It goes on,° I see,   419
As my soul prompts it. Spirit, fine spirit! I'll free thee
Within two days for this.
    FER.   Most sure, the goddess
On whom these airs attend!° Vouchsafe my prayer
May know if you remain upon this island,°
And that you will some good instruction give
How I may bear me° here. My prime request,   425
Which I do last pronounce, is, O you wonder!
If you be maid or no?°
    MIRA.   No wonder, sir,
But certainly a maid.
    FER.   My language! Heavens!
I am the best of them° that speak this speech,
Were I but where 'tis spoken.
    PRO.   How? The best?   430
What wert thou if the King of Naples heard thee?
    FER. A single° thing, as I am now, that wonders
To hear thee speak of Naples. He does hear me,
And that he does I weep. Myself am Naples,
Who with mine eyes, never since at ebb,° beheld
The King my father wrecked.
    MIRA.   Alack, for mercy!   436
    FER. Yes, faith, and all his lords, the Duke of
    Milan
And his brave son being twain.°
    PRO.   [*Aside*] The Duke of Milan
And his more braver daughter could control thee,
If now 'twere fit to do't. At the first sight   440
They have changed eyes.° Delicate Ariel,
I'll set thee free for this. [*To* FERDINAND] A word,
    good sir.
I fear you have done yourself some wrong. A word.
    MIRA. Why speaks my father so ungently? This
Is the third man that e'er I saw, the first   445
That e'er I sighed for. Pity move my father
To be inclined my way!

411. **brave form**: fine shape.   415. **canker**: maggot.   419. **It . . . on**: i.e., Prospero's plan that Miranda and Ferdinand shall fall in love.   422. **attend**: wait on.   422–23. **Vouchsafe . . . island**: grant my prayer, which is to know whether you inhabit this island.   425. **bear me**: behave myself.   427. **maid or no**: i.e., a mortal or a goddess.   429. **best of them**: i.e., I am now King of Naples since my father's death.   432. **single**: lonely.   435. **never . . . ebb**: i.e., have not ceased to flow.   438. **twain**: i.e., two of those drowned.   441. **changed eyes**: fallen in love.

370. **aches**: a two-syllable word, pronounced like "h's."
374. **vassal**: slave.   379. **whist**: silent.   380. **featly**: smartly.
381. **burden**: refrain.   382 s.d., **Dispersedly**: from different sides.   392. **passion**: emotion, sorrow.   407. **owes**: owns, possesses.   408. **advance**: raise.

FER.   Oh, if a virgin,
And your affection not gone forth,° I'll make you
The Queen of Naples.
    PRO.   Soft, sir! One word more.
[*Aside*] They are both in either's powers. But this
    swift business   450
I must uneasy make, lest too light winning
Make the prize light. [*To* FERDINAND] One word
    more. I charge thee
That thou attend me. Thou dost here usurp
The name thou owest not, and hast put thyself
Upon this island as a spy, to win it   455
From me, the lord on 't.
    FER.   No, as I am a man.
    MIRA. There's nothing ill can dwell in such a
    temple.°
If the ill spirit have so fair a house,
Good things will strive to dwell with 't.
    PRO.   Follow me.
Speak not you for him, he's a traitor. Come,   460
I'll manacle thy neck and feet together.
Sea water shalt thou drink, thy food shall be
The fresh-brook mussels, withered roots, and husks
Wherein the acorn cradled. Follow.
    FER.   No.
I will resist such entertainment till   465
Mine enemy has more power.
             [*Draws, and is charmed from moving.*]
    MIRA.   O dear Father,
Make not too rash a trial of him, for
He's gentle, and not fearful.°
    PRO.   What! I say,
My foot my tutor?° Put thy sword up, traitor,
Who makest a show but darest not strike, thy con-
    science   470
Is so possessed with guilt. Come from thy ward,°
For I can here disarm thee with this stick
And make thy weapon drop.
    MIRA.   Beseech you, Father.
    PRO. Hence! Hang not on my garments.
    MIRA.   Sir, have pity.
I'll be his surety.
    PRO.   Silence! One word more   475
Shall make me chide thee, if not hate thee. What!
An advocate for an impostor! Hush!
Thou think'st there is no more such shapes as he,
Having seen but him and Caliban. Foolish wench!
To the most of men this is a Caliban,   480
And they to him are angels.
    MIRA.   My affections
Are, then, most humble. I have no ambition
To see a goodlier man.

    PRO.   Come on, obey.
Thy nerves° are in their infancy again,
And have no vigor in them.
    FER.   So they are.   485
My spirits, as in a dream, are all bound up.
My father's loss, the weakness which I feel,
The wreck of all my friends, nor this man's threats,
To whom I am subdued, are but light to me
Might I but through my prison once a day   490
Behold this maid. All corners else o' th' earth
Let liberty make use of, space enough
Have I in such a prison.
    PRO.   [*Aside*] It works.
                          [*To* FERDINAND] Come on.
Thou hast done well, fine Ariel!
                          [*To* FERDINAND] Follow me.   494
[*To* ARIEL] Hark what thou else shalt do me.
    MIRA.   Be of comfort.
My father's of a better nature, sir,
Than he appears by speech. This is unwonted°
Which now came from him.
    PRO.   Thou shalt be as free
As mountain winds. But then exactly do
All points of my command.
    ARI.   To the syllable.   500
    PRO. Come, follow. Speak not for him. [*Exeunt.*]

Act II

SCENE I. *Another part of the island.*

[*Enter* ALONSO, SEBASTIAN, ANTONIO, GONZALO,
          ADRIAN, FRANCISCO, *and others.*]

    GON. Beseech you, sir, be merry. You have cause.
So have we all, of joy, for our escape
Is much beyond our loss. Our hint° of woe
Is common. Every day some sailor's wife,
The masters of some merchant,° and the merchant,°   4
Have just our theme of woe. But for the miracle —
I mean our preservation — few in millions
Can speak like us. Then wisely, good sir, weigh
Our sorrow with our comfort.
    ALON.   Prithee, peace.
    SEB. He receives comfort like cold porridge.   10
    ANT. The visitor° will not give him o'er so.
    SEB. Look, he's winding up the watch of his wit.
By and by it will strike.
    GON. Sir ——

---

448. gone forth: i.e., been bestowed on someone else. 457. temple:
i.e., beautiful body.   468. fearful: to be feared.   469. My . . .
tutor: The head is the tutor to the body, but Miranda (who is by
nature subordinate and so the foot) is trying to tell her father
what he should do.   471. ward: position of defense.

484. nerves: sinews.   497. unwonted: unusual.
    Act II, Sc. i: 3. hint: occasion. See I.ii.134.   5. masters . . .
merchant: captains of merchant ships. the merchant: i.e., the
owner.   11. visitor: visiting minister. See *T Night*, IV.ii.25–26.
Sebastian means that Gonzalo will insist on having his say
whether Alonso wishes to hear it or not.

SEB. One. Tell.°   15

GON. When every grief is entertained° that's of-
fered,
Comes to the entertainer ——

SEB. A dollar.

GON. Dolor comes to him, indeed. You have
spoken truer than you purposed.   20

SEB. You have taken it wiselier than I meant you
should.

GON. Therefore, my lord ——

ANT. Fie, what a spendthrift is he of his tongue!

ALON. I prithee, spare.   25

GON. Well, I have done. But yet ——

SEB. He will be talking.

ANT. Which, of he or Adrian, for a good wager,
first begins to crow?

SEB. The old cock.   30

ANT. The cockerel.

SEB. Done. The wager?

ANT. A laughter.°

SEB. A match!

ADR. Though this island seem to be desert ——

SEB. Ha, ha, ha! — So, you're paid.°   36

ADR. Uninhabitable, and almost inaccessible ——

SEB. Yet ——

ADR. Yet ——

ANT. He could not miss 't.°   40

ADR. It must needs be of subtle, tender, and deli-
cate temperance.

ANT. Temperance was a delicate wench.

SEB. Aye, and a subtle, as he most learnedly deliv-
ered.°   45

ADR. The air breathes upon us here most sweetly.

SEB. As if it had lungs, and rotten ones.

ANT. Or as 'twere perfumed by a fen.

GON. Here is everything advantageous to life.

ANT. True — save means to live.   50

SEB. Of that there's none, or little.

GON. How lush and lusty the grass looks! How
green!

ANT. The ground indeed is tawny.

SEB. With an eye° of green in 't.   55

ANT. He misses not much.

SEB. No, he doth but mistake the truth totally.

GON. But the rarity° of it is — which is indeed al-
most beyond credit° ——

SEB. As many vouched° rarities are.   60

GON. That our garments, being, as they were,
drenched in the sea, hold notwithstanding their
freshness and glosses, being rather new-dyed than
stained with salt water.

ANT. If but one of his pockets could speak,° would
it not say he lies?   66

SEB. Aye, or very falsely pocket up his report.

GON. Methinks our garments are now as fresh as
when we put them on first in Afric, at the marriage
of the King's fair daughter Claribel to the King of
Tunis.   71

SEB. 'Twas a sweet marriage, and we prosper well
in our return.

ADR. Tunis was never graced° before with such a
paragon to° their Queen.   75

GON. Not since Widow Dido's° time.

ANT. Widow! A pox° o' that! How came that
widow in?° Widow Dido!

SEB. What if he had said " Widower Aeneas " too?
Good Lord, how you take it!   80

ADR. "Widow Dido," said you? You make me
study of that. She was of Carthage, not of Tunis.

GON. This Tunis, sir, was Carthage.

ADR. Carthage?

GON. I assure you, Carthage.   85

ANT. His word is more than the miraculous harp.°

SEB. He hath raised the wall, and houses too.

ANT. What impossible matter will he make easy
next?

SEB. I think he will carry this island home in his
pocket, and give it his son for an apple.   91

ANT. And, sowing the kernels of it in the sea,
bring forth more islands.

GON. Aye.

ANT. Why, in good time.   95

GON. Sir, we were talking that our garments seem
now as fresh as when we were at Tunis at the mar-
riage of your daughter, who is now Queen.

ANT. And the rarest that e'er came there.

SEB. Bate,° I beseech you, Widow Dido.   100

ANT. Oh, Widow Dido! Aye, Widow Dido.

GON. Is not, sir, my doublet° as fresh as the first
day I wore it? I mean, in a sort.°

ANT. That sort was well fished for.°

GON. When I wore it at your daughter's mar-
riage?   105

ALON. You cram these words into mine ears
against

---

65. pockets . . . speak: i.e., his pockets are still wet.   74. graced:
honored.   75. to: for.   76. Widow Dido: Dido was the Queen of
Carthage (near the modern Tunis) who entertained Aeneas on his
way from Troy to Italy. She was a widow and had vowed eternal
fidelity to the memory of her husand, but she fell in love with
Aeneas. When he deserted her, she committed suicide.   77. pox:
plague; lit., venereal disease.   77–78. How . . . in: why do you
call her a widow?   86. His . . . harp: According to the legends
told by Ovid, the walls of Thebes came together at the music of
Amphion's harp. By a like miracle Gonzalo has erected a Car-
thage at Tunis.   100. Bate: except.   102. doublet: See Pl. 8b
and comment on p. 93a.   103. in a sort: after a fashion.   104. That
. . . for: i.e., he had to add "after a fashion."

---

15. Tell: count.   16. entertained: received.   33. A laughter:
the winner is to have the laugh on the loser, on the principle of
the proverb "He laughs that wins." Cf. *Oth.*, IV.i.126. (Kit-
tredge).   36. Ha . . . paid: F1 divides the speech: "*Sebastian:*
Ha, ha, ha. *Antonio:* So, you're paid"; i.e., you've had your laugh
as winner.   40. He . . . miss 't: i.e., if he begins the first clause
with "though," he is sure to follow it up with a "yet."   45. de-
livered: declared.   55. eye: tinge.   58. rarity: strange thing.
59. credit: belief.   60. vouched: guaranteed.

The stomach of my sense. Would I had never
Married my daughter there! For, coming thence,
My son is lost and, in my rate,° she too
Who is so far from Italy removed   110
I ne'er again shall see her. O thou mine heir
Of Naples and of Milan, what strange fish
Hath made his meal on thee?

FRAN.   Sir, he may live.
I saw him beat the surges° under him,
And ride upon their backs. He trod the water,   115
Whose enmity he flung aside, and breasted
The surge most swoln° that met him. His bold head
'Bove the contentious waves he kept, and oared
Himself with his good arms in lusty stroke
To the shore, that o'er his wave-worn basis bowed,°
As stooping to relieve him. I not doubt   121
He came alive to land.

ALON.   No, no, he's gone.

SEB. Sir, you may thank yourself for this great
    loss,
That would not bless our Europe with your
    daughter,
But rather lose her to an African.,   125
Where she, at least, is banished from your eye
Who hath cause to wet° the grief on 't.

ALON.   Prithee, peace.

SEB. You were kneeled to, and importuned other-
    wise,
By all of us, and the fair soul herself   129
Weighed° between loathness° and obedience, at
Which end o' the beam° should bow. We have lost
    your son,
I fear, forever. Milan and Naples have
Mo° widows in them of this business' making
Than we bring men to comfort them.
The fault's your own.

ALON.   So is the dear'st° o' the loss.   135

GON. My lord Sebastian,
The truth you speak doth lack some gentleness,
And time to speak it in. You rub the sore
When you should bring the plaster.

SEB.   Very well.

ANT. And most chirurgeonly.   140

GON. It is foul weather in us all, good sir,
When you are cloudy.

SEB.   Foul weather?

ANT.   Very foul.

GON. Had I plantation° of this isle, my lord ——

ANT. He'd sow 't with nettle seed.

SEB.   Or docks, or mallows.°

GON. And were the King on 't, what would I do?

SEB. 'Scape being drunk for want of wine.   146

GON. I' the commonwealth° I would by con-
    traries°
Execute all things, for no kind of traffic°
Would I admit, no name of magistrate.
Letters° should not be known; riches, poverty,   150
And use of service,° none; contract,° succession,°
Bourn,° bound° of land, tilth,° vineyard, none;
No use of metal,° corn, or wine, or oil;
No occupation° — all men idle, all;
And women too, but innocent and pure;   155
No sovereignty ——

SEB.   Yet he would be King on 't.

ANT. The latter end of his commonwealth forgets
the beginning.

GON. All things in common nature should pro-
    duce
Without sweat or endeavor. Treason, felony,   160
Sword, pike, knife, gun, or need of any engine°
Would I not have. But Nature should bring
    forth,
Of it° own kind, all foison,° all abundance,
To feed my innocent people.

SEB. No marrying 'mong his subjects?   165

ANT. None, man — all idle, whores and knaves.

GON. I would with such perfection govern, sir,
To excel the Golden Age.°

SEB.   'Save° His Majesty!

ANT. Long live Gonzalo!

GON.   And — do you mark me, sir?

ALON. Prithee, no more. Thou dost talk nothing to
me.   171

GON. I do well believe your Highness, and did it
to minister occasion° to these gentlemen, who are of
such sensible° and nimble lungs that they always use
to laugh at nothing.   175

ANT. 'Twas you we laughed at.

GON. Who in this kind of merry fooling am noth-
ing to you. So you may continue and laugh at noth-
ing still.

ANT. What a blow was there given!   180

SEB. An° it had not fallen flat-long.°

GON. You are gentlemen of brave mettle,° you
would lift the moon out of her sphere° if she would
continue in it five weeks without changing.

---

147. **I' . . . commonwealth:** For the origin of this passage see
Temp Intro. p. 1002b. **by contraries:** contrary to the usual plan.
148. **traffic:** trade.   150. **Letters:** learning.   151. **use of service:**
no one should have servants. **contract:** legal agreements. **suc-
cession:** right of inheritance.   152. **Bourn:** boundary. **bound:**
limit; i.e., private property rights. **tilth:** tillage.   153. **use of
metal:** i.e., exchange of money.   154. **occupation:** manual labor.
161. **engine:** instrument of warfare.   163. **it:** its. **foison:** plenty.
168. **Golden Age:** the days of perfect innocence at the beginning
of the world. **'Save:** God save.   173. **minister occasion:** provide
opportunity.   174. **sensible:** sensitive.   181. **An:** if. **flat-long:**
on the flat side of the sword.   182. **mettle:** material, stuff.
183. **sphere:** course.

---

109. **rate:** estimation.   114. **surges:** waves.   117. **swoln:** swol-
len.   120. **his . . . bowed:** hung over its base, which had been
worn away by the sea.   127. **wet:** weep for.   130. **Weighed:**
balanced. **loathness:** reluctance.   131. **end . . . beam:** which
scale should sink.   133. **Mo:** more.   135. **dear'st:** most griev-
ous.   140. **chirurgeonly:** like a good surgeon.   143. **plantation:**
colonization, but Antonio pretends to take it literally as "plant-
ing."   144. **docks or mallows:** common English weeds.

[*Enter* ARIEL (*invisible*) *playing solemn music.*]

SEB. We would so, and then go a-batfowling.°

ANT. Nay, good my lord, be not angry.   186

GON. No, I warrant you, I will not adventure my
discretion so weakly.° Will you laugh me asleep,
for I am very heavy?

ANT. Go sleep, and hear us.   190

[*All sleep except* ALONSO, SEBASTIAN, *and* ANTONIO.]

ALON. What, all so soon asleep! I wish mine eyes
Would, with themselves, shut up my thoughts. I find
They are inclined to do so.

SEB.   Please you, sir,
Do not omit the heavy offer° of it.
It seldom visits sorrow. When it doth,   195
It is a comforter.

ANT.   We two, my lord,
Will guard your person while you take your rest,
And watch your safety.

ALON.   Thank you. — Wondrous heavy.

[ALONSO *sleeps. Exit* ARIEL.]

SEB. What a strange drowsiness possesses them!

ANT. It is the quality° o' the climate.

SEB.   Why   200
Doth it not then our eyelids sink? I find not
Myself disposed to sleep.

ANT.   Nor I. My spirits are nimble.
They fell together all, as by consent,
They dropped as by a thunderstroke. What might,
Worthy Sebastian? — Oh, what might? — No
          more. —   205
And yet methinks I see it in thy face,
What thou shouldst be. The occasion speaks thee,°
          and
My strong imagination sees a crown
Dropping upon thy head.

SEB.   What, art thou waking?°

ANT. Do you not hear me speak?

SEB.   I do, and surely   210
It is a sleepy language, and thou speak'st
Out of thy sleep. What is it thou didst say?
This is a strange repose, to be asleep
With eyes wide-open — standing, speaking, moving,
And yet so fast asleep.

ANT.   Noble Sebastian,   215
Thou let'st thy fortune sleep — die, rather —
          wink'st
Whiles thou art waking.

SEB.   Thou dost snore distinctly.
There's meaning in thy snores.

ANT. I am more serious than my custom. You
Must be so too, if heed me,° which to do   220

Trebles thee o'er.°

SEB.   Well, I am standing water.°

ANT. I'll teach you how to flow.°

SEB.   Do so. To ebb
Hereditary sloth instructs me.

ANT.   Oh,
If you but knew how you the purpose cherish
Whiles thus you mock it! How, in stripping it,   225
You more invest it! Ebbing men, indeed,
Most often do so near the bottom run
By their own fear or sloth.°

SEB.   Prithee, say on.
The setting° of thine eye and cheek proclaim
A matter° from thee, and a birth, indeed,   230
Which throes thee much to yield.°

ANT.   Thus, sir.
Although this lord of weak remembrance, this,°
Who shall be of as little memory
When he is earthed, hath here almost persuaded —
For he's a spirit of persuasion, only   235
Professes to persuade — the King his son's alive,
'Tis as impossible that he's undrowned
As he that sleeps here swims.

SEB.   I have no hope
That he's undrowned.

ANT.   Oh, out of that "no hope"
What great hope have you! No hope that way is
Another way so high a hope that even   241
Ambition cannot pierce a wink beyond,
But doubt discovery there.° Will you grant with me
That Ferdinand is drowned?

SEB.   He's gone.

ANT.   Then tell me,
Who's the next heir of Naples?

SEB.   Claribel.   245

ANT. She that is Queen of Tunis, she that dwells
Ten leagues beyond man's life,° she that from
          Naples
Can have no note, unless the sun were post° —
The man i' the moon's too slow — till newborn
          chins
Be rough and razorable.° She that from whom   250
We all were sea-swallowed, though some cast° again,

221. **Trebles . . . o'er:** makes you three times the man you are.
standing water: i.e., at the turning of the tide, which for a while
neither ebbs nor flows. 222. **flow:** advance (like the rising tide).
224–28. **If . . . sloth:** if you would only realize how much you are
moved by the prospect of becoming King, even while you mock it;
how in stripping it of its glamour you make it more attractive.
Ebbing men (i.e., the lazy and unambitious) often run aground
through fear or sloth. 229. **setting:** expression. 230. **matter:**
something serious. 231. **throes . . . yield:** is very painful to bring
forth. 232. **this . . . this:** i.e., Francisco. See ll. 113–22.
240–43. **No . . . there:** i.e., your certainty that the true heir is
drowned gives you a greater hope in another direction (i.e., of
being King yourself), where even your ambition cannot look
higher. 247. **Ten . . . life:** ten leagues farther than a man could
travel in his lifetime. 248. **post:** messenger. 249–50. **newborn
. . . razorable:** i.e., newborn children are grown men. 251. **cast:**
vomited up.

185. **batfowling:** hunting for birds at night with the aid of torches
and sticks or bats. 187–88. **adventure . . . weakly:** risk my rep-
utation as a discreet man so easily, by showing anger at such as
you. 194. **omit . . . offer:** do not lose this chance of sleeping.
200. **quality:** nature. 207. **occasion . . . thee:** opportunity calls
you. 209. **waking:** awake. 220. **if . . . me:** if you will listen
to me.

And by that destiny, to perform an act
Whereof what's past is prologue, what to come,
In yours and my discharge.°

SEB.   What stuff is this! How say you?
'Tis true, my brother's daughter's Queen of Tunis,
So is she heir of Naples, 'twixt which regions   256
There is some space.

ANT.   A space whose every cubit
Seems to cry out, "How shall that Claribel
Measure us° back to Naples? Keep° in Tunis,
And let Sebastian wake." Say this were death   260
That now hath seized them — why, they were no
     worse
Than now they are. There be that can rule Naples
As well as he that sleeps, lords that can prate
As amply and unnecessarily
As this Gonzalo. I myself could make   265
A chough of as deep chat.° Oh, that you bore
The mind that I do! What a sleep were this
For your advancement! Do you understand me?

SEB. Methinks I do.

ANT.   And how does your content
Tender your own good fortune?

SEB.   I remember   270
You did supplant your brother Prospero.

ANT.   True.
And look how well my garments sit upon me,
Much feater° than before. My brother's servants
Were then my fellows,° now they are my men.°

SEB. But — for your conscience.   275

ANT. Aye, sir, where lies that? If 'twere a kibe,
'Twould put me to my slipper.° But I feel not
This deity in my bosom. Twenty consciences,
That stand 'twixt me and Milan, candied be they,
And melt ere they molest!° Here lies your brother,
No better than the earth he lies upon   281
If he were that which now he's like, that's dead.
Whom I, with this obedient steel, three inches of it,
Can lay to bed forever whiles you, doing thus,
To the perpetual wink° for aye might put   285
This ancient morsel, this Sir Prudence who
Should not upbraid our course. For all the rest,
They'll take suggestion as a cat laps milk,
They'll tell the clock to° any business that
We say befits the hour.

SEB.   Thy case, dear friend,   290
Shall be my precedent. As thou got'st Milan,
I'll come by Naples. Draw thy sword. One stroke

Shall free thee from the tribute which thou payest,
And I the King shall love thee.

ANT.   Draw together,
And when I rear my hand, do you the like,   295
To fall° it on Gonzalo.

SEB.   Oh, but one word. [*They talk apart.*]
[*Re-enter* ARIEL, *invisible.*]

ARI. My master through his art foresees the danger
That you, his friend, are in, and sends me forth —
For else his project dies — to keep them living.
[*Sings in* GONZALO'S *ear.*]
    "While you here do snoring lie,   300
       Open-eyed conspiracy
         His time° doth take.
      If of life you keep a care,
      Shake off slumber, and beware.
       Awake, awake!"   305

ANT. Then let us both be sudden.

GON.   Now, good angels
Preserve the King!   [*They wake.*]

ALON. Why, how now? Ho, awake! — Why are
you drawn?
Wherefore this ghastly looking?

GON.   What's the matter?

SEB. Whiles we stood here securing° your repose,
Even now, we heard a hollow burst of bellowing
Like bulls, or rather lions. Did 't not wake you?   312
It struck mine ear most terribly.

ALON.   I heard nothing.

ANT. Oh, 'twas a din to fright a monster's ear,
To make an earthquake! Sure, it was the roar   315
Of a whole herd of lions.

ALON.   Heard you this, Gonzalo?

GON. Upon mine honor, sir, I heard a humming,
And that a strange one too, which did awake me.
I shaked you, sir, and cried. As mine eyes opened
I saw their weapons drawn. — There was a noise,
That's verily.° 'Tis best we stand upon our guard,
Or that we quit this place. Let's draw our weapons.

ALON. Lead off this ground, and let's make further
search   323
For my poor son.

GON.   Heavens keep him from these beasts!
For he is sure i' th' island.

ALON.   Lead away.

ARI. Prospero my lord shall know what I have
done.
So, King, go safely on to seek thy son.   [*Exeunt.*]

SCENE II. *Another part of the island.*

[*Enter* CALIBAN *with a burden of wood. A noise of
thunder heard.*]

CAL. All the infections that the sun sucks up
From bogs, fens, flats, on Prosper fall, and make him

---

254. discharge: task to be performed.   259. Measure us: retrace
her journey after us. Keep: let her remain.   266. chough ...
chat: I could make a jackdaw (*chough*, rhyming with rough) talk
as profoundly as he does.   273. feater: more trimly.   274. fellows:
equals. men: servants.   276–77. kibe ... slipper: a chilblain which
would make me wear a slipper.   278–80. Twenty ... molest:
i.e., if twenty consciences had stood between me and the duke-
dom of Milan, I should have let them melt like candy before
they would have disturbed me. Other editors take "candied" to
mean "frozen."   285. perpetual wink: everlasting sleep.   289. tell
... to: say it is time for.

296. fall: let fall.   302. time: opportunity.   310. securing:
keeping safe.   321. verily: truth.

By inchmeal° a disease! His spirits hear me,
And yet I needs must curse. But they'll nor pinch,
Fright me with urchin shows,° pitch me i' the mire,
Nor lead me, like a firebrand,° in the dark   6
Out of my way, unless he bid 'em. But
For every trifle are they set upon me —
Sometime like apes, that mow° and chatter at me,
And after bite me; then like hedgehogs, which   10
Lie tumbling in my barefoot way and mount°
Their pricks at my footfall. Sometime am I
All wound with adders, who with cloven tongues
Do hiss me into madness.

       [*Enter* TRINCULO.] Lo, now, lo!
Here comes a spirit of his, and to torment me   15
For bringing wood in slowly. I'll fall flat.
Perchance he will not mind me.

  TRIN. Here's neither bush nor shrub to bear off
any weather at all, and another storm brewing, I
hear it sing i' the wind. Yond same black cloud,   20
yond huge one, looks like a foul bombard° that
would shed his liquor. If it should thunder as it did
before, I know not where to hide my head. Yond
same cloud cannot choose but fall by pailfuls. What
have we here? A man or a fish? Dead or alive?   25
A fish — he smells like a fish, a very ancient and fish-
like smell, a kind of not of the newest Poor John.° A
strange fish! Were I in England now, as once I was,
and had but this fish painted,° not a holiday fool
there but would give a piece of silver. There would
this monster make a man° — any strange beast   31
there makes a man. When they will not give a doit°
to relieve a lame beggar, they will lay out ten to see
a dead Indian. Legged like a man! And his fins like
arms! Warm, o' my troth! I do now let loose   35
my opinion, hold it no longer — this is no fish, but
an islander that hath lately suffered by a thunderbolt.
[*Thunder.*] Alas, the storm is come again! Best
way is to creep under his gaberdine,° there is no
other shelter hereabout. Misery acquaints a man   40
with strange bedfellows. I will here shroud° till the
dregs of the storm be past.

       [*Enter* STEPHANO, *singing, a bottle in his hand.*]
  STE.   " I shall no more to sea, to sea,
          Here shall I die ashore ——"   45
This is a very scurvy° tune to sing at a man's funeral.
Well, here's my comfort.   [*Drinks. Sings.*]
" The master, the swabber, the boatswain, and I,
    The gunner, and his mate,
Loved Mall, Meg, and Marian, and Margery,   50
    But none of us cared for Kate.

For she had a tongue with a tang,°
    Would cry to a sailor, Go hang!
She loved not the savor° of tar nor of pitch,   54
Yet a tailor might scratch her where'er she did itch.
    Then, to sea, boys, and let her go hang! "
This is a scurvy tune too, but here's my comfort.
                      [*Drinks.*]
  CAL. Do not torment me. — Oh!   58
  STE. What's the matter? Have we devils here? Do
you put tricks upon 's with salvages° and men of
Ind,° ha? I have not 'scaped drowning to be afeard
now of your four legs, for it hath been said,   62
As proper° a man as ever went on four legs cannot
make him give ground. And it shall be said so again
while Stephano breathes at nostrils.
  CAL. The spirit torments me. — Oh!   66
  STE. This is some monster of the isle with four
legs, who hath got, as I take it, an ague.° Where the
devil should he learn our language? I will give him
some relief, if it be but for that. If I can recover°
him, and keep him tame, and get to Naples with
him, he's a present for any emperor that ever trod on
neat's leather.°   73
  CAL. Do not torment me, prithee, I'll bring my
wood home faster.
  STE. He's in his fit now, and does not talk after
the wisest. He shall taste of my bottle. If he have
never drunk wine afore, it will go near to remove his
fit. If I can recover him, and keep him tame, I will
not take too much for him.° He shall pay for him
that hath him, and that soundly.   81
  CAL. Thou dost me yet but little hurt, thou wilt
anon, I know it by thy trembling.° Now Prosper
works upon thee.   84
  STE. Come on your ways. Open your mouth, here
is that which will give language to you, cat. Open
your mouth, this will shake your shaking, I can tell
you, and that soundly. You cannot tell who's your
friend. Open your chaps° again.   89
  TRIN. I should know that voice. It should be —
but he is drowned, and these are devils. — Oh, de-
fend me!   92
  STE. Four legs and two voices — a most delicate
monster! His forward voice, now, is to speak well of
his friend, his backward voice is to utter foul
speeches and to detract. If all the wine in my bottle
will recover him, I will help his ague. Come. —
Amen! I will pour some in thy other mouth.   99
  TRIN. Stephano!
  STE. Doth thy other mouth call me? Mercy, mercy!

Sc. ii: 3. inchmeal: by inches.   5. urchin shows: the appear-
ance of goblins. See I.ii.326.   6. firebrand: will-o'-the-wisp.
9. mow: make faces.   11. mount: raise.   21. bombard: large
black leathern jug. See Pl. 17f.   27. Poor John: dried salt hake.
29. had . . . painted: had a poster of this fish painted.   31. make
a man: i.e., his fortune.   32. doit: a small Dutch coin, a cent.
39. gaberdine: cloak.   41. shroud: cover myself.   46. scurvy:
"lousy."

52. tang: a sharp sound.   54. savor: taste.   60. salvages: sav-
ages.   60–61. men of Ind: natives of India.   63. proper: fine.
68. ague: fever, which makes him shiver.   71. recover: cure.
73. neat's leather: i.e., shoes.   79–80. I . . . him: I'll not take
even an excessive price.   83. trembling: Trinculo is the trembler,
for he believes that the voice of Stephano comes from a ghost.
Trinculo is a natural coward.   89. chaps: chops, jaws.

This is a devil and no monster. I will leave him, I have no long spoon.° 　103

TRIN. Stephano! If thou beest Stephano, touch me, and speak to me, for I am Trinculo — be not afeard — thy good friend Trinculo.

STE. If thou beest Trinculo, come forth. I'll pull thee by the lesser legs. If any be Trinculo's legs, these are they. Thou art very Trinculo indeed! How camest thou to be the siege° of this mooncalf?° Can he vent Trinculos? 　111

TRIN. I look him to be killed with a thunder-stroke. But art thou not drowned, Stephano? I hope, now, thou art not drowned. Is the storm overblown? I hid me under the dead mooncalf's gaberdine for fear of the storm. And art thou living, Stephano? O Stephano, two Neapolitans 'scaped! 　117

STE. Prithee do not turn me about, my stomach is not constant.°

CAL. [Aside] These be fine things, an if they be not sprites.
That's a brave god, and bears celestial liquor.
I will kneel to him. 　122

STE. How didst thou 'scape? How camest thou hither? Swear, by this bottle, how thou camest hither. I escaped upon a butt of sack,° which the sailors heaved o'erboard, by this bottle, which I made of the bark of a tree with mine own hands, since I was cast ashore. 　128

CAL. I'll swear upon that bottle to be thy true subject, for the liquor is not earthly.

STE. Here, swear, then, how thou escapedst.

TRIN. Swam ashore, man, like a duck. I can swim like a duck, I'll be sworn. 　133

STE. Here, kiss the book. Though thou canst swim like a duck, thou art made like a goose.

TRIN. O Stephano, hast any more of this?

STE. The whole butt, man. My cellar is in a rock by the seaside, where my wine is hid. How now, mooncalf! How does thine ague? 　139

CAL. Hast thou not dropped from Heaven?

STE. Out o' the moon, I do assure thee. I was the man 'i the moon when time was.° 　142

CAL. I have seen thee in her, and I do adore thee. My mistress showed me thee, and thy dog, and thy bush.°

STE. Come, swear to that, kiss the book. I will furnish it anon with new contents. Swear. 　147

TRIN. By this good light, this is a very shallow monster! I afeard of him! A very weak monster! The man i' the moon! A most poor credulous monster! Well drawn,° monster, in good sooth!° 　151

CAL. I'll show thee every fertile inch o' th' island, And I will kiss thy foot. I prithee be my god.

TRIN. By this light, a most perfidious and drunken monster! When's god's asleep, he'll rob his bottle.

CAL. I'll kiss thy foot, I'll swear myself thy subject.

STE. Come on, then, down, and swear.

TRIN. I shall laugh myself to death at this puppy-headed monster. A most scurvy monster! I could find in my heart to beat him —— 　160

STE. Come, kiss.

TRIN. But that the poor monster's in drink. An abominable monster!

CAL. I'll show thee the best springs, I'll pluck thee
berries,
I'll fish for thee, and get thee wood enough.
A plague upon the tyrant that I serve!
I'll bear him no more sticks, but follow thee,
Thou wondrous man.° 　168

TRIN. A most ridiculous monster, to make a wonder of a poor drunkard!

CAL. I prithee let me bring thee where crabs°
grow. 　171
And I with my long nails will dig thee pignuts,°
Show thee a jay's nest, and instruct thee how
To snare the nimble marmoset.° I'll bring thee
To clustering filberts, and sometimes I'll get thee
Young scamels° from the rock. Wilt thou go with
me? 　176

STE. I prithee now, lead the way, without any more talking. Trinculo, the King and all our company else being drowned, we will inherit here. Here, bear my bottle, fellow Trinculo, we'll fill him by and by again. 　181

CAL. [Sings drunkenly.]
"Farewell, master, farewell, farewell!"

TRIN. A howling monster, a drunken monster!

CAL. "No more dams I'll make for fish,
Nor fetch in firing 　185
At requiring,
Nor scrape trencher,° nor wash dish.
'Ban, 'Ban, Cacaliban
Has a new master. — Get a new man."
Freedom, heyday! Heyday, freedom! Freedom, hey-day, freedom! 　191

STE. O brave monster! Lead the way. [Exeunt.]

---

103. I . . . spoon: "He that sups with the Devil needs a long spoon" — a proverb from the time when men dipped into a common dish. A long spoon was needed, as the Devil's claws were long and sharp, and his table manners nasty. 110. siege: excrement. mooncalf: misshapen monster, freak. 119. constant: steady. Trinculo is pawing him all over, and turning him round in his excitement. 125. sack: a dry wine from Spain. For Falstaff on the merits of sack, see II Hen IV, IV.iii.102–35. 142. when . . . was: once upon a time. 144–45. thee . . . bush: the man in the moon had his dog and bush of thorns, as Quince knew. See MND, III.i.60.

151. drawn: sucked. sooth: truth. 168. Thou . . . man: See Temp Intro. p. 1004a. 171. crabs: crab apples. 172. pignut: called also earthnut, a plant producing edible tubers. 174. marmoset: kind of small monkey. 176. scamels: a much-discussed word which does not occur elsewhere and so has been variously interpreted or emended, the likeliest guess being seamel: sea gull. 187. trencher: wooden plate.

Act III

SCENE I. *Before* PROSPERO'S *cell.*

[*Enter* FERDINAND, *bearing a log.*]

FER. There be some sports are painful, and their labor
Delight in them sets off.° Some kinds of baseness
Are nobly undergone, and most poor matters
Point° to rich ends. This my mean task
Would be as heavy to me as odious, but   5
The mistress which I serve quickens° what's dead
And makes my labors pleasures. Oh, she is
Ten times more gentle than her father's crabbèd,
And he's composed of harshness. I must remove
Some thousands of these logs, and pile them up,   10
Upon a sore injunction.° My sweet mistress
Weeps when she sees me work, and says such baseness
Had never like executor.° I forget.
But these sweet thoughts do even refresh my labors,
Most busy lest when I do it.°

[*Enter* MIRANDA, *and* PROSPERO *at a distance,*° *unseen.*]

MIRA.   Alas, now, pray you   15
Work not so hard. I would the lightning had
Burned up those logs that you are enjoined to pile!
Pray set it down and rest you. When this burns,
'Twill weep° for having wearied you. My father
Is hard at study, pray now, rest yourself.   20
He's safe for these three hours.

FER.   O most dear mistress,
The sun will set before I shall discharge
What I must strive to do.

MIRA.   If you'll sit down,
I'll bear your logs the while. Pray give me that,
I'll carry it to the pile.

FER.   No, precious creature,   25
I had rather crack my sinews, break my back,
Than you should such dishonor undergo
While I sit lazy by.

MIRA.   It would become me
As well as it does you. And I should do it
With much more ease, for my goodwill is to it,   30
And yours it is against.

PRO.   Poor worm, thou art infected!

This visitation° shows it.

MIRA.   You look wearily.

FER. No, noble mistress, 'tis fresh morning with me
When you are by at night. I do beseech you —
Chiefly that I might set it in my prayers —   35
What is your name?

MIRA.   Miranda. — O my father,
I have broke your hest° to say so!

FER.   Admired Miranda!°
Indeed the top° of admiration! Worth
What's dearest to the world! Full many a lady
I have eyed with best regard, and many a time   40
The harmony of their tongues hath into bondage
Brought my too diligent ear. For several° virtues
Have I liked several women, never any
With so full soul but some defect in her
Did quarrel with the noblest grace she owed,   45
And put it to the foil.° But you, oh, you,
So perfect and so peerless, are created
Of every creature's best!

MIRA.   I do not know
One of my sex, no woman's face remember
Save, from my glass, mine own. Nor have I seen   50
More that I may call men than you, good friend,
And my dear father. How features are abroad,
I am skill-less of.° But, by my modesty,
The jewel in my dower, I would not wish
Any companion in the world but you,   55
Nor can imagination form a shape
Besides yourself to like of. But I prattle
Something too wildly, and my father's precepts
I therein do forget.

FER.   I am, in my condition,
A prince, Miranda, I do think, a king —   60
I would not so! — and would no more endure
This wooden slavery° than to suffer
The flesh fly blow° my mouth. Hear my soul speak.
The very instant that I saw you did
My heart fly to your service, there resides,   65
To make me slave to it, and for your sake
Am I this patient logman.

MIRA.   Do you love me?

FER. O Heaven, O earth, bear witness to this sound,
And crown what I profess with kind event°
If I speak true! If hollowly, invert   70
What best is boded° me to mischief! I,
Beyond all limit of what else i' the world,

Act III, Sc. i: 1–2. their . . . off: the delight which they bring
outweighs the fatigue. 4. Point: lead. 6. quickens: brings to
life. 11. injunction: a command enforced with penalties against
disobedience. 13. executor: performer. 15. Most . . . it: This
line has been much discussed and may be corrupt. It means
apparently "I am most busy when I am idle, for then I think
so many sweet thoughts." lest: least. s.d., and . . . distance: F1
simply reads "Enter Miranda and Prospero." They obviously do
not enter together, and on the Elizabethan stage probably Prospero entered on the balcony above, as later (III.iii.19). The balcony was a most convenient place for eavesdroppers. See Pl. 5b.
19. weep: i.e., drip with sap when burning.

32. visitation: visit. 37. hest: command. Admired Miranda: a
play on her name, for *miranda* in Latin means "she who ought to
be wondered at." "Admired" at this time had a stronger meaning
than today. 38. top: summit. 42. several: separate, individual.
46. put . . . foil: bring it to disgrace. 52–53. features . . . of: I
have no experience of how people look elsewhere. 62. wooden
slavery: i.e., task of having to carry wood. 63. blow: lay its eggs
on, foul. 69. event: result. 71. What . . . boded: the best
fate that is prophesied.

Do love, prize, honor you.

MIRA.   I am a fool
To weep at what I am glad of.

PRO.   Fair encounter
Of two most rare affections! Heavens rain grace   75
On that which breeds between 'em!

FER.   Wherefore weep you?

MIRA. At mine unworthiness, that dare not offer
What I desire to give, and much less take
What I shall die to want.° But this is trifling,
And all the more it seeks to hide itself,   80
The bigger bulk it shows. Hence, bashful cunning!
And prompt me, plain and holy innocence!
I am your wife, if you will marry me.
If not, I'll die your maid. To be your fellow°
You may deny me, but I'll be your servant,   85
Whether you will or no.

FER.   My mistress, dearest,
And I thus humble ever.

MIRA.   My husband, then?

FER. Aye, with a heart as willing°
As bondage e'er of freedom. Here's my hand.

MIRA. And mine, with my heart in 't. And now
     farewell   90
Till half an hour hence.

FER.   A thousand thousand!°

[*Exeunt* FERDINAND *and* MIRANDA *severally.*°]

PRO. So glad of this as they I cannot be,
Who° are surprised withal,° but my rejoicing
At nothing can be more. I'll to my book,
For yet ere suppertime must I perform   95
Much business appertaining.   [*Exit.*]

SCENE II. *Another part of the island.*

[*Enter* CALIBAN, STEPHANO, *and* TRINCULO.]

STE. Tell not me. — When the butt is out, we will
drink water, not a drop before. Therefore bear up,°
and board 'em. Servant-monster, drink to me.   4

TRIN. Servant-monster! The folly of this island!°
They say there's but five upon this isle. We are three
of them. If th' other two be brained like us, the state
totters.

STE. Drink, servant-monster, when I bid thee. Thy
eyes are almost set° in thy head.   10

TRIN. Where should they be set else? He were a
brave monster indeed if they were set in his tail.

STE. My man-monster hath drowned his tongue in
sack. For my part, the sea cannot drown me. I swam,

ere I could recover the shore, five and-thirty leagues°
off and on. By this light, thou shalt be my lieutenant,
monster, or my standard.°   17

TRIN. Your lieutenant, if you list. He's no stand-
ard.

STE. We'll not run, Monsieur Monster.

TRIN. Nor go neither, but you'll lie, like dogs, and
yet say nothing neither.

STE. Mooncalf, speak once in thy life, if thou beest
a good mooncalf.   25

CAL. How does thy Honor? Let me lick thy shoe.
I'll not serve him, he is not valiant.

TRIN. Thou liest, most ignorant monster. I am in
case° to jostle a constable. Why, thou deboshed° fish
thou, was there ever man a coward that hath drunk
so much sack as I today? Wilt thou tell a monstrous
lie, being but half a fish and half a monster?   33

CAL. Lo, how he mocks me! Wilt thou let him,
my lord?

TRIN. "Lord," quoth he! That a monster should
be such a natural!°

CAL. Lo, lo, again! Bite him to death, I prithee.

STE. Trinculo, keep a good tongue in your   40
head. If you prove a mutineer — the next tree! The
poor monster's my subject, and he shall not suffer
indignity.

CAL. I thank my noble lord. Wilt thou be pleased
to hearken once again to the suit I made to thee?   45

STE. Marry,° will I. Kneel and repeat it. I will
stand, and so shall Trinculo.

[*Enter* ARIEL, *invisible.*]

CAL. As I told thee before, I am subject to a tyrant,
a sorcerer, that by his cunning hath cheated me of
the island.   50

ARI. Thou liest.

CAL. Thou liest,° thou jesting monkey thou.
I would my valiant master would destroy thee!
I do not lie.

STE. Trinculo, if you trouble him any more in 's
tale, by this hand, I will supplant° some of your
teeth.   57

TRIN. Why, I said nothing.

STE. Mum, then, and no more. Proceed.

CAL. I say, by sorcery he got this isle.   60
From me he got it. If thy greatness will
Revenge it on him — for I know thou darest,
But this thing dare not——

STE. That's most certain.

CAL. Thou shalt be lord of it, and I'll serve thee.

STE. How now shall this be compassed?°   66
Canst thou bring me to the party?

---

79. want: be without.   84. fellow: equal. See II.i.274.   88. will-
ing: eager.   91. thousand thousand: i.e., farewells. s.d., sever-
ally: by different exits.   93. Who: i.e., Ferdinand and Miranda.
withal: therewith.
     Sc. ii: 2. bear up: crowd on more sail.   5. The . . . island:
what a silly place this island is.   10. set: closed, dazed with
drink.

15. league: three miles.   17. standard: standard-bearer (or en-
sign), the junior officer in the company, the others being the
captain and the lieutenant. Caliban is now too unsteady to be a
satisfactory *standard*.   29. in case: in a condition. deboshed:
debauched.   38. natural: born fool.   46. Marry: Mary, by the
Virgin.   52. Thou liest: Caliban supposes the voice to be Trin-
culo's.   56. supplant: displace.   66. compassed: brought about.

CAL. Yea, yea, my lord. I'll yield him thee asleep,
Where thou mayst knock a nail into his head.
ARI. Thou liest, thou canst not.   70
CAL. What a pied ninny's° this! Thou scurvy
patch!°
I do beseech thy greatness, give him blows,
And take his bottle from him. When that's gone,
He shall drink naught but brine, for I'll not show
him
Where the quick freshes° are.   75
STE. Trinculo, run into no further danger. Inter-
rupt the monster one word further and, by this
hand, I'll turn my mercy out o' doors and make a
stockfish° of thee.
TRIN. Why, what did I? I did nothing. I'll go
farther off.   81
STE. Didst thou not say he lied?
ARI. Thou liest.
STE. Do I so? Take thou that. [Beats him.] As
you like this, give me the lie° another time.   85
TRIN. I did not give the lie. Out o' your wits, and
hearing too? A pox o' your bottle! This can sack
and drinking do. A murrain° on your monster, and
the devil take your fingers!
CAL. Ha, ha, ha!   90
STE. Now, forward with your tale. — Prithee,
stand farther off.
CAL. Beat him enough. After a little time
I'll beat him too.
STE.   Stand farther. — Come, proceed.
CAL. Why, as I told thee, 'tis a custom with him
I' th' afternoon to sleep. There thou mayst brain
him,   96
Having first seized his books, or with a log
Batter his skull, or paunch° him with a stake,
Or cut his weasand° with thy knife. Remember
First to possess his books, for without them   100
He's but a sot, as I am, nor hath not
One spirit to command. They all do hate him
As rootedly° as I. Burn but his books.
He has brave utensils° — for so he calls them —
Which, when he has a house, he'll deck withal.   105
And that most deeply to consider is
The beauty of his daughter. He himself
Calls her a nonpareil.° I never saw a woman
But only Sycorax my dam and she,
But she as far surpasseth Sycorax   110
As great'st does least.
STE.   Is it so brave a lass?
CAL. Aye, lord, she will become thy bed, I warrant,

And bring thee forth brave brood.
STE. Monster, I will kill this man. His daughter
and I will be King and Queen — save our Graces! —
and Trinculo and thyself shall be Viceroys. Dost
thou like the plot, Trinculo?   117
TRIN. Excellent.
STE. Give me thy hand. I am sorry I beat thee, but
while thou livest keep a good tongue in thy head.
CAL. Within this half-hour will he be asleep.
Wilt thou destroy him then?
STE.   Aye, on mine honor.
ARI. This will I tell my master.
CAL. Thou makest me merry, I am full of pleasure.
Let us be jocund. Will you troll° the catch°   126
You taught me but whilere?°
STE. At thy request, monster, I will do reason,°
any reason. — Come on, Trinculo, let us sing.
[Sings.]   "Flout° 'em and scout° 'em,
    And scout 'em and flout 'em.   131
    Thought is free."
CAL. That's not the tune.
    [ARIEL plays the tune on a tabor° and pipe.]
STE. What is this same?
TRIN. This is the tune of our catch, played by the
picture of Nobody.°   136
STE. If thou beest a man, show thyself in thy like-
ness. If thou beest a devil, take 't as thou list.
TRIN. Oh, forgive me my sins!
STE. He that dies pays all debts. I defy thee. Mercy
upon us!   141
CAL. Art thou afeard?
STE. No, monster, not I.
CAL. Be not afeard. The isle is full of noises,°
Sounds and sweet airs that give delight and hurt not.
Sometimes a thousand twangling instruments   146
Will hum about mine ears, and sometime voices
That, if I then had waked after long sleep,
Will make me sleep again. And then, in dreaming,
The clouds methought would open and show riches
Ready to drop upon me, that when I waked,   151
I cried to dream again.
STE. This will prove a brave kingdom to me,
where I shall have my music for nothing.
CAL. When Prospero is destroyed.   155
STE. That shall be by and by.° I remember the
story.
TRIN. The sound is going away. Let's follow it,
and after do our work.
STE. Lead, monster, we'll follow. I would I could
see this taborer, he lays it on.   161
TRIN. Wilt come? I'll follow, Stephano. [Exeunt.]

71. pied ninny: patched fool, because Trinculo as a jester wears
motley, the "patched" or particolored dress of his profession. See
Pl. 13c. patch: fool.   75. quick freshes: running springs of fresh
water.   79. stockfish: dried cod, beaten to make it tender.
85. give . . . lie: call me a liar.   88. murrain: plague.   98. paunch:
stab him in the belly.   99. weasand: windpipe.   103. rootedly:
fixedly.   104. utensils: furnishings.   108. nonpareil: without
an equal.

126. troll: sing. catch: See T Night, II.iii.60,n. | 127. whilere:
just now.   128. reason: anything within reason.   130. Flout:
mock. scout: deride.   133 s.d., tabor: small drum. See Pl. 13d.
136. picture of Nobody: i.e., by an invisible player. There is a pic-
ture of Nobody in a play called Nobody and Some-body, printed
1606. It is all head and no body, like Humpty Dumpty.
144. noises: music.   156. by . . . by: in the near future.

SCENE III. *Another part of the island.*

[*Enter* ALONSO, SEBASTIAN, ANTONIO, GONZALO,
ADRIAN, FRANCISCO, *and others.*]

GON. By'r Lakin,° I can go no further, sir,
My old bones ache. Here's a maze trod, indeed,
Through forthrights and meanders!° By your pa-
tience,
I needs must rest me.

ALON.   Old lord, I cannot blame thee,
Who am myself attached with° weariness,   5
To the dulling of my spirits. Sit down and rest.
Even here I will put off my hope, and keep it
No longer for my flatterer. He is drowned
Whom thus we stray to find, and the sea mocks
Our frustrate° search on land. Well, let him go.   10

ANT. [*Aside to* SEBASTIAN] I am right glad that
he's so out of hope.
Do not, for one repulse, forgo the purpose
That you resolved to effect.

SEB. [*Aside to* ANTONIO] The next advantage
Will we take throughly.°

ANT. [*Aside to* SEBASTIAN] Let it be tonight,
For now they are oppressed with travel, they   15
Will not, nor cannot, use such vigilance
As when they are fresh.

SEB. [*Aside to* ANTONIO] I say tonight. No more.
                    [*Solemn and strange music.*]

ALON. What harmony is this? — My good friends,
hark!

GON. Marvelous sweet music!

[*Enter* PROSPERO *above, invisible. Enter several
strange Shapes, bringing in a banquet.*° *They dance
about it with gentle actions of salutation, and, invit-
ing the King, etc., to eat, they depart.*]

ALON. Give us kind keepers, Heavens! — What
were these?   20

SEB. A living drollery.° Now° I will believe
That there are unicorns, that in Arabia
There is one tree, the phoenix'° throne, one phoenix
At this hour reigning there.

ANT.   I'll believe both,
And what does else want credit,° come to me   25
And I'll be sworn 'tis true. Travelers ne'er did lie,
Though fools at home condemn 'em.

GON.   If in Naples
I should report this now, would they believe me?

If I should say I saw such islanders —
For, certes,° these are people of the island —   30
Who, though they are of monstrous shape, yet note,
Their manners are more gentle-kind than of
Our human generation° you shall find
Many — nay, almost any.

PRO.   [*Aside*] Honest lord,   34
Thou hast said well, for some of you there present
Are worse than devils.

ALON.   I cannot too much muse°
Such shapes, such gesture, and such sound, express-
ing —
Although they want the use of tongue — a kind
Of excellent dumb discourse.

PRO.   [*Aside*] Praise in departing.°

FRAN. They vanished strangely.

SEB.   No matter, since   40
They have left their viands behind, for we have
stomachs. —
Will 't please you taste of what is here?

ALON.   Not I.

GON. Faith, sir, you need not fear. When we were
boys,
Who would believe that there were mountaineers
Dewlapped° like bulls, whose throats had hanging
at 'em   45
Wallets of flesh? Or that there were such men
Whose heads stood in their breasts?° Which now
we find
Each putter-out of five for one° will bring us
Good warrant of.

ALON.   I will stand to and feed,
Although my last. No matter, since I feel   50
The best is past. Brother, my lord the Duke,
Stand to, and do as we.

[*Thunder and lightning. Enter* ARIEL, *like a harpy,*°
*claps his wings upon the table, and, with a quaint
device,*° *the banquet vanishes.*]

ARI. You are three men of sin, whom Destiny —
That hath to instrument this lower world

Sc. iii: 1. By'r Lakin: by Our Lady.   2–3. Here's . . . me-
anders: we have wandered as in a maze by straight paths (*forth-
rights*) and winding paths (*meanders*).   5. attached with: over-
come by; lit., arrested.   10. frustrate: vain.   14. throughly:
thoroughly.   19 s.d., banquet: light refreshments, such as fruit
and jellies.   21. drollery: puppet show.   21–27. Now . . . 'em:
i.e., after this we can believe any fantastic traveler's yarn.
23. phoenix: a mythical bird. According to the legend only one
phoenix was alive at a time. It lived for five hundred years. Then
it built itself a nest of spices, which were set alight by the rapid
beating of its wings. From the ashes a new phoenix was born.
25. want credit: is not believed.

30. certes: certainly.   33. generation: breed.   36. muse: won-
der at.   39. Praise in departing: a proverb meaning "Don't give
thanks for your entertainment until you see how it will end."
45. Dewlapped: having folds of loose skin hanging from the
throat.   46–47. men . . . breasts: Sir Walter Raleigh in his ac-
count of Guiana (1595) noted "a nation of people whose heads ap-
pear not above their shoulders; which though it may be thought a
mere fable, yet for mine own part I am resolved it is true, because
every child in the provinces of Arromaia and Canuri affirms the
same. They are called Ewaipanoma. They are reported to have
their eyes in their shoulders, and their mouths in the middle of
their breasts, and that a long train of hair groweth backward be-
tween their shoulders."   48. putter-out . . . one: In Shake-
speare's time voyages to distant and strange ports were so risky
that the traveler sometimes left a sum of money with a merchant
at home on condition that he should receive five times the amount
if he returned; if he did not, the premium was forfeited.   52 s.d.,
harpy: a foul creature, half bird of prey, half woman. This episode
was suggested by an event in Virgil's *Aeneid* when the harpies
seize and foul the food of Aeneas and his followers. quaint device:
piece of ingenious stage machinery.

And what is in 't° — the never-surfeited° sea   55
Hath caused to belch up you. And on this island,
Where man doth not inhabit — you 'mongst men
Being most unfit to live. I have made you mad,
And even with suchlike valor men hang and drown
Their proper° selves.

[*ALONZO, SEBASTIAN, etc., draw their swords.*]
               You fools! I and my fellows   60
Are ministers of Fate. The elements
Of whom your swords are tempered may as well
Wound the loud winds, or with bemocked-at stabs
Kill the still-closing° waters, as diminish
One dowle° that's in my plume.° My fellow minis-
    ters   65
Are like invulnerable. If you could hurt,
Your swords are now too massy° for your strengths,
And will not be uplifted. But remember —
For that's my business to you — that you three
From Milan did supplant good Prospero,   70
Exposed unto the sea, which hath requit° it,
Him and his innocent child. For which foul deed
The powers, delaying not forgetting, have
Incensed the seas and shores — yea, all the crea-
    tures —
Against your peace. Thee of thy son, Alonso,   75
They have bereft, and do pronounce by me
Lingering perdition° — worse than any death
Can be at once — shall step by step attend
You and your ways. Whose wraths to guard you
    from —
Which here, in this most desolate isle, else falls   80
Upon your heads — is nothing but° heart sorrow
And a clear° life ensuing.
[*He vanishes in thunder; then, to soft music, enter
the Shapes again, and dance, with mocks° and
mows,° and carrying out the table.*]

PRO. Bravely the figure of this harpy hast thou
Performed, my Ariel, a grace it had, devouring.°
Of my instruction hast thou nothing bated°   85
In what thou hadst to say. So, with good life°
And observation° strange,° my meaner ministers°
Their several kinds° have done. My high charms
    work,
And these mine enemies are all knit up°
In their distractions.° They now are in my power,

And in these fits I leave them while I visit   91
Young Ferdinand — whom they suppose is
    drowned —
And his and mine loved darling.   [*Exit above.*]
GON. I' the name of something holy, sir, why stand
    you
In this strange stare?
ALON.   Oh, it is monstrous, monstrous!   95
Methought the billows spoke, and told me of it,
The winds did sing it to me, and the thunder,
That deep and dreadful organ pipe, pronounced
The name of Prosper. It did bass my trespass.°
Therefore my son i' th' ooze is bedded, and   100
I'll seek him deeper than e'er plummet° sounded,
And with him there lie mudded.   [*Exit.*]
SEB.   But one fiend at a time,
I'll fight their legions o'er.
ANT.   I'll be thy second.
           [*Exeunt* SEBASTIAN *and* ANTONIO.]
GON. All three of them are desperate. Their great
    guilt,
Like poison given to work a great time after,   105
Now 'gins to bite the spirits. I do beseech you
That are of suppler joints, follow them swiftly,
And hinder them from what this ecstasy°
May now provoke them to.
ADR.   Follow, I pray you. [*Exeunt.*]

Act IV

SCENE I. *Before* PROSPERO's *cell.*

[*Enter* PROSPERO, FERDINAND, *and* MIRANDA.]
PRO. If I have too austerely punished you,
Your compensation makes amends. For I
Have given you here a third° of mine own life,
Or that for which I live, who once again
I tender° to thy hand. All thy vexations   5
Were but my trials of thy love, and thou
Hast strangely° stood the test. Here, afore Heaven,
I ratify this my rich gift. O Ferdinand,
Do not smile at me that I boast her off,°
For thou shalt find she will outstrip all praise   10
And make it halt° behind her.
FER.   I do believe it
Against an oracle.°

53–55. Destiny . . . in 't: Destiny (Providence), which uses this
world below and its powers as its instrument. **55. never-sur-
feited:** never overfull. A surfeit is an excess of food. Even the
sea, which can retain most things, cannot stomach Alonso and
his fellow sinners. **60. proper:** own. **64. still-closing:** always
closing up; i.e., which cannot be wounded. **65. dowle:** downy
feather. **plume:** wing. **67. massy:** heavy. **71. requit:** paid
back. **77. perdition:** destruction. **81. is . . . but:** i.e., only
repentance will guard you from destruction. **82. clear:** innocent.
s.d., mocks: mocking gestures. **mows:** grimaces. **84. grace . . .
devouring:** the action of devouring was splendidly (*bravely*) per-
formed. **85. bated:** abated, left out. **86. with . . . life:** real-
istically. **87. observation:** obedience. **strange:** unusual. **meaner
ministers:** lesser servants. **88. several kinds:** particular tasks.
89. knit up: entangled. **90. distractions:** fits of madness.

99. bass my trespass: proclaim my sin in a deep note. **101. plum-
met:** the lead weight at the end of a cord used by sailors to dis-
cover the depth of the water. **108. ecstasy:** mad fit. See *Haml.*,
III.iv.137–44.
    Act IV, Sc. i: 3. third: i.e., a great part of. **5. tender:** hand
over. **7. strangely:** exceptionally. **9. boast . . . off:** boast
about her. **11. halt:** come limping; i.e., she will excel all praise.
12. Against an oracle: i.e., even if a god had said the contrary

PRO. Then, as my gift, and thine own acquisition
Worthily purchased, take my daughter. But
If thou dost break her virgin knot before   15
All sanctimonious° ceremonies may
With full and holy rite be ministered,
No sweet aspersion° shall the Heavens let fall
To make this contract grow;° but barren hate,
Sour-eyed disdain, and discord shall bestrew   20
The union of your bed with weeds so loathly
That you shall hate it both. Therefore take heed,
As Hymen's° lamps shall light you.
FER.   As I hope
For quiet days, fair issue,° and long life,
With such love as 'tis now, the murkiest den,   25
The most opportune place, the strong'st suggestion°
Our worser genius° can, shall never melt
Mine honor into lust, to take away
The edge of that day's celebration
When I shall think or Phoebus' steeds are foundered,
Or Night kept chained below.°
PRO.   Fairly spoke.   31
Sit, then, and talk with her, she is thine own.
What, Ariel! My industrious servant, Ariel!

[Enter ARIEL.]

ARI. What would my potent master? Here I am.
PRO. Thou and thy meaner fellows your last
    service   35
Did worthily perform, and I must use you
In such another trick. Go bring the rabble,
O'er whom I give thee power, here to this place.
Incite them to quick motion, for I must
Bestow upon the eyes of this young couple   40
Some vanity° of mine art. It is my promise,
And they expect it from me.
ARI.   Presently?°
PRO. Aye, with a twink.°
ARI. Before you can say, "come," and "go,"
And breathe twice and cry, "so, so,"   45
Each one, tripping on his toe,
Will be here with mop° and mow.
Do you love me, master? No?   48
PRO. Dearly, my delicate Ariel. Do not approach
Till thou dost hear me call.
ARI.   Well, I conceive.° *[Exit.]*
PRO. Look thou be true. Do not give dalliance°
Too much the rein. The strongest oaths are straw
To the fire i' the blood. Be more abstemious,
Or else, good night your vow!
FER.   I warrant you, sir,

The white cold virgin snow upon my heart   55
Abates the ardor of my liver.°
PRO.   Well.
Now come, my Ariel! Bring a corollary°
Rather than want° a spirit. Appear, and pertly!°
No tongue! All eyes! Be silent.   *[Soft music.]*
                [Enter IRIS.°]

IRIS. Ceres,° most bounteous lady, thy rich leas°
Of wheat, rye, barley, vetches, oats, and pease;   61
Thy turfy mountains, where live nibbling sheep,
And flat meads° thatched with stover,° them to
    keep;
Thy banks with pioned and twilled brims,°
Which spongy April at thy hest° betrims°   65
To make cold nymphs chaste crowns; and thy
    broom° groves,
Whose shadow the dismissed° bachelor loves,
Being lasslorn;° thy pole-clipped° vineyard;
And thy sea marge,° sterile and rocky-hard,
Where thou thyself dost air — the Queen o' the Sky,°
Whose watery arch° and messenger am I,   71
Bids thee leave these, and with her sovereign grace,
Here on this grassplot, in this very place,
To come and sport. — Her peacocks° fly amain.°
Approach, rich Ceres, her to entertain.   75
                [Enter CERES.]

CER. Hail, many-colored messenger, that ne'er
Dost disobey the wife of Jupiter;
Who, with thy saffron° wings, upon my flowers
Diffusest honey drops, refreshing showers,
And with each end of thy blue bow dost crown   80
My bosky° acres and my unshrubbed down,°
Rich scarf° to my proud earth. — Why hath thy
    Queen
Summoned me hither, to this short-grassed green?
IRIS. A contract of true love to celebrate,
And some donation° freely to estate°   85
On the blest lovers.
CER.   Tell me, heavenly bow,

---

56. liver: passion. The liver was regarded as the seat of passion. **57. corollary:** excess; i.e., too many rather than too few. **58. want:** be without. **pertly:** briskly. **59 s.d., Enter Iris:** Prospero now produces a little wedding masque in honor not only of the lovers, Ferdinand and Miranda, but as a compliment to the Princess Elizabeth and her bridegroom. See *Temp.* Intro. p. 1001a and Gen. Intro. p. 47b. **Iris:** the female messenger of the gods, also the personification of the rainbow. **60. Ceres:** goddess of corn and plenty. **leas:** arable lands. **63. meads:** meadows. **thatched . . . stover:** covered over with grass for fodder. **64. pioned . . . brims:** a difficult phrase, much disputed and emended. The likeliest explanation is that *pioned* means dug, and *twilled,* heaped up; i.e., with high banks. **65. hest:** command. **betrims:** trims with wild flowers, especially kingcups, a kind of buttercup that grows by streams. **66. broom:** a shrub with yellow flowers. **67. dismissed:** rejected. **68. lasslorn:** without his girl. **pole-clipped:** poles embraced by vines. **69. sea marge:** seashore. **70. Queen . . . Sky:** the goddess Juno, wife of Jupiter. **71. watery arch:** i.e., the rainbow. **74. peacocks:** birds sacred to Juno. **amain:** swiftly. **78. saffron:** yellow. **81. bosky:** wooded. **unshrubbed down:** rolling open country, without shrubs. **82. scarf:** adornment. **85. donation:** present. **estate:** donate.

16. sanctimonious: religious. **18. aspersion:** blessing; lit., sprinkling. **19. grow:** prosper. **23. Hymen:** the god of marriage. **24. issue:** children. **26. suggestion:** temptation. **27. worser genius:** evil angel. **30–31. or . . . below:** either the horses of the Sun have fallen or Night has been imprisoned; i.e., my wedding day, when night seems never to come. **41. vanity:** display. **42. Presently:** at once. **43. twink:** the twinkling of an eye. **47. mop:** grimace. **50. conceive:** understand. **51. dalliance:** fondling.

If Venus or her son, as thou dost know,
Do now attend the Queen? Since they did plot
The means that dusky Dis° my daughter got,
Her and her blind boy's° scandaled° company   90
I have forsworn.

IRIS.   Of her society
Be not afraid. I met Her Deity
Cutting the clouds towards Paphos,° and her son
Dove-drawn° with her. Here thought they to have
   done
Some wanton charm upon this man and maid,   95
Whose vows are, that no bedright shall be paid
Till Hymen's torch° be lighted. But in vain,
Mars's hot minion° is returned again.
Her waspish-headed° son has broke his arrows,
Swears he will shoot no more, but play with spar-
   rows,   100
And be a boy right out.

CER.   High'st Queen of state,
Great Juno, comes. I know her by her gait.
            [*Enter* JUNO.]

JUNO. How does my bounteous sister? Go with
   me
To bless this twain, that they may prosperous be,
And honored in their issue.   105
       [*They sing.*]

JUNO.   "Honor, riches, marriage blessing,
         Long continuance, and increasing,
         Hourly joys be still° upon you!
         Juno sings her blessings on you."

CER.   "Earth's increase, foison° plenty,   110
         Barns and garners never empty,
         Vines with clustering bunches growing,
         Plants with goodly burden bowing,
         Spring come to you at the farthest
         In the very end of harvest!°   115
         Scarcity and want shall shun you,
         Ceres' blessing so is on you."

FER. This is a most majestic vision, and
Harmonious charmingly. May I be bold
To think these spirits?

PRO.   Spirits which by mine art   120
I have from their confines° called to enact
My present fancies.°

FER.   Let me live here ever.

89. **dusky Dis:** Pluto, god of the underworld, and so dark. He
seized Ceres' daughter Persephone and carried her down to his
kingdom.   90. **blind boy:** Cupid. **scandaled:** scandalous.   93. **Pa-
phos:** in Sicily, a town sacred to Venus.   94. **Dove-drawn:** in a
chariot drawn by doves.   97. **Hymen's torch:** The torches of the
wedding god were lit to escort bride and bridegroom to bed.
98. **Mars's . . . minion:** Mars' lusty darling; i.e., Venus.
99. **waspish-headed:** quick-tempered.   108. **still:** always.
110. **foison:** bounteous harvest.   114–15. **Spring . . . harvest:**
may spring follow autumn; i.e., may there be no bitterness of
winter in your lives. Cf. *Ant & Cleo*, V.ii.86–88 for a similar
image.   121. **confines:** places of confinement.   122. **fancies:**
devices of my imagination.

So rare a wondered° father and a wise
Makes this place Paradise.
      [JUNO *and* CERES *whisper, and send* IRIS
                        on employment.]

PRO.   Sweet, now silence!
Juno and Ceres whisper seriously,   125
There's something else to do. Hush, and be mute,
Or else our spell is marred.

IRIS. You nymphs, called Naiads,° of the win-
   dring° brooks,
With your sedged° crowns and ever-harmless looks,
Leave your crisp° channels, and on this green land
Answer your summons. Juno does command.   131
Come, temperate° nymphs, and help to celebrate
A contract of true love. Be not too late.
        [*Enter certain* NYMPHS.]
You sunburned sicklemen,° of August weary,
Come hither from the furrow, and be merry.   135
Make holiday, your rye-straw hats put on,
And these fresh nymphs encounter every one
In country footing.°
[*Enter certain* REAPERS, *properly habited. They join
with the* NYMPHS *in a graceful dance, towards the
end whereof* PROSPERO *starts suddenly, and speaks.
After which, to a strange, hollow, and confused
noise, they heavily° vanish.*]

PRO. [*Aside*] I had forgot that foul conspiracy
Of the beast Caliban and his confederates   140
Against my life. The minute of their plot
Is almost come. [*To the* SPIRITS] Well done! Avoid,°
   no more!

FER. This is strange. Your father's in some passion
That works him strongly.

MIRA.   Never till this day
Saw I him touched with anger so distempered.°

PRO. You do look, my son, in a movèd sort,°   146
As if you were dismayed. Be cheerful, sir.
Our revels now are ended. These our actors,
As I foretold you, were all spirits, and
Are melted into air, into thin air.   150
And, like the baseless fabric° of this vision,
The cloud-capped towers, the gorgeous palaces,
The solemn temples, the great globe itself —
Yea, all which it inherit — shall dissolve
And, like this insubstantial pageant faded,   155
Leave not a rack° behind. We are such stuff
As dreams are made on, and our little life
Is rounded° with a sleep. Sir, I am vexed.
Bear with my weakness, my old brain is troubled.

123. **wondered:** wonderful.   128. **Naiads:** water nymphs. **win-
dring:** wandering, winding.   129. **sedged:** covered with sedge, a
kind of water grass.   130. **crisp:** curled, rippling.   132. **temperate:**
chaste.   134. **sicklemen:** reapers, who cut the wheat with sickles.
138. **footing:** dancing. **s.d.:** *heavily:* sorrowfully.   142. **Avoid:** be
gone.   145. **distempered:** disturbed.   146. **moved sort:** as if you
were distressed.   151. **baseless fabric:** unreal stuff.   156. **rack:**
cloud.   158. **rounded:** completed; i.e., life is but a moment of
consciousness in an everlasting sleep.

Be not disturbed with my infirmity. 160
If you be pleased, retire into my cell,
And there repose. A turn or two I'll walk,
To still my beating° mind.

FER. & MIRA.   We wish your peace.   [*Exeunt.*]

PRO. Come with a thought. I thank thee, Ariel.
Come.

[*Enter* ARIEL.]

ARI. Thy thoughts I cleave to. What's thy pleasure?

PRO.   Spirit, 165
We must prepare to meet with Caliban.

ARI. Aye, my commander. When I presented°
Ceres,
I thought to have told thee of it, but I feared
Lest I might anger thee.

PRO. Say again, where didst thou leave these
varlets?° 170

ARI. I told you, sir, they were red-hot with drinking,
So full of valor that they smote the air
For breathing in their faces, beat the ground
For kissing of their feet, yet always bending°
Toward their project. Then I beat my tabor. 175
At which, like unbacked° colts, they pricked their
ears,
Advanced their eyelids, lifted up their noses
As° they smelt music. So I charmed their ears,
That, calflike, they my lowing followed through
Toothed briers, sharp furzes,° pricking goss,° and
thorns 180
Which entered their frail shins. At last I left them
I' the filthy-mantled° pool beyond your cell,
There dancing up to the chins, that the foul lake
O'erstunk their feet.

PRO.   This was well done, my bird.
Thy shape invisible retain thou still. 185
The trumpery° in my house, go bring it hither,
For stale° to catch these thieves.

ARI.   I go, I go.   [*Exit.*]

PRO. A devil, a born devil, on whose nature
Nurture° can never stick, on whom my pains,
Humanely taken, all, all lost, quite lost. 190
And as with age his body uglier grows,
So his mind cankers.° I will plague them all,
Even to roaring.

[*Re-enter* ARIEL, *loaden with glistering° apparel,*
etc.]

    Come, hang them on this line.°

[PROSPERO *and* ARIEL *remain, invisible. Enter*
CALIBAN, STEPHANO, *and* TRINCULO, *all wet.*]

CAL. Pray you, tread softly, that the blind mole
may not
Hear a footfall. We now are near his cell. 195

STE. Monster, your fairy, which you say is a harmless fairy, has done little better than played the jack°
with us.

TRIN. Monster, I do smell all horse piss, at which
my nose is in great indignation. 200

STE. So is mine. Do you hear, monster? If I should
take a displeasure against you, look you ——

TRIN. Thou wert but a lost monster.

CAL. Good my lord, give me thy favor still.
Be patient, for the prize I'll bring thee to 205
Shall hoodwink this mischance.° Therefore speak
softly.
All's hushed as midnight yet.

TRIN. Aye, but to lose our bottles in the pool ——

STE. There is not only disgrace and dishonor in
that, monster, but an infinite loss. 210

TRIN. That's more to me than my wetting. Yet
this is your harmless fairy, monster.

STE. I will fetch off° my bottle, though I be o'er
ears° for my labor. 214

CAL. Prithee, my King, be quiet. See'st thou here,
This is the mouth o' the cell. No noise, and enter.
Do that good mischief which may make this island
Thine own forever, and I, thy Caliban,
For aye thy footlicker.

STE. Give me thy hand. I do begin to have bloody
thoughts. 221

TRIN. O King Stephano!° O peer! O worthy
Stephano! Look what a wardrobe here is for thee!

CAL. Let it alone, thou fool, it is but trash.

TRIN. Oh ho, monster! We know what belongs to
a frippery.° O King Stephano! 226

STE. Put off that gown, Trinculo. By this hand,
I'll have that gown.

TRIN. Thy Grace shall have it.

CAL. The dropsy drown this fool! What do you
mean 230
To dote thus on such luggage?° Let 's alone,
And do the murder first. If he awake
From toe to crown he'll fill our skins with pinches,
Make us strange stuff. 234

STE. Be you quiet, monster. Mistress° line, is not
this my jerkin? Now is the jerkin under the line.
Now, jerkin, you are like to lose your hair and prove
a bald jerkin.

---

163. **beating:** throbbing. Cf. I.ii.176.   167. **presented:** either
introduced the masques or acted the part of Ceres. There is, however, very little time for a change of costume between Ariel's
exit at l. 50 and Ceres' entry at l. 75.   170. **varlets:** knaves.
174. **bending:** inclining.   176. **unbacked:** never saddled.
178. **As:** as if.   180. **furzes:** See I.i.72,n. **goss:** gorse.   182. **filthy-mantled:** covered with scum.   186. **trumpery:** cheap finery.
187. **stale:** bait.   189. **Nurture:** education.   192. **cankers:** grows
malignant.   193 s.d., **glistering:** glittering. **line:** lime tree.

197. **jack:** knave.   206. **hoodwink . . . mischance:** blindfold this
misfortune; i.e., make us forget it.   213. **fetch off:** rescue.
214. **o'er ears:** up to my ears in the pond.   222. **O . . . Stephano:**
The sight of all the clothes reminds Trinculo of the old ballad
"King Stephen was a worthy peer." See *Oth*, II.iii.92–99.
226. **frippery:** secondhand-clothes shop.   231. **luggage:** baggage,
which will hinder them.   235–40. **Mistress . . . Grace:** These
lines have mystified editors, and indeed elaborate Elizabethan

TRIN. Do, do. We steal by line and level, an 't like your Grace.   240

STE. I thank thee for that jest — here's a garment for 't. Wit shall not go unrewarded while I am King of this country. " Steal by line and level " is an excellent pass of pate° — there's another garment for 't.

TRIN. Monster come, put some lime° upon   246 your fingers, and away with the rest.

CAL. I will have none on 't. We shall lose our time, And all be turned to barnacles,° or to apes With foreheads villainous low.   250

STE. Monster, lay to your fingers. Help to bear this away where my hogshead of wine is, or I'll turn you out of my kingdom. Go to, carry this.

TRIN. And this.

STE. Aye, and this.   255

[*A noise of hunters heard. Enter divers* SPIRITS, *in shape of dogs and hounds, hunting them about,* PROSPERO *and* ARIEL *setting them on.*]

PRO. Hey, Mountain, hey!

ARI. Silver! There it goes, Silver!

PRO. Fury, Fury! There, Tyrant,° there! Hark, hark!

[CALIBAN, STEPHANO, *and* TRINCULO *are driven out.*]

Go charge my goblins that they grind their joints With dry convulsions. Shorten up their sinews   260 With agèd cramps,° and more pinch-spotted make them Then pard° or cat-o'-mountain.°

ARI.   Hark, they roar!

PRO. Let them be hunted soundly. At this hour Lie at my mercy all mine enemies. Shortly shall all my labors end, and thou   265 Shalt have the air at freedom. For a little Follow, and do me service.   [*Exeunt.*]

jokes, especially when made by a half-drunk butler, are not always easy to follow. Stephano begins by addressing the lime tree as "Mistress Line" as if he were talking to the dealer in an old-clothes shop. He appeals to her to decide whether the jerkin is his or Trinculo's. Having taken the jerkin for himself, he then puns on "under the line" (i.e., south of the Equator), where the various skin diseases common to long voyages in the tropics caused hair to fall out. Trinculo caps the remark by a further pun on "line and level"; i.e., "on the square," lit., by the bricklayer's instruments for ensuring perpendicular and horizontal exactness. **245. pass of pate:** sally of wit. **246. lime:** birdlime, to make them sticky, because Caliban disgustedly drops the garments. **249. barnacles:** tree geese. It was believed, even by serious botanists, that from the barnacles, which grow on rotten wood immersed in sea water, emerged creatures which grew into birds like geese. **256–58. Mountain . . . Silver . . . Fury . . . Tyrant:** the names of the hounds. **261. aged cramps:** the cramps which come with old age. **262. pard:** leopard. **cat-o'-mountain:** mountain cat.

Act V

SCENE I. *Before the cell of* PROSPERO.

[*Enter* PROSPERO *in his magic robes, and* ARIEL.]

PRO. Now does my project gather to a head. My charms crack not,° my spirits obey, and Time Goes upright with his carriage.° How's the day?

ARI. On the sixth hour, at which time, my lord, You said our work should cease.

PRO.   I did say so   5 When first I raised the tempest. Say, my spirit, How fares the King and 's followers?

ARI.   Confined together In the same fashion as you gave in charge, Just as you left them — all prisoners, sir, In the line grove° which weather-fends° your cell. They cannot budge till your release. The King,   11 His brother, and yours abide all three distracted, And the remainder mourning over them, Brimful of sorrow and dismay. But chiefly Him that you termed, sir, " The good old lord, Gonzalo."   15 His tears run down his beard like winter's drops From eaves of reeds.° Your charm so strongly works 'em That if you now beheld them, your affections Would become tender.

PRO.   Dost thou think so, spirit?

ARI. Mine would, sir, were I human.

PRO.   And mine shall.   20 Hast thou, which art but air, a touch, a feeling Of their afflictions, and shall not myself, One of their kind, that relish° all as sharply, Passion° as they, be kindlier moved than thou art? Though with their high wrongs I am struck to the quick,   25 Yet with my nobler reason 'gainst my fury Do I take part. The rarer action is In virtue than in vengeance.° They being penitent, The sole drift° of my purpose doth extend Not a frown further. Go release them, Ariel.   30 My charms I'll break, their senses I'll restore, And they shall be themselves.

ARI.   I'll fetch them, sir.   [*Exit.*]

PRO. Ye elves of hills, brooks, standing lakes, and groves, And ye that on the sands with printless foot° Do chase the ebbing Neptune° and do fly him   35

Act V, Sc. i: 2. crack not: do not break down. **2–3. Time . . . carriage:** Time bears his burden without stooping, because it has now grown so light. **10. line grove:** grove of lime trees. **weather-fends:** protects from the weather. **17. eaves of reeds:** a thatched roof. **23. relish:** feel. **24. Passion:** suffer emotion. **27–28. rarer . . . vengeance:** it is a finer action to be self-controlled than to take vengeance. **29. drift:** intention. **34. printless foot:** without leaving a footprint. **35. ebbing Neptune:** i.e., the outgoing tide.

When he comes back; you demipuppets° that
By moonshine do the green sour° ringlets° make,
Whereof the ewe not bites; and you whose pastime
Is to make midnight mushrooms° that rejoice
To hear the solemn curfew,° by whose aid —   40
Weak masters though ye be — I have bedimmed
The noontide sun, called forth the mutinous winds,
And 'twixt the green sea and the azured vault°
Set roaring war. To the dread rattling thunder
Have I given fire, and rifted° Jove's stout oak   45
With his own bolt. The strong-based promontory
Have I made shake, and by the spurs° plucked up
The pine and cedar. Graves at my command
Have waked their sleepers, oped, and let 'em forth
By my so potent art. But this rough magic   50
I here abjure, and when I have required
Some heavenly music — which even now I do —
To work mine end upon their senses, that
This airy charm is for, I'll break my staff,
Bury it certain fathoms in the earth,   55
And deeper than did ever plummet° sound
I'll drown my book.°   [Solemn music.]
[Re-enter ARIEL before; then ALONSO, with a frantic
    gesture, attended by GONZALO; SEBASTIAN and
    ANTONIO in like manner, attended by ADRIAN
    and FRANCISCO. They all enter the circle which
    PROSPERO had made, and there stand charmed,
    which PROSPERO observing, speaks:]
A solemn air,° and the best comforter
To an unsettled fancy, cure thy brains,
Now useless, boiled° within thy skull! There stand,
For you are spell-stopped.   61
Holy Gonzalo, honorable man,
Mine eyes, even sociable° to the show of thine,
Fall° fellowly° drops. The charm dissolves apace,°
And as the morning steals upon the night,   65
Melting the darkness, so their rising senses
Begin to chase the ignorant fumes° that mantle°
Their clearer reason. O good Gonzalo,
My true preserver, and a loyal sir
To him thou follow'st! I will pay thy graces   70
Home° both in word and deed. Most cruelly
Didst thou, Alonso, use me and my daughter.
Thy brother was a furtherer in the act.

Thou art pinched for 't now, Sebastian. Flesh and
    blood,
You, brother mine, that entertained ambition,   75
Expelled remorse° and nature, who with Sebas-
    tian —
Whose inward pinches therefore are most strong —
Would here have killed your King, I do forgive thee,
Unnatural though thou art. Their understanding
Begins to swell, and the approaching tide   80
Will shortly fill the reasonable shore°
That now lies foul and muddy. Not one of them
That yet looks on me, or would know me. Ariel,
Fetch me the hat and rapier in my cell.
I will disease° me, and myself present   85
As I was sometime Milan.° Quickly, spirit.
Thou shalt ere long be free.
    ARI. [Sings and helps to attire him.]
        "Where the bee sucks, there suck I.
            In a cowslip's bell I lie,
            There I couch° when owls do cry.   90
            On the bat's back I do fly
            After summer merrily.
        Merrily, merrily shall I live now
        Under the blossom that hangs on the bough."
    PRO. Why, that's my dainty Ariel! I shall miss
        thee,   95
But yet thou shalt have freedom. So, so, so.°
To the King's ship, invisible as thou art.
There shalt thou find the mariners asleep
Under the hatches. The master and the boatswain
Being awake, enforce them to this place,   100
And presently, I prithee.
    ARI. I drink the air before me, and return
Or ere your pulse twice beat.   [Exit.]
    GON. All torment, trouble, wonder, and amaze-
        ment
Inhabits here. Some heavenly power guide us   105
Out of this fearful country!
    PRO.   Behold, Sir King,
The wrongèd Duke of Milan, Prospero.
For more assurance that a living prince
Does now speak to thee, I embrace thy body,
And to thee and thy company I bid   110
A hearty welcome.
    ALON.   Whether thou be'st he or no,
Or some enchanted trifle° to abuse° me,
As late I have been, I not know. Thy pulse
Beats, as of° flesh and blood, and since I saw thee,
The affliction of my mind amends, with which,   115
I fear, a madness held me. This must crave —

36. demipuppets: tiny creatures, half the size of a puppet.
37. sour: i.e., unacceptable to the cattle. ringlets: fairy rings,
circles of grass of a darker green often seen in English meadows,
supposed to be caused by the fairies dancing in a ring. 39. mid-
night mushrooms: As mushrooms grow in a single night, they
were thought to be the work of fairies. 40. curfew: rung at
9 P.M. to warn people to go indoors. Thereafter the fairies can
work without interruption. 43. azured vault: blue sky.
45. rifted: split. 47. spurs: roots. 56. plummet: See III.iii.101,n.
57. book: i.e., of magic spells. 58. air: musical air. 60. boiled:
boiling. Cf. MND, V.i.4, "Lovers and madmen have such seeth-
ing brains." 63. sociable: of fellow feeling. 64. Fall: let fall.
fellowly: in sympathy. apace: quickly. 67. ignorant fumes:
mists of ignorance. mantle: cloak. 70–71. pay . . . Home: re-
ward your kind deeds fully.

76. remorse: pity. 81. reasonable shore: shore of reason; i.e.,
sanity is beginning to flow back like the incoming tide. 85. dis-
case: remove my outer garment. Prospero is still in his magic
robe and so not recognized by his former associates. 86. As . . .
Milan: as I was when I was Duke of Milan. 90. couch: lie.
96. So, so, so: "so," used thus, often indicates movement. Cf.
Lear, III.vi.90. 112. enchanted trifle: hallucination caused by
enchantment. abuse: deceive. 114. as of: as if composed of.

An if this be at all° — a most strange story.
Thy dukedom I resign, and do entreat
Thou pardon me my wrongs.° — But how should Prospero
Be living and be here?

PRO.   First, noble friend,   120
Let me embrace thine age, whose honor cannot
Be measured or confined.

GON.   Whether this be
Or be not, I'll not swear.

PRO.   You do yet taste
Some subtilties° o' the isle, that will not let you
Believe things certain. Welcome, my friends all!
[Aside to SEBASTIAN and ANTONIO] But you, my
      brace of lords, were I so minded,   126
I here could pluck His Highness' frown upon you,
And justify you traitors. At this time
I will tell no tales.

SEB.   [Aside] The Devil speaks in him.

PRO.   No.
For you, most wicked sir, whom to call brother   130
Would even infect my mouth, I do forgive
Thy rankest fault — all of them — and require
My dukedom of thee, which perforce I know
Thou must restore.

ALON.   If thou be'st Prospero,
Give us particulars of thy preservation —   135
How thou hast met us here, who three hours
      since
Were wrecked upon this shore, where I have lost —
How sharp the point of this remembrance is! —
My dear son Ferdinand.

PRO.   I am woe for't,° sir.

ALON. Irreparable is the loss, and Patience   140
Says it is past her cure.

PRO.   I rather think
You have not sought her help of whose soft grace
For the like loss I have her sovereign° aid,
And rest myself content.

ALON.   You the like loss!

PRO. As great to me as late, and, supportable   145
To make the dear loss, have I means much weaker
Than you may call to comfort you, for I
Have lost my daughter.

ALON.   A daughter?
O Heavens, that they were living both in Naples,
The King and Queen there! That they were, I wish
Myself were mudded in that oozy bed   151
Where my son lies. When did you lose your daugh-
      ter?

PRO. In this last tempest. I perceive these lords
At this encounter do so much admire°
That they devour their reason, and scarce think   155

Their eyes do offices of truth,° their words
Are natural breath. But howsoe'er you have
Been jostled from your senses, know for certain
That I am Prospero, and that very Duke
Which was thrust forth of Milan, who most strangely
Upon this shore where you were wrecked was
      landed,   161
To be the lord on 't. No more yet of this,
For 'tis a chronicle of day by day,
Not a relation for a breakfast, nor
Befitting this first meeting. Welcome, sir.   165
This cell's my Court. Here have I few attendants,
And subjects none abroad. Pray you look in.
My dukedom since you have given me again,
I will requite° you with as good a thing,
At least bring forth a wonder to content ye   170
As much as me my dukedom.
[Here PROSPERO discovers° FERDINAND and MIRANDA
                playing at chess.]

MIRA. Sweet lord, you play me false.

FER.   No, my dear'st love,
I would not for the world.

MIRA. Yes, for a score of kingdoms you should
      wrangle,
And I would call it fair play.

ALON.   If this prove   175
A vision of the island, one dear son
Shall I twice lose.

SEB.   A most high miracle!

FER. Though the seas threaten, they are merciful.
I have cursed them without cause.   [Kneels.]

ALON.   Now all the blessings
Of a glad father compass thee about!   180
Arise, and say how thou camest here.

MIRA.   Oh, wonder!
How many goodly creatures are there here!
How beauteous mankind is! Oh, brave new world,
That has such people in 't!

PRO.   'Tis new to thee.

ALON. What is this maid with whom thou wast at
      play?   185
Your eld'st° acquaintance cannot be three hours.
Is she the goddess that hath severed us,
And brought us thus together?

FER.   Sir, she is mortal,
But by immortal Providence she's mine.
I chose her when I could not ask my father   190
For his advice, nor thought I had one. She
Is daughter to this famous Duke of Milan,
Of whom so often I have heard renown
But never saw before, of whom I have
Received a second life, and second father   195
This lady makes him to me.

ALON.   I am hers.

---

117. An . . . all: if this is really true.   119. my wrongs: the
wrongs which I have committed.   123–24. You . . . subtilties:
you still have the taste of the magic nature.   139. woe for't: sorry
for it.   143. sovereign: all-powerful.   154. admire: wonder.

156. offices of truth: true service.   169. requite: pay back.
171. s.d., discovers: reveals by drawing back the curtain.
186. eld'st: longest.

But oh, how oddly will it sound that I
Must ask my child° forgiveness!

PRO.   There, sir, stop.
Let us not burden our remembrances with
A heaviness that's gone.

GON.   I have inly wept,   200
Or should have spoke ere this. Look down, you gods,
And on this couple drop a blessèd crown!
For it is you that have chalked forth° the way
Which brought us hither.

ALON.   I say Amen, Gonzalo!
GON. Was Milan thrust from Milan, that his issue
Should become Kings of Naples? Oh, rejoice   206
Beyond a common joy! And set it down
With gold on lasting pillars. In one voyage
Did Claribel her husband find at Tunis
And Ferdinand, her brother, found a wife   210
Where he himself was lost, Prospero his dukedom
In a poor isle, and all of us ourselves
When no man was his own.

ALON. [*To* FERDINAND *and* MIRANDA] Give me your
     hands.
Let grief and sorrow still embrace° his heart
That doth not wish you joy!

GON.   Be it so! Amen!   215
[*Re-enter* ARIEL, *with the* MASTER *and* BOATSWAIN
amazedly° *following.*]
Oh, look, sir, look, sir! Here is more of us.
I prophesied if a gallows were on land,
This fellow could not drown.° Now, blasphemy,°
That swear'st grace o'erboard,° not an oath on
     shore?   219
Hast thou no mouth by land? What is the news?
BOATS. The best news is that we have safely found
Our King and company. The next, our ship —
Which, but three glasses since, we gave out split —
Is tight and yare and bravely rigged as when
We first put out to sea.

ARI. [*Aside to* PROSPERO] Sir, all this service   225
Have I done since I went.

PRO.   [*Aside to* ARIEL] My tricksy° spirit!
ALON. These are not natural events, they
     strengthen
From strange to stranger. Say, how came you hither?
BOATS. If I did think, sir, I were well awake,
I'd strive to tell you. We were dead of sleep,   230
And — how we know not — all clapped° under
     hatches,
Where, but even now, with strange and several
     noises
Of roaring, shrieking, howling, jingling chains,

And mo diversity of sounds, all horrible,
We were awaked, straightway at liberty.   235
Where we, in all her trim, freshly beheld
Our royal, good, and gallant ship, our master
Capering° to eye her. — On a trice, so please you,
Even in a dream, were we divided from them,
And were brought moping hither.

ARI. [*Aside to* PROSPERO] Was 't well done?   240
PRO. [*Aside to* ARIEL] Bravely, my diligence. Thou
     shalt be free.
ALON. This is as strange a maze as e'er men trod,
And there is in this business more than nature
Was ever conduct of. Some oracle
Must rectify° our knowledge.

PRO.   Sir, my liege,   245
Do not infest your mind with beating on
The strangeness of this business. At picked leisure
Which shall be shortly, single° I'll resolve° you,
Which to you shall seem probable, of every
These happened accidents. Till when, be cheerful,
And think of each thing well. [*Aside to* ARIEL] Come
     hither, spirit.   251
Set Caliban and his companions free,
Untie the spell. [*Exit* ARIEL.] How fares my gracious
     sir?
There are yet missing of your company
Some few odd lads that you remember not.   255
[*Re-enter* ARIEL, *driving in* CALIBAN, STEPHANO, *and*
TRINCULO, *in their stolen apparel.*]
STE. Every man shift for all the rest, and let no
man take care for himself, for all is but fortune. —
Coragio,° bully-monster, coragio!
TRIN. If these be true spies° which I wear in my
head, here's a goodly sight.   260
CAL. Oh, Setebos, these be brave spirits indeed!
How fine my master is! I am afraid
He will chastise me.

SEB.   Ha, ha!
What things are these, my lord Antonio?
Will money buy 'em?

ANT.   Very like. One of them   265
Is a plain fish, and no doubt marketable.
PRO. Mark but the badges° of these men, my
     lords,
Then say if they be true. This misshapen knave,
His mother was a witch, and one so strong   269
That could control the moon, make flows and ebbs,
And deal in her command,° without her power.°
These three have robbed me, and this demidevil —
For he's a bastard one — had plotted with them
To take my life. Two of these fellows you

---

198. my child: i.e., Miranda, who is about to become his daughter-in-law.   203. chalked forth: marked out (as with a chalk line). 214. still embrace: always cling to.   215 s.d., amazedly: in amazement.   217–18. gallows . . . drown: see I.i.32–33. 218. blasphemy: you blasphemer.   219. That . . . o'erboard: that by your swearing drives the grace of God away. 226. tricksy: clever.   231. clapped: shut in.

238. Capering: dancing for joy.   245. rectify: prove true. 248. single: alone. resolve: inform.   258. Coragio: courage. 259. spies: eyes.   267. badges: A nobleman's servant wore a badge displaying his master's coat of arms.   271. deal . . . command: i.e., take over the moon's power of controlling the tides. without . . . power: without the aid of the moon.

Must know and own, this thing of darkness I   275
Acknowledge mine.

CAL.   I shall be pinched to death.

ALON. Is not this Stephano, my drunken butler?

SEB. He is drunk now. Where had he wine?

ALON. And Trinculo is reeling ripe. Where should
they   279
Find this grand liquor that hath gilded 'em?° —
How camest thou in this pickle?

TRIN. I have been in such a pickle since I saw you
last that I fear me will never out of my bones. I shall
not fear flyblowing.°

SEB. Why, how now, Stephano!   285

STE. Oh, touch me not. — I am not Stephano, but
a cramp.

PRO. You'd be King o' the isle, sirrah?

STE. I should have been a sore one, then.

ALON. This is a strange thing as e'er I looked on.
[*Pointing to* CALIBAN.]

PRO. He is as disproportioned in his manners°
As in his shape. Go, sirrah, to my cell.   291
Take with you your companions. As you look
To have my pardon, trim° it handsomely.

CAL. Aye, that I will, and I'll be wise hereafter,
And seek for grace.° What a thrice-double ass   295
Was I to take this drunkard for a god
And worship this dull fool!

PRO.   Go to, away!

ALON. Hence, and bestow your luggage where you
found it.

SEB. Or stole it, rather.   299
[*Exeunt* CALIBAN, STEPHANO, *and* TRINCULO.]

PRO. Sir, I invite your Highness and your train
To my poor cell, where you shall take your rest
For this one night. Which, part of it, I'll waste
With such discourse as I not doubt shall make it
Go quick away — the story of my life,
And the particular accidents° gone by   305
Since I came to this isle. And in the morn
I'll bring you to your ship, and so to Naples,
Where I have hope to see the nuptial
Of these our dear-belovèd solemnized,

And thence retire me to my Milan, where   310
Every third thought shall be my grave.

ALON.   I long
To hear the story of your life, which must
Take the ear strangely.

PRO.   I'll deliver all,
And promise you calm seas, auspicious° gales,
And sail so expeditious that shall catch   315
Your royal fleet far off. [*Aside to* ARIEL] My Ariel,
chick,
That is thy charge. Then to the elements
Be free, and fare thou well! Please you, draw near.
[*Exeunt.*]

EPILOGUE°

SPOKEN BY PROSPERO

Now my charms are all o'erthrown,
And what strength I have's mine own,
Which is most faint. Now, 'tis true,
I must be here confined by you,
Or sent to Naples. Let me not,   5
Since I have my dukedom got,
And pardoned the deceiver, dwell
In this bare island by your spell,
But release me from my bands°
With the help of your good hands.°   10
Gentle breath° of yours my sails
Must fill, or else my project fails,
Which was to please. Now I want°
Spirits to enforce, art to enchant,
And my ending is despair   15
Unless I be relieved by prayer
Which pierces so that it assaults
Mercy itself, and frees all faults.
As you from crimes would pardoned be,
Let your indulgence set me free.   20

280. gilded 'em: made them glow.   284. fear flyblowing: i.e.,
shall never go bad, for I have been so well pickled.   290. man-
ners: behavior.   293. trim: make tidy.   295. grace: favor.
305. accidents: events.

314. auspicious: favorable.
Epilogue: A concluding epilogue is fairly common in Eliza-
bethan plays, especially those performed before a Courtly audi-
ence. It is usually a conventional apology for the inadequacies of
the performance, and an appeal for applause. Cf. the epilogues
in *MND*, *AYLI*, and *II Hen IV*.   9. bands: bonds.   10. good
hands: i.e., by clapping.   11. Gentle breath: kindly criticism.
13. want: lack.

SONNETS

Introduction

Shakespeare's sonnets are the most discussed and disputed of all collections of poetry in the English language, and every conceivable view has been expressed about them. Most critics, however, tend to join one of two parties. Some agree with Wordsworth, who wrote:

Scorn not the Sonnet; Critic, you have frowned,
Mindless of its just honor; with this key
Shakespeare unlocked his heart.

Others follow Matthew Arnold, who said:

Others abide our question. Thou art free.
We ask and ask — Thou smilest and art still,
Out-topping knowledge.

These two observations sum up the main divisions between those who believe that Shakespeare was an inscrutable sphinx about whose personality we can know nothing and those who believe that Shakespeare has laid bare his heart in his plays and his sonnets.

There are indeed many lovers of poetry to whom all discussion of the personal and historical " problems " of the sonnets is distasteful, and who feel, not unreasonably, that such delicate works of art should not be dissected and anatomized. Such readers should leave these problems alone; indeed, theories about the sonnets are dreary unless the student studies the whole question for himself at first hand.

There are, however, certain indisputable facts. On May 20, 1609, Thomas Thorpe entered in the Stationers' Register " a Booke called Shakespeares sonnettes." On June 19, Edward Alleyn, in jotting down a list of purchases, noted " Shakspers Sonnets 5d." The title printed on Thorpe's quarto reads:

SHAKE-SPEARES
SONNETS

Neuer before Imprinted.

AT LONDON
By *G. Eld* for *T. T.* and are
to be solde by *Iohn Wright,* dwelling
at Christ Church gate.
1609.

The volume is dedicated in a curious and enigmatic way:

TO . THE . ONLIE . BEGETTER . OF .
THESE . INSVING . SONNETS .
Mʳ W. H. ALL . HAPPINESSE .
AND . THAT . ETERNITIE .
PROMISED .
BY .
OVR . EVER-LIVING . POET .
WISHETH .
THE . WELL-WISHING .
ADVENTVRER . IN .
SETTING .
FORTH .
T. T.

By 1609 some of the sonnets were at least eleven years old. In 1598 Meres, in his *Palladis Tamia* (see pp. 11b–12a), in writing of Shakespeare as a poet said: " As the soul of Euphorbus was thought to live in Pythagoras: so the sweet witty soul of Ovid lives in mellifluous and honey-tongued Shakespeare, witness his *Venus and Adonis,* his *Lucrece,* his sugared Sonnets among his private friends, &c." In 1599, William Jaggard had issued a little book called *" The Passionate Pilgrime. By W. Shakespeare."* It contained twenty short poems, of which the first two were versions of Sonnets 138 and 144, and Nos. 3, 5, 17, poems taken from *Love's Labor's Lost.* The rest of the poems in the volume were by other authors.

The volume of Shakespeare's *Sonnets* printed by Thorpe contains in all one hundred and fifty-four sonnets. As arranged in his edition, they tell a story of sorts. The first seventeen sonnets form a series. They are addressed to a beautiful youth and call on him to marry so that his type may be preserved and continued in his children. From Sonnet 18 to Sonnet 126, the poet addresses the youth on various topics and occasions and in a variety of moods. A sense of intimacy increases; admiration becomes love; but there is little method in the arrangement and no continuous story. The poet at first is shy and tongue-tied in the presence of his friend, and can only express himself in writing (23). The poet is separated from him by travel, but thinks continuously of the youth (27). He is outcast, but comforted by the thought of his love (29). He warns his friend not to honor him publicly, lest he become tainted with scandal (36). The friend steals the poet's mistress, but is forgiven (40–42). The poet has the youth's picture, which he wears at his breast on a journey (47–49). The poet is elderly (73). He is jealous because others seek the youth's patronage, especially one poet whose verse bears " proud full sail " (78–86). The poet gently rebukes the youth for wantonness (96). After a spring and a summer of separation the poet comes back to his friend (97–98). The poet congratulates the youth on his escape from a " confined doom " (107). He is reconciled after absence (109). He is disgusted with his profession (110–11). He defends himself against the charge of ingratitude (117). He apologizes for giving away the " tables " which the youth had given him (122). The last of this series is Sonnet 126.

Then follow twenty-six sonnets addressed to a dark woman, whom the poet has loved passionately but reluctantly. She is skillful in playing on the virginals, faithless, wanton, physically unattractive, false to her husband, and yet irresistibly desirable. The collection ends with two conventional love sonnets on Cupid.

There are thus a number of problems. If only we could answer any one of a dozen questions for certain, the enigma of the sonnets might be solved and our knowledge of Shakespeare greatly increased. The mysteries begin with the dedication. Even this has been interpreted in more than one way. Most assume that T. T. regards Mr. W. H. as the only begetter of the sonnets; but some read the dedication as implying that Mr. W. H. is wishing happiness to the only begetter.

Before considering these problems it is well to look at the probable date when Shakespeare's sonnets were written and at their place in Elizabethan poetry.

The Elizabethan sonnet is the most famous of all verse forms, but its vogue was very short-lived. The sonnet form had first been introduced into English through Wyatt and Surrey's translations from Petrarch, in the 1530's, and a few other English poets had written sonnets before 1590; but the popularity of the form was directly due to the publication of Sir Philip Sidney's *Astrophel and Stella* in the spring of 1591. Anything written by Sidney was eagerly read, and this series of sonnets was at times so personal and sincere that it revealed to English poets possibilities hitherto unrealized. The most important collections of sonnets — Daniel's *Delia*, Lodge's *Phyllis*, Constable's *Diana*, Drayton's *Idea*, Spenser's *Amoretti* — all appeared within the next five years, and thereafter for several years sonnets were seldom published. It is most likely, therefore, that most of Shakespeare's sonnets were written during this vogue; that is, not before 1592 and probably not much after 1598. In style, they are akin rather to *Venus and Adonis* and some of the earlier plays. The greatest number of parallels of phrase and idea are to be found in *Love's Labor's Lost, Two Gentlemen of Verona, Romeo and Juliet, Venus and Adonis, Lucrece, Richard the Second* and *Richard the Third,* all of which were written by 1595. Moreover, if the sonnets stand in approximately the order of their writing, it seems clear from Sonnet 104 that they cover a period of more than three years.

As for " Mr. W. H.," various candidates have been put forward. Sir Sidney Lee noted that an edition of the *Fourfold Meditations* of Father Robert Southwell, the Jesuit martyr, printed in 1606, was dedicated " To the Right Worshipful and Vertuous Gentleman, Matthew Saunders, Esquire. W. H. wisheth, with long life, a prosperous achievement of his good desires." Lee identified this W. H. with William Hall, a printer in a small way. Another guess is Sir William Harvey, who married the mother of the Earl of Southampton in 1598. If the Earl of Southampton was the beautiful youth, then this guess has much to recommend it; for Harvey was a likely person to have had access to the original manuscript. He has also a greater claim to be the " W. H." of Father Southwell's *Meditations,* for the Southampton family were strongly Catholic, whereas W. Hall, the printer, published anti-Catholic books.

A third candidate is William Herbert, Earl of Pembroke, but it seems unlikely that a nobleman of his standing would ever have been addressed as " Mr. W. H."

As for the fair youth, there are at present two main choices, Henry Wriothesley, Earl of Southampton, and William Herbert, Earl of Pembroke. Southampton was born on October 6,

1573 and succeeded to the title at the age of seven. He was therefore a ward (i.e., a minor needing a guardian) until he came of age. Lord Burleigh, Queen Elizabeth's great Minister, was his guardian. To Southampton Shakespeare dedicated *Venus and Adonis,* which was entered in the Stationers' Register on April 18, 1593 (see p. 10a). Just over a year later, Shakespeare dedicated *Lucrece* to Southampton in warmer terms (see p. 10a) which suggest that in the interval he had received considerable encouragement. As a young man Southampton was conspicuously handsome, but for some years he refused to marry, although Lord Burleigh himself proposed his own granddaughter as a suitable wife. In 1595, Southampton fell in love with Mistress Elizabeth Vernon, one of Queen Elizabeth's maids of honor, whom, to the Queen's great anger, he secretly married in 1598. Southampton was a personal friend and adoring follower of the Earl of Essex, and shared in his misfortune (see p. 24a–b).

The claims of William Herbert, Earl of Pembroke, are based principally on his initials and on the dedication to him and to his brother of the first folio in 1623, in which Heming and Condell declare " that their Lordships have been pleased to think these trifles somewhat heretofore, and have prosecuted both them and their Author living with so much favor." In 1595 there was a proposal to betroth Pembroke, then aged fifteen, to the daughter of Sir George Carey, son of the patron of the Lord Chamberlain's Company. Apart from this, there is no further known connection between him and Shakespeare.

With Pembroke, however, is linked the name of Mistress Mary Fitton, another of Queen Elizabeth's maids of honor. She was a lively lady who became the mother of three illegitimate children by different men, but afterward married richly and died very respectable. Pembroke was the father of her first child and there was much

scandal in court about their behavior. Mistress Fitton is a candidate for the doubtful honor of being considered the " Dark Lady"; she was not, however, conspicuously dark. This theory is known as the " Herbert theory." Its great glory is that it was itself the " only begetter " of George Bernard Shaw's play *The Dark Lady of the Sonnets,* and its preface.

Various other candidates have been put forward. Some take Sonnet 20, line 7, in its original spelling as a pointer:

A man in hew all *Hews* in his controwling.

There seems to be a pun in this line on the name Hughes. The theory is ancient, but Oscar Wilde championed it, claiming that the youth was a boy actor called William Hughes. The records of Elizabethan acting companies are fairly complete, and there is no trace of any actor of this name. There are many other theories, but until some further definite fact is indisputably established, they must remain theories, and the student of poetry can neglect them all.

The sonnet is one of the most difficult forms for sublime or permanent poetry. It is admirable for saying something short, pretty, effective, complimentary, but its very formality and rigidity are against it. There are very few perfect sonnets. The normal form is fixed at fourteen lines of iambic pentameters and a poet cannot always pack or expand his thoughts into so exact a mold. Moreover, Shakespeare chose the most difficult kind of sonnet pattern — three quatrains followed by a couplet. When successful, the couplet folds up the whole poem in a neat final conclusion, but too often the couplet is an awkward appendix to a twelve-line poem.

Shakespeare's sonnets, as poetry, are perhaps rather for private reading than public discussion, for they touch sensitive readers in secret ways. To such readers all discussion of the problems is impertinent and all criticism superfluous.

Sonnets

1

From fairest creatures we desire increase,
That thereby beauty's rose° might never die,
But as the riper should by time decrease,
His tender heir might bear his memory.
But thou, contracted to thine own bright eyes,° 5
Feed'st thy light's flame with self-substantial° fuel,
Making a famine where abundance lies,
Thyself thy foe, to thy sweet self too cruel.
Thou that art now the world's fresh ornament
And only herald to the gaudy spring, 10
Within thine own bud buriest thy content°
And, tender churl,° makest waste in niggarding.°
   Pity the world, or else this glutton be,
   To eat the world's due, by the grave and thee.°

2

When forty winters shall besiege thy brow
And dig deep trenches in thy beauty's field,
Thy youth's proud livery, so gazed on now,
Will be a tattered weed,° of small worth held.
Then being asked where all thy beauty lies, 5
Where all the treasure of thy lusty days,
To say within thine own deep-sunken eyes
Were an all-eating° shame and thriftless° praise.
How much more praise deserved thy beauty's use
If thou couldst answer, "This fair child of mine 10
Shall sum my count° and make my old excuse,"°
Proving his beauty by succession° thine!
   This were to be new-made when thou art old,
   And see thy blood warm when thou feel'st it cold.

3

Look in thy glass, and tell the face thou viewest
Now is the time that face should form another,
Whose fresh repair° if now thou not renewest,
Thou dost beguile the world, unbless some mother.

For where is she so fair whose uneared° womb 5
Disdains the tillage of thy husbandry?
Or who is he so fond° will be the tomb
Of his self-love,° to stop posterity?
Thou art thy mother's glass,° and she in thee
Calls back the lovely April of her prime. 10
So thou through windows of thine age shalt see,
Despite of wrinkles, this thy golden time.
   But if thou live, remembered not to be,°
   Die single, and thine image dies with thee.

4

Unthrifty loveliness, why dost thou spend
Upon thyself thy beauty's legacy?°
Nature's bequest gives nothing, but doth lend,
And being frank,° she lends to those are free.°
Then, beauteous niggard, why dost thou abuse 5
The bounteous largess° given thee to give?
Profitless usurer, why dost thou use
So great a sum of sums, yet canst not live?°
For having traffic with thyself alone,
Thou of thyself thy sweet self dost deceive. 10
Then how, when nature calls thee to be gone,
What ácceptable audit canst thou leave?
   Thy unused beauty must be tombed with thee,
   Which, used, lives th' executor° to be.

5

Those hours that with gentle work did frame
The lovely gaze° where every eye doth dwell
Will play the tyrants to the very same
And that unfair° which fairly doth excel.
For never-resting time leads summer on 5
To hideous winter and confounds° him there,
Sap checked with frost and lusty leaves quite gone,
Beauty o'ersnowed and bareness everywhere.
Then, were not summer's distillation° left,
A liquid prisoner pent in walls of glass, 10
Beauty's effect° with beauty were bereft,
Nor it, nor no remembrance what it was.

Sonnet 1: 2. beauty's rose: The rose is often used as a symbol of youthful perfection. Cf. *Haml*, III.i.160; *I Hen IV*, I.iii.175–76. 5. contracted . . . eyes: married to your own reflection. 6. self-substantial: of its own substance; i.e., consuming itself. 11. content: that which you contain; i.e., your child that might be. 12. churl: miser. niggarding: being niggardly. 14. To . . . thee: i.e., you and the grave will consume what is due to the world; viz., your posterity.
   Sonnet 2: 4. tattered weed: ragged garment. 8. all-eating: devouring. thriftless: unprofitable. 11. sum my count: balance my account. old excuse: excuse for being old. 12. succession: right of succession as your child.
   Sonnet 3: 3. repair: renewal.

5. uneared: unplowed. 7. fond: foolish. 8. Of . . . self-love: through sheer selfishness. 9. glass: reflection. 13. remembered . . . be: not to be remembered.
   Sonnet 4: 2. beauty's legacy: the beauty bestowed on you by your parents. 4. frank: liberal. free: generous. 6. largess: bounty. 8. live: survive. 14. th' executor: i.e., the survivor who carries out the wishes of the dead.
   Sonnet 5: 2. gaze: i.e., object. 4. unfair: make ugly. 6. confounds: destroys. 9. distillation: perfume distilled from summer's flowers. 11. effect: product; i.e., the perfume.

But flowers distilled, though they with winter meet,
Leese° but their show. Their substance still lives sweet.

6

Then let not winter's ragged hand deface
In thee thy summer, ere thou be distilled.
Make sweet some vial, treasure thou some place
With beauty's treasure, ere it be self-killed.
That use is not forbidden usury,°   5
Which happies° those that pay the willing loan.
That's for thyself to breed another thee,
Or ten times happier, be it ten for one.
Ten times thyself were happier than thou art
If ten of thine ten times refigured° thee.   10
Then what could death do if thou shouldst depart
Leaving thee living in posterity?
    Be not self-willed, for thou art much too fair
      To be death's conquest and make worms thine heir.

7

Lo, in the orient when the gracious light°
Lifts up his burning head, each undereye°
Doth homage to his new-appearing sight,
Serving with looks his sacred majesty.
And having climbed the steep-up heavenly hill,   5
Resembling strong youth in his middle age,
Yet mortal looks adore his beauty still,
Attending on his golden pilgrimage.
But when from highmost pitch,° with weary car,°
Like feeble age, he reeleth from the day,   10
The eyes, 'fore° duteous, now converted are
From his low tract,° and look another way.
    So thou, thyself outgoing° in thy noon,
    Unlooked on diest unless thou get° a son.

8

Music to hear,° why hear'st thou music sadly?
Sweets with sweets war not, joy delights in joy.

14. **Leese:** lose.

    Sonnet 6: 5. forbidden usury: Usury — the lending of money at excessive rates of interest — was regarded as un-Christian but the law allowed an interest rate of 10%.   **6. happies:** makes happy.   **10. refigured:** reproduced.

    Sonnet 7: 1. gracious light: i.e., the sun. The image of the sun in its course from dawn to sunset is sustained until l. 12. **2. undereye:** eye in the earth beneath.   **9. pitch:** zenith; lit., the highest point in the flight of a hawk. See App. 26. **car:** chariot. **11. 'fore:** before. **12. tract:** track. **13. outgoing:** going out, declining. **14. get:** beget.

    Sonnet 8: 1. Music to hear: you who are like music.

Why lovest thou that which thou receivest not gladly,
Or else receivest with pleasure thine annoy?°
If the true concord of well-tunèd sounds,   5
By unions married, do offend thine ear,
They do but sweetly chide thee, who confounds
In singleness the parts that thou shouldst bear.
Mark how one string, sweet husband to another,
Strikes each in each by mutual ordering,   10
Resembling sire and child and happy mother,
Who, all in one, one pleasing note do sing.
    Whose speechless song, being many, seeming one,
    Sings this to thee: "Thou single wilt prove none."

9

Is it for fear to wet a widow's eye
That thou consumest thyself in single life?
Ah, if thou issueless shalt hap to die,
The world will wail thee, like a makeless° wife.
The world will be thy widow, and still° weep   5
That thou no form° of thee hast left behind,
When every private widow well may keep
By children's eyes her husband's shape in mind.
Look what an unthrift in the world doth spend
Shifts but his place, for still the world enjoys it,°
But beauty's waste hath in the world an end,   11
And kept unused, the user so destroys it.
    No love toward others in that bosom sits
    That on himself such murderous shame commits.

10

For shame! Deny that thou bear'st love to any,
Who for thyself art so unprovident.
Grant, if thou wilt, thou art beloved of many,
But that thou none lovest is most evident.
For thou art so possessed with murderous hate   5
That 'gainst thyself thou stick'st not to conspire,
Seeking that beauteous roof° to ruinate°
Which to repair should be thy chief desire.
Oh, change thy thought, that I may change my mind!
Shall hate be fairer lodged than gentle love?   10
Be, as thy presence is, gracious and kind,
Or to thyself at least kindhearted prove.
    Make thee another self, for love of me,
    That beauty still may live in thine or thee.

4. **annoy:** harm.

    Sonnet 9: 4. makeless: without a mate.   **5. still:** always. **6. form:** shape. **9–10. Look . . . it:** i.e., the money which a waster (*unthrift*) spends remains in circulation.

    Sonnet 10: 7. roof: house; i.e., family. **ruinate:** destroy.

11

As fast as thou shalt wane, so fast thou grow'st
In one of thine, from that which thou departest,°
And that fresh blood which youngly thou bestow'st
Thou mayst call thine when thou from youth con-
  vertest.°
Herein lives wisdom, beauty, and increase;   5
Without this, folly, age, and cold decay.
If all were minded so, the times° should cease
And threescore year would make the world away.
Let those whom Nature hath not made for store,°
Harsh, featureless, and rude, barrenly perish.   10
Look whom she best endowed she gave the more,
Which bounteous gift thou shouldst in bounty
  cherish.
    She carved thee for her seal,° and meant thereby
    Thou shouldst print more, not let that copy die.

12

When I do count the clock that tells the time
And see the brave day sunk in hideous night,
When I behold the violet past prime
And sable° curls all silvered o'er with white;
When lofty trees I see barren of leaves   5
Which erst from heat did canopy the herd,
And summer's green all girded up in sheaves,
Borne on the bier with white and bristly beard° —
Then of thy beauty do I question° make,
That thou among the wastes of time must go,   10
Since sweets and beauties do themselves forsake
And die as fast as they see others grow.
    And nothing 'gainst Time's scythe can make de-
    fense
    Save breed,° to brave° him when he takes thee
    hence.

13

Oh, that you were yourself! But, love, you are
No longer yours than you yourself here live.
Against this coming end you should prepare,
And your sweet semblance to some other give.
So should that beauty which you hold in lease°   5
Find no determination.° Then you were
Yourself again after yourself's decease,

When your sweet issue your sweet form should bear.
Who lets so fair a house fall to decay,
Which husbandry° in honor might uphold   10
Against the stormy gusts of winter's day
And barren rage of death's eternal cold?
    Oh, none but unthrifts. Dear my love, you know
    You had a father. Let your son say so.

14°

Not from the stars do I my judgment pluck,
And yet methinks I have astronomy,°
But not to tell of good or evil luck,
Of plagues, of dearths, or seasons' quality.
Nor can I fortune to brief minutes tell,   5
Pointing to each his thunder, rain, and wind,
Or say with princes if it shall go well
By oft predict° that I in heaven find.
But from thine eyes my knowledge I derive,
And, constant stars, in them I read such art°   10
As truth and beauty shall together thrive,
If from thyself to store thou wouldst convert.°
    Or else of thee this I prognosticate:
    Thy end is truth's and beauty's doom and date.°

15

When I consider everything that grows
Holds in perfection but a little moment,
That this huge stage presenteth naught but shows
Whereon the stars in secret influence° comment;
When I perceive that men as plants increase,   5
Cheerèd and checked even by the selfsame sky,
Vaunt° in their youthful sap, at height decrease,
And wear their brave state out of memory —
Then the conceit° of this inconstant stay
Sets you most rich in youth before my sight,   10
Where wasteful Time debateth with Decay,
To change your day of youth to sullied° night.
    And all in war with Time for love of you,
    As he takes from you, I engraft° you new.

16

But wherefore do not you a mightier way
Make war upon this bloody tyrant, Time?
And fortify yourself in your decay

Sonnet 11: 1–2. As . . . departest: i.e., as you fade, your child
waxes toward that prime from which you are departing.   4. con-
vertest: change.   7. times: i.e., this generation.   9. store:
breeding.   13. seal: i.e., that which makes impressions of itself.
  Sonnet 12: 4. sable: black.   7–8. And . . . beard: i.e., the
barley, once green, now white and bearded, cut, stacked, and
carted.   9. question: matter for thought.   14. breed: offspring.
brave: taunt.
  Sonnet 13: 5. hold in lease: i.e., as a temporary tenant
6. determination: lit., the legal conclusion of a tenancy.

10. husbandry: good management.
  Sonnet 14: The whole sonnet sustains the image of astrological
predictions. See App. 1 and 2.   2. astronomy: astrology.   8. oft
predict: frequent signs.   10. art: knowledge.   12. store . . .
convert: breed progeny.   14. doom . . . date: Doomsday.
  Sonnet 15: 4. influence: See App. 1.   7. Vaunt: triumph.
9. conceit: thought.   12. sullied: dark.   14. engraft: i.e., graft
you into my verse.

With means more blessèd than my barren rhyme?
Now stand you on the top of happy hours,   5
And many maiden gardens, yet unset,
With virtuous wish would bear your living flowers
Much liker than your painted counterfeit.°
So should the lines of life° that life repair
Which this, Time's pencil, or my pupil pen,°   10
Neither in inward worth nor outward fair,°
Can make you live yourself in eyes of men.
    To give away yourself keeps yourself still,
    And you must live, drawn by your own sweet skill.

17°

Who will believe my verse in time to come
If it were filled with your most high deserts?
Though yet, Heaven knows, it is but as a tomb
Which hides your life and shows not half your
      parts.°
If I could write the beauty of your eyes   5
And in fresh numbers° number all your graces,
The age to come would say, "This poet lies,
Such heavenly touches ne'er touched earthly faces."
So should my papers, yellowed with their age,   9
Be scorned, like old men of less truth than tongue,
And your true rights be termed a poet's rage°
And stretchèd° meter of an antique song.
    But were some child of yours alive that time,
    You should live twice, in it and in my rhyme.

18

Shall I compare thee to a summer's day?
Thou art more lovely and more temperate.
Rough winds do shake the darling buds of May,
And summer's lease hath all too short a date.
Sometime too hot the eye of heaven° shines,   5
And often is his gold complexion dimmed.
And every fair from fair sometime declines,
By chance or nature's changing course untrimmed.°
But thy eternal summer shall not fade,
Nor lose possession of that fair thou owest,°   10
Nor shall Death brag thou wander'st in his shade

When in eternal lines to time thou grow'st.
    So long as men can breathe, or eyes can see,
    So long lives this, and this gives life to thee.°

19

Devouring Time, blunt thou the lion's paws,
And make the earth devour her own sweet brood.
Pluck the keen teeth from the fierce tiger's jaws,
And burn the long-lived phoenix° in her blood.
Make glad and sorry seasons as thou fleet'st,°   5
And do whate'er thou wilt, swift-footed Time,
To the wide world and all her fading sweets,
But I forbid thee one most heinous crime.
Oh, carve not with thy hours my love's fair brow,
Nor draw no lines there with thine antique pen.   10
Him in thy course untainted do allow
For beauty's pattern to succeeding men.
    Yet do thy worst, old Time. Despite thy wrong,
    My love shall in my verse ever live young.

20

A woman's face with Nature's own hand painted
Hast thou, the master-mistress of my passion,
A woman's gentle heart, but not acquainted
With shifting change, as is false women's fashion,
An eye more bright than theirs, less false in rolling,
Gilding the object whereupon it gazeth,°   6
A man in hue, all hues in his controlling,°
Which steals men's eyes and women's souls amazeth.
And for a woman wert thou first created,
Till Nature, as she wrought thee, fell a-doting,   10
And by addition me of thee defeated°
By adding one thing to my purpose nothing.
    But since she pricked thee out° for women's
      pleasure,
    Mine be thy love, and thy love's use their treasure.

21

So is it not with me as with that Muse°
Stirred° by a painted beauty to his verse,
Who Heaven itself for ornament doth use

Sonnet 16: 8. counterfeit: imitation, portrait.   9. lines of life: living lines; i.e., children.   10. Which . . . pen: which a portrait — Time's method of preserving a likeness — or my beginner's verse. Some editors read "this time's pencil"; i.e., artists of today.   11. fair: beauty.

Sonnet 17: This sonnet concludes the first series in which the young man is urged to marry.   4. parts: good qualities, physical and mental.   6. numbers: verses.   11. rage: enthusiasm.   12. stretched: exaggerated.

Sonnet 18: 5. eye of heaven: the sun.   8. untrimmed: shorn of beauty.   10. fair . . . owest: beauty you possess.

13–14. So . . . thee: This sentiment — that the poet is giving immortality to his subject — is a commonplace with sonneteers.

Sonnet 19: 4. phoenix: a mythical Arabian bird which lived for five hundred years. See *Temp*, III.iii.21–24,n.   5. fleet'st: pass rapidly.

Sonnet 20: 6. Gilding . . . gazeth: It was believed that the eye, like a searchlight, shot out a beam which enabled the gazer to see the object. Cf. *Tr & Cr*, III.iii.109–11.   7. A . . . controlling: See Sonnets Intro. p. 1034b.   11. defeated: cheated.   13. pricked . . . out: selected you.

Sonnet 21: 1. Muse: poet.   2. Stirred: roused.

And every fair with his fair doth rehearse,°
Making a couplement° of proud compare 5
With sun and moon, with earth and sea's rich gems,
With April's first-born flowers, and all things rare
That heaven's air in this huge rondure° hems.
Oh, let me, true in love, but truly write,
And then believe me, my love is as fair 10
As any mother's child, though not so bright
As those gold candles° fixed in heaven's air.
    Let them say more that like of hearsay well.
    I will not praise that purpose not to sell.°

22

My glass shall not persuade me I am old
So long as youth and thou are of one date,
But when in thee time's furrows I behold,
Then look I death my days should expiate.°
For all that beauty that doth cover thee 5
Is but the seemly raiment of my heart,
Which in thy breast doth live, as thine in me.
How can I then be elder than thou art?
Oh, therefore, love, be of thyself so wary
As I, not for myself, but for thee will, 10
Bearing thy heart, which I will keep so chary
As tender nurse her babe from faring ill.
    Presume not on thy heart when mine is slain.
    Thou gavest me thine, not to give back again.

23

As an unperfect actor on the stage,
Who with his fear is put besides his part,
Or some fierce thing replete with too much rage,
Whose strength's abundance weakens his own heart,
So I, for fear of trust, forget to say 5
The perfect ceremony of love's rite,°
And in mine own love's strength seem to decay,
O'ercharged with burden of mine own love's might.
Oh, let my books be then the eloquence
And dumb presagers° of my speaking breast, 10
Who plead for love, and look for recompense,
More than that tongue that more hath more ex-
    pressed.
    Oh, learn to read what silent love hath writ.
    To hear with eyes belongs to love's fine wit.

24

Mine eye hath played the painter and hath stelled°
Thy beauty's form in table° of my heart.
My body is the frame wherein 'tis held,
And pérspective it is best painter's art.
For through the painter must you see his skill, 5
To find where your true image pictured lies,
Which in my bosom's shop is hanging still,
That hath his windows glazèd with thine eyes.
Now see what good turns eyes for eyes have done.
Mine eyes have drawn thy shape, and thine for me
Are windows to my breast, wherethrough the sun
Delights to peep, to gaze therein on thee. 12
    Yet eyes this cunning want° to grace their art,
    They draw but what they see, know not the heart.

25

Let those who are in favor with their stars°
Of public honor and proud titles boast,
Whilst I, whom fortune of such triumph bars,
Unlooked for joy° in that I honor most.
Great princes' favorites their fair leaves spread 5
But as the marigold at the sun's eye,°
And in themselves their pride lies burièd,
For at a frown they in their glory die.
The painful° warrior famousèd for fight,
After a thousand victories once foiled, 10
Is from the book of honor razèd quite,
And all the rest forgot for which he toiled.
    Then happy I, that love and am beloved
    Where I may not remove nor be removed.

26°

Lord of my love, to whom in vassalage°
Thy merit hath my duty strongly knit,
To thee I send this written ambassage,
To witness duty, not to show my wit.
Duty so great, which wit so poor as mine 5
May make seem bare in wanting words to show it,
But that I hope some good conceit of thine
In thy soul's thought, all naked, will bestow it.
Till whatsoever star that guides my moving,
Points on me graciously with fair aspéct,° 10
And puts apparel on my tattered loving,

4. And . . . rehearse: compares his fair subject with every beauti-
ful thing. 5. couplement: union. 8. rondure: orb; i.e., the
earth. 12. gold candles: the stars. 14. I . . . sell: I do not
praise you because I want to sell you.
    Sonnet 22: 4. expiate: end.
    Sonnet 23: 5–6. So . . . rite: so I, being too diffident, forget
to show my love outwardly. 10. dumb presagers: like the
dumb show that explains the action which is to follow. See *Haml,*
III.ii.145.

Sonnet 24: 1. stelled: fixed. 2. table: the flat surface on
which a portrait is painted. 13. want: lack.
    Sonnet 25: 1. in . . . stars: lucky. 4. Unlooked . . . joy: re-
joice inconspicuously. 6. the . . . eye: i.e., which closes when
the sun ceases to shine on it. 9. painful: toiling.
    Sonnet 26: Written to accompany some offering of poetry,
possibly the *Rape of Lucrece.* See Gen. Intro. p. 10a. 1. vassal-
age: homage. 10. aspect; the "influence" of a star. See App. 1.

To show me worthy of thy sweet respect.
  Then may I dare to boast how I do love thee,
  Till then not show my head where thou mayst
    prove me.

27

Weary with toil, I haste me to my bed,
The dear repose for limbs with travel tired.
But then begins a journey in my head,
To work my mind, when body's work's expired.
For then my thoughts, from far where I abide,   5
Intend° a zealous pilgrimage to thee,
And keep my drooping eyelids open wide,
Looking on darkness which the blind do see.
Save that my soul's imaginary sight
Presents thy shadow° to my sightless view,   10
Which, like a jewel hung in ghastly night,
Makes black night beauteous and her old face new.
  Lo, thus by day my limbs, by night my mind,
  For thee and for myself no quiet find.

28

How can I then return in happy plight,
That am debarred the benefit of rest?
When day's oppression is not eased by night,
But day by night, and night by day, oppressed?
And each, though enemies to either's reign,   5
Do in consent shake hands to torture me,
The one by toil, the other to complain
How far I toil, still farther off from thee.
I tell the day, to please him° thou art bright,
And dost him grace when clouds do blot the heaven.
So flatter I the swart-complexioned night;   11
When sparkling stars twire° not thou gild'st the
    even.°
  But day doth daily draw my sorrows longer,
  And night doth nightly make grief's strength
    seem stronger.

29

When in disgrace with fortune and men's eyes
I all alone beweep my outcast state,
And trouble deaf Heaven with my bootless° cries,
And look upon myself and curse my fate,
Wishing me like to one more rich in hope,   5
Featured like him, like him with friends possessed,
Desiring this man's art and that man's scope,

With what I most enjoy contented least —
Yet in these thoughts myself almost despising,
Haply I think on thee, and then my state,   10
Like to the lark at break of day arising
From sullen earth, sings hymns at Heaven's gate.
  For thy sweet love remembered such wealth brings
  That then I scorn to change my state with kings.

30

When to the sessions° of sweet silent thought
I summon up remembrance of things past,
I sigh the lack of many a thing I sought,
And with old woes new wail my dear time's waste.
Then can I drown an eye, unused to flow,   5
For precious friends hid in death's dateless° night,
And weep afresh love's long since canceled woe,
And moan the expense° of many a vanished sight.
Then can I grieve at grievances foregone,°
And heavily from woe to woe tell o'er   10
The sad account of forebemoanèd moan,
Which I new-pay as if not paid before.
  But if the while I think on thee, dear friend,
  All losses are restored and sorrows end.

31°

Thy bosom is endearèd with all hearts,
Which I by lacking have supposèd dead.
And there reigns love, and all love's loving parts,
And all those friends which I thought burièd.
How many a holy and obsequious° tear   5
Hath dear religious love stol'n from mine eye,
As interest° of the dead, which now appear
But things removed that hidden in thee lie!
Thou art the grave where buried love doth live,
Hung with the trophies of my lovers° gone,   10
Who all their parts of me to thee did give,
That due of many now is thine alone.
  Their images I loved I view in thee,
  And thou, all they, hast all the all of me.

32

If thou survive my well-contented° day,
When that churl° Death my bones with dust shall
    cover,
And shalt by fortune once more resurvey

Sonnet 30: 1. **sessions**: lit., sittings of a law court.   6. **date-less**: everlasting.   8. **expense**: waste.   9. **foregone**: past.
    Sonnet 31: The poet's friend being absent is as dead. This reminds him of his dead friends whose qualities are combined in his friend.   5. **obsequious**: mourning.   7. **interest**: i.e., tribute due to.   10. **lovers**: dear friends.
    Sonnet 32: 1. **well-contented**: happy.   2. **churl**: boor.

Sonnet 27: 6. **Intend**: direct.   10. **shadow**: reflection, image.
    Sonnet 28: 9. **to . . . him**: to rejoice that.   12. **twire**: twinkle, peep. **even**: evening.
    Sonnet 29: 3. **bootless**: vain.

These poor rude lines of thy deceasèd lover,
Compare them with the bettering of the time,° 5
And though they be outstripped by every pen,
Reserve them for my love, not for their rhyme,
Exceeded by the height of happier men.
Oh, then vouchsafe me but this loving thought:
"Had my friend's Muse grown with this growing
    age, 10
A dearer birth than this his love had brought,
To march in ranks of better equipage.
    But since he died, and poets better prove,
    Theirs for their style I'll read, his for his love."

33

Full many a glorious morning have I seen
Flatter the mountaintops with sovereign° eye,
Kissing with golden face the meadows green,
Gilding pale streams with heavenly alchemy,°
Anon permit the basest clouds to ride 5
With ugly rack° on his celestial face
And from the forlorn world his visage hide,
Stealing unseen to west with this disgrace.
Even so my sun one early morn did shine
With all-triumphant splendor on my brow. 10
But out, alack! he was but one hour mine,
The region° cloud hath masked him from me now.
    Yet him for this my love no whit disdaineth.
    Suns of the world may stain when heaven's sun
    staineth.

34

Why didst thou° promise such a beauteous day,
And make me travel forth without my cloak,
To let base clouds o'ertake me in my way,
Hiding thy bravery° in their rotten smoke?°
'Tis not enough that through the cloud thou break
To dry the rain on my storm-beaten face, 6
For no man well of such a salve° can speak
That heals the wound and cures not the disgrace.
Nor can thy shame give physic to my grief.
Though thou repent, yet I have still the loss. 10
The offender's sorrow lends but weak relief
To him that bears the strong offense's cross.°
    Ah, but those tears are pearl which thy love sheds,
    And they are rich and ransom all ill deeds.

35

No more be grieved at that which thou hast done.
Roses have thorns, and silver fountains mud,
Clouds and eclipses stain both moon and sun,
And loathsome canker° lives in sweetest bud.
All men make faults, and even I in this, 5
Authorizing thy trespass with compare,°
Myself corrupting, salving thy amiss,
Excusing thy sins more than thy sins are.
For to thy sensual fault I bring in sense° —
Thy adverse party is thy advocate — 10
And 'gainst myself a lawful plea commence.
Such civil war is in my love and hate,
    That I an accessory needs must be
    To that sweet thief which sourly robs from me.

36

Let me confess that we two must be twain,
Although our undivided loves are one.
So shall those blots that do with me remain,
Without thy help, by me be borne alone.
In our two loves there is but one respect,° 5
Though in our lives a separable° spite,
Which though it alter not love's sole effect,°
Yet doth it steal sweet hours from love's delight.
I may not evermore acknowledge thee,
Lest my bewailèd guilt should do thee shame, 10
Nor thou with public kindness honor me,
Unless thou take that honor from thy name.
    But do not so. I love thee in such sort,
    As thou being mine, mine is thy good report.

37

As a decrepit father takes delight
To see his active child do deeds of youth,
So I, made lame by fortune's dearest° spite,
Take all my comfort of thy worth and truth.
For whether beauty, birth, or wealth, or wit, 5
Or any of these all, or all, or more,
Entitled in° thy parts do crownèd sit,
I make my love engrafted° to this store.
So then I am not lame, poor, nor despised
Whilst that this shadow doth such substance give 10
That I in thy abundance am sufficed

Sonnet 35: 4. canker: cankerworm. 6. Authorizing . . . compare: justifying your offense with my similes (e.g., of roses and thorns). 9. sense: reason (to allay my passion).
Sonnet 36: 5. respect: consideration. 6. separable: separating. 7. effect: result.
Sonnet 37: 3. dearest: bitterest. 7. Entitled in: having a right to. 8. engrafted: firmly joined.

5. bettering . . . time: finer verse which will then be written.
    Sonnet 33: 2. sovereign: supreme, glorious. 4. alchemy: transmutation of base metal to gold. See App. 21. 6. rack: mass of clouds. 12. region: of the air.
    Sonnet 34: 1. thou: i.e., the sun. 4. bravery: splendor.
smoke: mist. 7. salve: healing ointment. 12. cross: burden.

And by a part of all thy glory live.
  Look, what is best, that best I wish in thee.
  This wish I have, then ten times happy me!

38

How can my Muse want subject to invent
While thou dost breathe, that pour'st into my verse
Thine own sweet argument,° too excellent
For every vulgar paper to rehearse?
Oh, give thyself the thanks if aught in me   5
Worthy perusal stand against thy sight,
For who's so dumb that cannot write to thee
When thou thyself dost give invention° light?
Be thou the tenth Muse,° ten times more in worth
Than those old nine which rhymers invocate,   10
And he that calls on thee, let him bring forth
Eternal numbers to outlive long date.
  If my slight Muse do please these curious days,
  The pain be mine, but thine shall be the praise.

39

Oh, how thy worth with manners° may I sing,
When thou art all the better part of me?
What can mine own praise to mine own self bring?
And what is 't but mine own when I praise thee?
Even for this let us divided live,   5
And our dear love lose name of single one,
That by this separation I may give
That due to thee which thou deservest alone.
O absence, what a torment wouldst thou prove,
Were it not thy sour leisure gave sweet leave   10
To entertain the time with thoughts of love,
Which time and thoughts so sweetly doth deceive,°
  And that thou teachest how to make one twain°
  By praising him here who doth hence remain!

40

Take all my loves, my love, yea, take them all.
What hast thou then more than thou hadst before?
No love, my love, that thou mayst truelove call,

All mine was thine before thou hadst this more.
Then, if for my love thou my love receivest,°   5
I cannot blame thee for my love thou usest,
But yet be blamed if thou thyself deceivest
By willful taste of what thyself refusest.°
I do forgive thy robbery, gentle thief,
Although thou steal thee all my poverty.   10
And yet, love knows, it is a greater grief
To bear love's wrong than hate's known injury.
  Lascivious grace, in whom all ill well shows,
  Kill me with spites,° yet we must not be foes.

41°

Those pretty wrongs that liberty commits,
When I am sometime absent from thy heart,
Thy beauty and thy years full well befits,
For still temptation follows where thou art.
Gentle° thou art, and therefore to be won,   5
Beauteous thou art, therefore to be assailed.
And when a woman woos, what woman's son
Will sourly leave her till she have prevailed?
Aye me! but yet thou mightst my seat° forbear,
And chide thy beauty and thy straying youth,   10
Who lead thee in their riot even there
Where thou art forced to break a twofold truth°—
  Hers, by thy beauty tempting her to thee,
  Thine, by thy beauty being false to me.

42°

That thou hast her it is not all my grief,
And yet it may be said I loved her dearly.
That she hath thee is of my wailing chief,
A loss in love that touches me more nearly.
Loving offenders, thus I will excuse ye—   5
Thou dost love her, because thou know'st I love her,
And for my sake even so doth she abuse me,
Suffering my friend for my sake to approve° her.
If I lose thee, my loss is my love's° gain,
And losing her, my friend hath found that loss.   10
Both find each other, and I lose both twain,
And both for my sake lay on me this cross.
  But here's the joy—my friend and I are one.
  Sweet flattery! Then she loves but me alone.

Sonnet 38: 3. argument: topic for verse.   8. invention: the creative power.   9. tenth Muse: The Nine Muses were the patron goddesses of the different forms of art, particularly poetry, and were regarded by the ancients as directly inspiring the artist.
  Sonnet 39: 1. with manners: i.e., without immodesty.   12. deceive: beguile.   13. make . . . twain: make one person of two; i.e., though absent I am united with you in thought.

  Sonnet 40: 5. Then . . . receivest: if because you love me you take my mistress.   8. By . . . refusest: i.e., you take my love (mistress) but refuse my love (for you).   14. spites: vexations.
  Sonnet 41: (Continuing 40). 5. Gentle: of good birth. 9. seat: place.   12. truth: loyalty.
  Sonnet 42: (Continuing 41). 8. approve: make trial of. 9. love's: mistress's

43

When most I wink,° then do mine eyes best see,
For all the day they view things unrespected,°
But when I sleep, in dreams they look on thee,
And, darkly bright, are bright in dark° directed.
Then thou, whose shadow° shadows doth make bright, 5
How would thy shadow's form form happy show
To the clear day with thy much clearer light
When to unseeing eyes thy shade shines so!
How would, I say, mine eyes be blessèd made
By looking on thee in the living day, 10
When in dead night thy fair imperfect° shade
Through heavy sleep on sightless eyes doth stay!
　　All days are nights to see till I see thee,
　　And nights bright days when dreams do show thee me.

44°

If the dull substance° of my flesh were thought,
Injurious distance should not stop my way.
For then, despite of space, I would be brought
From limits far remote where thou dost stay.
No matter then although my foot did stand 5
Upon the farthest earth removed from thee,
For nimble thought can jump both sea and land
As soon as think the place where he would be.
But, ah, thought kills me, that I am not thought,
To leap large lengths of miles when thou art gone,
But that, so much of earth and water wrought,° 11
I must attend time's leisure with my moan,
　　Receiving naught by elements so slow
　　But heavy tears, badges of either's woe.

45°

The other two, slight air and purging fire,
Are both with thee, wherever I abide.
The first my thought, the other my desire,
These present-absent with swift motion slide.
For when these quicker elements are gone 5
In tender embassy of love to thee,
My life, being made of four, with two alone
Sinks down to death, oppressed with melancholy,
Until life's composition° be recured°

By those swift messengers returned from thee, 10
Who even but now come back again, assured
Of thy fair health, recounting it to me.
　　This told, I joy, but then no longer glad,
　　I send them back again, and straight grow sad.

46

Mine eye and heart are at a mortal° war
How to divide the conquest of thy sight.°
Mine eye my heart thy picture's sight would bar,
My heart mine eye the freedom of that right.
My heart doth plead that thou in him dost lie, 5
A closet never pierced with crystal eyes.
But the defendant doth that plea deny,
And says in him thy fair appearance lies.
To 'cide° this title is impanelèd
A quest° of thoughts, all tenants to the heart, 10
And by their verdict is determinèd
The clear eye's moiety° and the dear heart's part.
　　As thus: Mine eye's due is thine outward part,
　　And my heart's right thine inward love of heart.

47°

Betwixt mine eye and heart a league is took,
And each doth good turns now unto the other.
When that mine eye is famished for a look,
Or heart in love with sighs himself doth smother,
With my love's picture then my eye doth feast 5
And to the painted banquet bids my heart.
Another time mine eye is my heart's guest
And in his thoughts of love doth share a part.
So, either by thy picture or my love,
Thyself away art present still with me, 10
For thou not farther than my thoughts canst move,
And I am still with them and they with thee.
　　Or, if they sleep, thy picture in my sight
　　Awakes my heart to heart's and eye's delight.

48

How careful was I when I took my way,
Each trifle under truest bars to thrust,
That to my use it might unusèd stay
From hands of falsehood, in sure wards° of trust!

Sonnet 43: 1. wink: close my eyes in sleep. 2. unrespected: unnoticed. 4. bright in dark: i.e., see clearly because of your brightness. 5. shadow: appearance, image (as seen in a dream). 11. imperfect: i.e., unreal.

Sonnet 44: In this and the following sonnet the imagery is of the four elements. See App. 3. 1. dull substance: i.e., made of the two "dull" elements, earth and water. 11. so . . . wrought: I, being compounded (wrought) of these two elements.

Sonnet 45: (Continuing 44). 9. life's composition: i.e., the combination of all four elements. recured: restored.

Sonnet 46: 1. mortal: deadly. 2. the . . . sight: the right to gaze on your picture. 9. 'cide: decide. 10. quest: jury. 12. moiety: share.

Sonnet 47: (Continuing 46).

Sonnet 48: 4. wards: bolts.

But thou, to whom my jewels trifles are,   5
Most worthy comfort, now my greatest grief,
Thou, best of dearest and mine only care,
Art left the prey of every vulgar thief.
Thee have I not locked up in any chest,
Save where thou art not, though I feel thou art,   10
Within the gentle closure° of my breast,
From whence at pleasure thou mayst come and part.
    And even thence thou wilt be stol'n, I fear,
    For truth proves thievish for a prize so dear.

49

Against that time, if ever that time come,
When I shall see thee frown on my defects,
When as thy love hath cast his utmost sum,°
Called to that audit by advised respects° —   4
Against that time when thou shalt strangely° pass,
And scarcely greet me with that sun, thine eye,
When love, converted from the thing it was,
Shall reasons find of settled gravity° —
Against that time do I ensconce° me here
Within the knowledge of mine own desert,   10
And this my hand against myself uprear,
To guard the lawful reasons on thy part.
    To leave poor me thou hast the strength of laws,
    Since why to love I can allege no cause.

50

How heavy do I journey on the way
When what I seek, my weary travel's end,
Doth teach that ease and that repose to say,
" Thus far the miles are measured from thy friend! "
The beast that bears me, tired with my woe,   5
Plods dully on, to bear that weight in me,
As if by some instinct the wretch did know
His rider loved not speed, being made° from thee.
The bloody spur cannot provoke him on
That sometimes anger thrusts into his hide,   10
Which heavily he answers with a groan
More sharp to me than spurring to his side.
    For that same groan doth put this in my mind:
    My grief lies onward, and my joy behind.

51°

Thus can my love excuse the slow offense°
Of my dull bearer when from thee I speed.
From where thou art why should I haste me thence?
Till I return, of posting° is no need.
Oh, what excuse will my poor beast then find,   5
When swift extremity° can seem but slow?
Then should I spur, though mounted on the wind,
In wingèd speed no motion shall I know.
Then can no horse with my desire keep pace,
Therefore desire, of perfect'st love being made,   10
Shall neigh — no dull flesh — in his fiery race,
But love, for love, thus shall excuse my jade:°
    Since from thee going he went willful-slow,
    Toward thee I'll run and give him leave to go.°

52

So am I as the rich, whose blessèd key
Can bring him to his sweet uplockèd treasure,
The which he will not every hour survey,
For blunting the fine point of seldom pleasure.
Therefore are feasts so solemn and so rare,   5
Since, seldom coming, in the long year set°
Like stones of worth they thinly placèd are,
Or captain° jewels in the carcanet.°
So is the time that keeps you as my chest,
Or as the wardrobe which the robe doth hide,   10
To make some special instant special blest
By new-unfolding his imprisoned pride.
    Blessèd are you, whose worthiness gives scope,
    Being had, to triumph — being lacked, to hope.

53°

What is your substance, whereof are you made,
That millions of strange° shadows on you tend?
Since every one hath, every one, one shade,
And you, but one, can every shadow lend.°
Describe Adonis,° and the counterfeit°   5
Is poorly imitated after you.
On Helen's cheek all art of beauty set,

11. closure: enclosure.
   Sonnet 49: 3. cast . . . sum: balanced the last account.
4. advised respects: deliberate consideration of the differences be-
tween us.   5. strangely: like a stranger.   8. of . . . gravity: for
respectability; i.e., to dissociate yourself from me.   9. ensconce:
fortify.
   Sonnet 50: 8. being made: i.e., taking me away.

   Sonnet 51: (Continuing 50). 1. slow offense: offense caused
by its slowness.   4. posting: riding fast.   6. swift extremity:
extreme swiftness.   12. jade: nag, a poor-spirited horse.
14. go: walk.
   Sonnet 52: 6. in . . . set: once a year.   8. captain: chief.
carcanet: necklace.
   Sonnet 53: This sonnet plays with the different meanings
and ideas conveyed by "shadow" — the shape cast by a body
intercepting the sunlight; reflection; likeness or picture; symbol.
2. strange: i.e., not your own.   4. can . . . lend: i.e., on all you
bestow your reflection, which is made up of beauty of all kinds.
5. Adonis: the beautiful youth beloved of Venus. See Pl. 7a.
counterfeit: copy, picture, description.

And you in Grecian tires° are painted new.
Speak of the spring and foison° of the year,
The one doth shadow of your beauty show,   10
The other as your bounty doth appear,
And you in every blessèd shape we know.
  In all external grace you have some part,
  But you like none, none you, for constant heart.

54°

Oh, how much more doth beauty beauteous seem
By that sweet ornament which truth° doth give!
The rose looks fair, but fairer we it deem
For that sweet odor which doth in it live.
The canker blooms° have full as deep a dye   5
As the perfumèd tincture of the roses,
Hang on such thorns, and play as wantonly
When summer's breath their maskèd buds discloses.
But for° their virtue only is their show,
They live unwooed and unrespected fade,   10
Die to themselves. Sweet roses do not so.
Of their sweet deaths are sweetest odors made.
  And so of you, beauteous and lovely youth,
  When that shall vade,° by verse distills your truth.

55

Not marble, nor the gilded monuments
Of princes, shall outlive this powerful rhyme.
But you shall shine more bright in these contents
Than unswept stone,° besmeared with sluttish time.
When wasteful war shall statues overturn,   5
And broils root out the work of masonry,
Nor Mars his sword nor war's quick fire shall burn
The living record of your memory.
'Gainst death and all-oblivious enmity
Shall you pace forth. Your praise shall still find room
Even in the eyes of all posterity   11
That wear this world out to the ending doom.
  So, till the judgment° that° yourself arise,
  You live in this, and dwell in lovers' eyes.

56

Sweet love, renew thy force. Be it not said
Thy edge should blunter be than appetite,

8. tires: attire.   9. foison: plenty; i.e., autumn.
  Sonnet 54: (Continuing 53). 2. truth: constancy.   5. canker
blooms: wild roses, which are odorless, contrasted with the sweet-
scented garden rose.   9. for: since.   14. vade: fade.
  Sonnet 55: 4. unswept stone: the dusty inscribed slab over a
grave on the floor in a church.   13. judgment: Day of Judgment.
that: when.

Which but today by feeding is allayed,
Tomorrow sharpened in his former might.
So, love, be thou. Although today thou fill   5
Thy hungry eyes even till they wink with fullness,
Tomorrow see again, and do not kill
The spirit of love with a perpetual dullness.
Let this sad interim like the ocean be
Which parts the shore, where two contracted new°
Come daily to the banks, that when they see   11
Return of love, more blest may be the view.
  Or call it winter, which, being full of care,
  Makes summer's welcome thrice more wished,
    more rare.

57

Being your slave, what should I do but tend
Upon the hours and times of your desire?
I have no precious time at all to spend,
Nor services to do, till you require.
Nor dare I chide the world-without-end hour   5
Whilst I, my sovereign, watch the clock for you,
Nor think the bitterness of absence sour
When you have bid your servant once adieu.
Nor dare I question with my jealous thought
Where you may be, or your affairs suppose,°   10
But, like a sad slave, stay and think of naught
Save where you are how happy you make those.
  So true° a fool is love that in your will,
  Though you do anything, he thinks no ill.

58

That god forbid that made me first your slave,
I should in thought control your times of pleasure,
Or at your hand the account of hours to crave,
Being your vassal, bound to stay your leisure!
Oh, let me suffer, being at your beck,   5
The imprisoned absence of your liberty.°
And patience, tame to sufferance, bide each check°
Without accusing you of injury.
Be where you list, your charter is so strong
That you yourself may privilege your time   10
To what you will. To you it doth belong
Yourself to pardon of self-doing crime.
  I am to wait, though waiting so be Hell,
  Not blame your pleasure, be it ill or well.

  Sonnet 56: 10. contracted new: newly betrothed.
  Sonnet 57: 10. suppose: guess about.   13. true: faithful.
  Sonnet 58: 6. The . . . liberty: you are free to go as you
please, and your absence makes me a prisoner.   7. check:
rebuke.

59

If there be nothing new, but that which is
Hath been before, how are our brains beguiled,
Which, laboring for invention,° bear amiss
The second burden of a former child!°
Oh that recórd° could with a backward look,   5
Even of five hundred courses of the sun,
Show me your image in some antique book,
Since mind at first in character was done.°
That I might see what the old world could say
To this composèd wonder° of your frame —   10
Whether° we are mended, or whether better they,
Or whether revolution° be the same.
　　Oh, sure I am the wits of former days
　　To subjects worse have given admiring praise.

60

Like as the waves make toward the pebbled shore,
So do our minutes hasten to their end,
Each changing place with that which goes before,
In sequent toil all forward do contend.
Nativity,° once in the main of light,°   5
Crawls to maturity, wherewith being crowned,
Crookèd eclipses 'gainst his glory fight,
And Time that gave doth now his gift confound.
Time doth transfix the flourish set on youth
And delves the parallels in beauty's brow,   10
Feeds on the rarities of nature's truth,
And nothing stands but for his scythe to mow.
　　And yet to times in hope my verse shall stand,
　　Praising thy worth, despite his cruel hand.

61°

Is it thy will thy image should keep open
My heavy eyelids to the weary night?
Dost thou desire my slumbers should be broken
While shadows like to thee do mock my sight?
Is it thy spirit that thou send'st from thee   5
So far from home into my deeds to pry,
To find out shames and idle hours in me,
The scope and tenor° of thy jealousy?°
Oh, no! Thy love, though much, is not so great.
It is my love that keeps mine eye awake,   10

Mine own true love that doth my rest defeat,
To play the watchman ever for thy sake.
　　For thee watch I whilst thou dost wake elsewhere,
　　From me far off, with others all too near.

62

Sin of self-love possesseth all mine eye
And all my soul and all my every part,
And for this sin there is no remedy,
It is so grounded inward in my heart.
Methinks no face so gracious is as mine,   5
No shape so true, no truth of such account,
And for myself mine own worth do define,
As I all other in all worths surmount.
But when my glass shows me myself indeed,
Beated° and chopped° with tanned antiquity,   10
Mine own self-love quite contrary I read.
Self so self-loving were iniquity.
　　'Tis thee, myself,° that for myself I praise,
　　Painting my age with beauty of thy days.

63

Against° my love shall be, as I am now,
With Time's injurious hand crushed and o'erworn,
When hours have drained his blood and filled his
　　brow
With lines and wrinkles, when his youthful morn
Hath traveled on to age's steepy night,   5
And all those beauties whereof now he's king
Are vanishing or vanished out of sight,
Stealing away the treasure of his spring.
For such a time do I now fortify
Against confounding age's cruel knife,   10
That he shall never cut from memory
My sweet love's beauty, though my lover's life.
　　His beauty shall in these black lines be seen,
　　And they shall live, and he in them still green.

64°

When I have seen by Time's fell hand defaced
The rich-proud cost of outworn buried age;°
When sometime lofty towers I see down-razed,
And brass eternal slave to mortal rage;
When I have seen the hungry ocean gain   5
Advantage on the kingdom of the shore,

Sonnet 59: 3. invention: new creation.　4. The . . . child: a
notion which has already been expressed by another.　5. record:
research.　8. in . . . done: recorded in writing.　10. composed
wonder: marvel of construction.　11. Whether: pronounced
"whe'er."　12. revolution: change.
　Sonnet 60: 5. Nativity: the moment of birth; i.e., the newborn
infant. main of light: bright daylight.
　Sonnet 61: Cf. 43.　8. scope . . . tenor: aim and intention.
Jealousy: suspicion.

Sonnet 62: 10. Beated: overpowered. chopped: chapped,
roughened.　13. thee, myself: i.e., yourself, which is my other
self.
　Sonnet 63: 1. Against: anticipating the time when.
　Sonnet 64: (Continuing 63). 2. rich-proud . . . age: proud
costly memorials of a bygone age.

And the firm soil win of the watery main,
Increasing store with loss and loss with store;
When I have seen such interchange of state,
Or state itself confounded to decay —   10
Ruin hath taught me thus to ruminate,
That Time will come and take my love away.
　　This thought is as a death, which cannot choose
　　But weep to have that which it fears to lose.

65°

Since brass, nor stone, nor earth, nor boundless sea
But° sad mortality o'ersways° their power,
How with this rage shall beauty hold a plea,
Whose action is no stronger than a flower?
Oh, how shall summer's honey breath hold out   5
Against the wreckful siege of battering days
When rocks impregnable are not so stout,
Nor gates of steel so strong, but Time decays?
O fearful meditation! Where, alack,   9
Shall Time's best jewel from Time's chest lie hid?
Or what strong hand can hold his swift foot back?
Or who his spoil of beauty can forbid?
　　Oh, none, unless this miracle have might,
　　That in black ink my love may still shine bright.

66

Tired with all these, for restful death I cry,
As, to behold desert a beggar born,
And needy nothing trimmed in jollity,°
And purest faith unhappily forsworn,
And gilded honor shamefully misplaced,   5
And maiden virtue rudely strumpeted,
And right perfection wrongfully disgraced,
And strength by limping sway disabled,
And art° made tongue-tied by authority,
And folly, doctorlike,° controlling skill,   10
And simple truth miscalled simplicity,°
And captive good attending captain ill.
　　Tired with all these, from these would I be gone,
　　Save that, to die I leave my love alone.

67

Ah, wherefore with infection° should he live
And with his presence grace impiety,
That sin by him advantage should achieve

Sonnet 65: (Continuing 64). 1–2. Since . . . But: since there
is neither . . . but that. 2. o'ersways: overpowers.
　Sonnet 66: 3. needy . . . jollity: i.e., the beggar born clad in
gay clothes. 9. art: skill. 10. doctorlike: with the airs of a
scholar. 11. simplicity: silliness.
　Sonnet 67: 1. with infection: in these plaguey times.

And lace° itself with his society?
Why should false painting imitate his cheek,   5
And steal dead seeing° of his living hue?
Why should poor beauty indirectly seek
Roses of shadow,° since his rose is true?
Why should he live, now Nature bankrupt is,
Beggared of blood to blush through lively veins?
For she hath no exchequer now but his,°   11
And, proud of many, lives upon his gains.
　　Oh, him she stores, to show what wealth she had
　　In days long since, before these last so bad.

68

Thus is his cheek the map of days outworn,
When beauty lived and died as flowers do now.
Before these bastard signs of fair° were born
Or durst inhabit on a living brow;
Before the golden tresses of the dead,°   5
The right of sepulchers, were shorn away,
To live a second life on second head,
Ere beauty's dead fleece made another gay.
In him those holy antique hours are seen,
Without all ornament, itself° and true,   10
Making no summer of another's green,
Robbing no old to dress his beauty new.
　　And him as for a map° doth Nature store,°
　　To show false Art what beauty was of yore.

69

Those parts of thee that the world's eye doth view
Want nothing that the thought of hearts can mend.
All tongues, the voice of souls, give thee that due,
Uttering bare truth, even so as foes commend.°   4
Thy outward thus with outward praise is crowned,
But those same tongues that give thee so thine own
In other accents do this praise confound
By seeing farther than the eye hath shown.
They look into the beauty of thy mind,
And that, in guess, they measure by thy deeds.   10
Then, churls, their thoughts, although their eyes
　　　　were kind,
To thy fair flower add the rank smell of weeds.
　　But why° thy odor matcheth not thy show,
　　The soil° is this, that thou dost common° grow.

4. lace: ornament.　6. dead seeing: appearance of life which is
in reality dead.　8. Roses of shadow: i.e., imitation color.
11. exchequer . . . his: i.e., he is the only beautiful specimen of
nature now left.
　Sonnet 68: 3. bastard . . . fair: imitation beauty, cosmetics.
5. golden . . . dead: See M of Ven, III.ii.92–96,n.　10. itself:
i.e., pure.　13. map: pattern. store: hoard.
　Sonnet 69: 4. even . . . commend: i.e., which even an enemy
would grant.　13. But why: the reason why.　14. soil: blemish.
common: open to all comers.

70°

That thou art blamed shall not be thy defect.
For slander's mark was ever yet the fair.
The ornament of beauty is suspect,
A crow that flies in heaven's sweetest air.
So° thou be good, slander doth but approve°   5
Thy worth the greater, being wooed of time,
For canker vice the sweetest buds doth love,
And thou present'st a pure unstainèd prime.
Thou hast passed by the ambush of young days,
Either not assailed, or victor being charged.°   10
Yet this thy praise cannot be so thy praise,
To tie up envy evermore enlarged.°
    If some suspect° of ill masked° not thy show,
    Then thou alone kingdoms of hearts shouldst owe.

71

No longer mourn for me when I am dead
Than you shall hear the surly sullen bell°
Give warning to the world that I am fled
From this vile world, with vilest worms to dwell.
Nay, if you read this line, remember not   5
The hand that writ it, for I love you so
That I in your sweet thoughts would be forgot
If thinking on me then should make you woe.
Oh, if, I say, you look upon this verse
When I perhaps compounded am with clay,   10
Do not so much as my poor name rehearse,
But let your love even with my life decay,
    Lest the wise world should look into your moan,
    And mock you with me after I am gone.

72°

Oh, lest the world should task you to recite
What merit lived in me, that you should love
After my death, dear love, forget me quite.
For you in me can nothing worthy prove,
Unless you would devise some virtuous lie,   5
To do more for me than mine own desert,
And hang more praise upon deceasèd I
Than niggard truth would willingly impart.
Oh, lest your true love may seem false in this,
That you for love speak well of me untrue,   10
My name be buried where my body is,
And live no more to shame nor me nor you.
    For I am shamed by that which I bring forth,
    And so should you, to love things nothing worth.

73

That time of year thou mayst in me behold
When yellow leaves, or none, or few, do hang
Upon those boughs which shake against the cold,
Bare ruined choirs° where late the sweet birds sang.
In me thou see'st the twilight of such day   5
As after sunset fadeth in the west,
Which by and by black night doth take away,
Death's second self, that seals up° all in rest.
In me thou see'st the glowing of such fire,
That on the ashes of his youth doth lie   10
As the deathbed whereon it must expire,
Consumed with that which it was nourished by.
    This thou perceivest, which makes thy love more strong,
    To love that well which thou must leave ere long.

74°

But be contented. When that fell° arrest°
Without all bail shall carry me away,
My life hath in this line° some interest,
Which for memorial still with thee shall stay.
When thou reviewest this, thou dost review   5
The very part was consecrate to thee.
The earth can have but earth, which is his due,
My spirit is thine, the better part of me.
So then thou hast but lost the dregs of life,
The prey of worms, my body being dead,   10
The coward conquest of a wretch's knife,
Too base of thee to be rememberèd.
    The worth of that is that which it contains,
    And that is this, and this with thee remains.°

75

So are you to my thoughts as food to life,
Or as sweet-seasoned showers are to the ground.
And for the peace of you° I hold such strife
As 'twixt a miser and his wealth is found,
Now proud as an enjoyer, and anon   5
Doubting° the filching age will steal his treasure;
Now counting best to be with you alone,

Sonnet 73: 4. choirs: that part of a cathedral or large church in which the services are conducted. The image was suggested by the roofless choir of a ruined abbey, which resembles a leafless avenue of tall trees. See Pl. 6c.   8. seals up: concludes.
    Sonnet 74: (Continuing 73). 1. fell: fearful. arrest: Cf. *Haml,* V.ii.347–48.   3. this line: i.e., of verse.   13–14. The . . . remains: i.e, the worth of my body is the spirit which it contains, and this verse is my spirit, which stays with you.
    Sonnet 75: 3. peace of you: the peace which comes through your friendship.   6. Doubting: fearing.

Sonnet 70: (Continuing 69). 5. So: so long as. approve: prove. 10. charged: attacked.   12. enlarged: free to go to and fro. 13. suspect: suspicion. masked: concealed.
    Sonnet 71: 2. bell: See App. 19.
    Sonnet 72: (Continuing 71).

Then bettered° that the world may see my pleasure.
Sometime all full with feasting on your sight,
And by and by clean starvèd for a look,   10
Possessing or pursuing no delight
Save what is had or must from you be took.
  Thus do I pine and surfeit day by day,
  Or gluttoning on all or all away.

76

Why is my verse so barren of new pride,°
So far from variation or quick change?
Why with the time° do I not glance aside
To new-found methods and to compounds strange?°
Why write I still all one, ever the same,   5
And keep invention in a noted weed,°
That every word doth almost tell my name,
Showing their birth and where they did proceed?
Oh, know, sweet love, I always write of you,
And you and love are still my argument.°   10
So all my best is dressing old words new,
Spending again what is already spent.
  For as the sun is daily new and old,
  So is my love still telling what is told.

77°

Thy glass will show thee how thy beauties wear,
Thy dial° how thy precious minutes waste.
The vacant° leaves thy mind's imprint will bear,
And of this book this learning mayst thou taste.
The wrinkles which thy glass will truly show   5
Of mouthèd° graves will give thee memory.
Thou by thy dial's shady stealth° mayst know
Time's thievish progress to eternity.
Look, what thy memory cannot contain   9
Commit to these waste blanks, and thou shalt find
Those children nursed, delivered from thy brain,
To take a new acquaintance of thy mind.
  These offices, so oft as thou wilt look,
  Shall profit thee and much enrich thy book.

78

So oft have I invoked thee for° my Muse
And found such fair assistance in my verse

As° every alien pen hath got my use
And under thee° their poesy disperse.
Thine eyes, that taught the dumb on high to sing   5
And heavy ignorance aloft to fly,
Have added feathers to the learnèd's wing
And given grace a double majesty.
Yet be most proud of that which I compile,
Whose influence is thine and born of thee.   10
In others' works thou dost but mend the style,
And arts with thy sweet graces gracèd be,
  But thou art all my art, and dost advance
  As high as learning my rude ignorance.

79°

Whilst I alone did call upon thy aid,
My verse alone had all thy gentle grace,
But now my gracious numbers are decayed,
And my sick Muse doth give another place.
I grant, sweet love, thy lovely argument°   5
Deserves the travail of a worthier pen,
Yet what of thee thy poet doth invent
He robs thee of, and pays it thee again.
He lends thee virtue, and he stole that word
From thy behavior. Beauty doth he give,   10
And found it in thy cheek. He can afford
No praise to thee but what in thee doth live.
  Then thank him not for that which he doth say,
  Since what he owes thee thou thyself dost pay.

80

Oh, how I faint when I of you do write,
Knowing a better spirit° doth use your name,
And in the praise thereof spends all his might,
To make me tongue-tied, speaking of your fame!
But since your worth, wide as the ocean is,   5
The humble as the proudest sail doth bear,
My saucy bark,° inferior far to his,
On your broad main° doth willfully appear.
Your shallowest help will hold me up afloat,
Whilst he upon your soundless deep° doth ride,   10
Or, being wrecked, I am a worthless boat,°
He of tall° building and of goodly pride.
  Then if he thrive and I be cast away,
  The worst was this — my love was my decay.

---

8. bettered: made better.
  Sonnet 76: 1. new pride: novelty. 3. time: latest fashion.
4. compounds strange: fantastic compound words, such as some
poets were affecting. 6. noted weed: familiar garb. 10. argu-
ment: subject, theme.
  Sonnet 77: (Sent with the gift of a notebook). 2. dial: sundial.
3. vacant: empty. 6. mouthed: gaping. 7. shady stealth:
stealthy shadow.
  Sonnet 78: 1. for: to be.

3. As: that. 4. under thee: under your patronage.
  Sonnet 79: (Continuing 78). 5. thy . . . argument: the theme
of thy loveliness.
  Sonnet 80: 2. better spirit: greater poet. 7. bark: small
ship. 8. main: ocean. 10. soundless deep: a sea too deep to
be sounded. 11. boat: i.e., little boat. 12. tall: fine.

81

Or° I shall live your epitaph to make,
Or you survive when I in earth am rotten,
From hence° your memory death cannot take,
Although in me each part will be forgotten.
Your name from hence immortal life shall have, 5
Though I, once gone, to all the world must die.
The earth can yield me but a common grave,
When you entombèd in men's eyes shall lie.
Your monument shall be my gentle verse,
Which eyes not yet created shall o'erread, 10
And tongues to be your being shall rehearse°
When all the breathers of this world are dead.
　　You still shall live — such virtue hath my pen —
　　Where breath most breathes, even in the mouths
　　　　of men.

82

I grant thou wert not married° to my Muse,
And therefore mayst without attaint° o'erlook
The dedicated words° which writers use
Of their fair subject, blessing every book.
Thou art as fair in knowledge as in hue, 5
Finding thy worth a limit past my praise,
And therefore art enforced to seek anew
Some fresher stamp° of the time-bettering days.
And do so, love. Yet when they have devised
What strainèd touches rhetoric can lend, 10
Thou truly fair wert truly sympathized°
In true plain words by thy true-telling friend,
　　And their gross painting° might be better used
　　Where cheeks need blood — in thee it is abused.°

83

I never saw that you did painting need,
And therefore to your fair° no painting set.
I found, or thought I found, you did exceed
The barren tender° of a poet's debt.
And therefore have I slept in your report, 5
That you yourself, being extant, well might show
How far a modern° quill° doth come too short

Speaking of worth, what worth in you doth grow.
This silence for my sin you did impute,
Which shall be most my glory, being dumb, 10
For I impair not beauty being mute,
When others would give life and bring a tomb.°
　　There lives more life in one of your fair eyes
　　Than both your poets can in praise devise.

84°

Who is it that says most? Which can say more
Than this rich praise, that you alone are you?
In whose confine immurèd is the store
Which should example where your equal grew.°
Lean penury within that pen doth dwell 5
That to his subject lends not some small glory.
But he that writes of you, if he can tell
That you are you, so dignifies his story.
Let him but copy what in you is writ,
Not making worse what Nature made so clear, 10
And such a counterpart shall fame° his wit,
Making his style admirèd everywhere.
　　You to your beauteous blessings add a curse,
　　Being fond on° praise, which makes your praises
　　　　worse.

85

My tongue-tied Muse in manners holds her still,
While comments of your praise, richly compiled,
Reserve their character° with golden quill,
And precious phrase by all the Muses filed.°
I think good thoughts whilst other write good
　　words, 5
And, like unlettered clerk,° still cry "Amen"
To every hymn that able spirit affords,
In polished form of well-refinèd pen.
Hearing you praised, I say, "'Tis so, 'tis true,"
And to the most of praise add something more. 10
But that is in my thought, whose love to you,
Though words come hindmost, holds his rank be-
　　fore.
　　Then others for the breath of words respect,
　　Me for my dumb thoughts, speaking in effect.°

Sonnet 81: 1. Or: either.　3. hence: i.e., the epitaph.
11. rehearse: relate.
　Sonnet 82: 1. married: i.e., and therefore bound not to en-
courage others.　2. attaint: shame.　3. dedicated words: dedi-
cations (in books).　8. stamp: lit., that which makes an impres-
sion.　11. sympathized: expressed with feeling.　13. painting:
exaggeration.　14. abused: misused; i.e., your beauty needs no
exaggeration.
　Sonnet 83: (Continuing 82). 2. fair: beauty.　4. tender:
offering in repayment.　7. modern: slight. quill: pen.

11-12. For . . . tomb: I do not harm your beauty when I say
nothing, but others in trying to make it live destroy it.
　Sonnet 84: (Continuing 83). 3-4. In . . . grew: within your-
self is contained (immured; lit., walled in) the whole stock of
beauty from which other examples might have been chosen.
11. fame: make famous.　14. fond on: foolishly eager for.
　Sonnet 85: 3. Reserve . . . character: preserve this style
(character; lit., writing).　4. filed: polished.　6. clerk: The
clerk said the responses to the prayers read by the parson.
14. in effect: in act.

86°

Was it the proud full sail of his great verse,
Bound for the prize of all too precious you,
That did my ripe thoughts in my brain inhearse,°
Making their tomb the womb wherein they grew?
Was it his spirit, by spirits taught to write   5
Above a mortal pitch, that struck me dead?
No, neither he, nor his compeers° by night
Giving him aid, my verse astonishèd.
He, nor that affable familiar ghost°
Which nightly gulls° him with intelligence,°   10
As victors, of my silence cannot boast.
I was not sick of any fear from thence.
    But when your countenance filled up his line,
    Then lacked I matter. That enfeebled mine.

87

Farewell! Thou art too dear for my possessing,
And like enough thou know'st thy estimate.°
The charter° of thy worth gives thee releasing,
My bonds in thee are all determinate.°
For how do I hold thee but by thy granting?   5
And for that riches where is my deserving?
The cause of this fair gift in me is wanting,
And so my patent° back again is swerving.
Thyself thou gavest, thy own worth then not know-
        ing,
Or me, to whom thou gavest it, else mistaking.   10
So thy great gift, upon misprision° growing,
Comes home again, on better judgment making.
    Thus have I had thee, as a dream doth flatter,
    In sleep a king, but waking no such matter.

88

When thou shalt be disposed to set me light,°
And place my merit in the eye of scorn,
Upon thy side against myself I'll fight,
And prove thee virtuous, though thou art forsworn.
With mine own weakness being best acquainted,   5
Upon thy part I can set down a story
Of faults concealed, wherein I am attainted,°
That thou in losing me shalt win much glory.

Sonnet 86: (Continuing 85). The rival poet is by many be-
lieved to be George Chapman.   3. inhearse: entomb.   7. com-
peers: fellow students.   9. ghost: spirit.   10. gulls: cheats.
intelligence: news.
    Sonnet 87: 2. estimate: value.   3. charter: lit., a right to
perform certain actions.   4. determinate: ended.   8. patent:
privilege.   11. misprision: misunderstanding.
    Sonnet 88: 1. set me light: regard me lightly.   7. attainted:
dishonored.

And I by this will be a gainer too,
For bending all my loving thoughts on thee,   10
The injuries that to myself I do,
Doing thee vantage, double-vantage me.
    Such is my love, to thee I so belong
    That for thy right myself will bear all wrong.

89

Say that thou didst forsake me for some fault,
And I will comment upon that offense.
Speak of my lameness, and I straight will halt,
Against thy reasons making no defense.
Thou canst not, love, disgrace me half so ill,   5
To set a form° upon desirèd change,
As I'll myself disgrace. Knowing thy will,
I will acquaintance strangle° and look strange,
Be absent from thy walks, and in my tongue
Thy sweet belovèd name no more shall dwell,   10
Lest I, too much profane, should do it wrong,
And haply of our old acquaintance tell.
    For thee, against myself I'll vow debate,
    For I must ne'er love him whom thou dost hate.

90°

Then hate me when thou wilt. If ever, now,
Now while the world is bent my deeds to cross,
Join with the spite of fortune, make me bow,
And do not drop in for an afterloss.°
Ah, do not, when my heart hath 'scaped this sorrow,
Come in the rearward of a conquered woe.   6
Give not a windy night a rainy morrow,
To linger° out a purposed overthrow.
If thou wilt leave me, do not leave me last,
When other petty griefs have done their spite,   10
But in the onset come. So shall I taste
At first the very worst of fortune's might,
    And other strains of woe, which now seem woe,
    Compared with loss of thee will not seem so.

91

Some glory in their birth, some in their skill,
Some in their wealth, some in their body's force,
Some in their garments, though newfangled ill,°

Sonnet 89: 6. set a form: give a good appearance to
8. strangle: destroy.
    Sonnet 90: (Continuing 89). 4. afterloss: later misfortune.
8. linger: protract.
    Sonnet 91: 3. newfangled ill: i.e., the latest ugly fashion.

Some in their hawks and hounds, some in their
    horse.
And every humor° hath his adjunct° pleasure,   5
Wherein it finds a joy above the rest.
But these particulars are not my measure,
All these I better in one general best.
Thy love is better than high birth to me,
Richer than wealth, prouder than garments' cost,
Of more delight than hawks or horses be.   11
And having thee, of all men's pride I boast,
    Wretched in this alone, that thou mayst take
    All this away and me most wretched make.

92°

But do thy worst to steal thyself away,
For term of life thou art assurèd mine.
And life no longer than thy love will stay,
For it depends upon that love of thine.
Then need I not to fear the worst of wrongs,   5
When in the least of them my life hath end.
I see a better state to me belongs
Than that which on thy humor doth depend.
Thou canst not vex me with inconstant mind,
Since that my life on thy revolt doth lie.°   10
Oh, what a happy title do I find,
Happy to have thy love, happy to die!
    But what's so blessèd-fair that fears no blot?
    Thou mayst be false, and yet I know it not.

93

So shall I live, supposing thou art true,
Like a deceivèd husband. So love's face
May still seem love to me, though altered new,
Thy looks with me, thy heart in other place.
For there can live no hatred in thine eye,   5
Therefore in that I cannot know thy change.
In many's looks the false heart's history
Is writ in moods and frowns and wrinkles strange,
But Heaven in thy creation did decree
That in thy face sweet love should ever dwell,   10
Whate'er thy thoughts or thy heart's workings be,
Thy looks should nothing thence but sweetness tell.
    How like Eve's apple° doth thy beauty grow
    If thy sweet virtue answer not° thy show!

94

They that have power to hurt and will do none,
That do not do the thing they most do show,°
Who, moving others, are themselves as stone,
Unmovèd, cold, and to temptation slow —
They rightly do inherit Heaven's graces   5
And husband nature's riches from expense.°
They are the lords and owners of their faces,
Others but stewards° of their excellence.
The summer's flower is to the summer sweet,
Though to itself it only live and die,   10
But if that flower with base infection meet,
The basest weed outbraves his dignity.°
    For sweetest things turn sourest by their deeds.
    Lilies that fester smell far worse than weeds.

95

How sweet and lovely dost thou make the shame
Which, like a canker in the fragrant rose,
Doth spot the beauty of thy budding name!
Oh, in what sweets dost thou thy sins enclose!
That tongue that tells the story of thy days,   5
Making lascivious comments on thy sport,
Cannot dispraise but in a kind of praise.
Naming thy name blesses an ill report.
Oh, what a mansion have those vices got
Which for their habitation chose out thee,   10
Where beauty's veil doth cover every blot
And all things turn to fair that eyes can see!
    Take heed, dear heart, of this large privilege.°
    The hardest knife ill-used doth lose his edge.

96°

Some say thy fault is youth, some wantonness,
Some say thy grace is youth and gentle sport.
Both grace and faults are loved of more and less,
Thou makest faults graces that to thee resort.
As on the finger of a thronèd queen   5
The basest jewel will be well esteemed,
So are those errors that in thee are seen
To truths translated° and for true things deemed.
How many lambs might the stern wolf betray
If like a lamb he could his looks translate!°   10
How many gazers mightst thou lead away
If thou wouldst use the strength of all thy state!
    But do not so. I love thee in such sort
    As thou being mine, mine is thy good report.

5. **humor:** whim. See App. 3. **adjunct:** annexed.
    Sonnet 92: (Continuing 91). 9–10. **Thou . . . lie:** you cannot
torment me by being inconstant for when you desert me (*revolt*),
I die.
    Sonnet 93: 13. **Eve's apple:** i.e., lovely to look upon but dis-
astrous in its effects. 14. **answer not:** does not correspond with.

    Sonnet 94: 2. **show:** seem to do. 6. **expense:** waste.
8. **stewards:** hired overseers. 12. **dignity:** worth.
    Sonnet 95: 13. **large privilege:** freedom to go astray.
    Sonnet 96: (Continuing 95). 8. **translated:** transformed.
10. **like . . . translate:** make himself like a lamb.

97

How like a winter hath my absence been
From thee, the pleasure of the fleeting year!
What freezings have I felt, what dark days seen!
What old December's bareness everywhere!
And yet this time removed° was summer's time,　5
The teeming autumn, big with rich increase,
Bearing the wanton burden of the prime,
Like widowed wombs after their lords' decease.
Yet this abundant issue seemed to me
But hope of orphans and unfathered fruit,°　10
For summer and his pleasures wait on thee,
And, thou away, the very birds are mute,
　　Or if they sing, 'tis with so dull a cheer
　　That leaves look pale, dreading the winter's near.

98

From you have I been absent in the spring,
When proud-pied° April, dressed in all his trim,
Hath put a spirit of youth in everything,
That heavy Saturn° laughed and leaped with him.
Yet nor the lays of birds, nor the sweet smell　5
Of different flowers in odor and in hue,
Could make me any summer's story tell,
Or from their proud lap pluck them where they
　　grew.
Nor did I wonder at the lily's white,
Nor praise the deep vermilion in the rose.　10
They were but sweet, but figures of delight,
Drawn after you, you pattern of all those.°
　　Yet seemed it winter still and, you away,
　　As with your shadow° I with these did play.

99°

The forward° violet thus did I chide:
Sweet thief, whence didst thou steal thy sweet that
　　smells
If not from my love's breath? The purple pride
Which on thy soft cheek for complexion dwells
In my love's veins thou hast too grossly dyed.　5
The lily I condemnèd for thy hand,°
And buds of marjoram had stol'n thy hair.
The roses fearfully on thorns did stand,°
One blushing shame, another white despair,
A third, nor red nor white, had stol'n of both　10
And to his robbery had annexed thy breath.
But for his theft, in pride of all his growth
A vengeful canker eat him up to death.
　　More flowers I noted, yet I none could see
　　But sweet or color it had stol'n from thee.　15

100

Where art thou, Muse, that thou forget'st so long
To speak of that which gives thee all thy might?
Spend'st thou thy fury° on some worthless song,
Darkening thy power to lend base subjects light?
Return, forgetful Muse, and straight redeem　5
In gentle numbers time so idly spent,
Sing to the ear that doth thy lays esteem
And gives thy pen both skill and argument.
Rise, resty° Muse, my love's sweet face survey,
If Time have any wrinkle graven there.　10
If any, be a satire to° decay,
And make Time's spoils despisèd everywhere.
　　Give my love fame faster than Time wastes life.
　　So thou prevent'st° his scythe and crooked knife.

101°

O truant Muse, what shall be thy amends
For thy neglect of truth in beauty dyed?
Both truth and beauty on my love depends,
So dost thou too, and therein dignified.°
Make answer, Muse. Wilt thou not haply say,　5
"Truth needs no color with his color fixed,
Beauty no pencil, beauty's truth to lay,°
But best is best if never intermixed"?
Because he needs no praise, wilt thou be dumb?
Excuse not silence so, for 't lies in thee　10
To make him much outlive a gilded tomb
And to be praised of ages yet to be.
　　Then do thy office, Muse. I teach thee how
　　To make him seem long hence as he shows now.

Sonnet 97: 5. removed: of absence. 9–10. Yet . . . fruit: yet this promise of plenty seemed to me (like the widow's posthumous child) to be a promise also of children who should be fatherless orphans.

Sonnet 98: 2. proud-pied: exulting in the variety of its colors. 4. Saturn: the planet. Those born under its influence were heavy and saturnine. 11–12. They . . . those: i.e., their sweetness was nothing in itself; it was a symbol of you, the pattern of all loveliness. 14. shadow: symbol. See Sonnet 53.

Sonnet 99: (Continuing 98). This sonnet contains 15 lines, a fifth line having been added to the first quatrain. 1. forward: precocious. The violet is one of the first flowers to appear in the spring.

6. condemned . . . hand: accused of stealing the whiteness of your hand. 8. on . . . stand: i.e., uneasily, like anxious thieves. Cf. the phrase "on tenterhooks."

Sonnet 100: 3. fury: enthusiasm. 9. resty: sluggish. 11. be . . . to: write satires on. 14. prevent'st: anticipate.

Sonnet 101: (Continuing 100). 4. dignified: are dignified. 7. lay: paint.

102

My love is strengthened, though more weak in seeming,
I love not less, though less the show appear.
That love is merchandised° whose rich esteeming°
The owner's tongue doth publish everywhere.
Our love was new, and then but in the spring,   5
When I was wont to greet it with my lays,
As Philomel° in summer's front° doth sing,
And stops her pipe in growth of riper days.
Not that the summer is less pleasant now
Than when her mournful hymns did hush the night,
But that wild music burdens every bough,   11
And sweets grown common lose their dear delight.
  Therefore, like her, I sometime hold my tongue,
  Because I would not dull you with my song.

103

Alack, what poverty my Muse brings forth,
That having such a scope to show her pride,
The argument, all bare, is of more worth
Than when it hath my added praise beside!
Oh, blame me not if I no more can write!   5
Look in your glass, and there appears a face
That overgoes° my blunt invention quite,
Dulling my lines and doing me disgrace.
Were it not sinful then, striving to mend,
To mar the subject that before was well?   10
For to no other pass° my verses tend
Than of your graces and your gifts to tell,
  And more, much more, than in my verse can sit,
  Your own glass shows you when you look in it.

104°

To me, fair friend, you never can be old,
For as you were when first your eye I eyed,
Such seems your beauty still. Three winters cold
Have from the forests shook three summers' pride,
Three beauteous springs to yellow autumn turned
In process of the seasons have I seen,   6
Three April perfumes in three hot Junes burned,
Since first I saw you fresh, which yet are green.
Ah, yet doth beauty, like a dial hand,°
Steal from his figure, and no pace perceived.   10

So your sweet hue, which methinks still doth stand,
Hath motion, and mine eye may be deceived.
  For fear of which, hear this, thou age unbred —
  Ere you were born was beauty's summer dead.

105

Let not my love be called idolatry,
Nor my belovèd as an idol show,°
Since all alike my songs and praises be
To one, of one, still such, and ever so.
Kind is my love today, tomorrow kind,   5
Still constant in a wondrous excellence,
Therefore my verse to constancy confined,
One thing expressing, leaves out difference.°
"Fair, kind, and true" is all my argument,
"Fair, kind, and true" varying to other words,   10
And in this change° is my invention spent,
Three themes in one, which wondrous scope affords.
  "Fair, kind, and true" have often lived alone,
  Which three till now never kept seat in one.

106

When in the chronicle of wasted° time
I see descriptions of the fairest wights,°
And beauty making beautiful old rhyme
In praise of ladies dead and lovely knights,
Then, in the blazon° of sweet beauty's best,   5
Of hand, of foot, of lip, of eye, of brow,
I see their antique pen would have expressed
Even such a beauty as you master now.
So all their praises are but prophecies
Of this our time, all you prefiguring,   10
And, for° they looked but with divining° eyes,
They had not skill enough your worth to sing.
  For we, which now behold these present days,
  Have eyes to wonder, but lack tongues to praise.

107

Not mine own fears, nor the prophetic soul
Of the wide world dreaming on things to come,
Can yet the lease of my true love control,

Sonnet 102: 3. merchandised: bought and sold. esteeming:
value.   7. Philomel: the nightingale, whose song is chiefly heard
in May. front: early days.
  Sonnet 103: 7. overgoes: surpasses.   11. pass: end.
  Sonnet 104: In this sonnet the poet shows that the friendship
has lasted for three years.   9. like . . . hand: like the stealthy
movement of the shadow on the sundial.

Sonnet 105: 2. show: appear.   8. difference: the quality
which distinguishes different specimens of the same kind.
11. change: variety; lit., the different orders in which a peal of
bells can be rung. See App. 19.
  Sonnet 106: 1. wasted: passed, dead and gone.   2. wights:
men, a poetic word.   5. blazon: praise; lit., heraldic description
of a coat of arms.   11. for: except that. divining: foreseeing.

Supposed as forfeit to a cónfined doom.°
The mortal moon hath her eclipse endured,°   5
And the sad augurs° mock their own presage.
Incertainties now crown themselves assured,
And peace proclaims olives° of endless age.
Now with the drops of this most balmy time
My love looks fresh, and Death to me subscribes,°
Since, spite of him, I'll live in this poor rhyme   11
While he insults° o'er dull and speechless° tribes.
    And thou in this shalt find thy monument,
    When tyrants' crests and tombs of brass are spent.

108

What's in the brain that ink may character°
Which hath not figured to thee my true spirit?
What's new to speak, what new to register,
That may express my love, or thy dear merit?
Nothing, sweet boy. But yet, like prayers divine,   5
I must each day say o'er the very same,
Counting no old thing old, thou mine, I thine,
Even as when first I hallowed° thy fair name.
So that eternal love in love's fresh case°
Weighs not the dust and injury of age,   10
Nor gives to necessary wrinkles place,
But makes antiquity° for aye his page,°
    Finding the first conceit° of love there bred
    Where time and outward form would show it
      dead.

109

Oh, never say that I was false of heart,
Though absence seemed my flame to qualify.°
As easy might I from myself depart
As from my soul,° which in thy breast doth lie.
That is my home of love. If I have ranged,°   5
Like him that travels, I return again,

Just° to the time, not with the time exchanged,°
So that myself bring water for my stain.
Never believe, though in my nature reigned
All frailties that besiege all kinds of blood,   10
That it could so preposterously be stained,
To leave for nothing all thy sum of good.
    For nothing this wide universe I call,
    Save thou, my rose.° In it thou art my all.

110°

Alas, 'tis true I have gone here and there,
And made myself a motley° to the view,
Gored mine own thoughts, sold cheap what is most
    dear,
Made old offenses of affections new.°
Most true it is that I have looked on truth   5
Askance and strangely. But, by all above,
These blenches° gave my heart another youth,
And worse essays proved thee my best of love.
Now all is done, have what shall have no end.
Mine appetite I never more will grind   10
On newer proof, to try° an older friend,
A god in love, to whom I am confined.
    Then give me welcome, next my heaven the best,
    Even to thy pure and most most loving breast.

111

Oh, for my sake do you with Fortune chide,
The guilty goddess of my harmful deeds,
That did not better for my life provide
Than public means which public manners breeds.°
Thence comes it that my name receives a brand,°   5
And almost thence my nature is subdued
To what it works in, like the dyer's hand.
Pity me, then, and wish I were renewed,°
Whilst, like a willing patient, I will drink
Potions of eisel 'gainst my strong infection.°   10
No bitterness that I will bitter think,
Nor double penance, to correct correction.
    Pity me, then, dear friend, and I assure ye
    Even that your pity is enough to cure me.

Sonnet 107: 4. Supposed ... doom: if the *lease* is forfeit, the meaning of the quatrain is "those who declared that our love was ended have proved bad prophets." If *love* (i.e., my friend) is forfeit, the line means "believed to be condemned to imprisonment." **5. The ... endured:** The mortal moon is Queen Elizabeth, but it is disputable whether the line means "has passed through an eclipse and emerged safely" or has been permanently eclipsed; i.e., has died. The Queen died on March 24, 1603. **6. sad augurs:** i.e., those who prophesied disaster. **8. olives:** The olive is the symbol of peace. **10. subscribes:** yields. **12. insults:** triumphs. **speechless:** who cannot express themselves.
    Sonnet 108: 1. character: write. **8. hallowed:** made holy. **9. fresh case:** renewal. **12. antiquity:** old age. **page:** boy servant. **13. conceit:** thought.
    Sonnet 109: 2. qualify: moderate. **4. my soul:** i.e., you my love. Cf. *T Night*, I.v.288. **5. ranged:** roamed.

7. Just: exactly. **exchanged:** changed. **14. rose:** See Sonnet 1.2.
    Sonnet 110: (Continuing 109). **2. motley:** professional jester; lit., the fool's particolored dress. **4. Made ... new:** offended old friends by making new ones. **7. blenches:** glances aside. **11. try:** test.
    Sonnet 111: (Continuing 110). **4. public ... breeds:** living on vulgar applause which produces vulgar manners. **5. brand:** mark of shame. **8. renewed:** revived. **10. eisel ... infection:** vinegar, drunk as an antidote to the plague (*infection*).

112°

Your love and pity doth the impression fill°
Which vulgar scandal stamped upon my brow.
For what care I who calls me well or ill,
So you o'ergreen° my bad, my good allow?
You are my all the world, and I must strive   5
To know my shames and praises from your tongue,
None else to me, nor I to none alive,
That my steeled sense or changes right or wrong.°
In so profound abysm I throw all care
Of° others' voices, that my adder's sense°   10
To critic and to flatterer stoppèd are.
Mark how with my neglect I do dispense.°
   You are so strongly in my purpose bred
   That all the world besides methinks are dead.

113

Since I left you mine eye is in my mind,
And that which governs me to go about
Doth part his function° and is partly blind,
Seems seeing, but effectually° is out.
For it no form delivers to the heart   5
Of bird, of flower, or shape, which it doth latch.°
Of his quick objects hath the mind no part,
Nor his own vision holds what it doth catch.
For if it see the rudest or gentlest sight,
The most sweet favor° or deformed'st creature, 10
The mountain or the sea, the day or night,
The crow or dove, it shapes them to your feature.
   Incapable of more, replete with you,
   My most true mind thus maketh mine° untrue.

114°

Or whether° doth my mind, being crowned with
      you,
Drink up the monarch's plague, this flattery?°
Or whether shall I say mine eye saith true,
And that your love taught it this alchemy,°

To make of monsters and things indigest°   5
Such cherubins as your sweet self resemble,
Creating every bad a perfect best
As fast as objects to his beams° assemble?
Oh, 'tis the first, 'tis flattery in my seeing,
And my great mind most kingly drinks it up.   10
Mine eye well knows what with his gust° is 'gree-
      ing,
And to his palate doth prepare the cup.
   If it be poisoned, 'tis the lesser sin
   That mine eye loves it and doth first begin.

115

Those lines that I before have writ do lie,
Even those that said I could not love you dearer.
Yet then my judgment knew no reason why
My most full flame should afterward burn clearer.
But reckoning Time,° whose millioned accidents 5
Creep in 'twixt vows, and change decrees of kings,
Tan° sacred beauty, blunt the sharp'st intents,
Divert strong minds to the course of altering
      things —
Alas, why, fearing of Time's tyranny,
Might I not then say, "Now I love you best,"   10
When I was certain o'er incertainty,
Crowning the present, doubting of the rest?
   Love is a babe, then might I not say so,
   To give full growth to that which still doth grow?

116

Let me not to the marriage of true minds
Admit impediments. Love is not love
Which alters when it alteration finds,
Or bends with the remover to remove.°
Oh no! It is an ever-fixèd mark   5
That looks on tempests and is never shaken.
It is the star to every wandering bark,
Whose worth's unknown, although his height be
      taken.
Love's not Time's fool,° though rosy lips and cheeks
Within his bending sickle's compass come.   10
Love alters not with his brief hours and weeks,
But bears it out even to the edge of doom.°
   If this be error and upon me proved,
   I never writ, nor no man ever loved.

Sonnet 112: (Continuing 111). 1. impression fill: take away
the mark.   4. o'ergreen: cover over (as with new grass).
7–8. None . . . wrong: there is no one else for whom I care or
who cares for me that can change my firm feelings either to right
or wrong.   10. Of: for. adder's sense: an echo of Psalm 58:
The poison of the wicked "is like the poison of a serpent; they
are like the deaf adder that stoppeth her ear."   12. with . . .
dispense: I excuse my neglect.

Sonnet 113: 3. part . . . function: divides its functions; i.e.,
the eye's function is to perceive objects and convey the impres-
sion to the mind, but the poet's eye is now only able to perceive
without conveying.   4. effectually: actually.   6. latch: lay hold
of.   10. favor: face.   14. mine: i.e., eye.

Sonnet 114: (Continuing 113). 1. Or whether: is it that.
2. flattery: i.e., dressing up the truth to make it more palatable.
4. alchemy: power to transform. See App. 21.

5. indigest: shapeless.   8. beams: See Sonnet 20.6,n.   11. gust:
taste.

Sonnet 115: 5. reckoning Time: i.e., remembering Time's
power.   7. Tan: make brown.

Sonnet 116: 4. Or . . . remove: or wishes to change when the
loved one is inconstant.   9. Time's fool: i.e., mocked by Time.
Cf. I Hen IV, V.iv.81.   12. doom: Doomsday.

117

Accuse me thus: that I have scanted° all
Wherein I should your great deserts repay,
Forgot upon your dearest love to call,
Whereto all bonds do tie me day by day.
That I have frequent been with unknown minds, 5
And given to time your own dear-purchased right.
That I have hoisted sail to all the winds
Which should transport me farthest from your sight.
Book° both my willfulness and errors down,
And on just proof surmise accumulate.° 10
Bring me within the level° of your frown,
But shoot not at me in your wakened hate,
    Since my appeal says I did strive to prove
    The constancy and virtue of your love.

118°

Like as, to make our appetites more keen,
With eager° compounds we our palate urge—
As to prevent° our maladies unseen
We sicken° to shun sickness when we purge—
Even so, being full of your ne'er-cloying sweetness,
To bitter sauces did I frame my feeding, 6
And sick of welfare found a kind of meetness°
To be diseased, ere that there was true needing.
Thus policy in love, to anticipate
The ills that were not, grew to faults assured, 10
And brought to medicine° a healthful state,
Which, rank° of goodness, would by ill be cured.
    But thence I learn, and find the lesson true,
    Drugs poison him that so fell sick of you.

119

What potions have I drunk of Siren° tears,
Distilled from limbecks° foul as Hell within,
Applying fears to hopes and hopes to fears,
Still losing when I saw myself to win!
What wretched errors hath my heart committed 5
Whilst it hath thought itself so blessèd never!
How have mine eyes out of their spheres been fitted°
In the distraction of this madding fever!
O benefit of ill! Now I find true

That better is by evil still made better, 10
And ruined love, when it is built anew,
Grows fairer than at first, more strong, far greater.
    So I return rebuked to my content,
    And gain by ill thrice more than I have spent.

120

That you were once unkind befriends me now,
And for that sorrow which I then did feel
Needs must I under my transgression bow,
Unless my nerves° were brass or hammered steel.
For if you were by my unkindness shaken, 5
As I by yours, you've passed a hell of time,
And I, a tyrant, have no leisure taken
To weigh how once I suffered in your crime.
Oh, that our night of woe might have remembered°
My deepest sense, how hard true sorrow hits, 10
And soon to you, as you to me, then tendered
The humble salve° which wounded bosoms fits!
    But that your trespass now becomes a fee,
    Mine ransoms yours, and yours must ransom me.

121

'Tis better to be vile than vile esteemed,
When not to be receives reproach of being,
And the just pleasure lost, which is so° deemed
Not by our feeling, but by others' seeing.
For why should others' false adulterate eyes 5
Give salutation to° my sportive blood?
Or on my frailties why are frailer spies,
Which in their wills count bad what I think good?
No, I am that I am, and they that level
At my abuses reckon up their own. 10
I may be straight, though they themselves be bevel,°
By their rank thoughts my deeds must not be shown,
    Unless this general evil they maintain,
    All men are bad and in their badness reign.

122°

Thy gift, thy tables,° are within my brain
Full charactered° with lasting memory,
Which shall above that idle rank° remain
Beyond all date, even to eternity.

Sonnet 117: 1. scanted: neglected. 9. Book: record as a debit. 10. on . . . accumulate: add suspicion to proof. 11. level: aim.
Sonnet 118: (Continuing 117 but in the medical imagery of purging). 2. eager: bitter. 3. prevent: forestall. 4. sicken: deliberately make ourselves ill by taking medicine. 7. meetness: fitness. 11. brought to medicine: caused to be sick. 12. rank: overfull.
Sonnet 119: 1. Siren: temptress. The Sirens were creatures who by their beautiful songs lured mariners to their destruction. 2. limbecks: alembics, stills. 7. fitted: convulsed.

Sonnet 120: 4. nerves: sinews. 9. remembered: reminded. 12. salve: healing ointment.
Sonnet 121: 3. so: i.e., vile. 6. Give . . . to: salute as one of themselves. 11. bevel: slanting.
Sonnet 122: The poet excuses himself for giving away his friend's gift of a notebook. 1. tables: notebook. 2. charactered: inscribed. 3. idle rank: empty series (of leaves).

Or, at the least, so long as brain and heart   5
Have faculty by nature to subsist,
Till each to razed oblivion yield his part
Of thee, thy record never can be missed.
That poor retention° could not so much hold,
Nor need I tallies° thy dear love to score.°   10
Therefore to give them from me° was I bold,
To trust those tables that receive thee more.
    To keep an adjunct° to remember thee
    Were to import° forgetfulness in me.

123

No, Time, thou shalt not boast that I do change.
Thy pyramids built up with newer might
To me are nothing novel, nothing strange,
They are but dressings of a former sight.°
Our dates are brief, and therefore we admire°   5
What thou dost foist upon us that is old,
And rather make them born to our desire
Than think that we before have heard them told.
Thy registers and thee I both defy,
Not wondering at the present nor the past,   10
For thy recórds and what we see doth lie,
Made more or less by thy continual haste.
    This I do vow, and this shall ever be,
    I will be true, despite thy scythe and thee.

124

If my dear love were but the child of state,°
It might for Fortune's bastard be unfathered,°
As subject to Time's love or to Time's hate,
Weeds among weeds, or flowers with flowers
    gathered.
No, it was builded far from accident,   5
It suffers not in smiling pomp, nor falls
Under the blow of thrallèd discontent,°
Whereto the inviting time our fashion calls.°
It fears not policy, that heretic,
Which works on leases of short-numbered hours,
But all alone stands hugely politic,   11
That it nor grows with heat nor drowns with show-
    ers.

To this I witness call the fools of time,
Which die for goodness, who have lived for
    crime.°

125°

Were 't aught to me I bore the canopy,°
With my extern the outward honoring,
Or laid great bases for eternity,
Which prove more short than waste or ruining?
Have I not seen dwellers on form and favor°   5
Lose all, and more, by paying too much rent,
For compound sweet forgoing simple savor,
Pitiful thrivers, in their gazing spent?°
No, let me be obsequious in thy heart,
And take thou my oblation, poor but free,   10
Which is not mixed with seconds,° knows no art
But mutual render,° only me for thee.
    Hence, thou suborned° informer! A true soul
    When most impeached stands least in thy control.

126°

O thou, my lovely boy, who in thy power
Dost hold Time's fickle glass, his sickle, hour,
Who hast by waning grown,° and therein show'st
Thy lovers withering as thy sweet self grow'st,
If Nature, sovereign mistress over wrack,°   5
As thou goest onwards, still will pluck thee back,
She keeps thee to this purpose, that her skill
May time disgrace and wretched minutes kill.
Yet fear her, O thou minion° of her pleasure!
She may detain, but not still keep, her treasure.   10
Her audit, though delayed, answered must be,
And her quietus° is to render° thee.

127°

In the old age black was not counted fair,
Or if it were, it bore not beauty's name,

13–14. fools . . . crime: those foolish heretics who when executed
for crime declare that they are dying in a holy cause.
    Sonnet 125: (Continuing 124). 1. bore . . . canopy: paid out-
ward signs of respect. On state occasions, the sovereign walked or
was carried under a canopy carried by courtiers. See Pl. 3b.
5. dwellers . . . favor: hopeful flatterers who pay much attention
to ceremony and signs of favor.   8. Pitiful . . . spent: disap-
pointed losers who lose all while they gape for promotion.
11. seconds: ulterior aims.   12. render: surrender, exchange.
13. suborned: perjured.
    Sonnet 126: The last of the Sonnets to the fair youth, and
probably an envoy (or conclusion) to the whole series, written in
six rhymed couplets.   3. waning grown: i.e., growing more (and
not less) beautiful as you grow older.   5. wrack: ruin.   9. min-
ion: darling.   12. quietus: closing of the account. render: use
you as payment.
    Sonnet 127: The first of the series to the dark mistress.

9. retention: container; i.e., the book.   10. tallies: A tally was
a stick on which notches were cut as a record of sums of money
owed. score: record (a debt).   11. give . . . me: give away.
13. adjunct: object.   14. import: imply.
    Sonnet 123: 4. dressings . . . sight: repetitions of what we
have seen before.   5. admire: wonder at.
    Sonnet 124: 1. child of state: born of circumstances; i.e.,
accidental.   2. Fortune's . . . unfathered: be neglected as a mere
bastard.   7. thralled discontent: discontent held in subjugation.
8. the . . . calls: i.e., the discontent which is fashionable nowadays.

But now is black beauty's successive° heir,
And beauty slandered with a bastard shame.
For since each hand hath put on Nature's power, 5
Fairing the foul° with art's false borrowed face,
Sweet beauty hath no name, no holy bower,
But is profaned, if not lives in disgrace.
Therefore my mistress' eyes are raven-black,
Her eyes so suited,° and they mourners seem 10
At such who, not born fair, no beauty lack,°
Slandering creation with a false esteem.
　　Yet so they mourn, becoming of their woe,
　　That every tongue says beauty should look so.

128

How oft, when thou, my music, music play'st
Upon that blessèd wood° whose motion sounds
With thy sweet fingers, when thou gently sway'st
The wiry concord° that mine ear confounds,
Do I envy those jacks° that nimble leap 5
To kiss the tender inward of thy hand
Whilst my poor lips, which should that harvest reap,
At the wood's boldness by thee blushing stand!
To be so tickled, they would change their state
And situation with those dancing chips 10
O'er whom thy fingers walk with gentle gait,
Making dead wood more blest than living lips.
　　Since saucy jacks so happy are in this,
　　Give them thy fingers, me thy lips to kiss.

129

The expense of spirit in a waste of shame
Is lust in action, and till action, lust
Is perjured, murderous, bloody, full of blame,
Savage, extreme, rude, cruel, not to trust,
Enjoyed no sooner but despisèd straight, 5
Past reason hunted, and no sooner had,
Past reason hated, as a swallowed bait,
On purpose laid to make the taker mad.
Mad in pursuit, and in possession so,
Had, having, and in quest to have, extreme, 10
A bliss in proof, and proved,° a very woe.
Before, a joy proposed, behind, a dream.
　　All this the world well knows, yet none knows
　　　　well
　　To shun the Heaven that leads men to this Hell.

130

My mistress' eyes are nothing like the sun,
Coral is far more red than her lips' red.
If snow be white, why then her breasts are dun,
If hairs be wires, black wires grow on her head.
I have seen roses damasked,° red and white, 5
But no such roses see I in her cheeks.
And in some perfumes is there more delight
Than in the breath that from my mistress reeks.
I love to hear her speak, yet well I know
That music hath a far more pleasing sound. 10
I grant I never saw a goddess go,°
My mistress, when she walks, treads on the ground.
　　And yet, by Heaven, I think my love as rare
　　As any she belied with false compare.

131

Thou art as tyrannous, so as thou art,°
As those whose beauties proudly make them cruel.
For well thou know'st to my dear doting heart
Thou art the fairest and most precious jewel.
Yet, in good faith, some say that thee behold, 5
Thy face hath not the power to make love groan.
To say they err I dare not be so bold,
Although I swear it to myself alone.
And to be sure that is not false I swear,
A thousand groans, but thinking on thy face, 10
One on another's neck,° do witness bear
Thy face is fairest in my judgment's place.
　　In nothing art thou black save in thy deeds,
　　And thence this slander, as I think, proceeds.

132

Thine eyes I love, and they, as pitying me,
Knowing thy heart torments me with disdain,
Have put on black and loving mourners be,
Looking with pretty ruth° upon my pain.
And truly not the morning sun of heaven 5
Better becomes the gray cheeks of the east,
Nor that full star that ushers in the even
Doth half that glory to the sober west,
As those two mourning eyes become thy face.
Oh, let it then as well beseem° thy heart 10
To mourn for me, since mourning doth thee grace,
And suit thy pity° like in every part.
　　Then will I swear beauty herself is black,
　　And all they foul that thy complexion lack.

3. **successive:** in order of succession. 6. **Fairing . . . foul:** making beautiful the ugly. 10. **suited:** matching. 11. **no . . . lack:** i.e., because they have beautified themselves.
　Sonnet 128: 2. **wood:** i.e., the keys of the virginal. See Pl. 19f.
　4. **wiry concord:** harmony of wires. 5. **jacks:** keys.
　Sonnet 129: 11. **proved:** experienced.

　Sonnet 130: 5. **damasked:** variegated pink and white. 11. **go:** walk.
　Sonnet 131: 1. **so . . . art:** being what you are. 11. **One . . . neck:** one after the other.
　Sonnet 132: 4. **ruth:** pity. 10. **beseem:** be fitting for. 12. **suit . . . pity:** i.e., let your pity also wear black.

133°

Beshrew° that heart that makes my heart to groan
For that deep wound it gives my friend and me!
Is 't not enough to torture me alone,
But slave to slavery my sweet'st friend must be?
Me from myself thy cruel eye hath taken,   5
And my next self thou harder hast engrossed.°
Of him, myself, and thee I am forsaken,
A torment thrice threefold thus to be crossed.
Prison my heart in thy steel bosom's ward,°
But then my friend's heart let my poor heart bail.
Whoe'er keeps me, let my heart be his guard,   11
Thou canst not then use rigor in my jail.
    And yet thou wilt, for I, being pent in thee,
    Perforce am thine, and all that is in me.

134°

So, now I have confessed that he is thine
And I myself am mortgaged to thy will,
Myself I'll forfeit, so that other mine°
Thou wilt restore, to be my comfort still.
But thou wilt not, nor he will not be free,   5
For thou art covetous and he is kind.
He learned but surety-like to write° for me,
Under that bond that him as fast doth bind.
The statute of thy beauty thou wilt take,
Thou usurer, that put'st forth all to use,   10
And sue a friend came° debtor for my sake,
So him I lose through my unkind abuse.
    Him have I lost, thou hast both him and me.
    He pays the whole, and yet am I not free.

135

Whoever hath her wish, thou hast thy "Will,"°
And "Will" to boot,° and "Will" in overplus.
More than enough am I that vex thee still,
To thy sweet will making addition thus.
Wilt thou, whose will is large and spacious,   5
Not once vouchsafe to hide my will in thine?
Shall will in others seem right gracious
And in my will no fair acceptance shine?
The sea, all water, yet receives rain still,
And in abundance addeth to his store.   10
So thou, being rich in "Will," add to thy "Will"

One will of mine, to make thy large "Will" more.
    Let no unkind, no fair beseechers kill.
    Think all but one, and me in that one "Will."

136°

If thy soul check° thee that I come so near,
Swear to thy blind soul that I was thy "Will,"
And will, thy soul knows, is admitted there.
Thus far for love, my love suit, sweet, fulfill.
"Will" will fulfill the treasure of thy love —   5
Aye, fill it full with wills, and my will one.
In things of great receipt° with ease we prove
Among a number one is reckoned none.
Then in the number let me pass untold,
Though in thy store's account I one must be,   10
For nothing hold me, so it please thee hold
That nothing me, a something sweet to thee.
    Make but my name° thy love, and love that still,
    And then thou lovest me, for my name is "Will."

137

Thou blind fool, Love, what dost thou to mine eyes,
That they behold, and see not what they see?
They know what beauty is, see where it lies,
Yet what the best is take the worst to be.°
If eyes, corrupt by overpartial looks,   5
Be anchored in the bay where all men ride,
Why of eyes' falsehood° hast thou forgèd hooks
Whereto the judgment of my heart is tied?
Why should my heart think that a several° plot
Which my heart knows the wide world's common
        place?   10
Or mine eyes seeing this, say this is not,
To put fair truth upon so foul a face?
    In things right true my heart and eyes have erred,
    And to this false plague are they now transferred.

138

When my love swears that she is made of truth,
I do believe her, though I know she lies,
That she might think me some untutored youth,
Unlearnèd in the world's false subtleties.
Thus vainly thinking that she thinks me young,   5
Although she knows my days are past the best,
Simply I credit her false-speaking tongue.
On both sides thus is simple truth suppressed.

Sonnet 133: Cf. Sonnets 40, 42. 1. Beshrew: ill luck take.
6. engrossed: bought up wholesale. 9. ward: cell.
Sonnet 134: (Continuing 133). 3. other mine: my other self.
7. surety-like to write: to sign as surety. 11. came: who became.
Sonnet 135: 1. Will: desire, and Will Shakespeare. 2. to
boot: in addition.

Sonnet 136: (Continuing 135). 1. check: rebuke. 7. receipt:
capacity. 13. my name: i.e., Will (desire).
Sonnet 137: 4. what . . . be: take worst for the best. 7. false-
hood: deception. 9. several: private.

But wherefore says she not she is unjust?°
And wherefore say not I that I am old?   10
Oh, love's best habit° is in seeming trust,
And age in love loves not to have years told.°
 Therefore I lie with her and she with me,
 And in our faults by lies we flattered be.

139

Oh, call not me to justify the wrong
That thy unkindness lays upon my heart.
Wound me not with thine eye, but with thy tongue.
Use power with power,° and slay me not by art.°
Tell me thou lovest elsewhere, but in my sight,   5
Dear heart, forbear to glance thine eye aside.
What need'st thou wound with cunning when thy
  might
Is more than my o'erpressed defense can bide?
Let me excuse thee. Ah, my love well knows
Her pretty looks have been mine enemies,   10
And therefore from my face she turns my foes,
That they elsewhere might dart their injuries.
 Yet do not so, but since I am near slain,
 Kill me outright with looks, and rid my pain.

140

Be wise as thou art cruel. Do not press
My tongue-tied patience with too much disdain,
Lest sorrow lend me words and words express
The manner of my pity-wanting° pain.
If I might teach thee wit, better it were,   5
Though not to love, yet, love, to tell me so,
As testy sick men, when their deaths be near,
No news but health from their physicians know.°
For if I should despair, I should grow mad,
And in my madness might speak ill of thee.   10
Now this ill-wresting° world is grown so bad,
Mad slanderers by mad ears believèd be.
 That I may not be so, nor thou belied,
 Bear thine eyes straight, though thy proud heart
  go wide.

141

In faith, I do not love thee with mine eyes,
For they in thee a thousand errors note,
But 'tis my heart that loves what they despise,

Who, in despite of view, is pleased to dote.
Nor are mine ears with thy tongue's tune delighted,
Nor tender feeling, to base touches prone,   6
Nor taste, nor smell, desire to be invited
To any sensual feast with thee alone.
But my five wits nor my five senses can
Dissuade one foolish heart from serving thee   10
Who leaves unswayed° the likeness of a man,
Thy proud heart's slave and vassal° wretch to be.
 Only my plague thus far I count my gain,
 That she that makes me sin awards me pain.

142

Love is my sin, and thy dear virtue hate,
Hate of my sin, grounded on sinful loving.
Oh, but with mine compare thou thine own state,
And thou shalt find it merits not reproving,
Or if it do, not from those lips of thine,   5
That have profaned their scarlet ornaments
And sealed false bonds of love as oft as mine,
Robbed others' beds' revénues of their rents.
Be it lawful I love thee, as thou lovest those
Whom thine eyes woo as mine importune thee.   10
Root pity in thy heart, that, when it grows,
Thy pity may deserve to pitied be.
 If thou dost seek to have what thou dost hide,°
 By self-example mayst thou be denied!

143

Lo, as a careful housewife runs to catch
One of her feathered creatures broke away,
Sets down her babe, and makes all swift dispatch
In pursuit of the thing she would have stay
Whilst her neglected child holds her in chase,   5
Cries to catch her whose busy care is bent
To follow that which flies before her face,
Not prizing her poor infant's discontent —
So runn'st thou after that which flies from thee
Whilst I thy babe chase thee afar behind.   10
But if thou catch thy hope, turn back to me,
And play the mother's part, kiss me, be kind.
 So will I pray that thou mayst have thy " Will,"
 If thou turn back and my loud crying still.

144

Two loves I have of comfort and despair,
Which like two spirits do suggest° me still.
The better angel is a man right fair,

Sonnet 138: 9. unjust: untrue. 11. habit: garment. 12. told: counted.
Sonnet 139: 4. with power: powerfully. art: cunning; i.e., say outright that you do not love me.
Sonnet 140: 4. pity-wanting: lacking pity. 8. know: learn.
11. ill-wresting: that puts an evil interpretation on everything.

Sonnet 141: 11. unswayed: without self-control. 12. vassal: slave.
Sonnet 142: 13. what . . . hide: i.e., pity.
Sonnet 144: 2. suggest: tempt.

The worser spirit a woman colored ill.
To win me soon to Hell, my female evil   5
Tempteth my better angel from my side,
And would corrupt my saint to be a devil,
Wooing his purity with her foul pride.
And whether that my angel be turned fiend
Suspect I may, yet not directly tell,   10
But being both from me, both to each friend,°
I guess one angel in another's Hell.
   Yet this shall I ne'er know, but live in doubt
   Till my bad angel fire my good one out.

145°

Those lips that Love's own hand did make
Breathed forth the sound that said "I hate,"
To me that languished for her sake.
But when she saw my woeful state,
Straight in her heart did mercy come,   5
Chiding that tongue that ever sweet
Was used in giving gentle doom,
And taught it thus anew to greet.
"I hate" she altered with an end
That followed it as gentle day   10
Doth follow night, who, like a fiend,
From Heaven to Hell is flown away.
   "I hate" from hate away she threw,
   And saved my life, saying "not you."

146

Poor soul, the center° of my sinful earth,
My sinful earth,° these rebel powers that thee array,
Why dost thou pine within and suffer dearth,
Painting thy outward walls so costly gay?
Why so large cost, having so short a lease,   5
Dost thou upon thy fading mansion spend?
Shall worms, inheritors of this excess,
Eat up thy charge?° Is this thy body's end?
Then, soul, live thou upon thy servant's° loss,
And let that pine to aggravate° thy store.   10
Buy terms divine° in selling hours of dross,
Within be fed, without be rich no more.
   So shalt thou feed on Death, that feeds on men,
   And Death once dead, there's no more dying then.

11. to . . . friend: friends to each other.
   Sonnet 145: Written in an 8-syllable meter.
   Sonnet 146: 1. center: See App. 1.   2. My . . . earth: This is
the Q reading; the compositor has repeated "My sinful earth"
instead of the two syllables which should begin the line. There
have been many guesses. Some such word as "feeding" is re-
quired.   8. charge: what you have spent.   9. servant: i.e., the
body.   10. aggravate: increase.   11. terms divine: immortal life.

147

My love is as a fever, longing still°
For that which longer nurseth the disease,
Feeding on that which doth preserve the ill,
The uncertain sickly appetite to please.
My reason, the physician to my love,   5
Angry that his prescriptions are not kept,
Hath left me, and I desperate now approve°
Desire is death, which physic did except.°
Past cure I am, now reason is past care,
And frantic-mad with evermore unrest.   10
My thoughts and my discourse as madmen's are,
At random from the truth vainly expressed,
   For I have sworn thee fair, and thought thee
     bright,
   Who art as black as Hell, as dark as night.

148

Oh me, what eyes hath Love put in my head,
Which have no correspondence with true sight!
Or, if they have, where is my judgment fled,
That censures° falsely what they see aright?
If that be fair whereon my false eyes dote,   5
What means the world to say it is not so?
If it be not, then love doth well denote
Love's eye is not so true as all men's. No,
How can it? Oh, how can Love's eye be true,
That is so vexed with watching and with tears? 10
No marvel then, though I mistake my view.°
The sun itself sees not till heaven clears.
   O cunning Love! With tears thou keep'st me blind,
   Lest eyes well-seeing thy foul faults should find.

149

Canst thou, O cruel! say I love thee not,
When I against myself with thee partake?°
Do I not think on thee when I forgot
Am of myself, all tyrant,° for thy sake?
Who hateth thee that I do call my friend?   5
On whom frown'st thou that I do fawn upon?
Nay, if thou lour'st on me, do I not spend
Revenge upon myself with present moan?
What merit do I in myself respect,
That is so proud thy service to despise,   10
When all my best doth worship thy defect,°

Sonnet 147: 1. still: always.   7. approve: prove by experi-
ence.   8. except: forbid.
   Sonnet 148: 4. censures: judges.   11. view: what I see.
   Sonnet 149: 2. partake: take sides.   4. all tyrant: you com-
plete tyrant.   11. defect: lack of beauty.

Commanded by the motion of thine eyes?
  But, love, hate on, for now I know thy mind.
  Those that can see thou lovest, and I am blind.

150

Oh, from what power hast thou this powerful might
With insufficiency° my heart to sway?
To make me give the lie to my true sight,
And swear that brightness doth not grace the day?
Whence hast thou this becoming of things ill,° 5
That in the very refuse of thy deeds
There is such strength and warrantise° of skill
That, in my mind, thy worst all best exceeds?
Who taught thee how to make me love thee more,
The more I hear and see just cause of hate? 10
Oh, though I love what others do abhor,
With others thou shouldst not abhor my state.
  If thy unworthiness raised love in me,
  More worthy I to be beloved of thee.

151

Love is too young to know what conscience is,
Yet who knows not conscience is born of love?
Then, gentle cheater, urge° not my amiss,°
Lest guilty of my faults thy sweet self prove.
For, thou betraying me, I do betray 5
My nobler part to my gross body's treason.
My soul doth tell my body that he may
Triumph in love, flesh stays no farther reason,°
But rising at thy name doth point out thee
As his triumphant prize. Proud of this pride, 10
He is contented thy poor drudge to be,
To stand in thy affairs, fall by thy side.
  No want of conscience hold it that I call
  Her "love" for whose dear love I rise and fall.

152°

In loving thee thou know'st I am forsworn,
But thou art twice forsworn, to me love swearing,
In act thy bed vow° broke, and new faith torn,
In vowing new hate after new love bearing.
But why of two oaths' breach do I accuse thee 5

When I break twenty? I am perjured most,
For all my vows are oaths but to misuse° thee,
And all my honest faith in thee is lost.
For I have sworn deep oaths of thy deep kindness,
Oaths of thy love, thy truth, thy constancy, 10
And, to enlighten° thee, gave eyes to blindness,°
Or made them swear against the thing they see.
  For I have sworn thee fair, more perjured I,
  To swear against the truth so foul a lie!

153

Cupid laid by his brand° and fell asleep.
A maid of Dian's° this advantage found,
And his love-kindling fire did quickly steep
In a cold valley-fountain of that ground,
Which borrowed from this holy fire of Love 5
A dateless° lively heat, still to endure,
And grew a seething bath,° which yet men prove
Against strange maladies a sovereign cure.
But at my mistress' eye Love's brand new-fired,
The boy for trial needs would touch my breast. 10
I, sick withal, the help of bath desired,
And thither hied, a sad distempered guest,
  But found no cure. The bath for my help lies
  Where Cupid got new fire, my mistress' eyes.

154

The little Love god lying once asleep
Laid by his side his heart-inflaming brand
Whilst many nymphs that vowed chaste life to keep
Came tripping by. But in her maiden hand
The fairest votary° took up that fire 5
Which many legions of true hearts had warmed,
And so the general° of hot desire
Was sleeping by a virgin hand disarmed.
This brand she quenchèd in a cool well by,°
Which from Love's fire took heat perpetual, 10
Growing a bath and healthful remedy
For men diseased. But I, my mistress' thrall,
  Came there for cure, and this by that I prove,
  Love's fire heats water, water cools not love.

7. **misuse:** i.e., be false in saying that you are fair. 11. **enlighten:** make you appear light. **gave . . . blindness:** blinded my own eyes.
  Sonnet 153: 1. **brand:** torch. 2. **Dian:** Diana, goddess of virginity. 6. **dateless:** perpetual. 7. **seething bath:** hot bath; probably a reference to the natural hot springs of Bath, which were as famous in Shakespeare's day as in Roman times.
  Sonnet 154: 5. **votary:** one who has vowed to lead a chaste life. 7. **general:** commander; i.e., Love. 9. **by:** near by.

  Sonnet 150: 2. **With insufficiency:** in spite of your defects.
5. **becoming . . . ill:** power to make evil attractive. 7. **warrantise:** guarantee.
  Sonnet 151: 3. **urge:** stress. **amiss:** trespass. 8. **reason:** argument.
  Sonnet 152: (The last of the series to the dark mistress).
3. **bed vow:** marriage vow.

APPENDICES

Appendices

1. The Elizabethan Idea of the Universe

Although Copernicus's *De revolutionibus orbum Coelestium,* which first appeared in 1543, may be said to have revolutionized modern ideas about the physical structure of the universe, in Shakespeare's day the book was hardly known. Most Elizabethans still believed that the earth was the center of the universe and immovable, and that all matter on the earth was naturally drawn to its center, which was thus the absolute center of everything.

Around the earth moved the seven planets, each in its sphere, thus forming a series of concentric circles. Nearest was the moon; then came Mercury, Venus, Sol (the Sun), Mars, Jupiter, and Saturn. In an eighth circle were the fixed stars, which remained constant in their relationships to each other, and outside there was a ninth circle known as the *Primum Mobile,* or the First Mover. The *Primum Mobile* had the power to turn all the other circles around the earth from east to west once every twenty-four hours; yet each sphere had, at the same time, its own contrary motion as it moved from west to east in its own orbit.

The moon took twenty-eight days to complete its circle; Sol, Venus, and Mercury moved in a year; Mars in two years; Jupiter in twelve years; and Saturn in thirty. It was believed that the planets in their motion each made a musical note, the whole forming a perfect harmony of sound. Since the planets moved at different paces, their relationship to each other was constantly changing, and certain conjunctions of the planets were regarded as lucky, others as unlucky.

Planets were believed to give out a kind of ethereal fluid or "influence" (*influentia*), which greatly affected human beings. The moon, as the nearest and most easily observed, was known to affect the ebb and flow of tides and was believed to be peculiarly powerful. The other planets also were considered to have a direct bearing on the weather, and indeed on all earthly affairs. Accordingly, astrologers believed that as a result of their accumulation of observations they could by the pattern of the heavens decide what was likely to happen at any time. In the same way, by observing the various conjunctions of the heavenly bodies at the moment of a person's birth, a horoscope could be drawn up which would indicate the future course of his life. A man's fate was thus determined by the stars.

The movements of the heavenly bodies were usually discussed in terms of the zodiac. The zodiac is a belt of the heavens which lies eight degrees on either side of the sun's annual course. It forms a complete circle, which is divided into twelve houses or signs, each of thirty degrees. These signs are named Aries (the Ram), Taurus (the Bull), Gemini (the Twins), Cancer (the Crab), Leo (the Lion), Virgo (the Virgin), Libra (the Scales), Scorpio (the Scorpion), Sagittarius (the Archer), Capricornus (the Goat), Aquarius (the Water Carrier), and Pisces (the Fishes). During its annual course, the sun passes into and out of each house or sign. In astrological parlance, the season was described by the position of the sun in relation to the sign of the zodiac. Abnormal events in the heavens, and especially the appearance of a comet or an eclipse, were regarded as alarming portents of disaster.

2. The Almanac

Astrological language is common in Shakespeare and all Elizabethan writings, but much of the knowledge displayed came from no deeper source than the penny almanac, published annually. These little almanacs were of a pattern still preserved in the *Old Farmer's Almanac,* and gave miscellaneous information. Almanacs were printed in two colors, black for the text, with red for titles, special days, and other notable items. Thus Buckminster's *Almanac for the Year 1598* is described on the title page as:

An Almanacke and

Prognostication, for the
yeere of Christes incarnation
M. D. XCVIII.

Being the second after the leape yeere.

And the yeere of the worldes
creation. 5560

Seruing generally for all
England, but especially for the
Meridian of this honorable Citie
of London. Gathered and made by
Thomas Buckmynster.

Anno aetatis suae. 66.

imprinted at London by Richard
Watkins and James Roberts.

Cum priuilegio Regiæ Maiestatis

Next follows information of the movable feasts
of the Church (Easter, and so on). Then come
short notes for letting of blood, purging, bathing,
and so on; for example: " Let [that is, draw] the
melancholike blood when the Moone is in Libra
or Aquarius." Then comes a picture of a naked
man, showing the parts governed by the twelve
celestial signs.

The calendar proper follows, each month be-
ing given a page. The feasts of the Church are
noted, special feasts being printed in red, as is
also the day when the sun enters a new sign
of the zodiac. Thus in July it is noted that the sun
enters Leo on the thirteenth, and on the nine-
teenth " dog days " begin.

After the calendar follows the second part:

A Prognostication
for the yeere of
our Lord God.
M. D. XCVIII.

This contains certain notes on convenient times
for planting, for example: " You may sowe
seedes, especially in Gardens, betweene the
change and the full, when the Moone is in Virgo,
Sagittarius, or Pisces."

Then follow notes of the beginning and end
of the Law Terms; the dates when marriage may
not be solemnized without a license; the dates
of the two eclipses of the moon and one of the
sun which will occur during the year; a vague
prognostication of what is likely to happen in
each of the four quarters of the year; a table " to
know for ever how long the moon doth shine
every night "; and finally, a day-by-day weather
forecast for the whole year.

Astrologers and almanac-makers, needless to
say, were often mocked for their lack of success
as prophets. Their answer was that, though by
their science they could interpret the signs of the
heavens, they could not foresee the will of God,
which is unpredictable.

3. *The Humors*

It was believed that all matter in the universe
consisted of four elements or principles, each of
which was hostile to the other but could exist in
combination when in proper proportions. These
four elements were *earth, air, fire,* and *water.* It
followed that since the human body was also
matter, it must likewise be composed of the four
elements. Anatomy was much studied toward the
end of the sixteenth century, and the word be-
came popular in literary jargon to denote what
is now called analysis or psychology. When
learned men examined the human body, they
were impressed by its all-pervading *humor* or
quality of dampness. But the " humors " of the
body were obviously of different kinds, and on
the assumption that the physical body must be
composed of four elements, " earth " was identi-
fied as black bile, " air " as blood, " fire " as bile,
and " water " as phlegm. Each element produced
a corresponding temperament, which was indi-
cated outwardly by a man's complexion. Too
much earth produced the *melancholic* humor;
air, the *sanguine;* fire, the *choleric;* water, the
phlegmatic.

In a healthy body the four humors were accu-
rately balanced, one against the other; but if one
humor became predominant or deficient, the in-
dividual became mentally and physically unbal-
anced.

In the 1590's the word " humor " rapidly be-
came popular, as words sometimes will, and every
intelligent person began to talk of his humors.
Indeed, it became the mark of a would-be intel-
lectual to have a humor, preferably melancholic,
which was the sign of a great mind. The type is
thus described by Samuel Rowlands in *The Let-
ting of Humor's Blood in the Head-Vein:*

OF MASTER HUMORS
Ask Humors why a feather he doth wear?
" It is his humor, by the Lord," he'll swear.
Or what he doth with such a horsetail lock?
Or why upon a whore he spends his stock?
" He hath a humor doth determine so."

Why in that stop-throat fashion doth he go
With scarf about his neck? Hat without band?
" It is his humor, sweet sir, understand."
What cause his purse is so extreme distressed
That often times 'tis scarcely penny-blest?
" Only a humor." If you question why,
His tongue is ne'er unfurnished with a lie:
" It is his humor too," he doth protest.
Or why with sergeants he is so oppressed
That like to ghosts they haunt him every day?
A rascal humor doth not love to pay.
Object, why boots and spurs are still in season?
His humor answers; " humor is his reason."
If you perceive his wits in wetting shrunk,
It cometh of a humor to be drunk.
When you behold his looks pale, thin, and poor,
Th' occasion is his humor, and a whore.
And everything that he doth undertake,
It is a vein, for senseless humor's sake.

In Shakespeare's plays the word " humor " is very common and has a wide range of meanings. It may be used literally to mean moisture, or to imply one of the four humors, but its commonest meanings are whim, obsession, temperament, mood, temper, or inclination.

4. The Melancholic Humor

Of all kinds of humor the melancholic was the most often discussed. Melancholy characters appear fairly often in Elizabethan plays, and are usually treated seriously, though sometimes satirically. It is clear that in the late 1590's and early 1600's the melancholic intellectual was a common and recognized type. He was a man out of tune with his universe, who advertised himself by wearing a large black hat with the brim pulled down over his brow, a cloak, and a general air of moody aloofness.

Ben Jonson parodied the type in *Every Man in His Humor* (1598). Master Matheo, who tried to pose as an intellectual, was vastly impressed when he heard that Stephano, who was trying to learn fashionable behavior, was also melancholy, and he observed: " O Lord, sir, it's your only best humor, sir; your true melancholy breeds your perfect wit, sir. I am melancholy myself divers times, sir, and then do I no more but take your pen and paper presently, and write you your half score or your dozen of sonnets at a sitting." And he offers Stephano the use of his study. To which Stephano replies: " I thank you, sir; I shall be bold I warrant you. Have you a close stool there? " — for this piece of furniture was peculiarly devoted to melancholy contemplations.

Similarly John Davies in his epigram " On a Gull ":

See, yonder melancholy gentleman,
Which, hoodwinked with his hat, alone doth sit!
Think what he thinks, and tell me if you can
What great affairs troubles his little wit.
He thinks not of the war 'twixt France and Spain,
Whether it be for Europe's good or ill,
Nor whether the Empire can itself maintain
Against the Turkish power encroaching still;
Nor what great town in all the Netherlands,
The States determine to besiege this spring;
Nor how the Scottish policy now stands,
Nor what becomes of the Irish mutining.
But he doth seriously bethink him whether
Of the gulled people he be more esteemed
For his long cloak or for his great black feather,
By which each gull is now a gallant deemed.
Or of a journey he deliberates,
To Paris-garden, Cockpit or the Play;
Or how to steal a dog he meditates,
Or what he shall unto his mistress say.
    Yet with these thoughts he thinks himself most fit
    To be of counsel with a king for wit.

There were three main types of melancholic humor: lover's melancholy, politician's (or malcontent's) melancholy, and intellectual melancholy. The melancholy lover was thus described by Rosalind when she criticized Orlando for having none of the proper marks of a genuine specimen (*AYLI*, III.ii.391):

A lean cheek, which you have not, a blue eye and sunken, which you have not, an unquestionable spirit, which you have not, a beard neglected, which you have not; but I pardon you for that, for simply you having in beard, is a younger brother's revenue; then your hose should be ungartered, your bonnet unbanded, your sleeve unbuttoned, your shoe untied, and everything about you demonstrating a careless desolation.

The political or malcontent type was fairly common. Shakespeare's Thersites (in *Troilus and Cressida*) is a good example, but there were others in real life. For instance, Henry Cuffe, secretary and evil genius of the Earl of Essex, was described by Sir Henry Wotton, who at one time was his colleague, as " a man of secret ambitious ends of his own, and of proportionate counsels smothered under the habit of a scholar, and slubbered over with a certain rude and clownish fashion that had the semblance of integrity."

The third type was the intellectual melancholic; his was the true type of melancholic humor. Hamlet is Shakespeare's supreme example of this kind, and his famous soliloquy "To be or not to be" (III.i.56) sums up the intellectual's problems. He was a man who realized that the times were out of joint but could see no remedy or hope, either in this world or the next — if, indeed, there was a next. Most of the satirists suffered from this feeling of futility and frustration, and they revenged themselves on their fellows by snarling at their many follies.

Melancholy was recognized as a disease, and several treatises were written by physicians discussing its symptoms, causes, and cures. Special diets were prescribed or certain foods forbidden. The most elaborate study of the whole subject was *The Anatomy of Melancholy* that Robert Burton published in 1621.

One cause of melancholy was a foul smell. This led John Harington to connect melancholy with the Greek hero Ajax. Ajax (see *Troilus and Cressida*) was a great boaster, but he came to a sad end. After the death of Achilles, the armor which had been made for him by the god Vulcan was claimed both by Ulysses and by Ajax. When the armor was awarded to Ulysses, Ajax fell into such melancholy that he suffered hallucinations. He mistook a flock of sheep for his companions who had wronged him and he slaughtered them. In 1596 Harington wrote a Rabelaisian book called *The Metamorphosis of Ajax,* which was in fact a treatise on domestic sanitation and his invention of a primitive water closet. Harington used the name "Ajax" for the privy — a very foul-smelling convenience — and to describe his own invention of the first water closet. Thus, as he explained it, Ajax = A Jax = A Jakes (sometimes spelt Jaques); the word "jakes," it may be noted, was the coarse synonym for privy. Harington's book caused much scandalous amusement and was well known. Thereafter the name "Ajax" usually connoted at the same time both a privy and the melancholic humor. It is even possible that Shakespeare in giving the name "Jaques" to the melancholy philosopher in *As You Like It* was not unmindful of an anecdote in *The Metamorphosis:*

There was a very tall and serviceable gentleman, sometime Lieutenant of the Ordnance, called Master Jaques Wingfield, who coming one day, either of business or of kindness, to visit a great Lady of the Court, the Lady had her gentlewoman ask which of the Wingfields it was. He told her "Jaques Wingfield." The modest gentlewoman, that was not so well seen in the French to know that "Jaques" was but "James" in English, who so bashful, that to mend the matter (as she thought) she brought her Lady word not without blushing, that it was "Master Privy Wingfield," of which, I suppose the Lady then, I am sure the gentleman after, as long as he lived, was wont to make great sport.

Melancholy in its extreme form was also regarded as the cause of fearful visions and hallucinations. Thus Nashe in *Terrors of the Night* (1593) remarked:

Even as slime and dirt in a standing puddle engender toads and frogs and many other unsightly creatures, so this slimy melancholy humor still still thickening as it stands still engendreth many misshapen objects in our imaginations.

The term "melancholic humor" thus covered many forms of mental disturbance, from general depression to acute mania.

5. *Bearbaiting and Bullbaiting*

Among the Henslowe papers there is an advertisement which runs:

Tomorrowe beinge Thursdaie shalbe seen at the Beargardin on the banckside [See Pl. 2a] a greate mach plaid by the gamstirs of Essex who hath chalenged all comers what soeuer to plaie v dogges at the single beare for v pounds and also to wearie a bull dead at the stake and for your better content shall haue plasant sport with the horse and ape and whiping of the blind beare. Viuat Rex.

There are frequent references to the sport of bearbaiting, which took place twice a week, on Wednesday and Sunday, and Shakespeare used many poetic images drawn from it. Foreign visitors were particularly impressed by the sport.

In bearbaiting, the bear was tied by a long rope to a post. Four or five mastiffs were then let into the pit and attacked the bear, which retaliated fiercely. The surviving dogs, however, were pulled off before the bear had received fatal injuries. In bullbaiting, the bull was usually free, but the sport continued until the animal was worried to death.

Other forms of sport were mentioned in the advertisement. A pony was led into the ring with an ape fastened on its back. The amusement consisted in watching the pony, terrified by the screams of the ape, lashing out at the dogs which tried to pull it down.

For the whipping of the blind bear, half a dozen men armed with whips surrounded the bear, and beat it until they drew blood. The bear defended itself vigorously, striking the whips out of the hands of its tormentors and breaking them, and even clawing the men themselves.

For further details, see E. K. Chambers, *The Elizabethan Stage,* Vol. II, pp. 448–71.

6. *Letters and Seals*

LEGAL AGREEMENTS

There are many poetic images in Shakespeare's plays drawn from the preparation and the completion of legal documents. When a legal agreement was drawn up between two or more parties the different copies were written out on a single sheet of parchment, thus:

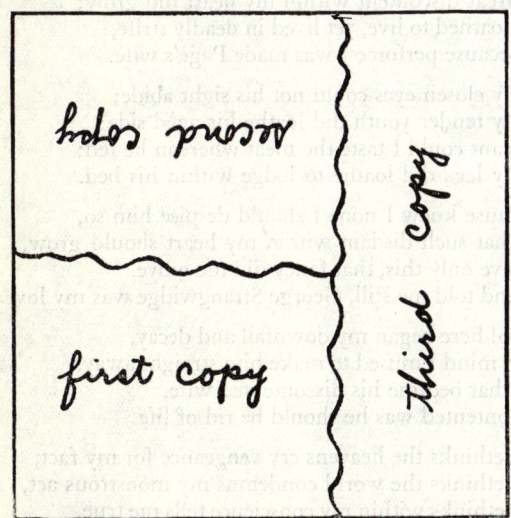

The copies were then cut apart with a wavy or indented cut; hence agreements were (and in legal language still are) known as *indentures* (see Pl. 11a). The purpose of the indentation was to prevent forgery. If the genuineness of any copy was called in question, it could be compared with and fitted against the other copy. When the

copies had been separated, about an inch of the parchment at the bottom of each was folded over, and through the folds slits were made. Ribbons, or "labels" of parchment, were then inserted, one for each of the parties to the agreement. These labels hung down some three or four inches. The parties signed their names on the folded portion across the upper end of the label. The bottom of the label was then enclosed in a small ball of softened wax, into which the party pressed his seal. The impressing of the seal was the final act in making the formal agreement. Normally indentures were made between two parties, but indentures "tripartite" were quite common.

LETTERS

The letters presented by messengers in modern stage performances of Shakespeare's plays usually resemble a college diploma — a rolled scroll tied with a ribbon. Actually, however, Elizabethan letters were not in this form. A letter of any importance was written with generous margins on a double sheet of paper. This was then folded over, with the writing inside, in such a way that at the back the top edge overlapped the lower. Thus two thicknesses of paper intervened between the writing and the outside. The address or superscription was written on the front. The back was then secured by sealing wax impressed with the sender's seal. An unbroken seal showed the recipient that the letter had not been opened in transit. Hence the reading of a letter is sometimes referred to as "breaking open." Envelopes had not yet been invented.

7. *Hats and Heads*

In Shakespeare's time, the outward signs of courtesy toward those of higher rank were strictly demanded and observed. In the presence of a superior, the inferior stood bareheaded, hat in hand, with his head slightly bent forward in an attitude of humility. The inferior, especially if a servant, also "made a leg," or curtsied. This was done by bending both knees, the right behind the left, as low as possible.

Great men wore their hats, indoors and out, on all ceremonial occasions as a sign of their importance; and the etiquette of rank was exact even in moments of crisis. Thus on the memorable occasion of Essex's rebellion (see Gen. Intro. p. 24a), a deputation consisting of the Lord Keeper of the Great Seal and other members of the Privy Council appeared at Essex House. They were admitted to the courtyard. The Lord Keeper removed his hat as a mark of respect to Essex, who was his senior in rank. Essex and his friends removed their hats in respect to the Lord Keeper as representing the Queen. When, however, the Lord Keeper began to speak in the Queen's name as her representative, he put on his hat and commanded Essex and his company on their allegiance to lay down their weapons. In reply to this command, Essex's party put on their hats as a deliberate sign of contempt. It is small wonder that so precise a courtier as Osric was embarrassed when Hamlet bade him " put his bonnet to its right use " (*Haml,* v.ii.94).

8. *Ballads*

Students of literature are accustomed to think of the ballad as a folk poem of early origin with certain metrical characteristics. In Shakespeare's time, the commonest form was the news ballad. Hundreds of these ballads were written on every manner of topic: battles and victories, royal progresses, grievances, marvelous events, crimes and executions (particularly in the form of a lament by the criminal for his wicked life and deserved end), and scandals of all kinds. The news ballad was a crude and popular form of publication that appealed to the kind of person who nowadays is interested only in comic strips or tabloids.

Wherever there was a crowd ballads were hawked by a ballad-singer, who first sang the ballad and then sold copies at a penny apiece. They were vilely printed on a single sheet of paper, headed with any woodcut, more or less appropriate, which happened to be available in the printer's workshop. A typical specimen by Thomas Deloney, one of the most famous ballad-writers, runs as follows:

The Lamentation of Mr. Page's Wife [1]

of Plymouth, who, being forced to wed him, consented to his
Murder, for the love of G. Strangwidge: for
which they suffered at Barnstable
in Devonshire.

[1] The case caused a great sensation. The parents of Ulalia forced her to marry a rich old man called Page, although her true love, George Strangwidge, was an entirely suitable husband. At

The Tune is Fortune my Foe, etc.

Unhappy she whom Fortune hath forlorn,
Despised of grace that proffered grace did scorn,
My lawless love hath luckless wrought my woe,
My discontent content did overthrow.

My loathèd life too late I do lament,
My woeful deeds in heart I do repent;
A wife I was that willful went awry,
And for that fault am here prepared to die.

In blooming years my father's greedy mind,
Against my will, a match for me did find.
Great wealth there was, yea, gold and silver store.
But yet my heart had chosen one before.

Mine eyes disliked my father's liking quite,
My heart did loathe my parent's fond delight;
My childish mind and fancy told to me,
That with his age my youth could not agree.

On knees I prayed they would not me constrain;
With tears I cried their purpose to refrain;
With sighs and sobs I did them often move,
I might not wed whereas I could not love.

But all in vain my speeches still I spent.
My mother's will my wishes did prevent.
Though wealthy Page possessed the outward part,
George Strangwidge still was lodgèd in my heart.

I wedded was and wrappèd all in woe;
Great discontent within my heart did grow;
I loathed to live, yet lived in deadly strife,
Because perforce I was made Page's wife.

My closen eyes could not his sight abide;
My tender youth did loathe his agèd side:
Scant could I taste the meat whereon he fed;
My legs did loathe to lodge within his bed.

Cause knew I none I should despise him so,
That such disdain within my heart should grow,
Save only this, that fancy did me move,
And told me still, George Strangwidge was my love.

Lo! here began my downfall and decay,
In mind I mused to make him straight away.
I that became his discontented wife,
Contented was he should be rid of life.

Methinks the heavens cry vengeance for my fact,
Methinks the world condemns my monstrous act,
Methinks within my conscience tells me true,
That for that deed hell-fire is my due.

My pensive soul doth sorrow for my sin,
For which offense my soul doth bleed within;

Ulalia's request, Strangwidge and two accomplices strangled Page in bed. All four were subsequently hanged. There was very general sympathy with the girl as the victim of her parents' stupid greed.

But mercy, Lord! for mercy still I cry:
Save thou my soul, and let my body die.

Well could I wish that Page enjoyed his life,
So that he had some other to his wife:
But never could I wish, of low or high,
A longer life than see sweet Strangwidge die.

Oh woe is me! that had no greater grace
To stay till he had run out Nature's race.
My deeds I rue, but I do repent
That to the same my Strangwidge gave consent.

You parents fond, that greedy-minded be,
And seek to graft upon the golden tree,
Consider well and rightful judges be,
And give you doom twixt parents' love and me.

I was their child, and bound for to obey,
Yet not to love where I no love could lay.
I married was to muck and endless strife;
But faith before had made me Strangwidge' wife.

O wretched world, who cankered rust doth blind!
And cursèd men who bear a greedy mind!
And hapless I, whom parents did force so,
To end my days in sorrow, shame, and woe.

You Denshire dames, and courteous Cornwall
      knights,
That here are come to visit woeful wights,
Regard my grief, and mark my woeful end,
But to your children be a better friend.

And thou, my dear, that for my fault must die,
Be not afraid the sting of death to try.
Like as we lived and loved together true,
So both at once we'll bid the world adieu.

Ulalia, thy friend, doth take her last farewell,
Whose soul with thee in Heaven shall ever dwell.
Sweet Saviour Christ, do thou my soul receive!
The world I do with all my heart forgive.

And parents now, whose greedy minds do show
Your heart's desire, and inward beauty woe,
Mourn you no more, for now my heart doth tell,
Ere day be done my soul shall be full well.

And Plymouth proud, I bid thee now farewell.
Take heed, you wives, let not your hands rebel.
And farewell, life, wherein such sorrow shows,
And welcome, death, that doth my corpse enclose.

And now, sweet Lord, forgive me my misdeeds!
Repentance cries for soul that inward bleeds.
My soul and body I commend to thee,
That with thy blood from death redeemèd me.

Lord! Bless our Queen with long and happy life,
And send true peace betwixt each man and wife;

And give all parents wisdom to foresee
The match is marred where minds do not agree.

T. D.

London. Printed by Thomas Scarlet 1591.

9. *Heralds and Heraldry*

Heralds, wearing their sleeveless coats embroidered with the royal arms, still have their place in state pageantry in England, but nowadays they are little more than a picturesque survival from the Middle Ages. Their greatest age was in the fourteenth century. Nevertheless in Shakespeare's time the heralds had an important place in the social and noble life, and a knowledge of the elaborate science of heraldry was part of the education of a gentleman. Heralds were under the control of the Earl Marshal, a court official of considerable importance. They were (and still are) organized in a College, in which each herald bore a romantic name. The three seniors were known as "Kings" — Garter King at Arms, Clarenceux King at Arms, and Norroy King at Arms. Under them were the heralds known as York, Richmond, Somerset, Lancaster, Chester, and Windsor, and four pursuivants, or junior heralds, called Rouge Dragon, Blue Mantle, Portcullis, and Rouge Croix.

The heralds were concerned with matters that affected the dignities and the honor of kings, noblemen, and gentlemen. They organized all important state ceremonies, especially those at the accession of kings, royal weddings, coronations, funerals, and the solemnities of the special orders of knighthood, such as the Garter or the Bath. In the Middle Ages they were also the official and inviolable messengers of kings in war and peace and as such read royal proclamations (see, for example, *Hen V,* III.vi.120; IV.iii.79–127). They directed proceedings at combats of honor (see, for example, *Rich II,* I.iii.), though trial by combat was no longer officially allowed in Shakespeare's time. Apart from their duties at Court they undertook to direct lesser ceremonies, particularly the funerals of noble or wealthy persons.

The most important function, however, of the College of Heralds was to preserve the records of noble families and to grant coats of arms to persons worthy to be considered gentlemen. From time to time, during visitations in the counties, they examined the claims of those who declared themselves to be of gentle birth, and recorded their findings. They thus acted as a kind of *Social Register* and *Who's Who* of the time.

The granting of a coat of arms was the official recognition that the recipient was a " gentleman." As might be expected, the privilege encouraged much petty snobbery. New-made gentlemen irritated alike those who lacked the privilege and those who had enjoyed it for many generations. Indeed in Shakespeare's time it was openly said, and with much truth, that any man with money could buy a coat of arms from the heralds quite regardless of a claim to merit. The truth is that in England the qualities that distinguish gentlemen from common men have always been very vague.

Heraldry was originally a means of distinguishing one warrior enclosed in armor from another. Each assumed a recognizable badge, which he painted on his shield. By the thirteenth century a regular system of recording and painting these badges had developed, and coats of arms were passed down from father to son. Coats of arms were not only useful in war; they are also a pleasing and picturesque form of decoration. In time, heraldry developed into an elaborate science with a considerable vocabulary to describe the colors, ornaments, and arrangement of innumerable devices in such a way that anyone could recognize or reproduce the design from the description.

Seven colors were used in painting (or *blazoning*) a shield, usually designated by French names, viz., *or* (yellow or gold), *argent* (white or silver), *gules* (red), *azure* (blue), *sable* (black), *vert* (green), *purpure* (purple). The shield was divided in many different ways, each of which had its technical name. Many shields contained only a geometrical pattern, but more commonly devices or *charges* were used, which were often appropriate to the name or the deeds of the first wearer. Coats of arms descended from father to children, but members of the same family often made a distinction in their coats by adding a border or changing the color of the background or making a slight variation in the device; this was known as a *difference*. Daughters bore the coats of arms of their fathers; and when a gentleman married the daughter of a distinguished house, especially if she was also an heiress, the coats of arms of the two families were combined, either by *impaling* (that is, by dividing the shield vertically and blazoning the two coats of arms side by side) or by *halving* (where

each coat was cut in two horizontally) or by quartering (when the shield was divided into four and the two coats repeated at the opposite corners).

A gentleman who was descended from several illustrious families often had a most elaborate shield subdivided into a dozen or more coats of arms. The expert in heraldry by reading the shield would be able to identify the wearer from the details of his descent thus set out. Coats of arms were not confined to noblemen or gentlemen; cities, corporations, bishops, universities, colleges, dioceses, guilds, were all entitled to appropriate arms.

In addition to the shield, the heralds granted a *crest*. This was originally a device worn on top of the helmet by a knight in full armor and was therefore something simple, such as an eagle, a lion, a swan's head.

The coat of arms and the crest granted to Shakespeare's father in 1596 will illustrate heraldic language. The coat was *Gold, on a bend sable, a spear of the first, steeled argent.* Gold (or yellow), the first color mentioned, is that of the background of the shield. The *bend* is a band running diagonally from the top right corner (i.e., the wearer's right); it is sable (or black). On the bend is a spear " of the first," that is, the first-mentioned color — gold, with its point silver. The spear is chosen as a pun on the name Shakespeare. The crest (or cognizance) was a *falcon, his wings displayed, argent, standing on a wreath of his colors;* that is, a silver falcon with wings outstretched standing on a silver wreath. Coat of arms and crest are illustrated on the title page of this book.

10. *Tortures and Punishments*

Torture was seldom practiced in England. Only in cases of high treason was the rack used to encourage a reluctant witness to talk. The *rack* was a large frame set out on the ground. At each end there were rollers around which a pair of ropes were wound. The hands and feet of the victim were fastened to these ropes and tension was applied by means of levers. The victim was thus stretched until he was persuaded to give the necessary information. In other countries other means of torture were used. The " strappado," several times mentioned by Shakespeare, was an

Italian torment. The victim was drawn up to a height by means of a rope passed through his elbows, and then let down with a jerk.

Various methods of punishment were used on convicted offenders. The court of the Star Chamber often sentenced an offender to stand in the *pillory*. This was a heavy framework of wood with holes through which the victim's hands and head were thrust. Thus fixed, he was subjected to the gaze and the abuse of the crowd. Over his head was fixed a paper setting out the details of his offense. Sometimes he was nailed to the pillory by one of his ears. The punishment of standing in the pillory often included the cutting off of one or both ears or slitting the nose. Petty malefactors and vagabonds were made to sit in the *stocks*. Here the legs were secured through holes in a heavy board. Rogues and vagabonds were whipped on the back until bloody. Convicted prostitutes were led through the streets tied to the back of a cart and whipped while metal basins were sounded to draw the attention of passers-by.

Debtors were imprisoned until the debt was discharged. The jailer was made responsible for producing his prisoner on demand, and if the prisoner escaped, the jailer himself had to pay the debt. Prisoners were obliged to pay for their keep and were not released until they had discharged their fees to the jailer. Poor prisoners were allowed to beg for the charity of passers-by; they would otherwise have starved, as no free rations were provided. It was not, however, usual to sentence an offender to long terms of imprisonment.

11. *Cuckolds and Horns*

Elizabethan plays abound in jokes about cuckolds and horns. A cuckold is a husband deceived by a faithless wife, and therefore regarded as an object of derision. The name derives from cuckoo, a bird of unusual and disorderly habits. It is a migrant which appears in northern Europe toward the end of April and disappears in July. It is remarkable for its distinctive and monotonous cry of "cuck-oo cuck-oo." It was and is regarded as a foolish bird, probably because of its cry, which is at first welcomed as a sign of spring but afterward disliked because of its irritating monotony. Unlike most birds, it makes no nest; instead it lays an egg in the nest of some smaller bird, who innocently hatches and feeds the foster child even after the latter has shouldered the legitimate offspring out of the nest. The origin of the name "cuckold" may thus be one who has been cheated by a cuckoo — an adulterer who has foisted his own offspring on an innocent victim. To "cry cuckoo" after a husband was to warn him that his wife's lover was near.

A cuckold was also supposed to wear a pair of invisible horns as a sign of his unhappy fate. The origin of this curious myth is unknown, though there have been many guesses, none very convincing. The simplest explanation is that horns are appropriate to a cuckold because he has shown himself to be a dull, stupid, oxlike creature. Once, however, a connection between horns and infidelity had been established, writers and wits showed endless ingenuity in making play on the word "horn" in all its possible meanings and uses.

12. *Signs*

In Elizabethan England the practice of numbering houses or shops in large towns had not yet been introduced. Instead each house or shop in a street displayed a sign jutting out at right angles, in the form of a painted board suspended from a bracket (see Pls. 3a, 6b). The sign was some simple and easily recognizable device, such as a bell, an angel, a white hart, a fox, or a green dragon. The sign of Cupid blindfolded denoted a brothel. The sign-painters' trade was therefore much in evidence. In England signs are still displayed over or beside inns.

As well as the pictorial signs, certain trades also had their own recognized symbols. The barber's shop was (and sometimes still is) designated by a pole painted spirally in red and white. A bush was the token of a wine shop, a garland of an ale house, while the lattice windows of a tavern were painted red.

13. *Bowls*

Shakespeare frequently used poetic imagery taken from the game of bowls. In that game a small bowl (or ball), called the *jack* or the *mistress,* was set as a mark at one end of the green; from the other end the players rolled their bowls toward the jack, the player whose bowl finally rested nearest the jack scoring highest. A bowl which touched the jack was said to "kiss."

The bowl was not a perfect sphere, but so made that one side somewhat protruded. This protrusion was called the *bias;* it caused the bowl to take a curving and indirect course. The game was played in bowling alleys and on greens; but the bowling green lacked the perfect and smooth surface of a modern green. Lumps and impediments in the turf which diverted the bowl were called *rubs.*

14. *The Great Household*

Some understanding of the organization of a great house is required to appreciate many of Shakespeare's plays. It was the fashion to employ as many servants as possible. A nobleman or a man of wealth lived in a small palace, and each department of the household had its own staff under the control of a gentleman, who was assisted by a yeoman. The "gentleman servingman" was usually the younger son of a man of good family, and employment in a great house was regarded as a normal occupation which carried with it no sense of social inferiority. Promising and ambitious young scholars, fresh from the universities, often took service as tutors or secretaries and in time rose to high positions. Similarly, the lady of the house was served by young gentlewomen of good family, who in this way learned polite behavior and domestic economy until such time as a marriage was arranged for them. Thus in *Twelfth Night,* Malvolio, Olivia's steward, was a man of good family, and Maria was a lady of birth and the social equal of Sir Toby.

15. *Marriage Customs*

In a marriage where all forms were observed the first step was the formal betrothal of the two parties. This was a private affair. Then came the publication of the banns: according to law, on three successive Sundays the minister must publicly announce in church the intention of the parties to be married and call on any person who knew any cause why the marriage should not lawfully be performed to come forward and declare it. If for any reason it was necessary to hasten the marriage, a special license was procured from the bishop of the diocese.

Elizabethan life was essentially a small-town or village affair. As a result, in most marriages the parties lived within walking distance of each other. A wedding celebrated with full ceremony was an uproarious all-day event. It began very early in the morning in the bride's house, when the bridesmaids awakened and dressed the bride. Soon the bridegroom, accompanied by his groomsmen, friends, and musicians, arrived to claim the bride. Then the whole party of friends and relations set out in procession to the church, the bride, dressed in white, with her hair loose, being the center of attraction.

After the ceremony had been performed, the party moved off to the bridegroom's house, where a great feast was prepared, and the guests settled down to enjoy themselves for the rest of the day with eating, drinking, dancing, and games. If there was a poet among the party, he would present an epithalamium, or wedding poem; or a masque or other form of entertainment might be given.

The merriment increased as night came on. At length the bridesmaids led the bride away to the wedding chamber, where she was undressed and put into bed. Then they took her garters and threw them among the bachelor guests, who scrambled for them. The bridegroom's friends then led him away, undressed him, and brought him to the wedding chamber, where he was put into bed with his bride, after which, with much noise, laughter, and coarse jesting, the two were sewed together into the sheets. Bridegroom and bride were then left alone to begin their married life while the guests went back to continue their revelry.

Early in the morning, the newly married couple were greeted with a song at their bedroom window. Thereafter, bride and bridegroom took their places among the married folk. There was no honeymoon.

A more idealized account of an Elizabethan wedding will be found in Spenser's *Epithalamium.*

16. *Funeral Customs*

Funeral customs in Shakespeare's time were elaborate. Great men were buried with much ceremonial, pomp, and ostentation. The body, enclosed in a coffin and covered with a pall, was borne to the grave by bearers wearing black, and followed by a long procession of mourners, friends, and servants, who wore hooded black cloaks which completely covered them. The coats of arms of the great man in the form of scutcheons painted on buckram and resembling stiff flags were carried in the procession, and the whole ceremony was elaborately ordered and arranged by one of the heralds, who drew a fee for his services. After the funeral the mourners were feasted, and sometimes money was given to the poor. To omit any of the proper ceremony was a sign of disrespect for the dead and cast a slur on his name and family, as Laertes complained when he heard that his father had been buried " hugger-mugger " (*Haml,* IV.v.213–17).

Of all state funerals during Shakespeare's life in London, that of Queen Elizabeth, on April 28, 1603, was the most elaborate and splendid. First came the Knight Marshal's men to clear the way; then two hundred and forty poor women, walking four and four; then servants of gentlemen, esquires, and knights, followed by the servants from the many departments of the Royal Household. In the next section of the procession walked the grooms of the household and the servants of earls and countesses. Then came two equerries, leading the Queen's horse, trapped with velvet; next the clerks and sergeants, the musicians, the apothecaries and surgeons, the Master of the Hall, the groom porter, the chief clerks. Next in ascending order were the clerks of the great Departments of State — the Privy Council, the Privy Seal, the Signet, the Parliament — doctors of physic, the Queen's chaplains. In the next section went the aldermen of London, the Solicitor General, the Attorney General, knights bachelors, the Lord Chief Baron, the Lord Chief Justice, knights ambassadors, and esquires of the body. After them came the Master of Requests, the agents for Venice and the States of the Low Countries, the Lord Mayor of London, Sir Robert Cecil (Principal Secretary), barons, bishops, viscounts, earls, marquises, the Lord Keeper of the Great Seal, the French Ambassador, and the Archbishop of Canterbury. They were followed by the heralds and gentlemen ushers, and then the chariot itself containing the body of the Queen, embalmed and enclosed in a lead coffin, surmounted by her recumbent effigy, crowned and in her Parliament robes. Over the chariot was a canopy borne by four noblemen, and immediately following the Earl of Worcester, Master of the Horse, leading the palfrey of honor. Next came the Lady Mar-

chioness of Northampton, who, as senior peeress, was the chief mourner, supported by the Lord Treasurer and the Lord Admiral. She was followed by the gentlewomen of the Queen's chamber, countesses, viscountesses, earls' daughters, baronesses, and maids of honor; and, last of all, Sir Walter Ralegh, Captain of the Guard, with all the guard following, five by five, with their halberds downward.

As the procession passed along, " the City of Westminster was surcharged with multitudes of all sorts of people in their streets, houses, windows, leads, and gutters, that came to see the obsequy; and when they beheld her statue or picture lying upon the coffin set forth in royal robes, having a crown upon the head thereof, and a ball and scepter in either hand, there was such a general sighing, groaning, and weeping as the like hath not been seen or known in the memory of man, neither doth any history mention any people, time, or state, to make like lamentation for the death of their Sovereign."

Sovereigns, noblemen, and men of wealth were buried inside the church beneath an elaborate monument, which they had usually taken care to erect for themselves while still living. Lesser men were buried more simply. The common man, indeed, was carried on a bier, uncoffined, and wrapped in a shroud which was simply a sheet knotted at head and foot, sometimes leaving the face exposed. He was buried in a shallow grave in the open churchyard. The practice of erecting headstones over graves had not yet come into fashion, and the dead were regarded only as temporary tenants of consecrated ground. After a time the grave would be used for some newcomer and the bones then thrown up were cast in the charnel house until they decayed or were thrown out.

Suicides were not permitted burial in holy ground. They were buried without ceremony in some open place, such as a crossroads (see *Haml,* V.i.).

17. The Post

There was in Elizabethan days no postal service for the general public. For official use, however, there was a regular system of post horses kept constantly ready by the local " postmaster " at various stages along the main highways. These saddle horses were available also for wealthy travelers who wished to make a fast journey, but they were intended mainly for official messengers, who carried their letters at top speed. In times of emergency the postmaster was empowered to impress riding horses as required. The post boy carried a horn which he blew to give warning of his approach. In Shakespeare's plays there are many images, usually denoting speed, derived from the post.

Some idea of the speed of the post boy can be gathered from the endorsements on letters. Thus a very urgent letter written by Essex on October 26, 1597, was dispatched from Plymouth about 10 A.M. It reached Ashburton (25 miles) at 4:30 P.M., Exeter (19 miles) after 8 P.M., Honiton (15 miles) at 10:30 P.M., Crewkerne (20 miles) at 1:30 A.M., Sherborne (12 miles) at 4:30 A.M., Shafton (14 miles) at 7 A.M., Salisbury (17 miles) at 9 A.M., Andover (16 miles) at noon, and Basingstoke (16 miles) at 3:30 P.M. This means that in less than 30 hours the letter was carried a distance of approximately 165 miles over unlit country roads, with nine pauses for change of horses.

18. *Nature and Art*

Nature and art are constantly contrasted by writers in the sixteenth and seventeenth centuries. In Elizabethan English, "nature" meant that which was born in a man — that is, natural ability; art was that which came with study and training. Ben Jonson in his conversations with the Scottish poet William Drummond of Hawthornden grumbled that Shakespeare "wanted art"; in his ode on Shakespeare, prefaced to the first folio (see Gen. Intro. p. 73a), he was more generous. By lack of art, Jonson meant that though Shakespeare had natural genius, he did not always take sufficient pains to design or polish his work or to observe the critical rules. Jonson himself was far more indebted to art than to nature, for his work was most conscientiously and deliberately wrought.

Art thus meant technical skill. Today the word "artist" implies also a touch of genius, and is confined chiefly to experts in painting, sculpture, music, literature, and acting. In Shakespeare's time an artist was a skilled craftsman. When Bacon contrasted "arts" and "sciences," he meant by "art" almost what is now called applied science and by "science," pure knowledge.

Art implied also study and conscious effort. Cassius admiring Brutus's stoic acceptance of the news of Portia's death says (*Caesar*, IV.iii.194):

> I have as much of this in art as you,
> But yet my nature could not bear it so.

Art and matter are likewise contrasted, "art" meaning style and "matter" content. When Polonius begins his lecture on Hamlet's madness, he is so pleased with his own style and artistic phrasing that the Queen interrupts him with (*Haml*, II.ii.95):

> More matter with less art.

Nature and Fortune also provide natural contrasts, as in the lighthearted argument between Celia and Rosalind (*AYLI*, I.ii.34–58): Nature bestows or withholds natural gifts such as ability, beauty, or goodness, which are born in a man; Fortune brings those accidental good or evil gifts which come to a man from without, such as wealth, friendship, promotion, poverty, or ill luck. Moreover, since Fortune is very capricious in her gifts, she is painted as a blind woman, as Ancient Pistol very learnedly explains (*Hen V*, III.vi.31–40).

19. *Bells*

Shakespeare constantly refers to church bells. They were rung on many occasions, to summon worshipers to church on Sunday and holy days, to announce good tidings, to give the alarm for fire or invasion, to celebrate the sovereign's accession, or for weddings and funerals. The bell was also tolled to announce the passing of a sick man, if possible at the moment of death, so that his soul might be accompanied by the prayers of his friends. It was tolled again at his funeral. In times of plague the sound of the passing bell was never still, and added to the general gloom. In many country churches there was a peal (or set) of bells, and bell-ringing was an art much practiced. For all joyous occasions peals of bells were rung, but one solitary bell was used for deaths and burials.

20. *Equivocation*

The theory of equivocation was much discussed between the years 1598 and 1606. In 1598 a great controversy arose among English Roman Catholics. Those who wished to practice their religion in peace realized that most of the bitter feeling against Catholics was caused by the actions of the English Jesuits on the Continent, who were regarded as being the instigators of the many plots against the life of Queen Elizabeth. The controversy led to a pamphlet war between the Jesuits and the Catholic secular priests in England, in which the Anglican Bishop of London took a hand, for he encouraged the seculars and even arranged for their pamphlets to be printed. One doctrine, hotly disputed and very generally abhorred by Protestant Englishmen, was the principle of equivocation by which a man might conceal the truth when giving evidence on oath. Equivocation was defended by Father Robert Parsons, the chief propagandist for the Jesuits, in a book called *A Brief Apology or Defense of the Catholic Ecclesiastical Hierarchy,* which appeared in 1602, wherein he claimed that in certain special circumstances " amphibology," or hiding the truth by dissimulation, was lawful. On March 28, 1606, Father Henry Garnet was tried and condemned to death for being accessory to the Gunpowder Plot. Equivocation was one of the major issues in the trial, for it was shown that some of the conspirators had deliberately concealed the truth when under oath. Garnet in his defense justified equivocation in particular cases. At his execution on May 6, he was urged not to equivocate with his last breath but to speak the truth. It is likely that the Porter's remarks in *Macbeth* (II.iii.9–12) are a direct reference to this event.

21. Alchemy

Chemistry as now studied was unknown in Shakespeare's time, but there was a considerable practical knowledge of chemical processes, especially among those who worked in the various metals. " Alchemists," basing their notions on the theories of the four humors (see App. 3), believed that all metals were composed of earth, water, and air in varying proportions; pure gold was the perfect metal in which all qualities were perfectly combined. On this assumption alchemists were concerned mainly with trying to find the " philosopher's stone " which would transmute baser metals into gold and would also produce the " elixir of life " or *aurum potabile* (tincture of

gold) which would reconcile the discords of the bodily humors and so be a cure for all diseases, including old age. The lure of boundless wealth attracted the credulous and the greedy, and there were many rascals ready to fleece them. Much magic and mystic symbolism were mingled with the study of alchemy, genuine and bogus. Ben Jonson's play *The Alchemist* gives an amusing picture of one group and contains much of the jargon actually used by alchemists. Nevertheless, many alchemists were genuine students; and even if they never succeeded in finding the philosopher's stone, they were at least conducting original experiments and not relying solely on tradition.

22. Time Problems

Critics, especially those who are not overfamiliar with the customs of the Elizabethan stage, are often disturbed by time problems in Shakespeare's plays. The most famous occurs in *Othello.* When the play is read carefully, there is a noticeable inconsistency. The action begins in Venice on the night of the runaway marriage of Othello and Desdemona. Almost at once Othello is summoned to the Council and dispatched forthwith to take command in Cyprus, leaving Desdemona to follow him. Cassio, Desdemona, and Othello reach Cyprus in different ships. Othello and Desdemona are reunited. That same night, Cassio is made drunk on guard by Iago and is immediately dismissed from his post by Othello. Early next morning, by Iago's advice Cassio comes to Desdemona to ask her to intercede for him with Othello, and directly afterwards — as Cassio is going out — Iago begins his plot to persuade Othello that Desdemona has deceived him and has long been Cassio's mistress. As the story is unfolded, there has been no possible chance or opportunity for Desdemona and Cassio even to have been alone together. This inconsistency in the story undoubtedly exists when the play is read and dissected; but *Othello,* and all Shakespeare's plays, were written for acting, and in the rush and excitement of events on the stage the difficulty passes unnoticed.

Shakespeare was indeed very free with time in a play. He was concerned with creating a succession of impressions in the minds of his audience, and not with presenting a series of mathematical problems of time. Months and even years pass unnoticed and unmentioned during the action of many Elizabethan plays. There are in fact other instances of compression of time, even in *Othello,* which disturb no one. Thus in II.i, the arrival of Cassio's ship in the harbor is announced at line 26; he enters at line 42. At line 51 another ship is sighted at sea; 14 lines later the arrival of Iago is announced, and he appears with Desdemona at line 81. The third ship is sighted at line 93, and Othello enters at line 183. Thus in a matter of less than a quarter of an hour of unbroken acting time three separate ships — and sailing ships at that — are sighted, enter the harbor, and are tied up. In real life the whole process between sighting and docking would have taken at least six hours.

Another instance which causes no comment is to be found in *Richard II.* In I.iv, Richard and Aumerle (who has just parted from Bolingbroke) discuss Bolingbroke's behavior as he went away to banishment. At line 52 Bushy announces that John of Gaunt is dying. Richard at once goes out to visit him, and arrives at II.i.68. Shortly afterward Gaunt is carried out, and his death is announced at line 147. Richard, having declared that he will seize Gaunt's wealth, makes his exit at line 223. At line 276 Northumberland announces that Bolingbroke has *already* gathered an expedition in Britanny to invade England.

These and many other apparent inconsistencies are quite unimportant on the stage. Indeed, the actual passing of time in drama is seldom noticed unless for some particular reason it obtrudes and causes a feeling of doubt or of questioning in the spectator.

23. *Witches and Witchcraft*

It is popularly supposed that in Shakespeare's England every Englishman believed in witches and that witchcraft was commonly practiced. Actually there were far more skeptics than believers, and the reports of the cases tried in the courts, of which there are many, make disappointingly unromantic reading.

The most famous and elaborate work on witchcraft to be published in Shakespeare's lifetime was Reginald Scot's *Discovery of Witchcraft* (1584). Scot had been greatly disturbed at the flimsy evidence offered at the trial of certain witches in his own part of the country, and he studied the subject carefully in many authorities, classical, foreign, and English. He set out to prove " that the compacts and contracts of witches with all Devils and all Infernal Spirits or Familiars are but erroneous novelties and imaginary conceptions." Scot's sturdy Protestant skepticism was not, however, acceptable to all his readers, because he made light of the evidence of the Bible.

In 1587 George Gifford, a minister of religion and a learned theologian, answered Scot in *A Discourse of the Subtle Practises of Devils by Witches and Sorcerers,* and six years later in a more popular *Dialogue Concerning Witches.* Gifford compromised between Scot's skepticism and vulgar credulity. In 1597 King James VI of Scotland, later King James I of England and patron of Shakespeare's company, published his *Daemonology,* to refute the " damnable opinions" of Scot. The book is well written in the form of a dialogue, and is a valuable summary of contemporary beliefs in the occult. King James had good reasons for his beliefs. In 1591 a number of Scottish witches of both sexes were brought to trial for endeavoring to murder him by witchcraft. King James was himself present at some of the examinations, and the evidence was sensational. When one of the witches named Agnes Sampson had made such strange confessions that the King exclaimed that they were all liars, she took him aside and " declared unto him the very words which passed between the King's Majesty and his Queen at Upslo in Norway the first night of their marriage; whereat the King wondered greatly and swore by the living God that he believed that all the devils in Hell could not have discovered the same." As a popular account of the trials was published in England in 1592, Shakespeare may have read it; the witches in *Macbeth* behave in much the same way as the witches in this case.

There is considerable evidence that in the Middle Ages and in Shakespeare's own time secret societies of witches flourished both in France and in Scotland. The members of these groups practiced an anti-Christian cult with various obscene rites, and they had a considerable knowledge of simple poisons. But there is little trace of any widespread witch cult in England. Individual witches, of both sexes, were accused of doing harm, sometimes resulting in death. If condemned, the witch was executed not for witchcraft, but for murder by witchcraft. For the most part the accused were lonely and malicious old women. Scot thus describes the type:

One sort of such as are said to be witches are women which be commonly old, lame, blear-eyed, pale, foul, and full of wrinkles; poor, sullen, superstitious, and papists; or such as know no religion: in whose drowsy minds the Devil hath gotten a fine seat; so as, what mischief, mischance, calamity, or slaughter is brought to pass, they are easily persuaded the same is done by themselves, imprinting in their minds an earnest and constant imagination thereof. They are lean and deformed, showing melancholy in their faces, to the horror of all that see them. They are doting, scolds, mad, devilish; and not much differing from them that are thought to be possessed with spirits; so firm and steadfast in their opinions, as whosoever shall only have respect to the constancy of their words uttered would easily believe they were true indeed.

These miserable wretches are so odious unto all their neighbors, and so feared, as few dare offend them, or deny them anything they ask. Whereby they take upon them — yea, and sometimes think that they can do — such things as are beyond the ability of human nature. These go from house to house, and from door to door, for a pot full of milk, yeast, drink, pottage, or some such relief; without the which they could hardly live; neither obtaining for their service and pains, nor by their art, nor yet at the Devil's hands (with whom they are said to make a perfect and visible bargain) either beauty, money, promotion, wealth, worship, pleasure, honor, knowledge, learning, or any other benefit whatsoever.

It falleth out many times that neither their necessities nor their expectation is answered or served, in those places where they beg or borrow; but rather their lewdness is by their neighbors reproved. And further, in tract of time the witch waxeth odious and tedious to her neighbors; and they again are despised and despited of her: so as sometimes she curseth one and sometimes another; and from that the master of the house, his wife, children, cattle, etc. to the little pig that lieth in the sty. Thus in process of time they have all displeased her, and she hath wished evil luck unto them all; perhaps with curses and imprecations made in form. Doubtless (at length) some of her neighbors die, or fall sick; or some of their children are visited with diseases that vex them strangely: as apoplexies, epilepsies, convulsions, hot fevers, worms, etc. Which by ignorant parents are supposed to be the vengeance of witches. Yea, and their opinions and conceits are confirmed and maintained by unskillful physicians: according to the common saying: *Inscitiæ pallium maleficium et incantatio,* Witchcraft and enchantment is the cloak of ignorance: whereas indeed evil humors, and not strange words, witches, or spirits are the causes of such diseases. Also some of their cattle perish, either by disease or mischance. Then they upon whom such adversities fall, weighing the fame that goeth upon this woman (her words, displeasure, and curses meeting so justly with their misfortune), do not only conceive, but also are resolved, that all their mishaps are brought to pass by her only means.

The witch, on the other side, expecting her neighbors' mischances, and seeing things sometimes come to pass according to her wishes, curses, and incantations (for *Bodin* himself confesseth that not one above two in a hundred of their witchings or wishings take effect) being called before a Justice, by due examination of the circumstances is driven to see her imprecations and desires and her neighbors' harms and losses to concur, and as it were to take effect: and so confesseth that she (as a goddess) hath brought such things to pass. Wherein not only she, but the accuser, and also the Justice, are fouly deceived and abused; as being through her confession and other circumstances persuaded (to the injury of God's glory) that she hath done, or can do, that which is proper only to God himself.

In general most Englishmen scoffed at witchcraft, but with the sneaking suspicion that " there might be something in it." An Elizabethan play about witches thus produced much the same reaction in an audience as a modern horror film.

24. *Dances*

Dancing[1] in the sixteenth century was as popular with all classes as today, and as severely condemned by extreme puritans. Of the dances practiced by gentlemen and their ladies, those most frequently mentioned by Shakespeare are:

THE MEASURE

The measure was a slow, solemn dance full of stately movement and suitable for the elderly and for formal occasions. It is thus described by Sir John Davies in *Orchestra, or The Poem of Dancing:*

But after these, as men more civil grew,
He [Love] did more grave and solemn measures frame,
With such fair order and proportion true,

[1] For a full note, see *Shakespeare's England,* Vol. II, pp. 437-50.

And correspondence every way the same,
That no faultfinding eye did ever blame;
   For every eye was movèd at the sight
   With sober wond'ring, and with sweet delight.

Not those old students of the heavenly book,
Atlas the great, Prometheus the wise,
Which on the stars did all their lifetime look,
Could ever find such measures in the skies,
So full of change and rare varieties;
   Yet all the feet whereon these measures go,
   Are only spondees, solemn, grave, and slow.

The measure was danced by Capulet's guests (*R & J*, I.iv.) and in *Much Ado*, II.i.

THE PAVAN

The pavan " was a stately, dignified, processional dance suitable to the gala mantles of princes and the robes of magistrates. ' Every pavane has its galliard ' says the Spanish proverb, as if to say every solemnity must have its moment of levity. The measured steps were two simple and a double one forward, and the same number backward, to the music of hautboys and trumpets." [2]

THE GALLIARD

The galliard, known also as a cinquepace or five-step, was a much quicker, livelier dance, of which Davies wrote:

But for more divers and more pleasing show,
A swift and wandering dance she did invent,
With passages uncertain to and fro,
Yet with a certain answer and consent
To the quick music of the instrument.
   Five was the number of the music's feet,
   Which still the dance did with five paces meet.

A gallant dance, that lively doth bewray
A spirit and a virtue masculine;
Impatient that her house on earth should stay
Since she herself is fiery and divine;
Oft doth she make her body upward fline [3]
   With lofty turns and capriols in the air,
   Which with the lusty tunes accordeth fair.

THE CAPRIOL

The capriol or caper was a movement that is still common in ballet dancing, where the dancer leaps upward beating the feet together while still in the air.

[2] *Shakespeare's England*, Vol. II, 444.   [3] That is, fly.

CORANTO AND LAVOLTA

The coranto and the lavolta were varieties of the galliard. In the coranto the movement was swift and gliding; in the lavolta the dancers leaped into the air. Davies describes them thus:

Coranto
What shall I name those current travases [4]
That on a triple dactile foot do run
Close by the ground with sliding passages,
Wherein that dancer greatest praise hath won
Which with best order can all orders shun;
   For everywhere he wantonly must range,
   And turn, and wind, with unexpected change.

Lavolta
Yet is there one, the most delightful kind,
A lofty jumping, or a leaping round,
Where arm in arm two dancers are entwined
And whirl themselves with strict embracements
   bound,
And still their feet an anapest do sound.
   An anapest is all their music's song,
   Whose first two feet are short, and third is long.

Much Ado ends with a coranto.

THE BRAWL

The brawl was originally a French dance in which a pair of dancers led the movement and the rest followed.

COUNTRY DANCES

Country dances were common, especially at holiday time. On Mayday the painted maypole was set up and boys and girls danced a round dance about it. Whitsun (Pentecost, which follows seven weeks after Easter, in May or June) was the time for morris dancing. The morris (originally Moorish) dance was a primitive kind of ballet in which the various dancers were in character, usually Robin Hood, Friar Tuck, Maid Marian, and Little John. There was also a member of the party who wore the hobbyhorse — a frame fastened to his waist resembling a horse, with trappings reaching down to the ground and concealing the human legs. Thus equipped, the dancer pranced and cavorted around. Morris dancers wore bells around their knees. See Pl. 13d.

[4] That is, traverses.

THE JIG

There were two kinds of jig, the one a lively round dance with movements like a Scottish reel, and the other danced after the performance of a play (see *Caesar* Intro. p. 529a). The stage jig was a pantomime dance performed by two or more dancers in character, often with dialogue and frequently very bawdy. Will Kempe, the clown of Shakespeare's company, was especially famous for dancing jigs.

25. *The Fencing Match in "Hamlet"*

THE BET

(V.ii.171–77)

Laertes fancies himself an expert fencer and is therefore prepared to give Hamlet a handicap. He has bet the King that he will hit Hamlet twelve times before Hamlet hits him nine times. Hamlet's handicap is, then, plus three in twelve hits.

THE MATCH

(V.ii.290–316)

Hamlet scores the first two hits and is thus two up. Laertes then presses his attack and scores a hit with his pointed foil. Both men are now roused. Hamlet, realizing from his wound that Laertes is fighting with a pointed foil, carries out a textbook movement to exchange rapiers. This is illustrated in Sainct-Didier's *Traicté contenant les secrets du premier livre sur l'espée seule* (see Pl. 13b), where the opponents are called the Lieutenant (=Laertes) and the Provost (=Hamlet). In the maneuver, the Lieutenant makes a short thrust. The Provost parries, drawing back his left foot; then with his foil he pushes the Lieutenant's blade to one side. Whereupon, bringing up his left foot, he swings round and with his left hand grasps the hilt of his opponent's foil and twists it backward. If the Lieutenant holds onto his own foil, it will be twisted out of his hand, and his fingers broken as well. His only answer to this movement is to drop his own foil and retaliate by similarly grasping the Provost's hilt with his left hand and twisting it out of his grasp. Each opponent now has the other's foil in his left hand. Each steps back, transfers the exchanged foil to the right hand, and resumes the contest.

Hamlet, having thus exchanged rapiers, now presses home the attack and scores his third hit with Laertes' pointed (and poisoned) rapier. At this moment the Queen swoons and the contest is broken off.

It may be noted that the stage direction in Q1 is "*They catch one another's Rapiers, and both are wounded.*" F1 reads "*In scuffling they change Rapiers.*" There is no stage direction in Q2.

26. *Hawks and Hawking*

Hawking, which was a very popular sport with gentlemen, had an elaborate vocabulary. Various types of hawk were used for the different kinds of game, the best being imported from the Continent. In training the hawk and keeping it in good condition, considerable skill and experience were necessary, and the professional falconer was an expert.

Hawks were not bred in captivity. They were captured wild and tamed. If taken from the nest (eyrie) they were called *eyasses,* and were brought up by hand. *Eyasses* were naturally more easily trained, but less skillful in taking the game. Mature wild hawks were called *haggards;* they were more difficult to tame, but having hunted naturally before capture, they needed less training.

The first stage in taming a wild hawk was to *seel* its eyes. This was done by passing a needle and thread through the lower eyelid of each eye; the thread was then tied over the head and the eyes could be closed at the will of the falconer. A blinded hawk does not resist handling. When the hawk was taken out, a hood was placed over its head, and little straps called *jesses,* by which the bird was held and controlled, were fastened to each leg. If the haggard remained wild it could usually be tamed by keeping it awake until it was exhausted. The process of taming a hawk was known as *manning.*

When the hawk was ready for field training, it was first induced to return to an artificial prey or bait known as a *lure.* When fully trained, the hawk was taken out and sent up to attack its *quarry.* Bells were attached to its legs, which enabled the falconer to locate his hawk if it brought down the quarry in thick country.

Of the various other technical words used in hawking the commonest were:

fly — to loose the hawk after the game

pitch — the highest point in the upward flight of the hawk as it hovers waiting for the game to be put up

stoop — the hawk's downward swoop on the quarry

bate — to flap the wings

imp — to insert a feather in a hawk's wing in place of one that was broken

For a fuller note see *Shakespeare's England*, Vol. II, pp. 351–66.

27. Money Values

One of the problems which confronts the student is to try to translate sums of Elizabethan English money into the equivalent in modern American dollars. This is exceedingly difficult, especially at the present time, when the purchasing power of the dollar is constantly shifting and when the value of the pound in dollars is equally unstable. In October 1951 the value of the pound was $2.80; at the beginning of the present century, when exchange was stable, £1 was worth $4.80; that is, one halfpenny was equivalent to one cent. To add to the difficulty, the actual value of coins in the sixteenth and seventeenth centuries varied from time to time as the relative value of gold and silver fluctuated. In Queen Elizabeth's time gold and silver coins contained their actual value of metal, though in earlier reigns the coinage had been debased. Paper money was unknown.

The English pound in Shakespeare's time (as today) contained 20 shillings; each shilling contained 12 pennies, and each penny 4 farthings. The pound was a gold coin, as were also the angel (10*s*.), the noble (6*s*. 4*d*., or one-third of a pound), and the crown (5*s*.). The commonest silver coins were shilling, sixpence, groat (fourpence), half-groat (twopence), and one penny (see Pl. 10a–e). The mark (13*s*. 4*d*., or two-thirds of a pound) was used as a sum in accounts, but there was no equivalent coin.

Historians from time to time make rough-and-ready calculations to express an approximate equivalent of the purchasing power of the pound at various dates. Thus £1 in 1600 was worth roughly £6 in 1914 and £10 in 1947. But this kind of calculation can never be at all accurate, because the values of commodities, wages, and needs have not changed uniformly. Moreover, modern men need far more. In Shakespeare's time automobiles, radios, cinemas, telephones, and social services (such as free education, public health, and sanitation) did not exist, so were not part of the individual's normal expenses. The standard of living, especially for those in the low-income brackets, was very low. It may, however, give a general idea of comparative standards of prices if the Elizabethan pound is taken as roughly equivalent in modern times to $40, the shilling as worth $2, and a penny as 16 cents.

Some actual figures from various sources will illustrate the changes in values:

SKILLED WORKERS' WAGES IN THE CITY OF LONDON

	In Elizabethan Money	Approximate Modern Equivalent
By the year, with maintenance:	£3 6*s*. 8*d*. to £6 13*s*. 4*d*.	$125 to $250
By the day with food and drink:	6*d*. to 9*d*.	$1 to $1.50
By the day without food and drink:	10*d*. to 14*d*.	$1.60 to $2.25

SOLDIERS' PAY

In 1596 the pay of the various ranks in the army serving in France was laid down as follows:

IN A COMPANY OF 200 MEN	In Elizabethan Money		Approximate Modern Equivalent	
	DAILY PAY	WEEKLY ALLOWANCE FOR MAINTENANCE	DAILY PAY	WEEKLY ALLOWANCE FOR MAINTENANCE
Captain	8*s*.	56*s*.	$16	$112
Lieutenant	4*s*.	28*s*.	$8	$56
Ensign	2*s*.	14*s*.	$4	$28
Sergeant Drummer Surgeon	12*d*.	7*s*.	$2	$14
Soldier	8*d*.	7*s*.	$1.30	$14

CEILING PRICES OF FOOD IN 1599

During the mobilization in August 1599 a scale of maximum prices was laid down which included the following:

	In Elizabethan Money	*Approximate Modern Equivalent*
Beer, best quality	1d. per quart	0.16
Beer, weak	½d. per quart	0.08
Butter	4d. per lb.	0.64
Cheese	1½d. to 2d. per lb.	0.24 to 0.32
Eggs, best quality	2d. for 7	0.54 per doz.
Beef, best quality	14d. for 8 lbs.	0.28 per lb.
A fat pig, best quality	16d.	$2.56
Fat chickens (capons)	20d. a pair	$1.60 each
Tallow candles	4d. per lb.	0.64

MISCELLANEOUS PRICES

Items (chiefly clothing) from Henslowe's *Diary* (see Gen. Intro. p. 38b):

	In Elizabethan Money	*Approximate Modern Equivalent*
A boy's wages	3s. a week	$ 6
An ordinary dinner	6d. to 9d. per person	$ 1 to 1.50
Soldier's sword and dagger	8s.	$ 16
Soldier's helmet	8s.	$ 16
A sackbut (musical instrument)	40s.	$ 80
Tailor's charges for making		
(a) a suit	18s.	$ 36
(b) woman's bodice and a pair of sleeves	6s. 7d.	$ 13
A short velvet cloak embroidered with bugles (beads) and a hood cape	£4	$160
Satin doublets (see Pl. 8b)	40s. to 45s. each	$ 80 to 90
A woman's gown	£10	$400
A woman's gray gown (a working dress)	20s.	$ 40
Two pile (second-grade) velvet of carnadine (red)	20s. a yard	$ 40
Satin	12s. a yard	$ 24
Taffeta	12s. 6d. a yard	$ 25
A plume of feathers	10s.	$ 20

PAYMENTS FOR PLAYS

	In Elizabethan Money	*Approximate Modern Equivalent*
To Jonson & Dekker for *Page of Plymouth*, 1599 (see Gen. Intro. p. 43b.)	£8	$320
To Drayton, Hathway, Munday, and Wilson for the two parts of *Sir John Oldcastle*, 1599 (see Gen. Intro. p. 43b.)	£14	$560
with a special present of 10s. at the first performance		$ 20
To Heywood for *A Woman Killed with Kindness*, 1603 (see Gen. Intro. p. 46b.)	£6	$240
Fee for licensing a play, paid to the Master of Revels	7s.	$ 14

As these figures show, food cost about the same as during the winter of 1947–48, clothing was more expensive, while wages, especially of workingmen, were very much less.

28. *The History Behind the History Plays*

RICHARD II, I AND II HENRY IV, HENRY V

Except for *King John* and *Henry VIII,* Shakespeare's ten history plays are concerned with one central theme — the rise and fall of the House of Lancaster. They cover a period of nearly a century of complex events.

Edward III reigned fifty years (1327–77). He had seven sons, of whom the eldest was Edward, the Black Prince. Both Edwards were passionately devoted to war and were constantly campaigning in France or Spain. In his later days, Edward III became senile, but he outlived his eldest son; the Black Prince died in 1376, Edward III a few months later, in 1377. Thereupon the King's eleven-year-old grandson, Richard II, son of the Black Prince, became King, under the regency of John of Gaunt, Duke of Lancaster, the eldest surviving son of Edward III. In 1381 occurred the Peasants' Revolt. The boy King behaved with great bravery and pacified the rebels by promises of redress of their grievances, promises which were afterward broken by his advisers. In 1382, at the age of sixteen, Richard married Anne of Bohemia. By this time, Gaunt had left the country and was warring in Spain; the control of the kingdom had passed to Thomas of Woodstock, Duke of Gloucester, sixth son of Edward III.

Richard was now growing up; to Gloucester's alarm, he formed a Court party of his own friends. Gloucester and his supporters (called the Lords Appellant), who included Henry Bolingbroke, Duke of Hereford (son of John of Gaunt), and Thomas Mowbray (Earl of Nottingham and afterward Duke of Norfolk), seized Richard's friends by force and executed them. In 1389, Richard suddenly declared that he was now of age, and Gloucester was obliged to resign his regency. Thereafter for some years Richard ruled competently and moderately; he even seemed to be reconciled with the Lords Appellant; but when Gloucester again began his intrigues he was arrested, sent to Calais (then an English possession), and there murdered.

Richard meanwhile had lost his first wife and had married again. His character changed. He became reckless and extravagant, and his Court was filled with favorites and parasites. As a result he was constantly in need of money, which he raised by forced loans, benevolences (" voluntary " gifts from wealthy men), and by farming out the taxes; that is, in return for cash down he granted some financier the right to collect the taxes — a system of raising money which led to great abuses.

In 1398, Bolingbroke and Norfolk quarreled. At this point, Shakespeare's *Richard II* begins. Richard banished both noblemen — Norfolk for life and Bolingbroke for six years — but with the promise that the great estates which should come to Bolingbroke on the death of his father (John of Gaunt, Duke of Lancaster), should not be violated. Nevertheless, when Gaunt died a few months later, Richard broke his promise and seized the Lancaster estates to pay for his expedition to subdue a rebellion in Ireland. While Richard was away, Bolingbroke landed in Yorkshire, declaring that he had come to recover his rights as Duke of Lancaster. The Percies of Northumberland — the greatest and most powerful family in the Northern parts — joined him, together with all Richard's enemies. When Richard returned to England, he found himself deserted. Bolingbroke now claimed the throne, and Richard was obliged to abdicate in favor of Bolingbroke, who became king as Henry IV. Plotting against the new King began almost at once. In 1400 Richard II was murdered. Here the play of *Richard II* ends.

The First Part of Henry IV covers the period of the next two and a half years, that is 1400–03.

Richard II left no children. The line of the Black Prince being thus extinct, the next heir to the throne by right of birth was therefore the senior surviving descendant of Lionel, Duke of Clarence (second son of Edward III). Lionel's daughter Phillipa had married Edmund Mortimer, third Earl of March. She had three children, Roger (who became fourth Earl of March), Elizabeth (who married Henry Percy, called " Hotspur," son of the Earl of Northumberland, and who is Lady Percy in the play), and Edmund. Roger had died in Ireland in 1398 and *his* son Edmund, fifth Earl of March, was thus the legal heir to the throne.

The reign of Henry IV was full of troubles. The first serious rebellion occurred in 1403 when Owen Glendower, a Welsh chieftain, led a national rising against the English. King **Henry**

Genealogical Tables

These tables show the complicated family relationship of the Houses of Lancaster, York, and Tudor. They have been much simplified and include only the major persons.

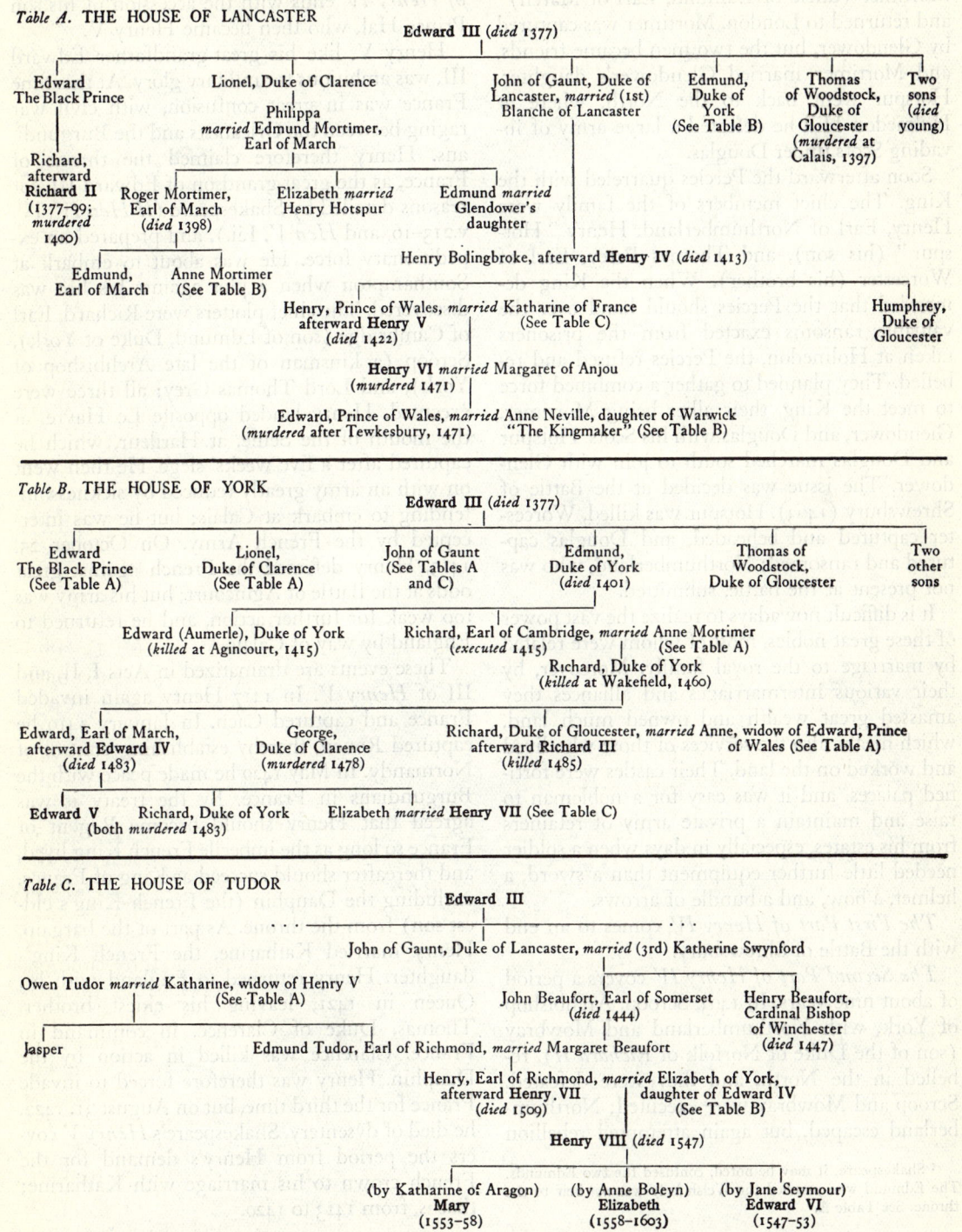

Table A. THE HOUSE OF LANCASTER

Edward III (*died* 1377)

- Edward The Black Prince
  - Richard, afterward **Richard II** (1377–99; *murdered* 1400)
- Lionel, Duke of Clarence
  - Philippa *married* Edmund Mortimer, Earl of March
    - Roger Mortimer, Earl of March (*died* 1398)
      - Edmund, Earl of March
      - Anne Mortimer (See Table B)
    - Elizabeth *married* Henry Hotspur
    - Edmund *married* Glendower's daughter
- John of Gaunt, Duke of Lancaster, *married* (1st) Blanche of Lancaster
  - Henry Bolingbroke, afterward **Henry IV** (*died* 1413)
    - Henry, Prince of Wales, *married* Katharine of France afterward **Henry V** (*died* 1422) (See Table C)
      - Henry VI *married* Margaret of Anjou (*murdered* 1471)
        - Edward, Prince of Wales, *married* Anne Neville, daughter of Warwick (*murdered* after Tewkesbury, 1471) "The Kingmaker" (See Table B)
    - Humphrey, Duke of Gloucester
- Edmund, Duke of York (See Table B)
- Thomas of Woodstock, Duke of Gloucester (*murdered* at Calais, 1397)
- Two sons (*died* young)

Table B. THE HOUSE OF YORK

Edward III (*died* 1377)

- Edward The Black Prince (See Table A)
- Lionel, Duke of Clarence (See Table A)
- John of Gaunt (See Tables A and C)
- Edmund, Duke of York (*died* 1401)
  - Edward (Aumerle), Duke of York (*killed* at Agincourt, 1415)
  - Richard, Earl of Cambridge, *married* Anne Mortimer (*executed* 1415) (See Table A)
    - Richard, Duke of York (*killed* at Wakefield, 1460)
      - Edward, Earl of March, afterward **Edward IV** (*died* 1483)
        - Edward V
        - Richard, Duke of York (both *murdered* 1483)
        - Elizabeth *married* **Henry VII** (See Table C)
      - George, Duke of Clarence (*murdered* 1478)
      - Richard, Duke of Gloucester, *married* Anne, widow of Edward, Prince of Wales afterward **Richard III** (*killed* 1485) (See Table A)
- Thomas of Woodstock, Duke of Gloucester
- Two other sons

Table C. THE HOUSE OF TUDOR

Edward III

- John of Gaunt, Duke of Lancaster, *married* (3rd) Katherine Swynford
  - John Beaufort, Earl of Somerset (*died* 1444)
    - Edmund Tudor, Earl of Richmond, *married* Margaret Beaufort
      - Henry, Earl of Richmond, afterward **Henry VII** (*died* 1509) *married* Elizabeth of York, daughter of Edward IV (See Table B)
        - Henry VIII (*died* 1547)
          - (by Katharine of Aragon) **Mary** (1553–58)
          - (by Anne Boleyn) **Elizabeth** (1558–1603)
          - (by Jane Seymour) **Edward VI** (1547–53)
  - Henry Beaufort, Cardinal Bishop of Winchester (*died* 1447)

- Owen Tudor *married* Katharine, widow of Henry V (See Table A)
  - Jasper
  - Edmund Tudor, Earl of Richmond, *married* Margaret Beaufort

went against him, but without success. He therefore left the command to Hotspur and Edmund Mortimer (uncle of Edmund, Earl of March) [1] and returned to London. Mortimer was captured by Glendower, but the two men became friends, and Mortimer married Glendower's daughter. Hotspur went back to the North, where at Holmedon Hill he defeated a large army of invading Scots under Douglas.

Soon afterward the Percies quarreled with the King. The chief members of the family were Henry, Earl of Northumberland, Henry "Hotspur" (his son), and Thomas Percy, Earl of Worcester (his brother). When the King demanded that the Percies should hand over the valuable ransoms exacted from the prisoners taken at Holmedon, the Percies refused and rebelled. They planned to gather a combined force to meet the King, their allies being Mortimer, Glendower, and Douglas with his Scots. Hotspur and Douglas marched south to join with Glendower. The issue was decided at the Battle of Shrewsbury (1403). Hotspur was killed, Worcester captured and beheaded, and Douglas captured and ransomed; Northumberland, who was not present at the battle, submitted.

It is difficult nowadays to realize the vast power of these great nobles, most of whom were related by marriage to the royal family. Moreover, by their various intermarriages and alliances they amassed great wealth and owned much land, which meant also the services of those who lived and worked on the land. Their castles were fortified palaces, and it was easy for a nobleman to raise and maintain a private army of retainers from his estates, especially in days when a soldier needed little further equipment than a sword, a helmet, a bow, and a bundle of arrows.

The First Part of Henry IV comes to an end with the Battle of Shrewsbury.

The Second Part of Henry IV covers a period of about nine years. In 1403, Scroop, Archbishop of York, with Northumberland and Mowbray (son of the Duke of Norfolk of *Richard II*), rebelled in the North, and they were defeated. Scroop and Mowbray were executed; Northumberland escaped, but again attempted rebellion

in 1408 and was killed. Henry IV, after a long period of sickness, died in 1413. *The Second Part of Henry IV* ends with the accession of his son Prince Hal, who then became Henry V.

Henry V, like his great-grandfather Edward III, was ambitious for military glory. At this time France was in great confusion, with civil war raging between the Orleanists and the Burgundians. Henry therefore claimed the throne of France, as the great-grandson of Edward III, for reasons detailed by Shakespeare (*II Hen IV*, IV. v.213–16, and *Hen V*, I.ii.), and prepared an expeditionary force. He was about to embark at Southampton when a plot against his life was discovered. The chief plotters were Richard, Earl of Cambridge (son of Edmund, Duke of York), Scroop (a kinsman of the late Archbishop of York), and Lord Thomas Grey; all three were executed. Henry landed opposite Le Havre, at the mouth of the Seine, at Harfleur, which he captured after a five weeks' siege. He then went on with an army greatly reduced by sickness, intending to embark at Calais; but he was intercepted by the French Army. On October 25, 1415, Henry defeated the French against great odds at the Battle of Agincourt; but his army was too weak for further action, and he returned to England by way of Calais.

These events are dramatized in Acts I, II, and III of *Henry V*. In 1417 Henry again invaded France and captured Caen. In January 1419 he captured Rouen, thereby establishing control of Normandy. In May 1420 he made peace with the Burgundians in France. By the treaty it was agreed that Henry should become Regent of France so long as the imbecile French King lived, and thereafter should succeed as King of France, excluding the Dauphin (the French King's eldest son) from the throne. As part of the bargain, Henry married Katharine, the French King's daughter. Henry returned to England with his Queen in 1421, leaving his eldest brother, Thomas, Duke of Clarence, in command in France. Clarence was killed in action by the Dauphin. Henry was therefore forced to invade France for the third time, but on August 31, 1422, he died of dysentery. Shakespeare's *Henry V* covers the period from Henry's demand for the French crown to his marriage with Katharine; that is, from 1413 to 1420.

---

[1] Shakespeare, it may be noted, confused the two Edmunds. The Edmund who married the Welsh lady was *not* heir to the throne. See Table A.

RICHARD III

English history from the death of Henry V (1422) to the accession of Henry VII (1485) was the theme of four of Shakespeare's earliest plays — the three parts of *Henry VI*, and *Richard III*. It was a period of constant strife, treachery, murder, and civil war between the various great noblemen who were descended from or closely related to the family of Edward III. When Henry V died in 1422, he left the throne to his son Henry VI, then an infant of nine months. Once more England was ruled by Regents and Protectors, each in turn striving to oust the other. Between them they lost all France except Calais, and then fell to squabbling and civil war at home.

Just before Henry V had set out for France, he discovered a conspiracy against himself (see above). It was led, among others, by Richard, Earl of Cambridge, who was the son of Edmund, Duke of York (fourth son of Edward III). Cambridge had married Anne, daughter of Roger Mortimer, the grandson of Lionel, Duke of Clarence (second son of Edward III; see Table B). The children of Richard, Earl of Cambridge, were thus in a more direct line of descent than was Henry V.

The First Part of Henry VI opens with the funeral of Henry V. The boy king, Henry VI, was at first ruled by his uncles, especially by Humphrey, Duke of Gloucester, son of Henry IV, and by the Beauforts — John, Earl of Somerset, and Henry, Cardinal Beaufort, sons of John of Gaunt by his third wife (see Table B). In 1445 Henry VI married Margaret of Anjou. In 1447 Gloucester was accused of treason by his enemies and murdered in prison. Failing an heir, the next in succession to Henry VI was Richard, Duke of York (son of Richard, Earl of Cambridge). The Beauforts grew jealous of him, and an open quarrel broke out between them. York took as his symbol a white rose; Somerset chose a red rose. The King favored the Beaufort party (see *I Hen VI*, ii.iv). From this point began the Wars of the Roses.

In 1453 Queen Margaret gave birth to a son, Prince Edward, who thus became heir to the throne; but in the next year Henry VI (who was always a saintly innocent and the mere puppet of the party in power) for a while became insane, and York was made Regent. When the King recovered, the Somerset party returned to power. York in self-protection raised an army and rebelled. At the Battle of St. Albans (1455) York defeated and killed Somerset and captured Henry VI. York thus again became Regent. Nevertheless, though the Lancastrians — that is, the Somerset party, called Lancastrians because of their descent from John of Gaunt, Duke of Lancaster — were defeated, Margaret of Anjou, a ferocious and ambitious woman, did not give up, even when her new forces were defeated in the first engagements. York then made formal claim to the throne for himself; but a few weeks later in an unlucky battle at Wakefield in Yorkshire (1460) he was defeated and killed by Margaret's forces. Margaret sent his head, crowned with a paper crown, to be set up in York.

York's son was Edward, fifth Earl of March. He carried on the fight, and in 1461 at the Battle of Towton he wiped out the Lancastrian army; but he failed to capture Margaret, who fled to France. Edward, Earl of March, now became King of England with the title of Edward IV. His chief supporter hitherto had been Richard Neville, Earl of Warwick, known as "Warwick the Kingmaker." Edward did not wish to be dependent on the Nevilles; and while Warwick was negotiating a French marriage for him, he secretly married a lady of no rank, Elizabeth Woodville, the widow of a Lancastrian knight. To strengthen his party, Edward IV promoted his wife's relatives to the greatest offices in the state. Warwick retaliated for this snub by arranging the marriage of his own daughter to George, Duke of Clarence (Edward IV's brother), who thus showed open hostility to the King.

In 1469 the Lancastrians were again gathering. Warwick deserted the Yorkists, and by persuasion of the French King, Louis XI, he was reconciled with Margaret, who was still an exile in France. Edward IV fled from England. Warwick then declared for Henry VI, and the new alliance between Warwick and Margaret was cemented by the marriage of Anne, Warwick's daughter, to Edward, the son of Margaret and Henry VI. Warwick's forces captured London; Henry VI was brought out of the Tower, where he had long been a prisoner, and was once more set on the throne.

Henry VI's second period as puppet King did not last long. Edward, aided by his brother Richard, Duke of Gloucester, landed at Ravenspur in Yorkshire with a small force. The little army marched southward. Clarence deserted Warwick and became reconciled to his brother Edward IV. The decisive battle was fought at Barnet, a few miles north of London, in 1471; Edward was victorious and Warwick was killed. The final defeat of the Lancastrians came a few weeks later at Tewkesbury in Gloucestershire, where Margaret's last army was utterly defeated. Among those captured was Edward, Margaret's son; he was murdered after the battle by Richard, Duke of Gloucester, and the surviving Lancastrian noblemen were executed. The only relic of the Lancastrian line now left was Henry Tudor, Earl of Richmond (see Table C).

So Edward IV once more returned to London as King; on the same day Henry VI was murdered in the Tower of London by Gloucester. At this point the third part of Shakespeare's *Henry VI* ends.

The play of *Richard III* begins shortly before the death of Edward IV in 1483 and covers a period of about two years. Edward was pleasure-loving and voluptuous, his love affair with Jane Shore, the wife of a London citizen, being particularly notorious. The King's brother Richard, Duke of Gloucester, who had married the widow of Prince Edward (whom he had murdered), was regarded as the strong man behind the throne; he had already amply shown his ruthless nature. Gloucester persuaded Edward that Clarence was again becoming dangerous. So Clarence was sent to the Tower and there murdered. But Gloucester had many enemies; the Queen's family and relations — the Woodvilles and the Greys — hated him; the King was ailing, and Gloucester knew that if they should retain their power after the King's death, his own chances of survival were small.

As soon as Edward IV was dead, Gloucester acted quickly. With the aid of the Duke of Buckingham, he captured the young King, Edward V, from his uncles, the Earl Rivers and Sir Richard Grey, whom he imprisoned and later caused to be beheaded. Then he was made Protector of the boy King. Gloucester was now aiming directly at the crown for himself, and when he found that the Lord Chamberlain, Lord Hastings, was not with him, he quarreled with Hastings at a meeting of the Council and ordered him to be beheaded out of hand.

Meanwhile the younger son of Edward IV, Richard, Duke of York, had been taken into sanctuary at Westminster by his mother. Gloucester persuaded her to release him to be a companion to his brother in the Tower. Gloucester was now ready for the next open step. Backed by Buckingham and his own retainers, he " accepted " the throne of England as Richard III when it was offered him by a deputation of London citizens; and to make his position more secure, he sent to have the two young Princes murdered in the Tower. However, Richard's ruthlessness caused general disgust, and his many enemies began plotting to bring in Henry of Richmond as King. Even Buckingham turned against him, but by bad luck he was captured and executed.

Richard's next plan was to get rid of his wife and marry his niece, Elizabeth of York, daughter of Edward IV; but before this scheme could be carried out Henry of Richmond landed in Wales. The last battle of the Wars of the Roses was fought at Bosworth near Leicester in 1485. Henry's chances seemed poor, for Richard's army was far larger; but in the battle many of Richard's supporters deserted to the other side, and Richard himself was killed fighting desperately. So Henry of Richmond became King as Henry VII, and by marrying Elizabeth of York united the White Rose and the Red.

The son of Henry VII was Henry VIII; Queen Elizabeth was his granddaughter. The last battles of the Wars of the Roses were almost as close to Shakespeare and his audiences as the American Civil War to modern times. Much of the fighting had occurred in places familiar to Shakespeare; Tewkesbury, where the most ghastly slaughter was made, is less than thirty miles from Stratford-on-Avon. Moreover, to Englishmen in those times it seemed only too likely that chaos would come again at the death of Queen Elizabeth. There was thus an immediate and keen interest in any play which told of the events and personalities of those brutal and not far distant days.